# BUTTERWORTHS
## RESIDENTIAL LANDLORD AND TENANT HANDBOOK

# BUTTERWORTHS
# RESIDENTIAL LANDLORD AND TENANT HANDBOOK

Fifth edition

Consultant Editor

*JAMES DRISCOLL, LLM, LLB, Solicitor*
*Consultant Solicitor, Trowers and Hamlins*
*Lawyer Chair, Residential Property Tribunal*
*Visiting Fellow, School of Law, University of Essex*
*Emeritus Professor of Property Law, London South Bank University*

# MEMBERS OF THE LEXISNEXIS GROUP WORLDWIDE

| | |
|---|---|
| United Kingdom | LexisNexis, a Division of Reed Elsevier (UK) Ltd, Halsbury House, 35 Chancery Lane, London, WC2A 1EL, and London House, 20–22 East London Street, Edinburgh EH7 4BQ |
| Australia | LexisNexis Butterworths, Chatswood, New South Wales |
| Austria | LexisNexis Verlag ARD Orac GmbH & Co KG, Vienna |
| Benelux | LexisNexis Benelux, Amsterdam |
| Canada | LexisNexis Canada, Markham, Ontario |
| China | LexisNexis China, Beijing and Shanghai |
| France | LexisNexis SA, Paris |
| Germany | LexisNexis Deutschland GmbH, Munster |
| Hong Kong | LexisNexis Hong Kong, Hong Kong |
| India | LexisNexis India, New Delhi |
| Italy | Giuffrè Editore, Milan |
| Japan | LexisNexis Japan, Tokyo |
| Malaysia | Malayan Law Journal Sdn Bhd, Kuala Lumpur |
| New Zealand | LexisNexis NZ Ltd, Wellington |
| Poland | Wydawnictwo Prawnicze LexisNexis Sp, Warsaw |
| Singapore | LexisNexis Singapore, Singapore |
| South Africa | LexisNexis Butterworths, Durban |
| USA | LexisNexis, Dayton, Ohio |

© Reed Elsevier (UK) Ltd 2009
Published by LexisNexis

This is a Butterworths title

A CIP Catalogue record for this book is available from the British Library.

ISBN: 978 1 4057 2890 4

Typeset by Columns Design Ltd, Reading, England

Printed in the UK by CPI William Clowes, Beccles, NR34 7TL

Visit LexisNexis Butterworths at www.lexisnexis.co.uk

# PREFACE TO THE FIFTH EDITION

Once again it is a pleasure to write the Preface to a new edition of this Handbook. Although it is only just over two years ago since the Fourth Edition was published, major amendments have been made to the Housing Act 1985, the Housing Act 1988, the Housing Act 1996 and other legislation. These are the changes made by Part 3 of the Housing and Regeneration Act 2008.

Amongst the most significant of the amendments are those to assured and secure tenancies. These change the law on the so-called 'tolerated trespasser' doctrine and possession orders. This doctrine has caused endless problems and complications to so many social landlords and their tenants (see: 'Tolerated trespassers: guidance for social landlords' Communities and Local Government, May 2009).

Turning to a different type of tenancy—long leases of flats and houses—there are changes as well. Amendments have been made to the Leasehold Reform Act 1967. Regulations have been made under these amended provisions in the 1967 Act. This is another of the changes made by Part 3 of the Housing and Regeneration Act 2008.

There are no amendments, though, to the enfranchisement and lease extension provisions in Part I of the Leasehold Reform, Housing and Urban Development Act 1993.

All of the available regulations made as a result of these changes under the Housing and Regeneration Act 2008 are included in this new edition. Regulations have yet to be made under section 21 of the Landlord and Tenant Act 1985 and section 42A of the Landlord and Tenant Act 1987. It is understood that these new sections will come into force on 6 April 2010. These modest reforms were first made by the Commonhold and Leasehold Reform Act 2002 but those amendments have never been brought into force. They are replaced by two new versions introduced into the 1985 and 1987 Acts by Part 3 of the Housing and Regeneration Act 2008. It is remarkable how long it has taken to implement these simple reforms.

On long leases, there are two other matters to report. First, are certain changes to the statutory right to manage (introduced under Part 2 of the Commonhold and Leasehold Reform Act 2002). Amendments to the regulations dealing with the constitution and related matters of RTM companies were made recently. These amendments are included in this new edition. The second matter relates to the RTE company amendments made to the 1993 Act. These were made by Part 2 of the 2002 Act but they have never been commenced. A consultation paper was published earlier this year ('A consultation paper on the right to enfranchise (RTE)' CLG, May 2009). Government is now of the view that the requirement that enfranchising flat leaseholders must form a special company to act as their nominee purchaser is unworkable. RTE will not be brought into force and the RTE amendments will be repealed in due course. One result of this is that flat leaseholders have no statutory right to participate in an enfranchisement claim (though they do in relation to the right to manage).

I am pleased that the publishers have found the space to include Parts 1 and 2 of the Housing and Regeneration Act 2008. These make fundamental changes to the funding and regulation of housing. For the first time, the funding and regulation of social housing has been split; the Housing Corporation is no more, and there are two new agencies. These are the Homes and Communities Agency and the new Social Housing Regulator (also known as the 'Tenant Services Authority'). It is understood that the new regulator will assume responsibility for regulating local authority housing in 2010 (see: 'The Housing and Regeneration Act 2008 (Registration of Local Authorities) Order: consultation' CLG, August 2009). This will be in addition to its current responsibilities to registered social landlords (renamed 'registered providers' as a result of the 2008 Act).

With the added emphasis this coverage brings to the social rented sector, it has also been decided to include the provisions under which social landlords owe duties to assist in housing the homeless.

Another change from the previous four editions is the inclusion of the legislation that regulates park homes: the Caravans Sites Act 1968 and the Mobile Homes Act 1983 (both amended by the Housing Act 2004). It is understood that certain disputes that may arise for a determination will be transferred in 2010 to the Residential Property Tribunal. This follows proposals in a consultation paper 'A new approach for resolving disputes and to procedures relating to Park Homes' CLG, May 2008). Unfortunately, the regulations relating thereto are not yet available.

In 2010 it is likely that there will be an increase to the maximum rent limit for assured tenancies from the current level of £25,000 to £100,000. This is one of the suggestions in 'The Government response to the Rugg Review' (CLG, May 2009). This proposal is made as the current upper limit has not been revised since it was introduced by the Housing Act 1988 as one the qualifications for a tenancy to be an assured tenancy. The thinking behind this proposal relates to the assured shorthold tenancies. These benefit from the statutory protections of tenancy deposits introduced under the Housing Act 2004. As rents for some rented accommodation now exceed the annual limit of £25,000, they are not, by definition, assured and cannot, therefore, benefit from the tenancy deposit schemes. It is unlikely that the legislative enactment to the current limit in the 1988 Act will be made until 2010.

This Handbook follows the standard Butterworths Handbooks style, with amendments made by new legislation incorporated into the text of existing legislation. The notes which follow a provision detail the changes that have been made to the text and list any prospective amendments. In the text:

- an ellipsis ( ... ) indicates that text has been repealed or revoked (or is outside the scope of this Handbook);

- square brackets denote text that has been inserted or substituted;

- italicised text is prospectively repealed or substituted, or repealed subject to savings.

The contents of this edition of the Handbook take into account the materials available as at 30 October 2009.

James Driscoll

Tower Hill, London EC3

30 October 2009

# PREFACE TO THE FOURTH EDITION

It is a pleasure to write the Preface to the Fourth Edition of this Handbook. I am very pleased that the publishers have decided to bring out a new edition even though it is just two years since the last one was published. This has allowed for the expansion of the Handbook to include, in particular, the important secondary legislation made under the Housing Act 2004, the principal reason for this new edition of the Handbook. This should be particularly useful for practitioners as so much of the workings of the 2004 Act depend on the content of these regulations which were not available when the Third Edition was being prepared. Almost all of the 2004 Act is in force though there continues to be delay in commencing the House in Multiple Occupation provisions in Part 2 of the 2004 Act as they apply to certain blocks of converted flats (s 257 of the Act). Those particular measures probably will not come into force until late 2007 in England and later still in Wales. In this edition, various statutory amendments to residential landlord and tenant legislation made since the Third Edition have also been incorporated.

It may seem remarkable that several of the reforms to residential leasehold law made by Part 2 of the Commonhold and Leasehold Reform Act 2002 are still not in force although it is now some five years since the measure had Royal Assent. As the preparation of this Handbook was being completed, regulations were laid which will bring into force in England new requirements that leaseholders are given a notice of their rights when either a service charge demand, or a demand for an administration charge, is made. These are the Service Charges (Summary of Rights and Obligations, and Transitional Provision) (England) Regulations 2007 and the Administration Charges (Summary of Rights and Obligations) (England) Regulations 2007. They are included in this new edition and come into force in England on 1 October 2007. The corresponding Welsh Regulations are, apparently, unlikely to appear until 2008. It is far from clear why it has taken so long for these reforms to be brought into force.

Unfortunately a number of the 2002 Act leasehold reforms have yet to be brought into force. These are:

- the requirements that flat leaseholders who wish to enfranchise must appoint as their nominee purchaser an RTE company (ss 4A to 4C and other references in the Leasehold Reform, Housing and Urban Development Act 1993);

- the revised requirements under s 21 of the Landlord and Tenant Act 1985 that landlords must give to leaseholders regular statements of account (accompanied by a right for the leaseholder to withhold the service charge if this requirement has not been complied with); and

- revised requirements under s 42A of the Landlord and Tenant Act 1987 relating to the holding by landlords of service charge contributions paid in advance in a designated account.

This new edition of the Handbook also adds material which was not previously included: for example, relevant extracts from the Human Rights Act 1998, the Contracts (Rights of Third Parties) Act 1999, the Rent Acts (Maximum Fair Rent) Order 1999 and the Unfair Terms in Consumer Contracts Regulations 1999. It also includes the Smoke-free (Exemptions and Vehicles) Regulations 2007 which apply to certain residential premises.

The contents of this edition of the Handbook take into account the materials available as at 21 May 2007.

James Driscoll

Tower Hill, London EC3

May 2007

# PREFACE TO THE THIRD EDITION

I am very pleased to write the Preface to the Third Edition of this Handbook. Some seven years have elapsed since publication of the Second Edition. During that period there have been several important items of legislation. This Edition was originally planned to take account of the enormous number of changes to residential landlord and tenant law made by Part 2 of the Commonhold and Leasehold Reform Act 2002, which has enacted a number of major leasehold reform measures. It was also decided to include the new Commonhold provisions in Part 1 of that Act in this Handbook as well. However, as much of the practical detail of both Parts of the 2002 Act are the subject of Regulations made under it, the decision was taken to delay publication until all of the secondary legislation was passed. This process took much longer than many expected. Eventually Commonhold, the new system for the ownership and management of interdependent buildings, such as blocks of flats, or commercial, or mixed-use premises was brought into force on 27th September 2004. The basic principles of Commonhold are in Part 1 of the 2002 Act; much of the practical detail is contained in the Commonhold Regulations 2004 that are also included in this work. There will be a further set of Commonhold Regulations to be made, but not until 2006. The second set of such Regulations will deal with shared ownership leases, compulsory purchase, Islamic mortgages and insolvency.

Part 2 of the 2002 Act has made a huge number of important changes to residential landlord and tenant law. Most of these changes have been made by amendments to existing legislation such as the Leasehold Reform Act 1967, the Landlord and Tenant Acts of 1985 and 1987, and Part 1 of the Leasehold Reform, Housing and Urban Development Act 1993. This Edition of the Handbook contains this body of legislation as it has been so amended, along with the available secondary legislation made under Part 2 of the 2002 Act. Whilst much of Part 2 of the 2002 Act made whole-scale changes to existing legislation, some of the provisions are new and free standing, notably the new statutory right to manage, and various other reforms. Unfortunately, there are a few provisions in Part 2 that have yet to come into force: these include the RTE company provisions relating to collective enfranchisement claims made under Part 1 of the 1993 Act; the revised provisions governing the keeping of advance service charge payments under new provisions inserted into the Landlord and Tenant Act 1987 and new provisions relating to service charge notices made by insertion of new provisions into the Landlord and Tenant Act 1985.

The delay in publication of this work has allowed the inclusion of the Housing Act 2004, one of the most important measures to affect private rented accommodation for many years. Most of the 2004 Act will not come into force until the end of 2005 but all the main provisions in the Act are included in this handbook. Also included is the Civil Partnership Act 2004 and the changes made by the Disability Discrimination Act 2005 as it affects residential landlord and tenant matters. Because of the sheer volume of legislative material, this Edition only includes provisions that are directly relevant to residential landlord and tenants. So, for example, the Human Rights Act 1998, the Contracts (Rights of Third Parties) Act 1999 and the Unfair Terms and Consumer Contracts Regulations 1999 are not included, although those consulting this volume will be well aware of their importance to property law generally. It is to be hoped that the publishers will be able to bring out a Fourth Edition of this work once all of the remaining provisions in Part 2 of the Commonhold and Leasehold Reform Act 2002, and those in the Housing Act 2004 and the Civil Partnerships Act 2004 have come into force. The contents of this Handbook take into account the materials available as at the 17 June 2005.

James Driscoll

Tower Hill, London EC3

July 2005

# PREFACE TO THE SECOND EDITION

I am delighted to write the Preface to the Second edition of this Handbook containing legislative source materials, the companion title to Butterworths Residential Landlord and Tenant Guide, which contains narrative guidance to the legislation. In the Preface to the First edition of this Handbook, I referred to the changes foreshadowed in the White Paper 'Our Future Homes' (Cm 2901) published in June 1995. Almost all the proposals contained in the White Paper were implemented in the Housing Act 1996. The law governing housing associations was re-enacted, with important changes, by Part I of the 1996 Act. Housing associations (now known as 'registered social landlords') continue to be the main source of new social housing for rent and the main recipients of transfers of local authority housing. Most of Part I of the 1996 Act deals with the registration and the regulation of registered social landlords and thus falls outside the scope of this book. The new right to acquire for tenants of registered social landlords is included in order to provide comparable coverage to the right to buy for secure tenants which is already covered in this book.

Part III of the Housing Act 1996 made significant changes to landlord and tenant law contained in the Landlord and Tenant Act 1985—namely reforms to residential long leases with new restrictions to the right of a landlord to forfeit for non-payment of service charges, redefined regulation of service charges (coupled with the transfer of jurisdiction of service charge disputes and applications for a manager to be appointed from the county court to the Leasehold Valuation Tribunal), a broader basis on which a manager can be appointed and a new right for lessees to appoint a surveyor to advise on service charges. Other far-reaching amendments were made to the Landlord and Tenant Act 1987, including the tightening up of lessees' rights of first refusal where a landlord wishes to dispose of an interest and the introduction of criminal liability where a landlord fails to comply with the new procedures. Further changes were also made to assured tenancies. With effect from 28 February 1997 almost all new tenancies are automatically assured shorthold tenancies with little further formality and this will hasten the deregulation of private sector rented accommodation. Part III also contains other provisions relating to other residential long leases: reforms to the low rent test and other changes to the right to enfranchisement and lease extension have increased the numbers of long leases which qualify for these rights with whole-scale amendments to the Leasehold Reform, Housing and Urban Development Act 1993 (and to a lesser extent, to the Leasehold Reform Act 1967). The provisions relating to the transfer of tenancies in divorce proceedings contained in the Family Law Act 1996 are also reproduced. The Housing Act 1996 (and the provisions relating to housing contained in the Housing Grants, Construction and Regeneration Act 1996) relates mainly to the public sector, which is outside the scope of this Handbook. However, the new provisions under which local housing authorities (and Housing Action Trusts) can elect to operate an introductory tenancy scheme are included as well as the measures introduced to deal with anti-social behaviour by tenants (such as a new nuisance possession ground and injunctions supported with a power of arrest).

Practitioners will probably welcome a period of respite from further legislative change. However, a proposal to limit increase in fair rents for regulated tenancies is under consideration as are proposals to change the 'cost floor rule' and to reduce the maximum discount available for purchases under the right to buy provisions. It is also expected that a Green Paper will be issued on residential long leases with recommendations for a new right for lessees to appoint a manager and further changes to enfranchisement and lease extensions. It is unlikely, however, that further primary legislation will appear until the new century.

James Driscoll

November 1998

# PREFACE TO THE FIRST EDITION

This Handbook and its companion volume *Business Landlord and Tenant Handbook* are the successors to the fourth edition of *Butterworths Landlord and Tenant Handbook* (1992). The material has been classified into its residential and commercial contexts. Most of the statutory material contained in this book applies exclusively to residential landlord and tenant law. In particular it contains statutes and statutory instruments relating to short-term lettings by both private and public sector landlords as well as to lettings by housing associations. Also included is the legislative material relating to the rights of long leaseholders of flats and houses, in both the private and the public sectors.

Those who practise and advise in the area of residential landlord and tenant law will no doubt be familiar with the way in which successive Acts of Parliament have phased out different statutory codes. The Housing Act 1988, Part I, contains a number of phasing out and transitional provisions which are likely to be relevant for a number of years. Section 34 of the 1988 Act provides that no tenancy created on or after 15 January 1989 can be protected by the Rent Act 1977. However, section 34 contains a limited number of exceptional cases where a new protected tenancy can be created after that date. Accordingly, for the foreseeable future the privately rented sector will include occupants who are protected by the Rent Act 1977, those who have an assured or an assured shorthold tenancy governed by the Housing Act 1988, and those who are excluded from any statutory regulation at all. Similarly, the granting of secure tenancies by registered housing associations is also being phased out, but again there are a number of important transitional provisions to bear in mind. The basic position is easy to state: on or after 15 January 1989, the grant of a new tenancy by a housing association will be either an assured or an assured shorthold tenancy (unless the agreement is one which is excluded because it falls within one of the categories set out in the Housing Act 1988, Schedule 1). In addition, the grant of tenancies or licences which are regulated by the Rent (Agriculture) Act 1976 is being phased out. A tenancy or a licence granted on or after 15 January 1989 will generally be on an assured agricultural occupancy.

Most tenants (and licensees) of a local authority or another public sector landlord will have a secure tenancy under the relevant provisions of the Housing Act 1985. Secure tenants enjoy security of tenure, the right to buy, and other statutory rights. However, if a local authority transfers dwellings to a housing association or another private landlord then the position of any tenants whose dwellings to a housing association or another private landlord then the position of any tenants whose dwellings are so transferred alters. This is a result of another transitional measure introduced by the Housing Act 1988, Part I. Following such a transfer, the tenants will cease to be secure tenants and will instead become assured tenants with a preserved right to buy.

In terms of long leases of houses, the right to enfranchise, contained in the Leasehold Reform Act 1967, was recently extended to high-value houses following amendments made to the principal legislation by the Leasehold Reform, Housing and Urban Development Act 1993. In addition, the 1993 Act introduced a collective right to enfranchise for qualifying groups of flat owners and an individual right to purchase an extended lease. These changes took effect from 1 November 1993.

The holder of a long lease of a flat who exercises the right to acquire a new lease under the 1993 Act will lose any right to obtain a statutory tenancy under the provisions of the Landlord and Tenant Act 1954, Part I. In this context, it should be noted that the right of a lessee to obtain a statutory tenancy at the end of a long lease of a flat or a house will be changed where the original long tenancy comes to an end on or after 15 January 1999. When this occurs the occupant may acquire an assured tenancy rather than a statutory tenancy. The same principle applies to long leases entered into on or after 1 April 1990.

Residential landlord and tenant is a rapidly changing area of law. At the time that this handbook is being prepared, a Disability Discrimination Bill is being considered in

Parliament and is expected to become law later in 1995. This Bill contains a number of provisions which will outlaw discrimination in the field of rented housing. Other important changes will occur if legislation is introduced to implement proposals announced in a Government White Paper on housing ("Our Future Homes: Opportunity, Choice, Responsibility: the Government's Housing Policies for England and Wales", Cm 2901), published on 27 June 1995. These proposals include changes to assured tenancies and a new right for housing association tenants to purchase their homes.

James Driscoll

London

August 1995

# CONTENTS

## PART II STATUTORY INSTRUMENTS

## PART III OTHER MATERIAL

## ALPHABETICAL LIST OF CONTENTS

# PART I
## STATUTES

# LAW OF PROPERTY ACT 1925

### (15 & 16 Geo 5 c 20)

### ARRANGEMENT OF SECTIONS

### PART I
#### GENERAL PRINCIPLES AS TO LEGAL ESTATES, EQUITABLE INTERESTS AND POWERS

### PART II
#### CONTRACTS, CONVEYANCES AND OTHER INSTRUMENTS

*Contracts*

*Conveyances and Other Instruments*

*Covenants*

### PART V
#### LEASES AND TENANCIES

### PART XI
#### MISCELLANEOUS

*Notices*

### PART XII
#### CONSTRUCTION, JURISDICTION, AND GENERAL PROVISIONS

SCHEDULES:

Second Schedule—Implied Covenants

Part VII—Covenant Implied in a Conveyance for valuable consideration, other than

*An Act to consolidate the enactments relating to Conveyancing and the Law of Property in England and Wales*

**[9 April 1925]**

**NOTES**

Modification: this Act (with the exception of s 75) has been modified by the Solicitors' Incorporated Practices Order 1991, SI 1991/2684, arts 2–5, Sch 1, so that any reference to a solicitor is to be construed as including a reference to a recognised body within the meaning of the Administration of Justice Act 1985, s 9.

## PART I
## GENERAL PRINCIPLES AS TO LEGAL ESTATES, EQUITABLE INTERESTS AND POWERS

### 1 Legal estates and equitable interests

(1) The only estates in land which are capable of subsisting or of being conveyed or created at law are—

    (a) An estate in fee simple absolute in possession;

    (b) A term of years absolute.

(2) The only interests or charges in or over land which are capable of subsisting or of being conveyed or created at law are—

    (a) An easement, right, or privilege in or over land for an interest equivalent to an estate in fee simple absolute in possession or a term of years absolute;

    (b) A rentcharge in possession issuing out of or charged on land being either perpetual or for a term of years absolute;

    (c) A charge by way of legal mortgage;

    (d) ... and any other similar charge on land which is not created by an instrument;

    (e) Rights of entry exercisable over or in respect of a legal term of years absolute, or annexed, for any purpose, to a legal rentcharge.

(3) All other estates, interests, and charges in or over land take effect as equitable interests.

(4) The estates, interests, and charges which under this section are authorised to subsist or to be conveyed or created at law are (when subsisting or conveyed or created at law) in this Act referred to as "legal estates," and have the same incidents as legal estates subsisting at the commencement of this Act; and the owner of a legal estate is referred to as "an estate owner" and his legal estate is referred to as his estate.

(5) A legal estate may subsist concurrently with or subject to any other legal estate in the same land in like manner as it could have done before the commencement of this Act.

(6) A legal estate is not capable of subsisting or of being created in an undivided share in land or of being held by an infant.

(7) Every power of appointment over, or power to convey or charge land or any interest therein, whether created by a statute or other instrument or implied by law, and whether created before or after the commencement of this Act (not being a power vested in a legal mortgagee or an estate owner in right of his estate and exercisable by him or by another person in his name and on his behalf), operates only in equity.

(8) Estates, interests, and charges in or over land which are not legal estates are in this Act referred to as "equitable interests", and powers which by this Act are to operate in equity only are in this Act referred to as "equitable powers".

(9) The provisions in any statute or other instrument requiring land to be conveyed to uses shall take effect as directions that the land shall (subject to creating or reserving thereout any legal estate authorised by this Act which may be required) be conveyed to a person of full age upon the requisite trusts.

(10) The repeal of the Statute of Uses (as amended) does not affect the operation thereof in regard to dealings taking effect before the commencement of this Act.

**[1]**

**NOTES**

Sub-s (2): words omitted repealed by the Finance Act 1963, s 73(8)(b), Sch 14, Pt IV and the Tithe Act 1936, s 48(3), Sch 9.

Statute of Uses Act (1535): repealed by the Law of Property Act 1922 and, in relation to transactions after 1926, by s 207 of, and Sch 7 to, this Act.

**2–4** *(Outside the scope of this work.)*

## 5 Satisfied terms, whether created out of freehold or leasehold land to cease

(1) Where the purposes of a term of years created or limited at any time out of freehold land, become satisfied either before or after the commencement of this Act (whether or not that term either by express declaration or by construction of law becomes attendant upon the freehold reversion) it shall merge in the reversion expectant thereon and shall cease accordingly.

(2) Where the purposes of a term of years created or limited, at any time, out of leasehold land, become satisfied after the commencement of this Act, that term shall merge in the reversion expectant thereon and shall cease accordingly.

(3) Where the purposes are satisfied only as respects part of the land comprised in a term, this section shall have effect as if a separate term had been created in regard to that part of the land.

[2]

## 6 Saving of lessors' and lessees' covenants

(1) Nothing in this Part of this Act affects prejudicially the right to enforce any lessor's or lessee's covenants, agreements or conditions (including a valid option to purchase or right of pre-emption over the reversion), contained in any such instrument as is in this section mentioned, the benefit or burden of which runs with the reversion or the term.

(2) This section applies where the covenant, agreement or condition is contained in any instrument—

(a)   creating a term of years absolute, or
(b)   varying the rights of the lessor or lessee under the instrument creating the term.

[3]

**7** *(Outside the scope of this work.)*

## 8 Saving of certain legal powers to lease

(1) All leases or tenancies at a rent for a term of years absolute authorised to be granted by a mortgagor or mortgagee or by the Settled Land Act 1925, or any other statute (whether or not extended by any instrument) may be granted in the name and on behalf of the estate owner by the person empowered to grant the same, whether being an estate owner or not, with the same effect and priority as if this Part of this Act had not been passed; but this section does not (except as respects the usual qualified covenant for quiet enjoyment) authorise any person granting a lease in the name of an estate owner to impose any personal liability on him.

(2) Where a rentcharge is held for a legal estate, the owner thereof may under the statutory power or under any corresponding power, create a legal term of years absolute for securing or compelling payment of the same; but in other cases terms created under any such power shall, unless and until the estate owner of the land charged gives legal effect to the transaction, take effect only as equitable interests.

[4]

**9–39**   *(Ss 9, 10, 12–15, 20–22, 24, 27, 31, 33, 34, 36–39 outside the scope of this work; s 11 repealed by the Law of Property Act 1969, s 16, Sch 2, Pt I; ss 16–18 repealed by the Finance Act 1975, ss 50, 52(2), (3), 59(5), Sch 13, Pt I; ss 19, 23, 25, 26, 28–30, 35 repealed by the Trusts of Land and Appointment of Trustees Act 1996, s 25(2), Sch 4 and s 32 repealed by ss 5(1), 25(2) of, and Sch 2, para 2, Sch 4 to, that Act, in relation to land purchased after on or after 1 January 1997 whether the trust or will in pursuance of which it is purchased comes into operation before or after that date, for savings see ss 2, 3, 18(3) 25(5) of, and Sch 1, para 1 to that Act.)*

PART II
CONTRACTS, CONVEYANCES AND OTHER INSTRUMENTS

*Contracts*

**40–43**   *(S 40 repealed by the Law of Property (Miscellaneous Provisions) Act 1989, ss 2(8), 4, Sch 2, except in relation to contracts made before 27 September 1989; ss 41–43 outside the scope of this work.)*

## 44 Statutory commencements of title

(1) After the commencement of this Act [fifteen years] shall be substituted for forty years as the period of commencement of title which a purchaser of land may require; nevertheless earlier title than [fifteen years] may be required in cases similar to those in which earlier title than forty years might immediately before the commencement of this Act be required.

(2)   Under a contract to grant or assign a term of years, whether derived or to be derived out of freehold or leasehold land, the intended lessee or assign shall not be entitled to call for the title to the freehold.

(3)   Under a contract to sell and assign a term of years derived out of a leasehold interest in land, the intended assign shall not have the right to call for the title to the leasehold reversion.

(4)   On a contract to grant a lease for a term of years to be derived out of a leasehold interest, with a leasehold reversion, the intended lessee shall not have the right to call for the title to that reversion.

[(4A)   Subsections (2) and (4) of this section do not apply to a contract to grant a term of years if the grant will be an event within section 4(1) of the Land Registration Act 2002 (events which trigger compulsory first registration of title).]

(5)   Where by reason of any of [subsections (2) to (4) of this section], an intending lessee or assign is not entitled to call for the title to the freehold or to a leasehold reversion, as the case may be, he shall not, where the contract is made after the commencement of this Act, be deemed to be affected with notice of any matter or thing of which, if he had contracted that such title should be furnished, he might have had notice.

(6)   Where land of copyhold or customary tenure has been converted into freehold by enfranchisement, then, under a contract to sell and convey the freehold, the purchaser shall not have the right to call for the title to make the enfranchisement.

(7)   Where the manorial incidents formerly affecting any land have been extinguished, then, under a contract to sell and convey the freehold, the purchaser shall not have the right to call for the title of the person entering into any compensation agreement or giving a receipt for the compensation money to enter into such agreement or to give such receipt, and shall not be deemed to be affected with notice of any matter or thing of which, if he had contracted that such title should be furnished, he might have had notice.

(8)   A purchaser shall not be deemed to be or ever to have been affected with notice of any matter or thing of which, if he had investigated the title or made enquiries in regard to matters prior to the period of commencement of title fixed by this Act, or by any other statute, or by any rule of law, he might have had notice, unless he actually makes such investigation or enquiries.

(9)   Where a lease whether made before or after the commencement of this Act, is made under a power contained in a settlement, will, Act of Parliament, or other instrument, any preliminary contract for or relating to the lease shall not, for the purpose of the deduction of title to an intended assign, form part of the title, or evidence of the title, to the lease.

(10)   This section, save where otherwise expressly provided, applies to contracts for sale whether made before or after the commencement of this Act, and applies to contracts for exchange in like manner as to contracts for sale, save that it applies only to contracts for exchange made after such commencement.

(11)   This section applies only if and so far as a contrary intention is not expressed in the contract.

[(12)   Nothing in this section applies in relation to registered land or to a term of years to be derived out of registered land.]

[5]

NOTES

Sub-s (1): words in square brackets substituted, in relation to contracts made on or after 1 January 1970, by the Law of Property Act 1969, s 23.

Sub-s (4A): inserted by the Land Registration Act 2002, s 133, Sch 11, para 2(1), (2).

Sub-s (5): words in square brackets substituted by the Land Registration Act 2002, s 133, Sch 11, para 2(1), (3).

Sub-s (12): added by the Land Registration Act 2002, s 133, Sch 11, para 2(1), (4).

**45–47**   (*Outside the scope of this work.*)

## 48 Stipulations preventing a purchaser, lessee, or underlessee from employing his own solicitor to be void

(1)   Any stipulation made on the sale of any interest in land after the commencement of this Act to the effect that the conveyance to, or the registration of the title of, the purchaser shall be prepared or carried out at the expense of the purchaser by a solicitor appointed by or acting for the vendor, and any stipulation which might restrict a purchaser in the selection of a solicitor to act on his behalf in relation to any interest in land agreed to be purchased, shall be void; and, if a sale is effected by demise or subdemise, then, for the purposes of this subsection, the instrument required for giving effect to the transaction shall be deemed to be a conveyance:

Provided that nothing in this subsection shall affect any right reserved to a vendor to furnish a form of conveyance to a purchaser from which the draft can be prepared, or to charge a reasonable fee therefor, or, where a perpetual rentcharge is to be reserved as the only consideration in money or money's worth, the right of a vendor to stipulate that the draft conveyance is to be prepared by his solicitor at the expense of the purchaser.

(2) Any covenant or stipulation contained in, or entered into with reference to any lease or underlease made before or after the commencement of this Act—

(a) whereby the right of preparing, at the expense of a purchaser, any conveyance of the estate or interest of the lessee or underlessee in the demised premises or in any part thereof, or of otherwise carrying out, at the expense of the purchaser, any dealing with such estate or interest, is expressed to be reserved to or vested in the lessor or underlessor or his solicitor; or

(b) which in any way restricts the right of the purchaser to have such conveyance carried out on his behalf by a solicitor appointed by him;

shall be void:

Provided that, where any covenant or stipulation is rendered void by this subsection, there shall be implied in lieu thereof a covenant or stipulation that the lessee or underlessee shall register with the lessor or his solicitor within six months from the date thereof, or as soon after the expiration of that period as may be practicable, all conveyances and devolutions (including probates or letters of administration) affecting the lease or underlease and pay a fee of one guinea in respect of each registration, and the power of entry (if any) on breach of any covenant contained in the lease or underlease shall apply and extend to the breach of any covenant so to be implied.

(3) Save where a sale is effected by demise or subdemise, this section does not affect the law relating to the preparation of a lease or underlease or the draft thereof.

(4) In this section "lease" and "underlease" include any agreement therefor or other tenancy, and "lessee" and "underlessee" and "lessor" and "underlessor" have corresponding meanings.

**[6]**

**NOTES**

Modifications: in this section any reference to a solicitor is to be construed as including a reference to a licensed conveyancer or to a body corporate for the time being recognised under the Administration of Justice Act 1985, s 32, see s 34(2) thereof; any reference to a solicitor is also to be construed as including a reference to a body corporate for the time being recognised under the Administration of Justice Act 1985, s 9, see Sch 2, para 37 thereto, and see further the Courts and Legal Services Act 1990, s 36.

**49, 50**    (*Outside the scope of this work.*)

*Conveyances and Other Instruments*

**51**    (*Outside the scope of this work.*)

## 52   Conveyances to be by deed

(1) All conveyances of land or of any interest therein are void for the purpose of conveying or creating a legal estate unless made by deed.

(2) This section does not apply to—

(a) assents by a personal representative;

(b) disclaimers made in accordance with [sections 178 to 180 or sections 315 to 319 of the Insolvency Act 1986], or not required to be evidenced in writing;

(c) surrenders by operation of law, including surrenders which may, by law, be effected without writing;

(d) leases or tenancies or other assurances not required by law to be made in writing;

(e) receipts [other than those falling within section 115 below];

(f) vesting orders of the court or other competent authority;

(g) conveyances taking effect by operation of law.

**[7]**

**NOTES**

Sub-s (2): words in square brackets in para (b) substituted by the Insolvency Act 1986, s 439(2), Sch 14; words in square brackets in para (e) substituted by the Law of Property (Miscellaneous Provisions) Act 1989, s 1(8), Sch 1, para 2, except in relation to instruments delivered as deeds before 31 July 1990.

**53**    (*Outside the scope of this work.*)

## 54   Creation of interests in land by parol

(1) All interests in land created by parol and not put in writing and signed by the persons so creating the same, or by their agents thereunto lawfully authorised in writing, have, notwithstanding any consideration having been given for the same, the force and effect of interests at will only.

(2)   Nothing in the foregoing provisions of this Part of this Act shall affect the creation by parol of leases taking effect in possession for a term not exceeding three years (whether or not the lessee is given power to extend the term) at the best rent which can be reasonably obtained without taking a fine.

[8]

## 55   Savings in regard to last two sections

Nothing in the last two foregoing sections shall—
  (a)   invalidate dispositions by will; or
  (b)   affect any interest validly created before the commencement of this Act; or
  (c)   affect the right to acquire an interest in land by virtue of taking possession; or
  (d)   affect the operation of the law relating to part performance.

[9]

## 56   Persons taking who are not parties and as to indentures

(1)   A person may take an immediate or other interest in land or other property, or the benefit of any condition, right of entry, covenant or agreement over or respecting land or other property, although he may not be named as a party to the conveyance or other instrument.

(2)   A deed between parties, to effect its objects, has the effect of an indenture though not indented or expressed to be an indenture.

[10]

**57–75**   (*Ss 57–72, 74, 74A, 75 outside the scope of this work; s 73 repealed by the Law of Property (Miscellaneous Provisions) Act 1989, s 4, Sch 2.*)

*Covenants*

**76**   (*Repealed by the Law of Property (Miscellaneous Provisions) Act 1994, ss 10(1), 21(2), (3), Sch 2, as regards dispositions of property made on or after 1 July 1995.*)

## 77   Implied covenants in conveyance subject to rents

(1)   In addition to the covenants implied under [Part I of the Law of Property (Miscellaneous Provisions) Act 1994], there shall in the several cases in this section mentioned, be deemed to be included and implied, a covenant to the effect in this section stated, by and with such persons as are hereinafter mentioned, that is to say:—
  (A)   In a conveyance for valuable consideration, other than a mortgage, of the entirety of the land affected by a rentcharge, a covenant by the grantee or joint and several covenants by the grantees, if more than one, with the conveying parties and with each of them, if more than one, in the terms set out in Part VII of the Second Schedule to this Act. Where a rentcharge has been apportioned in respect of any land, with the consent of the owner of the rentcharge, the covenants in this paragraph shall be implied in the conveyance of that land in like manner as if the apportioned rentcharge were the rentcharge referred to, and the document creating the rentcharge related solely to that land:
  (B)   In a conveyance for valuable consideration, other than a mortgage, of part of land affected by a rentcharge, subject to a part of that rentcharge which has been or is by that conveyance apportioned (but in either case without the consent of the owner of the rentcharge) in respect of the land conveyed:—
      (i)    A covenant by the grantee of the land or joint and several covenants by the grantees, if more than one, with the conveying parties and with each of them, if more than one, in the terms set out in paragraph (i) of Part VIII of the Second Schedule to this Act;
      (ii)   A covenant by a person who conveys or is expressed to convey as beneficial owner, or joint and several covenants by the persons who so convey or are expressed to so convey, if at the date of the conveyance any part of the land affected by such rentcharge is retained, with the grantees of the land and with each of them (if more than one) in the terms set out in paragraph (ii) of Part VIII of the Second Schedule to this Act:
  (C)   *In a conveyance for valuable consideration, other than a mortgage, of the entirety of the land comprised in a lease, for the residue of the term or interest created by the lease, a covenant by the assignee or joint and several covenants by the assignees (if more than one) with the conveying parties and with each of them (if more than one) in the terms set out in Part IX of the Second Schedule to this Act. Where a rent has been apportioned in respect of any land, with the consent of the lessor, the covenants in this paragraph shall be implied in the conveyance of that land in like manner as if the apportioned rent were the original rent reserved, and the lease related solely to that land:*
  (D)   *In a conveyance for valuable consideration, other than a mortgage, of part of the land comprised in a lease, for the residue of the term or interest created by the lease, subject*

*to a part of the rent which has been or is by the conveyance apportioned (but in either case without the consent of the lessor) in respect of the land conveyed:—*

    (i)    *A covenant by the assignee of the land, or joint and several covenants by the assignees, if more than one, with the conveying parties and with each of them, if more than one, in the terms set out in paragraph (i) of Part X of the Second Schedule to this Act;*

    (ii)   *A covenant by a person who conveys or is expressed to convey as beneficial owner, or joint and several covenants by the persons who so convey or are expressed to so convey, If at the date of the conveyance any part of the land comprised in the lease is retained, with the assignees of the land and with each of them (if more than one) in the terms set out in paragraph (ii) of Part X of the Second Schedule to this Act.*

[(2)   Where in a conveyance for valuable consideration, other than a mortgage, part of land affected by a rentcharge is, without the consent of the owner of the rentcharge, expressed to be conveyed subject to or charged with the entire rent, paragraph (B)(i) of subsection (1) of this section shall apply as if, in paragraph (i) of Part VIII of the Second Schedule to this Act—

    (a)    any reference to the apportioned rent were to the entire rent; and

    (b)    the words "(other than the covenant to pay the entire rent)" were omitted.

(2A)   Where in a conveyance for valuable consideration, other than a mortgage, part of land affected by a rentcharge is, without the consent of the owner of the rentcharge, expressed to be conveyed discharged or exonerated from the entire rent, paragraph (B)(ii) of subsection (1) of this section shall apply as if, in paragraph (ii) of Part VIII of the Second Schedule to this Act—

    (a)    any reference to the balance of the rent were to the entire rent; and

    (b)    the words ", other than the covenant to pay the entire rent," were omitted.]

(3)   In this section "conveyance" does not include a demise by way of lease at a rent.

(4)   Any covenant which would be implied under this section by reason of a person conveying or being expressed to convey as beneficial owner may, by express reference to this section, be implied, with or without variation, in a conveyance, whether or not for valuable consideration, by a person who conveys or is expressed to convey as settlor, or as trustee, or as mortgagee, or as personal representative of a deceased person, ... or under an order of the court.

(5)   The benefit of a covenant implied as aforesaid shall be annexed and incident to, and shall go with, the estate or interest of the implied covenantee, and shall be capable of being enforced by every person in whom that estate or interest is, for the whole or any part thereof, from time to time vested.

(6)   A covenant implied as aforesaid may be varied or extended by deed, and, as so varied or extended, shall. as far as may be, operate in the like manner, and with all the like incidents, effects and consequences, as if such variations or extensions were directed in this section to be implied.

(7)   In particular any covenant implied under this section may be extended by providing that—

    (a)    the land conveyed; or

    (b)    the part of the land affected by the rentcharge which remains vested in the covenantor: or

    (c)    *the part of the land demised which remains vested in the covenantor;*

shall, as the case may require, stand charged with the payment of all money which may become payable under the implied covenant.

(8)   This section applies only to conveyances made after the commencement of this Act.

**[11]**

---

**NOTES**

Sub-s (1): words in square brackets substituted for original words "the last preceding section" by the Law of Property (Miscellaneous Provisions) Act 1994, s 21(1), Sch 1, para 1, save in relation to any disposition of property to which, by virtue of s 10(1) or 11 of that Act, s 76 of this Act continues to apply; paras (C), (D) repealed by the Landlord and Tenant (Covenants) Act 1995, ss 14(a), 30(2), (3), Sch 2, except in relation to tenancies which are not new tenancies (as defined by ss 1, 28(1) of that Act at **[944]**, **[969]**).

Sub-ss (2), (2A): substituted for original sub-s (2) by the Landlord and Tenant (Covenants) Act 1995, s 30(1), (3), Sch 1, para 2, except in relation to tenancies which are not new tenancies (as defined by ss 1, 28(1) of that Act at **[944]**, **[969]**); the original sub-s (2) read as follows—

"(2)   Where in a conveyance for valuable consideration, other than a mortgage, part of land affected by a rentcharge, or part of land comprised in a lease is, without the consent of the owner of the rentcharge or of the lessor, as the case may be, expressed to be conveyed—

    (i)    subject to or charged with the entire rent—

        then paragraph (B)(ii) or (D)(i) of the last subsection, as the case may require, shall have effect as if the entire rent were the apportioned rent; or

    (ii)   discharged or exonerated from the entire rent—

        then paragraph (B)(ii) or (D)(ii) of the last subsection, as the case may require, shall have effect as if the entire rent were the balance of the rent, and the words "other than the covenant to pay the entire rent" had been omitted."

Sub-s (4): words omitted repealed by the Mental Health Act 1959, s 149(2), Sch 8, Pt 1.

Sub-s (7): para (c) and word "or" preceding it repealed by the Landlord and Tenant (Covenants) Act 1995, s 30(2), Sch 2, except in relation to tenancies which are not new tenancies (as defined by ss 1, 28(1) of that Act at **[944]**, **[969]**).

## 78  Benefit of covenants relating to land

(1)  A covenant relating to any land of the covenantee shall be deemed to be made with the covenantee and his successors in title and the persons deriving title under him or them, and shall have effect as if such successors and other persons were expressed.

For the purposes of this subsection in connexion with covenants restrictive of the user of land "successors in title" shall be deemed to include the owners and occupiers for the time being of the land of the covenantee intended to be benefited.

(2)  This section applies to covenants made after the commencement of this Act, but the repeal of section fifty-eight of the Conveyancing Act 1881 does not affect the operation of covenants to which that section applied.

**[12]**

**NOTES**

Modification: by virtue of the Landlord and Tenant (Covenants) Act 1995, s 30(4)(a) at **[971]**, this section is disapplied in relation to new tenancies (as defined by ss 1, 28(1) of that Act at **[944]**, **[969]**).

## 79  Burden of covenants relating to land

(1)  A covenant relating to any land of a covenantor or capable of being bound by him, shall, unless a contrary intention is expressed, be deemed to be made by the covenantor on behalf of himself his successors in title and the persons deriving title under him or them, and, subject as aforesaid, shall have effect as if such successors and other persons were expressed.

This subsection extends to a covenant to do some act relating to the land, notwithstanding that the subject-matter may not be in existence when the covenant is made.

(2)  For the purposes of this section in connexion with covenants restrictive of the user of land "successors in title" shall be deemed to include the owners and occupiers for the time being of such land.

(3)  This section applies only to covenants made after the commencement of this Act.

**[13]**

**NOTES**

Modification: by virtue of the Landlord and Tenant (Covenants) Act 1995, s 30(4)(a) at **[971]**, this section is disapplied in relation to new tenancies (as defined by ss 1, 28(1) of that Act at **[944]**, **[969]**).

## 80–83  (*Outside the scope of this work.*)

## [84  Power to discharge or modify restrictive covenants affecting land

(1)  The [Upper Tribunal] shall (without prejudice to any concurrent jurisdiction of the court) have power from time to time, on the application of any person interested in any freehold land affected by any restriction arising under covenant or otherwise as to the user thereof or the building thereon, by order wholly or partially to discharge or modify any such restriction on being satisfied—

(a)  that by reason of changes in the character of the property or the neighbourhood or other circumstances of the case which the [Upper Tribunal] may deem material, the restriction ought to be deemed obsolete; or

(aa)  that (in a case falling within subsection (1A) below) the continued existence thereof would impede some reasonable user of the land for public or private purposes or, as the case may be, would unless modified so impede such user; or

(b)  that the persons of full age and capacity for the time being or from time to time entitled to the benefit of the restriction, whether in respect of estates in fee simple or any lesser estates or interests in the property to which the benefit of the restriction is annexed, have agreed, either expressly or by implication, by their acts or omissions, to the same being discharged or modified; or

(c)  that the proposed discharge or modification will not injure the persons entitled to the benefit of the restriction;

and an order discharging or modifying a restriction under this subsection may direct the applicant to pay to any person entitled to the benefit of the restriction such sum by way of consideration as the Tribunal may think it just to award under one, but not both, of the following heads, that is to say, either—

(i)  a sum to make up for any loss or disadvantage suffered by that person in consequence of the discharge or modification; or

(ii) a sum to make up for any effect which the restriction had, at the time when it was imposed, in reducing the consideration then received for the land affected by it.

(1A) Subsection (1)(aa) above authorises the discharge or modification of a restriction by reference to its impeding some reasonable user of land in any case in which the [Upper Tribunal] is satisfied that the restriction, in impeding that user, either—

(a) does not secure to persons entitled to the benefit of it any practical benefits of substantial value or advantage to them; or

(b) is contrary to the public interest;

and that money will be an adequate compensation for the loss or disadvantage (if any) which any such person will suffer from the discharge or modification.

(1B) In determining whether a case is one falling within subsection (1A) above, and in determining whether (in any such case or otherwise) a restriction ought to be discharged or modified, the [Upper Tribunal] shall take into account the development plan and any declared or ascertainable pattern for the grant or refusal of planning permissions in the relevant areas, as well as the period at which and context in which the restriction was created or imposed and any other material circumstances.

(1C) It is hereby declared that the power conferred by this section to modify a restriction includes power to add such further provisions restricting the user of or the building on the land affected as appear to the [Upper Tribunal] to be reasonable in view of the relaxation of the existing provisions, and as may be accepted by the applicant; and the [Upper Tribunal] may accordingly refuse to modify a restriction without some such addition.

(2) The court shall have power on the application of any person interested—

(a) to declare whether or not in any particular case any freehold land is, or would in any given event be, affected by a restriction imposed by any instrument; or

(b) to declare what, upon the true construction of any instrument purporting to impose a restriction, is the nature and extent of the restriction thereby imposed and whether the same is, or would in any given event be, enforceable and if so by whom.

Neither subsections (7) and (11) of this section nor, unless the contrary is expressed, any later enactment providing for this section not to apply to any restrictions shall affect the operation of this subsection or the operation for purposes of this subsection of any other provisions of this section.

(3) The [Upper Tribunal] shall, before making any order under this section, direct such enquiries, if any, to be made of any government department or local authority, and such notices, if any, whether by way of advertisement or otherwise, to be given to such of the persons who appear to be entitled to the benefit of the restriction intended to be discharged, modified, or dealt with as, having regard to any enquiries, notices or other proceedings previously made, given or taken, the [Upper Tribunal] may think fit.

(3A) On an application to the [Upper Tribunal] under this section the [Upper Tribunal] shall give any necessary directions as to the persons who are or are not to be admitted (as appearing to be entitled to the benefit of the restriction) to oppose the application, and no appeal shall lie against any such direction; but [Tribunal Procedure Rules] shall make provision whereby, in cases in which there arises on such an application (whether or not in connection with the admission of persons to oppose) any such question as is referred to in subsection (2)(a) or (b) of this section, the proceedings on the application can and, if the rules so provide, shall be suspended to enable the decision of the court to be obtained on that question by an application under that subsection, ... or otherwise, as may be provided by those rules or by rules of court.

(5) Any order made under this section shall be binding on all persons, whether ascertained or of full age or capacity or not, then entitled or thereafter capable of becoming entitled to the benefit of any restriction, which is thereby discharged, modified or dealt with, and whether such persons are parties to the proceedings or have been served with notice or not.

(6) An order may be made under this section notwithstanding that any instrument which is alleged to impose the restriction intended to be discharged, modified, or dealt with, may not have been produced to the court or the [Upper Tribunal], and the court or the [Upper Tribunal] may act on such evidence of that instrument as it may think sufficient.

(7) This section applies to restrictions whether subsisting at the commencement of this Act or imposed thereafter, but this section does not apply where the restriction was imposed on the occasion of a disposition made gratuitously or for a nominal consideration for public purposes.

(8) This section applies whether the land affected by the restrictions is registered or not ...

(9) Where any proceedings by action or otherwise are taken to enforce a restrictive covenant, any person against whom the proceedings are taken, may in such proceedings apply to the court for an order giving leave to apply to the [Upper Tribunal] under this section, and staying the proceedings in the meantime.

(11) This section does not apply to restrictions imposed by the Commissioners of Works under any statutory power for the protection of any Royal Park or Garden or to restrictions of a like

character imposed upon the occasion of any enfranchisement effected before the commencement of this Act in any manor vested in His Majesty in right of the Crown or the Duchy of Lancaster, nor (subject to subsection (11A) below) to restrictions created or imposed—

    (a)    for naval, military or air force purposes,

    [(b)    for civil aviation purposes under the powers of the Air Navigation Act 1920, of section 19 or 23 of the Civil Aviation Act 1949 or of section 30 or 41 of the Civil Aviation Act 1982].

  (11A)    Subsection (11) of this section—

    (a)    shall exclude the application of this section to a restriction falling within subsection (11)(a), and not created or imposed in connection with the use of any land as an aerodrome, only so long as the restriction is enforceable by or on behalf of the Crown; and

    (b)    shall exclude the application of this section to a restriction falling within subsection (11)(b), or created or imposed in connection with the use of any land as an aerodrome, only so long as the restriction is enforceable by or on behalf of the Crown or any public or international authority.

  (12)    Where a term of more than forty years is created in land (whether before or after the commencement of this Act) this section shall, after the expiration of twenty-five years of the term, apply to restrictions affecting such leasehold land in like manner as it would have applied had the land been freehold:

Provided that this subsection shall not apply to mining leases.]

                                                                           **[14]**

**NOTES**

By virtue of the Law of Property Act 1969, s 28(1), this section has effect as set out in Sch 3 to that Act, incorporating the amendments made by the Landlord and Tenant Act 1954, s 52(1) and by s 28(1)–(9) of the 1969 Act (and the omission of repealed provisions), subject, however, to any other enactments affecting this section and to s 28(11) of the 1969 Act.

Sub-ss (1), (1A)–(1C), (3), (6), (9): words in square brackets substituted by the Transfer of Tribunal Functions (Lands Tribunal and Miscellaneous Amendments) Order 2009, SI 2009/1307, art 5(1), (2), Sch 1, para 5(a), subject to transitional provisions and savings in Sch 5 thereto.

Sub-s (3A): words substituted and words omitted repealed by SI 2009/1307, art 5(1), (2), Sch 1, para 5(b), subject to transitional provisions and savings in Sch 5 thereto.

Sub-s (8): words omitted repealed by the Land Registration Act 2002, ss 133, 135, Sch 11, para 2(1), (5), Sch 13.

Sub-s (11): para (b) substituted by the Civil Aviation Act 1982, s 109, Sch 15, para 1.

**85–138**    ((*Pts III, IV*) *outside the scope of this work.*)

PART V

LEASES AND TENANCIES

### 139  Effect of extinguishment of reversion

  (1)    Where a reversion expectant on a lease of land is surrendered or merged, the estate or interest which as against the lessee for the time being confers the next vested right to the land, shall be deemed the reversion for the purpose of preserving the same incidents and obligations as would have affected the original reversion had there been no surrender or merger thereof.

  (2)    This section applies to surrenders or mergers effected after the first day of October, eighteen hundred and forty-five.

                                                                           **[15]**

### 140  Apportionment of conditions on severance

  (1)    Notwithstanding the severance by conveyance, surrender, or otherwise of the reversionary estate in any land comprised in a lease, and notwithstanding the avoidance or cesser in any other manner of the term granted by a lease as to part only of the land comprised therein, every condition or right of re-entry, and every other condition contained in the lease, shall be apportioned, and shall remain annexed to the severed parts of the reversionary estate as severed, and shall be in force with respect to the term whereon each severed part is reversionary, or the term in the part of the land as to which the term has not been surrendered, or has not been avoided or has not otherwise ceased, in like manner as if the land comprised in each severed part, or the land as to which the term remains subsisting, as the case may be, had alone originally been comprised in the lease.

  (2)    In this section "right of re-entry" includes a right to determine the lease by notice to quit or otherwise; but where the notice is served by a person entitled to a severed part of the reversion so that it extends to part only of the land demised, the lessee may within one month determine the lease in regard to the rest of the land by giving to the owner of the reversionary estate therein a counter notice expiring at the same time as the original notice [ ... ]

(3)   This section applies to leases made before or after the commencement of this Act and whether the severance of the reversionary estate or the partial avoidance or cesser of the term was effected before or after such commencement:

Provided that, where the lease was made before the first day of January eighteen hundred and eighty-two nothing in this section shall affect the operation of a severance of the reversionary estate or partial avoidance or cesser of the term which was effected before the commencement of this Act.

**[16]**

**NOTES**

Sub-s (2): words omitted added by the Law of Property (Amendment) Act 1926, s 2 and repealed by the Agricultural Holdings Act 1948, ss 98, 100(1), Sch 8.

### 141   Rent and benefit of lessee's covenants to run with the reversion

(1)   Rent reserved by a lease, and the benefit of every covenant or provision therein contained, having reference to the subject-matter thereof, and on the lessee's part to be observed or performed, and every condition of re-entry and other condition therein contained, shall be annexed and incident to and shall go with the reversionary estate in the land, or in any part thereof, immediately expectant on the term granted by the lease, notwithstanding severance of that reversionary estate, and without prejudice to any liability affecting a covenantor or his estate.

(2)   Any such rent, covenant or provision shall be capable of being recovered, received, enforced, and taken advantage of, by the person from time to time entitled, subject to the term, to the income of the whole or any part, as the case may require, of the land leased.

(3)   Where that person becomes entitled by conveyance or otherwise, such rent, covenant or provision may be recovered, received, enforced or taken advantage of by him notwithstanding that he becomes so entitled after the condition of re-entry or forfeiture has become enforceable, but this subsection does not render enforceable any condition of re-entry or other condition waived or released before such person becomes entitled as aforesaid.

(4)   This section applies to leases made before or after the commencement of this Act, but does not affect the operation of—

    (a)   any severance of the reversionary estate; or

    (b)   any acquisition by conveyance or otherwise of the right to receive or enforce any rent covenant or provision;

effected before the commencement of this Act.

**[17]**

**NOTES**

Modification: by virtue of the Landlord and Tenant (Covenants) Act 1995, s 30(4)(b) at **[971]**, this section is disapplied in relation to new tenancies (as defined by ss 1, 28(1) of that Act at **[944]**, **[969]**).

### 142   Obligation of lessor's covenants to run with reversion

(1)   The obligation under a condition or of a covenant entered into by a lessor with reference to the subject-matter of the lease shall, if and as far as the lessor has power to bind the reversionary estate immediately expectant on the term granted by the lease, be annexed and incident to and shall go with that reversionary estate, or the several parts thereof, notwithstanding severance of that reversionary estate, and may be taken advantage of and enforced by the person in whom the term is from time to time vested by conveyance, devolution in law, or otherwise; and, if and as far as the lessor has power to bind the person from time to time entitled to that reversionary estate, the obligation aforesaid may be taken advantage of and entered against any person so entitled.

(2)   This section applies to leases made before or after the commencement of this Act, whether the severance of the reversionary estate was effected before or after such commencement:

Provided that, where the lease was made before the first day of January eighteen hundred and eighty-two, nothing in this section shall affect the operation of any severance of the reversionary estate effected before such commencement.

This section takes effect without prejudice to any liability affecting a covenantor or his estate.

**[18]**

**NOTES**

Modification: by virtue of the Landlord and Tenant (Covenants) Act 1995, s 30(4)(b) at **[971]**, this section is disapplied in relation to new tenancies (as defined by ss 1, 28(1) of that Act at **[944]**, **[969]**).

### 143   Effect of licences granted to lessees

(1)   Where a licence is granted to a lessee to do any act, the licence, unless otherwise expressed, extends only—

    (a)   to the permission actually given; or

    (b)   to the specific breach of any provision or covenant referred to; or

    (c)   to any other matter thereby specifically authorised to be done;

and the licence does not prevent any proceeding for any subsequent breach unless otherwise specified in the licence.

(2)   Notwithstanding any such licence—

    (a)   All rights under covenants and powers of re-entry contained in the lease remain in full force and are available as against any subsequent breach of covenant, condition or other matter not specifically authorised or waived, in the same manner as if no licence had been granted; and

    (b)   The condition or right of entry remains in force in all respects as if the licence had not been granted, save in respect of the particular matter authorised to be done.

(3)   Where in any lease there is a power or condition of re-entry on the lessee assigning, subletting or doing any other specified act without a licence, and a licence is granted—

    (a)   to any one of two or more lessees to do any act, or to deal with his equitable share or interest; or

    (b)   to any lessee, or to any one of two or more lessees to assign or underlet part only of the property, or to do any act in respect of part only of the property;

the licence does not operate to extinguish the right of entry in case of any breach of covenant or condition by the co-lessees of the other shares or interests in the property, or by the lessee or lessees of the rest of the property (as the case may be) in respect of such shares or interests or remaining property, but the right of entry remains in force in respect of the shares, interests or property not the subject of the licence.

This subsection does not authorise the grant after the commencement of this Act of a licence to create an undivided share in a legal estate.

(4)   This section applies to licences granted after the thirteenth day of August, eighteen hundred and fifty-nine.

[19]

## 144  No fine to be exacted for licence to assign

In all leases containing a covenant, condition, or agreement against assigning, underletting, or parting with the possession, or disposing of the land or property leased without licence or consent, such covenant, condition, or agreement shall, unless the lease contains an express provision to the contrary, be deemed to be subject to a proviso to the effect that no fine or sum of money in the nature of a fine shall be payable for or in respect of such licence or consent; but this proviso does not preclude the right to require the payment of a reasonable sum in respect of any legal or other expense incurred in relation to such licence or consent.

[20]

## 145  Lessee to give notice of ejectment to lessor

Every lessee to whom there is delivered any writ for the recovery of premises demised to or held by him, or to whose knowledge any such writ comes, shall forthwith give notice thereof to his lessor or his bailiff or receiver, and, if he fails so to do, he shall be liable to forfeit to the person of whom he holds the premises an amount equal to the value of three years' improved or rack rent of the premises, to be recovered by action in any court having jurisdiction in respect of claims for such an amount.

[21]

## 146  Restrictions on and relief against forfeiture of leases and underleases

(1)   A right of re-entry or forfeiture under any proviso or stipulation in a lease for a breach of any covenant or condition in the lease shall not be enforceable, by action or otherwise, unless and until the lessor serves on the lessee a notice—

    (a)   specifying the particular breach complained of; and

    (b)   if the breach is capable of remedy, requiring the lessee to remedy the breach; and

    (c)   in any case, requiring the lessee to make compensation in money for the breach;

and the lessee fails, within a reasonable time thereafter, to remedy the breach, if it is capable of remedy, and to make reasonable compensation in money, to the satisfaction of the lessor, for the breach.

(2)   Where a lessor is proceeding, by action or otherwise, to enforce such a right of re-entry or forfeiture, the lessee may, in the lessor's action, if any, or in any action brought by himself, apply to the court for relief; and the court may grant or refuse relief, as the court, having regard to the proceedings and conduct of the parties under the foregoing provisions of this section, and to all the other circumstances, thinks fit; and in case of relief may grant it on such terms, if any, as to costs, expenses, damages, compensation, penalty, or otherwise, including the granting of an injunction to restrain any like breach in the future, as the court, in the circumstances of each case, thinks fit.

(3)    A lessor shall be entitled to recover as a debt due to him from a lessee, and in addition to damages (if any), all reasonable costs and expenses properly incurred by the lessor in the employment of a solicitor and surveyor or valuer, or otherwise, in reference to any breach giving rise to a right of re-entry or forfeiture which, at the request of the lessee, is waived by the lessor, or from which the lessee is relieved, under the provisions of this Act.

(4)    Where a lessor is proceeding by action or otherwise to enforce a right of re-entry or forfeiture under any covenant, proviso, or stipulation in a lease, or for non-payment of rent, the court may, on application by any person claiming as under-lessee any estate or interest in the property comprised in the lease or any part thereof, either in the lessor's action (if any) or in any action brought by such person for that purpose, make an order vesting, for the whole term of the lease or any less term, the property comprised in the lease or any part thereof in any person entitled as under-lessee to any estate or interest in such property upon such conditions as to execution of any deed or other document, payment of rent, costs, expenses, damages, compensation, giving security, or otherwise, as the court in the circumstances of each case may think fit, but in no case shall any such under-lessee be entitled to require a lease to be granted to him for any longer term than he had under his original sub-lease.

(5)    For the purposes of this section—
   (a)    "Lease" includes an original or derivative under-lease; also an agreement for a lease where the lessee has become entitled to have his lease granted; also a grant at a fee farm rent, or securing a rent by condition;
   (b)    "Lessee" includes an original or derivative under-lessee, and the persons deriving title under a lessee; also a grantee under any such grant as aforesaid and the persons deriving title under him;
   (c)    "Lessor" includes an original or derivative under-lessor, and the persons deriving title under a lessor; also a person making such grant as aforesaid and the persons deriving title under him;
   (d)    "Under-lease" includes an agreement for an underlease where the underlessee has become entitled to have his underlease granted;
   (e)    "Underlessee" includes any person deriving title under an underlessee.

(6)    This section applies although the proviso or stipulation under which the right of re-entry or forfeiture accrues is inserted in the lease in pursuance of the directions of any Act of Parliament.

(7)    For the purposes of this section a lease limited to continue as long only as the lessee abstains from committing a breach of covenant shall be and take effect as a lease to continue for any longer term for which it could subsist, but determinable by a proviso for re-entry on such a breach.

(8)    This section does not extend—
   (i)    To a covenant or condition against assigning, underletting, parting with the possession, or disposing of the land leased where the breach occurred before the commencement of this Act; or
   (ii)   In the case of a mining lease, to a covenant or condition for allowing the lessor to have access to or inspect books, accounts, records, weighing machines or other things, or to enter or inspect the mine or the workings thereof.

(9)    This section does not apply to a condition for forfeiture on the bankruptcy of the lessee or on taking in execution of the lessee's interest if contained in a lease of—
   (a)    Agricultural or pastoral land;
   (b)    Mines or minerals;
   (c)    A house used or intended to be used as a public-house or beershop;
   (d)    A house let as a dwelling-house, with the use of any furniture, books, works of art, or other chattels not being in the nature of fixtures;
   (e)    Any property with respect to which the personal qualifications of the tenant are of importance for the preservation of the value or character of the property, or on the ground of neighbourhood to the lessor, or to any person holding under him.

(10)    Where a condition of forfeiture on the bankruptcy of the lessee or on taking in execution of the lessee's interest is contained in any lease, other than a lease of any of the classes mentioned in the last subsection, then—
   (a)    if the lessee's interest is sold within one year from the bankruptcy or taking in execution, this section applies to the forfeiture condition aforesaid;
   (b)    if the lessee's interest is not sold before the expiration of that year, this section only applies to the forfeiture condition aforesaid during the first year from the date of the bankruptcy or taking in execution.

(11)    This section does not, save as otherwise mentioned, affect the law relating to re-entry or forfeiture or relief in case of non-payment of rent.

(12)    This section has effect notwithstanding any stipulation to the contrary.

[(13)    The county court has jurisdiction under this section ... ]

NOTES
Sub-s (13): added by the County Courts Act 1984, s 148(1), Sch 2, Pt II, para 5; words omitted repealed by the High Court and County Courts Jurisdiction Order 1991, SI 1991/724, art 2(8), Schedule, Pt I.

## 147 Relief against notice to effect decorative repairs

(1)    After a notice is served on a lessee relating to the internal decorative repairs to a house or other building, he may apply to the court for relief, and if, having regard to all the circumstances of the case (including in particular the length of the lessee's term or interest remaining unexpired), the court is satisfied that the notice is unreasonable, it may, by order, wholly or partially relieve the lessee from liability for such repairs.

(2)    This section does not apply:—
    (i)    where the liability arises under an express covenant or agreement to put the property in a decorative state of repair and the covenant or agreement has never been performed;
    (ii)    to any matter necessary or proper—
        (a)    for putting or keeping the property in a sanitary condition, or
        (b)    for the maintenance or preservation of the structure;
    (iii)    to any statutory liability to keep a house in all respects reasonably fit for human habitation;
    (iv)    to any covenant or stipulation to yield up the house or other building in a specified state of repair at the end of the term.

(3)    In this section "lease" includes an underlease and an agreement for a lease, and "lessee" has a corresponding meaning and includes any person liable to effect the repairs.

(4)    This section applies whether the notice is served before or after the commencement of this Act, and has effect notwithstanding any stipulation to the contrary.

[(5)    The county court has jurisdiction under this section … ]

[23]

NOTES
Sub-s (5): added by the County Courts Act 1984, s 148(1), Sch 2, Pt II, para 6; words omitted repealed by the High Court and County Courts Jurisdiction Order 1991, SI 1991/724, art 2(8), Schedule, Pt I.

## 148 Waiver of a covenant in a lease

(1)    Where any actual waiver by a lessor or the persons deriving title under him of the benefit of any covenant or condition in any lease is proved to have taken place in any particular instance, such waiver shall not be deemed to extend to any instance, or to any breach of covenant or condition save that to which such waiver specially relates, nor operate as a general waiver of the benefit of any such covenant or condition.

(2)    This section applies unless a contrary intention appears and extends to waivers effected after the twenty-third day of July, eighteen hundred and sixty.

[24]

## 149 Abolition of interesse termini, and as to reversionary leases and leases for lives

(1)    The doctrine of interesse termini is hereby abolished.

(2)    As from the commencement of this Act all terms of years absolute shall, whether the interest is created before or after such commencement, be capable of taking effect at law or in equity, according to the estate interest or powers of the grantor, from the date fixed for commencement of the term, without actual entry.

(3)    A term, at a rent or granted in consideration of a fine, limited after the commencement of this Act to take effect more than twenty-one years from the date of the instrument purporting to create it, shall be void, and any contract made after such commencement to create such a term shall likewise be void: but this subsection does not apply to any term taking effect in equity under a settlement, or created out of an equitable interest under a settlement, or under an equitable power for mortgage, indemnity or other like purposes.

(4)    Nothing in subsections (1) and (2) of this section prejudicially affects the right of any person to recover any rent or to enforce or take advantage of any covenants or conditions or, as respects terms or interests created before the commencement of this Act, operates to vary any statutory or other obligations imposed in respect of such terms or interests.

(5)    Nothing in this Act affects the rule of law that a legal term, whether or not being a mortgage term, may be created to take effect in reversion expectant on a longer term, which rule is hereby confirmed.

(6)    Any lease or underlease, at a rent, or in consideration of a fine, for life or lives or for any term of years determinable with life or lives, or on the marriage of the lessee, [or on the formation of a civil partnership between the lessee and another person,] or any contract therefor, made before or

after the commencement of this Act, or created by virtue of Part V of the Law of Property Act 1922, shall take effect as a lease, underlease or contract therefor, for a term of ninety years determinable [after (as the case may be) the death or marriage of, or the formation of a civil partnership by, the original lessee or the survivor of the original lessees,] by at least one month's notice in writing given to determine the same on one of the quarter days applicable to the tenancy, either by the lessor or the persons deriving title under him, to the person entitled to the leasehold interest, or if no such person is in existence by affixing the same to the premises, or by the lessee or other persons in whom the leasehold interest is vested to the lessor or the persons deriving title under him:

Provided that—

   (a)   this subsection shall not apply to any term taking effect in equity under a settlement or created out of an equitable interest under a settlement for mortgage, indemnity, or other like purposes;

   (b)   the person in whom the leasehold interest is vested by virtue of Part V of the Law of Property Act 1922, shall, for the purposes of this subsection, be deemed an original lessee;

   (c)   if the lease, underlease, or contract therefor is made determinable on the dropping of the lives of persons other than or besides the lessees, then the notice shall be capable of being served after the death of any person or of the survivor of any persons (whether or not including the lessees) on the cesser of whose life or lives the lease, underlease, or contract is made determinable, instead of after the death of the original lessee or of the survivor of the original lessees;

   (d)   if there are no quarter days specially applicable to the tenancy, notice may be given to determine the tenancy on one of the usual quarter days.

[(7)   Subsection (8) applies where a lease, underlease or contract—

   (a)   relates to commonhold land, and

   (b)   would take effect by virtue of subsection (6) as a lease, underlease or contract of the kind mentioned in that subsection.

(8)   The lease, underlease or contract shall be treated as if it purported to be a lease, underlease or contract of the kind referred to in subsection (7)(b) (and sections 17 and 18 of the Commonhold and Leasehold Reform Act 2002 (residential and non-residential leases) shall apply accordingly).]

**[25]**

**NOTES**

Sub-s (6): words in first pair of square brackets inserted and words in second pair of square brackets substituted by the Civil Partnership Act 2004, s 81, Sch 8, para 1.

Sub-ss (7), (8): added by the Commonhold and Leasehold Reform Act 2002, s 68, Sch 5, para 3.

**150   Surrender of a lease, without prejudice to underleases with a view to the grant of a new lease**

(1)   A lease may be surrendered with a view to the acceptance of a new lease in place thereof, without a surrender of any under-lease derived thereout.

(2)   A new lease may be granted and accepted, in place of any lease so surrendered, without any such surrender of an under-lease as aforesaid, and the new lease operates as if all under-leases derived out of the surrendered lease had been surrendered before the surrender of that lease was effected.

(3)   The lessee under the new lease and any person deriving title under him is entitled to the same rights and remedies in respect of the rent reserved by and the covenants, agreements and conditions contained in any under-lease as if the original lease had not been surrendered but was or remained vested in him.

(4)   Each under-lessee and any person deriving title under him is entitled to hold and enjoy the land comprised in his under-lease (subject to the payment of any rent reserved by and to the observance of the covenants agreements and conditions contained in the under-lease) as if the lease out of which the under-lease was derived had not been surrendered.

(5)   The lessor granting the new lease and any person deriving title under him is entitled to the same remedies, *by distress or* entry in and upon the land comprised in any such under-lease for rent reserved by or for breach of any covenant, agreement or condition contained in the new lease (so far only as the rents reserved by or the covenants, agreements or conditions contained in the new lease do not exceed or impose greater burdens than those reserved by or contained in the original lease out of which the under-lease is derived) as he would have had—

   (a)   If the original lease had remained on foot; or

   (b)   If a new under-lease derived out of the new lease had been granted to the under-lessee or a person deriving title under him;

as the case may require.

(6)   This section does not affect the powers of the court to give relief against forfeiture.

**[26]**

PART I
STATUTES

**NOTES**

Sub-s (5): for the words in italics there are substituted the words "under section 72(1) of the Tribunals, Courts and Enforcement Act 2007 (commercial rent arrears recovery) or by" by the Tribunals, Courts and Enforcement Act 2007, s 86, Sch 14, paras 21, 24, as from a day to be appointed.

## 151 Provision as to attornments by tenants

(1)   Where land is subject to a lease—
    (a)    the conveyance of a reversion in the land expectant on the determination of the lease; or
    (b)    the creation or conveyance of a rentcharge to issue or issuing out of the land; shall be valid without any attornment of the lessee:
    Nothing in this subsection—
        (i)    affects the validity of any payment of rent by the lessee to the person making the conveyance or grant before notice of the conveyance or grant is given to him by the person entitled thereunder; or
        (ii)    renders the lessee liable for any breach of covenant to pay rent, on account of his failure to pay rent to the person entitled under the conveyance or grant before such notice is given to the lessee.

(2)   An attornment by the lessee in respect of any land to a person claiming to be entitled to the interest in the land of the lessor, if made without the consent of the lessor, shall be void.

This subsection does not apply to an attornment—
    (a)    made pursuant to a judgment of a court of competent jurisdiction; or
    (b)    to a mortgagee, by a lessee holding under a lease from the mortgagor where the right of redemption is barred; or
    (c)    to any other person rightfully deriving title under the lessor.

[27]

## 152 Leases invalidated by reason of non-compliance with terms of powers under which they are granted

(1)   Where in the intended exercise of any power of leasing, whether conferred by an Act of Parliament or any other instrument, a lease (in this section referred to as an invalid lease) is granted, which by reason of any failure to comply with the terms of the power is invalid, then—
    (a)    as against the person entitled after the determination of the interest of the grantor to the reversion; or
    (b)    as against any other person who, subject to any lease properly granted under the power, would have been entitled to the land comprised in the lease;
the lease, if it was made in good faith, and the lessee has entered thereunder, shall take effect in equity as a contract for the grant, at the request of the lessee, of a valid lease under the power, of like effect as the invalid lease, subject to such variations as may be necessary in order to comply with the terms of the power:

Provided that a lessee under an invalid lease shall not, by virtue of any such implied contract, be entitled to obtain a variation of the lease if the other persons who would have been bound by the contract are willing and able to confirm the lease without variation.

(2)   Where a lease granted in the intended exercise of such a power is invalid by reason of the grantor not having power to grant the lease at the date thereof, but the grantor's interest in the land comprised therein continues after the time when he might, in the exercise of the power, have properly granted a lease in the like terms, the lease shall take effect as a valid lease in like manner as if it had been granted at that time.

(3)   Where during the continuance of the possession taken under an invalid lease the person for the time being entitled, subject to such possession, to the land comprised therein or to the rents and profits thereof, is able to confirm the lease without variation, the lessee, or other person who would have been bound by the lease had it been valid, shall, at the request of the person so able to confirm the lease, be bound to accept a confirmation thereof, and thereupon the lease shall have effect and be deemed to have had effect as a valid lease from the grant thereof.

Confirmation under this subsection may be by a memorandum in writing signed by or on behalf of the persons respectively confirming and accepting the confirmation of the lease.

(4)   Where a receipt or a memorandum in writing confirming an invalid lease is, upon or before the acceptance of rent thereunder, signed by or on behalf of the person accepting the rent, that acceptance shall, as against that person, be deemed to be a confirmation of the lease.

(5)   The foregoing provisions of this section do not affect prejudicially—
    (a)    any right of action or other right or remedy to which, but for those provisions or any enactment replaced by those provisions, the lessee named in an invalid lease would or might have been entitled under any covenant on the part of the grantor for title or quiet enjoyment contained therein or implied thereby; or
    (b)    any right of re-entry or other right or remedy to which, but for those provisions or any

enactment replaced thereby, the grantor or other person for the time being entitled to the reversion expectant on the termination of the lease, would or might have been entitled by reason of any breach of the covenants, conditions or provisions contained in the lease and binding on the lessee.

(6)    Where a valid power of leasing is vested in or may be exercised by a person who grants a lease which, by reason of the determination of the interest of the grantor or otherwise, cannot have effect and continuance according to the terms thereof independently of the power, the lease shall for the purposes of this section be deemed to have been granted in the intended exercise of the power although the power is not referred to in the lease.

(7)    This section does not apply to a lease of land held on charitable, ecclesiastical or public trusts.

(8)    This section takes effect without prejudice to the provision in this Act for the grant of leases in the name and on behalf of the estate owner of the land affected.

**[28]**

### 153   Enlargement of residue of long terms into fee simple estates

(1)    Where a residue unexpired of not less than two hundred years of a term, which, as originally created, was for not less than three hundred years, is subsisting in land, whether being the whole land originally comprised in the term, or part only thereof,—

    (a)    without any trust or right of redemption affecting the term in favour of the freeholder, or other person entitled in reversion expectant on the term; and

    (b)    without any rent, or with merely a peppercorn rent or other rent having no money value, incident to the reversion, or having had a rent, not being merely a peppercorn rent or other rent having no money value, originally so incident, which subsequently has been released or has become barred by lapse of time, or has in any other way ceased to be payable;

the term may be enlarged into a fee simple in the manner, and subject to the restrictions in this section provided.

(2)    This section applies to and includes every such term as aforesaid whenever created, whether or not having the freehold as the immediate reversion thereon; but does not apply to—

    (i)    Any term liable to be determined by re-entry for condition broken; or

    (ii)   Any term created by subdemise out of a superior term, itself incapable of being enlarged into fee simple.

(3)    This section extends to mortgage terms, where the right of redemption is barred.

(4)    A rent not exceeding the yearly sum of one pound which has not been collected or paid for a continuous period of twenty years or upwards shall, for the purposes of this section, be deemed to have ceased to be payable:

    ...

(5)    Where a rent incident to a reversion expectant on a term to which this section applies is deemed to have ceased to be payable for the purposes aforesaid, no claim for such rent or for any arrears thereof shall be capable of being enforced.

(6)    Each of the following persons, namely—

    (i)    Any person beneficially entitled in right of the term, whether subject to any incumbrance or not, to possession of any land comprised in the term, and, in the case of a married woman without the concurrence of her husband, whether or not she is entitled for her separate use or as her separate property ... ;

    (ii)   Any person being in receipt of income as trustee, in right of the term, or having the term vested in him [as a trustee of land], whether subject to any incumbrance or not;

    (iii)  Any person in whom, as personal representative of any deceased person, the term is vested, whether subject to any incumbrance or not;

shall, so far as regards the land to which he is entitled, or in which he is interested in right of the term, in any such character as aforesaid, have power by deed to declare to the effect that, from and after the execution of the deed, the term shall be enlarged into a fee simple.

(7)    Thereupon, by virtue of the deed and of this Act, the term shall become and be enlarged accordingly, and the person in whom the term was previously vested shall acquire and have in the land a fee simple instead of the term.

(8)    The estate in fee simple so acquired by enlargement shall be subject to all the same trusts, powers, executory limitations over, rights and equities, and to all the same covenants and provisions relating to user and enjoyment, and to all the same obligations of every kind, as the term would have been subject to if it had not been so enlarged.

(9)    But where—

    (a)    any land so held for the residue of a term has been settled in trust by reference to other land, being freehold land, so as to go along with that other land, or, in the case of settlements coming into operation before the commencement of this Act, so as to go along with that other land as far as the law permits; and

(b)  at the time of enlargement, the ultimate beneficial interest in the term, whether subject to any subsisting particular estate or not, has not become absolutely and indefeasibly vested in any person, free from charges or powers of charging created by a settlement;

the estate in fee simple acquired as aforesaid shall, without prejudice to any conveyance for value previously made by a person having a contingent or defeasible interest in the term, be liable to be, and shall be, conveyed by means of a subsidiary vesting instrument and settled in like manner as the other land, being freehold land, aforesaid, and until so conveyed and settled shall devolve beneficially as if it had been so conveyed and settled.

(10)  The estate in fee simple so acquired shall, whether the term was originally created without impeachment of waste or not, include the fee simple in all mines and minerals which at the time of enlargement have not been severed in right or in fact, or have not been severed or reserved by an inclosure Act or award.

[29]

**NOTES**

Sub-s (4): words omitted repealed by the Statute Law (Repeals) Act 2004.
Sub-s (6): words omitted from para (i) repealed by the Married Women (Restraint upon Anticipation) Act 1949, s 1, Sch 2; words in square brackets in para (ii) substituted by the Trusts of Land and Appointment of Trustees Act 1996, s 25(1), Sch 3, para 4(1), (16), subject to savings in ss 3, 18(3), 25(5) of that Act.

## 154  Application Part V to existing leases

This part of this Act, except where otherwise expressly provided, applies to leases created before or after the commencement of this Act, and "lease" includes an under-lease or other tenancy.

[30]

**155–179**  ((Pts VI–X) outside the scope of this work.)

## PART XI
## MISCELLANEOUS

**180–195**  (Ss 180–190, 192–195 outside the scope of this work; s 191 repealed by the Rentcharges Act 1977, s 17(2), Sch 2.)

*Notices*

## 196  Regulations respecting notices

(1)  Any notice required or authorised to be served or given by this Act shall be in writing.

(2)  Any notice required or authorised by this Act to be served on a lessee or mortgagor shall be sufficient, although only addressed to the lessee or mortgagor by that designation, without his name, or generally to the persons interested, without any name, and notwithstanding that any person to be affected by the notice is absent, under disability, unborn, or unascertained.

(3)  Any notice required or authorised by this Act to be served shall be sufficiently served if it is left at the last-known place of abode or business in the United Kingdom of the lessee, lessor, mortgagee, mortgagor, or other person to be served, or, in case of a notice required or authorised to be served on a lessee or mortgagor, is affixed or left for him on the land or any house or building comprised in the lease or mortgage, or, in case of a mining lease, is left for the lessee at the office or counting-house of the mine.

(4)  Any notice required or authorised by this Act to be served shall also be sufficiently served, if it is sent by post in a registered letter addressed to the lessee, lessor, mortgagee, mortgagor, or other person to be served, by name, at the aforesaid place of abode or business, office, or counting-house, and if that letter is not returned [by the postal operator (within the meaning of the Postal Services Act 2000) concerned] undelivered; and that service shall be deemed to be made at the time at which the registered letter would in the ordinary course be delivered.

(5)  The provisions of this section shall extend to notices required to be served by any instrument affecting property executed or coming into operation after the commencement of this Act unless a contrary intention appears.

(6)  This section does not apply to notices served in proceedings in the court.

[31]

**NOTES**

Sub-s (4): words in square brackets substituted by the Postal Services Act 2000 (Consequential Modifications No 1) Order 2001, SI 2001/1149, art 3(1), Sch 1, para 7.

Modification: the reference to last known place of abode or business in sub-ss (3), (4) above is modified in its application to notices served by a tenant on a landlord of premises to which the Landlord and Tenant Act 1987, Pt VI applies by virtue of s 49 of that Act at **[708]**.

**197–200**   (*S 197 spent for certain purposes and repealed for certain purposes by the Law of Property Act 1969, s 16, Sch 2, Pt I and the Middlesex Deeds Act 1940, s 1; ss 198–200 outside the scope of this work.*)

## PART XII
## CONSTRUCTION, JURISDICTION, AND GENERAL PROVISIONS

**201–204**   (*Outside the scope of this work.*)

### 205   General definitions

(1)   In this Act unless the context otherwise requires, the following expressions have the meanings hereby assigned to them respectively, that is to say:—

(i)   "Bankruptcy" includes liquidation by arrangement; also in relation to a corporation means the winding up thereof;

(ii)   "Conveyance" includes a mortgage, charge, lease, assent, vesting declaration, vesting instrument, disclaimer, release and every other assurance of property or of an interest therein by any instrument, except a will; "convey" has a corresponding meaning; and "disposition" includes a conveyance and also a devise, bequest, or an appointment of property contained in a will; and "dispose of" has a corresponding meaning;

(iii)   "Building purposes" include the erecting and improving of, and the adding to, and the repairing of buildings; and a "building lease" is a lease for building purposes or purposes connected therewith;

[(iiiA)   … ]

(iv)   "Death duty" means estate duty, … and every other duty leviable or payable on a death;

(v)   "Estate owner" means the owner of a legal estate, but an infant is not capable of being an estate owner;

(vi)   "Gazette" means the London Gazette;

(vii)   "Incumbrance" includes a legal or equitable mortgage and a trust for securing money, and a lien, and a charge of a portion, annuity, or other capital or annual sum; and "incumbrancer" has a meaning corresponding with that of incumbrance, and includes every person entitled to the benefit of an incumbrance, or to require payment or discharge thereof;

(viii)   "Instrument" does not include a statute, unless the statute creates a settlement;

(ix)   "Land" includes land of any tenure, and mines and minerals, whether or not held apart from the surface, buildings or parts of buildings (whether the division is horizontal, vertical or made in any other way) and other corporeal hereditaments; also a manor, an advowson, and a rent and other incorporeal hereditaments, and an easement, right, privilege, or benefit in, over, or derived from land; … ; and "mines and minerals" include any strata or seam of minerals or substances in or under any land, and powers of working and getting the same … ; and "manor" includes a lordship, and reputed manor or lordship; and "hereditament" means any real property which on an intestacy occurring before the commencement of this Act might have devolved upon an heir;

(x)   "Legal estates" mean the estates, interests and charges, in or over land (subsisting or created at law) which are by this Act authorised to subsist or to be created as legal estates; "equitable interests" mean all the other interests and charges in or over land … ; an equitable interest "capable of subsisting as a legal estate" means such as could validly subsist or be created as a legal estate under this Act;

(xi)   "Legal powers" include the powers vested in a chargee by way of legal mortgage or in an estate owner under which a legal estate can be transferred or created; and "equitable powers" mean all the powers in or over land under which equitable interests or powers only can be transferred or created;

(xii)   "Limitation Acts" means the Real Property Limitation Acts 1833, 1837 and 1874, and "limitation" includes a trust;

[(xiii)   … ]

(xiv)   a "mining lease" means a lease for mining purposes, that is, the searching for, winning, working, getting, making merchantable, carrying away, or disposing of mines and minerals, or purposes connected therewith, and includes a grant or licence for mining purposes;

(xv)   "Minister" means [the Minister of Agriculture, Fisheries and Food];

(xvi)   "Mortgage" includes any charge or lien on any property for securing money or money's worth; "legal mortgage" means a mortgage by demise or subdemise or a charge by way of legal mortgage and "legal mortgagee" has a corresponding meaning; "mortgage money" means money or money's worth secured by a mortgage; "mortgagor" includes any person from time to time deriving title under the original mortgagor or entitled to redeem a mortgage according to his estate interest or right in the mortgaged property; "mortgagee" includes a chargee by way of legal mortgage and any person from time to time deriving title under the original mortgagee; and "mortgagee in possession" is, for the purposes of this Act, a mortgagee who, in right of the mortgage, has entered into and is in possession of the mortgaged property; and "right of redemption" includes an option to repurchase only if the option in effect creates a right of redemption;

(xvii)  "Notice" includes constructive notice;

(xviii)  "Personal representative" means the executor, original or by representation, or administrator for the time being of a deceased person, and as regards any liability for the payment of death duties includes any person who takes possession of or intermeddles with the property of a deceased person without the authority of the personal representatives or the court;

(xix)  "Possession" includes receipt of rents and profits or the right to receive the same, if any; and "income" includes rents and profits;

(xx)  "Property" includes any thing in action, and any interest in real or personal property;

(xxi)  "Purchaser" means a purchaser in good faith for valuable consideration and includes a lessee, mortgagee or other person who for valuable consideration acquires an interest in property except that in Part I of this Act and elsewhere where so expressly provided "purchaser" only means a person who acquires an interest in or charge on property for money or money's worth; and in reference to a legal estate includes a chargee by way of legal mortgage; and where the context so requires "purchaser" includes an intending purchaser; "purchase" has a meaning corresponding with that of "purchaser"; and "valuable consideration" includes marriage[, and formation of a civil partnership,] but does not include a nominal consideration in money;

(xxii)  "Registered land" has the same meaning as in the [Land Registration Act 2002;] …

(xxiii)  "Rent" includes a rent service or a rentcharge, or other rent, toll, duty, royalty, or annual or periodical payment in money or money's worth, reserved or issuing out of or charged upon land, but does not include mortgage interest; "rentcharge" includes a fee farm rent; "fine" includes a premium or foregift and any payment, consideration, or benefit in the nature of a fine, premium or foregift; "lessor" includes an underlessor and a person deriving title under a lessor or underlessor; and "lessee" includes an underlessee and a person deriving title under a lessee or underlessee, and "lease" includes an underlease or other tenancy;

(xxiv)  "Sale" includes an extinguishment of manorial incidents, but in other respects means a sale properly so called;

(xxv)  "Securities" include stocks, funds and shares

(xxvi)  "Tenant for life", "statutory owner", "settled land", "settlement", "vesting deed", "subsidiary vesting deed", "vesting order", "vesting instrument", "trust instrument", "capital money" and "trustees of the settlement" have the same meanings as in the Settled Land Act 1925;

(xxvii)  "Term of years absolute" means a term of years (taking effect either in possession or in reversion whether or not at a rent) with or without impeachment for waste, subject or not to another legal estate, and either certain or liable to determination by notice, re-entry, operation of law, or by a provision for cesser on redemption, or in any other event (other than the dropping of a life, or the determination of a determinable life interest); but does not include any term of years determinable with life or lives or with the cesser of a determinable life interest, nor, if created after the commencement of this Act, a term of years which is not expressed to take effect in possession within twenty-one years after the creation thereof where required by this Act to take effect within that period; and in this definition the expression "term of years" includes a term for less than a year, or for a year or years and a fraction of a year or from year to year;

(xxviii)  "Trust Corporation" means the Public Trustee or a corporation either appointed by the court in any particular case to be a trustee or entitled by rules made under subsection (3) of section four of the Public Trustee Act 1906 to act as custodian trustee;

(xxix)  "Trust for sale", in relation to land, means an immediate … trust for sale, whether or not exercisable at the request or with the consent of any person, … ; "trustees for sale" mean the persons (including a personal representative) holding land on trust for sale; …

(xxx)  "United Kingdom" means Great Britain and Northern Ireland;

(xxxi)  "Will" includes codicil.

[(1A)  Any reference in this Act to money being paid into court shall be construed as referring to the money being paid into the [Senior Courts] or any other court that has jurisdiction, and any reference in this Act to the court, in a context referring to the investment or application of money paid into court, shall be construed, in the case of money paid into the [Senior Courts], as referring to the High Court, and in the case of money paid into another court, as referring to that other court.]

(2)  Where an equitable interest in or power over property arises by statute or operation of law, references to the creation of an interest or power include references to any interest or power so arising.

(3)   References to registration under the Land Charges Act 1925 apply to any registration made under any other statute which is by the Land Charges Act 1925 to have effect as if the registration had been made under that Act.

[32]

**NOTES**

Sub-s (1): para (iiiA) inserted by the County Courts Act 1984, s 148(1), Sch 2, para 9, and repealed by the High Court and County Courts Jurisdiction Order 1991, SI 1991/724, art 2(8), Schedule, Pt I; in para (iv) words omitted repealed by the Finance Act 1949, s 52(9), (10), Sch 11, Pt IV; in paras (ix), (x), (xxix) words omitted repealed by the Trusts of Land and Appointment of Trustees Act 1996, s 25(2), Sch 4, for savings see ss 3, 18(3), 25(5) of that Act; para (xiii) substituted by the Mental Health Act 1959, s 149(1), Sch 7, Pt I and repealed by the Mental Capacity Act 2005, s 67(1), (2), Sch 6, para 4(1), (3), Sch 7; in para (xv) words in square brackets substituted by virtue of the Transfer of Functions (Ministry of Food) Order 1955, SI 1955/554; in para (xxi) words in square brackets inserted by the Civil Partnership Act 2004, s 261(1), Sch 27, para 7; in para (xxii) words in square brackets substituted and words omitted repealed by the Land Registration Act 2002, ss 133, 135, Sch 11, para 2(1), (13), Sch 13.

Sub-s (1A): inserted by the Administration of Justice Act 1965, ss 17, 18, Sch 1; words in square brackets substituted by the Constitutional Reform Act 2005, s 59(5), Sch 11, Pt 2, para 4(1), (3).

Modification: definition "Trust corporation" modified in relation to charities, by the Charities Act 1993, s 35.

County Courts Act 1959, s 192: see now the County Courts Act 1984, s 145.

Real Property Limitation Acts 1833, 1837 and 1874: see now the Limitation Act 1980.

Mental Health Act 1959, Pt VIII: repealed by (with the exception of s 120), and replaced by the Mental Health Act 1983.

Land Charges Act 1925: see now the Land Charges Act 1972 and the Local Land Charges Act 1975.

**206, 207**   (*S 206 repealed by the Statute Law (Repeals) Act 2004; s 207 outside the scope of this work.*)

**208   Application to the Crown**

(1)   Nothing in this Act shall be construed as rendering any property of the Crown subject to distress, or liable to be taken or disposed of by means of any distress.

(2)   This Act shall not in any manner (save as otherwise expressly provided and except so far as it relates to undivided shares, joint ownership, leases for lives or leases for years terminable with life or marriage) affect or alter the descent, devolution or tenure or the nature of the estates and interests of or in any land for the time being vested in His Majesty either in right of the Crown or of the Duchy of Lancaster or of or in any land for the time being belonging to the Duchy of Cornwall and held in right or in respect of the said Duchy, but so nevertheless that after the commencement of this Act, no estates, interests or charges in or over any such lands as aforesaid shall be conveyed or created, except such estates, interests or charges as are capable under this Act of subsisting or of being conveyed or created.

(3)   Subject as aforesaid the provisions of this Act bind the Crown.

[33]

**209   Short title, commencement, extent**

(1)   This Act may be cited as the Law of Property Act 1925.

(2)   …

(3)   This Act extends to England and Wales only.

[34]

**NOTES**

Sub-s (2): repealed by the Statute Law Revision Act 1950.

SCHEDULES

(*Sch 1 outside the scope of this work.*)

SECOND SCHEDULE
IMPLIED COVENANTS
Sections 76, 77

(*Parts I–VI repealed by the Law of Property (Miscellaneous Provisions) Act 1994, ss 10(1), 21(2), Sch 2, as regards dispositions of property made on or after 1 July 1995.*)

PART VII
COVENANT IMPLIED IN A CONVEYANCE FOR VALUABLE CONSIDERATION, OTHER THAN A MORTGAGE, OF THE ENTIRETY OF LAND AFFECTED BY A RENTCHARGE

That the grantees or the persons deriving title under them will at all times, from the date of the conveyance or other date therein stated, duly pay the said rentcharge and observe and perform all the covenants, agreements and conditions contained in the deed or other document creating the rentcharge, and thenceforth on the part of the owner of the land to be observed and performed:

And also will at all times, from the date aforesaid, save harmless and keep indemnified the conveying parties and their respective estates and effects, from and against all proceedings, costs, claims and expenses on account of any omission to pay the said rentcharge or any part thereof, or any breach of any of the said covenants, agreements and conditions.

[35]

### PART VIII
### COVENANTS IMPLIED IN A CONVEYANCE FOR VALUABLE CONSIDERATION, OTHER THAN A MORTGAGE, OR PART OF LAND AFFECTED BY A RENTCHARGE, SUBJECT TO A PART (NOT LEGALLY APPORTIONED) OF THAT RENTCHARGE

(i)   That the grantees, or the persons deriving title under them, will at all times, from the date of the conveyance or other date therein stated, pay the apportioned rent and observe and perform all the covenants (other than the covenant to pay the entire rent) and conditions contained in the deed or other document creating the rentcharge, so far as the same relate to the land conveyed:

And also will at all times, from the date aforesaid, save harmless and keep indemnified the conveying parties and their respective estates and effects, from and against all proceedings, costs, claims and expenses on account of any omission to pay the said apportioned rent, or any breach of any of the said covenants and conditions, so far as the same relate as aforesaid.

(ii)   That the conveying parties, or the persons deriving title under them, will at all times, from the date of the conveyance or other date therein stated, pay the balance of the rentcharge (after deducting the apportioned rent aforesaid, and any other rents similarly apportioned in respect of land not retained), and observe and perform all the covenants, other than the covenant to pay the entire rent, and conditions contained in the deed or other document creating the rentcharge, so far as the same relate to the land not included in the conveyance and remaining vested in the covenantors:

And also will at all times, from the date aforesaid, save harmless and keep indemnified the grantees and their estates and effects, from and against all proceedings, costs, claims and expenses on account of any omission to pay the aforesaid balance of the rentcharge, or any breach of any of the said covenants and conditions so far as they relate aforesaid.

[36]

*(Parts IX, X repealed by the Landlord and Tenant (Covenants) Act 1995, s 30(2), (3), Sch 2, except in relation to tenancies which are not new tenancies (as defined by ss 1, 28(1) of that Act at* **[944]**, **[969]**.)

*(Schs 3, 4 outside the scope of this work; Schs 5, 6 repealed by the Statute Law (Repeals) Act 2004; Sch 7 repealed by the Statute Law Revision Act 1950.)*

# ACCOMMODATION AGENCIES ACT 1953

## (1 & 2 Eliz 2 c 23)

*An Act to prohibit the taking of certain commissions in dealings with persons seeking houses or flats to let and the unauthorised advertisement for letting of houses and flats*

[14 July 1953]

### 1   Illegal commissions and advertisements

(1)   Subject to the provisions of this section, any person who, ... —

    (a)   demands or accepts payment of any sum of money in consideration of registering, or undertaking to register, the name or requirements of any person seeking the tenancy of a house;

    (b)   demands or accepts payment of any sum of money in consideration of supplying, or undertaking to supply, to any person addresses or other particulars of houses to let; or

    (c)   issues any advertisement, list or other document describing any house as being to let without the authority of the owner of the house or his agent,

shall be guilty of an offence.

(2)   A person shall not be guilty of an offence under this section by reason of his demanding or accepting payment from the owner of a house of any remuneration payable to him as agent for the said owner.

(3)   A person being a solicitor [or an authorised person] shall not be guilty of an offence under this section by reason of his demanding or accepting payment of any remuneration in respect of business done by him as such.

(4)   A person shall not be guilty of an offence under this section by reason of his demanding or accepting any payment in consideration of the display in a shop, or of the publication in a newspaper, of any advertisement or notice, or by reason of the display or publication as aforesaid of an advertisement or notice received for the purpose in the ordinary course of business.

(5)   Any person guilty of an offence under this section shall be liable on summary conviction to a fine not exceeding [level 3 on the standard scale] *or to imprisonment for a term not exceeding three months, or to both such fine and imprisonment.*

(6)   In this section the following expressions have the meanings hereby assigned to them that is to say:—

["authorised person" means a person (other than a solicitor) who, for the purposes of the Legal Services Act 2007, is an authorised person in relation to an activity which is a reserved legal activity (within the meaning of that Act);]

"house" includes any part of a building which is occupied or intended to be occupied as a dwelling;

"newspaper" includes any periodical or magazine;

"owner", in relation to a house, means the person having power to grant a lease of the house.

**[37]**

**NOTES**

Sub-s (1): words omitted repealed by the Expiring Laws Act 1969, s 1.

Sub-s (3): words in square brackets inserted by the Legal Services Act 2007, s 208(1), Sch 21, para 22(a), as from a day to be appointed.

Sub-s (5): words in square brackets substituted by virtue of the Criminal Justice Act 1982, ss 38, 46; words in italics repealed by the Criminal Justice Act 2003, s 332, Sch 37, Pt 9, as from a day to be appointed.

Sub-s (6): definition "authorised person" inserted by the Legal Services Act 2007, s 208(1), Sch 21, para 22(b), as from a day to be appointed.

Modification: any reference to solicitor(s) etc includes references to bodies recognised under the Administration of Justice Act 1985, s 9, by virtue of the Solicitors' Incorporated Practices Order 1991, SI 1991/2684, arts 4, 5, Sch 1.

**2   Short title, extent, commencement and duration**

(1)   This Act may be cited as the Accommodation Agencies Act 1953.

(2)   This Act shall not extend to Northern Ireland.

(3)   This Act shall come into operation one month after the date on which it is passed.

(4)   ...

**[38]**

**NOTES**

Sub-s (4): repealed by the Expiring Laws Act 1969, s 1.

# LANDLORD AND TENANT ACT 1954

(2 & 3 Eliz 2 c 56)

ARRANGEMENT OF SECTIONS

PART I
SECURITY OF TENURE FOR RESIDENTIAL TENANTS

*Security of tenure for tenants under ground leases, etc*

## PART IV
## MISCELLANEOUS AND SUPPLEMENTARY

*An Act to provide security of tenure for occupying tenants under certain leases of residential
property at low rents and for occupying sub-tenants of tenants under such leases; to enable
tenants occupying property for business, professional or certain other purposes to obtain new
tenancies in certain cases; to amend and extend the Landlord and Tenant Act 1927, the Leasehold
Property (Repairs) Act 1938, and section eighty-four of the Law of Property Act 1925; to confer
jurisdiction on the County Court in certain disputes between landlords and tenants; to make
provision for the termination of tenancies of derelict land; and for purposes connected with the
matters aforesaid*

[30 July 1954]

**NOTES**

Transfer of functions: as to the functions of Ministers of the Crown under this Act, so far as exercisable in
relation to Wales, being transferred to the National Assembly for Wales, see the National Assembly for Wales
(Transfer of Functions) Order 1999, SI 1999/672, art 2, Sch 1.

## PART I
## SECURITY OF TENURE FOR RESIDENTIAL TENANTS

**NOTES**

The Local Government and Housing Act 1989, Sch 10 at **[802]** applies, and s 1 of this Act at **[39]** does not
apply, to the tenancy of a dwelling-house, which is a long tenancy at a low rent and which is entered into on or
after 1 April 1990. otherwise than in pursuance of a contract made before that date. In the case of such tenancies
entered into before that date, the 1989 Act provides that where such a tenancy is in existence on 15 January 1999,
s 1 of this Act shall cease to apply and Sch 10 to the 1989 Act shall apply instead (unless, before that date, the
landlord has served notice specifying a date of termination earlier than 15 January 1999); see s 186(2), (3) of the
1989 Act at **[796]**. As to the application of provisions of this Act in relation to Sch 10 to the 1989 Act, see
s 186(5) of, and Sch 10, paras 19–21 to, that Act at **[802]**.

As to the disapplication of s 1 to a sub-lease directly or indirectly derived out of a lease granted under the Leasehold Reform, Housing and Urban Development Act 1993, s 56 at **[862]** after the term date of the lease, see s 59(2)(b) of the 1993 Act at **[866]**.

*Security of tenure for tenants under ground leases, etc*

## 1  Protection of residential tenants on termination of long tenancies at low rents

On the termination in accordance with the provisions of this Part of this Act of a tenancy to which this section applies the tenant shall be entitled to the protection of the [Rent Act] subject to and in accordance with those provisions.

**[39]**

**NOTES**
Words in square brackets substituted by the Rent Act 1968, s 117(2), Sch 15.
Rent Act: the Rent Act 1977.

## 2  Tenancies to which s 1 applies

(1)  The foregoing section applies to any long tenancy at a low rent, being a tenancy as respects which for the time being the following condition (hereinafter referred to as "the qualifying condition") is fulfilled, that is to say that the circumstances (as respects the property comprised in the tenancy, the use of that property, and all other relevant matters) are such that on the coming to an end of the tenancy at that time the tenant would, if the tenancy had not been one at a low rent, be entitled by virtue of the [Rent Act] to retain possession of the whole or part of the property comprised in the tenancy.

[(1A)  For the purpose only of determining whether the qualifying condition is fulfilled with respect to a tenancy which is entered into on or after 1st April 1990 (otherwise than, where the property comprised in the tenancy had a rateable value on 31st March 1990, in pursuance of a contract made before 1st April 1990), for section 4(4)(b) and (5) of that Act substitute—

"(b)   on the date the contract for the grant of the tenancy was made (or, if there was no such contract, on the date the tenancy was entered into) R exceeded £25,000 under the formula—

$$R = \frac{P \times I}{1 - (1 + I)^{-T}}$$

where—
P is the premium payable as a condition of the grant of the tenancy (and includes a payment of money's worth) or, where no premium is so payable, zero,
I is 0.06, and
T is the term, expressed in years, granted by the tenancy (disregarding any right to terminate the tenancy before the end of the term or to extend the tenancy).".]

(2)   At any time before, but not more than twelve months before, the term date application may be made to the court as respects any long tenancy at a low rent, not being at the time of the application a tenancy as respects which the qualifying condition is fulfilled, for an order declaring that the tenancy is not to be treated for the purposes of this Part of this Act as a tenancy to which the foregoing section applies; and where such an application is made—

(a)    the court, if satisfied that the tenancy is not likely, immediately before the term date, to be a tenancy to which the foregoing section applies, but not otherwise, shall make the order;

(b)    if the court makes the order, then notwithstanding anything in subsection (1) of this section the tenancy shall not thereafter be treated as a tenancy to which the foregoing section applies.

(3)   Anything authorised or required to be done under the following provisions of this Part of this Act in relation to tenancies to which the foregoing section applies shall, if done before the term date in relation to a long tenancy at a low rent, not be treated as invalid by reason only that at the time at which it was done the qualifying condition was not fulfilled as respects the tenancy.

(4)   In this Part of this Act the expression "long tenancy" means a tenancy granted for a term of years certain exceeding twenty-one years, whether or not subsequently extended by act of the parties or by any enactment.

[(5)   In this Part of this Act the expression "tenancy at a low rent" means a tenancy the rent payable in respect whereof (or, where that rent is a progressive rent, the maximum rent payable in respect whereof) is less than,—

(a)    where the tenancy was entered into before 1st April 1990 or (where the property comprised in the tenancy had a rateable value on 31st March 1990) is entered into on or after 1st April 1990 in pursuance of a contract made before that date, two-thirds of the rateable value of the property; and for the purposes of this subsection the rateable value of the property is that which would be taken as its rateable value for the purposes of section 5(1) of the Rent Act 1977; and,

(b)   where the tenancy is entered into on or after 1st April 1990 (otherwise than, where the property comprised in the tenancy had a rateable value on 31st March 1990, in pursuance of a contract made before 1st April 1990), is payable at a rate of,—

(i)   £1,000 or less a year if the property is in Greater London, and

(ii)   £250 or less a year if the property is elsewhere.]

(6)   In this Part of this Act the expression "term date", in relation to a tenancy granted for a term of years certain, means the date of expiry of the term.

[(7)   In determining whether a long tenancy is, or at any time was, a tenancy at a low rent there shall be disregarded such part (if any) of the sums payable by the tenant as is expressed (in whatever terms) to be payable in respect of rates [council tax], services, repairs, maintenance, or insurance, unless it could not have been regarded by the parties as a part so payable.

In this section "long tenancy" does not include a tenancy which is, or may become, terminable before the end of the term by notice given to the tenant.]

[(8)   The Secretary of State may by order replace any amount referred to in subsections (1A) and (5)(b) of this section and the number in the definition of "I" in subsection (1A) by such amount or number as is specified in the order; and such an order shall be made by statutory instrument which shall be subject to annulment in pursuance of a resolution of either House of Parliament.]

**[40]**

**NOTES**

Sub-s (1): words in square brackets substituted by the Rent Act 1968, s 117(2), Sch 15.

Sub-s (1A): inserted by the References to Rating (Housing) Regulations 1990, SI 1990/434, reg 2, Schedule, para 2.

Sub-s (5): substituted by SI 1990/434, reg 2, Schedule, para 3.

Sub-s (7): added by the Rent Act 1977, s 155, Sch 23, paras 12, 13; words in square brackets inserted by the Local Government Finance (Housing) (Consequential Amendments) Order 1993, SI 1993/651, art 2(1), Sch 1, para 1.

Sub-s (8): added by SI 1990/434, reg 2, Schedule, para 4.

This section was also amended by the Rent Act 1957, s 26(1), (3), Sch 6, para 15(1)–(3), Sch 8, Pt I, but by virtue of the Leasehold Reform Act 1967, s 39(2), Sch 5, para 2, those amendments are deemed never to have been made, subject to transitional provisions in s 39(2) of, and Sch 5, paras 5–8 to, that Act at **[134]**.

Rent Act: the Rent Act 1977.

*Continuation and termination of tenancies to which s 1 applies*

**3   Continuation of tenancies to which s 1 applies**

(1)   A tenancy which is current immediately before the term date and is then a tenancy to which section one of this Act applies shall not come to an end on that date except by being terminated under the provisions of this Part of this Act, and if not then so terminated shall subject to those provisions continue until so terminated and shall, while continuing by virtue of this section, be deemed (notwithstanding any change in circumstances) to be a tenancy to which section one of this Act applies.

(2)   Where by virtue of the last foregoing subsection a tenancy is continued after the term date, then—

(a)   if the premises qualifying for protection are the whole of the property comprised in the tenancy, the tenancy shall continue at the same rent and in other respects on the same terms as before the term date;

(b)   if the premises qualifying for protection are only part of the property comprised in the tenancy, the tenancy while continuing after the term date shall have effect as a tenancy of those premises to the exclusion of the remainder of the property, and at a rent to be ascertained by apportioning the rent payable before the term date as between those premises and the remainder of the property, and in other respects on the same terms (subject to any necessary modifications) as before the term date.

(3)   In this Part of this Act the expression "the premises qualifying for protection" means the aggregate of the premises of which, if the tenancy in question were not one at a low rent, the tenant would be entitled to retain possession by virtue of the [Rent Act] after the coming to an end of the tenancy at the term date.

(4)   Any question arising under paragraph (b) of subsection (2) of this section as to the premises comprised in a tenancy continuing as mentioned in that paragraph, as to the rent payable in respect of a tenancy so continuing, or as to any of the terms of such a tenancy, shall be determined by agreement between the landlord and the tenant or, on the application of either of them, by the court.

**[41]**

**NOTES**
Sub-s (3): words in square brackets substituted by the Rent Act 1968, s 117(2), Sch 15.
This section was also amended by the Rent Act 1957, s 26(1), Sch 6, para 15(1), (4), but by virtue of the Leasehold Reform Act 1967, s 39(2), Sch 5, para 2, those amendments are deemed never to have been made, subject to transitional provisions in s 39(2) of, and Sch 5, paras 5–8 to, that Act at **[134]**.
Rent Act: the Rent Act 1977.

## 4   Termination of tenancy by the landlord

(1)   The landlord may terminate a tenancy to which section one of this Act applies by notice given to the tenant in the prescribed form specifying the date at which the tenancy is to come to an end (hereinafter referred to as "the date of termination"), being either the term date of the tenancy or a later date:

Provided that this subsection has effect subject to the provisions of this Part of this Act as to the annulment of notices in certain cases and subject to the provisions of Part IV of this Act as to the interim continuation of tenancies pending the disposal of applications to the court.

(2)   A notice under the last foregoing subsection shall not have effect unless it is given not more than twelve nor less than six months before the date of termination specified therein.

(3)   A notice under subsection (1) of this section shall not have effect unless it specifies the premises which the landlord believes to be, or to be likely to be, the premises qualifying for protection and either—

(a)   it contains proposals for a statutory tenancy, as defined by subsection (3) of section seven of this Act, or

(b)   it contains notice that, if the tenant is not willing to give up possession at the date of termination of the tenancy, of all the property then comprised in the tenancy, the landlord proposes to apply to the court, on one or more of the grounds mentioned in section twelve of this Act, for possession of the property comprised in the tenancy, and states the ground or grounds on which he proposes to apply.

(4)   A notice under subsection (1) of this section shall invite the tenant, within two months after the giving of the notice, to notify the landlord in writing whether he is willing to give up possession as mentioned in paragraph (b) of the last foregoing subsection.

(5)   A notice under subsection (1) of this section containing proposals such as are mentioned in paragraph (a) of subsection (3) of this section is hereinafter referred to as a "landlord's notice proposing a statutory tenancy", and a notice under subsection (1) of this section not containing such proposals is hereinafter referred to as a "landlord's notice to resume possession".

(6)   References in this Part of this Act to an election by the tenant to retain possession are references to his notifying the landlord, in accordance with subsection (4) of this section, that he will not be willing to give up possession.

**[42]**

## 5   Termination of tenancy by the tenant

(1)   A tenancy to which section one of this Act applies may be brought to an end at the term date thereof by not less than one month's notice in writing given by the tenant to the immediate landlord.

(2)   A tenancy continuing after the term date thereof by virtue of section three of this Act may be brought to an end at any time by not less than one month's notice in writing given by the tenant to the immediate landlord, whether the notice is given after or before the term date of the tenancy.

(3)   The fact that the landlord has given a notice under subsection (1) of the last foregoing section, or that the tenant has elected to retain possession, shall not prevent the tenant from giving a notice terminating the tenancy at a date earlier than the date of termination specified in the landlord's notice.

**[43]**

*Statutory tenancies arising under Part I*

## 6   Application of Rent Acts where tenant retains possession

(1)   Where a tenancy is terminated by a landlord's notice proposing a statutory tenancy [the Rent Act shall apply], subject as hereinafter provided, as if the tenancy (hereinafter referred to as "the former tenancy")—

(a)   had been a tenancy of the dwelling-house, as hereinafter defined, and

[(b)   had not been a tenancy at a low rent and, except as regards the duration of the tenancy and the amount of the rent, had been a tenancy on the terms agreed or determined in accordance with the next following section and no other terms].

(2)   The [Rent Act] shall not apply as aforesaid, if at the end of the period of two months after the service of the landlord's notice the qualifying condition was not fulfilled as respects the tenancy, unless the tenant has elected to retain possession.

(3)   In this Part of this Act the expression "the dwelling-house" means the premises agreed between the landlord and the tenant or determined by the court,—

    (a)    if the agreement or determination is made on or after the term date of the former tenancy, to be the premises which as respects that tenancy are the premises qualifying for protection,

    (b)    if the agreement or determination is made before the term date of the former tenancy, to be the premises which are likely to be the premises qualifying for protection.

(4), (5)   ...

[44]

**NOTES**

Sub-s (1): words in first pair of square brackets substituted by the Rent Act 1968, s 117(2), Sch 15; para (b) substituted by the Leasehold Reform Act 1967, s 39(2), Sch 5, para 3(1)(a), subject to transitional provisions in Sch 5, paras 5–8 to that Act at **[134]**.

Sub-s (2): words in square brackets substituted by the Rent Act 1968, s 117(2), Sch 15.

Sub-s (4): repealed by the Leasehold Reform Act 1967, s 41(2), Sch 7, Pt I, subject to transitional provisions in Sch 5, paras 5–8 to that Act at **[134]**.

Sub-s (5): repealed by the Rent Act 1957, s 26(3), Sch 8, Pt I.

Rent Act: the Rent Act 1977.

## 7   Settlement of terms of statutory tenancy

(1)   The ... terms on which the tenant and any successor to his statutory tenancy may retain possession of the dwelling-house during that period [other than the amount of the rent] shall be such as may be agreed between the landlord and the tenant or determined by the court ...

(2)   A landlord's notice proposing a statutory tenancy and anything done in pursuance thereof shall cease to have effect if by the beginning of the period of two months ending with the date of termination specified in the notice any of the following matters, that is to say,—

    (a)    what premises are to constitute the dwelling-house;

    (b)    [as regards the rent] of the dwelling-house during the period of the statutory tenancy, the intervals at which instalments of that rent are to be payable, and whether they are to be payable in advance or in arrear;

    (c)    whether any, and if so what, initial repairs (as defined in the next following section) are to be carried out on the dwelling-house;

    (d)    whether initial repairs to be so carried out are to be carried out by the landlord or by the tenant, or which of them are to be carried out by the landlord and which by the tenant; and

    (e)    the matters required by the next following section to be agreed or determined in relation to repairs before the beginning of the period of the statutory tenancy,

has not been agreed between the landlord and the tenant and no application has been made by the beginning of the said period of two months for the determination by the court of such of those matters as have not been agreed:

Provided that this subsection shall not have effect if at the end of the period of two months after the service of the landlord's notice the qualifying condition was not fulfilled as respects the tenancy unless the tenant has elected to retain possession.

(3)   In paragraph (a) of subsection (3) of section four of this Act, the expression "proposals for a statutory tenancy" means [proposals as to the rent of the dwelling-house during the period of the statutory tenancy] proposals as to the matters specified in paragraphs (b) to (e) of the last foregoing subsection, and such other proposals (if any) as to the terms mentioned in subsection (1) of this section as the landlord may include in his notice.

(4)   Any such proposals—

    (a)    shall be made, and be expressed to be made, on the assumption that the dwelling-house will be the premises specified in the landlord's notice in accordance with subsection (3) of section four of this Act;

    (b)    shall not be treated as failing to satisfy the requirements of the said subsection (3) by reason only of a difference between the premises to which the proposals relate and the premises subsequently agreed or determined to be the dwelling-house,

and in the event of any such difference the landlord shall not be bound by his proposals notwithstanding that they may have been accepted by the tenant.

(5)   An application for securing a determination by the court in accordance with the foregoing provisions of this section shall be made by the landlord, and—

    (a)    shall be made during the currency of the landlord's notice proposing a statutory tenancy and not earlier than two months after the giving thereof, so however that if the tenant has elected to retain possession it may be made at a time not earlier than one month after the giving of the notice;

(b) subject to the provisions of the last foregoing subsection, shall not be made for the determination of any matter as to which agreement has already been reached between the landlord and the tenant.

(6) In this Part of this Act the expression "the period of the statutory tenancy" means the period beginning with the coming to an end of the former tenancy and ending with the earliest date by which the tenant, and any successor to his statutory tenancy, have ceased to retain possession of the dwelling-house by virtue of the [Rent Act].

**[45]**

**NOTES**

Sub-s (1): words omitted repealed by the Rent Act 1957, s 26(3), Sch 8, Pt I; words in square brackets inserted by the Leasehold Reform Act 1967, s 39(2), Sch 5, para 3(1)(b), subject to transitional provisions in Sch 5, paras 5–8 to that Act at **[134]**.

Sub-s (2): words in square brackets substituted by the Leasehold Reform Act 1967, s 39(2), Sch 5, para 3(1)(b), subject to transitional provisions in Sch 5, paras 5–8 to that Act at **[134]**.

Sub-s (3): words in square brackets inserted by the Leasehold Reform Act 1967, s 39(2), Sch 5, para 3(1)(b), subject to transitional provisions in Sch 5, paras 5–8 to that Act at **[134]**.

Sub-s (6): words in square brackets substituted by the Rent Act 1968, s 117(2), Sch 15.

Rent Act: the Rent Act 1977.

**8 Provisions as to repairs during period of statutory tenancy**

(1) Where it is agreed between the landlord and the tenant, or determined by the court, that the terms mentioned in subsection (1) of the last foregoing section shall include the carrying out of specified repairs (hereinafter referred to as "initial repairs"), and any of the initial repairs are required in consequence of failure by the tenant to fulfil his obligations under the former tenancy, the landlord shall be entitled to a payment (hereinafter referred to as a "payment for accrued tenant's repairs"), of an amount equal to the cost reasonably incurred by the landlord in ascertaining what repairs are required as aforesaid and in carrying out such of the initial repairs as are so required and as respects which it has been agreed or determined as aforesaid that they are to be carried out by the landlord, excluding any part of that cost which is recoverable by the landlord otherwise than from the tenant or his predecessor in title.

(2) A payment for accrued tenant's repairs may be made either by instalments or otherwise, as may be agreed or determined as aforesaid; and the provisions of the First Schedule to this Act shall have effect as to the time for, and method of, recovery of such payments, the persons from whom they are to be recoverable, and otherwise in relation thereto.

(3) The obligations of the landlord and the tenant as respects the repair of the dwelling-house during the period of the statutory tenancy shall, subject to the foregoing provisions of this section, be such as may be agreed between them or as may be determined by the court.

(4) The matters referred to in paragraph (e) of subsection (2) of the last foregoing section are:

(a) which of the initial repairs (if any) are required in consequence of failure by the tenant to fulfil his obligations under the former tenancy and, where there are any initial repairs so required, the amount to be included in the payment for accrued tenant's repairs in respect of the cost incurred by the landlord in ascertaining what initial repairs are so required;

(b) the estimated cost of the repairs so required, in so far as they are to be carried out by the landlord;

(c) whether any payment for accrued tenant's repairs is to be payable by instalments or otherwise, and if by instalments the amount of each instalment (subject to any necessary reduction of the last), the time at which the first is to be payable and the frequency of the instalments;

(d) whether there are to be any, and if so what, obligations as respects the repair of the dwelling-house during the period of the statutory tenancy, other than the execution of initial repairs.

(5) The provisions of the Second Schedule to this Act shall have effect as respects cases where the landlord or the tenant fails to carry out initial repairs, as to the cost of carrying out such repairs in certain cases and as to the making of a record, where required by the landlord or by the tenant, of the state of repair of the dwelling-house.

**[46]**

**9 Principles to be observed in determining terms of statutory tenancy as to repairs and rent**

(1) Where it falls to the court to determine what initial repairs (if any) should be carried out by the landlord, the court shall not, except with the consent of the landlord and the tenant, require the

carrying out of initial repairs in excess of what is required to bring the dwelling-house into good repair or the carrying out of any repairs not specified by the landlord in his application as repairs which he is willing to carry out.

(2)   In the last foregoing subsection the expression "good repair" means good repair as respects both structure and decoration, having regard to the age, character and locality of the dwelling-house.

(3)   Notwithstanding anything in subsection (1) of section seven of this Act, the court shall not have power to determine that any initial repairs shall be carried out by the tenant except with his consent.

(4)   Any obligations imposed by the court under this Part of this Act as to keeping the dwelling-house in repair during the period of the statutory tenancy shall not be such as to require the dwelling-house to be kept in a better state of repair than the state which may be expected to subsist after the completion of any initial repairs to be carried out or, in the absence of any agreement or determination requiring the carrying out of initial repairs, in a better state of repair than the state subsisting at the time of the court's determination of what obligations are to be imposed.

(5)   ...

[47]

**NOTES**
Sub-s (5): repealed by the Leasehold Reform Act 1967, s 41(2), Sch 7, Pt I, subject to transitional provisions in Sch 5, paras 5–8 to that Act at **[134]**.

**10   Provisions as to liabilities under tenant's covenants in former lease**

(1)   If on the termination of the former tenancy the tenant retains possession of the dwelling-house by virtue of section six of this Act, any liability, whether of the tenant or of any predecessor in title of his, arising under the terms of the former tenancy shall be extinguished:

Provided that this subsection shall not affect any liability—
(a)   for failure to pay rent or rates or to insure or keep insured, or
(b)   in respect of the use of any premises for immoral or illegal purposes,
or any liability under the terms of the former tenancy in so far as those terms related to property other than the dwelling-house.

(2)   During the period of the statutory tenancy no order shall be made for the recovery of possession of the dwelling-house from the tenant [in any of the circumstances specified in Cases 1 to 3 in [Schedule 15] to the Rent Act] (which relate to the recovery of possession where an obligation of the tenancy has been broken or where certain specified acts or defaults have been committed) by reason only of any act or default which occurred before the date of termination of the former tenancy.

[48]

**NOTES**
Sub-s (2): words in first (outer) pair of square brackets substituted by the Rent Act 1968, s 117(2), Sch 8; words in second (inner) pair of square brackets substituted by the Rent Act 1977, s 155, Sch 23, para 14.
Rent Act: the Rent Act 1977.

**11**   *(Repealed by the Rent Act 1957, s 26(3), Sch 8, Pt I.)*

*Provisions as to possession on termination of long tenancy*

**12   Grounds for resumption of possession by landlord**

(1)   The grounds on which a landlord may apply to the court for possession of the property comprised in a tenancy to which section one of this Act applies are the following:—
(a)   that for purposes of redevelopment after the termination of the tenancy the landlord proposes to demolish or reconstruct the whole or a substantial part of the relevant premises;
(b)   the grounds specified in the Third Schedule to this Act (which correspond, subject to the necessary modifications, to the [[Cases 1 to 9 in Schedule 15] to the Rent Act which specify circumstances in which a court may make an order for possession under that Act)].

(2)   In this section the expression "the relevant premises" means—
(a)   as respects any time after the term date, the premises of which, if the tenancy were not one at a low rent, the tenant would have been entitled to retain possession by virtue of the [Rent Act] after the coming to an end of the tenancy at the term date;
(b)   as respects any time before the term date, the premises agreed between the landlord and

the tenant or determined by the court to be likely to be the premises of which, if the tenancy were not one at a low rent, the tenant would be entitled to retain possession as aforesaid.

**[49]**

**NOTES**

Sub-s (1): words in first (outer) pair of square brackets substituted by the Rent Act 1968, s 117(2), Sch 15; words in second (inner) pair of square brackets substituted by the Rent Act 1977, s 155, Sch 23, para 15.

Sub-s (2): words in square brackets substituted by the Rent Act 1968, s 117(2), Sch 15.

This section was further amended by the Rent Act 1957, s 26(1), Sch 6, para 15(1), (5), but by virtue of the Leasehold Reform Act 1967, s 39(2), Sch 5, para 2, those amendments are deemed never to have been made, subject to transitional provisions in s 39(2) of, and Sch 5, paras 5–8 to, that Act at **[134]**.

Rent Act: the Rent Act 1977.

### 13   Landlord's application for possession

(1)   Where a landlord's notice to resume possession has been served and either—

    (a)   the tenant elects to retain possession, or

    (b)   at the end of the period of two months after the service of the landlord's notice the qualifying condition is fulfilled as respects the tenancy,

the landlord may apply to the court for an order under this section on such of the grounds mentioned in the last foregoing section as may be specified in the notice:

Provided that the application shall not be made later than two months after the tenant elects to retain possession, or, if he has not elected to retain possession, later than four months after the service of the notice.

(2)   Where the ground or one of the grounds for claiming possession specified in the landlord's notice was that mentioned in paragraph (a) of subsection (1) of the last foregoing section, then if on such an application the court is satisfied that the landlord has established that ground as respects premises specified in the application, and is further satisfied,—

    (a)   that on the said ground possession of the specified premises will be required by the landlord on the termination of the tenancy; and

    (b)   that the landlord has made such preparations (including the obtaining, or, if that is not reasonably practicable in the circumstances, preparations relating to the obtaining, of any requisite permission or consent, whether from any authority whose permission or consent is required under any enactment or from the owner of any interest in any property) for proceeding with the redevelopment as are reasonable in the circumstances,

the court shall order that the tenant shall, on the termination of the tenancy, give up possession of all the property then comprised in the tenancy.

(3)   Where in a case falling within the last foregoing subsection the court is not satisfied as therein mentioned, but would be satisfied if the date of termination of the tenancy had been such date (in this subsection referred to as "the postponed date") as the court may determine, being a date later, but not more than one year later, than the date of termination specified in the landlord's notice, the court shall, if the landlord so requires, make an order specifying the postponed date and otherwise to the following effect, that is to say:—

    (a)   that the tenancy shall not come to an end on the date of termination specified in the landlord's notice but shall continue thereafter, as respects the whole of the property comprised therein, at the same rent and in other respects on the same terms as before that date;

    (b)   that unless the tenancy comes to an end before the postponed date; the tenant shall on that date give up possession of all the property then comprised in the tenancy.

(4)   Where the ground or one of the grounds for claiming possession specified in the landlord's notice was one mentioned in the Third Schedule to this Act, then if on an application made in accordance with subsection (1) of this section the court is satisfied that the landlord has established that ground and that it is reasonable that the landlord should be granted possession, the court shall order that the tenant shall, on the termination of the tenancy, give up possession of all the property then comprised in the tenancy.

(5)   Nothing in the foregoing provisions of this section shall prejudice any power of the tenant under section five of this Act to terminate the tenancy; and subsection (2) of that section shall apply where the tenancy is continued by an order under subsection (3) of this section as it applies where the tenancy is continued by virtue of section three of this Act.

**[50]**

### 14   Provisions where tenant not ordered to give up possession

(1)   The provisions of this section shall have effect where in a case falling within paragraph (a) or (b) of subsection (1) of the last foregoing section the landlord does not obtain an order under the last foregoing section.

(2) If at the expiration of the period within which an application under the last foregoing section may be made the landlord has not made such an application, the landlord's notice, and anything done in pursuance thereof, shall thereupon cease to have effect.

(3) If before the expiration of the said period the landlord has made an application under the last foregoing section, but the result of the application, at the time when it is finally disposed of, is that no order is made, the landlord's notice shall cease to have effect; but if within one month after the application to the court is finally disposed of the landlord gives a landlord's notice proposing a statutory tenancy, the earliest date which may be specified therein as the date of termination shall, notwithstanding anything in subsection (2) of section four of this Act, be the expiration of three months from the giving of the subsequent notice.

(4) The reference in the last foregoing subsection to the time at which an application is finally disposed of shall be construed as a reference to the earliest time at which the proceedings on the application (including any proceedings on or in consequence of an appeal) have been determined and any time for appealing or further appealing has expired, except that if the application is withdrawn or any appeal is abandoned the reference shall be construed as a reference to the time of withdrawal or abandonment.

(5) A landlord's notice to resume possession may be withdrawn at any time by notice in writing served on the tenant (without prejudice, however, to the power of the court to make an order as to costs if the notice is withdrawn after the landlord has made an application under the last foregoing section); and if within one month of the withdrawal of a landlord's notice to resume possession the landlord gives a landlord's notice proposing a statutory tenancy, the earliest date which may be specified therein as the date of termination shall, notwithstanding anything in subsection (2) of section four of this Act, be the expiration of three months from the giving of the subsequent notice or six months from the giving of the withdrawn notice, whichever is the later.

(6) Where by virtue of subsection (3) or (5) of this section the landlord gives a landlord's notice proposing a statutory tenancy which specifies as the date of termination a date earlier than six months after the giving of the notice, subsection (2) of section seven of this Act shall apply in relation to the notice with the substitution, for references to the period of two months ending with the date of termination specified in the notice and the beginning of that period, of references to the period of three months beginning with the giving of the notice and the end of that period.

[51]

## [14A Compensation for possession obtained by misrepresentation

Where an order is made for possession of the property comprised in a tenancy to which section 1 of this Act applies and it is subsequently made to appear to the court that the order was obtained by misrepresentation or the concealment of material facts, the court may order the landlord to pay to the tenant such a sum as appears sufficient as compensation for damage or loss sustained by the tenant as the result of the order.]

[52]

**NOTES**

Inserted by the Regulatory Reform (Business Tenancies) (England and Wales) Order 2003, SI 2003/3096, art 28(1), Sch 5, paras 1, 2.

**15** (*Repealed by the Rent Act 1968, s 117(5), Sch 17.*)

*General and supplementary provisions*

## 16 Relief for tenant where landlord proceeding to enforce covenants

(1) The provisions of the next following subsection shall have effect where, in the case of a tenancy to which section one of this Act applies,—

    (a) the immediate landlord has brought proceedings to enforce a right of re-entry or forfeiture or a right to damages in respect of a failure to comply with any terms of the tenancy,

    (b) the tenant has made application in the proceedings for relief under this section, and

    (c) the court makes an order for the recovery from the tenant of possession of the property comprised in the tenancy or for the payment by the tenant of such damages as aforesaid, and the order is made at a time earlier than seven months before the term date of the tenancy.

(2) The operation of the order shall be suspended for a period of fourteen days from the making thereof, and if before the end of that period the tenant gives notice in writing to the immediate landlord that he desires that the provisions of the two following paragraphs shall have effect, and lodges a copy of the notice in the court,—

    (a) the order shall not have effect except if and in so far as it provides for the payment of costs and

(b)    the tenancy shall thereafter have effect, and this Part of this Act shall have effect in relation thereto, as if it had been granted for a term expiring at the expiration of seven months from the making of the order.

(3)    In any case falling within paragraphs (a) and (b) of subsection (1) of this section, the court shall not make any such order as is mentioned in paragraph (c) thereof unless the time of the making of the order falls earlier than seven months before the term date of the tenancy:

Provided that (without prejudice to section ten of this Act) this subsection shall not prevent the making of an order for the payment of damages in respect of a failure, as respects any premises, to comply with the terms of a tenancy if, at the time when the order is made, the tenancy has come to an end as respects those premises.

(4)    The foregoing provisions of this section shall not have effect in relation to a failure to comply with—

(a)    any term of a tenancy as to payment of rent or rates or as to insuring or keeping insured any premises, or

(b)    any term restricting the use of any premises for immoral or illegal purposes.

(5)    References in this section to proceedings to enforce a right to damages in respect of a failure to comply with any terms of a tenancy shall be construed as including references to proceedings for recovery from the tenant of expenditure incurred by or recovered from the immediate landlord in consequence of such a failure on the part of the tenant.

(6)    Nothing in the foregoing provisions of this section shall prejudice any right to apply for relief under any other enactment.

(7)    Subsection (3) of section two of this Act shall not have effect in relation to this section.

**[53]**

## 17 Prohibition of agreements excluding Part I

The provisions of this Part of this Act shall have effect notwithstanding any agreement to the contrary:

Provided that nothing in this Part of this Act shall be construed as preventing the surrender of a tenancy.

**[54]**

## 18 Duty of tenants of residential property to give information to landlords or superior landlords

(1)    Where the property comprised in a long tenancy at a low rent is or includes residential premises, then at any time during the last two years of the term of the tenancy, or (if the tenancy is being continued after the term date by subsection (1) of section three of this Act) at any time while the tenancy is being so continued, the immediate landlord or any superior landlord may give to the tenant or any sub-tenant of premises comprised in the long tenancy a notice in the prescribed form requiring him to notify the landlord or superior landlord, as the case may be,—

(a)    whether the interest of the person to whom the notice is given has effect subject to any sub-tenancy on which that interest is immediately expectant and, if so,

(b)    what premises are comprised in the sub-tenancy, for what term it has effect (or, if it is terminable by notice, by what notice it can be terminated), what is the rent payable thereunder, who is the sub-tenant and (to the best of the knowledge and belief of the person to whom the notice is given) whether the sub-tenant is in occupation of the premises comprised in the sub-tenancy or any part of those premises and, if not, what is the sub-tenant's address,

and it shall be the duty of the person to whom such a notice is given to comply therewith within one month of the giving of the notice.

(2)    In this section the expression "residential premises" means premises normally used, or adapted for use, as one or more dwellings, the expression "sub-tenant" in relation to a long tenancy means the owner of a tenancy created (whether immediately or derivatively) out of the long tenancy and includes a person retaining possession of any premises by virtue of the [Rent Act] after the coming to an end of a sub-tenancy, and the expression "sub-tenancy" includes a right so to retain possession.

**[55]**

---

**NOTES**

Sub-s (2): words in square brackets substituted by the Rent Act 1968, s 117(2), Sch 15.

This section was also amended by the Rent Act 1957, s 26(1), Sch 6, para 15(1), (3), but by virtue of the Leasehold Reform Act 1967, s 39(2), Sch 5, para 2, those amendments are deemed never to have been made, subject to transitional provisions in s 39(2) of, and Sch 5, paras 5–8 to, that Act at **[134]**.

Regulations: the Long Residential Tenancies (Supplemental Forms) Regulations 1997, SI 1997/3005 at **[3205]**.

Rent Act: the Rent Act 1977.

**19  Application of Part I to tenancies granted in continuation of long tenancies**

(1)  Where on the coming to an end of a tenancy at a low rent the person who was tenant thereunder immediately before the coming to an end thereof becomes (whether by grant or by implication of law) tenant of the whole or any part of the property comprised therein under another tenancy at a low rent, then if the first tenancy was a long tenancy or is deemed by virtue of this subsection to have been a long tenancy the second tenancy shall be deemed for the purposes of this Part of this Act to be a long tenancy irrespective of its terms.

(2)  In relation to a tenancy from year to year or other tenancy not granted for a term of years certain, being a tenancy which by virtue of the last foregoing subsection is to be deemed to be a long tenancy, this Part of this Act shall have effect subject to the modifications set out in the Fourth Schedule to this Act.

[56]

**NOTES**

This section was amended by the Rent Act 1957, s 26(1), (3), Sch 6, para 15(1), (3), (6), Sch 8, Pt I, but by virtue of the Leasehold Reform Act 1967, s 39(2), Sch 5, para 2, those amendments are deemed never to have been made, subject to transitional provisions in s 39(2) of, and Sch 5, paras 5–8 to, that Act at **[134]**.

**20  Assumptions on which court to determine future questions**

Where under this Part of this Act any question falls to be determined by the court by reference to the circumstances at a future date, the court shall have regard to all rights, interests and obligations under or relating to the tenancy as they subsist at the time of the determination and to all relevant circumstances as they then subsist and shall assume, except in so far as the contrary is shown, that those rights, interests, obligations and circumstances will continue to subsist unchanged until the said future date.

[57]

**21  Meaning of "the landlord" in Part I and provisions as to mesne landlords, etc**

(1)  Subject to the provisions of this section, in this Part of this Act the expression "the landlord", in relation to a tenancy (in this section referred to as "the relevant tenancy"), means the person (whether or not he is the immediate landlord) who is the owner of that interest in the property comprised in the relevant tenancy which for the time being fulfils the following conditions, that is to say—

    (a)    that it is an interest in reversion expectant (whether immediately or not) on the termination of the relevant tenancy, and

    (b)    that it is either the fee simple or a tenancy the duration of which is at least five years longer than that of the relevant tenancy,

and is not itself in reversion expectant (whether immediately or not) on an interest which fulfils those conditions

(2)  References in this Part of this Act to a notice to quit given by the landlord are references to a notice to quit given by the immediate landlord.

(3)  For the purposes of subsection (1) of this section the question whether a tenancy (hereinafter referred to as "the superior tenancy") is to be treated as having a duration at least five years longer than that of the relevant tenancy shall be determined as follows:—

    (a)    if the term date of the relevant tenancy has not passed, the superior tenancy shall be so treated unless it is due to expire at a time earlier than five years after the term date or can be brought to an end at such a time by notice to quit given by the landlord;

    (b)    if the term date of the relevant tenancy has passed, the superior tenancy shall be so treated unless it is due to expire within five years or can be brought to an end within five years by notice to quit given by the landlord.

(4)  In relation to the premises constituting the dwelling-house where the [Rent Act applies] by virtue of subsection (1) of section six of this Act, the expression "the landlord", as respects any time falling within the period of the statutory tenancy, means the person who as respects those premises is the landlord of the tenant for the purposes of the [Rent Act]:

Provided that in relation to the carrying out of initial repairs, and to any payment for accrued tenant's repairs, the said expression, as respects any time falling within that period, means the person whose interest in the dwelling-house fulfils the following conditions, that is to say:—

    (a)    that it is not due to expire within five years and is not capable of being brought to an end within five years by notice to quit given by the landlord, and

    (b)    that it is not itself in reversion expectant on an interest which is not due to expire or capable of being brought to an end as aforesaid.

(5)  The provisions of the Fifth Schedule to this Act shall have effect for the application of this Part of this Act to cases where the immediate landlord of the tenant is not the owner of the fee simple in respect of the premises in question.

(6)    Notwithstanding anything in subsection (1) of this section, if at any time the interest which apart from this subsection would be the interest of the landlord is an interest not bound by this Part of this Act and is not the interest of the immediate landlord, then as respects that time the expression "the landlord" means in this Part of this Act (subject to the provisions of subsection (2) of this section) the person (whether or not he is the immediate landlord) who has the interest in the property comprised in the relevant tenancy immediately derived out of the interest not bound by this Part of this Act.

[In this subsection "interest not bound by this Part of this Act" means an interest which belongs to Her Majesty in right of the Crown and is not under the management of the Crown Estate Commissioners or an interest belonging to a government department or held on behalf of Her Majesty for the purposes of a government department.]

**[58]**

NOTES
Sub-s (4): words in square brackets substituted by the Rent Act 1968, s 117(2), Sch 15.
Sub-s (6): words in square brackets substituted by the Housing Act 1980, s 73(4)(b).
Rent Act: the Rent Act 1977.

## 22   Interpretation of Part I

(1)    In this Part of this Act:—

"date of termination" has the meaning assigned to it by subsection (1) of section four of this Act;

"the dwelling-house" has the meaning assigned to it by subsection (3) of section six of this Act;

"election to retain possession" has the meaning assigned to it by subsection (6) of section four of this Act;

"former tenancy" has the meaning assigned to it by subsection (1) of section six of this Act;

"initial repairs" has the meaning assigned to it by subsection (1) of section eight of this Act;

"the landlord" has the meaning assigned to it by the last foregoing section;

"landlord's notice proposing a statutory tenancy" and "landlord's notice to resume possession" have the meanings assigned to them respectively by subsection (5) of section four of this Act;

"long tenancy" has the meaning assigned to it by subsection (4) of section two of this Act;

"order" includes judgment;

"payment for accrued tenant's repairs" has the meaning assigned to it by subsection (1) of section eight of this Act;

"the period of the statutory tenancy" has the meaning assigned to it by subsection (6) of section seven of this Act;

"premises qualifying for protection" has the meaning assigned to it by subsection (3) of section three of this Act;

"qualifying condition" has the meaning assigned to it by subsection (1) of section two of this Act;

["the Rent Act" means [the Rent Act 1977] as it applies to regulated tenancies but exclusive of [Parts II to V] thereof;]

"tenancy at a low rent" has the meaning assigned to it by subsection (5) of section two of this Act;

"term date" has the meaning assigned to it by subsection (6) of section two of this Act.

(2)    In relation to the premises constituting the dwelling-house the expression "the tenant" in this Part of this Act means the tenant under the former tenancy and, except as respects any payment for accrued tenant's repairs not payable by instalments, includes any successor to his statutory tenancy, and the expression "successor to his statutory tenancy", in relation to that tenant, means a person who after that tenant's death retains possession of the dwelling-house by virtue of the [Rent Act].

(3)    In determining, for the purposes of any provision of this Part of this Act, whether the property comprised in a tenancy, or any part of that property, was let as a separate dwelling, the nature of the property or part at the time of the creation of the tenancy shall be deemed to have been the same as its nature at the time in relation to which the question arises, and the purpose for which it was let under the tenancy shall be deemed to have been the same as the purpose for which it is or was used at the last-mentioned time.

**[59]**

NOTES
Sub-s (1): definitions omitted repealed by the Rent Act 1977, s 155, Sch 25; definition "the Rent Act" substituted by the Rent Act 1968, s 117(2), Sch 15, and words in square brackets therein substituted by the Rent Act 1977, s 155, Sch 23, para 16.
Sub-s (2): words in square brackets substituted by the Rent Act 1968, s 117(2), Sch 15.

**23–50**   *((Pts II, III) outside the scope of this work.)*

### PART IV
### MISCELLANEOUS AND SUPPLEMENTARY

**51, 52**   *(Outside the scope of this work.)*

### 53   Jurisdiction of county court where lessor refuses licence or consent

(1)   Where a landlord withholds his licence or consent—

   (a)   to an assignment of the tenancy or a sub-letting, charging or parting with the possession of the demised property or any part thereof, or

   (b)   to the making of an improvement on the demised property or any part thereof, or

   (c)   to a change in the use of the demised property or any part thereof, or to the making of a specified use of that property,

and the High Court has jurisdiction to make a declaration that the licence or consent was unreasonably withheld, then without prejudice to the jurisdiction of the High Court the county court shall have [the like jurisdiction whatever the net annual value for rating of the demised property is to be taken to be for the purposes of the County Courts Act 1984] and notwithstanding that the tenant does not seek any relief other than the declaration.

(2)   Where on the making of an application to the county court for such a declaration the court is satisfied that the licence or consent was unreasonably withheld, the court shall make a declaration accordingly.

(3)   The foregoing provisions of this section shall have effect whether the tenancy in question was created before or after the commencement of this Act and whether the refusal of the licence or consent occurred before or after the commencement of this Act.

(4)   Nothing in this section shall be construed as conferring jurisdiction on the county court to grant any relief other than such a declaration as aforesaid.

[60]

**NOTES**

Sub-s (1): words in square brackets substituted by the County Courts Act 1984, s 148(1), Sch 2, para 23.

### 54   Determination of tenancies of derelict land

Where a landlord, having power to serve a notice to quit, on an application to the county court satisfies the court—

   (a)   that he has taken all reasonable steps to communicate with the person last known to him to be the tenant, and has failed to do so,

   (b)   that during the period of six months ending with the date of the application neither the tenant nor any person claiming under him has been in occupation of the property comprised in the tenancy or any part thereof, and

   (c)   that during the said period either no rent was payable by the tenant or the rent payable has not been paid,

the court may if it thinks fit by order determine the tenancy as from the date of the order.

[61]

**55–62**   *(S 55 repealed by the Regulatory Reform (Business Tenancies) (England and Wales) Order 2003, SI 2003/3096, art 28(2), Sch 6, subject to transitional provisions in art 29(1), (2) thereof; ss 56–60, 60A outside the scope of this work; s 60B repealed, subject to transitional provisions, by the Government of Wales Act 1998, ss 131, 152, Sch 18, Pt IV; s 61 repealed by the Endowments and Glebe Measure 1976, s 47(4), Sch 8; s 62 repealed by the House of Commons Disqualification Act 1957, s 14(1), Sch 4, Pt I and the Industrial Expansion Act 1968, s 18(2), Sch 4.)*

### 63   Jurisdiction of court for purposes of Parts I and II and of Part I of Landlord and Tenant Act 1927

(1)   Any jurisdiction conferred on the court by any provision of Part I of this Act shall be exercised by the county court.

(2)   Any jurisdiction conferred on the court by any provision of Part II of this Act or conferred on the tribunal by Part I of the Landlord and Tenant Act 1927, shall, subject to the provisions of this section, be exercised [by the High Court or a County Court].

(3)   ...

(4)   The following provisions shall have effect as respects transfer of proceedings from or to the High Court or the county court, that is to say—

   (a)   where an application is made to the one but by virtue of [an Order under section 1 of the

Courts and Legal Services Act 1990] cannot be entertained except by the other, the application shall not be treated as improperly made but any proceedings thereon shall be transferred to the other court;

(b) any proceedings under the provisions of Part II of this Act or of Part I of the Landlord and Tenant Act 1927, which are pending before one of those courts may by order of that court made on the application of any person interested be transferred to the other court, if it appears to the court making the order that it is desirable that the proceedings and any proceedings before the other court should both be entertained by the other court.

(5) In any proceedings where in accordance with the foregoing provisions of this section the county court exercises jurisdiction the powers of the judge of summoning one or more assessors under subsection (1) of section eighty-eight of the County Courts Act 1934 may be exercised notwithstanding that no application is made in that behalf by any party to the proceedings.

(6) Where in any such proceedings an assessor is summoned by a judge under the said subsection (1),—

(a) he may, if so directed by the judge, inspect the land to which the proceedings relate without the judge and report to the judge in writing thereon;

(b) the judge may on consideration of the report and any observations of the parties thereon give such judgment or make such order in the proceedings as may be just;

(c) the remuneration of the assessor shall be at such rate as may be determined by the Lord Chancellor with the approval of the Treasury and shall be defrayed out of moneys provided by Parliament.

(7) In this section the expression "the holding"—

(a) in relation to proceedings under Part II of this Act, has the meaning assigned to it by subsection (3) of section twenty-three of this Act,

(b) in relation to proceedings under Part I of the Landlord and Tenant Act 1927, has the same meaning as in the said Part I.

(8) ...

(9) Nothing in this section shall prejudice the operation of [section 41 of the County Courts Act 1984] (which relates to the removal into the High Court of proceedings commenced in a county court).

(10) ...

                                                        **[62]**

**NOTES**

Sub-ss (2), (4), (9): words in square brackets substituted by the High Court and County Courts Jurisdiction Order 1991, SI 1991/724, art 2(1)(d), (8), Schedule, Pt I.

Sub-ss (3), (8): repealed by SI 1991/724, art 2(1)(d), (8), Schedule, Pt I.

Sub-s (10): substitutes the Landlord and Tenant Act 1927, s 21.

**64, 65** (*Outside the scope of this work.*)

**66 Provisions as to notices**

(1) Any form of notice required by this Act to be prescribed shall be prescribed by regulations made by [the Secretary of State] by statutory instrument.

(2) Where the form of a notice to be served on persons of any description is to be prescribed for any of the purposes of this Act, the form to be prescribed shall include such an explanation of the relevant provisions of this Act as appears to [the Secretary of State] requisite for informing persons of that description of their rights and obligations under those provisions.

(3) Different forms of notice may be prescribed for the purposes of the operation of any provision of this Act in relation to different cases.

(4) Section twenty-three of the Landlord and Tenant Act 1927 (which relates to the service of notices) shall apply for the purposes of this Act.

(5) Any statutory instrument under this section shall be subject to annulment in pursuance of a resolution of either House of Parliament.

                                                        **[63]**

**NOTES**

Sub-ss (1), (2): words in square brackets substituted by the Transfer of Functions (Lord Chancellor and Secretary of State) Order 1974, SI 1974/1896, arts 2, 3(2).

Regulations: the Landlord and Tenant (Notices) Regulations 1957, SI 1957/1157; the Landlord and Tenant Act 1954, Part II (Assured Tenancies) (Notices) Regulations 1986, SI 1986/2181 (made under this section as applied by the Housing Act 1980, s 58); the Leasehold Reform (Notices) Regulations 1997, SI 1997/640 at **[3176]**, (made under this section as applied by the Leasehold Reform Act 1967, s 22(5)); the Long Residential Tenancies (Supplemental Forms) Regulations 1997, SI 1997/3005 at **[3205]**; the Landlord and Tenant Act 1954, Part 2 (Notices) Regulations 2004, SI 2004/1005.

## 67 Provisions as to mortgagees in possession

Anything authorised or required by the provisions of this Act, other than subsection ... (3) of section forty, to be done at any time by, to or with the landlord, or a landlord of a specified description, shall, if at that time the interest of the landlord in question is subject to a mortgage and the mortgagee is in possession or a receiver appointed by the mortgagee or by the court is in receipt of the rents and profits, be deemed to be authorised or required to be done by, to or with the mortgagee instead of that landlord.

[64]

**NOTES**

Words omitted repealed by the Regulatory Reform (Business Tenancies) (England and Wales) Order 2003, SI 2003/3096, art 28(2), Sch 6, subject to transitional provisions in art 29(6) thereof.

## 68 (*Outside the scope of this work.*)

## 69 Interpretation

(1) In this Act the following expressions have the meanings hereby assigned to them respectively, that is to say:—

"agricultural holding" has the same meaning as in the [Agricultural Holdings Act 1986];

"development corporation" has the same meaning as in the New Towns Act 1946;

["farm business tenancy" has the same meaning as in the Agricultural Tenancies Act 1995;]

"local authority" [[means any local authority within the meaning of the Town and Country Planning Act 1990, any National Park authority, [an authority established for an area in England by an order under section 207 of the Local Government and Public Involvement in Health Act 2007 (joint waste authorities),] the Broads Authority[, the London Fire and Emergency Planning Authority] or] ... a joint authority established by Part IV of the Local Government Act 1985];

"mortgage" includes a charge or lien and "mortgagor" and "mortgagee" shall be construed accordingly;

"notice to quit" means a notice to terminate a tenancy (whether a periodical tenancy or a tenancy for a term of years certain) given in accordance with the provisions (whether express or implied) of that tenancy;

"repairs" includes any work of maintenance, decoration or restoration, and references to repairing, to keeping or yielding up in repair and to state of repair shall be construed accordingly;

"statutory undertakers" has the same meaning as in the Town and Country Planning Act 1947 ... ;

"tenancy" means a tenancy created either immediately or derivatively out of the freehold, whether by a lease or underlease, by an agreement for a lease or underlease or by a tenancy agreement or in pursuance of any enactment (including this Act), but does not include a mortgage term or any interest arising in favour of a mortgagor by his attorning tenant to his mortgagee, and references to the granting of a tenancy and to demised property shall be construed accordingly;

"terms", in relation to a tenancy, includes conditions.

(2) References in this Act to an agreement between the landlord and the tenant (except in section seventeen and subsections (1) and (2) of section thirty-eight thereof) shall be construed as references to an agreement in writing between them.

(3) References in this Act to an action for any relief shall be construed as including references to a claim for that relief by way of counterclaim in any proceedings.

[65]

**NOTES**

Sub-s (1): words in square brackets in definition "agricultural holding" substituted by the Agricultural Holdings Act 1986, s 100, Sch 14, para 22; definition "farm business tenancy" inserted by the Agricultural Tenancies Act 1995, s 40, Schedule, para 12; in definition "local authority", words in first (outer) pair of square brackets inserted by the Local Government Act 1985, s 84, Sch 14, Pt II, para 36, words in second (inner) pair of square brackets substituted by the Environment Act 1995, s 78, Sch 10, para 3, words in third (inner) pair of square brackets inserted by the Local Government and Public Involvement in Health Act 2007, s 209(2), Sch 13, Pt 2, para 25, words in fourth (inner) pair of square brackets inserted by the Greater London Authority Act 1999, s 328, Sch 29, Pt I, para 1, and words omitted repealed by the Education Reform Act 1988, s 237(2), Sch 13, Pt I; words omitted from definition "statutory undertakers" repealed by the Coal Industry Act 1994, s 67(1), (8), Sch 9, para 5, Sch 1, Pt II.

Modification: by virtue of the Waste Regulation and Disposal (Authorities) Order 1985, SI 1985/1884, art 10, Sch 3, the reference to a "joint authority" in the definition "local authority" includes references to a waste regulation or disposal authority established in that Order. The body corporate known as the Residuary Body for Wales is to be treated as a local authority for the purposes of this Act by virtue of the Local Government (Wales) Act 1994, Sch 13, para 20(a). The body corporate known as the Local Government Residuary Body (England) is to be treated as a local authority for the purposes of this Act by virtue of the Local Government Residuary Body (England) Order 1995, SI 1995/401, Schedule, para 2(a).

**70   Short title and citation, commencement and extent**

(1)   This Act may be cited as the Landlord and Tenant Act 1954, and the Landlord and Tenant Act 1927, and this Act may be cited together as the Landlord and Tenant Acts 1927 and 1954.

(2)   This Act shall come into operation on the first day of October, nineteen hundred and fifty-four.

(3)   This Act shall not extend to Scotland or to Northern Ireland.

**[66]**

## SCHEDULES

### FIRST SCHEDULE
### SUPPLEMENTARY PROVISIONS AS TO PAYMENTS FOR ACCRUED TENANT'S REPAIRS

Section 8

### PART I
### PROVISIONS AS TO MAKING OF PAYMENT IN LUMP SUM

1.   Subject to the provisions of this Part of this Schedule, a payment for accrued tenant's repairs which is to be payable otherwise than by instalments shall become payable when the relevant initial repairs have been completed unless the landlord and the tenant agree that it shall become payable wholly or in part at some other date.

2.   Where it is determined by the court that a payment for accrued tenant's repairs is to be payable otherwise than by instalments, the court may determine that any specified part of the payment shall become payable when any specified part of the relevant initial repairs has been completed.

3.   A payment for accrued tenant's repairs which is payable otherwise than by instalments, or any part of such a payment, shall be recoverable from the tenant.

4.—(1)   Where it has been agreed or determined that a payment for accrued tenant's repairs should be paid otherwise than by instalments, and the period of the statutory tenancy ends before the relevant initial repairs have been begun, or at a time when they have been begun but not completed, the following provisions shall have effect.

(2)   If the relevant initial repairs have not been begun and are no longer required, then notwithstanding anything in section eight of this Act no payment for accrued tenant's repairs shall be recoverable.

(3)   In any other case, the time for recovery of the payment for accrued tenant's repairs shall be the same as if all the relevant initial repairs had been completed immediately before the end of the period of the statutory tenancy, and the amount of the payment shall be as hereinafter provided:—

    (a)   if the relevant initial repairs have not been begun, the amount of the payment shall be the estimated cost of the repairs or of so much thereof as is still required;

    (b)   if the relevant initial repairs have been begun but not completed, the amount of the payment shall be an amount equal to the expenses reasonably incurred by the landlord for the purposes of so much of the relevant initial repairs as has been carried out together (unless the remainder is no longer required) with the estimated cost of the remainder or of so much thereof as is still required:

Provided that there shall be disregarded so much (if any) of the said expenses or estimated cost as is recoverable by the landlord otherwise than from the tenant or his predecessor in title.

(4)   Any question arising under this paragraph whether repairs are no longer required, whether any expenses were incurred, or reasonably incurred, by the landlord, or as to the amount of the estimated cost of any repairs shall be determined by agreement between the landlord and the tenant or by the court on the application of either of them.

(5)   For the purposes of this paragraph initial repairs shall be deemed to be no longer required after the end of the period of the statutory tenancy if, and only if, it is shown that the dwelling-house, in whatever state of repair it may then be, is at or shortly after the end of that period to be pulled down, or that such structural alterations are to be made in the dwelling-house as would render those repairs valueless if they were completed.

(6)   In a case falling within sub-paragraph (1) of this paragraph where a payment for accrued tenant's repairs would, apart from this paragraph, include an amount in respect of cost incurred by the landlord in ascertaining what initial repairs are required in consequence of failure by the tenant to fulfil his obligations under the former tenancy, the following provisions shall have effect—

    (a)   that amount shall be recoverable notwithstanding anything in sub-paragraph (2) of this paragraph;

(b) in a case falling within sub-paragraph (3) of this paragraph the said amount shall be recoverable in addition to the amount specified in that sub-paragraph;

(c) the time for recovery of the said amount shall, as well in a case falling within sub-paragraph (2) of this paragraph as in one falling within sub-paragraph (3) thereof, be that mentioned in the said sub-paragraph (3).

5. In relation to a case where the court exercises the power conferred by paragraph 2 of this Schedule references in the last foregoing paragraph to the relevant initial repairs shall be construed as references to any such part of those repairs as is referred to in the said paragraph 2, being a part which at the material time has not been begun or, as the case may be, has been begun but not completed, and references to the payment for accrued tenant's repairs shall be construed accordingly.

[67]

## PART II
### PROVISIONS AS TO MAKING OF PAYMENT BY INSTALMENTS

6. Subject to the provisions of this Part of this Schedule, where under Part I of this Act it is agreed or determined that a payment for accrued tenant's repairs is to be payable by instalments, the instalments shall become payable at the times so agreed or determined.

7. Any such instalment becoming payable at a time falling before the end of the period of the statutory tenancy shall be payable by the tenant.

8.—(1) Where the landlord is not the immediate landlord of the dwelling-house, the landlord and the immediate landlord may serve on the tenant a notice in the prescribed form requiring him to pay the instalments of the payment for accrued tenant's repairs to the immediate landlord for transmission to the landlord.

(2) A notice under the last foregoing sub-paragraph may be revoked by a subsequent notice given to the tenant by the landlord, with or without the concurrence of the immediate landlord.

9. Any instalment becoming payable at a time when the landlord is the immediate landlord or when a notice under sub-paragraph (1) of the last foregoing paragraph is in force shall be recoverable by the immediate landlord in the like manner and subject to the like provisions as the rent.

10. If the period of the statutory tenancy comes to an end before all instalments of the payment for accrued tenant's repairs have been paid, the remaining instalments shall become payable immediately after the end of that period, shall be recoverable by the person who immediately before the end thereof was the landlord, and shall be so recoverable from the person who immediately before the end thereof was the tenant.

11. In the application of the last foregoing paragraph to a case where the period of the statutory tenancy comes to an end before the relevant initial repairs have been begun, or at a time when they have been begun but not completed, the provisions of paragraph 4 of this Schedule shall have effect (with the necessary modifications) for limiting the recovery of any remaining instalments under the last foregoing paragraph.

12. Where, during the period of the statutory tenancy and before all instalments of the payment for accrued tenant's repairs have become payable, the interest of the landlord comes to an end or ceases to be an interest falling within paragraphs (a) and (b) of the proviso to subsection (4) of section twenty-one of this Act, he shall thereupon be entitled to recover from the person who thereupon becomes the landlord such amount (if any) as is equal to so much of the expenses reasonably incurred by the landlord—

(a) in ascertaining what initial repairs are required in consequence of failure by the tenant to fulfil his obligations under the former tenancy; and

(b) for the purposes of the relevant initial repairs;

as is recoverable from the tenant and has not been recovered.

[68]

---

**NOTES**

Para 9: amended by the Rent Act 1957, s 26(1), Sch 6, para 9, by the addition of certain words, but those words repealed by the Leasehold Reform Act 1967, s 41(2), Sch 7, Pt I, subject to transitional provisions in s 39(2) of, and Sch 5, paras 5–8 to, that Act at [134].

---

## PART III
### VARIATION OF AGREEMENT OR DETERMINATION AS TO TIME FOR MAKING PAYMENT

13. The tenant may apply to the court for the variation, on the grounds and to the extent hereinafter specified, of any agreement or determination for the making of a payment for accrued tenant's repairs.

14. The grounds on which an agreement or determination may be varied on an application under the last foregoing paragraph are the following:—
  (a) that the expenditure reasonably incurred by the landlord in carrying out the relevant initial repairs substantially exceeded the estimated cost thereof; or
  (b) that the applicant is not the person who was the tenant at the time of the previous agreement or determination and that there are considerations arising out of the personal circumstances of the applicant which ought to be taken into account in determining the manner of making the payment.

15. The extent to which an agreement or determination may be so varied on an application under paragraph 13 of this Schedule is the following:—
  (a) if the agreement or determination was for the making of the payment otherwise than by instalments, and the payment has not been fully made, by substituting therefor a determination that the payment or balance of the payment should be made by instalments;
  (b) if the agreement or determination was for the making of a payment by instalments, by substituting for the instalments agreed or determined instalments of such smaller amounts, payable at such times, as may be determined by the court.

16. Where an agreement or determination is varied under this Part of this Schedule, the foregoing provisions of this Schedule shall thereafter apply with the necessary modifications.

**[69]**

### PART IV
### SUPPLEMENTARY

17. Any failure by the tenant to make a payment for accrued tenant's repairs, or any part or instalment of such a payment, at the time when it becomes due shall be treated as a breach of the obligations of the tenancy for the purposes of [Case 1 in [Schedule 15] to the Rent Act] (which relates to recovery of possession where the rent has not been paid or any other obligation of the tenancy has not been performed).

18. Where any sum in respect of a payment for accrued tenant's repairs has been recovered in advance of the carrying out of the relevant initial repairs, then in any case where paragraph 4 or 11 of this Schedule applies such repayment shall be made as may be just.

19. In this Schedule the expression "immediate landlord" means the person who as respects the dwelling-house is the landlord of the tenant for the purposes of the [Rent Act] and the expression "relevant initial repairs" means the repairs in respect of which the payment for accrued tenant's repairs is payable.

**[70]**

**NOTES**
Para 17: words in first (outer) pair of square brackets substituted by the Rent Act 1968, s 117(2), Sch 15; words in second (inner) pair of square brackets substituted by the Rent Act 1977, s 155, Sch 23, para 19.
Para 19: words square brackets substituted by the Rent Act 1968, s 117(2), Sch 15.
Rent Act: the Rent Act 1977.

### SECOND SCHEDULE
### FURTHER PROVISIONS AS TO REPAIR WHERE TENANT RETAINS POSSESSION
Section 8

*Failure of landlord to carry out initial repairs*

1.—(1) Where—
  (a) the tenant retains possession of the dwelling-house by virtue of subsection (1) of section six of this Act, and
  (b) by virtue of an agreement or of a determination of the court the landlord is required to carry out initial repairs to the dwelling-house,

then if on an application made by the tenant during the period of the statutory tenancy the court is satisfied that the initial repairs have not been carried out within a reasonable time in accordance with the agreement or determination the court may by order direct that, until the discharge of the order as hereinafter provided or the end of the period of the statutory tenancy, whichever first occurs, the rent payable in respect of the dwelling-house shall be reduced to such amount specified in the order as the court may think just having regard to the extent to which the landlord has failed to comply with the agreement or determination.

(2) Where the court under the last foregoing sub-paragraph orders a reduction of rent, the court may further order that during the same period any instalments of a payment for accrued tenant's repairs shall be suspended.

(3) An order under this paragraph may include a provision that the reduction of rent shall take effect from a specified date before the making of the order, being such date as the court thinks just having regard to the landlord's delay in carrying out the initial repairs; and where an order contains

such a provision then, in addition to the reduction ordered by virtue of sub-paragraph (1) of this paragraph, such number of payments of rent next falling due after the date of the order shall be reduced by such amount as may be specified in the order for the purpose of giving effect to the said provision.

2.    Where an order under paragraph 1 of this Schedule is in force, and on an application by the landlord the court is satisfied that the initial repairs have been carried out in accordance with the agreement or with the determination of the court, as the case may be, the court shall discharge the order, but without prejudice to the operation thereof as respects any period before the date on which it is discharged or to any reduction ordered by virtue of sub-paragraph (3) of the last foregoing paragraph.

3.    If, while an order under paragraph 1 of this Schedule is in force, it is agreed between the landlord and the tenant that the initial repairs in question have been carried out as mentioned in the last foregoing paragraph, the order shall be discharged by virtue of that agreement in the like manner as if it had been discharged by the court.

### Failure of tenant to carry out initial repairs

4.    Where, by virtue of an agreement or of a determination of the court, the tenant is required to carry out initial repairs to the dwelling-house, failure by the tenant to carry out the repairs within a reasonable time in accordance with the agreement or determination shall be treated as a breach of the obligations of the tenancy for the purposes of [Case 1 in [Schedule 15] to the Rent Act] (which relates to recovery of possession where the rent has not been paid or any other obligation of the tenancy has not been performed).

### Expenses and receipts: mortgages, settlements, etc

5.    Any amount paid by a mortgagee in respect of expenses incurred in carrying out initial repairs in accordance with an agreement or determination under Part I of this Act, or in respect of any payment made in pursuance of a liability imposed by paragraph 12 of the First Schedule to this Act, shall be treated as if it were secured by the mortgage, with the like priority and with interest at the same rate as the mortgage money, so however that (without prejudice to the recovery of interest) any such amount shall not be recoverable from the mortgagor personally.

6.    The purposes authorised for the application of capital money by section seventy-three of the Settled Land Act 1925 …, and by section twenty-six of the Universities and College Estates Act 1925, and the purposes authorised by section seventy-one of the Settled Land Act 1925 … and by section [thirty] of the Universities and College Estates Act 1925, as purposes for which moneys may be raised by mortgage, shall include the payment of any such expenses as are mentioned in the last foregoing paragraph and the making of any such payment as is mentioned in that paragraph:

Provided that the like provisions shall have effect as to the repayment of capital money applied by virtue of this paragraph as have effect in the case of improvements authorised by Part II of the Third Schedule to the Settled Land Act 1925 (which specifies improvements the cost of which may be required to be replaced out of income).

### Record of state of repair of dwelling-house

7.    A landlord's notice proposing a statutory tenancy may contain a requirement that if the tenant retains possession by virtue of subsection (1) of section six of this Act a record shall be made of the state of repair of the dwelling-house.

8.    Where the landlord gives such a notice which does not contain such a requirement, then if the tenant elects to retain possession his notification in that behalf may include a requirement that a record shall be made of the state of repair of the dwelling-house.

9.    Where the tenant retains possession of the dwelling-house by virtue of subsection (1) of section six of this Act and either the landlord or the tenant has made such a requirement as is mentioned in either of the two last foregoing paragraphs, the record of the state of repair of the dwelling-house shall be made as soon as may be after the completion of any initial repairs to be carried out or, in the absence of any agreement or determination requiring the carrying out of initial repairs, as soon as may be after the beginning of the period of the statutory tenancy.

10.    Any record required to be made under the last foregoing paragraph shall be made by a person appointed, in default of agreement between the landlord and the tenant, by the President of the Royal Institution of Chartered Surveyors.

11.    The cost of making any such record as aforesaid shall, in default of agreement between the landlord and the tenant, be borne by them in equal shares.

[71]

**NOTES**

Para 1: amended by the Rent Act 1967, s 26(1), Sch 6, para 10, by the addition of certain words but those words repealed by the Leasehold Reform Act 1967, s 41(2), Sch 7, Pt I, subject to transitional provisions in s 39(2) of, and Sch 5, paras 5–8 to, that Act at **[134]**.

Para 4: words in first (outer) pair of square brackets substituted by the Rent Act 1968, s 117(2), Sch 15; words in second (inner) pair of square brackets substituted by the Rent Act 1977, s 155, Sch 23, para 19.

Para 6: words omitted repealed by the Trusts of Land and Appointment of Trustees Act 1996, s 25(2), Sch 4, subject to savings in s 25(3), (4) of that Act; word in square brackets substituted by the Universities and College Estates Act 1964, s 4(1), Sch 3, Pt II.

Rent Act: the Rent Act 1977.

## THIRD SCHEDULE
### GROUNDS FOR POSSESSION ON TERMINATION OF TENANCY
Sections 12, 13

1. The grounds referred to in paragraph (b) of subsection (1) of section twelve of this Act are the following, that is to say:—

    (a)    that suitable alternative accommodation will be available for the tenant at the date of termination of the tenancy;

    (b)    that the tenant has failed to comply with any term of the tenancy as to payment of rent or rates or as to insuring or keeping insured any premises;

    (c)    that the tenant or a person residing or lodging with him or being his sub-tenant has been guilty of conduct which is a nuisance or annoyance to adjoining occupiers, or has been convicted of using any premises comprised in the tenancy or allowing such premises to be used for an immoral or illegal purpose and, where the person in question is a lodger or sub-tenant, that the tenant has not taken such steps as he ought reasonably to have taken for the removal of the lodger or sub-tenant;

    (d)    ... ; and

    (e)    that premises comprised in the tenancy, and consisting of or including the relevant premises, are reasonably required by the landlord for occupation [as a residence for—

        (i)    himself,

        (ii)    any son or daughter of his over eighteen years of age,

        (iii)    his father or mother, or

        (iv)    the father, or mother, of his spouse or civil partner,

and] (if the landlord is not the immediate landlord) that he will be the immediate landlord at the date of termination:

Provided that the court shall not make an order under section thirteen of this Act on the grounds specified in sub-paragraph (e) of this paragraph—

    (a)    if the interest of the landlord, or an interest which has merged in that interest and but for the merger would be the interest of the landlord, was purchased or created after [the 18th February 1966]; or

    (b)    if the court is satisfied that having regard to all the circumstances of the case, including the question whether other accommodation is available for the landlord or the tenant, greater hardship would be caused by making the order than by refusing to make it.

[2. Part IV of [Schedule 15] to the Rent Act (which relates to the circumstances in which suitable accommodation is to be deemed to be available for the tenant) shall apply for the purposes of this Schedule as it applies for the purposes of [section 98(1)(a)] of that Act.]

**[72]**

**NOTES**

Para 1: sub-para (d) repealed by the Leasehold Reform Act 1967, s 41(2), Sch 7, Pt I, subject to transitional provisions in Sch 5, paras 5–8 to that Act at **[134]**; words in square brackets in sub-para (e) substituted by the Civil Partnership Act 2004, s 81, Sch 8, para 2; words in square brackets in para (a) of the proviso substituted by the Leasehold Reform Act 1967, s 39(2), Sch 5, para 1.

Para 2: substituted by the Rent Act 1968, s 117(2), Sch 15; words in square brackets therein substituted by the Rent Act 1977, s 155, Sch 23, para 20.

Rent Act: the Rent Act 1977.

## FOURTH SCHEDULE
### MODIFICATIONS OF PART I IN RELATION TO PERIODICAL TENANCIES
Section 19

1. In relation to such a tenancy as is mentioned in subsection (2) of section nineteen of this Act, Part I of this Act shall have effect subject to the following provisions of this Schedule.

2. For subsection (6) of section two there shall be substituted the following:—

    "(6)    In this Part of this Act the expression "term date", in relation to any such tenancy as is mentioned in subsection (2) of section nineteen of this Act, means the first date after the commencement of this Act on which apart from this Act the tenancy could have been brought to an end by notice to quit given by the landlord."

3.    For subsection (1) of section five there shall be substituted the following:—

> "(1)    A tenancy to which section one of this Act applies may be brought to an end at the term date thereof by notice in writing given by the tenant to the immediate landlord.
>
> The length of any such notice shall be not less than one month nor less than the length of the notice by which the tenant could apart from this Act have brought the tenancy to an end at the term date thereof."

4.    Notwithstanding anything in subsection (2) of section three, where by virtue of subsection (1) of that section the tenancy is continued after the term date thereof the provisions of Part I as to the termination of a tenancy by notice shall have effect in substitution for and not in addition to any such provisions included in the terms on which the tenancy had effect before the term date thereof.

5.    Where the tenancy is not terminated under the provisions of Part I of this Act at the term date thereof, then, whether or not it would have continued after that date apart from this Act, it shall be treated for the purposes of this Act as being continued by virtue of subsection (1) of section three thereof.

[73]

## FIFTH SCHEDULE
### PROVISIONS FOR PURPOSES OF PART I WHERE IMMEDIATE LANDLORD IS NOT THE FREEHOLDER

Section 21

### *Definitions*

1.—(1)    In this Schedule the following expressions have the meanings hereby assigned to them in relation to a tenancy (in this Schedule referred to as "the relevant tenancy"), that is to say:—

> "the competent landlord" means the person who in relation to the relevant tenancy is for the time being the landlord (as defined by section twenty-one of this Act) for the purposes of Part I of this Act;
>
> "mesne landlord" means a tenant whose interest is intermediate between the relevant tenancy and the interest of the competent landlord; and
>
> "superior landlord", except in paragraph 9 of this Schedule, means a person (whether the owner of the fee simple or a tenant) whose interest is superior to the interest of the competent landlord.

(2)    References in this Schedule to "other landlords" are references to persons who are either mesne landlords or superior landlords.

### *Acts of competent landlord binding on other landlords*

2.    Any notice given by the competent landlord under subsection (1) of section four of this Act, any agreement made under Part I of this Act between that landlord and the tenant under the relevant tenancy, and any determination of the court under the said Part I in proceedings between that landlord and that tenant, shall bind the interest of every other landlord (if any).

### *Provisions as to consent of other landlords to acts of competent landlord*

3.—(1)    Where in the four next following paragraphs reference is made to other landlords or to mesne landlords, the reference shall be taken not to include a mesne landlord whose interest is due to expire within the period of two months beginning with the relevant date or is terminable within that period by notice to quit given by his landlord.

(2)    In this paragraph the expression "the relevant date" means—

> (a)    if the term date of the relevant tenancy has not passed, that date;
> (b)    if that date has passed, and no notice has been given under subsection (1) of section four of this Act to terminate the relevant tenancy, the earliest date at which that tenancy could be brought to an end by such a notice;
> (c)    if such a notice has been given, the date of termination specified in the notice.

4.—(1)    If a notice is given by the competent landlord under subsection (1) of section four of this Act, or an agreement under Part I of this Act is made with the tenant by that landlord, without the written consent of every other landlord (if any), any other landlord whose written consent has not been given thereto shall, subject to the next following paragraph, be entitled to compensation from the competent landlord for any loss arising in consequence of the giving of the notice or the making of the agreement.

(2)    The amount of any compensation under this paragraph shall, in default of agreement, be determined by the court on the application of the person claiming it.

5.    The competent landlord may serve on any other landlord a notice in the prescribed form requiring him to consent to the giving or making of any such notice or agreement as aforesaid; and if within one month after the service of a notice under this paragraph—

> (a)    the consent has not been given, or

    (b)    conditions have been imposed on the giving of the consent which are in the opinion of the court unreasonable in all the circumstances,

the court, on an application by the competent landlord, may if it thinks fit order that the other landlord shall be deemed to have consented, either without qualification or subject to such conditions (including conditions as to the modification of the proposed notice or agreement or as to the payment of compensation by the competent landlord) as may be specified in the order.

6.—(1)   It may be made a condition either—

    (a)    of the giving of consent by a person whose consent is required under paragraph 4 of this Schedule, or

    (b)    of the making of an order under the last foregoing paragraph,

that the initial repairs which the competent landlord will agree to carry out, or which, as the case may be, he will specify in accordance with subsection (1) of section nine of this Act as repairs which he is willing to carry out, shall include such repairs as may be specified in the consent or order.

   (2)   In so far as any cost reasonably incurred by the competent landlord in carrying out repairs specified in accordance with the last foregoing sub-paragraph is not recovered by way of payment for accrued tenant's repairs and is not recoverable (apart from this sub-paragraph) otherwise than by way of such payment, it shall be recoverable by the competent landlord from the person whose consent was or is deemed to have been given subject to the condition or (if he is dead) from his personal representatives as a debt due from him at the time of his death.

7.—(1)   Where under Part I of this Act the competent landlord is required by an agreement, or by a determination of the court, to carry out initial repairs to any premises, he may serve on any mesne landlord a notice requiring him to pay to the competent landlord a contribution towards the cost reasonably incurred by the competent landlord in carrying out those repairs, if and in so far as that cost is not recovered by way of payment for accrued tenant's repairs and is not recoverable (apart from this sub-paragraph) otherwise than by way of such payment.

   (2)   Where a notice has been served under the last foregoing sub-paragraph, then in default of agreement between the competent landlord and the mesne landlord on whom the notice was served the court may order the mesne landlord to pay such a contribution as aforesaid.

   (3)   A contribution ordered under this paragraph shall be such as the court determines to be reasonable having regard to the difference between the rent under the relevant tenancy and the rent which, if the tenant retains possession, will be recoverable ... during the period of the statutory tenancy.

*Failure of competent landlord to carry out initial repairs*

8.   Where, in consequence of the failure of the competent landlord to carry out initial repairs, the amount of any payment of rent is reduced under paragraph 1 of the Second Schedule to this Act, and the competent landlord is not the immediate landlord of the tenant, the person who is for the time being the immediate landlord shall be entitled to recover from the competent landlord the amount of the reduction.

*Relief in proceedings by superior landlord*

9.—(1)   Where in the case of a tenancy to which section one of this Act applies—

    (a)    the interest of the immediate landlord is itself a tenancy (in this paragraph referred to as "the mesne tenancy"), and

    (b)    a superior landlord has brought proceedings to enforce a right of re-entry or forfeiture in respect of a failure to comply with any terms of the mesne tenancy or of a superior tenancy having effect subject to the mesne tenancy, and

    (c)    the court makes an order for the recovery by the superior landlord of possession of the property comprised in the tenancy,

the tenant shall not be required to give up possession of that property unless he has been a party to the proceedings or has been given notice of the order; and the provisions of the next following sub-paragraph shall have effect where he has been such a party or has been given such a notice:

    Provided that where the tenant has been a party to the proceedings the said provisions shall not apply unless he has at any time before the making of the order made application in the proceedings for relief under this paragraph.

   (2)   If the tenant within fourteen days after the making of the order, or where he has not been a party to the proceedings, within fourteen days after the said notice, gives notice in writing to the superior landlord that he desires that the following provisions of this sub-paragraph shall have effect and lodges a copy of the notice in the court—

    (a)    the tenant shall not be required to give up possession of the said property but the tenancy mentioned in head (b) of the last foregoing sub-paragraph shall be deemed as between the tenant and the superior landlord to have been surrendered on the date of the order; and

(b)  if the term date of the tenant's tenancy would otherwise fall later, it shall be deemed for the purposes of Part I of this Act to fall at the expiration of seven months from the making of the order.

(3)  Nothing in the foregoing provisions of this paragraph shall prejudice the operation of any order for the recovery of possession from the tenant under the mesne tenancy, or from the tenant under any superior tenancy having effect subject to the mesne tenancy.

(4)  Subsections (4), (6) and (7) of section sixteen of this Act shall with the necessary modifications apply for the purposes of this paragraph.

### *Relief for mesne landlord against damages for breach of covenant*

10.—(1)  The provisions of the next following sub-paragraph shall have effect where, in the case of a tenancy to which section one of this Act applies,—
- (a)  the competent landlord is not the immediate landlord, and
- (b)  the competent landlord has brought proceedings against a mesne landlord to enforce a right to damages in respect of a failure to comply with any terms of the mesne landlord's tenancy, and
- (c)  the mesne landlord has made application in the proceedings for relief under this paragraph, and
- (d)  the court makes an order for the payment by the mesne landlord of any such damages as aforesaid.

(2)  The operation of the order shall be suspended for a period of fourteen days from the making thereof, and if before the end of that period the mesne landlord gives notice in writing to the competent landlord that he desires that the provisions of heads (a) and (b) of this sub-paragraph shall have effect, and lodges a copy of the notice in the court—
- (a)  the order shall not be enforceable except if and in so far as it provides for the payment of costs, and
- (b)  the interest of the mesne landlord (unless it has then come to an end) shall be deemed to be surrendered, and his rights and liabilities thereunder to be extinguished, as from the date of the giving of the notice.

(3)  Subsections (4) to (7) of section sixteen of this Act shall with the necessary modifications apply for the purposes of this paragraph.

### *Provisions as to liabilities under tenants' covenants in superior leases*

11.—(1)  Where subsection (1) of section ten of this Act applies, any terms to which this paragraph applies shall cease to have effect in so far as they relate to the premises constituting the dwelling-house, and any liability of the competent landlord or any mesne landlord or of any predecessor in title of the competent landlord or of any mesne landlord, under any such terms, in so far as it related to those premises and was a liability subsisting at the termination of the relevant tenancy, shall be deemed to have been extinguished on the termination of that tenancy.

(2)  This paragraph applies to any terms of any tenancy owned by the competent landlord or by any other landlord, whether to be performed during that tenancy or on or after the expiration or determination thereof, except any such terms as are mentioned in paragraph (a) or (b) of the proviso to subsection (1) of section ten of this Act:

Provided that where any term to which this paragraph applies relates both to the dwelling-house and to other premises, nothing in this paragraph shall affect its operation in relation to the other premises.

(3)  Notwithstanding anything in sub-paragraph (1) of this paragraph, if the interest of the competent landlord, being a tenancy, or the interest of any mesne landlord, has not come to an end by the end of the period of the statutory tenancy, and the terms on which that interest was held included an obligation to repair or maintain the dwelling-house or the dwelling-house and other premises, then as from the end of the period of the statutory tenancy the instrument creating the interest of the competent landlord or mesne landlord shall be deemed to contain a covenant with the grantor of the interest that the grantee of the interest will at all times maintain the dwelling-house in a state of repair no less good than that in which it was after the completion of any initial repairs to be carried out thereon in accordance with the provisions of Part I of this Act, and will yield up possession of the dwelling-house in such a state on the coming to an end of the interest of the said landlord.

(4)  Where, in a case falling within sub-paragraph (1) of this paragraph, the competent landlord satisfies the court—
- (a)  that the obligations under the tenancy which in relation to him is the immediate mesne tenancy differ from the obligations under the relevant tenancy, and
- (b)  that if the obligations under the relevant tenancy had been the same as those under the first-mentioned tenancy he would have been entitled to recover any amount by way of payment for accrued tenant's repairs which he is not entitled to recover,

he shall be entitled to recover that amount from the tenant under the first-mentioned tenancy, or, if that tenancy has come to an end, from the person who was the tenant thereunder immediately before it came to an end.

(5) Where in accordance with the last foregoing sub-paragraph, or with that sub-paragraph as applied by the following provisions of this sub-paragraph, any sum is recoverable from a person, the last foregoing sub-paragraph shall with the necessary modifications apply as between him and the person entitled to the interest (if any) which in relation to him is the immediate mesne tenancy or, if such an interest formerly subsisted but has come to an end, as between him and the person last entitled to that interest.

(6) In this paragraph the expression "the immediate mesne tenancy", in relation to the competent landlord or to a mesne landlord, means the tenancy on which his interest in those premises is immediately expectant.

**[74]**

**NOTES**
Para 7: words omitted repealed by the Leasehold Reform Act 1967, s 41(2), Sch 7, Pt I, subject to transitional provisions in Sch 5, paras 5–8 to that Act at **[134]**.
Regulations: the Long Residential Tenancies (Supplemental Forms) Regulations 1997, SI 1997/3005 at **[3205]**.

(*Schs 6, 8, 9 outside the scope of this work; Sch 7 repealed by the Statute Law* (*Repeals*) *Act 1974.*)

# COSTS OF LEASES ACT 1958

(6 & 7 Eliz 2 c 52)

*An Act to make provision for the incidence of the costs of leases*

[23 July 1958]

**1 Costs of leases**

Notwithstanding any custom to the contrary, a party to a lease shall, unless the parties thereto agree otherwise in writing, be under no obligation to pay the whole or any part of any other party's solicitor's costs of the lease.

**[75]**

**NOTES**
Modification: the reference to a solicitor is modified to include a reference to bodies recognised under the Administration of Justice Act 1985, s 9, by virtue of the Solicitors' Incorporated Practices Order 1991, SI 1991/2684, arts 2–5, Sch 1.

**2 Interpretation**

In this Act—
 (a) "lease" includes an underlease and an agreement for a lease or underlease or for a tenancy or sub-tenancy;
 (b) "costs" includes fees, charges, disbursements (including stamp duty), expenses and remuneration.

**[76]**

**3 Short Title**

This Act may be cited as the Costs of Leases Act 1958.

**[77]**

# LEASEHOLD REFORM ACT 1967

(1967 c 88)

ARRANGEMENT OF SECTIONS

PART I
ENFRANCHISEMENT AND EXTENSION OF LONG LEASEHOLDS

*Right to enfranchisement or extension*

*An Act to enable tenants of houses held on long leases at low rents to acquire the freehold or an extended lease; to apply the Rent Acts to premises held on long leases at a rackrent, and to bring the operation of the Landlord and Tenant Act 1954 into conformity with the Rent Acts as so amended; to make other changes in the law in relation to premises held on long leases, including amendments of the Places of Worship (Enfranchisement) Act 1920; and for purposes connected therewith*

**[27 October 1967]**

**NOTES**
This Act is modified by the Housing Act 1985, ss 172–175 at **[544]–[546]**, in relation to leases granted under Pt V of that Act (the right to buy, ss 118–188 at **[461]–[559]**).
Transfer of functions: as to the functions of Ministers of the Crown under this Act, so far as exercisable in relation to Wales, being transferred to the National Assembly for Wales, see the National Assembly for Wales (Transfer of Functions) Order 1999, SI 1999/672, art 2, Sch 1.

PART I
ENFRANCHISEMENT AND EXTENSION OF LONG LEASEHOLDS
*Right to enfranchisement or extension*

**1   Tenants entitled to enfranchisement or extension**

(1)   This Part of this Act shall have effect to confer on a tenant of a leasehold house ... a right to acquire on fair terms the freehold or an extended lease of the house and premises where—
    [(a)   his tenancy is a long tenancy *at a low rent* and,—
        (i)   if the tenancy was entered into before 1st April 1990[, or on or after 1st April 1990 in pursuance of a contract made before that date, and the house and premises had a rateable value at the date of commencement of the tenancy or else at any time before 1st April 1990,] subject to subsections (5) and (6) below), the rateable value of the house and premises on the appropriate day was not more than £200 or, if it is in Greater London, than £400; and
        (ii)   if the tenancy [does not fall within sub-paragraph (i) above], on the date the contract for the grant of the tenancy was made or, if there was no such contract, on the date that the tenancy was entered into R did not exceed £25,000 under the formula—

$$R = \frac{P \times I}{1-(1+I)^{-T}}$$

        Where—
        P is the premium payable as a condition of the grant of the tenancy (and includes a payment of money's worth) or, where no premium is so payable, zero,
        I is 0.06, and
        T is the term, expressed in years, granted by the tenancy (disregarding any right to terminate the tenancy before the end of the term or to extend the tenancy);
    [(aa)   in the case of a right to acquire an extended lease, his long tenancy is a tenancy at a low rent;] and]

(b)    at the relevant time (that is to say, at the time when he gives notice in accordance with this Act of his desire to have the freehold or to have an extended lease, as the case may be) he has[—

    (i)   in the case of a right to acquire the freehold, been tenant of the house under a long tenancy for the last two years; and

    (ii)   in the case of a right to acquire an extended lease,]

been tenant of the house under a long tenancy at a low rent ... for the last [two years];

and to confer the like right in the other cases for which provision is made in this Part of this Act.

[(1ZA)   Where a house is for the time being let under two or more tenancies, a tenant under any of those tenancies which is superior to that held by any tenant on whom this Part of this Act confers a right does not have any right under this Part of this Act.

(1ZB)   Where a flat forming part of a house is let to a person who is a qualifying tenant of the flat for the purposes of Chapter 1 or 2 of Part 1 of the Leasehold Reform, Housing and Urban Development Act 1993 (c 28), a tenant of the house does not have any right under this Part of this Act unless, at the relevant time, he has been occupying the house, or any part of it, as his only or main residence (whether or not he has been using it for other purposes)—

(a)    for the last two years; or

(b)    for periods amounting to two years in the last ten years.]

[(1ZC)   The references in subsection (1)(a) and (b) to a long tenancy do not include a tenancy to which Part 2 of the Landlord and Tenant Act 1954 (business tenancies) applies unless—

(a)    it is granted for a term of years certain exceeding thirty-five years, whether or not it is (or may become) terminable before the end of that term by notice given by or to the tenant or by re-entry, forfeiture or otherwise,

(b)    it is for a term fixed by law under a grant with a covenant or obligation for perpetual renewal, unless it is a tenancy by sub-demise from one which is not a tenancy which falls within any of the paragraphs in this subsection,

(c)    it is a tenancy taking effect under section 149(6) of the Law of Property Act 1925 (c 20) (leases terminable after a death or marriage [or the formation of a civil partnership]), or

(d)    it is a tenancy which—

    (i)   is or has been granted for a term of years certain not exceeding thirty-five years, but with a covenant or obligation for renewal without payment of a premium (but not for perpetual renewal), and

    (ii)   is or has been once or more renewed so as to bring to more than thirty-five years the total of the terms granted (including any interval between the end of a tenancy and the grant of a renewal).

(1ZD)   Where this Part of this Act applies as if there were a single tenancy of property comprised in two or more separate tenancies, then, if each of the separate tenancies falls within any of the paragraphs of subsection (1ZC) above, that subsection shall apply as if the single tenancy did so.]

[(1A)   The references in *subsection (1)(a) and (b)* to a long tenancy *at a low rent* do not include a tenancy excluded from the operation of this Part by section 33A of and Schedule 4A to this Act.]

[(1B)   This Part of this Act shall not have effect to confer any right on the tenant of a house under a tenancy to which Part 2 of the Landlord and Tenant Act 1954 (c 56) (business tenancies) applies unless, at the relevant time, the tenant has been occupying the house, or any part of it, as his only or main residence (whether or not he has been using it for other purposes)—

(a)    for the last two years; or

(b)    for periods amounting to two years in the last ten years.]

(2)   ...

(3)   This Part of this Act shall not confer on the tenant of a house any right by reference to his [being a tenant of it] at any time when—

(a)    it is let to ... him with other land or premises to which it is ancillary; or

[(b)    it is comprised in—

    (i)   an agricultural holding within the meaning of the Agricultural Holdings Act 1986 held under a tenancy in relation to which that Act applies, or

    (ii)   the holding held under a farm business tenancy within the meaning of the Agricultural Tenancies Act 1995.]

[or, in the case of any right to which subsection (3A) below applies, at any time when the tenant's immediate landlord is a charitable housing trust and the house forms part of the housing accommodation provided by the trust in the pursuit of its charitable purposes].

[(3A)   For the purposes of subsection (3) above this subsection applies as follows—

(a)    where the tenancy was created after the commencement of Chapter III of Part I of the Leasehold Reform, Housing and Urban Development Act 1993, this subsection applies to any right to acquire the freehold of the house and premises; but

(b)    where the tenancy was created before that commencement, this subsection applies only to any such right exercisable by virtue of any one or more of the provisions of sections 1A*[, 1AA]* and 1B below;

and in that subsection "charitable housing trust" means a housing trust within the meaning of the Housing Act 1985 which is a charity within the meaning of the Charities Act 1993.]

(4)    In subsection (1)(a) above, "the appropriate day", in relation to any house and premises, means the 23rd March 1965 or such later day as by virtue of [section 25(3) of the Rent Act 1977] would be the appropriate day for purposes of that Act in relation to a dwelling house consisting of that house.

[(4A)    Schedule 8 to the Housing Act 1974 shall have effect to enable a tenant to have the rateable value of the house and premises reduced for purposes of this section in consequence of tenant's improvements.]

[(5)    If, in relation to any house and premises, the appropriate day for the purposes of subsection (1)(a) above falls on or after 1st April 1973 that subsection shall have effect in relation to the house and premises,—

(a)    in a case where the tenancy was created on or before 18th February 1966, as if for the sums of £200 and £400 specified in that subsection there were substituted respectively the sums of £750 and £1,500; and

(b)    in a case where the tenancy was created after 18th February 1966, as if for those sums of £200 and £400 there were substituted respectively the sums of £500 and £1,000.

(6)    If, in relation to any house and premises,—

(a)    the appropriate day for the purposes of subsection (1)(a) above falls before 1st April 1973, and

(b)    the rateable value of the house and premises on the appropriate day was more than £200 or, if it was then in Greater London, £400, and

(c)    the tenancy was created on or before 18th February 1966,

subsection (1)(a) above shall have effect in relation to the house and premises as if for the reference to the appropriate day there were substituted a reference to 1st April 1973 and as if for the sums of £200 and £400 specified in that subsection there were substituted respectively the sums of £750 and £1,500.]

[(7)    The Secretary of State may by order replace any amount referred to in subsection (1)(a)(ii) above and the number in the definition of "I" in that subsection by such amount or number as is specified in the order; and such an order shall be made by statutory instrument which shall be subject to annulment in pursuance of a resolution of either House of Parliament.]

**[78]**

---

**NOTES**

Sub-s (1): words omitted repealed and words in second pair of square brackets in para (b) substituted by the Commonhold and Leasehold Reform Act 2002, ss 138(1), 139(1), 180, Sch 14, except in relation to an application for enfranchisement or an extended lease of a house in respect of which notice was given under s 8 or 14 of this Act at **[90]**, **[97]**, or where an application was made under s 27 of this Act at **[110]**, before 26 July 2002 (in relation to England) or 1 January 2003 (in relation to Wales); para (a) substituted by the References to Rating (Housing) Regulations 1990, SI 1990/434, reg 2, Schedule, para 5; words in square brackets in para (a)(i), (ii) substituted by the Housing Act 1996, s 114, except in relation to cases where, before 1 October 1996, a notice was given under s 8 or 14 of this Act, or an application was made under s 27 of this Act; words in italics in para (a) repealed, para (aa) and words in first pair of square brackets in para (b) inserted by the Housing and Regeneration Act 2008, ss 300(1), 321(1), Sch 16, as from 7 September 2009 (in relation to England, subject to transitional provisions in SI 2009/2096, art 3) and as from a day to be appointed (in relation to Wales).

Sub-ss (1ZA), (1ZB): inserted by the Commonhold and Leasehold Reform Act 2002, s 138(2), subject to savings as noted above.

Sub-s (1ZC): inserted by the Commonhold and Leasehold Reform Act 2002, s 140, subject to savings as noted above; words in square brackets in para (c) inserted by the Civil Partnership Act 2004, s 81, Sch 8, para 3.

Sub-s (1ZD): inserted by the Commonhold and Leasehold Reform Act 2002, s 140, subject to savings as noted above.

Sub-s (1A): inserted by the Housing and Planning Act 1986, s 18, Sch 4, paras 3, 11; for the first words in italics there are substituted the words "subsection (1)" and second words in italics repealed by the Housing and Regeneration Act 2008, ss 300(2)(a), 321(1), Sch 16, as from 7 September 2009 (in relation to England, subject to transitional provisions in SI 2009/2096, art 3) and as from a day to be appointed (in relation to Wales).

Sub-s (1B): inserted by the Commonhold and Leasehold Reform Act 2002, s 139(2), subject to savings as noted above.

Sub-s (2): repealed by the Commonhold and Leasehold Reform Act 2002, s 180, Sch 14, subject to savings as noted above.

Sub-s (3): words in first pair of square brackets substituted and words omitted repealed by the Commonhold and Leasehold Reform Act 2002, ss 138(3), 180, Sch 14, subject to savings as noted above; para (b) substituted by the Agricultural Tenancies Act 1995, s 40, Schedule, para 22; words in third pair of square brackets added by the Leasehold Reform, Housing and Urban Development Act 1993, s 67(1), (2), except where the right to acquire the freehold of a house and premises arises other than by virtue of any one or more of the provisions of ss 1A, 1B of this Act at **[79]**, **[81]**, in relation to a lease created after 1 November 1993 pursuant to a contract entered into before that date.

Sub-s (3A): inserted by the Leasehold Reform, Housing and Urban Development Act 1993, s 67(1), (3), subject to savings as noted above; figure in square brackets in para (b) inserted by the Housing Act 1996, s 106, Sch 9, para 2(1), (2), except in a case where the house and premises are held under a tenancy which is a shared ownership lease within the meaning of the Housing Act 1985, s 622 at **[571]**, and was granted by a housing association, whether or not the interest of the landlord still belongs to such an association, nor does it have effect in a case where, before 1 April 1997, a notice was given under s 8 of this Act at **[90]**, or an application was made under s 27 of this Act at **[110]**, or a notice was given under the Leasehold Reform, Housing and Urban Development Act 1993, s 13 or 42 at **[817]**, **[848]**, or an application was made under s 26 or 50 of that Act at **[830]**, **[856]**; figure in italics repealed by the Housing and Regeneration Act 2008, s 321(1), Sch 16, as from 7 September 2009 (in relation to England, subject to transitional provisions in SI 2009/2096, art 3) and as from a day to be appointed (in relation to Wales).

Sub-s (4): words in square brackets substituted by the Rent Act 1977, s 155, Sch 23, para 42.

Sub-s (4A): inserted by the Housing Act 1980, s 141, Sch 21, para 2.

Sub-ss (5), (6): added by the Housing Act 1974, s 118(1), (3).

Sub-s (7): added by SI 1990/434, reg 2, Schedule, para 6.

## [1A  Right to enfranchisement only in case of houses whose value or rent exceeds applicable limit under s 1 or 4

(1)  Where subsection (1) of section 1 above would apply in the case of the tenant of a house but for the fact that the applicable financial limit specified in subsection (1)(a)(i) or (ii) or (as the case may be) subsection (5) or (6) of that section is exceeded, this Part of this Act shall have effect to confer on the tenant the same right to acquire the freehold of the house and premises as would be conferred by subsection (1) of that section if that limit were not exceeded.

(2)  *Where a tenancy of any property is not a tenancy at a low rent in accordance with section 4(1) below but is a tenancy falling within section 4A(1) below, the tenancy shall nevertheless be treated as a tenancy at a low rent for the purposes of this Part of this Act so far as it has effect for conferring on any person a right to acquire the freehold of a house and premises.]*

[79]

**NOTES**

Inserted by the Leasehold Reform, Housing and Urban Development Act 1993, s 63.

Sub-s (2): repealed by the Housing and Regeneration Act 2008, ss 300(2)(b)(i), 321(1), Sch 16, as from 7 September 2009 (in relation to England, subject to transitional provisions in SI 2009/2096, art 3) and as from a day to be appointed (in relation to Wales).

## [1AA  Additional right to enfranchisement only in case of houses whose rent exceeds applicable limit under section 4

(1)  Where—

    (a)    *section 1(1) above would apply in the case of the tenant of a house but for the fact that the tenancy is not a tenancy at a low rent, and*

    (b)    *the tenancy ... is not an excluded tenancy,*

this Part of this Act shall have effect to confer on the tenant the same right to acquire the freehold of the house and premises as would be conferred by section 1(1) above if it were a tenancy at a low rent.

(2)  ...

(3)  *A tenancy is an excluded tenancy for the purposes of subsection (1) above if—*

    (a)    *the house which the tenant occupies under the tenancy is in an area designated for the purposes of this provision as a rural area by order made by the Secretary of State,*

    (b)    *the freehold of that house is owned together with adjoining land which is not occupied for residential purposes and has been owned together with such land since [1st April 1997 (the date on which section 106 of the Housing Act 1996 came into force)], and*

    [(c)    *the tenancy either—*

        (i)    *was granted on or before that date, or*

        (ii)    *was granted after that date, but on or before the coming into force of section 141 of the Commonhold and Leasehold Reform Act 2002, for a term of years certain not exceeding thirty-five years.]*

(4)  ...

(5)  *The power to make an order under subsection (3) above shall be exercisable by statutory instrument which shall be subject to annulment in pursuance of a resolution of either House of Parliament.]*

[80]

**NOTES**

Inserted by the Housing Act 1996, s 106, Sch 9, para 1, except in a case where the house and premises are held under a tenancy which is a shared ownership lease within the meaning of the Housing Act 1985, s 622 at **[571]**, and was granted by a housing association, whether or not the interest of the landlord still belongs to such an association, nor does it have effect in a case where, before 1 April 1997, a notice was given under s 8 of this Act at **[90]**, or an application was made under s 27 of this Act at **[110]**, or a notice was given under the Leasehold Reform, Housing and Urban Development Act 1993, s 13 or 42 at **[817]**, **[848]**, or an application was made under s 26 or 50 of that Act at **[830]**, **[856]**.

Repealed by the Housing and Regeneration Act 2008, ss 300(2)(b)(ii), 321(1), Sch 16, as from 7 September 2009 (in relation to England, subject to transitional provisions in SI 2009/2096, art 3) and as from a day to be appointed (in relation to Wales).

Sub-s (1): words omitted repealed by the Commonhold and Leasehold Reform Act 2002, ss 141(1), (2)(a), 180, Sch 14, except in relation to an application for enfranchisement or an extended lease of a house in respect of which notice was given under s 8 or 14 of this Act at **[90]**, **[97]**, or where an application was made under s 27 of this Act at **[110]**, before 26 July 2002 (in relation to England) or 1 January 2003 (in relation to Wales).

Sub-ss (2), (4): repealed by the Commonhold and Leasehold Reform Act 2002, ss 141(1), (2)(b), 180, Sch 14, subject to savings as noted above.

Sub-s (3): words in square brackets in para (b) and the whole of para (c) substituted by the Commonhold and Leasehold Reform Act 2002, s 141(1), (3), subject to savings as noted above.

## [1B Right of enfranchisement only in case of certain tenancies terminable after death or marriage

Where a tenancy granted so as to become terminable by notice after [a death, a marriage or the formation of a civil partnership]—

(a)     is (apart from this section) a long tenancy in accordance with section 3(1) below, but

(b)     was granted before 18th April 1980 or in pursuance of a contract entered into before that date,

then (notwithstanding section 3(1)) the tenancy shall be a long tenancy for the purposes of this Part of this Act only so far as this Part has effect for conferring on any person a right to acquire the freehold of a house and premises.]

**[81]**

### NOTES

Inserted by the Leasehold Reform, Housing and Urban Development Act 1993, s 64(1).

Words in square brackets substituted by the Civil Partnership Act 2004, s 81, Sch 8, para 4.

## 2   Meaning of "house" and "house and premises", and adjustment of boundary

(1)     For purposes of this Part of this Act, "house" includes any building designed or adapted for living in and reasonably so called, notwithstanding that the building is not structurally detached, or was or is not solely designed or adapted for living in, or is divided horizontally into flats or maisonettes; and—

(a)     where a building is divided horizontally, the flats or other units into which it is so divided are not separate "houses", though the building as a whole may be; and

(b)     where a building is divided vertically the building as a whole is not a "house" though any of the units into which it is divided may be.

(2)     References in this Part of this Act to a house do not apply to a house which is not structurally detached and of which a material part lies above or below a part of the structure not comprised in the house.

(3)     Subject to the following provisions of this section, where in relation to a house let to … a tenant reference is made in this Part of this Act to the house and premises, the reference to premises is to be taken as referring to any garage, outhouse, garden, yard and appurtenances which at the relevant time are let to him with the house …

(4)     In relation to the exercise by a tenant of any right conferred by this Part of this Act there shall be treated as included in the house and premises any other premises let with the house and premises but not at the relevant time occupied and used [subject to a tenancy vested in him] (whether in consequence of an assignment of the term therein … or otherwise), if—

(a)     the landlord at the relevant time has an interest in the other premises and, not later than two months after the relevant time, gives to the tenant written notice objecting to the further severance of them from the house and premises; and

(b)     either the tenant agrees to their inclusion with the house and premises or the court is satisfied that it would be unreasonable to require the landlord to retain them without the house and premises.

(5)     In relation to the exercise by a tenant of any right conferred by this Part of this Act there shall be treated as not included in the house and premises any part of them which lies above or below other premises (not consisting only of underlying mines or minerals), if—

(a)     the landlord at the relevant time has an interest in the other premises and, not later than two months after the relevant time, gives to the tenant written notice objecting to the further severance from them of that part of the house and premises; and

(b)     either the tenant agrees to the exclusion of that part of the house and premises or the court is satisfied that any hardship or inconvenience likely to result to the tenant from the exclusion, when account is taken of anything that can be done to mitigate its effects and of any undertaking of the landlord to take steps to mitigate them, is out-weighed by the difficulties involved in the further severance from the other premises and any hardship or inconvenience likely to result from that severance to persons interested in those premises.

(6) The rights conferred on a tenant by this Part of this Act in relation to any house and premises shall not extend to underlying minerals comprised in the tenancy if the landlord requires that the minerals be excepted, and if proper provision is made for the support of the house and premises as they have been enjoyed during the tenancy and in accordance with its terms.

(7) Where by virtue of subsection (4) above a tenant of a house acquiring the freehold or an extended lease is required to include premises of which the tenancy is not vested in him, this Part of this Act shall apply for the purpose as if in the case of those premises a tenancy on identical terms were vested in him and the holder of the actual tenancy were a sub-tenant; and where by virtue of subsection (5) or (6) above a tenant of a house acquiring the freehold or an extended lease is required to exclude property of which the tenancy is vested in him, then unless the landlord and the tenant otherwise agree or the court for the protection of either of them from hardship or inconvenience otherwise orders, the grant to the tenant shall operate as a surrender of the tenancy in that property and the provision to be made by the grant shall be determined as if the surrender had taken place before the relevant time.

---

**NOTES**

Sub-s (3): words omitted repealed by the Commonhold and Leasehold Reform Act 2002, s 180, Sch 14, except in relation to an application for enfranchisement or an extended lease of a house in respect of which notice was given under s 8 or 14 of this Act at **[90]**, **[97]**, or where an application was made under s 27 of this Act at **[110]**, before 26 July 2002 (in relation to England) or 1 January 2003 (in relation to Wales).

Sub-s (4): words in square brackets substituted and words omitted repealed by the Commonhold and Leasehold Reform Act 2002, ss 138(4), 180, Sch 14, subject to savings as noted above.

---

**[82]**

## 3 Meaning of "long tenancy"

(1) In this Part of this Act "long tenancy" means, subject to the provisions of this section, a tenancy granted for a term of years certain exceeding twenty-one years, whether or not the tenancy is (or may become) terminable before the end of that term by notice given by or to the tenant or by re-entry, forfeiture or otherwise, and includes [both a tenancy taking effect under s 149(6) of the Law of Property Act 1925 (leases terminable after a death or marriage [or the formation of a civil partnership]) and] a tenancy for a term fixed by law under a grant with a covenant or obligation for perpetual renewal unless it is a tenancy by sub-demise from one which is not a long tenancy:

Provided that a tenancy granted so as to become terminable by notice after [a death, a marriage or the formation of a civil partnership] is not to be treated as a long tenancy [if—

    (a)    the notice is capable of being given at any time after the death or marriage of[, or the formation of a civil partnership by,] the tenant;

    (b)    the length of the notice is not more than three months; and

    (c)    the terms of the tenancy preclude both—

        (i)    its assignment otherwise than by virtue of section 92 of the Housing Act 1985 (assignments by way of exchange), and

        (ii)    the subletting of the whole of the premises comprised in it.]

(2) Where the tenant of any property under a long tenancy at a low rent [(other than a lease excluded from the operation of this Part by section 33A of and Schedule 4A to this Act)], on the coming to an end of that tenancy, becomes or has become tenant of the property or part of it under another tenancy (whether by express grant or by implication of law), then the later tenancy shall be deemed for the purposes of this Part of this Act, including any further application of this subsection, to be a long tenancy irrespective of its terms.

(3) Where the tenant of any property under a long tenancy, on the coming to an end of that tenancy, becomes or has become tenant of the property or part of it under another long tenancy, then in relation to the property or that part of it this Part of this Act [ ... ] shall apply as if there had been a single tenancy granted for a term beginning at the same time as the term under the earlier tenancy and expiring at the same time as the term under the later tenancy.

(4) Where a tenancy is or has been granted for a term of years certain not exceeding twenty-one years, but with a covenant or obligation for renewal without payment of a premium (but not for perpetual renewal), and the tenancy is or has been once or more renewed so as to bring to more than twenty-one years the total of the terms granted (including any interval between the end of a tenancy and the grant of a renewal), then this Part of this Act shall apply as it would apply if the term originally granted had been one exceeding twenty-one years.

(5) References in this Part of this Act to a long tenancy include any period during which the tenancy is or was continued under Part I or II of the Landlord and Tenant Act 1954 [under Schedule 10 to the Local Government and Housing Act 1989] or under the Leasehold Property (Temporary Provisions) Act 1951.

(6)   Where at any time there are separate tenancies, with the same landlord and the same tenant, of two or more parts of a house, or of a house or part of it and land or other premises occupied therewith, then in relation to the property comprised in such of those tenancies as are long tenancies this Part of this Act shall apply as it would if at that time there were a single tenancy of that property and the tenancy were a long tenancy, and for that purpose references in this Part of this Act to the commencement of the term or to the term date shall, if the separate tenancies commenced at different dates or have different term dates, have effect as references to the commencement or term date, as the case may be, of the tenancy comprising the house (or the earliest commencement or earliest term date of the tenancies comprising it):

Provided that this subsection shall have effect subject to the operation of subsections (2) to (5) above in relation to any of the separate tenancies.

**[83]**

**NOTES**
Sub-s (1): words in first (outer) pair of square brackets inserted and words in fourth (outer) pair of square brackets substituted by the Leasehold Reform, Housing and Urban Development Act 1993, s 64(2); words in second (inner) and fifth (inner) pairs of square brackets inserted and words in third pair of square brackets substituted by the Civil Partnership Act 2004, s 81, Sch 8, para 5.
Sub-s (2): words in square brackets inserted by the Housing and Planning Act 1986, s 18, Sch 4, paras 4, 11.
Sub-s (3): words omitted from square brackets inserted by the Housing Act 1996, s 106, Sch 9, para 2(1), (3) and repealed by the Commonhold and Leasehold Reform Act 2002, s 180, Sch 14, except in relation to an application for enfranchisement or an extended lease of a house in respect of which notice was given under s 8 or 14 of this Act at **[90]**, **[97]**, or where an application was made under s 27 of this Act at **[110]**, before 26 July 2002 (in relation to England) or 1 January 2003 (in relation to Wales).
Sub-s (5): words in square brackets inserted by the Local Government and Housing Act 1989, s 194(1), Sch 11, para 8.
Leasehold Property (Temporary Provisions) Act 1951: repealed by the Statute Law (Repeals) Act 1975.

### 4   Meaning of "low rent"

(1)   For purposes of this Part of this Act a tenancy of any property is a tenancy at a low rent at any time when rent is not payable under the tenancy in respect of the property at a yearly rate—
> [(i)   if the tenancy was entered into before 1st April 1990[, or on or after 1st April 1990 in pursuance of a contract made before that date, and the property had a rateable value other than nil at the date of the commencement of the tenancy or else at any time before 1st April 1990,] equal to or more than two-thirds of the rateable value of the property on the appropriate day or, if later, the first day of the term]
> [(ii)   if the tenancy [does not fall within paragraph (i) above,] more than £1,000 if the property is in Greater London and £250 if the property is elsewhere]:

Provided that a tenancy granted between the end of August 1939 and the beginning of April 1963 otherwise than by way of building lease (whether or not it is, by virtue of section 3(3) above, to be treated for other purposes as forming a single tenancy with a previous tenancy) shall not be regarded as a tenancy at a low rent if at the commencement of the tenancy the rent payable under the tenancy exceeded two-thirds of the letting value of the property (on the same terms).

For the purposes of this subsection—
> (a)   "appropriate day" means the 23rd March 1965 or such later day as by virtue of [section 25(3) of the Rent Act 1977] would be the appropriate day for purposes of that Act in relation to a dwelling-house consisting of the house in question [if the reference in paragraph (a) of that provision to a rateable value were to a rateable value other than nil]; and
> (b)   "rent" means rent reserved as such, and there shall be disregarded any part of the rent expressed to be payable in consideration of services to be provided, or of repairs, maintenance or insurance to be effected by the landlord, or to be payable in respect of the cost thereof to the landlord or a superior landlord; and
> (c)   there shall be disregarded any term of the tenancy providing for suspension or reduction of rent in the event of damage to property demised, or for any penal addition to the rent in the event of a contravention of or non-compliance with the terms of the tenancy or an agreement collateral thereto; and
> (d)   "building lease" means a lease granted in pursuance or in consideration of an agreement for the erection or the substantial re-building or reconstruction of the whole or part of the house in question or a building comprising it.

(2)   Where on a claim by the tenant of a house to exercise any right conferred by this Part of this Act a question arises under section 1(1) above whether his tenancy of the house is or was at any time a tenancy at a low rent, the question shall be determined by reference to the rent and rateable value of the house and premises as a whole, and in relation to a time before the relevant time shall be so determined whether or not the property then occupied with the house or any part of it was the same in all respects as that comprised in the house and premises for purposes of the claim; but, in a case where the tenancy derives (in accordance with section 3(6) above) from more than one separate

tenancy, the proviso to subsection (1) above shall have effect if, but only if, it applies to one of the separate tenancies which comprises the house or part of it.

(3)   Where on a claim by the tenant of a house to exercise any right conferred by this Part of this Act a question arises under section 3(2) above whether a tenancy is or was a long tenancy by reason of a previous tenancy having been a long tenancy at a low rent, the question whether the previous tenancy was one at a low rent shall be determined in accordance with subsection (2) above as if it were a question arising under section 1(1), and shall be so determined by reference to the rent and rateable value of the house and premises or the part included in the previous tenancy, exclusive of any other land or premises so included:

Provided that where an apportionment of rent or rateable value is required because the previous tenancy did not include the whole of the house and premises or included other property, the apportionment shall be made as at the end of the previous tenancy except in so far as, in the case of rent, an apportionment falls to be made at an earlier date under subsection (6) below.

(4)   For purposes of subsection (2) or (3) above a house and premises shall be taken as not including any premises which are to be or may be included under section 2(4) above in giving effect to the tenant's claim, and as including any part which is to be or may be excluded under section 2(5) or (6).

(5)   Where on a claim by the tenant of a house to exercise any right conferred by this Part of this Act a question arises whether a tenancy granted as mentioned in the proviso to subsection (1) above is or was at any time a tenancy at a low rent, it shall be presumed until the contrary is shown that the letting value referred to in that proviso was such that the proviso does not apply.

(6)   Any entire rent payable at any time in respect of both a house and premises or part thereof and of property not included in the house and premises shall for purposes of this section be apportioned as may be just according to the circumstances existing at the date of the severance giving rise to the apportionment, and references in this section to the rent of a house and premises or of part thereof shall be construed accordingly.

[(7)   Section 1(7) above applies to any amount referred to in subsection (1)(ii) above as it applies to the amount referred to in subsection (1)(a)(ii) of that section.]

[84]

**NOTES**
Sub-s (1): paras (i), (ii) inserted by the References to Rating (Housing) Regulations 1990, SI 1990/434, reg 2, Schedule, para 7; words in square brackets in paras (i), (ii) substituted and words in second pair of square brackets in para (a) added by the Housing Act 1996, s 105(1), except in relation to cases where, before 1 October 1996, a notice was given under s 8 or 14 of this Act at **[90]**, **[97]**, or an application was made under s 27 of this Act at **[110]**; words in first pair of square brackets in para (a) substituted by the Rent Act 1977, s 155, Sch 23, para 42.
Sub-s (7): added by SI 1990/434, reg 2, Schedule, para 8.

**[4A   Alternative rent limits for purposes of section 1A(2)**

(*1*)   *For the purposes of section 1A(2) above a tenancy of any property falls within this subsection if either no rent was payable under it in respect of the property during the initial year or the aggregate amount of rent so payable during that year did not exceed the following amount, namely—*

(*a*)   *where the tenancy was entered into before 1st April 1963, two-thirds of the letting value of the property (on the same terms) on the date of the commencement of the tenancy;*

(*b*)   *where—*

(*i*)   *the tenancy was entered into either on or after 1st April 1963 but before 1st April 1990, or on or after 1st April 1990 in pursuance of a contract made before that date, and*

[(*ii*)   *the property had a rateable value other than nil at the date of the commencement of the tenancy or else at any time before 1st April 1990,]*

(*c*)   *in any other case, £1,000 if the property is in Greater London or £250 if elsewhere.*

(*2*)   *For the purposes of subsection (1) above—*

(*a*)   *"the initial year", in relation to any tenancy, means the period of one year beginning with the date of the commencement of the tenancy;*

[(*b*)   *"the relevant date" means the date of the commencement of the tenancy or, if the property did not have a rateable value, or had a rateable value of nil, on that date, the date on which it first had a rateable value other than nil;]* and

(*c*)   *paragraphs (b) and (c) of section 4(1) above shall apply as they apply for the purposes of section 4(1);*

*and it is hereby declared that in subsection (1) above the reference to the letting value of any property is to be construed in like manner as the reference in similar terms which appears in the proviso to section 4(1) above.*

*(3)   Section 1(7) above applies to any amount referred to in subsection (1)(c) above as it applies to the amount referred to in subsection (1)(a)(ii) of that section.]*

**[85]**

**NOTES**
   Inserted by the Leasehold Reform, Housing and Urban Development Act 1993, s 65.
   Repealed by the Housing and Regeneration Act 2008, ss 300(2)(b)(iii), 321(1), Sch 16, as from 7 September 2009 (in relation to England, subject to transitional provisions in SI 2009/2096, art 3) and as from a day to be appointed (in relation to Wales).
   Sub-s (1): para (b)(ii) substituted by the Housing Act 1996, s 105(2)(a), except in relation to cases where, before 1 October 1996, a notice was given under s 8 or 14 of this Act at **[90]**, **[97]**, or an application was made under s 27 of this Act at **[110]**.
   Sub-s (2): para (b) substituted by the Housing Act 1996, s 105(2)(b), subject to savings as noted above.

**5   General provisions as to claims to enfranchisement or extension**

   (1)   Where under this Part of this Act a tenant of a house has the right to acquire the freehold or an extended lease and gives notice of his desire to have it, the rights and obligations of the landlord and the tenant arising from the notice shall inure for the benefit of and be enforceable against them, their executors, administrators and assigns to the like extent (but no further) as rights and obligations arising under a contract for a sale or lease freely entered into between the landlord and tenant; and accordingly, in relation to matters arising out of any such notice, references in this Part of this Act to the tenant and the landlord shall, in so far as the context permits, include their respective executors, administrators and assigns.

   (2)   Notwithstanding anything in subsection (1) above, the rights and obligations there referred to of a tenant shall be assignable with, but not capable of subsisting apart from, the tenancy of the entire house and premises; and if the tenancy is assigned without the benefit of the notice, or if the tenancy of one part of the house and premises is assigned to or vests in any person without the tenancy of another part, the notice shall accordingly cease to have effect, and the tenant shall be liable to make such compensation as may be just to the landlord in respect of the interference (if any) by the notice with the exercise by the landlord of his power to dispose of or deal with the house and premises or any neighbouring property.

   (3)   In the event of any default by the landlord or the tenant in carrying out the obligations arising from any such notice, the other of them shall have the like rights and remedies as in the case of a contract freely entered into.

   (4)   The provisions of Schedule 1 to this Act shall have effect in relation to the operation of this Part of this Act where a person gives notice of his desire to have the freehold or an extended lease of a house and premises, and either he does so in respect of a sub-tenancy or there is a tenancy reversionary on his tenancy; but any such notice given in respect of a tenancy granted by sub-demise out of a superior tenancy other than a long tenancy at a low rent shall be of no effect if the grant was made in breach of the terms of the superior tenancy and there has been no waiver of the breach by the superior landlord.

   (5)   No lease shall be registrable under the Land Charges Act 1925 or be deemed to be an estate contract within the meaning of that Act by reason of the rights conferred on the tenant by this Part of this Act to acquire the freehold or an extended lease of property thereby demised, nor shall any right of a tenant arising from a notice under this Act of his desire to have the freehold or to have an extended lease be [regarded for the purposes of the Land Registration Act 2002 as an interest falling within any of the paragraphs of Schedule 1 or 3 to that Act]; but any such notice shall be registrable under the Land Charges Act 1925 or may be the subject of a notice [under the Land Registration Act 2002], as if it were an estate contract.

   (6)   A notice of a person's desire to have the freehold or an extended lease of a house and premises under this Part of this Act—

   (a)   shall be of no effect if at the relevant time any person or body of persons who has or have been, or could be, authorised to acquire the whole or part of the house and premises compulsorily for any purpose has or have, with a view to its acquisition for that purpose, served notice to treat on the landlord or on the tenant, or entered into a contract for the purchase of the interest of either of them, and the notice to treat or contract remains in force; and

   (b)   shall cease to have effect if before the completion of the conveyance in pursuance of the tenant's notice any such person or body of persons serves notice to treat as aforesaid;

but where a tenant's notice ceases to have effect by reason of a notice to treat served on him or on the landlord, then on the occasion of the compulsory acquisition in question the compensation payable in respect of any interest in the house and premises (whether or not the one to which that notice to treat relates) shall be determined on the basis of the value of the interest subject to and with the benefit of the rights and obligations arising from the tenant's notice and affecting that interest.

   (7)   Where any such notice given by a tenant entitled to acquire the freehold or an extended lease has effect, then (without prejudice to the general law as to the frustration of contracts) the

landlord and all other persons shall be discharged from the further performance, so far as relates to the disposal in any manner of the landlord's interest in the house and premises or any part thereof, of any contract previously entered into and not providing for the eventuality of such a notice (including any such contract made in pursuance of the order of any court):

Provided that, in the case of a notice of the tenant's desire to have an extended lease, this subsection shall not apply to discharge a person from performance of a contract unless the contract was entered into on the basis, common to both parties, that vacant possession of the house and premises or part thereof would or might be obtainable on the termination of the existing tenancy.

(8) A tenant's notice of his desire to have an extended lease under this Part of this Act shall cease to have effect if afterwards (being entitled to do so) he gives notice of his desire to have the freehold.

[86]

---

**NOTES**

Sub-s (5): words in square brackets substituted by the Land Registration Act 2002, s 133, Sch 11, para 8(1), (2).

Land Charges Act 1925: see now the Land Charges Act 1972 and the Local Land Charges Act 1975.

---

## 6 Rights of trustees

(1) [A tenant of a house shall for purposes of this Part of this Act be treated as having been a tenant of it at any earlier time] if at that time—

    (a) the tenancy was settled land for purposes of the Settled Land Act 1925, and he was sole tenant for life within the meaning of that Act; or

    (b) the tenancy was vested in trustees and he, as a person beneficially interested (whether directly or derivatively) under the trusts, was entitled or permitted to occupy the house by reason of that interest.

References in this section to trustees include persons holding on [a trust arising under section 34 or section 36] of the Law of Property Act 1925 in cases of joint ownership or ownership in common.

(2) Where a tenancy of a house is settled land for purposes of the Settled Land Act 1925, a sole tenant for life within the meaning of that Act shall have the same rights under this Part of this Act ... as if the tenancy of it belonged to him absolutely, but without prejudice to his position under the settlement as a trustee for all parties entitled under the settlement; and—

    (a) the powers under that Act of a tenant for life shall include power to accept an extended lease under this Part of this Act; and

    (b) an extended lease granted under this Part of this Act to a tenant for life or statutory owner shall be treated as a subsidiary vesting deed in accordance with section 53(2) of that Act.

(3) *Where a tenancy of a house is vested in trustees (other than a sole tenant for life within the meaning of the Settled Land Act 1925), and a person beneficially interested (whether directly or derivatively) under the trusts is entitled or permitted by reason of his interest to occupy the house, then the trustees shall have the like rights under this Part of this Act in respect of his occupation as he would have if he were the tenant occupying in right of the tenancy.*

(4) Without prejudice to any powers exercisable under the Settled Land Act 1925 by tenants for life or statutory owners within the meaning of that Act, where a tenancy of a house is vested in trustees, then unless the instrument regulating the trusts (being made after the passing of this Act) contains an explicit direction to the contrary, the powers of the trustees under that instrument shall include power, with the like consent or on the like direction (if any) as may be required for the exercise of their powers (or ordinary powers) of investment, to acquire and retain the freehold or an extended lease under this Part of this Act.

(5) The purposes authorised for the application of capital money by section 73 of the Settled Land Act 1925 ... and the purposes authorised by section 71 of the Settled Land Act 1925 ... as purposes for which moneys may be raised by mortgage, shall include the payment of any expenses incurred by a tenant for life ... in or in connection with proceedings taken by him ... by virtue of subsection (2) *or* (3) above.

[87]

---

**NOTES**

Sub-s (1): words in first pair of square brackets substituted by the Commonhold and Leasehold Reform Act 2002, s 138(5), except in relation to an application for enfranchisement or an extended lease of a house in respect of which notice was given under s 8 or 14 of this Act at [90], [97], or where an application was made under s 27 of this Act at [110], before 26 July 2002 (in relation to England) or 1 January 2003 (in relation to Wales); words in second pair of square brackets substituted by the Trusts of Land and Appointment of Trustees Act 1996, s 25(1), Sch 3, para 10(a), subject to savings in s 25(4), (5) thereof.

Sub-s (2): words omitted repealed by the Commonhold and Leasehold Reform Act 2002, s 180, Sch 14, subject to savings as noted above.

Sub-s (3): repealed by the Commonhold and Leasehold Reform Act 2002, s 180, Sch 14, as from a day to be appointed.

Sub-s (5): words omitted in first and second places repealed by the Trusts of Land and Appointment of Trustees Act 1996, s 25(2), Sch 4, subject to savings in s 25(4), (5) thereof; words omitted in third and fourth places repealed by the Commonhold and Leasehold Reform Act 2002, s 180, Sch 14, subject to savings as noted above; words in italics repealed by the Commonhold and Leasehold Reform Act 2002, s 180, Sch 14, as from a day to be appointed.

## [6A   Rights of personal representatives

(1)   Where a tenant of a house dies and, immediately before his death, he had under this Part of this Act—

    (a)    the right to acquire the freehold, or

    (b)    the right to an extended lease,

the right is exercisable by his personal representatives while the tenancy is vested in them (but subject to subsection (2) below); and, accordingly, in such a case references in this Part of this Act to the tenant shall, in so far as the context permits, be to the personal representatives.

(2)   The personal representatives of a tenant may not give notice of their desire to have the freehold or an extended lease by virtue of subsection (1) above later than two years after the grant of probate or letters of administration.]

                                                                                         **[88]**

**NOTES**

Inserted by the Commonhold and Leasehold Reform Act 2002, s 142(1).

## 7   Rights of members of family succeeding to tenancy on death

(1)   Where the tenant of a house dies ..., and on his death a member of his family resident in the house becomes tenant of it under the same tenancy, then for the purposes of any claim by that member of the family to acquire the freehold or an extended lease under this Part of this Act he shall be treated as having been the tenant ... during any period when—

    (a)    he was resident in the house, and it was his only or main place of residence ...

    (b)    ...

(2)   For purposes of this section—

    (a)    a member of a tenant's family on whom the tenancy devolves on the tenant's death by virtue of a testamentary disposition or the law of intestate succession shall, on the tenancy vesting in him, be treated as having become tenant on the death; and

    (b)    a member of a tenant's family who, on the tenant's death, acquires the tenancy by the appropriation of it in or towards satisfaction of any legacy, share in residue, debt or other share in or claim against the tenant's estate, or by the purchase of it on a sale made by the tenant's personal representatives in the administration of the estate, shall be treated as a person on whom the tenancy devolved by direct bequest; and

    (c)    a person's interest in a tenancy as personal representative of a deceased tenant shall be disregarded, but references in paragraphs (a) and (b) above to a tenancy vesting in, or being acquired by, a member of a tenant's family shall apply also where, after the death of a member of the family, the tenancy vests in or is acquired by the personal representatives of that member.

(3)   Where a tenancy for a house is settled land for purposes of the Settled Land Act 1925, and on the death of a tenant for life within the meaning of that Act a member of his family resident [in the house] becomes entitled to the tenancy in accordance with the settlement or by any appropriation by or purchase from the personal representatives in respect of the settled land, this section shall apply as if the tenancy had belonged to the tenant for life absolutely and the trusts of the settlement taking effect after his death had been trusts of his will.

(4)   Where in a case not falling within subsection (3) above a tenancy of a house is held on trust and—

    (a)    a person beneficially interested (whether directly or derivatively) under the trust is entitled or permitted by reason of his interest to occupy the house; and

    (b)    on his death a member of his family resident [in the house] becomes tenant of the house in accordance with the terms of the trust or by any appropriation by or purchase from the trustees;

then this section shall apply as if the deceased person ... had been tenant of it ... , and as if after his death the trustees had held and dealt with the tenancy as his executors (the remaining trusts being trusts of his will).

(5)   Subsections (3) and (4) above shall apply, with any necessary adaptations, where a person becomes entitled to a tenancy on the termination of a settlement or trust as they would apply if he had become entitled in accordance with the settlement or trust.

(6)   ...

(7)　For purposes of this section a person is a member of another's family if that person is—

　(a)　the other's [spouse or civil partner]; or

　(b)　a son or daughter or a son-in-law or daughter-in-law of the other, or of the other's [spouse or civil partner]; or

　(c)　the father or mother of the other, or of the other's [spouse or civil partner].

In paragraph (b) above any reference to a person's son or daughter includes a reference to any stepson or stepdaughter, any illegitimate son or daughter ... of that person, and "son-in-law" and "daughter-in-law" shall be construed accordingly.

(8)　In Schedule 2 to the Intestates' Estates Act 1952 (which gives a surviving spouse a right to require the deceased's interest in the matrimonial home to be appropriated to the survivor's interest in the deceased's estate, but by paragraph 1(2) excludes tenancies terminating, or terminable by the landlord, within two years of the death), paragraph 1(2) shall not apply to a tenancy if—

　(a)　the surviving [spouse or civil partner] would in consequence of an appropriation in accordance with that paragraph become entitled by virtue of this section to acquire the freehold or an extended lease under this Part of this Act, either immediately on the appropriation or before the tenancy can determine or be determined as mentioned in paragraph 1(2); or

　(b)　the deceased [spouse or civil partner], being entitled to acquire the freehold or an extended lease under this Part of this Act, had given notice of his or her desire to have it and the benefit of that notice is appropriated with the tenancy.

(9)　This section shall have effect in relation to deaths occurring before this Act was passed as it has effect in relation to deaths occurring after.

[89]

**NOTES**

Sub-s (1): words omitted repealed by the Commonhold and Leasehold Reform Act 2002, s 180, Sch 14, except in relation to an application for enfranchisement or an extended lease of a house in respect of which notice was given under s 8 or 14 of this Act at [90], [97], or where an application was made under s 27 of this Act at [110], before 26 July 2002 (in relation to England) or 1 January 2003 (in relation to Wales).

Sub-s (3): words in square brackets substituted by the Commonhold and Leasehold Reform Act 2002, s 138(6), subject to savings as noted above.

Sub-s (4): words in square brackets substituted and words omitted repealed by the Commonhold and Leasehold Reform Act 2002, ss 138(6), 180, Sch 14, subject to savings as noted above.

Sub-s (6): repealed by the Commonhold and Leasehold Reform Act 2002, s 180, Sch 14, subject to savings as noted above.

Sub-s (7): words in square brackets substituted by the Civil Partnership Act 2004, s 81, Sch 8, para 6(1), (2); words omitted repealed by the Children Act 1975, s 108(1)(b), Sch 4, Pt I.

Sub-s (8): words in square brackets substituted by the Civil Partnership Act 2004, s 81, Sch 8, para 6(1), (3).

*Enfranchisement*

## 8　Obligation to enfranchise

(1)　Where a tenant of a house has under this Part of this Act a right to acquire the freehold, and gives to the landlord written notice of his desire to have the freehold, then except as provided by this Part of this Act the landlord shall be bound to make to the tenant, and the tenant to accept, (at the price and on the conditions so provided) a grant of the house and premises for an estate in fee simple absolute, subject to the tenancy and to tenant's incumbrances, but otherwise free of incumbrances.

(2)　For purposes of this Part of this Act "incumbrances" includes rent-charges and, subject to subsection (3) below, personal liabilities attaching in respect of the ownership of land or an interest in land though not charged on that land or interest; and "tenant's incumbrances" includes any interest directly or indirectly derived out of the tenancy, and any incumbrance on the tenancy or any such interest (whether or not the same matter is an incumbrance also on any interest reversionary on the tenancy).

(3)　Burdens originating in tenure, and burdens in respect of the upkeep or regulation for the benefit of any locality of any land, building, structure, works, ways or watercourse shall not be treated as incumbrances for purposes of this Part of this Act, but any conveyance executed to give effect to this section shall be made subject thereto except as otherwise provided by section 11 below.

(4)　A conveyance executed to give effect to this section—

　(a)　shall have effect under section 2(1) of the Law of Property Act 1925 to overreach any incumbrance capable of being overreached under that section as if, where the interest conveyed is settled land, the conveyance were made under the powers of the Settled Land Act 1925 and as if the requirements of section 2(1) as to payment of the capital money allowed any part of the purchase price paid or applied in accordance with sections 11 to 13 below to be so paid or applied;

　(b)　shall not be made subject to any incumbrance capable of being overreached by the conveyance, but shall be made subject (where they are not capable of being overreached) to rentcharges [redeemable under sections 8 to 10 of the Rentcharges Act 1977 and those falling within paragraphs (c) and (d) of section 2(3) of that Act (estate rentcharges and rentcharges imposed under certain enactments)], except as otherwise provided by section 11 below.

(5)   Notwithstanding that on a grant to a tenant of a house and premises under this section no payment or a nominal payment only is required from the tenant for the price of the house and premises, the tenant shall nevertheless be deemed for all purposes to be a purchaser for a valuable consideration in money or money's worth.

**[90]**

**NOTES**

Sub-s (4): words in square brackets substituted by the Rentcharges Act 1977, s 17(1), Sch 1, para 4(1).

**9   Purchase price and costs of enfranchisement, and tenant's right to withdraw**

(1)   Subject to subsection (2) below, the price payable for a house and premises on a conveyance under section 8 above shall be the amount which at the relevant time the house and premises, if sold in the open market by a willing seller [(with the tenant and members of his family ... not buying or seeking to buy)], might be expected to realise on the following assumptions:—

(a)   on the assumption that the vendor was selling for an estate in fee simple, subject to the tenancy but on the assumption that this Part of this Act conferred no right to acquire the freehold; and if the tenancy has not been extended under this Part of this Act, on the assumption that (subject to the landlord's rights under section 17 below) it was to be so extended;

(b)   on the assumption that (subject to paragraph (a) above) the vendor was selling subject, in respect of rentcharges ... to which section 11(2) below applies, to the same annual charge as the conveyance to the tenant is to be subject to, but the purchaser would otherwise be effectively exonerated until the termination of the tenancy from any liability or charge in respect of tenant's incumbrances; and

(c)   on the assumption that (subject to paragraphs (a) and (b) above) the vendor was selling with and subject to the rights and burdens with and subject to which the conveyance to the tenant is to be made, and in particular with and subject to such permanent or extended rights and burdens as are to be created in order to give effect to section 10 below.

[The reference in this subsection to members of the tenant's family shall be construed in accordance with section 7(7) of this Act.]

[(1A)   [Notwithstanding the foregoing subsection, the price payable for a house and premises,—

(i)   the rateable value of which was above £1,000 in Greater London and £500 elsewhere on 31st March 1990, or,

(ii)   which had no rateable value on that date and R exceeded £16,333 under the formula in section 1(1)(a) above (and section 1(7) above shall apply to that amount as it applies to the amount referred to in subsection (1)(a)(ii) of that section)

shall be the amount which at the relevant time the house and premises, if sold in the open market by a willing seller, might be expected to realise on the following assumptions:—]

(a)   on the assumption that the vendor was selling for an estate in fee simple, subject to the tenancy, but on the assumption that this Part of this Act conferred no right to acquire the freehold [or an extended lease ... ];

(b)   on the assumption that at the end of the tenancy the tenant has the right to remain in possession of the house and premises—

[(i)   if the tenancy is such a tenancy as is mentioned in subsection (2) or subsection (3) of section 186 of the Local Government and Housing Act 1989, or is a tenancy which is a long tenancy at a low rent for the purposes of Part I of the Landlord and Tenant Act 1954 in respect of which the landlord is not able to serve a notice under section 4 of that Act specifying a date of termination earlier than 15th January 1999, under the provisions of Schedule 10 to the Local Government and Housing Act 1989; and

(ii)   in any other case] under the provisions of Part I of the Landlord and Tenant Act 1954;

(c)   on the assumption that the tenant has no liability to carry out any repairs, maintenance or redecorations under the terms of the tenancy or Part I of the Landlord and Tenant Act 1954;

(d)   on the assumption that the price be diminished by the extent to which the value of the house and premises has been increased by any improvement carried out by the tenant or his predecessors in title at their own expense;

(e)   on the assumption that (subject to paragraph (a) above) the vendor was selling subject, in respect of rentcharges ... to which section 11(2) below applies, to the same annual charge as the conveyance to the tenant is to be subject to, but the purchaser would

PART I
STATUTES

otherwise be effectively exonerated until the termination of the tenancy from any liability or charge in respect of tenant's incumbrances; and

(f)    on the assumption that (subject to paragraphs (a) and (b) above) the vendor was selling with and subject to the rights and burdens with and subject to which the conveyance to the tenant is to be made, and in particular with and subject to such permanent or extended rights and burdens as are to be created in order to give effect to section 10 below.

[(1AA)   Where, in a case in which the price payable for a house and premises is to be determined in accordance with subsection (1A) above, the tenancy has been extended under this Part of this Act—

(a)    if the relevant time is on or before the original term date, the assumptions set out in that subsection apply as if the tenancy is to terminate on the original term date; and

(b)    if the relevant time is after the original term date, the assumptions set out in paragraphs (a), (c) and (e) of that subsection apply as if the tenancy had terminated on the original term date and the assumption set out in paragraph (b) of that subsection applies as if the words "at the end of the tenancy" were omitted.]

(1B)   For the purpose of determining whether the rateable value of the house and premises is above £1,000 in Greater London, or £500 elsewhere the rateable value shall be adjusted to take into account any tenant's improvements in accordance with Schedule 8 to the Housing Act 1974.]

[(1C)   Notwithstanding subsection (1) above, the price payable for a house and premises where the right to acquire the freehold arises by virtue of any one or more of the provisions of sections 1A[, *1AA*] and 1B above[, or where the tenancy of the house and premises has been extended under section 14 below and the notice under section 8(1) above was given (whether by the tenant or a sub-tenant) after the original term date of the tenancy,] shall be determined in accordance with subsection (1A) above; but in any such case—

(a)    ...

(b)    section 9A below has effect for determining whether any additional amount is payable by way of compensation under that section;

and in a case where the provision (or one of the provisions) by virtue of which the right to acquire the freehold arises is section 1A(1) above, subsection (1A) above shall apply with the omission of the assumption set out in paragraph (b) of that subsection.]

[(1D)   Where, in determining the price payable for a house and premises in accordance with this section, there falls to be taken into account any marriage value arising by virtue of the coalescence of the freehold and leasehold interests, the share of the marriage value to which the tenant is to be regarded as being entitled shall be one-half of it.]

[(1E)   But where at the relevant time the unexpired term of the tenant's tenancy exceeds eighty years, the marriage value shall be taken to be nil.]

(2)   The price payable for the house and premises shall be subject to such deduction (if any) in respect of any defect in the title to be conveyed to the tenant as on a sale in the open market might be expected to be allowed between a willing seller and a willing buyer.

(3)   On ascertaining the amount payable, or likely to be payable, as the price for a house and premises in accordance with this section (but not more than one month after the amount payable has been determined by agreement or otherwise), the tenant may give written notice to the landlord that he is unable or unwilling to acquire the house and premises at the price he must pay; and thereupon—

(a)    the notice under section 8 above of his desire to have the freehold shall cease to have effect, and he shall be liable to make such compensation as may be just to the landlord in respect of the interference (if any) by the notice with the exercise by the landlord of his power to dispose of or deal with the house and premises or any neighbouring property; and

(b)    any further notice given under that section with respect to the house or any part of it (with or without other property) shall be void if given within the following [twelve months].

(4)   Where a person gives notice of his desire to have the freehold of a house and premises under this Part of this Act, then unless the notice lapses under any provision of this Act excluding his liability, there shall be borne by him (so far as they are incurred in pursuance of the notice) the reasonable costs of or incidental to any of the following matters:—

(a)    any investigation by the landlord of that person's right to acquire the freehold;

(b)    any conveyance or assurance of the house and premises or any part thereof or of any *outstanding estate or interest therein*;

(c)    deducing, evidencing and verifying the title to the house and premises or any estate or interest therein;

(d)    making out and furnishing such abstracts and copies as the person giving the notice may require;

(e)   any valuation of the house and premises;

but so that this subsection shall not apply to any costs if on a sale made voluntarily a stipulation that they were to be borne by the purchaser would be void.

[(4A)   Subsection (4) above does not require a person to bear the costs of another person in connection with an application to a leasehold valuation tribunal.]

(5)   The landlord's lien (as vendor) on the house and premises for the price payable shall extend—

(a)   to any sums payable by way of rent or recoverable as rent in respect of the house and premises up to the date of the conveyance; and

(b)   to any sums for which the tenant is liable under subsection (4) above; and

(c)   to any other sums due and payable by him to the landlord under or in respect of the tenancy or any agreement collateral thereto.

**[91]**

PART I
STATUTES

## NOTES

Sub-s (1): words in square brackets inserted by the Housing Act 1969, s 82, and this Act is deemed always to have had effect subject to these amendments though the amendments do not have effect where the price was determined (by agreement or otherwise) before the passing of the 1969 Act (25 July 1969); words omitted in the first place repealed by the Commonhold and Leasehold Reform Act 2002, s 180, Sch 14, except in relation to an application for enfranchisement or an extended lease of a house in respect of which notice was given under s 8 or 14 of this Act at **[90]**, **[97]**, or where an application was made under s 27 of this Act at **[110]**, before 26 July 2002 (in relation to England) or 1 January 2003 (in relation to Wales); words omitted from para (b) repealed by the Rentcharges Act 1977, s 17(2), Sch 2.

Sub-s (1A): inserted by the Housing Act 1974, s 118(4); words in first pair of square brackets substituted by the References to Rating (Housing) Regulations 1990, SI 1990/434, reg 2, Schedule, para 9; in para (a), words in square brackets inserted by the Housing and Planning Act 1986, s 23(1), (3), and words omitted repealed by the Commonhold and Leasehold Reform Act 2002, s 180, Sch 14, subject to savings as noted above; words in square brackets in para (b) inserted by the Local Government and Housing Act 1989, s 194(1), Sch 11, para 9; words omitted from para (e) repealed by the Rentcharges Act 1977, s 17(2), Sch 2.

Sub-s (1AA): inserted by the Commonhold and Leasehold Reform Act 2002, s 143(4), subject to savings as noted above.

Sub-s (1B): inserted by the Housing Act 1974, s 118(4).

Sub-s (1C): inserted by the Leasehold Reform, Housing and Urban Development Act 1993, s 66(1); figure in first pair of square brackets inserted by the Housing Act 1996, s 106, Sch 9, para 2(1), (5), except in a case where the house and premises are held under a tenancy which is a shared ownership lease within the meaning of the Housing Act 1985, s 622 at **[571]**, and was granted by a housing association, whether or not the interest of the landlord still belongs to such an association, nor does it have effect in a case where, before 1 April 1997, a notice was given under s 8 of this Act at **[90]**, or an application was made under s 27 of this Act at **[110]**, or a notice was given under the Leasehold Reform, Housing and Urban Development Act 1993, s 13 or 42 at **[817]**, **[848]**, or an application was made under s 26 or 50 of that Act at **[830]**, **[856]**; figure in italics repealed by the Housing and Regeneration Act 2008, s 321(1), Sch 16, as from 7 September 2009 (in relation to England, subject to transitional provisions in SI 2009/2096, art 3) and as from a day to be appointed (in relation to Wales); words in second pair of square brackets inserted and para (a) repealed by the Commonhold and Leasehold Reform Act 2002, ss 145(1), (2), 147(1), 180, Sch 14, subject to savings as noted above.

Sub-s (1D): inserted by the Commonhold and Leasehold Reform Act 2002, s 145(1), (3), subject to savings as noted above.

Sub-s (1E): inserted by the Commonhold and Leasehold Reform Act 2002, s 146, subject to savings as noted above.

Sub-s (3): words in square brackets substituted by the Commonhold and Leasehold Reform Act 2002, s 139(3)(a), subject to savings as noted above.

Sub-s (4A): inserted by the Commonhold and Leasehold Reform Act 2002, s 176, Sch 13, paras 1, 2, except in relation to any application made to an LVT or any proceedings transferred to an LVT by a county court before 30 September 2003 (in relation to England) or 31 March 2004 (in relation to Wales).

## [9A   Compensation payable in cases where right to enfranchisement arises by virtue of section 1A or 1B

(1)   If, in a case where the right to acquire the freehold of a house and premises arises by virtue of any one or more of the provisions of sections 1A[, 1AA] and 1B above [or where the tenancy of the house and premises has been extended under section 14 below and the notice under section 8(1) above was given (whether by the tenant or a sub-tenant) after the original term date of the tenancy], the landlord will suffer any loss or damage to which this section applies, there shall be payable to him such amount as is reasonable to compensate him for that loss or damage.

(2)   This section applies to—

(a)   any diminution in value of any interest of the landlord in other property resulting from the acquisition of his interest in the house and premises; and

(b)   any other loss or damage which results therefrom to the extent that it is referable to his ownership of any interest in other property.

(3)   Without prejudice to the generality of paragraph (b) of subsection (2) above, the kinds of loss falling within that paragraph include loss of development value in relation to the house and premises to the extent that it is referable as mentioned in that paragraph.

(4)   In subsection (3) above "development value", in relation to the house and premises, means any increase in the value of the landlord's interest in the house and premises which is attributable to the possibility of demolishing, reconstructing, or carrying out substantial works of construction on, the whole or a substantial part of the house and premises.

(5)   In relation to any case falling within subsection (1) above—

    (a)    any reference (however expressed)—

        (i)    in section 8 or 9(3) or (5) above, or

        (ii)    in any of the following provisions of this Act,

        to the price payable under section 9 above shall be construed as including a reference to any amount payable to the landlord under this section; and

    (b)    for the purpose of determining any such separate price as is mentioned in paragraph 7(1)(b) of Schedule 1 to this Act, this section shall accordingly apply (with any necessary modifications) to each of the superior interests in question.]

**[92]**

---

**NOTES**

Inserted by the Leasehold Reform, Housing and Urban Development Act 1993, s 66(3).

Sub-s (1): figure in first pair of square brackets inserted by the Housing Act 1996, s 106, Sch 9, para 2(1), (5), except in a case where the house and premises are held under a tenancy which is a shared ownership lease within the meaning of the Housing Act 1985, s 622 at **[571]**, and was granted by a housing association, whether or not the interest of the landlord still belongs to such an association, nor does it have effect in a case where, before 1 April 1997, a notice was given under s 8 of this Act at **[90]**, or an application was made under s 27 of this Act at **[110]**, or a notice was given under the Leasehold Reform, Housing and Urban Development Act 1993, s 13 or 42 at **[817]**, **[848]**, or an application was made under s 26 or 50 of that Act at **[830]**, **[856]**; figure in italics repealed by the Housing and Regeneration Act 2008, s 321(1), Sch 16, as from 7 September 2009 (in relation to England, subject to transitional provisions in SI 2009/2096, art 3) and as from a day to be appointed (in relation to Wales); words in second pair of square brackets inserted by the Commonhold and Leasehold Reform Act 2002, s 147(2), except in relation to an application for enfranchisement or an extended lease of a house in respect of which notice was given under s 8 or 14 of this Act at **[90]**, **[97]**, or where an application was made under s 27 of this Act at **[110]**, before 26 July 2002 (in relation to England) or 1 January 2003 (in relation to Wales).

---

**10   Rights to be conveyed to tenant on enfranchisement**

(1)   Except for the purpose of preserving or recognising any existing interest of the landlord in tenant's incumbrances or any existing right or interest of any other person, a conveyance executed to give effect to section 8 above shall not be framed so as to exclude or restrict the general words implied in conveyances under section 62 of the Law of Property Act 1925, or the all-estate clause implied under section 63, unless the tenant consents to the exclusion or restriction; but the landlord shall not be bound to convey to the tenant any better title than that which he has or could require to be vested in him, …

[(1A)   The landlord shall not be required to enter into any covenant for title beyond those implied under Part I of the Law of Property (Miscellaneous Provisions) Act 1994 in a case where a disposition is expressed to be made with limited title guarantee; and in the absence of agreement to the contrary he shall be entitled to be indemnified by the tenant in respect of any costs incurred by him in complying with the covenant implied by virtue of section 2(1)(b) of that Act (covenant for further assurance).]

(2)   As regards rights of any of the following descriptions, that is to say,—

    (a)    rights of support for any building or part of a building;

    (b)    rights to the access of light and air to any building or part of a building;

    (c)    rights to the passage of water or of gas or other piped fuel, or to the drainage or disposal of water, sewage, smoke or fumes, or to the use or maintenance of pipes or other installations for such passage, drainage or disposal;

    (d)    rights to the use or maintenance of cables or other installations for the supply of electricity, for the telephone or for the receipt directly or by landline of visual or other wireless transmissions;

a conveyance executed to give effect to section 8 above shall by virtue of this subsection (but without prejudice to any larger operation it may have apart from this subsection) have effect—

    (i)    to grant with the house and premises all such easements and rights over other property, so far as the landlord is capable of granting them, as are necessary to secure to the tenant as nearly as may be the same rights as at the relevant time were available to him under or by virtue of the tenancy or any agreement collateral thereto, or under or by virtue of any grant, reservation or agreement made on the severance of the house and premises or any part thereof from other property then comprised in the same tenancy; and

    (ii)    to make the house and premises subject to all such easements and rights for the benefit of other property as are capable of existing in law and are necessary to secure to the person interested in the other property as nearly as may be the same rights as at the relevant time were available against the tenant under or by virtue of the tenancy or any agreement collateral thereto, or under or by virtue of any grant, reservation or agreement made as is mentioned in paragraph (i) above.

(3) As regards rights of way, a conveyance executed to give effect to section 8 above shall include—

(a) such provisions (if any) as the tenant may require for the purpose of securing to him rights of way over property not conveyed, so far as the landlord is capable of granting them, being rights of way which are necessary for the reasonable enjoyment of the house and premises as they have been enjoyed during the tenancy and in accordance with its provisions; and

(b) such provisions (if any) as the landlord may require for the purpose of making the property conveyed subject to rights of way necessary for the reasonable enjoyment of other property, being property in which at the relevant time the landlord has an interest, or to rights of way granted or agreed to be granted before the relevant time by the landlord or by the person then entitled to the reversion on the tenancy.

(4) As regards restrictive covenants (that is to say, any covenant or agreement restrictive of the user of any land or premises), a conveyance executed to give effect to section 8 above shall include—

(a) such provisions (if any) as the landlord may require to secure that the tenant is bound by, or to indemnify the landlord against breaches of, restrictive covenants which affect the house and premises otherwise than by virtue of the tenancy or any agreement collateral thereto and are enforceable for the benefit of other property; and

(b) such provisions (if any) as the landlord or the tenant may require to secure the continuance (with suitable adaptations) of restrictions arising by virtue of the tenancy or any agreement collateral thereto, being either—

(i) restrictions affecting the house and premises which are capable of benefiting other property and (if enforceable only by the landlord) are such as materially to enhance the value of the other property; or

(ii) restrictions affecting other property which are such as materially to enhance the value of the house and premises;

(c) such further provisions (if any) as the landlord may require to restrict the use of the house and premises in any way which will not interfere with the reasonable enjoyment of the house and premises as they have been enjoyed during the tenancy but will materially enhance the value of other property in which the landlord has an interest.

(5) Neither the landlord nor the tenant shall be entitled under subsection (3) or (4) above to require the inclusion in a conveyance of any provision which is unreasonable in all the circumstances, in view—

(a) of the date at which the tenancy commenced, and changes since that date which affect the suitability at the relevant time of the provisions of the tenancy; and

(b) where the tenancy is or was one of a number of tenancies of neighbouring houses, of the interests of those affected in respect of other houses.

(6) The landlord may be required to give to the tenant an acknowledgment within the meaning of section 64 of the Law of Property Act 1925 as regards any documents of which the landlord retains possession, but not an undertaking for the safe custody of any such documents; and where the landlord is required to enter into any covenant under subsection (4) above, the person entering into the covenant as landlord shall be entitled to limit his personal liability to breaches of the covenant for which he is responsible.

**[93]**

**NOTES**

Sub-s (1): words omitted repealed by the Law of Property (Miscellaneous Provisions) Act 1994, s 21(1), (2), (4), Sch 1, para 5(1), Sch 2, except in relation to a disposition of property to which the Law of Property Act 1925, s 76 or the Land Registration Act 1925, s 24(1)(a) continue to apply.

Sub-s (1A): inserted by the Law of Property (Miscellaneous Provisions) Act 1994, s 21(1), (4), Sch 1, para 5(1), subject to savings as noted above.

## 11 Exoneration from, or redemption of, rentcharges etc

(1) Where a house and premises are to be conveyed to a tenant in pursuance of section 8 above, section 8(4)(b) shall not preclude the landlord from releasing, or procuring the release of, the house and premises from any rentcharge ... ; and the conveyance may, with the tenant's agreement (which shall not be unreasonably withheld), provide in accordance with section 190(1) of the Law of Property Act 1925 that a rentcharge shall be charged exclusively on other land affected by it in exoneration of the house and premises, or be apportioned between other land affected by it and the house and premises.

(2) Where, but for this subsection, a conveyance of a house and premises to a tenant might in accordance with section 8 above be made subject, in respect of rents to which this subsection applies, to an annual charge exceeding the annual rent payable under the tenancy at the relevant

time, then the landlord shall be bound on or before the execution of the conveyance to secure that the house and premises are discharged from the whole or part of any rents in question to the extent necessary to secure that the annual charge shall not exceed the annual rent so payable; and for this purpose the annual rent shall be calculated in accordance with section 4(1)(b) and (c) and (6) above.

(3) For purposes of subsection (2) above the house and premises shall be treated as discharged from a rent to the extent to which—

    (a) the rent is charged on or apportioned to other land so as to confer on the tenant in respect of the house and premises the remedies against the other land provided for by section 190(2) of the Law of Property Act 1925; or

    (b) the landlord is otherwise entitled to be exonerated from or indemnified against liability for the rent in respect of the house and premises and the tenant will (in so far as the landlord's right is not a right against the tenant himself or his land) become entitled on the conveyance to the like exoneration or indemnity.

(4) Where for the purpose of complying with subsection (2) above the house and premises are to be discharged from a rent by redemption of it (with or without prior apportionment), and for any reason mentioned in section [13(2) below] difficulty arises in paying the redemption price, the tenant may, and if so required by the landlord shall, before execution of the conveyance pay into court on account of the price for the house and premises an amount not exceeding the appropriate amount to secure redemption of the rent; and if the amount so paid by the tenant is less than that appropriate amount, the landlord shall pay into court the balance.

(5) Where payment is made into court in accordance with subsection (4) above, the house and premises shall on execution of the conveyance be discharged from the rent, and any claim to the redemption money shall lie against the fund in court and not otherwise.

(6) For purposes of subsection (4) above "the appropriate amount to secure redemption" of a rent is (subject to subsection (7) below) the amount of redemption money agreed to be paid or in default of agreement, the amount [specified as the redemption price in instructions for redemption under section 9(4) of the Rentcharges Act 1977].

(7) Where a rent affects other property as well as the house and premises, and the other property is not exonerated or indemnified by means of a charge on the house and premises, then—

    (a) "the appropriate amount to secure redemption" of the rent for purposes of subsection (4) above shall, if no amount has been agreed or [specified] as mentioned in subsection (6), be such sum as, on an application under section [4 of the Rentcharges Act 1977] for the apportionment of the rent, may, pending the apportionment, be approved by the apportioning authority as suitable provision (with a reasonable margin) for the redemption money of the part likely to be apportioned to the house and premises; and

    (b) the apportionment, when made, shall be deemed to have had effect from the date of the payment into court, and if in respect of any property affected by the rent there has been any overpayment or underpayment, the amount shall be made good by abatement of or addition to the next payment after the apportionment and (if necessary) later payments.

(8) Subsection (2) above applies to rentcharges [redeemable under sections 8 to 10 of the Rentcharges Act 1977] which during the continuance of the tenancy are, or but for the termination of the tenancy before their commencement would have been, recoverable from the landlord without his having a right to be indemnified by the tenant.

[94]

---

**NOTES**

Sub-s (1): words omitted repealed by the Rentcharges Act 1977, s 17(1), (2), Sch 1, para 4(2), Sch 2.
Sub-ss (4), (6)–(8): words in square brackets substituted by the Rentcharges Act 1977, s 17(1), Sch 1, para 4(2).

---

## 12 Discharge of mortgages etc on landlord's estate

(1) Subject to the provisions of this section, a conveyance executed to give effect to section 8 above shall, as regards any charge on the landlord's estate (however created or arising) to secure the payment of money or the performance of any other obligation by the landlord or any other person, not being a charge subject to which the conveyance is required to be made or which would be overreached apart from this section, be effective by virtue of this section to discharge the house and premises from the charge, and from the operation of any order made by a court for the enforcement of the charge, and to extinguish any term of years created for the purposes of the charge, and shall do so without the persons entitled to or interested in the charge or in any such order or term of years becoming parties to or executing the conveyance.

(2) Where in accordance with subsection (1) above the conveyance to a tenant will be effective to discharge the house and premises from a charge to secure the payment of money, then except as otherwise provided by this section it shall be the duty of the tenant to apply the price payable for the house and premises, in the first instance, in or towards the redemption of any such charge (and, if there are more than one, then according to their priorities); and if any amount payable in accordance

with this subsection to the person entitled to the benefit of a charge is not so paid nor paid into court in accordance with section 13 below, then for the amount in question the house and premises shall remain subject to the charge, and to that extent subsection (1) above shall not apply.

(3)   For the purpose of determining the amount payable in respect of any charge under subsection (2) above a person entitled to the benefit of a charge to which that subsection applies shall not be permitted to exercise any right to consolidate that charge with a separate charge on other property; and if the landlord or the tenant is himself entitled to the benefit of a charge to which that subsection applies, it shall rank for payment as it would if another person were entitled to it, and the tenant shall be entitled to retain the appropriate amount in respect of any such charge of his.

(4)   For the purposes of discharging the house and premises from a charge to which subsection (2) above applies, a person may be required to accept three months or any longer notice of the intention to pay the whole or part of the principal secured by the charge, together with interest to the date of payment, notwithstanding that the terms of the security make other provision or no provision as to the time and manner of payment; but he shall be entitled, if he so requires, to receive such additional payment as is reasonable in the circumstances in respect of the costs of re-investment or other incidental costs and expenses and in respect of any reduction in the rate of interest obtainable on re-investment.

(5)   Subsection (2) above shall not apply to any debenture-holders' charge, that is to say, any charge, whether a floating charge or not, in favour of the holders of a series of debentures issued by a company or other body of persons, or in favour of trustees for such debenture-holders; and any such charge shall be disregarded in determining priorities for purposes of subsection (2):

Provided that this subsection shall not have effect in relation to a charge in favour of trustees for debenture holders which at the date of the conveyance to the tenant is (as regards the house and premises) a specific and not a floating charge.

(6)   Where the house and premises are discharged by this section from a charge (without the obligations secured by the charge being satisfied by the receipt of the whole or part of the price), the discharge of the house and premises shall not prejudice any right or remedy for the enforcement of those obligations against other property comprised in the same or any other security, nor prejudice any personal liability as principal or otherwise of the landlord or any other person.

(7)   Subsections (1) and (2) above shall not be taken to prevent a person from joining in the conveyance for the purpose of discharging the house and premises from any charge without payment or for a less payment than that to which he would otherwise be entitled; and, if he does so, the persons to whom the price ought to be paid shall be determined accordingly.

(8)   A charge on the landlord's estate to secure the payment of money or the performance of any other obligation shall not be treated for the purposes of this Part of this Act as a tenant's incumbrance by reason only of the grant of the tenancy being subsequent to the creation of the charge and not authorised as against the persons interested in the charge; and this section shall apply as if the persons so interested at the time of the grant had duly concurred in the grant for the purpose (but only for the purpose) of validating it despite the charge on the grantor's estate:

Provided that, where the tenancy is granted after the commencement of this Part of this Act (whether or not it is, by virtue of section 3(3) above, to be treated for other purposes as forming a single tenancy with a previous tenancy) and the tenancy has not by the time of the conveyance of the house and premises to the tenant become binding on the persons interested in the charge, the conveyance shall not by virtue of this section discharge the house and premises from the charge except so far as it is satisfied by the application or payment into court of the price payable for the house and premises.

(9)   Nothing in this section shall apply in relation to any charge falling within section 11 above, and for purposes of subsection (2) above the price payable for the house and premises shall be treated as reduced by any amount to be paid out of it before execution of the conveyance for the redemption of a rent in accordance with section 11(4).

**[95]**

### 13   Payment into court in respect of mortgages etc

(1)   Where under section 12(1) above a house and premises are, on a conveyance to the tenant, to be discharged of any charge falling within that subsection, and in accordance with section 12(2) a person is or may be entitled in respect of the charge to receive the whole or part of the price payable for the house and premises, then if—

(a)   for any reason difficulty arises in ascertaining how much is payable in respect of the charge; or

(b)   for any reason mentioned in subsection (2) below difficulty arises in making a payment in respect of the charge;

the tenant may pay into court on account of the price for the house and premises the amount, if known, of the payment to be made in respect of the charge or, if that amount is not known, the whole of the price or such less amount as the tenant thinks right in order to provide for that payment.

(2)   Payment may be made into court in accordance with subsection (1)(b) above where the difficulty arises for any of the following reasons:—

(a)   because a person who is or may be entitled to receive payment cannot be found or ascertained;

(b)   because any such person refuses or fails to make out a title, or to accept payment and give a proper discharge, or to take any steps reasonably required of him to enable the sum payable to be ascertained and paid; or

(c)   because a tender of the sum payable cannot, by reason of complications in the title to it or the want of two or more trustees or for other reasons, be effected, or not without incurring or involving unreasonable cost or delay.

(3)   Without prejudice to subsection (1)(a) above, the price payable for a house and premises on a conveyance under section 8 above shall be paid by the tenant into court if before execution of the conveyance written notice is given to him—

(a)   that the landlord or a person entitled to the benefit of a charge on the house and premises so requires for the purpose of protecting the rights of persons so entitled, or for reasons related to any application made or to be made under section 36 below, or to the bankruptcy or winding up of the landlord; or

(b)   that steps have been taken to enforce any charge on the landlord's interest in the house and premises by the bringing of proceedings in any court, or by the appointment of a receiver, or otherwise;

and where payment is to be made into court by reason only of a notice under this subsection, and the notice is given with reference to proceedings in a court specified in the notice other than the county court, payment shall be made into the court so specified.

(4)   For the purpose of computing the amount payable into court under this section, the price payable for the house and premises shall be treated as reduced by any amount to be paid out of it before execution of the conveyance for the redemption of a rent in accordance with section 11(4) above.

**[96]**

*Extension*

## 14   Obligation to grant extended lease

(1)   Where a tenant of a house has under this Part of this Act a right to an extended lease, and gives to the landlord written notice of his desire to have it, then except as provided by this Part of this Act the landlord shall be bound to grant to the tenant, and the tenant to accept, in substitution for the existing tenancy a new tenancy of the house and premises for a term expiring fifty years after the term date of the existing tenancy.

(2)   Where a person gives notice of his desire to have an extended lease of a house and premises under this Part of this Act, then unless the notice lapses under any provision of this Act excluding his liability, there shall be borne by him (so far as they are incurred in pursuance of the notice) the reasonable costs of or incidental to any of the following matters:—

(a)   any investigation by the landlord of that person's right to an extended lease;

(b)   any lease granting the new tenancy;

(c)   any valuation of the house and premises obtained by the landlord before the grant of the new tenancy for the purpose of fixing the rent payable under it in accordance with section 15 below.

[(2A)   Subsection (2) above does not require a person to bear the costs of another person in connection with an application to a leasehold valuation tribunal.]

(3)   A tenant shall not be entitled to require the execution of a lease granting a new tenancy under this section otherwise than on tender of the amount, so far as ascertained,—

(a)   of any sums payable by way of rent or recoverable as rent in respect of the house and premises up to the date of tender; and

(b)   of any sums for which at that date the tenant is liable under subsection (2) above; and

(c)   of any other sums due and payable by him to the landlord under or in respect of the existing tenancy or any agreement collateral thereto;

and, if the amount of any such sums is not or may not be fully ascertained, on offering reasonable security for the payment of such amount as may afterwards be found to be payable in respect of them.

(4)   This section shall have effect notwithstanding that the grant of the existing tenancy was subsequent to the creation of a charge on the landlord's estate and not authorised as against the persons interested in the charge; and a lease executed to give effect to this section shall be deemed to be authorised as against the persons interested in any charge on the landlord's estate, however created or arising, and shall be binding on them:

Provided that, where the existing tenancy is granted after the commencement of this Part of this Act (whether or not it is, by virtue of section 3(3) above, to be treated for other purposes as forming a single tenancy with a previous tenancy) and, the grant being subsequent to the creation of the charge on the landlord's estate, the existing tenancy is not binding on the persons interested in the charge, a lease executed to give effect to this section shall not by virtue of this subsection be binding on those persons.

(5) Where a lease is executed to give effect to this section, and any person having a charge on the landlord's estate is by reason thereof entitled to possession of the documents of title relating to that estate, the landlord shall within one month after execution of the lease deliver to that person a counterpart of it duly executed by the tenant, and the instrument creating or evidencing the charge shall apply in the event of his failing to deliver a counterpart in accordance with this subsection as if the obligation to do so were included in the terms of the charge as set out in that instrument.

(6) Where under a lease executed to give effect to this section the new tenancy takes effect subject to a subsisting charge on the existing tenancy, and at the time of its execution the person having the charge is by reason thereof entitled to possession of the documents of title relating to the existing tenancy, then he shall be similarly entitled to possession of the documents of title relating to the new tenancy and the tenant shall within one month of the execution of the lease deliver it to him, and the instrument creating or evidencing the charge shall apply in the event of the tenant failing to deliver the lease in accordance with this subsection as if the obligation to do so were included in the terms of the charge as set out in that instrument.

(7) A landlord granting a lease under this section shall be bound to take such steps as may be necessary to secure that it is not liable in accordance with the proviso to subsection (4) above to be defeated by persons interested in a charge on his estate; but a landlord is not obliged, in order to grant a lease under this section, to acquire a better title than he has or could require to be vested in him.

**[97]**

**NOTES**

Sub-s (2A): inserted by the Commonhold and Leasehold Reform Act 2002, s 176, Sch 13, paras 1, 3, except in relation to any application made to an LVT or any proceedings transferred to an LVT by a county court before 30 September 2003 (in relation to England) or 31 March 2004 (in relation to Wales).

## 15 Terms of tenancy to be granted on extension

(1) Subject to the provisions of this Part of this Act, the new tenancy to be granted under section 14 above shall be a tenancy on the same terms as the existing tenancy as those terms apply at the relevant time, but with such modifications as may be required or appropriate to take account—
   (a) of the omission from the new tenancy of property comprised in the existing tenancy; or
   (b) of alterations made to the property demised since the grant of the existing tenancy; or
   (c) in a case where the existing tenancy derives (in accordance with section 3(6) above) from more than one separate tenancies, of their combined effect and of the differences (if any) in their terms.

(2) The new tenancy shall provide that as from the original term date the rent payable for the house and premises shall be a rent ascertained or to be ascertained as follows:—
   (a) the rent shall be a ground rent in the sense that it shall represent the letting value of the site (without including anything for the value of buildings on the site) for the uses to which the house and premises have been put since the commencement of the existing tenancy, other than uses which by the terms of the new tenancy are not permitted or are permitted only with the landlord's consent;
   (b) the letting value for this purpose shall be in the first instance the letting value at the date from which the rent based on it is to commence, but as from the expiration of twenty-five years from the original term date the letting value at the expiration of those twenty-five years shall be substituted, if the landlord so requires, and a revised rent become payable accordingly;
   (c) the letting value at either of the times mentioned shall be determined not earlier than twelve months before that time (the reasonable cost of obtaining a valuation for the purpose being borne by the tenant), and there shall be no revision of the rent as provided by paragraph (b) above unless in the last of the twenty-five years there mentioned the landlord gives the tenant written notice claiming a revision.

(3) Where during the continuance of the new tenancy the landlord will be under any obligation for the provision of services, or for repairs, maintenance or insurance, the rent payable in accordance with subsection (2) above shall be in addition to any sums payable (whether as rent or otherwise) in consideration of those matters or in respect of the cost thereof to the landlord; and if the terms of the existing tenancy include no provision for the making of any such payments by the tenant, or provision only for the payment of a fixed amount, the terms of the new tenancy shall make, as from the time when rent becomes payable in accordance with subsection (2) above, such provision as may be just for the making by the tenant of payments related to the cost from time to time to the landlord, and for the tenant's liability to make those payments to be enforceable by *distress, re-entry or otherwise* in like manner as the liability for the rent.

(4) Subject to subsection (5) below, provision shall be made by the terms of the new tenancy or by an instrument collateral thereto for the continuance with any suitable adaptations of any agreement collateral to the existing tenancy.

(5) For purposes of subsections (1) and (4) above, there shall be excluded any term of the existing tenancy or any agreement collateral thereto in so far as that term provides for or relates to the renewal of the tenancy, or confers any option to purchase or right of pre-emption in relation to the house and premises, or provides for the termination of the tenancy before the term date otherwise than in the event of a breach of its terms; and there shall be made in the terms of the new tenancy or any instrument collateral thereto such modifications as may be required or appropriate to take account of the exclusion of any such term as aforesaid.

(6) Where the new tenancy is granted after the original term date, the first reference in subsection (2) above to that date shall have effect as a reference to the grant of the new tenancy; but on the grant of the new tenancy there shall be payable by the tenant to the landlord as an addition to the rent payable under the existing tenancy any amount by which for the period since the relevant time or the original term date (whichever is the later) the sums payable to the landlord in respect of the house and premises (after making any necessary apportionment) for rent and matters referred to in subsection (3) above fall short in total of the sums that would have been payable for rent and matters so referred to under the new tenancy, and section 14(3)(a) above shall apply accordingly.

(7) Subsections (1) to (6) above shall have effect subject to any agreement between the landlord and tenant as to the terms of the new tenancy or any agreement collateral thereto; and either of them may require that for purposes of the new tenancy there shall be excluded or modified any term of the existing tenancy or an agreement collateral thereto which it would be unreasonable in the circumstances to include unchanged in the new tenancy in view of the date at which the existing tenancy commenced and of changes since that date which affect the suitability at the relevant time of the provisions of that tenancy.

(8) The new tenancy shall make provision in accordance with section 16(4) below, and shall reserve to the landlord the right to resume possession in accordance with section 17.

[(9) In granting the new tenancy, the landlord shall not be bound to enter into any covenant for title beyond—
    (a)    those implied from the grant, and
    (b)    those implied under Part I of the Law of Property (Miscellaneous Provisions) Act 1994 in a case where a disposition is expressed to be made with limited title guarantee, but not including (in the case of a sub-tenancy) the covenant in section 4(1)(b) of that Act (compliance with terms of lease);
and in the absence of agreement to the contrary the landlord shall be entitled to be indemnified by the tenant in respect of any costs incurred by him in complying with the covenant implied by virtue of section 2(1)(b) of that Act (covenant for further assurance).

(9A) A person entering into any covenant required of him as landlord (under subsection (9) or otherwise) shall be entitled to limit his personal liability to breaches of that covenant for which he is responsible.]

(10) Nothing in this section shall affect the rights or obligations of the landlord under section 35 of and Schedule 1 to the Sexual Offences Act 1956 (which apply where the tenant or occupier of any premises is convicted of permitting the whole or part of them to be used as a brothel).

[98]

---

**NOTES**

Sub-s (3): for the words in italics there are substituted the words "re-entry or otherwise (subject to section 85 of the Tribunals, Courts and Enforcement Act 2007)" by the Tribunals, Courts and Enforcement Act 2007, s 86, Sch 14, para 29, as from a day to be appointed.

Sub-ss (9), (9A): substituted, for original sub-s (9), by the Law of Property (Miscellaneous Provisions) Act 1994, s 21(1), (4), Sch 1, para 5(2), except in relation to a disposition of property to which the Law of Property Act 1925, s 76 or the Land Registration Act 1925, s 24(1)(a) continue to apply.

---

## 16 Exclusion of further rights after extension

(1) Subject to subsections (2) and (3) below, where a tenancy of a house and premises has been extended under section 14 above, then as regards any property comprised in the extended tenancy—
    (a)    ...
    (b)    there shall be no further right to an extension of the tenancy under this Part of this Act; and
    (c)    neither section 1 of the Landlord and Tenant Act 1954 nor Part II of that Act shall apply to the tenancy; and
    (d)    after the extended term date neither section 1 of the Landlord and Tenant Act 1954 nor Part II of that Act shall apply to any sub-tenancy directly or indirectly derived out of the tenancy, nor shall a person be entitled by virtue of any such sub-tenancy to retain

possession under [[Part VII of the Rent Act 1977] or any enactment applying or extending that Part of that Act] [or under the Rent (Agriculture) Act 1976].

[(1A) The Rent Act 1977 shall not apply to a tenancy extended under section 14 above; but if when this provision comes into force a rent is registered under Part IV of the 1977 Act for a dwelling-house which is the subject of an extended tenancy, the tenant shall not be obliged to pay more than the registered rent under the extended tenancy until the next rental period (within the meaning of the 1977 Act) after the landlord has served on him a notice in writing that the registered rent no longer applies.]

[(1B) Schedule 10 to the Local Government and Housing Act 1989 applies to every tenancy extended under section 14 above (whether or not it is for the purposes of that Schedule a long tenancy at a low rent as respects which the qualifying condition is fulfilled).]

(2) Where—
  (a) a tenancy of a house and premises has been extended under section 14 above; and
  (b) any part other than the house of the property then comprised in that tenancy is afterwards (while so comprised) held ... with another house not so comprised;

subsection (1) ... (b) above shall not apply to exclude any right under this Part of this Act of a tenant of the other house to acquire ... an extended lease of that part as being at the relevant time comprised in his house and premises, unless the landlord objects in accordance with subsection (3) below.

(3) If, in a case falling within subsection (2) above, a tenant of the other house gives notice of his desire to have ... an extended lease under this Part of this Act, the landlord, not later than two months afterwards, may give him written notice objecting to the inclusion in his house and premises of the part in question; and, if the landlord does so, that part shall be treated as not so included and this Part of this Act shall apply as it applies where property is excluded from a house and premises under section 2(4):

...

(4) Where a tenancy has been extended under section 14 above, no long tenancy created immediately or derivatively by way of sub-demise under the tenancy shall confer on the sub-tenant, as against the tenant's landlord, any right under this Part of this Act to acquire ... an extended lease.

(5) Where a tenancy has been extended under section 14 above, and that tenancy and any subsequent tenancy at a low rent of property comprised in it (with or without intervening tenancies) are to be treated under section 3(3) above as a single tenancy of that property, the single tenancy shall be treated for purposes of this section as one which has been extended under section 14, and the instrument granting any such subsequent tenancy shall make provision in accordance with subsection (4) above.

(6) A person granting a sub-tenancy to which subsection (1)(d) above will apply, or negotiating with a view to the grant of such a sub-tenancy by him or by a person for whom he is acting as agent, shall inform the other party that the sub-tenancy is to be derived out of a tenancy extended under section 14 of this Act (or one treated for purposes of this section as so extended), unless either he knows that the other party is aware of it or he himself is unaware of it.

(7) Where an instrument extending a tenancy at a low rent, or granting a further tenancy at a low rent in substitution for or in continuance of such a tenancy, contains a statement to the effect that the tenancy is being or has been previously extended under this Part of this Act, the statement shall be conclusive for purposes of this section in favour of any person not being a party to the instrument, unless the statement appears from the instrument to be untrue.

(8) Any person who—
  (a) includes or causes to be included in an instrument a statement to the effect mentioned in subsection (7) above, knowing the statement to be untrue; or
  (b) executes, or with intent to deceive makes use of, any instrument, knowing that it contains such a statement and that the statement is untrue;

shall be liable on conviction on indictment to imprisonment for a term not exceeding two years, or on summary conviction to imprisonment for a term not exceeding three months or to a fine not exceeding [the prescribed sum], or to both.

**[99]**

---

**NOTES**

Sub-s (1): para (a) repealed by the Commonhold and Leasehold Reform Act 2002, ss 143(1)(a), 180, Sch 14, except in relation to an application for enfranchisement or an extended lease of a house in respect of which notice was given under s 8 or 14 of this Act at **[90]**, **[97]**, or where an application was made under s 27 of this Act at **[110]**, before 26 July 2002 (in relation to England) or 1 January 2003 (in relation to Wales); words in first (outer) pair of square brackets substituted by the Rent Act 1968, s 117(2), Sch 15; words in second (inner) pair of square brackets substituted by the Rent Act 1977, s 155, Sch 23, para 43; words in third pair of square brackets added by the Rent (Agriculture) Act 1976, s 40, Sch 8, para 17.

Sub-s (1A): inserted by the Housing Act 1980, s 141, Sch 21, para 4.

Sub-s (1B): inserted by the Local Government and Housing Act 1989, s 194(1), Sch 11, para 10; substituted by the Commonhold and Leasehold Reform Act 2002, s 143(2), subject to savings as noted above.

Sub-ss (2)–(4): words omitted repealed by the Commonhold and Leasehold Reform Act 2002, s 181, Sch 14, subject to savings as noted above.

Sub-s (8): words in square brackets substituted by virtue of the Magistrates' Courts Act 1980, s 32(2).

*Landlord's overriding rights*

## 17  Redevelopment rights (exclusion or termination of extension)

(1)  Where a tenancy of a house and premises has been extended under section 14 above, the landlord may, at any time not earlier than twelve months before the original term date of the tenancy, apply to the court for an order that he may resume possession of the property on the ground that for purposes of redevelopment he proposes to demolish or reconstruct the whole or a substantial part of the house and premises.

(2)  If on an application under subsection (1) above the court is satisfied that the landlord has established the ground mentioned in that subsection, then subject to the provisions of this section the court shall by order declare that the landlord is entitled as against the tenant to obtain possession of the house and premises and the tenant is entitled to be paid compensation by the landlord for the loss of the house and premises.

(3)  Where an order is made under subsection (2) above, the tenancy shall determine and the compensation become payable in accordance with Schedule 2 to this Act; and the provisions of that Schedule shall have effect as regards the measure of compensation under any such order and the effects of the order where there are sub-tenancies, and as regards other matters relating to applications and orders under this section.

(4)  Where the tenancy of a house and premises has not been extended under section 14 above, but the tenant has a right to an extended lease and gives notice of his desire to have one, then this section shall apply as if the lease had been extended under section 14; and—

    (a)    on the making by the landlord of an application under this section, the notice shall be suspended until the time when an order under subsection (2) or an order dismissing the application becomes final or the application is withdrawn; and

    (b)    on an order under subsection (2) becoming final, the notice shall cease to have effect, but section 14(2) above shall not apply to require the tenant to make any payment to the landlord in respect of costs incurred by reason of the notice.

(5)  For purposes of subsection (4) above, the reference in subsection (1) to the original term date shall have effect as a reference to the term date or, in a case where before the relevant time the landlord had given notice to quit terminating the tenancy at a date earlier than the term date, as a reference to the date specified in the notice to quit.

(6)  Where a landlord makes an application under subsection (1) above, then—

    (a)    if the tenant afterwards gives notice of his desire to have the freehold of the house and premises under this Part of this Act, that notice shall be of no effect if it is not given before the date of the order fixing the date for the termination of the tenancy (in accordance with Schedule 2 to this Act), or if the tenant's notice of his desire to have an extended lease was given within twelve months before the making of the landlord's application; and

    (b)    if a notice given by the tenant (before or after the making of the landlord's application) of his desire to have the freehold has effect, no order or further order shall be made on the landlord's application except as regards costs, but without prejudice to the making of a further application by the landlord if the tenant's notice lapses without effect being given to it.

[100]

## 18  Residential rights (exclusion of enfranchisement or extension)

(1)  Subject to subsection (2) below, where the tenancy of a house and premises has not been extended under section 14 above, but the tenant has a right to acquire the freehold or an extended lease and has given notice of his desire to have it, the landlord may, at any time before effect is given to the notice, apply to the court for an order that he may resume possession of the property on the ground that it or part of it is or will be reasonably required by him for occupation as the only or main residence of the landlord or of a person who is at the time of the application an adult member of the landlord's family.

(2)  A landlord shall not be entitled to apply to the court under this section if his interest in the house and premises, or an interest which has merged in that interest but would otherwise have had a duration extending at least five years longer than that of the tenancy, was purchased or created after the 18th February 1966; and for purposes of this subsection the duration of any interest in the house and premises (including the tenancy) shall be taken to be the period until it is due to expire or, if capable of earlier determination by notice given by a person as landlord the date or earliest date which has been or could be specified in such a notice.

(3) Where the landlord's interest is held on trust, subsection (1) above shall apply as if the reference to occupation as the residence of the landlord were a reference to the like occupation of a person having an interest under the trust (whether or not also a trustee), and the reference to a member of the landlord's family were a reference to the like member of such a person's family; and for purposes of subsection (1) a person is an adult member of another's family if that person is—

    (a)    the other's [spouse or civil partner]; or

    (b)    a son or daughter or a son-in-law or daughter-in-law of the other, or of the other's [spouse or civil partner], who has attained the age of eighteen; or

    (c)    the father or mother of the other, or of the other's [spouse or civil partner].

In paragraph (b) above any reference to a person's son or daughter includes a reference to any stepson or stepdaughter, any illegitimate son or daughter, ... of that person, and "son-in-law" and "daughter-in-law" shall be construed accordingly.

(4) If on an application under subsection (1) above the court is satisfied that the landlord has established the ground mentioned in that subsection and is not disentitled by subsection (2), the court shall by order declare that the landlord is entitled as against the tenant to obtain possession of the house and premises and the tenant is entitled to be paid compensation by the landlord for the loss of the house and premises:

Provided that the court shall not make an order under this subsection if the court is satisfied that having regard to all the circumstances of the case, including the question whether other accommodation is available for the landlord or the tenant, greater hardship would be caused by making the order than by refusing to make it.

(5) Where an order is made under subsection (4) above, the tenancy shall determine and the compensation become payable in accordance with Schedule 2 to this Act; and the provisions of that Schedule shall have effect as regards the measure of compensation under any such order and the effects of the order where there are sub-tenancies, and as regards other matters relating to applications and orders under this section.

(6) Where a landlord makes an application under this section,—

    (a)    any notice previously given by the tenant of his desire to have the freehold or an extended lease of the house and premises under this Part of this Act shall be suspended until the time when an order under subsection (4) or an order dismissing the application becomes final or the application is withdrawn; and

    (b)    on an order under subsection (4) becoming final, the notice shall cease to have effect, but section 9(4) or 14(2) above shall not apply to require the tenant to make any payment to the landlord in respect of costs incurred by reason of the notice;

and a notice of the tenant's desire to have the freehold shall be of no effect if given after the making of the application and before the time referred to in paragraph (a) above or after an order under subsection (4) above has become final.

**NOTES**

Sub-s (3): words in square brackets substituted by the Civil Partnership Act 2004, s 81, Sch 8, para 7; words omitted repealed by the Children Act 1975, s 108(1)(b), Sch 4, Pt I.

## 19 Retention of management powers for general benefit of neighbourhood

(1) Where, in the case of any area which is occupied directly or indirectly under tenancies held from one landlord (apart from property occupied by him or his licensees or for the time being unoccupied), the Minister on an application made within the two years beginning with the commencement of this Part of this Act grants a certificate that, in order to maintain adequate standards of appearance and amenity and regulate redevelopment in the area in the event of tenants acquiring the landlord's interest in their house and premises under this Part of this Act, it is in the Minister's opinion likely to be in the general interest that the landlord should retain powers of management in respect of the house and premises or have rights against the house and premises in respect of the benefits arising from the exercise elsewhere of his powers of management, then the High Court may, on an application made within one year of the giving of the certificate, approve a scheme giving the landlord such powers and rights as are contemplated by this subsection.

For purposes of this section "the Minister" means as regards areas within Wales and Monmouthshire the Secretary of State, and as regards other areas the Minister of Housing and Local Government.

(2) The Minister shall not give a certificate under this section unless he is satisfied that the applicant has, by advertisement or otherwise as may be required by the Minister, given adequate notice to persons interested, informing them of the application for a certificate and its purpose and inviting them to make representations to the Minister for or against the application within a time which appears to the Minister to be reasonable; and before giving a certificate the Minister shall consider any representations so made within that time, and if from those representations it appears to him that there is among the persons making them substantial opposition to the application, he

shall afford to those opposing the application, and on the same occasion to the applicant and such (if any) as the Minister thinks fit of those in favour of the application, an opportunity to appear and be heard by a person appointed by the Minister for the purpose, and shall consider the report of that person.

(3)　The Minister in considering whether to grant a certificate authorising a scheme for any area, and the High Court in considering whether to approve a scheme shall have regard primarily to the benefit likely to result from the scheme to the area as a whole (including houses likely to be acquired from the landlord under this Part of this Act), and the extent to which it is reasonable to impose, for the benefit of the area, obligations on tenants so acquiring their freeholds; but regard may also be had to the past development and present character of the area and to architectural or historical considerations, to neighbouring areas and to the circumstances generally.

(4)　If, having regard to the matters mentioned in subsection (3) above, to the provision which it is practicable to make by a scheme, and to any change of circumstances since the giving of the certificate under subsection (1), the High Court think it proper so to do, then the High Court may by order—

(a)　exclude from the scheme any part of the area certified under that subsection; or

(b)　declare that no scheme can be approved for the area;

and before submitting for approval a scheme for an area so certified a person may, if he sees fit, apply to the High Court for general directions as to the matters proper to be included in the scheme and for a decision whether an order should be made under paragraph (a) or (b) above.

(5)　Subject to subsections (3) and (4) above, on the submission of a scheme to the High Court, the High Court shall approve the scheme either as originally submitted or with any modifications proposed or agreed to by the applicant for the scheme, if the scheme (with those modifications, if any) appears to the court to be fair and practicable and not to give the landlord a degree of control out of proportion to that previously exercised by him or to that required for the purposes of the scheme; and the High Court shall not dismiss an application for the approval of a scheme, unless either—

(a)　the Court makes an order under subsection (4)(b) above; or

(b)　in the opinion of the Court the applicant is unwilling to agree to a suitable scheme or is not proceeding in the manner with due despatch.

(6)　A scheme under this section may make different provision for different parts of the area, and shall include provision for terminating or varying all or any of the provisions of the scheme, or excluding part of the area, if a change of circumstances makes it appropriate, or for enabling it to be done by or with the approval of the High Court.

(7)　Except as provided by the scheme, the operation of a scheme under this section shall not be affected by any disposition or devolution of the landlord's interest in the property within the area or part of that property; but the scheme—

(a)　shall include provision for identifying the person who is for the purposes of the scheme to be treated as the landlord for the time being; and

(b)　may include provision for transferring, or allowing the landlord for the time being to transfer, all or any of the powers and rights conferred by the scheme on the landlord for the time being to a local authority or other body, including a body constituted for the purpose.

In the following provisions of this section references to the landlord for the time being shall have effect, in relation to powers and rights transferred to a local authority or other body as contemplated by paragraph (b) above, as references to that authority or body.

(8)　Without prejudice to any other provision of this section, a scheme under it may provide for all or any of the following matters:—

(a)　for regulating the redevelopment, use or appearance of property of which tenants have acquired the landlord's interest under this Part of this Act; and

(b)　for empowering the landlord for the time being to carry out work for the maintenance or repair of any such property or carry out work to remedy a failure in respect of any such property to comply with the scheme, or for making the operation of any provisions of the scheme conditional on his doing so or on the provision or maintenance by him of services, facilities or amenities of any description; and

(c)　for imposing on persons from time to time occupying or interested in any such property obligations in respect of maintenance or repair of the property or of property used or enjoyed by them in common with others, or in respect of cost incurred by the landlord for the time being on any matter referred to in this paragraph or in paragraph (b) above;

(d)　for the inspection from time to time of any such property on behalf of the landlord for the time being, and for the recovery by him of sums due to him under the scheme in respect of any such property by means of a charge on the property;

and the landlord for the time being shall have, for the enforcement of any charge imposed under the scheme, the same powers and remedies under the Law of Property Act 1925 and otherwise as if he were a mortgagee by deed having powers of sale and leasing and of appointing a receiver.

(9)   A scheme under this section may extend to property in which the landlord's interest is disposed of otherwise than under this Part of this Act (whether residential property or not), so as to make that property, or allow it to be made, subject to any such provision as is or might be made by the scheme for property in which tenants acquire the landlord's interest under this Part of this Act.

(10)   A certificate given or scheme approved under this section [shall (notwithstanding section 2(a) or (b) of the Local Land Charges Act 1975) be a local land charge and for the purposes of that Act the landlord for the area to which it relates shall be treated as the originating authority as respects such charge; and where a scheme is registered in the appropriate local land charges register;]

(a)   the provisions of the scheme relating to property of any description shall, so far as they respectively affect the persons from time to time occupying or interested in that property, be enforceable by the landlord for the time being against them, as if each of them had covenanted with the landlord for the time being to be bound by the scheme; and

(b)   in relation to a house and premises in the area section 10 above shall have effect subject to the provisions of the scheme, and the price payable under section 9 shall be adjusted accordingly.

[(10A)   Section 10 of the Local Land Charges Act 1975 shall not apply in relation to schemes which, by virtue of this section, are local land charges.]

(11)   Subject to subsections (12) and (13) below, a certificate shall not be given nor a scheme approved under this section for any area except on the application of the landlord.

(12)   Where, on a joint application made by two or more persons as landlords of neighbouring areas, it appears to the Minister—

(a)   that a certificate could in accordance with subsection (1) above be given as regards those areas, treated as a unit, if the interests of those persons were held by a single person; and

(b)   that the applicants are willing to be bound by any scheme to co-operate in the management of their property in those areas and in the administration of the scheme;

the Minister may give a certificate under this section for those areas as a whole; and where a certificate is given by virtue of this subsection, this section shall apply accordingly, but so that any scheme made by virtue of the certificate shall be made subject to conditions (enforceable in such manner as may be provided by the scheme) for securing that the landlords and their successors co-operate as aforesaid.

(13)   Where it appears to the Minister—

(a)   that a certificate could be given under this section for any area or areas on the application of the landlord or landlords; and

(b)   that any body of persons is so constituted as to be capable of representing for purposes of this section the persons occupying or interested in property in the area or areas (other than the landlord or landlords), or such of them as are or may become entitled to acquire their landlord's interest under this Part of this Act, and is otherwise suitable;

then on an application made by that body either alone or jointly with the landlord or landlords a certificate may be granted accordingly; and where a certificate is so granted, whether to a representative body alone or to a representative body jointly with the landlord or landlords,—

(i)   an application for a scheme in pursuance of the certificate may be made by the representative body alone or by the landlord or landlords alone or by both jointly and, by leave of the High Court, may be proceeded with by the representative body or by the landlord or landlords though not the applicant or applicants; and

(ii)   without prejudice to subsection (7)(b) above, the scheme may, with the consent of the landlord or landlords or on such terms as to compensation or otherwise as appear to the High Court to be just, confer on the representative body any such rights or powers under the scheme as might be conferred on the landlord or landlords for the time being, or enable the representative body to participate in the administration of the scheme or in the management by the landlord or landlords of his or their property in the area or areas.

(14)   Where a certificate under this section has been given for an area, or an application for one is pending, then subject to subsection (15) below if (before or after the making of the application or the giving of the certificate) a tenant of a house in the area gives notice of his desire to have the freehold under this Part of this Act,—

(a)   no further proceedings need be taken in relation to the notice beyond those which appear to the landlord to be reasonable in the circumstances; but

(b)   the tenant may at any time withdraw the notice by a further notice in writing given to the landlord, and section 9(4) above shall not apply to require him to make any payment to the landlord in respect of costs incurred by reason of the notice withdrawn.

(15)   Subsection (14) above shall cease to have effect by virtue of an application for a certificate if the application is withdrawn or the certificate refused, and shall cease to have effect as regards the whole or part of an area to which a certificate relates—

(a)   on the approval of a scheme for the area or that part of it; or

(b)   on the expiration of one year from the giving of the certificate without an application having been made to the High Court for the approval of a scheme for the area or that part of it, or on the withdrawal of an application so made without a scheme being approved; or

(c)    on an order made under subsection (4) above with respect to the area or that part of it, or an order dismissing an application for the approval of a scheme for the area or that part of it, becoming final.

[102]

**NOTES**

Sub-s (10): words in square brackets substituted by the Local Land Charges Act 1975, s 17(2), Sch 1.

Sub-s (10A): inserted by the Local Land Charges Act 1975, s 17(2), Sch 1.

Minister of Housing and Local Government: functions transferred to the Secretary of State by the Secretary of State for the Environment Order 1970, SI 1970/1681.

*Determination of questions, procedure, etc*

## 20  Jurisdiction and special powers of county court

(1)    Subject to section 115 of the County Courts Act 1959, any jurisdiction expressed to be conferred on the court by this Part of this Act shall, unless the contrary intention appears, be exercised by the county court.

(2)    Except as provided by this section and section 21 below, there shall also be brought in the county court any proceedings under this Part of this Act of the following descriptions:—

(a)    proceedings for determining whether a person is entitled to acquire the freehold or an extended lease of a house and premises, or to what property his right extends;

(b)    proceedings for determining what provisions ought to be contained in a conveyance in accordance with section 10 or 29(1), or in a lease granting a new tenancy under section 14;

(c)    any other proceedings relating to the performance or discharge of obligations arising out of a tenant's notice of his desire to have the freehold or an extended lease, including proceedings for the recovery of damages or compensation in the event of the obligations not being performed;

(d)    any proceedings for determining the amount of a sub-tenant's share under Schedule 2 to this Act in compensation payable to a tenant under section 17 or 18, or for establishing or giving effect to his right to it.

(3)    Where in connection with any acquisition by a tenant of the freehold or an extended lease under this Part of this Act it is necessary to apportion between the house and premises (or part of them) and other property the rent payable under his tenancy or any superior or reversionary tenancy, then, subject to section 115 of the County Courts Act 1959 and to section 21 below, the apportionment shall be made by the county court.

(4)    Where it is made to appear to the court that the landlord or the tenant has been guilty of any unreasonable delay or default in the performance of obligations arising from a tenant's notice of his desire to have the freehold or an extended lease under this Part of this Act, then (without prejudice to any right to damages) the court may—

(a)    by order revoke or vary, and direct repayment of sums paid under, any provision made by a previous order as to payment of the costs of proceedings in the court in relation to the matter, or, where costs have not been awarded, award costs;

(b)    certify particulars of the delay or default to the [Upper Tribunal] with a view to enabling the Tribunal to exercise a like discretion in relation to costs of proceedings before the Tribunal.

[(4A)    Where the court certifies particulars of delay or default to the [Upper Tribunal] under subsection (4)(b) above, the [Upper Tribunal] may make any order as to costs of proceedings before the [Upper Tribunal] which the court may make in relation to proceedings in the court.]

(5)    Where a person gives notice of his desire to have the freehold or to have an extended lease of a house and premises under this Part of this Act, and the notice either is set aside by the court or withdrawn, or ceases to have effect, or would, if valid, cease to have effect, then if it is made to appear to the court—

(a)    that the notice was not given in good faith; or

(b)    that the person giving the notice attempted in any material respect to support it by misrepresentation or the concealment of material facts;

the court may, on the application of the landlord, order that person to pay to the landlord such sum as appears sufficient as compensation for damage or loss sustained by the landlord as the result of the giving of the notice.

(6)    In any case where under subsection (5) above the court has power, on the application of the landlord, to order a person to make a payment to the landlord, the court (whether or not it makes an order under that subsection) may, on the application of the landlord, order that any further notice

given by that person under this Part of this Act of his desire to have the freehold or an extended lease of the same house or any part of it, with or without other property, shall be void if given within the five years beginning with the date of the order.

(7)     Subsection (2)(c) above shall not prevent the bringing of proceedings in a court other than the county court where the claim is for damages or pecuniary compensation only.

**[103]**

**NOTES**

Sub-s (4): words in square brackets substituted by the Transfer of Tribunal Functions (Lands Tribunal and Miscellaneous Amendments) Order 2009, SI 2009/1307, art 5(1), (2), Sch 1, paras 82, 83, subject to transitional provisions and savings in Sch 5 thereto.

Sub-s (4A): inserted by the Commonhold and Leasehold Reform Act 2002, s 176, Sch 13, paras 1, 4, except in relation to any application made to an LVT or any proceedings transferred to an LVT by a county court before 30 September 2003 (in relation to England) or 31 March 2004 (in relation to Wales); words in square brackets substituted by SI 2009/1307, art 5(1), (2), Sch 1, paras 82, 83, subject to transitional provisions and savings in Sch 5 thereto.

County Courts Act 1959, s 115: repealed by the Supreme Court Act 1981, s 152(4), Sch 7, see now the County Courts Act 1984, s 41.

## 21    Jurisdiction of [leasehold valuation tribunals]

(1)     The following matters shall, in default of agreement, be determined by [a leasehold valuation tribunal] namely,—

(a)     the price payable for a house and premises under section 9 above;

(b)     the amount of the rent to be payable (whether originally or on a revision) for a house and premises in accordance with section 15(2);

[(ba)   the amount of any costs payable under section 9(4) or 14(2);]

(c)     the amount of any compensation payable to a tenant under section 17 or 18 for the loss of a house and premises;

[(cza) the amount of the appropriate sum to be paid into court under section 27(5);]

[(ca)   the amount of any costs payable under section 27A].

[(1A)    ... ]

[(1B)    No application may be made to a leasehold valuation tribunal under subsection (1) above to determine the price for a house and premises unless either—

(a)     the landlord has informed the tenant of the price he is asking; or

(b)     two months have elapsed without his doing so since the tenant gave notice of his desire to have the freehold under this Part of this Act.]

(2)     Notwithstanding section 20(2) or (3) above, [a leasehold valuation tribunal] shall have jurisdiction, either by agreement or in a case where an application is made to [a tribunal] under subsection (1) above with reference to the same transaction,—

(a)     to determine what provisions ought to be contained in a conveyance in accordance with section 10 or 29(1) of this Act, or in a lease granting a new tenancy under section 14; or

(b)     to apportion between the house and premises (or part of them) and other property the rent payable under any tenancy; or

(c)     to determine the amount of a sub-tenant's share under Schedule 2 to this Act in compensation payable to a tenant under section 17 or 18.

[(2A)    For the purposes of this Part of this Act a matter is to be treated as determined by (or on appeal from) a leasehold valuation tribunal—

(a)     if the decision on the matter is not appealed against, at the end of the period for bringing an appeal; or

(b)     if that decision is appealed against, at the time when the appeal is disposed of.

(2B)    An appeal is disposed of—

(a)     if it is determined and the period for bringing any further appeal has ended; or

(b)     if it is abandoned or otherwise ceases to have effect.]

(3), (4)   ...

[(4A)    ... ]

(5)   ...

**[104]**

**NOTES**

Section heading: words in square brackets substituted by the Transfer of Tribunal Functions (Lands Tribunal and Miscellaneous Amendments) Order 2009, SI 2009/1307, art 5(1), (2), Sch 1, paras 82, 84, subject to transitional provisions and savings in Sch 5 thereto.

Sub-s (1): words in first pair of square brackets substituted by the Housing Act 1980, s 142(3), Sch 22, Pt II, para 8(1); paras (ba), (ca) inserted by the Housing Act 1996, ss 115, 116, Sch 11, para 1(2), except (in the case of para (ba)) in relation to cases where, before 1 October 1996, a notice was given under s 8 or 14 of this Act at **[90]**, **[97]**, or an application was made under s 27 of this Act at **[110]**; para (cza) inserted by the Commonhold and Leasehold Reform Act 2002, s 149(2), except in relation to an application for enfranchisement made under this section before 30 September 2003 (in relation to England) or 31 March 2004 (in relation to Wales).

Sub-s (1A): inserted by the Housing Act 1980, s 142(3), Sch 22, Pt II, para 8(2); repealed by the Commonhold and Leasehold Reform Act 2002, s 180, Sch 14, except in relation to any application made to an LVT or any proceedings transferred to an LVT by a county court before 30 September 2003 (in relation to England) or 31 March 2004 (in relation to Wales).

Sub-s (1B): inserted by the Housing Act 1980, s 142(3), Sch 22, Pt II, para 8(2).

Sub-s (2): words in square brackets substituted by the Housing Act 1980, ss 142(3), Sch 22, Pt II, para 8(3), (4).

Sub-ss (2A), (2B): inserted by the Commonhold and Leasehold Reform Act 2002, s 176, Sch 13, paras 1, 5, except in relation to any application made to an LVT or any proceedings transferred to an LVT by a county court before 30 September 2003 (in relation to England) or 31 March 2004 (in relation to Wales).

Sub-ss (3), (4): repealed by the Commonhold and Leasehold Reform Act 2002, s 180, Sch 14, except in relation to any application made to an LVT or any proceedings transferred to an LVT by a county court before 30 September 2003 (in relation to England) or 31 March 2004 (in relation to Wales).

Sub-s (4A): inserted by the Housing Act 1980, s 142(3), Sch 22, Pt II, para 8(6); repealed by the Commonhold and Leasehold Reform Act 2002, s 180, Sch 14, except in relation to any application made to an LVT or any proceedings transferred to an LVT by a county court before 30 September 2003 (in relation to England) or 31 March 2004 (in relation to Wales).

Sub-s (5): repealed by the Housing Act 1980, ss 142(3), 152(3), Sch 22, Pt II, para 8(7), Sch 26.

## 22 Validity of tenants' notices, effect on Landlord and Tenant Act 1954 and on notices to quit, etc, and procedure generally

(1)    The provisions of Schedule 3 to this Act shall have effect—

    (a)    to exclude a tenant's right to acquire the freehold or an extended lease under this Part of this Act if a notice of his desire to have it is given too late; and

    (b)    to make a notice of a person's desire to have the freehold or an extended lease under this Part of this Act effectual where apart from the notice the tenancy would or might terminate by forfeiture or otherwise; and

    (c)    for adapting the procedure under Parts I and II of the Landlord and Tenant Act 1954, and for relating to one another proceedings under that Act and proceedings under this Part of this Act; and

    [(cc)    for adapting the procedure under Schedule 10 to the Local Government and Housing Act 1989, and for relating to one another proceedings under that Schedule and proceedings under this Part of this Act; and]

    (d)    generally for regulating the procedure under this Part of this Act.

(2)    Where a tenant having a right under this Part of this Act to acquire the freehold or an extended lease gives the landlord notice in accordance with this Part of this Act of his desire to have it, then except as otherwise provided by this Act the procedure for giving effect to the notice, and the rights and obligations of all parties in relation to the investigation of title and other matters arising in giving effect to the notice, shall be such as may be prescribed by regulations made by [the Secretary of State] by statutory instrument (which shall be subject to annulment in pursuance of a resolution of either House of Parliament), and subject to or in the absence of provision made by any such regulations as regards any matter shall be as nearly as may be the same as in the case of a contract of sale or leasing freely negotiated between the parties.

(3)    In relation to a claim to acquire the freehold, regulations under subsection (2) above may include provision—

    (a)    for a sum on account of the price payable for the house and premises and landlord's costs to be deposited with the landlord or with some person as his agent or as stakeholder, and for the return or forfeiture in any prescribed circumstances of the whole or part of the sum deposited;

    (b)    for enabling or requiring the tenant in any prescribed circumstances, instead of continuing to pay rent under the tenancy, to pay sums representing interest on the price payable or, at his option, either to pay such sums as aforesaid or to pay or deposit the price payable or the balance of it;

    (c)    for any matters incidental to or arising out of the matters mentioned above;

and in relation to any claim the regulations may provide for discharging the landlord or the tenant by reason of the other's default or delay from the obligations arising out of the claim.

(4)    In the case of a claim to acquire the freehold, subsection (2) above shall not be taken in any case as applying forms prescribed under section 46 of the Law of Property Act 1925 for contracts entered into by correspondence; but, without prejudice to the generality of that subsection section 49 (which provides for the determination of questions arising between vendor and purchaser) shall apply.

(5)    Section 66 of the Landlord and Tenant Act 1954 (which requires the prescribed form for a notice to be prescribed by regulations of [the Secretary of State], and makes provisions as to the contents of prescribed forms and as to the service of notices) shall have effect as if any reference therein to that Act were a reference also to this Part of this Act.

**NOTES**

Sub-s (1): para (cc) inserted by the Local Government and Housing Act 1989, s 194(1), Sch 11, para 11.

Sub-ss (2), (5) words in square brackets substituted by the Transfer of Functions (Lord Chancellor and Secretary of State) Order 1974, SI 1974/1896, art 3(2).

Regulations: the Leasehold Reform (Enfranchisement and Extension) Regulations 1967, SI 1967/1879 at **[3001]**; the Leasehold Reform (Notices) Regulations 1997, SI 1997/640 at **[3176]**, (made under the Landlord and Tenant Act 1954, s 66, as applied by sub-s (5) above).

*Supplementary*

## 23 Agreements excluding or modifying rights of tenant

(1) Except as provided by this section, any agreement relating to a tenancy (whether contained in the instrument creating the tenancy or not and whether made before the creation of the tenancy or not) shall be void in so far as it purports to exclude or modify any right to acquire the freehold or an extended lease or right to compensation under this Part of this Act, or provides for the termination or surrender of the tenancy in the event of a tenant acquiring or claiming any such right or for the imposition of any penalty or disability on the tenant in that event.

(2) Subsection (1) above shall not be taken to preclude a tenant from surrendering his tenancy, and shall not—

(a) invalidate any agreement for a tenant to acquire an interest superior to his tenancy or an extended lease on terms different from those provided for by this Part of this Act; or

(b) where a tenant has given notice of his desire to have the freehold or an extended lease under this Part of this Act, invalidate any agreement between the landlord and the tenant that that notice shall cease to be binding or any provision of such an agreement excluding or restricting for a period not exceeding [twelve months] the right to give a further notice of either kind with respect to the house or any part of it; or

(c) where a tenant's right to compensation has accrued, invalidate any agreement as to the amount of the compensation.

(3) Where—

(a) a person, being entitled as tenant of a house to acquire the freehold or an extended lease under this Part of this Act, enters into an agreement without the prior approval of the court for the surrender of his tenancy, or for the acquisition by him of an interest superior to his tenancy or of any extended lease; or

(b) a tenancy having been extended under this Part of this Act, the tenant, on the landlord claiming possession for purposes of redevelopment, enters into an agreement without the prior approval of the court for the surrender of the tenancy;

then on the application of the tenant the county court or any court in which proceedings are brought against him on the agreement may, if in the opinion of the court he is not adequately recompensed under the agreement for his rights under this Part of this Act, set aside or vary the agreement and give such other relief as appears to the court to be just, having regard to the situation and conduct of the parties.

(4) Where a tenant of a house is under this Part of this Act entitled to acquire the freehold or an extended lease, or entitled to the benefit of a previous tenant's notice of his desire to have the freehold or an extended lease, there may with the approval of the court be granted to him in satisfaction of that right a new tenancy on such terms as may be approved by the court; and, subject to [section 36 of the Charities Act 1993] and to section 31 below, a tenancy may be so granted by the landlord, and shall be binding on persons entitled to any interest in or charge on the landlord's estate, notwithstanding that it would not apart from this provision be authorised as against any such persons and notwithstanding any restriction imposed by statute or otherwise on the landlord's powers of leasing:

Provided that where the existing tenancy is granted after the commencement of this Part of this Act (whether or not it is, by virtue of section 3(3) above, to be treated for other purposes as forming a single tenancy with a previous tenancy) and, the grant being subsequent to the creation of a charge on the landlord's estate, the existing tenancy is not binding on the persons interested in the charge, a tenancy so granted shall not by virtue of this subsection be binding on those persons.

(5) Where a tenancy is granted by virtue of subsection (4) above,—

(a) the terms of the new tenancy may exclude any right to acquire the freehold under this Part of this Act; and

(b) [section 9(1) and (1A) above,] section 14(5) and (6) above and, except in so far as provision is made to the contrary by the terms of the new tenancy, section 16(1) to (6) and section 17(1) to (3) (together with Schedule 2 to this Act and, so far as relevant, subsections (1) to (3) above) shall apply as if the new tenancy were granted by way of extension under this Part of this Act.

(6) Where an instrument extending a tenancy at a low rent, or granting a further tenancy at a low rent in substitution for or in continuance of such a tenancy, contains a statement to the effect

that by virtue of subsection (4) above the tenancy is being or has previously been extended in satisfaction of the right to an extended lease under section 14 above, the statement shall be conclusive in favour of any person not being a party to the instrument, unless the statement appears from the instrument to be untrue.

(7)   Any person who—

(a)   includes or causes to be included in an instrument a statement to the effect mentioned in subsection (6) above, knowing the statement to be untrue; or

(b)   executes, or with intent to deceive makes use of, any instrument, knowing that it contains such a statement and that the statement is untrue;

shall be liable on conviction on indictment to imprisonment for a term not exceeding two years, or on summary conviction to imprisonment for a term not exceeding three months or to a fine not exceeding [the prescribed sum], or to both.

**[106]**

**NOTES**

Sub-s (2): words in square brackets in para (b) substituted by the Commonhold and Leasehold Reform Act 2002, s 139(3)(b), except in relation to an application for enfranchisement or an extended lease of a house in respect of which notice was given under s 8 or 14 of this Act at **[90]**, **[97]**, or where an application was made under s 27 of this Act at **[110]**, before 26 July 2002 (in relation to England) or 1 January 2003 (in relation to Wales).

Sub-s (4): words in square brackets substituted by the Charities Act 1993, s 98(1), Sch 6, para 8.

Sub-s (5): words in square brackets in para (b) inserted by the Housing and Planning Act 1986, s 23(1), (3).

Sub-s (7): words in square brackets substituted by virtue of the Magistrates' Courts Act 1980, s 32(2).

## 24   Application of price or compensation received by landlord, and charge of betterment levy on enfranchisement

(1)   Any sum received by the landlord by way of the price payable for a house and premises under section 9 above, or by way of compensation under any provision of this Part of this Act providing for compensation to be recovered by or awarded to a landlord,—

(a)   where the interest of the landlord is [subject to a trust of land] shall be dealt with as if it were proceeds of sale arising under the trust; and

(b)   where the landlord is a university or college to which the Universities and College Estates Act 1925 applies, shall be dealt with as if it were an amount payable as consideration on a sale effected under that Act.

(2)   …

**[107]**

**NOTES**

Sub-s (1): words in square brackets in para (a) substituted by the Trusts of Land and Appointment of Trustees Act 1996, s 25(1), Sch 3, para 10(b), subject to savings in s 25(4), (5) of that Act.

Sub-s (2): repealed by the Statute Law (Repeals) Act 1998.

## 25   Mortgagee in possession of landlord's interest

(1)   Where a landlord's interest is subject to a mortgage and the mortgagee is in possession, then subject to the provisions of this section all such proceedings arising out of a person's notice of his desire to have the freehold or an extended lease under this Part of this Act as would apart from this provision be taken by or in relation to the landlord shall, as regards his interest, be conducted by and through the mortgagee as if he were the landlord, and any conveyance to be executed under section 8 of this Act or lease to be executed under section 14 shall, if it requires execution by the landlord, either be executed by the landlord by the direction of the mortgagee or be executed by the mortgagee in the name and on behalf of the landlord; but this subsection shall not affect the operation in relation to the mortgage of sections 12 and 13 above.

(2)   Where a landlord's interest is subject to a mortgage and the mortgagee is in possession, then (without prejudice to subsection (1) above) any application under section 17 above shall be made by the mortgagee as if he were the landlord, and that section and Schedule 2 to this Act shall apply accordingly.

(3)   Any compensation paid by a mortgagee in accordance with section 17 above (whether possession is obtained under that section or without an application thereunder) shall be treated as if it were secured by the mortgage, with the like priority and with interest at the same rate as the mortgage money, so however that (without prejudice to the recovery of interest) the amount shall not be recoverable from the mortgagor personally.

(4)   Where a mortgagee is by virtue of this section acting as landlord and any case arises in which compensation may be recovered by or awarded to a landlord, compensation may be recovered by or awarded to the mortgagee accordingly, and shall be dealt with as if it were proceeds of sale of property subject to the mortgage.

(5)   Where a landlord's interest is subject to a mortgage, and a receiver appointed by the mortgagee or by the court is in receipt of the rents and profits,—

(a)   the landlord shall not make any application under section 17 or 18 above without the consent of the mortgagee; and

(b)   the mortgagee may by written notice given to the landlord require that this section shall apply, either generally or so far as relates to section 17 above, as if he were a mortgagee in possession.

(6)   In this section "mortgage" includes any charge or lien, and "mortgagor" and "mortgagee" shall be construed accordingly.

**[108]**

## 26   Person to act where landlord is custodian trustee or under disability

(1)   Where the interest of a landlord in any property is vested in a person as custodian trustee, the managing trustees or committee of management shall be deemed to be the landlord for the purposes of this Part of this Act and the interest be deemed to be vested in them, except as regards the execution of any instrument disposing of or affecting that interest.

[(2)   Where a landlord lacks capacity (within the meaning of the Mental Capacity Act 2005) to exercise his functions as a landlord, those functions are to be exercised—

(a)   by a donee of an enduring power of attorney or lasting power of attorney (within the meaning of the 2005 Act), or a deputy appointed for him by the Court of Protection, with power to exercise those functions, or

(b)   if no donee or deputy has that power, by a person authorised in that respect by that court.]

**[109]**

---

**NOTES**

Sub-s (2): substituted by the Mental Capacity Act 2005, s 67(1), Sch 6, para 13, except in relation to any proceedings pending at 1 October 2007 in which a receiver or a person authorised under Part 7 of the Mental Health Act 1983 is acting on behalf of the landlord.

---

## 27   Enfranchisement where landlord cannot be found

(1)   Where a tenant of a house having a right under this Part of this Act to acquire the freehold is prevented from giving notice of his desire to have the freehold because the person to be served with the notice cannot be found, or his identity cannot be ascertained, then on an application made by the tenant [the court] may, subject to and in accordance with the provisions of this section, make such order as [the court] thinks fit with a view to the house and premises being vested in him, his executors, administrators or assigns for the like estate and on the like terms (so far as the circumstances permit) as if he had at the date of his application to [the court] given notice of his desire to have the freehold.

(2)   Before making any such order [the court] may require the applicant to take such further steps by way of advertisement or otherwise as [the court] thinks proper for the purpose of tracing the landlord; and if after an application is made to [the court] and before the house and premises are vested in pursuance of the application the landlord is traced, then no further proceedings shall be taken with a view to the house and premises being so vested, but subject to subsection (7) below—

(a)   the rights and obligations of all parties shall be determined as if the applicant had, at the date of the application, duly given notice of his desire to have the freehold; and

(b)   [the court] may give such directions as [the court] thinks fit as to the steps to be taken for giving effect to those rights and obligations, including directions modifying or dispensing with any of the requirements of this Act or of regulations made under this Act.

(3)   Where a house and premises are to be vested in a person in pursuance of an application under this section, then on his paying into [court] the appropriate sum there shall be executed by such person as the [court] may designate a conveyance in a form approved by the [court] and containing such provisions as may be so approved for the purpose of giving effect so far as possible to the requirements of section 10 above; and that conveyance shall be effective to vest in the person to whom the conveyance is made the property expressed to be conveyed, subject as and in the manner in which it is expressed to be conveyed.

(4)   For the purpose of any conveyance to be executed in accordance with subsection (3) above, any question as to the property to be conveyed and the rights with or subject to which it is to be conveyed shall be determined by the [court], but it shall be assumed (unless the contrary is shown) that the landlord has no interest in property other than the property to be conveyed and, for the purpose of excepting them from the conveyance, any underlying minerals.

[(5)   The appropriate sum which, in accordance with subsection (3) above, is to be paid into court is the aggregate of—

    (a)    such amount as may be determined by (or on appeal from) a leasehold valuation tribunal to be the price payable in accordance with section 9 above; and

    (b)    the amount or estimated amount (as so determined) of any pecuniary rent payable for the house and premises up to the date of the conveyance which remains unpaid.]

(6)    Where a house and premises are vested in a person in accordance with this section, the payment into [court] of the appropriate sum shall be taken to have satisfied any claims against the tenant, his executors, administrators or assigns in respect of the price payable under this Part of this Act for the acquisition of the freehold in the house and premises.

(7)    An application under this section may be withdrawn at any time before execution of a conveyance under subsection (3) above and, after it is withdrawn, subsection (2)(a) shall not apply; but where any step is taken (whether by the landlord or the tenant) for the purpose of giving effect to subsection (2)(a) in the case of any application, the application shall not afterwards be withdrawn except with the landlord's consent or by leave of [the court], and [the court] shall not give leave unless it appears to [the court] just to do so by reason of matters coming to the knowledge of the applicant in consequence of the landlord being traced.

(8)    A conveyance executed under subsection (3) above shall have effect as provided by that subsection notwithstanding any interest of the Crown in the property expressed to be conveyed.

**[110]**

---

**NOTES**

Sub-ss (1)–(4), (6), (7): words in square brackets substituted by the Commonhold and Leasehold Reform Act 2002, s 148, except in relation to an application for enfranchisement made under this section before 30 September 2003 (in relation to England) or 31 March 2004 (in relation to Wales).

Sub-s (5): substituted by the Commonhold and Leasehold Reform Act 2002, s 149(1), except in relation to an application for enfranchisement made under this section before 30 September 2003 (in relation to England) or 31 March 2004 (in relation to Wales).

---

**[27A   Compensation for postponement of termination in connection with ineffective claims**

(1)    This section applies where, on or after 15th January 1999—

    (a)    a tenant of any property makes a claim to acquire the freehold or an extended lease of it, and

    (b)    the claim is not made at least two years before the term date of the tenancy in respect of which the claim is made ("the existing tenancy").

(2)    The tenant shall be liable to pay compensation if the claim is not effective and—

    (a)    the making of the claim caused a notice served under paragraph 4(1) of Schedule 10 to the Local Government and Housing Act 1989 to cease to have effect and the date on which the claim ceases to have effect is later than four months before the termination date specified in the notice,

    (b)    the making of the claim prevented the service of an effective notice under paragraph 4(1) of Schedule 10 to the Local Government and Housing Act 1989 (but did not cause a notice served under that provision to cease to have effect) and the date on which the claim ceases to have effect is a date later than six months before the term date of the tenancy, or

    (c)    the existing tenancy is continued under paragraph 3(1) of Schedule 3 to this Act by virtue of the claim.

(3)    Compensation under subsection (2) above shall become payable at the end of the appropriate period and be the right of the person who is the tenant's immediate landlord at that time.

(4)    The amount which the tenant is liable to pay under subsection (2) above shall be equal to the difference between—

    (a)    the rent for the appropriate period under the existing tenancy, and

    (b)    the rent which might reasonably be expected to be payable for that period were the property to which the existing tenancy relates let for a term equivalent to that period on the open market by a willing landlord on the following assumptions—

        (i)    that no premium is payable in connection with the letting,

        (ii)    that the letting confers no security of tenure, and

        (iii)    that, except as otherwise provided by this paragraph, the letting is on the same terms as the existing tenancy.

(5)    For the purposes of subsection (2) above, a claim to acquire the freehold or an extended lease is not effective if it ceases to have effect for any reason other than—

    (a)    the acquisition in pursuance of the claim of the interest to which it relates, or

    (b)    the lapsing of the claim under any provision of this Act excluding the tenant's liability for costs.

(6)    For the purposes of subsections (3) and (4) above, the appropriate period is—

    (a)    in a case falling within paragraph (a) of subsection (2) above, the period—

PART I
STATUTES

  (i) beginning with the termination date specified in the notice mentioned in that paragraph, and

  (ii) ending with the earliest date of termination which could have been specified in a notice under paragraph 4(1) of Schedule 10 to the Local Government and Housing Act 1989 served immediately after the date on which the claim ceases to have effect, or, if the existing tenancy is terminated before then, with the date of its termination;

 (b) in a case falling within paragraph (b) of subsection (2) above, the period—

  (i) beginning with the later of six months from the date on which the claim is made and the term date of the existing tenancy, and

  (ii) ending six months after the date on which the claim ceases to have effect, or, if the existing tenancy is terminated before then, with the date of its termination; and

 (c) in a case falling within paragraph (c) of subsection (2) above, the period for which the existing tenancy is continued under paragraph 3(1) of Schedule 3 to this Act.

 (7) For the purposes of this section—

 (a) references to a claim to acquire the freehold or an extended lease shall be taken as references to a notice of a person's desire to acquire it under Part I of this Act and as including a claim made by a tenant not entitled to acquire it, and

 (b) references to the date on which a claim ceases to have effect shall, in relation to a notice which is not a valid notice, be taken as references to the date on which the notice is set aside by the court or withdrawn or would, if valid, cease to have effect, that date being taken, where the notice is set aside, or would (if valid) cease to have effect, in consequence of a court order, to be the date when the order becomes final.]

                         **[111]**

**NOTES**

Inserted, together with s 27B, by the Housing Act 1996, s 116, Sch 11, para 1(1).

**[27B Modification of section 27A where change in immediate reversion**

 (1) Where a tenant's liability to pay compensation under section 27A above relates to a period during which there has been a change in the interest immediately expectant on the determination of his tenancy, that section shall have effect with the following modifications.

 (2) For subsections (3) and (4) there shall be substituted—

  "(3) Compensation under subsection (2) above shall become payable at the end of the appropriate period and there shall be a separate right to compensation in respect of each of the interests which, during that period, have been immediately expectant on the determination of the existing tenancy.

  (4) Compensation under subsection (2) above shall—

  (a) in the case of the interest which is immediately expectant on the determination of the existing tenancy at the end of the appropriate period, be the right of the person in whom that interest is vested at that time, and

  (b) in the case of an interest which ceases during the appropriate period to be immediately expectant on the determination of the existing tenancy, be the right of the person in whom the interest was vested immediately before it ceased to be so expectant.

  (4A) The amount which the tenant is liable to pay under subsection (2) above in respect of any interest shall be equal to the difference between—

  (a) the rent under the existing tenancy for the part of the appropriate period during which the interest was immediately expectant on the determination of that tenancy, and

  (b) the rent which might reasonably be expected to be payable for that part of that period were the property to which the existing tenancy relates let for a term equivalent to that part of that period on the open market by a willing landlord on the following assumptions—

   (i) that no premium is payable in connection with the letting,

   (ii) that the letting confers no security of tenure, and

   (iii) that, except as otherwise provided by this paragraph, the letting is on the same terms as the existing tenancy".

 (3) In subsection (6), for "(3) and (4)" there shall be substituted "(3) to (4A)".]

                         **[112]**

**NOTES**

Inserted as noted to s 27A at **[111]**.

*Land held for public purposes, ecclesiastical land, etc*

## 28 Retention or resumption of land required for public purposes

(1)   Where the landlord of any property is a body to which this section applies, and a Minister of the Crown certifies that the property will in ten years or less be required for relevant development, then—

(a)   a notice of a person's desire to have the freehold or an extended lease under this Part of this Act of a house comprised in the property shall be of no effect;

(b)   if the tenancy of any such house has not been extended under this Part of this Act, but the tenant, being entitled to acquire the freehold or an extended lease thereunder, either—

(i)   before a copy of the certificate has been served on him, has given notice of his desire to have the freehold or an extended lease; or

(ii)   not later than two months after a copy of the certificate is served on him, gives the landlord written notice, in the prescribed form, claiming to be so entitled;

then section 17 above shall apply as if the tenancy had been so extended;

(c)   for the purposes of any application by the landlord under section 17 above in relation to property comprised in the certificate (whether the application is made by virtue of paragraph (b) above or otherwise), the certificate shall be conclusive that the ground specified in section 17(1) is established.

(2)   Where by virtue of subsection (1)(b) above a tenancy of any property is to be treated as having been extended, then as regards that property the tenancy shall not terminate either by effluxion of time or in pursuance of any notice given by the landlord or the tenant or by the termination of a superior tenancy.

(3)   In the case of a tenancy to which Part II of the Landlord and Tenant Act 1954 applies, subsections (1) and (2) above shall have effect where a certificate is given under section 57 of that Act as they have effect where a certificate is given under this section; but where by virtue of subsection (1)(b) above a tenancy is to be treated as having been extended, no compensation shall be payable under section 59 of that Act in respect of the tenancy or any immediate or derivative sub-tenancy.

(4)   A Minister shall not give a certificate under this section with respect to any house, unless the landlord has given to the tenant of the house written notice stating—

(a)   that the question of giving such a certificate is under consideration by that Minister; and

(b)   that if within twenty-one days of the giving of the notice the tenant makes to that Minister representations in writing with respect to that question, they will be considered before the question is determined;

and if the tenant makes any such representations within those twenty-one days the Minister shall consider them before determining whether to give the certificate.

(5)   This section applies—

(a)   to any local authority, that is to say, the Mayor and commonalty and citizens of the City of London, ... any county council, borough council or district council, [ ... any joint authority established by Part IV of the Local Government Act 1985,] [any authority established for an area in England by an order under section 207 of the Local Government and Public Involvement in Health Act 2007 (joint waste authorities),] [the London Fire and Emergency Planning Authority,] any joint board in which all the constituent authorities are local authorities within this paragraph ... [any police authority established under [section 3 of the Police Act 1996] [and the Metropolitan Police Authority]; ... ]

[(aa)  to the Broads Authority; and]

[(ab)  to any National Park authority; and]

(b)   to the [new towns residuary body] and to any development corporation within the meaning of the New Towns Act 1965; and

[(bb) ... ]

[(bc) ... ]

(c)   to any university body, that is to say, any university, university college or college of a university, and for this purpose "college of a university" includes, in the case of a university organised on a collegiate basis, a constituent college or other society recognised by the university and, in the case of a London University, a college incorporated in the university or a school of the university; and

[(d)   to [any Strategic Health Authority,] any [[Local Health Board], any Special Health Authority][, any Primary Care Trust][, any National Health Service trust and any NHS foundation trust]; and]

(e)   to any body corporate established by or under any enactment for the purpose of carrying on under national ownership any industry or part of an industry or undertaking; and

[(ee)  to the [Environment Agency];]

(f) to any body not included above which is a harbour authority within the meaning of the Harbours Act 1964 ... , but in respect only of the body's functions as harbour authority ... [and

(g) a housing action trust established under Part III of the Housing Act 1988].

(6) In subsection (1) above "relevant development", in relation to any body to which this section applies, means development for purposes (other than investment purposes) of that body, but in relation to a local authority includes any development to be undertaken, whether or not by [that authority, in order to secure—

(a) the development or re-development of an area defined by a development plan under the [Planning and Compulsory Purchase Act 2004] as an area of comprehensive development; or

(b) the treatment as a whole, by development, re-development, or improvement, or partly by one and partly by another method, of any area in which the property is situated].

However—

(a) the purposes of a county council or ... council shall be taken to include the purposes of a police authority which is a committee of the council; and

(b) the purposes of a university body shall be taken to include the purposes of any related university body (a university and the colleges of that university within the meaning of subsection (5)(c) above being related to one another within the meaning of this paragraph); and

[(c) in the case of a [Strategic Health Authority,] [[Local Health Board], Special Health Authority][, Primary Care Trust][, National Health Service trust or NHS foundation trust], the purposes of the [the National Health Service Act 2006 or the National Health Service (Wales) Act 2006] shall be substituted for the purposes of the body.]

[(6A) In subsections (5) and (6) above, any reference to a county council shall be read, in relation to Wales, as including a reference to a county borough council.]

(7) If it appears to the Minister of Housing and Local Government or to the Secretary of State that this section should apply to any body or description of bodies having functions of a public nature but not included above, he may by order direct that this section shall apply to that body or description of bodies.

(8) The power to make orders under subsection (7) above shall include power to vary or revoke any order made for the purposes of that subsection, and shall be exercisable by statutory instrument of which a draft shall be laid before Parliament.

**[113]**

**NOTES**

Sub-s (5): in para (a), words omitted in the first place repealed and words in first pair of square brackets inserted by the Local Government Act 1985, ss 84, 102(2), Sch 14, para 43, Sch 17, words omitted in the second place repealed by the Education Reform Act 1988, s 237(2), Sch 13, Pt I, words in second pair of square brackets inserted by the Local Government and Public Involvement in Health Act 2007, s 209(2), Sch 13, Pt 2, para 27, words in third pair of square brackets inserted and word omitted in the third place repealed by the Greater London Authority Act 1999, ss 328, 423, Sch 29, para 8, Sch 34, Pt VII, words in fourth (outer) pair of square brackets substituted by the Police and Magistrates' Courts Act 1994, s 43, Sch 4, Pt II, para 48, words in fifth (inner) pair of square brackets substituted by the Police Act 1996, s 103(1), Sch 7, Pt I, para 1(1), (2)(d), words in sixth (inner) pair of square brackets inserted by the Greater London Authority Act 1999, s 325, Sch 27, para 21, and word omitted in the fourth place repealed by the Police Act 1997, s 134(2), Sch 10; para (aa) inserted by the Norfolk and Suffolk Broads Act 1988, s 21, Sch 6, para 6; para (ab) inserted by the Environment Act 1995, s 78, Sch 10, para 7; words in square brackets in para (b) substituted by the Housing and Regeneration Act 2008, s 56, Sch 8. paras 5, 6, subject to transitional provisions and savings in SI 2008/3068, arts 6–10 at **[3834B]–[3834F]**; para (bb) inserted by the Development of Rural Wales Act 1976, s 27, Sch 7, para 5(1), (2) and repealed by the Government of Wales Act 1998, ss 131, 152, Sch 18, Pt IV; para (bc) inserted by the Police Act 1997, s 134(1), Sch 9, para 16 and repealed by the Serious Organised Crime and Police Act 2005, ss 59, 174, Sch 4, para 17, Sch 17, Pt 2; para (d) substituted by the National Health Service Reorganisation Act 1973, ss 57, 58, Sch 4, para 111, words in first pair of square brackets inserted by the National Health Service Reform and Health Care Professions Act 2002 (Supplementary, Consequential etc Provisions) Regulations 2002, SI 2002/2469, reg 4, Sch 1, Pt 1, para 4(a), words in second (outer) pair of square brackets substituted by the Health Authorities Act 1995, s 2(1), Sch 1, Pt III, para 94(a), words in third (inner) pair of square brackets substituted by the References to Health Authorities Order 2007, SI 2007/961, art 3, Schedule, para 5, words in fourth pair of square brackets inserted by the Health Act 1999 (Supplementary, Consequential etc Provisions) Order 2000, SI 2000/90, art 3(1), Sch 1, para 7(a), words in fifth pair of square brackets substituted by the Health and Social Care (Community Health and Standards) Act 2003, s 34, Sch 4, paras 11, 12(a); para (ee) inserted and words omitted from para (f) repealed by the Water Act 1989, s 190(1), (3), Sch 25, para 35, Sch 27, Pt I; in para (ee) words in square brackets substituted by the Environment Act 1995 (Consequential Amendments) Regulations 1996, SI 1996/593, reg 2, Sch 1; para (g) and the word immediately preceding it added by the Housing Act 1988, s 140(1), Sch 17, Pt I, para 15.

Sub-s (6): words in first (outer) pair of square brackets substituted by the Planning (Consequential Provisions) Act 1990, ss 4, 5, Sch 2, para 17(1), Sch 3; words in square brackets in para (a) substituted by the Planning and Compulsory Purchase Act 2004, s 118(2), Sch 7, para 3; words omitted from para (a) of the proviso repealed by the Local Government Act 1972, s 272(1), Sch 30; para (c) of the proviso substituted by the National Health Service Reorganisation Act 1973, ss 57, 58, Sch 4, para 111; words in first pair of square brackets in para (c) of the proviso inserted by SI 2002/2469, reg 4, Sch 1, Pt 1, para 4(b); words in second (outer) pair of square brackets of para (c) of the proviso substituted by the Health Authorities Act 1995, s 2(1), Sch 1, Pt III, para 94(b); words in third (inner) pair of square brackets in para (c) of the proviso substituted by SI 2007/961, art 3, Schedule, para 5; words in fourth pair of square brackets in para (c) of the proviso inserted by SI 2000/90, art 3(1), Sch 1, para 7(b); words in fifth pair of square brackets in para (c) of the proviso substituted by the Health and Social Care (Community Health and Standards) Act 2003, s 34, Sch 4, paras 11, 12(b); words in sixth pair of square brackets in para (c) of the proviso substituted by the National Health Service (Consequential Provisions) Act 2006, s 2, Sch 1, paras 31, 32.

Sub-s (6A): inserted by the Local Government (Wales) Act 1994, s 22(2), Sch 8, para 1(1).

New Towns Act 1965: see now the New Towns Act 1981.

## 29 Reservation of future right to develop

(1)   Where a tenant of a house and premises acquires the freehold under this Part of this Act, the landlord being a local authority, there shall, if so required by the local authority, be included in the conveyance under section 8 above such covenants on the part of the tenant restricting the carrying out of development or clearing of land as are necessary to reserve the land for possible development by the authority.

(2)   Where a tenant of a house and premises acquires an extended lease under this Part of this Act, the landlord being a local authority, such covenants as are mentioned in subsection (1) above shall, if so required by the local authority, be included in the instrument extending the lease under section 14 above and, if so included, then in the terms of any subsequent tenancy at a low rent which is by virtue of section 3(3) above to be treated (with or without any intervening tenancies) as a single tenancy with that under the extended lease.

(3)   Where a covenant is entered into to give effect to subsection (1) or (2) above, it shall be expressed to be so entered into, and Part I of Schedule 4 to this Act shall have effect with respect to the operation and enforcement of any covenant so entered into.

(4)   Where a tenant of a house and premises acquires the freehold or an extended lease under this Part of this Act, the landlord being a local authority, and afterwards the local authority or any other person acquires compulsorily any interest in the property, then for the purpose of assessing compensation in accordance with the Land Compensation Act 1961 no account shall be taken of any increase in the value of that interest which is attributable to the carrying out of development in contravention of a covenant entered into to give effect to subsection (1) or (2) above, or to any prospect of carrying out any such development; and any compensation payable to a tenant under section 17 above shall be assessed without regard to any increase in the value of his interest which under this subsection would be disregarded on a compulsory purchase of that interest.

(5)   For purposes of this section "local authority" means a local authority as defined in section 28(5)(a) above.

(6)   Subsections (1) to (4) above shall have effect in relation—
   (a)   to the [new towns residuary body] and to any development corporation within the meaning of the New Towns Act 1965; and
   (b)   to any university body as defined in section 28(5)(c) above;

as if any reference in those subsections or in Part I of Schedule 4 to this Act to a local authority were a reference to [that residuary body], corporation or university body; ...

[(6A)   ... ]

[(6B)   Where the landlord is a university body, the possible development for which land may be reserved by a covenant entered into to give effect to subsection (1) or (2) above[—
   (a)   includes development by a related university body (within the meaning of section 28(6)(b) above); and
   (b)   must be development for the purposes (other than investment purposes) of the university body or any such related university body.]]

[(6C)   Subsection (1) to (4) above shall have effect in relation to a housing action trust as if any reference in those subsections or in Part I of Schedule 4 to this Act to a local authority were a reference to the trust.]

(7)   Part II of Schedule 4 to this Act shall have effect to enable property to be re-acquired compulsorily where it is subject to a covenant entered into to give effect to subsection (1) above with the [Welsh new towns residuary body] [ ... ] or a university body.

(8)   This section shall apply, with the necessary adaptations, where a new tenancy is granted in satisfaction of the right to an extended lease under this Part of this Act, as it applies where a lease is extended in accordance with this Part of this Act.

PART I
STATUTES

**NOTES**

Sub-s (6): words in square brackets substituted by the Housing and Regeneration Act 2008, s 56, Sch 8, paras 5, 7(1), (2), subject to transitional provisions and savings in SI 2008/3068, arts 6–10 at **[3834B]–[3834F]**; words omitted repealed by the Education and Inspections Act 2006, ss 177(1), (2), 184, Sch 18, Pt 2, subject to savings in s 177(4) thereof.

Sub-s (6A): inserted by the Development of Rural Wales Act 1976, s 27, Sch 7, para 5(1), (3); repealed by the Government of Wales Act 1998, ss 131, 152, Sch 18, Pt IV.

Sub-s (6B): inserted by the Housing Act 1980, s 141, Sch 21, para 5; paras (a), (b) substituted by the Education and Inspections Act 2006, s 177(1), (3), subject to savings in s 177(4) thereof.

Sub-s (6C): inserted by the Housing Act 1988, s 140(1), Sch 17, Pt I, para 16.

Sub-s (7): words in square brackets substituted by the Housing and Regeneration Act 2008, s 56, Sch 8, paras 5, 7(1), (3), subject to transitional provisions and savings in SI 2008/3068, arts 6–10 at **[3834B]–[3834F]**; words omitted inserted by the Development of Rural Wales Act 1976, s 27, Sch 7, para 5(1), (3) and repealed by the Government of Wales Act 1998, ss 131, 152, Sch 18, Pt IV.

New Towns Act 1965: see now the New Towns Act 1981.

**30  Reservation of right of pre-emption in new town or overspill area**

(1)   Where a tenant of a house and premises acquires the freehold under this Part of this Act, the landlord being a body to which this section applies, there shall, if so required by the landlord, be included in the conveyance under section 8 above the following covenants on the part of the tenant, that is to say,—

(a)    a covenant that no tenancy of the property comprised in the conveyance or any part of that property shall be granted except with the consent in writing of the landlord; and

(b)    such covenant as appears to the landlord to be requisite for securing that, in the event of any proposal to sell that property or any part of it, the landlord will have a right of pre-emption at the price mentioned in subsection (4) below.

(2)   Where a tenant of a house and premises acquires an extended lease under this Part of this Act, the landlord being a body to which this section applies, such covenants as are mentioned in subsection (1) above shall, if so required by the landlord, be included in the instrument extending the lease under section 14 above and, if so included, then in the terms of any subsequent tenancy at a low rent which is by virtue of section 3(3) above to be treated (with or without intervening tenancies) as a single tenancy with that under the extended lease.

(3)   Where a covenant is entered into to give effect to subsection (1) or (2) above, it shall be expressed to be so entered into, and Part I of Schedule 4 to this Act shall have effect, with respect to the operation and enforcement of any covenant so entered into as it applies in the case of a covenant entered into with the same body to give effect to section 29(1) or (2) above.

(4)   The price referred to in subsection (1)(b) above, in relation to an interest in any property, is a sum equal to (and, in default of agreement, to be determined in the like manner as) the compensation which would be payable for that interest if acquired by the execution, on such date as may be determined in accordance with the covenant, of a vesting declaration under Schedule 4 to this Act.

(5)   Section 19 of the Landlord and Tenant Act 1927 (covenants not to assign etc without licence or consent) shall not have effect in relation to any covenant entered into to give effect to subsection (2) above.

(6)   This section shall apply, with the necessary adaptations, where a new tenancy is granted in satisfaction of the right to an extended lease under this Part of this Act, as it applies where a lease is extended in accordance with this Part of this Act.

(7)   This section applies—

(a)    to the [new towns residuary body][ ... ] and to a development corporation within the meaning of the New Towns Act 1965; and

(b)    in respect of housing provided by them by virtue of section 5 of the Town Development Act 1952 (which authorises a council to exercise its powers for the purpose of relieving congestion or over-population outside their area), the council of any receiving district for purposes of that Act, ...

**[115]**

**NOTES**

Sub-s (7): words in square brackets substituted by the Housing and Regeneration Act 2008, s 56, Sch 8, paras 5, 8, subject to transitional provisions and savings in SI 2008/3068, arts 6–10 at **[3834B]–[3834F]**; words omitted from para (a) inserted by the Development of Rural Wales Act 1976, s 27, Sch 7, para 5(1), (4) and repealed by the Government of Wales Act 1998, ss 131, 152, Sch 18, Pt IV; words omitted from para (b) repealed by the Housing (Consequential Provisions) Act 1985, s 3, Sch 1.

New Towns Act 1965: see now the New Towns Act 1981, s 81, Sch 13.

### 31 Ecclesiastical property

(1) The provisions of this section shall have effect as regards the operation of this Part of this Act on tenancies (including subtenancies) of ecclesiastical property, that is to say, property belonging to a capitular body within the meaning of the Cathedrals Measure 1963 or belonging to [a diocesan board of finance as diocesan glebe land]; and in this section "ecclesiastical landlord" means the capitular body or [diocesan board of finance] having an interest as landlord in ecclesiastical property.

(2) In relation to an interest of an ecclesiastical landlord, the consent of the Church Commissioners shall be required to sanction—

   (a) the provisions to be contained in a conveyance in accordance with section 10 above, or in a lease granting a new tenancy under section 14, and the price or rent payable, except as regards matters determined by the court, [a leasehold valuation tribunal] or the [Upper Tribunal];

   (b) any exercise of the ecclesiastical landlord's rights under section 17 above, except as aforesaid, and any agreement for the payment of compensation to a tenant in accordance with that section without an application thereunder;

   (c) any grant of a tenancy in satisfaction of the right to an extended lease under this Part of this Act;

[provided that the consent of the Church Commissioners shall only be required if their consent would be required if the transaction were carried out under the Endowments and Glebe Measure 1976 or the Cathedrals Measure 1999].

(3) Where the ecclesiastical property forms part of the endowment of a cathedral church, any sum received by the capitular body by way of the price payable for the property under section 9 above, or by way of compensation under any provision of this Part of this Act providing for compensation to be recovered by or awarded to a landlord, shall be treated as part of that endowment; and the powers conferred by sections 21 and 23 of the Cathedrals Measure 1963 in relation to the investment in the acquisition of land of moneys forming part of the endowment of a cathedral church shall extend to the application of any such moneys in the payment of compensation in accordance with section 17 above (whether possession is obtained under that section or without an application thereunder).

(4) In the case of ecclesiastical property belonging to [a diocesan board of finance]—

   (a) no consent or concurrence other than that of the Church Commissioners under subsection (2) above shall be required to a disposition under this Part of this Act of the [interest of the diocesan board of finance] (including a grant of a tenancy in satisfaction of the right to an extended lease);

   (b) ...

   (c) any sum receivable by the [diocesan board of finance] by way of the price payable for the property under section 9 above, or of any such compensation as is mentioned in subsection (3) above, shall be paid to [the board] to be applied for purposes for which the proceeds of a sale by agreement of the property would be applicable under any enactment or Measure authorising such a sale or disposing of the proceeds of such a sale, and any sum required for the payment of compensation as mentioned in subsection (3) above may be paid by [the board] on behalf of the incumbent out of any moneys in [its] hands;

   (d) ...

[(5) In this section "diocesan board of finance" and "diocesan glebe land" have the same meaning as in the Endowments and Glebe Measure 1976.]

[116]

## 32 Saving for National Trust

This Part of this Act shall not prejudice the operation of section 21 of the National Trust Act 1907, and accordingly a person shall not be entitled under this Part of this Act to acquire the freehold of property if an interest in the property is under that section vested inalienably in the National Trust for Places of Historic Interest or Natural Beauty.

**[117]**

## [32A Property transferred for public benefit etc

(1)   A notice of a person's desire to have the freehold of a house and premises under this Part shall be of no effect if at the relevant time the whole or any part of the house and premises is qualifying property and either—

(a)   the tenancy was created after the commencement of Chapter III of Part I of the Leasehold Reform, Housing and Urban Development Act 1993; or

(b)   (where the tenancy was created before that commencement) the tenant would not be entitled to have the freehold if either or both of sections 1A and 1B above were not in force *[or if section 1AA above were not in force]*.

(2)   For the purposes of this section the whole or any part of the house and premises is qualifying property if—

(a)   it has been designated under section 31(1)(b), (c) or (d) of the Inheritance Tax Act 1984 (designation and undertakings relating to conditionally exempt transfers), whether with or without any other property, and no chargeable event has subsequently occurred with respect to it; or

(b)   an application to the Board for it to be so designated is pending; or

(c)   it is the property of a body not established or conducted for profit and a direction has been given in relation to it under section 26 of that Act (gifts for public benefit), whether with or without any other property; or

(d)   an application to the Board for a direction to be so given in relation to it is pending.

(3)   For the purposes of subsection (2) above an application is pending as from the time when it is made to the Board until such time as it is either granted or refused by the Board or withdrawn by the applicant; and for this purpose an application shall not be regarded as made unless and until the applicant has submitted to the Board all such information in support of the application as is required by the Board.

(4)   A notice of a person's desire to have the freehold of a house and premises under this Part shall cease to have effect if—

(a)   before completion of the conveyance in pursuance of the tenant's notice, the whole or any part of the house and premises becomes qualifying property; and

(b)   the condition set out in subsection (1)(a) or (as the case may be) subsection (1)(b) above is satisfied.

(5)   Where a tenant's notice ceases to have effect by virtue of subsection (4) above—

(a)   section 9(4) above shall not apply to require the tenant to make any payment to the landlord in respect of costs incurred by reason of the notice; and

(b)   the person who applied or is applying for designation or a direction shall be liable to the tenant for all reasonable costs incurred by the tenant in connection with his claim to acquire the freehold of the house and premises.

(6)   Where it is claimed that subsection (1) or (4) above applies in relation to a tenant's notice, the person making the claim shall, at the time of making it, furnish the tenant with evidence in support of it; and if he fails to do so he shall be liable for any costs which are reasonably incurred by the tenant in consequence of the failure.

(7)   In subsection (2) above—

(a)   paragraphs (a) and (b) apply to designation under section 34(1)(a), (b) or (c) of the Finance Act 1975 or section 77(1)(b), (c) or (d) of the Finance Act 1976 as they apply to designation under section 31(1)(b), (c) or (d) of the Inheritance Tax Act 1984; and

(b)   paragraphs (c) and (d) apply to a direction under paragraph 13 of Schedule 6 to the Finance Act 1975 as they apply to a direction under section 26 of that Act of 1984.

(8)   In this section—

"the Board" means the Commissioners of Inland Revenue;

"chargeable event" means—

(a)   any event which in accordance with any provision of Chapter II of Part II of the Inheritance Tax Act 1984 (exempt transfers) is a chargeable event, including any such provision as applied by section 78(3) of that Act (conditionally exempt occasions); or

(b)   any event which would have been a chargeable event in the circumstances mentioned in section 79(3) of that Act (exemption from ten-yearly charge).]

**[118]**

**NOTES**
Inserted by the Leasehold Reform, Housing and Urban Development Act 1993, s 68, except where the right to acquire the freehold of a house and premises arises other than by virtue of any one or more of the provisions of ss 1A, 1B of this Act at **[79]**, **[81]**, in relation to a lease created after 1 November 1993 pursuant to a contract entered into before that date.
Sub-s (1): words in square brackets in para (b) added by the Housing Act 1996, s 106, Sch 9, para 2(1), (6), except in a case where the house and premises are held under a tenancy which is a shared ownership lease within the meaning of the Housing Act 1985, s 622 at **[571]**, and was granted by a housing association, whether or not the interest of the landlord still belongs to such an association, nor does it have effect in a case where, before 1 April 1997, a notice was given under s 8 of this Act at **[90]**, or an application was made under s 27 of this Act at **[110]**, or a notice was given under the Leasehold Reform, Housing and Urban Development Act 1993, s 13 or 42 at **[817]**, **[848]**, or an application was made under s 26 or 50 of that Act at **[830]**, **[856]**; words in italics in para (b) repealed by the Housing and Regeneration Act 2008, s 321(1), Sch 16, as from 7 September 2009 (in relation to England, subject to transitional provisions in SI 2009/2096, art 3) and as from a day to be appointed (in relation to Wales).
Finance Act 1975, s 34, Sch 6; Finance Act 1976, s 77: repealed by the Inheritance Tax Act 1984, s 277, Sch 9 (then cited as the Capital Transfer Tax Act 1984).

## 33 Crown land

(1)    In the case of a tenancy from the Crown this Part of this Act shall apply in favour of the tenant as in the case of any other tenancy if there has ceased to be a Crown interest in the land, and as against a landlord holding a tenancy from the Crown shall apply also if either—

    (a)    his sub-tenant is seeking an extended lease and the landlord, or a superior landlord holding a tenancy from the Crown, has a sufficient interest to grant it and is entitled to do so without the concurrence of the appropriate authority; or

    (b)    the appropriate authority notifies the landlord that as regards any Crown interest affected the authority will grant or concur in granting the freehold or extended lease.

(2)    For purposes of this section "tenancy from the Crown" means a tenancy of land in which there is, or has during the subsistence of the tenancy been, a Crown interest superior to the tenancy, and "Crown interest" and "the appropriate authority" in relation to a Crown interest mean respectively—

    (a)    an interest comprised in the Crown Estate, and the Crown Estate Commissioners;

    (b)    an interest belonging to Her Majesty in right of the Duchy of Lancaster, and the Chancellor of the Duchy;

    (c)    an interest belonging to the Duchy of Cornwall, and such person as the Duke of Cornwall or the possessor for the time being of the Duchy appoints;

    (d)    any other interest belonging to a government department or held on behalf of Her Majesty for the purposes of a government department, and the Minister in charge of that department.

[(2A)    For the purposes of this Part of this Act, an interest belonging to the Welsh new towns residuary body in a tenancy of land is to be treated as if it were not an interest belonging to the Crown.]

(3)    The restriction imposed by section 3(2) of the Crown Estate Act 1961 on the term for which a lease may be granted by the Crown Estate Commissioners shall not apply where the lease is granted by way of extension of a long tenancy at a low rent and it appears to the Crown Estate Commissioners that, if the tenancy were not a tenancy from the Crown, there would be a right to an extended lease under this Part of this Act.

(4)    Where, in the case of land belonging to Her Majesty in right of the Duchy of Lancaster or to the Duchy of Cornwall, it appears to the appropriate authority that a tenant under a long lease at a low rent would, if the tenancy were not a tenancy from the Crown, be entitled to an extended lease under this Part of this Act, then a lease corresponding to that to which the tenant would be so entitled may be granted to take effect wholly or partly out of the Crown interest by the same person and with the same formalities as in the case of any other lease of such land.

(5)    In the case of land belonging to the Duchy of Cornwall, the purposes authorised by section 8 of the Duchy of Cornwall Management Act 1863 for the advancement of parts of such gross sums as are therein mentioned shall include the payment to tenants of sums corresponding to those which, if the tenancies were not tenancies from the Crown, would be payable by way of compensation under section 17 above.

**[119]**

**NOTES**
Sub-s (2A): inserted by the Housing and Regeneration Act 2008, s 56, Sch 8, paras 5, 9, subject to transitional provisions and savings in SI 2008/3068, arts 6–10 at **[3834B]–[3834F]**.

**[33A   Exclusion of certain shared ownership leases**

The provision of Schedule 4A to this Act shall have effect to exclude certain shared ownership leases from the operation of this Part of this Act.]

**[120]**

**NOTES**
Inserted by the Housing and Planning Act 1986, s 18, Sch 4, paras 5, 11, in relation to leases granted after 11 December 1987.

*Transitional*

**34, 35**   (*Repealed by the Statute Law (Repeals) Act 1993.*)

**36   Relief in respect of mortgages etc on landlord's estate**

(1)   Where at the passing of this Act—
   (a)   a house is held on a long tenancy not having more than twenty years unexpired, or on a long tenancy capable of being determined within twenty years by notice given by the landlord; and
   (b)   the estate of the immediate or a superior landlord is charged to secure payment of any sum (otherwise than by way of rentcharge), whether or not the landlord is personally liable as principal or otherwise for the payment of that sum;

then on an application under subsection (2) or (3) below the court may make such order authorised by the subsection as the court thinks proper for the purpose of avoiding or mitigating any financial hardship that might otherwise be caused by the rights conferred on tenants by this Part of this Act.

(2)   In any of the following cases, that is to say,—
   (a)   where the landlord proposes during the tenancy (including any extension thereof under this Act) to sell or realise any property which is subject to the charge, or a tenant of the house has given notice under this Part of this Act of his desire to have the freehold;
   (b)   where during the tenancy (including any such extension) the person entitled to the benefit of the charge has taken any steps to enforce the charge or demanded payment of the sum thereby secured or, if the house or any other property subject to the charge is subject also to another charge created or arising before the commencement of this Part of this Act, a person entitled to the benefit of the other charge has taken any steps to enforce the other charge or demanded payment of the sum thereby secured;

the court may on application of the landlord make an order providing for all or any of the following:—
   (i)    for discharging or modifying any liability in respect of the sum secured by the charge, whether of the landlord or of persons liable jointly with him or as surety for him;
   (ii)   for discharging or modifying the terms of the charge whether as respects the house or any other property subject to the charge, or the terms of any collateral charge;
   (iii)  for restricting the exercise of any right or remedy in respect of any such liability or charge.

(3)   In any of the cases mentioned in subsection (2)(a) and (b) above the court may on the application of the person entitled to the benefit of the charge make an order providing for all or any of the following:—
   (a)   for discharging or modifying the terms of any prior charge, whether as respects the house or any other property subject to the charge;
   (b)   for restricting the exercise of any right or remedy in respect of any prior charge on the house or other property subject to the charge.

(4)   Any order under this section may be made either unconditionally or subject to such terms and conditions, including conditions with respect to the payment of money, as the court may think just and equitable to impose.

(5)   Where steps are taken in a court other than the county court to enforce a charge or recover any sum thereby secured, that other court shall have the like powers under this section in relation to that or any other charge as the county court would have in consequence of those steps being taken or, if an application under this section is pending in the county court, may on such terms as the other court thinks just suspend the proceedings for the enforcement of the charge or recovery of the said sum or direct that they be transferred to the county court.

**[121]**

*Construction*

**37   Interpretation of Part I**

(1)   For the purposes of this Part of this Act—
   (a)   "the appointed day" means the day appointed for the coming into force of the provisions

of this Part of this Act other than sections 34 to 36, and references to the commencement of this Part of this Act shall be construed as referring to the commencement of those provisions;

(b) "incumbrance" and "tenant's incumbrance" have, subject to section 12(8) above, the meanings assigned to them by section 8;

[(ba) "new towns residuary body" means—

    (i) in relation to England, the Homes and Communities Agency so far as exercising functions in relation to anything transferred (or to be transferred) to it as mentioned in section 52(1)(a) to (d) of the Housing and Regeneration Act 2008; and

    (ii) in relation to Wales, means the Welsh Ministers so far as exercising functions in relation to anything transferred (or to be transferred) to them as mentioned in section 36(1)(a)(i) to (iii) of the New Towns Act 1981 (and references to the "Welsh new towns residuary body" shall be construed accordingly);]

(c) "notice to quit" means a notice to terminate a tenancy (whether a periodical tenancy or a tenancy for a term of years certain) given in accordance with the provisions (whether express or implied) of that tenancy;

(d) "relevant time" means, in relation to a person's claim to acquire the freehold or an extended lease under this Part of this Act, the time when he gives notice in accordance with this Act of his desire to have it;

(e) ... ;

(f) "tenancy" means a tenancy at law or in equity, but does not include a tenancy at will, nor any interest created by way of security and liable to termination by the exercise of any right of redemption or otherwise, nor any interest created by way of trust under a settlement, and "demise" shall be construed accordingly;

(g) "term date", in relation to a tenancy granted for a term of years certain, means the date of expiry of that term, and "extended term date" and "original term date" mean respectively the term date of a tenancy with and without an extension under this Part of this Act.

(2) A tenancy to which section 19(2) of the Landlord and Tenant Act 1954 [or paragraph 16(2) of Schedule 10 to the Local Government and Housing Act 1989] applies shall be treated for purposes of this Part of this Act as granted to expire at the date which is the term date for purposes of [the said Act of 1954 or, as the case may be, the said Schedule 10] (that is to say, the first date after the commencement of [the said Act of 1954 or, as the case may be, the coming into force of the said Schedule 10] on which, apart from [the said Act of 1954 or, as the case may be, the said Schedule 10], the tenancy could have been brought to an end by notice to quit given by the landlord).

(3) Subject to subsection (2) above, where under section 3(2) of this Act a tenancy created or arising as a tenancy from year to year or other periodical tenancy is to be treated as a long tenancy, the term date of that tenancy shall be taken to be the date (if any) at which the tenancy is to terminate by virtue of a notice to quit given by the landlord before the relevant time, or else the earliest date at which it could at that time (in accordance with its terms and apart from any enactment) be brought to an end by a notice to quit given by the landlord.

(4) Subject to subsection (2) above, in the case of a tenancy granted to continue as a periodical tenancy after the expiration of a term of years certain, or to continue as a periodical tenancy if not terminated at the expiration of such a term, any question whether the tenancy is at any time to be treated for purposes of this Part of this Act[ ... ] as a long tenancy, and (if so) with what term date, shall be determined as it would be if there had been two tenancies, as follows—

(a) one granted to expire at the earliest time (at or after the expiry of the said term of years) at which the tenancy could (in accordance with its terms and apart from any enactment) be brought to an end by notice to quit given by the landlord; and

(b) the other granted to commence at the expiration of the first (and not being one to which subsection (2) above applies).

(5) ... No reference in this Part of this Act to a person occupying property as his residence shall be taken to extend to any occupation of a company or other artificial person nor, where the tenant is a corporation sole, shall the corporator, while in occupation, be treated as occupying as tenant.

(6) [Section 25(1), (2) and (4) of the Rent Act 1977] shall apply to the ascertainment for purposes of this Part of this Act of the rateable value of a house and premises or any other property as they apply to the ascertainment of that of a dwelling-house for purposes of that Act.

(7) For purposes of this Part of this Act an order of a court is to be treated as becoming final—

(a) *if not appealed against, on the expiration of the time for bringing an appeal*; or

(b) if appealed against and not set aside in consequence of the appeal, at the time when the appeal and any further appeal is disposed of by the determination of it and the expiration of the time for bringing a further appeal (if any) or by its being abandoned or otherwise ceasing to have effect.

**[122]**

**NOTES**

Sub-s (1): para (ba) inserted by the Housing and Regeneration Act 2008, s 56, Sch 8, paras 5, 10, subject to transitional provisions and savings in SI 2008/3068, arts 6–10 at **[3834B]**–**[3834F]**; para (e) repealed by the Rent Act 1968, s 117(5), Sch 17.

Sub-s (2): words in first pair of square brackets inserted and words in second, third and fourth pairs of square brackets substituted by the Local Government and Housing Act 1989, s 194(1), Sch 11, para 12.

Sub-s (4): words omitted from square brackets inserted by the Housing Act 1996, s 106, Sch 9, para 2(1), (7) and repealed by the Commonhold and Leasehold Reform Act 2002, s 180, Sch 14, except in relation to an application for enfranchisement or an extended lease of a house in respect of which notice was given under s 8 or 14 of this Act at **[90]**, **[97]**, or where an application was made under s 27 of this Act at **[110]**, before 26 July 2002 (in relation to England) or 1 January 2003 (in relation to Wales).

Sub-s (5): words omitted repealed by the Commonhold and Leasehold Reform Act 2002, s 180, Sch 14, subject to savings as noted above.

Sub-s (6): words in square brackets substituted by the Rent Act 1977, s 155, Sch 23, para 44.

## PART II
## AMENDMENTS OF OTHER ACTS

### 38 Modification of right to possession under Landlord and Tenant Act 1954

(1) The grounds on which under section 13 of the Landlord and Tenant Act 1954 a landlord may apply to the court for possession of property comprised in a tenancy (and which may accordingly under section 4 be specified in a landlord's notice to resume possession), in the case of applications made after the commencement of this Part of this Act, shall not include the ground mentioned in section 12(1)(a) (redevelopment), except where the landlord seeking to obtain possession is a body to which section 28 above applies and the property is required for relevant development within the meaning of section 28; but on any application by such a body under section 13 of that Act for possession on that ground a certificate given by a Minister of the Crown as provided by section 28(1) above shall be conclusive that the property is so required.

(2) In section 57 of the Landlord and Tenant Act 1954 (under which a tenant's rights under Part II of that Act are curtailed if an authority within the section is the landlord or a superior landlord and obtains a certificate similar to that under section 28 above) references to a local authority shall apply to any body to which section 28 above applies and which is not otherwise within the said section 57.

(3) For purposes of this section, section 28(5) to (8) above shall have effect from the commencement of this Part of this Act.

**[123]**

### 39 Application of Rent Acts to long tenancies and adaptation of Landlord and Tenant Act 1954

(1) Section 21(2) of the Rent Act 1957 (which applies Part I of the Landlord and Tenant Act 1954 to long tenancies not at a low rent) shall cease to have effect; and—

(a)–(c) …

(2) Subsection (1) above shall have effect subject to the adaptations of Part I of the Landlord and Tenant Act 1954, and of the [Rent Act 1968] as it applies to a statutory tenancy arising by virtue of the said Part I, which are made by Schedule 5 to this Act; and the transitional and supplementary provisions made by that Schedule shall have effect in relation to subsection (1) above and to statutory tenancies so arising.

(3) …

**[124]**

**NOTES**

Sub-s (1): words omitted repealed by the Rent Act 1968, s 117(5), Sch 17 and the Counter-Inflation Act 1973, s 23(3), Sch 6.

Sub-s (2): words in square brackets substituted by the Rent Act 1968, s 117(2), Sch 15.

Sub-s (3): repealed by the Statute Law (Repeals) Act 1976.

Rent Act 1968: repealed and replaced by the Rent Act 1977.

### 40 Amendments of Places of Worship (Enfranchisement) Act 1920

(1)–(6) …

(7) In accordance with the provisions of this section the Places of Worship (Enfranchisement) Act 1920 shall, subject to subsection (8) below, have effect as set out in Schedule 6 to this Act.

(8) This section and the repeals made by Part II of Schedule 7 to this Act shall not affect the operation of the Places of Worship (Enfranchisement) Act 1920 where an interest has been acquired, or notice to treat for its acquisition has been served, under that Act before this section comes into force, except that section 4 of that Act shall cease to have effect for any purpose.

**[125]**

**NOTES**
Sub-ss (1)–(6): amend the Places of Worship (Enfranchisement) Act 1920, ss 1, 2, 5 and repeal s 4 of, and the Schedule to, that Act.

## 41 Short title, repeals, extent and commencement

(1) This Act may be cited as the Leasehold Reform Act 1967.

(2) The enactments mentioned in Schedule 7 to this Act are hereby repealed to the extent specified in the third column of that Schedule, but subject to the savings mentioned at the end of Parts I and II of the Schedule.

(3) This Act shall not extend to Scotland or Northern Ireland.

(4) Sections 34 to 36 of this Act shall come into force on the day it is passed; and, … the other provisions of Part I shall come into force on such day as the Minister of Housing and Local Government and the Secretary of State may appoint by order made by them jointly by statutory instrument, which shall be laid before Parliament after being made.

(5) Part II of this Act shall come into force at the end of one month following the day on which this Act is passed.

**[126]**

**NOTES**
Sub-s (4): words omitted repealed by the Statute Law (Repeals) Act 1993.
Orders: the Leasehold Reform Act 1967 Commencement Order 1967, SI 1967/1836.

## SCHEDULES

## SCHEDULE 1
### ENFRANCHISEMENT AND EXTENSION BY SUB-TENANTS
Section 5

*General*

1.—(1) Where a person (in this Schedule referred to as "the claimant") gives notice of his desire to have the freehold or an extended lease of a house and premises under Part I of this Act, and does so in respect of a sub-tenancy (in this Schedule referred to as "the tenancy in possession"), then except as otherwise provided by this Schedule—

    (a) the rights and obligations of the landlord under Part I of this Act shall, so far as their interests are affected, be rights and obligations respectively of the estate owner in respect of the fee simple and of each of the persons in whom is vested a concurrent tenancy superior to the tenancy in possession (and references to the landlord shall apply accordingly); and

    (b) the proceedings arising out of the notice, whether for resisting or giving effect to the claim to acquire the freehold or extended lease, shall be conducted, on behalf of all the persons referred to in (a) above, by and through that one of them who is identified by this Schedule as "the reversioner".

(2) Where there is a tenancy reversionary on a tenancy in respect of which a person gives notice as aforesaid, then (except in so far as special provision is made for such a reversionary tenancy) this Schedule shall apply as if the reversionary tenancy were a concurrent tenancy intermediate between the tenancy in possession and any interest superior to it.

(3) In the following provisions of this Schedule the persons for whom the reversioner is by this paragraph authorised to act are referred to as "other landlords"; and in this Schedule references to superior interests mean the estate in fee simple and any tenancy superior (or treated by sub-paragraph (2) above as superior) to the inferior interest in question.

2. Subject to paragraph 3 below, "the reversioner" shall be—

    (a) if any person has a tenancy of the house carrying an expectation of possession of thirty years or more, that person or, if there is more than one, that one of them to whose tenancy the other tenancies are superior;

    (b) if there is no such tenancy, the estate owner in respect of the fee simple of the house.

3.—(1) If it appears to the court, on an application made by any of the persons having an interest superior to the tenancy in possession,—

    (a) that the respective interests of those persons, the absence or incapacity of the person designated by paragraph 2 above or other special circumstances require that one of the other landlords should act as the reversioner instead of that person; or

(b)    that the person so designated is unwilling to act as the reversioner, and that one of the other landlords could appropriately replace him and is willing to do so; or

(c)    that by reason of complications in the title paragraph 2 above is inapplicable;

the court may, on such terms and conditions as it thinks fit, appoint such person as it thinks fit to be the reversioner.

(2)    The court may also, on the application of any of the other landlords or of the claimant, remove the reversioner and appoint another person in his place, if it appears to the court proper to do so by reason of any delay or default, actual or apprehended, on the part of the reversioner.

4.—(1)    Without prejudice to the generality of paragraph 1 above, the reversioner may on behalf and in the name of the other landlords—

(a)    execute any conveyance to give effect to section 8 of this Act, or any lease to give effect to section 14; and

(b)    take or defend any legal proceedings under Part I of this Act in respect of matters arising out of the claimant's notice.

(2)    Subject to paragraphs 5 and 6 below, in relation to all matters within the authority given to him by this Schedule the reversioner's acts shall be binding on the other landlords and on their interests in the house and premises or any other property; but in the event of dispute either the reversioner or any of the other landlords may apply to the court for directions as to the manner in which he should act on the matter in dispute.

(3)    If any of the other landlords cannot be found, or his identity cannot be ascertained, the reversioner shall apply to the court for directions, and the court may make such order in the matter as it thinks proper with a view to giving effect to the rights of the claimant and protecting the interests of other persons; but subject to the directions of the court—

(a)    the reversioner shall proceed as in other cases;

(b)    a conveyance or lease executed by the reversioner on behalf of that landlord by such description as will identify the interest intended to be conveyed or bound shall be of the same effect as if executed in his name;

(c)    if the freehold is to be conveyed to the claimant, any sum paid as the price for that landlord's interest shall be paid into court.

(4)    The reversioner, if he acts in good faith and with reasonable care and diligence, shall not be liable to any of the other landlords for any loss or damage caused by any act or omission in the exercise or intended exercise of the authority given to him by this Schedule.

5.—(1)    Notwithstanding anything in paragraph 4(2) above, any of the other landlords shall be entitled, if he so desires, to be separately represented in any legal proceedings in which his title to any property comes in question, or in any legal proceedings relating to the price payable for the house and premises under section 9 of this Act.

(2)    For the purpose of deducing, evidencing or verifying his title to any property, any of the other landlords, on giving written notice to the reversioner and to the claimant, may deal directly with the claimant, if he objects to disclosing his title to the reversioner; and he shall deal directly with the claimant if the claimant by written notice given to him and to the reversioner so requires.

(3)    For the purpose of agreeing the price payable for his interest under section 9 of this Act, any of the other landlords, on giving written notice to the reversioner and to the claimant, may deal directly with the claimant; and whether he does that or not, he may require the reversioner to apply to [a leasehold valuation tribunal] for the price to be determined by [a leasehold valuation tribunal].

(4)    Any of the other landlords shall be entitled to require that the price payable for his interest (or so much of it as is payable to him) shall be paid by the claimant to him or to a person authorised by him to receive it, instead of to the reversioner; but if, after being given proper notice of the time and place fixed for completion with the claimant, neither he nor a person so authorised attends to receive payment, and he has not made, and notified the reversioner of, other arrangements with the claimant to receive payment, the reversioner shall be authorised to receive it for him and the reversioner's written receipt for the amount payable shall be a complete discharge to the claimant.

(5)    It shall be the duty of each of the other landlords—

(a)    subject to sub-paragraphs (2) and (3) above, to give the reversioner all such information and assistance as he may reasonably require; and

(b)    after being given proper notice of the time and place fixed for completion with the claimant (if the claimant is acquiring the freehold), to ensure that all deeds and other documents that ought on his part to be delivered to the claimant on completion are available for the purpose, including in the case of registered land the land certificate and any other documents necessary to perfect the claimant's title;

and, if any of the other landlords fails to do so, he shall indemnify the reversioner against any liability incurred by the reversioner in consequence of the failure.

(6)    Each of the other landlords shall make such contribution as may be just to the costs and expenses incurred by the reversioner and not recoverable or not recovered from the claimant.

6.—(1)    The authority given by this Schedule to the reversioner shall not extend to the bringing of proceedings under section 17 or 18 or this Act on behalf of any of the other landlords, or preclude any of the other landlords from bringing proceedings under that section on his own behalf; and (without prejudice to the operation of paragraph 1(2) above) a person entitled to a tenancy reversionary on the tenancy in possession may make an application under section 17 (by virtue of subsection (4)) or section 18 as a landlord.

(2)    Sections 29 and 30 of this Act shall apply, and apply only, where the authority entitled to require the covenant under the section is the estate owner in respect of the fee simple and there is no tenancy carrying an expectation of possession of thirty years or more.

(3)    For purposes of section 3(6) of this Act separate tenancies shall be deemed to be tenancies with the same landlord if the immediate landlord is the same.

*Enfranchisement*

7.—(1)    Where a conveyance is executed to give effect to section 8 of this Act—
   (a)    section 10 shall have effect in relation to rights and restrictions arising by virtue of any tenancy superior to the tenancy in possession (or by virtue of an agreement collateral to such a tenancy), so far as they are directly or indirectly to the benefit of or enforceable against the claimant during the tenancy in possession, as if they arose by virtue of that tenancy[, and the reference in subsection (1A) of that section to the covenants for title implied under Part I of the Law of Property (Miscellaneous Provisions) Act 1994 shall be read as excluding the covenant in section 4(1)(b) of that Act (compliance with terms of lease)]; and
   (b)    [subject to paragraph 7A] a separate price shall be payable in accordance with section 9 for each of the interests superior to the tenancy in possession, and ... section 9 shall apply to the computation of that price with such modifications as are appropriate to relate it to a sale of the interest in question subject to any tenancies intermediate between that interest and the tenancy in possession, together with tenant's incumbrances relative to those tenancies; and
   (c)    so much of section 11 as relates to the application of the purchase price for redemption of rentcharges ... shall apply only to the price payable for the estate in fee simple; and
   (d)    so much of sections 12 and 13 as relates to the application of the price payable in or towards redemption of charges shall apply separately to the price payable for each interest together with the relative charges.

(2)    Where by reason of section 11(2) of this Act it is necessary to make (otherwise than out of the price payable for the house and premises) any payment for the redemption of a rentcharge ... , the reversioner, if he is not the landlord liable or primarily liable in respect of the rentcharge ... , shall not be required to make that payment otherwise than out of money made available for the purpose by that landlord, and it shall be the duty of that landlord to provide for the redemption; and similarly where by reason of section 12(8) proviso of this Act it is necessary to discharge the house and premises from a charge affecting the interest of any landlord.

[7A.—(1)    The price payable for a minor superior tenancy shall be calculated (except where it has been determined by agreement or otherwise before this paragraph comes into force) by applying the formula set out in sub-paragraph (5) instead of in accordance with section 9.

(2)    "A minor superior tenancy" means a superior tenancy having an expectation of possession of not more than one month and in respect of which the profit rent is not more than £5 per year.

(3)    "Profit rent" means an amount equal to that of the rent payable under the tenancy on which the minor superior tenancy is in immediate reversion, less that of the rent payable under the minor superior tenancy.

(4)    Where the minor superior tenancy or that on which it is in immediate reversion comprises property other than the house and premises, the reference in sub-paragraph (3) to the rent payable under it means so much of that rent as is apportioned to the house and premises.

(5)    The formula is—

$$P = \pounds\frac{R}{Y} - \frac{R}{Y(1+Y)^n}$$

where—
   P = the price payable;
   R = the profit rent;
   Y = the yield (expressed as a decimal fraction) from 2½ per cent Consolidated Stock;
   n = the period, expressed in years (taking any part of a year as a whole year) which the minor superior tenancy would have to run if it were not extinguished by enfranchisement.

(6). In calculating the yield from 2½ per cent Consolidated Stock, the price of that stock shall be taken to be the middle market price at the close of business on the last trading day in the week before the tenant gives notice in accordance with this Act of his desire to have the freehold.]

8. ...

9. Nothing in this Schedule shall be taken to entitle the claimant to give notice under section 9(3) of this Act of his inability or unwillingness to acquire particular interests superior to the tenancy in possession, but any such notice shall extend to all those interests.

*Extension*

10.—(1) Where a lease is executed to give effect to section 14 of this Act, then except as provided by paragraph 11 below the new tenancy shall be granted by the landlord having an interest sufficient in point of duration which is not superior to another such interest.

(2) Subject to paragraph 11 below, the lease shall have effect for the creation of the new tenancy, and for the operation of the rights and obligations conferred and imposed by it, as if there had been a surrender and re-grant of any subsisting tenancy intermediate between the interest of the landlord granting the new tenancy and the tenancy in possession, and the covenants and other provisions of the lease shall be framed and take effect accordingly.

(3) If there is no one landlord having such an interest in the whole of the house and premises as is referred to in sub-paragraph (1) above, then those having the appropriate interests in separate parts thereof shall instead grant the tenancy; and where it is necessary in accordance with this sub-paragraph for more than one landlord to join in granting the new tenancy, the lease shall have effect in accordance with sub-paragraph (2) above, but as if they had been jointly entitled to their interests and had become separately entitled by assignments taking effect immediately after the lease.

(4) The lease shall give effect to section 15(2) of this Act on the basis that the references there to the landlord include the landlord granting the new tenancy, the immediate landlord of whom the new tenancy will be held and any intermediate landlord, and shall give effect to section 15(3) on the basis that account is to be taken of obligations imposed on any of those landlords by virtue of the new tenancy or any superior tenancy; and section 16(4) of this Act shall apply on the basis that the reference there to the tenant's landlord includes the immediate landlord of whom the new tenancy will be held and all superior landlords, including any superior to the landlord granting the new tenancy.

11.—(1) Where a tenancy in the house and premises superior to the tenancy in possession is vested in the claimant or a trustee for him, the lease under section 14 of this Act shall include an actual surrender of that superior tenancy without a re-grant, and it shall accordingly be disregarded for purposes of paragraph 10 above.

(2) Where, apart from this provision, the effect of the lease under section 14 of this Act would be, as regards any tenancy superior to the new tenancy,—

(a) that the rent payable under that superior tenancy would be equal to or more than the rent payable under the tenancy on which it would be in immediate reversion (regard being had to the operation of this sub-paragraph in relation to any other tenancy); or

(b) that the difference between those rents would not be more than four pounds a year;

then the person entitled to that superior tenancy may by written notice given to his immediate landlord and, if neither of them is the reversioner, to the reversioner require that the lease shall include an actual surrender by him of his tenancy without a re-grant.

(3) Any person entitled to a tenancy superior to the new tenancy may by the like notice require that the lease shall confer on him the right to surrender his tenancy if by reason of any revision of the rent payable under the claimant's new tenancy (together with any consequent surrender under this provision of tenancies intermediate between the superior tenancy and that new tenancy) the rent payable under the superior tenancy will not thereafter be less by more than four pounds a year than the rent payable under the tenancy on which it will be in immediate reversion.

(4) Where a landlord required apart from this sub-paragraph (or by virtue of this sub-paragraph as it operates in relation to another landlord) to grant the new tenancy would do so by virtue of a tenancy in respect of which he claims, by the like notice, to have the benefit of sub-paragraph (2) or (3) above, he shall for purposes of paragraph 10 above be replaced, subject to any further operation of this sub-paragraph, by the next superior landlord.

(5) References in this paragraph to the rent payable under a tenancy mean, in relation to a tenancy comprising property other than the house and premises, so much of that rent as is apportionable to the house and premises, and any surrender or provision for the surrender of such a tenancy in accordance with this paragraph shall be limited to the house and premises.

12.—(1) No provision of any tenancy prohibiting, restricting or otherwise relating to a sub-demise by the tenant shall have effect with reference to any lease executed to give effect to section 14 of this Act.

(2)   Where by reason of section 14(4) proviso of this Act it is necessary to make any payment to discharge the house and premises from a charge affecting the interest of any landlord, the reversioner, if he is not the landlord liable or primarily liable in respect of the charge, shall not be required to make that payment otherwise than out of money made available for the purpose by that landlord, and it shall be the duty of that landlord to provide for the charge being discharged.

*Supplementary*

13.—(1)   For purposes of this Schedule the expectation of possession carried by a tenancy is the expectation which it carries at the relevant time of possession after the tenancy in possession, on the basis that—

(a)   subject to sub-paragraph (2) below, the tenancy in possession terminates at the relevant time if its term date fell before then, or else terminates at its term date or (in the case of a tenancy which has been extended) its original term date; and

(b)   a tenancy other than the tenancy in possession terminates at its term date.

(2)   In a case where before the relevant time the claimant's immediate landlord had given notice to quit terminating the tenancy in possession at a date earlier than the term date, the date specified in the notice to quit shall be substituted for the date in sub-paragraph (1)(a) above.

14.—(1)   This Schedule shall apply notwithstanding that the tenancy in possession is a tenancy from the Crown within the meaning of section 33 of this Act; and, where under section 33(1)(b) the appropriate authority gives notice that as regards a Crown interest the authority will grant or concur in granting the freehold or an extended lease, then in relation to the Crown interest and the person to whom it belongs this Schedule shall have effect as it has effect in relation to other landlords and their interests, but with the appropriate authority having power to act as reversioner or otherwise for purposes of this Schedule on behalf of that person:

Provided that paragraph 4(1)(a) above shall not apply to the execution of a conveyance or lease on behalf of the person to whom a Crown interest belongs.

(2)   A conveyance or lease executed in pursuance of paragraph 4(3) above shall be effective notwithstanding that the interest intended to be conveyed or bound is a Crown interest or a tenancy from the Crown.

[127]

**NOTES**

Para 5: words in square brackets in sub-para (3) substituted by the Housing Act 1980, s 142, Sch 22, Pt II, para 10.

Para 7: words in square brackets in sub-para (1)(a) inserted by the Law of Property (Miscellaneous Provisions) Act 1994, s 21(1), (4), Sch 1, para 5(3), except in relation to a disposition of property to which the Law of Property Act 1925, s 76 or the Land Registration Act 1925, s 24(1)(a) continue to apply; in sub-para (1)(b), words in square brackets inserted and words omitted repealed by the Housing Act 1980, ss 141, 152, Sch 21, para 6, Sch 26; words omitted from sub-paras (1)(c), (2) repealed by the Rentcharges Act 1977, s 17(2), (6), Sch 2.

Para 7A: inserted by the Housing Act 1980, s 141, Sch 21, para 6.

Para 8: repealed by the Rentcharges Act 1977, s 17(2), (6), Sch 2.

## SCHEDULE 2
### PROVISIONS SUPPLEMENTARY TO SECTIONS 17 AND 18 OF THIS ACT
Sections 17, 18, 20, 21, 23 and 25

1.—(1)   This Schedule has effect where a tenant of a house and premises is entitled to be paid compensation under section 17 or 18 of this Act, or would be so entitled on the landlord obtaining an order for possession, or where an application for such an order is dismissed or withdrawn; and for purposes of this Schedule—

(a)   "application for possession" means a landlord's application under section 17(1) or 18(1); and

(b)   "order for possession" means an order under section 17(2) or 18(4).

(2)   Where the tenancy has not been extended under section 14 of this Act, references in this Schedule to the original term date shall be construed as references to the term date or, in a case where before the relevant time the landlord had given notice to quit terminating the tenancy at a date earlier than the term date, as references to the date specified in the notice to quit.

2.—(1)   Where an order for possession is made, the tenancy shall determine, and the compensation payable to the tenant by virtue of the order shall become payable, on such date as may, when the *amount of that compensation is known*, be fixed by order of the court made on the application either of the landlord or of the tenant.

(2)   An order of the court under this paragraph shall not fix a date earlier than the original term date of the tenancy, nor shall it fix a date less than four months or more than twelve months after the date of the order unless the court sees special reason for doing so; and in a case under section 18 of

this Act an application to [a leasehold valuation tribunal] to determine the amount of the compensation payable to the tenant shall not be made more than twelve months before the original term date.

(3)  In fixing the date the court shall have regard to the conduct of the parties and, in a case under section 17 of this Act, to the extent to which the landlord has made reasonable preparations for proceeding with the redevelopment (including the obtaining of or preparations relating to the obtaining of any requisite permission or consent, whether from any authority whose permission or consent is required under any enactment or from the owner of an interest in any property).

(4)  The court may by order direct that the whole or part of the compensation payable to the tenant shall be paid into court, if the court thinks it expedient so to do for the purpose of ensuring that the sum paid is available for meeting charges on the tenant's interest in the house and premises, or for the purpose of division, or for any other purpose.

3.—(1)  On the termination of a tenancy under an order for possession there shall terminate also any immediate or derivative sub-tenancy, and the tenant shall be bound to give up possession of the house and premises to the landlord except in so far as he is precluded from doing so by the rights of other persons to retain possession under or by virtue of any enactment.

(2)  Where a sub-tenancy of property comprised in the tenancy has been created after the date of the application for possession (or any earlier date when, in the case of an application relying on section 28(1) of this Act, a copy of the Minister's certificate was served on the tenant), then no person shall in respect of that sub-tenancy be entitled under [[subsection (2) of section 137 of the Rent Act 1977] or any enactment (including [subsection (5)] of that section)] applying or extending it, [or under subsection (2) of section 9 of the Rent (Agriculture) Act 1976 as extended by subsection (5) of that section] to retain possession of that property after the termination of the tenancy under the order for possession.

(3)  In exercising its jurisdiction under section 17 or 18 of this Act or this Schedule the court shall assume that the landlord, having obtained an order for possession, will not be precluded from obtaining possession by the right of any person to retain possession by virtue of [[Part VII of the Rent Act 1977] or any enactment applying or extending that Part of that Act] [or of the Rent (Agriculture) Act 1976] or otherwise.

(4)  A person in occupation of the house and premises or part of them under a sub-tenancy liable to terminate under sub-paragraph (1) above may, with the leave of the court, appear and be heard on any application for possession or application under paragraph 2 above.

4.  Where an order has been made under paragraph 2 above, the court making the order or another county court shall have jurisdiction to hear and determine any proceedings brought by virtue of the order to recover possession of the property or to recover the compensation, notwithstanding that by reason of the value of the property or the amount of the compensation the proceedings are not within the jurisdiction conferred on county courts apart from this provision.

5.—(1)  The amount payable to a tenant, by virtue of an order for possession, by way of compensation for the loss of the house and premises shall be the amount which, if sections 17 and 18 of this Act had not been passed, the house and premises, if sold in the open market by a willing seller, might at the date when the order for possession becomes final be expected to realise, on the assumption that the vendor was selling the tenancy, and was selling—

(a)  subject to the rights of any person who will on the termination of the tenancy be entitled to retain possession as against the landlord, but otherwise with vacant possession; and

(b)  subject to any subsisting incumbrances which will not terminate with the tenancy and for which during the continuance of the tenancy the tenant is liable without having a right to be indemnified by the landlord, but otherwise free of incumbrances; and

(c)  subject to any restriction which would be required (in addition to any imposed by the terms of the tenancy) to limit the uses of the house and premises to those to which they have been put since the commencement of the tenancy and to preclude the erection of any new dwelling-house or any other building not ancillary to the house as a dwelling-house;

but there shall be left out of account any value attaching to the right to acquire the freehold under Part I of this Act.

(2)  The compensation payable in respect of a tenancy which has not been extended under section 14 of this Act shall be computed as if the tenancy was to be so extended.

6.—(1)  Part I of the Landlord and Tenant Act 1927 (compensation for improvements on termination of business tenancies) shall not apply on the termination of the tenancy or any sub-tenancy in accordance with this Schedule; and a request for a new tenancy under section 26 of the Landlord and Tenant Act 1954 in respect of the tenancy or any sub-tenancy shall be of no effect if made after the application for possession, or shall cease to have effect on the making of that application.

(2)  Where a sub-tenancy terminating with the tenancy in accordance with paragraph 3 above is one to which Part II of the Landlord and Tenant Act 1954 applies, the compensation payable to the

tenant shall be divided between him and the sub-tenant in such proportions as may be just, regard being had to their respective interests in the house and premises and to any loss arising from the termination of those interests and not incurred by imprudence.

(3)   Where the amount of the compensation payable to the tenant is agreed between him and the landlord without the consent of a sub-tenant entitled under sub-paragraph (2) above to a share in the compensation, and is shown by the sub-tenant to be less than might reasonably have been obtained by the tenant, the sub-tenant shall be entitled under sub-paragraph (2) above to recover from the tenant such increased share as may be just.

7.—(1)   The landlord shall not be concerned with the application of the amount payable to the tenant by way of compensation under an order for possession, but (subject to any statutory requirements as to payment of capital money arising under a settlement or [trust of land] and to any order under paragraph 2(4) above for payment into court) the written receipt of the tenant shall be a complete discharge for the amount payable.

(2)   The landlord shall be entitled to deduct from the amount so payable to the tenant—

(a)   the amount of any sum payable by way of rent or recoverable as rent in respect of the house and premises up to the termination of the tenancy; and

(b)   the amount of any other sums due and payable by the tenant to the landlord under or in respect of the tenancy or any agreement collateral thereto.

(3)   Where the tenancy is [subject to a trust of land], and compensation is paid in respect of it in accordance with section 17 or 18 of this Act (whether possession is obtained under that section or without any application for possession), the sum received shall be dealt with as if it were proceeds of sale arising under the trust.

8.—(1)   Where a landlord makes an application for possession, and it is made to appear to the court that in relation to matters arising out of that application (including the giving up of possession of the house and premises or the payment of compensation) the landlord or the tenant has been guilty of any unreasonable delay or default, the court may—

(a)   by order revoke or vary, and direct repayment of sums paid under, any provision made by a previous order as to payment of the costs of proceedings taken in the court on or with reference to the application, or, where costs have not been awarded, award costs;

(b)   certify particulars of the delay or default to the [Upper Tribunal] with a view to enabling the Tribunal to exercise a like discretion in relation to costs of proceedings before the Tribunal.

[(1A)   Where the court certifies particulars of delay or default to the [Upper Tribunal] under sub-paragraph (1)(b) above, the [Upper Tribunal] may make any order as to costs of proceedings before the [Upper Tribunal] which the court may make in relation to proceedings in the court.]

(2)   ...

(3)   Where an application for possession is dismissed or withdrawn, and it is made to appear to the court—

(a)   that the application was not made in good faith; or

(b)   that the landlord had attempted in any material respect to support by misrepresentation or the concealment of material facts a request to the tenant to deliver up possession without an application for possession;

the court may order that no further application for possession of the house and premises made by the landlord shall be entertained if it is made within the five years beginning with the date of the order.

9.—(1)   The purposes authorised for the application of capital money by section 73 of the Settled Land Act 1925 ... , and the purposes authorised by section 71 of the Settled Land Act 1925 ... as purposes for which moneys may be raised by mortgage, shall include the payment of compensation in accordance with section 17 or 18 of this Act (whether possession is obtained under that section or without any application for possession).

(2)   The purposes authorised for the application of capital money by section 26 of the Universities and College Estates Act 1925, and the purposes authorised by section 31 of that Act as purposes for which moneys may be raised by mortgage, shall include the payment of compensation in accordance with section 17 of this Act (whether possession is obtained under that section or without any application for possession).

[128]

**NOTES**

Para 2: words in square brackets in sub-para (2) substituted by the Housing Act 1980, s 142, Sch 22, Pt II, para 11.

Para 3: words in first (outer) pair of square brackets substituted by the Rent Act 1968, s 117(2), Sch 15; words in second (inner) pair of square brackets substituted by the Rent Act 1977, s 155, Sch 23, para 45; words in third (inner) pair of square brackets substituted and words in fourth pair of square brackets inserted by the Rent (Agriculture) Act 1976, s 40, Sch 8, para 18(a); words in the fifth (outer) pair of square brackets substituted by the Rent Act 1968, s 117(2), Sch 15; words in sixth (inner) pair of square brackets substituted by the Rent Act 1977, s 155(2), Sch 23, para 45; words in final pair of square brackets inserted by the Rent (Agriculture) Act 1976, s 40, Sch 8, para 18(b).

PART I
STATUTES

Para 7: words in square brackets substituted by the Trusts of Land and Appointment of Trustees Act 1996, s 25(1), Sch 3, para 10(c), subject to savings in s 25(4), (5) thereof.

Para 8: words in square brackets in paras (1), (1A) substituted by the Transfer of Tribunal Functions (Lands Tribunal and Miscellaneous Amendments) Order 2009, SI 2009/1307, art 5(1), (2), Sch 1, paras 82, 86, subject to transitional provisions and savings in Sch 5 thereto; sub-para (1A) inserted by the Commonhold and Leasehold Reform Act 2002, s 176, Sch 13, paras 1, 6, except in relation to any application made to an LVT or any proceedings transferred to an LVT by a county court before 30 September 2003 (in relation to England) or 31 March 2004 (in relation to Wales); sub-para (2) repealed by the Housing Act 1980, ss 142, 152, Sch 22, Pt II, para 12, Sch 26.

Para 9: words omitted repealed by the Trusts of Land and Appointment of Trustees Act 1996, s 25(2), Sch 4, subject to savings in s 25(4), (5) thereof.

## SCHEDULE 3
### VALIDITY OF TENANTS' NOTICES, EFFECT ON LANDLORD AND TENANT ACT 1954 ETC AND PROCEDURE GENERALLY
Sections 22 and 34

### PART I
#### RESTRICTIONS ON CLAIMS BY TENANT, AND EFFECT OF CLAIMS ON OTHER NOTICES, FORFEITURES, ETC

1.—(1)    A claim to acquire the freehold or an extended lease of any property shall be of no effect if made after the tenant has given notice terminating the tenancy of that property (not being a notice that has been superseded by the grant, express or implied, of a new tenancy), or if made during the subsistence of an agreement for a future tenancy to which section 28 of the Landlord and Tenant Act 1954 [or paragraph 17 of Schedule 10 to the Local Government and Housing Act 1989] applies.

(2)    A tenant's notice terminating the tenancy of any property, shall be of no effect if given during the currency of a claim made in respect of the tenancy to acquire the freehold or an extended lease of that property.

(3)    In sub-paragraphs (1) and (2) above references to a notice terminating a tenancy include a tenant's request for a new tenancy under section 26 of the Landlord and Tenant Act 1954, and a tenant's notice under section 27(1) of that Act that he does not desire the tenancy to be continued.

2.—[(1)    Sub-paragraphs (1A) to (1E) below apply where a landlord's notice terminating the tenancy of any property has been given under section 4 or 25 of the Landlord and Tenant Act 1954 or served under paragraph 4(1) of Schedule 10 to the Local Government and Housing Act 1989 (whether or not that notice has effect to terminate the tenancy).

(1A)    A claim to acquire the freehold or an extended lease of the property shall be of no effect if made after the relevant time, but this sub-paragraph is subject to sub-paragraphs (1D) and (1E) below.

(1B)    In this paragraph (but subject to sub-paragraph (1C) below) "the relevant time" is the end of the period of two months beginning with the date on which the landlord's notice terminating the tenancy has been given or served.

(1C)    Where—
  (a)    a landlord's notice terminating the tenancy has been given under section 25 of the Landlord and Tenant Act 1954, and
  (b)    the tenant applies to the court under section 24(1) of that Act for an order for the grant of a new tenancy before the end of the period of two months mentioned in sub-paragraph (1B) above,
"the relevant time" is the time when the application is made.

(1D)    Sub-paragraph (1A) above shall not apply where the landlord gives his written consent to the claim being made after the relevant time.

(1E)    Where a tenant, having given notice of a desire to have the freehold, gives after the relevant time a further notice under section 9(3) of this Act of his inability or unwillingness to acquire the house and premises at the price he must pay, he may with the notice under section 9(3) give a notice of his desire to have an extended lease (if he then has a right to such a lease).]

(2)    A landlord's notice terminating a tenancy of any property under section 4 or 25 of the Landlord and Tenant Act 1954 [or under paragraph 4(1) of Schedule 10 to the Local Government and Housing Act 1989] shall be of no effect if given [or served] during the currency of a claim made in respect of the tenancy to acquire the freehold or an extended lease of that property, and shall cease to have effect on the making of such a claim.

(3)    Where any such landlord's notice ceases (by virtue of sub-paragraph (2) above ... ) to have effect on the making of a claim, but the claim is not effective, then if within one month after the period of currency of that claim (or any subsequent claim made by virtue of the proviso to sub-paragraph (1) above) a landlord's notice terminating the tenancy is given under section 4 or 25

of the Landlord and Tenant Act 1954 [or served under paragraph 4(1) of Schedule 10 to the Local Government and Housing Act 1989], the earliest date which may be specified therein as the date of termination shall be—

  [(i) in the case of a notice given under the said Act of 1954] the date of termination specified in the previous notice or the expiration of three months from the giving of the new notice, whichever is the later

  [(ii) in the case of a notice served under the said Schedule 10, the date of termination specified in the previous notice or the expiration of the period of four months beginning on the date of service of the new notice, whichever is the later].

(4) Where by virtue of sub-paragraph (3) above a landlord's notice specifies as the date of termination of a tenancy a date earlier than six months after the giving of the notice, then—

  (a) if it is a notice proposing a statutory tenancy, section 7(2) of the Landlord and Tenant Act 1954 shall apply in relation to the notice with the substitution, for references to the period of two months ending with the date of termination specified in the notice and the beginning of that period, of references to the period of three months beginning with the giving of the notice and the end of that period; …

  (b) …

[2A.—(1) If—

  (a) the landlord commences proceedings under Part 2 of the Landlord and Tenant Act 1954; and

  (b) the tenant subsequently makes a claim to acquire the freehold or an extended lease of the property; and

  (c) paragraph 2 above does not render the claim of no effect,

no further steps shall be taken in the proceedings under Part 2 otherwise than for their dismissal and for the making of any consequential order.

(2) Section 64 of the Landlord and Tenant Act 1954 shall have no effect in a case to which sub-paragraph (1) above applies.]

3.—(1) Where a tenant makes a claim to acquire the freehold or an extended lease of any property, then during the currency of the claim and for three months thereafter the tenancy in that property shall not terminate either by effluxion of time or in pursuance of a notice to quit given by the landlord or by the termination of a superior tenancy; but if the claim is not effective, and but for this sub-paragraph the tenancy would have so terminated before the end of those three months, the tenancy shall so terminate at the end of the three months.

(2) Sub-paragraph (1) above shall not be taken to prevent an earlier termination of the tenancy in any manner not there mentioned, nor affect the power under section 146(4) of the Law of Property Act 1925 to grant a tenant relief against the termination of a superior tenancy, or any right of the tenant to relief under section 16(2) of the Landlord and Tenant Act 1954 or under paragraph 9 of Schedule 5 to that Act.

[(3) The reference in sub-paragraph (2) above to section 16(2) of, and paragraph 9 of Schedule 5 to, the Landlord and Tenant Act 1954 includes a reference to those provisions as they apply in relation to Schedule 10 to the Local Government and Housing Act 1989.]

4.—(1) Where a tenant makes a claim to acquire the freehold or an extended lease of any property, then during the currency of the claim no proceedings to enforce any right of re-entry or forfeiture terminating the tenancy shall be brought in any court without the leave of that court, and leave shall not be granted unless the court is satisfied that the claim was not made in good faith; but where leave is granted, the claim shall cease to have effect.

(2) Where a claim is made to acquire the freehold or an extended lease of property comprised in a tenancy, the tenancy shall be deemed for purposes of the claim to be a subsisting tenancy notwithstanding that the claim is made when proceedings are pending to enforce a right of re-entry or forfeiture terminating the tenancy and notwithstanding any order made afterwards in those proceedings, and if the claim is effective, the court in which the proceedings were brought may set aside or vary any such order to such extent and on such terms as appear to that court to be appropriate:

Provided that if it appears to that court that the claim is not made in good faith, or there has been unreasonable delay in making it, and that apart from the claim effect should be given to the right of re-entry or forfeiture, the court shall order that the tenancy shall not be treated as subsisting nor the claim as valid by virtue of this sub-paragraph.

(3) Where a court other than the county court—

  (a) grants leave under sub-paragraph (1) above; or

  (b) *makes an order under the proviso to* sub-paragraph (2) above on the ground that a claim was not made in good faith;

the court may make any such order as the county court is authorised to make by section 20(5) or (6) of this Act.

(4)   A tenant who, in proceedings to enforce a right of re-entry or forfeiture or a right to damages in respect of a failure to comply with any terms of the tenancy, applies for relief under section 16 of the Landlord and Tenant Act 1954 is not thereby precluded from making a claim to acquire the freehold or an extended lease; but if he gives notice under section 16(2) (under which the tenant is relieved from any order for recovery of possession or for payment of damages, but the tenancy is cut short), any claim made by him to acquire the freehold or an extended lease of property comprised in the tenancy, with or without other property, shall be of no effect, or, if already made, shall cease to have effect.

(5)   Sub-paragraph (4) above shall apply in relation to proceedings relating to a superior tenancy with the substitution for the references to section 16 and to section 16(2) of the Landlord and Tenant Act 1954 of references to paragraph 9 and to paragraph 9(2) of Schedule 5 to that Act.

[(6)   The references in this paragraph—
  (a)   to section 16 of the Landlord and Tenant Act 1954 and subsection (2) of that paragraph, and
  (b)   paragraph 9 of Schedule 5 to that Act and sub-paragraph (2) of that paragraph,
include references to those provisions as they apply in relation to Schedule 10 to the Local Government and Housing Act 1989.]

5.—(1)   For purposes of this Part of this Schedule—
  (a)   references to a claim to acquire the freehold or an extended lease shall be taken as references to a notice of a person's desire to acquire it under Part I of this Act and, except in so far as the contrary intention appears, as including a claim made by a tenant not entitled to acquire it and a claim made by a person who is not a tenant; and
  (b)   references to a claim being effective shall be taken as references to the freehold or an extended lease being acquired in pursuance of the claim; and
  (c)   references to the currency of a claim shall be taken as references to the period from the giving of a notice which has effect or would, if valid, have effect to the time when the notice is effective or ceases to have effect, or (not being a valid notice) is set aside by the court or withdrawn or would, if valid, cease to have effect, and those references shall include any period when the notice is suspended.

(2)   For purposes of sub-paragraph (1)(c) above the date when a notice ceases to have effect or is set aside or would, if valid, cease to have effect in consequence of an order of a court shall be taken to be the date when the order becomes final.

**[129]**

---

**NOTES**
  Para 1: words in square brackets inserted by the Local Government and Housing Act 1989, s 194(1), Sch 11, para 13(1).
  Para 2: sub-paras (1), (1A)–(1E) substituted for original sub-para (1), and sub-para (4)(b) and word omitted immediately preceding it repealed, by the Regulatory Reform (Business Tenancies) (England and Wales) Order 2003, SI 2003/3096, art 28, Sch 5, paras 10, 11, Sch 6, for transitional provisions see art 29(1) of that Order; words in square brackets in sub-paras (2), (3) inserted by the Local Government and Housing Act 1989, s 194(1), Sch 11, para 13(2); words omitted from sub-para (3) repealed by the Statute Law (Repeals) Act 1993.
  Para 2A: inserted by SI 2003/3096, art 28(1), Sch 5, paras 10, 12; for transitional provisions see art 29(1), (2) of that Order.
  Paras 3, 4: words in square brackets added by the Local Government and Housing Act 1989, s 194(1), Sch 11, para 13(3), (4).

---

## PART II
## PROCEDURAL PROVISIONS

6.—(1)   A tenant's notice under Part I of this Act of his desire to have the freehold or an extended lease of a house and premises shall be in the prescribed form, and shall contain the following particulars:—
  (a)   the address of the house, and sufficient particulars of the house and premises to identify the property to which the claim extends;
  (b)   such particulars of the tenancy and[, in the case of a tenancy falling within section 4(1)(i) of this Act,] of the rateable value of the house and premises as serve to identify the instrument creating the tenancy and show that
      [(i)   (apart from the operation, if any, of the proviso to section 4(1) of this Act) the tenancy is and has at the material times been a long tenancy at a low rent;
      [(ii)   at the material time the rateable value was within the limits specified for the purposes of section 1;]
  (c)   the date on which the tenant acquired the tenancy;
  (d)   ...
  [(e)   in the case of a tenancy falling within section 1(1)(a)(ii) of this Act, the premium payable as a condition of the grant of the tenancy.]

[(1A)   *Where the tenant gives the notice by virtue of section 1AA of this Act, sub-paragraph (1) above shall have effect with the substitution for paragraph (b) of—*

"(b) such particulars of the tenancy as serve to identify the instrument creating the tenancy and show that the tenancy is one in relation to which section 1AA(1) of this Act has effect to confer a right to acquire the freehold of the house and premises;".]

(2) Where the tenant gives the notice by virtue of section 6[, 6A] or 7 of this Act, sub-paragraph (1)(c) ... above shall apply with the appropriate modifications of references to the tenant, so that the notice shall show the particulars bringing the case within section 6[, 6A] or 7.

(3) The notice shall not be invalidated by any inaccuracy in the particulars required by this paragraph or any misdescription of the property to which the claim extends; and where the claim extends to property not properly included in the house and premises, or does not extend to property that ought to be so included, the notice may with the leave of the court, and on such terms as the court may see fit to impose, be amended so as to exclude or include that property.

7.—(1) Where a tenant of a house gives the landlord notice in accordance with Part I of this Act of the tenant's desire to have the freehold or an extended lease, the landlord shall within two months give the tenant a notice in reply in the prescribed form stating whether or not the landlord admits the tenant's right to have the freehold or extended lease (subject to any question as to the correctness of the particulars given in the tenant's notice of the house and premises); and if the landlord does not admit the tenant's right, the notice shall state the grounds on which it is not admitted.

(2) Subject to sub-paragraph (3) below, where under Part I of this Act the landlord may object to the inclusion of any part of the house and premises as described in the tenant's notice, or may object to the exclusion of other property, the notice of his objection shall be given with or before his notice in reply, unless the right to give it later is reserved by the notice in reply.

(3) If (on the assumption, where it is not admitted, that the tenant has the right claimed) it is intended to apply to the court for possession of the house and premises under section 17 or 18 of this Act, the notice in reply shall state that it is the intention to do so, and sub-paragraph (2) above shall not apply.

(4) Where a landlord's notice in reply admits the tenant's right to have the freehold or extended lease of a house and premises, the admission shall be binding on the landlord, so far as relates to the matters [relevant to the existence of that right], unless the landlord shows that he was induced to make the admission by misrepresentation or the concealment of material facts; but the admission shall not conclude any question whether the particulars of the house and premises in the tenant's notice are correct.

(5) The tenant shall not institute proceedings in the court with a view to the enforcement of his right to have the freehold or an extended lease before the landlord has given his notice in reply or two months have elapsed without his doing so since the giving of the tenant's notice.

8.—(1) Where a person ("the claimant") gives notice as tenant of a house of his desire to have the freehold or an extended lease under Part I of this Act,—

    (a) the notice shall be regarded as served on the landlord if it is served on any of the persons having an interest in the house and premises superior to the claimant's tenancy and references to the relevant time shall be construed accordingly;

    (b) copies of the notice shall be served by the claimant on any other persons known or believed by him to have such an interest;

    (c) the notice shall state whether copies are being served in accordance with paragraph (b) above on anyone other than the recipient and, if so, on whom;

    (d) a recipient of the notice or a copy of it (including a person receiving a copy under this paragraph), unless he is a person having no such interest, shall forthwith serve a copy on any person who is known or believed by him to have such an interest and is not stated in the recipient's copy of the notice or known by him to have received a copy;

    (e) a recipient of the notice or a copy of it shall, in any further copies served by him in accordance with paragraph (d) above, supplement the statement under paragraph (c) by adding any further persons on whom he is serving copies or who are known by him to have received one.

(2) Any recipient of any such notice or a copy of it—

    (a) if he serves further copies of it on other persons in accordance with sub-paragraph (1)(d) above, shall notify the claimant of the persons added by him to the statement under sub-paragraph (1)(c); and

    (b) if he knows who is, or believes himself to be, the person designated as the reversioner by paragraph 2 of Schedule 1 to this Act, shall give written notice to the claimant stating who is thought by him to be the reversioner, and shall serve copies of it on all persons known or believed by him to have an interest superior to the claimant's tenancy.

(3) Any person who fails without reasonable cause to comply with sub-paragraph (1) or (2) above, or is guilty of any unreasonable delay in doing so, shall be liable for any loss thereby occasioned to the claimant or to any person having an interest superior to the claimant's tenancy.

(4)   In this paragraph references to an interest superior to the claimant's tenancy mean the estate in fee simple and any tenancy superior to the claimant's tenancy, but shall apply also to a tenancy reversionary on the claimant's tenancy.

9.—(1)   Where the interest of a landlord is subject to a charge, and the person entitled to the benefit of the charge is in possession or a receiver appointed by him or by the court is in receipt of the rents and profits, a notice by a tenant of his desire to have the freehold or an extended lease under Part I of this Act shall be duly given if served either on the landlord or on that person or any such receiver; but the landlord or that person, if not the recipient of the notice, shall forthwith be sent the notice or a copy of it by the recipient:

Provided that in the case of a debenture-holders' charge within the meaning of section 12(5) of this Act this sub-paragraph shall not authorise the service of a notice on, or require a notice or copy to be sent to, the persons entitled to the benefit of the charge, other than trustees for the debenture-holders, but where the notice is served on the landlord and there is no trustee for the debenture-holders, he shall forthwith send it or a copy of it to any receiver appointed by virtue of the charge.

(2)   Where a tenant of a house gives notice of his desire to have the freehold or an extended lease under Part I of this Act, and the interest of the person to whom the notice is given, or of any person receiving a copy of it under paragraph 8 above, is subject to a charge to secure the payment of money, then subject to sub-paragraph (3) below the recipient of the notice or copy shall forthwith inform the person entitled to the benefit of the charge (unless the notice was served on him or a receiver appointed by virtue of the charge) that the notice has been given, and shall give him such further information as may from time to time be reasonably required from the recipient by him.

(3)   References in sub-paragraph (2) above to a charge shall not include a charge falling within section 11 of this Act or a debenture-holders' charge within the meaning of section 12(5) of this Act.

10.—(1)   This paragraph shall have effect in relation to a landlord's notice terminating a tenancy of a house under section 4 or 25 of the Landlord and Tenant Act 1954 [or under paragraph 4(1) of Schedule 10 to the Local Government and Housing Act 1989] if—

- (a)   no previous notice terminating the tenancy has been given under [any of those provisions]; and
- (b)   in the case of a notice under section 25, the tenancy is a long tenancy at a low rent, and the tenant is not a company or other artificial person.

(2)   The landlord's notice shall not have effect unless it states—

- (a)   that, if the tenant has a right under Part I of this Act to acquire the freehold or an extended lease of property comprised in the tenancy, notice of his desire to have the freehold or an extended lease cannot be given more than two months after the service of the landlord's notice; and
- (b)   that, in the event of a tenant having that right and giving such a notice within those two months, the landlord's notice will not operate; and
- (c)   that, in the event of the tenant giving such a notice within those two months, the landlord will be entitled to apply to the court under section 17 or 18 of this Act and proposes to do so or, as the case may be, will not be entitled or does not propose to do so.

[(2A)   If the landlord's notice is under section 25 of the Landlord and Tenant Act 1954, sub-paragraph (2) above shall effect in relation to it as if in paragraph (b), after the word "operate" there were inserted the words "and no further proceedings may be taken by him under Part 2 of the Landlord and Tenant Act 1954".]

(3)   The landlord shall also in the notice give the names and addresses of any other persons known or believed by him to have an interest superior to the tenancy terminated by the notice or to be the agent concerned with the property on behalf of a person having such an interest; and for this purpose "an interest superior to the tenancy terminated by the notice" means the estate in fee simple and any tenancy superior to that tenancy, but includes also a tenancy reversionary on that tenancy.

(4)   Where a tenant's notice of his desire to have the freehold or an extended lease of a house and premises under Part I of this Act is given after the service of a landlord's notice terminating the tenancy under section 4 or section 25 of the Landlord and Tenant Act 1954 [or under paragraph 4(1) of Schedule 10 to the Local Government and Housing Act 1989], and the landlord's notice does not comply with sub-paragraph (2) above, no application made under section 17 or 18 of this Act with respect to the house and premises by the landlord giving the notice shall be entertained by the court (other than an application under section 17 after the grant of an extended lease).

(5)   This paragraph shall not apply, ... to a landlord's notice given before the appointed day.

**[130]**

**NOTES**

Para 6: words in first pair of square brackets in sub-para (1)(b) inserted and sub-para (1)(e) added by the References to Rating (Housing) Regulations 1990, SI 1990/434, reg 2, Schedule, para 10; sub-para (1)(b)(i) numbered as such and sub-para (1)(b)(ii) inserted by the Housing Act 1980, s 141, Sch 21, para 7, as from a day to be appointed; sub-para (1)(d) and words omitted from sub-para (2) repealed by the Commonhold and

Leasehold Reform Act 2002, s 180, Sch 14, except in relation to an application for enfranchisement or an extended lease of a house in respect of which notice was given under s 8 or 14 of this Act at **[90]**, **[97]**, or where an application was made under s 27 of this Act at **[110]**, before 26 July 2002 (in relation to England) or 1 January 2003 (in relation to Wales); sub-para (1A) inserted by the Housing Act 1996, s 106, Sch 9, para 2(1), (8), except in a case where the house and premises are held under a tenancy which is a shared ownership lease within the meaning of the Housing Act 1985, s 622 at **[571]**, and was granted by a housing association, whether or not the interest of the landlord still belongs to such an association, nor does it have effect in a case where, before 1 April 1997, a notice was given under s 8 of this Act at **[90]**, or an application was made under s 27 of this Act at **[110]**, or a notice was given under the Leasehold Reform, Housing and Urban Development Act 1993, s 13 or 42 at **[817]**, **[848]**, or an application was made under s 26 or 50 of that Act at **[830]**, **[856]**; sub-para (1A) repealed by the Housing and Regeneration Act 2008, s 321(1), Sch 16, as from 7 September 2009 (in relation to England, subject to transitional provisions in SI 2009/2096, art 3) and as from a day to be appointed (in relation to Wales); words in square brackets in sub-para (2) inserted by the Commonhold and Leasehold Reform Act 2002, s 142(2).

Para 7: words in square brackets in sub-para (4) substituted by the Housing Act 1996, s 106, Sch 9, para 2(1), (9), except in a case where the house and premises are held under a tenancy which is a shared ownership lease within the meaning of the Housing Act 1985, s 622 at **[571]**, and was granted by a housing association, whether or not the interest of the landlord still belongs to such an association, nor does it have effect in a case where, before 1 April 1997, a notice was given under s 8 of this Act at **[90]**, or an application was made under s 27 of this Act at **[110]**, or a notice was given under the Leasehold Reform, Housing and Urban Development Act 1993, s 13 or 42 at **[817]**, **[848]**, or an application was made under s 26 or 50 of that Act at **[830]**, **[856]**.

Para 10: words in first and fourth pairs of square brackets inserted and words in second pair of square brackets substituted by the Local Government and Housing Act 1989, s 194(1), Sch 11, para 13(5); sub-para (2A) inserted by the Regulatory Reform (Business Tenancies) (England and Wales) Order 2003, SI 2003/3096, art 28(1), Sch 5, paras 10, 13; words omitted repealed by the Statute Law (Repeals) Act 1993.

Prescribed forms—paras 6, 7: prescribed by regulations under the Landlord and Tenant Act 1954, s 66; the relevant forms are now set out in the Schedule to the Leasehold Reform (Notices) Regulations 1997, SI 1997/640 at **[3176]**.

---

## SCHEDULE 4
### SPECIAL COVENANTS WITH LOCAL AUTHORITIES ETC ON ENFRANCHISEMENT OR EXTENSION
Sections 29 and 30

### PART I
### OPERATION AND ENFORCEMENT OF COVENANTS

1.—(1) A covenant entered into in accordance with section 29 or 30 of this Act (in this Part of this Schedule referred to as "a relevant covenant") shall not be enforceable by any means other than those provided by paragraphs 2 and 3 below.

(2) A relevant covenant affecting land other than registered land—

(a) may be registered under section 10 of the Land Charges Act 1925 as a restrictive covenant, if apart from this sub-paragraph it would not be registrable under that section as a restrictive covenant or as an estate contract; and

(b) subject to section 13 of that Act, shall be binding upon every successor of the covenantor, if apart from this sub-paragraph it would not be binding upon every such successor.

(3) Where a relevant covenant affects registered land,—

[(a) the covenant may be the subject of a notice in the register of title kept under the Land Registration Act 2002, if apart from this subsection it would not be capable of being the subject of such a notice; and]

(b) where [a notice in respect of the covenant has been entered in that register, it] shall be binding upon every successor of the covenantor, if apart from this subsection it would not be binding upon every such successor.

(4) In sub-paragraphs (2) and (3) above "successor of the covenantor", in relation to the covenants entered into on any disposition, means a person, other than the covenantor, who is for the time being entitled—

(a) to the interest disposed of, either in the whole or in part of the property comprised in the disposition; or

(b) to an interest consisting of a tenancy (whether of the whole or of part of that property) which has been created (directly or indirectly) out of the interest disposed of.

(5) Section 84 of the Law of Property Act 1925 (power to discharge or modify restrictive covenants affecting land) shall not have effect in relation to any relevant covenant.

(6) The rule against perpetuities and any enactment relating to that rule shall not apply to any right conferred by, or exercisable in relation to, a relevant covenant, if apart from this sub-paragraph it would apply to any such right.

(7) Where any such interest as is mentioned in sub-paragraph (4)(a) or (b) above is acquired (whether compulsorily or by agreement) by an authority possessing compulsory purchase powers within the meaning of the [Town and Country Planning Act 1990] (including any government

department), nothing in the enactment which authorises that acquisition, or in any other enactment conferring powers on that authority, shall be construed as relieving that authority from the obligation to comply with any relevant covenant to which that interest remains subject; but the rights of the covenantee shall for purposes of any such acquisition be treated as an interest in the land affected, and as capable of being, and liable to be, extinguished by being compulsorily acquired in like manner and subject to the like conditions as other interests of the covenantee would be.

2.—(1) Where it appears to a local authority that a relevant covenant entered into on a disposition by that authority has been broken, the authority may serve written notice under this paragraph on any one or more of the following persons, that is to say—

(a) any person for the time being entitled to the interest disposed of either in the whole or in part of the land comprised in the disposition (in this paragraph referred to as "the land under covenant"); and

(b) any person entitled to an interest consisting of a tenancy (whether of the whole or of part of the land under covenant) which has been created (directly or indirectly) out of the interest disposed of.

(2) A notice served on any person under sub-paragraph (1) above shall—

(a) specify the covenant and the matters in respect of which it is alleged by the authority that the covenant has been broken; and

(b) state that, after the end of such period (not being less than six weeks from the date of service of the notice) as may be specified in the notice, the authority propose to execute a vesting declaration under paragraph 3 below in respect of that person's interest in the land under covenant unless before the end of that period he serves on the authority a counter-notice under sub-paragraph (3) below.

(3) Any person on whom a notice is served under sub-paragraph (1) above may, before the end of the period specified in the notice in accordance with sub-paragraph (2)(b) serve on the authority a counter-notice in writing objecting to the notice on such one or more of the following grounds as may be specified in the counter-notice, that is to say—

(a) that the relevant covenant specified in the notice under sub-paragraph (1) above has not been broken as alleged in the notice;

(b) that, if that covenant has been so broken, the breach does not relate to any part of the land under covenant in which the person serving the counter-notice has an interest;

(c) that in the circumstances he ought to be relieved against the execution of a vesting declaration under paragraph 3 below in respect of his interest.

(4) Where a person has served a counter-notice under sub-paragraph (3) above and that counter-notice has not been withdrawn, the authority shall not execute a vesting declaration under paragraph 3 below in respect of his interest except with the leave of the court; and on any application for such leave—

(a) where the grounds of objection specified in the counter-notice consist of or include that which is specified in sub-paragraph (3)(a) or (b) above, the court shall not grant leave unless satisfied that the objection on that ground is not well-founded; and

(b) without prejudice to paragraph (a) above, where the grounds of objection specified in the counter-notice consist of or include that which is specified in sub-paragraph (3)(c) above, the court, if having regard to the conduct of the parties and to all the other circumstances it appears to the court to be just and equitable to do so, may refuse to grant leave, either unconditionally or on such terms (as to costs, damages or otherwise) as the court think fit.

3.—(1) Where a local authority have served on any person a notice under paragraph 2 above in respect of such an interest as is mentioned in paragraph 2(1)(a) or (b), then subject to paragraph 2(4) above and to the provisions of any order made under it, the authority may execute a vesting declaration under this paragraph in respect of that interest—

(a) at any time within the six months following the end of the period specified in the notice in accordance with paragraph 2(2)(b), if no counter-notice under paragraph 2(3) is served before the end of that period; or

(b) if such a counter-notice is so served but is withdrawn, at any time within the six months following the withdrawal of the counter-notice; or

(c) if such a counter-notice is so served and is not withdrawn, at any time within the six months following the time when the order giving leave under paragraph 2(4) becomes final.

(2) A vesting declaration under this paragraph in respect of an interest in land shall be in such form as may be prescribed by regulations made by statutory instrument by the Minister of Housing and Local Government.

(3) Where a vesting declaration is executed under this paragraph the interest to which it relates shall vest in the authority on such date as is specified in that behalf in the declaration.

(4) Any reference in the Land Compensation Act 1961 to the compulsory acquisition of land, or of an interest in land, shall be construed as including a reference to the execution of a vesting declaration under this paragraph in respect of an interest in land; and that Act shall apply in relation

to the execution of such a declaration as if the authority, having been duly authorised to acquire that interest compulsorily in accordance with the [Acquisition of Land Act 1981], had served notice to treat in respect of that interest on the date of execution of the declaration.

    (5)   In assessing compensation in accordance with the Land Compensation Act 1961 in respect of an interest in land vested in a local authority by a vesting declaration under this paragraph—

        (a)    nothing shall be included for damage sustained by reason that the land in which the interest subsists is severed from other land held therewith, or for disturbance or any other matter not directly based on the value of land or of an interest in land; and

        (b)    in a case where immediately before the execution of the declaration the interest is subject to a right of pre-emption under a covenant entered into in accordance with section 30(1)(b) of this Act, no account shall be taken of any diminution of the value of the interest which is attributable to that right.

[131]

**NOTES**

   Para 1: sub-para (3)(a) and words in square brackets in sub-para (3)(b) substituted by the Land Registration Act 2002, s 133, Sch 11, para 8(1), (3); words in square brackets in sub-para (7) substituted by the Planning (Consequential Provisions) Act 1990, s 4, Sch 2, para 17(2), subject to transitional provisions and savings in s 5 of, and Sch 3 to, that Act.

   Para 3: words in square brackets substituted by the Acquisition of Land Act 1981, s 34, Sch 4, para 1.

   Land Charges Act 1925, ss 10, 13: see now the Land Charges Act 1972, s 2(4), (5).

   Minister of Housing and Local Government: see the note to s 19 at [**102**].

<hr>

PART II

RE-ACQUISITION FOR DEVELOPMENT BY [WELSH NEW TOWNS RESIDUARY BODY] OR UNIVERSITY BODY

4.   Where a tenant of a house and premises acquires the freehold under Part I of this Act subject to a covenant entered into under section 29(1) with the [Welsh new towns residuary body], and the property or any part of it is afterwards required for development for purposes (other than investment purposes) of [that body, the body] may ... acquire the property or that part of it compulsorily; [and the Acquisition of Land Act 1981 shall apply to a compulsory purchase under this paragraph].

5.—(1)   Where a tenant of a house and premises acquires the freehold under Part I of this Act subject to a covenant entered into under section 29(1) with a university body, and the property or any part of it is afterwards required for development for the purposes (other than investment purposes) of that or a related university body, the Secretary of State for Education and Science may at the cost and on behalf of the university body for which it is required acquire the property or that part of it by compulsory purchase.

    [(2)   The Acquisition of Land Act 1981 shall apply to a compulsory purchase under this paragraph.]

    (3)   For purposes of this paragraph a university and the colleges of that university (within the meaning of section 28(5)(c) of this Act) are university bodies related to one another.

    [6.   ....]

[132]

**NOTES**

   Part heading: words in square brackets substituted by the Housing and Regeneration Act 2008, s 56, Sch 8, paras 5, 11(1), (2), subject to transitional provisions and savings in SI 2008/3068, arts 6–10 at [**3834B**]–[**3834F**].

   Para 4: words in first and second pairs of square brackets substituted and words omitted repealed by the Housing and Regeneration Act 2008, ss 56, 321(1), Sch 8, paras 5, 11(1), (3), Sch 16, subject to transitional provisions and savings in SI 2008/3068, arts 6–10 at [**3834B**]–[**3834F**]; words in third pair of square brackets substituted by the Acquisition of Land Act 1981, s 34, Sch 4, para 16(2).

   Para 5: sub-para (2) substituted by the Acquisition of Land Act 1981, s 34, Sch 4, para 16(3).

   Para 6: added by the Development of Rural Wales Act 1976, s 27, Sch 7, para 5(5); repealed by the Government of Wales Act 1998, ss 131, 152, Sch 18, Pt IV.

   Minister of Housing and Local Government: see the note to s 19 at [**102**].

<hr>

[SCHEDULE 4A

EXCLUSION OF CERTAIN SHARED OWNERSHIP LEASES

Section 33A

*Leases granted in pursuance of right to be granted a shared ownership lease*

1.   A lease granted in pursuance of the right to be granted a shared ownership lease under Part V of the Housing Act 1985 is excluded from the operation of this Part of this Act.

*Certain leases granted by certain public authorities*

2.—(1)   A lease which—

(a)    was granted at a premium by a body mentioned in sub-paragraph (2), and

(b)    complies with the conditions set out in sub-paragraph (3),

is excluded from the operation of this Part at any time when the interest of the landlord belongs to such a body[, to a registered social landlord] [or to a person who acquired that interest in exercise of the right conferred by Part IV of the Housing Act 1988].

(2)    The bodies are—

(a)    a county, [county borough,] district or London borough council, the Common Council of the City of London or the Council of the Isles of Scilly;

(b)    … a joint authority established by Part IV of the Local Government Act 1985;

[(bb) the London Fire and Emergency Planning Authority;]

(c)    the [new towns residuary body] or a development corporation established by an order made, or having effect as made, under the New Towns Act 1981;

(d)    an urban development corporation within the meaning of Part XVI of the Local Government, Planning and Land Act 1980;

(e)    … ;

[(f)   a housing action trust established under Part III of the Housing Act 1988.]

(3)    The conditions are that the lease—

(a)    provides for the tenant to acquire the freehold for a consideration which is to be calculated in accordance with the lease and which is reasonable, having regard to the premium or premiums paid by the tenant under the lease, and

(b)    states the landlord's opinion that by virtue of this paragraph the tenancy will be excluded from the operation of this Part of this Act at any time when the interest of the landlord belongs to a body mentioned in sub-paragraph (2) above [or to a registered social landlord].

(4)    If, in proceedings in which it falls to be determined whether a lease complies with the condition in sub-paragraph (3)(a), the question arises whether the consideration payable by the tenant on acquiring the freehold is reasonable, it is for the landlord to show that it is.

[(5)    In this paragraph "registered social landlord" has the same meaning as in Part 1 of the Housing Act 1996.]

*Certain leases granted by housing associations*

3.—(1)    A lease granted by a housing association and which complies with the conditions set out in sub-paragraph (2) is excluded from the operation of this Part of this Act, whether or not the interest of the landlord still belongs to such an association.

(2)    The conditions are that the lease—

(a)    was granted for a term of 99 years or more and is not (and cannot become) terminable except in pursuance of a provision for re-entry or forfeiture;

(b)    was granted at a premium, calculated by reference to the value of the house or the cost of providing it, of not less than 25 per cent, or such other percentage as may be prescribed, of the figure by reference to which it was calculated;

(c)    provides for the tenant to acquire additional shares in the house on terms specified in the lease and complying with such requirements as may be prescribed;

(d)    does not restrict the tenant's powers to … mortgage or charge his interest in the house;

(e)    if it enables the landlord to require payment for outstanding shares in the house, does so only in such circumstances as may be prescribed;

(f)    provides for the tenant to acquire the landlord's interest on terms specified in the lease and complying with such requirements as may be prescribed; and

(g)    states the landlord's opinion that by virtue of this paragraph the lease is excluded from the operation of this Part of this Act.

(3)    In any proceedings the court may, if of the opinion that it is just and equitable to do so, treat a lease as satisfying the conditions in sub-paragraph (2) notwithstanding that the condition specified in paragraph (g) of that sub-paragraph is not satisfied.

(4)    In this paragraph "housing association" has the same meaning as in the Housing Associations Act 1985.

[3A.—(1)    A lease which does not fall within paragraph 3 is excluded from the operation of this Part of this Act if the lease—

(a)    meets the conditions mentioned in sub-paragraph (2);

(b)    meets any other prescribed conditions; and

(c)    does not fall within any prescribed exemptions.

(2)    The conditions referred to in sub-paragraph (1)(a) are that the lease—

(a)    was granted for a term of 99 years or more and is not (and cannot become) terminable except in pursuance of a provision for re-entry or forfeiture;

(b)    was granted at a premium, calculated by reference to the value of the house or the cost of providing it, of not less than 25 per cent, or such other percentage as may be prescribed, of the figure by reference to which it was calculated;

(c)     provides for the tenant to acquire additional shares in the house on terms specified in the lease and complying with such requirements as may be prescribed;

(d)     does not restrict the tenant's powers to mortgage or charge his interest in the house;

(e)     if it enables the landlord to require payment for outstanding shares in the house, does so only in such circumstances as may be prescribed;

(f)     provides for the tenant to acquire the landlord's interest on terms specified in the lease and complying with such requirements as may be prescribed; and

(g)     states the landlord's opinion that by virtue of this paragraph the lease is excluded from the operation of this Part of this Act.]

(3)    In any proceedings the court may, if it considers that it is just and equitable to do so, treat a lease as meeting the conditions mentioned in sub-paragraph (2) despite the fact that the condition specified in paragraph (g) of that sub-paragraph is not met.]

### [Certain leases for the elderly]

4.—(1)    A lease for the elderly granted by a [registered social landlord] and which complies with the conditions set out in sub-paragraph (2) is excluded from the operation of this Part of this Act at any time when the interest of the landlord belongs to [a registered social landlord].

(2)    The conditions are that the lease—

(a)     is granted at a premium which is calculated by reference to a percentage of the value of the house or of the cost of providing it,

(b)     complies, at the time when it is granted, with such requirements as may be prescribed, and

(c)     states the landlord's opinion that by virtue of this paragraph the lease will be excluded from the operation of this Part of this Act at any time when the interest of the landlord belongs to a [registered social landlord].

(3)    In this paragraph—

"lease for the elderly" has such meaning as may be prescribed; and

["registered social landlord" has the same meaning as in the Housing Act 1985 (see section 5(4) and (5) of that Act).]

### [Certain leases in protected areas

4A.—(1)    A lease which does not fall within paragraph 3 or 3A is excluded from the operation of this Part of this Act if—

(a)     the lease meets the conditions mentioned in sub-paragraph (2);

(b)     any provision in the lease for the tenant to acquire the landlord's interest provides for the tenant to acquire the interest on terms specified in the lease and complying with such requirements as may be prescribed;

(c)     the lease meets any other prescribed conditions;

(d)     the lease does not fall within any prescribed exemptions; and

(e)     the house is in a protected area.

(2)    The conditions referred to in sub-paragraph (1)(a) are that the lease—

(a)     was granted for a term of 99 years or more and is not (and cannot become) terminable except in pursuance of a provision for re-entry or forfeiture;

(b)     was granted at a premium, calculated by reference to the value of the house or the cost of providing it, of not less than 25 per cent, or such other percentage as may be prescribed, of the figure by reference to which it was calculated;

(c)     provides for the tenant to acquire additional shares in the house on terms specified in the lease and complying with such requirements as may be prescribed;

(d)     does not restrict the tenant's powers to mortgage or charge his interest in the house;

(e)     if it enables the landlord to require payment for outstanding shares in the house, does so only in such circumstances as may be prescribed; and

(f)     states the landlord's opinion that by virtue of this paragraph the lease is excluded from the operation of this Part of this Act.

(3)    The appropriate national authority may by order made by statutory instrument designate an area as a protected area if it considers it appropriate to do so to support the provision in the area of houses, or descriptions of houses, which are available for occupation in accordance with shared ownership arrangements.

(4)    The appropriate national authority must publish the criteria for the time being in force which are to be taken into account by it in deciding whether to designate an area as a protected area.

(5)    Before making an order under sub-paragraph (3) the appropriate national authority must take such steps as it considers to be reasonable to consult those likely to be affected by the order.

(6)    In any proceedings the court may, if it considers that it is just and equitable to do so, treat a lease as meeting the conditions mentioned in sub-paragraph (2) despite the fact that the condition mentioned in paragraph (f) of that sub-paragraph is not met.

(7)    An order under this paragraph may contain such incidental, supplementary, transitory, transitional or saving provisions as the appropriate national authority considers appropriate.

(8)    In this paragraph "shared ownership arrangements" has the same meaning as in section 70 of the Housing and Regeneration Act 2008.

(9)    An instrument containing—
   (a)    an order of the Secretary of State under this paragraph is subject to annulment in pursuance of a resolution of either House of Parliament;
   (b)    an order of the Welsh Ministers under this paragraph is subject to annulment in pursuance of a resolution of the National Assembly for Wales.]

### Power to prescribe matters by regulations

5.—(1)    The *Secretary of State* may by regulations prescribe anything requiring to be prescribed for the purposes of this Schedule.

(2)    The regulations may—
   (a)    make different provision for different cases or descriptions of case, including different provision for different areas, and
   (b)    contain such incidental, supplementary or transitional provisions as the *Secretary of State* considers appropriate,

and shall be made by statutory instrument which[, in the case of regulations made by the Secretary of State,] shall be subject to annulment in pursuance of a resolution of either House of Parliament [and, in the case of regulations made by the Welsh Ministers, shall be subject to annulment in pursuance of a resolution of the National Assembly for Wales].

### Interpretation

6.    In this Schedule "lease" means a lease at law or in equity, and references to the grant of a lease shall be construed accordingly.

[7.    In this Schedule "appropriate national authority" means—
   (a)    in relation to England, the Secretary of State; and
   (b)    in relation to Wales, the Welsh Ministers.]]

**[133]**

---

**NOTES**
   Inserted by the Housing and Planning Act 1986, s 18, Sch 4, paras 6, 11, in relation to leases granted after 11 December 1987.
   Para 2: words in first pair of square brackets in sub-para (1), words in square brackets in sub-para (3)(b), and the whole of sub-para (5) inserted by the Commonhold and Leasehold Reform Act 2002, s 144(1), (2), except in relation to an application for enfranchisement or an extended lease of a house in respect of which notice was given under s 8 or 14 of this Act at **[90]**, **[97]**, or where an application was made under s 27 of this Act at **[110]**, before 26 July 2002 (in relation to England) or 1 January 2003 (in relation to Wales); words in second pair of square brackets in sub-para (1) inserted, and sub-para (2)(f) added by the Housing Act 1988, s 140(1), Sch 17, Pt I, para 17; words in square brackets in sub-para (2)(a) inserted by the Local Government (Wales) Act 1994, s 22(2), Sch 8, para 1(2); words omitted from sub-para (2)(b) repealed by the Education Reform Act 1988, s 237(2), Sch 13, Pt I; sub-para (2)(bb) inserted by the Greater London Authority Act 1999, s 328, Sch 29, Pt I, para 9; words in square brackets in sub-para (2)(c) substituted by the Housing and Regeneration Act 2008, s 56, Sch 8, paras 5, 12, subject to transitional provisions and savings in SI 2008/3068, arts 6–10 at **[3834B]**–**[3834F]**; sub-para (2)(e) repealed by the Government of Wales Act 1998, ss 131, 152, Sch 18, Pt IV.
   Para 3: for the heading immediately preceding para 3, there are substituted the words "Certain housing association and other leases" by the Housing and Regeneration Act 2008, s 301(2), as from 7 September 2009 (in relation to England) and as from a day to be appointed (in relation to Wales); word omitted repealed by the Commonhold and Leasehold Reform Act 2002, ss 144(1), (3), 180, Sch 14, subject to savings as noted above.
   Para 3A: inserted by the Housing and Regeneration Act 2008, s 301(1), as from 7 September 2009 (in relation to England) and as from a day to be appointed (in relation to Wales).
   Para 4: heading inserted by the Housing and Regeneration Act 2008, s 301(1), as from 7 September 2009 (in relation to England) and as from a day to be appointed (in relation to Wales); words in square brackets substituted by the Housing Act 1996 (Consequential Provisions) Order 1996, SI 1996/2325, art 5, Sch 2, para 1.
   Paras 4A, 7: inserted by the Housing and Regeneration Act 2008, s 302(1), (3), as from 7 September 2009 (in relation to England) and as from a day to be appointed (in relation to Wales).
   Para 5: for the words in italics there are substituted the words "appropriate national authority" and words in square brackets inserted by the Housing and Regeneration Act 2008, s 302(2), as from 7 September 2009 (in relation to England) and as from a day to be appointed (in relation to Wales).
   Regulations: the Housing Association Shared Ownership Leases (Exclusion from Leasehold Reform Act 1967 and Rent Act 1977) Regulations 1987, SI 1987/1940 at **[3067]**; the Housing (Shared Ownership Leases) (Exclusion from Leasehold Reform Act 1967) (England) Regulations 2009, SI 2009/2097 at **[3839]**; the Housing (Right to Enfranchise) (Designated Protected Areas) (England) Order 2009, SI 2009/2098 at **[3849]**.

---

## SCHEDULE 5
## LANDLORD AND TENANT ACT 1954 PART I (CONSEQUENTIAL AMENDMENTS, EFFECT OF RENT ACT 1965, ETC)

Section 39

*Consequential amendments of Landlord and Tenant Act 1954*

1.   ...

2.   The following provisions of the Landlord and Tenant Act 1954 shall have effect as if the amendments and repeals made in them by the Rent Act 1957 in consequence of the passing of section 21 of that Act had not been made, that is to say,—

(a)     section 2 (the words "at a low rent" being re-inserted in subsections (1), (2) and (3) after the words "long tenancy", and the words "if the tenancy had not been one at a low rent" being restored in place of the words "if the tenancy had not been a long tenancy and (in the case of a tenancy at a low rent) had not been a tenancy at a low rent");

(b)     section 3(3) (the words "if the tenancy in question were not one at a low rent" being restored in place of the words "if the tenancy in question were not a long tenancy and (in the case of a tenancy at a low rent) were not a tenancy at a low rent");

(c)     section 12(2)(*a*) and (*b*) (the words "if the tenancy were not one at a low rent" being in each case restored in place of the words "if the tenancy were not a long tenancy and (in the case of a tenancy at a low rent) were not a tenancy at a low rent");

(d)     section 18(1) (the words "at a low rent" being re-inserted after the words "long tenancy" where first occurring);

(e)     section 19(1) (the words "at a low rent" being re-inserted after the word "tenancy", where first occurring, and after the words "another tenancy", and there being omitted the words "and the second tenancy is a tenancy at a low rent").

*Regulated tenancies*

3.—(1)   The amount of the rent payable under a regulated tenancy arising by virtue of Part I of the Landlord and Tenant Act 1954 shall, subject to the provisions of that Act as to initial repairs and subject to the operation (as regards the fixing of a fair rent and otherwise) of the [Rent Act 1977], be such amount as may be agreed between the landlord and the tenant or, in default of agreement, the same amount as the rent last payable under the long tenancy ...

(2)   Where the rent payable under a statutory tenancy is arrived at in accordance with sub-paragraph (1) above, then the [Rent Act 1977] shall apply with the following adaptations:—

(a)     ...

(b)     [section 45(2)] (under which the rent payable for a statutory period of a tenancy is not to exceed that payable for the last contractual period) shall not apply;

(c)     [[sections 46 to 48 (which provide] for variations of rent in respect of changes in the burden on the landlord for rates, provision of services etc.) shall apply only if the rent is one arrived at by agreement, and shall then apply as if references to the last contractual period were references to the first statutory period.

4.—(1)   In relation to a rent registered or to be registered for a dwelling-house on an application made with reference to a regulated tenancy arising by virtue of Part I of the Landlord and Tenant Act 1954, the [Rent Act 1977] shall have effect subject to the provisions of this paragraph.

(2)   An application for the registration of a rent may be made by the landlord or the tenant, or jointly by the landlord and the tenant, before the commencement of the statutory tenancy, but not before the terms of that tenancy other than the amount of the rent have been agreed or determined in accordance with section 7 of the Landlord and Tenant Act 1954; and the provisions of the [Rent Act 1977] (including the provisions of [section 72] as to the date from which the registration takes effect) shall apply accordingly.

(3)   Where a rent is registered in pursuance of an application made by virtue of sub-paragraph (2) above, then a notice under [section 45(2)(*b*) of the Rent Act 1977] increasing the rent payable may, if the notice is given within four weeks after the date on which the rent is registered, specify as the date from which the increase is to take effect any date not earlier than the commencement of the tenancy nor earlier than the date from which the registration takes effect.

(4)   Where initial repairs (within the meaning of Part I of the Landlord and Tenant Act 1954) remain to be carried out to the dwelling-house, then in determining what rent is or would be a fair rent regard shall be had under [section 70(1) of the Rent Act 1977] to the state of repair which may be expected to subsist after the completion of the initial repairs.

(5)   The provisions of the [Rent Act 1977] as to the amount of the rent recoverable shall be taken as applying to the amount before account is taken of the provisions of the Landlord and Tenant Act 1954 as to initial repairs.

(6)   Any entry in the register of a rent or of its confirmation by the rent assessment committee shall indicate that the rent is registered on an application made with reference to a statutory tenancy arising by virtue of Part I of the Landlord and Tenant Act 1954.

*Transitional*

5.  In relation to a tenancy to which section 1 of the Landlord and Tenant Act 1954 applies immediately before the date of coming into operation of section 39 of this Act (in this and the following paragraphs referred to as "the operative date") , section 39 of this Act and paragraphs 1 to 4 above, together with the repeals made by Part I of Schedule 7 to this Act, shall not have effect if at the operative date there is in force a landlord's notice proposing a statutory tenancy and all the terms of the tenancy have been agreed or determined in accordance with section 7 of the Landlord and Tenant Act 1954 or an application for securing their determination by the court has been made.

6.—(1)   Subject to paragraph 7(1) below, where at the operative date (within the meaning of paragraph 5 above) a tenancy is continuing by virtue of section 3 of the Landlord and Tenant Act 1954, section 39 of this Act and paragraphs 1 to 4 above, together with the repeals made by Part I of Schedule 7 to this Act, shall apply to the tenancy only to the extent provided for by this paragraph.

(2)   Where at the operative date no notice under section 4 of the Landlord and Tenant Act 1954 terminating the tenancy is in force, Part I or, as the case may be, Part II of that Act shall apply as it would apply if the term date of the tenancy (within the meaning of Part I) had fallen on the operative date and if, in the case of a tenancy not at a low rent, it had been one at a low rent.

(3)   Where at the operative date there is in force a landlord's notice proposing a statutory tenancy, sub-paragraph (2) above shall apply as it applies in a case where there is no such notice, unless either—

    (a)    all the terms of the tenancy have been agreed or determined in accordance with section 7 of the Landlord and Tenant Act 1954 or an application for securing their determination by the court has been made; or

    (b)    Part II of that Act would in accordance with sub-paragraph (2) above apply to the tenancy.

(4)   Where a landlord's notice terminating the tenancy is in force at the operative date, and the notice ceases to have effect without the tenancy being terminated or a statutory tenancy arising, then sub-paragraph (2) above shall thereafter apply as it applies in a case where there is no such notice.

(5)   Where a statutory tenancy arises by virtue of Part I of the Landlord and Tenant Act 1954 as it applies in accordance with sub-paragraph (2) above the [Rent Act 1977] shall have effect in relation to the statutory tenancy accordingly.

(6)   Nothing in section 39 of this Act or in sub-paragraphs (2) to (5) above shall affect the operation of any notice given by a tenant under section 5 of the Landlord and Tenant Act 1954 to terminate the tenancy, if the notice is given while section 1 of the Act applies to the tenancy.

7.—(1)   This paragraph shall have effect in relation to tenancies of the following description, except where paragraph 5 above applies, and paragraph 6 shall not have effect in relation to them, that is to say, tenancies—

    (a)    to which section 1 of the Landlord and Tenant Act 1954 applies immediately before the operative date (within the meaning of paragraph 5 above); but

    (b)    to which in accordance with section 39 of this Act section 1 of the Landlord and Tenant Act 1954 can no longer apply because the rateable value of the dwelling-house on the appropriate day for purposes of the [Rent Act 1977] exceeds the amount specified in section 1(1) of that Act.

(2)   Where, on section 1 of the Landlord and Tenant Act 1954 ceasing by virtue of section 39 of this Act to apply to any such tenancy, Part II of that Act would not become applicable to it, then, if the term date falls or fell before the operative date or within the three months beginning with the operative date, the tenancy shall continue until the expiration of those three months unless sooner determined by a notice given by the tenant in accordance with section 5(1) or (2) of the Landlord and Tenant Act 1954 or by a landlord's notice to resume possession given before the operative date.

(3)   Where, on section 1 of the Landlord and Tenant Act 1954 ceasing by virtue of section 39 of this Act to apply to any such tenancy, Part II of that Act would become applicable to it, section 39 of this Act and paragraphs 1 to 4 above, together with the repeals made by Part I of Schedule 7 to this Act, shall not have effect in relation to the tenancy if at the operative date there is in force a landlord's notice to resume possession, or there is in force a notice given by the tenant in accordance with section 5(1) or (2) of the Landlord and Tenant Act 1954 to terminate the tenancy on a date within the three months beginning with the operative date:

Provided that this sub-paragraph shall cease to apply if the notice ceases to have effect without the tenancy being terminated.

8.—(1)   Where a statutory tenancy has by virtue of Part I of the Landlord and Tenant Act 1954 arisen before the operative date (within the meaning of paragraph 5 above), the operation of Part I of that Act in relation to the tenancy shall not be affected by section 39 of this Act and paragraphs 2 to 4 above, or the repeals made by Part I of Schedule 7 to this Act, except as provided by sub-paragraph (2) below.

(2)–(4) ...

9. ...

[10.—(1)  Section 74(2) of the Rent Act 1977 (which confers power by regulations to modify certain provisions of Part IV of that Act) shall apply also to this Schedule in so far as it affects section 67 or 72 of, or Schedule 11 to, that Act.

(2)  In so far as they relate to the Rent Act 1977, section 39 of this Act and this Schedule shall have effect subject to section 153 of that Act (which confers power to adapt the Act in its application to the Isles of Scilly) as if those provisions of this Act were contained in that Act.]

[134]

**NOTES**
Para 1: amends the Landlord and Tenant Act 1954, Sch 3, para 1 at [72].
Para 3: words omitted from sub-para (1) amend the Landlord and Tenant Act 1954, ss 6(1), 7 at [44], [45]; words in first (outer) pair of square brackets in sub-para (2)(c) substituted by the Rent Act 1968, s 117(2), Sch 15; all other words in square brackets substituted by the Rent Act 1977, s 155, Sch 23, para 46; sub-para (2)(a) repealed by the Housing Finance Act 1972, s 108(4), Sch 11, Pt II.
Paras 4, 6, 7: words in square brackets substituted by the Rent Act 1977, s 155, Sch 23, para 46.
Para 8: sub-paras (2), (3) repealed by the Housing Finance Act 1972, s 108(4), Sch 11, Pt II; sub-para (4) repealed by the Housing (Consequential Provisions) Act 1985, s 3, Sch 1, Pt I.
Para 9: repealed by the Rent Act 1968, s 117(5), Sch 17.
Para 10: substituted by the Rent Act 1977, s 155, Sch 23, para 46.

(*Sch 6 sets out the text of the Places of Worship (Enfranchisement) Act 1920, as amended; Sch 7 contains repeals only.*)

# CARAVAN SITES ACT 1968

## (1968 c 52)

### ARRANGEMENT OF SECTIONS

### PART I
### PROVISIONS FOR PROTECTION OF RESIDENTIAL OCCUPIERS

*An Act to restrict the eviction from caravan sites of occupiers of caravans and make other provision for the benefit of such occupiers; to secure the establishment of such sites by local authorities for the use of gipsies and other persons of nomadic habit, and control in certain areas the unauthorised occupation of land by such persons; to amend the definition of "caravan" in Part I of the Caravan Sites and Control of Development Act 1960; and for purposes connected with the matters aforesaid*

[26 July 1968]

### PART I
### PROVISIONS FOR PROTECTION OF RESIDENTIAL OCCUPIERS

**1    Application of Part I**

(1)  This Part of this Act applies in relation to any licence or contract (whether made before or after the passing of this Act) under which a person is entitled to station a caravan on a protected site (as defined by subsection (2) below) and occupy it as his residence, or to occupy as his residence a

caravan stationed on any such site; and any such licence or contract is in this Part referred to as a residential contract, and the person so entitled as the occupier.

(2) For the purposes of this Part of this Act a protected site is any land in respect of which a site licence is required under Part I of the Caravan Sites and Control of Development Act 1960 or would be so required if [paragraph 11 *or 11A of Schedule 1 to that Act* (*exemption of gypsy and other* local authority sites)] were omitted, not being land in respect of which the relevant planning permission or site licence—

    (a)    is expressed to be granted for holiday use only; or

    (b)    is otherwise so expressed or subject to such conditions that there are times of the year when no caravan may be stationed on the land for human habitation.

(3) References in this Part of this Act to the owner of a protected site are references to the person who is or would apart from any residential contract be entitled to possession of the land.

**[135]**

**NOTES**

Sub-s (2): words in square brackets substituted by the Housing Act 2004, s 209(1), (2), subject to s 209(3), (4) thereof; for the words in italics there are substituted the words "of Schedule 1 to that Act (exemption of" by the Housing (Scotland) Act 2006, s 171(1)(a), (2), in relation to Scotland only and except in relation to any conduct occurring before 28 May 2007.

## 2   Minimum length of notice

In any case where a residential contract is determinable by notice given by either party to the other, a notice so given shall be of no effect unless it is given not less than four weeks before the date on which it is to take effect.

**[136]**

## 3   Protection of occupiers against eviction and harassment

(1) Subject to the provisions of this section, a person shall be guilty of an offence under this section—

    (a)    if, during the subsistence of a residential contract, he unlawfully deprives the occupier of his occupation on the protected site of any caravan which the occupier is entitled by the contract to station and occupy, or to occupy, as his residence thereon;

    (b)    if, after the expiration or determination of a residential contract, he enforces, otherwise than by proceedings in the court, any right to exclude the occupier from the protected site or from any such caravan, or to remove or exclude any such caravan from the site;

    (c)    *if, whether during the subsistence or after the expiration or determination of a residential contract, with intent to cause the occupier—*

        (i)   *to abandon the occupation of the caravan or remove it from the site, or*

        (ii)   *to refrain from exercising any right or pursuing any remedy in respect thereof,*

    *he does acts [likely to interfere] with the peace or comfort of the occupier or persons residing with him, or persistently withdraws or withholds services or facilities reasonably required for the occupation of the caravan as a residence on the site.*

*[(1A) Subject to the provisions of this section, the owner of a protected site or his agent shall be guilty of an offence under this section if, whether during the subsistence or after the expiration or determination of a residential contract—*

    *(a)   he does acts likely to interfere with the peace or comfort of the occupier or persons residing with him, or*

    *(b)   he persistently withdraws or withholds services or facilities reasonably required for the occupation of the caravan as a residence on the site,*

*and (in either case) he knows, or has reasonable cause to believe, that that conduct is likely to cause the occupier to do any of the things mentioned in subsection (1)(c)(i) or (ii) of this section.*

*(1B)   References in subsection (1A) of this section to the owner of a protected site include references to a person with an estate or interest in the site which is superior to that of the owner.]*

(2) References in this section to the occupier include references to the person who was the occupier under a residential contract which has expired or been determined and, in the case of the death of the occupier (whether during the subsistence or after the expiration or determination of the contract), to any person then residing with the occupier being—

    (a)    the widow[, widower or surviving civil partner] of the occupier; or

    (b)    in default of a widow[, widower or surviving civil partner] so residing, any member of the occupier's family.

(3) A person guilty of an offence under this section shall, without prejudice to any liability or remedy to which he may be subject in civil proceedings, [be *liable—*

    (a)    *on summary conviction, to a fine not exceeding the statutory maximum or to imprisonment for a term not exceeding 12 months, or to both;*

    (*b*)    *on conviction on indictment, to a fine or to imprisonment for a term not exceeding 2 years, or to both].*

    (4)   In proceedings for an offence under paragraph (*a*) or (*b*) of subsection (1) of this section it shall be a defence to prove that the accused believed, and had reasonable cause to believe, that the occupier of the caravan had ceased to reside on the site.

    *[(4A)   In proceedings for an offence under subsection (1A) of this section it shall be a defence to prove that the accused had reasonable grounds for doing the acts or withdrawing or withholding the services or facilities in question.]*

    (5)   Nothing in this section applies to the exercise by any person of a right to take possession of a caravan of which he is the owner, other than a right conferred by or arising on the expiration or determination of a residential contract, or to anything done pursuant to the order of any court.

           **[137]**

**NOTES**

Sub-s (1): in para (c) words in square brackets substituted by the Housing Act 2004, s 210(1), (2), (6), except in relation to any conduct occurring before 18 January 2005; para (c) substituted by the Housing (Scotland) Act 2006, s 171(1)(b)(i), (2), in relation to Scotland only and except in relation to any conduct occurring before 28 May 2007, as follows:

    "(c)   if, whether during the subsistence or after the expiration or determination of a residential contract, the person—

        (i)   does anything likely to interfere with the peace or comfort of the occupier or persons residing with the occupier; or

        (ii)  persistently withdraws or withholds services or facilities reasonably required for the occupation of the caravan as a residence on the site,

    and (in either case) knows, or has reasonable cause to believe, that that conduct is likely to cause the occupier to abandon the occupation of the caravan or remove it from the site or to refrain from exercising any right or pursuing any remedy in relation to the caravan.".

Sub-ss (1A), (1B): inserted by the Housing Act 2004, s 210(1), (3), (6), except in relation to any conduct occurring before 18 January 2005; repealed by the Housing (Scotland) Act 2006, s 171(1)(b)(ii), (2), in relation to Scotland only and except in relation to any conduct occurring before 28 May 2007.

Sub-s (2): words in square brackets substituted by the Civil Partnership Act 2004, s 81, Sch 8, para 8.

Sub-s (3): words in square brackets substituted by the Housing Act 2004, s 210(1), (4), (6), except in relation to any conduct occurring before 18 January 2005; for the words in italics there are substituted the following words by the Housing (Scotland) Act 2006, s 171(1)(b)(iii), (2), in relation to Scotland only and except in relation to any conduct occurring before 28 May 2007:

    "liable on summary conviction—

       (a)   in the case of a first offence, to a fine not exceeding the statutory maximum;

       (b)   in the case of a second or subsequent offence, to a fine not exceeding the statutory maximum or to imprisonment for a term not exceeding 6 months, or to both".

Sub-s (4A): inserted by the Housing Act 2004, s 210(1), (5), (6), except in relation to any conduct occurring before 18 January 2005, and substituted by the Housing (Scotland) Act 2006, s 171(1)(b)(iv), (2), in relation to Scotland only and except in relation to any conduct occurring before 28 May 2007, as follows:

    "(4A)   In proceedings for an offence under subsection (1)(c) of this section it shall be a defence to prove that the accused had reasonable grounds for doing the acts or withdrawing or withholding the services or facilities in question.".

## 4   Provision for suspension of eviction orders

    (1)   If in proceedings by the owner of a protected site the court makes an order for enforcing in relation thereto any such right as is mentioned in paragraph (b) of subsection (1) of section 3 of this Act, the court may (without prejudice to any power apart from this section to postpone the operation or suspend the execution of an order, and subject to the following provisions of this section) suspend the enforcement of the order for such period not exceeding twelve months from the date of the order as the court thinks reasonable.

    (2)   Where the court by virtue of this section suspends the enforcement of an order, it may impose such terms and conditions, including conditions as to the payment of rent or other periodical payments or of arrears of such rent or payments, as the court thinks reasonable.

    (3)   The court may from time to time, on the application of either party, extend, reduce or terminate the period of suspension ordered by virtue of this section, or vary any terms or conditions imposed thereunder, but shall not extend the period of suspension for more than twelve months at a time.

    (4)   In considering whether or how to exercise its powers under this section, the court shall have regard to all the circumstances, and in particular to the questions—

       (a)   whether the occupier of the caravan has failed, whether before or after the expiration or determination of the relevant residential contract, to observe any terms or conditions of that contract, any conditions of the site licence, or any reasonable rules made by the owner for the management and conduct of the site or the maintenance of caravans thereon;

(b)    whether the occupier has unreasonably refused an offer by the owner to renew the residential contract or make another such contract for a reasonable period and on reasonable terms;

(c)    whether the occupier has failed to make reasonable efforts to obtain elsewhere other suitable accommodation for his caravan (or, as the case may be, another suitable caravan and accommodation for it).

(5)    Where the court makes such an order as is mentioned in subsection (1) of this section but suspends the enforcement of that order by virtue of this section, the court shall make no order for costs unless it appears to the court, having regard to the conduct of the owner or of the occupier, that there are special reasons for making such an order.

(6)    The court shall not suspend the enforcement of an order by virtue of this section [*if*—

(a)    *no site licence under Part 1 of that Act is in force in respect of the site, and*

(b)    *paragraph 11 or 11A of Schedule 1 to the Caravan Sites and Control of Development Act 1960 (c 2) does not apply;*]

and where a site licence in respect of the site is expressed to expire at the end of a specified period, the period for which enforcement may be suspended by virtue of this section shall not extend beyond the expiration of the licence.

**[138]**

**NOTES**

Sub-s (6): words in square brackets substituted by the Housing Act 2004, s 211, except in relation to proceedings begun before 18 January 2005; for the words in italics there are substituted the following words by the Housing (Scotland) Act 2006, s 171(1)(c), (3), in relation to Scotland only and except in relation to proceedings begun before 28 May 2007:

"if—

(a)    no site licence under Part 1 of the Caravan Sites and Control of Development Act 1960 (c 62) is in force in respect of the site; and

(b)    paragraph 11 of Schedule 1 to that Act does not apply;".

## 5   Supplementary

(1)    In this Part of this Act "the court" means the county court; and any powers of a county court in such proceedings as are mentioned in subsection (1) of section 4 of this Act may be exercised with the leave of the judge by any registrar of the court, except in so far as rules of court otherwise provide.

(2)    The power of the court under section 4 of this Act to suspend the enforcement of an order shall extend to any order made but not executed before the commencement of this Part of this Act.

(3)    Nothing in this Part of this Act shall affect the operation of section 13 of the Compulsory Purchase Act 1965.

(4)    Subsection (1) of section 12 of the Caravan Sites and Control of Development Act 1960 (power of site occupier to take possession and terminate a licence or tenancy in cases of contravention of section 1 of that Act) shall have effect subject to the foregoing provisions of this Part of this Act.

(5)    [The Protection from Eviction Act 1977] (protection against harassment and eviction without due process of law) shall not apply to any premises being a caravan stationed on a protected site.

**[139]**

**NOTES**

Sub-s (5): words in square brackets substituted by the Protection from Eviction Act 1977, s 12, Sch 1, para 3.

Modification: this section is modified in relation to Scotland by the Mobile Homes Act 1975, s 8, Schedule, Pt 2, para 2.

**6–12**    ((Pt 2) *Repealed by the Criminal Justice and Public Order Act 1994, ss 80(1), 168(3), Sch 11.*)

### PART III
### MISCELLANEOUS

## 13   Twin-unit caravans

(1)    A structure designed or adapted for human habitation which—

(a)    is composed of not more than two sections separately constructed and designed to be assembled on a site by means of bolts, clamps or other devices; and

(b)    is, when assembled, physically capable of being moved by road from one place to another (whether by being towed, or by being transported on a motor vehicle or trailer), shall not be treated as not being (or as not having been) a caravan within the meaning of Part I of the Caravan Sites and Control of Development Act 1960 by reason only that it cannot lawfully be so moved on a highway when assembled.

(2)   For the purposes of Part I of the Caravan Sites and Control of Development Act 1960, the expression "caravan" shall not include a structure designed or adapted for human habitation which falls within paragraphs (a) and (b) of the foregoing subsection if its dimensions when assembled exceed any of the following limits, namely—

    (a)   length (exclusive of any drawbar): [65.616] feet ([20] metres);

    (b)   width: [22.309] feet ([6.8] metres);

    (c)   overall height of living accommodation (measured internally from the floor at the lowest level to the ceiling at the highest level): [10.006] feet ([3.05] metres).

(3)   The Minister may by order made by statutory instrument after consultation with such persons or bodies as appear to him to be concerned substitute for any figure mentioned in subsection (2) of this section such other figure as may be specified in the order.

(4)   Any statutory instrument made by virtue of subsection (3) of this section shall be subject to annulment in pursuance of a resolution of either House of Parliament.

**[140]**

**NOTES**

Sub-s (2): in para (a) figures in square brackets substituted for original figures "60" and "18.288" respectively, in relation to England by the Caravan Sites Act 1968 and Social Landlords (Permissible Additional Purposes) (England) Order 2006 (Definition of Caravan) (Amendment) (England) Order 2006, SI 2006/2374, art 2(a) and in relation to Wales by the Caravan Sites Act 1968 (Amendment) (Wales) Order 2007, SI 2007/3163, art 2(a); in para (b) figures in square brackets substituted for original figures "20" and "6.096" respectively, in relation to England by SI 2006/2374, art 2(b) and in relation to Wales by SI 2007/3163, art 2(b); in para (c) figures in square brackets substituted for original figures "10" and "3.048" respectively, in relation to England by SI 2006/2374, art 2(c) and in relation to Wales by SI 2007/3163, art 2(c).

Transfer of functions: functions of the Minister, so far as exercisable in relation to Wales, are transferred to the National Assembly for Wales, by the National Assembly for Wales (Transfer of Functions) Order 1999, SI 1999/672, art 2, Sch 1.

**14   Offences**

(1)   Where an offence under this Act committed by a body corporate is proved to have been committed with the consent or connivance of or to be attributable to any neglect on the part of, any director, manager, secretary or other single officer of the body corporate or any person who is purporting to act in any such capacity, he as well as the body corporate shall be guilty of that offence and shall be liable to be proceeded against and punished accordingly.

(2)   Proceedings for an offence under this Act may be instituted by any local authority.

**[141]**

**15   Financial provision**

There shall be defrayed out of moneys provided by Parliament any increase which may arise in consequence of this Act in the sums payable out of money so provided in respect of rate support grant under the Local Government Act 1966.

**[142]**

**16   Interpretation**

In this Act the following expression have the following meanings that is to say—

    "caravan" has the same meaning as in Part I of the Caravan Sites and Control of Development Act 1960, as amended by this Act;

    *"gipsies" means persons of nomadic habit of life, whatever their race or origin, but does not include members of an organised group of travelling showmen, or of persons engaged in travelling circuses, travelling together as such;*

    "local authority" has the same meaning as in section 24 of the Caravan Sites and Control of Development Act 1960;

    "the Minister" means, in England other than Monmouthshire, the Minister of Housing and Local Government, and in Wales and Monmouthshire the Secretary of State;

    "planning permission" means permission under [Part III of the Town and Country Planning Act 1990].

**[143]**

**NOTES**

Definition "gipsies" repealed, except for the purposes of the definition of "protected site" in the Mobile Homes Act 1983, s 5(1), by the Criminal Justice and Public Order Act 1994, ss 80(1), (4), 168(3), Sch 11; in definition "planning permission" words in square brackets substituted by the Planning (Consequential Provisions) Act 1990, s 4, Sch 2, para 21(2).

Modification: this section is modified in relation to Scotland by the Mobile Homes Act 1975, s 8, Schedule, Pt 2, para 3.

Transfer of functions: functions of the Minister, so far as exercisable in relation to Wales, are transferred to the National Assembly for Wales, by the National Assembly for Wales (Transfer of Functions) Order 1999, SI 1999/672, art 2, Sch 1.

**17   Short title, commencement and extent**

(1)   This Act may be cited as the Caravan Sites Act 1968.

(2)   This Act, except Part II, shall come into force at the expiration of the period of one month beginning with the day on which it is passed, and Part II shall come into force on such date as the Minister may by order made by statutory instrument appoint.

[(3)   Part I and sections 13, 14(1), 16, subsection (1) above and this subsection shall extend to Scotland as read with section 8 of and the Schedule to the Mobile Homes Act 1975, but otherwise this Act does not extend to Scotland or Northern Ireland.]

**[144]**

NOTES

Sub-s (3): substituted by the Mobile Homes Act 1975, s 8, Schedule, Pt I, para 1.

# DEFECTIVE PREMISES ACT 1972

## (1972 c 35)

*An Act to impose duties in connection with the provision of dwellings and otherwise to amend the law of England and Wales as to liability for injury or damage caused to persons through defects in the state of premises*

[29 June 1972]

**1–3**   (*Outside the scope of this work.*)

**4   Landlord's duty of care in virtue of obligation or right to repair premises demised**

(1)   Where premises are let under a tenancy which puts on the landlord an obligation to the tenant for the maintenance or repair of the premises, the landlord owes to all persons who might reasonably be expected to be affected by defects in the state of the premises a duty to take such care as is reasonable in all the circumstances to see that they are reasonably safe from personal injury or from damage to their property caused by a relevant defect.

(2)   The said duty is owed if the landlord knows (whether as the result of being notified by the tenant or otherwise) or if he ought in all the circumstances to have known of the relevant defect.

(3)   In this section "relevant defect" means a defect in the state of the premises existing at or after the material time and arising from, or continuing because of, an act or omission by the landlord which constitutes or would if he had had notice of the defect, have constituted a failure by him to carry out his obligation to the tenant for the maintenance or repair of the premises; and for the purposes of the foregoing provision "the material time" means—

    (a)   where the tenancy commenced before this Act, the commencement of this Act; and

    (b)   in all other cases, the earliest of the following times, that is to say—

        (i)   the time when the tenancy commences;

        (ii)   the time when the tenancy agreement is entered into;

        (iii)   the time when possession is taken of the premises in contemplation of the letting.

(4)   Where premises are let under a tenancy which expressly or impliedly gives the landlord the right to enter the premises to carry out any description of maintenance or repair of the premises, then, as from the time when he first is, or by notice or otherwise can put himself, in a position to exercise the right and so long as he is or can put himself in that position, he shall be treated for the purposes of subsections (1) to (3) above (but for no other purpose) as if he were under an obligation to the tenant for that description of maintenance or repair of the premises; but the landlord shall not owe the tenant any duty by virtue of this subsection in respect of any defect in the state of the premises arising from, or continuing because of, a failure to carry out an obligation expressly imposed on the tenant by the tenancy.

(5)   For the purposes of this section obligations imposed or rights given by any enactment in virtue of a tenancy shall be treated as imposed or given by the tenancy.

(6)   This section applies to a right of occupation given by contract or any enactment and not amounting to a tenancy as if the right were a tenancy, and "tenancy" and cognate expressions shall be construed accordingly.

**NOTES**
Modification: this section is modified, where the RTM company has acquired the right to manage, by the Commonhold and Leasehold Reform Act 2002, s 102, Sch 7, para 2 at **[1266]**, **[1306]**.

**5** (*Outside the scope of this work.*)

**6 Supplemental**

(1) In this Act—
"disposal", in relation to premises, includes a letting, and an assignment or surrender of a tenancy, of the premises and the creation by contract of any other right to occupy the premises, and "dispose" shall be construed accordingly;

"personal injury" includes any disease and any impairment of a person's physical or mental condition;

"tenancy" means—

    (a) a tenancy created either immediately or derivatively out of the freehold, whether by a lease or underlease, by an agreement for a lease or underlease or by a tenancy agreement, but not including a mortgage term or any interest arising in favour of a mortgagor by his attorning tenant to his mortgagee; or

    (b) a tenancy at will or a tenancy on sufferance; or

    (c) a tenancy, whether or not constituting a tenancy at common law, created by or in pursuance of any enactment;

and cognate expressions shall be construed accordingly.

(2) Any duty imposed by or enforceable by virtue of any provision of this Act is in addition to any duty a person may owe apart from that provision.

(3) Any term of an agreement which purports to exclude or restrict, or has the effect of excluding or restricting, the operation of any of the provisions of this Act, or any liability arising by virtue of any such provision, shall be void.

(4) ...

**[146]**

**NOTES**
Sub-s (4): repeals the Occupiers' Liability Act 1957, s 4.

**7 Short title, commencement and extent**

(1) This Act may be cited as the Defective Premises Act 1972.

(2) This Act shall come into force on 1st January 1974.

(3) This Act does not extend to Scotland or Northern Ireland.

**[147]**

# HOUSING ACT 1974

(1974 c 44)

*An Act to extend the functions of the Housing Corporation and provide for the registration of, and the giving of financial assistance to, certain housing associations; to make further provision in relation to clearance areas and other areas in which living conditions are unsatisfactory or otherwise in need of improvement; to provide for the making of grants towards the improvement, repair and provision of housing accommodation and for the compulsory improvement of such accommodation; to amend the law relating to assistance for house purchase and improvement and expenditure in connection with the provision and improvement of housing accommodation and of hostels; to raise the rateable value limits under the Leasehold Reform Act 1967; to amend the Housing Finance Act 1972; to amend the law relating to the rights and obligations of landlords and tenants and the enforceability of certain covenants relating to the development of land; and for purposes connected therewith*

**[31 July 1974]**

**1–104** (*Ss 1–10, 12, 13, 15–30, 32–41, 43–49, 51, 56–78, 80–104 repealed by the Housing (Consequential Provisions) Act 1985, s 3, Sch 1, Pt I; s 11 repealed by the Taxation of Chargeable Gains Act 1992, s 290(3), Sch 12; ss 14, 31, 42, 50, 52–55, 79 repealed by the Housing Act 1980, ss 108(5), 109, 127(4), 130, 152, Sch 13, paras 2, 8, Sch 18, para 8, Sch 26.*)

# PART IX
## MISCELLANEOUS

**105–117**    *(Ss 105, 106, 108, 110–112, 114–117 repealed by the Housing (Consequential Provisions) Act 1985, s 3, Sch 1, Pt I; s 107 repealed by the Housing (Financial Provisions) (Scotland) Act 1978, s 16(2), Sch 3; s 109 repealed by the Housing Rents and Subsidies (Scotland) Act 1975, s 15, Sch 4; s 113 repealed by the Housing Rents and Subsidies Act 1975, s 17(5), Sch 6, Pt IV.)*

## 118    Rateable value limits for enfranchisement or extension under Leasehold Reform Act 1967

(1)    ...

(2)    In any case where, by virtue only of the amendments of section 1 of the Leasehold Reform Act 1967 effected by subsection (1) above, the right specified in subsection (1) of that section is conferred on a tenant, section 19 of that Act (retention of management powers for general benefit of neighbourhood) shall have effect in relation to the house and premises to which the tenant's right applies as if for the reference in subsection (1) of that section to an application made within two years beginning with the commencement of Part I of that Act there were substituted a reference to an application made within two years beginning with the date on which this Act is passed.

(3), (4)    ...

(5)    This section shall come into force on the passing of this Act.

**[148]**

**NOTES**

Sub-ss (1), (3), (4): amend the Leasehold Reform Act 1967, ss 1, 9 at **[78]**, **[91]**.

**119–130**    *(S 119 repealed by the Finance Act 1982, s 157, Sch 22, Pt V; s 120 repealed by the Income and Corporation Taxes Act 1988, s 844, Sch 31; ss 121, 122, 124, 125, 127–130 repealed by the Housing (Consequential Provisions) Act 1985, s 3, Sch 1, Pt I; s 123 repealed by the Protection from Eviction Act 1977, s 12, Sch 3; s 126 repealed by the Local Government (Miscellaneous Provisions) Act 1982, s 47, Sch 7, Pt XVI.)*

## 131    Short title, citation, commencement and extent

(1)    This Act may be cited as the Housing Act 1974.

(2)    ...

(3)    Except in so far as any provision of this Act otherwise provides, this Act shall come into operation on such day as the Secretary of State may by order appoint, and different days may be so appointed for different provisions and for different purposes.

(4)    Without prejudice to any express saving contained in Schedule 14 to this Act, an order under subsection (3) above appointing a day for the coming into operation of any provision of Schedule 13 or Schedule 15 to this Act may contain such savings with respect to the operation of that provision as appear to the Secretary of State to be appropriate [and an order under subsection (3) above may be revoked or varied by a further order under that subsection which may itself contain such savings with respect to the effect of the revocation or variation as appear to the Secretary of State to be appropriate].

(5)    ... in Part IX, sections ... [ ... 116], 118 ... of this Act extend to England and Wales only.

(6)    ...

(7)    This Act does not extend to Northern Ireland.

**[149]**

**NOTES**

Sub-s (2): repealed by the Housing (Consequential Provisions) Act 1985, s 3, Sch 1, Pt I.

Sub-s (4): words in square brackets added by the Local Government and Housing Act 1989, s 194(1), Sch 11, para 42.

Sub-s (5): figure in square brackets inserted by the Housing Rents and Subsidies (Scotland) Act 1975, s 17(4), Sch 5, para 24; words omitted repealed by the Housing (Consequential Provisions) Act 1985, s 3, Sch 1, Pt I.

Sub-s (6): applies to Scotland only.

Orders: the Housing (Revocation and Modification of Clearance Orders) Order 1990, SI 1990/1729.

SCHEDULES

*(Schs 1–7 repealed by the Housing (Consequential Provisions) Act 1985, s 3, Sch 1, Pt I.)*

SCHEDULE 8
REDUCTION OF RATEABLE VALUE IN CASE OF CERTAIN IMPROVEMENTS
Section 118

1.—(1)  Where the tenant, or any previous tenant, has made or contributed to the cost of an improvement on the premises comprised in the tenancy and the improvement is one to which this Schedule applies, then, if the tenant serves on the landlord a notice in the prescribed form requiring him to agree to a reduction under this Schedule, their rateable value as ascertained for the purposes of [section 1 of the Leasehold Reform Act 1967] shall be reduced by such amount, if any, as may be agreed or determined in accordance with the following provisions of this Schedule.

(2)  This Schedule applies to any improvement made by the execution of works amounting to structural alteration, extension or addition.

2.—(1)  The amount of any such reduction may at any time be agreed in writing between the landlord and the tenant.

(2)  Where, at the expiration of a period of six weeks from the service of a notice under paragraph 1 of this Schedule any of the following matters has not been agreed in writing between the landlord and the tenant, that is to say,—

    (a)    whether the improvement specified in the notice is an improvement to which this Schedule applies;

    (b)    what works were involved in it;

    (c)    whether the tenant or a previous tenant under the tenancy has made it or contributed to its cost; and

    (d)    what proportion his contribution, if any, bears to the whole cost;

the county court may on the application of the tenant determine that matter …

(3)  An application under the last foregoing sub-paragraph must be made within six weeks from the expiration of the period mentioned therein or such longer time as the court may allow.

3.—(1)  Where, after the service of a notice under paragraph 1 of this Schedule, it is agreed in writing between the landlord and tenant or determined by the county court—

    (a)    that the improvement specified in the notice is one to which this Schedule applies, and what works were involved in it, and

    (b)    that the tenant or a previous tenant under the tenancy has made it or contributed to its cost, and, in the latter case, what proportion his contribution bears to the whole cost, then if, at the expiration of a period of two weeks from the agreement or determination, it has not been agreed in writing between the landlord and the tenant whether any or what reduction is to be made under this Schedule, and the tenant, within four weeks from the expiration of that period, makes an application to the valuation officer for a certificate under the next following sub-paragraph, that question shall be determined in accordance with the certificate unless the landlord and the tenant otherwise agree in writing.

(2)  On any such application the valuation officer shall certify—

    (a)    whether or not the improvement has affected the rateable value on the 1st April, 1973 (as ascertained for the purposes of [section 1 of the Leasehold Reform Act 1967], of the hereditament of which the premises consist or, as the case may be, in which they are wholly or partly comprised, and

    (b)    if it has, the amount by which the rateable value would have been less if the improvement had not been made.

(3)  An application for such a certificate shall be in the prescribed form and shall state the name and address of the landlord, and the valuation officer shall send a copy of the certificate to the landlord.

(4)  Where the amount of the reduction under this Schedule falls to be determined in accordance with such a certificate, it shall be equal to the amount specified in pursuance of head (b) of sub-paragraph (2) of this paragraph, but proportionately reduced in any case where a proportion only of the cost was contributed by the tenant or a previous tenant under the tenancy.

(5)  Where at the time of an application for a certificate under this paragraph a proposal for an alteration in the valuation list relating to the hereditament is pending and the alteration would have effect from a date earlier than the 2nd April, 1973, the valuation officer shall not issue the certificate until the proposal is settled.

[4.  Where a notice under paragraph 1 of this Schedule is served on or after 21st December 1979, the tenant shall bear the reasonable costs incurred by the landlord in investigating any matter specified in it.]

FORM

*Leasehold Reform Act 1967*

Notice by Tenant to Landlord of Tenant's Improvements affecting Rateable Value

*Date*................

*To*.................... *landlord of*....................

PART I
STATUTES

1.　[I] [A previous tenant of the above mentioned premises under the tenancy] [made] [contributed to the cost of] the improvement[s] to the above mentioned premises particulars of which are set out in the First Schedule hereto [Note 1].

2.　I hereby require you to agree to a reduction in the rateable value of the premises for the purposes of the Leasehold Reform Act 1967.

3.　I propose that the rateable value shall be reduced to　　£　　(Note 2).

4.　If you do not agree to this reduction [Note 3], do you agree that—
   (a)　the improvement[s] [is] [are] [an] improvement[s] made by the execution of works amounting to the structural alteration or extension of the premises or a structural addition thereto;
   (b)　the works set out in the Second Schedule hereto were involved in the making of the improvement[s];
   (c)　[I] [A previous tenant under the tenancy] [made the improvement[s]] [contributed to the cost of the improvement[s]];
   (d)　the proportion of the cost borne by me or a previous tenant is] ...

Signature of tenant....................

*First Schedule*

Description of Improvement(s)

*Second Schedule*

Description of Works

Strike out words in square brackets if inapplicable.

Note 1
　　The improvement must be one made by the execution of works amounting to the structural alteration or extension of the premises or a structural addition thereto, e.g. the erection of a garage in the grounds.

Note 2
　　If the amount of the reduction is agreed in writing between the landlord and the tenant, the amount of the reduced rateable value as so agreed will be substituted for the purposes of the Leasehold Reform Act 1967, for the rateable value on 1st April, 1973.

Note 3
　　If the amount of the reduction is not agreed in writing between the landlord and the tenant, the Valuation Officer will have to decide whether the improvement has affected the rateable value of the premises, and if so, what that value would have been had the improvement not been made. The name and address of the Valuation Officer can be obtained from the local authority. Before, however, an application is made to the Valuation Officer, the Landlord and the tenant must try to agree in writing on the items mentioned at (a) to (d) of this paragraph, or such of those items as are material. If at the end of a period of six weeks after the service of this notice any of these items have not been agreed, the tenant may, within a further six weeks or so much longer time as the court may allow, apply to the county court to settle the matter.

　　If it has either been agreed or determined by the county court that there has been an improvement of the kind described in Note 1 involving specified works, and that the improvement was carried out by the tenant or a previous tenant, or that the tenant or a previous tenant contributed to its cost, and in the latter case what proportion the contribution bears to the whole cost of the works, then, if within a period of two weeks after the agreement or determination of the county court the landlord and the tenant have still not agreed in writing whether any or what reduction is to be made, the tenant has a further four weeks in which to make an application in the statutory form to the Valuation Officer for a certificate as to whether or not the improvement has affected the rateable value, and if so, the amount by which that value would have been less if the improvement had not been made.

# FORM

*Leasehold Reform Act 1967*

Application by Tenant to Valuation Officer for Certificate as to Reduction for the purposes of the Leasehold Reform Act 1967, in the Rateable Value of premises on account of Tenant's Improvements

Date...................

To the Valuation Officer.

1.   I am the tenant of                     , and my landlord is                     of

2.   It has been [agreed in writing between me and my landlord] [determined by the county court] that the improvement[s] specified in the First Schedule hereto [is an improvement] [are improvements] to which [Schedule 8 to the Housing Act 1974] applies, and that I or a previous tenant under the tenancy made the improvement[s] or contributed to [its] [their] cost, and that the works specified in the Second Schedule hereto were involved in the improvement[s].

3.   It has not been agreed between me and my landlord whether any or what reduction is to be made under said Schedule [8] in the rateable value of the premises for the purposes of the Leasehold Reform Act 1967, and I hereby make application to you for a certificate under paragraph 3(2) of the said Schedule Seven (Note 4).

Signature of Tenant................

*First Schedule*

Description of Improvement(s)

*Second Schedule*

Description of Works

Strike out words in square brackets if inapplicable.

Note 4
  If the Valuation Officer certifies that the rateable value would have been less but for the improvement by the amounts mentioned in the certificate, the rateable value will be reduced by those amounts for the purposes of the Leasehold Reform Act 1967 except in the case where a proportion only of the cost was contributed by the tenant, in which case the amounts of the reductions will be proportionately reduced accordingly.

**[150]**

---

**NOTES**
  Words in square brackets in paras 1(1) and 3(2)(a), and the references to "Schedule 8 to the Housing Act 1974" and "8" in paras 2, 3, respectively, of the second Form, substituted, words omitted from para 2(2) repealed, and para 4 inserted, by the Housing Act 1980, ss 141, 152, Sch 21, para 8, Sch 26. The remaining square brackets in the first and second Forms appear in the Queen's Printer's copy, and denote alternative versions of the respective Forms.

---

*(Schs 9, 10, 12, 14, 15 repealed by the Housing (Consequential Provisions) Act 1985, s 3, Sch 1, Pt I; Sch 11 repealed by the Finance Act 1982, s 157, Sch 22, Pt V; Sch 13 in part amends the Land Compensation Act 1973, ss 29, 37, 39, 43, in part applies to Scotland only, in part spent, remainder repealed by the Housing Rents and Subsidies Act 1975, s 17(5), Sch 6, Pt IV, the Housing Rents and Subsidies (Scotland) Act 1975, s 15(2), Sch 4, the Rent Act 1977, s 155(5), Sch 25, the Criminal Law Act 1977, s 65(5), Sch 13, and the Housing (Consequential Provisions) Act 1985, s 3, Sch 1, Pt I.)*

# MOBILE HOMES ACT 1975

(1975 c 49)

*An Act to amend the law in respect of mobile homes and residential caravan sites; and for purposes connected therewith*

[1 August 1975]

**1–6**   *(Repealed by the Mobile Homes Act 1983, s 6(2), Sch 2.)*

**7   Power to prescribe minimum standards**

 (1)   Without prejudice to his powers under section 5 (6) of the Act of 1960, the Secretary of State may by order prescribe minimum standards with respect to the layout of, and the provision of

facilities, services and equipment for protected sites within the meaning of Part I of the Act of 1968 on which there are mobile homes occupied as an only or main residence.

(2) An order made under subsection (1) above may apply generally or to a particular area or to protected sites in a particular category and may prescribe different minimum standards in relation to protected sites in different categories.

(3) The power of the Secretary of State to make orders under this section shall be exercisable by statutory instrument.

(4) An order under subsection (1) above shall be subject to annulment in pursuance of a resolution of either House of Parliament.

(5) Any power of the Secretary of State to make an order under any provision of this section shall include a power to make an order varying or revoking any order previously made under that provision.

**[151]**

**NOTES**
Transfer of functions: functions of the Secretary of State, so far as exercisable in relation to Wales, are transferred to the National Assembly for Wales, by the National Assembly for Wales (Transfer of Functions) Order 1999, SI 1999/672, art 2, Sch 1.

## 8   Extension of Act of 1968 to Scotland

Part I (relating to the protection of residential occupiers) and Part III (miscellaneous) of the Act of 1968 shall apply to Scotland subject to the modifications contained in the Schedule to this Act.

**[152]**

## 9   Interpretation

(1) In this Act the following expressions have the following meanings, that is to say—
"the Act of 1960" means the Caravan Sites and Control of Development Act 1960;
"the Act of 1968" means the Caravan Sites Act 1968;
.....
"mobile home" has the same meaning as "caravan" in Part I of the Act of 1960 as amended by the Act of 1968;
.....

(2) ...

**[153]**

**NOTES**
Sub-s (1): definitions "the court", "occupier", "owner", "planning permission", "protected site" and "site licence" repealed by the Mobile Homes Act 1983, s 6(2), Sch 2.
Sub-s (2): repealed by the Mobile Homes Act 1983, s 6(2), Sch 2.

## 10   Short title, commencement and extent

(1) This Act may be cited as the Mobile Homes Act 1975.

(2) This Act shall come into force at the expiration of the period of two months beginning with the day on which it is passed.

(3) This Act does not extend to Northern Ireland.

**[154]**

(*Part I of the Schedule substitutes the Caravan Sites Act 1968, s 17(3), in relation to Scotland only; Pt II substitutes the Caravan Sites Act 1968, ss 5, 16, in relation to Scotland only.*)

# RENT (AGRICULTURE) ACT 1976

(1976 c 80)

ARRANGEMENT OF SECTIONS

PART I
PRELIMINARY

*An Act to afford security of tenure for agricultural workers housed by their employers, and their successors; to make further provision as to the rents and other conditions of tenure of such persons, including amendments of the Rent Act 1968; to impose duties on housing authorities as respects agricultural workers and their successors; and for purposes connected with those matters*

[22 November 1976]

**NOTES**

Phasing out of protected occupancies and certain statutory tenancies: by the Housing Act 1988, s 34(4) at **[765]**, a licence or tenancy entered into on or after 15 January 1989 cannot be a relevant licence or relevant tenancy for the purposes of this Act unless it is entered into in pursuance of a contract made before that date or it is granted to an existing protected occupier or statutory tenant, within the meaning of this Act, and is so granted by the person who at that time was the landlord or licensor under the protected occupancy or statutory tenancy in question. In the case of tenancies and licences entered into on or after 15 January 1989, the protection afforded by this Act is superseded by that provided by Chapter III (ss 24, 25, Sch 3) of Pt I of the 1988 Act at **[760]**, **[761]** and **[790]**, which creates a variant of the assured tenancies created by Chapter I (ss 1–19, Schs 1, 2) of that Part of that Act at **[729]**–**[752]** and **[782]**–**[788]**. These new tenancies and licences are referred to as assured agricultural occupancies. Tenancies and licences entered into before 15 January 1989 are not assured agricultural occupancies, and agricultural workers who already have the protection of this Act will retain that protection. However, the licences and tenancies of certain serving or former agricultural workers, and licences and tenancies of qualifying successors of agricultural workers, fulfilling any of the conditions laid down in Sch 3 to the 1988 Act at **[790]** are to be assured agricultural occupancies. If they are also assured tenancies within s 1 of, and Sch 1 to, the 1988 Act at **[729]**, **[782]** they will be covered by Chapter I of Pt I of that Act, and if they are not assured tenancies they will be covered by that Chapter as applied, with modifications, by Chapter III of that Part of that Act to such assured agricultural occupancies.

Transfer of functions: as to the functions of Ministers of the Crown under this Act, so far as exercisable in relation to Wales, being transferred to the National Assembly for Wales, see the National Assembly for Wales (Transfer of Functions) Order 1999, SI 1999/672, art 2, Sch 1.

PART I
PRELIMINARY

**1 Interpretation and commencement**

(1) In this Act—

    (a) "agriculture" includes—

        (i) dairy-farming and livestock keeping and breeding (whether those activities involve the use of land or not);

        (ii) the production of any consumable produce which is grown for sale or for consumption or other use for the purposes of a trade or business or of any other undertaking (whether carried on for profit or not);

        (iii) the use of land as grazing, meadow or pasture land or orchard or osier land;

        (iv) the use of land for market gardens or nursery grounds; and

        (v) forestry;

    (b) "forestry" includes—

        (i) the use of land for nursery grounds for trees, and

        (ii) the use of land for woodlands where that use is ancillary to the use of land for other agricultural purposes.

(2) For the purposes of the definition in subsection (1)(a) above—

    "consumable produce" means produce grown for consumption or other use after severance or separation from the land or other growing medium on or in which it is grown;

    "livestock" includes any animal which is kept for the production of food, wool, skins or fur, or for the purpose of its use in the carrying on of any agricultural activity, and for the purposes of this definition "animal" includes bird but does not include fish.

(3) The expressions listed in column 1 of Schedule 1 to this Act have for the purposes of this Act the meanings given by the provisions shown in column 2 of the Schedule.

(4) In this Act "relevant licence" and "relevant tenancy" have the meanings given by Schedule 2 to this Act.

(5) Schedule 3 to this Act, of which—

    (a) Part I is for determining for the purposes of this Act—

        (i) whether a person is a qualifying worker,

        (ii)    whether a person is incapable of whole-time work in agriculture, or work in agriculture as a permit worker, in consequence of a qualifying injury or disease, and

        (iii)   whether a dwelling-house is in qualifying ownership,

  (b)    Part II postpones the operation of this Act in relation to certain persons employed in forestry, and

  (c)    Part III contains supplementary provisions,

shall have effect.

    (6)   This Act shall, subject to subsection (7) below, come into force on such date as the Secretary of State and the Minister of Agriculture, Fisheries and Food acting jointly may by order contained in a statutory instrument appoint, and that date is in this Act called "the operative date".

    (7)   Subsection (6) above has effect subject to the said Part II of Schedule 3 to this Act.

[155]

---

**NOTES**

  Orders: the Rent (Agriculture) Act 1976 (Commencement No 1) Order 1976, SI 1976/2124.

---

*Protected occupancies*

## 2  Protected occupiers in their own right

    (1)   Where a person has, in relation to a dwelling-house, a relevant licence or tenancy and the dwelling-house is in qualifying ownership, or has been in qualifying ownership at any time during the subsistence of the licence or tenancy (whether it was at the time a relevant licence or tenancy or not), he shall be a protected occupier of the dwelling-house if—

  (a)   he is a qualifying worker, or

  (b)   he has been a qualifying worker at any time during the subsistence of the licence or tenancy (whether it was at the time a relevant licence or tenancy or not).

    (2)   Where a person has, in relation to a dwelling-house, a relevant licence or tenancy and the dwelling-house is in qualifying ownership, or has been in qualifying ownership at any time during the subsistence of the licence or tenancy (whether it was at the time a relevant licence or tenancy or not), he shall be a protected occupier of the dwelling-house if and so long as he is incapable of whole-time work in agriculture, or work in agriculture as a permit worker, in consequence of a qualifying injury or disease.

    (3)   A person who has in relation to a dwelling-house a relevant licence or tenancy shall be a protected occupier of the dwelling-house if—

  (a)   immediately before the licence or tenancy was granted, he was a protected occupier or statutory tenant of the dwelling-house in his own right, or

  (b)   the licence or tenancy was granted in consideration of his giving up possession of another dwelling-house of which he was such an occupier or such a tenant.

    (4)   In this Act—

    "protected occupier in his own right" means a person who is a protected occupier by virtue of subsection (1), (2) or (3) above;

    "statutory tenant in his own right" means a person who is a statutory tenant by virtue of section 4(1) below and who, immediately before he became such a tenant, was a protected occupier in his own right.

[156]

---

**NOTES**

  By the Housing Act 1988, s 38 at **[769]**, where a tenancy entered into before, or in pursuance of a contract made before, 15 January 1989, is transferred on or after that date from a public body falling within sub-s (5) of that section or a housing association to different ownership, it will not be a protected occupancy within the meaning of this section. Such transferred tenancies will generally become assured tenancies under Chapter I of Pt I of the 1988 Act at **[729]**–**[752]**, or assured agricultural occupancies under Chapter III of that Part of that Act at **[760]**, **[761]**.

---

## 3  Protected occupiers by succession

    (1)   Subsection (2) or, as the case may be, subsection (3) below shall have effect for determining what person (if any) is a protected occupier of a dwelling-house after the death of a person ("the original occupier") who, immediately before his death, was a protected occupier of the dwelling-house in his own right.

    [(2)   Where the original occupier was a person who died leaving a surviving partner who was residing in the dwelling-house immediately before the original occupier's death then, after the original occupier's death, if the surviving partner has, in relation to the dwelling-house, a relevant licence or tenancy, the surviving partner shall be a protected occupier of the dwelling-house.]

    (3)   Where—

(a)    the original occupier was not a person who died leaving a [surviving partner] who was residing [in the dwelling-house immediately before [the original occupier's] death], but

(b)    one or more persons who were members of [the original occupier's] family were residing with [the original occupier] at the time of and for the period of six months immediately before [the original occupier's] death,

then, after [the original occupier's] death, if that person or, as the case may be, any of those persons has, in relation to the dwelling-house, a relevant licence or tenancy, that person or, as the case may be, such one of the persons having such a licence or tenancy as may be decided by agreement, or in default of agreement by the county court, shall be a protected occupier of the dwelling-house.

[(3A)    In subsections (2) and (3) above "surviving partner" means surviving spouse or surviving civil partner.]

(4)    A person who has, in relation to a dwelling-house, a relevant licence or tenancy shall be a protected occupier of the dwelling-house if—

(a)    immediately before the licence or tenancy was granted, he was a protected occupier or statutory tenant of the dwelling-house by succession, or

(b)    the licence or tenancy was granted in consideration of his giving up possession of another dwelling-house of which he was such an occupier or such a tenant.

(5)    In this Act—

"protected occupier by succession" means a person who is a protected occupier by virtue of subsection (2), (3) or (4) above;

"statutory tenant by succession" means a person who is a statutory tenant by virtue of section 4(1) below and who, immediately before he became such a tenant, was a protected occupier by succession, or a person who is a statutory tenant by virtue of section 4(3) or (4) below.

(6)    A dwelling-house is, in this Act, referred to as subject to a protected occupancy where there is a protected occupier of it.

**[157]**

---

**NOTES**

Sub-s (2): substituted by the Civil Partnership Act 2004, s 81, Sch 8, para 9(1), (2).

Sub-s (3): words in second (outer) pair of square brackets substituted by the Housing Act 1980, s 76(3); other words in square brackets substituted by the Civil Partnership Act 2004, s 81, Sch 8, para 9(1), (3).

Sub-s (3A): inserted by the Civil Partnership Act 2004, s 81, Sch 8, para 9(1), (4).

---

*Statutory tenancies*

## 4  Statutory tenants and tenancies

(1)    Subject to section 5 below, where a person ceases to be a protected occupier of a dwelling-house on the termination, whether by notice to quit or by virtue of section 16(3) of this Act or otherwise, of his licence or tenancy he shall, if and so long as he occupies the dwelling-house as his residence, be the statutory tenant of it.

(2)    Subject to section 5 below, subsection (3), … below shall have effect for determining what person (if any) is the statutory tenant of a dwelling-house at any time after the death of a person ("the original occupier") who was, immediately before his death, a protected occupier or statutory tenant of the dwelling-house in his own right.

[(3)    If the original occupier was a person who died leaving a surviving partner who was residing in the dwelling-house immediately before the original occupier's death then, after the original occupier's death, unless the surviving partner is a protected occupier of the dwelling-house by virtue of section 3(2) above, the surviving partner shall be the statutory tenant if and so long as he occupies the dwelling-house as his residence.]

(4)    Where—

(a)    the original occupier was not a person who died leaving a [surviving partner] who was residing [in the dwelling-house immediately before [the original occupier's] death], but

(b)    one or more persons who were members of [the original occupier's] family were residing with [the original occupier] [in the dwelling-house] at the time of and for the [period of 2 years] immediately before [the original occupier's] death.

then, after [the original occupier's] death, unless that person or, as the case may be, one of those persons is a protected occupier of the dwelling-house by virtue of section 3(3) above, that person or, as the case may be, such one of those persons as may be decided by agreement, or in default of agreement by the county court, shall be [entitled to an assured tenancy of the dwelling-house by succession].

(5)    In [subsections (1) and (3)] above the phrase "if and so long as he occupies the dwelling-house as his residence" shall be construed in accordance with [section 2(3) of the Rent Act 1977] (construction of that phrase in the corresponding provisions of that Act).

[(5ZA) In subsections (3) and (4) above "surviving partner" means surviving spouse or surviving civil partner.

(5A)　For the purposes of subsection (3) above—
　　(a)　a person who was living with the original occupier as his or her husband or wife shall be treated as the spouse of the original occupier, and
　　(b)　a person who was living with the original occupier as if they were civil partners shall be treated as the civil partner of the original occupier,

and, subject to subsection (5B) below, "surviving spouse" and "surviving civil partner" in subsection (5ZA) above shall be construed accordingly.]

[(5B)　If, immediately after the death of the original occupier, there is, by virtue of subsection (5A) above, more than one person who fulfils the conditions in subsection (3) above, such one of them as may be decided by agreement or, in default of agreement by the county court, shall be the statutory tenant by virtue of that subsection.

(5C)　If the original occupier died within the period of 18 months beginning on the operative date, then, for the purposes of subsection (3) above, a person who was residing in the dwelling-house with the original occupier at the time of his death and for the period which began 6 months before the operative date and ended at the time of his death shall be taken to have been residing with the original occupier for the period of 2 years immediately before his death; and in this subsection "the operative date" means the date on which Part I of the Housing Act 1988 came into force.]

(6)　A dwelling-house is, in this Act, referred to as subject to a statutory tenancy where there is a statutory tenant of it.

**[158]**

**NOTES**

Sub-s (2): words omitted repealed by the Housing Act 1988, s 39(4), Sch 4, Pt II, para 10, in relation to cases where the original occupier dies after 15 January 1989.

Sub-s (3): substituted by the Civil Partnership Act 2004, s 81, Sch 8, para 10(1), (2).

Sub-s (4): words in second (outer) pair of square brackets substituted by the Housing Act 1980, s 76(3); words in sixth pair of square brackets inserted and words in seventh and tenth pairs of square brackets substituted by the Housing Act 1988, s 39(4), Sch 4, Pt II, para 11, in relation to cases where the original occupier dies after 15 January 1989; other words in square brackets substituted by the Civil Partnership Act 2004, s 81, Sch 8, para 10(1), (3).

Sub-s (5): words in first pair of square brackets substituted by the Housing Act 1988, s 39(4), Sch 4, Pt II, para 12, in relation to cases where the original occupier dies after 15 January 1989; words in second pair of square brackets substituted by the Rent Act 1977, s 155, Sch 23, para 72.

Sub-ss (5ZA), (5A): substituted for sub-s (5A) (as originally inserted by the Housing Act 1988, s 39(4), Sch 4, Pt II, para 12), by the Civil Partnership Act 2004, s 81, Sch 8, para 10(1), (4).

Sub-ss (5B), (5C): inserted, together with original sub-s (5A), by the Housing Act 1988, s 39(4), Sch 4, Pt II, para 12, in relation to cases where the original occupier dies after 15 January 1989.

See further the Housing Act 1988, s 39(5) at **[770]**, which provides that where by virtue of the amendments made to this section by s 39(4) of the 1988 Act, a person becomes entitled to an assured tenancy within s 1 of, and Sch 1 to, that Act at **[729]**, **[782]**, by succession, the tenancy is to be an assured periodic tenancy and the provisions of s 39(6) of that Act apply thereto. By s 39(8) of that Act, if, immediately before his death, the predecessor was a protected occupier or statutory tenant within the meaning of this Act, the assured periodic tenancy of the successor is to be an assured agricultural occupancy within the Housing Act 1988, Pt I, Chapter III (ss 24, 25 and Sch 3) at **[760]**, **[761]** and **[790]**, whether or not it fulfils the conditions in s 24(1) of that Act.

## 5　No statutory tenancy where landlord's interest belongs to Crown or to local authority, etc

[(1)　A person shall not at any time be a statutory tenant of a dwelling-house if the interest of his immediate landlord would, at that time—
　　(a)　for Her Majesty for the purposes of a government department;
　　(b)　be held in trust for Her Majesty for the purposes of a government department

except that an interest belonging to Her Majesty in right of the Crown shall not prevent a person from being a statutory tenant if the interest is under the management of the Crown Estate Commissioners].

(2)　A person shall not at any time be a statutory tenant of a dwelling-house if the interest of his immediate landlord, would, at that time, belong to any of the bodies specified in subsection (3) below.

(3)　The bodies referred to in subsection (2) above are—
　　(a)　the council of a county[, county borough] or district or, in the application of this Act to the Isles of Scilly, the Council of those Isles;
　　(b)　... the council of a London borough or the Common Council of the City of London;
　　[(baa) a police authority established under [section 3 of the Police Act 1996][ ... ];]
　　[(ba) ...
　　(bb)　a joint authority established by Part IV of the Local Government Act 1985;]
　　[(bba)　an authority established for an area in England by an order under section 207 of the Local Government and Public Involvement in Health Act 2007 (joint waste authorities);]

[(bbb) the London Fire and Emergency Planning Authority;]

[(bc) the Broads Authority;]

[(bd) any National Park authority;]

(c) the [English new towns residuary body];

(d) the Housing Corporation;

[(da) ... ]

(e) a development corporation established by an order made, or having effect as if made, under the [New Towns Act 1981]; and

(f) a housing trust (as defined in [section 15(5) of the Rent Act 1977]) which is a charity within the meaning of [the Charities Act 1993].

[(3A)    In subsection (3)(c) above "English new towns residuary body" means the Homes and Communities Agency so far as exercising functions in relation to anything transferred (or to be transferred) to it as mentioned in section 52(1)(a) to (d) of the Housing and Regeneration Act 2008.]

(4)    If any of the conditions for the time being specified in [section 15(4) of the Rent Act 1977] (conditions for the operation of the corresponding provision of that Act) is fulfilled, a person shall not be a statutory tenant of a dwelling-house at any time if the interest of his immediate landlord would, at that time, [belong to a housing association which—

(a) is [a registered social landlord within the meaning of the Housing Act 1985 (see section 5(4) and (5) of that Act)], or

(b) is a co-operative housing association within the meaning of [the Housing Associations Act 1985].]

**[159]**

---

**NOTES**

Sub-s (1): substituted by the Housing Act 1980, s 73(3).

Sub-s (3): words in square brackets in para (a) inserted by the Local Government (Wales) Act 1994, s 22(2), Sch 8, para 2; words omitted from para (b) repealed by the Local Government Act 1985, s 102(2), Sch 17; para (baa) inserted by the Police and Magistrates' Courts Act 1994, s 43, Sch 4, Pt II, para 52, words in first pair of square brackets therein substituted by the Police Act 1996, s 103(1), Sch 7, Pt I, para 1(1), (2)(m), and words omitted from second pair of square brackets therein inserted by the Police Act 1997, s 134(1), Sch 9, para 38 and repealed by the Criminal Justice and Police Act 2001, ss 128(1), 137, Sch 6, Pt 3, para 62, Sch 7, Pt 5(1); para (ba) inserted by the Local Government Act 1985, s 84, Sch 14, Pt II, para 55 and repealed by the Education Reform Act 1988, s 237(2), Sch 13, Pt I; para (bb) inserted by the Local Government Act 1985, ss 84, Sch 14, Pt II, para 55; para (bba) inserted by the Local Government and Public Involvement in Health Act 2007, s 209(2), Sch 13, Pt 2, para 34; para (bbb) inserted by the Greater London Authority Act 1999, s 328, Sch 29, Pt I, para 25; para (bc) inserted by the Norfolk and Suffolk Broads Act 1988, s 21, Sch 6, para 17; para (bd) inserted by the Environment Act 1995, s 78, Sch 10, para 17; words in square brackets in para (c) substituted by the Housing and Regeneration Act 2008, s 56, Sch 8, para 22(1), (2); para (da) inserted by the Housing Act 1988, s 140(1), Sch 17, Pt II, para 98 and repealed by the Government of Wales Act 1998, ss 141, 152, Sch 18, Pt VI; words in square brackets in para (e) substituted by the New Towns Act 1981, s 81, Sch 12, para 23; in para (f) words in first pair of square brackets substituted by the Rent Act 1977, s 155, Sch 23, para 73, and words in second pair of square brackets substituted by the Charities Act 1993, s 98(1), Sch 6, para 30.

Sub-s (3A): inserted by the Housing and Regeneration Act 2008, s 56, Sch 8, para 22(1), (3).

Sub-s (4): words in first pair of square brackets substituted by the Rent Act 1977, s 155, Sch 23, para 73; words in second (outer) pair of square brackets substituted by the Housing (Consequential Provisions) Act 1985, s 4, Sch 2, para 33(1), (2) and words in third and fourth (inner) pairs of square brackets substituted by the Housing Act 1996 (Consequential Provisions) Order 1996, SI 1996/2325, art 5(1), Sch 2, para 5.

Modifications: "joint authority" includes an authority established for the purposes of waste regulation or disposal by virtue of the Waste Regulation and Disposal (Authorities) Order 1985, SI 1985/1884, art 10, Sch 3, para 4. A residuary body established by the Local Government Act 1985, s 57, and the Residuary Body for Wales established by the Local Government (Wales) Act 1994, s 39, are included among the bodies to which sub-s (2) above applies; see s 57(7) of, and Sch 13, para 14(c) to, the 1985 Act, and s 39(2) of, and Sch 13, para 24(e) to, the 1994 Act. In sub-s (3)(d) the reference to the Housing Corporation shall be treated as if it were a reference to the Regulator of Social Housing: see the Transfer of Housing Corporation Functions (Modifications and Transitional Provisions) Order 2008, SI 2008/2839, arts 1(2), 3, 6, Schedule.

---

## PART II
### SECURITY OF TENURE

*Protected occupancies and statutory tenancies*

## 6    Grounds for possession

(1)    A court shall not make an order for possession of a dwelling-house subject to a protected occupancy or statutory tenancy except in the Cases in Schedule 4 to this Act.

(2)    A landlord who obtains an order for possession of a dwelling-house as against a statutory tenant shall not be required to give to the statutory tenant any notice to quit.

(3)    Where in Case IX in the said Schedule a landlord obtains an order for possession of the dwelling-house, and it is subsequently made to appear to the court that the order was obtained by

misrepresentation or concealment of material facts, the court may order the landlord to pay to the former tenant such sum as appears sufficient as compensation for damage or loss sustained by the tenant as a result of the order.

(4)   In subsection (3) above and in Schedule 4 to this Act "tenant" means a protected occupier or a statutory tenant.

(5)   Section 7 below has effect as regards the Cases in Part I of the said Schedule.

(6)   If, apart from subsection (1) above, the landlord would be entitled to recover possession of a dwelling-house subject to a protected occupancy or statutory tenancy, the court shall make an order for possession if the circumstances of the case are as specified in any of the Cases in Part II of the said Schedule.

**[160]**

## 7   Discretion of court in giving possession

(1)   This section applies in the Cases in Part I of Schedule 4 to this Act.

(2)   In those Cases the court shall not make an order unless it considers it reasonable to do so.

[(2A)   In those cases the court may adjourn for such period or periods as it thinks fit.]

(3)   On the making of the order for possession, or at any time before execution of the order, the court may—
    (a)    stay or suspend execution of the order, or
    (b)    postpone the date of possession,
for such period or periods as the court thinks fit.

[(4)   On any such adjournment as is referred to in subsection (2A) above or any such stay, suspension or postponement as is referred to in subsection (3) above, the court shall, unless it considers that to do so would cause exceptional hardship to the tenant or would otherwise be unreasonable, impose conditions with regard to payment by the tenant of arrears of rent (if any) and rent or payments in respect of occupation after termination of the tenancy (mesne profits) and may impose such other conditions as it thinks fit.]

(5)   If conditions so imposed are complied with, the court may if it thinks fit discharge or rescind the order for possession,

[(5A)   Subsection (5B) below applies in any case where—
    (a)    proceedings are brought for possession of a dwelling-house which is subject to a protected occupancy or statutory tenancy;
    (b)    the tenant's spouse or former spouse, having rights of occupation under the Matrimonial Homes Act 1967, is then in occupation of the dwelling-house; and
    (c)    the tenancy is terminated as a result of those proceedings.

(5B)   In any case to which this subsection applies, the spouse or former spouse shall, so long as he or she remains in occupation, have the same rights in relation to or in connection with any such adjournment as is referred to in subsection (2A) above or any such stay, suspension or postponement as is referred to in subsection (3) above as he or she would have if those rights of occupation were not affected by the termination of the tenancy.]

(6)   In this section "tenant" means a protected occupier or a statutory tenant [and "tenancy" shall be construed accordingly].

**[161]**

### NOTES
Sub-ss (2A), (5A), (5B): inserted by the Housing Act 1980, s 75(4), (5), (7).
Sub-s (4): substituted by the Housing Act 1980, s 75(4), (6).
Sub-s (6): words in square brackets added by the Housing Act 1980, s 152(1), Sch 25, Pt I, para 23.
Matrimonial Homes Act 1967: mostly repealed and replaced by the Matrimonial Homes Act 1983 (itself repealed); by virtue of the Interpretation Act 1978, s 17(2)(a), the reference to the 1967 Act should be construed as a reference to the Family Law Act 1996.

## 8   Restriction on levy of distress for rent

*(1)   Subject to subsection (2) below, no distress for the rent of any dwelling-house subject to a protected occupancy or statutory tenancy shall be levied except with the leave of the county court; and the court shall, with respect to any application for such leave, have the same or similar powers with respect to adjournment, stay, suspension, postponement and otherwise as are conferred by section 7 of this Act, in relation to proceedings for possession of such a dwelling-house.*

*(2)   Nothing in subsection (1) above shall apply to distress levied under [section 102 of the County Courts Act 1984] (claims for rent where goods seized in execution).*

**[162]**

PART I STATUTES

**NOTES**

Repealed by the Tribunals, Courts and Enforcement Act 2007, ss 86, 146, Sch 14, para 31, Sch 23, Pt 4, as from a day to be appointed.

Sub-s (2): words in square brackets substituted by the County Courts Act 1984, s 144, Sch 2, Pt V, para 62.

## 9   Effect of determination of superior tenancy, etc

(1)   If a court makes an order for possession of a dwelling-house from a protected occupier or statutory tenant, or from a protected or statutory tenant for the purposes of the [Rent Act 1977], and the order is made by virtue of Part I of Schedule 4 to this Act or, as the case may be, [section 98 or 99(2)] of that Act, nothing in the order shall affect the right of any sub-tenant—

    (a)   to whom the dwelling-house or any part of it has been lawfully sublet before the commencement of the proceedings, and

    (b)   who is a protected occupier or statutory tenant thereof,

to retain possession by virtue of this Act, nor shall the order operate to give a right to possession against any such sub-tenant.

(2)   Where a statutorily protected tenancy of a dwelling-house is determined, either as a result of an order for possession or for any other reason, any sub-tenant—

    (a)   to whom the dwelling-house or any part of it has been lawfully sublet, and

    (b)   who is a protected occupier or statutory tenant thereof,

shall, subject to the provisions of this Act, be deemed to become the tenant of the landlord on the same terms as if the tenant's statutorily protected tenancy had continued.

(3)   Where a dwelling-house—

    (a)   forms part of premises which have been let as a whole on a superior tenancy but do not constitute a dwelling-house let on a statutorily protected tenancy; and

    (b)   is itself subject to a protected occupancy or statutory tenancy,

then, from the coming to an end of the superior tenancy, this Act shall apply in relation to the dwelling-house as if, in lieu of the superior tenancy, there had been separate tenancies of the dwelling-house and of the remainder of the premises, for the like purposes as under the superior tenancy, and at rents equal to the just proportion of the rent under the superior tenancy.

In this subsection "premises" includes an agricultural holding within the meaning of the [Agricultural Holdings Act 1986] [held under a tenancy in relation to which that Act applies and land comprised in a farm business tenancy within the meaning of the Agricultural Tenancies Act 1995.]

(4)   In subsections (2) and (3) above "statutorily protected tenancy" means—

    (a)   a protected occupancy or statutory tenancy;

    (b)   a protected or statutory tenancy for the purposes of the [Rent Act 1977],

    [(c)   a tenancy of an agricultural holding within the meaning of the Agricultural Holdings Act 1986 which is a tenancy in relation to which that Act applies; or

    (d)   a farm business tenancy within the meaning of the Agricultural Tenancies Act 1995.]

(5)   Subject to subsection (6) below, a long tenancy of a dwelling-house which is also a tenancy at a low rent but which, had it not been a tenancy at a low rent, would have been a protected tenancy for the purposes of the [Rent Act 1977], shall be treated for the purposes of subsection (2) above as a statutorily protected tenancy.

(6)   Notwithstanding anything in subsection (5) above, subsection (2) above shall not have effect where the sub-tenancy in question was created (whether immediately or derivatively) out of a long tenancy falling within subsection (5) above and, at the time of the creation of the sub-tenancy—

    (a)   a notice to terminate the long tenancy had been given under section 4(1) of the Landlord and Tenant Act 1954; or

    (b)   the long tenancy was being continued by section 3(1) of that Act;

unless the sub-tenancy was created with the consent in writing of the person who at the time when it was created was the landlord, within the meaning of Part I of that Act.

(7)   In subsections (5) and (6) above "long tenancy" means a tenancy granted for a term of years certain exceeding 21 years, whether or not subsequently extended by act of the parties or by any enactment; and in determining for the purposes of those subsections whether a long tenancy is a tenancy at a low rent, there shall be disregarded such part (if any) of the sums payable by the tenant as is expressed (in whatever terms) to be payable in respect of rates, [council tax,] service, repairs, maintenance or insurance, unless it would not have been regarded by the parties as so payable.

**[163]**

**NOTES**

Sub-ss (1), (5): words in square brackets substituted by the Rent Act 1977, s 155, Sch 23, para 74(a), (b).

Sub-s (3): words in first pair of square brackets substituted by the Agricultural Holdings Act 1986, s 100, Sch 14, para 54; words in second pair of square brackets inserted by the Agricultural Tenancies Act 1995, s 40, Schedule, para 25(1), (2).

Sub-s (4): words in first pair of square brackets substituted by the Rent Act 1977, s 155, Sch 23, para 74(b); words in second pair of square brackets substituted by the Agricultural Tenancies Act 1995, s 40, Schedule, para 25(1), (3).

Sub-s (7): words in square brackets inserted by the Local Government Finance (Housing) (Consequential Amendments) Order 1993, SI 1993/651, art 2(1), Sch 1, para 2.

*Statutory tenancies*

## 10 Terms and conditions

(1)    Schedule 5 to this Act contains provisions about the terms of a statutory tenancy.

(2)    Schedule 5 to this Act shall not impose any liability to pay rent under a statutory tenancy (whether the protected occupier was a tenant or a licensee), and accordingly no rent shall be payable under a statutory tenancy until rent becomes payable by virtue of an agreement under section 11 of this Act, or by virtue of a notice of increase under section 12 or 14 of this Act.

(3)    Rent under a statutory tenancy which is a weekly tenancy shall be payable weekly in arrear, except that—

(a)    if a rent or equivalent payment was payable under the protected occupancy, and was so payable otherwise than in arrear, rent under the statutory tenancy shall be payable in that other way, and

(b)    this subsection has effect subject to any agreement between the landlord and the tenant.

(4)    The day on which rent is payable weekly in arrear in accordance with subsection (3) above shall be—

(a)    where rent or any equivalent payment was payable weekly in arrear under the protected occupancy, the day on which it was so payable,

(b)    where paragraph (a) does not apply, and at the end of the protected occupancy the protected occupier was being paid weekly wages, the day on which the wages were paid,

(c)    in any other case such day as the landlord and tenant may agree, or in default of agreement, Friday in each week.

(5)    The covenants implied in the statutory tenancy shall include a covenant to pay rent in accordance with this Part of this Act.

**[164]**

## 11 Agreed rents

(1)    The landlord and the statutory tenant may by agreement fix the rent payable under a statutory tenancy (or may agree that no rent shall be payable under the statutory tenancy).

(2)    An agreement under this section may be made at any time, including a time before the beginning of the statutory tenancy, or a time when a rent is registered for the dwelling-house.

(3)    The rent so fixed shall not exceed—

(a)    where a rent is registered for the dwelling-house at the time when the agreement is made, the weekly or other periodical equivalent of the amount of the rent so registered,

(b)    where a rent is not so registered, the amount of the rent based on rateable value defined in the next following section.

(4)    Where a rent is registered for the dwelling-house at any time after the agreement is made, as from the date from which the registration takes effect the rent payable under the agreement shall not exceed the weekly or other periodical equivalent of the amount of the rent so registered.

(5)    If the rent payable under the agreement exceeds the limit imposed by subsections (3) or (4) above, the amount of the excess shall be irrecoverable from the tenant.

(6)    Unless the contrary intention appears from the agreement, it shall be terminable by the landlord or the tenant by notice in writing served on the other.

(7)    The notice shall specify the date from which the agreement is terminated, which shall be not earlier than four weeks after service of the notice.

(8)    Subject to subsection (3) above, an agreement made under this section may from time to time be varied by a further agreement so made, whether or not there has been a change in the persons who are landlord and tenant.

(9)    If and so long as, in the period following the termination of an agreement under this section, no notice of increase under section 12 or section 14 of this Act takes effect (and no subsequent agreement is in force), the rent payable under the statutory tenancy shall be the same as the rent payable, or last payable, under the agreement, and it shall be payable for equivalent rental periods, and in other respects in the same way as, the rent was payable, or last payable, under the agreement.

(10)    Where a rent is registered for the dwelling-house at any time after the termination of the agreement, as from the date from which the registration takes effect the rent payable under

subsection (9) above shall not exceed the weekly or other periodical equivalent of the amount of the rent so registered; and if the rent so payable exceeds the limit imposed by the foregoing provision of this subsection, the amount of the excess shall be irrecoverable from the tenant.

(11)  If the agreement mentioned in subsection (9) above provided that no rent was payable under the statutory tenancy, no rent shall be payable in the period for which that subsection applies.

**[165]**

## 12  Provisional rents

(1)  This section applies where a rent is not registered for a dwelling-house which is subject to a statutory tenancy.

(2)  If the rent payable for any period of the statutory tenancy would be less than the rent based on rateable value, it may be increased up to the amount of that rent by a notice of increase served by the landlord on the tenant.

(3)  The notice shall specify the amount of the rent based on rateable value, and set out the landlord's calculation of that amount.

(4)  The notice should also specify the date from which the notice is to take effect, which shall not be earlier than four weeks before service of the notice, and not at a time when an agreement under section 11 of this Act is in force.

(5)  If the notice takes effect from the termination of an agreement under section 11 of this Act, it shall state that fact, and specify the rent payable, or last payable, under that agreement.

(6)  If a notice is served under this section at a time when an agreement under section 11 of this Act is in force, and the date stated in the notice as that from which it is to take effect is—
   (a)  a date after service of the notice, and
   (b)  a date as at which the landlord could by notice served with the first-mentioned notice terminate the agreement,
the first-mentioned notice shall operate as a notice to terminate the agreement as at that date.

(7)  Where a rent is registered for the dwelling-house at any time after notice is served, as from the date from which the registration takes effect the rent payable in accordance with the notice shall not exceed the weekly or other periodical equivalent of the amount of the rent so registered.

(8)  If the rent payable in accordance with the notice exceeds the limit imposed by subsection (7) above, the amount of the excess shall be irrecoverable from the tenant.

(9)  In this section—
   (a)  "rent based on rateable value"[, where the dwelling-house had a rateable value on 31st March 1990,] means the weekly or other periodical equivalent of an annual amount equal to the prescribed multiple of the rateable value of the dwelling-house [on that date], and
   (b)  the "prescribed multiple" is 1.5, or such other number (whole or with a fraction) as the Secretary of State may by order prescribe[, and
   (c)  "rent based on rateable value", where the dwelling-house had no rateable value on 31st March 1990, means the weekly or other periodical equivalent of an annual amount equal to the rent at which it is estimated the dwelling-house might reasonably be expected to let from year to year if the tenant undertook to pay all usual tenant's rates and taxes and to bear the cost of the repairs and insurance and the other expenses (if any) necessary to maintain the dwelling-house in a state to command that rent.]

(10)  An order made under subsection (9) above—
   (a)  may contain such transitional and other supplemental and incidental provisions as appear to the Secretary of State expedient,
   (b)  may be varied or revoked by a subsequent order so made, and
   (c)  shall be contained in a statutory instrument subject to annulment in pursuance of a resolution of either House of Parliament.

(11)  The date as at which the rateable value [or the annual amount referred to in subsection (9)(c) above] is to be determined for the purposes of this section, and for the purposes of any agreement made under section 11 of this Act, shall be the date on which the notice is served, or as the case may be the date when the agreement was made[, or, if that date is after 31st March 1990 and the dwelling-house had a rateable value on that date, 31st March 1990].

(12)  If there is no separate rateable value for the dwelling-house [on the date as at which the rateable value is to be determined for the purposes of this section] the rateable value shall be ascertained by a proper apportionment or aggregation of the rateable value or values of the relevant hereditaments; and until the rateable value is so ascertained references in this section to the amount of the rent based on rateable value shall be construed as references to the amount of the rent based on the landlord's estimate of that value.

(13) Any question as to the proper apportionment or aggregation under subsection (12) above shall be determined by the county court, and the decision of the county court shall be final.

[166]

NOTES

Sub-ss (9), (11), (12): words in square brackets inserted by the References to Rating (Housing) Regulations 1990, SI 1990/434, reg 2, Schedule, paras 11–13.

## 13  Application for registration of rent

(1) There shall be a part of the register under Part IV of the [Rent Act 1977] in which rents may be registered for dwelling-houses which are subject to statutory tenancies (as defined in this Act).

(2) In relation to that part of the register the following provision of the [Rent Act 1977], that is—

[(a)  sections 67 [67A, 70 and 70A]
(b)  section 71, except subsection (3), and
(c)  Part I of Schedule 11,]

shall have effect as if for any reference in those provisions to a regulated tenancy there were substituted a reference to a statutory tenancy (as defined in this Act).

(3) The preceding provisions of this section shall not be taken as applying [sections ... , 71(3), 72 or 73 of the Rent Act 1977 ... ].

[(4) The registration of a rent in the said part of the register takes effect—
(a)  if the rent is determined by the rent officer, from the date when it is registered, and
(b)  if the rent is determined by a rent assessment committee, from the date when the committee make their decision.

(5) If the rent for the time being registered in the said part of the register is confirmed, the confirmation takes effect—
(a)  if it is made by the rent officer, from the date when it is noted in the register, and
(b)  if it is made by a rent assessment committee, from the date when the committee make their decision.

(6) If (by virtue of section 67(4) of the Rent Act 1977, as applied by subsection (2) above) an application for registration of a rent is made before the expiry of the period mentioned in section 67(3) and the resulting registration of a rent for the dwelling-house, or confirmation of the rent for the time being registered, would, but for this subsection, take effect before the expiry of that period it shall take effect on the expiry of that period.

(6A) The date from which the registration or confirmation of a rent takes effect shall be entered in the said part of the register.

(6B) As from the date on which the registration of a rent takes effect any previous registration of a rent for the dwelling-house ceases to have effect.]

(7) A rent registered in any part of the register for a dwelling-house which becomes, or ceases to be, one subject to a statutory tenancy shall be as effective as if it were registered in any other part of the register; but [section 67(3) of the Rent Act 1977] (no application for registration of a different rent to be made within [two years] of the last registration) shall not apply to an application for the registration, as respects a dwelling-house which is subject to a statutory tenancy, of a rent different from one which is registered in a part of the register other than the part mentioned in subsection (1) above.

[167]

NOTES

Sub-s (1): words in square brackets substituted by the Rent Act 1977, s 155, Sch 23, para 75(a).

Sub-s (2): words in first pair of square brackets and words in second (outer) pair of square brackets substituted by the Rent Act 1977, s 155, Sch 23, para 75(b); words in third (inner) pair of square brackets substituted by the Local Government Finance (Housing) (Consequential Amendments) Order 1993, SI 1993/651, art 2(2), Sch 2, para 1.

Sub-s (3): words in square brackets substituted by the Rent Act 1977, s 155, Sch 23, para 75(c); words omitted repealed by the Housing Act 1988, s 140(2), Sch 18.

Sub-ss (4)–(6), (6A), (6B): substituted, for original sub-ss (4)–(6), by the Housing Act 1980, s 61(2), subject to savings contained in s 61(8) of that Act at [360].

Sub-s (7): words in first pair of square brackets substituted by the Rent Act 1977, s 155, Sch 23, para 75(e); words in second pair of square brackets substituted by the Housing Act 1980, s 152(1), Sch 25, Pt I, para 33.

Regulations: the Rent Act 1977 (Forms etc) Regulations 1980, SI 1980/1697 at [3023].

## 14  Registered rents

(1) This section applies where a rent is registered for a dwelling-house subject to a statutory tenancy.

(2)   If the rent payable for any period of the statutory tenancy beginning on or after the date of registration would be less than the registered rent, it may be increased up to the amount of that rent by a notice of increase served by the landlord on the tenant.

(3)   The notice shall specify the amount of the registered rent, and the date from which the notice is to take effect, which shall not be earlier than four weeks before service of the notice, and not at a time when an agreement under section 11 of this Act is in force.

(4)   If the notice takes effect from the termination of an agreement under section 11 of this Act, it shall state that fact, and specify the rent payable, or last payable, under that agreement.

(5)   If a notice is served under this section at a time when an agreement under section 11 of this Act is in force, and the date stated in the notice as that from which it is to take effect is—
  (a)   a date after service of the notice, and
  (b)   a date as at which the landlord could by notice served with the first-mentioned notice terminate the agreement,
the first-mentioned notice shall operate as a notice to terminate the agreement as at that date.

**[168]**

**15**   *(Repealed by the Rent (Relief from Phasing) Order 1987, SI 1987/264.)*

**16   Notices of increase**

(1)   Any reference in the following provisions of this section to a notice is a reference to a notice of increase under section 12 or section 14 of this Act.

(2)   Notwithstanding that a notice relates to periods of a statutory tenancy it may be served before the statutory tenancy begins.

(3)   Where a notice is served before the statutory tenancy begins, and the protected occupancy could, by a notice to quit served at the same time, be brought to an end before the date specified in the notice of increase, the notice shall operate to terminate the protected occupancy as from that date.

(4)   If the county court is satisfied that any error or omission in a notice is due to a bona fide mistake on the part of the landlord, the court may by order amend the notice by correcting any errors or supplying any omission therein which, if not corrected or supplied, would render the notice invalid and if the court so directs, the notice as so amended shall have effect and be deemed to have had effect as a valid notice.

(5)   If [in a case to which section 12(12) applies] the county court is satisfied that—
  (a)   [on 31st March 1990] there was no separate rateable value for the dwelling-house, and
  (b)   the amount specified in the notice is the amount of the rent based on the landlord's estimate of the rateable value.
the court may by order amend the notice by substituting for the amount so specified the amount of the rent based on rateable value and, if the court so directs, the notice shall have effect and be deemed to have had effect and be deemed to have had effect as so amended.

(6)   Any amendment of a notice under subsection (4) or (5) above may be made on such terms and conditions with respect to arrears of rent or otherwise as appear to the court to be just and reasonable.

(7)   No increase of rent which becomes payable by reason of an amendment of a notice under subsection (4) or (5) above shall be recoverable in respect of any period of the statutory tenancy which ended more than six months before the date of the order making the amendment.

**[169]**

**NOTES**
  Sub-s (5): words in first pair of square brackets inserted and words in second pair of square brackets substituted by the References to Rating (Housing) Regulations 1990, SI 1990/434, reg 2, Schedule, para 14.

*General provisions*

**17   Adjustment for differences in lengths of rental periods**

In ascertaining for the purposes of this Part of this Act the weekly or other periodical equivalent of a registered rent, or of the annual amount mentioned in section 12(9) of this Act, a period of one month shall be treated as equivalent to one-twelfth of a year, and a period of a week as equivalent to one fifty-second of a year.

**[170]**

**18   Regulations**

(1)   The Secretary of State may make regulations prescribing the form of any notice or other document to be given or used in pursuance of this Part of this Act.

(2) Any such regulations shall be made by statutory instrument which shall be subject to annulment in pursuance of a resolution of either House of Parliament.

[171]

## 19 Interpretation of Part II

In this Part of this Act, unless the context otherwise requires—

"registered" means registered in the register under Part IV of [the Rent Act 1977],

"rent based on rateable value" has the meaning given by section 12(9) of this Act,

"rental period" means a period in respect of which a payment of rent, or in the case of a licence the equivalent of rent, falls to be made.

[172]

**NOTES**

Words in square brackets substituted by the Rent Act 1977, s 155, Sch 23, para 77.

## PART III

PROTECTED OCCUPANCIES AND STATUTORY TENANCIES: SUPPLEMENTAL

*Recovery of rent*

## 20 Avoidance of requirements for advance payment of rent

(1) Any requirement that rent under a protected occupancy, or under a statutory tenancy, shall be payable—

(a) before the beginning of the rental period in respect of which it is payable, or

(b) earlier than 6 months before the end of the rental period in respect of which it is payable (if that period is more than 6 months).

shall be void, and any requirement avoided by this section is referred to in this section as a "prohibited requirement".

(2) Rent for any rental period to which a prohibited requirement relates shall be irrecoverable from the tenant.

(3) A person who purports to impose a prohibited requirement shall be liable on summary conviction to a fine not exceeding [level 3 on the standard scale] and the court by which he is convicted may order the amount of rent paid in compliance with the prohibited requirement to be repaid to the person by whom it was paid.

(4) In this section "rental period" means a period in respect of which a payment of rent falls to be made.

(5) For the avoidance of doubt it is hereby declared that this section does not render any amount recoverable more than once.

[173]

**NOTES**

Sub-s (3): words in square brackets substituted by virtue of the Criminal Justice Act 1982, ss 38, 46.

## 21 Recovery from landlord of sums paid in excess of recoverable rent

(1) Where a tenant has paid on account of rent any amount which, by virtue of Part II of this Act or this Part, is irrecoverable by the landlord, then, subject to subsection (3) below, the tenant who paid it shall be entitled to recover that amount from the landlord who received it or his personal representatives.

(2) Subject to subsection (3) below, any amount which a tenant is entitled to recover under subsection (1) above may, without prejudice to any other method of recovery, be deducted by the tenant from any rent payable by him to the landlord.

(3) No amount which a tenant is entitled to recover under subsection (1) above shall be recoverable at any time after the expiry of two years from the date of payment.

(4) Any person who, in any rent book or similar document, makes an entry showing or purporting to show any tenant as being in arrears in respect of any sum on account of rent which is irrecoverable by virtue of Part II of this Act or this Part shall be liable on summary conviction to a fine not exceeding [level 3 on the standard scale], unless he proves that, at the time of the making of the entry, the landlord had a bona fide claim that the sum was recoverable.

(5) If, where any such entry has been made by or on behalf of any landlord, the landlord on being requested by or on behalf of the tenant to do so, refuses or neglects to cause the entry to be deleted within seven days, the landlord shall be liable on summary conviction to a fine not exceeding [level 3 on the standard scale], unless he proves that, at the time of the neglect or refusal to cause the entry to be deleted, he had a bona fide claim that the sum was recoverable.

[174]

**NOTES**

Sub-ss (4), (5): words in square brackets substituted by virtue of the Criminal Justice Act 1982, ss 38, 46.

## 22 Rectification of rent books in light of determination of recoverable rent

Where, in any proceedings, the recoverable rent of a dwelling-house subject to a statutory tenancy is determined by a court, then, on the application of the tenant (whether in those or in any subsequent proceedings) the court may call for the production of the rent book or any similar document relating to the dwelling-house and may direct the registrar or clerk of the court to correct any entries showing, or purporting to show, the tenant as being in arrears in respect of any sum which the court has determined to be irrecoverable.

**[175]**

*Miscellaneous*

## 23 Tenant sharing accommodation with persons other than landlord

(1)   Where a tenant has the exclusive occupation of any accommodation ("the separate accommodation"), and

 (a)   the terms as between the tenant and his landlord on which he holds the separate accommodation include the use of other accommodation (in this section referred to as "the shared accommodation") in common with another person or other persons, not being or including the landlord, and

 (b)   by reason only of the circumstances mentioned in paragraph (a) above, the separate accommodation would not, apart from this section, be a dwelling-house subject to a protected occupancy or statutory tenancy,

then, subject to subsection (2) below, the separate accommodation shall be deemed to be a dwelling-house subject to a protected occupancy or statutory tenancy as the case may be, and subsections (3) to (8) below shall have effect.

(2)   Subsection (1) above shall not apply in relation to accommodation which would, apart from this subsection, be deemed to be a dwelling-house subject to a protected tenancy if—

 (a)   the accommodation consists of only one room, and

 (b)   at the time when the tenancy was granted, not less than three other rooms in the same building were let, or were available for letting, as residential accommodation to separate tenants on such terms as are mentioned in subsection (1)(a) above.

(3)   For the avoidance of doubt it is hereby declared that where, for the purpose of determining the rateable value of the separate accommodation, it is necessary to make an apportionment under this Act, regard is to be had to the circumstances mentioned in subsection (1)(a) above.

(4)   Subject to subsection (5) below, while the tenant is in possession of the separate accommodation (whether as a protected occupier or statutory tenant), any term or condition of the contract of tenancy terminating or modifying, or providing for the termination or modification of, his right to the use of any of the shared accommodation which is living accommodation shall be of no effect.

(5)   Where the terms and conditions of the contract of tenancy are such that at any time during the tenancy the persons in common with whom the tenant is entitled to the use of the shared accommodation could be varied, or their number could be increased, nothing in subsection (4) above shall prevent those terms and conditions from having effect so far as they relate to any such variation or increase.

(6)   Subject to subsection (7) below and without prejudice to the enforcement of any order made thereunder, while the tenant is in possession of the separate accommodation, no order shall be made for possession of any of the shared accommodation, whether on the application of the immediate landlord of the tenant or on the application of any person under whom that landlord derives title, unless a like order has been made, or is made at the same time, in respect of the separate accommodation; and the provisions of section 6 of this Act shall apply accordingly.

(7)   On the application of the landlord, the county court may make such order, either terminating the right of the tenant to use the whole or any part of the shared accommodation other than living accommodation, or modifying his right to use the whole or any part of the shared accommodation, whether by varying the persons or increasing the number of persons entitled to the use of that accommodation, or otherwise, as the court thinks just:

Provided that no order shall be made under this subsection so as to effect any termination or modification of the rights of the tenant which, apart from subsection (4) above, could not be effected by or under the terms of the contract of tenancy.

(8)   In this section the expression "living accommodation" means accommodation of such a nature that the fact that it constitutes or is included in the shared accommodation is (or, if the tenancy has ended, was) sufficient, apart from this section, to prevent the tenancy from constituting a protected occupancy of a dwelling-house.

**[176]**

## 24   Certain sub-lettings, not to exclude any part of sub-lessor's premises from protection

(1)   Where the tenant of any premises, consisting of a house or part of a house, has sublet a part, but not the whole, of the premises, then, as against his landlord or any superior landlord, no part of the premises shall be treated as not being a dwelling-house subject to a protected occupancy or statutory tenancy by reason only that—

    (a)   the terms on which any person claiming under the tenant holds any part of the premises include the use of accommodation in common with other persons; or

    (b)   part of the premises is let to any such person at a rent which includes payments in respect of board or attendance.

(2)   Nothing in this section affects the rights against, and liabilities to, each other of the tenant and any person claiming under him, or of any two such persons.

**[177]**

## 25   Service of notices on landlord's agents

(1)   For the purposes of any proceedings arising out of Part I or II of this Act or this Part, a document shall be deemed to be duly served on the landlord of a dwelling-house if it is served—

    (a)   on any agent of the landlord named as such in the rent book or other similar document; or

    (b)   on the person who receives the rent of the dwelling-house.

(2)   If for the purpose of any proceedings (whether civil or criminal) arising out of Part I or II of this Act, or this Part, any person serves upon any such agent or other person as is referred to in paragraph (a) or paragraph (b) of subsection (1) above a notice in writing requiring the agent or other person to disclose to him the full name and place of abode or place of business of the landlord, that agent or other person shall forthwith comply with the notice.

(3)   If any such agent or other person as is referred to in subsection (2) above fails or refuses forthwith to comply with a notice served on him under that subsection, he shall be liable on summary conviction to a fine not exceeding [level 4 on the standard scale] unless he shows to the satisfaction of the court that he did not know, and could not with reasonable diligence have ascertained, such of the facts required by the notice to be disclosed as were not disclosed by him.

**[178]**

**NOTES**

Sub-s (3): words in square brackets substituted by virtue of the Criminal Justice Act 1982, ss 39, 46, Sch 3.

## 26   Jurisdiction and procedure

(1)   A county court shall have jurisdiction to determine—

    (a)   whether any person is or is not a protected occupier or a statutory tenant, or

    (b)   any question concerning the subject matter, terms or conditions of a statutory tenancy,

or any matter which is or may become material for determining a question under paragraph (a) or (b).

(2)   A county court shall have jurisdiction to deal with any claim or other proceedings arising out of Part I of this Act, or Part II of this Act, except Part II of Schedule 4, or this Part, notwithstanding that the case would not, apart from this subsection, be within the jurisdiction of a county court.

(3)   *If, on a claim arising under Part I of this Act, or Part II of this Act except Part II of Schedule 4, or this Part, a person takes proceedings in the High Court which he could have taken in the county court, he shall not be entitled to any costs.*

(4)   The jurisdiction conferred by subsection (1) above is exercisable either in the course of any proceedings relating to the dwelling-house, or on an application made for the purpose by the landlord or tenant.

(5)   ...

**[179]**

**NOTES**

Sub-s (3): repealed by the Courts and Legal Services Act 1990, s 125(7), Sch 20, as from a day to be appointed.

Sub-s (5): repealed by the Constitutional Reform Act 2005, ss 15(1), 146, Sch 4, Pt 1, para 88, Sch 18, Pt 2.

## PART IV
## REHOUSING

### 27   Applications to housing authority concerned

(1)   An application may be made by the occupier of land used for agriculture to the housing authority concerned ("the authority") on the ground that—

   (a)     vacant possession is or will be needed of a dwelling-house which is subject to a protected occupancy or statutory tenancy [or an assured agricultural occupancy], or which is let on or subject to a tenancy to which subsection (2) below applies, in order to house a person who is or is to be employed in agriculture by the applicant, and that person's family,

   (b)     the applicant is unable to provide, by any reasonable means, suitable alternative accommodation for the occupier of the dwelling-house, and

   (c)     the authority ought, in the interests of efficient agriculture, to provide the suitable alternative accommodation.

(2)   This subsection applies to any tenancy which is a protected or statutory tenancy for the purposes of [the Rent Act 1977] and which—

   (a)     if it were a tenancy at a low rent, and

   (b)     if (where relevant) any earlier tenancy granted to the tenant, or to a member of his family, had been a tenancy at a low rent,

would be a protected occupancy or statutory tenancy.

[(3)   In this Act "the housing authority concerned" is the local housing authority within the meaning of the Housing Act 1985 [and assured agricultural occupancy has the same meaning as in Chapter III of Part I of the Housing Act 1988].]

**[180]**

---

**NOTES**

Sub-s (1): words in square brackets inserted by the Housing Act 1988, s 26.

Sub-s (2): words in square brackets substituted by the Rent Act 1977, s 155, Sch 23, para 77.

Sub-s (3): substituted by the Housing (Consequential Provisions) Act 1985, s 4, Sch 2, para 33(1), (3); words in square brackets added by the Housing Act 1988, s 26.

---

### 28   Duty of housing authority concerned

(1)   An application to the authority shall be in writing and, if the authority so direct, shall be in such form as the authority direct; and there shall be a sufficient compliance with a direction under this subsection if the application is in a form substantially to that same effect as the form specified in the direction.

(2)   The authority shall, within seven days of their receiving the application, notify the occupier of the dwelling-house of which possession is sought ("the dwelling-house") that the application has been made.

(3)   The authority, or the applicant, or the occupier of the dwelling-house, may obtain advice on the case made by the applicant concerning the interests of efficient agriculture, and regarding the urgency of the application, by applying for the services of a committee under section 29 of this Act.

(4)   The committee shall tender its advice in writing to the authority, and make copies of it available for the applicant and the occupier of the dwelling-house.

(5)   In assessing the case made by the applicant and in particular the importance and degree of urgency of the applicant's need, the authority shall take full account of any advice tendered to them by the committee in accordance with section 29 of this Act, and in any legal proceedings relating to the duty imposed on the authority by this section, evidence shall be admissible of the advice so given.

[(6)   The authority shall notify their decision on the application in writing to the applicant, and to the occupier of the dwelling-house, within three months of their receiving the application or, if an application is made for the services of a committee under section 29 of this Act, within two months of their receiving the committee's advice.

(6A)   The notification shall state—

   (a)     if the authority are satisfied that the applicant's case is substantiated in accordance with section 27 above, what action they propose to take on the application;

   (b)     if they are not so satisfied, the reasons for their decision.]

(7)   If the authority are satisfied that the applicant's case is substantiated in accordance with section 27 above, they shall use their best endeavours to provide the suitable alternative accommodation; and in assessing under this subsection the priority to be given to meet the applicant's case, the authority shall take into account the urgency of the case, the competing claims on the accommodation which they can provide and the resources at their disposal.

PART I
STATUTES

(8)   Without prejudice to any other means of enforcing the duty imposed by subsection (7) above, that duty shall be enforceable, at the suit of the applicant, by an action against the authority for damages for breach of statutory duty.

(9)   The authority shall not be obliged to provide suitable alternative accommodation if at the time when the accommodation becomes available the person for whom it is to be provided is employed by the applicant in the same capacity as that in which he was employed by the applicant at the time when the application was made, and he will continue to be so employed if provided with the alternative accommodation.

(10)   The continuance of the obligation imposed on the authority by this section shall depend on compliance by the applicant with any reasonable request made by the authority for information about any change in circumstances which takes place after the making of the application, and which might affect the merits of the applicant's case.

(11)   Any material change of facts which have been stated to the authority, or to the committee, by the applicant or, in relation to the application, by the occupier of the dwelling-house, shall be notified to the authority as soon as practicable by the person making the statement unless before the change accommodation has been provided in accordance with the application, or the authority have decided that the applicant's case is not substantiated.

A person who without reasonable excuse fails to comply with this subsection shall be liable on summary conviction to a fine not exceeding [level 5 on the standard scale].

(12)   An application under this section shall lapse if the applicant ceases to be the occupier of the land used for agriculture, but without prejudice to the making of an application by any other person who is or becomes the occupier.

(13)   In this section and section 27 of this Act references to the authority providing housing accommodation are references to its provision by any means open to the authority, whether direct or indirect.

(14)   If in or in connection with an application under this section the applicant or any other person knowingly or recklessly makes a false statement for the purpose of inducing the authority to provide housing accommodation, he shall be liable on summary conviction to a fine not exceeding [level 5 on the standard scale].

[(14A)   Notwithstanding anything in section 127(1) of the Magistrates' Courts Act 1980, an information relating to an offence under this section may be tried if it is laid at any time within two years after the commission of the offence and within six months after the date on which evidence sufficient in the opinion of the housing authority concerned to justify the proceedings comes to its knowledge.]

[181]

**NOTES**

Sub-ss (6), (6A): substituted, for original sub-s (6), by the Rent (Agriculture) Amendment Act 1977, s 1.
Sub-ss (11), (14): words in square brackets substituted by virtue of the Criminal Justice Act 1982, ss 38, 46.
Sub-s (14A): inserted by the Housing Act 1988, s 140(1), Sch 17, Pt I, para 21.

## 29   Agricultural dwelling-house advisory committees

(1)   In the area of each agricultural wages committee established under the Agricultural Wages Act 1948 there shall be one or more agricultural dwelling-house advisory committees (in this section called "committees") to perform the functions given them under section 28 of this Act.

(2)   An application under section 28 of this Act for advice may be made to the chairman of the agricultural wages committee for the area in question for the appointment or designation of a committee to give the advice.

(3)   Each committee shall be appointed by the chairman of the agricultural wages committee, and he may include persons who are not members of the agricultural wages committee.

(4)   If there is no chairman, or if the chairman is unable to act, a vice-chairman of the agricultural wages committee may act in his place under this section.

(5)   Each committee shall be composed of an independent member, who is the chairman, a member representing employers and a member representing workers in agriculture.

(6)   The chairman of the committee shall be appointed from a panel of persons approved by the Minister.

(7)   All three members of a committee must be present at any meeting of the committee, and no meeting shall be held during a vacancy in the membership.

(8)   In carrying out their functions under section 28 of this Act committees shall act in accordance with any directions, whether general or specific, given to them by the Minister.

(9) The Minister may, if he thinks fit, make regulations contained in a statutory instrument regulating the procedure and meetings of committees, and may from time to time give directions, whether specific or general, regarding their procedure.

(10) Subject to regulations, or any direction, under subsection (9) above the procedure of any committee shall be such as the chairman of that committee may direct.

(11) The Minister may appoint a secretary for a committee, and there shall be paid to the members of a committee, and to the person who appoints or designates a committee, such fees and allowances by way of compensation for expenses incurred and time lost by them in the performance of their duties as the Minister may sanction with the consent of the Minister for the Civil Service.

(12) The Minister may with the consent of the Minister for the Civil Service make payments to persons other than members of a committee by way of fees or compensation for expenses incurred and time lost by them in or in connection with their giving, at the request of the committee, any advice or information.

(13) Payments made by the Minister under this section shall be defrayed out of money provided by Parliament.

(14) In this section "the Minister" means the Minister of Agriculture, Fisheries and Food.

**[182]**

## PART V
## POWER TO OBTAIN INFORMATION

### 30 Information about housing accommodation

(1) The Minister may exercise the powers conferred on him by section 31 of this Act for the purpose of obtaining information about the housing accommodation which is on, or held in connection with, or used for, agricultural or forestry land.

(2) The Minister may give information so obtained—
  (a) to the housing authority concerned for any part of the area to which the information relates, and
  (b) where, since the giving of the information, other land has come into common ownership or occupation with the first-mentioned land, to the housing authority concerned for any part of the other land,

and information so given may be transmitted to any other authority to whom the Minister may give it under this subsection.

(3) The Minister may also give the information so obtained to any agricultural dwelling-house advisory committee which is to give advice under section 29 of this Act concerning any part of the area to which the information relates.

(4) No information relating to any particular land or business which has been obtained under section 31 of this Act shall be published or otherwise disclosed without the previous consent in writing—
  (a) of the person giving the information, or
  (b) (if different) of any person who at the time of the disclosure is the owner or occupier of the land, or as the case may be, the owner of the business.

(5) Subsection (4) does not apply—
  (a) to disclosure under subsection (2) or (3) (but does apply to those to whom disclosure is so made),
  (b) to disclosure for the purposes of any criminal proceedings, or of any report of those proceedings.

(6) A person who contravenes subsection (4) shall be liable on summary conviction to a fine not exceeding [level 5 on the standard scale].

(7) In this section and in section 31 of this Act—
  "agricultural land" means land used for agriculture as defined in section 109 of the Agriculture Act 1947,
  "forestry land" does not include agricultural land,
  "occupier" includes a person responsible for the carrying on of any activity on agricultural or forestry land as servant or agent of the occupier,
  "owner" includes a person exercising, as servant or agent of the owner, functions of estate management in relation to the land.

(8) In this section and in section 31 of this Act references to the Minister are references to the Minister of Agriculture, Fisheries and Food and, so far as the reference relates to forestry land, to the Forestry Commissioners.

**[183]**

### 31 Kinds of information obtainable

(1)   The Minister may serve on any owner or occupier of agricultural or forestry land a notice requiring him to give such information as is specified in the notice concerning housing accommodation on, or held in connection with, or used for, the land, being information within section 30 of this Act.

(2)   The notice shall be complied with within such period, being not less than four weeks from service of the notice, as may be specified in the notice.

(3)   The notice may in particular require information about—
- (a)   the extent and nature of the accommodation,
- (b)   the condition and location of the accommodation, including the state of repair of any dwelling-house, and the means of access to it,
- (c)   whether any accommodation is wholly or partly occupied by a person who is or has been employed in agriculture or by a person who has been married to[, or has been the civil partner of,] such a person, or whether the accommodation is vacant, and any impending change in the state of occupation,
- (d)   so far as it lies within the knowledge of the person on whom the notice is served, facts about, or related to, housing accommodation on, or held in connection with, or used for, the land at some time or times prior to the service of the notice, or even prior to the operative date, but not at a time more than 5 years before the service of the notice.

(4)   If the person served is not the owner or occupier of the land, the notice may require him to give any information in his possession which may identify the true owner or occupier and his address, or to state that he has no such information.

(5)   The notice may be served either—
- (a)   by delivering it to the person on whom it is to be served, or
- (b)   by leaving it at the usual or last known place of abode of that person, or
- (c)   by sending it by the recorded delivery service or by registered post in a prepaid letter addressed to that person at his usual or last known place of abode, or
- (d)   in the case of an incorporated company or body, by delivering it to the secretary or clerk of the company or body at their registered or principal office or sending it, by the recorded delivery service or by registered post, in a prepaid letter addressed to the secretary or clerk of the company or body at that office, or
- (e)   if it is not practicable after reasonable inquiry to ascertain the name or address of an owner or occupier of the land, as being a person having any interest in the land or having particular functions or responsibilities, by addressing it to him by the description of the person having that interest in the land (naming it), or as the case may be having that function or responsibility (naming it), and delivering the notice to some responsible person on the land, or by affixing it, or a copy of it, to some conspicuous object on the land.

(6)   If any person—
- (a)   without reasonable excuse fails in any respect to comply with a notice under this section, or
- (b)   in purported compliance with a notice under this section knowingly or recklessly furnishes any information which is false in a material particular,

he shall be liable on summary conviction to a fine not exceeding [level 5 on the standard scale].

**[184]**

PART VI
MISCELLANEOUS AND SUPPLEMENTAL

**32**   (*Repealed by the Social Security and Housing Benefits Act 1982, s 48(6), Sch 5.*)

### 33 Suspension of condition attached to planning permission

(1)   This section applies where planning permission as respects a dwelling-house is or has been granted subject to a condition that the occupation of the dwelling-house is limited to a person employed in agriculture or forestry.

(2)   If and so long as the dwelling-house is subject to a protected occupancy or statutory tenancy, or is let on or subject to [an assured agricultural occupancy, within the meaning of Chapter III of Part I of the Housing Act 1988, or] a tenancy to which subsection (3) below applies, the condition shall be suspended.

(3)   This subsection applies to any tenancy which is a protected or statutory tenancy for the purposes of [the Rent Act 1977] and which—
  (a)   if it were a tenancy at a low rent, and
  (b)   if (where relevant) any earlier tenancy granted to the tenant, or to a member of his family, had been a tenancy at a low rent,
would be a protected occupancy or statutory tenancy.

(4)   Suspension of the condition shall not affect the operation of [section 73A of the Town and Country Planning Act 1990].

(5)   Subsection (1) applies irrespective of the degree to which the condition circumscribes the employment in agriculture or forestry, irrespective of the other persons covered by the condition, and irrespective of the way in which agriculture or forestry is defined.

**[185]**

**NOTES**
  Sub-s (2): words in square brackets inserted by the Local Government and Housing Act 1989, s 194(1), Sch 11, para 49.
  Sub-s (3): words in square brackets substituted by the Rent Act 1977, s 155, Sch 23, para 77.
  Sub-s (4): words in square brackets substituted by the Planning and Compensation Act 1991, s 32, Sch 7, para 4.

## 34   Interpretation

(1)   In this Act, unless the context otherwise requires—
  "landlord" includes any person from time to time deriving title under the original landlord and also includes, in relation to any dwelling-house, any person other than the tenant who is, or but for Part II of this Act would be, entitled to possession of the dwelling-house,
  "licence" means any contract whereby (whether or not the contract contains other terms) one person grants to another, whether or not for any consideration, the right to occupy a dwelling-house as a residence, and references to the granting of a licence shall be construed accordingly,
  "rates" includes water rates and charges and an occupier's drainage rate, "tenancy" includes sub-tenancy,
  "tenancy at a low rent" means a tenancy under which either no rent is payable or the rent payable is less than two-thirds of the rateable value which is or was the rateable value of the dwelling-house on the appropriate day for the purposes of [the Rent Act 1977],
  "tenant" includes statutory tenant and also includes a sub-tenant and any person deriving title under the original tenant or sub-tenant.

(2)   In this Act reference to tenancies include, unless the context otherwise requires, references to licences, and cognate expressions, including those in subsection (1) above, shall be construed accordingly.

(3)   For the purposes of this Act a dwelling-house may be a house or part of a house.

(4)   It is hereby declared that any power of giving directions conferred by this Act includes power to vary or revoke directions so given.

(5)   Except in so far as the context otherwise requires, any reference in this Act to any other enactment shall be taken as referring to that enactment as amended by or under any other enactment, including this Act.

**[186]**

**NOTES**
  Sub-s (1): words in square brackets substituted by the Rent Act 1977, s 155, Sch 23, para 77.

## 35   Isles of Scilly

(1)   The Secretary of State and the Minister of Agriculture, Fisheries and Food acting jointly may by order direct that any of the provisions of this Act shall, in their application to the Isles of Scilly, have effect subject to such exceptions, adaptations and modifications as may be specified in the order.

(2)   An order under this section shall be made by statutory instrument subject to annulment in pursuance of a resolution of either House of Parliament and may be varied or revoked by a subsequent order so made.

**[187]**

## 36  Application to Crown property

(1)  Subject to section 5(1) of this Act, this Act shall apply in relation to premises in which there subsists, or at any material time subsisted, a Crown interest as it applies in relation to premises in which no such interest subsists or ever subsisted.

(2)  In this section "Crown interest" means any interest which belongs to Her Majesty in right of the Crown or of the Duchy of Lancaster or to the Duchy of Cornwall or to a Government department, or which is held in trust for Her Majesty for the purposes of a Government department.

**[188]**

## 37  Offences by bodies corporate

(1)  Where an offence under this Act which has been committed by a body corporate is proved to have been committed with the consent or connivance of, or to be attributable to any neglect on the part of, a director, manager, secretary or other similar officer of the body corporate, or any person who was purporting to act in any such capacity, he as well as the body corporate shall be guilty of that offence and be liable to be proceeded against and punished accordingly.

(2)  Where the affairs of a body corporate are managed by its members, subsection (1) above shall apply in relation to the acts and defaults of a member in connection with his functions of management as if he were a director of the body corporate.

**[189]**

## 38  Prosecution of offences

Without prejudice to section 222 of the Local Government Act 1972 (power of local authorities to prosecute or defend legal proceedings), proceedings for an offence under any provision of this Act except section 31(6) may be instituted by the housing authority concerned.

**[190]**

## 39  Expenses

There shall be paid out of moneys provided by Parliament—

    (a)    any expenses incurred by a Minister, or Government department, in consequence of the provisions of this Act, and

    (b)    any increase in sums so payable under any other Act which is attributable to the provisions of this Act.

**[191]**

## 40  Short title, etc

(1)  This Act may be cited as the Rent (Agriculture) Act 1976.

(2)  Schedule 8 to this Act contains consequential and minor amendments of other Acts.

(3)  Schedule 9 to this Act contains transitional provisions.

(4)  …

(5)  This Act shall not extend to Scotland or Northern Ireland.

**[192]**

---

**NOTES**

Sub-s (4): repealed by the Rent Act 1977, s 155, Sch 25.

---

## SCHEDULES

### SCHEDULE 1
### INDEX OF GENERAL DEFINITIONS

Section 1

| *Expression defined* | *Provisions in Act* |
| --- | --- |
| Agricultural dwelling-house advisory committee | Section 29(1). |
| Agriculture | Section 1(1). |
| Date of operation for forestry workers | Schedule 3, Part II. |
| Dwelling-house | Section 34(3). |
| Dwelling-house in qualifying ownership | Schedule 3, Part I. |
| Forestry | Section 1(1). |
| Housing authority concerned | Section 27(3). |

| Expression defined | Provisions in Act |
|---|---|
| Incapable of whole-time work in agriculture, or work in agriculture as a permit worker, in consequence of a qualifying injury or disease | Schedule 3, Part I. |
| Landlord | Section 34(1). |
| Licence | Section 34(1). |
| Operative date | Section 1(6). |
| Protected occupier | Sections 2 and 3. |
| Protected occupier by succession | Section 3(5). |
| Protected occupier in his own right | Section 2(4). |
| Rates | Section 34(1). |
| Relevant licence | Schedule 2. |
| Relevant tenancy | Schedule 2. |
| Qualifying worker | Schedule 3, Part I. |
| Statutory tenant | Sections 4 and 5. |
| Statutory tenant by succession | Section 3(5). |
| Statutory tenant in his own right | Section 2(4). |
| Subject to a protected occupancy | Section 3(6). |
| Subject to a statutory tenancy | Section 4(6). |
| Tenancy | Section 34(1). |
| Tenancy at a low rent | Section 34(1). |
| Tenant | Section 34(1). |

PART I<br>STATUTES

**[193]**

## SCHEDULE 2
### MEANING OF "RELEVANT LICENCE" AND "RELEVANT TENANCY"
Section 1

#### *Relevant licence*

1. In this Act "relevant licence" means any licence under which a person has the exclusive occupation of a dwelling-house as a separate dwelling and which—
  (a) if it were a tenancy, and
  [(b) if the provisions of Part I of the Rent Act 1977 relating to exceptions to the definition of "protected tenancy" were modified as mentioned in paragraph 3 below,]
would be a protected tenancy for the purposes of that Act.

#### *Relevant tenancy*

2. In this Act "relevant tenancy" means any tenancy under which a dwelling-house is let as a separate dwelling and which—
  (a) is not a protected tenancy for the purposes of [the Rent Act 1977], but
  (b) would be such a tenancy if [the provisions of the Act mentioned in paragraph 1(b) above] were modified as mentioned in paragraph 3 below,
other than a tenancy to which Part I or Part II of the Landlord and Tenant Act 1954 applies [a tenancy to which Schedule 10 to the Local Government and Housing Act 1989 applies][, a tenancy of an agricultural holding within the meaning of the Agricultural Holdings Act 1986 which is a *tenancy in relation to* which that Act applies, and a farm business tenancy within the meaning of the Agricultural Tenancies Act 1995.]

[3.—(1) For the purposes of this Schedule the modifications of Part I of the Rent Act 1977 are as follows.

 (2) Omit sections 5 (tenancies at low rents) and 10 (tenancy of a dwelling-house comprised in any agricultural holding etc).

 [(2A) In section 5A (exclusion of certain shared ownership leases), in subsection (2)(g) (condition that lease states landlord's opinion that 1977 Act does not apply) for the reference to the 1977 Act substitute a reference to this Act.]

 (3) For section 7 (payments for board or attendance) substitute:—

"7.—(1)   A tenancy is not a protected tenancy if it is a bona fide term of the tenancy that the landlord provides the tenant with board or attendance.

(2)   For the avoidance of doubt it is hereby declared that meals provided in the course of a person's employment in agriculture do not constitute board for the purposes of this section; and a term that the landlord provides the tenant with attendance shall not be taken to be a bona fide term for those purposes unless, having regard to its value to the tenant, the attendance is substantial."

4.   The other provisions of [the Rent Act 1977] which are relevant for the purposes of the above definitions, and which are therefore also applied by this Schedule, include—

section 1 (definition of "protected tenancy");
[section 13] (no protected or statutory tenancy where landlord's interest belongs to Crown);
[sections 14 to 16] (no protected or statutory tenancy where landlord's interest belongs to local authority, etc);
[section 12] (no protected tenancy in certain cases where landlord's interest belongs to resident landlord);
[section 25] (rateable value and appropriate day).

**[194]**

**NOTES**
Para 1: words in square brackets substituted by the Rent Act 1977, s 155, Sch 23, para 78.
Para 2: words in first and second pairs of square brackets substituted by the Rent Act 1977, s 155, Sch 23, para 79; words in the third pair of square brackets inserted by the Local Government and Housing Act 1989, s 194(1), Sch 11, para 50; words in fourth pair of square brackets substituted by the Agricultural Tenancies Act 1995, s 40, Schedule, para 26.
Para 3: inserted by the Rent Act 1977, s 155, Sch 23, para 80; sub-para (2A) inserted by the Housing and Planning Act 1986, s 18, Sch 4, paras 2, 11(1).
Para 4: words in square brackets substituted by the Rent Act 1977, s 155, Sch 23, para 81.

## SCHEDULE 3
## PROTECTED OCCUPIERS IN THEIR OWN RIGHT

Section 1

## PART I
## DEFINITIONS

### *Qualifying worker*

1.   A person is a qualifying worker for the purposes of this Act at any time if, at that time, he has worked whole-time in agriculture, or has worked in agriculture as a permit worker, for not less than 91 out of the last 104 weeks.

### *Incapable of whole-time work in agriculture, or work in agriculture as a permit worker, in consequence of a qualifying injury or disease*

2.—(1)   A person is, for the purposes of this Act, incapable of whole-time work in agriculture in consequence of a qualifying injury or disease if—
(a)   he is incapable of such work in consequence of—
  (i)   an injury or disease prescribed in relation to him, by reason of his employment in agriculture, under section 76(2) of the Social Security Act 1975, or
  (ii)   an injury caused by an accident arising out of and in the course of his employment in agriculture, and
(b)   at the time when he became so incapable, he was employed in agriculture as a whole-time worker.

(2)   A person is, for the purposes of this Act, incapable of work in agriculture as a permit worker in consequence of a qualifying injury or disease if—
(a)   he is incapable of such work in consequence of any such injury or disease as is mentioned in sub-paragraph (1) above, and
(b)   at the time when he became so incapable, he was employed in agriculture as a permit worker.

(3)   Where—
(a)   a person has died in consequence of any such injury or disease as is mentioned in sub-paragraph (1) above, and
(b)   immediately before his death, he was employed in agriculture as a whole-time worker, or as a permit worker,

he shall be regarded for the purposes of this Act as having been, immediately before his death, incapable of whole-time work in agriculture, or work in agriculture as a permit worker, in consequence of a qualifying injury or disease.

*Dwelling-house in qualifying ownership*

3.—(1) A dwelling-house in relation to which a person ("the occupier") has a licence or tenancy is in qualifying ownership for the purposes of this Act at any time if, at that time, the occupier is employed in agriculture and the occupier's employer either—

(a) is the owner of the dwelling-house, or

(b) has made arrangements with the owner of the dwelling-house for it to be used as housing accommodation for persons employed by him in agriculture.

(2) In this paragraph—

"employer", in relation to the occupier, means the person or, as the case may be, one of the persons by whom he is employed in agriculture;

"owner", in relation to the dwelling-house, means the occupier's immediate landlord or, where the occupier is a licensee, the person who would be the occupier's immediate landlord if the licence were a tenancy.

*Supplemental*

4.—(1) The provisions of this paragraph shall have effect for determining what is whole-time work in agriculture for the purposes of this Part of this Schedule.

(2) A person works whole-time in agriculture for any week in which—

(a) he is employed to work in agriculture, and

(b) the number of hours for which he works in agriculture, or in activities incidental to agriculture, for the person or persons by whom he is so employed is not less than the standard number of hours.

(3) Where a person is employed in agriculture as a whole-time worker, any week in which by agreement with his employer or, where he has two or more employers, by agreement with the employer or employers concerned he works less than the standard number of hours shall count as a week of whole-time work in agriculture.

(4) If in any week a person who is employed in agriculture as a whole-time worker is, for the whole or part of the week—

(a) absent from work in agriculture by reason of his taking a holiday to which he is entitled, or

(b) absent from work in agriculture with the consent of his employer or, where he has two or more employers, with the consent of the employer or employers concerned, or

(c) incapable of whole-time work in agriculture in consequence of an injury or disease (whether a qualifying injury or disease or not),

that week shall count as a week of whole-time work in agriculture.

(5) If in any week a person (whether employed in agriculture as a whole-time worker or not) is, for the whole or part of the week, incapable of whole-time work in agriculture in consequence of a qualifying injury or disease, that week shall count as a week of whole-time work in agriculture.

5.—(1) The provisions of this paragraph shall have effect for determining what is work in agriculture as a permit worker for the purposes of this Part of this Schedule.

(2) A person works in agriculture as a permit worker for any week in which he works in agriculture as an employee for the whole or part of the week and there is in force in relation to him a permit granted under section 5 of the Agricultural Wages Act 1948.

(3) If in any week a person who is employed in agriculture as a permit worker is, for the whole or part of the week—

(a) absent from work in agriculture by reason of his taking a holiday to which he is entitled, or

(b) absent from work in agriculture with the consent of his employer or, where he has two or more employers, with the consent of the employer or employers concerned, or

(c) incapable of work in agriculture as a permit worker in consequence of an injury or disease (whether a qualifying injury or disease or not),

that week shall count as a week of work in agriculture as a permit worker.

(4) If in any week a person (whether employed in agriculture as a permit worker or not) is, for the whole or part of the week, incapable of work in agriculture as a permit worker in consequence of a qualifying injury or disease, that week shall count as a week of work in agriculture as a permit worker.

6. For the purposes of this Part of this Schedule a person is employed in agriculture as a whole-time worker if he is employed to work in agriculture by the week, or by any period longer than a week, and the number of hours for which he is employed to work in agriculture, or in activities incidental to agriculture, in any week is not less than the standard number of hours.

7.   For the purposes of this Part of this Schedule, a person is employed in agriculture as a permit worker if he is employed in agriculture and there is in force in relation to him a permit granted under section 5 of the Agricultural Wages Act 1948.

**[195]**

**NOTES**

Social Security Act 1975, s 76(2): repealed by the Social Security (Consequential Provisions) Act 1992, s 3, Sch 1; by virtue of the Social Security (Consequential Provisions) Act 1992, s 2(2), regulations prescribing injuries or diseases under s 76(2) of the 1975 Act take effect under the Social Security Contributions and Benefits Act 1992, s 108.

## PART II
### TEMPORARY PROVISIONS AS RESPECTS CERTAIN FORESTRY WORKERS

8.   In this Act "the date of operation for forestry workers" means such date after the operative date as the Secretary of State and the Minister of Agriculture, Fisheries and Food acting jointly may appoint by order contained in a statutory instrument.

9.—(1)   Whole-time work in forestry, and work in forestry as a permit worker, shall be left out of account in determining for the purposes of this Act whether, at a date before the date of operation for forestry workers, a person is a qualifying worker.

   (2)   Employment in forestry as a whole-time worker, or as a permit worker, shall be left out of account in determining for the purposes of this Act whether, at a date before the date of operation for forestry workers, a person is incapable of whole-time work in agriculture, or work in agriculture as a permit worker, in consequence of a qualifying injury or disease.

10.—(1)   The question of what is whole-time work in forestry, or work in forestry as a permit worker, for the purposes of this Part of this Schedule shall be determined in the same way as what is whole-time work in agriculture, or work in agriculture as a permit worker, is determined for the purposes of Part I of this Schedule, and for that purpose all work which is not work in forestry shall be disregarded.

   (2)   For the purposes of this Part of this Schedule a person is employed in forestry as a whole-time worker if he is employed to work in forestry by the week, or by any period longer than a week, and the number of hours for which he is employed to work in forestry, or in activities incidental to forestry, in any week is not less than the standard number of hours.

   (3)   For the purposes of this Part of this Schedule a person is employed in forestry as a permit worker if he is employed in forestry and there is in force in relation to him a permit granted under section 5 of the Agricultural Wages Act 1948.

**[196]**

**NOTES**

Orders: the Rent (Agriculture) Act 1976 (Commencement No 2) Order 1977, SI 1977/1268.

## PART III
### SUPPLEMENTAL

11.—(1)   In this Schedule "employment" means employment under one or more contracts of employment, and cognate expressions shall be construed accordingly.

   (2)   For the purposes of the definition in sub-paragraph (1) above "contract of employment" means a contract of employment or apprenticeship (whether express or implied and, if express, whether oral or in writing).

12.—(1)   In this Schedule "the standard number of hours" means 35 hours or such other number of hours as may be specified in an order made by the Secretary of State and the Minister of Agriculture, Fisheries and Food acting jointly.

   (2)   An order under this paragraph shall be made by statutory instrument which shall be subject to annulment in pursuance of a resolution of either House of Parliament.

   (3)   An order made under this paragraph—
   (a)   may contain transitional and other supplemental and incidental provisions, and
   (b)   may be varied or revoked by a subsequent order so made.

13.   Any reference in this Schedule, to work in agriculture or in forestry, or to employment in agriculture or in forestry, is a reference to such work or such employment, in the United Kingdom (including the Channel Islands and the Isle of Man) or in the territory of any other State which is a member of the European Economic Community.

**[197]**

## SCHEDULE 4
## GROUNDS FOR POSSESSION OF DWELLING-HOUSE SUBJECT TO PROTECTED OCCUPANCY OR STATUTORY TENANCY

Section 6

### PART I
### CASES WHERE COURT HAS A DISCRETION

*Case I*
*Alternative accommodation not provided or arranged by housing authority*

1.   The court is satisfied that suitable alternative accommodation is available for the tenant, or will be available for him when the order for possession takes effect.

2.—[(1)]   Accommodation shall be deemed suitable in this Case if it consists of—
   (a)   premises which are to be let as a separate dwelling such that they will then be let on a protected tenancy within the meaning of [the Rent Act 1977], or
   (b)   premises which are to be let as a separate dwelling on terms which will, in the opinion of the court, afford to the tenant security of tenure reasonably equivalent to the security afforded by [Part VII of the Rent Act 1977] in the case of a protected tenancy,

and, in the opinion of the court, the accommodation fulfils the conditions in paragraph 3 below.

  [(2)   … ]

3.—(1)   The accommodation must be reasonably suitable to the needs of the tenant and his family as regards proximity to place of work and either—
   (a)   similar as regards rental and extent to the accommodation afforded by dwelling-houses provided in the neighbourhood by the housing authority concerned for persons whose needs as regards extent are similar to those of the tenant and his family, or
   (b)   reasonably suitable to the means of the tenant, and to the needs of the tenant and his family as regards extent and character.

  (2)   For the purposes of sub-paragraph (1)(a) above, a certificate of the housing authority concerned stating—
   (a)   the extent of the accommodation afforded by dwelling-houses provided by the authority to meet the needs of tenants with families of such number as may be specified in the certificate, and
   (b)   the amount of the rent charged by the housing authority concerned for dwelling-houses affording accommodation of that extent,

shall be conclusive evidence of the facts so stated.

  (3)   If any furniture was provided by the landlord for use under the tenancy, furniture must be provided for use in the alternative accommodation which is either similar, or is reasonably suitable to the needs of the tenant and his family.

4.   Accommodation shall not be deemed to be suitable to the needs of the tenant and his family if the result of their occupation of the accommodation would be that it would be an overcrowded dwelling-house for the purposes of [Part X of the Housing Act 1985].

5.   Any document purporting to be a certificate of the housing authority concerned issued for the purposes of this Case and to be signed by the proper officer of the authority shall be received in evidence and, unless the contrary is shown, shall be deemed to be such a certificate without further proof.

6.   In this Case no account shall be taken of accommodation as respects which an offer has been made, or notice has been given, as mentioned in paragraph 1 of Case II below.

*Case II*
*Alternative accommodation provided or arranged by housing authority*

1.   The housing authority concerned have made an offer in writing to the tenant of alternative accommodation which appears to them to be suitable, specifying the date when the accommodation will be available and the date (not being less than 14 days from the date of offer) by which the offer must be accepted.

  OR

The housing authority concerned have given notice in writing to the tenant that they have received from a person specified in the notice an offer in writing to rehouse the tenant in alternative accommodation which appears to the housing authority concerned to be suitable, and the notice specifies both the date when the accommodation will be available and the date (not being less than 14 days from the date when the notice was given to the tenant) by which the offer must be accepted.

2.   The landlord shows that the tenant accepted the offer (by the housing authority or other person) within the time duly specified in the offer.

  OR

The landlord shows that the tenant did not so accept the offer, and the tenant does not satisfy the court that he acted reasonably in failing to accept the offer.

3.—(1) The accommodation offered must in the opinion of the court fulfil the conditions in this paragraph.

(2) The accommodation must be reasonably suitable to the needs of the tenant and his family as regards proximity to place of work.

(3) The accommodation must be reasonably suitable to the means of the tenant, and to the needs of the tenant and his family as regards extent.

4. If the accommodation offered is available for a limited period only, the housing authority's offer or notice under paragraph 1 above must contain an assurance that other accommodation—

- (a) the availability of which is not so limited,
- (b) which appears to them to be suitable, and
- (c) which fulfils the conditions in paragraph 3 above, will be offered to the tenant as soon as practicable.

## Case III

Rent lawfully due from the tenant has not been paid,

OR

Any other lawful obligation of the tenancy, whether or not it is an obligation created by this Act, has been broken or not performed.

## Case IV

The tenant, or any person residing or lodging with him or sub-tenant of his, has been guilty of conduct which is a nuisance or annoyance to adjoining occupiers, or has been convicted of using the dwelling-house, or allowing the dwelling-house to be used, for immoral or illegal purposes.

## Case V

1. The condition of the dwelling-house has, in the opinion of the court, deteriorated owing to acts of waste by, or the neglect or default of, the tenant or any person residing or lodging with him, or any sub-tenant of his.

2. If the person at fault is not the tenant, the court must be satisfied that the tenant has not, before the making of the order for possession, taken such steps as he ought reasonably to have taken for the removal of the person at fault.

## Case VI

1. The condition of any furniture provided by the landlord for use under the tenancy has, in the opinion of the court, deteriorated owing to ill-treatment by the tenant or any person residing or lodging with him, or any sub-tenant of his.

2. If the person at fault is not the tenant, the court must be satisfied that the tenant has not, before the making of the order for possession, taken such steps as he ought reasonably to have taken for the removal of the person at fault.

## Case VII

1. The tenant has given notice to quit and in consequence of that notice the landlord has contracted to sell or let the dwelling-house, or has taken any other steps as a result of which he would, in the opinion of the court, be seriously prejudiced if he could not obtain possession.

2. This Case does not apply where the tenant has given notice to terminate his employment and that notice has operated to terminate the tenancy.

## Case VIII

1. The tenant has, without the consent of the landlord, assigned, sub-let or parted with possession of the dwelling-house, or any part of it.

2. This Case does not apply if the assignment, sub-letting or parting with possession was effected before the operative date.

## Case IX

1. The dwelling-house is reasonably required by the landlord for occupation as a residence for—

- (a) himself, or
- (b) any son or daughter of his over 18 years of age, or
- (c) his father or mother, or the father or mother of his wife, or husband [or civil partner], or
- (d) his grandfather or grandmother, or the grandfather or grandmother of his wife, or husband [or civil partner],

and the landlord did not become landlord by purchasing the dwelling-house, or any interest in it, after 12th April 1976.

2. The court, having regard to all the circumstances of the case, including the question whether other accommodation is available for the landlord or tenant, is satisfied that no greater hardship would be caused by granting the order than by refusing to grant it.

### Case X

1. Any part of the dwelling-house is sublet.

2. The court is satisfied that the rent charged by the tenant is or was in excess of the maximum rent recoverable for that part, having regard to the provisions of [ ... Part III or Part V of the Rent Act 1977] or Part II of this Act, as the case may require.

3. Paragraph 2 does not apply to a rental period beginning before the operative date.

**[198]**

### NOTES

Case I: para 2(1) numbered as such and para 2(2) added by the Housing and Planning Act 1986, s 13(3); para 2(2) subsequently repealed by the Housing Act 1988, s 140(2), Sch 18; words in square brackets in para 2(1)(a), (b) substituted by the Rent Act 1977, s 155, Sch 23, para 82(a), (b); words in square brackets in para 4 substituted by the Housing (Consequential Provisions) Act 1985, s 4, Sch 2, para 33(1), (4)(a).

Case IX: words in square brackets inserted by the Civil Partnership Act 2004, s 81, Sch 8, para 12.

Case X: words in square brackets substituted by the Rent Act 1977, s 155, Sch 23, para 82(c); words omitted repealed by the Housing Act 1980, s 152, Sch 26.

## PART II
## CASES IN WHICH COURT MUST ORDER POSSESSION

### Case XI

1. The person who granted the tenancy or, as the case may be, the original tenancy ("the original occupier") was, prior to granting it, occupying the dwelling house as his residence.

2. The court is satisfied that the dwelling-house is required as a residence for the original occupier or any member of his family who resided with the original occupier when he last occupied the dwelling-house as his residence.

3. Not later than the relevant date the original occupier gave notice in writing to the tenant that possession might be recovered under this Case.

4. The dwelling-house has not since the operative date been let by the original occupier to a tenant as respects whom the condition mentioned in paragraph 3 above was not satisfied.

5. The court may dispense with the requirements of either or both of paragraphs 3 and 4 if of opinion that it is just and equitable so to do.

6. In this Case and in Case XII below—
    "original tenancy", in relation to a statutory tenancy, means the tenancy on the termination of which the statutory tenancy arose;
    "the relevant date" means the date of the commencement of the tenancy, or as the case may be, the original tenancy, or the expiration of the period of six months beginning with the operative date, whichever is the later.

### Case XII

1. The person who granted the tenancy, or, as the case may be, the original tenancy ("the owner") acquired the dwelling-house or any interest in it, with a view to occupying it as his residence at such time as he should retire from regular employment.

2. The court is satisfied—
   (a)   that the owner has retired from regular employment and requires the dwelling-house as his residence, or
   (b)   that the owner has died and the dwelling-house is required as a residence for a member of his family who was residing with him at the time of his death.

3. Not later than the relevant date the owner gave notice in writing to the tenant that possession might be recovered under this Case.

4. The dwelling-house has not since the operative date been let by the owner to a tenant as respects whom the condition mentioned in paragraph 3 above was not satisfied.

5. The court may dispense with the requirements of either or both of paragraphs 3 and 4 if of opinion that it is just and equitable so to do.

*Case XIII*

The dwelling-house is overcrowded, within the meaning of [Part X of the Housing Act 1985], in such circumstances as to render the occupier guilty of an offence.

**[199]**

**NOTES**

Case XIII: words in square brackets substituted by the Housing (Consequential Provisions) Act 1985, s 4, Sch 2, para 33(1), (4)(b).

## SCHEDULE 5
### TERMS OF THE STATUTORY TENANCY

Section 10

*Preliminary*

1.—(1)   In this Schedule the "original contract", in relation to a statutory tenancy, means the licence or tenancy on the termination of which the statutory tenancy arose.

(2)   No account shall be taken for the purposes of this Schedule of any term of the original contract under which the right of occupation depended, or which itself depended, on the occupier being employed in agriculture or in some other way.

(3)   In this Schedule "term", in relation to the statutory tenancy, or in relation to the original contract, includes a condition of the tenancy or contract.

*Terms derived from the original licence or tenancy*

2.—(1)   So long as he retains possession, the statutory tenant shall observe, and be entitled to the benefit of, all the terms of the original contract.

(2)   Sub-paragraph (1) applies whether or not the terms are express or implied or statutory.

(3)   Sub-paragraph (1) applies subject to the provisions of this Schedule, and of Part II of this Act.

*Tenancy derived from licence*

3.   If the original contract was a licence, the statutory tenancy shall be a weekly tenancy.

*Covenant for quiet enjoyment, etc*

4.—(1)   If the original contract was a licence, the terms of the statutory tenancy shall include any term which would be implied if the contract had been a contract of tenancy.

(2)   This applies in particular to the landlord's covenant for quiet enjoyment and the tenant's obligation to use the premises in a tenant-like manner, which are implied in any tenancy.

*Non-contractual arrangements*

5.—(1)   It shall be a term of the statutory tenancy that the landlord provides the tenant with any services or facilities—
- (a)   which the landlord was providing for the occupier before the beginning of the statutory tenancy, though not under the original contract, or which he had provided for the occupier, but was not providing when the original contract terminated, and
- (b)   which are reasonably necessary for any person occupying the dwelling-house as a statutory tenant, but which such a tenant cannot reasonably be expected to provide for himself.

(2)   This paragraph may apply, for example, where the only convenient electricity or water supplies, or the only convenient sewage disposal facilities, are those provided by the landlord from his own installations.

*Landlord's obligation to repair*

6.—(1)   [Section 11 of the Landlord and Tenant Act 1985] shall apply to the dwelling-house so long as it is subject to the statutory tenancy.

(2)   This paragraph is without prejudice to the operation of paragraph 2 above where the original contract was a tenancy to which [the said section 11] applied.

*Tenant's obligations*

7.—(1)   It shall be a condition of the statutory tenancy that the tenant will not use the dwelling-house, or any part of it, for purposes other than those of a private dwelling-house.

(2)   It shall be a condition of the statutory tenancy that the tenant will not assign, sub-let, or part with possession of, the dwelling-house, or any part of it.

(3)   Sub-paragraph (2) does not affect anything lawfully done before the beginning of the statutory tenancy.

### Access by landlord

8.   It shall be a condition of the statutory tenancy that the tenant will afford to the landlord access to the dwelling-house and all reasonable facilities for executing therein any repairs which the landlord is entitled to execute.

### Access by tenant

9.—(1)   The landlord shall afford any such right of access to the dwelling-house as is reasonable in the circumstances.

(2)   In applying sub-paragraph (1) account shall be taken of any right of access to be afforded under paragraph 2 or 4 of this Schedule.

(3)   Without prejudice to the definition of original contract in paragraph 1 of this Schedule, any right of access to be afforded under paragraph 2 of this Schedule shall be confined to such right of access to the dwelling-house as is reasonable in the circumstances, and without regard to any right of access afforded wholly or mainly because the occupier of the dwelling-house, or his predecessor, was employed on the land.

(4)   Paragraph 5 of this Schedule shall not apply to facilities for access to the dwelling-house.

(5)   If it is reasonably necessary in order to prevent the spread of disease which might otherwise affect livestock or crops, whether on the landlord's land or elsewhere, the landlord may temporarily restrict access to the dwelling-house made available in pursuance of this Schedule so long as suitable alternative access is available or is made available.

(6)   If it is reasonably necessary in the interests of efficient agriculture, the landlord may permanently or temporarily deprive the dwelling-house of access made available in pursuance of this Schedule so long as suitable alternative access is available or is made available.

### Notice to quit served on landlord

10.—(1)   If the original contract—
  (a)   was not a tenancy, or
  (b)   was a tenancy the provisions of which did not require the tenant to give notice to quit before giving up possession,
the statutory tenant shall be entitled to give up possession of the dwelling-house if, and only if, he gives not less than four weeks' notice to quit.

(2)   If the original contract required the tenant to give notice to quit before giving up possession, the statutory tenant shall be entitled to give up possession of the dwelling-house, if, and only if, he gives that notice, or, if longer, the notice required by [section 5 of the Protection from Eviction Act 1977] (four weeks' notice).

### Rates, water rates, etc

11.—(1)   Paragraph 2 of this Schedule shall not impose any liability on the tenant to make payments to the landlord in respect of rates borne by the landlord or a superior landlord.

(2)   The following provisions of this paragraph shall apply as respects any rental period of the statutory tenancy, including one as respects which an agreement under section 11 of this Act either fixes the rent or provides that no rent is payable.

(3)   Subject to sub-paragraph (4) below, where any rates in respect of the dwelling-house are borne by the landlord or a superior landlord, the amount of the rates for the rental period, as ascertained in accordance with [Schedule 5 to the Rent Act 1977], shall be recoverable from the statutory tenant as if it were rent payable under the statutory tenancy.

(4)   The tenant's liability under sub-paragraph (3) above shall not arise unless notice in writing to that effect is served by the landlord on the tenant, and that notice shall take effect from such as may be specified in the notice, which shall not be earlier than four weeks before service of the *notice*.

(5)   If the dwelling-house forms part only of a hereditament in respect of which any rates are charged, the proportion for which the statutory tenant is liable under this paragraph shall be such as may be agreed by him with the landlord, or as may be determined by the county court; and the decision of the county court shall be final.

(6)   In this paragraph "rental period" means in relation to a statutory tenancy under which no rent is payable, any period of the statutory tenancy which would be a rental period if a rent were payable under that tenancy; and in [Schedule 5 to the Rent Act 1977] as applied by sub-paragraph (3) above any reference to a rental period, or to a rating period during which the rent for a rental period is payable, shall be construed accordingly.

*Variation of statutory tenancy*

12.—(1)   Subject to the provisions of this paragraph, the landlord and the statutory tenant may by agreement in writing vary any of the provisions of the statutory tenancy.

(2)   An agreement under this paragraph may be made at any time, including a time before the beginning of the statutory tenancy.

(3)   So far as a variation of the provisions of the statutory tenancy concerns rent it shall be effected in accordance with section 11 of this Act, and no agreement under that section may conflict with any of the provisions of this Act.

(4)   This paragraph shall not authorise an agreement which results in—
(a)   a substantial addition to the land or premises which the statutory tenant is entitled to occupy, or
(b)   the breach of any obligation implied by law, and in particular the breach of the obligation imposed by [section 11 of the Landlord and Tenant Act 1985] (landlord's obligation to repair), or
(c)   the circumstances in which the statutory tenant can give notice to quit, or
(d)   the inclusion of any term which relates to the employment by the landlord of the tenant, or of any other term unrelated to the occupation of the dwelling-house.

(5)   The following bind any successor of the landlord or the tenant under a statutory tenancy to the same extent as they bind the landlord, or as the case may be the tenant—
(a)   an agreement under this paragraph,
(b)   an agreement under section 10(3)(b) or section 11 of this Act,
(c)   section 11(9) (rent payable after termination of agreement),
(d)   a notice of increase by the landlord under section 12 or section 14 of this Act,
(e)   a notice under paragraph 11 of this Schedule (rates recoverable by landlord from statutory tenant).

[200]

**NOTES**
Paras 6, 12: words in square brackets substituted by the Housing (Consequential Provisions) Act 1985, s 4, Sch 2, para 33(1), (5).
Para 10: words in square brackets substituted by the Protection from Eviction Act 1977, s 12, Sch 1, para 4.
Para 11: words in square brackets substituted by the Rent Act 1977, s 155, Sch 23, para 83.

*(Sch 6 repealed by the Rent (Relief from Phasing) Order 1987, SI 1987/264; Sch 7 repealed by the Social Security and Housing Benefits Act 1982, s 48(6), Sch 5; Sch 8 contains amendments which, in so far as within the scope of this work, have been incorporated at the appropriate place.)*

SCHEDULE 9
TRANSITIONAL

Section 40

*Licence or tenancy granted before operative date: resident landlord on and after that date*

1.   A licence or tenancy which was granted before the operative date shall not be a relevant licence or tenancy if, on the assumption—
(a)   that it was granted on the operative date, and
(b)   that the condition in paragraph (b) of subsection (1) of section 5A of the Rent Act 1968 (no protected tenancy in certain cases where landlord's interest belongs to resident landlord) was fulfilled,
it would be precluded from being a relevant licence or tenancy by virtue of the said section 5A as applied by Schedule 2 to this Act.

*Protected occupancy arising on or after operative date*

2.—(1)   This paragraph applies as respects the question whether at any date which is on or after the operative date a person who has in relation to a dwelling-house a relevant licence or tenancy is a protected occupier of the dwelling-house.

(2)   So far as the question depends on prior circumstances, they shall be taken into account even if occurring before the operative date.

(3)   In applying this paragraph to section 2(3) or to section 3 of this Act (so that the question whether a person is a protected occupier depends on whether he or another person was, at a time before the material date, a protected occupier or statutory tenant) it shall be assumed that this Act and the provisions of the Rent Act 1968 which are applied by Schedule 2 to this Act, including (where relevant) any amendments to those provisions, were in force at all material times before the operative date.

*Statutory tenancy arising on operative date*

3.  A person who is occupying a dwelling-house as his residence on the operative date shall become the statutory tenant of the dwelling-house if, on the assumption that this Act and the provisions of the Rent Act 1968 which are applied by Schedule 2 to this Act, including (where relevant) any amendments to those provisions, were in force at all material times before that date, he would be a statutory tenant of the dwelling-house on that date, and this Act shall thereafter apply to him, and by reference to him, on that assumption.

*Statutory tenancy: order for possession before operative date*

4.—(1)  Where before the operative date a court has made an order for possession of a dwelling-house which on the operative date is subject to a statutory tenancy and the order has not been executed, the court may, on the application of the person against whom the order was made, rescind or vary the order in such manner as the court thinks fit for the purpose of giving effect to this Act.

(2)  If proceedings for possession of the dwelling-house are pending on the operative date, Part II of this Act shall apply as it would apply to proceedings commenced on the operative date.

*Dwelling subject to Part VI contract: pending notice to quit*

5.—(1)  In any case where—
  (a)   before the operative date a notice to quit has been served in respect of a dwelling to which a Part VI contract then related, and
  (b)   the period at the end of which that notice to quit takes effect had, before the operative date, been extended under Part VI of the Rent Act 1968, and
  (c)   that period had not expired before the operative date, and
  (d)   on the operative date the Part VI contract becomes a protected occupancy,
the notice to quit shall take effect on the day following the operative date (whenever it would otherwise take effect) and, accordingly, on that day the protected occupancy shall become a statutory tenancy.

(2)  In this paragraph "Part VI contract" has the meaning given by section 70(6) of the Rent Act 1968.

*Section 10A tenancy: order for possession before operative date*

6.—(1)  This paragraph applies to a dwelling-house which is let on or subject to a tenancy which is a protected or statutory tenancy for the purposes of the Rent Act 1968 and which—
  (a)   if it were a tenancy at a low rent, and
  (b)   if (where relevant) any earlier tenancy granted to the tenant, or to a member of his family, had been a tenancy at a low rent,
would be a protected occupancy or statutory tenancy (that is to say a tenancy to which section 10A of that Act, inserted by this Act, applies).

(2)  Where—
  (a)   before the operative date a court has made an order for possession of the dwelling-house, and
  (b)   the order has not been executed, and
  (c)   the order was made under Case 7, 12, 13 or 14 of Schedule 3 to the Rent Act 1968,
the court shall on the application of the person against whom the order was made rescind the order, or vary it in such manner as the court thinks fit for the purposes of giving effect to the said section 10A.

(3)  If proceedings for an order for possession of a dwelling-house are pending on the operative date, the said section 10A shall apply to the proceedings as it would apply to proceedings commenced on the operative date.

*Forestry workers*

7.—(1)  This paragraph applies to a person—
  (a)   who becomes a protected occupier or statutory tenant at a time on or after the date of operation for forestry workers, and
  (b)   who, if the date of operation for forestry workers fell after that time, would not at that time (having regard to the provisions of paragraph 9 of Schedule 3 to this Act) have become a protected occupier or statutory tenant.

(2)  In relation to such a person references to the operative date in—
  (a)   Classes VIII, X, XI and XII of Schedule 4, and
  (b)   paragraphs 4 and 5 of this Schedule,
shall be taken as references to the date of operation for forestry workers.

(3)   In determining in accordance with paragraphs 1, 2 and 3 of this Schedule whether a person is a protected occupier or statutory tenant who would be a person to whom this paragraph applies, references in those paragraphs to the operative date shall be taken as references to the date of operation for forestry workers.

(4)   If, on the assumptions in paragraphs (a) and (b) of paragraph 6(1) of this Schedule the tenant would be a person to whom this paragraph applies, references to the operative date in sub-paragraphs (2) and (3) of that paragraph shall be taken as references to the date of operation for forestry workers.

**[201]**

**NOTES**
Rent Act 1968: repealed and replaced by the Rent Act 1977.

# RENT ACT 1977

### (1977 c 42)

## ARRANGEMENT OF SECTIONS

### PART I
### PRELIMINARY

*Protected and statutory tenancies*

### PART III
### RENTS UNDER REGULATED TENANCIES

*Regulation of rent*

## PART IV
### REGISTRATION OF RENTS UNDER REGULATED TENANCIES

## PART V
### RENTS UNDER RESTRICTED CONTRACTS

### *Control of rents*

### *Miscellaneous and general*

## PART VI
### RENT LIMIT FOR DWELLINGS LET BY HOUSING ASSOCIATIONS, HOUSING TRUSTS AND THE HOUSING CORPORATION

### *Registration of rents*

*An Act to consolidate the Rent Act 1968, Parts III, IV and VIII of the Housing Finance Act 1972, the
Rent Act 1974, sections 7 to 10 of the Housing Rents and Subsidies Act 1975, and certain related
enactments, with amendments to give effect to recommendations of the Law Commission*
[29 July 1977]

**NOTES**
Transfer of functions: as to the functions of Ministers of the Crown under this Act, so far as exercisable in
relation to Wales, being transferred to the National Assembly for Wales, see the National Assembly for Wales
(Transfer of Functions) Order 1999, SI 1999/672, art 2, Sch 1.

PART I
STATUTES

# PART I
# PRELIMINARY

**NOTES**

Phasing out of protected and statutory tenancies: the Housing Act 1988, s 34 at **[765]**, provides that no tenancy which is entered into on or after 15 January 1989 can be a protected tenancy for the purposes of this Act unless it is entered into under a contract made before that date, or it falls within one of the classes set out in s 34(1)(b)–(d) of the 1988 Act, which relate to new tenancies granted to existing protected or statutory tenants (but not a tenant under a protected shorthold tenancy), tenancies granted as suitable alternative accommodation in cases where the court has directed that the tenancy shall be protected under this Act, and certain former new town corporation tenancies. The Housing Act 1988, Pt I, Chapter I (ss 1–19, Schs 1, 2) at **[729]**–**[752]** and **[782]**–**[788]**, creates a new form of assured tenancy, which, generally, does not apply to tenancies entered into before, or under a contract made before, 15 January 1989. A protected tenancy within the meaning of s 1 of this Act at **[202]** cannot be an assured tenancy within the meaning of s 1 of, and Sch 1 to, the 1988 Act at **[729]**, **[782]**, but tenancies which, by virtue of s 34 of the 1988 Act, are not protected under this Act will generally become assured tenancies under Pt I, Chapter I of the 1988 Act except where s 34(3) thereof applies, in which case they will become assured shorthold tenancies under Pt I, Chapter II of that Act (ss 19A–23, Sch 2A) at **[753]**–**[759]** and **[789]**, whether or not, in the case of a tenancy to which the provision applies, the conditions in s 20(1) thereof at **[754]**, are fulfilled.

*Protected and statutory tenancies*

## 1 Protected tenants and tenancies

Subject to this Part of this Act, a tenancy under which a dwelling-house (which may be a house or part of a house) is let as a separate dwelling is a protected tenancy for the purposes of this Act.

Any reference in this Act to a protected tenant shall be construed accordingly.

**[202]**

## 2 Statutory tenants and tenancies

(1) Subject to this Part of this Act—

    (a) after the termination of a protected tenancy of a dwelling-house the person who, immediately before that termination, was the protected tenant of the dwelling-house shall, if and so long as he occupies the dwelling-house as his residence, be the statutory tenant of it; and

    (b) Part I of Schedule 1 to this Act shall have effect for determining what person (if any) is the statutory tenant of a dwelling-house [or, as the case may be, is entitled to an assured tenancy of a dwelling-house by succession] at any time after the death of a person who, immediately before his death, was either a protected tenant of the dwelling-house or the statutory tenant of it by virtue of paragraph (a) above.

(2) In this Act a dwelling-house is referred to as subject to a statutory tenancy when there is a statutory tenant of it.

(3) In subsection (1)(a) above and in Part I of Schedule 1, the phrase "if and so long as he occupies the dwelling-house as his residence" shall be construed as it was immediately before the commencement of this Act (that is to say, in accordance with section 3(2) of the Rent Act 1968).

(4) A person who becomes a statutory tenant of a dwelling-house as mentioned in subsection (1)(a) above is, in this Act, referred to as a statutory tenant by virtue of his previous protected tenancy.

(5) A person who becomes a statutory tenant as mentioned in subsection (1)(b) above is, in this Act, referred to as a statutory tenant by succession.

**[203]**

**NOTES**

Sub-s (1): words in square brackets inserted by the Housing Act 1988, s 39(1).

Rent Act 1968, s 3(2): repealed by s 155(5) of, and Sch 25 to, this Act.

## 3 Terms and conditions of statutory tenancies

(1) So long as he retains possession, a statutory tenant shall observe and be entitled to the benefit of all the terms and conditions of the original contract of tenancy, so far as they are consistent with the provisions of this Act.

(2) It shall be a condition of a statutory tenancy of a dwelling-house that the statutory tenant shall afford to the landlord access to the dwelling-house and all reasonable facilities for executing therein any repairs which the landlord is entitled to execute.

(3) Subject to section 5 of the Protection from Eviction Act 1977 (under which at least 4 weeks' notice to quit is required), a statutory tenant of a dwelling-house shall be entitled to give up possession of the dwelling-house if, and only if, he gives such notice as would have been required under the provisions of the original contract of tenancy, or, if no notice would have been so required, on giving not less than 3 months' notice.

(4)    Notwithstanding anything in the contract of tenancy, a landlord who obtains an order for possession of a dwelling-house as against a statutory tenant shall not be required to give to the statutory tenant any notice to quit.

(5)    Part II of Schedule 1 to this Act shall have effect in relation to the giving up of possession of statutory tenancies and the changing of statutory tenants by agreement.

**[204]**

*Exceptions*

### 4   Dwelling-houses above certain rateable values

(1)    A tenancy [which is entered into before 1st April 1990 or (where the dwelling-house had a rateable value on 31st March 1990) is entered into on or after 1st April 1990 in pursuance of a contract made before that date] is not a protected tenancy if the dwelling-house falls within one of the Classes set out in subsection (2) below.

(2)    Where alternative rateable values are mentioned in this subsection, the higher applies if the dwelling-house is in Greater London and the lower applies if it is elsewhere.

#### Class A

The appropriate day in relation to the dwelling-house falls or fell on or after 1st April 1973 and the dwelling-house on the appropriate day has or had a rateable value exceeding £1,500 or £750.

#### Class B

The appropriate day in relation to the dwelling-house fell on or after 22nd March 1973, but before 1st April 1973, and the dwelling-house—
    (a)    on the appropriate day had a rateable value exceeding £600 or £300, and
    (b)    on 1st April 1973 had a rateable value exceeding £1,500 or £750.

#### Class C

The appropriate day in relation to the dwelling-house fell before 22nd March 1973 and the dwelling-house—
    (a)    on the appropriate day had a rateable value exceeding £400 or £200, and
    (b)    on 22nd March 1973 had a rateable value exceeding £600 or £300, and
    (c)    on 1st April 1973 had a rateable value exceeding £1,500 or £750.

(3)    If any question arises in any proceedings whether a dwelling-house falls within a Class in subsection (2) above, by virtue of its rateable value at any time, it shall be deemed not to fall within that Class unless the contrary is shown.

[(4)    A tenancy is not a protected tenancy if—
    (a)    it is entered into on or after 1st April 1990 (otherwise than, where the dwelling-house had a rateable value on 31st March 1990, in pursuance of a contract made before 1st April 1990), and
    (b)    under it the rent payable for the time being is payable at a rate exceeding £25,000 a year.

(5)    In subsection (4) above "rent" does not include any sum payable by the tenant as is expressed (in whatever terms) to be payable in respect of rates [council tax], services, repairs, maintenance or insurance, unless it could not have been regarded by the parties as a sum so payable.

(6)    If any question arises in any proceedings whether a tenancy is precluded from being a protected tenancy by subsection (4) above, the tenancy shall be deemed to be a protected tenancy unless the contrary is shown.

(7)    The Secretary of State may by order replace the amount referred to in subsection (4) above by an amount specified in the order; and such an order shall be made by statutory instrument which shall be subject to annulment in pursuance of a resolution of either House of Parliament.]

**[205]**

**NOTES**
    Sub-s (1): words in square brackets inserted by the References to Rating (Housing) Regulations 1990, SI 1990/434, reg 2, Schedule, para 15.
    Sub-ss (4), (6), (7): added by SI 1990/434, reg 2, Schedule, para 16.
    Sub-s (5): added by SI 1990/434, reg 2, Schedule, para 16; words in square brackets inserted by the Local Government Finance (Housing) (Consequential Amendments) Order 1993, SI 1993/651, art 2(1), Sch 1, para 3.

### 5   Tenancies at low rents

(1)    A tenancy [which was entered into before 1st April 1990 or (where the dwelling-house had a rateable value on 31st March 1990) is entered into on or after 1st April 1990 in pursuance of a contract made before that date] is not a protected tenancy if under the tenancy either no rent is payable or, … , the rent payable is less than two-thirds of the rateable value which is or was the rateable value of the dwelling-house on the appropriate day.

(2) Where—

    (a)    the appropriate day in relation to a dwelling-house fell before 22nd March 1973, and

    (b)    the dwelling-house had on the appropriate day a rateable value exceeding, if it is in Greater London, £400 or, if it is elsewhere, £200,

subsection (1) above shall apply in relation to the dwelling-house as if the reference to the appropriate day were a reference to 22nd March 1973.

[(2A)    A tenancy is not a protected tenancy if—

    (a)    it is entered into on or after 1st April 1990 (otherwise than, where the dwelling-house had a rateable value on 31st March 1990, in pursuance of a contract made before 1st April 1990), and

    (b)    under the tenancy for the time being either no rent is payable or the rent is payable at a rate of, if the dwelling-house is in Greater London, £1,000 or less a year, and, if the dwelling-house is elsewhere, £250 or less a year.

(2B)    Subsection (7) of section 4 above shall apply to any amount referred to in subsection (2A) above as it applies to the amount referred to in subsection (4) of that section.]

(3)    In this Act a tenancy falling within subsection (1) above, is referred to as a "tenancy at a low rent".

(4)    In determining whether a long tenancy is a tenancy at a low rent, there shall be disregarded such part (if any) of the sums payable by the tenant as is expressed (in whatever terms) to be payable in respect of rates [council tax], services, repairs, maintenance, or insurance, unless it could not have been regarded by the parties as a part so payable.

(5)    In subsection (4) above "long tenancy" means a tenancy granted for a term certain exceeding 21 years, other than a tenancy which is, or may become, terminable before the end of that term by notice given to the tenant.

**[206]**

### NOTES

Sub-s (1): words in square brackets inserted by the References to Rating (Housing) Regulations 1990, SI 1990/434, reg 2, Schedule, para 17; words omitted repealed by the Housing Act 1980, s 152, Sch 26, subject to savings in Sch 25, Pt II, para 75 thereof at **[392]**.

Sub-ss (2A), (2B): inserted by SI 1990/434, reg 2, Schedule, para 18.

Sub-s (4): words in square brackets inserted by the Local Government Finance (Housing) (Consequential Amendments) Order 1993, SI 1993/651, art 2(1), Sch 1, para 4.

### [5A    Certain shared ownership leases

(1)    A tenancy is not a protected tenancy if it is a qualifying shared ownership lease, that is—

    (a)    a lease granted in pursuance of the right to be granted a shared ownership lease under Part V of the Housing Act 1985, or

    (b)    a lease granted by a housing association and which complies with the conditions set out in subsection (2) below.

(2)    The conditions referred to in subsection (1)(b) above are that the lease—

    (a)    was granted for a term of 99 years or more and is not (and cannot become) terminable except in pursuance of a provision for re-entry or forfeiture;

    (b)    was granted at a premium, calculated by reference to the value of the dwelling-house or the cost of providing it, of not less than 25 per cent, or such other percentage as may be prescribed, of the figure by reference to which it was calculated;

    (c)    provides for the tenant to acquire additional shares in the dwelling-house on terms specified in the lease and complying with such requirements as may be prescribed;

    (d)    does not restrict the tenant's powers to assign, mortgage or charge his interest in the dwelling-house;

    (e)    if it enables the landlord to require payment for outstanding shares in the dwelling-house, does so only in such circumstances as may be prescribed;

    (f)    provides, in the case of a house, for the tenant to acquire the landlord's interest on terms specified in the lease and complying with such requirements as may be prescribed; and

    (g)    states the landlord's opinion that by virtue of this section the lease is excluded from the operation of this Act.

(3)    The Secretary of State may by regulations prescribe anything requiring to be prescribed for the purposes of subsection (2) above.

(4)    The regulations may—

    (a)    make different provision for different cases or descriptions of case, including different provision for different areas, and

    (b)    contain such incidental, supplementary or transitional provisions as the Secretary of State considers appropriate,

and shall be made by statutory instrument which shall be subject to annulment in pursuance of a resolution of either House of Parliament.

(5) In any proceedings the court may, if of opinion that it is just and equitable to do so, treat a lease as a qualifying shared ownership lease notwithstanding that the condition specified in subsection (2)(g) above is not satisfied.

(6) In this section—
"house" has the same meaning as in Part I of the Leasehold Reform Act 1967;
"housing association" has the same meaning as in the Housing Associations Act 1985; and
"lease" includes an agreement for a lease, and references to the grant of a lease shall be construed accordingly.]

**[207]**

**NOTES**
Inserted by the Housing and Planning Act 1986, s 18, Sch 4, paras 1(2), 11(1), in relation to leases granted after 11 December 1987.
Housing Act 1985, Pt V: the right to be granted a shared ownership lease was conferred by s 143 et seq as originally enacted. The right is abolished by the Leasehold Reform, Housing and Urban Development Act 1993, s 107(c) at **[906]**, subject to savings.
Regulations: the Housing Association Shared Ownership Leases (Exclusion from Leasehold Reform Act 1967 and Rent Act 1977) Regulations 1987, SI 1987/1940 at **[3067]**.

## 6 Dwelling-houses let with other land

Subject to section 26 of this Act, a tenancy is not a protected tenancy if the dwelling-house which is subject to the tenancy is let together with land other than the site of the dwelling-house.

**[208]**

## 7 Payments for board or attendance

(1) A tenancy is not a protected tenancy if under the tenancy the dwelling-house is bona fide let at a rent which includes payments in respect of board or attendance.

(2) For the purposes of subsection (1) above, a dwelling-house shall not be taken to be bona fide let at a rent which includes payments in respect of attendance unless the amount of rent which is fairly attributable to attendance, having regard to the value of the attendance to the tenant, forms a substantial part of the whole rent.

**[209]**

## 8 Lettings to students

(1) A tenancy is not a protected tenancy if it is granted to a person who is pursuing, or intends to pursue, a course of study provided by a specified educational institution and is so granted either by that institution or by another specified institution or body of persons.

(2) In subsection (1) above "specified" means specified, or of a class specified, for the purposes of this section by regulations made by the Secretary of State by statutory instrument.

(3) A statutory instrument containing any such regulations shall be subject to annulment in pursuance of a resolution of either House of Parliament.

**[210]**

**NOTES**
Regulations: the Assured and Protected Tenancies (Lettings to Students) Regulations 1998, SI 1998/1967 at **[3214]**.

## 9 Holiday lettings

A tenancy is not a protected tenancy if the purpose of the tenancy is to confer on the tenant the right to occupy the dwelling-house for a holiday.

**[211]**

## [10 Agricultural holdings etc

(1) A tenancy is not a protected tenancy if—
(a) the dwelling-house is comprised in an agricultural holding and is occupied by the person responsible for the control (whether as tenant or as servant or agent of the tenant) of the farming of the holding, or
(b) the dwelling-house is comprised in the holding held under a farm business tenancy and is occupied by the person responsible for the control (whether as tenant or as servant or agent of the tenant) of the management of the holding.

(2) In subsection (1) above—
"agricultural holding" means any agricultural holding within the meaning of the Agricultural Holdings Act 1986 held under a tenancy in relation to which that Act applies, and
"farm business tenancy" and "holding" in relation to such a tenancy, have the same meaning as in the Agricultural Tenancies Act 1995.]

**[212]**

**NOTES**
Substituted by the Agricultural Tenancies Act 1995, s 40, Schedule, para 27.

## 11  Licensed premises

A tenancy of a dwelling-house which consists of or comprises [premises which, by virtue of a premises licence under the Licensing Act 2003, may be used for the supply of alcohol (within the meaning of section 14 of that Act)] for consumption on the premises shall not be a protected tenancy, nor shall such a dwelling-house be the subject of a statutory tenancy.

**NOTES**
Words in square brackets substituted by the Licensing Act 2003, s 198(1), Sch 6, para 67.

**[213]**

## 12  Resident landlords

(1)   Subject to subsection (2) below, a tenancy of a dwelling-house granted on or after 14th August 1974 shall not be a protected tenancy at any time if—

[(a)   the dwelling-house forms part only of a building and, except in a case where the dwelling-house also forms part of a flat, the building is not a purpose-built block of flats; and

(b)   the tenancy was granted by a person who, at the time when he granted it, occupied as his residence another dwelling-house which—

(i)   in the case mentioned in paragraph (a) above, also forms part of the flat; or

(ii)   in any other case, also forms part of the building; and

(c)   subject to paragraph 1 of Schedule 2 to this Act, at all times since the tenancy was granted the interest of the landlord under the tenancy has belonged to a person who, at the time he owned that interest, occupied as his residence another dwelling-house which—

(i)   in the case mentioned in paragraph (a) above, also formed part of the flat; or

(ii)   in any other case, also formed part of the building].

[(2)   This section does not apply to a tenancy of a dwelling-house which forms part of a building if the tenancy is granted to a person who, immediately before it was granted, was a protected or statutory tenant of that dwelling-house or of any other dwelling-house in that building.]

(4)   Schedule 2 to this Act shall have effect for the purpose of supplementing this section.

**[214]**

**NOTES**
Sub-s (1): paras (a)–(c) substituted by the Housing Act 1980, s 65(1).
Sub-s (2): substituted, for original sub-ss (2), (3), by the Housing Act 1980, s 69(4).

## [13  Landlord's interest belonging to Crown

(1)   Except as provided by subsection (2) below—

(a)   a tenancy shall not be a protected tenancy at any time when the interest of the landlord under the tenancy belongs to Her Majesty in right of the Crown or to a government department or is held in trust for Her Majesty for the purposes of a government department; and

(b)   a person shall not at any time be a statutory tenant of a dwelling-house if the interest of his immediate landlord would at that time belong or be held as mentioned in paragraph (a) above.

(2)   An interest belonging to Her Majesty in right of the Crown shall not prevent a tenancy from being a protected tenancy or a person from being a statutory tenant if the interest is under the management of the Crown Estate Commissioners.]

**[215]**

**NOTES**
Substituted by the Housing Act 1980, s 73(1).

## 14  Landlord's interest belonging to local authority, etc

[(1)]   A tenancy shall not be a protected tenancy at any time when the interest of the landlord under that tenancy belongs to—

(a)   the council of a county [or county borough];

(b)   the council of a district or, in the application of this Act to the Isles of Scilly, the Council of the Isles of Scilly;

[(bb)  the Broads Authority;]

[(bc)  a National Park authority;]

(c)     ... the council of a London borough or the Common Council of the City of London;
[(caa) a police authority established under [section 3 of the Police Act 1996];]
[(caaa) ... ]
[(ca) ... ;
(cb)    a joint authority established by Part IV of the Local Government Act 1985;]
[(cba)an authority established for an area in England by an order under section 207 of the
        Local Government and Public Involvement in Health Act 2007 (joint waste authorities);]
[(cc)   the London Fire and Emergency Planning Authority;]
(d)     the [English new towns residuary body];
(e)     a development corporation established by an order made, or having effect as if made,
        under the [New Towns Act 1981]; or
(f)     ... [or
(g)     an urban development corporation within the meaning of Part XVI of the Local
        Government, Planning and Land Act 1980;]
[(h)    a housing action trust established under Part III of the Housing Act 1988];
[(i)    The Residuary Body for Wales (Corff Gweddilliol Cymru;]

nor shall a person at any time be a statutory tenant of a dwelling-house if the interest of his immediate landlord would belong at that time to any of those bodies.

[(2)    In subsection (1)(d) "English new towns residuary body" means the Homes and Communities Agency so far as exercising functions in relation to anything transferred (or to be transferred) to it as mentioned in section 52(1)(a) to (d) of the Housing and Regeneration Act 2008.]

**[216]**

**NOTES**

Sub-s (1): numbered as such by the Housing and Regeneration Act 2008, s 56, Sch 8, para 23(1), (2), and is amended as follows:
   words in square brackets in para (a) inserted by the Local Government (Wales) Act 1994, s 22(2), Sch 8, para 3(1);
   para (bb) inserted by the Norfolk and Suffolk Broads Act 1988, s 21, Sch 6, para 18;
   para (bc) inserted by the Environment Act 1995, s 78, Sch 10, para 18;
   words omitted from para (c) repealed by the Local Government Act 1985, s 102(2), Sch 17;
   para (caa) inserted by the Police and Magistrates' Courts Act 1994, s 43, Sch 4, Pt II, para 53 and words in square brackets substituted by the Police Act 1996, s 103(1), Sch 7, Pt I, para 1(1), (2);
   para (caaa) inserted by the Police Act 1997, s 134(1), Sch 9, para 39 and repealed by the Criminal Justice and Police Act 2001, ss 128(1), 137, Sch 6, Pt 3, para 63, Sch 7, Pt 5(1);
   para (ca) inserted by the Local Government Act 1985, s 84, Sch 14, Pt II, para 56 and repealed by the Education Reform Act 1988, s 237(2), Sch 13, Pt I;
   para (cb) inserted by the Local Government Act 1985, s 84, Sch 14, Pt II, para 56;
   para (cba) inserted by the Local Government and Public Involvement in Health Act 2007, s 209(2), Sch 13, Pt 2, para 35;
   para (cc) inserted by the Greater London Authority Act 1999, s 328, Sch 29, Pt I, para 26;
   words in square brackets in para (d) substituted by the Housing and Regeneration Act 2008, s 56, Sch 8, para 23(1), (3);
   words in square brackets in para (e) substituted by the New Towns Act 1981, s 81, Sch 12, para 24;
   para (f) repealed by the Government of Wales Act 1998, s 152, Sch 18, Pt IV;
   para (g) inserted by the Local Government, Planning and Land Act 1980, s 155(1);
   para (h) inserted by the Housing Act 1988, s 62(7);
   para (i) inserted by the Local Government (Wales) Act 1994, s 39(2), Sch 13, para 28;
Sub-s (2): inserted by the Housing and Regeneration Act 2008, s 56, Sch 8, para 23(1), (4).
Modification: in sub-s (1)(cb), "joint authority" includes an authority established for the purposes of waste regulation or disposal by virtue of the Waste Regulation and Disposal (Authorities) Order 1985, SI 1985/1884, art 10, Sch 3, para 4.

## 15  Landlord's interest belonging to housing association, etc

(1)    A tenancy ... shall not be a protected tenancy at any time when the interest of the landlord under that tenancy belongs to a housing association falling within subsection (3) below; nor shall a person at any time be a statutory tenant of a dwelling-house if the interest of his immediate landlord would belong at that time to such a housing association.

(2)    A tenancy shall not be a protected tenancy at any time when the interest of the landlord under that tenancy belongs to—
(a)     the Housing Corporation
[(aa) ... ]; or
(b)     a housing trust which is a charity within the meaning of the [Charities Act 1993];

nor shall a person at any time be a statutory tenant of a dwelling-house if the interest of his immediate landlord would belong at that time to any of those bodies.

[(3)    A housing association falls within this subsection if—
(a)     it is [a registered social landlord within the meaning of the Housing Act 1985 (see
        section 5(4) and (5) of that Act)], or

PART I<br/>STATUTES

(b)　it is a co-operative housing association within the meaning of [the Housing Associations Act 1985].]

(4)　...

[(5)　In subsection (2) above "housing trust" means a corporation or body of persons which—

(a)　is required by the terms of its constituent instrument to use the whole of its funds, including any surplus which may arise from its operations, for the purpose of providing housing accommodation; or

(b)　is required by the terms of its constituent instrument to devote the whole, or substantially the whole, of its funds to charitable purposes and in fact uses the whole, or substantially the whole, of its funds for the purpose of providing housing accommodation.]

(6)　...

**[217]**

**NOTES**

Sub-s (1): words omitted repealed by the Housing Act 1980, ss 74(1), 152(3), Sch 26.

Sub-s (2): para (aa) inserted by the Housing Act 1988, s 140(1), Sch 17, Pt II, para 99 and repealed by the Government of Wales Act 1998, ss 141, 152, Sch 18, Pt VI; words in square brackets in para (b) substituted by the Charities Act 1993, s 98(1), Sch 6, para 30.

Sub-s (3): substituted by the Housing (Consequential Provisions) Act 1985, s 4, Sch 2, para 35(1), (2); words in square brackets substituted by the Housing Act 1996 (Consequential Provisions) Order 1996, SI 1996/2325, art 5, Sch 2, para 6.

Sub-s (4): repealed by the Housing Act 1980, ss 74, 152(3), Sch 26, with a saving in respect of protected or statutory tenancies which would otherwise cease to be such by virtue of the repeal of sub-s (4)(f); see Sch 9, Sch 25, Pt II, para 68 thereof at [390], [392].

Sub-s (5): substituted by the Housing Act 1980, s 74(2).

Sub-s (6): repealed by the Housing Act 1980, s 152(3), Sch 26.

Modification: in sub-s (2)(a) the reference to the Housing Corporation shall be treated as if it were a reference to the Regulator of Social Housing: see the Transfer of Housing Corporation Functions (Modifications and Transitional Provisions) Order 2008, SI 2008/2839, arts 1(2), 3, 6, Schedule.

## 16　Landlord's interest belonging to housing co-operative

A tenancy shall not be a protected tenancy at any time when the interest of the landlord under that tenancy belongs to a housing co-operative, [within the meaning of section 27B of the Housing Act 1985 (agreements with housing co-operatives under certain superseded provisions) and the dwelling-house is comprised in a housing co-operative agreement within the meaning of that section].

**[218]**

**NOTES**

Words in square brackets substituted by the Housing and Planning Act 1986, s 24(2), Sch 5, Pt II, para 15.

**16A**　*(Inserted by the Housing Act 1980, s 56(5), (6); repealed, subject to savings, by the Housing Act 1988, s 140(2), Sch 18.)*

*Controlled and regulated tenancies*

**17**　*(Repealed by the Housing Act 1980, s 152(3), Sch 26.)*

## 18　Regulated tenancies

(1)　Subject to sections 24(3) and 143 of this Act, a "regulated tenancy" is, for the purposes of this Act, a protected or statutory tenancy ...

(2)　Where a regulated tenancy is followed by a statutory tenancy of the same dwelling-house, the two shall be treated for the purposes of this Act as together constituting one regulated tenancy.

(3), (4)　...

**[219]**

**NOTES**

Sub-s (1): words omitted repealed by the Housing Act 1980, s 152(1), (3), Sch 25, Pt I, para 35, Sch 26.

Sub-ss (3), (4): repealed by the Housing Act 1980, s 152(1), (3), Sch 25, Pt I, para 35, Sch 26.

## [18A　Modification of Act for controlled tenancies converted into regulated tenancies

*Schedule 17 to this Act applies for the purpose of modifying the provisions of this Act in relation to a tenancy which, by virtue of any of the following enactments, was converted from a controlled tenancy into a regulated tenancy, that is to say—*

(a)　section 18(3) of this Act;

(b)　paragraph 5 of Schedule 2 to the Rent Act 1968 (which was superseded by section 18(3));

(c)  Part VIII of this Act;

(d)  Part III of the Housing Finance Act 1972 (which was superseded by Part VIII);

(e)  Part IV of the Act of 1972 (conversion by reference to rateable values);

(f)  section 64 of the Housing Act 1980 (conversion of remaining controlled tenancies into regulated tenancies).]

**[220]**

**NOTES**

Inserted by the Housing Act 1980, s 152(1), Sch 25, Pt I, para 35.

**19, 20**   *(Repealed, subject to savings, by the Housing Act 1988, s 140(2), Sch 18.)*

*Shared accommodation*

**21**   *(Repealed, subject to savings, by the Housing Act 1988, s 140(2), Sch 18.)*

**22  Tenant sharing accommodation with persons other than landlord**

(1)  Where a tenant has the exclusive occupation of any accommodation ("the separate accommodation") and—

(a)  the terms as between the tenant and his landlord on which he holds the separate accommodation include the use of other accommodation ("the shared accommodation") in common with another person or other persons, not being or including the landlord, and

(b)  by reason only of the circumstances mentioned in paragraph (a) above, the separate accommodation would not, apart from this section, be a dwelling-house let on or subject to a protected or statutory tenancy,

the separate accommodation shall be deemed to be a dwelling-house let on a protected tenancy or, as the case may be, subject to a statutory tenancy and the following provisions of this section shall have effect.

(2)  For the avoidance of doubt it is hereby declared that where, for the purpose of determining the rateable value of the separate accommodation, it is necessary to make an apportionment under this Act, regard is to be had to the circumstances mentioned in subsection (1)(a) above.

(3)  While the tenant is in possession of the separate accommodation (whether as a protected or statutory tenant), any term or condition of the contract of tenancy terminating or modifying, or providing for the termination or modification of, his right to the use of any of the shared accommodation which is living accommodation shall be of no effect.

(4)  Where the terms and conditions of the contract of tenancy are such that at any time during the tenancy the persons in common with whom the tenant is entitled to the use of the shared accommodation could be varied, or their number could be increased, nothing in subsection (3) above shall prevent those terms and conditions from having effect so far as they relate to any such variation or increase.

(5)  Without prejudice to the enforcement of any order made under subsection (6) below, while the tenant is in possession of the separate accommodation, no order shall be made for possession of any of the shared accommodation, whether on the application of the immediate landlord of the tenant or on the application of any person under whom that landlord derives title, unless a like order has been made, or is made at the same time, in respect of the separate accommodation; and the provisions of section 98(1) of this Act shall apply accordingly.

(6)  On the application of the landlord, the county court may make such order either—

(a)  terminating the right of the tenant to use the whole or any part of the shared accommodation other than living accommodation, or

(b)  modifying his right to use the whole or any part of the shared accommodation, whether by varying the persons or increasing the number of persons entitled to the use of that accommodation, or otherwise,

as the court thinks just.

(7)  No order shall be made under subsection (6) above so as to effect any termination or modification of the rights of the tenant which, apart from subsection (3) above, could not be effected by or under the terms of the contract of tenancy.

(8)  In this section "living accommodation" means accommodation of such a nature that the fact that it constitutes or is included in the shared accommodation is (or, if the tenancy has ended, was) sufficient, apart from this section, to prevent the tenancy from constituting a protected tenancy of a dwelling-house.

**[221]**

*Sublettings*

## 23 Certain sublettings not to exclude any part of sub-lessor's premises from protection

(1)   Where the tenant of any premises, consisting of a house or part of a house, has sublet a part but not the whole of the premises, then, as against his landlord or any superior landlord, no part of the premises shall be treated as not being a dwelling-house let on or subject to a protected or statutory tenancy by reason only that—

    (a)    the terms on which any person claiming under the tenant holds any part of the premises include the use of accommodation in common with other persons; or

    (b)    part of the premises is let to any such person at a rent which includes payments in respect of board or attendance.

(2)   Nothing in this section shall affect the rights against, and liabilities to, each other of the tenant and any person claiming under him, or of any 2 such persons.

[222]

*Business premises*

## 24 Premises with a business use

(1), (2)   ...

(3)   A tenancy shall not be a regulated tenancy if it is a tenancy to which Part II of the Landlord and Tenant Act 1954 applies (but this provision is without prejudice to the application of any other provision of this Act to a sub-tenancy of any part of the premises comprised in such a tenancy).

[223]

**NOTES**

    Sub-ss (1), (2): repealed by the Housing Act 1980, s 152(3), Sch 26.

*Miscellaneous*

## 25 Rateable value and meaning of "appropriate day"

(1)   Except where this Act otherwise provides, the rateable value on any day of a dwelling-house shall be ascertained for the purposes of this Act as follows:—

    (a)    if the dwelling-house is a hereditament for which a rateable value is then shown in the valuation list, it shall be that rateable value;

    (b)    if the dwelling-house forms part only of such a hereditament or consists of or forms part of more than one such hereditament, its rateable value shall

be taken to be such value as is found by a proper apportionment or aggregation of the rateable value or values so shown.

(2)   Any question arising under this section as to the proper apportionment or aggregation of any value or values shall be determined by the county court, and the decision of the county court shall be final.

(3)   In this Act "the appropriate day"—

    (a)    in relation to any dwelling-house which, on 23rd March 1965, was or formed part of a hereditament for which a rateable value was shown in the valuation list then in force, or consisted or formed part of more than one such hereditament, means that date, and

    (b)    in relation to any other dwelling-house, means the date on which such a value is or was first shown in the valuation list.

(4)   Where, after the date which is the appropriate day in relation to any dwelling-house, the valuation list is altered so as to vary the rateable value of the hereditament of which the dwelling-house consists or forms part and the alteration has effect from a date not later than the appropriate day, the rateable value of the dwelling-house on the appropriate day shall be ascertained as if the value shown in the valuation list on the appropriate day had been the value shown in the list as altered.

(5)   This section applies in relation to any other land as it applies in relation to a dwelling-house.

[224]

## 26 Land and premises let with dwelling-house

(1)   For the purposes of this Act, any land or premises let together with a dwelling-house shall, unless it consists of agricultural land exceeding 2 acres in extent, be treated as part of the dwelling-house.

(2)   For the purposes of subsection (1) above "agricultural land" has the meaning set out in section 26(3)(a) of the General Rate Act 1967 (exclusion of agricultural land and premises from liability for rating).

[225]

**NOTES**

General Rate Act 1967: repealed by the Local Government Finance Act 1988, ss 117, 149, Sch 13, Pt I, with effect for financial years beginning in or after 1990, but subject to savings in regulations made under s 117(8) of that Act.

**27–43** *((Pt II) Repealed by the Housing Act 1980, s 152(3), Sch 26.)*

## PART III
## RENTS UNDER REGULATED TENANCIES

**NOTES**

Application of this Act: provision as to the amount of rent payable under a regulated tenancy arising by virtue of the Landlord and Tenant Act 1954, Pt I at **[39]**–**[59]**, is made by the Leasehold Reform Act 1967, s 39(2) and Sch 5, para 3(1) at **[124]**, **[134]**. By para 3(2) of that Schedule, where the rent payable under a statutory tenancy is arrived at in that way, this Act applies subject to adaptations affecting ss 46–48 at **[228]**, **[229]** and excluding s 45(2) at **[227]**. Moreover, in relation to a rent registered or to be registered under Pt IV of this Act on an application made with reference to a regulated tenancy arising by virtue of Pt I of the 1954 Act, this Act is to have effect subject to the provisions of Sch 5, para 4 to the 1967 Act.

*Regulation of rent*

**44 Limit of rent during contractual periods**

(1) Where a rent for a dwelling-house is registered under Part IV of this Act, the rent recoverable for any contractual period of a regulated tenancy of the dwelling-house shall be limited to the rent so registered.

This subsection is subject to the following provisions of this Act: subsection (4) below, [section 71(3)], paragraph 1(3) of Schedule 7, ... and paragraph 3 of Schedule 20.

(2) Where a limit is imposed by subsection (1) above on the rent recoverable in relation to any contractual period of a regulated tenancy, the amount by which the rent payable under the tenancy exceeds that limit shall, notwithstanding anything in any agreement, be irrecoverable from the tenant.

(3) In this Part of this Act "contractual rent limit" means the limit specified in subsection (1) above.

(4) Schedule 7 to this Act shall have effect for the purpose of providing a special rent limit in relation to certain tenancies which became regulated tenancies by virtue of section 14 of the Counter-Inflation Act 1973.

**[226]**

**NOTES**

Sub-s (1): words in square brackets substituted by the Rent (Relief from Phasing) Order 1987, SI 1987/264, art 2(3), Sch 1; words omitted repealed by the Housing Act 1980, s 152(3), Sch 26.

Counter-Inflation Act 1973, s 14: repealed by s 155(5) of, and Sch 25 to, this Act and partly replaced by s 4(2), (3) at **[205]**.

**45 Limit of rent during statutory periods**

(1) Except as otherwise provided by this Part of this Act, where the rent payable for any statutory period of a regulated tenancy of a dwelling-house would exceed the rent recoverable for the last contractual period thereof, the amount of the excess shall, notwithstanding anything in any agreement, be irrecoverable from the tenant.

(2) Where a rent for the dwelling-house is registered under Part IV of this Act, the following provisions shall apply with respect to the rent for any statutory period of a regulated tenancy of the dwelling-house:—

    (a) if the rent payable for any statutory period would exceed the rent so registered, the amount of the excess shall, notwithstanding anything in any agreement, be irrecoverable from the tenant; and

    (b) if the rent payable for any statutory period would be less than the rent so registered, it may be increased up to the amount of that rent by a notice of increase served by the landlord on the tenant and specifying the date from which the increase is to take effect.

This subsection is subject to the following provisions of this Act: [section 71(3)], paragraph 1(3) of Schedule 7, ... , ... and paragraph 3 of Schedule 20.

(3) The date specified in a notice of increase under subsection (2)(b) above shall not be earlier than the date [from which the registration of the rent took effect] nor earlier than 4 weeks before the service of the notice.

(4)   Where no rent for the dwelling-house is registered under Part IV of this Act, sections 46 [and 47] of this Act shall have effect with respect to the rent recoverable for any statutory period under a regulated tenancy of the dwelling-house.

**[227]**

---

**NOTES**

Sub-s (2): words in square brackets substituted and words omitted in the first place repealed by the Rent (Relief from Phasing) Order 1987, SI 1987/264, art 2(3), Sch 1; words omitted in the second place repealed by the Housing Act 1980, s 152(3), Sch 26.

Sub-ss (3), (4): words in square brackets substituted by the Housing Act 1980, ss 61(4), 152(1), Sch 25, Pt I, para 37, subject to savings in s 61(8) thereof at **[360]**.

---

**46   Adjustment, with respect to rates, of recoverable rent for statutory periods before registration**

(1)   Where—

    (a)   section 45(4) of this Act applies, and

    (b)   any rates in respect of the dwelling-house are, or were during the last contractual period, borne by the landlord or a superior landlord,

then, for any statutory period for which the amount of the rates (ascertained in accordance with Schedule 5 to this Act) differs from the amount, so ascertained, of the rates for the last contractual period, the recoverable rent shall be increased or decreased by the amount of the difference.

(2)   Where the amount of the recoverable rent is increased by virtue of this section, the increase shall not take effect except in pursuance of a notice of increase served by the landlord on the tenant and specifying the increase and the date from which it is to take effect.

(3)   The date specified in a notice of increase under subsection (2) above shall be not earlier than 6 weeks before the service of the notice, and if it is earlier than the service of the notice any rent unpaid shall become due on the day after the service of the notice.

**[228]**

**47   Adjustment, with respect to services and furniture, of recoverable rent for statutory periods before registration**

(1)   Where section 45(4) of this Act applies and for any statutory period there is with respect to—

    (a)   the provision of services for the tenant by the landlord or a superior landlord, or

    (b)   the use of furniture by the tenant,

or any circumstances relating thereto any difference, in comparison with the last contractual period, such as to affect the amount of the rent which it is reasonable to charge, the recoverable rent for the statutory period shall be increased or decreased by an appropriate amount.

(2)   Any question whether, or by what amount, the recoverable rent for any period is increased or decreased by virtue of this section shall be determined by agreement in writing between the landlord and the tenant or by the county court; and any such determination—

    (a)   may be made so as to relate to past statutory periods; and

    (b)   shall have effect with respect to statutory periods subsequent to the periods to which it relates until revoked or varied by any such agreement as is referred to in this subsection or by the county court.

**[229]**

**48**   (*Repealed by the Housing Act 1980, ss 63, 152(2), (3), Sch 26, subject to savings in Sch 25, Pt II, para 64 thereto at* **[392]**.)

**49   Notices of increase**

(1)   Any reference in this section to a notice of increase is a reference to a notice of increase under section 45(2), [or 46] of this Act.

(2)   A notice of increase must be in the prescribed form.

(3)   Notwithstanding that a notice of increase relates to statutory periods, it may be served during a contractual period.

(4)   Where a notice of increase is served during a contractual period and the protected tenancy could, by a notice to quit served by the landlord at the same time, be brought to an end before the date specified in the notice of increase, the notice of increase shall operate to convert the protected tenancy into a statutory tenancy as from that date.

(5)   If the county court is satisfied that any error or omission in a notice of increase is due to a bona fide mistake on the part of the landlord, the court may by order amend the notice by correcting any errors or supplying any omission therein which, if not corrected or supplied, would render the notice invalid and, if the court so directs, the notice as so amended shall have effect and be deemed to have had effect as a valid notice.

(6) Any amendment of a notice of increase under subsection (5) above may be made on such terms and conditions with respect to arrears of rent or otherwise as appear to the court to be just and reasonable.

(7) No increase of rent which becomes payable by reason of an amendment of a notice of increase under subsection (5) above shall be recoverable in respect of any statutory period which ended more than 6 months before the date of the order making the amendment.

**[230]**

**NOTES**

Sub-s (1): words in square brackets substituted by the Housing Act 1980, s 152(1), Sch 25, Pt I, para 38. Regulations: the Rent Act 1977 (Forms etc) Regulations 1980, SI 1980/1697 at **[3023]**.

**50** (*Repealed by the Housing Act 1980, ss 63, 152(3), Sch 26.*)

*Rent agreements with tenants having security of tenure*

## 51 Protection of tenants with security of tenure

(1) In this Part of this Act a "rent agreement with a tenant having security of tenure" means—
   (a) an agreement increasing the rent payable under a protected tenancy which is a regulated tenancy, or
   (b) the grant to the tenant under a regulated tenancy, or to any person who might succeed him as a statutory tenant, of another regulated tenancy of the dwelling-house at a rent exceeding the rent under the previous tenancy.

(2) Where any rates in respect of the dwelling-house are borne by the landlord or a superior landlord, any increase of rent shall be disregarded for the purposes of the definition in subsection (1) above if the increase is no more than one corresponding to an increase in the rates borne by the landlord or a superior landlord in respect of the dwelling-house.

(3) If—
   (a) a rent agreement with a tenant having security of tenure takes effect on or after the commencement of this Act, and was made at a time when no rent was registered for the dwelling-house under Part IV of this Act, …
   (b) …
the requirements of subsection (4) below shall be observed as respects the agreement.

(4) The requirements are that—
   (a) the agreement is in writing signed by the landlord and the tenant, and
   (b) the document containing the agreement contains a statement, in characters not less conspicuous than those used in any other part of the agreement—
      (i) that the tenant's security of tenure under this Act will not be affected if he refuses to enter into the agreement, and
      [(ia) … ]
      (ii) that entry into the agreement will not deprive the tenant or landlord of the right to apply at any time to the rent officer for the registration of a fair rent under Part IV of this Act.
      or words to that effect, and
   (c) the statement mentioned in paragraph (b) above is set out at the head of the document containing the agreement.

**[231]**

**NOTES**

Sub-s (3): words omitted repealed by the Housing Act 1980, s 152(3), Sch 26.
Sub-s (4): para (b)(ia) inserted by the Housing Act 1980, s 68(1) and repealed by the Rent (Relief from Phasing) Order 1987, SI 1987/264, art 2(3), Sch 1.

## [52 Protection: special provisions following conversion

(1) This section applies to an agreement with a tenant having security of tenure which is entered into after the commencement of section 68(2) of the Housing Act 1980 if the tenancy has become or, as the case may be, the previous tenancy became a regulated tenancy by conversion.

(2) Any such agreement which purports to increase the rent payable under a protected tenancy shall, if entered into at a time when no rent is registered for the dwelling-house under Part IV of this Act, be void.

(3) If any such agreement constitutes a grant of a regulated tenancy and is made at a time when no rent is so registered, any excess of the rent payable under the tenancy so granted (for any contractual or statutory period of the tenancy) over the rent limit applicable to the previous tenancy, shall be irrecoverable from the tenant; but this subsection ceases to apply if a rent is subsequently so registered.

(4)   For the purposes of this section a tenancy is a regulated tenancy by conversion if it has become a regulated tenancy by virtue of—

(a)   Part VIII of this Act, section 43 of the Housing Act 1969 or Part III or IV of the Housing Finance Act 1972 (conversion of controlled tenancies into regulated tenancies); or

(b)   section 18(3) of this Act or paragraph 5 of Schedule 2 to the Rent Act 1968 (conversion on death of first successor); or

(c)   section 64 of the Housing Act 1980 (conversion of all remaining controlled tenancies).

(5)   This section does not apply to any agreement where the tenant is neither the person who, at the time of the conversion, was the tenant nor a person who might succeed the tenant at that time as a statutory tenant.

(6)   Where a rent is registered for the dwelling-house and the registration is subsequently cancelled, this section shall not apply to the agreement submitted to the rent officer in connection with the cancellation nor to any agreement made so as to take effect after the cancellation.]

[232]

**NOTES**

Substituted by the Housing Act 1980, s 68(2).

Housing Act 1969, s 43: repealed by the Housing Finance Act 1972, s 108(4), Sch 11, Pt VI.

Housing Finance Act 1972, Pts III, IV: Pt III repealed by s 155(5) of, and Sch 25 to, this Act; the provisions of Pt IV providing for conversion of controlled tenancies into regulated tenancies (ie ss 35, 36) were repealed by the Housing Rents and Subsidies Act 1975, s 17(5), Sch 6, Pt III.

Rent Act 1968, Sch 2, para 5: repealed by s 155(5) of, and Sch 25 to, this Act.

**53**   *(Repealed by the Housing Act 1980, s 152(3), Sch 26.)*

**54   Failure to comply with provisions for protection of tenants**

(1)   If, in the case of a variation of the terms of a regulated tenancy, there is a failure to observe any of the requirements of section 51, ... of this Act, any excess of the rent payable under the terms as varied over the terms without the variation shall be irrecoverable from the tenant.

(2)   If, in the case of the grant of a tenancy, there is a failure to observe any of those requirements, any excess of the rent payable under the tenancy so granted (for any contractual or any statutory period of the tenancy) over the previous limit shall be irrecoverable from the tenant.

(3)   In subsection (2) above the "previous limit" shall be taken to be the amount which (taking account of any previous operation of this section or of section 46 of the Housing Finance Act 1972, which is superseded by this section) was recoverable by way of rent for the last period of the previous tenancy of the dwelling-house, or which would have been so recoverable if all notices of increase authorised by this Act, the Rent Act 1968 and section 37(3) of the Act of 1972 had been served.

(4), (5)   ...

[233]

**NOTES**

Sub-s (1): words omitted repealed by the Housing Act 1980, s 152(3), Sch 26.

Sub-ss (4), (5): repealed by the Housing Act 1980, s 152(3), Sch 26.

Rent Act 1968; Housing Finance Act 1972, ss 37(3), 46: repealed by s 155(5) of, and Sch 25 to, this Act.

**55, 56**   *(S 55 repealed by the Rent (Relief from Phasing) Order 1987, SI 1987/264, art 2(1)(a); s 56 repealed by the Housing Act 1980, ss 60(4), 152(3), Sch 26.)*

*Enforcement provisions*

**57   Recovery from landlord of sums paid in excess of recoverable rent, etc**

(1)   Where a tenant has paid on account of rent any amount which, by virtue of this Part of this Act, is irrecoverable by the landlord, the tenant who paid it shall be entitled to recover that amount from the landlord who received it or his personal representatives.

(2)   Any amount which a tenant is entitled to recover under subsection (1) above may, without prejudice to any other method of recovery, be deducted by the tenant from any rent payable by him to the landlord.

[(3)   No amount which a tenant is entitled to recover under subsection (1) above shall be recoverable at any time after the expiry of—

(a)   one year, in the case of an amount which is irrecoverable by virtue of section 54 of this Act; or

(b)   two years, in any other case.]

(4)   Any person who, in any rent book or similar document, makes an entry showing or purporting to show any tenant as being in arrears in respect of any sum on account of rent which is

irrecoverable by virtue of this Part of this Act shall be liable to a fine not exceeding [level 3 on the standard scale], unless he proves that, at the time of the making of the entry, the landlord had a bona fide claim that the sum was recoverable.

(5)   If, where any such entry has been made by or on behalf of any landlord, the landlord on being requested by or on behalf of the tenant to do so, refuses or neglects to cause the entry to be deleted within 7 days, the landlord shall be liable to a fine not exceeding [level 3 on the standard scale], unless he proves that, at the time of the neglect or refusal to cause the entry to be deleted, he had a bona fide claim that the sum was recoverable.

**[234]**

**NOTES**
Sub-s (3): substituted by the Housing Act 1980, s 68(3).
Sub-ss (4), (5): words in square brackets substituted by virtue of the Criminal Justice Act 1982, ss 38, 46.

## 58   Rectification of rent books in light of determination of recoverable rent

Where, in any proceedings, the recoverable rent of a dwelling-house subject to a regulated tenancy is determined by a court, then, on the application of the tenant (whether in those or in any subsequent proceedings) the court may call for the production of the rent book or any similar document relating to the dwelling-house and may direct the registrar or clerk of the court to correct any entries showing, or purporting to show, the tenant as being in arrears in respect of any sum which the court has determined to be irrecoverable.

**[235]**

*General provisions*

## 59   Adjustment for differences in lengths of rental periods

In ascertaining for the purposes of this Part of this Act whether there is any difference with respect to rents or rates between one rental period and another (whether of the same tenancy or not) or the amount of any such difference, any necessary adjustment shall be made to take account of periods of different lengths; and for the purposes of such an adjustment a period of one month shall be treated as equivalent to one-twelfth of a year and a period of a week as equivalent to one-fifty-second of a year.

**[236]**

## 60   Regulations

(1)   The Secretary of State may make regulations—
    (a)   prescribing the form of any notice or other document to be given or used in pursuance of this Part of this Act; and
    (b)   prescribing anything required or authorised to be prescribed by this Part of this Act.

(2)   Any such regulations shall be made by statutory instrument which shall be subject to annulment in pursuance of a resolution of either House of Parliament.

**[237]**

**NOTES**
Regulations: the Rent Act 1977 (Forms etc) Regulations 1980, SI 1980/1697 at **[3023]**.

## 61   Interpretation of Part III

(1)   In this Part of this Act, except where the context otherwise requires—
    "contractual period" means a rental period of a regulated tenancy which is a period beginning before the expiry or termination of the protected tenancy;
    "contractual rent limit" has the meaning assigned to it by section 44(3) of this Act;
    .....
    "prescribed" means prescribed by regulations under section 60 of this Act and references to a prescribed form include references to a form substantially to the same effect as the prescribed form;
    "recoverable rent" means rent which, under a regulated tenancy, is or was for the time being recoverable, having regard to the provisions of this Part of this Act;
    "rent agreement with a tenant having security of tenure" has the meaning assigned to it by section 51 of this Act;
    "statutory period" means any rental period of a regulated tenancy which is not a contractual period.

(2)   References in this Part of this Act to rates, in respect of a dwelling-house, include references to such proportion of any rates in respect of a hereditament of which the dwelling-house forms part as may be agreed in writing between the landlord and the tenant or determined by the county court.

**[238]**

**NOTES**

Sub-s (1): words omitted repealed by the Housing Act 1980, s 152(3), Sch 26.

## PART IV
## REGISTRATION OF RENTS UNDER REGULATED TENANCIES

**NOTES**

As to the application of this Part in relation to a regulated tenancy under the Landlord and Tenant Act 1954, Pt I at **[39]–[59]**, see the note preceding s 44 of this Act at **[226]**.

## 62 Registration areas

(1) [Except so far as different provision is made by an order under section 17 of the Local Government Act 1992 [or Part 1 of the Local Government and Public Involvement in Health Act 2007 (orders constituting new local government areas etc)],] the registration areas for the purpose of this Part of this Act [in England] [are—
    (a)    counties, [ ... ]
    (b)    London boroughs, and
    (c)    the City of London].

[(1A)    Wales is a registration area for the purposes of this Part of this Act.]

(2)    For the purposes of this Part or this Act—
    (a)    ... the City of London shall be deemed to include the Inner Temple and the Middle Temple, and
    (b)    the Isles of Scilly shall be a registration area and the Council of the Isles of Scilly shall be the local authority for that registration area.

        **[239]**

**NOTES**

Sub-s (1): words in first (outer) pair of square brackets inserted by the Local Government Changes (Rent Act) Regulations 1995, SI 1995/2451, regs 2, 3; words in second (inner) pair of square brackets inserted by the Local Government and Public Involvement in Health Act 2007, s 22, Sch 1, Pt 2, para 13; words in third pair of square brackets inserted, in relation to Wales, by the Administration of the Rent Officer Service (Wales) Order 2003, SI 2003/973, art 10(a); words in fourth (outer) pair of square brackets substituted by the Local Government Act 1985, s 16, Sch 8, para 13(1), (2); words omitted from square brackets in para (a) inserted by the Local Government (Wales) Act 1994, s 22(2), Sch 8, para 3(2) and repealed by SI 2003/973, art 10(b).

Sub-s (1A): inserted by SI 2003/973, art 10(c).

Sub-s (2): words omitted repealed by the Local Government Act 1985, s 16, Sch 8, para 13(1), (2).

## 63 Schemes for appointment of rent officers

(1)    The Secretary of State shall for every registration area make, after consultation with the local authority, a scheme providing for the appointment by the proper officer of the local authority—
    (a)    of such number of rent officers for the area as may be determined by or in accordance with the scheme, ...
    (b)    ...

(2)    A scheme under this section—
    (a)    shall provide for the payment by the local authority to rent officers ... of remuneration and allowances in accordance with scales approved by the Secretary of State ... ;
    (b)    shall prohibit the dismissal of a rent officer ... except by the proper officer of the local authority on the direction, or with the consent, of the Secretary of State;
    (c)    shall require the local authority to provide for the rent officers office accommodation and clerical and other assistance;
    (d)    shall allocate, or confer on the proper officer of the local authority the duty of allocating, work as between the rent officers and shall confer on the proper officer the duty of supervising the conduct of rent officers ...
    [(e)    ... ].

[(2A)    A scheme under this section may make all or any of the following provisions—
    (a)    provision requiring the consent of the Secretary of State to the appointment of rent officers;
    (b)    provision with respect to the appointment of rent officers for fixed periods;
    (c)    provision for the proper officer of the local authority, in such circumstances and subject to such conditions (as to consent or otherwise) as may be specified in the scheme,—
        (i)    to designate a person appointed or to be appointed a rent officer as chief rent officer and to designate one or more such persons as senior rent officers;
        (ii)    to delegate to a person so designated as chief rent officer such functions as may be specified in the scheme; and

      (iii)   to revoke a designation under sub-paragraph (i) above and to revoke or vary a delegation under sub-paragraph (ii) above;

  (d)   provision with respect to the delegation of functions by a chief rent officer to other rent officers (whether designated as senior rent officers or not);

  (e)   provision as to the circumstances in which and the terms on which a rent officer appointed by the scheme may undertake functions outside the area to which the scheme relates in accordance with paragraph (f) below;

  (f)   provision under which a rent officer appointed for an area other than that to which the scheme relates may undertake functions in the area to which the scheme relates and for such a rent officer to be treated for such purposes as may be specified in the scheme (which may include the purposes of paragraphs (c) and (d) above and paragraphs (c) and (d) of subsection (2) above) as if he were a rent officer appointed under the scheme; and

  (g)   provision conferring functions on the proper officer of a local authority with respect to the matters referred to in paragraphs (d) to (f) above.]

(3)   For the purposes of any local Act scheme, within the meaning of section 8 of the Superannuation Act 1972, rent officers ... appointed in pursuance of a scheme under this section shall be deemed to be officers in the employment of the local authority for whose area the scheme is made; and for the purposes of—

  (a)   Part III of the [Pension Schemes Act 1993], and

  (b)   the Social Security Act 1975,

they shall be deemed to be in that employment under a contract of service.

[(4)   In this Part "the rent officer" means—

  (a)   in relation to any area not specified in an order made under section 64B of this Act, any rent officer appointed for the area who is authorised to act in accordance with a scheme under this section;

  (b)   in relation to any area or areas so specified, any rent officer appointed by the [Commissioners for Her Majesty's Revenue and Customs] [or, in relation to Wales, any rent officer appointed by the National Assembly for Wales].]

(5)   A scheme under this section may be varied or revoked by a subsequent scheme made thereunder.

(6)   The Secretary of State shall, in respect of each financial year, make to any local authority incurring expenditure which is of a kind mentioned in subsection (7) below, a grant equal to that expenditure.

(7)   The expenditure mentioned in subsection (6) above is any expenditure—

  (a)   attributable to this section [or an order under section 122 of the Housing Act 1996], or

  (b)   incurred in respect of pensions, allowances or gratuities payable to or in respect of rent officers ... (appointed in pursuance of a scheme under this section) by virtue of regulations under section 7 [or section 24] of the Superannuation Act 1972 [or]

  [(c)  incurred in respect of increases of pensions payable to or in respect of rent officers (so appointed) by virtue of the Pensions (Increase) Act 1971].

(8)   Any expenditure incurred by the Secretary of State by virtue of subsection (6) above shall be paid out of money provided by Parliament.

[(9)   In the case of a registration area in respect of which there is more than one local authority, this section shall apply as if—

  (a)   the first reference to "the local authority" in subsection (1) were a reference to each of those local authorities which is—

      (i)   the county council for a county in England; or

      (ii)  the council for a district in England which is not in a county having a county council; and

  (b)   the second reference to "the local authority" in that subsection, the references to "the local authority" in subsections (2) and (2A)(c), the reference to "a local authority" in subsection (2A)(g), and the reference to "the local authority for whose area the scheme is made" in subsection (3) were references to such one of those authorities as has been designated by the scheme.]

**[240]**

---

**NOTES**

Sub-s (1): words omitted repealed by the Housing Act 1988, ss 120, 140(2), Sch 14, Pt I, para 1, Sch 18.

Sub-s (2): words omitted in the first place from para (a) and from paras (b), (d) repealed by the Housing Act 1988, ss 120, 140(2), Sch 14, Pt I, para 2(a)–(c), Sch 18; words omitted in the second place from para (a) repealed by the Housing Act 1996, ss 222, 227, Sch 18, Pt IV, para 22(1)(a), Sch 19, Pt XIII; para (e) added by the Housing Act 1980, s 59(1) and repealed by the Housing Act 1988, ss 120, 140(2), Sch 14, Pt I, para 2(d), Sch 18.

Sub-s (2A): inserted by the Housing Act 1988, s 120, Sch 14, Pt I, para 3.

Sub-s (3): words omitted repealed by the Housing Act 1988, ss 120, 140(2), Sch 14, Pt I, para 4, Sch 18; words in square brackets substituted by the Pension Schemes Act 1993, s 190, Sch 8, para 10 (but note that this substitution is purportedly made to s 653(3) of this Act).

Sub-s (4): substituted by the Administration of the Rent Officer Service (England) Order 1999, SI 1999/2403, art 7(a); words in first pair of square brackets substituted by the Transfer of Functions (Administration of Rent Officer Service in England) Order 2008, SI 2008/3134, art 6, Schedule, para 1; words in second pair of square brackets inserted by the Rent Officer Service (Wales) Order 2003, SI 2003/973, art 11.

Sub-s (7): words in square brackets in para (a) added by the Housing Act 1988, s 121(3) and substituted by the Housing Act 1996, s 123, Sch 13, para 1; words omitted from para (b) repealed, words in first pair of square brackets in para (b) inserted, word in second pair of square brackets in para (b) substituted and para (c) added by the Housing Act 1988, ss 120, 140(2), Sch 14, Pt I, paras 3, 5, Sch 18.

Sub-s (9): added by the Local Government Act 1985, s 16, Sch 8, para 13(3); substituted by the Local Government Changes (Rent Act) Regulations 1995, SI 1995/2451, regs 2, 4.

Social Security Act 1975: repealed by the Social Security (Consequential Provisions) Act 1992, s 3, Sch 1, and consolidated in the Social Security Contributions and Benefits Act 1992 and the Social Security Administration Act 1992.

## 64   Default powers of Secretary of State

(1)   If the Secretary of State is of opinion that a local authority have failed to carry out any function conferred on them by a scheme under section 63 of this Act he may, after such enquiry as he thinks fit, by order revoke the scheme and, without consulting the local authority, make another scheme under that section.

(2)   A scheme made by virtue of subsection (1) above may confer functions otherwise exercisable by the local authority or the proper officer of the local authority on a person appointed by the Secretary of State and that person may, if another local authority consent, be that other local authority or, as the case may be, the proper officer of that other local authority.

(3)   If the Secretary of State is of opinion that the proper officer of the local authority has failed to carry out any functions conferred on the proper officer by a scheme under section 63 he may (after consultation with the local authority) exercise his power under subsection (5) of that section by making a scheme providing for all or any of the functions otherwise exercisable by the proper officer to be exercised by some other person.

(4)   A scheme made by virtue of this section may contain such incidental and transitional provisions as appear to the Secretary of State to be necessary or expedient.

[241]

## [64A   Amalgamation schemes

(1)   If the Secretary of State is of the opinion—
- (a)   that there is at any time insufficient work in two or more registration areas to justify the existence of a separate service of rent officers for each area, or
- (b)   that it would at any time be beneficial for the efficient administration of the service provided by rent officers in two or more registration areas,

he may, after consultation with the local authorities concerned, make a scheme under section 63 above designating as an amalgamated registration area the areas of those authorities and making provision accordingly for that amalgamated area.

(2)   Any reference in the following provisions of this Chapter to a registration area includes a reference to an amalgamated registration area and, in relation to such an area, "the constituent authorities" means the local authorities whose areas make up the amalgamated area.

(3)   A scheme under section 63 above made for an amalgamated registration area—
- (a)   shall confer on the proper officer of one of the constituent authorities all or any of the functions which, in accordance with section 63 above, fall to be exercisable by the proper officer of the local authority for the registration area;
- (b)   may provide that any rent officer previously appointed for the area of any one of the constituent authorities shall be treated for such purposes as may be specified in the scheme as a rent officer appointed for the amalgamated registration area; and
- (c)   shall make such provision as appears to the Secretary of State to be appropriate for the payment by one or more of the constituent authorities of the remunerations, allowances and other expenditure which under section 63 above is to be paid by the local authority for the area.

(4)   A scheme under section 63 above made for an amalgamated registration area may contain such incidental, transitional and supplementary provisions as appear to the Secretary of State to be *necessary or expedient.*]

[242]

## NOTES

Inserted, together with s 64B, by the Housing Act 1988, s 120, Sch 14, Pt II.

**[64B   New basis for administration of rent officer service**

(1)   If, with respect to registration areas generally or any particular registration area or areas, it appears to the Secretary of State that it is no longer appropriate for the appointment, remuneration and administration of rent officers to be a function of local authorities, he may by order—

    (a)    provide that no scheme under section 63 above shall be made for the area or areas specified in the order; and

    (b)    make, with respect to the area or areas so specified, such provision as appears to him to be appropriate with respect to the appointment, remuneration and administration of rent officers and the payment of pensions, allowances or gratuities to or in respect of them.

(2)   An order under this section shall make provision for any expenditure attributable to the provisions of the order to be met by the Secretary of State in such manner as may be specified in the order (whether by way of grant, reimbursement or otherwise); and any expenditure incurred by the Secretary of State by virtue of this subsection shall be paid out of money provided by Parliament.

(3)   An order under this section—

    (a)    may contain such incidental, transitional and supplementary provisions as appear to the Secretary of State to be appropriate, including provisions amending this Part of this Act; and

    (b)    shall be made by statutory instrument which shall be subject to annulment in pursuance of a resolution of either House of Parliament.]

**[243]**

**NOTES**

Inserted as noted to s 64A at **[242]**.

Orders: the Administration of the Rent Officer Service (England) Order 1999, SI 1999/2403; the Administration of the Rent Officer Service (Wales) Order 2003, SI 2003/973.

## 65   Rent assessment committees

Rent assessment committees shall be constituted in accordance with Schedule 10 to this Act.

**[244]**

## 66   Register of rents

[(1)   For each registration area, a register for the purposes of this Part of this Act shall be prepared and kept up to date by the rent officer.

(1A)   The rent officer shall make the register available for inspection in such place or places and in such manner—

    (a)    if the area is not specified in an order made under section 64B of this Act, as may be provided by the scheme made for the area under section 63 of this Act;

    (b)    if the area is so specified, as the Secretary of State [or in relation to Wales, the National Assembly for Wales] may direct.]

(2)   The register shall contain, in addition to the rent payable under a regulated tenancy of a dwelling-house—

    (a)    the prescribed particulars with regard to the tenancy; and

    (b)    a specification of the dwelling-house.

(3)   A copy of an entry in the register certified under the hand of the rent officer or any person duly authorised by him shall be receivable in evidence in any court and in any proceedings.

(4)   A person requiring such a certified copy shall be entitled to obtain it on payment of the prescribed fee.

[(5)   In relation to Wales, references in this section to the rent officer are to the rent officer or rent officers designated for the purposes of this section by the National Assembly for Wales.]

**[245]**

**NOTES**

Sub-s (1): substituted, together with sub-s (1A), for original sub-s (1), by the Administration of the Rent Officer Service (England) Order 1999, SI 1999/2403, art 7(b).

Sub-s (1A): substituted as noted to sub-s (1) above; words in square brackets inserted by the Administration of the Rent Officer Service (Wales) Order 2003, SI 2003/973, art 12(a).

Sub-s (5): added by SI 2003/973, art 12(b).

Regulations: the Rent Act 1977 (Forms etc) Regulations 1980, SI 1980/1697 at **[3023]**; the Rent Act 1977 (Forms etc) (Welsh Forms and Particulars) Regulations 1993, SI 1993/1511.

## 67   Application for registration of rent

(1)   An application for the registration of a rent for a dwelling-house may be made to the rent officer by the landlord or the tenant, or jointly by the landlord and the tenant, under a regulated tenancy of the dwelling-house.

[(2)   Any such application must be in the prescribed form and must—

   (a)   specify the rent which it is sought to register;

   (b)   where the rent includes any sum payable by the tenant to the landlord for services and the application is made by the landlord, specify that sum and be accompanied by details of the expenditure incurred by the landlord in providing those services; and

   (c)   contain such other particulars as may be prescribed.]

(3)   Subject to subsection (4) below [and sections 67A and 70A of this Act], where a rent for a dwelling-house has been registered under this Part of this Act, no application by the tenant alone or by the landlord alone for the registration of a different rent for that dwelling-house shall be entertained before the expiry of [2 years] from the relevant date (as defined in subsection (5) below) except on the ground that, since that date, there has been such a change in—

   (a)   the condition of the dwelling-house (including the making of any improvement therein),

   (b)   the terms of the tenancy,

   (c)   the quantity, quality or condition of any furniture provided for use under the tenancy (deterioration by fair wear and tear excluded), or

   (d)   any other circumstances taken into consideration when the rent was registered or confirmed,

as to make the registered rent no longer a fair rent.

[(3A)   If the dwelling-house forms part of a hereditament in respect of which the landlord or a superior landlord is, or was on the relevant date, liable under Part I of the Local Government Finance Act 1992 to pay council tax, then, in determining for the purposes of subsection (3) above whether since the relevant date there has been such a change falling within paragraph (d) of that subsection as to make the registered rent no longer a fair rent, any change in the amount of council tax payable in respect of the hereditament shall be disregarded unless it is attributable to—

   (a)   the fact that the hereditament has become, or has ceased to be, an exempt dwelling,

   (b)   an alteration in accordance with regulations under section 24 of the Local Government Finance Act 1992 of the valuation band shown in a valuation list as applicable to the hereditament, or

   (c)   the compilation of a new valuation list in consequence of an order of the Secretary of State under section 5(4)(b) of that Act.

(3B)   In subsection (3A) above "hereditament" means a dwelling within the meaning of Part I of the Local Government Finance Act 1992 and, subject to that, expressions used in subsection (3A) and in Part I of that Act have the same meaning in that subsection as in that Part.]

(4)   Notwithstanding anything in subsection (3) above, an application such as is mentioned in that subsection which is made by the landlord alone and is so made within the last 3 months of the period of [2 years] referred to in that subsection may be entertained notwithstanding that that period has not expired.

[(5)   In this section … "relevant date", in relation to a rent which has been registered under this Part of this Act, means the date from which the registration took effect or, in the case of a registered rent which has been confirmed, the date from which the confirmation (or, where there have been two or more successive confirmations, the last of them) took effect] [but for the purposes of this subsection any registration or confirmation by virtue of section 70A of this Act shall be disregarded.]

(6)   …

(7)   … , the provisions of Part I of Schedule 11 to this Act [as modified by the Regulated Tenancies (Procedure) Regulations 1980] shall have effect with respect to the procedure to be followed on applications for the registration of rents.

**[246]**

**NOTES**

   Sub-s (2): substituted by the Housing Act 1980, s 59(2).

   Sub-s (3): words in first pair of square brackets inserted by the Local Government Finance (Housing) (Consequential Amendments) Order 1993, SI 1993/651, art 2(2), Sch 2, para 2(a); words in second pair of square brackets substituted by the Housing Act 1980, s 60(1), except in any case where, on the determination or confirmation of a rent by the rent officer, the rent determined by him is registered, or his confirmation is noted in the register, before 28 November 1980.

   Sub-ss (3A), (3B): inserted by SI 1993/651, art 2(1), Sch 1, para 5.

   Sub-s (4): words in square brackets substituted by the Housing Act 1980, s 60(1), except in any case where, on the determination or confirmation of a rent by the rent officer, the rent determined by him is registered, or his confirmation is noted in the register, before 28 November 1980.

   Sub-s (5): substituted by the Housing Act 1980, s 61(5), subject to savings in s 61(8) thereof at **[360]**; words omitted repealed by the Housing Act 1988, s 140(2), Sch 18; words in square brackets added by SI 1993/651, art 2(2), Sch 2, para 2(b).

   Sub-s (6): repealed by the Housing Act 1980, s 152(3), Sch 26.

   Sub-s (7): words omitted repealed by the Housing Act 1988, s 140(2), Sch 18, except in relation to an application for a certificate of fair rent under s 69(1) (repealed) made before 15 January 1989 or a certificate of fair rent issued pursuant to such an application; words in square brackets inserted by the Regulated Tenancies (Procedure) Regulations 1980, SI 1980/1696, reg 2, in respect of applications made after 28 November 1980.

Modification: this section has effect as if references to a regulated tenancy were references to a statutory tenancy, by virtue of the Rent (Agriculture) Act 1976, s 13(2), (6), (7) at **[167]**.

Regulations: the Rent Act 1977 (Forms etc) Regulations 1980, SI 1980/1697 at **[3023]**; the Rent Act 1977 (Forms etc) (Welsh Forms and Particulars) Regulations 1993, SI 1993/1511.

**[67A   Application before 1st April 1994 for interim increase of rent in certain cases where landlord liable for council tax**

(1)   Subject to subsection (4) below, an application under this section for the registration under section 70A of this Act of an increased rent for a dwelling-house may be made by the landlord or the tenant, or jointly by the landlord and the tenant, under a regulated tenancy of the dwelling-house in any case where—

    (a)   under Part I of the Local Government Finance Act 1992 the landlord or a superior landlord is liable to pay council tax in respect of a dwelling (within the meaning of that Part of that Act) which includes the dwelling-house,

    (b)   under the terms of the tenancy (or an agreement collateral to the tenancy) the tenant is liable to make payments to the landlord in respect of council tax,

    (c)   the case falls within subsection (2) or subsection (3) below, and

    (d)   no previous application has been made under this section in relation to the dwelling-house.

(2)   The case falls within this subsection if—

    (a)   a rent has been registered under this Part of this Act before 1st April 1993,

    (b)   the period of two years from the relevant date has not yet expired, and

    (c)   since the relevant date there has been no such change in circumstances of a kind mentioned in paragraphs (a) to (d) of section 67(3) of this Act (other than circumstances relating to council tax) as to make the registered rent no longer a fair rent.

(3)   The case falls within this subsection if an application under section 67 of this Act has been made before 1st April 1993 but has not been disposed of before that date.

(4)   No application may be made under this section after 31st March 1994.

(5)   Any such application must be in the prescribed form and must—

    (a)   specify the rent which it is sought to register to take into account the tenant's liability to make payments to the landlord in respect of council tax; and

    (b)   contain such other particulars as may be prescribed.

(6)   The provisions of Part I of Schedule 11 to this Act (as modified by the Regulated Tenancies (Procedure) Regulations 1980 and by the Rent Assessment Committees (England and Wales) (Amendment) Regulations 1981) shall have effect with respect to the procedure to be followed on applications for the registration of rents.

(7)   In this section "relevant date", in relation to a rent which has been registered under this Part of this Act, has the same meaning as in section 67 of this Act.]

**[247]**

**NOTES**

Inserted by the Local Government Finance (Housing) (Consequential Amendments) Order 1993, SI 1993/651, art 2(2), Sch 2, para 3.

Modification: this section has effect as if references to a regulated tenancy were references to a statutory tenancy, by virtue of the Rent (Agriculture) Act 1976, s 13(2), (6), (7) at **[167]**.

Regulations: the Rent Act 1977 (Forms etc) (Welsh Forms and Particulars) Regulations 1993, SI 1993/1511.

**68, 69**   *(Repealed by the Housing Act 1980, s 140, Sch 17, Pt I, para 22, Sch 18.)*

**70   Determination of fair rent**

(1)   In determining, for the purposes of this Part of this Act, what rent is or would be a fair rent under a regulated tenancy of a dwelling-house, regard shall be had to all the circumstances (other than personal circumstances) and in particular to—

    (a)   the age, character, locality and state of repair of the dwelling-house, …

    (b)   if any furniture is provided for use under the tenancy, the quantity, quality and condition of the furniture[, and

    (c)   any premium, or sum in the nature of a premium, which has been or may be lawfully required or received on the grant, renewal, continuance or assignment of the tenancy].

(2)   For the purposes of the determination it shall be assumed that the number of persons seeking to become tenants of similar dwelling-houses in the locality on the terms (other than those relating to rent) of the regulated tenancy is not substantially greater than the number of such dwelling-houses in the locality which are available for letting on such terms.

(3)   There shall be disregarded—

    (a)   any disrepair or other defect attributable to a failure by the tenant under the regulated tenancy or any predecessor in title of his to comply with any terms thereof;

(b) any improvement carried out, otherwise than in pursuance of the terms of the tenancy, by the tenant under the regulated tenancy or any predecessor in title of his;

(c), (d) ...

(e) if any furniture is provided for use under the regulated tenancy, any improvement to the furniture by the tenant under the regulated tenancy or any predecessor in title of his or, as the case may be, any deterioration in the condition of the furniture due to any ill-treatment by the tenant, any person residing or lodging with him, or any sub-tenant of his.

[(3A) In any case where under Part I of the Local Government Finance Act 1992 the landlord or a superior landlord is liable to pay council tax in respect of a hereditament ("the relevant hereditament") of which the dwelling-house forms part, regard shall also be had to the amount of council tax which, as at the date on which the application to the rent officer was made, was set by the billing authority—

(a) for the financial year in which that application was made, and

(b) for the category of dwellings within which the relevant hereditament fell on that date,

but any discount or other reduction affecting the amount of council tax payable shall be disregarded.

(3B) In subsection (3A) above—

(a) "hereditament" means a dwelling within the meaning of Part I of the Local Government Finance Act 1992,

(b) "billing authority" has the same meaning as in that Part of that Act, and

(c) "category of dwellings" has the same meaning as in section 30(1) and (2) of that Act.]

(4) In this section "improvement" includes the replacement of any fixture or fitting.

[(4A) In this section "premium" has the same meaning as in Part IX of this Act, and "sum in the nature of a premium" means—

(a) any such loan as is mentioned in section 119 or 120 of this Act,

(b) any such excess over the reasonable price of furniture as is mentioned in section 123 of this Act, and

(c) any such advance payment of rent as is mentioned in section 126 of this Act.]

(5) ...

**[248]**

**NOTES**

Sub-s (1): words omitted repealed and para (c) added by the Housing and Planning Act 1986, s 17(1), (2), (4), in relation to every decision made by a rent officer or rent assessment committee after 7 January 1987 irrespective of when the application or decision was made.

Sub-s (3): paras (c), (d) repealed by the Housing Act 1980, s 152(1), (3), Sch 25, Pt I, para 41, Sch 26.

Sub-ss (3A), (3B): inserted by the Local Government Finance (Housing) (Consequential Amendments) Order 1993, SI 1993/651, art 2(1), Sch 1, para 6.

Sub-s (4A): inserted by the Housing and Planning Act 1986, s 17(1), (3), (4), in relation to every decision made by a rent officer or rent assessment committee after 7 January 1987 irrespective of when the application or decision was made.

Sub-s (5): repealed by the Housing Act 1980, s 152(1), (3), Sch 25, Pt I, para 41, Sch 26.

Modification: this section has effect as if references to a regulated tenancy were references to a statutory tenancy, by virtue of the Rent (Agriculture) Act 1976, s 13(2), (6), (7) at **[167]**.

## [70A Interim determination of fair rent on application under section 67A

(1) Where an application is made under section 67A of this Act—

(a) the rent officer shall determine the amount by which, having regard to the provisions of section 70(3A) of this Act, the existing registered rent might reasonably be increased to take account of the tenant's liability to make payments to the landlord in respect of council tax; and

(b) the amount to be registered as the rent of the dwelling-house shall be the existing registered rent plus the amount referred to in paragraph (a) above.

(2) Where in a case falling within section 67A(3) of this Act a rent officer has before him at the same time an application under section 67 and an application under section 67A of this Act and the rent officer proposes to entertain the two applications together, the rent officer shall make a determination in relation to the application under section 67 before making his determination in relation to the application under section 67A; and the reference in subsection (1)(a) above to the existing registered rent shall have effect as a reference to the rent determined on the application under section 67.]

**[249]**

**NOTES**

Inserted by the Local Government Finance (Housing) (Consequential Amendments) Order 1993, SI 1993/651, art 2(2), Sch 2, para 4.

Modification: this section has effect as if references to a regulated tenancy were references to a statutory tenancy, by virtue of the Rent (Agriculture) Act 1976, s 13(2), (6), (7) at **[167]**.

### 71   Amount to be registered as rent

(1)   The amount to be registered as the rent of any dwelling-house shall include any sums payable by the tenant to the landlord [in respect of council tax or] for the use of furniture or for services, whether or not those sums are separate from the sums payable for the occupation of the dwelling-house or are payable under separate agreements.

(2)   Where any rates in respect of a dwelling-house are borne by the landlord or a superior landlord, the amount to be registered under this Part of this Act as the rent of the dwelling-house shall be the same as if the rates were not so borne; but the fact that they are so borne shall be noted on the register.

(3)   Where subsection (2) above applies, the amount of the rates for any rental period, ascertained in accordance with Schedule 5 to this Act—
  (a)   shall ... be added to the limit imposed by section 44(1) of this Act ... ; and
  (b)   if the rental period is a statutory period, as defined in section 61 of this Act, shall be recoverable, without service of any notice of increase, in addition to the sums recoverable from the tenant apart from this subsection.

(4)   Where, under a regulated tenancy, the sums payable by the tenant to the landlord include any sums varying according to the cost from time to time of—
  (a)   any services provided by the landlord or a superior landlord, or
  (b)   any works of maintenance or repair carried out by the landlord or a superior landlord,
the amount to be registered under this Part of this Act as rent may, if the rent officer is satisfied or, as the case may be, the rent assessment committee are satisfied, that the terms as to the variation are reasonable, be entered as an amount variable in accordance with those terms.

**[250]**

**NOTES**
  Sub-s (1): words in square brackets inserted by the Local Government Finance (Housing) (Consequential Amendments) Order 1993, SI 1993/651, art 2(1), Sch 1, para 7.
  Sub-s (3): words omitted in the first place repealed by the Housing Act 1980, s 152(3), Sch 26; words omitted in the second place repealed by the Rent (Relief from Phasing) Order 1987, SI 1987/264, art 2(3), Sch 1.
  Modification: this section (except sub-s (3)) has effect as if references to a regulated tenancy were references to a statutory tenancy, by virtue of the Rent (Agriculture) Act 1976, s 13(2), (6), (7) at **[167]**.

### [72   Effect of registration of rent

(1)   The registration of a rent for a dwelling-house takes effect—
  (a)   if the rent is determined by the rent officer, from the date when it is registered, and
  (b)   if the rent is determined by a rent assessment committee, from the date when the committee make their decision.

(2)   If the rent for the time being registered is confirmed, the confirmation takes effect—
  (a)   if it is made by the rent officer, from the date when it is noted in the register, and
  (b)   if it is made by a rent assessment committee, from the date when the committee make their decision.

(3)   If (by virtue of section 67(4) of this Act) an application for registration of a rent is made before the expiry of the period mentioned in section 67(3) and the resulting registration of a rent for the dwelling-house, or confirmation of the rent for the time being registered, would, but for this subsection, take effect before the expiry of that period it shall take effect on the expiry of that period.

(4)   The date from which the registration or confirmation of a rent takes effect shall be entered in the register.

(5)   As from the date on which the registration of a rent takes effect any previous registration of a rent for the dwelling-house ceases to have effect.

(6)   Where a valid notice of increase under any provision of Part III of this Act has been served on a tenant and, in consequence of the registration of a rent, part but not the whole of the increase specified in the notice becomes irrecoverable from the tenant, the registration shall not invalidate the notice, but the notice shall, as from the date from which the registration takes effect, have effect as if it specified such part only of the increase as has not become irrecoverable.]

**[251]**

**NOTES**
  Substituted by the Housing Act 1980, s 61(1), subject to savings in s 61(8) thereof at **[360]**.

**[72A Amounts attributable to services**

In order to assist authorities to give effect to the housing benefit scheme under Part VII of the Social Security Contributions and Benefits Act 1992, where a rent is registered, there shall be noted on the register the amount (if any) of the registered rent which, in the opinion of the rent officer or rent assessment committee, is fairly attributable to the provision of services, except any amount which is negligible in the opinion of the officer or, as the case may be, the committee.]

**[252]**

**NOTES**
Inserted by the Social Security (Consequential Provisions) Act 1992, s 4, Sch 2, para 47.

**73 Cancellation of registration of rent**

(1) An application may be made in accordance with this section for the cancellation of the registration of a rent for a dwelling-house where—

    (a) a rent agreement as respects the dwelling-house takes effect, or is to take effect, after the expiration of a period of [2 years] beginning with the relevant date (as defined in section 67(5) of this Act), and

    (b) the period for which the tenancy has effect cannot end, or be brought to an end by the landlord (except for non-payment of rent or a breach of the terms of the tenancy), earlier than 12 months after the date of the application, and

    (c) the application is made jointly by the landlord and the tenant under the agreement.

[(1A) Such an application may also be made where—

    (a) not less than two years have elapsed since the relevant date (as defined in section 67(5) of this Act); and

    (b) the dwelling-house is not for the time being subject to a regulated tenancy; and

    (c) the application is made by the person who would be the landlord if the dwelling-house were let on such a tenancy.]

(2) The rent agreement may be one providing that the agreement does not take effect unless the application for cancellation of registration is granted.

[(3) An application under this section must—

    (a) be in the form prescribed for the application concerned and contain the prescribed particulars; and

    (b) be accompanied, in the case of an application under subsection (1) above, by a copy of the rent agreement.]

(4) If [the application is made under subsection (1) above and] the rent officer is satisfied that the rent, or the highest rent, payable under the rent agreement does not exceed a fair rent for the dwelling-house, he shall cancel the registration [and he shall also cancel the registration if the application is made under subsection (1A) above].

(5) Where [the application is made under subsection (1) above and] under the terms of the rent agreement the sums payable by the tenant to the landlord include any sums varying according to the cost from time to time of any services provided by the landlord or a superior landlord, or of any works of maintenance or repair carried out by the landlord or a superior landlord, the rent officer shall not cancel the registration unless he is satisfied that those terms are reasonable.

(6) [A cancellation made in pursuance of an application under subsection (1) above] shall not take effect until the date when the agreement takes effect; and if the cancellation is registered before that date, the date on which it is to take effect shall be noted on the register.

(7) The cancellation of the registration shall be without prejudice to a further registration of a rent at any time after cancellation.

(8) The rent officer shall notify the applicants of his decision to grant, or to refuse, any application under this section.

(9) In this section "rent agreement" means—

    (a) an agreement increasing the rent payable under a protected tenancy which is a regulated tenancy, or

    (b) where a regulated tenancy is terminated, and a new regulated tenancy is granted at a rent exceeding the rent under the previous tenancy, the grant of the new tenancy.

**[253]**

**NOTES**
Sub-s (1): words in square brackets substituted by the Housing Act 1980, s 152, Sch 25, Pt I, para 40, except in relation to a case where, on a determination or confirmation of rent by a rent officer, the determination or confirmation is noted in the register before 28 November 1980.
Sub-s (1A): inserted by the Housing Act 1980, s 62(1), (2).
Sub-s (3): substituted by the Housing Act 1980, s 62(1), (3).
Sub-ss (4), (5): words in square brackets inserted by the Housing Act 1980, s 62(1), (4), (5).
Sub-s (6): words in square brackets substituted by the Housing Act 1980, s 62(1), (6).

Regulations: the Rent Act 1977 (Forms etc) Regulations 1980, SI 1980/1697 at **[3023]**; the Rent Act 1977 (Forms etc) (Welsh Forms and Particulars) Regulations 1993, SI 1993/1511.

**74  Regulations**

(1)   The Secretary of State may make regulations—
   (a)   prescribing the form of any notice, application, register or other document to be given, made or used in pursuance of this Part of this Act;
   (b)   regulating the procedure to be followed—
      [(i)   by rent officers under this Act; and
      (ii)   by rent assessment committees whether under this Act or otherwise; and]
   (c)   prescribing anything required or authorised to be prescribed by this Part of this Act.

(2)   Regulations under subsection (1)(b) above may contain provisions modifying the following provisions of this Act:—
   (a)   Section 67, ... or 72;
   (b)   Part I ... of Schedule 11;
   (c)   ... ;

but no regulations containing such provisions shall have effect unless approved by a resolution of each House of Parliament.

(3)   Regulations made under this section shall be made by statutory instrument which, except in a case falling within subsection (2) above, shall be subject to annulment in pursuance of a resolution of either House of Parliament.

**[254]**

**NOTES**

Sub-s (1): words in square brackets substituted by the Leasehold Reform, Housing and Urban Development Act 1993, s 187(1), Sch 21, para 7.

Sub-s (2): words omitted repealed by the Housing Act 1988, s 140(2), Sch 18.

Regulations: the Regulated Tenancies (Procedure) Regulations 1980, SI 1980/1696; the Rent Act (Forms etc) Regulations 1980, SI 1980/1697 at **[3023]**; the Rent Regulation (Cancellation of Registration of Rent) Regulations 1980, SI 1980/1698 at **[3035]**; the Rent Assessment Committees (England and Wales) (Rent Tribunal) Regulations 1980, SI 1980/1700 at **[3040]**; the Rent Act 1977 (Forms etc) (Welsh Forms and Particulars) Regulations 1993, SI 1993/1511. In addition, by virtue of s 155(3) of, and Sch 24, para 1 to, this Act, the Rent Assessment Committees (England and Wales) Regulations 1971, SI 1971/1065 at **[3007]** have effect as if made under this section.

Extension of regulation making powers: the power to make regulations conferred by this section is extended by the Leasehold Reform Act 1967, s 39(2), Sch 5, para 10 at **[124]**, **[134]**, and the Leasehold Reform, Housing and Urban Development Act 1993, s 91(5).

**75  Interpretation of Part IV**

(1)   In this Part of this Act, except where the context otherwise requires—
   "improvement" includes structural alteration, extension or addition and the provision of additional fixtures or fittings, but does not include anything done by way of decoration or repair;
   "prescribed" means prescribed by regulations under section 74 of this Act, and references to a prescribed form include references to a form substantially to the same effect as the prescribed form.

(2)   References in this Part of this Act to rates, in respect of a dwelling-house, include references to such proportion of any rates in respect of a hereditament of which the dwelling-house forms part as may be agreed in writing between the landlord and the tenant or determined by the county court.

**[255]**

**PART V**
**RENTS UNDER RESTRICTED CONTRACTS**

**NOTES**

Phasing out of restricted contracts: the Housing Act 1988, s 36 at **[767]**, provides that a tenancy or other contract entered into on or after 15 January 1989 cannot be a restricted contract for the purposes of this Act and accordingly covered by the special regime applying to such contracts in this Part and in ss 102A–106A at **[281]**–**[286]**, unless it is entered into under a contract made before that date.

**76**   (*Repealed by the Housing Act 1980, ss 72(1), 152(3), Sch 26.*)

*Control of rents*

## 77 Reference of contracts to rent tribunals and obtaining by them of information

(1) Either the lessor or the lessee under a restricted contract ... may refer the contract to the rent tribunal ...

(2) Where a restricted contract is referred to a rent tribunal under subsection (1) above they may, by notice in writing served on the lessor, require him to give to them, within such period (not less than 7 days from the date of the service of the notice) as may be specified in the notice, such information as they may reasonably require regarding such of the prescribed particulars relating to the contract as are specified in the notice.

(3) If, within the period specified in a notice under subsection (2) above, the lessor fails without reasonable cause to comply with the provisions of the notice he shall be liable [to a fine not exceeding level 3 on the standard scale].

(4) Proceedings for an offence under this section shall not be instituted otherwise than by the local authority.

[256]

**NOTES**

Sub-s (1): words omitted in the first place repealed by the Housing Act 1988, s 140, Sch 17, Pt I, para 23, Sch 18; words omitted in the second place repealed by the Housing Act 1980, s 152(3), Sch 26.

Sub-s (3): words in square brackets substituted by virtue of the Criminal Justice Act 1982, ss 38, 46.

Regulations: the Rent Act 1977 (Forms etc) Regulations 1980, SI 1980/1697 at **[3023]**.

## 78 Powers of rent tribunals on reference of contracts

(1) Where a restricted contract is referred to a rent tribunal and the reference is not, before the tribunal have entered upon consideration of it, withdrawn by the party or authority who made it, the tribunal shall consider it.

(2) After making such inquiry as they think fit and giving to—
  (a) each party to the contract, and
  (b) if the general management of the dwelling is vested in and exercisable by a housing authority, that authority,
an opportunity of being heard or, at his or their option, of submitting representations in writing, the tribunal, subject to subsections (3) and (4) below,—
  (i) shall approve the rent payable under the contract, or
  (ii) shall reduce or increase the rent to such sum as they may, in all the circumstances, think reasonable, or
  (iii) may, if they think fit in all the circumstances, dismiss the reference, and shall notify the parties ... of their decision.

[(2A) In any case where under Part I of the Local Government Finance Act 1992 the lessor, or any person having any title superior to that of the lessor, is liable to pay council tax in respect of a hereditament ("the relevant hereditament") of which the dwelling forms part, the tribunal shall have regard to the amount of council tax which, as at the date on which the reference to the tribunal was made, was set by the billing authority—
  (a) for the financial year in which that reference was made, and
  (b) for the category of dwellings within which the relevant hereditament fell on that date,
but any discount or other reduction affecting the amount of council tax payable shall be disregarded.

(2B) In subsection (2A) above—
  (a) "hereditament" means a dwelling within the meaning of Part I of the Local Government Finance Act 1992,
  (b) "billing authority" has the same meaning as in that Part of that Act, and
  (c) "category of dwellings" has the same meaning as in section 30(1) and (2) of that Act.]

(3) On the reference of a restricted contract relating to a dwelling for which a rent is registered under Part IV of this Act, the rent tribunal may not reduce the rent payable under the contract below the amount which would be recoverable from the tenant under a regulated tenancy of the dwelling.

(4) An approval, reduction or increase under this section may be limited to rent payable in respect of a particular period.

(5) In [subsection (2)] above, "housing authority" [means a local housing authority within the meaning of the Housing Act 1985].

[257]

**NOTES**

Sub-s (2): words omitted repealed by the Housing Act 1980, s 152(3), Sch 26.

Sub-ss (2A), (2B): inserted by the Local Government Finance (Housing) (Consequential Amendments) Order 1993, SI 1993/651, art 2(1), Sch 1, para 8.

PART I
STATUTES

Sub-s (5): words in first pair of square brackets substituted by the Housing Act 1980, s 152(1), Sch 25, Pt I, para 42; words in second pair of square brackets substituted by the Housing (Consequential Provisions) Act 1985, s 4, Sch 2, para 35(1), (4).

### 79 Register of rents under restricted contracts

(1)   The [president of every rent assessment panel] shall prepare and keep up to date a register for the purposes of this Part of this Act and shall make the register available for inspection in such place or places and in such manner as the Secretary of State may direct.

(2)   The register shall be so prepared and kept up to date as to contain, with regard to any contract relating to a dwelling situated in the area of the [rent assessment panel] and under which a rent is payable which has been approved, reduced or increased under section 78 of this Act, entries of—

    (a)   the prescribed particulars with regard to the contract;

    (b)   a specification of the dwelling to which the contract relates; and

    (c)   the rent as approved, reduced or increased by the rent tribunal, and in a case in which the approval, reduction or increase is limited to rent payable in respect of a particular period, a specification of that period.

(3)   Where any rates in respect of a dwelling are borne by the lessor or any person having any title superior to that of the lessor, the amount to be entered in the register under this section as the rent payable for the dwelling shall be the same as if the rates were not so borne; but the fact that they are so borne shall be noted in the register.

[(3A)   The amount to be entered in the register under this section as the rent payable for a dwelling shall include any sums payable by the lessee to the lessor in respect of council tax, whether or not those sums are separate from the sums payable for the occupation of the dwelling or are payable under separate agreements.]

(4)   ...

(5)   A copy of an entry in the register certified under the hand of an officer duly authorised in that behalf by the [president of the rent assessment panel concerned] shall be receivable in evidence in any court and in any proceedings.

(6)   A person requiring such a certified copy shall be entitled to obtain it on payment of the prescribed fee.

[(6A)   Every local authority shall, before the expiry of the period of three months beginning with the commencement of paragraph 44 of Schedule 25 to the Housing Act 1980, send to the president of the appropriate rent assessment panel the register previously kept by the authority under this section.]

**[258]**

---

**NOTES**

Sub-ss (1), (2), (5): words in square brackets substituted by the Housing Act 1980, s 152(1), Sch 25(1), para 43(a), (b), (d).

Sub-s (3A): inserted by the Local Government Finance (Housing) (Consequential Amendments) Order 1993, SI 1993/651, art 2(1), Sch 1, para 9.

Sub-s (4): repealed by the Housing Act 1980, s 152(1), (3), Sch 25, Pt I, para 43(c), Sch 26.

Sub-s (6A): inserted by the Housing Act 1980, s 152(1), Sch 25, Pt I, para 44.

Regulations: the Rent Act 1977 (Forms etc) Regulations 1980, SI 1980/1697 at **[3023]**; the Rent Act 1977 (Forms etc) (Welsh Forms and Particulars) Regulations 1993, SI 1993/1511.

---

### 80 Reconsideration of rent after registration

(1)   Where the rent payable for any dwelling has been entered in the register under section 79 of this Act the lessor or the lessee ... may refer the case to the rent tribunal for reconsideration of the rent so entered.

(2)   Where the rent under a restricted contract has been registered under section 79 of this Act, a rent tribunal shall not be required to entertain a reference, made otherwise than by the lessor and the lessee jointly, for the registration of a different rent for the dwelling concerned before the expiry of the period of [2 years] beginning on the date on which the rent was last considered by the tribunal, except on the ground that, since that date, there has been such a change in—

    (a)   the condition of the dwelling,

    (b)   the furniture or services provided,

    (c)   the terms of the contract, or

    (d)   any other circumstances taken into consideration when the rent was last considered,

as to make the registered rent no longer a reasonable rent.

[(3)   If the dwelling forms part of a hereditament in respect of which the lessor, or any person having any title superior to that of the lessor, is liable under Part I of the Local Government Finance Act 1992 to pay council tax or was so liable on the date on which the rent was last considered by the tribunal, then, in determining for the purposes of subsection (2) above whether since that date there has been such a change falling within paragraph (d) of that subsection as to make the registered rent no longer a reasonable rent, any change in the amount of council tax payable in respect of the hereditament shall be disregarded unless it is attributable to—

(a)  the fact that the hereditament has become, or has ceased to be, an exempt dwelling,

(b)  an alteration in accordance with regulations under section 24 of the Local Government Finance Act 1992 of the valuation band shown in a valuation list as applicable to the hereditament, or

(c)  the compilation of a new valuation list in consequence of an order of the Secretary of State under section 5(4)(b) of that Act.

(4)  In subsection (3) above "hereditament" means a dwelling within the meaning of Part I of the Local Government Finance Act 1992 and, subject to that, expressions used in subsection (3) and in Part I of that Act (other than "dwelling") have the same meaning in that subsection as in that Part.]

**[259]**

**NOTES**

Sub-s (1): words omitted repealed by the Housing Act 1988, s 140(2), Sch 18.

Sub-s (2): words in square brackets substituted by the Housing Act 1980, s 70(1), subject to savings in s 70(2) thereof at **[364]**.

Sub-ss (3), (4): added by the Local Government Finance (Housing) (Consequential Amendments) Order 1993, SI 1993/651, art 2(1), Sch 1, para 10.

### [80A  Reference before 1st April 1994 for interim increase of rent in certain cases where lessor liable for council tax

(1)  In any case where—

(a)  under Part I of the Local Government Finance Act 1992 the lessor under a restricted contract or any person having any title superior to that of the lessor is liable to pay council tax in respect of a hereditament which includes the dwelling to which the restricted contract relates,

(b)  under the terms of the restricted contract (or an agreement collateral to the contract) the lessee is liable to make payments to the lessor in respect of council tax,

(c)  the case falls within subsection (2) or subsection (3) below, and

(d)  no previous reference under this section in relation to the dwelling has been made to the rent tribunal,

the lessor or the lessee may, subject to subsection (4) below, refer the contract to the rent tribunal under this section for consideration of an increased rent.

(2)  The case falls within this subsection if—

(a)  a rent has been entered in the register under section 79 of this Act before 1st April 1993,

(b)  the period of two years beginning on the date on which the rent was last considered by the tribunal has not yet expired, and

(c)  since that date there has been no such change in circumstances of the kind mentioned in paragraphs (a) to (d) of section 80 of this Act (other than circumstances relating to council tax) as to make the registered rent no longer a reasonable rent.

(3)  The case falls within this subsection if a reference under section 77 or 80 of this Act has been made before 1st April 1993 but has not been disposed of before that date.

(4)  No reference may be made under this section after 31st March 1994.

(5)  Where a reference is made under this section—

(a)  the rent tribunal shall (after making such inquiry as they think fit and giving to each party to the contract an opportunity of being heard or of submitting representations in writing) increase the amount of the existing registered rent by such amount as is reasonable, having regard to the provisions of section 78(2A) of this Act, to take account of the lessee's liability to make payments to the lessor in respect of the council tax, and

(b)  the amount to be registered under section 79 of this Act as the rent of the dwelling shall be the existing registered rent plus the amount referred to in paragraph (a) above.

(6)  Where in a case to which subsection (3) above applies a rent tribunal have before them at the same time a reference under section 77 or 80 of this Act and a reference under this section and the rent tribunal propose to entertain the two references together, the tribunal shall approve, reduce or increase the rent under the reference under section 77 or 80 before making their increase in relation to the reference under this section; and the reference in subsection (5)(a) above to the existing registered rent shall have effect as a reference to the rent determined on the reference under section 77 or 80.

(7)  In this section "hereditament" means a dwelling within the meaning of Part I of the Local Government Finance Act 1992.]

**[260]**

PART I
STATUTES

**NOTES**

Inserted by the Local Government Finance (Housing) (Consequential Amendments) Order 1993, SI 1993/651, art 2(2), Sch 2, para 5.

---

### 81 Effect of registration of rent

(1)   Where the rent payable for any dwelling is entered in the register under section 79 of this Act, it shall not be lawful to require or receive on account of rent for that dwelling under a restricted contract payment of any amount in excess of the rent so registered—

    (a)   in respect of any period subsequent to the date of the entry, or

    (b)   where a particular period is specified in the register, in respect of that period.

(2)   Where subsection (3) of section 79 applies, the amount entered in the register under that section shall be treated for the purposes of this section as increased for any rental period by the amount of the rates for that period, ascertained in accordance with Schedule 5 to this Act.

(3)   Where any payment has been made or received in contravention of this section, the amount of the excess shall be recoverable by the person by whom it was paid.

(4)   Any person who requires or receives any payment in contravention of this section shall be liable to a fine not exceeding [level 3 on the standard scale] or to imprisonment for a term not exceeding 6 months or both, and, without prejudice to any other method of recovery, the court by which a person is found guilty of an offence under this subsection may order the amount paid in excess to be repaid to the person by whom the payment was made.

(5)   Proceedings for an offence under this section shall not be instituted otherwise than by the local authority.

**[261]**

---

**NOTES**

Sub-s (4): words in square brackets substituted by virtue of the Criminal Justice Act 1982, ss 38, 46.

---

### [81A   Cancellation of registration of rent

(1)   Where the rent payable for any dwelling is entered in the register under section 79 of this Act, the rent tribunal shall cancel the entry, on an application made under this section, if—

    (a)   ...

    (b)   the dwelling is not for the time being subject to a restricted contract; and

    (c)   the application is made by the person who would be the lessor if the dwelling were subject to a restricted contract.

(2)   An application under this section must be in the prescribed form, and contain the prescribed particulars.

(3)   Cancellation of the registration shall be without prejudice to a further registration of a rent at any time after the cancellation.

(4)   The rent tribunal shall notify the applicant of their decision to grant, or to refuse, any application under this section.]

**[262]**

---

**NOTES**

Inserted by the Housing Act 1980, s 71(1).
Sub-s (1): para (a) repealed by the Housing Act 1988, ss 36(4), 140(2), Sch 18.
Regulations: the Rent Act 1977 (Forms etc) Regulations 1980, SI 1980/1697 at **[3023]**.

---

*Miscellaneous and general*

### 82   Jurisdiction of rent tribunals

Where a restricted contract is referred to a rent tribunal under this Part, or Part VII, of this Act and—

    (a)   the contract relates to a dwelling consisting of or comprising part only of a hereditament, and

    (b)   no apportionment of the rateable value of the hereditament has been made under section 25 of this Act,

then, unless the lessor in the course of the proceedings requires that such an apportionment shall be made and, within 2 weeks of making the requirement, brings proceedings in the county court for the making of the apportionment, the rent tribunal shall have jurisdiction to deal with the reference if it appears to them that, had the apportionment been made, they would have had jurisdiction.

**[263]**

---

### 83   Local authorities for Part V

(1)   For the purposes of this Part of this Act, the local authority shall be—

    [(a)   in a London borough or district, the council of the London borough or district in question or, where the district is in a county in England and does not have a district council, the council of the county in question; and]

[(aa) in a Welsh county or county borough, the council of the county or county borough in question,]

(b) in the City of London, the Common Council.

(2) The local authority shall have power to publish information regarding the provisions of this Part, and sections 103 to 106, of this Act.

[264]

**NOTES**

Sub-s (1): para (a) substituted by the Local Government Changes (Rent Act) Regulations 1995, SI 1995/2451, regs 2, 5; para (aa) inserted by the Local Government (Wales) Act 1994, s 22(2), Sch 8, para 3(3).

## 84 Regulations

The Secretary of State may by statutory instrument make regulations—

(a), (b) ...

(c) for prescribing anything which is required by this Part of this Act to be prescribed; and

(d) generally for carrying into effect the provisions of this Part, and sections 103 to 106, of this Act.

[265]

**NOTES**

Paras (a), (b): repealed by the Housing Act 1980, s 152(3), Sch 26.
Regulations: the Rent Act 1977 (Forms etc) Regulations 1980, SI 1980/1697 at **[3023]**.

## 85 Interpretation of Part V

(1) In this Part of this Act, except where the context otherwise requires,—

"dwelling" means a house or part of a house;

"lessee" means the person to whom is granted, under a restricted contract, the right to occupy the dwelling in question as a residence and any person directly or indirectly deriving title from the grantee;

"lessor" means the person who, under a restricted contract, grants to another the right to occupy the dwelling in question as a residence and any person directly or indirectly deriving title from the grantor;

"register" means the register kept by the [president of the rent assessment panel concerned] in pursuance of section 79 of this Act;

"rent tribunal" [shall be construed in accordance with section 72 of the Housing Act 1980];

"services" includes attendance, the provision of heating or lighting, the supply of hot water and any other privilege or facility connected with the occupancy of a dwelling, other than a privilege or facility requisite for the purposes of access, cold water supply or sanitary accommodation.

(2) References in this Part of this Act to a party to a contract include references to any person directly or indirectly deriving title from such a party.

(3) Where separate sums are payable by the lessee of any dwelling to the lessor for any two or more of the following:—

(a) occupation of the dwelling,

(b) use of furniture, and

(c) services,

any reference in this Part of this Act to "rent" in relation to that dwelling is a reference to the aggregate of those sums and, where those sums are payable under separate contracts, those contracts shall be deemed to be one contract.

(4) The references in sections 79(3) and 81(2) of this Act to rates, in respect of a dwelling, include references to such proportion of any rates in respect of a hereditament of which the dwelling forms part as may be agreed in writing between the lessor and the lessee or determined by the county court.

[266]

**NOTES**

Sub-s (1): words in square brackets substituted by the Housing Act 1980, s 152(1), Sch 25, Pt I, para 45.

## PART VI
## RENT LIMIT FOR DWELLINGS LET BY HOUSING ASSOCIATIONS, HOUSING TRUSTS AND THE HOUSING CORPORATION

**NOTES**

Phasing out of housing association tenancies: the Housing Act 1988 s 35 at **[766]**, provides that no tenancy entered into on or after 15 January 1989 can be a housing association tenancy and accordingly covered by the special regime applying to such tenancies under this Part of this Act unless it (i) is entered into under a contract made before that date, (ii) is granted to an existing housing association tenant, (iii) is granted as suitable alternative accommodation in a case where the court has directed that the tenancy shall be a housing association tenancy, or (iv) is a former new town corporation tenancy. Protected or statutory tenancies under this Act as respects which a housing association, housing trust, etc, becomes the landlord on or after 15 January 1989 may also still become housing association tenancies for the purposes of this Part of this Act; see s 35(5) of the 1988 Act. Special provision is made to ensure that where a registered social landlord buys back a dwelling from an occupier who was a former secure tenant and grants a new tenancy to that occupier, the tenancy can be a secure tenancy at a fair rent, see the Housing Act 1985, s 554(2A). Tenancies which, by virtue of s 35 of the 1988 Act, do not become housing association tenancies for the purposes of this Part will generally become assured tenancies under Pt I, Chapter I (ss 1–19 and Schs 1, 2) of the 1988 Act at **[729]**–**[752]** and **[782]**–**[788]**.

*Registration of rents*

### 86   Tenancies to which Part VI applies

(1)   In this Part of this Act "housing association tenancy" means a tenancy to which this Part of this Act applies.

(2)   This Part of this Act applies to a tenancy [(other than a co-ownership tenancy)] where—

(a)   the interest of the landlord under that tenancy belongs to a housing association or housing trust, or to the Housing Corporation [or to the Secretary of State where that interest belongs to him as the result of the exercise by him of functions under Part III of the Housing Associations Act 1985] [ … ], and

(b)   the tenancy would be a protected tenancy but for section [13 or] 15 or 16 of this Act, and is not a tenancy to which Part II of the Landlord and Tenant Act 1954 applies.

(3)   In this Part of this Act "housing association" [has the same meaning as in the Housing Associations Act 1985].

[(3A)   For the purposes of this section a tenancy is a "co-ownership tenancy" if—

(a)   it was granted by a housing association which [is a co-operative housing association within the meaning of the Housing Associations Act 1985]; and

(b)   the tenant (or his personal representatives) will, under the terms of the tenancy agreement or of the agreement under which he became a member of the association, be entitled, on his ceasing to be a member and subject to any conditions stated in either agreement, to a sum calculated by reference directly or indirectly to the value of the dwelling-house.]

[(4)   In this Part of this Act "housing trust" has the same meaning as in section 15 of this Act.]

(5)   …

**[267]**

**NOTES**

Sub-s (2): words in first pair of square brackets inserted by the Housing Act 1980, s 77, Sch 10, para 1(1), (2); words in first pair of square brackets in para (a) and words in square brackets in para (b) inserted by the Government of Wales Act 1998 (Housing) (Amendments) Order 1999, SI 1999/61, art 2, Schedule, para 1(1)–(3); words omitted from second pair of square brackets in para (a) inserted by the Housing Act 1988, s 140(1), Sch 17, Pt II, para 100 and repealed by the Government of Wales Act 1998, ss 141, 152, Sch 18, Pt VI.

Sub-s (3): words in square brackets substituted by the Housing (Consequential Provisions) Act 1985, s 4, Sch 2, para 35(1), (5)(a).

Sub-s (3A): inserted by the Housing Act 1980, s 77, Sch 10, para 1(1), (4); words in square brackets in para (a) substituted by the Housing (Consequential Provisions) Act 1985, s 4, Sch 2, para 35(1), (5)(b).

Sub-s (4): substituted by the Housing Act 1980, s 77, Sch 10, para 1(1), (5).

Sub-s (5): repealed by the Housing Act 1980, s 152(3), Sch 26.

Modification: in sub-s (2)(a) the reference to the Housing Corporation shall be treated as if it were a reference to the Regulator of Social Housing: see the Transfer of Housing Corporation Functions (Modifications and Transitional Provisions) Order 2008, SI 2008/2839, arts 1(2), 3, 6, Schedule.

### 87   Rents to be registrable

(1)   There shall be a part of the register under Part IV of this Act in which rents may be registered for dwelling-houses which are let, or are, or are to be, available for letting under a housing association tenancy.

(2)   In relation to that part of the register the following (and no other) provisions of this Act:—

(a)   sections 67, … [, [67A, 70, 70A] and 72],

(b)   section 71, except subsection (3), and

(c)   Schedules 11 … ,

shall apply in relation to housing association tenancies, and in their application to such tenancies shall have effect as if for any reference in those provisions to a regulated tenancy there were substituted a reference to a housing association tenancy.

(3)–(5)  ...

(6)   A rent registered in any part of the register for a dwelling-house which becomes, or ceases to be, one subject to a housing association tenancy, shall be as effective as if it were registered in any other part of the register.

**[268]**

---

**NOTES**

Sub-s (2): words omitted repealed by the Housing Act 1988, s 140(2), Sch 18, except in relation to an application for a certificate of fair rent under s 69(1) (repealed) made before 15 January 1989 or a certificate of fair rent issued pursuant to such an application; words in first (outer) pair of square brackets substituted by the Housing Act 1980, s 61(3); figures in second (inner) pair of square brackets substituted by the Local Government Finance (Housing) (Consequential Amendments) Order 1993, SI 1993/651, art 2(2), Sch 2, para 6.

Sub-ss (3)–(5): repealed by the Housing Act 1980, ss 61(3), 152(3), Sch 26, subject to savings in s 61(8) thereof at **[360]**.

---

*Rent limit*

**88   Rent limit**

(1)   Where the rent payable under a tenancy would exceed the rent limit determined in accordance with this Part of this Act, the amount of the excess shall be irrecoverable from the tenant.

(2)   Where a rent for the dwelling-house is registered, ... the rent limit is the rent so registered.

(3)   Where any rates in respect of the dwelling-house are borne by the landlord, or a superior landlord, the amount of those rates for any rental period, ascertained in accordance with Schedule 5 to this Act, shall be added to the limit imposed by subsection (2) above, and in this Part of this Act references to the amount of the registered rent include any amount to be added under this subsection.

(4)   Where no rent for the dwelling-house is registered, then, subject to subsection (5) below, the rent limit shall be determined as follows:—

(a)   if the lease or agreement creating the tenancy was made before 1st January 1973, the rent limit is the rent recoverable under the tenancy, as varied by any agreement made before that date (but not as varied by any later agreement);

(b)   if paragraph (a) above does not apply, and, not more than [2 years] before the tenancy began, the dwelling-house was subject to another tenancy (whether before 1973 or later) the rent limit is the rent recoverable under that other tenancy (or if there was more than one, the last of them) for the last rental period thereof;

(c)   if paragraphs (a) and (b) above do not apply, the rent limit is the rent payable under the terms of the lease or agreement creating the tenancy (and not the rent so payable under those terms as varied by any subsequent agreement).

(5)   The reference in subsection (4)(b) above to another tenancy includes, in addition to a housing association tenancy, a regulated tenancy—

(a)   which subsisted at any time after 1st April 1975; and

(b)   under which, immediately before it came to an end, the interest of the landlord belonged to a housing association.

(6)   Where for any period there is a difference between the amount (if any) of the rates borne by the landlord or a superior landlord in respect of the dwelling-house and the amount (if any) so borne in the rental period on which the rent limit is based, the rent limit under this Part of this Act shall be increased or decreased by the amount of the difference.

(7)   A tenancy commencing (whether before or after the coming into force of this Act) while there is in operation a condition imposed under any of the following enactments:—

(a)   section 2 of the Housing (Financial Provisions) Act 1924;

[(b)   paragraph 2 of Part II of Schedule 16 to the Housing Act 1985, or any corresponding earlier enactment];

(c)   section 23 of the Housing Act 1949; and

[(d)   section 33 of the Housing Act 1985, or any corresponding earlier enactment];

[which impose a rent limit in respect of the dwelling-house] shall be disregarded for the purposes of subsection (4)(b) above in determining the rent limit under any subsequent tenancy of the dwelling-house.

**[269]**

---

**NOTES**

Sub-s (2): words omitted repealed by the Housing Act 1988, s 140, Sch 17, Pt I, para 24, Sch 18.

Sub-s (4): words in square brackets substituted, subject to savings, by the Housing Act 1980, s 152(1), Sch 25, Pt I, para 40.

Sub-s (7): words in square brackets substituted by the Housing (Consequential Provisions) Act 1985, s 4, Sch 2, para 35(1), (6).

Housing (Financial Provisions) Act 1924, s 2: repealed with savings by the Housing (Financial Provisions) Act 1958, s 59, Sch 6. The whole of the 1958 Act was repealed by the Housing (Consequential Provisions) Act 1985, s 3, Sch 1, Pt I, and any remaining operation is further saved by s 5(2) of, and Sch 4, para 2 to, the 1985 Act.

Housing Act 1949, s 23: repealed with savings by the Housing (Financial Provisions) Act 1958, s 59, Sch 6, and replaced by s 33 of, and Sch 4 to, the 1958 Act. Those provisions of the 1958 Act were repealed by the Housing Act 1969, s 89(3), Sch 10, subject to the savings in s 89(2) of, and Sch 9, para 1 to, that Act. Section 89(2) of, and Sch 9 to, the 1969 Act were repealed by the Housing (Consequential Provisions) Act 1985, s 3, Sch 1, Pt I, and any remaining operation is further saved by s 5(2) of, and Sch 4, para 2 to, the 1985 Act.

**89–91**    *(S 89 repealed by the Housing Act 1988, s 140, Sch 17, Pt I, para 24, Sch 18, subject to savings; ss 90, 91 repealed by the Housing Act 1980, ss 77, 152(3), Sch 10, para 3, Sch 26, subject to savings in relation to s 90, in Sch 25, Pt II, para 77 to that Act at* **[392]***.)*

### Conversion to regulated tenancies

## 92   Conversion of housing association tenancies into regulated tenancies

(1)   If at any time, by virtue of subsections (1) and (3) of section 15 of this Act, a tenancy ceases to be one to which this Part of this Act applies and becomes a protected tenancy, that tenancy shall be a regulated tenancy and the housing association which is the landlord under that tenancy shall give notice in writing to the tenant, … , informing him that his tenancy is no longer excluded from protection under this Act.

(2)   If, without reasonable excuse, a housing association fails to give notice to a tenant under subsection (1) above within the period of 21 days beginning on the day on which his tenancy becomes a protected tenancy, the association shall be liable to a fine not exceeding [level 3 on the standard scale].

(3)   Where an offence under subsection (2) above committed by a body corporate is proved to have been committed with the consent or connivance of, or to be attributable to any neglect on the part of, any director, manager or secretary or other similar officer of the body corporate or any person who was purporting to act in any such capacity, he as well as the body corporate shall be guilty of that offence and shall be liable to be proceeded against and punished accordingly.

(4)   Schedule 14 to this Act shall have effect for supplementing this section.

(5)   In this section—
"housing association" has the same meaning as in [the Housing Associations Act 1985]; …

(6), (7)   …

[270]

**NOTES**

Sub-s (1): words omitted repealed by the Housing Act 1980, ss 77, 152(3), Sch 10, para 4, Sch 26.

Sub-s (2): words in square brackets substituted by virtue of the Criminal Justice Act 1982, ss 38, 46.

Sub-s (5): words in square brackets substituted by the Housing (Consequential Provisions) Act 1985, s 4, Sch 2, para 35(1), (7); words omitted repealed by the Housing Act 1980, s 152(3), Sch 26.

Sub-ss (6), (7): repealed by the Housing Act 1980, s 152(3), Sch 26.

### Miscellaneous

## 93   Increase of rent without notice to quit

(1)   Subject to subsections (2) and (3) below, where a housing association tenancy is a weekly or other periodical tenancy, the rent payable to the housing association or, as the case may be, the housing trust or the Housing Corporation [or the Secretary of State] [ … ] (in this section called "the landlord") may, without the tenancy being terminated, be increased with effect from the beginning of any rental period by a written notice of increase [specifying the date on which the increase is to take effect and given by the landlord to the tenant not later than four weeks before that date].

[(2)   Where a notice of increase is given under subsection (1) above and the tenant, before the date specified in the notice of increase, gives a valid notice to quit, the notice of increase does not take effect unless the tenant, with the written agreement of the landlord, withdraws his notice to quit before that date.]

(3)   …

(4)   This section shall apply to a tenancy notwithstanding that the letting took place before the coming into force of this Act.

(5)   Nothing in this section shall authorise any rent to be increased above the rent limit, and any reference in section 88 of this Act to the variation by agreement of the rent recoverable under a tenancy shall include a reference to variation under this section.

[271]

## NOTES

Sub-s (1): words in first pair of square brackets inserted by the Government of Wales Act 1998 (Housing) (Amendments) Order 1999, SI 1999/61, art 2, Schedule, para 1(1), (4); words omitted from second pair of square brackets inserted by the Housing Act 1988, s 140(1), Sch 17, Pt II, para 100 and repealed by the Government of Wales Act 1998, ss 141, 152, Sch 18, Pt VI; words in third pair of square brackets substituted by the Housing Act 1980, s 77, Sch 10, para 5(1), (2), (5), in relation to notices of increase given after 28 November 1980.

Sub-s (2): substituted by the Housing Act 1980, s 77, Sch 10, para 5(1), (3), (5), in relation to notices of increase given after 28 November 1980.

Sub-s (3): repealed by the Housing Act 1980, ss 77, 152(3), Sch 10, para 5(1), (4), (5), Sch 26, in relation to notices of increase given after 28 November 1980.

Modification: in sub-s (1) the reference to the Housing Corporation shall be treated as if it were a reference to the Regulator of Social Housing: see the Transfer of Housing Corporation Functions (Modifications and Transitional Provisions) Order 2008, SI 2008/2839, arts 1(2), 3, 6, Schedule.

## 94  Recovery from landlord of sums paid in excess of recoverable rent, etc

(1)    Where a tenant has paid on account of rent any amount which, by virtue of this Part of this Act, is irrecoverable by the landlord, the tenant who paid it shall be entitled to recover that amount from the landlord who received it or his personal representatives.

(2)    Any amount which a tenant is entitled to recover under subsection (1) above may, without prejudice to any other method of recovery, be deducted by the tenant from any rent payable by him to the landlord.

(3)    No amount which a tenant is entitled to recover under subsection (1) above shall be recoverable at any time after the expiry of 2 years from the date of payment.

(4)    Any person who, in any rent book or similar document, makes an entry showing or purporting to show any tenant as being in arrears in respect of any sum on account of rent which is irrecoverable by virtue of this Part of this Act shall be liable to a fine not exceeding [level 3 on the standard scale], unless he proves that, at the time of the making of the entry, the landlord had a bona fide claim that the sum was recoverable.

(5)    If, where any such entry has been made by or on behalf of any landlord, the landlord on being requested by or on behalf of the tenant to do so, refuses or neglects to cause the entry to be deleted within 7 days, the landlord shall be liable to a fine not exceeding [level 3 on the standard scale], unless he proves that, at the time of the neglect or refusal to cause the entry to be deleted, he had a bona fide claim that the sum was recoverable.

[272]

## NOTES

Sub-ss (4), (5): words in square brackets substituted by virtue of the Criminal Justice Act 1982, ss 38, 46.

## 95  Duty of landlord to supply statement of rent under previous tenancy

(1)    Where the rent payable under a tenancy is subject to the rent limit specified in section 88(4)(b) of this Act, the landlord shall, on being so requested in writing by the tenant, supply him with a statement in writing of the rent which was payable for the last rental period of the other tenancy referred to in that subsection.

(2)    If, without reasonable excuse, a landlord who has received such a request—
  (a)    fails to supply the statement referred to in subsection (1) above within 21 days of receiving the request, or
  (b)    supplies a statement which is false in any material particular,
he shall be liable [to a fine not exceeding level 3 on the standard scale].

(3)    Where an offence under this section committed by a body corporate is proved to have been committed with the consent or connivance of, or to be attributable to any neglect on the part of, any director, manager or secretary or other similar officer of the body corporate or any person who was purporting to act in any such capacity, he as well as the body corporate shall be guilty of that offence and shall be liable to be proceeded against and punished accordingly.

[273]

## NOTES

Sub-s (2): words in square brackets substituted by virtue of the Criminal Justice Act 1982, ss 38, 46.

## 96  Supplemental

(1), (2)    ...

(3)    A county court shall have jurisdiction, either in the course of any proceedings relating to a dwelling-house or on an application made for the purpose by the landlord or the tenant, to determine any question as to the rent limit under this Part of this Act, or as to any matter which is or may become material for determining any such question.

(4)   In ascertaining for the purposes of this Part of this Act whether there is any difference with respect to rents or rates between one rental period and another (whether of the same tenancy or not) or the amount of any such difference, any necessary adjustments shall be made to take account of periods of different lengths.

(5)   For the purposes of such an adjustment a period of one month shall be treated as equivalent to one-twelfth of a year and a period of a week as equivalent to one-fifty-second of a year.

[274]

**NOTES**

Sub-ss (1), (2): repealed by the Housing Act 1980, ss 61(3), 152(3), Sch 26, subject to savings in s 61(8) thereof at **[360]**.

### 97   Interpretation of Part VI

(1)   In this Part of this Act, except where the context otherwise requires—
  "housing association", "housing association tenancy" and "housing trust" have the meanings assigned to them by section 86 of this Act; and
  "tenancy" means a housing association tenancy.

(2)   In this Part of this Act references to registration are, subject to section 87(5) of this Act and unless the context otherwise requires, references to registration pursuant to section 87.

(3)   It is hereby declared that any power of giving directions conferred on the Secretary of State by this Part of this Act includes power to vary or revoke directions so given.

[275]

PART VII
SECURITY OF TENURE

*Limitations on recovery of possession of dwelling-houses let on protected tenancies or subject to statutory tenancies*

### 98   Grounds for possession of certain dwelling-houses

(1)   Subject to this Part of this Act, a court shall not make an order for possession of a dwelling-house which is for the time being let on a protected tenancy or subject to a statutory tenancy unless the court considers it reasonable to make such an order and either—
  (a)   the court is satisfied that suitable alternative accommodation is available for the tenant or will be available for him when the order in question takes effect, or
  (b)   the circumstances are as specified in any of the Cases in Part I of Schedule 15 to this Act.

(2)   If, apart from subsection (1) above, the landlord would be entitled to recover possession of a dwelling-house which is for the time being let on or subject to a regulated tenancy, the court shall make an order for possession if the circumstances of the case are as specified in any of the Cases in Part II of Schedule 15.

(3)   Part III of Schedule 15 shall have effect in relation to Case 9 in that Schedule and for determining the relevant date for the purposes of the Cases in Part II of that Schedule.

(4)   Part IV of Schedule 15 shall have effect for determining whether, for the purposes of subsection (1)(a) above, suitable alternative accommodation is or will be available for a tenant.

[(5)   Part V of Schedule 15 shall have effect for the purpose of setting out conditions which are relevant to Cases 11 and 12 of that Schedule.]

[276]

**NOTES**

Sub-s (5): added by the Housing Act 1980, s 66(3), subject to savings in s 66(5), (6) thereof at **[363]**.

### 99   Grounds for possession of certain dwelling-houses let to agricultural workers, etc

(1)   This section applies to any protected or statutory tenancy which—
  (a)   if it were a tenancy at a low rent, and
  (b)   if (where relevant) any earlier tenancy granted to the tenant, or to a member of his family, had been a tenancy at a low rent,
would be a protected occupancy or statutory tenancy as defined in the Rent (Agriculture) Act 1976.

(2)   Notwithstanding anything in section 98 of this Act, the court shall not make an order for possession of a dwelling-house which is for the time being let on or subject to a tenancy to which this section applies unless the court considers it reasonable to make such an order and the circumstances are as specified in any of the Cases (except Case 8) in Part I of Schedule 15 to this Act or in either of the Cases in Schedule 16 to this Act.

(3)   If, apart from subsection (2) above, the landlord would be entitled to recover possession of a dwelling-house which is for the time being let on or subject to a tenancy to which this section applies, the court shall make an order for possession if the circumstances are as specified in any of the Cases (except Cases 16 to 18) in Part II of Schedule 15 to this Act.

[277]

## 100   Extended discretion of court in claims for possession of certain dwelling-houses

(1)   Subject to subsection (5) below, a court may adjourn, for such period or periods as it thinks fit, proceedings for possession of a dwelling-house which is let on a protected tenancy or subject to a statutory tenancy.

(2)   On the making of an order for possession of such a dwelling-house, or at any time before the execution of such an order (whether made before or after the commencement of this Act), the court, subject to subsection (5) below, may—

    (a)   stay or suspend execution of the order, or
    (b)   postpone the date of possession,

for such period or periods as the court thinks fit.

[(3)   On any such adjournment as is referred to in subsection (1) above or any such stay, suspension or postponement as is referred to in subsection (2) above, the court shall, unless it considers that to do so would cause exceptional hardship to the tenant or would otherwise be unreasonable, impose conditions with regard to payment by the tenant of arrears of rent (if any) and rent or payments in respect of occupation after termination of the tenancy (mesne profits) and may impose such other conditions as it thinks fit.]

(4)   If any such conditions as are referred to in subsection (3) above are complied with, the court may, if it thinks fit, discharge or rescind any such order as is referred to in subsection (2) above.

[(4A)   Subsection (4B) below applies in any case where—

    (a)   proceedings are brought for possession of a dwelling-house which is let on a protected tenancy or subject to a statutory tenancy;
    (b)   the tenant's spouse or former spouse, having rights of occupation under the Matrimonial Homes Act 1967, is then in occupation of the dwelling-house; and
    (c)   the tenancy is terminated as a result of those proceedings.

(4B)   In any case to which this subsection applies, the spouse or former spouse shall, so long as he or she remains in occupation, have the same rights in relation to, or in connection with, any such adjournment as is referred to in subsection (1) above or any such stay, suspension or postponement as is referred to in subsection (2) above, as he or she would have if those rights of occupation were not affected by the termination of the tenancy.]

(5)   This section shall not apply if the circumstances are as specified in any of the Cases in Part II of Schedule 15.

[278]

**NOTES**
  Sub-s (3): substituted by the Housing Act 1980, s 75(1), (2).
  Sub-ss (4A), (4B): inserted by the Housing Act 1980, s 75(1), (3).
  Matrimonial Homes Act 1967: mostly repealed by the Matrimonial Homes Act 1983, s 12(2), Sch 3, and replaced by provisions of that Act, which is itself repealed, subject to savings, by the Family Law Act 1996, s 66(2), (3), Sch 9, paras 5, 8–10, Sch 10.

## [101   Overcrowded dwelling-houses

At any time when a dwelling-house is overcrowded within the meaning of Part X of the Housing Act 1985 in such circumstances as to render the occupier guilty of an offence, nothing in this Part of this Act shall prevent the immediate landlord of the occupier from obtaining possession of the dwelling-house.]

[279]

**NOTES**
  Substituted by the Housing (Consequential Provisions) Act 1985, ss 4, 5(1), Sch 2, para 35(1), (8), Sch 3, para 3, in relation to cases where the tenant (or statutory tenant) occupies the dwelling-house under (or by virtue of) a tenancy granted on or after 1 April 1986.

## 102   Compensation for misrepresentation or concealment in Cases 8 and 9

Where, in such circumstances as are specified in Case 8 or Case 9 in Schedule 15 to this Act, a landlord obtains an order for possession of a dwelling-house let on a protected tenancy or subject to a statutory tenancy and it is subsequently made to appear to the court that the order was obtained by misrepresentation or concealment of material facts, the court may order the landlord to pay to the former tenant such sum as appears sufficient as compensation for damage or loss sustained by that tenant as a result of the order.

[280]

*Restricted contracts*

**NOTES**

As to the phasing out of restricted contracts, see the note preceding s 77 at **[256]**.

**[102A   Restricted application of sections 103 to 106**

Sections 103 to 106 of this Act apply only to restricted contracts entered into before the commencement of section 69 of the Housing Act 1980.]

**[281]**

**NOTES**

Inserted by the Housing Act 1980, s 69(3).

**103   Notice to quit served after reference of contract to rent tribunal**

(1)   If, after a restricted contract has been referred to a rent tribunal by the lessee ... under section 77 or 80 of this Act, a notice to quit the dwelling to which the contract relates is served by the lessor on the lessee at any time before the decision of the tribunal is given or within the period of 6 months thereafter, then, subject to sections 105 and 106 of this Act, the notice shall not take effect before the expiry of that period.

(2)   In a case falling within subsection (1) above—,

    (a)   the rent tribunal may, if they think fit, direct that a shorter period shall be substituted for the period of 6 months specified in that subsection; and

    (b)   if the reference to the rent tribunal is withdrawn, the period during which the notice to quit is not to take effect shall end on the expiry of 7 days from the withdrawal of the reference.

**[282]**

**NOTES**

Sub-s (1): words omitted repealed by the Housing Act 1988, s 140(2), Sch 18, except in relation to an application under s 77 or 80 made before 15 January 1989.

**104   Application to tribunal for security of tenure where notice to quit is served**

(1)   Subject to sections 105 and 106(3) of this Act, where—

    (a)   a notice to quit a dwelling the subject of a restricted contract has been served, and

    (b)   the restricted contract has been referred to a rent tribunal under section 77 or 80 of this Act (whether before or after the service of the notice to quit) and the reference has not been withdrawn, and

    (c)   the period at the end of which the notice to quit takes effect (whether by virtue of the contract, of section 103 of this Act or of this section) has not expired,

the lessee may apply to the rent tribunal for the extension of that period.

(2)   Where an application is made under this section, the notice to quit to which the application relates shall not have effect before the determination of the application unless the application is withdrawn.

(3)   On an application under this section, the rent tribunal, after making such inquiry as they think fit and giving to each party an opportunity of being heard or, at his option, of submitting representations in writing, may direct that the notice to quit shall not have effect until the end of such period, not exceeding 6 months from the date on which the notice to quit would have effect apart from the direction, as may be specified in the direction.

(4)   If the rent tribunal refuse to give a direction under this section,—

    (a)   the notice to quit shall not have effect before the expiry of 7 days from the determination of the application; and

    (b)   no subsequent application under this section shall be made in relation to the same notice to quit.

(5)   On coming to a determination on an application under this section, the rent tribunal shall notify the parties of their determination.

**[283]**

**105   Notices to quit served by owner-occupiers**

Where a person who has occupied a dwelling as a residence (in this section referred to as "the owner-occupier") has, by virtue of a restricted contract, granted the right to occupy the dwelling to another person and—

    (a)   at or before the time when the right was granted (or, if it was granted before 8th December 1965, not later than 7th June 1966) the owner-occupier has given notice in writing to that other person that he is the owner-occupier within the meaning of this section, and

(b)    if the dwelling is part of a house, the owner-occupier does not occupy any other part of the house as his residence,

neither section 103 nor 104 of this Act shall apply where a notice to quit the dwelling is served if, at the time the notice is to take effect, the dwelling is required as a residence for the owner-occupier or any member of his family who resided with him when he last occupied the dwelling as a residence.

**[284]**

## 106    Reduction of period of notice on account of lessee's default

(1)    Subsections (2) and (3) below apply where a restricted contract has been referred to a rent tribunal and the period at the end of which a notice to quit will take effect has been determined by virtue of section 103 of this Act or extended under section 104.

(2)    If, in a case where this subsection applies, it appears to the rent tribunal, on an application made by the lessor for a direction under this section,—

(a)    that the lessee has not complied with the terms of the contract, or

(b)    that the lessee or any person residing or lodging with him has been guilty of conduct which is a nuisance or annoyance to adjoining occupiers or has been convicted of using the dwelling, or allowing the dwelling to be used, for an immoral or illegal purpose, or

(c)    that the condition of the dwelling has deteriorated owing to any act or neglect of the lessee or any person residing or lodging with him, or

(d)    that the condition of any furniture provided for the use of the lessee under the contract has deteriorated owing to any ill-treatment by the lessee or any person residing or lodging with him,

the rent tribunal may direct that the period referred to in subsection (1) above shall be reduced so as to end at a date specified in the direction.

(3)    No application may be made under section 104 of this Act with respect to a notice to quit if a direction has been given under subsection (2) above reducing the period at the end of which the notice is to take effect.

(4)    In any case where—

(a)    a notice to quit a dwelling which is the subject of a restricted contract has been served, and

(b)    the period at the end of which the notice to quit takes effect is for the time being extended by virtue of section 103 or 104 of this Act, and

(c)    at some time during that period the lessor institutes proceedings in the county court for the recovery of possession of the dwelling, and

(d)    in those proceedings the county court is satisfied that any of paragraphs (a) and (d) of subsection (2) above applies,

the court may direct that the period referred to in paragraph (b) above shall be reduced so as to end at a date specified in the direction.

**[285]**

## [106A    Discretion of court in certain proceedings for possession

(1)    This section applies to any dwelling-house which is the subject of a restricted contract entered into after the commencement of section 69 of the Housing Act 1980.

(2)    On the making of an order for possession of such a dwelling-house, or at any time before the execution of such an order, the court may—

(a)    stay or suspend execution of the order, or

(b)    postpone the date of possession,

for such period or periods as, subject to subsection (3) below, the court thinks fit.

(3)    Where a court makes an order for possession of such a dwelling-house, the giving up of possession shall not be postponed (whether by the order or any variation, suspension or stay of execution) to a date later than 3 months after the making of the order.

(4)    On any such stay, suspension or postponement as is referred to in subsection (2) above, the court shall, unless it considers that to do so would cause exceptional hardship to the lessee or would otherwise be unreasonable, impose conditions with regard to payment by the lessee of arrears of rent (if any) and rent or payments in respect of occupation after termination of the tenancy (mesne profits) and may impose such other conditions as it thinks fit.

(5)    Subsection (6) below applies in any case where—

(a)    proceedings are brought for possession of such a dwelling-house;

(b)    the lessee's spouse or former spouse, having rights of occupation under the Matrimonial Homes Act 1967, is then in occupation of the dwelling-house; and

(c)    the restricted contract is terminated as a result of those proceedings.

(6)    In any case to which this subsection applies, the spouse or former spouse shall, so long as he or she remains in occupation, have the same rights in relation to, or in connection with, any such

stay, suspension or postponement as is referred to in subsection (2) above, as he or she would have if those rights of occupation were not affected by the termination of the restricted contract.]

**[286]**

**NOTES**
Inserted by the Housing Act 1980, s 69(2).
Matrimonial Homes Act 1967: mostly repealed by the Matrimonial Homes Act 1983, s 12(2), Sch 3, and replaced by provisions of that Act, which is itself repealed, subject to savings, by the Family Law Act 1996, s 66(2), (3), Sch 9, paras 5, 8–10, Sch 10.

*Miscellaneous*

## 107 Interpretation of Part VII

(1)    In this Part of this Act, except where the context otherwise requires—
"dwelling" means a house or part of a house;
"lessee" means the person to whom is granted, under a restricted contract, the right to occupy the dwelling in question as a residence and any person directly or indirectly deriving title from the grantee; and
"lessor" means the person who, under a restricted contract, grants to another the right to occupy the dwelling in question as a residence and any person directly or indirectly deriving title from the grantor.

(2)    References in this Part of this Act to a party to a contract include references to any person directly or indirectly deriving title from such a party.

**[287]**

## PART VIII
## CONVERSION OF CONTROLLED TENANCIES INTO REGULATED TENANCIES

**108–114**    *(Repealed, with savings for s 114, by the Housing Act 1980, ss 60(4), 152(2), (3), Sch 25, Pt II, para 63, Sch 26.)*

*Miscellaneous*

**115**    *(Repealed by the Housing Act 1980, s 152(1), (3), Sch 25, Pt I, para 35, Sch 26.)*

## 116   Consent of tenant

[(1)    This section applies where a dwelling-house is subject to a statutory tenancy and the landlord wishes to carry out works which cannot be carried out without the consent of the tenant.]

(2)    If the tenant is unwilling to give his consent, then, if [either of the conditions specified in subsections (3) and (3A)] below is satisfied, the county court may, on the application of the landlord, make an order empowering him to enter and carry out the works.

[(3)    The [first of the conditions referred to in subsection (2) above] is that the works were specified in an application for a … grant under Chapter I of Part I of the Housing Grants, Construction and Regeneration Act 1996 and the application has been approved.]

[(3A)    The second of those conditions is that assistance was or is to be provided in relation to the carrying out of the works under article 3 of the Regulatory Reform (Housing Assistance) (England and Wales) Order 2002.]

(4)    An order under subsection (2) above may be made subject to such conditions as to the time at which the works are to be carried out and as to any provision to be made for the accommodation of the tenant and his household while they are carried out as the court may think fit.

(5)    Where such an order is made subject to any condition as to time, compliance with that condition shall be deemed to be also compliance with any condition imposed by the [local housing authority [under section 37 of the Housing Grants, Construction and Regeneration Act 1996]].

(6)    In determining whether to make such an order and, if it is made, what (if any) conditions it should be subject to, the court shall have regard to all the circumstances and in particular to—
(a)    any disadvantage to the tenant that might be expected to result from the works, and
(b)    the accommodation that might be available for him whilst the works are carried out, and
(c)    the age and health of the tenant,
but the court shall not take into account the means or resources of the tenant.

**[288]**

**NOTES**
Sub-s (1): substituted by the Housing Act 1980, s 152(1), Sch 25, Pt I, para 47(1), (2).
Sub-s (2): words in square brackets substituted by the Regulatory Reform (Housing Assistance) (England and Wales) Order 2002, SI 2002/1860, art 9, Sch 1, para 1(1), (2).

Sub-s (3): substituted by the Housing Grants, Construction and Regeneration Act 1996, s 103, Sch 1, para 1(1), (3); words in square brackets substituted and words omitted repealed by SI 2002/1860, arts 9, 12, 15(1), Sch 1, para 1(1), (3), Sch 4, para 1, Sch 6.

Sub-s (3A): inserted by SI 2002/1860, art 9, Sch 1, para 1(1), (4).

Sub-s (5): words in first (outer) pair of square brackets substituted by the Housing (Consequential Provisions) Act 1985, s 4, Sch 2, para 35(1), (9); words in second (inner) pair of square brackets substituted by the Housing Grants, Construction and Regeneration Act 1996, s 103, Sch 1, para 1(1), (4).

**117, 118** *(S 117 repealed by the Housing Act 1980, s 152(3), Sch 26; s 118 repealed by the Housing (Consequential Provisions) Act 1985, s 3, Sch 1, Pt I.)*

## PART IX
## PREMIUMS, ETC

### 119 Prohibition of premiums and loans on grant of protected tenancies

(1)   Any person who, as a condition of the grant, renewal or continuance of a protected tenancy, requires, in addition to the rent, the payment of any premium or the making of any loan (whether secured or unsecured) shall be guilty of an offence.

(2)   Any person who, in connection with the grant, renewal or continuance of a protected tenancy, receives any premium in addition to the rent shall be guilty of an offence.

(3)   A person guilty of an offence under this section shall be liable to a fine not exceeding [level 3 on the standard scale].

(4)   The court by which a person is convicted of an offence under this section relating to requiring or receiving any premium may order the amount of the premium to be repaid to the person by whom it was paid.

[289]

**NOTES**

Sub-s (3): words in square brackets substituted by virtue of the Criminal Justice Act 1982, ss 38, 46.

### 120 Prohibition of premiums and loans on assignment of protected tenancies

(1)   Subject to section 121 of this Act, any person who, as a condition of the assignment of a protected tenancy, requires the payment of any premium or the making of any loan (whether secured or unsecured) shall be guilty of an offence.

(2)   Subject to section 121 of this Act, any person who, in connection with the assignment of a protected tenancy, receives any premium shall be guilty of an offence.

(3)   Notwithstanding anything in subsections (1) and (2) above, an assignor of a protected tenancy of a dwelling-house may, if apart from this section he would be entitled to do so, require the payment by the assignee or receive from the assignee a payment—

(a)   of so much of any outgoings discharged by the assignor as is referable to any period after the assignment takes effect;

(b)   of a sum not exceeding the amount of any expenditure reasonably incurred by the assignor in carrying out any structural alteration of the dwelling-house or in providing or improving fixtures therein, being fixtures which, as against the landlord, he is not entitled to remove;

(c)   where the assignor became a tenant of the dwelling-house by virtue of an assignment of the protected tenancy, of a sum not exceeding any reasonable amount paid by him to his assignor in respect of expenditure incurred by that assignor, or by any previous assignor of the tenancy, in carrying out any such alteration or in providing or improving any such fixtures as are mentioned in paragraph (b) above; or

(d)   where part of the dwelling-house is used as a shop or office, or for business, trade or professional purposes, of a reasonable amount in respect of any goodwill of the business, trade or profession, being goodwill transferred to the assignee in connection with the assignment or accruing to him in consequence thereof.

(4)   Without prejudice to subsection (3) above, the assignor shall not be guilty of an offence under this section by reason only that—

(a)   any payment of outgoings required or received by him on the assignment was a payment of outgoings referable to a period before the assignment took effect; or

(b)   any expenditure which he incurred in carrying out structural alterations of the dwelling-house or in providing or improving fixtures therein and in respect of which he required or received the payment of any sum on the assignment was not reasonably incurred; or

(c)   any amount paid by him as mentioned in subsection (3)(c) above was not a reasonable amount; or

(d)   any amount which he required to be paid, or which he received, on the assignment in respect of goodwill was not a reasonable amount.

(5) Notwithstanding anything in subsections (1) and (2) above, Part I of Schedule 18 to this Act shall have effect in relation to the assignment of protected tenancies which are regulated tenancies in cases where a premium was lawfully required or received at the commencement of the tenancy.

(6) A person guilty of an offence under this section shall be liable to a fine not exceeding [level 3 on the standard scale].

(7) The court by which a person is convicted of an offence under this section relating to requiring or receiving any premium may order the amount of the premium, or so much of it as cannot lawfully be required or received under this section (including any amount which, by virtue of subsection (4) above, does not give rise to any offence) to be repaid to the person by whom it was paid.

**[290]**

**NOTES**
    Sub-s (6): words in square brackets substituted by virtue of the Criminal Justice Act 1982, ss 38, 46.

### 121 Tenancies which became regulated by virtue of Counter-Inflation Act 1973

Part II of Schedule 18 to this Act shall have effect where a premium was lawfully required and paid on the grant, renewal or continuance of a regulated tenancy—
    (a)    which was granted before 8th March 1973, and
    (b)    which would not have been a regulated tenancy, but for section 14(1) of the Counter-Inflation Act 1973 (which brought certain tenancies of dwelling-houses with high rateable values within the protection of the Rent Act 1968).

**[291]**

**NOTES**
    Counter-Inflation Act 1973, s 14(1): repealed by s 155(5) of, and Sch 25 to, this Act, and replaced by s 4(2) at **[205]**.
    Rent Act 1968: repealed by s 155(5) of, and Sch 25 to, this Act.

### 122 Prohibition of premiums on grant or assignment of rights under restricted contracts

(1) This section applies in relation to any premises if—
    (a)    under Part V of this Act, a rent is registered for those premises in the register kept in pursuance of section 79 of this Act; and
    (b)    in a case where the approval, reduction or increase of the rent by the rent tribunal is limited to rent payable in respect of a particular period, that period has not expired.

(2) Any person who, as a condition of the grant, renewal, continuance or assignment of rights under a restricted contract, requires the payment of any premium shall be guilty of an offence.

(3) Nothing in subsection (2) above shall prevent a person from requiring—
    (a)    that there shall be paid so much of any outgoings discharged by a grantor or assignor as is referable to any period after the grant or assignment takes effect; or
    (b)    that there shall be paid a reasonable amount in respect of goodwill of a business, trade, or profession, where the goodwill is transferred to a grantee or assignee in connection with the grant or assignment or accrues to him in consequence thereof.

(4) A person guilty of an offence under this section shall be liable to a fine not exceeding [level 3 on the standard scale].

(5) The court by which a person is convicted of an offence under this section may order the amount of the premium, or so much of it as cannot lawfully be required under this section, to be repaid to the person by whom it was paid.

**[292]**

**NOTES**
    Sub-s (4): words in square brackets substituted by virtue of the Criminal Justice Act 1982, ss 38, 46.

### 123 Excessive price for furniture to be treated as premium

Where the purchase of any furniture has been required as a condition of the grant, renewal, continuance or assignment—
    (a)    of a protected tenancy, or
    (b)    of rights under a restricted contract which relates to premises falling within section 122(1) of this Act,

then, if the price exceeds the reasonable price of the furniture, the excess shall be treated, for the purposes of this Part of this Act, as if it were a premium required to be paid as a condition of the grant, renewal, continuance or assignment of the protected tenancy or, as the case may be, the rights under the restricted contract.

**[293]**

## 124 Punishment of attempts to obtain from prospective tenants excessive prices for furniture

(1)  Any person who, in connection with the proposed grant, renewal, continuance or assignment, on terms which require the purchase of furniture, of a protected tenancy—

(a)  offers the furniture at a price which he knows or ought to know is unreasonably high, or otherwise seeks to obtain such a price for the furniture, or

(b)  fails to furnish, to any person seeking to obtain or retain accommodation whom he provides with particulars of the tenancy, a written inventory of the furniture, specifying the price sought for each item,

shall be liable to a fine not exceeding [level 3 on the standard scale].

(2)  Where a local authority have reasonable grounds for suspecting that an offence under subsection (1)(a) above has been committed with respect to a protected tenancy or proposed protected tenancy of a dwelling-house, they may give notice to the person entitled to possession of the dwelling-house or his agent that, on such date as may be specified in the notice, which shall not be earlier than—

(a)  24 hours after the giving of the notice, or

(b)  if the dwelling-house is unoccupied, the expiry of such period after the giving of the notice as may be reasonable in the circumstances,

facilities will be required for entry to the dwelling-house and inspection of the furniture therein.

(3)  A notice under this section may be given by post.

(4)  Where a notice is given under this section, any person authorised by the local authority may avail himself of any facilities for such entry and inspection as are referred to in subsection (2) above which are provided on the specified date but shall, if so required, produce some duly authenticated document showing that he is authorised by the local authority.

(5)  If it is shown to the satisfaction of a justice of the peace, on sworn information in writing, that a person required to give facilities under this section has failed to give them, the justice may, by warrant under his hand, empower the local authority, by any person authorised by them, to enter the dwelling-house in question, if need be by force, and inspect the furniture therein.

(6)  A person empowered by or under the preceding provisions of this section to enter a dwelling-house may take with him such other persons as may be necessary and, if the dwelling-house is unoccupied, shall leave it as effectively secured against trespassers as he found it.

(7)  Any person who wilfully obstructs a person acting in pursuance of a warrant issued under subsection (5) above shall be liable [to a fine not exceeding level 3 on the standard scale].

(8)  In this section "local authority" means [the council of a district (or, in a county in England in which there are no districts having a district council, the council of the county) or the council of a London borough] or the Common Council of the City of London [or, in Wales, the council of a county or county borough].

**[294]**

**NOTES**

Sub-ss (1), (7): words in square brackets substituted by virtue of the Criminal Justice Act 1982, ss 38, 46.

Sub-s (8): words in first pair of square brackets substituted by the Local Government Changes (Rent Act) Regulations 1995, SI 1995/2451, regs 2, 6; words in second pair of square brackets added by the Local Government (Wales) Act 1994, s 22(2), Sch 8, para 3(4).

## 125 Recovery of premiums and loans unlawfully required or received

(1)  Where under any agreement (whether made before or after the commencement of this Act) any premium is paid after the commencement of this Act and the whole or any part of the premium could not lawfully be required or received under the preceding provisions of this Part of this Act, the amount of the premium, or, as the case may be, so much of it as could not lawfully be required or received, shall be recoverable by the person by whom it was paid.

(2)  Nothing in section 119 or 120 of this Act shall invalidate any agreement for the making of a loan or any security issued in pursuance of such an agreement but, notwithstanding anything in the agreement for the loan, any sum lent in circumstances involving a contravention of either of those sections shall be repayable to the lender on demand.

**[295]**

## 126 Avoidance of requirements for advance payment of rent in certain cases

(1)  Where a protected tenancy which is a regulated tenancy is granted, continued or renewed, any requirement that rent shall be payable—

(a)  before the beginning of the rental period in respect of which it is payable, or

(b)  earlier than 6 months before the end of the rental period in respect of which it is payable (if that period is more than 6 months),

shall be void, whether the requirement is imposed as a condition of the grant, renewal or continuance of the tenancy or under the terms thereof.

(2)   Any requirement avoided by subsection (1) above is, in this section, referred to as a "prohibited requirement".

(3)   Rent for any rental period to which a prohibited requirement relates shall be irrecoverable from the tenant.

(4)   Any person who purports to impose any prohibited requirement shall be liable to a fine not exceeding [level 3 on the standard scale], and the court by which he is convicted may order any amount of rent paid in compliance with the prohibited requirement to be repaid to the person by whom it was paid.

(5)   Where a tenant has paid on account of rent any amount which, by virtue of this section, is irrecoverable the tenant shall be entitled to recover that amount from the landlord who received it or his personal representatives.

(6)   Any amount which a tenant is entitled to recover under subsection (5) above may, without prejudice to any other method of recovery, be deducted by the tenant from any rent payable by him to the landlord.

(7)   No amount which a tenant is entitled to recover under subsection (5) above shall be recoverable at any time after the expiry of 2 years from the date of payment.

(8)   Any person who, in any rent book or similar document makes an entry showing or purporting to show any tenant as being in arrears in respect of any sum on account of rent which is irrecoverable by virtue of this section shall be liable to a fine not exceeding [level 3 on the standard scale], unless he proves that, at the time of the making of the entry, the landlord had a bona fide claim that the sum was recoverable.

(9)   If, where any such entry has been made by or on behalf of any landlord, the landlord on being requested by or on behalf of the tenant to do so, refuses or neglects to cause the entry to be deleted within 7 days, the landlord shall be liable to a fine not exceeding [level 3 on the standard scale], unless he proves that, at the time of the neglect or refusal to cause the entry to be deleted, he had a bona fide claim that the sum was recoverable.

**[296]**

**NOTES**

Sub-ss (4), (8), (9): words in square brackets substituted by virtue of the Criminal Justice Act 1982, ss 38, 46.

### 127   Allowable premiums in relation to certain long tenancies

(1)   Where a tenancy is both a long tenancy within the meaning of Part I of the Landlord and Tenant Act 1954 and a protected tenancy, then—

(a)   if the conditions specified in subsection (2) below are satisfied with respect to it, nothing in this Part of this Act or in Part VII of the Rent Act 1968 (provisions superseded by this Part) or the enactments replaced by the said Part VII shall apply or be deemed ever to have applied to the tenancy;

(b)   if any of those conditions are not satisfied with respect to it, Part II of Schedule 18 to this Act shall apply and, if the tenancy was granted before the passing of this Act, be deemed always to have applied to it.

[(2)   The conditions mentioned in subsection (1)(a) above are—

(a)   that the landlord has no power to determine the tenancy at any time within twenty years beginning on the date when it was granted; and

(b)   that the terms of the tenancy do not inhibit both the assignment and the underletting of the whole of the premises comprised in the tenancy;

but for the purpose of paragraph (b) above there shall be disregarded any term of the tenancy which inhibits assignment and underletting only during a period which is or falls within the final seven years of the term for which the tenancy was granted.

(3)   The reference in subsection (2) above to a power of the landlord to determine a tenancy does not include a reference to a power of re-entry or forfeiture for breach of any term or condition of the tenancy.]

[(3A)   If the conditions in subsection (3B) below are satisfied in respect of a tenancy, this Part of this Act shall not apply to that tenancy and, together with Part VII of the Rent Act 1968 and the enactments replaced by Part VII, shall be deemed never to have applied to it.

(3B)   The conditions are that—

(a)   the tenancy was granted before 16th July 1980;

(b)   a premium was lawfully required and paid on the grant of the tenancy;

(c)   the tenancy was, at the time when it was granted, a tenancy at a low rent; and

(d)   the terms of the tenancy do not inhibit both the assignment and the underletting of the whole of the premises comprised in the tenancy.]

[(3C), (3D)   ... ]

(4) Nothing in this section shall affect the recovery, in pursuance of any judgment given or order or agreement made before 20th May 1969, of any amount which it was not lawful to receive under the law in force at the time it was received.

(5) In this section "grant" includes continuance and renewal [and for the purposes of subsections [(2)(b)] and (3B)(d) above the terms of a tenancy inhibit an assignment or underletting if they—

- (a) preclude it; or
- (b) permit it subject to a consent but exclude section 144 of the Law of Property Act 1925 (no payment in nature of fine); or
- (c) permit it subject to a consent but require in connection with a request for consent the making of an offer to surrender the tenancy].

**[297]**

**NOTES**

Sub-ss (2), (3): substituted by the Housing Act 1988, s 115, with respect to any premium received or required to be paid after 15 January 1989, or any loan required to be made after that date.

Sub-ss (3A), (3B): inserted, with retrospective effect, by the Housing Act 1980, s 78.

Sub-ss (3C), (3D): inserted, with retrospective effect, by the Housing Act 1980, s 78; repealed by the Housing Act 1988, s 115, with respect to any premium received or required to be paid after 15 January 1989.

Sub-s (5): words in first (outer) pair of square brackets inserted, with retrospective effect, by the Housing Act 1980, s 78; figure in second (inner) pair of square brackets substituted by the Housing Act 1988, s 115, with respect to any premium received or required to be paid after 15 January 1989, or any loan required to be made after that date.

Rent Act 1968, Pt VII: repealed by s 155(5) of, and Sch 25 to, this Act, and replaced by the provisions in this Part.

## 128 Interpretation of Part IX

(1) In this Part of this Act, unless the context otherwise requires,—

"furniture" includes fittings and other articles; and

["premium" includes—

- (a) any fine or other like sum;
- (b) any other pecuniary consideration in addition to rent; and
- (c) any sum paid by way of a deposit, other than one which does not exceed one-sixth of the annual rent and is reasonable in relation to the potential liability in respect of which it is paid].

(2) For the avoidance of doubt it is hereby declared that nothing in this Part of this Act shall render any amount recoverable more than once.

**[298]**

**NOTES**

Sub-s (1): definition "premium" substituted by the Housing Act 1980, s 79.

## PART X
## MORTGAGES

## 129 Mortgages to which Part X applies

(1) This Part of this Act is concerned with mortgages which—

- (a) were created before the relevant date, and
- [(b) are regulated mortgages as defined in section 131 of this Act].

(2) For the purposes of this Part of this Act, "relevant date"—

- (a) in a case where, on 28th November 1967, land consisting of or including a dwelling-house was subject to a long tenancy which became a regulated tenancy on that date by virtue of section 39 of the Leasehold Reform Act 1967, means, in relation to that land, 28th November 1967;
- (b) in a case where, on 22nd March 1973, land consisting of or including a dwelling-house was subject to a tenancy which became a regulated tenancy by virtue of section 14 of the Counter-Inflation Act 1973, means, in relation to that land, 22nd March 1973;
- (c) in the case of land consisting of or including a dwelling-house subject to a regulated furnished tenancy, means, in relation to that land, 14th August 1974; and
- (d) in any other case, means 8th December 1965.

**[299]**

**NOTES**

Sub-s (1): para (b) substituted by the Housing Act 1980, s 152, Sch 25, Pt I, para 48.

Counter-Inflation Act 1973, s 14: repealed by s 155(5) of, and Sch 25 to, this Act, and partly replaced by s 4(2), (3) at **[205]**.

**130**　　(*Repealed by the Housing Act 1980, s 152(3), Sch 26.*)

### 131　Regulated mortgages

(1)　Subject to subsection (2) below, a mortgage which falls within section 129(1)(a) of this Act ... is a regulated mortgage if—

(a)　it is a legal mortgage of land consisting of or including a dwelling-house which is let on or subject to a regulated tenancy; and

(b)　the regulated tenancy is binding on the mortgagee.

(2)　Notwithstanding that a mortgage falls within subsection (1) above, it is not a regulated mortgage if—

(a)　the rateable value on the appropriate day of the dwelling-house which falls within subsection (1)(a) above, or if there is more than one such dwelling-house comprised in the mortgage, the aggregate of the rateable values of those dwelling-houses on the appropriate day is less than one-tenth of the rateable value on the appropriate day of the whole of the land comprised in the mortgage, or

(b)　the mortgagor is in breach of covenant, but for this purpose a breach of the covenant for the repayment of the principal money otherwise than by instalments shall be disregarded.

(3)　Subsection (2)(a) above shall have effect, in the case of land consisting of or including a dwelling-house which on 22nd March 1973, was subject to a tenancy which became a regulated tenancy by virtue of section 14 of the Counter-Inflation Act 1973, as if for the reference to the appropriate day there were substituted a reference to 7th March 1973.

(4)　In this section "legal mortgage" includes a charge by way of legal mortgage.

(5)　Any reference in this Part of this Act to a regulated mortgage shall be construed in accordance with this section.

**[300]**

---

NOTES

Sub-s (1): words omitted repealed by the Housing Act 1980, s 152(3), Sch 26.

Counter-Inflation Act 1973, s 14: repealed by s 155(5) of, and Sch 25 to, this Act, and partly replaced by s 4(2), (3) at **[205]**.

### 132　Powers of court to mitigate hardship to mortgagors under regulated mortgages

(1)　The powers of the court under this section [become exercisable, in relation to a regulated mortgage] only on an application made by the mortgagor within 21 days, or such longer time as the court may allow, after the occurrence of one of the following events:—

(a)　the rate of interest payable in respect of the mortgage is increased; or

(b)　a rent for a dwelling-house comprised in the mortgage is registered under Part IV of this Act and the rent so registered is lower than the rent which was payable immediately before the registration; or

(c)　the mortgagee, not being a mortgagee who was in possession on the relevant date demands payment of the principal money secured by the mortgage or takes any steps for exercising any right of foreclosure or sale or for otherwise enforcing his security.

Paragraph (b) above shall not apply to a case falling within section 129(2)(b) of this Act.

(2)　If the court is satisfied on any such application that, by reason of the event in question and of the operation of this Act, the mortgagor would suffer severe financial hardship unless relief were given under this section, the court may by order make such provision—

(a)　limiting the rate of interest,

(b)　extending the time for the repayment of the principal money, or

(c)　otherwise varying the terms of the mortgage or imposing any limitation or condition on the exercise of any right or remedy in respect thereof,

as it thinks appropriate.

(3)　Where the court makes an order under subsection (2) above in relation to a mortgage which comprises other land as well as a dwelling-house or dwelling-houses subject to a regulated tenancy the order may, if the mortgagee so requests, make provision for apportioning the money secured by the mortgage between that other land and the dwelling-house or dwelling-houses.

(4)　Where such an apportionment is made, the other provisions of the order made by the court shall not apply in relation to the other land referred to in that subsection and the money secured by the other land, and the mortgage shall have effect for all purposes as two separate mortgages of the apportioned parts.

(5)　Where the court has made an order under this section it may vary or revoke it by a subsequent order.

(6)    The court for the purposes of this section is a county court, except that where an application under subsection (1) above is made in pursuance of any step taken by the mortgagee in the High Court, it is the High Court.

[301]

---

**NOTES**

Sub-s (1): words in square brackets substituted by the Housing Act 1980, s 152, Sch 25, Pt I, para 49.

---

**133–135**    *(Repealed by the Housing Act 1980, s 152(3), Sch 26.)*

### 136   Interpretation of Part X

In this Part of this Act, except where the context otherwise requires—
(a)    "mortgagee" and "mortgagor" include any person from time to time deriving title under the original mortgagee or mortgagor; and
(b)    "legal mortgage" in relation to regulated mortgages, [includes] any [registered charge (within the meaning of the Land Registration Act 2002)].

[302]

---

**NOTES**

Word in first pair of square brackets substituted by the Housing Act 1980, s 152(1), Sch 25, Pt I, para 50; words in second pair of square brackets substituted by the Land Registration Act 2002, s 133, Sch 11, para 14.

---

PART XI

GENERAL

*Sublettings*

### 137   Effect on sub-tenancy of determination of superior tenancy

(1)    If a court makes an order for possession of a dwelling-house from—
(a)    a protected or statutory tenant, or
(b)    a protected occupier or statutory tenant as defined in the Rent (Agriculture) Act 1976,

and the order is made by virtue of section 98(1) or 99(2) of this Act or, as the case may be, under Part I of Schedule 4 to that Act, nothing in the order shall affect the right of any sub-tenant to whom the dwelling-house or any part of it has been lawfully sublet before the commencement of the proceedings to retain possession by virtue of … this Act, nor shall the order operate to give a right to possession against any such sub-tenant.

(2)    Where a statutorily protected tenancy of a dwelling-house is determined, either as a result of an order for possession or for any other reason, any sub-tenant to whom the dwelling-house or any part of it has been lawfully sublet shall, subject to this Act, be deemed to become the tenant of the landlord on the same terms as if the tenant's statutorily protected tenancy has continued.

(3)    Where a dwelling-house—
(a)    forms part of premises which have been let as a whole on a superior tenancy but do not constitute a dwelling-house let on a statutorily protected tenancy; and
(b)    is itself subject to a protected or statutory tenancy,

then, from the coming to an end of the superior tenancy, this Act shall apply in relation to the dwelling-house as if, in lieu of the superior tenancy, there had been separate tenancies of the dwelling-house and of the remainder of the premises, for the like purposes as under the superior tenancy, and at rents equal to the just proportion of the rent under the superior tenancy.

In this subsection "premises" includes, if the sub-tenancy in question is a protected or statutory tenancy to which section 99 of this Act applies, an agricultural holding within the meaning of the [Agricultural Holdings Act 1986] [held under a tenancy to which that Act applies and land comprised in a farm business tenancy within the meaning of the Agricultural Tenancies Act 1995.]

(4)    In subsections (2) and (3) above "statutorily protected tenancy" means—
(a)    a protected or statutory tenancy;
(b)    a protected occupancy or statutory tenancy as defined in the Rent (Agriculture) Act 1976; or
(c)    if the sub-tenancy in question is a protected or statutory tenancy to which section 99 of this Act [applies—
(i)    a tenancy of an agricultural holding within the meaning of the Agricultural Holdings Act 1986 which is a tenancy in relation to which that Act applies; or
(ii)    a farm business tenancy within the meaning of the Agricultural Tenancies Act 1995.]

(5)    Subject to subsection (6) below, a long tenancy of a dwelling-house which is also a tenancy at a low rent but which, had it not been a tenancy at a low rent, would have been a protected tenancy

[or an assured tenancy, within the meaning of Part I of the Housing Act 1988], shall be treated for the purposes of subsection (2) above as a statutorily protected tenancy.

(6)   Notwithstanding anything in subsection (5) above, subsection (2) above shall not have effect where the sub-tenancy in question was created (whether immediately or derivatively) out of a long tenancy falling within subsection (5) above and, at the time of the creation of the sub-tenancy—

(a)   a notice to terminate the long tenancy had been given under section 4(1) of the Landlord and Tenant Act 1954 [or, as the case may be, served under paragraph 4(1) of Schedule 10 to the Local Government and Housing Act 1989]; or

(b)   the long tenancy was being continued by section 3(1) of [the said Act of 1954 or, as the case may be, paragraph 3 of the said Schedule 10];

unless the sub-tenancy was created with the consent in writing of the person who at the time when it was created was the landlord, within the meaning of [Part I of the said Act of 1954 or, as the case may be, the said Schedule 10].

(7)   This section shall apply equally where a protected occupier of a dwelling-house, or part of a dwelling-house, has a relevant licence as defined in the Rent (Agriculture) Act 1976, and in this section "tenancy" and all cognate expressions shall be construed accordingly.

**[303]**

**NOTES**

Sub-s (1): words omitted repealed by the Housing Act 1988, s 140, Sch 17, Pt I, para 25, Sch 18.

Sub-s (3): words in first pair of square brackets substituted by the Agricultural Holdings Act 1986, s 100, Sch 14, para 60; words in second pair of square brackets inserted by the Agricultural Tenancies Act 1995, s 40, Schedule, para 28(1), (2).

Sub-s (4): words in square brackets substituted by the Agricultural Tenancies Act 1995, s 40, Schedule, para 28(1), (3).

Sub-s (5): words in square brackets inserted by the Local Government and Housing Act 1989, s 194, Sch 11, para 53(1).

Sub-s (6): words in first pair of square brackets inserted and words in second and third pairs of square brackets substituted by the Local Government and Housing Act 1989, s 194, Sch 11, para 53(2).

**138   Effect on furnished sub-tenancy of determination of superior unfurnished tenancy**

(1)   If, in a case where section 137(2) of this Act applies the conditions mentioned in subsection (2) below are fulfilled, the terms on which the sub-tenant is, by virtue of section 137(2), deemed to become the tenant of the landlord shall not include any terms as to the provision by the landlord of furniture or services.

(2)   The conditions are:—

(a)   that the statutorily protected tenancy which is determined as mentioned in section 137(2) was neither a protected furnished tenancy nor a statutory furnished tenancy; and

(b)   that, immediately before the determination of that statutorily protected tenancy, the sub-tenant referred to in section 137(2) was the tenant under a protected furnished tenancy or a statutory furnished tenancy; and

(c)   that the landlord, within the period of 6 weeks beginning with the day on which the statutorily protected tenancy referred to in section 137(2) is determined, serves notice on the sub-tenant that this section is to apply to his tenancy or statutory tenancy.

(3)   In this section "statutorily protected tenancy" has the [same meaning as it has for the purposes of section 137(2) of this Act].

**[304]**

**NOTES**

Sub-s (3): words in square brackets substituted, with retrospective effect, by the Housing Act 1980, s 152(1), Sch 25, Pt I, para 51.

**139   Obligation to notify sublettings of dwelling-houses let on or subject to protected or statutory tenancies**

(1)   If the tenant of a dwelling-house let on or subject to a protected or statutory tenancy sublets any part of the dwelling-house on a protected tenancy, then, subject to subsection (2) below, he shall, within 14 days after the subletting, supply the landlord with a statement in writing of the subletting giving particulars of occupancy including the rent charged.

(2)   Subsection (1) above shall not require the supply of a statement in relation to a subletting of any part of a dwelling-house if the particulars which would be required to be included in the statement as to the rent and other conditions of the sub-tenancy would be the same as in the last statement supplied in accordance with that subsection with respect to a previous subletting of that part.

(3)   A tenant who is required to supply a statement in accordance with subsection (1) above and who, without reasonable excuse—

    (a)    fails to supply a statement, or

    (b)    supplies a statement which is false in any material particular,

shall be liable to a fine not exceeding [level 2 on the standard scale].

    (4)   In this section—

    (a)    "protected tenancy" includes a protected occupancy under the Rent (Agriculture) Act 1976;

    (b)    "statutory tenancy" includes a statutory tenancy under that Act.

**[305]**

**NOTES**

Sub-s (3): words in square brackets substituted by virtue of the Criminal Justice Act 1982, ss 38, 46.

**140**    *(Repealed by the Regulatory Reform (Fire Safety) Order 2005, SI 2005/1541, art 53(1), (2), Sch 2, para 13, Sch 4.)*

### Jurisdiction and procedure

### 141  County court jurisdiction

    (1)   A county court shall have jurisdiction either in the course of any proceedings relating to a dwelling or on an application made for the purpose by the landlord or the tenant, to determine any question—

    (a)    as to whether a tenancy is a protected tenancy or whether any person is a statutory tenant of a dwelling-house, ... ; or

    (b)    as to the rent limit; or

    (c)    ...

    (d)    as to the application of Part V and sections 103 to 106 of this Act to a contract; or

    (e)    as to whether a protected, statutory or regulated tenancy is a protected, statutory or regulated furnished tenancy;

or as to any matter which is or may become material for determining any such question.

    (2)   ...

    (3)   A county court shall have jurisdiction to deal with any claim or other proceedings arising out of any of the provisions of this Act specified in subsection (5) below, notwithstanding that by reason of the amount of the claim or otherwise the case would not, apart from this subsection, be within the jurisdiction of a county court.

    (4)   *If, under any of the provisions of this Act specified in subsection (5) below, a person takes proceedings in the High Court which he could have taken in the county court, he shall not be entitled to recover any costs.*

    (5)   The provisions referred to in subsections (3) and (4) above are—

    (a)    ...

    (b)    in Part III, section 57;

    (c)    Part VII, except sections 98(2) and 101;

    (d)    in Part IX, sections 125 and 126;

    (e)    in Part X, sections 133(1), 134 and 135; and

    (f)    in this Part of this Act, sections 145 and 147.

**[306]**

**NOTES**

Sub-s (1): words omitted repealed by the Housing Act 1980, s 152(3), Sch 26.

Sub-s (2): repealed by the Housing Act 1980, s 152(3), Sch 26.

Sub-s (4): repealed by the Courts and Legal Services Act 1990, s 125(7), Sch 20, as from a day to be appointed.

Sub-s (5): repealed by the Courts and Legal Services Act 1990, s 125(7), Sch 20, as from a day to be appointed; para (a) repealed by the Housing Act 1980, s 152(3), Sch 26; in para (f), for the words "sections 145 and 147" there are substituted the words "section 145" by virtue of the Tribunals, Courts and Enforcement Act 2007, s 86, Sch 14, paras 32, 33, as from a day to be appointed.

**142**    *(Repealed by the Constitutional Reform Act 2005, ss 15(1), 146, Sch 4, Pt 1, para 94, Sch 18, Pt 2.)*

### Release from provisions of Act

### 143  Release from rent regulation

    (1)   Where the Secretary of State is satisfied with respect to every part of any area that the number of persons seeking to become tenants there—

    (a)    of dwelling-houses exceeding a specified rateable value, or (b)	of any class or description of dwelling-house or of dwelling-house exceeding a specified rateable value,

is not substantially greater than the number of such dwelling-houses in that part, he may by order provide that no such dwelling-house in the area shall be the subject of a regulated tenancy or the subject of a protected occupancy or statutory tenancy under the Rent (Agriculture) Act 1976.

(2)	An order under this section may contain such transitional provisions, including provisions to avoid or mitigate hardship, as appear to the Secretary of State to be desirable.

(3)	The power to make an order under this section shall be exercisable by statutory instrument and no such order shall have effect unless it is approved by a resolution of each House of Parliament.

**[307]**

### 144	Release from restricted contract provisions

(1)	The Secretary of State may by order provide that, as from such date as may be specified in the order, section 19 of this Act shall not apply to a dwelling the rateable value of which on such day as may be specified in the order exceeds such amount as may be so specified.

(2)	An order under this section—
(a)	may be made so as to relate to the whole of England and Wales or to such area in England and Wales as may be specified in the order, and so as to apply generally or only to, or except to, such classes or descriptions of dwellings as may be specified in the order; and
(b)	may contain such transitional provisions as appear to the Secretary of State to be desirable.

(3)	The power to make an order under this section shall be exercisable by statutory instrument and no such order shall have effect unless it is approved by a resolution of each House of Parliament.

**[308]**

**145**	*(Repealed by the Housing (Consequential Provisions) Act 1985, s 3, Sch 1, Pt I.)*

*Miscellaneous*

### 146	Long tenancies at a low rent

(1)	In determining whether a long tenancy was, at any time,—
(a)	a tenancy at a low rent within the meaning of the Rent Act 1968; or
(b)	a tenancy to which, by virtue of section 12 (7) of the Act of 1920, the Rent Acts did not apply;

there shall be disregarded such part (if any) of the sums payable by the tenant as is expressed (in whatever terms) to be payable in respect of rates [council tax], services, repairs, maintenance, or insurance, unless it could not have been regarded by the parties as a part so payable.

(2)	In subsection (1) above—
"long tenancy" means a tenancy granted for a term certain exceeding 21 years, other than a tenancy which is, or may become, terminable before the end of that term by notice given to the tenant;
"the Act of 1920" means the Increase of Rent and Mortgage Interest (Restrictions) Act 1920; and
"the Rent Acts" means the Rent and Mortgage Interest Restrictions Acts 1920 to 1939.

**[309]**

**NOTES**
Sub-s (1): words in square brackets inserted by the Local Government Finance (Housing) (Consequential Amendments) Order 1993, SI 1993/651, art 2(1), Sch 1, para 11.
Rent Act 1968: repealed by s 155(5) of, and Sch 25 to, this Act.
Rent and Mortgage Interest (Restrictions) Acts 1920 to 1939: repealed by the Rent Act 1968, s 117(5), Sch 17.

### 147	Restriction on levy of distress for rent

*(1)	No distress for the rent of any dwelling-house let on a protected tenancy or subject to a statutory tenancy shall be levied except with the leave of the county court; and the court shall, with respect to any application for such leave, have the same or similar powers with respect to adjournment, stay, suspension, postponement and otherwise as are conferred by section 100 of this Act in relation to proceedings for possession of such a dwelling-house.*

*(2)	Nothing in subsection (1) above shall apply to distress levied under [section 102 of the County Courts Act 1984].*

**[310]**

## 148  Implied term in all protected tenancies

It shall be a condition of a protected tenancy of a dwelling-house that the tenant shall afford to the landlord access to the dwelling-house and all reasonable facilities for executing therein any repairs which the landlord is entitled to execute.

[311]

*Supplemental*

## 149  Powers of local authorities for the purposes of giving information

(1)   Any local authority to which this section applies shall have power—
    (a)    to publish information, for the assistance of landlords and tenants and others, as to their rights and duties under—
        [(i)    sections 4 to 7 (provision of rent books) and sections 18 to 30 (service charges) of the Landlord and Tenant Act 1985,]
        (ii)   the Protection from Eviction Act 1977,
        [(iii)  Part II ... , of the Housing Act 1980,]
        (iv)   this Act,
        [(v)   Chapters I to III of Part I of the Housing Act 1988]
        and as to the procedure for enforcing those rights or securing the performance of those duties, and
    (b)    to publish information, for the assistance of owners and occupiers of dwelling-houses and others, as to their rights and duties under the Rent (Agriculture) Act 1976 and as to the procedure for enforcing those rights or securing the performance of those duties, and
    (c)    to make any such information as is mentioned in paragraph (a) or (b) above available in any other way, and
    (d)    to furnish particulars as to the availability, extent and character of alternative accommodation.

(2)   This section applies to the following local authorities:—
    (a)    councils of districts[, councils of counties in England in which there are no districts having district councils and councils] of London boroughs;
    [(aa)  councils of Welsh counties or county boroughs;]
    (b)    the Common Council of the City of London; and
    (c)    the Council of the Isles of Scilly.

[312]

## 150  Prosecution of offences

(1)   Offences under this Act are punishable summarily.

(2)   Proceedings for an offence under this Act ... may be instituted by any local authority to which section 149 of this Act applies.

[313]

## 151  Service of notices on landlord's agents

(1)   Any document required or authorised by this Act to be served by the tenant of a dwelling-house on the landlord thereof shall be deemed to be duly served on him if it is served—
    (a)    on any agent of the landlord named as such in the rent book or other similar document; or
    (b)    on the person who receives the rent of the dwelling-house.

(2)   Where a dwelling-house is subject to a regulated tenancy, subsection (1) above shall apply also in relation to any document required or authorised by this Act to be served on the landlord by a person other than the tenant.

(3)   If for the purpose of any proceedings (whether civil or criminal) brought or intended to be brought under this Act, any person serves upon any such agent or other person as is referred to in paragraph (a) or paragraph (b) of subsection (1) above a notice in writing requiring the agent or other person to disclose to him the full name and place of abode or place of business of the landlord, that agent or other person shall forthwith comply with the notice.

(4)   If any such agent or other person as is referred to in subsection (3) above fails or refuses forthwith to comply with a notice served on him under that subsection, he shall be liable to a fine not exceeding [level 4 on the standard scale], unless he shows to the satisfaction of the court that he did not know, and could not with reasonable diligence have ascertained, such of the facts required by the notice to be disclosed as were not disclosed by him.

(5)   So far as this section relates to Part V or IX or sections 103 to 107, of this Act, references to a landlord and to a tenant shall respectively include references to a lessor and to a lessee as defined by section 85 of this Act.

[314]

**NOTES**

Sub-s (4): words in square brackets substituted by virtue of the Criminal Justice Act 1982, ss 39, 46, Sch 3.

## 152   Interpretation

(1)   In this Act, except where the context otherwise requires,—
"the appropriate day" has the meaning assigned to it by section 25(3) of this Act;

   .....

"landlord" includes any person from time to time deriving title under the original landlord and also includes, in relation to any dwelling-house, any person other than the tenant who is, or but for Part VII of this Act would be, entitled to possession of the dwelling-house;
"let" includes "sublet";
"long tenancy" means a tenancy granted for a term of years certain exceeding 21 years, whether or not subsequently extended by act of the parties or by any enactment;
"protected furnished tenancy", "regulated furnished tenancy" and "statutory furnished tenancy" mean a protected or, as the case may be, regulated or statutory tenancy—
   (a)   under which the dwelling-house concerned is bona fide let at a rent which includes payments in respect of furniture, and
   (b)   in respect of which the amount of rent which is fairly attributable to the use of furniture, having regard to the value of that use to the tenant, forms a substantial part of the whole rent;
"protected tenant" and "protected tenancy" shall be construed in accordance with section 1 of this Act;
"rates" includes water rates and charges but does not include an owner's drainage rate as defined in section 63(2)(a) of the Land Drainage Act 1976;
"rateable value" shall be construed in accordance with section 25 of this Act;
"regulated tenancy" shall be construed in accordance with section 18 of this Act;
"rent tribunal" has the meaning given by section 76(1) of this Act;
"rental period" means a period in respect of which a payment of rent falls to be made;
"restricted contract" shall be construed in accordance with section 19 of this Act;
"statutory tenant" and "statutory tenancy" shall be construed in accordance with section 2 of this Act;
"tenant" includes statutory tenant and also includes a sub-tenant and any person deriving title under the original tenant or sub-tenant;
"tenancy" includes "sub-tenancy";
"tenancy at a low rent" has the meaning assigned to it by section 5 of this Act.

(2)   Except in so far as the context otherwise requires, any reference in this Act to any other enactment shall be taken as referring to that enactment as amended by or under any other enactment, including this Act.

[315]

**NOTES**

Sub-s (1): words omitted repealed by the Housing Act 1980, s 152(3), Sch 26.
Land Drainage Act 1976, s 63(2)(a): repealed, subject to savings, by the Water Consolidation (Consequential Provisions) Act 1991, ss 2(2), 3(1), Sch 2, Pt II, para 15, Sch 3, Pt I.

## 153   Application to Isles of Scilly

(1)   With the exception of Part V, and sections [102A to 106A], of this Act (which do not apply to the Isles of Scilly) this Act applies to the Isles subject to such exceptions, adaptations and modifications as the Secretary of State may by order direct.

(2)   The power to make an order under this section shall be exercisable by statutory instrument which shall be subject to annulment in pursuance of a resolution of either House of Parliament.

(3)   An order under this section may be varied or revoked by a subsequent order.

[316]

NOTES

Sub-s (1): words in square brackets substituted by the Housing Act 1980, s 152(1), Sch 25, Pt I, para 54.

## 154   Application to Crown property

(1)   Subject to sections 13 and 19(5)(b) of this Act this Act shall apply in relation to premises in which there subsists, or at any material time subsisted, a Crown interest as it applies in relation to premises in which no such interest subsists or ever subsisted.

(2)   In this section "Crown interest" means an interest which belongs to Her Majesty in right of the Crown or of the Duchy of Lancaster or to the Duchy of Cornwall, or to a government department, or which is held in trust for Her Majesty for the purposes of a government department.

[317]

## 155   Modifications, amendments, transitional provisions, repeals etc

(1)   ...

(2)   Subject to subsection (3) below, the enactments specified in Schedule 23 to this Act shall have effect subject to the amendments specified in that Schedule.

(3)   The savings and transitional provisions in Schedule 24 to this Act shall have effect.

(4)   The inclusion in this Act of any express saving, transitional provision or amendment shall not be taken as prejudicing the operation of section 38 of the Interpretation Act 1889 (which relates to the effect of repeals).

(5)   Subject to subsection (3) above, the enactments specified in Schedule 25 to this Act (which include enactments which were spent before the passing of this Act) are hereby repealed to the extent specified in the third column of that Schedule.

[318]

NOTES

Sub-s (1): repealed by the Housing Act 1980, s 152(1), (3), Sch 25, Pt I, para 55, Sch 26.
Interpretation Act 1889, s 38: repealed by the Interpretation Act 1978, s 25, Sch 3, and replaced by ss 16(1), 17(2)(a) of, and Sch 2, para 3 to, that Act.

## 156   Short title, commencement and extent

(1)   This Act may be cited as the Rent Act 1977.

(2)   This Act shall come into force on the expiry of the period of one month beginning with the date on which it is passed.

(3)   This Act does not extend to Scotland or Northern Ireland.

[319]

## SCHEDULES

## SCHEDULE 1
## STATUTORY TENANCIES

Sections 2, 3

## PART I
## STATUTORY TENANTS BY SUCCESSION

1.   Paragraph 2 ... below shall have effect, subject to section 2(3) of this Act, for the purpose of determining who is the statutory tenant of a dwelling-house by succession after the death of the person (in this Part of this Schedule referred to as "the original tenant") who, immediately before his death, was a protected tenant of the dwelling-house or the statutory tenant of it by virtue of his previous protected tenancy.

[2.—[(1)]   The surviving spouse[, or surviving civil partner,] (if any) of the original tenant, if residing in the dwelling-house immediately before the death of the original tenant, shall after the death be the statutory tenant if and so long as he or she occupies the dwelling-house as his or her residence.

   [(2)   For the purposes of this paragraph—
      (a)   a person who was living with the original tenant as his or her wife or husband shall be treated as the spouse of the original tenant, and
      (b)   a person who was living with the original tenant as if they were civil partners shall be treated as the civil partner of the original tenant.]

[(3)  If, immediately after the death of the original tenant, there is, by virtue of sub-paragraph (2) above, more than one person who fulfils the conditions in sub-paragraph (1) above, such one of them as may be decided by agreement or, in default of agreement, by the county court [shall for the purposes of this paragraph be treated (according to whether that one of them is of the opposite sex to, or of the same sex as, the original tenant) as the surviving spouse or the surviving civil partner].]

3.—[(1)  Where paragraph 2 above does not apply, but a person who was a member of the original tenant's family was residing with him [in the dwelling-house] at the time of and for the [period of 2 years] immediately before his death then, after his death, that person or if there is more than one such person such one of them as may be decided by agreement, or in default of agreement by the county court, shall be [entitled to an assured tenancy of the dwelling-house by succession].

[(2)  If the original tenant dies within the period of 18 months beginning on the operative date, then, for the purposes of this paragraph, a person who was residing in the dwelling-house with the original tenant at the time of his death and for the period which began 6 months before the operative date and ended at the time of his death shall be taken to have been residing with the original tenant for the period of 2 years immediately before his death.]

4.  A person who becomes the statutory tenant of a dwelling-house by virtue of paragraph 2 ... above is in this Part of this Schedule referred to as "the first successor".

5.  If, immediately before his death, the first successor was still a statutory tenant, paragraph 6 [below shall have effect], for the purpose of determining who is [entitled to an assured tenancy of the dwelling-house by succession] after the death of the first successor.

[6.—(1)  Where a person who—
   (a)  was a member of the original tenant's family immediately before that tenant's death, and
   (b)  was a member of the first successor's family immediately before the first successor's death,

was residing in the dwelling-house with the first successor at the time of, and for a period of 2 years immediately before, the first successor's death, that person or, if there is more than one such person, such one of them as may be decided by agreement or, in default of agreement, by the county court shall be entitled to an assured tenancy of the dwelling-house by succession.

(2)  If the first successor died within the period of 18 months beginning on the operative date, then, for the purposes of this paragraph, a person who was residing in the dwelling-house with the first successor at the time of his death and for the period which began 6 months before the operative date and ended at the time of his death shall be taken to have been residing with the first successor for the period of 2 years immediately before his death.]

7, 8.  ...

9.  Paragraphs 5 to 8 above do not apply where the statutory tenancy of the original tenant arose by virtue of section 4 of the Requisitioned Houses and Housing (Amendment) Act 1955 or section 20 of the Rent Act 1965.

10.—(1)  Where after a succession the successor becomes the tenant of the dwelling-house by the grant to him of another tenancy, "the original tenant" and "the first successor" in this Part of this Schedule shall, in relation to that other tenancy, mean the persons who were respectively the original tenant and the first successor at the time of the succession, and accordingly—
   (a)  if the successor was the first successor, and, immediately before his death he was still the tenant (whether protected or statutory), [paragraph 6] above shall apply on his death,
   (b)  if the successor was not the first successor, no person shall become a statutory tenant on his death by virtue of this Part of this Schedule.

(2)  Sub-paragraph (1) above applies—
   (a)  even if a successor enters into more than one other tenancy of the dwelling-house, and
   (b)  even if both the first successor and the successor on his death enter into other tenancies of the dwelling-house.

(3)  In this paragraph "succession" means the occasion on which a person becomes the statutory tenant of a dwelling-house by virtue of this Part of this Schedule and "successor" shall be construed accordingly.

(4)  This paragraph shall apply as respects a succession which took which place before 27th August 1972 if, and only if, the tenancy granted after the succession, or the first of those tenancies, was granted on or after that date, and where it does not apply as respects a succession, no account should be taken of that succession in applying this paragraph as respects any later succession.

11.—(1)  Paragraphs 5 to 8 above do not apply where—
   (a)  the tenancy of the original tenant was granted on or after the operative date within the meaning of the Rent (Agriculture) Act 1976, and
   (b)  both that tenancy and the statutory tenancy of the first successor were tenancies to which section 99 of this Act applies.

(2)    If the tenants under both of the tenancies falling within sub-paragraph (1)(b) above were persons to whom paragraph 7 of Schedule 9 to the Rent (Agriculture) Act 1976 applies, the reference in sub-paragraph (1)(a) above to the operative date shall be taken as a reference to the date of operation for forestry workers within the meaning of that Act.

[11A.    In this Part of this Schedule "the operative date" means the date on which Part I of the Housing Act 1988 came into force.]

**[320]**

---

**NOTES**

Paras 1, 4: words omitted repealed by the Housing Act 1988, ss 39, 140, Sch 4, Pt I, paras 1, 4, Sch 18, in relation to cases where the original tenant dies on or after 15 January 1989, and in relation to cases where the original tenant died before 15 January 1989 and the first successor dies on or after that date.

Para 2: substituted by the Housing Act 1980, s 76, in relation to deaths occurring after 28 November 1980; sub-para (1) numbered as such by virtue of, and sub-paras (2), (3) inserted by, the Housing Act 1988, s 39, Sch 4, Pt I, para 2, in relation to cases where the original tenant dies on or after 15 January 1989, and in relation to cases where the original tenant died before 15 January 1989 and the first successor dies on or after that date; words in square brackets in sub-para (1) inserted, sub-para (2) substituted, and words in square brackets in sub-para (3) substituted by the Civil Partnership Act 2004, s 81, Sch 8, para 13.

Para 3: sub-para (1) numbered as such by virtue of, words in first pair of square brackets inserted, words in second and third pairs of square brackets substituted, and sub-para (2) added by the Housing Act 1988, s 39, Sch 4, Pt I, para 3, in relation to cases where the original tenant dies on or after 15 January 1989, and in relation to cases where the original tenant died before 15 January 1989 and the first successor dies on or after that date.

Para 5: words in square brackets substituted by the Housing Act 1988, s 39, Sch 4, Pt I, para 5, in relation to cases where the original tenant dies on or after 15 January 1989, and in relation to cases where the original tenant died before 15 January 1989 and the first successor dies on or after that date.

Para 6: substituted by the Housing Act 1988, s 39, Sch 4, Pt I, para 6, in relation to cases where the original tenant dies on or after 15 January 1989, and in relation to cases where the original tenant died before 15 January 1989 and the first successor dies on or after that date.

Para 7: repealed by the Housing Act 1988, ss 39, 140, Sch 4, Pt I, para 7, Sch 18, in relation to cases where the original tenant dies on or after 15 January 1989, and in relation to cases where the original tenant died before 15 January 1989 and the first successor dies on or after that date.

Para 8: repealed by the Housing Act 1980, s 152(3), Sch 26.

Para 10: words in square brackets substituted by the Housing Act 1988, s 39, Sch 4, Pt I, para 8, in relation to cases where the original tenant dies on or after 15 January 1989, and in relation to cases where the original tenant died before 15 January 1989 and the first successor dies on or after that date.

Para 11A: inserted by the Housing Act 1988, s 39, Sch 4, Pt I, para 9, in relation to cases where the original tenant dies on or after 15 January 1989, and in relation to cases where the original tenant died before 15 January 1989 and the first successor dies on or after that date.

By the Housing Act 1988, s 39(5) at **[770]**, where, by virtue of the amendments to this Part of this Schedule, a person becomes entitled to an assured tenancy of a dwelling-house (ie an assured tenancy within the meaning of the Housing Act 1988, Pt I, Ch I at **[729]**–**[752]**) by succession, that tenancy is to be an assured periodic tenancy and the provisions of s 39(6) of the 1988 Act apply to that tenancy. By s 39(7), (8) of that Act, if, immediately before the death of the predecessor, the dwelling-house was let under a protected shorthold tenancy and the landlord might have recovered possession under Case 19 in Sch 15 at **[330]**, the assured periodic tenancy to which the successor becomes entitled is to be an assured shorthold tenancy falling within the Housing Act 1988, Pt I, Ch II at **[753]**–**[759]**, whether or not, in the case of a tenancy to which the provision applies, it fulfils the conditions in s 20(1) of that Act at **[754]**. If, before that time, he was a protected occupier or statutory tenant within the meaning of the Rent (Agriculture) Act 1976 at **[155]** et seq, the assured periodic tenancy of the successor is to be an assured agricultural occupancy within the Housing Act 1988, Pt I, Ch III at **[760]**, **[761]**, whether or not it fulfils the conditions in s 24(1) of the 1988 Act. Where, immediately before his death, the predecessor was a tenant under a fixed term tenancy, as defined in s 45(1) of the 1988 Act at **[777]**, the provisions in s 6 of that Act at **[734]**, relating to fixing the terms of the periodic tenancy arising by virtue of s 5 of that Act at **[733]**, apply in relation to the assured periodic tenancy arising on the predecessor's death, with the modifications set out in s 39(9) of the 1988 Act.

Requisitioned Houses and Housing (Amendment) Act 1955, s 4: repealed by the Statute Law (Repeals) Act 1978; but note the provisions of s 155(3) of, and Sch 24, paras 3(1), 4, 9 to, this Act at **[318]**, **[338]**.

Rent Act 1965, s 20: repealed by the Rent Act 1968, s 117(5), Sch 17; but see s 155(3) of, and Sch 24, paras 3(2), 14 to, this Act at **[318]**, **[338]**.

---

## PART II
## RELINQUISHING TENANCIES AND CHANGING TENANTS

*Payments demanded by statutory tenants as a condition of giving up possession*

12.—(1)    A statutory tenant of a dwelling-house who, as a condition of giving up possession of the dwelling-house, asks for or receives the payment of any sum, or the giving of any other consideration, by any person other than the landlord, shall be guilty of an offence.

(2)    Where a statutory tenant of a dwelling-house requires that furniture or other articles shall be purchased as a condition of his giving up possession of the dwelling-house, the price demanded shall, at the request of the person on whom the demand is made, be stated in writing, and if the price exceeds the reasonable price of the articles the excess shall be treated, for the purposes of sub-paragraph (1) above, as a sum asked to be paid as a condition of giving up possession.

(3)    A person guilty of an offence under this paragraph shall be liable to a fine not exceeding [level 3 on the standard scale].

(4)    The court by which a person is convicted of an offence under this paragraph may order the payment—

(a)    to the person who made any such payment, or gave any such consideration, as is referred to in sub-paragraph (1) above, of the amount of that payment or the value of that consideration, or

(b)    to the person who paid any such price as is referred to in sub-paragraph (2) above, of the amount by which the price paid exceeds the reasonable price.

### Change of statutory tenant by agreement

13.—(1)    Where it is so agreed in writing between a statutory tenant ("the outgoing tenant") and a person proposing to occupy the dwelling ("the incoming tenant"), the incoming tenant shall be deemed to be the statutory tenant of the dwelling as from such date as may be specified in the agreement ("the transfer date").

(2)    Such an agreement shall not have effect unless the landlord is a party thereto, and, if the consent of any superior landlord would have been required to an assignment of the previous contractual tenancy, the agreement shall not have effect unless the superior landlord is a party thereto.

(3)    If the outgoing tenant is the statutory tenant by virtue of his previous protected tenancy, then, subject to sub-paragraph (6) below, this Act shall have effect, on and after the transfer date, as if the incoming tenant had been a protected tenant and had become the statutory tenant by virtue of his previous protected tenancy.

(4)    Subject to sub-paragraphs (5) and (6) below, if the outgoing tenant is a statutory tenant by succession, then, on and after the transfer date—

(a)    this Act shall have effect as if the incoming tenant were a statutory tenant by succession, and

(b)    the incoming tenant shall be deemed to have become a statutory tenant by virtue of that paragraph of Part I of this Schedule by virtue of which the outgoing tenant became (or is deemed to have become) a statutory tenant.

(5)    If the outgoing tenant is a statutory tenant by succession, the agreement may provide that, notwithstanding anything in sub-paragraph (4) above, on and after the transfer date, this Act shall have effect, subject to sub-paragraph (6) below, as if the incoming tenant had been a protected tenant and had become the statutory tenant by virtue of his previous protected tenancy.

(6)    Unless the incoming tenant is deemed, by virtue of sub-paragraph (4)(b) above, to have become a statutory tenant by virtue of paragraph 6 or 7 of Part I of this Schedule, paragraphs 5 to 7 of that Part shall not apply where a person has become a statutory tenant by virtue of this paragraph.

(7)    In this paragraph "the dwelling" means the aggregate of the premises comprised in the statutory tenancy of the outgoing tenant.

### No pecuniary consideration to be required on change of tenant under paragraph 13

14.—(1)    Any person who requires the payment of any pecuniary consideration for entering into such an agreement as is referred to in paragraph 13(1) above shall be liable to a fine not exceeding [level 3 on the standard scale].

(2)    The court by which a person is convicted of an offence under sub-paragraph (1) above may order the amount of the payment to be repaid by the person to whom it was paid.

(3)    Without prejudice to sub-paragraph (2) above, the amount of any such payment as is referred to in sub-paragraph (1) above shall be recoverable by the person by whom it was made either by proceedings for its recovery or, if it was made to the landlord by a person liable to pay rent to the landlord, by deduction from any rent so payable.

(4)    Notwithstanding anything in sub-paragraph (1) above, if apart from this paragraph he would be entitled to do so, the outgoing tenant may require the payment by the incoming tenant—

(a)    of so much of any outgoings discharged by the outgoing tenant as is referable to any period after the transfer date;

(b)    of a sum not exceeding the amount of any expenditure reasonably incurred by the outgoing tenant in carrying out any structural alteration of the dwelling or in providing or improving fixtures therein, being fixtures which, as against the landlord, the outgoing tenant is not entitled to remove;

(c)    where the outgoing tenant became a tenant of the dwelling by virtue of an assignment of the previous protected tenancy, of a sum not exceeding any reasonable amount paid by him to his assignor in respect of expenditure incurred by the assignor, or by any previous assignor of the tenancy, in carrying out any such alteration or in providing or improving any such fixtures as are mentioned in paragraph (b) above; or

(d)    where part of the dwelling is used as a shop or office, or for business, trade or professional purposes, of a reasonable amount in respect of any goodwill of the business, trade or profession, being goodwill transferred to the incoming tenant in connection with his becoming a statutory tenant of the dwelling or accruing to him in consequence thereof.

(5) In this paragraph "outgoing tenant", "incoming tenant", "the transfer date" and "the dwelling" have the same meanings as in paragraph 13 above.

[321]

**NOTES**

Paras 12, 14: words in square brackets substituted by virtue of the Criminal Justice Act 1982, ss 38, 46.

## SCHEDULE 2
## RESIDENT LANDLORDS

Section 12(4)

## PART I
## PROVISIONS FOR DETERMINING APPLICATION OF SECTION 12

1. In determining whether the condition in section 12(1)(c) of this Act is at any time fulfilled with respect to a tenancy, there shall be disregarded—

    (a) any period of not more than [28 days] beginning with the date on which the interest of the landlord under the tenancy becomes vested at law and in equity in an individual who, during that period, does not occupy as his residence another dwelling-house which forms part of the building [or, as the case may be, flat] concerned;

    (b) if, within a period falling within paragraph (a) above, the individual concerned notifies the tenant in writing of his intention to occupy as his residence another [dwelling-house in the building or, as the case may be, flat concerned], the period beginning with the date on which the interest of the landlord under the tenancy becomes vested in that individual as mentioned in that paragraph and ending—

        (i) at the expiry of the period of 6 months beginning on that date, or

        (ii) on the date on which that interest ceases to be so vested, or

        (iii) on the date on which the condition in section 12(1)(c) again applies, whichever is the earlier; and

    (c) any period of not more than [2 years] beginning with the date on which the interest of the landlord under the tenancy becomes, and during which it remains, vested—

        (i) ...

        (ii) in trustees as such; or

        (iii) by virtue of section 9 of the Administration of Estates Act 1925, in [the Probate Judge or the Public Trustee].

2. During any period when—

    (a) the interest of the landlord under the tenancy referred to in section 12(1) is vested in trustees as such, and

    (b) that interest is ... held on trust for any person who occupies as his residence a dwelling-house which forms part of the building [or, as the case may be, flat] referred to in section 12(1)(a),

the condition in section 12(1)(c) shall be deemed to be fulfilled and, accordingly, no part of that period shall be disregarded by virtue of paragraph 1 above.

[2A.—(1) The tenancy referred to in section 12(1) falls within this paragraph if the interest of the landlord under the tenancy becomes vested in the personal representatives of a deceased person acting in that capacity.

(2) If the tenancy falls within this paragraph, the condition in section 12(1)(c) shall be deemed to be fulfilled for any period, beginning with the date on which the interest becomes vested in the personal representatives and not exceeding two years, during which the interest of the landlord remains so vested.]

3. Throughout any period which, by virtue of paragraph 1 above, falls to be disregarded for the purpose of determining whether the condition in section 12(1)(c) is fulfilled with respect to a tenancy, no order shall be made for possession of the dwelling-house subject to that tenancy, other than an order which might be made if that tenancy were or, as the case may be, had been a regulated tenancy.

4. For the purposes of section 12, a building is a purpose-built block of flats if as constructed it contained, and it contains, 2 or more flats; and for this purpose "flat" means dwelling-house which—

    (a) forms part only of a building; and

    (b) is separated horizontally from another dwelling-house which forms part of the same building.

5.　For the purposes of section 12, a person shall be treated as occupying a dwelling-house as his residence if, so far as the nature of the case allows, he fulfils the same conditions as, by virtue of section 2(3) of this Act, are required to be fulfilled by a statutory tenant of a dwelling-house.

**[322]**

**NOTES**

Para 1: words in first pair of square brackets in sub-para (a), words in square brackets in sub-para (b) and words in first pair of square brackets in sub-para (c) substituted, words in second pair of square brackets in sub-para (a) inserted, and words omitted from sub-para (c) repealed by the Housing Act 1980, ss 65(2)–(4), 152(3), Sch 26, subject to savings in s 65(6), (7) thereof at **[362]**; words in second pair of square brackets in sub-para (c) substituted by the Law of Property (Miscellaneous Provisions) Act 1994, s 21(1), Sch 1, para 8.

Para 2: words omitted repealed by the Trusts of Land and Appointment of Trustees Act 1996, s 25(2), Sch 4, subject to savings in s 25(4), (5) thereof; words in square brackets substituted by the Housing Act 1980, s 65(2), (4), (6), in relation to tenancies granted before as well as those granted after 28 November 1980.

Para 2A: inserted by the Housing Act 1980, s 65(5), subject to savings in s 65(6), (7) thereof at **[362]**.

## PART II
## TENANCIES CEASING TO FALL WITHIN SECTION 12

6.—(1)　In any case where—

　　(a)　a tenancy which, by virtue only of section 12, was precluded from being a protected tenancy ceases to be so precluded and accordingly becomes a protected tenancy and,

　　(b)　before it became a protected tenancy a rent was registered for the dwelling concerned under Part V of this Act,

the amount which is so registered shall be deemed to be registered under Part IV of this Act as the rent for the dwelling-house which is let on that tenancy, and that registration shall be deemed to take effect on the day the tenancy becomes a protected tenancy.

　　(2)　Section 67(3) of this Act shall not apply to an application for the registration under Part IV of a rent different from that which is deemed to be registered as mentioned in sub-paragraph (1) above.

　　(3)　…

　　(4)　If, immediately before a tenancy became a protected tenancy as mentioned in sub-paragraph (1)(a) above, the rates in respect of the dwelling-house concerned were borne as mentioned in subsection (3) of section 79 of this Act and the fact that they were so borne was noted as required by that subsection, then, in the application of Part IV in relation to the protected tenancy, section 71(2) of this Act shall be deemed to apply.

7.　If, in a case where a tenancy becomes a protected tenancy as mentioned in sub-paragraph (1)(a) above—

　　(a)　a notice to quit had been served in respect of the dwelling concerned before the date on which the tenancy became a protected tenancy, and

　　(b)　the period at the end of which that notice to quit takes effect had, before that date, been extended under Part VII of this Act, and

　　(c)　that period has not expired before that date,

the notice to quit shall take effect on the day following that date (whenever it would otherwise take effect) and, accordingly, on that day the protected tenancy shall become a statutory tenancy.

**[323]**

**NOTES**

Para 6: sub-para (3) repealed by the Housing Act 1988, s 140(2), Sch 18.

*(Schs 3, 4 repealed by the Housing Act 1980, s 152(3), Sch 26.)*

## SCHEDULE 5
## CALCULATION OF AMOUNT OF RATES

Section 27

1.　For the purposes of this Act, the amount of rates for any rental period shall be taken, subject to this Schedule, to be an amount which bears to the total rates payable during the relevant rating period the same proportion as the length of the rental period bears to the length of the relevant rating period.

2.　In this Schedule "the relevant rating period", in relation to a rental period, means the rating period during which the rent for that rental period is payable.

3.　The amount of the rates for any rental period which precedes the making, by the authority levying the rates, of their first demand for, or for an instalment of, the rates for the relevant rating period shall be calculated on the basis that the rates for that rating period will be the same as for the last preceding rating period.

4.—(1) On the making, by the authority levying the rates, of their first such demand, and on the making by them of any subsequent such demand, the amount of the rates for any rental period shall if necessary be recalculated on the basis that the rates for the relevant rating period will be such as appears from the information given in the demand and any previous demands.

(2) Any such recalculation shall not affect the ascertainment of the rates for any rental period beginning more than 6 weeks before the date of the service of the demand giving rise to the recalculation.

5. If, as a result of the settlement of a proposal, the rates payable for the relevant rating period are decreased, the amount of the rates for a rental period shall be recalculated so as to give effect to the decrease; but any such recalculation shall not affect the ascertainment of the rates for any rental period beginning more than 6 weeks before the date of the settlement of the proposal.

6. In computing the rates for any rental period for the purposes of this Schedule, any discount, and any allowance made under any of the enactments relating to allowances given where rates are paid by the owner instead of by the occupier, shall be left out of account, and accordingly those rates shall be computed as if no such discount or allowance had fallen to be, or had been, allowed or made.

[324]

**NOTES**

Section 27 of this Act, which introduced this Schedule, was repealed by the Housing Act 1980, s 152(3), Sch 26, but this Schedule, unlike the other Schedules to this Act repealed by the 1980 Act, is not specifically repealed.

*(Sch 6 repealed by the Housing Act 1980, s 152(3), Sch 26.)*

## SCHEDULE 7
### RENT LIMIT FOR CERTAIN TENANCIES FIRST REGULATED BY VIRTUE OF THE COUNTER-INFLATION ACT 1973

Section 44(4)

*Special rent limit*

1.—(1) This paragraph applies to a regulated tenancy—
   (a) which was granted before 8th March 1973, and
   (b) which would not have been a regulated tenancy but for section 14(1) of the Counter-Inflation Act 1973 (which brought certain tenancies of dwelling-houses with high rateable values within the protection of the Rent Act 1968).

(2) Subject to this Schedule, the recoverable rent for any contractual period of a tenancy to which this paragraph applies shall not exceed the limit specified in paragraph 2 below, and the amount of any excess shall, notwithstanding anything in any agreement, be irrecoverable from the tenant.

(3) Where a rent for the dwelling-house is registered under Part IV of this Act which is less than the limit specified in paragraph 2 below, neither section 44(1) nor section 45(2) of this Act shall apply to a tenancy to which this paragraph applies.

(4) Sub-paragraphs (2) and (3) above shall cease to apply if the landlord and the tenant so provide by an agreement conforming with the requirements of section 51(4) of this Act.

(5) Sub-paragraph (2) above shall not apply where a rent for the dwelling-house is registered under Part IV of this Act which is not less than the limit specified in paragraph 2 below.

2.—(1) Where, at 22nd March 1973, Article 10 of the Counter-Inflation (Rents) (England and Wales) Order 1972 applied to the rent under the tenancy (to which paragraph 1 above applies), the said limit is the rent payable under the tenancy as limited by the said Article 10 immediately before that date.

(2) In any other case the said limit is the rent payable under the terms of the tenancy (to which paragraph 1 above applies) at 22nd March 1973.

*Adjustment for repairs, services or rates*

3.—(1) This paragraph applies to a contractual period the rent for which is subject to paragraph 1(2) above.

(2) In this paragraph "the previous terms" means the terms of the tenancy (to which paragraph 1 above applies) as at 22nd March 1973, and "the limit" means the limit in paragraph 2 above.

(3) Where under the terms of the tenancy there is with respect to—
   (a) the responsibility for any repairs, or
   (b) the provision of services by the landlord or any superior landlord, or
   (c) the use of furniture by the tenant,

any difference compared with the previous terms, such as to affect the amount of the rent which it is reasonable to charge, the limit shall be increased by an appropriate amount.

(4)   Where for the contractual period there is a difference between the amount (if any) of the rates borne by the landlord or a superior landlord in respect of the dwelling-house and the amount (if any) so borne during the first rental period for which the previous terms were agreed, the limit shall be increased or decreased by the difference.

(5)   Where for the contractual period there is an increase in the cost of the provision of the services (if any) provided for the tenant by the landlord or a superior landlord compared with that cost at the time when the previous terms were agreed, such as to affect the amount of the rent which it is reasonable to charge, the limit shall be increased by an appropriate amount.

(6)   Where the previous terms provide for a variation of the rent in any of the circumstances mentioned in this paragraph, the limit shall not be further varied under this paragraph by reason of the same circumstances.

(7)   Any question whether, or by what amount, the limit is increased or decreased by sub-paragraph (3) or (5) above shall be determined by the county court, and any such determination—

(a)   may be made so as to relate to past rental periods, and

(b)   shall have effect with respect to rental periods subsequent to the periods to which it relates until revoked or varied by a subsequent determination.

4.   ...

**[325]**

**NOTES**

Para 4: repealed by the Housing Act 1980, s 152(3), Sch 26.
Counter-Inflation Act 1973, s 14(1): repealed by s 155(5) of, and Sch 25 to, this Act and replaced by s 4(2) at **[205]**.
Rent Act 1968: repealed by s 155(5) of, and Sch 25 to, this Act.
Counter-Inflation (Rents) (England and Wales) Order 1972: SI 1972/1851: revoked in part by the Counter-Inflation Act 1973, s 23(3), Sch 6, and the remainder lapsed.

(*Sch 8 repealed in part by the Rent (Relief from Phasing) Order 1987, SI 1987/264; remainder repealed by the Housing Act 1988, s 140, Sch 17, Pt I, para 24, Sch 18, except in relation to an increase in rent up to, or towards, a registered rent in relation to which the relevant date for the purposes of this Schedule falls before 15 January 1989, or pursuant to the first application under s 67 hereof at* **[246]**, *or s 68 (repealed) relating to a regulated tenancy which has been converted from a controlled tenancy and for which no rent was registered under Pt IV of this Act before 4 May 1987; Sch 9 repealed with savings by the Housing Act 1980, ss 60(4), 152, Sch 25, Pt II, para 63, Sch 26.*)

## SCHEDULE 10
## RENT ASSESSMENT COMMITTEES

Section 65

1.   The Secretary of State shall draw up and from time to time revise panels of persons to act as chairmen and other members of rent assessment committees for such areas, comprising together every registration area, as the Secretary of State may from time to time determine.

2.   Each panel shall consist of a number of persons appointed by the Lord Chancellor and a number of persons appointed by the Secretary of State ...

[2A.   No appointment of a person to any panel by the Lord Chancellor shall be such as to extend beyond the day on which the person attains the age of seventy years; but this sub-paragraph is subject to section 26(4) to (6) of the Judicial Pensions and Retirement Act 1993 (Lord Chancellor's power to authorise continuance in office up to the age of seventy-five years).]

3.   The Secretary of State shall nominate one of the persons appointed by the Lord Chancellor to act as president of the panel, and one or more such persons to act as vice-president or vice-presidents.

4.   Subject to this Schedule, the number of rent assessment committees to act for an area and the constitution of those committees shall be determined by the president of the panel formed for that area or, in the case of the president's absence or incapacity, by the vice-president or, as the case may be, one of the vice-presidents.

5.   Subject to [paragraphs 6 and 6A] below, each rent assessment committee shall consist of a chairman and one or two other members, and the chairman shall be either the president or vice-president (or, as the case may be one of the vice-presidents) of the panel or one of the other members appointed by the Lord Chancellor.

6.   The president of the panel may, if he thinks fit, direct that when dealing with such cases or dealing with a case in such circumstances as may be specified in the direction, the chairman sitting alone may, with the consent of the parties, exercise the functions of a rent assessment committee.

[6A.   When dealing with an application under section 81A of this Act a rent assessment committee carrying out the functions of a rent tribunal shall consist of the chairman of the committee sitting alone.]

7.   There shall be paid to members of panels such remuneration and allowances as the Secretary of State, … , may determine.

[7A.   The Secretary of State may, … , provide for the payment of pensions, allowances or gratuities to or in respect of any person nominated to act as president or vice-president of a panel.]

8.   The president of the panel may appoint, with the approval of the Secretary of State as to numbers, such clerks and other officers and servants of rent assessment committees as he thinks fit, and there shall be paid to the clerks and other officers and servants such salaries and allowances as the Secretary of State, … , may determine.

9.   There shall be paid out of moneys provided by Parliament—
    (a)    the remuneration and allowances of members of panels;
    (b)    the salaries and allowances of clerks and other officers and servants appointed under this Schedule; and
    (c)    such other expenses of a panel as [the Secretary of State] may determine.

10.   …

[326]

---

**NOTES**

Para 2: words omitted repealed by the Housing Act 1980, s 152(1), (3), Sch 25, Pt I, para 56, Sch 26.
Para 2A: inserted by the Judicial Pensions and Retirement Act 1993, s 26(10), Sch 6, para 56, subject to savings in ss 26(11), 27 of, and Sch 7 to, that Act.
Para 5: words in square brackets substituted by the Housing Act 1980, s 71(2).
Para 6A: inserted by the Housing Act 1980, s 71(2).
Paras 7, 8: words omitted repealed by the Housing Act 1996, ss 222, 227, Sch 18, Pt IV, para 22(1)(a), Sch 19, Pt XIII.
Para 7A: inserted by the Housing Act 1980, s 148; words omitted repealed by the Housing Act 1996, ss 222, 227, Sch 18, Pt IV, para 22(1)(a), Sch 19, Pt XIII.
Para 9: words in square brackets substituted by the Housing Act 1996, s 222, Sch 18, para 22(2).
Para 10: repealed by the Housing Act 1980, s 152, Sch 25(1), (3), para 56, Sch 26.

---

## SCHEDULE 11
## APPLICATIONS FOR REGISTRATION OF RENT
Section 67

### PART I
### APPLICATION UNSUPPORTED BY CERTIFICATE OF FAIR RENT

*Procedure on application to rent officer*

1.   On receiving any application for the registration of a rent, the rent officer may, by notice in writing served on the landlord or on the tenant (whether or not the applicant or one of the applicants) require him to give to the rent officer, within such period of not less than 7 days from the service of the notice as may be specified in the notice, such information as he may reasonably require regarding such of the particulars contained in the application as may be specified in the notice.

[2.—(1)   Where the application is made jointly by the landlord and the tenant and it appears to the rent officer, after making such inquiry, if any, as he thinks fit and considering any information supplied to him in pursuance of paragraph 1 above, that the rent specified in the application is a fair rent, he may register that rent without further proceedings.

(2)   Where the rent officer registers a rent under this paragraph he shall notify the landlord and tenant accordingly.

3.—(1)   In the case of an application which does not fall within paragraph 2 above, the rent officer shall serve on the landlord and on the tenant a notice inviting the person on whom the notice is served to state in writing, within a period of not less than seven days after the service of the notice, whether he wishes the rent officer to consider, in consultation with the landlord and the tenant, what rent ought to be registered for the dwelling-house.

(2)   A notice served under sub-paragraph (1) above on the person who did not make the application shall be accompanied—
    (a)    by a copy of the application; and
    (b)    where, in pursuance of section 67(2)(b), the application was accompanied by details of the landlord's expenditure in connection with the provisions of services, by a copy of those details.

3A.   If, after service of a notice by the rent officer under paragraph 3 above, no request in writing is made within the period specified in the notice for the rent to be considered as mentioned in that paragraph, the rent officer after considering what rent ought to be registered or, as the case may be, whether a different rent ought to be registered, may—

(a)    determine a fair rent and register it as the rent for the dwelling-house; or
(b)    confirm the rent for the time being registered and note the confirmation in the register; or
(c)    serve a notice under paragraph 4(2) below.]

4.—[(1)    Where, in response to a notice served by the rent officer under paragraph 3(1) above, the landlord or the tenant states in writing that he wishes the rent to be considered as mentioned in that paragraph, the rent officer shall serve a notice under this paragraph.]

(2)    A notice under this paragraph shall be served on the landlord and on the tenant informing them that the rent officer proposes, at a time (which shall not be earlier than 7 days after the service of the [notice, or 14 days in a case falling within paragraph 3(2)(b) above)] and place specified in the notice, to consider in consultation with the landlord and the tenant, or such of them as may appear at that time and place, what rent ought to be registered for the dwelling-house or, as the case may be, whether a different rent ought to be so registered.

(3)    At any such consultation the landlord and the tenant may each be represented by a person authorised by him in that behalf, whether or not that person is of counsel or a solicitor.

[(4)    The rent officer may, where he considers it appropriate, arrange for consultations in respect of one dwelling-house to be held together with consultations in respect of one or more other dwelling-houses.]

5.    After considering, in accordance with paragraph 4 above, what rent ought to be registered or, as the case may be, whether a different rent ought to be registered, the rent officer shall, as the case may require,—
(a)    determine a fair rent and register it as the rent for the dwelling-house; or
(b)    confirm the rent for the time being registered and note the confirmation in the register.

[5A.    Where a rent has been registered or confirmed by the rent officer under paragraph 3A or 5 above, he shall] notify the landlord and the tenant accordingly by a notice stating that if, within 28 days of the service of the notice or such longer period as he or a rent assessment committee may allow, an objection in writing is received by the rent officer from the landlord or the tenant the matter will be referred to a rent assessment committee.

6.—(1)    If such an objection as is mentioned in paragraph [5A] above is received then—
(a)    if it is received within the period of 28 days specified in that paragraph or a rent assessment committee so direct, the rent officer shall refer the matter to a rent assessment committee;
(b)    if it is received after the expiry of that period the rent officer may either refer the matter to a rent assessment committee or seek the directions of a rent assessment committee whether so to refer it.

(2)    The rent officer shall indicate in the register whether the matter has been referred to a rent assessment committee in pursuance of this paragraph.

*Determination of fair rent by rent assessment committee*

7.—(1)    The rent assessment committee to whom a matter is referred under paragraph 6 above—
(a)    may by notice in the prescribed form served on the landlord or the tenant require him to give to the committee, within such period of not less than 14 days from the service of the notice as may be specified in the notice, such further information, in addition to any given to the rent officer in pursuance of paragraph 1 above, as they may reasonably require; and
(b)    shall serve on the landlord and on the tenant a notice specifying a period of not less than [7 days] from the service of the notice during which either representations in writing or a request to make oral representations may be made by him to the committee.

(2)    If any person fails without reasonable cause to comply with any notice served on him under sub-paragraph (1)(a) above, he shall be liable [to a fine not exceeding level 3 on the standard scale].

(3)    Where an offence under sub-paragraph (2) above committed by a body corporate is proved to have been committed with the consent or connivance of, or to be attributable to any neglect on the part of, any director, manager or secretary or other similar officer of the body corporate or any person who was purporting to act in any such capacity, he as well as the body corporate shall be guilty of that offence and shall be liable to be proceeded against and punished accordingly.

8.    Where, within the period specified in paragraph 7(1)(b) above, or such further period as the committee may allow, the landlord or the tenant requests to make oral representations the committee shall give him an opportunity to be heard either in person or by a person authorised by him in that behalf, whether or not that person is of counsel or a solicitor.

9.—(1)    The committee shall make such inquiry, if any, as they think fit and consider any information supplied or representation made to them in pursuance of paragraph 7 or paragraph 8 above and—
(a)    if it appears to them that the rent registered or confirmed by the rent officer is a fair rent, they shall confirm that rent;

(b)   if it does not appear to them that that rent is a fair rent, they shall determine a fair rent for the dwelling-house.

(2)   Where the committee confirm or determine a rent under this paragraph they shall notify the landlord, the tenant and the rent officer [of their decision and of the date on which it was made].

(3)   On receiving the notification, the rent officer shall, as the case may require, either indicate in the register that the rent has been confirmed or register the rent determined by the committee as the rent for the dwelling-house.

### [*Interim registration of rent*

9A.   In this Schedule references to a fair rent in relation to an application under section 67A of this Act are references to the amount to be registered under section 70A(1)(b) of this Act.]

### [*Maximum Fair Rent*

9B.   This Schedule has effect subject to article 2 of the Rent Acts (Maximum Fair Rent) Order 1999 and accordingly—
    (a)   the rent officer, in considering what rent ought to be registered, shall consider whether that article applies; and
    (b)   where a matter is referred to them, the committee shall consider whether that article applies and, where it does apply, they shall not, subject to paragraph (5) of that article, confirm or determine a rent for the dwelling-house that exceeds the maximum fair rent calculated in accordance with that article.]

[327]

---

**NOTES**

Paras 2, 3, 3A: substituted, for original paras 2, 3, by the Regulated Tenancies (Procedure) Regulations 1980, SI 1980/1696, reg 2, Sch 1, para 1, in relation to an application for the registration of a rent made after 28 November 1980.

Para 4: sub-para (1) and words in square brackets in sub-para (2) substituted and sub-para (4) added by SI 1980/1696, reg 2, Sch 1, paras 2–4, in relation to an application for the registration of a rent made after 28 November 1980.

Para 5A: words from "5A" to "he shall" in square brackets substituted for part of the original para 5 by SI 1980/1696, reg 2, Sch 1, para 5, in relation to an application for the registration of a rent made after 28 November 1980.

Para 6: figure in square brackets substituted by SI 1980/1696, reg 2, Sch 1, para 6, in relation to an application for the registration of a rent made after 28 November 1980.

Para 7: words in first pair of square brackets substituted by the Rent Assessment Committees (England and Wales) (Amendment) Regulations 1981, SI 1981/1783, reg 3, as respects matters referred after 1 January 1982; words in second pair of square brackets substituted by virtue of the Criminal Justice Act 1982, ss 38, 46.

Para 9: words in square brackets substituted by the Housing Act 1980, s 61(7).

Para 9A: inserted by the Local Government Finance (Housing) (Consequential Amendments) Order 1993, SI 1993/651, art 2(2), Sch 2, para 7.

Para 9B: inserted by the Rent Acts (Maximum Fair Rent) Order 1999, SI 1999/6, art 3, Schedule.

This Schedule is amended by the Housing Act 1980, s 59(3), Sch 6, as from a day to be appointed under s 153(4) of that Act, but that Schedule will not now be brought into force. The amendments made to this Schedule by the Regulated Tenancies (Procedure) Regulations 1980, SI 1980/1696 are broadly the same as those in Sch 6 to the 1980 Act, but differ in that they do not require the rent officer to supply an applicant with information or documents already supplied by him.

Modification: this section has effect as if references to a regulated tenancy were references to a statutory tenancy by virtue of the Rent (Agriculture) Act 1976, s 13(2), (6), (7) at **[167]**.

---

(*Sch 11, Pt II, Sch 12 repealed by the Housing Act 1988, s 140, Sch 17, Pt I, para 22, Sch 18, except in relation to an application under s 69(1) of this Act (repealed) made before 15 January 1989 or a certificate of fair rent issued pursuant to such an application; Sch 11, Pt III, Sch 13 repealed by the Housing Act 1980, s 152(3), Sch 26.*)

### SCHEDULE 14
### CONVERSION OF HOUSING ASSOCIATION TENANCIES INTO REGULATED TENANCIES

Section 92

1.—(1)   This paragraph applies in any case where—
    (a)   a tenancy of a dwelling-house under which the interest of the landlord belonged to a housing association came to an end at a time before 1st April 1975, and
    (b)   on the date when it came to an end, the tenancy was one to which Part VIII of the 1972 Act (which is superseded by Part VI of this Act) applied, and
    (c)   if the tenancy had come to an end on 1st April 1975 it would, by virtue of section 18(1) of the 1974 Act have then been a protected tenancy for the purposes of the Rent Act 1968.

(2)   If on 1st April 1975 a person who was the tenant under the tenancy which came to an end duly retained possession of the dwelling-house, he shall be deemed to have done so as a statutory

tenant under a regulated tenancy and as a person who became a statutory tenant on the termination of a protected tenancy under which he was the tenant.

(3)    If on 1st April 1975 a person duly retained possession of the dwelling-house as being a person who, in the circumstances described in sub-paragraph (5) below, would have been the first successor, within the meaning of Schedule 1 to the Rent Act 1968, he shall be deemed to have done so as the statutory tenant under a regulated tenancy and as a person who became a statutory tenant by virtue of paragraph 2 or 3 of Schedule 1 to this Act.

(4)    If on 1st April 1975 a person duly retained possession of the dwelling-house as being a person who, in the circumstances described in sub-paragraph (5) below, would have become the statutory tenant on the death of a first successor, he shall be deemed to have done so as a statutory tenant under a regulated tenancy and as a person who became a statutory tenant by virtue of paragraph 6 or 7 of Schedule 1 to this Act.

(5)    The circumstances mentioned in sub-paragraphs (3) and (4) above are that—
    (a)    the tenant under the tenancy, or any person to whom the dwelling-house or any part thereof had been lawfully sublet has died; and
    (b)    if the deceased had been the original tenant within the meaning of Schedule 1 to the Rent Act 1968, the person duly retaining possession of the dwelling-house would have been the first successor within the meaning of that Schedule or would have become the statutory tenant on the death of that first successor.

(6)    References in this paragraph to a person duly retaining possession of a dwelling-house are references to his retaining possession without any order for possession having been made or, where such an order has been made—
    (a)    during any period while its operation is postponed or its execution is suspended; or
    (b)    after it has been rescinded.

(7)    Subject to sub-paragraph (8) below, the tenancy referred to in sub-paragraph (1) above shall be treated as the original contract of tenancy for the purposes of section 3 of this Act in relation to a statutory tenancy imposed by any of sub-paragraphs (2) to (4) above.

(8)    The High Court or the county court may by order vary all or any of the terms of a statutory tenancy imposed by any of sub-paragraphs (2) to (4) above in any way appearing to the court to be just and equitable (and whether or not in a way authorised by sections 46 and 47 of this Act).

2.—(1)    If, in a case where either a tenancy has become a protected tenancy by virtue of section 18(1) of the 1974 Act or by virtue of subsections (1) and (3) of section 15 of this Act or a statutory tenancy has been imposed by virtue of paragraph 1 above—
    (a)    a rent (the "previous registered rent") was registered for the dwelling-house at a time when Part VIII of the 1972 Act or Part VI of this Act applied to that tenancy or, as the case may be, to the tenancy referred to in paragraph 1(1) above; and
    (b)    a rent has subsequently been registered for the dwelling-house under Part IV of this Act but the rent so registered is less than the previous registered rent,

then subject to paragraph 4 below, until such time as a rent is registered under Part IV which is higher than the previous registered rent, the contractual rent limit or, as the case may be, the maximum rent recoverable during any statutory period of the regulated tenancy concerned shall be the previous registered rent.

(2)    If in a case falling within sub-paragraph (1) above, the Secretary of State has, in a direction under section 90 of this Act, specified a rent limit for the dwelling-house higher than the previous registered rent, then, during the period for which that direction has effect as mentioned in that section, sub-paragraph (1) above shall have effect with the substitution for any reference to the previous registered rent of a reference to the rent limit so specified.

(3)    Nothing in this paragraph shall affect the operation of section 73 of this Act and, accordingly, where the registration of a rent is cancelled in accordance with that section, sub-paragraph (1) above shall cease to apply in relation to the rent of the dwelling-house concerned.

3.—(1)    This paragraph applies for the purposes of the application of Part III of this Act in relation to—
    (a)    a tenancy which has become a protected tenancy by virtue of section 18(1) of the 1974 Act or by virtue of subsections (1) and (3) of section 15 of this Act,
    (b)    a statutory tenancy arising on the termination of such a tenancy, and
    (c)    a statutory tenancy imposed by virtue of paragraph 1 above,

in any case where at the time when Part VIII of the 1972 Act or Part VI of this Act applied to the tenancy referred to in paragraph (a) above or, as the case may require, paragraph 1(1) above, section 83(3) of the 1972 Act or section 88(4) of this Act, applied.

(2)    Where this paragraph applies, the rent limit applicable to the tenancy or statutory tenancy referred to in sub-paragraph (1) above shall be deemed to be (or, as the case may be, to have been) the contractual rent limit under the relevant tenancy, but without prejudice to the subsequent

registration of a rent for the dwelling-house under Part IV of this Act or (during the currency of a protected tenancy) the making of an agreement under section 51 of this Act increasing the rent payable.

(3) Sub-paragraph (2) above shall have effect notwithstanding the repeal by the 1972 Act of section 20(3) of the Rent Act 1968 (contractual rent limit before registration), but nothing in this paragraph shall be taken as applying any provisions of section 88 of this Act to a tenancy at a time when it is a protected tenancy.

(4) In this paragraph "the relevant tenancy" means—
  (a)  in the case of a tenancy falling within sub-paragraph (1)(a) above, that tenancy;
  (b)  in the case of a statutory tenancy falling within sub-paragraph (1)(b) above, the tenancy referred to in sub-paragraph (1)(a) above; and
  (c)  in the case of a statutory tenancy falling within sub-paragraph (1)(c) above, the protected tenancy referred to in sub-paragraph (2) of paragraph 1 above or, in a case where sub-paragraph (3) or (4) of that paragraph applies, a notional protected tenancy which, when taken with that regulated tenancy would, by virtue of section 18(2) of this Act, be treated for the purposes of this Act as constituting one regulated tenancy when taken together with the statutory tenancy.

4. ...

5.—(1) This paragraph has effect with respect to the application of Schedule 9 to this Act in relation to a regulated tenancy consisting of—
  (a)  a tenancy which has become a protected tenancy by virtue of section 18(1) of the 1974 Act or by virtue of subsections (1) and (3) of section 15 of this Act, or
  (b)  a statutory tenancy imposed by virtue of paragraph 1 above,
together with any subsequent statutory tenancy which, when taken with that regulated tenancy, is by virtue of section 18(2) of this Act treated for the purposes of this Act as constituting one regulated tenancy.

(2) For the purposes of paragraph 1(1)(b) of Schedule 9, a tenancy falling within sub-paragraph (1)(a) above shall be deemed to have been a regulated tenancy throughout the period when Part VIII of the 1972 Act or Part VI of this Act applied to it.

(3) In the case of a regulated tenancy falling within sub-paragraph (1)(b) above, paragraph 1(1)(b) of Schedule 9 shall have effect as if the reference to the completion of works during the existence of the regulated tenancy included a reference to their completion during the period beginning on the day on which Part VIII of the 1972 Act or Part VI of this Act first applied to the tenancy referred to in paragraph 1(1) above and ending on the day on which the regulated tenancy came into existence.

(4) The reference in paragraph 3(1) of Schedule 9 to notices of increase authorised by this Act shall include a reference to notices of increase under section 87 of the 1972 Act.

6. ...

7. In the application of section 70 of this Act in relation to a tenancy which has become a protected tenancy by virtue of section 18(1) of the 1974 Act or by virtue of subsections (1) and (3) of section 15 of this Act or a statutory tenancy which is imposed by virtue of paragraph 1 above, the reference in subsection (3) to a failure to comply with any terms of a regulated tenancy or to carrying out an improvement includes a reference to a failure occurring or an improvement carried out before the tenancy became a regulated tenancy or, as the case may be, before the statutory tenancy was imposed.

8. In this Schedule "the 1972 Act" means the Housing Finance Act 1972 and "the 1974 Act" means the Housing Act 1974.

[328]

**NOTES**
Para 4: repealed by the Housing Act 1988, s 140(2), Sch 18.
Para 6: repealed by the Housing Act 1980, s 152(3), Sch 26.
Rent Act 1968: repealed by s 155(5) of, and Sch 25 to, this Act.
Housing Finance Act 1972, Pt VIII: repealed by s 155(5) of, and Sch 25 to, this Act.
Housing Act 1974, s 18(1): partly repealed by s 155(5) of, and Sch 25 to, this Act and replaced by s 15(1), (3), as originally enacted.

## SCHEDULE 15
## GROUNDS FOR POSSESSION OF DWELLING-HOUSES LET ON OR SUBJECT TO PROTECTED OR STATUTORY TENANCIES

Section 98

### PART I
### CASES IN WHICH COURT MAY ORDER POSSESSION

*Case 1*

Where any rent lawfully due from the tenant has not been paid, or any obligation of the protected or statutory tenancy which arises under this Act, or—

   (a)   in the case of a protected tenancy, any other obligation of the tenancy, in so far as is consistent with the provisions of Part VII of this Act, or

   (b)   in the case of a statutory tenancy, any other obligation of the previous protected tenancy which is applicable to the statutory tenancy,

has been broken or not performed.

*Case 2*

Where the tenant or any person residing or lodging with him or any sub-tenant of his has been guilty of conduct which is a nuisance or annoyance to adjoining occupiers, or has been convicted of using the dwelling-house or allowing the dwelling-house to be used for immoral or illegal purposes.

*Case 3*

Where the condition of the dwelling-house has, in the opinion of the court, deteriorated owing to acts of waste by, or the neglect or default of, the tenant or any person residing or lodging with him or any sub-tenant of his and, in the case of any act of waste by, or the neglect or default of, a person lodging with the tenant or a sub-tenant of his, where the court is satisfied that the tenant has not, before the making of the order in question, taken such steps as he ought reasonably to have taken for the removal of the lodger or sub-tenant, as the case may be.

*Case 4*

Where the condition of any furniture provided for use under the tenancy has, in the opinion of the court, deteriorated owing to ill-treatment by the tenant or any person residing or lodging with him or any sub-tenant of his and, in the case of any ill-treatment by a person lodging with the tenant or a sub-tenant of his, where the court is satisfied that the tenant has not, before the making of the order in question, taken such steps as he ought reasonably to have taken for the removal of the lodger or sub-tenant, as the case may be.

*Case 5*

Where the tenant has given notice to quit and, in consequence of that notice, the landlord has contracted to sell or let the dwelling-house or has taken any other steps as the result of which he would, in the opinion of the court, be seriously prejudiced if he could not obtain possession.

*Case 6*

Where, without the consent of the landlord, the tenant has, at any time after—

   (a)   ...

   (b)   22nd March 1973, in the case of a tenancy which became a regulated tenancy by virtue of section 14 of the Counter-Inflation Act 1973;

   [(bb)   the commencement of section 73 of the Housing Act 1980, in the case of a tenancy which became a regulated tenancy by virtue of that section;]

   (c)   14th August 1974, in the case of a regulated furnished tenancy; or

   (d)   8th December 1965, in the case of any other tenancy,

assigned or sublet the whole of the dwelling-house or sublet part of the dwelling-house, the remainder being already sublet.

*Case 7*

...

*Case 8*

Where the dwelling-house is reasonably required by the landlord for occupation as a residence for some person engaged in his whole-time employment, or in the whole-time employment of some tenant from him or with whom, conditional on housing being provided, a contract for such employment has been entered into, and the tenant was in the employment of the landlord or a former landlord, and the dwelling-house was let to him in consequence of that employment and he has ceased to be in that employment.

## Case 9

Where the dwelling-house is reasonably required by the landlord for occupation as a residence for—
- (a)  himself, or
- (b)  any son or daughter of his over 18 years of age, or
- (c)  his father or mother, or
- (d)  if the dwelling-house is let on or subject to a regulated tenancy, the father or mother of his [spouse or civil partner],

and the landlord did not become landlord by purchasing the dwelling-house or any interest therein after—
- (i)  7th November 1956, in the case of a [tenancy which was then a controlled tenancy];
- (ii)  8th March 1973, in the case of a tenancy which became a regulated tenancy by virtue of section 14 of the Counter-Inflation Act 1973;
- (iii)  24th May 1974, in the case of a regulated furnished tenancy; or
- (iv)  23rd March 1965, in the case of any other tenancy.

## Case 10

Where the court is satisfied that the rent charged by the tenant—
- (a)  for any sublet part of the dwelling-house which is a dwelling-house let on a protected tenancy or subject to a statutory tenancy is or was in excess of the maximum rent for the time being recoverable for that part, having regard to … Part III of this Act, or
- (b)  for any sublet part of the dwelling-house which is subject to a restricted contract is or was in excess of the maximum (if any) which it is lawful for the lessor, within the meaning of Part V of this Act to require or receive having regard to the provisions of that Part.

**[329]**

**NOTES**

Case 6: para (a) repealed and para (bb) inserted by the Housing Act 1980, ss 73, 152(3), Sch 8, para 2, Sch 26.
Case 7: repealed by the Housing Act 1980, s 152(3), Sch 26.
Case 9: words in first pair of square brackets substituted by the Civil Partnership Act 2004, s 81, Sch 8, para 14; words in second pair of square brackets substituted by the Housing Act 1980, s 152(1), Sch 25, Pt I, para 57.
Case 10: words omitted repealed by the Housing Act 1980, s 152(3), Sch 26.
Counter-Inflation Act 1973, s 14: repealed by s 155(5) of, and Sch 25 to, this Act, and partly replaced by s 4(2), (3) at **[205]**.

## PART II
### CASES IN WHICH COURT MUST ORDER POSSESSION WHERE DWELLING-HOUSE SUBJECT TO REGULATED TENANCY

## Case 11

[Where a person (in this Case referred to as "the owner-occupier") who let the dwelling-house on a regulated tenancy had, at any time before the letting, occupied it as his residence] and—
- (a)  not later than the relevant date the landlord gave notice in writing to the tenant that possession might be recovered under this Case, and
- (b)  the dwelling-house has not, since—
    - (i)  22nd March 1973, in the case of a tenancy which became a regulated tenancy by virtue of section 14 of the Counter-Inflation Act 1973;
    - (ii)  14th August 1974, in the case of a regulated furnished tenancy; or
    - (iii)  8th December 1965, in the case of any other tenancy,
    been let by the owner-occupier on a protected tenancy with respect to which the condition mentioned in paragraph (a) above was not satisfied, and
- [(c)  the court is of the opinion that of the conditions set out in Part V of this Schedule one of those in paragraphs (a) and (c) to (f) is satisfied].

If the court is of the opinion that, notwithstanding that the condition in paragraph (a) or (b) above is not complied with, it is just and equitable to make an order for possession of the dwelling-house, the court may dispense with the requirements of either or both of those paragraphs, as the case may require.

The giving of a notice before 14th August 1974 under section 79 of the Rent Act 1968 shall be treated, in the case of a regulated furnished tenancy, as compliance with paragraph (a) of this Case.

[Where the dwelling-house has been let by the owner-occupier on a protected tenancy (in this paragraph referred to as "the earlier tenancy") granted on or after 16th November 1984 but not later than the end of the period of two months beginning with the commencement of the Rent (Amendment) Act 1985 and either—
- (i)  the earlier tenancy was granted for a term certain (whether or not to be followed by a

further term or to continue thereafter from year to year or some other period) and was during that term a protected shorthold tenancy as defined in section 52 of the Housing Act 1980, or

(ii)    the conditions mentioned in paragraphs (a) to (c) of Case 20 were satisfied with respect to the dwelling-house and the earlier tenancy,

then for the purposes of paragraph (b) above the condition in paragraph (a) above is to be treated as having been satisfied with respect to the earlier tenancy.]

PART 1
STATUTES

### Case 12

[Where the landlord (in this Case referred to as "the owner") intends to occupy the dwelling-house as his residence at such time as he might retire from regular employment and has let] it on a regulated tenancy before he has so retired and—

(a)    not later than the relevant date the landlord gave notice in writing to the tenant that possession might be recovered under this Case; and

(b)    the dwelling-house has not, since 14th August 1974, been let by the owner on a protected tenancy with respect to which the condition mentioned in paragraph (a) above was not satisfied; and

[(c)    the court is of the opinion that of the conditions set out in Part V of this Schedule one of those in paragraphs (b) to (e) is satisfied].

If the court is of the opinion that, notwithstanding that the condition in paragraph (a) or (b) above is not complied with, it is just and equitable to make an order for possession of the dwelling-house, the court may dispense with the requirements of either or both of those paragraphs, as the case may require.

### Case 13

Where the dwelling-house is let under a tenancy for a term of years certain not exceeding 8 months and—

(a)    not later than the relevant date the landlord gave notice in writing to the tenant that possession might be recovered under this Case; and

(b)    the dwelling-house was, at some time within the period of 12 months ending on the relevant date, occupied under a right to occupy it for a holiday.

For the purposes of this Case a tenancy shall be treated as being for a term of years certain notwithstanding that it is liable to determination by re-entry or on the happening of any event other than the giving of notice by the landlord to determine the term.

### Case 14

Where the dwelling-house is let under a tenancy for a term of years certain not exceeding 12 months and—

(a)    not later than the relevant date the landlord gave notice in writing to the tenant that possession might be recovered under this Case; and

(b)    at some time within the period of 12 months ending on the relevant date, the dwelling-house was subject to such a tenancy as is referred to in section 8(1) of this Act.

For the purposes of this Case a tenancy shall be treated as being for a term of years certain notwithstanding that it is liable to determination by re-entry or on the happening of any event other than the giving of notice by the landlord to determine the term.

### Case 15

Where the dwelling-house is held for the purpose of being available for occupation by a minister of religion as a residence from which to perform the duties of his office and—

(a)    not later than the relevant date the tenant was given notice in writing that possession might be recovered under this Case, and

(b)    the court is satisfied that the dwelling-house is required for occupation by a minister of religion as such a residence.

### Case 16

Where the dwelling-house was at any time occupied by a person under the terms of his employment as a person employed in agriculture, and

(a)    the tenant neither is nor at any time was so employed by the landlord and is not the widow of a person who was so employed, and

(b)    not later than the relevant date, the tenant was given notice in writing that possession might be recovered under this Case, and

(c)    the court is satisfied that the dwelling-house is required for occupation by a person employed, or to be employed, by the landlord in agriculture.

For the purposes of this Case "employed", "employment" and "agriculture" have the same meanings as in the Agricultural Wages Act 1948.

## Case 17

Where proposals for amalgamation, approved for the purposes of a scheme under section 26 of the Agriculture Act 1967, have been carried out and, at the time when the proposals were submitted, the dwelling-house was occupied by a person responsible (whether as owner, tenant, or servant or agent of another) for the control of the farming of any part of the land comprised in the amalgamation and

(a) after the carrying out of the proposals, the dwelling-house was let on a regulated tenancy otherwise than to, or to the widow of, either a person ceasing to be so responsible as part of the amalgamation or a person who is, or at any time was, employed by the landlord in agriculture, and

(b) not later than the relevant date the tenant was given notice in writing that possession might be recovered under this Case, and

(c) the court is satisfied that the dwelling-house is required for occupation by a person employed, or to be employed, by the landlord in agriculture, and

(d) the proceedings for possession are commenced by the landlord at any time during the period of 5 years beginning with the date on which the proposals for the amalgamation were approved or, if occupation of the dwelling-house after the amalgamation continued in, or was first taken by, a person ceasing to be responsible as mentioned in paragraph (a) above or his widow, during a period expiring 3 years after the date on which the dwelling-house next became unoccupied.

For the purposes of this Case "employed" and "agriculture" have the same meanings as in the Agricultural Wages Act 1948 and "amalgamation" has the same meaning as in Part II of the Agriculture Act 1967.

## Case 18

Where—

(a) the last occupier of the dwelling-house before the relevant date was a person, or the widow of a person, who was at some time during his occupation responsible (whether as owner, tenant, or servant or agent of another) for the control of the farming of land which formed, together with the dwelling-house, an agricultural unit within the meaning of the Agriculture Act 1947, and

(b) the tenant is neither—

   (i) a person, or the widow of a person, who is or has at any time been responsible for the control of the farming of any part of the said land, nor

   (ii) a person, or the widow of a person, who is or at any time was employed by the landlord in agriculture, and

(c) the creation of the tenancy was not preceded by the carrying out in connection with any of the said land of an amalgamation approved for the purposes of a scheme under section 26 of the Agriculture Act 1967, and

(d) not later than the relevant date the tenant was given notice in writing that possession might be recovered under this Case, and

(e) the court is satisfied that the dwelling-house is required for occupation either by a person responsible or to be responsible (whether as owner, tenant, or servant or agent of another) for the control of the farming of any part of the said land or by a person employed or to be employed by the landlord in agriculture, and

(f) in a case where the relevant date was before 9th August 1972, the proceedings for possession are commenced by the landlord before the expiry of 5 years from the date on which the occupier referred to in paragraph (a) above went out of occupation.

For the purposes of this Case "employed" and "agriculture" have the same meanings as in the Agricultural Wages Act 1948 and "amalgamation" has the same meaning as in Part II of the Agriculture Act 1967.

## [Case 19

Where the dwelling-house was let under a protected shorthold tenancy (or is treated under section 55 of the Housing Act 1980 as having been so let) and—

(a) there either has been no grant of a further tenancy of the dwelling-house since the end of the protected shorthold tenancy or, if there was such a grant, it was to a person who immediately before the grant was in possession of the dwelling-house as a protected or statutory tenant; and

(b) the proceedings for possession were commenced after appropriate notice by the landlord to the tenant and not later than 3 months after the expiry of the notice.

A notice is appropriate for this Case if—

   (i) it is in writing and states that proceedings for possession under this Case may be brought after its expiry; and

   (ii) it expires not earlier than 3 months after it is served nor, if, when it is served, the tenancy is a periodic tenancy, before that periodic tenancy could be brought to an end by a notice to quit served by the landlord on the same day;

   (iii) it is served—

    (a)    in the period of 3 months immediately preceding the date on which the protected shorthold tenancy comes to an end; or

    (b)    if that date has passed, in the period of 3 months immediately preceding any anniversary of that date; and

(iv)   in a case where a previous notice has been served by the landlord on the tenant in respect of the dwelling-house, and that notice was an appropriate notice, it is served not earlier than 3 months after the expiry of the previous notice.]

### [Case 20

Where the dwelling-house was let by a person (in this Case referred to as "the owner") at any time after the commencement of section 67 of the Housing Act 1980 and—

    (a)    at the time when the owner acquired the dwelling-house he was a member of the regular armed forces of the Crown;

    (b)    at the relevant date the owner was a member of the regular armed forces of the Crown;

    (c)    not later than the relevant date the owner gave notice in writing to the tenant that possession might be recovered under this Case;

    (d)    the dwelling-house has not, since the commencement of section 67 of the Act of 1980 been let by the owner on a protected tenancy with respect to which the condition mentioned in paragraph (c) above was not satisfied; and

    (e)    the court is of the opinion that—

        (i)    the dwelling-house is required as a residence for the owner; or

        (ii)    of the conditions set out in Part V of this Schedule one of those in paragraphs (c) to (f) is satisfied.

If the court is of the opinion that, notwithstanding that the condition in paragraph (c) or (d) above is not complied with, it is just and equitable to make an order for possession of the dwelling-house, the court may dispense with the requirements of either or both of these paragraphs, as the case may require.

For the purposes of this Case "regular armed forces of the Crown" has the same meaning as in section 1 of the House of Commons Disqualification Act 1975.]

                                                                     **[330]**

**NOTES**

Case 11: words in first pair of square brackets substituted and words in third pair of square brackets added by the Rent (Amendment) Act 1985, s 1(1), (2), (4); words in second pair of square brackets substituted by the Housing Act 1980, s 66(1), subject to savings in s 66(5), (6) thereof at **[363]**.

Case 12: words in square brackets substituted by the Housing Act 1980, s 66(2), (4), subject to savings in s 66(5), (6) thereof at **[363]**.

Case 19: added by the Housing Act 1980, s 55(1).

Case 20: added by the Housing Act 1980, s 67.

Counter-Inflation Act 1973, s 14: repealed by s 155(5) of, and Sch 25 to, this Act and partly replaced by s 4(2), (3) at **[205]**.

Rent Act 1968, s 79: repealed by s 155(5) of, and Sch 25 to, this Act.

Housing Act 1980, s 52: repealed with savings by the Housing Act 1988, s 140(2), Sch 18.

### PART III
### PROVISIONS APPLICABLE TO CASE 9 AND PART II OF THIS SCHEDULE

#### *Provision for Case 9*

1.   A court shall not make an order for possession of a dwelling-house by reason only that the circumstances of the case fall within Case 9 in Part I of this Schedule if the court is satisfied that, having regard to all the circumstances of the case, including the question whether other accommodation is available for the landlord or the tenant, greater hardship would be caused by granting the order than by refusing to grant it.

#### *Provision for Part II*

2.   Any reference in Part II of this Schedule to the relevant date shall be construed as follows:—

    (a)    except in a case falling within paragraph (b) or (c) below, if the protected tenancy, or, in the case of a statutory tenancy, the previous contractual tenancy, was created before 8th December 1965, the relevant date means 7th June 1966; and

    (b)    except in a case falling within paragraph (c) below, if the tenancy became a regulated tenancy by virtue of section 14 of the Counter-Inflation Act 1973 and the tenancy or, in the case of a statutory tenancy, the previous contractual tenancy, was created before 22nd March 1973, the relevant date means 22nd September 1973; and

    (c)    in the case of a regulated furnished tenancy, if the tenancy or, in the case of a statutory furnished tenancy, the previous contractual tenancy was created before 14th August 1974, the relevant date means 13th February 1975; and

(d)   in any other case, the relevant date means the date of the commencement of the regulated tenancy in question.

[331]

---

**NOTES**

Counter-Inflation Act 1973, s 14: repealed by s 155(5) of, and Sch 25 to, this Act and partly replaced by s 4(2), (3) at **[205]**.

---

PART IV
## SUITABLE ALTERNATIVE ACCOMMODATION

3.   For the purposes of section 98(1)(a) of this Act, a certificate of the [local housing authority] for the district in which the dwelling-house in question is situated, certifying that the authority will provide suitable alternative accommodation for the tenant by a date specified in the certificate, shall be conclusive evidence that suitable alternative accommodation will be available for him by that date.

4.—[(1)]   Where no such certificate as is mentioned in [paragraph 3] above is produced to the court, accommodation shall be deemed to be suitable for the purposes of section 98(1)(a) of this Act if it consists of either—

(a)   premises which are to be let as a separate dwelling such that they will then be let on a protected tenancy [(other than one under which the landlord might recover possession of the dwelling-house under one of the Cases in Part II of this Schedule)], or

(b)   premises to be let as a separate dwelling on terms which will, in the opinion of the court, afford to the tenant security of tenure reasonably equivalent to the security afforded by Part VII of this Act in the case of a protected tenancy [of a kind mentioned in paragraph (a) above],

and, in the opinion of the court, the accommodation fulfils the relevant conditions as defined in paragraph 5 below.

[(2)   ... ]

5.—(1)   For the purposes of paragraph 4 above, the relevant conditions are that the accommodation is reasonably suitable to the needs of the tenant and his family as regards proximity to place of work, and either—

(a)   similar as regards rental and extent to the accommodation afforded by dwelling-houses provided in the neighbourhood by any [local housing authority] for persons whose needs as regards extent are, in the opinion of the court, similar to those of the tenant and of his family; or

(b)   reasonably suitable to the means of the tenant and to the needs of the tenant and his family as regards extent and character; and

that if any furniture was provided for use under the protected or statutory tenancy in question, furniture is provided for use in the accommodation which is either similar to that so provided or is reasonably suitable to the needs of the tenant and his family.

(2)   For the purposes of sub-paragraph (1)(a) above, a certificate of a [local housing authority] stating—

(a)   the extent of the accommodation afforded by dwelling-houses provided by the authority to meet the needs of tenants with families of such number as may be specified in the certificate, and

(b)   the amount of the rent charged by the authority for dwelling-houses affording accommodation of that extent,

shall be conclusive evidence of the facts so stated.

6.   Accommodation shall not be deemed to be suitable to the needs of the tenant and his family if the result of their occupation of the accommodation would be that it would be an overcrowded dwelling-house for the purposes of the [Part X of the Housing Act 1985].

7.   Any document purporting to be a certificate of a [local housing authority] named therein issued for the purposes of this Schedule and to be signed by the proper officer of that authority shall be received in evidence and, unless the contrary is shown, shall be deemed to be such a certificate without further proof.

[8.   In this Part "local housing authority" and "district" in relation to such an authority have the same meaning as in the Housing Act 1985.]

[332]

---

**NOTES**

Paras 3, 5–7: words in square brackets substituted by the Housing (Consequential Provisions) Act 1985, s 4, Sch 2, para 35(1), (11).

Para 4: sub-para (1) numbered as such and sub-para (2) added by the Housing and Planning Act 1986, s 13(2); sub-para (2) repealed by the Housing Act 1988, s 140(2), Sch 18; words in square brackets in sub-para (1) substituted and added by the Housing Act 1980, s 152(1), Sch 25, Pt I, para 58.

Para 8: substituted by the Housing (Consequential Provisions) Act 1985, s 4, Sch 2, para 35(1), (11).

---

[PART V
PROVISIONS APPLYING TO CASES 11, 12 AND 20

1.    In this Part of this Schedule—
"mortgage" includes a charge and "mortgagee" shall be construed accordingly;
"owner" means, in relation to Case 11, the owner-occupier; and
"successor in title" means any person deriving title from the owner, other than a purchaser for value or a person deriving title from a purchaser for value.

2.    The conditions referred to in paragraph (c) in each of Cases 11 and 12 and in paragraph (e)(ii) of Case 20 are that—
  (a)    the dwelling-house is required as a residence for the owner or any member of his family who resided with the owner when he last occupied the dwelling-house as a residence;
  (b)    the owner has retired from regular employment and requires the dwelling-house as a residence;
  (c)    the owner has died and the dwelling-house is required as a residence for a member of his family who was residing with him at the time of his death;
  (d)    the owner has died and the dwelling-house is required by a successor in title as his residence or for the purpose of disposing of it with vacant possession;
  (e)    the dwelling-house is subject to a mortgage, made by deed and granted before the tenancy, and the mortgagee—
    (i)    is entitled to exercise a power of sale conferred on him by the mortgage or by section 101 of the Law of Property Act 1925; and
    (ii)    requires the dwelling-house for the purpose of disposing of it with vacant possession in exercise of that power; and
  (f)    the dwelling-house is not reasonably suitable to the needs of the owner, having regard to his place of work, and he requires it for the purpose of disposing of it with vacant possession and of using the proceeds of that disposal in acquiring, as his residence, a dwelling-house which is more suitable to those needs.]

**[333]**

**NOTES**
Inserted by the Housing Act 1980, s 66(3), Sch 7, subject to savings in s 66(5), (6) thereof at **[363]**.

SCHEDULE 16
FURTHER GROUNDS FOR POSSESSION OF DWELLING-HOUSES LET ON OR SUBJECT TO TENANCIES TO WHICH SECTION 99 APPLIES
Section 99

CASE I

*Alternative accommodation not provided or arranged by housing authority*

1.    The court is satisfied that suitable alternative accommodation is available for the tenant, or will be available for him when the order for possession takes effect.

2.    Accommodation shall be deemed suitable in this Case if it consists of—
  (a)    premises which are to be let as a separate dwelling such that they will then be let on a protected tenancy, or
  (b)    premises which are to be let as a separate dwelling on terms which will, in the opinion of the court, afford to the tenant security of tenure reasonably equivalent to the security afforded by Part VII of this Act in the case of a protected tenancy,

and, in the opinion of the court, the accommodation fulfils the conditions in paragraph 3 below.

3.—(1)    The accommodation must be reasonably suitable to the needs of the tenant and his family as regards proximity to place of work and either—
  (a)    similar as regards rental and extent to the accommodation afforded by dwelling-houses provided in the neighbourhood by [the local housing authority] for persons whose needs as regards extent are similar to those of the tenant and his family, or
  (b)    reasonably suitable to the means of the tenant, and to the needs of the tenant and his family as regards extent and character.

(2)    For the purposes of sub-paragraph (1)(a) above, a certificate of [the local housing authority] stating—
  (a)    the extent of the accommodation afforded by dwelling-houses provided by the authority to meet the needs of tenants with families of such number as may be specified in the certificate, and
  (b)    the amount of the rent charged by [the local housing authority] for dwelling-houses affording accommodation of that extent,

shall be conclusive evidence of the facts so stated.

(3)   If any furniture was provided by the landlord for use under the tenancy, furniture must be provided for use in the alternative accommodation which is either similar, or is reasonably suitable to the needs of the tenant and his family.

4.   Accommodation shall not be deemed to be suitable to the needs of the tenant and his family if the result of their occupation of the accommodation would be that it would be an overcrowded dwelling-house for the purposes of [Part X of the Housing Act 1985].

5.   Any document purporting to be a certificate of [the local housing authority] issued for the purposes of this Case and to be signed by the proper officer of the authority shall be received in evidence and, unless the contrary is shown, shall be deemed to be such a certificate without further proof.

6.   In this Case no account shall be taken of accommodation as respects which an offer has been made, or notice has been given, as mentioned in paragraph 1 of Case II below.

[7.   In this Case and in Case II below "the local housing authority" has the same meaning as in the Housing Act 1985.]

## CASE II

### *Alternative accommodation provided or arranged by housing authority*

1.   [The local housing authority] have made an offer in writing to the tenant of alternative accommodation which appears to them to be suitable, specifying the date when the accommodation will be available and the date (not being less than 14 days from the date of offer) by which the offer must be accepted.

*OR*

[The local housing authority] have given notice in writing to the tenant that they have received from a person specified in the notice an offer in writing to rehouse the tenant in alternative accommodation which appears to [the local housing authority] to be suitable, and the notice specifies both the date when the accommodation will be available and the date (not being less than 14 days from the date when the notice was given to the tenant) by which the offer must be accepted

2.   The landlord shows that the tenant accepted the offer (by the housing authority or other person) within the time duly specified in the offer.

*OR*

The landlord shows that the tenant did not so accept the offer, and the tenant does not satisfy the court that he acted reasonably in failing to accept the offer.

3.—(1)   The accommodation offered must in the opinion of the court fulfil the conditions of this paragraph.

(2)   The accommodation must be reasonably suitable to the needs of the tenant and his family as regards proximity to place of work.

(3)   The accommodation must be reasonably suitable to the means of the tenant, and to the needs of the tenant and his family as regards extent.

4.   If the accommodation offered is available for a limited period only, the [local housing authority's offer] or notice under paragraph 1 of this Case must contain an assurance that other accommodation—

    (a)   the availability of which is not so limited,
    (b)   which appears to them to be suitable, and
    (c)   which fulfils the conditions in paragraph 3 above,

will be offered to the tenant as soon as practicable.

[334]

**NOTES**

Words in square brackets substituted by the Housing (Consequential Provisions) Act 1985, s 4, Sch 2, para 35(1), (12).

## SCHEDULE 17
### CONVERTED TENANCIES: MODIFICATION OF ACT

Section 18A

1.   In this Schedule—

    "converted tenancy" means a tenancy which has become a regulated tenancy by virtue of [any of the enactments mentioned in section 18A of this Act.]

    "the conversion" means the time when the tenancy became a regulated tenancy.

2.   In relation to any rental period beginning after the conversion, sections 45 to 47 of this Act shall have effect as if references therein to the last contractual period were references to the last rental period beginning before the conversion.

3, 4.   ...

5.   Section 5(1) of this Act shall not apply to the converted tenancy after the conversion.

6.   Section 70 of this Act shall apply in relation to the converted tenancy as if the references in subsection (3) of that section to the tenant under the regulated tenancy included references to the tenant under the tenancy before the conversion.

7.   [None of the enactments mentioned in section 18A of this Act shall] be taken as affecting any court proceedings, instituted under this Act (or, as the case may be, the Rent Act 1968) before the conversion, which may affect the recoverable rent before the conversion, or the rent under the regulated tenancy after the conversion so far as that depends on the previous rent.

8.   Any court order in any proceedings to which paragraph 7 above applies which is made after the conversion may exclude from the effect of the order rent for any rental period beginning before the conversion, or for any later rental period beginning before the making of the order.

9.   Any right conferred on a tenant by section 38 of, or paragraph 6(4) of Schedule 6 to, this Act to recover any amount by deducting it from rent shall be exercisable by deducting it from rent for any rental period beginning after the conversion to the same extent as the right would have been exercisable if the conversion had not taken place.

10, 11.   ...

**[335]**

**NOTES**

Paras 1, 7: words in square brackets substituted by the Housing Act 1980, s 152(1), Sch 25, Pt I, para 59.

Paras 3, 4: repealed by the Housing Act 1980, s 152, Sch 25, Pt I, para 59, Sch 26, subject to savings in Sch 25, Pt II, para 78 thereto at **[392]**.

Paras 10, 11: repealed by the Housing Act 1980, s 152(3), Sch 26.

Rent Act 1968: repealed by s 155(5) of, and Sch 25 to, this Act.

SCHEDULE 18

ALLOWABLE PREMIUMS

Sections 120(5), 121, 127 (1)

PART I

PREMIUM ALLOWED ON ASSIGNMENT OF TENANCY WHERE PREMIUM LAWFULLY PAID ON GRANT

1.—(1)   This Part of this Schedule applies where—

(a)   a premium was lawfully required and paid, or lawfully received, in respect of the grant, renewal or continuance of a protected tenancy of a dwelling-house which is a regulated tenancy; and

(b)   since that grant, renewal or continuance the landlord has not granted a tenancy of the dwelling-house under which, as against the landlord, a person became entitled to possession, other than the person who was so entitled to possession of the dwelling-house immediately before that tenancy began; and

(c)   a rent for the dwelling-house is registered under Part IV of this Act and the rent so registered is higher than the rent payable under the tenancy.

(2)   Any reference in this Part of this Schedule to a premium does not include a premium which consisted only of any such outgoings, sum or amount as fall within section 120(3) of this Act and, in the case of a premium which included any such outgoings, sum or amount, so much only of the premium as does not consist of those outgoings, sum or amount shall be treated as the premium for the purposes of this Part of this Schedule.

2.   In a case where this Part of this Schedule applies, nothing in section 120 of this Act shall prevent any person from requiring or receiving, on an assignment of the protected tenancy referred to in paragraph 1(1)(a) above or any subsequent protected tenancy of the same dwelling-house, a premium which does not exceed an amount calculated (subject to paragraph 4 below) in accordance with the formula—

$$\frac{P \times A}{G}$$

where

P is the premium referred to in paragraph 1(1)(a) above;

A is the length of the period beginning on the date on which the assignment in question takes effect and ending on the relevant date; and

G is the length of the period beginning on the date of the grant, renewal or continuance in respect of which the premium was paid and ending on the relevant date.

3.—(1)   If, although the registered rent is higher than the rent payable under the tenancy, the lump sum equivalent of the difference is less than the premium, paragraph 2 above shall have effect as if P were the lump sum equivalent.

(2)   For the purposes of this Part of this Schedule, the lump sum equivalent of the difference between the two rents referred to in sub-paragraph (1) above shall be taken to be that difference multiplied by the number of complete rental periods falling within the period beginning with the grant, renewal or continuance in respect of which the premium was paid and ending on the relevant date.

4.   Where any rates in respect of the dwelling-house are borne by the landlord or a superior landlord, the amount of the registered rent shall be taken, for the purposes of this Part of this Schedule, to be increased by the amount of the rates so borne in respect of the rental period comprising the date from which the registration took effect.

5.—(1)   Any reference in this Part of this Schedule to the relevant date shall be construed in accordance with this paragraph.

(2)   Where the tenancy referred to in paragraph 1(1)(a) above was granted, renewed or continued for a term of years certain exceeding 7 years and that term has not expired when the assignment takes effect, the relevant date is the date of the expiry of that term.

(3)   In any other case, the relevant date is the date of the expiry of 7 years from the commencement of the term, or, as the case may be, the renewal or continuance of the term in respect of which the premium was paid.

(4)   For the purposes of this paragraph—
   (a)   a term of years shall be treated as certain notwithstanding that it is liable to determination by re-entry or on the happening of any event other than the giving of notice by the landlord to determine the term; and
   (b)   a term of years determinable by the landlord giving notice to determine it shall be treated as a term of years certain expiring on the earliest date on which such a notice given after the date of the assignment would be capable of taking effect.

**[336]**

## PART II
### PREMIUM ALLOWED UNDER SECTIONS 121 AND 127

6.—(1)   Where this Part of this Schedule applies to any tenancy and a premium was lawfully required and paid on the grant or an assignment of the tenancy, nothing in section 120 of this Act shall prevent any person from requiring or receiving, on an assignment of the tenancy, the fraction of the premium specified below (without prejudice, however, to his requiring or receiving a greater sum in a case where he may lawfully do so under Part I of this Schedule).

(2)   If there was more than one premium, sub-paragraph (1) above shall apply to the last of them.

7.—(1)   The fraction

$$\frac{x}{y}$$

is where—
   X is the residue of the term of the tenancy at the date of the assignment, and
   Y is the term for which the tenancy was granted.

(2)   Sub-paragraph (1) above shall apply where a tenancy has been assigned as it applies where a tenancy has been granted and then Y in the fraction shall be the residue, at the date of that assignment, of the term for which the tenancy was granted.

8.   Where the tenancy was granted on the surrender of a previous tenancy, and a premium had been lawfully required and paid on the grant or an assignment of the previous tenancy, the surrender value of the previous tenancy shall be treated, for the purposes of this Part of this Schedule, as a premium or, as the case may be, as part of the premium, paid on the grant of the tenancy.

9.   For the purposes of paragraph 8 above, the surrender value of the previous tenancy shall be taken to be the amount which, had the previous tenancy been assigned instead of being surrendered and had this Part of this Schedule applied to it, would have been the amount that could have been required and received on the assignment in pursuance of this Part of this Schedule.

10.   In determining for the purposes of this Part of this Schedule the amount which may or could have been required and received on the assignment of a tenancy terminable, before the end of the term for which it was granted, by notice to the tenant, that term shall be taken to be a term expiring at the earliest date on which such a notice given after the date of the assignment would have been capable of taking effect.

11.   In this Part of this Schedule "grant" includes continuance and renewal.

**[337]**

*(Sch 19 repealed by the Housing Act 1980, s 152(3), Sch 26; Sch 20 repealed by the Regulatory Reform (Fire Safety) Order 2005, SI 2005/1541, art 53(1), (2), Sch 2, para 13, Sch 4; Schs 21, 22 repealed by the Housing Act 1980, s 152(3), Sch 26; Sch 23 contains amendments which, in so far as within the scope of this work, have been incorporated at the appropriate place.)*

## SCHEDULE 24
## SAVINGS AND TRANSITIONAL PROVISIONS
Section 155(3)

### General transitional provisions

1.—(1)  In so far as anything done, or having effect as if done, under an enactment repealed by this Act could have been done under a corresponding provision in this Act, it shall not be invalidated by the repeal but shall have effect as if done under that provision.

(2)  Sub-paragraph (1) above applies, in particular, to any regulation, order, scheme, agreement, dissent, election, application, reference, representation, appointment or apportionment made, notice served, certificate issued, statement supplied, undertaking or direction given or rent registered.

(3)  Subject to this Schedule, any document made, served or issued before the passing of this Act or at any time thereafter (whether before or after the commencement of this Act) and containing a reference to an enactment repealed by this Act, or having effect as if containing such a reference, shall, except in so far as a contrary intention appears, be construed as referring, or as the context requires, as including a reference, to the corresponding provision of this Act.

(4)  Where a period of time specified in an enactment repealed by this Act is current at the commencement of this Act, this Act shall have effect as if the corresponding provision thereof had been in force when that period began to run.

(5)  Nothing in this Act shall affect the enactments repealed thereby in their operation in relation to offences committed before the commencement of this Act.

(6)  A conviction for an offence under an enactment repealed by this Act shall be treated for the purposes of this Act as a conviction of an offence under the corresponding provision of this Act.

(7)  Subject to the provisions of this Act, any reference in any document or enactment to a dwelling-house which is let on or subject to a protected or statutory tenancy (including any reference which, immediately before the commencement of this Act, was to be construed as such a reference by virtue of paragraph 5 of Schedule 16 to the Rent Act 1968) shall be construed, except in so far as the context otherwise requires, as a reference to a dwelling-house let on or subject to a protected or statutory tenancy within the meaning of this Act.

(8)  Subject to the provisions of this Act, any reference in any document or enactment to a Part VI contract (within the meaning of Part VI of the Rent Act 1968) shall be construed, except in so far as the context otherwise requires, as a reference to a restricted contract.

### Existing statutory tenants

2.—(1)  If, immediately before the commencement of this Act, a person (the "existing statutory tenant") was a statutory tenant of a dwelling-house by virtue of any enactment repealed by this Act (a "repealed enactment") that person shall, on the commencement of this Act, be a statutory tenant of the dwelling-house for the purposes of this Act.

(2)  If, immediately before the existing statutory tenant became a statutory tenant, he was a tenant of the dwelling-house under a tenancy then, for the purposes of this Act, he shall be the statutory tenant by virtue of his previous protected tenancy.

(3)  If the existing statutory tenant became a statutory tenant on the death of a person who was himself a tenant or statutory tenant of the dwelling-house then, for the purposes of this Act, the existing statutory tenant shall be a statutory tenant by succession; and, unless he became a statutory tenant by virtue of section 13 of the Rent Act 1965, or paragraph 6 or 7 of Schedule 1 to the Rent Act 1968, he shall be deemed to be the first successor within the meaning of Schedule 1 to this Act.

(4)  If the existing statutory tenant became a statutory tenant by virtue of an exchange under section 17 of the Rent Act 1957 or section 14 of the Rent Act 1968 then, for the purposes of this Act, he shall be deemed to be the statutory tenant by virtue of his previous protected tenancy or, as the case may be, a statutory tenant by succession, if immediately before the commencement of this Act he was so deemed for the purposes of the Rent Act 1968.

(5)  If, by virtue of sub-paragraph (4) above, the existing statutory tenant is for the purposes of this Act a statutory tenant by succession, he shall be deemed to be the first successor, within the meaning of Schedule 1 to this Act if, and only if, the person who was a statutory tenant immediately before the date of exchange was not a statutory tenant by virtue of section 13 of the Rent Act 1965 or paragraph 6 or 7 of Schedule 1 to the Rent Act 1968.

(6)  Without prejudice to the case where by virtue of sub-paragraph (4) or (5) above, the existing statutory tenant is deemed to be a statutory tenant by succession but is not deemed to be the first successor, within the meaning of Schedule 1 to this Act, paragraphs 5 to 7 of that Schedule shall

not apply where the existing statutory tenant, or the person on whose death he became a statutory tenant, became a statutory tenant by virtue of an exchange under section 17 of the Rent Act 1957 or section 14 of the Rent Act 1968.

3.—(1)  A person who, at any time before the commencement of this Act, became a statutory tenant of a dwelling-house by virtue of—

(a)  section 12(10) of the Increase of Rent and Mortgage Interest (Restrictions) Act 1920 (under which workmen housed in certain dwelling-houses taken over by the Government during the 1914–18 war were to be treated as tenants of the landlords of those houses); and

(b)  section 4 of the Requisitioned Houses and Housing (Amendment) Act 1955 (under which certain requisitioned dwelling-houses were returned to their owners on condition that the owners accepted the existing licensees as statutory tenants),

(and not by way of succession to a previous statutory tenancy) shall be treated for the purposes of this Act as having become the statutory tenant of that dwelling-house on the expiry of a protected tenancy thereof.

(2)  A person who, on or after the commencement of the Rent Act 1965, retained possession of a dwelling-house by virtue of section 20 of that Act (which made transitional provisions in relation to tenancies which expired before the commencement of that Act) shall be deemed to have done so under a statutory tenancy arising on the termination of a tenancy which was a regulated tenancy, and the terms as to rent and otherwise of that tenancy shall be deemed to have been the same, subject to any variation specified by the court, as those of the tenancy mentioned in subsection (1) of that section (that is to say, the tenancy which ended before the commencement of the Rent Act 1965 but which would have been a regulated tenancy if that Act had then been in force).

4.  A statutory tenancy subsisting at the commencement of this Act under section 4 of the Requisitioned Houses and Housing (Amendment) Act 1955 shall be treated, for the purposes of this Act—

(a)  as a regulated tenancy if, by virtue of section 10 of the Rent Act 1965, it fell to be treated as a regulated tenancy after 31st March 1966; and

(b)  in any other case, as a controlled tenancy.

### Tenancies which ended before passing of Counter-Inflation Act 1973 (c 9)

5.—(1)  This paragraph applies where the tenancy of a dwelling-house came to an end at a time before 22nd March 1973 and the tenancy would have been a regulated tenancy, for the purposes of the Rent Act 1968, if section 14 of the Counter-Inflation Act 1973 had been in force at that time.

(2)  If the tenant under the tenancy which came to an end duly retained possession of the dwelling-house after 22nd March 1973 without any order for possession having been made, or after the rescission of such an order, he shall be deemed to have done so under a statutory tenancy arising on the termination of the tenancy which came to an end and, subject to sub-paragraph (6) below, the terms of that tenancy (including the rent) shall be deemed to have been the same as those of the tenancy which came to an end.

(3)  Any statutory tenancy arising by virtue of sub-paragraph (2) above, shall be treated as a statutory tenancy arising on the termination of a protected tenancy which was a regulated tenancy.

(4)  Where Article 10 of the Counter-Inflation (Rents) (England and Wales) Order 1972 applied to the rent under the tenancy, the rent under the tenancy imposed by sub-paragraph (2) above shall be the rent as limited by Article 10.

(5)  Schedule 7 to this Act shall not apply to a statutory tenancy arising under sub-paragraph (2) above.

(6)  The High Court or the county court may by order vary all or any of the terms of the tenancy imposed by sub-paragraph (2) above in any way appearing to the court to be just and equitable (and whether or not in a way authorised by the provisions of sections 46 and 47 of this Act).

(7)  If at 22nd March 1973 the dwelling-house was occupied by a person who would, if the tenancy had been a regulated tenancy, have been the "first-successor" within the meaning of paragraph 4 of Schedule 1 to the Rent Act 1968 (which is re-enacted in Schedule 1 to this Act), sub-paragraphs (2), (4) and (5) above shall apply where that person retained possession as they apply where the tenant retained possession.

### Protected furnished tenancies

6.—(1)  In any case where—

(a)  before 14th August 1974 a dwelling was subject to a tenancy which was a Part VI contract within the meaning of the Rent Act 1968, and

(b)  the dwelling forms part only of a building, and that building is not a purpose-built block of flats within the meaning of section 12 of this Act, and

(c)  on that date the interest of the lessor, within the meaning of Part VI of the Rent Act 1968, under the tenancy—

21. Subject to the provisions of this Act, any reference in any document or enactment to a Part VI letting (within the meaning of Part II of the Housing Finance Act 1972) shall be construed, except in so far as the context otherwise requires, as a reference to a restricted letting (within the meaning of Part II as amended by this Act).

### Transitional provisions from Rent Act 1957

22. If the rent recoverable under a controlled tenancy for any rental period beginning immediately before the commencement of this Act was, by virtue of section 1(4) of the Rent Act 1957 and paragraph 15 of Schedule 16 to the Rent Act 1968, the same as the rent recoverable for the rental period comprising the commencement of the Act of 1957 then, after the commencement of this Act, that rent shall remain the rent recoverable under that tenancy for any rental period for which it is neither increased nor reduced under Part II of this Act (but without prejudice to paragraph 1 of this Schedule).

23. If, immediately before the commencement of this Act, an agreement or determination of a tribunal made or given for the purposes of paragraph (b) of section 24(3) of the Housing Repairs and Rents Act 1954 was deemed, by virtue of paragraph 1 of Schedule 7 to the Rent Act 1957 and paragraph 16 of Schedule 16 to the Rent Act 1968, to be an agreement or determination made under paragraph (c) of section 52(1) of the Act of 1968 then, after the commencement of this Act, that agreement or determination shall, until an agreement or determination is made as is mentioned in paragraph (c) of section 27(1) of this Act, be deemed to be an agreement or determination made as mentioned in paragraph (c) of section 27(1).

24.—(1) If, immediately before the commencement of this Act, the rent limit under a controlled tenancy of a dwelling was increased, by virtue of paragraph 2 of Schedule 7 to the Rent Act 1957 and paragraph 17 of Schedule 16 to the Rent Act 1968, on account of an improvement, or a notice of increase relating to an improvement, completed before the commencement of the Act of 1957, the like increase shall apply after the commencement of this Act to the rent limit under that controlled tenancy.

(2) In sub-paragraph (1) above, "the rent limit", in relation to any time before the commencement of this Act, has the same meaning as in the Rent Act 1968, and in relation to any time after that commencement, has the same meaning as in Part II of this Act.

25.—(1) If, immediately before the commencement of this Act a certificate of a local authority under section 26(1) of the Housing Repairs and Rents Act 1954 or a certificate of a sanitary authority having effect as if it were a certificate under Part II of that Act had effect, by virtue of paragraph 3 of Schedule 7 to the Rent Act 1957 and paragraph 18 of Schedule 16 to the Rent Act 1968, as a certificate of disrepair under Schedule 9 to the Act of 1968, then, after the commencement of this Act, the certificate shall have effect, to the like extent as before that commencement, as if it were a certificate of disrepair under Schedule 6 to this Act.

(2) Where any such certificate ceases to have effect (whether by virtue of an order of the court or in consequence of being cancelled by the local authority) sections 27 and 28 of this Act shall have effect, in relation to any rental period beginning after the date as from which the certificate ceases to have effect as if it had ceased to have effect immediately before the basic rental period (within the meaning of Part II of this Act).

26. Where any increase in the rent recoverable under a controlled tenancy current on 6th July 1957 took effect before that date but after the beginning of the basic rental period (within the meaning of Part II of this Act), section 27 of this Act shall have effect as if for references to the rent recoverable for the basic rental period there were substituted references to the rent which would have been recoverable for that period if the increase had taken effect before the beginning thereof.

### Savings

27.—(1) Notwithstanding the repeal by this Act of the Rent Act 1968 and section 42 of the Housing Finance Act 1972:—
  (a) sections 20(3) and 21 of the Rent Act 1968 (rent limit where no registered rent) shall continue to apply in relation to a regulated tenancy granted before 1st January 1973 if the rent under the tenancy, as varied by any agreement made before that date, exceeded the rent limit under section 20(3) with any adjustment under section 21);
  (b) sections 30 (certain regulated tenancies to be disregarded in determining contractual rent limit) and 35 (duty of landlord to supply statement of rent under previous tenancy) of the Rent Act 1968 shall continue to apply in any case where section 20(3)(a) applies by virtue of this paragraph.

(2) In any case to which section 21 of the Rent Act 1968 applies by virtue of sub-paragraph (1) above, the reference in subsection (5) of that section to the amount expended on the improvement shall be construed as a reference to that amount diminished by the amount of any grant or repayment of the kind mentioned in section 48(2)(a) or (b) of this Act.

(3)  This paragraph shall cease to apply if the landlord and the tenant enter into an agreement which is a rent agreement with a tenant having security of tenure (within the meaning of section 51 of this Act) which complies with the requirements of subsection (4) of that section, or if they provide that this paragraph is not to apply by an agreement conforming with those requirements.

28.—(1)  Section 47 of the Housing Act 1969 (first registration of a rent after issue of qualification certificate) shall continue to have effect as respects an application for the first registration of a rent where the tenancy became a regulated tenancy before the date of the repeal of Part III of that Act by the Housing Finance Act 1972, but with the substitution, for the references to Part IV of the Rent Act 1968 and Schedule 6 to that Act, of references respectively to Part IV of, and Part II of Schedule 11 to, this Act.

(2)  Paragraph 3 of Schedule 17 to this Act shall apply to a conversion under the said Part III as it applies to a conversion under Part VIII of this Act.

(3)  Notwithstanding the said repeal, section 51(2)(a) of the Act of 1969 shall continue to have effect.

(4)  Sections 45 to 47 of this Act shall have effect in relation to a tenancy which has become a regulated tenancy by virtue of the said Part III as if references therein to the last contractual period were references to the last rental period beginning before the tenancy became a regulated tenancy.

29.  Subsections (2) and (5) of section 48 of this Act shall have effect, in relation to any grant paid under section 30 of the Housing (Financial Provisions) Act 1958 (improvement grants) or section 4 of the House Purchase and Housing Act 1959 (standard grants) in pursuance of an application made before 25th August 1969, as they have effect in relation to any of the grants mentioned in those subsections.

30.  Notwithstanding the repeal by this Act of the Rent Act 1968, the amendments made in other enactments ("the amended enactments") by that Act shall, to the extent that they had effect immediately before the coming into force of this Act, continue to have effect subject to any amendment of any of the amended enactments by this Act.

31.  Any registration of a rent made before the commencement of this Act—
 (a)  in the part of the register provided for by section 82 of the Housing Finance Act 1972, and
 (b)  in reliance on subsection (3A) of section 44 of the Rent Act 1968,
shall be as valid, and shall have effect, as if this Act had then been in force.

32.  Notwithstanding the repeal by this Act of paragraphs 20 to 26 of Schedule 16 to the Rent Act 1968 (miscellaneous savings) any enactment which, immediately before the commencement of this Act, had effect by virtue of any of those paragraphs shall continue to have effect; and this Act shall have effect in relation to cases falling within any of those paragraphs as the Act of 1968 had effect immediately before the commencement of this Act.

**[338]**

**NOTES**
 Paras 6, 16: words in square brackets substituted by the Housing Act 1980, s 152(1), Sch 25, Pt I, para 60.
 Para 8: sub-para (3) repealed by the Housing Act 1988, s 140, Sch 18.
 Para 19: spent.
 Administration of Estates Act 1925, s 9: substituted by the Law of Property (Miscellaneous Provisions) Act 1994, s 14; references to the Probate Judge in para 6 should be construed as references to the Public Trustee.
 Public Health Act 1875, s 150; Private Street Works Act 1892: repealed by the Highways Act 1959, s 312(2), Sch 25.
 Increase of Rent and Mortgage Interest (Restrictions) Act 1920: repealed by the Rent Act 1968, s 117(5), Sch 17.
 Housing Repairs and Rents Act 1954, Pt II: repealed by the Rent Act 1957, s 26(3), Sch 8, Pt I and the Rent Act 1968, s 117(5), Sch 17.
 Requisitioned Houses and Housing (Amendment) Act 1955, s 4: repealed by the Statute Law (Repeals) Act 1978.
 Rent Act 1957: ss 1(4), 17 and Sch 7, paras 1–3 repealed by the Rent Act 1968, s 117(5), Sch 17.
 Housing (Financial Provisions) Act 1958, s 30; House Purchase and Housing Act 1959, s 4: repealed by the Housing Act 1969, s 89(3), Sch 10.
 Rent Act 1965, ss 10, 13, 20: repealed by the Rent Act 1968, s 117(5), Sch 17.
 Rent Act 1968: repealed by s 155(5) of, and Sch 25 to, this Act.
 Housing Act 1969, Pt III, ss 47, 51(2)(a): Pt III repealed by the Housing Finance Act 1972, s 108, Sch 11, Pt VI.
 Housing Finance Act 1972: ss 42, 43, 44(5), 45 and 82 repealed by s 155(5) of, and Sch 25 to, this Act.
 Counter-Inflation Act 1973, s 14: repealed by s 155(5) of, and Sch 25 to, this Act and partly replaced by s 4(2), (3) at **[205]**.
 Housing Act 1974, Sch 13, para 33: repealed by s 155(5) of, and Sch 25 to, this Act.
 Rent Act 1974: repealed in relation to England and Wales by s 155(5) of, and Sch 25 to, this Act.
 Housing Rents and Subsidies Act 1975, Schs 2, 3: repealed by s 155(5) of, and Sch 25 to, this Act.
 Defence (General) Regulations 1939, reg 68CB: revoked by SI 1954/1558.

*(Sch 25 contains repeals only.)*

# PROTECTION FROM EVICTION ACT 1977

(1977 c 43)

## ARRANGEMENT OF SECTIONS

### PART I
### UNLAWFUL EVICTION AND HARASSMENT

### PART II
### NOTICE TO QUIT

### PART III
### SUPPLEMENTAL PROVISIONS

*An Act to consolidate section 16 of the Rent Act 1957 and Part III of the Rent Act 1965, and related enactments*

[29 July 1977]

**NOTES**

Transfer of functions: as to the functions of Ministers of the Crown under this Act, so far as exercisable in relation to Wales, being transferred to the National Assembly for Wales, see the National Assembly for Wales (Transfer of Functions) Order 1999, SI 1999/672, art 2, Sch 1.

### PART I
### UNLAWFUL EVICTION AND HARASSMENT

**1 Unlawful eviction and harassment of occupier**

(1) In this section "residential occupier", in relation to any premises, means a person occupying the premises as a residence, whether under a contract or by virtue of any enactment or rule of law giving him the right to remain in occupation or restricting the right of any other person to recover possession of the premises.

(2) If any person unlawfully deprives the residential occupier of any premises of his occupation of the premises or any part thereof, or attempts to do so, he shall be guilty of an offence unless he proves that he believed, and had reasonable cause to believe, that the residential occupier had ceased to reside in the premises.

(3) If any person with intent to cause the residential occupier of any premises—

    (a)    to give up the occupation of the premises or any part thereof; or

    (b)    to refrain from exercising any right or pursuing any remedy in respect of the premises or part thereof;

does acts [likely] to interfere with the peace or comfort of the residential occupier or members of his household, or persistently withdraws or withholds services reasonably required for the occupation of the premises as a residence, he shall be guilty of an offence.

[(3A) Subject to subsection (3B) below, the landlord of a residential occupier or an agent of the landlord shall be guilty of an offence if—

    (a)    he does acts likely to interfere with the peace or comfort of the residential occupier or members of his household, or

    (b)    he persistently withdraws or withholds services reasonably required for the occupation of the premises in question as a residence, and (in either case) he knows, or has reasonable cause to believe, that that conduct is likely to cause the residential occupier to give up the occupation of the whole or part of the premises or to refrain from exercising any right or pursuing any remedy in respect of the whole or part of the premises.

(3B)    A person shall not be guilty of an offence under subsection (3A) above if he proves that he had reasonable grounds for doing the acts or withdrawing or withholding the services in question.

(3C)    In subsection (3A) above "landlord", in relation to a residential occupier of any premises, means the person who, but for—

    (a)    the residential occupier's right to remain in occupation of the premises, or

    (b)    a restriction on the person's right to recover possession of the premises,

would be entitled to occupation of the premises and any superior landlord under whom that person derives title.]

(4)    A person guilty of an offence under this section shall be liable—

    (a)    on summary conviction, to a fine not exceeding [the prescribed sum] or to imprisonment for a term not exceeding 6 months or to both;

    (b)    on conviction on indictment, to a fine or to imprisonment for a term not exceeding 2 years or to both.

(5)    Nothing in this section shall be taken to prejudice any liability or remedy to which a person guilty of an offence thereunder may be subject in civil proceedings.

(6)    Where an offence under this section committed by a body corporate is proved to have been committed with the consent or connivance of, or to be attributable to any neglect on the part of, any director, manager or secretary or other similar officer of the body corporate or any person who was purporting to act in any such capacity, he as well as the body corporate shall be guilty of that offence and shall be liable to be proceeded against and punished accordingly.

**[339]**

---

**NOTES**

Sub-s (3): word in square brackets substituted by the Housing Act 1988, s 29(1), with respect to acts done after 15 January 1989.

Sub-ss (3A)–(3C): inserted by the Housing Act 1988, s 29(2), with respect to acts done after 15 January 1989.

Sub-s (4): words in square brackets substituted by virtue of the Magistrates' Court Act 1980, s 32(2).

---

## 2  Restriction on re-entry without due process of law

Where any premises are let as a dwelling on a lease which is subject to a right of re-entry or forfeiture it shall not be lawful to enforce that right otherwise than by proceedings in the court while any person is lawfully residing in the premises or part of them.

**[340]**

## 3  Prohibition of eviction without due process of law

(1)    Where any premises have been let as a dwelling under a tenancy which is [neither a statutorily protected tenancy nor an excluded tenancy] and—

    (a)    the tenancy (in this section referred to as the former tenancy) has come to an end, but

    (b)    the occupier continues to reside in the premises or part of them,

it shall not be lawful for the owner to enforce against the occupier, otherwise than by proceedings in the court, his right to recover possession of the premises.

(2)    In this section "the occupier", in relation to any premises, means any person lawfully residing in the premises or part of them at the termination of the former tenancy.

[(2A)    Subsections (1) and (2) above apply in relation to any restricted contract (within the meaning of the Rent Act 1977) which—

    (a)    creates a licence; and

    (b)    is entered into after the commencement of section 69 of the Housing Act 1980;

as they apply in relation to a restricted contract which creates a tenancy.]

[(2B)    Subsections (1) and (2) above apply in relation to any premises occupied as a dwelling under a licence, other than an excluded licence, as they apply in relation to premises let as a dwelling under a tenancy, and in those subsections the expressions "let" and "tenancy" shall be construed accordingly.

(2C)    References in the preceding provisions of this section and section 4(2A) below to an excluded tenancy do not apply to—

    (a)    a tenancy entered into before the date on which the Housing Act 1988 came into force, or

    (b)    a tenancy entered into on or after that date but pursuant to a contract made before that date,

but, subject to that, "excluded tenancy" and "excluded licence" shall be construed in accordance with section 3A below.]

(3)   This section shall, with the necessary modifications, apply where the owner's right to recover possession arises on the death of the tenant under a statutory tenancy within the meaning of the Rent Act 1977 or the Rent (Agriculture) Act 1976.

**[341]**

**NOTES**

Sub-s (1): words in square brackets substituted by the Housing Act 1988, s 30(1).
Sub-ss (2A): inserted by the Housing Act 1980, s 69(1).
Sub-ss (2B), (2C): inserted by the Housing Act 1988, s 30(2).

### [3A   Excluded tenancies and licences

(1)   Any reference in this Act to an excluded tenancy or an excluded licence is a reference to a tenancy or licence which is excluded by virtue of any of the following provisions of this section.

(2)   A tenancy or licence is excluded if—
  (a)   under its terms the occupier shares any accommodation with the landlord or licensor; and
  (b)   immediately before the tenancy or licence was granted and also at the time it comes to an end, the landlord or licensor occupied as his only or principal home premises of which the whole or part of the shared accommodation formed part.

(3)   A tenancy or licence is also excluded if—
  (a)   under its terms the occupier shares any accommodation with a member of the family of the landlord or licensor;
  (b)   immediately before the tenancy or licence was granted and also at the time it comes to an end, the member of the family of the landlord or licensor occupied as his only or principal home premises of which the whole or part of the shared accommodation formed part; and
  (c)   immediately before the tenancy or licence was granted and also at the time it comes to an end, the landlord or licensor occupied as his only or principal home premises in the same building as the shared accommodation and that building is not a purpose-built block of flats.

(4)   For the purposes of subsections (2) and (3) above, an occupier shares accommodation with another person if he has the use of it in common with that person (whether or not also in common with others) and any reference in those subsections to shared accommodation shall be construed accordingly, and if, in relation to any tenancy or licence, there is at any time more than one person who is the landlord or licensor, any reference in those subsections to the landlord or licensor shall be construed as a reference to any one of those persons.

(5)   In subsections (2) to (4) above—
  (a)   "accommodation" includes neither an area used for storage nor a staircase, passage, corridor or other means of access;
  (b)   "occupier" means, in relation to a tenancy, the tenant and, in relation to a licence, the licensee; and
  (c)   "purpose-built block of flats" has the same meaning as in Part III of Schedule 1 to the Housing Act 1988;

and section 113 of the Housing Act 1985 shall apply to determine whether a person is for the purposes of subsection (3) above a member of another's family as it applies for the purposes of Part IV of that Act.

(6)   A tenancy or licence is excluded if it was granted as a temporary expedient to a person who entered the premises in question or any other premises as a trespasser (whether or not, before the beginning of that tenancy or licence, another tenancy or licence to occupy the premises or any other premises had been granted to him).

(7)   A tenancy or licence is excluded if—
  (a)   it confers on the tenant or licensee the right to occupy the premises for a holiday only, or
  (b)   it is granted otherwise than for money or money's worth.

[(7A)   A tenancy or licence is excluded if it is granted in order to provide accommodation [under section 4 or Part VI of the Immigration and Asylum Act 1999].]

[(7B)   Section 32 of the Nationality, Immigration and Asylum Act 2002 (accommodation centre: tenure) provides for a resident's licence to occupy an accommodation centre to be an excluded licence.]

[(7C)   A tenancy or licence is excluded if it is granted in order to provide accommodation under the Displaced Persons (Temporary Protection) Regulations 2005.]

(8)   A licence is excluded if it confers rights of occupation in a hostel, within the meaning of the Housing Act 1985, which is provided by—
  (a)   the council of a county, [county borough,] district or London Borough, the Common Council of the City of London, the Council of the Isles of Scilly, the Inner London

Education Authority, [the London Fire and Emergency Planning Authority,] a joint authority within the meaning of the Local Government Act 1985 or a residuary body within the meaning of that Act;

(b) a development corporation within the meaning of the New Towns Act 1981;

(c) the [new towns residuary body];

(d) an urban development corporation established by an order under section 135 of the Local Government, Planning and Land Act 1980;

(e) a housing action trust established under Part III of the Housing Act 1988;

(f) ...

(g) the Housing Corporation ... ;

[(ga) the Secretary of State under section 8 of the Housing Associations Act 1985;]

[(h) a housing trust (within the meaning of the Housing Associations Act 1985) which is a charity or a registered social landlord (within the meaning of the Housing Act 1985); or]

(i) any other person who is, or who belongs to a class of person which is, specified in an order made by the Secretary of State.

[(8A) In subsection (8)(c) above "new towns residuary body" means—

(a) in relation to England, the Homes and Communities Agency so far as exercising functions in relation to anything transferred (or to be transferred) to it as mentioned in section 52(1)(a) to (d) of the Housing and Regeneration Act 2008; and

(b) in relation to Wales, means the Welsh Ministers so far as exercising functions in relation to anything transferred (or to be transferred) to them as mentioned in section 36(1)(a)(i) to (iii) of the New Towns Act 1981.]

(9) The power to make an order under subsection (8)(i) above shall be exercisable by statutory instrument which shall be subject to annulment in pursuance of a resolution of either House of Parliament.]

**[342]**

**NOTES**

Inserted by the Housing Act 1988, s 31.

Sub-s (7A): inserted by the Immigration and Asylum Act 1999, s 169(1), Sch 14, para 73; words in square brackets substituted by the Immigration, Asylum and Nationality Act 2006, s 43(4)(a).

Sub-s (7B): inserted by the Nationality, Immigration and Asylum Act 2002, s 32(5), as from a day to be appointed.

Sub-s (7C): inserted by the Displaced Persons (Temporary Protection) Regulations 2005, SI 2005/1379, Schedule, para 1.

Sub-s (8): words in first pair of square brackets in para (a) inserted by the Local Government (Wales) Act 1994, s 22(2), Sch 8, para 4(1); words in second pair of square brackets in para (a) inserted by the Greater London Authority Act 1999, s 328, Sch 29, Pt I, para 27; words in square brackets in para (c) substituted by the Housing and Regeneration Act 2008, s 56, Sch 8, para 24(1), (2); para (f) and words omitted from para (g) repealed and para (ga) inserted by the Government of Wales Act 1998, ss 131, 140(1), 141, 152, Sch 16, para 2, Sch 18, Pts IV, VI; para (h) substituted by the Housing Act 1996 (Consequential Provisions) Order 1996, SI 1996/2325, art 5, Sch 2, para 7.

Sub-s (8A): inserted by the Housing and Regeneration Act 2008, s 56, Sch 8, para 24(1), (3).

Modification: in sub-s (8)(g) the reference to the Housing Corporation shall be treated as if it were a reference to the Regulator of Social Housing: see the Transfer of Housing Corporation Functions (Modifications and Transitional Provisions) Order 2008, SI 2008/2839, arts 1(2), 3, 6, Schedule.

Orders: the Protection from Eviction (Excluded Licences) Order 1991, SI 1991/1943.

## 4 Special provisions for agricultural employees

(1) This section shall apply where the tenant under the former tenancy (within the meaning of section 3 of this Act) occupied the premises under the terms of his employment as a person employed in agriculture, as defined in section 1 of the Rent (Agriculture) Act 1976, but is not a statutory tenant as defined in that Act.

(2) In this section "the occupier", in relation to any premises, means—

(a) the tenant under the former tenancy; or

(b) the [surviving spouse or surviving civil partner] of the tenant under the former tenancy residing with him at his death or, if the former tenant leaves no such [surviving spouse or surviving civil partner], any member of his family residing with him at his death.

[(2A) In accordance with section 3(2B) above, any reference in subsections (1) and (2) above to the tenant under the former tenancy includes a reference to the licensee under a licence (other than an excluded licence) which has come to an end (being a licence to occupy premises as a dwelling); and in the following provisions of this section the expressions "tenancy" and "rent" and any other expressions referable to a tenancy shall be construed accordingly.]

(3) Without prejudice to any power of the court apart from this section to postpone the operation or suspend the execution of an order for possession, if in proceedings by the owner against the occupier the court makes an order for the possession of the premises the court may suspend the execution of the order on such terms and conditions, including conditions as to the payment by the occupier of arrears of rent, mesne profits and otherwise as the court thinks reasonable.

(4)   Where the order for possession is made within the period of 6 months beginning with the date when the former tenancy came to an end, then, without prejudice to any powers of the court under the preceding provisions of this section or apart from this section to postpone the operation or suspend the execution of the order for a longer period, the court shall suspend the execution of the order for the remainder of the said period of 6 months unless the court—

    (a)    is satisfied either—

        (i)    that other suitable accommodation is, or will within that period be made, available to the occupier; or

        (ii)    that the efficient management of any agricultural land or the efficient carrying on of any agricultural operations would be seriously prejudiced unless the premises are available for occupation by a person employed or to be employed by the owner; or

        (iii)    that greater hardship (being hardship in respect of matters other than the carrying on of such a business as aforesaid) would be caused by the suspension of the order until the end of that period than by its execution within that period; or

        (iv)    that the occupier, or any person residing or lodging with the occupier, has been causing damage to the premises or has been guilty of conduct which is a nuisance or annoyance to persons occupying other premises; and

    (b)    considers that it would be reasonable not to suspend the execution of the order for the remainder of that period.

(5)   Where the court suspends the execution of an order for possession under subsection (4) above it shall do so on such terms and conditions, including conditions as to the payment by the occupier of arrears of rent, mesne profits and otherwise as the court thinks reasonable.

(6)   A decision of the court not to suspend the execution of the order under subsection (4) above shall not prejudice any other power of the court to postpone the operation or suspend the execution of the order for the whole or part of the period of 6 months mentioned in that subsection.

(7)   Where the court has, under the preceding provisions of this section, suspended the execution of an order for possession, it may from time to time vary the period of suspension or terminate it and may vary any terms or conditions imposed by virtue of this section.

(8)   In considering whether or how to exercise its powers under subsection (3) above, the court shall have regard to all the circumstances and, in particular, to—

    (a)    whether other suitable accommodation is or can be made available to the occupier;

    (b)    whether the efficient management of any agricultural land or the efficient carrying on of any agricultural operations would be seriously prejudiced unless the premises were available for occupation by a person employed or to be employed by the owner; and

    (c)    whether greater hardship would be caused by the suspension of the execution of the order than by its execution without suspension or further suspension.

(9)   Where in proceedings for the recovery of possession of the premises the court makes an order for possession but suspends the execution of the order under this section, it shall make no order for costs, unless it appears to the court, having regard to the conduct of the owner or of the occupier, that there are special reasons for making such an order.

(10)   Where, in the case of an order for possession of the premises to which subsection (4) above applies, the execution of the order is not suspended under that subsection or, the execution of the order having been so suspended, the suspension is terminated, then, if it is subsequently made to appear to the court that the failure to suspend the execution of the order or, as the case may be, the termination of the suspension was—

    (a)    attributable to the provisions of paragraph (a)(ii) of subsection (4), and

    (b)    due to misrepresentation or concealment of material facts by the owner of the premises,

the court may order the owner to pay to the occupier such sum as appears sufficient as compensation for damage or loss sustained by the occupier as a result of that failure or termination.

**[343]**

---

**NOTES**

Sub-s (2): words in square brackets substituted by the Civil Partnership Act 2004, s 81, Sch 8, para 15.

Sub-s (2A): inserted by the Housing Act 1988, s 30(3).

---

## PART II
## NOTICE TO QUIT

### 5   Validity of notices to quit

(1)   [Subject to subsection (1B) below] no notice by a landlord or a tenant to quit any premises let (whether before or after the commencement of this Act) as a dwelling shall be valid unless—

    (a)    it is in writing and contains such information as may be prescribed, and

    (b)    it is given not less than 4 weeks before the date on which it is to take effect.

[(1A)   Subject to subsection (1B) below, no notice by a licensor or a licensee to determine a periodic licence to occupy premises as a dwelling (whether the licence was granted before or after the passing of this Act) shall be valid unless—
(a)   it is in writing and contains such information as may be prescribed, and
(b)   it is given not less than 4 weeks before the date on which it is to take effect.

(1B)   Nothing in subsection (1) or subsection (1A) above applies to—
(a)   premises let on an excluded tenancy which is entered into on or after the date on which the Housing Act 1988 came into force unless it is entered into pursuant to a contract made before that date; or
(b)   premises occupied under an excluded licence.]

(2)   In this section "prescribed" means prescribed by regulations made by the Secretary of State by statutory instrument, and a statutory instrument containing any such regulations shall be subject to annulment in pursuance of a resolution of either House of Parliament.

(3)   Regulations under this section may make different provision in relation to different descriptions of lettings and different circumstances.

**[344]**

**NOTES**
Sub-s (1): words in square brackets inserted by the Housing Act 1988, s 32(1).
Sub-ss (1A), (1B): inserted by the Housing Act 1988, s 32(2).
Regulations: the Notices to Quit etc (Prescribed Information) Regulations 1988, SI 1988/2201 at **[3078]**.

## PART III
## SUPPLEMENTAL PROVISIONS

### 6   Prosecution of offences

Proceedings for an offence under this Act may be instituted by any of the following authorities—
(a)   councils of districts and London boroughs;
[(aa)   councils of Welsh counties and county boroughs;]
(b)   the Common Council of the City of London;
(c)   the Council of the Isles of Scilly.

**[345]**

**NOTES**
Para (aa): inserted by the Local Government (Wales) Act 1994, s 22(2), Sch 8, para 4(2).

### 7   Service of notices

(1)   If for the purpose of any proceedings (whether civil or criminal) brought or intended to be brought under this Act, any person serves upon—
(a)   any agent of the landlord named as such in the rent book or other similar document, or
(b)   the person who receives the rent of the dwelling,
a notice in writing requiring the agent or other person to disclose to him the full name and place of abode or place of business of the landlord, that agent or other person shall forthwith comply with the notice.

(2)   If any agent or other person as is referred to in subsection (1) above fails or refuses forthwith to comply with a notice served on him under that subsection, he shall be liable on summary conviction to a fine not exceeding [level 4 on the standard scale] unless he shows to the satisfaction of the court that he did not know, and could not with reasonable diligence have ascertained, such of the facts required by the notice to be disclosed as were not disclosed by him.

(3)   In this section "landlord" includes—
(a)   any person from time to time deriving title under the original landlord,
(b)   in relation to any dwelling-house, any person other than the tenant who is or, but for Part VII of the Rent Act 1977 would be, entitled to possession of the dwelling-house, and
(c)   any person who, ... grants to another the right to occupy the dwelling in question as a residence and any person directly or indirectly deriving title from the grantor.

**[346]**

**NOTES**
Sub-s (2): words in square brackets substituted by virtue of the Criminal Justice Act 1982, ss 39, 46, Sch 3.
Sub-s (3): words omitted repealed by the Housing Act 1988, s 140, Sch 17, Pt I, para 26, Sch 18.

### 8   Interpretation

(1)   In this Act "statutorily protected tenancy" means—

(a)    a protected tenancy within the meaning of the Rent Act 1977 or a tenancy to which Part I of the Landlord and Tenant Act 1954 applies;

(b)    a protected occupancy or statutory tenancy as defined in the Rent (Agriculture) Act 1976;

(c)    a tenancy to which Part II of the Landlord and Tenant Act 1954 applies;

(d)    a tenancy of an agricultural holding within the meaning of the [Agricultural Holdings Act 1986] [which is a tenancy in relation to which that Act applies];

[(e)    an assured tenancy or assured agricultural occupancy under Part I of the Housing Act 1988;]

[(f)    a tenancy to which Schedule 10 of the Local Government and Housing Act 1989 applies;]

[(g)    a farm business tenancy within the meaning of the Agricultural Tenancies Act 1995].

(2)   For the purposes of Part I of this Act a person who, under the terms of his employment, had exclusive possession of any premises other than as a tenant shall be deemed to have been a tenant and the expressions "let" and "tenancy" shall be construed accordingly.

(3)   In Part I of this Act "the owner", in relation to any premises, means the person who, as against the occupier, is entitled to possession thereof.

[(4)   In this Act "excluded tenancy" and "excluded licence" have the meaning assigned by section 3A of this Act.

(5)   If, on or after the date on which the Housing Act 1988 came into force, the terms of an excluded tenancy or excluded licence entered into before that date are varied, then—

(a)    if the variation affects the amount of the rent which is payable under the tenancy or licence, the tenancy or licence shall be treated for the purposes of sections 3(2C) and 5(1B) above as a new tenancy or licence entered into at the time of the variation; and

(b)    if the variation does not affect the amount of the rent which is so payable, nothing in this Act shall affect the determination of the question whether the variation is such as to give rise to a new tenancy or licence.

(6)   Any reference in subsection (5) above to a variation affecting the amount of the rent which is payable under a tenancy or licence does not include a reference to—

(a)    a reduction or increase effected under Part III or Part VI of the Rent Act 1977 (rents under regulated tenancies and housing association tenancies), section 78 of that Act (power of rent tribunal in relation to restricted contracts) or sections 11 to 14 of the Rent (Agriculture) Act 1976; or

(b)    a variation which is made by the parties and has the effect of making the rent expressed to be payable under the tenancy or licence the same as a rent for the dwelling which is entered in the register under Part IV or section 79 of the Rent Act 1977.]

**[347]**

---

NOTES

Sub-s (1): words in first pair of square brackets in para (d) substituted by the Agricultural Holdings Act 1986, s 100, Sch 14, para 61; words in second pair of square brackets in para (d) inserted and para (g) added by the Agricultural Tenancies Act 1995, s 40, Schedule, para 29; para (e) added by the Housing Act 1988, s 33(1), (2); para (f) added by the Local Government and Housing Act 1989, s 194(1), Sch 11, para 54.

Sub-ss (4)–(6): added by the Housing Act 1988, s 33(1), (3).

---

## 9   The court for purposes of Part I

(1)   The court for the purposes of Part I of this Act shall, subject to this section, be—

(a)    the county court, in relation to premises with respect to which the county court has for the time being jurisdiction in actions for the recovery of land; and

(b)    the High Court, in relation to other premises.

(2)   Any powers of a county court in proceedings for the recovery of possession of any premises in the circumstances mentioned in section 3(1) of this Act may be exercised with the leave of the judge by any registrar of the court, except in so far as rules of court otherwise provide.

(3)   Nothing in this Act shall affect the jurisdiction of the High Court in proceedings to enforce a lessor's right of re-entry or forfeiture or to enforce a mortgagee's right of possession in a case where the former tenancy was not binding on the mortgagee.

(4)   Nothing in this Act shall affect the operation of—

(a)    section 59 of the Pluralities Act 1838;

(b)    section 19 of the Defence Act 1842;

(c)    section 6 of the Lecturers and Parish Clerks Act 1844;

(d)    paragraph 3 of Schedule 1 to the Sexual Offences Act 1956; or

(e)    section 13 of the Compulsory Purchase Act 1965.

**[348]**

**NOTES**

Lecturers and Parish Clerks Act 1844, s 6: repealed by the Church of England (Miscellaneous Provisions) Measure 1992, s 17(2), Sch 4, Pt I.

## 10 Application to Crown

In so far as this Act requires the taking of proceedings in the court for the recovery of possession or confers any powers on the court it shall (except in the case of section 4(10)) be binding on the Crown.

[349]

## 11 Application to Isles of Scilly

(1)   In its application to the Isles of Scilly, this Act (except in the case of section 5) shall have effect subject to such exceptions, adaptations and modifications as the Secretary of State may by order direct.

(2)   The power to make an order under this section shall be exercisable by statutory instrument which shall be subject to annulment, in pursuance of a resolution of either House of Parliament.

(3)   An order under this section may be varied or revoked by a subsequent order.

[350]

## 12 Consequential amendments, etc

(1)   Schedule 1 to this Act contains amendments consequential on the provisions of this Act.

(2)   Schedule 2 to this Act contains transitional provisions and savings.

(3)   The enactments mentioned in Schedule 3 to this Act are hereby repealed to the extent specified in the third column of that Schedule.

(4)   The inclusion in this Act of any express savings, transitional provisions or amendment shall not be taken to affect the operation in relation to this Act of section 38 of the Interpretation Act 1889 (which relates to the effect of repeals).

[351]

**NOTES**

Interpretation Act 1889, s 38: repealed by the Interpretation Act 1978, s 25, Sch 3, and replaced by ss 16(1), 17(2)(a) of, and Sch 2, para 3 to, that Act.

## 13 Short title, etc

(1)   This Act may be cited as the Protection from Eviction Act 1977.

(2)   This Act shall come into force on the expiry of the period of one month beginning with the date on which it is passed.

(3)   This Act does not extend to Scotland or Northern Ireland.

(4)   References in this Act to any enactment are references to that enactment as amended, and include references thereto as applied by any other enactment including, except where the context otherwise requires, this Act.

[352]

## SCHEDULES

(*Sch 1, para 1 amends the Reserve and Auxiliary Forces (Protection of Civil Interests) Act 1951, s 22; para 2 repealed by the County Courts Act 1984, s 148(3), Sch 4; para 3 amends the Caravan Sites Act 1968, s 5; para 4 amends the Rent (Agriculture) Act 1976, Sch 5 at* [200].)

## SCHEDULE 2
### TRANSITIONAL PROVISIONS AND SAVINGS

Section 12

1.—(1)   In so far as anything done under an enactment repealed by this Act could have been done under a corresponding provision of this Act, it shall not be invalidated by the repeal but shall have effect as if done under that provision.

(2)   Sub-paragraph (1) above applies, in particular, to any regulation, rule, notice or order.

2.   The enactments mentioned in Schedule 6 to the Rent Act 1965 shall, notwithstanding the repeal of that Act by this Act, continue to have effect as they had effect immediately before the commencement of this Act.

[353]

PART I
STATUTES

**NOTES**

Rent Act 1965, Sch 6: repealed by s 12 of, and Sch 3 to, this Act.

*(Sch 3 contains repeals only.)*

# LEASEHOLD REFORM ACT 1979

## (1979 c 44)

*An Act to provide further protection, for a tenant in possession claiming to acquire the freehold under the Leasehold Reform Act 1967, against artificial inflation of the price he has to pay*

[4 April 1979]

## 1 Price to tenant on enfranchisement

(1)   As against a tenant in possession claiming under section 8 of the Leasehold Reform Act 1967, the price payable on a conveyance for giving effect to that section cannot be made less favourable by reference to a transaction since 15th February 1979 involving the creation or transfer of an interest superior to (whether or not preceding) his own, or an alteration since that date of the terms on which such an interest is held.

(2)   References in this section to a tenant claiming are to his giving notice under section 8 of his desire to have the freehold.

(3)   Subsection (1) applies to any claim made on or after the commencement date (which means the date of the passing of this Act), and also to a claim made before that date unless by then the price has been determined by agreement or otherwise.

**[354]**

## 2 Citation and extent

(1)   This Act may be cited as the Leasehold Reform Act 1979; and the 1967 Act and this Act may be cited together as the Leasehold Reform Acts 1967 and 1979.

(2)   This Act extends to England and Wales only.

**[355]**

**NOTES**

1967 Act: the Leasehold Reform Act 1967 at **[78]** et seq.

# HOUSING ACT 1980

## (1980 c 51)

### ARRANGEMENT OF SECTIONS

### PART II
### PRIVATE SECTOR TENANTS

*Protected shorthold tenancies*

*An Act to give security of tenure, and the right to buy their homes, to tenants of local authorities and other bodies; to make other provision with respect to those and other tenants; to amend the law about housing finance in the public sector; to make other provision with respect to housing; to restrict the discretion of the court in making orders for possession of land; and for connected purposes*

[8 August 1980]

**NOTES**

Transfer of functions: as to the functions of Ministers of the Crown under this Act, so far as exercisable in relation to Wales, being transferred to the National Assembly for Wales, see the National Assembly for Wales (Transfer of Functions) Order 1999, SI 1999/672, art 2, Sch 1.

**1–50**    (*Repealed by the Housing (Consequential Provisions) Act 1985, s 3, Sch 1, Pt I.*)

## PART II
## PRIVATE SECTOR TENANTS

*Protected shorthold tenancies*

### 51 Preliminary

Sections 53 to 55 below modify the operation of the 1977 Act in relation to protected shorthold tenancies as defined in section 52 below.

**[356]**

---

**NOTES**

1977 Act: Rent Act 1977.

---

**52** (*Repealed by the Housing Act 1988, s 140(2), Sch 18, except in relation to any tenancy entered into before 15 January 1989, or any tenancy which, having regard to s 34 of that Act at* **[765]**, *can be a protected shorthold tenancy.*)

### 53 Right of tenant to terminate protected shorthold tenancy

(1) A protected shorthold tenancy may be brought to an end (by virtue of this section and notwithstanding anything in the terms of the tenancy) before the expiry of the term certain by notice in writing of the appropriate length given by the tenant to the landlord; and the appropriate length of the notice is—

    (a)   one month if the term certain is two years or less; and

    (b)   three months if it is more than two years.

(2) Any agreement relating to a protected shorthold tenancy (whether or not contained in the instrument creating the tenancy) shall be void in so far as it purports to impose any penalty or disability on the tenant in the event of his giving a notice under this section.

**[357]**

### 54 Subletting or assignment

(1) Where the whole or part of a dwelling-house let under a protected shorthold tenancy has been sublet at any time during the continuous period specified in subsection (3) below, and, during that period, the landlord becomes entitled, as against the tenant, to possession of the dwelling-house, he shall also be entitled to possession against the sub-tenant and section 137 of the 1977 Act shall not apply.

(2) A protected shorthold tenancy of a dwelling-house and any protected tenancy of the same dwelling-house granted during the continuous period specified in subsection (3) below shall not be capable of being assigned, [except in pursuance of an order under—

    (a)   *section 24* of the Matrimonial Causes Act 1973 (property adjustment orders in connection with matrimonial proceedings),

    (b)   section 17(1) of the Matrimonial and Family Proceedings Act 1984 (property adjustment orders after overseas divorce, &c), ...

    (c)   paragraph 1 of Schedule 1 to the Children Act 1989 (orders for financial relief against parents)][, or

    (d)   Part 2 of Schedule 5, or paragraph 9(2) or (3) of Schedule 7, to the Civil Partnership Act 2004 (property adjustment orders in connection with civil partnership proceedings or after overseas dissolution of civil partnership, etc)].

(3) The continuous period mentioned in subsections (1) and (2) above is the period beginning with the grant of the protected shorthold tenancy and continuing until either—

    (a)   no person is in possession of the dwelling-house as a protected or statutory tenant; or

    (b)   a protected tenancy of the dwelling-house is granted to a person who is not, immediately before the grant, in possession of the dwelling-house as a protected or statutory tenant.

**[358]**

---

**NOTES**

Sub-s (2): words in first pair of square brackets substituted by the Housing Act 1996, s 222, Sch 18, Pt III, para 7; for the words in italics in para (a) there are substituted the words "sections 23A or 24" by the Family Law Act 1996, s 66(1), Sch 8, Pt I, para 29, as from a day to be appointed; word omitted from para (b) repealed and para (d) and word "or" immediately preceding it inserted by the Civil Partnership Act 2004, ss 81, 261(4), Sch 8, para 16, Sch 30.

1977 Act: Rent Act 1977.

---

### 55 Orders for possession

(1) ...

(2) If, in proceedings for possession under Case 19 set out above, the court is of opinion that, notwithstanding that the condition of paragraph (b) or (c) of section 52(1) above is not satisfied, it is

just and equitable to make an order for possession, it may treat the tenancy under which the dwelling-house was let as a protected shorthold tenancy.

[359]

**NOTES**
Sub-s (1): amends the Rent Act 1977, Sch 15, Pt II at [330].

**56, 56A–56D, 57, 58**  (*Repealed by the Housing Act 1988, ss 1(4), 140(2), Sch 18, as from 15 January 1989 except in relation to a tenancy to which, by virtue of s 37(2) of that Act at [768], s 1(3) of that Act at [729], does not apply.*)

*Rents*

**59, 60**  (*S 59(1) repealed by the Housing Act 1988, s 140(2), Sch 18; s 59(2) substitutes the Rent Act 1977, s 67(2) at [246]; s 59(3) spent; s 60 repealed by the Housing Act 1988, s 140(2), Sch 18.*)

**61  Effect of registration of rent etc**

(1)–(7)  ...

(8)  Subsections (1) to (5) above do not apply in any case where, on the determination or confirmation of a rent by the rent officer, the rent determined by him is registered, or his confirmation is noted in the register, before the commencement of this section.

[360]

**NOTES**
Sub-s (1): substitutes the Rent Act 1977, s 72 at [251].
Sub-s (2): amends the Rent (Agriculture) Act 1976, s 13 at [167].
Sub-s (3)–(5), (7): amend the Rent Act 1977, ss 45, 67, 87, 96, Sch 11, para 9 at [227], [246], [268], [274], [327].
Sub-s (6): amends the Rent (Agriculture) Act 1976, Sch 6, and the Rent Act 1977, Sch 8.

**62, 63**  (*S 62 amends the Rent Act 1977, s 73 at [253]; s 63 repeals ss 48, 50 of that Act.*)

*Conversion of controlled tenancies*

**64  Conversion of controlled tenancies into regulated tenancies**

(1)  At the commencement of this section every controlled tenancy shall cease to be a controlled tenancy and become a regulated tenancy, except in the case mentioned in subsection (2) below.

(2)  If the controlled tenancy is one to which Part I of the Landlord and Tenant Act 1954 would apply, apart from section 24(2) of the 1977 Act, or would so apply if it were a tenancy within the meaning of the Act of 1954, it shall, when it ceases to be a controlled tenancy, be treated as a tenancy continuing by virtue of section 24 of the Act of 1954 after the expiry of a term of years certain.

[361]

**NOTES**
1977 Act: Rent Act 1977.

*Regulated tenancies*

**65  Resident landlords**

(1)–(5)  ...

(6)  Subject to subsection (7) below, this section, except subsection (1), applies to tenancies granted before as well as those granted after the commencement of this section.

(7)  In any case where the interest of the landlord under a tenancy vested in the personal representatives (acting in that capacity) of a person who died before the commencement of this section, Schedule 2 to the 1977 Act applies as if paragraph 2A had not been inserted and paragraph 1(c)(i) had not been repealed.

[362]

**NOTES**
Sub-ss (1)–(5): amend the Rent Act 1977, s 12(1), Sch 2, Pt I at [214], [322].
1977 Act: Rent Act 1977.

**66  Amendment of Cases 11 and 12 of Schedule 15 to Rent Act 1977**

(1), (2)  ...

(3)    There are inserted in Schedule 15, as a new Part V, the provisions set out in Schedule 7 to this Act; ...

(4)    ...

(5)    Subject to subsection (6) below, Cases 11 and 12, as amended by this section, apply to tenancies granted before, as well as those granted after, the commencement of this section; and nothing in this section invalidates a notice that possession might be recovered under Case 11 or Case 12 which was duly given to a tenant before then.

(6)    Paragraphs (c) and (d) of Part V of Schedule 15 do not apply to Case 11 if the tenancy was granted, and the owner died, before the commencement of this section; and paragraph (d) does not apply to Case 12 in any such case.

**[363]**

**NOTES**
Sub-ss (1), (2), (4): amend the Rent Act 1977, Sch 15, Pt II at **[330]**.
Sub-s (3): words omitted amend the Rent Act 1977, s 98 at **[276]**.

**67–69**    (*S 67 amends the Rent Act 1977, Sch 15, Pt II at* **[330]**; *s 68 in part spent, remainder substitutes ss 52, 57(3) of that Act at* **[232]**, **[234]**; *s 69(1) inserts the Protection from Eviction Act 1977, s 3(2A) at* **[341]**; *s 69(2), (3) inserts the Rent Act 1977, ss 102A, 106A at* **[281]**, **[286]**; *s 69(4) substitutes s 12(2), (3) of that Act at* **[214]**.)

*Restricted contracts*

**70   Reconsideration of registered rents under Part V of Rent Act 1977**

(1)    ...

(2)    This section does not apply in any case where the date from which the period during which no application for registration can be made is to be calculated falls before the commencement of this section.

**[364]**

**NOTES**
Sub-s (1): amends the Rent Act 1977, s 80(2) at **[259]**.

**71**    (*Sub-s (1) inserts the Rent Act 1977, s 81A at* **[262]**; *sub-s (2) amends Sch 10 to that Act at* **[326]**.)

**72   Functions of rent tribunals**

(1)    Rent tribunals, as constituted for the purposes of the 1977 Act, are hereby abolished ...

(2)    As from the commencement of this section the functions which, under the 1977 Act, are conferred on rent tribunals shall be carried out by rent assessment committees.

(3)    A rent assessment committee shall, when constituted to carry out functions so conferred, be known as a rent tribunal.

**[365]**

**NOTES**
Sub-s (1): words omitted repeal the Rent Act 1977, s 76.
1977 Act: Rent Act 1977.

*Miscellaneous*

**73   Dwellings forming part of Crown Estate or belonging to Duchies**

(1)–(4)    ...

(5)    Schedule 8 to this Act has effect for making certain provisions consequential on this section.

**[366]**

**NOTES**
Sub-s (1): substitutes the Rent Act 1977, s 13 at **[215]**.
Sub-s (2): repealed by the Housing Act 1988, s 140(2), Sch 18.
Sub-s (3): substitutes the Rent (Agriculture) Act 1976, s 5(1) at **[159]**.
Sub-s (4): amends the Landlord and Tenant Act 1954, s 21 at **[58]**, and s 56.

**74 Housing association and housing trust tenancies under Rent Act 1977**

(1), (2)   ...

(3)    Schedule 9 to this Act has effect for the purpose of supplementing this section.

[367]

**NOTES**
Sub-ss (1), (2): amend the Rent Act 1977, s 15 at [217].

**75** *(Sub-ss (1)–(3) amend the Rent Act 1977, s 100 at* [278]*; sub-ss (4)–(7) amend the Rent (Agriculture) Act 1976, s 7 at* [161]*.)*

**76 Statutory tenancies by succession**

(1)–(3)   ...

(4)    The amendments made by this section have effect only in relation to deaths occurring after the commencement of the subsection concerned.

[368]

**NOTES**
Sub-s (1): substitutes the Rent Act 1977, Sch 1, para 2 at [320].
Sub-s (2): repealed by the Housing Act 1988, s 140(2), Sch 18.
Sub-s (3): amends the Rent (Agriculture) Act 1976, ss 3, 4 at [157], [158].

**77   Amendment of Part VI of Rent Act 1977**

Part VI of the 1977 Act (rent limit for dwellings let by housing associations, housing trusts and the Housing Corporation) is amended in accordance with the provisions of Schedule 10 to this Act.

[369]

**NOTES**
1977 Act: Rent Act 1977.

**78, 79**    *(S 78 in part spent, remainder amends the Rent Act 1977, s 127 at* [297]*; s 79 amends s 128(1) of that Act at* [298]*.)*

PART III
TENANT'S REPAIRS AND IMPROVEMENTS

**80**    *(Repealed by the Housing (Consequential Provisions) Act 1985, s 3, Sch 1, Pt I.)*

**81   Tenant's improvements**

(1)    The following provisions of this section have effect with respect to ... , protected tenancies and statutory tenancies in place of section 19(2) of the Landlord and Tenant Act 1927.

(2)    It is by virtue of this section a term of every such tenancy that the tenant will not make any improvement without the written consent of the landlord.

(3)    The consent required by virtue of subsection (2) above is not to be unreasonably withheld and, if unreasonably withheld, shall be treated as given.

(4)    Subsections (1) to (3) above do not apply in any case where the tenant has been given a notice—

(a)    of a kind mentioned in one of Cases 11 to 18 and 20 in Schedule 15 to the 1977 Act (notice that possession might be recovered under that Case); or

(b)    under section 52(1)(b) of this Act (notice that a tenancy is to be a protected shorthold tenancy);

unless the tenant proves that, at the time when the landlord gave the notice, it was unreasonable for the landlord to expect to be able in due course to recover possession of the dwelling-house under that Case or, as the case may be, Case 19 of Schedule 15 (added by section 55 of this Act).

(5)    In Part I, and in this Part, of this Act "improvement" means any alteration in, or addition to, a dwelling-house and includes—

(a)    any addition to, or alteration in, landlord's fixtures and fittings and any addition or alteration connected with the provision of any services to a dwelling-house;

(b)    the erection of any wireless or television aerial; and

(c)    the carrying out of external decoration;

but paragraph (c) above does not apply in relation to a protected or statutory tenancy if the landlord is under an obligation to carry out external decoration or to keep the exterior of the dwelling-house in repair.

[370]

PART I
STATUTES

## 82 Provisions as to consents required by section 81

(1)   If any question arises whether the withholding of a consent required by virtue of section 81 above was unreasonable it is for the landlord to show that it was not; and in determining that question the court shall, in particular, have regard to the extent to which the improvement would be likely—

(a)   to make the dwelling-house, or any other premises, less safe for occupiers;

(b)   to cause the landlord to incur expenditure which it would be unlikely to incur if the improvement were not made; or

(c)   to reduce the price which the dwelling-house would fetch if sold on the open market or the rent which the landlord would be able to charge on letting the dwelling-house.

(2)   A consent required by virtue of section 81 may be validly given notwithstanding that it follows, instead of preceding, the action requiring it and may be given subject to a condition.

(3)   Where the tenant has applied in writing for a consent which is required by virtue of section 81 then—

(a)   if the landlord refuses to give the consent it shall give to the tenant a written statement of the reasons why the consent was refused; and

(b)   if the landlord neither gives nor refuses to give the consent within a reasonable time, the consent shall be taken to have been withheld, and if the landlord gives the consent but subject to an unreasonable condition, the consent shall be taken to have been unreasonably withheld.

(4)   If any question arises whether a condition attached to a consent was reasonable, it is for the landlord to show that it was.

[371]

## 83 Conditional consent to tenant's improvements

Any failure by ... a protected tenant or a statutory tenant to satisfy any reasonable condition imposed by his landlord in giving consent to an improvement which the tenant proposes to make, or has made, shall be treated ... for the purposes of the 1977 Act as a breach by the tenant of an obligation of his tenancy or, as the case may be, of an obligation of the previous protected tenancy which is applicable to the statutory tenancy.

[372]

## 84 Exclusion of certain housing associations from Part III

This Part of this Act does not apply in relation to a housing association which falls within paragraph (d) of section 15(3) of the 1977 Act (certain societies registered under the Industrial and Provident Societies Act 1965).

[373]

## 85 Interpretation and application of Part III

(1)   In this Part of this Act any expression used ... in the 1977 Act has the same meaning as ... that Act.

(2)   This Part of this Act applies to tenancies granted before as well as tenancies granted after the commencement of this Part of this Act.

[374]

## PART IV
## JURISDICTION AND PROCEDURE

### 86 Jurisdiction of county court and rules of procedure

[(1)   A county court has jurisdiction to determine any question arising under Part III of this Act (tenant's improvements) and to entertain any proceedings brought thereunder.

(2)   The jurisdiction conferred by this section includes jurisdiction to entertain proceedings on any question whether any consent required by section 81 was withheld or unreasonably withheld, notwithstanding that no other relief is sought than a declaration.]

(3)   *If a person takes proceedings in the High Court which, by virtue of this section, he could have taken in the county court he is not entitled to recover any costs.*

(4)–(6)   ...

[375]

**NOTES**
   Sub-ss (1), (2): substituted by the Housing (Consequential Provisions) Act 1985, s 4, Sch 2, para 44(1), (2).
   Sub-s (3): repealed by the Courts and Legal Services Act 1990, s 125(7), Sch 20, as from a day to be appointed.
   Sub-ss (4)–(6): repealed by the Constitutional Reform Act 2005, ss 15(1), 146, Sch 4, Pt 1, para 104, Sch 18, Pt 2.

### 87   *(Repealed by the Housing (Consequential Provisions) Act 1985, s 3, Sch 1, Pt I.)*

### 88 Discretion of court in certain proceedings for possession

(1)   Where, under the terms of a rental purchase agreement, a person has been let into possession of a dwelling-house and, on the termination of the agreement or of his right to possession under it, proceedings are brought for the possession of the dwelling-house, the court may—
   (a)   adjourn the proceedings; or
   (b)   on making an order for the possession of the dwelling-house, stay or suspend execution of the order or postpone the date of possession;
for such period or periods as the court thinks fit.

(2)   On any such adjournment, stay, suspension or postponement the court may impose such conditions with regard to payments by the person in possession in respect of his continued occupation of the dwelling-house and such other conditions as the court thinks fit.

(3)   The court may revoke or from time to time vary any condition imposed by virtue of this section.

(4)   In this section "rental purchase agreement" means an agreement for the purchase of a dwelling-house (whether freehold or leasehold property) under which the whole or part of the purchase price is to be paid in three or more instalments and the completion of the purchase is deferred until the whole or a specified part of the purchase price has been paid.

(5)   This section extends to proceedings for the possession of a dwelling-house which were begun before the commencement of this section unless an order for the possession of the dwelling-house was made in the proceedings and executed before the commencement of this section.

[376]

### 89 Restriction on discretion of court in making orders for possession of land

(1)   Where a court makes an order for the possession of any land in a case not falling within the exceptions mentioned in subsection (2) below, the giving up of possession shall not be postponed (whether by the order or any variation, suspension or stay of execution) to a date later than fourteen days after the making of the order, unless it appears to the court that exceptional hardship would be caused by requiring possession to be given up by that date; and shall not in any event be postponed to a date later than six weeks after the making of the order.

(2)   The restrictions in subsection (1) above do not apply if—
   (a)   the order is made in an action by a mortgagee for possession; or
   (b)   the order is made in an action for forfeiture of a lease; or
   (c)   the court had power to make the order only if it considered it reasonable to make it; or
   (d)   the order relates to a dwelling-house which is the subject of a restricted contract (within the meaning of section 19 of the 1977 Act); or
   (e)   the order is made in proceedings brought as mentioned in section 88(1) above.

[377]

**NOTES**
   1977 Act: Rent Act 1977: section 19 repealed with savings by the Housing Act 140(2), Sch 18.

**90–133**    (*Ss 90–113, 120–133 repealed by the Housing (Consequential Provisions) Act 1985, s 3, Sch 1, Pt I; ss 114–116 repealed by the Finance Act 1982, s 157, Sch 22, Pt V; ss 117–119 repealed by the Social Security and Housing Benefits Act 1982, ss 32(7)(a), 48(6), Sch 5.*)

### PART IX
### GENERAL

**134–136**    (*Repealed by the Housing (Consequential Provisions) Act 1985, s 3, Sch 1, Pt I.*)

*Miscellaneous*

**137–140**    (*Ss 137, 139 repealed by the Housing (Consequential Provisions) Act 1985, s 3, Sch 1, Pt I; s 138 amends the Land Compensation Act 1973, s 42(1); s 140 repealed, with savings in relation to leases granted before 11 December 1987, by the Housing and Planning Act 1986, s 18, Sch 4, paras 7, 11(2).*)

### 141   Amendments of Leasehold Reform Act 1967 etc

Sections 1, ... 9, 16, 23 and 29 of, and Schedules 1 and 3 to, the Leasehold Reform Act 1967 and Schedule 8 to the 1974 Act are amended as shown in Schedule 21 to this Act.

**[378]**

**NOTES**

Figure omitted repealed by the Leasehold Reform, Housing and Urban Development Act 1993, s 187(2), Sch 22.

1974 Act: Housing Act 1974.

### 142   Leasehold valuation tribunals

(1)    Any matter which under section 21(1), (2) or (3) of the Leasehold Reform Act 1967 is to be determined by the Lands Tribunal shall instead be determined by a [leasehold valuation tribunal].

(2)    ...

(3)    ... the 1967 Act is amended in accordance with [Schedule 22 to this Act].

**[379]**

**NOTES**

Sub-s (1): words in square brackets substituted by the Commonhold and Leasehold Reform Act 2002, s 176, Sch 13, para 7(1), (2), except in relation to any application made to an LVT or any proceedings transferred to an LVT by a county court before 30 September 2003 (in relation to England) or 31 March 2004 (in relation to Wales).

Sub-s (2): repealed by the Commonhold and Leasehold Reform Act 2002, s 180, Sch 14, except in relation to any application made to an LVT or any proceedings transferred to an LVT by a county court before 30 September 2003 (in relation to England) or 31 March 2004 (in relation to Wales).

Sub-s (3): words omitted repealed and words in square brackets substituted by the Commonhold and Leasehold Reform Act 2002, ss 176, 180, Sch 13, para 7(1), (3), Sch 14, except in relation to any application made to an LVT or any proceedings transferred to an LVT by a county court before 30 September 2003 (in relation to England) or 31 March 2004 (in relation to Wales).

### 143   Apportionment of rents

(1)    ...

(2)    The Secretary of State may by order vary the amount there mentioned.

(3)    ...

**[380]**

**NOTES**

Sub-ss (1), (3): amend the Landlord and Tenant Act 1927, s 20.

**144–149**    (*Ss 144–147, 149 repealed by the Housing (Consequential Provisions) Act 1985, s 3, Sch 1, Pt I; s 148 inserts the Rent Act 1977, Sch 10, para 7A at* **[326]**.)

*Supplemental*

### 150   Interpretation

In this Act—

     "protected tenant" and "statutory tenant" have the same meanings as in the 1977 Act;

     "secure tenant" means the tenant under a secure tenancy and "secure tenancy" has the meaning
         given by section 28;

                     .....

     "the 1977 Act" means the Rent Act 1977;

[ ..... ]

[381]

**NOTES**
Words omitted (which in the second place had been added by the Housing and Building Control Act 1984, s 64, Sch 11, para 29) repealed by the Housing (Consequential Provisions) Act 1985, s 3, Sch 1, Pt I.

## 151 Regulations and orders

(1) Any power of the Secretary of State to make an order or regulations under this Act shall be exercisable by statutory instrument subject, except in the case of regulations under section ... 52(3), 56(7) ... or an order under section [ ... ] 52(4), 60 or 153 to annulment in pursuance of a resolution of either House of Parliament.

(2) No order under section 52(4) or 60 shall be made unless a draft of it has been laid before Parliament and approved by a resolution of each House of Parliament.

(3) Any order or regulation under this Act may make different provision with respect to different cases or descriptions of cases, including different provision for different areas.

(4) ...

[382]

**NOTES**
Sub-s (1): words omitted (which in the third place had been inserted by the Housing and Building Control Act 1984, s 64, Sch 11, para 30) repealed by the Housing (Consequential Provisions) Act 1985, s 3, Sch 1, Pt I.
Sub-s (4): repealed by the Housing (Consequential Provisions) Act 1985, s 3, Sch 1, Pt I.
Regulations: the Assured Tenancies (Notice to Tenant) Regulations 1981, SI 1981/591 at **[3049]**.

## 152 Amendments, savings, transitional provisions and repeals

(1) The enactments mentioned in Part I of Schedule 25 to this Act shall have effect subject to the amendments specified in that Schedule.

(2) The savings and transitional provisions in Part II of that Schedule shall have effect.

(3) The enactments specified in the first column of Schedule 26 to this Act are hereby repealed to the extent specified in column 3 of that Schedule.

[383]

## 153 Commencement

(1), (2) ...

(3) Sections ... 140, 150, 151, 152(2) and 153 to 155 shall come into operation on the passing of this Act.

(4) The remaining provisions of this Act shall come into operation on such day as the Secretary of State may by order appoint; and—
   (a) different days may be appointed for different provisions; and
   (b) any provision may be brought into force on different days for England, Wales and Scotland.

[384]

**NOTES**
Sub-ss (1), (2): repealed by the Housing (Consequential Provisions) Act 1985, s 3, Sch 1, Pt I.
Sub-s (3): words omitted repealed by the Housing (Consequential Provisions) Act 1985, s 3, Sch 1, Pt I.
Orders: the Housing Act 1980 (Commencement No 1) Order 1980, SI 1980/1406; the Housing Act 1980 (Commencement No 2) Order 1980, SI 1980/1466; the Housing Act 1980 (Commencement No 3) Order 1980, SI 1980/1557; the Housing Act 1980 (Commencement No 4) Order 1980, SI 1980/1693; the Housing Act 1980 (Commencement No 5) Order 1980, SI 1980/1706; the Housing Act 1980 (Commencement No 6) Order 1980, SI 1980/1781; the Housing Act 1980 (Commencement No 7) Order 1981, SI 1981/119; the Housing Act 1980 (Commencement No 8) Order 1981, SI 1981/296.

## 154 Expenses and receipts

(1) There shall be paid out of moneys provided by Parliament the administrative expenses of the Secretary of State under this Act and any increase attributable to this Act in the sums so payable under any other enactment.

(2) ...

[385]

**NOTES**
Sub-s (2): repealed by the Housing (Consequential Provisions) Act 1985, s 3, Sch 1, Pt I.

**155  Short title and extent**

(1)   This Act may be cited as the Housing Act 1980.

(2)   …

(3)   Sections [111(8),] 152(1), 153, this section and paragraphs 11, 12, 18 and 19 of Part I of Schedule 25 extend to Northern Ireland; but this Act does not otherwise so extend.

**[386]**

---

**NOTES**

Sub-s (2): repealed by the Housing (Scotland) Act 1987, s 339(3), Sch 24.
Sub-s (3): figure in square brackets substituted by the Housing (Northern Ireland Consequential Amendments) Order 1983, SI 1983/1122.

---

## SCHEDULES

*(Schs 1–4, 4A repealed by the Housing (Consequential Provisions) Act 1985, s 3, Sch 1, Pt I; Sch 5 repealed by virtue of the Housing Act 1988, ss 1(4), 140(2), Sch 18, as from 15 January 1989, except in relation to a tenancy to which, by virtue of s 37(2) of that Act at* **[768]**, *s 1(3) of that Act at* **[729]**, *does not apply; Sch 6 spent; Sch 7 adds the Rent Act 1977, Sch 15, Pt V at* **[333]**.)

## SCHEDULE 8
## CROWN ESTATE AND DUCHIES—CONSEQUENTIAL PROVISIONS
Section 73

### PART I
### RENT ACT 1977

1.   Where a tenancy granted before the commencement of section 73 of this Act becomes, or would but for its low rent become, a protected tenancy by virtue of that section, section 5 of the 1977 Act applies as if in relation to the dwelling-house the appropriate day were the commencement of that section.

2.   …

3.   In Part II of Schedule 15 to the 1977 Act any reference to the relevant date shall (notwithstanding paragraph 2 of Part III of that Schedule) be construed, in the case of a tenancy which becomes a regulated tenancy by virtue of section 73 of this Act as meaning the date falling six months after the passing of this Act.

4.—(1)   Part II of Schedule 18 to the 1977 Act applies to a tenancy which becomes a regulated tenancy by virtue of section 73 of this Act (unless it is a tenancy falling within sub-paragraph (2) below).

(2)   Nothing in Part IX of the 1977 Act applies to the assignment, before the end of the year 1990, of a tenancy which falls within this sub-paragraph; and a tenancy falls within this sub-paragraph if it was granted for a term certain and its terms do not inhibit both the assignment and the underletting of the whole of the premises comprised in the tenancy, and either—

(a)   it was granted before the commencement of section 73 of this Act and became a regulated tenancy by virtue of that section; or

(b)   it is a regulated tenancy by virtue of that section and was granted to a person who, at the time of the grant, was the tenant of the premises comprised in it under a regulated tenancy which also fell within this sub-paragraph.

(3)   For the purposes of sub-paragraph (2) above the terms of a tenancy inhibit an assignment or underletting if they—

(a)   preclude it; or

(b)   permit it subject to a consent but exclude section 144 of the Law of Property Act 1925 (no payment in nature of fine); or

(c)   permit it subject to a consent but require in connection with a request for consent the making of an offer to surrender the tenancy.

**[387]**

---

**NOTES**

Para 2: amends the Rent Act 1977, Sch 15, Pt I at **[329]**.
1977 Act: Rent Act 1977.

---

### PART II
### RENT (AGRICULTURE) ACT 1976

5.   Where the question whether a person is a qualifying worker for the purposes of the Rent (Agriculture) Act 1976 arises by virtue of section 73 of this Act, Part II of Schedule 3 to that Act applies as if the date of operation for forestry workers were the commencement of that section.

6.   Where a protected occupancy or statutory tenancy within the meaning of the Rent (Agriculture) Act 1976 arises at the commencement of section 73 of this Act, Cases VIII and X in Schedule 4 to that Act apply in relation to it as if the operative date were that commencement.

7.   For the purpose of determining whether, at the commencement of section 73 of this Act, a person becomes a statutory tenant for the purposes of the Rent (Agriculture) Act 1976 and of applying that Act to him if he does, paragraph 3 of Schedule 9 to that Act applies as if the operative date were that commencement.

8.   Paragraphs 6 and 7 above apply in relation to forestry workers as they apply in relation to other persons and paragraph 7 of Schedule 9 to the Rent (Agriculture) Act 1976 does not apply.

**[388]**

## PART III
## GENERAL

9.   Where an interest belongs to Her Majesty in right of the Duchy of Lancaster, then, for the purposes of Part I of the Landlord and Tenant Act 1954, the Rent (Agriculture) Act 1976 or the 1977 Act, the Chancellor of the Duchy of Lancaster shall be deemed to be the owner of the interest.

10.   Where an interest belongs to the Duchy of Cornwall, then, for the purposes of Part I of the Landlord and Tenant Act 1954, the Rent (Agriculture) Act 1976 or the 1977 Act, the Secretary of the Duchy of Cornwall shall be deemed to be the owner of the interest.

**[389]**

**NOTES**
1977 Act: Rent Act 1977.

## SCHEDULE 9
## PROVISIONS SUPPLEMENTING SECTION 74
Section 74

1.   Paragraphs 2 to 6 below apply to any tenancy which was a protected or statutory tenancy but which, by virtue of the landlord becoming a "housing trust" within the meaning of section 15 of the 1977 Act, has ceased to be such a tenancy.

2.   …

3.   Registration of a rent, or of a different rent, for the dwelling-house shall be effected in pursuance of section 87 of the 1977 Act; but until such time as a rent is so registered—
   (a)   the rent recoverable under the tenancy; and
   (b)   where a rent was registered for the dwelling-house under Part IV of the 1977 Act, the time at which an application for a different registered rent may be made;
shall be determined as if the tenancy had continued to be a regulated tenancy.

4.   If the tenant was a successor within the meaning of Schedule 1 to the 1977 Act he shall not be treated as a successor for the purposes of [Part IV of the Housing Act 1985 (secure tenancies)].

5.   [Section 83 of the Housing Act 1985 (notice of proceedings for possession)] does not apply in any case where proceedings for possession were begun before the tenancy ceased to be a protected or statutory tenancy; but in such a case the court shall allow the parties to take such steps in relation to the proceedings as it considers appropriate in consequence of the tenancy becoming a secure tenancy.

6.—(1)   This paragraph applies in any case where—
   (a)   the tenant died before the date on which the tenancy ceased to be a protected or statutory tenancy; and
   (b)   there was then more than one member of his family entitled to succeed him as statutory tenant but no decision had, by that date, been reached as to which of them was to succeed.

   (2)   In a case to which this paragraph applies, the person who is to be the secure tenant of the dwelling-house on the tenancy becoming a secure tenancy shall be selected by the landlord from among those mentioned in sub-paragraph (1)(b) above notwithstanding that the question may have been referred to the county court in accordance with paragraph 1(7) of Schedule 1 to the 1977 Act.

**[390]**

**NOTES**
Para 2: repealed by the Housing Act 1988, s 140(2), Sch 18.
Paras 4, 5: words in square brackets substituted by the Housing (Consequential Provisions) Act 1985, s 4, Sch 2, para 44(4).
1977 Act: Rent Act 1977.

*(Sch 10 repealed in part by the Housing (Consequential Provisions) Act 1985, s 3, Sch 1, Pt I and the Housing Act 1988, s 140(2), Sch 18, remainder amends the Rent Act 1977, ss 86, 92, 93(1), (2)*

at **[267]**, **[270]**, **[271]**, *repeals ss 90, 91 of that Act, and repeals s 93(3) of that Act, in relation to notices of increase given after 28 November 1980; Schs 11–13, 16–20 repealed by the Housing (Consequential Provisions) Act 1985, s 3, Sch 1, Pt I; Sch 14 repealed by the Finance Act 1982, s 157, Sch 22; Sch 15 repealed by the Social Security and Housing Benefit Act 1982, s 48(6), Sch 5; Sch 21 repealed in part by the Leasehold Reform, Housing and Urban Development Act 1993, s 187(2), Sch 22, remainder amends the Leasehold Reform Act 1967, ss 1, 16, 29, Sch 1 at* **[78]**, **[99]**, **[114]**, **[127]** *and the Housing Act 1974, Sch 8; Sch 22, Pt I repealed by the Commonhold and Leasehold Reform Act 2002, s 180, Sch 14, except in relation to any application made to an LVT or any proceedings transferred to an LVT by a county court before 30 September 2003 (in relation to England) or 31 March 2004 (in relation to Wales); Sch 22, Pt II amends the Leasehold Reform Act 1967, ss 21, 31(2), Sch 1, para 5, Sch 2, paras 2, 8 at* **[104]**, **[116]**, **[127]**, **[128]**; *Schs 23, 24 repealed by the Housing (Consequential Provisions) Act 1985, s 3, Sch 1, Pt I.*

PART I<br>STATUTES

### SCHEDULE 25
### MINOR AND CONSEQUENTIAL AMENDMENTS, TRANSITIONAL PROVISIONS AND SAVINGS
Section 152

### PART I
### MINOR AND CONSEQUENTIAL AMENDMENTS

1–56.   ...

57.   In Schedule 15 to the 1977 Act (grounds for possession of dwelling-houses), in paragraph (i) in Case 9, for the words "controlled tenancy" there are substituted the words "tenancy which was then a controlled tenancy".

Case 9 has effect, as so amended, in relation to any tenancy which was a controlled tenancy on the date mentioned in paragraph (i) notwithstanding that it ceased to be a controlled tenancy before the commencement of this paragraph.

58–60.   ...

*Protection from Eviction Act 1977 (c 43)*

61.   The Protection from Eviction Act 1977 shall apply, where a person has been let into possession of a dwelling-house under the terms of a rental purchase agreement (within the meaning of section 88 of this Act) as if—
   (a)   the dwelling-house had been let to him as a dwelling under a tenancy which is not a statutorily protected tenancy (within the meaning of section 3 of that Act); and
   (b)   that tenancy had come to an end on the termination of the agreement or of his right to possession under it.

**[391]**

**NOTES**
Paras 1–56, 58–60: repealed in part by the Matrimonial Homes and Property Act 1981, s 10(2), Sch 3, the Supreme Court Act 1981, s 152(4), Sch 7, the Matrimonial Homes Act 1983, s 12(2), Sch 3, the Housing (Consequential Provisions) Act 1985, s 3, Sch 1, Pt I and the Housing Act 1988, s 140(2), Sch 18; remainder contains consequential amendments which, in so far as within the scope of this work, have been incorporated at the appropriate place.
1977 Act: Rent Act 1977.

### PART II
### TRANSITIONAL PROVISIONS AND SAVINGS

62, 63.   ...

64.   Where the recoverable rent for any statutory period has been increased by a notice under section 48 of the 1977 Act, nothing in section 63 of this Act affects that increase or the operation of subsections (4) and (5) of section 48 in relation to the notice.

65.   In a case where, by virtue of subsection (4) of section 52 of the 1977 Act, that section would not have applied to an agreement with a tenant having security of tenure had it not been replaced by the section substituted by section 68(2) of this Act, the substituted section 52 shall also not apply in relation to that agreement.

66.   The repeal by this Act of subsections (4) and (5) of section 54 of the 1977 Act does not affect the operation of those subsections in relation to defaults occurring before the commencement of section 68 of this Act.

67.   Where, immediately before the commencement of section 69(4) of this Act, a tenancy was, by virtue of section 12(2)(b) of the 1977 Act, a protected tenancy and not a restricted contract, the 1977 Act shall continue to apply in relation to that tenancy as if section 69(4) had not been enacted.

68.　The repeals made by section 74 of this Act in section 15 of the 1977 Act shall not affect any tenancy which was, immediately before the commencement of section 74(1), a protected or statutory tenancy but which would, were it not for this paragraph, have ceased to be such a tenancy by virtue of the repeal of section 15(4)(f).

69–74.　…

75.　Section 5 of the 1977 Act (tenancies at low rents) shall continue not to apply to any tenancy which, immediately before the repeal by this Act of section 17 of the 1977 Act (categories of controlled tenancies) was a controlled tenancy by virtue of subsection (2) of section 17.

76.　…

77.　Section 90 of the 1977 Act continues to have effect, notwithstanding its repeal by this Act, in relation to any direction given by the Secretary of State under that section.

78.　Paragraphs 3 and 4 of Schedule 17 to the 1977 Act continue to have effect, notwithstanding paragraph 59 of this Schedule, in relation to a notice of increase served under paragraph 4 before the commencement of paragraph 59.

**[392]**

**NOTES**

Paras 62, 69, 71, 74, 76: repealed by the Housing (Consequential Provisions) Act 1985, s 3, Sch 1, Pt I.
Para 63: repealed by the Housing Act 1988, s 140(2), Sch 18.
Para 70: spent on the repeal of s 114 of this Act by the Finance Act 1982, s 157, Sch 22, Pt V.
Para 72: relates to notices given after 31 March 1980 but before 3 October 1980 in relation to certain tenancies excepted from being secure tenancies, and is now considered to be spent.
Para 73: adds a further category to the tenancies excepted from being secure tenancies in relation to a tenancy or licence granted before 8 May 1980, and is now considered to be spent.

*(Sch 26 contains repeals.)*

# [SENIOR COURTS ACT 1981]

### (1981 c 54)

*An Act to consolidate with amendments the Supreme Court of Judicature (Consolidation) Act 1925 and other enactments relating to the Supreme Court in England and Wales and the administration of justice therein; to repeal certain obsolete or unnecessary enactments so relating; to amend Part VIII of the Mental Health Act 1959, the Courts-Martial (Appeals) Act 1968, the Arbitration Act 1979 and the law relating to county courts; and for connected purposes*

**[28 July 1981]**

**NOTES**

Act title: the Supreme Court Act 1981 was renamed the Senior Courts Act 1981 by the Constitutional Reform Act 2005, s 59(5), Sch 11, Pt 1, para 1(1), as from 1 October 2009.

**1–14**　((*Pt I*) *outside the scope of this work.*)

## PART II
## JURISDICTION

**15–18**　(*Outside the scope of this work.*)

## THE HIGH COURT

**19–31**　(*Outside the scope of this work.*)

### *Powers*

**32–37**　(*Outside the scope of this work.*)

## 38　Relief against forfeiture for non-payment of rent

(1)　In any action in the High Court for the forfeiture of a lease for non-payment of rent, the court shall have power to grant relief against forfeiture in a summary manner, and may do so subject to the same terms and conditions as to the payment of rent, costs or otherwise as could have been imposed by it in such an action immediately before the commencement of this Act.

(2)    Where the lessee or a person deriving title under him is granted relief under this section, he shall hold the demised premises in accordance with the terms of the lease without the necessity for a new lease.

**[393]**

**39–128**    (*Ss 39–52, ss 53–87 (Pt III), ss 88–104 (Pt IV), ss 105–128 (Pt V) outside the scope of this work.*)

## PART VI
## MISCELLANEOUS AND SUPPLEMENTARY

**129–150**    (*Ss 129–138, 138A, 138B, 139–142, 145–147, 150 outside the scope of this work; s 143 repealed by the Administration of Justice Act 1982, s 75, Sch 9, Pt I; s 144 repealed by the Mental Health Act 1983, s 148(3), Sch 6; s 148 repealed by the Arbitration Act 1996, s 107(2), Sch 4; s 149 repealed by the County Courts Act 1984, s 148(3), Sch 4.*)

### *Supplementary*

**151, 152**    (*Outside the scope of this work.*)

### 153   Citation, commencement and extent

(1)    This Act may be cited as the [Senior Courts Act 1981].

(2)    This Act, except the provisions mentioned in subsection (3), shall come into force on 1st January 1982; and references to the commencement of this Act shall be construed as references to the beginning of that day.

(3)    ...

(4)    In this Act—

...

but, save as aforesaid, the provisions of this Act, other than those mentioned in subsection (5), extend to England and Wales only.

(5)    The provisions of this Act whose extent is not restricted by subsection (4) are—
    section 27;
    section 150;
    section 151(1);
    section 152(4) and Schedule 7 as far as they relate to the Naval Prize Act 1864, the Prize Courts Act 1915 and section 56 of the Administration of Justice Act 1956;
    this section;
    paragraph 1 of Schedule 4.

**[394]**

---

**NOTES**

Sub-s (1): words in square brackets substituted by the Constitutional Reform Act 2005, s 59(5), Sch 11, Pt 1, para 1(2).

Sub-s (3): outside the scope of this work.

Sub-s (4): words omitted apply to Scotland and Northern Ireland only.

---

(*Schs 1–7 outside the scope of this work.*)

# MOBILE HOMES ACT 1983

### (1983 c 34)

### ARRANGEMENT OF SECTIONS

[13 May 1983]

## [1 Particulars of agreements

(1)   This Act applies to any agreement under which a person ("the occupier") is entitled—
    (a)   to station a mobile home on land forming part of a protected site; and
    (b)   to occupy the mobile home as his only or main residence.

(2)   Before making an agreement to which this Act applies, the owner of the protected site ("the owner") shall give to the proposed occupier under the agreement a written statement which—
    (a)   specifies the names and addresses of the parties;
    (b)   includes particulars of the land on which the proposed occupier is to be entitled to station the mobile home that are sufficient to identify that land;
    (c)   sets out the express terms to be contained in the agreement;
    (d)   sets out the terms to be implied by section 2(1) below; and
    (e)   complies with such other requirements as may be prescribed by regulations made by the appropriate national authority.

(3)   The written statement required by subsection (2) above must be given—
    (a)   not later than 28 days before the date on which any agreement for the sale of the mobile home to the proposed occupier is made, or
    (b)   (if no such agreement is made before the making of the agreement to which this Act applies) not later than 28 days before the date on which the agreement to which this Act applies is made.

(4)   But if the proposed occupier consents in writing to that statement being given to him by a date ("the chosen date") which is less than 28 days before the date mentioned in subsection (3)(a) or (b) above, the statement must be given to him not later than the chosen date.

(5)   If any express term—
    (a)   is contained in an agreement to which this Act applies, but
    (b)   was not set out in a written statement given to the proposed occupier in accordance with subsections (2) to (4) above,
the term is unenforceable by the owner or any person within section 3(1) below.

This is subject to any order made by the court under section 2(3) below.

(6)   If the owner has failed to give the occupier a written statement in accordance with subsections (2) to (4) above, the occupier may, at any time after the making of the agreement, apply to the court for an order requiring the owner—
    (a)   to give him a written statement which complies with paragraphs (a) to (e) of subsection (2) (read with any modifications necessary to reflect the fact that the agreement has been made), and
    (b)   to do so not later than such date as is specified in the order.

(7)   A statement required to be given to a person under this section may be either delivered to him personally or sent to him by post.

(8)   Any reference in this section to the making of an agreement to which this Act applies includes a reference to any variation of an agreement by virtue of which the agreement becomes one to which this Act applies.

(9)   Regulations under this section—
    (a)   shall be made by statutory instrument;
    (b)   if made by the Secretary of State, shall be subject to annulment in pursuance of a resolution of either House of Parliament; and
    (c)   may make different provision with respect to different cases or descriptions of case, including different provision for different areas.]

[395]

---

**NOTES**

Commencement: 18 January 2005 (in relation to England and Wales); 28 May 2007 (in relation to Scotland).

Substituted, in relation to England and Wales, by the Housing Act 2004, s 206(1) (for effect see s 206(4), (5) thereof) and in relation to Scotland by the Housing (Scotland) Act 2006, s 167.

Transfer of Functions: functions of the Secretary of State, so far as exercisable in relation to Wales, are transferred to the National Assembly for Wales by the National Assembly for Wales (Transfer of Functions) Order 1999, SI 1999/672, art 2, Sch 1.

Regulations: the Mobile Homes (Written Statement) (England) Regulations 2006, SI 2006/2275 at **[3725]**; the Mobile Homes (Written Statement) (Wales) Regulations 2007, SI 2007/3164 at **[3778]**.

**2   Terms of agreements**

(1)    In any agreement to which this Act applies there shall be implied the terms set out in Part I of Schedule 1 to this Act; and this subsection shall have effect notwithstanding any express term of the agreement.

(2)    The court may, on the application of either party made [within the relevant period], order that there shall be implied in the agreement terms concerning the matters mentioned in Part II of Schedule 1 to this Act.

[(3)    The court may, on the application of either party made within the relevant period, make an order—

    (a)   varying or deleting any express term of the agreement;

    (b)   in the case of any express term to which section 1(6) above applies, provide for the term to have full effect or to have such effect subject to any variation specified in the order.

(3A)    In subsections (2) and (3) above "the relevant period" means the period beginning with the date on which the agreement is made and ending—

    (a)   six months after that date, or

    (b)   where a written statement relating to the agreement is given to the occupier after that date (whether or not in compliance with an order under section 1(6) above), six months after the date on which the statement is given;

and section 1(8) above applies for the purposes of this subsection as it applies for the purposes of section 1.]

(4)    On an application under this section, the court shall make such provision as the court considers just and equitable in the circumstances.

[(5)    The supplementary provisions in Part 3 of Schedule 1 to this Act have effect for the purposes of paragraphs 8 and 9 of Part 1 of that Schedule.]

**[396]**

**NOTES**

Sub-s (2): words in square brackets substituted, in relation to England and Wales, by the Housing Act 2004, s 206(2)(a), and in relation to Scotland by the Housing (Scotland) Act 2006, s 168(a).

Sub-ss (3), (3A): substituted, for original sub-s (3), in relation to England and Wales, by the Housing Act 2004, s 206(2)(b), and in relation to Scotland by the Housing (Scotland) Act 2006, s 168(b).

Sub-s (5): inserted, in relation to England and Wales, by the Housing Act 2004, s 265(1), Sch 15, para 9.

**[2A    Power to amend implied terms**

(1)    The appropriate national authority may by order make such amendments of Part 1 or 2 of Schedule 1 to this Act as the authority considers appropriate.

(2)    An order under this section—

    (a)   shall be made by statutory instrument;

    (b)   may make different provision with respect to different cases or descriptions of case, including different provision for different areas;

    (c)   may contain such incidental, supplementary, consequential, transitional or saving provisions as the authority making the order considers appropriate.

(3)    Without prejudice to the generality of subsections (1) and (2), an order under this section may—

    (a)   make provision for or in connection with the determination by the court of such questions, or the making by the court of such orders, as are specified in the order;

    (b)   make such amendments of any provision of this Act as the authority making the order considers appropriate in consequence of any amendment made by the order in Part 1 or 2 of Schedule 1.

(4)    The first order made under this section in relation to England or Wales respectively may provide for all or any of its provisions to apply in relation to agreements to which this Act applies that were made at any time before the day on which the order comes into force (as well as in relation to such agreements made on or after that day).

(5)    No order may be made by the appropriate national authority under this section unless the authority has consulted—

    (a)   such organisations as appear to it to be representative of interests substantially affected by the order; and

    (b)   such other persons as it considers appropriate.

(6)    No order may be made by the Secretary of State under this section unless a draft of the order has been laid before, and approved by a resolution of, each House of Parliament.]

**[397]**

**NOTES**

Inserted, in relation to England and Wales, by the Housing Act 2004, s 208(1); for effect see s 208(2) thereof.

PART I
STATUTES

Orders: the Mobile Homes Act 1983 (Amendment of Schedule 1) (England) Order 2006, SI 2006/1755; the Mobile Homes Act 1983 (Amendment of Schedule 1) (Wales) Order 2007, SI 2007/3151.

### [2B  Power to amend implied terms: Scotland

(1)   The Scottish Ministers may by order make such amendments of Part 1 or 2 of Schedule 1 to this Act as they consider appropriate.

(2)   An order under this section—
- (a)   shall be made by statutory instrument;
- (b)   may make different provision with respect to different cases or descriptions of case;
- (c)   may contain such incidental, supplementary, consequential, transitional or saving provisions as the Scottish Ministers consider appropriate.

(3)   Without prejudice to the generality of subsections (1) and (2), an order under this section may—
- (a)   make provision for or in connection with the determination by the court of such questions, or the making by the court of such orders, as are specified in the order;
- (b)   make such amendments of any provision of this Act as the Scottish Ministers consider appropriate in consequence of any amendment made by the order in Part 1 or 2 of Schedule 1.

(4)   The first order made under this section may provide for all or any of its provisions to apply in relation to agreements to which this Act applies that were made at any time before the day on which the order comes into force (as well as in relation to such agreements made on or after that day).

(5)   No order may be made under this section unless the Scottish Ministers have consulted—
- (a)   such organisations as appear to them to be representative of interests substantially affected by the order; and
- (b)   such other persons as they consider appropriate.

(6)   No order may be made under this section unless a draft of the order has been laid before, and approved by a resolution of, the Scottish Parliament.]

**[398]**

**NOTES**
Commencement: 28 May 2007.
Inserted by the Housing (Scotland) Act 2006, s 170(1); for effect see s 170(2) thereof.

### 3   Successors in title

(1)   An agreement to which this Act applies shall be binding on and enure for the benefit of any successor in title of the owner and any person claiming through or under the owner or any such successor.

(2)   Where an agreement to which this Act applies is lawfully assigned to any person, the agreement shall enure for the benefit of and be binding on that person.

(3)   Where a person entitled to the benefit of and bound by an agreement to which this Act applies dies at a time when he is occupying the mobile home as his only or main residence, the agreement shall enure for the benefit of and be binding on—
- (a)   any person residing with that person ("the deceased") at that time being—
  - (i)    the widow[, widower or surviving civil partner] of the deceased; or
  - (ii)   in default of a widow[, widower or surviving civil partner] so residing, any member of the deceased's family; or
- (b)   in default of any such person so residing, the person entitled to the mobile home by virtue of the deceased's will or under the law relating to intestacy but subject to subsection (4) below.

(4)   An agreement to which this Act applies shall not enure for the benefit of or be binding on a person by virtue of subsection 3(*b*) above in so far as—
- (a)   it would, but for this subsection, enable or require that person to occupy the mobile home; or
- (b)   it includes terms implied by virtue of paragraph 5 or 9 of Part I of Schedule 1 to this Act.

**[399]**

**NOTES**
Sub-s (3): words in square brackets substituted by the Civil Partnership Act 2004, s 261(1), Sch 27, para 87.

### 4   Jurisdiction of the court
The court shall have jurisdiction to determine any question arising under this Act or any agreement to which it applies, and to entertain any proceedings brought under this Act or any such agreement.

**[400]**

**5 Interpretation**

(1) In this Act, unless the context otherwise requires—

["the appropriate national authority" means—

    (a) in relation to England, the Secretary of State, and

    (b) in relation to Wales, the National Assembly for Wales;]

"the court" means—

    (a) in relation to England and Wales, the county court for the district in which the protected site is situated or, where the parties have agreed in writing to submit any question arising under this Act or, as the case may be, any agreement to which it applies to arbitration, the arbitrator;

    (b) in relation to Scotland, the sheriff having jurisdiction where the protected site is situated or, where the parties have so agreed, the arbiter;

"local authority" has the same meaning as in Part I of the Caravan Sites and Control of Development Act 1960;

"mobile home" has the same meaning as "caravan" has in that Part of that Act;

"owner", in relation to a protected site, means the person who, by virtue of an estate or interest held by him, is entitled to possession of the site or would be so entitled but for the rights of any persons to station mobile homes on land forming part of the site;

"planning permission" means permission under [Part III of the Town and Country Planning Act 1990] or [Part III of the Town and Country Planning (Scotland) Act 1997];

"protected site" *does not include any land occupied by a local authority as a caravan site providing accommodation for gipsies or, in Scotland, for persons to whom section 24(8A) of the Caravan Sites and Control of Development Act 1960 applies but, subject to that,* has the same meaning as in Part I of the Caravan Sites Act 1968.

(2) In relation to an agreement to which this Act applies—

    (a) any reference in this Act to the owner includes a reference to any person who is bound by and entitled to the benefit of the agreement by virtue of subsection (1) of section 3 above; and

    (b) subject to subsection (4) of that section, any reference in this Act to the occupier includes a reference to any person who is entitled to the benefit of and bound by the agreement by virtue of subsection (2) or (3) of that section.

(3) A person is a member of another's family within the meaning of this Act if he is his spouse, [civil partner,] parent, grandparent, child, grandchild, brother, sister, uncle, aunt, nephew or niece; treating—

    (a) any relationship by marriage [or civil partnership] as a relationship by blood, any relationship of the half blood as a relationship of the whole blood and the stepchild of any person as his child; and

    (b) an illegitimate person as the legitimate child of his mother and reputed father;

or if they live together as husband and wife [or as if they were civil partners].

[(4) In relation to land in Scotland, any reference in this Act to an "estate or interest" shall be construed as a reference to a right in, or to, the land.]

[401]

---

**NOTES**

Sub-s (1): definition "the appropriate national authority" inserted, in relation to England and Wales, by the Housing Act 2004, s 206(3) (for effect see s 206(4), (5) thereof); in definition "planning permission" words in first pair of square brackets substituted by the Planning (Consequential Provisions) Act 1990, s 4, Sch 2, para 59 and words in second pair of square brackets substituted by the Planning (Consequential Provisions) (Scotland) Act 1997, s 4, Sch 2, para 36; in definition "protected site" words in italics repealed by the Housing and Regeneration Act 2008, ss 318, 321(1), Sch 16, as from a day to be appointed.

Sub-s (3): words in square brackets inserted by the Civil Partnership Act 2004, s 261(1), Sch 27, para 88.

Sub-s (4): inserted by the Abolition of Feudal Tenure etc (Scotland) Act 2000, s 76(1), Sch 12, para 44.

---

**6 Short title, repeals, commencement and extent**

(1) This Act may be cited as the Mobile Homes Act 1983.

(2) The enactments mentioned in Schedule 2 to this Act are hereby repealed to the extent specified in the third column of that Schedule.

(3) This Act shall come into force on the expiry of the period of one week beginning with the day on which it is passed.

(4) This Act does not extend to Northern Ireland.

[402]

## SCHEDULE 1
## AGREEMENTS UNDER ACT
Section 2

### PART I
### TERMS IMPLIED BY ACT

#### *Duration of Agreement*

1.   Subject to paragraph 2 below, the right to station the mobile home on land forming part of the protected site shall subsist until the agreement is determined under paragraph 3, 4, 5 or 6 below.

2.—(1)   If the owner's estate or interest is insufficient to enable him to grant the right for an indefinite period, the period for which the right subsists shall not extend beyond the date when the owner's estate or interest determines.

   (2)   If planning permission for the use of the protected site as a site for mobile homes has been granted in terms such that it will expire at the end of a specified period, the period for which the right subsists shall not extend beyond the date when the planning permission expires.

   (3)   If before the end of a period determined by this paragraph there is a change in circumstances which allows a longer period, account shall be taken of that change.

#### *Termination by occupier*

3.   The occupier shall be entitled to terminate the agreement by notice in writing given to the owner not less than four weeks before the date on which it is to take effect.

4.   The owner shall be entitled to terminate the agreement forthwith if, on the application of the owner, the court—
   (a)   is satisfied that the occupier has breached a term of the agreement and, after service of a notice to remedy the breach, has not complied with the notice within a reasonable time; and
   (b)   considers it reasonable for the agreement to be terminated.

5.   The owner shall be entitled to terminate the agreement forthwith if, on the application of the owner, [the court—
   (a)   is satisfied that the occupier is not occupying the mobile home as his only or main residence; and
   (b)   considers it reasonable for the agreement to be terminated].

6.—(1)   The owner shall be entitled to terminate the agreement [forthwith] if, on the application of the owner, the court is satisfied that, having regard to its ... condition, the mobile home—
   (a)   is having a detrimental effect on the amenity of the site; [; and]
   [(b)   the court considers it reasonable for the agreement to be terminated].

   (2)   ...

   [(3)   Sub-paragraphs (4) and (5) below apply if, on an application under sub-paragraph (1) above—
   (a)   the court considers that, having regard to the present condition of the mobile home, paragraph (a) ... of that sub-paragraph applies to it, but
   (b)   it also considers that it would be reasonably practicable for particular repairs to be carried out on the mobile home that [would result in sub-paragraph (1)(a) not applying to it], and
   (c)   the occupier indicates that he intends to carry out those repairs.

   (4)   In such a case the court may make an order adjourning proceedings on the application for such period specified in the order as the court considers reasonable to allow the repairs to be carried out.
The repairs must be set out in the order.

   (5)   If the court makes such an order, the application shall not be further proceeded with unless the court is satisfied that the specified period has expired without the repairs having been carried out.]

#### *Recovery of overpayments by occupier*

7.   Where the agreement is terminated as mentioned in paragraph 3, 4, 5 or 6 above, the occupier shall be entitled to recover from the owner so much of any payment made by him in pursuance of the agreement as is attributable to a period beginning after the termination.

#### *Sale of mobile home*

8.—(1)   The occupier shall be entitled to sell the mobile home, and to assign the agreement, to a person approved of by the owner, whose approval shall not be unreasonably withheld.

[(1A)    The occupier may serve on the owner a request for the owner to approve a person for the purposes of sub-paragraph (1) above.

(1B)    Where the owner receives such a request, he must, within the period of 28 days beginning with the date on which he received the request—
  (a)    approve the person, unless it is reasonable for him not to do so, and
  (b)    serve on the occupier notice of his decision whether or not to approve the person.

[(1C)    The owner may not give his approval subject to conditions.]

[(1D)    If the approval is withheld, the notice under sub-paragraph (1B) above must specify the reasons for withholding it.]

(1E)    If the owner fails to notify the occupier as required by [sub-paragraph (1B) (and, if applicable, sub-paragraph (1D))] above, the occupier may apply to the court for an order declaring that the person is approved for the purposes of sub-paragraph (1) above; and the court may make such an order if it thinks fit.

(1F)    It is for the owner—
  (a)    if he served a notice as mentioned in [sub-paragraph (1B) (and, if applicable, sub-paragraph (1D)] and the question arises whether he served the notice within the required period of 28 days, to show that he did;
  (b)    ...
  (c)    if he did not give his approval and the question arises whether it was reasonable for him not to do so, to show that it was reasonable.

(1G)    A request or notice under this paragraph—
  (a)    must be in writing, and
  (b)    may be served by post.]

(2)    Where the occupier sells the mobile home, and assigns the agreement, as mentioned in sub-paragraph (1) above, the owner shall be entitled to receive a commission on the sale at a rate not exceeding such rate as may be specified by an order made by [the appropriate national authority].

[(2A)    Except to the extent mentioned in sub-paragraph (2) above, the owner may not require any payment to be made (whether to himself or otherwise) in connection with the sale of the mobile home, and the assignment of the agreement, as mentioned in sub-paragraph (1) above.]

(3)    An order under this paragraph—
  (a)    shall be made by statutory instrument which [(if made by the Secretary of State)] shall be subject to annulment in pursuance of a resolution of either House of Parliament; and
  (b)    may make different provision for different areas or for sales at different prices.

*Gift of mobile home*

9.—[(1)]    The occupier shall be entitled to give the mobile home, and to assign the agreement, to a member of his family approved by the owner, whose approval shall not be unreasonably withheld.

[(2)    Sub-paragraphs (1A) to (1G) of paragraph 8 above shall apply in relation to the approval of a person for the purposes of sub-paragraph (1) above as they apply in relation to the approval of a person for the purposes of sub-paragraph (1) of that paragraph.]

[(3)    The owner may not require any payment to be made (whether to himself or otherwise) in connection with the gift of the mobile home, and the assignment of the agreement, as mentioned in sub-paragraph (1) above.]

*[Re-siting of mobile home*

10.—(1)    The owner shall be entitled to require that the occupier's right to station the mobile home is exercisable for any period in relation to another pitch forming part of the protected site ("the other pitch") if (and only if)—
  (a)    on the application of the owner, the court is satisfied that the other pitch is broadly comparable to the occupier's original pitch and that it is reasonable for the mobile home to be stationed on the other pitch for that period; or
  (b)    the owner needs to carry out essential repair or emergency works that can only be carried out if the mobile home is moved to the other pitch for that period, and the other pitch is broadly comparable to the occupier's original pitch.

(2)    If the owner requires the occupier to station the mobile home on the other pitch so that he can replace, or carry out repairs to, the base on which the mobile home is stationed, he must if the occupier so requires, or the court on the application of the occupier so orders, secure that the mobile home is returned to the original pitch on the completion of the replacement or repairs.

(3)    The owner shall pay all the costs and expenses incurred by the occupier in connection with his mobile home being moved to and from the other pitch.

(4)    In this paragraph and in paragraph 13 below, "essential repair or emergency works" means—

(a) repairs to the base on which the mobile home is stationed;
(b) works or repairs needed to comply with any relevant legal requirements; or
(c) works or repairs in connection with restoration following flood, landslide or other natural disaster.

### Quiet enjoyment of the mobile home

11. The occupier shall be entitled to quiet enjoyment of the mobile home together with the pitch during the continuance of the agreement, subject to paragraphs 10, 12, 13 and 14.

### Owner's right of entry to the pitch

12. The owner may enter the pitch without prior notice between the hours of 9 am and 6 pm
(a) to deliver written communications, including post and notices, to the occupier; and
(b) to read any meter for gas, electricity, water, sewerage or other services supplied by the owner.

13. The owner may enter the pitch to carry out essential repair or emergency works on giving as much notice to the occupier (whether in writing or otherwise) as is reasonably practicable in the circumstances.

14. Unless the occupier has agreed otherwise, the owner may enter the pitch for a reason other than one specified in paragraph 12 or 13 only if he has given the occupier at least 14 clear days' written notice of the date, time and reason for his visit.

15. The rights conferred by paragraphs 12 to 14 above do not extend to the mobile home.

### The pitch fee

16. The pitch fee can only be changed in accordance with paragraph 17, either—
(a) with the agreement of the occupier, or
(b) if the court, on the application of the owner or the occupier, considers it reasonable for the pitch fee to be changed and makes an order determining the amount of the new pitch fee.

17.—(1) The pitch fee shall be reviewed annually as at the review date.

(2) At least 28 clear days before the review date the owner shall serve on the occupier a written notice setting out his proposals in respect of the new pitch fee.

(3) If the occupier agrees to the proposed new pitch fee, it shall be payable as from the review date.

(4) If the occupier does not agree to the proposed new pitch fee—
(a) the owner may apply to the court for an order under paragraph 16(b) determining the amount of the new pitch fee;
(b) the occupier shall continue to pay the current pitch fee to the owner until such time as the new pitch fee is agreed by the occupier or an order determining the amount of the new pitch fee is made by the court under paragraph 16(b); and
(c) the new pitch fee shall be payable as from the review date but the occupier shall not be treated as being in arrears until the 28th day after the date on which the new pitch fee is agreed or, as the case may be, the 28th day after the date of the court order determining the amount of the new pitch fee.

(5) An application under sub-paragraph (4)(a) may be made at any time after the end of the period of 28 days beginning with the review date.

(6) Sub-paragraphs (7) to (10) apply if the owner—
(a) has not served the notice required by sub-paragraph (2) by the time by which it was required to be served, but
(b) at any time thereafter serves on the occupier a written notice setting out his proposals in respect of a new pitch fee.

(7) If (at any time) the occupier agrees to the proposed pitch fee, it shall be payable as from the 28th day after the date on which the owner serves the notice under sub-paragraph (6)(b).

(8) If the occupier has not agreed to the proposed pitch fee—
(a) the owner may apply to the court for an order under paragraph 16(b) determining the amount of the new pitch fee;
(b) the occupier shall continue to pay the current pitch fee to the owner until such time as the new pitch fee is agreed by the occupier or an order determining the amount of the new pitch fee is made by the court under paragraph 16(b); and
(c) if the court makes such an order, the new pitch fee shall be payable as from the 28th day after the date on which the owner serves the notice under sub-paragraph (6)(b).

(9) An application under sub-paragraph (8) may be made at any time after the end of the period of 56 days beginning with date on which the owner serves the notice under sub-paragraph (6)(b).

(10) The occupier shall not be treated as being in arrears—

    (a)    where sub-paragraph (7) applies, until the 28th day after the date on which the new pitch fee is agreed; or

    (b)    where sub-paragraph (8)(b) applies, until the 28th day after the date on which the new pitch fee is agreed or, as the case may be, the 28th day after the date of the court order determining the amount of the new pitch fee.

18.—(1)    When determining the amount of the new pitch fee particular regard shall be had to—

    (a)    any sums expended by the owner since the last review date on improvements—

        (i)    which are for the benefit of the occupiers of mobile homes on the protected site;

        (ii)    which were the subject of consultation in accordance with paragraph 22(e) and (f) below; and

        (iii)    to which a majority of the occupiers have not disagreed in writing or which, in the case of such disagreement, the court, on the application of the owner, has ordered should be taken into account when determining the amount of the new pitch fee;

    (b)    any decrease in the amenity of the protected site since the last review date; and

    (c)    the effect of any enactment, other than an order made under paragraph 8(2) above, which has come into force since the last review date.

(2)    When calculating what constitutes a majority of the occupiers for the purposes of sub-paragraph (1)(b)(iii) each mobile home is to be taken to have only one occupier and, in the event of there being more than one occupier of a mobile home, its occupier is to be taken to be the occupier whose name first appears on the agreement.

(3)    In a case where the pitch fee has not been previously reviewed, references in this paragraph to the last review date are to be read as references to the date when the agreement commenced.

19.    When determining the amount of the new pitch fee, any costs incurred by the owner in connection with expanding the protected site shall not be taken into account.

20.—(1)    There is a presumption that the pitch fee shall increase or decrease by a percentage which is no more than any percentage increase or decrease in the retail prices index since the last review date, unless this would be unreasonable having regard to paragraph 18(1) above.

(2)    Paragraph 18(3) above applies for the purposes of this paragraph as it applies for the purposes of paragraph 18.

*Occupier's obligations*

21.    The occupier shall—

    (a)    pay the pitch fee to the owner;

    (b)    pay to the owner all sums due under the agreement in respect of gas, electricity, water, sewerage or other services supplied by the owner;

    (c)    keep the mobile home in a sound state of repair;

    (d)    maintain—

        (i)    the outside of the mobile home, and

        (ii)    the pitch, including all fences and outbuildings belonging to, or enjoyed with, it and the mobile home,

    in a clean and tidy condition; and

    (e)    if requested by the owner, provide him with documentary evidence of any costs or expenses in respect of which the occupier seeks reimbursement.

*Owner's obligations*

22.    The owner shall—

    (a)    if requested by the occupier, and on payment by the occupier of a charge of not more than £30, provide accurate written details of—

        (i)    the size of the pitch and the base on which the mobile home is stationed; and

        (ii)    the location of the pitch and the base within the protected site;

    and such details must include measurements between identifiable fixed points on the protected site and the pitch and the base;

    (b)    if requested by the occupier, provide (free of charge) documentary evidence in support and explanation of—

        (i)    any new pitch fee;

        (ii)    any charges for gas, electricity, water, sewerage or other services payable by the occupier to the owner under the agreement; and

        (iii)    any other charges, costs or expenses payable by the occupier to the owner under the agreement;

    (c)    be responsible for repairing the base on which the mobile home is stationed and for maintaining any gas, electricity, water, sewerage or other services supplied by the owner to the pitch or to the mobile home;

    (d)    maintain in a clean and tidy condition those parts of the protected site, including access ways, site boundary fences and trees, which are not the responsibility of any occupier of a mobile home stationed on the protected site;

    (e)    consult the occupier about improvements to the protected site in general, and in particular about those which the owner wishes to be taken into account when determining the amount of any new pitch fee; and

    (f)    consult a qualifying residents' association, if there is one, about all matters which relate to the operation and management of, or improvements to, the protected site and may affect the occupiers either directly or indirectly.

23.    The owner shall not do or cause to be done anything which may adversely affect the ability of the occupier to perform his obligations under paragraph 21(c) and (d) above.

24.    For the purposes of paragraph 22(e) above, to "consult" the occupier means—

    (a)    to give the occupier at least 28 clear days' notice in writing of the proposed improvements which—

        (i)    describes the proposed improvements and how they will benefit the occupier in the long and short term;

        (ii)    details how the pitch fee may be affected when it is next reviewed; and

        (iii)    states when and where the occupier can make representations about the proposed improvements; and

    (b)    to take into account any representations made by the occupier about the proposed improvements, in accordance with paragraph (a)(iii), before undertaking them.

25.    For the purposes of paragraph 22(f) above, to "consult" a qualifying residents' association means—

    (a)    to give the association at least 28 clear days' notice in writing of the matters referred to in paragraph 22(f) which—

        (i)    describes the matters and how they may affect the occupiers either directly or indirectly in the long and short term; and

        (ii)    states when and where the association can make representations about the matters; and

    (b)    to take into account any representations made by the association, in accordance with paragraph (a)(ii), before proceeding with the matters.

*Owner's name and address*

26.—(1)    The owner shall by notice inform the occupier and any qualifying residents' association of the address in England or Wales at which notices (including notices of proceedings) may be served on him by the occupier or a qualifying residents' association.

    (2)    If the owner fails to comply with sub-paragraph (1), then (subject to sub-paragraph (5) below) any amount otherwise due from the occupier to the owner in respect of the pitch fee shall be treated for all purposes as not being due from the occupier to the owner at any time before the owner does so comply.

    (3)    Where in accordance with the agreement the owner gives any written notice to the occupier or (as the case may be) a qualifying residents' association, the notice must contain the following information—

    (a)    the name and address of the owner; and

    (b)    if that address is not in England or Wales, an address in England or Wales at which notices (including notices of proceedings) may be served on the owner.

    (4)    Subject to sub-paragraph (5) below, where—

    (a)    the occupier or a qualifying residents' association receives such a notice, but

    (b)    it does not contain the information required to be contained in it by virtue of sub-paragraph (3) above,

    the notice shall be treated as not having been given until such time as the owner gives the information to the occupier or (as the case may be) the association in respect of the notice.

    (5)    An amount or notice within sub-paragraph (2) or (4) (as the case may be) shall not be treated as mentioned in relation to any time when, by virtue of an order of any court or tribunal, there is in force an appointment of a receiver or manager whose functions include receiving from the occupier the pitch fee, payments for services supplied or other charges.

    (6)    Nothing in sub-paragraphs (3) to (5) applies to any notice containing a demand to which paragraph 27(1) below applies.

27.—(1)    Where the owner makes any demand for payment by the occupier of the pitch fee, or in respect of services supplied or other charges, the demand must contain—

    (a)    the name and address of the owner; and

    (b)    if that address is not in England or Wales, an address in England or Wales at which notices (including notices of proceedings) may be served on the owner.

    (2)    Subject to sub-paragraph (3) below, where—

    (a)    the occupier receives such a demand, but

    (b)    it does not contain the information required to be contained in it by virtue of sub-paragraph (1), the amount demanded shall be treated for all purposes as not being due from the occupier to the owner at any time before the owner gives that information to the occupier in respect of the demand.

(3) The amount demanded shall not be so treated in relation to any time when, by virtue of an order of any court or tribunal, there is in force an appointment of a receiver or manager whose functions include receiving from the occupier the pitch fee, payments for services supplied or other charges.

*Qualifying residents' association*

28.—(1) A residents' association is a qualifying residents' association in relation to a protected site if—

(a) it is an association representing the occupiers of mobile homes on that site;

(b) at least 50 per cent of the occupiers of the mobile homes on that site are members of the association;

(c) it is independent from the owner, who together with any agent or employee of his is excluded from membership;

(d) subject to paragraph (c) above, membership is open to all occupiers who own a mobile home on that site;

(e) it maintains a list of members which is open to public inspection together with the rules and constitution of the residents' association;

(f) it has a chairman, secretary and treasurer who are elected by and from among the members;

(g) with the exception of administrative decisions taken by the chairman, secretary and treasurer acting in their official capacities, decisions are taken by voting and there is only one vote for each mobile home; and

(h) the owner has acknowledged in writing to the secretary that the association is a qualifying residents' association, or, in default of this, the court has so ordered.

(2) When calculating the percentage of occupiers for the purpose of sub-paragraph (1)(b) above, each mobile home shall be taken to have only one occupier and, in the event of there being more than one occupier of a mobile home, its occupier is to be taken to be the occupier whose name first appears on the agreement.

*Interpretation*

29. In this Schedule—

"pitch" means the land, forming part of the protected site and including any garden area, on which the occupier is entitled to station the mobile home under the terms of the agreement;

"pitch fee" means the amount which the occupier is required by the agreement to pay to the owner for the right to station the mobile home on the pitch and for use of the common areas of the protected site and their maintenance, but does not include amounts due in respect of gas, electricity, water and sewerage or other services, unless the agreement expressly provides that the pitch fee includes such amounts;

"retail prices index" means the general index (for all items) published by the [Statistics Board] or, if that index is not published for a relevant month, any substituted index or index figures published by [the Board];

"review date" means the date specified in the written statement as the date on which the pitch fee will be reviewed in each year, or if no such date is specified, each anniversary of the date the agreement commenced; and

"written statement" means the written statement that the owner of the protected site is required to give to the occupier by section 1(2) of this Act.]

**[403]**

NOTES

Para 5: words in square brackets substituted in relation to England by the Mobile Homes Act 1983 (Amendment of Schedule 1) (England) Order 2006, SI 2006/1755, art 2(1), (2), subject to transitional provisions and savings, and in relation to Wales by the Mobile Homes Act 1983 (Amendment of Schedule 1) (Wales) Order 2007, SI 2007/3151, art 2(1), (2), subject to transitional provisions and savings.

Para 6: words in square brackets substituted, sub-para (2) and words omitted from sub-para (3) repealed in relation to England by SI 2006/1755, art 2(1), (3), subject to transitional provisions and savings, and in relation to Wales by SI 2007/3151, art 2(1), (3), subject to transitional provisions and savings; words omitted from sub-para (1) repealed in relation to England and Wales by the Housing Act 2004, ss 207(1), (2)(a), 266, Sch 16 (for effect see s 207(6), (7) thereof), and in relation to Scotland by the Housing (Scotland) Act 2006, s 169(1), (2)(a) (for effect see s 169(5), (6)(a) thereof); sub-paras (3)–(5) inserted, in relation to England and Wales, by the Housing Act 2004, s 207(1), (2)(b) (for effect see s 207(6), (7) thereof), and in relation to Scotland by the Housing (Scotland) Act 2006, s 169(1), (2)(b) (for effect see s 169(5), (6)(a) thereof).

Para 8: sub-paras (1A)–(1G) inserted, in relation to England and Wales, by the Housing Act 2004, s 207(2), (3)(a) (for effect see s 207(6), (7) thereof), and in relation to Scotland by the Housing (Scotland) Act 2006, s 169(1), (3)(a) (for effect see s 169(5), (6)(a) thereof); sub-paras (1C), (1D) substituted, words in square brackets in sub-paras (1E), (1F) substituted, words omitted from sub-para (1F) repealed and sub-para (2A) inserted in relation to England by SI 2006/1755, art 2(1), (4), subject to transitional provisions and savings, and in relation to Wales by SI 2007/3151, art 2(1), (4), subject to transitional provisions and savings;

words in square brackets in sub-para (2) substituted in relation to England and Wales, by the Housing Act 2004, s 207(1), (3)(b) (for effect see s 207(6), (7) thereof), and in relation to Scotland by the Housing (Scotland) Act 2006, s 169(1), (3)(b) (for effect see s 169(5), (6)(a) thereof); words in square brackets in sub-para (3) inserted, in relation to England and Wales, by the Housing Act 2004, s 207(1), (3)(c) (for effect see s 270(6) thereof).

Para 9: sub-para (1) numbered as such and sub-para (2) inserted, in relation to England and Wales, by the Housing Act 2004, s 207(1), (4) (for effect see s 207(6), (7)) thereof) and in relation to Scotland by the Housing (Scotland) Act 2006, s 169(1), (4) (for effect see s 169(5), (6)(a) thereof); sub-para (3) inserted in relation to England by SI 2006/1755, art 2(1), (5), subject to transitional provisions and savings, and in relation to Wales by SI 2007/3151, art 2(1), (5), subject to transitional provisions and savings.

Paras 10–29: substituted (with preceding cross-heading) for original para 10, in relation to England by SI 2006/1755, art 2(1), (6), subject to transitional provisions and savings, and in relation to Wales by SI 2007/3151, art 2(1), (6), subject to transitional provisions and savings.

Para 29: in definition "retail prices index" words in square brackets substituted by the Statistics and Registration Service Act 2007, s 60(1), Sch 3, para 2.

Order: the Mobile Homes (Commissions) Order 1983, SI 1983/748 at **[3054]**.

## PART II
## MATTERS CONCERNING WHICH TERMS MAY BE IMPLIED BY COURT

1.    ...

2.    The sums payable by the occupier in pursuance of the agreement and the times at which they are to be paid.

3.    The review at yearly intervals of the sums so payable.

4.    The provision or improvement of services available on the protected site, and the use by the occupier of such services.

5.    The preservation of the amenity of the protected site.

6, 7.    ...

**[404]**

**NOTES**

Paras 1, 6, 7: repealed in relation to England by the Mobile Homes Act 1983 (Amendment of Schedule 1) (England) Order 2006, SI 2006/1755, art 3, subject to transitional provisions and savings, and in relation to Wales by the Mobile Homes Act 1983 (Amendment of Schedule 1) (Wales) Order 2007, SI 2007/3151, art 3, subject to transitional provisions and savings.

Transfer of Functions: functions of the Secretary of State, so far as exercisable in relation to Wales, are transferred to the National Assembly for Wales, by the National Assembly for Wales (Transfer of Functions) Order 1999, SI 1999/672, art 2, Sch 1.

## [PART III
## SUPPLEMENTARY PROVISIONS

*Duty to forward requests under paragraph 8 or 9 of Part 1*

1.—(1)    This paragraph applies to—

    (a)    a request by the occupier for the owner to approve a person for the purposes of paragraph 8(1) of Part 1 (see paragraph 8(1A)), or

    (b)    a request by the occupier for the owner to approve a person for the purposes of paragraph 9(1) of Part 1 (see paragraph 8(1A) as applied by paragraph 9(2)).

    (2)    If a person ("the recipient") receives such a request and he—

    (a)    though not the owner, has an estate or interest in the protected site, and

    (b)    believes that another person is the owner (and that the other person has not received such a request),

the recipient owes a duty to the occupier to take such steps as are reasonable to secure that the other person receives the request within the period of 28 days beginning with the date on which the recipient receives it.

    (3)    In paragraph 8(1B) of Part 1 of this Schedule (as it applies to any request within sub-paragraph (1) above) any reference to the owner receiving such a request includes a reference to his receiving it in accordance with sub-paragraph (2) above.

*Action for breach of duty under paragraph 1*

2.—(1)    A claim that a person has broken the duty under paragraph 1(2) above may be made the subject of civil proceedings in like manner as any other claim in tort for breach of statutory duty.

    (2)    The right conferred by sub-paragraph (1) is in addition to any right to bring proceedings, in respect of a breach of any implied term having effect by virtue of paragraph 8 or 9 of Part 1 of this Schedule, against a person bound by that term.]

**[405]**

**NOTES**
Commencement: 18 January 2005.
Inserted, in relation to England and Wales, by the Housing Act 2004, s 207(5); for effect see s 207(6), (7)(b) thereof.

(*Sch 2 repeals the Mobile Homes Act 1975, ss 1–6 and repeals in part s 9 thereof at* **[153]**.)

# COUNTY COURTS ACT 1984

## (1984 c 28)

### ARRANGEMENT OF SECTIONS

### PART IX
### MISCELLANEOUS AND GENERAL

*Forfeiture for non-payment of rent*

*An Act to consolidate certain enactments relating to county courts*

[26 June 1984]

**1–127** ((*Pts I–VIII*) *outside the scope of this work.*)

### PART IX
### MISCELLANEOUS AND GENERAL

**128–137** (*Outside the scope of this work.*)

*Forfeiture for non-payment of rent*

### 138 Provisions as to forfeiture for non-payment of rent

(1) This section has effect where a lessor is proceeding by action in a county court (being an action in which the county court has jurisdiction) to enforce against a lessee a right of re-entry or forfeiture in respect of any land for non-payment of rent.

(2) If the lessee pays into court [or to the lessor] not less than 5 clear days before the return day all the rent in arrear and the costs of the action, the action shall cease, and the lessee shall hold the land according to the lease without any new lease.

(3) If—
    (a) the action does not cease under subsection (2); and
    (b) the court at the trial is satisfied that the lessor is entitled to enforce the right of re-entry or forfeiture,
the court shall order possession of the land to be given to the lessor at the expiration of such period, not being less than 4 weeks from the date of the order, as the court thinks fit, unless within that period the lessee pays into court [or to the lessor] all the rent in arrear and the costs of the action.

(4) The court may extend the period specified under subsection (3) at any time before possession of the land is recovered in pursuance of the order under that subsection.

(5) ... if—
    (a) within the period specified in the order; or
    (b) within that period as extended under subsection (4),
the lessee pays into court [or to the lessor]—
    (i) all the rent in arrear; and
    (ii) the costs of the action,
he shall hold the land according to the lease without any new lease.

(6)    Subsection (2) shall not apply where the lessor is proceeding in the same action to enforce a right of re-entry or forfeiture on any other ground as well as for non-payment of rent, or to enforce any other claim as well as the right of re-entry or forfeiture and the claim for arrears of rent.

(7)    If the lessee does not—
    (a)    within the period specified in the order; or
    (b)    within that period as extended under subsection (4), pay into court [or to the lessor]—
        (i)    all the rent in arrear; and
        (ii)    the costs of the action,
the order shall be [enforceable] in the prescribed manner and so long as the order remains unreversed the lessee shall[, subject to subsections (8) and (9A),] be barred from all relief.

(8)    The extension under subsection (4) of a period fixed by a court shall not be treated as relief from which the lessee is barred by subsection (7) if he fails to pay into court [or to the lessor] all the rent in arrear and the costs of the action within that period.

(9)    Where the court extends a period under subsection (4) at a time when—
    (a)    that period has expired; and
    (b)    a warrant has been issued for the possession of the land, the court shall suspend the warrant for the extended period; and, if, before the expiration period, the lessee pays into court [or to the lessor] all the rent in arrear and all the costs of the action, the court shall cancel the warrant.

[(9A)    Where the lessor recovers possession of the land at any time after the making of the order under subsection (3) (whether as a result of the enforcement of the order or otherwise) the lessee may, at any time within six months from the date on which the lessor recovers possession, apply to the court for relief; and on any such application the court may, if it thinks fit, grant to the lessee such relief, subject to such terms and conditions, as it thinks fit.

(9B)    Where the lessee is granted relief on an application under subsection (9A) he shall hold the land according to the lease without any new lease.

(9C)    An application under subsection (9A) may be made by a person with an interest under a lease of the land derived (whether immediately or otherwise) from the lessee's interest therein in like manner as if he were the lessee; and on any such application the court may make an order which (subject to such terms and conditions as the court thinks fit) vests the land in such a person, as lessee of the lessor, for the remainder of the term of the lease under which he has any such interest as aforesaid, or for any lesser term.

In this subsection any reference to the land includes a reference to a part of the land.]

(10)    Nothing in this section or section 139 shall be taken to affect—
    (a)    the power of the court to make any order which it would otherwise have power to make as respects a right of re-entry or forfeiture on any ground other than non-payment of rent; or
    (b)    section 146(4) of the Law of Property Act 1925 (relief against forfeiture).

[406]

**NOTES**
Sub-ss (2), (3), (8), (9): words in square brackets inserted by the Courts and Legal Services Act 1990, s 125(2), Sch 17, para 17.
Sub-s (5): words omitted repealed by the Administration of Justice Act 1985, ss 55(2), 67(2), Sch 8, Pt III; words in square brackets inserted by the Courts and Legal Services Act 1990, s 125(2), Sch 17, para 17.
Sub-s (7): words in first pair of square brackets inserted by the Courts and Legal Services Act 1990, s 125(2), Sch 17, para 17; words in second pair of square brackets substituted and words in third pair of square brackets inserted by the Administration of Justice Act 1985, s 55(3).
Sub-ss (9A)–(9C): inserted by the Administration of Justice Act 1985, s 55(4).

## 139    Service of summons and re-entry

(1)    In a case where section 138 has effect, if—
    (a)    one-half-year's rent is in arrear at the time of the commencement of the action; and
    (b)    the lessor has a right to re-enter for non-payment of that rent; and
    (c)    *no sufficient distress is to be found on the premises countervailing the arrears then due,*
the service of the summons in the action in the prescribed manner shall stand in lieu of a demand and re-entry.

(2)    Where a lessor has enforced against a lessee, by re-entry without action, a right of re-entry or forfeiture as respects any land for non-payment of rent, the lessee may ... at any time within six months from the date on which the lessor re-entered apply to the county court for relief, and on any such application the court may, if it thinks fit, grant to the lessee such relief as the High Court could have granted.

[(3) Subsections (9B) and (9C) of section 138 shall have effect in relation to an application under subsection (2) of this section as they have effect in relation to an application under subsection (9A) of that section.]

[407]

**NOTES**

Sub-s (1): para (c) substituted by new paras (c), (d), by the Tribunals, Courts and Enforcement Act 2007, s 86, Sch 14, paras 38, 40, as from a day to be appointed, as follows:

"(c)   the power under section 72(1) of the Tribunals, Courts and Enforcement Act 2007 (commercial rent arrears recovery) is exercisable to recover the arrears; and

(d)   there are not sufficient goods on the premises to recover the arrears by that power,".

Sub-s (2): words omitted repealed by the High Court and County Courts Jurisdiction Order 1991, SI 1991/724, art 2(8), Schedule, Pt I.

Sub-s (3): added by the Administration of Justice Act 1985, s 55(5).

## 140   Interpretation of sections 138 and 139

For the purposes of sections 138 and 139—

"lease" includes—

(a)   an original or derivative under-lease;

(b)   an agreement for a lease where the lessee has become entitled to have his lease granted; and

(c)   a grant at a fee farm rent, or under a grant securing a rent by condition;

"lessee" includes—

(a)   an original or derivative under-lessee;

(b)   the persons deriving title under a lessee;

(c)   a grantee under a grant at a fee farm rent, or under a grant securing a rent by condition; and

(d)   the persons deriving title under such a grantee;

"lessor" includes—

(a)   an original or derivative under-lessor;

(b)   the persons deriving title under a lessor;

(c)   a person making a grant at a fee farm rent, or a grant securing a rent by condition; and

(d)   the persons deriving title under such a grantor;

"under-lease" includes an agreement for an under-lease where the under-lessee has become entitled to have his underlease granted; and

"under-lessee" includes any person deriving title under an under-lessee.

[408]

**141–145**   (*S 141 repealed by the Statute Law (Repeals) Act 1986; ss 142–145 outside the scope of this work.*)

*General*

**146–148**   (*Outside the scope of this work.*)

## 149   Extent

(1), (2)   (*Outside the scope of this work.*)

(3)   Subject to subsections (1) and (2), this Act extends to England and Wales only.

[409]

## 150   Commencement

This Act shall come into force on 1st August 1984.

[410]

## 151   Short title

This Act may be cited as the County Courts Act 1984.

[411]

(*Schs 1–4 outside the scope of this work.*)

# RENT (AMENDMENT) ACT 1985

(1985 c 24)

*An Act to make further provision as to the circumstances in which possession of a dwelling-house is recoverable under Case 11 in Schedule 15 to the Rent Act 1977 and Case 11 in Schedule 2 to the*

*Rent (Scotland) Act 1984 and as to the parliamentary procedure applicable to an Order in Council under paragraph 1(1) of Schedule 1 to the Northern Ireland Act 1974 which states that it is made for corresponding purposes*

[23 May 1985]

**1 Recovery in possession under Case 11**

(1)–(3)  ...

(4)   Case 11 in Schedule 15 to the Rent Act 1977 and Case 11 in Schedule 2 to the Rent (Scotland) Act 1984, as those cases have effect by virtue of this section, apply to tenancies granted and notices given before, as well as after, the commencement of this Act.

[412]

**NOTES**

Sub-ss (1)–(3): amend the Rent Act 1977, Sch 15, Pt II at **[330]**, and the Rent (Scotland) Act 1984, Sch 2.

**2  Northern Ireland**

An Order in Council under paragraph 1(1)(b) of Schedule 1 to the Northern Ireland Act 1974 (legislation for Northern Ireland in the interim period) which states that it is made only for purposes corresponding to those of section 1 of this Act—

(a)   shall not be subject to paragraph 1(4) and (5) of that Schedule (affirmative resolution of both Houses of Parliament); but

(b)   shall be subject to annulment in pursuance of a resolution of either House.

[413]

**3  Short title and extent**

(1)   This Act may be cited as the Rent (Amendment) Act 1985.

(2)   Only section 2 of this Act extends to Northern Ireland.

[414]

# HOUSING ACT 1985

(1985 c 68)

## ARRANGEMENT OF SECTIONS

### PART IV
### SECURE TENANCIES AND RIGHTS OF SECURE TENANTS

*Security of tenure*

PART V
THE RIGHT TO BUY

*An Act to consolidate the Housing Acts (except those provisions consolidated in the Housing Associations Act 1985 and the Landlord and Tenant Act 1985), and certain related provisions, with amendments to give effect to recommendations of the Law Commission*

[30 October 1985]

**NOTES**

Transfer of functions: as to the functions of Ministers of the Crown under this Act, so far as exercisable in relation to Wales, being transferred to the National Assembly for Wales, see the National Assembly for Wales (Transfer of Functions) Order 1999, SI 1999/672, art 2, Sch 1.

**1–78**  ((*Pts I–III*) *outside the scope of this work.*)

## PART IV
## SECURE TENANCIES AND RIGHTS OF SECURE TENANTS

*Security of tenure*

**NOTES**

Phasing out of certain secure tenancies: the Housing Act 1988, s 35(4) at **[766]**, provides that (subject to s 38(4A)) no tenancy or licence entered into on or after 15 January 1989 can be a secure tenancy and accordingly be covered by the special regime applying to such tenancies under this Part and the right to buy provisions in Pt V at **[461]** et seq, unless it satisfies one of the conditions set out in that subsection. Tenancies which by virtue of s 35 of the 1988 Act do not become secure tenancies will generally become assured tenancies under Chapter I of Pt I of that Act at **[729]** et seq. For further provision with regard to the transfer of existing tenancies from the public to the private sector, see s 38 of the 1988 Act at **[769]**.

## 79  Secure tenancies

(1)  A tenancy under which a dwelling-house is let as a separate dwelling is a secure tenancy at any time when the conditions described in sections 80 and 81 as the landlord condition and the tenant condition are satisfied.

(2)  Subsection (1) has effect subject to—
  (a)  the exceptions in Schedule 1 (tenancies which are not secure tenancies),
  (b)  sections 89(3) and (4) and 90(3) and (4) (tenancies ceasing to be secure after death of tenant), and
  (c)  sections 91(2) and 93(2) (tenancies ceasing to be secure in consequence of assignment or subletting).

(3)  The provisions of this Part apply in relation to a licence to occupy a dwelling-house (whether or not granted for a consideration) as they apply in relation to a tenancy.

(4)  Subsection (3) does not apply to a licence granted as a temporary expedient to a person who entered the dwelling-house or any other land as a trespasser (whether or not, before the grant of that licence, another licence to occupy that or another dwelling-house had been granted to him).

[415]

## 80  The landlord condition

(1)  The landlord condition is that the interest of the landlord belongs to one of the following authorities or bodies—
    a local authority,
    a [development] corporation,
    [a housing action trust]
    an urban development corporation, [in the case of a tenancy falling within subsections (2A) to (2E), the Homes and Communities Agency or the Welsh Ministers (as the case may be),]
    ...

...

a housing trust which is a charity, or

a ... housing co-operative to which this section applies.

(2) ...

[(2A)    A tenancy falls within this subsection if the interest of the landlord is transferred to—
  (a)    the Homes and Communities Agency as mentioned in section 52(1)(a) to (d) of the Housing and Regeneration Act 2008, or
  (b)    the Welsh Ministers as mentioned in section 36(1)(a)(i) to (iii) of the New Towns Act 1981.

(2B)    A tenancy falls within this subsection if it is entered into pursuant to a contract under which the rights and liabilities of the prospective landlord are transferred to the Homes and Communities Agency or the Welsh Ministers as mentioned in subsection (2A)(a) or (b) (as the case may be).

(2C)    A tenancy falls within this subsection if it is granted by the Homes and Communities Agency or the Welsh Ministers to a person (alone or jointly with others) who, immediately before it was entered into, was a secure tenant of the Homes and Communities Agency or the Welsh Ministers (as the case may be).

(2D)    A tenancy falls within this subsection if—
  (a)    it is granted by the Homes and Communities Agency or the Welsh Ministers to a person (alone or jointly with others),
  (b)    before the grant of the tenancy, an order for possession of a dwelling-house let under a secure tenancy was made against the person (alone or jointly with others) and in favour of the Homes and Communities Agency or the Welsh Ministers (as the case may be) on the court being satisfied as mentioned in section 84(2)(b) or (c), and
  (c)    the tenancy is of the premises which constitute the suitable accommodation as to which the court was so satisfied.

(2E)    A tenancy falls within this subsection if it is granted by the Homes and Communities Agency or the Welsh Ministers pursuant to an obligation under section 554(2A).]

(3)    If a co-operative housing association ceases to be [a registered social landlord], it shall, within the period of 21 days beginning with the date on which it ceases to be [a registered social landlord], notify each of its tenants who thereby becomes a secure tenant, in writing, that he has become a secure tenant.

[(4)    This section applies to a housing co-operative within the meaning of section 27B (agreements under certain superseded provisions) where the dwelling-house is comprised in a housing co-operative agreement within the meaning of that section.]

[(5)    In this Act and in any provision made under this Act, or made by or under any other enactment, a reference to—
  (a)    a person within section 80 or 80(1) of this Act, or
  (b)    a person who satisfies the landlord condition under this section,

includes a reference to the Homes and Communities Agency or to the Welsh Ministers so far as acting in their capacity as landlord (or, in the case of disposals, former landlord) in respect of a tenancy which falls within subsections (2A) to (2E) above but, subject to this, does not include the Homes and Communities Agency or the Welsh Ministers.

(6)    Subsection (5)—
  (a)    applies whether the person is described as an authority, body or landlord or in any other way and whether the reference is otherwise expressed in a different way, and
  (b)    is subject to any provision to the contrary.]

**[416]**

---

NOTES

Sub-s (1): word in first pair of square brackets substituted and words in third pair of square brackets inserted by the Housing and Regeneration Act 2008 (Consequential Provisions) Order 2008, SI 2008/3002, art 4, Sch 1, paras 2, 10(1), (2), subject to transitional provisions and savings in art 5, Sch 2 thereto; words in second pair of square brackets inserted by the Housing Act 1988, s 83(1), (2); words omitted in the first place repealed by the Government of Wales Act 1998, s 152, Sch 18, Pt IV; other words omitted repealed by the Housing Act 1988, s 140(2), Sch 18, subject to the savings noted below.

Sub-s (2): repealed by the Housing Act 1988, s 140(2), Sch 18, subject to the savings noted below.

Sub-ss (2A)–(2E): inserted by SI 2008/3002, art 4, Sch 1, paras 2, 10(1), (3), subject to transitional provisions and savings in art 5, Sch 2 thereto.

Sub-s (3): words in square brackets substituted by the Housing Act 1996 (Consequential Provisions) Order 1996, SI 1996/2325, art 5, Sch 2, para 14.

Sub-s (4): substituted by the Housing and Planning Act 1986, s 24(2), Sch 5, Pt II, para 26.

Sub-ss (5), (6): inserted by SI 2008/3002, art 4, Sch 1, paras 2, 10(1), (4), subject to transitional provisions and savings in art 5, Sch 2 thereto.

Savings: the repeals made to this section by the Housing Act 1988, s 140(2), Sch 18 apply (subject to s 35(5) of that Act at **[766]**) in relation to any tenancy or licence entered into before 15 January 1989, unless, immediately before that date, the landlord (or licensor) is a body which, in accordance with the repeals, would cease to be within this section (ie, the Housing Corporation, charitable housing trusts and a housing association). The repeals also do not have effect in relation to (i) a tenancy or licence entered into on or after that date if it falls within any of the conditions specified in s 35(4)(c)–(f) of the 1988 Act; (ii) a tenancy while it is a housing association tenancy. The repealed text, in so far as it is saved, is amended by SI 1996/2325, art 5, Sch 2, para 14 and the Government of Wales Act 1998, s 140, Sch 16, paras 4, 5.

Modifications: the body corporate known as the Residuary Body for Wales is to be treated as a local authority for the purposes of this section, by virtue of the Local Government (Wales) Act 1994, s 39, Sch 13, para 21(c).

The body corporate known as the Residuary Body for England is to be treated as a local authority for the purposes of this Part (and Pt V), by virtue of the Local Government Residuary Body (England) Order 1995, SI 1995/401, art 18, Schedule, para 8.

## 81 The tenant condition

The tenant condition is that the tenant is an individual and occupies the dwelling-house as his only or principal home; or, where the tenancy is a joint tenancy, that each of the joint tenants is an individual and at least one of them occupies the dwelling-house as his only or principal home.

**[417]**

## 82 Security of tenure

(1)   A secure tenancy which is either—
   (a)   a weekly or other periodic tenancy, or
   (b)   a tenancy for a term certain but subject to termination by the landlord,
cannot be brought to an end by the landlord except [as] [mentioned in subsection (1A)].

[(1A)   The tenancy may be brought to an end by the landlord—
   (a)   obtaining—
      (i)   an order of the court for the possession of the dwelling-house, and
      (ii)   the execution of the order,
   (b)   obtaining an order under subsection (3), or
   (c)   obtaining a demotion order under section 82A.

(2)   In the case mentioned in subsection (1A)(a), the tenancy ends when the order is executed.]

(3)   Where a secure tenancy is a tenancy for a term certain but with a provision for re-entry or forfeiture, the court shall not order possession of the dwelling-house in pursuance of that provision, but in a case where the court would have made such an order it shall instead make an order terminating the tenancy on a date specified in the order and section 86 (periodic tenancy arising on termination of fixed term) shall apply.

(4)   Section 146 of the Law of Property Act 1925 (restriction on and relief against forfeiture), except subsection (4) (vesting in under-lessee), and any other enactment or rule of law relating to forfeiture, shall apply in relation to proceedings for an order under subsection (3) of this section as if they were proceedings to enforce a right of re-entry or forfeiture.

**[418]**

**NOTES**
Sub-s (1): word in first pair of square brackets substituted by the Housing and Regeneration Act 2008, s 299, Sch 11, Pt 1, paras 1, 2(1), (2), subject to transitional provisions in Sch 11, Pt 1, para 14 thereto at **[1891]**; words in second pair of square brackets substituted by the Anti-social Behaviour Act 2003, s 14(1)(a).

Sub-s (1A): inserted by the Anti-social Behaviour Act 2003, s 14(1)(b); substituted by the Housing and Regeneration Act 2008, s 299, Sch 11, Pt 1, paras 1, 2(1), (3), subject to transitional provisions in Sch 11, Pt 1, para 14 thereto at **[1891]**.

Sub-s (2): substituted by the Housing and Regeneration Act 2008, s 299, Sch 11, Pt 1, paras 1, 2(1), (3), subject to transitional provisions in Sch 11, Pt 1, para 14 thereto at **[1891]**.

## [82A   Demotion because of anti-social behaviour

(1)   This section applies to a secure tenancy if the landlord is—
   (a)   a local housing authority;
   (b)   a housing action trust;
   (c)   a registered social landlord.

(2)   The landlord may apply to a county court for a demotion order.

(3)   A demotion order has the following effect—
   (a)   the secure tenancy is terminated with effect from the date specified in the order;
   (b)   if the tenant remains in occupation of the dwelling-house after that date a demoted tenancy is created with effect from that date;
   (c)   it is a term of the demoted tenancy that any arrears of rent payable at the termination of the secure tenancy become payable under the demoted tenancy;
   (d)   it is also a term of the demoted tenancy that any rent paid in advance or overpaid at the termination of the secure tenancy is credited to the tenant's liability to pay rent under the demoted tenancy.

(4)   The court must not make a demotion order unless it is satisfied—

 (a) that the tenant or a person residing in or visiting the dwelling-house has engaged or has threatened to [engage in—
  (i) housing-related anti-social conduct, or
  (ii) conduct to which section 153B of the Housing Act 1996 (use of premises for unlawful purposes) applies, and]
 (b) that it is reasonable to make the order.

 (5) Each of the following has effect in respect of a demoted tenancy at the time it is created by virtue of an order under this section as it has effect in relation to the secure tenancy at the time it is terminated by virtue of the order—
 (a) the parties to the tenancy;
 (b) the period of the tenancy;
 (c) the amount of the rent;
 (d) the dates on which the rent is payable.

 (6) Subsection (5)(b) does not apply if the secure tenancy was for a fixed term and in such a case the demoted tenancy is a weekly periodic tenancy.

 (7) If the landlord of the demoted tenancy serves on the tenant a statement of any other express terms of the secure tenancy which are to apply to the demoted tenancy such terms are also terms of the demoted tenancy.

 [(7A) In subsection (4)(a) "housing-related anti-social conduct" has the same meaning as in section 153A of the Housing Act 1996.]

 (8) For the purposes of this section a demoted tenancy is—
 (a) a tenancy to which section 143A of the Housing Act 1996 applies if the landlord of the secure tenancy is a local housing authority or a housing action trust;
 (b) a tenancy to which section 20B of the Housing Act 1988 applies if the landlord of the secure tenancy is a registered social landlord.]

**[419]**

**NOTES**

Commencement: 30 June 2004 (in relation to England); 30 September 2004 (in relation to Wales for the purpose of making regulations); 30 April 2005 (otherwise).

Inserted by the Anti-social Behaviour Act 2003, s 14(2).

Sub-s (4): words in square brackets substituted for original words "engage in conduct to which section 153A or 153B of the Housing Act 1996 (anti-social behaviour or use of premises for unlawful purposes) applies, and" by the Police and Justice Act 2006, s 52, Sch 14, para 12(1), (2), except in relation to any application for a demotion order or a suspension order made by a landlord (other than a relevant Welsh landlord) made before 6 April 2007.

Sub-s (7A): inserted by the Police and Justice Act 2006, s 52, Sch 14, para 12(1), (3), except in relation to any application for a demotion order or a suspension order made by a landlord (other than a relevant Welsh landlord) made before 6 April 2007.

---

**[83 Proceedings for possession or termination: notice requirements**

 (1) The court shall not entertain proceedings for [an order mentioned in section 82(1A)] unless—
 (a) the landlord has served a notice on the tenant complying with the provisions of this section, or
 (b) the court considers it just and equitable to dispense with the requirement of such a notice.

 (2) A notice under this section shall—
 (a) be in a form prescribed by regulations made by the Secretary of State,
 (b) specify the ground on which the court will be asked to make [the order], and
 (c) give particulars of that ground.

 (3) Where the tenancy is a periodic tenancy and the ground or one of the grounds specified in the notice is Ground 2 in Schedule 2 (nuisance or other anti-social behaviour), the notice—
 (a) shall also—
  (i) state that proceedings for the possession of the dwelling-house may be begun immediately, and
  (ii) specify the date sought by the landlord as the date on which the tenant is to give up possession of the dwelling-house, and
 (b) ceases to be in force twelve months after the date so specified.

 (4) Where the tenancy is a periodic tenancy and Ground 2 in Schedule 2 is not specified in the notice, the notice—
 (a) shall also specify the date after which proceedings for the possession of the dwelling-house may be begun, and
 (b) ceases to be in force twelve months after the date so specified.

 [(4A) If the proceedings are for a demotion order under section 82A the notice—

(a)    must specify the date after which the proceedings may be begun;

(b)    ceases to be in force twelve months after the date so specified.]

(5)    The date specified in accordance with subsection (3), [(4) or (4A)] must not be earlier than the date on which the tenancy could, apart from this Part, be brought to an end by notice to quit given by the landlord on the same date as the notice under this section.

(6)    Where a notice under this section is served with respect to a secure tenancy for a term certain, it has effect also with respect to any periodic tenancy arising on the termination of that tenancy by virtue of section 86; and subsections (3) to (5) of this section do not apply to the notice.

(7)    Regulations under this section shall be made by statutory instrument and may make different provision with respect to different cases or descriptions of case, including different provision for different areas.]

**[420]**

**NOTES**
Substituted, together with s 83A for original s 83, by the Housing Act 1996, s 147(1), except in relation to notices served before 12 February 1997.
Sub-s (1): words in square brackets substituted by the Anti-social Behaviour Act 2003, s 14(3)(a).
Sub-s (2): words in square brackets in para (b) substituted by the Anti-social Behaviour Act 2003, s 14(3)(b).
Sub-s (4A): inserted by the Anti-social Behaviour Act 2003, s 14(3)(c).
Sub-s (5): words in square brackets substituted by the Anti-social Behaviour Act 2003, s 14(3)(d).
Regulations: by virtue of the Interpretation Act 1978, s 17(2)(b), the Secure Tenancies (Notices) Regulations 1987, SI 1987/755 at **[3064]**, have effect as if made under this section.

**[83A    Additional requirements in relation to certain proceedings for possession**

(1)    Where a notice under section 83 has been served on a tenant containing the information mentioned in subsection (3)(a) of that section, the court shall not entertain proceedings for the possession of the dwelling-house unless they are begun at a time when the notice is still in force.

(2)    Where—

(a)    a notice under section 83 has been served on a tenant, and

(b)    a date after which proceedings may be begun has been specified in the notice in accordance with subsection (4)(a) of that section,

the court shall not entertain proceedings for the possession of the dwelling-house unless they are begun after the date so specified and at a time when the notice is still in force.

(3)    Where—

(a)    the ground or one of the grounds specified in a notice under section 83 is Ground 2A in Schedule 2 (domestic violence), and

(b)    the partner who has left the dwelling-house as mentioned in that ground is not a tenant of the dwelling-house,

the court shall not entertain proceedings for the possession of the dwelling-house unless it is satisfied that the landlord has served a copy of the notice on the partner who has left or has taken all reasonable steps to serve a copy of the notice on that partner.

This subsection has effect subject to subsection (5).

(4)    Where—

(a)    Ground 2A in Schedule 2 is added to a notice under section 83 with the leave of the court after proceedings for possession are begun, and

(b)    the partner who has left the dwelling-house as mentioned in that ground is not a party to the proceedings,

the court shall not continue to entertain the proceedings unless it is satisfied that the landlord has served a notice under subsection (6) on the partner who has left or has taken all reasonable steps to serve such a notice on that partner.

This subsection has effect subject to subsection (5).

(5)    Where subsection (3) or (4) applies and Ground 2 in Schedule 2 (nuisance or other anti-social behaviour) is also specified in the notice under section 83, the court may dispense with the requirements as to service in relation to the partner who has left the dwelling-house if it considers it just and equitable to do so.

(6)    A notice under this subsection shall—

(a)    state that proceedings for the possession of the dwelling-house have begun,

(b)    specify the ground or grounds on which possession is being sought, and

(c)    give particulars of the ground or grounds.]

**[421]**

**NOTES**
Substituted as noted to s 83 at **[420]**.

**84   Grounds and orders for possession**

(1)   The court shall not make an order for the possession of a dwelling-house let under a secure tenancy except on one or more of the grounds set out in Schedule 2.

(2)   The court shall not make an order for possession—
    (a)   on the grounds set out in Part I of that Schedule (grounds 1 to 8), unless it considers it reasonable to make the order,
    (b)   on the grounds set out in Part II of that Schedule (grounds 9 to 11), unless it is satisfied that suitable accommodation will be available for the tenant when the order takes effect,
    (c)   on the grounds set out in Part III of that Schedule (grounds 12 to 16), unless it both considers it reasonable to make the order and is satisfied that suitable accommodation will be available for the tenant when the order takes effect;

and Part IV of that Schedule has effect for determining whether suitable accommodation will be available for a tenant.

[(3)   Where a notice under section 83 has been served on the tenant, the court shall not make such an order on any of those grounds above unless the ground is specified in the notice; but the grounds so specified may be altered or added to with the leave of the court.

(4)   Where a date is specified in a notice under section 83 in accordance with subsection (3) of that section, the court shall not make an order which requires the tenant to give up possession of the dwelling-house in question before the date so specified.]

**[422]**

**NOTES**

Sub-ss (3), (4): substituted, for original sub-s (3), by the Housing Act 1996, s 147(2), except in relation to notices served under s 83, before 12 February 1997.

**85   Extended discretion of court in certain proceedings for possession**

(1)   Where proceedings are brought for possession of a dwelling-house let under a secure tenancy on any of the grounds set out in Part I or Part III of Schedule 2 (grounds 1 to 8 and 12 to 16: cases in which the court must be satisfied that it is reasonable to make a possession order), the court may adjourn the proceedings for such period or periods as it thinks fit.

(2)   On the making of an order for possession of such a dwelling-house on any of those grounds, or at any time before the execution of the order, the court may—
    (a)   stay or suspend the execution of the order, or
    (b)   postpone the date of possession,

for such period or periods as the court thinks fit.

(3)   On such an adjournment, stay, suspension or postponement the court—
    (a)   shall impose conditions with respect to the payment by the tenant of arrears of rent (if any) and rent … unless it considers that to do so would cause exceptional hardship to the tenant or would otherwise be unreasonable, and
    (b)   may impose such other conditions as it thinks fit.

*(4)   If the conditions are complied with, the court may, if it thinks fit, discharge or rescind the order for possession.*

(5)   …

[(5A)   … ]

**[423]**

**NOTES**

Sub-s (3): words omitted repealed by the Housing and Regeneration Act 2008, ss 299, 321(1), Sch 11, Pt 1, paras 1, 3(1), (2), Sch 16, subject to transitional provisions in Sch 11, Pt 1, para 14 thereto at **[1891]**.

Sub-s (4): substituted by the Housing and Regeneration Act 2008, s 299, Sch 11, Pt 1, paras 1, 3(1), (3), subject to transitional provisions in Sch 11, Pt 1, para 14 thereto at **[1891]**, as from a day to be appointed, as follows:

"(4)   The court may discharge or rescind the order for possession if it thinks it appropriate to do so having had regard to—
    (a)   any conditions imposed under subsection (3), and
    (b)   the conduct of the tenant in connection with those conditions.".

Sub-s (5): repealed by the Housing and Regeneration Act 2008, ss 299, 321(1), Sch 11, Pt 1, paras 1, 3(1), (4), Sch 16, subject to transitional provisions in Sch 11, Pt 1, para 14 thereto at **[1891]**.

Sub-s (5A): added by the Family Law Act 1996, s 66(1), Sch 8, Pt III, para 53, subject to savings in s 66(2) of, and Sch 9, paras 8–10 to, that Act; repealed by the Housing and Regeneration Act 2008, ss 299, 321(1), Sch 11, Pt 1, paras 1, 3(1), (4), Sch 16, subject to transitional provisions in Sch 11, Pt 1, para 14 thereto at **[1891]**.

**[85A Proceedings for possession: anti-social behaviour**

(1) This section applies if the court is considering under section 84(2)(a) whether it is reasonable to make an order for possession on ground 2 set out in Part 1 of Schedule 2 (conduct of tenant or other person).

(2) The court must consider, in particular—

    (a)   the effect that the nuisance or annoyance has had on persons other than the person against whom the order is sought;

    (b)   any continuing effect the nuisance or annoyance is likely to have on such persons;

    (c)   the effect that the nuisance or annoyance would be likely to have on such persons if the conduct is repeated.]

                                                                     **[424]**

**NOTES**

Inserted by the Anti-social Behaviour Act 2003, s 16(1), except in relation to any proceedings for the possession of a dwelling-house begun before 30 June 2004 (in relation to England) and 30 September 2004 (in relation to Wales).

**86 Periodic tenancy arising on termination of fixed term**

(1) Where a secure tenancy ("the first tenancy") is a tenancy for a term certain and comes to an end—

    (a)   by effluxion of time, or

    (b)   by an order of the court under section 82(3) (termination in pursuance of provision for re-entry or forfeiture),

a periodic tenancy of the same dwelling-house arises by virtue of this section, unless the tenant is granted another secure tenancy of the same dwelling-house (whether a tenancy for a term certain or a periodic tenancy) to begin on the coming to an end of the first tenancy.

(2) Where a periodic tenancy arises by virtue of this section—

    (a)   the periods of the tenancy are the same as those for which rent was last payable under the first tenancy, and

    (b)   the parties and the terms of the tenancy are the same as those of the first tenancy at the end of it;

except that the terms are confined to those which are compatible with a periodic tenancy and do not include any provision for re-entry or forfeiture.

                                                                       **[425]**

*Succession on death of tenant*

**87 Persons qualified to succeed tenant**

A person is qualified to succeed the tenant under a secure tenancy if he occupies the dwelling-house as his only or principal home at the time of the tenant's death and either—

    (a)   he is the tenant's spouse [or civil partner], or

    (b)   he is another member of the tenant's family and has resided with the tenant throughout the period of twelve months ending with the tenant's death;

unless, in either case, the tenant was himself a successor, as defined in section 88.

                                                                       **[426]**

**NOTES**

Words in square brackets inserted by the Civil Partnership Act 2004, s 81, Sch 8, para 20.

**88 Cases where the tenant is a successor**

(1) The tenant is himself a successor if—

    (a)   the tenancy vested in him by virtue of section 89 (succession to a periodic tenancy), or

    (b)   he was a joint tenant and has become the sole tenant, or

    (c)   the tenancy arose by virtue of section 86 (periodic tenancy arising on ending of term certain) and the first tenancy there mentioned was granted to another person or jointly to him and another person, or

    (d)   he became the tenant on the tenancy being assigned to him (but subject to subsections [(2) to (3)]), or

    (e)   he became the tenant on the tenancy being vested in him on the death of the previous tenant [or

    (f)   the tenancy was previously an introductory tenancy and he was a successor to the introductory tenancy.]

(2) A tenant to whom the tenancy was assigned in pursuance of an order under *section 24* of the Matrimonial Causes Act 1973 (property adjustment orders in connection with matrimonial

proceedings) [or section 17(1) of the Matrimonial and Family Proceedings Act 1984 (property adjustment orders after overseas divorce, &c)] is a successor only if the other party to the marriage was a successor.

[(2A)   A tenant to whom the tenancy was assigned in pursuance of an order under Part 2 of Schedule 5, or paragraph 9(2) or (3) of Schedule 7, to the Civil Partnership Act 2004 (property adjustment orders in connection with civil partnership proceedings or after overseas dissolution of civil partnership, etc) is a successor only if the other civil partner was a successor.]

(3)   A tenant to whom the tenancy was assigned by virtue of section 92 (assignments by way of exchange) is a successor only if he was a successor in relation to the tenancy which he himself assigned by virtue of that section.

(4)   Where within six months of the coming to an end of a secure tenancy which is a periodic tenancy ("the former tenancy") the tenant becomes a tenant under another secure tenancy which is a periodic tenancy, and—
    (a)   the tenant was a successor in relation to the former tenancy, and
    (b)   under the other tenancy either the dwelling-house or the landlord, or both, are the same as under the former tenancy,
the tenant is also a successor in relation to the other tenancy unless the agreement creating that tenancy otherwise provides.

**[427]**

**NOTES**
Sub-s (1): words in square brackets in para (d) substituted by the Civil Partnership Act 2004, s 81, Sch 8, para 21(1), (2); para (f) and the word immediately preceding it inserted by the Housing Act 1996, s 141(1), Sch 14, para 1.
Sub-s (2): for the words in italics there are substituted the words "section 23A or 24" by the Family Law Act 1996, s 66(1), Sch 8, Pt I, para 34, as from a day to be appointed, subject to savings in s 66(2) of, and Sch 9, para 5 to, that Act; words in square brackets inserted by the Housing Act 1996, s 222, Sch 18, Pt III, para 9.
Sub-s (2A): inserted by the Civil Partnership Act 2004, s 81, Sch 8, para 21(1), (3).

---

**89   Succession to periodic tenancy**

(1)   This section applies where a secure tenant dies and the tenancy is a periodic tenancy.

(2)   Where there is a person qualified to succeed the tenant, the tenancy vests by virtue of this section in that person, or if there is more than one such person in the one to be preferred in accordance with the following rules—
    (a)   the tenant's spouse [or civil partner] is to be preferred to another member of the tenant's family;
    (b)   of two or more other members of the tenant's family such of them is to be preferred as may be agreed between them or as may, where there is no such agreement, be selected by the landlord.

[(3)   Where there is no person qualified to succeed the tenant, the tenancy ceases to be a secure tenancy—
    (a)   when it is vested or otherwise disposed of in the course of the administration of the tenant's estate, unless the vesting or other disposal is in pursuance of an order made under—
        (i)   *section 24* of the Matrimonial Causes Act 1973 (property adjustment orders made in connection with matrimonial proceedings),
        (ii)   section 17(1) of the Matrimonial and Family Proceedings Act 1984 (property adjustment orders after overseas divorce, &c), ...
        (iii)   paragraph 1 of Schedule 1 to the Children Act 1989 (orders for financial relief against parents); [or
        (iv)   Part 2 of Schedule 5, or paragraph 9(2) or (3) of Schedule 7, to the Civil Partnership Act 2004 (property adjustment orders in connection with civil partnership proceedings or after overseas dissolution of civil partnership, etc)]; or
    (b)   when it is known that when the tenancy is so vested or disposed of it will not be in pursuance of such an order.]

(4)   A tenancy which ceases to be a secure tenancy by virtue of this section cannot subsequently become a secure tenancy.

**[428]**

**NOTES**
Sub-s (2): words in square brackets inserted by the Civil Partnership Act 2004, s 81, Sch 8, para 22(1), (2).
Sub-s (3): substituted by the Housing Act 1996, s 222, Sch 18, Pt III, para 10; for the words in italics in para (a)(i) there are substituted the words "section 23A or 24" by the Family Law Act 1996, s 66(1), Sch 8, Pt I, para 34, as from a day to be appointed, subject to savings in s 66(2) of, and Sch 9, para 5 to, that Act; word omitted from para (a)(ii) repealed and para (a)(iv) and word immediately preceding it added by the Civil Partnership Act 2004, ss 81, 261(4), Sch 8, para 22(1), (3), Sch 30.

**90 Devolution of term certain**

(1)   This section applies where a secure tenant dies and the tenancy is a tenancy for a term certain.

(2)   The tenancy remains a secure tenancy until—
  (a)   it is vested or otherwise disposed of in the course of the administration of the tenant's estate, as mentioned in subsection (3), or
  (b)   it is known that when it is so vested or disposed of it will not be a secure tenancy.

(3)   The tenancy ceases to be a secure tenancy on being vested or otherwise disposed of in the course of administration of the tenant's estate, unless—
  [(a)   the vesting or other disposal is in pursuance of an order made under—
    (i)   *section 24* of the Matrimonial Causes Act 1973 (property adjustment orders in connection with matrimonial proceedings),
    (ii)   section 17(1) of the Matrimonial and Family Proceedings Act 1984 (property adjustment orders after overseas divorce, &c), ...
    (iii)   paragraph 1 of Schedule 1 to the Children Act 1989 (orders for financial relief against parents), or
    [(iv)   Part 2 of Schedule 5, or paragraph 9(2) or (3) of Schedule 7, to the Civil Partnership Act 2004 (property adjustment orders in connection with civil partnership proceedings or after overseas dissolution of civil partnership, etc), or]]
  (b)   the vesting or other disposal is to a person qualified to succeed the tenant.

(4)   A tenancy which ceases to be a secure tenancy by virtue of this section cannot subsequently become a secure tenancy.

**[429]**

**NOTES**
Sub-s (3): para (a) substituted by the Housing Act 1996, s 222, Sch 18, Pt III, para 11; for the words in italics in para (a)(i) there are substituted the words "section 23A or 24" by the Family Law Act 1996, s 66(1), Sch 8, Pt I, para 34, as from a day to be appointed, subject to savings in s 66(2) of, and Sch 9, para 5 to, that Act; word omitted from para (a)(ii) repealed and para (a)(iv) added by the Civil Partnership Act 2004, ss 81, 261(4), Sch 8, para 23, Sch 30.

*Assignment, lodgers and subletting*

**91 Assignment in general prohibited**

(1)   A secure tenancy which is—
  (a)   a periodic tenancy, or
  (b)   a tenancy for a term certain granted on or after 5th November 1982,
is not capable of being assigned except in the cases mentioned in subsection (3).

(2)   If a secure tenancy for a term certain granted before 5th November 1982 is assigned, then, except in the cases mentioned in subsection (3), it ceases to be a secure tenancy and cannot subsequently become a secure tenancy.

(3)   The exceptions are—
  (a)   an assignment in accordance with section 92 (assignment by way of exchange);
  [(b)   an assignment in pursuance of an order made under—
    (i)   *section 24* of the Matrimonial Causes Act 1973 (property adjustment orders in connection with matrimonial proceedings),
    (ii)   section 17(1) of the Matrimonial and Family Proceedings Act 1984 (property adjustment orders after overseas divorce, &c), ...
    (iii)   paragraph 1 of Schedule 1 to the Children Act 1989 (orders for financial relief against parents)[, or
    (iv)   Part 2 of Schedule 5, or paragraph 9(2) or (3) of Schedule 7, to the Civil Partnership Act 2004 (property adjustment orders in connection with civil partnership proceedings or after overseas dissolution of civil partnership, etc)];]
  (c)   an assignment to a person who would be qualified to succeed the tenant if the tenant died immediately before the assignment.

**[430]**

**NOTES**
Sub-s (3): para (b) substituted by the Housing Act 1996, s 222, Sch 18, Pt III, para 12; for the words in italics in para (b)(i) there are substituted the words "section 23A or 24" by the Family Law Act 1996, s 66(1), Sch 8, Pt I, para 34, as from a day to be appointed, subject to savings in s 66(2) of, and Sch 9, para 5 to, that Act; word omitted from para (b)(ii) repealed and para (b)(iv) and word immediately preceding it added by the Civil Partnership Act 2004, ss 81, 261(4), Sch 8, para 24, Sch 30.

**92   Assignments by way of exchange**

(1)   It is a term of every secure tenancy that the tenant may, with the written consent of the landlord, assign the tenancy to another secure tenant who satisfies the condition in subsection (2) [or to an assured tenant who satisfies the conditions in subsection (2A)].

(2)   The condition is that the other secure tenant has the written consent of his landlord to an assignment of his tenancy either to the first-mentioned tenant or to another secure tenant who satisfies the condition in this subsection.

[(2A)   The conditions to be satisfied with respect to an assured tenant are—
  (a)   that the landlord under his assured tenancy is either the Housing Corporation, ... a [registered social landlord] or a housing trust which is a charity; and
  (b)   that he intends to assign his assured tenancy to the secure tenant referred to in subsection (1) or to another secure tenant who satisfies the condition in subsection (2).]

(3)   The consent required by virtue of this section shall not be withheld except on one or more of the grounds set out in Schedule 3, and if withheld otherwise than on one of those grounds shall be treated as given.

(4)   The landlord may not rely on any of the grounds set out in Schedule 3 unless he has, within 42 days of the tenant's application for the consent, served on the tenant a notice specifying the ground and giving particulars of it.

(5)   Where rent lawfully due from the tenant has not been paid or an obligation of the tenancy has been broken or not performed, the consent required by virtue of this section may be given subject to a condition requiring the tenant to pay the outstanding rent, remedy the breach or perform the obligation.

(6)   Except as provided by subsection (5), a consent required by virtue of this section cannot be given subject to a condition, and a condition imposed otherwise than as so provided shall be disregarded.

**[431]**

**NOTES**

Sub-s (1): words in square brackets added by the Local Government and Housing Act 1989, s 163(1), (2).

Sub-s (2A): inserted by the Local Government and Housing Act 1989, s 163(1), (3); words omitted repealed by the Government of Wales Act 1998, ss 140, 152, Sch 16, paras 4, 10, Sch 18, Pt VI; words in square brackets substituted by the Housing Act 1996 (Consequential Provisions) Order 1996, SI 1996/2325, art 5, Sch 2, para 14(1), (9).

Modification: in sub-s (2A)(a) the reference to the Housing Corporation shall be treated as a reference to the Regulator of Social Housing: see the Transfer of Housing Corporation Functions (Modifications and Transitional Provisions) Order 2008, SI 2008/2839, arts 1(2), 2, 3, 6, Schedule, para 2(1).

**93   Lodgers and subletting**

(1)   It is a term of every secure tenancy that the tenant—
  (a)   may allow any persons to reside as lodgers in the dwelling-house, but
  (b)   will not, without the written consent of the landlord, sublet or part with possession of part of the dwelling-house.

(2)   If the tenant under a secure tenancy parts with the possession of the dwelling-house or sublets the whole of it (or sublets first part of it and then the remainder), the tenancy ceases to be a secure tenancy and cannot subsequently become a secure tenancy.

**[432]**

**94   Consent to subletting**

(1)   This section applies to the consent required by virtue of section 93(1)(b) (landlord's consent to subletting of part of dwelling-house).

(2)   Consent shall not be unreasonably withheld (and if unreasonably withheld shall be treated as given), and if a question arises whether the witholding of consent was unreasonable it is for the landlord to show that it was not.

(3)   In determining that question the following matters, if shown by the landlord, are among those to be taken into account—
  (a)   that the consent would lead to overcrowding of the dwelling-house within the meaning of Part X (overcrowding);
  (b)   that the landlord proposes to carry out works on the dwelling-house, or on the building of which it forms part, and that the proposed works will affect the accommodation likely to be used by the sub-tenant who would reside in the dwelling-house as a result of the consent.

(4)   Consent may be validly given notwithstanding that it follows, instead of preceding, the action requiring it.

(5)   Consent cannot be given subject to a condition (and if purporting to be given subject to a condition shall be treated as given unconditionally).

(6)   Where the tenant has applied in writing for consent, then—
    (a)   if the landlord refuses to give consent, it shall give the tenant a written statement of the reasons why consent was refused, and
    (b)   if the landlord neither gives nor refuses to give consent within a reasonable time, consent shall be taken to have been withheld.

[433]

## 95   Assignment or subletting where tenant condition not satisfied

(1)   This section applies to a tenancy which is not a secure tenancy but would be if the tenant condition referred to in section 81 (occupation by the tenant) were satisfied.

(2)   Sections 91 and 93(2) (restrictions on assignment or subletting of whole dwelling-house) apply to such a tenancy as they apply to a secure tenancy, except that—
    (a)   section 91(3)(b) and (c) (assignments excepted from restrictions) do not apply to such a tenancy for a term certain granted before 5th November 1982, and
    (b)   references to the tenancy ceasing to be secure shall be disregarded, without prejudice to the application of the remainder of the provisions in which those references occur.

[434]

*Repairs and improvements*

## [96   Right to have repairs carried out

(1)   The Secretary of State may make regulations for entitling secure tenants whose landlords are local housing authorities, subject to and in accordance with the regulations, to have qualifying repairs carried out, at their landlords' expense, to the dwelling-houses of which they are such tenants.

(2)   The regulations may make all or any of the following provisions, namely—
    (a)   provision that, where a secure tenant makes an application to his landlord for a qualifying repair to be carried out, the landlord shall issue a repair notice—
        (i)   specifying the nature of the repair, the listed contractor by whom the repair is to be carried out and the last day of any prescribed period; and
        (ii)   containing such other particulars as may be prescribed;
    (b)   provision that, if the contractor specified in a repair notice fails to carry out the repair within a prescribed period, the landlord shall issue a further repair notice specifying such other listed contractor as the tenant may require; and
    (c)   provision that, if the contractor specified in a repair notice fails to carry out the repair within a prescribed period, the landlord shall pay to the tenant such

sum by way of compensation as may be determined by or under the regulations.

(3)   The regulations may also make such procedural, incidental, supplementary and transitional provisions as may appear to the Secretary of State necessary or expedient, and may in particular—
    (a)   require a landlord to take such steps as may be prescribed to make its secure tenants aware of the provisions of the regulations;
    (b)   require a landlord to maintain a list of contractors who are prepared to carry out repairs for which it is responsible under the regulations;
    (c)   provide that, where a landlord issues a repair notice, it shall give to the tenant a copy of the notice and the prescribed particulars of at least two other listed contractors who are competent to carry out the repair;
    (d)   provide for questions arising under the regulations to be determined by the county court; and
    (e)   enable the landlord to set off against any compensation payable under the regulations any sums owed to it by the tenant.

(4)   Nothing in subsection (2) or (3) shall be taken as prejudicing the generality of subsection (1).

(5)   Regulations under this section—
    (a)   may make different provision with respect to different cases or descriptions of case, including different provision for different areas, and
    (b)   shall be made by statutory instrument which shall be subject to annulment in pursuance of a resolution of either House of Parliament.

(6)   In this section—
    "listed contractor", in relation to a landlord, means any contractor (which may include the landlord) who is specified in the landlord's list of contractors;
    "qualifying repair", in relation to a dwelling-house, means any repair of a prescribed description which the landlord is obliged by a repairing covenant to carry out;

"repairing covenant", in relation to a dwelling-house, means a covenant, whether express or implied, obliging the landlord to keep in repair the dwelling-house or any part of the dwelling-house;

and for the purposes of this subsection a prescribed description may be framed by reference to any circumstances whatever.]

**[435]**

**NOTES**
Substituted by the Leasehold Reform, Housing and Urban Development Act 1993, s 121, except in cases where a notice was served in accordance with the Secure Tenancies (Right to Repair Scheme) Regulations 1985, SI 1985/1493, Schedule, para 3, before 1 April 1994.
Regulations: the Secure Tenants of Local Housing Authorities (Right to Repair) Regulations 1994, SI 1994/133 at **[3106]**. Also, by virtue of the Housing (Consequential Provisions) Act 1985, s 2(2), the Secure Tenancies (Right to Repair Scheme) Regulations 1985, SI 1985/1493, have effect as if made under this section.

## 97　Tenant's improvements require consent

(1)　It is a term of every secure tenancy that the tenant will not make any improvement without the written consent of the landlord.

(2)　In this Part "improvement" means any alteration in, or addition to, a dwelling-house, and includes—

(a)　any addition to or alteration in landlord's fixtures and fittings,
(b)　any addition or alteration connected with the provision of services to the dwelling-house,
(c)　the erection of a wireless or television aerial, and
(d)　the carrying out of external decoration.

(3)　The consent required by virtue of subsection (1) shall not be unreasonably withheld, and if unreasonably withheld shall be treated as given.

(4)　The provisions of this section have effect, in relation to secure tenancies, in place of section 19(2) of the Landlord and Tenant Act 1927 (general provisions as to covenants, etc not to make improvements without consent).

**[436]**

## 98　Provisions as to consents required by s 97

(1)　If a question arises whether the withholding of a consent required by virtue of section 97 (landlord's consent to improvements) was unreasonable, it is for the landlord to show that it was not.

(2)　In determining that question the court shall, in particular, have regard to the extent to which the improvement would be likely—

(a)　to make the dwelling-house, or any other premises, less safe for occupiers,
(b)　to cause the landlord to incur expenditure which it would be unlikely to incur if the improvement were not made, or
(c)　to reduce the price which the dwelling-house would fetch if sold on the open market or the rent which the landlord would be able to charge on letting the dwelling-house.

(3)　A consent required by virtue of section 97 may be validly given notwithstanding that it follows, instead of preceding, the action requiring it.

(4)　Where a tenant has applied in writing for a consent which is required by virtue of section 97—

(a)　the landlord shall if it refuses consent give the tenant a written statement of the reason why consent was refused, and
(b)　if the landlord neither gives nor refuses to give consent within a reasonable time, consent shall be taken to have been withheld.

**[437]**

## 99　Conditional consent to improvements

(1)　Consent required by virtue of section 97 (landlord's consent to improvements) may be given subject to conditions.

(2)　If the tenant has applied in writing for consent and the landlord gives consent subject to an unreasonable condition, consent shall be taken to have been unreasonably withheld.

(3)　If a question arises whether a condition was reasonable, it is for the landlord to show that it was.

(4)　A failure by a secure tenant to satisfy a reasonable condition imposed by his landlord in giving consent to an improvement which the tenant proposes to make, or has made, shall be treated for the purposes of this Part as a breach by the tenant of an obligation of his tenancy.

**[438]**

**[99A Right to compensation for improvements**

(1) The powers conferred by this section shall be exercisable as respects cases where a secure tenant has made an improvement and—

    (a) the work on the improvement was begun not earlier than the commencement of section 122 of the Leasehold Reform, Housing and Urban Development Act 1993,

    (b) the landlord, or a predecessor in title of the landlord (being a local authority), has given its written consent to the improvement or is to be treated as having given its consent, and

    (c) at the time when the tenancy comes to an end the landlord is a local authority and the tenancy is a secure tenancy.

(2) The Secretary of State may make regulations for entitling the qualifying person or persons (within the meaning given by section 99B)—

    (a) at the time when the tenancy comes to an end, and

    (b) subject to and in accordance with the regulations,

to be paid compensation by the landlord in respect of the improvement.

(3) The regulations may provide that compensation shall be not payable if—

    (a) the improvement is not of a prescribed description,

    (b) the tenancy comes to an end in prescribed circumstances,

    (c) compensation has been paid under section 100 in respect of the improvement, or

    (d) the amount of any compensation which would otherwise be payable is less than a prescribed amount;

and for the purposes of this subsection a prescribed description may be framed by reference to any circumstances whatever.

(4) The regulations may provide that the amount of any compensation payable shall not exceed a prescribed amount but, subject to that, shall be determined by the landlord, or calculated, in such manner, and taking into account such matters, as may be prescribed.

(5) The regulations may also make such procedural, incidental, supplementary and transitional provisions as may appear to the Secretary of State necessary or expedient, and may in particular—

    (a) provide for the manner in which and the period within which claims for compensation under the regulations are to be made, and for the procedure to be followed in determining such claims,

    (b) prescribe the form of any document required to be used for the purposes of or in connection with such claims,

    (c) provide for questions arising under the regulations to be determined by the district valuer or the county court, and

    (d) enable the landlord to set off against any compensation payable under the regulations any sums owed to it by the qualifying person or persons.

(6) Nothing in subsections (3) to (5) shall be taken as prejudicing the generality of subsection (2).

(7) Regulations under this section—

    (a) may make different provision with respect to different cases or descriptions of case, including different provision for different areas, and

    (b) shall be made by statutory instrument which (except in the case of regulations making only such provision as is mentioned in subsection (5)(b)) shall be subject to annulment in pursuance of a resolution of either House of Parliament.

(8) For the purposes of this section and section 99B, a tenancy shall be treated as coming to an end if—

    (a) it ceases to be a secure tenancy by reason of the landlord condition no longer being satisfied, or

    (b) it is assigned, with the consent of the landlord—

        (i) to another secure tenant who satisfies the condition in subsection (2) of section 92 (assignments by way of exchange), or

        (ii) to an assured tenant who satisfies the conditions in subsection (2A) of that section.]

**[439]**

**NOTES**

Inserted, together with s 99B, by the Leasehold Reform, Housing and Urban Development Act 1993, s 122, except in cases where work on the improvement had begun before 1 April 1994.

Regulations: the Secure Tenants of Local Authorities (Compensation for Improvements) Regulations 1994, SI 1994/613 at **[3118]**.

**[99B Persons qualifying for compensation**

(1) A person is a qualifying person for the purposes of section 99A(2) if—

(a)    he is, at the time when the tenancy comes to an end, the tenant or, in the case of a joint tenancy at that time, one of the tenants, and

(b)    he is a person to whom subsection (2) applies.

(2)    This subsection applies to—

(a)    the improving tenant;

(b)    a person who became a tenant jointly with the improving tenant;

(c)    a person in whom the tenancy was vested, or to whom the tenancy was disposed of, under section 89 (succession to periodic tenancy) or section 90 (devolution of term certain) on the death of the improving tenant or in the course of the administration of his estate;

(d)    a person to whom the tenancy was assigned by the improving tenant and who would have been qualified to succeed him if he had died immediately before the assignment;

[(e)    a person to whom the tenancy was assigned by the improving tenant in pursuance of an order made under—

    (i)    *section 24* of the Matrimonial Causes Act 1973 (property adjustment orders in connection with matrimonial proceedings),

    (ii)    section 17(1) of the Matrimonial and Family Proceedings Act 1984 (property adjustment orders after overseas divorce, &c), ...

    (iii)    paragraph 1 of Schedule 1 to the Children Act 1989 (orders for financial relief against parents)[, or

    (iv)    Part 2 of Schedule 5, or paragraph 9(2) or (3) of Schedule 7, to the Civil Partnership Act 2004 (property adjustment orders in connection with civil partnership proceedings or after overseas dissolution of civil partnership, etc)];]

[(f)    a spouse, former spouse, [civil partner, former civil partner,] cohabitant or former cohabitant of the improving tenant to whom the tenancy has been transferred by an order made under Schedule 1 to the Matrimonial Homes Act 1983 or Schedule 7 to the Family Law Act 1996;]

(3)    Subsection (2)(c) does not apply in any case where the tenancy ceased to be a secure tenancy by virtue of section 89(3) or, as the case may be, section 90(3).

(4)    Where, in the case of two or more qualifying persons, one of them ("the missing person") cannot be found—

(a)    a claim under regulations made under section 99A may be made by, and compensation under those regulations may be paid to, the other qualifying person or persons; but

(b)    the missing person shall be entitled to recover his share of any compensation so paid from that person or those persons.

(5)    In this section "the improving tenant" means—

(a)    the tenant by whom the improvement mentioned in section 99A(1) was made, or

(b)    in the case of a joint tenancy at the time when the improvement was made, any of the tenants at that time.]

**[440]**

**NOTES**

Inserted as noted to s 99A at **[439]**.

Sub-s (2): para (e) substituted by the Housing Act 1996, s 222, Sch 18, Pt III, para 13; for the words in italics in para (e)(i) there are substituted the words "section 23A or 24" by the Family Law Act 1996, s 66(1), Sch 8, Pt I, para 34, as from a day to be appointed (for savings see s 66(2) of, and Sch 9, paras 5, 8–10 to, that Act) and para (f) substituted by s 66(1) of, and Sch 8, Pt III, para 54 to, that Act; word omitted from para (e)(ii) repealed, para (e)(iv) and word immediately preceding it added, and words in square brackets in para (f) inserted by the Civil Partnership Act 2004, ss 81, 82, 261(4), Sch 8, para 25, Sch 9, Pt 2, para 19, Sch 30, subject to transitional provisions in Sch 9, Pt 3, para 25 to that Act at **[1328]**.

Matrimonial Homes Act 1983: repealed by the Family Law Act 1996, s 66(3), Sch 10, subject to savings contained in s 66(2) of, and Sch 9, paras 5, 8–15 to, that Act.

---

**100  Power to reimburse cost of tenant's improvements**

(1)    Where a secure tenant has made an improvement and—

(a)    the work on the improvement was begun on or after 3rd October 1980,

(b)    the landlord, or a predecessor in title of the landlord, has given its written consent to the improvement or is treated as having given its consent, and

(c)    the improvement has materially added to the price which the dwelling-house may be expected to fetch if sold on the open market, or the rent which the landlord may be expected to be able to charge on letting the dwelling-house,

the landlord may, at or after the end of the tenancy, make to the tenant (or his personal representatives) such payment in respect of the improvement as the landlord considers to be appropriate.

(2)  ...

[(2A)   ... ]

(3) The power conferred by this section to make such payments as are mentioned in subsection (1) is in addition to any other power of the landlord to make such payments.

[441]

**NOTES**
Sub-s (2): repealed by the Regulatory Reform (Housing Assistance) (England and Wales) Order 2002, SI 2002/1860, arts 12, 15(1), Sch 4, para 2(1), (2), Sch 6, except in relation to advances made by a local authority under s 435(1)(d) of this Act and applications approved before 18 July 2003.
Sub-s (2A): inserted by the Local Government and Housing Act 1989, s 194(1), Sch 11, para 66; repealed by the Housing Grants, Construction and Regeneration Act 1996, ss 103, 147, Sch 1, para 4(2), Sch 3, Pt I.

## 101 Rent not to be increased on account of tenant's improvements

(1) This section applies where a person (the "improving tenant") who is or was the secure tenant of a dwelling-house has lawfully made an improvement and has borne the whole or part of its cost; and for the purposes of this section a person shall be treated as having borne any cost which he would have borne but for a [renovation grant or common parts grant under Chapter I of Part I of the Housing Grants, Construction and Regeneration Act 1996 (grants for renewal of private sector housing).]

[(1A) ... ]

(2) In determining, at any time whilst the improving tenant or his qualifying successor is a secure tenant of the dwelling-house, whether or to what extent to increase the rent, the landlord shall treat the improvement as justifying only such part of an increase which would otherwise be attributable to the improvement as corresponds to the part of the cost which was not borne by the tenant (and accordingly as not justifying an increase if he bore the whole cost).

(3) The following are qualifying successors of an improving tenant—
[(a) a person in whom the tenancy was vested, or to whom the tenancy was disposed of, under section 89 (succession to periodic tenancy) or section 90 (devolution of term certain) on the death of the tenant or in the course of the administration of his estate;]
(b) a person to whom the tenancy was assigned by the tenant and who would have been qualified to succeed him if he had died immediately before the assignment;
[(c) a person to whom the tenancy was assigned by the tenant in pursuance of an order made under—
  (i) *section 24* of the Matrimonial Causes Act 1973 (property adjustment orders in connection with matrimonial proceedings),
  (ii) section 17(1) of the Matrimonial and Family Proceedings Act 1984 (property adjustment orders after overseas divorce, &c), ...
  (iii) paragraph 1 of Schedule 1 to the Children Act 1989 (orders for financial relief against parents)[, or
  (iv) Part 2 of Schedule 5, or paragraph 9(2) or (3) of Schedule 7, to the Civil Partnership Act 2004 (property adjustment orders in connection with civil partnership proceedings or after overseas dissolution of civil partnership, etc)];]
[(d) a spouse, former spouse, [civil partner, former civil partner,] cohabitant or former cohabitant of the tenant to whom the tenancy has been transferred by an order made under Schedule 1 to the Matrimonial Homes Act 1983 or Schedule 7 to the Family Law Act 1996;]

(4) This section does not apply to an increase of rent attributable to rates [or to council tax].

[442]

**NOTES**
Sub-s (1): words in square brackets substituted by the Housing Grants, Construction and Regeneration Act 1996, s 103, Sch 1, para 5(1).
Sub-s (1A): inserted by the Local Government and Housing Act 1989, s 194(1), Sch 11, para 67; repealed by the Housing Grants, Construction and Regeneration Act 1996, ss 103, 147, Sch 1, para 5(2), Sch 3, Pt I.
Sub-s (3): para (a) substituted by the Leasehold Reform, Housing and Urban Development Act 1993, s 187(1), Sch 21, para 10; para (c) substituted by the Housing Act 1996, s 222, Sch 18, Pt III, para 14; para (d) substituted by the Family Law Act 1996, s 66(1), Sch 8, Pt III, para 55, and for the words in italics in para (c)(i) there are substituted the words "section 23A or 24" by s 66(1) of, and Sch 8, Pt I, para 34 to, that Act, as from a day to be appointed, subject to savings in s 66(2) of, and Sch 9, paras 5, 8–10 to, that Act; word omitted from para (c)(ii) repealed, para (c)(iv) and word immediately preceding it added and words in square brackets in para (d) inserted by the Civil Partnership Act 2004, ss 81, 82, 261(4), Sch 8, para 26, Sch 9, Pt 2, para 20, Sch 30 (for transitional provisions in relation to para (d) see Sch 9, Pt 3, para 25 to that Act at [**1328**]).
Sub-s (4): words in square brackets inserted by the Local Government Finance (Housing) (Consequential Amendments) Order 1993, SI 1993/651, art 2(1), Sch 1, para 12.
Matrimonial Homes Act 1983: repealed by the Family Law Act 1996, s 66(3), Sch 10, subject to savings contained in s 66(2) of, and Sch 9, paras 5, 8–15 to, that Act.

*Variation of terms of tenancy*

## 102 Variation of terms of secure tenancy

(1) The terms of a secure tenancy may be varied in the following ways, and not otherwise—
   (a) by agreement between the landlord and the tenant;
   (b) to the extent that the variation relates to rent or to payments in respect of rates[, council tax] or services, by the landlord or the tenant in accordance with a provision in the lease or agreement creating the tenancy, or in an agreement varying it;
   (c) in accordance with section 103 (notice of variation of periodic tenancy).

(2) References in this section and section 103 to variation include addition and deletion; and for the purposes of this section the conversion of a monthly tenancy into a weekly tenancy, or a weekly tenancy into a monthly tenancy, is a variation of a term of the tenancy, but a variation of the premises let under a tenancy is not.

(3) This section and section 103 do not apply to a term of a tenancy which—
   (a) is implied by an enactment, or
   (b) may be varied under section 93 of the Rent Act 1977 (housing association and other tenancies: increase of rent without notice to quit).

(4) This section and section 103 apply in relation to the terms of a periodic tenancy arising by virtue of section 86 (periodic tenancy arising on termination of a fixed term) as they would have applied to the terms of the first tenancy mentioned in that section had that tenancy been a periodic tenancy.

**[443]**

**NOTES**

Sub-s (1): words in square brackets inserted by the Local Government Finance (Housing) (Consequential Amendments) Order 1993, SI 1993/651, art 2(1), Sch 1, para 13.

## 103 Notice of variation of periodic tenancy

(1) The terms of a secure tenancy which is a periodic tenancy may be varied by the landlord by a notice of variation served on the tenant.

(2) Before serving a notice of variation on the tenant the landlord shall serve on him a preliminary notice—
   (a) informing the tenant of the landlord's intention to serve a notice of variation,
   (b) specifying the proposed variation and its effect, and
   (c) inviting the tenant to comment on the proposed variation within such time, specified in the notice, as the landlord considers reasonable;

and the landlord shall consider any comments made by the tenant within the specified time.

(3) Subsection (2) does not apply to a variation of the rent, or of payments in respect of services or facilities provided by the landlord or of payments in respect of rates.

(4) The notice of variation shall specify—
   (a) the variation effected by it, and
   (b) the date on which it takes effect;

and the period between the date on which it is served and the date on which it takes effect must be at least four weeks or the rental period, whichever is the longer.

(5) The notice of variation, when served, shall be accompanied by such information as the landlord considers necessary to inform the tenant of the nature and effect of the variation.

(6) If after the service of a notice of variation the tenant, before the date on which the variation is to take effect, gives a valid notice to quit, the notice of variation shall not take effect unless the tenant, with the written agreement of the landlord, withdraws his notice to quit before that date.

**[444]**

*Provision of information and consultation*

## 104 Provision of information about tenancies

(1) Every body which lets dwelling-houses under secure tenancies shall from time to time publish information about its secure tenancies, in such form as it considers best suited to explain in simple terms, and so far as it considers it appropriate, the effect of—
   (a) the express terms of its secure tenancies,
   (b) the provisions of this Part ... , and
   (c) the provisions of sections 11 to 16 of the Landlord and Tenant Act 1985 (landlord's repairing obligations),

and shall ensure that so far as is reasonably practicable the information so published is kept up to date.

(2) The landlord under a secure tenancy shall supply the tenant with—

(a)   a copy of the information for secure tenants published by it under subsection (1), and

(b)   a written statement of the terms of the tenancy, so far as they are neither expressed in the lease or written tenancy agreement (if any) nor implied by law;

and the statement required by paragraph (b) shall be supplied [when the secure tenancy arises] or as soon as practicable afterwards.

[(3)   A local authority which is the landlord under a secure tenancy shall supply the tenant, at least once in every relevant year, with a copy of such information relating to the provisions mentioned in subsection (1)(b) and (c) as was last published by it; and in this subsection "relevant year" means any period of twelve months beginning with an anniversary of the date of such publication.]

[445]

**NOTES**

Sub-s (1): words omitted from para (b) repealed by the Housing Act 2004, ss 189(2), 266, Sch 16.

Sub-s (2): words in square brackets substituted by the Housing Act 1996, s 141(1), Sch 14, para 2.

Sub-s (3): added by the Leasehold Reform, Housing and Urban Development Act 1993, s 123.

## 105   Consultation on matters of housing management

(1)   A landlord authority shall maintain such arrangements as it considers appropriate to enable those of its secure tenants who are likely to be substantially affected by a matter of housing management to which this section applies—

(a)   to be informed of the authority's proposals in respect of the matter, and

(b)   to make their views known to the authority within a specified period;

and the authority shall, before making any decision on the matter, consider any representations made to it in accordance with those arrangements.

(2)   For the purposes of this section, a matter is one of housing management if, in the opinion of the landlord authority, it relates to—

(a)   the management, maintenance, improvement or demolition of dwelling-houses let by the authority under secure tenancies, or

(b)   the provision of services or amenities in connection with such dwellinghouses;

but not so far as it relates to the rent payable under a secure tenancy or to charges for services or facilities provided by the authority.

(3)   This section applies to matters of housing management which, in the opinion of the landlord authority, represent—

(a)   a new programme of maintenance, improvement or demolition, or

(b)   a change in the practice or policy of the authority,

and are likely substantially to affect either its secure tenants as a whole or a group of them who form a distinct social group or occupy dwelling-houses which constitute a distinct class (whether by reference to the kind of dwelling-house, or the housing estate or other larger area in which they are situated).

(4)   In the case of a landlord authority which is a local housing authority, the reference in subsection (2) to the provision of services or amenities is a reference only to the provision of services or amenities by the authority acting in its capacity as landlord of the dwelling-houses concerned.

(5)   A landlord authority shall publish details of the arrangements which it makes under this section, and a copy of the documents published under this subsection shall—

(a)   be made available at the authority's principal office for inspection at all reasonable hours, without charge, by members of the public, and

(b)   be given, on payment of a reasonable fee, to any member of the public who asks for one.

(6)   A landlord authority which is a [registered social landlord] shall, instead of complying with paragraph (a) of subsection (5), send a copy of any document published under that subsection—

(a)   to the [Relevant Authority], and

(b)   to the council of any district[, Welsh county or county borough] or London borough in which there are dwelling-houses let by the [landlord authority] under secure tenancies;

and a council to whom a copy is sent under this subsection shall make it available at its principal office for inspection at all reasonable hours, without charge, by members of the public.

[(7)   For the purposes of this section—

(a)   secure tenants include demoted tenants within the meaning of section 143A of the Housing Act 1996;

(b)   secure tenancies include demoted tenancies within the meaning of that section.]

[446]

PART I
STATUTES

**NOTES**

Sub-s (6): words in first and fourth pairs of square brackets substituted by the Housing Act 1996 (Consequential Provisions) Order 1996, SI 1996/2325, art 5, Sch 2, para 14(1), (10); words in second pair of square brackets substituted by the Government of Wales Act 1998, s 140, Sch 16, paras 4, 5; words in third pair of square brackets inserted by the Local Government (Wales) Act 1994, s 22(2), Sch 8, para 5(7).

Sub-s (7): added by the Anti-social Behaviour Act 2003, s 14(5), Sch 1, para 2(1), (2).

## 106 Information about housing allocation

(1)   A landlord authority shall publish a summary of its rules—

   (a)   for determining priority as between applicants in the allocation of its housing accommodation, and

   (b)   governing cases where secure tenants wish to move (whether or not by way of exchange of dwelling-houses) to other dwelling-houses let under secure tenancies by that authority or another body.

(2)   A landlord authority shall—

   (a)   maintain a set of the rules referred to in subsection (1) and of the rules which it has laid down governing the procedure to be followed in allocating its housing accommodation, and

   (b)   make them available at its principal office for inspection at all reasonable hours, without charge, by members of the public.

(3)   A landlord authority which is a [registered social landlord] shall, instead of complying with paragraph (b) of subsection (2), send a set of the rules referred to in paragraph (a) of that subsection—

   (a)   to the [Relevant Authority], and

   (b)   to the council of any district[, Welsh county or county borough] or London borough in which there are dwelling-houses let or to be let by the [landlord authority] under secure tenancies;

and a council to whom a set of rules is sent under this subsection shall make it available at its principal office for inspection at all reasonable hours, without charge, by members of the public.

(4)   A copy of the summary published under subsection (1) shall be given without charge, and a copy of the set of rules maintained under subsection (2) shall be given on payment of a reasonable fee, to any member of the public who asks for one.

(5)   At the request of a person who has applied to it for housing accommodation, a landlord authority shall make available to him, at all reasonable times and without charge, details of the particulars which he has given to the authority about himself and his family and which the authority has recorded as being relevant to his application for accommodation.

[(6)   The provisions of this section do not apply to a landlord authority which is a local housing authority so far as they impose requirements corresponding to those to which such an authority is subject under [section] 168 of the Housing Act 1996 (provision of information about … allocation schemes).]

**[447]**

**NOTES**

Sub-s (3): words in first and fourth pairs of square brackets substituted by the Housing Act 1996 (Consequential Provisions) Order 1996, SI 1996/2325, art 5, Sch 2, para 14(1), (11); words in second pair of square brackets substituted by the Government of Wales Act 1998, s 140, Sch 16, paras 4, 5; words in third pair of square brackets inserted by the Local Government (Wales) Act 1994, s 22(2), Sch 8, para 5(7).

Sub-s (6): added by the Housing Act 1996, s 173, Sch 16, para 1; word in square brackets substituted and words omitted repealed by the Homelessness Act 2002, s 18, Sch 1, para 1, Sch 2.

## [106A   Consultation before disposal to private sector landlord

(1)   The provisions of Schedule 3A have effect with respect to the duties of—

   (a)   a local authority proposing to dispose of dwelling-houses subject to secure tenancies [or introductory tenancies], and

   (b)   the Secretary of State in considering whether to give his consent to such a disposal,

to have regard to the views of tenants liable as a result of the disposal to cease to be secure tenants [or introductory tenants].

(2)   In relation to a disposal to which that Schedule applies, the provisions of that Schedule apply in place of the provisions of section 105 (consultation on matters of housing management) [in the case of secure tenants and section 137 of the Housing Act 1996 (consultation on matters of housing management) in the case of introductory tenants].

[(3)   That Schedule, and this section, do not apply in relation to any disposal of an interest in land by a local authority if—

   (a)   the interest has been acquired by the authority (whether compulsorily or otherwise) following the making of an order for compulsory purchase under any enactment, other than section 290 (acquisition of land for clearance),

(b)   the order provides that the interest is being acquired for the purpose of disposal to a registered social landlord, and

(c)   such a disposal is made within one year of the acquisition.

(4)   In this section "registered social landlord" has the same meaning as in Part I of the Housing Act 1996.]]

[448]

**NOTES**

Inserted by the Housing and Planning Act 1986, s 6, in relation to disposals after 11 March 1988.
Sub-ss (1), (2): words in square brackets inserted by the Housing Act 1996 (Consequential Amendments) Order 1997, SI 1997/74, art 2, Schedule, para 3(a), (h).
Sub-ss (3), (4): added by the Housing Act 1996, s 222, Sch 18, Pt IV, para 23.

*Miscellaneous*

**107**   *(Repealed by the Local Government and Housing Act 1989, ss 168(4), 194(4), Sch 12, Pt II.)*

### 108   Heating charges

(1)   This section applies to secure tenants of dwelling-houses to which a heating authority supply heat produced at a heating installation.

(2)   The Secretary of State may by regulations require heating authorities to adopt such methods for determining heating charges payable by such tenants as will secure that the proportion of heating costs borne by each of those tenants is no greater than is reasonable.

(3)   The Secretary of State may by regulations make provision for entitling such tenants, subject to and in accordance with the regulations, to require the heating authority—

(a)   to give them, in such form as may be prescribed by the regulations, such information as to heating charges and heating costs as may be so prescribed, and

(b)   where such information has been given, to afford them reasonable facilities for inspecting the accounts, receipts and other documents supporting the information and for taking copies or extracts from them.

(4)   Regulations under this section—

(a)   may make different provision with respect to different cases or descriptions of case, including different provision for different areas;

(b)   may make such procedural, incidental, supplementary and transitional provision as appears to the Secretary of State to be necessary or expedient, and may in particular provide for any question arising under the regulations to be referred to and determined by the county court; and

(c)   shall be made by statutory instrument which shall be subject to annulment in pursuance of a resolution of either House of Parliament.

(5)   In this section—

(a)   "heating authority" means a housing authority [or housing action trust] who operate a heating installation and supply to premises heat produced at the installation;

(b)   "heating installation" means a generating station or other installation for producing heat;

(c)   references to heat produced at an installation include steam produced from, and air and water heated by, heat so produced;

(d)   "heating charge" means an amount payable to a heating authority in respect of heat produced at a heating installation and supplied to premises, including in the case of heat supplied to premises let by the authority such an amount payable as part of the rent;

(e)   "heating costs" means expenses incurred by a heating authority in operating a heating installation.

[449]

**NOTES**

Sub-s (5): words in square brackets inserted by the Housing Act 1988, s 83(1), (3).

### 109   Provisions not applying to tenancies of co-operative housing associations

Sections 91 to 108 (assignment and subletting, repairs and improvements, variation of terms, provision of information and consultation, contributions to costs of transfers and heating charges) do not apply to a tenancy when the interest of the landlord belongs to a co-operative housing association.

[450]

*Supplementary provisions*

## [109A Acquisition of dwelling-house subject to statutory tenancy

Where an authority or body within section 80 (the landlord condition for secure tenancies) becomes the landlord of a dwelling-house subject to a statutory tenancy, the tenancy shall be treated for all purposes as if it were a contractual tenancy on the same terms, and the provisions of this Part apply accordingly.]

**[451]**

**NOTES**

Inserted by the Housing and Planning Act 1986, s 24(1)(b), Sch 5, Pt I, para 2.

## 110　Jurisdiction of county court

(1)　A county court has jurisdiction to determine questions arising under this Part and to entertain proceedings brought under this Part and claims, for whatever amount, in connection with a secure tenancy.

(2)　That jurisdiction includes jurisdiction to entertain proceedings on the following questions—

   (a)　whether a consent required by section 92 (assignment by way of exchange) was withheld otherwise than on one or more of the grounds set out in Schedule 3,

   (b)　whether a consent required by section 93(1)(b) or 97(1) (landlord's consent to subletting of part of dwelling-house or to carrying out of improvements) was withheld or unreasonably withheld, or

   (c)　whether a statement supplied in pursuance of section 104(2)(b) (written statement of certain terms of tenancy) is accurate,

notwithstanding that no other relief is sought than a declaration.

*(3)　If a person takes proceedings in the High Court which, by virtue of this section, he could have taken in the county court, he is not entitled to recover any costs.*

**[452]**

**NOTES**

Sub-s (3): repealed by the Courts and Legal Services Act 1990, s 125(7), Sch 20, as from a day to be appointed.

**111**　*(Repealed by the Constitutional Reform Act 2005, ss 15(1), 146, Sch 4, Pt 1, paras 180, 181, Sch 18, Pt 2.)*

## [111A　Introductory tenancies

Sections 102(1), (2) and (3)(a), 103 and 108 apply in relation to introductory tenancies as they apply in relation to secure tenancies.]

**[453]**

**NOTES**

Inserted by the Housing Act 1996 (Consequential Amendments) Order 1997, SI 1997/74, art 2, Schedule, para 3(a), (i).

## 112　Meaning of "dwelling-house"

(1)　For the purposes of this Part a dwelling-house may be a house or a part of a house.

(2)　Land let together with a dwelling-house shall be treated for the purposes of this Part as part of the dwelling-house unless the land is agricultural land (as defined in section 26(3)(a) of the General Rate Act 1967) exceeding two acres.

**[454]**

**NOTES**

General Rate Act 1967: repealed by the Local Government Finance Act 1988, ss 117(1), 149, Sch 13, Pt I, with effect for financial years beginning in or after 1990.

## 113　Members of a person's family

(1)　A person is a member of another's family within the meaning of this Part if—

   (a)　he is the spouse [or civil partner] of that person, or he and that person live together as husband and wife [or as if they were civil partners], or

   (b)　he is that person's parent, grandparent, child, grandchild, brother, sister, uncle, aunt, nephew or niece.

(2)　For the purpose of subsection (1)(b)—

   (a)　a relationship by marriage [or civil partnership] shall be treated as a relationship by blood,

(b)    a relationship of the half-blood shall be treated as a relationship of the whole blood,

(c)    the stepchild of a person shall be treated as his child, and

(d)    an illegitimate child shall be treated as the legitimate child of his mother and reputed father.

**[455]**

**NOTES**

Words in square brackets inserted by the Civil Partnership Act 2004, s 81, Sch 8, para 27.

## 114 Meaning of "landlord authority"

(1)    In this Part "landlord authority" means—

a local housing authority,

a [registered social landlord] other than a co-operative housing association,

a housing trust which is a charity,

a development corporation,

[a housing action trust][, or]

an urban development corporation, ...

other than an authority in respect of which an exemption certificate has been issued.

(2)    The Secretary of State may, on an application duly made by the authority concerned, issue an exemption certificate to—

a development corporation,

[a housing action trust][, or]

an urban development corporation, ...

if he is satisfied that it has transferred, or otherwise disposed of, at least three-quarters of the dwellings which have at any time before the making of the application been vested in it.

(3)    The application shall be in such form and shall be accompanied by such information as the Secretary of State may, either generally or in relation to a particular case, direct.

**[456]**

**NOTES**

Sub-s (1): words in first pair of square brackets substituted by the Housing Act 1996 (Consequential Provisions) Order 1996, SI 1996/2325, art 5, Sch 2, para 14(1), (12); words in second pair of square brackets inserted by the Housing Act 1988, s 83(1), (4); word in third pair of square brackets inserted and words omitted repealed by the Government of Wales Act 1998, ss 129, 152, Sch 15, para 10, Sch 18, Pt IV.

Sub-s (2): words in first pair of square brackets inserted by the Housing Act 1988, s 83(1), (4); word in second pair of square brackets inserted and words omitted repealed by the Government of Wales Act 1998, ss 129, 152, Sch 15, para 10, Sch 18, Pt IV.

## 115 Meaning of "long tenancy"

(1)    The following are long tenancies for the purposes of this Part, subject to subsection (2)—

(a)    a tenancy granted for a term certain exceeding 21 years, whether or not it is (or may become) terminable before the end of that term by notice given by the tenant or by re-entry or forfeiture;

(b)    a tenancy for a term fixed by law under a grant with a covenant or obligation for perpetual renewal, other than a tenancy by sub-demise from one which is not a long tenancy;

(c)    any tenancy granted in pursuance of Part V (the right to buy)[, including any tenancy granted in pursuance of that Part as it has effect by virtue of section 17 of the Housing Act 1996 (the right to acquire)].

(2)    A tenancy granted so as to become terminable by notice after a death is not a long tenancy for the purposes of this Part, unless—

(a)    it is granted by a housing association which at the time of the grant is [a registered social landlord],

(b)    it is granted at a premium calculated by reference to a percentage of the value of the dwelling-house or of the cost of providing it, and

(c)    at the time it is granted it complies with the requirements of the regulations then in force under section 140(4)(b) of the Housing Act 1980 [or paragraph 4(2)(b) of Schedule 4A to the Leasehold Reform Act 1967] (conditions for exclusion of shared ownership leases from Part I of the Leasehold Reform Act 1967) or, in the case of a tenancy granted before any such regulations were brought into force, with the first such regulations to be in force.

**[457]**

**NOTES**

Sub-s (1): words in square brackets inserted by the Housing Act 1996 (Consequential Amendments) (No 2) Order 1997, SI 1997/627, art 2, Schedule, para 3(1), (2).

Sub-s (2): words in first pair of square brackets substituted by the Housing Act 1996 (Consequential Provisions) Order 1996, SI 1996/2325, art 5, Sch 2, para 14(1), (13); words in second pair of square brackets inserted by the Housing Act 1988, s 140(1), Sch 17, Pt I, para 40.

Housing Act 1980, s 140(4)(b): repealed, with savings in relation to leases granted before 11 December 1987, by the Housing and Planning Act 1986, s 18, Sch 4, paras 7, 11(2).

### [115A   Meaning of "introductory tenancy"

In this Part "introductory tenancy" has the same meaning as in Chapter I of Part V of the Housing Act 1996.]

**[458]**

**NOTES**

Inserted by the Housing Act 1996, s 141(1), Sch 14, para 3.

### 116   Minor definitions

In this Part—

"common parts", in relation to a dwelling-house let under a tenancy, means any part of a building comprising the dwelling-house and any other premises which the tenant is entitled under the terms of the tenancy to use in common with the occupiers of other dwelling-houses let by the landlord;

"housing purposes" means the purposes for which dwelling-houses are held by local housing authorities under Part II (provision of housing) or purposes corresponding to those purposes;

"rental period" means a period in respect of which a payment of rent falls to be made;

"term", in relation to a secure tenancy, includes a condition of the tenancy.

**[459]**

### 117   Index of defined expressions: Part IV

The following Table shows provisions defining or otherwise explaining expressions used in this Part (other than provisions defining or explaining an expression in the same section or paragraph):—

| | |
|---|---|
| [assured tenancy | section 622] |
| cemetery | section 622 |
| charity | section 622 |
| common parts (in relation to a dwelling-house let under a tenancy) | section 116 |
| [consent (in Schedule 3A) | paragraph 2(3) of that Schedule] |
| co-operative housing association | section 5(2) |
| [ ... | ... ] |
| development corporation | section 4(c) |
| dwelling-house | section 112 |
| family (member of) | section 113 |
| housing association | section 5(1) |
| housing authority | section 4(a) |
| housing purposes | section 116 |
| housing trust | section 6 |
| improvement | section 97(2) |
| [introductory tenancy | section 115A] |
| landlord authority | section 114 |
| [landlord (in Part V of Schedule 2) | paragraph 7 of that Part] |
| local authority | section 4(e) |
| local housing authority | sections 1, 2(2) |
| long tenancy | section 115 |
| [management agreement and manager | sections 27(2) and 27B(4)] |
| new town corporation | section 4(b) |

PART I
STATUTES

| | |
|---|---|
| qualified to succeed (on the death of a secure tenant) | section 87 |
| [registered social landlord | section 5(4) and (5)] |
| [the Relevant Authority | section 6A] |
| rental period | section 116 |
| secure tenancy | section 79 |
| term (in relation to a secure tenancy) | section 116 |
| urban development corporation | section 4(d) |
| variation (of the terms of a secure tenancy) | section 102(2) |

**[460]**

**NOTES**

Entry "assured tenancy" inserted by the Local Government and Housing Act 1989, s 163(1), (4); entries "consent" and "management agreement and manager" inserted by the Housing and Planning Act 1986, s 24(2), Sch 5, Pt II, para 27, and entry "landlord (in Part V of Schedule 2)" inserted by those provisions, as from a day to be appointed; entry "the Corporation" (omitted) inserted by the Housing Act 1988, s 140(1), Sch 17, Pt II, para 109 and repealed by the Government of Wales Act 1998, ss 140, 152, Sch 16, paras 4, 11(a), Sch 18, Pt VI; entry "introductory tenancy" inserted by the Housing Act 1996, s 141(1), Sch 14, para 4; entry "registered social landlord" substituted by the Housing Act 1996 (Consequential Provisions) Order 1996, SI 1996/2325, art 5, Sch 2, para 14(1), (14); entry "the Relevant Authority" inserted by the Government of Wales Act 1998, s 140, Sch 16, paras 4, 11(b).

## PART V
## THE RIGHT TO BUY

### *The right to buy*

**NOTES**

Most tenants of registered social landlords do not have the right to buy. A secure tenant of such a landlord will not, in most cases, have the right to buy because of the exceptions set out in Sch 5 to this Act at **[584]**. An assured tenant of a registered social landlord does not have the right to buy, unless the tenant has a preserved right to buy under ss 171A–171H of this Act at **[536]**–**[543]**. Note however, that all tenants of registered social landlords (whether assured, other than an assured shorthold tenant, or secure) have the right to acquire their dwelling if it was provided with public money and meets other specified statutory conditions (see the Housing Act 1996, ss 16, 17 at **[1002]**, **[1004]**).

### 118 The right to buy

(1)   A secure tenant has the right to buy, that is to say, the right, in the circumstances and subject to the conditions and exceptions stated in the following provisions of this Part—

  (a)   if the dwelling-house is a house and the landlord owns the freehold, to acquire the freehold of the dwelling-house;

  (b)   if the landlord does not own the freehold or if the dwelling-house is a flat (whether or not the landlord owns the freehold), to be granted a lease of the dwelling-house.

(2)   Where a secure tenancy is a joint tenancy then, whether or not each of the joint tenants occupies the dwelling-house as his only or principal home, the right to buy belongs jointly to all of them or to such one or more of them as may be agreed between them; but such an agreement is not valid unless the person or at least one of the persons to whom the right to buy is to belong occupies the dwelling-house as his only or principal home.

[(3)   For the purposes of this Part, a dwelling-house which is a commonhold unit (within the meaning of the Commonhold and Leasehold Reform Act 2002) shall be treated as a house and not as a flat.]

**[461]**

**NOTES**

Sub-s (3): added by the Commonhold and Leasehold Reform Act 2002, s 68, Sch 5, para 5.

### 119 Qualifying period for right to buy

(1)   The right to buy does not arise unless the period which, in accordance with Schedule 4, is to be taken into account for the purposes of this section is at least [five] years.

(2)   Where the secure tenancy is a joint tenancy the condition in subsection (1) need be satisfied with respect to one only of the joint tenants.

**[462]**

**NOTES**

Sub-s (1): word in square brackets substituted by the Housing Act 2004, s 180(1), except in relation to a secure tenancy where the tenancy was entered into before, or in pursuance of an agreement made before, 18 January 2005, or where the tenant is a public sector tenant on that day.

## 120   Exceptions to the right to buy

The right to buy does not arise in the cases specified in Schedule 5 (exceptions to the right to buy).
**[463]**

## 121   Circumstances in which the right to buy cannot be exercised

[(1)   The right to buy cannot be exercised if the tenant is subject to an order of the court for possession of the dwelling-house.]

(2)   The right to buy cannot be exercised if the person, or one of the persons, to whom the right to buy belongs—
- (a)   has a bankruptcy petition pending against him,
- (b)   ...
- (c)   is an undischarged bankrupt, or
- (d)   has made a composition or arrangement with his creditors the terms of which remain to be fulfilled.

[(3)   The right to buy cannot be exercised at any time during the suspension period under an order made under section 121A in respect of the secure tenancy.]
**[464]**

**NOTES**

Sub-s (1): substituted by the Housing and Regeneration Act 2008, s 304, except where the tenant has served a notice under s 122 of this Act before 22 September 2008 and the notice is not withdrawn.

Sub-s (2): para (b) repealed by the Insolvency Act 1985, s 235(3), Sch 10, Pt III.

Sub-s (3): added by the Housing Act 2004, s 192(1).

## [121A   Order suspending right to buy because of anti-social behaviour

(1)   The court may, on the application of the landlord under a secure tenancy, make a suspension order in respect of the tenancy.

(2)   A suspension order is an order providing that the right to buy may not be exercised in relation to the dwelling-house during such period as is specified in the order ("the suspension period").

(3)   The court must not make a suspension order unless it is satisfied—
- (a)   that the tenant, or a person residing in or visiting the dwelling-house, has engaged or threatened to [engage in—
  - (i)   housing-related anti-social conduct, or
  - (ii)   conduct to which section 153B of the Housing Act 1996 (use of premises for unlawful purposes) applies, and]
- (b)   that it is reasonable to make the order.

(4)   When deciding whether it is reasonable to make the order, the court must consider, in particular—
- (a)   whether it is desirable for the dwelling-house to be managed by the landlord during the suspension period; and
- (b)   where the conduct mentioned in subsection (3)(a) consists of conduct by a person which is capable of causing nuisance or annoyance, the effect that the conduct (or the threat of it) has had on other persons, or would have if repeated.

(5)   Where a suspension order is made—
- (a)   any existing claim to exercise the right to buy in relation to the dwelling-house ceases to be effective as from the beginning of the suspension period, and
- (b)   section 138(1) shall not apply to the landlord, in connection with such a claim, at any time after the beginning of that period, but
- (c)   the order does not affect the computation of any period in accordance with Schedule 4.

(6)   The court may, on the application of the landlord, make (on one or more occasions) a further order which extends the suspension period under the suspension order by such period as is specified in the further order.

(7)   The court must not make such a further order unless it is satisfied—
- (a)   that, since the making of the suspension order (or the last order under subsection (6)), the tenant, or a person residing in or visiting the dwelling-house, has engaged or threatened to [engage in—
  - (i)   housing-related anti-social conduct, or

(ii)   conduct to which section 153B of the Housing Act 1996 (use of premises for unlawful purposes) applies, and]

(b)   that it is reasonable to make the further order.

(8)   When deciding whether it is reasonable to make such a further order, the court must consider, in particular—

(a)   whether it is desirable for the dwelling-house to be managed by the landlord during the further period of suspension; and

(b)   where the conduct mentioned in subsection (7)(a) consists of conduct by a person which is capable of causing nuisance or annoyance, the effect that the conduct (or the threat of it) has had on other persons, or would have if repeated.

(9)   In this section any reference to the tenant under a secure tenancy is, in relation to a joint tenancy, a reference to any of the joint tenants.

[(10)   In this section "housing-related anti-social conduct" has the same meaning as in section 153A of the Housing Act 1996.]]

**[465]**

**NOTES**

Commencement: 6 June 2005 (in relation to England); 25 November 2005 (in relation to Wales).
Inserted by the Housing Act 2004, s 192(2).
Sub-s (3): words in square brackets substituted for original words "engage in conduct to which section 153A or 153B of the Housing Act 1996 applies (anti-social behaviour or use of premises for unlawful purposes), and" by the Police and Justice Act 2006, s 52, Sch 14, para 13(1), (2), except in relation to any application for a demotion order or a suspension order made by a landlord (other than a relevant Welsh landlord) made before 6 April 2007.
Sub-s (7): words in square brackets substituted for original words "engage in conduct to which section 153A or 153B of the Housing Act 1996 applies, and" by the Police and Justice Act 2006, s 52, Sch 14, para 13(1), (2), except in relation to any application for a demotion order or a suspension order made by a landlord (other than a relevant Welsh landlord) made before 6 April 2007.
Sub-s (10): added by the Police and Justice Act 2006, s 52, Sch 14, para 13(1), (3), except in relation to any application for a demotion order or a suspension order made by a landlord (other than a relevant Welsh landlord) made before 6 April 2007.

## [121AA   Information to help tenants decide whether to exercise right to buy etc

(1)   Every body which lets dwelling-houses under secure tenancies shall prepare a document that contains information for its secure tenants about such matters as are specified in an order made by the Secretary of State.

(2)   The matters that may be so specified are matters which the Secretary of State considers that it would be desirable for secure tenants to have information about when considering whether to exercise the right to buy or the right to acquire on rent to mortgage terms.

(3)   The information contained in the document shall be restricted to information about the specified matters, and the information about those matters—

(a)   shall be such as the body concerned considers appropriate, but

(b)   shall be in a form which the body considers best suited to explaining those matters in simple terms.

(4)   Once a body has prepared the document required by subsection (1), it shall revise it as often as it considers necessary in order to ensure that the information contained in it—

(a)   is kept up to date so far as is reasonably practicable, and

(b)   reflects any changes in the matters for the time being specified in an order under this section.

(5)   An order under this section shall be made by statutory instrument which shall be subject to annulment in pursuance of a resolution of either House of Parliament.

**[466]**

**NOTES**

Commencement: 18 January 2005.
Inserted, together with s 121B, by the Housing Act 2004, s 189(1).
Orders: the Housing (Right to Buy) (Information to Secure Tenants) (England) Order 2005, SI 2005/1735 at **[3549]**; the Housing (Right to Buy) (Information to Secure Tenants) (Wales) Order 2005, SI 2005/2681 at **[3574]**.

## [121B   Provision of information

(1)   This section sets out when the document prepared by a body under section 121AA is to be published or otherwise made available.

(2)   The body shall—

(a)   publish the document (whether in its original or a revised form), and

(b)   supply copies of it to the body's secure tenants,

at such times as may be prescribed by, and otherwise in accordance with, an order made by the Secretary of State.

(3)    The body shall make copies of the current version of the document available to be supplied, free of charge, to persons requesting them.

(4)    The copies must be made available for that purpose—
(a)    at the body's principal offices, and
(b)    at such other places as it considers appropriate,
at reasonable hours.

(5)    The body shall take such steps as it considers appropriate to bring to the attention of its secure tenants the fact that copies of the current version of the document can be obtained free of charge from the places where, and at the times when, they are made available in accordance with subsection (4).

(6)    In this section any reference to the current version of the document is to the version of the document that was last published by the body in accordance with subsection (2)(a).

(7)    An order under this section shall be made by statutory instrument which shall be subject to annulment in pursuance of a resolution of either House of Parliament.]

**[467]**

---

**NOTES**
Commencement: 18 January 2005.
Inserted as noted to s 121AA at **[466]**.
Orders: the Housing (Right to Buy) (Information to Secure Tenants) (England) Order 2005, SI 2005/1735 at **[3549]**; the Housing (Right to Buy) (Information to Secure Tenants) (Wales) Order 2005, SI 2005/2681 at **[3574]**.

---

*Claim to exercise right to buy*

**122  Tenant's notice claiming to exercise right to buy**

(1)    A secure tenant claims to exercise the right to buy by written notice to that effect served on the landlord.

(2)    In this Part "the relevant time", in relation to an exercise of the right to buy, means the date on which that notice is served.

(3)    The notice may be withdrawn at any time by notice in writing served on the landlord.
**[468]**

**123  Claim to share right to buy with members of family**

(1)    A secure tenant may in his notice under section 122 require that not more than three members of his family who are not joint tenants but occupy the dwelling-house as their only or principal home should share the right to buy with him.

(2)    He may validly do so in the case of any such member only if—
(a)    that member is his spouse[, is his civil partner] or has been residing with him throughout the period of twelve months ending with the giving of the notice, or
(b)    the landlord consents.

(3)    Where by such a notice any members of the tenant's family are validly required to share the right to buy with the tenant, the right to buy belongs to the tenant and those members jointly and he and they shall be treated for the purposes of this Part as joint tenants.
**[469]**

---

**NOTES**
Sub-s (2): words in square brackets inserted by the Civil Partnership Act 2004, s 81, Sch 8, para 28.

---

**124  Landlord's notice admitting or denying right to buy**

(1)    Where a notice under section 122 (notice claiming to exercise right to buy) has been served by the tenant, the landlord shall, unless the notice is withdrawn, serve on the tenant within the period specified in subsection (2) a written notice either—
(a)    admitting his right, or
(b)    denying it and stating the reasons why, in the opinion of the landlord, the tenant does not have the right to buy.

(2)    The period for serving a notice under this section is four weeks where the requirement of section 119 (qualifying period for the right to buy) is satisfied by a period or periods during which the landlord was the landlord on which the tenant's notice under section 122 was served, and eight weeks in any other case.

(3)    ...

**[470]**

**NOTES**
Sub-s (3): repealed by the Leasehold Reform, Housing and Urban Development Act 1993, s 187(2), Sch 22, except in relation to a case where a notice under s 122 at **[468]**, is served before 11 October 1993 or in relation to the operation of this Part of this Act as applied by the Local Government Reorganisation (Preservation of the Right to Buy) Order 1986, SI 1986/2092.

### 125 Landlord's notice of purchase price and other matters

(1)   Where a secure tenant has claimed to exercise the right to buy and that right has been established (whether by the landlord's admission or otherwise), the landlord shall—

   (a)   within eight weeks where the right is that mentioned in section 118(1)(a) (right to acquire freehold), and

   (b)   within twelve weeks where the right is that mentioned in section 118(1)(b) (right to acquire leasehold interest),

serve on the tenant a notice complying with this section.

(2)   The notice shall describe the dwelling-house, shall state the price at which, in the opinion of the landlord, the tenant is entitled to have the freehold conveyed or, as the case may be, the lease granted to him and shall, for the purpose of showing how the price has been arrived at, state—

   (a)   the value at the relevant time,

   (b)   the improvements disregarded in pursuance of section 127 (improvements to be disregarded in determining value), and

   (c)   the discount to which the tenant is entitled, stating the period to be taken into account under section 129 (discount) and, where applicable, the amount mentioned in section 130(1) (reduction for previous discount) or section 131(1) or (2) (limits on amount of discount).

(3)   The notice shall state the provisions which, in the opinion of the landlord, should be contained in the conveyance or grant.

[(4)   Where the notice states provisions which would enable the landlord to recover from the tenant—

   (a)   service charges, or

   (b)   improvement contributions,

the notice shall also contain the estimates and other information required by section 125A (service charges) or 125B (improvement contributions).]

[(4A)   The notice shall contain a description of any structural defect known to the landlord affecting the dwelling-house or the building in which it is situated or any other building over which the tenant will have rights under the conveyance or lease.]

[(5)   The notice shall also inform the tenant of—

   (a)   the effect of sections 125D and 125E(1) and (4) (tenant's notice of intention, landlord's notice in default and effect of failure to comply),

   (b)   his right under section 128 to have the value of the dwelling-house at the relevant time determined or re-determined by the district valuer,

   (c)   the effect of section 136(2) (change of tenant after service of notice under section 125),

   (d)   the effect of sections 140 and 141(1), (2) and (4) (landlord's notices to complete and effect of failure to comply),

   (e)   the effect of the provisions of this Part relating to the right to acquire on rent to mortgage terms, and

   (f)   the relevant amount and multipliers for the time being declared by the Secretary of State for the purposes of section 143B.]

**[471]**

**NOTES**
Sub-s (4): substituted by the Housing and Planning Act 1986, s 4(1), (6), except in relation to cases where both the tenant's notice claiming to exercise the right to buy, and the landlord's notice under this section, were served before 7 January 1987 (but without prejudice to the tenant's right to withdraw the notice served before that date and serve a new notice).
Sub-s (4A): inserted by the Housing and Planning Act 1986, s 24(1)(c), Sch 5, Pt I, para 3.
Sub-s (5): substituted by the Leasehold Reform, Housing and Urban Development Act 1993, s 104, except in relation to a case where a notice under s 122 at **[468]**, is served before 11 October 1993 or in relation to the operation of this Part of this Act as applied by the Local Government Reorganisation (Preservation of the Right to Buy) Order 1986, SI 1986/2092.

### [125A   Estimates and information about service charges

(1)   A landlord's notice under section 125 shall state as regards service charges (excluding, in the case of a flat, charges to which subsection (2) applies)—

   (a)   the landlord's estimate of the average annual amount (at current prices) which would be payable in respect of each head of charge in the reference period, and

    (b)    the aggregate of those estimated amounts,

and shall contain a statement of the reference period adopted for the purpose of the estimates.

    (2)    A landlord's notice under section 125 given in respect of a flat shall, as regards service charges in respect of repairs (including works for the making good of structural defects), contain—

    (a)    the estimates required by subsection (3), together with a statement of the reference period adopted for the purpose of the estimates, and

    (b)    a statement of the effect of—

         paragraph 16B of Schedule 6 (which restricts by reference to the estimates the amounts payable by the tenant), and

         section 450A and the regulations made under that section (right to a loan in respect of certain service charges).

    (3)    The following estimates are required for works in respect of which the landlord considers that costs may be incurred in the reference period—

    (a)    for works itemised in the notice, estimates of the amount (at current prices) of the likely cost of, and of the tenant's likely contribution in respect of, each item, and the aggregate amounts of those estimated costs and contributions, and

    (b)    for works not so itemised, an estimate of the average annual amount (at current prices) which the landlord considers is likely to be payable by the tenant.]

**[472]**

**NOTES**

Inserted, together with ss 125B, 125C, by the Housing and Planning Act 1986, s 4(2), (6), except in relation to cases where both the tenant's notice claiming to exercise the right to buy, and the landlord's notice under s 125 at **[471]**, were served before 7 January 1987 (but without prejudice to the tenant's right to withdraw the notice served before that date and serve a new notice).

### [125B    Estimates and information about improvement contributions

    (1)    A landlord's notice under section 125 given in respect of a flat, shall, as regards improvement contributions, contain—

    (a)    the estimates required by this section, together with a statement of the reference period adopted for the purpose of the estimates, and

    (b)    a statement of the effect of paragraph 16C of Schedule 6 (which restricts by reference to the estimates the amounts payable by the tenant).

    (2)    Estimates are required for works in respect of which the landlord considers that costs may be incurred in the reference period.

    (3)    The words to which the estimates relate shall be itemised and the estimates shall show—

    (a)    the amount (at current prices) of the likely cost of, and of the tenant's likely contribution in respect of, each item, and

    (b)    the aggregate amounts of those estimated costs and contributions.]

**[473]**

**NOTES**

Inserted as noted to s 125A at **[472]**.

### [125C    Reference period for purposes of ss 125A and 125B

    (1)    The reference period for the purposes of the estimates required by section 125A or 125B is the period—

    (a)    beginning on such date not more than six months after the notice is given as the landlord may reasonably specify as being a date by which the conveyance will have been made or the lease granted, and

    (b)    ending five years after that date or, where the notice states that the conveyance or lease will provide for a service charge or improvement contribution to be calculated by reference to a specified annual period, with the end of the fifth such period beginning after that date.

    (2)    For the purpose of the estimates it shall be assumed that the conveyance will be made or the lease granted at the beginning of the reference period on the terms stated in the notice.]

**[474]**

**NOTES**

Inserted as noted to s 125A at **[472]**.

### [125D    Tenant's notice of intention

    (1)    Where a notice under section 125 has been served on a secure tenant, he shall within the period specified in subsection (2) either—

(a)     serve a written notice on the landlord stating either that he intends to pursue his claim to exercise the right to buy or that he withdraws that claim, or

(b)     serve a notice under section 144 claiming to exercise the right to acquire on rent to mortgage terms.

(2)     The period for serving a notice under subsection (1) is the period of twelve weeks beginning with whichever of the following is the later—

(a)     the service of the notice under section 125, ...

(b)     where the tenant exercises his right to have the value of the dwelling-house determined or re-determined by the district valuer [(or where the landlord exercises his right to have the value of the dwelling-house re-determined by the district valuer), the relevant event].

[(3)     In subsection (2)(b) "the relevant event" means—

(a)     where a review notice was capable of being served under section 128A in relation to the determination or re-determination but no such notice was served during the period permitted by that section, the service of the notice under section 128(5) stating the effect of the determination or re-determination,

(b)     where a review notice was served under section 128A in relation to the determination or re-determination and section 128B(3) applied, the service on the tenant of the notice under section 128B(3), and

(c)     where a review notice was served under section 128A in relation to the determination or re-determination and section 128B(5) applied, the service of the notice under section 128B(7).]]

**[475]**

**NOTES**
Inserted, together with s 125E, by the Leasehold Reform, Housing and Urban Development Act 1993, s 105(1), except in relation to a case where a notice under s 122 at **[468]**, is served before 11 October 1993 or in relation to the operation of this Part of this Act as applied by the Local Government Reorganisation (Preservation of the Right to Buy) Order 1986, SI 1986/2092.
Sub-s (2): word omitted repealed by the Housing and Regeneration Act 2008, s 321(1), Sch 16, and words in square brackets substituted by the Housing and Regeneration Act 2008, s 306(1), (3), (12), except in relation to any determination or re-determination under s 128 of this Act which was required before 22 September 2008.
Sub-s (3): inserted by the Housing and Regeneration Act 2008, s 306(1), (4), (12), except in relation to any determination or re-determination under s 128 of this Act which was required before 22 September 2008.

**[125E     Landlord's notice in default**

(1)     The landlord may, at any time after the end of the period specified in section 125D(2) or, as the case may require, section 136(2), serve on the tenant a written notice—

(a)     requiring him, if he has failed to serve the notice required by section 125D(1), to serve that notice within 28 days, and

(b)     informing him of the effect of this subsection and subsection (4).

(2)     At any time before the end of the period mentioned in subsection (1)(a) (or that period as previously extended) the landlord may by written notice served on the tenant extend it (or further extend it).

(3)     If at any time before the end of that period (or that period as extended under subsection (2)) the circumstances are such that it would not be reasonable to expect the tenant to comply with a notice under this section, that period (or that period as so extended) shall by virtue of this subsection be extended (or further extended) until 28 days after the time when those circumstances no longer obtain.

(4)     If the tenant does not comply with a notice under this section, the notice claiming to exercise the right to buy shall be deemed to be withdrawn at the end of that period (or, as the case may require, that period as extended under subsection (2) or (3)).]

**[476]**

**NOTES**
Inserted as noted to s 125D at **[475]**.

*Purchase price*

**126     Purchase price**

(1)     The price payable for a dwelling-house on a conveyance or grant in pursuance of this Part is—

(a)     the amount which under section 127 is to be taken as its value at the relevant time, less

(b)     the discount to which the purchaser is entitled under this Part.

(2)     References in this Part to the purchase price include references to the consideration for the grant of a lease.

**[477]**

**127    Value of dwelling-house**

(1)    The value of a dwelling-house at the relevant time shall be taken to be the price which at that time it would realise if sold on the open market by a willing vendor—

  (a)    on the assumptions stated for a conveyance in subsection (2) and for a grant in subsection (3), ...

  (b)    disregarding any improvements made by any of the persons specified in subsection (4) and any failure by any of those persons to keep the dwelling-house in good internal repair[, and

  (c)    on the assumption that any service charges or improvement contributions payable will not be less than the amounts to be expected in accordance with the estimates contained in the landlord's notice under section 125].

(2)    For a conveyance the assumptions are—

  (a)    that the vendor was selling for an estate in fee simple with vacant possession,

  (b)    that neither the tenant nor a member of his family residing with him wanted to buy, and

  (c)    that the dwelling-house was to be conveyed with the same rights and subject to the same burdens as it would be in pursuance of this Part.

(3)    For the grant of a lease the assumptions are—

  (a)    that the vendor was granting a lease with vacant possession for the appropriate term defined in paragraph 12 of Schedule 6 (but subject to sub-paragraph (3) of that paragraph),

  (b)    that neither the tenant nor a member of his family residing with him wanted to take the lease,

  (c)    that the ground rent would not exceed £10 per annum, and

  (d)    that the grant was to be made with the same rights and subject to the same burdens as it would be in pursuance of this Part.

(4)    The persons referred to in subsection (1)(b) are—

  (a)    the secure tenant,

  (b)    any person who under the same tenancy was a secure tenant [or an introductory tenant] before him, and

  [(c)    any member of his family who, immediately before the secure tenancy was granted (or, where an introductory tenancy has become the secure tenancy, immediately before the introductory tenancy was granted), was a secure tenant or, an introductory tenant of the same dwelling-house under another tenancy,]

but do not include, in a case where the secure tenant's tenancy has at any time been assigned by virtue of section 92 (assignments by way of exchange), a person who under that tenancy was a secure tenant [or an introductory tenant] before the assignment.

[(5)    In this section "introductory tenant" and "introductory tenancy" have the same meaning as in Chapter I of Part V of the Housing Act 1996.]

**[478]**

**NOTES**

Sub-s (1): word omitted from para (a) repealed and para (c) and the word "and" immediately preceding it added by the Housing and Planning Act 1986, ss 4(3), (6), 24(2), (3), Sch 5, Pt II, para 28, Sch 12, Pt I, except in relation to cases where both the tenant's notice claiming to exercise the right to buy, and the landlord's notice under s 125 at **[471]**, were served before 7 January 1987 (but without prejudice to the tenant's right to withdraw the notice served before that date and serve a new notice).

Sub-s (4): words in first and third pairs of square brackets inserted and para (c) substituted by the Housing Act 1996 (Consequential Amendments) Order 1997, SI 1997/74, art 2, Schedule, para 3(a), (j).

Sub-s (5): added by SI 1997/74, art 2, Schedule, para 3(a), (k).

**128    Determination of value by district valuer**

(1)    Any question arising under this Part as to the value of a dwelling-house at the relevant time shall be determined by the district valuer in accordance with this section.

(2)    A tenant may require that value to be determined ... by a notice in writing served on the landlord not later than three months after the service on him of the notice under section 125 (landlord's notice of purchase price and other matters) or, if proceedings are then pending between the landlord and the tenant for the determination of any other question arising under this Part, within three months of the final determination of the proceedings.

(3)    If such proceedings are begun after a previous determination under this section—

  (a)    the tenant may, by notice in writing served on the landlord within four weeks of the final determination of the proceedings, require the value of the dwelling-house at the relevant time to be re-determined, and

  (b)    the landlord may at any time within those four weeks, whether or not a notice under paragraph (a) is served, require the district valuer to re-determine that value;

and where the landlord requires a re-determination to be made in pursuance of this subsection, it shall serve on the tenant a notice stating that the requirement is being or has been made.

(4) Before making a determination or re-determination in pursuance of this section, the district valuer shall consider any representation made to him by the landlord or the tenant within four weeks from the service of the tenant's notice under this section or, as the case may be, from the service of the landlord's notice under subsection (3).

(5) As soon as practicable after a determination or re-determination has been made in pursuance of this section, the landlord shall serve on the tenant a notice [stating—
   (a)   the effect of the determination or re-determination,
   (b)   the matters mentioned in section 125(2) and (3) (terms for exercise of right to buy), and
   (c)   the effect of section 128A(2) (right of district valuer to serve review notice and of landlord and tenant to request that such a notice is served).]

[(5A) The landlord shall, as soon as practicable, serve a copy of the notice on the district valuer if—
   (a)   the district valuer requests it; or
   (b)   the landlord requests a review of the determination or re-determination under section 128A(2)(b).

(5B) The tenant shall, as soon as practicable, serve a copy of the notice on the district valuer if the tenant requests a review of the determination or re-determination under section 128A(2)(b).

(5C) For the purposes of subsections (5A) and (5B) it does not matter whether the request in question was made before, on or after the service of the notice in accordance with subsection (5).]

(6) ...

[479]

---

**NOTES**

Sub-s (2): words omitted repealed by the Housing and Regeneration Act 2008, ss 306(1), (5), (12), 321(1), Sch 16, except in relation to any determination or re-determination under s 128 of this Act which was required before 22 September 2008.

Sub-s (5): words in square brackets substituted by the Housing and Regeneration Act 2008, s 306(1), (6), (12), except in relation to any determination or re-determination under s 128 of this Act which was required before 22 September 2008.

Sub-ss (5A)–(5C): inserted by the Housing and Regeneration Act 2008, s 306(1), (7), (12), except in relation to any determination or re-determination under s 128 of this Act which was required before 22 September 2008.

Sub-s (6): repealed by the Leasehold Reform, Housing and Urban Development Act 1993, s 187(2), Sch 22, except in relation to a case where a notice under s 122 at [468], is served before 11 October 1993 or in relation to the operation of this Part of this Act as applied by the Local Government Reorganisation (Preservation of the Right to Buy) Order 1986, SI 1986/2092.

---

**[128A   Determination of value: review notices**

(1) Subsection (2) applies if the value of a dwelling-house has been determined or re-determined under section 128 ("the section 128 determination").

(2) The district valuer may—
   (a)   on the valuer's own initiative; or
   (b)   at the request of the landlord or the tenant of the dwelling-house;
   serve on the landlord and the tenant a notice of intention to review the section 128 determination giving reasons for the intention ("a review notice").

(3) A request under subsection (2)(b) must—
   (a)   be in writing;
   (b)   state the reason it is being made; and
   (c)   confirm that the landlord has not made to the tenant a grant of the kind mentioned in section 138(1) in respect of the claim by the tenant to exercise the right to buy in respect of the dwelling-house.

(4) The landlord or the tenant may not make a request under subsection (2)(b) after the end of the period of 28 days beginning with the section 128(5) service date.

(5) The district valuer must, before the end of the period of 14 days beginning with the day on which such a request is made, serve on the landlord and the tenant—
   (a)   a review notice; or
   (b)   a notice stating—
      (i)   that the request was made;
      (ii)   that the district valuer has decided not to comply with it; and
      (iii)   the reasons for the decision.

(6) A review notice may not be served after the end of the period of 42 days beginning with the section 128(5) service date.

(7)   A review notice may not be served in relation to a determination which is subject to a re-determination required in pursuance of section 128(3) (but this does not prevent the service of a review notice in relation to the re-determination).

(8)   A review notice may not be served if the landlord has made a grant of the kind mentioned in subsection (3)(c).

(9)   A person who makes a request under subsection (2)(b) must inform the district valuer if a grant of the kind mentioned in subsection (3)(c) is made during the period of 14 days mentioned in subsection (5).

(10)   Subsection (11) applies if the district valuer is considering whether to serve a review notice on the valuer's own initiative.

(11)   The landlord or the tenant must, if requested by the district valuer, inform the valuer whether a grant of the kind mentioned in subsection (3)(c) has been made.

(12)   In this section and section 128B—
"a review notice" has the meaning given by subsection (2);
"the section 128 determination" has the meaning given by subsection (1);
"the section 128(5) service date" means the day on which the landlord serves a notice on the tenant under section 128(5) in relation to the section 128 determination.]

**[480]**

**NOTES**
Commencement: 22 September 2008.
Inserted, together with s 128B, by the Housing and Regeneration Act 2008, s 306(1), (2), (12), except in relation to any determination or re-determination under s 128 of this Act which was required before 22 September 2008.

## [128B   Review of determination of value

(1)   The district valuer must review the section 128 determination as soon as reasonably practicable after serving a review notice.

(2)   Subsection (3) applies if, following the review, the district valuer decides that neither of the withdrawal conditions is met.

(3)   The district valuer must, as soon as reasonably practicable, serve on the landlord and the tenant a notice stating—
   (a)   the decision;
   (b)   the reasons for it; and
   (c)   that no further determination or (as the case may be) re-determination is to be made under this section.

(4)   Subsection (5) applies if, following the review, the district valuer decides that either withdrawal condition is met or both are met.

(5)   The district valuer must—
   (a)   as soon as reasonably practicable, withdraw the section 128 determination by serving a further determination notice on the landlord and the tenant; and
   (b)   make a further determination or (as the case may be) re-determination of the value of the dwelling-house at the relevant time.

(6)   Before making such a determination or re-determination, the district valuer must consider any representation made to the valuer by the landlord or the tenant before the end of the period of 14 days beginning with the day on which the further determination notice was served.

(7)   As soon as practicable after such a determination or re-determination has been made, the landlord must serve on the tenant a determination effect notice.

(8)   A determination effect notice is a notice stating—
   (a)   the effect of the further determination or (as the case may be) re-determination; and
   (b)   the matters mentioned in section 125(2) and (3).

(9)   For the purposes of this section, the withdrawal conditions are—
   (a)   that a significant error was made in the section 128 determination; or
   (b)   that the district valuer did not comply with section 128(4) in relation to the section 128 determination.

(10)   This section does not apply to a determination which is subject to a re-determination required in pursuance of section 128(3) (but this does not prevent this section applying to the re-determination).

(11)   In this section—
"a further determination notice" is a notice stating—
   (a)   that the section 128 determination is withdrawn;
   (b)   the reasons for the withdrawal; and

(c) that a further determination or (as the case may be) re-determination of the value of the dwelling-house at the relevant time will be made;

"significant error", in relation to the section 128 determination, means an error of fact, or a number of such errors, made in the section 128 determination as a result of which the value of the dwelling-house determined or (as the case may be) re-determined was at least 5% more or less than it would otherwise have been.]

[481]

NOTES

Commencement: 22 September 2008.

Inserted as noted to s 128A at **[480]**.

## 129 Discount

[(1) Subject to the following provisions of this Part, a person exercising the right to buy is entitled to a discount of a percentage calculated by reference to the period which is to be taken into account in accordance with Schedule 4 (qualifying period for right to buy and discount).

(2) The discount is, subject to any order under subsection (2A)—

(a) in the case of a house, [35 per cent] plus one per cent for each complete year by which the qualifying period exceeds [five] years, up to a maximum of 60 per cent;

(b) in the case of a flat, [50 per cent] plus two per cent for each complete year by which the qualifying period exceeds [five] years, up to a maximum of 70 per cent.

(2A) The Secretary of State may by order made with the consent of the Treasury provide that, in such cases as may be specified in the order—

(a) the minimum percentage discount,

(b) the percentage increase for each complete year of the qualifying period after the first [five], or

(c) the maximum percentage discount,

shall be such percentage, higher than that specified in subsection (2), as may be specified in the order.

(2B) An order—

(a) may make different provision with respect to different cases or descriptions of case,

(b) may contain such incidental, supplementary or transitional provisions as appear to the Secretary of State to be necessary or expedient, and

(c) shall be made by statutory instrument and shall not be made unless a draft of it has been laid before and approved by resolution of each House of Parliament.]

(3) Where joint tenants exercise the right to buy, Schedule 4 shall be construed as if for the secure tenant there were substituted that one of the joint tenants whose substitution will produce the largest discount.

[482]

NOTES

Sub-ss (1), (2B): substituted, together with sub-ss (2), (2A), for original sub-ss (1), (2), by the Housing and Planning Act 1986, s 2(1), (2).

Sub-ss (2), (2A): substituted, together with sub-ss (1), (2B), for original sub-ss (1), (2), by the Housing and Planning Act 1986, s 2(1), (2); words in square brackets substituted by the Housing Act 2004, s 180(2)–(4), except in relation to a secure tenancy where the tenancy was entered into before, or in pursuance of an agreement made before, 18 January 2005, or where the tenant is a public sector tenant on that day.

## 130 Reduction of discount where previous discount given

(1) There shall be deducted from the discount an amount equal to any previous discount qualifying, or the aggregate of previous discounts qualifying, under the provisions of this section.

(2) A "previous discount" means a discount given before the relevant time—

(a) on conveyance of the freehold, or a grant or assignment of a long lease, of a dwelling-house by a person within paragraph 7 [or 7A] of Schedule 4 (public sector landlords) or, in such circumstances as may be prescribed by order of the Secretary of State, by a person so prescribed, or

[(aa) on conveyance of the freehold, or a grant or assignment of a long lease of a dwelling-house by a person against whom the right to buy was exercisable by virtue of section 171A (preservation of right to buy on disposal to private sector landlord) to a person who was a qualifying person for the purposes of the preserved right to buy and in relation to whom that dwelling-house was the qualifying dwelling-house, or]

[(ab) in pursuance of the provision required by paragraphs 3 to 5 or paragraph 7 of Schedule 6A (redemption of landlord's share), or]

(b) in pursuance of the provision required by paragraph 1 of Schedule 8 (terms of shared ownership lease: right to acquire additional shares), or any other provision to the like effect [or

(c) in pursuance of any provision of, or required by, this Part as it has effect by virtue of section 17 of the Housing Act 1996 (the right to acquire).]

(3) A previous discount qualifies for the purposes of this section if it was given—

(a) to the person or one of the persons exercising the right to buy, or

(b) to the spouse[, or civil partner,] of that person or one of those persons (if they are living together at the relevant time), or

(c) to a deceased spouse[, or deceased civil partner,] of that person or one of those persons (if they were living together at the time of the death);

and where a previous discount was given to two or more persons jointly, this section has effect as if each of them had been given an equal proportion of the discount.

(4) Where the whole or part of a previous discount has been recovered by the person by whom it was given (or a successor in title of his)—

(a) by the receipt of a payment determined by reference to the discount, or

(b) by a reduction so determined of any consideration given by that person (or a successor in title of his), or

(c) in any other way,

then, so much of the discount as has been so recovered shall be disregarded for the purposes of this section.

(5) An order under this section—

(a) may make different provision with respect to different cases or descriptions of case, including different provision for different areas, and

(b) shall be made by statutory instrument which shall be subject to annulment in pursuance of a resolution of either House of Parliament.

(6) In this section "dwelling-house" includes any yard, garden, outhouses and appurtenances belonging to the dwelling-house or usually enjoyed with it.

**[483]**

**NOTES**

Sub-s (2): words in square brackets in para (a) and para (aa) inserted by the Housing and Planning Act 1986, s 24(2), Sch 5, Pt II, para 29, except in cases where notice was served before 17 August 1992 under s 122 at **[468]**; para (ab) inserted by the Leasehold Reform, Housing and Urban Development Act 1993, s 187(1), Sch 21, para 11, except in relation to a case where a notice under s 122 is served before 11 October 1993 or in relation to the operation of this Part of this Act as applied by the Local Government Reorganisation (Preservation of the Right to Buy) Order 1986, SI 1986/2092; para (c) and the preceding word added by the Housing Act 1996 (Consequential Amendments) (No 2) Order 1997, SI 1997/627, art 2, Schedule, para 3(1), (3).

Sub-s (3): words in square brackets inserted by the Civil Partnership Act 2004, s 81, Sch 8, para 29.

Orders: the Housing (Right to Buy) (Prescribed Persons) Order 1992, SI 1992/1703.

### 131 Limits on amount of discount

(1) Except where the Secretary of State so determines, the discount shall not reduce the price below the amount which, in accordance with a determination made by him, is to be taken as representing so much of the costs incurred in respect of the dwelling-house as, in accordance with the determination—

[(a) is to be treated as incurred at or after the beginning of that period of account of the landlord in which falls the date which is eight years, or such other period of time as may be specified in an order made by the Secretary of State, earlier than the relevant time, and]

(b) is to be treated as relevant for the purposes of this subsection;

and if the price before discount is below that amount, there shall be no discount.

[(1A) In subsection (1)(a) above "period of account", in relation to any costs, means the period for which the landlord made up those of its accounts in which account is taken of those costs.]

(2) The discount shall not in any case reduce the price by more than such sum as the Secretary of State may by order prescribe.

(3) An order or determination under this section may make different provision for different cases or descriptions of case, including different provision for different areas.

(4) An order under this section shall be made by statutory instrument which shall be subject to annulment in pursuance of a resolution of either House of Parliament.

**[484]**

**NOTES**

Sub-s (1): para (a) substituted by the Housing Act 1988, s 122(1), (2), with effect in accordance with s 122(4) of that Act.

Sub-s (1A): inserted by the Housing Act 1988, s 122(1), (3), with effect in accordance with s 122(4) of that Act.

Orders: the Housing (Right to Buy) (Limits on Discount) Order 1998, SI 1998/2997; the Housing (Right to Buy) (Limits on Discount) (Wales) Order 1999, SI 1999/292.

**132–135** *(Repealed by the Leasehold Reform, Housing and Urban Development Act 1993, s 187(2), Sch 22, except in relation to a case where a notice under s 122 at* **[468]***, is served before 11 October 1993 or in relation to the operation of this Part of this Act as applied by the Local Government Reorganisation (Preservation of the Right to Buy) Order 1986, SI 1986/2092.)*

*Change of tenant or landlord after service of notice claiming right to buy*

### 136 Change of secure tenant after notice claiming right to buy

(1) Where, after a secure tenant ("the former tenant") has given a notice claiming the right to buy, another person ("the new tenant")—

  (a) becomes the secure tenant under the same secure tenancy, otherwise than on an assignment made by virtue of section 92 (assignments by way of exchange), or

  (b) becomes the secure tenant under a periodic tenancy arising by virtue of section 86 (periodic tenancy arising on termination of fixed term) on the coming to an end of the secure tenancy,

the new tenant shall be in the same position as if the notice had been given by him and he had been the secure tenant at the time it was given.

[(2) If a notice under section 125 (landlord's notice of purchase price and other matters) has been served on the former tenant, then, whether or not the former tenant has served a notice under subsection (1) of section 125D (tenant's notice of intention), the new tenant shall serve a notice under that subsection within the period of twelve weeks beginning with whichever of the following is the later—

  (a) his becoming the secure tenant, ...

  (b) where the right to have the value of the dwelling-house determined or re-determined by the district valuer is or has been exercised by him or the former tenant [(or where the right to have the value of the dwelling-house re-determined by the district valuer is or has been exercised by the landlord), the relevant event].]

[(2A) In subsection (2)(b) "the relevant event" means—

  (a) where a review notice was capable of being served under section 128A in relation to the determination or re-determination but no such notice was served during the period permitted by that section, the service of the notice under section 128(5) stating the effect of the determination or re-determination,

  (b) where a review notice was served under section 128A in relation to the determination or re-determination and section 128B(3) applied, the service on the new tenant or (as the case may be) the former tenant of the notice under section 128B(3), and

  (c) where a review notice was served under section 128A in relation to the determination or re-determination and section 128B(5) applied, the service of the notice under section 128B(7).]

(6) The preceding provisions of this section do not confer any right on a person required in pursuance of section 123 (claim to share right to buy with members of family) to share the right to buy, unless he could have been validly so required had the notice claiming to exercise the right to buy been given by the new tenant.

(7) The preceding provisions of this section apply with the necessary modifications if there is a further change in the person who is the secure tenant.

[485]

**NOTES**

Sub-s (2): substituted, for original sub-ss (2)–(5), by the Leasehold Reform, Housing and Urban Development Act 1993, s 105(2), except in relation to a case where a notice under s 122 at **[468]**, is served before 11 October 1993 or in relation to the operation of this Part of this Act as applied by the Local Government Reorganisation (Preservation of the Right to Buy) Order 1986, SI 1986/2092; word omitted repealed by the Housing and Regeneration Act 2008, s 321(1), Sch 16 and words in square brackets substituted by the Housing and Regeneration Act 2008, s 306(1), (8), (12), except in relation to any determination or re-determination under s 128 of this Act which was required before 22 September 2008.

Sub-s (2A): inserted by the Housing and Regeneration Act 2008, s 306(1), (9), (12), except in relation to any determination or re-determination under s 128 of this Act which was required before 22 September 2008.

### 137 Change of landlord after notice claiming right to buy or right to a mortgage

[(1)] Where the interest of the landlord in the dwelling-house passes from the landlord to another body after a secure tenant has given a notice claiming to exercise the right to buy ... , all parties shall[, subject to subsection (2),] be in the same position as if the other body had become the landlord before the notice was given and had been given that notice and any further notice given by the tenant to the landlord and had taken all steps which the landlord had taken.

[(2)  If the circumstances after the disposal differ in any material respect, as for example where—

    (a)    the interest of the disponee in the dwelling-house after the disposal differs from that of the disponor before the disposal, or

    (b)    ...

    (c)    any of the provisions of Schedule 5 (exceptions to the right to buy) becomes or ceases to be applicable,

all those concerned shall, as soon as practicable after the disposal, take all such steps (whether by way of amending or withdrawing and re-serving any notice or extending any period or otherwise) as may be requisite for the purpose of securing that all parties are, as nearly as may be, in the same position as they would have been if those circumstances had obtained before the disposal.]

**[486]**

**NOTES**

Sub-s (1): numbered as such and words in square brackets inserted by the Housing and Planning Act 1986, s 24(1)(d), Sch 5, Pt I, para 4; words omitted repealed by the Leasehold Reform, Housing and Urban Development Act 1993, s 187(2), Sch 22, except in relation to a case where a notice under s 122 at **[468]**, is served before 11 October 1993 or in relation to the operation of this Part of this Act as applied by the Local Government Reorganisation (Preservation of the Right to Buy) Order 1986, SI 1986/2092.

Sub-s (2): added by the Housing and Planning Act 1986, s 24(1)(d), Sch 5, Pt I, para 4; para (b) repealed by the Leasehold Reform, Housing and Urban Development Act 1993, s 187(2), Sch 22, subject to savings as noted above.

---

*Completion of purchase in pursuance of right to buy*

## 138  Duty of landlord to convey freehold or grant lease

(1)  Where a secure tenant has claimed to exercise the right to buy and that right has been established, then, as soon as all matters relating to the grant ... have been agreed or determined, the landlord shall make to the tenant—

    (a)    if the dwelling-house is a house and the landlord owns the freehold, a grant of the dwelling-house for an estate in fee simple absolute, or

    (b)    if the landlord does not own the freehold or if the dwelling-house is a flat (whether or not the landlord owns the freehold), a grant of a lease of the dwelling-house,

in accordance with the following provisions of this Part.

(2)  If the tenant has failed to pay the rent or any other payment due from him as a tenant for a period of four weeks after it has been lawfully demanded from him, the landlord is not bound to comply with subsection (1) while the whole or part of that payment remains outstanding.

[(2A)  Subsection (2B) applies if an application is pending before any court—

    (a)    for a demotion order or Ground 2 possession order to be made in respect of the tenant, or

    (b)    for a suspension order to be made in respect of the tenancy.

(2B)  The landlord is not bound to comply with subsection (1) until such time (if any) as the application is determined without—

    (a)    a demotion order or an operative Ground 2 possession order being made in respect of the tenant, or

    (b)    a suspension order being made in respect of the tenancy,

or the application is withdrawn.

(2C)  For the purposes of subsection (2A) and (2B)—

    "demotion order" means a demotion order under section 82A;

    "Ground 2 possession order" means an order for possession under Ground 2 in Schedule 2;

    "operative Ground 2 possession order" means an order made under that Ground which requires possession of the dwelling-house to be given up on a date specified in the order;

    "suspension order" means a suspension order under section 121A.

(2D)  Subsection (1) has effect subject to section 121A(5) (disapplication of subsection (1) where suspension order is made).]

[(2E)  Subsection (1) also has effect subject to—

    (a)    section 138A(2) (operation of subsection (1) suspended while initial demolition notice is in force), and

    (b)    section 138B(2) (subsection (1) disapplied where final demolition notice is served).]

(3)  The duty imposed on the landlord by subsection (1) is enforceable by injunction.

**[487]**

---

**NOTES**

Sub-s (1): words omitted repealed by the Leasehold Reform, Housing and Urban Development Act 1993, s 187(2), Sch 22, except in relation to a case where a notice under s 122 at **[468]**, is served before 11 October 1993 or in relation to the operation of this Part of this Act as applied by the Local Government Reorganisation (Preservation of the Right to Buy) Order 1986, SI 1986/2092.

Sub-ss (2A)–(2D): inserted by the Housing Act 2004, s 193(1), except in relation to any case where the tenant's notice under section 122 of this Act at **[468]**, was served before 6 June 2005 (in relation to England) and 25 November 2005 (in relation to Wales).

Sub-s (2E): inserted by the Housing Act 2004, s 183(1), except in relation to any case where the tenant's notice under s 122 of this Act at **[468]**, was served before 18 January 2005.

## [138A Effect of initial demolition notice served before completion

(1)   This section applies where—
- (a)   an initial demolition notice is served on a secure tenant under Schedule 5A, and
- (b)   the notice is served on the tenant before the landlord has made to him such a grant as is required by section 138(1) in respect of a claim by the tenant to exercise the right to buy.

(2)   In such a case the landlord is not bound to comply with section 138(1), in connection with any such claim by the tenant, so long as the initial demolition notice remains in force under Schedule 5A.

(3)   Section 138C provides a right to compensation in certain cases where this section applies.]

**[488]**

**NOTES**

Commencement: 18 January 2005.
Inserted, together with ss 138B, 138C, by the Housing Act 2004, s 183(2), except in relation to any case where the tenant's notice under s 122 of this Act at **[468]**, was served before 18 January 2005.

## [138B Effect of final demolition notice served before completion

(1)   This section applies where—
- (a)   a secure tenant has claimed to exercise the right to buy, but
- (b)   before the landlord has made to the tenant such a grant as is required by section 138(1) in respect of the claim, a final demolition notice is served on the tenant under paragraph 13 of Schedule 5.

(2)   In such a case—
- (a)   the tenant's claim ceases to be effective as from the time when the final demolition notice comes into force under that paragraph, and
- (b)   section 138(1) accordingly does not apply to the landlord, in connection with the tenant's claim, at any time after the notice comes into force.

(3)   Section 138C provides a right to compensation in certain cases where this section applies.]

**[489]**

**NOTES**

Commencement: 18 January 2005.
Inserted as noted to s 138A at **[488]**.

## [138C Compensation where demolition notice served

(1)   This section applies where—
- (a)   a secure tenant has claimed to exercise the right to buy,
- (b)   before the landlord has made to the tenant such a grant as is required by section 138(1) in respect of the claim, either an initial demolition notice is served on the tenant under Schedule 5A or a final demolition notice is served on him under paragraph 13 of Schedule 5, and
- (c)   the tenant's claim is established before that notice comes into force under Schedule 5A or paragraph 13 of Schedule 5 (as the case may be).

(2)   If, within the period of three months beginning with the date when the notice comes into force ("the operative date"), the tenant serves on the landlord a written notice claiming an amount of compensation under subsection (3), the landlord shall pay that amount to the tenant.

(3)   Compensation under this subsection is compensation in respect of expenditure reasonably incurred by the tenant before the operative date in respect of legal and other fees, and other professional costs and expenses, payable in connection with the exercise by him of the right to buy.

(4)   A notice under subsection (2) must be accompanied by receipts or other documents showing that the tenant incurred the expenditure in question.]

**[490]**

**NOTES**

Commencement: 18 January 2005.
Inserted as noted to s 138A at **[488]**.

### 139   Terms and effect of conveyance or grant and mortgage

(1)   A conveyance of the freehold executed in pursuance of the right to buy shall conform with Parts I and II of Schedule 6; a grant of a lease so executed shall conform with Parts I and III of that Schedule; and Part IV of that Schedule has effect in relation to certain charges.

(2)   The secure tenancy comes to an end on the grant to the tenant of an estate in fee simple, or of a lease, in pursuance of the provisions of this Part relating to the right to buy; and if there is then a subtenancy section 139 of the Law of Property Act 1925 (effect of extinguishment of reversion) applies as on a merger or surrender.

(3)   ...

**[491]**

---

**NOTES**

Sub-s (3): repealed by the Leasehold Reform, Housing and Urban Development Act 1993, s 187(2), Sch 22, except in relation to a case where a notice under s 122 at **[468]**, is served before 11 October 1993 or in relation to the operation of this Part of this Act as applied by the Local Government Reorganisation (Preservation of the Right to Buy) Order 1986, SI 1986/2092.

---

### 140   Landlord's first notice to complete

(1)   The landlord may, subject to the provisions of this section, serve on the tenant at any time a written notice requiring him—

    (a)   if all relevant matters have been agreed or determined, to complete the transaction within a period stated in the notice, or

    (b)   if any relevant matters are outstanding, to serve on the landlord within that period a written notice to that effect specifying the matters,

and informing the tenant of the effect of this section and of section 141(1), (2) and (4) (landlord's second notice to complete).

(2)   The period stated in a notice under this section shall be such period (of at least 56 days) as may be reasonable in the circumstances.

[(3)   A notice under this section shall not be served earlier than [three] months after—

    (a)   the service of the landlord's notice under section 125 (notice of purchase price and other matters), or

    (b)   where a notice has been served under section 146 (landlord's notice admitting or denying right to acquire on rent to mortgage terms), the service of that notice.]

(4)   A notice under this section shall not be served if—

    (a)   a requirement for the determination or re-determination of the value of the dwelling-house by the district valuer has not been complied with,

    [(aa)   a review notice (within the meaning of section 128A) has been served in relation to such a determination or re-determination, section 128B applies and the district valuer has neither—

        (i)   served a notice under section 128B(3) (refusal to make further determination), nor

        (ii)   served a notice under section 128B(7) (a determination effect notice),

    (ab)   no such review notice has been served but such a notice may still be served under section 128A,]

    (b)   proceedings for the determination of any other relevant matter have not been disposed of, or

    (c)   any relevant matter stated to be outstanding in a written notice served on the landlord by the tenant has not been agreed in writing or determined.

(5)   In this section "relevant matters" means matters relating to the grant ...

**[492]**

---

**NOTES**

Sub-s (3): substituted by the Leasehold Reform, Housing and Urban Development Act 1993, s 187(1), Sch 21, para 12, except in relation to a case where a notice under s 122 at **[468]**, is served before 11 October 1993 or in relation to the operation of this Part of this Act as applied by the Local Government Reorganisation (Preservation of the Right to Buy) Order 1986, SI 1986/2092; word in square brackets substituted by the Housing Act 2004, s 184(1), (2), except in relation to any case where the tenant's notice under s 122 of this Act was served before 18 January 2005.

Sub-s (4): paras (aa), (ab) inserted by the Housing and Regeneration Act 2008, s 306(1), (10), (12), except in relation to any determination or re-determination under s 128 of this Act which was required before 22 September 2008.

Sub-s (5): words omitted repealed by the Leasehold Reform, Housing and Urban Development Act 1993, s 187(2), Sch 22, subject to savings as noted above.

---

### 141   Landlord's second notice to complete

(1)   If the tenant does not comply with a notice under section 140 (landlord's first notice to complete), the landlord may serve on him a further written notice—

(a)    requiring him to complete the transaction within a period stated in the notice, and

(b)    informing him of the effect of this section in the event of his failing to comply.

(2)    The period stated in a notice under this section shall be such period (of at least 56 days) as may be reasonable in the circumstances.

(3)    At any time before the end of that period (or that period as previously extended) the landlord may by a written notice served on the tenant extend it (or further extend it).

(4)    If the tenant does not comply with a notice under this section the notice claiming to exercise the right to buy shall be deemed to be withdrawn at the end of that period (or as the case may require, that period as extended under subsection (3)).

(5)    If a notice under this section has been served on the tenant and by virtue of section 138(2) (failure of tenant to pay rent, etc) the landlord is not bound to complete, the tenant shall be deemed not to comply with the notice.

**[493]**

**142**    (*Repealed by the Leasehold Reform, Housing and Urban Development Act 1993, s 187(2), Sch 22, except in relation to a case where a notice under s 122 at* **[468]**, *is served before 11 October 1993 or in relation to the operation of this Part of this Act as applied by the Local Government Reorganisation (Preservation of the Right to Buy) Order 1986, SI 1986/2092, and except in relation to the provisions of this Part of this Act relating to the preserved right to buy in a case where a person has the preserved right to buy (as defined in s 171A at* **[536]**) *before 11 October 1993.*)

*[Right to acquire on rent to mortgage terms]*

**NOTES**

Cross-heading: substituted, together with ss 143, 143A, 143B for original s 143, by the Leasehold Reform, Housing and Urban Development Act 1993, s 108, except in relation to a case where a notice under s 122 at **[468]**, is served before 11 October 1993 or in relation to the operation of this Part of this Act as applied by the Local Government Reorganisation (Preservation of the Right to Buy) Order 1986, SI 1986/2092.

**[142A    Termination of the right to acquire on rent to mortgage terms**

(1)    As from the termination date, the right to acquire on rent to mortgage terms is not exercisable except in pursuance of a notice served under section 144 before that date.

(2)    In this section "the termination date" means the date falling 8 months after the date of the passing of the Housing Act 2004.]

**[494]**

**NOTES**

Inserted by the Housing Act 2004, s 190(1).

**[143    Right to acquire on rent to mortgage terms**

(1)    Subject to subsection (2) and sections [142A,] 143A and 143B, where—

(a)    a secure tenant has claimed to exercise the right to buy, and

(b)    his right to buy has been established and his notice claiming to exercise it remains in force,

he also has the right to acquire on rent to mortgage terms in accordance with the following provisions of this Part.

(2)    The right to acquire on rent to mortgage terms cannot be exercised if the exercise of the right to buy is precluded by section 121 (circumstances in which right to buy cannot be exercised).

(3)    Where the right to buy belongs to two or more persons jointly, the right to acquire on rent to mortgage terms also belongs to them jointly.]

**[495]**

**NOTES**

Substituted, together with the cross-heading preceding s 142A and ss 143A, 143B, for original s 143, by the Leasehold Reform, Housing and Urban Development Act 1993, s 108, except in relation to a case where a notice under s 122 at **[468]**, is served before 11 October 1993 or in relation to the operation of this Part of this Act as applied by the Local Government Reorganisation (Preservation of the Right to Buy) Order 1986, SI 1986/2092.

Sub-s (1): reference in square brackets inserted by the Housing Act 2004, s 190(2).

**[143A    Right excluded by entitlement to housing benefit**

(1)    The right to acquire on rent to mortgage to terms cannot be exercised if—

(a)    it has been determined that the tenant is or was entitled to housing benefit in respect of any part of the relevant period, or

(b) a claim for housing benefit in respect of any part of that period has been made (or is treated as having been made) by or on behalf of the tenant and has not been determined or withdrawn.

(2) In this section "the relevant period" means the period—
(a) beginning twelve months before the day on which the tenant claims to exercise the right to acquire on rent to mortgage terms, and
(b) ending with the day on which the conveyance or grant is executed in pursuance of that right.]

**[496]**

---

**NOTES**

Substituted as noted to s 143 at **[495]**.

---

**[143B Right excluded if minimum initial payment exceeds maximum initial payment**

(1) The right to acquire on rent to mortgage terms cannot be exercised if the minimum initial payment in respect of the dwelling-house exceeds the maximum initial payment in respect of it.

(2) The maximum initial payment in respect of a dwelling-house is 80 per cent of the price which would be payable if the tenant were exercising the right to buy.

(3) Where, in the case of a dwelling-house which is a house, the weekly rent at the relevant time did not exceed the relevant amount, the minimum initial payment shall be determined by the formula—

$$P = R \times M$$

where—

P = the minimum initial payment;
R = the amount of the weekly rent at the relevant time;
M = the multiplier which at that time was for the time being declared by the Secretary of State for the purposes of this subsection.

(4) Where, in the case of a dwelling-house which is a house, the weekly rent at the relevant time exceeded the relevant amount, the minimum initial payment shall be determined by the formula—

$$P = Q + (E \times M)$$

where—

P = the minimum initial payment;
Q = the qualifying maximum for the year of assessment which included the relevant time;
E = the amount by which the weekly rent at that time exceeded the relevant amount;
M = the multiplier which at that time was for the time being declared by the Secretary of State for the purposes of this subsection.

(5) The minimum initial payment in respect of a dwelling-house which is a flat is 80 per cent of the amount which would be the minimum initial payment in respect of the dwelling-house if it were a house.

(6) The relevant amount and multipliers for the time being declared for the purposes of this section shall be such that, in the case of a dwelling-house which is a house, they will produce a minimum initial payment equal to the capital sum which, in the opinion of the Secretary of State, could be raised on a 25 year repayment mortgage in the case of which the net amount of the monthly mortgage payments was equal to the rent at the relevant time calculated on a monthly basis.

(7) For the purposes of subsection (6) the Secretary of State shall assume—
(a) that the interest rate applicable throughout the 25 year term were the standard national rate for the time being declared by the Secretary of State under paragraph 2 of Schedule 16 (local authority mortgage interest rates); and
(b) that the monthly mortgage payments represented payments of capital and interest only.

(8) In this section—
"net amount", in relation to monthly mortgage payments, means the amount of such payments after deduction of tax under section 369 of the Income and Corporation Taxes Act 1988 (mortgage interest payable under deduction of tax);
"qualifying maximum" means the qualifying maximum defined in section 367(5) of that Act (limit on relief for interest on certain loans);
"relevant amount" means the amount which at the relevant time was for the time being declared by the Secretary of State for the purposes of this section;
"relevant time" means the time of the service of the landlord's notice under section 146 (landlord's notice admitting or denying right);
"rent" means rent payable under the secure tenancy, but excluding any element which is expressed to be payable for services, repairs, maintenance or insurance or the landlord's costs of management.]

**[497]**

**NOTES**
Substituted as noted to s 143 at **[495]**.

**[144  Tenant's notice claiming right**

(1)   [Subject to section 142A, a secure tenant] claims to exercise the right to acquire on rent to mortgage terms by written notice to that effect served on the landlord.

(2)   The notice may be withdrawn at any time by notice in writing served on the landlord.

(3)   On the service of a notice under this section, any notice served by the landlord under section 140 or 141 (landlord's notices to complete purchase in pursuance of right to buy) shall be deemed to have been withdrawn; and no such notice may be served by the landlord whilst a notice under this section remains in force.

(4)   Where a notice under this section is withdrawn, the tenant may complete the transaction in accordance with the provisions of this Part relating to the right to buy.]

**[498]**

**NOTES**
Substituted, for original ss 144, 145, by the Leasehold Reform, Housing and Urban Development Act 1993, s 109, except in relation to a case where a notice under s 122 at **[468]**, is served before 11 October 1993 or in relation to the operation of this Part of this Act as applied by the Local Government Reorganisation (Preservation of the Right to Buy) Order 1986, SI 1986/2092.
Sub-s (1): words in square brackets substituted by the Housing Act 2004, s 190(3).

**[146  Landlord's notice admitting or denying right**

(1)   Where a notice under section 144 (notice claiming to exercise the right to acquire on rent to mortgage terms) has been served by the tenant, the landlord shall, unless the notice is withdrawn, serve on the tenant as soon as practicable a written notice either—

(a)   admitting the tenant's right and informing him of the matters mentioned in subsection (2), or

(b)   denying it and stating the reasons why, in the opinion of the landlord, the tenant does not have the right to acquire on rent to mortgage terms.

(2)   The matters are—

(a)   the relevant amount and multipliers for the time being declared by the Secretary of State for the purposes of section 143B;

(b)   the amount of the minimum initial payment;

(c)   the proportion which that amount bears to the price which would be payable if the tenant exercised the right to buy;

(d)   the landlord's share on the assumption that the tenant makes the minimum initial payment;

(e)   the amount of the initial discount on that assumption; and

(f)   the provisions which, in the landlord's opinion, should be contained in the conveyance or grant and the mortgage required by section 151B (mortgage for securing redemption of landlord's share).]

**[499]**

**NOTES**
Substituted by the Leasehold Reform, Housing and Urban Development Act 1993, s 110, except in relation to a case where a notice under s 122 at **[468]**, is served before 11 October 1993 or in relation to the operation of this Part of this Act as applied by the Local Government Reorganisation (Preservation of the Right to Buy) Order 1986, SI 1986/2092.

**[146A  Tenant's notice of intention**

(1)   Where a notice under section 146 has been served on a secure tenant, he shall within the period specified in subsection (2) serve a written notice on the landlord stating either—

(a)   that he intends to pursue his claim to exercise the right to acquire on rent to mortgage terms and the amount of the initial payment which he proposes to make, or

(b)   that he withdraws that claim and intends to pursue his claim to exercise the right to buy, or

(c)   that he withdraws both of those claims.

(2)   The period for serving a notice under subsection (1) is the period of twelve weeks beginning with the service of the notice under section 146.

(3)   The amount stated in a notice under subsection (1)(a)—

(a)   shall not be less than the minimum initial payment and not more than the maximum initial payment, and

(b)   may be varied at any time by notice in writing served on the landlord.]

**[500]**

**NOTES**

Inserted, together with s 146B, by the Leasehold Reform, Housing and Urban Development Act 1993, s 111, except in relation to a case where a notice under s 122 at **[468]**, is served before 11 October 1993 or in relation to the operation of this Part of this Act as applied by the Local Government Reorganisation (Preservation of the Right to Buy) Order 1986, SI 1986/2092.

**[146B   Landlord's notice in default**

(1)   The landlord may, at any time after the end of the period specified in section 146A(2), serve on the tenant a written notice—

(a)   requiring him, if he has failed to serve the notice required by section 146A(1), to serve that notice within 28 days, and

(b)   informing him of the effect of this subsection and subsection (4).

(2)   At any time before the end of the period mentioned in subsection (1)(a) (or that period as previously extended) the landlord may by written notice served on the tenant extend it (or further extend it).

(3)   If at any time before the end of that period (or that period as extended under subsection (2)) the circumstances are such that it would not be reasonable to expect the tenant to comply with a notice under this section, that period (or that period as so extended) shall by virtue of this subsection be extended (or further extended) until 28 days after the time when those circumstances no longer obtain.

(4)   If the tenant does not comply with a notice under this section the notice claiming to exercise the right to acquire on rent to mortgage terms shall be deemed to be withdrawn at the end of that period (or, as the case may require, that period as extended under subsection (2) or (3)).]

**[501]**

**NOTES**

Inserted as noted to s 146A at **[500]**.

**[147   Notice of landlord's share and initial discount**

(1)   Where a secure tenant has served—

(a)   a notice under section 146A(1)(a) stating that he intends to pursue his claim to exercise the right to acquire on rent to mortgage terms, and the amount of the initial payment which he proposes to make, or

(b)   a notice under section 146A(3)(b) varying the amount stated in a notice under section 146A(1)(a),

the landlord shall, as soon as practicable, serve on the tenant a written notice complying with this section.

(2)   The notice shall state—

(a)   the landlord's share on the assumption that the amount of the tenant's initial payment is that stated in the notice under section 146A(1)(a) or, as the case may be, section 146A(3)(b), and

(b)   the amount of the initial discount on that assumption,

determined in each case in accordance with section 148.]

**[502]**

**NOTES**

Substituted by the Leasehold Reform, Housing and Urban Development Act 1993, s 112, except in relation to a case where a notice under s 122 at **[468]**, is served before 11 October 1993 or in relation to the operation of this Part of this Act as applied by the Local Government Reorganisation (Preservation of the Right to Buy) Order 1986, SI 1986/2092.

**[148   Determination of landlord's share, initial discount etc**

The landlord's share shall be determined by the formula—

$$S = \frac{P - IP}{P} \times 100$$

the amount of the initial discount shall be determined by the formula—

$$ID = \frac{IP}{P} \times D$$

and the amount of any previous discount which will be recovered by virtue of the transaction shall be determined by the formula—

$$RD = \frac{IP}{P} \times PD$$

where—

S = the landlord's share expressed as a percentage;

P = the price which would be payable if the tenant were exercising the right to buy;

IP = the amount of the tenant's initial payment (but disregarding any reduction in pursuance of section 153B(3));

ID = the amount of the initial discount;

D = the amount of the discount which would be applicable if the tenant were exercising the right to buy;

RD = the amount of any previous discount which will be recovered by virtue of the transaction;

PD = the amount of any previous discount which would be recovered if the tenant were exercising the right to buy.]

**[503]**

**NOTES**

Substituted by the Leasehold Reform, Housing and Urban Development Act 1993, s 113, except in relation to a case where a notice under s 122 at **[468]**, is served before 11 October 1993 or in relation to the operation of this Part of this Act as applied by the Local Government Reorganisation (Preservation of the Right to Buy) Order 1986, SI 1986/2092.

**[149   Change of landlord after notice claiming right**

(1)   Where the interest of the landlord in the dwelling-house passes from the landlord to another body after a secure tenant has given a notice claiming to exercise the right to acquire on rent to mortgage terms, all parties shall subject to subsection (2) be in the same position as if the other body—

(a)   had become the landlord before the notice was given, and

(b)   had been given that notice and any further notice given by the tenant to the landlord, and

(c)   had taken all steps which the landlord had taken.

(2)   If the circumstances after the disposal differ in any material respect, as for example where—

(a)   the interest of the disponee in the dwelling-house after the disposal differs from that of the disponor before the disposal, or

(b)   any of the provisions of Schedule 5 (exceptions to the right to buy) becomes or ceases to be applicable,

all those concerned shall, as soon as practicable after the disposal, take all such steps (whether by way of amending or withdrawing and re-serving any notice or extending any period or otherwise) as may be requisite for the purpose of securing that all parties are, as nearly as may be, in the same position as they would have been if those circumstances had obtained before the disposal.]

**[504]**

**NOTES**

Substituted by the Leasehold Reform, Housing and Urban Development Act 1993, s 114, except in relation to a case where a notice under s 122 at **[468]**, is served before 11 October 1993 or in relation to the operation of this Part of this Act as applied by the Local Government Reorganisation (Preservation of the Right to Buy) Order 1986, SI 1986/2092.

**[150   Duty of landlord to convey freehold or grant lease**

(1)   Where a secure tenant has claimed to exercise the right to acquire on rent to mortgage terms and that right has been established, then, as soon as all matters relating to the grant and to securing the redemption of the landlord's share have been agreed or determined, the landlord shall make to the tenant—

(a)   if the dwelling-house is a house and the landlord owns the freehold, a grant of the dwelling-house for an estate in fee simple absolute, or

(b)   if the landlord does not own the freehold or if the dwelling-house is a flat (whether or not the landlord owns the freehold), a grant of a lease of the dwelling-house,

in accordance with the following provisions of this Part.

(2)   If the tenant has failed to pay the rent or any other payment due from him as a tenant for a period of four weeks after it has been lawfully demanded from him, the landlord is not bound to comply with subsection (1) while the whole or part of that payment remains outstanding.

(3)   The duty imposed on the landlord by subsection (1) is enforceable by injunction.]

**[505]**

**NOTES**
 Substituted by the Leasehold Reform, Housing and Urban Development Act 1993, s 115, except in relation to a case where a notice under s 122 at **[468]**, is served before 11 October 1993 or in relation to the operation of this Part of this Act as applied by the Local Government Reorganisation (Preservation of the Right to Buy) Order 1986, SI 1986/2092.

**[151   Terms and effect of conveyance or grant: general**

   (1)   A conveyance of the freehold executed in pursuance of the right to acquire on rent to mortgage terms shall conform with Parts I and II of Schedule 6; a grant of a lease so executed shall conform with Parts I and III of that Schedule; and Part IV of that Schedule applies to such a conveyance or lease as it applies to a conveyance or lease executed in pursuance of the right to buy.

   (2)   The secure tenancy comes to an end on the grant to the tenant of an estate in fee simple, or of a lease, in pursuance of the right to acquire on rent to mortgage terms; and if there is then a sub-tenancy section 139 of the Law of Property Act 1925 (effect of extinguishment of reversion) applies as on a merger or surrender.]

**[506]**

**NOTES**
 Substituted by the Leasehold Reform, Housing and Urban Development Act 1993, s 116(1), except in relation to a case where a notice under s 122 at **[468]**, is served before 11 October 1993 or in relation to the operation of this Part of this Act as applied by the Local Government Reorganisation (Preservation of the Right to Buy) Order 1986, SI 1986/2092.

**[151A   Redemption of landlord's share**

Schedule 6A (which makes provision for the redemption of the landlord's share) shall have effect; and a conveyance of the freehold or a grant of a lease executed in pursuance of the right to acquire on rent to mortgage terms shall conform with that Schedule.]

**[507]**

**NOTES**
 Inserted by the Leasehold Reform, Housing and Urban Development Act 1993, s 117(1), except in relation to a case where a notice under s 122 at **[468]**, is served before 11 October 1993 or in relation to the operation of this Part of this Act as applied by the Local Government Reorganisation (Preservation of the Right to Buy) Order 1986, SI 1986/2092.

**[151B   Mortgage for securing redemption of landlord's share**

   (1)   The liability that may arise under the covenant required by paragraph 1 of Schedule 6A (covenant for the redemption of the landlord's share in the circumstances there mentioned) shall be secured by a mortgage.

   (2)   Subject to subsections (3) and (4), the mortgage shall have priority immediately after any legal charge securing an amount advanced to the secure tenant by an approved lending institution for the purpose of enabling him to exercise the right to acquire on rent to mortgage terms.

   (3)   The following, namely—
      (a)   any advance which is made otherwise than for the purpose mentioned in subsection (2) and is secured by a legal charge having priority to the mortgage, and
      (b)   any further advance which is so secured,
shall rank in priority to the mortgage if, and only if, the landlord by written notice served on the institution concerned gives its consent; and the landlord shall so give its consent if the purpose of the advance or further advance is an approved purpose.

   (4)   The landlord may at any time by written notice served on an approved lending institution postpone the mortgage to any advance or further advance which—
      (a)   is made to the tenant by that institution, and
      (b)   is secured by a legal charge not having priority to the mortgage;
and the landlord shall serve such a notice if the purpose of the advance or further advance is an approved purpose.

   (5)   The approved lending institutions for the purposes of this section are—
      the [Relevant Authority],
      [an authorised deposit taker
      an authorised insurer],
      [an authorised mortgage lender.]

   (6)   The approved purposes for the purposes of this section are—
      (a)   to enable the tenant to make an interim or final payment,
      (b)   to enable the tenant to defray, or to defray on his behalf, any of the following—
         (i)   the cost of any works to the dwelling-house,

(ii)    any service charge payable in respect of the dwelling-house for works, whether or not to the dwelling-house, and

(iii)    any service charge or other amount payable in respect of the dwelling-house for insurance, whether or not of the dwelling-house, and

(c)   to enable the tenant to discharge, or to discharge on his behalf, any of the following—

(i)    so much as is still outstanding of any advance or further advance which ranks in priority to the mortgage,

(ii)    any arrears of interest on such an advance or further advance, and

(iii)    any costs and expenses incurred in enforcing payment of any such interest, or repayment (in whole or in part) of any such advance or further advance.

(7)   Where different parts of an advance or further advance are made for different purposes, each of those parts shall be regarded as a separate advance or further advance for the purposes of this section.

(8)   The Secretary of State may by order prescribe—

(a)   matters for which the deed by which the mortgage is effected must make provision, and

(b)   terms which must, or must not, be contained in that deed,

but only in relation to deeds executed after the order comes into force.

(9)   The deed by which the mortgage is effected may contain such other provisions as may be—

(a)   agreed between the mortgagor and the mortgagee, or

(b)   determined by the county court to be reasonably required by the mortgagor or the mortgagee.

(10)   An order under this section—

(a)   may make different provision with respect to different cases or descriptions of case, including different provision for different areas, and

(b)   shall be made by statutory instrument which shall be subject to annulment in pursuance of a resolution of either House of Parliament.]

**[508]**

---

**NOTES**

Inserted by the Leasehold Reform, Housing and Urban Development Act 1993, s 118, except in relation to a case where a notice under s 122 at **[468]**, is served before 11 October 1993 or in relation to the operation of this Part of this Act as applied by the Local Government Reorganisation (Preservation of the Right to Buy) Order 1986, SI 1986/2092.

Sub-s (5): words in first pair of square brackets substituted by the Government of Wales Act 1998, s 140, Sch 16, paras 4, 5; words in second pair of square brackets substituted by the Financial Services and Markets Act 2000 (Consequential Amendments and Repeals) Order 2001, SI 2001/3649, art 299(1), (3); words in third pair of square brackets substituted by the Housing and Regeneration Act 2008, s 307(5).

Modification: this section is modified by the Transfer of Housing Corporation Functions (Modifications and Transitional Provisions) Order 2008, SI 2008/2839, art 3, Schedule.

Transfer of Functions: functions of the Housing Corporation under this section are transferred to the Homes and Communities Agency by the Transfer of Housing Corporation Functions (Modifications and Transitional Provisions) Order 2008, SI 2008/2839, arts 1(2), 2, 6.

---

**152  Landlord's first notice to complete**

(1)   The landlord may, subject to the provisions of this section, serve on the tenant at any time a written notice requiring him—

(a)   if all relevant matters have been agreed or determined, to complete the transaction within a period stated in the notice, or

(b)   if any relevant matters are outstanding, to serve on the landlord within that period a written notice to that effect specifying the matters,

and informing the tenant of the effect of this section and of section 153(1), (2) and (4) (landlord's second notice to complete and its effect).

(2)   The period stated in a notice under this section shall be such period (of at least 56 days) as may be reasonable in the circumstances.

[(3)   A notice under this section shall not be served earlier than twelve months after the service of the notice under section 146 (landlord's notice admitting or denying right).]

(4)   A notice under this section shall not be served if—

(a)   a requirement for the determination or re-determination of the value of the dwelling-house by the district valuer has not been complied with,

(b)   proceedings for the determination of any other relevant matter have not been disposed of, or

(c)   any relevant matter stated to be outstanding in a written notice served on the landlord by the tenant has not been agreed in writing or determined.

(5)   In this section "relevant matters" means matters relating to the grant and to [securing the redemption of the landlord's share].

**[509]**

PART 1
STATUTES

**NOTES**

Sub-s (3): substituted by the Leasehold Reform, Housing and Urban Development Act 1993, s 119(1), except in relation to a case where a notice under s 122 at **[468]**, is served before 11 October 1993 or in relation to the operation of this Part of this Act as applied by the Local Government Reorganisation (Preservation of the Right to Buy) Order 1986, SI 1986/2092.

Sub-s (5): words in square brackets substituted by the Leasehold Reform, Housing and Urban Development Act 1993, s 119(2), subject to savings as noted above.

## 153 Landlord's second notice to complete

(1)  If the tenant does not comply with a notice under section 152 (landlord's first notice to complete), the landlord may serve on him a further written notice—

    (a)   requiring him to complete the transaction within a period stated in the notice, and

    (b)   informing him of the effect of this section in the event of his failing to comply.

(2)  The period stated in a notice under this section shall be such period (of at least 56 days) as may be reasonable in the circumstances.

(3)  At any time before the end of that period (or that period as previously extended) the landlord may by a written notice served on the tenant extend it (or further extend it).

(4)  If the tenant does not comply with a notice under this section, the notice claiming to exercise [the right to acquire on rent to mortgage terms] and the notice claiming to exercise the right to buy shall be deemed to have been withdrawn at the end of that period (or, as the case may require, that period as extended under subsection (3)).

(5)  If a notice under this section has been served on the tenant and by virtue of section 150(2) (failure of tenant to pay rent, etc) the landlord is not bound to complete, the tenant shall be deemed not to comply with the notice.

**[510]**

**NOTES**

Sub-s (4): words in square brackets substituted by the Leasehold Reform, Housing and Urban Development Act 1993, s 119(3), except in relation to a case where a notice under s 122 at **[468]**, is served before 11 October 1993 or in relation to the operation of this Part of this Act as applied by the Local Government Reorganisation (Preservation of the Right to Buy) Order 1986, SI 1986/2092.

*[Tenant's sanction for landlord's delays]*

**NOTES**

Cross-heading inserted by the Leasehold Reform, Housing and Urban Development Act 1993, s 187, Sch 21, para 13(1), except in relation to a case where a notice under s 122 at **[468]**, is served before 11 October 1993 or in relation to the operation of this Part of this Act as applied by the Local Government Reorganisation (Preservation of the Right to Buy) Order 1986, SI 1986/2092.

## [153A  Tenant's notices of delay

(1)  Where a secure tenant has claimed to exercise the right to buy, he may serve on his landlord a notice (in this section referred to as an "initial notice of delay") in any of the following cases, namely,—

    (a)   where the landlord has failed to serve a notice under section 124 within the period appropriate under subsection (2) of that section;

    (b)   where the tenant's right to buy has been established and the landlord has failed to serve a notice under section 125 within the period appropriate under subsection (1) of that section;

    (c), (d) ...

    (e)   where the tenant considers that delays on the part of the landlord are preventing him from exercising expeditiously his right to buy or his [right to acquire on rent to mortgage terms];

and where an initial notice of delay specifies [either of the cases in paragraphs (a) and (b)], any reference in this section or section 153B to the default date is a reference to the end of the period referred to in the paragraph in question or, if it is later, the day appointed for the coming into force of section 124 of the Housing Act 1988.

(2)  An initial notice of delay—

    (a)   shall specify the most recent action of which the tenant is aware which has been taken by the landlord pursuant to this Part of this Act; and

    (b)   shall specify a period (in this section referred to as "the response period"), not being less than one month, beginning on the date of service of the notice, within which the service by the landlord of a counter notice under subsection (3) will have the effect of cancelling the initial notice of delay.

(3)    Within the response period specified in an initial notice of delay or at any time thereafter, the landlord may serve on the tenant a counter notice in either of the following circumstances—

(a)    if the initial notice specifies [either of the cases in paragraphs (a) and (b)] of subsection (1) and the landlord has served, or is serving together with the counter notice, the required notice under section 124, [or section 125], as the case may be; or

(b)    if the initial notice specifies the case in subsection (1)(e) and there is no action under this Part which, at the beginning of the response period, it was for the landlord to take in order to allow the tenant expeditiously to exercise his right to buy or his [right to acquire on rent to mortgage terms] and which remains to be taken at the time of service of the counter notice.

(4)    A counter notice under subsection (3) shall specify the circumstances by virtue of which it is served.

(5)    At any time when—

(a)    the response period specified in an initial notice of delay has expired, and

(b)    the landlord has not served a counter notice under subsection (3),

the tenant may serve on the landlord a notice (in this section and section 153B referred to as an "operative notice of delay") which shall state that section 153B will apply to payments of rent made by the tenant on or after the default date or, if the initial notice of delay specified the case in subsection (1)(e), the date of the service of the notice.

(6)    If, after a tenant has served an initial notice of delay, a counter notice has been served under subsection (3), then, whether or not the tenant has also served an operative notice of delay, if any of the cases in subsection (1) again arises, the tenant may serve a further initial notice of delay and the provisions of this section shall apply again accordingly.]

[511]

## NOTES

Inserted, together with s 153B, by the Housing Act 1988, s 124.

Sub-s (1): paras (c), (d) repealed and words in square brackets substituted by the Leasehold Reform, Housing and Urban Development Act 1993, s 187, Sch 21, para 13(2), Sch 22, except in relation to a case where a notice under s 122 at **[468]**, is served before 11 October 1993 or in relation to the operation of this Part of this Act as applied by the Local Government Reorganisation (Preservation of the Right to Buy) Order 1986, SI 1986/2092.

Sub-s (3): words in square brackets substituted by the Leasehold Reform, Housing and Urban Development Act 1993, s 187(1), Sch 21, para 13(3), subject to savings as noted above.

## [153B    Payments of rent attributable to purchase price etc

(1)    Where a secure tenant has served on his landlord an operative notice of delay, this section applies to any payment of rent which is made on or after the default date or, as the case may be, the date of the service of the notice and before the occurrence of any of the following events (and, if more than one event occurs, before the earliest to occur)—

(a)    the service by the landlord of a counter notice under section 153A(3);

(b)    the date on which the landlord makes to the tenant the grant required by section 138 or, as the case may be, section 150;

(c)    …

(d)    the date on which the tenant withdraws or is deemed to have withdrawn the notice claiming to exercise the right to buy or, as the case may be, the notice claiming to exercise the [right to acquire on rent to mortgage terms]; and

(e)    the date on which the tenant ceases to be entitled to exercise the right to buy.

(2)    Except where this section ceases to apply on a date determined under [paragraph (d) or (e)] of subsection (1), so much of any payment of rent to which this section applies as does not consist of—

(a)    a sum due on account of rates [or council tax], or

(b)    a service charge (as defined in section 621A),

shall be treated not only as a payment of rent but also as a payment on account by the tenant which is to be taken into account in accordance with subsection (3).

(3)    In a case where subsection (2) applies, the amount which, apart from this section, would be the purchase price or, as the case may be, [the tenant's initial payment] shall be reduced by an amount equal to the aggregate of—

(a)    the total of any payments on account treated as having been paid by the tenant by virtue of subsection (2); and

(b)    if those payments on account are derived from payments of rent referable to a period of more than twelve months, a sum equal to the appropriate percentage of the total referred to in paragraph (a).

(4)    In subsection (3)(b) "the appropriate percentage" means 50 per cent or such other percentage as may be prescribed.]

[512]

**NOTES**

Inserted as noted to s 153A at **[511]**.

Sub-s (1): para (c) repealed and words in square brackets in para (d) substituted by the Leasehold Reform, Housing and Urban Development Act 1993, s 187, Sch 21, para 14, Sch 22, except in relation to a case where a notice under s 122 at **[468]**, is served before 11 October 1993 or in relation to the operation of this Part of this Act as applied by the Local Government Reorganisation (Preservation of the Right to Buy) Order 1986, SI 1986/2092. Note also that the repeal of para (c) does not apply in relation to the provisions of this Part of this Act relating to the preserved right to buy in a case where a person has the preserved right to buy (as defined in s 171A at **[536]**) before 11 October 1993.

Sub-s (2): words in first pair of square brackets substituted by the Leasehold Reform, Housing and Urban Development Act 1993, s 187(1), Sch 21, para 14, subject to savings as noted above; words in second pair of square brackets inserted by the Local Government Finance (Housing) (Consequential Amendments) Order 1993, SI 1993/651, art 2(1), Sch 1, para 14.

Sub-s (3): words in square brackets substituted by the Leasehold Reform, Housing and Urban Development Act 1993, s 187(1), Sch 21, para 14, subject to savings as noted above.

*Registration of title*

**154 Registration of title**

(1)   ...

(2)   Where the landlord's title to the dwelling-house is not registered, the landlord shall give the tenant a certificate stating that the landlord is entitled to convey the freehold or make the grant subject only to such incumbrances, rights and interests as are stated in the conveyance or grant or summarised in the certificate.

(3)   Where the landlord's interest in the dwelling-house is a lease, the certificate under subsection (2) shall also state particulars of that lease and, with respect to each superior title—

(a)   where it is registered, the title number;

(b)   where it is not registered, whether it was investigated in the usual way on the grant of the landlord's lease.

(4)   A certificate under subsection (2) shall be—

(a)   in a form approved by the Chief Land Registrar, and

(b)   signed by such officer of the landlord or such other person as may be approved by the Chief Land Registrar.

(5)   The Chief Land Registrar shall, for the purpose of the registration of title, accept such a certificate as sufficient evidence of the facts stated in it; but if as a result he has to meet a claim against him under the [Land Registration Act 2002] the landlord is liable to indemnify him.

(6), [(7)]   ...

**[513]**

**NOTES**

Sub-ss (1), (6): repealed by the Land Registration Act 2002, s 135, Sch 13.

Sub-s (5): words in square brackets substituted by the Land Registration Act 2002, s 133, Sch 11, para 18(1), (3).

Sub-s (7): added by the Land Registration Act 1986, s 2(3), (4); repealed by the Land Registration Act 2002, s 135, Sch 13.

*Provisions affecting future disposals*

**155 Repayment of discount on early disposal**

(1)   A conveyance of the freehold or grant of a lease in pursuance of this Part shall contain (unless, in the case of a conveyance or grant in pursuance of the right to buy, there is no discount) a covenant binding on the secure tenant and his successors in title to the following effect.

[(2)   In the case of a conveyance or grant in pursuance of the right to buy, the covenant shall be to pay the landlord such sum (if any) as the landlord may demand in accordance with section 155A on the occasion of the first relevant disposal (other than an exempted disposal) which takes place within the period of five years beginning with the conveyance or grant.

(3)   In the case of a conveyance or grant in pursuance of the right to acquire on rent to mortgage terms, the covenant shall be to pay the landlord such sum (if any) as the landlord may demand in accordance with section 155B on the occasion of the first relevant disposal (other than an exempted disposal) which takes place within the period of five years beginning with the making of the initial payment.]

[(3A)   Where a secure tenant has served on his landlord an operative notice of delay, as defined in section 153A,—

(a)   the [five years] referred to in subsection (2) shall begin from a date which precedes the date of the conveyance of the freehold or grant of the lease by a period equal to the time (or, if there is more than one such notice, the aggregate of the times) during which, by virtue of section 153B, any payment of rent falls to be taken into account in accordance with subsection (3) of that section; and

[(b)  any reference in subsection (3) (other than paragraph (a) thereof) to the making of the initial payment shall be construed as a reference to the date which precedes that payment by the period referred to in paragraph (a) of this subsection].]

**[514]**

**NOTES**
Sub-ss (2), (3): substituted by the Housing Act 2004, s 185(1), (2); for effect see s 185(5)–(8) of that Act at **[1471]**.
Sub-s (3A): added by the Housing Act 1988, s 140(1), Sch 17, Pt I, para 41; words in square brackets in para (a) substituted by the Housing Act 2004, s 185(1), (3), for effect see s 185(5)–(8) of that Act at **[1471]**; para (b) substituted by the Leasehold Reform, Housing and Urban Development Act 1993, s 120(2).

**[155A  Amount of discount which may be demanded by landlord: right to buy**

(1)  For the purposes of the covenant mentioned in section 155(2), the landlord may demand such sum as he considers appropriate, up to and including the maximum amount specified in this section.

(2)  The maximum amount which may be demanded by the landlord is a percentage of the price or premium paid for the first relevant disposal which is equal to the discount to which the secure tenant was entitled, where the discount is expressed as a percentage of the value which under section 127 was taken as the value of the dwelling-house at the relevant time.

(3)  But for each complete year which has elapsed after the conveyance or grant and before the disposal the maximum amount which may be demanded by the landlord is reduced by one-fifth.

(4)  This section is subject to section 155C.]

**[515]**

**NOTES**
Commencement: 18 January 2005.
Inserted, together with s 155B, by the Housing Act 2004, s 185(4); for effect see s 185(5)–(8) of that Act at **[1471]**.

**[155B  Amount of discount which may be demanded by landlord: right to acquire on rent to mortgage terms**

(1)  For the purposes of the covenant mentioned in section 155(3), the landlord may demand such sum as he considers appropriate, up to and including the maximum amount specified in this section.

(2)  The maximum amount which may be demanded by the landlord is the discount (if any) to which the tenant was entitled on the making of—
(a)  the initial payment,
(b)  any interim payment made before the disposal, or
(c)  the final payment if so made,

reduced, in each case, by one-fifth for each complete year which has elapsed after the making of the initial payment and before the disposal.]

**[516]**

**NOTES**
Commencement: 18 January 2005.
Inserted as noted to s 155A at **[515]**.

**[155C  Increase attributable to home improvements**

(1)  In calculating the maximum amount which may be demanded by the landlord under section 155A, such amount (if any) of the price or premium paid for the disposal which is attributable to improvements made to the dwelling-house—
(a)  by the person by whom the disposal is, or is to be, made, and
(b)  after the conveyance or grant and before the disposal,
shall be disregarded.

(2)  The amount to be disregarded under this section shall be such amount as may be agreed between the parties or determined by the district valuer.

(3)  The district valuer shall not be required by virtue of this section to make a determination for the purposes of this section unless—
(a)  it is reasonably practicable for him to do so; and
(b)  his reasonable costs in making the determination are paid by the person by whom the disposal is, or is to be, made.

(4)   If the district valuer does not make a determination for the purposes of this section (and in default of an agreement), no amount is required to be disregarded under this section.]

**[517]**

**NOTES**
Commencement: 18 January 2005.
Inserted by the Housing Act 2004, s 186(1).

### 156   Liability to repay is a charge on the premises

(1)   The liability that may arise under the covenant required by section 155 is a charge on the dwelling-house, taking effect as if it had been created by deed expressed to be by way of legal mortgage.

[(2)   Subject to subsections (2A) and (2B), the charge has priority as follows—
  (a)   if it secures the liability that may arise under the covenant required by section 155(2), immediately after any legal charge securing an amount advanced to the secure tenant by an approved lending institution for the purpose of enabling him to exercise the right to buy;
  (b)   if it secures the liability that may arise under the covenant required by section 155(3), immediately after the mortgage—
    (i)   which is required by section 151B (mortgage for securing redemption of landlord's share), and
    (ii)   which, by virtue of subsection (2) of that section, has priority immediately after any legal charge securing an amount advanced to the secure tenant by an approved lending institution for the purpose of enabling him to exercise the right to acquire on rent to mortgage terms.

(2A)   The following, namely—
  (a)   any advance which is made otherwise than for the purpose mentioned in paragraph (a) or (b) of subsection (2) and is secured by a legal charge having priority to the charge taking effect by virtue of this section, and
  (b)   any further advance which is so secured,
shall rank in priority to that charge if, and only if, the landlord by written notice served on the institution concerned gives its consent; and the landlord shall so give its consent if the purpose of the advance or further advance is an approved purpose.

(2B)   The landlord may at any time by written notice served on an approved lending institution postpone the charge taking effect by virtue of this section to any advance or further advance which—
  (a)   is made to the tenant by that institution, and
  (b)   is secured by a legal charge not having priority to that charge;
and the landlord shall serve such a notice if the purpose of the advance or further advance is an approved purpose.]

(3)   ...

[(3A)   The covenant required by section 155 (covenant for repayment of discount) does not, by virtue of its binding successors in title of the tenant, bind a person exercising rights under a charge having priority over the charge taking effect by virtue of this section, or a person deriving title under him; and a provision of the conveyance or grant, or of a collateral agreement, is void in so far as it purports to authorise a forfeiture, or to impose a penalty or disability, in the event of any such person failing to comply with that covenant.]

(4)   The approved lending institutions for the purposes of this section are—
  the [Relevant Authority],
  [an authorised deposit taker
  an authorised insurer],
  [an authorised mortgage lender.]

[(4A)   The approved purposes for the purposes of this section are—
  (a)   to enable the tenant to make an interim or final payment,
  (b)   to enable the tenant to defray, or to defray on his behalf, any of the following—
    (i)   the cost of any works to the dwelling-house,
    (ii)   any service charge payable in respect of the dwelling-house for works, whether or not to the dwelling-house, and
    (iii)   any service charge or other amount payable in respect of the dwelling-house for insurance, whether or not of the dwelling-house, and
  (c)   to enable the tenant to discharge, or to discharge on his behalf, any of the following—
    (i)   so much as is still outstanding of any advance or further advance which ranks in priority to the charge taking effect by virtue of this section,
    (ii)   any arrears of interest on such an advance or further advance, and

PART I
STATUTES

(iii) any costs and expenses incurred in enforcing payment of any such interest, or repayment (in whole or in part) of any such advance or further advance.

(4B) Where different parts of an advance or further advance are made for different purposes, each of those parts shall be regarded as a separate advance or further advance for the purposes of this section.]

(5), (6) ...

**[518]**

**NOTES**

Sub-ss (2)–(2B): substituted, for original sub-s (2), by the Leasehold Reform, Housing and Urban Development Act 1993, s 120(3), (4), except in relation to a case where a notice under s 122 at **[468]**, is served before 11 October 1993 or in relation to the operation of this Part of this Act as applied by the Local Government Reorganisation (Preservation of the Right to Buy) Order 1986, SI 1986/2092.

Sub-s (3): repealed by the Land Registration Act 2002, s 135, Sch 13.

Sub-s (3A): inserted by the Housing and Planning Act 1987, s 24(1), Sch 5, para 1.

Sub-s (4): words in first pair of square brackets substituted by the Government of Wales Act 1998, s 140, Sch 16, paras 4, 5; words in second pair of square brackets substituted by the Financial Services and Markets Act 2000 (Consequential Amendments and Repeals) Order 2001, SI 2001/3649, art 299(1), (4); words in third pair of square brackets substituted by the Housing and Regeneration Act 2008, s 307(1)(a).

Sub-ss (4A), (4B): inserted by the Leasehold Reform, Housing and Urban Development Act 1993, s 120(3), (4), subject to savings as noted above.

Sub-ss (5), (6): repealed by the Housing and Regeneration Act 2008, ss 307(1)(b), 321(1), Sch 16.

Modification: this section is modified by the Transfer of Housing Corporation Functions (Modifications and Transitional Provisions) Order 2008, SI 2008/2839, art 3, Schedule.

Transfer of Functions: functions of the Housing Corporation under this section are transferred to the Homes and Communities Agency by the Transfer of Housing Corporation Functions (Modifications and Transitional Provisions) Order 2008, SI 2008/2839, arts 1(2), 2, 6.

Orders: the Housing (Right to Buy) (Priority of Charges) Order 1987, SI 1987/1203; the Housing (Right to Buy) (Priority of Charges) (No 2) Order 1987, SI 1987/1810; the Housing (Right to Buy) (Priority of Charges) (No 1) Order 1988, SI 1988/85; the Housing (Right to Buy) (Priority of Charges) (No 2) Order 1988, SI 1988/1726; the Housing (Right to Buy) (Priority of Charges) Order 1989, SI 1989/958; the Housing (Right to Buy) (Priority of Charges) (No 2) Order 1989, SI 1989/2102; the Housing (Right to Buy) (Priority of Charges) (No 3) Order 1989, SI 1989/2329; the Housing (Right to Buy) (Priority of Charges) Order 1990, SI 1990/1388; the Housing (Right to Buy) (Priority of Charges) (No 2) Order 1990, SI 1990/2390; the Housing (Right to Buy) (Priority of Charges) Order 1991, SI 1991/619; the Housing (Right to Buy) (Priority of Charges) (No 2) Order 1991, SI 1991/2052; the Housing (Right to Buy) (Priority of Charges) Order 1992, SI 1992/2317; the Housing (Right to Buy) (Priority of Charges) Order 1993, SI 1993/303; the Housing (Right to Buy) (Priority of Charges) (No 2) Order 1993, SI 1993/2757; the Housing (Right to Buy) (Priority of Charges) Order 1994, SI 1994/1762; the Housing (Right to Buy) (Priority of Charges) Order 1995, SI 1995/211; the Housing (Right to Buy) (Priority of Charges) (No 2) Order 1995, SI 1995/2066; the Housing (Right to Buy) (Priority of Charges) Order 1996, SI 1996/162; the Housing (Right to Buy) (Priority of Charges) Order 1997, SI 1997/945; the Housing (Right to Buy) (Priority of Charges) (No 2) Order 1997, SI 1997/2327; the Housing (Right to Buy) (Priority of Charges) Order 1998, SI 1998/320; the Housing (Right to Buy) (Priority of Charges) (No 2) Order 1998, SI 1998/2015; the Housing (Right to Buy) (Priority of Charges) (England) Order 1999, SI 1999/2919; the Housing (Right to Buy) (Priority of Charges) (Wales) Order 2000, SI 2000/349; the Housing (Right to Buy) (Priority of Charges) (England) Order 2001, SI 2001/205; the Housing (Right to Buy) (Priority of Charges) (Wales) Order 2001, SI 2001/1786; the Housing (Right to Buy) (Priority of Charges) (England) (No 2) Order 2001, SI 2001/3219; the Housing (Right to Buy) (Priority of Charges) (England) (No 3) Order 2001, SI 2001/3874; the Housing (Right to Buy) (Priority of Charges) (Wales) Order 2002, SI 2002/763; the Housing (Right to Buy) (Priority of Charges) (England) Order 2003, SI 2003/1083; the Housing (Right to Buy) (Priority of Charges) (Wales) Order 2003, SI 2003/1853; the Housing (Right to Buy) (Priority of Charges) (England) Order 2004, SI 2004/1071; the Housing (Right to Buy) (Priority of Charges) (Wales) Order 2004, SI 2004/1806; the Housing (Right to Buy) (Priority of Charges) (England) Order 2005, SI 2005/92; the Housing (Right to Buy) (Priority of Charges) (England) (No 2) Order 2005, SI 2005/407; the Housing (Right to Buy) (Priority of Charges) (Wales) Order 2005, SI 2005/1351; the Housing (Right to Buy) (Priority of Charges) (England) Order 2006, SI 2006/950; the Housing (Right to Buy) (Priority of Charges) (England) Order 2006, SI 2006/1263; the Housing (Right to Buy) (Priority of Charges) (England) (No 2) Order 2006, SI 2006/2563; the Housing (Right to Buy) (Priority of Charges) (England) (No 3) Order 2006, SI 2006/3242; the Housing (Right to Buy) (Priority of Charges) (Wales) Order 2008, SI 2008/371.

Also, by virtue of the Housing (Consequential Provisions) Act 1985, s 2(2), the Housing (Right to Buy) (Priority of Charges) Order 1984, SI 1984/1554 at **[3056]**, and the Housing (Right to Buy) (Priority of Charges) Order 1985, SI 1985/1979, have effect as if made under this section.

**[156A Right of first refusal for landlord etc**

(1) A conveyance of the freehold or grant of a lease in pursuance of this Part shall contain the following covenant, which shall be binding on the secure tenant and his successors in title.

This is subject to subsection (8).

(2) The covenant shall be to the effect that, until the end of the period of ten years beginning with the conveyance or grant, there will be no relevant disposal which is not an exempted disposal, unless the prescribed conditions have been satisfied in relation to that or a previous such disposal.

(3) In subsection (2) "the prescribed conditions" means such conditions as are prescribed by regulations under this section at the time when the conveyance or grant is made.

(4) The Secretary of State may by regulations prescribe such conditions as he considers appropriate for and in connection with conferring on—

    (a) a landlord who has conveyed a freehold or granted a lease to a person ("the former tenant") in pursuance of this Part, or

    (b) such other person as is determined in accordance with the regulations,

a right of first refusal to have a disposal within subsection (5) made to him for such consideration as is mentioned in section 158.

(5) The disposals within this subsection are—

    (a) a reconveyance or conveyance of the dwelling-house; and

    (b) a surrender or assignment of the lease.

(6) Regulations under this section may, in particular, make provision—

    (a) for the former tenant to offer to make such a disposal to such person or persons as may be prescribed;

    (b) for a prescribed recipient of such an offer to be able either to accept the offer or to nominate some other person as the person by whom the offer may be accepted;

    (c) for the person who may be so nominated to be either a person of a prescribed description or a person whom the prescribed recipient considers, having regard to any prescribed matters, to be a more appropriate person to accept the offer;

    (d) for a prescribed recipient making such a nomination to give a notification of the nomination to the person nominated, the former tenant and any other prescribed person;

    (e) for authorising a nominated person to accept the offer and for determining which acceptance is to be effective where the offer is accepted by more than one person;

    (f) for the period within which the offer may be accepted or within which any other prescribed step is to be, or may be, taken;

    (g) for the circumstances in which the right of first refusal lapses (whether following the service of a notice to complete or otherwise) with the result that the former tenant is able to make a disposal on the open market;

    (h) for the manner in which any offer, acceptance or notification is to be communicated.

(7) In subsection (6) any reference to the former tenant is a reference to the former tenant or his successor in title.

Nothing in that subsection affects the generality of subsection (4).

(8) In a case to which section 157(1) applies—

    (a) the conveyance or grant may contain a covenant such as is mentioned in subsections (1) and (2) above instead of a covenant such as is mentioned in section 157(1), but

    (b) it may do so only if the Secretary of State or, where the conveyance or grant is executed by a housing association within section 6A(3) or (4), the Relevant Authority consents.

(9) Consent may be given in relation to—

    (a) a particular disposal, or

    (b) disposals by a particular landlord or disposals by landlords generally,

and may, in any case, be given subject to conditions.

(10) Regulations under this section—

    (a) may make different provision with respect to different cases or descriptions of case; and

    (b) shall be made by statutory instrument which shall be subject to annulment in pursuance of a resolution of either House of Parliament.

(11) The limitation imposed by a covenant within subsection (2) (whether the covenant is imposed in pursuance of subsection (1) or (8)) is a local land charge.

(12) The Chief Land Registrar must enter in the register of title a restriction reflecting the limitation imposed by any such covenant.]

**[519]**

---

**NOTES**

Commencement: 18 January 2005.

Inserted by the Housing Act 2004, s 188(1); for effect see s 188(5), (6) of that Act at **[1472]**.

Regulations: the Housing (Right of First Refusal) (England) Regulations 2005, SI 2005/1917 at **[3555]**; the Housing (Right of First Refusal) (Wales) Regulations 2005, SI 2005/2680 at **[3573]**.

---

**157 Restriction on disposal of dwelling-houses in National Parks, etc**

(1) Where in pursuance of this Part a conveyance or grant is executed by a local authority ... or a housing association ("the landlord") of a dwelling-house situated in—

    (a) a National Park,

    (b) an area designated under [section 82 of the Countryside and Rights of Way Act 2000] as an area of outstanding natural beauty, or

    (c) an area designated by order of the Secretary of State as a rural area, the conveyance or grant may [(subject to section 156A(8)] contain a covenant limiting the freedom of the tenant (including any successor in title of his and any person deriving title under him or such a successor) to dispose of the dwelling-house in the manner specified below.

(2)    The limitation is ... that until such time (if any) as may be notified in writing by the landlord to the tenant or a successor in title of his,

[(a)]    there will be no relevant disposal which is not an exempted disposal without the written consent of the landlord; but that consent shall not be withheld if the disposal is to a person satisfying the condition stated in subsection (3) [and—

(b)      there will be no disposal by way of tenancy or licence without the written consent of the landlord unless the disposal is to a person satisfying that condition or by a person whose only or principal home is and, throughout the duration of the tenancy or licence, remains the dwelling-house].

(3)    The condition is that the person to whom the disposal is made (or, if it is made to more than one person, at least one of them) has, throughout the period of three years immediately preceding the application for consent [or, in the case of a disposal by way of tenancy or licence, preceding the disposal]—

(a)      had his place of work in a region designated by order of the Secretary of State which, or part of which, is comprised in the National Park or area, or

(b)      had his only or principal home in such a region;

or has had the one in part or parts of that period and the other in the remainder; but the region need not have been the same throughout the period.

(4), (5)    ...

(6)    A disposal in breach of such a covenant as is mentioned in subsection (1) is void [and, so far as it relates to disposals by way of tenancy or licence, such a covenant may be enforced by the landlord as if—

(a)      the landlord were possessed of land adjacent to the house concerned; and

(b)      the covenant were expressed to be made for the benefit of such adjacent land].

[(6A)    Any reference in the preceding provisions of this section to a disposal by way of tenancy or licence does not include a reference to a relevant disposal or an exempted disposal.]

(7)    Where such a covenant imposes the limitation specified in subsection (2), the limitation is a local land charge and the Chief Land Registrar shall enter [a restriction in the register of title reflecting the limitation].

(8)    An order under this section—

(a)      may make different provision with respect to different cases or descriptions of case, including different provision for different areas, and

(b)      shall be made by statutory instrument which shall be subject to annulment in pursuance of a resolution of either House of Parliament.

**[520]**

---

**NOTES**

Sub-s (1): words omitted repealed by the Government of Wales Act 1998, s 152, Sch 18, Pt IV; words in square brackets in para (b) substituted by the Countryside and Rights of Way Act 2000, s 93, Sch 15, Pt I, para 9; words in second pair of square brackets inserted by the Housing Act 2004, s 188(2)(a), for effect see s 188(5), (6) of that Act at **[1472]**.

Sub-s (2): words omitted repealed by the Housing Act 2004, ss 188(2)(b), 266, Sch 16, for effect see s 188(5), (6) of that Act at **[1472]**; para (a) numbered as such and para (b) added by the Housing Act 1988, s 126, in relation to cases where the conveyance or grant referred to in sub-s (1) above is executed on or after 15 January 1989.

Sub-s (3): words in square brackets inserted by the Housing Act 1988, s 126, in relation to cases where the conveyance or grant referred to in sub-s (1) above is executed on or after 15 January 1989.

Sub-ss (4), (5): repealed by the Housing Act 2004, ss 188(2)(c), 266, Sch 16, for effect see s 188(5), (6) of that Act at **[1472]**.

Sub-s (6): words in square brackets added by the Housing Act 1988, s 126, in relation to cases where the conveyance or grant referred to in sub-s (1) above is executed on or after 15 January 1989.

Sub-s (6A): inserted by the Housing Act 1988, s 126, in relation to cases where the conveyance or grant referred to in sub-s (1) above is executed on or after 15 January 1989.

Sub-s (7): words in square brackets substituted by the Land Registration Act 2002, s 133, Sch 11, para 18(1), (4).

Orders: the Housing (Right to Buy) (Designated Rural Areas and Designated Regions) (England) Order 1986, SI 1986/1695; the Housing (Right to Buy) (Designated Rural Areas and Designated Region) (England) Order 1988, SI 1988/2057; the Housing (Right to Buy) (Designated Rural Areas and Designated Regions) (England) Order 1990, SI 1990/1282; the Housing (Right to Buy) (Designated Rural Areas and Designated Regions) (England) Order 2002, SI 2002/1769; the Housing (Right to Acquire and Right to Buy) (Designated Rural Areas and Designated Regions) (Wales) Order 2003, SI 2003/54; the Housing (Right to Buy) (Designated Rural Areas and Designated Region) (England) Order 2003, SI 2003/1105; the Housing (Right to Buy) (Designated Rural Areas and Designated Regions) (England) Order 2004, SI 2004/418; the Housing (Right to Buy) (Designated Rural Areas and Designated Regions) (England) (No 2) Order 2004, SI 2004/2681; the Housing (Right to Buy) (Designated Rural Areas and Designated Regions) (England) Order 2005, SI 2005/1995;

the Housing (Right to Buy) (Designated Rural Areas and Designated Regions) (England) (No 2) Order 2005, SI 2005/2908; the Housing (Right to Buy) (Designated Rural Areas and Designated Region) (England) Order 2006, SI 2006/1948.

Also, by virtue of the Housing (Consequential Provisions) Act 1985, s 2(2), the following orders have effect as if made under this section: the Housing (Right to Buy) (Designated Regions) Order 1980, SI 1980/1345 at **[3020]**; the Housing (Right to Buy) (Designated Rural Areas and Designated Regions) (England) Order 1981, SI 1981/397; the Housing (Right to Buy) (Designated Rural Areas and Designated Regions) (England) (No 2) Order 1981, SI 1981/940; the Housing (Right to Buy) (Designated Rural Areas and Designated Regions) (England) Order 1982, SI 1982/21; and the Housing (Right to Buy) (Designated Rural Areas and Designated Regions) (England) (No 2) Order 1982, SI 1982/187.

## 158 Consideration for [disposal under section 156A]

[(1) The consideration for such a disposal as is mentioned in section 156A(4) shall be such amount as may be agreed between the parties, or determined by the district valuer, as being the amount which is to be taken to be the value of the dwelling-house at the time when the offer is made (as determined in accordance with regulations under that section).]

(2) That value shall be taken to be the price which, at that time, the interest to be reconveyed[, conveyed, surrendered or assigned] would realise if sold on the open market by a willing vendor, on the assumption that any liability under—

    (a)   the covenant required by section 155 (repayment of discount on early disposal), and

    [(aa)  any covenant required by paragraph 1 of Schedule 6A (obligation to redeem landlord's share where conveyance or grant executed in pursuance of right to acquire on rent to mortgage terms), and]

    (b)   any covenant required by paragraph 6 of Schedule 8 (payment for outstanding share on disposal of dwelling-house subject to shared ownership lease),

would be discharged by the vendor.

(3) If [the offer is accepted in accordance with regulations under section 156A,] no payment shall be required in pursuance of any such covenant as is mentioned in subsection (2), but the consideration shall be reduced[, subject to subsection (4),] by such amount (if any) as, on a disposal made at the time the offer was made, being a relevant disposal which is not an exempted disposal, would fall to be paid under that covenant.

[(4) Where there is a charge on the dwelling-house having priority over the charge to secure payment of the sum due under the covenant mentioned in subsection (2), the consideration shall not be reduced under subsection (3) below the amount necessary to discharge the outstanding sum secured by the first-mentioned charge at the date of the offer [(as determined in accordance with regulations under section 156A).]]

**[521]**

### NOTES

Section heading: words in square brackets substituted by the Housing Act 2004, s 188(3)(a); for effect see s 188(5), (6) of that Act at **[1472]**.

Sub-s (1): substituted by the Housing Act 2004, s 188(3)(b); for effect see s 188(5), (6) of that Act at **[1472]**.

Sub-s (2): words in first pair of square brackets substituted by the Housing Act 2004, s 188(3)(c), for effect see s 188(5), (6) of that Act at **[1472]**; para (aa) inserted by the Leasehold Reform, Housing and Urban Development Act 1993, s 187(1), Sch 21, para 15, except in relation to a case where a notice under s 122 at **[468]**, is served before 11 October 1993 or in relation to the operation of this Part of this Act as applied by the Local Government Reorganisation (Preservation of the Right to Buy) Order 1986, SI 1986/2092.

Sub-s (3): words in first pair of square brackets substituted by the Housing Act 2004, s 188(3)(d), for effect see s 188(5), (6) of that Act at **[1472]**; words in second pair of square brackets inserted by the Housing and Planning Act 1986, s 24(1)(a), Sch 5, Pt I, para 1, in relation to covenants entered into before or after 7 January 1987.

Sub-s (4): added by the Housing and Planning Act 1986, s 24(1)(a), Sch 5, Pt I, para 1, in relation to covenants entered into before or after 7 January 1987; words in square brackets substituted by the Housing Act 2004, s 188(3)(e), for effect see s 188(5), (6) of that Act at **[1472]**.

## 159 Relevant disposals

(1) A disposal, whether of the whole or part of the dwelling-house, is a relevant disposal for the purposes of this Part if it is—

    (a)   a further conveyance of the freehold or an assignment of the lease, or

    (b)   the grant of a lease (other than a mortgage term) for a term of more than 21 years otherwise than at a rack rent.

(2) For the purposes of subsection (1)(b) it shall be assumed—

    (a)   that any option to renew or extend a lease or sub-lease, whether or not forming part of a series of options, is exercised, and

    (b)   that any option to terminate a lease or sub-lease is not exercised.

**[522]**

## 160 Exempted disposals

(1) A disposal is an exempted disposal for the purposes of this Part if—

(a)     it is a disposal of the whole of the dwelling-house and a further conveyance of the freehold or an assignment of the lease and the person or each of the persons to whom it is made is a qualifying person (as defined in subsection (2));

(b)     it is a vesting of the whole of the dwelling-house in a person taking under a will or on an intestacy;

[(c)     it is a disposal of the whole of the dwelling-house in pursuance of any such order as is mentioned in subsection (3);]

(d)     it is a compulsory disposal (as defined in section 161); or

(e)     it is a disposal of property consisting of land included in the dwelling-house by virtue of section 184 (land let with or used for the purposes of the dwelling-house).

(2)     For the purposes of subsection (1)(a), a person is a qualifying person in relation to a disposal if—

(a)     he is the person, or one of the persons, by whom the disposal is made,

(b)     he is the spouse or a former spouse[, or the civil partner or a former civil partner,] of that person, or one of those persons, or

(c)     he is a member of the family of that person, or one of those persons, and has resided with him throughout the period of twelve months ending with the disposal.

[(3)     The orders referred to in subsection (1)(c) are orders under—

(a)     *section 24 or 24A of the Matrimonial Causes Act 1973* (property adjustment orders or orders for the sale of property in connection with matrimonial proceedings),

(b)     section 2 of the Inheritance (Provision for Family and Dependants) Act 1975 (orders as to financial provision to be made from estate),

(c)     section 17 of the Matrimonial and Family Proceedings Act 1984 (property adjustment orders or orders for the sale of property after overseas divorce, &c), ...

(d)     paragraph 1 of Schedule 1 to the Children Act 1989 (orders for financial relief against parents)[, or

(e)     Part 2 or 3 of Schedule 5, or paragraph 9 of Schedule 7, to the Civil Partnership Act 2004 (property adjustment orders, or orders for the sale of property, in connection with civil partnership proceedings or after overseas dissolution of civil partnership, etc)].]

**[523]**

**NOTES**
Sub-s (1): para (c) substituted by the Housing Act 1996, s 222, Sch 18, Pt III, para 15.
Sub-s (2): words in square brackets in para (b) inserted by the Civil Partnership Act 2004, s 81, Sch 8, para 18.
Sub-s (3): added by the Housing Act 1996, s 222, Sch 18, Pt III, para 15; for the words in italics in para (a) there are substituted the words "section 23A or 24" by virtue of the Family Law Act 1996, s 66(1), Sch 8, Pt I, para 34, as from a day to be appointed, subject to savings in s 66(2) of, and Sch 9, para 5 to, that Act; word omitted from para (c) repealed and para (e) and word immediately preceding it added by the Civil Partnership Act 2004, ss 81, 261(4), Sch 8, para 30, Sch 30.
It should be noted that the amendment made to sub-s (1)(c) of this section as originally enacted by the Family Law Act 1996, s 66(1), Sch 8, Pt I, para 34, as from a day to be appointed under s 67(3) of that Act, has been superseded by the substitution of that paragraph and the addition of sub-s (3) as noted above.

## 161   Meaning of "compulsory disposal"

In this Part a "compulsory disposal" means a disposal of property which is acquired compulsorily, or is acquired by a person who has made or would have made, or for whom another person has made or would have made, a compulsory purchase order authorising its compulsory purchase for the purposes for which it is acquired.

**[524]**

## 162   Exempted disposals which end liability under covenants

Where there is a relevant disposal which is an exempted disposal by virtue of section 160(1)(d) or (e) (compulsory disposals or disposals of land let with or used for purposes of dwelling-house)—

(a)     the covenant required by section 155 (repayment of discount on early disposal) is not binding on the person to whom the disposal is made or any successor in title of his, and that covenant and the charge taking effect by virtue of section 156 cease to apply in relation to the property disposed of, and

[(aa)     the covenant required by section 156A (right of first refusal for landlord etc) is not binding on the person to whom the disposal is made or any successor in title of his, and that covenant ceases to apply in relation to the property disposed of, and]

(b)     any such covenant as is mentioned in section 157 (restriction on disposal of dwelling-houses in National Parks, etc) ceases to apply in relation to the property disposed of.

**NOTES**
Para (aa) inserted by the Housing Act 2004, s 188(4); for effect see s 188(5), (6) of that Act at **[1472]**.

**[525]**

**163 Treatment of options**

(1)  For the purposes of this Part the grant of an option enabling a person to call for a relevant disposal which is not an exempted disposal shall be treated as such a disposal made to him.

(2)  For the purposes of section 157(2) (requirement of consent to disposal of dwelling-house in National Park, etc) a consent to such a grant shall be treated as a consent to a disposal in pursuance of the option.

**[526]**

**[163A  Treatment of deferred resale agreements for purposes of section 155**

(1)  If a secure tenant or his successor in title enters into an agreement within subsection (3), any liability arising under the covenant required by section 155 shall be determined as if a relevant disposal which is not an exempted disposal had occurred at the appropriate time.

(2)  In subsection (1) "the appropriate time" means—
  (a)  the time when the agreement is entered into, or
  (b)  if it was made before the beginning of the discount repayment period, immediately after the beginning of that period.

(3)  An agreement is within this subsection if it is an agreement between the secure tenant or his successor in title and any other person—
  (a)  which is made (expressly or impliedly) in contemplation of, or in connection with, the tenant exercising, or having exercised, the right to buy,
  (b)  which is made before the end of the discount repayment period, and
  (c)  under which a relevant disposal (other than an exempted disposal) is or may be required to be made to any person after the end of that period.

(4)  Such an agreement is within subsection (3)—
  (a)  whether or not the date on which the disposal is to take place is specified in the agreement, and
  (b)  whether or not any requirement to make the disposal is or may be made subject to the fulfilment of any condition.

(5)  The Secretary of State may by order provide—
  (a)  for subsection (1) to apply to agreements of any description specified in the order in addition to those within subsection (3);
  (b)  for subsection (1) not to apply to agreements of any description so specified to which it would otherwise apply.

(6)  An order under subsection (5)—
  (a)  may make different provision with respect to different cases or descriptions of case; and
  (b)  shall be made by statutory instrument which shall be subject to annulment in pursuance of a resolution of either House of Parliament.

(7)  In this section—
  "agreement" includes arrangement;
  "the discount repayment period" means the period of three or five years that applies for the purposes of section 155(2) or (3) (depending on whether the tenant's notice under section 122 was given before or on or after the date of the coming into force of section 185 of the Housing Act 2004).]

**[527]**

---

**NOTES**

Commencement: 18 January 2005.

Inserted by the Housing Act 2004, s 187(1), except in relation to any agreement or arrangement made before 18 January 2005.

---

*Powers of Secretary of State*

**164  Secretary of State's general power to intervene**

(1)  The Secretary of State may use his powers under this section where it appears to him that tenants generally, a tenant or tenants of a particular landlord, or tenants of a description of landlords, have or may have difficulty in exercising effectively and expeditiously the right to buy or the [right to acquire on rent to mortgage terms].

(2)  The powers may be exercised only after he has given the landlord or landlords notice in writing of his intention to do so and while the notice is in force.

(3)  Such a notice shall be deemed to be given 72 hours after it has been sent.

(4)  Where a notice under this section has been given to a landlord or landlords, no step taken by the landlord or any of the landlords while the notice is in force or before it was given has any effect in relation to the exercise by a secure tenant of the right to buy, [or the right to acquire on rent to mortgage terms], except in so far as the notice otherwise provides.

(5) While a notice under this section is in force the Secretary of State may do all such things as appear to him necessary or expedient to enable secure tenants of the landlord or landlords to which the notice was given to exercise the right to buy, [and the right to acquire on rent to mortgage terms]; and he is not bound to take the steps which the landlord would have been bound to take under this Part.

(6) ...

[528]

**NOTES**

Sub-ss (1), (4), (5): words in square brackets substituted by the Leasehold Reform, Housing and Urban Development Act 1993, s 187, Sch 21, para 16, except in relation to a case where a notice under s 122 at **[468]**, is served before 11 October 1993 or in relation to the operation of this Part of this Act as applied by the Local Government Reorganisation (Preservation of the Right to Buy) Order 1986, SI 1986/2092.

Sub-s (6): repealed by the Leasehold Reform, Housing and Urban Development Act 1993, s 187, Sch 22, subject to savings as noted above.

## 165 Vesting orders for purposes of s 164

(1) For the purpose of conveying a freehold or granting a lease in the exercise of his powers under section 164 the Secretary of State may execute a document, to be known as a vesting order, containing such provisions as he may determine; and for the purposes of stamp duty the vesting order shall be treated as a document executed by the landlord.

(2) A vesting order has the like effect, except so far as it otherwise provides, as a conveyance or grant duly executed in pursuance of this Part, and, in particular, binds both the landlord and its successors in title and the tenant and his successors in title (including any person deriving title under him or them) to the same extent as if the covenants contained in it and expressed to be made on their behalf had been entered into by them.

(3) If the landlord's title to the dwelling-house in respect of which a vesting order is made is not registered, the vesting order shall contain a certificate stating that the freehold conveyed or grant made by it is subject only to such incumbrances, rights and interests as are stated elsewhere in the vesting order or summarised in the certificate.

(4) The Chief Land Registrar shall, on a vesting order being presented to him, register the tenant as proprietor of the title concerned; and if the title has not previously been registered—

    (a) he shall so register him with an absolute title, or as the case may require a good leasehold title, and

    (b) he shall, for the purpose of the registration, accept any such certificate as is mentioned in subsection (3) as sufficient evidence of the facts stated in it.

(5) ...

(6) If a person suffers loss in consequence of a registration under this section in circumstances in which he would have been entitled to be indemnified under [Schedule 8 to the Land Registration Act 2002] by the Chief Land Registrar had the registration of the tenant as proprietor of the title been effected otherwise than under this section, he is instead entitled to be indemnified by the Secretary of State and section 166(4) of this Act (recovery of Secretary of State's costs from landlord) applies accordingly.

[529]

**NOTES**

Sub-s (5): repealed by the Land Registration Act 1988, ss 1(2)(d), 2, Schedule.

Sub-s (6): words in square brackets substituted by the Land Registration Act 2002, s 133, Sch 11, para 18(1), (5).

## 166 Other provisions supplementary to s 164

(1) A notice under section 164 may be withdrawn by a further notice in writing, either completely or in relation to a particular landlord or a particular case or description of case.

(2) The further notice may give such directions as the Secretary of State may think fit for the completion of a transaction begun before the further notice was given; and such directions are binding on the landlord, and may require the taking of steps different from those which the landlord would have been required to take if the Secretary of State's powers under section 164 had not been used.

(3) Where in consequence of the exercise of his powers under section 164 the Secretary of State receives sums due to a landlord, he may retain them while a notice under that section is in force in relation to the landlord and is not bound to account to the landlord for interest accruing on them.

(4) Where the Secretary of State exercises his powers under section 164 with respect to secure tenants of a landlord, he may—

(a)     calculate, in such manner and on such assumptions as he may determine, the costs incurred by him in doing so, and

(b)     certify a sum as representing those costs;

and a sum so certified is a debt from the landlord to the Secretary of State payable on a date specified in the certificate, together with interest from that date at a rate so specified.

(5)     Sums payable under subsection (4) may, without prejudice to any other method of recovery, be recovered from the landlord by the withholding of sums due from the Secretary of State, including sums payable to the landlord and received by the Secretary of State in consequence of his exercise of his powers under section 164.

(6)   ...

**[530]**

**NOTES**

Sub-s (6): repealed by the Leasehold Reform, Housing and Urban Development Act 1993, s 187(2), Sch 22, except in relation to a case where a notice under s 122 at **[468]**, is served before 11 October 1993 or in relation to the operation of this Part of this Act as applied by the Local Government Reorganisation (Preservation of the Right to Buy) Order 1986, SI 1986/2092.

### 167    Power to give directions as to covenants and conditions

(1)     Where it appears to the Secretary of State that, if covenants or conditions of any kind were included in conveyances or grants of dwelling-houses of any description executed in pursuance of this Part—

(a)     the conveyances would not conform with Parts I and II of Schedule 6, or

(b)     the grants would not conform with Parts I and III of that Schedule, [or

(c)     in the case of conveyances or grants executed in pursuance of the right to acquire on rent to mortgage terms, the conveyances or grants would not conform with Schedule 6A,]

he may direct landlords generally, landlords of a particular description or particular landlords not to include covenants or conditions of that kind in such conveyances or grants executed on or after a date specified in the direction.

(2)     A direction under this section may be varied or withdrawn by a subsequent direction.

**[531]**

**NOTES**

Sub-s (1): para (c) and the word immediately preceding it inserted by the Leasehold Reform, Housing and Urban Development Act 1993, s 187(1), Sch 21, para 17, except in relation to a case where a notice under s 122 at **[468]**, is served before 11 October 1993 or in relation to the operation of this Part of this Act as applied by the Local Government Reorganisation (Preservation of the Right to Buy) Order 1986, SI 1986/2092.

### 168    Effect of direction under s 167 on existing covenants and conditions

(1)     If a direction under section 167 so provides, the provisions of this section shall apply in relation to a covenant or condition which—

(a)     was included in a conveyance or grant executed before the date specified in the direction, and

(b)     could not have been so included if the conveyance or grant had been executed on or after that date.

(2)     The covenant or condition shall be discharged or (if the direction so provides) modified, as from the specified date, to such extent or in such manner as may be provided by the direction; and the discharge or modification is binding on all persons entitled or capable of becoming entitled to the benefit of the covenant or condition.

(3)     The landlord by whom the conveyance or grant was executed shall, within such period as may be specified in the direction—

(a)     serve on the person registered as the proprietor of the dwelling-house, and on any person registered as the proprietor of a charge affecting the dwelling-house, a written notice informing him of the discharge or modification, and

(b)     on behalf of the person registered as the proprietor of the dwelling-house, apply to the Chief Land Registrar (and pay the appropriate fee) for notice of the discharge or modification to be entered in the register.

(4), (5)   ...

**[532]**

**NOTES**

Sub-s (4): repealed by the Land Registration Act 1988, s 2, Schedule.

Sub-s (5): repealed by the Land Registration Act 2002, s 135, Sch 13.

**169  Power to obtain information, etc**

(1)  Where it appears to the Secretary of State necessary or expedient for the purpose of determining whether his powers under section 164 or 166 (general power to intervene) or section 167 or 168 (power to give directions as to covenants and conditions) are exercisable, or for or in connection with the exercise of those powers, he may by notice in writing to a landlord require it—

    (a)    at such time and at such place as may be specified in the notice, to produce any document, or

    (b)    within such period as may be so specified or such longer period as the Secretary of State may allow, to furnish a copy of any document or supply any information.

(2)  Any officer of the landlord designated in the notice for that purpose or having custody or control of the document or in a position to give that information shall, without instructions from the landlord, take all reasonable steps to ensure that the notice is complied with.

(3)  In this section references to a landlord include—

    (a)    a landlord by whom a conveyance or grant was executed in pursuance of this Part, ...

    (b)    ...

**[533]**

**NOTES**

Sub-s (3): words omitted repealed by the Leasehold Reform, Housing and Urban Development Act 1993, s 187(2), Sch 22, except in relation to a case where a notice under s 122 at **[468]**, is served before 11 October 1993 or in relation to the operation of this Part of this Act as applied by the Local Government Reorganisation (Preservation of the Right to Buy) Order 1986, SI 1986/2092.

**170  Power to give assistance in connection with legal proceedings**

(1)  This section applies to—

    (a)    proceedings under this Part or to determine a question arising under or in connection with this Part, and

    (b)    proceedings to determine a question arising under or in connection with a conveyance or grant executed in pursuance of this Part,

other than proceedings to determine a question as to the value of a dwelling-house (or part of a dwelling-house).

(2)  A party or prospective party to proceedings or prospective proceedings to which this section applies, who—

    (a)    has claimed to exercise or has exercised the right to buy or the [right to acquire on rent to mortgage terms], or

    (b)    is a successor in title of a person who has exercised either of those rights,

may apply to the Secretary of State for assistance under this section.

(3)  The Secretary of State may grant the application if he thinks fit to do so on the ground—

    (a)    that the case raises a question of principle, or

    (b)    that it is unreasonable having regard to the complexity of the case, or to any other matter, to expect the applicant to deal with it without such assistance,

or by reason of any other special consideration.

(4)  Assistance by the Secretary of State under this section may include—

    (a)    giving advice,

    (b)    procuring or attempting to procure the settlement of the matter in dispute,

    (c)    arranging for the giving of advice or assistance by a solicitor or counsel,

    (d)    arranging for representation by a solicitor or counsel, including such assistance as is usually given by a solicitor or counsel in the steps preliminary or incidental to any proceedings, or in arriving at or giving effect to a compromise to avoid or bring to an end any proceedings, and

    (e)    any other form of assistance which the Secretary of State may consider appropriate;

but paragraph (d) does not affect the law and practice regulating the descriptions of persons who may appear in, conduct, defend and address the court in any proceedings.

(5)  In so far as expenses are incurred by the Secretary of State in providing the applicant with assistance under this section, the recovery of those expenses (as taxed or assessed in such manner as may be prescribed by rules of court) shall constitute a first charge for the benefit of the Secretary of State—

    (a)    on any costs which (whether by virtue of a judgment or order of a court or an agreement or otherwise) are payable to the applicant by any other person in respect of the matter in connection with which the assistance was given, and

    (b)    so far as relates to any costs, on his rights under any compromise or settlement arrived at in connection with that matter to avoid or bring to an end any proceedings;

but subject to any charge [imposed by section 10(7) of the Access to Justice Act 1999 and any provision in, or made under, Part I of that Act for the payment of any sum to the Legal Services Commission].

 (6) References in this section to a solicitor include the Treasury Solicitor.

**[534]**

PART I
STATUTES

---

**NOTES**

 Sub-s (2): words in square brackets substituted by the Leasehold Reform, Housing and Urban Development Act 1993, s 187(1), Sch 21, para 18, except in relation to a case where a notice under s 122 at **[468]**, is served before 11 October 1993 or in relation to the operation of this Part of this Act as applied by the Local Government Reorganisation (Preservation of the Right to Buy) Order 1986, SI 1986/2092.

 Sub-s (5): words in square brackets substituted by the Access to Justice Act 1999, s 24, Sch 4, para 37, with savings in relation to existing cases.

 Modifications: references to a Solicitor include references to a "recognised body" under the Administration of Justice Act 1985, s 9; see the Solicitors' Incorporated Practices Order 1991, SI 1991/2684, arts 2–5, Sch 1.

---

*Power to extend right to buy, etc*

### 171 Power to extend right to buy, etc

 (1) The Secretary of State may by order provide that, where there are in a dwelling-house let on a secure tenancy one or more interests to which this section applies, this Part and Part IV (secure tenancies) have effect with such modifications as are specified in the order.

 (2) This section applies to an interest held by—

> a local authority,
> a new town corporation,
> [a housing action trust]
> an urban development corporation,
> ...
> the [Housing Corporation or Scottish Homes], or
> a [registered social landlord],

which is immediately superior to the interest of the landlord or to another interest to which this section applies.

 (3) An order under this section—

  (a) may make different provision with respect to different cases or descriptions of case;

  (b) may contain such consequential, supplementary or transitional provisions as appear to the Secretary of State to be necessary or expedient; and

  (c) shall be made by statutory instrument which shall be subject to annulment in pursuance of a resolution of either House of Parliament.

**[535]**

---

**NOTES**

 Sub-s (2): words in first pair of square brackets inserted by the Housing Act 1988, s 83(5); words omitted repealed and words in second pair of square brackets substituted by the Government of Wales Act 1998, ss 140, 152, Sch 16, para 13, Sch 18, Pt IV; words in third pair of square brackets substituted by the Housing Act 1996 (Consequential Provisions) Order 1996, SI 1996/2325, art 5, Sch 2, para 14(1), (15).

 Modification: in sub-s (2) the reference to the Housing Corporation shall be treated as a reference to the Regulator of Social Housing: see the Transfer of Housing Corporation Functions (Modifications and Transitional Provisions) Order 2008, SI 2008/2839, arts 1(2), 2, 3, 6, Schedule.

 Orders: the Housing (Extension of Right to Buy) Order 1993, SI 1993/2240.

---

*[Preservation of right to buy on disposal to private sector landlord*

### 171A Cases in which right to buy is preserved

 (1) The provisions of this Part continue to apply where a person ceases to be a secure tenant of a dwelling-house by reason of the disposal by the landlord of an interest in the dwelling-house to a person who is not an authority or body within section 80 (the landlord condition for secure tenancies).

 (2) In the following provisions of this Part—

  (a) references to the preservation of the right to buy and to a person having the preserved right to buy are to the continued application of the provisions of this Part by virtue of this section and to a person in relation to whom those provisions so apply;

  (b) "qualifying disposal" means a disposal in relation to which this section applies, and

  (c) the "former secure tenant" and the "former landlord" are the persons mentioned in subsection (1),

 (3) This section does not apply—

  (a) where the former landlord was a person against whom the right to buy could not be exercised by virtue of paragraph 1, 2 or 3 of Schedule 5 (charities and certain housing associations), or

   (b)   in such other cases as may be excepted from the operation of this section by order of the Secretary of State.

(4)   Orders under subsection (3)(b)—

   (a)   may relate to particular disposals and may make different provision with respect to different cases or descriptions of case, including different provision for different areas, and

   (b)   shall be made by statutory instrument which shall be subject to annulment in pursuance of a resolution of either House of Parliament.]

**[536]**

**NOTES**

Inserted, together with the preceding cross-heading and ss 171B–171H, in relation to qualifying disposals made on or after 5 April 1989, by the Housing and Planning Act 1986, s 8(1), (3).

## [171B   Extent of preserved right: qualifying persons and dwelling-houses

(1)   A person to whom this section applies has the preserved right to buy so long as he occupies the relevant dwelling-house as his only or principal home, subject to the following provisions of this Part.

[(1A)   A person to whom this section applies ceases to have the preserved right to buy if the tenancy of a relevant dwelling-house becomes a demoted tenancy by virtue of a demotion order under section 6A of the Housing Act 1988.]

(2)   References in this Part to a "qualifying person" and "qualifying dwellinghouse", in relation to the preserved right to buy, are to a person who has that right and to a dwelling-house in relation to which a person has that right.

(3)   The following are the persons to whom this section applies—

   (a)   the former secure tenant, or in the case of a joint tenancy, each of them;

   (b)   a qualifying successor as defined in subsection (4); and

   (c)   a person to whom a tenancy of a dwelling-house is granted jointly with a person who has the preserved right to buy in relation to that dwelling-house.

(4)   The following are qualifying successors for this purpose—

   [(a)   where the former secure tenancy was not a joint tenancy and, immediately before his death, the former secure tenant was tenant under an assured tenancy of a dwelling-house in relation to which he had the preserved right to buy, a member of the former secure tenant's family who acquired that assured tenancy under the will or intestacy of the former secure tenant [or in whom that assured tenancy vested under section 17 of the Housing Act 1988 (statutory succession to assured tenancy)];

   (aa)   where the former secure tenancy was not a joint tenancy, a member of the former secure tenant's family to whom the former secure tenant assigned his assured tenancy of a dwelling-house in relation to which, immediately before the assignment, he had the preserved right to buy];

   (b)   a person who becomes the tenant of a dwelling-house in pursuance of—

      (i)   a property adjustment order under *section 24* of the Matrimonial Causes Act 1973, or

      (ii)   an order under Schedule 1 to the Matrimonial Homes Act 1983 [or Schedule 7 to the Family Law Act 1996] transferring the tenancy, [or

      (iii)   a property adjustment order under section 17(1) of the Matrimonial and Family Proceedings Act 1984 (property adjustment orders after overseas divorce, &c), or

      (iv)   an order under paragraph 1 of Schedule 1 to the Children Act 1989 (orders for financial relief against parents),] [or

      (v)   an order under Part 2 of Schedule 5, or a property adjustment order under paragraph 9(2) or (3) of Schedule 7, to the Civil Partnership Act 2004 (property adjustment orders in connection with civil partnership proceedings or after overseas dissolution of civil partnership, etc),]

in place of a person who had the preserved right to buy in relation to that dwelling-house.

(5)   The relevant dwelling-house is in the first instance—

   (a)   in relation to a person within paragraph (a) of subsection (3), the dwelling-house which was the subject of the qualifying disposal;

   (b)   in relation to a person within paragraph (b) of that subsection, the dwelling-house of which he became the statutory tenant or tenant as mentioned in [subsection (4)];

   (c)   in relation to a person within paragraph (c) of subsection (3), the dwelling-house of which he became a joint tenant as mentioned in that paragraph.

(6)   If a person having the preserved right to buy becomes the tenant of another dwelling-house in place of the relevant dwelling-house (whether the new dwelling-house is entirely different or partly or substantially the same as the previous dwelling-house) and the landlord is the same person

as the landlord of the previous dwelling-house or, where that landlord was a company, is a connected company, the new dwelling-house becomes the relevant dwelling-house for the purposes of the preserved right to buy.

For this purpose "connected company" means a subsidiary or holding company within the meaning of [section 1159 of the Companies Act 2006].]

**[537]**

**NOTES**
Inserted as noted to s 171A at **[536]**.
Sub-s (1A): inserted by the Anti-social Behaviour Act 2003, s 14(5), Sch 1, para 2(1), (3).
Sub-s (4): paras (a), (aa) substituted, for original para (a), by the Housing Act 1988, s 127(1); words in square brackets in para (a) added (in relation to qualifying disposals made on or after 24 September 1996), and sub-paras (b)(iii), (iv) and the word "or" immediately preceding them added by the Housing Act 1996, s 222, Sch 18, Pt III, para 16, Pt IV, para 26; for the words in italics in sub-para (b)(i) there are substituted the words "section 23A or 24" by the Family Law Act 1996, s 66(1), Sch 8, Pt I, para 34, as from a day to be appointed, and words in square brackets in para (b)(ii) inserted by s 66(1) of, and Sch 8, Pt III, para 56 to, that Act (for savings see s 66(2) of that Act, and Sch 9, paras 5, 8–10 thereto); para (b)(v) and the word "or" immediately preceding it added by the Civil Partnership Act 2004, s 81, Sch 8, para 31.
Sub-s (5): words in square brackets substituted by the Housing Act 1996, s 222, Sch 18, Pt IV, para 26.
Sub-s (6): words in square brackets substituted by the Companies Act 2006 (Consequential Amendments, Transitional Provisions and Savings) Order 2009, SI 2009/1941, art 2(1), Sch 1, para 62(1), (5).
Matrimonial Homes Act 1983: repealed by the Family Law Act 1996, s 66(3), Sch 10, subject to savings contained in s 66(2) of, and Sch 9, paras 5, 8–15 to, that Act.

**[171C   Modifications of this Part in relation to preserved right**

(1)   Where the right to buy is preserved, the provisions of this Part have effect subject to such exceptions, adaptations and other modifications as may be prescribed by regulations made by the Secretary of State.

(2)   The regulations may in particular provide—
    (a)   that paragraphs [1, 3 and] 5 to 11 of Schedule 5 (certain exceptions to the right to buy) do not apply;
    (b)   …
    (c)   that the provisions of this Part relating to the [right to acquire on rent to mortgage terms] do not apply; and
    (d)   that the landlord is not required to but may include a covenant for the repayment of discount, provided its terms are no more onerous than those of the covenant provided for in section 155.

(3)   The prescribed exceptions, adaptations and other modifications shall take the form of textual amendments of the provisions of this Part as they apply in cases where the right to buy is preserved; and the first regulations, and any subsequent consolidating regulations, shall set out the provisions of this Part as they so apply.

(4)   The regulations—
    (a)   may make different provision for different cases or descriptions of case, including different provision for different areas,
    (b)   may contain such incidental, supplementary and transitional provisions as the Secretary of State considers appropriate, and
    (c)   shall be made by statutory instrument which shall be subject to annulment in pursuance of a resolution of either House of Parliament.

[(5)   The disapplication by the regulations of paragraph 1 of Schedule 5 shall not be taken to authorise any action on the part of a charity which would conflict with the trusts of the charity.]]

**[538]**

**NOTES**
Inserted as noted to s 171A at **[536]**.
Sub-s (2): words in first pair of square brackets inserted by the Housing Act 1988, s 127(2); para (b) repealed and words in second pair of square brackets substituted by the Leasehold Reform, Housing and Urban Development Act 1993, s 187, Sch 21, para 19, Sch 22, except in relation to a case where a notice under s 122 at **[468]**, is served before 11 October 1993 or in relation to the operation of this Part of this Act as applied by the Local Government Reorganisation (Preservation of the Right to Buy) Order 1986, SI 1986/ 2092.
Sub-s (5): added by the Housing Act 1988, s 127(3).
Regulations: the Housing (Preservation of Right to Buy) Regulations 1993, SI 1993/2241; the Housing (Right of First Refusal) (England) Regulations 2005, SI 2005/1917 at **[3555]**; the Housing (Right of First Refusal) (Wales) Regulations 2005, SI 2005/2680 at **[3573]**.

**[171D   Subsequent dealings: disposal of landlord's interest in qualifying dwelling-house**

(1)   The disposal by the landlord of an interest in the qualifying dwelling-house, whether his whole interest or a lesser interest, does not affect the preserved right to buy, unless—

    (a)    as a result of the disposal an authority or body within section 80(1) (the landlord condition for secure tenancies) becomes the landlord of the qualifying person or persons, or

    (b)    paragraph 6 of Schedule 9A applies (effect of failure to register entry protecting preserved right to buy),

in which case the right to buy ceases to be preserved.

    (2)    The disposal by the landlord of a qualifying dwelling-house of less than his whole interest as landlord of the dwelling-house, or in part of it, requires the consent of the *Secretary of State*, unless the disposal is to the qualifying person or persons.

    [(2A)    "The appropriate authority" means—

    (a)    in relation to a disposal of land in England by a registered provider of social housing, the Regulator of Social Housing,

    (b)    in relation to any other disposal of land in England, the Secretary of State, and

    (c)    in relation to a disposal of land in Wales, the Welsh Ministers.]

    (3)    Consent may be given in relation to a particular disposal or generally in relation to disposals of a particular description and may, in either case, be given subject to conditions.

    (4)    A disposal made without the consent required by subsection (2) is void, except in a case where, by reason of a failure to make the entries on the land register or land charges register required by Schedule 9A, the preserved right to buy does not bind the person to whom the disposal is made.]

**[539]**

**NOTES**

Inserted as noted to s 171A at **[536]**.

Sub-s (2): for the words in italics there are substituted the words "appropriate authority" by the Housing and Regeneration Act 2008, s 191(1)(a), as from a day to be appointed.

Sub-s (2A): inserted by the Housing and Regeneration Act 2008, s 191(1)(b), as from a day to be appointed.

**[171E   Subsequent dealings: termination of landlord's interest in qualifying dwelling-house**

    (1)    On the termination of the landlord's interest in the qualifying dwelling-house—

    (a)    on the occurrence of an event determining his estate or interest, or by re-entry on a breach of condition or forfeiture, or

    (b)    where the interest is a leasehold interest, by notice given by him or a superior landlord, on the expiry or surrender of the term, or otherwise (subject to subsection (2)),

the right to buy ceases to be preserved.

    (2)    The termination of the landlord's interest by merger on his acquiring a superior interest, or on the acquisition by another person of the landlord's interest together with a superior interest, does not affect the preserved right to buy, unless—

    (a)    as a result of the acquisition an authority or body within section 80(1) (the landlord condition for secure tenancies) becomes the landlord of the qualifying person or persons, or

    (b)    paragraph 6 of Schedule 9A applies (effect of failure to register entry protecting preserved right to buy),

in which case the right to buy ceases to be preserved.

    (3)    Where the termination of the landlord's interest as mentioned in subsection (1) is caused by the act or omission of the landlord, a qualifying person who is thereby deprived of the preserved right to buy is entitled to be compensated by him.]

**[540]**

**NOTES**

Inserted as noted to s 171A at **[536]**.

**[171F   Subsequent dealings: transfer of qualifying person to alternative accommodation**

The court shall not order a qualifying person to give up possession of the qualifying dwelling-house in pursuance of section 98(1)(a) of the Rent Act 1977 [or on Ground 9 in Schedule 2 to the Housing Act 1988] (suitable alternative accommodation) unless the court is satisfied—

    (a)    that the preserved right to buy will, by virtue of section 171B(6) (accommodation with same landlord or connected company), continue to be exercisable in relation to the dwelling-house offered by way of alternative accommodation and that the interest of the landlord in the new dwelling-house will be—

        (i)    where the new dwelling-house is a house, not less than the interest of the landlord in the existing dwelling-house, or

(ii)  where the new dwelling-house is a flat, not less than the interest of the landlord in the existing dwelling-house or a term of years of which 80 years or more remain unexpired, whichever is the less; or

(b)  that the landlord of the new dwelling-house will be an authority or body within section 80(1) (the landlord condition for secure tenancies).]

[541]

**NOTES**
Inserted as noted to s 171A at [536].
Words in square brackets inserted by the Housing Act 1988, s 140(1), Sch 17, Pt I, para 42.

## [171G  Land registration and related matters

Schedule 9A has effect with respect to registration of title and related matters arising in connection with the preservation of the right to buy.]

[542]

**NOTES**
Inserted as noted to s 171A at [536].

## [171H  Disposal after notice claiming to exercise right to buy, etc

(1)  Where notice has been given in respect of a dwelling-house claiming to exercise the right to buy ... and before the completion of the exercise of that right the dwelling-house is the subject of—

(a)  a qualifying disposal, or
(b)  a disposal to which section 171D(1)(a) or 171E(2)(a) applies (disposal to authority or body satisfying landlord condition for secure tenancies),

all parties shall, subject to subsection (2), be in the same position as if the disponee had become the landlord before the notice was given and had been given that notice and any further notice given by the tenant to the landlord and had taken all steps which the landlord had taken.

(2)  If the circumstances after the disposal differ in any material respect, as for example where—

(a)  the interest of the disponee in the dwelling-house after the disposal differs from that of the disponor before the disposal, or
(b)  ...
(c)  any of the provisions of Schedule 5 (exceptions to the right to buy) becomes or ceases to be applicable,

all those concerned shall, as soon as practicable after the disposal, take all such steps (whether by way of amending or withdrawing and re-serving any notice or extending any period or otherwise) as may be requisite for the purpose of securing that all parties are, as nearly as may be, in the same position as they would have been if those circumstances had obtained before the disposal.]

[543]

**NOTES**
Inserted as noted to s 171A at [536].
Sub-ss (1), (2): words omitted repealed by the Leasehold Reform, Housing and Urban Development Act 1993, s 187(2), Sch 22, except in relation to a case where a notice under s 122 at [468], is served before 11 October 1993 or in relation to the operation of this Part of this Act as applied by the Local Government Reorganisation (Preservation of the Right to Buy) Order 1986, SI 1986/2092.

*Modifications of Leasehold Reform Act 1967 in relation to leases granted under this Part*

## 172  Exclusion of leases where landlord is housing association and freeholder is a charity

(1)  Part I of the Leasehold Reform Act 1967 (enfranchisement and extension of long leaseholds) does not apply where, in the case of a tenancy or sub-tenancy to which this section applies, the landlord is a housing association and the freehold is owned by a body of persons or trust established for charitable purposes only.

(2)  This section applies to a tenancy created by the grant of a lease in pursuance of this Part of a dwelling-house which is a house.

(3)  Where Part I of the 1967 Act applies as if there had been a single tenancy granted for a term beginning at the same time as the term under a tenancy falling within subsection (2) and expiring at the same time as the term under a later tenancy, this section also applies to that later tenancy.

(4)  This section applies to any sub-tenancy directly or indirectly derived out of a tenancy within subsection (2) or (3).

[544]

**173**  (*Repealed by the Statute Law (Repeals) Act 1998, s 1(1), Sch 1, Pt X.*)

## 174  Leases granted under this Part to be treated as long leases at a low rent

For the purposes of Part I of the Leasehold Reform Act 1967 (enfranchisement and extension of long leaseholds)—

    (a)    a tenancy created by the grant of a lease in pursuance of this Part of a dwelling-house which is a house shall be treated as being a long tenancy notwithstanding that it is granted for a term of 21 years or less, ...

    (b)    ...

**[545]**

**NOTES**

Words omitted repealed by the Statute Law (Repeals) Act 1998, s 1(1), Sch 1, Pt X.

## 175  Determination of price payable

(1)    Where, in the case of a tenancy or sub-tenancy to which this section applies, the tenant exercises his right to acquire the freehold under Part I of the Leasehold Reform Act 1967, the price payable for the dwelling-house shall be determined in accordance with section 9(1A) of that Act notwithstanding that [the circumstances specified in that section do not apply].

(2)    This section applies to a tenancy created by the grant of a lease in pursuance of this Part of a dwelling-house which is a house.

(3)    Where Part I of the 1967 Act applies as if there had been a single tenancy granted for a term beginning at the same time as the term under a tenancy falling within subsection (2) and expiring at the same time as the term under a later tenancy, this section also applies to that later tenancy.

(4)    This section applies to any sub-tenancy directly or indirectly derived out of a tenancy falling within subsection (2) or (3).

(5)    This section also applies to a tenancy granted in substitution for a tenancy or sub-tenancy falling within subsections (2) to (4) in pursuance of Part I of the 1967 Act.

**[546]**

**NOTES**

Sub-s (1): words in square brackets substituted by the References to Rating (Housing) Regulations 1990, SI 1990/434, reg 2, Schedule, para 19.

*Supplementary provisions*

## 176  Notices

(1)    The Secretary of State may by regulations prescribe the form of any notice under this Part and the particulars to be contained in the notice.

(2)    Where the form of, and the particulars to be contained in, a notice under this Part are so prescribed, a tenant who proposes to claim, or has claimed, to exercise the right to buy may request the landlord to supply him with a form for use in giving such notice; and the landlord shall do so within seven days of the request.

(3)    A notice under this Part may be served by sending it by post.

(4)    Where the landlord is a housing association, a notice to be served by the tenant on the landlord under this Part may be served by leaving it at, or sending it to, the principal office of the association or the office of the association with which the tenant usually deals.

(5)    Regulations under this section—

    (a)    may make different provision with respect to different cases or descriptions of case, including different provision for different areas, and

    (b)    shall be made by statutory instrument.

**[547]**

**NOTES**

Regulations: the Housing (Right to Buy) (Prescribed Forms) Regulations 1986, SI 1986/2194 at **[3057]**; the Housing (Right to Buy Delay Procedure) (Prescribed Forms) Regulations 1989, SI 1989/240 at **[3081]**; the Housing (Right to Buy Delay Procedure) (Prescribed Forms) (Welsh Forms) Regulations 1994, SI 1994/2931; the Housing (Right to Buy) (Prescribed Forms) (Welsh Forms) Regulations 1994, SI 1994/2932.

## 177  Errors and omissions in notices

(1)    A notice served by a tenant under this Part is not invalidated by an error in, or omission from, the particulars which are required by regulations under section 176 to be contained in the notice.

(2)    Where as a result of such an error or omission—

    (a)    the landlord has mistakenly admitted or denied the right to buy or the [right to acquire on rent to mortgage terms] in a notice under section 124 or 146, or

(b)    the landlord ... has formed a mistaken opinion as to any matter required to be stated in a
notice by any of the provisions mentioned in subsection (3) and has stated that opinion
in the notice,

the parties shall, as soon as practicable after they become aware of the mistake, take all such steps
(whether by way of amending, withdrawing or re-serving any notice or extending any period or
otherwise) as may be requisite for the purpose of securing that all parties are, as nearly as may be, in
the same position as they would have been if the mistake had not been made.

(3)    The provisions referred to in subsection (2)(b) are—
section 125 (notice of purchase price, etc),
...
[section 146 (landlord's notice admitting or denying right to acquire on rent to mortgage
terms).]
...

(4)    Subsection (2) does not apply where the tenant has exercised the right to which the notice
relates before the parties become aware of the mistake.

**[548]**

**NOTES**
Sub-ss (2), (3): words in square brackets substituted and words omitted repealed by the Leasehold Reform,
Housing and Urban Development Act 1993, s 187, Sch 21, para 20, Sch 22, except in relation to a case where a
notice under s 122 at **[468]**, is served before 11 October 1993 or in relation to the operation of this Part of this
Act as applied by the Local Government Reorganisation (Preservation of the Right to Buy) Order 1986,
SI 1986/2092.

**[178   Costs**

An agreement between the landlord and a tenant claiming to exercise—
(a)    the right to buy,
(b)    the right to acquire on rent to mortgage terms, or
(c)    any such right as is mentioned in paragraph 2(1) or 6(1) of Schedule 6A (redemption of
landlord's share: right to make final or interim payment),

is void in so far as it purports to oblige the tenant to bear any part of the costs incurred by the
landlord in connection with the tenant's exercise of that right.]

**[549]**

**NOTES**
Substituted by the Leasehold Reform, Housing and Urban Development Act 1993, s 187(1), Sch 21, para 21,
except in relation to a case where a notice under s 122 at **[468]**, is served before 11 October 1993 or in relation
to the operation of this Part of this Act as applied by the Local Government Reorganisation (Preservation of the
Right to Buy) Order 1986, SI 1986/2092.

**179   Provisions restricting right to buy, etc of no effect**

(1)    A provision of a lease held by the landlord or a superior landlord, or of an agreement
(whenever made), is void in so far as it purports to prohibit or restrict—
(a)    the grant of a lease in pursuance of the right to buy or the [right to acquire on rent to
mortgage terms], or
(b)    the subsequent disposal (whether by way of assignment, sub-lease or otherwise) of a
lease so granted

or to authorise a forfeiture, or impose on the landlord or superior landlord a penalty or disability, in
the event of such a grant or disposal.

(2)    Where a dwelling-house let on a secure tenancy is land held—
(a)    for the purposes of section 164 of the Public Health Act 1875 (pleasure grounds), or
(b)    in accordance with section 10 of the Open Spaces Act 1906 (duty of local authority to
maintain open spaces and burial grounds),

then, for the purposes of this Part, the dwelling-house shall be deemed to be freed from any trust
arising solely by virtue of its being land held in trust for enjoyment by the public in accordance with
section 164 or, as the case may be, section 10.

**[550]**

**NOTES**
Sub-s (1): words in square brackets substituted by the Leasehold Reform, Housing and Urban Development
Act 1993, s 187(1), Sch 21, para 22, except in relation to a case where a notice under s 122 at **[468]**, is served
before 11 October 1993 or in relation to the operation of this Part of this Act as applied by the Local Government
Reorganisation (Preservation of the Right to Buy) Order 1986, SI 1986/2092.

PART 1
STATUTES

**180  Statutory declarations**

A landlord, ... or the Secretary of State may, if the landlord, .... or Secretary of State thinks fit, accept a statutory declaration made for the purposes of this Part as sufficient evidence of the matters declared in it.

**[551]**

**NOTES**

Words omitted repealed by the Leasehold Reform, Housing and Urban Development Act 1993, s 187(2), Sch 22, except in relation to a case where a notice under s 122 at **[468]**, is served before 11 October 1993 or in relation to the operation of this Part of this Act as applied by the Local Government Reorganisation (Preservation of the Right to Buy) Order 1986, SI 1986/2092.

**181  Jurisdiction of county court**

(1)  A county court has jurisdiction—
 (a)  to entertain any proceedings brought under this Part, and
 (b)  to determine any question arising under this Part or under [a conveyance or grant executed in pursuance of the right to acquire on rent to mortgage terms];

but subject to sections 128[, 128B][, 155C and 158] ... (which provide for matters of valuation to be determined by the district valuer).

(2)  The jurisdiction conferred by this section includes jurisdiction to entertain proceedings on any such question as is mentioned in subsection (1)(b) notwithstanding that no other relief is sought than a declaration.

(3)  *If a person takes proceedings in the High Court which, by virtue of this section, he could have taken in the county court, he is not entitled to recover any costs.*

(4), (5)  ...

**[552]**

**NOTES**

Sub-s (1): words in first pair of square brackets substituted and words omitted repealed by the Leasehold Reform, Housing and Urban Development Act 1993, s 187, Sch 21, para 23, Sch 22, except in relation to a case where a notice under s 122 at **[468]**, is served before 11 October 1993 or in relation to the operation of this Part of this Act as applied by the Local Government Reorganisation (Preservation of the Right to Buy) Order 1986, SI 1986/2092; figure in second pair of square brackets inserted by the Housing and Regeneration Act 2008, s 306(1), (11), (12), except in relation to any determination or re-determination under s 128 of this Act which was required before 22 September 2008; words in third pair of square brackets substituted by the Housing Act 2004, s 186(2).

Sub-s (3): repealed by the Courts and Legal Services Act 1990, s 125(7), Sch 20, as from a day to be appointed.

Sub-ss (4), (5): repealed by the Constitutional Reform Act 2005, ss 15(1), 146, Sch 4, Pt 1, paras 180, 182, Sch 18, Pt 2.

**182  Power to repeal or amend local Acts**

(1)  The Secretary of State may by order repeal or amend a provision of a local Act passed before 8th August 1980 where it appears to him that the provision is inconsistent with a provision of this Part relating to the right to buy ...

(2)  Before making an order under this section the Secretary of State shall consult any local housing authority appearing to him to be concerned.

(3)  An order made under this section may contain such transitional, incidental or supplementary provisions as the Secretary of State considers appropriate.

(4)  An order under this section—
 (a)  may make different provision with respect to different cases or descriptions of case, including different provision for different areas, and
 (b)  shall be made by statutory instrument which shall be subject to annulment in pursuance of a resolution of either House of Parliament.

**[553]**

**NOTES**

Sub-s (1): words omitted repealed by the Leasehold Reform, Housing and Urban Development Act 1993, s 187(2), Sch 22, except in relation to a case where a notice under s 122 at **[468]**, is served before 11 October 1993 or in relation to the operation of this Part of this Act as applied by the Local Government Reorganisation (Preservation of the Right to Buy) Order 1986, SI 1986/2092.

**183  Meaning of "house", "flat" and "dwelling-house"**

(1)  The following provisions apply to the interpretation of "house", "flat" and "dwelling-house" when used in this Part.

(2)   A dwelling-house is a house if, and only if, it (or so much of it as does not consist of land included by virtue of section 184) is a structure reasonably so called; so that—
   (a)   where a building is divided horizontally, the flats or other units into which it is divided are not houses;
   (b)   where a building is divided vertically, the units into which it is divided may be houses;
   (c)   where a building is not structurally detached, it is not a house if a material part of it lies above or below the remainder of the structure.

(3)   A dwelling-house which is not a house is a flat.

[554]

## 184   Land let with or used for purposes of dwelling-house

(1)   For the purpose of this Part land let together with a dwelling-house shall be treated as part of the dwelling-house, unless the land is agricultural land (within the meaning set out in section 26(3)(a) of the General Rate Act 1967) exceeding two acres.

(2)   There shall be treated as included in a dwelling-house any land which is not within subsection (1) but is or has been used for the purpose of the dwelling-house if—
   (a)   the tenant, by a written notice served on the landlord at any time before he exercises the right to buy or the [right to acquire on rent to mortgage terms], requires the land to be included in the dwelling-house, and
   (b)   it is reasonable in all the circumstances for the land to be so included.

(3)   A notice under subsection (2) may be withdrawn by a written notice served on the landlord at any time before the tenant exercises the right to buy or the [right to acquire on rent to mortgage terms].

(4)   Where a notice under subsection (2) is served or withdrawn after the service of the notice under section 125 (landlord's notice of purchase price, etc), the parties shall, as soon as practicable after the service or withdrawal, take all such steps (whether by way of amending, withdrawing or re-serving any notice or extending any period or otherwise) as may be requisite for the purpose of securing that all parties are, as nearly as may be, in the same position as they would have been in if the notice under subsection (2) had been served or withdrawn before the service of the notice under section 125.

[555]

**NOTES**
Sub-ss (2), (3): words in square brackets substituted by the Leasehold Reform, Housing and Urban Development Act 1993, s 187(1), Sch 21, para 24, except in relation to a case where a notice under s 122 at [468], is served before 11 October 1993 or in relation to the operation of this Part of this Act as applied by the Local Government Reorganisation (Preservation of the Right to Buy) Order 1986, SI 1986/2092.
General Rate Act 1967: repealed by the Local Government Finance Act 1988, ss 117(1), 149, Sch 13, Pt I, with effect for financial years beginning in or after 1 April 1990, but subject to any savings in regulations made under s 117(8) of that Act.

## 185   Meaning of "secure tenancy" and "secure tenant"

(1)   References in this Part to a secure tenancy or a secure tenant in relation to a time before 26th August 1984 are to a tenancy which would have been a secure tenancy if Chapter II of Part I of the Housing Act 1980 and Part I of the Housing and Building Control Act 1984 had then been in force or to a person who would then have been a secure tenant.

(2)   For the purpose of determining whether a person would have been a secure tenant and his tenancy a secure tenancy—
   (a)   a predecessor of a local authority shall be deemed to have been such an authority, and
   (b)   a housing association shall be deemed to have been registered if it is or was [a registered social landlord] at any later time.

[556]

**NOTES**
Sub-s (2): words in square brackets substituted by the Housing Act 1996 (Consequential Provisions) Order 1996, SI 1996/2325, art 5, Sch 2, para 14(1), (16).
Housing Act 1980, Pt I, Ch II; Housing and Building Control Act 1984, Pt I: repealed by the Housing (Consequential Provisions) Act 1985, s 3, Sch 1, Pt I.

## 186   Members of a person's family

(1)   A person is a member of another's family within the meaning of this Part if—
   (a)   he is the spouse [or civil partner] of that person, or he and that person live together as husband and wife [or as if they were civil partners], or
   (b)   he is that person's parent, grandparent, child, grandchild, brother, sister, uncle, aunt, nephew or niece.

(2)   For the purposes of subsection (1)(b)—

(a) a relationship by marriage [or civil partnership] shall be treated as a relationship by blood,

(b) a relationship of the half-blood shall be treated as a relationship of the whole blood,

(c) the stepchild of a person shall be treated as his child, and

(d) an illegitimate child shall be treated as the legitimate child of his mother and reputed father.

[557]

---

**NOTES**

Words in square brackets inserted by the Civil Partnership Act 2004, s 81, Sch 8, para 27.

---

## 187 Minor definitions

In this Part—

"improvement" means[, in relation to a dwelling-house,] any alteration in, or addition to, [the dwelling-house] and includes—

    (a) any addition to, or alteration in, landlord's fixtures and fittings and any addition or alteration connected with the provision of services to [the dwelling-house],

    (b) the erection of a wireless or television aerial, and

    (c) the carrying out of external decoration;

[and shall be similarly construed in relation to any other building or land;]

["improvement contribution" means an amount payable by a tenant of a flat in respect of improvements to the flat, the building in which it is situated or any other building or land, other than works carried out in discharge of any such obligations as are referred to in paragraph 16A(1) of Schedule 6 (obligations to repair, reinstate, etc);]

"long tenancy" means—

    (a) a long tenancy within the meaning of Part IV,

    (b) ... , or

    (c) a tenancy falling within paragraph 1 of Schedule 2 to the Housing (Northern Ireland) Order 1983;

and "long lease" shall be construed accordingly;

.....

[558]

---

**NOTES**

In definition "improvement" words in first pair of square brackets inserted, words in second and third pairs of square brackets substituted, and words in fourth pair of square brackets added by the Housing and Planning Act 1986, s 24(2), Sch 5, Pt II, para 30.

Definition "improvement contribution" inserted by the Housing and Planning Act 1986, s 24(2), Sch 5, Pt II, para 30.

In definition "long tenancy" para (b) repealed by the Housing (Scotland) Act 1987, s 339(2), (3), Sch 23, para 30(2), Sch 24.

Definition "total share" (omitted) repealed by the Leasehold Reform, Housing and Urban Development Act 1993, s 187(2), Sch 22, except in relation to a case where a notice under s 122 at [**468**], is served before 11 October 1993 or in relation to the operation of this Part of this Act as applied by the Local Government Reorganisation (Preservation of the Right to Buy) Order 1986, SI 1986/2092.

---

## 188 Index of defined expressions: Part V

The following Table shows provisions defining or otherwise explaining expressions used in this Part (other than provisions defining or explaining an expression used in the same section or paragraph):—

...

| | |
|---|---|
| bank | section 622 |
| building society | section 622 |
| cemetery | section 622 |
| charity | section 622 |
| compulsory disposal | section 161 |
| co-operative housing association | section 5(2) |
| [ ... | ... ] |
| [disposal and instrument effecting disposal (in Schedule 9A) | paragraph 10 of that Schedule] |
| [district valuer | section 622] |

| | |
|---|---|
| dwelling-house | sections 183 and 184 |
| ... | |
| exempted disposal | section 160 |
| family (member of) | section 186 |
| [final payment | paragraph 1 of Schedule 6A] |
| flat | section 183 |
| [former landlord and former secure tenant (in relation to a qualifying disposal) | section 171A(2)(c)] |
| friendly society | section 622 |
| ... | |
| house | section 183 |
| housing association | section 5(1) |
| housing trust | section 6 |
| improvement | section 187 |
| [improvement contribution | section 187] |
| incumbrances | paragraph 7 of Schedule 6 |
| [initial payment and interim payment | section 143B and paragraph 6 of Schedule 6A] |
| ... | |
| insurance company | section 622 |
| [landlord's share | section 148 and paragraph 7 of Schedule 6A] |
| lease | section 621 |
| local authority | section 4(e) |
| local housing authority | section 1, 2(2) |
| long tenancy (and long lease) | section 187 |
| [minimum initial payment and maximum initial payment | section 143B] |
| new town corporation | section 4(b) |
| [prescribed | section 614] |
| ... | |
| [preserved right to buy | section 171A(2)(a)] |
| public sector tenancy (and public sector tenant) | paragraphs 6 to 10 of Schedule 4 |
| purchase price | section 126 |
| [qualifying disposal (in relation to the preserved right to buy) | section 171A(2)(b)] |
| [qualifying dwelling-house and qualifying person (in relation to the preserved right to buy) | section 171B(1)] |
| [reference period (for purposes of s 125A or 125B) | section 125C] |
| [registered social landlord | section 5(4) and (5)] |
| regular armed forces of the Crown | section 622 |
| [the Relevant Authority | section 6A] |
| relevant disposal | section 159 (and see section 452(3)) |
| relevant time | section 122(2) |
| [right to acquire on rent to mortgage terms | section 143] |
| ... | |
| right to buy | section 118(1) |

...

| | |
|---|---|
| secure tenancy and secure tenant | sections 79 and 185 |
| [service charge | section 621A] |
| tenant's incumbrance | paragraph 7 of Schedule 6 |

...

| | |
|---|---|
| trustee savings bank | section 622 |
| urban development corporation | section 4(d) |

**[559]**

**NOTES**

Entries relating to "additional share and additional contribution", "effective discount", "full mortgage", "initial share and initial contributions", "prescribed percentage", "right to be granted a shared ownership lease", "right to further advances" and "right to a mortgage" and "total share" repealed and entries relating to "district valuer", "final payment", "initial payment and interim payment", "landlord's share", "minimum initial payment and maximum initial payment", "prescribed" and "right to acquire on rent to mortgage terms" inserted by the Leasehold Reform, Housing and Urban Development Act 1993, s 187, Sch 21, para 25, Sch 22, except in relation to a case where a notice under s 122 at **[468]**, is served before 11 October 1993 or in relation to the operation of this Part of this Act as applied by the Local Government Reorganisation (Preservation of the Right to Buy) Order 1986, SI 1986/2092.

Entry "the Corporation" omitted from first pair of square brackets inserted by the Housing Act 1988, s 140(1), Sch 17, Pt II, para 110 and repealed by the Government of Wales Act 1998, ss 140, 152, Sch 16, para 14(a), Sch 18, Pt VI.

Entries relating to "disposal and instrument effecting disposal", "former landlord and former secure tenant", "improvement contribution", "preserved right to buy", "qualifying disposal", "qualifying dwelling-house and qualifying person", "reference period" and "service charge" inserted by the Housing and Planning Act 1986, s 24(2), Sch 5, Pt II, para 31.

Entry relating to "registered social landlord" substituted by the Housing Act 1996 (Consequential Provisions) Order 1996, SI 1996/2325, art 5, Sch 2, para 14(1), (17).

Entry relating to "the Relevant Authority" inserted by the Government of Wales Act 1998, s 140, Sch 16, para 14(b).

---

**189–603** *((Pts VI–XVII) outside the scope of this work.)*

## PART XVIII
## MISCELLANEOUS AND GENERAL PROVISIONS

**604–611** *(Outside the scope of this work.)*

*General provisions*

### 612 Exclusion of Rent Act protection

Nothing in the Rent Acts [or Part I of the Housing Act 1988] prevents possession being obtained of a [dwelling-house] of which possession is required for the purpose of enabling a local housing authority to exercise their powers under any enactment relating to housing.

**[560]**

---

**NOTES**

Words in first pair of square brackets inserted by the Housing Act 1988, s 140(1), Sch 17, Pt I, para 63; words in second pair of square brackets substituted by the Local Government and Housing Act 1989, s 165(1), Sch 9, Pt V, para 89.

---

### 613 Liability of directors, etc in case of offence by body corporate

(1) Where an offence under this Act committed by a body corporate is proved to have been committed with the consent or connivance of, or to be attributable to any neglect on the part of, a director, manager, secretary or other similar officer of the body corporate, or a person purporting to act in any such capacity, he, as well as the body corporate, is guilty of an offence and liable to be proceeded against and punished accordingly.

(2) Where the affairs of a body corporate are managed by its members, subsection (1) applies in relation to the acts and defaults of a member in connection with his functions of management as if he were a director of the body corporate.

**[561]**

### 614 Power to prescribe forms etc

(1) The Secretary of State may by regulations prescribe—

(a) anything which by this Act is to be prescribed; or

(b)   the form of any notice, advertisement, statement or other document which is required or authorised to be used under or for the purposes of this Act.

(2)   The regulations shall be made by statutory instrument which shall be subject to annulment in pursuance of a resolution of either House of Parliament.

(3)   The power conferred by this section is not exercisable where specific provision for prescribing a thing, or the form of a document, is made elsewhere.

**[562]**

**NOTES**
Regulations: the Housing (Prescribed Forms) Regulations 1990, SI 1990/447; the Housing (Prescribed Forms) (No 2) Regulations 1990, SI 1990/1730; the Housing (Prescribed Forms) (No 2) (Welsh Forms) Regulations 1991, SI 1991/974.

### 615 Dispensation with advertisements and notices

(1)   The Secretary of State may dispense with the publication of advertisements or the service of notices required to be published or served by a local authority under this Act if he is satisfied that there is reasonable cause for dispensing with the publication or service.

(2)   A dispensation may be given by the Secretary of State—
(a)   either before or after the time at which the advertisement is required to be published or the notice is required to be served, and
(b)   either unconditionally or upon such conditions, as to the publication of other advertisements or the service of other notices or otherwise, as the Secretary of State thinks fit,

due care being taken by him to prevent the interests of any persons being prejudiced by the dispensation.

**[563]**

### 616 Local inquiries

For the purposes of the execution of his powers and duties under this Act, the Secretary of State may cause such local inquiries to be held as he may think fit.

**[564]**

### 617 Service of notices

(1)   Where under any provision of this Act it is the duty of a local housing authority to serve a document on a person who is to the knowledge of the authority—
(a)   a person having control of premises, however defined, or
(b)   a person managing premises, however defined, or
(c)   a person having an estate or interest in premises, whether or not restricted to persons who are owners or lessees or mortgagees or to any other class of those having an estate or interest in premises,
the authority shall take reasonable steps to identify the person or persons coming within the description in that provision.

(2)   A person having an estate or interest in premises may for the purposes of any provision to which subsection (1) applies give notice to the local housing authority of his interest in the premises and they shall enter the notice in their records.

(3)   A document required or authorised by this Act to be served on a person as being a person having control of premises (however defined) may, if it is not practicable after reasonable enquiry to ascertain the name or address of that person, be served by—
(a)   addressing it to him by the description of "person having control of" the premises (naming them) to which it relates, and
(b)   delivering it to some person on the premises or, if there is no person on the premises to whom it can be delivered, by affixing it, or a copy of it, to some conspicuous part of the premises.

(4)   Where under any provision of this Act a document is to be served on—
(a)   the person having control of premises, however defined, or
(b)   the person managing premises, however defined, or
(c)   the owner of premises, however defined,
and more than one person comes within the description in the enactment, the document may be served on more than one of those persons.

**[565]**

### 618 The Common Council of the City of London

(1)   The Common Council of the City of London may appoint a committee, consisting of so many persons as they think fit, for any purposes of this Act or the Housing Associations Act 1985 which in their opinion may be better regulated and managed by means of a committee.

(2)   A committee so appointed—

(a)   shall consist as to a majority of its members of members of the Common Council, and

(b)   shall not be authorised to borrow money or to make a rate,

and shall be subject to any regulations and restrictions which may be imposed by the Common Council.

(3)   A person is not, by reason only of the fact that he occupies a house at a rental from the Common Council, disqualified from being elected or being a member of that Council or any committee of that Council; but no person shall vote as a member of that Council, or any such committee, on a resolution or question which is proposed or arises in pursuance of this Act or the Housing Associations Act 1985 and relates to land in which he is beneficially interested.

(4)   A person who votes in contravention of subsection (3) commits a summary offence and is liable on conviction to a fine not exceeding [level 4 on the standard scale]; but the fact of his giving the vote does not invalidate any resolution or proceeding of the authority.

**[566]**

**NOTES**

Sub-s (4): words in square brackets substituted by the Housing and Planning Act 1986, s 24(1)(f), Sch 5, Pt I, para 6, in relation to offences committed on or after 7 January 1987.

### 619   The Inner and Middle Temples

(1)   ...

(2)   [The provisions of Parts I to XI and XIII to XVIII of this Act] are among those for which provision may be made by Order in Council under section 94 of the Local Government Act 1985 (general power to provide for exercise of local authority functions as respects the Temples).

**[567]**

**NOTES**

Sub-s (1): repealed by the Housing Act 1996, s 227, Sch 19, Pt II.

Sub-s (2): words in square brackets substituted by the Housing Act 1996, s 80(2)(a).

### 620   The Isles of Scilly

(1)   This Act applies to the Isles of Scilly subject to such exceptions, adaptations and modifications as the Secretary of State may by order direct.

(2)   An order shall be made by statutory instrument which shall be subject to annulment in pursuance of a resolution of either House of Parliament.

**[568]**

**NOTES**

Orders: by virtue of the Housing (Consequential Provisions) Act 1985, s 2(2), the Isles of Scilly (Housing) Order 1972, SI 1972/1204 and the Isles of Scilly (Housing) Order 1975, SI 1975/512, have effect as if made under this section.

### 621   Meaning of "lease" and "tenancy" and related expressions

(1)   In this Act "lease" and "tenancy" have the same meaning.

(2)   Both expressions include—

(a)   a sub-lease or sub-tenancy, and

(b)   an agreement for a lease or tenancy (or sub-lease or sub-tenancy).

(3)   The expressions "lessor" and "lessee" and "landlord" and "tenant", and references to letting, to the grant of a lease or to covenants or terms, shall be construed accordingly.

**[569]**

### [621A   Meaning of "service charge" and related expressions

(1)   In this Act "service charge" means an amount payable by a purchaser or lessee of premises—

(a)   which is payable, directly or indirectly, for services, repairs, maintenance or insurance or the vendor's or lessor's costs of management, and

(b)   the whole or part of which varies or may vary according to the relevant costs.

(2)   The relevant costs are the costs or estimated costs incurred or to be incurred by or on behalf of the payee, or (in the case of a lease) a superior landlord, in connection with the matters for which the service charge is payable.

(3)   For this purpose—

(a)   "costs" includes overheads, and

(b) costs are relevant costs in relation to a service charge whether they are incurred, or to be incurred, in the period for which the service charge is payable or in an earlier or later period.

(4) In relation to a service charge—

(a) the "payee" means the person entitled to enforce payment of the charge, and

(b) the "payer" means the person liable to pay it.

[(5) But this section does not apply in relation to Part 14.]]

**[570]**

---

**NOTES**

Inserted by the Housing and Planning Act 1986, s 24(2), Sch 5, Pt II, para 39.
Sub-s (5): added by the Commonhold and Leasehold Reform Act 2002, s 150, Sch 9, paras 1, 6.

---

### 622 Minor definitions: general

[(1)] In this Act—

["assured tenancy" has the same meaning as in Part I of the Housing Act 1988;

"assured agricultural occupancy" has the same meaning as in Part I of the Housing Act 1988;]

["authorised deposit taker" means—

(a) a person who has permission under Part 4 of the Financial Services and Markets Act 2000 to accept deposits, or

(b) an EEA firm of the kind mentioned in paragraph 5(b) of Schedule 3 to that Act who has permission under paragraph 15 of that Schedule (as a result of qualifying for authorisation under paragraph [12] of that Schedule) to accept deposits;

"authorised insurer" means—

(a) a person who has permission under Part 4 of the Financial Services and Markets Act 2000 to effect or carry out contracts of insurance, or

(b) an EEA firm of the kind mentioned in paragraph 5(b) of Schedule 3 to that Act who has permission under paragraph 15 of that Schedule (as a result of qualifying for authorisation under paragraph [12] of that Schedule) to effect or carry out contracts of insurance;]

["authorised mortgage lender" means—

(a) a person who has permission under Part 4 of the Financial Services and Markets Act 2000 to enter into a regulated mortgage contract as lender,

(b) an EEA firm of the kind mentioned in paragraph (5)(b) of Schedule 3 to that Act who has permission under paragraph 15 of that Schedule (as a result of qualifying for authorisation under paragraph 12 of that Schedule) to enter into a regulated mortgage contract as lender, or

(c) a Treaty firm within the meaning of Schedule 4 to that Act who has permission under paragraph 4 of that Schedule (as a result of qualifying for authorisation under paragraph 2 of that Schedule) to enter into a regulated mortgage contract as lender;]

. . . . .

"building regulations" means—

(a) building regulations made under Part I of the Building Act 1984,

(b) . . . , or

(c) any provision of a local Act, or of a byelaw made under a local Act, dealing with the construction and drainage of new buildings and the laying out and construction of new streets;

. . . . .

"cemetery" has the same meaning as in section 214 of the Local Government Act 1972;

"charity" has the same meaning as in [the Charities Act 1993];

["district valuer", in relation to any land in the district of a local housing authority, means an officer of the Commissioners of Inland Revenue appointed by them for the purpose of exercising, in relation to that district, the functions of the district valuer under this Act;]

"friendly society" means a friendly society, or a branch of a friendly society, registered under the Friendly Societies Act 1974 or earlier legislation;

"general rate fund" means—

(a) in relation to the Council of the Isles of Scilly, the general fund of that council;

(b) in relation to the Common Council of the City of London, that council's general rate;

"hostel" means a building in which is provided, for persons generally or for a class or classes of persons—

(a) residential accommodation otherwise than in separate and self-contained sets of premises, and

(b) either board or facilities for the preparation of food adequate to the needs of those persons, or both;

"protected occupancy" and "protected occupier" have the same meaning as in the Rent (Agriculture) Act 1976;

"protected tenancy" has the same meaning as in the Rent Act 1977;

["regular armed forces of the Crown" means the regular forces as defined by section 374 of the Armed Forces Act 2006;]

"the Rent Acts" means the Rent Act 1977 and the Rent (Agriculture) Act 1976;

"restricted contract" has the same meaning as in the Rent Act 1977;

"shared ownership lease" means a lease—

    (a)    granted on payment of a premium calculated by reference to a percentage of the value of the dwelling or of the cost of providing it, or

    (b)    under which the tenant (or his personal representatives) will or may be entitled to a sum calculated by reference, directly or indirectly, to the value of the dwelling;

"statutory tenancy" and "statutory tenant" mean a statutory tenancy or statutory tenant within the meaning of the Rent Act 1977 or the Rent (Agriculture) Act 1976;

"street" includes any court, alley, passage, square or row of houses, whether a thoroughfare or not;

"subsidiary" has [the meaning given by] [section 1159 of the Companies Act 2006];

[(2)    The definitions of "authorised deposit taker"[, "authorised insurer" and "authorised mortgage lender"] in subsection (1) must be read with—

    (a)    section 22 of the Financial Services and Markets Act 2000;

    (b)    any relevant order under that section; and

    (c)    Schedule 2 to that Act.]

[571]

**NOTES**

Sub-s (1): numbered as such, definitions "authorised deposit taker" and "authorised insurer" inserted and definitions "bank", "building society", "insurance company", "trustee savings bank" (all omitted) repealed by the Financial Services and Markets Act 2000 (Consequential Amendments and Repeals) Order 2001, SI 2001/3649, art 300(1)–(4); definitions "assured tenancy" and "assured agricultural occupancy" inserted by the Housing Act 1988, s 140(1), Sch 17, Pt I, para 64; figures in square brackets in definitions "authorised deposit taker" and "authorised insurer" substituted by the Housing and Regeneration Act 2008, s 316, except for the purpose of defining "approved lending institutions" in ss 36(4), 151B(5) and 156(4) of this Act, where the advance concerned was made before 7 September 2009 (see SI 2009/2096, art 3(3)); definition "authorised mortgage lender" inserted by the Housing and Regeneration Act 2008, s 307(2); in definition "building regulations" para (b) repealed by the Planning and Compensation Act 1991, s 84(6), Sch 19, Pt V, subject to the savings provisions set out in s 81(2) of that Act; in definition "charity" words in square brackets substituted by the Charities Act 1993, s 98(1), Sch 6, para 30; definition "district valuer" substituted by the References to Rating (Housing) Regulations 1990, SI 1990/434, reg 2, Schedule, para 23; definition "regular armed forces of the Crown" substituted by the Armed Forces Act 2006, s 378(1), Sch 16, para 108; definitions "standard scale" and "statutory maximum" repealed by the Statute Law (Repeals) Act 1993; in definition "subsidiary" words in first pair of square brackets substituted by the Companies Act 1989, s 144(4), Sch 18, para 40 and words in second pair of square brackets substituted by the Companies Act 2006 (Consequential Amendments, Transitional Provisions and Savings) Order 2009, SI 2009/1941, art 2(1), Sch 1, para 62(1), (6).

Sub-s (2): added by SI 2001/3649, art 300(1), (5); words in square brackets substituted by the Housing and Regeneration Act 2008, s 307(3).

**623  Minor definitions: Part XVIII**

[(1)]    In this Part—

["dwelling-house" … shall be construed in accordance with subsection (2);
… ]

"owner", in relation to premises—

    (a)    means a person (other than a mortgagee not in possession) who is for the time being entitled to dispose of the fee simple absolute in the premises, whether in possession or in reversion, and

    (b)    includes also a person holding or entitled to the rents and profits of the premises under a lease of which the unexpired term exceeds three years.

[(2)    For the purposes of this Part, "dwelling-house" includes any yard, garden, outhouses and appurtenances belonging to it or usually enjoyed with it and section 183 shall have effect to determine whether a dwelling-house is a flat.]

[572]

**NOTES**

Sub-s (1): numbered as such by virtue of, and words in square brackets substituted by, the Local Government and Housing Act 1989, s 165(1), Sch 9, Pt V, para 90; words omitted repealed by the Housing Act 2004, s 266, Sch 16.

Sub-s (2): added by the Local Government and Housing Act 1989, s 165(1), Sch 9, Pt V, para 90.

**624   Index of defined expressions: Part XVIII**

The following Table shows provisions defining or otherwise explaining expressions used in this Part (other than provisions defining or explaining an expression used in the same section):—

| | |
|---|---|
| clearance area | section 289 |
| district (of a local housing authority) | section 2(1) |
| [dwelling-house | section 623] |
| [ ... | ... ] |
| [ ... | ... ] |
| ... | ... |
| [ ... | ... ] |
| lease and let | section 621 |
| local housing authority | section 1, 2(2) |
| owner | section 623 |
| Rent Acts | section 622 |
| standard scale (in reference to the maximum fine on summary conviction) | section 622 |
| street | section 622 |
| unfit for human habitation | section 604 |

**[573]**

---

**NOTES**

   Entry "dwelling-house" inserted and entry "house" (omitted) repealed by the Local Government and Housing Act 1989, ss 165(1), 194(4), Sch 9, Pt V, para 91, Sch 12, Pt II; entries "flat", "flat in multiple occupation", "house in multiple occupation" (omitted from square brackets) inserted by the Local Government and Housing Act 1989, s 165(1), Sch 9, Pt V, para 91, and repealed by the Housing Act 2004, s 266, Sch 16.

   Note: it is thought that the entry "standard scale" should be ignored as s 622 no longer contains a reference to the standard scale.

---

*Final provisions*

**625   Short title, commencement and extent**

   (1)   This Act may be cited as the Housing Act 1985.

   (2)   This Act comes into force on 1st April 1986.

   (3)   This Act extends to England and Wales only.

**[574]**

## SCHEDULES

## SCHEDULE 1
### TENANCIES WHICH ARE NOT SECURE TENANCIES

Section 79

*Long leases*

1.   A tenancy is not a secure tenancy if it is a long tenancy.

*[Introductory tenancies*

1A.   A tenancy is not a secure tenancy if it is an introductory tenancy or a tenancy which has ceased to be an introductory tenancy—

   (a)   by virtue of section 133(3) of the Housing Act 1996 (disposal on death to non-qualifying person), or

   (b)   by virtue of the tenant, or in the case of a joint tenancy every tenant, ceasing to occupy the dwelling-house as his only or principal home.]

[1B.   A tenancy is not a secure tenancy if it is a demoted tenancy within the meaning of section 143A of the Housing Act 1996.]

*Premises occupied in connection with employment*

2.—(1)  [Subject to sub-paragraph (4B)] a tenancy is not a secure tenancy if the tenant is an employee of the landlord or of—

> a local authority,
>
> a new town corporation,
>
> [a housing action trust]
>
> an urban development corporation,
>
> ... , or
>
> the governors of an aided school,

and his contract of employment requires him to occupy the dwelling-house for the better performance of his duties.

(2)  [Subject to sub-paragraph (4B)] a tenancy is not a secure tenancy if the tenant is a member of a police force and the dwelling-house is provided for him free of rent and rates in pursuance of regulations made under [section 50 of the Police Act 1996] (general regulations as to government, administration and conditions of service of police forces).

(3)  [Subject to sub-paragraph (4B)] a tenancy is not a secure tenancy if the tenant is an employee of a [fire and rescue authority] and—

(a)  his contract of employment requires him to live in close proximity to a particular fire station, and

(b)  the dwelling-house was let to him by the authority in consequence of that requirement.

(4)  [Subject to sub-paragraph (4A) and (4B)] a tenancy is not a secure tenancy if—

(a)  within the period of three years immediately preceding the grant the conditions mentioned in sub-paragraph (1), (2) or (3) have been satisfied with respect to a tenancy of the dwelling-house, and

(b)  before the grant the landlord notified the tenant in writing of the circumstances in which this exception applies and that in its opinion the proposed tenancy would fall within this exception,

...

[(4A)  Except where the landlord is a local housing authority, a tenancy under sub-paragraph (4) shall become a secure tenancy when the periods during which the conditions mentioned in sub-paragraph (1), (2) or (3) are not satisfied with respect to the tenancy amount in aggregate to more than three years.

(4B)  Where the landlord is a local housing authority, a tenancy under sub-paragraph (1), (2), (3) or (4) shall become a secure tenancy if the authority notify the tenant that the tenancy is to be regarded as a secure tenancy.]

(5)  In this paragraph "contract of employment" means a contract of service or apprenticeship, whether express or implied and (if express) whether oral or in writing.

*Land acquired for development*

3.—(1)  A tenancy is not a secure tenancy if the dwelling-house is on land which has been acquired for development and the dwelling-house is used by the landlord, pending development of the land, as temporary housing accommodation.

(2)  In this paragraph "development" has the meaning given by [section 55 of the Town and Country Planning Act 1990] (general definition of development for purposes of that Act).

*[Accommodation for homeless persons*

4.  A tenancy granted in pursuance of any function under Part VII of the Housing Act 1996 (homelessness) is not a secure tenancy unless the local housing authority concerned have notified the tenant that the tenancy is to be regarded as a secure tenancy.]

*[Family intervention tenancies*

4ZA.—(1)  A tenancy is not a secure tenancy if it is a family intervention tenancy.

(2)  But a tenancy mentioned in sub-paragraph (1) becomes a secure tenancy if the landlord notifies the tenant that it is to be regarded as a secure tenancy.

(3)  In this paragraph "a family intervention tenancy" means, subject to sub-paragraph (4), a tenancy granted by a local housing authority in respect of a dwelling-house—

(a)  to a person ("the new tenant") against whom a possession order under section 84 in respect of another dwelling-house—

(i)  has been made, in relation to a secure tenancy, on ground 2 or 2A of Part 1 of Schedule 2;

(ii)  could, in the opinion of the authority, have been so made in relation to such a tenancy; or

     (iii)   could, in the opinion of the authority, have been so made if the person had had such a tenancy; and

  (b)   for the purposes of the provision of behaviour support services.

(4)   A tenancy is not a family intervention tenancy for the purposes of this paragraph if the local housing authority has failed to serve a notice under sub-paragraph (5) on the new tenant before the new tenant entered into the tenancy.

(5)   A notice under this sub-paragraph is a notice stating—

  (a)   the reasons for offering the tenancy to the new tenant;

  (b)   the dwelling-house in respect of which the tenancy is to be granted;

  (c)   the other main terms of the tenancy (including any requirements on the new tenant in respect of behaviour support services);

  (d)   the security of tenure available under the tenancy and any loss of security of tenure which is likely to result from the new tenant agreeing to enter into the tenancy;

  (e)   that the new tenant is not obliged to enter into the tenancy or (unless otherwise required to do so) to surrender any existing tenancy or possession of a dwelling-house;

  (f)   any likely action by the local housing authority if the new tenant does not enter into the tenancy or surrender any existing tenancy or possession of a dwelling-house.

(6)   The appropriate national authority may by regulations made by statutory instrument amend sub-paragraph (5).

(7)   A notice under sub-paragraph (5) must contain advice to the new tenant as to how the new tenant may be able to obtain assistance in relation to the notice.

(8)   The appropriate national authority may by regulations made by statutory instrument make provision about the type of advice to be provided in such notices.

(9)   Regulations under this paragraph may contain such transitional, transitory or saving provision as the appropriate national authority considers appropriate.

(10)   A statutory instrument containing (whether alone or with other provision) regulations under this paragraph which amend or repeal any of paragraphs (a) to (f) of sub-paragraph (5) may not be made—

  (a)   by the Secretary of State unless a draft of the instrument has been laid before, and approved by a resolution of, each House of Parliament; and

  (b)   by the Welsh Ministers unless a draft of the instrument has been laid before, and approved by a resolution of, the National Assembly for Wales.

(11)   Subject to this, a statutory instrument containing regulations made under this paragraph—

  (a)   by the Secretary of State is subject to annulment in pursuance of a resolution of either House of Parliament; and

  (b)   by the Welsh Ministers is subject to annulment in pursuance of a resolution of the National Assembly for Wales.

(12)   In this paragraph—

"appropriate national authority"—

     (a)   in relation to England, means the Secretary of State; and

     (b)   in relation to Wales, means the Welsh Ministers;

"behaviour support agreement" means an agreement in writing about behaviour and the provision of support services made between the new tenant and the local housing authority concerned (or between persons who include those persons);

"behaviour support services" means relevant support services to be provided by any person to—

     (a)   the new tenant; or

     (b)   any person who is to reside with the new tenant;

for the purpose of addressing the kind of behaviour which led to the new tenant falling within sub-paragraph (3)(a);

"family intervention tenancy" has the meaning given by sub-paragraph (3);

"the new tenant" has the meaning given by sub-paragraph (3)(a);

"relevant support services" means support services of a kind identified in a behaviour support agreement and designed to meet such needs of the recipient as are identified in the agreement.]

*[Accommodation for asylum-seekers*

4A.—(1)   A tenancy is not a secure tenancy if it is granted in order to provide accommodation [under section 4 or Part VI of the Immigration and Asylum Act 1999].

(2)   A tenancy mentioned in sub-paragraph (1) becomes a secure tenancy if the landlord notifies the tenant that it is to be regarded as a secure tenancy.]

*[Accommodation for persons with Temporary Protection*

4B.　A tenancy is not a secure tenancy if it is granted in order to provide accommodation under the Displaced Persons (Temporary Protection) Regulations 2005.]

*Temporary accommodation for persons taking up employment*

5.—(1)　[Subject to sub-paragraphs (1A) and (1B), a tenancy is not a secure tenancy] if—
- (a)　the person to whom the tenancy was granted was not, immediately before the grant, resident in the district in which the dwelling-house is situated,
- (b)　before the grant of the tenancy, he obtained employment, or an offer of employment, in the district or its surrounding area,
- (c)　the tenancy was granted to him for the purpose of meeting his need for temporary accommodation in the district or its surrounding area in order to work there, and of enabling him to find permanent accommodation there, and
- (d)　the landlord notified him in writing of the circumstances in which this exception applies and that in its opinion the proposed tenancy would fall within this exception;

...

[(1A)　Except where the landlord is a local housing authority, a tenancy under sub-paragraph (1) shall become a secure tenancy on the expiry of one year from the grant or on earlier notification by the landlord to the tenant that the tenancy is to be regarded as a secure tenancy.

(1B)　Where the landlord is a local housing authority, a tenancy under sub-paragraph (1) shall become a secure tenancy if at any time the authority notify the tenant that the tenancy is to be regarded as a secure tenancy.]

(2)　In this paragraph—
　"district" means district of a local housing authority; and
　"surrounding area", in relation to a district, means the area consisting of each district that adjoins it.

*Short-term arrangements*

6.　A tenancy is not a secure tenancy if—
- (a)　the dwelling-house has been leased to the landlord with vacant possession for use as temporary housing accommodation,
- (b)　the terms on which it has been leased include provision for the lessor to obtain vacant possession from the landlord on the expiry of a specified period or when required by the lessor,
- (c)　the lessor is not a body which is capable of granting secure tenancies, and
- (d)　the landlord has no interest in the dwelling-house other than under the lease in question or as a mortgagee.

*Temporary accommodation during works*

7.　A tenancy is not a secure tenancy if—
- (a)　the dwelling-house has been made available for occupation by the tenant (or a predecessor in title of his) while works are carried out on the dwelling-house which he previously occupied as his home, and
- (b)　the tenant or predecessor was not a secure tenant of that other dwelling-house at the time when he ceased to occupy it as his home.

*[Agricultural holdings etc*

8.—(1)　A tenancy is not a secure tenancy if—
- (a)　the dwelling-house is comprised in an agricultural holding and is occupied by the person responsible for the control (whether as tenant or as servant or agent of the tenant) of the farming of the holding, or
- (b)　the dwelling-house is comprised in the holding held under a farm business tenancy and is occupied by the person responsible for the control (whether as tenant or as servant or agent of the tenant) of the management of the holding.

(2)　In sub-paragraph (1) above—
- (a)　"agricultural holding" means any agricultural holding within the meaning of the Agricultural Holdings Act 1986 held under a tenancy in relation to which that Act applies, and
- (b)　"farm business tenancy", and "holding" in relation to such a tenancy, have the same meaning as in the Agricultural Tenancies Act 1995.]

*Licensed premises*

9.   A tenancy is not a secure tenancy if the dwelling-house consists of or includes [premises which, by virtue of a premises licence under the Licensing Act 2003, may be used for the supply of alcohol (within the meaning of section 14 of that Act)] for consumption on the premises.

*Student lettings*

10.—(1)   [Subject to sub-paragraphs (2A) and (2B), a tenancy of a dwelling-house is not a secure tenancy] if—

    (a)   it is granted for the purpose of enabling the tenant to attend a designated course at an educational establishment, and

    (b)   before the grant of the tenancy the landlord notified him in writing of the circumstances in which this exception applies and that in its opinion the proposed tenancy would fall within this exception;

    ...

(2)   A landlord's notice under sub-paragraph (1)(b) shall specify the educational establishment which the person concerned proposes to attend.

[(2A)   Except where the landlord is a local housing authority, a tenancy under sub-paragraph (1) shall become a secure tenancy on the expiry of the period specified in sub-paragraph (3) or on earlier notification by the landlord to the tenant that the tenancy is to be regarded as a secure tenancy.

(2B)   Where the landlord is a local housing authority, a tenancy under sub-paragraph (1) shall become a secure tenancy if at any time the authority notify the tenant that the tenancy is to be regarded as a secure tenancy.]

(3)   The period referred to in [sub-paragraph (2A)] is—

    (a)   in a case where the tenant attends a designated course at the educational establishment specified in the landlord's notice, the period ending six months after the tenant ceases to attend that (or any other) designated course at that establishment;

    (b)   in any other case, the period ending six months after the grant of the tenancy.

(4)   In this paragraph—

    "designated course" means a course of any kind designated by regulations made by the Secretary of State for the purposes of this paragraph;

    "educational establishment" means a university or [institution which provides higher education or further education (or both); and for the purposes of this definition "higher education" and "further education" have the same meaning as in [the Education Act 1996]].

(5)   Regulations under sub-paragraph (4) shall be made by statutory instrument and may make different provision with respect to different cases or descriptions of case, including different provision for different areas.

*1954 Act tenancies*

11.   A tenancy is not a secure tenancy if it is one to which Part II of the Landlord and Tenant Act 1954 applies (tenancies of premises occupied for business purposes).

*Almshouses*

[12.   A licence to occupy a dwelling-house is not a secure tenancy if—

    (a)   the dwelling-house is an almshouse, and

    (b)   the licence was granted by or on behalf of a charity which—

        (i)   is authorised under its trusts to maintain the dwelling-house as an almshouse, and

        (ii)   has no power under its trusts to grant a tenancy of the dwelling-house;

and in this paragraph "almshouse" means any premises maintained as an almshouse, whether they are called an almshouse or not; and "trusts", in relation to a charity, means the provisions establishing it as a charity and regulating its purposes and administration, whether those provisions take effect by way of trust or not.]

**[575]**

---

**NOTES**

Para 1A: inserted by the Housing Act 1996, s 141(1), Sch 14, para 5.

Para 1B: inserted by the Anti-social Behaviour Act 2003, s 14(5), Sch 1, para 2(1), (4).

Para 2: words in first pair of square brackets in sub-paras (1)–(3), words in square brackets in sub-para (4), and the whole of sub-paras (4A), (4B) inserted, and words omitted from sub-para (4) repealed by the Housing Act 1996, ss 173, 227, Sch 16, para 2(1)–(4), Sch 19, Pt VII, except in relation to a tenancy granted before 1 April 1997; words omitted from sub-para (1) repealed by the Government of Wales Act 1998, s 152, Sch 18, Pt IV; words in second pair of square brackets in sub-para (1) inserted by the Housing Act 1988, s 83(1), (6)(a); words in second pair of square brackets in sub-para (2) substituted by the Police Act 1996, s 103(1), Sch 7, Pt II, para 40; words in second pair of square brackets in sub-para (3) substituted by the Fire and Rescue Services Act 2004, s 53(1), Sch 1, para 62(1), (3).

Para 3: words in square brackets substituted by the Planning (Consequential Provisions) Act 1990, s 4, Sch 2, para 71(6), subject to transitional provisions and savings in s 5 of, and Sch 3 to, that Act.

Para 4: substituted by the Housing Act 1996, s 216(3), Sch 17, para 3, subject to transitional provisions in s 216(2) of that Act.

Para 4ZA: inserted by the Housing and Regeneration Act 2008, s 297(1), (3), as from 1 January 2009 in relation to England, except in relation to any tenancy granted before that date, and as from a day to be appointed in relation to Wales.

Para 4A: inserted by the Immigration and Asylum Act 1999, s 169(1), Sch 14, para 81; words in square brackets substituted by the Immigration, Asylum and Nationality Act 2006, s 43(4)(d).

Para 4B: inserted by the Displaced Persons (Temporary Protection) Regulations 2005, SI 2005/1379, Schedule, para 4.

Para 5: words in square brackets in sub-para (1) substituted, words omitted from sub-para (1) repealed and sub-paras (1A), (1B) inserted by the Housing Act 1996, ss 173, 227, Sch 16, para 2(1), (5), (6), Sch 19, Pt VII, except in relation to a tenancy granted before 1 April 1997.

Para 8: substituted by the Agricultural Tenancies Act 1995, s 40, Schedule, para 30.

Para 9: words in square brackets substituted by the Licensing Act 2003, Sch 6, paras 102, 104.

Para 10: words in square brackets in sub-paras (1), (3) substituted, words omitted repealed and sub-paras (2A), (2B) inserted by the Housing Act 1996, ss 173, 227, Sch 16, para 2(1), (7)–(9), Sch 19, Pt VII, except in relation to a tenancy granted before 1 April 1997; in sub-para (4) words in first (outer) pair of square brackets substituted by the Education Reform Act 1988, s 237(1), Sch 12, Pt III, para 95, words in second (inner) pair of square brackets substituted by the Education Act 1996, s 582(1), Sch 37, Pt I, para 62.

Para 12: substituted by the Charities Act 1992, s 78(1), Sch 6, para 12.

Regulations: by virtue of the Housing (Consequential Provisions) Act 1985, s 2(2), the Secure Tenancies (Designated Courses) Regulations 1980, SI 1980/1407 at **[3021]**, have effect as if made under para 10.

## SCHEDULE 2
## GROUNDS FOR POSSESSION OF DWELLING-HOUSES LET UNDER SECURE TENANCIES

Section 84

## PART I
## GROUNDS ON WHICH COURT MAY ORDER POSSESSION IF IT CONSIDERS IT REASONABLE

### *Ground 1*

Rent lawfully due from the tenant has not been paid or an obligation of the tenancy has been broken or not performed.

### *[Ground 2*

The tenant or a person residing in or visiting the dwelling-house—
    (a)   has been guilty of conduct causing or likely to cause a nuisance or annoyance to a person residing, visiting or otherwise engaging in a lawful activity in the locality, or
    (b)   has been convicted of—
        (i)   using the dwelling-house or allowing it to be used for immoral or illegal purposes, or
        (ii)   an [indictable] offence committed in, or in the locality of, the dwelling-house.]

### *[Ground 2A*

The dwelling-house was occupied (whether alone or with others) by [a married couple, a couple who are civil partners of each other,] a couple living together as husband and wife [or a couple living together as if they were civil partners] and—
    (a)   one or both of the partners is a tenant of the dwelling-house,
    (b)   one partner has left because of violence or threats of violence by the other towards—
        (i)   that partner, or
        (ii)   a member of the family of that partner who was residing with that partner immediately before the partner left, and
    (c)   the court is satisfied that the partner who has left is unlikely to return.]

### *Ground 3*

The condition of the dwelling-house or of any of the common parts has deteriorated owing to acts of waste by, or the neglect or default of, the tenant or a person residing in the dwelling-house and, in the case of an act of waste by, or the neglect or default of, a person lodging with the tenant or a sub-tenant of his, the tenant has not taken such steps as he ought reasonably to have taken for the removal of the lodger or sub-tenant.

### *Ground 4*

The condition of furniture provided by the landlord for use under the tenancy, or for use in the common parts, has deteriorated owing to ill-treatment by the tenant or a person residing in the dwelling-house and, in the case of ill-treatment by a person lodging with the tenant or a sub-tenant of his, the tenant has not taken such steps as he ought reasonably to have taken for the removal of the lodger or sub-tenant.

### Ground 5

The tenant is the person, or one of the persons, to whom the tenancy was granted and the landlord was induced to grant the tenancy by a false statement made knowingly or recklessly [by—

    (a)    the tenant, or

    (b)    a person acting at the tenant's instigation].

### Ground 6

The tenancy was assigned to the tenant, or to a predecessor in title of his who is a member of his family and is residing in the dwelling-house, by an assignment made by virtue of section 92 (assignments by way of exchange) and a premium was paid either in connection with that assignment or the assignment which the tenant or predecessor himself made by virtue of that section.

In this paragraph "premium" means any fine or other like sum and any other pecuniary consideration in addition to rent.

### Ground 7

The dwelling-house forms part of, or is within the curtilage of, a building which, or so much of it as is held by the landlord, is held mainly for purposes other than housing purposes and consists mainly of accommodation other than housing accommodation, and—

    (a)    the dwelling-house was let to the tenant or a predecessor in title of his in consequence of the tenant or predecessor being in the employment of the landlord, or of—

        a local authority,

        a [development] corporation,

        [a housing action trust]

        an urban development corporation,

        … , or

        the governors of an aided school, and

    (b)    the tenant or a person residing in the dwelling-house has been guilty of conduct such that, having regard to the purpose for which the building is used, it would not be right for him to continue in occupation of the dwelling-house.

### Ground 8

The dwelling-house was made available for occupation by the tenant (or a predecessor in title of his) while works were carried out on the dwelling-house which he previously occupied as his only or principal home and—

    (a)    the tenant (or predecessor) was a secure tenant of the other dwelling-house at the time when he ceased to occupy it as his home,

    (b)    the tenant (or predecessor) accepted the tenancy of the dwelling-house of which possession is sought on the understanding that he would give up occupation when, on completion of the works, the other dwelling-house was again available for occupation by him under a secure tenancy, and

    (c)    the works have been completed and the other dwelling-house is so available.

**[576]**

---

**NOTES**

Ground 2: substituted by the Housing Act 1996, s 144, except in relation to a case where a notice under s 83 at **[420]**, was served before 12 February 1997; word in square brackets substituted by the Serious Organised Crime and Police Act 2005, s 111, Sch 7, Pt 3, para 45.

Ground 2A: inserted by the Housing Act 1996, s 145, subject to savings as noted above; words in first pair of square brackets substituted and words in second pair of square brackets inserted by the Civil Partnership Act 2004, s 81, Sch 8, para 33.

Ground 5: words in square brackets substituted by the Housing Act 1996, s 146, subject to savings as noted above.

Ground 7: word in first pair of square brackets substituted by the Housing and Regeneration Act 2008 (Consequential Provisions) Order 2008, SI 2008/3002, art 4, Sch 1, paras 2, 29(1), (2), subject to transitional provisions and savings in art 5, Sch 2 thereto; words in second pair of square brackets inserted by the Housing Act 1988, s 83(1), (6)(b); words omitted repealed by the Government of Wales Act 1998, s 152, Sch 18, Pt IV.

## PART II
## GROUNDS ON WHICH THE COURT MAY ORDER POSSESSION IF SUITABLE ALTERNATIVE ACCOMMODATION IS AVAILABLE

### Ground 9

The dwelling-house is overcrowded, within the meaning of Part X, in such circumstances as to render the occupier guilty of an offence.

### Ground 10

The landlord intends, within a reasonable time of obtaining possession of the dwelling-house—
  (a)  to demolish or reconstruct the building or part of the building comprising the dwelling-house, or
  (b)  to carry out work on that building or on land let together with, and thus treated as part of, the dwelling-house,
and cannot reasonably do so without obtaining possession of the dwelling-house.

### [Ground 10A

The dwelling-house is in an area which is the subject of a redevelopment scheme approved by the Secretary of State or the [Housing Corporation or Scottish Homes] in accordance with Part V of this Schedule and the landlord intends within a reasonable time of obtaining possession to dispose of the dwelling-house in accordance with the scheme.

or

Part of the dwelling-house is in such an area and the landlord intends within a reasonable time of obtaining possession to dispose of that part in accordance with the scheme and for that purpose reasonably requires possession of the dwelling-house.]

### Ground 11

The landlord is a charity and the tenant's continued occupation of the dwelling-house would conflict with the objects of the charity.

[577]

**NOTES**

Ground 10A: inserted by the Housing and Planning Act 1986, s 9(1); words in square brackets substituted by the Government of Wales Act 1998, s 140, Sch 16, para 21(1), (2).

Modification: in Ground 10A the reference to the Housing Corporation shall be treated as a reference to the Regulator of Social Housing; see the Transfer of Housing Corporation Functions (Modifications and Transitional Provisions) Order 2008, SI 2008/2839, arts 1(2), 2, 3, 6, Schedule.

## PART III
## GROUNDS ON WHICH THE COURT MAY ORDER POSSESSION IF IT CONSIDERS IT REASONABLE AND SUITABLE ALTERNATIVE ACCOMMODATION IS AVAILABLE

### Ground 12

The dwelling-house forms part of, or is within the curtilage of, a building which, or so much of it as is held by the landlord, is held mainly for purposes other than housing purposes and consists mainly of accommodation other than housing accommodation, or is situated in a cemetery, and—
  (a)  the dwelling-house was let to the tenant or a predecessor in title of his in consequence of the tenant or predecessor being in the employment of the landlord or of—
      a local authority,
      a [development] corporation,
      [a housing action trust]
      an urban development corporation,
      … , or
      the governors of an aided school,
      and that employment has ceased, and
  (b)  the landlord reasonably requires the dwelling-house for occupation as a residence for some person either engaged in the employment of the landlord, or of such a body, or with whom a contract for such employment has been entered into conditional on housing being provided.

### Ground 13

The dwelling-house has features which are substantially different from those of ordinary dwelling-houses and which are designed to make it suitable for occupation by a physically disabled person who requires accommodation of a kind provided by the dwelling-house and—
  (a)  there is no longer such a person residing in the dwelling-house, and

(b)   the landlord requires it for occupation (whether alone or with members of his family) by such a person.

### Ground 14

The landlord is a housing association or housing trust which lets dwelling-houses only for occupation (whether alone or with others) by persons whose circumstances (other than merely financial circumstances) make it especially difficult for them to satisfy their need for housing, and—

(a)   either there is no longer such a person residing in the dwelling-house or the tenant has received from a local housing authority an offer of accommodation in premises which are to be let as a separate dwelling under a secure tenancy, and

(b)   the landlord requires the dwelling-house for occupation (whether alone or with members of his family) by such a person.

### Ground 15

The dwelling-house is one of a group of dwelling-houses which it is the practice of the landlord to let for occupation by persons with special needs and—

(a)   a social service or special facility is provided in close proximity to the group of dwelling-houses in order to assist persons with those special needs,

(b)   there is no longer a person with those special needs residing in the dwelling-house, and

(c)   the landlord requires the dwelling-house for occupation (whether alone or with members of his family) by a person who has those special needs.

### Ground 16

The accommodation afforded by the dwelling-house is more extensive than is reasonably required by the tenant and—

(a)   the tenancy vested in the tenant by virtue of section 89 (succession to periodic tenancy), the tenant being qualified to succeed by virtue of section 87(b) (members of family other than spouse), and

(b)   notice of the proceedings for possession was served under section 83 [(or, where no such notice was served, the proceedings for possession were begun)] more than six months but less than twelve months after the date of the previous tenant's death.

The matters to be taken into account by the court in determining whether it is reasonable to make an order on this ground include—

(a)   the age of the tenant,

(b)   the period during which the tenant has occupied the dwelling-house as his only or principal home, and

(c)   any financial or other support given by the tenant to the previous tenant.

**[578]**

**NOTES**

   Ground 12: word in first pair of square brackets substituted by the Housing and Regeneration Act 2008 (Consequential Provisions) Order 2008, SI 2008/3002, art 4, Sch 1, paras 2, 29(1), (3), subject to transitional provisions and savings in art 5, Sch 2 thereto; words in second pair of square brackets inserted by the Housing Act 1988, s 83(1), (6)(b); words omitted repealed by the Government of Wales Act 1998, s 152, Sch 18, Pt IV.

   Ground 16: words in square brackets inserted by the Housing Act 1996, s 147(3), except in relation to notices served under s 83 at **[420]**, before 12 February 1997.

### PART IV
### SUITABILITY OF ACCOMMODATION

1.   For the purposes of section 84(2)(b) and (c) (case in which court is not to make an order for possession unless satisfied that suitable accommodation will be available) accommodation is suitable if it consists of premises—

(a)   which are to be let as a separate dwelling under a secure tenancy, or

(b)   which are to be let as a separate dwelling under a protected tenancy, not being a tenancy under which the landlord might recover possession under one of the Cases in Part II of Schedule 15 to the Rent Act 1977 (cases where court must order possession), [or

(c)   which are to be let as a separate dwelling under an assured tenancy which is neither an assured shorthold tenancy, within the meaning of Part I of the Housing Act 1988, nor a tenancy under which the landlord might recover possession under any of Grounds 1 to 5 in Schedule 2 to that Act]

and, in the opinion of the court, the accommodation is reasonably suitable to the needs of the tenant and his family.

2.   In determining whether the accommodation is reasonably suitable to the needs of the tenant and his family, regard shall be had to—

(a)   the nature of the accommodation which it is the practice of the landlord to allocate to persons with similar needs;

PART I STATUTES

   (b)   the distance of the accommodation available from the place of work or education of the tenant and of any members of his family;

   (c)   its distance from the home of any member of the tenant's family if proximity to it is essential to that member's or the tenant's well-being;

   (d)   the needs (as regards extent of accommodation) and means of the tenant and his family;

   (e)   the terms on which the accommodation is available and the terms of the secure tenancy;

   (f)   if furniture was provided by the landlord for use under the secure tenancy, whether furniture is to be provided for use in the other accommodation, and if so the nature of the furniture to be provided.

3.　Where possession of a dwelling-house is sought on ground 9 (overcrowding such as to render occupier guilty of offence), other accommodation may be reasonably suitable to the needs of the tenant and his family notwithstanding that the permitted number of persons for that accommodation, as defined in section 326(3) (overcrowding: the space standard), is less than the number of persons living in the dwelling-house of which possession is sought.

4.—(1)　A certificate of the appropriate local housing authority that they will provide suitable accommodation for the tenant by a date specified in the certificate is conclusive evidence that suitable accommodation will be available for him by that date.

(2)　The appropriate local housing authority is the authority for the district in which the dwelling-house of which possession is sought is situated.

(3)　This paragraph does not apply where the landlord is a local housing authority.

[579]

**NOTES**

Para 1: words in square brackets inserted by the Housing Act 1988, s 140(1), Sch 17, Pt I, para 65.

### [PART V
### APPROVAL OF REDEVELOPMENT SCHEMES FOR PURPOSES OF GROUND 10A

1.—(1)　The Secretary of State may, on the application of the landlord, approve for the purposes of ground 10A in Part II of this Schedule a scheme for the disposal and redevelopment of an area of land consisting of or including the whole or part of one or more dwelling-houses.

(2)　For this purpose—

   (a)   "disposal" means a disposal of any interest in the land (including the grant of an option), and

   (b)   "redevelopment" means the demolition or reconstruction of buildings or the carrying out of other works to buildings or land;

and it is immaterial whether the disposal is to precede or follow the redevelopment.

(3)　The Secretary of State may on the application of the landlord approve a variation of a scheme previously approved by him and may, in particular, approve a variation adding land to the area subject to the scheme.

2.—(1)　Where a landlord proposes to apply to the Secretary of State for the approval of a scheme or variation it shall serve a notice in writing on any secure tenant of a dwelling-house affected by the proposal stating—

   (a)   the main features of the proposed scheme or, as the case may be, the scheme as proposed to be varied,

   (b)   that the landlord proposes to apply to the Secretary of State for approval of the scheme or variation, and

   (c)   the effect of such approval, by virtue of section 84 and ground 10A in Part II of this Schedule, in relation to proceedings for possession of the dwelling-house,

and informing the tenant that he may, within such period as the landlord may allow (which shall be at least 28 days from service of the notice), make representations to the landlord about the proposal.

(2)　The landlord shall not apply to the Secretary of State until it has considered any representations made to it within that period.

(3)　In the case of a landlord to which section 105 applies (consultation on matters of housing management) the provisions of this paragraph apply in place of the provisions of that section in relation to the approval or variation of a redevelopment scheme.

3.—(1)　In considering whether to give his approval to a scheme or variation the Secretary of State shall take into account, in particular—

   (a)   the effect of the scheme on the extent and character of housing accommodation in the neighbourhood,

   (b)   over what period of time it is proposed that the disposal and redevelopment will take place in accordance with the scheme, and

   (c)   to what extent the scheme includes provision for housing provided under the scheme to be sold or let to existing tenants or persons nominated by the landlord;

and he shall take into account any representations made to him and, so far as they are brought to his notice, any representations made to the landlord.

(2)   The landlord shall give to the Secretary of State such information as to the representations made to it, and other relevant matters, as the Secretary of State may require.

4.   The Secretary of State shall not approve a scheme or variation so as to include in the area subject to the scheme—
   (a)   part only of one or more dwelling-houses, or
   (b)   one or more dwelling-houses not themselves affected by the works involved in redevelopment but which are proposed to be disposed of along with other land which is so affected,
unless he is satisfied that the inclusion is justified in the circumstances.

5.—(1)   Approval may be given subject to conditions and may be expressed to expire after a specified period.

(2)   The Secretary of State, on the application of the landlord or otherwise, may vary an approval so as to—
   (a)   add, remove or vary conditions to which the approval is subject; or
   (b)   extend or restrict the period after which the approval is to expire.

(3)   Where approval is given subject to conditions, the landlord may serve a notice under section 83 (notice of proceedings for possession) specifying ground 10A notwithstanding that the conditions are not yet fulfilled but the court shall not make an order for possession on that ground unless satisfied that they are or will be fulfilled.

6.   Where the landlord is a [social landlord registered in the register maintained by the Housing Corporation under section 1 of the Housing Act 1996 or a housing association registered in the register maintained by Scottish Homes under section 3 of the Housing Associations Act 1985, the Housing Corporation, or Scottish Homes, (and not the Secretary of State)] has the functions conferred by this Part of this Schedule.

7.   In this Part of this Schedule references to the landlord of a dwelling-house include any authority or body within section 80 (the landlord condition for secure tenancies) having an interest of any description in the dwelling-house.]

**[580]**

**NOTES**
   Added by the Housing and Planning Act 1986, s 9(2).
   Para 6: words in square brackets substituted by the Government of Wales Act 1998, s 140, Sch 16, para 21(1), (3).
   Modification: in para 6 the reference to the Housing Corporation shall be treated as a reference to the Regulator of Social Housing; see the Transfer of Housing Corporation Functions (Modifications and Transitional Provisions) Order 2008, SI 2008/2839, arts 1(2), 2, 3, 6, Schedule.

## SCHEDULE 3
GROUNDS FOR WITHHOLDING CONSENT TO ASSIGNMENT BY WAY OF EXCHANGE
Section 92

### [Ground 1]

The tenant or the proposed assignee is subject to an order of the court for the possession of the dwelling-house of which he is the secure tenant.]

### Ground 2

Proceedings have been begun for possession of the dwelling-house of which the tenant or the proposed assignee is the secure tenant on one or more of grounds 1 to 6 in Part I of Schedule 2 (grounds on which possession may be ordered despite absence of suitable alternative accommodation), or there has been served on the tenant or the proposed assignee a notice under section 83 (notice of proceedings for possession) which specifies one or more of those grounds and is still in force.

### [Ground 2A

Either—
   (a)   a relevant order or suspended Ground 2 or 14 possession order is in force, or
   (b)   an application is pending before any court for a relevant order, a demotion order or a Ground 2 or 14 possession order to be made,
in respect of the tenant or the proposed assignee or a person who is residing with either of them.

A "relevant order" means—
   an injunction under section 152 of the Housing Act 1996 (injunctions against anti-social behaviour);

an injunction to which a power of arrest is attached by virtue of section 153 of that Act (other injunctions against anti-social behaviour);

an injunction under section 153A, 153B or 153D of that Act (injunctions against anti-social behaviour on application of certain social landlords);

an anti-social behaviour order under section 1 of the Crime and Disorder Act 1998; or

an injunction to which a power of arrest is attached by virtue of section 91 of the Anti-social Behaviour Act 2003.

A "demotion order" means a demotion order under section 82A of this Act or section 6A of the Housing Act 1988.

A "Ground 2 or 14 possession order" means an order for possession under Ground 2 in Schedule 2 to this Act or Ground 14 in Schedule 2 to the Housing Act 1988.

Where the tenancy of the tenant or the proposed assignee is a joint tenancy, any reference to that person includes (where the context permits) a reference to any of the joint tenants.]

### Ground 3

The accommodation afforded by the dwelling-house is substantially more extensive than is reasonably required by the proposed assignee.

### Ground 4

The extent of the accommodation afforded by the dwelling-house is not reasonably suitable to the needs of the proposed assignee and his family.

### Ground 5

The dwelling-house—

(a) forms part of or is within the curtilage of a building which, or so much of it as is held by the landlord, is held mainly for purposes other than housing purposes and consists mainly of accommodation other than housing accommodation, or is situated in a cemetery, and

(b) was let to the tenant or a predecessor in title of his in consequence of the tenant or predecessor being in the employment of—

the landlord,

a local authority,

a [development] corporation,

[a housing action trust]

...

an urban development corporation, or

the governors of an aided school.

### Ground 6

The landlord is a charity and the proposed assignee's occupation of the dwelling-house would conflict with the objects of the charity.

### Ground 7

The dwelling-house has features which are substantially different from those of ordinary dwelling-houses and which are designed to make it suitable for occupation by a physically disabled person who requires accommodation of the kind provided by the dwelling-house and if the assignment was made there would no longer be such a person residing in the dwelling-house.

### Ground 8

The landlord is a housing association or housing trust which lets dwelling-houses only for occupation (alone or with others) by persons whose circumstances (other than merely financial circumstances) make it especially difficult for them to satisfy their need for housing and if the assignment were made there would no longer be such a person residing in the dwelling-house.

### Ground 9

The dwelling-house is one of a group of dwelling-houses which it is the practice of the landlord to let for occupation by persons with special needs and a social service or special facility is provided in close proximity to the group of dwelling-houses in order to assist persons with those special needs and if the assignment were made there would no longer be a person with those special needs residing in the dwelling-house.

### [Ground 10

The dwelling-house is the subject of a management agreement under which the manager is a housing association of which at least half the members are tenants of dwelling-houses subject to the agreement, at least half the tenants of the dwelling-houses are members of the association and the proposed assignee is not, and is not willing to become, a member of the association.]

**[581]**

**NOTES**

Ground 1: substituted by the Housing and Regeneration Act 2008, s 299, Sch 11, Pt 1, paras 1, 4, subject to transitional provisions in Sch 11, Pt 1, para 14 thereto at **[1891]**.

Ground 2A: inserted by the Housing Act 2004, s 191(1), in relation to applications for consent under section 92 of this Act which are made on or after 6 June 2005 (in relation to England) and 14 July 2005 (in relation to Wales).

Ground 5: in para (b), word in first pair of square brackets substituted by the Housing and Regeneration Act 2008 (Consequential Provisions) Order 2008, SI 2008/3002, art 4, Sch 1, paras 2, 30, subject to transitional provisions and savings in art 5, Sch 2 thereto, words in second pair square brackets inserted by the Housing Act 1988, s 83(1), (6)(e), and words omitted repealed by the Government of Wales Act 1998, s 152, Sch 18, Pt IV.

Ground 10: added by the Housing and Planning Act 1986, s 24(1)(g), Sch 5, Pt I, para 7.

## [SCHEDULE 3A
### CONSULTATION BEFORE DISPOSAL TO PRIVATE SECTOR LANDLORD
Section 106A

*Disposals to which this Schedule applies*

1.—(1)   This Schedule applies to the disposal by a local authority of an interest in land as a result of which a secure tenant [or an introductory tenant] of the authority will become the tenant of a private sector landlord.

(2)   For the purposes of this Schedule the grant of an option which if exercised would result in a secure tenant [or an introductory tenant] of a local authority becoming the tenant of a private sector landlord shall be treated as a disposal of the interest which is the subject of the option.

(3)   Where a disposal of land by a local authority is in part a disposal to which this Schedule applies, the provisions of this Schedule apply to that part as to a separate disposal.

(4)   In this paragraph "private sector landlord" means a person other than an authority or body within section 80 (the landlord condition for secure tenancies).

*Application for Secretary of State's consent*

2.—(1)   The Secretary of State shall not entertain an application for his consent to a disposal to which this Schedule applies unless the authority certify either—
    (a)    that the requirements of paragraph 3 as to consultation have been complied with, or
    (b)    that the requirements of that paragraph as to consultation have been complied with except in relation to tenants expected to have vacated the dwelling-house in question before the disposal;
and the certificate shall be accompanied by a copy of the notices given by the authority in accordance with that paragraph.

(2)   Where the certificate is in the latter form, the Secretary of State shall not determine the application until the authority certify as regards the tenants not originally consulted—
    (a)    that they have vacated the dwelling-house in question, or
    (b)    that the requirements of paragraph 3 as to consultation have been complied with;
and a certificate under sub-paragraph (b) shall be accompanied by a copy of the notices given by the authority in accordance with paragraph 3.

(3)   References in this Schedule to the Secretary of State's consent to a disposal are to the consent required by section 32 or 43 (general requirement of consent for disposal of houses or land held for housing purposes).

*Requirements as to consultation*

3.—(1)   The requirements as to consultation referred to above are as follows.

(2)   The authority shall serve notice in writing on the tenant informing him of—
    (a)    such details of their proposal as the authority consider appropriate, but including the identity of the person to whom the disposal is to be made,
    (b)    the likely consequences of the disposal for the tenant, and
    (c)    the effect of the provisions of this Schedule and[, in the case of a secure tenant,] of sections 171A to 171H (preservation of right to buy on disposal to private sector landlord),
and informing him that he may, within such reasonable period as may be specified in the notice, make representations to the authority.

(3)   The authority shall consider any representations made to them within that period and shall serve a further written notice on the tenant informing him—

(a)  of any significant changes in their proposal, and
(b)  that he may within such period as is specified (which must be at least 28 days after the service of the notice) communicate to the Secretary of State his objection to the proposal,

and informing him of the effect of paragraph 5 (consent to be withheld if majority of tenants are opposed).

[(4)  When a notice has been served under sub-paragraph (3) the authority shall arrange a ballot of the tenants in accordance with sub-paragraph (5) to establish whether or not the tenants wish the disposal to proceed.

(5)  The authority shall—
(a)  make arrangements for such person as they consider appropriate to conduct the ballot in such manner as that person considers appropriate; or
(b)  conduct the ballot themselves.

(6)  After the ballot has been held the authority shall serve a notice on each tenant (whether or not he voted in the ballot) informing him—
(a)  of the ballot result; and
(b)  if the authority intend to proceed with the disposal, that he may within 28 days after the service of the notice make representations to the Secretary of State or (as the case may be) the Welsh Ministers.]

*Power to require further consultation*

4.  The Secretary of State may require the authority to carry out such further consultation with their tenants, and to give him such information as to the results of that consultation, as he may direct.

*Consent to be withheld if majority of tenants are opposed*

5.—(1)  The Secretary of State shall not give his consent if [the result of a ballot arranged under paragraph 3(4) shows] that a majority of the tenants of the dwelling-houses to which the application relates [who voted in the ballot] do not wish the disposal to proceed; but this does not affect his general discretion to refuse consent on grounds relating to whether a disposal has the support of the tenants or on any other ground.

(2)  In making his decision the Secretary of State may have regard to any information available to him; and the local authority shall give him such information as to the representations made to them by tenants and others, and other relevant matters, as he may require.

*[Guidance*

5A.—(1)  The appropriate person must give guidance to local authorities about complying with the requirements of paragraph 3 as to consultation.

(2)  The appropriate person must publish guidance given under this paragraph as soon as reasonably practicable after giving it.

(3)  Local authorities must, in complying with the requirements of paragraph 3 as to consultation, have regard to the guidance for the time being in force under this paragraph.

(4)  The appropriate person may revoke guidance given under this paragraph.

(5)  References in this paragraph to giving guidance include references to giving guidance by varying existing guidance.

(6)  In this paragraph "the appropriate person" means—
(a)  in relation to England, the Secretary of State, and
(b)  in relation to Wales, the Welsh Ministers.]

*Protection of purchasers*

6.  The Secretary of State's consent to a disposal is not invalidated by a failure on his part or that of the local authority to comply with the requirements of this Schedule.]

**[582]**

**NOTES**
Inserted by the Housing and Planning Act 1986, s 6(2), (3), Sch 1, in relation to disposals after 11 March 1988.
Para 1: words in square brackets inserted by the Housing Act 1996 (Consequential Amendments) Order 1997, SI 1997/74, art 2, Schedule, para 3(a), (l)(i).
Para 3: words in square brackets in sub-para (2) inserted by the Housing Act 1996 (Consequential Amendments) Order 1997, SI 1997/74, art 2, Schedule, para 3(a), (l)(ii); sub-paras (4)–(6) inserted by the Housing and Regeneration Act 2008, s 294(1), (2), (5), (6), except in relation to consultations begun before 22 September 2008.

Para 5: words in first pair of square brackets substituted and words in second pair of square brackets inserted by the Housing and Regeneration Act 2008, s 294(1), (3), (5), (6), except in relation to consultations begun before 22 September 2008.

Para 5A: inserted by the Housing and Regeneration Act 2008, s 294(1), (4)–(6), except in relation to consultations begun before 22 September 2008.

PART 1<br>STATUTES

## SCHEDULE 4
### QUALIFYING PERIOD FOR RIGHT TO BUY AND DISCOUNT
Sections 119 and 129

*Introductory*

1.    The period to be taken into account—
     (a)    for the purposes of section 119 (qualification for right to buy), and
     (b)    for the purposes of section 129 (discount).

is the period qualifying, or the aggregate of the periods qualifying, under the following provisions of this Schedule.

*Periods occupying accommodation subject to public sector tenancy*

2.    A period qualifies under this paragraph if it is a period during which, before the relevant time—
     (a)    the secure tenant, or
     (b)    his spouse [or civil partner] (if they are living together at the relevant time), or
     (c)    a deceased spouse[, or deceased civil partner,] of his (if they were living together at the time of the death),

was a public sector tenant or was the spouse [or civil partner] of a public sector tenant and occupied as his only or principal home the dwelling-house of which the spouse [or civil partner] was such a tenant.

3.    For the purposes of paragraph 2 a person who, as a joint tenant under a public sector tenancy, occupied a dwelling-house as his only or principal home shall be treated as having been the public sector tenant under that tenancy.

4.—(1)    This paragraph applies where the public sector tenant of a dwelling-house died or otherwise ceased to be a public sector tenant of the dwelling-house, and thereupon a child of his who occupied the dwelling-house as his only or principal home (the "new tenant") became the public sector tenant of the dwelling-house (whether under the same or under another public sector tenancy).

     (2)    A period during which the new tenant, since reaching the age of 16, occupied as his only or principal home a dwelling-house of which a parent of his was the public sector tenant or one of joint tenants under a public sector tenancy, being either—
     (a)    the period at the end of which he became the public sector tenant, or
     (b)    an earlier period ending two years or less before the period mentioned in paragraph (a) or before another period within this paragraph,

shall be treated for the purposes of paragraph 2 as a period during which he was a public sector tenant.

     (3)    For the purposes of this paragraph two persons shall be treated as parent and child if they would be so treated under section 186(2) (members of a person's family: relationships other than those of the whole blood).

*Periods occupying forces accommodation*

5.    A period qualifies under this paragraph if it is a period during which, before the relevant time—
     (a)    the secure tenant, or
     (b)    his spouse [or civil partner] (if they are living together at the relevant time), or
     (c)    a deceased spouse[, or deceased civil partner,] of his (if they were living together at the time of the death),

occupied accommodation provided for him as a member of the regular armed forces of the Crown or was the spouse [or civil partner] of a person occupying accommodation so provided and also occupied that accommodation.

*[Periods during which right to buy is preserved*

5A.    A period qualifies under this paragraph if it is a period during which, before the relevant time—
     (a)    the [qualifying person], or
     (b)    his spouse [or civil partner] (if they are living together at the relevant time), or
     (c)    a deceased spouse[, or deceased civil partner,] of his (if they were living together at the time of the death),

was a qualifying person for the purposes of the preserved right to buy or was the spouse [or civil partner] of such a person and occupied the qualifying dwelling-house as his only or principal home.]

*Meaning of "public sector tenant"*

6.—(1)   In this Schedule a "public sector tenant" means a tenant under a public sector tenancy.

(2)   For the purposes of this Schedule, a tenancy, other than a long tenancy, under which a dwelling-house was let as a separate dwelling was a public sector tenancy at any time when the conditions described below as the landlord condition and the tenant condition were satisfied.

(3)   The provisions of this Schedule apply in relation to a licence to occupy a dwelling-house (whether or not granted for a consideration) as they apply in relation to a tenancy.

(4)   Sub-paragraph (3) does not apply to a licence granted as a temporary expedient to a person who entered the dwelling-house or any other land as a trespasser (whether or not, before the grant of that licence, another licence to occupy that or another dwelling-house had been granted to him).

*The landlord condition*

7.—(1)   The landlord condition is, subject to [paragraphs 7A and 7B and] any order under paragraph 8, that the interest of the landlord belonged to, or to a predecessor of—

a local authority,
a [development] corporation,
[a housing action trust]
the Development Board for Rural Wales,
an urban development corporation,
[the Commission for the New Towns,]
the [Housing Corporation or Housing for Wales],
a [registered social landlord] which is not a co-operative housing association,
[the Secretary of State where that interest belonged to him as the result of the exercise by him of functions under Part III of the Housing Associations Act 1985]
… ,

or to, or to a predecessor of, an authority or other body falling within sub-paragraph (2) or (3) (corresponding authorities and bodies in Scotland and Northern Ireland).

(2)   The corresponding authorities and bodies in Scotland are—
a [council constituted under section 2 of the Local Government etc (Scotland) Act 1994],
a joint board or joint committee of such a council, the common good of such a council or a trust under its control,
a development corporation established by an order made or having effect as if made under the New Towns (Scotland) Act 1968,
[Scottish Homes],
a housing association which falls within [section 61(2)(a)(vi) of the Housing (Scotland) Act 1987] but is not a registered society within the meaning of section [45] of that Act, and
…

(3)   The corresponding authorities and bodies in Northern Ireland are—
a district council within the meaning of the Local Government Act (Northern Ireland) 1972, the Northern Ireland Housing Executive, and
a registered housing association within the meaning of Chapter II of Part II of the Housing (Northern Ireland) Order 1983.

[7A.—(1)   The landlord condition shall be treated as having been satisfied in the case of a dwelling-house comprised in a housing co-operative agreement made—
   (a)   in England and Wales, by a local housing authority, new town corporation or the Development Board for Rural Wales, or
   (b)   in Scotland, by [a local housing authority],
if the interest of the landlord belonged to the housing co-operative.

(2)   In sub-paragraph (1) "housing co-operative agreement" and "housing co-operative"—
   (a)   as regards England and Wales have the same meaning as in section 27B (agreements with housing co-operatives under superseded provisions), and
   (b)   *(applies to Scotland only).*]

[7B.   The landlord condition shall be treated as having been satisfied in the case of a dwelling-house let under a tenancy falling within section 80(2A) to (2E) at any time if, at that time, the interest of the landlord belonged to—
   (a)   the Homes and Communities Agency, or
   (b)   the Welsh Ministers.]

8.—(1)   The landlord condition shall also be treated as having been satisfied, in such circumstances as may be prescribed for the purposes of this paragraph by order of the Secretary of State, if the interest of the landlord belonged to a person who is so prescribed.

(2)   An order under this paragraph—
   (a)   may make different provision with respect to different cases or descriptions of case, including different provision for different areas, and

PART I
STATUTES

(b)   shall be made by statutory instrument which shall be subject to annulment in pursuance of a resolution of either House of Parliament.

### The tenant condition

9.   The tenant condition is that the tenant was an individual and occupied the dwelling-house as his only or principal home; or, where the tenancy was a joint tenancy, that each of the joint tenants was an individual and at least one of them occupied the dwelling-house as his only or principal home.

[9A.   The tenant condition is not met during any period when a tenancy is a demoted tenancy by virtue of section 20B of the Housing Act 1988 or section 143A of the Housing Act 1996.]

### Application to certain housing association tenancies

10.   For the purpose of determining whether at any time a tenant of a housing association was a public sector tenant and his tenancy a public sector tenancy, the association shall be deemed to have been registered at that time, under [Part I of the Housing Act 1996 or Part I of the Housing Associations Act 1985 or under] the corresponding Northern Ireland legislation, if it was so registered at any later time.

**[583]**

---

**NOTES**

Paras 2, 5: words in square brackets inserted by the Civil Partnership Act 2004, s 81, Sch 8, para 34.

Para 5A: inserted, together with the preceding cross-heading, by the Housing and Planning Act 1986, s 24(2), Sch 5, Pt II, para 40(1), (2), except in a case where a notice under s 122(1) at **[468]** was served before 17 August 1992; words in first pair of square brackets substituted by the Housing (Preservation of Right to Buy) (Amendment) Regulations 1992, SI 1992/1709, reg 2; words in second, third and fourth pairs of square brackets inserted by the Civil Partnership Act 2004, s 81, Sch 8, para 34.

Para 7: in sub-para (1), words in first and second pairs of square brackets substituted and words in fourth pair of square brackets inserted by the Housing and Regeneration Act 2008 (Consequential Provisions) Order 2008, SI 2008/3002, art 4, Sch 1, paras 2, 31(1), (2), subject to transitional provisions and savings in art 5, Sch 2 thereto, words in third pair of square brackets inserted by the Housing Act 1988, s 83(7), words in fifth pair of square brackets substituted by the Government of Wales Act 1998, s 140, Sch 16, para 22, words in sixth pair of square brackets substituted by the Housing Act 1996 (Consequential Provisions) Order 1996, SI 1996/2325, art 5, Sch 2, para 14(1), (32), words in seventh pair of square brackets inserted by the Government of Wales Act 1998 (Housing) (Amendments) Order 1999, SI 1999/61, art 2, Schedule, para 2; words omitted from sub-paras (1), (2) repealed by the Housing and Planning Act 1986, s 24(3), Sch 12, Pt I; in sub-para (2), words in first pair of square brackets substituted by the Local Government etc (Scotland) Act 1994, s 180(1), Sch 13, para 142(1), (3); words in second pair of square brackets substituted by the Housing (Scotland) Act 1988, ss 1, 3(3), Sch 2, para 1; words in third and fourth pairs of square brackets substituted by the Housing (Scotland) Act 1987, s 339(2), Sch 23, para 30(4).

Para 7A: inserted by the Housing and Planning Act 1986, s 24(2), Sch 5, Pt II, para 40(1), (4), except in a case where a notice under s 122(1) at **[468]**, was served before 17 August 1992; words in square brackets substituted by the Local Government etc (Scotland) Act 1994, s 180(1), Sch 13, para 142(1), (3).

Para 7B: inserted by SI 2008/3002, art 4, Sch 1, paras 2, 31(1), (3), subject to transitional provisions and savings in art 5, Sch 2 thereto.

Para 9A: inserted by the Anti-social Behaviour Act 2003, s 14(5), Sch 1, para 2(1), (5).

Para 10: words in square brackets substituted by SI 1996/2325, art 5, Sch 2, para 14(1), (32).

Modification: in para 7(1), the reference to the Housing Corporation shall be treated as a reference to the Regulator of Social Housing; see the Transfer of Housing Corporation Functions (Modifications and Transitional Provisions) Order 2008, SI 2008/2839, arts 1(2), 2, 3, 6, Schedule.

Orders: the Housing (Right to Buy) (Prescribed Persons) Order 1992, SI 1992/1703.

---

## SCHEDULE 5
## EXCEPTIONS TO THE RIGHT TO BUY

Section 120

### Charities

1.   The right to buy does not arise if the landlord is a housing trust or a housing association and is a charity.

### Certain housing associations

2.   The right to buy does not arise if the landlord is a co-operative housing association.

3.   The right to buy does not arise if the landlord is a housing association which at no time received a grant under—

   any enactment mentioned in paragraph 2 of Schedule 1 to the Housing Associations Act 1985 (grants under enactments superseded by the Housing Act 1974),
   section 31 of the Housing Act 1974 (management grants),
   section 41 of the Housing Associations Act 1985 (housing association grants),
   section 54 of that Act (revenue deficit grants),
   section 55 of that Act (hostel deficit grants), ...
   [section 58] of that Act (grants by local authorities)

[section 50 of the Housing Act 1988 (housing association grants), ...
section 51 of that Act (revenue deficit grants)][,
section 18 of the Housing Act 1996 (social housing grants)][, or
section 22 of [that Act] (grants by local authorities for registered social landlords)][, or
section 19 of the Housing and Regeneration Act 2008 (financial assistance) which was a grant
    made on condition that the housing association provides social housing (and "provides
    social housing" has the same meaning as in Part 1 of that Act).]

*Landlord with insufficient interest in the property*

4.   The right to buy does not arise unless the landlord owns the freehold or has an interest sufficient
to grant a lease in pursuance of this Part for—
    (a)   where the dwelling-house is a house, a term exceeding 21 years, or
    (b)   where the dwelling-house is a flat, a term of not less than 50 years,
commencing, in either case, with the date on which the tenant's notice claiming to exercise the right
to buy is served.

*Dwelling-houses let in connection with employment*

5.—(1)   The right to buy does not arise if the dwelling-house—
    (a)   forms part of, or is within the curtilage of, a building which, or so much of it as is held
        by the landlord, is held mainly for purposes other than housing purposes and consists
        mainly of accommodation other than housing accommodation, or is situated in a
        cemetery, and
    (b)   was let to the tenant or a predecessor in title of his in consequence of the tenant or
        predecessor being in the employment of the landlord or of—
        a local authority,
        a [development] corporation,
        [a housing action trust]
        ...
        an urban development corporation, or
        the governors of an aided school.

    (2)   In sub-paragraph (1)(a) "housing purposes" means the purposes for which dwelling-houses
are held by local housing authorities under Part II (provision of housing) or purposes corresponding
to those purposes.

*Certain dwelling-houses for the disabled*

6.   ...

7.   The right to buy does not arise if the dwelling-house has features which are substantially
different from those of ordinary dwelling-houses and are designed to make it suitable for occupation
by physically disabled persons, and—
    (a)   it is one of a group of dwelling-houses which it is the practice of the landlord to let for
        occupation by physically disabled persons, and
    (b)   a social service or special facilities are provided in close proximity to the group of
        dwelling-houses wholly or partly for the purpose of assisting those persons.

8.   ...

9.—(1)   The right to buy does not arise if—
    (a)   the dwelling-house is one of a group of dwelling-houses which it is the practice of the
        landlord to let for occupation by persons who are suffering or have suffered from a
        mental disorder, and
    (b)   a social service or special facilities are provided wholly or partly for the purpose of
        assisting those persons.

    (2)   In sub-paragraph (1)(a) "mental disorder" has the same meaning as in the Mental Health
Act 1983.

*Certain dwelling-houses for persons of pensionable age*

10.—(1)   The right to buy does not arise if the dwelling-house is one of a group of dwelling-
houses—
    (a)   which are particularly suitable, having regard to their location, size, design, heating
        systems and other features, for occupation by [elderly persons], and
    (b)   which it is the practice of the landlord to let for occupation by [persons aged 60 or
        more], or for occupation by such persons and physically disabled persons,
and special facilities such as are mentioned in sub-paragraph (2) are provided wholly or mainly for
the purposes of assisting those persons.

    (2)   The facilities referred to above are facilities which consist of or include—
    (a)   the services of a resident warden, or

(b)    the services of a non-resident warden, a system for calling him and the use of a common room in close proximity to the group of dwelling-houses.

[11.—(1)    The right to buy does not arise if the dwelling-house—

    (a)    is particularly suitable, having regard to its location, size, design, heating system and other features, for occupation by elderly persons, and

    (b)    was let to the tenant or a predecessor in title of his for occupation by a person who was aged 60 or more (whether the tenant or predecessor or another person).

(2)    In determining whether a dwelling is particularly suitable, no regard shall be had to the presence of any feature provided by the tenant or a predecessor in title of his.

(3)    Notwithstanding anything in section 181 (jurisdiction of county court), any question arising under this paragraph shall be determined as follows.

(4)    If an application for the purpose is made by the tenant to *the Secretary of State* before the end of the period of 56 days beginning with the service of the landlord's notice under section 124, the question shall be determined by *the Secretary of State*.

(5)    If no such application is so made, the question shall be deemed to have been determined in favour of the landlord.

[(5A)    In this paragraph "the appropriate tribunal or authority" means—

    (a)    in relation to England, a residential property tribunal; and

    (b)    in relation to Wales, the Secretary of State.

(5B)    [Section 231(1), (2), (3) and (5)] of the Housing Act 2004 (appeals to [Upper Tribunal]) does not apply to any decision of a residential property tribunal under this paragraph.]

(6)    This paragraph does not apply unless the dwelling-house concerned was first let before 1st January 1990.]

### Dwelling-houses held on Crown tenancies

12.—(1)    The right to buy does not arise if the dwelling-house is held by the landlord on a tenancy from the Crown, unless—

    (a)    the landlord is entitled to grant a lease in pursuance of this Part without the concurrence of the appropriate authority, or

    (b)    the appropriate authority notifies the landlord that as regards any Crown interest affected the authority will give its consent to the granting of such a lease.

(2)    In this paragraph "tenancy from the Crown" means a tenancy of land in which there is a Crown interest superior to the tenancy, and "Crown interest" and "appropriate authority" mean respectively—

    (a)    an interest comprised in the Crown Estate, and the Crown Estate Commissioners or other government department having the management of the land in question;

    (b)    an interest belonging to Her Majesty in right of the Duchy of Lancaster, and the Chancellor of the Duchy;

    (c)    an interest belonging to the Duchy of Cornwall, and such person as the Duke of Cornwall or the possessor for the time being of the Duchy appoints;

    (d)    any other interest belonging to a government department or held on behalf of Her Majesty for the purposes of a government department, and that department.

(3)    Section 179(1) (which renders ineffective certain provisions restricting the grant of leases under this Part) shall be disregarded for the purposes of sub-paragraph (1)(a).

### [Dwelling-house due to be demolished within 24 months

13.—(1)    The right to buy does not arise if a final demolition notice is in force in respect of the dwelling-house.

(2)    A "final demolition notice" is a notice—

    (a)    stating that the landlord intends to demolish the dwelling-house or (as the case may be) the building containing it ("the relevant premises"),

    (b)    setting out the reasons why the landlord intends to demolish the relevant premises,

    (c)    specifying—

        (i)    the date by which he intends to demolish those premises ("the proposed demolition date"), and

        (ii)    the date when the notice will cease to be in force (unless extended under paragraph 15),

    (d)    stating that one of conditions A to C in paragraph 14 is satisfied in relation to the notice (specifying the condition concerned), and

    (e)    stating that the right to buy does not arise in respect of the dwelling-house while the notice is in force.

(3)   If, at the time when the notice is served, there is an existing claim to exercise the right to buy in respect of the dwelling-house, the notice shall (instead of complying with sub-paragraph (2)(e)) state—

    (a)    that that claim ceases to be effective on the notice coming into force, but

    (b)    that section 138C confers a right to compensation in respect of certain expenditure,

and the notice shall also give details of that right to compensation and of how it may be exercised.

(4)   The proposed demolition date must fall within the period of 24 months beginning with the date of service of the notice on the tenant.

(5)   For the purposes of this paragraph a final demolition notice is in force in respect of the dwelling-house concerned during the period of 24 months mentioned in sub-paragraph (4), but this is subject to—

    (a)    compliance with the conditions in sub-paragraphs (6) and (7) (in a case to which they apply), ...,

    (b)    the provisions of paragraph 15(1) to [(7A)][, and

    (c)    the provisions of paragraph 15A].

(6)   If—

    (a)    the dwelling-house is contained in a building which contains one or more other dwelling-houses, and

    (b)    the landlord intends to demolish the whole of the building,

the landlord must have served a final demolition notice on the occupier of each of the dwelling-houses contained in it (whether addressed to him by name or just as "the occupier").

An accidental omission to serve a final demolition notice on one or more occupiers does not prevent the condition in this sub-paragraph from being satisfied.

(7)   A notice stating that the landlord intends to demolish the relevant premises must have appeared—

    (a)    in a local or other newspaper circulating in the locality in which those premises are situated (other than one published by the landlord), and

    (b)    in any newspaper published by the landlord, and

    (c)    on the landlord's website (if he has one).

(8)   The notice mentioned in sub-paragraph (7) must contain the following information—

    (a)    sufficient information to enable identification of the premises that the landlord intends to demolish;

    (b)    the reasons why the landlord intends to demolish those premises;

    (c)    the proposed demolition date;

    (d)    the date when any final demolition notice or notices relating to those premises will cease to be in force, unless extended or revoked under paragraph 15;

    (e)    that the right to buy will not arise in respect of those premises or (as the case may be) in respect of any dwelling-house contained in them;

    (f)    that there may be a right to compensation under section 138C in respect of certain expenditure incurred in respect of any existing claim.

(9)   In this paragraph and paragraphs 14 and 15 [(other than paragraph 15(7A))] any reference to the landlord, in the context of a reference to an intention or decision on his part to demolish or not to demolish any premises, or of a reference to the acquisition or transfer of any premises, includes a reference to a superior landlord.

14.—(1)   A final demolition notice may only be served for the purposes of paragraph 13 if one of conditions A to C is satisfied in relation to the notice.

(2)   Condition A is that the proposed demolition of the dwelling-house does not form part of a scheme involving the demolition of other premises.

(3)   Condition B is that—

    (a)    the proposed demolition of the dwelling-house does form part of a scheme involving the demolition of other premises, but

    (b)    none of those other premises needs to be acquired by the landlord in order for the landlord to be able to demolish them.

(4)   Condition C is that—

    (a)    the proposed demolition of the dwelling-house does form part of a scheme involving demolition of other premises, and

    (b)    one or more of those premises need to be acquired by the landlord in order for the landlord to be able to demolish them, but

    (c)    in each case arrangements for their acquisition are in place.

(5)   For the purposes of sub-paragraph (4) arrangements for the acquisition of any premises are in place if—

    (a)    an agreement under which the landlord is entitled to acquire the premises is in force, or

    (b)    a notice to treat has been given in respect of the premises under section 5 of the Compulsory Purchase Act 1965, or

PART I
STATUTES

(c)    a vesting declaration has been made in respect of the premises under section 4 of the Compulsory Purchase (Vesting Declarations) Act 1981.

(6)    In this paragraph—
"premises" means premises of any description;
"scheme" includes arrangements of any description.

15.—(1)    The Secretary of State may, on an application by the landlord, give a direction extending or further extending the period during which a final demolition notice is in force in respect of a dwelling-house.

(2)    A direction under sub-paragraph (1) may provide that any extension of that period is not to have effect unless the landlord complies with such requirements relating to the service of further notices as are specified in the direction.

(3)    A direction under sub-paragraph (1) may only be given at a time when the demolition notice is in force (whether by virtue of paragraph 13 or this paragraph).

(4)    If, while a final demolition notice is in force, the landlord decides not to demolish the dwelling-house in question, he must, as soon as is reasonably practicable, serve a notice ("a revocation notice") on the tenant which informs him—
(a)    of the landlord's decision, and
(b)    that the demolition notice is revoked as from the date of service of the revocation notice.

(5)    If, while a final demolition notice is in force, it appears to the Secretary of State that the landlord has no intention of demolishing the dwelling-house in question, he may serve a notice ("a revocation notice") on the tenant which informs him—
(a)    of the Secretary of State's conclusion, and
(b)    that the demolition notice is revoked as from the date of service of the revocation notice.

Section 169 applies in relation to the Secretary of State's power under this sub-paragraph as it applies in relation to his powers under the provisions mentioned in subsection (1) of that section.

(6)    But the Secretary of State may not serve a revocation notice unless he has previously served a notice on the landlord which informs him of the Secretary of State's intention to serve the revocation notice.

(7)    Where a revocation notice is served under sub-paragraph (4) or (5), the demolition notice ceases to be in force as from the date of service of the revocation notice.

[(7A)    Sub-paragraphs (4) to (7) do not apply if the landlord is selling or otherwise transferring his interest as landlord to another person or is offering it for sale or for other transfer.]

(8)    Once a final demolition notice [("the earlier notice")] has (for any reason) ceased to be in force in respect of a dwelling-house without it being demolished, no further final demolition notice [(and no initial demolition notice)] may be served in respect of it[, by the landlord who served the earlier notice or any landlord who served a continuation notice in respect of the earlier notice,] during the period of 5 years following the time when the [earlier] notice ceases to be in force, unless—
(a)    [the further final demolition notice (or, as the case may be, the initial demolition notice)] is served with the consent of the Secretary of State, and
(b)    it states that it is so served.

(9)    The Secretary of State's consent under sub-paragraph (8) may be given subject to compliance with such conditions as he may specify.

[(10)    In sub-paragraph (8) "initial demolition notice" has the meaning given by paragraph 1 of Schedule 5A (initial demolition notices).]

[15A.—(1)    This paragraph applies if—
(a)    a final demolition notice is in force in respect of a dwelling-house, and
(b)    the landlord transfers his interest as landlord to another person.

(2)    The final demolition notice ("the original notice") continues in force but this is subject to—
(a)    paragraphs 13(5) and 15, and
(b)    the following provisions of this paragraph.

(3)    Sub-paragraph (4) applies if the transferee—
(a)    intends to demolish the dwelling-house, but
(b)    has not—
(i)    served a continuation notice, and
(ii)    complied with the conditions in sub-paragraphs (8) and (10),
within the period of 2 months beginning with the date of transfer.

(4)    The transferee must proceed under paragraph 15(4) as if the transferee has decided not to demolish the dwelling-house (and paragraph 15(5) to (7) applies on the same basis).

(5)    A continuation notice is a notice—
(a)    stating that the transferee—
(i)    has acquired the interest concerned, and

(ii) intends to demolish the dwelling-house or (as the case may be) the building containing it ("the relevant premises"),

(b) setting out the reasons why the transferee intends to demolish the relevant premises,

(c) stating that one of conditions A to C in paragraph 14 is satisfied in relation to the original notice (specifying the condition concerned),

(d) stating that the original notice is to continue in force, and

(e) explaining the continued effect of the original notice.

(6) A continuation notice may not vary the proposed demolition date in the original notice nor the date when the original notice will cease to be in force.

(7) Sub-paragraph (8) applies if—

(a) the dwelling-house is contained in a building which contains one or more other dwelling-houses, and

(b) the transferee intends to demolish the whole of the building.

(8) The transferee must serve a continuation notice on the occupier of each of the dwelling-houses contained in the building (whether addressed to him by name or just as "the occupier").

(9) An accidental omission to serve a continuation notice on one or more occupiers does not prevent the condition in sub-paragraph (8) from being satisfied.

(10) Paragraph 13(7) and (8) apply in relation to the transferee's intention to demolish so as to impose a condition on the transferee for a notice to appear within the period of 2 months beginning with the date of transfer.

(11) Sub-paragraphs (7) to (10) above apply instead of paragraph 13(6) to (8) in relation to a final demolition notice so far as continued in force under this paragraph.]

16.—(1) Any notice under paragraph 13[, 15 or 15A] may be served on a person—

(a) by delivering it to him, by leaving it at his proper address or by sending it by post to him at that address, or

(b) if the person is a body corporate, by serving it in accordance with paragraph (a) on the secretary of the body.

(2) For the purposes of this section and section 7 of the Interpretation Act 1978 (service of documents by post) the proper address of a person on whom a notice is to be served shall be—

(a) in the case of a body corporate or its secretary, that of the registered or principal office of the body, and

(b) in any other case, the last known address of that person.]

**[584]**

---

**NOTES**

Para 3: word omitted in the first place repealed and words in second (outer) pair of square brackets added by the Housing Act 1988, s 140, Sch 17, Pt I, para 66, Sch 18; words in first pair of square brackets substituted, word "or" omitted in the second place repealed in relation to England and Wales only and words in fourth (inner) pair of square brackets added by the Housing Act 1996 (Consequential Provisions) Order 1996, SI 1996/2325, arts 4, 5, Sch 1, Pt I, Sch 2, para 14(1), (33); words in third (inner) pair of square brackets inserted and words in fifth (inner) pair of square brackets substituted by the Housing Act 1996 (Consequential Amendments) (No 2) Order 1997, SI 1997/627, art 2, Schedule, para 3(1), (4); words in final pair of square brackets inserted by the Housing and Regeneration Act 2008, s 56, Sch 8, para 35, as from a day to be appointed.

Para 5: word in first pair of square brackets substituted by the Housing and Regeneration Act 2008 (Consequential Provisions) Order 2008, SI 2008/3002, art 4, Sch 1, paras 2, 32, subject to transitional provisions and savings in art 5, Sch 2 thereto; words in second pair of square brackets inserted by the Housing Act 1988, s 83(1), (6)(d); words omitted repealed by the Government of Wales Act 1998, s 152, Sch 18, Pt IV.

Paras 6, 8: repealed by the Housing Act 1988, ss 123, 140(2), Sch 18, except in relation to cases where the tenant's notice claiming to exercise his right to buy was served before from 15 January 1989.

Para 10: words in square brackets substituted by the Leasehold Reform, Housing and Urban Development Act 1993, s 106, except where the tenant's notice claiming to exercise the right to buy was served before 11 October 1993 (no account being taken of any steps taken under s 177 of this Act at **[548]**). By the Leasehold Reform, Housing and Urban Development Act 1993 (Commencement and Transitional Provisions No 1) Order 1993, SI 1993/2134, art 4, Sch 1, para 4, these amendments do not have effect in relation to the operation of Pt V as applied by the Local Government Reorganisation (Preservation of Right to Buy) Order 1986, SI 1986/2092.

Para 11: substituted by the Leasehold Reform, Housing and Urban Development Act 1993, s 106, subject to savings as noted above; for the words in italics in both places they appear in sub-para (4) there are substituted the words "the appropriate tribunal or authority" and sub-paras (5A), (5B) inserted, by the Housing Act 2004, s 181(1)–(3), as from 4 July 2005 (in relation to England) and as from a day to be appointed (in relation to Wales); for effect see s 181(4)–(6) of that Act, and the notes thereto at **[1470]**; in sub-para (5B), words in first pair of square brackets substituted by the Housing and Regeneration Act 2008, s 310(1), subject to savings in s 310(2) thereof, and words in second pair of square brackets substituted by the Transfer of Tribunal Functions (Lands Tribunal and Miscellaneous Amendments) Order 2009, SI 2009/1307, art 5(1), (2), Sch 1, paras 171, 176, subject to transitional provisions and savings in Sch 5 thereto.

Para 13: added by the Housing Act 2004, s 182(1), except in relation to any case where the tenant's notice under section 122 of this Act at **[468]**, was served before 18 January 2005; word omitted from sub-para (5) repealed, reference in first pair of square brackets in sub-para (5) substituted, and words in second pair of square brackets in sub-para (5) and words in square brackets in sub-para (9) inserted by the Housing and Regeneration Act 2008, ss 305, 321(1), Sch 13, paras 1, 2, 14, Sch 16, except in relation to notices served before 22 September 2008.

Para 14: added by the Housing Act 2004, s 182(1), except in relation to any case where the tenant's notice under section 122 of this Act at [**468**], was served before 18 January 2005.

Para 15: added by the Housing Act 2004, s 182(1), except in relation to any case where the tenant's notice under section 122 of this Act at [**468**], was served before 18 January 2005; sub-paras (7A), (10) inserted, in sub-para (8), words in first, second, third and fourth pairs of square brackets inserted and words in fifth pair of square brackets substituted by the Housing and Regeneration Act 2008, s 305, Sch 13, paras 1, 3, 14, except in relation to notices served before 22 September 2008.

Para 15A: inserted by the Housing and Regeneration Act 2008, s 305, Sch 13, paras 1, 4, 14, except in relation to notices served before 22 September 2008.

Para 16: added by the Housing Act 2004, s 182(1), except in relation to any case where the tenant's notice under section 122 of this Act at [**468**], was served before 18 January 2005; words in square brackets substituted by the Housing and Regeneration Act 2008, s 305, Sch 13, paras 1, 5, 14, except in relation to notices served before 22 September 2008

[SCHEDULE 5A
## INITIAL DEMOLITION NOTICES

Section 138A

### *Initial demolition notices*

1.—(1)  For the purposes of this Schedule an "initial demolition notice" is a notice served on a secure tenant—
- (a)  stating that the landlord intends to demolish the dwelling-house or (as the case may be) the building containing it ("the relevant premises"),
- (b)  setting out the reasons why the landlord intends to demolish the relevant premises,
- (c)  specifying the period within which he intends to demolish those premises, and
- (d)  stating that, while the notice remains in force, he will not be under any obligation to make such a grant as is mentioned in section 138(1) in respect of any claim made by the tenant to exercise the right to buy in respect of the dwelling-house.

(2)  An initial demolition notice must also state—
- (a)  that the notice does not prevent—
  - (i)  the making by the tenant of any such claim, or
  - (ii)  the taking of steps under this Part in connection with any such claim up to the point where section 138(1) would otherwise operate in relation to the claim, or
  - (iii)  the operation of that provision in most circumstances where the notice ceases to be in force, but
- (b)  that, if the landlord subsequently serves a final demolition notice in respect of the dwelling-house, the right to buy will not arise in respect of it while that notice is in force and any existing claim will cease to be effective.

(3)  If, at the time when an initial demolition notice is served, there is an existing claim to exercise the right to buy in respect of the dwelling-house, the notice shall—
- (a)  state that section 138C confers a right to compensation in respect of certain expenditure, and
- (b)  give details of that right to compensation and of how it may be exercised.

(4)  The period specified in accordance with sub-paragraph (1)(c) must not—
- (a)  allow the landlord more than what is, in the circumstances, a reasonable period to carry out the proposed demolition of the relevant premises (whether on their own or as part of a scheme involving the demolition of other premises); or
- (b)  in any case expire more than [seven] years after the date of service of the notice on the tenant.

### *Period of validity of initial demolition notice*

2.—(1)  For the purposes of this Schedule an initial demolition notice—
- (a)  comes into force in respect of the dwelling-house concerned on the date of service of the notice on the tenant, and
- (b)  ceases to be so in force at the end of the period specified in accordance with paragraph 1(1)(c),

but this is subject to compliance with the conditions mentioned in sub-paragraph (2) (in a case to which they apply) and to [paragraphs 3 and 3A].

(2)  The conditions in sub-paragraphs (6) and (7) of paragraph 13 of Schedule 5 (publicity for final demolition notices) shall apply in relation to an initial demolition notice as they apply in relation to a final demolition notice.

(3)  The notice mentioned in paragraph 13(7) (as it applies in accordance with sub-paragraph (2) above) must contain the following information—

(a)  sufficient information to enable identification of the premises that the landlord intends to demolish,

(b)  the reasons why the landlord intends to demolish those premises,

(c)  the period within which the landlord intends to demolish those premises,

(d)  the date when any initial demolition notice or notices relating to those premises will cease to be in force, unless revoked or otherwise terminated under or by virtue of paragraph 3 below,

(e)  that, during the period of validity of any such notice or notices, the landlord will not be under any obligation to make such a grant as is mentioned in section 138(1) in respect of any claim to exercise the right to buy in respect of any dwelling-house contained in those premises,

(f)  that there may be a right to compensation under section 138C in respect of certain expenditure incurred in respect of any existing claim.

### *Revocation or termination of initial demolition notices*

3.—(1)  Paragraph 15(4) to [(7A)] of Schedule 5 (revocation notices) shall apply in relation to an initial demolition notice as they apply in relation to a final demolition notice.

(2)  If a compulsory purchase order has been made for the purpose of enabling the landlord to demolish the dwelling-house in respect of which he has served an initial demolition notice (whether or not it would enable him to demolish any other premises as well) and—

(a)  a relevant decision within sub-paragraph (3)(a) becomes effective while the notice is in force, or

(b)  a relevant decision within sub-paragraph (3)(b) becomes final while the notice is in force,

the notice ceases to be in force as from the date when the decision becomes effective or final.

(3)  A "relevant decision" is—

(a)  a decision under Part 2 of the Acquisition of Land Act 1981 to confirm the order with modifications, or not to confirm the whole or part of the order, or

(b)  a decision of the High Court to quash the whole or part of the order under section 24 of that Act,

where the effect of the decision is that the landlord will not be able, by virtue of that order, to carry out the demolition of the dwelling-house.

(4)  A relevant decision within sub-paragraph (3)(a) becomes effective—

(a)  at the end of the period of 16 weeks beginning with the date of the decision, if no application for judicial review is made in respect of the decision within that period, or

(b)  if such an application is so made, at the time when—

(i)  a decision on the application which upholds the relevant decision becomes final, or

(ii)  the application is abandoned or otherwise ceases to have effect.

(5)  A relevant decision within sub-paragraph (3)(b), or a decision within sub-paragraph (4)(b), becomes final—

(a)  if not appealed against, at the end of the period for bringing an appeal, or

(b)  if appealed against, at the time when the appeal (or any further appeal) is disposed of.

(6)  An appeal is disposed of—

(a)  if it is determined and the period for bringing any further appeal has ended, or

(b)  if it is abandoned or otherwise ceases to have effect.

(7)  Where an initial demolition notice ceases to be in force under sub-paragraph (2), the landlord must, as soon as is reasonably practicable, serve a notice on the tenant which informs him—

(a)  that the notice has ceased to be in force as from the date in question, and

(b)  of the reason why it has ceased to be in force.

(8)  If, while an initial demolition notice is in force in respect of a dwelling-house, a final demolition notice comes into force under paragraph 13 of Schedule 5 in respect of that dwelling-house, the initial demolition notice ceases to be in force as from the date when the final demolition notice comes into force.

(9)  In such a case the final demolition notice must state that it is replacing the initial demolition notice.

### *[Transfer of initial demolition notices*

3A.—(1)  This paragraph applies if—

(a)  an initial demolition notice is in force in respect of a dwelling-house, and

(b)  the landlord transfers his interest as landlord to another person.

(2)  The initial demolition notice ("the original notice") continues in force but this is subject to—

    (a)   paragraphs 2 and 3, and

    (b)   the following provisions of this paragraph.

  (3)   Sub-paragraph (4) applies if the transferee—

    (a)   intends to demolish the dwelling-house, but

    (b)   has not—

        (i)   served a continuation notice, and

        (ii)   complied with the conditions in sub-paragraphs (8) and (10),

        within the period of 2 months beginning with the date of transfer.

  (4)   The transferee must proceed under paragraph 15(4) of Schedule 5 as applied by paragraph 3(1) above as if the transferee has decided not to demolish the dwelling-house (and paragraph 15(5) to (7) of that Schedule as so applied applies on the same basis).

  (5)   A continuation notice is a notice—

    (a)   stating that the transferee—

        (i)   has acquired the interest concerned, and

        (ii)   intends to demolish the dwelling-house or (as the case may be) the building containing it ("the relevant premises"),

    (b)   setting out the reasons why the transferee intends to demolish the relevant premises,

    (c)   stating that the original notice is to continue in force, and

    (d)   explaining the continued effect of the original notice.

  (6)   A continuation notice may not vary the period specified in the original notice in accordance with paragraph 1(1)(c).

  (7)   Sub-paragraph (8) applies if—

    (a)   the dwelling-house is contained in a building which contains one or more other dwelling-houses, and

    (b)   the transferee intends to demolish the whole of the building.

  (8)   The transferee must serve a continuation notice on the occupier of each of the dwelling-houses contained in the building (whether addressed to him by name or just as "the occupier").

  (9)   An accidental omission to serve a continuation notice on one or more occupiers does not prevent the condition in sub-paragraph (8) from being satisfied.

  (10)   Paragraph 13(7) of Schedule 5 applies in relation to the transferee's intention to demolish so as to impose a condition on the transferee for a notice to appear within the period of 2 months beginning with the date of transfer; and paragraph 2(3) above applies for this purpose.

  (11)   Sub-paragraphs (7) to (10) above apply instead of paragraph 2(2) and (3) in relation to an initial demolition notice so far as continued in force under this paragraph.]

### *Restriction on serving further demolition notices*

4.—(1)   This paragraph applies where an initial demolition notice ("the relevant notice") has (for any reason) ceased to be in force in respect of a dwelling-house without it being demolished.

  (2)   No further initial demolition notice may be served in respect of the dwelling-house[, by the landlord who served the relevant notice or any landlord who served a continuation notice in respect of the relevant notice,] during the period of 5 years following the time when the relevant notice ceases to be in force, unless—

    (a)   [the further notice] is served with the consent of the Secretary of State, and

    (b)   it states that it is so served.

  (3)   Subject to sub-paragraph (4), no final demolition notice may be served in respect of the dwelling-house[, by the landlord who served the relevant notice or any landlord who served a continuation notice in respect of the relevant notice,] during the period of 5 years following the time when the relevant notice ceases to be in force, unless—

    (a)   [the final demolition notice] is served with the consent of the Secretary of State, and

    (b)   it states that it is so served.

  (4)   Sub-paragraph (3) does not apply to a final demolition notice which is served at a time when an initial demolition notice served in accordance with sub-paragraph (2) is in force.

  (5)   The Secretary of State's consent under sub-paragraph (2) or (3) may be given subject to compliance with such conditions as he may specify.

### *Service of notices*

5.   Paragraph 16 of [Schedule 5] (service of notices) applies in relation to notices under this Schedule as it applies in relation to notices under paragraph 13[, 15 or 15A] of that Schedule.

*Interpretation*

6.—(1)   In this Schedule [(other than paragraph 3A)] any reference to the landlord, in the context of a reference to the demolition or intended demolition of any premises, includes a reference to a superior landlord.

(2)   In this Schedule—

"final demolition notice" means a final demolition notice served under paragraph 13 of Schedule 5;

"premises" means premises of any description;

"scheme" includes arrangements of any description.]

**[585]**

**NOTES**

Commencement: 18 January 2005.

Inserted by the Housing Act 2004, s 183(3), Sch 9, except in relation to any case where the tenant's notice under s 122 of this Act at **[468]**, was served before 18 January 2005.

Para 1: word in square brackets in sub-para (4)(b)substituted by the Housing and Regeneration Act 2008, s 305, Sch 13, paras 6, 7, 14, except in relation to notices served before 22 September 2008.

Para 2: words in square brackets in sub-para (1) substituted by the Housing and Regeneration Act 2008, s 305, Sch 13, paras 6, 8, 14, except in relation to notices served before 22 September 2008.

Para 3: reference in square brackets in sub-para (1) substituted by the Housing and Regeneration Act 2008, s 305, Sch 13, paras 6, 9, 14, except in relation to notices served before 22 September 2008.

Para 3A: inserted by the Housing and Regeneration Act 2008, s 305, Sch 13, paras 6, 10, 14, except in relation to notices served before 22 September 2008.

Para 4: words in first and third pairs of square brackets inserted and words in second and fourth pairs of square brackets substituted by the Housing and Regeneration Act 2008, s 305, Sch 13, paras 6, 11, 14, except in relation to notices served before 22 September 2008.

Para 5: words in first pair of square brackets substituted by the Housing and Regeneration Act 2008, s 310(3), and words in second pair of square brackets substituted by s 305 of, and Sch 13, paras 6, 12, 14 to that Act, except in relation to notices served before 22 September 2008.

Para 6: words in square brackets in sub-para (1) inserted by the Housing and Regeneration Act 2008, s 305, Sch 13, paras 6, 13, 14, except in relation to notices served before 22 September 2008.

SCHEDULE 6
CONVEYANCE OF FREEHOLD AND GRANT OF LEASE IN PURSUANCE OF RIGHT TO BUY

Sections 139 and 151

PART I
COMMON PROVISIONS

*Rights to be conveyed or granted—general*

1.   The conveyance or grant shall not exclude or restrict the general words implied under section 62 of the Law of Property Act 1925, unless the tenant consents or the exclusion or restriction is made for the purpose of preserving or recognising an existing interest of the landlord in tenant's incumbrances or an existing right or interest of another person.

*Rights of support, passage of water, etc*

2.—(1)   The conveyance or grant shall, by virtue of this Schedule, have the effect stated in sub-paragraph (2) as regards—

(a)   rights of support for a building or part of a building;

(b)   rights to the access of light and air to a building or part of a building;

(c)   rights to the passage of water or of gas or other piped fuel, or to the drainage or disposal of water, sewage, smoke or fumes, or to the use or maintenance of pipes or other installations for such passage, drainage or disposal;

(d)   rights to the use or maintenance of cables or other installations for the supply of electricity, for the telephone or for the receipt directly or by landline of visual or other wireless transmissions.

(2)   The effect is—

(a)   to grant with the dwelling-house all such easements and rights over other property, so far as the landlord is capable of granting them, as are necessary to secure to the tenant as nearly as may be the same rights as at the relevant time were available to him under or by virtue of the secure tenancy or an agreement collateral to it, or under or by virtue of a grant, reservation or agreement made on the severance of the dwelling-house from other property then comprised in the same tenancy; and

(b)   to make the dwelling-house subject to all such easements and rights for the benefit of other property as are capable of existing in law and are necessary to secure to the person interested in the other property as nearly as may be the same rights as at the relevant time were available against the tenant under or by virtue of the secure tenancy or an agreement collateral to it, or under or by virtue of a grant, reservation or agreement made as mentioned in paragraph (a).

(3)    This paragraph—
    (a)    does not restrict any wider operation which the conveyance or grant may have apart from this paragraph; but
    (b)    is subject to any provision to the contrary that may be included in the conveyance or grant with the consent of the tenant.

### Rights of way

3.    The conveyance or grant shall include—
    (a)    such provisions (if any) as the tenant may require for the purpose of securing to him rights of way over land not comprised in the dwelling-house, so far as the landlord is capable of granting them, being rights of way that are necessary for the reasonable enjoyment of the dwelling-house; and
    (b)    such provisions (if any) as the landlord may require for the purpose of making the dwelling-house subject to rights of way necessary for the reasonable enjoyment of other property, being property in which at the relevant time the landlord has an interest, or to rights of way granted or agreed to be granted before the relevant time by the landlord or by the person then entitled to the reversion on the tenancy.

### Covenants and conditions

4.    The conveyance or grant shall include such provisions (if any) as the landlord may require to secure that the tenant is bound by, or to indemnify the landlord against breaches of, restrictive covenants (that is to say, covenants or agreements restrictive of the use of any land or premises) which affect the dwelling-house otherwise than by virtue of the secure tenancy or an agreement collateral to it and are enforceable for the benefit of other property.

[4A.    The conveyance or grant shall be expressed to be made by the landlord with full title guarantee (thereby implying the covenants for title specified in Part I of the Law of Property (Miscellaneous Provisions) Act 1994.]

5.    Subject to paragraph 6, and to Parts II and III of this Schedule, the conveyance or grant may include such [other covenants] and conditions as are reasonable in the circumstances.

### No charge to be made for landlord's consent or approval

6.    A provision of the conveyance or lease is void in so far as it purports to enable the landlord to charge the tenant a sum for or in connection with the giving of a consent or approval.

### Meaning of "incumbrances" and "tenant's incumbrance"

7.    In this Schedule—
     "incumbrances" includes personal liabilities attaching in respect of the ownership of land or an interest in land though not charged on the land or interest; and
     "tenant's incumbrance" means—
    (a)    an incumbrance on the secure tenancy which is also an incumbrance on the reversion, and
    (b)    an interest derived, directly or indirectly, out of the secure tenancy.

**[586]**

---

**NOTES**

Para 4A: inserted by the Law of Property (Miscellaneous Provisions) Act 1994, s 21(1), (4), Sch 1, para 9(1), (2), except in relation to any disposition of property to which, by virtue of s 10(1) or 11 of that Act, the Law of Property Act 1925, s 76, or the Land Registration Act 1925, s 24(1)(a), continue to apply.

Para 5: words in square brackets substituted the Law of Property (Miscellaneous Provisions) Act 1994, s 21(1), (4), Sch 1, para 9(1), (3), subject to savings as noted above.

---

### PART II
### CONVEYANCE OF FREEHOLD

### General

8.    The conveyance shall not exclude or restrict the all estate clause implied under section 63 of the Law of Property Act 1925, unless the tenant consents or the exclusion or restriction is made for the purpose of preserving or recognising an existing interest of the landlord in tenant's incumbrances or an existing right or interest of another person.

9.—(1)    The conveyance shall be of an estate in fee simple absolute, subject to—
    (a)    tenant's incumbrances,

(b)    burdens (other than burdens created by the conveyance) in respect of the upkeep or regulation for the benefit of any locality of any land, building, structure, works, ways or watercourses;

but otherwise free from incumbrances.

(2)    Nothing in sub-paragraph (1) shall be taken as affecting the operation of paragraph 5 of this Schedule (reasonable covenants and conditions).

10.    ...

[587]

**NOTES**

Para 10: repealed by the Law of Property (Miscellaneous Provisions) Act 1994, s 21(1), (2), (4), Sch 1, para 9(1), (4), Sch 2, except in relation to any disposition of property to which, by virtue of s 10(1) or 11 of that Act, the Law of Property Act 1925, s 76, or the Land Registration Act 1925, s 24(1)(a), continue to apply.

## PART III
## LEASES
### General

11.    A lease shall be for the appropriate term defined in paragraph 12 (but subject to sub-paragraph (3) of that paragraph) and at a rent not exceeding £10 per annum, and the following provisions have effect with respect to the other terms of the lease.

### The appropriate term

12.—(1)    If at the time the grant is made the landlord's interest in the dwelling-house is not less than a lease for a term of which more than 125 years and five days are unexpired, the appropriate term is a term of not less than 125 years.

(2)    In any other case the appropriate term is a term expiring five days before the term of the landlord's lease of the dwelling-house (or, as the case may require, five days before the first date on which the term of any lease under which the landlord holds any part of the dwelling-house) is to expire.

(3)    If the dwelling-house is a flat contained in a building which also contains one or more other flats and the landlord has, since 8th August 1980, granted a lease of one or more of them for the appropriate term, the lease of the dwelling-house may be for a term expiring at the end of the term for which the other lease (or one of the other leases) was granted.

### Common use of premises and facilities

13.    Where the dwelling-house is a flat and the tenant enjoyed, during the secure tenancy, the use in common with others of any premises, facilities or services, the lease shall include rights to the like enjoyment, so far as the landlord is capable of granting them, unless otherwise agreed between the landlord and the tenant.

### Covenants by the landlord

14.—(1)    This paragraph applies where the dwelling-house is a flat.

(2)    There are implied covenants by the landlord—

(a)    to keep in repair the structure and exterior of the dwelling-house and of the building in which it is situated (including drains, gutters and external pipes) and to make good any defect affecting that structure;

(b)    to keep in repair any other property over or in respect of which the tenant has rights by virtue of this Schedule;

(c)    to ensure, so far as practicable, that services which are to be provided by the landlord and to which the tenant is entitled (whether by himself or in common with others) are maintained at a reasonable level and to keep in repair any installation connected with the provision of those services;

...

(3)    [There is an implied covenant] that the landlord shall rebuild or reinstate the dwelling-house and the building in which it is situated in the case of destruction or damage by fire, tempest, flood or any other cause against the risk of which it is normal practice to insure.

[(3A)    Sub-paragraphs (2) and (3) have effect subject to paragraph 15(3) (certain obligations not to be imposed, where landlord's title is leasehold, by reason of provisions of superior lease).]

(4)    The county court may, by order made with the consent of the parties, authorise the inclusion in the lease or in an agreement collateral to it of provisions excluding or modifying the obligations of the landlord under the covenants implied by this paragraph, if it appears to the court that it is reasonable to do so.

15.—(1)  This paragraph applies where the landlord's interest in the dwelling-house is leasehold.

(2)  There is implied a covenant by the landlord to pay the rent reserved by the landlord's lease and, except in so far as they fall to be discharged by the tenant, to discharge its obligations under the covenants contained in that lease.

(3)  A covenant implied by virtue of paragraph 14 (implied covenants where dwelling-house is a flat) shall not impose on the landlord an obligation which the landlord is not entitled to discharge under the provisions of the landlord's lease or a superior lease.

(4)  Where the landlord's lease or a superior lease, or an agreement collateral to the landlord's lease or a superior lease, contains a covenant by a person imposing obligations which, but for sub-paragraph (3), would be imposed by a covenant implied by virtue of paragraph 14, there is implied a covenant by the landlord to use its best endeavours to secure that that person's obligations under the first-mentioned covenant are discharged.

*Covenant by tenant*

16.  Unless otherwise agreed between the landlord and the tenant, there is implied a covenant by the tenant—

    (a)    where the dwelling-house is a house, to keep the dwelling-house in good repair (including decorative repair);

    (b)    where the dwelling-house is a flat, to keep the interior of the dwelling-house in such repair.

*[Service charges and other contributions payable by the tenant*

16A.—(1)  The lease may require the tenant to bear a reasonable part of the costs incurred by the landlord—

    (a)    in discharging or insuring against the obligations imposed by the covenants implied by virtue of paragraph 14(2) (repairs, making good structural defects, provision of services, etc), or

    (b)    in insuring against the obligations imposed by the covenant implied by virtue of paragraph 14(3) (rebuilding or reinstatement, etc),

and to the extent that by virtue of paragraph 15(3) (effect of provision of superior lease) such obligations are not imposed on the landlord, to bear a reasonable part of the costs incurred by the landlord in contributing to costs incurred by a superior landlord or other person in discharging or, as the case may be, insuring against obligations to the like effect.

(2)  Where the lease requires the tenant to contribute to the costs of insurance, it shall provide that the tenant is entitled to inspect the relevant policy at such reasonable times as may be specified in the lease.

(3)  Where the landlord does not insure against the obligations imposed by the covenant implied by virtue of paragraph 14(3), or, as the case may be, the superior landlord or other person does not insure against his obligations to the like effect, the lease may require the tenant to pay a reasonable sum in place of the contribution he could be required to make if there were insurance.

(4)  Where in any case the obligations imposed by the covenants implied by virtue of paragraph 14(2) or (3) are modified in accordance with paragraph 14(4) (power of county court to authorise modification), the references in this paragraph are to the obligations as so modified.

(5)  This paragraph has effect subject to paragraph 16B (restrictions in certain cases as regards costs incurred in the initial period of the lease).

16B.—(1)  Where a lease of a flat requires the tenant to pay service charges in respect of repairs (including works for the making good of structural defects), his liability in respect of costs incurred in the initial period of the lease is restricted as follows.

(2)  He is not required to pay in respect of works itemised in the estimates contained in the landlord's notice under section 125 any more than the amount shown as his estimated contribution in respect of that item, together with an inflation allowance.

(3)  He is not required to pay in respect of works not so itemised at a rate exceeding—

    (a)    as regards parts of the initial period falling within the reference period for the purposes of the estimates contained in the landlord's notice under section 125, the estimated annual average amount shown in the estimates;

    (b)    as regards parts of the initial period not falling within that reference period, the average rate produced by averaging over the reference period all works for which estimates are contained in the notice;

together, in each case, with an inflation allowance.

(4)  The initial period of the lease for the purposes of this paragraph begins with the grant of the lease and ends five years after the grant, except that—

(a) if the lease includes provision for service charges to be payable in respect of costs incurred in a period before the grant of the lease, the initial period begins with the beginning of that period;

(b) if the lease provides for service charges to be calculated by reference to a specified annual period, the initial period continues until the end of the fifth such period beginning after the grant of the lease; ...

(c) ...

16C.—(1) Where a lease of a flat requires the tenant to pay improvement contributions, his liability in respect of costs incurred in the initial period of the lease is restricted as follows.

(2) He is not required to make any payment in respect of works for which no estimate was given in the landlord's notice under section 125.

(3) He is not required to pay in respect of works for which an estimate was given in that notice any more than the amount shown as his estimated contribution in respect of that item, together with an inflation allowance.

(4) The initial period of the lease for the purposes of this paragraph begins with the grant of the lease and ends five years after the grant, except that—

(a) if the lease includes provision for improvement contributions to be payable in respect of costs incurred in a period before the grant of the lease, the initial period begins with the beginning of that period;

(b) if the lease provides for improvement contributions to be calculated by reference to a specified annual period, the initial period continues until the end of the fifth such period beginning after the grant of the lease; ...

(c) ...

16D.—(1) The Secretary of State may by order prescribe—

(a) the method by which inflation allowances for the purposes of paragraph 16B or 16C are to be calculated by reference to published statistics; and

(b) the information to be given to a tenant when he is asked to pay a service charge or improvement contribution to which the provisions of paragraph 16B or 16C are or may be relevant.

(2) An order—

(a) may make different provision for different cases or descriptions of case, including different provision for different areas;

(b) may contain such incidental, supplementary or transitional provisions as the Secretary of State thinks appropriate; and

(c) shall be made by statutory instrument which shall be subject to annulment in pursuance of a resolution of either House of Parliament.]

[16E.—(1) Where a lease of a flat granted in pursuance of the right to acquire on rent to mortgage terms requires the tenant to pay—

(a) service charges in respect of repairs (including works for the making good of structural defects), or

(b) improvement contributions,

his liability in respect of costs incurred at any time before the final payment is made is restricted as follows.

(2) He is not required to pay any more than the amount determined by the formula—

$$M = P \times \frac{100 - S}{100}$$

where—

M = the maximum amount which he is required to pay;

P = the amount which, but for this paragraph, he would be required to pay;

S = the landlord's share at the time expressed as a percentage.]

### Avoidance of certain provisions

17.—(1) A provision of the lease, or of an agreement collateral to it, is void in so far as it purports to prohibit or restrict the assignment of the lease or the subletting, wholly or in part, of the dwelling-house.

(2) Sub-paragraph (1) has effect subject to section 157 (restriction on disposal of dwelling-houses in National Parks, etc).

[18. Where the dwelling-house is a flat, a provision of the lease or of an agreement collateral to it is void in so far as it purports—

(a) to authorise the recovery of such a charge as is mentioned in paragraph 16A (contributions in respect of repairs, etc) otherwise than in accordance with that paragraph and paragraph 16B (restrictions in initial period of lease); or

(b)     to authorise the recovery of any charge in respect of costs incurred by the landlord—

       (i)     in discharging the obligations imposed by the covenant implied by paragraph 14(3) (rebuilding or reinstatement, &c), or those obligations as modified in accordance with paragraph 14(4), or

       (ii)     in contributing to costs incurred by a superior landlord or other person in discharging obligations to the like effect; or

(c)     to authorise the recovery of an improvement contribution otherwise than in accordance with paragraph 16C (restrictions in initial period of lease).]

19.     A provision of the lease, or of an agreement collateral to it, is void in so far as it purports to authorise a forfeiture, or to impose on the tenant a penalty or disability, in the event of his enforcing or relying on the preceding provisions of this Schedule.

**[588]**

PART I
STATUTES

---

**NOTES**

Para 14: words omitted repealed, words in square brackets in sub-para (3) substituted and sub-para (3A) inserted by the Housing and Planning Act 1986, s 24(2), (3), Sch 5, Pt II, para 41, Sch 12, Pt I.

Paras 16A, 16D: inserted, together with the preceding cross-heading and paras 16B, 16C, by the Housing and Planning Act 1986, s 4(4), (6), except in relation to cases where both the tenant's notice claiming to exercise the right to buy, and the landlord's notice under s 125 at **[471]**, were served before 7 January 1987 (but without prejudice to the tenant's right to withdraw the notice served before that date and serve a new notice).

Paras 16B, 16C: inserted, together with paras 16A, 16D, by the Housing and Planning Act 1986, s 4(4), (6), subject to savings as noted above; words omitted repealed by the Leasehold Reform, Housing and Urban Development Act 1993, s 187(2), Sch 22, except in relation to a case where a notice under s 122 at **[468]**, is served before 11 October 1993 or in relation to the operation of Pt V of this Act as applied by the Local Government Reorganisation (Preservation of the Right to Buy) Order 1986, SI 1986/2092. Note also that these repeals do not apply in relation to the provisions of Pt V of this Act relating to the preserved right to buy in a case where a person has the preserved right to buy (as defined in s 171A at **[536]**) before 11 October 1993.

Para 16E: inserted by the Leasehold Reform, Housing and Urban Development Act 1993, s 116(2), except in relation to a case where a notice under s 122 at **[468]**, is served before 11 October 1993 or in relation to the operation of Pt V of this Act as applied by SI 1986/2092.

Para 18: substituted by the Housing and Planning Act 1986, s 4(5), (6), subject to savings as noted to paras 16A, 16D above.

Orders: the Housing (Right to Buy) (Service Charges) Order 1986, SI 1986/2195.

---

### PART IV
### CHARGES

#### *Grant of Lease*

20.     A charge (however created or arising) on the interest of the landlord which is not a tenant's incumbrance does not affect a lease granted in pursuance of the right to buy.

#### *Conveyance of freehold*

21.—(1)     This paragraph applies to a charge (however created or arising) on the freehold where the freehold is conveyed in pursuance of the right to buy.

(2)     If the charge is not a tenant's incumbrance and is not a rentcharge the conveyance is effective to release the freehold from the charge; but the release does not affect the personal liability of the landlord or any other person in respect of any obligation which the charge was created to secure.

(3)     If the charge is a rentcharge the conveyance shall be made subject to the charge; but if the rentcharge also affects other land—

(a)     the conveyance shall contain a covenant by the landlord to indemnify the tenant and his successors in title in respect of any liability arising under the rentcharge, and

(b)     if the rentcharge is of a kind which may be redeemed under the Rentcharges Act 1977 the landlord shall immediately after the conveyance take such steps as are necessary to redeem the rentcharge so far as it affects land owned by him.

(4)     In this paragraph "rentcharge" has the same meaning as in the Rentcharges Act 1977; and—

(a)     for the purposes of sub-paragraph (3) land is owned by a person if he is the owner of it within the meaning of section 13(1) of that Act, and

(b)     for the purposes of that sub-paragraph and that Act land which has been conveyed by the landlord in pursuance of the right to buy but subject to the rentcharge shall be treated as if it had not been so conveyed but had continued to be owned by him.

**[589]**

[SCHEDULE 6A
REDEMPTION OF LANDLORD'S SHARE

Section 151A

*Obligation to redeem landlord's share in certain circumstances*

1.—(1) The conveyance or grant shall contain a covenant binding on the secure tenant and his successors in title to make to the landlord, immediately after—

    (a)   the making of a relevant disposal which is not an excluded disposal, or

    (b)   the expiry of the period of one year beginning with a relevant death,

(whichever first occurs), a final payment, that is to say, a payment of the amount required to redeem the landlord's share.

    (2)   A disposal is an excluded disposal for the purposes of this paragraph if—

    (a)   it is a further conveyance of the freehold or an assignment of the lease and the person or each of the persons to whom it is made is, or is the spouse [or civil partner] of, the person or one of the persons by whom it is made;

    (b)   it is a vesting in a person taking under a will or intestacy; or

    [(c)   it is a disposal in pursuance of an order under—

        (i)   *section 24* or 24A of the Matrimonial Causes Act 1973 (property adjustment orders or orders for the sale of property in connection with matrimonial proceedings),

        (ii)   section 2 of the Inheritance (Provision for Family and Dependants) Act 1975 (orders as to financial provision to be made from estate),

        (iii)   section 17 of the Matrimonial and Family Proceedings Act 1984 (property adjustment orders or orders for the sale of property after overseas divorce, &c), ...

        (iv)   paragraph 1 of Schedule 1 to the Children Act 1989 (orders for financial relief against parents), [or

        (v)   Part 2 or 3 of Schedule 5, or paragraph 9 of Schedule 7, to the Civil Partnership Act 2004 (property adjustment orders, or orders for the sale of property, in connection with civil partnership proceedings or after overseas dissolution of civil partnership, etc),]]

and (in any case) an interest to which this paragraph applies subsists immediately after the disposal.

    (3)   In this paragraph "relevant death" means the death of a person who immediately before his death was the person or, as the case may be, the last remaining person entitled to an interest to which this paragraph applies.

    (4)   A beneficial interest in the dwelling-house is an interest to which this paragraph applies if the person entitled to it is—

    (a)   the secure tenant or, as the case may be, one of the secure tenants, or

    (b)   a qualifying person.

*Right to redeem landlord's share at any time*

2.—(1) The conveyance or grant shall include provision entitling the secure tenant and his successors in title to make a final payment at any time.

    (2)   The right shall be exercisable by written notice served on the landlord claiming to make a final payment.

    (3)   The notice may be withdrawn at any time by written notice served on the landlord.

    (4)   If the final payment is not tendered to the landlord before the end of the period of three months beginning with the time when the value of the dwelling-house is agreed or determined in accordance with paragraph 8, the notice claiming to make a final payment shall be deemed to have been withdrawn.

*Value of landlord's share and amount of final payment*

3.   The value of the landlord's share shall be determined by the formula—

$$VS = \frac{V \times S}{100}$$

and the amount required to redeem that share shall be determined by the formula—

$$R = VS - D$$

where—

    VS = the value of the landlord's share;

    V = the value of the dwelling-house (agreed or determined in accordance with paragraph 8);

    S = the landlord's share expressed as a percentage;

    R = the amount required to redeem the landlord's share;

D = the amount of the final discount (if any) which is applicable under paragraphs 4 and 5.

*Final discount*

4.—(1)   Where a final payment is made by, or by two or more persons who include—

(a)   the secure tenant or, as the case may be, one of the secure tenants, or

(b)   a qualifying person,

the person or persons making the payment are entitled, subject to the following provisions of this paragraph and paragraph 5, to a final discount equal to 20 per cent of the value of the landlord's share.

(2)   Sub-paragraph (1) shall not apply if the final payment is made after the end of the protection period, that is to say, the period of two years beginning with the time when there ceases to be an interest to which this sub-paragraph applies.

(3)   A beneficial interest in the dwelling-house is an interest to which sub-paragraph (2) applies if the person entitled to it is—

(a)   the secure tenant or, as the case may be, one of the secure tenants, or

(b)   a [qualifying partner].

(4)   The Secretary of State may by order made with the consent of the Treasury provide that the percentage discount shall be such percentage as may be specified in the order.

(5)   An order under this paragraph—

(a)   may make different provision with respect to different cases or descriptions of case, including different provision for different areas,

(b)   may contain such incidental, supplementary or transitional provisions as appear to the Secretary of State necessary or expedient, and

(c)   shall be made by statutory instrument and shall not be made unless a draft of the order has been laid before and approved by resolution of each House of Parliament.

*Restrictions on and deductions from final discount*

5.—(1)   Except where the Secretary of State so determines, a final discount shall not reduce the total purchase price, that is to say, the aggregate of the initial payment, the final payment and any interim payments, below the amount which would be applicable under section 131(1) in respect of the dwelling-house if the relevant time were the time when the value of the dwelling-house is agreed or determined.

(2)   The total discount, that is to say, the aggregate of the initial discount, the final discount and any interim discounts, shall not in any case reduce the total purchase price by more than the sum prescribed for the purposes of section 131(2) at the time when the value of the dwelling-house is agreed or determined.

(3)   If a final payment is made after the end of the first twelve months of the protection period, there shall be deducted from any final discount given by paragraph 4 and the preceding provisions of this paragraph an amount equal to 50 per cent of that discount.

(4)   There shall be deducted from any final discount given by paragraph 4 and the preceding provisions of this paragraph an amount equal to any previous discount qualifying or, the aggregate of any previous discounts qualifying, under the provisions of section 130.

(5)   A determination under this paragraph may make different provision for different cases or descriptions of case, including different provision for different areas.

*Right to make interim payment at any time*

6.—(1)   The conveyance or grant shall include provision entitling the secure tenant and his successors in title at any time to make to the landlord an interim payment, that is to say, a payment which—

(a)   is less than the amount required to redeem the landlord's share; but

(b)   is not less than 10 per cent of the value of the dwelling-house (agreed or determined in accordance with paragraph 8).

(2)   The right shall be exercisable by written notice served on the landlord, claiming to make an interim payment and stating the amount of the interim payment proposed to be made.

(3)   The notice may be withdrawn at any time by written notice served on the landlord.

(4)   If the interim payment is not tendered to the landlord before the end of the period of three months beginning with the time when the value of the dwelling-house is agreed or determined in accordance with paragraph 8, the notice claiming to make an interim payment shall be deemed to have been withdrawn.

*Landlord's reduced share and interim discount*

7.   The landlord's share after the making of an interim payment shall be determined by the formula—

$$S = \frac{R - IP}{R} \times PS$$

the amount of the interim discount shall be determined by the formula—

$$ID = \frac{PS \times V}{100} - \frac{S \times V}{100} - IP$$

and the amount of any previous discount which will be recovered by virtue of the making of an interim payment shall be determined by the formula—

$$RD = \frac{IP}{R} \times PD$$

where—
S = the landlord's share expressed as a percentage;
R = the amount which would have been required to redeem the landlord's share immediately before the interim payment was made;
IP = the amount of the interim payment;
PS = the landlord's share immediately before the interim payment was made also expressed as a percentage;
ID = the amount of the interim discount;
V = the value of the dwelling-house (agreed or determined in accordance with paragraph 8);
RD = the amount of any previous discount which will be recovered by virtue of the making of the interim payment;
PD = the amount of any previous discount which would be recovered if the tenant were making the final payment.

*Value of dwelling-house*

8.—(1)   For the purposes of the final payment or any interim payment, the value of a dwelling-house is the amount which for those purposes—
   (a)   is agreed at any time between the parties, or
   (b)   in default of such agreement, is determined at any time by an independent valuer,
as the amount which, in accordance with this paragraph, is to be taken as its value at that time.

   (2)   Subject to sub-paragraph (6), that value shall be taken to be the price which the interest of the secure tenant in the dwelling-house would realise if sold on the open market by a willing vendor—
   (a)   on the assumption that the liabilities mentioned in sub-paragraph (3) would be discharged by the vendor, and
   (b)   disregarding the matters specified in sub-paragraph (4).

   (3)   The liabilities referred to in sub-paragraph (2)(a) are—
   (a)   any mortgages of the interest of the secure tenant,
   (b)   the liability under the covenant required by paragraph 1, and
   (c)   any liability under the covenant required by section 155(3) (repayment of discount on early disposal).

   (4)   The matters to be disregarded in pursuance of sub-paragraph (2)(b) are—
   (a)   any interests or rights created over the dwelling-house by the secure tenant,
   (b)   any improvements made by the secure tenant or any of the persons mentioned in section 127(4) (certain predecessors as secure tenant), and
   (c)   any failure by the secure tenant or any of those persons—
      (i)   where the dwelling-house is a house, to keep the dwelling-house in good repair (including decorative repair);
      (ii)   where the dwelling-house is a flat, to keep the interior of the dwelling-house in such repair.

   (5)   Sub-paragraph (6) applies where, at the time when the value of the dwelling-house is agreed or determined, the dwelling-house—
   (a)   has been destroyed or damaged by fire, tempest, flood or any other cause against the risk of which it is normal practice to insure, and
   (b)   has not been fully rebuilt or reinstated.

   (6)   That value shall be taken to include the value of such of the following as are applicable, namely—

(a)　　any sums paid or falling to be paid to the secure tenant under a relevant policy in so far as they exceed the cost of any rebuilding or reinstatement which has been carried out;

(b)　　any rights of the secure tenant under the covenant implied by paragraph 14(3) of Schedule 6 (covenant to rebuild or reinstate); and

(c)　　any rights of the secure tenant under the covenant implied by paragraph 15(4) of that Schedule (covenant to use best endeavours to secure rebuilding or reinstatement).

(7)　In sub-paragraph (6) "relevant policy" means a policy insuring the secure tenant against the risk of fire, tempest or flood or any other risk against which it is normal practice to insure.

(8)　References in this paragraph to the secure tenant include references to his successors in title.

### Costs of independent valuation

9.　The conveyance or grant shall include provision requiring any sums falling to be paid to an independent valuer (whether by way of fees or expenses or otherwise) to be paid by the secure tenant or his successors in title.

### No charges to be made by landlord

10.　A provision of the conveyance or grant is void in so far as it purports to enable the landlord to charge the tenant or his successors in title a sum in respect of or in connection with the making of a final or interim payment.

### Other covenants and provisions

11.　Subject to the provisions of this Schedule, the conveyance or grant may include such covenants and provisions as are reasonable in the circumstances.

### Interpretation

12.—(1)　In this Schedule—
　　　"independent valuer" means an independent valuer appointed in pursuance of provisions in that behalf contained in the conveyance or grant;
　　　"protection period" has the meaning given by paragraph 4(2);
　　　"qualifying person" means a [qualifying partner] or a qualifying resident.

(2)　A person is a [qualifying partner] for the purposes of this Schedule if—

(a)　　he is entitled to a beneficial interest in the dwelling-house immediately after the time when there ceases to be an interest to which this paragraph applies;

(b)　　he is occupying the dwelling-house as his only or principal home immediately before that time; and

[(c)　　he—
　　　(i)　is the spouse, the civil partner, a former spouse, a former civil partner, the surviving spouse, the surviving civil partner, a surviving former spouse or a surviving former civil partner of the person who immediately before that time was entitled to the interest to which this paragraph applies or, as the case may be, the last remaining such interest, or
　　　(ii)　is the surviving spouse, the surviving civil partner, a surviving former spouse or a surviving former civil partner of a person who immediately before his death was entitled to such an interest.]

(3)　A person is a qualifying resident for the purposes of this Schedule if—

(a)　　he is entitled to a beneficial interest in the dwelling-house immediately after the time when there ceases to be an interest to which this paragraph applies;

(b)　　he is occupying the dwelling-house as his only or principal home immediately before that time;

(c)　　he has resided throughout the period of twelve months ending with that time—
　　　(i)　with the person who immediately before that time was entitled to the interest to which this paragraph applies or, as the case may be, the last remaining such interest, or
　　　(ii)　with two or more persons in succession each of whom was throughout the period of residence with him entitled to such an interest; and

(d)　　he is not a [qualifying partner].

(4)　A beneficial interest in the dwelling-house is an interest to which this paragraph applies if the person entitled to it is the secure tenant or, as the case may be, one of the secure tenants.

(5)　References in this Schedule to the secure tenant are references to the secure tenant or tenants to whom the conveyance or grant is made and references to the secure tenant or, as the case may be, one of the secure tenants shall be construed accordingly.

(6) References in this Schedule to the secure tenant's successors in title do not include references to any person entitled to a legal charge having priority to the mortgage required by section 151B (mortgage for securing redemption of landlord's share) or any person whose title derives from such a charge.]

**[590]**

**NOTES**

Inserted by the Leasehold Reform, Housing and Urban Development Act 1993, s 117(2), Sch 16, except in relation to a case where a notice under s 122 at **[468]**, is served before 11 October 1993 or in relation to the operation of Pt V of this Act as applied by the Local Government Reorganisation (Preservation of the Right to Buy) Order 1986, SI 1986/2092.

Para 1: words in square brackets in sub-para (2)(a) and sub-para (2)(c)(v) and word immediately preceding it inserted and word omitted from sub-para (2)(c)(iii) repealed by the Civil Partnership Act 2004, ss 81, 261(4), Sch 8, para 35(1)–(3), Sch 30; sub-para (2)(c) substituted by the Housing Act 1996, s 222, Sch 18, Pt III, para 17; for the words in italics in sub-para (2)(c) there are substituted the words "section 23A or 24" by the Family Law Act 1996, s 66(1), Sch 8, Pt I, para 34, as from a day to be appointed, subject to savings in s 66(2) of, and Sch 9, para 5 to, that Act.

Para 4: words in square brackets substituted by the Civil Partnership Act 2004, s 81, Sch 8, para 35(1), (4).

Para 12: words in square brackets substituted by the Civil Partnership Act 2004, s 81, Sch 8, para 35(1), (4), (5).

*(Schs 7–9 repealed by the Leasehold Reform, Housing and Urban Development Act 1993, s 187(2), Sch 22, except in relation to a case where a notice under s 122 at **[468]**, is served before 11 October 1993 or in relation to the operation of Pt V of this Act as applied by the Local Government Reorganisation (Preservation of the Right to Buy) Order 1986, SI 1986/2092.)*

[SCHEDULE 9A

## LAND REGISTRATION AND RELATED MATTERS WHERE RIGHT TO BUY PRESERVED
Section 171G

### *Statement to be contained in instrument effecting qualifying disposal*

1. On a qualifying disposal, the disponor shall secure that the instrument effecting the disposal—
   (a) states that the disposal is, so far as it relates to dwelling-houses occupied by secure tenants, a disposal to which section 171A applies (preservation of right to buy on disposal to private landlord), and
   (b) lists, to the best of the disponor's knowledge and belief, the dwelling-houses to which the disposal relates which are occupied by secure tenants.

### *Registration of title on qualifying disposal*

2.—(1) ...

(2) [Where on a qualifying disposal the disponor's title to the dwelling-house is not registered, the disponor] shall give the disponee a certificate stating that the disponor is entitled to effect the disposal subject only to such incumbrances, rights and interests as are stated in the instrument effecting the disposal or summarised in the certificate.

(3) Where the disponor's interest in the dwelling-house is a lease, the certificate shall also state particulars of the lease and, with respect to each superior title—
   (a) where it is registered, the title number;
   (b) where it is not registered, whether it was investigated in the usual way on the grant of the disponor's lease.

(4) The certificate shall be—
   (a) in a form approved by the Chief Land Registrar, and
   (b) signed by such officer of the disponor or such other person as may be approved by the Chief Land Registrar,

and the Chief Registrar shall, for the purpose of registration of title, accept the certificate as sufficient evidence of the facts stated in it.

3. ...

### *Entries on register protecting preserved right to buy*

[4.—(1) This paragraph applies where the Chief Land Registrar approves an application for registration of—
   (a) a disposition of registered land, or
   (b) the disponee's title under a disposition of unregistered land,

and the instrument effecting the disposition contains the statement required by paragraph 1.

(2) The Chief Land Registrar must enter in the register—
   (a) a notice in respect of the rights of qualifying persons under this Part in relation to dwelling-houses comprised in the disposal, and
   (b) a restriction reflecting the limitation under section 171D(2) on subsequent disposal.]

### Change of qualifying dwelling-house

5.—(1)   This paragraph applies where by virtue of section 171B(6) a new dwelling-house becomes the qualifying dwelling-house which—

 (a)   is entirely different from the previous qualifying dwelling-house, or

 (b)   includes new land,

and applies to the new dwelling-house or the new land, as the case may be.

 [(2)   If the landlord's title is registered, the landlord shall apply for the entry in the register of—

 (a)   a notice in respect of the rights of the qualifying person or persons under the provisions of this Part, and

 (b)   a restriction reflecting the limitation under section 171D(2) on subsequent disposal.]

 (3)   ...

 (4)   If the landlord's title is not registered, the rights of the qualifying person or persons under the provisions of this Part are registrable under the Land Charges Act 1972 in the same way as an estate contract and the landlord shall, and a qualifying person may, apply for such registration.

### Effect of non-registration

6.—[(1)   The rights of a qualifying person under this Part in relation to the qualifying dwelling house shall not be regarded as falling within Schedule 3 to the Land Registration Act 2002 (and so are liable to be postponed under section 29 of that Act, unless protected by means of a notice in the register).]

 (2)   Where by virtue of paragraph 5(4) the rights of a qualifying person under this Part in relation to the qualifying dwelling-house are registrable under the Land Charges Act 1972 in the same way as an estate contract, section 4(6) of that Act (under which such a contract may be void against a purchaser unless registered) applies accordingly, with the substitution for the reference to the contract being void of a reference to the right to buy ceasing to be preserved.

### Statement required on certain disposals on which right to buy ceases to be preserved

7.—(1)   A conveyance of the freehold or grant of a lease of the qualifying dwelling-house to a qualifying person in pursuance of the right to buy shall state that it is made in pursuance of the provisions of this Part as they apply by virtue of section 171A (preservation of the right to buy).

 (2)   Where on a conveyance of the freehold or grant of a lease of the qualifying dwelling-house to a qualifying person otherwise than in pursuance of the right to buy the dwelling-house ceases to be subject to any rights arising under this Part, the conveyance or grant shall contain a statement to that effect.

 (3)   Where on a disposal of an interest in a qualifying dwelling-house the dwelling-house ceases to be subject to the rights of a qualifying person under this Part by virtue of section 171D(1)(a) or 171E(2)(a) (qualifying person becoming tenant of authority or body satisfying landlord condition for secure tenancies), the instrument by which the disposal is effected shall state that the dwelling-house ceases as a result of the disposal to be subject to any rights arising by virtue of section 171A (preservation of the right to buy).

### Removal of entries on land register

8.   Where the registered title to land contains an entry made by virtue of this Schedule, the Chief Land Registrar shall, for the purpose of removing or amending the entry, accept as sufficient evidence of the facts stated in it a certificate by the registered proprietor that the whole or a specified part of the land is not subject to any rights of a qualifying person under this Part.

### Liability to compensate or indemnify

9.—(1)   An action for breach of statutory duty lies where—

 (a)   the disponor on a qualifying disposal fails to comply with paragraph 1 (duty to secure inclusion of statement in instrument effecting disposal), or

 (b)   the landlord on a change of the qualifying dwelling-house fails to comply with paragraph 5(2) or (4) (duty to apply for registration protecting preserved right to buy),

and a qualifying person is deprived of the preserved right to buy by reason of the non-registration of the matters which would have been registered if that duty had been complied with.

 (2)   If the Chief Land Registrar has to meet a claim under the [Land Registration Act 2002] as a result of acting upon—

 (a)   a certificate given in pursuance of paragraph 2 (certificate of title on first registration),

 (b)   a statement made in pursuance of paragraph 7 (statements required on disposal on which right to buy ceases to be preserved), or

 (c)   a certificate given in pursuance of paragraph 8 (certificate that dwelling-house has ceased to be subject to rights under this Part),

the person who gave the certificate or made the statement shall indemnify him.

*Meaning of "disposal" and "instrument effecting disposal"*

10. References in this Schedule to a disposal or to the instrument effecting a disposal are to the conveyance, transfer, grant or assignment, as the case may be.]

**[591]**

---

**NOTES**

Inserted by the Housing and Planning Act 1986, s 8(2), (3), Sch 2, in relation to qualifying disposals made on or after 5 April 1989.

Para 2: sub-para (1) repealed and words in square brackets in sub-para (2) substituted by the Land Registration Act 2002, ss 133, 135, Sch 11, para 18(1), (6), Sch 13.

Para 3: repealed by the Land Registration Act 2002, s 135, Sch 13.

Para 4: substituted by the Land Registration Act 2002, s 133, Sch 11, para 18(1), (7).

Para 5: sub-para (2) substituted and sub-para (3) repealed by the Land Registration Act 2002, ss 133, 135, Sch 11, para 18(1), (8), (9), Sch 13.

Para 6: sub-para (1) substituted by the Land Registration Act 2002, s 133, Sch 11, para 18(1), (10).

Para 9: words in square brackets in sub-para (2) substituted by the Land Registration Act 2002, s 133, Sch 11, para 18(1), (11).

---

*(Schs 10–24, in so far as unrepealed, outside the scope of this work.)*

# LANDLORD AND TENANT ACT 1985

(1985 c 70)

## ARRANGEMENT OF SECTIONS

*Information to be given to tenant*

*Provision of rent books*

*Implied terms as to fitness for human habitation*

*Repairing obligations*

*Service charges*

*An Act to consolidate certain provisions of the law of landlord and tenant formerly found in the Housing Acts, together with the Landlord and Tenant Act 1962, with amendments to give effect to recommendations of the Law Commission*

[30 October 1985]

**NOTES**

Transfer of functions: as to the functions of Ministers of the Crown under this Act, so far as exercisable in relation to Wales, being transferred to the National Assembly for Wales, see the National Assembly for Wales (Transfer of Functions) Order 1999, SI 1999/672, art 2, Sch 1.

*Information to be given to tenant*

## 1   Disclosure of landlord's identity

(1)   If the tenant of premises occupied as a dwelling makes a written request for the landlord's name and address to—

    (a)   any person who demands, or the last person who received, rent payable under the tenancy, or

    (b)   any other person for the time being acting as agent for the landlord, in relation to the tenancy,

that person shall supply the tenant with a written statement of the landlord's name and address within the period of 21 days beginning with the day on which he receives the request.

(2)   A person who, without reasonable excuse, fails to comply with subsection (1) commits a summary offence and is liable on conviction to a fine not exceeding level 4 on the standard scale.

(3)   In this section and section 2—

    (a)   "tenant" includes a statutory tenant; and

    (b)   "landlord" means the immediate landlord.

[592]

## 2   Disclosure of directors, etc of corporate landlord

(1)   Where a tenant is supplied under section 1 with the name and address of his landlord and the landlord is a body corporate, he may make a further written request to the landlord for the name and address of every director and of the secretary of the landlord.

(2)   The landlord shall supply the tenant with a written statement of the information requested within the period of 21 days beginning with the day on which he receives the request.

(3)   A request under this section is duly made to the landlord if it is made to—
  (a)   an agent of the landlord, or
  (b)   a person who demands the rent of the premises concerned;
and any such agent or person to whom such a request is made shall forward it to the landlord as soon as may be.

(4)   A landlord who, without reasonable excuse, fails to comply with a request under this section, and a person who, without reasonable excuse, fails to comply with a requirement imposed on him by subsection (3), commits a summary offence and is liable on conviction to a fine not exceeding level 4 on the standard scale.

[593]

### 3   Duty to inform tenant of assignment of landlord's interest

(1)   If the interest of the landlord under a tenancy of premises which consist of or include a dwelling is assigned, the new landlord shall give notice in writing of the assignment, and of his name and address, to the tenant not later than the next day on which rent is payable under the tenancy or, if that is within two months of the assignment, the end of that period of two months.

(2)   If trustees constitute the new landlord, a collective description of the trustees as the trustees of the trust in question may be given as the name of the landlord, and where such a collective description is given—
  (a)   the address of the new landlord may be given as the address from which the affairs of the trust are conducted, and
  (b)   a change in the persons who are for the time being the trustees of the trust shall not be treated as an assignment of the interest of the landlord.

(3)   A person who is the new landlord under a tenancy falling within subsection (1) and who fails, without reasonable excuse, to give the notice required by that subsection, commits a summary offence and is liable on conviction to a fine not exceeding level 4 on the standard scale.

[(3A)   The person who was the landlord under the tenancy immediately before the assignment ("the old landlord") shall be liable to the tenant in respect of any breach of any covenant, condition or agreement under the tenancy occurring before the end of the relevant period in like manner as if the interest assigned were still vested in him; and where the new landlord is also liable to the tenant in respect of any such breach occurring within that period, he and the old landlord shall be jointly and severally liable in respect of it.

(3B)   In subsection (3A) "the relevant period" means the period beginning with the date of the assignment and ending with the date when—
  (a)   notice in writing of the assignment, and of the new landlord's name and address, is given to the tenant by the new landlord (whether in accordance with subsection (1) or not), or
  (b)   notice in writing of the assignment, and of the new landlord's name and last-known address, is given to the tenant by the old landlord,
whichever happens first.]

(4)   In this section—
  (a)   "tenancy" includes a statutory tenancy, and
  (b)   references to the assignment of the landlord's interest include any conveyance other than a mortgage or charge.

[594]

---

**NOTES**
Sub-ss (3A), (3B): inserted by the Landlord and Tenant Act 1987, s 50.

---

### [3A   Duty to inform tenant of possible right to acquire landlord's interest

(1)   Where a new landlord is required by section 3(1) to give notice to a tenant of an assignment to him, then if—
  (a)   the tenant is a qualifying tenant within the meaning of Part I of the Landlord and Tenant Act 1987 (tenants' rights of first refusal), and
  (b)   the assignment was a relevant disposal within the meaning of that Part affecting premises to which at the time of the disposal that Part applied,
the landlord shall give also notice in writing to the tenant to the following effect.

(2)   The notice shall state—
  (a)   that the disposal to the landlord was one to which Part I of the Landlord and Tenant Act 1987 applied;
  (b)   that the tenant (together with other qualifying tenants) may have the right under that Part—
     (i)   to obtain information about the disposal, and

     (ii)    to acquire the landlord's interest in the whole or part of the premises in which the tenant's flat is situated; and

    (c)    the time within which any such right must be exercised, and the fact that the time would run from the date of receipt of notice under this section by the requisite majority of qualifying tenants (within the meaning of that Part).

(3)    A person who is required to give notice under this section and who fails, without reasonable excuse, to do so within the time allowed for giving notice under section 3(1) commits a summary offence and is liable on conviction to a fine not exceeding level 4 on the standard scale.]

**[595]**

**NOTES**
Inserted by the Housing Act 1996, s 93(1).

*Provision of rent books*

### 4  Provision of rent books

(1)    Where a tenant has a right to occupy premises as a residence in consideration of a rent payable weekly, the landlord shall provide a rent book or other similar document for use in respect of the premises.

(2)    Subsection (1) does not apply to premises if the rent includes a payment in respect of board and the value of that board to the tenant forms a substantial proportion of the whole rent.

(3)    In this section and sections 5 to 7—
    (a)    "tenant" includes a statutory tenant and a person having a contractual right to occupy the premises; and
    (b)    "landlord", in relation to a person having such a contractual right, means the person who granted the right or any successor in title of his, as the case may require.

**[596]**

### 5  Information to be contained in rent books

(1)    A rent book or other similar document provided in pursuance of section 4 shall contain notice of the name and address of the landlord of the premises and—
    (a)    if the premises are occupied by virtue of a restricted contract, particulars of the rent and of the other terms and conditions of the contract and notice of such other matters as may be prescribed;
    (b)    if the premises are let on or subject to a protected or statutory tenancy [or let on an assured tenancy within the meaning of Part I of the Housing Act 1988], notice of such matters as may be prescribed.

(2)    If the premises are occupied by virtue of a restricted contract or let on or subject to a protected or statutory tenancy [or let on an assured tenancy within the meaning of Part I of the Housing Act 1988], the notice and particulars required by this section shall be in the prescribed form.

(3)    In this section "prescribed" means prescribed by regulations made by the Secretary of State, which—
    (a)    may make different provision for different cases, and
    (b)    shall be made by statutory instrument which shall be subject to annulment in pursuance of a resolution of either House of Parliament.

**[597]**

**NOTES**
Sub-ss (1), (2): words in square brackets inserted by the Housing Act 1988, s 140(1), Sch 17, Pt I, para 67(1), (2).
Regulations: by virtue of the Housing (Consequential Provisions) Act 1985, s 2(2), the Rent Book (Forms of Notice) Regulations 1982, SI 1982/1474 at **[3051]** have effect as if made under this section.

### 6  Information to be supplied by companies

(1)    Where the landlord of premises to which section 4(1) applies (premises occupied as a residence at a weekly rent) is a company, and the tenant serves on the landlord a request in writing to that effect, the landlord shall give the tenant in writing particulars of the name and address of every director and of the secretary of the company.

(2)    A request under this section is duly served on the landlord if it is served—
    (a)    on an agent of the landlord named as such in the rent book or other similar document, or
    (b)    on the person who receives the rent of the premises;
and a person on whom a request is so served shall forward it to the landlord as soon as may be.

**[598]**

## 7 Offences

(1) If the landlord of premises to which section 4(1) applies (premises occupied as a residence at a weekly rent) fails to comply with any relevant requirement of—

section 4 (provision of rent book),

section 5 (information to be contained in rent book), or

section 6 (information to be supplied by companies),

he commits a summary offence and is liable on conviction to a fine not exceeding level 4 on the standard scale.

(2) If a person demands or receives rent on behalf of the landlord of such premises while any relevant requirement of—

section 4 (provision of rent book), or

section 5 (information to be contained in rent book),

is not complied with, then, unless he shows that he neither knew nor had reasonable cause to suspect that any such requirement had not been complied with, he commits a summary offence and is liable to a fine not exceeding level 4 on the standard scale.

(3) If a person fails to comply with a requirement imposed on him by section 6(2) (duty to forward request to landlord), he commits a summary offence and is liable on conviction to a fine not exceeding level 4 on the standard scale.

(4) If a default in respect of which—

    (a)    a landlord is convicted of an offence under subsection (1), or

    (b)    another person is convicted of an offence under subsection (3),

continues for more than 14 days after the conviction, the landlord or other person commits a further offence under that subsection in respect of the default.

**[599]**

*Implied terms as to fitness for human habitation*

## 8 Implied terms as to fitness for human habitation

(1) In a contract to which this section applies for the letting of a house for human habitation there is implied, notwithstanding any stipulation to the contrary—

    (a)    a condition that the house is fit for human habitation at the commencement of the tenancy, and

    (b)    an undertaking that the house will be kept by the landlord fit for human habitation during the tenancy.

(2) The landlord, or a person authorised by him in writing, may at reasonable times of the day, on giving 24 hours' notice in writing to the tenant or occupier, enter premises to which this section applies for the purpose of viewing their state and condition.

(3) This section applies to a contract if—

    (a)    the rent does not exceed the figure applicable in accordance with subsection (4), and

    (b)    the letting is not on such terms as to the tenant's responsibility as are mentioned in subsection (5).

(4) The rent limit for the application of this section is shown by the following Table, by reference to the date of making of the contract and the situation of the premises:

TABLE

| Date of making of contract | Rent limit |
| --- | --- |
| Before 31st July 1923. | In London: £40. |
| | Elsewhere: £26 or £16 (see Note 1). |
| On or after 31st July 1923 and before 6th July 1957. | In London: £40. |
| | Elsewhere: £26. |
| On or after 6th July 1957. | In London: £80. |
| | Elsewhere: £52. |

NOTES

1. The applicable figure for contracts made before 31st July 1923 is £26 in the case of premises situated in a borough or urban district which at the date of the contract had according to the last published census a population of 50,000 or more. In the case of a house situated elsewhere, the figure is £16.

2. The references to "London" are, in relation to contracts made before 1st April 1965, to the administrative county of London and, in relation to contracts made on or after that date, to Greater London exclusive of the outer London boroughs.

(5) This section does not apply where a house is let for a term of three years or more (the lease not being determinable at the option of either party before the expiration of three years) upon terms that the tenant puts the premises into a condition reasonably fit for human habitation.

(6) In this section "house" includes—
    (a)    a part of a house, and
    (b)    any yard, garden, outhouses and appurtenances belonging to the house or usually enjoyed with it.

**[600]**

## 9   Application of s 8 to certain houses occupied by agricultural workers

(1) Where under the contract of employment of a worker employed in agriculture the provision of a house for his occupation forms part of his remuneration and the provisions of section 8 (implied terms as to fitness for human habitation) are inapplicable by reason only of the house not being let to him—
    (a)    there are implied as part of the contract of employment, notwithstanding any stipulation to the contrary, the like condition and undertaking as would be implied under that section if the house were so let, and
    (b)    the provisions of that section apply accordingly, with the substitution of "employer" for "landlord" and such other modifications as may be necessary.

(2) This section does not affect any obligation of a person other than the employer to repair a house to which this section applies, or any remedy for enforcing such an obligation.

(3) In this section "house" includes—
    (a)    a part of a house, and
    (b)    any yard, garden, outhouses and appurtenances belonging to the house or usually enjoyed with it.

**[601]**

## 10   Fitness for human habitation

In determining for the purposes of this Act whether a house is unfit for human habitation, regard shall be had to its condition in respect of the following matters—
    repair,
    stability,
    freedom from damp,
    internal arrangement,
    natural lighting,
    ventilation,
    water supply,
    drainage and sanitary conveniences,
    facilities for preparation and cooking of food and for the disposal of waste water;
and the house shall be regarded as unfit for human habitation if, and only if, it is so far defective in one or more of those matters that it is not reasonably suitable for occupation in that condition.

**[602]**

*Repairing obligations*

## 11   Repairing obligations in short leases

(1) In a lease to which this section applies (as to which, see sections 13 and 14) there is implied a covenant by the lessor—
    (a)    to keep in repair the structure and exterior of the dwelling-house (including drains, gutters and external pipes),
    (b)    to keep in repair and proper working order the installations in the dwelling-house for the supply of water, gas and electricity and for sanitation (including basins, sinks, baths and sanitary conveniences, but not other fixtures, fittings and appliances for making use of the supply of water, gas or electricity), and
    (c)    to keep in repair and proper working order the installations in the dwelling-house for space heating and heating water.

[(1A)  If a lease to which this section applies is a lease of a dwelling-house which forms part only of a building, then, subject to subsection (1B), the covenant implied by subsection (1) shall have effect as if—

    (a)    the reference in paragraph (a) of that subsection to the dwelling-house included a reference to any part of the building in which the lessor has an estate or interest; and

    (b)    any reference in paragraphs (b) and (c) of that subsection to an installation in the dwelling-house included a reference to an installation which, directly or indirectly, serves the dwelling-house and which either—

        (i)    forms part of any part of a building in which the lessor has an estate or interest; or

        (ii)    is owned by the lessor or under his control.

(1B)  Nothing in subsection (1A) shall be construed as requiring the lessor to carry out any works or repairs unless the disrepair (or failure to maintain in working order) is such as to affect the lessee's enjoyment of the dwelling-house or of any common parts, as defined in section 60(1) of the Landlord and Tenant Act 1987, which the lessee, as such, is entitled to use.]

(2)  The covenant implied by subsection (1) ("the lessor's repairing covenant") shall not be construed as requiring the lessor—

    (a)    to carry out works or repairs for which the lessee is liable by virtue of his duty to use the premises in a tenant-like manner, or would be so liable but for an express covenant on his part,

    (b)    to rebuild or reinstate the premises in the case of destruction or damage by fire, or by tempest, flood or other inevitable accident, or

    (c)    to keep in repair or maintain anything which the lessee is entitled to remove from the dwelling-house.

(3)  In determining the standard of repair required by the lessor's repairing covenant, regard shall be had to the age, character and prospective life of the dwelling-house and the locality in which it is situated.

[(3A)  In any case where—

    (a)    the lessor's repairing covenant has effect as mentioned in subsection (1A), and

    (b)    in order to comply with the covenant the lessor needs to carry out works or repairs otherwise than in, or to an installation in, the dwelling-house, and

    (c)    the lessor does not have a sufficient right in the part of the building or the installation concerned to enable him to carry out the required works or repairs,

then, in any proceedings relating to a failure to comply with the lessor's repairing covenant, so far as it requires the lessor to carry out the works or repairs in question, it shall be a defence for the lessor to prove that he used all reasonable endeavours to obtain, but was unable to obtain, such rights as would be adequate to enable him to carry out the works or repairs.]

(4)  A covenant by the lessee for the repair of the premises is of no effect so far as it relates to the matters mentioned in subsection (1)(a) to (c), except so far as it imposes on the lessee any of the requirements mentioned in subsection (2)(a) or (c).

(5)  The reference in subsection (4) to a covenant by the lessee for the repair of the premises includes a covenant—

    (a)    to put in repair or deliver up in repair,

    (b)    to paint, point or render,

    (c)    to pay money in lieu of repairs by the lessee, or

    (d)    to pay money on account of repairs by the lessor.

(6)  In a lease in which the lessor's repairing covenant is implied there is also implied a covenant by the lessee that the lessor, or any person authorised by him in writing, may at reasonable times of the day and on giving 24 hours' notice in writing to the occupier, enter the premises comprised in the lease for the purpose of viewing their condition and state of repair.

**[603]**

**NOTES**

Sub-ss (1A), (1B), (3A): inserted by the Housing Act 1988, s 116(1)–(4), except with respect to a lease entered into before 15 January 1989 or a lease entered into pursuant to a contract made before that date.

Modified, where the RTM company has acquired the right to manage, by the Commonhold and Leasehold Reform Act 2002, s 102, Sch 7, para 3 at **[1266]**, **[1306]**.

**12  Restriction on contracting out of s 11**

(1)  A covenant or agreement, whether contained in a lease to which section 11 applies or in an agreement collateral to such a lease, is void in so far as it purports—

    (a)    to exclude or limit the obligations of the lessor or the immunities of the lessee under that section, or

    (b)    to authorise any forfeiture or impose on the lessee any penalty, disability or obligation in the event of his enforcing or relying upon those obligations or immunities,

unless the inclusion of the provision was authorised by the county court.

(2)   The county court may, by order made with the consent of the parties, authorise the inclusion in a lease, or in an agreement collateral to a lease, of provisions excluding or modifying in relation to the lease, the provisions of section 11 with respect to the repairing obligations of the parties if it appears to the court that it is reasonable to do so, having regard to all the circumstances of the case, including the other terms and conditions of the lease.

**[604]**

**NOTES**

Modified, where the RTM company has acquired the right to manage, by the Commonhold and Leasehold Reform Act 2002, s 102, Sch 7, para 3 at **[1266]**, **[1306]**.

## 13   Leases to which s 11 applies: general rule

(1)   Section 11 (repairing obligations) applies to a lease of a dwelling-house granted on or after 24th October 1961 for a term of less than seven years.

(2)   In determining whether a lease is one to which section 11 applies—

(a)   any part of the term which falls before the grant shall be left out of account and the lease shall be treated as a lease for a term commencing with the grant,

(b)   a lease which is determinable at the option of the lessor before the expiration of seven years from the commencement of the term shall be treated as a lease for a term of less than seven years, and

(c)   a lease (other than a lease to which paragraph (b) applies) shall not be treated as a lease for a term of less than seven years if it confers on the lessee an option for renewal for a term which, together with the original term, amounts to seven years or more.

(3)   This section has effect subject to—

section 14 (leases to which section 11 applies: exceptions), and

section 32(2) (provisions not applying to tenancies within Part II of the Landlord and Tenant Act 1954).

**[605]**

## 14   Leases to which s 11 applies: exceptions

(1)   Section 11 (repairing obligations) does not apply to a new lease granted to an existing tenant, or to a former tenant still in possession, if the previous lease was not a lease to which section 11 applied (and, in the case of a lease granted before 24th October 1961, would not have been if it had been granted on or after that date).

(2)   In subsection (1)—

"existing tenant" means a person who is when, or immediately before, the new lease is granted, the lessee under another lease of the dwelling-house;

"former tenant still in possession" means a person who—

(a)   was the lessee under another lease of the dwelling-house which terminated at some time before the new lease was granted, and

(b)   between the termination of that other lease and the grant of the new lease was continuously in possession of the dwelling-house or of the rents and profits of the dwelling-house; and

"the previous lease" means the other lease referred to in the above definitions.

(3)   Section 11 does not apply to a lease of a dwelling-house which is a tenancy of an agricultural holding within the meaning of the [Agricultural Holdings Act 1986] [and in relation to which that Act applies or to a farm business tenancy within the meaning of the Agricultural Tenancies Act 1995].

(4)   Section 11 does not apply to a lease granted on or after 3rd October 1980 to—

a local authority,

[a National Park authority]

a new town corporation,

an urban development corporation,

the Development Board for Rural Wales,

a [registered social landlord],

a co-operative housing association, or

an educational institution or other body specified, or of a class specified, by regulations under section 8 of the Rent Act 1977 [or paragraph 8 of Schedule 1 to the Housing Act 1988] (bodies making student lettings)

[a housing action trust established under Part III of the Housing Act 1988].

(5)   Section 11 does not apply to a lease granted on or after 3rd October 1980 to—

(a)   Her Majesty in right of the Crown (unless the lease is under the management of the Crown Estate Commissioners), or

(b)    a government department or a person holding in trust for Her Majesty for the purposes of a government department.

[606]

**NOTES**

Sub-s (3): words in first pair of square brackets substituted by the Agricultural Holdings Act 1986, s 100, Sch 14, para 64; words in second pair of square brackets added by the Agricultural Tenancies Act 1995, s 40, Schedule, para 31.

Sub-s (4): words in first pair of square brackets inserted by the Environment Act 1995, s 78, Sch 10, para 25(1); words in second pair of square brackets substituted by the Housing Act 1996 (Consequential Provisions) Order 1996, SI 1996/2325, art 5, Sch 2, para 16(1), (2); words in third pair of square brackets inserted by the Local Government and Housing Act 1989, s 194(1), Sch 11, para 89; words in fourth pair of square brackets added by the Housing Act 1988, s 116(3), (4), except with respect to a lease entered into before 15 January 1989 or a lease entered into in pursuance of a contract made before that date.

## 15   Jurisdiction of county court

The county court has jurisdiction to make a declaration that section 11 (repairing obligations) applies, or does not apply, to a lease—

(a)    whatever the net annual value of the property in question, and

(b)    notwithstanding that no other relief is sought than a declaration.

[607]

## 16   Meaning of "lease" and related expressions

In sections 11 to 15 (repairing obligations in short leases)—

(a)    "lease" does not include a mortgage term;

(b)    "lease of a dwelling-house" means a lease by which a building or part of a building is let wholly or mainly as a private residence, and "dwelling-house" means that building or part of a building;

(c)    "lessee" and "lessor" mean, respectively, the person for the time being entitled to the term of a lease and to the reversion expectant on it.

[608]

## 17   Specific performance of landlord's repairing obligations

(1)    In proceedings in which a tenant of a dwelling alleges a breach on the part of his landlord of a repairing covenant relating to any part of the premises in which the dwelling is comprised, the court may order specific performance of the covenant whether or not the breach relates to a part of the premises let to the tenant and notwithstanding any equitable rule restricting the scope of the remedy, whether on the basis of a lack of mutuality or otherwise.

(2)    In this section—

(a)    "tenant" includes a statutory tenant,

(b)    in relation to a statutory tenant the reference to the premises let to him is to the premises of which he is a statutory tenant,

(c)    "landlord", in relation to a tenant, includes any person against whom the tenant has a right to enforce a repairing covenant, and

(d)    "repairing covenant" means a covenant to repair, maintain, renew, construct or replace any property.

[609]

*Service charges*

## 18   Meaning of "service charge" and "relevant costs"

(1)    In the following provisions of this Act "service charge" means an amount payable by a tenant of a [dwelling] as part of or in addition to the rent—

(a)    which is payable, directly or indirectly, for services, repairs, maintenance[, improvements] or insurance or the landlord's costs of management, and

(b)    the whole or part of which varies or may vary according to the relevant costs.

(2)    The relevant costs are the costs or estimated costs incurred or to be incurred by or on behalf of the landlord, or a superior landlord, in connection with the matters for which the service charge is payable.

(3)    For this purpose—

(a)    "costs" includes overheads, and

(b)    costs are relevant costs in relation to a service charge whether they are incurred, or to be incurred, in the period for which the service charge is payable or in an earlier or later period.

[610]

**NOTES**

Sub-s (1): word in first pair of square brackets substituted by the Landlord and Tenant Act 1987, s 41(1), Sch 2, para 1; word in second pair of square brackets inserted by the Commonhold and Leasehold Reform Act 2002, s 150, Sch 9, para 7, except in relation to costs incurred before 30 September 2003 (in relation to England) or 31 March 2004 (in relation to Wales) in connection with matters for which a service charge is payable.

Modified, where the RTM company has acquired the right to manage, by the Commonhold and Leasehold Reform Act 2002, s 102, Sch 7, para 4 at **[1266]**, **[1306]**.

## 19   Limitation of service charges: reasonableness

(1)   Relevant costs shall be taken into account in determining the amount of a service charge payable for a period—

     (a)   only to the extent that they are reasonably incurred, and

     (b)   where they are incurred on the provision of services or the carrying out of works, only if the services or works are of a reasonable standard;

and the amount payable shall be limited accordingly.

(2)   Where a service charge is payable before the relevant costs are incurred, no greater amount than is reasonable is so payable, and after the relevant costs have been incurred any necessary adjustment shall be made by repayment, reduction or subsequent charges or otherwise.

[(2A)–(2C)], (3), (4)   ...

*[(5)   If a person takes any proceedings in the High Court in pursuance of any of the provisions of this Act relating to service charges and he could have taken those proceedings in the county court, he shall not be entitled to recover any costs.]*

**[611]**

**NOTES**

Sub-ss (2A)–(2C): inserted by the Housing Act 1996, s 83(1); repealed by the Commonhold and Leasehold Reform Act 2002, s 180, Sch 14, except in relation to any application made to an LVT under these sub-ss or any proceedings relating to a service charge transferred to an LVT by a county court before 30 September 2003 (in relation to England) or 31 March 2004 (in relation to Wales).

Sub-s (3): repealed by the Commonhold and Leasehold Reform Act 2002, s 180, Sch 14, except in relation to any application made to an LVT under sub-ss (2A), (2B) above or any proceedings relating to a service charge transferred to an LVT by a county court before 30 September 2003 (in relation to England) or 31 March 2004 (in relation to Wales).

Sub-s (4): repealed by the Housing Act 1996, s 227, Sch 19, Pt III.

Sub-s (5): added by the Landlord and Tenant Act 1987, s 41(1), Sch 2, para 2; repealed by the Courts and Legal Services Act 1990, s 125(7), Sch 20, as from a day to be appointed.

Modified, where the RTM company has acquired the right to manage, by the Commonhold and Leasehold Reform Act 2002, s 102, Sch 7, para 4 at **[1266]**, **[1306]**.

## [20   Limitation of service charges: consultation requirements

(1)   Where this section applies to any qualifying works or qualifying long term agreement, the relevant contributions of tenants are limited in accordance with subsection (6) or (7) (or both) unless the consultation requirements have been either—

     (a)   complied with in relation to the works or agreement, or

     (b)   dispensed with in relation to the works or agreement by (or on appeal from) a leasehold valuation tribunal.

(2)   In this section "relevant contribution", in relation to a tenant and any works or agreement, is the amount which he may be required under the terms of his lease to contribute (by the payment of service charges) to relevant costs incurred on carrying out the works or under the agreement.

(3)   This section applies to qualifying works if relevant costs incurred on carrying out the works exceed an appropriate amount.

(4)   The Secretary of State may by regulations provide that this section applies to a qualifying long term agreement—

     (a)   if relevant costs incurred under the agreement exceed an appropriate amount, or

     (b)   if relevant costs incurred under the agreement during a period prescribed by the regulations exceed an appropriate amount.

(5)   An appropriate amount is an amount set by regulations made by the Secretary of State; and the regulations may make provision for either or both of the following to be an appropriate amount—

     (a)   an amount prescribed by, or determined in accordance with, the regulations, and

     (b)   an amount which results in the relevant contribution of any one or more tenants being an amount prescribed by, or determined in accordance with, the regulations.

(6)    Where an appropriate amount is set by virtue of paragraph (a) of subsection (5), the amount of the relevant costs incurred on carrying out the works or under the agreement which may be taken into account in determining the relevant contributions of tenants is limited to the appropriate amount.

(7)    Where an appropriate amount is set by virtue of paragraph (b) of that subsection, the amount of the relevant contribution of the tenant, or each of the tenants, whose relevant contribution would otherwise exceed the amount prescribed by, or determined in accordance with, the regulations is limited to the amount so prescribed or determined.]

**[612]**

---

**NOTES**

Substituted, together with s 20ZA, for original s 20, by the Commonhold and Leasehold Reform Act 2002, s 151, subject to savings in relation to certain qualifying works: see the Commonhold and Leasehold Reform Act 2002 (Commencement No 2 and Savings) (England) Order 2003, SI 2003/1986, art 3(2)–(7) and the Commonhold and Leasehold Reform Act 2002 (Commencement No 2 and Savings) (Wales) Order 2004, SI 2004/669, art 2(d).

Section 20 and the notes relating to it, prior to its substitution by the Commonhold and Leasehold Reform Act 2002 as noted above (and as substituted by the Landlord and Tenant Act 1987, s 41, Sch 2, para 3), read as follows—

**"[20    Limitation of service charges: estimates and consultation**

(1)    Where relevant costs incurred on the carrying out of any qualifying works exceed the limit specified in subsection (3), the excess shall not be taken into account in determining the amount of a service charge unless the relevant requirements have been either—
    (a)    complied with, or
    (b)    dispensed with by the court in accordance with subsection (9);
and the amount payable shall be limited accordingly.

(2)    In subsection (1) "qualifying works", in relation to a service charge, means works (whether on a building or on any other premises) to the costs of which the tenant by whom the service charge is payable may be required under the terms of his lease to contribute by the payment of such a charge.

(3)    The limit is whichever is the greater of—
    (a)    £25, or such other amount as may be prescribed by order of the Secretary of State, multiplied by the number of dwellings let to the tenants concerned; or
    (b)    £500, or such other amount as may be so prescribed.

(4)    The relevant requirements in relation to such of the tenants concerned as are not represented by a recognised tenants' association are—
    (a)    At least two estimates for the works shall be obtained, one of them from a person wholly unconnected with the landlord.
    (b)    A notice accompanied by a copy of the estimates shall be given to each of those tenants or shall be displayed in or more places where it is likely to come to the notice of all those tenants.
    (c)    The notice shall describe the works to be carried out and invite observations on them and on the estimates and shall state the name and the address in the United Kingdom of the person to whom the observations may be sent and the date by which they are to be received.
    (d)    The date stated in the notice shall not be earlier than one month after the date on which the notice is given or displayed as required by paragraph (b).
    (e)    The landlord shall have regard to any observations received in pursuance of the notice; and unless the works are urgently required they shall not be begun earlier than the date specified in the notice.

(5)    The relevant requirements in relation to such of the tenants concerned as are represented by a recognised tenants' association are—
    (a)    The landlord shall give to the secretary of the association a notice containing a detailed specification of the works in question and specifying a reasonable period within which the association may propose to the landlord the names of one or more persons from whom estimates for the works should in its view be obtained by the landlord.
    (b)    At least two estimates for the works shall be obtained, one of them from a person wholly unconnected with the landlord.
    (c)    A copy of each of the estimates shall be given to the secretary of the association.
    (d)    A notice shall be given to each of the tenants concerned represented by the association, which shall—
        (i)    describe briefly the works to be carried out,
        (ii)    summarise the estimates,
        (iii)    inform the tenant that he has a right to inspect and take copies of a detailed specification of the works to be carried out and of the estimates,
        (iv)    invite observations on those works and on the estimates, and
        (v)    specify the name and the address in the United Kingdom of the person to whom the observations may be sent and the date by which they are to be received.
    (e)    The date stated in the notice shall not be earlier than one month after the date on which the notice is given as required by paragraph (d).
    (f)    If any tenant to whom the notice is given so requests, the landlord shall afford him reasonable facilities for inspecting a detailed specification of the works to be carried out and the estimates, free of charge, and for taking copies of them on payment of such reasonable charge as the landlord may determine.
    (g)    The landlord shall have regard to any observations received in pursuance of the notice and, unless the works are urgently required, they shall not be begun earlier than the date specified in the notice.

(6)   Paragraphs (d)(ii) and (iii) and (f) of subsection (5) shall not apply to any estimate of which a copy is enclosed with the notice given in pursuance of paragraph (d).

(7)   The requirement imposed on the landlord by subsection (5)(f) to make any facilities available to a person free of charge shall not be construed as precluding the landlord from treating as part of his costs of management any costs incurred by him in connection with making those facilities so available.

(8)   In this section "the tenants concerned" means all the landlord's tenants who may be required under the terms of their leases to contribute to the costs of the works in question by the payment of service charges.

(9)   In proceedings relating to a service charge the court may, if satisfied that the landlord acted reasonably, dispense with all or any of the relevant requirements.

(10)   An order under this section—
    (a)   may make different provision with respect to different cases or descriptions of case, including different provision for different areas, and
    (b)   shall be made by statutory instrument which shall be subject to annulment in pursuance of a resolution of either House of Parliament.]".

**Notes**
Figures of £50 and £1000 were prescribed for the purposes of sub-s (3)(a), (b) respectively by the Service Charge (Estimates and Consultation) Order 1988, SI 1988/1285 (now lapsed).

Modified, where the RTM company has acquired the right to manage, by the Commonhold and Leasehold Reform Act 2002, s 102, Sch 7, para 4 at **[1266]**, **[1306]**.
Regulations: the Service Charges (Consultation Requirements) (England) Regulations 2003, SI 2003/1987 at **[3287]**; the Service Charges (Consultation Requirements) (Wales) Regulations 2004, SI 2004/684 at **[3365]**.

### [20ZA   Consultation requirements: supplementary

(1)   Where an application is made to a leasehold valuation tribunal for a determination to dispense with all or any of the consultation requirements in relation to any qualifying works or qualifying long term agreement, the tribunal may make the determination if satisfied that it is reasonable to dispense with the requirements.

(2)   In section 20 and this section—
    "qualifying works" means works on a building or any other premises, and
    "qualifying long term agreement" means (subject to subsection (3)) an agreement entered into, by or on behalf of the landlord or a superior landlord, for a term of more than twelve months.

(3)   The Secretary of State may by regulations provide that an agreement is not a qualifying long term agreement—
    (a)   if it is an agreement of a description prescribed by the regulations, or
    (b)   in any circumstances so prescribed.

(4)   In section 20 and this section "the consultation requirements" means requirements prescribed by regulations made by the Secretary of State.

(5)   Regulations under subsection (4) may in particular include provision requiring the landlord—
    (a)   to provide details of proposed works or agreements to tenants or the recognised tenants' association representing them,
    (b)   to obtain estimates for proposed works or agreements,
    (c)   to invite tenants or the recognised tenants' association to propose the names of persons from whom the landlord should try to obtain other estimates,
    (d)   to have regard to observations made by tenants or the recognised tenants' association in relation to proposed works or agreements and estimates, and
    (e)   to give reasons in prescribed circumstances for carrying out works or entering into agreements.

(6)   Regulations under section 20 or this section—
    (a)   may make provision generally or only in relation to specific cases, and
    (b)   may make different provision for different purposes.

(7)   Regulations under section 20 or this section shall be made by statutory instrument which shall be subject to annulment in pursuance of a resolution of either House of Parliament.]

**[613]**

**NOTES**
Substituted as noted to s 20 at **[612]**.
Modified, where the RTM company has acquired the right to manage, by the Commonhold and Leasehold Reform Act 2002, s 102, Sch 7, para 4 at **[1266]**, **[1306]**.
Regulations: the Service Charges (Consultation Requirements) (England) Regulations 2003, SI 2003/1987 at **[3287]**; the Service Charges (Consultation Requirements) (Wales) Regulations 2004, SI 2004/684 at **[3365]**.

### [20A   Limitation of service charges: grant-aided works

[(1)]   Where relevant costs are incurred or to be incurred on the carrying out of works in respect of which a grant has been or is to be paid under [section 523 of the Housing Act 1985 (assistance for provision of separate service pipe for water supply) or any provision of Part I of the Housing Grants, Construction and Regeneration Act 1996 (grants, &c for renewal of private sector housing) or any corresponding earlier enactment] [or article 3 of the Regulatory Reform (Housing Assistance) (England and Wales) Order 2002 (power of local housing authorities to provide assistance)], the amount of the grant shall be deducted from the costs and the amount of the service charge payable shall be reduced accordingly.

   [(2)   In any case where—
- (a)   relevant costs are incurred or to be incurred on the carrying out of works which are included in the external works specified in a group repair scheme, within the meaning of [Part I of the Housing Grants, Construction and Regeneration Act 1996], and
- (b)   the landlord participated or is participating in that scheme as an assisted participant,

the amount which, in relation to the landlord, is [the balance of the cost determined in accordance with section 69(3) of the Housing Grants, Construction and Regeneration Act 1996] shall be deducted from the costs, and the amount of the service charge payable shall be reduced accordingly.]]

**[614]**

---

**NOTES**

Inserted by the Housing and Planning Act 1986, s 24(1)(i), Sch 5, Pt I, para 9(1).

Sub-s (1): numbered as such by virtue of the Local Government and Housing Act 1989, s 194(1), Sch 11, para 90; words in first pair of square brackets substituted by the Housing Grants, Construction and Regeneration Act 1996, s 103, Sch 1, para 11(1); words in second pair of square brackets inserted by the Regulatory Reform (Housing Assistance) (England and Wales) Order 2002, SI 2002/1860, art 9, Sch 1, para 2.

Sub-s (2): added by the Local Government and Housing Act 1989, s 194(1), Sch 11, para 90; words in square brackets substituted by the Housing Grants, Construction and Regeneration Act 1996, s 103, Sch 1, para 11(2).

Modified, where the RTM company has acquired the right to manage, by the Commonhold and Leasehold Reform Act 2002, s 102, Sch 7, para 4 at **[1266]**, **[1306]**.

---

**[20B  Limitation of service charges: time limit on making demands**

   (1)   If any of the relevant costs taken into account in determining the amount of any service charge were incurred more than 18 months before a demand for payment of the service charge is served on the tenant, then (subject to subsection (2)), the tenant shall not be liable to pay so much of the service charge as reflects the costs so incurred.

   (2)   Subsection (1) shall not apply if, within the period of 18 months beginning with the date when the relevant costs in question were incurred, the tenant was notified in writing that those costs had been incurred and that he would subsequently be required under the terms of his lease to contribute to them by the payment of a service charge.]

**[615]**

---

**NOTES**

Inserted by the Landlord and Tenant Act 1987, s 41(1), Sch 2, para 4.

Modified, where the RTM company has acquired the right to manage, by the Commonhold and Leasehold Reform Act 2002, s 102, Sch 7, para 4 at **[1266]**, **[1306]**.

---

**[20C  Limitation of service charges: costs of proceedings**

   (1)   A tenant may make an application for an order that all or any of the costs incurred, or to be incurred, by the landlord in connection with proceedings before a court[, residential property tribunal] or leasehold valuation tribunal, or the [Upper Tribunal], or in connection with arbitration proceedings, are not to be regarded as relevant costs to be taken into account in determining the amount of any service charge payable by the tenant or any other person or persons specified in the application.

   (2)   The application shall be made—
- (a)   in the case of court proceedings, to the court before which the proceedings are taking place or, if the application is made after the proceedings are concluded, to a county court;
- [(aa)  in the case of proceedings before a residential property tribunal, to a leasehold valuation tribunal;]
- (b)   in the case of proceedings before a leasehold valuation tribunal, to the tribunal before which the proceedings are taking place or, if the application is made after the proceedings are concluded, to any leasehold valuation tribunal;
- (c)   in the case of proceedings before the [Upper Tribunal], to the tribunal;
- (d)   in the case of arbitration proceedings, to the arbitral tribunal or, if the application is made after the proceedings are concluded, to a county court.

   (3)   The court or tribunal to which the application is made may make such order on the application as it considers just and equitable in the circumstances.]

**[616]**

**NOTES**
 Inserted by the Landlord and Tenant Act 1987, s 41(1), Sch 2, para 4.
 Substituted by the Housing Act 1996, s 83(4).
 Sub-s (1): words in first pair of square brackets inserted by the Housing Act 2004, s 265(1), Sch 15, para 32(1), (2); words in second pair of square brackets substituted by the Transfer of Tribunal Functions (Lands Tribunal and Miscellaneous Amendments) Order 2009, SI 2009/1307, art 5(1), (2), Sch 1, para 177, subject to transitional provisions and savings in Sch 5 thereto.
 Sub-s (2): para (aa) inserted by the Housing Act 2004, s 265(1), Sch 15, para 32(1), (3); words in square brackets in para (c) substituted by SI 2009/1307, art 5(1), (2), Sch 1, para 177, subject to transitional provisions and savings in Sch 5 thereto.
 Modified, where the RTM company has acquired the right to manage, by the Commonhold and Leasehold Reform Act 2002, s 102, Sch 7, para 4 at **[1266]**, **[1306]**.

### 21  Request for summary of relevant costs

 *(1)   A tenant may require the landlord in writing to supply him with a written summary of the costs incurred—*
   *(a)   if the relevant accounts are made up for periods of twelve months, in the last such period ending not later than the date of the request, or*
   *(b)   if the accounts are not so made up, in the period of twelve months ending with the date of the request,*
 *and which are relevant costs in relation to the service charges payable or demanded as payable in that or any other period.*

 *(2)   If [the tenant is represented by a recognised tenants' association and he] consents, the request may be made by the secretary of the association instead of by the tenant and may then be for the supply of the summary to the secretary.*

 *(3)   A request is duly served on the landlord if it is served on—*
   *(a)   an agent of the landlord named as such in the rent book or similar document, or*
   *(b)   the person who receives the rent on behalf of the landlord;*
 *and a person on whom a request is so served shall forward it as soon as may be to the landlord.*

 *(4)   The landlord shall comply with the request within one month of the request or within six months of the end of the period referred to in subsection (1)(a) or (b) whichever is the later.*

 *(5)   The summary shall [state whether any of the costs relate to works in respect of which a grant has been or is to be paid under [section 523 of the Housing Act 1985 (assistance for provision of separate service pipe for water supply) or any provision of Part I of the Housing Grants, Construction and Regeneration Act 1996 (grants, &c for renewal of private sector housing) or any corresponding earlier enactment], and] set out the costs in a way showing [how they have been or will be reflected in demands for service charges and, in addition, shall summarise each of the following items, namely—*
   *(a)   any of the costs in respect of which no demand for payment was received by the landlord within the period referred to in subsection (1)(a) or (b).*
   *(b)   any of the costs in respect of which—*
       *(i)   a demand for payment was so received, but*
       *(ii)   no payment was made by the landlord within that period, and*
   *(c)   any of the costs in respect of which—*
       *(i)   a demand for payment was so received, and*
       *(ii)   payment was made by the landlord within that period,*
 *and specify the aggregate of any amounts received by the landlord down to the end of that period on account of service charges in respect of relevant dwellings and still standing to the credit of the tenants of those dwellings at the end of that period.*

 *(5A)   In subsection (5) "relevant dwelling" means a dwelling whose tenant is either—*
   *(a)   the person by or with the consent of whom the request was made, or*
   *(b)   a person whose obligations under the terms of his lease as regards contributing to relevant costs relate to the same costs as the corresponding obligations of the person mentioned in paragraph (a) above relate to].*

 *[(5B)   The summary shall state whether any of the costs relate to works which are included in the external works specified in a group repair scheme, within the meaning of [Chapter II of Pt I of the Housing Grants, Construction and Regeneration Act 1996 or any corresponding earlier enactment], in which the landlord participated or is participating as an assisted participant.]*

 *(6)   [If the service charges in relation to which the costs are relevant costs as mentioned in subsection (1) are payable by the tenants of more than four dwellings], the summary shall be certified by a qualified accountant as—*
   *(a)   in this opinion a fair summary complying with the [requirements] of subsection (5), and*

    (*b*)    *being sufficiently supported by accounts, receipts and other documents which have been produced to him.*

**[617]**

**NOTES**

Substituted, together with new s 21A at **[618]**, by the Commonhold and Leasehold Reform Act 2002, s 152, as from 26 July 2002 (in relation to England for the purpose of making regulations), 1 January 2003 (in relation to Wales for the purpose of making regulations), and otherwise as from a day to be appointed, as follows:

**"21  Regular statements of account**

(1)   The landlord must supply to each tenant by whom service charges are payable, in relation to each accounting period, a written statement of account dealing with—

    (a)    service charges of the tenant and the tenants of dwellings associated with his dwelling,

    (b)    relevant costs relating to those service charges,

    (c)    the aggregate amount standing to the credit of the tenant and the tenants of those dwellings—

        (i)   at the beginning of the accounting period, and

        (ii)  at the end of the accounting period, and

    (d)    related matters.

(2)   The statement of account in relation to an accounting period must be supplied to each such tenant not later than six months after the end of the accounting period.

(3)   Where the landlord supplies a statement of account to a tenant he must also supply to him—

    (a)    a certificate of a qualified accountant that, in the accountant's opinion, the statement of account deals fairly with the matters with which it is required to deal and is sufficiently supported by accounts, receipts and other documents which have been produced to him, and

    (b)    a summary of the rights and obligations of tenants of dwellings in relation to service charges.

(4)   The Secretary of State may make regulations prescribing requirements as to the form and content of—

    (a)    statements of account,

    (b)    accountants' certificates, and

    (c)    summaries of rights and obligations,

required to be supplied under this section.

(5)   The Secretary of State may make regulations prescribing exceptions from the requirement to supply an accountant's certificate.

(6)   If the landlord has been notified by a tenant of an address in England and Wales at which he wishes to have supplied to him documents required to be so supplied under this section, the landlord must supply them to him at that address.

(7)   And the landlord is to be taken to have been so notified if notification has been given to—

    (a)    an agent of the landlord named as such in the rent book or similar document, or

    (b)    the person who receives the rent on behalf of the landlord;

and where notification is given to such an agent or person he must forward it as soon as may be to the landlord.

(8)   For the purposes of this section a dwelling is associated with another dwelling if the obligations of the tenants of the dwellings under the terms of their leases as regards contributing to relevant costs relate to the same costs.

(9)   In this section "accounting period" means such period—

    (a)    beginning with the relevant date, and

    (b)    ending with such date, not later than twelve months after the relevant date,

as the landlord determines.

(10)   In the case of the first accounting period in relation to any dwellings, the relevant date is the later of—

    (a)    the date on which service charges are first payable under a lease of any of them, and

    (b)    the date on which section 152 of the Commonhold and Leasehold Reform Act 2002 comes into force,

and, in the case of subsequent accounting periods, it is the date immediately following the end of the previous accounting period.

(11)   Regulations under subsection (4) may make different provision for different purposes.

(12)   Regulations under this section shall be made by statutory instrument which shall be subject to annulment in pursuance of a resolution of either House of Parliament.".

Sub-s (2): words in square brackets substituted by the Landlord and Tenant Act 1987, s 41(1), Sch 2, para 5(1), (2).

Sub-s (5): words in first (outer) pair of square brackets inserted by the Housing and Planning Act 1986, s 24(1)(i), Sch 5, Pt I, para 9(2); words in second (inner) pair of square brackets substituted by the Housing Grants, Construction and Regeneration Act 1996, s 103, Sch 1, para 12; words in third pair of square brackets substituted by the Landlord and Tenant Act 1987, s 41(1), Sch 2, para 5.

Sub-s (5A): inserted by the Landlord and Tenant Act 1987, s 41(1), Sch 2, para 5(1), (3).

Sub-s (5B): inserted by the Local Government and Housing Act 1989, s 194(1), Sch 11, para 91(2); words in square brackets substituted by the Housing Grants, Construction and Regeneration Act 1996, s 103, Sch 1, para 12.

Sub-s (6): words in square brackets substituted by the Landlord and Tenant Act 1987, s 41, Sch 2, para 5(1), (4).

Modified, where the RTM company has acquired the right to manage, by the Commonhold and Leasehold Reform Act 2002, s 102, Sch 7, para 4 at **[1266]**, **[1306]**.

This section (as substituted by the Commonhold and Leasehold Reform Act 2002, s 152, as noted above) is further substituted by the Housing and Regeneration Act 2008, s 303, Sch 12, paras 1, 2, as from 1 December 2008 (for the purpose of enabling the Secretary of State to make regulations), and as from a day to be appointed (for remaining purposes), as follows:

**"21   Service charge information**

(1)    The appropriate national authority may make regulations about the provision, by landlords of dwellings to each tenant by whom service charges are payable, of information about service charges.

(2)    The regulations must, subject to any exceptions provided for in the regulations, require the landlord to provide information about—
    (a)    the service charges of the tenant,
    (b)    any associated service charges, and
    (c)    relevant costs relating to service charges falling within paragraph (a) or (b).

(3)    The regulations must, subject to any exceptions provided for in the regulations, require the landlord to provide the tenant with a report by a qualified person on information which the landlord is required to provide by virtue of this section.

(4)    The regulations may make provision about—
    (a)    information to be provided by virtue of subsection (2),
    (b)    other information to be provided (whether in pursuance of a requirement or otherwise),
    (c)    reports of the kind mentioned in subsection (3),
    (d)    the period or periods in relation to which information or reports are to be provided,
    (e)    the times at or by which information or reports are to be provided,
    (f)    the form and manner in which information or reports are to be provided (including in particular whether information is to be contained in a statement of account),
    (g)    the descriptions of persons who are to be qualified persons for the purposes of subsection (3).

(5)    Subsections (2) to (4) do not limit the scope of the power conferred by subsection (1).

(6)    Regulations under this section may—
    (a)    make different provision for different cases or descriptions of case or for different purposes,
    (b)    contain such supplementary, incidental, consequential, transitional, transitory or saving provision as the appropriate national authority considers appropriate.

(7)    Regulations under this section are to be made by statutory instrument which, subject to subsections (8) and (9)—
    (a)    in the case of regulations made by the Secretary of State, is to be subject to annulment in pursuance of a resolution of either House of Parliament, and
    (b)    in the case of regulations made by the Welsh Ministers, is to be subject to annulment in pursuance of a resolution of the National Assembly for Wales.

(8)    The Secretary of State may not make a statutory instrument containing the first regulations made by the Secretary of State under this section unless a draft of the instrument has been laid before, and approved by a resolution of, each House of Parliament.

(9)    The Welsh Ministers may not make a statutory instrument containing the first regulations made by the Welsh Ministers under this section unless a draft of the instrument has been laid before, and approved by a resolution of, the National Assembly for Wales.

(10)    In this section—
    "the appropriate national authority"—
        (a)    in relation to England, means the Secretary of State, and
        (b)    in relation to Wales, means the Welsh Ministers,
    "associated service charges", in relation to a tenant by whom a contribution to relevant costs is payable as a service charge, means service charges of other tenants so far as relating to the same costs.".

**[21A   Withholding of service charges**

*(1)    A tenant may withhold payment of a service charge if—*
    *(a)    the landlord has not supplied a document to him by the time by which he is required to supply it under section 21, or*
    *(b)    the form or content of a document which the landlord has supplied to him under that section (at any time) does not conform exactly or substantially with the requirements prescribed by regulations under subsection (4) of that section.*

(2)    The maximum amount which the tenant may withhold is an amount equal to the aggregate of—
    *(a)    the service charges paid by him in the accounting period to which the document concerned would or does relate, and*
    *(b)    so much of the aggregate amount required to be dealt with in the statement of account for that accounting period by section 21(1)(c)(i) as stood to his credit.*

(3)    An amount may not be withheld under this section—
    *(a)    in a case within paragraph (a) of subsection (1), after the document concerned has been supplied to the tenant by the landlord, or*
    *(b)    in a case within paragraph (b) of that subsection, after a document conforming exactly or substantially with the requirements prescribed by regulations under section 21(4) has been supplied to the tenant by the landlord by way of replacement of the one previously supplied.*

(4)  If, on an application made by the landlord to a leasehold valuation tribunal, the tribunal determines that the landlord has a reasonable excuse for a failure giving rise to the right of a tenant to withhold an amount under this section, the tenant may not withhold the amount after the determination is made.

(5)  Where a tenant withholds a service charge under this section, any provisions of the tenancy relating to non-payment or late payment of service charges do not have effect in relation to the period for which he so withholds it.]

**[618]**

**NOTES**
Commencement: to be appointed.
Substituted as noted to s 21 at **[617]**.
Sub-s (1): substituted by the Housing and Regeneration Act 2008, s 303, Sch 12, paras 1, 3(1), (2), as from 1 December 2008 (for the purpose of enabling the Secretary of State to make regulations), and as from a day to be appointed (for remaining purposes), as follows:
"(1)  A tenant may withhold payment of a service charge if—
  (a)  the landlord has not provided him with information or a report—
     (i)   at the time at which, or
     (ii)  (as the case may be) by the time by which,
     he is required to provide it by virtue of section 21, or
  (b)  the form or content of information or a report which the landlord has provided him with by virtue of that section (at any time) does not conform exactly or substantially with the requirements prescribed by regulations under that section.".

Sub-s (2): for the words in italics in para (a) there are substituted the words "period to which the information or report" and para (b) substituted as follows, by the Housing and Regeneration Act 2008, s 303, Sch 12, paras 1, 3(1), (3), as from 1 December 2008 (for the purpose of enabling the Secretary of State to make regulations), and as from a day to be appointed (for remaining purposes):
  "(b)  amounts standing to the tenant's credit in relation to the service charges at the beginning of that period.".

Sub-s (3): for the words in italics in para (a) there are substituted the words "information or report concerned has been provided" and para (b) substituted as follows, by the Housing and Regeneration Act 2008, s 303, Sch 12, paras 1, 3(1), (4), as from 1 December 2008 (for the purpose of enabling the Secretary of State to make regulations), and as from a day to be appointed (for remaining purposes):
  "(b)  in a case within paragraph (b) of that subsection, after information or a report conforming exactly or substantially with requirements prescribed by regulations under section 21 has been provided to the tenant by the landlord by way of replacement of that previously provided.".

Modified, where the RTM company has acquired the right to manage, by the Commonhold and Leasehold Reform Act 2002, s 102, Sch 7, para 4 at **[1266]**, **[1306]**.

**[21B  Notice to accompany demands for service charges]**

(1)  A demand for the payment of a service charge must be accompanied by a summary of the rights and obligations of tenants of dwellings in relation to service charges.

(2)  The Secretary of State may make regulations prescribing requirements as to the form and content of such summaries of rights and obligations.

(3)  A tenant may withhold payment of a service charge which has been demanded from him if subsection (1) is not complied with in relation to the demand.

(4)  Where a tenant withholds a service charge under this section, any provisions of the lease relating to non-payment or late payment of service charges do not have effect in relation to the period for which he so withholds it.

(5)  Regulations under subsection (2) may make different provision for different purposes.

(6)  Regulations under subsection (2) shall be made by statutory instrument which shall be subject to annulment in pursuance of a resolution of either House of Parliament.]

**[619]**

**NOTES**
Commencement: 26 July 2002 (in relation to England for the purpose of making regulations); 1 January 2003 (in relation to Wales for the purpose of making regulations); 1 October 2007 (in relation to England for remaining purposes); 30 November 2007 (in relation to Wales for remaining purposes).
Inserted by the Commonhold and Leasehold Reform Act 2002, s 153.
Modified, where the RTM company has acquired the right to manage, by the Commonhold and Leasehold Reform Act 2002, s 102, Sch 7, para 4 at **[1266]**, **[1306]**.
Regulations: the Service Charges (Summary of Rights and Obligations, and Transitional Provision) (England) Regulations 2007, SI 2007/1257 at **[3759]**; the Service Charges (Summary of Rights and Obligations, and Transitional Provisions) (Wales) Regulations 2007, SI 2007/3160 at **[3776]**.

**22 Request to inspect supporting accounts, etc**

*(1) This section applies where a tenant, or the secretary of a recognised tenants' association, has obtained such a summary as is referred to in section 21(1) (summary of relevant costs), whether in pursuance of that section or otherwise.*

*(2) The tenant, or the secretary with the consent of the tenant, may within six months of obtaining the summary require the landlord in writing to afford him reasonable facilities—*
  *(a) for inspecting the accounts, receipts and other documents supporting the summary, and*
  *(b) for taking copies or extracts from them.*

*(3) A request under this section is duly served on the landlord if it is served on—*
  *(a) an agent of the landlord named as such in the rent book or similar document, or*
  *(b) the person who receives the rent on behalf of the landlord;*
*and a person on whom a request is so served shall forward it as soon as may be to the landlord.*

*(4) The landlord shall make such facilities available to the tenant or secretary for a period of two months beginning not later than one month after the request is made.*

*[(5) The landlord shall—*
  *(a) where such facilities are for the inspection of any documents, make them so available free of charge;*
  *(b) where such facilities are for the taking of copies or extracts, be entitled to make them so available on payment of such reasonable charge as he may determine.*

*(6) The requirement imposed on the landlord by subsection (5)(a) to make any facilities available to a person free of charge shall not be construed as precluding the landlord from treating as part of his costs of management any costs incurred by him in connection with making those facilities so available.]*

**[620]**

---

**NOTES**
Sub-ss (5), (6): added by the Landlord and Tenant Act 1987, s 41(1), Sch 2, para 6.
Modified, where the RTM company has acquired the right to manage, by the Commonhold and Leasehold Reform Act 2002, s 102, Sch 7, para 4 at **[1266]**, **[1306]**.
This section is substituted by the Commonhold and Leasehold Reform Act 2002, s 154, as from a day to be appointed, and subsequently amended as noted below, as follows—

**"22 Inspection etc of documents**

(1) A tenant may by notice in writing require the landlord—
  (a) to afford him reasonable facilities for inspecting accounts, receipts or other documents relevant to *the matters which must be dealt with in a statement of account required to be supplied to him under* section 21 and for taking copies of or extracts from them, or
  (b) to take copies of or extracts from any such accounts, receipts or other documents and either send them to him or afford him reasonable facilities for collecting them (as he specifies).

(2) If the tenant is represented by a recognised tenants' association and he consents, the notice may be served by the secretary of the association instead of by the tenant (and in that case any requirement imposed by it is to afford reasonable facilities, or to send copies or extracts, to the secretary).

(3) A notice under this section may not be served after the end of the period of six months beginning with the date by which the tenant is required to be *supplied with the statement of account under* section 21.

(4) But if—
  (a) the *statement of account* is not *supplied* to the tenant on or before that date, or
  (b) the *statement of account* so *supplied* does not conform exactly or substantially with the requirements prescribed by regulations under section *21(4)*,
the six month period mentioned in subsection (3) does not begin until any later date on which the *statement of account* (conforming exactly or substantially with those requirements) is *supplied* to him.

(5) A notice under this section is duly served on the landlord if it is served on—
  (a) an agent of the landlord named as such in the rent book or similar document, or
  (b) the person who receives the rent on behalf of the landlord;
and a person on whom such a notice is so served must forward it as soon as may be to the landlord.

(6) The landlord must comply with a requirement imposed by a notice under this section within the period of twenty-one days beginning with the day on which he receives the notice.

(7) To the extent that a notice under this section requires the landlord to afford facilities for inspecting documents—
  (a) he must do so free of charge, but
  (b) he may treat as part of his costs of management any costs incurred by him in doing so.

(8) The landlord may make a reasonable charge for doing anything else in compliance with a requirement imposed by a notice under this section.".

Sub-s (1): for the words in italics in para (a) there are substituted the words "information required to be provided to him by virtue of" by the Housing and Regeneration Act 2008, s 303, Sch 12, paras 1, 4(1), (2), as from 1 December 2008 (for the purpose of enabling the Secretary of State to make regulations), and as from a day to be appointed (for remaining purposes).

Sub-s (3): for the words in italics there are substituted the words "provided with the information concerned by virtue of" by the Housing and Regeneration Act 2008, s 303, Sch 12, paras 1, 4(1), (3), as from 1 December 2008 (for the purpose of enabling the Secretary of State to make regulations), and as from a day to be appointed (for remaining purposes).

Sub-s (4): for "statement of account" in each place it appears in italics there is substituted "information", for "supplied" in each place it appears in italics there is substituted "provided", and for "21(4)" in italics there is substituted "21" by the Housing and Regeneration Act 2008, s 303, Sch 12, paras 1, 4(1), (4), as from 1 December 2008 (for the purpose of enabling the Secretary of State to make regulations), and as from a day to be appointed (for remaining purposes).

## 23 Request relating to information held by superior landlord

*(1) If a request under section 21 (request for summary of relevant costs) relates in whole or in part to relevant costs incurred by or on behalf of a superior landlord, and the landlord to whom the request is made is not in possession of the relevant information—*

    *(a) he shall in turn make a written request for the relevant information to the person who is his landlord (and so on, if that person is not himself the superior landlord),*

    *(b) the superior landlord shall comply with that request within a reasonable time, and*

    *(c) the immediate landlord shall then comply with the tenant's or secretary's request, or that part of it which relates to the relevant costs incurred by or on behalf of the superior landlord, within the time allowed by section 21 or such further time, if any, as is reasonable in the circumstances.*

*(2) If a request under section 22 (request for facilities to inspect supporting accounts, etc) relates to a summary of costs incurred by or on behalf of a superior landlord—*

    *(a) the landlord to whom the request is made shall forthwith inform the tenant or secretary of that fact and of the name and address of the superior landlord, and*

    *(b) section 22 shall then apply to the superior landlord as it applies to the immediate landlord.*

**[621]**

**NOTES**

Substituted by the Commonhold and Leasehold Reform Act 2002, s 157, Sch 10, para 1, as from a day to be appointed, and subsequently amended as noted below, as follows—

**"23 Information held by superior landlord**

(1) If *a statement of account which the landlord is required to supply under* section 21 relates to matters concerning a superior landlord and the landlord is not in possession of the relevant information [which relates to those matters]—

    (a) he may by notice in writing require the person who is his landlord to give him the relevant information (and so on, if that person is not himself the superior landlord), and

    (b) the superior landlord must comply with the requirement within a reasonable time.

(2) If a notice under section 22 imposes a requirement in relation to documents held by a superior landlord—

    (a) the landlord shall immediately inform the tenant or secretary of that fact and of the name and address of the superior landlord, and

    (b) section 22 then applies in relation to the superior landlord (as in relation to the landlord).".

Sub-s (1) (as substituted): for the words in italics there are substituted the words "information which the landlord is required to provide by virtue of" and words in square brackets inserted by the Housing and Regeneration Act 2008, s 303, Sch 12, paras 1, 5, as from 1 December 2008 (for the purpose of enabling the Secretary of State to make regulations), and as from a day to be appointed (for remaining purposes).

Modified, where the RTM company has acquired the right to manage, by the Commonhold and Leasehold Reform Act 2002, s 102, Sch 7, para 4 at **[1266]**, **[1306]**.

## [23A Effect of change of landlord

(1) This section applies where, at a time when a duty imposed on the landlord or a superior landlord by or by virtue of any of sections 21 to 23 remains to be discharged by him, he disposes of the whole or part of his interest as landlord or superior landlord to another person.

(2) If the landlord or superior landlord is, despite the disposal, still in a position to discharge the duty to any extent, he remains responsible for discharging it to that extent.

(3) If the other person is in a position to discharge the duty to any extent, he is responsible for discharging it to that extent.

(4) Where the other person is responsible for discharging the duty to any extent (whether or not the landlord or superior landlord is also responsible for discharging it to that or any other extent)—

    (a) references to the landlord or superior landlord in sections 21 to 23 [and any regulations under section 21] are to, or include, the other person so far as is appropriate to reflect his responsibility for discharging the duty to that extent, but

    (b) in connection with its discharge by the other person, section 22(6) applies as if the reference to the day on which the landlord receives the notice were to the date of the disposal referred to in subsection (1); [and

   (c)     any regulations under section 21 apply subject to any modifications contained in the regulations.]]

**NOTES**

Commencement: to be appointed.

Inserted by the Commonhold and Leasehold Reform Act 2002, s 157, Sch 10, para 2.

Sub-s (4): words in square brackets inserted by the Housing and Regeneration Act 2008, s 303, Sch 12, paras 1, 6, as from 1 December 2008 (for the purpose of enabling the Secretary of State to make regulations), and as from a day to be appointed (for remaining purposes).

Modified, where the RTM company has acquired the right to manage, by the Commonhold and Leasehold Reform Act 2002, s 102, Sch 7, para 4 at **[1266]**, **[1306]**.

### 24   Effect of assignment on request

*The assignment of a tenancy does not affect the validity of a request made under section 21, 22 or 23 before the assignment; but a person is not obliged to provide a summary or make facilities available more than once for the same [dwelling] and for the same period.*

**NOTES**

Substituted by the Commonhold and Leasehold Reform Act 2002, s 157, Sch 10, para 3, as from a day to be appointed, as follows—

#### "24   Effect of assignment

The assignment of a tenancy does not affect any duty imposed by or by virtue of any of sections 21 to 23A; but a person is not required to comply with more than a reasonable number of requirements imposed by any one person.".

Word in square brackets substituted by the Landlord and Tenant Act 1987, s 41(1), Sch 2, para 7.

Modified, where the RTM company has acquired the right to manage, by the Commonhold and Leasehold Reform Act 2002, s 102, Sch 7, para 4 at **[1266]**, **[1306]**.

### 25   Failure to comply with s 21, 22, or 23 an offence

   (1)    It is a summary offence for a person to fail, without reasonable excuse, to perform a duty imposed on him *by section 21, 22 or 23*.

   (2)    A person committing such an offence is liable on conviction to a fine not exceeding level 4 on the standard scale.

**NOTES**

Sub-s (1): for the words in italics there are substituted the words "by or by virtue of any of sections 21 to 23A" by the Commonhold and Leasehold Reform Act 2002, s 157, Sch 10, para 4, as from a day to be appointed.

Modified, where the RTM company has acquired the right to manage, by the Commonhold and Leasehold Reform Act 2002, s 102, Sch 7, para 4 at **[1266]**, **[1306]**.

### 26   Exception: tenants of certain public authorities

   (1)    Sections 18 to 25 (limitation on service charges *and requests for information about costs*) do not apply to a service charge payable by a tenant of—

         a local authority,

         [a National Park authority [or]]

         a new town corporation, or

         ...

unless the tenancy is a long tenancy, in which case sections 18 to 24 apply but section 25 (offence of failure to comply) does not.

   (2)    The following are long tenancies for the purposes of subsection (1), subject to subsection (3)—

      (a)    a tenancy granted for a term certain exceeding 21 years, whether or not it is (or may become) terminable before the end of that term by notice given by the tenant or by re-entry or forfeiture;

      (b)    a tenancy for a term fixed by law under a grant with a covenant or obligation for perpetual renewal, other than a tenancy by sub-demise from one which is not a long tenancy;

      (c)    any tenancy granted in pursuance of Part V of the Housing Act 1985 (the right to buy)[, including any tenancy granted in pursuance of that Part as it has effect by virtue of section 17 of the Housing Act 1996 (the right to acquire)].

   (3)    A tenancy granted so as to become terminable by notice after a death is not a long tenancy for the purposes of subsection (1), unless—

    (a)    it is granted by a housing association which at the time of the grant is [a registered social landlord],

    (b)    it is granted at a premium calculated by reference to a percentage of the value of the dwelling-house or the cost of providing it, and

    (c)    at the time it is granted it complied with the requirements of the regulations then in force under section 140(4)(b) of the Housing Act 1980 [or paragraph 4(2)(b) of Schedule 4A to the Leasehold Reform Act 1967] (conditions for exclusion of shared ownership leases from Part I of Leasehold Reform Act 1967) or, in the case of a tenancy granted before any such regulations were brought into force, with the first such regulations to be in force.

**[625]**

**NOTES**

Sub-s (1): for the words in italics there are substituted the words ", statements of account and inspection etc of documents)" by the Commonhold and Leasehold Reform Act 2002, s 157, Sch 10, para 5, as from a day to be appointed, and subsequently for the words "statements of account" there are substituted the words "service charge information, reports on such information" by the Housing and Regeneration Act 2008, s 303, Sch 12, paras 1, 7, as from 1 December 2008 (for the purpose of enabling the Secretary of State to make regulations), and as from a day to be appointed (for remaining purposes); words in first (outer) pair of square brackets inserted by the Environment Act 1995, s 78, Sch 10, para 25(1); word in second (inner) pair of square brackets inserted and words omitted repealed by the Government of Wales Act 1998, ss 129(2), 131, 152, Sch 15, paras 11, 12, Sch 18, Pt IV.

Sub-s (2): words in square brackets added by the Housing Act 1996 (Consequential Amendments) (No 2) Order 1997, SI 1997/627, art 2, Schedule, para 4.

Sub-s (3): words in first pair of square brackets substituted by the Housing Act 1996 (Consequential Provisions) Order 1996, SI 1996/2325, art 5, Sch 2, para 16(1), (3); words in second pair of square brackets inserted by the Housing Act 1988, s 140(1), Sch 17, Pt I, para 68.

Modified, where the RTM company has acquired the right to manage, by the Commonhold and Leasehold Reform Act 2002, s 102, Sch 7, para 4 at **[1266]**, **[1306]**.

Housing Act 1980, s 140(4)(b): repealed by the Housing and Planning Act 1986, ss 18, 24(3), Sch 4, para 7, Sch 12, Pt I; see now the Leasehold Reform Act 1967, s 33A, Sch 4A.

## 27  Exception: rent registered and not entered as variable

Sections 18 to 25 (limitation on service charges *and requests for information about costs*) do not apply to a service charge payable by the tenant of a [dwelling] the rent of which is registered under Part IV of the Rent Act 1977, unless the amount registered is, in pursuance of section 71(4) of that Act, entered as a variable amount.

**[626]**

**NOTES**

For the words in italics there are substituted the words ", statements of account and inspection etc of documents)" by the Commonhold and Leasehold Reform Act 2002, s 157, Sch 10, para 5, as from a day to be appointed, and subsequently for the words "statements of account" there are substituted the words "service charge information, reports on such information" by the Housing and Regeneration Act 2008, s 303, Sch 12, paras 1, 8, as from 1 December 2008 (for the purpose of enabling the Secretary of State to make regulations), and as from a day to be appointed (for remaining purposes); word in square brackets substituted by the Landlord and Tenant Act 1987, s 41(1), Sch 2, para 8.

Modified, where the RTM company has acquired the right to manage, by the Commonhold and Leasehold Reform Act 2002, s 102, Sch 7, para 4 at **[1266]**, **[1306]**.

## [27A  Liability to pay service charges: jurisdiction

(1)    An application may be made to a leasehold valuation tribunal for a determination whether a service charge is payable and, if it is, as to—

    (a)    the person by whom it is payable,

    (b)    the person to whom it is payable,

    (c)    the amount which is payable,

    (d)    the date at or by which it is payable, and

    (e)    the manner in which it is payable.

(2)    Subsection (1) applies whether or not any payment has been made.

(3)    An application may also be made to a leasehold valuation tribunal for a determination whether, if costs were incurred for services, repairs, maintenance, improvements, insurance or management of any specified description, a service charge would be payable for the costs and, if it would, as to—

    (a)    the person by whom it would be payable,

    (b)    the person to whom it would be payable,

    (c)    the amount which would be payable,

    (d)    the date at or by which it would be payable, and

    (e)    the manner in which it would be payable.

(4)    No application under subsection (1) or (3) may be made in respect of a matter which—

(a)  has been agreed or admitted by the tenant,
(b)  has been, or is to be, referred to arbitration pursuant to a post-dispute arbitration agreement to which the tenant is a party,
(c)  has been the subject of determination by a court, or
(d)  has been the subject of determination by an arbitral tribunal pursuant to a post-dispute arbitration agreement.

(5)  But the tenant is not to be taken to have agreed or admitted any matter by reason only of having made any payment.

(6)  An agreement by the tenant of a dwelling (other than a post-dispute arbitration agreement) is void in so far as it purports to provide for a determination—
(a)  in a particular manner, or
(b)  on particular evidence,
of any question which may be the subject of an application under subsection (1) or (3).

(7)  The jurisdiction conferred on a leasehold valuation tribunal in respect of any matter by virtue of this section is in addition to any jurisdiction of a court in respect of the matter.]

**[627]**

**NOTES**

Inserted by the Commonhold and Leasehold Reform Act 2002, 155(1), except in relation to any application made to an LVT under s 19(2A) or (2B) of this Act or any proceedings relating to a service charge transferred to an LVT by a county court before 30 September 2003 (in relation to England) or 31 March 2004 (in relation to Wales).

Modified, where the RTM company has acquired the right to manage, by the Commonhold and Leasehold Reform Act 2002, s 102, Sch 7, para 4 at **[1266]**, **[1306]**.

## 28  Meaning of "qualified accountant"

*(1)    The reference to a "qualified accountant" in section 21(6) (certification of summary of information about relevant costs) is to a person who, in accordance with the following provisions, has the necessary qualification and is not disqualified from acting.*

*[(2)    A person has the necessary qualification if he is eligible for appointment as a [statutory auditor under Part 42 of the Companies Act 2006]].*

*(3)    ...*

*(4)    The following are disqualified from acting—*
*(a)    ...*
*(b)    an officer[, employee or partner] of the landlord or, where the landlord is a company, of an associated company;*
*(c)    a person who is a partner or employee of any such officer or employee;*
*[(d)   an agent of the landlord who is a managing agent for any premises to which any of the costs covered by the summary in question relate;*
*(e)    an employee or partner of any such agent].*

*(5)    For the purposes of subsection (4)(b) a company is associated with a landlord company if it is (within the meaning of [section 1159 of the Companies Act 2006]) the landlord's holding company, a subsidiary of the landlord or another subsidiary of the landlord's holding company.*

*[(5A)    For the purposes of subsection (4)(d) a person is a managing agent for any premises to which any costs relate if he has been appointed to discharge any of the landlord's obligations relating to the management by him of the premises and owed to the tenants who may be required under the terms of their leases to contribute to those costs by the payment of service charges.]*

*(6)    Where the landlord is [an emanation of the Crown,] a local authority, [National Park authority] [or a new town corporation]—*
*(a)    the persons who have the necessary qualification include members of the Chartered Institute of Public Finance and Accountancy, and*
*(b)    subsection (4)(b) (disqualification of officers and employees of landlord) does not apply.*

**[628]**

**NOTES**

Repealed by the Housing and Regeneration Act 2008, ss 303, 321(1), Sch 12, paras 1, 9, Sch 16, as from 1 December 2008 (for the purpose of enabling the Secretary of State to make regulations), and as from a day to be appointed (for remaining purposes).

Sub-s (1): for the words "21(6) (certification of summary of information about relevant costs)" there are substituted the words "21(3)(a) (certification of statements of account)" by the Commonhold and Leasehold Reform Act 2002, s 157, Sch 10, para 6(1), (2), as from a day to be appointed.

Sub-s (2): substituted by the Companies Act 1989 (Eligibility for Appointment as Company Auditor) (Consequential Amendments) Regulations 1991, SI 1991/1997, regs 2, 4, Schedule, para 60(a); words in square brackets substituted by the Companies Act 2006 (Consequential Amendments etc) Order 2008, SI 2008/948, arts 3(1)(a), 6, Sch 1, Pt 1, para 1(jj), subject to transitional provisions and savings in arts 6, 12 thereof.

Sub-s (3): repealed by SI 1991/1997, regs 2, 4, Schedule, para 60(b).

Sub-s (4): para (a) repealed by SI 1991/1997, regs 2, 4, Schedule, para 60(c); words in square brackets in para (b) substituted and paras (d), (e) added by the Landlord and Tenant Act 1987, s 41(1), Sch 2, para 9(1), (2); in para (d) for the words "any of the costs covered by the summary in question relate" there are substituted the words "the statement of account in question relates" by the Commonhold and Leasehold Reform Act 2002, s 157, Sch 10, para 6(1), (3), as from a day to be appointed.

Sub-s (5): words in square brackets substituted by the Companies Act 2006 (Consequential Amendments, Transitional Provisions and Savings) Order 2009, SI 2009/1941, art 2(1), Sch 1, para 64.

Sub-s (5A): inserted by the Landlord and Tenant Act 1987, s 41(1), Sch 2, para 9(1), (3); for the words "any costs relate" and "those costs" there are substituted the words "a statement of account relates" and "costs covered by the statement of account" respectively, by the Commonhold and Leasehold Reform Act 2002, s 157, Sch 10, para 6(1), (4), as from a day to be appointed.

Sub-s (6): words in first pair of square brackets inserted by the Commonhold and Leasehold Reform Act 2002, s 157, Sch 10, para 6(1), (5), as from a day to be appointed; words in second pair of square brackets inserted by the Environment Act 1995, s 78, Sch 10, para 25(2); words in third pair of square brackets substituted by the Government of Wales Act 1998, ss 129(2), 131, Sch 15, paras 11, 13.

Modified, where the RTM company has acquired the right to manage, by the Commonhold and Leasehold Reform Act 2002, s 102, Sch 7, para 4 at **[1266]**, **[1306]**.

## 29 Meaning of "recognised tenants' association"

(1)   A recognised tenants' association is an association of [qualifying tenants (whether with or without other tenants)] which is recognised for the purposes of the provisions of this Act relating to service charges either—

    (a)   by notice in writing given by the landlord to the secretary of the association, or

    (b)   by a certificate of a member of the local rent assessment committee panel.

(2)   A notice given under subsection (1)(a) may be withdrawn by the landlord by notice in writing given to the secretary of the association not less than six months before the date on which it is to be withdrawn.

(3)   A certificate given under subsection (1)(b) may be cancelled by any member of the local rent assessment committee panel.

(4)   In this section the "local rent assessment committee panel" means the persons appointed by the Lord Chancellor under the Rent Act 1977 to the panel of persons to act as members of a rent assessment committee for the registration area in which [the dwellings let to the qualifying tenants are situated, and for the purposes of this section a number of tenants are qualifying tenants if each of them may be required under the terms of his lease to contribute to the same costs by the payment of a service charge].

[(5)   The Secretary of State may by regulations specify—

    (a)   the procedure which is to be followed in connection with an application for, or for the cancellation of, a certificate under subsection (1)(b);

    (b)   the matters to which regard is to be had in giving or cancelling such a certificate;

    (c)   the duration of such a certificate; and

    (d)   any circumstances in which a certificate is not to be given under subsection (1)(b).]

(6)   Regulations under subsection (5)—

    (a)   may make different provisions with respect to different cases or descriptions of case, including different provision for different areas, and

    (b)   shall be made by statutory instrument which shall be subject to annulment in pursuance of a resolution of either House of Parliament.

**[629]**

**NOTES**

Sub-ss (1), (4): words in square brackets substituted by the Landlord and Tenant Act 1987, s 41(1), Sch 2, para 10(1)–(3).

Sub-s (5): substituted by the Landlord and Tenant Act 1987, s 41(1), Sch 2, para 10(1), (4).

Modified, where the RTM company has acquired the right to manage, by the Commonhold and Leasehold Reform Act 2002, s 102, Sch 7, para 4 at **[1266]**, **[1306]**.

## 30 Meaning of "flat", "landlord" and "tenant"

In the provisions of this Act relating to service charges—

    .....

    "landlord" includes any person who has a right to enforce payment of a service charge;

    "tenant" includes—

        (a)   a statutory tenant, and

        (b)   where the [dwelling] or part of it is sub-let, the sub-tenant.

**[630]**

**NOTES**

Definition omitted repealed and word in square brackets in definition "tenant" substituted by the Landlord and Tenant Act 1987, ss 41(1), 61(2), Sch 2, para 11, Sch 5.

Modified, where the RTM company has acquired the right to manage, by the Commonhold and Leasehold Reform Act 2002, s 102, Sch 7, para 4 at **[1266]**, **[1306]**.

## *[Insurance*

### 30A Rights of tenants with respect to insurance

The Schedule to this Act (which confers on tenants certain rights with respect to the insurance of their dwellings) shall have effect.]

**[631]**

**NOTES**

Inserted, together with preceding cross-heading, by the Landlord and Tenant Act 1987, s 43(1).

Modified, where the RTM company has acquired the right to manage, by the Commonhold and Leasehold Reform Act 2002, s 102, Sch 7, para 5 at **[1266]**, **[1306]**.

## *[Managing agents*

### 30B Recognised tenants' associations to be consulted about managing agents

(1)    A recognised tenants' association may at any time serve a notice on the landlord requesting him to consult the association in accordance with this section on matters relating to the appointment or employment by him of a managing agent for any relevant premises.

(2)    Where, at the time when any such notice is served by a recognised tenants' association, the landlord does not employ any managing agent for any relevant premises, the landlord shall, before appointing such a managing agent, serve on the association a notice specifying—

(a)    the name of the proposed managing agent;

(b)    the landlord's obligations to the tenants represented by the association which it is proposed that the managing agent should be required to discharge on his behalf; and

(c)    a period of not less than one month beginning with the date of service of the notice within which the association may make observations on the proposed appointment.

(3)    Where, at the time when a notice is served under subsection (1) by a recognised tenants' association, the landlord employs a managing agent for any relevant premises, the landlord shall, within the period of one month beginning with the date of service of that notice, serve on the association a notice specifying—

(a)    the landlord's obligations to the tenants represented by the association which the managing agent is required to discharge on his behalf; and

(b)    a reasonable period within which the association may make observations on the manner in which the managing agent has been discharging those obligations, and on the desirability of his continuing to discharge them.

(4)    Subject to subsection (5), a landlord who has been served with a notice by an association under subsection (1) shall, so long as he employs a managing agent for any relevant premises—

(a)    serve on that association at least once in every five years a notice specifying—

(i)    any change occurring since the date of the last notice served by him on the association under this section in the obligations which the managing agent has been required to discharge on his behalf; and

(ii)    a reasonable period within which the association may make observations on the manner in which the managing agent has discharged those obligations since that date, and on the desirability of his continuing to discharge them;

(b)    serve on that association, whenever he proposes to appoint any new managing agent for any relevant premises, a notice specifying the matters mentioned in paragraphs (a) to (c) of subsection (2).

(5)    A landlord shall not, by virtue of a notice served by an association under subsection (1), be required to serve on the association a notice under subsection (4)(a) or (b) if the association subsequently serves on the landlord a notice withdrawing its request under subsection (1) to be consulted by him.

(6)    Where—

(a)    a recognised tenants' association has served a notice under subsection (1) with respect to any relevant premises, and

(b)    the interest of the landlord in those premises becomes vested in a new landlord,

that notice shall cease to have effect with respect to those premises (without prejudice to the service by the association on the new landlord of a fresh notice under that subsection with respect to those premises).

(7)    Any notice served by a landlord under this section shall specify the name and the address in the United Kingdom of the person to whom any observations made in pursuance of the notice are to be sent; and the landlord shall have regard to any such observations that are received by that person within the period specified in the notice.

(8) In this section—

"landlord", in relation to a recognised tenants' association, means the immediate landlord of the tenants represented by the association or a person who has a right to enforce payment of service charges payable by any of those tenants;

"managing agent", in relation to any relevant premises, means an agent of the landlord appointed to discharge any of the landlord's obligations to the tenants represented by the recognised tenants' association in question which relate to the management by him of those premises; and

"tenant" includes a statutory tenant;

and for the purposes of this section any premises (whether a building or not) are relevant premises in relation to a recognised tenants' association if any of the tenants represented by the association may be required under the terms of their leases to contribute by the payment of service charges to costs relating to those premises.]

**[632]**

**NOTES**

Inserted, together with preceding cross-heading, by the Landlord and Tenant Act 1987, s 44.

Modified, where the RTM company has acquired the right to manage, by the Commonhold and Leasehold Reform Act 2002, s 102, Sch 7, para 6 at **[1266]**, **[1306]**.

*Miscellaneous*

## 31 Reserve power to limit rents

(1) The Secretary of State may by order provide for—

(a) restricting or preventing increases of rent for dwellings which would otherwise take place, or

(b) restricting the amount of rent which would otherwise be payable on new lettings of dwellings;

and may so provide either generally or in relation to any specified description of dwelling.

(2) An order may contain supplementary or incidental provisions, including provisions excluding, adapting or modifying any provision made by or under an enactment (whenever passed) relating to rent or the recovery of overpaid rent.

(3) In this section—

"new letting" includes any grant of a tenancy, whether or not the premises were previously let, and any grant of a licence;

"rent" includes a sum payable under a licence, but does not include a sum attributable to rates or [council tax or], in the case of dwellings of local authorities [National Park authorities] or new town corporations, to the use of furniture, or the provision of services;

and for the purposes of this section an increase in rent takes place at the beginning of the rental period for which the increased rent is payable.

(4) An order under this section shall be made by statutory instrument which shall be subject to annulment in pursuance of a resolution of either House of Parliament.

**[633]**

**NOTES**

Sub-s (3): words in first pair of square brackets inserted by the Local Government Finance (Housing) (Consequential Amendments) Order 1993, SI 1993/651, art 2(1), Sch 1, para 16; words in second pair of square brackets inserted by the Environment Act 1995, s 78, Sch 10, para 25(3).

Order: the Rent Acts (Maximum Fair Rent) Order 1999, SI 1999/6 at **[3222]**.

*Supplementary provisions*

**31A–31C** *(Inserted by the Housing Act 1996, s 83(3); repealed by the Commonhold and Leasehold Reform Act 2002, s 180, Sch 14, except in relation to any application made to an LVT or any proceedings transferred to an LVT by a county court before 30 September 2003 (in relation to England) or 31 March 2004 (in relation to Wales).)*

## 32 Provisions not applying to tenancies within Part II of the Landlord and Tenant Act 1954

(1) The following provisions do not apply to a tenancy to which Part II of the Landlord and Tenant Act 1954 (business tenancies) applies—

[sections 1 to 3A] (information to be given to tenant),

section 17 (specific performance of landlord's repairing obligations).

(2) Section 11 (repairing obligations) does not apply to a new lease granted to an existing tenant, or to a former tenant still in possession, if the new lease is a tenancy to which Part II of the Landlord and Tenant Act 1954 applies and the previous lease either is such a tenancy or would be but for section 28 of that Act (tenancy not within Part II if renewal agreed between the parties).

In this subsection "existing tenant", "former tenant still in possession" and "previous lease" have the same meaning as in section 14(2).

(3) Section 31 (reserve power to limit rents) does not apply to a dwelling forming part of a property subject to a tenancy to which Part II of the Landlord and Tenant Act 1954 applies; but without prejudice to the application of that section in relation to a sub-tenancy of a part of the premises comprised in such a tenancy.

**[634]**

**NOTES**

Sub-s (1): words in square brackets substituted by the Housing Act 1996, s 93(2).

### 33 Liability of directors, etc for offences by body corporate

(1) Where an offence under this Act which has been committed by a body corporate is proved—
   (a) to have been committed with the consent or connivance of a director, manager, secretary or other similar officer of the body corporate, or a person purporting to act in any such capacity, or
   (b) to be attributable to any neglect on the part of such an officer or person,

he, as well as the body corporate, is guilty of an offence and liable to be proceeded against and punished accordingly.

(2) Where the affairs of a body corporate are managed by its members, subsection (1) applies in relation to the acts and defaults of a member in connection with his functions of management as if he were a director of the body corporate.

**[635]**

### 34 Power of local housing authority to prosecute

Proceedings for an offence under any provision of this Act may be brought by a local housing authority.

**[636]**

### 35 Application to Isles of Scilly

(1) This Act applies to the Isles of Scilly subject to such exceptions, adaptations and modifications as the Secretary of State may by order direct.

(2) An order shall be made by statutory instrument which shall be subject to annulment in pursuance of a resolution of either House of Parliament.

**[637]**

### 36 Meaning of "lease" and "tenancy" and related expressions

(1) In this Act "lease" and "tenancy" have the same meaning.

(2) Both expressions include—
   (a) a sub-lease or sub-tenancy, and
   (b) an agreement for a lease or tenancy (or sub-lease or sub-tenancy).

(3) The expressions "lessor" and "lessee" and "landlord" and "tenant", and references to letting, to the grant of a lease or to covenants or terms, shall be construed accordingly.

**[638]**

### 37 Meaning of "statutory tenant" and related expressions

In this Act—
   (a) "statutory tenancy" and "statutory tenant" mean a statutory tenancy or statutory tenant within the meaning of the Rent Act 1977 or the Rent (Agriculture) Act 1976; and
   (b) "landlord", in relation to a statutory tenant, means the person who, apart from the statutory tenancy, would be entitled to possession of the premises.

**[639]**

**NOTES**

Phasing out of certain statutory tenancies: see the notes preceding the Rent (Agriculture) Act 1976, s 1 at **[155]** and preceding the Rent Act 1977, s 1 at **[202]**.

### 38 Minor definitions

In this Act—
   "address" means a person's place of abode or place of business or, in the case of a company, its registered office;
   ["arbitration agreement", "arbitration proceedings" and "arbitral tribunal" have the same meaning as in Part I of the Arbitration Act 1996 [and post-dispute arbitration agreement, in relation to any matter, means an arbitration agreement made after a dispute about the matter has arisen];]

"co-operative housing association" has the same meaning as in the Housing Associations Act 1985;

"dwelling" means a building or part of a building occupied or intended to be occupied as a separate dwelling, together with any yard, garden, outhouses and appurtenances belonging to it or usually enjoyed with it;

"housing association" has the same meaning as in the Housing Associations Act 1985;

"local authority" means a district, county[, county borough] or London borough council, the Common Council of the City of London or the Council of the Isles of Scilly and in sections 14(4), 26(1) and 28(6) includes ... [the Broads Authority][, a police authority established under [section 3 of the Police Act 1996][, the Metropolitan Police Authority][ ... ] ... ] ... a joint authority established by Part IV of the Local Government Act 1985 [, an authority established for an area in England by an order under section 207 of the Local Government and Public Involvement in Health Act 2007 (joint waste authorities)] [and the London Fire and Emergency Planning Authority];

"local housing authority" has the meaning given by section 1 of the Housing Act 1985;

"new town corporation" means—

(a)     a development corporation established by an order made, or treated as made, under the New Towns Act 1981,

[(b)     the Homes and Communities Agency so far as exercising functions in relation to anything transferred (or to be transferred) to it as mentioned in section 52(1)(a) to (d) of the Housing and Regeneration Act 2008, or

(c)     the Welsh Ministers so far as exercising functions in relation to anything transferred (or to be transferred) to them as mentioned in section 36(1)(a)(i) to (iii) of the New Towns Act 1981;]

"protected tenancy" has the same meaning as in the Rent Act 1977;

["registered social landlord" has the same meaning as in the Housing Act 1985 (see section 5(4) and (5) of that Act);]

"restricted contract" has the same meaning as in the Rent Act 1977;

"urban development corporation" has the same meaning as in Part XVI of the Local Government, Planning and Land Act 1980.

**[640]**

---

**NOTES**

Definitions "arbitration agreement", "arbitration proceedings" and "arbitral proceedings" inserted by the Housing Act 1996, s 83(5); words in square brackets inserted by the Commonhold and Leasehold Reform Act 2002, s 155(2), except in relation to any application made to an LVT under s 19(2A) or (2B) of this Act or any proceedings relating to a service charge transferred to an LVT by a county court before 30 September 2003 (in relation to England) or 31 March 2004 (in relation to Wales).

In definition "local authority" words in first pair of square brackets inserted by the Local Government (Wales) Act 1994, s 22(2), Sch 8, para 7; words omitted in the first and final places repealed by the Education Reform Act 1988, s 237(2), Sch 13, Pt I; words in second pair of square brackets substituted by the Norfolk and Suffolk Broads Act 1988, s 21, Sch 6, para 26; words in third (outer) pair of square brackets inserted by the Police and Magistrates' Courts Act 1994, s 43, Sch 4, Pt II, para 60; words in fourth (inner) pair of square brackets inserted by the Police Act 1996, s 103(1), Sch 7, Pt I, para 1(1), (2)(x); words in fifth (inner) and eighth pairs of square brackets inserted, and words omitted in the third place repealed, by the Greater London Authority Act 1999, ss 325, 328, 423, Sch 27, para 53, Sch 29, Pt I, para 44, Sch 34, Pt VIII; words omitted in the second place from sixth (inner) pair of square brackets inserted by the Police Act 1997, s 134(1), Sch 9, para 51 and repealed by the Criminal Justice and Police Act 2001, ss 128(1), 137, Sch 6, Pt 3, para 69, Sch 7, Pt 5(1); words in seventh pair of square brackets inserted by the Local Government and Public Involvement in Health Act 2007, s 209(2), Sch 13, Pt 2, para 42.

In definition "new town corporation" paras (b), (c) substituted for original para (b), by the Housing and Regeneration Act 2008, s 56, Sch 8, para 36, subject to transitional provisions and savings in SI 2008/3068, arts 6–10 at **[3834B]–[3834F]**.

Definition "registered social landlord" substituted, for original definition "registered", by the Housing Act 1996 (Consequential Provisions) Order 1996, SI 1996/2325, art 5, Sch 2, para 16(1), (4).

Modifications: a residuary body established by the Local Government Act 1985, Pt VII, is to be treated as a local authority for the purposes of ss 14(4), 18–30 of, and Schedule, para 9(1) to, this Act; see Sch 13, para 24 to the 1985 Act.

The Residuary Body for Wales, established under the Local Government (Wales) Act 1994, s 39, Sch 13, is to be treated as a local authority for the purposes of ss 14(4), 18–30 of, and Schedule, para 9(1) to, this Act; see para 23 of that Schedule, to the 1994 Act.

The Local Government Residuary Body (England), established under the Local Government Act 1992, s 22 and the Local Government Residuary Body (England) Order 1995, SI 1995/401, is to be treated as a local authority for the purposes of ss 14(4), 18–30 of, and Schedule, para 9(1) to, this Act; see art 18 of, and para 10 of the Schedule to, the 1995 Order.

A housing action trust established under the Housing Act 1988, Pt III, is to be treated as a local authority for the purposes of ss 18–30; see s 79(12) of the 1988 Act.

---

**39   Index of defined expressions**

The following Table shows provisions defining or otherwise explaining expressions used in this Act (other than provisions defining or explaining an expression in the same section)—

| | |
|---|---|
| address | section 38 |
| [arbitration agreement, arbitration proceedings[, arbitral tribunal and post-dispute arbitration agreement] | section 38] |
| co-operative housing association | section 38 |
| dwelling | section 38 |
| dwelling-house (in the provisions relating to repairing obligations) | section 16 |
| fit for human habitation | section 10 |
| … | |
| housing association | section 38 |
| landlord— | |
| (generally) | section 36(3) |
| (in sections 1 and 2) | section 1(3) |
| (in the provisions relating to rent books) | section 4(3) |
| (in the provisions relating to service charges) | |
| (in relation to a statutory tenancy) | section 37(b) |
| lease, lessee and lessor— | |
| (generally) | section 36 |
| (in the provisions relating to repairing obligations) | section 16 |
| local authority | section 38 |
| local housing authority | section 38 |
| new town corporation | section 38 |
| protected tenancy | section 38 |
| *qualified accountant (for the purposes of section 21(6))* | *section 28* |
| [registered social landlord] | section 38 |
| recognised tenants' association | section 29 |
| relevant costs (in relation to a service charge) | section 18(2) |
| restricted contract | section 38 |
| service charge | section 18(1) |
| statutory tenant | section 37(a) |
| tenancy and tenant— | |
| (generally) | section 36 |
| (in sections 1 and 2) | section 1(3) |
| (in the provisions relating to rent books) | section 4(3) |
| (in the provisions relating to service charges) | section 30 |
| urban development corporation | section 38 |

**[641]**

**NOTES**

Entry beginning "arbitration agreement" inserted by the Housing Act 1996, s 83(6); words in square brackets therein substituted by the Commonhold and Leasehold Reform Act 2002, s 155(3), except in relation to any application made to an LVT under s 19(2A) or (2B) of this Act or any proceedings relating to a service charge transferred to an LVT by a county court before 30 September 2003 (in relation to England) or 31 March 2004 (in relation to Wales).

Entry "flat" (omitted) repealed by the Commonhold and Leasehold Reform Act 2002, s 180, Sch 14.

Entry "qualified accountant" repealed by the Housing and Regeneration Act 2008, ss 303, 321(1), Sch 12, paras 1, 10, Sch 16, as from 1 December 2008 (for the purpose of enabling the Secretary of State to make regulations), and as from a day to be appointed (for remaining purposes); for the reference to "21(6)" there is substituted "21(3)(a)" by the Commonhold and Leasehold Reform Act 2002, s 157, Sch 10, para 7, as from a day to be appointed.

In entry "registered social landlord" words in square brackets substituted by the Housing Act 1996 (Consequential Provisions) Order 1996, SI 1996/2325, art 5, Sch 2, para 16(1), (5).

*Final provisions*

## 40  Short title, commencement and extent

(1)  This Act may be cited as the Landlord and Tenant Act 1985.

(2)  This Act comes into force on 1st April 1986.

(3)  This Act extends to England and Wales.

**[642]**

[SCHEDULE
RIGHTS OF TENANTS WITH RESPECT TO INSURANCE

Section 30A

*Construction*

1.  In this Schedule—
"landlord", in relation to a tenant by whom a service charge is payable which includes an amount payable directly or indirectly for insurance, includes any person who has a right to enforce payment of that service charge;
"relevant policy", in relation to a dwelling, means any policy of insurance under which the dwelling is insured (being, in the case of a flat, a policy covering the building containing it); and
"tenant" includes a statutory tenant.

*… Summary of insurance cover*

2.—(1)  Where a service charge is payable by the tenant of a dwelling which consists of or includes an amount payable directly or indirectly for insurance, the tenant may [by notice in writing] require the landlord] to supply him with a written summary of the insurance for the time being effected in relation to the dwelling.

(2)  If the tenant is represented by a recognised tenants' association and he consents, the [notice may be served] by the secretary of the association instead of by the tenant and may then be for the supply of the summary to the secretary.

(3)  A [notice under this paragraph is duly] served on the landlord if it is served on—
(a)  an agent of the landlord named as such in the rent book or similar document, or
(b)  the person who receives the rent on behalf of the landlord;
and a person on [whom such a notice] is so served shall forward it as soon as may be to the landlord.

(4)  The landlord shall, within [the period of twenty-one days beginning with the day on which he receives the notice,] comply with it by supplying to the tenant or the secretary of the recognised tenants' association (as the case may require) such a summary as is mentioned in sub-paragraph (1), which shall include—
(a)  the insured amount or amounts under any relevant policy, and
(b)  the name of the insurer under any such policy, and
(c)  the risks in respect of which the dwelling or (as the case may be) the building containing it is insured under any such policy.

(5)  In sub-paragraph (4)(a) "the insured amount or amounts", in relation to a relevant policy, means—
(a)  in the case of a dwelling other than a flat, the amount for which the dwelling is insured under the policy; and
(b)  in the case of a flat, the amount for which the building containing it is insured under the policy and, if specified in the policy, the amount for which the flat is insured under it.

(6)  The landlord shall be taken to have complied with the [notice] if, within the period mentioned in sub-paragraph (4), he instead supplies to the tenant or the secretary (as the case may require) a copy of every relevant policy.

(7)  In a case where two or more buildings are insured under any relevant policy, the summary or copy supplied under sub-paragraph (4) or (6) so far as relating to that policy need only be of such parts of the policy as relate—
(a)  to the dwelling, and
(b)  if the dwelling is a flat, to the building containing it.

*[Inspection of insurance policy etc*

3.—(1)  Where a service charge is payable by the tenant of a dwelling which consists of or includes an amount payable directly or indirectly for insurance, the tenant may by notice in writing require the landlord—
(a)  to afford him reasonable facilities for inspecting any relevant policy or associated documents and for taking copies of or extracts from them, or

(b)    to take copies of or extracts from any such policy or documents and either send them to him or afford him reasonable facilities for collecting them (as he specifies).

(2)    If the tenant is represented by a recognised tenants' association and he consents, the notice may be served by the secretary of the association instead of by the tenant (and in that case any requirement imposed by it is to afford reasonable facilities, or to send copies or extracts, to the secretary).

(3)    A notice under this paragraph is duly served on the landlord if it is served on—
   (a)    an agent of the landlord named as such in the rent book or similar document, or
   (b)    the person who receives the rent on behalf of the landlord;
and a person on whom such a notice is so served shall forward it as soon as may be to the landlord.

(4)    The landlord shall comply with a requirement imposed by a notice under this paragraph within the period of twenty-one days beginning with the day on which he receives the notice.

(5)    To the extent that a notice under this paragraph requires the landlord to afford facilities for inspecting documents—
   (a)    he shall do so free of charge, but
   (b)    he may treat as part of his costs of management any costs incurred by him in doing so.

(6)    The landlord may make a reasonable charge for doing anything else in compliance with a requirement imposed by a notice under this paragraph.

(7)    In this paragraph—
"relevant policy" includes a policy of insurance under which the dwelling was insured for the period of insurance immediately preceding that current when the notice is served (being, in the case of a flat, a policy covering the building containing it), and
"associated documents" means accounts, receipts or other documents which provide evidence of payment of any premiums due under a relevant policy in respect of the period of insurance which is current when the notice is served or the period of insurance immediately preceding that period.]

*…… Insurance effected by superior landlord*

4.—(1)    If [a notice is served] under paragraph 2 in a case where a superior landlord has effected, in whole or in part, the insurance of the dwelling in question and the landlord [on whom the notice is served] is not in possession of the relevant information—
   (a)    he shall in turn [by notice in writing require the person who is his landlord to give him the relevant information] (and so on, if that person is not himself the superior landlord),
   (b)    the superior landlord shall comply with [the notice] within a reasonable time, and
   (c)    the immediate landlord shall then comply with the tenant's or [secretary's notice] in the manner provided by sub-paragraphs (4) to (7) of paragraph 2 within the time allowed by that paragraph or such further time, if any, as is reasonable in the circumstances.

(2)    If, in a case where a superior landlord has effected, in whole or in part, the insurance of the dwelling in question, a [notice under paragraph 3 imposes a requirement relating] to any policy of insurance effected by the superior landlord—
   (a)    the landlord [on whom the notice is served] shall forthwith inform the tenant or secretary of that fact and of the name and address of the superior landlord, and
   (b)    that paragraph shall then apply to the superior landlord in relation to that policy as it applies to the immediate landlord.

*[Effect of change of landlord*

4A.—(1)    This paragraph applies where, at a time when a duty imposed on the landlord or a superior landlord by virtue of any of paragraphs 2 to 4 remains to be discharged by him, he disposes of the whole or part of his interest as landlord or superior landlord).

(2)    If the landlord or superior landlord is, despite the disposal, still in a position to discharge the duty to any extent, he remains responsible for discharging it to that extent.

(3)    If the other person is in a position to discharge the duty to any extent, he is responsible for discharging it to that extent.

(4)    Where the other person is responsible for discharging the duty to any extent (whether or not the landlord or superior landlord is also responsible for discharging it to that or any other extent)—
   (a)    references to the landlord or superior landlord in paragraphs 2 to 4 are to, or include, the other person so far as is appropriate to reflect his responsibility for discharging the duty to that extent, but
   (b)    in connection with its discharge by that person, paragraphs 2(4) and 3(4) apply as if the reference to the day on which the landlord receives the notice were to the date of the disposal referred to in sub-paragraph (1).]

*Effect of assignment ...*

5. The assignment of a tenancy does not affect [any duty imposed by virtue of any of paragraphs 2 to 4A; but a person is not required to comply with more than a reasonable number of requirements imposed by any one person].

*[Offence of failure to comply]*

6.—(1) It is a summary offence for a person to fail, without reasonable excuse, to perform a duty imposed on him by or by virtue of [any of paragraphs 2 to 4A].

(2) A person committing such an offence is liable on conviction to a fine not exceeding level 4 on the standard scale.

*Tenant's right to notify insurers of possible claim*

7.—(1) This paragraph applies to any dwelling in respect of which the tenant pays to the landlord a service charge consisting of or including an amount payable directly or indirectly for insurance.

(2) Where—
    (a) it appears to the tenant of any such dwelling that damage has been caused—
        (i) to the dwelling, or
        (ii) if the dwelling is a flat, to the dwelling or to any other part of the building containing it,
      in respect of which a claim could be made under the terms of a policy of insurance, and
    (b) it is a term of that policy that the person insured under the policy should give notice of any claim under it to the insurer within a specified period,
the tenant may, within that specified period, serve on the insurer a notice in writing stating that it appears to him that damage has been caused as mentioned in paragraph (a) and describing briefly the nature of the damage.

(3) Where—
    (a) any such notice is served on an insurer by a tenant in relation to any such damage, and
    (b) the specified period referred to in sub-paragraph (2)(b) would expire earlier than the period of six months beginning with the date on which the notice is served,
the policy in question shall have effect as regards any claim subsequently made in respect of that damage by the person insured under the policy as if for the specified period there were substituted that period of six months.

(4) Where the tenancy of a dwelling to which this paragraph applies is held by joint tenants, a single notice under this paragraph may be given by any one or more of those tenants.

(5) The Secretary of State may by regulations prescribe the form of notices under this paragraph and the particulars which such notices must contain.

(6) Any such regulations—
    (a) may make different provision with respect to different cases or descriptions of case, including different provision for different areas, and
    (b) shall be made by statutory instrument.

*Right to challenge landlord's choice of insurers*

[8.—(1) This paragraph applies where a tenancy of a dwelling requires the tenant to insure the dwelling with an insurer nominated [or approved] by the landlord.

(2) The tenant or landlord may apply to a county court or leasehold valuation tribunal for a determination whether—
    (a) the insurance which is available from the nominated [or approved] insurer for insuring the tenant's dwelling is unsatisfactory in any respect, or
    (b) the premiums payable in respect of any such insurance are excessive.

(3) No such application may be made in respect of a matter which—
    (a) has been agreed or admitted by the tenant,
    (b) under an arbitration agreement to which the tenant is a party is to be referred to arbitration, or
    (c) has been the subject of determination by a court or arbitral tribunal.

(4) On an application under this paragraph the court or tribunal may make—
    (a) an order requiring the landlord to nominate [or approve] such other insurer as is specified in the order, or
    (b) an order requiring him to nominate [or approve] another insurer who satisfies such requirements in relation to the insurance of the dwelling as are specified in the order.

(5) ...

(6) An agreement by the tenant of a dwelling (other than an arbitration agreement) is void in so far as it purports to provide for a determination in a particular manner, or on particular evidence, of any question which may be the subject of an application under this paragraph.]

*Exception for tenants of certain public authorities*

9.—(1)  Paragraphs 2 to 8 do not apply to a tenant of—
a local authority,
[a National Park authority [or]]
a new town corporation ...

unless the tenancy is a long tenancy, in which case paragraphs 2 to 5 and 7 and 8 apply but paragraph 6 does not.

(2)  Subsections (2) and (3) of section 26 shall apply for the purposes of sub-paragraph (1) as they apply for the purposes of subsection (1) of that section.]

**[643]**

PART I
STATUTES

---

**NOTES**

Added by the Landlord and Tenant Act 1987, s 43(2), Sch 3.

Para 2: words omitted from cross-heading repealed and words in square brackets substituted by the Commonhold and Leasehold Reform Act 2002, ss 157, 180, Sch 10, para 8, Sch 14, except in relation to a request made under this Schedule before 30 September 2003 (in relation to England) or 31 March 2004 (in relation to Wales).

Para 3: substituted, together with preceding cross-heading, by the Commonhold and Leasehold Reform Act 2002, s 157, Sch 10, para 9, except in relation to a request made under this Schedule before 30 September 2003 (in relation to England) or 31 March 2004 (in relation to Wales).

Para 4: words omitted from cross-heading repealed and words in square brackets substituted by the Commonhold and Leasehold Reform Act 2002, ss 157, 180, Sch 10, para 10, Sch 14, except in relation to a request made under this Schedule before 30 September 2003 (in relation to England) or 31 March 2004 (in relation to Wales).

Para 4A: inserted, together with preceding cross-heading, by the Commonhold and Leasehold Reform Act 2002, s 157, Sch 10, para 11, except in relation to a request made under this Schedule before 30 September 2003 (in relation to England) or 31 March 2004 (in relation to Wales).

Para 5: words omitted from cross-heading repealed and words in square brackets substituted by the Commonhold and Leasehold Reform Act 2002, ss 157, 180, Sch 10, para 12, Sch 14, except in relation to a request made under this Schedule before 30 September 2003 (in relation to England) or 31 March 2004 (in relation to Wales).

Para 6: cross-heading and words in square brackets substituted by the Commonhold and Leasehold Reform Act 2002, s 157, Sch 10, para 13, except in relation to a request made under this Schedule before 30 September 2003 (in relation to England) or 31 March 2004 (in relation to Wales).

Para 8: substituted by the Housing Act 1996, s 83(2); words in square brackets in sub-paras (1), (2), (4) inserted by the Commonhold and Leasehold Reform Act 2002, s 165; sub-para (5) repealed by s 180 of, and Sch 14 to, the 2002 Act, except in relation to any application made to an LVT or any proceedings transferred to an LVT by a county court before 30 September 2003 (in relation to England) or 31 March 2004 (in relation to Wales).

Para 9: words in first (outer) pair of square brackets inserted by the Environment Act 1995, s 78, Sch 10, para 25(1); word in second (inner) pair of square brackets inserted and words omitted repealed by the Government of Wales Act 1998, ss 129(2), 152, Sch 15, paras 11, 14, Sch 18, Pt IV.

---

# LANDLORD AND TENANT ACT 1987

### (1987 c 31)

### ARRANGEMENT OF SECTIONS

### PART I
### TENANTS' RIGHTS OF FIRST REFUSAL

*Preliminary*

*Rights of first refusal*

## PART II
### APPOINTMENT OF MANAGERS BY A LEASEHOLD VALUATION TRIBUNAL

## PART III
### COMPULSORY ACQUISITION BY TENANTS OF THEIR LANDLORD'S INTEREST

## PART IV
### VARIATION OF LEASES

*Applications relating to flats*

*Orders varying leases*

*An Act to confer on tenants of flats rights with respect to the acquisition by them of their landlord's reversion; to make provision for the appointment of a manager at the instance of such tenants and for the variation of long leases held by such tenants; to make further provision with respect to service charges payable by tenants of flats and other dwellings; to make other provision with respect to such tenants; to make further provision with respect to the permissible purposes and objects of registered housing associations as regards the management of leasehold property; and for connected purposes*

**[15 May 1987]**

**NOTES**

Transfer of functions: as to the functions of Ministers of the Crown under this Act, so far as exercisable in relation to Wales, being transferred to the National Assembly for Wales, see the National Assembly for Wales (Transfer of Functions) Order 1999, SI 1999/672, art 2, Sch 1.

**PART I**
**TENANTS' RIGHTS OF FIRST REFUSAL**

*Preliminary*

## 1   Qualifying tenants to have rights of first refusal on disposals by landlord

(1)     A landlord shall not make a relevant disposal affecting any premises to which at the time of the disposal this Part applies unless—

     (a)     he has in accordance with section 5 previously served a notice under that section with respect to the disposal on the qualifying tenants of the flats contained in those premises (being a notice by virtue of which rights of first refusal are conferred on those tenants); and

     (b)     the disposal is made in accordance with the requirements of sections 6 to 10.

(2)     Subject to subsections (3) and (4), this Part applies to premises if—

     (a)     they consist of the whole or part of a building; and

  (b)   they contain two or more flats held by qualifying tenants; and
  (c)   the number of flats held by such tenants exceeds 50 per cent of the total number of flats contained in the premises.

  (3)   This Part does not apply to premises falling within subsection (2) if—
  (a)   any part or parts of the premises is or are occupied or intended to be occupied otherwise than for residential purposes; and
  (b)   the internal floor area of that part or those parts (taken together) exceeds 50 per cent of the internal floor area of the premises (taken as a whole);

and for the purposes of this subsection the internal floor area of any common parts shall be disregarded.

  (4)   This Part also does not apply to any such premises at a time when the interest of the landlord in the premises is held by an exempt landlord or a resident landlord.

  (5)   The Secretary of State may by order substitute for the percentage for the time being specified in subsection (3)(b) such other percentage as is specified in the order.

[644]

## 2   Landlords for the purposes of Part I

  (1)   Subject to subsection (2) [and section 4(1A)], a person is for the purposes of this Part the landlord in relation to any premises consisting of the whole or part of a building if he is—
  (a)   the immediate landlord of the qualifying tenants of the flats contained in those premises, or
  (b)   where any of those tenants is a statutory tenant, the person who, apart from the statutory tenancy, would be entitled to possession of the flat in question.

  (2)   Where the person who is, in accordance with subsection (1), the landlord in relation to any such premises for the purposes of this Part ("the immediate landlord") is himself a tenant of those premises under a tenancy which is either—
  (a)   a tenancy for a term of less than seven years, or
  (b)   a tenancy for a longer term but terminable within the first seven years at the option of the person who is the landlord under that tenancy ("the superior landlord"),

the superior landlord shall also be regarded as the landlord in relation to those premises for the purposes of this Part and, if the superior landlord is himself a tenant of those premises under a tenancy falling within paragraph (a) or (b) above, the person who is the landlord under that tenancy shall also be so regarded (and so on).

[645]

### NOTES
Sub-s (1): words in square brackets inserted by the Housing Act 1988, s 119, Sch 13, para 1, except in relation to a disposal made in pursuance of a contract entered into before 15 January 1989 or where the offer notice was served, or treated as served, under s 5 of this Act at **[649]**, before that date.

## 3   Qualifying tenants

  (1)   Subject to the following provisions of this section, a person is for the purposes of this Part a qualifying tenant of a flat if he is the tenant of the flat under a tenancy other than—
  (a)   a protected shorthold tenancy as defined in section 52 of the Housing Act 1980;
  (b)   a tenancy to which Part II of the Landlord and Tenant Act 1954 (business tenancies) applies; ...
  (c)   a tenancy terminable on the cessation of his employment [or
  (d)   an assured tenancy or assured agricultural occupancy within the meaning of Part I of the Housing Act 1988].

  (2)   A person is not to be regarded as being a qualifying tenant of any flat contained in any particular premises consisting of the whole or part of a building if [by virtue of one or more tenancies none of which falls within paragraphs (a) to (d) of subsection (1), he is the tenant not only of the flat in question but also of at least two other flats contained in those premises].

  (3)   For the purposes of subsection [(2)] any tenant of a flat contained in the premises in question who is a body corporate shall be treated as the tenant of any other flat so contained and let to an associated company.

  (4)   A tenant of a flat whose landlord is a qualifying tenant of that flat is not to be regarded as being a qualifying tenant of that flat.

[646]

### NOTES
Sub-s (1): words omitted repealed by the Housing Act 1988, ss 119, 140(2), Sch 13, para 2(1), Sch 18, except in relation to a disposal made in pursuance of a contract entered into before 15 January 1989 or where the offer notice was served, or treated as served, under s 5 of this Act at **[649]**, before that date; words in square brackets added by the Housing Act 1988, s 119, Sch 13, para 2(1).

Sub-s (2): words in square brackets substituted by the Housing Act 1988, s 119, Sch 13, para 2(2), subject to savings as noted above.

Sub-s (3): figure in square brackets substituted by the Housing Act 1988, s 119, Sch 13, para 2(2), subject to savings as noted above.

## 4  Relevant disposals

(1)  In this Part references to a relevant disposal affecting any premises to which this Part applies are references to the disposal by the landlord of any estate or interest (whether legal or equitable) in any such premises, including the disposal of any such estate or interest in any common parts of any such premises but excluding—

    (a)   the grant of any tenancy under which the demised premises consist of a single flat (whether with or without any appurtenant premises); and

    (b)   any of the disposals falling within subsection (2).

[(1A)  Where an estate or interest of the landlord has been mortgaged, the reference in subsection (1) above to the disposal of an estate or interest by the landlord includes a reference to its disposal by the mortgagee in exercise of a power of sale or leasing, whether or not the disposal is made in the name of the landlord; and, in relation to such a proposed disposal by the mortgagee, any reference in the following provisions of this Part to the landlord shall be construed as a reference to the mortgagee.]

(2)  The disposals referred to in subsection (1)(b) are—

    (a)   a disposal of—

        (i)   any interest of a beneficiary in settled land within the meaning of the Settled Land Act 1925, [or]

        (ii)   ...

        (iii)   any incorporeal hereditament;

    [(aa)   a disposal ... by way of security for a loan]

    (b)   a disposal to a trustee in bankruptcy or to the liquidator of a company;

    [(c)   a disposal in pursuance of an order made under—

        (i)   *section 24* of the Matrimonial Causes Act 1973 (property adjustment orders in connection with matrimonial proceedings),

        (ii)   section 24A of the Matrimonial Causes Act 1973 (orders for the sale of property in connection with matrimonial proceedings) where the order includes provision requiring the property concerned to be offered for sale to a person or class of persons specified in the order,

        (iii)   section 2 of the Inheritance (Provision for Family and Dependants) Act 1975 (orders as to financial provision to be made from estate),

        (iv)   section 17(1) of the Matrimonial and Family Proceedings Act 1984 (property adjustment orders after overseas divorce, &c),

        (v)   section 17(2) of the Matrimonial and Family Proceedings Act 1984 (orders for the sale of property after overseas divorce, &c) where the order includes provision requiring the property concerned to be offered for sale to a person or class of persons specified in the order, ...

        (vi)   paragraph 1 of Schedule 1 to the Children Act 1989 (orders for financial relief against parents);

        [(vii)   Part 2 of Schedule 5, or paragraph 9(2) or (3) of Schedule 7, to the Civil Partnership Act 2004 (property adjustment orders in connection with civil partnership proceedings or after overseas dissolution of a civil partnership, etc), or

        (viii)   Part 3 of Schedule 5, or paragraph 9(4) of Schedule 7, to the Civil Partnership Act 2004 (orders for the sale of property in connection with civil partnership proceedings or after overseas dissolution of a civil partnership, etc) where the order includes provision requiring the property concerned to be offered for sale to a person or class of persons specified in the order;]]

    (d)   a disposal in pursuance of a compulsory purchase order or in pursuance of an agreement entered into in circumstances where, but for the agreement, such an order would have been made or (as the case may be) carried into effect;

    [(da)   a disposal of any freehold or leasehold interest in pursuance of Chapter I of Part I of the Leasehold Reform, Housing and Urban Development Act 1993;]

    (e)   a disposal by way of gift to a member of the landlord's family or to a charity;

    (f)   a disposal by one charity to another of an estate or interest in land which prior to the disposal is functional land of the first-mentioned charity and which is intended to be functional land of the other charity once the disposal is made;

    (g)   a disposal consisting of the transfer of an estate or interest held on trust for any person where the disposal is made in connection with the appointment of a new trustee or in connection with the discharge of any trustee;

    (h)   a disposal consisting of a transfer by two or more persons who are members of the same family either—

        (i)    to fewer of their number, or

        (ii)   to a different combination of members of the family (but one that includes at least one of the transferors);

[(i)    a disposal in pursuance of a contract, option or right of pre-emption binding on the landlord (except as provided by section 8D (application of sections 11 to 17 to disposal in pursuance of option or right of pre-emption));]

(j)    a disposal consisting of the surrender of a tenancy in pursuance of any covenant, condition or agreement contained in it;

(k)   a disposal to the Crown; and

[(l)    a disposal by a body corporate to a company which has been an associated company of that body for at least two years.]

    (3)   In this Part "disposal" means a disposal whether by the creation or the transfer of an estate or interest and—

        (a)   includes the surrender of a tenancy and the grant of an option or right of pre-emption, but

        (b)   excludes a disposal under the terms of a will or under the law relating to intestacy;

and references in this Part to the transferee in connection with a disposal shall be construed accordingly.

    (4)   In this section "appurtenant premises", in relation to any flat, means any yard, garden, outhouse or appurtenance (not being a common part of the building containing the flat) which belongs to, or is usually enjoyed with, the flat.

    (5)   A person is a member of another's family for the purposes of this section if—

        (a)   that person is the spouse [or civil partner] of that other person, or the two of them live together as husband and wife [or as if they were civil partners], or

        (b)   that person is that other person's parent, grandparent, child, grandchild, brother, sister, uncle, aunt, nephew or niece.

    (6)   For the purposes of subsection (5)(b)—

        (a)   a relationship by marriage [or civil partnership] shall be treated as a relationship by blood,

        (b)   a relationship of the half-blood shall be treated as a relationship of the whole blood,

        (c)   the stepchild of a person shall be treated as his child, and

        (d)   the illegitimate child shall be treated as the legitimate child of his mother and reputed father.

**[647]**

## NOTES

Sub-s (1A): inserted by the Housing Act 1988, s 119, Sch 13, para 3(1), except in relation to a disposal made in pursuance of a contract entered into before 15 January 1989 or where the offer notice was served, or treated as served, under s 5 of this Act at **[649]**, before that date.

Sub-s (2): word in square brackets in para (a)(i) added, para (a)(ii) repealed and para (aa) inserted by the Housing Act 1988, ss 119, 140(2), Sch 13, para 3(2), Sch 18, subject to savings as noted above; words omitted from para (aa) repealed and paras (c), (i) substituted by the Housing Act 1996, ss 89(2), 92(1), 222, 227, Sch 6, Pt IV, para 1, Sch 18, Pt III, para 18, Sch 19, Pt III; for the words in italics in para (c)(i) there are substituted the words "section 23A, 24" by the Family Law Act 1996, s 66(1), Sch 8, Pt I, para 38, as from a day to be appointed, subject to savings in s 66(2) of, and Sch 9, para 5 to, that Act; word omitted from para (c)(v) repealed and para (c)(vii), (viii) inserted by the Civil Partnership Act 2004, ss 81, 261(4), Sch 8, para 40(1), (2), Sch 30; para (da) inserted by the Leasehold Reform, Housing and Urban Development Act 1993, s 187(1), Sch 21, para 26; para (l) substituted by the Housing Act 1996, s 90, except in relation to disposals made in pursuance of an obligation entered into before 1 October 1996.

Sub-ss (5), (6): words in square brackets inserted by the Civil Partnership Act 2004, s 81, Sch 8, para 40(1), (3), (4).

## [4A Application of provisions to contracts

    (1)   The provisions of this Part apply to a contract to create or transfer an estate or interest in land, whether conditional or unconditional and whether or not enforceable by specific performance, as they apply in relation to a disposal consisting of the creation or transfer of such an estate or interest.

As they so apply—

        (a)   references to a disposal of any description shall be construed as references to a contract to make such a disposal;

        (b)   references to making a disposal of any description shall be construed as references to entering into a contract to make such a disposal; and

        (c)   references to the transferee under the disposal shall be construed as references to the other party to the contract and include a reference to any other person to whom an estate or interest is to be granted or transferred in pursuance of the contract.

(2)   The provisions of this Part apply to an assignment of rights under such a contract as is mentioned in subsection (1) as they apply in relation to a disposal consisting of the transfer of an estate or interest in land.

As they so apply—

(a)   references to a disposal of any description shall be construed as references to an assignment of rights under a contract to make such a disposal;

(b)   references to making a disposal of any description shall be construed as references to making an assignment of rights under a contract to make such a disposal;

(c)   references to the landlord shall be construed as references to the assignor; and

(d)   references to the transferee under the disposal shall be construed as references to the assignee of such rights.

(3)   The provisions of this Part apply to a contract to make such an assignment as is mentioned in subsection (2) as they apply (in accordance with subsection (1)) to a contract to create or transfer an estate or interest in land.

(4)   Nothing in this section affects the operation of the provisions of this Part relating to options or rights of pre-emption.]

**[648]**

---

**NOTES**

Inserted by the Housing Act 1996, s 89(1).

---

*[Rights of first refusal*

## 5   Landlord required to serve offer notice on tenants

(1)   Where the landlord proposes to make a relevant disposal affecting premises to which this Part applies, he shall serve a notice under this section (an "offer notice") on the qualifying tenants of the flats contained in the premises (the "constituent flats").

(2)   An offer notice must comply with the requirements of whichever is applicable of the following sections—

section 5A (requirements in case of contract to be completed by conveyance, &c),

section 5B (requirements in case of sale at auction),

section 5C (requirements in case of grant of option or right of pre-emption),

section 5D (requirements in case of conveyance not preceded by contract, &c);

and in the case of a disposal to which section 5E applies (disposal for non-monetary consideration) shall also comply with the requirements of that section.

(3)   Where a landlord proposes to effect a transaction involving the disposal of an estate or interest in more than one building (whether or not involving the same estate or interest), he shall, for the purpose of complying with this section, sever the transaction so as to deal with each building separately.

(4)   If, as a result of the offer notice being served on different tenants on different dates, the period specified in the notice as the period for accepting the offer would end on different dates, the notice shall have effect in relation to all the qualifying tenants on whom it is served as if it provided for that period to end with the latest of those dates.

(5)   A landlord who has not served an offer notice on all of the qualifying tenants on whom it was required to be served shall nevertheless be treated as having complied with this section—

(a)   if he has served an offer notice on not less than 90% of the qualifying tenants on whom such a notice was required to be served, or

(b)   where the qualifying tenants on whom it was required to be served number less than ten, if he has served such a notice on all but one of them.]

**[649]**

---

**NOTES**

Substituted, together with preceding cross-heading and ss 5A–5E, 6–8, 8A–8E, 9A, 9B, 10, for original ss 5–10, by the Housing Act 1996, s 92(1), Sch 6, Pt I.

Modified, where the RTM company has acquired the right to manage, by the Commonhold and Leasehold Reform Act 2002, s 102, Sch 7, para 7 at **[1266]**, **[1306]**.

---

## [5A   Offer notice: requirements in case of contract to be completed by conveyance, &c

(1)   The following requirements must be met in relation to an offer notice where the disposal consists of entering into a contract to create or transfer an estate or interest in land.

(2)   The notice must contain particulars of the principal terms of the disposal proposed by the landlord, including in particular—

(a)   the property, and the estate or interest in that property, to which the contract relates,

(b)   the principal terms of the contract (including the deposit and consideration required).

(3) The notice must state that the notice constitutes an offer by the landlord to enter into a contract on those terms which may be accepted by the requisite majority of qualifying tenants of the constituent flats.

(4) The notice must specify a period within which that offer may be so accepted, being a period of not less than two months which is to begin with the date of service of the notice.

(5) The notice must specify a further period of not less than two months within which a person or persons may be nominated by the tenants under section 6.

(6) This section does not apply to the grant of an option or right of pre-emption (see section 5C).]

[650]

**NOTES**
Substituted as noted to s 5 at **[649]**.

## [5B Offer notice: requirements in case of sale by auction

(1) The following requirements must be met in relation to an offer notice where the landlord proposes to make the disposal by means of a sale at a public auction held in England and Wales.

(2) The notice must contain particulars of the principal terms of the disposal proposed by the landlord, including in particular the property to which it relates and the estate or interest in that property proposed to be disposed of.

(3) The notice must state that the disposal is proposed to be made by means of a sale at a public auction.

(4) The notice must state that the notice constitutes an offer by the landlord, which may be accepted by the requisite majority of qualifying tenants of the constituent flats, for the contract (if any) entered into by the landlord at the auction to have effect as if a person or persons nominated by them, and not the purchaser, had entered into it.

(5) The notice must specify a period within which that offer may be so accepted, being a period of not less than two months beginning with the date of service of the notice.

(6) The notice must specify a further period of not less than 28 days within which a person or persons may be nominated by the tenants under section 6.

(7) The notice must be served not less than four months or more than six months before the date of the auction; and—
    (a)    the period specified in the notice as the period within which the offer may be accepted must end not less than two months before the date of the auction, and
    (b)    the period specified in the notice as the period within which a person may be nominated under section 6 must end not less than 28 days before the date of the auction.

(8) Unless the time and place of the auction and the name of the auctioneers are stated in the notice, the landlord shall, not less than 28 days before the date of the auction, serve on the requisite majority of qualifying tenants of the constituent flats a further notice stating those particulars.]

[651]

**NOTES**
Substituted as noted to s 5 at **[649]**.

## [5C Offer notice: requirements in case of grant or option or right of pre-emption

(1) The following requirements must be met in relation to an offer notice where the disposal consists of the grant of an option or right of pre-emption.

(2) The notice must contain particulars of the principal terms of the disposal proposed by the landlord, including in particular—
    (a)    the property, and the estate or interest in that property, to which the option or right of pre-emption relates,
    (b)    the consideration required by the landlord for granting the option or right of pre-emption, and
    (c)    the principal terms on which the option or right of pre-emption would be exercisable, including the consideration payable on its exercise.

(3) The notice must state that the notice constitutes an offer by the landlord to grant an option or right of pre-emption on those terms which may be accepted by the requisite majority of qualifying tenants of the constituent flats.

(4) The notice must specify a period within which that offer may be so accepted, being a period of not less than two months which is to begin with the date of service of the notice.

(5)    The notice must specify a further period of not less than two months within which a person or persons may be nominated by the tenants under section 6.]

**NOTES**
Substituted as noted to s 5 at **[649]**.

**[5D    Offer notice: requirements in case of conveyance not preceded by contract, &c**

(1)    The following requirements must be met in relation to an offer notice where the disposal is not made in pursuance of a contract, option or right of pre-emption binding on the landlord.

(2)    The notice must contain particulars of the principal terms of the disposal proposed by the landlord, including in particular—
> (a)    the property to which it relates and the estate or interest in that property proposed to be disposed of, and
> (b)    the consideration required by the landlord for making the disposal.

(3)    The notice must state that the notice constitutes an offer by the landlord to dispose of the property on those terms which may be accepted by the requisite majority of qualifying tenants of the constituent flats.

(4)    The notice must specify a period within which that offer may be so accepted, being a period of not less than two months which is to begin with the date of service of the notice.

(5)    The notice must specify a further period of not less than two months within which a person or persons may be nominated by the tenants under section 6.]

**NOTES**
Substituted as noted to s 5 at **[649]**.

**[5E    Offer notice: disposal for non-monetary consideration**

(1)    This section applies where, in any case to which section 5 applies, the consideration required by the landlord for making the disposal does not consist, or does not wholly consist, of money.

(2)    The offer notice, in addition to complying with whichever is applicable of sections 5A to 5D, must state—
> (a)    that an election may be made under section 8C (explaining its effect), and
> (b)    that, accordingly, the notice also constitutes an offer by the landlord, which may be accepted by the requisite majority of qualifying tenants of the constituent flats, for a person or persons nominated by them to acquire the property in pursuance of sections 11 to 17.

(3)    The notice must specify a period within which that offer may be so accepted, being a period of not less than two months which is to begin with the date of service of the notice.]

**NOTES**
Substituted as noted to s 5 at **[649]**.

**[6    Acceptance of landlord's offer: general provisions**

(1)    Where a landlord has served an offer notice, he shall not during—
> (a)    the period specified in the notice as the period during which the offer may be accepted, or
> (b)    such longer period as may be agreed between him and the requisite majority of the qualifying tenants of the constituent flats,

dispose of the protected interest except to a person or persons nominated by the tenants under this section.

(2)    Where an acceptance notice is duly served on him, he shall not during the protected period (see subsection (4) below) dispose of the protected interest except to a person duly nominated for the purposes of this section by the requisite majority of qualifying tenants of the constituent flats (a "nominated person").

(3)    An "acceptance notice" means a notice served on the landlord by the requisite majority of qualifying tenants of the constituent flats informing him that the persons by whom it is served accept the offer contained in his notice.

An acceptance notice is "duly served" if it is served within—
> (a)    the period specified in the offer notice as the period within which the offer may be accepted, or

(b)   such longer period as may be agreed between the landlord and the requisite majority of qualifying tenants of the constituent flats.

(4)   The "protected period" is the period beginning with the date of service of the acceptance notice and ending with—

(a)   the end of the period specified in the offer notice as the period for nominating a person under this section, or

(b)   such later date as may be agreed between the landlord and the requisite majority of qualifying tenants of constituent flats.

(5)   A person is "duly nominated" for the purposes of this section if he is nominated at the same time as the acceptance notice is served or at any time after that notice is served and before the end of—

(a)   the period specified in the offer notice as the period for nomination, or

(b)   such longer period as may be agreed between the landlord and the requisite majority of qualifying tenants of the constituent flats.

(6)   A person nominated for the purposes of this section by the requisite majority of qualifying tenants of the constituent flats may be replaced by another person so nominated if, and only if, he has (for any reason) ceased to be able to act as a nominated person.

(7)   Where two or more persons have been nominated and any of them ceases to act without being replaced, the remaining person or persons so nominated may continue to act.]

**[655]**

**NOTES**
Substituted as noted to s 5 at **[649]**.

**[7   Failure to accept landlord's offer or to make nomination**

(1)   Where a landlord has served an offer notice on the qualifying tenants of the constituent flats and—

(a)   no acceptance notice is duly served on the landlord, or

(b)   no person is nominated for the purposes of section 6 during the protected period,

the landlord may, during the period of 12 months beginning with the end of that period, dispose of the protected interest to such person as he thinks fit, but subject to the following restrictions.

(2)   Where the offer notice was one to which section 5B applied (sale by auction), the restrictions are—

(a)   that the disposal is made by means of a sale at a public auction, and

(b)   that the other terms correspond to those specified in the offer notice.

(3)   In any other case the restrictions are—

(a)   that the deposit and consideration required are not less than those specified in the offer notice, and

(b)   that the other terms correspond to those specified in the offer notice.

(4)   The entitlement of a landlord, by virtue of this section or any other corresponding provision of this Part, to dispose of the protected interest during a specified period of 12 months extends only to a disposal of that interest, and accordingly the requirements of section 1(1) must be satisfied with respect to any other disposal by him during that period of 12 months (unless the disposal is not a relevant disposal affecting any premises to which at the time of the disposal this Part applies).]

**[656]**

**NOTES**
Substituted as noted to s 5 at **[649]**.

**[8   Landlord's obligations in case of acceptance and nomination**

(1)   This section applies where a landlord serves an offer notice on the qualifying tenants of the constituent flat and—

(a)   an acceptance notice is duly served on him, and

(b)   a person is duly nominated for the purposes of section 6,

by the requisite majority of qualifying tenants of the constituent flats.

(2)   Subject to the following provisions of this Part, the landlord shall not dispose of the protected interest except to the nominated person.

(3)   The landlord shall, within the period of one month beginning with the date of service of notice of nomination, either—

(a)   serve notice on the nominated person indicating an intention no longer to proceed with the disposal of the protected interest, or

(b)   be obliged to proceed in accordance with the following provisions of this Part.

(4)    A notice under subsection (3)(a) is a notice of withdrawal for the purposes of section 9B(2) to (4) (consequences of notice of withdrawal by landlord).

(5)    Nothing in this section shall be taken as prejudicing the application of the provisions of this Part to any further offer notice served by the landlord on the qualifying tenants of the constituent flats.]

**[657]**

**NOTES**
Substituted as noted to s 5 at **[649]**.

### [8A   Landlord's obligation: general provisions

(1)    This section applies where the landlord is obliged to proceed and the offer notice was not one to which section 5B applied (sale by auction).

(2)    The landlord shall, within the period of one month beginning with the date of service of the notice of nomination, send to the nominated person a form of contract for the acquisition of the protected interest on the terms specified in the landlord's offer notice.

(3)    If he fails to do so, the following provisions of this Part apply as if he had given notice under section 9B (notice of withdrawal by landlord) at the end of that period.

(4)    If the landlord complies with subsection (2), the nominated person shall, within the period of two months beginning with the date on which it is sent or such longer period beginning with that date as may be agreed between the landlord and that person, either—

(a)    serve notice on the landlord indicating an intention no longer to proceed with the acquisition of the protected interest, or

(b)    offer an exchange of contracts, that is to say, sign the contract and send it to the landlord, together with the requisite deposit.

In this subsection "the requisite deposit" means a deposit of an amount determined by or under the contract or an amount equal to 10 per cent of the consideration, whichever is the less.

(5)    If the nominated person—

(a)    serves notice in pursuance of paragraph (a) of subsection (4), or

(b)    fails to offer an exchange of contracts within the period specified in that subsection,

the following provisions of this Part apply as if he had given notice under section 9A (withdrawal by nominated person) at the same time as that notice or, as the case may be, at the end of that period.

(6)    If the nominated person offers an exchange of contracts within the period specified in subsection (4), but the landlord fails to complete the exchange within the period of seven days beginning with the day on which he received that person's contract, the following provisions of this Part apply as if the landlord had given notice under section 9B (withdrawal by landlord) at the end of that period.]

**[658]**

**NOTES**
Substituted as noted to s 5 at **[649]**.

### [8B   Landlord's obligation: election in case of sale at auction

(1)    This section applies where the landlord is obliged to proceed and the offer notice was one to which section 5B applied (sale by auction).

(2)    The nominated person may, by notice served on the landlord not less than 28 days before the date of the auction, elect that the provisions of this section shall apply.

(3)    If a contract for the disposal is entered into at the auction, the landlord shall, within the period of seven days beginning with the date of the auction, send a copy of the contract to the nominated person.

(4)    If, within the period of 28 days beginning with the date on which such a copy is so sent, the nominated person—

(a)    serves notice on the landlord accepting the terms of the contract, and

(b)    fulfils any conditions falling to be fulfilled by the purchaser on entering into the contract,

the contract shall have effect as if the nominated person, and not the purchaser, had entered into the contract.

(5)    Unless otherwise agreed, any time limit in the contract as it has effect by virtue of subsection (4) shall start to run again on the service of notice under that subsection; and nothing in the contract as it has effect by virtue of a notice under this section shall require the nominated person to complete the purchase before the end of the period of 28 days beginning with the day on which he is deemed to have entered into the contract.

(6)　If the nominated person—

(a)　does not serve notice on the landlord under subsection (2) by the time mentioned in that subsection, or

(b)　does not satisfy the requirements of subsection (4) within the period mentioned in that subsection,

the following provisions of this Part apply as if he had given notice under section 9A (withdrawal by nominated person) at the end of that period.]

[659]

**NOTES**

Substituted as noted to s 5 at **[649]**.

**[8C　Election in case of disposal for non-monetary consideration**

(1)　This section applies where an acceptance notice is duly served on the landlord indicating an intention to accept the offer referred to in section 5E (offer notice: disposal for non-monetary consideration).

(2)　The requisite majority of qualifying tenants of the constituent flats may, by notice served on the landlord within—

(a)　the period specified in the offer notice for nominating a person or persons for the purposes of section 6, or

(b)　such longer period as may be agreed between the landlord and the requisite majority of qualifying tenants of the constituent flats,

elect that the following provisions shall apply.

(3)　Where such an election is made and the landlord disposes of the protected interest on terms corresponding to those specified in his offer notice in accordance with section 5A, 5B, 5C or 5D, sections 11 to 17 shall have effect as if—

(a)　no notice under section 5 had been served;

(b)　in section 11A(3) (period for serving notice requiring information, &c), the reference to four months were a reference to 28 days; and

(c)　in section 12A(2) and 12B(3) (period for exercise of tenants' rights against purchaser) each reference to six months were a reference to two months.

(4)　For the purposes of sections 11 to 17 as they have effect by virtue of subsection (3) so much of the consideration for the original disposal as did not consist of money shall be treated as such amount in money as was equivalent to its value in the hands of the landlord.

The landlord or the nominated person may apply to have that amount determined by a leasehold valuation tribunal.]

[660]

**NOTES**

Substituted as noted to s 5 at **[649]**.

**[8D　Disposal in pursuance of option or right of pre-emption**

(1)　Where—

(a)　the original disposal was the grant of an option or right of pre-emption, and

(b)　in pursuance of the option or right, the landlord makes another disposal affecting the premises ("the later disposal") before the end of the period specified in subsection (2),

sections 11 to 17 shall have effect as if the later disposal, and not the original disposal, were the relevant disposal.

(2)　The period referred to in subsection (1)(b) is the period of four months beginning with the date by which—

(a)　notices under section 3A of the Landlord and Tenant Act 1985 (duty of new landlord to inform tenants of rights) relating to the original disposal, or

(b)　where that section does not apply, documents of any other description—

(i)　indicating that the original disposal has taken place, and

(ii)　alerting the tenants to the existence of their rights under this Part and the time within which any such rights must be exercised,

have been served on the requisite majority of qualifying tenants of the constituent flats.]

[661]

**NOTES**

Substituted as noted to s 5 at **[649]**.

### [8E   Covenant, &c affecting landlord's power to dispose

(1)   Where the landlord is obliged to proceed but is precluded by a covenant, condition or other obligation from disposing of the protected interest to the nominated person unless the consent of some other person is obtained—

    (a)   he shall use his best endeavours to secure that the consent of that person to that disposal is given, and

    (b)   if it appears to him that that person is obliged not to withhold his consent unreasonably but has nevertheless so withheld it, he shall institute proceedings for a declaration to that effect.

(2)   Subsection (1) ceases to apply if a notice of withdrawal is served under section 9A or 9B (withdrawal of either party from transaction) or if notice is served under section 10 (lapse of landlord's offer: premises ceasing to be premises to which this Part applies).

(3)   Where the landlord has discharged any duty imposed on him by subsection (1) but any such consent as is there mentioned has been withheld, and no such declaration as is there mentioned has been made, the landlord may serve a notice on the nominated person stating that to be the case.

When such a notice has been served, the landlord may, during the period of 12 months beginning with the date of service of the notice, dispose of the protected interest to such person as he thinks fit, but subject to the following restrictions.

(4)   Where the offer notice was one to which section 5B applied (sale by auction), the restrictions are—

    (a)   that the disposal is made by means of a sale at a public auction, and

    (b)   that the other terms correspond to those specified in the offer notice.

(5)   In any other case the restrictions are—

    (a)   that the deposit and consideration required are not less than those specified in the offer notice or, if higher, those agreed between the landlord and the nominated person (subject to contract), and

    (b)   that the other terms correspond to those specified in the offer notice.

(6)   Where notice is given under subsection (3), the landlord may recover from the nominated party and the qualifying tenants who served the acceptance notice any costs reasonably incurred by him in connection with the disposal between the end of the first four weeks of the nomination period and the time when that notice is served by him.

Any such liability of the nominated person and those tenants is a joint and several liability.]

                                                                     **[662]**

---

**NOTES**

Substituted as noted to s 5 at **[649]**.

---

### [9A   Notice of withdrawal by nominated person

(1)   Where the landlord is obliged to proceed, the nominated person may serve notice on the landlord (a "notice of withdrawal") indicating his intention no longer to proceed with the acquisition of the protected interest.

(2)   If at any time the nominated person becomes aware that the number of the qualifying tenants of the constituent flats desiring to proceed with the acquisition of the protected interest is less than the requisite majority of qualifying tenants of those flats, he shall forthwith serve a notice of withdrawal.

(3)   Where notice of withdrawal is given by the nominated person under this section, the landlord may, during the period of 12 months beginning with the date of service of the notice, dispose of the protected interest to such person as he thinks fit, but subject to the following restrictions.

(4)   Where the offer notice was one to which section 5B applied (sale by auction), the restrictions are—

    (a)   that the disposal is made by means of a sale at a public auction, and

    (b)   that the other terms correspond to those specified in the offer notice.

(5)   In any other case the restrictions are—

    (a)   that the deposit and consideration required are not less than those specified in the offer notice or, if higher, those agreed between the landlord and the nominated person (subject to contract), and

    (b)   that the other terms correspond to those specified in the offer notice.

(6)   If notice of withdrawal is served under this section before the end of the first four weeks of the nomination period specified in the offer notice, the nominated person and the qualifying tenants who served the acceptance notice are not liable for any costs incurred by the landlord in connection with the disposal.

(7)   If notice of withdrawal is served under this section after the end of those four weeks, the landlord may recover from the nominated person and the qualifying tenants who served the acceptance notice any costs reasonably incurred by him in connection with the disposal between the end of those four weeks and the time when the notice of withdrawal was served on him.

Any such liability of the nominated person and those tenants is a joint and several liability.

(8)   This section does not apply after a binding contract for the disposal of the protected interest—

    (a)   has been entered into by the landlord and the nominated person, or

    (b)   has otherwise come into existence between the landlord and the nominated person by virtue of any provision of this Part.]

[663]

**NOTES**

Substituted as noted to s 5 at **[649]**.

## [9B   Notice of withdrawal by landlord

(1)   Where the landlord is obliged to proceed, he may serve notice on the nominated person (a "notice of withdrawal") indicating his intention no longer to proceed with the disposal of the protected interest.

(2)   Where a notice of withdrawal is given by the landlord, he is not entitled to dispose of the protected interest during the period of 12 months beginning with the date of service of the notice.

(3)   If a notice of withdrawal is served before the end of the first four weeks of the nomination period specified in the offer notice, the landlord is not liable for any costs incurred in connection with the disposal by the nominated person and the qualifying tenants who served the acceptance notice.

(4)   If a notice of withdrawal is served after the end of those four weeks, the nominated person and the qualifying tenants who served the acceptance notice may recover from the landlord any costs reasonably incurred by them in connection with the disposal between the end of those four weeks and the time when the notice of withdrawal was served.

(5)   This section does not apply after a binding contract for the disposal of the protected interest—

    (a)   has been entered into by the landlord and the nominated person, or

    (b)   has otherwise come into existence between the landlord and the nominated person by virtue of any provision of this Part.]

[664]

**NOTES**

Substituted as noted to s 5 at **[649]**.

## [10   Lapse of landlord's offer

(1)   If after a landlord has served an offer notice the premises concerned cease to be premises to which this Part applies, the landlord may serve a notice on the qualifying tenants of the constituent flats stating—

    (a)   that the premises have ceased to be premises to which this Part applies, and

    (b)   that the offer notice, and anything done in pursuance of it, is to be treated as not having been served or done;

and on the service of such a notice the provisions of this Part cease to have effect in relation to that disposal.

(2)   A landlord who has not served such a notice on all of the qualifying tenants of the constituent flats shall nevertheless be treated as having duly served a notice under subsection (1)—

    (a)   if he has served such a notice on not less than 90% of those tenants, or

    (b)   where those qualifying tenants number less than ten, if he has served such a notice on all but one of them.

(3)   Where the landlord is entitled to serve a notice under subsection (1) but does not do so, this Part shall continue to have effect in relation to the disposal in question as if the premises in question were still premises to which this Part applies.

(4)   The above provisions of this section do not apply after a binding contract for the disposal of the protected interest—

    (a)   has been entered into by the landlord and the nominated person, or

    (b)   has otherwise come into existence between the landlord and the nominated person by virtue of any provision of this Part.

(5)   Where a binding contract for the disposal of the protected interest has been entered into between the landlord and the nominated person but it has been lawfully rescinded by the landlord,

the landlord may, during the period of 12 months beginning with the date of the rescission of the contract, dispose of that interest to such person (and on such terms) as he thinks fit.]

**[665]**

**NOTES**
  Substituted as noted to s 5 at **[649]**.

**[10A    Offence of failure to comply with requirements of Part I**

  (1)    A landlord commits an offence if, without reasonable excuse, he makes a relevant disposal affecting premises to which this Part applies—

     (a)    without having first complied with the requirements of section 5 as regards the service of notices on the qualifying tenants of flats contained in the premises, or

     (b)    in contravention of any prohibition or restriction imposed by sections 6 to 10.

  (2)    A person guilty of an offence under this section is liable on summary conviction to a fine not exceeding level 5 on the standard scale.

  (3)    Where an offence under this section committed by a body corporate is proved—

     (a)    to have been committed with the consent or connivance of a director, manager, secretary or other similar officer of the body corporate, or a person purporting to act in such a capacity, or

     (b)    to be due to any neglect on the part of such an officer or person,

he, as well as the body corporate, is guilty of the offence and liable to be proceeded against and punished accordingly.

  Where the affairs of a body corporate are managed by its members, the above provision applies in relation to the acts and defaults of a member in connection with his functions of management as if he were a director of the body corporate.

  (4)    Proceedings for an offence under this section may be brought by a local housing authority (within the meaning of section 1 of the Housing Act 1985).

  (5)    Nothing in this section affects the validity of the disposal.]

**[666]**

**NOTES**
  Inserted by the Housing Act 1996, s 91, except in relation to disposals made in pursuance of an obligation entered into before 1 October 1996.

*[Enforcement by tenants of rights against purchaser*

**11    Circumstances in which tenants' rights enforceable against purchaser**

  (1)    The following provisions of this Part apply where a landlord has made a relevant disposal affecting premises to which at the time of the disposal this Part applied ("the original disposal"), and either—

     (a)    no notice was served by the landlord under section 5 with respect to that disposal, or

     (b)    the disposal was made in contravention of any provision of sections 6 to 10, and the premises are still premises to which this Part applies.

  (2)    In those circumstances the requisite majority of the qualifying tenants of the flats contained in the premises affected by the relevant disposal (the "constituent flats") have the rights conferred by the following provisions—

     section 11A (right to information as to terms of disposal, &c),
     section 12A (right of qualifying tenants to take benefit of contract),
     section 12B (right of qualifying tenants to compel sale, &c by purchaser), and
     section 12C (right of qualifying tenants to compel grant of new tenancy by superior landlord).

  (3)    In those sections the transferee under the original disposal (or, in the case of the surrender of a tenancy, the superior landlord) is referred to as "the purchaser".

  This shall not be read as restricting the operation of those provisions to disposals for consideration.]

**[667]**

**NOTES**
  Substituted, together with preceding cross-heading and ss 11A, 12A–12D, 13, 14, for original ss 11–15, by the Housing Act 1996, s 92(1), Sch 6, Pt II.

**[11A    Right to information as to terms of disposal, &c**

  (1)    The requisite majority of qualifying tenants of the constituent flats may serve a notice on the purchaser requiring him—

(a) to give particulars of the terms on which the original disposal was made (including the deposit and consideration required) and the date on which it was made, and

(b) where the disposal consisted of entering into a contract, to provide a copy of the contract.

(2) The notice must specify the name and address of the person to whom (on behalf of the tenants) the particulars are to be given, or the copy of the contract provided.

(3) Any notice under this section must be served before the end of the period of four months beginning with the date by which—

(a) notices under section 3A of the Landlord and Tenant Act 1985 (duty of new landlord to inform tenants of rights) relating to the original disposal, or

(b) where that section does not apply, documents of any other description—

(i) indicating that the original disposal has taken place, and

(ii) alerting the tenants to the existence of their rights under this Part and the time within which any such rights must be exercised,

have been served on the requisite majority of qualifying tenants of the constituent flats.

(4) A person served with a notice under this section shall comply with it within the period of one month beginning with the date on which it is served on him.]

**[668]**

**NOTES**
Substituted as noted to s 11 at **[667]**.

**[12A Right of qualifying tenants to take benefit of contract**

(1) Where the original disposal consisted of entering into a contract, the requisite majority of qualifying tenants of the constituent flats may by notice to the landlord elect that the contract shall have effect as if entered into not with the purchaser but with a person or persons nominated for the purposes of this section by the requisite majority of qualifying tenants of the constituent flats.

(2) Any such notice must be served before the end of the period of six months beginning—

(a) if a notice was served on the purchaser under section 11A (right to information as to terms of disposal, &c), with the date on which the purchaser complied with that notice;

(b) in any other case, with the date by which documents of any description—

(i) indicating that the original disposal has taken place, and

(ii) alerting the tenants to the existence of their rights under this Part and the time within which any such rights must be exercised,

have been served on the requisite majority of qualifying tenants of the constituent flats.

(3) The notice shall not have effect as mentioned in subsection (1) unless the nominated person—

(a) fulfils any requirements as to the deposit required on entering into the contract, and

(b) fulfils any other conditions required to be fulfilled by the purchaser on entering into the contract.

(4) Unless otherwise agreed, any time limit in the contract as it has effect by virtue of a notice under this section shall start to run again on the service of that notice; and nothing in the contract as it has effect by virtue of a notice under this section shall require the nominated person to complete the purchase before the end of the period of 28 days beginning with the day on which he is deemed to have entered into the contract.

(5) Where the original disposal related to other property in addition to premises to which this Part applied at the time of the disposal—

(a) a notice under this section has effect only in relation to the premises to which this Part applied at the time of the original disposal, and

(b) the terms of the contract shall have effect with any necessary modifications.

In such a case the notice under this section may specify the subject-matter of the disposal, and the terms on which the disposal is to be made (whether doing so expressly or by reference to the original disposal), or may provide for that estate or interest, or any such terms, to be determined by a leasehold valuation tribunal.]

**[669]**

**NOTES**
Substituted as noted to s 11 at **[667]**.

**[12B Right of qualifying tenants to compel sale, &c by purchaser**

(1) This section applies where—

(a) the original disposal consisted of entering into a contract and no notice has been served under section 12A (right of qualifying tenants to take benefit of contract), or

(b) the original disposal did not consist of entering into a contract.

(2)   The requisite majority of qualifying tenants of the constituent flats may serve a notice (a "purchase notice") on the purchaser requiring him to dispose of the estate or interest that was the subject-matter of the original disposal, on the terms on which it was made (including those relating to the consideration payable), to a person or persons nominated for the purposes of this section by any such majority of qualifying tenants of those flats.

(3)   Any such notice must be served before the end of the period of six months beginning—

(a)   if a notice was served on the purchaser under section 11A (right to information as to terms of disposal, &c), with the date on which the purchaser complied with that notice;

(b)   in any other case, with the date by which—

(i)   notices under section 3A of the Landlord and Tenant Act 1985 (duty of new landlord to inform tenants of rights) relating to the original disposal, or

(ii)   where that section does not apply, documents of any other description indicating that the original disposal has taken place, and alerting the tenants to the existence of their rights under this Part and the time within which any such rights must be exercised,

have been served on the requisite majority of qualifying tenants of the constituent flats.

(4)   A purchase notice shall where the original disposal related to other property in addition to premises to which this Part applied at the time of the disposal—

(a)   require the purchaser only to make a disposal relating to those premises, and

(b)   require him to do so on the terms referred to in subsection (2) with any necessary modifications.

In such a case the purchase notice may specify the subject-matter of the disposal, and the terms on which the disposal is to be made (whether doing so expressly or by reference to the original disposal), or may provide for those matters to be determined by a leasehold valuation tribunal.

(5)   Where the property which the purchaser is required to dispose of in pursuance of the purchase notice has since the original disposal become subject to any charge or other incumbrance, then, unless the court by order directs otherwise—

(a)   in the case of a charge to secure the payment of money or the performance of any other obligation by the purchaser or any other person, the instrument by virtue of which the property is disposed of by the purchaser to the person or persons nominated for the purposes of this section shall (subject to the provisions of Part I of Schedule 1) operate to discharge the property from that charge; and

(b)   in the case of any other incumbrance, the property shall be so disposed of subject to the incumbrance but with a reduction in the consideration payable to the purchaser corresponding to the amount by which the existence of the incumbrance reduces the value of the property.

(6)   Subsection (5)(a) and Part I of Schedule 1 apply, with any necessary modifications, to mortgages and liens as they apply to charges; but nothing in those provisions applies to a rentcharge.

(7)   Where the property which the purchaser is required to dispose of in pursuance of the purchase notice has since the original disposal increased in monetary value owing to any change in circumstances (other than a change in the value of money), the amount of the consideration payable to the purchaser for the disposal by him of the property in pursuance of the purchase notice shall be the amount that might reasonably have been obtained on a corresponding disposal made on the open market at the time of the original disposal if the change in circumstances had already taken place.]

**[670]**

---

**NOTES**

Substituted as noted to s 11 at **[667]**.

---

**[12C   Right of qualifying tenants to compel grant of new tenancy by superior landlord**

(1)   This section applies where the original disposal consisted of the surrender by the landlord of a tenancy held by him ("the relevant tenancy").

(2)   The requisite majority of qualifying tenants of the constituent flats may serve a notice on the purchaser requiring him to grant a new tenancy of the premises which were subject to the relevant tenancy, on the same terms as those of the relevant tenancy and so as to expire on the same date as that tenancy would have expired, to a person or persons nominated for the purposes of this section by any such majority of qualifying tenants of those flats.

(3)   Any such notice must be served before the end of the period of six months beginning—

(a)   if a notice was served on the purchaser under section 11A (right to information as to terms of disposal, &c), with the date on which the purchaser complied with that notice;

(b)   in any other case, with the date by which documents of any description—

(i)   indicating that the original disposal has taken place, and

(ii)   alerting the tenants to the existence of their rights under this Part and the time within which any such rights must be exercised, have been served on the requisite majority of qualifying tenants of the constituent flats.

(4) If the purchaser paid any amount to the landlord as consideration for the surrender by him of that tenancy, the nominated person shall pay that amount to the purchaser.

(5) Where the premises subject to the relevant tenancy included premises other than premises to which this Part applied at the time of the disposal, a notice under this section shall—

(a) require the purchaser only to grant a new tenancy relating to the premises to which this Part then applied, and

(b) require him to do so on the terms referred to in subsection (2) subject to any necessary modifications.

(6) The purchase notice may specify the subject-matter of the disposal, and the terms on which the disposal is to be made (whether doing so expressly or by reference to the original disposal), or may provide for those matters to be determined by a leasehold valuation tribunal.]

**[671]**

**NOTES**
Substituted as noted to s 11 at **[667]**.

**[12D Nominated persons: supplementary provisions**

(1) The person or persons initially nominated for the purposes of section 12A, 12B or 12C shall be nominated in the notice under that section.

(2) A person nominated for those purposes by the requisite majority of qualifying tenants of the constituent flats may be replaced by another person so nominated if, and only if, he has (for any reason) ceased to be able to act as a nominated person.

(3) Where two or more persons have been nominated and any of them ceases to act without being replaced, the remaining person or persons so nominated may continue to act.

(4) Where, in the exercise of its power to award costs, the court or the [Upper Tribunal] makes, in connection with any proceedings arising under or by virtue of this Part, an award of costs against the person or persons so nominated, the liability for those costs is a joint and several liability of that person or those persons together with the qualifying tenants by whom the relevant notice was served.]

**[672]**

**NOTES**
Substituted as noted to s 11 at **[667]**.
Sub-s (4): words in square brackets substituted by the Transfer of Tribunal Functions (Lands Tribunal and Miscellaneous Amendments) Order 2009, SI 2009/1307, art 5(1), (2), Sch 1, paras 180, 181, subject to transitional provisions and savings in Sch 5 thereto.

**[13 Determination of questions by leasehold valuation tribunal**

(1) A leasehold valuation tribunal has jurisdiction to hear and determine—

(a) any question arising in relation to any matters specified in a notice under section 12A, 12B or 12C, and

(b) any question arising for determination as mentioned in section 8C(4), 12A(5) or 12B(4) (matters left for determination by tribunal).

(2) On an application under this section the interests of the persons by whom the notice was served under section 12A, 12B or 12C shall be represented by the nominated person; and accordingly the parties to any such application shall not include those persons.

**[673]**

**NOTES**
Substituted as noted to s 11 at **[667]**.

**[14 Withdrawal of nominated person from transaction under s 12B or 12C**

(1) Where notice has been duly served on the landlord under—
section 12B (right of qualifying tenants to compel sale, &c by purchaser), or
section 12C (right of qualifying tenants to compel grant of new tenancy by superior landlord),
the nominated person may at any time before a binding contract is entered into in pursuance of the notice, serve notice under this section on the purchaser (a "notice of withdrawal") indicating an intention no longer to proceed with the disposal.

(2) If at any such time the nominated person becomes aware that the number of qualifying tenants of the constituent flats desiring to proceed with the disposal is less than the requisite majority of those tenants, he shall forthwith serve a notice of withdrawal.

(3)   If a notice of withdrawal is served under this section the purchaser may recover from the nominated person any costs reasonably incurred by him in connection with the disposal down to the time when the notice is served on him.

(4)   If a notice of withdrawal is served at a time when proceedings arising under or by virtue of this Part are pending before the court or the [Upper Tribunal], the liability of the nominated person for any costs incurred by the purchaser as mentioned in subsection (3) shall be such as may be determined by the court or (as the case may be) by the Tribunal.

(5)   The costs that may be recovered by the purchaser under this section do not include any costs incurred by him in connection with an application to a leasehold valuation tribunal.]

**[674]**

**NOTES**

Substituted as noted to s 11 at **[667]**.

Sub-s (4): words in square brackets substituted by the Transfer of Tribunal Functions (Lands Tribunal and Miscellaneous Amendments) Order 2009, SI 2009/1307, art 5(1), (2), Sch 1, paras 180, 182, subject to transitional provisions and savings in Sch 5 thereto.

*[Enforcement by tenants of rights against subsequent purchasers*

**16   Rights of qualifying tenants against subsequent purchaser**

(1)   This section applies where, at the time when a notice is served on the purchaser under section 11A, 12A, 12B or 12C, he no longer holds the estate or interest that was the subject-matter of the original disposal.

(2)   In the case of a notice under section 11A (right to information as to terms of disposal, &c) the purchaser shall, within the period for complying with that notice—

(a)   serve notice on the person specified in the notice as the person to whom particulars are to be provided of the name and address of the person to whom he has disposed of that estate or interest ("the subsequent purchaser"), and

(b)   serve on the subsequent purchaser a copy of the notice under section 11A and of the particulars given by him in response to it.

(3)   In the case of a notice under section 12A, 12B or 12C the purchaser shall forthwith—

(a)   forward the notice to the subsequent purchaser, and

(b)   serve on the nominated person notice of the name and address of the subsequent purchaser.

(4)   Once the purchaser serves a notice in accordance with subsection (2)(a) or (3)(b), sections 12A to 14 shall, instead of applying to the purchaser, apply to the subsequent purchaser as if he were the transferee under the original disposal.

(5)   Subsections (1) to (4) have effect, with any necessary modifications, in a case where, instead of disposing of the whole of the estate or interest referred to in subsection (1) to another person, the purchaser has disposed of it in part or in parts to one or more other persons.

In such a case, sections 12A to 14—

(a)   apply to the purchaser in relation to any part of that estate or interest retained by him, and

(b)   in relation to any part of that estate or interest disposed of to any other person, apply to that other person instead as if he were (as respects that part) the transferee under the original disposal.]

**[675]**

**NOTES**

Substituted, together with s 17 and the preceding cross-headings, by the Housing Act 1996, s 92(1), Sch 6, Pt III.

*[Termination of rights against purchasers or subsequent purchasers*

**17   Termination of rights against purchaser or subsequent purchaser**

(1)   If, at any time after a notice has been served under section 11A, 12A, 12B or 12C, the premises affected by the original disposal cease to be premises to which this Part applies, the purchaser may serve a notice on the qualifying tenants of the constituent flats stating—

(a)   that the premises have ceased to be premises to which this Part applies, and

(b)   that any such notice served on him, and anything done in pursuance of it, is to be treated as not having been served or done.

(2)   A landlord who has not served such a notice on all of the qualifying tenants of the constituent flats shall nevertheless be treated as having duly served a notice under subsection (1)—

(a)   if he has served such a notice on not less than 90% of those tenants, or

(b)   where those qualifying tenants number less than ten, if he has served such a notice on all but one of them.

(3)   Where a period of three months beginning with the date of service of a notice under section 12A, 12B or 12C on the purchaser has expired—

(a)   without any binding contract having been entered into between the purchaser and the nominated person, and

(b)   without there having been made any application in connection with the notice to the court or to a leasehold valuation tribunal,

the purchaser may serve on the nominated person a notice stating that the notice, and anything done in pursuance of it, is to be treated as not having been served or done.

(4)   Where any such application as is mentioned in subsection (3)(b) was made within the period of three months referred to in that subsection, but—

(a)   a period of two months beginning with the date of the determination of that application has expired,

(b)   no binding contract has been entered into between the purchaser and the nominated person, and

(c)   no other such application as is mentioned in subsection (3)(b) is pending,

the purchaser may serve on the nominated person a notice stating that any notice served on him under section 12A, 12B or 12C, and anything done in pursuance of any such notice, is to be treated as not having been served or done.

(5)   Where the purchaser serves a notice in accordance with subsection (1), (3) or (4), this Part shall cease to have effect in relation to him in connection with the original disposal.

(6)   Where a purchaser is entitled to serve a notice under subsection (1) but does not do so, this Part shall continue to have effect in relation to him in connection with the original disposal as if the premises in question were still premises to which this Part applies.

(7)   References in this section to the purchaser include a subsequent purchaser to whom sections 12A to 14 apply by virtue of section 16(4) or (5).]

[676]

**NOTES**
Substituted as noted to s 16 at [675].

*Notices served by prospective purchasers*

## 18   Notices served by prospective purchasers to ensure that rights of first refusal do not arise

(1)   Where—

(a)   any disposal of an estate or interest in any premises consisting of the whole or part of a building is proposed to be made by a landlord, and

(b)   it appears to the person who would be the transferee under that disposal ("the purchaser") that any such disposal would, or might, be a relevant disposal affecting premises to which this Part applies,

the purchaser may serve notices under this subsection on the tenants of the flats contained in the premises referred to in paragraph (a) ("the flats affected").

(2)   Any notice under subsection (1) shall—

(a)   inform the person on whom it is served of the general nature of the principal terms of the proposed disposal, including in particular—

(i)   the property to which it would relate and the estate or interest in that property proposed to be disposed of by the landlord, and

(ii)   the consideration required by him for making the disposal;

(b)   invite that person to serve a notice on the purchaser stating—

(i)   whether the landlord has served on him, or on any predecessor in title of his, a notice under section 5 with respect to the disposal, and

(ii)   if the landlord has not so served any such notice, whether he is aware of any reason why he is not entitled to be served with any such notice by the landlord, and

(iii)   if he is not so aware, whether he would wish to avail himself of the right of first refusal conferred by any such notice if it were served; and

(c)   inform that person of the effect of the following provisions of this section.

(3)   Where the purchaser has served notices under subsection (1) on at least 80 per cent of the tenants of the flats affected and—

(a)   not more than 50 per cent of the tenants on whom those notices have been served by the purchaser have served notices on him in pursuance of subsection (2)(b) by the end of the period of [two months] beginning with the date on which the last of them was served by him with a notice under this section, or

(b)   more than 50 per cent of the tenants on whom those notices have been served by the purchaser have served notices on him in pursuance of subsection (2)(b) but the notices in each case indicate that the tenant serving it either—

      (i)   does not regard himself as being entitled to be served by the landlord with a notice under section 5 with respect to the disposal, or

      (ii)   would not wish to avail himself of the right of first refusal conferred by such a notice if it were served,

the premises affected by the disposal shall, in relation to the disposal, be treated for the purposes of this Part as premises to which this Part does not apply.

    (4)   For the purposes of subsection (3) each of the flats affected shall be regarded as having one tenant, who shall count towards any of the percentages specified in that subsection whether he is a qualifying tenant of the flat or not.

**[677]**

**NOTES**

    Sub-s (3): words in square brackets substituted by the Tenants' Rights of First Refusal (Amendment) Regulations 1996, SI 1996/2371, in relation to any disposal in a case where the purchaser has served a notice under sub-s (1) above, after 3 October 1996.

*Supplementary*

## [18A  The requisite majority of qualifying tenants

    (1)   In this Part "the requisite majority of qualifying tenants of the constituent flats" means qualifying tenants of constituent flats with more than 50 per cent of the available votes.

    (2)   The total number of available votes shall be determined as follows—

    (a)   where an offer notice has been served under section 5, that number is equal to the total number of constituent flats let to qualifying tenants on the date when the period specified in that notice as the period for accepting the offer expires;

    (b)   where a notice is served under section 11A without a notice having been previously served under section 5, that number is equal to the total number of constituent flats let to qualifying tenants on the date of service of the notice under section 11A;

    (c)   where a notice is served under section 12A, 12B or 12C without a notice having been previously served under section 5 or section 11A, that number is equal to the total number of constituent flats let to qualifying tenants on the date of service of the notice under section 12A, 12B or 12C, as the case may be.

    (3)   There is one available vote in respect of each of the flats so let on the date referred to in the relevant paragraph of subsection (2), which shall be attributed to the qualifying tenant to whom it is let.

    (4)   The persons constituting the requisite majority of qualifying tenants for one purpose may be different from the persons constituting such a majority for another purpose.]

**[678]**

**NOTES**

    Inserted by the Housing Act 1996, s 92(1), Sch 6, Pt IV, para 2.

## 19  Enforcement of obligations under Part I

    (1)   The court may, on the application of any person interested, make an order requiring any person who has made default in complying with any duty imposed on him by any provision of this Part to make good the default within such time as is specified in the order.

    (2)   An application shall not be made under subsection (1) unless—

    (a)   a notice has been previously served on the person in question requiring him to make good the default, and

    (b)   more than 14 days have elapsed since the date of service of that notice without his having done so.

    (3)   The restriction imposed by section 1(1) may be enforced by an injunction granted by the court.

**[679]**

## 20  Construction of Part I and power of Secretary of State to prescribe modifications

    (1)   In this Part—

    ["acceptance notice" has the meaning given by section 6(3);]

    "associated company", in relation to a body corporate, means another body corporate which is (within the meaning of [section 1159 of the Companies Act 2006]) that body's holding company, a subsidiary of that body or another subsidiary of that body's holding company;

    ["constituent flat" shall be construed in accordance with section 5(1) or 11(2), as the case may require;]

"disposal" [shall be construed in accordance with section 4(3) and section 4A (application of provisions to contracts)], and references to the acquisition of an estate or interest shall be construed accordingly;

"landlord", in relation to any premises, shall be construed in accordance with section 2;

.....

["the nominated person" means the person or persons for the time being nominated by the requisite majority of the qualifying tenants of the constituent flats for the purposes of section 6, 12A, 12B or 12C, as the case may require;]

"offer notice" means a notice served by a landlord under section 5;

"the original disposal" means the relevant disposal referred to in section 11(1);

["the protected interest" means the estate, interest or other subject-matter of an offer notice;]

["the protected period" has the meaning given by section 6(4);]

["purchase notice" has the meaning given by section 12B(2);]

["purchaser" has the meaning given by section 11(3);]

"qualifying tenant", in relation to a flat, shall be construed in accordance with section 3;

"relevant disposal" shall be construed in accordance with section 4;

"the requisite majority", in relation to qualifying tenants, shall be construed in accordance with [section 18A];

"transferee", in relation to a disposal, shall be construed in accordance with section 4(3).

(2)   In this Part—
(a)   any reference to an offer ... is a reference to an offer ... made subject to contract, and
(b)   any reference to the acceptance of an offer ... is a reference to its acceptance subject to contract.

(3)   Any reference in this Part to a tenant of a particular description shall be construed, in relation to any time when the interest under his tenancy has ceased to be vested in him, as a reference to the person who is for the time being the successor in title to that interest.

(4)   The Secretary of State may by regulations make such modifications of any of the provisions of sections 5 to 18 as he considers appropriate, and any such regulations may contain such incidental, supplemental or transitional provisions as he considers appropriate in connection with the regulations.

(5)   In subsection (4) "modifications" includes additions, omissions and alterations.

[680]

**NOTES**
Sub-s (1): definitions "acceptance notice", "constituent flat", "the protected interest" and "purchase notice" substituted, words in square brackets in definitions "disposal" and "the requisite majority" substituted, definitions "the nominated person", "the protected period" and "the purchaser" inserted, and definition "the new landlord" (omitted) repealed by the Housing Act 1996, ss 89(3), 92(1), 227, Sch 6, Pt IV, para 3, Sch 19, Pt III; words in square brackets in definition "associated company" substituted by the Companies Act 2006 (Consequential Amendments, Transitional Provisions and Savings) Order 2009, SI 2009/1941, art 2(1), Sch 1, para 88.
Sub-s (2): words omitted repealed by the Housing Act 1996, ss 92(1), 227, Sch 6, Pt IV, para 4, Sch 19, Pt III.

PART II
APPOINTMENT OF MANAGERS BY [A LEASEHOLD VALUATION TRIBUNAL]

**NOTES**
Part heading: words in square brackets substituted by virtue of the Housing Act 1996, s 86(1), (2).

**21   Tenant's right to apply to [tribunal] for appointment of manager**

(1)   The tenant of a flat contained in any premises to which this Part applies may, subject to the following provisions of this Part, apply to [a leasehold valuation tribunal] for an order under section 24 appointing a manager to act in relation to those premises.

(2)   Subject to subsection (3), this Part applies to premises consisting of the whole or part of a building if the building or part contains two or more flats.

(3)   This Part does not apply to any such premises at a time when—
(a)   the interest of the landlord in the premises is held by[—
(i)]   an exempt landlord or a resident landlord, [or
(ii)   the Welsh Ministers in their new towns residuary capacity,] or
(b)   the premises are included within the functional land of any charity.

[(3A)   But this Part is not prevented from applying to any premises because the interest of the landlord in the premises is held by a resident landlord if at least one-half of the flats contained in the premises are held on long leases which are not tenancies to which Part 2 of the Landlord and Tenant Act 1954 (c 56) applies.]

(4)   An application for an order under section 24 may be made—

(a) jointly by tenants of two or more flats if they are each entitled to make such an application by virtue of this section, and

(b) in respect of two or more premises to which this Part applies;

and, in relation to any such joint application as is mentioned in paragraph (a), references in this Part to a single tenant shall be construed accordingly.

(5) Where the tenancy of a flat contained in any such premises is held by joint tenants, an application for an order under section 24 in respect of those premises may be made by any one or more of those tenants.

(6) An application to the court for it to exercise in relation to any premises [any jurisdiction] to appoint a receiver or manager shall not be made by a tenant (in his capacity as such) in any circumstances in which an application could be made by him for an order under section 24 appointing a manager to act in relation to those premises.

(7) References in this Part to a tenant do not include references to a tenant under a tenancy to which Part II of the Landlord and Tenant Act 1954 applies.

**[681]**

---

**NOTES**

Section heading, sub-ss (1), (6): words in square brackets substituted by the Housing Act 1996, s 86.

Sub-s (3): words in square brackets inserted by the Housing and Regeneration Act 2008, s 56, Sch 8, paras 37, 38, subject to transitional provisions and savings in SI 2008/3068, arts 6–10 at **[3834B]–[3834F]**.

Sub-s (3A): inserted by the Commonhold and Leasehold Reform Act 2002, s 161, except in relation to applications made under Part II of this Act at **[681]–[684]**, before 26 July 2002 (in relation to England) or 1 January 2003 (in relation to Wales).

Modification: sub-ss (1), (2), (3A)–(7) are modified, where the RTM company has acquired the right to manage, by the Commonhold and Leasehold Reform Act 2002, s 102, Sch 7, para 8 at **[1266]**, **[1306]**.

---

## 22 Preliminary notice by tenant

(1) Before an application for an order under section 24 is made in respect of any premises to which this Part applies by a tenant of a flat contained in those premises, a notice under this section must (subject to subsection (3)) be served [by the tenant on—

(i) the landlord, and

(ii) any person (other than the landlord) by whom obligations relating to the management of the premises or any part of them are owed to the tenant under his tenancy].

(2) A notice under this section must—

(a) specify the tenant's name, the address of his flat and an address in England and Wales (which may be the address of his flat) at which [any person on whom the notice is served] may serve notices, including notices in proceedings, on him in connection with this Part;

(b) state that the tenant intends to make an application for an order under section 24 to be made by [a leasehold valuation tribunal] in respect of such premises to which this Part applies as are specified in the notice, but (if paragraph (d) is applicable) that he will not do so if the [requirement specified in pursuance of that paragraph is complied with];

(c) specify the grounds on which [the tribunal] would be asked to make such an order and the matters that would be relied on by the tenant for the purpose of establishing those grounds;

(d) where those matters are capable of being remedied by [any person on whom the notice is served, require him], within such reasonable period as is specified in the notice, to take such steps for the purpose of remedying them as are so specified; and

(e) contain such information (if any) as the Secretary of State may by regulations prescribe.

(3) [A leasehold valuation tribunal] may (whether on the hearing of an application for an order under section 24 or not) by order dispense with the requirement to serve a notice under this section [on a person] in a case where it is satisfied that it would not be reasonably practicable to serve such a notice on the [person], but [the tribunal] may, when doing so, direct that such other notices are served, or such other steps are taken, as it thinks fit.

(4) In a case where—

(a) a notice under this section has been served on the landlord, and

(b) his interest in the premises specified in pursuance of subsection (2)(b) is subject to a mortgage,

the landlord shall, as soon as is reasonably practicable after receiving the notice, serve on the mortgagee a copy of the notice.

**[682]**

**NOTES**

Sub-s (1): words in square brackets substituted by the Commonhold and Leasehold Reform Act 2002, s 160(1), (2)(a), except in relation to applications made under Part II of this Act at **[681]–[684]**, before 26 July 2002 (in relation to England) or 1 January 2003 (in relation to Wales).

Sub-s (2): words in square brackets in paras (a), (d) and words in second pair of square brackets in para (b) substituted by the Commonhold and Leasehold Reform Act 2002, s 160(1), (2)(b)–(d), except in relation to applications made under Part II of this Act at **[681]–[684]**, before 26 July 2002 (in relation to England) or 1 January 2003 (in relation to Wales); words in first pair of square brackets in para (b) and words in square brackets in para (c) substituted by the Housing Act 1996, s 86(1), (2).

Sub-s (3): words in first and fourth pairs of square brackets substituted by the Housing Act 1996, s 86(1), (2); words in second pair of square brackets inserted and word in third pair of square brackets substituted by the Commonhold and Leasehold Reform Act 2002, s 160(1), (2)(e), except in relation to applications made under Part II of this Act at **[681]–[684]**, before 26 July 2002 (in relation to England) or 1 January 2003 (in relation to Wales).

Modified, where the RTM company has acquired the right to manage, by the Commonhold and Leasehold Reform Act 2002, s 102, Sch 7, para 8 at **[1266]**, **[1306]**.

## 23 Application to [tribunal] for appointment of manager

(1) No application for an order under section 24 shall be made to [a leasehold valuation tribunal] unless—

    (a)    in a case where a notice has been served under section 22, either—

        (i)    the period specified in pursuance of paragraph (d) of subsection (2) of that section has expired without the [person required to take steps in pursuance of that paragraph having taken them], or

        (ii)    that paragraph was not applicable in the circumstances of the case; or

    (b)    in a case where the requirement to serve such a notice has been dispensed with by an order under subsection (3) of that section, either—

        (i)    any notices required to be served, and any other steps required to be taken, by virtue of the order have been served or (as the case may be) taken, or

        (ii)    no direction was given by [the tribunal] when making the order.

(2)  ...

                                                            **[683]**

**NOTES**

Section heading: word in square brackets substituted by virtue of the Housing Act 1996, s 86(1), (2).

Sub-s (1): words in first and third pairs of square brackets substituted by the Housing Act 1996, s 86(1), (2), (4); words in second pair of square brackets substituted by the Commonhold and Leasehold Reform Act 2002, s 160(1), (3), except in relation to applications made under Part II of this Act at **[681]–[684]**, before 26 July 2002 (in relation to England) or 1 January 2003 (in relation to Wales).

Sub-s (2): repealed by the Commonhold and Leasehold Reform Act 2002, s 180, Sch 14, except in relation to any application made to an LVT or any proceedings transferred to an LVT by a county court before 30 September 2003 (in relation to England) or 31 March 2004 (in relation to Wales).

Modified, where the RTM company has acquired the right to manage, by the Commonhold and Leasehold Reform Act 2002, s 102, Sch 7, para 8 at **[1266]**, **[1306]**.

## 24 Appointment of manager by [a leasehold valuation tribunal]

(1) [A leasehold valuation tribunal] may, on an application for an order under this section, by order (whether interlocutory or final) appoint a manager to carry out in relation to any premises to which this Part applies—

    (a)    such functions in connection with the management of the premises, or

    (b)    such functions of a receiver,

or both, as [the tribunal] thinks fit.

(2) [A leasehold valuation tribunal] may only make an order under this section in the following circumstances, namely—

    (a)    where [the tribunal] is satisfied—

        (i)    that [any relevant person] either is in breach of any obligation owed by him to the tenant under his tenancy and relating to the management of the premises in question or any part of them or (in the case of an obligation dependent on notice) would be in breach of any such obligation but for the fact that it has not been reasonably practicable for the tenant to give him the appropriate notice, and

        (ii)    ...

        (iii)    that it is just and convenient to make the order in all the circumstances of the case;

    [(ab)  where [the tribunal] is satisfied—

        (i)    that unreasonable service charges have been made, or are proposed or likely to be made, and

        (ii)    that it is just and convenient to make the order in all the circumstances of the case;

    [(aba)  where the tribunal is satisfied—

(i) that unreasonable variable administration charges have been made, or are proposed or likely to be made, and

(ii) that it is just and convenient to make the order in all the circumstances of the case;]

[(abb) where the tribunal is satisfied—

(i) that there has been a failure to comply with a duty imposed by or by virtue of section 42 or 42A of this Act, and

(ii) that it is just and convenient to make the order in all the circumstances of the case;]

(ac) where [the tribunal] is satisfied—

(i) that [any relevant person] has failed to comply with any relevant provision of a code of practice approved by the Secretary of State under section 87 of the Leasehold Reform, Housing and Urban Development Act 1993 (codes of management practice), and

(ii) that it is just and convenient to make the order in all the circumstances of the case;] or

(b) where [the tribunal] is satisfied that other circumstances exist which make it just and convenient for the order to be made.

[(2ZA) In this section "relevant person" means a person—

(a) on whom a notice has been served under section 22, or

(b) in the case of whom the requirement to serve a notice under that section has been dispensed with by an order under subsection (3) of that section.]

[(2A) For the purposes of subsection (2)(ab) a service charge shall be taken to be unreasonable—

(a) if the amount is unreasonable having regard to the items for which it is payable,

(b) if the items for which it is payable are of an unnecessarily high standard, or

(c) if the items for which it is payable are of an insufficient standard with the result that additional service charges are or may be incurred.

In that provision and this subsection "service charge" means a service charge within the meaning of section 18(1) of the Landlord and Tenant Act 1985, other than one excluded from that section by section 27 of that Act (rent of dwelling registered and not entered as variable).]

[(2B) In subsection (2)(aba) "variable administration charge" has the meaning given by paragraph 1 of Schedule 11 to the Commonhold and Leasehold Reform Act 2002.]

(3) The premises in respect of which an order is made under this section may, if [the tribunal] thinks fit, be either more or less extensive than the premises specified in the application on which the order is made.

(4) An order under this section may make provision with respect to—

(a) such matters relating to the exercise by the manager of his functions under the order, and

(b) such incidental or ancillary matters,

as [the tribunal] thinks fit; and, on any subsequent application made for the purpose by the manager, [the tribunal] may give him directions with respect to any such matters.

(5) Without prejudice to the generality of subsection (4), an order under this section may provide—

(a) for rights and liabilities arising under contracts to which the manager is not a party to become rights and liabilities of the manager;

(b) for the manager to be entitled to prosecute claims in respect of causes of action (whether contractual or tortious) accruing before or after the date of his appointment;

(c) for remuneration to be paid to the manager by [any relevant person], or by the tenants of the premises in respect of which the order is made or by all or any of those persons;

(d) for the manager's functions to be exercisable by him (subject to subsection (9)) either during a specified period or without limit of time.

(6) Any such order may be granted subject to such conditions as [the tribunal] thinks fit, and in particular its operation may be suspended on terms fixed by [the tribunal].

(7) In a case where an application for an order under this section was preceded by the service of a notice under section 22, [the tribunal] may, if it thinks fit, make such an order notwithstanding—

(a) that any period specified in the notice in pursuance of subsection (2)(d) of that section was not a reasonable period, or

(b) that the notice failed in any other respect to comply with any requirement contained in subsection (2) of that section or in any regulations applying to the notice under section 54(3).

(8) The Land Charges Act 1972 and the [Land Registration Act 2002] shall apply in relation to an order made under this section as they apply in relation to an order appointing a receiver or sequestrator of land.

(9)   [A leasehold valuation tribunal] may, on the application of any person interested, vary or discharge (whether conditionally or unconditionally) an order made under this section; and if the order has been protected by an entry registered under the Land Charges Act 1972 or the [Land Registration Act 2002], [the tribunal] may by order direct that the entry shall be cancelled.

[(9A)   The [tribunal] shall not vary or discharge an order under subsection (9) on [the application of any relevant person] unless it is satisfied—

(a)   that the variation or discharge of the order will not result in a recurrence of the circumstances which led to the order being made, and

(b)   that it is just and convenient in all the circumstances of the case to vary or discharge the order.]

(10)   An order made under this section shall not be discharged by [a leasehold valuation tribunal] by reason only that, by virtue of section 21(3), the premises in respect of which the order was made have ceased to be premises to which this Part applies.

(11)   References in this [Part] to the management of any premises include references to the repair, maintenance[, improvement] or insurance of those premises.

**[684]**

**NOTES**

Section heading: words in square brackets substituted by virtue of the Housing Act 1996, s 86(1), (2).

Sub-ss (1), (3), (4), (6), (7), (10): words in square brackets substituted by the Housing Act 1996, s 86(1), (2).

Sub-s (2): words in square brackets in sub-paras (a)(i), (ac)(i) substituted by the Commonhold and Leasehold Reform Act 2002, s 160(1), (4)(a), except in relation to applications made under Part II of this Act at **[681]–[684]**, before 26 July 2002 (in relation to England) or 1 January 2003 (in relation to Wales); para (aba) inserted, except in relation to an application made under this section before 30 September 2003 (in relation to England) or 31 March 2004 (in relation to Wales), by s 158 of, and Sch 11, Pt 2, paras 7, 8(1), (2) to, the 2002 Act, and para (abb) inserted by s 157 of, and Sch 10, para 14 to, the 2002 Act, as from a day to be appointed; sub-para (a)(ii) repealed, paras (ab), (ac) inserted and other words in square brackets substituted by the Housing Act 1996, ss 85(1)–(3), (5), 86(1), (2), 227, Sch 19, Pt III.

Sub-s (2ZA): inserted by the Commonhold and Leasehold Reform Act 2002, s 160(1), (4)(b), except in relation to applications made under Part II of this Act at **[681]–[684]**, before 26 July 2002 (in relation to England) or 1 January 2003 (in relation to Wales).

Sub-s (2A): inserted by the Housing Act 1996, s 85(1), (4), (5), in relation to applications for an order under this section after 24 September 1996.

Sub-s (2B): inserted by the Commonhold and Leasehold Reform Act 2002, s 158, Sch 11, Pt 2, paras 7, 8(1), (3), except in relation to an application made under this section before 30 September 2003 (in relation to England) or 31 March 2004 (in relation to Wales).

Sub-s (5): words in square brackets substituted by the Commonhold and Leasehold Reform Act 2002, s 160(1), (4)(c), except in relation to applications made under Part II of this Act at **[681]–[684]**, before 26 July 2002 (in relation to England) or 1 January 2003 (in relation to Wales).

Sub-s (8): words in square brackets substituted by the Land Registration Act 2002, s 133, Sch 11, para 20.

Sub-s (9): words in first and third pairs of square brackets substituted by the Housing Act 1996, s 86(1), (2); words in second pair of square brackets substituted by the Land Registration Act 2002, s 133, Sch 11, para 20.

Sub-s (9A): inserted by the Housing Act 1996, s 85(1), (6); words in square brackets substituted by the Commonhold and Leasehold Reform Act 2002, ss 160(1), (4)(d), 176, Sch 13, paras 8, 9 except in relation to any application made to an LVT or any proceedings transferred to an LVT by a county court before 30 September 2003 (in relation to England) or 31 March 2004 (in relation to Wales).

Sub-s (11): word in first pair of square brackets substituted, except in relation to applications made under Part II of this Act at **[681]–[684]**, before 26 July 2002 (in relation to England) or 1 January 2003 (in relation to Wales), and word in second pair of square brackets inserted, except in relation to an application made under this section before 30 September 2003 (in relation to England) or 31 March 2004 (in relation to Wales) by the Commonhold and Leasehold Reform Act 2002, ss 150, 160(1), (4)(e), Sch 9, para 8.

Modified, where the RTM company has acquired the right to manage, by the Commonhold and Leasehold Reform Act 2002, s 102, Sch 7, para 8 at **[1266]**, **[1306]**.

**24A, 24B**   *(Inserted by the Housing Act 1996, s 83(3); repealed by the Commonhold and Leasehold Reform Act 2002, s 180, Sch 14, except in relation to any application made to an LVT or any proceedings transferred to an LVT by a county court before 30 September 2003 (in relation to England) or 31 March 2004 (in relation to Wales).)*

**PART III**
**COMPULSORY ACQUISITION BY TENANTS OF THEIR LANDLORD'S INTEREST**

**25   Compulsory acquisition of landlord's interest by qualifying tenants**

(1)   This Part has effect for the purpose of enabling qualifying tenants of flats contained in any premises to which this Part applies to make an application to the court for an order providing for a person nominated by them to acquire their landlord's interest in the premises without his consent; and any such order is referred to in this Part as "an acquisition order".

(2)   Subject to subsections (4) and (5), this Part applies to premises if—

(a)   they consist of the whole or part of a building; and

    (b)      they contain two or more flats held by tenants of the landlord who are qualifying tenants; and

    [(c)      the total number of flats held by such tenants is not less than two-thirds of the total number of flats contained in the premises.]

    (3)   ...

    (4)      This Part does not apply to premises falling within subsection (2) if—

    (a)      any part or parts of the premises is or are occupied or intended to be occupied otherwise than for residential purposes; and

    (b)      the internal floor area of that part or those parts (taken together) exceeds 50 per cent of the internal floor area of the premises (taken as a whole);

and for the purposes of this subsection the internal floor area of any common parts shall be disregarded.

    (5)      This Part also does not apply to any such premises at a time when—

    (a)      the interest of the landlord in the premises is held by an exempt landlord or a resident landlord, or

    (b)      the premises are included within the functional land of any charity.

    (6)      The Secretary of State may by order substitute for the percentage for the time being specified in subsection (4)(b) such other percentage as is specified in the order.

**[685]**

**NOTES**

    Sub-s (2): para (c) substituted by the Leasehold Reform, Housing and Urban Development Act 1993, s 85(1), (2)(a).

    Sub-s (3): repealed by the Leasehold Reform, Housing and Urban Development Act 1993, ss 85(1), (2)(b), 187(2), Sch 22.

    Modified, where the RTM company has acquired the right to manage, by the Commonhold and Leasehold Reform Act 2002, s 102, Sch 7, para 9 at **[1266]**, **[1306]**.

## 26   Qualifying tenants

    (1)      Subject to subsections (2) and (3), a person is a qualifying tenant of a flat for the purposes of this Part if he is the tenant of the flat under a long lease other than one constituting a tenancy to which Part II of the Landlord and Tenant Act 1954 applies.

    (2)      A person is not to be regarded as being a qualifying tenant of a flat contained in any particular premises consisting of the whole or part of a building if [by virtue of one or more long leases none of which constitutes a tenancy to which Part II of the Landlord and Tenant Act 1954 applies, he is the tenant not only of the flat in question but also of at least two other flats contained in those premises].

    (3)      A tenant of a flat under a long lease whose landlord is a qualifying tenant of that flat is not to be regarded as being a qualifying tenant of that flat.

    [(4)      For the purposes of subsection (2) any tenant of a flat contained in the premises in question who is a body corporate shall be treated as the tenant of any other flat so contained and let to an associated company, as defined in section 20(1).]

**[686]**

**NOTES**

    Sub-s (2): words in square brackets substituted by the Housing Act 1988, s 119, Sch 13, para 4(1), except in relation to an application made to the court before 15 January 1989.

    Sub-s (4): added by the Housing Act 1988, s 119, Sch 13, para 4, subject to savings as noted above.

    Modified, where the RTM company has acquired the right to manage, by the Commonhold and Leasehold Reform Act 2002, s 102, Sch 7, para 9 at **[1266]**, **[1306]**.

## 27   Preliminary notice by tenants

    (1)      Before an application for an acquisition order is made in respect of any premises to which this Part applies, a notice under this section must (subject to subsection (3)) be served on the landlord by qualifying tenants of the flats contained in the premises who, at the date when it is served, constitute the requisite majority of such tenants.

    (2)      A notice under this section must—

    (a)      specify the names of the qualifying tenants by whom it is served, the addresses of their flats and the name and the address in England and Wales of a person on whom the landlord may serve notices (including notices in proceedings) in connection with this Part instead of serving them on those tenants;

    (b)      state that those tenants intend to make an application for an acquisition order to be made by the court in respect of such premises to which this Part applies as are specified in the notice, but (if paragraph (d) is applicable) that they will not do so if the landlord complies with the requirement specified in pursuance of that paragraph;

   (c)    specify the grounds on which the court would be asked to make such an order and the matters that would be relied on by the tenants for the purpose of establishing those grounds;

   (d)    where those matters are capable of being remedied by the landlord, require the landlord, within such reasonable period as is specified in the notice, to take such steps for the purpose of remedying them as are so specified; and

   (e)    contain such information (if any) as the Secretary of State may by regulations prescribe.

(3)   The court may by order dispense with the requirement to serve a notice under this section in a case where it is satisfied that it would not be reasonably practicable to serve such a notice on the landlord, but the court may, when doing so, direct that such other notices are served, or such other steps are taken, as it thinks fit.

(4)   Any reference in this Part to the requisite majority of qualifying tenants of the flats contained in any premises is a reference to qualifying tenants of the flats so contained with [not less than two-thirds] of the available votes; and for the purposes of this subsection—

   (a)    the total number of available votes shall correspond to the total number of those flats for the time being let to qualifying tenants; and

   (b)    there shall be one available vote in respect of each of the flats so let which shall be attributed to the qualifying tenant to whom it is let.

(5)   Nothing in this Part shall be construed as requiring the persons constituting any such majority in any one context to be the same as the persons constituting any such majority in any other context.

                                                              **[687]**

**NOTES**

Sub-s (4): words in square brackets substituted by the Leasehold Reform, Housing and Urban Development Act 1993, s 85(1), (3).

Modified, where the RTM company has acquired the right to manage, by the Commonhold and Leasehold Reform Act 2002, s 102, Sch 7, para 9 at **[1266]**, **[1306]**.

## 28  Applications for acquisition orders

(1)   An application for an acquisition order in respect of any premises to which this Part applies must be made by qualifying tenants of the flats contained in the premises who, at the date when it is made, constitute the requisite majority of such tenants.

(2)   No such application shall be made to the court unless—

   (a)    in a case where a notice has been served under section 27, either—

        (i)    the period specified in pursuance of paragraph (d) of subsection (2) of that section has expired without the landlord having taken the steps that he was required to take in pursuance of that provision, or

        (ii)   that paragraph was not applicable in the circumstances of the case; or

   (b)    in a case where the requirement to serve such a notice has been dispensed with by an order under subsection (3) of that section, either—

        (i)    any notices required to be served, and any other steps required to be taken, by virtue of the order have been served or (as the case may be) taken, or

        (ii)   no direction was given by the court when making the order.

(3)   An application for an acquisition order may, subject to the preceding provisions of this Part, be made in respect of two or more premises to which this Part applies.

(4)   Rules of court shall make provision—

   (a)    for requiring notice of an application for an acquisition order in respect of any premises to be served on such descriptions of persons as may be specified in the rules; and

   (b)    for enabling persons served with any such notice to be joined as parties to the proceedings.

(5)   The Land Charges Act 1972 and the [Land Registration Act 2002] shall apply in relation to an application for an acquisition order as they apply in relation to other pending land actions.

(6)   ...

                                                              **[688]**

**NOTES**

Sub-s (5): words in square brackets substituted by the Land Registration Act 2002, s 133, Sch 11, para 20.

Sub-s (6): repealed by the Land Registration Act 2002, s 135, Sch 13.

Modified, where the RTM company has acquired the right to manage, by the Commonhold and Leasehold Reform Act 2002, s 102, Sch 7, para 9 at **[1266]**, **[1306]**.

## 29  Conditions for making acquisition orders

(1)   The court may, on an application for an acquisition order, make such an order in respect of any premises if—

(a)    the court is satisfied—
    (i)    that those premises were, at the date of service on the landlord of the notice (if any) under section 27 and on the date when the application was made, premises to which this Part applies, and
    (ii)    that they have not ceased to be such premises since the date when the application was made, and
(b)    either of the conditions specified in subsections (2) and (3) is fulfilled with respect to those premises, and
(c)    the court considers it appropriate to make the order in the circumstances of the case.

(2)    The first of the conditions referred to in subsection (1)(b) is that the court is satisfied—
(a)    that the landlord either is in breach of any obligation owed by him to the applicants under their leases and relating to the ... management of the premises in question, or any part of them, or (in the case of an obligation dependent on notice) would be in breach of any such obligation but for the fact that it has not been reasonably practicable for the tenant to give him the appropriate notice, and
(b)    that the circumstances by virtue of which he is (or would be) in breach of any such obligation are likely to continue, ...
(c)    ...

[(2A)    The reference in subsection (2) to the management of any premises includes a reference to the repair, maintenance, improvement or insurance of those premises.]

(3)    The second of those conditions is that, both at the date when the application was made and throughout the period of [two years] immediately preceding that date, there was in force an appointment under Part II of a person to act as manager in relation to the premises in question [which was made by reason of an act or omission on the part of the landlord].

(4)    An acquisition order may, if the court thinks fit—
(a)    include any yard, garden, outhouse or appurtenance belonging to, or usually enjoyed with, the premises specified in the application on which the order is made;
(b)    exclude any part of the premises so specified.

(5)    Where—
(a)    the premises in respect of which an application for an acquisition order is made consist of part only of more extensive premises in which the landlord has an interest, and
(b)    it appears to the court that the landlord's interest in the latter premises is not reasonably capable of being severed, either in the manner contemplated by the application or in any manner authorised by virtue of subsection (4)(b),

then, notwithstanding that paragraphs (a) and (b) of subsection (1) apply, the court shall not make an acquisition order on the application.

(6)    In a case where an application for an acquisition order was preceded by the service of a notice under section 27, the court may, if it thinks fit, make such an order notwithstanding—
(a)    that any period specified in the notice in pursuance of subsection (2)(d) of that section was not a reasonable period, or
(b)    that the notice failed in any other respect to comply with any requirement contained in subsection (2) of that section or in any regulations applying to the notice under section 54(3).

(7)    Where any premises are premises to which this Part applies at the time when an application for an acquisition order is made in respect of them, then, for the purposes of this section and the following provisions of this Part, they shall not cease to be such premises by reason only that—
(a)    the interest of the landlord in them subsequently becomes held by[—
    (i)]    an exempt landlord or a resident landlord, [or
    (ii)    the Welsh Ministers in their new towns residuary capacity,] or
(b)    they subsequently become included within the functional land of any charity.

**[689]**

---

**NOTES**

Sub-s (2): words omitted from para (a) repealed by the Commonhold and Leasehold Reform Act 2002, ss 150, 180, Sch 9, para 9(1), (2), Sch 14, except in relation to an application made under this section before 30 September 2003 (in relation to England) or 31 March 2004 (in relation to Wales); para (c) and word immediately preceding it repealed by the Leasehold Reform, Housing and Urban Development Act 1993, ss 85(1), (4), 187(2), Sch 22.

Sub-s (2A): inserted by the Commonhold and Leasehold Reform Act 2002, s 150, Sch 9, para 9(1), (3), except in relation to an application made under this section before 30 September 2003 (in relation to England) or 31 March 2004 (in relation to Wales).

Sub-s (3): words in first pair of square brackets substituted by the Housing Act 1996, s 88; words in second pair of square brackets inserted by the Commonhold and Leasehold Reform Act 2002, s 160(1), (5), except in relation to applications made under Part II of this Act at **[681]–[684]**, before 26 July 2002 (in relation to England) or 1 January 2003 (in relation to Wales).

Sub-s (7): words in square brackets inserted by the Housing and Regeneration Act 2008, s 56, Sch 8, paras 37, 39, subject to transitional provisions and savings in SI 2008/3068, arts 6–10 at **[3834B]–[3834F]**.

PART I
STATUTES

Modified, where the RTM company has acquired the right to manage, by the Commonhold and Leasehold Reform Act 2002, s 102, Sch 7, para 9 at **[1266]**, **[1306]**.

## 30 Content of acquisition orders

(1) Where an acquisition order is made by the court, the order shall (except in a case falling within section 33(1)) provide for the nominated person to be entitled to acquire the landlord's interest in the premises specified in the order on such terms as may be determined—
    (a) by agreement between the landlord and the qualifying tenants in whose favour the order is made, or
    (b) in default of agreement, by a rent assessment committee under section 31.

(2) An acquisition order may be granted subject to such conditions as the court thinks fit, and in particular its operation may be suspended on terms fixed by the court.

(3) References in this Part, in relation to an acquisition order, to the nominated person are references to such person or persons as may be nominated for the purposes of this Part by the persons applying for the order.

(4) Those persons must secure that the nominated person is joined as a party to the application, and no further nomination of a person for the purposes of this Part shall be made by them after the order is made (whether in addition to, or in substitution for, the existing nominated person) except with the approval of the court.

(5) Where the landlord is, by virtue of any covenant, condition or other obligation, precluded from disposing of his interest in the premises in respect of which an acquisition order has been made unless the consent of some other person is obtained—
    (a) he shall use his best endeavours to secure that the consent of that person to that disposal is obtained and, if it appears to him that that person is obliged not to withhold his consent unreasonably but has nevertheless so withheld it, shall institute proceedings for a declaration to that effect; but
    (b) if—
        (i) the landlord has discharged any duty imposed on him by paragraph (a), and
        (ii) the consent of that person has been withheld, and
        (iii) no such declaration has been made,
    the order shall cease to have effect.

(6) The Land Charges Act 1972 and the [Land Registration Act 2002] shall apply in relation to an acquisition order as they apply in relation to an order affecting land made by the court for the purpose of enforcing a judgment or recognisance.

**[690]**

### NOTES
Sub-s (6): words in square brackets substituted by the Land Registration Act 2002, s 133, Sch 11, para 20.
Modified, where the RTM company has acquired the right to manage, by the Commonhold and Leasehold Reform Act 2002, s 102, Sch 7, para 9 at **[1266]**, **[1306]**.

## 31 Determination of terms by [leasehold valuation tribunals]

(1) A [leasehold valuation tribunal] shall have jurisdiction to determine the terms on which the landlord's interest in the premises specified in an acquisition order may be acquired by the nominated person to the extent that those terms have not been determined by agreement between the landlord and either—
    (a) the qualifying tenants in whose favour the order was made, or
    (b) the nominated person;
and (subject to subsection (2)) [the tribunal] shall determine any such terms on the basis of what appears to them to be fair and reasonable.

(2) Where an application is made under this section for [the tribunal] to determine the consideration payable for the acquisition of a landlord's interest in any premises, [the tribunal] shall do so by determining an amount equal to the amount which, in their opinion, that interest might be expected to realise if sold on the open market by a willing seller on the appropriate terms and on the assumption that none of the tenants of the landlord of any premises comprised in those premises was buying or seeking to buy that interest.

(3) In subsection (2) "the appropriate terms" means all the terms to which the acquisition of the landlord's interest in pursuance of the order is to be subject (whether determined by agreement as mentioned in subsection (1) or on an application under this section) apart from those relating to the consideration payable.

(4) On any application under this section the interests of the qualifying tenants in whose favour the acquisition order was made shall be represented by the nominated person, and accordingly the parties to any such application shall not include those tenants.

(5) ...

(6)   Nothing in this section shall be construed as authorising a [leasehold valuation tribunal] to determine any terms dealing with matters in relation to which provision is made by section 32 or 33.

**[691]**

**NOTES**

Section heading: words in square brackets substituted by the Housing Act 1996, s 92(1), Sch 6, Pt IV, para 5.
Sub-ss (1), (2), (6): words in square brackets substituted by the Housing Act 1996, s 92(1), Sch 6, Pt IV, para 5.
Sub-s (5): repealed by the Housing Act 1996, ss 92(1), 227, Sch 6, Pt IV, para 5, Sch 19, Pt III.
Modified, where the RTM company has acquired the right to manage, by the Commonhold and Leasehold Reform Act 2002, s 102, Sch 7, para 9 at **[1266]**, **[1306]**.

## 32   Discharge of existing mortgages

(1)   Where the landlord's interest in any premises is acquired in pursuance of an acquisition order, the instrument by virtue of which it is so acquired shall (subject to subsection (2) and Part II of Schedule 1) operate to discharge the premises from any charge on that interest to secure the payment of money or the performance of any other obligation by the landlord or any other person.

(2)   Subsection (1) does not apply to any such charge if—
  (a)   it has been agreed between the landlord and either—
      (i)   the qualifying tenants in whose favour the order was made, or
      (ii)   the nominated person,
      that the landlord's interest should be acquired subject to the charge, or
  (b)   the court is satisfied, whether on the application for the order or on an application made by the person entitled to the benefit of the charge, that in the exceptional circumstances of the case it would be fair and reasonable that the landlord's interest should be so acquired, and orders accordingly.

(3)   This section and Part II of Schedule 1 shall apply, with any necessary modifications, to mortgages and liens as they apply to charges; but nothing in those provisions shall apply to a rentcharge.

**[692]**

**NOTES**

Modified, where the RTM company has acquired the right to manage, by the Commonhold and Leasehold Reform Act 2002, s 102, Sch 7, para 9 at **[1266]**, **[1306]**.

## 33   Acquisition order where landlord cannot be found

(1)   Where an acquisition order is made by the court in a case where the landlord cannot be found, or his identity cannot be ascertained, the order shall provide for the landlord's interest in the premises specified in the order to vest in the nominated person on the following terms, namely—
  (a)   such terms as to payment as are specified in subsection (2), and
  (b)   such other terms as the court thinks fit, being terms which, in the opinion of the court, correspond so far as possible to those on which the interest might be expected to be transferred if it were being transferred by the landlord.

(2)   The terms as to payment referred to in subsection (1)(a) are terms requiring the payment into court of—
  (a)   such amount as a surveyor selected by the [Senior President of Tribunals] may certify to be in his opinion the amount which the landlord's interest might be expected to realise if sold as mentioned in section 31(2); and
  (b)   any amounts or estimated amounts remaining due to the landlord from any tenants of his of any premises comprised in the premises in respect of which the order is made, being amounts or estimated amounts determined by the court as being due from those persons under the terms of their leases.

(3)   Where any amount or amounts required by virtue of subsection (2) to be paid into court are so paid, the landlord's interest shall, by virtue of this section, vest in the nominated person in accordance with the order.

**[693]**

**NOTES**

Sub-s (2): words in square brackets substituted by the Transfer of Tribunal Functions (Lands Tribunal and Miscellaneous Amendments) Order 2009, SI 2009/1307, art 5(1), (2), Sch 1, paras 180, 183, subject to transitional provisions and savings in Sch 5 thereto.
Modified, where the RTM company has acquired the right to manage, by the Commonhold and Leasehold Reform Act 2002, s 102, Sch 7, para 9 at **[1266]**, **[1306]**.

## 34  Discharge of acquisition order and withdrawal by tenants

(1)  If, on an application by a landlord in respect of whose interest an acquisition order has been made, the court is satisfied—

    (a)    that the nominated person has had a reasonable time within which to effect the acquisition of that interest in pursuance of the order but has not done so, or

    (b)    that the number of qualifying tenants of flats contained in the premises in question who desire to proceed with the acquisition of the landlord's interest is less than the requisite majority of qualifying tenants of the flats contained in those premises, or

    (c)    that the premises in question have ceased to be premises to which this Part applies,

the court may discharge the order.

(2)  Where—

    (a)    a notice is served on the landlord by the qualifying tenants by whom a notice has been served under section 27 or (as the case may be) by whom an application has been made for an acquisition order, or by the person nominated for the purposes of this Part by any such tenants, and

    (b)    the notice indicates an intention no longer to proceed with the acquisition of the landlord's interest in the premises in question,

the landlord may (except in a case where subsection (4) applies) recover under this subsection any costs reasonably incurred by him in connection with the disposal by him of that interest down to the time when the notice is served; and, if the notice is served after the making of an acquisition order, that order shall cease to have effect.

(3)  If (whether before or after the making of an acquisition order) the nominated person becomes aware—

    (a)    that the number of qualifying tenants of flats contained in the premises in question who desire to proceed with the acquisition of the landlord's interest is less than the requisite majority of qualifying tenants of the flats contained in those premises, or

    (b)    that those premises have ceased to be premises to which this Part applies,

he shall forthwith serve on the landlord a notice indicating an intention no longer to proceed with the acquisition of that interest, and subsection (2) shall apply accordingly.

(4)  If, at any time when any proceedings taken under or by virtue of this Part are pending before the court or the [Upper Tribunal]—

    (a)    such a notice as is mentioned in subsection (2) or (3) is served on the landlord, or

    (b)    the nominated person indicates that he is no longer willing to act in the matter and nobody is nominated for the purposes of this Part in his place, or

    (c)    the number of qualifying tenants of flats contained in the premises in question who desire to proceed with the acquisition of the landlord's interest falls below the requisite majority of qualifying tenants of the flats contained in those premises, or

    (d)    those premises cease to be premises to which this Part applies,

or if the court discharges an acquisition order under subsection (1), the landlord may recover such costs incurred by him in connection with the disposal by him of his interest in those premises as the court or (as the case may be) the Tribunal may determine.

(5)  The costs that may be recovered by the landlord under subsection (2) or (4) include costs incurred by him in connection with any proceedings under this Part (other than proceedings before a rent assessment committee).

(6)  Any liability for costs arising under this section shall be the joint and several liability of the following persons, namely—

    (a)    where the liability arises before the making of an application for an acquisition order, the tenants by whom a notice was served under section 27, or

    (b)    where the liability arises after the making of such an application, the tenants by whom the application was made,

together with (in either case) any person nominated by those tenants for the purposes of this Part.

(7)  In relation to any time when a tenant falling within paragraph (a) or (b) of subsection (6) has ceased to have vested in him the interest under his lease, that paragraph shall be construed as applying instead to the person who is for the time being the successor in title to that interest.

(8)  Nothing in this section shall be construed as authorising the court to discharge an acquisition order where the landlord's interest has already been acquired in pursuance of the order.

(9)  If—

    (a)    an acquisition order is discharged, or ceases to have effect, by virtue of any provision of this Part, and

    (b)    the order has been protected by an entry registered under the Land Charges Act 1972 or the [Land Registration Act 2002],

the court may by order direct that that entry shall be cancelled.

[694]

PART I
STATUTES

**NOTES**

Sub-s (4): words in square brackets substituted by the Transfer of Tribunal Functions (Lands Tribunal and Miscellaneous Amendments) Order 2009, SI 2009/1307, art 5(1), (2), Sch 1, paras 180, 184, subject to transitional provisions and savings in Sch 5 thereto.

Sub-s (9): words in square brackets in para (b) substituted by the Land Registration Act 2002, s 133, Sch 11, para 20.

Modified, where the RTM company has acquired the right to manage, by the Commonhold and Leasehold Reform Act 2002, s 102, Sch 7, para 9 at **[1266]**, **[1306]**.

## PART IV
## VARIATION OF LEASES

### *Applications relating to flats*

## 35 Application by party to lease for variation of lease

(1) Any party to a long lease of a flat may make an application to [a leasehold valuation tribunal] for an order varying the lease in such manner as is specified in the application.

(2) The grounds on which any such application may be made are that the lease fails to make satisfactory provision with respect to one or more of the following matters, namely—

- (a) the repair or maintenance of—
  - (i) the flat in question, or
  - (ii) the building containing the flat, or
  - (iii) any land or building which is let to the tenant under the lease or in respect of which rights are conferred on him under it;
- [(b) the insurance of the building containing the flat or of any such land or building as is mentioned in paragraph (a)(iii);]
- (c) the repair or maintenance of any installations (whether they are in the same building as the flat or not) which are reasonably necessary to ensure that occupiers of the flat enjoy a reasonable standard of accommodation;
- (d) the provision or maintenance of any services which are reasonably necessary to ensure that occupiers of the flat enjoy a reasonable standard of accommodation (whether they are services connected with any such installations or not, and whether they are services provided for the benefit of those occupiers or services provided for the benefit of the occupiers of a number of flats including that flat);
- (e) the recovery by one party to the lease from another party to it of expenditure incurred or to be incurred by him, or on his behalf, for the benefit of that other party or of a number of persons who include that other party;
- (f) the computation of a service charge payable under the lease;
- [(g) such other matters as may be prescribed by regulations made by the Secretary of State].

(3) For the purposes of subsection (2)(c) and (d) the factors for determining, in relation to the occupiers of a flat, what is a reasonable standard of accommodation may include—

- (a) factors relating to the safety and security of the flat and its occupiers and of any common parts of the building containing the flat; and
- (b) other factors relating to the condition of any such common parts.

[(3A) For the purposes of subsection (2)(e) the factors for determining, in relation to a service charge payable under a lease, whether the lease makes satisfactory provision include whether it makes provision for an amount to be payable (by way of interest or otherwise) in respect of a failure to pay the service charge by the due date.]

(4) For the purposes of subsection (2)(f) a lease fails to make satisfactory provision with respect to the computation of a service charge payable under it if—

- (a) it provides for any such charge to be a proportion of expenditure incurred, or to be incurred, by or on behalf of the landlord or a superior landlord; and
- (b) other tenants of the landlord are also liable under their leases to pay by way of service charges proportions of any such expenditure; and
- (c) the aggregate of the amounts that would, in any particular case, be payable by reference to the proportions referred to in paragraphs (a) and (b) would [either exceed or be less than] the whole of any such expenditure.

(5) [Procedure regulations under Schedule 12 to the Commonhold and Leasehold Reform Act 2002] shall make provision—

- (a) for requiring notice of any application under this Part to be served by the person making the application, and by any respondent to the application, on any person who the applicant, or (as the case may be) the respondent, knows or has reason to believe is likely to be affected by any variation specified in the application, and
- (b) for enabling persons served with any such notice to be joined as parties to the proceedings.

[(6) For the purposes of this Part a long lease shall not be regarded as a long lease of a flat if—
    (a) the demised premises consist of or include three or more flats contained in the same building; or
    (b) the lease constitutes a tenancy to which Part II of the Landlord and Tenant Act 1954 applies.]

(8) In this section "service charge" has the meaning given by section 18(1) of the 1985 Act.
**[695]**

---

**NOTES**

Sub-ss (1), (5): words in square brackets substituted by the Commonhold and Leasehold Reform Act 2002, s 163(1), (2), except in relation to an application made to the court under Part IV of this Act at **[695]**–**[700]**, before 30 September 2003 (in relation to England) or 31 March 2004 (in relation to Wales).

Sub-s (2): para (b) substituted and para (g) inserted by the Commonhold and Leasehold Reform Act 2002, s 162(1)–(3), except in relation to applications made under Part II of this Act at **[681]**–**[684]**, before 26 July 2002 (in relation to England) or 1 January 2003 (in relation to Wales).

Sub-s (3A): inserted by the Commonhold and Leasehold Reform Act 2002, s 162(1), (4), except in relation to applications made under Part II of this Act at **[681]**–**[684]**, before 26 July 2002 (in relation to England) or 1 January 2003 (in relation to Wales).

Sub-s (4): words in square brackets in para (c) substituted by the Leasehold Reform, Housing and Urban Development Act 1993, s 86, except in relation to a case where an application under sub-s (1) above was made before 1 November 1993.

Sub-s (6): substituted, for original sub-ss (6), (7), by the Housing Act 1988, s 119, Sch 13, para 5, except in relation to an application made to the court before 15 January 1989.

Modified, where the RTM company has acquired the right to manage, by the Commonhold and Leasehold Reform Act 2002, s 102, Sch 7, para 10 at **[1266]**, **[1306]**.

1985 Act: Landlord and Tenant Act 1985.

Regulations: the Leasehold Valuation Tribunals (Procedure) (England) Regulations 2003, SI 2003/2099 at **[3319]**; the Leasehold Valuation Tribunals (Procedure) (Wales) Regulations 2004, SI 2004/681 at **[3363]**.

---

**36 Application by respondent for variation of other leases**

(1) Where an application ("the original application") is made under section 35 by any party to a lease, any other party to the lease may make an application to the [tribunal] asking it, in the event of its deciding to make an order effecting any variation of the lease in pursuance of the original application, to make an order which effects a corresponding variation of each of such one or more other leases as are specified in the application.

(2) Any lease so specified—
    (a) must be a long lease of a flat under which the landlord is the same person as the landlord under the lease specified in the original application; but
    (b) need not be a lease of a flat which is in the same building as the flat let under that lease, nor a lease drafted in terms identical to those of that lease.

(3) The grounds on which an application may be made under this section are—
    (a) that each of the leases specified in the application fails to make satisfactory provision with respect to the matter or matters specified in the original application; and
    (b) that, if any variation is effected in pursuance of the original application, it would be in the interests of the person making the application under this section, or in the interests of the other persons who are parties to the leases specified in that application, to have all of the leases in question (that is to say, the ones specified in that application together with the one specified in the original application) varied to the same effect.
**[696]**

---

**NOTES**

Sub-s (1): word in square brackets substituted by the Commonhold and Leasehold Reform Act 2002, s 163(1), (3), except in relation to an application made to the court under Part IV of this Act at **[695]**–**[700]**, before 30 September 2003 (in relation to England) or 31 March 2004 (in relation to Wales).

Modified, where the RTM company has acquired the right to manage, by the Commonhold and Leasehold Reform Act 2002, s 102, Sch 7, para 10 at **[1266]**, **[1306]**.

---

**37 Application by majority of parties for variation of leases**

(1) Subject to the following provisions of this section, an application may be made to [a leasehold valuation tribunal] in respect of two or more leases for an order varying each of those leases in such manner as is specified in the application.

(2) Those leases must be long leases of flats under which the landlord is the same person, but they need not be leases of flats which are in the same building, nor leases which are drafted in identical terms.

(3) The grounds on which an application may be made under this section are that the object to be achieved by the variation cannot be satisfactorily achieved unless all the leases are varied to the same effect.

(4)   An application under this section in respect of any leases may be made by the landlord or any of the tenants under the leases.

(5)   Any such application shall only be made if—
  (a)   in a case where the application is in respect of less than nine leases, all, or all but one, of the parties concerned consent to it; or
  (b)   in a case where the application is in respect of more than eight leases, it is not opposed for any reason by more than 10 per cent of the total number of the parties concerned and at least 75 per cent of that number consent to it.

(6)   For the purposes of subsection (5)—
  (a)   in the case of each lease in respect of which the application is made, the tenant under the lease shall constitute one of the parties concerned (so that in determining the total number of the parties concerned a person who is the tenant under a number of such leases shall be regarded as constituting a corresponding number of the parties concerned); and
  (b)   the landlord shall also constitute one of the parties concerned.

**[697]**

**NOTES**

Sub-s (1): words in square brackets substituted by the Commonhold and Leasehold Reform Act 2002, s 163(1), (4), except in relation to an application made to the court under Part IV of this Act at **[695]**–**[700]**, before 30 September 2003 (in relation to England) or 31 March 2004 (in relation to Wales).

*Orders varying leases*

### 38   Orders ... varying leases

(1)   If, on an application under section 35, the grounds on which the application was made are established to the satisfaction of the [tribunal], the [tribunal] may (subject to subsections (6) and (7)) make an order varying the lease specified in the application in such manner as is specified in the order.

(2)   If—
  (a)   an application under section 36 was made in connection with that application, and
  (b)   the grounds set out in subsection (3) of that section are established to the satisfaction of the [tribunal] with respect to the leases specified in the application under section 36,

the [tribunal] may (subject to subsections (6) and (7)) also make an order varying each of those leases in such manner as is specified in the order.

(3)   If, on an application under section 37, the grounds set out in subsection (3) of that section are established to the satisfaction of the [tribunal] with respect to the leases specified in the application, the [tribunal] may (subject to subsections (6) and (7)) make an order varying each of those leases in such manner as is specified in the order.

(4)   The variation specified in an order under subsection (1) or (2) may be either the variation specified in the relevant application under section 35 or 36 or such other variation as the [tribunal] thinks fit.

(5)   If the grounds referred to in subsection (2) or (3) (as the case may be) are established to the satisfaction of the [tribunal] with respect to some but not all of the leases specified in the application, the power to make an order under that subsection shall extend to those leases only.

(6)   [A tribunal] shall not make an order under this section effecting any variation of a lease if it appears to [the tribunal]—
  (a)   that the variation would be likely substantially to prejudice—
    (i)   any respondent to the application, or
    (ii)   any person who is not a party to the application,
    and that an award under subsection (10) would not afford him adequate compensation, or
  (b)   that for any other reason it would not be reasonable in the circumstances for the variation to be effected.

(7)   [A tribunal] shall not, on an application relating to the provision to be made by a lease with respect to insurance, make an order under this section effecting any variation of the lease—
  (a)   which terminates any existing right of the landlord under its terms to nominate an insurer for insurance purposes; or
  (b)   which requires the landlord to nominate a number of insurers from which the tenant would be entitled to select an insurer for those purposes; or
  (c)   which, in a case where the lease requires the tenant to effect insurance with a specified insurer, requires the tenant to effect insurance otherwise than with another specified insurer.

(8)   [A tribunal] may, instead of making an order varying a lease in such manner as is specified in the order, make an order directing the parties to the lease to vary it in such manner as is so

specified; and accordingly any reference in this Part (however expressed) to an order which effects any variation of a lease or to any variation effected by an order shall include a reference to an order which directs the parties to a lease to effect a variation of it or (as the case may be) a reference to any variation effected in pursuance of such an order.

(9)   [A tribunal] may by order direct that a memorandum of any variation of a lease effected by an order under this section shall be endorsed on such documents as are specified in the order.

(10)   Where [a tribunal] makes an order under this section varying a lease [the tribunal] may, if it thinks fit, make an order providing for any party to the lease to pay, to any other party to the lease or to any other person, compensation in respect of any loss or disadvantage that [the tribunal] considers he is likely to suffer as a result of the variation.

**[698]**

**NOTES**

Words omitted repealed, except in relation to any application made to an LVT or any proceedings transferred to an LVT by a county court before 30 September 2003 (in relation to England) or 31 March 2004 (in relation to Wales), and words in square brackets substituted, except in relation to an application made to the court under Part IV of this Act at **[695]**–**[700]**, before 30 September 2003 (in relation to England) or 31 March 2004 (in relation to Wales), by the Commonhold and Leasehold Reform Act 2002, ss 163(1), (5), 180, Sch 14.

Modified, where the RTM company has acquired the right to manage, by the Commonhold and Leasehold Reform Act 2002, s 102, Sch 7, para 10 at **[1266]**, **[1306]**.

### 39   Effect of orders varying leases: applications by third parties

(1)   Any variation effected by an order under section 38 shall be binding not only on the parties to the lease for the time being but also on other persons (including any predecessors in title of those parties), whether or not they were parties to the proceedings in which the order was made or were served with a notice by virtue of section 35(5).

(2)   Without prejudice to the generality of subsection (1), any variation effected by any such order shall be binding on any surety who has guaranteed the performance of any obligation varied by the order; and the surety shall accordingly be taken to have guaranteed the performance of that obligation as so varied.

(3)   Where any such order has been made and a person was, by virtue of section 35(5), required to be served with a notice relating to the proceedings in which it was made, but he was not so served, he may—

   (a)   bring an action for damages for breach of statutory duty against the person by whom any such notice was so required to be served in respect of that person's failure to serve it;

   (b)   apply to [a leasehold valuation tribunal] for the cancellation or modification of the variation in question.

(4)   [A tribunal] may, on an application under subsection (3)(b) with respect to any variation of a lease—

   (a)   by order cancel that variation or modify it in such manner as is specified in the order, or

   (b)   make such an order as is mentioned in section 38(10) in favour of the person making the application,

as it thinks fit.

(5)   Where a variation is cancelled or modified under paragraph (a) of subsection (4)—

   (a)   the cancellation or modification shall take effect as from the date of the making of the order under that paragraph or as from such later date as may be specified in the order, and

   (b)   the [tribunal] may by order direct that a memorandum of the cancellation or modification shall be endorsed on such documents as are specified in the order;

and, in a case where a variation is so modified, subsections (1) and (2) above shall, as from the date when the modification takes effect, apply to the variation as modified.

**[699]**

**NOTES**

Sub-ss (3)–(5): words in square brackets substituted by the Commonhold and Leasehold Reform Act 2002, s 163(1), (6), except in relation to an application made to the court under Part IV of this Act at **[695]**–**[700]**, before 30 September 2003 (in relation to England) or 31 March 2004 (in relation to Wales).

Modified, where the RTM company has acquired the right to manage, by the Commonhold and Leasehold Reform Act 2002, s 102, Sch 7, para 10 at **[1266]**, **[1306]**.

*Applications relating to dwellings other than flats*

### 40   Application for variation of insurance provisions of lease of dwelling other than a flat

(1)   Any party to a long lease of a dwelling may make an application to [a leasehold valuation tribunal] for an order varying the lease, in such manner as is specified in the application, on the

grounds that the lease fails to make satisfactory provision with respect to any matter relating to the insurance of the dwelling, including the recovery of the costs of such insurance.

(2)   Sections 36 and 38 shall apply to an application under subsection (1) subject to the modifications specified in subsection (3).

(3)   Those modifications are as follows—
    (a)   in section 36—
        (i)   in section (1), the reference to section 35 shall be read as a reference to subsection (1) above, and
        (ii)   in subsection (2), any reference to a flat shall be read as a reference to a dwelling; and
    (b)   in section 38—
        (i)   any reference to an application under section 35 shall be read as a reference to an application under subsection (1) above, and
        (ii)   any reference to an application under section 36 shall be read as a reference to an application under section 36 as applied by subsection (2) above.

[(4)   For the purpose of this section, a long lease shall not be regarded as a long lease of a dwelling if—
    (a)   the demised premises consist of three or more dwellings; or
    (b)   the lease constitutes a tenancy to which Part II of the Landlord and Tenant Act 1954 applies.

(4A)   Without prejudice to subsection (4), an application under subsection (1) may not be made by a person who is a tenant under a long lease of a dwelling if, by virtue of that lease and one or more other long leases of dwellings, he is also a tenant from the same landlord of at least two other dwellings.

(4B)   For the purposes of subsection (4A), any tenant of a dwelling who is a body corporate shall be treated as a tenant of any other dwelling held from the same landlord which is let under a long lease to an associated company, as defined in section 20(1).]

(5)   In this section "dwelling" means a dwelling other than a flat.

**[700]**

**NOTES**
Sub-s (1): words in square brackets substituted by the Commonhold and Leasehold Reform Act 2002, s 163(1), (7), except in relation to an application made to the court under Part IV of this Act at **[695]**–**[700]**, before 30 September 2003 (in relation to England) or 31 March 2004 (in relation to Wales).
Sub-ss (4), (4A), (4B): substituted, for original sub-s (4), by the Housing Act 1988, s 119, Sch 13, para 6, except in relation to an application made to the court before 15 January 1989.

## PART V
## MANAGEMENT OF LEASEHOLD PROPERTY

### *Service charges*

### 41   Amendments relating to service charges

(1)   Sections 18 to 30 of the 1985 Act (regulation of service charges payable by tenants) shall have effect subject to the amendments specified in Schedule 2 (which include amendments—
    (a)   extending the provisions of those sections to dwellings other than flats, and
    (b)   introducing certain additional limitations on service charges).

(2)   Sections 45 to 51 of the Housing Act 1985 (which are, so far as relating to dwellings let on long leases, superseded by sections 18 to 30 of the 1985 Act as amended by Schedule 2) shall cease to have effect in relation to dwellings so let.

**[701]**

**NOTES**
1985 Act: Landlord and Tenant Act 1985.

### 42   Service charge contributions to be held in trust

(1)   This section applies where the tenants of two or more dwellings may be required under the terms of their leases to contribute to the same costs[, or the tenant of a dwelling may be required under the terms of his lease to contribute to costs to which no other tenant of a dwelling may be required to contribute,] by the payment of service charges; and in this section—
    "the contributing tenants" means those tenants [and "the sole contributing tenant" means that tenant];
    "the payee" means the landlord or other person to whom any such charges are payable by those tenants[, or that tenant, under the terms of their leases, or his lease];
    "relevant service charges" means any such charges;

"service charge" has the meaning given by section 18(1) of the 1985 Act, except that it does not include a service charge payable by the tenant of a dwelling the rent of which is registered under Part IV of the Rent Act 1977, unless the amount registered is, in pursuance of section 71(4) of that Act, entered as a variable amount;

"tenant" does not include a tenant of an exempt landlord; and

"trust fund" means the fund, or (as the case may be) any of the funds, mentioned in subsection (2) below.

(2)   Any sums paid to the payee by the contributing tenants[, or the sole contributing tenant,] by way of relevant service charges, *and any investments representing those sums,* shall (together with any income accruing thereon) be held by the payee either as a single fund or, if he thinks fit, in two or more separate funds.

(3)   The payee shall hold any trust fund—

(a)   on trust to defray costs incurred in connection with the matters for which the relevant service charges were payable (whether incurred by himself or by any other person), and

(b)   subject to that, on trust for the persons who are the contributing tenants for the time being[, or the person who is the sole contributing tenant for the time being].

(4)   Subject to subsections (6) to (8), the contributing tenants shall be treated as entitled by virtue of subsection (3)(b) to such shares in the residue of any such fund as are proportionate to their respective liabilities to pay relevant service charges [or the sole contributing tenant shall be treated as so entitled to the residue of any such fund].

(5)   *If the Secretary of State by order so provides, any sums standing to the credit of any trust fund may, instead of being invested in any other manner authorised by law, be invested in such manner as may be specified in the order; and any such order may contain such incidental, supplemental or transitional provisions as the Secretary of State considers appropriate in connection with the order.*

(6)   On the termination of the lease of [any of the contributing tenants] the tenant shall not be entitled to any part of any trust fund, and (except where subsection (7) applies) any part of any such fund which is attributable to relevant service charges paid under the lease shall accordingly continue to be held on the trusts referred to in subsection (3).

(7)   [On the termination of the lease of the last of the contributing tenants, or of the lease of the sole contributing tenant,] any trust fund shall be dissolved as at the date of the termination of the lease, and any assets comprised in the fund immediately before its dissolution shall—

(a)   if the payee is the landlord, be retained by him for his own use and benefit, and

(b)   in any other case, be transferred to the landlord by the payee.

(8)   Subsections (4), (6) and (7) shall have effect in relation to [any of the contributing tenants, or the sole contributing tenant,] subject to any express terms of his lease [(whenever it was granted)] which relate to the distribution, either before or (as the case may be) at the termination of the lease, of amounts attributable to relevant service charges paid under its terms (*whether the lease was granted before or after the commencement of this section*).

(9)   Subject to subsection (8), the provisions of this section shall prevail over the terms of any express or implied trust created by a lease so far as inconsistent with those provisions, other than an express trust so created[, in the case of a lease of any of the contributing tenants,] before the commencement of this section [or, in the case of the lease of the sole contributing tenant, before the commencement of paragraph 15 of Schedule 10 to the Commonhold and Leasehold Reform Act 2002].

[702]

**NOTES**

Sub-s (1): words in first pair of square brackets and words in square brackets in definition "the contributing tenants" inserted, and words in square brackets in definition "the payee" substituted by the Commonhold and Leasehold Reform Act 2002, s 157, Sch 10, para 15(1), (2).

Sub-s (2): words in square brackets inserted by the Commonhold and Leasehold Reform Act 2002, s 157, Sch 10, para 15(1), (3), and words in italics repealed by s 180 of, and Sch 14 to, that Act, as from a day to be appointed.

Sub-ss (3), (4), (9): words in square brackets inserted by the Commonhold and Leasehold Reform Act 2002, s 157, Sch 10, para 15(1), (4), (5), (9).

Sub-s (5): repealed by the Commonhold and Leasehold Reform Act 2002, s 180, Sch 14, as from a day to be appointed.

Sub-s (6): words in square brackets substituted by the Commonhold and Leasehold Reform Act 2002, s 157, Sch 10, para 15(1), (6).

Sub-s (7): words in square brackets substituted by the Commonhold and Leasehold Reform Act 2002, s 157, Sch 10, para 15(1), (7).

Sub-s (8): words in first pair of square brackets substituted and words in second pair of square brackets inserted by the Commonhold and Leasehold Reform Act 2002, s 157, Sch 10, para 15(1), (8), and words in italics repealed by s 180 of, and Sch 14 to, that Act, as from a day to be appointed.

Modified, where the RTM company has acquired the right to manage, by the Commonhold and Leasehold Reform Act 2002, s 102, Sch 7, para 11 at **[1266]**, **[1306]**.

Orders: the Service Charge Contributions (Authorised Investments) Order 1988, SI 1988/1284.
1985 Act: Landlord and Tenant Act 1985.

### [42A  Service charge contributions to be held in designated account

(1)    The payee must hold any sums standing to the credit of any trust fund in a designated account at a relevant financial institution.

(2)    An account is a designated account in relation to sums standing to the credit of a trust fund if—

    (a)    the relevant financial institution has been notified in writing that sums standing to the credit of the trust fund are to be (or are) held in it, and

    (b)    *no other funds are held in the account,*

and the account is an account of a description specified in regulations made by the *Secretary of State*.

[(2A)    The appropriate national authority may by regulations ensure that a payee who holds more than one trust fund in the same designated account cannot move any of those funds to another designated account unless conditions specified in the regulations are met.]

(3)    Any of the contributing tenants, or the sole contributing tenant, may by notice in writing require the payee—

    (a)    to afford him reasonable facilities for inspecting documents evidencing that subsection (1) is[, or regulations under subsection (2A) are,] complied with and for taking copies of or extracts from *them*, or

    (b)    to take copies of or extracts from any such documents and either send them to him or afford him reasonable facilities for collecting them (as he specifies).

(4)    If the tenant is represented by a recognised tenants' association and he consents, the notice may be served by the secretary of the association instead of by the tenant (and in that case any requirement imposed by it is to afford reasonable facilities, or to send copies or extracts, to the secretary).

(5)    A notice under *this section* is duly served on the payee if it is served on—

    (a)    an agent of the payee named as such in the rent book or similar document, or

    (b)    the person who receives the rent on behalf of the payee;

and a person on whom such a notice is so served must forward it as soon as may be to the payee.

(6)    The payee must comply with a requirement imposed by a notice under *this section* within the period of twenty-one days beginning with the day on which he receives the notice.

(7)    To the extent that a notice under *this section* requires the payee to afford facilities for inspecting documents—

    (a)    he must do so free of charge, but

    (b)    he may treat as part of his costs of management any costs incurred by him in doing so.

(8)    The payee may make a reasonable charge for doing anything else in compliance with a requirement imposed by a notice under *this section*.

(9)    Any of the contributing tenants, or the sole contributing tenant, may withhold payment of a service charge if he has reasonable grounds for believing that the payee has failed to comply with the duty imposed on him by subsection (1); and any provisions of his tenancy relating to non-payment or late payment of service charges do not have effect in relation to the period for which he so withholds it.

[(9A)    Regulations under subsection (2A) may include provision about—

    (a)    the circumstances in which a contributing tenant who has reasonable grounds for believing that the payee has not complied with a duty imposed on him by the regulations may withhold payment of a service charge,

    (b)    the period for which payment may be so withheld,

    (c)    the amount of service charge that may be so withheld;

and the regulations may provide that any provisions of the contributing tenant's tenancy relating to non-payment or late payment of service charge do not have effect in relation to the period for which the payment is so withheld.]

(10)    Nothing in this section [or in regulations under subsection (2A)] applies to the payee if the circumstances are such as are specified in regulations made by the *Secretary of State*.

[(10A)    Regulations under this section may—

    (a)    make different provision for different cases, including different provision for different areas,

    (b)    contain such supplementary, incidental, consequential, transitional, transitory or saving provision as the appropriate national authority considers appropriate.

(10B)    Regulations under this section are to be made by statutory instrument which—

(a) in the case of regulations made by the Secretary of State, is to be subject to annulment in pursuance of a resolution of either House of Parliament, and

(b) in the case of regulations made by the Welsh Ministers, is to be subject to annulment in pursuance of a resolution of the National Assembly for Wales.]

(11) In this section—

["the appropriate national authority"—

(a) in relation to England, means the Secretary of State, and

(b) in relation to Wales, means the Welsh Ministers,]

"recognised tenants' association" has the same meaning as in the 1985 Act, and

"relevant financial institution" has the meaning given by regulations made by the *Secretary of State*;

and expressions used both in section 42 and this section have the same meaning as in that section.]

**[703]**

---

**NOTES**

Commencement: 26 July 2002 (in relation to England for the purpose of making regulations); 1 January 2003 (in relation to Wales for the purpose of making regulations); to be appointed (otherwise).

Inserted, together with s 42B, by the Commonhold and Leasehold Reform Act 2002, s 156(1).

Sub-s (2): para (b) substituted as follows, and for the words in italics there are substituted the words "appropriate national authority" by the Housing and Regeneration Act 2008, s 303, Sch 12, paras 11, 12(1), (2), as from 1 December 2008 (for the purpose of enabling the Secretary of State to make regulations) and as from a day to be appointed (for remaining purposes):

"(b) any other sums held in the account are sums standing to the credit of one or more other trust funds,".

Sub-ss (2A), (9A), (10A), (10B): inserted by the Housing and Regeneration Act 2008, s 303, Sch 12, paras 11, 12(1), (3), (6), (8), as from 1 December 2008 (for the purpose of enabling the Secretary of State to make regulations) and as from a day to be appointed (for remaining purposes).

Sub-s (3): words in square brackets inserted and for the word in italics there are substituted the words "such documents" by the Housing and Regeneration Act 2008, s 303, Sch 12, paras 11, 12(1), (4), as from 1 December 2008 (for the purpose of enabling the Secretary of State to make regulations) and as from a day to be appointed (for remaining purposes).

Sub-ss (5)–(8): for the words "this section" in italics in each place they appear there are substituted the words "subsection (3)" by the Housing and Regeneration Act 2008, s 303, Sch 12, paras 11, 12(1), (5), as from 1 December 2008 (for the purpose of enabling the Secretary of State to make regulations) and as from a day to be appointed (for remaining purposes).

Sub-s (10): words in square brackets inserted and for the words in italics there are substituted the words "appropriate national authority" by the Housing and Regeneration Act 2008, s 303, Sch 12, paras 11, 12(1), (7), as from 1 December 2008 (for the purpose of enabling the Secretary of State to make regulations) and as from a day to be appointed (for remaining purposes).

Sub-s (11): definition "the appropriate national authority" inserted and for the words in italics in definition "relevant financial institution" there are substituted the words "appropriate national authority" by the Housing and Regeneration Act 2008, s 303, Sch 12, paras 11, 12(1), (9), as from 1 December 2008 (for the purpose of enabling the Secretary of State to make regulations) and as from a day to be appointed (for remaining purposes).

Modified, where the RTM company has acquired the right to manage, by the Commonhold and Leasehold Reform Act 2002, s 102, Sch 7, para 11 at **[1266]**, **[1306]**.

---

**[42B Failure to comply with section 42A**

(1) If a person fails, without reasonable excuse, to comply with a duty imposed on him by or by virtue of section 42A he commits an offence.

(2) A person guilty of an offence under this section is liable on summary conviction to a fine not exceeding level 4 on the standard scale.

(3) Where an offence under this section committed by a body corporate is proved—

(a) to have been committed with the consent or connivance of a director, manager, secretary or other similar officer of the body corporate, or a person purporting to act in such a capacity, or

(b) to be due to any neglect on the part of such an officer or person,

he, as well as the body corporate, is guilty of the offence and liable to be proceeded against and punished accordingly.

(4) Where the affairs of a body corporate are managed by its members, subsection (3) applies in relation to the acts and defaults of a member in connection with his functions of management as if he were a director of the body corporate.

(5)Proceedings for an offence under this section may be brought by a local housing authority (within the meaning of section 1 of the Housing Act 1985 (c 68)).]

**[704]**

**NOTES**

Commencement: to be appointed.

Inserted as noted to s 42A at **[703]**.

Modified, where the RTM company has acquired the right to manage, by the Commonhold and Leasehold Reform Act 2002, s 102, Sch 7, para 11 at **[1266]**, **[1306]**.

**43–45**    (*S 43 inserts the Landlord and Tenant Act 1985, s 30A, Schedule at* **[631]**, **[643]**; *s 44 inserts s 30B of that Act at* **[632]**; *s 45 repealed by the Housing Act 1988, s 140(2), Sch 18.*)

PART VI

INFORMATION TO BE FURNISHED TO TENANTS

**46   Application of Part VI, etc**

(1)    This Part applies to premises which consist of or include a dwelling and are not held under a tenancy to which Part II of the Landlord and Tenant Act 1954 applies.

(2)    In this Part "service charge" has the meaning given by section 18(1) of the 1985 Act.

[(3)    In this Part "administration charge" has the meaning given by paragraph 1 of Schedule 11 to the Commonhold and Leasehold Reform Act 2002.]

**[705]**

**NOTES**

Sub-s (3): added by the Commonhold and Leasehold Reform Act 2002, s 158, Sch 11, Pt 2, paras 7, 9.

Modified, where the RTM company has acquired the right to manage, by the Commonhold and Leasehold Reform Act 2002, s 102, Sch 7, para 12 at **[1266]**, **[1306]**.

1985 Act: Landlord and Tenant Act 1985.

**47   Landlord's name and address to be contained in demands for rent etc**

(1)    Where any written demand is given to a tenant of premises to which this Part applies, the demand must contain the following information, namely—

    (a)    the name and address of the landlord, and

    (b)    if that address is not in England and Wales, an address in England and Wales at which notices (including notices in proceedings) may be served on the landlord by the tenant.

(2)    Where—

    (a)    a tenant of any such premises is given such a demand, but

    (b)    it does not contain any information required to be contained in it by virtue of subsection (1),

then (subject to subsection (3)) any part of the amount demanded which consists of a service charge [or an administration charge] ("the relevant amount") shall be treated for all purposes as not being due from the tenant to the landlord at any time before that information is furnished by the landlord by notice given to the tenant.

(3)    The relevant amount shall not be so treated in relation to any time when, by virtue of an order of any court [or tribunal], there is in force an appointment of a receiver or manager whose functions include the receiving of service charges [or (as the case may be) administration charges] from the tenant.

(4)    In this section "demand" means a demand for rent or other sums payable to the landlord under the terms of the tenancy.

**[706]**

**NOTES**

Sub-s (2): words in first pair of square brackets inserted and words in second pair of square brackets inserted except in relation to any application made to an LVT or any proceedings transferred to an LVT by a county court before 30 September 2003 (in relation to England) or 31 March 2004 (in relation to Wales), by the Commonhold and Leasehold Reform Act 2002, ss 158, 176, Sch 11, Pt 2, paras 7, 10(1), (2), Sch 13, paras 8, 10.

Sub-s (3): words in square brackets inserted by the Commonhold and Leasehold Reform Act 2002, s 158, Sch 11, Pt 2, paras 7, 10(1), (3).

Modified, where the RTM company has acquired the right to manage, by the Commonhold and Leasehold Reform Act 2002, s 102, Sch 7, para 12 at **[1266]**, **[1306]**.

**48   Notification by landlord of address for service of notices**

(1)    A landlord of premises to which this Part applies shall by notice furnish the tenant with an address in England and Wales at which notices (including notices in proceedings) may be served on him by the tenant.

(2)    Where a landlord of any such premises fails to comply with subsection (1), any rent[, service charge or administration charge] otherwise due from the tenant to the landlord shall (subject to subsection (3)) be treated for all purposes as not being due from the tenant to the landlord at any time before the landlord does comply with that subsection.

(3)   Any such rent[, service charge or administration charge] shall not be so treated in relation to any time when, by virtue of an order of any court [or tribunal], there is in force an appointment of a receiver or manager whose functions include the receiving of rent[, service charges or (as the case may be) administration charges] from the tenant.

[707]

NOTES

Sub-s (2): words in square brackets substituted by the Commonhold and Leasehold Reform Act 2002, s 158, Sch 11, Pt 2, paras 7, 11(1), (2).

Sub-s (3): words in first and third pairs of square brackets substituted, and words in second pair of square brackets inserted except in relation to any application made to an LVT or any proceedings transferred to an LVT by a county court before 30 September 2003 (in relation to England) or 31 March 2004 (in relation to Wales), by the Commonhold and Leasehold Reform Act 2002, ss 158, 176, Sch 11, Pt 2, paras 7, 11(1), (3), Sch 13, paras 8, 11.

Modified, where the RTM company has acquired the right to manage, by the Commonhold and Leasehold Reform Act 2002, s 102, Sch 7, para 12 at [**1266**], [**1306**].

### 49   Extension of circumstances in which notices are sufficiently served

In section 196 of the Law of Property Act 1925 (regulations respecting notices), any reference in subsection (3) or (4) to the last known place of abode or business of the person to be served shall have effect, in its application to a notice to be served by a tenant on a landlord of premises to which this Part applies, as if that reference included a reference to—

(a)   the address last furnished to the tenant by the landlord in accordance with section 48, or

(b)   if no address has been so furnished in accordance with section 48, the address last furnished to the tenant by the landlord in accordance with section 47.

[708]

**50, 51**   *(S 50 inserts the Landlord and Tenant Act 1985, s 3(3A), (3B) at* [**594**]*; s 51 repealed by the Land Registration Act 1988, s 2, Schedule.)*

### PART VII
### GENERAL

### 52   Jurisdiction of county courts

(1)   A county court shall have jurisdiction to hear and determine any question arising under any provision to which this section applies (other than a question falling within the jurisdiction of a [leasehold valuation tribunal] by virtue of section 13(1) or 31(1)).

(2)   This section applies to—

(a)   any provision of [Parts I, [and III]];

(b)   any provision of section 42; and

(c)   any provision of sections 46 to 48.

(3)   Where any proceedings under any provision to which this section applies are being taken in a county court, the county court shall have jurisdiction to hear and determine any other proceedings joined with those proceedings, notwithstanding that the other proceedings would, apart from this subsection, be outside the court's jurisdiction.

(4)   *If a person takes any proceedings under any such provision in the High Court he shall not be entitled to recover any more costs of those proceedings than those to which he would have been entitled if the proceedings had been taken in a county court; and in any such case the taxing master shall have the same power of directing on what county court scale costs are to be allowed, and of allowing any item of costs, as the judge would have had if the proceedings had been taken in a county court.*

(5)   *Subsection (4) shall not apply where the purpose of taking the proceedings in the High Court was to enable them to be joined with any proceedings already pending before that court (not being proceedings taken under any provision to which this section applies).*

[709]

NOTES

Sub-s (1): words in square brackets substituted by the Housing Act 1996, s 92(1), Sch 6, Pt IV, para 6.

Sub-s (2): in para (a), words in first (outer) pair of square brackets substituted by the Housing Act 1996, s 86(1), (6); words in second (inner) pair of square brackets substituted by the Commonhold and Leasehold Reform Act 2002, s 163(1), (8), except in relation to an application made to the court under Part IV of this Act at [**695**]–[**700**], before 30 September 2003 (in relation to England) or 31 March 2004 (in relation to Wales).

Sub-ss (4), (5): repealed by the Courts and Legal Services Act 1990, s 125(7), Sch 20, as from a day to be appointed.

**52A**   *(Inserted by the Housing Act 1996, s 92(1), Sch 6, Pt IV, para 7; repealed by the Commonhold and Leasehold Reform Act 2002, s 180, Sch 14, except in relation to any application* *made to an LVT or any proceedings transferred to an LVT by a county court before 30 September 2003 (in relation to England) or 31 March 2004 (in relation to Wales).)*

### 53  Regulations and orders

(1)   Any power of the Secretary of State to make an order or regulations under this Act shall be exercisable by statutory instrument and may be exercised so as to make different provision for different cases, including different provision for different areas.

(2)   A statutory instrument containing—
    (a)    an order made under section 1(5), 25(6), *42(5)* or 55, or
    (b)    any regulations made … under section 20(4) [or 35(2)(g)] *[or 42A]*,

shall be subject to annulment in pursuance of a resolution of either House of Parliament.

[(3)   This section does not apply to any power to make regulations under section 42A.]

**[710]**

#### NOTES

Sub-s (2): reference in italics in para (a) repealed and words in second pair of square brackets in para (b) inserted by the Commonhold and Leasehold Reform Act 2002, ss 156(2), 180, Sch 14, as from a day to be appointed; in para (b) words omitted repealed except in relation to any application made to an LVT or any proceedings transferred to an LVT by a county court before 30 September 2003 (in relation to England) or 31 March 2004 (in relation to Wales) and words in first pair of square brackets inserted except in relation to applications made under s 35 of this Act at **[695]**, before 26 July 2002 (in relation to England) or 1 January 2003 (in relation to Wales) by ss 156(2), 180 of, and Sch 14 to, the 2002 Act; reference in italics in para (b) repealed by the Housing and Regeneration Act 2008, ss 303, 321(1), Sch 12, paras 11, 13(1), (2), Sch 16, as from 1 December 2008 (for the purpose of enabling the Secretary of State to make regulations) and as from a day to be appointed (for remaining purposes).

Sub-s (3): added by the Housing and Regeneration Act 2008, s 303, Sch 12, paras 11, 13(1), (3), as from 1 December 2008 (for the purpose of enabling the Secretary of State to make regulations) and as from a day to be appointed (for remaining purposes).

### 54  Notices

(1)   Any notice required or authorised to be served under this Act—
    (a)    shall be in writing; and
    (b)    may be sent by post.

(2)   Any notice purporting to be a notice served under any provision of Part I or III by the requisite majority of any qualifying tenants (as defined for the purposes of that provision) shall specify the names of all of the persons by whom it is served and the addresses of the flats of which they are qualifying tenants.

(3)   The Secretary of State may by regulations prescribe—
    (a)    the form of any notices required or authorised to be served under or in pursuance of any provision of Parts I to III, and
    (b)    the particulars which any such notices must contain (whether in addition to, or in substitution for, any particulars required by virtue of the provision in question).

(4)   Subsection (3)(b) shall not be construed as authorising the Secretary of State to make regulations under subsection (3) varying [any of the periods specified in section 5A(4) or (5), 5B(5) or (6), 5C(4) or (5), 5D(4) or (5) or 5E(3)] (which accordingly can only be varied by regulations under section 20(4)).

**[711]**

#### NOTES

Sub-s (4): words in square brackets substituted by the Housing Act 1996, s 92(1), Sch 6, Pt IV, para 9.

### 55  Application to Isles of Scilly

This Act shall apply to the Isles of Scilly subject to such exceptions, adaptations and modifications as the Secretary of State may by order direct.

**[712]**

### 56  Crown land

(1)   [Parts 1 and 3 and sections 42 to 42B (and so much of this Part as relates to those provisions)] shall apply to a tenancy from the Crown if there has ceased to be a Crown interest in the land subject to it.

(2)   …

(3)   Where there exists a Crown interest in any land subject to a tenancy from the Crown and the person holding that tenancy is himself the landlord under any other tenancy whose subject-matter comprises the whole or part of that land, [the provisions mentioned in subsection (1)] shall apply to that other tenancy, and to any derivative sub-tenancy, notwithstanding the existence of that interest.

(4)   For the purposes of this section "tenancy from the Crown" means a tenancy of land in which there is, or has during the subsistence of the tenancy been, a Crown interest superior to the tenancy, and "Crown interest" means—

(a)   an interest comprised in the Crown Estate;
(b)   an interest belonging to Her Majesty in right of the Duchy of Lancaster;
(c)   an interest belonging to the Duchy of Cornwall;
(d)   any other interest belonging to a government department or held on behalf of Her Majesty for the purposes of a government department.

[713]

**NOTES**
Sub-ss (1), (3): words in square brackets substituted for original words "this Act", except so far as relating to ss 42A, 42B of this Act, by the Commonhold and Leasehold Reform Act 2002, s 172(6). In relation to ss 42A, 42B those words are substituted as from a day to be appointed.
Sub-s (2): repealed by the Commonhold and Leasehold Reform Act 2002, s 180, Sch 14.

## 57  Financial provision

There shall be paid out of money provided by Parliament any increase attributable to this Act in the sums payable out of money so provided under any other Act.

[714]

## 58  Exempt landlords and resident landlords

(1)   In this Act "exempt landlord" means a landlord who is one of the following bodies, namely—

(a)   a district, county[, county borough] or London borough council, the Common Council of the City of London, [the London Fire and Emergency Planning Authority,] the Council of the Isles of Scilly, [a police authority established under [section 3 of the Police Act 1996]] [ ... ] ... , or a joint authority established by Part IV of the Local Government Act 1985;
(b)   ... a development corporation established by an order made (or having effect as if made) under the New Towns Act 1981;
(c)   an urban development corporation within the meaning of Part XVI of the Local Government, Planning and Land Act 1980;
[(ca) a housing action trust established under Part III of the Housing Act 1988]
(d)   ... ;
[(dd) the Broads Authority;]
[(de) a National Park authority;]
[(df) the Homes and Communities Agency;]
(e)   the Housing Corporation;
[(ea) ... ]
(f)   a housing trust (as defined in section 6 of the Housing Act 1985) which is a charity;
[(g)   a registered social landlord, or a fully mutual housing association which is not a registered social landlord; or]
(h)   an authority established under section 10 of the Local Government Act 1985 (joint arrangements for waste disposal functions).

[(1A)   In subsection (1)(g)—

"fully mutual housing association" has the same meaning as in the Housing Associations Act 1985 (see section 1(1) and (2) of that Act); and

"registered social landlord" has the same meaning as in the Housing Act 1985 (see section 5(4) and (5) of that Act).]

(2)   For the purposes of this Act the landlord of any premises consisting of the whole or part of a building is a resident landlord of those premises at any time if—

(a)   the premises are not, and do not form part of, a purpose-built block of flats; and
(b)   at that time the landlord occupies a flat contained in the premises as his only or principal residence; and
(c)   he has so occupied such a flat throughout a period of not less than 12 months ending with that time.

(3)   In subsection (2) "purpose-built block of flats" means a building which contained as constructed, and contains, two or more flats.

[715]

**NOTES**
Sub-s (1): in para (a), words in first pair of square brackets inserted by the Local Government (Wales) Act 1994, s 22(2), Sch 8, para 8, words in second pair of square brackets inserted by the Greater London Authority Act 1999, s 328, Sch 29, Pt I, para 48, words in third (outer) pair of square brackets substituted by the Police and Magistrates' Courts Act 1994, s 43, Sch 4, Pt II, para 61, words in fourth (inner) pair of square brackets substituted by the Police Act 1996, s 103(1), Sch 7, Pt I, para 1(1), (2)(z), words omitted from fifth pair

of square brackets inserted by the Police Act 1997, s 134(1), Sch 9, para 52 and repealed by the Criminal Justice and Police Act 2001, ss 128(1), 137, Sch 6, Pt 3, para 70, Sch 7, Pt 5(1), words omitted in second place from para (a) repealed by the Education Reform Act 1988, s 237(2), Sch 13, Pt I; words omitted from para (b) repealed and para (df) inserted by the Housing and Regeneration Act 2008, ss 56, 321(1), Sch 8, paras 37, 40, Sch 16, subject to transitional provisions and savings in SI 2008/3068, arts 6–10 at **[3834B]–[3834F]**; paras (ca), (ea) inserted by the Housing Act 1988, ss 119, 140(1), Sch 13, para 7, Sch 17, Pt II, para 114, and para (ea) repealed, together with para (d), by the Government of Wales Act 1998, ss 131, 141, 152, Sch 18, Pts IV, VI; para (dd) inserted by the Norfolk and Suffolk Broads Act 1988, s 21, Sch 6, para 28; para (de) inserted by the Environment Act 1995, s 78, Sch 10, para 2; para (g) substituted by the Housing Act 1996 (Consequential Provisions) Order 1996, SI 1996/2325, art 5, Sch 2, para 17(1), (2).

Sub-s (1A): inserted by SI 1996/2325, art 5, Sch 2, para 17(1), (3).

Modification: in sub-s (1)(e) the reference to the Housing Corporation shall be treated as if it were a reference to the Regulator of Social Housing: see the Transfer of Housing Corporation Functions (Modifications and Transitional Provisions) Order 2008, SI 2008/2839, arts 1(2), 3, 6, Schedule.

See further: a residuary body established by the Local Government Act 1985, Pt VII, is included among the bodies specified in sub-s (1) above; see Sch 13, para 25 to that Act. The Residuary Body for Wales, established under the Local Government (Wales) Act 1994, s 39, Sch 13, is included among the bodies specified in sub-s (1) above; see para 25(b) of that Schedule. The Local Government Residuary Body (England), established under the Local Government Act 1992, s 22, and the Local Government Residuary Body (England) Order 1995, SI 1995/401, is included among the bodies specified in sub-s (1) above; see art 18 of, and para 11 of the Schedule to, the 1995 Order.

## 59    Meaning of "lease", "long lease" and related expressions

(1)    In this Act "lease" and "tenancy" have the same meaning; and both expressions include—

    (a)    a sub-lease or sub-tenancy, and

    (b)    an agreement for a lease or tenancy (or for a sub-lease or sub-tenancy).

(2)    The expressions "landlord" and "tenant", and references to letting, to the grant of a lease or to covenants or the terms of a lease shall be construed accordingly.

(3)    In this Act "long lease" means—

    (a)    a lease granted for a term certain exceeding 21 years, whether or not it is (or may become) terminable before the end of that term by notice given by the tenant or by re-entry or forfeiture;

    (b)    a lease for a term fixed by law under a grant with a covenant or obligation for perpetual renewal, other than a lease by sub-demise from one which is not a long lease; or

    (c)    a lease granted in pursuance of Part V of the Housing Act 1985 (the right to buy)[, including a lease granted in pursuance of that Part as it has effect by virtue of section 17 of the Housing Act 1996 (the right to acquire)].

**[716]**

**NOTES**

Sub-s (3): words in square brackets added by the Housing Act 1996 (Consequential Amendments) (No 2) Order 1997, SI 1997/627, art 2, Schedule, para 5.

## 60    General interpretation

(1)    In this Act—

"the 1985 Act" means the Landlord and Tenant Act 1985;

"charity" means a charity within the meaning of [the Charities Act 1993], and "charitable purposes", in relation to a charity, means charitable purposes whether of that charity or of that charity and other charities;

"common parts", in relation to any building or part of a building, includes the structure and exterior of that building or part and any common facilities within it;

"the court" means the High Court or a county court;

"dwelling" means a building or part of a building occupied or intended to be occupied as a separate dwelling, together with any yard, garden, outhouses and appurtenances belonging to it or usually enjoyed with it;

"exempt landlord" has the meaning given by section 58(1);

"flat" means a separate set of premises, whether or not on the same floor, which—

    (a)    forms part of a building, and

    (b)    is divided horizontally from some other part of that building, and

    (c)    is constructed or adapted for use for the purposes of a dwelling;

"functional land", in relation to a charity, means land occupied by the charity, or by trustees for it, and wholly or mainly used for charitable purposes;

"landlord" (except for the purposes of Part I) means the immediate landlord or, in relation to a statutory tenant, the person who, apart from the statutory tenancy, would be entitled to possession of the premises subject to the tenancy;

"lease" and related expressions shall be construed in accordance with section 59(1) and (2);

"long lease" has the meaning given by section 59(3);

"mortgage" includes any charge or lien, and references to a mortgagee shall be construed accordingly;

"notices in proceedings" means notices or other documents served in, or in connection with, any legal proceedings;

.....

"resident landlord" shall be construed in accordance with section 58(2);

"statutory tenancy" and "statutory tenant" mean a statutory tenancy or statutory tenant within the meaning of the Rent Act 1977 or the Rent (Agriculture) Act 1976;

"tenancy" includes a statutory tenancy.

[(1A)   In this Act a reference to the Welsh Ministers in their new towns residuary capacity means the Welsh Ministers so far as exercising functions in relation to anything transferred (or to be transferred) to them as mentioned in section 36(1)(a)(i) to (iii) of the New Towns Act 1981.]

(2)   ...

[717]

**NOTES**
Sub-s (1): words in square brackets in definition "charity" substituted by the Charities Act 1993, s 98(1), Sch 6, para 30; definition "rent assessment committee" (omitted) repealed by the Housing Act 1996, ss 92(1), 227, Sch 6, Pt IV, para 10, Sch 19, Pt III.
Sub-s (1A): inserted by the Housing and Regeneration Act 2008, s 56, Sch 8, paras 37, 41, subject to transitional provisions and savings in SI 2008/3068, arts 6–10 at **[3834B]–[3834F]**.
Sub-s (2): repealed by the Housing Act 1988, s 140(2), Sch 18, except in relation to a disposal made in pursuance of a contract entered into before 15 January 1989 or where the offer notice was served, or treated as served, under s 5 of this Act at **[649]**, before that date.
Phasing out of certain statutory tenancies: see the notes preceding the Rent (Agriculture) Act 1976, s 1 at **[155]** and preceding the Rent Act 1977, s 1 at **[202]**.

**61   Consequential amendments and repeals**

(1)   The enactments mentioned in Schedule 4 shall have effect subject to the amendments there specified (being amendments consequential on the preceding provisions of this Act).

(2)   The enactments mentioned in Schedule 5 are hereby repealed to the extent specified in the third column of that Schedule.

[718]

**62   Short title, commencement and extent**

(1)   This Act may be cited as the Landlord and Tenant Act 1987.

(2)   This Act shall come into force on such day as the Secretary of State may by order appoint.

(3)   An order under subsection (2)—
   (a)   may appoint different days for different provisions or for different purposes; and
   (b)   may make such transitional, incidental, supplemental or consequential provision or saving as the Secretary of State considers necessary or expedient in connection with the coming into force of any provision of this Act or the operation of any enactment which is repealed or amended by a provision of this Act during any period when the repeal or amendment is not wholly in force.

(4)   This Act extends to England and Wales only.

[719]

**NOTES**
Orders: the Landlord and Tenant Act 1987 (Commencement No 1) Order 1987, SI 1987/2177; the Landlord and Tenant Act 1987 (Commencement No 2) Order 1988, SI 1988/480; the Landlord and Tenant Act 1987 (Commencement No 3) Order 1988, SI 1988/1283.

SCHEDULES

SCHEDULE 1
DISCHARGE OF MORTGAGES ETC: SUPPLEMENTARY PROVISIONS
Sections 12 and 32

PART I
DISCHARGE IN PURSUANCE OF PURCHASE NOTICES

*Construction*

1.   In this Part of this Schedule—
   "the consideration payable" means the consideration payable to [the purchaser] for the disposal by him of the property referred to in [section 12B(7)];
   "[the purchaser]" has the same meaning as in section 12, and accordingly includes any person to whom that section applies by virtue of [section 16(4) or (5)]; and
   "the nominated person" means the person or persons nominated as mentioned in [section 12B(2)].

### Duty of nominated person to redeem mortgages

2.—(1)   Where in accordance with [section 12B(5)(a)] an instrument will operate to discharge any property from a charge to secure the payment of money, it shall be the duty of the nominated person to apply the consideration payable, in the first instance, in or towards the redemption of any such charge (and, if there are more than one, then according to their priorities).

(2)   Where sub-paragraph (1) applies to any charge or charges, then if (and only if) the consideration payable is applied by the nominated person in accordance with that sub-paragraph or paid into court by him in accordance with paragraph 4, the instrument in question shall operate as mentioned in sub-paragraph (1) notwithstanding that the consideration payable is insufficient to enable the charge or charges to be redeemed in its or their entirety.

(3)   Subject to sub-paragraph (4), sub-paragraph (1) shall not apply to a charge which is a debenture holders' charge, that is to say, a charge (whether a floating charge or not) in favour of the holders of a series of debentures issued by a company or other body of persons, or in favour of trustees for such debenture holders; and any such charge shall be disregarded in determining priorities for the purposes of sub-paragraph (1).

(4)   Sub-paragraph (3) above shall not have effect in relation to a charge in favour of trustees for debenture holders which at the date of the instrument by virtue of which the property is disposed of by [the purchaser] is (as regards that property) a specific and not a floating charge.

### Determination of amounts due in respect of mortgages

3.—(1)   For the purpose of determining the amount payable in respect of any charge under paragraph 2(1), a person entitled to the benefit of a charge to which that provision applies shall not be permitted to exercise any right to consolidate that charge with a separate charge on other property.

(2)   For the purpose of discharging any property from a charge to which paragraph 2(1) applies, a person may be required to accept three months or any longer notice of the intention to pay the whole or part of the principal secured by the charge, together with interest to the date of payment, notwithstanding that the terms of the security make other provision or no provision as to the time and manner of payment; but he shall be entitled, if he so requires, to receive such additional payment as is reasonable in the circumstances in respect of the costs of re-investment or other incidental costs and expenses and in respect of any reduction in the rate of interest obtainable on re-investment.

### Payments into court

4.—(1)   Where under [section 12B(5)(a)] any property is to be discharged from a charge and, in accordance with paragraph 2(1), a person is or may be entitled in respect of the charge to receive the whole or part of the consideration payable, then if—

  (a)   for any reason difficulty arises in ascertaining how much is payable in respect of the charge, or

  (b)   for any reason mentioned in sub-paragraph (2) below difficulty arises in making a payment in respect of the charge,

the nominated person may pay into court on account of the consideration payable the amount, if known, of the payment to be made in respect of the charge or, if that amount is not known, the whole of that consideration or such lesser amount as the nominated person thinks right in order to provide for that payment.

(2)   Payment may be made into court in accordance with sub-paragraph (1)(b) where the difficulty arises for any of the following reasons, namely—

  (a)   because a person who is or may be entitled to receive payment cannot be found or ascertained;

  (b)   because any such person refuses or fails to make out a title, or to accept payment and give a proper discharge, or to take any steps reasonably required of him to enable the sum payable to be ascertained and paid; or

  (c)   because a tender of the sum payable cannot, by reason of complications in the title to it or the want of two or more trustees or for other reasons, be effected, or not without incurring or involving unreasonable cost or delay.

(3)   Without prejudice to sub-paragraph (1)(a), the whole or part of the consideration payable shall be paid into court by the nominated person if, before execution of the instrument referred to in paragraph 2(1), notice is given to him—

  (a)   that [the purchaser] or a person entitled to the benefit of a charge on the property in question requires him to do so for the purpose of protecting the rights of persons so entitled, or for reasons related to the bankruptcy or winding up of [the purchaser], or

  (b)   that steps have been taken to enforce any charge on [the purchaser's] interest in that property by the bringing of proceedings in any court, or by the appointment of a receiver or otherwise;

and where payment into court is to be made by reason only of a notice under this sub-paragraph, and the notice is given with reference to proceedings in a court specified in the notice other than a county court, payment shall be made into the court so specified.

### Savings

5.—(1)   Where any property is discharged by [section 12B(5)(a)] from a charge (without the obligations secured by the charge being satisfied by the receipt of the whole or part of the consideration payable), the discharge of that property from the charge shall not prejudice any right or remedy for the enforcement of those obligations against other property comprised in the same or any other security, nor prejudice any personal liability as principal or otherwise of [the purchaser] or any other person.

(2)   Nothing in this Schedule shall be construed as preventing a person from joining in the instrument referred to in paragraph 2(1) for the purpose of discharging the property in question from any charge without payment or for a lesser payment than that to which he would otherwise be entitled; and, if he does so, the persons to whom the consideration payable ought to be paid shall be determined accordingly.

[720]

**NOTES**
Paras 1, 2, 4, 5: words in square brackets substituted by the Housing Act 1996, s 92(1), Sch 6, Pt IV, para 11.

### PART II
## DISCHARGE IN PURSUANCE OF ACQUISITION ORDERS

### Construction

6.   In this Part of this Schedule—
   "the consideration payable" means the consideration payable for the acquisition of the landlord's interest referred to in section 32(1); and
   "the nominated person" means the person or persons nominated for the purposes of Part III by the persons who applied for the acquisition order in question.

### Duty of nominated person to redeem mortgages

7.—(1)   Where in accordance with section 32(1) an instrument will operate to discharge any premises from a charge to secure the payment of money, it shall be the duty of the nominated person to apply the consideration payable, in the first instance, in or towards the redemption of any such charge (and, if there are more than one, then according to their priorities).

(2)   Where sub-paragraph (1) applies to any charge or charges, then if (and only if) the consideration payable is applied by the nominated person in accordance with that sub-paragraph or paid into court by him in accordance with paragraph 9, the instrument in question shall operate as mentioned in sub-paragraph (1) notwithstanding that the consideration payable is insufficient to enable the charge or charges to be redeemed in its or their entirety.

(3)   Subject to sub-paragraph (4), sub-paragraph (1) shall not apply to a charge which is a debenture holders' charge within the meaning of paragraph 2(3) in Part I of this Schedule; and any such charge shall be disregarded in determining priorities for the purposes of sub-paragraph (1).

(4)   Sub-paragraph (3) above shall not have effect in relation to a charge in favour of trustees for debenture holders which at the date of the instrument by virtue of which the landlord's interest in the premises in question is acquired is (as regards those premises) a specific and not a floating charge.

### Determination of amounts due in respect of mortgages

8.—(1)   For the purpose of determining the amount payable in respect of any charge under paragraph 7(1), a person entitled to the benefit of a charge to which that provision applies shall not be permitted to exercise any right to consolidate that charge with a separate charge on other property.

(2)   For the purpose of discharging any premises from a charge to which paragraph 7(1) applies, a person may be required to accept three months or any longer notice of the intention to pay the whole or part of the principal secured by the charge, together with interest to the date of payment, notwithstanding that the terms of the security make other provision or no provision as to the time and manner of payment; but he shall be entitled, if he so requires, to receive such additional payment as is reasonable in the circumstances in respect of the costs of re-investment or other incidental costs and expenses and in respect of any reduction in the rate of interest obtainable on re-investment.

*Payments into court*

9.—(1)   Where under section 32 any premises are to be discharged from a charge and, in accordance with paragraph 7(1), a person is or may be entitled in respect of the charge to receive the whole or part of the consideration payable, then if—

(a)   for any reason difficulty arises in ascertaining how much is payable in respect of the charge, or

(b)   for any reason mentioned in sub-paragraph (2) below difficulty arises in making a payment in respect of the charge,

the nominated person may pay into court on account of the consideration payable the amount, if known, of the payment to be made in respect of the charge or, if that amount is not known, the whole of that consideration or such lesser amount as the nominated person thinks right in order to provide for that payment.

(2)   Payment may be made into court in accordance with sub-paragraph (1)(b) where the difficulty arises for any of the following reasons, namely—

(a)   because a person who is or may be entitled to receive payment cannot be found or ascertained;

(b)   because any such person refuses or fails to make out a title, or to accept payment and give a proper discharge, or to take any steps reasonably required of him to enable the sum payable to be ascertained and paid; or

(c)   because a tender of the sum payable cannot, by reason of complications in the title to it or the want of two or more trustees or for other reasons, be effected, or not without incurring or involving unreasonable cost or delay.

(3)   Without prejudice to sub-paragraph (1)(a), the whole or part of the consideration payable shall be paid into court by the nominated person if, before execution of the instrument referred to in paragraph 7(1), notice is given to him—

(a)   that the landlord or a person entitled to the benefit of a charge on the premises in question requires him to do so for the purpose of protecting the rights of persons so entitled, or for reasons related to the bankruptcy or winding up of the landlord, or

(b)   that steps have been taken to enforce any charge on the landlord's interest in those premises by the bringing of proceedings in any court, or by the appointment of a receiver or otherwise;

and where payment into court is to be made by reason only of a notice under this sub-paragraph, and the notice is given with reference to proceedings in a court specified in the notice other than a county court, payment shall be made into the court so specified.

*Savings*

10.—(1)   Where any premises are discharged by section 32 from a charge (without the obligations secured by the charge being satisfied by the receipt of the whole or part of the consideration payable), the discharge of those premises from the charge shall not prejudice any right or remedy for the enforcement of those obligations against other property comprised in the same or any other security, nor prejudice any personal liability as principal or otherwise of the landlord or any other person.

(2)   Nothing in this Schedule shall be construed as preventing a person from joining in the instrument referred to in paragraph 7(1) for the purpose of discharging the premises in question from any charge without payment or for a lesser payment than that to which he would otherwise be entitled; and, if he does so, the persons to whom the consideration payable ought to be paid shall be determined accordingly.

**[721]**

**NOTES**

Modified, where the RTM company has acquired the right to manage, by the Commonhold and Leasehold Reform Act 2002, s 102, Sch 7, para 9 at **[1266]**, **[1306]**.

*(Sch 2 contains consequential amendments which, in so far as within the scope of this work, have been incorporated at the appropriate place; Sch 3 adds the Landlord and Tenant Act 1985, Schedule at* **[643]***; Sch 4 outside the scope of this work; Sch 5 contains repeals only.)*

# LANDLORD AND TENANT ACT 1988

(1988 c 26)

## ARRANGEMENT OF SECTIONS

*An Act to make new provision for imposing statutory duties in connection with covenants in tenancies against assigning, underletting, charging or parting with the possession of premises without consent*

[29 July 1988]

## 1  Qualified duty to consent to assigning, underletting etc of premises

(1)   This section applies in any case where—
   (a)   a tenancy includes a covenant on the part of the tenant not to enter into one or more of the following transactions, that is—
      (i)   assigning,
      (ii)   underletting,
      (iii)   charging, or
      (iv)   parting with the possession of,
      the premises comprised in the tenancy or any part of the premises without the consent of the landlord or some other person, but
   (b)   the covenant is subject to the qualification that the consent is not to be unreasonably withheld (whether or not it is also subject to any other qualification).

(2)   In this section and section 2 of this Act—
   (a)   references to a proposed transaction are to any assignment, underletting, charging or parting with possession to which the covenant relates, and
   (b)   references to the person who may consent to such a transaction are to the person who under the covenant may consent to the tenant entering into the proposed transaction.

(3)   Where there is served on the person who may consent to a proposed transaction a written application by the tenant for consent to the transaction, he owes a duty to the tenant within a reasonable time—
   (a)   to give consent, except in a case where it is reasonable not to give consent,
   (b)   to serve on the tenant written notice of his decision whether or not to give consent specifying in addition—
      (i)   if the consent is given subject to conditions, the conditions,
      (ii)   if the consent is withheld, the reasons for withholding it.

(4)   Giving consent subject to any condition that is not a reasonable condition does not satisfy the duty under subsection (3)(a) above.

(5)   For the purposes of this Act it is reasonable for a person not to give consent to a proposed transaction only in a case where, if he withheld consent and the tenant completed the transaction, the tenant would be in breach of a covenant.

(6)   It is for the person who owed any duty under subsection (3) above—
   (a)   if he gave consent and the question arises whether he gave it within a reasonable time, to show that he did,
   (b)   if he gave consent subject to any condition and the question arises whether the condition was a reasonable condition, to show that it was,
   (c)   if he did not give consent and the question arises whether it was reasonable for him not to do so, to show that it was reasonable,

and, if the question arises whether he served notice under that subsection within a reasonable time, to show that he did.

[722]

**NOTES**
   Modified, where the RTM company has acquired the right to manage, by the Commonhold and Leasehold Reform Act 2002, s 102, Sch 7, para 13(1), (2) at **[1266]**, **[1306]**.

## 2  Duty to pass on applications

(1)   If, in a case where section 1 of this Act applies, any person receives a written application by the tenant for consent to a proposed transaction and that person—
   (a)   is a person who may consent to the transaction or (though not such a person) is the landlord, and
   (b)   believes that another person, other than a person who he believes has received the application or a copy of it, is a person who may consent to the transaction,

he owes a duty to the tenant (whether or not he owes him any duty under section 1 of this Act) to take such steps as are reasonable to secure the receipt within a reasonable time by the other person of a copy of the application.

(2)   The reference in section 1(3) of this Act to the service of an application on a person who may consent to a proposed transaction includes a reference to the receipt by him of an application or a copy of an application (whether it is for his consent or that of another).

**[723]**

### 3   Qualified duty to approve consent by another

(1)   This section applies in any case where—

   (a)   a tenancy includes a covenant on the part of the tenant not without the approval of the landlord to consent to the sub-tenant—
      (i)   assigning,
      (ii)   underletting,
      (iii)   charging, or
      (iv)   parting with the possession of,
      the premises comprised in the sub-tenancy or any part of the premises, but
   (b)   the covenant is subject to the qualification that the approval is not to be unreasonably withheld (whether or not it is also subject to any other qualification).

(2)   Where there is served on the landlord a written application by the tenant for approval or a copy of a written application to the tenant by the sub-tenant for consent to a transaction to which the covenant relates the landlord owes a duty to the sub-tenant within a reasonable time—

   (a)   to give approval, except in a case where it is reasonable not to give approval,
   (b)   to serve on the tenant and the sub-tenant written notice of his decision whether or not to give approval specifying in addition—
      (i)   if approval is given subject to conditions, the conditions,
      (ii)   if approval is withheld, the reasons for withholding it.

(3)   Giving approval subject to any condition that is not a reasonable condition does not satisfy the duty under subsection (2)(a) above.

(4)   For the purposes of this section it is reasonable for the landlord not to give approval only in a case where, if he withheld approval and the tenant gave his consent, the tenant would be in breach of covenant.

(5)   It is for a landlord who owed any duty under subsection (2) above—

   (a)   if he gave approval and the question arises whether he gave it within a reasonable time, to show that he did,
   (b)   if he gave approval subject to any condition and the question arises whether the condition was a reasonable condition, to show that it was,
   (c)   if he did not give approval and the question arises whether it was reasonable for him not to do so, to show that it was reasonable,

and, if the question arises whether he served notice under that subsection within a reasonable time, to show that he did.

**[724]**

---

**NOTES**

Modification: sub-ss (2), (4), (5) are modified, where the RTM company has acquired the right to manage, by the Commonhold and Leasehold Reform Act 2002, s 102, Sch 7, para 13(1), (3) at **[1266]**, **[1306]**.

---

### 4   Breach of duty

A claim that a person has broken any duty under this Act may be made the subject of civil proceedings in like manner as any other claim in tort for breach of statutory duty.

**[725]**

### 5   Interpretation

(1)   In this Act—

   "covenant" includes condition and agreement, "consent" includes licence,
   "landlord" includes any superior landlord from whom the tenant's immediate landlord directly or indirectly holds,
   "tenancy", subject to subsection (3) below, means any lease or other tenancy (whether made before or after the coming into force of this Act) and includes—
      (a)   a sub-tenancy, and
      (b)   an agreement for a tenancy
      and references in this Act to the landlord and to the tenant are to be interpreted accordingly, and
   "tenant", where the tenancy is affected by a mortgage (within the meaning of the Law of Property Act 1925) and the mortgagee proposes to exercise his statutory or express power of sale, includes the mortgagee.

PART I
STATUTES

(2)   An application or notice is to be treated as served for the purposes of this Act if—

(a)   served in any manner provided in the tenancy, and

(b)   in respect of any matter for which the tenancy makes no provision, served in any manner provided by section 23 of the Landlord and Tenant Act 1927.

(3)   This Act does not apply to a secure tenancy (defined in section 79 of the Housing Act 1985) [or to an introductory tenancy (within the meaning of Chapter I of Part V of the Housing Act 1996)].

(4)   This Act applies only to applications for consent or approval served after its coming into force.

**[726]**

---

**NOTES**

Sub-s (3): words in square brackets added by the Housing Act 1996 (Consequential Amendments) Order 1997, SI 1997/74, art 2, Schedule, para 5.

---

## 6   Application to Crown

This Act binds the Crown; but as regards the Crown's liability in tort shall not bind the Crown further than the Crown is made liable in tort by the Crown Proceedings Act 1947.

**[727]**

## 7   Short title, commencement and extent

(1)   This Act may be cited as the Landlord and Tenant Act 1988.

(2)   This Act shall come into force at the end of the period of two months beginning with the day on which it is passed.

(3)   This Act extends to England and Wales only.

**[728]**

# HOUSING ACT 1988

## (1988 c 50)

### ARRANGEMENT OF SECTIONS

### PART I
### RENTED ACCOMMODATION

### CHAPTER I
### ASSURED TENANCIES

*Meaning of assured tenancy etc*

*An Act to make further provision with respect to dwelling-houses let on tenancies or occupied under licences; to amend the Rent Act 1977 and the Rent (Agriculture) Act 1976; to establish a body, Housing for Wales, having functions relating to housing associations; to amend the Housing Associations Act 1985 and to repeal and re-enact with amendments certain provisions of Part II of that Act; to make provision for the establishment of housing action trusts for areas designated by the Secretary of State; to confer on persons approved for the purpose the right to acquire from public sector landlords certain dwelling-houses occupied by secure tenants; to make further provision about rent officers, the administration of housing benefit and rent allowance subsidy, the right to buy, repair notices and certain disposals of land and the application of capital money arising thereon; to make provision consequential upon the Housing (Scotland) Act 1988; and for connected purposes*

[15 November 1988]

**NOTES**

Transfer of functions: as to the functions of Ministers of the Crown under this Act, so far as exercisable in relation to Wales, being transferred to the National Assembly for Wales, see the National Assembly for Wales (Transfer of Functions) Order 1999, SI 1999/672, art 2, Sch 1.

PART I
RENTED ACCOMMODATION

CHAPTER I
ASSURED TENANCIES

*Meaning of assured tenancy etc*

**1  Assured tenancies**

(1)   A tenancy under which a dwelling-house is let as a separate dwelling is for the purposes of this Act an assured tenancy if and so long as—
    (a)    the tenant or, as the case may be, each of the joint tenants is an individual; and
    (b)    the tenant or, as the case may be, at least one of the joint tenants occupies the dwelling-house as his only or principal home; and
    (c)    the tenancy is not one which, by virtue of subsection (2) or subsection (6) below, cannot be an assured tenancy.

(2)   Subject to subsection (3) below, if and so long as a tenancy falls within any paragraph in Part I of Schedule 1 to this Act, it cannot be an assured tenancy; and in that Schedule—
    (a)    "tenancy" means a tenancy under which a dwelling-house is let as a separate dwelling;
    (b)    Part II has effect for determining the rateable value of a dwelling-house for the purposes of Part I; and
    (c)    Part III has effect for supplementing paragraph 10 in Part I.

[(2A)   The Secretary of State may by order replace any amount referred to in paragraphs 2 and 3A of Schedule 1 to this Act by such amount as is specified in the order; and such an order shall be made by statutory instrument which shall be subject to annulment in pursuance of a resolution of either House of Parliament.]

(3)   Except as provided in Chapter V below, at the commencement of this Act, a tenancy—
    (a)    under which a dwelling-house was then let as a separate dwelling, and
    (b)    which immediately before that commencement was an assured tenancy for the purposes of sections 56 to 58 of the Housing Act 1980 (tenancies granted by approved bodies),
shall become an assured tenancy for the purposes of this Act.

(4)   In relation to an assured tenancy falling within subsection (3) above—
    (a)    Part I of Schedule 1 to this Act shall have effect, subject to subsection (5) below, as if it consisted only of paragraphs 11 and 12; and
    (b)    sections 56 to 58 of the Housing Act 1980 (and Schedule 5 to that Act) shall not apply after the commencement of this Act.

(5)   In any case where—
    (a)    immediately before the commencement of this Act the landlord under a tenancy is a fully mutual housing association, and
    (b)    at the commencement of this Act the tenancy becomes an assured tenancy by virtue of subsection (3) above,

then, so long as that association remains the landlord under that tenancy (and under any statutory periodic tenancy which arises on the coming to an end of that tenancy), paragraph 12 of Schedule 1 to this Act shall have effect in relation to that tenancy with the omission of sub-paragraph (1)(h).

(6), (7)    ...

**[729]**

---

**NOTES**

Sub-s (2A): inserted by the References to Rating (Housing) Regulations 1990, SI 1990/434, reg 2, Schedule, para 27.

Sub-ss (6), (7): repealed by the Housing Act 1996, s 227, Sch 19, Pt VIII, except in relation to an applicant whose application for accommodation or assistance in obtaining accommodation was made before 20 January 1997.

---

## 2   Letting of a dwelling-house together with other land

(1)    If, under a tenancy, a dwelling-house is let together with other land, then, for the purposes of this Part of this Act,—

(a)    if and so long as the main purpose of the letting is the provision of a home for the tenant or, where there are joint tenants, at least one of them, the other land shall be treated as part of the dwelling-house; and

(b)    if and so long as the main purpose of the letting is not as mentioned in paragraph (a) above, the tenancy shall be treated as not being one under which a dwelling-house is let as a separate dwelling.

(2)    Nothing in subsection (1) above affects any question whether a tenancy is precluded from being an assured tenancy by virtue of any provision of Schedule 1 to this Act.

**[730]**

## 3   Tenant sharing accommodation with persons other than landlord

(1)    Where a tenant has the exclusive occupation of any accommodation (in this section referred to as "the separate accommodation") and—

(a)    the terms as between the tenant and his landlord on which he holds the separate accommodation include the use of other accommodation (in this section referred to as "the shared accommodation") in common with another person or other persons, not being or including the landlord, and

(b)    by reason only of the circumstances mentioned in paragraph (a) above, the separate accommodation would not, apart from this section, be a dwelling-house let on an assured tenancy,

the separate accommodation shall be deemed to be a dwelling-house let on an assured tenancy and the following provisions of this section shall have effect.

(2)    For the avoidance of doubt it is hereby declared that where, for the purpose of determining the rateable value of the separate accommodation, it is necessary to make an apportionment under Part II of Schedule 1 to this Act, regard is to be had to the circumstances mentioned in subsection (1)(a) above.

(3)    While the tenant is in possession of the separate accommodation, any term of the tenancy terminating or modifying, or providing for the termination or modification of, his right to the use of any of the shared accommodation which is living accommodation shall be of no effect.

(4)    Where the terms of the tenancy are such that, at any time during the tenancy, the persons in common with whom the tenant is entitled to the use of the shared accommodation could be varied or their number could be increased, nothing in subsection (3) above shall prevent those terms from having effect so far as they relate to any such variation or increase.

(5)    In this section "living accommodation" means accommodation of such a nature that the fact that it constitutes or is included in the shared accommodation is sufficient, apart from this section, to prevent the tenancy from constituting an assured tenancy of a dwelling-house.

**[731]**

## 4   Certain sublettings not to exclude any part of sub-lessor's premises from assured tenancy

(1)    Where the tenant of a dwelling-house has sub-let a part but not the whole of the dwelling-house, then, as against his landlord or any superior landlord, no part of the dwelling-house shall be treated as excluded from being a dwelling-house let on an assured tenancy by reason only that the terms on which any person claiming under the tenant holds any part of the dwelling-house include the use of accommodation in common with other persons.

(2)    Nothing in this section affects the rights against, and liabilities to, each other of the tenant and any person claiming under him, or of any two such persons.

**[732]**

**5  Security of tenure**

[(1)    An assured tenancy cannot be brought to an end by the landlord except by—

(a)    obtaining—

(i)    an order of the court for possession of the dwelling-house under section 7 or 21, and

(ii)    the execution of the order,

(b)    obtaining an order of the court under section 6A (demotion order), or

(c)    in the case of a fixed term tenancy which contains power for the landlord to determine the tenancy in certain circumstances, by the exercise of that power,

and, accordingly, the service by the landlord of a notice to quit is of no effect in relation to a periodic assured tenancy.

(1A)    Where an order of the court for possession of the dwelling-house is obtained, the tenancy ends when the order is executed.]

(2)    If an assured tenancy which is a fixed term tenancy comes to an end otherwise than by virtue of—

(a)    an order of the court [of the kind mentioned in subsection (1)(a) or (b) or any other order of the court], or

(b)    a surrender or other action on the part of the tenant,

then, subject to section 7 and Chapter II below, the tenant shall be entitled to remain in possession of the dwelling-house let under that tenancy and, subject to subsection (4) below, his right to possession shall depend upon a periodic tenancy arising by virtue of this section.

(3)    The periodic tenancy referred to in subsection (2) above is one—

(a)    taking effect in possession immediately on the coming to an end of the fixed term tenancy;

(b)    deemed to have been granted by the person who was the landlord under the fixed term tenancy immediately before it came to an end to the person who was then the tenant under that tenancy;

(c)    under which the premises which are let are the same dwelling-house as was let under the fixed term tenancy;

(d)    under which the periods of the tenancy are the same as those for which rent was last payable under the fixed term tenancy; and

(e)    under which, subject to the following provisions of this Part of this Act, the other terms are the same as those of the fixed term tenancy immediately before it came to an end, except that any term which makes provision for

determination by the landlord or the tenant shall not have effect while the tenancy remains an assured tenancy.

(4)    The periodic tenancy referred to in subsection (2) above shall not arise if, on the coming to an end of the fixed term tenancy, the tenant is entitled, by virtue of the grant of another tenancy, to possession of the same or substantially the same dwelling-house as was let to him under the fixed term tenancy.

(5)    If, on or before the date on which a tenancy is entered into or is deemed to have been granted as mentioned in subsection (3)(b) above, the person who is to be the tenant under that tenancy—

(a)    enters into an obligation to do any act which (apart from this subsection) will cause the tenancy to come to an end at a time when it is an assured tenancy, or

(b)    executes, signs or gives any surrender, notice to quit or other document which (apart from this subsection) has the effect of bringing the tenancy to an end at a time when it is an assured tenancy,

the obligation referred to in paragraph (a) above shall not be enforceable or, as the case may be, the surrender, notice to quit or other document referred to in paragraph (b) above shall be of no effect.

[(5A)    Nothing in subsection (5) affects any right of pre-emption—

(a)    which is exercisable by the landlord under a tenancy in circumstances where the tenant indicates his intention to dispose of the whole of his interest under the tenancy, and

(b)    in pursuance of which the landlord would be required to pay, in respect of the acquisition of that interest, an amount representing its market value.

"Dispose" means dispose by assignment or surrender, and "acquisition" has a corresponding meaning.]

(6)    If, by virtue of any provision of this Part of this Act, Part I of Schedule 1 to this Act has effect in relation to a fixed term tenancy as if it consisted only of paragraphs 11 and 12, that Part shall have the like effect in relation to any periodic tenancy which arises by virtue of this section on the coming to an end of the fixed term tenancy.

(7)  Any reference in this Part of this Act to a statutory periodic tenancy is a reference to a periodic tenancy arising by virtue of this section.

[733]

---

**NOTES**

Sub-ss (1), (1A): substituted for original sub-s (1), by the Housing and Regeneration Act 2008, s 299, Sch 11, Pt 1, paras 5, 6(1), (2), subject to transitional provisions in Sch 11, Pt 1, para 14 thereto at **[1891]**.

Sub-s (2): words in square brackets inserted by the Housing and Regeneration Act 2008, s 299, Sch 11, Pt 1, paras 5, 6(1), (3), subject to transitional provisions in Sch 11, Pt 1, para 14 thereto at **[1891]**.

Sub-s (5A): inserted by the Housing Act 2004, s 222(1), except in relation to any right of pre-emption granted before 18 January 2005.

---

## 6  Fixing of terms of statutory periodic tenancy

(1)  In this section, in relation to a statutory periodic tenancy,—
  (a)  "the former tenancy" means the fixed term tenancy on the coming to an end of which the statutory periodic tenancy arises; and
  (b)  "the implied terms" means the terms of the tenancy which have effect by virtue of section 5(3)(e) above, other than terms as to the amount of the rent;

but nothing in the following provisions of this section applies to a statutory periodic tenancy at a time when, by virtue of paragraph 11 or paragraph 12 in Part I of Schedule 1 to this Act, it cannot be an assured tenancy.

(2)  Not later than the first anniversary of the day on which the former tenancy came to an end, the landlord may serve on the tenant, or the tenant may serve on the landlord, a notice in the prescribed form proposing terms of the statutory periodic tenancy different from the implied terms and, if the landlord or the tenant considers it appropriate, proposing an adjustment of the amount of the rent to take account of the proposed terms.

(3)  Where a notice has been served under subsection (2) above,—
  (a)  within the period of three months beginning on the date on which the notice was served on him, the landlord or the tenant, as the case may be, may, by an application in the prescribed form, refer the notice to a rent assessment committee under subsection (4) below; and
  (b)  if the notice is not so referred, then, with effect from such date, not falling within the period referred to in paragraph (a) above, as may be specified in the notice, the terms proposed in the notice shall become terms of the tenancy in substitution for any of the implied terms dealing with the same

subject matter and the amount of the rent shall be varied in accordance with any adjustment so proposed.

(4)  Where a notice under subsection (2) above is referred to a rent assessment committee, the committee shall consider the terms proposed in the notice and shall determine whether those terms, or some other terms (dealing with the same subject matter as the proposed terms), are such as, in the committee's opinion, might reasonably be expected to be found in an assured periodic tenancy of the dwelling-house concerned, being a tenancy—
  (a)  which begins on the coming to an end of the former tenancy; and
  (b)  which is granted by a willing landlord on terms which, except in so far as they relate to the subject matter of the proposed terms, are those of the statutory periodic tenancy at the time of the committee's consideration.

(5)  Whether or not a notice under subsection (2) above proposes an adjustment of the amount of the rent under the statutory periodic tenancy, where a rent assessment committee determine any terms under subsection (4) above, they shall, if they consider it appropriate, specify such an adjustment to take account of the terms so determined.

(6)  In making a determination under subsection (4) above, or specifying an adjustment of an amount of rent under subsection (5) above, there shall be disregarded any effect on the terms or the amount of the rent attributable to the granting of a tenancy to a sitting tenant.

(7)  Where a notice under subsection (2) above is referred to a rent assessment committee, then, unless the landlord and the tenant otherwise agree, with effect from such date as the committee may direct—
  (a)  the terms determined by the committee shall become terms of the statutory periodic tenancy in substitution for any of the implied terms dealing with the same subject matter; and
  (b)  the amount of the rent under the statutory periodic tenancy shall be altered to accord with any adjustment specified by the committee;

but for the purposes of paragraph (b) above the committee shall not direct a date earlier than the date specified, in accordance with subsection (3)(b) above, in the notice referred to them.

(8) Nothing in this section requires a rent assessment committee to continue with a determination under subsection (4) above if the landlord and tenant give notice in writing that they no longer require such a determination or if the tenancy has come to an end.

[734]

NOTES

Regulations: the Assured Tenancies and Agricultural Occupancies (Forms) Regulations 1997, SI 1997/194 at [3169].

**[6A Demotion because of anti-social behaviour**

(1)    This section applies to an assured tenancy if the landlord is a registered social landlord.

(2)    The landlord may apply to a county court for a demotion order.

(3)    A demotion order has the following effect—
    (a)    the assured tenancy is terminated with effect from the date specified in the order;
    (b)    if the tenant remains in occupation of the dwelling-house after that date a demoted tenancy is created with effect from that date;
    (c)    it is a term of the demoted tenancy that any arrears of rent payable at the termination of the assured tenancy become payable under the demoted tenancy;
    (d)    it is also a term of the demoted tenancy that any rent paid in advance or overpaid at the termination of the assured tenancy is credited to the tenant's liability to pay rent under the demoted tenancy.

(4)    The court must not make a demotion order unless it is satisfied—
    (a)    that the tenant or a person residing in or visiting the dwelling-house has engaged or has threatened to *engage in conduct to which section 153A or 153B of the Housing Act 1996 (anti-social behaviour or use of premises for unlawful purposes) applies, and*
    (b)    that it is reasonable to make the order.

(5)    The court must not entertain proceedings for a demotion order unless—
    (a)    the landlord has served on the tenant a notice under subsection (6), or
    (b)    the court thinks it is just and equitable to dispense with the requirement of the notice.

(6)    The notice must—
    (a)    give particulars of the conduct in respect of which the order is sought;
    (b)    state that the proceedings will not begin before the date specified in the notice;
    (c)    state that the proceedings will not begin after the end of the period of twelve months beginning with the date of service of the notice.

(7)    The date specified for the purposes of subsection (6)(b) must not be before the end of the period of two weeks beginning with the date of service of the notice.

(8)    Each of the following has effect in respect of a demoted tenancy at the time it is created by virtue of an order under this section as it has effect in relation to the assured tenancy at the time it is terminated by virtue of the order—
    (a)    the parties to the tenancy;
    (b)    the period of the tenancy;
    (c)    the amount of the rent;
    (d)    the dates on which the rent is payable.

(9)    Subsection (8)(b) does not apply if the assured tenancy was for a fixed term and in such a case the demoted tenancy is a weekly periodic tenancy.

(10)    If the landlord of the demoted tenancy serves on the tenant a statement of any other express terms of the assured tenancy which are to apply to the demoted tenancy such terms are also terms of the demoted tenancy.

[(10A)    In subsection (4)(a) "housing-related anti-social conduct" has the same meaning as in section 153A of the Housing Act 1996.]

(11)    For the purposes of this section a demoted tenancy is a tenancy to which section 20B of the Housing Act 1988 applies.]

[735]

NOTES

Commencement: 30 June 2004 (in relation to England); 30 April 2005 (in relation to Wales).
Inserted by the Anti-social Behaviour Act 2003, s 14(4).
Sub-s (4): for the words in italics there are substituted the following words by the Police and Justice Act 2006, s 52, Sch 14, para 15(1), (2), as from a day to be appointed—
    "engage in—
        (i)    housing-related anti-social conduct, or
        (ii)    conduct to which section 153B of the Housing Act 1996 (use of premises for unlawful purposes) applies, and".

Sub-s (10A): inserted by the Police and Justice Act 2006, s 52, Sch 14, para 15(1), (3), as from a day to be appointed.

## 7 Orders for possession

(1) The court shall not make an order for possession of a dwelling-house let on an assured tenancy except on one or more of the grounds set out in Schedule 2 to this Act; but nothing in this Part of this Act relates to proceedings for possession of such a dwelling-house which are brought by a mortgagee, within the meaning of the Law of Property Act 1925, who has lent money on the security of the assured tenancy.

(2) The following provisions of this section have effect, subject to section 8 below, in relation to proceedings for the recovery of possession of a dwelling-house let on an assured tenancy.

(3) If the court is satisfied that any of the grounds in Part I of Schedule 2 to this Act is established then, subject to [subsections (5A) and (6)] below, the court shall make an order for possession.

(4) If the court is satisfied that any of the grounds in Part II of Schedule 2 to this Act is established, then, subject to [subsections (5A) and (6)] below, the court may make an order for possession if it considers it reasonable to do so.

(5) Part III of Schedule 2 to this Act shall have effect for supplementing Ground 9 in that Schedule and Part IV of that Schedule shall have effect in relation to notices given as mentioned in Grounds 1 to 5 of that Schedule.

[(5A) The court shall not make an order for possession of a dwelling-house let on an assured periodic tenancy arising under Schedule 10 to the Local Government and Housing Act 1989 on any of the following grounds, that is to say—
   (a)   Grounds 1, 2 and 5 in Part I of Schedule 2 to this Act;
   (b)   Ground 16 in Part II of that Schedule; and
   (c)   if the assured periodic tenancy arose on the termination of a former 1954 Act tenancy, within the meaning of the said Schedule 10, Ground 6 in Part I of Schedule 2 to this Act.]

(6) The court shall not make an order for possession of a dwelling-house to take effect at a time when it is let on an assured fixed term tenancy unless—
   (a)   the ground for possession is Ground 2 or Ground 8 in Part I of Schedule 2 to this Act or any of the grounds in Part II of that Schedule, other than Ground 9 or Ground 16; and
   (b)   the terms of the tenancy make provision for it to be brought to an end on the ground in question (whether that provision takes the form of a provision for re-entry, for forfeiture, for determination by notice or otherwise).

(7) Subject to the preceding provisions of this section, the court may make an order for possession of a dwelling-house on grounds relating to a fixed term tenancy which has come to an end; and where an order is made in such circumstances, any statutory periodic tenancy which has arisen on the ending of the fixed term tenancy shall end (without any notice and regardless of the period) [in accordance with section 5(1A)].

[736]

## NOTES
Sub-ss (3), (4): words in square brackets substituted by the Local Government and Housing Act 1989, s 194, Sch 11, para 101(1), (2).
Sub-s (5A): inserted by the Local Government and Housing Act 1989, s 194, Sch 11, para 101(3).
Sub-s (7): words in square brackets substituted by the Housing and Regeneration Act 2008, s 299, Sch 11, Pt 1, paras 5, 7, subject to transitional provisions in Sch 11, Pt 1, para 14 thereto at [1891].

## 8 Notice of proceedings for possession

(1) The court shall not entertain proceedings for possession of a dwelling-house let on an assured tenancy unless—
   (a)   the landlord or, in the case of joint landlords, at least one of them has served on the tenant a notice in accordance with this section and the proceedings are begun within the time limits stated in the notice in accordance with [subsections (3) to (4B)] below; or
   (b)   the court considers it just and equitable to dispense with the requirement of such a notice.

(2) The court shall not make an order for possession on any of the grounds in Schedule 2 to this Act unless that ground and particulars of it are specified in the notice under this section; but the grounds specified in such a notice may be altered or added to with the leave of the court.

(3) A notice under this section is one in the prescribed form informing the tenant that—
   (a)   the landlord intends to begin proceedings for possession of the dwelling-house on one or more of the grounds specified in the notice; and

(b) those proceedings will not begin earlier than a date specified in the notice [in accordance with subsections (4) to (4B) below]; and

(c) those proceedings will not begin later than twelve months from the date of service of the notice.

[(4) If a notice under this section specifies in accordance with subsection (3)(a) above Ground 14 in Schedule 2 to this Act (whether with or without other grounds), the date specified in the notice as mentioned in subsection (3)(b) above shall not be earlier than the date of the service of the notice.

(4A) If a notice under this section specifies in accordance with subsection (3)(a) above, any of Grounds 1, 2, 5 to 7, 9 and 16 in Schedule 2 to this Act (whether without other grounds or with any ground other than Ground 14), the date specified in the notice as mentioned in subsection (3)(b) above shall not be earlier than—

(a) two months from the date of service of the notice; and

(b) if the tenancy is a periodic tenancy, the earliest date on which, apart from section 5(1) above, the tenancy could be brought to an end by a notice to quit given by the landlord on the same date as the date of service of the notice under this section.

(4B) In any other case, the date specified in the notice as mentioned in subsection (3)(b) above shall not be earlier than the expiry of the period of two weeks from the date of the service of the notice.]

(5) The court may not exercise the power conferred by subsection (1)(b) above if the landlord seeks to recover possession on Ground 8 in Schedule 2 to this Act.

(6) Where a notice under this section—

(a) is served at a time when the dwelling-house is let on a fixed term tenancy, or

(b) is served after a fixed term tenancy has come to an end but relates (in whole or in part) to events occurring during that tenancy,

the notice shall have effect notwithstanding that the tenant becomes or has become tenant under a statutory periodic tenancy arising on the coming to an end of the fixed term tenancy.

[737]

**NOTES**
Sub-ss (1), (3): words in square brackets substituted by the Housing Act 1996, s 151(1)–(3).
Sub-ss (4)–(4B): substituted, for original sub-s (4), by the Housing Act 1996, s 151(1), (4).
Regulations: the Assured Tenancies and Agricultural Occupancies (Forms) Regulations 1997, SI 1997/194 at [3169].

**[8A Additional notice requirements: ground of domestic violence**

(1) Where the ground specified in a notice under section 8 (whether with or without other grounds) is Ground 14A in Schedule 2 to this Act and the partner who has left the dwelling-house as mentioned in that ground is not a tenant of the dwelling-house, the court shall not entertain proceedings for possession of the dwelling-house unless—

(a) the landlord or, in the case of joint landlords, at least one of them has served on the partner who has left a copy of the notice or has taken all reasonable steps to serve a copy of the notice on that partner, or

(b) the court considers it just and equitable to dispense with such requirements as to service.

(2) Where Ground 14A in Schedule 2 to this Act is added to a notice under section 8 with the leave of the court after proceedings for possession are begun and the partner who has left the dwelling-house as mentioned in that ground is not a party to the proceedings, the court shall not continue to entertain the proceedings unless—

(a) the landlord or, in the case of joint landlords, at least one of them has served a notice under subsection (3) below on the partner who has left or has taken all reasonable steps to serve such a notice on that partner, or

(b) the court considers it just and equitable to dispense with the requirement of such a notice.

(3) A notice under this subsection shall—

(a) state that proceedings for the possession of the dwelling-house have begun,

(b) specify the ground or grounds on which possession is being sought, and

(c) give particulars of the ground or grounds.]

[738]

**NOTES**
Inserted by the Housing Act 1996, s 150.

**9 Extended discretion of court in possession claims**

(1) Subject to subsection (6) below, the court may adjourn for such period or periods as it thinks fit proceedings for possession of a dwelling-house let on an assured tenancy.

(2)   On the making of an order for possession of a dwelling-house let on an assured tenancy or at any time before the execution of such an order, the court, subject to subsection (6) below, may—

    (a)   stay or suspend execution of the order, or

    (b)   postpone the date of possession,

for such period or periods as the court thinks just.

(3)   On any such adjournment as is referred to in subsection (1) above or on any such stay, suspension or postponement as is referred to in subsection (2) above, the court, unless it considers that to do so would cause exceptional hardship to the tenant or would otherwise be unreasonable, shall impose conditions with regard to payment by the tenant of arrears of rent (if any) and rent … and may impose such other conditions as it thinks fit.

(4)   *If any such conditions as are referred to in subsection (3) above are complied with, the court may, if it thinks fit, discharge or rescind any such order as is referred to in subsection (2) above.*

(5)   …

[(5A)   … ]

(6)   This section does not apply if the court is satisfied that the landlord is entitled to possession of the dwelling-house—

    (a)   on any of the grounds in Part I of Schedule 2 to this Act; or

    (b)   by virtue of subsection (1) or subsection (4) of section 21 below.

**[739]**

**NOTES**

Sub-s (3): words omitted repealed by the Housing and Regeneration Act 2008, ss 299, 321(1), Sch 11, Pt 1, paras 5, 8(1), (2), Sch 16, subject to transitional provisions in Sch 11, Pt 1, para 14 thereto at **[1891]**.

Sub-s (4): substituted by the Housing and Regeneration Act 2008, s 299, Sch 11, Pt 1, paras 5, 8(1), (3), subject to transitional provisions in Sch 11, Pt 1, para 14 thereto at **[1891]**, as from a day to be appointed, as follows:

"(4)   The court may discharge or rescind any such order as is referred to in subsection (2) if it thinks it appropriate to do so having had regard to—

    (a)   any conditions imposed under subsection (3), and

    (b)   the conduct of the tenant in connection with those conditions.".

Sub-s (5): repealed by the Housing and Regeneration Act 2008, ss 299, 321(1), Sch 11, Pt 1, paras 5, 8(1), (4), Sch 16, subject to transitional provisions in Sch 11, Pt 1, para 14 thereto at **[1891]**.

Sub-s (5A): inserted by the Family Law Act 1996, s 66(1), Sch 8, Pt III, para 59(1), (3); repealed by the Housing and Regeneration Act 2008, ss 299, 321(1), Sch 11, Pt 1, paras 5, 8(1), (4), Sch 16, subject to transitional provisions in Sch 11, Pt 1, para 14 thereto at **[1891]**.

**[9A   Proceedings for possession: anti-social behaviour**

(1)   This section applies if the court is considering under section 7(4) whether it is reasonable to make an order for possession on ground 14 set out in Part 2 of Schedule 2 (conduct of tenant or other person).

(2)   The court must consider, in particular—

    (a)   the effect that the nuisance or annoyance has had on persons other than the person against whom the order is sought;

    (b)   any continuing effect the nuisance or annoyance is likely to have on such persons;

    (c)   the effect that the nuisance or annoyance would be likely to have on such persons if the conduct is repeated.]

**[740]**

**NOTES**

Inserted by the Anti-social Behaviour Act 2003, s 16(2), except in relation to any proceedings for the possession of a dwelling-house begun before 30 June 2004 (in relation to England) and 30 September 2004 (in relation to Wales).

**10   Special provisions applicable to shared accommodation**

(1)   This section applies in a case falling within subsection (1) of section 3 above and expressions used in this section have the same meaning as in that section.

(2)   Without prejudice to the enforcement of any order made under subsection (3) below, while the tenant is in possession of the separate accommodation, no order shall be made for possession of any of the shared accommodation, whether on the application of the immediate landlord of the tenant or on the application of any person under whom that landlord derives title, unless a like order has been made, or is made at the same time, in respect of the separate accommodation; and the provisions of section 6 above shall have effect accordingly.

(3)   On the application of the landlord, the court may make such order as it thinks just either—

(a)  terminating the right of the tenant to use the whole or any part of the shared accommodation other than living accommodation; or

(b)  modifying his right to use the whole or any part of the shared accommodation, whether by varying the persons or increasing the number of persons entitled to the use of that accommodation or otherwise.

(4)  No order shall be made under subsection (3) above so as to effect any termination or modification of the rights of the tenant which, apart from section 3(3) above, could not be effected by or under the terms of the tenancy.

[741]

## 11  Payment of removal expenses in certain cases

(1)  Where a court makes an order for possession of a dwelling-house let on an assured tenancy on Ground 6 or Ground 9 in Schedule 2 to this Act (but not on any other ground), the landlord shall pay to the tenant a sum equal to the reasonable expenses likely to be incurred by the tenant in removing from the dwelling-house.

(2)  Any question as to the amount of the sum referred to in subsection (1) above shall be determined by agreement between the landlord and the tenant or, in default of agreement, by the court.

(3)  Any sum payable to a tenant by virtue of this section shall be recoverable as a civil debt due from the landlord.

[742]

## 12  Compensation for misrepresentation or concealment

Where a landlord obtains an order for possession of a dwelling-house let on an assured tenancy on one or more of the grounds in Schedule 2 to this Act and it is subsequently made to appear to the court that the order was obtained by misrepresentation or concealment of material facts, the court may order the landlord to pay to the former tenant such sum as appears sufficient as compensation for damage or loss sustained by that tenant as a result of the order.

[743]

*Rent and other terms*

## 13  Increases of rent under assured periodic tenancies

(1)  This section applies to—

(a)  a statutory periodic tenancy other than one which, by virtue of paragraph 11 or paragraph 12 in Part I of Schedule 1 to this Act, cannot for the time being be an assured tenancy; and

(b)  any other periodic tenancy which is an assured tenancy, other than one in relation to which there is a provision, for the time being binding on the tenant, under which the rent for a particular period of the tenancy will or may be greater than the rent for an earlier period.

(2)  For the purpose of securing an increase in the rent under a tenancy to which this section applies, the landlord may serve on the tenant a notice in the prescribed form proposing a new rent to take effect at the beginning of a new period of the tenancy specified in the notice, being a period beginning not earlier than—

(a)  the minimum period after the date of the service of the notice; and

(b)  except in the case of a statutory periodic [tenancy—

(i)  in the case of an assured agricultural occupancy, the first anniversary of the date on which the first period of the tenancy began;

(ii)  in any other case, on the date that falls 52 weeks after the date on which the first period of the tenancy began; and]

(c)  if the rent under the tenancy has previously been increased by virtue of a notice under this subsection or a determination under section 14 [below—

(i)  in the case of an assured agricultural occupancy, the first anniversary of the date on which the increased rent took effect;

(ii)  in any other case, the appropriate date].

(3)  The minimum period referred to in subsection (2) above is—

(a)  in the case of a yearly tenancy, six months;

(b)  in the case of a tenancy where the period is less than a month, one month; and

(c)  in any other case, a period equal to the period of the tenancy.

[(3A)  The appropriate date referred to in subsection (2)(c)(ii) above is—

(a)  in a case to which subsection (3B) below applies, the date that falls 53 weeks after the date on which the increased rent took effect;

(b)  in any other case, the date that falls 52 weeks after the date on which the increased rent took effect.

(3B)  This subsection applies where—

(a)  the rent under the tenancy has been increased by virtue of a notice under this section or a determination under section 14 below on at least one occasion after the coming into force of the Regulatory Reform (Assured Periodic Tenancies) (Rent Increases) Order 2003; and

(b)  the fifty-third week after the date on which the last such increase took effect begins more than six days before the anniversary of the date on which the first such increase took effect.]

(4)  Where a notice is served under subsection (2) above, a new rent specified in the notice shall take effect as mentioned in the notice unless, before the beginning of the new period specified in the notice,—

(a)  the tenant by an application in the prescribed form refers the notice to a rent assessment committee; or

(b)  the landlord and the tenant agree on a variation of the rent which is different from that proposed in the notice or agree that the rent should not be varied.

(5)  Nothing in this section (or in section 14 below) affects the right of the landlord and the tenant under an assured tenancy to vary by agreement any term of the tenancy (including a term relating to rent).

**[744]**

**NOTES**

Sub-s (2): words in square brackets substituted by the Regulatory Reform (Assured Periodic Tenancies) (Rent Increases) Order 2003, SI 2003/259, arts 1, 2(a), in respect of notices served under sub-s (2) after 10 February 2003.

Sub-ss (3A), (3B): inserted by SI 2003/259, arts 1, 2(b), in respect of notices served under sub-s (2) after 10 February 2003.

Regulations: the Assured Tenancies and Agricultural Occupancies (Forms) Regulations 1997, SI 1997/194 at **[3169]**.

## 14  Determination of rent by rent assessment committee

(1)  Where, under subsection (4)(a) of section 13 above, a tenant refers to a rent assessment committee a notice under subsection (2) of that section, the committee shall determine the rent at which, subject to subsections (2) and (4) below, the committee consider that the dwelling-house concerned might reasonably be expected to be let in the open market by a willing landlord under an assured tenancy—

(a)  which is a periodic tenancy having the same periods as those of the tenancy to which the notice relates;

(b)  which begins at the beginning of the new period specified in the notice;

(c)  the terms of which (other than relating to the amount of the rent) are the same as those of the tenancy to which the notice relates; and

(d)  in respect of which the same notices, if any, have been given under any of Grounds 1 to 5 of Schedule 2 to this Act, as have been given (or have effect as if given) in relation to the tenancy to which the notice relates.

(2)  In making a determination under this section, there shall be disregarded—

(a)  any effect on the rent attributable to the granting of a tenancy to a sitting tenant;

(b)  any increase in the value of the dwelling-house attributable to a relevant improvement carried out by a person who at the time it was carried out was the tenant, if the improvement—

(i)  was carried out otherwise than in pursuance of an obligation to his immediate landlord, or

(ii)  was carried out pursuant to an obligation to his immediate landlord being an obligation which did not relate to the specific improvement concerned but arose by reference to consent given to the carrying out of that improvement; and

(c)  any reduction in the value of the dwelling-house attributable to a failure by the tenant to comply with any terms of the tenancy.

(3)  For the purposes of subsection (2)(b) above, in relation to a notice which is referred by a tenant as mentioned in subsection (1) above, an improvement is a relevant improvement if either it was carried out during the tenancy to which the notice relates or the following conditions are satisfied, namely—

(a)  that it was carried out not more than twenty-one years before the date of service of the notice; and

(b)  that, at all times during the period beginning when the improvement was carried out and ending on the date of service of the notice, the dwelling-house has been let under an assured tenancy; and

(c)  that, on the coming to an end of an assured tenancy at any time during that period, the tenant (or, in the case of joint tenants, at least one of them) did not quit.

[(3A)   In making a determination under this section in any case where under Part I of the Local Government Finance Act 1992 the landlord or superior landlord is liable to pay council tax in respect of a hereditament ("the relevant hereditament") of which the dwelling-house forms part, the rent assessment committee shall have regard to the amount of council tax which, as at the date on which the notice under section 13(2) above was served, was set by the billing authority—

(a)   for the financial year in which that notice was served, and

(b)   for the category of dwellings within which the relevant hereditament fell on that date,

but any discount or other reduction affecting the amount of council tax payable shall be disregarded.

(3B)   In subsection (3A) above—

(a)   "hereditament" means a dwelling within the meaning of Part I of the Local Government Finance Act 1992,

(b)   "billing authority" has the same meaning as in that Part of that Act, and

(c)   "category of dwellings" has the same meaning as in section 30(1) and (2) of that Act.]

(4)   In this section "rent" does not include any service charge, within the meaning of section 18 of the Landlord and Tenant Act 1985, but, subject to that, includes any sums payable by the tenant to the landlord on account of the use of furniture[, in respect of council tax] or for any of the matters referred to in subsection (1)(a) of that section, whether or not those sums are separate from the sums payable for the occupation of the dwelling-house concerned or are payable under separate agreements.

(5)   Where any rates in respect of the dwelling-house concerned are borne by the landlord or a superior landlord, the rent assessment committee shall make their determination under this section as if the rates were not so borne.

(6)   In any case where—

(a)   a rent assessment committee have before them at the same time the reference of a notice under section 6(2) above relating to a tenancy (in this subsection referred to as "the section 6 reference") and the reference of a notice under section 13(2) above relating to the same tenancy (in this subsection referred to as "the section 13 reference"), and

(b)   the date specified in the notice under section 6(2) above is not later than the first day of the new period specified in the notice under section 13(2) above, and

(c)   the committee propose to hear the two references together,

the committee shall make a determination in relation to the section 6 reference before making their determination in relation to the section 13 reference and, accordingly, in such a case the reference in subsection (1)(c) above to the terms of the tenancy to which the notice relates shall be construed as a reference to those terms as varied by virtue of the determination made in relation to the section 6 reference.

(7)   Where a notice under section 13(2) above has been referred to a rent assessment committee, then, unless the landlord and the tenant otherwise agree, the rent determined by the committee (subject, in a case where subsection (5) above applies, to the addition of the appropriate amount in respect of rates) shall be the rent under the tenancy with effect from the beginning of the new period specified in the notice or, if it appears to the rent assessment committee that that would cause undue hardship to the tenant, with effect from such later date (not being later than the date the rent is determined) as the committee may direct.

(8)   Nothing in this section requires a rent assessment committee to continue with their determination of a rent for a dwelling-house if the landlord and tenant give notice in writing that they no longer require such a determination or if the tenancy has come to an end.

[(9)   This section shall apply in relation to an assured shorthold tenancy as if in subsection (1) the reference to an assured tenancy were a reference to an assured shorthold tenancy.]

[745]

---

**NOTES**

Sub-ss (3A), (3B): inserted by the Local Government Finance (Housing) (Consequential Amendments) Order 1993, SI 1993/651, arts 1(2), 2(1), Sch 1, para 17(1), (2), but not so as to affect the determination of rent under this section on a reference which relates to a notice served under s 13(2) of this Act before 1 April 1993.

Sub-s (4): words in square brackets inserted by SI 1993/651, arts 1(2), 2(1), Sch 1, para 17(1), (3), but not so as to affect the determination of rent under this section on a reference which relates to a notice served under s 13(2) of this Act before 1 April 1993.

Sub-s (9): added by the Housing Act 1996, s 104, Sch 8, para 2(1), (2).

Modification: sub-ss (2), (4), (5) are modified in relation to their application to the determination of rent under the Local Government and Housing Act 1989, Sch 10, para 6(3) or 11(5); see Sch 10, paras 6(4)–(6), 11(6)–(8) and 12 to the 1989 Act at [802].

---

**[14A   Interim increase before 1st April 1994 of rent under assured periodic tenancies in certain cases where landlord liable for council tax**

(1)   In any case where—

(a)   under Part I of the Local Government Finance Act 1992 the landlord of a dwelling-house

PART I
STATUTES

let under an assured tenancy to which section 13 above applies or a superior landlord is liable to pay council tax in respect of a dwelling (within the meaning of that Part of that Act) which includes that dwelling-house,

(b)   under the terms of the tenancy (or an agreement collateral to the tenancy) the tenant is liable to make payments to the landlord in respect of council tax,

(c)   the case falls within subsection (2) or subsection (3) below, and

(d)   no previous notice under this subsection has been served in relation to the dwelling-house,

the landlord may serve on the tenant a notice in the prescribed form proposing an increased rent to take account of the tenant's liability to make payments to the landlord in respect of council tax, such increased rent to take effect at the beginning of a new period of the tenancy specified in the notice being a period beginning not earlier than one month after the date on which the notice was served.

(2)   The case falls within this subsection if—

(a)   the rent under the tenancy has previously been increased by virtue of a notice under section 13(2) above or a determination under section 14 or above, and

(b)   the first anniversary of the date on which the increased rent took effect has not yet occurred.

(3)   The case falls within this subsection if a notice has been served under section 13(2) above before 1st April 1993 but no increased rent has taken effect before that date.

(4)   No notice may be served under subsection (1) above after 31st March 1994.

(5)   Where a notice is served under subsection (1) above, the new rent specified in the notice shall take effect as mentioned in the notice unless, before the beginning of the new period specified in the notice—

(a)   the tenant by an application in the prescribed form refers the notice to a rent assessment committee, or

(b)   the landlord and the tenant agree on a variation of the rent which is different from that proposed in the notice or agree that the rent should not be varied.

(6)   Nothing in this section (or in section 14B below) affects the rights of the landlord and the tenant under an assured tenancy to vary by agreement any term of the tenancy (including a term relating to rent).]

[746]

---

**NOTES**

Inserted, together with s 14B, by the Local Government Finance (Housing) (Consequential Amendments) Order 1993, SI 1993/651, art 2(2), Sch 2, para 8.

---

## [14B Interim determination of rent by rent assessment committee

(1)   Where, under subsection (5)(a) of section 14A above, a tenant refers to a rent assessment committee a notice under subsection (1) of that section, the committee shall determine the amount by which, having regard to the provisions of section 14(3A) above, the existing rent might reasonably be increased to take account of the tenant's liability to make payments to the landlord in respect of council tax.

(2)   Where a notice under section 14A(1) above has been referred to a rent assessment committee, then, unless the landlord and the tenant otherwise agree, the existing rent shall be increased by the amount determined by the committee with effect from the beginning of the new period specified in the notice or, if it appears to the committee that that would cause undue hardship to the tenant, with effect from such later date (not being later than the date the increase is determined) as the committee may direct.

(3)   In any case where—

(a)   a rent assessment committee have before them at the same time the reference of a notice under section 13(2) above relating to a tenancy (in this subsection referred to as "the section 13 reference") and the reference of a notice under section 14A(1) above relating to the same tenancy (in this subsection referred to as "the section 14A reference"); and

(b)   the committee propose to hear the two references together,

the committee shall make a determination in relation to the section 13 reference before making their determination in relation to the section 14A reference, and if in such a case the date specified in the notice under section 13(2) above is later than the date specified in the notice under section 14A(1) above, the rent determined under the section 14A reference shall not take effect until the date specified in the notice under section 13(2).

(4)   In this section "rent" has the same meaning as in section 14 above; and section 14(4) above applies to a determination under this section as it applies to a determination under that section.]

[747]

**15 Limited prohibition on assignment etc without consent**

(1)   Subject to subsection (3) below, it shall be an implied term of every assured tenancy which is a periodic tenancy that, except with the consent of the landlord, the tenant shall not—

    (a)   assign the tenancy (in whole or in part); or

    (b)   sub-let or part with possession of the whole or any part of the dwelling-house let on the tenancy.

(2)   Section 19 of the Landlord and Tenant Act 1927 (consents to assign not to be unreasonably withheld etc) shall not apply to a term which is implied into an assured tenancy by subsection (1) above.

(3)   In the case of a periodic tenancy which is not a statutory periodic tenancy [or an assured periodic tenancy arising under Schedule 10 to the Local Government and Housing Act 1989] subsection (1) above does not apply if—

    (a)   there is a provision (whether contained in the tenancy or not) under which the tenant is prohibited (whether absolutely or conditionally) from assigning or sub-letting or parting with possession or is permitted (whether absolutely or conditionally) to assign, sub-let or part with possession; or

    (b)   a premium is required to be paid on the grant or renewal of the tenancy.

(4)   In subsection (3)(b) above "premium" includes—

    (a)   any fine or other like sum;

    (b)   any other pecuniary consideration in addition to rent; and

    (c)   any sum paid by way of deposit, other than one which does not exceed one-sixth of the annual rent payable under the tenancy immediately after the grant or renewal in question.

**[748]**

NOTES
Sub-s (3): words in square brackets inserted by the Local Government and Housing Act 1989, s 194(1), Sch 11, para 102.

**16 Access for repairs**

It shall be an implied term of every assured tenancy that the tenant shall afford to the landlord access to the dwelling-house let on the tenancy and all reasonable facilities for executing therein any repairs which the landlord is entitled to execute.

**[749]**

*Miscellaneous*

**17 Succession to assured periodic tenancy by spouse**

(1)   In any case where—

    (a)   the sole tenant under an assured periodic tenancy dies, and

    (b)   immediately before the death, the tenant's spouse [or civil partner] was occupying the dwelling-house as his or her only or principal home, and

    (c)   the tenant was not himself a successor, as defined in subsection (2) or subsection (3) below,

then, on the death, the tenancy vests by virtue of this section in the spouse [or civil partner] (and, accordingly, does not devolve under the tenant's will or intestacy).

(2)   For the purposes of this section, a tenant is a successor in relation to a tenancy if—

    (a)   the tenancy became vested in him either by virtue of this section or under the will or intestacy of a previous tenant; or

    (b)   at some time before the tenant's death the tenancy was a joint tenancy held by himself and one or more other persons and, prior to his death, he became the sole tenant by survivorship; or

    (c)   he became entitled to the tenancy as mentioned in section 39(5) below.

(3)   For the purposes of this section, a tenant is also a successor in relation to a tenancy (in this subsection referred to as "the new tenancy") which was granted to him (alone or jointly with others) if—

    (a)   at some time before the grant of the new tenancy, he was, by virtue of subsection (2) above, a successor in relation to an earlier tenancy of the same or substantially the same dwelling-house as is let under the new tenancy; and

    (b)   at all times since he became such a successor he has been a tenant (alone or jointly with others) of the dwelling-house which is let under the new tenancy or of a dwelling-house which is substantially the same as that dwelling-house.

[(4) For the purposes of this section—
    (a) a person who was living with the tenant as his or her wife or husband shall be treated as the tenant's spouse, and
    (b) a person who was living with the tenant as if they were civil partners shall be treated as the tenant's civil partner.]

(5) If, on the death of the tenant, there is, by virtue of subsection (4) above, more than one person who fulfils the condition in subsection (1)(b) above, such one of them as may be decided by agreement or, in default of agreement, by the county court [shall for the purposes of this section be treated (according to whether that one of them is of the opposite sex to, or of the same sex as, the tenant) as the tenant's spouse or the tenant's civil partner.]

**[750]**

**NOTES**
  Sub-s (1): words in square brackets inserted by the Civil Partnership Act 2004, s 81, Sch 8, para 41(1), (2).
  Sub-s (4): substituted by the Civil Partnership Act 2004, s 81, Sch 8, para 41(1), (3).
  Sub-s (5): words in square brackets substituted by the Civil Partnership Act 2004, s 81, Sch 8, para 41(1), (4).

## 18 Provisions as to reversions on assured tenancies

(1) If at any time—
    (a) a dwelling-house is for the time being lawfully let on an assured tenancy, and
    (b) the landlord under the assured tenancy is himself a tenant under a superior tenancy; and
    (c) the superior tenancy comes to an end,
then, subject to subsection (2) below, the assured tenancy shall continue in existence as a tenancy held of the person whose interest would, apart from the continuance of the assured tenancy, entitle him to actual possession of the dwelling-house at that time.

(2) Subsection (1) above does not apply to an assured tenancy if the interest which, by virtue of that subsection, would become that of the landlord, is such that, by virtue of Schedule 1 to this Act, the tenancy could not be an assured tenancy.

(3) Where, by virtue of any provision of this Part of this Act, an assured tenancy which is a periodic tenancy (including a statutory periodic tenancy) continues beyond the beginning of a reversionary tenancy which was granted (whether before, on or after the commencement of this Act) so as to begin on or after—
    (a) the date on which the previous contractual assured tenancy came to an end, or
    (b) a date on which, apart from any provision of this Part, the periodic tenancy could have been brought to an end by the landlord by notice to quit,
the reversionary tenancy shall have effect as if it had been granted subject to the periodic tenancy.

(4) The reference in subsection (3) above to the previous contractual assured tenancy applies only where the periodic tenancy referred to in that subsection is a statutory periodic tenancy and is a reference to the fixed-term tenancy which immediately preceded the statutory periodic tenancy.

**[751]**

## 19 Restriction on levy of distress for rent

*(1) Subject to subsection (2) below, no distress for the rent of any dwelling-house let on an assured tenancy shall be levied except with the leave of the county court; and, with respect to any application for such leave, the court shall have the same powers with respect to adjournment, stay, suspension, postponement and otherwise as are conferred by section 9 above in relation to proceedings for possession of such a dwelling-house.*

*(2) Nothing in subsection (1) above applies to distress levied under section 102 of the County Courts Act 1984.*

**[752]**

**NOTES**
  Repealed by the Tribunals, Courts and Enforcement Act 2007, ss 86, 146, Sch 14, para 45, Sch 23, Pt 4, as from a day to be appointed.

CHAPTER II
ASSURED SHORTHOLD TENANCIES

**[19A Assured shorthold tenancies: post-Housing Act 1996 tenancies**
An assured tenancy which—
    (a) is entered into on or after the day on which section 96 of the Housing Act 1996 comes into force (otherwise than pursuant to a contract made before that day), or

(b)    comes into being by virtue of section 5 above on the coming to an end of an assured
        tenancy within paragraph (a) above,

is an assured shorthold tenancy unless it falls within any paragraph in Schedule 2A to this Act.]

[753]

NOTES
    Inserted by the Housing Act 1996, s 96(1).

## [20   Assured shorthold tenancies: pre-Housing Act 1996 tenancies

(1)    Subject to subsection (3) below, an assured tenancy which is not one to which section 19A
above applies is an assured shorthold tenancy if—
    (a)    it is a fixed term tenancy granted for a term certain of not less than six months,
    (b)    there is no power for the landlord to determine the tenancy at any time earlier than six
            months from the beginning of the tenancy, and
    (c)    a notice in respect of it is served as mentioned in subsection (2) below.]

(2)    The notice referred to in subsection (1)(c) above is one which—
    (a)    is in such form as may be prescribed;
    (b)    is served before the assured tenancy is entered into;
    (c)    is served by the person who is to be the landlord under the assured tenancy on the person
            who is to be the tenant under that tenancy; and
    (d)    states that the assured tenancy to which it relates is to be a shorthold tenancy.

(3)    Notwithstanding anything in subsection (1) above, where—
    (a)    immediately before a tenancy (in this subsection referred to as "the new tenancy") is
            granted, the person to whom it is granted or, as the case may be, at least one of the
            persons to whom it is granted was a tenant under an assured tenancy which was not a
            shorthold tenancy, and
    (b)    the new tenancy is granted by the person who, immediately before the beginning of the
            tenancy, was the landlord under the assured tenancy referred to in paragraph (a) above,

the new tenancy cannot be an assured shorthold tenancy.

(4)    Subject to subsection (5) below, if, on the coming to an end of an assured shorthold tenancy
(including a tenancy which was an assured shorthold but ceased to be assured before it came to an
end), a new tenancy of the same or substantially the same premises comes into being under which
the landlord and the tenant are the same as at the coming to an end of the earlier tenancy, then, if and
so long as the new tenancy is an assured tenancy, it shall be an assured shorthold tenancy, whether or
not it fulfils the conditions in paragraphs (a) to (c) of subsection (1) above.

(5)    Subsection (4) above does not apply if, before the new tenancy is entered into (or, in the
case of a statutory periodic tenancy, takes effect in possession), the landlord serves notice on the
tenant that the new tenancy is not to be a shorthold tenancy.

[(5A)    Subsections (3) and (4) above do not apply where the new tenancy is one to which
section 19A above applies.]

(6)    In the case of joint landlords—
    (a)    the reference in subsection (2)(c) above to the person who is to be the landlord is a
            reference to at least one of the persons who are to be joint landlords; and
    (b)    the reference in subsection (5) above to the landlord is a reference to at least one of the
            joint landlords.

(7)    ...

[754]

NOTES
    Sub-s (1): substituted, together with section heading, by the Housing Act 1996, s 104, Sch 8, para 2(1), (3).
    Sub-s (5A): inserted by the Housing Act 1996, s 104, Sch 8, para 2(1), (4).
    Sub-s (7): repealed by the Housing Act 1996, s 227, Sch 19, Pt IV.

## [20A   Post-Housing Act 1996 tenancies: duty of landlord to provide statement as to terms of tenancy

(1)    Subject to subsection (3) below, a tenant under an assured shorthold tenancy to which
section 19A above applies may, by notice in writing, require the landlord under that tenancy to
provide him with a written statement of any term of the tenancy which—
    (a)    falls within subsection (2) below, and
    (b)    is not evidenced in writing.

(2)    The following terms of a tenancy fall within this subsection, namely—
    (a)    the date on which the tenancy began or, if it is a statutory periodic tenancy or a tenancy
            to which section 39(7) below applies, the date on which the tenancy came into being,
    (b)    the rent payable under the tenancy and the dates on which that rent is payable,

    (c)    any term providing for a review of the rent payable under the tenancy, and

    (d)    in the case of a fixed term tenancy, the length of the fixed term.

(3)    No notice may be given under subsection (1) above in relation to a term of the tenancy if—

    (a)    the landlord under the tenancy has provided a statement of that term in response to an earlier notice under that subsection given by the tenant under the tenancy, and

    (b)    the term has not been varied since the provision of the statement referred to in paragraph (a) above.

(4)    A landlord who fails, without reasonable excuse, to comply with a notice under subsection (1) above within the period of 28 days beginning with the date on which he received the notice is liable on summary conviction to a fine not exceeding level 4 on the standard scale.

(5)    A statement provided for the purposes of subsection (1) above shall not be regarded as conclusive evidence of what was agreed by the parties to the tenancy in question.

(6)    Where—

    (a)    a term of a statutory periodic tenancy is one which has effect by virtue of section 5(3)(e) above, or

    (b)    a term of a tenancy to which subsection (7) of section 39 below applies is one which has effect by virtue of subsection (6)(e) of that section,

subsection (1) above shall have effect in relation to it as if paragraph (b) related to the term of the tenancy from which it derives.

(7)    In subsections (1) and (3) above—

    (a)    references to the tenant under the tenancy shall, in the case of joint tenants, be taken to be references to any of the tenants, and

    (b)    references to the landlord under the tenancy shall, in the case of joint landlords, be taken to be references to any of the landlords.]

**[755]**

---

**NOTES**

Inserted by the Housing Act 1996, s 97.

---

**[20B    Demoted assured shorthold tenancies**

(1)    An assured tenancy is an assured shorthold tenancy to which this section applies (a demoted assured shorthold tenancy) if—

    (a)    the tenancy is created by virtue of an order of the court under section 82A of the Housing Act 1985 or section 6A of this Act (a demotion order), and

    (b)    the landlord is a registered social landlord.

(2)    At the end of the period of one year starting with the day when the demotion order takes effect a demoted assured shorthold tenancy ceases to be an assured shorthold tenancy unless subsection (3) applies.

(3)    This subsection applies if before the end of the period mentioned in subsection (2) the landlord gives notice of proceedings for possession of the dwelling house.

(4)    If subsection (3) applies the tenancy continues to be a demoted assured shorthold tenancy until the end of the period mentioned in subsection (2) or (if later) until one of the following occurs—

    (a)    the notice of proceedings for possession is withdrawn;

    (b)    the proceedings are determined in favour of the tenant;

    (c)    the period of six months beginning with the date on which the notice is given ends and no proceedings for possession have been brought.

(5)    Registered social landlord has the same meaning as in Part 1 of the Housing Act 1996.]

**[756]**

---

**NOTES**

Commencement: 30 June 2004 (in relation to England): 30 April 2005 (in relation to Wales).
Inserted by the Anti-social Behaviour Act 2003, s 15(1).

---

**21    Recovery of possession on expiry or termination of assured shorthold tenancy**

(1)    Without prejudice to any right of the landlord under an assured shorthold tenancy to recover possession of the dwelling-house let on the tenancy in accordance with Chapter I above, on or after the coming to an end of an assured shorthold tenancy which was a fixed term tenancy, a court shall make an order for possession of the dwelling-house if it is satisfied—

    (a)    that the assured shorthold tenancy has come to an end and no further assured tenancy (whether shorthold or not) is for the time being in existence, other than [an assured shorthold periodic tenancy (whether statutory or not)]; and

    (b)    the landlord or, in the case of joint landlords, at least one of them has given to the tenant not less than two months' notice [in writing] stating that he requires possession of the dwelling-house.

(2) A notice under paragraph (b) of subsection (1) above may be given before or on the day on which the tenancy comes to an end; and that subsection shall have effect notwithstanding that on the coming to an end of the fixed term tenancy a statutory periodic tenancy arises.

(3) Where a court makes an order for possession of a dwelling-house by virtue of subsection (1) above, any statutory periodic tenancy which has arisen on the coming to an end of the assured shorthold tenancy shall end (without further notice and regardless of the period) [in accordance with section 5(1A)].

(4) Without prejudice to any such right as is referred to in subsection (1) above, a court shall make an order for possession of a dwelling-house let on an assured shorthold tenancy which is a periodic tenancy if the court is satisfied—

    (a)    that the landlord or, in the case of joint landlords, at least one of them has given to the tenant a notice [in writing] stating that, after a date specified in the notice, being the last day of a period of the tenancy and not earlier than two months after the date the notice was given, possession of the dwelling-house is required by virtue of this section; and

    (b)    that the date specified in the notice under paragraph (a) above is not earlier than the earliest day on which, apart from section 5(1) above, the tenancy could be brought to an end by a notice to quit given by the landlord on the same date as the notice under paragraph (a) above.

[(4A) Where a court makes an order for possession of a dwelling-house by virtue of subsection (4) above, the assured shorthold tenancy shall end in accordance with section 5(1A).]

[(5) Where an order for possession under subsection (1) or (4) above is made in relation to a dwelling-house let on a tenancy to which section 19A above applies, the order may not be made so as to take effect earlier than—

    (a)    in the case of a tenancy which is not a replacement tenancy, six months after the beginning of the tenancy, and

    (b)    in the case of a replacement tenancy, six months after the beginning of the original tenancy.

[(5A) Subsection (5) above does not apply to an assured shorthold tenancy to which section 20B (demoted assured shorthold tenancies) applies.]

(6) In subsection (5)(b) above, the reference to the original tenancy is—

    (a)    where the replacement tenancy came into being on the coming to an end of a tenancy which was not a replacement tenancy, to the immediately preceding tenancy, and

    (b)    where there have been successive replacement tenancies, to the tenancy immediately preceding the first in the succession of replacement tenancies.

(7) For the purposes of this section, a replacement tenancy is a tenancy—

    (a)    which comes into being on the coming to an end of an assured shorthold tenancy, and

    (b)    under which, on its coming into being—

        (i)    the landlord and tenant are the same as under the earlier tenancy as at its coming to an end, and

        (ii)    the premises let are the same or substantially the same as those let under the earlier tenancy as at that time.]

        **[757]**

---

**NOTES**

Sub-s (1): words in square brackets in para (a) substituted by the Local Government and Housing Act 1989, s 194(1), Sch 11, para 103; words in square brackets in para (b) inserted by the Housing Act 1996, s 98(1), (2).

Sub-s (3): words in square brackets substituted by the Housing and Regeneration Act 2008, s 299, Sch 11, Pt 1, paras 5, 9(1), (2), subject to transitional provisions in Sch 11, Pt 1, para 14 thereto at **[1891]**.

Sub-s (4): words in square brackets in para (a) inserted by the Housing Act 1996, s 98(1), (3).

Sub-s (4A): inserted by the Housing and Regeneration Act 2008, s 299, Sch 11, Pt 1, paras 5, 9(1), (3), subject to transitional provisions in Sch 11, Pt 1, para 14 thereto at **[1891]**.

Sub-ss (5)–(7): added by the Housing Act 1996, s 99.

Sub-s (5A): inserted by the Anti-social Behaviour Act 2003, s 15(2).

---

**22 Reference of excessive rents to rent assessment committee**

(1) Subject to section 23 and subsection (2) below, the tenant under an assured shorthold tenancy … may make an application in the prescribed form to a rent assessment committee for a determination of the rent which, in the committee's opinion, the landlord might reasonably be expected to obtain under the assured shorthold tenancy.

(2) No application may be made under this section if—

    (a)    the rent payable under the tenancy is a rent previously determined under this section; …

[(aa)    the tenancy is one to which section 19A above applies and more than six months have elapsed since the beginning of the tenancy or, in the case of a replacement tenancy, since the beginning of the original tenancy; or]

(b)    the tenancy is an assured shorthold tenancy falling within subsection (4) of section 20 above (and, accordingly, is one in respect of which notice need not have been served as mentioned in subsection (2) of that section).

(3)   Where an application is made to a rent assessment committee under subsection (1) above with respect to the rent under an assured shorthold tenancy, the committee shall not make such a determination as is referred to in that subsection unless they consider—

(a)    that there is a sufficient number of similar dwelling-houses in the locality let on assured tenancies (whether shorthold or not); and

(b)    that the rent payable under the assured shorthold tenancy in question is significantly higher than the rent which the landlord might reasonably be expected to be able to obtain under the tenancy, having regard to the level of rents payable under the tenancies referred to in paragraph (a) above.

(4)   Where, on an application under this section, a rent assessment committee make a determination of a rent for an assured shorthold tenancy—

(a)    the determination shall have effect from such date as the committee may direct, not being earlier than the date of the application;

(b)    if, at any time on or after the determination takes effect, the rent which, apart from this paragraph, would be payable under the tenancy exceeds the rent so determined, the excess shall be irrecoverable from the tenant; and

(c)    no notice may be served under section 13(2) above with respect to a tenancy of the dwelling-house in question until after the first anniversary of the date on which the determination takes effect.

(5)   Subsections (4), (5) and (8) of section 14 above apply in relation to a determination of rent under this section as they apply in relation to a determination under that section and, accordingly, where subsection (5) of that section applies, any reference in subsection (4)(b) above to rent is a reference to rent exclusive of the amount attributable to rates.

[(5A)   Where—

(a)    an assured tenancy ceases to be an assured shorthold tenancy by virtue of falling within paragraph 2 of Schedule 2A to this Act, and

(b)    at the time when it so ceases to be an assured shorthold tenancy there is pending before a rent assessment committee an application in relation to it under this section,

the fact that it so ceases to be an assured shorthold tenancy shall, in relation to that application, be disregarded for the purposes of this section.]

[(6)   In subsection (2)(aa) above, the references to the original tenancy and to a replacement tenancy shall be construed in accordance with subsections (6) and (7) respectively of section 21 above.]

**[758]**

**NOTES**

Sub-s (1): words omitted repealed by the Housing Act 1996, ss 104, 227, Sch 8, para 2(1), (5), Sch 19, Pt IV.

Sub-s (2): word omitted repealed and para (aa) inserted by the Housing Act 1996, ss 100(1), (2), 227, Sch 19, Pt IV.

Sub-ss (5A), (6): inserted by the Housing Act 1996, ss 100(1), (6), 104, Sch 8, para 2(1), (6).

Regulations: the Assured Tenancies and Agricultural Occupancies (Forms) Regulations 1997, SI 1997/194 at **[3169]**.

### 23   Termination of rent assessment committee's functions

(1)   If the Secretary of State by order made by statutory instrument so provides, section 22 above shall not apply in such cases or to tenancies of dwelling-houses in such areas or in such other circumstances as may be specified in the order.

(2)   An order under this section may contain such transitional, incidental and supplementary provisions as appear to the Secretary of State to be desirable.

(3)   No order shall be made under this section unless a draft of the order has been laid before, and approved by a resolution of, each House of Parliament.

**[759]**

CHAPTER III
ASSURED AGRICULTURAL OCCUPANCIES

### 24   Assured agricultural occupancies

(1)   A tenancy or licence of a dwelling-house is for the purposes of this Part of this Act an "assured agricultural occupancy" if—

(a)   it is of a description specified in subsection (2) below; and

(b)   by virtue of any provision of Schedule 3 to this Act the agricultural worker condition is for the time being fulfilled with respect to the dwelling-house subject to the tenancy or licence.

(2)   The following are the tenancies and licences referred to in subsection (1)(a) above—

(a)   an assured tenancy which is not an assured shorthold tenancy;

(b)   a tenancy which does not fall within paragraph (a) above by reason only of paragraph 3[, 3A, 3B] or paragraph 7 of Schedule 1 to this Act ([or more than one of those paragraphs]) [and is not an excepted tenancy]; and

(c)   a licence under which a person has the exclusive occupation of a dwelling-house as a separate dwelling and which, if it conferred a sufficient interest in land to be a tenancy, would be a tenancy falling within paragraph (a) or paragraph (b) above.

[(2A)   For the purposes of subsection (2)(b) above, a tenancy is an excepted tenancy if it is—

(a)   a tenancy of an agricultural holding within the meaning of the Agricultural Holdings Act 1986 in relation to which that Act applies, or

(b)   a farm business tenancy within the meaning of the Agricultural Tenancies Act 1995.]

(3)   For the purposes of Chapter I above and the following provisions of this Chapter, every assured agricultural occupancy which is not an assured tenancy shall be treated as if it were such a tenancy and any reference to a tenant, a landlord or any other expression appropriate to a tenancy shall be construed accordingly; but the provisions of Chapter I above shall have effect in relation to every assured agricultural occupancy subject to the provisions of this Chapter.

(4)   Section 14 above shall apply in relation to an assured agricultural occupancy as if in subsection (1) of that section the reference to an assured tenancy were a reference to an assured agricultural occupancy.

**[760]**

**NOTES**

Sub-s (2): words in first pair of square brackets inserted and words in second pair of square brackets substituted by the References to Rating (Housing) Regulations 1990, SI 1990/434, reg 2, Schedule, para 28; words in third pair of square brackets inserted by the Housing Act 1996, s 103.

Sub-s (2A): inserted by the Housing Act 1996, s 103.

## 25  Security of tenure

(1)   If a statutory periodic tenancy arises on the coming to an end of an assured agricultural occupancy—

(a)   it shall be an assured agricultural occupancy as long as, by virtue of any provision of Schedule 3 to this Act, the agricultural worker condition is for the time being fulfilled with respect to the dwelling-house in question; and

(b)   if no rent was payable under the assured agricultural occupancy which constitutes the fixed term tenancy referred to in subsection (2) of section 5 above, subsection (3)(d) of that section shall apply as if for the words "the same as those for which rent was last payable under" there were substituted "monthly beginning on the day following the coming to an end of".

(2)   In its application to an assured agricultural occupancy, Part II of Schedule 2 to this Act shall have effect with the omission of Ground 16.

(3)   In its application to an assured agricultural occupancy, Part III of Schedule 2 to this Act shall have effect as if any reference in paragraph 2 to an assured tenancy included a reference to an assured agricultural occupancy.

(4)   If the tenant under an assured agricultural occupancy gives notice to terminate his employment then, notwithstanding anything in any agreement or otherwise, that notice shall not constitute a notice to quit as respects the assured agricultural occupancy.

(5)   Nothing in subsection (4) above affects the operation of an actual notice to quit given in respect of an assured agricultural occupancy.

**[761]**

**26**   (*Amends the Rent* (*Agriculture*) *Act 1976, s 27 at* **[180]**.)

## CHAPTER IV
## PROTECTION FROM EVICTION

## 27  Damages for unlawful eviction

(1)   This section applies if, at any time after 9th June 1988, a landlord (in this section referred to as "the landlord in default") or any person acting on behalf of the landlord in default unlawfully deprives the residential occupier of any premises of his occupation of the whole or part of the premises.

(2)   This section also applies if, at any time after 9th June 1988, a landlord (in this section referred to as "the landlord in default") or any person acting on behalf of the landlord in default—

- (a)   attempts unlawfully to deprive the residential occupier of any premises of his occupation of the whole or part of the premises, or
- (b)   knowing or having reasonable cause to believe that the conduct is likely to cause the residential occupier of any premises—
    - (i)   to give up his occupation of the premises or any part thereof, or
    - (ii)   to refrain from exercising any right or pursuing any remedy in respect of the premises or any part thereof,

    does acts likely to interfere with the peace or comfort of the residential occupier or members of his household, or persistently withdraws or withholds services reasonably required for the occupation of the premises as a residence,

and, as a result, the residential occupier gives up his occupation of the premises as a residence.

(3)   Subject to the following provisions of this section, where this section applies, the landlord in default shall, by virtue of this section, be liable to pay to the former residential occupier, in respect of his loss of the right to occupy the premises in question as his residence, damages assessed on the basis set out in section 28 below.

(4)   Any liability arising by virtue of subsection (3) above—

- (a)   shall be in the nature of a liability in tort; and
- (b)   subject to subsection (5) below, shall be in addition to any liability arising apart from this section (whether in tort, contract or otherwise).

(5)   Nothing in this section affects the right of a residential occupier to enforce any liability which arises apart from this section in respect of his loss of the right to occupy premises as his residence; but damages shall not be awarded both in respect of such a liability and in respect of a liability arising by virtue of this section on account of the same loss.

(6)   No liability shall arise by virtue of subsection (3) above if—

- (a)   before the date on which proceedings to enforce the liability are finally disposed of, the former residential occupier is reinstated in the premises in question in such circumstances that he becomes again the residential occupier of them; or
- (b)   at the request of the former residential occupier, a court makes an order (whether in the nature of an injunction or otherwise) as a result of which he is reinstated as mentioned in paragraph (a) above;

and, for the purposes of paragraph (a) above, proceedings to enforce a liability are finally disposed of on the earliest date by which the proceedings (including any proceedings on or in consequence of an appeal) have been determined and any time for appealing or further appealing has expired, except that if any appeal is abandoned, the proceedings shall be taken to be disposed of on the date of the abandonment.

(7)   If, in proceedings to enforce a liability arising by virtue of subsection (3) above, it appears to the court—

- (a)   that, prior to the event which gave rise to the liability, the conduct of the former residential occupier or any person living with him in the premises concerned was such that it is reasonable to mitigate the damages for which the landlord in default would otherwise be liable, or
- (b)   that, before the proceedings were begun, the landlord in default offered to reinstate the former residential occupier in the premises in question and either it was unreasonable of the former residential occupier to refuse that offer or, if he had obtained alternative accommodation before the offer was made, it would have been unreasonable of him to refuse that offer if he had not obtained that accommodation,

the court may reduce the amount of damages which would otherwise be payable to such amount as it thinks appropriate.

(8)   In proceedings to enforce a liability arising by virtue of subsection (3) above, it shall be a defence for the defendant to prove that he believed, and had reasonable cause to believe—

- (a)   that the residential occupier had ceased to reside in the premises in question at the time when he was deprived of occupation as mentioned in subsection (1) above or, as the case may be, when the attempt was made or the acts were done as a result of which he gave up his occupation of those premises; or
- (b)   that, where the liability would otherwise arise by virtue only of the doing of acts or the withdrawal or withholding of services, he had reasonable grounds for doing the acts or withdrawing or withholding the services in question.

(9)   In this section—

- (a)   "residential occupier", in relation to any premises, has the same meaning as in section 1 of the 1977 Act;
- (b)   "the right to occupy", in relation to a residential occupier, includes any restriction on the right of another person to recover possession of the premises in question;

PART I
STATUTES

   (c)   "landlord", in relation to a residential occupier, means the person who, but for the occupier's right to occupy, would be entitled to occupation of the premises and any superior landlord under whom that person derives title;

   (d)   "former residential occupier", in relation to any premises, means the person who was the residential occupier until he was deprived of or gave up his occupation as mentioned in subsection (1) or subsection (2) above (and, in relation to a former residential occupier, "the right to occupy" and "landlord" shall be construed accordingly).

**[762]**

**NOTES**
1977 Act: Protection from Eviction Act 1977.

## 28  The measure of damages

(1)   The basis for the assessment of damages referred to in section 27(3) above is the difference in value, determined as at the time immediately before the residential occupier ceased to occupy the premises in question as his residence, between—

   (a)   the value of the interest of the landlord in default determined on the assumption that the residential occupier continues to have the same right to occupy the premises as before that time; and

   (b)   the value of that interest determined on the assumption that the residential occupier has ceased to have that right.

(2)   In relation to any premises, any reference in this section to the interest of the landlord in default is a reference to his interest in the building in which the premises in question are comprised (whether or not that building contains any other premises) together with its curtilage.

(3)   For the purposes of the valuations referred to in subsection (1) above, it shall be assumed—

   (a)   that the landlord in default is selling his interest on the open market to a willing buyer;

   (b)   that neither the residential occupier nor any member of his family wishes to buy; and

   (c)   that it is unlawful to carry out any substantial development of any of the land in which the landlord's interest subsists or to demolish the whole or part of any building on that land.

(4)   In this section "the landlord in default" has the same meaning as in section 27 above and subsection (9) of that section applies in relation to this section as it applies in relation to that.

(5)   Section 113 of the Housing Act 1985 (meaning of "members of a person's family") applies for the purposes of subsection (3)(b) above.

(6)   The reference in subsection (3)(c) above to substantial development of any of the land in which the landlord's interest subsists is a reference to any development other than—

   (a)   development for which planning permission is granted by a general development order for the time being in force and which is carried out so as to comply with any condition or limitation subject to which planning permission is so granted; or

   (b)   a change of use resulting in the building referred to in subsection (2) above or any part of it being used as, or as part of, one or more dwelling-houses;

and in this subsection "general development order" [has the same meaning given in section 56(6) of the Town and Country Planning Act 1990] and other expressions have the same meaning as in that Act.

**[763]**

**NOTES**
Sub-s (6): words in square brackets substituted by the Planning (Consequential Provisions) Act 1990, s 4, Sch 2, para 79(1).

**29–32**   (*Ss 29, 30 amend the Protection from Eviction Act 1977, ss 1, 3, 4 at* **[339]**, **[341]**, **[343]***; s 31 inserts s 3A of that Act at* **[342]***; s 32 amends s 5 of that Act at* **[344]**.)

## 33  Interpretation of Chapter IV and the 1977 Act

(1)   In this Chapter "the 1977 Act" means the Protection from Eviction Act 1977.

(2), (3)   ...

**[764]**

**NOTES**
Sub-ss (2), (3): amend the Protection from Eviction Act 1977, s 8 at **[347]**.

CHAPTER V
## PHASING OUT OF RENT ACTS AND OTHER TRANSITIONAL PROVISIONS

**34  New protected tenancies and agricultural occupancies restricted to special cases**

(1)   A tenancy which is entered into on or after the commencement of this Act cannot be a protected tenancy, unless—

(a)   it is entered into in pursuance of a contract made before the commencement of this Act; or

(b)   it is granted to a person (alone or jointly with others) who, immediately before the tenancy was granted, was a protected or statutory tenant and is so granted by the person who at that time was the landlord (or one of the joint landlords) under the protected or statutory tenancy; or

(c)   it is granted to a person (alone or jointly with others) in the following circumstances—

(i)   prior to the grant of the tenancy, an order for possession of a dwelling-house was made against him (alone or jointly with others) on the court being satisfied as mentioned in section 98(1)(a) of, or Case 1 in Schedule 16 to, the Rent Act 1977 or Case 1 in Schedule 4 to the Rent (Agriculture) Act 1976 (suitable alternative accommodation available); and

(ii)   the premises which constitute the suitable alternative accommodation as to which the court was so satisfied; and

(iii)   in the proceedings for possession the court considered that, in the circumstances, the grant of an assured tenancy would not afford the required security and, accordingly, directed that the tenancy would be a protected tenancy; or

[(d)   it is a tenancy under which the interest of the landlord was at the time the tenancy was granted held by [the Commission for the New Towns or a development] corporation, within the meaning of section 80 of the Housing Act 1985, and, before the date which has effect by virtue of paragraph (a) or paragraph (b) of subsection (4) of section 38 below, ceased to be so held by virtue of a disposal by the Commission for the New Towns made pursuant to a direction under section 37 of the New Towns Act 1981].

(2)   In subsection (1)(b) above "protected tenant" and "statutory tenant" do not include—

(a)   a tenant under a protected shorthold tenancy;

(b)   a protected or statutory tenant of a dwelling-house which was let under a protected shorthold tenancy which ended before the commencement of this Act and in respect of which at that commencement either there has been no grant of a further tenancy or any grant of a further tenancy has been to the person who, immediately before the grant, was in possession of the dwelling-house as a protected or statutory tenant;

and in this subsection "protected shorthold tenancy" includes a tenancy which, in proceedings for possession under Case 19 in Schedule 15 to the Rent Act 1977, is treated as a protected shorthold tenancy.

(3)   In any case where—

(a)   by virtue of subsections (1) and (2) above, a tenancy entered into on or after the commencement of this Act is an assured tenancy, but

(b)   apart from subsection (2) above, the effect of subsection (1)(b) above would be that the tenancy would be a protected tenancy, and

(c)   the landlord and the tenant under the tenancy are the same as at the coming to an end of the protected or statutory tenancy which, apart from subsection (2) above, would fall within subsection (1)(b) above,

the tenancy shall be an assured shorthold tenancy (whether or not[, in the case of a tenancy to which the provision applies,] it fulfils the conditions in section 20(1) above) unless, before the tenancy is entered into, the landlord serves notice on the tenant that it is not to be a shorthold tenancy.

(4)   A licence or tenancy which is entered into on or after the commencement of this Act cannot be a relevant licence or relevant tenancy for the purposes of the Rent (Agriculture) Act 1976 (in this subsection referred to as "the 1976 Act") unless—

(a)   it is entered into in pursuance of a contract made before the commencement of this Act; or

(b)   it is granted to a person (alone or jointly with others) who, immediately before the licence or tenancy was granted, was a protected occupier or statutory tenant, within the meaning of the 1976 Act, and is so granted by the person who at that time was the landlord or licensor (or one of the joint landlords or licensors) under the protected occupancy or statutory tenancy in question.

(5)   Except as provided in subsection (4) above, expressions used in this section have the same meaning as in the Rent Act 1977.

**NOTES**
Sub-s (1): para (d) substituted by the Local Government and Housing Act 1989, s 194(1), Sch 11, para 104; words in square brackets in para (d) substituted by the Housing and Regeneration Act 2008 (Consequential Provisions) Order 2008, SI 2008/3002, art 4, Sch 1, paras 36, 37, subject to transitional provisions and savings in Sch 2 thereto.
Sub-s (3): words in square brackets inserted by the Housing Act 1996, s 104, Sch 8, para 2(1), (7).

### 35 Removal of special regimes for tenancies of housing associations etc

(1) In this section "housing association tenancy" has the same meaning as in Part VI of the Rent Act 1977.

(2) A tenancy which is entered into on or after the commencement of this Act cannot be a housing association tenancy unless—

(a) it is entered into in pursuance of a contract made before the commencement of this Act; or

(b) it is granted to a person (alone or jointly with others) who, immediately before the tenancy was granted, was a tenant under a housing association tenancy and is so granted by the person who at that time was the landlord under that housing association tenancy; or

(c) it is granted to a person (alone or jointly with others) in the following circumstances—

    (i) prior to the grant of the tenancy, an order for possession of a dwelling-house was made against him (alone or jointly with others) on the court being satisfied as mentioned in paragraph (b) or paragraph (c) of subsection (2) of section 84 of the Housing Act 1985; and

    (ii) the tenancy is of the premises which constitute the suitable accommodation as to which the court was so satisfied; and

    (iii) in the proceedings for possession the court directed that the tenancy would be a housing association tenancy; or

[(d) it is a tenancy under which the interest of the landlord was at the time the tenancy was granted held by [the Commission for the New Towns or a development] corporation, within the meaning of section 80 of the Housing Act 1985, and, before the date which has effect by virtue of paragraph (a) or paragraph (b) of subsection (4) of section 38 below, ceased to be so held by virtue of a disposal by the Commission for the New Towns made pursuant to a direction under section 37 of the New Towns Act 1981].

(3) Where, on or after the commencement of this Act, a [registered social landlord, within the meaning of the Housing Act 1985 (see section 5(4) and (5) of that Act)], grants a secure tenancy pursuant to an obligation under section 554(2A) of the Housing Act 1985 (as set out in Schedule 17 to this Act) then, in determining whether that tenancy is a housing association tenancy, it shall be assumed for the purposes only of section 86(2)(b) of the Rent Act 1977 (tenancy would be a protected tenancy but for section 15 or 16 of that Act) that the tenancy was granted before the commencement of this Act.

(4) [Subject to section 38(4A) below] a tenancy or licence which is entered into on or after the commencement of this Act cannot be a secure tenancy unless—

(a) the interest of the landlord belongs to a local authority, a [development] corporation or an urban development corporation, all within the meaning of section 80 of the Housing Act 1985, [or a housing action trust established under Part III of this Act]; or

(b) the interest of the landlord belongs to a housing co-operative within the meaning of section 27B of the Housing Act 1985 (agreements between local housing authorities and housing co-operatives) and the tenancy or licence is of a dwelling-house comprised in a housing co-operative agreement falling within that section; or

[(ba) the interest of the landlord belongs to the Homes and Communities Agency or the Welsh Ministers and the tenancy or licence falls within section 80(2A) to (2E) of the Housing Act 1985; or]

(c) it is entered into in pursuance of a contract made before the commencement of this Act; or

(d) it is granted to a person (alone or jointly with others) who, immediately before it was entered into, was a secure tenant and is so granted by the body which at that time was the landlord or licensor under the secure tenancy; or

(e) it is granted to a person (alone or jointly with others) in the following circumstances—

    (i) prior to the grant of the tenancy or licence, an order for possession of a dwelling-house was made against him (alone or jointly with others) on the court being satisfied as mentioned in paragraph (b) or paragraph (c) of subsection (2) of section 84 of the Housing Act 1985; and

    (ii) the tenancy or licence is of the premises which constitute the suitable accommodation as to which the court was so satisfied; and

    (iii) in the proceedings for possession the court considered that, in the circumstances, the grant of an assured tenancy would not afford the required security and, accordingly, directed that the tenancy or licence would be a secure tenancy; or

(f)    it is granted pursuant to an obligation under section 554(2A) of the Housing Act 1985 (as set out in Schedule 17 to this Act).

(5)    If, on or after the commencement of this Act, the interest of the landlord under a protected or statutory tenancy becomes held by a housing association, a housing trust [or the Housing Corporation], [or, where that interest becomes held by him as the result of the exercise by him of functions under Part III of the Housing Association Act 1985, the Secretary of State,] nothing in the preceding provisions of this section shall prevent the tenancy from being a housing association tenancy or a secure tenancy and, accordingly, in such a case section 80 of the Housing Act 1985 (and any enactment which refers to that section) shall have effect without regard to the repeal of provisions of that section effected by this Act.

(6)    In subsection (5) above "housing association" and "housing trust" have the same meaning as in the Housing Act 1985.

**[766]**

**NOTES**

Sub-s (2): para (d) substituted by the Local Government and Housing Act 1989, s 194(1), Sch 11, para 105; words in square brackets in para (d) substituted by the Housing and Regeneration Act 2008 (Consequential Provisions) Order 2008, SI 2008/3002, art 4, Sch 1, paras 36, 38(1), (2), subject to transitional provisions and savings in Sch 2 thereto.

Sub-s (3): words in square brackets substituted by the Housing Act 1996 (Consequential Provisions) Order 1996, SI 1996/2325, art 5, Sch 2, para 18(1), (2).

Sub-s (4): words in first pair of square brackets inserted by the Local Government and Housing Act 1989, s 194(1), Sch 11, para 105(2); word in second pair of square brackets substituted and para (ba) inserted by SI 2008/3002, art 4, Sch 1, paras 36, 38(1), (3), subject to transitional provisions and savings in Sch 2 thereto; words in third pair of square brackets substituted by the Government of Wales Act 1998, s 129, Sch 15, para 60.

Sub-s (5): words in first pair of square brackets substituted by the Government of Wales Act 1998, s 140(1), Sch 16, paras 59, 60; words in second pair of square brackets inserted by the Government of Wales Act 1998 (Housing) (Amendments) Order 1999, SI 1999/61, art 2, Schedule, para 3(1), (2).

Modification: in sub-s (5) the reference to the Housing Corporation shall be treated as a reference to the Regulator of Social Housing: see the Transfer of Housing Corporation Functions (Modifications and Transitional Provisions) Order 2008, SI 2008/2839, arts 1(2), 3, 6, Schedule.

## 36    New restricted contracts limited to transitional cases

(1)    A tenancy or other contract entered into after the commencement of this Act cannot be a restricted contract for the purposes of the Rent Act 1977 unless it is entered into in pursuance of a contract made before the commencement of this Act.

(2)    If the terms of a restricted contract are varied after this Act comes into force then, subject to subsection (3) below,—

(a)    if the variation affects the amount of the rent which, under the contract, is payable for the dwelling in question, the contract shall be treated as a new contract entered into at the time of the variation (and subsection (1) above shall have effect accordingly); and

(b)    if the variation does not affect the amount of the rent which, under the contract, is so payable, nothing in this section shall affect the determination of the question whether the variation is such as to give rise to a new contract.

(3)    Any reference in subsection (2) above to a variation affecting the amount of the rent which, under a contract, is payable for a dwelling does not include a reference to—

(a)    a reduction or increase effected under section 78 of the Rent Act 1977 (power of rent tribunal); or

(b)    a variation which is made by the parties and has the effect of making the rent expressed to be payable under the contract the same as the rent for the dwelling which is entered in the register under section 79 of the Rent Act 1977.

(4)    ...

(5)    In this section "rent" has the same meaning as in Part V of the Rent Act 1977.

**[767]**

**NOTES**

Sub-s (4): amends the Rent Act 1977, s 81A at **[262]**.

## 37    No further assured tenancies under Housing Act 1980

(1)    A tenancy which is entered into on or after the commencement of this Act cannot be an assured tenancy for the purposes of sections 56 to 58 of the Housing Act 1980 (in this section referred to as a "1980 Act tenancy").

(2)    In any case where—

PART I
STATUTES

(a) before the commencement of this Act, a tenant under a 1980 Act tenancy made an application to the court under section 24 of the Landlord and Tenant Act 1954 (for the grant of a new tenancy), and

(b) at the commencement of this Act the 1980 Act tenancy is continuing by virtue of that section or of any provision of Part IV of the said Act of 1954,

section 1(3) of this Act shall not apply to the 1980 Act tenancy.

(3) If, in a case falling within subsection (2) above, the court makes an order for the grant of a new tenancy under section 29 of the Landlord and Tenant Act 1954, that tenancy shall be an assured tenancy for the purposes of this Act.

(4) In any case where—

(a) before the commencement of this Act a contract was entered into for the grant of a 1980 Act tenancy, but

(b) at the commencement of this Act the tenancy had not been granted,

the contract shall have effect as a contract for the grant of an assured tenancy (within the meaning of this Act).

(5) In relation to an assured tenancy falling within subsection (3) above or granted pursuant to a contract falling within subsection (4) above, Part I of Schedule 1 to this Act shall have effect as if it consisted only of paragraphs 11 and 12; and, if the landlord granting the tenancy is a fully mutual housing association, then, so long as that association remains the landlord under that tenancy (and under any statutory periodic tenancy which arises on the coming to an end of that tenancy), the said paragraph 12 shall have effect in relation to that tenancy with the omission of sub-paragraph (1)(h).

(6) Any reference in this section to a provision of the Landlord and Tenant Act 1954 is a reference only to that provision as applied by section 58 of the Housing Act 1980.

**[768]**

---

**NOTES**

Housing Act 1980, ss 56–58: repealed by s 140(2) of, and Sch 18 to, this Act, except in relation to any tenancy to which, by virtue of sub-s (2) above, s 1(3) at **[729]** does not apply.

## 38 Transfer of existing tenancies from public to private sector

(1) The provisions of subsection (3) below apply in relation to a tenancy which was entered into before, or pursuant to a contract made before, the commencement of this Act if,—

(a) at that commencement or, if it is later, at the time it is entered into, the interest of the landlord is held by a public body (within the meaning of subsection (5) below); and

(b) at some time after that commencement, the interest of the landlord ceases to be so held.

(2) The provisions of subsection (3) below also apply in relation to a tenancy which was entered into before, or pursuant to a contract made before, the commencement of this Act if,—

(a) at the commencement of this Act or, if it is later, at the time it is entered into, it is a housing association tenancy; and

(b) at some time after that commencement, it ceases to be such a tenancy.

(3) [Subject to subsections (4), [[(4ZA), (4A), (4BA)]] and (4B),] below] on and after the time referred to in subsection (1)(b) or, as the case may be, subsection (2)(b) above—

(a) the tenancy shall not be capable of being a protected tenancy, a protected occupancy or a housing association tenancy;

(b) the tenancy shall not be capable of being a secure tenancy unless (and only at a time when) the interest of the landlord under the tenancy is (or is again) held by a public body; and

(c) paragraph 1 of Schedule 1 to this Act shall not apply in relation to it, and the question whether at any time thereafter it becomes (or remains) an assured tenancy shall be determined accordingly.

(4) In relation to a tenancy under which, at the commencement of this Act or, if it is later, at the time the tenancy is entered into, the interest of the landlord is held by [the Commission for the New Towns or a development] corporation, within the meaning of section 80 of the Housing Act 1985 [and which subsequently ceases to be so held by virtue of a disposal by the Commission for the New Towns made pursuant to a direction under section 37 of the New Towns Act 1981], subsections (1) and (3) above shall have effect as if any reference in subsection (1) above to the commencement of this Act were a reference to—

(a) the date on which expires the period of two years beginning on the day this Act is passed; or

(b) if the Secretary of State by order made by statutory instrument within that period so provides, such other date (whether earlier or later) as may be specified by the order for the purposes of this subsection.

[(4ZA) In relation to any time on or after the coming into force of this subsection, subsection (4) applies as if—

(a)  the references to the Commission for the New Towns were references to the new towns residuary body;

(b)  in the case of a disposal by the English new towns residuary body, the reference to section 37 of the New Towns Act 1981 were a reference to section 47 of the Housing and Regeneration Act 2008; and

(c)  in the case of a disposal by the Welsh new towns residuary body, the words "made pursuant to a direction under section 37 of the New Towns Act 1981" were omitted.]

[(4A)  Where, by virtue of a disposal falling within subsection (4) above and made before the date which has effect by virtue of paragraph (a) or paragraph (b) of that subsection, the interest of the landlord under a tenancy passes to a [registered social landlord (within the meaning of the Housing Act 1985 (see section 5(4) and (5) of that Act))], then, notwithstanding anything in subsection (3) above, so long as the tenancy continues to be held by a body which would have been specified in subsection (1) of section 80 of the Housing Act 1985 if the repeal of provisions of that section effected by this Act had not been made, the tenancy shall continue to be a secure tenancy and to be capable of being a housing association tenancy.]

[(4B)  Where, by virtue of a disposal by the Secretary of State made in the exercise by him of functions under Part III of the Housing Associations Act 1985, the interest of the landlord under a secure tenancy passes to a registered social landlord (within the meaning of the Housing Act 1985) then, notwithstanding anything in subsection (3) above, so long as the tenancy continues to be held by a body which would have been specified in subsection (1) of section 80 of the Housing Act 1985 if the repeal of provisions of that section effected by this Act had not been made, the tenancy shall continue to be a secure tenancy and to be capable of being a housing association tenancy.]

[(4BA)  The references in subsections (4A) and (4B) to a body which would have been specified in subsection (1) of section 80 of the Housing Act 1985 if the repeal of provisions of that section effected by this Act had not been made includes a reference to the new towns residuary body.]

(5)  For the purposes of this section, the interest of a landlord under a tenancy is held by a public body at a time when—

(a)  it belongs to a local authority, a [development] corporation or an urban development corporation, all within the meaning of section 80 of the Housing Act 1985 [or to the English new towns residuary body]; or

(b)  it belongs to a housing action trust established under Part III of this Act; or

(c)  …

(d)  it belongs to Her Majesty in right of the Crown or to a government department or is held in trust for Her Majesty for the purposes of a government department.

[(5A)  In this section "new towns residuary body" means—

(a)  in relation to times before the coming into force of this subsection, the Commission for the New Towns; and

(b)  in relation to other times—

  (i)  in relation to England, the Homes and Communities Agency so far as exercising functions in relation to anything transferred (or to be transferred) to it as mentioned in section 52(1)(a) to (d) of the Housing and Regeneration Act 2008 (and any reference to the English new towns residuary body shall be construed accordingly); and

  (ii)  in relation to Wales, the Welsh Ministers so far as exercising functions in relation to anything transferred (or to be transferred) to them as mentioned in section 36(1)(a)(i) to (iii) of the New Towns Act 1981 (and any reference to the Welsh new towns residuary body shall be construed accordingly).]

(6)  In this section—

(a)  "housing association tenancy" means a tenancy to which Part VI of the Rent Act 1977 applies;

(b)  "protected tenancy" has the same meaning as in that Act; and

(c)  "protected occupancy" has the same meaning as in the Rent (Agriculture) Act 1976.

**[769]**

---

**NOTES**

Sub-s (3): words in first (outer) pair of square brackets inserted by the Local Government and Housing Act 1989, s 194(1), Sch 11, para 106(1); words in second (inner) pair of square brackets substituted by the Government of Wales Act 1998 (Housing) (Amendments) Order 1999, SI 1999/61, art 2, Schedule, para 3(1), (3)(a); references in third (inner) pair of square brackets substituted by the Housing and Regeneration Act 2008 (Consequential Provisions) Order 2008, SI 2008/3002, art 4, Sch 1, paras 36, 39(1), (2), subject to transitional provisions and savings in Sch 2 thereto.

Sub-s (4): words in first pair of square brackets substituted by SI 2008/3002, art 4, Sch 1, paras 36, 39(1), (3), subject to transitional provisions and savings in Sch 2 thereto; words in second pair of square brackets inserted by the Local Government and Housing Act 1989, s 194(1), Sch 11, para 106(2).

Sub-ss (4ZA), (4BA), (5A): inserted by SI 2008/3002, art 4, Sch 1, paras 36, 39(1), (4), (5), (7), subject to transitional provisions and savings in Sch 2 thereto.

Sub-s (4A): inserted by the Local Government and Housing Act 1989, s 194(1), Sch 11, para 106; words in square brackets substituted by the Housing Act 1996 (Consequential Provisions) Order 1996, SI 1996/2325, art 5, Sch 2, para 18(1), (3).

Sub-s (4B): inserted by SI 1999/61, art 2, Schedule, para 3(1), (3)(b).

Sub-s (5): in para (a), word in first pair of square brackets substituted and words in second pair of square brackets inserted by SI 2008/3002, art 4, Sch 1, paras 36, 39(1), (6), subject to transitional provisions and savings in Sch 2 thereto; para (c) repealed by the Government of Wales Act 1998, ss 131, 152, Sch 18, Pt IV.

Order: the Commission for the New Towns (Specified Date) (Tenancies) Order 1990, SI 1990/1980 (specifying 31 March 1996 as the "specified date" for the purposes of sub-s (4)(b) above).

## 39 Statutory tenants: succession

(1) ...

(2) Where the person who is the original tenant, within the meaning of Part I of Schedule 1 to the Rent Act 1977, dies after the commencement of this Act, that Part shall have effect subject to the amendments in Part I of Schedule 4 to this Act.

(3) Where subsection (2) above does not apply but the person who is the first successor, within the meaning of Part I of Schedule 1 to the Rent Act 1977, dies after the commencement of this Act, that Part shall have effect subject to the amendments in paragraphs 5 to 9 of Part I of Schedule 4 to this Act.

(4) In any case where the original occupier, within the meaning of section 4 of the Rent (Agriculture) Act 1976 (statutory tenants and tenancies) dies after the commencement of this Act, that section shall have effect subject to the amendments in Part II of Schedule 4 to this Act.

(5) In any case where, by virtue of any provision of—

    (a)   Part I of Schedule 1 to the Rent Act 1977, as amended in accordance with subsection (2) or subsection (3) above, or

    (b)   section 4 of the Rent (Agriculture) Act 1976, as amended in accordance with subsection (4) above,

a person (in the following provisions of this section referred to as "the successor") becomes entitled to an assured tenancy of a dwelling-house by succession, that tenancy shall be a periodic tenancy arising by virtue of this section.

(6) Where, by virtue of subsection (5) above, the successor becomes entitled to an assured periodic tenancy, that tenancy is one—

    (a)   taking effect in possession immediately after the death of the protected or statutory tenant or protected occupier (in the following provisions of this section referred to as "the predecessor") on whose death the successor became so entitled;

    (b)   deemed to have been granted to the successor by the person who, immediately before the death of the predecessor, was the landlord of the predecessor under his tenancy;

    (c)   under which the premises which are let are the same dwelling-house as, immediately before his death, the predecessor occupied under his tenancy;

    (d)   under which the periods of the tenancy are the same as those for which rent was last payable by the predecessor under his tenancy;

    (e)   under which, subject to sections 13 to 15 above, the other terms are the same as those on which, under his tenancy, the predecessor occupied the dwelling-house immediately before his death; and

    (f)   which, for the purposes of section 13(2) above, is treated as a statutory periodic tenancy;

and in paragraphs (b) to (e) above "under his tenancy", in relation to the predecessor, means under his protected tenancy or protected occupancy or in his capacity as a statutory tenant.

(7) If, immediately before the death of the predecessor, the landlord might have recovered possession of the dwelling-house under Case 19 in Schedule 15 to the Rent Act 1977, the assured periodic tenancy to which the successor becomes entitled shall be an assured shorthold tenancy (whether or not[, in the case of a tenancy to which the provision applies,] it fulfils the conditions in section 20(1) above).

(8) If, immediately before his death, the predecessor was a protected occupier or statutory tenant within the meaning of the Rent (Agriculture) Act 1976, the assured periodic tenancy to which the successor becomes entitled shall be an assured agricultural occupancy (whether or not it fulfils the conditions in section 24(1) above).

(9) Where, immediately before his death, the predecessor was a tenant under a fixed term tenancy, section 6 above shall apply in relation to the assured periodic tenancy to which the successor becomes entitled on the predecessor's death subject to the following modifications—

    (a)   for any reference to a statutory periodic tenancy there shall be substituted a reference to the assured periodic tenancy to which the successor becomes so entitled;

    (b)   in subsection (1) of that section, paragraph (a) shall be omitted and the reference in paragraph (b) to section 5(3)(e) above shall be construed as a reference to subsection (6)(e) above; and

(c)    for any reference to the coming to an end of the former tenancy there shall be substituted a reference to the date of the predecessor's death.

(10)    If and so long as a dwelling-house is subject to an assured tenancy to which the successor has become entitled by succession, section 7 above and Schedule 2 to this Act shall have effect subject to the modifications in Part III of Schedule 4 to this Act; and in that Part "the predecessor" and "the successor" have the same meaning as in this section.

[770]

**NOTES**

Sub-s (1): amends the Rent Act 1977, s 2 at **[203]**.
Sub-s (7): words in square brackets inserted by the Housing Act 1996, s 104, Sch 8, para 2(1), (8).

## CHAPTER VI
## GENERAL PROVISIONS

### 40  Jurisdiction of county courts

(1)    A county court shall have jurisdiction to hear and determine any question arising under any provision of—

    (a)    Chapters I to III and V above, or

    (b)    sections 27 and 28 above,

other than a question falling within the jurisdiction of a rent assessment committee by virtue of any such provision.

(2)    ...

(3)    Where any proceedings under any provision mentioned in subsection (1) above are being taken in a county court, the court shall have jurisdiction to hear and determine any other proceedings joined with those proceedings, notwithstanding that, apart from this subsection, those other proceedings would be outside the court's jurisdiction.

(4)    *If any person takes any proceedings under any provision mentioned in subsection (1) above in the High Court, he shall not be entitled to recover any more costs of those proceedings than those to which he would have been entitled if the proceedings had been taken in a county court: and in such a case the taxing master shall have the same power of directing on what county court scale costs are to be allowed, and of allowing any item of costs, as the judge would have had if the proceedings had been taken in a county court.*

(5)    *Subsection (4) above shall not apply where the purpose of taking the proceedings in the High Court was to enable them to be joined with any proceedings already pending before that court (not being proceedings taken under any provision mentioned in subsection (1) above).*

[771]

**NOTES**

Sub-s (2): repealed by the High Court and County Courts Jurisdiction Order 1991, SI 1991/724, art 2(8), Schedule, Pt I.
Sub-ss (4), (5): repealed by the Courts and Legal Services Act 1990, s 125(7), Sch 20, as from a day to be appointed.

### 41  Rent assessment committees: procedure and information powers

(1)    ...

(2)    The rent assessment committee to whom a matter is referred under Chapter I or Chapter II above may by notice in the prescribed form served on the landlord or the tenant require him to give to the committee, within such period of not less than fourteen days from the service of the notice as may be specified in the notice, such information as they may reasonably require for the purposes of their functions.

(3)    If any person fails without reasonable excuse to comply with a notice served on him under subsection (2) above, he shall be liable on summary conviction to a fine not exceeding level 3 on the standard scale.

(4)    Where an offence under subsection (3) above committed by a body corporate is proved to have been committed with the consent or connivance of, or to be attributable to any neglect on the part of, any director, manager or secretary or other similar officer of the body corporate or any person who was purporting to act in any such capacity, he as well as the body corporate shall be guilty of that offence and shall be liable to be proceeded against and punished accordingly.

[772]

**NOTES**

Sub-s (1): repealed by the Leasehold Reform, Housing and Urban Development Act 1993, s 187(2), Sch 22.

Regulations: the Assured Tenancies and Agricultural Occupancies (Forms) Regulations 1997, SI 1997/194 at **[3169]**.

## [41A Amounts attributable to services

In order to assist authorities to give effect to the housing benefit scheme under Part VII of the Social Security Contributions and Benefits Act 1992, where a rent is determined under section 14 or 22 above, the rent assessment committee shall note in their determination the amount (if any) of the rent which, in the opinion of the committee, is fairly attributable to the provision of services, except where that amount is in their opinion negligible; and the amount so noted may be included in the information specified in an order under section 42 below.]

**[773]**

**NOTES**
Inserted by the Social Security (Consequential Provisions) Act 1992, s 4, Sch 2, para 103.

## [41B Provision of information as to exemption from council tax

A billing authority within the meaning of Part I of the Local Government Finance Act 1992 shall, if so requested in writing by a rent officer or rent assessment committee in connection with his or their functions under any enactment, inform the rent officer or rent assessment committee in writing whether or not a particular dwelling (within the meaning of Part I of the Local Government Finance Act 1992) is, or was at any time specified in the request, an exempt dwelling for the purposes of that Part of that Act.]

**[774]**

**NOTES**
Inserted by the Local Government Finance (Housing) (Consequential Amendments) Order 1993, SI 1993/651, art 2(1), Sch 1, para 18, as substituted by SI 1993/1120.

## 42 Information as to determinations of rents

(1) The President of every rent assessment panel shall keep and make publicly available, in such manner as is specified in an order made by the Secretary of State, such information as may be so specified with respect to rents under assured tenancies and assured agricultural occupancies which have been the subject of references or applications to, or determinations by, rent assessment committees.

(2) A copy of any information certified under the hand of an officer duly authorised by the President of the rent assessment panel concerned shall be receivable in evidence in any court and in any proceedings.

(3) An order under subsection (1) above—
  (a) may prescribe the fees to be charged for the supply of a copy, including a certified copy, of any of the information kept by virtue of that subsection; and
  (b) may make different provision with respect to different cases or descriptions of case, including different provision for different areas.

(4) The power to make an order under subsection (1) above shall be exercisable by statutory instrument which shall be subject to annulment in pursuance of a resolution of either House of Parliament.

**[775]**

**NOTES**
Orders: the Assured Tenancies and Agricultural Occupancies (Rent Information) Order 1988, SI 1988/2199 at **[3072]**.

**43** (*Amends the Rent Act 1977, s 149 at* **[312]**.)

## 44 Application to Crown Property

(1) Subject to paragraph 11 of Schedule 1 to this Act and subsection (2) below, Chapters I to IV above apply in relation to premises in which there subsists, or at any material time subsisted, a Crown interest as they apply in relation to premises in relation to which no such interest subsists or ever subsisted.

(2) In Chapter IV above—
  (a) sections 27 and 28 do not bind the Crown; and
  (b) the remainder binds the Crown to the extent provided for in section 10 of the Protection from Eviction Act 1977.

(3) In this section "Crown interest" means an interest which belongs to Her Majesty in right of the Crown or of the Duchy of Lancaster or to the Duchy of Cornwall, or to a government department, or which is held in trust for Her Majesty for the purposes of a government department.

(4)   Where an interest belongs to Her Majesty in right of the Duchy of Lancaster, then, for the purposes of Chapters I to IV above, the Chancellor of the Duchy of Lancaster shall be deemed to be the owner of the interest.

[776]

### 45   Interpretation of Part I

(1)   In this Part of this Act, except where the context otherwise requires,—

"dwelling-house" may be a house or part of a house;

"fixed term tenancy" means any tenancy other than a periodic tenancy;

"fully mutual housing association" has the same meaning as in Part I of the Housing Associations Act 1985;

"landlord" includes any person from time to time deriving title under the original landlord and also includes, in relation to a dwelling-house, any person other than a tenant who is, or but for the existence of an assured tenancy would be, entitled to possession of the dwelling-house;

"let" includes "sub-let";

"prescribed" means prescribed by regulations made by the Secretary of State by statutory instrument;

"rates" includes water rates and charges but does not include an owner's drainage rate, as defined in section 63(2)(a) of the Land Drainage Act 1976;

"secure tenancy" has the meaning assigned by section 79 of the Housing Act 1985;

"statutory periodic tenancy" has the meaning assigned by section 5(7) above;

"tenancy" includes a sub-tenancy and an agreement for a tenancy or sub-tenancy; and

"tenant" includes a sub-tenant and any person deriving title under the original tenant or sub-tenant.

(2)   Subject to paragraph 11 of Schedule 2 to this Act, any reference in this Part of this Act to the beginning of a tenancy is a reference to the day on which the tenancy is entered into or, if it is later, the day on which, under the terms of any lease, agreement or other document, the tenant is entitled to possession under the tenancy.

(3)   Where two or more persons jointly constitute either the landlord or the tenant in relation to a tenancy, then, except where this Part of this Act otherwise provides, any reference to the landlord or to the tenant is a reference to all the persons who jointly constitute the landlord or the tenant, as the case may require.

(4)   For the avoidance of doubt, it is hereby declared that any reference in this Part of this Act (however expressed) to a power for a landlord to determine a tenancy does not include a reference to a power of re-entry or forfeiture for breach of any term or condition of the tenancy.

(5)   Regulations under subsection (1) above may make different provision with respect to different cases or descriptions of case, including different provision for different areas.

[777]

---

**NOTES**

Land Drainage Act 1976, s 63(2)(a): repealed, with savings, by the Water Consolidation (Consequential Provisions) Act 1991, s 3(1), Sch 3, Pt I.

Regulations: the Assured Tenancies and Agricultural Occupancies (Forms) Regulations 1997, SI 1997/194 at **[3169]** (made by virtue of the definition of "prescribed" in sub-s (1) above).

**46–114**   ((*Pts II–IV*) *in so far as unrepealed outside the scope of this work.*)

PART V
MISCELLANEOUS AND GENERAL

**115–119**   (*S 115 amends the Rent Act 1977, s 127 at* **[297]**; *s 116 amends the Landlord and Tenant Act 1985, ss 11, 14 at* **[603]**, **[606]**; *ss 117, 119 outside the scope of this work; s 118 applies to Scotland only.*)

*Rent officers*

**120**   (*Outside the scope of this work.*)

### 121   Rent officers: additional functions relating to housing benefit etc

(*1*)   *The Secretary of State may by order require rent officers to carry out such functions as may be specified in the order in connection with housing benefit and rent allowance subsidy [and applications to which [section 31 of the Housing Grants, Construction and Regeneration Act 1996 applies]].*

(*2*)   *An order under this section—*

(a)    shall be made by statutory instrument which, except in the case of the first order to be made, shall be subject to annulment in pursuance of a resolution of either House of Parliament;

(b)    may make different provision for different cases or classes of case and for different areas; and

(c)    may contain such transitional, incidental and supplementary provisions as appear to the Secretary of State to be desirable;

and the first order under this section shall not be made unless a draft of it has been laid before, and approved by a resolution of, each House of Parliament.

(3)–(6)   ...

[(7)   In this section—

"housing benefit" means housing benefit under Part VII of the Social Security Contributions and Benefits Act 1992; and

"rent allowance subsidy" has the meaning assigned to it by section 135 of the Social Security Administration Act 1992.]

**[778]**

**NOTES**

Repealed by the Housing Act 1996, s 227, Sch 19, Pt VI, except for the purposes of any benefit subsidy in relation to any benefit paid or claimed in respect of any benefit before 1 April 1997, and except in so far as it has effect for the purposes of the Housing Grants, Construction and Regeneration Act 1996, s 31; see the Housing Act 1996 (Commencement No 10 and Transitional Provisions) Order 1997, SI 1997/618, Schedule, paras 4, 6.

Sub-s (1): words in first (outer) pair of square brackets added by the Local Government and Housing Act 1989, s 110; words in second (inner) pair of square brackets substituted by the Housing Grants, Construction and Regeneration Act 1996, s 103, Sch 1, para 13.

Sub-s (3): amends the Rent Act 1977, s 63 at **[240]**.

Sub-ss (4), (6): repealed by the Social Security (Consequential Provisions) Act 1992, s 3(1), Sch 1.

Sub-s (5): repealed by the Social Security Act 1989, s 31(2), Sch 9, and repealed again by the Social Security (Consequential Provisions) Act 1992, s 3(1), Sch 1.

Sub-s (7): substituted by the Social Security (Consequential Provisions) Act 1992, s 4, Sch 2, para 104.

Social Security Administration Act 1992, s 135: repealed by the Housing Act 1996, s 227, Sch 19, Pt VI, and replaced by the Social Security Administration Act 1992, ss 140A–140D.

Orders: the Rent Officers (Housing Renewal Grants Functions) Order 1997, SI 1997/778.

**122–137**   (Ss 122, 123, 129–133, 136, 137 in so far as unrepealed outside the scope of this work; s 124 inserts the Housing Act 1985, ss 153A, 153B at **[511]**, **[512]**; s 125 amends s 37 of the 1985 Act; s 126 amends s 157 of the 1985 Act at **[520]**; s 127 amends ss 171B, 171C of that Act at **[537]**, **[538]**; ss 128, 134, 135 apply to Scotland only.)

*Supplementary*

**138   Financial provisions**

(1)   There shall be paid out of money provided by Parliament—

(a), (b) (*outside the scope of this work.*)

(c)    any other expenses of the Secretary of State under this Act; and

(d)    any increase attributable to this Act in the sums so payable under any other enactment.

(2)   Any sums received by the Secretary of State under this Act, other than those required to be paid into the National Loans Fund, shall be paid into the Consolidated Fund.

**[779]**

**139   Application to Isles of Scilly**

(1)   This Act applies to the Isles of Scilly subject to such exceptions, adaptations and modifications as the Secretary of State may by order direct.

(2)   The power to make an order under this section shall be exercisable by statutory instrument which shall be subject to annulment in pursuance of a resolution of either House of Parliament

**[780]**

**140**   (*Outside the scope of this work.*)

**141   Short title, commencement and extent**

(1)   This Act may be cited as the Housing Act 1988.

(2)   The provisions of Parts II and IV of this Act and sections 119, 122, 124, 128, 129, 135 and 140 above shall come into force on such day as the Secretary of State may by order made by statutory instrument appoint, and different days may be so appointed for different provisions or for different purposes.

(3)   Part I and this Part of this Act, other than sections 119, 122, 124, 128, 129, 132, 133, 134, 135 and 138 onwards, shall come into force at the expiry of the period of two months beginning on the day it is passed; and any reference in those provisions to the commencement of this Act shall be construed accordingly.

(4)   An order under subsection (2) above may make such transitional provisions as appear to the Secretary of State necessary or expedient in connection with the provisions brought into force by the order.

(5)   Parts I, III and IV of this Act and this Part, except sections 118, 128, 132, 134, 135 and 137 onwards, extend to England and Wales only.

(6)   This Act does not extend to Northern Ireland.

[781]

**NOTES**
   Orders: the Housing Act 1988 (Commencement No 1) Order 1988, SI 1988/2056; the Housing Act 1988 (Commencement No 2) Order 1988, SI 1988/2152; the Housing Act 1988 (Commencement No 3) Order 1989, SI 1989/203; the Housing Act 1988 (Commencement No 4) Order 1989, SI 1989/404; the Housing Act 1988 (Commencement No 5 and Transitional Provisions) Order 1991, SI 1991/324; the Housing Act 1988 (Commencement No 6) Order 1992, SI 1992/324.

## SCHEDULES

## SCHEDULE 1
### TENANCIES WHICH CANNOT BE ASSURED TENANCIES
Section 1

### PART I
### THE TENANCIES
*Tenancies entered into before commencement*

1.   A tenancy which is entered into before, or pursuant to a contract made before, the commencement of this Act.

*Tenancies of dwelling-houses with high rateable values*

[2.—(1)   A tenancy—
   (a)   which is entered into on or after 1st April 1990 (otherwise than, where the dwelling-house had a rateable value on 31st March 1990, in pursuance of a contract made before 1st April 1990), and
   (b)   under which the rent payable for the time being is payable at a rate exceeding £25,000 a year.

(2)   In sub-paragraph (1) "rent" does not include any sum payable by the tenant as is expressed (in whatever terms) to be payable in respect of rates, [council tax,] services, management, repairs, maintenance or insurance, unless it could not have been regarded by the parties to the tenancy as a sum so payable.

2A.   A tenancy—
   (a)   which was entered into before 1st April 1990 or on or after that date in pursuance of a contract made before that date, and
   (b)   under which the dwelling-house had a rateable value on the 31st March 1990 which, if it is in Greater London, exceeded £1,500 and, if it is elsewhere, exceeded £750.]

*Tenancies at a low rent*

[3.   A tenancy under which for the time being no rent is payable.

3A.   A tenancy—
   (a)   which is entered into on or after 1st April 1990 (otherwise than, where the dwelling-house had a rateable value on 31st March 1990, in pursuance of a contract made before 1st April 1990), and
   (b)   under which the rent payable for the time being is payable at a rate of, if the dwelling-house is in Greater London, £1,000 or less a year and, if it is elsewhere, £250 or less a year.

3B.   A tenancy—
   (a)   which was entered into before 1st April 1990 or where the dwelling-house had a rateable value on 31st March 1990, on or after 1st April 1990 in pursuance of a contract made before that date, and
   (b)   under which the rent for the time being payable is less than two-thirds of the rateable value of the dwelling-house on 31st March 1990.

3C.   Paragraph 2(2) above applies for the purposes of paragraphs 3, 3A and 3B as it applies for the purposes of paragraph 2(1).]

### Business tenancies

4.   A tenancy to which Part II of the Landlord and Tenant Act 1954 applies (business tenancies).

### Licensed premises

5.   A tenancy under which the dwelling-house consists of or comprises [premises which, by virtue of a premises licence under the Licensing Act 2003, may be used for the supply of alcohol (within the meaning of section 14 of that Act)] for consumption on the premises.

### Tenancies of agricultural land

6.—(1)   A tenancy under which agricultural land, exceeding two acres, is let together with the dwelling-house.

(2)   In this paragraph "agricultural land" has the meaning set out in section 26(3)(a) of the General Rate Act 1967 (exclusion of agricultural land and premises from liability for rating).

### [Tenancies of agricultural holdings etc

7.—(1)   A tenancy under which the dwelling-house—
   (a)   is comprised in an agricultural holding, and
   (b)   is occupied by the person responsible for the control (whether as tenant or as servant or agent of the tenant) of the farming of the holding.

(2)   A tenancy under which the dwelling-house—
   (a)   is comprised in the holding held under a farm business tenancy, and
   (b)   is occupied by the person responsible for the control (whether as tenant or as servant or agent of the tenant) of the management of the holding.

(3)   In this paragraph—
   "agricultural holding" means any agricultural holding within the meaning of the Agricultural Holdings Act 1986 held under a tenancy in relation to which that Act applies, and
   "farm business tenancy" and "holding", in relation to such a tenancy, have the same meaning as in the Agricultural Tenancies Act 1995.]

### Lettings to students

8.—(1)   A tenancy which is granted to a person who is pursuing, or intends to pursue, a course of study provided by a specified educational institution and is so granted either by that institution or by another specified institution or body of persons.

(2)   In sub-paragraph (1) above "specified" means specified, or of a class specified, for the purposes of this paragraph by regulations made by the Secretary of State by statutory instrument.

(3)   A statutory instrument made in the exercise of the power conferred by sub-paragraph (2) above shall be subject to annulment in pursuance of a resolution of either House of Parliament.

### Holiday lettings

9.   A tenancy the purpose of which is to confer on the tenant the right to occupy the dwelling-house for a holiday.

### Resident landlords

10.—(1)   A tenancy in respect of which the following conditions are fulfilled—
   (a)   that the dwelling-house forms part only of a building and, except in a case where the dwelling-house also forms part of a flat, the building is not a purpose-built block of flats; and
   (b)   that, subject to Part III of this Schedule, the tenancy was granted by an individual who, at the time when the tenancy was granted, occupied as his only or principal home another dwelling-house which,—
      (i)   in the case mentioned in paragraph (a) above, also forms part of the flat; or
      (ii)   in any other case, also forms part of the building; and
   (c)   that, subject to Part III of this Schedule, at all times since the tenancy was granted the interest of the landlord under the tenancy has belonged to an individual who, at the time he owned that interest, occupied as his only or principal home another dwelling-house which,—
      (i)   in the case mentioned in paragraph (a) above, also formed part of the flat; or
      (ii)   in any other case, also formed part of the building; and
   (d)   that the tenancy is not one which is excluded from this sub-paragraph by sub-paragraph (3) below.

(2)    If a tenancy was granted by two or more persons jointly, the reference in sub-paragraph (1)(b) above to an individual is a reference to any one of those persons and if the interest of the landlord is for the time being held by two or more persons jointly, the reference in sub-paragraph (1)(c) above to an individual is a reference to any one of those persons.

(3)    A tenancy (in this sub-paragraph referred to as "the new tenancy") is excluded from sub-paragraph (1) above if—

(a)    it is granted to a person (alone, or jointly with others) who, immediately before it was granted, was a tenant under an assured tenancy (in this sub-paragraph referred to as "the former tenancy") of the same dwelling-house or of another dwelling-house which forms part of the building in question; and

(b)    the landlord under the new tenancy and under the former tenancy is the same person or, if either of those tenancies is or was granted by two or more persons jointly, the same person is the landlord or one of the landlords under each tenancy.

*Crown tenancies*

11.—(1)    A tenancy under which the interest of the landlord belongs to Her Majesty in right of the Crown or to a government department or is held in trust for Her Majesty for the purposes of a government department.

(2)    The reference in sub-paragraph (1) above to the case where the interest of the landlord belongs to Her Majesty in right of the Crown does not include the case where that interest is under the management of the Crown Estate Commissioners [or it is held by the Secretary of State as the result of the exercise by him of functions under Part III of the Housing Associations Act 1985].

*Local authority tenancies etc*

12.—(1)    A tenancy under which the interest of the landlord belongs to—

(a)    a local authority, as defined in sub-paragraph (2) below;
(b)    the Commission for the New Towns;
(c)    …
(d)    an urban development corporation established by an order under section 135 of the Local Government, Planning and Land Act 1980;
(e)    a development corporation, within the meaning of the New Towns Act 1981;
(f)    an authority established under section 10 of the Local Government Act 1985 (waste disposal authorities);
[(fa)    an authority established for an area in England by an order under section 207 of the Local Government and Public Involvement in Health Act 2007 (joint waste authorities);]
(g)    a residuary body, within the meaning of the Local Government Act 1985;
[(gg)    the Residuary Body for Wales (Corff Gweddilliol Cymru);]
(h)    a fully mutual housing association; or
(i)    a housing action trust established under Part III of this Act.

(2)    The following are local authorities for the purposes of sub-paragraph (1)(a) above—

(a)    the council of a county, [county borough,] district or London borough;
(b)    the Common Council of the City of London;
(c)    the Council of the Isles of Scilly;
(d)    the Broads Authority;
[(da)    a National Park authority;]
[(ee)    the London Fire and Emergency Planning Authority;]
(e)    the Inner London Education Authority; and
(f)    a joint authority, within the meaning of the Local Government Act 1985 [and
(g)    a police authority established under [section 3 of the Police Act 1996] [ … ].]

*[Family intervention tenancies*

12ZA.—(1)    A family intervention tenancy.

(2)    But a family intervention tenancy becomes an assured tenancy if the landlord notifies the tenant that it is to be regarded as an assured tenancy.

(3)    In this paragraph "a family intervention tenancy" means, subject to sub-paragraph (4), a tenancy granted by a registered provider of social housing or a registered social landlord ("the landlord") in respect of a dwelling-house—

(a)    to a person ("the new tenant") against whom a possession order under section 7 in respect of another dwelling-house—
(i)    has been made, in relation to an assured tenancy, on ground 14 or 14A of Part 2 of Schedule 2;
(ii)    could, in the opinion of the landlord, have been so made in relation to such a tenancy; or
(iii)    could, in the opinion of the landlord, have been so made if the person had had such a tenancy; and

(b)    for the purposes of the provision of behaviour support services.

(4)    A tenancy is not a family intervention tenancy for the purposes of this paragraph if the landlord has failed to serve a notice under sub-paragraph (5) on the new tenant before the new tenant entered into the tenancy.

(5)    A notice under this sub-paragraph is a notice stating—
   (a)    the reasons for offering the tenancy to the new tenant;
   (b)    the dwelling-house in respect of which the tenancy is to be granted;
   (c)    the other main terms of the tenancy (including any requirements on the new tenant in respect of behaviour support services);
   (d)    the security of tenure available under the tenancy and any loss of security of tenure which is likely to result from the new tenant agreeing to enter into the tenancy;
   (e)    that the new tenant is not obliged to enter into the tenancy or (unless otherwise required to do so) to surrender any existing tenancy or possession of a dwelling-house;
   (f)    any likely action by the landlord if the new tenant does not enter into the tenancy or surrender any existing tenancy or possession of a dwelling-house.

(6)    The appropriate national authority may by regulations made by statutory instrument amend sub-paragraph (5).

(7)    A notice under sub-paragraph (5) must contain advice to the new tenant as to how the new tenant may be able to obtain assistance in relation to the notice.

(8)    The appropriate national authority may by regulations made by statutory instrument make provision about the type of advice to be provided in such notices.

(9)    Regulations under this paragraph may contain such transitional, transitory or saving provision as the appropriate national authority considers appropriate.

(10)    A statutory instrument containing (whether alone or with other provision) regulations under this paragraph which amend or repeal any of paragraphs (a) to (f) of sub-paragraph (5) may not be made—
   (a)    by the Secretary of State unless a draft of the instrument has been laid before, and approved by a resolution of, each House of Parliament; and
   (b)    by the Welsh Ministers unless a draft of the instrument has been laid before, and approved by a resolution of, the National Assembly for Wales.

(11)    Subject to this, a statutory instrument containing regulations made under this paragraph—
   (a)    by the Secretary of State is subject to annulment in pursuance of a resolution of either House of Parliament; and
   (b)    by the Welsh Ministers is subject to annulment in pursuance of a resolution of the National Assembly for Wales.

(12)    In this paragraph—
   "appropriate national authority"—
      (a)    in relation to England, means the Secretary of State; and
      (b)    in relation to Wales, means the Welsh Ministers;
   "behaviour support agreement" means an agreement in writing about behaviour and the provision of support services made between the new tenant, the landlord and the local housing authority for the district in which the dwelling-house which is to be subject to the new tenancy is situated (or between persons who include those persons);
   "behaviour support services" means relevant support services to be provided by any person to—
      (a)    the new tenant; or
      (b)    any person who is to reside with the new tenant;
   for the purpose of addressing the kind of behaviour which led to the new tenant falling within sub-paragraph (3)(a);
   "family intervention tenancy" has the meaning given by sub-paragraph (3);
   "landlord" has the meaning given by sub-paragraph (3);
   "local housing authority" (and the reference to its district) has the same meaning as in the Housing Act 1985 (see sections 1 and 2(1) of that Act);
   "the new tenant" has the meaning given by sub-paragraph (3)(a);
   "registered social landlord" has the same meaning as in Part 1 of the Housing Act 1996;
   "relevant support services" means support services of a kind identified in a behaviour support agreement and designed to meet such needs of the recipient as are identified in the agreement.]

*[Accommodation for asylum-seekers*

12A.—(1)    A tenancy granted by a private landlord under arrangements for the provision of support for asylum-seekers or dependants of asylum-seekers made [under section 4 or Part VI of the Immigration and Asylum Act 1999].

(2)    "Private landlord" means a landlord who is not within section 80(1) of the Housing Act 1985.]

*[Accommodation for persons with Temporary Protection*

12B.—(1)   A tenancy granted by a private landlord under arrangements for the provision of accommodation for persons with temporary protection made under the Displaced Persons (Temporary Protection) Regulations 2005.

(2)   "Private landlord" means a landlord who is not within section 80(1) of the Housing Act 1985.]

*Transitional cases*

13.—(1)   A protected tenancy, within the meaning of the Rent Act 1977.

(2)   A housing association tenancy, within the meaning of Part VI of that Act.

(3)   A secure tenancy.

(4)   Where a person is a protected occupier of a dwelling-house, within the meaning of the Rent (Agriculture) Act 1976, the relevant tenancy, within the meaning of that Act, by virtue of which he occupies the dwelling-house.

**[782]**

**NOTES**
   Para 2: substituted, together with para 2A, for original para 2, by the References to Rating (Housing) Regulations 1990, SI 1990/434, reg 2, Schedule, para 29; words in square brackets inserted by the Local Government Finance (Housing) (Consequential Amendments) Order 1993, SI 1993/651, art 2(1), Sch 1, para 19.
   Para 2A: substituted, together with para 2, for original para 2, by SI 1990/434, reg 2, Schedule, para 29.
   Paras 3, 3A–3C: substituted, for original para 3, by SI 1990/434, reg 2, Schedule, para 30.
   Para 5: words in square brackets substituted by the Licensing Act 2003, s 198(1), Sch 6, para 108.
   Para 7: substituted, together with the preceding cross-heading, by the Agricultural Tenancies Act 1995, s 40, Schedule, para 34.
   Para 11: words in square brackets inserted by the Government of Wales Act 1998 (Housing) (Amendments) Order 1999, SI 1999/61, art 2, Schedule, para 3(1), (4).
   Para 12: sub-para (1)(c) repealed by the Government of Wales Act 1998, ss 131, 152, Sch 18, Pt IV; sub-para (1)(fa) inserted by the Local Government and Public Involvement in Health Act 2007, s 209(2), Sch 13, Pt 2, para 44; sub-para (1)(gg) and words in square brackets in sub-para (2)(a) inserted by the Local Government (Wales) Act 1994, ss 22(2), 39(2), Sch 8, para 9(2), Sch 13, para 31; sub-para (2)(da) inserted by the Environment Act 1995, s 78, Sch 10, para 28; sub-para (2)(ee) inserted by the Greater London Authority Act 1999, s 328(8), Sch 29, Pt I, para 53; sub-para (2)(g) and word "and" preceding it inserted by the Police and Magistrates' Courts Act 1994, s 43, Sch 4, Pt II, para 62, words in first pair of square brackets therein substituted by the Police Act 1996, s 103(1), Sch 7, Pt I, para 1(1), (2)(zc), words omitted from second pair of square brackets inserted by the Greater London Authority Act 1999, s 325, Sch 27, para 59 and the Police Act 1997, s 134(1), Sch 9, para 57 and repealed by the Police Reform Act 2002, ss 100(2), 107(2), Sch 8.
   Para 12ZA: inserted by the Housing and Regeneration Act 2008, s 297(2), (3), as from 1 January 2009 in relation to England, except in relation to any tenancy granted before that date, and as from a day to be appointed in relation to Wales.
   Para 12A: inserted, together with the preceding cross-heading, by the Immigration and Asylum Act 1999, s 169(1), Sch 14, para 88; words in square brackets substituted by the Immigration, Asylum and Nationality Act 2006, s 43(4)(f).
   Para 12B: inserted, together with the preceding cross-heading, by the Displaced Persons (Temporary Protection) Regulations 2005, SI 2005/1379, Schedule, para 6.
   Regulations: the Assured and Protected Tenancies (Lettings to Students) Regulations 1998, SI 1998/1967 at **[3214]**.

PART II
RATEABLE VALUES

14.—(1)   The rateable value of a dwelling-house at any time shall be ascertained for the purposes of Part I of this Schedule as follows—

(a)   if the dwelling-house is a hereditament for which a rateable value is then shown in the valuation list, it shall be that rateable value;

(b)   if the dwelling-house forms part only of such a hereditament or consists of or forms part of more than one such hereditament, its rateable value shall be taken to

be such value as is found by a proper apportionment or aggregation of the rateable value or values so shown.

(2)   Any question arising under this Part of this Schedule as to the proper apportionment or aggregation of any value or values shall be determined by the county court and the decision of that court shall be final.

15.   Where, after the time at which the rateable value of a dwelling-house is material for the purposes of any provision of Part I of this Schedule, the valuation list is altered so as to vary the rateable value of the hereditament of which the dwelling-house consists (in whole or in part) or forms part and the alteration has effect from that time or from an earlier time, the rateable value of the dwelling-house at the material time shall be ascertained as if the value shown in the valuation list at the material time had been the value shown in the list as altered.

16.    Paragraphs 14 and 15 above apply in relation to any other land which, under section 2 of this Act, is treated as part of a dwelling-house as they apply in relation to the dwelling-house itself.

**[783]**

## PART III
### PROVISIONS FOR DETERMINING APPLICATION OF PARAGRAPH 10
### (RESIDENT LANDLORDS)

17.—(1)    In determining whether the condition in paragraph 10(1)(c) above is at any time fulfilled with respect to a tenancy, there shall be disregarded—

(a)    any period of not more than twenty-eight days, beginning with the date on which the interest of the landlord under the tenancy becomes vested at law and in equity in an individual who, during that period, does not occupy as his only or principal home another dwelling-house which forms part of the building or, as the case may be, flat concerned;

(b)    if, within a period falling within paragraph (a) above, the individual concerned notifies the tenant in writing of his intention to occupy as his only or principal home another dwelling-house in the building or, as the case may be, flat concerned, the period beginning with the date on which the interest of the landlord under the tenancy becomes vested in that individual as mentioned in that paragraph and ending—

(i)    at the expiry of the period of six months beginning on that date, or

(ii)    on the date on which that interest ceases to be so vested, or

(iii)    on the date on which that interest becomes again vested in such an individual as is mentioned in paragraph 10(1)(c) or the condition in that paragraph becomes deemed to be fulfilled by virtue of paragraph 18(1) or paragraph 20 below, whichever is the earlier; and

(c)    any period of not more than two years beginning with the date on which the interest of the landlord under the tenancy becomes, and during which it remains, vested—

(i)    in trustees as such; or

(ii)    by virtue of section 9 of the Administration of Estates Act 1925, in [the Probate Judge or the Public Trustee].

(2)    Where the interest of the landlord under a tenancy becomes vested at law and in equity in two or more persons jointly, of whom at least one was an individual, sub-paragraph (1) above shall have effect subject to the following modifications—

(a)    in paragraph (a) for the words from "an individual" to "occupy" there shall be substituted "the joint landlords if, during that period none of them occupies"; and

(b)    in paragraph (b) for the words "the individual concerned" there shall be substituted "any of the joint landlords who is an individual" and for the words "that individual" there shall be substituted "the joint landlords".

18.—(1)    During any period when—

(a)    the interest of the landlord under the tenancy referred to in paragraph 10 above is vested in trustees as such, and

(b)    that interest is … held on trust for any person who or for two or more persons of whom at least one occupies as his only or principal home a dwelling-house which form part of the building or, as the case may be, flat referred to in paragraph 10(1)(a),

the condition in paragraph 10(1)(c) shall be deemed to be fulfilled and accordingly, no part of that period shall be disregarded by virtue of paragraph 17 above.

(2)    If a period during which the condition in paragraph 10(1)(c) is deemed to be fulfilled by virtue of sub-paragraph (1) above comes to an end on the death of a person who was in occupation of a dwelling-house as mentioned in paragraph (b) of that sub-paragraph, then, in determining whether that condition is at any time thereafter fulfilled, there shall be disregarded any period—

(a)    which begins on the date of the death;

(b)    during which the interest of the landlord remains vested as mentioned in sub-paragraph (1)(a) above; and

(c)    which ends at the expiry of the period of two years beginning on the date of the death or on any earlier date on which the condition in paragraph 10(1)(c) becomes again deemed to be fulfilled by virtue of sub-paragraph (1) above.

19.    In any case where—

(a)    immediately before a tenancy comes to an end the condition in paragraph 10(1)(c) is deemed to be fulfilled by virtue of paragraph 18(1) above, and

(b)    on the coming to an end of that tenancy the trustees in whom the interest of the landlord is vested grant a new tenancy of the same or substantially the same dwelling-house to a person (alone or jointly with others) who was the tenant or one of the tenants under the previous tenancy,

the condition in paragraph 10(1)(b) above shall be deemed to be fulfilled with respect to the new tenancy.

20.—(1)   The tenancy referred to in paragraph 10 above falls within this paragraph if the interest of the landlord under the tenancy becomes vested in the personal representatives of a deceased person acting in that capacity.

(2)   If the tenancy falls within this paragraph, the condition in paragraph 10(1)(c) shall be deemed to be fulfilled for any period, beginning with the date on which the interest becomes vested in the personal representatives and not exceeding two years, during which the interest of the landlord remains so vested.

21.   Throughout any period which, by virtue of paragraph 17 or paragraph 18(2) above, falls to be disregarded for the purpose of determining whether the condition in paragraph 10(1)(c) is fulfilled with respect to a tenancy, no order shall be made for possession of the dwelling-house subject to that tenancy, other than an order which might be made if that tenancy were or, as the case may be, had been an assured tenancy.

22.   For the purposes of paragraph 10 above, a building is a purpose-built block of flats if as constructed it contained, and it contains, two or more flats; and for this purpose "flat" means a dwelling-house which—
- (a)   forms part only of a building; and
- (b)   is separated horizontally from another dwelling-house which forms part of the same building.

**[784]**

**NOTES**

Para 17: words in square brackets in sub-para (1)(c) substituted by the Law of Property (Miscellaneous Provisions) Act 1994, s 21(1), Sch 1, para 11.

Para 18: words omitted from sub-para (1)(b) repealed, subject to savings, by the Trusts of Land and Appointment of Trustees Act 1996, s 25(2), (4), (5).

## SCHEDULE 2
### GROUNDS FOR POSSESSION OF DWELLING-HOUSES LET ON ASSURED TENANCIES
Section 7

### PART I
#### GROUNDS ON WHICH COURT MUST ORDER POSSESSION

*Ground 1*

Not later than the beginning of the tenancy the landlord gave notice in writing to the tenant that possession might be recovered on this ground or the court is of the opinion that it is just and equitable to dispense with the requirement of notice and (in either case)—
- (a)   at some time before the beginning of the tenancy, the landlord who is seeking possession or, in the case of joint landlords seeking possession, at least one of them occupied the dwelling-house as his only or principal home; or
- (b)   the landlord who is seeking possession or, in the case of joint landlords seeking possession, at least one of them requires the dwelling-house as [his, his spouse's or his civil partner's] only or principal home and neither the landlord (or, in the case of joint landlords, any one of them) nor any other person who, as landlord, derived title under the landlord who gave the notice mentioned above acquired the reversion on the tenancy for money or money's worth.

*Ground 2*

The dwelling-house is subject to a mortgage granted before the beginning of the tenancy and—
- (a)   the mortgagee is entitled to exercise a power of sale conferred on him by the mortgage or by section 101 of the Law of Property Act 1925; and
- (b)   the mortgagee requires possession of the dwelling-house for the purpose of disposing of it with vacant possession in exercise of that power; and
- (c)   either notice was given as mentioned in Ground 1 above or the court is satisfied that it is just and equitable to dispense with the requirement of notice;

and for the purposes of this ground "mortgage" includes a charge and "mortgagee" shall be construed accordingly.

*Ground 3*

The tenancy is a fixed term tenancy for a term not exceeding eight months and—
- (a)   not later than the beginning of the tenancy the landlord gave notice in writing to the tenant that possession might be recovered on this ground; and
- (b)   at some time within the period of twelve months ending with the beginning of the tenancy, the dwelling-house was occupied under a right to occupy it for a holiday.

*Ground 4*

The tenancy is a fixed term tenancy for a term not exceeding twelve months and—

    (a)    not later than the beginning of the tenancy the landlord gave notice in writing to the tenant that possession might be recovered on this ground; and

    (b)    at some time within the period of twelve months ending with the beginning of the tenancy, the dwelling-house was let on a tenancy falling within paragraph 8 of Schedule 1 to this Act.

*Ground 5*

The dwelling-house is held for the purpose of being available for occupation by a minister of religion as a residence from which to perform the duties of his office and—

    (a)    not later than the beginning of the tenancy the landlord gave notice in writing to the tenant that possession might be recovered on this ground; and

    (b)    the court is satisfied that the dwelling-house is required for occupation by a minister of religion as such a residence.

*Ground 6*

The landlord who is seeking possession or, if that landlord is a [registered social landlord] or charitable housing trust, a superior landlord intends to demolish or reconstruct the whole or a substantial part of the dwelling-house or to carry out substantial works on the dwelling-house or any part thereof or any building of which it forms part and the following conditions are fulfilled—

    (a)    the intended work cannot reasonably be carried out without the tenant giving up possession of the dwelling-house because—

        (i)    the tenant is not willing to agree to such a variation of the terms of the tenancy as would give such access and other facilities as would permit the intended work to be carried out, or

        (ii)    the nature of the intended work is such that no such variation is practicable, or

        (iii)    the tenant is not willing to accept an assured tenancy of such part only of the dwelling-house (in this sub-paragraph referred to as "the reduced part") as would leave in the possession of his landlord so much of the dwelling-house as would be reasonable to enable the intended work to be carried out and, where appropriate, as would give such access and other facilities over the reduced part as would permit the intended work to be carried out, or

        (iv)    the nature of the intended work is such that such a tenancy is not practicable;

    (b)    either the landlord seeking possession acquired his interest in the dwelling-house before the grant of the tenancy or that interest was in existence at the time of that grant and neither that landlord (or, in the case of joint landlords, any of them) nor any other person who, alone or jointly with others, has acquired that interest since that time acquired it for money or money's worth; and

    (c)    the assured tenancy on which the dwelling-house is let did not come into being by virtue of any provision of Schedule 1 to the Rent Act 1977, as amended by Part I of Schedule 4 to this Act or, as the case may be, section 4 of the Rent (Agriculture) Act 1976, as amended by Part II of that Schedule.

For the purposes of this ground, if, immediately before the grant of the tenancy, the tenant to whom it was granted or, if it was granted to joint tenants, any of them was the tenant or one of the joint tenants [of the dwelling-house concerned] under an earlier assured tenancy [or, as the case may be, under a tenancy to which Schedule 10 to the Local Government and Housing Act 1989 applied], any reference in paragraph (b) above to the grant of the tenancy is a reference to the grant of that earlier assured tenancy [or, as the case may be, to the grant of the tenancy to which the said Schedule 10 applied].

For the purposes of this ground ["registered housing association" has the same meaning as in the Housing Act 1985 (see section 5(4) and (5) of that Act)] and "charitable housing trust" means a housing trust, within the meaning of [the Housing Associations Act 1985], which is a charity, within the meaning of [the Charities Act 1993].

    [ ... ]

*Ground 7*

The tenancy is a periodic tenancy (including a statutory periodic tenancy) which has devolved under the will or intestacy of the former tenant and the proceedings for the recovery of possession are begun not later than twelve months after the death of the former tenant or, if the court so directs, after the date on which, in the opinion of the court, the landlord or, in the case of joint landlords, any one of them became aware of the former tenant's death.

For the purposes of this ground, the acceptance by the landlord of rent from a new tenant after the death of the former tenant shall not be regarded as creating a new periodic tenancy, unless the landlord agrees in writing to a change (as compared with the tenancy before the death) in the amount of the rent, the period of the tenancy, the premises which are let or any other term of the tenancy.

### Ground 8

Both at the date of the service of the notice under section 8 of this Act relating to the proceedings for possession and at the date of the hearing—

    (a)   if rent is payable weekly or fortnightly, at least [eight weeks'] rent is unpaid;

    (b)   if rent is payable monthly, at least [two months'] rent is unpaid;

    (c)   if rent is payable quarterly, at least one quarter's rent is more than three months in arrears; and

    (d)   if rent is payable yearly, at least three months' rent is more than three months in arrears;

and for the purpose of this ground "rent" means rent lawfully due from the tenant.

**[785]**

**NOTES**

Ground 1: words in square brackets substituted by the Civil Partnership Act 2004, s 81, Sch 8, para 43(1), (2).

Ground 6: words in first, fifth and sixth pairs of square brackets substituted by the Housing Act 1996 (Consequential Provisions) Order 1996, SI 1996/2325, art 5, Sch 2, para 18(1), (13); words in second and fourth pairs of square brackets inserted and words in third pair of square brackets substituted by the Local Government and Housing Act 1989, s 194(1), Sch 11, para 108; words in seventh pair of square brackets substituted by the Charities Act 1993, s 98(1), Sch 6, para 30; words omitted from eighth pair of square brackets added by the Local Government Act 1989, s 194(1), Sch 11, para 109 and repealed, subject to a saving in relation to applications under s 96 of this Act which had not been disposed of before 1 October 1996, by the Housing Act 1996, s 227, Sch 19, Pt IX.

Ground 8: words in square brackets in paras (a), (b) substituted by the Housing Act 1996, s 101.

### PART II
### GROUNDS ON WHICH COURT MAY ORDER POSSESSION

### Ground 9

Suitable alternative accommodation is available for the tenant or will be available for him when the order for possession takes effect.

### Ground 10

Some rent lawfully due from the tenant—

    (a)   is unpaid on the date on which the proceedings for possession are begun; and

    (b)   except where subsection (1)(b) of section 8 of this Act applies, was in arrears at the date of the service of the notice under that section relating to those proceedings.

### Ground 11

Whether or not any rent is in arrears on the date on which proceedings for possession are begun, the tenant has persistently delayed paying rent which has become lawfully due.

### Ground 12

Any obligation of the tenancy (other than one related to the payment of rent) has been broken or not performed.

### Ground 13

The condition of the dwelling-house or any of the common parts has deteriorated owing to acts of waste by, or the neglect or default of, the tenant or any other person residing in the dwelling-house and, in the case of an act of waste by, or the neglect or default of, a person lodging with the tenant or a sub-tenant of his, the tenant has not taken such steps as he ought reasonably to have taken for the removal of the lodger or sub-tenant.

For the purposes of this ground, "common parts" means any part of a building comprising the dwelling-house and any other premises which the tenant is entitled under the terms of the tenancy to use in common with the occupiers of other dwelling-houses in which the landlord has an estate or interest.

### [Ground 14

The tenant or a person residing in or visiting the dwelling-house—

    (a)   has been guilty of conduct causing or likely to cause a nuisance or annoyance to a person residing, visiting or otherwise engaging in a lawful activity in the locality, or

    (b)   has been convicted of—

(i)   using the dwelling-house or allowing it to be used for immoral or illegal purposes, or

(ii)   an [indictable] offence committed in, or in the locality of, the dwelling house.]

## [Ground 14A

The dwelling-house was occupied (whether alone or with others) by [a married couple, a couple who are civil partners of each other,] or a couple living together as husband and wife [or a couple living together as if they were civil partners] and—

(a)   one or both of the partners is a tenant of the dwelling-house,

(b)   the landlord who is seeking possession is a registered social landlord or a charitable housing trust,

(c)   one partner has left the dwelling-house because of violence or threats of violence by the other towards—

    (i)   that partner, or

    (ii)   a member of the family of that partner who was residing with that partner immediately before the partner left, and

(d)   the court is satisfied that the partner who has left is unlikely to return.

For the purposes of this ground "registered social landlord" and "member of the family" have the same meaning as in Part I of the Housing Act 1996 and "charitable housing trust" means a housing trust, within the meaning of the Housing Associations Act 1985, which is a charity within the meaning of the Charities Act 1993.]

## Ground 15

The condition of any furniture provided for use under the tenancy has, in the opinion of the court, deteriorated owing to ill-treatment by the tenant or any other person residing in the dwelling-house and, in the case of ill-treatment by a person lodging with the tenant or by a sub-tenant of his, the tenant has not taken such steps as he ought reasonably to have taken for the removal of the lodger or sub-tenant.

## Ground 16

The dwelling-house was let to the tenant in consequence of his employment by the landlord seeking possession or a previous landlord under the tenancy and the tenant has ceased to be in that employment.

[For the purposes of this ground, at a time when the landlord is or was the Secretary of State, employment by a health service body, as defined in section 60(7) of the National Health Service and Community Care Act 1990, [or by a Local Health Board] shall be regarded as employment by the Secretary of State.]

## [Ground 17

The tenant is the person, or one of the persons, to whom the tenancy was granted and the landlord was induced to grant the tenancy by a false statement made knowingly or recklessly by—

(a)   the tenant, or

(b)   a person acting at the tenant's instigation.]

**[786]**

---

**NOTES**

Ground 14: substituted by the Housing Act 1996, s 148; word in square brackets substituted by the Serious Organised Crime and Police Act 2005, s 111, Sch 7, Pt 3, para 46.

Ground 14A: inserted by the Housing Act 1996, s 149; words in first pair of square brackets substituted and words in second pair of square brackets inserted by the Civil Partnership Act 2004, s 81, Sch 8, para 43(1), (3)(a).

Ground 16: words in first (outer) pair of square brackets added by the National Health Service and Community Care Act 1990, s 60, Sch 8, para 10; words in second (inner) pair of square brackets inserted by the National Health Service Reform and Health Care Professions Act 2002, s 6(2), Sch 5, para 28.

Ground 17: added by the Housing Act 1996, s 102.

---

## PART III
### SUITABLE ALTERNATIVE ACCOMMODATION

1.   For the purposes of Ground 9 above, a certificate of the local housing authority for the district in which the dwelling-house in question is situated, certifying that the authority will provide suitable alternative accommodation for the tenant by a date specified in the certificate, shall be conclusive evidence that suitable alternative accommodation will be available for him by that date.

2.   Where no such certificate as is mentioned in paragraph 1 above is produced to the court, accommodation shall be deemed to be suitable for the purposes of Ground 9 above if it consists of either—

(a)    premises which are to be let as a separate dwelling such that they will then be let on an assured tenancy, other than—

      (i)   a tenancy in respect of which notice is given not later than the beginning of the tenancy that possession might be recovered on any of Grounds 1 to 5 above, or

      (ii)  an assured shorthold tenancy, within the meaning of Chapter II of Part I of this Act, or

(b)    premises to be let as a separate dwelling on terms which will, in the opinion of the court, afford to the tenant security of tenure reasonably equivalent to the security afforded by Chapter I of Part I of this Act in the case of an assured tenancy of a kind mentioned in sub-paragraph (a) above,

and, in the opinion of the court, the accommodation fulfils the relevant conditions as defined in paragraph 3 below.

3.—(1)    For the purposes of paragraph 2 above, the relevant conditions are that the accommodation is reasonably suitable to the needs of the tenant and his family as regards proximity to place of work, and either—

(a)    similar as regards rental and extent to the accommodation afforded by dwelling-houses provided in the neighbourhood by any local housing authority for persons whose needs as regards extent are, in the opinion of the court, similar to those of the tenant and of his family; or

(b)    reasonably suitable to the means of the tenant and to the needs of the tenant and his family as regards extent and character; and

that if any furniture was provided for use under the assured tenancy in question, furniture is provided for use in the accommodation which is either similar to that so provided or is reasonable to the needs of the tenant and his family.

(2)    For the purposes of sub-paragraph (1)(a) above, a certificate of a local housing authority stating—

(a)    the extent of the accommodation afforded by dwelling-houses provided by the authority to meet the needs of tenants with families of such number as may be specified in the certificate, and

(b)    the amount of the rent charged by the authority for dwelling-houses affording accommodation of that extent,

shall be conclusive evidence of the facts so stated.

4.    Accommodation shall not be deemed to be suitable to the needs of the tenant and his family if the result of their occupation of the accommodation would be that it would be an overcrowded dwelling-house for the purposes of Part X of the Housing Act 1985.

5.    Any document purporting to be a certificate of a local housing authority named therein issued for the purposes of this Part of this Schedule and to be signed by the proper officer of that authority shall be received in evidence and, unless the contrary is shown, shall be deemed to be such a certificate without further proof.

6.    In this Part of this Schedule "local housing authority" and "district", in relation to such an authority, have the same meaning as in the Housing Act 1985.

**[787]**

## PART IV
### NOTICES RELATING TO RECOVERY OF POSSESSION

7.    Any reference in Grounds 1 to 5 in Part I of this Schedule or in the following provisions of this Part to the landlord giving a notice in writing to the tenant is, in the case of joint landlords, a reference to at least one of the joint landlords giving such a notice.

8.—(1)    If, not later than the beginning of a tenancy (in this paragraph referred to as "the earlier tenancy"), the landlord gives such a notice in writing to the tenant as is mentioned in any of Grounds 1 to 5 in Part I of this Schedule, then for the purposes of the ground in question and any further application of this paragraph, that notice shall also have effect as if it had been given immediately before the beginning of any later tenancy falling within sub-paragraph (2) below.

(2)    Subject to sub-paragraph (3) below, sub-paragraph (1) above applies to a later tenancy—

(a)    which takes effect immediately on the coming to an end of the earlier tenancy; and

(b)    which is granted (or deemed to be granted) to the person who was the tenant under the earlier tenancy immediately before it came to an end; and

(c)    which is of substantially the same dwelling-house as the earlier tenancy.

(3)    Sub-paragraph (1) above does not apply in relation to a later tenancy if, not later than the beginning of the tenancy, the landlord gave notice in writing to the tenant that the tenancy is not one in respect of which possession can be recovered on the ground in question.

9.   Where paragraph 8(1) above has effect in relation to a notice given as mentioned in Ground 1 in Part I of this Schedule, the reference in paragraph (b) of that ground to the reversion on the tenancy is a reference to the reversion on the earlier tenancy and on any later tenancy falling within paragraph 8(2) above.

10.   Where paragraph 8(1) above has effect in relation to a notice given as mentioned in Ground 3 or Ground 4 in Part I of this Schedule, any second or subsequent tenancy in relation to which the notice has effect shall be treated for the purpose of that ground as beginning at the beginning of the tenancy in respect of which the notice was actually given.

11.   Any reference in Grounds 1 to 5 in Part I of this Schedule to a notice being given not later than the beginning of the tenancy is a reference to its being given not later than the day on which the tenancy is entered into and, accordingly, section 45(2) of this Act shall not apply to any such reference.

[788]

## [SCHEDULE 2A
## ASSURED TENANCIES: NON-SHORTHOLDS

Section 19A

### *Tenancies excluded by notice*

1.—(1)   An assured tenancy in respect of which a notice is served as mentioned in sub-paragraph (2) below.

(2)   The notice referred to in sub-paragraph (1) above is one which—
   (a)   is served before the assured tenancy is entered into,
   (b)   is served by the person who is to be the landlord under the assured tenancy on the person who is to be the tenant under that tenancy, and
   (c)   states that the assured tenancy to which it relates is not to be an assured shorthold tenancy.

2.—(1)   An assured tenancy in respect of which a notice is served as mentioned in sub-paragraph (2) below.

(2)   The notice referred to in sub-paragraph (1) above is one which—
   (a)   is served after the assured tenancy has been entered into,
   (b)   is served by the landlord under the assured tenancy on the tenant under that tenancy, and
   (c)   states that the assured tenancy to which it relates is no longer an assured shorthold tenancy.

### *Tenancies containing exclusions provision*

3.   An assured tenancy which contains a provision to the effect that the tenancy is not an assured shorthold tenancy.

### *Tenancies under section 39*

4.   An assured tenancy arising by virtue of section 39 above, other than one to which subsection (7) of that section applies.

### *Former secure tenancies*

5.   An assured tenancy which became an assured tenancy on ceasing to be a secure tenancy.

### [*Former demoted tenancies*

5A.   An assured tenancy which ceases to be an assured shorthold tenancy by virtue of section 20B(2) or (4).]

### *Tenancies under Schedule 10 to the Local Government and Housing Act 1989*

6.   An assured tenancy arising by virtue of Schedule 10 to the Local Government and Housing Act 1989 (security of tenure on ending of long residential tenancies).

### *Tenancies replacing non-shortholds*

7.—(1)   An assured tenancy which—
   (a)   is granted to a person (alone or jointly with others) who, immediately before the tenancy was granted, was the tenant (or, in the case of joint tenants, one of the tenants) under an assured tenancy other than a shorthold tenancy ("the old tenancy"),
   (b)   is granted (alone or jointly with others) by a person who was at that time the landlord (or one of the joint landlords) under the old tenancy, and
   (c)   is not one in respect of which a notice is served as mentioned in sub-paragraph (2) below.

(2)   The notice referred to in sub-paragraph (1)(c) above is one which—

(a)   is in such form as may be prescribed,

(b)   is served before the assured tenancy is entered into,

(c)   is served by the person who is to be the tenant under the assured tenancy on the person who is to be the landlord under that tenancy (or, in the case of joint landlords, on at least one of the persons who are to be joint landlords), and

(d)   states that the assured tenancy to which it relates is to be a shorthold tenancy.

8.   An assured tenancy which comes into being by virtue of section 5 above on the coming to an end of an assured tenancy which is not a shorthold tenancy.

### Assured agricultural occupancies

9.—(1)   An assured tenancy—

(a)   in the case of which the agricultural worker condition is, by virtue of any provision of Schedule 3 to this Act, for the time being fulfilled with respect to the dwelling-house subject to the tenancy, and

(b)   which does not fall within sub-paragraph (2) or (4) below.

(2)   An assured tenancy falls within this sub-paragraph if—

(a)   before it is entered into, a notice—

(i)   in such form as may be prescribed, and

(ii)   stating that the tenancy is to be a shorthold tenancy,

is served by the person who is to be the landlord under the tenancy on the person who is to be the tenant under it, and

(b)   it is not an excepted tenancy.

(3)   For the purposes of sub-paragraph (2)(b) above, an assured tenancy is an excepted tenancy if—

(a)   the person to whom it is granted or, as the case may be, at least one of the persons to whom it is granted was, immediately before it is granted, a tenant or licensee under an assured agricultural occupancy, and

(b)   the person by whom it is granted or, as the case may be, at least one of the persons by whom it is granted was, immediately before it is granted, a landlord or licensor under the assured agricultural occupancy referred to in paragraph (a) above.

(4)   An assured tenancy falls within this sub-paragraph if it comes into being by virtue of section 5 above on the coming to an end of a tenancy falling within sub-paragraph (2) above.]

**[789]**

---

**NOTES**

Inserted by the Housing Act 1996, s 96(2), Sch 7.

Para 5A: inserted by the Anti-social Behaviour Act 2003, s 15(3).

Regulations: the Assured Tenancies and Agricultural Occupancies (Forms) Regulations 1997, SI 1997/194 at **[3169]**.

---

### SCHEDULE 3
### AGRICULTURAL WORKER CONDITIONS
Section 24

### Interpretation

1.—(1)   In this Schedule—

"the 1976 Act" means the Rent (Agriculture) Act 1976;

"agriculture" has the same meaning as in the 1976 Act; and

"relevant tenancy or licence" means a tenancy or licence of a description specified in section 24(2) of this Act.

(2)   In relation to a relevant tenancy or licence—

(a)   "the occupier" means the tenant or licensee; and

(b)   "the dwelling-house" means the dwelling-house which is let under the tenancy or, as the case may be, is occupied under the licence.

(3)   Schedule 3 to the 1976 Act applies for the purposes of this Schedule as it applies for the purposes of that Act and, accordingly, shall have effect to determine—

(a)   whether a person is a qualifying worker;

(b)   whether a person is incapable of whole-time work in agriculture, or work in agriculture as a permit worker, in consequence of a qualifying injury of disease; and

(c)   whether a dwelling-house is in qualifying ownership.

### The conditions

2.   The agricultural worker condition is fulfilled with respect to a dwelling-house subject to a relevant tenancy or licence if—

(a)    the dwelling-house is or has been in qualifying ownership at any time during the subsistence of the tenancy or licence (whether or not it was at that time a relevant tenancy or licence); and

(b)    the occupier or, where there are joint occupiers, at least one of them—
    (i)    is a qualifying worker or has been a qualifying worker at any time during the subsistence of the tenancy or licence (whether or not it was at that time a relevant tenancy or licence); or
    (ii)    is incapable of whole-time work in agriculture or work in agriculture as a permit worker in consequence of a qualifying injury or disease.

3.—(1)    The agricultural worker condition is also fulfilled with respect to a dwelling-house subject to a relevant tenancy or licence if—

(a)    that condition was previously fulfilled with respect to the dwelling-house but the person who was then the occupier or, as the case may be, a person who was one of the joint occupiers (whether or not under the same relevant tenancy or licence) had died; and

(b)    that condition ceased to be fulfilled on the death of the occupier referred to in paragraph (a) above (hereinafter referred to as "the previous qualifying occupier"); and

(c)    the occupier is either—
    (i)    the qualifying [surviving partner] of the previous qualifying occupier; or
    (ii)    the qualifying member of the previous qualifying occupier's family.

[(2)    For the purposes of sub-paragraph (1)(c)(i) above and sub-paragraph (3) below—

(a)    "surviving partner" means widow, widower or surviving civil partner; and

(b)    a surviving partner of the previous qualifying occupier of the dwelling-house is a qualifying surviving partner if that surviving partner was residing in the dwelling-house immediately before the previous qualifying occupier's death.]

(3)    Subject to sub-paragraph (4) below, for the purposes of sub-paragraph (1)(c)(ii) above, a member of the family of the previous qualifying occupier of the dwelling-house is the qualifying member of the family if—

(a)    on the death of the previous qualifying occupier there was no qualifying [surviving partner]; and

(b)    the member of the family was residing in the dwelling-house with the previous qualifying occupier at the time of, and for the period of two years before, his death.

(4)    Not more than one member of the previous qualifying occupier's family may be taken into account in determining whether the agricultural worker condition is fulfilled by virtue of this paragraph and, accordingly, if there is more than one member of the family—

(a)    who is the occupier in relation to the relevant tenancy or licence, and

(b)    who, apart from this sub-paragraph, would be the qualifying member of the family by virtue of sub-paragraph (3) above,

only that one of those members of the family who may be decided by agreement or, in default of agreement by the county court, shall be the qualifying member.

[(5)    For the purposes of sub-paragraph (2)(a) above—

(a)    a person who, immediately before the previous qualifying occupier's death, was living with the previous occupier as his or her wife or husband shall be treated as the widow or widower of the previous occupier, and

(b)    a person who, immediately before the previous qualifying occupier's death, was living with the previous occupier as if they were civil partners shall be treated as the surviving civil partner of the previous occupier.]

(6)    If, immediately before the death of the previous qualifying occupier, there is, by virtue of sub-paragraph (5) above, more than one person who falls within sub-paragraph (1)(c)(i) above, such one of them as may be decided by agreement or, in default of agreement, by the county court shall be treated as the qualifying [surviving partner] for the purposes of this paragraph.

4.    The agricultural worker condition is also fulfilled with respect to a dwelling-house subject to a relevant tenancy or licence if—

(a)    the tenancy or licence was granted to the occupier or, where there are joint occupiers, at least one of them in consideration of his giving up possession of another dwelling-house of which he was then occupier (or one of joint occupiers) under another relevant tenancy or licence; and

(b)    immediately before he gave up possession of that dwelling-house, as a result of his occupation the agricultural worker condition was fulfilled with respect to it (whether by virtue of paragraph 2 or paragraph 3 above or this paragraph);

and the reference in paragraph (a) above to a tenancy or licence granted to the occupier or at least one of joint occupiers includes a reference to the case where the grant is to him together with one or more other persons.

5.—(1)    This paragraph applies where—

(a)    by virtue of any of paragraphs 2 to 4 above, the agricultural worker condition is fulfilled with respect to a dwelling-house subject to a relevant tenancy or licence (in this paragraph referred to as "the earlier tenancy or licence"); and

(b)     another relevant tenancy or licence of the same dwelling-house (in this paragraph referred to as "the later tenancy or licence") is granted to the person who, immediately before the grant, was the occupier or one of the joint occupiers under the earlier tenancy or licence and as a result of whose occupation the agricultural worker condition was fulfilled as mentioned in paragraph (a) above;

and the reference in paragraph (b) above to the grant of the later tenancy or licence to the person mentioned in that paragraph includes a reference to the case where the grant is to that person together with one or more other persons.

(2)     So long as a person as a result of whose occupation of the dwelling-house the agricultural worker condition was fulfilled with respect to the earlier tenancy or licence continues to be the occupier, or one of the joint occupiers, under the later tenancy or licence, the agricultural worker condition shall be fulfilled with respect to the dwelling-house.

(3)     For the purposes of paragraphs 3 and 4 above and any further application of this paragraph, where sub-paragraph (2) above has effect, the agricultural worker condition shall be treated as fulfilled so far as concerns the later tenancy or licence by virtue of the same paragraph of this Schedule as was applicable (or, as the case may be, last applicable) in the case of the earlier tenancy or licence.

**[790]**

**NOTES**
    Para 3: words in square brackets in sub-paras (1), (3), (6), and the whole of sub-paras (2), (5) substituted by the Civil Partnership Act 2004, s 81, Sch 8, para 44.

SCHEDULE 4
STATUTORY TENANTS: SUCCESSION
Section 39

*(Pt I (paras 1–9) amends the Rent Act 1977, Sch 1 at* **[320]***; Pt II (paras 10–12) amends the Rent (Agriculture) Act 1976, s 4 at* **[158]***.)*

PART III
MODIFICATIONS OF SECTION 7 AND SCHEDULE 2

13.—(1)     Subject to sub-paragraph (2) below, in relation to the assured tenancy to which the successor becomes entitled by succession, section 7 of this Act shall have effect as if in subsection (3) after the word "established" there were inserted the words "or that the circumstances are as specified in any of Cases 11, 12, 16, 17, 18 and 20 in Schedule 15 to the Rent Act 1977".

(2)     Sub-paragraph (1) above does not apply if, by virtue of section 39(8) of this Act, the assured tenancy to which the successor becomes entitled is an assured agricultural occupancy.

14.     If by virtue of section 39(8) of this Act, the assured tenancy to which the successor becomes entitled is an assured agricultural occupancy, section 7 of this Act shall have effect in relation to that tenancy as if in subsection (3) after the word "established" there were inserted the words "or that the circumstances are as specified in Case XI or Case XII of the Rent (Agriculture) Act 1976".

15.—(1)     In relation to the assured tenancy to which the successor becomes entitled by succession, any notice given to the predecessor for the purposes of Case 13, Case 14 or Case 15 in Schedule 15 to the Rent Act 1977 shall be treated as having been given for the purposes of whichever of Grounds 3 to 5 in Schedule 2 to this Act corresponds to the Case in question.

(2)     Where sub-paragraph (1) above applies, the regulated tenancy of the predecessor shall be treated, in relation to the assured tenancy of the successor, as "the earlier tenancy" for the purposes of Part IV of Schedule 2 to this Act.

**[791]**

*(Sch 5 repealed by the Government of Wales Act 1998, ss 140, 141, 152, Sch 16, paras 59, 73, Sch 18, Pt VI; Schs 6–12, 15 outside the scope of this work; Sch 13 amends the Landlord and Tenant Act 1987, ss 2, 3, 4, 26, 35, 40, 58 at* **[645]**, **[646]**, **[647]**, **[686]**, **[695]**, **[700]**, **[715]***; Sch 14 amends the Rent Act 1977, s 63 at* **[240]***, and inserts ss 64A, 64B of that Act at* **[242]**, **[243]***; Sch 16 applies to Scotland only; Sch 17 contains minor and consequential amendments; Sch 18 contains repeals only.)*

PART I
STATUTES

# LAW OF PROPERTY (MISCELLANEOUS PROVISIONS) ACT 1989

(1989 c 34)

*An Act to make new provisions with respect to deeds and their execution and contracts for the sale or other disposition of interests in land; and to abolish the rule of law known as the rule in Bain v Fothergill*

[27 July 1989]

**1** *(Outside the scope of this work.)*

## 2  Contracts for sale etc of land to be made by signed writing

(1)   A contract for the sale or other disposition of an interest in land can only be made in writing and only by incorporating all the terms which the parties have expressly agreed in one document or, where contracts are exchanged, in each.

(2)   The terms may be incorporated in a document either by being set out in it or by reference to some other document.

(3)   The document incorporating the terms or, where contracts are exchanged, one of the documents incorporating them (but not necessarily the same one) must be signed by or on behalf of each party to the contract.

(4)   Where a contract for the sale or other disposition of an interest in land satisfies the conditions of this section by reason only of the rectification of one or more documents in pursuance of an order of a court, the contract shall come into being, or be deemed to have come into being, at such time as may be specified in the order.

(5)   This section does not apply in relation to—
    (a)   a contract to grant such a lease as is mentioned in section 54(2) of the Law of Property Act 1925 (short leases);
    (b)   a contract made in the course of a public auction; or
    [(c)   a contract regulated under the Financial Services and Markets Act 2000, other than a regulated mortgage contract[, *a regulated home reversion plan or a regulated home purchase plan*];]

and nothing in this section affects the creation or operation of resulting, implied or constructive trusts.

(6)   In this section—
    "disposition" has the same meaning as in the Law of Property Act 1925;
    "interest in land" means any estate, interest or charge in or over land …
    ["regulated mortgage contract"[, "regulated home reversion plan" *and* "*regulated home purchase plan*"] must be read with—
        (a)   section 22 of the Financial Services and Markets Act 2000,
        (b)   any relevant order under that section, and
        (c)   Schedule 22 to that Act].

(7)   Nothing in this section shall apply in relation to contracts made before this section comes into force.

(8)   …

[792]

**NOTES**

Sub-s (5): para (c) substituted by the Financial Services and Markets Act 2000 (Consequential Amendments and Repeals) Order 2001, SI 2001/3649, art 317(1), (2); words in square brackets in para (c) inserted by the Financial Services and Markets Act 2000 (Regulated Activities) (Amendment) (No 2) Order 2006, SI 2006/2383, art 27(a), subject to transitional provisions in arts 37–39 thereof; for the words in italics in para (c) there are substituted the words "a regulated home reversion plan, a regulated home purchase plan or a regulated sale and rent back agreement" by the Financial Services and Markets Act 2000 (Regulated Activities) (Amendment) Order 2009, SI 2009/1342, art 24(a), as from 1 July 2009 for certain purposes and 30 June 2010 for remaining purposes (see SI 2009/1342, art 1(2)).

Sub-s (6): words omitted from definition "interest in land" repealed by the Trusts of Land and Appointment of Trustees Act 1996, s 25(2), Sch 4, subject to savings contained in ss 3, 18(3), 25(5) of that Act; definition "regulated mortgage" inserted by SI 2001/3649, art 317(1), (3); words in square brackets therein inserted by SI 2006/2383, art 27(b), subject to transitional provisions in arts 37–39 thereof; for the words in italics therein there are substituted the words ", "regulated home purchase plan" and "regulated sale and rent back agreement"" by SI 2009/1342, art 24(b), as from 1 July 2009 for certain purposes and 30 June 2010 for remaining purposes (see SI 2009/1342, art 1(2)).

Sub-s (8): repeals the Law of Property Act 1925, s 40.

**3, 4**   *(Outside the scope of this work.)*

**5 Commencement**

(1) The provisions of this Act to which this subsection applies shall come into force on such day as the Lord Chancellor may by order made by statutory instrument appoint.

(2) The provisions to which subsection (1) above applies are—
  (a) section 1 above; and
  (b) section 4 above, except so far as it relates to section 40 of the Law of Property Act 1925.

(3) The provisions of this Act to which this subsection applies shall come into force at the end of the period of two months beginning with the day on which this Act is passed.

(4) The provisions of this Act to which subsection (3) above applies are—
  (a) sections 2 and 3 above; and
  (b) section 4 above, so far as it relates to section 40 of the Law of Property Act 1925.

**[793]**

**NOTES**
Order: the Law of Property (Miscellaneous Provisions) Act 1989 (Commencement) Order 1990, SI 1990/1175.

**6 Citation**

(1) This Act may be cited as the Law of Property (Miscellaneous Provisions) Act 1989.

(2) This Act extends to England and Wales only.

**[794]**

*(Sch 1 amends the Law of Property Act 1925, s 52 at* **[7]** *and contains other amendments outside the scope of this work; Sch 2 contains repeals only.)*

# LOCAL GOVERNMENT AND HOUSING ACT 1989

(1989 c 42)

ARRANGEMENT OF SECTIONS

PART IX
MISCELLANEOUS AND GENERAL

*Local Government Finance Act 1988, local finance (Scotland) and block grants*

*An Act to make provision with respect to the members, officers and other staff and the procedure of local authorities; to amend Part III of the Local Government Act 1974 and Part II of the Local Government (Scotland) Act 1975 and to provide for a national code of local government conduct; to make further provision about the finances and expenditure of local authorities (including provision with respect to housing subsidies) and about companies in which local authorities have interests; to make provision for and in connection with renewal areas, grants towards the cost of improvement and repair of housing accommodation and the carrying out of works of maintenance, repair and improvement; to amend the Housing Act 1985 and Part III of the Local Government Finance Act 1982; to make amendments of and consequential upon Parts I, II and IV of the Housing Act 1988; to amend the Local Government Finance Act 1988 and the Abolition of Domestic Rates Etc (Scotland) Act 1987 and certain enactments relating, as respects Scotland, to rating and valuation, and to provide for the making of grants; to make provision with respect to the imposition of charges by local authorities; to make further provision about certain existing grants and about financial assistance to and planning by local authorities in respect of emergencies; to amend sections 102 and 211 of the Local Government (Scotland) Act 1973; to amend the Local Land Charges Act 1975; to enable local authorities in Wales to be known solely by Welsh language names; to provide for the transfer of new town housing stock; to amend certain of the provisions of the Housing (Scotland) Act 1987 relating to a secure tenant's right to purchase his house; to amend section 47 of the Race Relations Act 1976; to confer certain powers on the Housing Corporation, Housing for Wales and Scottish Homes; to make provision about security of tenure for certain tenants under long tenancies; to provide for the making of grants and giving of guarantees in respect of certain activities carried on in relation to the construction industry; to provide for the repeal of certain enactments relating to improvement notices, town development and education support grants; to make, as respects Scotland, further provision in relation to the phasing of progression to registered rent for houses let by housing associations or Scottish Homes and in relation to the circumstances in which rent increases under assured tenancies may be secured; and for connected purposes*

[16 November 1989]

**1–138**   ((*Pts I–VIII*) *in so far as unrepealed outside the scope of this work.*)

## PART IX
## MISCELLANEOUS AND GENERAL

*Local Government Finance Act 1988, local finance (Scotland) and block grants*

**139–148**   (*S 139 outside the scope of this work; ss 140–144, 146 repealed, with savings, by the Local Government Finance Act 1992, ss 117(2), 118, Sch 14 (as from a day to be appointed in the case of ss 142–144); s 145 applies to Scotland only; ss 147, 148 repealed by the Statute Law (Repeals) Act 2004.*)

**149   Statutory references to rating**

(1)–(5)   (*Outside the scope of this work.*)

(6)   Without prejudice to the generality of the powers conferred by this section, section 37 of the Landlord and Tenant Act 1954 (which provides for compensation by reference to rateable values) shall be amended in accordance with Schedule 7 to this Act.

**[795]**

**150–181**   (*Ss 150–158, 161(1), 162, 165, 166, 168, 169, 171–173, 175, outside the scope of this work; ss 159, 161(2), 170, 176–179, 181, apply to Scotland only; s 160 repealed by the Local Government Reorganisation (Wales) (Consequential Amendments No 3) Order 1996, SI 1996/3071, art 2, Schedule, para 3(10); s 163 amends the Housing Act 1985, ss 92, 117 at* **[431]**, **[460]**; *s 164 repealed by the Leasehold Reform, Housing and Urban Development Act 1993, s 187(2), Sch 22; s 167 repealed by the Housing Act 2004, ss 227, 266, Sch 16; s 174 repealed by the Housing Act 1996, s 227, Sch 19, Pt IX; s 180 repealed by the Equality Act 2006, s 91, Sch 4.*)

*Other provisions*

**182–185**   (*S 182 repealed in relation to England and Wales by the Housing Act 1996, s 227, Sch 19, Pt I; s 183 outside the scope of this work; s 184 repealed by the National Health Service and Community Care Act 1990, s 66(2), Sch 10 and the Audit Commission Act 1998, s 54(3), Sch 5; s 185 applies to Scotland only.*)

**186   Security of tenure on ending of long residential tenancies**

(1)   Schedule 10 to this Act shall have effect (in place of Part I of the Landlord and Tenant Act 1954) to confer security of tenure on certain tenants under long tenancies and, in particular, to establish assured periodic tenancies when such long tenancies come to an end.

(2)   Schedule 10 to this Act applies, and section 1 of the Landlord and Tenant Act 1954 does not apply, to a tenancy of a dwelling-house—

(a)   which is a long tenancy at a low rent, as defined in Schedule 10 to this Act; and

(b)   which is entered into on or after the day appointed for the coming into force of this section, otherwise than in pursuance of a contract made before that day.

(3)   If a tenancy—

(a)   is in existence on 15th January 1999, and

(b)   does not fall within subsection (2) above, and

(c)   immediately before that date was, or was deemed to be, a long tenancy at a low rent for the purposes of Part I of the Landlord and Tenant Act 1954,

then, on and after that date (and so far as concerns any notice specifying a date of termination on or after that date and any steps taken in consequence thereof), section 1 of that Act shall cease to apply to it and Schedule 10 to this Act shall apply to it unless, before that date, the landlord has served a notice under section 4 of that Act specifying a date of termination which is earlier than that date.

(4) The provisions of Schedule 10 to this Act have effect notwithstanding any agreement to the contrary, but nothing in this subsection or that Schedule shall be construed as preventing the surrender of a tenancy.

(5) Section 18 of the Landlord and Tenant Act 1954 (duty of tenants of residential property to give information to landlords or superior landlords) shall apply in relation to property comprised in a long tenancy at a low rent, within the meaning of Schedule 10 to this Act, as it applies to property comprised in a long tenancy at a low rent within the meaning of Part I of that Act, except that the reference in that section to subsection (1) of section 3 of that Act shall be construed as a reference to sub-paragraph (1) of paragraph 3 of Schedule 10 to this Act.

(6) Where, by virtue of subsection (3) above, Schedule 10 to this Act applies to a tenancy which is not a long tenancy at a low rent as defined in that Schedule, it shall be deemed to be such a tenancy for the purposes of that Schedule.

**[796]**

**187–189**    *(S 187 outside the scope of this work; s 188 repealed by the Education Act 1996, s 582(2), Sch 38, Pt I; s 189 repealed by the Criminal Justice Act 1991, s 101(2), Sch 13.)*

*Supplementary*

## 190 Regulations

(1) Under any power to make regulations conferred by any provision of this Act, different provision may be made for different cases and different descriptions of cases (including different provision for different areas).

(2) Any power to make regulations conferred by any provision of this Act shall be exercisable by statutory instrument which, except in the case of a statutory instrument containing regulations under section 150 or section 151 or Schedule 10, shall be subject to annulment in pursuance of a resolution of either House of Parliament.

**[797]**

## 191 Separate provisions for Wales

(1) Where any provision of this Act which extends to England and Wales confers (directly or by amendment of another Act) a power on the Secretary of State to make regulations, orders, rules or determinations or to give directions or specify any matter, the power may be exercised differently for England and Wales, whether or not it is exercised separately.

(2) This section is without prejudice to section 190(1) above and to any other provision of this Act or of any Act amended by this Act by virtue of which powers may be exercised differently in different cases or in any other circumstances.

**[798]**

**NOTES**

Transfer of functions: the functions of the Secretary of State, so far as exercisable in relation to Wales, are transferred to the National Assembly for Wales, by the National Assembly for Wales (Transfer of Functions) Order 1999, SI 1999/672, art 2, Sch 1.

**192**    *(Outside the scope of this work.)*

## 193 Application to Isles of Scilly

(1) This Act applies to the Isles of Scilly subject to such exceptions, adaptations and modifications as the Secretary of State may by order direct.

(2) The power to make an order under this section shall be exercisable by statutory instrument which shall be subject to annulment in pursuance of a resolution of either House of Parliament.

**[799]**

**194**    *(Outside the scope of this work.)*

## 195 Short title, commencement and extent

(1) This Act may be cited as the Local Government and Housing Act 1989.

(2) The provisions of sections 1 and 2, 9, 10, 13 to 20 above, Parts II to V (with the exception in Part II of section 24), VII and VIII and (in this Part) sections 140 to 145, 156, 159, 160, 162, 164, 165, [168] to 173, 175 to 180, 182 and 183, 185, 186 and 194, except in so far as it relates to paragraphs 104 to 106 of Schedule 11, shall come into force on such day as the Secretary of State may by order made by statutory instrument appoint, and different days may be so appointed for different provisions or for different purposes.

(3)   An order under subsection (2) above may contain such transitional provisions and savings (whether or not involving the modification of any statutory provision) as appear to the Secretary of State necessary or expedient in connection with the provisions brought into force by the order.

(4)   Subject to subsection (5) below, this Act, except Parts I and II and sections 36(9), 140 to 145, 150 to 152, 153, 155, 157, 159, 161, 166, 168, 170, 171, 176 to 182, 185, 190, 192, 194(1), 194(4) and this section, extends to England and Wales only.

(5)   (*Applies to Scotland only.*)

(6)   This Act does not extend to Northern Ireland.

[800]

**NOTES**

Sub-s (2): figure in square brackets substituted by the Housing Act 2004, s 265(1), Sch 15, para 35.

Orders: the Local Government and Housing Act 1989 (Commencement No 1) Order 1989, SI 1989/2180; the Local Government and Housing Act 1989 (Commencement No 2) Order 1989, SI 1989/2186; the Local Government and Housing Act 1989 (Commencement No 3) Order 1989, SI 1989/2445; the Local Government and Housing Act 1989 (Commencement No 4) Order 1990, SI 1990/191; the Local Government and Housing Act 1989 (Commencement No 5 and Transitional Provisions) Order 1990, SI 1990/431, as amended by SI 1990/762; the Local Government and Housing Act 1989 (Commencement No 6 and Miscellaneous Provisions) Order 1990, SI 1990/762, the Local Government and Housing Act 1989 (Commencement No 7) Order 1990, SI 1990/961; the Local Government and Housing Act 1989 (Commencement No 8 and Transitional Provisions) Order 1990, SI 1990/1274, as amended by SI 1990/1335; the Local Government and Housing Act 1989 (Commencement No 9 and Saving) Order 1990, SI 1990/1552; the Local Government and Housing Act 1989 (Commencement No 10) Order 1990, SI 1990/2581; the Local Government and Housing Act 1989 (Commencement No 11 and Savings) Order 1991, SI 1991/344; the Local Government and Housing Act 1989 (Commencement No 12) Order 1991, SI 1991/953; the Local Government and Housing Act 1989 (Commencement No 13) Order 1991, SI 1991/2940; the Local Government and Housing Act 1989 (Commencement No 14) Order 1992, SI 1992/760; the Local Government and Housing Act 1989 (Commencement No 15) Order 1993, SI 1993/105; the Local Government and Housing Act 1989 (Commencement No 16) Order 1993, SI 1993/2410; the Local Government and Housing Act 1989 (Commencement No 17) Order 1995, SI 1995/841; the Local Government and Housing Act 1989 (Commencement No 18) Order 1996, SI 1996/1857.

## SCHEDULES

(*Schs 1, 2, 4, 5 outside the scope of this work; Sch 3 repealed by the Local Government Act 2003, s 127(2), Sch 8, Pt 1; Sch 6 applies to Scotland only.*)

## SCHEDULE 7
## COMPENSATION PROVISIONS OF LANDLORD AND TENANT ACT 1954, PART II
Section 149

1.   Any reference in this Schedule to a section which is not otherwise identified is a reference to that section of the Landlord and Tenant Act 1954, Part II of which relates to security of tenure for business, professional and other tenants.

2.   ....

3.   The amendments made by paragraph 2 above do not have effect unless the date which, apart from paragraph 4 below, is relevant for determining the rateable value of the holding under subsection (5) of section 37 is on or after 1st April 1990.

4.—(1)   Subject to paragraph 3 above and paragraph 5 below, in any case where—
   (a)   the tenancy concerned was entered into before 1st April 1990 or was entered into on or after that date in pursuance of a contract made before that date, and
   (b)   the landlord's notice under section 25 or, as the case may be, section 26(6) is given before 1st April 2000, and
   (c)   within the period referred to in section 29(3) for the making of an application under section 24(1), the tenant gives notice to the landlord that he wants the special basis of compensation provided for by this paragraph,
the amendments made by paragraph 2 above shall not have effect and section 37 shall, instead, have effect with the modification specified in sub-paragraph (2) below.

(2)   The modification referred to in sub-paragraph (1) above is that the date which is relevant for the purposes of determining the rateable value of the holding under subsection (5) of section 37 shall be 31st March 1990 instead of the date on which the landlord's notice is given.

5.   In any case where—
   (a)   paragraph 4(1)(a) above applies, and
   (b)   on 31st March 1990, the rateable value of the holding could be determined only in accordance with paragraph (c) of subsection (5) of section 37,
no notice may be given under paragraph 4(1)(b) above.

[801]

**NOTES**

Para 2: amends the Landlord and Tenant Act 1954, s 37.

*(Sch 8 repealed by the Local Government Reorganisation (Wales) (Consequential Amendments No 3) Order 1996, SI 1996/3071, art 2, Schedule, para 3(11); Sch 9 outside the scope of this work.)*

## SCHEDULE 10
SECURITY OF TENURE ON ENDING OF LONG RESIDENTIAL TENANCIES

Section 186

*Preliminary*

1.—(1) This Schedule applies to a long tenancy of a dwelling-house at a low rent as respects which for the time being the following condition (in this Schedule referred to as "the qualifying condition") is fulfilled, that is to say, that the circumstances (as respects the property let under the tenancy, the use of that property and all other relevant matters) are such that, if the tenancy were not at a low rent, it would at that time be an assured tenancy within the meaning of Part I of the Housing Act 1988.

(2) For the purpose only of determining whether the qualifying condition is fulfilled with respect to a tenancy, Schedule 1 to the Housing Act 1988 (tenancies which cannot be assured tenancies) shall have effect with the omission of paragraph 1 (which excludes tenancies entered into before, or pursuant to contracts made before, the coming into force of Part I of that Act).

[(2A) For the purpose only of determining whether the qualifying condition is fulfilled with respect to a tenancy which is entered into on or after 1st April 1990 (otherwise than, where the dwelling-house has a rateable value on 31st March 1990, in pursuance of a contract made before 1st April 1990), for paragraph 2(1)(b) and (2) of Schedule 1 to the Housing Act 1988 there shall be substituted—

"(b) where (on the date the contract for the grant of the tenancy was made or, if there was no such contract, on the date the tenancy was entered into) R exceeded £25,000 under the formula—

$$R = \frac{P \times I}{1 - (1+I)^{-T}}$$

where—
P is the premium payable as a condition of the grant of the tenancy (and includes a payment of money's worth) or, where no premium is so payable, zero,
I is 0·06,
T is the term, expressed in years, granted by the tenancy (disregarding any right to terminate the tenancy before the end of the term or to extend the tenancy).".]

(3) At any time within the period of twelve months ending on the day preceding the term date, application may be made to the court as respects any long tenancy of a dwelling-house at a low rent, not being at the time of the application a tenancy as respects which the qualifying condition is fulfilled, for an order declaring that the tenancy is not to be treated as a tenancy to which this Schedule applies.

(4) Where an application is made under sub-paragraph (3) above—
(a) the court, if satisfied that the tenancy is not likely immediately before the term date to be a tenancy to which this Schedule applies but not otherwise, shall make the order; and
(b) if the court makes the order, then, notwithstanding anything in sub-paragraph (1) above the tenancy shall not thereafter be treated as a tenancy to which this Schedule applies.

(5) A tenancy to which this Schedule applies is hereinafter referred to as a long residential tenancy.

(6) Anything authorised or required to be done under the following provisions of this Schedule in relation to a long residential tenancy shall, if done before the term date in relation to a long tenancy of a dwelling-house at a low rent, not be treated as invalid by reason only that at the time at which it was done the qualifying condition was not fulfilled as respects the tenancy.

(7) In determining for the purposes of any provision of this Schedule whether the property let under a tenancy was let as a separate dwelling, the nature of the property at the time of the creation of the tenancy shall be deemed to have been the same as its nature at the time in relation to which the question arises, and the purpose for which it was let under the tenancy shall be deemed to have been the same as the purpose for which it is or was used at the last-mentioned time.

[(8) The Secretary of State may by order replace the number in the definition of "I" in sub-paragraph (2A) above and any amount referred to in that sub-paragraph and paragraph 2(4)(b) below by such number or amount as is specified in the order; and such an order shall be made by statutory instrument which shall be subject to annulment in pursuance of a resolution of either House of Parliament.]

PART 1
STATUTES

2.—(1) This paragraph has effect for the interpretation of certain expressions used in this Schedule.

(2) Except where the context otherwise requires, expressions to which a meaning is assigned for the purposes of the 1988 Act or Part I of that Act have the same meaning in this Schedule.

(3) "Long tenancy" means a tenancy granted for a term of years certain exceeding 21 years, whether or not subsequently extended by act of the parties or by any enactment, but excluding any tenancy which is, or may become, terminable before the end of the term by notice given to the tenant.

[(4) A tenancy is "at a low rent" if under the tenancy—
  (a) no rent is payable,
  (b) where the tenancy is entered into on or after 1st April 1990 (otherwise than, where the dwelling-house had a rateable value on 31st March 1990, in pursuance of a contract made before 1st April 1990), the maximum rent payable at any time is payable at a rate of—
    (i) £1,000 or less a year if the dwelling-house is in Greater London and,
    (ii) £250 or less a year if the dwelling-house is elsewhere, or,
  (c) where the tenancy was entered into before 1st April 1990 or (where the dwelling-house had a rateable value on 31st March 1990) is entered into on or after 1st April 1990 in pursuance of a contract made before that date, and the maximum rent payable at any time under the tenancy is less than two-thirds of the rateable value of the dwelling-house on 31st March 1990.]

(5) [Paragraph 2(2)] of Schedule 1 to the 1988 Act applies to determine whether the rent under a tenancy falls within sub-paragraph (4) above and Part II of that Schedule applies to determine the rateable value of a dwelling-house for the purposes of that sub-paragraph.

(6) "Long residential tenancy" and "qualifying condition" have the meaning assigned by paragraph 1 above and the following expressions shall be construed as follows—
  "the 1954 Act" means the Landlord and Tenant Act 1954;
  "the 1988 Act" means the Housing Act 1988;
  "assured periodic tenancy" shall be construed in accordance with paragraph 9(4) below;
  "the date of termination" has the meaning assigned by paragraph 4(4) below;
  "disputed terms" shall be construed in accordance with paragraph 11(1)(a) below;
  "election by the tenant to retain possession" shall be construed in accordance with paragraph 4(7) below;
  "former 1954 Act tenancy" means a tenancy to which, by virtue of section 186(3) of this Act, this Schedule applies on and after 15th January 1999;
  "the implied terms" shall be construed in accordance with paragraph 4(5)(a) below;
  "landlord" shall be construed in accordance with paragraph 19(1) below;
  "landlord's notice" means a notice under sub-paragraph (1) of paragraph 4 below and such a notice is—
    (a) a "landlord's notice proposing an assured tenancy" if it contains such proposals as are mentioned in sub-paragraph (5)(a) of that paragraph; and
    (b) a "landlord's notice to resume possession" if it contains such proposals as are referred to in sub-paragraph (5)(b) of that paragraph;
  "specified date of termination", in relation to a tenancy in respect of which a landlord's notice is served, means the date specified in the notice as mentioned in paragraph 4(1)(a) below;
  "tenant's notice" shall be construed in accordance with paragraph 10(1)(a) below;
  "term date", in relation to a tenancy granted for a term of years certain, means the date of expiry of that term; and
  "the terms of the tenancy specified in the landlord's notice" shall be construed in accordance with paragraph 4(6) below; and
  "undisputed terms" shall be construed in accordance with paragraph 11(2) below.

*Continuation of long residential tenancies*

3.—(1) A tenancy which, immediately before the term date, is a long residential tenancy shall not come to an end on that date except by being terminated under the provisions of this Schedule, and, if not then so terminated, shall subject to those provisions continue until so terminated and, while continuing by virtue of this paragraph, shall be deemed to be a long residential tenancy (notwithstanding any change in circumstances).

(2) Sub-paragraph (1) above does not apply in the case of a former 1954 Act tenancy the term date of which falls before 15th January 1999 but if, in the case of such a tenancy,—
  (a) the tenancy is continuing immediately before that date by virtue of section 3 of the 1954 Act, and
  (b) on that date the qualifying condition (as defined in paragraph 1(1) above) is fulfilled,
then, subject to the provisions of this Schedule, the tenancy shall continue until terminated under those provisions and, while continuing by virtue of this paragraph, shall be deemed to be a long residential tenancy (notwithstanding any change in circumstances).

(3)    Where by virtue of this paragraph a tenancy continues after the term date, the tenancy shall continue at the same rent and in other respects on the same terms as before the term date.

*Termination of tenancy by the landlord*

4.—(1)    Subject to sub-paragraph (2) below and the provisions of this Schedule as to the annulment of notices in certain cases, the landlord may terminate a long residential tenancy by a notice in the prescribed form served on the tenant—

    (a)    specifying the date at which the tenancy is to come to an end, being either the term date or a later date; and

    (b)    so served not more than twelve nor less than six months before the date so specified.

(2)    In any case where—

    (a)    a landlord's notice has been served, and

    (b)    an application has been made to the court or a rent assessment committee under the following provisions of this Schedule other than paragraph 6, and

    (c)    apart from this paragraph, the effect of the notice would be to terminate the tenancy before the expiry of the period of three months beginning with the date on which the application is finally disposed of,

the effect of the notice shall be to terminate the tenancy at the expiry of the said period of three months and not at any other time.

(3)    The reference in sub-paragraph (2)(c) above to the date on which the application is finally disposed of shall be construed as a reference to the earliest date by which the proceedings on the application (including any proceedings on or in consequence of an appeal) have been determined and any time for appealing or further appealing has expired, except that if the application is withdrawn or any appeal is abandoned the reference shall be construed as a reference to the date of withdrawal or abandonment.

(4)    In this Schedule "the date of termination", in relation to a tenancy in respect of which a landlord's notice is served, means,—

    (a)    where the tenancy is continued as mentioned in sub-paragraph (2) above, the last day of the period of three months referred to in that sub-paragraph; and

    (b)    in any other case, the specified date of termination.

(5)    A landlord's notice shall not have effect unless—

    (a)    it proposes an assured monthly periodic tenancy of the dwelling-house and a rent for that tenancy (such that it would not be a tenancy at a low rent) and, subject to sub-paragraph (6) below, states that the other terms of the tenancy shall be the same as those of the long residential tenancy immediately before it is terminated (in this Schedule referred to as "the implied terms"); or

    (b)    it gives notice that, if the tenant is not willing to give up possession at the date of termination of the property let under the tenancy, the landlord proposes to apply to the court, on one or more of the grounds specified in paragraph 5(1) below, for the possession of the property let under the tenancy and states the ground or grounds on which he proposes to apply.

(6)    In the landlord's notice proposing an assured tenancy the landlord may propose terms of the tenancy referred to in sub-paragraph (5)(a) above different from the implied terms; and any reference in the following provisions of this Schedule to the terms of the tenancy specified in the landlord's notice is a reference to the implied terms or, if the implied terms are varied by virtue of this sub-paragraph, to the implied terms as so varied.

(7)    A landlord's notice shall invite the tenant, within the period of two months beginning on the date on which the notice was served, to notify the landlord in writing whether,—

    (a)    in the case of a landlord's notice proposing an assured tenancy, the tenant wishes to remain in possession; and

    (b)    in the case of a landlord's notice to resume possession, the tenant is willing to give up possession as mentioned in sub-paragraph (5)(b) above;

and references in this Schedule to an election by the tenant to retain possession are references to his notifying the landlord under this sub-paragraph that he wishes to remain in possession or, as the case may be, that he is not willing to give up possession.

5.—(1)    Subject to the following provisions of this paragraph, the grounds mentioned in paragraph 4(5)(b) above are—

    (a)    Ground 6 in, and those in Part II of, Schedule 2 to the 1988 Act, other than Ground 16;

    (b)    the ground that, for the purposes of redevelopment after the termination of the tenancy, the landlord proposes to demolish or reconstruct the whole or a substantial part of the premises; and

    (c)    the ground that the premises or part of them are reasonably required by the landlord for occupation [as a residence for—

        (i)    himself,

        (ii)    any son or daughter of his over eighteen years of age,

(iii)   his father or mother, or

(iv)   the father, or mother, of his spouse or civil partner, and,] if the landlord is not the immediate landlord, that he will be at the specified date of termination.

(2)   Ground 6 in Schedule 2 to the 1988 Act may not be specified in a landlord's notice to resume possession if the tenancy is a former 1954 Act tenancy; and in the application of that Ground in accordance with sub-paragraph (1) above in any other case, paragraph (c) shall be omitted.

(3)   In its application in accordance with sub-paragraph (1) above, Ground 10 in Schedule 2 to the 1988 Act shall have effect as if, in paragraph (b)—

(a)   the words "except where subsection (1)(b) of section 8 of this Act applies" were omitted; and

(b)   for the words "notice under that section relating to those proceedings" there were substituted "landlord's notice to resume possession (within the meaning of Schedule 10 to the Local Government and Housing Act 1989)".

(4)   The ground mentioned in sub-paragraph (1)(b) above may not be specified in a landlord's notice to resume possession unless the landlord is a body to which section 28 of the Leasehold Reform Act 1967 applies and the premises are required for relevant development within the meaning of that section; and on any application by such a body under paragraph 13 below for possession on that ground, a certificate given by a Minister of the Crown as provided by subsection (1) of that section shall be conclusive evidence that the premises are so required.

(5)   The ground mentioned in sub-paragraph (1)(c) above may not be specified in a landlord's notice to resume possession if the interest of the landlord, or an interest which is merged in that interest and but for the merger would be the interest of the landlord, was purchased or created after 18th February 1966.

### *Interim rent*

6.—(1)   On the date of service of a landlord's notice proposing an assured tenancy, or at any time between that date and the date of termination, the landlord may serve a notice on the tenant in the prescribed form proposing an interim monthly rent to take effect from a date specified in the notice, being not earlier than the specified date of termination, and to continue while the tenancy is continued by virtue of the preceding provisions of this Schedule.

(2)   Where a notice has been served under sub-paragraph (1) above,—

(a)   within the period of two months beginning on the date of service, the tenant may refer the interim monthly rent proposed in the notice to a rent assessment committee; and

(b)   if the notice is not so referred, then, with effect from the date specified in the notice or, if it is later, the expiry of the period mentioned in paragraph (a) above, the interim monthly rent proposed in the notice shall be the rent under the tenancy.

(3)   Where, under sub-paragraph (2) above, the rent specified in a landlord's notice is referred to a rent assessment committee, the committee shall determine the monthly rent at which, subject to sub-paragraph (4) below, the committee consider that the premises let under the tenancy might reasonably be expected to be let on the open market by a willing landlord under a monthly periodic tenancy—

(a)   which begins on the day following the specified date of termination;

(b)   under which the other terms are the same as those of the existing tenancy at the date on which was given the landlord's notice proposing an assured tenancy; and

(c)   which affords the tenant security of tenure equivalent to that afforded by Chapter I of Part I of the 1988 Act in the case of an assured tenancy (other than an assured shorthold tenancy) in respect of which possession may not be recovered under any of Grounds 1 to 5 in Part I of Schedule 2 to that Act.

(4)   Subsections (2), [(3A),] (4) and (5) of section 14 of the 1988 Act shall apply in relation to a determination of rent under sub-paragraph (3) above as they apply in relation to a determination under that section subject to the modifications in sub-paragraph (5) below; and in this paragraph "rent" shall be construed in accordance with subsection (4) of that section.

(5)   The modifications of section 14 of the 1988 Act referred to in sub-paragraph (4) above are that in subsection (2), the reference in paragraph (b) to a relevant improvement being carried out shall be construed as a reference to an improvement being carried out during the long residential tenancy and the reference in paragraph (c) to a failure to comply with any term of the tenancy shall be construed as a reference to a failure to comply with any term of the long residential tenancy.

(6)   Where a reference has been made to a rent assessment committee under sub-paragraph (2) above, then, the rent determined by the committee (subject, in a case where section 14(5) of the 1988 Act applies, to the addition of the appropriate amount in respect of rates) shall be the rent under the tenancy with effect from the date specified in the notice served under sub-paragraph (1) above or, if it is later, the expiry of the period mentioned in paragraph (a) of sub-paragraph (2) above.

7.—(1)  Nothing in paragraph 6 above affects the right of the landlord and the tenant to agree the interim monthly rent which is to have effect while the tenancy is continued by virtue of the preceding provisions of this Schedule and the date from which that rent is to take effect; and, in such a case,—

    (a)   notwithstanding the provisions of paragraph 6 above, that rent shall be the rent under the tenancy with effect from that date; and

    (b)   no steps or, as the case may be, no further steps may be taken by the landlord or the tenant under the provisions of that paragraph.

(2)  Nothing in paragraph 6 above requires a rent assessment committee to continue with a determination under sub-paragraph (3) of that paragraph—

    (a)   if the tenant gives notice in writing that he no longer requires such a determination; or

    (b)   if the long residential tenancy has come to an end on or before the specified date of termination.

(3)  Notwithstanding that a tenancy in respect of which an interim monthly rent has effect in accordance with paragraph 6 above or this paragraph is no longer at a low rent, it shall continue to be regarded as a tenancy at a low rent and, accordingly, shall continue to be a long residential tenancy.

### Termination of tenancy by the tenant

8.—(1)  A long residential tenancy may be brought to an end at the term date by not less than one month's notice in writing given by the tenant to his immediate landlord.

(2)  A tenancy which is continuing after the term date by virtue of paragraph 3 above may be brought to an end at any time by not less than one month's notice in writing given by the tenant to his immediate landlord, whether the notice is given before or after the term date of the tenancy.

(3)  The fact that the landlord has served a landlord's notice or that there has been an election by the tenant to retain possession shall not prevent the tenant from giving notice under this paragraph terminating the tenancy at a date earlier than the specified date of termination.

### The assured periodic tenancy

9.—(1)  Where a long residential tenancy (in this paragraph referred to as "the former tenancy") is terminated by a landlord's notice proposing an assured tenancy, then, subject to sub-paragraph (3) below, the tenant shall be entitled to remain in possession of the dwelling-house and his right to possession shall depend upon an assured periodic tenancy arising by virtue of this paragraph.

(2)  The assured periodic tenancy referred to in sub-paragraph (1) above is one—

    (a)   taking effect in possession on the day following the date of termination;

    (b)   deemed to have been granted by the person who was the landlord under the former tenancy on the date of termination to the person who was then the tenant under that tenancy;

    (c)   under which the premises let are the dwelling-house;

    (d)   under which the periods of the tenancy, and the intervals at which rent is to be paid, are monthly beginning on the day following the date of termination;

    (e)   under which the rent is determined in accordance with paragraphs 10 to 12 below; and

    (f)   under which the other terms are determined in accordance with paragraphs 10 to 12 below.

(3)  If, at the end of the period of two months beginning on the date of service of the landlord's notice, the qualifying condition was not fulfilled as respects the tenancy, the tenant shall not be entitled to remain in possession as mentioned in sub-paragraph (1) above unless there has been an election by the tenant to retain possession; and if, at the specified date of termination, the qualifying condition is not fulfilled as respects the tenancy, then, notwithstanding that there has been such an election, the tenant shall not be entitled to remain in possession as mentioned in that sub-paragraph.

(4)  Any reference in the following provisions of this Schedule to an assured periodic tenancy is a reference to an assured periodic tenancy arising by virtue of this paragraph.

### Initial rent under and terms of assured periodic tenancy

10.—(1)  Where a landlord's notice proposing an assured tenancy has been served on the tenant,—

    (a)   within the period of two months beginning on the date of service of the notice, the tenant may serve on the landlord a notice in the prescribed form proposing either or both of the following, that is to say,—

        (i)   a rent for the assured periodic tenancy different from that proposed in the landlord's notice; and

        (ii)  terms of the tenancy different from those specified in the landlord's notice, and such a notice is in this Schedule referred to as a "tenant's notice"; and

    (b)   if a tenant's notice is not so served, then, with effect from the date on which the assured periodic tenancy takes effect in possession,—

        (i)   the rent proposed in the landlord's notice shall be the rent under the tenancy; and

(ii)   the terms of the tenancy specified in the landlord's notice shall be terms of the tenancy.

(2)   Where a tenant's notice has been served on the landlord under sub-paragraph (1) above—

    (a)   within the period of two months beginning on the date of service of the notice, the landlord may by an application in the prescribed form refer the notice to a rent assessment committee; and

    (b)   if the notice is not so referred, then, with effect from the date on which the assured periodic tenancy takes effect in possession,—

        (i)   the rent (if any) proposed in the tenant's notice, or, if no rent is so proposed, the rent proposed in the landlord's notice, shall be the rent under the tenancy; and

        (ii)   the other terms of the tenancy (if any) proposed in the tenant's notice and, in so far as they do not conflict with the terms so proposed, the terms specified in the landlord's notice shall be terms of the tenancy.

11.—(1)   Where, under sub-paragraph (2) of paragraph 10 above, a tenant's notice is referred to a rent assessment committee, the committee, having regard only to the contents of the landlord's notice and the tenant's notice, shall decide—

    (a)   whether there is any dispute as to the terms (other than those relating to the amount of the rent) of the assured periodic tenancy (in this Schedule referred to as "disputed terms") and, if so, what the disputed terms are; and

    (b)   whether there is any dispute as to rent under the tenancy;

and where the committee decide that there are disputed terms and that there is a dispute as to the rent under the tenancy, they shall make a determination under sub-paragraph (3) below before they make a determination under sub-paragraph (5) below.

(2)   Where, under paragraph 10(2) above, a tenant's notice is referred to a rent assessment committee, any reference in this Schedule to the undisputed terms is a reference to those terms (if any) which—

    (a)   are proposed in the landlord's notice or the tenant's notice; and

    (b)   do not relate to the amount of the rent; and

    (c)   are not disputed terms.

(3)   If the rent assessment committee decide that there are disputed terms, they shall determine whether the terms in the landlord's notice, the terms in the tenant's notice, or some other terms, dealing with the same subject matter as the disputed terms are such as, in the committee's opinion, might reasonably be expected to be found in an assured monthly periodic tenancy of the dwelling-house (not being an assured shorthold tenancy)—

    (a)   which begins on the day following the date of termination;

    (b)   which is granted by a willing landlord on terms which, except so far as they relate to the subject matter of the disputed terms, are the undisputed terms; and

    (c)   in respect of which possession may not be recovered under any of Grounds 1 to 5 in Part I of Schedule 2 to the 1988 Act;

and the committee shall, if they consider it appropriate, specify an adjustment of the undisputed terms to take account of the terms so determined and shall, if they consider it appropriate, specify an adjustment of the rent to take account of the terms so determined and, if applicable, so adjusted.

(4)   In making a determination under sub-paragraph (3) above, or specifying an adjustment of the rent or undisputed terms under that sub-paragraph, there shall be disregarded any effect on the terms or the amount of rent attributable to the granting of a tenancy to a sitting tenant.

(5)   If the rent assessment committee decide that there is a dispute as to the rent under the assured periodic tenancy, the committee shall determine the monthly rent at which, subject to sub-paragraph (6) below, the committee consider that the dwelling-house might reasonably be expected to be let in the open market by a willing landlord under an assured tenancy (not being an assured shorthold tenancy)—

    (a)   which is a monthly periodic tenancy;

    (b)   which begins on the day following the date of termination;

    (c)   in respect of which possession may not be recovered under any of Grounds 1 to 5 in Part I of Schedule 2 to the 1988 Act; and

    (d)   the terms of which (other than those relating to the amount of the rent) are the same as—

        (i)   the undisputed terms; or

        (ii)   if there has been a determination under sub-paragraph (3) above, the terms determined by the committee under that sub-paragraph and the undisputed terms (as adjusted, if at all, under that sub-paragraph).

(6)   Subsections (2), [(3A),] (4) and (5) of section 14 of the 1988 Act shall apply in relation to a determination of rent under sub-paragraph (5) above as they apply in relation to a determination under that section subject to the modifications in sub-paragraph (7) below; and in this paragraph "rent" shall be construed in accordance with subsection (4) of that section.

(7)   The modifications of section 14 of the 1988 Act referred to in sub-paragraph (6) above are that in subsection (2), the reference in paragraph (b) to a relevant improvement being carried out

shall be construed as a reference to an improvement being carried out during the long residential tenancy and the reference in paragraph (c) to a failure to comply with any term of the tenancy shall be construed as a reference to a failure to comply with any term of the long residential tenancy.

(8)   Where a reference has been made to a rent assessment committee under sub-paragraph (2) of paragraph 10 above, then,—

(a)   if the committee decide that there are no disputed terms and that there is no dispute as to the rent, paragraph 10(2)(b) above shall apply as if the notice had not been so referred,

(b)   where paragraph (a) above does not apply then, so far as concerns the amount of the rent under the tenancy, if there is a dispute as to the rent, the rent determined by the committee (subject, in a case where section 14(5) of the 1988 Act applies, to the addition of the appropriate amount in respect of rates) and, if there is no dispute as to the rent, the rent specified in the landlord's notice or, as the case may be, the tenant's notice (subject to any adjustment under sub-paragraph (3) above) shall be the rent under the tenancy, and

(c)   where paragraph (a) above does not apply and there are disputed terms, then, so far as concerns the subject matter of those terms, the terms determined by the committee under sub-paragraph (3) above shall be terms of the tenancy and, so far as concerns any undisputed terms, those terms (subject to any adjustment under sub-paragraph (3) above) shall also be terms of the tenancy,

with effect from the date on which the assured periodic tenancy takes effect in possession.

(9)   Nothing in this Schedule affects the right of the landlord and the tenant under the assured periodic tenancy to vary by agreement any term of the tenancy (including a term relating to rent).

12.—(1)   Subsections (2) to (4) of section 41 of the 1988 Act (rent assessment committees: information powers) shall apply where there is a reference to a rent assessment committee under the preceding provisions of this Schedule as they apply where a matter is referred to such a committee under Chapter I or Chapter II of Part I of the 1988 Act.

(2)   Nothing in paragraph 10 or paragraph 11 above affects the right of the landlord and the tenant to agree any terms of the assured periodic tenancy (including a term relating to the rent) before the tenancy takes effect in possession (in this sub-paragraph referred to as "the expressly agreed terms"); and, in such case,—

(a)   the expressly agreed terms shall be terms of the tenancy in substitution for any terms dealing with the same subject matter which would otherwise, by virtue of paragraph 10 or paragraph 11 above, be terms of the tenancy; and

(b)   where a reference has already been made to a rent assessment committee under sub-paragraph (2) of paragraph 10 above but there has been no determination by the committee under paragraph 11 above,—

(i)   the committee shall have regard to the expressly agreed terms, as notified to them by the landlord and the tenant, in deciding, for the purposes of paragraph 11 above, what the disputed terms are and whether there is any dispute as to the rent; and

(ii)   in making any determination under paragraph 11 above the committee shall not make any adjustment of the expressly agreed terms, as so notified.

(3)   Nothing in paragraph 11 above requires a rent assessment committee to continue with a determination under that paragraph—

(a)   if the long residential tenancy has come to an end; or

(b)   if the landlord serves notice in writing on the committee that he no longer requires such a determination;

and, where the landlord serves notice as mentioned in paragraph (b) above, then, for the purposes of sub-paragraph (2) of paragraph 10 above, the landlord shall be treated as not having made a reference under paragraph (a) of that sub-paragraph and, accordingly, paragraph (b) of that sub-paragraph shall, subject to sub-paragraph (2) above, have effect for determining rent and other terms of the assured periodic tenancy.

*Landlord's application for possession*

13.—(1)   Where a landlord's notice to resume possession has been served on the tenant and either—

(a)   there is an election by the tenant to retain possession, or

(b)   at the end of the period of two months beginning on the date of service of the notice, the qualifying condition is fulfilled as respects the tenancy,

the landlord may apply to the court for an order under this paragraph on such of the grounds mentioned in paragraph 5(1) above as may be specified in the notice.

(2)   The court shall not entertain an application under sub-paragraph (1) above unless the application is made—

(a)   within the period of two months beginning on the date of the election by the tenant to retain possession; or

(b)    if there is no election by the tenant to retain possession, within the period of four months beginning on the date of service of the landlord's notice.

(3)    Where the ground or one of the grounds for claiming possession specified in the landlord's notice is Ground 6 in Part I of Schedule 2 to the 1988 Act, then, if on an application made under sub-paragraph (1) above the court is satisfied that the landlord has established that ground, the court shall order that the tenant shall, on the date of termination, give up possession of the property then let under the tenancy.

(4)    Subject to sub-paragraph (6) below, where the ground or one of the grounds for claiming possession specified in the landlord's notice is any of Grounds 9 to 15 in Part II of Schedule 2 to the 1988 Act or the ground mentioned in paragraph 5(1)(c) above, then, if on an application made under sub-paragraph (1) above the court is satisfied that the landlord has established that ground and that it is reasonable that the landlord should be granted possession, the court shall order that the tenant shall, on the date of termination, give up possession of the property then let under the tenancy.

(5)    Part III of Schedule 2 to the 1988 Act shall have effect for supplementing Ground 9 in that Schedule (as that ground applies in relation to this Schedule) as it has effect for supplementing that ground for the purposes of that Act, subject to the modification that in paragraph 3(1), in the words following paragraph (b) the reference to the assured tenancy in question shall be construed as a reference to the long residential tenancy in question.

(6)    Where the ground or one of the grounds for claiming possession specified in the landlord's notice is that mentioned in paragraph 5(1)(c) above, the court shall not make the order mentioned in sub-paragraph (4) above on that ground if it is satisfied that, having regard to all the circumstances of the case, including the question whether other accommodation is available for the landlord or the tenant, greater hardship would be caused by making the order than by refusing to make it.

(7)    Where the ground or one of the grounds for claiming possession specified in the landlord's notice is that mentioned in paragraph 5(1)(b) above, then, if on an application made under sub-paragraph (1) above the court is satisfied that the landlord has established that ground and is further satisfied—

(a)    that on that ground possession of those premises will be required by the landlord on the date of termination, and

(b)    that the landlord has made such preparations (including the obtaining or, if that is not reasonably practicable in the circumstances, preparations relating to the obtaining of any requisite permission or consent, whether from any authority whose permission or consent is required under any enactment or from the owner of any interest in any property) for proceeding with the redevelopment as are reasonable in the circumstances,

the court shall order that the tenant shall, on the date of termination, give up possession of the property then let under the tenancy.

14.—(1)    Where, in a case falling within sub-paragraph (7) of paragraph 13 above, the court is not satisfied as mentioned in that sub-paragraph but would be satisfied if the date of termination of the tenancy had been such date (in this paragraph referred to as "the postponed date") as the court may determine, being a date later, but not more than one year later, than the specified date of termination, the court shall, if the landlord so requires, make an order as mentioned in sub-paragraph (2) below.

(2)    The order referred to in sub-paragraph (1) above is one by which the court specifies the postponed date and orders—

(a)    that the tenancy shall not come to an end on the date of termination but shall continue thereafter, as respects the whole of the property let under the tenancy, at the same rent and in other respects on the same terms as before that date; and

(b)    that, unless the tenancy comes to an end before the postponed date, the tenant shall on that date give up possession of the property then let under the tenancy.

(3)    Notwithstanding the provisions of paragraph 13 above and the preceding provisions of this paragraph and notwithstanding that there has been an election by the tenant to retain possession, if the court is satisfied, at the date of the hearing, that the qualifying condition is not fulfilled as respects the tenancy, the court shall order that the tenant shall, on the date of termination, give up possession of the property then let under the tenancy.

(4)    Nothing in paragraph 13 above or the preceding provisions of this paragraph shall prejudice any power of the tenant under paragraph 8 above to terminate the tenancy; and sub-paragraph (2) of that paragraph shall apply where the tenancy is continued by an order under sub-paragraph (2) above as it applies where the tenancy is continued by virtue of paragraph 3 above.

*Provisions where tenant not ordered to give up possession*

15.—(1)    The provisions of this paragraph shall have effect where the landlord is entitled to make an application under sub-paragraph (1) of paragraph 13 above but does not obtain an order under that paragraph or paragraph 14 above.

(2)　If at the expiration of the period within which an application under paragraph 13(1) above may be made the landlord has not made such an application, the landlord's notice to resume possession, and anything done in pursuance thereof, shall cease to have effect.

(3)　If before the expiration of the period mentioned in sub-paragraph (2) above the landlord has made an application under paragraph 13(1) above but the result of the application, at the time when it is finally disposed of, is that no order is made, the landlord's notice to resume possession shall cease to have effect.

(4)　In any case where sub-paragraph (3) above applies, then, if within the period of one month beginning on the date that the application to the court is finally disposed of the landlord serves on the tenant a landlord's notice proposing an assured tenancy, the earliest date which may be specified in the notice as the date of termination shall, notwithstanding anything in paragraph 4(1)(b) above, be the day following the last day of the period of four months beginning on the date of service of the subsequent notice.

(5)　The reference in sub-paragraphs (3) and (4) above to the time at which an application is finally disposed of shall be construed as a reference to the earliest time at which the proceedings on the application (including any proceedings on or in consequence of an appeal) have been determined and any time for appealing or further appealing has expired, except that if the application is withdrawn or any appeal is abandoned the reference shall be construed as a reference to the time of withdrawal or abandonment.

(6)　A landlord's notice to resume possession may be withdrawn at any time by notice in writing served on the tenant (without prejudice, however, to the power of the court to make an order as to costs if the notice is withdrawn after the landlord has made an application under paragraph 13(1) above).

(7)　In any case where sub-paragraph (6) above applies, then, if within the period of one month beginning on the date of withdrawal of the landlord's notice to resume possession the landlord serves on the tenant a landlord's notice proposing an assured tenancy, the earliest date which may be specified in the notice as the date of termination shall, notwithstanding anything in paragraph 4(1)(b) above, be the day following the last day of the period of four months beginning on the date of service of the subsequent notice or the day following the last day of the period of six months beginning on the date of service of the withdrawn notice, whichever is the later.

### *Tenancies granted in continuation of long tenancies*

16.—(1)　Where on the coming to the end of a tenancy at a low rent the person who was the tenant immediately before the coming to an end thereof becomes (whether by grant or by implication of the law) the tenant under another tenancy at a low rent of a dwelling-house which consists of the whole or any part of the property let under the previous tenancy, then, if the previous tenancy was a long tenancy or is deemed by virtue of this paragraph to have been a long tenancy, the new tenancy shall be deemed for the purposes of this Schedule to be a long tenancy, irrespective of its terms.

(2)　In relation to a tenancy from year to year or other tenancy not granted for a term of years certain, being a tenancy which by virtue of sub-paragraph (1) above is deemed for the purposes of this Schedule to be a long tenancy, the preceding provisions of this Schedule shall have effect subject to the modifications set out below.

(3)　In sub-paragraph (6) of paragraph 2 above for the expression beginning "term date" there shall be substituted—

"""term date", in relation to any such tenancy as is mentioned in paragraph 16(2) below, means the first date after the coming into force of this Schedule on which, apart from this Schedule, the tenancy could have been brought to an end by notice to quit given by the landlord".

(4)　Notwithstanding anything in sub-paragraph (3) of paragraph 3 above, where by virtue of that paragraph the tenancy is continued after the term date, the provisions of this Schedule as to the termination of a tenancy by notice shall have effect, subject to sub-paragraph (5) below, in substitution for and not in addition to any such provisions included in the terms on which the tenancy had effect before the term date.

(5)　The minimum period of notice referred to in paragraph 8(1) above shall be one month or such longer period as the tenant would have been required to give to bring the tenancy to an end at the term date.

(6)　Where the tenancy is not terminated under paragraph 4 or paragraph 8 above at the term date, then, whether or not it would have continued after that date apart from the provisions of this Schedule, it shall be treated for the purposes of those provisions as being continued by virtue of paragraph 3 above.

## Agreements as to the grant of new tenancies

17.   In any case where, prior to the date of termination of a long residential tenancy, the landlord and the tenant agree for the grant to the tenant of a future tenancy of the whole or part of the property let under the tenancy at a rent other than a low rent and on terms and from a date specified in the agreement, the tenancy shall continue until that date but no longer; and, in such a case, the provisions of this Schedule shall cease to apply in relation to the tenancy with effect from the date of the agreement.

## Assumptions on which to determine future questions

18.   Where under this Schedule any question falls to be determined by the court or a rent assessment committee by reference to circumstances at a future date, the court or committee shall have regard to all rights, interests and obligations under or relating to the tenancy as they subsist at the time of the determination and to all relevant circumstances as those then subsist and shall assume, except in so far as the contrary is shown, that those rights, interests, obligations and circumstances will continue to subsist unchanged until that future date.

## Landlords and mortgagees in possession

19.—(1)   Section 21 of the 1954 Act (meaning of "the landlord" and provisions as to mesne landlords) shall apply in relation to this Schedule as it applies in relation to Part I of that Act but subject to the following modifications—

    (a)    any reference to Part I of that Act shall be construed as a reference to this Schedule; and
    (b)    subsection (4) (which relates to statutory tenancies arising under that Part) shall be omitted.

(2)   Section 67 of the 1954 Act (mortgagees in possession) applies for the purposes of this Schedule except that for the reference to that Act there shall be substituted a reference to this Schedule.

(3)   In accordance with sub-paragraph (1) above, Schedule 5 to the 1954 Act shall also apply for the purpose of this Schedule but subject to the following modifications—

    (a)    any reference to Part I of the 1954 Act shall be construed as a reference to the provisions of this Schedule (other than this sub-paragraph);
    (b)    any reference to section 21 of the 1954 Act shall be construed as a reference to that section as it applies in relation to this Schedule;
    (c)    any reference to subsection (1) of section 4 of that Act shall be construed as a reference to sub-paragraph (1) of paragraph 4 above;
    (d)    any reference to the court includes a reference to a rent assessment committee;
    (e)    paragraphs 6 to 8 and 11 shall be omitted;
    (f)    any reference to a particular subsection of section 16 of the 1954 Act shall be construed as a reference to that subsection as it applies in relation to this Schedule;
    (g)    any reference to a tenancy to which section 1 of the 1954 Act applies shall be construed as a reference to a long residential tenancy; and
    (h)    expressions to which a meaning is assigned by any provision of this Schedule (other than this sub-paragraph) shall be given that meaning.

## Application of other provisions of the 1954 Act

20.—(1)   Section 16 of the 1954 Act (relief for tenant where landlord proceeding to enforce covenants) shall apply in relation to this Schedule as it applies in relation to Part I of that Act but subject to the following modifications—

    (a)    in subsection (1) the reference to a tenancy to which section 1 of the 1954 Act applies shall be construed as a reference to a long residential tenancy;
    (b)    in subsection (2) the reference to Part I of that Act shall be construed as a reference to this Schedule;
    (c)    subsection (3) shall have effect as if the words "(without prejudice to section ten of this Act)" were omitted; and
    (d)    in subsection (7) the reference to subsection (3) of section 2 of the 1954 Act shall be construed as a reference to paragraph 1(6) above.

(2)   Section 55 of the 1954 Act (compensation for possession obtained by misrepresentation) shall apply in relation to this Schedule as it applies in relation to Part I of that Act.

(3)   Section 63 of the 1954 Act (jurisdiction of court for purposes of Parts I and II of the 1954 Act and of Part I of the Landlord and Tenant Act 1927) shall apply in relation to this Schedule and section 186 of this Act as it applies in relation to Part I of that Act.

(4)   Section 65 of the 1954 Act (provisions as to reversions) applies for the purposes of this Schedule except that for any reference to that Act there shall be substituted a reference to this Schedule.

(5)   Subsection (4) of section 66 of the 1954 Act (service of notices) shall apply in relation to this Schedule as it applies in relation to that Act.

21.—(1)   Where this Schedule has effect in relation to a former 1954 Act tenancy the term date of which falls before 15th January 1999, any reference (however expressed) in the preceding provisions of this Schedule to the dwelling-house (or the property) let under the tenancy shall have effect as a reference to the premises qualifying for protection, within the meaning of the 1954 Act.

(2)   Notwithstanding that at any time section 1 of the 1954 Act does not, and this Schedule does, apply to a former 1954 Act tenancy, any question of what are the premises qualifying for protection or (in that context) what is the tenancy shall be determined for the purposes of this Schedule in accordance with Part I of that Act.

*Crown application*

22.—(1)   This Schedule shall apply where—
  (a)   there is an interest belonging to Her Majesty in right of the Crown and that interest is under the management of the Crown Estate Commissioners, or
  (b)   there is an interest belonging to Her Majesty in right of the Duchy of Lancaster or belonging to the Duchy of Cornwall,
as if it were an interest not so belonging.

(2)   Where an interest belongs to Her Majesty in right of the Duchy of Lancaster, then, for the purposes of this Schedule, the Chancellor of the Duchy of Lancaster shall be deemed to be the owner of the interest.

(3)   Where an interest belongs to the Duchy of Cornwall, then, for the purposes of this Schedule, such person as the Duke of Cornwall, or other possessor for the time being of the Duchy of Cornwall, appoints shall be deemed to be the owner of the interest.

**[802]**

**NOTES**
  Para 1: sub-para (2A) inserted and sub-para (8) added by the References to Rating (Housing) Regulations 1990, SI 1990/434, reg 2, Schedule, paras 31, 32.
  Para 2: sub-para (4) and words in square brackets in sub-para (5) substituted by SI 1990/434, reg 2, Schedule, paras 33, 34.
  Para 5: words in square brackets in sub-para (1)(c) substituted by the Civil Partnership Act 2004, s 81, Sch 8, para 46.
  Paras 6, 11: figures in square brackets inserted by the Local Government Finance (Housing) (Consequential Amendments) Order 1993, SI 1993/651, art 2(1), Sch 1, para 20.
  Transfer of functions: the functions of the Secretary of State and the Treasury, so far as exercisable in relation to Wales, are transferred to the National Assembly for Wales, by the National Assembly for Wales (Transfer of Functions) Order 1999, SI 1999/672, art 2, Sch 1.
  Regulations: the Long Residential Tenancies (Principal Forms) Regulations 1997, SI 1997/3008 at **[3208]**.

*(Sch 11 contains minor and consequential amendments; Sch 12 contains repeals only.)*

# LEASEHOLD REFORM, HOUSING AND URBAN DEVELOPMENT ACT 1993

## (1993 c 28)

### ARRANGEMENT OF SECTIONS

### PART I
### LANDLORD AND TENANT

### CHAPTER I
### COLLECTIVE ENFRANCHISEMENT IN CASE OF TENANTS OF FLATS

*Preliminary*

## CHAPTER II
### INDIVIDUAL RIGHT OF TENANT OF FLAT TO ACQUIRE NEW LEASE

#### Preliminary

CHAPTER IV
ESTATE MANAGEMENT SCHEMES IN CONNECTION WITH ENFRANCHISEMENT

CHAPTER V
TENANTS' RIGHT TO MANAGEMENT AUDIT

*An Act to confer rights to collective enfranchisement and lease renewal on tenants of flats; to make further provision with respect to enfranchisement by tenants of houses; to make provision for auditing the management, by landlords or other persons, of residential property and for the approval of codes of practice relating thereto; to amend Parts III and IV of the Landlord and Tenant Act 1987; to confer jurisdiction on leasehold valuation tribunals as respects Crown land; to make provision for rendering void agreements preventing the occupation of leasehold property by persons with mental disorders; to amend Parts II, IV and V of the Housing Act 1985, Schedule 2 to the Housing Associations Act 1985, Parts I and III and sections 248 and 299 of the Housing (Scotland) Act 1987, Part III of the Housing Act 1988, and Part VI of the Local Government and Housing Act 1989; to make provision with respect to certain disposals requiring consent under Part II of the Housing Act 1985, including provision for the payment of a levy; to alter the basis of certain contributions by the Secretary of State under section 569 of that Act; to establish and confer functions on a body to replace the English Industrial Estates Corporation and to be known as the Urban Regeneration Agency; to provide for the designation of certain urban and other areas and to make provision as to the effect of such designation; to amend section 23 of the Land Compensation Act 1961, section 98 of the Local Government, Planning and Land Act 1980 and section 27 of the Housing and Planning Act 1986; to make further provision with respect to urban development corporations and urban development areas; and for connected purposes*

**[20 July 1993]**

**NOTES**

Transfer of functions: as to the functions of Ministers of the Crown under this Act, so far as exercisable in relation to Wales, being transferred to the National Assembly for Wales, see the National Assembly for Wales (Transfer of Functions) Order 1999, SI 1999/672, art 2, Sch 1.

# PART I
## LANDLORD AND TENANT

### CHAPTER I
### COLLECTIVE ENFRANCHISEMENT IN CASE OF TENANTS OF FLATS
*Preliminary*

**1 The right to collective enfranchisement**

(1)   This Chapter has effect for the purpose of conferring *on qualifying tenants of flats contained in premises to which this Chapter applies on the relevant date the right, exercisable subject to and in accordance with this Chapter, to have the freehold of those premises acquired on their behalf*—
    (a)   by a person or persons appointed by them for the purpose, and
    (b)   at a price determined in accordance with this Chapter;
and that right is referred to in this Chapter as "the right to collective enfranchisement".

(2)   Where the right to collective enfranchisement is exercised in relation to any such premises ("the relevant premises")—
    (a)   *the qualifying tenants by whom the right is exercised shall be entitled, subject to and in accordance with this Chapter, to have acquired*, in like manner, the freehold of any property which is not comprised in the relevant premises but to which this paragraph applies by virtue of subsection (3); and
    (b)   section 2 has effect with respect to the acquisition of leasehold interests to which paragraph (a) or (b) of subsection (1) of that section applies.

(3)   Subsection (2)(a) applies to any property if … at the relevant date either—
    (a)   it is appurtenant property which is demised by the lease held by a qualifying tenant of a flat contained in the relevant premises; or
    (b)   it is property which any such tenant is entitled under the terms of the lease of his flat to use in common with the occupiers of other premises (whether those premises are contained in the relevant premises or not).

(4)   The right of acquisition in respect of the freehold of any such property as is mentioned in subsection (3)(b) shall, however, be taken to be satisfied with respect to that property if, on the acquisition of the relevant premises in pursuance of this Chapter, either—
    (a)   there are granted by the [person who owns the freehold of that property]—
        (i)   over that property, or
        (ii)   over any other property,
    such permanent rights as will ensure that thereafter the occupier of the flat referred to in that provision has as nearly as may be the same rights as those enjoyed in relation to that property on the relevant date by the qualifying tenant under the terms of his lease; or
    (b)   there is acquired from the [person who owns the freehold of that property] the freehold of any other property over which any such permanent rights may be granted.

(5)   A claim by *qualifying tenants* to exercise the right to collective enfranchisement may be made in relation to any premises to which this Chapter applies despite the fact that those premises are less extensive than the entirety of the premises in relation to which *those tenants are* entitled to exercise that right.

(6)   Any right or obligation under this Chapter to acquire any interest in property shall not extend to underlying minerals in which that interest subsists if—
    (a)   the owner of the interest requires the minerals to be excepted, and
    (b)   proper provision is made for the support of the property as it is enjoyed on the relevant date.

(7)   In this section—
"appurtenant property", in relation to a flat, means any garage, outhouse, garden, yard or appurtenances belonging to, or usually enjoyed with, the flat;
.....
"the relevant premises" means any such premises as are referred to in subsection (2).

(8)   In this Chapter "the relevant date", in relation to any claim to exercise the right to collective enfranchisement, means the date on which notice of the claim is given under section 13.

[803]

**NOTES**

Sub-s (1): words in italics substituted by the words "the right to acquire the freehold of premises to which this Chapter applies on the relevant date, at a price determined in accordance with this Chapter, exercisable subject to and in accordance with this Chapter by a company (referred to in this Chapter as a RTE company) of which qualifying tenants of flats contained in the premises are members;" by the Commonhold and Leasehold Reform Act 2002, s 124, Sch 8, paras 2, 3(1), (2), as from a day to be appointed.

Sub-s (2): words in italics substituted by the words "the RTE company by which the right to collective enfranchisement is exercised is entitled, subject to and in accordance with this Chapter, to acquire," by the Commonhold and Leasehold Reform Act 2002, s 124, Sch 8, paras 2, 3(1), (3), as from a day to be appointed.

Sub-ss (3), (7): words omitted repealed by the Housing Act 1996, ss 107(3), 227, Sch 19, Pt V, except in relation to a case where, before 1 October 1996, a notice was given under s 13 or 42 of this Act at **[817]**, **[848]**, or an application was made to court under s 26 or 50 of this Act at **[830]**, **[856]**.

Sub-s (4): words in square brackets substituted by the Housing Act 1996, s 107(4), Sch 10, paras 1, 2, subject to savings as noted above.

Sub-s (5): words in italics in the first place substituted by the words "a RTE company" and words in italics in the second place substituted by the words "the RTE company is" by the Commonhold and Leasehold Reform Act 2002, s 124, Sch 8, paras 2, 3(1), (4), as from a day to be appointed.

## 2   Acquisition of leasehold interests

(*1*)   *Where the right to collective enfranchisement is exercised in relation to any premises to which this Chapter applies ("the relevant premises"), then, subject to and in accordance with this Chapter—*

    (*a*)   *there shall be acquired on behalf of the qualifying tenants by whom the right is exercised every interest to which this paragraph applies by virtue of subsection (2); and*

    (*b*)   *those tenants shall be entitled to have acquired on their behalf any interest to which this paragraph applies by virtue of subsection (3); and any interest so acquired on behalf of those tenants shall be acquired in the manner mentioned in paragraphs (a) and (b) of section 1(1).*

(2)   Paragraph (a) of subsection (1) above applies to the interest of the tenant under any lease which is superior to the lease held by a qualifying tenant of a flat contained in the relevant premises.

(3)   Paragraph (b) of subsection (1) above applies to the interest of the tenant under any lease (not falling within subsection (2) above) under which the demised premises consist of or include—

    (a)   any common parts of the relevant premises, or

    (b)   any property falling within section 1(2)(a) which is to be acquired by virtue of that provision,

where the acquisition of that interest is reasonably necessary for the proper management or maintenance of those common parts, or (as the case may be) that property, *on behalf of the tenants by whom the right to collective enfranchisement is exercised.*

(4)   Where the demised premises under any lease falling within subsection (2) or (3) include any premises other than—

    (a)   a flat contained in the relevant premises which is held by a qualifying tenant,

    (b)   any common parts of those premises, or

    (c)   any such property as is mentioned in subsection (3)(b),

the obligation or (as the case may be) right under subsection (1) above to acquire the interest of the tenant under the lease shall not extend to his interest under the lease in any such other premises.

(5)   Where the qualifying tenant of a flat is a public sector landlord and the flat is let under a secure tenancy [or an introductory tenancy], then if—

    (a)   the condition specified in subsection (6) is satisfied, and

    (b)   the lease of the qualifying tenant is directly derived out of a lease under which the tenant is a public sector landlord,

the interest of that public sector landlord as tenant under that lease shall not be liable to be acquired by virtue of subsection (1) to the extent that it is an interest in the flat or in any appurtenant property; and the interest of a public sector landlord as tenant under any lease out of which the qualifying tenant's lease is indirectly derived shall, to the like extent, not be liable to be so acquired (so long as the tenant under every lease intermediate between that lease and the qualifying tenant's lease is a public sector landlord).

(6)   The condition referred to in subsection (5)(a) is that either—

    (a)   the qualifying tenant is the immediate landlord under the secure tenancy [or, as the case may be, the introductory tenancy], or

    (b)   he is the landlord under a lease which is superior to the secure tenancy [or, as the case may be, the introductory tenancy] and the tenant under that lease, and the tenant under every lease (if any) intermediate between it and the secure tenancy [or the introductory tenancy], is also a public sector landlord;

and in subsection (5) "appurtenant property" has the same meaning as in section 1.

(7)   In this section "the relevant premises" means any such premises as are referred to in subsection (1).

**[804]**

---

**NOTES**

Sub-s (1): substituted by the Commonhold and Leasehold Reform Act 2002, s 124, Sch 8, paras 2, 4, as from a day to be appointed, as follows—

"(1)   Where the right to collective enfranchisement is exercised by a RTE company in relation to any premises to which this Chapter applies ("the relevant premises"), then, subject to and in accordance with this Chapter—
>    (a)   there shall be acquired by the RTE company every interest to which this paragraph applies by virtue of subsection (2); and
>    (b)   the RTE company shall be entitled to acquire any interest to which this paragraph applies by virtue of subsection (3);

and any interest which the RTE company so acquires shall be acquired in the manner mentioned in section 1(1).".

Sub-s (3): words in italics repealed by the Commonhold and Leasehold Reform Act 2002, s 180, Sch 14, as from a day to be appointed.

Sub-ss (5), (6): words in square brackets inserted by the Housing Act 1996 (Consequential Amendments) Order 1997, SI 1997/74, art 2, Schedule, para 9(a).

## 3   Premises to which this Chapter applies

(1)   Subject to section 4, this Chapter applies to any premises if—
>    (a)   they consist of a self-contained building or part of a building ... ;
>    (b)   they contain two or more flats held by qualifying tenants; and
>    (c)   the total number of flats held by such tenants is not less than two thirds of the total number of flats contained in the premises.

(2)   For the purposes of this section a building is a self-contained building if it is structurally detached, and a part of a building is a self-contained part of a building if—
>    (a)   it constitutes a vertical division of the building and the structure of the building is such that that part could be redeveloped independently of the remainder of the building; and
>    (b)   the relevant services provided for occupiers of that part either—
>> (i)   are provided independently of the relevant services provided for occupiers of the remainder of the building, or
>> (ii)   could be so provided without involving the carrying out of any works likely to result in a significant interruption in the provision of any such services for occupiers of the remainder of the building;

and for this purpose "relevant services" means services provided by means of pipes, cables or other fixed installations.

**[805]**

**NOTES**

Sub-s (1): words omitted repealed by the Housing Act 1996, ss 107(1), 227, Sch 19, Pt V, except in relation to a case where, before 1 October 1996, a notice was given under s 13 or 42 of this Act at **[817]**, **[848]**, or an application was made to court under s 26 or 50 of this Act at **[830]**, **[856]**.

## 4   Premises excluded from right

(1)   This Chapter does not apply to premises falling within section 3(1) if—
>    (a)   any part or parts of the premises is or are neither—
>> (i)   occupied, or intended to be occupied, for residential purposes, nor
>> (ii)   comprised in any common parts of the premises; and
>    (b)   the internal floor area of that part or of those parts (taken together) exceeds [25 per cent] of the internal floor area of the premises (taken as a whole).

(2)   Where in the case of any such premises any part of the premises (such as, for example, a garage, parking space or storage area) is used, or intended for use, in conjunction with a particular dwelling contained in the premises (and accordingly is not comprised in any common parts of the premises), it shall be taken to be occupied, or intended to be occupied, for residential purposes.

(3)   For the purpose of determining the internal floor area of a building or of any part of a building, the floor or floors of the building or part shall be taken to extend (without interruption) throughout the whole of the interior of the building or part, except that the area of any common parts of the building or part shall be disregarded.

[(3A)   Where different persons own the freehold of different parts of premises within subsection (1) of section 3, this Chapter does not apply to the premises if any of those parts is a self-contained part of a building for the purposes of that section.]

(4)   This Chapter does not apply to premises falling within section 3(1) if the premises are premises with a resident landlord and do not contain more than four units.

[(5)   This Chapter does not apply to premises falling within section 3(1) if the freehold of the premises includes track of an operational railway; and for the purposes of this subsection—
>    (a)   "track" includes any land or other property comprising the permanent way of a railway (whether or not it is also used for other purposes) and includes any bridge, tunnel, culvert, retaining wall or other structure used for the support of, or otherwise in connection with, track,
>    (b)   "operational" means not disused, and

(c)   "railway" has the same meaning as in any provision of Part 1 of the Railways Act 1993 (c 43) for the purposes of which that term is stated to have its wider meaning.]

**[806]**

**NOTES**

Sub-s (1): words in square brackets substituted by the Commonhold and Leasehold Reform Act 2002, s 115, except in relation to an application for collective enfranchisement in respect of which notice was given under s 13 of this Act at **[817]**, or where an application was made for an order under s 26 of this Act at **[830]**, before 26 July 2002 (in relation to England) or 1 January 2003 (in relation to Wales).

Sub-s (3A): inserted by the Housing Act 1996, s 107(2), except in relation to a case where, before 1 October 1996, a notice was given under s 13 or 42 of this Act at **[817]**, **[848]**, or an application was made to court under s 26 or 50 of this Act at **[830]**, **[856]**.

Sub-s (5): added by the Commonhold and Leasehold Reform Act 2002, s 116, subject to savings as noted above.

### [4A   RTE companies

(1)   A company is a RTE company in relation to premises if—
    (a)   it is a private company limited by guarantee, and
    (b)   its [articles of association state] that its object, or one of its objects, is the exercise of the right to collective enfranchisement with respect to the premises.

(2)   But a company is not a RTE company if it is a commonhold association (within the meaning of Part 1 of the Commonhold and Leasehold Reform Act 2002).

(3)   And a company is not a RTE company in relation to premises if another company which is a RTE company in relation to—
    (a)   the premises, or
    (b)   any premises containing or contained in the premises,
has given a notice under section 13 with respect to the premises, or any premises containing or contained in the premises, and the notice continues in force in accordance with subsection (11) of that section.]

**[807]**

**NOTES**

Commencement: to be appointed.

Inserted, together with ss 4B, 4C, by the Commonhold and Leasehold Reform Act 2002, s 122.

Sub-s (1): words in square brackets in para (b) substituted by the Companies Act 2006 (Consequential Amendments, Transitional Provisions and Savings) Order 2009, SI 2009/1941, art 2(1), Sch 1, para 140(1), (2).

### [4B   RTE companies: membership

(1)   Before the execution of a relevant conveyance to a company which is a RTE company in relation to any premises the following persons are entitled to be members of the company—
    (a)   qualifying tenants of flats contained in the premises, and
    (b)   if the company is also a RTM company which has acquired the right to manage the premises, landlords under leases of the whole or any part of the premises.

(2)   In this section—
"relevant conveyance" means a conveyance of the freehold of the premises or of any premises containing or contained in the premises; and
"RTM company" has the same meaning as in Chapter 1 of Part 2 of the Commonhold and Leasehold Reform Act 2002.

(3)   On the execution of a relevant conveyance to the RTE company, any member of the company who is not a participating member ceases to be a member.

(4)   In this Chapter "participating member", in relation to a RTE company, means a person who is a member by virtue of subsection (1)(a) of this section and who—
    (a)   has given a participation notice to the company before the date when the company gives a notice under section 13 or during the participation period, or
    (b)   is a participating member by virtue of either of the following two subsections.

(5)   A member who is the assignee of a lease by virtue of which a participating member was a qualifying tenant of his flat is a participating member if he has given a participation notice to the company within the period beginning with the date of the assignment and ending 28 days later (or, if earlier, on the execution of a relevant conveyance to the company).

(6)   And if the personal representatives of a participating member are a member, they are a participating member if they have given a participation notice to the company at any time (before the execution of a relevant conveyance to the company).

(7)   In this section "participation notice", in relation to a member of the company, means a notice stating that he wishes to be a participating member.

(8) For the purposes of this section a participation notice given to the company during the period—

    (a)    beginning with the date when the company gives a notice under section 13, and

    (b)    ending immediately before a binding contract is entered into in pursuance of the notice under section 13,

is of no effect unless a copy of the participation notice has been given during that period to the person who (in accordance with section 9) is the reversioner in respect of the premises.

(9) For the purposes of this section "the participation period" is the period beginning with the date when the company gives a notice under section 13 and ending—

    (a)    six months, or such other time as the Secretary of State may by order specify, after that date, or

    (b)    immediately before a binding contract is entered into in pursuance of the notice under section 13,

whichever is the earlier.

(10) In this section references to assignment include an assent by personal representatives, and assignment by operation of law where the assignment is to a trustee in bankruptcy or to a mortgagee under section 89(2) of the Law of Property Act 1925 (c 20) (foreclosure of leasehold mortgage); and references to an assignee shall be construed accordingly.]

                                                                 **[808]**

**NOTES**

Commencement: to be appointed.

Inserted as noted to s 4A at **[807]**.

## [4C RTE companies: regulations

(1) The Secretary of State shall by regulations make provision about the content and form of the [articles of association] of RTE companies.

(2) A RTE company may adopt provisions of the regulations for its [articles].

(3) The regulations may include provision which is to have effect for a RTE company whether or not it is adopted by the company.

(4) A provision of the [articles] of a RTE company has no effect to the extent that it is inconsistent with the regulations.

(5) The regulations have effect in relation to [articles]—

    (a)    irrespective of the date of [the articles], but

    (b)    subject to any transitional provisions of the regulations.

[(6) Section 20 of the Companies Act 2006 (default application of model articles) does not apply to a RTE company.]]

                                                                 **[809]**

**NOTES**

Commencement: 26 July 2002 (in relation to England for the purpose of making regulations); 1 January 2003 (in relation to Wales for the purpose of making regulations); to be appointed (otherwise).

Inserted as noted to s 4A at **[807]**.

Sub-ss (1), (2), (4), (5): words in square brackets substituted by the Companies Act 2006 (Consequential Amendments, Transitional Provisions and Savings) Order 2009, SI 2009/1941, art 2(1), Sch 1, para 140(1), (3)(a)–(c).

Sub-s (6): substituted by SI 2009/1941, art 2(1), Sch 1, para 140(1), (3)(d).

## 5 Qualifying tenants

(1) Subject to the following provisions of this section, a person is a qualifying tenant of a flat for the purposes of this Chapter if he is tenant of the flat under a long lease …

(2) Subsection (1) does not apply where—

    (a)    the lease is a business lease; or

    (b)    the immediate landlord under the lease is a charitable housing trust and the flat forms part of the housing accommodation provided by it in the pursuit of its charitable purposes; or

    (c)    the lease was granted by sub-demise out of a superior lease other than a long lease … [ … ], the grant was made in breach of the terms of the superior lease, and there has been no waiver of the breach by the superior landlord;

and in paragraph (b) "charitable housing trust" means a housing trust within the meaning of the Housing Act 1985 which is a charity within the meaning of the Charities Act 1993.

(3) No flat shall have more than one qualifying tenant at any one time.

(4) Accordingly—

    (a)    where a flat is for the time being let under two or more leases to which subsection (1) applies, any tenant under any of those leases which is superior to that held by any other such tenant shall not be a qualifying tenant of the flat for the purposes of this Chapter; and

(b) where a flat is for the time being let to joint tenants under a lease to which subsection (1) applies, the joint tenants shall (subject to paragraph (a) and subsection (5)) be regarded for the purposes of this Chapter as jointly constituting the qualifying tenant of the flat.

(5) Where apart from this subsection—

(a) a person would be regarded for the purposes of this Chapter as being (or as being among those constituting) the qualifying tenant of a flat contained in any particular premises consisting of the whole or part of a building, but

(b) that person would also be regarded for those purposes as being (or as being among those constituting) the qualifying tenant of each of two or more other flats contained in those premises,

then, whether that person is tenant of the flats referred to in paragraphs (a) and (b) under a single lease or otherwise, there shall be taken for those purposes to be no qualifying tenant of any of those flats.

(6) For the purposes of subsection (5) in its application to a body corporate any flat let to an associated company (whether alone or jointly with any other person or persons) shall be treated as if it were so let to that body; and for this purpose "associated company" means another body corporate which is (within the meaning of [section 1159 of the Companies Act 2006]) that body's holding company, a subsidiary of that body or another subsidiary of that body's holding company.

**[810]**

**NOTES**

Sub-s (1): words omitted repealed by the Commonhold and Leasehold Reform Act 2002, ss 117(1), 180, Sch 14, except in relation to an application for collective enfranchisement in respect of which notice was given under s 13 at **[817]**, or where an application was made for an order under s 26 at **[830]**, or in relation to applications for a new lease of flats in respect of which a notice was given under s 42 at **[848]**, or an order was made under s 50 at **[856]**, before 26 July 2002 (in relation to England) or 1 January 2003 (in relation to Wales).

Sub-s (2): words omitted from square brackets inserted by the Housing Act 1996, s 106, Sch 9, para 3(1), (2)(b) and repealed, together with other words omitted, by the Commonhold and Leasehold Reform Act 2002, s 180, Sch 14, subject to savings as noted above.

Sub-s (6): words in square brackets substituted by the Companies Act 2006 (Consequential Amendments, Transitional Provisions and Savings) Order 2009, SI 2009/1941, art 2(1), Sch 1, para 140(1), (4).

**6** (*Repealed by the Commonhold and Leasehold Reform Act 2002, s 180, Sch 14, except in relation to an application for collective enfranchisement in respect of which notice was given under s 13 of this Act at* **[817]**, *or where an application was made for an order under s 26 of this Act at* **[830]**, *before 26 July 2002* (*in relation to England*) *or 1 January 2003* (*in relation to Wales*).)

**7 Meaning of "long lease"**

(1) In this Chapter "long lease" means (subject to the following provisions of this section)—

(a) a lease granted for a term of years certain exceeding 21 years, whether or not it is (or may become) terminable before the end of that term by notice given by or to the tenant or by re-entry, forfeiture or otherwise;

(b) a lease for a term fixed by law under a grant with a covenant or obligation for perpetual renewal (other than a lease by sub-demise from one which is not a long lease) or a lease taking effect under section 149(6) of the Law of Property Act 1925 (leases terminable after a death and marriage [or the formation of a civil partnership]);

(c) a lease granted in pursuance of the right to buy conferred by Part V of the Housing Act 1985 or in pursuance of the right to acquire on rent to mortgage terms conferred by that Part of that Act; ...

(d) a shared ownership lease, whether granted in pursuance of that Part of that Act or otherwise, where the tenant's total share is 100 per cent; [or

(e) a lease granted in pursuance of that Part of that Act as it has effect by virtue of section 17 of the Housing Act 1996 (the right to acquire)].

(2) A lease terminable by notice after [a death, a marriage or the formation of a civil partnership] is not to be treated as a long lease for the purposes of this Chapter if—

(a) the notice is capable of being given at any time after the death or marriage of[, or the formation of a civil partnership by,] the tenant;

(b) the length of the notice is not more than three months; and

(c) the terms of the lease preclude both—

(i) its assignment otherwise than by virtue of section 92 of the Housing Act 1985 (assignments by way of exchange), and

(ii) the sub-letting of the whole of the premises comprised in it.

(3) Where the tenant of any property under a long lease ... , on the coming to an end of that lease, becomes or has become tenant of the property or part of it under any subsequent tenancy

(whether by express grant or by implication of law), then that tenancy shall be deemed for the purposes of this Chapter (including any further application of this subsection) to be a long lease irrespective of its terms.

(4)  Where—

    (a)  a lease is or has been granted for a term of years certain not exceeding 21 years, but with a covenant or obligation for renewal without payment of a premium (but not for perpetual renewal), and

    (b)  the lease is or has been renewed on one or more occasions so as to bring to more than 21 years the total of the terms granted (including any interval between the end of a lease and the grant of a renewal),

this Chapter shall apply as if the term originally granted had been one exceeding 21 years.

(5)  References in this Chapter to a long lease include—

    (a)  any period during which the lease is or was continued under Part I of the Landlord and Tenant Act 1954 or under Schedule 10 to the Local Government and Housing Act 1989;

    (b)  any period during which the lease was continued under the Leasehold Property (Temporary Provisions) Act 1951.

(6)  Where in the case of a flat there are at any time two or more separate leases, with the same landlord and the same tenant, and—

    (a)  the property comprised in one of those leases consists of either the flat or a part of it (in either case with or without any appurtenant property), and

    (b)  the property comprised in every other lease consists of either a part of the flat (with or without any appurtenant property) or appurtenant property only,

then in relation to the property comprised in such of those leases as are long leases, this Chapter shall apply as it would if at that time—

    (i)  there were a single lease of that property, and

    (ii)  that lease were a long lease;

but this subsection has effect subject to the operation of subsections (3) to (5) in relation to any of the separate leases.

(7)  In this section—

"appurtenant property" has the same meaning as in section 1;

"shared ownership lease" means a lease—

    (a)  granted on payment of a premium calculated by reference to a percentage of the value of the demised premises or the cost of providing them, or

    (b)  under which the tenant (or his personal representatives) will or may be entitled to a sum calculated by reference, directly or indirectly, to the value of those premises; and

"total share", in relation to the interest of a tenant under a shared ownership lease, means his initial share plus any additional share or shares in the demised premises which he has acquired.

**[811]**

**NOTES**

Sub-s (1): words in square brackets in para (b) inserted by the Civil Partnership Act 2004, s 81, Sch 8, para 47(1), (2); word omitted from para (c) repealed and para (e) and word immediately preceding it added by the Housing Act 1996 (Consequential Amendments) (No 2) Order 1997, SI 1997/627, art 2, Schedule, para 7.

Sub-s (2): words in first pair of square brackets substituted and words in square brackets inserted by the Civil Partnership Act 2004, s 81, Sch 8, para 47(1), (3).

Sub-s (3): words omitted repealed by the Commonhold and Leasehold Reform Act 2002, s 180, Sch 14, except in relation to an application for collective enfranchisement in respect of which notice was given under s 13 of this Act at **[817]**, or where an application was made for an order under s 26 of this Act at **[830]**, or in relation to an application for a new lease in respect of which notice was given under s 42 of this Act at **[848]**, or an application was made for an order under s 50 of this Act at **[856]**, before 26 July 2002 (in relation to England) or 1 January 2003 (in relation to Wales).

Leasehold (Temporary Provisions) Act 1951: repealed.

**8, 8A**  (*S 8 repealed by the Commonhold and Leasehold Reform Act 2002, s 180, Sch 14, except in relation to an application for collective enfranchisement in respect of which notice was given under s 13 of this Act at* **[817]**, *or where an application was made for an order under s 26 of this Act at* **[830]**, *or in relation to an application for a new lease in respect of which notice was given under s 42 of this Act at* **[848]**, *or an application was made for an order under s 50 of this Act at* **[856]**, *before 26 July 2002 (in relation to England) or 1 January 2003 (in relation to Wales); s 8A inserted by the Housing Act 1996, s 106, Sch 9, para 3(1), (3) and repealed as noted to s 8.*)

**9   The reversioner and other relevant landlords for the purpose of this Chapter**

(1)   Where, in connection with any claim to exercise the right to collective enfranchisement in relation to any premises [the freehold of the whole of which is owned by the same person], it is not proposed to acquire any interests other than—

(a)   the freehold of the premises, or

(b)   any other interests of the person who owns the freehold of the premises,

that person shall be the reversioner in respect of the premises for the purposes of this Chapter.

(2)   Where, in connection with any such claim [as is mentioned in subsection (1)], it is proposed to acquire interests of persons other than the person who owns the freehold of the premises to which the claim relates, then—

(a)   the reversioner in respect of the premises shall for the purposes of this Chapter be the person identified as such by Part I of Schedule 1 to this Act; and

(b)   the person who owns the freehold of the premises, [every person who owns any freehold interest which it is proposed to acquire by virtue of section 1(2)(a)] and every person who owns any leasehold interest which it is proposed to acquire under or by virtue of section 2(1)(a) or (b), shall be a relevant landlord for those purposes.

[(2A)   In the case of any claim to exercise the right to collective enfranchisement in relation to any premises the freehold of the whole of which is not owned by the same person—

(a)   the reversioner in respect of the premises shall for the purposes of this Chapter be the person identified as such by Part IA of Schedule 1 to this Act, and

(b)   every person who owns a freehold interest in the premises, every person who owns any freehold interest which it is proposed to acquire by virtue of section 1(2)(a), and every person who owns any leasehold interest which it is proposed to acquire under or by virtue of section 2(1)(a) or (b), shall be a relevant landlord for those purposes.]

(3)   Subject to the provisions of Part II of Schedule 1, the reversioner in respect of any premises shall, in a case to which subsection (2) [or (2A)] applies, conduct on behalf of all the relevant landlords all proceedings arising out of any notice given with respect to the premises under section 13 (whether the proceedings are for resisting or giving effect to the claim in question).

(4)   Schedule 2 (which makes provision with respect to certain special categories of landlords) has effect for the purposes of this Chapter.

**[812]**

**NOTES**

Sub-ss (1), (2), (3): words in square brackets inserted by the Housing Act 1996, s 107(4), Sch 10, paras 1, 3(2), (3), (5), except in relation to a case where, before 1 October 1996, a notice was given under s 13 or 42 of this Act at **[817]**, **[848]**, or an application was made to court under s 26 or 50 of this Act at **[830]**, **[856]**.

Sub-s (2A): inserted by the Housing Act 1996, s 107(4), Sch 10, paras, 1, 3(4), subject to savings as noted above.

**10   Premises with a resident landlord**

[(1)   For the purposes of this Chapter any premises falling within section 3(1) are premises with a resident landlord at any time if—

(a)   the premises are not, and do not form part of, a purpose-built block of flats;

(b)   the same person has owned the freehold of the premises since before the conversion of the premises into two or more flats or other units; and

(c)   he, or an adult member of his family, has occupied a flat or other unit contained in the premises as his only or principal home throughout the period of twelve months ending with that time.]

(2), (3)   ...

[(4)   Where the freehold of any premises is held on trust, subsection (1) applies as if—

(a)   the requirement in paragraph (b) were that the same person has had an interest under the trust (whether or not also a trustee) since before the conversion of the premises, and

(b)   paragraph (c) referred to him or an adult member of his family.]

[(4A)   ... ]

(5)   For the purposes of this section a person is an adult member of another's family if that person is—

(a)   the other's [spouse or civil partner]; or

(b)   a son or daughter or a son-in-law or daughter-in-law of the other, or of the other's [spouse or civil partner], who has attained the age of 18; or

(c)   the father or mother of the other, or of the other's [spouse or civil partner];

and in paragraph (b) any reference to a person's son or daughter includes a reference to any stepson or stepdaughter of that person, and "son-in-law" and "daughter-in-law" shall be construed accordingly.

(6)   In this section—

"purpose-built block of flats" means a building which as constructed contained two or more flats.

[ ..... ]

**NOTES**

Sub-s (1): substituted by the Commonhold and Leasehold Reform Act 2002, s 118(1), (2), except in relation to an application for collective enfranchisement in respect of which notice was given under s 13 of this Act at **[817]**, or where an application was made for an order under s 26 of this Act at **[830]**, before 26 July 2002 (in relation to England) or 1 January 2003 (in relation to Wales).

Sub-ss (2), (3): repealed by the Commonhold and Leasehold Reform Act 2002, s 180, Sch 14, subject to savings as noted above.

Sub-s (4): substituted by the Commonhold and Leasehold Reform Act 2002, s 118(1), (3), subject to savings as noted above.

Sub-s (4A): inserted by the Housing Act 1996, s 107(4), Sch 10, paras, 1, 4(1), (5); repealed by the Commonhold and Leasehold Reform Act 2002, s 180, Sch 14, subject to savings as noted above.

Sub-s (5): words in square brackets substituted by the Civil Partnership Act 2004, s 81, Sch 8, para 48.

Sub-s (6): definition "the freeholder" (omitted) repealed by the Housing Act 1996, s 227, Sch 19, Pt V; definition "qualifying flat" (omitted) inserted by the Housing Act 1996, s 107(4), Sch 10, paras 1, 4(1), (6) and repealed by the Commonhold and Leasehold Reform Act 2002, s 180, Sch 14, subject to savings as noted above.

*Preliminary inquiries by tenants*

**11 Right of qualifying tenant to obtain information about superior interests etc**

(1)   A qualifying tenant of a flat may give—
   (a)   to [any immediate landlord of his], or
   (b)   to any person receiving rent on behalf of [any immediate landlord of his],
a notice requiring the recipient to give the tenant (so far as known to the recipient) the name and address of [every person who owns a freehold interest in] the relevant premises and the name and address of every other person who has an interest to which subsection (2) applies.

(2)   In relation to a qualifying tenant of a flat, this subsection applies to the following interests, namely—
   (a)   the freehold of any property not contained in the relevant premises—
      (i)   which is demised by the lease held by the tenant, or
      (ii)   which the tenant is entitled under the terms of his lease to use in common with other persons; and
   (b)   any leasehold interest in the relevant premises or in any such property which is superior to that of [any immediate landlord of the tenant].

(3)   Any qualifying tenant of a flat may give to [any person who owns a freehold interest in] the relevant premises a notice requiring him to give the tenant (so far as known to him) the name and address of every person, apart from the tenant, who is—
   (a)   a tenant of the whole of the relevant premises, or
   (b)   a tenant or licensee of any separate set or sets of premises contained in the relevant premises, or
   (c)   a tenant or licensee of the whole or any part of any common parts so contained or of any property not so contained—
      (i)   which is demised by the lease held by a qualifying tenant of a flat contained in the relevant premises, or
      (ii)   which any such qualifying tenant is entitled under the terms of his lease to use in common with other persons.

(4)   Any such qualifying tenant may also give—
   [(a)   to any person who owns a freehold interest in the relevant premises,
   (aa)   to any person who owns a freehold interest in any such property as is mentioned in subsection (3)(c),]
   (b)   to any person falling within subsection (3)(a), (b) or (c),
a notice requiring him to give the tenant—
      (i)   such information relating to his interest in the relevant premises or (as the case may be) in any such property ... , or
      (ii)   (so far as known to him) such information relating to any interest derived (whether directly or indirectly) out of that interest,
as is specified in the notice, where the information is reasonably required *by the tenant in connection with the making* of a claim to exercise the right to collective enfranchisement in relation to the whole or part of the relevant premises.

(5)   Where a notice is given by a qualifying tenant under subsection (4), the following rights shall be exercisable by him in relation to the recipient of the notice, namely—

   (a)    a right, on giving reasonable notice, to be provided with a list of documents to which subsection (6) applies;

   (b)    a right to inspect, at any reasonable time and on giving reasonable notice, any documents to which that subsection applies; and

   (c)    a right, on payment of a reasonable fee, to be provided with a copy of any documents which are contained in any list provided under paragraph (a) or have been inspected under paragraph (b).

(6)    This subsection applies to any document in the custody or under the control of the recipient of the notice under subsection 4—

   (a)    sight of which is reasonably required *by the qualifying tenant* in connection with the making of such a claim as is mentioned in that subsection; and

   (b)    which, on a proposed sale by a willing seller to a willing buyer of the recipient's interest in the relevant premises or (as the case may be) in any such property as is mentioned in subsection (3)(c), the seller would be expected to make available to the buyer (whether at or before contract or completion).

(7)    Any person who—

   (a)    is required by a notice under any of subsections (1) to (4) to give any information to a qualifying tenant, or

   (b)    is required by a qualifying tenant under subsection (5) to supply any list of documents, to permit the inspection of any documents or to supply a copy of any documents,

shall comply with that requirement within the period of 28 days beginning with the date of the giving of the notice referred to in paragraph (a) or (as the case may be) with the date of the making of the requirement referred to in paragraph (b).

(8)    Where—

   (a)    a person has received a notice under subsection (4), and

   (b)    within the period of six months beginning with the date of receipt of the notice, he—

        (i)    disposes of any interest (whether legal or equitable) in the relevant premises [or in any such property as is mentioned in subsection (3)(c)] otherwise than by the creation of an interest by way of security for a loan, or

        (ii)    acquires any such interest (otherwise than by way of security for a loan),

then (unless that disposal or acquisition has already been notified to the qualifying tenant in accordance with subsection (7)) he shall notify the qualifying tenant of that disposal or acquisition within the period of 28 days beginning with the date when it occurred.

(9)    In this section—

   ["document" means anything in which information of any description is recorded, and in relation to a document in which information is recorded otherwise than in legible form any reference to sight of the document is to sight of the information in legible form;]

   "the relevant premises", in relation to any qualifying tenant of a flat, means—

   (a)    if the person who owns the freehold interest in the flat owns[, or the persons who own the freehold interests in the flat own,] the freehold of the whole of the building in which the flat is contained, that building, or

   (b)    if that person owns[, or those persons own,] the freehold of part only of that building, that part of that building;

and any reference to an interest in the relevant premises includes an interest in part of those premises.

**[814]**

---

**NOTES**

Sub-ss (1)–(3): words in square brackets substituted by the Housing Act 1996, s 107(4), Sch 10, paras 1, 5(1)–(4), except in relation to a case where, before 1 October 1996, a notice was given under s 13 or 42 of this Act at **[817]**, **[848]**, or an application was made to court under s 26 or 50 of this Act at **[830]**, **[856]**.

Sub-s (4): paras (a), (aa) substituted, for original para (a), and words omitted repealed by the Housing Act 1996, ss 107(4), 227, Sch 10, paras 1, 5(1), (5), Sch 19, Pt V, subject to savings as noted above; for the words in italics there are substituted the words "in connection with the making by a RTE company" by the Commonhold and Leasehold Reform Act 2002, s 124, Sch 8, paras 2, 5, as from a day to be appointed.

Sub-s (6): words in italics repealed by the Commonhold and Leasehold Reform Act 2002, s 180, Sch 14, as from a day to be appointed.

Sub-s (8): words in square brackets inserted by the Housing Act 1996, s 107(4), Sch 10, paras 1, 5(1), (6), subject to savings as noted above.

Sub-s (9): definition "document" substituted by the Civil Evidence Act 1995, s 15(1), Sch 1, para 17; in definition "the relevant premises" words in square brackets inserted by the Housing Act 1996, s 107(4), Sch 10, paras 1, 5(1), (7), subject to savings as noted above.

---

## 12  Right of qualifying tenant to obtain information about other matters

(1)    Any notice given by a qualifying tenant under section 11(4) shall, in addition to any other requirement imposed in accordance with that provision, require the recipient to give the tenant—

   (a)    *the information specified in subsection (2) below; and*

   (b)    (so far as known to the recipient) the information specified in subsection (3) below.

(2)   *The information referred to in subsection (1)(a) is—*
   (a)    *whether the recipient has received in respect of any premises containing the tenant's flat—*
        (i)   *a notice under section 13 in the case of which the relevant claim is still current, or*
        (ii)   *a copy of such a notice; and*
   (b)    *if so, the date on which the notice under section 13 was given and the name and address of the nominee purchaser for the time being appointed for the purposes of section 15 in relation to that claim.*

(3)   The information referred to in subsection (1)(b) is—
   (a)    whether the tenant's flat is comprised in any property in the case of which any of paragraphs (a) to (d) of section 31(2) is applicable; and
   (b)    if paragraph (b) or (d) of that provision is applicable, the date of the application in question.

(4)   *Where—*
   (a)    *within the period of six months beginning with the date of receipt of a notice given by a tenant under section 11(4), the recipient of the notice receives in respect of any premises containing the tenant's flat—*
        (i)   *a notice under section 13, or*
        (ii)   *a copy of such a notice, and*
   (b)    *the tenant is not one of the qualifying tenants by whom the notice under section 13 is given,*

*the recipient shall, within the period of 28 days beginning with the date of receipt of the notice under section 13 or (as the case may be) the copy, notify the tenant of the date on which the notice was given and of the name and address of the nominee purchaser for the time being appointed for the purposes of section 15 in relation to the relevant claim.*

(5)   Where—
   (a)    the recipient of a notice given by a tenant under section 11(4) has, in accordance with subsection (1) above, informed the tenant of any such application as is referred to in subsection (3)(b) above; and
   (b)    within the period of six months beginning with the date of receipt of the notice, the application is either granted or refused by the Commissioners of Inland Revenue or is withdrawn by the applicant,

the recipient shall, within the period of 28 days beginning with the date of the granting, refusal or withdrawal of the application, notify the tenant that it has been granted, refused or withdrawn.

(6)   *In this section "the relevant claim", in relation to a notice under section 13, means the claim in respect of which that notice is given; and for the purposes of subsection (2) above any such claim is current if—*
   (a)    *that notice continues in force in accordance with section 13(11), or*
   (b)    *a binding contract entered into in pursuance of that notice remains in force, or*
   (c)    *where an order has been made under section 24(4)(a) or (b) or 25(6)(a) or (b) with respect to any such premises as are referred to in subsection (2)(a) above, any interests which by virtue of the order fall to be vested in the nominee purchaser have yet to be so vested.*

                                                  **[815]**

**NOTES**

Sub-s (1): para (a) repealed by the Commonhold and Leasehold Reform Act 2002, s 180, Sch 14, as from a day to be appointed.

Sub-ss (2), (4), (6): repealed by the Commonhold and Leasehold Reform Act 2002, s 180, Sch 14, as from a day to be appointed.

*[The notice of invitation to participate*

## 12A  Notice by RTE company inviting participation

(1)   Before making a claim to exercise the right to collective enfranchisement with respect to any premises, a RTE company must give notice to each person who at the time when the notice is given—
   (a)    is the qualifying tenant of a flat contained in the premises, but
   (b)    neither is nor has agreed to become a participating member of the RTE company.

(2)   A notice given under this section (a "notice of invitation to participate") must—
   (a)    state that the RTE company intends to exercise the right to collective enfranchisement with respect to the premises,
   (b)    state the names of the participating members of the RTE company,
   (c)    explain the rights and obligations of the members of the RTE company with respect to

the exercise of the right (including their rights and obligations in relation to meeting the price payable in respect of the freehold, and any other interests to be acquired in pursuance of this Chapter, and associated costs),

(d) include an estimate of that price and those costs, and

(e) invite the recipients of the notice to become participating members of the RTE company.

(3) A notice of invitation to participate must either—

(a) be accompanied by a copy of the [articles of association] of the RTE company, or

(b) include a statement about inspection and copying of the [articles of association] of the RTE company.

(4) A statement under subsection (3)(b) must—

(a) specify a place (in England or Wales) at which the [articles of association] may be inspected,

(b) specify as the times at which they may be inspected periods of at least two hours on each of at least three days (including a Saturday or Sunday or both) within the seven days beginning with the day following that on which the notice is given,

(c) specify a place (in England or Wales) at which, at any time within those seven days, a copy of the [articles of association] may be ordered, and

(d) specify a fee for the provision of an ordered copy, not exceeding the reasonable cost of providing it.

(5) Where a notice given to a person includes a statement under subsection (3)(b), the notice is to be treated as not having been given to him if he is not allowed to undertake an inspection, or is not provided with a copy, in accordance with the statement.

(6) A notice of invitation to participate shall not be invalidated by any inaccuracy in any of the particulars required by or by virtue of this section.]

**[816]**

**NOTES**

Commencement: to be appointed.

Inserted, together with preceding cross-heading, by the Commonhold and Leasehold Reform Act 2002, s 123(1).

Sub-ss (3), (4): words in square brackets substituted by the Companies Act 2006 (Consequential Amendments, Transitional Provisions and Savings) Order 2009, SI 2009/1941, art 2(1), Sch 1, para 140(1), (5).

*The initial notice*

## 13 Notice by qualifying tenants of claim to exercise right

(1) A claim to exercise the right to collective enfranchisement with respect to any premises is made by the giving of notice of the claim under this section.

(2) A notice given under this section ("the initial notice")—

(a) must

[(i) in a case to which section 9(2) applies,] be given to the reversioner in respect of those premises; [and

(ii) in a case to which section 9(2A) applies, be given to the person specified in the notice as the recipient;] and

(b) must be given by [a RTE company which has among its participating members] a number of qualifying tenants of flats contained in the premises as at the relevant date which—

(i) ...

(ii) is not less than one-half of the total number of flats so contained;

...

[(2ZA) But in a case where, at the relevant date, there are only two qualifying tenants of flats contained in the premises, subsection (2)(b) is not satisfied unless both are participating members of the RTE company.]

[(2ZB) The initial notice may not be given unless each person required to be given a notice of invitation to participate has been given such a notice at least 14 days before.]

[(2A) In a case to which section 9(2A) applies, the initial notice must specify—

(a) a person who owns a freehold interest in the premises, or

(b) if every person falling within paragraph (a) is a person who cannot be found or whose identity cannot be ascertained, a relevant landlord,

as the recipient of the notice.]

(3) The initial notice must—

(a) specify and be accompanied by a plan showing—

(i) the premises of which the freehold is proposed to be acquired by virtue of section 1(1),

    (ii)    any property of which the freehold is proposed to be acquired by virtue of section 1(2)(a), and

    (iii)   any property ... over which it is proposed that rights (specified in the notice) should be granted ... in connection with the acquisition of the freehold of the specified premises or of any such property so far as falling within section 1(3)(a);

(b)    contain a statement of the grounds on which it is claimed that the specified premises are, on the relevant date, premises to which this Chapter applies;

(c)    specify—

    (i)    any leasehold interest proposed to be acquired under or by virtue of section 2(1)(a) or (b), and

    (ii)   any flats or other units contained in the specified premises in relation to which it is considered that any of the requirements in Part II of Schedule 9 to this Act are applicable;

(d)    specify the proposed purchase price for each of the following, namely—

    (i)    the freehold interest in the specified premises [or, if the freehold of the whole of the specified premises is not owned by the same person, each of the freehold interests in those premises],

    (ii)   the freehold interest in any property specified under paragraph (a)(ii), and

    (iii)  any leasehold interest specified under paragraph (c)(i);

(e)    state the full names of all the qualifying tenants of flats contained in the specified premises [who are participating members of the RTE company] and the addresses of their flats, and contain ... in relation to each of those tenants ... —

    (i)    such particulars of his lease as are sufficient to identify it, including the date on which the lease was entered into, the term for which it was granted and the date of the commencement of the term,

    (ii), (iii) ...

(f)    *state the full name or names of the person or persons appointed as the nominee purchaser for the purposes of section 15, and an address in England and Wales at which notices may be given to that person or those persons under this Chapter; and*

(g)    specify the date by which the reversioner must respond to the notice by giving a counter-notice under section 21.

(4)   ...

(5)   The date specified in the initial notice in pursuance of subsection (3)(g) must be a date falling not less than two months after the relevant date.

[(5A)   A copy of a notice under this section must be given to each person who at the relevant date is the qualifying tenant of a flat contained in the premises specified under subsection (3)(a)(i).]

(6), (7)   ...

(8)   Where any premises have been specified in a notice under this section, no subsequent notice which specifies the whole or part of those premises may be given under this section so long as the earlier notice continues in force.

(9)   Where any premises have been specified in a notice under this section and—

(a)    that notice has been withdrawn, or is deemed to have been withdrawn, under or by virtue of any provision of this Chapter or under section 74(3), or

(b)    in response to that notice, an order has been applied for and obtained under section 23(1),

no subsequent notice which specifies the whole or part of those premises may be given under this section within the period of twelve months beginning with the date of the withdrawal or deemed withdrawal of the earlier notice or with the time when the order under section 23(1) becomes final (as the case may be).

(10)   In subsections (8) and (9) any reference to a notice which specifies the whole or part of any premises includes a reference to a notice which specifies any premises which contain the whole or part of those premises; and in those subsections and this "specifies" means specifies under subsection (3)(a)(i).

(11)   Where a notice is given in accordance with this section, then for the purposes of this Chapter the notice continues in force as from the relevant date—

(a)    until a binding contract is entered into in pursuance of the notice, or an order is made under section 24(4)(a) or (b) or 25(6)(a) or (b) providing for the vesting of interests in the *nominee purchaser*;

(b)    if the notice is withdrawn or deemed to have been withdrawn under or by virtue of any provision of this Chapter or under section 74(3), until the date of the withdrawal or deemed withdrawal, or

(c)    until such other time as the notice ceases to have effect by virtue of any provision of this Chapter.

(12)	In this Chapter "the specified premises", in relation to a claim made under this Chapter, means—

(a)	the premises specified in the initial notice under subsection (3)(a)(i), or

(b)	if it is subsequently agreed or determined under this Chapter that any less extensive premises should be acquired in pursuance of the notice in satisfaction of the claim, those premises;

and similarly references to any property or interest specified in the initial notice under subsection (3)(a)(ii) or (c)(i) shall, if it is subsequently agreed or determined under this Chapter that any less extensive property or interest should be acquired in pursuance of the notice, be read as references to that property or interest.

(13)	Schedule 3 to this Act (which *contains restrictions on participating in the exercise of the right to collective enfranchisement*, and makes further provision in connection with the giving of notices under this section) shall have effect.

[817]

**NOTES**

Sub-s (2): words in square brackets in para (a) inserted by the Housing Act 1996, s 107(4), Sch 10, paras 1, 6(1), (2), except in relation to a case where, before 1 October 1996, a notice was given under this section or s 42 of this Act at [848], or an application was made to court under s 26 or 50 of this Act at [830], [856]; words in square brackets in para (b) inserted by the Commonhold and Leasehold Reform Act 2002, s 121(1), (2), as from a day to be appointed, and words omitted repealed by ss 119, 120, 180 of, and Sch 14 to, that Act; for transitional provisions in relation to applications for collective enfranchisement where notice was given under this section (including cases made under sub-s (2)(b) above before the Commonhold and Leasehold Reform Act 2002, ss 121–124 come into force) and applications for orders under s 26 of this Act, see the Commonhold and Leasehold Reform Act 2002 (Commencement No 1, Savings and Transitional Provisions) (England) Order 2002, SI 2002/1912, Sch 2, paras 1, 2 and the Commonhold and Leasehold Reform Act 2002 (Commencement No 1, Savings and Transitional Provisions) (Wales) Order 2002, SI 2002/3012, Sch 2, paras 1, 2.

Sub-s (2ZA): inserted by the Commonhold and Leasehold Reform Act 2002, s 121(1), (3), as from a day to be appointed.

Sub-s (2ZB): inserted by the Commonhold and Leasehold Reform Act 2002, s 123(2), as from a day to be appointed.

Sub-s (2A): inserted by the Housing Act 1996, s 107(4), Sch 10, paras 1, 6(1), (3), subject to savings as noted above.

Sub-s (3): words omitted from para (a)(iii) repealed and words in square brackets in para (d) inserted by the Housing Act 1996, ss 107(4), 227, Sch 10, paras 1, 6(4), Sch 19, Pt V, subject to savings as noted above; words omitted from para (e) repealed by the Commonhold and Leasehold Reform Act 2002, s 180, Sch 14, except in relation to an application for collective enfranchisement in respect of which notice was given under this section, or where an application was made for an order under s 26 of this Act at [830] before 26 July 2002 (in relation to England) or 1 January 2003 (in relation to Wales); words in square brackets in para (e) inserted and para (f) substituted by s 124 of, and Sch 8, paras 2, 6(1), (2) to, the 2002 Act, as from a day to be appointed, as follows—

"(f)	state the name and registered office of the RTE company;".

Sub-ss (4), (6), (7): repealed by the Housing Act 1996, ss 108, 227, Sch 19, Part V, except in relation to a case where, before 1 April 1997, a notice was given under this section or s 42 of this Act at [848], or an application was made to court under s 26 or 50 of this Act at [830], [856].

Sub-s (5A): inserted by the Commonhold and Leasehold Reform Act 2002, s 124, Sch 8, paras 2, 6(1), (3), as from a day to be appointed.

Sub-s (11): words in italics in para (a) substituted by the words "RTE company" by the Commonhold and Leasehold Reform Act 2002, s 124, Sch 8, paras 2, 6(1), (4), as from a day to be appointed.

Sub-s (13): words in italics substituted by the words "specifies circumstances in which the fact that a qualifying tenant is a member of a RTE company is to be disregarded when considering whether the requirement in subsection (2)(b) is satisfied" by the Commonhold and Leasehold Reform Act 2002, s 124, Sch 8, paras 2, 6(1), (5), as from a day to be appointed.

Regulations: the Collective Enfranchisement and Tenants' Audit (Qualified Surveyors) Regulations 1994, SI 1994/1263 at [3137].

*Participating tenants and nominee purchaser*

## 14	The participating tenants

(*1*)	*In relation to any claim to exercise the right to collective enfranchisement, the participating tenants are (subject to the provisions of this section and Part I of Schedule 3) the following persons, namely—*

(*a*)	*in relation to the relevant date, the qualifying tenants by whom the initial notice is given; and*

(*b*)	*in relation to any time falling after that date, such of those qualifying tenants as for the time being remain qualifying tenants of flats contained in the specified premises.*

(*2*)	*Where the lease by virtue of which a participating tenant is a qualifying tenant of his flat is assigned to another person, the assignee of the lease shall, within the period of 14 days beginning with the date of the assignment, notify the nominee purchaser—*

(*a*)	*of the assignment, and*

(*b*)	*as to whether or not the assignee is electing to participate in the proposed acquisition.*

(*3*)	*Where a qualifying tenant of a flat contained in the specified premises—*

    (*a*)   is not one of the persons by whom the initial notice was given, and

    (*b*)   is not such an assignee of the lease of a participating tenant as is mentioned in subsection (2),

then (*subject to paragraph 8 of Schedule 3*) he may elect to participate in the proposed acquisition, but only with the agreement of all the persons who are for the time being participating tenants; and, if he does so elect, he shall notify the nominee purchaser forthwith of his election.

    (*4*)   Where a person notifies the nominee purchaser under subsection (2) or (3) of his election to participate in the proposed acquisition, he shall be regarded as a participating tenant for the purposes of this Chapter—

    (*a*)   as from the date of the assignment or agreement referred to in that subsection; and

    (*b*)   so long as he remains a qualifying tenant of a flat contained in the specified premises.

    (*5*)   Where a participating tenant dies, his personal representatives shall, within the period of 56 days beginning with the date of death, notify the nominee purchaser—

    (*a*)   of the death of the tenant, and

    (*b*)   as to whether or not the personal representatives are electing to withdraw from participation in the proposed acquisition;

and, unless the personal representatives of a participating tenant so notify the nominee purchaser that they are electing to withdraw from participation in that acquisition, they shall be regarded as a participating tenant for the purposes of this Chapter—

    (*i*)   as from the date of the death of the tenant, and

    (*ii*)   so long as his lease remains vested in them.

    (*6*)   Where in accordance with subsection (4) or (5) any assignee or personal representatives of a participating tenant ("*the tenant*") is or are to be regarded as a participating tenant for the purposes of this Chapter, any arrangements made between the nominee purchaser and the participating tenants and having effect immediately before the date of the assignment or (*as the case may be*) the date of death shall have effect as from that date—

    (*a*)   with such modifications as are necessary for substituting the assignee or (*as the case may be*) the personal representatives as a party to the arrangements in the place of the tenant; or

    (*b*)   in the case of an assignment by a person who remains a qualifying tenant of a flat contained in the specified premises, with such modifications as are necessary for adding the assignee as a party to the arrangements.

    (*7*)   Where the nominee purchaser receives a notification under subsection (2), (3) or (5), he shall, within the period of 28 days beginning with the date of receipt of the notification—

    (*a*)   give a notice under subsection (8) to the reversioner in respect of the specified premises, and

    (*b*)   give a copy of that notice to every other relevant landlord.

    (*8*)   A notice under this subsection is a notice stating—

    (*a*)   in the case of a notification under subsection (2)—

        (*i*)   the date of the assignment and the name and address of the assignee,

        (*ii*)   that the assignee has or (*as the case may be*) has not become a participating tenant in accordance with subsection (4), and

        (*iii*)   if he has become a participating tenant (*otherwise than in a case to which subsection (6)(b) applies*), that he has become such a tenant in place of his assignor;

    (*b*)   in the case of a notification under subsection (3), the name and address of the person who has become a participating tenant in accordance with subsection (4); and

    (*c*)   in the case of a notification under subsection (5)—

        (*i*)   the date of death of the deceased tenant,

        (*ii*)   the names and addresses of the personal representatives of the tenant, and

        (*iii*)   that in accordance with that subsection those persons are or (*as the case may be*) are not to be regarded as a participating tenant.

    (*9*)   Every notice under subsection (8)—

    (*a*)   shall identify the flat with respect to which it is given; and

    (*b*)   if it states that any person or persons is or are to be regarded as a participating tenant, shall be signed by the person or persons in question.

    (*10*)   In this section references to assignment include an assent by personal representatives and assignment by operation of law, where the assignment is—

    (*a*)   to a trustee in bankruptcy, or

    (*b*)   to a mortgagee under section 89(2) of the *Law of Property Act 1925* (*foreclosure of leasehold mortgage*),

and references to an assignee shall be construed accordingly.

*(11)   Nothing in this section has effect for requiring or authorising anything to be done at any time after a binding contract is entered into in pursuance of the initial notice.*

**[818]**

**NOTES**
Repealed by the Commonhold and Leasehold Reform Act 2002, s 180, Sch 14, as from a day to be appointed.

## 15   The nominee purchaser: appointment and replacement

*(1)   The nominee purchaser shall conduct on behalf of the participating tenants all proceedings arising out of the initial notice, with a view to the eventual acquisition by him, on their behalf, of such freehold and other interests as fall to be so acquired under a contract entered into in pursuance of that notice.*

*(2)   In relation to any claim to exercise the right to collective enfranchisement with respect to any premises, the nominee purchaser shall be such person or persons as may for the time being be appointed for the purposes of this section by the participating tenants; and in the first instance the nominee purchaser shall be the person or persons specified in the initial notice in pursuance of section 13(3)(f).*

*(3)   The appointment of any person as the nominee purchaser, or as one of the persons constituting the nominee purchaser, may be terminated by the participating tenants by the giving of a notice stating that that person's appointment is to terminate on the date on which the notice is given.*

*(4)   Any such notice must be given—*
  *(a)   to the person whose appointment is being terminated, and*
  *(b)   to the reversioner in respect of the specified premises.*

*(5)   Any such notice must in addition either—*
  *(a)   specify the name or names of the person or persons constituting the nominee purchaser as from the date of the giving of the notice, and an address in England and Wales at which notices may be given to that person or those persons under this Chapter; or*
  *(b)   state that the following particulars will be contained in a further notice given to the reversioner within the period of 28 days beginning with that date, namely—*
    *(i)   the name of the person or persons for the time being constituting the nominee purchaser,*
    *(ii)   if falling after that date, the date of appointment of that person or of each of those persons, and*
    *(iii)   an address in England and Wales at which notices may be given to that person or those persons under this Chapter;*

*and the appointment of any person by way of replacement for the person whose appointment is being terminated shall not be valid unless his name is specified, or is one of those specified, under paragraph (a) or (b).*

*(6)   Where the appointment of any person is terminated in accordance with this section, anything done by or in relation to the nominee purchaser before the date of termination of that person's appointment shall be treated, so far as necessary for the purpose of continuing its effect, as having been done by or in relation to the nominee purchaser as constituted on or after that date.*

*(7)   Where the appointment of any person is so terminated, he shall not be liable under section 33 for any costs incurred in connection with the proposed acquisition under this Chapter at any time after the date of termination of his appointment; but if—*
  *(a)   at any such time he is requested by the nominee purchaser for the time being to supply to the nominee purchaser, at an address in England and Wales specified in the request, all or any documents in his custody or under his control that relate to that acquisition, and*
  *(b)   he fails without reasonable cause to comply with any such request or is guilty of any unreasonable delay in complying with it,*

*he shall be liable for any costs which are incurred by the nominee purchaser, or for which the nominee purchaser is liable under section 33, in consequence of the failure.*

*(8)   Where—*
  *(a)   two or more persons together constitute the nominee purchaser, and*
  *(b)   the appointment of any (but not both or all) of them is terminated in accordance with this section without any person being appointed by way of immediate replacement,*

*the person or persons remaining shall for the time being constitute the nominee purchaser.*

*(9)   Where—*
  *(a)   a notice given under subsection (3) contains such a statement as is mentioned in subsection (5)(b), and*
  *(b)   as a result of the termination of the appointment in question there is no nominee purchaser for the time being,*

PART I
STATUTES

*the running of any period which—*

    (i)    *is prescribed by or under this Part for the giving of any other notice or the making of any application, and*

    (ii)    *would otherwise expire during the period beginning with the date of the giving of the notice under subsection (3) and ending with the date when the particulars specified in subsection (5)(b) are notified to the reversioner,*

*shall (subject to subsection (10)) be suspended throughout the period mentioned in paragraph (ii).*

    (10)   *If—*

    (a)    *the circumstances are as mentioned in subsection (9)(a) and (b), but*

    (b)    *the particulars specified in subsection (5)(b) are not notified to the reversioner within the period of 28 days specified in that provision,*

*the initial notice shall be deemed to have been withdrawn at the end of that period.*

    (11)   *A copy of any notice given under subsection (3) or (5)(b) shall be given by the participating tenants to every relevant landlord (other than the reversioner) to whom the initial notice or a copy of it was given in accordance with section 13 and Part II of Schedule 3; and, where a notice under subsection (3) terminates the appointment of a person who is one of two or more persons together constituting the nominee purchaser, a copy of the notice shall also be so given to every other person included among those persons.*

    (12)   *Nothing in this section applies in relation to the termination of the appointment of the nominee purchaser (or of any of the persons constituting the nominee purchaser) at any time after a binding contract is entered into in pursuance of the initial notice; and in this Chapter references to the nominee purchaser, so far as referring to anything done by or in relation to the nominee purchaser at any time falling after such a contract is so entered into, are references to the person or persons constituting the nominee purchaser at the time when the contract is entered into or such other person as is for the time being the purchaser under the contract.*

**[819]**

**NOTES**

    Repealed by the Commonhold and Leasehold Reform Act 2002, s 180, Sch 14, as from a day to be appointed.

## 16  The nominee purchaser: retirement or death

    (1)   *The appointment of any person as the nominee purchaser, or as one of the persons constituting the nominee purchaser, may be terminated by that person by the giving of a notice stating that he is resigning his appointment with effect from 21 days after the date of the notice.*

    (2)   *Any such notice must be given—*

    (a)    *to each of the participating tenants; and*

    (b)    *to the reversioner in respect of the specified premises.*

    (3)   *Where the participating tenants have received any such notice, they shall, within the period of 56 days beginning with the date of the notice, give to the reversioner a notice informing him of the resignation and containing the following particulars, namely—*

    (a)    *the name or names of the person or persons for the time being constituting the nominee purchaser,*

    (b)    *if falling after that date, the date of appointment of that person or of each of those persons, and*

    (c)    *an address in England and Wales at which notices may be given to that person or those persons under this Chapter;*

*and the appointment of any person by way of replacement for the person resigning his appointment shall not be valid unless his name is specified, or is one of those specified, under paragraph (a).*

    (4)   *Subsections (6) to (8) of section 15 shall have effect in connection with a person's resignation of his appointment in accordance with this section as they have effect in connection with the termination of a person's appointment in accordance with that section.*

    (5)   *Where the person, or one of the persons, constituting the nominee purchaser dies, the participating tenants shall, within the period of 56 days beginning with the date of death, give to the reversioner a notice informing him of the death and containing the following particulars, namely—*

    (a)    *the name or names of the person or persons for the time being constituting the nominee purchaser,*

    (b)    *if falling after that date, the date of appointment of that person or of each of those persons, and*

    (c)    *an address in England and Wales at which notices may be given to that person or those persons under this Chapter;*

*and the appointment of any person by way of replacement for the person who has died shall not be valid unless his name is specified, or is one of those specified, under paragraph (a).*

(6)　Subsections (6) and (8) of section 15 shall have effect in connection with the death of any such person as they have effect in connection with the termination of a person's appointment in accordance with that section.

(7)　If—
　(a)　the participating tenants are required to give a notice under subsection (3) or (5), and
　(b)　as a result of the resignation or death referred to in that subsection there is no nominee purchaser for the time being,
the running of any period which—
　(i)　is prescribed by or under this Part for the giving of any other notice or the making of any application, and
　(ii)　would otherwise expire during the period beginning with the relevant date and ending with the date when the particulars specified in that subsection are notified to the reversioner,
shall (subject to subsection (8)) be suspended throughout the period mentioned in paragraph (ii); and for this purpose "the relevant date" means the date of the notice of resignation under subsection (1) or the date of death (as the case may be).

(8)　If—
　(a)　the circumstances are as mentioned in subsection (7)(a) and (b), but
　(b)　the participating tenants fail to give a notice under subsection (3) or (as the case may be) subsection (5) within the period of 56 days specified in that subsection,
the initial notice shall be deemed to have been withdrawn at the end of that period.

(9)　Where a notice under subsection (1) is given by a person who is one of two or more persons together constituting the nominee purchaser, a copy of the notice shall be given by him to every other person included among those persons; and a copy of any notice given under subsection (3) or (5) shall be given by the participating tenants to every relevant landlord (other than the reversioner) to whom the initial notice or a copy of it was given in accordance with section 13 and Part II of Schedule 3.

(10)　Nothing in this section applies in relation to the resignation or death of the nominee purchaser (or any of the persons together constituting the nominee purchaser) at any time after a binding contract is entered into in pursuance of the initial notice.

**[820]**

**NOTES**

Repealed by the Commonhold and Leasehold Reform Act 2002, s 180, Sch 14, as from a day to be appointed.

*Procedure following giving of initial notice*

## 17　[Rights of access]

(1)　Once the initial notice or a copy of it has been given in accordance with section 13 or Part II of Schedule 3 to the reversioner or to any other relevant landlord, that person and any person authorised to act on his behalf shall, in the case of—
　(a)　any part of the specified premises, or
　(b)　any part of any property specified in the notice under section 13(3)(a)(ii),
in which he has a freehold or leasehold interest which is included in the proposed acquisition by the *nominee purchaser*, have a right of access thereto for the purpose of enabling him to obtain a valuation of that interest in connection with the notice [or if it is reasonable in connection with any other matter arising out of the claim to exercise the right to collective enfranchisement].

(2)　Once the initial notice has been given in accordance with section 13, the *nominee purchaser* and any person authorised to act on *his* behalf shall have a right of access to—
　(a)　any part of the specified premises, or
　(b)　any part of any property specified in the notice under section 13(3)(a)(ii),
where such access is reasonably required by the *nominee purchaser* in connection with any matter arising out of the notice.

(3)　A right of access conferred by this section shall be exercisable at any reasonable time and on giving not less than 10 days' notice to the occupier of any premises to which access is sought (or, if those premises are unoccupied, to the person entitled to occupy them).

**[821]**

**NOTES**

Section heading: words in square brackets substituted by the Commonhold and Leasehold Reform Act 2002, s 125(2), except in relation to an application for collective enfranchisement in respect of which notice was given under s 13 of this Act at **[817]**, or where an application was made for an order under s 26 of this Act at **[830]**, before 26 July 2002 (in relation to England) or 1 January 2003 (in relation to Wales).

Sub-s (1): words in italics substituted by the words "RTE company" by the Commonhold and Leasehold Reform Act 2002, s 124, Sch 8, paras 2, 7(1), (2), as from a day to be appointed, and words in square brackets inserted by s 125(1) of that Act, subject to savings as noted above.

Sub-s (2): words "nominee purchaser" in italics substituted in both places by the words "RTE company" and word "his" in italics substituted by the word "its" by the Commonhold and Leasehold Reform Act 2002, s 124, Sch 8, paras 2, 7(1), (3), as from a day to be appointed.

## 18 Duty of nominee purchaser to disclose existence of agreements affecting specified premises etc

(1) If at any time during the period beginning with the relevant date and ending with the [time when a binding contract is entered into in pursuance of the initial notice]—

    (a)    there subsists between the *nominee purchaser* and a person other than a participating *tenant* any agreement (of whatever nature) providing for the disposal of a relevant interest, *or*

    (b)    *if the nominee purchaser is a company, any person other than a participating tenant holds any share in that company by virtue of which a relevant interest may be acquired,*

the existence of that agreement *or shareholding* shall be notified to the reversioner by the *nominee purchaser* as soon as possible after the agreement *or shareholding* is made *or established* or, if in existence on the relevant date, as soon as possible after that date.

(2) If—

    (a)    the *nominee purchaser* is required to give any notification under subsection (1) but fails to do so before the price payable to the reversioner or any other relevant landlord in respect of the acquisition of any interest of his by the *nominee purchaser* is determined for the purposes of Schedule 6, and

    (b)    it may reasonably be assumed that, had the *nominee purchaser* given the notification, it would have resulted in the price so determined being increased by an amount referable to the existence of any agreement *or shareholding* falling within subsection (1)(a) *or (b)*,

the *nominee purchaser* and the participating *tenants* shall be jointly and severally liable to pay the amount to the reversioner or (as the case may be) the other relevant landlord.

(3) In subsection (1) "relevant interest" means any interest in, or in any part of the specified premises or any property specified in the initial notice under section 13(3)(a)(ii).

(4) Paragraph (a) of subsection (1) does not, however, apply to an agreement if the only disposal of such an interest for which it provides is one consisting in the creation of an interest by way of security for a loan.

**[822]**

**NOTES**

Sub-s (1): words in square brackets substituted by the Commonhold and Leasehold Reform Act 2002, s 126(2), except in relation to a notice given under s 13 of this Act at **[817]**, or an application made under s 26 of this Act at **[830]**, before 28 February 2005 (in relation to England) or 31 May 2005 (in relation to Wales), and words "nominee purchaser" in italics substituted in both places by the words "RTE company", word "tenant" in italics in para (a) substituted by the word "member", para (b) and word "or" immediately preceding it and words "or shareholding" in both places and "or established" in italics repealed by ss 124, 180 of, and Sch 8, paras 2, 8(1), (2), Sch 14 to, the 2002 Act, as from a day to be appointed.

Sub-s (2): words "nominee purchaser" in italics substituted in each place by the words "RTE company", words "or shareholding" and "or (b)" in italics repealed and word "tenants" in italics substituted by the word "members" by the Commonhold and Leasehold Reform Act 2002, ss 124, 180, Sch 8, paras 2, 8(1), (3), Sch 14, as from a day to be appointed.

## 19 Effect of initial notice as respects subsequent transactions by freeholder etc

(1) Where the initial notice has been registered in accordance with section 97(1), then so long as it continues in force—

    (a)    [any person who owns the freehold of the whole or any part of the specified premises or the freehold of any property specified in the notice under section 13(3)(a)(ii)] shall not—

        (i)    make any disposal severing his interest in those premises or in [that property] or

        (ii)    grant out of that interest any lease under which, if it had been granted before the relevant date, the interest of the tenant would to any extent have been liable on that date to acquisition by virtue of section 2(1)(a) or (b); and

    (b)    no other relevant landlord shall grant out of his interest in the specified premises or in any property so specified any such lease as is mentioned in paragraph (a)(ii);

and any transaction shall be void to the extent that it purports to effect any such disposal or any such grant of a lease as is mentioned in paragraph (a) or (b).

(2) Where the initial notice has been so registered and at any time when it continues in force—

    [(a)    any person who owns the freehold of the whole or any part of the specified premises or the freehold of any property specified in the notice under section 13(3)(a)(ii) disposes of his interest in those premises or that property,]

    (b)    any other relevant landlord disposes of any interest of his specified in the notice under section 13(3)(c)(i),

subsection (3) below shall apply in relation to that disposal.

    (3)    Where this subsection applies in relation to any such disposal as is mentioned in subsection (2)(a) or (b), all parties shall for the purposes of this Chapter be in the same position as if the person acquiring the interest under the disposal—

    (a)    had become its owner before the initial notice was given (and was accordingly a relevant landlord in place of the person making the disposal), and

    (b)    had been given any notice or copy of a notice given under this Chapter to that person, and

    (c)    had taken all steps which that person had taken;

and, if any subsequent disposal of that interest takes place at any time when the initial notice continues in force, this subsection shall apply in relation to that disposal as if any reference to the person making the disposal included any predecessor in title of his.

    (4)    Where immediately before the relevant date there is in force a binding contract relating to the disposal to any extent—

    [(a)    by any person who owns the freehold of the whole or any part of the specified premises or the freehold of any property specified in the notice under section 13(3)(a)(ii),] or

    (b)    by any other relevant landlord,

of any interest of his falling within subsection (2)(a) or (b), then, so long as the initial notice continues in force, the operation of the contract shall be suspended so far as it relates to any such disposal.

    (5)    Where—

    (a)    the operation of a contract has been suspended under subsection (4) ("the suspended contract"), and

    (b)    a binding contract is entered into in pursuance of the initial notice,

then (without prejudice to the general law as to the frustration of contracts) the person referred to in paragraph (a) or (b) of that subsection shall, together with all other persons, be discharged from the further performance of the suspended contract so far as it relates to any such disposal as is mentioned in subsection (4).

    (6)    In subsections (4) and (5) any reference to a contract (except in the context of such a contract as is mentioned in subsection (5)(b)) includes a contract made in pursuance of an order of any court; but those subsections do not apply to any contract providing for the eventuality of a notice being given under section 13 in relation to the whole or part of the property in which any such interest as is referred to in subsection (4) subsists.

**[823]**

---

**NOTES**

    Sub-ss (1), (2), (4): words in square brackets substituted by the Housing Act 1996, s 107(4), Sch 10, paras 1, 7, except in relation to a case where, before 1 October 1996, a notice was given under s 13 or 42 of this Act at **[817]**, **[848]**, or an application was made to court under s 26 or 50 of this Act at **[830]**, **[856]**.

---

## 20  Right of reversioner to require evidence of tenant's right to participate

    (1)    The reversioner in respect of the specified premises may, within the period of 21 days beginning with the relevant date, give the *nominee purchaser a notice requiring him, in the case of any person by whom the initial notice was given, to deduce the title of that person* to the lease by virtue of which it is claimed that he is a qualifying tenant of a flat contained in the specified premises.

    (2)    The *nominee purchaser* shall comply with any such requirement within the period of 21 days beginning with the date of the giving of the notice.

    (3)    Where—

    (a)    the *nominee purchaser* fails to comply with a requirement under subsection (1) in the case of any *person* within the period mentioned in subsection (2), and

    (b)    the initial notice would not have been given in accordance with section 13(2)(b) if—

        (i)    that *person*, and

        (ii)    any other *person* in the case of whom a like failure by the *nominee purchaser* has occurred,

        had been neither *included among the persons who gave the notice* nor included among the qualifying tenants of the flats referred to in that provision,

the initial notice shall be deemed to have been withdrawn at the end of that period.

**[824]**

---

**NOTES**

    Sub-s (1): words in italics substituted by the words "RTE company a notice requiring it, in the case of any qualifying tenant of a flat contained in the specified premises who was a participating member of the company at the relevant time, to deduce the title of that qualifying tenant" by the Commonhold and Leasehold Reform Act 2002, s 124, Sch 8, paras 2, 9(1), (2), as from a day to be appointed.

Sub-s (2): words in italics substituted by the words "RTE company" by the Commonhold and Leasehold Reform Act 2002, s 124, Sch 8, paras 2, 9(1), (3), as from a day to be appointed.

Sub-s (3): words "nominee purchaser" in italics substituted in both places by the words "RTE company", word "person" in italics substituted in each place by the words "qualifying tenant" and words in italics in the sixth place substituted by the words "members of the RTE company" by the Commonhold and Leasehold Reform Act 2002, s 124, Sch 8, paras 2, 9(1), (4), as from a day to be appointed.

## 21  Reversioner's counter-notice

(1)  The reversioner in respect of the specified premises shall give a counter-notice under this section to the *nominee purchaser* by the date specified in the initial notice in pursuance of section 13(3)(g).

(2)  The counter-notice must comply with one of the following requirements, namely—

    (a)    state that the reversioner admits that the *participating tenants were* on the relevant date entitled to exercise the right to collective enfranchisement in relation to the specified premises;

    (b)    state that, for such reasons as are specified in the counter-notice, the reversioner does not admit that the *participating tenants were* so entitled;

    (c)    contain such a statement as is mentioned in paragraph (a) or (b) above but state that an application for an order under subsection (1) of section 23 is to be made by such appropriate landlord (within the meaning of that section) as is specified in the counter-notice, on the grounds that he intends to redevelop the whole or a substantial part of the specified premises.

(3)  If the counter-notice complies with the requirement set out in subsection (2)(a), it must in addition—

    (a)    state which (if any) of the proposals contained in the initial notice are accepted by the reversioner and which (if any) of those proposals are not so accepted, and specify—

        (i)    in relation to any proposal which is not so accepted, the reversioner's counter-proposal, and

        (ii)    any additional leaseback proposals by the reversioner;

    (b)    if (in a case where any property specified in the initial notice under section 13(3)(a)(ii) is property falling within section 1(3)(b)) any such counter-proposal relates to the grant of rights or the disposal of any freehold interest in pursuance of section 1(4), specify—

        (i)    the nature of those rights and the property over which it is proposed to grant them, or

        (ii)    the property in respect of which it is proposed to dispose of any such interest,

    as the case may be;

    (c)    state which interests (if any) the *nominee purchaser* is to be required to acquire in accordance with subsection (4) below;

    (d)    state which rights (if any) [any] relevant landlord, desires to retain—

        (i)    over any property in which he has any interest which is included in the proposed acquisition by the *nominee purchaser*, or

        (ii)    over any property in which he has any interest which the *nominee purchaser* is to be required to acquire in accordance with subsection (4) below,

    on the grounds that the rights are necessary for the proper management or maintenance of property in which he is to retain a freehold or leasehold interest; and

    (e)    include a description of any provisions which the reversioner or any other relevant landlord considers should be included in any conveyance to the *nominee purchaser* in accordance with section 34 and Schedule 7.

(4)  The *nominee purchaser may be required to acquire on behalf of the participating tenants* the interest in any property of [any] relevant landlord, if the property—

    (a)    would for all practical purposes cease to be of use and benefit to him, or

    (b)    would cease to be capable of being reasonably managed or maintained by him,

in the event of his interest in the specified premises or (as the case may be) in any other property being acquired *by the nominee purchaser* under this Chapter.

(5)  Where a counter-notice specifies any interest in pursuance of subsection (3)(c), the *nominee purchaser* or any person authorised to act on *his* behalf shall, in the case of any part of the property in which that interest subsists, have a right of access thereto for the purpose of enabling the *nominee purchaser* to obtain, in connection with the proposed acquisition by *him*, a valuation of that interest; and subsection (3) of section 17 shall apply in relation to the exercise of that right as it applies in relation to the exercise of a right of access conferred by that section.

(6)  Every counter-notice must specify an address in England and Wales at which notices may be given to the reversioner under this Chapter.

(7)   The reference in subsection (3)(a)(ii) to additional leaseback proposals is a reference to proposals which relate to the leasing back, in accordance with section 36 and Schedule 9, of flats or other units contained in the specified premises and which are made either—

    (a)   in respect of flats or other units in relation to which Part II of that Schedule is applicable but which were not specified in the initial notice under section 13(3)(c)(ii), or

    (b)   in respect of flats or other units in relation to which Part III of that Schedule is applicable.

(8)   Schedule 4 (which imposes requirements as to the furnishing of information by the reversioner about the exercise of rights under Chapter II with respect to flats contained in the specified premises) shall have effect.

**[825]**

**NOTES**

Sub-s (1): words in italics in para (a) substituted by the words "RTE company" by the Commonhold and Leasehold Reform Act 2002, s 124, Sch 8, paras 2, 10(1), (2), as from a day to be appointed.

Sub-s (2): words in italics in paras (a), (b) substituted by the words "RTE company was" by the Commonhold and Leasehold Reform Act 2002, s 124, Sch 8, paras 2, 10(1), (3), as from a day to be appointed.

Sub-s (3): words in italics substituted in each place by the words "RTE company" by the Commonhold and Leasehold Reform Act 2002, s 124, Sch 8, paras 2, 10(1), (4), as from a day to be appointed; word in square brackets substituted by the Housing Act 1996, s 107(4), Sch 10, paras 1, 8(1), (2), except in relation to a case where, before 1 October 1996, a notice was given under s 13 or 42 of this Act at **[817]**, **[848]**, or an application was made to court under s 26 or 50 of this Act at **[830]**, **[856]**.

Sub-s (4): words in italics in the first place substituted by the words "RTE company may be required to acquire" and words in italics in the second place substituted by the words "by the RTE company" by the Commonhold and Leasehold Reform Act 2002, s 124, Sch 8, paras 2, 10(1), (5), as from a day to be appointed; word in square brackets substituted by the Housing Act 1996, s 107(4), Sch 10, paras 1, 8(1), (3), subject to savings as noted above.

Sub-s (5): words "nominee purchaser" in italics substituted in both places by the words "RTE company", word "his" in italics substituted by the words "its" and word "him" in italics substituted by the word "it" by the Commonhold and Leasehold Reform Act 2002, s 124, Sch 8, paras 2, 10(1), (6), as from a day to be appointed.

*Applications to court or leasehold valuation tribunal*

## 22   Proceedings relating to validity of initial notice

(1)   Where—

    (a)   the reversioner in respect of the specified premises has given the *nominee purchaser* a counter-notice under section 21 which (whether it complies with the requirement set out in subsection (2)(b) or (c) of that section) contains such a statement as is mentioned in subsection (2)(b) of that section, but

    (b)   the court is satisfied, on an application made by the *nominee purchaser, that the participating tenants were* on the relevant date entitled to exercise the right to collective enfranchisement in relation to the specified premises,

the court shall by order make a declaration to that effect.

(2)   Any application for an order under subsection (1) must be made not later than the end of the period of two months beginning with the date of the giving of the counter-notice to the *nominee purchaser.*

(3)   If on any such application the court makes an order under subsection (1), then (subject to subsection (4)) the court shall make an order—

    (a)   declaring that the reversioner's counter-notice shall be of no effect, and

    (b)   requiring the reversioner to give a further counter-notice to the *nominee purchaser* by such date as is specified in the order.

(4)   Subsection (3) shall not apply if—

    (a)   the counter-notice complies with the requirement set out in section 21(2)(c), and

    (b)   either—

        (i)   an application for an order under section 23(1) is pending, or

        (ii)   the period specified in section 23(3) as the period for the making of such an application has not expired.

(5)   Subsections (3) to (5) of section 21 shall apply to any further counter-notice required to be given by the reversioner under subsection (3) above as if it were a counter-notice under that section complying with the requirement set out in subsection (2)(a) of that section.

(6)   If an application by the *nominee purchaser* for an order under subsection (1) is dismissed by the court, the initial notice shall cease to have effect at the time when the order dismissing the application becomes final.

**NOTES**
Sub-s (1): words in italics in para (a) substituted by the words "RTE company" and words in italics in para (b) substituted by the words "RTE company, that it was" by the Commonhold and Leasehold Reform Act 2002, s 124, Sch 8, paras 2, 11(1), (2), as from a day to be appointed.
Sub-ss (2), (3), (6): words in italics substituted in each place by the words "RTE company" by the Commonhold and Leasehold Reform Act 2002, s 124, Sch 8, paras 2, 11(1), (3), as from a day to be appointed.

### 23 Tenants' claim liable to be defeated where landlord intends to redevelop

(1)   Where the reversioner in respect of the specified premises has given a counter-notice under section 21 which complies with the requirement set out in subsection (2)(c) of that section, the court may, on the application of any appropriate landlord, by order declare that the right to collective enfranchisement shall not be exercisable in relation to those premises by reason of that landlord's intention to redevelop the whole or a substantial part of the premises.

(2)   The court shall not make an order under subsection (1) unless it is satisfied—
   (a)   that not less than two-thirds of all the long leases on which flats contained in the specified premises are held are due to terminate within the period of five years beginning with the relevant date; and
   (b)   that for the purposes of redevelopment the applicant intends, once the leases in question have so terminated—
      (i)   to demolish or reconstruct, or
      (ii)   to carry out substantial works of construction on,
      the whole or a substantial part of the specified premises; and
   (c)   that he could not reasonably do so without obtaining possession of the flats demised by those leases.

(3)   Any application for an order under subsection (1) must be made within the period of two months beginning with the date of the giving of the counter-notice to the *nominee purchaser*; but, where the counter-notice is one falling within section 22(1)(a), such an application shall not be proceeded with until such time (if any) as an order under section 22(1) becomes final.

(4)   Where an order under subsection (1) is made by the court, the initial notice shall cease to have effect on the order becoming final.

(5)   Where an application for an order under subsection (1) is dismissed by the court, the court shall make an order—
   (a)   declaring that the reversioner's counter-notice shall be of no effect, and
   (b)   requiring the reversioner to give a further counter-notice to the *nominee purchaser* by such date as is specified in the order.

(6)   Where—
   (a)   the reversioner has given such a counter-notice as is mentioned in subsection (1), but
   (b)   either—
      (i)   no application for an order under that subsection is made within the period referred to in subsection (3), or
      (ii)   such an application is so made but is subsequently withdrawn,
then (subject to subsection (8)), the reversioner shall give a further counter-notice to the *nominee purchaser* within the period of two months beginning with the appropriate date.

(7)   In subsection (6) "the appropriate date" means—
   (a)   if subsection (6)(b)(i) applies, the date immediately following the end of the period referred to in subsection (3); and
   (b)   if subsection (6)(b)(ii) applies, the date of withdrawal of the application.

(8)   Subsection (6) shall not apply if any application has been made by the *nominee purchaser* under section 22(1).

(9)   Subsections (3) to (5) of section 21 shall apply to any further counter-notice required to be given by the reversioner under subsection (5) or (6) above as if it were a counter-notice under that section complying with the requirement set out in subsection (2)(a) of that section.

(10)   In this section "appropriate landlord", in relation to the specified premises, means—
   (a)   the reversioner or any other relevant landlord; or
   (b)   any two or more persons falling within paragraph (a) who are acting together.

[827]

**NOTES**
Sub-ss (3), (5), (6), (8): words in italics substituted in each place by the words "RTE company" by the Commonhold and Leasehold Reform Act 2002, s 124, Sch 8, paras 2, 12, as from a day to be appointed.

**24  Applications where terms in dispute or failure to enter contract**

(1)  Where the reversioner in respect of the specified premises has given the *nominee purchaser*—

    (a)    a counter-notice under section 21 complying with the requirement set out in subsection (2)(a) of that section, or

    (b)    a further counter-notice required by or by virtue of section 22(3) or section 23(5) or (6),

but any of the terms of acquisition remain in dispute at the end of the period of two months beginning with the date on which the counter-notice or further counter-notice was so given, a leasehold valuation tribunal may, on the application of either the *nominee purchaser* or the reversioner, determine the matters in dispute.

(2)  Any application under subsection (1) must be made not later than the end of the period of six months beginning with the date on which the counter-notice or further counter-notice was given to the *nominee purchaser*.

(3)  Where—

    (a)    the reversioner has given the *nominee purchaser* such a counter-notice or further counter-notice as is mentioned in subsection (1)(a) or (b), and

    (b)    all of the terms of acquisition have been either agreed between the parties or determined by a leasehold valuation tribunal under subsection (1),

but a binding contract incorporating those terms has not been entered into by the end of the appropriate period specified in subsection (6), the court may, on the application of either the *nominee purchaser* or the reversioner, make such order under subsection (4) as it thinks fit.

(4)  The court may under this subsection make an order—

    (a)    providing for the interests to be acquired by the *nominee purchaser* to be vested in *him* on the terms referred to in subsection (3);

    (b)    providing for those interests to be vested in *him* on those terms, but subject to such modifications as—

        (i)    may have been determined by a leasehold valuation tribunal, on the application of either the *nominee purchaser* or the reversioner, to be required by reason of any change in circumstances since the time when the terms were agreed or determined as mentioned in that subsection, and

        (ii)    are specified in the order; or

    (c)    providing for the initial notice to be deemed to have been withdrawn at the end of the appropriate period specified in subsection (6);

and Schedule 5 shall have effect in relation to any such order as is mentioned in paragraph (a) or (b) above.

(5)  Any application for an order under subsection (4) must be made not later than the end of the period of two months beginning immediately after the end of the appropriate period specified in subsection (6).

(6)  For the purposes of this section the appropriate period is—

    (a)    where all of the terms of acquisition have been agreed between the parties, the period of two months beginning with the date when those terms were finally so agreed;

    (b)    where all or any of those terms have been determined by a leasehold valuation tribunal under subsection (1)—

        (i)    the period of two months beginning with the date when the decision of the tribunal under that subsection becomes final, or

        (ii)    such other period as may have been fixed by the tribunal when making its determination.

(7)  In this section "the parties" means the *nominee purchaser* and the reversioner and any relevant landlord who has given to those persons a notice for the purposes of paragraph 7(1)(a) of Schedule 1.

(8)  In this Chapter "the terms of acquisition", in relation to a claim made under this Chapter, means the terms of the proposed acquisition by the *nominee purchaser*, whether relating to—

    (a)    the interests to be acquired,

    (b)    the extent of the property to which those interests relate or the rights to be granted over any property,

    (c)    the amounts payable as the purchase price for such interests,

    (d)    the apportionment of conditions or other matters in connection with the severance of any reversionary interest, or

    (e)    the provisions to be contained in any conveyance,

or otherwise, and includes any such terms in respect of any interest to be acquired in pursuance of section 1(4) or 21(4).

**NOTES**
Sub-ss (1)–(3), (7), (8): words in italics substituted in each place by the words "RTE company" by the Commonhold and Leasehold Reform Act 2002, s 124, Sch 8, paras 2, 13(1)–(4), (6), as from a day to be appointed.
Sub-s (4): words "nominee purchaser" in italics substituted in both places by the words "RTE company" and word "him" in italics substituted in both places by the word "it" by the Commonhold and Leasehold Reform Act 2002, s 124, Sch 8, paras 2, 13(1), (5), as from a day to be appointed.

## 25 Applications where reversioner fails to give counter-notice or further counter-notice

(1)   Where the initial notice has been given in accordance with section 13 but—

 (a) the reversioner has failed to give the *nominee purchaser* a counter-notice in accordance with section 21(1), or

 (b) if required to give the *nominee purchaser* a further counter-notice by or by virtue of section 22(3) or section 23(5) or (6), the reversioner has failed to comply with that requirement,

the court may, on the application of the *nominee purchaser*, make an order determining the terms on which *he* is to acquire, in accordance with the proposals contained in the initial notice, such interests and rights as are specified in it under section 13(3).

(2)   The terms determined by the court under subsection (1) shall, if Part II of Schedule 9 is applicable, include terms which provide for the leasing back, in accordance with section 36 and that Part of that Schedule, of flats or other units contained in the specified premises.

(3)   The court shall not make any order on an application made by virtue of paragraph (a) of subsection (1) unless it is satisfied—

 (a) that the *participating tenants were* on the relevant date entitled to exercise the right to collective enfranchisement in relation to the specified premises; and

 (b) if applicable, that the requirements of Part II of Schedule 3 were complied with as respects the giving of copies of the initial notice.

(4)   Any application for an order under subsection (1) must be made not later than the end of the period of six months beginning with the date by which the counter-notice or further counter-notice referred to in that subsection was to be given to the *nominee purchaser*.

(5)   Where—

 (a) the terms of acquisition have been determined by an order of the court under subsection (1), but

 (b) a binding contract incorporating those terms has not been entered into by the end of the appropriate period specified in subsection (8),

the court may, on the application of either the *nominee purchaser* or the reversioner, make such order under subsection (6) as it thinks fit.

(6)   The court may under this subsection make an order—

 (a) providing for the interests to be acquired by the *nominee purchaser* to be vested in *him* on the terms referred to in subsection (5);

 (b) providing for those interests to be vested in *him* on those terms, but subject to such modifications as—

  (i) may have been determined by a leasehold valuation tribunal, on the application of either the *nominee purchaser* or the reversioner, to be required by reason of any change in circumstances since the time when the terms were determined as mentioned in that subsection, and

  (ii) are specified in the order; or

 (c) providing for the initial notice to be deemed to have been withdrawn at the end of the appropriate-period specified in subsection (8);

and Schedule 5 shall have effect in relation to any such order as is mentioned in paragraph (a) or (b) above.

(7)   Any application for an order under subsection (6) must be made not later than the end of the period of two months beginning immediately after the end of the appropriate period specified in subsection (8).

(8)   For the purposes of this section the appropriate period is—

 (a) the period of two months beginning with the date when the order of the court under subsection (1) becomes final, or

 (b) such other period as may have been fixed by the court when making that order.

**[829]**

**NOTES**
Sub-ss (1), (4), (5): words in italics substituted in each place by the words "RTE company" by the Commonhold and Leasehold Reform Act 2002, s 124, Sch 8, paras 2, 14(1), (2), (4), as from a day to be appointed.

Sub-s (3): words in italics substituted by the words "RTE company was" by the Commonhold and Leasehold Reform Act 2002, s 124, Sch 8, paras 2, 14(1), (3), as from a day to be appointed.

Sub-s (6): words "nominee purchaser" in italics substituted in both places by the words "RTE company" and word "him" in italics substituted in both places by the word "it" by the Commonhold and Leasehold Reform Act 2002, s 124, Sch 8, paras 2, 14(1), (5), as from a day to be appointed.

## 26 Applications where relevant landlord cannot be found

(1)   Where *not less than two-thirds of the qualifying tenants of flats contained in any premises to which this Chapter applies desire to make a claim to exercise the right to collective enfranchisement in relation to those premises* but—

    (a)   (in a case to which section 9(1) applies) the person who owns the freehold of the premises cannot be found or his identity cannot be ascertained, or

    (b)   (in a case to which section 9(2) [or (2A)] applies) each of the relevant landlords is someone who cannot be found or whose identity cannot be ascertained,

the court may, on the application of the *qualifying tenants in question*, make a vesting order under this subsection—

    (i)   with respect to any interests of that person (whether in those premises or in any other property) which are liable to acquisition *on behalf of those tenants* by virtue of section 1(1) or (2)(a) or section 2(1), or

    (ii)   with respect to any interests of those landlords which are so liable to acquisition by virtue of any of those provisions,

as the case may be.

(2)   Where in a case to which section 9(2) applies—

    (a)   *not less than two-thirds of the qualifying tenants of flats contained in any premises to which this Chapter applies desire to make a claim to exercise the right to collective enfranchisement in relation to those premises,* and

    (b)   paragraph (b) of subsection (1) does not apply, but

    (c)   a notice of that claim or (as the case may be) a copy of such a notice cannot be given in accordance with section 13 or Part II of Schedule 3 to any person to whom it would otherwise be required to be so given because he cannot be found or his identity cannot be ascertained,

the court may, on the application of the *qualifying tenants in question*, make an order dispensing with the need to give such a notice or (as the case may be) a copy of such a notice to that person.

(3)   If[, in a case to which section 9(2) applies] that person is the person who owns the freehold of the premises, then on the application of *those tenants*, the court may, in connection with an order under subsection (2), make an order appointing any other relevant landlord to be the reversioner in respect of the premises in place of that person; and if it does so references in this Chapter to the reversioner shall apply accordingly.

[(3A)   Where in a case to which section 9(2A) applies—

    (a)   *not less than two-thirds of the qualifying tenants of flats contained in any premises to which this Chapter applies desire to make a claim to exercise the right to collective enfranchisement in relation to those premises,* and

    (b)   paragraph (b) of subsection (1) does not apply, but

    (c)   a copy of a notice of that claim cannot be given in accordance with Part II of Schedule 3 to any person to whom it would otherwise be required to be so given because he cannot be found or his identity cannot be ascertained,

the court may, on the application of the *qualifying tenants in question*, make an order dispensing with the need to give a copy of such a notice to that person.]

(4)   The court shall not make an order on any application under subsection (1)[, (2) or (3A)] unless it is satisfied—

    (a)   that on the date of the making of the application the premises to which the application relates were premises to which this Chapter applies; and

    (b)   that on that date the *applicants* would not have been precluded by any provision of this Chapter from giving a valid notice under section 13 with respect to those premises

[and that the RTE company has given notice of the application to each person who is the qualifying tenant of a flat contained in those premises.]

(5)   Before making any such order the court may require the *applicants* to take such further steps by way of advertisement or otherwise as the court thinks proper for the purpose of tracing the person or persons in question; and if, after an application is made for a vesting order under subsection (1) and before any interest is vested in pursuance of the application, the person or (as the case may be) any of the persons referred to in paragraph (a) or (b) of that subsection is traced, then no further proceedings shall be taken with a view to any interest being so vested, but (subject to subsection (6))—

    (a)   the rights and obligations of all parties shall be determined as if the *applicants* had, at the date of the application, duly given notice under section 13 of *their* claim to exercise the right to collective enfranchisement in relation to the premises to which the application relates; and

(b)    the court may give such directions as the court thinks fit as to the steps to be taken for giving effect to those rights and obligations, including directions modifying or dispensing with any of the requirements of this Chapter or of regulations made under this Part.

(6)   An application for a vesting order under subsection (1) may be withdrawn at any time before execution of a conveyance under section 27(3) and, after it is withdrawn, subsection (5)(a) above shall not apply; but where any step is taken (whether by the *applicants* or otherwise) for the purpose of giving effect to subsection (5)(a) in the case of any application, the application shall not afterwards be withdrawn except—

(a)    with the consent of every person who is the owner of any interest the vesting of which is sought by the *applicants*, or

(b)    by leave of the court,

and the court shall not give leave unless it appears to the court just to do so by reason of matters coming to the knowledge of the *applicants* in consequence of the tracing of any such person.

(7)   Where an order has been made under subsection (2) [or (3A)] dispensing with the need to give a notice under section 13, or a copy of such a notice, to a particular person with respect to any particular premises, then if—

(a)    a notice is subsequently given under that section with respect to those premises, and

(b)    in reliance on the order, the notice or a copy of the notice is not to be given to that person,

the notice must contain a statement of the effect of the order.

(8)   Where a notice under section 13 contains such a statement in accordance with subsection (7) above, then in determining for the purposes of any provision of this Chapter whether the requirements of section 13 or Part II of Schedule 3 have been complied with in relation to the notice, those requirements shall be deemed to have been complied with so far as relating to the giving of the notice or a copy of it to the person referred to in subsection (7) above.

(9)   Rules of court shall make provision—

(a)    for requiring notice of any application under subsection (3) to be served by the *persons making the application on any person who the applicants know or have* reason to believe is a relevant landlord; and

(b)    for enabling persons served with any such notice to be joined as parties to the proceedings.

**[830]**

---

**NOTES**

Sub-s (1): words in italics in the first place substituted by the words "a RTE company which satisfies the requirement in section 13(2)(b) wishes to make a claim to exercise the right to collective enfranchisement", words in italics in the second place substituted by the words "RTE company" and words in italics in the third place substituted by the words "by the RTE company" by the Commonhold and Leasehold Reform Act 2002, s 124, Sch 8, paras 2, 15(1), (2), as from a day to be appointed; words in square brackets in para (a) inserted by the Housing Act 1996, s 107(4), Sch 10, paras 1, 9(1), (2), except in relation to a case where, before 1 October 1996, a notice was given under s 13 or 42 of this Act at **[817]**, **[848]**, or an application was made to court under this section or s 50 of this Act at **[856]**.

Sub-s (2): words in italics in the first place substituted by the words "a RTE company which satisfies the requirement in section 13(2)(b) wishes to make a claim to exercise the right to collective enfranchisement" and words in italics in the second place substituted by the words "RTE company" by the Commonhold and Leasehold Reform Act 2002, s 124, Sch 8, paras 2, 15(1), (3), as from a day to be appointed.

Sub-s (3): words in square brackets inserted by the Housing Act 1996, s 107(4), Sch 10, paras 1, 9(1), (3), subject to savings as noted above; words in italics substituted by the words "the RTE company" by the Commonhold and Leasehold Reform Act 2002, s 124, Sch 8, paras 2, 15(1), (4), as from a day to be appointed.

Sub-s (3A): inserted by the Housing Act 1996, s 107(4), Sch 10, paras 1, 9(1), (4), subject to savings as noted above; words in italics in the first place substituted by the words "a RTE company which satisfies the requirement in section 13(2)(b) wishes to make a claim to exercise the right to collective enfranchisement" and words in italics in the second place substituted by the words "RTE company" by the Commonhold and Leasehold Reform Act 2002, s 124, Sch 8, paras 2, 15(1), (5), as from a day to be appointed.

Sub-s (4): words in first pair of square brackets substituted by the Housing Act 1996, s 107(4), Sch 10, paras 1, 9(1), (5), subject to savings as noted above; word in italics substituted by the words "RTE company" and words in second pair of square brackets inserted by the Commonhold and Leasehold Reform Act 2002, s 124, Sch 8, paras 2, 15(1), (6), as from a day to be appointed.

Sub-s (5): words "applicants" in italics substituted in both places by the words "RTE company" and word "their" in italics substituted by the word "its" by the Commonhold and Leasehold Reform Act 2002, s 124, Sch 8, paras 2, 15(1), (7), as from a day to be appointed.

Sub-s (6): words "applicants" in italics substituted in each place by the words "RTE company" by the Commonhold and Leasehold Reform Act 2002, s 124, Sch 8, paras 2, 15(1), (8), as from a day to be appointed.

Sub-s (7): words in square brackets inserted by the Housing Act 1996, s 107(4), Sch 10, paras 1, 9(1), (6), subject to savings as noted above.

Sub-s (9): words in italics substituted by the words "RTE company on any person who it knows or has" by the Commonhold and Leasehold Reform Act 2002, s 124, Sch 8, paras 2, 15(1), (9), as from a day to be appointed.

**27   Supplementary provisions relating to vesting orders under section 26(1)**

(1)   A vesting order under section 26(1) is an order providing for the vesting of any such interests as are referred to in paragraph (i) or (ii) of that provision—

(a)   in *such person or persons as may be appointed for the purpose by the applicants for the order*, and

(b)   on such terms as may be determined by a leasehold valuation tribunal to be appropriate with a view to the interests being vested in *that person or those persons* in like manner (so far as the circumstances permit) as if the *applicants had*, at the date of *their* application, given notice under section 13 of *their* claim to exercise the right to collective enfranchisement in relation to the premises with respect to which the order is made.

(2)   If a leasehold valuation tribunal so determines in the case of a vesting order under section 26(1), the order shall have effect in relation to interests which are less extensive than those specified in the application on which the order was made.

(3)   Where any interests are to be vested in *any person or persons* by virtue of a vesting order under section 26(1), then on *his or their* paying into court the appropriate sum in respect of each of those interests there shall be executed by such person as the court may designate a conveyance which—

(a)   is in a form approved by a leasehold valuation tribunal, and

(b)   contains such provisions as may be so approved for the purpose of giving effect so far as possible to the requirements of section 34 and Schedule 7;

and that conveyance shall be effective to vest in the *person or persons to whom the conveyance is made* the interests expressed to be conveyed, subject to and in accordance with the terms of the conveyance.

(4)   In connection with the determination by a leasehold valuation tribunal of any question as to the interests to be conveyed by any such conveyance, or as to the rights with or subject to which they are to be conveyed, it shall be assumed (unless the contrary is shown) that any person whose interests are to be conveyed ("the transferor") has no interest in property other than those interests and, for the purpose of excepting them from the conveyance, any minerals underlying the property in question.

(5)   The appropriate sum which in accordance with subsection (3) is to be paid into court in respect of any interest is the aggregate of—

(a)   such amount as may be determined by a leasehold valuation tribunal to be the price which would be payable in respect of that interest in accordance with Schedule 6 if the interest were being acquired in pursuance of such a notice as is mentioned in subsection (1)(b); and

(b)   any amounts or estimated amounts determined by such a tribunal as being, at the time of execution of the conveyance, due to the transferor from any tenants of his of premises comprised in the premises in which that interest subsists (whether due under or in respect of their leases or under or in respect of agreements collateral thereto).

(6)   Where any interest is vested in *any person or persons* in accordance with this section, the payment into court of the appropriate sum in respect of that interest shall be taken to have satisfied any claims against the *applicants for the vesting order under section 26(1), their personal representatives or assigns* in respect of the price payable under this Chapter for the acquisition of that interest.

(7)   Where any interest is so vested in *any person or persons*, section 32(5) shall apply in relation to *his or their acquisition of that interest as it applies in relation to the acquisition of any interest by a nominee purchaser.*

**[831]**

**NOTES**

Sub-s (1): words in italics in the first and second places substituted by the words "the RTE company", words in italics in the third place substituted by the words "RTE company had" and word "their" in italics substituted in both places by the word "its" by the Commonhold and Leasehold Reform Act 2002, s 124, Sch 8, paras 2, 16(1), (2), as from a day to be appointed.

Sub-s (3): words in italics in the first place substituted by the words "the RTE company", words "his or their" in italics substituted by the word "its" and words in italics in the third place substituted by the words "RTE company" by the Commonhold and Leasehold Reform Act 2002, s 124, Sch 8, paras 2, 16(1), (3), as from a day to be appointed.

Sub-s (6): words in italics in the first place substituted by the words "the RTE company" and words in italics in the second place substituted by the words "RTE company" by the Commonhold and Leasehold Reform Act 2002, s 124, Sch 8, paras 2, 16(1), (4), as from a day to be appointed.

Sub-s (7): words in italics in the first place substituted by the words "the RTE company" and words in italics in the second place substituted by the words "its acquisition of that interest." by the Commonhold and Leasehold Reform Act 2002, s 124, Sch 8, paras 2, 16(1), (5), as from a day to be appointed.

*Termination of acquisition procedures*

## 28 Withdrawal from acquisition by *participating tenants*

(1)    At any time before a binding contract is entered into in pursuance of the initial notice, the *participating tenants* may withdraw that notice by the giving of a notice to that effect under this section ("a notice of withdrawal").

(2)    *A notice of withdrawal must be given—*
  (a)    *to the nominee purchaser;*
  (b)    *to the reversioner in respect of the specified premises; and*
  (c)    *to every other relevant landlord who is known or believed by the participating tenants to have given to the nominee purchaser a notice under paragraph 7(1) or (4) of Schedule 1;*

*and, if by virtue of paragraph (c) a notice of withdrawal falls to be given to any person falling within that paragraph, it shall state that he is a recipient of the notice.*

(3)    *The nominee purchaser shall, on receiving a notice of withdrawal, give a copy of it to every relevant landlord who—*
  (a)    *has given to the nominee purchaser such a notice as is mentioned in subsection (2)(c); and*
  (b)    *is not stated in the notice of withdrawal to be a recipient of it.*

(4)    Where a notice of withdrawal is given by the *participating tenants under subsection (1)—*
  (a)    *those persons, and*
  (b)    *(subject to subsection (5)) every other person who is not a participating tenant for the time being but has at any time been such a tenant,*

shall be liable—
  (i)    to the reversioner, and
  (ii)    to every other relevant landlord,

for all relevant costs incurred by him in pursuance of the initial notice down to the time when the notice of withdrawal or a copy of it is given to him in accordance with subsection (2) *or (3).*

(5)    A person falling within paragraph (b) of subsection (4) shall not be liable for any costs by virtue of that subsection if—
  (a)    the lease in respect of which he was a *participating* tenant has been assigned to another person; and
  (b)    that other person has become a participating *tenant in accordance with section 14(4);*

and in paragraph (a) above the reference to an assignment *shall be construed in accordance with section 14(10).*

(6)    Where any liability for costs arises under subsection (4)—
  (a)    it shall be a joint and several liability of the persons concerned; and
  (b)    the *nominee purchaser* shall not be liable for any costs under section 33.

(7)    In subsection (4) "relevant costs", in relation to the reversioner or any other relevant landlord, means costs for which the *nominee purchaser* would (apart from subsection (6)) be liable to that person under section 33.

**[832]**

## NOTES

Section heading: words in italics substituted by the words "RTE company" by the Commonhold and Leasehold Reform Act 2002, s 124, Sch 8, paras 2, 17(1), (7), as from a day to be appointed.

Sub-ss (1), (6), (7): words in italics substituted in each place by the words "RTE company" by the Commonhold and Leasehold Reform Act 2002, s 124, Sch 8, paras 2, 17(1), (2), (6), as from a day to be appointed.

Sub-s (2): substituted by the Commonhold and Leasehold Reform Act 2002, s 124, Sch 8, paras 2, 17(1), (3), as from a day to be appointed, as follows—

"(2)    A notice of withdrawal must be given to—
  (a)    each person who is the qualifying tenant of a flat contained in the specified premises;
  (b)    the reversioner in respect of the specified premises; and
  (c)    every other relevant landlord who has given to the RTE company a notice under paragraph 7(1) or (4) of Schedule 1.".

Sub-s (3): repealed by the Commonhold and Leasehold Reform Act 2002, s 180, Sch 14, as from a day to be appointed.

Sub-s (4): words in italics in the second place repealed and words in italics in the first place substituted by the Commonhold and Leasehold Reform Act 2002, ss 124, 180, Sch 8, paras 2, 17(1), (4), Sch 14, as from a day to be appointed, as follows—

"RTE company under subsection (1)—

(a)   the company, and
(b)   (subject to subsection (5)) every person who is, or has at any time been, a participating member of the company,".

Sub-s (5): word in italics in para (a) substituted by the word "qualifying", words in italics in para (b) substituted by the words "member of the RTE company" and words in italics in the third place substituted by the words "includes an assent by personal representatives, and assignment by operation of law where the assignment is to a trustee in bankruptcy or to a mortgagee under section 89(2) of the Law of Property Act 1925 (c 20) (foreclosure of leasehold mortgage)" by the Commonhold and Leasehold Reform Act 2002, s 124, Sch 8, paras 2, 17(1), (5), as from a day to be appointed.

## 29   Deemed withdrawal of initial notice

(1)   Where, in a case falling within paragraph (a) of subsection (1) of section 22—
   (a)   no application for an order under that subsection is made within the period specified in subsection (2) of that section, or
   (b)   such an application is so made but is subsequently withdrawn, the initial notice shall be deemed to have been withdrawn—
      (i)   (if paragraph (a) above applies) at the end of that period, or
      (ii)   (if paragraph (b) above applies) on the date of the withdrawal of the application.

(2)   Where—
   (a)   in a case to which subsection (1) of section 24 applies, no application under that subsection is made within the period specified in subsection (2) of that section, or
   (b)   in a case to which subsection (3) of that section applies, no application for an order under subsection (4) of that section is made within the period specified in subsection (5) of that section,

the initial notice shall be deemed to have been withdrawn at the end of the period referred to in paragraph (a) or (b) above (as the case may be).

(3)   Where, in a case falling within paragraph (a) or (b) of subsection (1) of section 25, no application for an order under that subsection is made within the period specified in subsection (4) of that section, the initial notice shall be deemed to have been withdrawn at the end of that period.

(4)   Where, in a case to which subsection (5) of section 25 applies, no application for an order under subsection (6) of that section is made within the period specified in subsection (7) of that section, the initial notice shall be deemed to have been withdrawn at the end of that period.

[(4A)   The initial notice shall be deemed to have been withdrawn if—
   (a)   a winding-up order ... is made, or a resolution for voluntary winding up is passed, with respect to the RTE company, [or the RTE company enters administration,]
   (b)   a receiver or a manager of the RTE company's undertaking is duly appointed, or possession is taken, by or on behalf of the holders of any debentures secured by a floating charge, of any property of the RTE company comprised in or subject to the charge,
   (c)   a voluntary arrangement proposed in the case of the RTE company for the purposes of Part 1 of the Insolvency Act 1986 (c 45) is approved under that Part of that Act, or
   (d)   the RTE company's name is struck off the register under [section 1000, 1001 or 1003 of the Companies Act 2006].]

(5)   The following provisions, namely—
   (*a*)   *section 15(10),*
   (*b*)   *section 16(8),*
   (c)   section 20(3),
   (d)   section 24(4)(c), and
   (e)   section 25(6)(c),

also make provision for a notice under section 13 to be deemed to have been withdrawn at a particular time.

(6)   Where the initial notice is deemed to have been withdrawn at any time by virtue of any provision of this Chapter, subsections (4) and (5) of section 28 shall apply for the purposes of this section in like manner as they apply where a notice of withdrawal is given under that section, but as if the reference in subsection (4) of that section to the time when a notice or copy is given as there mentioned were a reference to the time when the initial notice is so deemed to have been withdrawn.

(7)   *Where the initial notice is deemed to have been withdrawn by virtue of section 15(10) or 16(8)—*
   (*a*)   *the liability for costs arising by virtue of subsection (6) above shall be a joint and several liability of the persons concerned; and*
   (*b*)   *the nominee purchaser shall not be liable for any costs under section 33.*

(8)    In the provisions applied by subsection (6), "relevant costs", in relation to the reversioner or any other relevant landlord, means costs for which the *nominee purchaser is, or would (apart from subsection (7)) be,* liable to that person under section 33.

[833]

## 30 Effect on initial notice or subsequent contract of institution of compulsory acquisition procedures

(1)    A notice given under section 13 shall be of no effect if on the relevant date—
  (a)    any acquiring authority has, with a view to the acquisition of the whole or part of the specified premises for any authorised purpose—
      (i)    served notice to treat on any relevant person, or
      (ii)    entered into a contract for the purchase of the interest of any such person in the premises or part of them, and
  (b)    the notice to treat or contract remains in force.

(2)    In subsection (1) "relevant person", in relation to the specified premises, means—
  (a)    the person who owns the freehold of the premises [or, where the freehold of the whole of the premises is not owned by the same person, any person who owns the freehold of part of them]; or
  (b)    any other person who owns any leasehold interest in the premises which is specified in the initial notice under section 13(3)(c)(i).

(3)    A notice given under section 13 shall not specify under subsection (3)(a)(ii) or (c)(i) of that section any property or leasehold interest in property if on the relevant date—
  (a)    any acquiring authority has, with a view to the acquisition of the whole or part of the property for any authorised purpose—
      (i)    served notice to treat on the person who owns the freehold of, or any such leasehold interest in, the property, or
      (ii)    entered into a contract for the purchase of the interest of any such person in the property or part of it, and
  (b)    the notice to treat or contract remains in force.

(4)    A notice given under section 13 shall cease to have effect if before a binding contract is entered into in pursuance of the notice, any acquiring authority serves, with a view to the acquisition of the whole or part of the specified premises for any authorised purpose, notice to treat as mentioned in subsection (1)(a).

(5)    Where any such authority so serves notice to treat at any time after a binding contract is entered into in pursuance of the notice given under section 13 but before completion of the acquisition by the *nominee purchaser* under this Chapter, then (without prejudice to the general law as to the frustration of contracts) the parties to the contract shall be discharged from the further performance of the contract.

(6)    Where subsection (4) or (5) applies in relation to the initial notice or any contract entered into in pursuance of it, then on the occasion of the compulsory acquisition in question the compensation payable in respect of any interest in the specified premises (whether or not the one to which the relevant notice to treat relates) shall be determined on the basis of the value of the interest—
  (a)    (if subsection (4) applies) subject to and with the benefit of the rights and obligations arising from the initial notice and affecting that interest; or
  (b)    (if subsection (5) applies) subject to and with the benefit of the rights and obligations arising from the contract and affecting that interest.

(7)    In this section—

(a)     "acquiring authority", in relation to the specified premises or any other property, means any person or body of persons who has or have been, or could be, authorised to acquire the whole or part of those premises or that property compulsorily for any purpose; and

(b)     "authorised purpose", in relation to any acquiring authority, means any such purpose.

[834]

**NOTES**

Sub-s (2): words in square brackets inserted by the Housing Act 1996, s 107(4), Sch 10, paras 1, 10, except in relation to a case where, before 1 October 1996, a notice was given under s 13 or 42 of this Act at [817], [848], or an application was made to court under s 26 or 50 of this Act at [830], [856].

Sub-s (5): words in italics substituted by the words "RTE company" by the Commonhold and Leasehold Reform Act 2002, s 124, Sch 8, paras 2, 19, as from a day to be appointed.

### 31   Effect on initial notice of designation for inheritance tax purposes and applications for designation

(1)     A notice given under section 13 shall be of no effect if on the relevant date the whole or any part of—

(a)     the specified premises, or

(b)     any property specified in the notice under section 13(3)(a)(ii), is qualifying property.

(2)     For the purposes of this section the whole or any part of the specified premises, or of any property specified as mentioned in subsection (1), is qualifying property if—

(a)     it has been designated under section 31(1)(b), (c) or (d) of the Inheritance Tax Act 1984 (designation and undertakings relating to conditionally exempt transfers), whether with or without any other property, and no chargeable event has subsequently occurred with respect to it; or

(b)     an application to the Board for it to be so designated is pending; or

(c)     it is the property of a body not established or conducted for profit and a direction has been given in relation to it under section 26 of that Act (gifts for public benefit), whether with or without any other property; or

(d)     an application to the Board for a direction to be so given in relation to it is pending.

(3)     For the purposes of subsection (2) an application is pending as from the time when it is made to the Board until such time as it is either granted or refused by the Board or withdrawn by the applicant; and for this purpose an application shall not be regarded as made unless and until the applicant has submitted to the Board all such information in support of the application as is required by the Board.

(4)     A notice given under section 13 shall cease to have effect if, before a binding contract is entered into in pursuance of the notice, the whole or any part of—

(a)     the specified premises, or

(b)     any property specified in the notice under section 13(3)(a)(ii), becomes qualifying property.

(5)     Where a notice under section 13 ceases to have effect by virtue of subsection (4) above—

(a)     the *nominee purchaser* shall not be liable for any costs under section 33; and

(b)     the person who applied or is applying for designation or a direction shall be *liable*—

(i)     *to the qualifying tenants by whom the notice was given for all reasonable costs incurred by them in the preparation and giving of the notice; and*

(ii)    *to the nominee purchaser for all reasonable costs incurred in pursuance of the notice by him or by any other person who has acted as the nominee purchaser.*

(6)     Where it is claimed that subsection (1) or (4) applies in relation to a notice under section 13, the person making the claim shall, at the time of making it, furnish the *nominee purchaser* with evidence in support of it; and if he fails to do so he shall be liable for any costs which are reasonably incurred by the *nominee purchaser* in consequence of the failure.

(7)     In subsection (2)—

(a)     paragraphs (a) and (b) apply to designation under section 34(1)(a), (b) or (c) of the Finance Act 1975 or section 77(1)(b), (c) or (d) of the Finance Act 1976 as they apply to designation under section 31(1)(b), (c) or (d) of the Inheritance Tax Act 1984; and

(b)     paragraphs (c) and (d) apply to a direction under paragraph 13 of Schedule 6 to the Finance Act 1975 as they apply to a direction under section 26 of that Act of 1984.

(8)     In this section—

"the Board" means the Commissioners of Inland Revenue;

"chargeable event" means—

(a)     any event which in accordance with any provision of Chapter II of Part II of the Inheritance Tax Act 1984 (exempt transfers) is a chargeable event, including any such provision as applied by section 78(3) of that Act (conditionally exempt occasions); or

(b)  any event which would have been a chargeable event in the circumstances mentioned in section 79(3) of that Act (exemption from ten-yearly charge).

**[835]**

NOTES

Sub-s (5): words in italics in para (a) substituted by the words "RTE company" and words in italics in para (b) substituted by the words "liable to the RTE company for all reasonable costs incurred in the preparation or giving of the notice or in pursuance of it." by the Commonhold and Leasehold Reform Act 2002, s 124, Sch 8, paras 2, 20(1), (2), as from a day to be appointed.

Sub-s (6): words in italics substituted by the words "RTE company" by the Commonhold and Leasehold Reform Act 2002, s 124, Sch 8, paras 2, 20(1), (3), as from a day to be appointed.

Finance Act 1975, s 34, Sch 6; Finance Act 1976, s 77: repealed by the Inheritance Tax Act 1984, s 277, Sch 9 (then cited as the Capital Transfer Tax Act 1984).

*Determination of price and costs of enfranchisement*

## 32  Determination of price

(1)  Schedule 6 to this Act (which relates to the determination of the price payable by the *nominee purchaser* in respect of each of the freehold and other interests to be acquired by *him* in pursuance of this Chapter) shall have effect.

(2)  The lien of the owner of any such interest (as vendor) on the specified premises, or (as the case may be) on any other property, for the price payable shall extend—

(a)  to any amounts which, at the time of the conveyance of that interest, are due to him from any tenants of his premises comprised in the premises in which that interest subsists (whether due under or in respect of their leases or under or in respect of agreements collateral thereto); and

(b)  to any amount payable to him by virtue of section 18(2); and

(c)  to any costs payable to him by virtue of section 33.

(3)  Subsection (2)(a) does not apply in relation to amounts due to the owner of any such interest from tenants of any premises which are to be comprised in the premises demised by a lease granted in accordance with section 36 and Schedule 9.

(4)  In subsection (2) the reference to the specified premises or any other property includes a reference to a part of those premises or that property.

(5)  Despite the fact that in accordance with Schedule 6 no payment or only a nominal payment is payable by the *nominee purchaser* in respect of the acquisition by *him* of any interest *he* shall nevertheless be deemed for all purposes to be a purchaser of that interest for a valuable consideration in money or money's worth.

**[836]**

NOTES

Sub-s (1): words "nominee purchaser" in italics substituted by the words "RTE company" and word "him" in italics substituted by the word "it" by the Commonhold and Leasehold Reform Act 2002, s 124, Sch 8, paras 2, 21(1), (2), as from a day to be appointed.

Sub-s (5): words "nominee purchaser" in italics substituted by the words "RTE company" and words "him" and "he" in italics substituted in both places by the word "it" by the Commonhold and Leasehold Reform Act 2002, s 124, Sch 8, paras 2, 21(1), (3), as from a day to be appointed.

## 33  Costs of enfranchisement

(1)  Where a notice is given under section 13, then (subject to the provisions of this section and sections 28(6), 29(7) and 31(5)) the *nominee purchaser* shall be liable, to the extent that they have been incurred in pursuance of the notice by the reversioner or by any other relevant landlord, for the reasonable costs of and incidental to any of the following matters, namely—

(a)  any investigation reasonably undertaken—

(i)  of the question whether any interest in the specified premises or other property is liable to acquisition in pursuance of the initial notice, or

(ii)  of any other question arising out of that notice;

(b)  deducing, evidencing and verifying the title to any such interest;

(c)  making out and furnishing such abstracts and copies as the *nominee purchaser* may require;

(d)  any valuation of any interest in the specified premises or other property;

(e)  any conveyance of any such interest;

but this subsection shall not apply to any costs if on a sale made voluntarily a stipulation that they were to be borne by the purchaser would be void.

(2)  For the purposes of subsection (1) any costs incurred by the reversioner or any other relevant landlord in respect of professional services rendered by any person shall only be regarded

as reasonable if and to the extent that costs in respect of such services might reasonably be expected to have been incurred by him if the circumstances had been such that he was personally liable for all such costs.

(3) Where by virtue of any provision of this Chapter the initial notice ceases to have effect at any time, then (subject to subsection (4)) the *nominee purchaser's* liability under this section for costs incurred by any person shall be a liability for costs incurred by *him* down to that time.

(4) The *nominee purchaser* shall not be liable for any costs under this section if the initial notice ceases to have effect by virtue of section 23(4) or 30(4).

(5) The *nominee purchaser* shall not be liable under this section for any costs which a party to any proceedings under this Chapter before a leasehold valuation tribunal incurs in connection with the proceedings.

(6) *In this section references to the nominee purchaser include references to any person whose appointment has terminated in accordance with section 15(3) or 16(1); but this section shall have effect in relation to such a person subject to section 15(7).*

(7) *Where by virtue of this section, or of this section and section 29(6) taken together, two or more persons are liable for any costs, they shall be jointly and severally liable for them.*

**[837]**

**NOTES**

Sub-s (1): reference to "29(7)" in italics repealed and words "nominee purchaser" in italics substituted in both places by the words "RTE company" by the Commonhold and Leasehold Reform Act 2002, ss 124, 180, Sch 8, paras 2, 22(1), (2), Sch 14, as from a day to be appointed.

Sub-s (3): words "nominee purchaser's" in italics substituted by the words "RTE company's" and word "him" in italics substituted by the word "it" by the Commonhold and Leasehold Reform Act 2002, s 124, Sch 8, paras 2, 22(1), (3), as from a day to be appointed.

Sub-ss (4), (5): words "nominee purchaser" in italics substituted by the words "RTE company" by the Commonhold and Leasehold Reform Act 2002, s 124, Sch 8, paras 2, 22(1), (4), as from a day to be appointed.

Sub-ss (6), (7): repealed by the Commonhold and Leasehold Reform Act 2002, s 180, Sch 14, as from a day to be appointed.

*Completion of acquisition*

### 34 Conveyance to *nominee purchaser*

(1) Any conveyance executed for the purposes of this Chapter, being a conveyance to the *nominee purchaser* of the freehold of the specified premises[, of a part of those premises] or of any other property, shall grant to the *nominee purchaser* an estate in fee simple absolute in those premises[, that part of those premises] or that property, subject only to such incumbrances as may have been agreed or determined under this Chapter to be incumbrances subject to which that estate should be granted, having regard to the following provisions of this Chapter.

(2) Any such conveyance shall, where the *nominee purchaser* is to acquire any leasehold interest in the specified premises[, the part of the specified premises] or (as the case may be) in the other property to which the conveyance relates, provide for the disposal to the *nominee purchaser* of any such interest.

(3) Any conveyance executed for the purposes of this Chapter shall have effect under section 2(1) of the Law of Property Act 1925 (conveyances overreaching certain equitable interests etc) to overreach any incumbrance capable of being overreached under section 2(1)—

 (a) as if, where the interest conveyed is settled land for the purposes of the Settled Land Act 1925, the conveyance were made under the powers of that Act, and

 (b) as if the requirements of section 2(1) as to payment of the capital money allowed any part of the purchase price paid or applied in accordance with section 35 below or Schedule 8 to this Act to be so paid or applied.

(4) For the purposes of this section "incumbrances" includes—

 (a) rentcharges, and

 (b) (subject to subsection (5)) personal liabilities attaching in respect of the ownership of land or an interest in land though not charged on that land or interest.

(5) Burdens originating in tenure, and burdens in respect of the upkeep or regulation for the benefit of any locality of any land, building, structure, works, ways or watercourse shall not be treated as incumbrances for the purposes of this section; but any conveyance executed for the purposes of this Chapter shall be made subject to any such burdens.

(6) A conveyance executed for the purposes of this Chapter shall not be made subject to any incumbrance capable of being overreached by the conveyance, but shall be made subject (where they are not capable of being overreached) to—

 (a) rentcharges redeemable under sections 8 to 10 of the Rentcharges Act 1977, and

 (b) those falling within paragraphs (c) and (d) of section 2(3) of that Act (estate rentcharges and rentcharges imposed under certain enactments), except as otherwise provided by subsections (7) and (8) below.

(7)   Where any land is to be conveyed to the *nominee purchaser* by a conveyance executed for the purposes of this Chapter, subsection (6) shall not preclude the person who owns the freehold interest in the land from releasing, or procuring the release of, the land from any rentcharge.

(8)   The conveyance of any such land ("the relevant land") may, with the agreement of the *nominee purchaser* (which shall not be unreasonably withheld), provide in accordance with section 190(1) of the Law of Property Act 1925 (charging of rentcharges on land without rent owner's consent) that a rentcharge—

(a)   shall be charged exclusively on other land affected by it in exoneration of the relevant land, or

(b)   shall be apportioned between other land affected by it and the relevant land.

(9)   Except to the extent that any departure is agreed to by the *nominee purchaser* and the person whose interest is to be conveyed, any conveyance executed for the purposes of this Chapter shall—

(a)   as respects the conveyance of any freehold interest, conform with the provisions of Schedule 7, and

(b)   as respects the conveyance of any leasehold interest, conform with the provisions of paragraph 2 of that Schedule (any reference in that paragraph to the freeholder being read as a reference to the person whose leasehold interest is to be conveyed[, and with the reference to the covenants for title implied under Part I of the Law of Property (Miscellaneous Provisions) Act 1994 being read as excluding the covenant in section 4(1)(b) of that Act (compliance with terms of lease)]).

(10)   Any such conveyance shall in addition contain a statement that it is a conveyance executed for the purposes of this Chapter; and any such statement shall comply with such requirements as may be prescribed by [land registration rules under the Land Registration Act 2002].

**[838]**

---

**NOTES**

Section heading: words in italics substituted by the words "RTE company" by the Commonhold and Leasehold Reform Act 2002, s 124, Sch 8, paras 2, 23, as from a day to be appointed.

Sub-ss (1), (2): words in italics substituted in each place by the words "RTE company" by the Commonhold and Leasehold Reform Act 2002, s 124, Sch 8, paras 2, 23, as from a day to be appointed; words in square brackets inserted by the Housing Act 1996, s 107(4), Sch 10, paras 1, 11, except in relation to a case where, before 1 October 1996, a notice was given under s 13 or 42 of this Act at **[817]**, **[848]**, or an application was made to court under s 26 or 50 of this Act at **[830]**, **[856]**.

Sub-ss (7), (8): words in italics substituted in each place by the words "RTE company" by the Commonhold and Leasehold Reform Act 2002, s 124, Sch 8, paras 2, 23, as from a day to be appointed.

Sub-s (9): words in italics substituted by the words "RTE company" by the Commonhold and Leasehold Reform Act 2002, s 124, Sch 8, paras 2, 23, as from a day to be appointed; words in square brackets inserted by the Law of Property (Miscellaneous Provisions) Act 1994, s 21(1), (4), Sch 1, para 12(1), save in relation to any disposition of property to which, by virtue of ss 10, 11 of that Act, the Law of Property Act 1925, s 76, or the Land Registration Act 1925, s 24(1)(a), continues to apply.

Sub-s (10): words in square brackets substituted by the Land Registration Act 2002, s 133, Sch 11, para 30(1), (2).

Rules: the Land Registration Rules 2003, SI 2003/1417.

---

## 35   Discharge of existing mortgages on transfer to *nominee purchaser*

(1)   Subject to the provisions of Schedule 8, where any interest is acquired by the *nominee purchaser* in pursuance of this Chapter, the conveyance by virtue of which it is so acquired shall, as regards any mortgage to which this section applies, be effective by virtue of this section—

(a)   to discharge the interest from the mortgage, and from the operation of any order made by a court for the enforcement of the mortgage, and

(b)   to extinguish any term of years created for the purposes of the mortgage,

and shall do so without the persons entitled to or interested in the mortgage or in any such order or term of years becoming parties to or executing the conveyance.

(2)   Subject to subsections (3) and (4), this section applies to any mortgage of the interest so acquired (however created or arising) which—

(a)   is a mortgage to secure the payment of money or the performance of any other obligation by the person from whom the interest is so acquired or any other person; and

(b)   is not a mortgage which would be overreached apart from this section.

(3)   This section shall not apply to any such mortgage if it has been agreed between the *nominee purchaser* and the reversioner or (as the case may be) any other relevant landlord that the interest in question should be acquired subject to the mortgage.

(4)   In this section and Schedule 8 "mortgage" includes a charge or lien; but neither this section nor that Schedule applies to a rentcharge.

**[839]**

PART I
STATUTES

**NOTES**

Section heading: words in italics substituted by the words "RTE company" by the Commonhold and Leasehold Reform Act 2002, s 124, Sch 8, paras 2, 24, as from a day to be appointed.

Sub-ss (1), (3): words in italics substituted by the words "RTE company" by the Commonhold and Leasehold Reform Act 2002, s 124, Sch 8, paras 2, 24, as from a day to be appointed.

### 36 *Nominee purchaser* required to grant leases back to former freeholder in certain circumstances

(1)    In connection with the acquisition by *him* of [a freehold interest in] the specified premises, the *nominee purchaser* shall grant to the person from whom the [interest] is acquired such leases of flats or other units contained in those premises as are required to be so granted by virtue of Part II or III of Schedule 9.

(2)    Any such lease shall be granted so as to take effect immediately after the acquisition by the *nominee purchaser* of the freehold [interest concerned].

(3)    Where any flat or other unit demised under any such lease ("the relevant lease") is at the time of that acquisition subject to any existing lease, the relevant lease shall take effect as a lease of the freehold reversion in respect of the flat or other unit.

(4)    Part IV of Schedule 9 has effect with respect to the terms of a lease granted in pursuance of Part II or III of that Schedule.

**[840]**

**NOTES**

Section heading: words in italics substituted by the words "RTE company" by the Commonhold and Leasehold Reform Act 2002, s 124, Sch 8, paras 2, 25(1), (4), as from a day to be appointed.

Sub-s (1): word "him" in italics substituted by the word "it" and words "nominee purchaser" in italics substituted by the words "RTE company" by the Commonhold and Leasehold Reform Act 2002, s 124, Sch 8, paras 2, 25(1), (2), as from a day to be appointed; words in square brackets substituted by the Housing Act 1996, s 107(4), Sch 10, paras 1, 12(1), (2), except in relation to a case where, before 1 October 1996, a notice was given under s 13 or 42 of this Act at **[817]**, **[848]**, or an application was made to court under s 26 or 50 of this Act at **[830]**, **[856]**.

Sub-s (2): words in italics substituted by the words "RTE company" by the Commonhold and Leasehold Reform Act 2002, s 124, Sch 8, paras 2, 25(1), (3), as from a day to be appointed; words in square brackets substituted by the Housing Act 1996, s 107(4), Sch 10, paras 1, 12(1), (3), except in relation to a case where, before 1 October 1996, a notice was given under s 13 or 42 of this Act at **[817]**, **[848]**, or an application was made to court under s 26 or 50 of this Act at **[830]**, **[856]**.

### 37 Acquisition of interests from local authorities etc

Schedule 10 to this Act (which makes provision with respect to the acquisition of interests from local authorities etc in pursuance of this Chapter) shall have effect.

**[841]**

*[Landlord's right to compensation in relation to ineffective claims*

### 37A Compensation for postponement of termination in connection with ineffective claims

(1)    This section applies where a claim to exercise the right to collective enfranchisement in respect of any premises is made on or after 15th January 1999 by *tenants of flats contained in the premises* and the claim is not effective.

(2)    A *person who is a participating tenant* immediately before the claim ceases to have effect shall be liable to pay compensation if—

(a)    the claim was not made at least two years before the term date of the lease by virtue of which he is a qualifying tenant ("the existing lease"), and

(b)    any of the conditions mentioned in subsection (3) is met.

(3)    The conditions referred to above are—

(a)    that the making of the claim caused a notice served under paragraph 4(1) of Schedule 10 to the Local Government and Housing Act 1989 in respect of the existing lease to cease to have effect and the date on which the claim ceases to have effect is later than four months before the termination date specified in the notice,

(b)    that the making of the claim prevented the service of an effective notice under paragraph 4(1) of Schedule 10 to the Local Government and Housing Act 1989 in respect of the existing lease (but did not cause a notice served under that provision in respect of that lease to cease to have effect) and the date on which the claim ceases to have effect is a date later than six months before the term date of the existing lease, and

(c)    that the existing lease has been continued under paragraph 6(1) of Schedule 3 by virtue of the claim.

(4)    Compensation under subsection (2) shall become payable at the end of the appropriate period and be the right of the person who is the tenant's immediate landlord at that time.

(5)    The amount which a tenant is liable to pay under subsection (2) shall be equal to the difference between—

    (a)    the rent for the appropriate period under the existing lease, and

    (b)    the rent which might reasonably be expected to be payable for that period were the property to which the existing lease relates let for a term equivalent to that period on the open market by a willing landlord on the following assumptions—

        (i)    that no premium is payable in connection with the letting,

        (ii)    that the letting confers no security of tenure, and

        (iii)    that, except as otherwise provided by this paragraph, the letting is on the same terms as the existing lease.

(6)    For the purposes of subsections (4) and (5), the appropriate period is—

    (a)    in a case falling within paragraph (a) of subsection (3), the period—

        (i)    beginning with the termination date specified in the notice mentioned in that paragraph, and

        (ii)    ending with the earliest date of termination which could have been specified in a notice under paragraph 4(1) of Schedule 10 to the Local Government and Housing Act 1989 in respect of the existing lease served immediately after the date on which the claim ceases to have effect, or, if the existing lease is terminated before then, with the date of its termination;

    (b)    in a case falling within paragraph (b) of subsection (3), the period—

        (i)    beginning with the later of six months from the date on which the claim is made and the term date of the existing lease, and

        (ii)    ending six months after the date on which the claim ceases to have effect, or, if the existing lease is terminated before then, with the date of its termination; and

    (c)    in a case falling within paragraph (c) of subsection (3), the period for which the existing lease is continued under paragraph 6(1) of Schedule 3.

(7)    *In the case of a person who becomes a participating tenant by virtue of an election under section 14(3), the references in subsections (3)(a) and (b) and (6)(b)(i) to the making of the claim shall be construed as references to the making of the election.*

(8)    For the purposes of this section—

    (a)    references to a claim to exercise the right to collective enfranchisement shall be taken as references to a notice given, or purporting to be given (*whether by persons who are qualifying tenants or not*), under section 13,

    (b)    references to the date on which a claim ceases to have effect shall, in the case of a claim made by a notice which is not a valid notice under section 13, be taken as references to the date on which the notice is set aside by the court or is withdrawn or would, if valid, cease to have effect or be deemed to have been withdrawn, that date being taken, where the notice is set aside, or would, if valid, cease to have effect, in consequence of a court order, to be the date when the order becomes final, and

    (c)    a claim to exercise the right to collective enfranchisement is not effective if it ceases to have effect for any reason other than—

        (i)    the application of section 23(4), 30(4) or 31(4),

        (ii)    the entry into a binding contract for the acquisition of the freehold and other interests falling to be acquired in pursuance of the claim, or

        (iii)    the making of an order under section 24(4)(a) or (b) or 25(6)(a) or (b) which provides for the vesting of those interests.]

[842]

**NOTES**

    Inserted, together with s 37B and preceding cross-heading, by the Housing Act 1996, s 116, Sch 11, para 2(1).

    Sub-s (1): words in italics substituted by the words "a RTE company" by the Commonhold and Leasehold Reform Act 2002, s 124, Sch 8, paras 2, 26(1), (2), as from a day to be appointed.

    Sub-s (2): words in italics substituted by the words "qualifying tenant who is a participating member of the RTE company" by the Commonhold and Leasehold Reform Act 2002, s 124, Sch 8, paras 2, 26(1), (3), as from a day to be appointed.

    Sub-s (7): repealed by the Commonhold and Leasehold Reform Act 2002, s 180, Sch 14, as from a day to be appointed.

    Sub-s (8): words in italics repealed by the Commonhold and Leasehold Reform Act 2002, s 180, Sch 14, as from a day to be appointed.

**[37B    Modification of section 37A where change in immediate reversion**

(1)    Where a tenant's liability to pay compensation under section 37A relates to a period during which there has been a change in the interest immediately expectant on the determination of his lease, that section shall have effect with the following modifications.

(2)    For subsections (4) and (5) there shall be substituted—

"(4)    Compensation under subsection (2) shall become payable at the end of the appropriate period and there shall be a separate right to compensation in respect of each of the interests which, during that period, have been immediately expectant on the determination of the existing lease.

(5)    Compensation under subsection (2) above shall—

(a)    in the case of the interest which is immediately expectant on the determination of the existing lease at the end of the appropriate period, be the right of the person in whom that interest is vested at that time, and

(b)    in the case of an interest which ceases during the appropriate period to be immediately expectant on the determination of the existing lease, be the right of the person in whom the interest was vested immediately before it ceased to be so expectant.

(5A)    The amount which the tenant is liable to pay under subsection (2) above in respect of any interest shall be equal to the difference between—

(a)    the rent under the existing lease for the part of the appropriate period during which the interest was immediately expectant on the determination of that lease, and

(b)    the rent which might reasonably be expected to be payable for that part of that period were the property to which the existing lease relates let for a term equivalent to that part of that period on the open market by a willing landlord on the following assumptions—

(i)    that no premium is payable in connection with the letting,

(ii)    that the letting confers no security of tenure, and

(iii)    that, except as otherwise provided by this paragraph, the letting is on the same terms as the existing lease."

(3)    In subsection (6), for "(4) and (5)" there shall be substituted "(4) to (5A)".]

**[843]**

**NOTES**
Inserted as noted to s 37A at **[842]**.

*Supplemental*

## 38    Interpretation of Chapter I

(1)    In this Chapter (unless the context otherwise requires)—

"conveyance" includes assignment, transfer and surrender, and related expressions shall be construed accordingly;

"the initial notice" means the notice given under section 13;

["introductory tenancy" has the same meaning as in Chapter I of Part V of the Housing Act 1996,]

["participating member" has the meaning given by section 4B;

"the notice of invitation to participate" means the notice given under section 12A;]

*"the nominee purchaser" shall be construed in accordance with section 15;*

*"the participating tenants" shall be construed in accordance with section 14;*

"premises with a resident landlord" shall be construed in accordance with section 10;

"public sector landlord" means any of the persons listed in section 171(2) of the Housing Act 1985;

"qualifying tenant" shall be construed in accordance with section 5;

"the relevant date" has the meaning given by section 1(8);

"relevant landlord" and "the reversioner" shall be construed in accordance with section 9;

"the right to collective enfranchisement" means the right specified in section 1(1);

["RTE company" shall be construed in accordance with sections 1(1) and 4A;]

"secure tenancy" has the meaning given by section 79 of the Housing Act 1985;

"the specified premises" shall be construed in accordance with section 13(12);

"the terms of acquisition" has the meaning given by section 24(8);

"unit" means—

(a)    a flat;

(b)    any other separate set of premises which is constructed or adapted for use for the purposes of a dwelling; or

(c)    a separate set of premises let, or intended for letting, on a business lease.

(2)    Any reference in this Chapter (however expressed) to the acquisition or proposed acquisition by *the nominee purchaser* is a reference to the acquisition or proposed acquisition by the *nominee purchaser, on behalf of the participating tenants,* of such freehold and other interests as fall to be so acquired under a contract entered into in pursuance of the initial notice.

(3)    Any reference in this Chapter to the interest of a relevant landlord in the specified premises is a reference to the interest in those premises by virtue of which he is, in accordance with section 9(2)(b) [or (2A)(b)], a relevant landlord.

(4) Any reference in this Chapter to agreement in relation to all or any of the terms of acquisition is a reference to agreement subject to contract.

[844]

**NOTES**

Sub-s (1): definition "introductory tenancy" inserted by the Housing Act 1996 (Consequential Amendments) Order 1997, SI 1997/74, art 2, Schedule, para 9(b); definitions "participating member", "the notice of invitation to participate", and "RTE company" inserted and definitions in italics repealed by the Commonhold and Leasehold Reform Act 2002, ss 124, 180, Sch 8, paras 2, 27(1)–(3), Sch 14, as from a day to be appointed.

Sub-s (2): words in italics in the first place substituted by the words "a RTE company" and words in italics in the second place substituted by the words "RTE company" by the Commonhold and Leasehold Reform Act 2002, s 124, Sch 8, paras 2, 27(1), (4), as from a day to be appointed.

Sub-s (3): words in square brackets inserted by the Housing Act 1996, s 107(4), Sch 10, paras 1, 13, except in relation to a case where, before 1 October 1996, a notice was given under s 13 or 42 of this Act at [817], [848], or an application was made to court under s 26 or 50 of this Act at [830], [856].

## CHAPTER II
## INDIVIDUAL RIGHT OF TENANT OF FLAT TO ACQUIRE NEW LEASE

*Preliminary*

### 39 Right of qualifying tenant of flat to acquire new lease

(1) This Chapter has effect for the purpose of conferring on a tenant of a flat, in the circumstances mentioned in subsection (2), the right, exercisable subject to and in accordance with this Chapter, to acquire a new lease of the flat on payment of a premium determined in accordance with this Chapter.

(2) Those circumstances are that on the relevant date for the purposes of this Chapter—
    (a) the tenant [has for the last two years been] a qualifying tenant of the flat; ...
    [(b) ...

(2A), (2B) ... ]

(3) The following provisions, namely—
    (a) section 5 (with the omission of subsections (5) and (6)),
    (b) section 7, ...
    (c) ... [ ...
    (d) ... ]

shall apply for the purposes of this Chapter as they apply for the purposes of Chapter I; and references in this Chapter to a qualifying tenant of a flat shall accordingly be construed by reference to those provisions.

[(3A) On the death of a person who has for the two years before his death been a qualifying tenant of a flat, the right conferred by this Chapter is exercisable, subject to and in accordance with this Chapter, by his personal representatives; and, accordingly, in such a case references in this Chapter to the tenant shall, in so far as the context permits, be to the personal representatives.]

(4) For the purposes of this Chapter a person can be (or be among those constituting) the qualifying tenant of each of two or more flats at the same time, whether he is tenant of those flats under one lease or under two or more separate leases.

[(4A) ... ]

(5), (6) ...

(7) The right conferred by this Chapter on a tenant to acquire a new lease shall not extend to underlying minerals comprised in his existing lease if—
    (a) the landlord requires the minerals to be excepted, and
    (b) proper provision is made for the support of the premises demised by that existing lease as they are enjoyed on the relevant date.

(8) In this Chapter "the relevant date", in relation to a claim by a tenant under this Chapter, means the date on which notice of the claim is given to the landlord under section 42.

[845]

**NOTES**

Sub-s (2): words in first pair of square brackets substituted and word omitted in the first place repealed by the Commonhold and Leasehold Reform Act 2002, s 130(1), (2) except in relation to an application for a new lease of a flat in respect of which notice was given under s 42 of this Act at [848], or where an application was made for an order under s 50 of this Act at [856], before 26 July 2002 (in relation to England) or 1 January 2003 (in relation to Wales); para (b) substituted, together with sub-ss (2A), (2B) for original para (b), by the Housing Act 1996, s 112(1), (2) and repealed by ss 130(1), (3), 180 of, and Sch 14 to, the 2002 Act, subject to savings as noted above.

Sub-ss (2A), (2B): substituted, together with sub-s (2)(b) for original sub-s (2)(b), by the Housing Act 1996, s 112(1), (2); repealed by the Commonhold and Leasehold Reform Act 2002, ss 130(1), (3), 180, Sch 14, subject to savings as noted above.

Sub-s (3): word omitted in the first place repealed by the Housing Act 1996, s 227, Sch 19, Pt V; para (d) and the word "and" immediately preceding it inserted by the Housing Act 1996, s 106, Sch 9, para 4(1), (2) and repealed, together with para (c), by the Commonhold and Leasehold Reform Act 2002, ss 131, 180, Sch 14, subject to savings as noted above.

Sub-s (3A): inserted by the Commonhold and Leasehold Reform Act 2002, s 132(1).

Sub-s (4A): inserted by the Housing Act 1996, s 112(1), (3); repealed by the Commonhold and Leasehold Reform Act 2002, s 180, Sch 14, subject to savings as noted above.

Sub-s (5): repealed by the Commonhold and Leasehold Reform Act 2002, s 180, Sch 14, subject to savings as noted above.

Sub-s (6): repealed by the Housing Act 1996, s 227, Sch 19, Pt V.

### 40　The landlord for the purposes of this Chapter

(1)　In this Chapter "the landlord", in relation to the lease held by a qualifying tenant of a flat, means the person who is the owner of that interest in the flat which for the time being fulfils the following conditions, namely—

(a)　it is an interest in reversion expectant (whether immediately or not) on the termination of the tenant's lease, and

(b)　it is either a freehold interest or a leasehold interest whose duration is such as to enable that person to grant a new lease of that flat in accordance with this Chapter,

and is not itself expectant (whether immediately or not) on an interest which fulfils those conditions.

(2)　Where in accordance with subsection (1) the immediate landlord under the lease of a qualifying tenant of a flat is not the landlord in relation to that lease for the purposes of this Chapter, the person who for those purposes is the landlord in relation to it shall conduct on behalf of all the other landlords all proceedings arising out of any notice given by the tenant with respect to the flat under section 42 (whether the proceedings are for resisting or giving effect to the claim in question).

(3)　Subsection (2) has effect subject to the provisions of Schedule 11 to this Act (which makes provision in relation to the operation of this Chapter in cases to which that subsection applies).

(4)　In this section and that Schedule—

(a)　"the tenant" means any such qualifying tenant as is referred to in subsection (2) and "the tenant's lease" means the lease by virtue of which he is a qualifying tenant;

(b)　"the competent landlord" means the person who, in relation to the tenant's lease, is the landlord (as defined by subsection (1)) for the purposes of this Chapter;

(c)　"other landlord" means any person (other than the tenant or a trustee for him) in whom there is vested a concurrent tenancy intermediate between the interest of the competent landlord and the tenant's lease.

(5)　Schedule 2 (which makes provision with respect to certain special categories of landlords) has effect for the purposes of this Chapter.

**[846]**

*Preliminary inquiries by qualifying tenant*

### 41　Right of qualifying tenant to obtain information about superior interests etc

(1)　A qualifying tenant of a flat may give—

(a)　to his immediate landlord, or

(b)　to any person receiving rent on behalf of his immediate landlord,

a notice requiring the recipient to state whether the immediate landlord is the owner of the freehold interest in the flat and, if not, to give the tenant such information as is mentioned in subsection (2) (so far as known to the recipient).

(2)　That information is—

(a)　the name and address of the person who owns the freehold interest in the flat;

(b)　the duration of the leasehold interest in the flat of the tenant's immediate landlord and the extent of the premises in which it subsists; and

(c)　the name and address of every person who has a leasehold interest in the flat which is superior to that of the tenant's immediate landlord, the duration of any such interest and the extent of the premises in which it subsists.

(3)　If the immediate landlord of any such qualifying tenant is not the owner of the freehold interest in the flat, the tenant may also—

(a)　give to the person who is the owner of that interest a notice requiring him to give the tenant such information as is mentioned in paragraph (c) of subsection (2) (so far as known to that person);

(b)　give to any person falling within that paragraph a notice requiring him to give the tenant—

(i)　particulars of the duration of his leasehold interest in the flat and the extent of the premises in which it subsists, and

(ii)　(so far as known to him) such information as is mentioned in paragraph (a) of that subsection and, as regards any other person falling within paragraph (c) of that subsection, such information as is mentioned in that paragraph.

(4) Any notice given by a qualifying tenant under this section shall, in addition to any other requirement imposed in accordance with subsections (1) to (3), require the recipient to state—

(a) whether he has received in respect of any premises containing the tenant's flat—

(i) a notice under section 13 in the case of which the relevant claim under Chapter I is still current, or

(ii) a copy of such a notice; and

(b) if so, the date on which the notice under section 13 was given and the name and *address of the nominee purchaser for the time being appointed for the purposes of section 15 in relation to that claim.*

(5) For the purposes of subsection (4)—

(a) "the relevant claim under Chapter I", in relation to a notice under section 13, means the claim in respect of which that notice is given; and

(b) any such claim is current if—

(i) that notice continues in force in accordance with section 13(11), or

(ii) a binding contract entered into in pursuance of that notice remains in force, or

(iii) where an order has been made under section 24(4)(a) or (b) or 25(6)(a) or (b) with respect to any such premises as are referred to in subsection (4)(a) above, any interests which by virtue of the order fall to be vested in the *nominee purchaser* for the purposes of Chapter I have yet to be so vested.

(6) Any person who is required to give any information by virtue of a notice under this section shall give that information to the qualifying tenant within the period of 28 days beginning with the date of the giving of the notice.

**[847]**

**NOTES**

Sub-s (4): words in italics substituted by the words "registered office of the RTE company by which it was given." by the Commonhold and Leasehold Reform Act 2002, s 124, Sch 8, paras 2, 28(1), (2), as from a day to be appointed.

Sub-s (5): words in italics substituted by the words "RTE company" by the Commonhold and Leasehold Reform Act 2002, s 124, Sch 8, paras 2, 28(1), (3), as from a day to be appointed.

*The tenant's notice*

## 42 Notice by qualifying tenant of claim to exercise right

(1) A claim by a qualifying tenant of a flat to exercise the right to acquire a new lease of the flat is made by the giving of notice of the claim under this section.

(2) A notice given by a tenant under this section ("the tenant's notice") must be given—

(a) to the landlord, and

(b) to any third party to the tenant's lease.

(3) The tenant's notice must—

(a) state the full name of the tenant and the address of the flat in respect of which he claims a new lease under this Chapter;

(b) contain the following particulars, namely—

(i) sufficient particulars of that flat to identify the property to which the claim extends,

(ii) such particulars of the tenant's lease as are sufficient to identify it, including the date on which the lease was entered into, the term for which it was granted and the date of the commencement of the term,

(iii), (iv) ...

(c) specify the premium which the tenant proposes to pay in respect of the grant of a new lease under this Chapter and, where any other amount will be payable by him in accordance with any provision of Schedule 13, the amount which he proposes to pay in accordance with that provision;

(d) specify the terms which the tenant proposes should be contained in any such lease;

(e) state the name of the person (if any) appointed by the tenant to act for him in connection with his claim, and an address in England and Wales at which notices may be given to any such person under this Chapter; and

(f) specify the date by which the landlord must respond to the notice by giving a counter-notice under section 45.

(4) ...

[(4A) A notice under this section may not be given by the personal representatives of a tenant later than two years after the grant of probate or letters of administration.]

(5)    The date specified in the tenant's notice in pursuance of subsection (3)(f) must be a date falling not less than two months after the date of the giving of the notice.

(6)    Where a notice under this section has been given with respect to any flat, no subsequent notice may be given under this section with respect to the flat so long as the earlier notice continues in force.

(7)    Where a notice under this section has been given with respect to a flat and—

(a)    that notice has been withdrawn, or is deemed to have been withdrawn, under or by virtue of any provision of this Chapter, or

(b)    in response to that notice, an order has been applied for and obtained under section 47(1),

no subsequent notice may be given under this section with respect to the flat within the period of twelve months beginning with the date of the withdrawal or deemed withdrawal of the earlier notice or with the time when the order under section 47(1) becomes final (as the case may be).

(8)    Where a notice is given in accordance with this section, then for the purposes of this Chapter the notice continues in force as from the relevant date—

(a)    until a new lease is granted in pursuance of the notice;

(b)    if the notice is withdrawn, or is deemed to have been withdrawn, under or by virtue of any provision of this Chapter, until the date of the withdrawal or deemed withdrawal; or

(c)    until such other time as the notice ceases to have effect by virtue of any provision of this Chapter;

but this subsection has effect subject to section 54.

(9)    Schedule 12 (which contains restrictions on terminating a tenant's lease where he has given a notice under this section and makes other provision in connection with the giving of notices under this section) shall have effect.

**[848]**

---

**NOTES**

Sub-s (3): para (b)(iii), (iv) repealed by the Commonhold and Leasehold Reform Act 2002, s 180, Sch 14, except in relation to an application for a new lease of a flat in respect of which notice was given under this section, or where an application was made for an order under s 50 of this Act at **[856]**, before 26 July 2002 (in relation to England) or 1 January 2003 (in relation to Wales).

Sub-s (4): repealed by the Commonhold and Leasehold Reform Act 2002, s 180, Sch 14, subject to savings as noted above.

Sub-s (4A): inserted by the Commonhold and Leasehold Reform Act 2002, s 132(2).

---

### 43    General provisions as respects effect of tenant's notice

(1)    Where a notice has been given under section 42 with respect to any flat, the rights and obligations of the landlord and the tenant arising from the notice shall enure for the benefit of and be enforceable against them, their personal representatives and assigns to the like extent (but no further) as rights and obligations arising under a contract for leasing freely entered into between the landlord and the tenant.

(2)    Accordingly, in relation to matters arising out of any such notice, references in this Chapter to the landlord and the tenant shall, in so far as the context permits, include their respective personal representatives and assigns.

(3)    Notwithstanding anything in subsection (1), the rights and obligations of the tenant shall be assignable with, but shall not be capable of subsisting apart from, the lease of the entire flat; and, if the tenant's lease is assigned without the benefit of the notice, the notice shall accordingly be deemed to have been withdrawn by the tenant as at the date of the assignment.

(4)    In the event of any default by the landlord or the tenant in carrying out the obligations arising from the tenant's notice, the other of them shall have the like rights and remedies as in the case of a contract freely entered into.

(5)    In a case to which section 40(2) applies, the rights and obligations of the landlord arising out of the tenant's notice shall, so far as their interests are affected, be rights and obligations respectively of the competent landlord and of each of the other landlords, and references to the landlord in subsections (1) and (2) above shall apply accordingly.

(6)    In subsection (5) "competent landlord" and "other landlord" have the meaning given by section 40(4); and subsection (5) has effect without prejudice to the operation of section 40(2) or Schedule 11.

**[849]**

*Procedure following giving of tenant's notice*

### 44    Access by landlords for valuation purposes

(1)    Once the tenant's notice or a copy of it has been given in accordance with section 42 or Part I of Schedule 11—

(a)  to the landlord for the purposes of this Chapter, or

(b)  to any other landlord (as defined by section 40(4)),

that landlord and any person authorised to act on his behalf shall have a right of access to the flat to which the notice relates for the purpose of enabling that landlord to obtain, in connection with the notice, a valuation of his interest in the flat.

(2)  That right shall be exercisable at any reasonable time and on giving not less than 3 days' notice to the tenant.

**[850]**

### 45  Landlord's counter-notice

(1)  The landlord shall give a counter-notice under this section to the tenant by the date specified in the tenant's notice in pursuance of section 42(3)(f).

(2)  The counter-notice must comply with one of the following requirements—

(a)  state that the landlord admits that the tenant had on the relevant date the right to acquire a new lease of his flat;

(b)  state that, for such reasons as are specified in the counter-notice, the landlord does not admit that the tenant had such a right on that date;

(c)  contain such a statement as is mentioned in paragraph (a) or (b) above but state that the landlord intends to make an application for an order under section 47(1) on the grounds that he intends to redevelop any premises in which the flat is contained.

(3)  If the counter-notice complies with the requirement set out in subsection (2)(a), it must in addition—

(a)  state which (if any) of the proposals contained in the tenant's notice are accepted by the landlord and which (if any) of those proposals are not so accepted; and

(b)  specify, in relation to each proposal which is not accepted, the landlord's counter-proposal.

(4)  The counter-notice must specify an address in England and Wales at which notices may be given to the landlord under this Chapter.

(5)  Where the counter-notice admits the tenant's right to acquire a new lease of his flat, the admission shall be binding on the landlord as to the matters mentioned in section 39(2)(a) ... , unless the landlord shows that he was induced to make the admission by misrepresentation or the concealment of material facts; but the admission shall not conclude any question whether the particulars of the flat stated in the tenant's notice in pursuance of section 42(3)(b)(i) are correct.

**[851]**

**NOTES**

Sub-s (5): words omitted repealed by the Commonhold and Leasehold Reform Act 2002, s 180, Sch 14, except in relation to an application for a new lease of a flat in respect of which notice was given under s 42 of this Act at **[848]**, or where an application was made for an order under s 50 of this Act at **[856]**, before 26 July 2002 (in relation to England) or 1 January 2003 (in relation to Wales).

*Applications to court or leasehold valuation tribunal*

### 46  Proceedings relating to validity of tenant's notice

(1)  Where—

(a)  the landlord has given the tenant a counter-notice under section 45 which (whether it complies with the requirement set out in subsection (2)(b) or (c) of that section) contains such a statement as is mentioned in subsection (2)(b) of that section, and

(b)  the court is satisfied, on an application made by the landlord, that on the relevant date the tenant had no right under this Chapter to acquire a new lease of his flat,

the court shall by order make a declaration to that effect.

(2)  Any application for an order under subsection (1) must be made not later than the end of the period of two months beginning with the date of the giving of the counter-notice to the tenant; and if, in a case falling within paragraph (a) of that subsection, either—

(a)  no application for such an order is made by the landlord within that period, or

(b)  such an application is so made but is subsequently withdrawn,

section 49 shall apply as if the landlord had not given the counter-notice.

(3)  If on any such application the court makes such a declaration as is mentioned in subsection (1), the tenant's notice shall cease to have effect on the order becoming final.

(4)  If, however, any such application is dismissed by the court, then (subject to subsection (5)) the court shall make an order—

(a)  declaring that the landlord's counter-notice shall be of no effect, and

(b)  requiring the landlord to give a further counter-notice to the tenant by such date as is specified in the order.

(5)   Subsection (4) shall not apply if—
  (a)   the counter-notice complies with the requirement set out in section 45(2)(c), and
  (b)   either—
     (i)   an application for an order under section 47(1) is pending, or
     (ii)   the period specified in section 47(3) as the period for the making of such an application has not expired.

(6)   Subsection (3) of section 45 shall apply to any further counter-notice required to be given by the landlord under subsection (4) above as if it were a counter-notice under that section complying with the requirement set out in subsection (2)(a) of that section.

**[852]**

### 47   Application to defeat tenant's claim where landlord intends to redevelop

(1)   Where the landlord has given the tenant a counter-notice under section 45 which complies with the requirement set out in subsection (2)(c) of that section, the court may, on the application of the landlord, by order declare that the right to acquire a new lease shall not be exercisable by the tenant by reason of the landlord's intention to redevelop any premises in which the tenant's flat is contained; and on such an order becoming final the tenant's notice shall cease to have effect.

(2)   The court shall not make an order under subsection (1) unless it is satisfied—
  (a)   that the tenant's lease of his flat is due to terminate within the period of five years beginning with the relevant date; and
  (b)   that for the purposes of redevelopment the landlord intends, once the lease has so terminated—
     (i)   to demolish or reconstruct, or
     (ii)   to carry out substantial works of construction on,
     the whole or a substantial part of any premises in which the flat is contained; and
  (c)   that he could not reasonably do so without obtaining possession of the flat.

(3)   Any application for an order under subsection (1) must be made within the period of two months beginning with the date of the giving of the counter-notice to the tenant; but, where the counter-notice is one falling within section 46(1)(a), such an application shall not be proceeded with until such time (if any) as any order dismissing an application under section 46(1) becomes final.

(4)   Where an application for an order under subsection (1) is dismissed by the court, the court shall make an order—
  (a)   declaring that the landlord's counter-notice shall be of no effect, and
  (b)   requiring the landlord to give a further counter-notice to the tenant by such date as is specified in the order.

(5)   Where—
  (a)   the landlord has given such a counter-notice as is mentioned in subsection (1), but
  (b)   either—
     (i)   no application for an order under that subsection is made within the period referred to in subsection (3), or
     (ii)   such an application is so made but is subsequently withdrawn,
then (subject to subsection (7)), the landlord shall give a further counter-notice to the tenant within the period of two months beginning with the appropriate date.

(6)   In subsection (5) "the appropriate date" means—
  (a)   if subsection (5)(b)(i) applies, the date immediately following the end of the period referred to in subsection (3); and
  (b)   if subsection (5)(b)(ii) applies, the date of withdrawal of the application.

(7)   Subsection (5) shall not apply if any application has been made by the landlord for an order under section 46(1).

(8)   Subsection (3) of section 45 shall apply to any further counter-notice required to be given by the landlord under subsection (4) or (5) above as if it were a counter-notice under that section complying with the requirement set out in subsection (2)(a) of that section.

**[853]**

### 48   Applications where terms in dispute or failure to enter into new lease

(1)   Where the landlord has given the tenant—
  (a)   a counter-notice under section 45 which complies with the requirement set out in subsection (2)(a) of that section, or
  (b)   a further counter-notice required by or by virtue of section 46(4) or section 47(4) or (5),
but any of the terms of acquisition remain in dispute at the end of the period of two months beginning with the date when the counter-notice or further counter-notice was so given, a leasehold valuation tribunal may, on the application of either the tenant or the landlord, determine the matters in dispute.

(2)    Any application under subsection (1) must be made not later than the end of the period of six months beginning with the date on which the counter-notice or further counter-notice was given to the tenant.

(3)    Where—
(a)    the landlord has given the tenant such a counter-notice or further counter-notice as is mentioned in subsection (1)(a) or (b), and
(b)    all the terms of acquisition have been either agreed between those persons or determined by a leasehold valuation tribunal under subsection (1),

but a new lease has not been entered into in pursuance of the tenant's notice by the end of the appropriate period specified in subsection (6), the court may, on the application of either the tenant or the landlord, make such order as it thinks fit with respect to the performance or discharge of any obligations arising out of that notice.

(4)    Any such order may provide for the tenant's notice to be deemed to have been withdrawn at the end of the appropriate period specified in subsection (6).

(5)    Any application for an order under subsection (3) must be made not later than the end of the period of two months beginning immediately after the end of the appropriate period specified in subsection (6).

(6)    For the purposes of this section the appropriate period is—
(a)    where all of the terms of acquisition have been agreed between the tenant and the landlord, the period of two months beginning with the date when those terms were finally so agreed; or
(b)    where all or any of those terms have been determined by a leasehold valuation tribunal under subsection (1)—
(i)    the period of two months beginning with the date when the decision of the tribunal under subsection (1) becomes final, or
(ii)    such other period as may have been fixed by the tribunal when making its determination.

(7)    In this Chapter "the terms of acquisition", in relation to a claim by a tenant under this Chapter, means the terms on which the tenant is to acquire a new lease of his flat, whether they relate to the terms to be contained in the lease or to the premium or any other amount payable by virtue of Schedule 13 in connection with the grant of the lease, or otherwise.

[854]

## 49  Applications where landlord fails to give counter-notice or further counter-notice

(1)    Where the tenant's notice has been given in accordance with section 42 but—
(a)    the landlord has failed to give the tenant a counter-notice in accordance with section 45(1), or
(b)    if required to give a further counter-notice to the tenant by or by virtue of section 46(4) or section 47(4) or (5), the landlord has failed to comply with that requirement,

the court may, on the application of the tenant, make an order determining, in accordance with the proposals contained in the tenant's notice, the terms of acquisition.

(2)    The court shall not make such an order on an application made by virtue of paragraph (a) of subsection (1) unless it is satisfied—
(a)    that on the relevant date the tenant had the right to acquire a new lease of his flat; and
(b)    if applicable, that the requirements of Part I of Schedule 11 were complied with as respects the giving of copies of the tenant's notice.

(3)    Any application for an order under subsection (1) must be made not later than the end of the period of six months beginning with the date by which the counter-notice or further counter-notice referred to in that subsection was required to be given.

(4)    Where—
(a)    the terms of acquisition have been determined by an order of the court under this section, but
(b)    a new lease has not been entered into in pursuance of the tenant's notice by the end of the appropriate period specified in subsection (7),

the court may, on the application of either the tenant or the landlord, make such order as it thinks fit with respect to the performance or discharge of any obligations arising out of that notice.

(5)    Any such order may provide for the tenant's notice to be deemed to have been withdrawn at the end of the appropriate period specified in subsection (7).

(6)    Any application for an order under subsection (4) must be made not later than the end of the period of two months beginning immediately after the end of the appropriate period specified in subsection.

(7)    For the purposes of this section the appropriate period is—

(a)   the period of two months beginning with the date when the order of the court under subsection (1) becomes final, or
(b)   such other period as may have been fixed by the court when making that order.

[855]

## 50   Applications where landlord cannot be found

(1)   Where—
  (a)   a qualifying tenant of a flat desires to make a claim to exercise the right to acquire a new lease of his flat, but
  (b)   the landlord cannot be found or his identity cannot be ascertained,

the court may, on the application of the tenant, make a vesting order under this subsection.

(2)   Where—
  (a)   a qualifying tenant of a flat desires to make such a claim as is mentioned in subsection (1), and
  (b)   paragraph (b) of that subsection does not apply, but
  (c)   a copy of a notice of that claim cannot be given in accordance with Part I of Schedule 11 to any person to whom it would otherwise be required to be so given because that person cannot be found or his identity cannot be ascertained,

the court may, on the application of the tenant, make an order dispensing with the need to give a copy of such a notice to that person.

(3)   The court shall not make an order on any application under subsection (1) or (2) unless it is satisfied—
  (a)   that on the date of the making of the application the tenant had the right to acquire a new lease of his flat; and
  (b)   that on that date he would not have been precluded by any provision of this Chapter from giving a valid notice under section 42 with respect to his flat.

(4)   Before making any such order the court may require the tenant to take such further steps by way of advertisement or otherwise as the court thinks proper for the purpose of tracing the person in question; and if, after an application is made for a vesting order under subsection (1) and before any lease is executed in pursuance of the application, the landlord is traced, then no further proceedings shall be taken with a view to a lease being so executed, but (subject to subsection (5))—
  (a)   the rights and obligations of all parties shall be determined as if the tenant had, at the date of the application, duly given notice under section 42 of his claim to exercise the right to acquire a new lease of his flat; and
  (b)   the court may give such directions as the court thinks fit as to the steps to be taken for giving effect to those rights and obligations, including directions modifying or dispensing with any of the requirements of this Chapter or of regulations made under this Part.

(5)   An application for a vesting order under subsection (1) may be withdrawn at any time before execution of a lease under section 51(3) and, after it is withdrawn, subsection (4)(a) above shall not apply; but where any step is taken (whether by the landlord or the tenant) for the purpose of giving effect to subsection (4)(a) in the case of any application, the application shall not afterwards be withdrawn except—
  (a)   with the consent of the landlord, or
  (b)   by leave of the court,

and the court shall not give leave unless it appears to the court just to do so by reason of matters coming to the knowledge of the tenant in consequence of the tracing of the landlord.

(6)   Where an order has been made under subsection (2) dispensing with the need to give a copy of a notice under section 42 to a particular person with respect to any flat, then if—
  (a)   a notice is subsequently given under that section with respect to that flat, and
  (b)   in reliance on the order, a copy of the notice is not to be given to that person,

the notice must contain a statement of the effect of the order.

(7)   Where a notice under section 42 contains such a statement in accordance with subsection (6) above, then in determining for the purposes of any provision of this Chapter whether the requirements of Part I of Schedule 11 have been complied with in relation to the notice, those requirements shall be deemed to have been complied with so far as relating to the giving of a copy of the notice to the person referred to in subsection (6) above.

[856]

## 51   Supplementary provisions relating to vesting orders under section 50(1)

(1)   A vesting order under section 50(1) is an order providing for the surrender of the tenant's lease of his flat and for the granting to him of a new lease of it on such terms as may be determined by a leasehold valuation tribunal to be appropriate with a view to the lease being granted to him in like manner (so far as the circumstances permit) as if he had, at the date of his application, given notice under section 42 of his claim to exercise the right to acquire a new lease of his flat.

(2) If a leasehold valuation tribunal so determines in the case of a testing order under section 50(1), the order shall have effect in relation to property which is less extensive than that specified in the application on which the order was made.

(3) Where any lease is to be granted to a tenant by virtue of a vesting order under section 50(1), then on his paying into court the appropriate sum there shall be executed by such person as the court may designate a lease which—

    (a) is in a form approved by a leasehold valuation tribunal, and

    (b) contains such provisions as may be so approved for the purpose of giving effect so far as possible to section 56(1) and section 57 (as that section applies in accordance with subsections (7) and (8) below);

and that lease shall be effective to vest in the person to whom it is granted the property expressed to be demised by it, subject to and in accordance with the terms of the lease.

(4) In connection with the determination by a leasehold valuation tribunal of any question as to the property to be demised by any such lease, or as to the rights with or subject to which it is to be demised, it shall be assumed (unless the contrary is shown) that the landlord has no interest in property other than the property to be demised and, for the purpose of excepting them from the lease, any minerals underlying that property.

(5) The appropriate sum to be paid into court in accordance with subsection (3) is the aggregate of—

    (a) such amount as may be determined by a leasehold valuation tribunal to be the premium which is payable under Schedule 13 in respect of the grant of the new lease;

    (b) such other amount or amounts (if any) as may be determined by such a tribunal to be payable by virtue of that Schedule in connection with the grant of that lease; and

    (c) any amounts or estimated amounts determined by such a tribunal as being, at the time of execution of that lease, due to the landlord from the tenant (whether due under or in respect of the tenant's lease of his flat or under or in respect of an agreement collateral thereto).

(6) Where any lease is granted to a person in accordance with this section, the payment into court of the appropriate sum shall be taken to have satisfied any claims against the tenant, his personal representatives or assigns in respect of the premium and any other amounts payable as mentioned in subsection (5)(a) and (b).

(7) Subject to subsection (8), the following provisions, namely—

    (a) sections 57 to 59, and

    (b) section 61 and Schedule 14,

shall, so far as capable of applying to a lease granted in accordance with this section, apply to such a lease as they apply to a lease granted under section 56; and subsections (6) and (7) of that section shall apply in relation to a lease granted in accordance with this section as they apply in relation to a lease granted under that section.

(8) In its application to a lease granted in accordance with this section—

    (a) section 57 shall have effect as if—

        (i) any reference to the relevant date were a reference to the date of the application under section 50(1) in pursuance of which the vesting order under that provision was made, and

        (ii) in subsection (5) the reference to section 56(3)(a) were a reference to subsection (5)(c) above; and

    (b) section 58 shall have effect as if—

        (i) in subsection (3) the second reference to the landlord were a reference to the person designated under subsection (3) above, and

        (ii) subsections (6)(a) and (7) were omitted.

[857]

*Termination or suspension of acquisition procedures*

## 52 Withdrawal by tenant from acquisition of new lease

(1) At any time before a new lease is entered into in pursuance of the tenant's notice, the tenant may withdraw that notice by the giving of a notice to that effect under this section ("a notice of withdrawal").

(2) A notice of withdrawal must be given—

    (a) to the landlord for the purposes of this Chapter;

    (b) to every other landlord (as defined by section 40(4)); and

    (c) to any third party to the tenant's lease.

(3)   Where a notice of withdrawal is given by the tenant to any person in accordance with subsection (2), the tenant's liability under section 60 for costs incurred by that person shall be a liability for costs incurred by him down to the time when the notice is given to him.

**[858]**

### 53   Deemed withdrawal of tenant's notice

(1)   Where—
- (a)   in a case to which subsection (1) of section 48 applies, no application under that subsection is made within the period specified in subsection (2) of that section, or
- (b)   in a case to which subsection (3) of that section applies, no application for an order under that subsection is made within the period specified in subsection (5) of that section,

the tenant's notice shall be deemed to have been withdrawn at the end of the period referred to in paragraph (a) or (b) above (as the case may be).

(2)   Where, in a case falling within paragraph (a) or (b) of subsection (1) of section 49, no application for an order under that subsection is made within the period specified in subsection (3) of that section, the tenant's notice shall be deemed to have been withdrawn at the end of that period.

(3)   Where, in a case to which subsection (4) of section 49 applies, no application for an order under that subsection is made within the period specified in subsection (6) of that section, the tenant's notice shall be deemed to have been withdrawn at the end of that period.

(4)   The following provisions, namely—
- (a)   section 43(3),
- (b)   section 48(4), and
- (c)   section 49(5),

also make provision for a notice under section 42 to be deemed to have been withdrawn at a particular time.

**[859]**

### 54   Suspension of tenant's notice during currency of claim under Chapter I

(1)   If, at the time when the tenant's notice is given—
- (a)   a notice has been given under section 13 with respect to any premises containing the tenant's flat, and
- (b)   the relevant claim under Chapter I is still current,

the operation of the tenant's notice shall be suspended during the currency of that claim; and so long as it is so suspended no further notice shall be given, and no application shall be made, under this Chapter with a view to resisting or giving effect to the tenant's claim.

(2)   If, at any time when the tenant's notice continues in force, a notice is given under section 13 with respect to any premises containing the tenant's flat, then, as from the date which is the relevant date for the purposes of Chapter I in relation to that notice under section 13, the operation of the tenant's notice shall be suspended during the currency of the relevant claim under Chapter I; and so long as it is so suspended no further notice shall be given, and no application shall be made or proceeded with, under this Chapter with a view to resisting or giving effect to the tenant's claim.

(3)   Where the operation of the tenant's notice is suspended by virtue of subsection (1) or (2), the landlord shall give the tenant a notice informing him of its suspension—
- (a)   (if it is suspended by virtue of subsection (1)) not later than the date specified in the tenant's notice in pursuance of section 42(3)(f); or
- (b)   (if it is suspended by virtue of subsection (2)) as soon as possible after the date referred to in that subsection;

and any such notice shall in addition inform the tenant of the date on which the notice under section 13 was given and of the name and *address of the nominee purchaser for the time being appointed for the purposes of section 15 in relation to the relevant claim under Chapter I.*

(4)   Where—
- (a)   the operation of the tenant's notice is suspended by virtue of subsection (1), and
- (b)   as a result of the relevant claim under Chapter I ceasing to be current, the operation of the tenant's notice subsequently ceases to be so suspended and the tenant's notice thereupon continues in force in accordance with section 42(8),

then, as from the date when that claim ceases to be current ("the termination date"), this Chapter shall apply as if there were substituted for the date specified in the tenant's notice in pursuance of section 42(3)(f) such date as results in the period of time intervening between the termination date and that date being equal to the period of time intervening between the relevant date and the date originally so specified.

(5)   Where—
- (a)   the operation of the tenant's notice is suspended by virtue of subsection (2), and
- (b)   its suspension began in circumstances falling within subsection (6), and

(c) as a result of the relevant claim under Chapter I ceasing to be current, the operation of the tenant's notice subsequently ceases to be so suspended and the tenant's notice thereupon continues in force in accordance with section 42(8),

any relevant period shall be deemed to have begun on the date when that claim ceases to be current.

(6) The circumstances referred to in subsection (5)(b) are that the suspension of the operation of the tenant's notice began—

(a) before the date specified in the tenant's notice in pursuance of section 42(3)(f) and before the landlord had given the tenant a counter-notice under section 45; or

(b) after the landlord had given the tenant a counter-notice under section 45 complying with the requirement set out in subsection (2)(b) or (c) of that section but—

(i) before any application had been made for an order under section 46(1) or 47(1), and

(ii) before the period for making any such application had expired; or

(c) after an order had been made under section 46(4) or 47(4) but—

(i) before the landlord had given the tenant a further counter-notice in accordance with the order, and

(ii) before the period for giving any such counter-notice had expired.

(7) Where—

(a) the operation of the tenant's notice is suspended by virtue of subsection (2), and

(b) its suspension began otherwise than in circumstances falling within subsection (6), and

(c) as a result of the relevant claim under Chapter I ceasing to be current, the operation of the tenant's notice subsequently ceases to be so suspended and the tenant's notice thereupon continues in force in accordance with section 42(8),

any relevant period shall be deemed to have begun on the date on which the tenant is given a notice under subsection (8) below or, if earlier, the date on which the tenant gives the landlord a notice informing him of the circumstances by virtue of which the operation of the tenant's notice has ceased to be suspended.

(8) Where subsection (4), (5) or (7) applies, the landlord shall, as soon as possible after becoming aware of the circumstances by virtue of which the operation of the tenant's notice has ceased to be suspended as mentioned in that subsection, give the tenant a notice informing him that, as from the date when the relevant claim under Chapter I ceased to be current, the operation of his notice is no longer suspended.

(9) Subsection (8) shall not, however, require the landlord to give any such notice if he has received a notice from the tenant under subsection (7).

(10) In subsections (5) and (7) "relevant period" means any period which—

(a) is prescribed by or under this Part for the giving of any notice, or the making of any application, in connection with the tenant's notice; and

(b) was current at the time when the suspension of the operation of the tenant's notice began.

(11) For the purposes of this section—

(a) "the relevant claim under Chapter I", in relation to a notice under section 13, means the claim in respect of which that notice is given; and

(b) any such claim is current if—

(i) that notice continues in force in accordance with section 13(11), or

(ii) a binding contract entered into in pursuance of that notice remains in force, or

(iii) where an order has been made under section 24(4)(a) or (b) or 25(6)(a) or (b) with respect to any such premises as are referred to in subsection (1) or (2) above (as the case may be), any interests which by virtue of the order fall to be vested in the *nominee purchaser* for the purposes of Chapter I have yet to be so vested.

[860]

---

**NOTES**

Sub-s (3): words in italics substituted by the words "registered office of the RTE company by which it was given." by the Commonhold and Leasehold Reform Act 2002, s 124, Sch 8, paras 2, 29(1), (2), as from a day to be appointed.

Sub-s (11): words in italics substituted by the words "RTE company" by the Commonhold and Leasehold Reform Act 2002, s 124, Sch 8, paras 2, 29(1), (3), as from a day to be appointed.

---

## 55 Effect on tenant's notice of institution of compulsory acquisition procedures

(1) A notice given by a tenant under section 42 shall be of no effect if on the relevant date—

(a) any person or body of persons who has or have been, or could be, authorised to acquire the whole or part of the tenant's flat compulsorily for any purpose has or have, with a view to its acquisition for that purpose—

(i) served notice to treat on the landlord or the tenant, or

        (ii)    entered into a contract for the purchase of the interest of either of them in the flat or part of it, and

  (b)    the notice to treat or contract remains in force.

(2)    A notice given by a tenant under section 42 shall cease to have effect if, before a new lease is entered into in pursuance of it, any such person or body of persons as is mentioned in subsection (1) serves or serve notice to treat as mentioned in that subsection.

(3)    Where subsection (2) applies in relation to a notice given by a tenant under section 42, then on the occasion of the compulsory acquisition in question the compensation payable in respect of any interest in the tenant's flat (whether or not the one to which the relevant notice to treat relates) shall be determined on the basis of the value of the interest subject to and with the benefit of the rights and obligations arising from the tenant's notice and affecting that interest.

**[861]**

### Grant of new lease

### 56   Obligation to grant new lease

(1)    Where a qualifying tenant of a flat has under this Chapter a right to acquire a new lease of the flat and gives notice of his claim in accordance with section 42, then except as provided by this Chapter the landlord shall be bound to grant to the tenant, and the tenant shall be bound to accept—

  (a)    in substitution for the existing lease, and

  (b)    on payment of the premium payable under Schedule 13 in respect of the grant,

a new lease of the flat at a peppercorn rent for a term expiring 90 years after the term date of the existing lease.

(2)    In addition to any such premium there shall be payable by the tenant in connection with the grant of any such new lease such amounts to the owners of any intermediate leasehold interests (within the meaning of Schedule 13) as are so payable by virtue of that Schedule.

(3)    A tenant shall not be entitled to require the execution of any such new lease otherwise than on tendering to the landlord, in addition to the amount of any such premium and any other amounts payable by virtue of Schedule 13, the amount so far as ascertained—

  (a)    of any sums payable by him by way of rent or recoverable from him as rent in respect of the flat up to the date of tender;

  (b)    of any sums for which at that date the tenant is liable under section 60 in respect of costs incurred by any relevant person (within the meaning of that section); and

  (c)    of any other sums due and payable by him to any such person under or in respect of the existing lease;

and, if the amount of any such sums is not or may not be fully ascertained, on offering reasonable security for the payment of such amount as may afterwards be found to be payable in respect of them.

(4)    To the extent that any amount tendered to the landlord in accordance with subsection (3) is an amount due to a person other than the landlord, that amount shall be payable to that person by the landlord; and that subsection has effect subject to paragraph 7(2) of Schedule 11.

(5)    No provision of any lease prohibiting, restricting or otherwise relating to a sub-demise by the tenant under the lease shall have effect with reference to the granting of any lease under this section.

(6)    It is hereby declared that nothing in any of the provisions specified in paragraph 1(2) of Schedule 10 (which impose requirements as to consent or consultation or other restrictions in relation to disposals falling within those provisions) applies to the granting of any lease under this section.

(7)    For the purposes of subsection (6), paragraph 1(2) of Schedule 10 has effect as if the reference to section 79(2) of the Housing Act 1988 (which is not relevant in the context of subsection (6)) were omitted.

**[862]**

### 57   Terms on which new lease is to be granted

(1)    Subject to the provisions of this Chapter (and in particular to the provisions as to rent and duration contained in section 56(1)), the new lease to be granted to a tenant under section 56 shall be a lease on the same terms as those of the existing lease, as they apply on the relevant date, but with such modifications as may be required or appropriate to take account—

  (a)    of the omission from the new lease of property included in the existing lease but not comprised in the flat;

  (b)    of alterations made to the property demised since the grant of the existing lease; or

  (c)    in a case where the existing lease derives (in accordance with section 7(6) as it applies in accordance with section 39(3)) from more than one separate leases, of their combined effect and of the differences (if any) in their terms.

(2)  Where during the continuance of the new lease the landlord will be under any obligation for the provision of services, or for repairs, maintenance or insurance—

  (a)  the new lease may require payments to be made by the tenant (whether as rent or otherwise) in consideration of those matters or in respect of the cost thereof to the landlord; and

  (b)  (if the terms of the existing lease do not include any provision for the making of any such payments by the tenant or include provision only for the payment of a fixed amount) the terms of the new lease shall make, as from the term date of the existing lease, such provision as may be just—

    (i)  for the making by the tenant of payments related to the cost from time to time to the landlord, and

    (ii)  for the tenant's liability to make those payments to be enforceable by *distress, re-entry or otherwise* in like manner as if it were a liability for payment of rent.

(3)  Subject to subsection (4), provision shall be made by the terms of the new lease or by an agreement collateral thereto for the continuance, with any suitable adaptations, of any agreement collateral to the existing lease.

(4)  For the purposes of subsections (1) and (3) there shall be excluded from the new lease any term of the existing lease or of any agreement collateral thereto in so far as that term—

  (a)  provides for or relates to the renewal of the lease,

  (b)  confers any option to purchase or right of pre-emption in relation to the flat demised by the existing lease, or

  (c)  provides for the termination of the existing lease before its term date otherwise than in the event of a breach of its terms;

and there shall be made in the terms of the new lease or any agreement collateral thereto such modifications as may be required or appropriate to take account of the exclusion of any such term.

(5)  Where the new lease is granted after the term date of the existing lease, then on the grant of the new lease there shall be payable by the tenant to the landlord, as an addition to the rent payable under the existing lease, any amount by which, for the period since the term date or the relevant date (whichever is the later), the sums payable to the landlord in respect of the flat (after making any necessary apportionment) for the matters referred to in subsection (2) fall short in total of the sums that would have been payable for such matters under the new lease if it had been granted on that date; and section 56(3)(a) shall apply accordingly.

(6)  Subsections (1) to (5) shall have effect subject to any agreement between the landlord and tenant as to the terms of the new lease or an agreement collateral thereto; and either of them may require that for the purposes of the new lease any term of the existing lease shall be excluded or modified in so far as—

  (a)  it is necessary to do so in order to remedy a defect in the existing lease; or

  (b)  it would be unreasonable in the circumstances to include, or include without modification, the term in question in view of changes occurring since the date of commencement of the existing lease which affect the suitability on the relevant date of the provisions of that lease.

(7)  The terms of the new lease shall—

  (a)  make provision in accordance with section 59(3); and

  (b)  reserve to the person who is for the time being the tenant's immediate landlord the right to obtain possession of the flat in question in accordance with section 61.

[(8)  In granting the new lease the landlord shall not be bound to enter into any covenant for title beyond—

  (a)  those implied from the grant, and

  (b)  those implied under Part I of the Law of Property (Miscellaneous Provisions) Act 1994 in a case where a disposition is expressed to be made with limited title guarantee, but not including (in the case of an underlease) the covenant in section 4(1)(b) of that Act (compliance with terms of lease);

and in the absence of agreement to the contrary the landlord shall be entitled to be indemnified by the tenant in respect of any costs incurred by him in complying with the covenant implied by virtue of section 2(1)(b) of that Act (covenant for further assurance).

(8A)  A person entering into any covenant required of him as landlord (under subsection (8) or otherwise) shall be entitled to limit his personal liability to breaches of that covenant for which he is responsible.]

(9)  Where any person—

  (a)  is a third party to the existing lease, or

  (b)  (not being the landlord or tenant) is a party to any agreement collateral thereto,

then (subject to any agreement between him and the landlord and the tenant) he shall be made a party to the new lease or (as the case may be) to an agreement collateral thereto, and shall accordingly join in its execution; but nothing in this section has effect so as to require the new lease or (as the case may be) any such collateral agreement to provide for him to discharge any function at any time after the term date of the existing lease.

(10)   Where—

(a)   any such person ("the third party") is in accordance with subsection (9) to discharge any function down to the term date of the existing lease, but

(b)   it is necessary or expedient in connection with the proper enjoyment by the tenant of the property demised by the new lease for provision to be made for the continued discharge of that function after that date,

the new lease or an agreement collateral thereto shall make provision for that function to be discharged after that date (whether by the third party or by some other person).

(11)   The new lease shall contain a statement that it is a lease granted under section 56; and any such statement shall comply with such requirements as may be prescribed by [land registration rules under the Land Registration Act 2002].

**[863]**

---

**NOTES**

Sub-s (2): for the words in italics in para (b)(ii) there are substituted the words "re-entry or otherwise (subject to section 85 of the Tribunals, Courts and Enforcement Act 2007)" by the Tribunals, Courts and Enforcement Act 2007, s 86, Sch 14, para 47, as from a day to be appointed.

Sub-ss (8), (8A): substituted, for original sub-s (8), by the Law of Property (Miscellaneous Provisions) Act 1994, s 21(1), Sch 1, para 12(2), save in relation to any disposition of property to which, by virtue of ss 10, 11 of that Act, the Law of Property Act 1925, s 76, or the Land Registration Act 1925, s 24(1)(a), continues to apply.

Sub-s (11): words in square brackets substituted by the Land Registration Act 2002, s 133, Sch 11, para 30(1), (2).

Rules: the Land Registration Rules 2003, SI 2003/1417.

---

## 58   Grant of new lease where interest of landlord or tenant is subject to a mortgage

(1)   Subject to subsection (2), a qualifying tenant shall be entitled to be granted a new lease under section 56 despite the fact that the grant of the existing lease was subsequent to the creation of a mortgage on the landlord's interest and not authorised as against the persons interested in the mortgage; and a lease granted under that section—

(a)   shall be deemed to be authorised as against the persons interested in any mortgage on the landlord's interest (however created or arising), and

(b)   shall be binding on those persons.

(2)   A lease granted under section 56 shall not, by virtue of subsection (1) above, be binding on the persons interested in any such mortgage if the existing lease—

(a)   is granted after the commencement of this Chapter, and

(b)   being granted subsequent to the creation of the mortgage, would not, apart from that subsection, be binding on the persons interested in the mortgage.

(3)   Where—

(a)   a lease is granted under section 56, and

(b)   any person having a mortgage on the landlord's interest is thereby entitled to possession of the documents of title relating to that interest,

the landlord shall, within one month of the execution of the lease, deliver to that person a counterpart of it duly executed by the tenant.

(4)   Where the existing lease is, immediately before its surrender on the grant of a lease under section 56, subject to any mortgage, the new lease shall take effect subject to the mortgage in substitution for the existing lease; and the terms of the mortgage, as set out in the instrument creating or evidencing it, shall accordingly apply in relation to the new lease in like manner as they applied in relation to the existing lease.

(5)   Where—

(a)   a lease granted under section 56 takes effect subject to any such subsisting mortgage on the existing lease, and

(b)   at the time of execution of the new lease the person having the mortgage is thereby entitled to possession of the documents of title relating to the existing lease,

he shall be similarly entitled to possession of the documents of title relating to the new lease; and the tenant shall deliver the new lease to him within one month of the date on which the lease is received from Her Majesty's Land Registry following its registration.

(6)   Where—

(a)   the landlord fails to deliver a counterpart of the new lease in accordance with subsection (3), or

(b)   the tenant fails to deliver the new lease in accordance with subsection (5), the instrument creating or evidencing the mortgage in question shall apply as if the obligation to deliver a counterpart or (as the case may be) deliver the lease were included in the terms of the mortgage as set out in that instrument.

(7) A landlord granting a lease under section 56 shall be bound to take such steps as may be necessary to secure that the lease is not liable in accordance with subsection (2) to be defeated by persons interested in a mortgage on his interest; but a landlord is not obliged, in order to grant a lease for the purposes of that section, to acquire a better title than he has or could require to be vested in him.

[864]

**[58A Priority of interests on grant of new lease**

(1) Where a lease granted under section 56 takes effect subject to two or more interests to which the existing lease was subject immediately before its surrender, the lease was subject immediately before its surrender, interests shall have the same priority in relation to one another on the grant of the new lease as they had immediately before the surrender of the existing lease.

(2) Subsection (1) is subject to agreement to the contrary.

(3) Where a person who is entitled on the grant of a lease under section 56 to rights of occupation in relation to the flat comprised in that lease was entitled immediately before the surrender of the existing lease to rights of occupation in relation to the flat comprised in that lease, the rights to which he is entitled on the grant of the new lease shall be treated as a continuation of the rights to which he was entitled immediately before the surrender of the existing lease.

(4) In this section—

"the existing lease", in relation to a lease granted under section 56, means the lease surrendered on the grant of the new lease, and

"rights of occupation" has the same meaning as in the Matrimonial Homes Act 1983.]

[865]

**NOTES**

Inserted by the Housing Act 1996, s 117.

**59 Further renewal, but no security of tenure, after grant of new lease**

(1) The right to acquire a new lease under this Chapter may be exercised in relation to a lease of a flat despite the fact that the lease is itself a lease granted under section 56; and the provisions of this Chapter shall, with any necessary modifications, apply for the purposes of or in connection with any claim to exercise that right in relation to a lease so granted as they apply for the purposes of or in connection with any claim to exercise that right in relation to a lease which has not been so granted.

(2) Where a lease has been granted under section 56—

(a) none of the statutory provisions relating to security of tenure for tenants shall apply to the lease;

(b) after the term date of the lease none of the following provisions, namely—

(i) section 1 of the Landlord and Tenant Act 1954 or Schedule 10 to the Local Government and Housing Act 1989 (which make provision for security of tenure on the ending of long residential tenancies), or

(ii) Part II of that Act of 1954 (business tenancies),

shall apply to any sub-lease directly or indirectly derived out of the lease; and

(c) after that date no person shall be entitled by virtue of any such sub-lease to retain possession under—

(i) Part VII of the Rent Act 1977 (security of tenure for protected tenancies etc) or any enactment applying or extending that Part of that Act,

(ii) the Rent (Agriculture) Act 1976, or

(iii) Part I of the Housing Act 1988 (assured tenancies etc).

(3) Where a lease has been granted under section 56, no long lease created immediately or derivatively by way of sub-demise under the lease shall confer on the sub-tenant, as against the tenant's landlord, any right under this Chapter to acquire a new lease (and for this purpose "long lease" shall be construed in accordance with section 7).

(4) Any person who—

(a) grants a sub-lease to which subsection (2)(b) and (c) will apply, or

(b) negotiates with a view to the grant of such a sub-lease by him or by a person for whom he is acting as agent,

shall inform the other party that the sub-lease is to be derived out of a lease granted under section 56, unless either he knows that the other party is aware of it or he himself is unaware of it.

(5)   Where any lease contains a statement to the effect that it is a lease granted under section 56, the statement shall be conclusive for the purposes of subsections (2) to (4) in favour of any person who is not a party to the lease, unless the statement appears from the lease to be untrue.

**[866]**

### *Costs incurred in connection with new lease*

## 60   Costs incurred in connection with new lease to be paid by tenant

(1)   Where a notice is given under section 42, then (subject to the provisions of this section) the tenant by whom it is given shall be liable, to the extent that they have been incurred by any relevant person in pursuance of the notice, for the reasonable costs of and incidental to any of the following matters, namely—

   (a)   any investigation reasonably undertaken of the tenant's right to a new lease;

   (b)   any valuation of the tenant's flat obtained for the purpose of fixing the premium or any other amount payable by virtue of Schedule 13 in connection with the grant of a new lease under section 56;

   (c)   the grant of a new lease under that section;

but this subsection shall not apply to any costs if on a sale made voluntarily a stipulation that they were to be borne by the purchaser would be void.

(2)   For the purposes of subsection (1) any costs incurred by a relevant person in respect of professional services rendered by any person shall only be regarded as reasonable if and to the extent that costs in respect of such services might reasonably be expected to have been incurred by him if the circumstances had been such that he was personally liable for all such costs.

(3)   Where by virtue of any provision of this Chapter the tenant's notice ceases to have effect, or is deemed to have been withdrawn, at any time, then (subject to subsection (4)) the tenant's liability under this section for costs incurred by any person shall be a liability for costs incurred by him down to that time.

(4)   A tenant shall not be liable for any costs under this section if the tenant's notice ceases to have effect by virtue of section 47(1) or 55(2).

(5)   A tenant shall not be liable under this section for any costs which a party to any proceedings under this Chapter before a leasehold valuation tribunal incurs in connection with the proceedings.

(6)   In this section "relevant person", in relation to a claim by a tenant under this Chapter, means the landlord for the purposes of this Chapter, any other landlord (as defined by section 40(4)) or any third party to the tenant's lease.

**[867]**

### *Landlord's right to terminate new lease*

## 61   Landlord's right to terminate new lease on grounds of redevelopment

(1)   Where a lease of a flat ("the new lease") has been granted under section 56 but the court is satisfied, on an application made by the landlord—

   (a)   that for the purposes of redevelopment the landlord intends—

      (i)   to demolish or reconstruct, or

      (ii)   to carry out substantial works of construction on,

      the whole or a substantial part of any premises in which the flat is contained, and

   (b)   that he could not reasonably do so without obtaining possession of the flat,

the court shall by order declare that the landlord is entitled as against the tenant to obtain possession of the flat and the tenant is entitled to be paid compensation by the landlord for the loss of the flat.

(2)   An application for an order under this section may be made—

   (a)   at any time during the period of 12 months ending with the term date of the lease in relation to which the right to acquire a new lease was exercised; and

   (b)   at any time during the period of five years ending with the term date of the new lease.

(3)   Where the new lease is not the first lease to be granted under section 56 in respect of a flat, subsection (2) shall apply as if paragraph (b) included a reference to the term date of any previous lease granted under that section in respect of the flat, but paragraph (a) shall be taken to be referring to the term date of the lease in relation to which the right to acquire a new lease was first exercised.

(4)   Where an order is made under this section, the new lease shall determine, and compensation shall become payable, in accordance with Schedule 14 to this Act; and the provisions of that Schedule shall have effect as regards the measure of compensation payable by virtue of any such order and the effects of any such order where there are sub-leases, and as regards other matters relating to orders and applications under this section.

(5)   Except in subsection (1)(a) or (b), any reference in this section to the flat held by the tenant under the new lease includes any premises let with the flat under that lease.

**[868]**

*[Landlord's right to compensation in relation to ineffective claims*

### 61A Compensation for postponement of termination in connection with ineffective claims

(1) This section applies where, on or after 15th January 1999—

   (a) a tenant of a flat makes a claim to acquire a new lease of the flat, and

   (b) the claim is not made at least two years before the term date of the lease in respect of which the claim is made ("the existing lease").

(2) The tenant shall be liable to pay compensation if the claim is not effective and—

   (a) the making of the claim caused a notice served under paragraph 4(1) of Schedule 10 to the Local Government and Housing Act 1989 to cease to have effect and the date on which the claim ceases to have effect is later than four months before the termination date specified in the notice,

   (b) the making of the claim prevented the service of an effective notice under paragraph 4(1) of Schedule 10 to the Local Government and Housing Act 1989 (but did not cause a notice served under that provision to cease to have effect) and the date on which the claim ceases to have effect is a date later than six months before the term date of the existing lease, or

   (c) the existing lease is continued under paragraph 5(1) of Schedule 12 by virtue of the claim.

(3) Compensation under subsection (2) shall become payable at the end of the appropriate period and be the right of the person who is the tenant's immediate landlord at that time.

(4) The amount which the tenant is liable to pay under subsection (2) shall be equal to the difference between—

   (a) the rent for the appropriate period under the existing lease, and

   (b) the rent which might reasonably be expected to be payable for that period were the property to which the existing lease relates let for a term equivalent to that period on the open market by a willing landlord on the following assumptions—

      (i) that no premium is payable in connection with the letting,

      (ii) that the letting confers no security of tenure, and

      (iii) that, except as otherwise provided by this paragraph, the letting is on the same terms as the existing lease.

(5) For the purposes of subsections (3) and (4), the appropriate period is—

   (a) in a case falling within paragraph (a) of subsection (2), the period—

      (i) beginning with the termination date specified in the notice mentioned in that paragraph, and

      (ii) ending with the earliest date of termination which could have been specified in a notice under paragraph 4(1) of Schedule 10 to the Local Government and Housing Act 1989 served immediately after the date on which the claim ceases to have effect, or, if the existing lease is terminated before then, with the date on which it is terminated;

   (b) in a case falling within paragraph (b) of subsection (2), the period—

      (i) beginning with the later of six months from the date on which the claim is made and the term date of the existing lease, and

      (ii) ending six months after the date on which the claim ceases to have effect, or, if the existing lease is terminated before then, with the date of its termination; and

   (c) in a case falling within paragraph (c) of subsection (2), the period for which the existing lease is continued under paragraph 5(1) of Schedule 12.

(6) For the purposes of subsection (2), a claim to a new lease is not effective if it ceases to have effect for any reason other than—

   (a) the application of section 47(1) or 55(2), or

   (b) the acquisition of the new lease in pursuance of the claim.

(7) For the purposes of this section—

   (a) references to a claim to acquire a new lease shall be taken as references to a notice given, or purporting to be given (whether by a qualifying tenant or not), under section 42, and

   (b) references to the date on which a claim ceases to have effect shall, in the case of a claim made by a notice which is not a valid notice under section 42, be taken as references to the date on which the notice is set aside by the court or is withdrawn or would, if valid, cease to have effect or be deemed to have been withdrawn, that date being taken, where the notice is set aside, or would, if valid, cease to have effect, in consequence of a court order, to be the date when the order becomes final.]

**[869]**

**NOTES**

Inserted, together with s 61B and preceding cross-heading, by the Housing Act 1996, s 116, Sch 11, para 3(1).

**[61B　Modification of section 61A where change in immediate reversion**

(1)　Where a tenant's liability to pay compensation under section 61A relates to a period during which there has been a change in the interest immediately expectant on the determination of his lease, that section shall have effect with the following modifications.

(2)　For subsections (3) and (4) there shall be substituted—

"(3)　Compensation under subsection (2) shall become payable at the end of the appropriate period and there shall be a separate right to compensation in respect of each of the interests which, during that period, have been immediately expectant on the determination of the existing lease.

(4)　Compensation under subsection (2) above shall—

(a)　in the case of the interest which is immediately expectant on the determination of the existing lease at the end of the appropriate period, be the right of the person in whom that interest is vested at that time, and

(b)　in the case of an interest which ceases during the appropriate period to be immediately expectant on the determination of the existing lease, be the right of the person in whom the interest was vested immediately before it ceased to be so expectant.

(4A)　The amount which the tenant is liable to pay under subsection (2) above in respect of any interest shall be equal to the difference between—

(a)　the rent under the existing lease for the part of the appropriate period during which the interest was immediately expectant on the determination of that lease, and

(b)　the rent which might reasonably be expected to be payable for that part of that period were the property to which the existing lease relates let for a term equivalent to that part of that period on the open market by a willing landlord on the following assumptions—

(i)　that no premium is payable in connection with the letting,

(ii)　that the letting confers no security of tenure, and

(iii)　that, except as otherwise provided by this paragraph, the letting is on the same terms as the existing lease."

(3)　In subsection (5), for "(3) and (4)" there shall be substituted "(3) to (4A)".]

**[870]**

**NOTES**

Inserted as noted to s 61A at **[869]**.

*Supplemental*

**62　Interpretation of Chapter II**

(1)　In this Chapter—

"the existing lease", in relation to a claim by a tenant under this Chapter, means the lease in relation to which the claim is made;

"the landlord", in relation to such a claim, has the meaning given by section 40(1);

"mortgage" includes a charge or lien;

"qualifying tenant" shall be construed in accordance with section 39(3);

"the relevant date" (unless the context otherwise requires) has the meaning given by section 39(8);

"the tenant's notice" means the notice given under section 42;

"the terms of acquisition" shall be construed in accordance with section 48(7);

"third party", in relation to a lease, means any person who is a party to the lease apart from the tenant under the lease and his immediate landlord.

(2)　Subject to subsection (3), references in this Chapter to a flat, in relation to a claim by a tenant under this Chapter, include any garage, outhouse, garden, yard and appurtenances belonging to, or usually enjoyed with, the flat and let to the tenant with the flat on the relevant date (or, in a case where an application is made under section 50(1), on the date of the making of the application).

(3)　Subsection (2) does not apply—

(a)　to any reference to a flat in section 47 or 55(1); or

(b)　to any reference to a flat (not falling within paragraph (a) above) which occurs in the context of a reference to any premises containing the flat.

(4)　...

**[871]**

PART I
STATUTES

**NOTES**

Sub-s (4): repealed by the Commonhold and Leasehold Reform Act 2002, s 180, Sch 14, except in relation to an application for a new lease of a flat in respect of which notice was given under s 42 of this Act at **[848]**, or where an application was made for an order under s 50 of this Act at **[856]**, before 26 July 2002 (in relation to England) or 1 January 2003 (in relation to Wales).

**63–68** (*S 63 inserts the Leasehold Reform Act 1967, s 1A at* **[79]**; *s 64(1) inserts s 1B of that Act at* **[81]**; *s 64(2) amends s 3(1) of that Act at* **[83]**; *s 65 inserts s 4A of that Act at* **[85]**; *s 66(1) amends s 9 of that Act at* **[91]**; *s 66(2) introduces Sch 15 to this Act; s 66(3) inserts s 9A of the 1967 Act at* **[92]**; *s 67 amends s 1 of that Act at* **[78]**; *s 68 inserts s 32A of that Act at* **[118]**.)

## CHAPTER IV
### ESTATE MANAGEMENT SCHEMES IN CONNECTION WITH ENFRANCHISEMENT

### 69 Estate management schemes

(1)  For the purposes of this Chapter an estate management scheme is a scheme which (subject to sections 71 and 73) is approved by a leasehold valuation tribunal under section 70 for an area occupied directly or indirectly under leases held from one landlord (apart from property occupied by him or his licensees or for the time being unoccupied) and which is designed to secure that in the event of tenants—

[(a)  acquiring the landlord's interest in their house and premises ("the house") under Part I of the Leasehold Reform Act 1967 by virtue of the provisions of section 1AA of that Act (as inserted by paragraph 1 of Schedule 9 to the Housing Act 1996), or

(b)  acquiring the landlord's interest in any premises ("the premises") in accordance with Chapter I of this Part of this Act [in circumstances in which, but for section 117(1) of the Commonhold and Leasehold Reform Act 2002 and the repeal by that Act of paragraph 3 of Schedule 9 to the Housing Act 1996, they would have been entitled to acquire it by virtue of the amendments of that Chapter made by that paragraph],]

the landlord will—

(i)  retain powers of management in respect of the house or premises, and

(ii)  have rights against the house or premises in respect of the benefits arising from the exercise elsewhere of his powers of management.

(2)  An estate management scheme may make different provision for different parts of the area of the scheme, and shall include provision for terminating or varying all or any of the provisions of the scheme, or excluding part of the area, if a change of circumstances makes it appropriate, or for enabling it to be done by or with the approval of a leasehold valuation tribunal.

(3)  Without prejudice to any other provision of this section, an estate management scheme may provide for all or any of the following matters—

(a)  for regulating the redevelopment, use or appearance of property in which tenants have acquired the landlord's interest as mentioned in subsection (1)(a) or (b);

(b)  for empowering the landlord for the time being to carry out works of maintenance, repair, renewal or replacement in relation to any such property or carry out work to remedy a failure in respect of any such property to comply with the scheme, or for making the operation of any provisions of the scheme conditional on his doing so or on the provision or maintenance by him of services, facilities or amenities of any description;

(c)  for imposing on persons from time to time occupying or interested in any such property obligations in respect of the carrying out of works of maintenance, repair, renewal or replacement in relation to the property or property used or enjoyed by them in common with others, or in respect of costs incurred by the landlord for the time being on any matter referred to in this paragraph or in paragraph (b) above;

(d)  for the inspection from time to time of any such property on behalf of the landlord for the time being, and for the recovery by him of sums due to him under the scheme in respect of any such property by means of a charge on the property;

and the landlord for the time being shall have, for the enforcement of any charge imposed under the scheme, the same powers and remedies under the Law of Property Act 1925 and otherwise as if he were a mortgagee by deed having powers of sale and leasing and of appointing a receiver.

(4)  Except as provided by the scheme, the operation of an estate management scheme shall not be affected by any disposition or devolution of the landlord's interest in the property within the area of the scheme or in parts of that property; but the scheme—

(a)  shall include provision for identifying the person who is for the purposes of the scheme to be treated as the landlord for the time being; and

(b)  shall also include provision for transferring, or allowing the landlord for the time being to transfer, all or any of the powers and rights conferred by the scheme on the landlord for the time being to a local authority or other body, including a body constituted for the purpose.

(5) Without prejudice to the generality of paragraph (b) of subsection (4), an estate management scheme may provide for the operation of any provision for transfer included in the scheme in accordance with that paragraph to be dependent—

    (a)    on a determination of a leasehold valuation tribunal effecting or approving the transfer;

    (b)    on such other circumstances as the scheme may provide.

(6) An estate management scheme may extend to property in which the landlord's interest is disposed of otherwise than as mentioned in subsection (1)(a) or (b) (whether residential property or not), so as to make that property, or allow it to be made, subject to any such provision as is or might be made by the scheme for property in which tenants acquire the landlord's interest as mentioned in either of those provisions.

(7) In this Chapter references to the landlord for the time being shall have effect, in relation to powers and rights transferred to a local authority or other body as contemplated by subsection (4)(b) above, as references to that authority or body.

**[872]**

**NOTES**

Sub-s (1): paras (a), (b) substituted by the Housing Act 1996, s 118(1), (2), except in relation to a case where, before 1 April 1997, an application was made to the leasehold valuation tribunal under any of ss 70–73 of this Act at **[873]**–**[876]**; words in square brackets in para (b) substituted by the Commonhold and Leasehold Reform Act 2002, s 117(2), except in relation to an application for collective enfranchisement in respect of which notice was given under s 13 of this Act at **[817]**, or where an application was made for an order under s 26 of this Act at **[830]**, before 26 July 2002 (in relation to England) or 1 January 2003 (in relation to Wales).

## 70   Approval by leasehold valuation tribunal of estate management scheme

(1) A leasehold valuation tribunal may, on an application made by a landlord for the approval of a scheme submitted by him to the tribunal, approve the scheme as an estate management scheme for such area falling within section 69(1) as is specified in the scheme; but any such application must (subject to section 72) be made within the period of [two years beginning with the coming into force of section 118 of the Housing Act 1996].

(2) A leasehold valuation tribunal shall not approve a scheme as an estate management scheme for any area unless it is satisfied that, in order to maintain adequate standards of appearance and amenity and regulate redevelopment within the area in the event of tenants acquiring the interest of the landlord in any property as mentioned in section 69(1)(a) or (b), it is in the general interest that the landlord should retain such powers of management and have such rights falling within section 69(1)(i) and (ii) as are conferred by the scheme.

(3) In considering whether to approve a scheme as an estate management scheme for any area, a leasehold valuation tribunal shall have regard primarily to—

    (a)    the benefit likely to result from the scheme to the area as a whole (including houses or premises likely to be acquired from the landlord as mentioned in section 69(1)(a) or (b)); and

    (b)    the extent to which it is reasonable to impose, for the benefit of the area, obligations on tenants so acquiring the interest of their landlord;

but the tribunal shall also have regard to the past development and present character of the area and to architectural or historical considerations, to neighbouring areas and to the circumstances generally.

(4) A leasehold valuation tribunal shall not consider any application for it to approve a scheme unless it is satisfied that the applicant has, by advertisement or otherwise, given adequate notice to persons interested—

    (a)    informing them of the application for approval of the scheme and the provision intended to be made by the scheme, and

    (b)    inviting them to make representations to the tribunal about the application within a time which appears to the tribunal to be reasonable.

(5) In subsection (4) "persons interested" includes, in particular, in relation to any application for the approval of a scheme for any area ("the scheme area") within a conservation area—

    (a)    each local planning authority within whose area any part of the scheme area falls, and

    (b)    if the whole of the scheme area is in England, the Historic Buildings and Monuments Commission for England.

[(6) Where the application is to be considered in an oral hearing, the tribunal shall afford to any person making representations under subsection (4)(b) about the application an opportunity to appear at the hearing.]

(7)   Subject to the preceding provisions of this section, a leasehold valuation tribunal shall, after considering the application, approve the scheme in question either—

(a)   as originally submitted, or

(b)   with any relevant modifications proposed or agreed to by the applicant,

if the scheme (with those modifications, if any) appears to the tribunal—

(i)   to be fair and practicable, and

(ii)   not to give the landlord a degree of control out of proportion to that previously exercised by him or to that required for the purposes of the scheme.

(8)   In subsection (7) "relevant modifications" means modifications relating to the extent of the area to which the scheme is to apply or to the provisions contained in it.

(9)   If, having regard to—

(a)   the matters mentioned in subsection (3), and

(b)   the provision which it is practicable to make by a scheme,

the tribunal thinks it proper to do so, the tribunal may declare that no scheme can be approved for the area in question in pursuance of the application.

(10)   A leasehold valuation tribunal shall not dismiss an application for the approval of a scheme unless—

(a)   it makes such a declaration as is mentioned in subsection (9); or

(b)   in the opinion of the tribunal the applicant is unwilling to agree to a suitable scheme or is not proceeding in the matter with due despatch.

[(10A)   Any person who makes representations under subsection (4)(b) about an application for the approval of a scheme may appeal from a decision of the tribunal in proceedings on the application.]

(11)   A scheme approved under this section as an estate management scheme for an area shall be a local land charge, notwithstanding section 2(a) or (b) of the Local Land Charges Act 1975 (matters which are not local land charges), and for the purposes of that Act the landlord for that area shall be treated as the originating authority as respects any such charge.

(12)   Where such a scheme is registered in the appropriate local land charges register—

(a)   the provisions of the scheme relating to property of any description shall so far as they respectively affect the persons from time to time occupying or interested in that property be enforceable by the landlord for the time being against them, as if each of them had covenanted with the landlord for the time being to be bound by the scheme; and

(b)   in relation to any acquisition such as is mentioned in section 69(1)(a) above, section 10 of the Leasehold Reform Act 1967 (rights to be conveyed on enfranchisement) shall have effect subject to the provisions of the scheme, and the price payable under section 9 of that Act shall be adjusted so far as is appropriate (if at all); and

(c)   in relation to any acquisition such as is mentioned in section 69(1)(b) above, section 34 of, and Schedule 7 to, this Act shall have effect subject to the provisions of the scheme, and any price payable under Schedule 6 to this Act shall be adjusted so far as is appropriate (if at all).

(13)   Section 10 of the Local Land Charges Act 1975 (compensation for non-registration etc) shall not apply to schemes which, by virtue of subsection (11) above, are local land charges.

(14)   In this section and in section 73 "conservation area" and "local planning authority" have the same meaning as in the Planning (Listed Buildings and Conservation Areas) Act 1990; and in connection with the latter expression—

(a)   the expression "the planning Acts" in the Town and Country Planning Act 1990 shall be treated as including this Act; and

(b)   paragraphs 4 and 5 of Schedule 4 to the Planning (Listed Buildings and Conservation Areas) Act 1990 (further provisions as to exercise of functions by different authorities) shall apply in relation to functions under or by virtue of this section or section 73 of this Act as they apply in relation to functions under section 69 of that Act.

**[873]**

**NOTES**

Sub-s (1): words in square brackets substituted by the Housing Act 1996, s 118(1), (3), except in relation to a case where, before 1 April 1997, an application was made to the leasehold valuation tribunal under this section or ss 71–73 of this Act at **[874]–[876]**.

Sub-s (6): substituted by the Commonhold and Leasehold Reform Act 2002, s 176, Sch 13, paras 12, 13(1), (2), except in relation to any application made to an LVT or any proceedings transferred to an LVT by a county court before 30 September 2003 (in relation to England) or 31 March 2004 (in relation to Wales).

Sub-s (10A): inserted by the Commonhold and Leasehold Reform Act 2002, s 176, Sch 13, paras 12, 13(1), (3), subject to savings as noted above.

### 71  Applications by two or more landlords or by representative bodies

(1)   Where, on a joint application made by two or more persons as landlords of neighbouring areas, it appears to a leasehold valuation tribunal—

(a)   that a scheme could in accordance with subsections (1) and (2) of section 70 be approved as an estate management scheme for those areas, treated as a unit, if the interests of those persons were held by a single person, and

(b)   that the applicants are willing to be bound by the scheme to co-operate in the management of their property in those areas and in the administration of the scheme,

the tribunal may (subject to the provisions of section 70 and subsection (2) below) approve the scheme under that section as an estate management scheme for those areas as a whole.

(2)   Any such scheme shall be made subject to conditions (enforceable in such manner as may be provided by the scheme) for securing that the landlords and their successors co-operate as mentioned in subsection (1)(b) above.

(3)   Where it appears to a leasehold valuation tribunal—

(a)   that a scheme could, on the application of any landlord or landlords, be approved under section 70 as an estate management scheme for any area or areas, and

(b)   that any body of persons—

(i)   is so constituted as to be capable of representing for the purposes of the scheme the persons occupying or interested in property in the area or areas (other than the landlord or landlords or his or their licensees), or such of them as are or may become entitled to acquire their landlord's interest as mentioned in section 69(1)(a) or (b), and

(ii)   is otherwise suitable,

an application for the approval of the scheme under section 70 may be made to the tribunal by the representative body alone or by the landlord or landlords alone or by both jointly and, by leave of the tribunal, may be proceeded with by the representative body or by the landlord or landlords despite the fact that the body or landlord or landlords in question did not make the application.

(4)   Without prejudice to section 69(4)(b), any such scheme may with the consent of the landlord or landlords, or on such terms as to compensation or otherwise as appear to the tribunal to be just—

(a)   confer on the representative body any such rights or powers under the scheme as might be conferred on the landlord or landlords for the time being, or

(b)   enable the representative body to participate in the administration of the scheme or in the management by the landlord or landlords of his or their property in the area or areas.

(5)   Where any such scheme confers any rights or powers on the representative body in accordance with subsection (4) above, section 70(11) and (12)(a) shall have effect with such modifications (if any) as are provided for in the scheme.

**[874]**

### 72  Applications after expiry of two-year period

(1)   An application for the approval of a scheme for an area under section 70 (including an application in accordance with section 71(1) or (3)) may be made after the expiry of the period mentioned in subsection (1) of that section if the Secretary of State has, not more than six months previously, consented to the making of such an application for that area or for an area within which that area falls.

(2)   The Secretary of State may give consent under subsection (1) to the making of an application ("the proposed application") only where he is satisfied—

(a)   that either or both of the conditions mentioned in subsection (3) apply; and

(b)   that adequate notice has been given to persons interested informing them of the request for consent and the purpose of the request.

(3)   The conditions referred to in subsection (2)(a) are—

(a)   that the proposed application could not have been made before the expiry of the period mentioned in section 70(1); and

(b)   that—

(i)   any application for the approval under section 70 of a scheme for the area, or part of the area, to which the proposed application relates would probably have been dismissed under section 70(10)(a) had it been made before the expiry of that period; but

(ii)   because of a change in any of the circumstances required to be considered under section 70(3) the proposed application would, if made following the giving of consent by the Secretary of State, probably be granted.

(4)   A request for consent under subsection (1) must be in writing and must comply with such requirements (if any) as to the form of, or the particulars to be contained in, any such request as the Secretary of State may by regulations prescribe.

(5)   The procedure for considering a request for consent under subsection (1) shall be such as may be prescribed by regulations made by the Secretary of State.

[875]

## 73   Applications by certain public bodies

(1)   Where it appears to a leasehold valuation tribunal after the expiry of the period mentioned in section 70(1) that a scheme could, on the application of any landlord or landlords within that period, have been approved under section 70 as an estate management scheme for any area or areas within a conservation area, an application for the approval of the scheme under that section may, subject to subsections (2) and (3) below, be made to the tribunal by one or more bodies constituting the relevant authority for the purposes of this section.

(2)   An application under subsection (1) may only be made if—
- (a)   no scheme has been approved under section 70 for the whole or any part of the area or areas to which the application relates ("the scheme area"); and
- (b)   any application which has been made in accordance with section 70(1), 71(1) or 71(3) for the approval of a scheme for the whole or any part of the scheme area has been withdrawn or dismissed; and
- (c)   no request for consent under section 72(1) which relates to the whole or any part of the scheme area is pending or has been granted within the last six months.

(3)   An application under subsection (1) above must be made within the period of six months beginning—
- (a)   with the date on which the period mentioned in section 70(1) expires, or
- (b)   if any application has been made as mentioned in subsection (2)(b) above, with the date (or, as the case may be, the latest date) on which any such application is withdrawn or dismissed,

whichever is the later; but if at any time during that period of six months a request of a kind mentioned in subsection (2)(c) above is pending or granted, an application under subsection (1) above may, subject to subsection (2) above, be made within the period of—
- (i)   six months beginning with the date on which the request is withdrawn or refused, or
- (ii)   twelve months beginning with the date on which the request is granted,

as the case may be.

(4)   A scheme approved on an application under subsection (1) may confer on the applicant or applicants any such rights or powers under the scheme as might have been conferred on the landlord or landlords for the time being.

(5)   For the purposes of this section the relevant authority for the scheme area is—
- (a)   where that area falls wholly within the area of a local planning authority—
  - (i)   that authority; or
  - (ii)   subject to subsection (6), that authority acting jointly with the Historic Buildings and Monuments Commission for England ("the Commission"); or
  - (iii)   subject to subsection (6), the Commission; or
- (b)   in any other case—
  - (i)   all of the local planning authorities within each of whose areas any part of the scheme area falls, acting jointly; or
  - (ii)   subject to subsection (6), one or more of those authorities acting jointly with the Commission; or
  - (iii)   subject to subsection (6), the Commission.

(6)   The Commission may make, or join in the making of, an application under subsection (1) only if—
- (a)   the whole of the scheme area is in England; and
- (b)   they have consulted any local planning authority within whose area the whole or any part of the scheme area falls.

(7)   Where a scheme is approved on an application under subsection (1) by two or more bodies acting jointly, the scheme shall, if the tribunal considers it appropriate, be made subject to conditions (enforceable in such manner as may be provided by the scheme) for securing that those bodies co-operate in the administration of the scheme.

(8)   Where a scheme is approved on an application under subsection (1)—
- (a)   section 70(11) and (12)(a) shall (subject to subsection (9) below) have effect as if any reference to the landlord, or the landlord for the time being, for the area for which an estate management scheme has been approved were a reference to the applicant or applicants; and
- (b)   section 70(12)(b) and (c) shall each have effect with the omission of so much of that provision as relates to the adjustment of any such price as is there mentioned.

(9)   A scheme so approved shall not be enforceable by a local planning authority in relation to any property falling outside the authority's area; and in the case of a scheme approved on a joint

application made by one or more local planning authorities and the Commission, the scheme may provide for any of its provisions to be enforceable in relation to property falling within the area of a local planning authority either by the authority alone, or by the Commission alone, or by the authority and the Commission acting jointly, as the scheme may provide.

    (10)    For the purposes of—

        (a)    section 9(1A) of the Leasehold Reform Act 1967 (purchase price on enfranchisement) as it applies in relation to any acquisition such as is mentioned in section 69(1)(a) above, and

        (b)    paragraph 3 of Schedule 6 to this Act as it applies in relation to any acquisition such as is mentioned in section 69(1)(b) above (including that paragraph as it applies by virtue of paragraph 7 or 11 of that Schedule),

it shall be assumed that any scheme approved under subsection (1) and relating to the property in question had not been so approved, and accordingly any application for such a scheme to be approved, and the possibility of such an application being made, shall be disregarded.

    (11)    Section 70(14) applies for the purposes of this section.

**[876]**

## 74  Effect of application for approval on claim to acquire freehold

    (1)    Subject to subsections (5) and (6), this subsection applies where—

        (a)    an application ("the scheme application") is made for the approval of a scheme as an estate management scheme for any area or a request ("the request for consent") is made for consent under section 72(1) in relation to any area, and

        (b)    whether before or after the making of the application or request—

            (i)    the tenant of a house in that area gives notice of his desire to have the freehold under Part I of the Leasehold Reform Act 1967, ...

            (ii)    a notice is given under section 13 above in respect of any premises in the area [and

        (c)    in the case of an application for the approval of a scheme as an estate management scheme, the scheme would extend to the house or premises if acquired in pursuance of the notice].

    (2)    Where subsection (1) applies by virtue of paragraph (b)(i) of that subsection, then—

        (a)    no further steps need be taken towards the execution of a conveyance to give effect to section 10 of the 1967 Act beyond those which appear to the landlord to be reasonable in the circumstances; and

        (b)    if the notice referred to in subsection (1)(b)(i) ("the tenant's notice") was given before the making of the scheme application or the request for consent, that notice may be withdrawn by a further notice given by the tenant to the landlord.

    (3)    Where subsection (1) applies by virtue of paragraph (b)(ii) of that subsection, then—

        (a)    if the notice referred to in that provision ("the initial notice") was given before the making of the scheme application or the request for consent, the notice may be withdrawn by a further notice given by the *nominee purchaser* to the reversioner;

        (b)    unless the initial notice is so withdrawn, the reversioner shall, if he has not already given the *nominee purchaser* a counter-notice under section 21, give *him* by the date referred to in subsection (1) of that section a counter-notice which complies with one of the requirements set out in subsection (2) of that section (but in relation to which subsection (3) of that section need not be complied with); and

        (c)    no proceedings shall be brought under Chapter I in pursuance of the initial notice otherwise than under section 22 or 23, and, if the court under either of those sections makes an order requiring the reversioner to give a further counter-notice to the *nominee purchaser*, the date by which it is to be given shall be such date as falls two months after subsection (1) above ceases to apply;

but no other counter-notice need be given under Chapter I, and (subject to the preceding provisions of this subsection) no further steps need be taken towards the final determination (whether by agreement or otherwise) of the terms of the proposed acquisition by the *nominee purchaser* beyond those which appear to the reversioner to be reasonable in the circumstances.

    (4)    If the tenant's notice or the initial notice is withdrawn in accordance with subsection (2) or (3) above, section 9(4) of the 1967 Act or (as the case may be) section 33 above shall not have effect to require the payment of any costs incurred in pursuance of that notice.

    (5)    Where the scheme application is withdrawn or dismissed, subsection (1) does not apply at any time falling after—

        (a)    the date of the withdrawal of the application, or

        (b)    the date when the decision of the tribunal dismissing the application becomes final,

as the case may be; and subsection (1) does not apply at any time falling after the date on which a scheme is approved for the area referred to in that subsection, or for any part of it, in pursuance of the scheme application.

(6)   Where the request for consent is withdrawn or refused, subsection (1) does not apply at any time falling after the date on which the request is withdrawn or refused, as the case may be; and where the request is granted, subsection (1) does not apply at any time falling more than six months after the date on which it is granted (unless that subsection applies by virtue of an application made in reliance on the consent).

(7)   Where, in accordance with subsection (5) or (6), subsection (1) ceases to apply as from a particular date, it shall do so without prejudice to—
   (a)   the effect of anything done before that date in pursuance of subsection (2) or (3); or
   (b)   the operation of any provision of this Part, or of regulations made under it, in relation to anything so done.

(8)   If, however, no notice of withdrawal has been given in accordance with subsection (3) before the date when subsection (1) so ceases to apply and before that date either—
   (a)   the reversioner has given the *nominee purchaser* a counter-notice under section 21 complying with the requirement set out in subsection (2)(a) of that section, or
   (b)   section 23(6) would (but for subsection (3) above) have applied to require the reversioner to give a further counter-notice to the *nominee purchaser*,

the reversioner shall give a further counter-notice to the *nominee purchaser* within the period of two months beginning with the date when subsection (1) ceases to apply.

(9)   Subsections (3) to (5) of section 21 shall apply to any further counter-notice required to be given by the reversioner under subsection (8) above as if it were a counter-notice under that section complying with the requirement set out in subsection (2)(a) of that section; and sections 24 and 25 shall apply in relation to any such counter-notice as they apply in relation to one required by section 22(3).

(10)   In this section—
   "the 1967 Act" means the Leasehold Reform Act 1967; and
   "the *nominee purchaser*" and "the reversioner" have the same meaning as in Chapter I of this Part of this Act;

and references to the approval of a scheme for any area include references to the approval of a scheme for two or more areas in accordance with section 71 or 73 above.

[877]

**NOTES**
Sub-s (1): words omitted repealed and para (c) and the word "and" preceding it added by the Housing Act 1996, s 118(1), (4), except in relation to a case where, before 1 April 1997, an application was made to the leasehold valuation tribunal under any of ss 70–73 of this Act at [873]–[876].
Sub-s (3): words "nominee purchaser" in italics substituted in each place by the words "RTE company" and in para (b) word "him" in italics substituted by the word "it" by the Commonhold and Leasehold Reform Act 2002, s 124, Sch 8, paras 2, 30(1)–(3), as from a day to be appointed.
Sub-ss (8), (10): words in italics substituted in each place by the words "RTE company" by the Commonhold and Leasehold Reform Act 2002, s 124, Sch 8, paras 2, 30(1), (2), as from a day to be appointed.

## 75   Variation of existing schemes

(1)   Where a scheme under section 19 of the Leasehold Reform Act 1967 (estate management schemes in connection with enfranchisement under that Act) includes, in pursuance of subsection (6) of that section, provision for enabling the termination or variation of the scheme, or the exclusion of part of the area of the scheme, by or with the approval of the High Court, that provision shall have effect—
   (a)   as if any reference to the High Court were a reference to a leasehold valuation tribunal, and
   (b)   with such modifications (if any) as are necessary in consequence of paragraph (a).

(2)   A scheme under that section may be varied by or with the approval of a leasehold valuation tribunal for the purpose of, or in connection with, extending the scheme to property within the area of the scheme in which the landlord's interest may be acquired as mentioned in section 69(1)(a) above.

(3)   Where any such scheme has been varied in accordance with subsection (2) above, section 19 of that Act shall apply as if the variation had been effected under provisions included in the scheme in pursuance of subsection (6) of that section (and accordingly the scheme may be further varied under provisions so included).

(4), (5)   ...

[878]

**NOTES**
Sub-ss (4), (5): repealed by the Commonhold and Leasehold Reform Act 2002, s 180, Sch 14, except in relation to any application made to an LVT or any proceedings transferred to an LVT by a county court before 30 September 2003 (in relation to England) or 31 March 2004 (in relation to Wales).

## CHAPTER V
## TENANTS' RIGHT TO MANAGEMENT AUDIT

### 76 Right to audit management by landlord

(1) This Chapter has effect to confer on two or more qualifying tenants of dwellings held on leases from the same landlord the right, exercisable subject to and in accordance with this Chapter, to have an audit carried out on their behalf which relates to the management of the relevant premises and any appurtenant property by or on behalf of the landlord.

(2) That right shall be exercisable—
   (a) where the relevant premises consist of or include two dwellings let to qualifying tenants of the same landlord, by either or both of those tenants; and
   (b) where the relevant premises consist of or include three or more dwellings let to qualifying tenants of the same landlord, by not less than two-thirds of those tenants;

and in this Chapter the dwellings let to those qualifying tenants are referred to as "the constituent dwellings".

(3) In relation to an audit on behalf of two or more qualifying tenants—
   (a) "the relevant premises" means so much of—
      (i) the building or buildings containing the dwellings let to those tenants, and
      (ii) any other building or buildings,
      as constitutes premises in relation to which management functions are discharged in respect of the costs of which common service charge contributions are payable under the leases of those qualifying tenants; and
   (b) "appurtenant property" means so much of any property not contained in the relevant premises as constitutes property in relation to which any such management functions are discharged.

(4) This Chapter also has effect to confer on a single qualifying tenant of a dwelling the right, exercisable subject to and in accordance with this Chapter, to have an audit carried out on his behalf which relates to the management of the relevant premises and any appurtenant property by or on behalf of the landlord.

(5) That right shall be exercisable by a single qualifying tenant of a dwelling where the relevant premises contain no other dwelling let to a qualifying tenant apart from that let to him.

(6) In relation to an audit on behalf of a single qualifying tenant—
   (a) "the relevant premises" means so much of—
      (i) the building containing the dwelling let to him, and
      (ii) any other building or buildings,
      as constitutes premises in relation to which management functions are discharged in respect of the costs of which a service charge is payable under his lease (whether as a common service charge contribution or otherwise); and
   (b) "appurtenant property" means so much of any property not contained in the relevant premises as constitutes property in relation to which any such management functions are discharged.

(7) The provisions of sections 78 to 83 shall, with any necessary modifications, have effect in relation to an audit on behalf of a single qualifying tenant as they have effect in relation to an audit on behalf of two or more qualifying tenants.

(8) For the purposes of this section common service charge contributions are payable by two or more persons under their leases if they may be required under the terms of those leases to contribute to the same costs by the payment of service charges.

**[879]**

**NOTES**

Modified, where the RTM company has acquired the right to manage, by the Commonhold and Leasehold Reform Act 2002, s 102, Sch 7, para 14 at **[1266]**, **[1306]**.

### 77 Qualifying tenants

(1) Subject to the following provisions of this section, a tenant is a qualifying tenant of a dwelling for the purposes of this Chapter if—
   (a) he is a tenant of the dwelling under a long lease other than a business lease; and
   (b) any service charge is payable under the lease.

(2) For the purposes of subsection (1) a lease is a long lease if—
   (a) it is a lease falling within any of paragraphs (a) to (c) of subsection (1) of section 7; or
   (b) it is a shared ownership lease (within the meaning of that section), whether granted in pursuance of Part V of the Housing Act 1985 or otherwise and whatever the share of the tenant under it.

(3) No dwelling shall have more than one qualifying tenant at any one time.

(4) Accordingly—

    (a) where a dwelling is for the time being let under two or more leases falling within subsection (1), any tenant under any of those leases which is superior to that held by any other such tenant shall not be a qualifying tenant of the dwelling for the purposes of this Chapter; and

    (b) where a dwelling is for the time being let to joint tenants under a lease falling within subsection (1), the joint tenants shall (subject to paragraph (a)) be regarded for the purposes of this Chapter as jointly constituting the qualifying tenant of the dwelling.

(5) A person can, however, be (or be among those constituting) the qualifying tenant of each of two or more dwellings at the same time, whether he is tenant of those dwellings under one lease or under two or more separate leases.

(6) Where two or more persons constitute the qualifying tenant of a dwelling in accordance with subsection (4)(b), any one or more of those persons may sign a notice under section 80 on behalf of both or all of them.

**[880]**

---

**NOTES**

Modified, where the RTM company has acquired the right to manage, by the Commonhold and Leasehold Reform Act 2002, s 102, Sch 7, para 14 at **[1266]**, **[1306]**.

## 78 Management audits

(1) The audit referred to in section 76(1) is an audit carried out for the purpose of ascertaining—

    (a) the extent to which the obligations of the landlord which—

        (i) are owed to the qualifying tenants of the constituent dwellings, and

        (ii) involve the discharge of management functions in relation to the relevant premises or any appurtenant property,

        are being discharged in an efficient and effective manner; and

    (b) the extent to which sums payable by those tenants by way of service charges are being applied in an efficient and effective manner;

and in this Chapter any such audit is referred to as a "management audit".

(2) In determining whether any such obligations as are mentioned in subsection (1)(a) are being discharged in an efficient and effective manner, regard shall be had to any applicable provisions of any code of practice for the time being approved by the Secretary of State under section 87.

(3) A management audit shall be carried out by a person who—

    (a) is qualified for appointment by virtue of subsection (4); and

    (b) is appointed—

        (i) in the circumstances mentioned in section 76(2)(a), by either or both of the qualifying tenants of the constituent dwellings, or

        (ii) in the circumstances mentioned in section 76(2)(b), by not less than two-thirds of the qualifying tenants of the constituent dwellings;

and in this Chapter any such person is referred to as "the auditor".

(4) A person is qualified for appointment for the purposes of subsection (3) above if—

    (*a*) *he has the necessary qualification (within the meaning of subsection (1) of section 28 of the 1985 Act (meaning of "qualified accountant")) or is a qualified surveyor;*

    (*b*) *he is not disqualified from acting (within the meaning of that subsection); and*

    (*c*) he is not a tenant of any premises contained in the relevant premises.

(5) For the purposes of subsection (4)(a) above a person is a qualified surveyor if he is a fellow or professional associate of the Royal Institution of Chartered Surveyors or of the Incorporated Society of Valuers and Auctioneers or satisfies such other requirement or requirements as may be prescribed by regulations made by the Secretary of State.

[(5A) For the purposes of subsection (4)(b)(i) above a company is associated with a landlord company if it is the landlord's holding company, a subsidiary of the landlord or another subsidiary of the landlord's holding company.

(5B) Subsection (4)(b)(i) does not apply where the landlord is a relevant landlord.

(5C) For the purposes of subsection (4)(b)(iii) above a person is a managing agent for any premises if he has been appointed to discharge any of the landlord's obligations relating to the management by the landlord of the premises.]

(6) The auditor may appoint such persons to assist him in carrying out the audit as he thinks fit.

[(7) In this section—

"holding company" and "subsidiary" have the meanings given by section 1159 of the Companies Act 2006;

"relevant landlord" means—

(a)     a local authority (within the meaning of the Landlord and Tenant Act 1985);

(b)     a National Park authority; or

(c)     a new town corporation (within the meaning of the Act of 1985).]

**[881]**

### NOTES

Sub-s (4): paras (a), (b) substituted by the Housing and Regeneration Act 2008, s 303, Sch 12, paras 14, 15(1), (2), as from a day to be appointed, as follows:

"(a)     he is—

    (i)     a member of a body which is a recognised supervisory body for the purposes of Part 42 of the Companies Act 2006;

    (ii)     a qualified surveyor; or

    (iii)     where the landlord is a relevant landlord, a member of the Chartered Institute of Public Finance and Accountancy;

(b)     he is not any of the following—

    (i)     an officer, employee or partner of the landlord or, where the landlord is a company, of an associated company;

    (ii)     a person who is a partner or employee of any such officer or employee;

    (iii)     an agent of the landlord who is a managing agent for any premises to which the audit in question relates; or

    (iv)     an employee or partner of any such agent; and".

Sub-ss (5A)–(5C): inserted by the Housing and Regeneration Act 2008, s 303, Sch 12, paras 14, 15(1), (3), as from a day to be appointed.

Sub-s (7): inserted by the Housing and Regeneration Act 2008, s 303, Sch 12, paras 14, 15(1), (4), as from a day to be appointed.

Modified, where the RTM company has acquired the right to manage, by the Commonhold and Leasehold Reform Act 2002, s 102, Sch 7, para 14 at **[1266]**, **[1306]**.

1985 Act: Landlord and Tenant Act 1985.

Regulations: the Collective Enfranchisement and Tenants' Audit (Qualified Surveyors) Regulations 1994, SI 1994/1263 at **[3137]**.

### 79    Rights exercisable in connection with management audits

(1)     Where the qualifying tenants of any dwellings exercise under section 80 their right to have a management audit carried out on their behalf, the rights conferred on the auditor by *subsection (2)* below shall be exercisable by him in connection with the audit.

(2)     *The rights conferred on the auditor by this subsection are—*

(a)     *a right to require the landlord—*

    (i)     *to supply him with such a summary as is referred to in section 21(1) of the 1985 Act (request for summary of relevant costs) in connection with any service charges payable by the qualifying tenants of the constituent dwellings, and*

    (ii)     *to afford him reasonable facilities for inspecting, or taking copies of or extracts from, the accounts, receipts and other documents supporting any such summary;*

(b)     *a right to require the landlord or any relevant person to afford him reasonable facilities for inspecting any other documents sight of which is reasonably required by him for the purpose of carrying out the audit; and*

(c)     *a right to require the landlord or any relevant person to afford him reasonable facilities for taking copies of or extracts from any documents falling within paragraph (b).*

(3)     The rights conferred on the auditor by *subsection (2)* shall be exercisable by him—

(a)     in relation to the landlord, by means of a notice under section 80; and

(b)     in relation to any relevant person, by means of a notice given to that person at (so far as is reasonably practicable) the same time as a notice under section 80 is given to the landlord;

and, where a notice is given to any relevant person in accordance with paragraph (b) above, a copy of that notice shall be given to the landlord by the auditor.

(4)     The auditor shall also be entitled, on giving notice in accordance with section 80, to carry out an inspection of any common parts comprised in the relevant premises or any appurtenant property.

(5)     *The landlord or (as the case may be) any relevant person shall—*

(a)     *where facilities for the inspection of any documents are required under subsection (2)(a)(ii) or (b), make those facilities available free of charge;*

(b)     *where any documents are required to be supplied under subsection (2)(a)(i) or facilities for the taking of copies or extracts are required under subsection (2)(a)(ii) or (c), be entitled to supply those documents or (as the case may be) make those facilities available on payment of such reasonable charge as he may determine.*

(6)     *The requirement imposed on the landlord by subsection (5)(a) to make any facilities available free of charge shall not be construed as precluding the landlord from treating as part of his costs of management any costs incurred by him in connection with making those facilities so available.*

(7)   In this Chapter "relevant person" means a person (other than the landlord) who—
   (a)   is charged with responsibility—
      (i)   for the discharge of any such obligations as are mentioned in section 78(1)(a), or
      (ii)   for the application of any such service charges as are mentioned in section 78(1)(b); or
   (b)   has a right to enforce payment of any such service charges.

(8)   In this Chapter references to the auditor in the context of—
   (a)   *being afforded any such facilities as are mentioned in subsection* (2), or
   (b)   the carrying out of any inspection under subsection (4),
shall be read as including a person appointed by the auditor under section 78(6).

[882]

NOTES

Sub-s (1): words in italics substituted by the words "subsections (2) and (2A)" by the Commonhold and Leasehold Reform Act 2002, s 157, Sch 10, para 16(1), (2), as from a day to be appointed.

Sub-s (2): substituted by sub-ss (2), (2A) by the Commonhold and Leasehold Reform Act 2002, s 157, Sch 10, para 16(1), (3), as from a day to be appointed, and in the substituted sub-s (2) below, for the first words in italics there are substituted the words "information required to be provided" and for the second word in italics there are substituted the words "by virtue of" by the Housing and Regeneration Act 2008, s 303, Sch 12, paras 14, 16, as from a day to be appointed, as follows—

   "(2)   The right conferred on the auditor by this subsection is a right to require the landlord—
   (a)   to afford him reasonable facilities for inspecting accounts, receipts or other documents relevant to *the matters which must be shown in any statement of account required to be supplied* to the qualifying tenants of the constituent dwellings *under* section 21 of the 1985 Act and for taking copies of or extracts from them, or
   (b)   to take copies of or extracts from any such accounts, receipts or other documents and either send them to him or afford him reasonable facilities for collecting them (as he specifies).

   (2A)   The right conferred on the auditor by this subsection is a right to require the landlord or any relevant person—
   (a)   to afford him reasonable facilities for inspecting any other documents sight of which is reasonably required by him for the purpose of carrying out the audit and for taking copies of or extracts from them, or
   (b)   to take copies of or extracts from any such documents and either send them to him or afford him reasonable facilities for collecting them (as the auditor specifies).".

Sub-s (3): words in italics substituted by the words "subsections (2) and (2A)" by the Commonhold and Leasehold Reform Act 2002, s 157, Sch 10, para 16(1), (4), as from a day to be appointed.

Sub-ss (5), (6): substituted by the Commonhold and Leasehold Reform Act 2002, s 157, Sch 10, para 16(1), (5), as from a day to be appointed, as follows—

   "(5)   To the extent that a requirement imposed under this section on the landlord or any relevant person requires him to afford facilities for inspecting documents, he shall do so free of charge; but the landlord may treat as part of his costs of management any costs incurred by him in doing so.

   (6)   The landlord or a relevant person may make a reasonable charge for doing anything else in compliance with such a requirement.".

Sub-s (8): in para (a) words in italics substituted by the words "a requirement imposed under subsection (2) or (2A)" by the Commonhold and Leasehold Reform Act 2002, s 157, Sch 10, para 16(1), (6), as from a day to be appointed.

Modified, where the RTM company has acquired the right to manage, by the Commonhold and Leasehold Reform Act 2002, s 102, Sch 7, para 14 at **[1266]**, **[1306]**.

1985 Act: Landlord and Tenant Act 1985.

## 80   Exercise of right to have a management audit

(1)   The right of any qualifying tenants to have a management audit carried out on their behalf shall be exercisable by the giving of a notice under this section.

(2)   A notice given under this section—
   (a)   must be given to the landlord by the auditor, and
   (b)   must be signed by each of the tenants on whose behalf it is given.

(3)   Any such notice must—
   (a)   state the full name of each of those tenants and the address of the dwelling of which he is a qualifying tenant;
   (b)   state the name and address of the auditor;
   (c)   *specify any documents or description of documents—*
      (i)   *which the landlord is required to supply to the auditor under section 79(2)(a)(i), or*
      (ii)   *in respect of which he is required to afford the auditor facilities for inspection or for taking copies or extracts under any other provision of section 79(2); and*
   (d)   if the auditor proposes to carry out an inspection under section 79(4), state the date on which he proposes to carry out the inspection.

(4)   The date specified under subsection (3)(d) must be a date falling not less than one month nor more than two months after the date of the giving of the notice.

(5)   A notice is duly given under this section to the landlord of any qualifying tenants if it is given to a person who receives on behalf of the landlord the rent payable by any such tenants; and a person to whom such a notice is so given shall forward it as soon as may be to the landlord.

**[883]**

**NOTES**
Sub-s (3): para (c) substituted by the Commonhold and Leasehold Reform Act 2002, s 157, Sch 10, para 17, as from a day to be appointed, as follows—
   "(c)   specify any documents or description of documents in respect of which a requirement is imposed on him under section 79(2) or (2A); and".

Modified, where the RTM company has acquired the right to manage, by the Commonhold and Leasehold Reform Act 2002, s 102, Sch 7, para 14 at **[1266]**, **[1306]**.

### 81   Procedure following giving of notice under section 80

(1)   Where the landlord is given a notice under section 80, then within the period of one month beginning with the date of the giving of the notice, he shall—
   (a)   *supply the auditor with any document specified under subsection (3)(c)(i) of that section, and afford him, in respect of any document falling within section 79(2)(a)(ii), any facilities specified in relation to it under subsection (3)(c)(ii) of section 80;*
   (b)   *in the case of every other document or description of documents specified in the notice under subsection (3)(c)(ii) of that section, either—*
      (i)   *afford the auditor facilities for inspection or (as the case may be) taking copies or extracts in respect of that document or those documents, or*
      (ii)   *give the auditor a notice stating that he objects to doing so for such reasons as are specified in the notice; and*
   (c)   if a date is specified in the notice under subsection (3)(d) of that section, either approve the date or propose another date for the carrying out of an inspection under section 79(4).

(2)   Any date proposed by the landlord under subsection (1)(c) must be a date falling not later than the end of the period of two months beginning with the date of the giving of the notice under section 80.

(3)   Where a relevant person is given a notice under section 79 *requiring him to afford the auditor facilities for inspection or taking copies or extracts in respect of any documents or description of documents specified in the notice, then within the period of one month beginning with the date of the giving of the notice, he shall, in the case of every such document or description of documents, either—*
   (a)   *afford the auditor the facilities required by him; or*
   (b)   *give the auditor a notice stating that he objects to doing so for such reasons as are specified in the notice.*

(4)   If by the end of the period of two months beginning with—
   (a)   the date of the giving of the notice under section 80, or
   (b)   the date of the giving of such a notice under section 79 as is mentioned in subsection (3) above,
the landlord or (as the case may be) a relevant person has failed to comply with any requirement of the notice, the court may, on the application of the auditor, make an order requiring the landlord or (as the case may be) the relevant person to comply with that requirement within such period as is specified in the order.

(5)   The court shall not make an order under subsection (4) in respect of any document or documents unless it is satisfied that the document or documents falls or fall within *paragraph (a) or (b) of section 79(2).*

(6)   If by the end of the period of two months specified in subsection (2) no inspection under section 79(4) has been carried out by the auditor, the court may, on the application of the auditor, make an order providing for such an inspection to be carried out on such date as is specified in the order.

(7)   Any application for an order under subsection (4) or (6) must be made before the end of the period of four months beginning with—
   (a)   in the case of an application made in connection with a notice given under section 80, the date of the giving of that notice; or
   (b)   in the case of an application made in connection with such a notice under section 79 as is mentioned in subsection (3) above, the date of the giving of that notice.

**[884]**

## NOTES

Sub-s (1): paras (a), (b) substituted by the Commonhold and Leasehold Reform Act 2002, s 157, Sch 10, para 18(1), (2), as from a day to be appointed, as follows—

"(a)   comply with it so far as it relates to documents within section 79(2);
(b)   either—
    (i)   comply with it, or
    (ii)   give the auditor a notice stating that he objects to doing so for such reasons as are specified in the notice,
    so far as it relates to documents within section 79(2A); and".

Sub-s (3): for the words in italics there are substituted the following words, by the Commonhold and Leasehold Reform Act 2002, s 157, Sch 10, para 18(1), (3), as from a day to be appointed—

", then within the period of one month beginning with the date of the giving of the notice, he shall either—
(a)   comply with it, or
(b)   give the auditor a notice stating that he objects to doing so for such reasons as are specified in the notice,
in the case of every document or description of document specified in the notice".

Sub-s (5): words in italics substituted by the words "section 79(2) or (2A)" by the Commonhold and Leasehold Reform Act 2002, s 157, Sch 10, para 18(1), (4), as from a day to be appointed.

Modified, where the RTM company has acquired the right to manage, by the Commonhold and Leasehold Reform Act 2002, s 102, Sch 7, para 14 at **[1266]**, **[1306]**.

## 82   Requirement relating to information etc held by superior landlord

*(1)   Where the landlord is required by a notice under section 80 to supply any summary falling within section 79(2)(a), and any information necessary for complying with the notice so far as relating to any such summary is in the possession of a superior landlord—*

*(a)   the landlord shall make a written request for the relevant information to the person who is his landlord (and so on, if that person is himself not the superior landlord);*

*(b)   the superior landlord shall comply with that request within the period of one month beginning with the date of the making of the request; and*

*(c)   the landlord who received the notice shall then comply with it so far as relating to any such summary within the time allowed by section 81(1) or such further time, if any, as is reasonable.*

*(2)   Where—*

*(a)   the landlord is required by a notice under section 80 to afford the auditor facilities for inspection or taking copies or extracts in respect of any documents or description of documents specified in the notice, and*

*(b)   any of the documents in question is in the custody or under the control of a superior landlord,*

*the landlord shall on receiving the notice inform the auditor as soon as may be of that fact and of the name and address of the superior landlord, and the auditor may then give the superior landlord a notice requiring him to afford the facilities in question in respect of the document.*

(3)   Subsections (3) to (5) and (7) of section 81 shall, with any necessary modifications, have effect in relation to a notice given to a superior landlord under subsection (2) above as they have effect in relation to any such notice given to a relevant person as is mentioned in subsection (3) of that section.

**[885]**

## NOTES

Sub-ss (1), (2): substituted by the Commonhold and Leasehold Reform Act 2002, s 157, Sch 10, para 19, as from a day to be appointed, as follows—

"(1)   Where the landlord is given a notice under section 80 imposing on him a requirement relating to any documents which are held by a superior landlord, he shall inform the auditor as soon as may be of that fact and of the name and address of the superior landlord.

(2)   The auditor may then give the superior landlord a notice requiring him to comply with the requirement.".

Modified, where the RTM company has acquired the right to manage, by the Commonhold and Leasehold Reform Act 2002, s 102, Sch 7, para 14 at **[1266]**, **[1306]**.

## 83   Supplementary provisions

(1)   Where—

(a)   a notice has been given to a landlord under section 80, and

(b)   at a time when any obligations arising out of the notice remain to be discharged by him—

    (i)   he disposes of the whole or part of his interest as landlord of the qualifying tenants of the constituent dwellings, and

(ii)    the person acquiring any such interest of the landlord is in a position to discharge any of those obligations to any extent,

that person shall be responsible for discharging those obligations to that extent, as if he had been given the notice under that section.

(2)    If the landlord is, despite any such disposal, still in a position to discharge those obligations to the extent referred to in subsection (1), he shall remain responsible for so discharging them; but otherwise the person referred to in that subsection shall be responsible for so discharging them to the exclusion of the landlord.

(3)    Where a person is so responsible for discharging any such obligations (whether with the landlord or otherwise)

(a)    references to the landlord in section 81 shall be read as including, or as, references to that person to such extent as is appropriate to reflect his responsibility for discharging those obligations; but

(b)    in connection with the discharge of any such obligations by that person, that section shall apply as if any reference to the date of the giving of the notice under section 80 were a reference to the date of the disposal referred to in subsection (1).

(4)    Where—

(a)    a notice has been given to a relevant person under section 79, and

(b)    at a time when any obligations arising out of the notice remain to be discharged by him, he ceases to be a relevant person, but

(c)    he is, despite ceasing to be a relevant person, still in a position to discharge those obligations to any extent,

he shall nevertheless remain responsible for discharging those obligations to that extent; and section 81 shall accordingly continue to apply to him as if he were still a relevant person.

(5)    Where—

(a)    a notice has been given to a landlord under section 80, or

(b)    a notice has been given to a relevant person under section 79,

then during the period of twelve months beginning with the date of that notice, no subsequent such notice may be given to the landlord or (as the case may be) that person on behalf of any persons who, in relation to the earlier notice, were qualifying tenants of the constituent dwellings.

**[886]**

**NOTES**

Modified, where the RTM company has acquired the right to manage, by the Commonhold and Leasehold Reform Act 2002, s 102, Sch 7, para 14 at **[1266]**, **[1306]**.

## 84    Interpretation of Chapter V

In this Chapter—

"the 1985 Act" means the Landlord and Tenant Act 1985;

"appurtenant property" shall be construed in accordance with section 76(3) or (6);

"the auditor", in relation to a management audit, means such a person as is mentioned in section 78(3);

"the constituent dwellings" means the dwellings referred to in section 76(2)(a) or (b) (as the case may be);

"landlord" means immediate landlord;

"management audit" means such an audit as is mentioned in section 78(1);

"management functions" includes functions with respect to the provision of services or the repair, maintenance[, improvement] or insurance of property;

"relevant person" has the meaning given by section 79(7);

"the relevant premises" shall be construed in accordance with section 76(3) or (6);

"service charge" has the meaning given by section 18(1) of the 1985 Act.

**[887]**

**NOTES**

In definition "management functions" word in square brackets inserted by the Commonhold and Leasehold Reform Act 2002, s 150, Sch 9, para 10, except in relation to an application made under s 80 of this Act at **[883]**, before 30 September 2003 (in relation to England) or 31 March 2004 (in relation to Wales).

Modified, where the RTM company has acquired the right to manage, by the Commonhold and Leasehold Reform Act 2002, s 102, Sch 7, para 14 at **[1266]**, **[1306]**.

## CHAPTER VI
## MISCELLANEOUS

**85, 86**    (*S 85 substitutes the Landlord and Tenant Act 1987, s 25 at* **[685]**, *and amends ss 27, 29 of that Act at* **[687]**, **[689]**; *s 86 amends s 35 of that Act at* **[695]**.)

*Codes of practice*

## 87 Approval by Secretary of State of codes of management practice

(1) The Secretary of State may, if he considers it appropriate to do so, by order—

    (a) approve any code of practice—

        (i) which appears to him to be designed to promote desirable practices in relation to any matter or matters directly or indirectly concerned with the management of residential property by relevant persons; and

        (ii) which has been submitted to him for his approval;

    (b) approve any modifications of any such code which have been so submitted; or

    (c) withdraw his approval for any such code or modifications.

(2) The Secretary of State shall not approve any such code or any modifications of any such code unless he is satisfied that arrangements have been made for the text of the code or the modifications to be published in such manner as he considers appropriate for bringing the provisions of the code or the modifications to the notice of those likely to be affected by them (which, in the case of modifications of a code, may include publication of a text of the code incorporating the modifications).

(3) The power of the Secretary of State under this section to approve a code of practice which has been submitted to him for his approval includes power to approve a part of any such code; and references in this section to a code of practice may accordingly be read as including a reference to a part of a code of practice.

(4) At any one time there may be two or more codes of practice for the time being approved under this section.

(5) A code of practice approved under this section may make different provision with respect to different cases or descriptions of cases, including different provision for different areas.

(6) Without prejudice to the generality of subsections (1) and (5)—

    (a) a code of practice approved under this section may, in relation to any such matter as is referred to in subsection (1), make provision in respect of relevant persons who are under an obligation to discharge any function in connection with that matter as well as in respect of relevant persons who are not under such an obligation; and

    (b) any such code may make provision with respect to—

        (i) the resolution of disputes with respect to residential property between relevant persons and the tenants of such property;

        (ii) competitive tendering for works in connection with such property; and

        (iii) the administration of trusts in respect of amounts paid by tenants by way of service charges.

(7) A failure on the part of any person to comply with any provision of a code of practice for the time being approved under this section shall not of itself render him liable to any proceedings; but in any proceedings before a court or tribunal—

    (a) any code of practice approved under this section shall be admissible in evidence; and

    (b) any provision of any such code which appears to the court or tribunal to be relevant to any question arising in the proceedings shall be taken into account in determining that question.

(8) For the purposes of this section—

    (a) "relevant person" means any landlord of residential property or any person who discharges management functions in respect of such property, and for this purpose "management functions" includes functions with respect to the provision of services or the repair, maintenance[, improvement] or insurance of such property;

    (b) "residential property" means any building or part of a building which consists of one or more dwellings let on leases, but references to residential property include—

        (i) any garage, outhouse, garden, yard and appurtenances belonging to or usually enjoyed with such dwellings,

        (ii) any common parts of any such building or part, and

        (iii) any common facilities which are not within any such building or part; and

    (c) "service charge" means an amount payable by a tenant of a dwelling as part of or in addition to the rent—

        (i) which is payable, directly or indirectly, for services, repairs, maintenance[, improvements] or insurance or any relevant person's costs of management, and

        (ii) the whole or part of which varies or may vary according to the costs or estimated costs incurred or to be incurred by any relevant person in connection with the matters mentioned in sub-paragraph (i).

(9) This section applies in relation to dwellings let on licences to occupy as it applies in relation to dwellings let on leases, and references in this section to landlords and tenants of residential property accordingly include references to licensors and licensees of such property.

[888]

**NOTES**

Sub-s (8): words in square brackets inserted by the Commonhold and Leasehold Reform Act 2002, s 159, Sch 9, para 11.

Orders: the Approval of Codes of Management Practice (Residential Property) Order 1996, SI 1996/2839 at **[3149]**; the Approval of Codes of Management Practice (Residential Property) (England) Order 2004, SI 2004/1802 at **[3375]**; the Approval of Code of Management Practice (Private Retirement Housing) (England) Order 2005, SI 2005/3307 at **[3594]**; the Approval of Codes of Management Practice (Residential Property) (Wales) Order 2006, SI 2006/178; the Approval of Code of Practice (Private Retirement Housing) (Wales) Order 2007, SI 2007/578 at **[3753]**; the Approval of Code of Management Practice (Residential Management) (Service Charges) (England) Order 2009, SI 2009/512 at **[3835]**.

*Jurisdiction of leasehold valuation tribunals in relation to enfranchisement etc of Crown land*

**88　Jurisdiction of leasehold valuation tribunals in relation to enfranchisement etc of Crown land**

(1)　This section applies where any tenant under a lease from the Crown is proceeding with a view to acquiring the freehold or an extended lease of a house and premises in circumstances in which, but for the existence of any Crown interest in the land subject to the lease, he would be entitled to acquire the freehold or such an extended lease under Part I of the Leasehold Reform Act 1967.

(2)　Where—

  (a)　this section applies in accordance with subsection (1), and

  (b)　any question arises in connection with the acquisition of the freehold or an extended lease of the house and premises which is such that, if the tenant were proceeding as mentioned in that subsection in pursuance of a claim made under Part I of that Act, a leasehold valuation tribunal … would have jurisdiction to determine it in proceedings under that Part, and

  (c)　it is agreed between—

    (i)　the appropriate authority and the tenant, and

    (ii)　all other persons (if any) whose interests would fall to be represented in proceedings brought under that Part for the determination of that question by such a tribunal,

  that that question should be determined by such a tribunal,

a [leasehold valuation tribunal] constituted for the purposes of this section shall have jurisdiction to determine that question.

(3)–(5)　…

(6)　For the purposes of this section "lease from the Crown" means a lease of land in which there is, or has during the subsistence of the lease been, a Crown interest superior to the lease; and "Crown interest" and "the appropriate authority" in relation to a Crown interest mean respectively—

  (a)　an interest comprised in the Crown Estate, and the Crown Estate Commissioners;

  (b)　an interest belonging to Her Majesty in right of the Duchy of Lancaster, and the Chancellor of the Duchy;

  (c)　an interest belonging to the Duchy of Cornwall, and such person as the Duke of Cornwall or the possessor for the time being of the Duchy appoints;

  (d)　any other interest belonging to a government department or held on behalf of Her Majesty for the purposes of a government department, and the Minister in charge of that department.

(7)　…

**[889]**

**NOTES**

Sub-s (2): words omitted from para (b) repealed and words in square brackets substituted by the Commonhold and Leasehold Reform Act 2002, ss 176, 180, Sch 13, paras 12, 14, Sch 14, except in relation to any application made to an LVT or any proceedings transferred to an LVT by a county court before 30 September 2003 (in relation to England) or 31 March 2004 (in relation to Wales).

Sub-ss (3)–(5), (7): repealed by the Commonhold and Leasehold Reform Act 2002, s 180, Sch 14, subject to savings as noted above.

*Provision of accommodation for persons with mental disorders*

**89　Avoidance of provisions preventing occupation of leasehold property by persons with mental disorders**

(1)　Any agreement relating to a lease of any property which comprises or includes a dwelling (whether contained in the instrument creating the lease or not and whether made before the creation of the lease or not) shall be void in so far as it would otherwise have the effect of prohibiting or imposing any restriction on—

(a)   the occupation of the dwelling, or of any part of the dwelling, by persons with mental disorders (within the meaning of the Mental Health Act 1983), or

(b)   the provision of accommodation within the dwelling for such persons.

(2)   Subsection (1) applies to any agreement made after the coming into force of this section.

**[890]**

## CHAPTER VII
## GENERAL

### 90   Jurisdiction of county courts

(1)   Any jurisdiction expressed to be conferred on the court by this Part shall be exercised by a county court.

(2)   There shall also be brought in a county court any proceedings for determining any question arising under or by virtue of any provision of Chapter I or II or this Chapter which is not a question falling within its jurisdiction by virtue of subsection (1) or one falling within the jurisdiction of a leasehold valuation tribunal by virtue of section 91.

(3)   Where, however, there are brought in the High Court any proceedings which, apart from this subsection, are proceedings within the jurisdiction of the High Court, the High Court shall have jurisdiction to hear and determine any proceedings joined with those proceedings which are proceedings within the jurisdiction of a county court by virtue of subsection (1) or (2).

(4)   Where any proceedings are brought in a county court by virtue of subsection (1) or (2), the court shall have jurisdiction to hear and determine any other proceedings joined with those proceedings, despite the fact that, apart from this subsection, those other proceedings would be outside the court's jurisdiction.

**[891]**

### 91   Jurisdiction of leasehold valuation tribunals

(1)   ... any question arising in relation to any of the matters specified in subsection (2) shall, in default of agreement, be determined by [a leasehold valuation tribunal].

(2)   Those matters are—

(a)   the terms of acquisition relating to—

(i)   any interest which is to be acquired by a *nominee purchaser* in pursuance of Chapter I, or

(ii)   any new lease which is to be granted to a tenant in pursuance of Chapter II, including in particular any matter which needs to be determined for the purposes of any provision of Schedule 6 or 13;

(b)   the terms of any lease which is to be granted in accordance with section 36 and Schedule 9;

(c)   the amount of any payment falling to be made by virtue of section 18(2);

[(ca)  the amount of any compensation payable under section 37A;]

[(cb)  the amount of any compensation payable under section 61A;]

(d)   the amount of any costs payable by any person or persons by virtue of any provision of Chapter I or II and, in the case of costs to which section 33(1) or 60(1) applies, the liability of any person or persons by virtue of any such provision to pay any such costs; and

(e)   the apportionment between two or more persons of any amount (whether of costs or otherwise) payable by virtue of any such provision.

(3)–(8)   ...

(9)   A leasehold valuation tribunal may, when determining the property in which any interest is to be acquired in pursuance of a notice under section 13 or 42, specify in its determination property which is less extensive than that specified in that notice.

(10)   ...

(11)   In this section—

"*the nominee purchaser*" and "*the participating tenants*" have the same meaning as in Chapter I;

"the terms of acquisition" shall be construed in accordance with section 24(8) or section 48(7), as appropriate;

...

**[892]**

---

**NOTES**

Sub-s (1): words omitted repealed and words in square brackets substituted by the Commonhold and Leasehold Reform Act 2002, ss 176, 180, Sch 13, paras 12, 15, Sch 14, except in relation to any application made to an LVT or any proceedings transferred to an LVT by a county court before 30 September 2003 (in relation to England) or 31 March 2004 (in relation to Wales).

Sub-s (2): words in italics in para (a) substituted by the words "RTE company" by the Commonhold and Leasehold Reform Act 2002, s 124, Sch 8, paras 2, 31(1), (2), as from a day to be appointed; paras (ca), (cb) inserted by the Housing Act 1996, s 116, Sch 11, paras 2(2), 3(2).

Sub-ss (3)–(8), (10): repealed by the Commonhold and Leasehold Reform Act 2002, s 180, Sch 14, except in relation to any application made to an LVT or any proceedings transferred to an LVT by a county court before 30 September 2003 (in relation to England) or 31 March 2004 (in relation to Wales).

Sub-s (11): words in italics substituted by the words '"RTE company" has' by the Commonhold and Leasehold Reform Act 2002, s 124, Sch 8, paras 2, 31(1), (3), as from a day to be appointed, and words omitted repealed by s 180 of, and Sch 14 to, that Act, except in relation to any application made to an LVT or any proceedings transferred to an LVT by a county court before 30 September 2003 (in relation to England) or 31 March 2004 (in relation to Wales).

## 92  Enforcement of obligations under Chapters I and II

(1)   The court may, on the application of any person interested, make an order requiring any person who has failed to comply with any requirement imposed on him under or by virtue of any provision of Chapter I or II to make good the default within such time as is specified in the order.

(2)   An application shall not be made under subsection (1) unless—

    (a)    a notice has been previously given to the person in question requiring him to make good the default, and

    (b)    more than 14 days have elapsed since the date of the giving of that notice without his having done so.

[893]

## 93  Agreements excluding or modifying rights of tenant under Chapter I and II

(1)   Except as provided by this section, any agreement relating to a lease (whether contained in the instrument creating the lease or not and whether made before the creation of the lease or not) shall be void in so far as it—

    (a)    purports to exclude or modify—

        (i)    any entitlement to *participate in the making of a claim to exercise* the right to collective enfranchisement under Chapter I,

        (ii)   any right to acquire a new lease under Chapter II, or

        (iii)  any right to compensation under section 61; or

    (b)    provides for the termination or surrender of the lease in the event of the tenant becoming *a participating tenant for the purposes of Chapter I or* giving a notice under section 42; or

    (c)    provides for the imposition of any penalty or disability *on the tenant in that event.*

(2)   Subsection (1) shall not be taken to preclude a tenant from surrendering his lease, and shall not—

    (a)    invalidate any agreement for the acquisition on behalf of a tenant of an interest superior to his lease, or for the acquisition by a tenant of a new lease, on terms different from those provided by Chapters I and II; or

    (b)    where a tenant has *become a participating tenant for the purposes of Chapter I or has* given a notice under section 42, invalidate—

        (i)    any agreement that the notice given under *section 13 or* (*as the case may be*) section 42 shall cease to have effect, or

        (ii)   any provision of such an agreement excluding or restricting for a period not exceeding three years any such *entitlement or* right as is mentioned in subsection (1)(a)(*i*) *or* (ii); or

    (c)    where a tenant's right to compensation under section 61 has accrued, invalidate any agreement as to the amount of the compensation.

(3)   Where—

    (a)    a tenant having the right to acquire a new lease under Chapter II—

        (i)    has entered into an agreement for the surrender of his lease without the prior approval of the court, or

        (ii)   has entered into an agreement for the grant of a new lease without any of the terms of acquisition (within the meaning of that Chapter) having been determined by a leasehold valuation tribunal under that Chapter, or

    (b)    a tenant has been granted a new lease under Chapter II or by virtue of subsection (4) below and, on his landlord claiming possession for the purposes of redevelopment, enters into an agreement without the prior approval of the court for the surrender of the lease,

then on the application of the tenant a county court, or any court in which proceedings are brought on the agreement, may, if in its opinion the tenant is not adequately recompensed under the agreement for his rights under Chapter II, set aside or vary the agreement and give such other relief as appears to it to be just having regard to the situation and conduct of the parties.

(4)   Where a tenant has the right to acquire a new lease under Chapter II, there may with the approval of the court be granted to him in satisfaction of that right a new lease on such terms as may be approved by the court, which may include terms excluding or modifying—

(a)   any entitlement to *participate in the making of a claim to exercise* the right to collective enfranchisement under Chapter I, or

(b)   any right to acquire a further lease under Chapter II.

(5)   Subject to the provisions specified in subsection (6) and to subsection (7), a lease may be granted by virtue of subsection (4), and shall if so granted be binding on persons entitled to any interest in or charge on the landlord's estate—

(a)   despite the fact that, apart from this subsection, it would not be authorised against any such persons, and

(b)   despite any statutory or other restrictions on the landlord's powers of leasing.

(6)   The provisions referred to in subsection (5) are—

(a)   section 36 of the Charities Act 1993 (restrictions on disposition of charity land); and

(b)   paragraph 8(2)(c) of Schedule 2 to this Act.

(7)   Where the existing lease of the tenant is granted after the commencement of Chapter II and, the grant being subsequent to the creation of a charge on the landlord's estate, the existing lease is not binding on the persons interested in the charge, a lease granted by virtue of subsection (4) shall not be binding on those persons.

(8)   Where a lease is granted by virtue of subsection (4), then except in so far as provision is made to the contrary by the terms of the lease, the following provisions shall apply in relation to the lease as they apply in relation to a lease granted under section 56, namely—

(a)   section 58(3), (5) and (6);

(b)   section 59(2) to (5); and

(c)   section 61 and Schedule 14;

and subsections (5) to (7) of section 56 shall apply in relation to the lease as they apply in relation to a lease granted under that section.

[894]

---

**NOTES**

Sub-s (1): words in italics in para (a) substituted by the words "be, or do any thing as, a member of a RTE company for the purpose of the exercise of", words in italics in para (b) substituted by the words ", or doing any thing as, a member of a RTE company (within the meaning of Chapter 1) or of such a RTE company doing any thing or in the event of a tenant" and words in italics in para (c) substituted by the words "in the event of a tenant becoming, or doing any thing as, a member of such a RTE company or of such a RTE company doing any thing" by the Commonhold and Leasehold Reform Act 2002, s 124, Sch 8, paras 2, 32(1), (2), as from a day to be appointed.

Sub-s (2): words in italics repealed by the Commonhold and Leasehold Reform Act 2002, s 180, Sch 14, as from a day to be appointed.

Sub-s (4): words in italics in para (a) substituted by the words "be, or do any thing as, a member of a RTE company for the purpose of the exercise of" by the Commonhold and Leasehold Reform Act 2002, s 124, Sch 8, paras 2, 32(1), (3), as from a day to be appointed.

---

**[93A   Powers of trustees in relation to rights under Chapters I and II**

(1)   Where trustees are a qualifying tenant of a flat for the purposes of Chapter I or II, their powers under the instrument regulating the trusts shall include power to *participate in* the exercise of the right to collective enfranchisement under Chapter I or, as the case may be, to exercise the right to a new lease under Chapter II.

(2)   Subsection (1) shall not apply where the instrument regulating the trusts—

(a)   is made on or after the day on which section 113 of the Housing Act 1996 comes into force, and

(b)   contains an explicit direction to the contrary.

(3)   The powers conferred by subsection (1) shall be extricable with the like consent or on the like direction (if any) as may be required for the exercise of the trustees' powers (or ordinary powers) of investment.

(4)   The following purposes, namely—

(a)   those authorised for the application of capital money by section 73 of the Settled Land Act 1925 ... , and

(b)   those authorised by section 71 of the Settled Land Act 1925 ... as purposes for which moneys may be raised by mortgage,

shall include the payment of any expenses incurred by a tenant for life or statutory owners ... , as the case may be, in or in connection with *participation in* the exercise of the right to collective enfranchisement under Chapter I or in connection with the exercise of the right to a new lease under Chapter II.]

[895]

**NOTES**

Inserted by the Housing Act 1996, s 113, except in relation to a case where, before 1 October 1996, a notice was given under s 13 or 42 of this Act at **[817]**, **[848]**, or an application was made to court under s 26 or 50 of this Act at **[830]**, **[856]**.

Sub-s (1): words in italics substituted by the words "become a member (and participating member) of a RTE company for the purpose of" by the Commonhold and Leasehold Reform Act 2002, s 124, Sch 8, paras 2, 33(1), (2), as from a day to be appointed.

Sub-s (4): words omitted repealed by the Trusts of Land and Appointment of Trustees Act 1996, s 25(2), Sch 4, subject to savings set out in s 25(3), (4) of that Act; words in italics substituted by the words "becoming a member (or participating member) of a RTE company for the purpose of" by the Commonhold and Leasehold Reform Act 2002, s 124, Sch 8, paras 2, 33(1), (3), as from a day to be appointed.

## 94   Crown land

(1)   Subject to subsection (2), Chapters I and II shall apply to a lease from the Crown if (and only if) there has ceased to be a Crown interest in the land subject to it.

[(2)   Chapter 2 applies as against a landlord under a lease from the Crown if—

   (a)    a sub-tenant is seeking a new lease under that Chapter and the landlord, or a superior landlord under a lease from the Crown, is entitled to grant such a new lease without the concurrence of the appropriate authority, or

   (b)    the appropriate authority notifies the landlord that, as regards any Crown interest affected, it will grant or concur in granting such a new lease.]

(3)   The restriction imposed by section 3(2) of the Crown Estate Act 1961 (general provisions as to management) on the term for which a lease may be granted by the Crown Estate Commissioners shall not apply where—

   (a)    the lease is granted by way of renewal of a long lease … , and

   (b)    it appears to the Crown Estate Commissioners that, but for the existence of any Crown interest, there would be a right to acquire a new lease under Chapter II of this Part of this Act.

(4)   Where, in the case of land belonging—

   (a)    to Her Majesty in right of the Duchy of Lancaster, or

   (b)    to the Duchy of Cornwall,

it appears to the appropriate authority that a tenant under a long lease … would, but for the existence of any Crown interest, be entitled to acquire a new lease under Chapter II, then a lease corresponding to that to which the tenant would be so entitled may be granted to take effect wholly or partly out of the Crown interest by the same person and with the same formalities as in the case of any other lease of such land.

(5)   In the case of land belonging to the Duchy of Cornwall, the purposes authorised by section 8 of the Duchy of Cornwall Management Act 1863 for the advancement of parts of such gross sums as are there mentioned shall include the payment to tenants under leases from the Crown of sums corresponding to those which, but for the existence of any Crown interest, would be payable by way of compensation under section 61 above.

(6)   The appropriate authority in relation to any area occupied under leases from the Crown may make an application for the approval under section 70 of a scheme for that area which is designed to secure that, in the event of tenants under those leases acquiring freehold interests in such circumstances as are mentioned in subsection (7) below, the authority will—

   (a)    retain powers of management in respect of the premises in which any such freehold interests are acquired, and

   (b)    have rights against any such premises in respect of the benefits arising from the exercise elsewhere of the authority's powers of management.

(7)   The circumstances mentioned in subsection (6) are circumstances in which, but for the existence of any Crown interest, the tenants acquiring any such freehold interests would be entitled to acquire them as mentioned in section 69(1)(a) or (b).

(8)   Subject to any necessary modifications—

   (a)    subsections (2) to (7) of section 69 shall apply in relation to any such scheme as is mentioned in subsection (6) above as they apply in relation to an estate management scheme; and

   (b)    section 70 shall apply in relation to the approval of such a scheme as it applies in relation to the approval of a scheme as an estate management scheme.

(9)   Subsection (10) applies where—

   (a)    any tenants under leases from the Crown are proceeding with a view to acquiring the freehold of any premises in circumstances in which, but for the existence of any Crown interest, they would be entitled to acquire the freehold under Chapter I, or

   (b)    any tenant under a lease from the Crown is proceeding with a view to acquiring a new lease of his flat in circumstances in which, but for the existence of any Crown interest, he would be entitled to acquire such a lease under Chapter II.

(10) Where—

    (a) this subsection applies in accordance with subsection (9), and

    (b) any question arises in connection with the acquisition of the freehold of those premises or any such new lease which is such that, if the tenants or tenant were proceeding as mentioned in that subsection in pursuance of a claim made under Chapter I or (as the case may be) Chapter II, a leasehold valuation tribunal would have jurisdiction to determine it in proceedings under that Chapter, and

    (c) it is agreed between—

        (i) the appropriate authority and the tenants or tenant, and

        (ii) all other persons (if any) whose interests would fall to be represented in proceedings brought under that Chapter for the determination of that question by a leasehold valuation tribunal,

that that question should be determined by such a tribunal,

a leasehold valuation tribunal shall have jurisdiction to determine that question; ...

(11) For the purposes of this section "lease from the Crown" means a lease of land in which there is, or has during the subsistence of the lease been, a Crown interest superior to the lease; and "Crown interest" and "the appropriate authority" in relation to a Crown interest mean respectively—

    (a) an interest comprised in the Crown Estate, and the Crown Estate Commissioners;

    (b) an interest belonging to Her Majesty in right of the Duchy of Lancaster, and the Chancellor of the Duchy;

    (c) an interest belonging to the Duchy of Cornwall, and such person as the Duke of Cornwall or the possessor for the time being of the Duchy appoints;

    (d) any other interest belonging to a government department or held on behalf of Her Majesty for the purposes of a government department, and the Minister in charge of that department.

[(12) For the purposes of this section "long lease ..." shall be construed in accordance with sections 7 ... ]

**[896]**

---

**NOTES**

Sub-s (2): substituted by the Commonhold and Leasehold Reform Act 2002, s 133.

Sub-ss (3), (4): words omitted repealed by the Commonhold and Leasehold Reform Act 2002, s 180, Sch 14, except in relation to an application for a new lease of a flat in respect of which notice was given under s 42 of this Act at **[848]**, or where an application was made for an order under s 50 of this Act at **[856]**, before 26 July 2002 (in relation to England) or 1 January 2003 (in relation to Wales).

Sub-s (10): words omitted repealed by the Commonhold and Leasehold Reform Act 2002, s 180, Sch 14, except in relation to any application made to an LVT or any proceedings transferred to an LVT by a county court before 30 September 2003 (in relation to England) or 31 March 2004 (in relation to Wales).

Sub-s (12): substituted by the Housing Act 1996, s 106, Sch 9, para 5(1), (4), except in relation to a case where, before 1 April 1997, a notice was given under s 13 or 42 of this Act at **[817]**, **[848]**, or an application was made to court under s 26 or 50 of this Act at **[830]**, **[856]**; words omitted repealed by the Commonhold and Leasehold Reform Act 2002, s 180, Sch 14, subject to savings as noted to sub-ss (3), (4) above.

---

### 95 Saving for National Trust

Chapters I and II shall not prejudice the operation of section 21 of the National Trust Act 1907, and accordingly there shall be no right under Chapter I or II to acquire any interest in or new lease of any property if an interest in the property is under that section vested inalienably in the National Trust for Places of Historic Interest or Natural Beauty.

**[897]**

### 96 Property within cathedral precinct

There shall be no right under Chapter I or II to acquire any interest in or lease of any property which for the purposes of the Care of Cathedrals Measure 1990 is within the precinct of a cathedral church.

**[898]**

### 97 Registration of notices, applications and orders under Chapters I and II

(1) No lease shall be registrable under the Land Charges Act 1972 or be taken to be an estate contract within the meaning of that Act by reason of any rights or obligations of *the tenant* or landlord which may arise under Chapter I or II, and any right of *a tenant* arising from a notice given under section 13 or 42 shall not be [capable of falling within paragraph 2 of Schedule 1 or 3 to the Land Registration Act 2002]; but a notice given under section 13 or 42 shall be registrable under the Land Charges Act 1972, or may be the subject of a notice [under the Land Registration Act 2002], as if it were an estate contract.

(2) The Land Charges Act 1972 and the [Land Registration Act 2002]—

PART I
STATUTES

(a)    shall apply in relation to an order made under section 26(1) or 50(1) as they apply in relation to an order affecting land which is made by the court for the purpose of enforcing a judgment or recognisance; and

(b)    shall apply in relation to an application for such an order as they apply in relation to other pending land actions.

(3)    ...

**[899]**

**NOTES**

Sub-s (1): words "the tenant" in italics substituted by the words "a RTE company, tenant" and words "a tenant" in italics substituted by the words "a RTE company or tenant" by the Commonhold and Leasehold Reform Act 2002, s 124, Sch 8, paras 2, 34, as from a day to be appointed; words in square brackets substituted by the Land Registration Act 2002, s 133, Sch 11, para 30(1), (3).

Sub-s (2): words in square brackets substituted by the Land Registration Act 2002, s 133, Sch 11, para 30(1), (4).

Sub-s (3): repealed by the Land Registration Act 2002, s 135, Sch 13.

## 98   Power to prescribe procedure under Chapters I and II

(1)    Where a claim to exercise the right to collective enfranchisement under Chapter I is made by the giving of a notice under section 13, or a claim to exercise the right to acquire a new lease under Chapter II is made by the giving of a notice under section 42, then except as otherwise provided by Chapter I or (as the case may be) Chapter II—

(a)    the procedure for giving effect to the notice, and

(b)    the rights and obligations of all parties in relation to the investigation of title and other matters arising in giving effect to the notice,

shall be such as may be prescribed by regulations made by the Secretary of State and, subject to or in the absence of provision made by any such regulations, shall be as nearly as may be the same as in the case of a contract of sale or leasing freely negotiated between the parties.

(2)    Regulations under this section may, in particular, make provision—

(a)    for a person to be discharged from performing any obligations arising out of a notice under section 13 or 42 by reason of the default or delay of some other person;

(b)    for the payment of a deposit—

(i)    by a *nominee purchaser* (within the meaning of Chapter I) on exchange of contracts, or

(ii)    by a tenant who has given a notice under section 42; and

(c)    with respect to the following matters, namely—

(i)    the person with whom any such deposit is to be lodged and the capacity in which any such person is to, hold it, and

(ii)    the circumstances in which the whole or part of any such deposit is to be returned or forfeited.

**[900]**

**NOTES**

Sub-s (2): words in italics in para (b) substituted by the words "RTE company" by the Commonhold and Leasehold Reform Act 2002, s 124, Sch 8, paras 2, 35, as from a day to be appointed.

Regulations: the Leasehold Reform (Collective Enfranchisement and Lease Renewal) Regulations 1993, SI 1993/2407 at **[3100]**.

## 99   Notices

(1)    Any notice required or authorised to be given under this Part—

(a)    shall be in writing; and

(b)    may be sent by post.

(2)    Where in accordance with Chapter I or II an address in England and Wales is specified as an address at which notices may be given to any person or persons under that Chapter—

(a)    any notice required or authorised to be given to that person or those persons under that Chapter may (without prejudice to the operation of subsection (3)) be given to him or them at the address so specified; but

(b)    if a new address in England and Wales is so specified in substitution for that address by the giving of a notice to that effect, any notice so required or authorised to be given may be given to him or them at that new address instead.

(3)    Where a tenant is required or authorised to give any notice under Chapter I or II to a person who

(a)    is the tenant's immediate landlord, and

(b)    is such a landlord in respect of premises to which Part VI of the Landlord and Tenant Act 1987 (information to be furnished to tenants) applies, the tenant may, unless he has been subsequently notified by the landlord of a different address in England and Wales for the purposes of this section, give the notice to the landlord—

    (i)    at the address last furnished to the tenant as the landlord's address for service in accordance with section 48 of that Act (notification of address for service of notices on landlord); or

    (ii)    if no such address has been furnished, at the address last furnished to the tenant as the landlord's address in accordance with section 47 of that Act (landlord's name and address to be contained in demands for rent).

(4)    Subsections (2) and (3) apply to notices in proceedings under Chapter I or II as they apply to notices required or authorised to be given under that Chapter.

(5)    Any notice which is given under Chapter I or II by any tenants or tenant must—

    (a)    if it is a notice given under section *13 or* 42, be signed *by each of the tenants, or* (*as the case may be*) by the tenant, by whom it is given; and

    (b)    in any other case, be signed by or on behalf of each of the tenants, or (as the case may be) by or on behalf of the tenant, by whom it is given.

(6)    The Secretary of State may by regulations prescribe—

    (a)    the form of any notice required or authorised to be given under this Part; and

    (b)    the particulars which any such notice must contain (whether in addition to, or in substitution for, any particulars required by virtue of any provision of this Part).

**[901]**

**NOTES**

Sub-s (5): words in italics repealed by the Commonhold and Leasehold Reform Act 2002, s 180, Sch 14, as from a day to be appointed.

Regulations: the Leasehold Reform (Collective Enfranchisement) (Counter-notices) (England) Regulations 2002, SI 2002/3208 at **[3271]**; the Leasehold Reform (Collective Enfranchisement) (Counter-notices) (Wales) Regulations 2003, SI 2003/990 at **[3280]**.

## 100  Orders and regulations

(1)    Any power of the Secretary of State to make orders or regulations under this Part—

    (a)    may be so exercised as to make different provision for different cases or descriptions of cases, including different provision for different areas; and

    (b)    includes power to make such procedural, incidental, supplementary and transitional provision as may appear to the Secretary of State necessary or expedient.

(2)    Any power of the Secretary of State to make orders or regulations under this Part shall be exercisable by statutory instrument which (except in the case of regulations making only such provision as is mentioned in section 99(6)) shall be subject to annulment in pursuance of a resolution of either House of Parliament.

**[902]**

## 101  General interpretation of Part I

(1)    In this Part—

"business lease" means a tenancy to which Part II of the Landlord and Tenant Act 1954 applies;

"common parts", in relation to any building or part of a building, includes the structure and exterior of that building or part and any common facilities within it;

"the court" (unless the context otherwise requires) means, by virtue of section 90(1), a county court;

"disposal" means a disposal whether by the creation or the transfer of an interest, and includes the surrender of a lease and the grant of an option or right of pre-emption, and "acquisition" shall be construed accordingly (as shall expressions related to either of these expressions);

"dwelling" means any building or part of a building occupied or intended to be occupied as a separate dwelling;

"flat" means a separate set of premises (whether or not on the same floor)—

    (a)    which forms part of a building, and

    (b)    which is constructed or adapted for use for the purposes of a dwelling, and

    (c)    either the whole or a material part of which lies above or below some other part of the building;

"interest" includes estate;

"lease" and "tenancy", and related expressions, shall be construed in accordance with subsection (2);

...

"the term date", in relation to a lease granted for a term of years certain, means (subject to subsection (6)) the date of expiry of that term, and, in relation to a tenancy to which any of the provisions of section 102 applies, shall be construed in accordance with those provisions.

(2)  In this Part "lease" and "tenancy" have the same meaning, and both expressions include (where the context so permits)—

(a)  a sub-lease or sub-tenancy, and

(b)  an agreement for a lease or tenancy (or for a sub-lease or sub-tenancy),

but do not include a tenancy at will or at sufferance; and the expressions "landlord" and "tenant", and references to letting, to the grant of a lease or to covenants or the terms of a lease, shall be construed accordingly.

(3)  In this Part any reference (however expressed) to the lease held by a qualifying tenant of a flat is a reference to a lease held by him under which the demised premises consist of or include the flat (whether with or without one or more other flats).

(4)  Where two or more persons jointly constitute either the landlord or the tenant or qualifying tenant in relation to a lease of a flat, any reference in this Part to the landlord or to the tenant or qualifying tenant is (unless the context otherwise requires) a reference to both or all of the persons who jointly constitute the landlord or the tenant or qualifying tenant, as the case may require.

(5)  Any reference in this Part to the date of the commencement of a lease is a reference to the date of the commencement of the term of the lease.

(6)  In the case of a lease which derives (in accordance with section 7(6)) from more than one separate leases, references in this Part to the date of the commencement of the lease or to the term date shall, if the terms of the separate leases commenced at different dates or those leases have different term dates, have effect as references to the date of the commencement, or (as the case may be) to the term date, of the lease comprising the flat in question (or the earliest date of commencement or earliest term date of the leases comprising it).

(7)  For the purposes of this Part property is let with other property if the properties are let either under the same lease or under leases which, in accordance with section 7(6), are treated as a single lease.

(8)  For the purposes of this Part any lease which is reversionary on another lease shall be treated as if it were a concurrent lease intermediate between that other lease and any interest superior to that other lease.

(9)  For the purposes of this Part an order of a court or a decision of a leasehold valuation tribunal is to be treated as becoming final—

(a)  if not appealed against, on the expiry of the time for bringing an appeal; or

(b)  if appealed against and not set aside in consequence of the appeal, at the time when the appeal and any further appeal is disposed of—

(i)  by the determination of it and the expiry of the time for bringing a further appeal (if any), or

(ii)  by its being abandoned or otherwise ceasing to have effect.

**NOTES**

Sub-s (1): definition "rent assessment committee" repealed by the Commonhold and Leasehold Reform Act 2002, s 180, Sch 14, except in relation to any application made to an LVT or any proceedings transferred to an LVT by a county court before 30 September 2003 (in relation to England) or 31 March 2004 (in relation to Wales).

**[903]**

## 102  Term date and other matters relating to periodical tenancies

(1)  Where either of the following provisions (which relate to continuation tenancies) applies to a tenancy, namely—

(a)  section 19(2) of the Landlord and Tenant Act 1954 ("the 1954 Act"), or

(b)  paragraph 16(2) of Schedule 10 to the Local Government and Housing Act 1989 ("the 1989 Act"),

the tenancy shall be treated for the relevant purposes of this Part as granted to expire—

(i)  on the date which is the term date for the purposes of the 1954 Act (namely, the first date after the commencement of the 1954 Act on which, apart from the 1954 Act, the tenancy could have been brought to an end by a notice to quit given by the landlord under the tenancy), or

(ii)  on the date which is the term date for the purposes of Schedule 10 to the 1989 Act (namely, the first date after the commencement of Schedule 10 to the 1989 Act on which, apart from that Schedule, the tenancy could have been brought to an end by such a notice to quit),

as the case may be.

(2)  Subject to subsection (1), where under section 7(3) a tenancy created or arising as a tenancy from year to year or other periodical tenancy is to be treated as a long lease, then for the relevant purposes of this Part, the term date of that tenancy shall be taken to be the date (if any) on which the tenancy is to terminate by virtue of a notice to quit given by the landlord under the tenancy before

the relevant date for those purposes, or else the earliest date on which it could as at that date (in accordance with its terms and apart from any enactment) be brought to an end by such a notice to quit.

(3) Subject to subsection (1), in the case of a tenancy granted to continue as a periodical tenancy after the expiry of a term of years certain, or to continue as a periodical tenancy if not terminated at the expiry of such a term, any question whether the tenancy is at any time to be treated for the relevant purposes of this Part as a long lease, and (if so) with what term date, shall be determined as it would be if there had been two tenancies, as follows—

    (a)    one granted to expire at the earliest time (at or after the expiry of that term of years certain) at which the tenancy could (in accordance with its terms and apart from any enactment) be brought to an end by a notice to quit given by the landlord under the tenancy; and

    (b)    the other granted to commence at the expiry of the first (and not being one to which subsection (1) applies).

(4) In this section "the relevant purposes of this Part" means the purposes of Chapter I or, to the extent that section 7 has effect for the purposes of Chapter II in accordance with section 39(3), the purposes of that Chapter.

**[904]**

### 103 Application of Part I to Isles of Scilly

This Part applies to the Isles of Scilly subject to such exceptions, adaptations and modifications as the Secretary of State may by order direct.

**[905]**

## PART II
## PUBLIC SECTOR HOUSING

### CHAPTER I
### ENGLAND AND WALES

**104–106**     *(S 104 substitutes the Housing Act 1985, s 125(5) at* **[471]***; s 105 inserts ss 125D, 125E of that Act at* **[475]**, **[476]** *and substitutes s 136(2)–(5) of that Act at* **[485]***; s 106 amends Sch 5 to that Act at* **[584]***.)*

*Abolition of certain ancillary rights*

### 107 Abolition of right to a mortgage, right to defer completion and right to be granted a shared ownership lease

The following rights ancillary to the right to buy are hereby abolished, namely—

    (a)    the right to a mortgage conferred by sections 132 to 135 of the 1985 Act;

    (b)    the right to defer completion conferred by section 142 of that Act; and

    (c)    the right to be granted a shared ownership lease conferred by sections 143 to 151 of that Act.

**[906]**

**NOTES**

    1985 Act: Housing Act 1985. Ss 132–135, 142 are repealed by s 187(2) of, and Sch 22 to, this Act. Ss 143–151, as originally enacted, are replaced by new provisions introduced by this Act (ie, ss 143, 143A, 143B, 144, 146, 146A, 146B, 147–151, 151A, 151B at **[495]**–**[508]**).

**108–125**     *(Ss 108–123 amend the Housing Act 1985 at* **[415]** *et seq, and these amendments have been incorporated at the appropriate place in this work; s 124(1)–(3) amend the Housing Act 1988, ss 79(2), 84; s 124(4)–(6) repealed by the Housing Act 1996, s 227, Sch 19, Pt IX; s 125 amends the Housing Act 1988, s 84 and inserts s 84A of that Act.)*

*Housing welfare services*

**126, 127**     *(Outside the scope of this work.)*

### 128 Power to repeal provisions made by sections 126 and 127

(1) The Secretary of State may at any time by order made by statutory instrument provide that, on such day or in relation to such periods as may be appointed by the order, the provisions made by sections 126 and 127—

    (a)    shall cease to have effect; or

    (b)    shall cease to apply for such purposes as may be specified in the order.

(2) An order under this section—

(a)    may appoint different days or periods for different provisions or purposes or for different authorities or descriptions of authority, and

(b)    may contain such incidental, supplementary or transitional provisions as appear to the Secretary of State to be necessary or expedient.

**[907]**

**NOTES**

Orders: the Housing (Welfare Services) Order 1994, SI 1994/42; the Housing (Welfare Services) (Wales) Order 1995, SI 1995/2720.

**129–134**    (*S 129, 132, 133 outside the scope of this work; ss 130, 131, 134 repealed by the Housing Act 1996, s 227, Sch 19.*)

*Disposals of dwelling-houses by local authorities*

**135**    (*Repealed by the Housing and Regeneration Act 2008, ss 311, 321(1), Sch 14, para 3(1), (2), Sch 16.*)

**136  Levy on disposals**

(1)    For the purposes of this section a disposal of one or more dwelling-houses by a local authority to any person is a qualifying disposal if—

    (a)    it requires the consent of the Secretary of State under section 32 of the 1985 Act (power to dispose of land held for the purposes of Part II), or section 43 of that Act (consent required for certain disposals not within section 32); and

    (b)    the aggregate of the following, namely—

        (i)    the number of dwelling-houses included in the disposal; and

        (ii)    the number of dwelling-houses which, within any relevant period, have been previously or are subsequently disposed of by the authority to that person, or that person and any associates of his taken together,

    exceeds 499 or, if the Secretary of State by order so provides, such other number as may be specified in the order.

(2)    In subsection (1) "relevant period" means—

    (a)    any period of five years beginning after the commencement of this section and including the date of the disposal; or

    (b)    if the Secretary of State by order so provides, any such other period beginning after that commencement and including that date as may be specified in the order.

(3)    A local authority which after the commencement of this section makes a disposal which is or includes, or which subsequently becomes or includes, a qualifying disposal shall be liable to pay to the Secretary of State a levy of an amount calculated in accordance with the formula—

$$L = (CR - D) \times P$$

where—

L = the amount of the levy;

[CR = the aggregate of—

        (i)    any sums received by the authority in respect of the disposal which are capital receipts for the purposes of Chapter 1 of Part 1 of the Local Government Act 2003 (capital finance etc) and do not fall within a description determined by the Secretary of State; and

        (ii)    any capital receipts which the authority is treated as having by virtue of the application, in relation to the disposal, of regulations under section 10 of the Local Government Act 2003 (power to make provision about disposal consideration not received by the person making the disposal or not received in the form of money).]

D = such amount as may be calculated in accordance with such formula as the Secretary of State may determine;

P = 20 per cent or, if the Secretary of State by order so provides, such other percentage as may be specified in the order.

(4)    A formula determined for the purposes of item D in subsection (3) may include any variable which is included in a determination made for the purposes of section 80 of the 1989 Act (calculation of Housing Revenue Account subsidy).

[(4A)    The power of the Secretary of State to determine a formula for the purposes of item D in subsection (3) shall include power to determine that, in such cases as he may determine, item D is to be taken to be equal to item CR.]

(5)    The administrative arrangements for the payment of any levy under this section shall be such as may be specified in a determination made by the Secretary of State, and such a determination may in particular make provision as to—

(a)   the information to be supplied by authorities;

(b)   the form and manner in which, and the time within which, the information is to be supplied;

(c)   the payment of the levy in stages in such circumstances as may be provided in the determination;

(d)   the date on which payment of the levy (or any stage payment of the levy) is to be made;

(e)   the adjustment of any levy which has been paid in such circumstances as may be provided in the determination;

(f)   the payment of interest in such circumstances as may be provided in the determination; and

(g)   the rate or rates (whether fixed or variable, and whether or not calculated by reference to some other rate) at which such interest is to be payable;

and any such administrative arrangements shall be binding on local authorities.

(6)   Any amounts by way of levy or interest which are not paid to the Secretary of State as required by the arrangements mentioned in subsection (5) shall be recoverable in a court of competent jurisdiction.

(7)–(9)   ...

(10)   Any sums received by the Secretary of State under this section shall be paid into the Consolidated Fund; and any sums paid by the Secretary of State by way of adjustment of levies paid under this section shall be paid out of money provided by Parliament.

(11)   Before making an order or determination under this section, the Secretary of State shall consult such representatives of local government as appear to him to be appropriate.

(12)   An order ... under this section—

(a)   shall be made by statutory instrument which shall be subject to annulment in pursuance of a resolution of either House of Parliament;

(b)   may make different provision for different cases or descriptions of case, or for different authorities or descriptions of authority; and

(c)   may contain such transitional and supplementary provisions as the Secretary of State considers necessary or expedient.

(13)   Any determination under this section—

(a)   may make different provision for different cases or descriptions of case, or for different authorities or descriptions of authority; and

(b)   may be varied or revoked by a subsequent determination.

[(14)   In this section—

"the 1989 Act" means the Local Government and Housing Act 1989;

"dwelling-house" has the same meaning as in Part 5 of the 1985 Act except that it does not include a hostel (as defined in section 622 of that Act) or any part of a hostel;

"local authority" has the meaning given by section 4 of that Act;

"long lease" means a lease for a term of years certain exceeding 21 years other than a lease which is terminable before the end of that term by notice given by or to the landlord;

"subsidiary" has the same meaning as in section 61 of the Housing Act 1996 but as if references in subsection (2) of that section and section 60 of that Act to registered social landlords and landlords were references to housing associations (within the meaning of the Housing Associations Act 1985).

(15)   For the purposes of this section—

(a)   a disposal of any dwelling-house is to be disregarded if at the time of the disposal the local authority's interest in the dwelling-house is or was subject to a long lease;

(b)   two persons are associates of each other if—

(i)   one of them is a subsidiary of the other;

(ii)   they are both subsidiaries of some other person; or

(iii)   there exists between them such relationship or other connection as may be specified in a determination made by the Secretary of State; and

(c)   a description of authority may be framed by reference to any circumstances whatever.]

**[908]**

**NOTES**

Sub-s (3): definition "CR" substituted by the Local Authorities (Capital Finance) (Consequential, Transitional and Saving Provisions) Order 2004, SI 2004/533, art 5(a).

Sub-s (4A): inserted by the Finance Act 1997, s 109, and is deemed always to have had effect.

Sub-ss (7)–(9): repealed by SI 2004/533, art 5(b).

Sub-s (12): words omitted repealed by SI 2004/533, art 5(c).

Sub-ss (14), (15): substituted for original sub-s (14), by the Housing and Regeneration Act 2008, s 311, Sch 14, para 3(1), (3), (5).

1985 Act: Housing Act 1985.

### 137 Disposals: transitional provisions

(1)–(3)  …

(4)   If before the commencement of section 136 any statement was made by or on behalf of the Secretary of State—

(a)   that, if that section were then in force, he would make under that section such determinations as are set out in the statement, and

(b)   that, when that section comes into force, he is to be regarded as having made under that section the determinations set out in the statement,

those determinations shall have effect as if they had been validly made under that section at the time of the statement.

(5)   Any consultation undertaken—

(a)   before the commencement of section 136,

(b)   before the making of such a statement as is mentioned in subsection (4), and

(c)   in connection with determinations proposed to be set out in the statement,

shall be as effective, in relation to those determinations, as if that section had been in force at the time the consultation was undertaken.

**[909]**

**NOTES**

Sub-ss (1)–(3): repealed by the Housing and Regeneration Act 2008, ss 311, 321(1), Sch 14, para 3(1), (4), Sch 16.

*Expenses on defective housing*

**138**   (*Amends the Local Government and Housing Act 1989, s 157.*)

### 139 Contributions in respect of certain pre-April 1989 expenses

(1)   Where—

(a)   before 1st April 1989 a local housing authority incurred any such expense as is referred to in subsection (1) of section 569 of the 1985 Act (assistance by way of reinstatement grant, repurchase or payments for owners of defective housing); and

(b)   before 1st January 1993, the Secretary of State has not made in respect of that expense any contribution of such a description as is referred to in subsection (2) of that section, as amended by section 157(8) of the Local Government and Housing Act 1989 (single commuted contributions),

any contributions in respect of that expense which are made under section 569 on or after 1st January 1993 shall be annual payments calculated and payable in accordance with the following provisions of this section.

(2)   The amount of the annual payment in respect of any relevant financial year shall be a sum equal to the relevant percentage of the annual loan charges referable to the amount of the expense incurred.

(3)   Notwithstanding that annual loan charges are calculated by reference to a 20 year period, annual payments made by virtue of this section shall be made only in respect of relevant financial years ending at or before the end of the period of 20 years beginning with the financial year in which, as the case may be—

(a)   the work in respect of which the reinstatement grant was payable was completed;

(b)   the acquisition of the interest concerned was completed; or

(c)   the payment referred to in subsection (1)(c) of section 569 was made.

(4)   Subsections (3) and (4) of section 569 (which determine the relevant percentage and the amount of the expense incurred) apply for the purposes of the preceding provisions of this section as they apply for the purposes of that section.

(5)   Nothing in this section affects the operation of subsection (6) of section 569 (terms etc for payment of contributions).

(6)   In this section—

"the annual loan charges referable to the amount of the expense incurred" means the annual sum which, in the opinion of the Secretary of State, would fall to be provided by a local housing authority for the payment of interest on, and the repayment of, a loan of that amount repayable over a period of 20 years;

"relevant financial year" means the financial year beginning on 1st April 1991 and each successive financial year.

(7)   This section shall be deemed to have come into force on 1st January 1993.

**[910]**

**NOTES**
1985 Act: the Housing Act 1985.

**140–185** *(S 140 amends the Local Government and Housing Act 1989, s 80; ss 141–157 in so far as unrepealed apply to Scotland only; ss 158–185 (Pt III) in so far as unrepealed outside the scope of this work.)*

## PART IV
## SUPPLEMENTAL

### 186 Financial provisions

(1) There shall be paid out of money provided by Parliament—
  (a) any expenses of the Secretary of State incurred in consequence of this Act; and
  (b) any increase attributable to this Act in the sums payable out of money so provided under any other enactment.

(2) There shall be paid into the Consolidated Fund any increase attributable to this Act in the sums payable into that Fund under any other enactment.

**[911]**

### 187 Amendments and repeals

(1) The enactments mentioned in Schedule 21 to this Act shall have effect subject to the amendments there specified (being minor amendments and amendments consequential on the provisions of this Act).

(2) The enactments mentioned in Schedule 22 to this Act (which include some that are spent or no longer of practical utility) are hereby repealed to the extent specified in the third column of that Schedule.

**[912]**

### 188 Short title, commencement and extent

(1) This Act may be cited as the Leasehold Reform, Housing and Urban Development Act 1993.

(2) This Act, except—
  (a) this section;
  (b) sections 126 and 127, 135 to 140, 149 to 151, 181(1), (2) and (4) and 186; and
  (c) the repeal in section 80(1) of the Local Government and Housing Act 1989,
shall come into force on such day as the Secretary of State may by order made by statutory instrument appoint; and different days may be so appointed for different provisions or for different purposes.

(3) An order under subsection (2) may contain such transitional provisions and savings (whether or not involving the modification of any statutory provision) as appear to the Secretary of State necessary or expedient in connection with the provisions thereby brought into force by the order.

(4) The following, namely—
  (a) Part I of this Act;
  (b) Chapter I of Part II of this Act; and
  (c) subject to subsection (6), Part III of this Act,
extend to England and Wales only.

(5) Chapter II of Part II of this Act extends to Scotland only.

(6) In Part III of this Act—
  (a) sections … 179 and 180 also extend to Scotland; …
  (b) …

(7) This Part, except this section, paragraph 3 of Schedule 21 and the repeals in the House of Commons Disqualification Act 1975 and the Northern Ireland Assembly Disqualification Act 1975, does not extend to Northern Ireland.

**[913]**

**NOTES**
Sub-s (6): figure omitted from para (a) repealed by the Housing Grants, Construction and Regeneration Act 1996, s 147, Sch 3, Pt III; para (b) and word immediately preceding it repealed by the Housing and Regeneration Act 2008, ss 56, 321(1), Sch 8, para 63(1), (3), Sch 16, subject to transitional provisions and savings in SI 2008/3068, arts 6–10 at **[3834B]–[3834F]**.
  Orders: the Leasehold Reform, Housing and Urban Development Act 1993 (Commencement and Transitional Provisions No 1) Order 1993, SI 1993/2134; the Leasehold Reform, Housing and Urban Development Act 1993 (Commencement No 2) (Scotland) Order 1993, SI 1993/2163; the Leasehold Reform, Housing and Urban

Development Act 1993 (Commencement and Transitional Provisions No 3) Order 1993, SI 1993/2762; the Leasehold Reform, Housing and Urban Development Act 1993 (Commencement No 4) Order 1994, SI 1994/935.

## SCHEDULES

### SCHEDULE 1
## CONDUCT OF PROCEEDINGS BY REVERSIONER ON BEHALF OF OTHER LANDLORDS
Section 9

### PART I
### THE REVERSIONER

#### *Freeholder to be reversioner*

1.   Subject to paragraphs 2 to 4, [in a case to which section 9(2) applies,] the reversioner in respect of any premises is the person who owns the freehold of those premises.

#### *Replacement of freeholder by other relevant landlord*

2.   The court may, on the application of all the relevant landlords of any premises, appoint to be the reversioner in respect of those premises (in place of the person designated by paragraph 1) such person as may have been determined by agreement between them.

3.   If it appears to the court, on the application of a relevant landlord of any premises—
   (a)   that the respective interests of the relevant landlords of those premises, the absence or incapacity of the person referred to in paragraph 1 or other special circumstances require that some person other than the person there referred to should act as the reversioner in respect of the premises, or
   (b)   that the person referred to in that paragraph is unwilling to act as the reversioner,
the court may appoint to be the reversioner in respect of those premises (in place of the person designated by paragraph 1) such person as it thinks fit.

4.   The court may also, on the application of any of the relevant landlords or of the *nominee purchaser*, remove the reversioner in respect of any premises and appoint another person in his place, if it appears to the court proper to do so by reason of any delay or default, actual or apprehended, on the part of the reversioner.

5.   A person appointed by the court under any of paragraphs 2 to 4—
   (a)   must be a relevant landlord; but
   (b)   may be so appointed on such terms and conditions as the court thinks fit.

**[914]**

**NOTES**
   Para 1: words in square brackets inserted by the Housing Act 1996, s 107(4), Sch 10, paras 1, 14, except in relation to a case where, before 1 October 1996, a notice was given under s 13 or 42 of this Act at **[817]**, **[848]**, or an application was made to court under s 26 or 50 of this Act at **[830]**, **[856]**.
   Para 4: words in italics substituted by the words "RTE company" by the Commonhold and Leasehold Reform Act 2002, s 124, Sch 8, paras 2, 36(1), (2), as from a day to be appointed.

### [PART IA
### THE REVERSIONER: PREMISES WITH MULTIPLE FREEHOLDERS

#### *Initial reversioner*

5A.   Subject to paragraphs 5B to 5D, in a case to which section 9(2A) applies, the reversioner in respect of any premises is the person specified in the initial notice in accordance with section 13(2A) as the recipient.

#### *Change of reversioner*

5B.   The court may, on the application of all the relevant landlords of any premises, appoint to be the reversioner in respect of those premises (in place of the person designated by paragraph 5A) such person as may have been determined by agreement between them.

5C.   If it appears to the court, on the application of a relevant landlord of any premises—
   (a)   that the respective interests of the relevant landlords of those premises, the absence or incapacity of the person referred to in paragraph 5A or other special circumstances require that some person other than the person there referred to should act as the reversioner in respect of the premises, or
   (b)   that the person referred to in that paragraph is unwilling to act as the reversioner,
the court may appoint to be the reversioner in respect of those premises (in place of the person designated by paragraph 5A) such person as it thinks fit.

5D.   The court may also, on the application of any of the relevant landlords or of the *nominee purchaser*, remove the reversioner in respect of any premises and appoint another person in his place, if it appears to the court proper to do so by reason of any delay or default, actual or apprehended, on the part of the reversioner.

5E.   A person appointed by the court under any of paragraphs 5B to 5D—
   (a)   must be a relevant landlord; but
   (b)   may be so appointed on such terms and conditions as the court thinks fit.]

**[915]**

**NOTES**
   Inserted by the Housing Act 1996, s 107(4), Sch 10, paras 1, 15, except in relation to a case where, before 1 October 1996, a notice was given under s 13 or 42 of this Act at **[817]**, **[848]**, or an application was made to court under s 26 or 50 of this Act at **[830]**, **[856]**.
   Para 5D: words in italics substituted by the words "RTE company" by the Commonhold and Leasehold Reform Act 2002, s 124, Sch 8, paras 2, 36(1), (2), as from a day to be appointed.

## PART II
## CONDUCT OF PROCEEDINGS ON BEHALF OF OTHER LANDLORDS

### *Acts of reversioner binding on other landlords*
6.—(1)   Without prejudice to the generality of section 9(3)—
   (a)   any notice given by or to the reversioner under this Chapter or section 74(3) following the giving of the initial notice shall be given or received by him on behalf of all the relevant landlords; and
   (b)   the reversioner may on behalf and in the name of all or (as the case may be) any of those landlords—
      (i)   deduce, evidence or verify the title to any property;
      (ii)   negotiate and agree with the *nominee purchaser* the terms of acquisition;
      (iii)   execute any conveyance for the purpose of transferring an interest to the *nominee purchaser*;
      (iv)   receive the price payable for the acquisition of any interest;
      (v)   take or defend any legal proceedings under this Chapter in respect of matters arising out of the initial notice.

   (2)   Subject to paragraph 7—
   (a)   the reversioner's acts in relation to matters within the authority conferred on him by section 9(3), and
   (b)   any determination of the court or a leasehold valuation tribunal under this Chapter in proceedings between the reversioner and the *nominee purchaser*,
shall be binding on the other relevant landlords and on their interests in the specified premises or any other property; but in the event of dispute the reversioner or any of the other relevant landlords may apply to the court for directions as to the manner in which the reversioner should act in the dispute.

   (3)   If any of the other relevant landlords cannot be found, or his identity cannot be ascertained, the reversioner shall apply to the court for directions and the court may make such order as it thinks proper with a view to giving effect to the rights of the *participating tenants* and protecting the interests of other persons, but subject to any such directions—
   (a)   the reversioner shall proceed as in other cases;
   (b)   any conveyance executed by the reversioner on behalf of that relevant landlord which identifies the interest to be conveyed shall have the same effect as if executed in his name; and
   (c)   any sum paid as the price for the acquisition of that relevant landlord's interest, and any other sum payable to him by virtue of Schedule 6, shall be paid into court.

   (4)   The reversioner, if he acts in good faith and with reasonable care and diligence, shall not be liable to any of the other relevant landlords for any loss or damage caused by any act or omission in the exercise or intended exercise of the authority conferred on him by section 9(3).

### *Other landlords acting independently*
7.—(1)   Notwithstanding anything in section 9(3) or paragraph 6, any of the other relevant landlords shall, at any time after the giving by the reversioner of a counter-notice under section 21 and on giving notice of his intention to do so to both the reversioner and the *nominee purchaser*, be entitled—
   (a)   to deal directly with the *nominee purchaser* in connection with any of the matters mentioned in sub-paragraphs (i) to (iii) of paragraph 6(1)(b) so far as relating to the acquisition of any interest of his;
   (b)   to be separately represented in any legal proceedings in which his title to any property

comes in question, or in any legal proceedings relating to the terms of acquisition so far as relating to the acquisition of any interest of his.

(2)   If the *nominee purchaser* so requires by notice given to the reversioner and any of the other relevant landlords, that landlord shall deal directly with the *nominee purchaser* for the purpose of deducing, evidencing or verifying the landlord's title to any property.

(3)   Any of the other relevant landlords may by notice given to the reversioner require him to apply to a leasehold valuation tribunal for the determination by the tribunal of any of the terms of acquisition so far as relating to the acquisition of any interest of the landlord.

(4)   Any of the other relevant landlords may also, on giving notice to the reversioner and the *nominee purchaser*, require that the price payable for the acquisition of his interest shall be paid by the *nominee purchaser* to him, or to a person authorised by him to receive it, instead of to the reversioner; but if, after being given proper notice of the time and method of completion with the *nominee purchaser*, either—

    (a)   he fails to notify the reversioner of the arrangements made with the *nominee purchaser* to receive payment, or

    (b)   having notified the reversioner of those arrangements, the arrangements are not duly implemented,

the reversioner shall be authorised to receive the payment for him, and the reversioner's written receipt for the amount payable shall be a complete discharge to the *nominee purchaser.*

*Obligations of other landlords to reversioner*

8.—(1)   It shall be the duty of each of the other relevant landlords—

    (a)   (subject to paragraph 7) to give the reversioner all such information and assistance as he may reasonably require; and

    (b)   after being given proper notice of the time and method of completion with the *nominee purchaser*, to ensure that all deeds and other documents that ought on his part to be delivered to the *nominee purchaser* on completion are available for the purpose, including in the case of registered land the land certificate and any other documents necessary to perfect the *nominee purchaser's* title;

and, if any of the other relevant landlords fails to comply with this sub-paragraph, that relevant landlord shall indemnify the reversioner against any liability incurred by the reversioner in consequence of the failure.

(2)   Each of the other relevant landlords shall make such contribution as shall be just to the costs and expenses properly incurred by the reversioner in pursuance of section 9(3) which are not recoverable or not recovered from the *nominee purchaser* or any other person.

*Applications made by other landlords under section 23(1)*

9.   The authority given to the reversioner by section 9(3) shall not extend to the bringing of proceedings under section 23(1) on behalf of any of the other relevant landlords, or preclude any of those landlords from bringing proceedings under that provision on his own behalf.

**[916]**

---

**NOTES**

Paras 6, 7: words in italics substituted in each place by the words "RTE company" by the Commonhold and Leasehold Reform Act 2002, s 124, Sch 8, paras 2, 36, as from a day to be appointed.

Para 8: words "nominee purchaser" in italics substituted in each place by the words "RTE company" and words "nominee purchaser's" in italics substituted by the words "RTE company's" by the Commonhold and Leasehold Reform Act 2002, s 124, Sch 8, paras 2, 36(1), (2), as from a day to be appointed.

---

SCHEDULE 2<br>SPECIAL CATEGORIES OF LANDLORDS

Sections 9 and 40

*Interpretation*

1.—(1)   In this Schedule—

    "Chapter I landlord" means a person who is, in relation to a claim made under Chapter I, [a] relevant landlord within the meaning of that Chapter;

    "Chapter II landlord" means a person who is, in relation to a claim made under Chapter II, the landlord within the meaning of that Chapter or any of the other landlords (as defined by section 40(4));

    "debenture holders' charge" means a charge (whether a floating charge or not) in favour of the holders of a series of debentures issued by a company or other body of persons, or in favour of trustees for such debenture holders;

    "mortgage" includes a charge or lien, and related expressions shall be construed accordingly;

    "the relevant notice" means—

        (a)   in relation to a Chapter I landlord, the notice given under section 13, and

    (b)   in relation to a Chapter II landlord, the notice given under section 42.

(2)   In paragraphs 5 to 8 any reference to a premium payable on the grant of lease includes a reference to any other amount payable by virtue of Schedule 13 in connection with its grant.

### Mortgagee in possession of landlord's interest

2.—(1)   Where—
    (a)   the interest of a Chapter I or Chapter II landlord is subject to mortgage, and
    (b)   the mortgagee is in possession,

all such proceedings arising out of the relevant notice as would apart from this sub-paragraph be taken by or in relation to that landlord ("the mortgagor") shall, as regards his interest, be conducted by and through the mortgagee as if he were that landlord; but this sub-paragraph shall not, in its application to a Chapter I landlord, affect the operation in relation to the mortgagee of section 35 or Schedule 8.

(2)   Where sub-paragraph (1) above applies to a Chapter I landlord, then (without prejudice to the generality of that sub-paragraph) any application under section 23(1) that would otherwise be made by the mortgagor (whether alone or together with any other person or persons) shall be made by the mortgagee as if he were the mortgagor.

(3)   Where—
    (a)   the interest of a Chapter I landlord is subject to a mortgage, and
    (b)   a receiver appointed by the mortgagee or by order of any court is in receipt of the rents and profits,

the person referred to in paragraph (a) shall not make any application under section 23(1) without the consent of the mortgagee, and the mortgagee may by notice given to that person require that, as regards his interest, this paragraph shall apply, either generally or so far as it relates to section 23, as if the mortgagee were a mortgagee in possession.

(4)   Where—
    (a)   the interest of a Chapter I or Chapter II landlord is subject to a mortgage, and
    (b)   the mortgagee is in possession or a receiver appointed by the mortgagee or by order of any court is in receipt of the rents and profits,

the relevant notice or a copy of it shall be regarded as duly given to that landlord if it is given to the mortgagee or to any such receiver; but whichever of the landlord, the mortgagee and any such receiver are not the recipient of the notice shall be given a copy of it by the recipient.

(5)   Sub-paragraph (4) has effect in relation to a debenture holders' charge as if any reference to the mortgagee were a reference to the trustees for the debenture holders; but, where the relevant notice is given to a Chapter I or Chapter II landlord whose interest is subject to any such charge and there is no trustee for the debenture holders, the landlord shall forthwith send it or a copy of it to any receiver appointed by virtue of the charge.

(6)   Where—
    (a)   a Chapter I or Chapter II landlord is given the relevant notice or a copy of it, and
    (b)   his interest is subject to a mortgage to secure the payment of money,

then (subject to sub-paragraph (7)), the landlord shall forthwith inform the mortgagee (unless the notice was given to him or a receiver appointed by virtue of the mortgage) that the notice has been given, and shall give him such further information as may from time to time be reasonably required from the landlord by the mortgagee.

(7)   Sub-paragraph (6) does not apply to a debenture holders' charge.

### Landlord's interest vested in custodian trustee

3.   Where the interest of a Chapter I or Chapter II landlord is vested in a person as custodian trustee, then for the purposes of Chapter I or (as the case may be) Chapter II the interest shall be deemed to be vested in the managing trustees or committee of management as owners of that interest, except as regards the execution of any instrument disposing of or otherwise affecting that interest.

### Landlord under a disability

[4.—(1)   This paragraph applies where a Chapter I or Chapter II landlord lacks capacity (within the meaning of the Mental Capacity Act 2005) to exercise his functions as a landlord.

(2)   For the purposes of the Chapter concerned, the landlord's place is to be taken—
    (a)   by a donee of an enduring power of attorney or lasting power of attorney (within the meaning of the 2005 Act), or a deputy appointed for him by the Court of Protection, with power to exercise those functions, or
    (b)   if no deputy or donee has that power, by a person authorised in that respect by that court.]

*Landlord's interest held [in trust]*

5.—(1)   Where the interest of a Chapter I landlord is [subject to a trust for land], any sum payable to the landlord by way of the price payable for the interest on its acquisition in pursuance of Chapter I shall be dealt with as if it were proceeds of sale arising under the trust.

(2)   Where the interest of a Chapter II landlord is [subject to a trust of land]—

   (a)   any sum payable to the landlord by way of a premium on the grant of a new lease under Chapter II or section 93(4) shall be dealt with as if it were proceeds of sale arising under the trust; ...

   (b)   ...

shall include the payment of compensation by the landlord on the termination of a new lease granted under Chapter II or section 93(4) (whether the payment is made in pursuance of an order under section 61 or in pursuance of an agreement made in conformity with paragraph 5 of Schedule 14 without an application having been made under that section).

*Landlord's interest subject to a settlement*

6.   Where the interest of a Chapter II landlord is subject to a settlement (within the meaning of the Settled Land Act 1925), the purposes authorised—

   (a)   by section 73 of that Act for the application of capital money, and

   (b)   by section 71 of that Act as purposes for which money may be raised by mortgage,

shall include the payment of compensation [by the landlord on the termination of a new lease granted under Chapter II or section 93(4) (whether the payment is made in pursuance of an order under section 61 or in pursuance of an agreement made in conformity with paragraph 5 of Schedule 14 without an application having been made under that section)].

*University or college landlords*

7.—(1)   Where a Chapter I landlord is a university or college to which the Universities and College Estates Act 1925 applies, any sum payable to the landlord by way of the price payable for any interest on its acquisition in pursuance of Chapter I shall be dealt with as if it were an amount payable by way of consideration on a sale effected under that Act.

(2)   Where a Chapter II landlord is a university or college to which that Act applies—

   (a)   any sum payable to the landlord by way of a premium on the grant of a new lease under Chapter II or section 93(4) shall be dealt with as if it were an amount payable by way of consideration on a sale effected under that Act; and

   (b)   the purposes authorised—

      (i)   by section 26 of that Act for the application of capital money, and

      (ii)   by section 31 of that Act as purposes for which money may be raised by mortgage,

      shall include the payment of compensation as mentioned in paragraph [6] above.

*Ecclesiastical landlords*

8.—(1)   The provisions of this paragraph shall have effect as regards Chapter I or Chapter II landlords who are ecclesiastical landlords; and in this paragraph "ecclesiastical landlord" means—

   (a)   a capitular body within the meaning of the Cathedrals Measure 1963 having an interest as landlord in property, or

   (b)   a diocesan board of finance having an interest as landlord in property belonging to the board as diocesan glebe land.

(2)   In relation to an interest of an ecclesiastical landlord, the consent of the Church Commissioners shall be required[, if their consent would be required if the transaction were carried out under the Cathedrals Measure 1999 or the Endowments and Glebe Measure 1976,] to sanction—

   (a)   the provisions to be contained in a conveyance in accordance with section 34 and Schedule 7, or in any lease granted under section 56, and the price or premium payable, except as regards matters determined by the court or a leasehold valuation tribunal;

   (b)   any exercise of the ecclesiastical landlord's rights under section 61, except as aforesaid, and any agreement for the payment of compensation to a tenant in conformity with paragraph 5 of Schedule 14 without an application having been made under that section; and

   (c)   any grant of a lease in pursuance of section 93(4);

...

(3)   Where a capitular body has an interest in property which forms part of the endowment of a cathedral church—

   (a)   any sum payable to that body by way of—

      (i)   the price payable for any interest in the property on its acquisition in pursuance of Chapter I, or

      (ii)   a premium on the grant of a new lease under Chapter II or section 93(4), shall be treated as part of that endowment; and

(b) the powers conferred by sections 21 and 23 of the Cathedrals Measure 1963 in relation to the investment in the acquisition of land of money forming part of the endowment of a cathedral church shall extend to the application of any such money in the payment of compensation as mentioned in paragraph [6] above.

(4) In the case of a diocesan board of finance—

(a) no consent or concurrence other than that of the Church Commissioners under sub-paragraph (2) above shall be required to a disposition under this Part of the interest of the diocesan board of finance in property (including a grant of a new lease in pursuance of section 93(4));

(b) any sum payable to the diocesan board of finance by way of—

(i) the price payable for any interest in property on its acquisition in pursuance of Chapter I, or

(ii) a premium on the grant of a new lease of property under Chapter II or section 93(4),

shall be paid to the [Diocesan Board of Finance in which the land is vested] to be applied for purposes for which the proceeds of any such disposition of property by agreement would be applicable under any enactment or Measure authorising such a disposition or disposing of the proceeds of such a disposition; and

(c) any sum required for the payment of compensation as mentioned in paragraph [6] above may be paid by the [Diocesan Board of Finance out of any money held by it].

(5) In this paragraph "diocesan board of finance" and "diocesan glebe land" have the same meaning as in the Endowments and Glebe Measure 1976.

**[917]**

NOTES

Para 1: word in square brackets substituted by the Housing Act 1996, s 107(4), Sch 10, paras 1, 16.

Para 4: substituted by the Mental Capacity Act 2005, s 67(1), Sch 6, para 39, except in relation to any proceedings pending at 1 October 2007 in which a receiver or a person authorised under the Mental Health Act 1983, Pt 7 is acting on behalf of the landlord.

Para 5: words in square brackets substituted and words omitted repealed by the Trusts of Land and Appointment of Trustees Act 1996, s 25(1), (2), Sch 3, para 27, Sch 4, subject to savings in s 25(4), (5) of that Act.

Paras 6, 7: words in square brackets substituted by the Trusts of Land and Appointment of Trustees Act 1996, s 25(1), Sch 3, para 27(1), (2), subject to savings in s 25(4), (5) of that Act.

Para 8: in sub-para (2), words in square brackets inserted and words omitted repealed, and words in square brackets in sub-para (4)(b),(c) substituted by the Church of England (Miscellaneous Provisions) Measure 2006, s 14, Sch 5, para 31; figure in square brackets in sub-paras (3)(b), (4)(c) substituted by the Trusts of Land and Appointment of Trustees Act 1996, s 25(1), Sch 3, para 27(1), (2), subject to savings in s 25(4), (5) of that Act.

Modification: by virtue of the Cathedrals Measure 1999, ss 36(2), (6), 38(1)–(3), references in para 8 to a capitular body are, except in relation to Westminster Abbey, St George's Chapel, Windsor or the cathedral church of Christ in Oxford, and subject to transitional provision in relation to cathedrals existing on 30 June 1999, to be construed as references to the corporate body of the cathedral.

## SCHEDULE 3
## THE INITIAL NOTICE: SUPPLEMENTARY PROVISIONS
Section 13

## PART I
## RESTRICTIONS ON PARTICIPATION BY INDIVIDUAL TENANTS, EFFECT OF CLAIMS ON OTHER NOTICES, FORFEITURES ETC

*Prior notice by tenant terminating lease*

1. A qualifying tenant of a flat shall *not participate in the giving of* a relevant notice of claim if the notice is given—

(a) after the tenant has given notice terminating the lease of the flat (other than a notice that has been superseded by the grant, express or implied, of a new tenancy); or

(b) during the subsistence of an agreement for the grant to the tenant of a future tenancy of the flat, where the agreement is one to which paragraph 17 of Schedule 10 to the Local Government and Housing Act 1989 applies.

*Prior notice by landlord terminating lease*

2.—(1) A qualifying tenant of a flat shall *not participate in the giving of* a relevant notice of claim if the notice is given more than four months after a landlord's notice terminating the tenant's lease of the flat has been given under section 4 of the Landlord and Tenant Act 1954 or served under paragraph 4(1) of Schedule 10 to the Local Government and Housing Act 1989 (whether or not the notice has effect to terminate the lease).

(2) Where in the case of any qualifying tenant of a flat—

(a) any such landlord's notice is given or served as mentioned in sub-paragraph (1), but

(b)    that notice was not given or served more than four months before the date when a relevant notice of claim is given,

the landlord's notice shall cease to have effect on that date.

(3)    If—

(a)    any such landlord's notice ceases to have effect by virtue of sub-paragraph (2), but

(b)    the claim made in pursuance of the relevant notice of claim is not effective,

then sub-paragraph (4) shall apply to any landlord's notice terminating the tenant's lease of the flat which—

    (i)    is given under section 4 of the Landlord and Tenant Act 1954 or served under paragraph 4(1) of Schedule 10 to the Local Government and Housing Act 1989, and

    (ii)    is so given or served within one month after the expiry of the period of currency of that claim.

(4)    Where this sub-paragraph applies to a landlord's notice, the earliest date which may be specified in the notice as the date of termination shall be—

(a)    in the case of a notice given under section 4 of that Act of 1954—

    (i)    the date of termination specified in the previous notice, or

    (ii)    the date of expiry of the period of three months beginning with the date of the giving of the new notice,

    whichever is the later; or

(b)    in the case of a notice served under paragraph 4(1) of Schedule 10 to that Act of 1989—

    (i)    the date of termination specified in the previous notice, or

    (ii)    the date of expiry of the period of four months beginning with the date of service of the new notice,

    whichever is the later.

(5)    Where—

(a)    by virtue of sub-paragraph (4) a landlord's notice specifies as the date of termination of a lease a date earlier than six months after the date of the giving of the notice, and

(b)    the notice proposes a statutory tenancy,

section 7(2) of the Landlord and Tenant Act 1954 shall apply in relation to the notice with the substitution, for references to the period of two months ending with the date of termination specified in the notice and the beginning of that period, of references to the period of three months beginning with the date of the giving of the notice and the end of that period.

*Orders for possession and pending proceedings for forfeiture etc*

3.—(1)    A qualifying tenant of a flat shall *not participate in the giving of* a relevant notice of claim if at the time when it is given he is obliged to give up possession of his flat in pursuance of an order of a court or will be so obliged at a date specified in such an order.

(2)    Except with the leave of the court, a qualifying tenant of a flat shall *not participate in the giving of* a relevant notice of claim at a time when any proceedings are pending to enforce a right of re-entry or forfeiture terminating his lease of the flat.

(3)    Leave shall only be granted under sub-paragraph (2) if the court is satisfied that the tenant does not wish *to participate in the giving of such a notice of claim* solely or mainly for the purpose of avoiding the consequences of the breach of the terms of his lease in respect of which proceedings are pending.

(4)    If—

(a)    leave is so granted, and

(b)    a relevant notice of claim is given,

the tenant's lease shall be deemed for the purposes of the claim to be a subsisting lease despite the existence of those proceedings and any order made afterwards in those proceedings; and, if the claim is effective, the court in which those proceedings were brought may set aside or vary any such order to such extent and on such terms as appear to that court to be appropriate.

*Institution of compulsory purchase procedures*

4.—(1)    A qualifying tenant of a flat shall *not participate in the giving of* a relevant notice of claim if on the date when the notice is given—

(a)    any person or body of persons who has or have been, or could be, authorised to acquire the whole or part of the flat compulsorily for any purpose has or have, with a view to its acquisition for that purpose—

    (i)    served a notice to treat on that tenant, or

    (ii)    entered into a contract for the purchase of his interest in the whole or part of the flat; and

(b)    the notice to treat or contract remains in force.

(2)    Where—

(a)    a relevant notice of claim is given, and

(b)   during the currency of the claim any such person or body of persons as is mentioned in sub-paragraph (1)(a) serves or serve, in relation to the flat held by a *participating* tenant, notice to treat as mentioned in that provision,

the tenant shall cease to be *entitled to participate in the making of the claim by virtue of being a qualifying tenant of the flat, and shall accordingly cease to be participating tenant in respect of the flat.*

### Notice terminating lease given by tenant or landlord during currency of claim

5.   Where a relevant notice of claim is given, any notice terminating the lease of any flat held by a *participating tenant*, whether it is—

(a)   a notice given by the tenant, or

(b)   a landlord's notice given under section 4 of the Landlord and Tenant Act 1954 or served under paragraph 4(1) of Schedule 10 to the Local Government and Housing Act 1989,

shall be of no effect if it is given or served during the currency of the claim.

### Initial notice operates to prevent termination of tenant's lease by other means

6.—(1)   Where a relevant notice of claim is given, then during the currency of the claim and for three months thereafter the lease of any flat held by a *participating tenant* shall not terminate—

(a)   by effluxion of time, or

(b)   in pursuance of a notice to quit given by the landlord, or

(c)   by the termination of a superior lease;

but if the claim is not effective, and but for this sub-paragraph the lease would have so terminated before the end of those three months, the lease shall so terminate at the end of those three months.

(2)   Sub-paragraph (1) shall not be taken to prevent an earlier termination of the lease in any manner not mentioned in that sub-paragraph, and shall not affect—

(a)   the power under section 146(4) of the Law of Property Act 1925 (relief against forfeiture of leases) to grant a tenant relief against the termination of a superior lease, or

(b)   any right of the tenant to relief under section 16(2) of the Landlord and Tenant Act 1954 (relief where landlord proceeding to enforce covenants) or under paragraph 9 of Schedule 5 to that Act (relief in proceedings brought by superior landlord).

(3)   The reference in sub-paragraph (2) to section 16(2) of, and paragraph 9 of Schedule 5 to, the Landlord and Tenant Act 1954 includes a reference to those provisions as they apply in relation to Schedule 10 to the Local Government and Housing Act 1989.

### Restriction on proceedings against participating tenant to enforce right of re-entry or forfeiture

7.—(1)   Where a relevant notice of claim is given, then during the currency of the claim—

(a)   no proceedings to enforce any right of re-entry or forfeiture terminating the lease of any flat held by a *participating tenant* shall be brought in any court without the leave of that court; and

(b)   leave shall only be granted if the court is satisfied that the *tenant is participating in the making of the claim* solely or mainly for the purpose of avoiding the consequences of the breach of the terms of his lease in respect of which proceedings are proposed to be brought.

(2)   If leave is granted under sub-paragraph (1), the tenant shall cease to be *entitled to participate in the making of the claim by virtue of being a qualifying tenant of the flat referred to in that sub-paragraph, and shall accordingly cease to be a participating tenant in respect of the flat.*

### Restrictions for purposes of s 14(3) on tenant electing to become participating tenant during currency of claim

8.—(1)   *Where a relevant notice of claim is given, a qualifying tenant of a flat may not subsequently make an election under section 14(3)—*

(a)   *if he was prohibited from participating in the giving of the notice by virtue of paragraph 1, 2(1), 3(1) or 4(1) above; or*

(b)   *at a time when he would be so prohibited from participating in the giving of a relevant notice of claim, if such a notice were to be given then.*

(2)   *Where a relevant notice of claim is given, then except with the leave of the court, a qualifying tenant of a flat may not subsequently make an election under section 14(3) at a time when any proceedings are pending to enforce a right of re-entry or forfeiture terminating his lease of the flat.*

(3)   *Leave shall only be granted under sub-paragraph (2) if the court is satisfied that the tenant does not wish to make such an election solely or mainly for the purpose of avoiding the consequences of the breach of the terms of his lease in respect of which proceedings are pending.*

(4)   *If—*

(a)   *leave is so granted, and*

(b)   *the tenant makes such an election,*

*the tenant's lease shall be deemed for the purposes of the claim to be a subsisting lease despite the existence of those proceedings and any order made afterwards in those proceedings; and, if the claim is effective, the court in which those proceedings were brought may set aside or vary any such order to such extent and on such terms as appear to that court to be appropriate.*

(5)   *References in this paragraph and paragraph 9 below to making an election under section 14(3) are references to making such an election to participate in the making of the claim in respect of which the relevant notice of claim is given.*

*Effect of tenant's election on certain notices given by landlord*

9.—(1)   *This paragraph applies to a qualifying tenant of a flat who, following the giving of a relevant notice of claim, makes an election under section 14(3).*

(2)   *Where in the case of any such tenant—*

(a)   *a landlord's notice terminating the tenant's lease of the flat has been given or served as mentioned in paragraph 2(1) above (whether or not the notice has effect to terminate the lease), but*

(b)   *that notice was not given or served more than four months before the date when the tenant makes his election under section 14(3),*

*the landlord's notice shall cease to have effect on that date.*

(3)   *If—*

(a)   *any such landlord's notice ceases to have effect by virtue of sub-paragraph (2) above, but*

(b)   *the claim made in pursuance of the relevant notice of claim is not effective,*

*then paragraph 2(4) above shall apply to any landlord's notice terminating the tenant's lease of the flat which—*

(i)   *is given under section 4 of the Landlord and Tenant Act 1954 or served under paragraph 4(1) of Schedule 10 to the Local Government and Housing Act 1989, and*

(ii)   *is so given or served within one month after the expiry of the period of currency of that claim;*

*and paragraph 2(5) above shall apply accordingly.*

(4)   *Paragraph 8(5) above applies for the purposes of this paragraph.*

*Interpretation*

10.—(1)   For the purposes of this Part of this Schedule—

(a)   "relevant notice of claim", in relation to any flat, means a notice under section 13 in the case of which the specified premises contain that flat, *and references to participating in the giving of such a notice are references to being one of the persons by whom the notice is given*;

(b)   references to a notice under section 13 include, in so far as the context permits, references to a notice purporting to be given under that section (*whether by persons who are qualifying tenants or not*);

(c)   references to a claim being effective are references to a binding contract being entered into for the acquisition of the freehold and other interests falling to be acquired in pursuance of the claim or to the making of an order under section 24(4)(a) or (b) or 25(6)(a) or (b) which provides for the vesting of those interests; and

(d)   references to the currency of a claim are—

(i)   where the claim is made by a valid notice under section 13, references to the period during which the notice continues in force in accordance with subsection (11) of that section, or

(ii)   where the claim is made by a notice which is not a valid notice under section 13, references to the period beginning with the giving of the notice and ending with the time when the notice is set aside by the court or is withdrawn or when it would (if valid) cease to have effect or be deemed to have been withdrawn.

(2)   For the purposes of sub-paragraph (1)(d) the date when a notice is set aside, or would (if valid) cease to have effect, in consequence of an order of a court shall be taken to be the date when the order becomes final.

**[918]**

**NOTES**

Paras 1, 2: words in italics substituted by the words "be disregarded when considering whether the requirement in section 13(2)(b) is satisfied in relation to" by the Commonhold and Leasehold Reform Act 2002, s 124, Sch 8, paras 2, 37(1), (2), as from a day to be appointed.

Para 3: words in italics in sub-paras (1), (2) substituted by the words "be disregarded when considering whether the requirement in section 13(2)(b) is satisfied in relation to" and words in italics in sub-para (3) substituted by the words "such a notice of claim to be given" by the Commonhold and Leasehold Reform Act 2002, s 124, Sch 8, paras 2, 37(1)–(3), as from a day to be appointed.

Para 4: words in italics in sub-para (1) substituted by the words "be disregarded when considering whether the requirement in section 13(2)(b) is satisfied in relation to", word in italics in sub-para (2)(b) substituted by the word "qualifying" and words in italics in the third place substituted by the words "a member of the RTE company." by the Commonhold and Leasehold Reform Act 2002, s 124, Sch 8, paras 2, 37(1), (2), (4), as from a day to be appointed.

Paras 5, 6: words in italics substituted by the words "participating member of the RTE company" by the Commonhold and Leasehold Reform Act 2002, s 124, Sch 8, paras 2, 37(1), (5), as from a day to be appointed.

Para 7: words "against participating tenant" in the cross-heading repealed, in sub-para (1) words in italics in the first place substituted by the words "participating member of the RTE company", words in italics in the second place substituted by the words "member is a participating member", and words in italics in sub-para (2) substituted by the words "a member of the RTE company." by the Commonhold and Leasehold Reform Act 2002, ss 124, 180, Sch 8, paras 2, 37(1), (6), Sch 14, as from a day to be appointed.

Paras 8, 9: repealed by the Commonhold and Leasehold Reform Act 2002, s 180, Sch 14, as from a day to be appointed.

Para 10: words in italics repealed by the Commonhold and Leasehold Reform Act 2002, s 180, Sch 14, as from a day to be appointed.

## PART II
## PROCEDURE FOR GIVING COPIES TO RELEVANT LANDLORDS

### *Application of Part II*

11.  This Part of this Schedule has effect where a notice under section 13 is given in a case to which section 9(2) [or (2A)] applies.

### *Qualifying tenants to give copies of initial notice*

12.—(1)  [In a case to which section 9(2) applies,] The *qualifying tenants* by whom the initial notice is given shall, in addition to giving the initial notice to the reversioner in respect of the specified premises, give a copy of the notice to every other person known or believed by *them* to be a relevant landlord of those premises.

(2)  The initial notice shall state whether copies are being given in accordance with sub-paragraph (1) to anyone other than the recipient and, if so, to whom.

[12A.—(1)  In a case to which section 9(2A) applies, the *qualifying tenants* by whom the initial notice is given shall, in addition to giving the initial notice to the person specified in it as the recipient, give a copy of the notice to every other person known or believed by *them* to be a relevant landlord of the specified premises.

(2)  The initial notice shall state whether copies are being given in accordance with sub-paragraph (1) to anyone other than the person specified in it as the recipient and, if so, to whom.]

### *Recipient of notice or copy to give further copies*

13.—(1)  Subject to sub-paragraph (2), a recipient of the initial notice or of a copy of it (including a person receiving a copy under this sub-paragraph) shall forthwith give a copy to any person who—
   (a)   is known or believed by him to be a relevant landlord, and
   (b)   is not stated in the recipient's copy of the notice, or known by him, to have received a copy.

(2)  Sub-paragraph (1) does not apply where the recipient is neither the reversioner nor another relevant landlord.

(3)  Where a person gives any copies of the initial notice in accordance with sub-paragraph (1), he shall—
   (a)   supplement the statement under paragraph 12(2) [or, as the case may be, 12A(2)] by adding any further persons to whom he is giving copies or who are known to him to have received one; and
   (b)   notify the *qualifying tenants by whom* the initial notice is given of the persons added by him to that statement.

### *Consequences of failure to comply with paragraph 12 or 13*

14.—(1)  Where—
   (a)   a relevant landlord of the specified premises does not receive a copy of the initial notice before the end of the period specified in it in pursuance of section 13(3)(g), but
   (b)   he was given a notice under section 11 by *any of the qualifying tenants by whom* the initial notice was given and, in response to the notice under that section, notified the tenant in question of his interest in the specified premises,
the initial notice shall cease to have effect at the end of that period.

(2)  Where—
   (a)   sub-paragraph (1) does not apply, but

(b)     any person fails without reasonable cause to comply with paragraph 12[, 12A] or 13 above, or is guilty of any unreasonable delay in complying with [any] of those paragraphs,

he shall be liable for any loss thereby occasioned to the *qualifying tenants by whom* the initial notice was given or to the reversioner or any other relevant landlord.

**[919]**

**NOTES**

Para 11: words in square brackets inserted by the Housing Act 1996, s 107(4), Sch 10, paras 1, 17(1), (2), except in relation to a case where, before 1 October 1996, a notice was given under s 13 or 42 of this Act at **[817]**, **[848]**, or an application was made to court under s 26 or 50 of this Act at **[830]**, **[856]**.

Para 12: words "qualifying tenants" in the heading and sub-para (1) substituted by the words "RTE company" and word "them" in italics substituted by the word "it" by the Commonhold and Leasehold Reform Act 2002, s 124, Sch 8, paras 2, 37(1), (7), as from a day to be appointed; words in square brackets inserted by the Housing Act 1996, s 107(4), Sch 10, paras 1, 17(1), (3), subject to savings as noted above.

Para 12A: inserted by the Housing Act 1996, s 107(4), Sch 10, paras 1, 17(1), (4), subject to savings as noted above; words "qualifying tenants" substituted by the words "RTE company" and word "them" in italics substituted by the word "it" by the Commonhold and Leasehold Reform Act 2002, s 124, Sch 8, paras 2, 37(1), (8), as from a day to be appointed.

Para 13: words in square brackets inserted by the Housing Act 1996, s 107(4), Sch 10, paras 1, 17(1), (5), subject to savings as noted above; words in italics substituted by the words "RTE company by which" by the Commonhold and Leasehold Reform Act 2002, s 124, Sch 8, paras 2, 37(1), (9), as from a day to be appointed.

Para 14: words in italics in sub-para (1) substituted by the words "a qualifying tenant who was a member of the RTE company by which" and words in italics in sub-para (2) substituted by the words "RTE company by which" by the Commonhold and Leasehold Reform Act 2002, s 124, Sch 8, paras 2, 37(1), (10), as from a day to be appointed; figure in square brackets inserted and word in square brackets substituted by the Housing Act 1996, s 107(4), Sch 10, paras 1, 17(1), (6), subject to savings as noted above.

PART III
OTHER PROVISIONS

Inaccuracies or misdescription in initial notice

15.—(1)     The initial notice shall not be invalidated by any inaccuracy in any of the particulars required by [or by virtue of] section 13(3) or by any misdescription of any of the property to which the claim extends.

(2)     Where the initial notice—
(a)     specifies any property or interest which was not liable to acquisition under or by virtue of section 1 or 2, or
(b)     fails to specify any property or interest which is so liable to acquisition,

the notice may, with the leave of the court and on such terms as the court may think fit, be amended so as to exclude or include the property or interest in question.

(3)     Where the initial notice is so amended as to exclude any property or interest, references to the property or interests specified in the notice under any provision of section 13(3) shall be construed accordingly; and, where it is so amended as to include any property or interest, the property or interest shall be treated as if it had been specified under the provision of that section under which it would have fallen to be specified if its acquisition had been proposed at the relevant date.

Effect on initial notice of tenant's lack of qualification to participate

*16.—(1)     It is hereby declared that, where at the relevant date any of the persons by whom the initial notice is given—*
*(a)     is not a qualifying tenant of a flat contained in the specified premises, or*
*(b)     is such a qualifying tenant but is prohibited from participating in the giving of the notice by virtue of Part I of this Schedule, or*
*(c)     (if it is claimed in the notice that he satisfies the residence condition) does not satisfy that condition,*

*the notice shall not be invalidated on that account, so long as the notice was in fact properly given by a sufficient number of qualifying tenants of flats contained in the premises as at the relevant date, and not less than one-half of the qualifying tenants by whom it was so given then satisfied the residence condition.*

*(2)     For the purposes of sub-paragraph (1) a sufficient number is a number which—*
*(a)     is not less than two-thirds of the total number of qualifying tenants of flats contained in the specified premises as at the relevant date, and*
*(b)     is not less than one-half of the total number of flats so contained.*

**[920]**

**NOTES**

Para 15: words in square brackets inserted by the Commonhold and Leasehold Reform Act 2002, s 124, Sch 8, paras 2, 37(1), (11), as from a day to be appointed.

Para 16: substituted, together with preceding cross-heading, by the Commonhold and Leasehold Reform Act 2002, s 124, Sch 8, paras 2, 37(1), (12), as from a day to be appointed, as follows—

### "*Effect on initial notice of member's lack of qualification*

16.   Where any of the members of the RTE company by which an initial notice is given was not the qualifying tenant of a flat contained in the premises at the relevant date even though his name was stated in the notice, the notice is not invalidated on that account, so long as a sufficient number of qualifying tenants of flats contained in the premises were members of the company at that date; and for this purpose a "sufficient number" is a number (greater than one) which is not less than one-half of the total number of flats contained in the premises at that date.".

## SCHEDULE 4
### INFORMATION TO BE FURNISHED BY REVERSIONER ABOUT EXERCISE OF RIGHTS UNDER CHAPTER II
Section 21

### *Information to accompany counter-notice*

1.—(1)   This paragraph applies where before the date of the giving of a counter-notice under section 21 the reversioner or any other relevant landlord—

(a)   has received—

  (i)   a notice given under section 42 with respect to any flat contained in the specified premises (being a notice to which section 54(1) or (2) applies on that date), or

  (ii)   a copy of such a notice, or

(b)   has given any counter-notice under section 45 in response to any such notice.

(2)   A copy of every notice which, or a copy of which, has been received as mentioned in sub-paragraph (1)(a), and a copy of every counter-notice which has been given as mentioned in sub-paragraph (1)(b), shall either—

(a)   accompany any counter-notice given under section 21, or

(b)   be given to the *nominee purchaser* by the reversioner as soon as possible after the date of the giving of any such counter-notice.

### *Continuing duty to furnish information*

2.—(1)   Subject to sub-paragraph (3), this paragraph applies where on or after the date of the giving of a counter-notice under section 21 the reversioner or any other relevant landlord receives—

(a)   a notice given under section 42 with respect to any flat contained in the specified premises or a copy of such a notice, or

(b)   any notice of withdrawal given under section 52 and relating to any notice under section 42 of which a copy has already been furnished to the *nominee purchaser* under this Schedule.

(2)   A copy of every notice which, or a copy of which, is received as mentioned in sub-paragraph (1)(a) or (b) shall be given to the *nominee purchaser* by the reversioner as soon as possible after the time when the notice or copy is received by the reversioner or (as the case may be) the other relevant landlord.

(3)   This paragraph does not apply if the notice or copy is received by the reversioner or (as the case may be) the other relevant landlord otherwise than at a time when—

(a)   the initial notice continues in force, or

(b)   a binding contract entered into in pursuance of that notice remains in force, or

(c)   where an order has been made under section 24(4)(a) or (b) or 25(6)(a) or (b) with respect to the specified premises, any interests which by virtue of the order fall to be vested in the *nominee purchaser* have yet to be so vested.

### *Duty of other landlords to furnish copies to reversioner*

3.—(1)   Without prejudice to the generality of paragraph 8(1)(a) of Schedule 1, the duty imposed by that provision shall extend to requiring any relevant landlord (other than the reversioner) who—

(a)   receives a relevant notice or a copy of such a notice, or

(b)   gives a relevant counter-notice,

to furnish a copy of the notice or counter-notice to the reversioner as soon as possible after the time when the notice or copy is received or (as the case may be) the counter-notice is given by the relevant landlord.

(2) In this paragraph "relevant notice" and "relevant counter-notice" mean respectively any notice of which a copy is required to be given to the *nominee purchaser* by the reversioner in accordance with this Schedule and any counter-notice of which a copy is required to be so given.

**[921]**

---

**NOTES**

Paras 1–3: words in italics substituted in each place by the words "RTE company" by the Commonhold and Leasehold Reform Act 2002, s 124, Sch 8, paras 2, 38, as from a day to be appointed.

---

## SCHEDULE 5
### VESTING ORDERS UNDER SECTIONS 24 AND 25

Sections 24 and 25

*Interpretation*

1.—(1) In this Schedule "a vesting order" means an order made by the court under section 24(4)(a) or (b) or section 25(6)(a) or (b).

(2) In this Schedule "the relevant terms of acquisition", in relation to any such order, means the terms of acquisition referred to in section 24(4)(a) or (b) or section 25(6)(a) or (b), as the case may be.

*Execution of conveyance*

2.—(1) Where any interests are to be vested in the *nominee purchaser* by virtue of a vesting order, then on his paying into court the appropriate sum in respect of each of those interests there shall be executed by such person as the court may designate a conveyance which—

   (a)    is in a form approved by a leasehold valuation tribunal, and

   (b)    contains such provisions as may be so approved for the purpose of giving effect to the relevant terms of acquisition.

(2) The conveyance shall be effective to vest in the *nominee purchaser* the interests expressed to be conveyed, subject to and in accordance with the terms of the conveyance.

*The appropriate sum*

3.—(1) In the case of any vesting order, the appropriate sum which in accordance with paragraph 2(1) is to be paid into court in respect of any interest is the aggregate of—

   (a)    such amount as is fixed by the relevant terms of acquisition as the price which is payable in accordance with Schedule 6 in respect of that interest; and

   (b)    any amounts or estimated amounts determined by a leasehold valuation tribunal as being, at the time of execution of the conveyance, due to the transferor from any tenants of his of premises comprised in the premises in which that interest subsists (whether due under or in respect of their leases or under or in respect of agreements collateral thereto).

(2) In this paragraph "the transferor", in relation to any interest, means the person from whom the interest is to be acquired by the *nominee purchaser*.

*Effect of payment of appropriate sum into court*

4. Where any interest is vested in the *nominee purchaser* in accordance with this Schedule, the payment into court of the appropriate sum in respect of that interest shall be taken to have satisfied any claims against the *nominee purchaser* or *the participating tenants*, or the personal representatives or assigns of any of them, in respect of the price payable under this Chapter for the acquisition of that interest.

*Supplemental*

5.—(1) In the provisions specified in sub-paragraph (2) references to a binding contract being entered into in pursuance of the initial notice shall be read as including references to the making of a vesting order.

(2) Those provisions are—

   (a)    section 14(11);

   (b)    section 15(12) (*except so far as it provides for the interpretation of references to the nominee purchaser*);

   (c)    section 16(10);

   (d)    section 19(5)(b);

   (e)    section 28(1);

   (f)    section 30(4); and

   (g)    section 31(4).

(3)   Where, at any time after a vesting order is made but before the interests falling to be vested in the *nominee purchaser* by virtue of the order have been so vested, any acquiring authority (within the meaning of section 30) serves notice to treat as mentioned in subsection (1)(a) of that section, the vesting order shall cease to have effect.

(4)   Where sub-paragraph (3) applies to any vesting order, then on the occasion of the compulsory acquisition in question the compensation payable in respect of any interest in the specified premises (whether or not the one to which the notice to treat relates) shall be determined on the basis of the value of the interest subject to and with the benefit of the rights and obligations arising from the initial notice and affecting the interest.

(5)   In section 38(2) (except so far as it provides for the interpretation of references to the proposed acquisition by the *nominee purchaser*) the reference to a contract entered into in pursuance of the initial notice shall be read as including a reference to a vesting order.

[922]

**NOTES**
   Paras 2, 3: words "nominee purchaser" in italics substituted in each place by the words "RTE company" by the Commonhold and Leasehold Reform Act 2002, s 124, Sch 8, paras 2, 39(1), (2), as from a day to be appointed.
   Para 4: words "nominee purchaser" in italics substituted in each place by the words "RTE company" and words "the participating tenants" in italics substituted by the words "its members" by the Commonhold and Leasehold Reform Act 2002, s 124, Sch 8, paras 2, 39, as from a day to be appointed.
   Para 5: sub-paras (2)(a)–(c) repealed and words "nominee purchaser" in italics substituted in both places by the words "RTE company" by the Commonhold and Leasehold Reform Act 2002, ss 124, 180, Sch 8, paras 2, 39(1), (2), Sch 14, as from a day to be appointed.

## SCHEDULE 6
## PURCHASE PRICE PAYABLE BY *NOMINEE PURCHASER*

Section 32

### PART I
### GENERAL

*Interpretation and operation of Schedule*

1.—(1)   In this Schedule—

   .....
   "intermediate leasehold interest" means the interest of the tenant under a lease which is superior to the lease held by a qualifying tenant of a flat contained in the specified premises, to the extent that—
   (a)   any such interest is to be acquired by the *nominee purchaser* by virtue of section 2(1)(a), and
   (b)   it is an interest in the specified premises;
   .....

(2)   Parts II to IV of this Schedule have effect subject to the provisions of Parts V and VI (which relate to interests with negative values).

[923]

**NOTES**
   Schedule heading: words in italics substituted by the words "RTE company" by the Commonhold and Leasehold Reform Act 2002, s 124, Sch 8, paras 2, 40(1), (2), as from a day to be appointed.
   Para 1: definition "the freeholder" (omitted) repealed by the Housing Act 1996, ss 107(4), 227, Sch 10, para 18(2)(a), Sch 19, Pt V, except in relation to a case where, before 1 October 1996, a notice was given under s 13 or 42 of this Act at [817], [848], or an application was made to court under s 26 or 50 of this Act at [830], [856]; definition "the valuation date" (omitted) repealed by the Commonhold and Leasehold Reform Act 2002, s 180, Sch 14, and in definition "intermediate leasehold interest", words in italics substituted by the words "RTE company", by s 124 of, and Sch 8, paras 2, 40(1), (2) to, that Act, as from a day to be appointed.

### PART II
### FREEHOLD OF SPECIFIED PREMISES

*Price payable for freehold of specified premises*

2.—(1)   Subject to the provisions of this paragraph, [where the freehold of the whole of the specified premises is owned by the same person] the price payable by the *nominee purchaser* for the freehold of [those] premises shall be the aggregate of—
   (a)   the value of the freeholder's interest in the premises as determined in accordance with paragraph 3,
   (b)   the freeholder's share of the marriage value as determined in accordance with paragraph 4, and
   (c)   any amount of compensation payable to the freeholder under paragraph 5.

(2)    Where the amount arrived at in accordance with sub-paragraph (1) is a negative amount, the price payable by the *nominee purchaser* for the freehold shall be nil.

### Value of freeholder's interest

3.—(1)    Subject to the provisions of this paragraph, the value of the freeholder's interest in the specified premises is the amount which at [the relevant date] that interest might be expected to realise if sold on the open market by a willing seller (with [no person who falls within sub-paragraph (1A)] buying or seeking to buy) on the following assumptions—

(a)    on the assumption that the vendor is selling for an estate in fee simple—

    (i)    subject to any leases subject to which the freeholder's interest in the premises is to be acquired by the *nominee purchaser*, but

    (ii)    subject also to any intermediate or other leasehold interests in the premises which are to be acquired by the *nominee purchaser*;

(b)    on the assumption that this Chapter and Chapter II confer no right to acquire any interest in the specified premises or to acquire any new lease (except that this shall not preclude the taking into account of a notice given under section 42 with respect to a flat contained in the specified premises where it is given by a person other than a *participating tenant*);

(c)    on the assumption that any increase in the value of any flat held by a *participating tenant* which is attributable to an improvement carried out at his own expense by *the tenant* or by any predecessor in title is to be disregarded; and

(d)    on the assumption that (subject to paragraphs (a) and (b)) the vendor is selling with and subject to the rights and burdens with and subject to which the conveyance to the *nominee purchaser* of the freeholder's interest is to be made, and in particular with and subject to such permanent or extended rights and burdens as are to be created in order to give effect to Schedule 7.

[(1A)    A person falls within this sub-paragraph if he is—

(a)    the *nominee purchaser*, or

(b)    a tenant of premises contained in the specified premises, or

[(ba)    an owner of an interest which the *nominee purchaser* is to acquire in pursuance of section 1(2)(a), or]

(c)    an owner of an interest which the *nominee purchaser* is to acquire in pursuance of section 2(1)(b).]

(2)    It is hereby declared that the fact that sub-paragraph (1) requires assumptions to be made as to the matters specified in paragraphs (a) to (d) of that sub-paragraph does not preclude the making of assumptions as to other matters where those assumptions are appropriate for determining the amount which at [the relevant date] the freeholder's interest in the specified premises might be expected to realise if sold as mentioned in that sub-paragraph.

(3)    In determining that amount there shall be made such deduction (if any) in respect of any defect in title as on a sale of the interest on the open market might be expected to be allowed between a willing seller and a willing buyer.

(4)    Where a lease of any flat or other unit contained in the specified premises is to be granted to the freeholder in accordance with section 36 and Schedule 9, the value of his interest in those premises at [the relevant date] so far as relating to that flat or other unit shall be taken to be the difference as at that date between—

(a)    the value of his freehold interest in it, and

(b)    the value of his interest in it under that lease, assuming it to have been granted to him at that date;

and each of those values shall, so far as is appropriate, be determined in like manner as the value of the freeholder's interest in the whole of the specified premises is determined for the purposes of paragraph 2(1)(a).

(5)    The value of the freeholder's interest in the specified premises shall not be increased by reason of—

(a)    any transaction which—

    (i)    is entered into on or after the date of the passing of this Act (otherwise than in pursuance of a contract entered into before that date), and

    (ii)    involves the creation or transfer of an interest superior to (whether or not preceding) any interest held by a qualifying tenant of a flat contained in the specified premises; or

(b)    any alteration on or after that date of the terms on which any such superior interest is held.

(6)    Sub-paragraph (5) shall not have the effect of preventing an increase in value of the freeholder's interest in the specified premises in a case where the increase is attributable to any such leasehold interest with a negative value as is mentioned in paragraph 14(2).

*Freeholder's share of marriage value*

4.—(1)   The marriage value is the amount referred to in sub-paragraph (2), and the freeholder's share of the marriage value is [50 per cent of that amount].

(2)   [Subject to sub-paragraph (2A),] the marriage value is any increase in the aggregate value of the freehold and every intermediate leasehold interest in the specified premises, when regarded as being (in consequence of their being acquired by the *nominee purchaser*) interests under the control of the *participating tenants, as* compared with the aggregate value of those interests when held by the persons from whom they are to be so acquired, being an increase in value—

(a)   which is attributable to the potential ability of the *participating tenants, once* those interests have been so acquired, to have new leases granted to them without payment of any premium and without restriction as to length of term, and

(b)   which, if those interests were being sold to the *nominee purchaser* on the open market by willing sellers, the *nominee purchaser* would have to agree to share with the sellers in order to reach agreement as to price.

[(2A)   Where at the relevant date the unexpired term of the lease held by any of those participating members exceeds eighty years, any increase in the value of the freehold or any intermediate leasehold interest in the specified premises which is attributable to his potential ability to have a new lease granted to him as mentioned in sub-paragraph (2)(a) is to be ignored.]

(3)   For the purposes of sub-paragraph (2) the value of the freehold or any intermediate leasehold interest in the specified premises when held by the person from whom it is to be acquired by the *nominee purchaser* and its value when acquired by the *nominee purchaser*—

(a)   shall be determined on the same basis as the value of the interest is determined for the purposes of paragraph 2(1)(a) or (as the case may be) paragraph 6(1)(b)(i); and

(b)   shall be so determined as at [the relevant date].

(4)   Accordingly, in so determining the value of an interest when acquired by the *nominee purchaser*—

(a)   the same assumptions shall be made under paragraph 3(1) (or, as the case may be, under paragraph 3(1) as applied by paragraph 7(1)) as are to be made under that provision in determining the value of the interest when held by the person from whom it is to be acquired by the *nominee purchaser*; and

(b)   any merger or other circumstances affecting the interest on its acquisition by the *nominee purchaser* shall be disregarded.

*Compensation for loss resulting from enfranchisement*

5.—(1)   Where the freeholder will suffer any loss or damage to which this paragraph applies, there shall be payable to him such amount as is reasonable to compensate him for that loss or damage.

(2)   This paragraph applies to—

(a)   any diminution in value of any interest of the freeholder in other property resulting from the acquisition of his interest in the specified premises; and

(b)   any other loss or damage which results therefrom to the extent that it is referable to his ownership of any interest in other property.

(3)   Without prejudice to the generality of paragraph (b) of sub-paragraph (2), the kinds of loss falling within that paragraph include loss of development value in relation to the specified premises to the extent that it is referable as mentioned in that paragraph.

(4)   In sub-paragraph (3) "development value", in relation to the specified premises, means any increase in the value of the freeholder's interest in the premises which is attributable to the possibility of demolishing, reconstructing or carrying out substantial works of construction on, the whole or a substantial part of the premises.

(5)   Where the freeholder will suffer loss or damage to which this paragraph applies, then in determining the amount of compensation payable to him under this paragraph, it shall not be material that—

(a)   the loss or damage could to any extent be avoided or reduced by the grant to him, in accordance with section 36 and Schedule 9, of a lease granted in pursuance of Part III of that Schedule, and

(b)   he is not requiring the *nominee purchaser* to grant any such lease.

[*Price payable for freehold of part of specified premises*

5A.—(1)   Where different persons own the freehold of different parts of the specified premises—

(a)   a separate price shall be payable by the *nominee purchaser* for the freehold of each of those parts, and

(b)   sub-paragraph (2) shall apply to determine the price so payable.

(2)   Subject to sub-paragraph (3), the price payable by the *nominee purchaser* for the freehold of part of the specified premises shall be the aggregate of—

    (a)   the value of the freeholder's interest in the part as determined in accordance with paragraph 3, modified as mentioned in paragraph 5B, and

    (b)   the freeholder's share of the marriage value as determined in accordance with paragraph 4, modified as mentioned in paragraph 5C, and

    (c)   any amount of compensation payable to the freeholder under paragraph 5.

    (3)   Where the amount arrived at in accordance with sub-paragraph (2) is a negative amount, the price payable by the *nominee purchaser* for the freehold of the part shall be nil.

**5B.**—(1)   In its application in accordance with paragraph 5A(2)(a), paragraph 3 shall have effect with the following modifications.

    (2)   In sub-paragraph (1)(a)(ii), there shall be inserted at the end "so far as relating to the part of the premises in which the freeholder's interest subsists".

    (3)   In sub-paragraph (1A), after paragraph (a) there shall be inserted—

       "(aa) an owner of a freehold interest in the specified premises, or".

    (4)   In sub-paragraph (4)—

    (a)   the words "the whole of" shall be omitted, and

    (b)   for "2(1)(a)" there shall be substituted "5A(2)(a)".

**5C.**—(1)   In its application in accordance with paragraph 5A(2)(b), paragraph 4 shall have effect with the following modifications.

    (2)   In sub-paragraph (2)—

    (a)   after "the specified premises" there shall be inserted "so far as relating to the part of the premises in which the freeholder's interest subsists",

    (b)   after "*participating tenants*", where it first occurs, there shall be inserted "in whose flats the freeholder's interest subsists", and

    (c)   in paragraph (a), for "the", where it second occurs, there shall be substituted "those".

    (3)   In sub-paragraph (3)—

    (a)   after "the specified premises" there shall be inserted "so far as relating to the part of the premises in which the freeholder's interest subsists", and

    (b)   in paragraph (a), for "2(1)(a)" there shall be substituted "5A(2)(a)".

    (4)   In sub-paragraph (4)(a), after "3(1)", where it first occurs, there shall be inserted "as applied by paragraph 5A(2)(a)".]

**[924]**

---

**NOTES**

    Para 2: words in first pair of square brackets inserted and words in second pair of square brackets substituted by the Housing Act 1996, s 107(4), Sch 10, paras 1, 18(1), (3), except in relation to a case where, before 1 October 1996, a notice was given under s 13 or 42 of this Act at **[817]**, **[848]**, or an application was made to court under s 26 or 50 of this Act at **[830]**, **[856]**; words in italics substituted in both places by the words "RTE company" by the Commonhold and Leasehold Reform Act 2002, s 124, Sch 8, paras 2, 40(1), (2), as from a day to be appointed.

    Para 3: words "the relevant date" in square brackets substituted in each place by the Commonhold and Leasehold Reform Act 2002, s 126(1), except in relation to a notice given under s 13 of this Act at **[817]**, or an application made under s 26 of this Act at **[830]**, before 28 February 2005 (in relation to England) or 31 May 2005 (in relation to Wales), and words "nominee purchaser" in italics substituted in each place by the words "RTE company", words "participating tenant" in italics substituted in each place by the words "participating member of the RTE company" and words "the tenant" in italics substituted by the words "the member" by s 124 of, and Sch 8, paras 2, 40(1)–(4) to, the 2002 Act, as from a day to be appointed; words in second pair of square brackets in sub-para (1) substituted, sub-para (1A) inserted and para (ba) therein inserted by the Housing Act 1996, ss 107(4), 109(1)–(3), Sch 10, paras 1, 18(1), (4), subject to savings as noted above.

    Para 4: words in square brackets in sub-para (1) substituted (except in relation to a notice given under s 13 of this Act at **[817]**, or an application made under s 26 of this Act at **[830]**), before 26 July 2002 (in relation to England) or 1 January 2003 (in relation to Wales)), and words in square brackets in sub-para (2) and the whole of sub-para (2A) inserted, by the Commonhold and Leasehold Reform Act 2002, ss 127, 128 (for savings and transitional provisions, see the Commonhold and Leasehold Reform Act 2002 (Commencement No 1, Savings and Transitional Provisions) (England) Order 2002, SI 2002/1912, and the Commonhold and Leasehold Reform Act 2002 (Commencement No 1, Savings and Transitional Provisions) (Wales) Order 2002, SI 2002/3012), words "nominee purchaser" in italics substituted in each place by the words "RTE company", words "participating tenants, as" in italics substituted by the words "persons who are participating members of the RTE company immediately before a binding contract is entered into in pursuance of the initial notice, as" and words "participating tenants, once" in italics substituted by the words "those participating members, once" by s 124 of, and Sch 8, paras 2, 40(1), (2), (5) to, the 2002 Act, as from a day to be appointed, and in sub-para (3) words "the relevant date" in square brackets substituted by s 126(1) of the 2002 Act, except in relation to a notice given under s 13 of this Act at **[817]**, or an application made under s 26 of this Act at **[830]**, before 28 February 2005 (in relation to England) or 31 May 2005 (in relation to Wales).

    Para 5: words in italics in sub-para (5) substituted by the words "RTE company" by the Commonhold and Leasehold Reform Act 2002, s 124, Sch 8, paras 2, 40(1), (2), as from a day to be appointed.

    Paras 5A: inserted, together with paras 5B, 5C, by the Housing Act 1996, s 107(4), Sch 10, paras 1, 18(1), (5), subject to savings as noted above; words "nominee purchaser" in italics substituted in each place by the words "RTE company" by the Commonhold and Leasehold Reform Act 2002, s 124, Sch 8, paras 2, 40(1), (2), as from a day to be appointed.

Para 5B: inserted, together with paras 5A, 5C, by the Housing Act 1996, s 107(4), Sch 10, paras 1, 18(1), (5), subject to savings as noted above.

Para 5C: inserted, together with paras 5A, 5B, by the Housing Act 1996, s 107(4), Sch 10, paras 1, 18(1), (5), subject to savings as noted above; words in italics substituted by the words "participating member[s] of the RTE company" by virtue of the Commonhold and Leasehold Reform Act 2002, s 124, Sch 8, paras 2, 40(1), (3), as from a day to be appointed.

## PART III
### INTERMEDIATE LEASEHOLD INTERESTS
#### *Price payable for intermediate leasehold interests*

6.—(1)   Where the *nominee purchaser* is to acquire one or more intermediate leasehold interests—

    (a)    a separate price shall be payable for each of those interests, and

    (b)    (subject to the provisions of this paragraph) that price shall be the aggregate of—

        (i)    the value of the interest as determined in accordance with paragraph 7, and

        (ii)    any amount of compensation payable to the owner of that interest in accordance with paragraph 8.

(2)   Where in the case of any intermediate leasehold interest the amount arrived at in accordance with sub-paragraph (1)(b) is a negative amount, the price payable by the *nominee purchaser* for the interest shall be nil.

#### *Value of intermediate leasehold interests*

7.—(1)   Subject to sub-paragraph (2), paragraph 3 shall apply for determining the value of any intermediate leasehold interest for the purposes of paragraph 6(1)(b)(i) with such modifications as are appropriate to relate that paragraph to a sale of the interest in question subject (where applicable) to any leases intermediate between that interest and any lease held by a qualifying tenant of a flat contained in the specified premises.

[(1A)   In its application in accordance with sub-paragraph (1), paragraph 3(1A) shall have effect with the addition after paragraph (a) of—

    "(aa) an owner of a freehold interest in the specified premises, or".]

(2)   The value of an intermediate leasehold interest which is the interest of the tenant under a minor intermediate lease shall be calculated by applying the formula set out in sub-paragraph (7) instead of in accordance with sub-paragraph (1).

(3)   "A minor intermediate lease" means a lease complying with the following requirements, namely—

    (a)    it must have an expectation of possession of not more than one month, and

    (b)    the profit rent in respect of the lease must be not more than £5 per year;

and, in the case of a lease which is in immediate reversion on two or more leases, those requirements must be complied with in connection with each of the sub-leases.

(4)   Where a minor intermediate lease is in immediate reversion on two or more leases—

    (a)    the formula set out in sub-paragraph (7) shall be applied in relation to each of those sub-leases (and sub-paragraphs (5) and (6) shall also so apply); and

    (b)    the value of the interest of the tenant under the minor intermediate lease shall accordingly be the aggregate of the amounts calculated by so applying the formula.

(5)   "Profit rent" means an amount equal to that of the rent payable under the lease on which the minor intermediate lease is in immediate reversion, less that of the rent payable under the minor intermediate lease.

(6)   Where the minor intermediate lease or that on which it is in immediate reversion comprises property other than a flat held by a qualifying tenant, then in sub-paragraph (5) the reference to the rent payable under it means so much of that rent as is apportioned to any such flat.

(7)   The formula is—

$$P = £\frac{R}{Y} - \frac{R}{Y(1+Y)^n}$$

where—

    $P$ = the price payable;

    $R$ = the profit rent;

    $Y$ = the yield (expressed as a decimal fraction) from 2½ per cent Consolidated Stock;

    $n$ = the period, expressed in years (taking any part of a year as a whole year), of the remainder of the term of the minor intermediate lease as at [the relevant date].

(8)   In calculating the yield from 2½ per cent Consolidated Stock, the price of that stock shall be taken to be the middle market price at the close of business on the last trading day in the week before [the relevant date].

(4) Where the owner of an intermediate leasehold interest is entitled in accordance with sub-paragraph (2) to any part of the amount payable to the freeholder in respect of the freeholder's share of the marriage value, the amount to which he is so entitled shall be payable to him by the freeholder.]

**[925]**

**NOTES**

Para 6: words in italics substituted in both places by the words "RTE company" by the Commonhold and Leasehold Reform Act 2002, s 124, Sch 8, paras 2, 40(1), (2), as from a day to be appointed.

Para 7: sub-para (1A) inserted by the Housing Act 1996, s 109(1), (4), except in relation to a case where, before 1 October 1996, a notice was given under s 13 or 42 of this Act at **[817]**, **[848]**, or an application was made to court under s 26 or 50 of this Act at **[830]**, **[856]**; words "the relevant date" in square brackets in sub-paras (7)–(9) substituted by the Commonhold and Leasehold Reform Act 2002, s 126(1), for savings see the Commonhold and Leasehold Reform Act 2002 (Commencement No 5 and Saving and Transitional Provision) Order 2004, SI 2004/3056, art 4(1A) at **[3434]**, and the Commonhold and Leasehold Reform Act 2002 (Commencement No 3 and Saving and Transitional Provision) (Wales) Order 2005, SI 2005/1353, art 3(2) at **[3449]**.

Para 8: substituted by the Housing Act 1996, s 107(4), Sch 10, paras 1, 18(1), (6), subject to savings as noted above.

Para 9: words in square brackets inserted by the Housing Act 1996, ss 109(1), (4), 107(4), Sch 10, paras 1, 18(1), (7), subject to savings as noted above; words in italics substituted by the words "RTE company" by the Commonhold and Leasehold Reform Act 2002, s 124, Sch 8, paras 2, 40(1), (2), as from a day to be appointed.

Para 9A: inserted by the Housing Act 1996, s 107(4), Sch 10, paras 1, 18(1), (8), subject to savings as noted above; words in italics substituted by the words "RTE company" by the Commonhold and Leasehold Reform Act 2002, s 124, Sch 8, paras 2, 40(1), (2), as from a day to be appointed.

## PART IV
## OTHER INTERESTS TO BE ACQUIRED

### *Price payable for other interests*

10.—(1) Where the *nominee purchaser* is to acquire any freehold interest in pursuance of section 1(2)(a) or (4) or section 21(4), then (subject to sub-paragraph (3) below) the price payable for that interest shall be the aggregate of—

    (a)    the value of the interest as determined in accordance with paragraph 11,

    (b)    any share of the marriage value to which the owner of the interest is entitled under paragraph 12, and

    (c)    any amount of compensation payable to the owner of the interest in accordance with paragraph 13.

(2) Where the *nominee purchaser* is to acquire any leasehold interest by virtue of section 2(1) other than an intermediate leasehold interest, or *he* is to acquire any leasehold interest in pursuance of section 21(4), then (subject to sub-paragraph (3) below) the price payable for that interest shall be the aggregate of—

    (a)    the value of the interest as determined in accordance with paragraph 11, and

    (b)    any amount of compensation payable to the owner of the interest in accordance with paragraph 13.

(3) Where in the case of any interest the amount arrived at in accordance with sub-paragraph (1) or (2) is a negative amount, the price payable by the *nominee purchaser* for the interest shall be nil.

### *Value of other interests*

11.—(1) In the case of any such freehold interest as is mentioned in paragraph 10(1), paragraph 3 shall apply for determining the value of the interest with such modifications as are appropriate to relate it to a sale of the interest subject (where applicable) to any leases intermediate between that interest and any lease held by a qualifying tenant of a flat contained in the specified premises.

(2) In the case of any such leasehold interest as is mentioned in paragraph 10(2), then—

    (a)    (unless paragraph (b) below applies) paragraph 3 shall apply as mentioned in sub-paragraph (1) above;

    (b)    if it is the interest of the tenant under a minor intermediate lease within the meaning of paragraph 7, sub-paragraphs (2) to (10) of that paragraph shall apply with such modifications as are appropriate for determining the value of the interest.

(3) In its application in accordance with sub-paragraph (1) or (2) above, paragraph 3(6) shall have effect as if the reference to paragraph 14(2) were a reference to paragraph 18(2).

[(4) In its application in accordance with sub-paragraph (2) above, paragraph 3(1A) shall have effect with the addition after paragraph (a) of—

    "(aa) an owner of a freehold interest in the specified premises, or".]

(9)  For the purposes of this paragraph the expectation of possession carried by a lease in relation to a lease ("the sub-lease") on which it is in immediate reversion is the expectation of possession which it carries at [the relevant date] after the sub-lease, on the basis that—

    (a)   (subject to sub-paragraph (10)) where the sub-lease is a lease held by a qualifying tenant of a flat contained in the specified premises, it terminates at [the relevant date] if its term date fell before then, or else it terminates on its term date; and

    (b)   in any other case, the sub-lease terminates on its term date.

(10)  In a case where before the relevant date for the purposes of this Chapter the landlord of any such qualifying tenant as is mentioned in sub-paragraph (9)(a) had given notice to quit terminating the tenant's sub-lease on a date earlier than that date, the date specified in the notice to quit shall be substituted for the date specified in that provision.

PART I
STATUTES

### *Compensation for loss on acquisition of interest*

[8.—(1)  Where the owner of the intermediate leasehold interest will suffer any loss or damage to which this paragraph applies, there shall be payable to him such amount as is reasonable to compensate him for that loss or damage.

(2)  This paragraph applies to—

    (a)   any diminution in value of any interest of the owner of the intermediate leasehold interest in other property resulting from the acquisition of his interest in the specified premises; and

    (b)   any other loss or damage which results therefrom to the extent that it is referable to his ownership of any interest in other property.

(3)  Without prejudice to the generality of paragraph (b) of sub-paragraph (2), the kinds of loss falling within that paragraph include loss of development value in relation to the specified premises to the extent that it is referable as mentioned in that paragraph.

(4)  In sub-paragraph (3) "development value", in relation to the specified premises, means any increase in the value of the interest in the premises of the owner of the intermediate leasehold interest which is attributable to the possibility of demolishing, reconstructing or carrying out substantial works of construction on, the whole or a substantial part of the premises.]

### *Owners of intermediate interests entitled to part of marriage value*

9.—(1)  This paragraph applies where [paragraph 2 applies and]—

    (a)   the price payable for the freehold of the specified premises includes an amount in respect of the freeholder's share of the marriage value, and

    (b)   the *nominee purchaser* is to acquire any intermediate leasehold interests.

(2)  The amount payable to the freeholder in respect of his share of the marriage value shall be divided between the freeholder and the owners of the intermediate leasehold interests in proportion to the value of their respective interests in the specified premises (as determined for the purposes of paragraph 2(1)(a) or paragraph 6(1)(b)(i), as the case may be).

(3)  Where the owner of an intermediate leasehold interest is entitled in accordance with sub-paragraph (2) to any part of the amount payable to the freeholder in respect of the freeholder's share of the marriage value, the amount to which he is so entitled shall be payable to him by the freeholder.

[9A.—(1)  This paragraph applies where paragraph 5A applies and—

    (a)   the price payable for the freehold of a part of the specified premises includes an amount in respect of the freeholder's share of the marriage value, and

    (b)   the *nominee purchaser* is to acquire any intermediate leasehold interests which subsist in that part.

(2)  The amount payable to the freeholder of the part in respect of his share of the marriage value shall be divided between the freeholder and the owners of the intermediate leasehold interests which subsist in that part in proportion to the value of their respective interests in the part (as determined for the purposes of paragraph 5A(2)(a) or paragraph 6(1)(b)(i), as the case may be).

(3)  Where an intermediate leasehold interest subsists not only in the part of the specified premises in which the freeholder's interest subsists ("the relevant part") but also in another part of those premises—

    (a)   the value of the intermediate leasehold interest as determined for the purposes of paragraph 6(1)(b)(i) shall be apportioned between the relevant part and the other part of the specified premises in which it subsists, and

    (b)   sub-paragraph (2) shall have effect as if the reference to the value of the intermediate leasehold interest in the relevant part as determined for the purposes of paragraph 6(1)(b)(i) were to the value of that interest as determined on an apportionment in accordance with paragraph (a).

*Marriage value*

12.—(1)   Where any such freehold interest as is mentioned in paragraph 10(1) is an interest in any such property as is mentioned in section 1(3)(a)—

(a)   sub-paragraphs (2) to (4) of paragraph 4 shall apply with such modifications as are appropriate for determining the marriage value in connection with the acquisition by the *nominee purchaser* of that interest; and

(b)   sub-paragraph (1) of that paragraph shall apply with such modifications as are appropriate for determining the share of the marriage value to which the owner of that interest is entitled.

(2)   Where—

(a)   the owner of any such freehold interest is entitled to any share of the marriage value in respect of any such property, and

(b)   the *nominee purchaser* is to acquire any leasehold interests in that property superior to any lease held by a *participating tenant*,

the amount payable to the owner of the freehold interest in respect of his share of the marriage value in respect of that property shall be divided between the owner of that interest and the owners of the leasehold interests in proportion to the value of their respective interests in that property (as determined for the purposes of paragraph 10(1) or (2), as the case may be).

(3)   Where the owner of any such leasehold interest ("the intermediate landlord") is entitled in accordance with sub-paragraph (2) to any part of the amount payable to the owner of any freehold interest in respect of his share of the marriage value in respect of any property, the amount to which the intermediate landlord is so entitled shall be payable to him by the owner of that freehold interest.

*Compensation for loss on acquisition of interest*

[13.—(1)   Where the owner of any such freehold or leasehold interest as is mentioned in paragraph 10(1) or (2) ("relevant interest") will suffer any loss or damage to which this paragraph applies, there shall be payable to him such amount as is reasonable to compensate him for that loss or damage.

(2)   This paragraph applies to—

(a)   any diminution in value of any interest in other property belonging to the owner of a relevant interest, being diminution resulting from the acquisition of the property in which the relevant interest subsists; and

(b)   any other loss or damage which results therefrom to the extent that it is referable to his ownership of any interest in other property.

(3)   Without prejudice to the generality of paragraph (b) of sub-paragraph (2), the kinds of loss falling within that paragraph include loss of development value in relation to the property in which the relevant interest subsists to the extent that it is referable to his ownership of any interest in other property.

(4)   In sub-paragraph (3) "development value", in relation to the property in which the relevant interest subsists, means any increase in the value of the relevant interest which is attributable to the possibility of demolishing, reconstructing or carrying out substantial works of construction on, the whole or a substantial part of the property.]

**[926]**

**NOTES**

Para 10: words "nominee purchaser" in italics substituted in each place by the words "RTE company" and word "he" in italics substituted by the word "it" by the Commonhold and Leasehold Reform Act 2002, s 124, Sch 8, paras 2, 40(1), (2), (6), as from a day to be appointed.

Para 11: sub-para (4) added by the Housing Act 1996, s 109(1), (5), except in relation to a case where, before 1 October 1996, a notice was given under s 13 or 42 of this Act at **[817]**, **[848]**, or an application was made to court under s 26 or 50 of this Act at **[830]**, **[856]**.

Para 12: words "nominee purchaser" in italics substituted in each place by the words "RTE company" and words "participating tenant" in italics substituted by the words "participating member of the RTE company" by the Commonhold and Leasehold Reform Act 2002, s 124, Sch 8, paras 2, 40(1)–(3), as from a day to be appointed.

Para 13: substituted by the Housing Act 1996, s 107(4), Sch 10, paras 1, 18(1), (9), subject to savings as noted above.

## PART V
VALUATION ETC OF INTERESTS IN SPECIFIED PREMISES WITH NEGATIVE VALUES

*Valuation of freehold and intermediate leasehold interests*

14.—(1)   Where—

(a)   the value of the freeholder's interest in [a] specified premises (as determined [for the relevant purposes]), or

(b)     the value of any intermediate leasehold interest (as determined [for the relevant purposes]),

is a negative amount, the value of the interest for [those] purposes shall be nil.

(2)     Where sub-paragraph (1) applies to any intermediate leasehold interest whose value is a negative amount ("the negative interest"), then for the relevant purposes any interests in the specified premises superior to the negative interest and having a positive value shall be reduced in value—

(a)     beginning with the interest which is immediately superior to the negative interest and continuing (if necessary) with any such other superior interests in order of proximity to the negative interest;

(b)     until the aggregate amount of the reduction is equal to the negative amount in question; and

(c)     without reducing the value of any interest to less than nil.

(3)     In a case where sub-paragraph (1) applies to two or more intermediate leasehold interests whose values are negative amounts, sub-paragraph (2) shall apply separately in relation to each of those interests—

(a)     beginning with the interest which is inferior to every other of those interests and then in order of proximity to that interest; and

(b)     with any reduction in the value of any interest for the relevant purposes by virtue of any prior application of sub-paragraph (2) being taken into account.

[(3A)     Where sub-paragraph (2) applies—

(a)     for the purposes of paragraph 5A(2)(a), and

(b)     in relation to an intermediate leasehold interest in relation to which there is more than one immediately superior interest,

any reduction in value made under that sub-paragraph shall be apportioned between the immediately superior interests.]

(4)     For the purposes of sub-paragraph (2) an interest has a positive value if (apart from that sub-paragraph) its value for the relevant purposes is a positive amount.

(5)     In this Part of this Schedule "the relevant purposes"—

(a)     as respects [a] freeholder's interest in the specified premises, means the purposes of paragraph 2(1)(a) [or, as the case may be, 5A(2)(a)]; and

(b)     as respects any intermediate leasehold interest, means the purposes of paragraph 6(1)(b)(i).

*Calculation of marriage value*

15.—(1)     Where (as determined in accordance with paragraph 4(3) and (4)) the value of any interest—

(a)     when held by the person from whom it is to be acquired by the *nominee purchaser*, or

(b)     when acquired by the *nominee purchaser*,

is a negative amount, then for the purposes of paragraph 4(2) the value of the interest when so held or acquired shall be nil.

(2)     Where sub-paragraph (1) above applies to any intermediate leasehold interest whose value when held or acquired as mentioned in paragraph (a) or (b) of that sub-paragraph is a negative amount, paragraph 14(2) to (4) shall apply for determining for the purposes of paragraph 4(2) the value when so held or acquired of other interests in the specified premises, as if—

(a)     any reference to paragraph 14(1) were a reference to sub-paragraph (1) above; and

(b)     any reference to the relevant purposes were, as respects any interest, a reference to the purposes of paragraph 4(2) as it applies to the interest when so held or acquired.

(3)     References in paragraph 16 or 17 to paragraph 14(2) or (3) do not extend to that provision as it applies in accordance with sub-paragraph (2) above.

[(4)     References in this paragraph to paragraph 4(2), (3) or (4) extend to that provision as it applies in accordance with paragraph 5A(2)(b).]

*Apportionment of marriage value*

16.—(1)     Where paragraph 14(1) applies to an interest, the value of the interest for the purposes of paragraph 9(2) shall be nil, unless sub-paragraph (2) below applies.

(2)     In a case where paragraph 14(1) applies to [a] freeholder's interest in the specified premises and to every intermediate leasehold interest—

(a)     sub-paragraph (1) above shall not apply for the purposes of paragraph 9(2); and

(b)     any division falling to be made on the proportional basis referred to in paragraph 9(2) shall be so made in such a way as to secure that the greater the negativity of an interest's value the smaller the share in respect of the interest.

(3)     In a case where—

(a)    paragraph 14(2) operates to reduce the value of any such superior interest as is there mentioned ("the superior interest"), and

(b)    after the operation of that provision there remains any interest whose value for the relevant purposes is a positive amount,

the value of the superior interest for the purposes of paragraph 9(2) shall be the value which (in accordance with paragraph 14(2)) it has for the relevant purposes.

(4)    In a case where—

(a)    paragraph 14(2) operates to reduce the value of any such superior interest as is there mentioned ("the superior interest"), but

(b)    after the operation of that provision there remains no such interest as is mentioned in sub-paragraph (3)(b) above,

the value of the superior interest for the purposes of paragraph 9(2) shall be the value which it has for the relevant purposes apart from paragraph 14(2).

*Adjustment of compensation*

17.—(1)    Where—

(a)    paragraph 14(2) operates to reduce the value of any such superior interest as is there mentioned ("the superior interest"), and

(b)    apart from this paragraph any amount of compensation is payable under paragraph 8 to the owner of any relevant inferior interest in respect of that interest,

there shall be payable to the owner of the superior interest so much of the amount of compensation as is equal to the amount of the reduction or, if less than that amount, the whole of the amount of compensation.

(2)    Where—

(a)    paragraph 14(2) operates to reduce the value of two or more such superior interests as are there mentioned ("the superior interests"), and

(b)    apart from this paragraph any amount of compensation is payable under paragraph 8 to the owner of any relevant inferior interest in respect of that interest,

sub-paragraph (1) shall apply in the first instance as if the reference to the owner of the superior interest were to the owner of such of the superior interests as is furthest from the negative interest, and then, as respects any remaining amount of compensation, as if that reference were to the owner of such of the superior interests as is next furthest from the negative interest, and so on.

(3)    In sub-paragraph (1) or (2) "relevant inferior interest", in relation to any interest whose value is reduced as mentioned in that sub-paragraph ("the superior interest"), means—

(a)    the negative interest on account of which any such reduction is made, or

(b)    any other interest intermediate between that negative interest and the superior interest;

but sub-paragraph (1) shall apply in the first instance in relation to any amount of compensation payable to the owner of that negative interest, and then, for the purpose of offsetting (so far as possible) any reduction remaining to be offset in accordance with sub-paragraph (1) or (2), in relation to any amount of compensation payable to the owner of the interest immediately superior to that negative interest, and so on in order of proximity to it.

(4)    To the extent that an amount of compensation is payable to the owner of any interest by virtue of this paragraph—

(a)    paragraph 2(1)(c)[, 5A(2)(c)] or 6(1)(b)(ii) shall have effect as if it were an amount of compensation payable to him, as owner of that interest, in accordance with paragraph 5 or 8, as the case may be; and

(b)    the person who would otherwise have been entitled to it in accordance with paragraph 8 shall accordingly not be so entitled.

(5)    In a case where paragraph 14(2) applies separately in relation to two or more negative interests in accordance with paragraph 14(3), the preceding provisions of this paragraph shall similarly apply separately in relation to the reductions made on account of each of those interests, and shall so apply—

(a)    according to the order determined by paragraph 14(3)(a); and

(b)    with there being taken into account any reduction in the amount of compensation payable to any person under paragraph 8 which results from the prior application of the preceding provisions of this paragraph.

[(6)    Where any reduction in value under sub-paragraph (2) of paragraph 14 is apportioned in accordance with sub-paragraph (3A) of that paragraph, any amount of compensation payable by virtue of this paragraph shall be similarly apportioned.]

**[927]**

---

**NOTES**

Para 14: words in square brackets in sub-para (1) and word in first pair of square brackets in sub-para (5) substituted, and sub-para (3A) and words in second pair of square brackets in sub-para (5) inserted by the

Housing Act 1996, s 107(4), Sch 10, paras 1, 18(1), (10)–(12), except in relation to a case where, before 1 October 1996, a notice was given under s 13 or 42 of this Act at **[817]**, **[848]**, or an application was made to court under s 26 or 50 of this Act at **[830]**, **[856]**.

Para 15: words in italics in sub-para (1) substituted in both places by the words "RTE company" by the Commonhold and Leasehold Reform Act 2002, s 124, Sch 8, paras 2, 40(1), (2), as from a day to be appointed; sub-para (4) added by the Housing Act 1996, s 107(4), Sch 10, paras 1, 18(1), (13), subject to savings as noted above.

Para 16: word in square brackets substituted by the Housing Act 1996, s 107(4), Sch 10, paras 1, 18(1), (14), subject to savings as noted above.

Para 17: figure in square brackets in sub-para (4) inserted and sub-para (6) added by the Housing Act 1996, s 107(4), Sch 10, paras 1, 18(1), (16), subject to savings as noted above.

## PART VI
## VALUATION ETC OF OTHER INTERESTS WITH NEGATIVE VALUES

### Valuation of freehold and leasehold interests

18.—(1)  Where—
   (a)  the value of any freehold interest (as determined in accordance with paragraph 11(1)), or
   (b)  the value of any leasehold interest (as determined in accordance with paragraph 11(2)),
is a negative amount, the value of the interest for the relevant purposes shall be nil.

(2)  Where, in the case of any property, sub-paragraph (1) applies to any leasehold interest in the property whose value is a negative amount ("the negative interest"), then for the relevant purposes any interests in the property superior to the negative interest and having a positive value shall, if they are interests which are to be acquired by the *nominee purchaser*, be reduced in value—
   (a)  beginning with the interest which is nearest to the negative interest and continuing (if necessary) with any such other superior interests in order of proximity to the negative interest;
   (b)  until the aggregate amount of the reduction is equal to the negative amount in question; and
   (c)  without reducing the value of any interest to less than nil.

(3)  In a case where sub-paragraph (1) applies to two or more leasehold interests in any property whose values are negative amounts, sub-paragraph (2) shall apply separately in relation to each of those interests—
   (a)  beginning with the interest which is inferior to every other of those interests and then in order of proximity to that interest; and
   (b)  with any reduction in the value of any interest for the relevant purposes by virtue of any prior application of sub-paragraph (2) being taken into account.

(4)  For the purposes of sub-paragraph (2) an interest has a positive value if (apart from that sub-paragraph) its value for the relevant purposes is a positive amount.

(5)  In this Part of this Schedule "the relevant purposes"—
   (a)  as respects any freehold interest, means the purposes of paragraph 10(1)(a); and
   (b)  as respects any leasehold interest, means the purposes of paragraph 10(2)(a).

### Calculation of marriage value

19.—(1)  Where (as determined in accordance with paragraph 4(3) and (4)) the value of any interest—
   (a)  when held by the person from whom it is to be acquired by the *nominee purchaser*, or
   (b)  when acquired by the *nominee purchaser*,
is a negative amount, then for the purposes of paragraph 4(2) the value of the interest when so held or acquired shall be nil.

(2)  Where, in the case of any property, sub-paragraph (1) above applies to any leasehold interest in the property whose value when held or acquired as mentioned in paragraph (a) or (b) of that sub-paragraph is a negative amount, paragraph 18(2) to (4) shall apply for determining for the purposes of paragraph 4(2) the value when so held or acquired of other interests in the property, as if—
   (a)  any reference to paragraph 18(1) were a reference to sub-paragraph (1) above; and
   (b)  any reference to the relevant purposes were, as respects any interest, a reference to the purposes of paragraph 4(2) as it applies to the interest when so held or acquired.

(3)  In this paragraph any reference to any provision of paragraph 4 is a reference to that provision as it applies in accordance with paragraph 12(1).

(4)  References in paragraph 20 or 21 to paragraph 18(2) or (3) do not extend to that provision as it applies in accordance with sub-paragraph (2) above.

*Apportionment of marriage value*

20.—(1)    Where paragraph 18(1) applies to any interest in any property to which paragraph 12(1) applies, the value of the interest for the purposes of paragraph 12(2) shall be nil, unless sub-paragraph (2) below applies.

(2)    Where, in the case of any property, paragraph 18(1) applies to every interest which is to be acquired by the *nominee purchaser*—
    (a)    sub-paragraph (1) above shall not apply for the purposes of paragraph 12(2); and
    (b)    any division falling to be made on the proportional basis referred to in paragraph 12(2) shall be so made in such a way as to secure that the greater the negativity of an interest's value the smaller the share in respect of the interest.

(3)    Where in the case of any property—
    (a)    paragraph 18(2) operates to reduce the value of any such superior interest as is there mentioned ("the superior interest"), and
    (b)    after the operation of that provision there remains any interest which is to be acquired by the *nominee purchaser* and whose value for the relevant purposes is a positive amount,
the value of the superior interest for the purposes of paragraph 12(2) shall be the value which (in accordance with paragraph 18(2)) it has for the relevant purposes.

(4)    Where in the case of any property—
    (a)    paragraph 18(2) operates to reduce the value of any such superior interest as is there mentioned ("the superior interest"), but
    (b)    after the operation of that provision there remains no such interest as is mentioned in sub-paragraph (3)(b) above,
the value of the superior interest for the purposes of paragraph 12(2) shall be the value which it has for the relevant purposes apart from paragraph 18(2).

*Adjustment of compensation*

21.—(1)    Where in the case of any property—
    (a)    paragraph 18(2) operates to reduce the value of any such superior interest as is there mentioned ("the superior interest"), and
    (b)    apart from this paragraph any amount of compensation is payable by virtue of paragraph 13 to the owner of any relevant inferior interest in respect of that interest,
there shall be payable to the owner of the superior interest so much of the amount of compensation as is equal to the amount of the reduction or, if less than that amount, the whole of the amount of compensation.

(2)    Where in the case of any property—
    (a)    paragraph 18(2) operates to reduce the value of two or more such superior interests as are there mentioned ("the superior interests"), and
    (b)    apart from this paragraph any amount of compensation is payable by virtue of paragraph 13 to the owner of any relevant inferior interest in respect of that interest,
sub-paragraph (1) shall apply in the first instance as if the reference to the owner of the superior interest were to the owner of such of the superior interests as is furthest from the negative interest, and then, as respects any remaining amount of compensation, as if that reference were to the owner of such of the superior interests as is next furthest from the negative interest, and so on.

(3)    In sub-paragraph (1) or (2) "relevant inferior interest", in relation to any interest whose value is reduced as mentioned in that sub-paragraph ("the superior interest"), means—
    (a)    the negative interest on account of which any such reduction is made, or
    (b)    any other interest in the property in question which is to be acquired by the *nominee purchaser* and is intermediate between that negative interest and the superior interest;
but sub-paragraph (1) shall apply in the first instance in relation to any amount of compensation payable to the owner of that negative interest, and then, for the purpose of offsetting (so far as possible) any reduction remaining to be offset in accordance with sub-paragraph (1) or (2), in relation to any amount of compensation payable to the owner of such interest falling within paragraph (b) above as is nearest to that negative interest, and so on in order of proximity to it.

(4)    To the extent that an amount of compensation is payable to the owner of any interest by virtue of this paragraph—
    (a)    paragraph 10(1)(c) or (as the case may be) paragraph 10(2)(b) shall have effect as if it were an amount of compensation payable to him, as owner of that interest, in accordance with paragraph 13; and
    (b)    the person who would otherwise have been entitled to it in accordance with paragraph 13 shall accordingly not be so entitled.

(5)    In a case where paragraph 18(2) applies separately in relation to two or more negative interests in accordance with paragraph 18(3), the preceding provisions of this paragraph shall similarly apply separately in relation to the reductions made on account of each of those interests, and shall so apply—

(a)   according to the order determined by paragraph 18(3)(a); and
(b)   with there being taken into account any reduction in the amount of compensation payable to any person by virtue of paragraph 13 which results from the prior application of the preceding provisions of this paragraph.

**[928]**

**NOTES**
Paras 18–21: words in italics substituted in each place by the words "RTE company" by the Commonhold and Leasehold Reform Act 2002, s 124, Sch 8, paras 2, 40(1), (2), as from a day to be appointed.

## SCHEDULE 7
### CONVEYANCE TO *NOMINEE PURCHASER* ON ENFRANCHISEMENT
Section 34

*Interpretation*

1.   In this Schedule—
[(a)   "the relevant premises" means, in relation to the conveyance of any interest, the premises in which the interest subsists;
(b)   "the freeholder" means, in relation to the conveyance of a freehold interest, the person whose interest is to be conveyed;]
(c)   "other property" means property of which the freehold is not to be acquired by the *nominee purchaser* under this Chapter; and
[(d)   "the appropriate time" means, in relation to the conveyance of a freehold interest, the time when the interest is to be conveyed to the *nominee purchaser*].

*General*

2.—(1)   The conveyance shall not exclude or restrict the general words implied in conveyances under section 62 of the Law of Property Act 1925, or the all-estate clause implied under section 63 of that Act, unless—
(a)   the exclusion or restriction is made for the purpose of preserving or recognising any existing interest of the freeholder in tenant's incumbrances or any existing right or interest of any other person, or
(b)   the *nominee purchaser* consents to the exclusion or restriction.

(2)   The freeholder shall not be bound—
(a)   to convey to the *nominee purchaser* any better title than that which he has or could require to be vested in him, or
[(b)   to enter into any covenant for title beyond those implied under Part I of the Law of Property (Miscellaneous Provisions) Act 1994 in a case where a disposition is expressed to be made with limited title guarantee;
and in the absence of agreement to the contrary the freeholder shall be entitled to be indemnified by the *nominee purchaser* in respect of any costs incurred by him in complying with the covenant implied by virtue of section 2(1)(b) of that Act (covenant for further assurance).]

(3)   In this paragraph "tenant's incumbrances" includes any interest directly or indirectly derived out of a lease, and any incumbrance on a lease or any such interest (whether or not the same matter is an incumbrance also on any interest reversionary on the lease); and "incumbrances" has the same meaning as it has for the purposes of section 34 of this Act.

*Rights of support, passage of water etc*

3.—(1)   This paragraph applies to rights of any of the following descriptions, namely—
(a)   rights of support for a building or part of a building;
(b)   rights to the access of light and air to a building or part of a building;
(c)   rights to the passage of water or of gas or other piped fuel, or to the drainage or disposal of water, sewage, smoke or fumes, or to the use or maintenance of pipes or other installations for such passage, drainage or disposal;
(d)   rights to the use or maintenance of cables or other installations for the supply of electricity, for the telephone or for the receipt directly or by landline of visual or other wireless transmissions;
and the provisions required to be included in the conveyance by virtue of sub-paragraph (2) are accordingly provisions relating to any such rights.

(2)   The conveyance shall include provisions having the effect of—
(a)   granting with the relevant premises (so far as the freeholder is capable of granting them—
    (i)   all such easements and rights over other property as are necessary to secure as nearly as may be for the benefit of the relevant premises the same rights as exist for the benefit of those premises immediately before the appropriate time, and

(ii)    such further easements and rights (if any) as are necessary for the reasonable enjoyment of the relevant premises; and

(b)    making the relevant premises subject to the following easements and rights (so far as they are capable of existing in law), namely—

(i)    all easements and rights for the benefit of other property to which the relevant premises are subject immediately before the appropriate time, and

(ii)    such further easements and rights (if any) as are necessary for the reasonable enjoyment of other property, being property in which the freeholder has an interest at the relevant date.

### Rights of way

4.    Any such conveyance shall include—

(a)    such provisions (if any) as the *nominee purchaser* may require for the purpose of securing to *him* and the persons deriving title under *him* rights of way over other property, so far as the freeholder is capable of granting them, being rights of way that are necessary for the reasonable enjoyment of the relevant premises; and

(b)    such provisions (if any) as the freeholder may require for the purpose of making the relevant premises subject to rights of way necessary for the reasonable enjoyment of other property, being property in which he is to retain an interest after the acquisition of the relevant premises.

### Restrictive covenants

5.—(1)    As regards restrictive covenants, the conveyance shall include—

(a)    such provisions (if any) as the freeholder may require to secure that the *nominee purchaser* is bound by, or to indemnify the freeholder against breaches of, restrictive covenants which—

(i)    affect the relevant premises otherwise than by virtue of any lease subject to which the relevant premises are to be acquired or any agreement collateral to any such lease, and

(ii)    are immediately before the appropriate time enforceable for the benefit of other property; and

(b)    such provisions (if any) as the freeholder or the *nominee purchaser* may require to secure the continuance (with suitable adaptations) of restrictions arising by virtue of any such lease or collateral agreement as is mentioned in paragraph (a)(i), being either—

(i)    restrictions affecting the relevant premises which are capable of benefiting other property and (if enforceable only by the freeholder) are such as materially to enhance the value of the other property, or

(ii)    restrictions affecting other property which are such as materially to enhance the value of the relevant premises; and

(c)    such further restrictions as the freeholder may require to restrict the use of the relevant premises in a way which—

(i)    will not interfere with the reasonable enjoyment of those premises as they have been enjoyed during the currency of the leases subject to which they are to be acquired, but

(ii)    will materially enhance the value of other property in which the freeholder has an interest at the relevant date.

(2)    In this paragraph "restrictive covenant" means a covenant or agreement restrictive of the user of any land or building.

**[929]**

---

**NOTES**

Schedule heading: words "nominee purchaser" in italics substituted by the words "RTE company" by the Commonhold and Leasehold Reform Act 2002, s 124, Sch 8, paras 2, 41(1), (2), as from a day to be appointed.

Para 1: sub-paras (a), (b), (d) substituted by the Housing Act 1996, s 107(4), Sch 10, paras 1, 19, except in relation to a case where, before 1 October 1996, a notice was given under s 13 or 42 of this Act at **[817]**, **[848]**, or an application was made to court under s 26 or 50 of this Act at **[830]**, **[856]**; words in italics substituted in both places by the words "RTE company" by the Commonhold and Leasehold Reform Act 2002, s 124, Sch 8, paras 2, 41(1), (2), as from a day to be appointed.

Para 2: words in square brackets in sub-para (2) substituted by the Law of Property (Miscellaneous Provisions) Act 1994, s 21(1), (4), Sch 1, para 12(3), except in relation to any disposition of property to which, by virtue of ss 10, 11 of the 1994 Act, the Law of Property Act 1925, s 76 or the Land Registration Act 1925, s 24(1)(a) continues to apply; words in italics substituted in each place by the words "RTE company" by the Commonhold and Leasehold Reform Act 2002, s 124, Sch 8, paras 2, 41(1), (2), as from a day to be appointed.

Para 4: words "nominee purchaser" in italics substituted by the words "RTE company" and word "him" in italics substituted in both places by the word "it" by the Commonhold and Leasehold Reform Act 2002, s 124, Sch 8, paras 2, 41, as from a day to be appointed.

Para 5: words in italics substituted in each place by the words "RTE company" by the Commonhold and Leasehold Reform Act 2002, s 124, Sch 8, paras 2, 41(1), (2), as from a day to be appointed.

## SCHEDULE 8
## DISCHARGE OF MORTGAGES ETC: SUPPLEMENTARY PROVISIONS
Section 35

### *Construction*

1.   In this Schedule—

   "the consideration payable" means the consideration payable for the acquisition of the relevant interest;

   "the landlord" means the person from whom the relevant interest is being acquired;

   "the relevant interest" means any such interest as is mentioned in paragraph 2(1).

### *Duty of nominee purchaser to redeem mortgages*

2.—(1)   Where in accordance with section 35(1) a conveyance will operate to discharge any interest from a mortgage to secure the payment of money, it shall be the duty of the *nominee purchaser* to apply the consideration payable, in the first instance, in or towards the redemption of any such mortgage (and, if there are more than one, then according to their priorities).

(2)   If any amount payable in accordance with sub-paragraph (1) to the person entitled to the benefit of a mortgage is not so paid, nor paid into court in accordance with paragraph 4, the relevant interest shall remain subject to the mortgage as regards the amount in question, and to that extent section 35(1) shall not apply.

(3)   Subject to sub-paragraph (4), sub-paragraph (1) shall not apply to a debenture holders' charge, that is to say, a charge (whether a floating charge or not) in favour of the holders of a series of debentures issued by a company or other body of persons, or in favour of trustees for such debenture holders; and any such charge shall be disregarded in determining priorities for the purposes of sub-paragraph (1).

(4)   Sub-paragraph (3) shall not have effect in relation to a charge in favour of trustees for debenture holders which, at the date of the conveyance by virtue of which the relevant interest is acquired by the *nominee purchaser*, is (as regards that interest) a specific and not a floating charge.

### *Determination of amounts due in respect of mortgages*

3.—(1)   For the purpose of determining the amount payable in respect of any mortgage under paragraph 2(1)—

   (a)   a person entitled to the benefit of a mortgage to which that provision applies shall not be permitted to exercise any right to consolidate that mortgage with a separate mortgage on other property; and

   (b)   if the landlord or *any participating tenant* is himself entitled to the benefit of a mortgage to which that provision applies, it shall rank for payment as it would if another person were entitled to it, and the *nominee purchaser* shall be entitled to retain the appropriate amount in respect of any such mortgage of *a participating tenant*.

(2)   For the purpose of discharging any interest from a mortgage to which paragraph 2(1) applies, a person may be required to accept three months or any longer notice of the intention to pay the whole or part of the principal secured by the mortgage, together with interest to the date of payment, notwithstanding that the terms of the security make other provision or no provision as to the time and manner of payment; but he shall be entitled, if he so requires, to receive such additional payment as is reasonable in the circumstances—

   (a)   in respect of the costs of re-investment or other incidental costs and expenses; and

   (b)   in respect of any reduction in the rate of interest obtainable on reinvestment.

### *Payments into court*

4.—(1)   Where under section 35(1) any interest is to be discharged from a mortgage and, in accordance with paragraph 2(1), a person is or may be entitled in respect of the mortgage to receive the whole or part of the consideration payable, then if—

   (a)   for any reason difficulty arises in ascertaining how much is payable in respect of the mortgage, or

   (b)   for any reason mentioned in sub-paragraph (2) below difficulty arises in making a payment in respect of the mortgage,

the *nominee purchaser* may pay into court on account of the consideration payable the amount, if known, of the payment to be made in respect of the mortgage or, if that amount is not known, the whole of that consideration or such lesser amount as the *nominee purchaser* thinks right in order to provide for that payment.

(2)   Payment may be made into court in accordance with sub-paragraph (1)(b) where the difficulty arises for any of the following reasons, namely—

   (a)   because a person who is or may be entitled to receive payment cannot be found or his identity cannot be ascertained;

(b)    because any such person refuses or fails to make out a title, or to accept payment and give a proper discharge, or to take any steps reasonably required of him to enable the sum payable to be ascertained and paid; or

(c)    because a tender of the sum payable cannot, by reason of complications in the title to it or the want of two or more trustees or for other reasons, be effected, or not without incurring or involving unreasonable cost or delay.

(3)    Without prejudice to sub-paragraph (1)(a), the whole or part of the consideration payable shall be paid into court by the *nominee purchaser* if, before execution of the conveyance referred to in paragraph 2(1), notice is given to *him*—

(a)    that the landlord, or a person entitled to the benefit of a mortgage on the relevant interest, requires *him* to do so for the purpose of protecting the rights of persons so entitled, or for reasons related to the bankruptcy or winding up of the landlord, or

(b)    that steps have been taken to enforce any mortgage on the relevant interest by the bringing of proceedings in any court, or by the appointment of a receiver, or otherwise;

and where payment into court is to be made by reason only of a notice under this sub-paragraph, and the notice is given with reference to proceedings in a court specified in the notice other than a county court, payment shall be made into the court so specified.

*Savings*

5.—(1)    Where any interest is discharged by section 35(1) from a mortgage (without the obligations secured by the mortgage being satisfied by the receipt of the whole or part of the consideration payable), the discharge of that interest from the mortgage shall not prejudice any right or remedy for the enforcement of those obligations against other property comprised in the same or any other security, nor prejudice any personal liability as principal or otherwise of the landlord or any other person.

(2)    Nothing in this Schedule or section 35 shall be construed as preventing a person from joining in the conveyance referred to in paragraph 2(1) for the purpose of discharging the relevant interest from any mortgage without payment or for a lesser payment than that to which he would otherwise be entitled; and, if he does so, the persons to whom the consideration payable ought to be paid shall be determined accordingly.

**[930]**

**NOTES**

Para 2: words "nominee purchaser" in italics substituted in each place (including the preceding cross-heading) by the words "RTE company" by the Commonhold and Leasehold Reform Act 2002, s 124, Sch 8, paras 2, 42(1), (2), as from a day to be appointed.

Para 3: words "any participating tenant" in italics substituted by the words "any member of the RTE company", words "nominee purchaser" in italics substituted by the words "RTE company" and words "a participating tenant" substituted by the words "any of its members" by the Commonhold and Leasehold Reform Act 2002, s 124, Sch 8, paras 2, 42(1)–(3), as from a day to be appointed.

Para 4: words "nominee purchaser" in italics substituted in each place by the words "RTE company" and word "him" substituted in both places by the word "it" by the Commonhold and Leasehold Reform Act 2002, s 124, Sch 8, paras 2, 42(1), (2), (4), as from a day to be appointed.

SCHEDULE 9
GRANT OF LEASES BACK TO THE FORMER FREEHOLDER

Section 36

PART I
GENERAL

1.—(1)    In this Schedule—

["the appropriate time", in relation to a flat or other unit contained in the specified premises, means the time when the freehold of the flat or other unit is acquired by the *nominee purchaser*;]

"the demised premises", in relation to a lease granted or to be granted in pursuance of Part II or III of this Schedule, means—

(a)    the flat or other unit demised or to be demised under the lease, or

(b)    in the case of such a lease under which two or more units are demised, both or all of those units or (if the context so permits) any of them;

["the freeholder", in relation to a flat or other unit contained in the specified premises, means the person who owns the freehold of the flat or other unit immediately before the appropriate time;]

"housing association" has the meaning given by section 1(1) of the Housing Associations Act 1985;

"intermediate landlord", in relation to a flat or other unit let to a tenant, means a person who holds a leasehold interest in the flat or other unit which is superior to that held by the tenant's immediate landlord;

"other property" means property other than the demised premises.

(2)   In this Schedule any reference to a flat or other unit, in the context of the grant of a lease of it, includes any yard, garden, garage, outhouses and appurtenances belonging to or usually enjoyed with it and let with it immediately before the appropriate time.

**[931]**

**NOTES**
Definitions "the appropriate time" and "the freeholder" substituted by the Housing Act 1996, s 107(4), Sch 10, paras 1, 20(1), (2), except in relation to a case where, before 1 October 1996, a notice was given under s 13 or 42 of this Act at **[817]**, **[848]**, or an application was made to court under s 26 or 50 of this Act at **[830]**, **[856]**; in definition "the appropriate time" words in italics substituted by the words "RTE company" by the Commonhold and Leasehold Reform Act 2002, s 124, Sch 8, paras 2, 43, as from a day to be appointed.

## PART II
## MANDATORY LEASEBACK

### *Flats etc let under secure tenancies*

2.—(1)   This paragraph applies where immediately before the appropriate time any flat [falling within sub-paragraph (1A)] is let under a secure tenancy [or an introductory tenancy] and either—
   (a)   the freeholder is the tenant's immediate landlord, or
   (b)   the freeholder is a public sector landlord and every intermediate landlord of the flat (as well as the immediate landlord under the secure tenancy [or the introductory tenancy]) is also a public sector landlord.

[(1A)   A flat falls within this sub-paragraph if—
   (a)   the freehold of the whole of it is owned by the same person, and
   (b)   it is contained in the specified premises.]

(2)   Sub-paragraph (1)(b) has effect whether any such intermediate landlord, or the immediate landlord under the secure tenancy [or the introductory tenancy], is or is not a qualifying tenant of the flat.

(3)   Where this paragraph applies, the *nominee purchaser* shall grant to the freeholder a lease of the flat in accordance with section 36 and paragraph 4 below.

(4)   In this paragraph any reference to a flat includes a reference to a unit (other than a flat) which is used as a dwelling.

### *Flats etc let by housing associations under tenancies other than secure tenancies*

3.—(1)   This paragraph applies where immediately before the appropriate time any flat [falling within sub-paragraph (1A)] is let by a housing association under a tenancy other than a secure tenancy and—
   (a)   the housing association is the freeholder, and
   (b)   the tenant is not a qualifying tenant of the flat.

[(1A)   A flat falls within this sub-paragraph if—
   (a)   the freehold of the whole of it is owned by the same person, and
   (b)   it is contained in the specified premises.]

(2)   Where this paragraph applies, the *nominee purchaser* shall grant to the freeholder (that is to say, the housing association) a lease of the flat in accordance with section 36 and paragraph 4 below.

(3)   In this paragraph any reference to a flat includes a reference to a unit (other than a flat) which is used as a dwelling.

### *Provisions as to terms of lease*

4.—(1)   Any lease granted to the freeholder in pursuance of paragraph 2 or 3, and any agreement collateral to it, shall conform with the provisions of Part IV of this Schedule except to the extent that any departure from those provisions is agreed to by the *nominee purchaser* and the freeholder with the approval of a leasehold valuation tribunal.

(2)   A leasehold valuation tribunal shall not approve any such departure from those provisions unless it appears to the tribunal that it is reasonable in the circumstances.

(3)   In determining whether any such departure is reasonable in the circumstances, the tribunal shall have particular regard to the interests of the tenant under the secure tenancy [or introductory tenancy] referred to in paragraph 2(1) or (as the case may be) under the housing association tenancy referred to in paragraph 3(1).

(4)   Subject to the preceding provisions of this paragraph, any such lease or agreement as is mentioned in sub-paragraph (1) may include such terms as are reasonable in the circumstances.

**[932]**

PART I
STATUTES

**NOTES**

Para 2: words in first pair of square brackets substituted and sub-para (1A) inserted by the Housing Act 1996, s 107(4), Sch 10, paras 1, 20(1), (3), except in relation to a case where, before 1 October 1996, a notice was given under s 13 or 42 of this Act at **[817]**, **[848]**, or an application was made to court under s 26 or 50 of this Act at **[830]**, **[856]**; other words in square brackets inserted by the Housing Act 1996 (Consequential Amendments) Order 1997, SI 1997/74, art 2, Schedule, para 9(d)(i), (ii); words in italics in sub-para (3) substituted by the words "RTE company" by the Commonhold and Leasehold Reform Act 2002, s 124, Sch 8, paras 2, 43, as from a day to be appointed.

Para 3: words in first pair of square brackets substituted and sub-para (1A) inserted by the Housing Act 1996, s 107(4), Sch 10, paras 1, 20(1), (4), subject to savings as noted above; words in italics in sub-para (2) substituted by the words "RTE company" by the Commonhold and Leasehold Reform Act 2002, s 124, Sch 8, paras 2, 43, as from a day to be appointed.

Para 4: words in italics in sub-para (1) substituted by the words "RTE company" by the Commonhold and Leasehold Reform Act 2002, s 124, Sch 8, paras 2, 43, as from a day to be appointed; words in square brackets in sub-para (3) inserted by SI 1997/74, art 2, Schedule, para 9(d)(iii).

## PART III
## RIGHT OF FREEHOLDER TO REQUIRE LEASEBACK OF CERTAIN UNITS

### *Flats without qualifying tenants and other units*

**5.**—(1)   Subject to sub-paragraph (3), this paragraph applies to any unit [falling within sub-paragraph (1A)] which is not immediately before the appropriate time a flat let to a person who is a qualifying tenant of it.

[(1A)   A unit falls within this sub-paragraph if—
   (a)   the freehold of the whole of it is owned by the same person, and
   (b)   it is contained in the specified premises.]

(2)   Where this paragraph applies, the *nominee purchaser* shall, if the freeholder by notice requires him to do so, grant to the freeholder a lease of the unit in accordance with section 36 and paragraph 7 below.

(3)   This paragraph does not apply to a flat or other unit to which paragraph 2 or 3 applies.

### *Flat etc occupied by resident landlord*

**6.**—[(1)   Sub-paragraph (2) applies where, immediately before the freehold of a flat or other unit contained in the specified premises is acquired by the *nominee purchaser*—
   (a)   those premises are premises with a resident landlord by virtue of the occupation of the flat or other unit by the freeholder of it, and
   (b)   the freeholder of the flat or other unit is a qualifying tenant of it.

(2)   If the freeholder of the flat or other unit ("the relevant unit") by notice requires the *nominee purchaser* to do so, the *nominee purchaser* shall grant to the freeholder a lease of the relevant unit in accordance with section 36 and paragraph 7 below; and, on the grant of such a lease to the freeholder, he shall be deemed to have surrendered any lease of the relevant unit held by him immediately before the appropriate time.]

(3)   Sections 5, 7 and 8 shall apply for the purpose of determining whether, for the purposes of sub-paragraph [(1)(b)] above, the freeholder is a qualifying tenant of a unit other than a flat as they apply for the purpose of determining whether a person is a qualifying tenant of a flat.

### *Provisions as to terms of lease*

**7.**—(1)   Any lease granted to the freeholder in pursuance of paragraph 5 or 6, and any agreement collateral to it, shall conform with the provisions of Part IV of this Schedule except to the extent that any departure from those provisions—
   (a)   is agreed to by the *nominee purchaser* and the freeholder; or
   (b)   is directed by a leasehold valuation tribunal on an application made by either of those persons.

(2)   A leasehold valuation tribunal shall not direct any such departure from those provisions unless it appears to the tribunal that it is reasonable in the circumstances.

(3)   In determining whether any such departure is reasonable in the circumstances, the tribunal shall have particular regard to the interests of any person who will be the tenant of the flat or other unit in question under a lease inferior to the lease to be granted to the freeholder.

(4)   Subject to the preceding provisions of this paragraph, any such lease or agreement as is mentioned in sub-paragraph (1) may include such terms as are reasonable in the circumstances.

**[933]**

**NOTES**

Para 5: words in first pair of square brackets substituted and sub-para (1A) inserted by the Housing Act 1996, s 107(4), Sch 10, paras 1, 20(1), (5), except in relation to a case where, before 1 October 1996, a notice was given under s 13 or 42 of this Act at **[817]**, **[848]**, or an application was made to court under s 26 or 50 of this Act at **[830]**, **[856]**; words "nominee purchaser" in italics in sub-para (2) substituted by the words "RTE company" by the Commonhold and Leasehold Reform Act 2002, s 124, Sch 8, paras 2, 43, as from a day to be appointed.

Para 6: sub-paras (1), (2) and number in square brackets in sub-para (3) substituted by the Housing Act 1996, s 107, Sch 10, para 20(1), (6), (7), subject to savings as noted above; words in italics substituted in each place by the words "RTE company" by the Commonhold and Leasehold Reform Act 2002, s 124, Sch 8, paras 2, 43, as from a day to be appointed.

Para 7: words in italics substituted by the words "RTE company" by the Commonhold and Leasehold Reform Act 2002, s 124, Sch 8, paras 2, 43, as from a day to be appointed.

### PART IV
### TERMS OF LEASE GRANTED TO FREEHOLDER
*Duration of lease and rent*

8.    The lease shall be a lease granted for a term of 999 years at a peppercorn rent.

*General rights to be granted*

9.    The lease shall not exclude or restrict the general words implied under section 62 of the Law of Property Act 1925, unless the exclusion or restriction is made for the purpose of preserving or recognising an existing right or interest of any person.

*[Covenants for title*

9A.    The lessor shall not be bound to enter into any covenant for title beyond—
    (a)    those implied from the grant, and
    (b)    those implied under Part I of the Law of Property (Miscellaneous Provisions) Act 1994 in a case where a disposition is expressed to be made with limited title guarantee.]

10.—(1)    This paragraph applies to rights of any of the following descriptions, namely—
    (a)    rights of support for a building or part of a building;
    (b)    rights to the access of light and air to a building or part of a building;
    (c)    rights to the passage of water or of gas or other piped fuel, or to the drainage or disposal of water, sewage, smoke or fumes, or to the use or maintenance of pipes or other installations for such passage, drainage or disposal; and
    (d)    rights to the use or maintenance of cables or other installations for the supply of electricity, for the telephone or for the receipt directly or by landline of visual or other wireless transmissions;

and the provisions required to be included in the lease by virtue of sub-paragraph (2) are accordingly provisions relating to any such rights.

(2)    The lease shall include provisions having the effect of—
    (a)    granting with the demised premises (so far as the lessor is capable of granting them)—
        (i)    all such easements and rights over other property as are necessary to secure as nearly as may be for the benefit of the demised premises the same rights as exist for the benefit of those premises immediately before the appropriate time, and
        (ii)    such further easements and rights (if any) as are necessary for the reasonable enjoyment of the demised premises; and
    (b)    making the demised premises subject to the following easements and rights (so far as they are capable of existing in law), namely—
        (i)    all easements and rights for the benefit of other property to which the demised premises are subject immediately before the appropriate time, and
        (ii)    such further easements and rights (if any) as are necessary for the reasonable enjoyment of other property, being property in which the lessor acquires an interest at the appropriate time.

*Rights of way*

11.    The lease shall include—
    (a)    such provisions (if any) as the lessee may require for the purpose of securing to him, and persons deriving title under him, rights of way over other property (so far as the lessor is capable of granting them), being rights of way that are necessary for the reasonable enjoyment of the demised premises; and
    (b)    such provisions (if any) as the lessor may require for the purpose of making the demised premises subject to rights of way necessary for the reasonable enjoyment of other property, being property in which the lessor acquires an interest at the appropriate time.

*Common use of premises and facilities*

12.    The lease shall include, so far as the lessor is capable of granting them, the like rights to use in common with others any premises, facilities or services as are enjoyed immediately before the appropriate time by any tenant of the demised premises.

*Covenants affecting demised premises*

13.    The lease shall include such provisions (if any) as the lessor may require to secure that the lessee is bound by, or to indemnify the lessor against breaches of, restrictive covenants (that is to say, covenants or agreements restrictive of the use of any land or premises) affecting the demised premises immediately before the appropriate time and enforceable for the benefit of other property.

*Covenants by lessor*

14.—(1)    The lease shall include covenants by the lessor—

   (a)    to keep in repair the structure and exterior of the demised premises and of the specified premises (including drains, gutters and external pipes) and to make good any defect affecting that structure;

   (b)    to keep in repair any other property over or in respect of which the lessee has rights by virtue of this Schedule;

   (c)    to ensure, so far as practicable, that the services which are to be provided by the lessor and to which the lessee is entitled (whether alone or in common with others) are maintained at a reasonable level, and to keep in repair any installation connected with the provision of any of those services.

(2)    The lease shall include a covenant requiring the lessor—

   (a)    to insure the specified premises for their full reinstatement value against destruction or damage by fire, tempest, flood or any other cause against the risk of which it is the normal practice to insure;

   (b)    to rebuild or reinstate the demised premises or the specified premises in the case of any such destruction or damage.

*Covenants by lessee*

15.    The lease shall include a covenant by the lessee to ensure that the interior of the demised premises is kept in good repair (including decorative repair).

*Contributions by lessee*

16.—(1)    The lease may require the lessee to bear a reasonable part of the costs incurred by the lessor in discharging or insuring against the obligations imposed by the covenants required by paragraph 14(1) or in discharging the obligation imposed by the covenant required by paragraph 14(2)(a).

(2)    Where a covenant required by paragraph 14(1) or (2)(a) has been modified to any extent in accordance with paragraph 4 or 7, the reference in sub-paragraph (1) above to the obligations or (as the case may be) the obligation imposed by that covenant shall be read as a reference to the obligations or obligation imposed by that covenant as so modified.

*Assignment and sub-letting of premises*

17.—(1)    Except where the demised premises consist of or include any unit let or intended for letting on a business lease, the lease shall not include any provision prohibiting or restricting the assignment of the lease or the sub-letting of the whole or part of the demised premises.

(2)    Where the demised premises consist of or include any such unit as is mentioned in sub-paragraph (1), the lease shall contain a prohibition against—

   (a)    assigning or sub-letting the whole or part of any such unit, or

   (b)    altering the user of any such unit,

without the prior written consent of the lessor (such consent not to be unreasonably withheld).

*Restriction on terminating lease*

18.    The lease shall not include any provision for the lease to be terminated otherwise than by forfeiture on breach of any term of the lease by the lessee.

**[934]**

---

**NOTES**

Para 9A: inserted, together with preceding cross-heading, by the Law of Property (Miscellaneous Provisions) Act 1994, s 21(1), (4), Sch 1, para 12(4), except in relation to any disposition of property to which, by virtue of ss 10, 11 of the 1994 Act, the Law of Property Act 1925, s 76 or the Land Registration Act 1925, s 24(1)(a) continues to apply.

## SCHEDULE 10
### ACQUISITION OF INTERESTS FROM LOCAL AUTHORITIES ETC
Section 37

*Disapplication of provisions relating to disposals by local authorities etc*

1.—(1)   It is hereby declared that nothing in any of the provisions specified in sub-paragraph (2) (which impose requirements as to consent or consultation or other restrictions in relation to disposals falling within those provisions) applies to any disposal of a freehold or leasehold interest in any premises which is made in pursuance of this Chapter.

(2)   The provisions referred to in sub-paragraph (1) are—
    (a)    sections 32 and 43 of the Housing Act 1985 (disposals of land by local authorities) and section 133 of the Housing Act 1988 (certain subsequent disposals);
    [(b)    section 9 and 42 of the Housing Act 1996 and section 9 of the Housing Associations Act 1985 (disposals by registered social landlords and other housing associations);]
    (c)    section 79(1) and (2) of the Housing Act 1988 (disposals by housing action trusts) and section 81 of that Act (certain subsequent disposals); and
    (d)    ...

*Provisions relating to secure tenants following leaseback*

2.—(1)   This paragraph applies where a lease is granted to a public sector landlord in pursuance of paragraph 2 of Schedule 9.

(2)   Where—
    (a)    immediately before the appropriate time the public sector landlord was the immediate landlord under a secure tenancy [or an introductory tenancy] of a flat contained in the demised premises, and
    (b)    that tenancy continues in force after the grant of the lease referred to in sub-paragraph (1),

the tenant shall be deemed to have continued without interruption as tenant of the landlord under the secure tenancy [or, as the case may be, the introductory tenancy], despite the disposal of the landlord's interest which immediately preceded the grant of the lease referred to in that sub-paragraph.

(3)   Where—
    (a)    immediately before the appropriate time a person was a successor in relation to a secure tenancy [or an introductory tenancy] of a flat contained in the demised premises, and
    (b)    that person is, in connection with the grant of the lease referred to in sub-paragraph (1), granted a new secure tenancy of that flat which is a tenancy for a term certain,

then for the purposes of sections 87 to 90 of the Housing Act 1985 (succession on death of tenant) that person shall also be a successor in relation to the new tenancy.

(4)   Where—
    (a)    immediately before the appropriate time a person was the tenant under a secure tenancy [or an introductory tenancy] of a flat contained in the demised premises, and
    (b)    that person is, in connection with the grant of the lease referred to in sub-paragraph (1), granted a new secure tenancy [or introductory tenancy] of that flat,

then, for the purpose of determining whether either of the conditions referred to in sub-paragraph (5) is satisfied, the new tenancy shall not be regarded as a new letting of the flat but shall instead be regarded as a continuation of the secure tenancy [or introductory tenancy] referred to in paragraph (a) above.

(5)   Those conditions are—
    (a)    the condition specified in sub-paragraph (1)(b) of paragraph 5 of Schedule 5 to the Housing Act 1985 (exception to the right to buy in case of letting in connection with employment); and
    (b)    the condition specified in sub-paragraph (1)(b) of paragraph 11 of that Schedule (exception to the right to buy in case of letting for occupation by person of pensionable age etc).

(6)   In this paragraph—
    (a)    any reference to a secure tenancy [or an introductory tenancy] of a flat is a reference to a secure tenancy [or an introductory tenancy] of a flat whether with or without any yard, garden, garage, outhouses or appurtenances belonging to or usually enjoyed with it; and
    (b)    any reference to a flat includes a reference to a unit (other than a flat) which is used as a dwelling.

(7)   In this paragraph—
    (a)    "the appropriate time" and "the demised premises" have the same meaning as in Schedule 9; and

(b)　"successor" has the same meaning as in section 88 of the Housing Act 1985 [in relation to a secure tenancy and as in section 132 of the Housing Act 1996 in relation to an introductory tenancy].

**[935]**

**NOTES**
Para 1: sub-para (2)(b) substituted by the Housing Act 1996 (Consequential Provisions) Order 1996, SI 1996/2325, art 5, Sch 2, para 21(1), (3); sub-para (2)(d) repealed by the Housing Act 1996, s 227, Sch 19, Pt IX.
Para 2: words in square brackets inserted by the Housing Act 1996 (Consequential Amendments) Order 1997, SI 1997/74, art 2, Schedule, para 9(e).

SCHEDULE 11
PROCEDURE WHERE COMPETENT LANDLORD IS NOT TENANT'S
IMMEDIATE LANDLORD
Section 40

PART I
PROCEDURE IN RELATION TO TENANT'S NOTICE

*Tenant's notice may be given to any of the other landlords*

1.　The tenant's notice under section 42 shall be regarded as given to the competent landlord for the purposes of subsection (2)(a) of that section if it is given to any of the other landlords instead; and references in this Chapter to the relevant date shall be construed accordingly.

*Tenant to give copies of notice*

2.—(1)　Where the tenant's notice is given to the competent landlord, the tenant shall give a copy of the notice to every person known or believed by him to be one of the other landlords.

(2)　Where the tenant's notice is, in accordance with paragraph 1, given to one of the other landlords, the tenant shall give a copy of the notice to every person (apart from the recipient of the notice) known or believed by the tenant to be either the competent landlord or one of the other landlords.

(3)　The tenant's notice shall state whether copies are being given in accordance with this paragraph to anyone other than the recipient and, if so, to whom.

*Recipient of notice or copy to give further copies*

3.—(1)　Subject to sub-paragraph (2), a recipient of the tenant's notice or of a copy of it (including a person receiving a copy under this sub-paragraph—
　　(a)　shall forthwith give a copy to any person who—
　　　　(i)　is known or believed by him to be the competent landlord or one of the other landlords, and
　　　　(ii)　is not stated in the recipient's copy of the notice, or known by him, to have received a copy; and
　　(b)　if he knows who is, or he believes himself to be, the competent landlord, shall—
　　　　(i)　give a notice to the tenant stating who is the person thought by him to be the competent landlord, and
　　　　(ii)　give a copy of it to that person (if not himself) and to every person known or believed by him to be one of the other landlords.

(2)　Sub-paragraph (1) does not apply where the recipient is neither the competent landlord nor one of the other landlords.

(3)　Where a person gives any copies of the tenant's notice in accordance with sub-paragraph (1)(a), he shall—
　　(a)　supplement the statement under paragraph 2(3) by adding any further persons to whom he is giving copies or who are known by him to have received one; and
　　(b)　notify the tenant of the persons added by him to that statement.

*Consequences of failure to comply with paragraph 2 or 3*

4.—(1)　Where—
　　(a)　the competent landlord or any of the other landlords does not receive a copy of the tenant's notice before the end of the period specified in it in pursuance of section 42(3)(f), but
　　(b)　he was given a notice under section 41 by the tenant and, in response to the notice under that section, notified the tenant of his interest in the tenant's flat,
the tenant's notice shall cease to have effect at the end of that period.

(2)　Where—

(a)     sub-paragraph (1) does not apply, but
(b)     any person fails without reasonable cause to comply with paragraph 2 or 3 above, or is guilty of any unreasonable delay in complying with either of those paragraphs,

he shall be liable for any loss thereby occasioned to the tenant or to the competent landlord or any of the other landlords.

**[936]**

## PART II
### CONDUCT OF PROCEEDINGS BY COMPETENT LANDLORD ON BEHALF OF OTHER LANDLORDS

#### *Counter-notice to specify other landlords*

5.    Any counter-notice given to the tenant by the competent landlord must specify the other landlords on whose behalf he is acting.

#### *Acts of competent landlord binding on other landlords*

6.—(1)    Without prejudice to the generality of section 40(2)—
(a)     any notice given under this Chapter by the competent landlord to the tenant,
(b)     any agreement for the purposes of this Chapter between that landlord and the tenant, and
(c)     any determination of the court or a leasehold valuation tribunal under this Chapter in proceedings between that landlord and the tenant,

shall be binding on the other landlords and on their interests in the property demised by the tenant's lease or any other property; but in the event of dispute the competent landlord or any of the other landlords may apply to the court for directions as to the manner in which the competent landlord should act in the dispute.

(2)    Subject to paragraph 7(2), the authority given to the competent landlord by section 40(2) shall extend to receiving on behalf of any other landlord any amount payable to that person by virtue of Schedule 13.

(3)    If any of the other landlords cannot be found, or his identity cannot be ascertained, the competent landlord shall apply to the court for directions and the court may make such order as it thinks proper with a view to giving effect to the rights of the tenant and protecting the interests of other persons; but, subject to any such directions, the competent landlord shall proceed as in other cases.

(4)    The competent landlord, if he acts in good faith and with reasonable care and diligence, shall not be liable to any of the other landlords for any loss or damage caused by any act or omission in the exercise or intended exercise of the authority given to him by section 40(2).

#### *Other landlords acting independently*

7.—(1)    Notwithstanding anything in section 40(2), any of the other landlords shall, at any time after the giving by the competent landlord of a counter-notice under section 45 and on giving notice to both the competent landlord and the tenant of his intention to be so represented, be entitled to be separately represented—
(a)     in any legal proceedings in which his title to any property comes in question, or
(b)     in any legal proceedings relating to the determination of any amount payable to him by virtue of Schedule 13.

(2)    Any of the other landlords may also, on giving notice to the competent landlord and the tenant, require that any amount payable to him by virtue of Schedule 13 shall be paid by the tenant to him, or to a person authorised by him to receive it, instead of to the competent landlord; but if, after being given proper notice of the time and method of completion with the tenant, either—
(a)     he fails to notify the competent landlord of the arrangements made with the tenant to receive payment, or
(b)     having notified the competent landlord of those arrangements, the arrangements are not duly implemented,

the competent landlord shall be authorised to receive the payment for him, and the competent landlord's written receipt for the amount payable shall be a complete discharge to the tenant.

#### *Obligations of other landlords to competent landlord*

8.—(1)    It shall be the duty of each of the other landlords (subject to paragraph 7) to give the competent landlord all such information and assistance as he may reasonably require; and, if any of the other landlords fails to comply with this sub-paragraph, that landlord shall indemnify the competent landlord against any liability incurred by him in consequence of the failure.

(2)    Each of the other landlords shall make such contribution as shall be just to costs and expenses which are properly incurred by the competent landlord in pursuance of section 40(2) but are not recoverable or not recovered from the tenant.

### *Applications made by other landlords under section 47(1)*

9.—(1)    The authority given to the competent landlord by section 40(2) shall not extend to the bringing of proceedings under section 47(1) on behalf of any of the other landlords, or preclude any of those landlords from bringing proceedings under that provision on his own behalf as if he were the competent landlord.

(2)    In section 45(2)(c) any reference to the competent landlord shall include a reference—

    (a)    to any of the other landlords, or

    (b)    to any two or more of the following, namely the competent landlord and the other landlords, acting together;

and in section 47(1) and (2) references to the landlord shall be construed accordingly; but if any of the other landlords intends to make such an application as is mentioned in section 45(2)(c), whether alone or together with any other person or persons, his name shall be stated in the counter-notice.

### *Deemed surrender and re-grant of leases of other landlords*

10.—(1)    Where a lease is executed under section 56 or 93(4) or in pursuance of any order made under this Chapter, then (subject to sub-paragraph (3)) that instrument shall have effect for the creation of the tenant's new lease of his flat, and for the operation of the rights and obligations conferred and imposed by it, as if there had been a surrender and re-grant of any subsisting lease intermediate between the interest of the competent landlord and the existing lease; and the covenants and other provisions of that instrument shall be framed and take effect accordingly.

(2)    Section 57(2) shall apply to the new lease on the basis that account is to be taken of obligations imposed on any of the other landlords by virtue of that or any superior lease; and section 59(3) shall apply on the basis that the reference there to the tenant's landlord includes the immediate landlord from whom the new lease will be held and all superior landlords, including any superior to the competent landlord.

(3)    Where a lease of the tenant's flat superior to the existing lease is vested in the tenant or a trustee for him, the new lease shall include an actual surrender of that superior lease without a re-grant, and it shall accordingly be disregarded for the purposes of the preceding provisions of this paragraph.

### *Discharge of existing mortgages*

11.    Where by reason of section 58(2) it is necessary to make any payment to discharge the tenant's flat from a mortgage affecting the interest of any landlord, then if the competent landlord is not the landlord liable or primarily liable in respect of the mortgage, he shall not be required to make that payment otherwise than out of money made available for the purpose by the landlord so liable, and it shall be the duty of that landlord to provide for the mortgage being discharged.

**[937]**

## SCHEDULE 12
## THE TENANT'S NOTICE: SUPPLEMENTARY PROVISIONS

Section 42

## PART I
## EFFECT OF TENANT'S NOTICE ON OTHER NOTICES, FORFEITURES ETC

### *Prior notice by tenant terminating lease*

1.    A notice given by a qualifying tenant of a flat under section 42 shall be of no effect if it is given—

    (a)    after the tenant has given notice terminating the lease of the flat (other than a notice that has been superseded by the grant, express or implied, of a new tenancy); or

    (b)    during the subsistence of an agreement for the grant to the tenant of a future tenancy of the flat, where the agreement is one to which paragraph 17 of Schedule 10 to the Local Government and Housing Act 1989 applies.

### *Prior notice by landlord terminating lease*

2.—(1)    Subject to sub-paragraph (2), a notice given by a qualifying tenant of a flat under section 42 shall be of no effect if it is given more than two months after a landlord's notice terminating the tenant's lease of the flat has been given under section 4 of the Landlord and Tenant Act 1954 or served under paragraph (1) of Schedule 10 to the Local Government and Housing Act 1989 (whether or not the notice has effect to terminate the lease).

(2)    Sub-paragraph (1) does not apply where the landlord gives his written consent to a notice being given under section 42 after the end of those two months.

(3)    Where in the case of a qualifying tenant of a flat who gives a notice under section 42—

    (a)    any such landlord's notice is given or served as mentioned in sub-paragraph (1), but

    (b)    that notice was not given or served more than two months before the date on which the notice under section 42 is given to the landlord,

the landlord's notice shall cease to have effect on that date.

    (4)   If—

    (a)    any such landlord's notice ceases to have effect by virtue of sub-paragraph (3), but

    (b)    the claim made by the tenant by the giving of his notice under section 42 is not effective,

then sub-paragraph (5) shall apply to any landlord's notice terminating the tenant's lease of the flat which—

    (i)   is given under section 4 of the Landlord and Tenant Act 1954 or served under paragraph 4(1) of Schedule 10 to the Local Government and Housing Act 1989, and

    (ii)   is so given or served within one month after the expiry of the period of currency of that claim.

    (5)   Where this sub-paragraph applies to a landlord's notice, the earliest date which may be specified in the notice as the date of termination shall be—

    (a)    in the case of a notice given under section 4 of that Act of 1954—

       (i)   the date of termination specified in the previous notice, or

       (ii)   the date of expiry of the period of three months beginning with the date of the giving of the new notice,

      whichever is the later; or

    (b)    in the case of a notice served under paragraph 4(1) of Schedule 10 to that Act of 1989—

       (i)   the date of termination specified in the previous notice, or

       (ii)   the date of expiry of the period of four months beginning with the date of service of the new notice,

      whichever is the later.

    (6)   Where—

    (a)    by virtue of sub-paragraph (5) a landlord's notice specifies as the date of termination of a lease a date earlier than six months after the date of the giving of the notice, and

    (b)    the notice proposes a statutory tenancy,

section 7(2) of the Landlord and Tenant Act 1954 shall apply in relation to the notice with the substitution, for references to the period of two months ending with the date of termination specified in the notice and the beginning of that period, of references to the period of three months beginning with the date of the giving of the notice and the end of that period.

### *Orders for possession and pending proceedings for forfeiture etc*

3.—(1)   A notice given by a qualifying tenant of a flat under section 42 shall be of no effect if at the time when it is given he is obliged to give up possession of his flat in pursuance of an order of a court or will be so obliged at a date specified in such an order.

    (2)   Except with the leave of the court, a qualifying tenant of a flat shall not give a notice under section 42 at a time when any proceedings are pending to enforce a right of re-entry or forfeiture terminating his lease of the flat.

    (3)   Leave shall only be granted under sub-paragraph (2) if the court is satisfied that the tenant does not wish to give such a notice solely or mainly for the purpose of avoiding the consequences of the breach of the terms of his lease in respect of which proceedings are pending.

    (4)   If—

    (a)    leave is so granted, and

    (b)    the tenant by such a notice makes a claim to acquire a new lease of his flat,

the tenant's lease shall be deemed for the purposes of the claim to be a subsisting lease despite the existence of those proceedings and any order made afterwards in those proceedings; and, if the claim is effective, the court in which those proceedings were brought may set aside or vary any such order to such extent and on such terms as appear to that court to be appropriate.

### *Notice terminating lease given by tenant or landlord during currency of claim*

4.   Where by a notice given under section 42 a tenant makes a claim to acquire a new lease of a flat, any notice terminating the tenant's lease of the flat, whether it is—

    (a)    a notice given by the tenant, or

    (b)    a landlord's notice given under section 4 of the Landlord and Tenant Act 1954 or served under paragraph 4(1) of Schedule 10 to the Local Government and Housing Act 1989,

shall be of no effect if it is given or served during the currency of the claim.

### *Tenant's notice operates to prevent termination of lease*

5.—(1)   Where by a notice under section 42 a tenant makes a claim to acquire a new lease of a flat, then during the currency of the claim and for three months thereafter the lease of the flat shall not terminate—

    (a)    by effluxion of time, or

(b)     in pursuance of a notice to quit given by the immediate landlord of the tenant, or

(c)     by the termination of a superior lease;

but if the claim is not effective, and but for this sub-paragraph the lease would have so terminated before the end of those three months, the lease shall so terminate at the end of those three months.

(2)     Sub-paragraph (1) shall not be taken to prevent an earlier termination of the lease in any manner not mentioned in that sub-paragraph, and shall not affect—

(a)     the power under section 146(4) of the Law of Property Act 1925 (relief against forfeiture of leases) to grant a tenant relief against the termination of a superior lease, or

(b)     any right of the tenant to relief under section 16(2) of the Landlord and Tenant Act 1954 (relief where landlord proceeding to enforce covenants) or under paragraph 9 of Schedule 5 to that Act (relief in proceedings brought by superior landlord).

*Restriction on proceedings to enforce right of re-entry or forfeiture*

6.     Where by a notice under section 42 a tenant makes a claim to acquire a new lease of a flat, then during the currency of the claim—

(a)     no proceedings to enforce any right of re-entry or forfeiture terminating the lease of the flat shall be brought in any court without the leave of that court, and

(b)     leave shall only be granted if the court is satisfied that the notice was given solely or mainly for the purpose of avoiding the consequences of the breach of the terms of the tenant's lease in respect of which proceedings are proposed to be brought;

but where leave is granted, the notice shall cease to have effect.

*Effect of notice under section 16(2) of Landlord and Tenant Act 1954 on tenant's notice*

7.—(1)     A tenant who, in proceedings to enforce a right of re-entry or forfeiture or a right to damages in respect of a failure to comply with any terms of his lease, applies for relief under section 16 of the Landlord and Tenant Act 1954 is not thereby precluded from making a claim to acquire a new lease under this Chapter; but if he gives notice under section 16(2) of that Act (under which the tenant is relieved from any order for recovery of possession or for payment of damages, but the tenancy is cut short), any notice given by him under section 42 with respect to property comprised in his lease shall be of no effect or, if already given, shall cease to have effect.

(2)     Sub-paragraph (1) shall apply in relation to proceedings relating to a superior tenancy with the substitution for the references to section 16 and to section 16(2) of the Landlord and Tenant Act 1954 of references to paragraph 9 and to paragraph 9(2) of Schedule 5 to that Act.

*Interpretation*

8.—(1)     For the purposes of this Part of this Schedule—

(a)     references to a notice under section 42 include, in so far as the context permits, references to a notice purporting to be given under that section (whether by a qualifying tenant or not), and references to the tenant by whom a notice is given shall be construed accordingly;

(b)     references to a claim being effective are references to a new lease being acquired in pursuance of the claim; and

(c)     references to the currency of a claim are—

(i)     where the claim is made by a valid notice under section 42, references to the period during which the notice continues in force in accordance with subsection (8) of that section, or

(ii)     where the claim is made by a notice which is not a valid notice under section 42, references to the period beginning with the giving of the notice and ending with the time when the notice is set aside by the court or is withdrawn or when it would (if valid) cease to have effect or be deemed to have been withdrawn.

(2)     For the purposes of sub-paragraph (1)(c) the date when a notice is set aside, or would (if valid) cease to have effect, in consequence of an order of a court shall be taken to be the date when the order becomes final.

(3)     The references in this Schedule—

(a)     to section 16 of the Landlord and Tenant Act 1954 and subsection (2) of that section, and

(b)     to paragraph 9 of Schedule 5 to that Act and sub-paragraph (2) of that paragraph,

include references to those provisions as they apply in relation to Schedule 10 to the Local Government and Housing Act 1989 (security of tenure on ending of long residential tenancies).

**[938]**

# PART II
## OTHER PROVISIONS

9.—(1)     The tenant's notice shall not be invalidated by any inaccuracy in any of the particulars required by section 42(3) or by any misdescription of any of the property to which the claim extends.

(2) Where the tenant's notice—
    (a)    specifies any property which he is not entitled to have demised to him under a new lease granted in pursuance of this Chapter, or
    (b)    fails to specify any property which he is entitled to have so demised to him,

the notice may, with the leave of the court and on such terms as the court may think fit, be amended so as to exclude or include the property in question.

**[939]**

## SCHEDULE 13
## PREMIUM AND OTHER AMOUNTS PAYABLE BY TENANT ON GRANT OF NEW LEASE
Section 56

### PART I
### GENERAL

1.    In this Schedule—
    "intermediate leasehold interest" means the interest of any person falling within section 40(4)(c), to the extent that it is an interest in the tenant's flat subsisting immediately before the grant of the new lease;
    .....

**[940]**

**NOTES**
Definition "the valuation date" (omitted) repealed by the Commonhold and Leasehold Reform Act 2002, s 180, Sch 14, except in relation to an application for a new lease of a flat in respect of which notice was given under s 42 of this Act at **[848]**, or where an application was made for an order under s 50 of this Act at **[856]**, before 26 July 2002 (in relation to England) or 1 January 2003 (in relation to Wales).

### PART II
### PREMIUM PAYABLE IN RESPECT OF GRANT OF NEW LEASE

*Premium payable by tenant*

2.    The premium payable by the tenant in respect of the grant of the new lease shall be the aggregate of—
    (a)    the diminution in value of the landlord's interest in the tenant's flat as determined in accordance with paragraph 3,
    (b)    the landlord's share of the marriage value as determined in accordance with paragraph 4, and
    (c)    any amount of compensation payable to the landlord under paragraph 5.

*Diminution in value of landlord's interest*

3.—(1)    The diminution in value of the landlord's interest is the difference between—
    (a)    the value of the landlord's interest in the tenant's flat prior to the grant of the new lease; and
    (b)    the value of his interest in the flat once the new lease is granted.

(2)    Subject to the provisions of this paragraph, the value of any such interest of the landlord as is mentioned in sub-paragraph (1)(a) or (b) is the amount which at [the relevant date] that interest might be expected to realise if sold on the open market by a willing seller (with [neither the tenant nor any owner of an intermediate leasehold interest] buying or seeking to buy) on the following assumptions—
    (a)    on the assumption that the vendor is selling for an estate in fee simple or (as the case may be) such other interest as is held by the landlord, subject to the relevant lease and any intermediate leasehold interests;
    (b)    on the assumption that Chapter I and this Chapter confer no right to acquire any interest in any premises containing the tenant's flat or to acquire any new lease;
    (c)    on the assumption that any increase in the value of the flat which is attributable to an improvement carried out at his own expense by the tenant or by any predecessor in title is to be disregarded; and
    (d)    on the assumption that (subject to paragraph (b)) the vendor is selling with and subject to the rights and burdens with and subject to which the relevant lease has effect or (as the case may be) is to be granted.

(3)    In sub-paragraph (2) "the relevant lease" means either the tenant's existing lease or the new lease, depending on whether the valuation is for the purposes of paragraph (a) or paragraph (b) of sub-paragraph (1).

(4)    It is hereby declared that the fact that sub-paragraph (2) requires assumptions to be made as to the matters specified in paragraphs (a) to (d) of that sub-paragraph does not preclude the making of assumptions as to other matters where those assumptions are appropriate for determining the

amount which at [the relevant date] any such interest of the landlord as is mentioned in sub-paragraph (1)(a) or (b) might be expected to realise if sold as mentioned in sub-paragraph (2).

(5)    In determining any such amount there shall be made such deduction (if any) in respect of any defect in title as on a sale of that interest on the open market might be expected to be allowed between a willing seller and a willing buyer.

(6)    The value of any such interest of the landlord as is mentioned in sub-paragraph (1)(a) or (b) shall not be increased by reason of—
    (a)    any transaction which—
        (i)    is entered into on or after the date of the passing of this Act (otherwise than in pursuance of a contract entered into before that date), and
        (ii)    involves the creation or transfer of an interest superior to (whether or not preceding) any interest held by the tenant; or
    (b)    any alteration on or after that date of the terms on which any such superior interest is held.

### Landlord's share of marriage value

4.—(1)    The marriage value is the amount referred to in sub-paragraph (2), and the landlord's share of the marriage value is [50 per cent of that amount].

(2)    [Subject to sub-paragraph (2A),] the marriage value is the difference between the following amounts, namely—
    (a)    the aggregate of—
        (i)    the value of the interest of the tenant under his existing lease,
        (ii)    the value of the landlord's interest in the tenant's flat prior to the grant of the new lease, and
        (iii)    the values prior to the grant of that lease of all intermediate leasehold interests (if any); and
    (b)    the aggregate of—
        (i)    the value of the interest to be held by the tenant under the new lease,
        (ii)    the value of the landlord's interest in the tenant's flat once the new lease is granted, and
        (iii)    the values of all intermediate leasehold interests (if any) once that lease is granted.

[(2A)    Where at the relevant date the unexpired term of the tenant's existing lease exceeds eighty years, the marriage value shall be taken to be nil.]

(3)    For the purposes of sub-paragraph (2)—
    [(a)    the value of the interest of the tenant under his existing lease shall be determined in accordance with paragraph 4A;
    (aa)    the value of the interest to be held by the tenant under the new lease shall be determined in accordance with paragraph 4B;]
    (b)    the value of any such interest of the landlord as is mentioned in paragraph (a) or paragraph (b) of [sub-paragraph (2)] is the amount determined for the purposes of paragraph 3(1)(a) or paragraph 3(1)(b) (as the case may be); and
    (c)    the value of any intermediate leasehold interest shall be determined in accordance with paragraph 8, and shall be so determined as at [the relevant date].

[4A.—(1)    Subject to the provisions of this paragraph, the value of the interest of the tenant under the existing lease is the amount which at [the relevant date] that interest might be expected to realise if sold on the open market by a willing seller (with neither the landlord nor any owner of an intermediate leasehold interest buying or seeking to buy) on the following assumptions—
    (a)    on the assumption that the vendor is selling such interest as is held by the tenant subject to any interest inferior to the interest of the tenant;
    (b)    on the assumption that Chapter I and this Chapter confer no right to acquire any interest in any premises containing the tenant's flat or to acquire any new lease;
    (c)    on the assumption that any increase in the value of the flat which is attributable to an improvement carried out at his own expense by the tenant or by any predecessor in title is to be disregarded; and
    (d)    on the assumption that (subject to paragraph (b)) the vendor is selling with and subject to the rights and burdens with and subject to which any interest inferior to the existing lease of the tenant has effect.

(2)    It is hereby declared that the fact that sub-paragraph (1) requires assumptions to be made in relation to particular matters does not preclude the making of assumptions as to other matters where those assumptions are appropriate for determining the amount which at [the relevant date] the interest of the tenant under his existing lease might be expected to realise if sold as mentioned in that sub-paragraph.

(3)　In determining any such amount there shall be made such deduction (if any) in respect of any defect in title as on a sale of that interest on the open market might be expected to be allowed between a willing seller and a willing buyer,

(4)　Subject to sub-paragraph (5), the value of the interest of the tenant under his existing lease shall not be increased by reason of—

(a)　any transaction which—
　　(i)　is entered into after 19th January 1996, and
　　(ii)　involves the creation or transfer of an interest inferior to the tenant's existing lease; or
(b)　any alteration after that date of the terms on which any such inferior interest is held.

(5)　Sub-paragraph (4) shall not apply to any transaction which falls within paragraph (a) of that sub-paragraph if—

(a)　the transaction is entered into in pursuance of a contract entered into on or before the date mentioned in that paragraph; and
(b)　the amount of the premium payable by the tenant in respect of the grant of the new lease was determined on or before that date either by agreement or by a leasehold valuation tribunal under this Chapter.

4B.—(1)　Subject to the provisions of this paragraph, the value of the interest to be held by the tenant under the new lease is the amount which at [the relevant date] that interest (assuming it to have been granted to him at that date) might be expected to realise if sold on the open market by a willing seller (with the owner of any interest superior to the interest of the tenant not buying or seeking to buy) on the following assumptions—

(a)　on the assumption that the vendor is selling such interest as is to be held by the tenant under the new lease subject to the inferior interests to which the tenant's existing lease is subject at [the relevant date];
(b)　on the assumption that Chapter I and this Chapter confer no right to acquire any interest in any premises containing the tenant's flat or to acquire any new lease;
(c)　on the assumption that there is to be disregarded any increase in the value of the flat which would fall to be disregarded under paragraph (c) of sub-paragraph (1) of paragraph 4A in valuing in accordance with that sub-paragraph the interest of the tenant under his existing lease; and
(d)　on the assumption that (subject to paragraph (b)) the vendor is selling with and subject to the rights and burdens with and subject to which any interest inferior to the tenant's existing lease at [the relevant date] then has effect.

(2)　It is hereby declared that the fact that sub-paragraph (1) requires assumptions to be made in relation to particular matters does not preclude the making of assumptions as to other matters where those assumptions are appropriate for determining the amount which at [the relevant date] the interest to be held by the tenant under the new lease might be expected to realise if sold as mentioned in that sub-paragraph.

(3)　In determining any such amount there shall be made such deduction (if any) in respect of any defect in title as on a sale of that interest on the open market might be expected to be allowed between a willing seller and a willing buyer.

(4)　Subject to sub-paragraph (5), the value of the interest to be held by the tenant under the new lease shall not be decreased by reason of—

(a)　any transaction which—
　　(i)　is entered into after 19th January 1996, and
　　(ii)　involves the creation or transfer of an interest inferior to the tenant's existing lease; or
(b)　any alteration after that date of the terms on which any such inferior interest is held.

(5)　Sub-paragraph (4) shall not apply to any transaction which falls within paragraph (a) of that sub-paragraph if—

(a)　the transaction is entered into in pursuance of a contract entered into on or before the date mentioned in that paragraph; and
(b)　the amount of the premium payable by the tenant in respect of the grant of the new lease was determined on or before that date either by agreement or by a leasehold valuation tribunal under this Chapter.]

*Compensation for loss arising out of grant of new lease*

5.—(1)　Where the landlord will suffer any loss or damage to which this paragraph applies, there shall be payable to him such amount as is reasonable to compensate him for that loss or damage.

(2)　This paragraph applies to—

(a)　any diminution in value of any interest of the landlord in any property other than the tenant's flat which results from the grant to the tenant of the new lease; and
(b)　any other loss or damage which results therefrom to the extent that it is referable to the landlord's ownership of any such interest.

(3)    Without prejudice to the generality of paragraph (b) of sub-paragraph (2), the kinds of loss falling within that paragraph include loss of development value in relation to the tenant's flat to the extent that it is referable as mentioned in that paragraph.

(4)    In sub-paragraph (3) "development value", in relation to the tenant's flat, means any increase in the value of the landlord's interest in the flat which is attributable to the possibility of demolishing, reconstructing, or carrying out substantial works of construction affecting, the flat (whether together with any other premises or otherwise).

**[941]**

**NOTES**
    Para 3: words in first pair of square brackets in sub-para (2) and words in square brackets in sub-para (4) substituted by the Commonhold and Leasehold Reform Act 2002, s 134, except in relation to an application for a new lease of a flat in respect of which notice was given under s 42 of this Act at **[848]**, or where an application was made for an order under s 50 of this Act at **[856]**, before 26 July 2002 (in relation to England) or 1 January 2003 (in relation to Wales); words in second pair of square brackets in sub-para (2) substituted the Housing Act 1996, s 110(1), (2), (5), in relation to any claim made after 19 January 1996 by the giving of notice under s 42 of this Act unless the amount of the premium payable in pursuance of the claim was, either by agreement or by a leasehold valuation tribunal under Chapter II of Part II of this Act before 24 July 1996.
    Para 4: words in square brackets in sub-paras (1), (3)(c) substituted, and words in square brackets in sub-para (2) and the whole of sub-para (2A) inserted, by the Commonhold and Leasehold Reform Act 2002, ss 134–136, subject to savings as noted above; sub-para (3)(a), (aa) substituted, for original sub-para (3)(a), and words in square brackets in sub-para (3)(b) substituted by the Housing Act 1996, s 110(1), (3), (5), subject to savings as noted above.
    Paras 4A, 4B: inserted by the Housing Act 1996, s 110(1), (4), (5), subject to savings as noted above; words in square brackets substituted by the Commonhold and Leasehold Reform Act 2002, s 134, subject to savings as noted above.

## PART III
### AMOUNTS PAYABLE TO OWNERS OF INTERMEDIATE LEASEHOLD INTERESTS
#### *Amount payable to owner of intermediate interest*

6.    In connection with the grant of the new lease to the tenant there shall be payable by the tenant to the owner of any intermediate leasehold interest an amount which is the aggregate of—
    (a)    the diminution in value of that interest as determined in accordance with paragraph 7; and
    (b)    any amount of compensation payable to him under paragraph 9.

#### *Diminution in value of intermediate interest*

7.—(1)    The diminution in value of any intermediate leasehold interest is the difference between—
    (a)    the value of that interest prior to the grant of the new lease; and
    (b)    the value of that interest once the new lease is granted.

(2)    Each of those values shall be determined, as at [the relevant date], in accordance with paragraph 8.

#### *Value of intermediate interests*

8.—(1)    Subject to sub-paragraph (2), paragraph 3(2) to (6) shall apply for determining the value of any intermediate leasehold interest for the purposes of any provision of this Schedule with such modifications as are appropriate to relate those provisions of paragraph 3 to a sale of the interest in question subject to the tenant's lease for the time being and to any leases intermediate between the interest in question and that lease.

(2)    The value of an intermediate leasehold interest which is the interest of the tenant under a minor intermediate lease shall be calculated by applying the formula set out in sub-paragraph (6) instead of in accordance with sub-paragraph (1).

(3)    "A minor intermediate lease" means a lease complying with the following requirements, namely—
    (a)    it must have an expectation of possession of not more than one month, and
    (b)    the profit rent in respect of the lease must be not more than £5 per year.

(4)    "Profit rent" means an amount equal to that of the rent payable under the lease on which the minor intermediate lease is in immediate reversion, less that of the rent payable under the minor intermediate lease.

(5)    Where the minor intermediate lease or that on which it is in immediate reversion comprises property other than the tenant's flat, then in sub-paragraph (4) the reference to the rent payable under it means so much of that rent as is apportioned to that flat.

(6)    The formula is—

$$P = £\frac{R}{Y} - \frac{R}{Y(1+Y)^n}$$

where—

P = the price payable;

R = the profit rent;

Y = the yield (expressed as a decimal fraction) from 2½ per cent Consolidated Stock;

n = the period, expressed in years (taking any part of a year as a whole year), of the remainder of the term of the minor intermediate lease as at [the relevant date].

(7)    In calculating the yield from 2½ per cent Consolidated Stock, the price of that stock shall be taken to be the middle market price at the close of business on the last trading day in the week before [the relevant date].

(8)    For the purposes of this paragraph the expectation of possession carried by a lease is the expectation which it carries at [the relevant date] of possession after the tenant's lease, on the basis that—

(a)    (subject to sub-paragraph (9)) the tenant's lease terminates at [the relevant date] if its term date fell before then, or else it terminates on its term date; and

(b)    any other lease terminates on its term date.

(9)    In a case where before the relevant date for the purposes of this Chapter the immediate landlord of the tenant had given notice to quit terminating the tenant's lease on a date earlier than that date, the date specified in the notice to quit shall be substituted for the date specified in sub-paragraph (8)(a) above.

### Compensation for loss arising out of grant of new lease

9.    Paragraph 5 shall apply in relation to the owner of any intermediate leasehold interest as it applies in relation to the landlord.

### Owners of intermediate interests entitled to part of marriage value

10.—(1)    This paragraph applies in a case where—

(a)    the premium payable by the tenant in respect of the grant of the new lease includes an amount in respect of the landlord's share of the marriage value, and

(b)    there are any intermediate leasehold interests.

(2)    The amount payable to the landlord in respect of his share of the marriage value shall be divided between the landlord and the owners of any such intermediate interests in proportion to the amounts by which the values of their respective interests in the flat will be diminished in consequence of the grant of the new lease.

(3)    For the purposes of sub-paragraph (2)—

(a)    the amount by which the value of the landlord's interest in the flat will be so diminished is the diminution in value of that interest as determined for the purposes of paragraph 2(a); and

(b)    the amount by which the value of any intermediate leasehold interest will be so diminished is the diminution in value of that interest as determined for the purposes of paragraph 6(a).

(4)    Where the owner of any intermediate leasehold interest is entitled in accordance with sub-paragraph (2) to any part of the amount payable to the landlord in respect of the landlord's share of the marriage value, the amount to which he is so entitled shall be payable to him by the landlord.

**[942]**

---

**NOTES**

Paras 7, 8: words in square brackets substituted by the Commonhold and Leasehold Reform Act 2002, s 134, except in relation to an application for a new lease of a flat in respect of which notice was given under s 42 of this Act at **[848]**, or where an application was made for an order under s 50 of this Act at **[856]**, before 26 July 2002 (in relation to England) or 1 January 2003 (in relation to Wales).

---

## SCHEDULE 14
### PROVISIONS SUPPLEMENTARY TO SECTION 61

Section 61

1.—(1)    This Schedule has effect where a tenant of a flat is entitled to be paid compensation under section 61, or would be so entitled on the landlord obtaining an order for possession, or where an application for such an order is dismissed or withdrawn.

(2)    In this Schedule—

"application for possession" means a landlord's application under section 61;

"the new lease" has the same meaning as in that section; and

"order for possession" means an order made under that section;

and (except in the case of the reference in paragraph 5(1)(b) to the flat as a dwelling) references to the flat held by the tenant under the new lease shall be construed in accordance with subsection (5) of that section.

2.—(1)   Where an order for possession is made—

    (a)   the new lease shall determine, and

    (b)   the compensation payable to the tenant by virtue of the order shall become payable,

on such date as may, when the amount of compensation has been determined either by agreement between the landlord and the tenant or by a leasehold valuation tribunal, be fixed by order of the court made on the application of either the landlord or the tenant.

(2)   Where the application for possession was made by virtue of section 61(2)(a), then—

    (a)   (unless paragraph (b) below applies) an order of the court under this paragraph shall not fix a date earlier than the term date of the lease in relation to which the right to acquire a new lease was exercised;

    (b)   in a case where section 61(2)(a) applies in accordance with section 61(3), an order of the court under this paragraph shall not fix a date earlier than the term date of the lease in relation to which that right was first exercised.

(3)   In fixing the date referred to in sub-paragraph (1) the court shall have regard to the conduct of the parties and to the extent to which the landlord has made reasonable preparations for proceeding with the redevelopment (including the obtaining of, or preparations relating to the obtaining of, any requisite permission or consent, whether from any authority whose permission or consent is required under any enactment or from the owner of an interest in any property).

(4)   The court may by order direct that the whole or part of the compensation payable to the tenant shall be paid into court, if the court thinks it expedient to do so for the purpose of ensuring that the sum paid is available for meeting any mortgage on the tenant's interest in the flat in question, or for the purpose of division, or for any other purpose.

3.—(1)   On the termination of a lease under an order for possession there shall terminate also any immediate or derivative sub-lease, and the tenant shall be bound to give up possession of the flat in question to the landlord except in so far as he is precluded from doing so by the rights of other persons to retain possession under or by virtue of any enactment.

(2)   Where a sub-lease of property comprised in the lease has been created after the date of the application for possession, no person shall in respect of that sub-lease be entitled under any of the following provisions (which relate to retaining possession on the termination of a superior tenancy), namely—

    (a)   subsection (2) of section 137 of the Rent Act 1977, or any enactment (including subsection (5) of that section) applying or extending it,

    (b)   subsection (2) of section 9 of the Rent (Agriculture) Act 1976 as extended by subsection (5) of that section, or

    (c)   section 18(1) of the Housing Act 1988,

to retain possession of that property after the termination of the lease under the order for possession.

(3)   In exercising its jurisdiction under section 61 or this Schedule the court shall assume that the landlord, having obtained an order for possession, will not be precluded from obtaining possession by the right of any person to retain possession by virtue of—

    (a)   Part VII of the Rent Act 1977 or any enactment applying or extending that Part of that Act,

    (b)   the Rent (Agriculture) Act 1976, or

    (c)   Part I of the Housing Act 1988,

or otherwise.

(4)   A person in occupation of any property under a sub-lease liable to terminate under sub-paragraph (1) may, with the leave of the court, appear and be heard on any application for possession or any application under paragraph 2.

4.   Where an order has been made by a county court under paragraph 2, that court or another county court shall have jurisdiction to hear and determine any proceedings brought by virtue of the order to recover possession of the property or to recover the compensation.

5.—(1)   The amount payable to a tenant, by virtue of an order for possession, by way of compensation for loss of his flat shall be the amount which at the valuation date the new lease, if sold on the open market by a willing seller, might be expected to realise on the following assumptions—

    (a)   on the assumption that Chapter I and this Chapter confer no right to acquire any interest in any premises containing the tenant's flat or to acquire any new lease;

    (b)   on the assumption that the vendor is selling—

        (i)   subject to the rights of any person who will on the termination of the lease be entitled to retain possession as against the landlord, but otherwise with vacant possession, and

        (ii)   subject to any restriction that would be required (in addition to any imposed by the terms of the lease) to limit the uses of the flat to those to which it has been put since the commencement of the lease and to preclude the erection of any new dwelling or any other building not ancillary to the flat as a dwelling; and

(c)    on the assumption that (subject to paragraphs (a) and (b)) the vendor is selling with and subject to the rights and burdens with and subject to which the flat will be held by the landlord on the termination of the lease.

(2)    It is hereby declared that the fact that sub-paragraph (1) requires assumptions to be made as to the matters specified in paragraphs (a) to (c) of that sub-paragraph does not preclude the making of assumptions as to other matters where those assumptions are appropriate for determining the amount which at the valuation date the new lease might be expected to realise if sold as mentioned in that sub-paragraph.

(3)    In determining any such amount there shall be made such deduction (if any) in respect of any defect in title as on a sale of that interest on the open market might be expected to be allowed between a willing seller and a willing buyer.

(4)    In this paragraph "the valuation date" means the date when the amount of the compensation payable to the tenant is determined as mentioned in paragraph 2(1).

6.—(1)    Part I of the Landlord and Tenant Act 1927 (compensation for improvements on termination of business tenancies) shall not apply on the termination of the new lease or any sub-lease in accordance with this Schedule; and a request for a new tenancy under section 26 of the Landlord and Tenant Act 1954 in respect of the new lease or any sub-lease shall be of no effect if made after the application for possession, or, if already made, shall cease to have effect on the making of that application.

(2)    Where a sub-lease terminating with the new lease in accordance with paragraph 3 is one to which Part II of the Landlord and Tenant Act 1954 applies, the compensation payable to the tenant shall be divided between him and the sub-tenant in such proportions as may be just, regard being had to their respective interests in the flat in question and to any loss arising from the termination of those interests and not incurred by imprudence.

(3)    Where the amount of the compensation payable to the tenant is agreed between him and the landlord without the consent of a sub-tenant entitled under sub-paragraph (2) to a share in the compensation, and is shown by the sub-tenant to be less than might reasonably have been obtained by the tenant, the sub-tenant shall be entitled under sub-paragraph (2) to recover from the tenant such increased share as may be just.

7.—(1)    The landlord shall not be concerned with the application of the amount payable to the tenant by way of compensation under an order for possession, but (subject to any statutory requirements as to payment of capital money arising under a settlement or a [trust of land] and to any order under paragraph 2(4) for payment into court) the written receipt of the tenant shall be a complete discharge for the amount payable.

(2)    The landlord shall be entitled to deduct from the amount so payable to the tenant—

(a)    the amount of any sum recoverable as rent in respect of the flat up to the termination of the new lease; and

(b)    the amount of any other sums due and payable by the tenant to the landlord under or in respect of the lease or any agreement collateral thereto.

8.—(1)    Where a landlord makes an application for possession, and it is made to appear to the court that in relation to matters arising out of that application (including the giving up of possession of the flat or the payment of compensation) the landlord or the tenant has been guilty of any unreasonable delay or default, the court may—

(a)    by order revoke or vary, and direct repayment of sums paid under, any provision made by a previous order as to payment of the costs of proceedings taken in the court on or with reference to the application; or

(b)    where costs have not been awarded, award costs.

(2)    Where an application for possession is dismissed or withdrawn, and it is made to appear to the court—

(a)    that the application was not made in good faith, or

(b)    that the landlord had attempted in any material respect to support by misrepresentation or the concealment of material facts a request to the tenant to deliver up possession without an application for possession,

the court may order that no further application for possession of the flat made by the landlord shall be entertained if it is made within the period of five years beginning with the date of the order.

9.    Where—

(a)    the new lease is [subject to a trust of land], and

(b)    compensation is paid by the landlord on the termination of the new lease (whether the payment is made in pursuance of an order for possession or in pursuance of an agreement made in conformity with paragraph 5 above without an application having been made under section 61), the sum received shall be dealt with as if it were proceeds of sale arising under the trust.

10.   Where—
    (a)   the tenant under the new lease is a university or college to which the Universities and College Estates Act 1925 applies, and
    (b)   compensation is paid as mentioned in paragraph 9(b) above,

the sum received shall be dealt with as if it were an amount payable by way of consideration on a sale effected under that Act.

11.   Where—
    (a)   the tenant under the new lease is a capitular body within the meaning of the Cathedrals Measure 1963 and the lease comprises property which forms part of the endowment of a cathedral church, and
    (b)   compensation is paid as mentioned in paragraph 9(b) above,

the sum received shall be treated as part of that endowment.

12.—(1)   Where—
    (a)   the tenant under the new lease is a diocesan board of finance and the lease comprises diocesan glebe land, and
    (b)   compensation is paid as mentioned in paragraph 9(b) above,

the sum received shall be paid to the Church Commissioners to be applied for purposes for which the proceeds of any disposition of property by agreement would be applicable under any enactment or Measure authorising such a disposition or disposing of the proceeds of such a disposition.

(2)   In this paragraph "diocesan board of finance" and "diocesan glebe land" have the same meaning as in the Endowments and Glebe Measure 1976.

**[943]**

**NOTES**

   Paras 7, 9: words in square brackets substituted by the Trusts of Land and Appointment of Trustees Act 1996, s 25(1), Sch 3, para 27(1), (3), subject to savings in s 25(4), (5) thereof.

   Modification: by virtue of the Cathedrals Measure 1999, ss 36(2), (6), 38(1)–(3), the reference in para 11 to a capitular body is, except in relation to Westminster Abbey, St George's Chapel, Windsor or the cathedral church of Christ in Oxford, and subject to transitional provision in relation to cathedrals existing on 30 June 1999, to be construed as a reference to the corporate body of the cathedral.

*(Sch 15 sets out the text of the Leasehold Reform Act 1967, s 9 at [91], as amended by s 66 of this Act, with the omission of the repealed provisions; Sch 16 inserts the Housing Act 1985, Sch 6A at [590]; Schs 17–20 repealed by the Housing and Regeneration Act 2008, ss 56, 321(1), Sch 8, para 63(1), (2)(b), Sch 16, subject to transitional provisions in SI 2009/803, arts 4–6; Sch 21 contains minor and consequential amendments; Sch 22 contains repeals only.)*

# LANDLORD AND TENANT (COVENANTS) ACT 1995

### (1995 c 30)

### ARRANGEMENT OF SECTIONS

*Preliminary*

*Transmission of covenants*

*Release of covenants on assignment*

*Apportionment of liability between assignor and assignee*

*An Act to make provision for persons bound by covenants of a tenancy to be released from such covenants on the assignment of the tenancy, and to make other provision with respect to rights and liabilities arising under such covenants; to restrict in certain circumstances the operation of rights of re-entry, forfeiture and disclaimer; and for connected purposes*

[19 July 1995]

*Preliminary*

## 1   Tenancies to which the Act applies

(1)   Sections 3 to 16 and 21 apply only to new tenancies.

(2)   Sections 17 to 20 apply to both new and other tenancies.

(3)   For the purposes of this section a tenancy is a new tenancy if it is granted on or after the date on which this Act comes into force otherwise than in pursuance of—

(a)   an agreement entered into before that date, or
(b)   an order of a court made before that date.

(4)   Subsection (3) has effect subject to section 20(1) in the case of overriding leases granted under section 19.

(5)   Without prejudice to the generality of subsection (3), that subsection applies to the grant of a tenancy where by virtue of any variation of a tenancy there is a deemed surrender and regrant as it applies to any other grant of a tenancy.

(6)   Where a tenancy granted on or after the date on which this Act comes into force is so granted in pursuance of an option granted before that date, the tenancy shall be regarded for the purposes of subsection (3) as granted in pursuance of an agreement entered into before that date (and accordingly is not a new tenancy), whether or not the option was exercised before that date.

(7)   In subsection (6) "option" includes right of first refusal.

**[944]**

## 2   Covenants to which the Act applies

(1)   This Act applies to a landlord covenant or a tenant covenant of a tenancy—
  (a)   whether or not the covenant has reference to the subject matter of the tenancy, and
  (b)   whether the covenant is express, implied or imposed by law,
but does not apply to a covenant falling within subsection (2).

(2)   Nothing in this Act affects any covenant imposed in pursuance of—
  (a)   section 35 or 155 of the Housing Act 1985 (covenants for repayment of discount on early disposals);
  (b)   paragraph 1 of Schedule 6A to that Act (covenants requiring redemption of landlord's share); or
  (c)   [section 11 or 13 of the Housing Act 1996 or] paragraph 1 or 3 of Schedule 2 to the Housing Associations Act 1985 (covenants for repayment of discount on early disposals or for restricting disposals).

**[945]**

### NOTES

Sub-s (2): words in square brackets inserted by the Housing Act 1996 (Consequential Provisions) Order 1996, SI 1996/2325, art 5, Sch 2, para 22.

*Transmission of covenants*

## 3   Transmission of benefit and burden of covenants

(1)   The benefit and burden of all landlord and tenant covenants of a tenancy—
  (a)   shall be annexed and incident to the whole, and to each and every part, of the premises demised by the tenancy and of the reversion in them, and
  (b)   shall in accordance with this section pass on an assignment of the whole or any part of those premises or of the reversion in them.

(2)   Where the assignment is by the tenant under the tenancy, then as from the assignment the assignee—
  (a)   becomes bound by the tenant covenants of the tenancy except to the extent that—
    (i)    immediately before the assignment they did not bind the assignor, or
    (ii)   they fall to be complied with in relation to any demised premises not comprised in the assignment; and
  (b)   becomes entitled to the benefit of the landlord covenants of the tenancy except to the extent that they fall to be complied with in relation to any such premises.

(3)   Where the assignment is by the landlord under the tenancy, then as from the assignment the assignee—
  (a)   becomes bound by the landlord covenants of the tenancy except to the extent that—
    (i)    immediately before the assignment they did not bind the assignor, or
    (ii)   they fall to be complied with in relation to any demised premises not comprised in the assignment; and
  (b)   becomes entitled to the benefit of the tenant covenants of the tenancy except to the extent that they fall to be complied with in relation to any such premises.

(4)   In determining for the purposes of subsection (2) or (3) whether any covenant bound the assignor immediately before the assignment, any waiver or release of the covenant which (in whatever terms) is expressed to be personal to the assignor shall be disregarded.

(5)   Any landlord or tenant covenant of a tenancy which is restrictive of the user of land shall, as well as being capable of enforcement against an assignee, be capable of being enforced against any other person who is the owner or occupier of any demised premises to which the covenant relates, even though there is no express provision in the tenancy to that effect.

(6)   Nothing in this section shall operate—
  (a)   in the case of a covenant which (in whatever terms) is expressed to be personal to any person, to make the covenant enforceable by or (as the case may be) against any other person; or
  (b)   to make a covenant enforceable against any person if, apart from this section, it would not be enforceable against him by reason of its not having been registered under the [Land Registration Act 2002] or the Land Charges Act 1972.

(7)   To the extent that there remains in force any rule of law by virtue of which the burden of a covenant whose subject matter is not in existence at the time when it is made does not run with the land affected unless the covenantor covenants on behalf of himself and his assigns, that rule of law is hereby abolished in relation to tenancies.

**[946]**

NOTES
Sub-s (6): words in square brackets substituted by the Land Registration Act 2002, s 133, Sch 11, para 33(1), (2).

## 4 Transmission of rights of re-entry

The benefit of a landlord's right of re-entry under a tenancy—

    (a)    shall be annexed and incident to the whole, and to each and every part, of the reversion in the premises demised by the tenancy, and

    (b)    shall pass on an assignment of the whole or any part of the reversion in those premises.

**[947]**

*Release of covenants on assignment*

## 5 Tenant released from covenants on assignment of tenancy

    (1)    This section applies where a tenant assigns premises demised to him under a tenancy.

    (2)    If the tenant assigns the whole of the premises demised to him, he—

    (a)    is released from the tenant covenants of the tenancy, and

    (b)    ceases to be entitled to the benefit of the landlord covenants of the tenancy,

as from the assignment.

    (3)    If the tenant assigns part only of the premises demised to him, then as from the assignment he—

    (a)    is released from the tenant covenants of the tenancy, and

    (b)    ceases to be entitled to the benefit of the landlord covenants of the tenancy,

only to the extent that those covenants fall to be complied with in relation to that part of the demised premises.

    (4)    This section applies as mentioned in subsection (1) whether or not the tenant is tenant of the whole of the premises comprised in the tenancy.

**[948]**

## 6 Landlord may be released from covenants on assignment of reversion

    (1)    This section applies where a landlord assigns the reversion in premises of which he is the landlord under a tenancy.

    (2)    If the landlord assigns the reversion in the whole of the premises of which he is the landlord—

    (a)    he may apply to be released from the landlord covenants of the tenancy in accordance with section 8; and

    (b)    if he is so released from all of those covenants, he ceases to be entitled to the benefit of the tenant covenants of the tenancy as from the assignment.

    (3)    If the landlord assigns the reversion in part only of the premises of which he is the landlord—

    (a)    he may apply to be so released from the landlord covenants of the tenancy to the extent that they fall to be complied with in relation to that part of those premises; and

    (b)    if he is, to that extent, so released from all of those covenants, then as from the assignment he ceases to be entitled to the benefit of the tenant covenants only to the extent that they fall to be complied with in relation to that part of those premises.

    (4)    This section applies as mentioned in subsection (1) whether or not the landlord is landlord of the whole of the premises comprised in the tenancy.

**[949]**

## 7 Former landlord may be released from covenants on assignment of reversion

    (1)    This section applies where—

    (a)    a landlord assigns the reversion in premises of which he is the landlord under a tenancy, and

    (b)    immediately before the assignment a former landlord of the premises remains bound by a landlord covenant of the tenancy ("the relevant covenant").

    (2)    If immediately before the assignment the former landlord does not remain the landlord of any other premises demised by the tenancy, he may apply to be released from the relevant covenant in accordance with section 8.

    (3)    In any other case the former landlord may apply to be so released from the relevant covenant to the extent that it falls to be complied with in relation to any premises comprised in the assignment.

    (4)    If the former landlord is so released from every landlord covenant by which he remained bound immediately before the assignment, he ceases to be entitled to the benefit of the tenant covenants of the tenancy.

(5)　If the former landlord is so released from every such landlord covenant to the extent that it falls to be complied with in relation to any premises comprised in the assignment, he ceases to be entitled to the benefit of the tenant covenants of the tenancy to the extent that they fall to be so complied with.

(6)　This section applies as mentioned in subsection (1)—

    (a)　whether or not the landlord making the assignment is landlord of the whole of the premises comprised in the tenancy; and

    (b)　whether or not the former landlord has previously applied (whether under section 6 or this section) to be released from the relevant covenant.

**[950]**

## 8　Procedure for seeking release from a covenant under section 6 or 7

(1)　For the purposes of section 6 or 7 an application for the release of a covenant to any extent is made by serving on the tenant, either before or within the period of four weeks beginning with the date of the assignment in question, a notice informing him of—

    (a)　the proposed assignment or (as the case may be) the fact that the assignment has taken place, and

    (b)　the request for the covenant to be released to that extent.

(2)　Where an application for the release of a covenant is made in accordance with subsection (1), the covenant is released to the extent mentioned in the notice if—

    (a)　the tenant does not, within the period of four weeks beginning with the day on which the notice is served, serve on the landlord or former landlord a notice in writing objecting to the release, or

    (b)　the tenant does so serve such a notice but the court, on the application of the landlord or former landlord, makes a declaration that it is reasonable for the covenant to be so released, or

    (c)　the tenant serves on the landlord or former landlord a notice in writing consenting to the release and, if he has previously served a notice objecting to it, stating that that notice is withdrawn.

(3)　Any release from a covenant in accordance with this section shall be regarded as occurring at the time when the assignment in question takes place.

(4)　In this section—

    (a)　"the tenant" means the tenant of the premises comprised in the assignment in question (or, if different parts of those premises are held under the tenancy by different tenants, each of those tenants);

    (b)　any reference to the landlord or the former landlord is a reference to the landlord referred to in section 6 or the former landlord referred to in section 7, as the case may be; and

    (c)　"the court" means a county court.

**[951]**

*Apportionment of liability between assignor and assignee*

## 9　Apportionment of liability under covenants binding both assignor and assignee of tenancy or reversion

(1)　This section applies where—

    (a)　a tenant assigns part only of the premises demised to him by a tenancy;

    (b)　after the assignment both the tenant and his assignee are to be bound by a non-attributable tenant covenant of the tenancy; and

    (c)　the tenant and his assignee agree that as from the assignment liability under the covenant is to be apportioned between them in such manner as is specified in the agreement.

(2)　This section also applies where—

    (a)　a landlord assigns the reversion in part only of the premises of which he is the landlord under a tenancy;

    (b)　after the assignment both the landlord and his assignee are to be bound by a non-attributable landlord covenant of the tenancy; and

    (c)　the landlord and his assignee agree that as from the assignment liability under the covenant is to be apportioned between them in such manner as is specified in the agreement.

(3)　Any such agreement as is mentioned in subsection (1) or (2) may apportion liability in such a way that a party to the agreement is exonerated from all liability under a covenant.

(4)　In any case falling within subsection (1) or (2) the parties to the agreement may apply for the apportionment to become binding on the appropriate person in accordance with section 10.

(5)　In any such case the parties to the agreement may also apply for the apportionment to become binding on any person (other than the appropriate person) who is for the time being entitled to enforce the covenant in question; and section 10 shall apply in relation to such an application as it applies in relation to an application made with respect to the appropriate person.

(6)   For the purposes of this section a covenant is, in relation to an assignment, a "non-attributable" covenant if it does not fall to be complied with in relation to any premises comprised in the assignment.

(7)   In this section "the appropriate person" means either—
   (a)   the landlord of the entire premises referred to in subsection (1)(a) (or, if different parts of those premises are held under the tenancy by different landlords, each of those landlords), or
   (b)   the tenant of the entire premises referred to in subsection (2)(a) (or, if different parts of those premises are held under the tenancy by different tenants, each of those tenants), depending on whether the agreement in question falls within subsection (1) or subsection (2).

**[952]**

## 10   Procedure for making apportionment bind other party to lease

(1)   For the purposes of section 9 the parties to an agreement falling within subsection (1) or (2) of that section apply for an apportionment to become binding on the appropriate person if, either before or within the period of four weeks beginning with the date of the assignment in question, they serve on that person a notice informing him of—
   (a)   the proposed assignment or (as the case may be) the fact that the assignment has taken place;
   (b)   the prescribed particulars of the agreement; and
   (c)   their request that the apportionment should become binding on him.

(2)   Where an application for an apportionment to become binding has been made in accordance with subsection (1), the apportionment becomes binding on the appropriate person if—
   (a)   he does not, within the period of four weeks beginning with the day on which the notice is served under subsection (1), serve on the parties to the agreement a notice in writing objecting to the apportionment becoming binding on him, or
   (b)   he does so serve such a notice but the court, on the application of the parties to the agreement, makes a declaration that it is reasonable for the apportionment to become binding on him, or
   (c)   he serves on the parties to the agreement a notice in writing consenting to the apportionment becoming binding on him and, if he has previously served a notice objecting thereto, stating that the notice is withdrawn.

(3)   Where any apportionment becomes binding in accordance with this section, this shall be regarded as occurring at the time when the assignment in question takes place.

(4)   In this section—
   "the appropriate person" has the same meaning as in section 9;
   "the court" means a county court;
   "prescribed" means prescribed by virtue of section 27.

**[953]**

*Excluded assignments*

## 11   Assignments in breach of covenant or by operation of law

(1)   This section provides for the operation of sections 5 to 10 in relation to assignments in breach of a covenant of a tenancy or assignments by operation of law ("excluded assignments").

(2)   In the case of an excluded assignment subsection (2) or (3) of section 5—
   (a)   shall not have the effect mentioned in that subsection in relation to the tenant as from that assignment, but
   (b)   shall have that effect as from the next assignment (if any) of the premises assigned by him which is not an excluded assignment.

(3)   In the case of an excluded assignment subsection (2) or (3) of section 6 or 7—
   (a)   shall not enable the landlord or former landlord to apply for such a release as is mentioned in that subsection as from that assignment, but
   (b)   shall apply on the next assignment (if any) of the reversion assigned by the landlord which is not an excluded assignment so as to enable the landlord
or former landlord to apply for any such release as from that subsequent assignment.

(4)   Where subsection (2) or (3) of section 6 or 7 does so apply—
   (a)   any reference in that section to the assignment (except where it relates to the time as from which the release takes effect) is a reference to the excluded assignment; but
   (b)   in that excepted case and in section 8 as it applies in relation to any application under

that section made by virtue of subsection (3) above, any reference to the assignment or proposed assignment is a reference to any such subsequent assignment as is mentioned in that subsection.

(5)   In the case of an excluded assignment section 9—

(a)   shall not enable the tenant or landlord and his assignee to apply for an agreed apportionment to become binding in accordance with section 10 as from that assignment, but

(b)   shall apply on the next assignment (if any) of the premises or reversion assigned by the tenant or landlord which is not an excluded assignment so as to enable him and his assignee to apply for such an apportionment to become binding in accordance with section 10 as from that subsequent assignment.

(6)   Where section 9 does so apply—

(a)   any reference in that section to the assignment or the assignee under it is a reference to the excluded assignment and the assignee under that assignment; but

(b)   in section 10 as it applies in relation to any application under section 9 made by virtue of subsection (5) above, any reference to the assignment or proposed assignment is a reference to any such subsequent assignment as is mentioned in that subsection.

(7)   If any such subsequent assignment as is mentioned in subsection (2), (3) or (5) above comprises only part of the premises assigned by the tenant or (as the case may be) only part of the premises the reversion in which was assigned by the landlord on the excluded assignment—

(a)   the relevant provision or provisions of section 5, 6, 7 or 9 shall only have the effect mentioned in that subsection to the extent that the covenants or covenant in question fall or falls to be complied with in relation to that part of those premises; and

(b)   that subsection may accordingly apply on different occasions in relation to different parts of those premises.

**[954]**

*Third party covenants*

## 12   Covenants with management companies etc

(1)   This section applies where—

(a)   a person other than the landlord or tenant ("the third party") is under a covenant of a tenancy liable (as principal) to discharge any function with respect to all or any of the demised premises ("the relevant function"); and

(b)   that liability is not the liability of a guarantor or any other financial liability referable to the performance or otherwise of a covenant of the tenancy by another party to it.

(2)   To the extent that any covenant of the tenancy confers any rights against the third party with respect to the relevant function, then for the purposes of the transmission of the benefit of the covenant in accordance with this Act it shall be treated as if it were—

(a)   a tenant covenant of the tenancy to the extent that those rights are exercisable by the landlord; and

(b)   a landlord covenant of the tenancy to the extent that those rights are exercisable by the tenant.

(3)   To the extent that any covenant of the tenancy confers any rights exercisable by the third party with respect to the relevant function, then for the purposes mentioned in subsection (4), it shall be treated as if it were—

(a)   a tenant covenant of the tenancy to the extent that those rights are exercisable against the tenant; and

(b)   a landlord covenant of the tenancy to the extent that those rights are exercisable against the landlord.

(4)   The purposes mentioned in subsection (3) are—

(a)   the transmission of the burden of the covenant in accordance with this Act; and

(b)   any release from, or apportionment of liability in respect of, the covenant in accordance with this Act.

(5)   In relation to the release of the landlord from any covenant which is to be treated as a landlord covenant by virtue of subsection (3), section 8 shall apply as if any reference to the tenant were a reference to the third party.

**[955]**

*Joint liability under covenants*

## 13   Covenants binding two or more persons

(1)   Where in consequence of this Act two or more persons are bound by the same covenant, they are so bound both jointly and severally.

(2)   Subject to section 24(2), where by virtue of this Act—

(a) two or more persons are bound jointly and severally by the same covenant, and

(b) any of the persons so bound is released from the covenant,

the release does not extend to any other of those persons.

(3) For the purpose of providing for contribution between persons who, by virtue of this Act, are bound jointly and severally by a covenant, the Civil Liability (Contribution) Act 1978 shall have effect as if—

(a) liability to a person under a covenant were liability in respect of damage suffered by that person;

(b) references to damage accordingly included a breach of a covenant of a tenancy; and

(c) section 7(2) of that Act were omitted.

**[956]**

**14** *(Repeals the Law of Property Act 1925, s 77(1)(C), (D) and the Land Registration Act 1925, s 24(1)(b), (2).)*

*Enforcement of covenants*

## 15 Enforcement of covenants

(1) Where any tenant covenant of a tenancy, or any right of re-entry contained in a tenancy, is enforceable by the reversioner in respect of any premises demised by the tenancy, it shall also be so enforceable by—

(a) any person (other than the reversioner) who, as the holder of the immediate reversion in those premises, is for the time being entitled to the rents and profits under the tenancy in respect of those premises, or

(b) any mortgagee in possession of the reversion in those premises who is so entitled.

(2) Where any landlord covenant of a tenancy is enforceable against the reversioner in respect of any premises demised by the tenancy, it shall also be so enforceable against any person falling within subsection (1)(a) or (b).

(3) Where any landlord covenant of a tenancy is enforceable by the tenant in respect of any premises demised by the tenancy, it shall also be so enforceable by any mortgagee in possession of those premises under a mortgage granted by the tenant.

(4) Where any tenant covenant of a tenancy, or any right of re-entry contained in a tenancy, is enforceable against the tenant in respect of any premises demised by the tenancy, it shall also be so enforceable against any such mortgagee.

(5) Nothing in this section shall operate—

(a) in the case of a covenant which (in whatever terms) is expressed to be personal to any person, to make the covenant enforceable by or (as the case may be) against any other person; or

(b) to make a covenant enforceable against any person if, apart from this section, it would not be enforceable against him by reason of its not having been registered under the [Land Registration Act 2002] or the Land Charges Act 1972.

(6) In this section—

"mortgagee" and "mortgage" include "chargee" and "charge" respectively;

"the reversioner", in relation to a tenancy, means the holder for the time being of the interest of the landlord under the tenancy.

**[957]**

**NOTES**

Sub-s (5): words in square brackets substituted by the Land Registration Act 2002, s 133, Sch 11, para 33(1), (2).

*Liability of former tenant etc in respect of covenants*

## 16 Tenant guaranteeing performance of covenant by assignee

(1) Where on an assignment a tenant is to any extent released from a tenant covenant of a tenancy by virtue of this Act ("the relevant covenant"), nothing in this Act (and in particular section 25) shall preclude him from entering into an authorised guarantee agreement with respect to the performance of that covenant by the assignee.

(2) For the purposes of this section an agreement is an authorised guarantee agreement if—

(a) under it the tenant guarantees the performance of the relevant covenant to any extent by the assignee; and

(b) it is entered into in the circumstances set out in subsection (3); and

(c) its provisions conform with subsections (4) and (5).

(3) Those circumstances are as follows—

(a)    by virtue of a covenant against assignment (whether absolute or qualified) the assignment cannot be effected without the consent of the landlord under the tenancy or some other person;

(b)    any such consent is given subject to a condition (lawfully imposed) that the tenant is to enter into an agreement guaranteeing the performance of the covenant by the assignee; and

(c)    the agreement is entered into by the tenant in pursuance of that condition.

(4)    An agreement is not an authorised guarantee agreement to the extent that it purports—

(a)    to impose on the tenant any requirement to guarantee in any way the performance of the relevant covenant by any person other than the assignee; or

(b)    to impose on the tenant any liability, restriction or other requirement (of whatever nature) in relation to any time after the assignee is released from that covenant by virtue of this Act.

(5)    Subject to subsection (4), an authorised guarantee agreement may—

(a)    impose on the tenant any liability as sole or principal debtor in respect of any obligation owed by the assignee under the relevant covenant;

(b)    impose on the tenant liabilities as guarantor in respect of the assignee's performance of that covenant which are no more onerous than those to which he would be subject in the event of his being liable as sole or principal debtor in respect of any obligation owed by the assignee under that covenant;

(c)    require the tenant, in the event of the tenancy assigned by him being disclaimed, to enter into a new tenancy of the premises comprised in the assignment—

     (i)    whose term expires not later than the term of the tenancy assigned by the tenant, and

     (ii)    whose tenant covenants are no more onerous than those of that tenancy;

(d)    make provision incidental or supplementary to any provision made by virtue of any of paragraphs (a) to (c).

(6)    Where a person ("the former tenant") is to any extent released from a covenant of a tenancy by virtue of section 11(2) as from an assignment and the assignor under the assignment enters into an authorised guarantee agreement with the landlord with respect to the performance of that covenant by the assignee under the assignment—

(a)    the landlord may require the former tenant to enter into an agreement under which he guarantees, on terms corresponding to those of that authorised guarantee agreement, the performance of that covenant by the assignee under the assignment; and

(b)    if its provisions conform with subsections (4) and (5), any such agreement shall be an authorised guarantee agreement for the purposes of this section; and

(c)    in the application of this section in relation to any such agreement—

     (i)    subsections (2)(b) and (c) and (3) shall be omitted, and

     (ii)    any reference to the tenant or to the assignee shall be read as a reference to the former tenant or to the assignee under the assignment.

(7)    For the purposes of subsection (1) it is immaterial that—

(a)    the tenant has already made an authorised guarantee agreement in respect of a previous assignment by him of the tenancy referred to in that subsection, it having been subsequently revested in him following a disclaimer on behalf of the previous assignee, or

(b)    the tenancy referred to in that subsection is a new tenancy entered into by the tenant in pursuance of an authorised guarantee agreement;

and in any such case subsections (2) to (5) shall apply accordingly.

(8)    It is hereby declared that the rules of law relating to guarantees (and in particular those relating to the release of sureties) are, subject to its terms, applicable in relation to any authorised guarantee agreement as in relation to any other guarantee agreement.

**[958]**

## 17   Restriction on liability of former tenant or his guarantor for rent or service charge etc

(1)    This section applies where a person ("the former tenant") is as a result of an assignment no longer a tenant under a tenancy but—

(a)    (in the case of a tenancy which is a new tenancy) he has under an authorised guarantee agreement guaranteed the performance by his assignee of a tenant covenant of the tenancy under which any fixed charge is payable; or

(b)    (in the case of any tenancy) he remains bound by such a covenant.

(2)    The former tenant shall not be liable under that agreement or (as the case may be) the covenant to pay any amount in respect of any fixed charge payable under the covenant unless, within the period of six months beginning with the date when the charge becomes due, the landlord serves on the former tenant a notice informing him—

(a)    that the charge is now due; and

PART I.
STATUTES

(b)   that in respect of the charge the landlord intends to recover from the former tenant such amount as is specified in the notice and (where payable) interest calculated on such basis as is so specified.

(3)   Where a person ("the guarantor") has agreed to guarantee the performance by the former tenant of such a covenant as is mentioned in subsection (1), the guarantor shall not be liable under the agreement to pay any amount in respect of any fixed charge payable under the covenant unless, within the period of six months beginning with the date when the charge becomes due, the landlord serves on the guarantor a notice informing him—

(a)   that the charge is now due; and

(b)   that in respect of the charge the landlord intends to recover from the guarantor such amount as is specified in the notice and (where payable) interest calculated on such basis as is so specified.

(4)   Where the landlord has duly served a notice under subsection (2) or (3), the amount (exclusive of interest) which the former tenant or (as the case may be) the guarantor is liable to pay in respect of the fixed charge in question shall not exceed the amount specified in the notice unless—

(a)   his liability in respect of the charge is subsequently determined to be for a greater amount,

(b)   the notice informed him of the possibility that that liability would be so determined, and

(c)   within the period of three months beginning with the date of the determination, the landlord serves on him a further notice informing him that the landlord intends to recover that greater amount from him (plus interest, where payable).

(5)   For the purposes of subsection (2) or (3) any fixed charge which has become due before the date on which this Act comes into force shall be treated as becoming due on that date; but neither of those subsections applies to any such charge if before that date proceedings have been instituted by the landlord for the recovery from the former tenant of any amount in respect of it.

(6)   In this section—

"fixed charge", in relation to tenancy, means—

(a)   rent,

(b)   any service charge as defined by section 18 of the Landlord and Tenant Act 1985 (the words "of a dwelling" being disregarded for this purpose), and

(c)   any amount payable under a tenant covenant of the tenancy providing for the payment of a liquidated sum in the event of a failure to comply with any such covenant;

"landlord", in relation to a fixed charge, includes any person who has a right to enforce payment of the charge.

[959]

## 18 Restriction of liability of former tenant or his guarantor where tenancy subsequently varied

(1)   This section applies where a person ("the former tenant") is as a result of an assignment no longer a tenant under a tenancy but—

(a)   (in the case of a new tenancy) he has under an authorised guarantee agreement guaranteed the performance by his assignee of any tenant covenant of the tenancy; or

(b)   (in the case of any tenancy) he remains bound by such a covenant.

(2)   The former tenant shall not be liable under the agreement or (as the case may be) the covenant to pay any amount in respect of the covenant to the extent that the amount is referable to any relevant variation of the tenant covenants of the tenancy effected after the assignment.

(3)   Where a person ("the guarantor") has agreed to guarantee the performance by the former tenant of a tenant covenant of the tenancy, the guarantor (where his liability to do so is not wholly discharged by any such variation of the tenant covenants of the tenancy) shall not be liable under the agreement to pay any amount in respect of the covenant to the extent that the amount is referable to any such variation.

(4)   For the purposes of this section a variation of the tenant covenants of a tenancy is a "relevant variation" if either—

(a)   the landlord has, at the time of the variation, an absolute right to refuse to allow it; or

(b)   the landlord would have had such a right if the variation had been sought by the former tenant immediately before the assignment by him but, between the time of that assignment and the time of the variation, the tenant covenants of the tenancy have been so varied as to deprive the landlord of such a right.

(5)   In determining whether the landlord has or would have had such a right at any particular time regard shall be had to all the circumstances (including the effect of any provision made by or under any enactment).

(6)   Nothing in this section applies to any variation of the tenant covenants of a tenancy effected before the date on which this Act comes into force.

(7)   In this section "variation" means a variation whether effected by deed or otherwise.

**[960]**

*Overriding leases*

## 19   Right of former tenant or his guarantor to overriding lease

(1)   Where in respect of any tenancy ("the relevant tenancy") any person ("the claimant") makes full payment of an amount which he has been duly required to pay in accordance with section 17, together with any interest payable, he shall be entitled (subject to and in accordance with this section) to have the landlord under that tenancy grant him an overriding lease of the premises demised by the tenancy.

(2)   For the purposes of this section "overriding lease" means a tenancy of the reversion expectant on the relevant tenancy which—

    (a)    is granted for a term equal to the remainder of the term of the relevant tenancy plus three days or the longest period (less than three days) that will not wholly displace the landlord's reversionary interest expectant on the relevant tenancy, as the case may require; and

    (b)    (subject to subsections (3) and (4) and to any modifications agreed to by the claimant and the landlord) otherwise contains the same covenants as the relevant tenancy, as they have effect immediately before the grant of the lease.

(3)   An overriding lease shall not be required to reproduce any covenant of the relevant tenancy to the extent that the covenant is (in whatever terms) expressed to be a personal covenant between the landlord and the tenant under that tenancy.

(4)   If any right, liability or other matter arising under a covenant of the relevant tenancy falls to be determined or otherwise operates (whether expressly or otherwise) by reference to the commencement of that tenancy—

    (a)    the corresponding covenant of the overriding lease shall be so framed that that right, liability or matter falls to be determined or otherwise operates by reference to the commencement of that tenancy; but

    (b)    the overriding lease shall not be required to reproduce any covenant of that tenancy to the extent that it has become spent by the time that that lease is granted.

(5)   A claim to exercise the right to an overriding lease under this section is made by the claimant making a request for such a lease to the landlord; and any such request—

    (a)    must be made to the landlord in writing and specify the payment by virtue of which the claimant claims to be entitled to the lease ("the qualifying payment"); and

    (b)    must be so made at the time of making the qualifying payment or within the period of 12 months beginning with the date of that payment.

(6)   Where the claimant duly makes such a request—

    (a)    the landlord shall (subject to subsection (7)) grant and deliver to the claimant an overriding lease of the demised premises within a reasonable time of the request being received by the landlord; and

    (b)    the claimant—

        (i)    shall thereupon deliver to the landlord a counterpart of the lease duly executed by the claimant, and

        (ii)    shall be liable for the landlord's reasonable costs of and incidental to the grant of the lease.

(7)   The landlord shall not be under any obligation to grant an overriding lease of the demised premises under this section at a time when the relevant tenancy has been determined; and a claimant shall not be entitled to the grant of such a lease if at the time when he makes his request—

    (a)    the landlord has already granted such a lease and that lease remains in force; or

    (b)    another person has already duly made a request for such a lease to the landlord and that request has been neither withdrawn nor abandoned by that person.

(8)   Where two or more requests are duly made on the same day, then for the purposes of subsection (7)—

    (a)    a request made by a person who was liable for the qualifying payment as a former tenant shall be treated as made before a request made by a person who was so liable as a guarantor; and

    (b)    a request made by a person whose liability in respect of the covenant in question commenced earlier than any such liability of another person shall be treated as made before a request made by that other person.

(9)   Where a claimant who has duly made a request for an overriding lease under this section subsequently withdraws or abandons the request before he is granted such a lease by the landlord,

the claimant shall be liable for the landlord's reasonable costs incurred in pursuance of the request down to the time of its withdrawal or abandonment; and for the purposes of this section—

    (a)    a claimant's request is withdrawn by the claimant notifying the landlord in writing that he is withdrawing his request; and

    (b)    a claimant is to be regarded as having abandoned his request if—

        (i)    the landlord has requested the claimant in writing to take, within such reasonable period as is specified in the landlord's request, all or any of the remaining steps required to be taken by the claimant before the lease can be granted, and

        (ii)    the claimant fails to comply with the landlord's request,

    and is accordingly to be regarded as having abandoned it at the time when that period expires.

(10)    Any request or notification under this section may be sent by post.

(11)    The preceding provisions of this section shall apply where the landlord is the tenant under an overriding lease granted under this section as they apply where no such lease has been granted; and accordingly there may be two or more such leases interposed between the first such lease and the relevant tenancy.

**[961]**

## 20  Overriding leases: supplementary provisions

(1)    For the purposes of section 1 an overriding lease shall be a new tenancy only if the relevant tenancy is a new tenancy.

(2)    Every overriding lease shall state—

    (a)    that it is a lease granted under section 19, and

    (b)    whether it is or is not a new tenancy for the purposes of section 1;

and any such statement shall comply with such requirements as may be prescribed by [land registration rules under the Land Registration Act 2002].

(3)    A claim that the landlord has failed to comply with subsection (6)(a) of section 19 may be made the subject of civil proceedings in like manner as any other claim in tort for breach of statutory duty; and if the claimant under that section fails to comply with subsection (6)(b)(i) of that section he shall not be entitled to exercise any of the rights otherwise exercisable by him under the overriding lease.

(4)    An overriding lease—

    (a)    shall be deemed to be authorised as against the persons interested in any mortgage of the landlord's interest (however created or arising); and

    (b)    shall be binding on any such persons;

and if any such person is by virtue of such a mortgage entitled to possession of the documents of title relating to the landlord's interest—

        (i)    the landlord shall within one month of the execution of the lease deliver to that person the counterpart executed in pursuance of section 19(6)(b)(i); and

        (ii)    if he fails to do so, the instrument creating or evidencing the mortgage shall apply as if the obligation to deliver a counterpart were included in the terms of the mortgage as set out in that instrument.

(5)    It is hereby declared—

    (a)    that the fact that an overriding lease takes effect subject to the relevant tenancy shall not constitute a breach of any covenant of the lease against subletting or parting with possession of the premises demised by the lease or any part of them; and

    (b)    that each of sections 16, 17 and 18 applies where the tenancy referred to in subsection (1) of that section is an overriding lease as it applies in other cases falling within that subsection.

(6)    No tenancy shall be registrable under the Land Charges Act 1972 or be taken to be an estate contract within the meaning of that Act by reason of any right or obligation that may arise under section 19, and any right arising from a request made under that section shall not be [capable of falling within paragraph 2 of Schedule 1 or 3 to the Land Registration Act 2002]; but any such request shall be registrable under the Land Charges Act 1972, or may be the subject of a notice [under the Land Registration Act 2002], as if it were an estate contract.

(7)    In this section—

    (a)    "mortgage" includes "charge"; and

    (b)    any expression which is also used in section 19 has the same meaning as in that section.

**[962]**

**NOTES**

Sub-ss (2), (6): words in square brackets substituted by the Land Registration Act 2002, s 133, Sch 11, para 33(1), (3), (4).

*Forfeiture and disclaimer*

## 21   Forfeiture or disclaimer limited to part only of demised premises

(1)   Where—

(a)   as a result of one or more assignments a person is the tenant of part only of the premises demised by a tenancy, and

(b)   under a proviso or stipulation in the tenancy there is a right of re-entry or forfeiture for a breach of a tenant covenant of the tenancy, and

(c)   the right is (apart from this subsection) exercisable in relation to that part and other land demised by the tenancy,

the right shall nevertheless, in connection with a breach of any such covenant by that person, be taken to be a right exercisable only in relation to that part.

(2)   Where—

(a)   a company which is being wound up, or a trustee in bankruptcy, is as a result of one or more assignments the tenant of part only of the premises demised by a tenancy, and

(b)   the liquidator of the company exercises his power under section 178 of the Insolvency Act 1986, or the trustee in bankruptcy exercises his power under section 315 of that Act, to disclaim property demised by the tenancy,

the power is exercisable only in relation to the part of the premises referred to in paragraph (a).

**[963]**

## 22   *(Inserts the Landlord and Tenant Act 1927, s 19(1A)–(1E).)*

*Supplemental*

## 23   Effects of becoming subject to liability under, or entitled to benefit of, covenant etc

(1)   Where as a result of an assignment a person becomes, by virtue of this Act, bound by or entitled to the benefit of a covenant, he shall not by virtue of this Act have any liability or rights under the covenant in relation to any time falling before the assignment.

(2)   Subsection (1) does not preclude any such rights being expressly assigned to the person in question.

(3)   Where as a result of an assignment a person becomes, by virtue of this Act, entitled to a right of re-entry contained in a tenancy, that right shall be exercisable in relation to any breach of a covenant of the tenancy occurring before the assignment as in relation to one occurring thereafter, unless by reason of any waiver or release it was not so exercisable immediately before the assignment.

**[964]**

## 24   Effects of release from liability under, or loss of benefit of, covenant

(1)   Any release of a person from a covenant by virtue of this Act does not affect any liability of his arising from a breach of the covenant occurring before the release.

(2)   Where—

(a)   by virtue of this Act a tenant is released from a tenant covenant of a tenancy, and

(b)   immediately before the release another person is bound by a covenant of the tenancy imposing any liability or penalty in the event of a failure to comply with that tenant covenant,

then, as from the release of the tenant, that other person is released from the covenant mentioned in paragraph (b) to the same extent as the tenant is released from that tenant covenant.

(3)   Where a person bound by a landlord or tenant covenant of a tenancy—

(a)   assigns the whole or part of his interest in the premises demised by the tenancy, but

(b)   is not released by virtue of this Act from the covenant (with the result that subsection (1) does not apply),

the assignment does not affect any liability of his arising from a breach of the covenant occurring before the assignment.

(4)   Where by virtue of this Act a person ceases to be entitled to the benefit of a covenant, this does not affect any rights of his arising from a breach of the covenant occurring before he ceases to be so entitled.

**[965]**

## 25   Agreement void if it restricts operation of the Act

(1)   Any agreement relating to a tenancy is void to the extent that—

(a)   it would apart from this section have effect to exclude, modify or otherwise frustrate the operation of any provision of this Act, or

(b)   it provides for—

(i)   the termination or surrender of the tenancy, or

(ii)    the imposition on the tenant of any penalty, disability or liability, in the event of the operation of any provision of this Act, or

(c)    it provides for any of the matters referred to in paragraph (b)(i) or (ii) and does so (whether expressly or otherwise) in connection with, or in consequence of, the operation of any provision of this Act.

(2)    To the extent that an agreement relating to a tenancy constitutes a covenant (whether absolute or qualified) against the assignment, or parting with the possession, of the premises demised by the tenancy or any part of them—

(a)    the agreement is not void by virtue of subsection (1) by reason only of the fact that as such the covenant prohibits or restricts any such assignment or parting with possession; but

(b)    paragraph (a) above does not otherwise affect the operation of that subsection in relation to the agreement (and in particular does not preclude its application to the agreement to the extent that it purports to regulate the giving of, or the making of any application for, consent to any such assignment or parting with possession).

(3)    In accordance with section 16(1) nothing in this section applies to any agreement to the extent that it is an authorised guarantee agreement; but (without prejudice to the generality of subsection (1) above) an agreement is void to the extent that it is one falling within section 16(4)(a) or (b).

(4)    This section applies to an agreement relating to a tenancy whether or not the agreement is—

(a)    contained in the instrument creating the tenancy; or

(b)    made before the creation of the tenancy.

**[966]**

## 26  Miscellaneous savings etc

(1)    Nothing in this Act is to be read as preventing—

(a)    a party to a tenancy from releasing a person from a landlord covenant or a tenant covenant of the tenancy; or

(b)    the parties to a tenancy from agreeing to an apportionment of liability under such a covenant.

(2)    Nothing in this Act affects the operation of section 3(3A) of the Landlord and Tenant Act 1985 (preservation of former landlord's liability until tenant notified of new landlord).

(3)    No apportionment which has become binding in accordance with section 10 shall be affected by any order or decision made under or by virtue of any enactment not contained in this Act which relates to apportionment.

**[967]**

## 27  Notices for the purposes of the Act

(1)    The form of any notice to be served for the purposes of section 8, 10 or 17 shall be prescribed by regulations made by the Lord Chancellor by statutory instrument.

(2)    The regulations shall require any notice served for the purposes of section 8(1) or 10(1) ("the initial notice") to include—

(a)    an explanation of the significance of the notice and the options available to the person on whom it is served;

(b)    a statement that any objections to the proposed release, or (as the case may be) to the proposed binding effect of the apportionment, must be made by notice in writing served on the person or persons by whom the initial notice is served within the period of four weeks beginning with the day on which the initial notice is served; and

(c)    an address in England and Wales to which any such objections may be sent.

(3)    The regulations shall require any notice served for the purposes of section 17 to include an explanation of the significance of the notice.

(4)    If any notice purporting to be served for the purposes of section 8(1), 10(1) or 17 is not in the prescribed form, or in a form substantially to the same effect, the notice shall not be effective for the purposes of section 8, section 10 or section 17 (as the case may be).

(5)    Section 23 of the Landlord and Tenant Act 1927 shall apply in relation to the service of notices for the purposes of section 8, 10 or 17.

(6)    Any statutory instrument made under this section shall be subject to annulment in pursuance of a resolution of either House of Parliament.

**[968]**

**NOTES**

Regulations: the Landlord and Tenant (Covenants) Act 1995 (Notices) Regulations 1995, SI 1995/2964 at **[3141]**.

## 28　Interpretation

(1)　In this Act (unless the context otherwise requires—

"assignment" includes equitable assignment and in addition (subject to section 11) assignment in breach of a covenant of a tenancy or by operation of law;

"authorised guarantee agreement" means an agreement which is an authorised guarantee agreement for the purposes of section 16;

"collateral agreement", in relation to a tenancy, means any agreement collateral to the tenancy, whether made before or after its creation;

"consent" includes licence;

"covenant" includes term, condition and obligation, and references to a covenant (or any description of covenant) of a tenancy include a covenant (or a covenant of that description) contained in a collateral agreement;

"landlord" and "tenant", in relation to a tenancy, mean the person for the time being entitled to the reversion expectant on the term of the tenancy and the person so entitled to that term respectively;

"landlord covenant", in relation to a tenancy, means a covenant falling to be complied with by the landlord of premises demised by the tenancy;

"new tenancy" means a tenancy which is a new tenancy for the purposes of section 1;

"reversion" means the interest expectant on the termination of a tenancy;

"tenancy" means any lease or other tenancy and includes—
　(a)　a sub-tenancy, and
　(b)　an agreement for a tenancy,
　but does not include a mortgage term;

"tenant covenant", in relation to a tenancy, means a covenant falling to be complied with by the tenant of premises demised by the tenancy.

(2)　For the purposes of any reference in this Act to a covenant falling to be complied with in relation to a particular part of the premises demised by a tenancy, a covenant falls to be so complied with if—
　(a)　it in terms applies to that part of the premises, or
　(b)　in its practical application it can be attributed to that part of the premises (whether or not it can also be so attributed to other individual parts of those premises).

(3)　Subsection (2) does not apply in relation to covenants to pay money; and, for the purposes of any reference in this Act to a covenant falling to be complied with in relation to a particular part of the premises demised by a tenancy, a covenant of a tenancy which is a covenant to pay money falls to be so complied with if—
　(a)　the covenant in terms applies to that part; or
　(b)　the amount of the payment is determinable specifically by reference—
　　(i)　to that part, or
　　(ii)　to anything falling to be done by or for a person as tenant or occupier of that part (if it is a tenant covenant), or
　　(iii)　to anything falling to be done by or for a person as landlord of that part (if it is a landlord covenant).

(4)　Where two or more persons jointly constitute either the landlord or the tenant in relation to a tenancy, any reference in this Act to the landlord or the tenant is a reference to both or all of the persons who jointly constitute the landlord or the tenant, as the case may be (and accordingly nothing in section 13 applies in relation to the rights and liabilities of such persons between themselves).

(5)　References in this Act to the assignment by a landlord of the reversion in the whole or part of the premises demised by a tenancy are to the assignment by him of the whole of his interest (as owner of the reversion) in the whole or part of those premises.

(6)　For the purposes of this Act—
　(a)　any assignment (however effected) consisting in the transfer of the whole of the landlord's interest (as owner of the reversion) in any premises demised by a tenancy shall be treated as an assignment by the landlord of the reversion in those premises even if it is not effected by him; and
　(b)　any assignment (however effected) consisting in the transfer of the whole of the tenant's interest in any premises demised by a tenancy shall be treated as an assignment by the tenant of those premises even if it is not effected by him.

**[969]**

## 29　Crown application

This Act binds the Crown.

**[970]**

## 30 Consequential amendments and repeals

(1)    The enactments specified in Schedule 1 are amended in accordance with that Schedule, the amendments being consequential on the provisions of this Act.

(2)    The enactments specified in Schedule 2 are repealed to the extent specified.

(3)    Subsections (1) and (2) do not affect the operation of—

   (a)    section 77 of, or Part IX or X of Schedule 2 to, the Law of Property Act 1925, or

   (b)    section 24(1)(b) or (2) of the Land Registration Act 1925,

in relation to tenancies which are not new tenancies.

(4)    In consequence of this Act nothing in the following provisions, namely—

   (a)    sections 78 and 79 of the Law of Property Act 1925 (benefit and burden of covenants relating to land), and

   (b)    sections 141 and 142 of that Act (running of benefit and burden of covenants with reversion),

shall apply in relation to new tenancies.

(5)    The Lord Chancellor may by order made by statutory instrument make, in the case of such enactments as may be specified in the order, such amendments or repeals in, or such modifications of, those enactments as appear to him to be necessary or expedient in consequence of any provision of this Act.

(6)    Any statutory instrument made under subsection (5) shall be subject to annulment in pursuance of a resolution of either House of Parliament.

**[971]**

## 31 Commencement

(1)    The provisions of this Act come into force on such day as the Lord Chancellor may appoint by order made by statutory instrument.

(2)    An order under this section may contain such transitional provisions and savings (whether or not involving the modification of any enactment) as appear to the Lord Chancellor necessary or expedient in connection with the provisions brought into force by the order.

**[972]**

### NOTES

Orders: the Landlord and Tenant (Covenants) Act 1995 (Commencement) Order 1995, SI 1995/2963.

## 32 Short title and extent

(1)    This Act may be cited as the Landlord and Tenant (Covenants) Act 1995.

(2)    This Act extends to England and Wales only.

**[973]**

*(Sch 1 amends the Trustee Act 1925, s 26, the Law of Property Act 1925, s 77 at* **[11]***, and the Landlord and Tenant Act 1954, ss 34, 35; Sch 2 contains repeals only.)*

# DISABILITY DISCRIMINATION ACT 1995

## (1995 c 50)

### ARRANGEMENT OF SECTIONS

### PART III
### DISCRIMINATION IN OTHER AREAS

*Premises*

## PART VIII
## MISCELLANEOUS

*An Act to make it unlawful to discriminate against disabled persons in connection with employment, the provision of goods, facilities and services or the disposal or management of premises; to make provision about the employment of disabled persons; and to establish a National Disability Council*

**[8 November 1995]**

**1–18E**    *((Pts I, II) outside the scope of this work.)*

## PART III
## DISCRIMINATION IN OTHER AREAS

**19–21J**    *(Outside the scope of this work.)*

*Premises*

### 22   Discrimination in relation to premises

(1)    It is unlawful for a person with power to dispose of any premises to discriminate against a disabled person—

     (a)    in the terms on which he offers to dispose of those premises to the disabled person;

     (b)    by refusing to dispose of those premises to the disabled person; or

     (c)    in his treatment of the disabled person in relation to any list of persons in need of premises of that description.

(2)    Subsection (1) does not apply to a person who owns an estate or interest in the premises and wholly occupies them unless, for the purpose of disposing of the premises, he—

     (a)    uses the services of an estate agent, or

     (b)    publishes an advertisement or causes an advertisement to be published.

(3)    It is unlawful for a person managing any premises to discriminate against a disabled person occupying those premises—

     (a)    in the way he permits the disabled person to make use of any benefits or facilities;

     (b)    by refusing or deliberately omitting to permit the disabled person to make use of any benefits or facilities; or

     (c)    by evicting the disabled person, or subjecting him to any other detriment.

[(3A)    Regulations may make provision, for purposes of subsection (3)—

     (a)    as to who is to be treated as being, or as to who is to be treated as not being, a person who manages premises;

     (b)    as to who is to be treated as being, or as to who is to be treated as not being, a person occupying premises.]

(4)    It is unlawful for any person whose licence or consent is required for the disposal of any premises comprised in, or (in Scotland) the subject of, a tenancy to discriminate against a disabled person by withholding his licence or consent for the disposal of the premises to the disabled person.

(5)    Subsection (4) applies to tenancies created before as well as after the passing of this Act.

(6)    In this section—

     "advertisement" includes every form of advertisement or notice, whether to the public or not;

     "dispose", in relation to premises, includes granting a right to occupy the premises, and, in relation to premises comprised in, or (in Scotland) the subject of, a tenancy, includes—

         (a)     assigning the tenancy, and

         (b)     sub-letting or parting with possession of the premises or any part of the premises;

and "disposal" shall be construed accordingly;

"estate agent" means a person who, by way of profession or trade, provides services for the purpose of finding premises for persons seeking to acquire them or assisting in the disposal of premises; and

"tenancy" means a tenancy created—

    (a)    by a lease or sub-lease,

    (b)    by an agreement for a lease or sub-lease,

    (c)    by a tenancy agreement, or

    (d)    in pursuance of any enactment.

(7)    In the case of an act which constitutes discrimination by virtue of section 55, this section also applies to discrimination against a person who is not disabled.

(8)    This section applies only in relation to premises in the United Kingdom.

**[974]**

**NOTES**

Sub-s (3A): inserted by the Disability Discrimination Act 2005, s 19(1), Sch 1, Pt 1, paras 1, 16.
Regulations: the Disability Discrimination (Premises) Regulations 2006, SI 2006/887.

**[22A  Commonholds**

(1)    It is unlawful for any person whose licence or consent is required for the disposal of an interest in a commonhold unit by the unit-holder to discriminate against a disabled person by withholding his licence or consent for the disposal of the interest in favour of, or to, the disabled person.

(2)    Where it is not possible for an interest in a commonhold unit to be disposed of by the unit-holder unless some other person is a party to the disposal of the interest, it is unlawful for that other person to discriminate against a disabled person by deliberately not being a party to the disposal of the interest in favour of, or to, the disabled person.

(3)    Regulations may provide for subsection (1) or (2) not to apply, or to apply only, in cases of a prescribed description.

(4)    Regulations may make provision, for purposes of this section-

    (a)    as to what is, or as to what is not, to be included within the meaning of "dispose" (and "disposal");

    (b)    as to what is, or as to what is not, to be included within the meaning of "interest in a commonhold unit".

(5)    In this section "commonhold unit", and "unit-holder" in relation to such a unit, have the same meaning as in Part 1 of the Commonhold and Leasehold Reform Act 2002.

(6)    In the case of an act which constitutes discrimination by virtue of section 55, this section also applies to discrimination against a person who is not disabled.

(7)    This section applies only in relation to premises in England and Wales.]

**[975]**

**NOTES**

Commencement: 30 June 2005 (for the purpose of making regulations); 4 December 2006 (otherwise).
Inserted by the Disability Discrimination Act 2005, s 19(1), Sch 1, Pt 1, paras 1, 17.
Regulations: the Disability Discrimination (Premises) Regulations 2006, SI 2006/887.

**23  Exemption for small dwellings**

(1)    Where the conditions mentioned in subsection (2) are satisfied, subsection (1), (3) or (as the case may be) (4) of section 22 does not apply.

(2)    The conditions are that—

    (a)    the relevant occupier resides, and intends to continue to reside, on the premises;

    (b)    the relevant occupier shares accommodation on the premises with persons who reside on the premises and are not members of his household;

    (c)    the shared accommodation is not storage accommodation or a means of access; and

    (d)    the premises are small premises.

(3)    For the purposes of this section, premises are "small premises" if they fall within subsection (4) or (5).

(4)    Premises fall within this subsection if—

    (a)    only the relevant occupier and members of his household reside in the accommodation occupied by him;

    (b)    the premises comprise, in addition to the accommodation occupied by the relevant occupier, residential accommodation for at least one other household;

    (c)    the residential accommodation for each other household is let, or available for letting, on a separate tenancy or similar agreement; and (d)　　there are not normally more than two such other households.

(5)　　Premises fall within this subsection if there is not normally residential accommodation on the premises for more than six persons in addition to the relevant occupier and any members of his household.

(6)　　For the purposes of this section "the relevant occupier" means—

(a)　　in a case falling within section 22(1), the person with power to dispose of the premises, or a near relative of his;

[(aa)　in a case falling within section 22(3), the person managing the premises, or a near relative of his;]

(b)　　in a case falling within section 22(4), the person whose licence or consent is required for the disposal of the premises, or a near relative of his.

(7)　　For the purposes of this section—

"near relative" means a person's spouse [or civil partner], partner, parent, child, grandparent, grandchild, or brother or sister (whether of full or half blood or [by marriage or civil partnership)]; and

["partner" means the other member of a couple consisting of—

(a)　　a man and a woman who are not married to each other but are living together as husband and wife, or

(b)　　two people of the same sex who are not civil partners of each other but are living together as if they were civil partners.]

**[976]**

---

**NOTES**

Sub-s (6): para (aa) inserted by the Disability Discrimination Act 2005, s 19(1), Sch 1, Pt 1, paras 1, 18.

Sub-s (7): in definition "near relative" words in first pair of square brackets inserted, words in second pair of square brackets substituted, and definition "partner" substituted by the Civil Partnership Act 2004, s 261(1), Sch 27, para 150(1)–(3).

---

**24　Meaning of "discrimination"**

(1)　　For the purposes of [sections 22 and 22A], a person ("A") discriminates against a disabled person if—

(a)　　for a reason which relates to the disabled person's disability, he treats him less favourably than he treats or would treat others to whom that reason does not or would not apply; and

(b)　　he cannot show that the treatment in question is justified.

(2)　　For the purposes of this section, treatment is justified only if—

(a)　　in A's opinion, one or more of the conditions mentioned in subsection (3) are satisfied; and

(b)　　it is reasonable, in all the circumstances of the case, for him to hold that opinion.

(3)　　The conditions are that—

(a)　　in any case, the treatment is necessary in order not to endanger the health or safety of any person (which may include that of the disabled person);

(b)　　in any case, the disabled person is incapable of entering into an enforceable agreement, or of giving an informed consent, and for that reason the treatment is reasonable in that case;

(c)　　in a case falling within section 22(3)(a), the treatment is necessary in order for the disabled person or the occupiers of other premises forming part of the building to make use of the benefit or facility;

(d)　　in a case falling within section 22(3)(b), the treatment is necessary in order for the occupiers of other premises forming part of the building to make use of the benefit or facility

[(e)　in a case to which subsection (3A) applies, the terms are less favourable in order to recover costs which—

(i)　　as a result of the disabled person having a disability, are incurred in connection with the disposal of the premises, and

(ii)　　are not costs incurred in connection with taking steps to avoid liability under section 24G(1);

(f)　　in a case to which subsection (3B) applies, the disabled person is subjected to the detriment in order to recover costs which—

(i)　　as a result of the disabled person having a disability, are incurred in connection with the management of the premises, and

(ii)　　are not costs incurred in connection with taking steps to avoid liability under section 24A(1) or 24G(1).]

[(3A)　This subsection applies to a case if—

(a)　　the case falls within section 22(1)(a);

(b)    the premises are to let;

(c)    the person with power to dispose of the premises is a controller of them; and

(d)    the proposed disposal of the premises would involve the disabled person becoming a person to whom they are let.

(3B)    This subsection applies to a case if—

(a)    the case falls within section 22(3)(c);

(b)    the detriment is not eviction;

(c)    the premises are let premises;

(d)    the person managing the premises is a controller of them; and

(e)    the disabled person is a person to whom the premises are let or, although not a person to whom they are let, is lawfully under the letting an occupier of them.

(3C)    Section 24G(3) and (4) apply for the purposes of subsection (3A) as for those of section 24G; and section 24A(3) and (4) apply for the purposes of subsection (3B) as for those of section 24A.]

(4)    Regulations may make provision, for purposes of this section, as to circumstances in which—

(a)    it is reasonable for a person to hold the opinion mentioned in subsection 2(a);

(b)    it is not reasonable for a person to hold that opinion.

[(4A)    Regulations may make provision for the condition specified in subsection (3)(b) not to apply in prescribed circumstances.]

(5)    Regulations may make provision, for purposes of this section, as to circumstances (other than those mentioned in subsection (3)) in which treatment is to be taken to be justified.

**[977]**

**NOTES**

Sub-s (1): words in square brackets substituted by the Disability Discrimination Act 2005, s 19(1), Sch 1, Pt 1, paras 1, 19(1), (2).

Sub-s (3): paras (e), (f) added by the Disability Discrimination Act 2005, s 19(1), Sch 1, Pt 1, paras 1, 19(1), (3).

Sub-ss (3A)–(3C): inserted by the Disability Discrimination Act 2005, s 19(1), Sch 1, Pt 1, paras 1, 19(1), (4).

Sub-s (4A): inserted by the Disability Discrimination Act 2005, s 19(1), Sch 1, Pt 1, paras 1, 19(1), (5).

Regulations: the Disability Discrimination (Premises) Regulations 2006, SI 2006/887.

**[24A    Let premises: discrimination in failing to comply with duty**

(1)    It is unlawful for a controller of let premises to discriminate against a disabled person—

(a)    who is a person to whom the premises are let; or

(b)    who, although not a person to whom the premises are let, is lawfully under the letting an occupier of the premises.

(2)    For the purposes of subsection (1), a controller of let premises discriminates against a disabled person if—

(a)    he fails to comply with a duty under section 24C or 24D imposed on him by reference to the disabled person; and

(b)    he cannot show that failure to comply with the duty is justified (see section 24K).

(3)    For the purposes of this section and sections 24B to 24F, a person is a controller of let premises if he is—

(a)    a person by whom the premises are let; or

(b)    a person who manages the premises.

(4)    For the purposes of this section and sections 24B to 24F—

(a)    "let" includes sub-let; and

(b)    premises shall be treated as let by a person to another where a person has granted another a contractual licence to occupy them.

(5)    This section applies only in relation to premises in the United Kingdom.]

**[978]**

**NOTES**

Commencement: 4 December 2006.

Inserted, together with ss 24B–24H, 24J–24L, by the Disability Discrimination Act 2005, s 13.

**[24B    Exceptions to section 24A(1)**

(1)    Section 24A(1) does not apply if—

(a)    the premises are, or have at any time been, the only or principal home of an individual who is a person by whom they are let; and

(b)    since entering into the letting-

(i)    the individual has not, and

(ii)    where he is not the sole person by whom the premises are let, no other person by whom they are let has,

used for the purpose of managing the premises the services of a person who, by profession or trade, manages let premises.

(2)    Section 24A(1) does not apply if the premises are of a prescribed description.

(3)    Where the conditions mentioned in section 23(2) are satisfied, section 24A(1) does not apply.

(4)    For the purposes of section 23 "the relevant occupier" means, in a case falling within section 24A(1), a controller of the let premises, or a near relative of his; and "near relative" has here the same meaning as in section 23.]

**[979]**

---

**NOTES**

Commencement: 4 December 2006.

Inserted as noted to s 24A at **[978]**.

---

**[24C    Duty for purposes of section 24A(2) to provide auxiliary aid or service**

(1)    Subsection (2) applies where—
   (a)    a controller of let premises receives a request made by or on behalf of a person to whom the premises are let;
   (b)    it is reasonable to regard the request as a request that the controller take steps in order to provide an auxiliary aid or service; and
   (c)    either the first condition, or the second condition, is satisfied.

(2)    It is the duty of the controller to take such steps as it is reasonable, in all the circumstances of the case, for him to have to take in order to provide the auxiliary aid or service (but see section 24E(1)).

(3)    The first condition is that—
   (a)    the auxiliary aid or service-
      (i)    would enable a relevant disabled person to enjoy, or facilitate such a person's enjoyment of, the premises, but
      (ii)    would be of little or no practical use to the relevant disabled person concerned if he were neither a person to whom the premises are let nor an occupier of them; and
   (b)    it would, were the auxiliary aid or service not to be provided, be impossible or unreasonably difficult for the relevant disabled person concerned to enjoy the premises.

(4)    The second condition is that—
   (a)    the auxiliary aid or service-
      (i)    would enable a relevant disabled person to make use, or facilitate such a person's making use, of any benefit, or facility, which by reason of the letting is one of which he is entitled to make use, but
      (ii)    would be of little or no practical use to the relevant disabled person concerned if he were neither a person to whom the premises are let nor an occupier of them; and
   (b)    it would, were the auxiliary aid or service not to be provided, be impossible or unreasonably difficult for the relevant disabled person concerned to make use of any benefit, or facility, which by reason of the letting is one of which he is entitled to make use.]

**[980]**

---

**NOTES**

Commencement: 4 December 2006.

Inserted as noted to s 24A at **[978]**.

---

**[24D    Duty for purposes of section 24A(2) to change practices, terms etc**

(1)    Subsection (3) applies where—
   (a)    a controller of let premises has a practice, policy or procedure which has the effect of making it impossible, or unreasonably difficult, for a relevant disabled person-
      (i)    to enjoy the premises, or
      (ii)    to make use of any benefit, or facility, which by reason of the letting is one of which he is entitled to make use, or
   (b)    a term of the letting has that effect,

and (in either case) the conditions specified in subsection (2) are satisfied.

(2)    Those conditions are—

(a)   that the practice, policy, procedure or term would not have that effect if the relevant disabled person concerned did not have a disability;

(b)   that the controller receives a request made by or on behalf of a person to whom the premises are let; and

(c)   that it is reasonable to regard the request as a request that the controller take steps in order to change the practice, policy, procedure or term so as to stop it having that effect.

(3)   It is the duty of the controller to take such steps as it is reasonable, in all the circumstances of the case, for him to have to take in order to change the practice, policy, procedure or term so as to stop it having that effect (but see section 24E(1)).]

**[981]**

**NOTES**

Commencement: 4 December 2006.
Inserted as noted to s 24A at **[978]**.

**[24E   Sections 24C and 24D: supplementary and interpretation**

(1)   For the purposes of sections 24C and 24D, it is never reasonable for a controller of let premises to have to take steps consisting of, or including, the removal or alteration of a physical feature.

(2)   Sections 24C and 24D impose duties only for the purpose of determining whether a person has, for the purposes of section 24A, discriminated against another; and accordingly a breach of any such duty is not actionable as such.

(3)   In sections 24C and 24D "relevant disabled person", in relation to let premises, means a particular disabled person—

(a)   who is a person to whom the premises are let; or

(b)   who, although not a person to whom the premises are let, is lawfully under the letting an occupier of the premises.

(4)   For the purposes of sections 24C and 24D, the terms of a letting of premises include the terms of any agreement which relates to the letting of the premises.]

**[982]**

**NOTES**

Commencement: 4 December 2006.
Inserted as noted to s 24A at **[978]**.

**[24F   Let premises: victimisation of persons to whom premises are let**

(1)   Where a duty under section 24C or 24D is imposed on a controller of let premises by reference to a person who, although not a person to whom the premises are let, is lawfully under the letting an occupier of the premises, it is unlawful for a controller of the let premises to discriminate against a person to whom the premises are let.

(2)   For the purposes of subsection (1), a controller of the let premises discriminates against a person to whom the premises are let if—

(a)   the controller treats that person ("T") less favourably than he treats or would treat other persons whose circumstances are the same as T's; and

(b)   he does so because of costs incurred in connection with taking steps to avoid liability under section 24A(1) for failure to comply with the duty.

(3)   In comparing T's circumstances with those of any other person for the purposes of subsection (2)(a), the following (as well as the costs' having been incurred) shall be disregarded—

(a)   the making of the request that gave rise to the imposition of the duty; and

(b)   the disability of each person who-

(i)   is a disabled person or a person who has had a disability, and

(ii)   is a person to whom the premises are let or, although not a person to whom the premises are let, is lawfully under the letting an occupier of the premises.]

**[983]**

**NOTES**

Commencement: 4 December 2006.
Inserted as noted to s 24A at **[978]**.

**[24G   Premises that are to let: discrimination in failing to comply with duty**

(1)   Where—

(a)   a person has premises to let, and

(b)   a disabled person is considering taking a letting of the premises,

it is unlawful for a controller of the premises to discriminate against the disabled person.

(2)    For the purposes of subsection (1), a controller of premises that are to let discriminates against a disabled person if—

    (a)   he fails to comply with a duty under section 24J imposed on him by reference to the disabled person; and

    (b)   he cannot show that failure to comply with the duty is justified (see section 24K).

(3)    For the purposes of this section and sections 24H and 24J, a person is a controller of premises that are to let if he is—

    (a)   a person who has the premises to let; or

    (b)   a person who manages the premises.

(4)    For the purposes of this section and sections 24H and 24J—

    (a)   "let" includes sub-let;

    (b)   premises shall be treated as to let by a person to another where a person proposes to grant another a contractual licence to occupy them;

and references to a person considering taking a letting of premises shall be construed accordingly.

(5)    This section applies only in relation to premises in the United Kingdom.]

                                                            **[984]**

**NOTES**

    Commencement: 4 December 2006.

    Inserted as noted to s 24A at **[978]**.

### [24H    Exceptions to section 24G(1)

(1)    Section 24G(1) does not apply in relation to premises that are to let if the premises are, or have at any time been, the only or principal home of an individual who is a person who has them to let and—

    (a)   the individual does not use, and

    (b)   where he is not the sole person who has the premises to let, no other person who has the premises to let uses,

the services of an estate agent (within the meaning given by section 22(6)) for the purposes of letting the premises.

(2)    Section 24G(1) does not apply if the premises are of a prescribed description.

(3)    Where the conditions mentioned in section 23(2) are satisfied, section 24G(1) does not apply.

(4)    For the purposes of section 23 "the relevant occupier" means, in a case falling within section 24G(1), a controller of the premises that are to let, or a near relative of his; and "near relative" has here the same meaning as in section 23.]

                                                           **[985]**

**NOTES**

    Commencement: 4 December 2006.

    Inserted as noted to s 24A at **[978]**.

### [24J    Duties for purposes of section 24G(2)

(1)    Subsection (2) applies where—

    (a)   a controller of premises that are to let receives a request made by or on behalf of a relevant disabled person;

    (b)   it is reasonable to regard the request as a request that the controller take steps in order to provide an auxiliary aid or service;

    (c)   the auxiliary aid or service—

        (i)   would enable the relevant disabled person to become, or facilitate his becoming, a person to whom the premises are let, but

        (ii)   would be of little or no practical use to him if he were not considering taking a letting of the premises; and

    (d)   it would, were the auxiliary aid or service not to be provided, be impossible or unreasonably difficult for the relevant disabled person to become a person to whom the premises are let.

(2)    It is the duty of the controller to take such steps as it is reasonable, in all the circumstances of the case, for the controller to have to take in order to provide the auxiliary aid or service (but see subsection (5)).

(3)    Subsection (4) applies where—

    (a)   a controller of premises that are to let has a practice, policy or procedure which has the effect of making it impossible, or unreasonably difficult, for a relevant disabled person to become a person to whom the premises are let;

   (b)    the practice, policy or procedure would not have that effect if the relevant disabled person did not have a disability;

   (c)    the controller receives a request made by or on behalf of the relevant disabled person; and

   (d)    it is reasonable to regard the request as a request that the controller take steps in order to change the practice, policy or procedure so as to stop it having that effect.

(4)   It is the duty of the controller to take such steps as it is reasonable, in all the circumstances of the case, for him to have to take in order to change the practice, policy or procedure so as to stop it having that effect (but see subsection (5)).

(5)   For the purposes of this section, it is never reasonable for a controller of premises that are to let to have to take steps consisting of, or including, the removal or alteration of a physical feature.

(6)   In this section "relevant disabled person", in relation to premises that are to let, means a particular disabled person who is considering taking a letting of the premises.

(7)   This section imposes duties only for the purpose of determining whether a person has, for the purposes of section 24G, discriminated against another; and accordingly a breach of any such duty is not actionable as such.]

**[986]**

**NOTES**
Commencement: 4 December 2006.
Inserted as noted to s 24A at **[978]**.

**[24K   Let premises and premises that are to let: justification**

(1)   For the purposes of sections 24A(2) and 24G(2), a person's failure to comply with a duty is justified only if—

   (a)    in his opinion, a condition mentioned in subsection (2) is satisfied; and

   (b)    it is reasonable, in all the circumstances of the case, for him to hold that opinion.

(2)   The conditions are—

   (a)    that it is necessary to refrain from complying with the duty in order not to endanger the health or safety of any person (which may include that of the disabled person concerned);

   (b)    that the disabled person concerned is incapable of entering into an enforceable agreement, or of giving informed consent, and for that reason the failure is reasonable.

(3)   Regulations may—

   (a)    make provision, for purposes of this section, as to circumstances in which it is, or as to circumstances in which it is not, reasonable for a person to hold the opinion mentioned in subsection (1)(a);

   (b)    amend or omit a condition specified in subsection (2) or make provision for it not to apply in prescribed circumstances;

   (c)    make provision, for purposes of this section, as to circumstances (other than any for the time being mentioned in subsection (2)) in which a failure is to be taken to be justified.]

**[987]**

**NOTES**
Commencement: 30 June 2005 (for the purpose of making regulations); 4 December 2006 (otherwise).
Inserted as noted to s 24A at **[978]**.
Regulations: the Disability Discrimination (Premises) Regulations 2006, SI 2006/887.

**[24L   Sections 24 to 24K: power to make supplementary provision**

(1)   Regulations may make provision, for purposes of sections 24(3A) and (3B) and 24A to 24K—

   (a)    as to circumstances in which premises are to be treated as let to a person;

   (b)    as to circumstances in which premises are to be treated as not let to a person;

   (c)    as to circumstances in which premises are to be treated as being, or as not being, to let;

   (d)    as to who is to be treated as being, or as to who is to be treated as not being, a person who, although not a person to whom let premises are let, is lawfully under the letting an occupier of the premises;

   (e)    as to who is to be treated as being, or as to who is to be treated as not being, a person by whom premises are let;

   (f)    as to who is to be treated as having, or as to who is to be treated as not having, premises to let;

   (g)    as to who is to be treated as being, or as to who is to be treated as not being, a person who manages premises;

   (h)    as to things which are, or as to things which are not, to be treated as auxiliary aids or services;

(i)    as to what is, or as to what is not, to be included within the meaning of "practice, policy or procedure";

(j)    as to circumstances in which it is, or as to circumstances in which it is not, reasonable for a person to have to take steps of a prescribed description;

(k)    as to steps which it is always, or as to steps which it is never, reasonable for a person to have to take;

(l)    as to circumstances in which it is, or as to circumstances in which it is not, reasonable to regard a request as being of a particular kind;

(m)    as to things which are, or as to things which are not, to be treated as physical features;

(n)    as to things which are, or as to things which are not, to be treated as alterations of physical features.

(2)    Regulations under subsection (1)(a) may (in particular) provide for premises to be treated as let to a person where they are a commonhold unit of which he is a unit-holder; and "commonhold unit", and "unit-holder" in relation to such a unit, have here the same meaning as in Part 1 of the Commonhold and Leasehold Reform Act 2002.

(3)    The powers under subsections (1)(j) and (k) are subject to sections 24E(1) and 24J(5).]

**[988]**

---

**NOTES**

Commencement: 30 June 2005 (for the purpose of making regulations); 4 December 2006 (otherwise).
Inserted as noted to s 24A at **[978]**.
Regulations: the Disability Discrimination (Premises) Regulations 2006, SI 2006/887.

---

**[24M   Premises provisions do not apply where other provisions operate**

(1)    Sections 22 to 24L do not apply—

(a)    in relation to the provision of premises by a provider of services where he provides the premises in providing services to members of the public;

(b)    in relation to the provision, in the course of a Part 2 relationship, of premises by the regulated party to the other party;

(c)    in relation to the provision of premises to a student or prospective student—

(i)    by a responsible body within the meaning of Chapter 1 or 2 of Part 4, or

(ii)    by an authority in discharging any functions mentioned in section 28F(1); or

(d)    to anything which is unlawful under section 21F or which would be unlawful under that section but for the operation of any provision in or made under this Act.

(2)    Subsection (1)(a) has effect subject to any prescribed exceptions.

(3)    In subsection (1)(a) "provider of services", and providing services, have the same meaning as in section 19.

(4)    For the purposes of subsection (1)(b)—

(a)    "Part 2 relationship" means a relationship during the course of which an act of discrimination against, or harassment of, one party to the relationship by the other party to it is unlawful under sections 4 to 15C; and

(b)    in relation to a Part 2 relationship, "regulated party" means the party whose acts of discrimination, or harassment, are made unlawful by sections 4 to 15C.

(5)    In subsection (1)(c) "student" includes pupil.]

**[989]**

---

**NOTES**

Commencement: 4 December 2006.
Inserted by the Disability Discrimination Act 2005, s 19(1), Sch 1, Pt 1, paras 1, 20.

---

*Enforcement, etc*

**25   Enforcement, remedies and procedure**

(1)    A claim by any person that another person—

(a)    has discriminated against him in a way which is unlawful under this Part; or

(b)    is by virtue of section 57 or 58 to be treated as having discriminated against him in such a way,

may be made the subject of civil proceedings in the same way as any other claim in tort or (in Scotland) in reparation for breach of statutory duty.

(2)    For the avoidance of doubt it is hereby declared that damages in respect of discrimination in a way which is unlawful under this Part may include compensation for injury to feelings whether or not they include compensation under any other head.

(3)    Proceedings in England and Wales shall be brought only in a county court.

(4)    Proceedings in Scotland shall be brought only in a sheriff court.

(5)   The remedies available in such proceedings are those which are available in the High Court or (as the case may be) the Court of Session.

(6)   Part II of Schedule 3 makes further provision about the enforcement of this Part and about procedure.

[(6A)   Subsection (1) does not apply in relation to a claim by a person that another person—
  (a)   has discriminated against him in relation to the provision under a group insurance arrangement of facilities by way of insurance; or
  (b)   is by virtue of section 57 or 58 to be treated as having discriminated against him in relation to the provision under such an arrangement of such facilities.]

[[(7)   Subsection (1) does not apply in relation to a claim by a person that another person—
  (a)   has discriminated against him in relation to the provision of employment services; or
  (b)   is by virtue of section 57 or 58 to be treated as having discriminated against him in relation to the provision of employment services.

(8)   A claim—
  (a)   of the kind referred to in subsection (6A) or (7), or
  (b)   by a person that another—
      (i)   has subjected him to harassment in a way which is unlawful under section 21A(2), or
      (ii)   is by virtue of section 57 or 58 to be treated as having subjected him to harassment in such a way,

may be presented as a complaint to an employment tribunal.]

(9)   Section 17A(1A) to (7) and paragraphs 3 and 4 of Schedule 3 apply in relation to a complaint under subsection (8) as if it were a complaint under section 17A(1) (and paragraphs 6 to 8 of Schedule 3 do not apply in relation to such a complaint).]

**[990]**

**NOTES**

Sub-s (6A): inserted by the Disability Discrimination Act 2005, s 11(2).

Sub-ss (7), (8): added, together with sub-s (9), by the Disability Discrimination Act 1995 (Amendment) Regulations 2003, SI 2003/1673, regs 3(1), 19(2); substituted by the Disability Discrimination Act 2005, s 19(1), Sch 1, Pt 1, paras 1, 21.

Sub-s (9): added, together with original sub-ss (7), (8), by SI 2003/1673, regs 3(1), 19(2).

## 26   Validity and revision of certain agreements

(1)   Any term in a contract for the provision of goods, facilities or services or in any other agreement is void so far as it purports to—
  (a)   require a person to do anything which would contravene any provision of, or made under, this Part,
  (b)   exclude or limit the operation of any provision of this Part, or
  (c)   prevent any person from making a claim under this Part.

[(1A)   Subsection (1) does not apply to—
  (a)   any term in a contract for the provision of employment services;
  (b)   any term in a contract which is a group insurance arrangement; or
  (c)   a term which—
      (i)   is in an agreement which is not a contract of either of those kinds, and
      (ii)   relates to the provision of employment services or the provision under a group insurance arrangement of facilities by way of insurance.]

(2)   Paragraphs (b) and (c) of subsection (1) do not apply to an agreement settling a claim to which section 25 applies.

(3)   On the application of any person interested in an agreement to which subsection (1) applies, a county court or a sheriff court may make such order as it thinks just for modifying the agreement to take account of the effect of subsection (1).

(4)   No such order shall be made unless all persons affected have been—
  (a)   given notice of the application; and
  (b)   afforded an opportunity to make representations to the court.

(5)   Subsection (4) applies subject to any rules of court providing for that notice to be dispensed with.

(6)   An order under subsection (3) may include provision as respects any period before the making of the order.

**[991]**

PART I
STATUTES

**NOTES**

Sub-s (1A): inserted by the Disability Discrimination Act 1995 (Amendment) Regulations 2003, SI 2003/1673, regs 3(1), 19(3); substituted by the Disability Discrimination Act 2005, s 19(1), Sch 1, Pt 1, paras 1, 22.

### 27 Alterations to premises occupied under leases

(1)   This section applies where—

    (a)   a provider of services[, a public authority (within the meaning given by section 21B) or an association to which section 21F applies] ("the occupier") occupies premises under a lease;

    (b)   but for this section, [the occupier] would not be entitled to make a particular alteration to the premises; and

    (c)   the alteration is one which the occupier proposes to make in order to comply with a section 21 duty [or a duty imposed under section 21E or 21H].

(2)   Except to the extent to which it expressly so provides, the lease shall have effect by virtue of this subsection as if it provided—

    (a)   for the occupier to be entitled to make the alteration with the written consent of the lessor;

    (b)   for the occupier to have to make a written application to the lessor for consent if he wishes to make the alteration;

    (c)   if such an application is made, for the lessor not to withhold his consent unreasonably; and

    (d)   for the lessor to be entitled to make his consent subject to reasonable conditions.

(3)   In this section—

"lease" includes a tenancy, sub-lease or sub-tenancy and an agreement for a lease, tenancy, sub-lease or sub-tenancy; and

"sub-lease" and "sub-tenancy" have such meaning as may be prescribed.

(4)   If the terms and conditions of a lease—

    (a)   impose conditions which are to apply if the occupier alters the premises, or

    (b)   entitle the lessor to impose conditions when consenting to the occupier's altering the premises,

the occupier is to be treated for the purposes of subsection (1) as not being entitled to make the alteration.

(5)   Part II of Schedule 4 supplements the provisions of this section.

**[992]**

**NOTES**

Sub-s (1): words in square brackets in paras (a), (c) inserted and words in square brackets in para (b) substituted by the Disability Discrimination Act 2005, s 19(1), Sch 1, Pt 1, paras 1, 23.

Modification: this section is modified, in relation to any case where the occupier occupies premises under a sub-lease or sub-tenancy, by the Disability Discrimination (Providers of Services) (Adjustment of Premises) Regulations 2001, SI 2001/3253, reg 9(1)–(3).

Regulations: the Disability Discrimination (Providers of Services) (Adjustment of Premises) Regulations 2001, SI 2001/3253; the Disability Discrimination (Service Providers and Public Authorities Carrying Out Functions) Regulations 2005, SI 2005/2901.

**28–59A**   *(S 28 repealed by the Equality Act 2006, ss 40, 91, Sch 3, paras 41, 45, Sch 4; ss 28A–59A (Pts IV–VII) outside the scope of this work.)*

### PART VIII
### MISCELLANEOUS

**60–69**   *(Outside the scope of this work.)*

### 70 Short title, commencement, extent etc

(1)   This Act may be cited as the Disability Discrimination Act 1995.

(2)   This section (apart from subsections (4), (5) and (7)) comes into force on the passing of this Act.

[(2A)]   *(Outside the scope of this work.)*

(3)   The other provisions of this Act come into force on such day as the Secretary of State may by order appoint and different days may be appointed for different purposes.

(4)   Schedule 6 makes consequential amendments.

(5)   The repeals set out in Schedule 7 shall have effect.

[(5A), (5B)]   (*Outside the scope of this work*).

(6)   [Subject to subsections (5A) and (5B), this Act extends to England and Wales, Scotland and Northern Ireland;] but in their application to Northern Ireland the provisions of this Act mentioned in Schedule 8 shall have effect subject to the modifications set out in that Schedule.

(7)   (*Outside the scope of this work*).

(8)   Consultations which are required by any provision of this Act to be held by the Secretary of State may be held by him before the coming into force of that provision.

**[993]**

**NOTES**

Sub-s (6): words in square brackets substituted by the Disability Discrimination Act 1995 (Amendment) Regulations 2003, SI 2003/1673, regs 3(1), 28(b).

Orders: the Disability Discrimination Act 1995 (Commencement No 1) Order 1995, SI 1995/3330; the Disability Discrimination Act 1995 (Commencement No 2) Order 1996, SI 1996/1336; the Disability Discrimination Act 1995 (Commencement No 3 and Saving and Transitional Provisions) Order 1996, SI 1996/1474; the Disability Discrimination Act 1995 (Commencement No 4) Order 1996, SI 1996/3003; the Disability Discrimination Act 1995 (Commencement No 5) Order 1998, SI 1998/1282; the Disability Discrimination Act 1995 (Commencement Order No 6) Order 1999, SI 1999/1190; the Disability Discrimination Act 1995 (Commencement No 7) Order 2000, SI 2000/1969; the Disability Discrimination Act 1995 (Commencement No 8) Order 2000, SI 2000/2989; the Disability Discrimination Act 1995 (Commencement No 9) Order 2001, SI 2001/2030; the Disability Discrimination Act 1995 (Commencement No 10) (Scotland) Order 2003, SI 2003/215; the Disability Discrimination Act 1995 (Commencement No 11) Order 2005, SI 2005/1122.

## SCHEDULES

(*Schs 1, 2 outside the scope of this work.*)

## SCHEDULE 3
## ENFORCEMENT AND PROCEDURE
Sections [17A(8)], 25(6)[, 31ADA]

**NOTES**

Figure in first pair of square brackets substituted by the Disability Discrimination Act 1995 (Amendment) Regulations 2003, SI 2003/1673, regs 3(1), 29(2)(a); figure in second pair of square brackets inserted by the Disability Discrimination Act 1995 (Amendment etc) (General Qualifications Bodies) (Alteration of Premises and Enforcement) Regulations 2007, SI 2007/2405, regs 2(1), 4(1), (2).

(*Pt I outside the scope of this work.*)

## PART II
## DISCRIMINATION IN OTHER AREAS
*Restriction on proceedings for breach of Part III*

5.—(1)   Except as provided by section 25 no civil or criminal proceedings may be brought against any person in respect of an act merely because the act is unlawful under Part III.

(2)   Sub-paragraph (1) does not prevent the making of an application for judicial review.

*Period within which proceedings must be brought*

6.—(1)   A county court or a sheriff court shall not consider a claim under section 25 unless proceedings in respect of the claim are instituted before the end of the period of six months beginning when the act complained of was done.

[(2)   Where, in relation to proceedings or prospective proceedings under section 25, the dispute concerned is referred for conciliation in pursuance of arrangements under section 27 of the Equality Act 2006 before the end of the period of six months mentioned in sub-paragraph (1), the period allowed by that sub-paragraph shall be extended by three months.]

(3)   A court may consider any claim under section 25 which is out of time if, in all the circumstances of the case, it considers that it is just and equitable to do so.

(4)   For the purposes of sub-paragraph (1)—
   (a)   where an unlawful act of discrimination is attributable to a term in a contract, that act is to be treated as extending throughout the duration of the contract;
   (b)   any act extending over a period shall be treated as done at the end of that period; and
   (c)   a deliberate omission shall be treated as done when the person in question decided upon it.

(5)   In the absence of evidence establishing the contrary, a person shall be taken for the purposes of this paragraph to decide upon an omission—

> (a) when he does an act inconsistent with doing the omitted act; or
> (b) if he has done no such inconsistent act, when the period expires within which he might reasonably have been expected to do the omitted act if it was to be done.

*[Staying or sisting proceedings on section 21B claim affecting criminal matters*

6A.—(1) Sub-paragraph (2) applies where a party to proceedings under section 25 which have arisen by virtue of section 21B(1) has applied for a stay or sist of those proceedings on the grounds of prejudice to—

> (a) particular criminal proceedings;
> (b) a criminal investigation; or
> (c) a decision to institute criminal proceedings.

(2) The court shall grant the stay or sist unless it is satisfied that the continuance of the proceedings under section 25 would not result in the prejudice alleged.

*Restriction of remedies for section 21B claim relating to criminal matters*

6B.—(1) Sub-paragraph (2) applies to a remedy other than—

> (a) damages; or
> (b) a declaration or, in Scotland, a declarator.

(2) In proceedings under section 25, the remedy shall be obtainable in respect of a relevant discriminatory act only if the court is satisfied that—

> (a) no criminal investigation,
> (b) no decision to institute criminal proceedings, and
> (c) no criminal proceedings,

would be prejudiced by the remedy.

(3) In sub-paragraph (2) "relevant discriminatory act" means an act—

> (a) which is done, or by virtue of section 57 or 58 is treated as done, by a person-
>> (i) in carrying out public investigator functions, or
>> (ii) in carrying out functions as a public prosecutor; and
> (b) which is unlawful by virtue of section 21B(1).]

*Compensation for injury to feelings*

7. In any proceedings under section 25, the amount of any damages awarded as compensation for injury to feelings shall not exceed the prescribed amount.

*Evidence*

8.—(1) In any proceedings under section 25, a certificate signed by or on behalf of a Minister of the Crown and certifying—

> (a) that any conditions or requirements specified in the certificate were imposed by a Minister of the Crown and were in operation at a time or throughout a time so specified, or
> (b) that an act specified in the certificate was done for the purpose of safeguarding national security,

shall be conclusive evidence of the matters certified.

(2) A document purporting to be such a certificate shall be received in evidence and, unless the contrary is proved, be deemed to be such a certificate.

[(3) In any proceedings under section 25, a certificate signed by or on behalf of the Scottish Ministers and certifying that any conditions or requirements specified in the certificate—

> (a) were imposed by a member of the Scottish Executive, and
> (b) were in operation at a time or throughout a time so specified,

shall be conclusive evidence of the matters certified.

(4) In any proceedings under section 25, a certificate signed by or on behalf of the [Welsh Ministers] and certifying that any conditions or requirements specified in the certificate—

> (a) were imposed by the [National Assembly for Wales constituted by the Government of Wales Act 1998, the Welsh Ministers, the First Minister for Wales or the Counsel General to the Welsh Assembly Government], and
> (b) were in operation at a time or throughout a time so specified,

shall be conclusive evidence of the matters certified.

(5) A document purporting to be such a certificate as is mentioned in sub-paragraph (3) or (4) shall be received in evidence and, unless the contrary is proved, be deemed to be such a certificate.]

**[994]**

**NOTES**

Para 6: sub-para (2) substituted by the Equality Act 2006, s 40, Sch 3, paras 41, 56(1).

Paras 6A, 6B: inserted, together with preceding cross-headings, by the Disability Discrimination Act 2005, s 19(1), Sch 1, Pt 1, paras 1, 38(1), (5).

Para 8: sub-paras (3)–(5) added by the Disability Discrimination Act 2005, s 19(1), Sch 1, Pt 1, paras 1, 38(1), (6); words in square brackets in sub-para (4) substituted by the Government of Wales Act 2006 (Consequential Modifications and Transitional Provisions) Order 2007, SI 2007/1388, art 3, Sch 1, paras 47, 63(1), (3).

*(Sch 3, Pts 3–5, Sch 3A outside the scope of this work.)*

## SCHEDULE 4
### PREMISES OCCUPIED UNDER LEASES

Sections [18A(5)], 27(5)[, 31ADB]

**NOTES**

Figure in first pair of square brackets substituted by the Disability Discrimination Act 1995 (Amendment) Regulations 2003, SI 2003/1673, regs 3(1), 29(3)(a); figure in second pair of square brackets inserted by the Disability Discrimination Act 1995 (Amendment etc) (General Qualifications Bodies) (Alteration of Premises and Enforcement) Regulations 2007, SI 2007/2405, regs 2(1), 6(1), (2).

*(Pt I outside the scope of this work.)*

### PART II
### OCCUPATION BY [PERSONS SUBJECT TO A DUTY UNDER SECTION 21, 21E OR 21H]

*Failure to obtain consent to alteration*

5. If any question arises as to whether the occupier has failed to comply with the section 21 duty [or a duty imposed under section 21E or 21H], by failing to make a particular alteration to premises, any constraint attributable to the fact that he occupies the premises under a lease is to be ignored unless he has applied to the lessor in writing for consent to the making of the alteration.

*Reference to court*

6.—(1) If the occupier has applied in writing to the lessor for consent to the alteration and—
    (a) that consent has been refused, or
    (b) the lessor has made his consent subject to one or more conditions,
the occupier or a disabled person who has an interest in the proposed alteration to the premises being made, may refer the matter to a county court or, in Scotland, to the sheriff.

(2) In the following provisions of this Schedule "court" includes "sheriff".

(3) On such a reference the court shall determine whether the lessor's refusal was unreasonable or (as the case may be) whether the condition is, or any of the conditions are, unreasonable.

(4) If the court determines—
    (a) that the lessor's refusal was unreasonable, or
    (b) that the condition is, or any of the conditions are, unreasonable,
it may make such declaration as it considers appropriate or an order authorising the occupier to make the alteration specified in the order.

(5) An order under sub-paragraph (4) may require the occupier to comply with conditions specified in the order.

*Joining lessors in proceedings under section 25*

7.—(1) In any proceedings on a claim [under section 25 in a case to which section 27 applies, other than a claim presented as a complaint under section 25(8),] the plaintiff, the pursuer or the occupier concerned may ask the court to direct that the lessor be joined or sisted as a party to the proceedings.

(2) The request shall be granted if it is made before the hearing of the claim begins.

(3) The court may refuse the request if it is made after the hearing of the claim begins.

(4) The request may not be granted if it is made after the court has determined the claim.

(5) Where a lessor has been so joined or sisted as a party to the proceedings, the court may determine—
    (a) whether the lessor has—
        (i) refused consent to the alteration, or
        (ii) consented subject to one or more conditions, and
    (b) if so, whether the refusal or any of the conditions was unreasonable.

(6) If, under sub-paragraph (5), the court determines that the refusal or any of the conditions was unreasonable it may take one or more of the following steps—
    (a) make such declaration as it considers appropriate;

    (b)    make an order authorising the occupier to make the alteration specified in the order;

    (c)    order the lessor to pay compensation to the complainant.

(7)    An order under sub-paragraph (6)(b) may require the occupier to comply with conditions specified in the order.

(8)    If the court orders the lessor to pay compensation it may not order the occupier to do so.

*[Joining lessors in proceedings relating to group insurance or employment services*

**7A.**—(1)    In any proceedings on a complaint under section 25(8) in a case to which section 27 applies, the complainant or the occupier may ask the tribunal hearing the complaint to direct that the lessor be joined or sisted as a party to the proceedings.

(2)    The request shall be granted if it is made before the hearing of the complaint begins.

(3)    The tribunal may refuse the request if it is made after the hearing of the complaint begins.

(4)    The request may not be granted if it is made after the tribunal has determined the complaint.

(5)    Where a lessor has been so joined or sisted as a party to the proceedings, the tribunal may determine—

    (a)    whether the lessor has—

        (i)    refused consent to the alteration, or

        (ii)    consented subject to one or more conditions; and

    (b)    if so, whether the refusal or any of the conditions was unreasonable.

(6)    If, under sub-paragraph (5), the tribunal determines that the refusal or any of the conditions was unreasonable it may take one or more of the following steps—

    (a)    make such declaration as it considers appropriate;

    (b)    make an order authorising the occupier to make the alteration specified in the order;

    (c)    order the lessor to pay compensation to the complainant.

(7)    An order under sub-paragraph (6)(b) may require the occupier to comply with conditions specified in the order.

(8)    Any step taken by the tribunal under sub-paragraph (6) may be in substitution for, or in addition to, any step taken by the tribunal under section 17A(2).

(9)    If the tribunal orders the lessor to pay compensation it may not make an order under section 17A(2) ordering the occupier to do so.]

*Regulations*

8.    Regulations may make provision as to circumstances in which—

    (a)    a lessor is to be taken, for the purposes of section 27 and this Part of this Schedule to have—

        (i)    withheld his consent;

        (ii)    withheld his consent unreasonably;

        (iii)    acted reasonably in withholding his consent;

    (b)    a condition subject to which a lessor has given his consent is to be taken to be reasonable;

    (c)    a condition subject to which a lessor has given his consent is to be taken to be unreasonable.

*Sub-leases etc*

9.    The Secretary of State may by regulations make provision supplementing, or modifying, the provision made by section 27 or any provision made by or under this Part of this Schedule in relation to cases where the occupier occupies premises under a sub-lease or sub-tenancy.

**[995]**

---

**NOTES**

Part heading: words in square brackets substituted by the Disability Discrimination Act 2005, s 19(1), Sch 1, Pt 1, paras 1, 40(1), (3).

Para 5: words in square brackets inserted by the Disability Discrimination Act 2005, s 19(1), Sch 1, Pt 1, paras 1, 40(1), (4).

Para 7: words in square brackets in sub-para (1) substituted by the Disability Discrimination Act 2005, s 19(1), Sch 1, Pt 1, paras 1, 40(1), (5).

Para 7A: inserted, together with preceding cross-heading, by the Disability Discrimination Act 2005, s 19(1), Sch 1, Pt 1, paras 1, 40(1), (6).

Modification: modified, in relation to any case where the occupier occupies premises under a sub-lease or sub-tenancy, by the Disability Discrimination (Providers of Services) (Adjustment of Premises) Regulations 2001, SI 2001/3253, reg 9(1), (4)–(7).

Regulations: the Disability Discrimination (Providers of Services) (Adjustment of Premises) Regulations 2001, SI 2001/3253; the Disability Discrimination (Service Providers and Public Authorities Carrying Out Functions) Regulations 2005, SI 2005/2901.

---

*(Sch 4, Pts 3, 4, Schs 4A–8 outside the scope of this work.)*

# FAMILY LAW ACT 1996

## (1996 c 27)

### ARRANGEMENT OF SECTIONS

#### PART IV
#### FAMILY HOMES AND DOMESTIC VIOLENCE

*Rights to occupy matrimonial or civil partnership home*

*Transfer of tenancies*

#### PART V
#### SUPPLEMENTAL

*An Act to make provision with respect to: divorce and separation; legal aid in connection with mediation in disputes relating to family matters; proceedings in cases where marriages have broken down; rights of occupation of certain domestic premises; prevention of molestation; the inclusion in certain orders under the Children Act 1989 of provisions about the occupation of a dwelling-house; the transfer of tenancies between spouses and persons who have lived together as husband and wife; and for connected purposes*

**[4 July 1996]**

**1–29**   (*(Pts I–III) in so far as unrepealed outside the scope of this work.*)

### PART IV
### FAMILY HOMES AND DOMESTIC VIOLENCE

*Rights to occupy matrimonial [or civil partnership] home*

## 30   Rights concerning [home where one spouse or civil partner] has no estate, etc

(1)   This section applies if—
  (a)   one spouse [or civil partner ("A")] is entitled to occupy a dwelling-house by virtue of—
     (i)   a beneficial estate or interest or contract; or
     (ii)   any enactment giving [A] the right to remain in occupation; and
  (b)   the other spouse [or civil partner ("B")] is not so entitled.

(2)   Subject to the provisions of this Part, [B] has the following rights (["home rights"])—
  (a)   if in occupation, a right not to be evicted or excluded from the dwelling-house or any part of it by [A] except with the leave of the court given by an order under section 33;
  (b)   if not in occupation, a right with the leave of the court so given to enter into and occupy the dwelling-house.

(3)   If [B] is entitled under this section to occupy a dwelling-house or any part of a dwelling-house, any payment or tender made or other thing done by [B] in or towards satisfaction of any liability of [A] in respect of rent, mortgage payments or other outgoings affecting the dwelling-house is, whether or not it is made or done in pursuance of an order under section 40, as good as if made or done by [A].

(4)   [B's] occupation by virtue of this section—
  (a)   is to be treated, for the purposes of the Rent (Agriculture) Act 1976 and the Rent Act 1977 (other than Part V and sections 103 to 106 of that Act), as occupation [by A as A's] residence, and
  (b)   if [B occupies the dwelling-house as B's] only or principal home, is to be treated, for the purposes of the Housing Act 1985[, Part I of the Housing Act 1988 and Chapter I of Part V of the Housing Act 1996], as occupation [by A as A's] only or principal home.

(5)   If [B]—
  (a)   is entitled under this section to occupy a dwelling-house or any part of a dwelling-house, and

(b)　makes any payment in or towards satisfaction of any liability of [A] in respect of mortgage payments affecting the dwelling-house,

the person to whom the payment is made may treat it as having been made by [A], but the fact that that person has treated any such payment as having been so made does not affect any claim of [B against A] to an interest in the dwelling-house by virtue of the payment.

(6)　If [B] is entitled under this section to occupy a dwelling-house or part of a dwelling-house by reason of an interest of [A] under a trust, all the provisions of subsections (3) to (5) apply in relation to the trustees as they apply in relation to [A].

(7)　This section does not apply to a dwelling-house [which—
(a)　in the case of spouses, has at no time been, and was at no time intended by them to be, a matrimonial home of theirs; and
(b)　in the case of civil partners, has at no time been, and was at no time intended by them to be, a civil partnership home of theirs.]

(8)　[B's home rights] continue—
(a)　only so long as the marriage [or civil partnership] subsists, except to the extent that an order under section 33(5) otherwise provides; and
(b)　only so long as [A] is entitled as mentioned in subsection (1) to occupy the dwelling-house, except where provision is made by section 31 for those rights to be a charge on an estate or interest in the dwelling-house.

(9)　It is hereby declared that [a person]—
(a)　who has an equitable interest in a dwelling-house or in its proceeds of sale, but
(b)　is not [a person] in whom there is vested (whether solely or as joint tenant) a legal estate in fee simple or a legal term of years absolute in the dwelling-house,

is to be treated, only for the purpose of determining whether he has [home rights], as not being entitled to occupy the dwelling-house by virtue of that interest.

**[996]**

**NOTES**

Section heading: words in square brackets substituted, and words in square brackets in preceding cross-heading inserted, by the Civil Partnership Act 2004, s 82, Sch 9, Pt 1, para 1(1), (11), subject to transitional provisions in s 82 of, and Sch 9, Pt 3 to, that Act at **[1324]**, **[1328]**.

Sub-s (1): words in first and third pairs of square brackets inserted and reference in second pair of square brackets substituted by the Civil Partnership Act 2004, s 82, Sch 9, Pt 1, para 1(1), (2), subject to transitional provisions as noted above.

Sub-s (2): words in square brackets substituted by the Civil Partnership Act 2004, s 82, Sch 9, Pt 1, para 1(1), (3), subject to transitional provisions as noted above.

Sub-s (3): references in square brackets substituted by the Civil Partnership Act 2004, s 82, Sch 9, Pt 1, para 1(1), (4), subject to transitional provisions as noted above.

Sub-s (4): reference in first pair of square brackets, words in square brackets in para (a), and words in first and third pairs of square brackets in para (b) substituted by the Civil Partnership Act 2004, s 82, Sch 9, Pt 1, para 1(1), (5), subject to transitional provisions as noted above; words in second pair of square brackets in para (b) substituted by the Housing Act 1996 (Consequential Amendments) Order 1997, SI 1997/74, art 2, Schedule, para 10(a).

Sub-ss (5)–(7): references and words in square brackets substituted by the Civil Partnership Act 2004, s 82, Sch 9, Pt 1, para 1(1), (6)–(8), subject to transitional provisions as noted above.

Sub-s (8): words in first and third pairs of square brackets substituted and words in second pair of square brackets inserted by the Civil Partnership Act 2004, s 82, Sch 9, Pt 1, para 1(1), (9), subject to transitional provisions as noted above.

Sub-s (9): words in square brackets substituted by the Civil Partnership Act 2004, s 82, Sch 9, Pt 1, para 1(1), (10), subject to transitional provisions as noted above.

**31–52**　(*Outside the scope of this work.*)

*Transfer of tenancies*

## 53　Transfer of certain tenancies

Schedule 7 makes provision in relation to the transfer of certain tenancies on divorce etc or on separation of cohabitants.

**[997]**

**54–63S**　(*Ss 54–63, ss 63A–63S (Pt IVA) outside the scope of this work.*)

PART V
SUPPLEMENTAL

**64–66**　(*Outside the scope of this work.*)

## 67 Short title, commencement and extent

(1)   This Act may be cited as the Family Law Act 1996.

(2)   Section 65 and this section come into force on the passing of this Act.

(3)   The other provisions of this Act come into force on such day as the Lord Chancellor may by order appoint; and different days may be appointed for different purposes.

(4)   This Act, other than section 17, extends only to England and Wales, except that—
   (a)   in Schedule 8—
       (i)   the amendments of section 38 of the Family Law Act 1986 extend also to Northern Ireland;
       (ii)   the amendments of the Judicial Proceedings (Regulation of Reports) Act 1926 extend also to Scotland; and
       (iii)   the amendments of the Maintenance Orders Act 1950, the Civil Jurisdiction and Judgments Act 1982, the Finance Act 1985 and sections 42 and 51 of the Family Law Act 1986 extend also to both Northern Ireland and Scotland; and
   (b)   in Schedule 10, the repeal of section 2(1)(b) of the Domestic and Appellate Proceedings (Restriction of Publicity) Act 1968 extends also to Scotland.

**[998]**

**NOTES**

Orders: the Family Law Act 1996 (Commencement No 1) Order 1997, SI 1997/1077; the Family Law Act 1996 (Commencement No 2) Order 1997, SI 1997/1892; the Family Law Act 1996 (Commencement) (No 3) Order 1998, SI 1998/2572.

## SCHEDULES

*(Schs 1–6 outside the scope of this work.)*

### SCHEDULE 7
### TRANSFER OF CERTAIN TENANCIES ON DIVORCE ETC OR ON SEPARATION OF COHABITANTS

Section 53

### PART I
### GENERAL

*Interpretation*

1.   In this Schedule—
   ["civil partner", except in paragraph 2, includes (where the context requires) former civil partner;]
   "cohabitant", except in paragraph 3, includes (where the context requires) former cohabitant;
   "the court" does not include a magistrates' court,
   "landlord" includes—
       (a)   any person from time to time deriving title under the original landlord; and
       (b)   in relation to any dwelling-house, any person other than the tenant who is, or (but for Part VII of the Rent Act 1977 or Part II of the Rent (Agriculture) Act 1976) would be, entitled to possession of the dwelling-house;
   "Part II order" means an order under Part II of this Schedule;
   "a relevant tenancy" means—
       (a)   a protected tenancy or statutory tenancy within the meaning of the Rent Act 1977;
       (b)   a statutory tenancy within the meaning of the Rent (Agriculture) Act 1976;
       (c)   a secure tenancy within the meaning of section 79 of the Housing Act 1985; ...
       (d)   an assured tenancy or assured agricultural occupancy within the meaning of Part I of the Housing Act 1988; [or
       (e)   an introductory tenancy within the meaning of Chapter I of Part V of the Housing Act 1996;]
   "spouse", except in paragraph 2, includes (where the context requires) former spouse; and
   "tenancy" includes sub-tenancy.

*Cases in which the court may make an order*

2.—(1)   This paragraph applies if one spouse [or civil partner] is entitled, either in his own right or jointly with the other spouse [or civil partner], to occupy a dwelling-house by virtue of a relevant tenancy.

   [(2)   The court may make a Part II order—
       (a)   on granting a decree of divorce, a decree of nullity of marriage or a decree of judicial separation or at any time thereafter (whether, in the case of a decree of divorce or nullity of marriage, before or after the decree is made absolute), or

(b)    at any time when it has power to make a property adjustment order under Part 2 of Schedule 5 to the Civil Partnership Act 2004 with respect to the civil partnership.]

3.—(1)   This paragraph applies if one cohabitant is entitled, either in his own right or jointly with the other cohabitant, to occupy a dwelling-house by virtue of a relevant tenancy.

(2)   If the cohabitants cease [to cohabit], the court may make a Part II order.

4.   The court shall not make a Part II order unless the dwelling-house is or was—
- (a)    in the case of spouses, a matrimonial home; ...
- [(aa)   in the case of civil partners, a civil partnership home; or]
- (b)    in the case of cohabitants, a home in which they [cohabited].

### Matters to which the court must have regard

5.   In determining whether to exercise its powers under Part II of this Schedule and, if so, in what manner, the court shall have regard to all the circumstances of the case including—
- (a)    the circumstances in which the tenancy was granted to either or both of the spouses[, civil partners] or cohabitants or, as the case requires, the circumstances in which either or both of them became tenant under the tenancy;
- (b)    the matters mentioned in section 33(6)(a), (b) and (c) and, where the parties are cohabitants and only one of them is entitled to occupy the dwelling-house by virtue of the relevant tenancy, the further matters mentioned in section 36(6)(e), (f), (g) and (h); and
- (c)    the suitability of the parties as tenants.

[999]

**NOTES**

Para 1: definition "civil partner" inserted by the Civil Partnership Act 2004, s 82, Sch 9, Pt 1, para 16(1), (2), subject to transitional provisions in s 82 of, and Sch 9, Pt 3 to, that Act at **[1324]**, **[1328]**; in definition "a relevant tenancy" word omitted from para (c) repealed and para (e) and word immediately preceding it added by the Housing Act 1996 (Consequential Amendments) Order 1997, SI 1997/74, art 2, Schedule, para 10(b)(i).

Para 2: words in square brackets in sub-para (1) inserted and sub-para (2) substituted by the Civil Partnership Act 2004, s 82, Sch 9, Pt 1, para 16(1), (3), (4), subject to transitional provisions as noted above.

Para 3: words in square brackets substituted by the Domestic Violence, Crime and Victims Act 2004, s 58(1), Sch 10, para 42(1), (2).

Para 4: word omitted from sub-para (a) repealed and sub-para (aa) inserted by the Civil Partnership Act 2004, ss 82, 261(4), Sch 9, Pt 1, para 16(1), (5), Sch 30, subject to transitional provisions as noted above; word in square brackets in sub-para (b) substituted by the Domestic Violence, Crime and Victims Act 2004, s 58(1), Sch 10, para 42(1), (3).

Para 5: words in square brackets inserted by the Civil Partnership Act 2004, s 82, Sch 9, Pt 1, para 16(1), (6), subject to transitional provisions as noted above.

### PART II
### ORDERS THAT MAY BE MADE

#### References to entitlement to occupy

6.   References in this Part of this Schedule to a spouse[, a civil partner] or a cohabitant being entitled to occupy a dwelling-house by virtue of a relevant tenancy apply whether that entitlement is in his own right or jointly with the other spouse[, civil partner] or cohabitant.

#### Protected, secure or assured tenancy or assured agricultural occupancy

7.—(1)   If a spouse[, civil partner] or cohabitant is entitled to occupy the dwelling-house by virtue of a protected tenancy within the meaning of the Rent Act 1977, a secure tenancy within the meaning of the Housing Act 1985[, an assured tenancy] or assured agricultural occupancy within the meaning of Part I of the Housing Act 1988 [or an introductory tenancy within the meaning of Chapter I of Part V of the Housing Act 1996], the court may by order direct that, as from such date as may be specified in the order, there shall, by virtue of the order and without further assurance, be transferred to, and vested in, the other spouse[, civil partner] or cohabitant—
- (a)    the estate or interest which the spouse[, civil partner] or cohabitant so entitled had in the dwelling-house immediately before that date by virtue of the lease or agreement creating the tenancy and any assignment of that lease or agreement, with all rights, privileges and appurtenances attaching to that estate or interest but subject to all covenants, obligations, liabilities and incumbrances to which it is subject; and
- (b)    where the spouse[, civil partner] or cohabitant so entitled is an assignee of such lease or agreement, the liability of that spouse[, civil partner] or cohabitant under any covenant of indemnity by the assignee express or implied in the assignment of the lease or agreement to that spouse[, civil partner] or cohabitant.

(2)   If an order is made under this paragraph, any liability or obligation to which the spouse[, civil partner] or cohabitant so entitled is subject under any covenant having reference to the

PART I<br>STATUTES

dwelling-house in the lease or agreement, being a liability or obligation falling due to be discharged or performed on or after the date so specified, shall not be enforceable against that spouse[, civil partner] or cohabitant.

[(3)   If the spouse, civil partner or cohabitant so entitled is a successor within the meaning of Part 4 of the Housing Act 1985—

    (a)   his former spouse (or, in the case of judicial separation, his spouse),

    (b)   his former civil partner (or, if a separation order is in force, his civil partner), or

    (c)   his former cohabitant,

is to be deemed also to be a successor within the meaning of that Part.

(3A)   If the spouse, civil partner or cohabitant so entitled is a successor within the meaning of section 132 of the Housing Act 1996—

    (a)   his former spouse (or, in the case of judicial separation, his spouse),

    (b)   his former civil partner (or, if a separation order is in force, his civil partner), or

    (c)   his former cohabitant,

is to be deemed also to be a successor within the meaning of that section.

(4)   If the spouse, civil partner or cohabitant so entitled is for the purposes of section 17 of the Housing Act 1988 a successor in relation to the tenancy or occupancy—

    (a)   his former spouse (or, in the case of judicial separation, his spouse),

    (b)   his former civil partner (or, if a separation order is in force, his civil partner), or

    (c)   his former cohabitant,

is to be deemed to be a successor in relation to the tenancy or occupancy for the purposes of that section.]

(5)   If the transfer under sub-paragraph (1) is of an assured agricultural occupancy, then, for the purposes of Chapter III of Part I of the Housing Act 1988—

    (a)   the agricultural worker condition is fulfilled with respect to the dwelling-house while the spouse[, civil partner] or cohabitant to whom the assured agricultural occupancy is transferred continues to be the occupier under that occupancy, and

    (b)   that condition is to be treated as so fulfilled by virtue of the same paragraph of Schedule 3 to the Housing Act 1988 as was applicable before the transfer.

(6)   ...

### *Statutory tenancy within the meaning of the Rent Act 1977*

8.—(1)   This paragraph applies if the spouse[, civil partner] or cohabitant is entitled to occupy the dwelling-house by virtue of a statutory tenancy within the meaning of the Rent Act 1977.

(2)   The court may by order direct that, as from the date specified in the order—

    (a)   that spouse[, civil partner] or cohabitant is to cease to be entitled to occupy the dwelling-house; and

    (b)   the other spouse[, civil partner] or cohabitant is to be deemed to be the tenant or, as the case may be, the sole tenant under that statutory tenancy.

(3)   The question whether the provisions of paragraphs 1 to 3, or (as the case may be) paragraphs 5 to 7 of Schedule 1 to the Rent Act 1977, as to the succession by the surviving spouse [or surviving civil partner] of a deceased tenant, or by a member of the deceased tenant's family, to the right to retain possession are capable of having effect in the event of the death of the person deemed by an order under this paragraph to be the tenant or sole tenant under the statutory tenancy is to be determined according as those provisions have or have not already had effect in relation to the statutory tenancy.

### *Statutory tenancy within the meaning of the Rent (Agriculture) Act 1976*

9.—(1)   This paragraph applies if the spouse[, civil partner] or cohabitant is entitled to occupy the dwelling-house by virtue of a statutory tenancy within the meaning of the Rent (Agriculture) Act 1976.

(2)   The court may by order direct that, as from such date as may be specified in the order—

    (a)   that spouse[, civil partner] or cohabitant is to cease to be entitled to occupy the dwelling-house; and

    (b)   the other spouse[, civil partner] or cohabitant is to be deemed to be the tenant or, as the case may be, the sole tenant under that statutory tenancy.

(3)   A spouse[, civil partner] or cohabitant who is deemed under this paragraph to be the tenant under a statutory tenancy is (within the meaning of that Act) a statutory tenant in his own right, or a statutory tenant by succession, according as the other spouse[, civil partner] or cohabitant was a statutory tenant in his own right or a statutory tenant by succession.

**[1000]**

PART I
STATUTES

**NOTES**

Paras 6, 8, 9: words in square brackets inserted by the Civil Partnership Act 2004, s 82, Sch 9, Pt 1, para 16(1), (7), (12)–(14), subject to transitional provisions in s 82 of, and Sch 9, Pt 3 to, that Act at **[1324]**, **[1328]**.

Para 7: in sub-para (1) words in second pair of square brackets substituted, words in third pair of square brackets inserted and sub-para (3A) inserted by the Housing Act 1996 (Consequential Amendments) Order 1997, SI 1997/74, art 2, Schedule, para 10(b)(ii), (iii); in sub-paras (1), (2), (5), words ", civil partner" inserted in each place, sub-paras (3), (3A), (4) substituted and sub-para (6) repealed by the Civil Partnership Act 2004, ss 82, 261(4), Sch 9, Pt 1, para 16(1), (8)–(11), Sch 30, subject to transitional provisions as noted above.

## PART III
## SUPPLEMENTARY PROVISIONS

### *Compensation*

10.—(1)   If the court makes a Part II order, it may by the order direct the making of a payment by the spouse[, civil partner] or cohabitant to whom the tenancy is transferred ("the transferee") to the other spouse[, civil partner] or cohabitant ("the transferor").

(2)   Without prejudice to that, the court may, on making an order by virtue of sub-paragraph (1) for the payment of a sum—
   (a)   direct that payment of that sum or any part of it is to be deferred until a specified date or until the occurrence of a specified event, or
   (b)   direct that that sum or any part of it is to be paid by instalments.

(3)   Where an order has been made by virtue of sub-paragraph (1), the court may, on the application of the transferee or the transferor—
   (a)   exercise its powers under sub-paragraph (2), or
   (b)   vary any direction previously given under that sub-paragraph,
at any time before the sum whose payment is required by the order is paid in full.

(4)   In deciding whether to exercise its powers under this paragraph and, if so, in what manner, the court shall have regard to all the circumstances including—
   (a)   the financial loss that would otherwise be suffered by the transferor as a result of the order;
   (b)   the financial needs and financial resources of the parties; and
   (c)   the financial obligations which the parties have, or are likely to have in the foreseeable future, including financial obligations to each other and to any relevant child.

(5)   The court shall not give any direction under sub-paragraph (2) unless it appears to it that immediate payment of the sum required by the order would cause the transferee financial hardship which is greater than any financial hardship that would be caused to the transferor if the direction were given.

### *Liabilities and obligations in respect of the dwelling-house*

11.—(1)   If the court makes a Part II order, it may by the order direct that both spouses[, civil partners] or cohabitants are to be jointly and severally liable to discharge or perform any or all of the liabilities and obligations in respect of the dwelling-house (whether arising under the tenancy or otherwise) which—
   (a)   have at the date of the order fallen due to be discharged or performed by one only of them; or
   (b)   but for the direction, would before the date specified as the date on which the order is to take effect fall due to be discharged or performed by one only of them.

(2)   If the court gives such a direction, it may further direct that either spouse[, civil partner] or cohabitant is to be liable to indemnify the other in whole or in part against any payment made or expenses incurred by the other in discharging or performing any such liability or obligation.

### *[Date when order made between spouses or civil partners takes effect*

12.   The date specified in a Part II order as the date on which the order is to take effect must not be earlier than—
   (a)   in the case of a marriage in respect of which a decree of divorce or nullity has been granted, the date on which the decree is made absolute;
   (b)   in the case of a civil partnership in respect of which a dissolution or nullity order has been made, the date on which the order is made final.

### *Effect of remarriage or subsequent civil partnership*

13.—(1)   If after the grant of a decree dissolving or annulling a marriage either spouse remarries or forms a civil partnership, that spouse is not entitled to apply, by reference to the grant of that decree, for a Part II order.

(2)    If after the making of a dissolution or nullity order either civil partner forms a subsequent civil partnership or marries, that civil partner is not entitled to apply, by reference to the making of that order, for a Part II order.

(3)    In sub-paragraphs (1) and (2)—

(a)    the references to remarrying and marrying include references to cases where the marriage is by law void or voidable, and

(b)    the references to forming a civil partnership include references to cases where the civil partnership is by law void or voidable.]

### *Rules of court*

14.—(1)    Rules of court shall be made requiring the court, before it makes an order under this Schedule, to give the landlord of the dwelling-house to which the order will relate an opportunity of being heard.

(2)    Rules of court may provide that an application for a Part II order by reference to an order or decree may not, without the leave of the court by which that order was made or decree was granted, be made after the expiration of such period from the order or grant as may be prescribed by the rules.

### *Saving for other provisions of Act*

15.—(1)    If a spouse [or civil partner] is entitled to occupy a dwelling-house by virtue of a tenancy, this Schedule does not affect the operation of sections 30 and 31 in relation to the other [spouse's or civil partner's home rights].

(2)    If a spouse[, civil partner] or cohabitant is entitled to occupy a dwelling-house by virtue of a tenancy, the court's powers to make orders under this Schedule are additional to those conferred by sections 33, 35 and 36.

**[1001]**

**NOTES**

Paras 10, 11: words in square brackets inserted by the Civil Partnership Act 2004, s 82, Sch 9, Pt 1, para 16(1), (14)–(16), subject to transitional provisions in s 82 of, and Sch 9, Pt 3 to, that Act at **[1324]**, **[1328]**.

Paras 12, 13: substituted, together with preceding cross-headings, by the Civil Partnership Act 2004, s 82, Sch 9, Pt 1, para 16(1), (17), (18), subject to transitional provisions as noted above.

Para 15: words in first and third pairs of square brackets inserted and words in second pair of square brackets substituted by the Civil Partnership Act 2004, s 82, Sch 9, Pt 1, para 16(1), (19), (20), subject to transitional provisions as noted above.

*(Schs 8, 9 outside the scope of this work; Sch 10 contains repeals only.)*

# HOUSING ACT 1996

### (1996 c 52)

### ARRANGEMENT OF SECTIONS

### PART I
### SOCIAL RENTED SECTOR

### CHAPTER II
### DISPOSAL OF LAND AND RELATED MATTERS

#### *Right of tenant to acquire dwelling*

### PART III
### LANDLORD AND TENANT

### CHAPTER I
### TENANTS' RIGHTS

#### *Forfeiture*

PART VIII
MISCELLANEOUS AND GENERAL PROVISIONS

*Miscellaneous*

*General*

*An Act to make provision about housing, including provision about the social rented sector, houses
in multiple occupation, landlord and tenant matters, the administration of housing benefit, the
conduct of tenants, the allocation of housing accommodation by local housing authorities and
homelessness; and for connected purposes*

**[24 July 1996]**

**NOTES**
Transfer of functions: as to the functions of Ministers of the Crown under this Act, so far as exercisable in
relation to Wales, being transferred to the National Assembly for Wales, see the National Assembly for Wales
(Transfer of Functions) Order 1999, SI 1999/672, art 2, Sch 1.

## PART I
### *SOCIAL RENTED SECTOR*

**NOTES**
Part heading: for the words in italics there are substituted the words "Social Rented Sector in Wales" by the
Housing and Regeneration Act 2008, s 61(1), as from a day to be appointed.

**A1–7**   (*Outside the scope of this work.*)

### CHAPTER II
### DISPOSAL OF LAND AND RELATED MATTERS

**8–15A**   (*Outside the scope of this work.*)

*Right of tenant to acquire dwelling*

## 16   Right of tenant to acquire dwelling

(*1*)   A tenant of a registered social landlord has the right to acquire the dwelling of which he is
a tenant if—
  (*a*)   he is a tenant under an assured tenancy, other than an assured shorthold tenancy or a
       long tenancy, or under a secure tenancy,
  (*b*)   the dwelling was provided with public money and has remained in the social rented
       sector, and
  (*c*)   he satisfies any further qualifying conditions applicable under Part V of the Housing
       Act 1985 (*the right to buy*) as it applies in relation to the right conferred by this section.

(2)   For this purpose a dwelling shall be regarded as provided with public money if—
  (a)   it was provided or acquired wholly or in part by means of a grant under section 18
       (social housing grant),
  (b)   it was provided or acquired wholly or in part by applying or appropriating sums standing
       in the disposal proceeds fund of a registered social landlord (see section 25), or
  (c)   it was acquired by a registered social landlord [or a registered provider of social
       housing] after the commencement of this paragraph on a disposal by a public sector
       landlord at a time when it was capable of being let as a separate dwelling.

(3)   A dwelling shall be regarded for the purposes of this section as having remained within the
social rented sector if, since it was so provided or acquired—
  (a)   the person holding the freehold interest in the dwelling has been either a registered
       social landlord[, a registered provider of social housing] or a public sector landlord; and
  (b)   any person holding an interest as lessee (otherwise than as mortgagee) in the dwelling
       has been—
       (i)   an individual holding otherwise than under a long tenancy; or
       (ii)   a registered social landlord[, a registered provider of social housing] or a public
            sector landlord.

[(3A)   In subsection (3)(a) the reference to the freehold interest in the dwelling includes a
reference to such an interest in the dwelling as is held by the landlord under a lease granted in
pursuance of paragraph 3 of Schedule 9 to the Leasehold Reform, Housing and Urban Development
Act 1993 (mandatory leaseback to former freeholder on collective enfranchisement).]

(4)    A dwelling shall be regarded for the purposes of this section as provided by means of a grant under section 18 (social housing grant) if, and only if, *the [Relevant Authority]* when making the grant notified the recipient that the dwelling was to be so regarded.

*The [Relevant Authority]* shall before making the grant inform the applicant that *it proposes* to give such a notice and allow him an opportunity to withdraw his application within a specified time.

[(5)    But notice must be taken to be given to a registered social landlord under subsection (4) by the Housing Corporation if it is sent using electronic communications to such number or address as the registered social landlord has for the time being notified to the Housing Corporation for that purpose.

(6)    The means by which notice is sent by virtue of subsection (5) must be such as to enable the registered social landlord to reproduce the notice by electronic means in a form which is visible and legible.

(7)    An electronic communication is a communication transmitted (whether from one person to another, from one device to another, or from a person to a device or vice versa)—
 (a)    by means of [an electronic communications network]; or
 (b)    by other means but while in an electronic form.]

**[1002]**

---

**NOTES**

Sub-s (1): substituted by the Housing and Regeneration Act 2008, s 185(1)(a), as from a day to be appointed, as follows:

"(1)    The tenant of a dwelling in Wales has a right to acquire the dwelling if—
 (a)    the landlord is a registered social landlord or a registered provider of social housing,
 (b)    the tenancy is—
   (i)    an assured tenancy, other than an assured shorthold tenancy or a long tenancy, or
   (ii)    a secure tenancy,
 (c)    the dwelling was provided with public money and has remained in the social rented sector, and
 (d)    the tenant satisfies any further qualifying conditions applicable under Part V of the Housing Act 1985 (the right to buy) as it applies in relation to the right conferred by this section.".

Sub-ss (2), (3): words in square brackets inserted by the Housing and Regeneration Act 2008, s 185(1)(b), (c), as from a day to be appointed.
Sub-s (3A): inserted by the Housing Act 2004, s 202(1), (2); for effect see s 202(3) of that Act at **[1475]**.
Sub-s (4): words in square brackets substituted by the Government of Wales Act 1998, ss 140, 141, Sch 16, paras 81, 82; for the first, second and third words in italics there are substituted the words "the Welsh Ministers", "The Welsh Ministers" and "they propose" respectively by the Housing and Regeneration Act 2008, s 61(1), (7), as from a day to be appointed.
Sub-ss (5), (6): inserted, together with sub-s (7), in relation to England, by the Housing (Right to Acquire) (Electronic Communications) (England) Order 2001, SI 2001/3257, art 2.
Sub-s (7): inserted, together with sub-ss (5), (6), in relation to England, by SI 2001/3257, art 2; words in square brackets substituted by the Communications Act 2003, s 406(1), Sch 17, para 136.
Transfer of Functions: functions of the Housing Corporation under this section transferred to the Homes and Communities Agency: see the Transfer of Housing Corporation Functions (Modifications and Transitional Provisions) Order 2008, SI 2008/2839, arts 1(2), 2, 3, 6, Schedule, para 5(2), (3).
Many housing associations register with the Housing Corporation under provisions formerly to be found in the Housing Associations Act 1985. These provisions have been re-enacted, with modifications, in Pt I of this Act. Now, a housing association (and certain other bodies) which is registered with the Housing Corporation is known as a "registered social landlord" (see s 1 of this Act). As to which bodies are eligible for registration, see s 2 of this Act.

---

**[16A    Extension of section 16 to dwellings funded by grants under section 27A**

(1)    Section 16 applies in relation to a dwelling [in Wales] ("a funded dwelling") provided or acquired wholly or in part by means of a grant under section 27A (grants to bodies other than registered social landlords) with the following modifications.

(2)    In section 16(1) the reference to a registered social landlord includes a reference to any person to whom a grant has been paid under section 27A.

(3)    In section 16(2) and (4) any reference to section 18 includes a reference to section 27A.

(4)    For the purposes of section 16 a funded dwelling is to be regarded as having remained within the social rented sector in relation to any relevant time if, since it was acquired or provided as mentioned in subsection (1) above, it was used—
 (a)    by the recipient of the grant mentioned in that subsection, or
 (b)    if section 27B applies in relation to the grant, by each person to whom the grant was, or is treated as having been, paid,

exclusively for the purposes for which the grant was made or any other purposes agreed to by *the Relevant Authority.*

(5)    In subsection (4) "relevant time" means a time when the dwelling would not be treated as being within the social rented sector by virtue of section 16(3).]

**[1003]**

**NOTES**
Commencement: 17 February 2005 (in relation to England); to be appointed (in relation to Wales).
Inserted by the Housing Act 2004, s 221.
Sub-s (1): words in square brackets inserted by the Housing and Regeneration Act 2008, s 185(2), as from a day to be appointed.
Sub-s (4): for the words in italics there are substituted the words "the Welsh Ministers" by the Housing and Regeneration Act 2008, s 61(1), (7), as from a day to be appointed.
Transfer of Functions: Functions of the Housing Corporation under this section transferred to the Homes and Communities Agency: see the Transfer of Housing Corporation Functions (Modifications and Transitional Provisions) Order 2008, SI 2008/2839, arts 1(2), 2, 3, 6, Schedule, para 5(2).

## 17 Right of tenant to acquire dwelling: supplementary provisions

(1) The *Secretary of State* may by order—

    (a) specify the amount or rate of discount to be given on the exercise of the right conferred by section 16; and

    (b) designate rural areas in relation to dwellings in which the right conferred by that section does not arise.

(2) The provisions of Part V of the Housing Act 1985 apply in relation to the right to acquire under section 16—

    (a) subject to any order under subsection (1) above, and

    (b) subject to such other exceptions, adaptations and other modifications as may be specified by regulations made by the *Secretary of State*.

(3) The regulations may provide—

    (a) that the powers of the Secretary of State under sections 164 to 170 of that Act (powers to intervene, give directions or assist) do not apply,

    (b) that paragraphs 1 and 3 (exceptions for charities and certain housing associations), and paragraph 11 (right of appeal to Secretary of State), of Schedule 5 to that Act do not apply,

    (c) that the provisions of Part V of that Act relating to the right to acquire on rent to mortgage terms do not apply,

    (d) that the provisions of that Part relating to restrictions on disposals in National Parks, &c do not apply, and

    (e) that the provisions of that Part relating to the preserved right to buy do not apply.

Nothing in this subsection affects the generality of the power conferred by subsection (2).

(4) The specified exceptions, adaptations and other modifications shall take the form of textual amendments of the provisions of Part V of that Act as they apply in relation to the right to buy under that Part; and the first regulations, and any subsequent consolidating regulations, shall set out the provisions of Part V as they so apply.

(5) An order or regulations under this section—

    (a) may make different provision for different cases or classes of case including different areas, and

    (b) may contain such incidental, supplementary and transitional provisions as the *Secretary of State considers* appropriate.

(6) Before making an order which would have the effect that an area ceased to be designated under subsection (1)(b), the *Secretary of State* shall consult—

    (a) the local housing authority or authorities in whose district the area or any part of it is situated or, if the order is general in its effect, local housing authorities in general, and

    (b) such bodies appearing to *him* to be representative of registered social landlords as *he considers* appropriate.

(7) An order or regulations under this section shall be made by statutory instrument which shall be subject to annulment in pursuance of a resolution of *either House of Parliament*.

**[1004]**

**NOTES**
Sub-ss (1), (2): for the words in italics there are substituted the words "Welsh Ministers" by the Housing and Regeneration Act 2008, s 62(a), as from a day to be appointed.
Sub-s (5): for the words in italics there are substituted the words "Welsh Ministers consider" by the Housing and Regeneration Act 2008, s 62(a), (e), as from a day to be appointed.
Sub-s (6): for the first, second and third words in italics there are substituted the words "Welsh Ministers", "them" and "they consider" respectively by the Housing and Regeneration Act 2008, s 62(a), (c)–(e), as from a day to be appointed.
Sub-s (7): for the words in italics there are substituted the words "the National Assembly for Wales" by the Housing and Regeneration Act 2008, s 63, as from a day to be appointed.
Orders: the Housing (Right to Acquire) (Discount) (Wales) Order 1997, SI 1997/569; the Leasehold Reform and Housing (Excluded Tenancies) (Designated Rural Areas) (Wales) Order 1997, SI 1997/685; the Housing (Right to Acquire or Enfranchise) (Designated Rural Areas) Order 1999, SI 1999/1307; the Housing (Right to

Acquire) (Discount) Order 2002, SI 2002/1091; the Housing (Right to Acquire and Right to Buy) (Designated Rural Areas and Designated Regions) (Wales) Order 2003, SI 2003/54.

Regulations: the Housing (Right to Acquire) Regulations 1997, SI 1997/619; the Housing (Right of First Refusal) (England) Regulations 2005, SI 2005/1917 at **[3555]**; the Housing (Right of First Refusal) (Wales) Regulations 2005, SI 2005/2680 at **[3573]**.

**18–80** (*Ss 18–64 (Chs III–V), ss 65–80 (Pt II) in so far as unrepealed outside the scope of this work.*)

PART III
LANDLORD AND TENANT

CHAPTER I
TENANTS' RIGHTS

*Forfeiture*

**81 Restriction on termination of tenancy for failure to pay service charge**

(1) A landlord may not, in relation to premises let as a dwelling, exercise a right of re-entry or forfeiture for failure [by a tenant to pay a service charge or administration charge unless—

(a) it is finally determined by (or on appeal from) a leasehold valuation tribunal or by a court, or by an arbitral tribunal in proceedings pursuant to a post-dispute arbitration agreement, that the amount of the service charge or administration charge is payable by him, or

(b) the tenant has admitted that it is so payable].

[(2) The landlord may not exercise a right of re-entry or forfeiture by virtue of subsection (1)(a) until after the end of the period of 14 days beginning with the day after that on which the final determination is made.]

[(3) For the purposes of this section it is finally determined that the amount of a service charge or administration charge is payable—

(a) if a decision that it is payable is not appealed against or otherwise challenged, at the end of the time for bringing an appeal or other challenge, or

(b) if such a decision is appealed against or otherwise challenged and not set aside in consequence of the appeal or other challenge, at the time specified in subsection (3A).

(3A) The time referred to in subsection (3)(b) is the time when the appeal or other challenge is disposed of—

(a) by the determination of the appeal or other challenge and the expiry of the time for bringing a subsequent appeal (if any), or

(b) by its being abandoned or otherwise ceasing to have effect.]

(4) The reference in subsection (1) to premises let as a dwelling does not include premises let on—

(a) a tenancy to which Part II of the Landlord and Tenant Act 1954 applies (business tenancies),

(b) a tenancy of an agricultural holding within the meaning of the Agricultural Holdings Act 1986 in relation to which that Act applies, or

(c) a farm business tenancy within the meaning of the Agricultural Tenancies Act 1995.

[(4A) References in this section to the exercise of a right of re-entry or forfeiture include the service of a notice under section 146(1) of the Law of Property Act 1925 (restriction on re-entry or forfeiture).]

(5) In this section

[(a) "administration charge" has the meaning given by Part 1 of Schedule 11 to the Commonhold and Leasehold Reform Act 2002,

(b) "arbitration agreement" and "arbitral tribunal" have the same meaning as in Part 1 of the Arbitration Act 1996 (c 23) and "post-dispute arbitration agreement", in relation to any matter, means an arbitration agreement made after a dispute about the matter has arisen,

(c) "dwelling" has the same meaning as in the Landlord and Tenant Act 1985 (c 70), and

(d)] "service charge" means a service charge within the meaning of section 18(1) of the Landlord and Tenant Act 1985, other than one excluded from that section by section 27 of that Act (rent of dwelling registered and not entered as variable).

[(5A) Any order of a court to give effect to a determination of a leasehold valuation tribunal shall be treated as a determination by the court for the purposes of this section.]

(6) Nothing in this section affects the exercise of a right of re-entry or forfeiture on other grounds.

**NOTES**

Sub-s (1): words in square brackets substituted by the Commonhold and Leasehold Reform Act 2002, s 170(1), (2), except in relation to notices served under the Law of Property Act 1925, s 146(1) at **[22]**, before 28 February 2005 (in relation to England) or 31 May 2005 (in relation to Wales).

Sub-s (2): substituted by the Commonhold and Leasehold Reform Act 2002, s 170(1), (3), subject to savings as noted above.

Sub-ss (3), (3A): substituted for original sub-s (3) by the Commonhold and Leasehold Reform Act 2002, s 170(1), (4), subject to savings as noted above.

Sub-s (4A): inserted by the Commonhold and Leasehold Reform Act 2002, s 170(1), (5), subject to savings as noted above.

Sub-s (5): paras (a)–(c) inserted and para (d) numbered as such by the Commonhold and Leasehold Reform Act 2002, s 170(1), (6), subject to savings as noted above.

Sub-s (5A): inserted by the Commonhold and Leasehold Reform Act 2002, s 176, Sch 13, para 16, subject to savings as noted above.

---

**82** (*Repealed by the Commonhold and Leasehold Reform Act 2002, s 180, Sch 14.*)

*Service charges*

**83** (*Inserts the Landlord and Tenant Act 1985, ss 19(2A)–(2C), 31A–31C, substitutes s 20C of, and Schedule, para 8 to, the 1985 Act at* **[616]**, **[643]**, *and amends ss 38, 39 of that Act at* **[640]**, **[641]**; *repealed in part by the Commonhold and Leasehold Reform Act 2002, s 180, Sch 14.*)

**84 Right to appoint surveyor to advise on matters relating to service charges**

(1) A recognised tenants' association may appoint a surveyor for the purposes of this section to advise on any matters relating to, or which may give rise to, service charges payable to a landlord by one or more members of the association.

The provisions of Schedule 4 have effect for conferring on a surveyor so appointed rights of access to documents and premises.

(2) A person shall not be so appointed unless he is a qualified surveyor.

For this purpose "qualified surveyor" has the same meaning as in section 78(4)(a) of the Leasehold Reform, Housing and Urban Development Act 1993 (persons qualified for appointment to carry out management audit).

(3) The appointment shall take effect for the purposes of this section upon notice in writing being given to the landlord by the association stating the name and address of the surveyor, the duration of his appointment and the matters in respect of which he is appointed.

(4) An appointment shall cease to have effect for the purposes of this section if the association gives notice in writing to the landlord to that effect or if the association ceases to exist.

(5) A notice is duly given under this section to a landlord of any tenants if it is given to a person who receives on behalf of the landlord the rent payable by those tenants; and a person to whom such a notice is so given shall forward it as soon as may be to the landlord.

(6) In this section—

"recognised tenants' association" has the same meaning as in the provisions of the Landlord and Tenant Act 1985 relating to service charges (see section 29 of that Act); and

"service charge" means a service charge within the meaning of section 18(1) of that Act, other than one excluded from that section by section 27 of that Act (rent of dwelling registered and not entered as variable).

**[1006]**

---

**NOTES**

Modified, where the RTM company has acquired the right to manage, by the Commonhold and Leasehold Reform Act 2002, s 102, Sch 7, para 15 at **[1266]**, **[1306]**.

---

**85–93** (*S 85 amends the Landlord and Tenant Act 1987, s 24 at* **[684]**; *s 86 amends the Landlord and Tenant Act 1987, ss 21–24, 52(2) at* **[681]**–**[684]**, **[709]**, *and inserts ss 24A, 24B of that Act; s 87 introduces Sch 5 to this Act; s 88 amends s 29(3) of the 1987 Act at* **[689]**; *s 89 amends ss 4(2), 20(1) of the 1987 Act at* **[647]**, **[680]**, *and inserts s 4A of that Act at* **[648]**; *s 90 amends s 4(2) of the 1987 Act; s 91 adds s 10A of the 1987 Act at* **[666]**; *s 92 introduces Sch 6 to this Act; s 93 adds the Landlord and Tenant Act 1985, s 3A at* **[595]**, *and amends s 32(1) of that Act at* **[634]**.)

*General [advice etc]*

---

**NOTES**

Words in square brackets substituted by the Housing and Regeneration Act 2008, s 312(2).

**94  Provision of general [advice etc] about residential tenancies**

(1)   The Secretary of State may give financial assistance to any person in relation to the provision by that person of [information, training or] general advice about[, or a dispute resolution service in connection with]—

(a)   any aspect of the law of landlord and tenant, so far as relating to residential tenancies,

[(aa) any other matter relating to residential tenancies,] or

(b)   [any matter relating to] Chapter IV of Part I of the Leasehold Reform, Housing and Urban Development Act 1993 (estate management schemes in connection with enfranchisement).

(2)   Financial assistance under this section may be given in such form and on such terms as the Secretary of State considers appropriate.

(3)   The terms on which financial assistance under this section may be given may, in particular, include provision as to the circumstances in which the assistance must be repaid or otherwise made good to the Secretary of State and the manner in which that is to be done.

**[1007]**

**NOTES**

Section heading: words in square brackets substituted by the Housing and Regeneration Act 2008, s 312(2).
Sub-s (1): words in square brackets inserted by the Housing and Regeneration Act 2008, s 312(1).

*Supplementary*

**95  Jurisdiction of county courts**

(1)   Any jurisdiction expressed by a provision to which this section applies to be conferred on the court shall be exercised by a county court.

(2)   There shall also be brought in a county court any proceedings for determining any question arising under or by virtue of any provision to which this section applies.

(3)   Where, however, other proceedings are properly brought in the High Court, that court has jurisdiction to hear and determine proceedings to which subsection (1) or (2) applies which are joined with those proceedings.

(4)   Where proceedings are brought in a county court by virtue of subsection (1) or (2), that court has jurisdiction to hear and determine other proceedings joined with those proceedings despite the fact that they would otherwise be outside its jurisdiction.

(5)   The provisions to which this section applies are—

(a)   section 81 (restriction on termination of tenancy for failure to pay service charge), and

(b)   section 84 (right to appoint surveyor to advise on matters relating to service charges) and Schedule 4 (rights exercisable by surveyor appointed by tenants' association).

**[1008]**

**96–104**   (*S 96 inserts the Housing Act 1988, s 19A at* **[753]** *and introduces Sch 7 to this Act; s 97 inserts the Housing Act 1988, s 20A at* **[755]***; ss 98–103 amend ss 21, 22, 24 of the 1988 Act at* **[757]**, **[758]**, **[760]**, *and Sch 2, Pts I, II to that Act at* **[785]**, **[786]***; s 104 introduces Sch 8 to this Act.*)

CHAPTER III
LEASEHOLD REFORM

**105–113**   (*S 105 amends the Leasehold Reform Act 1967, ss 4(1), 4A at* **[84]**, **[85]**, *and the Leasehold Reform, Housing and Urban Development Act 1993, s 8(1), (2), and is repealed in part by the Commonhold and Leasehold Reform Act 2002, s 180, Sch 14; s 106 introduces Sch 9 to this Act; s 107 amends the Leasehold Reform, Housing and Urban Development Act 1993, ss 1(3), 3(1), 4 at* **[803]**, **[805]**, **[806]**, *and introduces Sch 10 to this Act; ss 108, 109 amend s 13 of the 1993 Act at* **[817]**, *and Sch 6 to that Act at* **[923]***; s 110 amends Sch 13 to the 1993 Act at* **[940]***; ss 111, 112 repealed by the Commonhold and Leasehold Reform Act 2002, s 180, Sch 14; s 113 inserts the Leasehold Reform, Housing and Urban Development Act 1993, s 93A at* **[895]**.)

*Miscellaneous*

**114–119**   (*Ss 114, 115 amend the Leasehold Reform Act 1967, s 1(1), 21(1) at* **[78]**, **[104]***; s 116 introduces Sch 11 to this Act; s 117 inserts the Leasehold Reform, Housing and Urban Development Act 1993, s 58A at* **[865]***; s 118 amends ss 69(1), 70, 74(1), 94 of the 1993 Act at* **[872]**, **[873]**, **[877]**, **[896]**, *amends the National Heritage Act 1983, s 33, and amends the Planning (Listed Buildings and Conservation Areas) Act 1990, s 72; s 119 repealed by the Commonhold and Leasehold Reform Act 2002, s 180, Sch 14.*)

**120–123** ((*Pt IV*) *outside the scope of this work.*)

## PART V
## CONDUCT OF TENANTS

### CHAPTER I
### INTRODUCTORY TENANCIES

*General provisions*

### 124  Introductory tenancies

(1)  A local housing authority or a housing action trust may elect to operate an introductory tenancy regime.

(2)  When such an election is in force, every periodic tenancy of a dwelling-house entered into or adopted by the authority or trust shall, if it would otherwise be a secure tenancy, be an introductory tenancy, unless immediately before the tenancy was entered into or adopted the tenant or, in the case of joint tenants, one or more of them was—

(a)  a secure tenant of the same or another dwelling-house, or

(b)  an assured tenant of a registered social landlord (otherwise than under an assured shorthold tenancy) in respect of the same or another dwelling-house.

(3)  Subsection (2) does not apply to a tenancy entered into or adopted in pursuance of a contract made before the election was made.

(4)  For the purposes of this Chapter a periodic tenancy is adopted by a person if that person becomes the landlord under the tenancy, whether on a disposal or surrender of the interest of the former landlord.

(5)  An election under this section may be revoked at any time, without prejudice to the making of a further election.

[1009]

### 125  Duration of introductory tenancy

(1)  A tenancy remains an introductory tenancy until the end of the trial period, unless one of the events mentioned in subsection (5) occurs before the end of that period.

(2)  The "trial period" is the period of one year beginning with—

(a)  in the case of a tenancy which was entered into by a local housing authority or housing action trust—

   (i)  the date on which the tenancy was entered into, or

   (ii)  if later, the date on which a tenant was first entitled to possession under the tenancy; or

(b)  in the case of a tenancy which was adopted by a local housing authority or housing action trust, the date of adoption;

[but this is subject to subsections (3) and (4) and to section 125A (extension of trial period by 6 months).]

(3)  Where the tenant under an introductory tenancy was formerly a tenant under another introductory tenancy, or held an assured shorthold tenancy from a registered social landlord, any period or periods during which he was such a tenant shall count towards the trial period, provided—

(a)  if there was one such period, it ended immediately before the date specified in subsection (2), and

(b)  if there was more than one such period, the most recent period ended immediately before that date and each period succeeded the other without interruption.

(4)  Where there are joint tenants under an introductory tenancy, the reference in subsection (3) to the tenant shall be construed as referring to the joint tenant in whose case the application of that subsection produces the earliest starting date for the trial period.

(5)  A tenancy ceases to be an introductory tenancy if, before the end of the trial period—

(a)  the circumstances are such that the tenancy would not otherwise be a secure tenancy,

(b)  a person or body other than a local housing authority or housing action trust becomes the landlord under the tenancy,

(c)  the election in force when the tenancy was entered into or adopted is revoked, or

(d)  the tenancy ceases to be an introductory tenancy by virtue of section 133(3) (succession).

(6)  A tenancy does not come to an end merely because it ceases to be an introductory tenancy, but a tenancy which has once ceased to be an introductory tenancy cannot subsequently become an introductory tenancy.

(7) This section has effect subject to section 130 (effect of beginning proceedings for possession).

**[1010]**

PART I
STATUTES

**NOTES**
  Sub-s (2): words in square brackets substituted by the Housing Act 2004, s 179(1), (2), except in relation to any tenancy entered into before, or in pursuance of an agreement made before 6 June 2005 (in relation to England) and 25 November 2005 (in relation to Wales).

### [125A Extension of trial period by 6 months

(1) If both of the following conditions are met in relation to an introductory tenancy, the trial period is extended by 6 months.

(2) The first condition is that the landlord has served a notice of extension on the tenant at least 8 weeks before the original expiry date.

(3) The second condition is that either—
  (a) the tenant has not requested a review under section 125B in accordance with subsection (1) of that section, or
  (b) if he has, the decision on the review was to confirm the landlord's decision to extend the trial period.

(4) A notice of extension is a notice—
  (a) stating that the landlord has decided that the period for which the tenancy is to be an introductory tenancy should be extended by 6 months, and
  (b) complying with subsection (5).

(5) A notice of extension must—
  (a) set out the reasons for the landlord's decision, and
  (b) inform the tenant of his right to request a review of the landlord's decision and of the time within which such a request must be made.

(6) In this section and section 125B "the original expiry date" means the last day of the period of one year that would apply as the trial period apart from this section.]

**[1011]**

**NOTES**
  Commencement: 6 June 2005 (in relation to England); 25 November 2005 (in relation to Wales).
  Inserted, together with s 125B, by the Housing Act 2004, s 179(1), (3), except in relation to any tenancy entered into before, or in pursuance of an agreement made before, the commencement of this section.

### [125B Review of decision to extend trial period

(1) A request for review of the landlord's decision that the trial period for an introductory tenancy should be extended under section 125A must be made before the end of the period of 14 days beginning with the day on which the notice of extension is served.

(2) On a request being duly made to it, the landlord shall review its decision.

(3) The Secretary of State may make provision by regulations as to the procedure to be followed in connection with a review under this section.

Nothing in the following provisions affects the generality of this power.

(4) Provision may be made by regulations—
  (a) requiring the decision on review to be made by a person of appropriate seniority who was not involved in the original decision, and
  (b) as to the circumstances in which the person concerned is entitled to an oral hearing, and whether and by whom he may be represented at such a hearing.

(5) The landlord shall notify the tenant of the decision on the review.

If the decision is to confirm the original decision, the landlord shall also notify him of the reasons for the decision.

(6) The review shall be carried out and the tenant notified before the original expiry date.]

**[1012]**

**NOTES**
  Commencement: 6 June 2005 (in relation to England); 25 November 2005 (in relation to Wales).
  Inserted as noted to s 125A at **[1011]**, except in relation to any tenancy entered into before, or in pursuance of an agreement made before, the commencement of this section.
  Regulations: the Introductory Tenancies (Review of Decisions to Extend a Trial Period) (England) Regulations 2006, SI 2006/1077; the Introductory Tenancies (Review of Decisions to Extend a Trial Period) (Wales) Regulations 2006, SI 2006/2983.

**126 Licences**

(1)   The provisions of this Chapter apply in relation to a licence to occupy a dwelling-house (whether or not granted for a consideration) as they apply in relation to a tenancy.

(2)   Subsection (1) does not apply to a licence granted as a temporary expedient to a person who entered the dwelling-house or any other land as a trespasser (whether or not, before the grant of that licence, another licence to occupy that or another dwelling-house had been granted to him).

**[1013]**

*Proceedings for possession*

**127   Proceedings for possession**

(1)   The landlord may only bring an introductory tenancy to an end by obtaining[—
   (a)   an order of the court for the possession of the dwelling-house, and
   (b)   the execution of the order.]

   [(1A)   In such a case, the tenancy ends when the order is executed.]

(2)   The court shall make [an order of the kind mentioned in subsection (1)(a)] unless the provisions of section 128 apply.

(3)   ...

**[1014]**

**NOTES**
Sub-s (1): words in square brackets substituted by the Housing and Regeneration Act 2008, s 299, Sch 11, Pt 1, paras 10, 11(1), (2), subject to transitional provisions in Sch 11, Pt 1, para 14 thereto at **[1891]**.
Sub-s (1A): inserted by the Housing and Regeneration Act 2008, s 299, Sch 11, Pt 1, paras 10, 11(1), (3), subject to transitional provisions in Sch 11, Pt 1, para 14 thereto at **[1891]**.
Sub-s (2): words in square brackets substituted by the Housing and Regeneration Act 2008, s 299, Sch 11, Pt 1, paras 10, 11(1), (4), subject to transitional provisions in Sch 11, Pt 1, para 14 thereto at **[1891]**.
Sub-s (3): repealed by the Housing and Regeneration Act 2008, ss 299, 321(1), Sch 11, Pt 1, paras 10, 11(1), (5), Sch 16, subject to transitional provisions in Sch 11, Pt 1, para 14 thereto at **[1891]**.

**128   Notice of proceedings for possession**

(1)   The court shall not entertain proceedings for the possession of a dwelling-house let under an introductory tenancy unless the landlord has served on the tenant a notice of proceedings complying with this section.

(2)   The notice shall state that the court will be asked to make an order for the possession of the dwelling-house.

(3)   The notice shall set out the reasons for the landlord's decision to apply for such an order.

(4)   The notice shall specify a date after which proceedings for the possession of the dwelling-house may be begun.

   The date so specified must not be earlier than the date on which the tenancy could, apart from this Chapter, be brought to an end by notice to quit given by the landlord on the same date as the notice of proceedings.

(5)   The court shall not entertain any proceedings for possession of the dwelling-house unless they are begun after the date specified in the notice of proceedings.

(6)   The notice shall inform the tenant of his right to request a review of the landlord's decision to seek an order for possession and of the time within which such a request must be made.

(7)   The notice shall also inform the tenant that if he needs help or advice about the notice, and what to do about it, he should take it immediately to a Citizens' Advice Bureau, a housing aid centre, a law centre or a solicitor.

**[1015]**

**129   Review of decision to seek possession**

(1)   A request for review of the landlord's decision to seek an order for possession of a dwelling-house let under an introductory tenancy must be made before the end of the period of 14 days beginning with the day on which the notice of proceedings is served.

(2)   On a request being duly made to it, the landlord shall review its decision.

(3)   The Secretary of State may make provision by regulations as to the procedure to be followed in connection with a review under this section.

   Nothing in the following provisions affects the generality of this power.

(4)   Provision may be made by regulations—
   (a)   requiring the decision on review to be made by a person of appropriate seniority who was not involved in the original decision, and
   (b)   as to the circumstances in which the person concerned is entitled to an oral hearing, and whether and by whom he may be represented at such a hearing.

(5)   The landlord shall notify the person concerned of the decision on the review.

If the decision is to confirm the original decision, the landlord shall also notify him of the reasons for the decision.

(6)   The review shall be carried out and the tenant notified before the date specified in the notice of proceedings as the date after which proceedings for the possession of the dwelling-house may be begun.

**[1016]**

**NOTES**

Regulations: the Introductory Tenants (Review) Regulations 1997, SI 1997/72 at **[3159]**.

**130   Effect of beginning proceedings for possession**

(1)   This section applies where the landlord has begun proceedings for the possession of a dwelling-house let under an introductory tenancy and—

    (a)   the trial period ends, or

    (b)   any of the events specified in section 125(5) occurs (events on which a tenancy ceases to be an introductory tenancy).

(2)   Subject to the following provisions, the tenancy remains an introductory tenancy until—

    (a)   the tenancy comes to an end [in accordance with section 127(1A)], or

    (b)   the proceedings are otherwise finally determined.

(3)   If any of the events specified in section 125(5)(b) to (d) occurs, the tenancy shall thereupon cease to be an introductory tenancy but—

    (a)   the landlord (or, as the case may be, the new landlord) may continue the proceedings, and

    (b)   if he does so, section [127(1A) and (2)] (termination by landlord) apply as if the tenancy had remained an introductory tenancy.

(4)   Where in accordance with subsection (3) a tenancy ceases to be an introductory tenancy and becomes a secure tenancy, the tenant is not entitled to exercise the right to buy under Part V of the Housing Act 1985 unless and until the proceedings are finally determined on terms such that he is not required to give up possession of the dwelling-house.

(5)   For the purposes of this section proceedings shall be treated as finally determined if they are withdrawn or any appeal is abandoned or the time for appealing expires without an appeal being brought.

**[1017]**

**NOTES**

Sub-s (2): words in square brackets substituted by the Housing and Regeneration Act 2008, s 299, Sch 11, Pt 1, paras 10, 12(1), (2), subject to transitional provisions in Sch 11, Pt 1, para 14 thereto at **[1891]**.

Sub-s (3): words in square brackets substituted by the Housing and Regeneration Act 2008, s 299, Sch 11, Pt 1, paras 10, 12(1), (3), subject to transitional provisions in Sch 11, Pt 1, para 14 thereto at **[1891]**.

*Succession on death of tenant*

**131   Persons qualified to succeed tenant**

A person is qualified to succeed the tenant under an introductory tenancy if he occupies the dwelling-house as his only or principal home at the time of the tenant's death and either—

    (a)   he is the tenant's spouse [or civil partner], or

    (b)   he is another member of the tenant's family and has resided with the tenant throughout the period of twelve months ending with the tenant's death;

unless, in either case, the tenant was himself a successor, as defined in section 132.

**[1018]**

**NOTES**

Words in square brackets inserted by the Civil Partnership (Family Proceedings and Housing Consequential Amendments) Order 2005, SI 2005/3336, art 20.

**132   Cases where the tenant is a successor**

(1)   The tenant is himself a successor if—

    (a)   the tenancy vested in him by virtue of section 133 (succession to introductory tenancy),

    (b)   he was a joint tenant and has become the sole tenant,

    (c)   he became the tenant on the tenancy being assigned to him (but subject to subsections (2) and (3)), or

    (d)   he became the tenant on the tenancy being vested in him on the death of the previous tenant.

(2) A tenant to whom the tenancy was assigned in pursuance of an order under section 24 of the Matrimonial Causes Act 1973 (property adjustment orders in connection with matrimonial proceedings) or section 17(1) of the Matrimonial and Family Proceedings Act 1984 (property adjustment orders after overseas divorce, &c) is a successor only if the other party to the marriage was a successor.

[(2A) A tenant to whom the tenancy was assigned in pursuance of an order under Part 2 of Schedule 5, or paragraph 9(2) or (3) of Schedule 7, to the Civil Partnership Act 2004 (property adjustment orders in connection with civil partnership proceedings or after overseas dissolution of civil partnership, etc) is a successor only if the other civil partner was a successor.]

(3) Where within six months of the coming to an end of an introductory tenancy ("the former tenancy") the tenant becomes a tenant under another introductory tenancy, and—

    (a) the tenant was a successor in relation to the former tenancy, and

    (b) under the other tenancy either the dwelling-house or the landlord, or both, are the same as under the former tenancy,

the tenant is also a successor in relation to the other tenancy unless the agreement creating that tenancy otherwise provides.

**[1019]**

**NOTES**

Sub-s (2A): inserted by the Civil Partnership Act 2004, s 81, Sch 8, para 52.

## 133 Succession to introductory tenancy

(1) This section applies where a tenant under an introductory tenancy dies.

(2) Where there is a person qualified to succeed the tenant, the tenancy vests by virtue of this section in that person, or if there is more than one such person in the one to be preferred in accordance with the following rules—

    (a) the tenant's spouse [or civil partner] is to be preferred to another member of the tenant's family;

    (b) of two or more other members of the tenant's family such of them is to be preferred as may be agreed between them or as may, where there is no such agreement, be selected by the landlord.

(3) Where there is no person qualified to succeed the tenant, the tenancy ceases to be an introductory tenancy—

    (a) when it is vested or otherwise disposed of in the course of the administration of the tenant's estate, unless the vesting or other disposal is in pursuance of an order made under—

        (i) section 24 of the Matrimonial Causes Act 1973 (property adjustment orders made in connection with matrimonial proceedings),

        (ii) section 17(1) of the Matrimonial and Family Proceedings Act 1984 (property adjustment orders after overseas divorce, &c), ...

        (iii) paragraph 1 of Schedule 1 to the Children Act 1989 (orders for financial relief against parents)[, or

        (iv) Part 2 of Schedule 5, or paragraph 9(2) or (3) of Schedule 7, to the Civil Partnership Act 2004 (property adjustment orders in connection with civil partnership proceedings or after overseas dissolution of civil partnership, etc)]; or

    (b) when it is known that when the tenancy is so vested or disposed of it will not be in pursuance of such an order.

**[1020]**

**NOTES**

Sub-s (2): words in square brackets inserted by the Civil Partnership Act 2004, s 81, Sch 8, para 53(1), (2).

Sub-s (3): word omitted from para (a)(ii) repealed and para (a)(iv) and word immediately preceding it inserted by the Civil Partnership Act 2004, ss 81, 261(4), Sch 8, para 53(1), (3), Sch 30.

*Assignment*

## 134 Assignment in general prohibited

(1) An introductory tenancy is not capable of being assigned except in the cases mentioned in subsection (2).

(2) The exceptions are—

    (a) an assignment in pursuance of an order made under—

        (i) section 24 of the Matrimonial Causes Act 1973 (property adjustment orders in connection with matrimonial proceedings),

        (ii) section 17(1) of the Matrimonial and Family Proceedings Act 1984 (property adjustment orders after overseas divorce, &c), ...

(iii)    paragraph 1 of Schedule 1 to the Children Act 1989 (orders for financial relief against parents)[, or;

(iv)    Part 2 of Schedule 5, or paragraph 9(2) or (3) of Schedule 7, to the Civil Partnership Act 2004 (property adjustment orders in connection with civil partnership proceedings or after overseas dissolution of civil partnership, etc)];

(b)    an assignment to a person who would be qualified to succeed the tenant if the tenant died immediately before the assignment.

(3)    Subsection (1) also applies to a tenancy which is not an introductory tenancy but would be if the tenant, or where the tenancy is a joint tenancy, at least one of the tenants, were occupying or continuing to occupy the dwelling-house as his only or principal home.

**[1021]**

**NOTES**

Sub-s (2): word omitted from para (a)(ii) repealed and para (a)(iv) and word immediately preceding it inserted by the Civil Partnership Act 2004, ss 81, 261(4), Sch 8, para 54, Sch 30.

*Repairs*

## 135 Right to carry out repairs

The Secretary of State may by regulations under section 96 of the Housing Act 1985 (secure tenants: right to carry out repairs) apply to introductory tenants any provision made under that section in relation to secure tenants.

**[1022]**

*Provision of information and consultation*

## 136 Provision of information about tenancies

(1)    Every local housing authority or housing action trust which lets dwelling-houses under introductory tenancies shall from time to time publish information about its introductory tenancies, in such form as it considers best suited to explain in simple terms, and, so far as it considers it appropriate, the effect of—

(a)    the express terms of its introductory tenancies,

(b)    the provisions of this Chapter, and

(c)    the provisions of sections 11 to 16 of the Landlord and Tenant Act 1985 (landlord's repairing obligations),

and shall ensure that so far as is reasonably practicable the information so published is kept up to date.

(2)    The landlord under an introductory tenancy shall supply the tenant with—

(a)    a copy of the information for introductory tenants published by it under subsection (1), and

(b)    a written statement of the terms of the tenancy, so far as they are neither expressed in the lease or written tenancy agreement (if any) nor implied by law;

and the statement required by paragraph (b) shall be supplied on the grant of the tenancy or as soon as practicable afterwards.

**[1023]**

## 137 Consultation on matters of housing management

(1)    This section applies in relation to every local housing authority and housing action trust which lets dwelling-houses under introductory tenancies and which is a landlord authority for the purposes of Part IV of the Housing Act 1985 (secure tenancies).

(2)    The authority or trust shall maintain such arrangements as it considers appropriate to enable those of its introductory tenants who are likely to be substantially affected by a relevant matter of housing management—

(a)    to be informed of the proposals of the authority or trust in respect of the matter, and

(b)    to make their views known to the authority or trust within a specified period;

and the authority or trust shall, before making a decision on the matter, consider any representations made to it in accordance with those arrangements.

(3)    A matter is one of housing management if, in the opinion of the authority or trust concerned, it relates to—

(a)    the management, improvement, maintenance or demolition of dwelling-houses let by the authority or trust under introductory or secure tenancies, or

(b)    the provision of services or amenities in connection with such dwelling-houses;

but not so far as it relates to the rent payable under an introductory or secure tenancy or to charges for services or facilities provided by the authority or trust.

(4)    A matter is relevant if, in the opinion of the authority or trust concerned, it represents—

    (a)    a new programme of maintenance, improvement or demolition, or

    (b)    a change in the practice or policy of the authority or trust,

and is likely substantially to affect either its introductory tenants as a whole or a group of them who form a distinct social group or occupy dwelling-houses which constitute a distinct class (whether by reference to the kind of dwelling-house, or the housing estate or other larger area in which they are situated).

(5)    In the case of a local housing authority, the reference in subsection (3) to the provision of services or amenities is a reference only to the provision of services or amenities by the authority acting in its capacity as landlord of the dwelling-houses concerned.

(6)    The authority or trust shall publish details of the arrangements which it makes under this section, and a copy of the documents published under this subsection shall—

    (a)    be made available at its principal office for inspection at all reasonable hours, without charge, by members of the public, and

    (b)    be given, on payment of a reasonable fee, to any member of the public who asks for one.

**[1024]**

## *Supplementary*

### 138  Jurisdiction of county court

(1)    A county court has jurisdiction to determine questions arising under this Chapter and to entertain proceedings brought under this Chapter and claims, for whatever amount, in connection with an introductory tenancy.

(2)    That jurisdiction includes jurisdiction to entertain proceedings as to whether a statement supplied in pursuance of section 136(2)(b) (written statement of certain terms of tenancy) is accurate notwithstanding that no other relief is sought than a declaration.

(3)    If a person takes proceedings in the High Court which, by virtue of this section, he could have taken in the county court, he is not entitled to recover any costs.

(4)–(6)  ...

**[1025]**

**NOTES**

Sub-ss (4)–(6): repealed by the Constitutional Reform Act 2005, ss 15(1), 146, Sch 4, paras 256, 257, Sch 18, Pt 2.

### 139  Meaning of "dwelling-house"

(1)    For the purposes of this Chapter a dwelling-house may be a house or a part of a house.

(2)    Land let together with a dwelling-house shall be treated for the purposes of this Chapter as part of the dwelling-house unless the land is agricultural land which would not be treated as part of a dwelling-house for the purposes of Part IV of the Housing Act 1985 (see section 112(2) of that Act).

**[1026]**

### 140  Members of a person's family: Chapter I

(1)    A person is a member of another's family within the meaning of this Chapter if—

    (a)    he is the spouse [or civil partner] of that person, or he and that person live together as husband and wife [or as if they were civil partners], or

    (b)    he is that person's parent, grandparent, child, grandchild, brother, sister, uncle, aunt, nephew or niece.

(2)    For the purpose of subsection (1)(b)—

    (a)    a relationship by marriage [or civil partnership] shall be treated as a relationship by blood,

    (b)    a relationship of the half-blood shall be treated as a relationship of the whole blood, and

    (c)    the stepchild of a person shall be treated as his child.

**[1027]**

**NOTES**

Words in square brackets inserted by the Civil Partnership Act 2004, s 81, Sch 8, para 51.

### 141  Consequential amendments: introductory tenancies

(1)    The enactments mentioned in Schedule 14 have effect with the amendments specified there which are consequential on the provisions of this Chapter.

(2)    The Secretary of State may by order make such other amendments or repeals of any enactment as appear to him necessary or expedient in consequence of the provisions of this Chapter.

(3)   Without prejudice to the generality of subsection (2), an order under that subsection may make such provision in relation to an enactment as the Secretary of State considers appropriate as regards its application (with or without modifications) or non-application in relation to introductory tenants or introductory tenancies.

**[1028]**

## NOTES

Orders: the Housing Act 1996 (Consequential Amendments) Order 1997, SI 1997/74.

## 142   Regulations and orders

Any regulations or orders under this Part—
(a)   may contain such incidental, supplementary or transitional provisions, or savings, as the Secretary of State thinks fit, and
(b)   shall be made by statutory instrument which shall be subject to annulment in pursuance of a resolution of either House of Parliament.

**[1029]**

## 143   Index of defined expressions: introductory tenancies

The following Table shows provisions defining or otherwise explaining provisions used in this Chapter (other than provisions defining or explaining an expression in the same section)—

| | |
|---|---|
| adopt (in relation to periodic tenancy) | section 124(4) |
| assured tenancy and assured shorthold tenancy | section 230 |
| dwelling-house | section 139 |
| housing action trust | section 230 |
| introductory tenancy and introductory tenant | section 124 |
| local housing authority | section 230 |
| member of family | section 140 |
| registered social landlord | section 2 |
| secure tenancy and secure tenant | section 230 |

**[1030]**

## [CHAPTER 1A
## DEMOTED TENANCIES

*General provisions*

## 143A   Demoted tenancies

(1)   This section applies to a periodic tenancy of a dwelling-house if each of the following conditions is satisfied.

(2)   The first condition is that the landlord is either a local housing authority or a housing action trust.

(3)   The second condition is that the tenant condition in section 81 of the Housing Act 1985 is satisfied.

(4)   The third condition is that the tenancy is created by virtue of a demotion order under section 82A of that Act.

(5)   In this Chapter—
(a)   a tenancy to which this section applies is referred to as a demoted tenancy;
(b)   references to demoted tenants must be construed accordingly.]

**[1031]**

## NOTES

Commencement: 30 June 2004 (in relation to England); 30 September 2004 (in relation to Wales for the purpose of making regulations); 30 April 2005 (otherwise).
Chapter 1A (ss 143A–143P) inserted by the Anti-social Behaviour Act 2003, s 14(5), Sch 1, para 1.

## [143B   Duration of demoted tenancy

(1)   A demoted tenancy becomes a secure tenancy at the end of the period of one year (the demotion period) starting with the day the demotion order takes effect; but this is subject to subsections (2) to (5).

(2)   A tenancy ceases to be a demoted tenancy if any of the following paragraphs applies—
  (a)   either of the first or second conditions in section 143A ceases to be satisfied;
  (b)   the demotion order is quashed;
  (c)   the tenant dies and no one is entitled to succeed to the tenancy.

(3)   If at any time before the end of the demotion period the landlord serves a notice of proceedings for possession of the dwelling-house subsection (4) applies.

(4)   The tenancy continues as a demoted tenancy until the end of the demotion period or (if later) until any of the following occurs—
  (a)   the notice of proceedings is withdrawn by the landlord;
  (b)   the proceedings are determined in favour of the tenant;
  (c)   the period of 6 months beginning with the date on which the notice is served ends and no proceedings for possession have been brought.

(5)   A tenancy does not come to an end merely because it ceases to be a demoted tenancy.]

**[1032]**

**NOTES**
Commencement: 30 June 2004 (in relation to England); 30 September 2004 (in relation to Wales for the purpose of making regulations); 30 April 2005 (otherwise).
Inserted as noted to s 143A at **[1031]**.

## [143C   Change of landlord

(1)   A tenancy continues to be a demoted tenancy for the duration of the demotion period if—
  (a)   at the time the demoted tenancy is created the interest of the landlord belongs to a local housing authority or a housing action trust, and
  (b)   during the demotion period the interest of the landlord transfers to another person who is a local housing authority or a housing action trust.

(2)   Subsections (3) and (4) apply if—
  (a)   at the time the demoted tenancy is created the interest of the landlord belongs to a local housing authority or a housing action trust, and
  (b)   during the demotion period the interest of the landlord transfers to a person who is not such a body.

(3)   If the new landlord is a registered social landlord or a person who does not satisfy the landlord condition the tenancy becomes an assured shorthold tenancy.

(4)   If the new landlord is not a registered social landlord and does satisfy the landlord condition the tenancy becomes a secure tenancy.

(5)   The landlord condition must be construed in accordance with section 80 of the Housing Act 1985.]

**[1033]**

**NOTES**
Commencement: 30 June 2004 (in relation to England); 30 September 2004 (in relation to Wales for the purpose of making regulations); 30 April 2005 (otherwise).
Inserted as noted to s 143A at **[1031]**.

*[Proceedings for possession*

## 143D   Proceedings for possession

(1)   The landlord may only bring a demoted tenancy to an end by obtaining[—
  (a)   an order of the court for the possession of the dwelling-house, and
  (b)   the execution of the order.]

[(1A)   In such a case, the tenancy ends when the order is executed.]

(2)   The court must make an order for possession unless it thinks that the procedure under sections 143E and 143F has not been followed.

(3)   ... ]

**[1034]**

**NOTES**
Commencement: 30 June 2004 (in relation to England); 30 September 2004 (in relation to Wales for the purpose of making regulations); 30 April 2005 (otherwise).
Inserted as noted to s 143A at **[1031]**.
Sub-s (1): words in square brackets substituted by the Housing and Regeneration Act 2008, s 299, Sch 11, Pt 1, paras 10, 13(1), (2), subject to transitional provisions in Sch 11, Pt 1, para 14 thereto at **[1891]**.
Sub-s (1A): inserted by the Housing and Regeneration Act 2008, s 299, Sch 11, Pt 1, paras 10, 13(1), (3), subject to transitional provisions in Sch 11, Pt 1, para 14 thereto at **[1891]**.

Sub-s (3): repealed by the Housing and Regeneration Act 2008, ss 299, 321(1), Sch 11, Pt 1, paras 10, 13(1), (4), Sch 16, subject to transitional provisions in Sch 11, Pt 1, para 14 thereto at **[1891]**.

PART I
STATUTES

### [143E   Notice of proceedings for possession

(1)   Proceedings for possession of a dwelling-house let under a demoted tenancy must not be brought unless the landlord has served on the tenant a notice of proceedings under this section.

(2)   The notice must—
  (a)   state that the court will be asked to make an order for the possession of the dwelling-house;
  (b)   set out the reasons for the landlord's decision to apply for the order;
  (c)   specify the date after which proceedings for the possession of the dwelling-house may be begun;
  (d)   inform the tenant of his right to request a review of the landlord's decision and of the time within which the request must be made.

(3)   The date specified under subsection (2)(c) must not be earlier than the date on which the tenancy could (apart from this Chapter) be brought to an end by notice to quit given by the landlord on the same date as the notice of proceedings.

(4)   The court must not entertain proceedings begun on or before the date specified under subsection (2)(c).

(5)   The notice must also inform the tenant that if he needs help or advice—
  (a)   about the notice, or
  (b)   about what to do about the notice,

he must take the notice immediately to a Citizen's Advice Bureau, a housing aid centre, a law centre or a solicitor.]

**[1035]**

#### NOTES
Commencement: 30 June 2004 (in relation to England); 30 September 2004 (in relation to Wales for the purpose of making regulations); 30 April 2005 (otherwise).
Inserted as noted to s 143A at **[1031]**.

### [143F   Review of decision to seek possession

(1)   Before the end of the period of 14 days beginning with the date of service of a notice for possession of a dwelling-house let under a demoted tenancy the tenant may request the landlord to review its decision to seek an order for possession.

(2)   If a request is made in accordance with subsection (1) the landlord must review the decision.

(3)   The Secretary of State may by regulations make provision as to the procedure to be followed in connection with a review under this section.

(4)   The regulations may include provision—
  (a)   requiring the decision on review to be made by a person of appropriate seniority who was not involved in the original decision;
  (b)   as to the circumstances in which the tenant is entitled to an oral hearing, and whether and by whom he may be represented at the hearing.

(5)   The landlord must notify the tenant—
  (a)   of the decision on the review;
  (b)   of the reasons for the decision.

(6)   The review must be carried out and notice given under subsection (5) before the date specified in the notice of proceedings as the date after which proceedings for possession of the dwelling-house may be begun.]

**[1036]**

#### NOTES
Commencement: 30 June 2004 (in relation to England); 30 September 2004 (in relation to Wales for the purpose of making regulations); 30 April 2005 (otherwise).
Inserted as noted to s 143A at **[1031]**.
Regulations: the Demoted Tenancies (Review of Decisions) (England) Regulations 2004, SI 2004/1679 at **[3366]**; the Demoted Tenancies (Review of Decisions) (Wales) Regulations 2005, SI 2005/1228 at **[3445]**.

### [143G   Effect of proceedings for possession

(1)   This section applies if the landlord has begun proceedings for the possession of a dwelling-house let under a demoted tenancy and—
  (a)   the demotion period ends, or

(b)    any of paragraphs (a) to (c) of section 143B(2) applies (circumstances in which a tenancy ceases to be a demoted tenancy).

(2)    If any of paragraphs (a) to (c) of section 143B(2) applies the tenancy ceases to be a demoted tenancy but the landlord (or the new landlord as the case may be) may continue the proceedings.

(3)    Subsection (4) applies if in accordance with subsection (2) a tenancy ceases to be a demoted tenancy and becomes a secure tenancy.

(4)    The tenant is not entitled to exercise the right to buy unless—
(a)    the proceedings are finally determined, and
(b)    he is not required to give up possession of the dwelling-house.

(5)    The proceedings must be treated as finally determined if—
(a)    they are withdrawn;
(b)    any appeal is abandoned;
(c)    the time for appealing expires without an appeal being brought.]

**[1037]**

NOTES
Commencement: 30 June 2004 (in relation to England); 30 September 2004 (in relation to Wales for the purpose of making regulations); 30 April 2005 (otherwise).
Inserted as noted to s 143A at **[1031]**.

*[Succession*

**143H    Succession to demoted tenancy**

(1)    This section applies if the tenant under a demoted tenancy dies.

(2)    If the tenant was a successor, the tenancy—
(a)    ceases to be a demoted tenancy, but
(b)    does not become a secure tenancy.

(3)    In any other case a person is qualified to succeed the tenant if—
(a)    he occupies the dwelling-house as his only or principal home at the time of the tenant's death,
(b)    he is a member of the tenant's family, and
(c)    he has resided with the tenant throughout the period of 12 months ending with the tenant's death.

(4)    If only one person is qualified to succeed under subsection (3) the tenancy vests in him by virtue of this section.

(5)    If there is more than one such person the tenancy vests by virtue of this section in the person preferred in accordance with the following rules—
(a)    the tenant's [spouse or civil partner or (if the tenant has neither spouse nor civil partner)] the person mentioned in section 143P(1)(b) is to be preferred to another member of the tenant's family;
(b)    if there are two or more other members of the tenant's family the person preferred may be agreed between them or (if there is no such agreement) selected by the landlord.]

**[1038]**

NOTES
Commencement: 30 June 2004 (in relation to England); 30 September 2004 (in relation to Wales for the purpose of making regulations); 30 April 2005 (otherwise).
Inserted as noted to s 143A at **[1031]**.
Sub-s (5): words in square brackets substituted by the Civil Partnership Act 2004, s 81, Sch 8, para 55.

**[143I    No successor tenant: termination**

(1)    This section applies if the demoted tenant dies and no person is qualified to succeed to the tenancy as mentioned in section 143H(3).

(2)    The tenancy ceases to be a demoted tenancy if either subsection (3) or (4) applies.

(3)    This subsection applies if the tenancy is vested or otherwise disposed of in the course of the administration of the tenant's estate unless the vesting or other disposal is in pursuance of an order under—
(a)    section 23A or 24 of the Matrimonial Causes Act 1973 (property adjustment orders in connection with matrimonial proceedings);
(b)    section 17(1) of the Matrimonial and Family Proceedings Act 1984 (property adjustment orders after overseas divorce, etc);
(c)    paragraph 1 of Schedule 1 to the Children Act 1989 (orders for financial relief against parents);
[(d)    Part 2 of Schedule 5, or paragraph 9(2) or (3) of Schedule 7, to the Civil Partnership

Act 2004 (property adjustment orders in connection with civil partnership proceedings or after overseas dissolution of civil partnership, etc)].

(4) This subsection applies if it is known that when the tenancy is vested or otherwise disposed of in the course of the administration of the tenant's estate it will not be in pursuance of an order mentioned in subsection (3).

(5) A tenancy which ceases to be a demoted tenancy by virtue of this section cannot subsequently become a secure tenancy.]

**[1039]**

**NOTES**

Commencement: 30 June 2004 (in relation to England); 30 September 2004 (in relation to Wales for the purpose of making regulations); 30 April 2005 (otherwise).
Inserted as noted to s 143A at **[1031]**.
Sub-s (3): para (d) inserted by the Civil Partnership Act 2004, s 81, Sch 8, para 56.

## [143J Successor tenants

(1) This section applies for the purpose of sections 143H and 143I.

(2) A person is a successor to a secure tenancy which is terminated by a demotion order if any of subsections (3) to (6) applies to him.

(3) The tenancy vested in him—
   (a) by virtue of section 89 of the Housing Act 1985 or section 133 of this Act;
   (b) under the will or intestacy of the preceding tenant.

(4) The tenancy arose by virtue of section 86 of the Housing Act 1985 and the original fixed term was granted—
   (a) to another person, or
   (b) to him jointly with another person.

(5) He became the tenant on the tenancy being assigned to him unless—
   [(a) the tenancy was assigned—
      (i) in proceedings under section 24 of the Matrimonial Causes Act 1973 (property adjustment orders in connection with matrimonial proceedings) or section 17(1) of the Matrimonial and Family Proceedings Act 1984 (property adjustment orders after overseas divorce, etc), or
      (ii) in proceedings under Part 2 of Schedule 5, or paragraph 9(2) or (3) of Schedule 7, to the Civil Partnership Act 2004 (property adjustment orders in connection with civil partnership proceedings or after overseas dissolution of civil partnership, etc),
   (b) where the tenancy was assigned as mentioned in paragraph (a)(i), neither he nor the other party to the marriage was a successor, and
   (c) where the tenancy was assigned as mentioned in paragraph (a)(ii), neither he nor the other civil partner was a successor.]

(6) He became the tenant on assignment under section 92 of the Housing Act 1985 if he himself was a successor to the tenancy which he assigned in exchange.

(7) A person is the successor to a demoted tenancy if the tenancy vested in him by virtue of section 143H(4) or (5).

(8) A person is the successor to a joint tenancy if he has become the sole tenant.]

**[1040]**

**NOTES**

Commencement: 30 June 2004 (in relation to England); 30 September 2004 (in relation to Wales for the purpose of making regulations); 30 April 2005 (otherwise).
Inserted as noted to s 143A at **[1031]**.
Sub-s (5): paras (a)–(c) substituted for original paras (a), (b), by the Civil Partnership Act 2004, s 81, Sch 8, para 57.

*[Assignment*

## 143K Restriction on assignment

(1) A demoted tenancy is not capable of being assigned except as mentioned in subsection (2).

(2) The exceptions are assignment in pursuance of an order made under—
   (a) section 24 of the Matrimonial Causes Act 1973 (property adjustment orders in connection with matrimonial proceedings);
   (b) section 17(1) of the Matrimonial and Family Proceedings Act 1984 (property adjustment orders after overseas divorce, etc.);
   (c) paragraph 1 of Schedule 1 to the Children Act 1989 (orders for financial relief against parents);

[(d) Part 2 of Schedule 5, or paragraph 9(2) or (3) of Schedule 7, to the Civil Partnership Act 2004 (property adjustment orders in connection with civil partnership proceedings or after overseas dissolution of civil partnership, etc)].]

**[1041]**

**NOTES**
Commencement: 30 June 2004 (in relation to England); 30 September 2004 (in relation to Wales for the purpose of making regulations); 30 April 2005 (otherwise).
Inserted as noted to s 143A at **[1031]**.
Sub-s (2): para (d) added by the Civil Partnership Act 2004, s 81, Sch 8, para 58.

*[Repairs*

**143L Right to carry out repairs**
The Secretary of State may by regulations under section 96 of the Housing Act 1985 (secure tenants: right to carry out repairs) apply to demoted tenants any provision made under that section in relation to secure tenants.]

**[1042]**

**NOTES**
Commencement: 30 June 2004 (in relation to England); 30 September 2004 (in relation to Wales for the purpose of making regulations); 30 April 2005 (otherwise).
Inserted as noted to s 143A at **[1031]**.

*[Provision of information*

**143M Provision of information**
(1) This section applies to a local housing authority or a housing action trust if it is the landlord of a demoted tenancy.

(2) The landlord must from time to time publish information about the demoted tenancy in such form as it thinks best suited to explain in simple terms and so far as it considers appropriate the effect of—
   (a) the express terms of the demoted tenancy;
   (b) the provisions of this Chapter;
   (c) the provisions of sections 11 to 16 of the Landlord and Tenant Act 1985 (landlord's repairing obligations).

(3) The landlord must ensure that information published under subsection (2) is, so far as is reasonably practicable, kept up to date.

(4) The landlord must supply the tenant with—
   (a) a copy of the information published under subsection (2);
   (b) a written statement of the terms of the tenancy, so far as they are neither expressed in the lease or written tenancy agreement (if any) nor implied by law.

(5) The statement required by subsection (4)(b) must be supplied on the grant of the tenancy or as soon as practicable afterwards.]

**[1043]**

**NOTES**
Commencement: 30 June 2004 (in relation to England); 30 September 2004 (in relation to Wales for the purpose of making regulations); 30 April 2005 (otherwise).
Inserted as noted to s 143A at **[1031]**.

*[Supplementary*

**143N Jurisdiction of county court**
(1) A county court has jurisdiction—
   (a) to determine questions arising under this Chapter;
   (b) to entertain proceedings brought under this Chapter;
   (c) to determine claims (for whatever amount) in connection with a demoted tenancy.

(2) The jurisdiction includes jurisdiction to entertain proceedings as to whether a statement supplied in pursuance of section 143M(4)(b) (written statement of certain terms of tenancy) is accurate.

(3) For the purposes of subsection (2) it is immaterial that no relief other than a declaration is sought.

(4) If a person takes proceedings in the High Court which, by virtue of this section, he could have taken in the county court he is not entitled to recover any costs.

(5)–(7) ... ]

**[1044]**

PART I
STATUTES

**NOTES**

Commencement: 30 June 2004 (in relation to England); 30 September 2004 (in relation to Wales for the purpose of making regulations); 30 April 2005 (otherwise).

Inserted as noted to s 143A at **[1031]**.

Sub-ss (5)–(7): repealed by the Constitutional Reform Act 2005, ss 15(1), 146, Sch 4, Pt 1, paras 256, 258, Sch 18, Pt 2.

## [143O    Meaning of dwelling house

(1)    For the purposes of this Chapter a dwelling-house may be a house or a part of a house.

(2)    Land let together with a dwelling-house must be treated for the purposes of this Chapter as part of the dwelling-house unless the land is agricultural land which would not be treated as part of a dwelling-house for the purposes of Part 4 of the Housing Act 1985.]

**[1045]**

**NOTES**

Commencement: 30 June 2004 (in relation to England); 30 September 2004 (in relation to Wales for the purpose of making regulations); 30 April 2005 (otherwise).

Inserted as noted to s 143A at **[1031]**.

## [143P    Members of a person's family

(1)    For the purposes of this Chapter a person is a member of another's family if—
- (a)    he is the spouse [or civil partner] of that person;
- (b)    he and that person live together as a couple in an enduring family relationship, but he does not fall within paragraph (c);
- (c)    he is that person's parent, grandparent, child, grandchild, brother, sister, uncle, aunt, nephew or niece.

(2)    For the purposes of subsection (1)(b) it is immaterial that two persons living together in an enduring family relationship are of the same sex.

(3)    For the purposes of subsection (1)(c)—
- (a)    a relationship by marriage [or civil partnership] must be treated as a relationship by blood;
- (b)    a relationship of the half-blood must be treated as a relationship of the whole blood;
- (c)    a stepchild of a person must be treated as his child.]

**[1046]**

**NOTES**

Commencement: 30 June 2004 (in relation to England); 30 September 2004 (in relation to Wales for the purpose of making regulations); 30 April 2005 (otherwise).

Inserted as noted to s 143A at **[1031]**.

Sub-ss (1), (3): words in square brackets inserted by the Civil Partnership Act 2004, s 81, Sch 8, para 59.

**144–151**    ((*Ch II) ss 144–146 amend the Housing Act 1985, Sch 2, Pt I at* **[576]***; s 147 substitutes ss 83, 83A of that Act, for original s 83 at* **[420]**, **[421]**, *and amends s 84 of, and Sch 2, Pt III to, that Act at* **[422]**, **[578]***; ss 148, 149 amend the Housing Act 1988, Sch 2, Pt II at* **[786]***; s 150 inserts s 8A of the 1988 Act at* **[738]***; s 151 amends s 8 of the 1988 Act at* **[737]**.)

## CHAPTER III
## INJUNCTIONS AGAINST ANTI-SOCIAL BEHAVIOUR

**152, 153**    (*Repealed by the Anti-social Behaviour Act 2003, ss 13(1), (2), 92, Sch 3; for savings see the Anti-social Behaviour Act 2003 (Commencement No 3 and Savings) Order 2004, SI 2004/1502, art 2, Schedule, para 1 and the Anti-social Behaviour Act 2003 (Commencement No 2 and Savings) (Wales) Order 2004, SI 2004/2557, art 2, Schedule, para 1.)*

## [153A    Anti-social behaviour injunction

(1)    In this section—

"anti-social behaviour injunction" means an injunction that prohibits the person in respect of whom it is granted from engaging in housing-related anti-social conduct of a kind specified in the injunction;

"anti-social conduct" means conduct capable of causing nuisance or annoyance to some person (who need not be a particular identified person);

"conduct" means conduct anywhere;

"housing-related" means directly or indirectly relating to or affecting the housing management functions of a relevant landlord.

(2)   The court on the application of a relevant landlord may grant an anti-social behaviour injunction if the condition in subsection (3) is satisfied.

(3)   The condition is that the person against whom the injunction is sought is engaging, has engaged or threatens to engage in housing-related conduct capable of causing a nuisance or annoyance to—

(a)   a person with a right (of whatever description) to reside in or occupy housing accommodation owned or managed by a relevant landlord,

(b)   a person with a right (of whatever description) to reside in or occupy other housing accommodation in the neighbourhood of housing accommodation mentioned in paragraph (a),

(c)   a person engaged in lawful activity in, or in the neighbourhood of, housing accommodation mentioned in paragraph (a), or

(d)   a person employed (whether or not by a relevant landlord) in connection with the exercise of a relevant landlord's housing management functions.

(4)   Without prejudice to the generality of the court's power under subsection (2), a kind of conduct may be described in an anti-social behaviour injunction by reference to a person or persons and, if it is, may (in particular) be described by reference—

(a)   to persons generally,

(b)   to persons of a description specified in the injunction, or

(c)   to persons, or a person, specified in the injunction.]

**[1047]**

**NOTES**
Commencement: 6 April 2007.
Inserted, together with ss 153B–153E, by the Anti-social Behaviour Act 2003, s 13(1), (3) (subject to savings in the Anti-social Behaviour Act 2003 (Commencement No 3 and Savings) Order 2004, SI 2004/1502, art 2, Schedule, para 1 and the Anti-social Behaviour Act 2003 (Commencement No 2 and Savings) (Wales) Order 2004, SI 2004/2557, art 2, Schedule, para 1); substituted by the Police and Justice Act 2006, s 26, except in relation to any application for an injunction by a relevant landlord (other than a relevant Welsh landlord) made before 6 April 2007.

**[153B   Injunction against unlawful use of premises**

(1)   This section applies to conduct which consists of or involves using or threatening to use housing accommodation owned or managed by a relevant landlord for an unlawful purpose.

(2)   The court on the application of the relevant landlord may grant an injunction prohibiting the person in respect of whom the injunction is granted from engaging in conduct to which this section applies.]

**[1048]**

**NOTES**
Inserted, together with original s 153A and ss 153C–153E, by the Anti-social Behaviour Act 2003, s 13(1), (3); for savings see the Anti-social Behaviour Act 2003 (Commencement No 3 and Savings) Order 2004, SI 2004/1502, art 2, Schedule, para 1 and the Anti-social Behaviour Act 2003 (Commencement No 2 and Savings) (Wales) Order 2004, SI 2004/2557, art 2, Schedule, para 1.

**[153C   Injunctions: exclusion order and power of arrest**

(1)   This section applies if the court grants an injunction under subsection (2) of section 153A or 153B and it thinks that either of the following paragraphs applies—

(a)   the conduct consists of or includes the use or threatened use of violence;

(b)   there is a significant risk of harm to a person mentioned in [any of paragraphs (a) to (d) of section 153A(3)].

(2)   The court may include in the injunction a provision prohibiting the person in respect of whom it is granted from entering or being in—

(a)   any premises specified in the injunction;

(b)   any area specified in the injunction.

(3)   The court may attach a power of arrest to any provision of the injunction.]

**[1049]**

**NOTES**
Inserted as noted to s 153B at **[1048]**.
Sub-s (1): words in square brackets substituted for original words "section 153A(4)" by the Police and Justice Act 2006, s 52, Sch 14, para 32(a), except in relation to any application for an injunction by a relevant landlord (other than a relevant Welsh landlord) made before 6 April 2007.

**[153D    Injunction against breach of tenancy agreement**

(1)    This section applies if a relevant landlord applies for an injunction against a tenant in respect of the breach or anticipated breach of a tenancy agreement on the grounds that the tenant—

   (a)    is engaging or threatening to engage in conduct that is capable of causing nuisance or annoyance to any person, or

   (b)    is allowing, inciting or encouraging any other person to engage or threaten to engage in such conduct.

(2)    The court may proceed under subsection (3) or (4) if it is satisfied—

   (a)    that the conduct includes the use or threatened use of violence, or

   (b)    that there is a significant risk of harm to any person.

(3)    The court may include in the injunction a provision prohibiting the person in respect of whom it is granted from entering or being in—

   (a)    any premises specified in the injunction;

   (b)    any area specified in the injunction.

(4)    The court may attach a power of arrest to any provision of the injunction.

(5)    Tenancy agreement includes any agreement for the occupation of residential accommodation owned or managed by a relevant landlord.]

**[1050]**

---

**NOTES**

Inserted as noted to s 153B at **[1048]**.

---

**[153E    Injunctions: supplementary**

(1)    This section applies for the purposes of sections 153A to 153D.

(2)    An injunction may—

   (a)    be made for a specified period or until varied or discharged;

   (b)    have the effect of excluding a person from his normal place of residence.

(3)    An injunction may be varied or discharged by the court on an application by—

   (a)    the person in respect of whom it is made;

   (b)    the relevant landlord.

(4)    If the court thinks it just and convenient it may grant or vary an injunction without the respondent having been given such notice as is otherwise required by rules of court.

(5)    If the court acts under subsection (4) it must give the person against whom the injunction is made an opportunity to make representations in relation to the injunction as soon as it is practicable for him to do so.

(6)    The court is the High Court or a county court.

(7)    Each of the following is a relevant landlord—

   (a)    a housing action trust;

   (b)    a local authority (within the meaning of the Housing Act 1985);

   (c)    a registered social landlord.

(8)    A charitable housing trust which is not a registered social landlord is also a relevant landlord for the purposes of section 153D.

(9)    Housing accommodation includes—

   (a)    flats, lodging-houses and hostels;

   (b)    any yard, garden, outhouses and appurtenances belonging to the accommodation or usually enjoyed with it;

   (c)    in relation to a neighbourhood, the whole of the housing accommodation owned or managed by a relevant landlord in the neighbourhood and any common areas used in connection with the accommodation.

(10)    A landlord owns housing accommodation if either of the following paragraphs applies to him—

   (a)    he is a person (other than a mortgagee not in possession) who is for the time being entitled to dispose of the fee simple in the premises, whether in possession or in reversion;

   (b)    he is a person who holds or is entitled to the rents and profits of the premises under a lease which (when granted) was for a term of not less than three years.

(11)    The housing management functions of a relevant landlord include—

   (a)    functions conferred by or under any enactment;

   (b)    the powers and duties of the landlord as the holder of an estate or interest in housing accommodation.

(12)    Harm includes serious ill-treatment or abuse (whether physical or not).]

**[1051]**

**NOTES**
Inserted as noted to s 153B at **[1048]**.

### 154   Powers of arrest: ex parte applications for injunctions

(1)   In determining whether to exercise its power under [section 153C(3) or 153D(4)] to attach a power of arrest to an injunction which it intends to grant on an ex-parte application, the High Court or a county court shall have regard to all the circumstances including—

(a)   whether it is likely that the applicant will be deterred or prevented from seeking the exercise of the power if the power is not exercised immediately, and

(b)   whether there is reason to believe that the respondent is aware of the proceedings for the injunction but is deliberately evading service and that the applicant or any person of a description mentioned in [any of paragraphs (a) to (d) of section 153A(3)] (as the case may be) will be seriously prejudiced if the decision as to whether to exercise the power were delayed until substituted service is effected.

(2)   Where the court exercises its power as mentioned in subsection (1), it shall afford the respondent an opportunity to make representations relating to the exercise of the power as soon as just and convenient at a hearing of which notice has been given to all the parties in accordance with rules of court.

**[1052]**

**NOTES**
Sub-s (1): words in first pair of square brackets substituted by the Anti-social Behaviour Act 2003, s 13(1), (4)(a) (for savings see the Anti-social Behaviour Act 2003 (Commencement No 3 and Savings) Order 2004, SI 2004/1502, art 2, Schedule, para 1 and the Anti-social Behaviour Act 2003 (Commencement No 2 and Savings) (Wales) Order 2004, SI 2004/2557, art 2, Schedule, para 1); words in second pair of square brackets substituted for words "section 153A(4)" (as previously substituted by the Anti-social Behaviour Act 2003, s 13(1), (4)(b), subject to savings as noted above) by the Police and Justice Act 2006, s 52, Sch 14, para 32(b), except in relation to any application for an injunction by a relevant landlord (other than a relevant Welsh landlord) made before 6 April 2007.

### 155   Arrest and remand

(1)   If a power of arrest is attached to certain provisions of an injunction by virtue of [section 153C(3) or 153D(4)], a constable may arrest without warrant a person whom he has reasonable cause for suspecting to be in breach of any such provision or otherwise in contempt of court in relation to a breach of any such provision.

A constable shall after making any such arrest forthwith inform the person on whose application the injunction was granted.

(2)   Where a person is arrested under subsection (1)—

(a)   he shall be brought before the relevant judge within the period of 24 hours beginning at the time of his arrest, and

(b)   if the matter is not then disposed of forthwith, the judge may remand him.

In reckoning for the purposes of this subsection any period of 24 hours no account shall be taken of Christmas Day, Good Friday or any Sunday.

(3)   If the court has granted an injunction in circumstances such that a power of arrest could have been attached under [section 153C(3) or 153D(4)] but—

(a)   has not attached a power of arrest under the section in question to any provisions of the injunction, or

(b)   has attached that power only to certain provisions of the injunction,

then, if at any time the applicant considers that the respondent has failed to comply with the injunction, he may apply to the relevant judge for the issue of a warrant for the arrest of the respondent.

(4)   The relevant judge shall not issue a warrant on an application under subsection (3) unless—

(a)   the application is substantiated on oath, and

(b)   he has reasonable grounds for believing that the respondent has failed to comply with the injunction.

(5)   If a person is brought before a court by virtue of a warrant issued under subsection (4) and the court does not dispose of the matter forthwith, the court may remand him.

(6)   Schedule 15 (which makes provision corresponding to that applying in magistrates' courts in civil cases under sections 128 and 129 of the Magistrates' Courts Act 1980) applies in relation to the powers of the High Court and a county court to remand a person under this section.

(7)   If a person remanded under this section is granted bail by virtue of subsection (6), he may be required by the relevant judge to comply, before release on bail or later, with such requirements as appear to the judge to be necessary to secure that he does not interfere with witness or otherwise obstruct the course of justice.

**[1053]**

**NOTES**
Sub-ss (1), (3): words in square brackets substituted by the Anti-social Behaviour Act 2003, s 13(1), (5); for savings see the Anti-social Behaviour Act 2003 (Commencement No 3 and Savings) Order 2004, SI 2004/1502, art 2, Schedule, para 1 and the Anti-social Behaviour Act 2003 (Commencement No 2 and Savings) (Wales) Order 2004, SI 2004/2557, art 2, Schedule, para 1.

### 156   Remand for medical examination and report

(1)   If the relevant judge has reason to consider that a medical report will be required, any power to remand a person under section 155 may be exercised for the purpose of enabling a medical examination and report to be made.

(2)   If such a power is so exercised the adjournment shall not be for more than 4 weeks at a time unless the judge remands the accused in custody.

(3)   If the judge so remands the accused, the adjournment shall not be for more than 3 weeks at a time.

(4)   If there is reason to suspect that a person who has been arrested—
    (a)    under section 155(1), or
    (b)    under a warrant issued under section 155(4),
is suffering from [mental disorder within the meaning of the Mental Health Act 1983], the relevant judge shall have the same power to make an order under section 35 of [that Act] (remand for report on accused's mental condition) as the Crown Court has under [that section] in the case of an accused person within the meaning of that section.

**[1054]**

**NOTES**
Sub-s (4): words in square brackets substituted by the Mental Health Act 2007, s 1(4), Sch 1, Pt 2, para 21, subject to transitional provisions and savings in Sch 10, paras 1, 2(1)–(3), (4)(a) thereto.

### 157   Powers of arrest: supplementary provisions

(1)   If in exercise of its power under [section 153C(3) or 153D(4)] the High Court or a county court attaches a power of arrest to any provisions of an injunction, it may provide that the power of arrest is to have effect for a shorter period than the other provisions of the injunction.

(2)   Any period specified for the purposes of subsection (1) may be extended by the court (on one or more occasions) on an application to vary or discharge the injunction.

(3)   If a power of arrest has been attached to certain provisions of an injunction by virtue of [section 153C(3) or 153D(4)], the court may vary or discharge the injunction in so far as it confers a power of arrest (whether or not any application has been made to vary or discharge any other provision of the injunction).

(4)   An injunction may be varied or discharged under subsection (3) on an application by the respondent or the person on whose application the injunction was made.

**[1055]**

**NOTES**
Sub-ss (1), (3): words in square brackets substituted by the Anti-social Behaviour Act 2003, s 13(1), (6); for savings see the Anti-social Behaviour Act 2003 (Commencement No 3 and Savings) Order 2004, SI 2004/1502, art 2, Schedule, para 1 and the Anti-social Behaviour Act 2003 (Commencement No 2 and Savings) (Wales) Order 2004, SI 2004/2557, art 2, Schedule, para 1.

### 158   Interpretation: Chapter III

(1)   For the purposes of this Chapter—
    "charitable housing trust" means a housing trust, within the meaning of the Housing Associations Act 1985, which is a charity within the meaning of the Charities Act 1993;
    .....
    "relevant judge", in relation to an injunction, means—
        (a)    where the injunction was granted by the High Court, a judge of that court,
        (b)    where the injunction was granted by a county court, a judge or district judge of that or any other county court;
    "tenancy" includes a licence, and "tenant" and "landlord" shall be construed accordingly.

(2)   ...

**[1056]**

**NOTES**

Sub-s (1): definitions omitted repealed by the Anti-social Behaviour Act 2003, ss 13(1), (7)(a), 92, Sch 3; for savings see the Anti-social Behaviour Act 2003 (Commencement No 3 and Savings) Order 2004, SI 2004/1502, art 2, Schedule, para 1 and the Anti-social Behaviour Act 2003 (Commencement No 2 and Savings) (Wales) Order 2004, SI 2004/2557, art 2, Schedule, para 1.

Sub-s (2): repealed by the Anti-social Behaviour Act 2003, ss 13(1), (7)(b), 92, Sch 3, subject to savings as noted above.

## PART VI
## ALLOCATION OF HOUSING ACCOMMODATION

*Introductory*

### 159   Allocation of housing accommodation

(1)   A local housing authority shall comply with the provisions of this Part in allocating housing accommodation.

(2)   For the purposes of this Part a local housing authority allocate housing accommodation when they—

(a)   select a person to be a secure or introductory tenant of housing accommodation held by them,

(b)   nominate a person to be a secure or introductory tenant of housing accommodation held by another person, or

(c)   nominate a person to be an assured tenant of housing accommodation held by a registered social landlord.

(3)   The reference in subsection (2)(a) to selecting a person to be a secure tenant includes deciding to exercise any power to notify an existing tenant or licensee that his tenancy or licence is to be a secure tenancy.

(4)   The references in subsection (2)(b) and (c) to nominating a person include nominating a person in pursuance of any arrangements (whether legally enforceable or not) to require that housing accommodation, or a specified amount of housing accommodation, is made available to a person or one of a number of persons nominated by the authority.

[(5)   The provisions of this Part do not apply to an allocation of housing accommodation to a person who is already a secure or introductory tenant unless the allocation involves a transfer of housing accommodation for that person and is made on his application.]

(7)   Subject to the provisions of this Part, a local housing authority may allocate housing accommodation in such manner as they consider appropriate.

**[1057]**

**NOTES**

Sub-s (5): substituted, for original sub-ss (5), (6), by the Homelessness Act 2002, s 13.

See further, in relation to functions of a local housing authority conferred under this Part: Local Authorities (Contracting Out of Allocation of Housing and Homelessness Functions) Order 1996, SI 1996/3205, reg 2, Sch 1.

### 160   Cases where provisions about allocation do not apply

(1)   The provisions of this Part about the allocation of housing accommodation do not apply in the following cases.

(2)   They do not apply where a secure tenancy—

(a)   vests under section 89 of the Housing Act 1985 (succession to periodic secure tenancy on death of tenant),

(b)   remains a secure tenancy by virtue of section 90 of that Act (devolution of term certain of secure tenancy on death of tenant),

(c)   is assigned under section 92 of that Act (assignment of secure tenancy by way of exchange),

(d)   is assigned to a person who would be qualified to succeed the secure tenant if the secure tenant died immediately before the assignment, or

(e)   vests or is otherwise disposed of in pursuance of an order made under—

(i)   section 24 of the Matrimonial Causes Act 1973 (property adjustment orders in connection with matrimonial proceedings),

(ii)   section 17(1) of the Matrimonial and Family Proceedings Act 1984 (property adjustment orders after overseas divorce, &c), ...

(iii)   paragraph 1 of Schedule 1 to the Children Act 1989 (orders for financial relief against parents)[, or

(iv)   Part 2 of Schedule 5, or paragraph 9(2) or (3) of Schedule 7, to the Civil

Partnership Act 2004 (property adjustment orders in connection with civil partnership proceedings or after overseas dissolution of civil partnership, etc)].

(3)   They do not apply where an introductory tenancy—
  (a)   becomes a secure tenancy on ceasing to be an introductory tenancy,
  (b)   vests under section 133(2) (succession to introductory tenancy on death of tenant),
  (c)   is assigned to a person who would be qualified to succeed the introductory tenant if the introductory tenant died immediately before the assignment, or
  (d)   vests or is otherwise disposed of in pursuance of an order made under—
    (i)   section 24 of the Matrimonial Causes Act 1973 (property adjustment orders in connection with matrimonial proceedings),
    (ii)   section 17(1) of the Matrimonial and Family Proceedings Act 1984 (property adjustment orders after overseas divorce, &c), ...
    (iii)   paragraph 1 of Schedule 1 to the Children Act 1989 (orders for financial relief against parents)[, or
    (iv)   Part 2 of Schedule 5, or paragraph 9(2) or (3) of Schedule 7, to the Civil Partnership Act 2004 (property adjustment orders in connection with civil partnership proceedings or after overseas dissolution of civil partnership, etc)].

(4)   They do not apply in such other cases as the Secretary of State may prescribe by regulations.

(5)   The regulations may be framed so as to make the exclusion of the provisions of this Part about the allocation of housing accommodation subject to such restrictions or conditions as may be specified.

In particular, those provisions may be excluded—
  (a)   in relation to specified descriptions of persons, or
  (b)   in relation to housing accommodation of a specified description or a specified proportion of housing accommodation of any specified description.

**[1058]**

**NOTES**
  Sub-s (2): word omitted from para (e)(ii) repealed and para (e)(iv) and word immediately preceding it inserted by the Civil Partnership Act 2004, ss 81, 261(4), Sch 8, para 60, Sch 30.
  Sub-s (3): word omitted from para (d)(ii) repealed and para (d)(iv) and word immediately preceding it inserted by the Civil Partnership Act 2004, ss 81, 261(4), Sch 8, para 60, Sch 30.
  Regulations: the Allocation of Housing (England) Regulations 2002, SI 2002/3264 at **[3276]**; the Allocation of Housing (Wales) Regulations 2003, SI 2003/239 at **[3279]**.

*[Eligibility for allocation of housing accommodation*

### 160A   Allocation only to eligible persons

(1)   A local housing authority shall not allocate housing accommodation—
  (a)   to a person from abroad who is ineligible for an allocation of housing accommodation by virtue of subsection (3) or (5);
  (b)   to a person who the authority have decided is to be treated as ineligible for such an allocation by virtue of subsection (7); or
  (c)   to two or more persons jointly if any of them is a person mentioned in paragraph (a) or (b).

(2)   Except as provided by subsection (1), any person may be allocated housing accommodation by a local housing authority (whether on his application or otherwise).

(3)   A person subject to immigration control within the meaning of the Asylum and Immigration Act 1996 (c 49) is (subject to subsection (6)) ineligible for an allocation of housing accommodation by a local housing authority unless he is of a class prescribed by regulations made by the Secretary of State.

(4)   No person who is excluded from entitlement to housing benefit by section 115 of the Immigration and Asylum Act 1999 (c 33) (exclusion from benefits) shall be included in any class prescribed under subsection (3).

(5)   The Secretary of State may by regulations prescribe other classes of persons from abroad who are (subject to subsection (6)) ineligible for an allocation of housing accommodation, either in relation to local housing authorities generally or any particular local housing authority.

(6)   Nothing in subsection (3) or (5) affects the eligibility of a person who is already—
  (a)   a secure or introductory tenant;
  (b)   an assured tenant of housing accommodation allocated to him by a local housing authority.

(7)   A local housing authority may decide that an applicant is to be treated as ineligible for an allocation of housing accommodation by them if they are satisfied that—

(a)  he, or a member of his household, has been guilty of unacceptable behaviour serious enough to make him unsuitable to be a tenant of the authority; and

(b)  in the circumstances at the time his application is considered, he is unsuitable to be a tenant of the authority by reason of that behaviour.

(8)  The only behaviour which may be regarded by the authority as unacceptable for the purposes of subsection (7)(a) is—

(a)  behaviour of the person concerned which would (if he were a secure tenant of the authority) entitle the authority to a possession order under section 84 of the Housing Act 1985 (c 68) on any ground mentioned in Part 1 of Schedule 2 to that Act (other than ground 8); or

(b)  behaviour of a member of his household which would (if he were a person residing with a secure tenant of the authority) entitle the authority to such a possession order.

(9)  If a local housing authority decide that an applicant for housing accommodation—

(a)  is ineligible for an allocation by them by virtue of subsection (3) or (5); or

(b)  is to be treated as ineligible for such an allocation by virtue of subsection (7),

they shall notify the applicant of their decision and the grounds for it.

(10)  That notice shall be given in writing and, if not received by the applicant, shall be treated as having been given if it is made available at the authority's office for a reasonable period for collection by him or on his behalf.

(11)  A person who is being treated by a local housing authority as ineligible by virtue of subsection (7) may (if he considers that he should no longer be treated as ineligible by the authority) make a fresh application to the authority for an allocation of housing accommodation by them.]

**[1059]**

**NOTES**

Inserted, together with preceding cross heading, by the Homelessness Act 2002, s 14(2); for effect see s 14(3), (4) thereof.

Regulations: the Allocation of Housing (England) Regulations 2002, SI 2002/3264 at **[3276]**; the Allocation of Housing (Wales) Regulations 2003, SI 2003/239 at **[3279]**; the Allocation of Housing and Homelessness (Eligibility) (England) Regulations 2006, SI 2006/1294 at **[3703]**; the Allocation of Housing and Homelessness (Miscellaneous Provisions) (England) Regulations 2006, SI 2006/2527 at **[3733]**; the Allocation of Housing and Homelessness (Eligibility) (Wales) Regulations 2009, SI 2009/393.

**161–165**  (*Repealed by the Homelessness Act 2002, ss 14(1), 18(2), Sch 2; for effect see s 14(3), (4) thereof.*)

*[Applications for housing accommodation*

## 166  Applications for housing accommodation

(1)  A local housing authority shall secure that—

(a)  advice and information is available free of charge to persons in their district about the right to make an application for an allocation of housing accommodation; and

(b)  any necessary assistance in making such an application is available free of charge to persons in their district who are likely to have difficulty in doing so without assistance.

(2)  A local housing authority shall secure that an applicant for an allocation of housing accommodation is informed that he has the rights mentioned in section 167(4A).

(3)  Every application made to a local housing authority for an allocation of housing accommodation shall (if made in accordance with the procedural requirements of the authority's allocation scheme) be considered by the authority.

(4)  The fact that a person is an applicant for an allocation of housing accommodation shall not be divulged (without his consent) to any other member of the public.

(5)  In this Part "district" in relation to a local housing authority has the same meaning as in the Housing Act 1985 (c 68).]

**[1060]**

**NOTES**

Substituted, together with preceding cross heading, by the Homelessness Act 2002, s 15.

*The allocation scheme*

## 167  Allocation in accordance with allocation scheme

(1)  Every local housing authority shall have a scheme (their "allocation scheme") for determining priorities, and as to the procedure to be followed, in allocating housing accommodation.

For this purpose "procedure" includes all aspects of the allocation process, including the persons or descriptions of persons by whom decisions are to be taken.

[(1A) The scheme shall include a statement of the authority's policy on offering people who are to be allocated housing accommodation—
- (a) a choice of housing accommodation; or
- (b) the opportunity to express preferences about the housing accommodation to be allocated to them.]

[(2) As regards priorities, the scheme shall[, subject to subsection (2ZA),] be framed so as to secure that reasonable preference is given to—
- (a) people who are homeless (within the meaning of Part 7);
- (b) people who are owed a duty by any local housing authority under section 190(2), 193(2) or 195(2) (or under section 65(2) or 68(2) of the Housing Act 1985) or who are occupying accommodation secured by any such authority under section 192(3);
- (c) people occupying insanitary or overcrowded housing or otherwise living in unsatisfactory housing conditions;
- (d) people who need to move on medical or welfare grounds [(including grounds relating to a disability)]; and
- (e) people who need to move to a particular locality in the district of the authority, where failure to meet that need would cause hardship (to themselves or to others).

The scheme may also be framed so as to give additional preference to particular descriptions of people within this subsection (being descriptions of people with urgent housing needs).

[(2ZA) People are to be disregarded for the purposes of subsection (2) if they would not have fallen within paragraph (a) or (b) of that subsection without the local housing authority having had regard to a restricted person (within the meaning of Part 7).]

(2A) The scheme may contain provision for determining priorities in allocating housing accommodation to people within subsection (2); and the factors which the scheme may allow to be taken into account include—
- (a) the financial resources available to a person to meet his housing costs;
- (b) any behaviour of a person (or of a member of his household) which affects his suitability to be a tenant;
- (c) any local connection (within the meaning of section 199) which exists between a person and the authority's district.

(2B) Nothing in subsection (2) requires the scheme to provide for any preference to be given to people the authority have decided are people to whom subsection (2C) applies.

(2C) This subsection applies to a person if the authority are satisfied that—
- (a) he, or a member of his household, has been guilty of unacceptable behaviour serious enough to make him unsuitable to be a tenant of the authority; and
- (b) in the circumstances at the time his case is considered, he deserves by reason of that behaviour not to be treated as a member of a group of people who are to be given preference by virtue of subsection (2).

(2D) Subsection (8) of section 160A applies for the purposes of subsection (2C)(a) above as it applies for the purposes of subsection (7)(a) of that section.

(2E) Subject to subsection (2), the scheme may contain provision about the allocation of particular housing accommodation—
- (a) to a person who makes a specific application for that accommodation;
- (b) to persons of a particular description (whether or not they are within subsection (2)).]

(3) The Secretary of State may by regulations—
- (a) specify further descriptions of people to whom preference is to be given as mentioned in subsection (2), or
- (b) amend or repeal any part of subsection (2).

(4) The Secretary of State may by regulations specify factors which a local housing authority shall not take into account in allocating housing accommodation.

[(4A) The scheme shall be framed so as to secure that an applicant for an allocation of housing accommodation—
- (a) has the right to request such general information as will enable him to assess—
  - (i) how his application is likely to be treated under the scheme (including in particular whether he is likely to be regarded as a member of a group of people who are to be given preference by virtue of subsection (2)); and
  - (ii) whether housing accommodation appropriate to his needs is likely to be made available to him and, if so, how long it is likely to be before such accommodation becomes available for allocation to him;
- (b) is notified in writing of any decision that he is a person to whom subsection (2C) applies and the grounds for it;
- (c) has the right to request the authority to inform him of any decision about the facts of his case which is likely to be, or has been, taken into account in considering whether to allocate housing accommodation to him; and

    (d)    has the right to request a review of a decision mentioned in paragraph (b) or (c), or in section 160A(9), and to be informed of the decision on the review and the grounds for it.]

(5)    As regards the procedure to be followed, the scheme shall be framed in accordance with such principles as the Secretary of State may prescribe by regulations.

(6)    Subject to the above provisions, and to any regulations made under them, the authority may decide on what principles the scheme is to be framed.

(7)    Before adopting an allocation scheme, or making an alteration to their scheme reflecting a major change of policy, a local housing authority shall—
    (a)    send a copy of the draft scheme, or proposed alteration, to every registered social landlord with which they have nomination arrangements (see section 159(4)), and
    (b)    afford those persons a reasonable opportunity to comment on the proposals.

(8)    A local housing authority shall not allocate housing accommodation except in accordance with their allocation scheme.

**[1061]**

**NOTES**
Sub-s (1A): inserted by the Homelessness Act 2002, s 16(1), (2).
Sub-s (2): substituted, together with sub-ss (2A)–(2E) for original sub-s (2). by the Homelessness Act 2002, s 16(1), (3); words in first pair of square brackets inserted by the Housing and Regeneration Act 2008, s 314, Sch 15, Pt 1, paras 1, 2(1), (2), except in relation to applications for an allocation of social housing or housing assistance (homelessness) or for accommodation made before 2 March 2009; words in square brackets in para (d) inserted by the Housing Act 2004, s 223, as from a day to be appointed in relation to Wales.
Sub-s (2ZA): inserted by the Housing and Regeneration Act 2008, s 314, Sch 15, Pt 1, paras 1, 2(1), (3), except in relation to applications for an allocation of social housing or housing assistance (homelessness) or for accommodation made before 2 March 2009.
Sub-ss (2A)–(2E): substituted, together with sub-s (2) for original sub-s (2), by the Homelessness Act 2002, s 16(1), (3).
Sub-s (4A): inserted by the Homelessness Act 2002, s 16(1), (4).
Regulations: the Local Housing Authorities (Prescribed Principles for Allocation Schemes) (Wales) Regulations 1997, SI 1997/45 at **[3155]**; the Allocation of Housing (Procedure) Regulations 1997, SI 1997/483 at **[3173]**; the Allocation of Housing (Reasonable and Additional Preference) Regulations 1997, SI 1997/1902 at **[3180]**.

## 168    Information about allocation scheme

(1)    A local housing authority shall publish a summary of their allocation scheme and provide a copy of the summary free of charge to any member of the public who asks for one.

(2)    The authority shall make the scheme available for inspection at their principal office and shall provide a copy of the scheme, on payment of a reasonable fee, to any member of the public who asks for one.

(3)    When the authority make an alteration to their scheme reflecting a major change of policy, they shall within a reasonable period of time [take such steps as they consider reasonable to bring the effect of the alteration to the attention of those likely to be affected by it].

**[1062]**

**NOTES**
Sub-s (3): words in square brackets substituted by the Homelessness Act 2002, s 18(1), Sch 1, paras 2, 4.

*Supplementary*

## 169    Guidance to authorities by the Secretary of State

(1)    In the exercise of their functions under this Part, local housing authorities shall have regard to such guidance as may from time to time be given by the Secretary of State.

(2)    The Secretary of State may give guidance generally or to specified descriptions of authorities.

**[1063]**

## 170    Co-operation between registered social landlords and local housing authorities

Where a local housing authority so request, a registered social landlord shall co-operate to such extent as is reasonable in the circumstances in offering accommodation to [people with priority under the authority's allocation scheme].

**[1064]**

**NOTES**
Words in square brackets substituted by the Homelessness Act 2002, s 18(1), Sch 1, paras 2, 5.

**171 False statements and withholding information**

(1) A person commits an offence if, in connection with the exercise by a local housing authority of their functions under this Part—

(a) he knowingly or recklessly makes a statement which is false in a material particular, or

(b) he knowingly withholds information which the authority have reasonably required him to give in connection with the exercise of those functions.

(2) A person guilty of an offence under this section is liable on summary conviction to a fine not exceeding level 5 on the standard scale.

**[1065]**

**172 Regulations**

(1) Regulations under this Part shall be made by statutory instrument.

(2) No regulations shall be made under section 167(3) (regulations amending provisions about priorities in allocating housing accommodation) unless a draft of the regulations has been laid before and approved by a resolution of each House of Parliament.

(3) Any other regulations under this Part shall be subject to annulment in pursuance of a resolution of either House of Parliament.

(4) Regulations under this Part may contain such incidental, supplementary and transitional provisions as appear to the Secretary of State appropriate, and may make different provision for different cases including different provision for different areas.

**[1066]**

**173 Consequential amendments: Part VI**

The enactments mentioned in Schedule 16 have effect with the amendments specified there which are consequential on the provisions of this Part.

**[1067]**

**174 Index of defined expressions: Part VI**

The following Table shows provisions defining or otherwise explaining expressions used in this Part (other than provisions defining or explaining an expression used in the same section)—

| | |
|---|---|
| allocation (of housing) | section 159(2) |
| allocation scheme | section 167 |
| assured tenancy | section 230 |
| [district (of local housing authority) | section 166(5)] |
| ... | ... |
| introductory tenancy and introductory tenant | section 230 and 124 |
| local housing authority | section 230 |
| ... | ... |
| registered social landlord | section 230 and 2 |
| secure tenancy and secure tenant | section 230 |

**[1068]**

**NOTES**

Entry "district (of local housing authority)" inserted and entries "housing register" and "qualifying person" (omitted) repealed by the Homelessness Act 2002, s 18, Sch 1, paras 2, 6, Sch 2.

PART VII
HOMELESSNESS

*Homelessness and threatened homelessness*

**175 Homelessness and threatened homelessness**

(1) A person is homeless if he has no accommodation available for his occupation, in the United Kingdom or elsewhere, which he—

(a) is entitled to occupy by virtue of an interest in it or by virtue of an order of a court,

(b) has an express or implied licence to occupy, or

(c) occupies as a residence by virtue of any enactment or rule of law giving him the right to remain in occupation or restricting the right of another person to recover possession.

(2)   A person is also homeless if he has accommodation but—

(a)   he cannot secure entry to it, or

(b)   it consists of a moveable structure, vehicle or vessel designed or adapted for human habitation and there is no place where he is entitled or permitted both to place it and to reside in it.

(3)   A person shall not be treated as having accommodation unless it is accommodation which it would be reasonable for him to continue to occupy.

(4)   A person is threatened with homelessness if it is likely that he will become homeless within 28 days.

**[1069]**

## 176   Meaning of accommodation available for occupation

Accommodation shall be regarded as available for a person's occupation only if it is available for occupation by him together with—

(a)   any other person who normally resides with him as a member of his family, or

(b)   any other person who might reasonably be expected to reside with him.

References in this Part to securing that accommodation is available for a person's occupation shall be construed accordingly.

**[1070]**

## 177   Whether it is reasonable to continue to occupy accommodation

(1)   It is not reasonable for a person to continue to occupy accommodation if it is probable that this will lead to domestic violence [or other violence] against him, or against—

(a)   a person who normally resides with him as a member of his family, or

(b)   any other person who might reasonably be expected to reside with him.

[(1A)   For this purpose "violence" means—

(a)   violence from another person; or

(b)   threats of violence from another person which are likely to be carried out;

and violence is "domestic violence" if it is from a person who is associated with the victim.]

(2)   In determining whether it would be, or would have been, reasonable for a person to continue to occupy accommodation, regard may be had to the general circumstances prevailing in relation to housing in the district of the local housing authority to whom he has applied for accommodation or for assistance in obtaining accommodation.

(3)   The Secretary of State may by order specify—

(a)   other circumstances in which it is to be regarded as reasonable or not reasonable for a person to continue to occupy accommodation, and

(b)   other matters to be taken into account or disregarded in determining whether it would be, or would have been, reasonable for a person to continue to occupy accommodation.

**[1071]**

---

**NOTES**

Sub-s (1): words in square brackets inserted by the Homelessness Act 2002, s 10(1)(a).

Sub-s (1A): substituted, for the original sub-s (1) proviso, by the Homelessness Act 2002, s 10(1)(b).

Order: the Homelessness (Suitability of Accommodation) Order 1996, SI 1996/3204 at **[3152]**.

## 178   Meaning of associated person

(1)   For the purposes of this Part, a person is associated with another person if—

(a)   they are or have been married to each other;

[(aa)   they are or have been civil partners of each other;]

(b)   they are cohabitants or former cohabitants;

(c)   they live or have lived in the same household;

(d)   they are relatives;

(e)   they have agreed to marry one another (whether or not that agreement has been terminated);

[(ea)   they have entered into a civil partnership agreement between them (whether or not that agreement has been terminated);]

(f)   in relation to a child, each of them is a parent of the child or has, or has had, parental responsibility for the child.

(2)   If a child has been adopted or [falls within subsection (2A)], two persons are also associated with each other for the purposes of this Part if—

(a)   one is a natural parent of the child or a parent of such a natural parent, and

(b)   the other is the child or a person—

(i)   who has become a parent of the child by virtue of an adoption order or who has applied for an adoption order, or

(ii)   with whom the child has at any time been placed for adoption.

[(2A)    A child falls within this subsection if—

   (a)    an adoption agency, within the meaning of section 2 of the Adoption and Children Act 2002, is authorised to place him for adoption under section 19 of that Act (placing children with parental consent) or he has become the subject of an order under section 21 of that Act (placement orders), or

   (b)    he is freed for adoption by virtue of an order made—

      (i)    in England and Wales, under section 18 of the Adoption Act 1976,

      (ii)    in Scotland, under section 18 of the Adoption (Scotland) Act 1978, or

      (iii)    in Northern Ireland, under Article 17(1) or 18(1) of the Adoption (Northern Ireland) Order 1987.]

   (3)    In this section—

["adoption order" means an adoption order within the meaning of section 72(1) of the Adoption Act 1976 or section 46(1) of the Adoption and Children Act 2002;]

"child" means a person under the age of 18 years;

["civil partnership agreement" has the meaning given by section 73 of the Civil Partnership Act 2004;]

["cohabitants" means—

   (a)    a man and a woman who, although not married to each other, are living together as husband and wife, or

   (b)    two people of the same sex who, although not civil partners of each other, are living together as if they were civil partners;

and "former cohabitants" shall be construed accordingly;]

"parental responsibility" has the same meaning as in the Children Act 1989; and

"relative", in relation to a person, means—

   (a)    the father, mother, stepfather, stepmother, son, daughter, stepson, stepdaughter, grandmother, grandfather, grandson or granddaughter of that person or of that person's [spouse, civil partner, former spouse or former civil partner], or

   (b)    the brother, sister, uncle, aunt, niece or nephew (whether of the full blood or of the half blood or by [marriage or civil partnership]) of that person or of that person's [spouse, civil partner, former spouse or former civil partner],

and includes, in relation to a person who is living or has lived with another person as husband and wife, a person who would fall within paragraph (a) or (b) if the parties were married to each other.

**[1072]**

---

**NOTES**

Sub-s (1): paras (aa), (ea) inserted by the Civil Partnership Act 2004, s 81, Sch 8, para 61(1)–(3).

Sub-s (2): words in square brackets substituted by the Adoption and Children Act 2002, s 139(1), Sch 3, paras 89, 90.

Sub-s (2A): inserted by the Adoption and Children Act 2002, s 139(1), Sch 3, paras 89, 91.

Sub-s (3): definition "adoption order" substituted by the Adoption and Children Act 2002, s 139(1), Sch 3, paras 89, 92; definition "civil partnership agreement" inserted, definition "cohabitants" substituted and words in square brackets in definition "relative" substituted by the Civil Partnership Act 2004, s 81, Sch 8, para 61(1), (4)–(7).

---

*General functions in relation to homelessness or threatened homelessness*

## 179    Duty of local housing authority to provide advisory services

   (1)    Every local housing authority shall secure that advice and information about homelessness, and the prevention of homelessness, is available free of charge to any person in their district.

   (2)    The authority may give to any person by whom such advice and information is provided on behalf of the authority assistance by way of grant or loan.

   (3)    A local housing authority may also assist any such person—

   (a)    by permitting him to use premises belonging to the authority,

   (b)    by making available furniture or other goods, whether by way of gift, loan or otherwise, and

   (c)    by making available the services of staff employed by the authority.

**[1073]**

## 180    Assistance for voluntary organisations

   (1)    The Secretary of State or a local housing authority may give assistance by way of grant or loan to voluntary organisations concerned with homelessness or matters relating to homelessness.

   (2)    A local housing authority may also assist any such organisation—

   (a)    by permitting them to use premises belonging to the authority,

   (b)    by making available furniture or other goods, whether by way of gift, loan or otherwise, and

   (c)    by making available the services of staff employed by the authority.

(3)  A "voluntary organisation" means a body (other than a public or local authority) whose activities are not carried on for profit.

[1074]

## 181  Terms and conditions of assistance

(1)  This section has effect as to the terms and conditions on which assistance is given under section 179 or 180.

(2)  Assistance shall be on such terms, and subject to such conditions, as the person giving the assistance may determine.

(3)  No assistance shall be given unless the person to whom it is given undertakes—

(a)  to use the money, furniture or other goods or premises for a specified purpose, and

(b)  to provide such information as may reasonably be required as to the manner in which the assistance is being used.

The person giving the assistance may require such information by notice in writing, which shall be complied with within 21 days beginning with the date on which the notice is served.

(4)  The conditions subject to which assistance is given shall in all cases include conditions requiring the person to whom the assistance is given—

(a)  to keep proper books of account and have them audited in such manner as may be specified,

(b)  to keep records indicating how he has used the money, furniture or other goods or premises, and

(c)  to submit the books of account and records for inspection by the person giving the assistance.

(5)  If it appears to the person giving the assistance that the person to whom it was given has failed to carry out his undertaking as to the purpose for which the assistance was to be used, he shall take all reasonable steps to recover from that person an amount equal to the amount of the assistance.

(6)  He must first serve on the person to whom the assistance was given a notice specifying the amount which in his opinion is recoverable and the basis on which that amount has been calculated.

[1075]

## 182  Guidance by the Secretary of State

(1)  In the exercise of their functions relating to homelessness and the prevention of homelessness, a local housing authority or social services authority shall have regard to such guidance as may from time to time be given by the Secretary of State.

(2)  The Secretary of State may give guidance either generally or to specified descriptions of authorities.

[1076]

*Application for assistance in case of homelessness or threatened homelessness*

## 183  Application for assistance

(1)  The following provisions of this Part apply where a person applies to a local housing authority for accommodation, or for assistance in obtaining accommodation, and the authority have reason to believe that he is or may be homeless or threatened with homelessness.

(2)  In this Part—

"applicant" means a person making such an application,

"assistance under this Part" means the benefit of any function under the following provisions of this Part relating to accommodation or assistance in obtaining accommodation, and

"eligible for assistance" means not excluded from such assistance by section 185 (persons from abroad not eligible for housing assistance) *or section 186 (asylum seekers and their dependants)*.

(3)  Nothing in this section or the following provisions of this Part affects a person's entitlement to advice and information under section 179 (duty to provide advisory services).

[1077]

**NOTES**

Sub-s (2): in definition "eligible for assistance" words in italics repealed by the Immigration and Asylum Act 1999, s 169(1), (3), Sch 14, para 116, Sch 16, as from a day to be appointed.

## 184  Inquiry into cases of homelessness or threatened homelessness

(1)  If the local housing authority have reason to believe that an applicant may be homeless or threatened with homelessness, they shall make such inquiries as are necessary to satisfy themselves—

(a) whether he is eligible for assistance, and

(b) if so, whether any duty, and if so what duty, is owed to him under the following provisions of this Part.

(2) They may also make inquiries whether he has a local connection with the district of another local housing authority in England, Wales or Scotland.

(3) On completing their inquiries the authority shall notify the applicant of their decision and, so far as any issue is decided against his interests, inform him of the reasons for their decision.

[(3A) If the authority decide that a duty is owed to the applicant under section 193(2) or 195(2) but would not have done so without having had regard to a restricted person, the notice under subsection (3) must also—

(a) inform the applicant that their decision was reached on that basis,

(b) include the name of the restricted person,

(c) explain why the person is a restricted person, and

(d) explain the effect of section 193(7AD) or (as the case may be) section 195(4A).]

(4) If the authority have notified or intend to notify another local housing authority under section 198 (referral of cases), they shall at the same time notify the applicant of that decision and inform him of the reasons for it.

(5) A notice under subsection (3) or (4) shall also inform the applicant of his right to request a review of the decision and of the time within which such a request must be made (see section 202).

(6) Notice required to be given to a person under this section shall be given in writing and, if not received by him, shall be treated as having been given to him if it is made available at the authority's office for a reasonable period for collection by him or on his behalf.

[(7) In this Part "a restricted person" means a person—

(a) who is not eligible for assistance under this Part,

(b) who is subject to immigration control within the meaning of the Asylum and Immigration Act 1996, and

(c) either—

   (i) who does not have leave to enter or remain in the United Kingdom, or

   (ii) whose leave to enter or remain in the United Kingdom is subject to a condition to maintain and accommodate himself, and any dependants, without recourse to public funds.]

**[1078]**

**NOTES**

Sub-s (3A): inserted by the Housing and Regeneration Act 2008, s 314, Sch 15, Pt 1, paras 1, 3(1), (2), except in relation to applications for an allocation of social housing or housing assistance (homelessness) or for accommodation made before 2 March 2009.

Sub-s (7): inserted by the Housing and Regeneration Act 2008, s 314, Sch 15, Pt 1, paras 1, 3(1), (3), except in relation to applications for an allocation of social housing or housing assistance (homelessness) or for accommodation made before 2 March 2009.

*Eligibility for assistance*

## 185 Persons from abroad not eligible for housing assistance

(1) A person is not eligible for assistance under this Part if he is a person from abroad who is ineligible for housing assistance.

(2) A person who is subject to immigration control within the meaning of the Asylum and Immigration Act 1996 is not eligible for housing assistance unless he is of a class prescribed by regulations made by the Secretary of State.

[(2A) No person who is excluded from entitlement to housing benefit by section 115 of the Immigration and Asylum Act 1999 (exclusion from benefits) shall be included in any class prescribed under subsection (2).]

(3) The Secretary of State may make provision by regulations as to other descriptions of persons who are to be treated for the purposes of this Part as persons from abroad who are ineligible for housing assistance.

(4) A person from abroad who is not eligible for housing assistance shall be disregarded in determining for the purposes of this Part whether [a person falling within subsection (5)]—

(a) is homeless or threatened with homelessness, or

(b) has a priority need for accommodation.

[(5) A person falls within this subsection if the person—

(a) falls within a class prescribed by regulations made under subsection (2); but

(b) is not a national of an EEA State or Switzerland.]

**[1079]**

**NOTES**
Sub-s (2A): inserted by the Immigration and Asylum Act 1999, s 117(4); substituted by the Homelessness Act 2002, s 18(1), Sch 1, paras 2, 7(1).
Sub-s (4): words in square brackets substituted by the Housing and Regeneration Act 2008, s 314, Sch 15, Pt 1, paras 1, 4(1), (2), except in relation to applications for an allocation of social housing or housing assistance (homelessness) or for accommodation made before 2 March 2009.
Sub-s (5): inserted by the Housing and Regeneration Act 2008, s 314, Sch 15, Pt 1, paras 1, 4(1), (3), except in relation to applications for an allocation of social housing or housing assistance (homelessness) or for accommodation made before 2 March 2009.
Regulations: the Allocation of Housing and Homelessness (Eligibility) (England) Regulations 2006, SI 2006/1294 at **[3703]**; the Allocation of Housing and Homelessness (Miscellaneous Provisions) (England) Regulations 2006, SI 2006/2527 at **[3733]**; the Homelessness (Wales) Regulations 2006, SI 2006/2646 at **[3736]**; the Allocation of Housing and Homelessness (Eligibility) (Wales) Regulations 2009, SI 2009/393.

## 186 Asylum-seekers and their dependants

*(1)   An asylum-seeker, or a dependant of an asylum-seeker who is not by virtue of section 185 a person from abroad who is ineligible for housing assistance, is not eligible for assistance under this Part if he has any accommodation in the United Kingdom, however temporary, available for his occupation.*

*(2)   For the purposes of this section a person who makes a claim for asylum—*
   *(a)   becomes an asylum-seeker at the time when his claim is recorded by the Secretary of State as having been made, and*
   *(b)   ceases to be an asylum-seeker at the time when his claim is recorded by the Secretary of State as having been finally determined or abandoned.*

*(3)   For the purposes of this section a person—*
   *(a)   becomes a dependant of an asylum-seeker at the time when he is recorded by the Secretary of State as being a dependant of the asylum-seeker, and*
   *(b)   ceases to be a dependant of an asylum-seeker at the time when the person whose dependant he is ceases to be an asylum-seeker or, if it is earlier, at the time when he is recorded by the Secretary of State as ceasing to be a dependant of the asylum-seeker.*

*(4)   In relation to an asylum-seeker, "dependant" means a person—*
   *(a)   who is his spouse or a child of his under the age of eighteen, and*
   *(b)   who has neither a right of abode in the United Kingdom nor indefinite leave under the Immigration Act 1971 to enter or remain in the United Kingdom.*

*(5)   In this section a "claim for asylum" means a claim made by a person that it would be contrary to the United Kingdom's obligations under the Convention relating to the Status of Refugees done at Geneva on 28th July 1951 and the Protocol to that Convention for him to be removed from, or required to leave, the United Kingdom.*

**[1080]**

**NOTES**
Repealed by the Immigration and Asylum Act 1999, ss 117(5), 169(3), Sch 16, as from a day to be appointed.

## 187 Provision of information by Secretary of State

(1)   The Secretary of State shall, at the request of a local housing authority, provide the authority with such information as they may require—
   (a)   as to whether a person is [a person to whom section 115 of the Immigration and Asylum Act 1999 (exclusion from benefits) applies], and
   (b)   to enable them to determine whether such a person is eligible for assistance under this Part under section 185 (persons from abroad not eligible for housing assistance).

(2)   Where that information is given otherwise than in writing, the Secretary of State shall confirm it in writing if a written request is made to him by the authority.

(3)   If it appears to the Secretary of State that any application, decision or other change of circumstances has affected the status of a person about whom information was previously provided by him to a local housing authority under this section, he shall inform the authority in writing of that fact, the reason for it and the date on which the previous information became inaccurate.

**[1081]**

**NOTES**
Sub-s (1): words in square brackets in para (a) substituted by the Immigration and Asylum Act 1999, s 117(6).

*Interim duty to accommodate*

## 188 Interim duty to accommodate in case of apparent priority need

(1)   If the local housing authority have reason to believe that an applicant may be homeless, eligible for assistance and have a priority need, they shall secure that accommodation is available for his occupation pending a decision as to the duty (if any) owed to him under the following provisions of this Part.

(2)   The duty under this section arises irrespective of any possibility of the referral of the applicant's case to another local housing authority (see sections 198 to 200).

(3)   The duty ceases when the authority's decision is notified to the applicant, even if the applicant requests a review of the decision (see section 202).

The authority may [secure] that accommodation is available for the applicant's occupation pending a decision on a review.

**[1082]**

**NOTES**
Sub-s (3): word in square brackets substituted by the Homelessness Act 2002, s 18(1), Sch 1, paras 2, 8.

## 189 Priority need for accommodation

(1)   The following have a priority need for accommodation—
  (a)   a pregnant woman or a person with whom she resides or might reasonably be expected to reside;
  (b)   a person with whom dependent children reside or might reasonably be expected to reside;
  (c)   a person who is vulnerable as a result of old age, mental illness or handicap or physical disability or other special reason, or with whom such a person resides or might reasonably be expected to reside;
  (d)   a person who is homeless or threatened with homelessness as a result of an emergency such as flood, fire or other disaster.

(2)   The Secretary of State may by order—
  (a)   specify further descriptions of persons as having a priority need for accommodation, and
  (b)   amend or repeal any part of subsection (1).

(3)   Before making such an order the Secretary of State shall consult such associations representing relevant authorities, and such other persons, as he considers appropriate.

(4)   No such order shall be made unless a draft of it has been approved by resolution of each House of Parliament.

**[1083]**

**NOTES**
Orders: the Homeless Persons (Priority Need) (Wales) Order 2001, SI 2001/607 at **[3252]**; the Homelessness (Priority Need for Accommodation) (England) Order 2002, SI 2002/2051 at **[3259]**.

*Duties to persons found to be homeless or threatened with homelessness*

## 190 Duties to persons becoming homeless intentionally

(1)   This section applies where the local housing authority are satisfied that an applicant is homeless and is eligible for assistance but are also satisfied that he became homeless intentionally.

(2)   If the authority are satisfied that the applicant has a priority need, they shall—
  (a)   secure that accommodation is available for his occupation for such period as they consider will give him a reasonable opportunity of securing accommodation for his occupation, and
  (b)   provide him with [(or secure that he is provided with) advice and assistance] in any attempts he may make to secure that accommodation becomes available for his occupation.

(3)   If they are not satisfied that he has a priority need, they shall provide him with [(or secure that he is provided with) advice and assistance] in any attempts he may make to secure that accommodation becomes available for his occupation.

[(4)   The applicant's housing needs shall be assessed before advice and assistance is provided under subsection (2)(b) or (3).

(5)   The advice and assistance provided under subsection (2)(b) or (3) must include information about the likely availability in the authority's district of types of accommodation appropriate to the applicant's housing needs (including, in particular, the location and sources of such types of accommodation).]

**[1084]**

NOTES

Sub-s (2): words in square brackets in para (b) substituted by the Homelessness Act 2002, s 18(1), Sch 1, paras 2, 9.

Sub-s (3): words in square brackets substituted by the Homelessness Act 2002, s 18(1), Sch 1, paras 2, 9.

Sub-ss (4), (5): inserted by the Homelessness Act 2002, s 18(1), Sch 1, paras 2, 10.

## 191 Becoming homeless intentionally

(1) A person becomes homeless intentionally if he deliberately does or fails to do anything in consequence of which he ceases to occupy accommodation which is available for his occupation and which it would have been reasonable for him to continue to occupy.

(2) For the purposes of subsection (1) an act or omission in good faith on the part of a person who was unaware of any relevant fact shall not be treated as deliberate.

(3) A person shall be treated as becoming homeless intentionally if—

(a) he enters into an arrangement under which he is required to cease to occupy accommodation which it would have been reasonable for him to continue to occupy, and

(b) the purpose of the arrangement is to enable him to become entitled to assistance under this Part,

and there is no other good reason why he is homeless.

(4) ...

[1085]

NOTES

Sub-s (4): repealed by the Homelessness Act 2002, s 18(2), Sch 2.

## 192 Duty to persons not in priority need who are not homeless intentionally

(1) This section applies where the local housing authority—

(a) are satisfied that an applicant is homeless and eligible for assistance, and

(b) are not satisfied that he became homeless intentionally,

but are not satisfied that he has a priority need.

(2) The authority shall provide the applicant with [(or secure that he is provided with) advice and assistance] in any attempts he may make to secure that accommodation becomes available for his occupation.

[(3) The authority may secure that accommodation is available for occupation by the applicant.]

[(4) The applicant's housing needs shall be assessed before advice and assistance is provided under subsection (2).

(5) The advice and assistance provided under subsection (2) must include information about the likely availability in the authority's district of types of accommodation appropriate to the applicant's housing needs (including, in particular, the location and sources of such types of accommodation).]

[1086]

NOTES

Sub-s (2): words in square brackets substituted by the Homelessness Act 2002, s 18(1), Sch 1, paras 2, 11.

Sub-ss (3)–(5): inserted by the Homelessness Act 2002, ss 5(1), 18(1), Sch 1, paras 2, 12.

## 193 Duty to persons with priority need who are not homeless intentionally

(1) This section applies where the local housing authority are satisfied that an applicant is homeless, eligible for assistance and has a priority need, and are not satisfied that he became homeless intentionally.

...

(2) Unless the authority refer the application to another local housing authority (see section 198), they shall secure that accommodation is available for occupation by the applicant.

[(3) The authority are subject to the duty under this section until it ceases by virtue of any of the following provisions of this section.]

[(3A) The authority shall, on becoming subject to the duty under this section [in a case which is not a restricted case], give the applicant a copy of the statement included in their allocation scheme by virtue of section 167(1A) (policy on offering choice to people allocated housing accommodation under Part 6).]

[(3B) In this section "a restricted case" means a case where the local housing authority would not be satisfied as mentioned in subsection (1) without having had regard to a restricted person.]

(5)   The local housing authority shall cease to be subject to the duty under this section if the applicant, having been informed by the authority of the possible consequence of refusal [and of his right to request a review of the suitability of the accommodation], refuses an offer of accommodation which the authority are satisfied is suitable for him and the authority notify him that they regard themselves as having discharged their duty under this section.

(6)   The local housing authority shall cease to be subject to the duty under this section if the applicant—
    (a)    ceases to be eligible for assistance,
    (b)    becomes homeless intentionally from the accommodation made available for his occupation,
    (c)    accepts an offer of accommodation under Part VI (allocation of housing), or
    [(cc)  accepts an offer of an assured tenancy (other than an assured shorthold tenancy) from a private landlord,]
    (d)    otherwise voluntarily ceases to occupy as his only or principal home the accommodation made available for his occupation.

[(7)   The local housing authority shall also cease to be subject to the duty under this section if the applicant, having been informed of the possible consequence of refusal and of his right to request a review of the suitability of the accommodation, refuses a final offer of accommodation under Part 6.

(7A)   An offer of accommodation under Part 6 is a final offer for the purposes of subsection (7) if it is made in writing and states that it is a final offer for the purposes of subsection (7).]

[(7AA)   In a restricted case the authority shall also cease to be subject to the duty under this section if the applicant, having been informed of the matters mentioned in subsection (7AB)—
    (a)    accepts a private accommodation offer, or
    (b)    refuses such an offer.

(7AB)   The matters are—
    (a)    the possible consequence of refusal of the offer, and
    (b)    that the applicant has the right to request a review of the suitability of the accommodation.

(7AC)   For the purposes of this section an offer is a private accommodation offer if—
    (a)    it is an offer of an assured shorthold tenancy made by a private landlord to the applicant in relation to any accommodation which is, or may become, available for the applicant's occupation,
    (b)    it is made, with the approval of the authority, in pursuance of arrangements made by the authority with the landlord with a view to bringing the authority's duty under this section to an end, and
    (c)    the tenancy being offered is a fixed term tenancy (within the meaning of Part 1 of the Housing Act 1988) for a period of at least 12 months.

(7AD)   In a restricted case the authority shall, so far as reasonably practicable, bring their duty under this section to an end as mentioned in subsection (7AA).]

[(7B)   [In a case which is not a restricted case,] the authority shall also cease to be subject to the duty under this section if the applicant accepts a qualifying offer of an assured shorthold tenancy which is made by a private landlord in relation to any accommodation which is, or may become, available for the applicant's occupation.

(7C)   [In a case which is not a restricted case,] the applicant is free to reject a qualifying offer without affecting the duty owed to him under this section by the authority.

(7D)   For the purposes of subsection (7B) an offer of an assured shorthold tenancy is a qualifying offer if—
    (a)    it is made, with the approval of the authority, in pursuance of arrangements made by the authority with the landlord with a view to bringing the authority's duty under this section to an end;
    (b)    the tenancy being offered is a fixed term tenancy (within the meaning of Part 1 of the Housing Act 1988 (c 50)); and
    (c)    it is accompanied by a statement in writing which states the term of the tenancy being offered and explains in ordinary language that—
        (i)   there is no obligation to accept the offer, but
        (ii)  if the offer is accepted the local housing authority will cease to be subject to the duty under this section in relation to the applicant.

(7E)   An acceptance of a qualifying offer is only effective for the purposes of subsection (7B) if the applicant signs a statement acknowledging that he has understood the statement mentioned in subsection (7D).

(7F)   The local housing authority shall not—
    (a)    make a final offer of accommodation under Part 6 for the purposes of subsection (7);

[(ab)  approve a private accommodation offer;] or

(b)  approve an offer of an assured shorthold tenancy for the purposes of subsection (7B),

unless they are satisfied that the accommodation is suitable for the applicant and that it is reasonable for him to accept the offer.]

(8)  For the purposes of [subsection (7F)] an applicant may reasonably be expected to accept an offer … even though he is under contractual or other obligations in respect of his existing accommodation, provided he is able to bring those obligations to an end before he is required to take up the offer.

(9)  A person who ceases to be owed the duty under this section may make a fresh application to the authority for accommodation or assistance in obtaining accommodation.

**[1087]**

---

**NOTES**

Sub-s (1): words omitted repealed by the Homelessness Act 2002, s 18(2), Sch 2.

Sub-s (3): substituted, for original sub-ss (3), (4), by the Homelessness Act 2002, s 6(1); for effect see s 6(2) thereof.

Sub-s (3A): inserted by the Homelessness Act 2002, s 18(1), Sch 1, paras 2, 13; words in square brackets inserted by the Housing and Regeneration Act 2008, s 314, Sch 15, Pt 1, paras 1, 5(1), (2), except in relation to applications for an allocation of social housing or housing assistance (homelessness) or for accommodation made before 2 March 2009.

Sub-s (3B): inserted by the Housing and Regeneration Act 2008, s 314, Sch 15, Pt 1, paras 1, 5(1), (3), except in relation to applications for an allocation of social housing or housing assistance (homelessness) or for accommodation made before 2 March 2009.

Sub-s (5): words in square brackets inserted by the Homelessness Act 2002, s 8(1).

Sub-s (6): para (cc) inserted by the Homelessness Act 2002, s 7(1), (2); for effect see s 7(6) thereof.

Sub-ss (7), (7A): substituted, for original sub-s (7), by the Homelessness Act 2002, s 7(1), (3); for effect see s 7(6) thereof.

Sub-ss (7AA)–(7AD): inserted by the Housing and Regeneration Act 2008, s 314, Sch 15, Pt 1, paras 1, 5(1), (4), except in relation to applications for an allocation of social housing or housing assistance (homelessness) or for accommodation made before 2 March 2009.

Sub-s (7B): inserted by the Homelessness Act 2002, s 7(1), (4); for effect see s 7(6) thereof; words in square brackets inserted by the Housing and Regeneration Act 2008, s 314, Sch 15, Pt 1, paras 1, 5(1), (5), except in relation to applications for an allocation of social housing or housing assistance (homelessness) or for accommodation made before 2 March 2009.

Sub-s (7C): inserted by the Homelessness Act 2002, s 7(1), (4); for effect see s 7(6) thereof; words in square brackets inserted by the Housing and Regeneration Act 2008, s 314, Sch 15, Pt 1, paras 1, 5(1), (5), except in relation to applications for an allocation of social housing or housing assistance (homelessness) or for accommodation made before 2 March 2009.

Sub-ss (7D), (7E): inserted by the Homelessness Act 2002, s 7(1), (4); for effect see s 7(6) thereof.

Sub-s (7F): inserted by the Homelessness Act 2002, s 7(1), (4); for effect see s 7(6) thereof; para (ab) inserted by the Housing and Regeneration Act 2008, s 314, Sch 15, Pt 1, paras 1, 5(1), (6), except in relation to applications for an allocation of social housing or housing assistance (homelessness) or for accommodation made before 2 March 2009.

Sub-s (8): words in square brackets substituted and words omitted repealed by the Homelessness Act 2002, ss 7(1), (5), 18(2), Sch 2; for effect see s 7(6) thereof.

---

**194**  (*Repealed by the Homelessness Act 2002, ss 6(3), 18(2), Sch 2; for effect see s 6(4) thereof.*)

**195  Duties in case of threatened homelessness**

(1)  This section applies where the local housing authority are satisfied that an applicant is threatened with homelessness and is eligible for assistance.

(2)  If the authority—

(a)  are satisfied that he has a priority need, and

(b)  are not satisfied that he became threatened with homelessness intentionally,

they shall take reasonable steps to secure that accommodation does not cease to be available for his occupation.

…

(3)  Subsection (2) does not affect any right of the authority, whether by virtue of a contract, enactment or rule of law, to secure vacant possession of any accommodation.

[(3A)  The authority shall, on becoming subject to the duty under this section [in a case which is not a restricted threatened homelessness case], give the applicant a copy of the statement included in their allocation scheme by virtue of section 167(1A) (policy on offering choice to people allocated housing accommodation under Part 6).]

(4)  Where[, in a case which is not a restricted threatened homelessness case,] in pursuance of the duty under subsection (2) the authority secure that accommodation other than that occupied by the applicant when he made his application is available for occupation by him, the provisions of section 193(3) to (9) (period for which duty owed) … apply, with any necessary modifications, in

relation to the duty under this section as they apply in relation to the duty under section 193 [in a case which is not a restricted case (within the meaning of that section)].

[(4A) Where, in a restricted threatened homelessness case, in pursuance of the duty under subsection (2) the authority secure that accommodation other than that occupied by the applicant when he made his application is available for occupation by him, the provisions of section 193(3) to (9) (period for which duty owed) apply, with any necessary modifications, in relation to the duty under this section as they apply in relation to the duty under section 193 in a restricted case (within the meaning of that section).

(4B) In subsections (3A) to (4A) "a restricted threatened homelessness case" means a case where the local housing authority would not be satisfied as mentioned in subsection (1) without having had regard to a restricted person.]

(5) If the authority—
  (a) are not satisfied that the applicant has a priority need, or
  (b) are satisfied that he has a priority need but are also satisfied that he became threatened with homelessness intentionally,

they shall [provide him with (or secure that he is provided with) advice and assistance] in any attempts he may make to secure that accommodation does not cease to be available for his occupation.

[(6) The applicant's housing needs shall be assessed before advice and assistance is provided under subsection (5).

(7) The advice and assistance provided under subsection (5) must include information about the likely availability in the authority's district of types of accommodation appropriate to the applicant's housing needs (including, in particular, the location and sources of such types of accommodation).]

[(8) If the authority decide that they owe the applicant the duty under subsection (5) by virtue of paragraph (b) of that subsection, they may, pending a decision on a review of that decision—
  (a) secure that accommodation does not cease to be available for his occupation; and
  (b) if he becomes homeless, secure that accommodation is so available.]

[(9) If the authority—
  (a) are not satisfied that the applicant has a priority need; and
  (b) are not satisfied that he became threatened with homelessness intentionally,

the authority may take reasonable steps to secure that accommodation does not cease to be available for the applicant's occupation.]

**[1088]**

**NOTES**

Sub-s (2): words omitted repealed by the Homelessness Act 2002, s 18(2), Sch 2.

Sub-s (3A): inserted by the Homelessness Act 2002, s 18(1), Sch 1, paras 2, 14(a); words in square brackets inserted by the Housing and Regeneration Act 2008, s 314, Sch 15, Pt 1, paras 1, 6(1), (2), except in relation to applications for an allocation of social housing or housing assistance (homelessness) or for accommodation made before 2 March 2009.

Sub-s (4): words in square brackets inserted by the Housing and Regeneration Act 2008, s 314, Sch 15, Pt 1, paras 1, 6(1), (3), except in relation to applications for an allocation of social housing or housing assistance (homelessness) or for accommodation made before 2 March 2009; words omitted repealed by the Homelessness Act 2002, s 18(2), Sch 2.

Sub-ss (4A), (4B): inserted by the Housing and Regeneration Act 2008, s 314, Sch 15, Pt 1, paras 1, 6(1), (4), except in relation to applications for an allocation of social housing or housing assistance (homelessness) or for accommodation made before 2 March 2009.

Sub-s (5): words in square brackets substituted by the Homelessness Act 2002, s 18(1), Sch 1, paras 2, 14(b).

Sub-ss (6)–(9): inserted by the Homelessness Act 2002, ss 5(2), 18(1), Sch 1, paras 2, 14(c), (d).

## 196 Becoming threatened with homelessness intentionally

(1) A person becomes threatened with homelessness intentionally if he deliberately does or fails to do anything the likely result of which is that he will be forced to leave accommodation which is available for his occupation and which it would have been reasonable for him to continue to occupy.

(2) For the purposes of subsection (1) an act or omission in good faith on the part of a person who was unaware of any relevant fact shall not be treated as deliberate.

(3) A person shall be treated as becoming threatened with homelessness intentionally if—
  (a) he enters into an arrangement under which he is required to cease to occupy accommodation which it would have been reasonable for him to continue to occupy, and
  (b) the purpose of the arrangement is to enable him to become entitled to assistance under this Part,

and there is no other good reason why he is threatened with homelessness.

(4) ...

**[1089]**

**NOTES**

Sub-s (4): repealed by the Homelessness Act 2002, s 18(2), Sch 2.

**197** *(Repealed by the Homelessness Act 2002, ss 9(1), 18(2), Sch 2; for effect see s 9(2), (3) thereof.)*

*Referral to another local housing authority*

## 198 Referral of case to another local housing authority

(1) If the local housing authority would be subject to the duty under section 193 (accommodation for those with priority need who are not homeless intentionally) but consider that the conditions are met for referral of the case to another local housing authority, they may notify that other authority of their opinion.

...

(2) The conditions for referral of the case to another authority are met if—

    (a) neither the applicant nor any person who might reasonably be expected to reside with him has a local connection with the district of the authority to whom his application was made,

    (b) the applicant or a person who might reasonably be expected to reside with him has a local connection with the district of that other authority, and

    (c) neither the applicant nor any person who might reasonably be expected to reside with him will run the risk of domestic violence in that other district.

[(2A) But the conditions for referral mentioned in subsection (2) are not met if—

    (a) the applicant or any person who might reasonably be expected to reside with him has suffered violence (other than domestic violence) in the district of the other authority; and

    (b) it is probable that the return to that district of the victim will lead to further violence of a similar kind against him.

(3) For the purposes of subsections (2) and (2A) "violence" means—

    (a) violence from another person; or

    (b) threats of violence from another person which are likely to be carried out;

and violence is "domestic violence" if it is from a person who is associated with the victim.]

(4) The conditions for referral of the case to another authority are also met if—

    (a) the applicant was on a previous application made to that other authority placed (in pursuance of their functions under this Part) in accommodation in the district of the authority to whom his application is now made, and

    (b) the previous application was within such period as may be prescribed of the present application.

(5) The question whether the conditions for referral of a case are satisfied shall be decided by agreement between the notifying authority and the notified authority or, in default of agreement, in accordance with such arrangements as the Secretary of State may direct by order.

(6) An order may direct that the arrangements shall be—

    (a) those agreed by any relevant authorities or associations of relevant authorities, or

    (b) in default of such agreement, such arrangements as appear to the Secretary of State to be suitable, after consultation with such associations representing relevant authorities, and such other persons, as he thinks appropriate.

(7) No such order shall be made unless a draft of the order has been approved by a resolution of each House of Parliament.

**[1090]**

**NOTES**

Sub-s (1): words omitted repealed by the Homelessness Act 2002, s 18(2), Sch 2.

Sub-ss (2A), (3): substituted, for original sub-s (3), by the Homelessness Act 2002, s 10(2).

Modified, in relation to asylum-seekers who are eligible for housing assistance under s 185(2) of the Housing Act 1996, and who are not made ineligible by s 186 (or any other provision) of that Act, in relation to England only, by the Homelessness (Asylum-Seekers) (Interim Period) (England) Order 1999, SI 1999/3126, arts 1(2), 2, 3.

Orders: the Homelessness (Decisions on Referrals) Order 1998, SI 1998/1578 at **[3211]**; the Allocation of Housing and Homelessness (Miscellaneous Provisions) (England) Regulations 2006, SI 2006/2527 at **[3733]**.

## 199 Local connection

(1) A person has a local connection with the district of a local housing authority if he has a connection with it—

    (a) because he is, or in the past was, normally resident there, and that residence is or was of his own choice,

(b)   because he is employed there,

(c)   because of family associations, or

(d)   because of special circumstances.

(2)   *A person is not employed in a district if he is serving in the regular armed forces of the Crown.*

(3)   Residence in a district is not of a person's own choice if—

(a)   *he becomes resident there because he, or a person who might reasonably be expected to reside with him, is serving in the regular armed forces of the Crown, or*

(b)   he, or a person who might reasonably be expected to reside with him, becomes resident there because he is detained under the authority of an Act of Parliament.

(4)   *In subsections (2) and (3) "regular armed forces of the Crown" means [the regular forces as defined by section 374 of the Armed Forces Act 2006].*

(5)   The Secretary of State may by order specify *other* circumstances in which—

(a)   a person is not to be treated as employed in a district, or

(b)   residence in a district is not to be treated as of a person's own choice.

[(6)   A person has a local connection with the district of a local housing authority if he was (at any time) provided with accommodation in that district under section 95 of the Immigration and Asylum Act 1999 (support for asylum seekers).

(7)   But subsection (6) does not apply—

(a)   to the provision of accommodation for a person in a district of a local housing authority if he was subsequently provided with accommodation in the district of another local housing authority under section 95 of that Act, or

(b)   to the provision of accommodation in an accommodation centre by virtue of section 22 of the Nationality, Immigration and Asylum Act 2002 (c 41) (use of accommodation centres for section 95 support).]

**[1091]**

**NOTES**

Sub-s (2): repealed by the Housing and Regeneration Act 2008, ss 315(a), 321(1), Sch 16, as from 1 December 2008 (in relation to England for certain purposes), 30 March 2009 (in relation to Wales for certain purposes) and from a day to be appointed (for remaining purposes).

Sub-s (3): para (a) repealed by the Housing and Regeneration Act 2008, ss 315(b), 321(1), Sch 16, as from 1 December 2008 (in relation to England for certain purposes), 30 March 2009 (in relation to Wales for certain purposes) and from a day to be appointed (for remaining purposes).

Sub-s (4): repealed by the Housing and Regeneration Act 2008, ss 315(c), 321(1), Sch 16, as from 1 December 2008 (in relation to England for certain purposes), 30 March 2009 (in relation to Wales for certain purposes) and from a day to be appointed (for remaining purposes); words in square brackets substituted by the Armed Forces Act 2006, s 378(1), Sch 16, para 139.

Sub-s (5): word in italics repealed by the Housing and Regeneration Act 2008, ss 315(d), 321(1), Sch 16, as from 1 December 2008 (in relation to England for certain purposes), 30 March 2009 (in relation to Wales for certain purposes) and from a day to be appointed (for remaining purposes).

Sub-ss (6), (7): inserted by the Asylum and Immigration (Treatment of Claimants, etc) Act 2004, s 11(1).

**200   Duties to the applicant whose case is considered for referral or referred**

(1)   Where a local housing authority notify an applicant that they intend to notify or have notified another local housing authority of their opinion that the conditions are met for the referral of his case to that other authority—

(a)   they cease to be subject to any duty under section 188 (interim duty to accommodate in case of apparent priority need), and

(b)   they are not subject to any duty under section 193 (the main housing duty),

but they shall secure that accommodation is available for occupation by the applicant until he is notified of the decision whether the conditions for referral of his case are met.

(2)   When it has been decided whether the conditions for referral are met, the notifying authority shall notify the applicant of the decision and inform him of the reasons for it.

The notice shall also inform the applicant of his right to request a review of the decision and of the time within which such a request must be made.

[(3)   If it is decided that the conditions for referral are not met, the notifying authority are subject to the duty under section 193 (the main housing duty).

(4)   If it is decided that those conditions are met, the notified authority are subject to the duty under section 193 (the main housing duty).]

(5)   The duty under subsection (1), ... ceases as provided in that subsection even if the applicant requests a review of the authority's decision (see section 202).

The authority may [secure] that accommodation is available for the applicant's occupation pending the decision on a review.

(6)   Notice required to be given to an applicant under this section shall be given in writing and, if not received by him, shall be treated as having been given to him if it is made available at the authority's office for a reasonable period for collection by him or on his behalf.

**[1092]**

**NOTES**
    Sub-ss (3), (4): substituted by the Homelessness Act 2002, s 18(1), Sch 1, paras 2, 15(a).
    Sub-s (5): words omitted repealed and word in square brackets substituted by the Homelessness Act 2002, s 18, Sch 1, paras 2, 15(b), Sch 2.

**201   Application of referral provisions to cases arising in Scotland**

Sections 198 and 200 (referral of application to another local housing authority and duties to applicant whose case is considered for referral or referred) apply—
    (a)    to applications referred by a local authority in Scotland in pursuance of sections 33 and 34 of the Housing (Scotland) Act 1987, and
    (b)    to persons whose applications are so transferred,
as they apply to cases arising under this Part (the reference in section 198 to this Part being construed as a reference to Part II of that Act).

**[1093]**

*Right to request review of decision*

**202   Right to request review of decision**

    (1)   An applicant has the right to request a review of—
    (a)    any decision of a local housing authority as to his eligibility for assistance,
    (b)    any decision of a local housing authority as to what duty (if any) is owed to him under sections 190 to 193 and 195 [and 196] (duties to persons found to be homeless or threatened with homelessness),
    (c)    any decision of a local housing authority to notify another authority under section 198(1) (referral of cases),
    (d)    any decision under section 198(5) whether the conditions are met for the referral of his case,
    (e)    any decision under section 200(3) or (4) (decision as to duty owed to applicant whose case is considered for referral or referred), ...
    (f)    any decision of a local housing authority as to the suitability of accommodation offered to him in discharge of their duty under any of the provisions mentioned in paragraph (b) or (e) [or as to the suitability of accommodation offered to him as mentioned in section 193(7)][, or
    (g)    any decision of a local housing authority as to the suitability of accommodation offered to him by way of a private accommodation offer (within the meaning of section 193)].

[(1A)   An applicant who is offered accommodation as mentioned in section 193(5)[, (7) or (7AA)] may under subsection (1)(f) [or (as the case may be) (g)] request a review of the suitability of the accommodation offered to him whether or not he has accepted the offer.]

    (2)   There is no right to request a review of the decision reached on an earlier review.

    (3)   A request for review must be made before the end of the period of 21 days beginning with the day on which he is notified of the authority's decision or such longer period as the authority may in writing allow.

    (4)   On a request being duly made to them, the authority or authorities concerned shall review their decision.

**[1094]**

**NOTES**
    Sub-s (1): words in square brackets in para (b) substituted and words in square brackets in para (f) inserted by the Homelessness Act 2002, ss 8(2)(a), 18(1), Sch 1, paras 2, 16; word omitted from para (e) repealed by the Housing and Regeneration Act 2008, s 321(1), Sch 16; para (g) and word immediately preceding it inserted by the Housing and Regeneration Act 2008, s 314, Sch 15, Pt 1, paras 1, 7(1), (2), except in relation to applications for an allocation of social housing or housing assistance (homelessness) or for accommodation made before 2 March 2009.
    Sub-s (1A): inserted by the Homelessness Act 2002, s 8(2)(b); words in first pair of square brackets substituted and words in second pair of square brackets inserted by the Housing and Regeneration Act 2008, s 314, Sch 15, Pt 1, paras 1, 7(1), (3), except in relation to applications for an allocation of social housing or housing assistance (homelessness) or for accommodation made before 2 March 2009.

**203   Procedure on a review**

    (1)   The Secretary of State may make provision by regulations as to the procedure to be followed in connection with a review under section 202.

Nothing in the following provisions affects the generality of this power.

(2)   Provision may be made by regulations—

(a)   requiring the decision on review to be made by a person of appropriate seniority who was not involved in the original decision, and

(b)   as to the circumstances in which the applicant is entitled to an oral hearing, and whether and by whom he may be represented at such a hearing.

(3)   The authority, or as the case may be either of the authorities, concerned shall notify the applicant of the decision on the review.

(4)   If the decision is—

(a)   to confirm the original decision on any issue against the interests of the applicant, or

(b)   to confirm a previous decision—

(i)   to notify another authority under section 198 (referral of cases), or

(ii)   that the conditions are met for the referral of his case,

they shall also notify him of the reasons for the decision.

(5)   In any case they shall inform the applicant of his right to appeal to a county court on a point of law, and of the period within which such an appeal must be made (see section 204).

(6)   Notice of the decision shall not be treated as given unless and until subsection (5), and where applicable subsection (4), is complied with.

(7)   Provision may be made by regulations as to the period within which the review must be carried out and notice given of the decision.

(8)   Notice required to be given to a person under this section shall be given in writing and, if not received by him, shall be treated as having been given if it is made available at the authority's office for a reasonable period for collection by him or on his behalf.

**[1095]**

**NOTES**

Regulations: the Allocation of Housing and Homelessness (Review Procedures) Regulations 1999, SI 1999/71 at **[3225]**.

## 204   Right of appeal to county court on point of law

(1)   If an applicant who has requested a review under section 202—

(a)   is dissatisfied with the decision on the review, or

(b)   is not notified of the decision on the review within the time prescribed under section 203,

he may appeal to the county court on any point of law arising from the decision or, as the case may be, the original decision.

(2)   An appeal must be brought within 21 days of his being notified of the decision or, as the case may be, of the date on which he should have been notified of a decision on review.

[(2A)   The court may give permission for an appeal to be brought after the end of the period allowed by subsection (2), but only if it is satisfied—

(a)   where permission is sought before the end of that period, that there is a good reason for the applicant to be unable to bring the appeal in time; or

(b)   where permission is sought after that time, that there was a good reason for the applicant's failure to bring the appeal in time and for any delay in applying for permission.]

(3)   On appeal the court may make such order confirming, quashing or varying the decision as it thinks fit.

(4)   Where the authority were under a duty under section 188, 190 or 200 to secure that accommodation is available for the applicant's occupation[, or had the power under section 195(8) to do so, they may] secure that accommodation is so available—

(a)   during the period for appealing under this section against the authority's decision, and

(b)   if an appeal is brought, until the appeal (and any further appeal) is finally determined.

**[1096]**

**NOTES**

Sub-s (2A): inserted by the Homelessness Act 2002, s 18(1), Sch 1, paras 2, 17(a), except in relation to any case in England where an appeal is brought under sub-s (1) before 30 September 2002.

Sub-s (4): words in square brackets substituted by the Homelessness Act 2002, s 18(1), Sch 1, paras 2, 17(b).

## [204A   Section 204(4): appeals

(1)   This section applies where an applicant has the right to appeal to the county court against a local housing authority's decision on a review.

(2)   If the applicant is dissatisfied with a decision by the authority—

(a)   not to exercise their power under section 204(4) ("the section 204(4) power") in his case;

    (b)    to exercise that power for a limited period ending before the final determination by the county court of his appeal under section 204(1) ("the main appeal"); or

    (c)    to cease exercising that power before that time,

he may appeal to the county court against the decision.

(3)    An appeal under this section may not be brought after the final determination by the county court of the main appeal.

(4)    On an appeal under this section the court—

    (a)    may order the authority to secure that accommodation is available for the applicant's occupation until the determination of the appeal (or such earlier time as the court may specify); and

    (b)    shall confirm or quash the decision appealed against,

and in considering whether to confirm or quash the decision the court shall apply the principles applied by the High Court on an application for judicial review.

(5)    If the court quashes the decision it may order the authority to exercise the section 204(4) power in the applicant's case for such period as may be specified in the order.

(6)    An order under subsection (5)—

    (a)    may only be made if the court is satisfied that failure to exercise the section 204(4) power in accordance with the order would substantially prejudice the applicant's ability to pursue the main appeal;

    (b)    may not specify any period ending after the final determination by the county court of the main appeal.]

**[1097]**

**NOTES**

Inserted by the Homelessness Act 2002, s 11, except in relation to any case in England where an appeal is brought under s 204(1) before 30 September 2002.

*Supplementary provisions*

## 205   Discharge of functions: introductory

(1)    The following sections have effect in relation to the discharge by a local housing authority of their functions under this Part to secure that accommodation is available for the occupation of a person—

    section 206 (general provisions),

    ...

    section 208 (out-of-area placements),

    section 209 (arrangements with private landlord).

(2)    In [sections 206 and 208] those functions are referred to as the authority's "housing functions under this Part".

**[1098]**

**NOTES**

Sub-s (1): words omitted repealed by the Homelessness Act 2002, s 18(2), Sch 2.

Sub-s (2): words in square brackets substituted by the Homelessness Act 2002, s 18(1), Sch 1, paras 2, 18.

See further, in relation to functions of a local housing authority conferred under this Part: Local Authorities (Contracting Out of Allocation of Housing and Homelessness Functions) Order 1996, SI 1996/3205, reg 3, Sch 2.

## 206   Discharge of functions by local housing authorities

(1)    A local housing authority may discharge their housing functions under this Part only in the following ways—

    (a)    by securing that suitable accommodation provided by them is available,

    (b)    by securing that he obtains suitable accommodation from some other person, or

    (c)    by giving him such advice and assistance as will secure that suitable accommodation is available from some other person.

(2)    A local housing authority may require a person in relation to whom they are discharging such functions—

    (a)    to pay such reasonable charges as they may determine in respect of accommodation which they secure for his occupation (either by making it available themselves or otherwise), or

    (b)    to pay such reasonable amount as they may determine in respect of sums payable by them for accommodation made available by another person.

**[1099]**

**NOTES**

Modified, in relation to asylum-seekers who are eligible for housing assistance under s 185(2) of the Housing Act 1996, and who are not made ineligible by s 186 (or any other provision) of that Act, in relation to England only, by the Homelessness (Asylum-Seekers) (Interim Period) (England) Order 1999, SI 1999/3126, arts 1(2), 2, 4.

**207**    (*Repealed by the Homelessness Act 2002, s 18(2), Sch 2.*)

**208    Discharge of functions: out-of-area placements**

(1)    So far as reasonably practicable a local housing authority shall in discharging their housing functions under this Part secure that accommodation is available for the occupation of the applicant in their district.

(2)    If they secure that accommodation is available for the occupation of the applicant outside their district, they shall give notice to the local housing authority in whose district the accommodation is situated.

(3)    The notice shall state—
- (a)    the name of the applicant,
- (b)    the number and description of other persons who normally reside with him as a member of his family or might reasonably be expected to reside with him,
- (c)    the address of the accommodation,
- (d)    the date on which the accommodation was made available to him, and
- (e)    which function under this Part the authority was discharging in securing that the accommodation is available for his occupation.

(4)    The notice must be in writing, and must be given before the end of the period of 14 days beginning with the day on which the accommodation was made available to the applicant.

**[1100]**

**NOTES**

Modified, in relation to asylum-seekers who are eligible for housing assistance under s 185(2) of the Housing Act 1996, and who are not made ineligible by s 186 (or any other provision) of that Act, in relation to England only, by the Homelessness (Asylum-Seekers) (Interim Period) (England) Order 1999, SI 1999/3126, arts 1(2), 2, 5.

**[209    Discharge of interim duties: arrangements with private landlord**

(1)    This section applies where in pursuance of any of their housing functions under section 188, 190, 200 or 204(4) (interim duties) a local housing authority make arrangements with a private landlord to provide accommodation.

(2)    A tenancy granted to the applicant in pursuance of the arrangements cannot be an assured tenancy before the end of the period of twelve months beginning with—
- (a)    the date on which the applicant was notified of the authority's decision under section 184(3) or 198(5); or
- (b)    if there is a review of that decision under section 202 or an appeal to the court under section 204, the date on which he is notified of the decision on review or the appeal is finally determined,

unless, before or during that period, the tenant is notified by the landlord (or in the case of joint landlords, at least one of them) that the tenancy is to be regarded as an assured shorthold tenancy or an assured tenancy other than an assured shorthold tenancy.]

**[1101]**

**NOTES**

Substituted by the Homelessness Act 2002, s 18(1), Sch 1, paras 2, 19.

**210    Suitability of accommodation**

(1)    In determining for the purposes of this Part whether accommodation is suitable for a person, the local housing authority shall have regard to [Parts 9 and 10] of the Housing Act 1985 (slum clearance [and overcrowding) and Parts 1 to 4 of the Housing Act 2004]).

(2)    The Secretary of State may by order specify—
- (a)    circumstances in which accommodation is or is not to be regarded as suitable for a person, and
- (b)    matters to be taken into account or disregarded in determining whether accommodation is suitable for a person.

**[1102]**

**NOTES**

Sub-s (1): words in square brackets substituted by the Housing Act 2004, s 265(1), Sch 15, paras 40, 43.

Modified, in relation to asylum-seekers who are eligible for housing assistance under s 185(2) of the Housing Act 1996, and who are not made ineligible by s 186 (or any other provision) of that Act, in relation to England only, by the Homelessness (Asylum-Seekers) (Interim Period) (England) Order 1999, SI 1999/3126, arts 1(2), 2, 6.

Orders: the Homelessness (Suitability of Accommodation) Order 1996, SI 1996/3204 at **[3152]**; the Homelessness (Suitability of Accommodation) (England) Order 2003, SI 2003/3326 at **[3352]**; the Homelessness (Suitability of Accommodation) (Wales) Order 2006, SI 2006/650 at **[3639]**.

## 211   Protection of property of homeless persons and persons threatened with homelessness

(1)   This section applies where a local housing authority have reason to believe that—
   (a)   there is danger of loss of, or damage to, any personal property of an applicant by reason of his inability to protect it or deal with it, and
   (b)   no other suitable arrangements have been or are being made.

(2)   If the authority have become subject to a duty towards the applicant under—
   section 188 (interim duty to accommodate),
   section 190, 193 or 195 (duties to persons found to be homeless or threatened with homelessness), or
   section 200 (duties to applicant whose case is considered for referral or referred),
then, whether or not they are still subject to such a duty, they shall take reasonable steps to prevent the loss of the property or prevent or mitigate damage to it.

(3)   If they have not become subject to such a duty, they may take any steps they consider reasonable for that purpose.

(4)   The authority may decline to take action under this section except upon such conditions as they consider appropriate in the particular case, which may include conditions as to—
   (a)   the making and recovery by the authority of reasonable charges for the action taken, or
   (b)   the disposal by the authority, in such circumstances as may be specified, of property in relation to which they have taken action.

(5)   References in this section to personal property of the applicant include personal property of any person who might reasonably be expected to reside with him.

(6)   Section 212 contains provisions supplementing this section.

**[1103]**

## 212   Protection of property: supplementary provisions

(1)   The authority may for the purposes of section 211 (protection of property of homeless persons or persons threatened with homelessness)—
   (a)   enter, at all reasonable times, any premises which are the usual place of residence of the applicant or which were his last usual place of residence, and
   (b)   deal with any personal property of his in any way which is reasonably necessary, in particular by storing it or arranging for its storage.

(2)   Where the applicant asks the authority to move his property to a particular location nominated by him, the authority—
   (a)   may, if it appears to them that his request is reasonable, discharge their responsibilities under section 211 by doing as he asks, and
   (b)   having done so, have no further duty or power to take action under that section in relation to that property.

If such a request is made, the authority shall before complying with it inform the applicant of the consequence of their doing so.

(3)   If no such request is made (or, if made, is not acted upon) the authority cease to have any duty or power to take action under section 211 when, in their opinion, there is no longer any reason to believe that there is a danger of loss of or damage to a person's personal property by reason of his inability to protect it or deal with it.

But property stored by virtue of their having taken such action may be kept in store and any conditions upon which it was taken into store continue to have effect, with any necessary modifications.

(4)   Where the authority—
   (a)   cease to be subject to a duty to take action under section 211 in respect of an applicant's property, or
   (b)   cease to have power to take such action, having previously taken such action,
they shall notify the applicant of that fact and of the reason for it.

(5)   The notification shall be given to the applicant—
   (a)   by delivering it to him, or
   (b)   by leaving it, or sending it to him, at his last known address.

(6)   References in this section to personal property of the applicant include personal property of any person who might reasonably be expected to reside with him.

**[1104]**

### 213   Co-operation between relevant housing authorities and bodies

(1)   Where a local housing authority—

   (a)   request another relevant housing authority or body, in England, Wales or Scotland, to assist them in the discharge of their functions under this Part, or

   (b)   request a social services authority, in England, Wales or Scotland, to exercise any of their functions in relation to a case which the local housing authority are dealing with under this Part,

the authority or body to whom the request is made shall co-operate in rendering such assistance in the discharge of the functions to which the request relates as is reasonable in the circumstances.

(2)   In subsection (1)(a) "relevant housing authority or body" means—

   (a)   in relation to England and Wales, a local housing authority, a new town corporation, a registered social landlord or a housing action trust;

   (b)   in relation to Scotland, a local authority, a development corporation, a registered housing association or Scottish Homes.

Expressions used in paragraph (a) have the same meaning as in the Housing Act 1985; and expressions used in paragraph (b) have the same meaning as in the Housing (Scotland) Act 1987.

(3)   Subsection (1) above applies to a request by a local authority in Scotland under section 38 of the Housing (Scotland) Act 1987 as it applies to a request by a local housing authority in England and Wales (the references to this Part being construed, in relation to such a request, as references to Part II of that Act).

**[1105]**

### [213A   Co-operation in certain cases involving children

(1)   This section applies where a local housing authority have reason to believe that an applicant with whom a person under the age of 18 normally resides, or might reasonably be expected to reside—

   (a)   may be ineligible for assistance;

   (b)   may be homeless and may have become so intentionally; or

   (c)   may be threatened with homelessness intentionally.

(2)   A local housing authority shall make arrangements for ensuring that, where this section applies—

   (a)   the applicant is invited to consent to the referral of the essential facts of his case to the social services authority for the district of the housing authority (where that is a different authority); and

   (b)   if the applicant has given that consent, the social services authority are made aware of those facts and of the subsequent decision of the housing authority in respect of his case.

(3)   Where the local housing authority and the social services authority for a district are the same authority (a "unitary authority"), that authority shall make arrangements for ensuring that, where this section applies—

   (a)   the applicant is invited to consent to the referral to the social services department of the essential facts of his case; and

   (b)   if the applicant has given that consent, the social services department is made aware of those facts and of the subsequent decision of the authority in respect of his case.

(4)   Nothing in subsection (2) or (3) affects any power apart from this section to disclose information relating to the applicant's case to the social services authority or to the social services department (as the case may be) without the consent of the applicant.

(5)   Where a social services authority—

   (a)   are aware of a decision of a local housing authority that the applicant is ineligible for assistance, became homeless intentionally or became threatened with homelessness intentionally, and

   (b)   request the local housing authority to provide them with advice and assistance in the exercise of their social services functions under Part 3 of the Children Act 1989,

the local housing authority shall provide them with such advice and assistance as is reasonable in the circumstances.

(6)   A unitary authority shall make arrangements for ensuring that, where they make a decision of a kind mentioned in subsection (5)(a), the housing department provide the social services department with such advice and assistance as the social services department may reasonably request.

(7)   In this section, in relation to a unitary authority—

"the housing department" means those persons responsible for the exercise of their housing functions; and

"the social services department" means those persons responsible for the exercise of their social services functions under Part 3 of the Children Act 1989.]

**[1106]**

---

**NOTES**

Inserted by the Homelessness Act 2002, s 12.

*General provisions*

### 214 False statements, withholding information and failure to disclose change of circumstances

(1) It is an offence for a person, with intent to induce a local housing authority to believe in connection with the exercise of their functions under this Part that he or another person is entitled to accommodation or assistance in accordance with the provisions of this Part, or is entitled to accommodation or assistance of a particular description—

(a) knowingly or recklessly to make a statement which is false in a material particular, or

(b) knowingly to withhold information which the authority have reasonably required him to give in connection with the exercise of those functions.

(2) If before an applicant receives notification of the local housing authority's decision on his application there is any change of facts material to his case, he shall notify the authority as soon as possible.

The authority shall explain to every applicant, in ordinary language, the duty imposed on him by this subsection and the effect of subsection (3).

(3) A person who fails to comply with subsection (2) commits an offence unless he shows that he was not given the explanation required by that subsection or that he had some other reasonable excuse for non-compliance.

(4) A person guilty of an offence under this section is liable on summary conviction to a fine not exceeding level 5 on the standard scale.

**[1107]**

### 215 Regulations and orders

(1) In this Part "prescribed" means prescribed by regulations of the Secretary of State.

(2) Regulations or an order under this Part may make different provision for different purposes, including different provision for different areas.

(3) Regulations or an order under this Part shall be made by statutory instrument.

(4) Unless required to be approved in draft, regulations or an order under this Part shall be subject to annulment in pursuance of a resolution of either House of Parliament.

**[1108]**

### 216 Transitional and consequential matters

(1) The provisions of this Part have effect in place of the provisions of Part III of the Housing Act 1985 (housing the homeless) and shall be construed as one with that Act.

(2) Subject to any transitional provision contained in an order under section 232(4) (power to include transitional provision in commencement order), the provisions of this Part do not apply in relation to an applicant whose application for accommodation or assistance in obtaining accommodation was made before the commencement of this Part.

(3) The enactments mentioned in Schedule 17 have effect with the amendments specified there which are consequential on the provisions of this Part.

**[1109]**

### 217 Minor definitions: Part VII

(1) In this Part, subject to subsection (2)—

["private landlord" means a landlord who is not within section 80(1) of the Housing Act 1985 (c 68) (the landlord condition for secure tenancies);]

"relevant authority" means a local housing authority or a social services authority; and

"social services authority" means a local authority for the purposes of the Local Authority Social Services Act 1970, as defined in section 1 of that Act.

(2) In this Part, in relation to Scotland—

(a) "local housing authority" means a local authority within the meaning of the Housing (Scotland) Act 1988, and

(b) "social services authority" means a local authority for the purposes of the Social Work (Scotland) Act 1968.

(3) References in this Part to the district of a local housing authority—
  (a) have the same meaning in relation to an authority in England or Wales as in the Housing Act 1985, and
  (b) in relation to an authority in Scotland, mean the area of the local authority concerned.

**[1110]**

**NOTES**
Sub-s (1): definition "private landlord" inserted by the Homelessness Act 2002, s 18(1), Sch 1, paras 2, 20.

## 218 Index of defined expressions: Part VII

The following Table shows provisions defining or otherwise explaining expressions used in this Part (other than provisions defining or explaining an expression used in the same section)—

| | |
|---|---|
| accommodation available for occupation | section 176 |
| applicant | section 183(2) |
| assistance under this Part | section 183(2) |
| associated (in relation to a person) | section 178 |
| assured tenancy and assured shorthold tenancy | section 230 |
| district (of local housing authority) | section 217(3) |
| eligible for assistance | section 183(2) |
| homeless | section 175(1) |
| housing functions under this Part (in sections [206 and 208]) | section 205(2) |
| intentionally homeless | section 191 |
| intentionally threatened with homelessness | section 196 |
| local connection | section 199 |
| local housing authority— | |
| – in England and Wales | section 230 |
| – in Scotland | section 217(2)(a) |
| … | … |
| Prescribed | section 215(1) |
| priority need | section 189 |
| [private landlord | section 217(1)] |
| Reasonable to continue to occupy accommodation | section 177 |
| registered social landlord | section 230 |
| relevant authority | section 217(1) |
| [restricted person | section 184(7)] |
| social services authority | section 217(1) and (2)(b) |
| threatened with homelessness | section 175(4) |

**[1111]**

**NOTES**
In entry "housing functions under this Part" words in square brackets substituted, entry "minimum period" (omitted) repealed, and entry "private landlord" inserted by the Homelessness Act 2002, s 18, Sch 1, paras 2, 21, Sch 2; entry "restricted person" inserted by the Housing and Regeneration Act 2008, s 314, Sch 15, Pt 1, paras 1, 8, except in relation to applications for an allocation of social housing or housing assistance (homelessness) or for accommodation made before 2 March 2009.

### PART VIII
### MISCELLANEOUS AND GENERAL PROVISIONS

*Miscellaneous*

## [218A Anti-social behaviour: landlords' policies and procedures

(1) This section applies to the following landlords—
  (a) a local housing authority;

    (b)    a housing action trust;

    (c)    a registered social landlord.

(2)    The landlord must prepare—

    (a)    a policy in relation to anti-social behaviour;

    (b)    procedures for dealing with occurrences of anti-social behaviour.

(3)    The landlord must not later than 6 months after the commencement of section 12 of the Anti-social Behaviour Act 2003 publish a statement of the policy and procedures prepared under subsection (2).

(4)    The landlord must from time to time keep the policy and procedures under review and, when it thinks appropriate, publish a revised statement.

(5)    A copy of a statement published under subsection (3) or (4)—

    (a)    must be available for inspection at all reasonable hours at the landlord's principal office;

    (b)    must be provided on payment of a reasonable fee to any person who requests it.

(6)    The landlord must also—

    (a)    prepare a summary of its current policy and procedures;

    (b)    provide without charge a copy of the summary to any person who requests it.

(7)    In preparing and reviewing the policy and procedures the landlord must have regard to guidance issued—

    (a)    by the Secretary of State in the case of a local housing authority or a housing action trust;

    (b)    by the Relevant Authority under section 36 in the case of a registered social landlord.

[(8)    Anti-social behaviour is—

    (a)    any housing-related anti-social conduct, or

    (b)    any conduct to which section 153B applies.

(8A)    Housing-related anti-social conduct has the same meaning as in section 153A.]

(9)    Relevant Authority has the same meaning as in Part 1.]

**[1112]**

---

**NOTES**

Commencement: 30 June 2004 (in relation to England); 30 April 2005 (in relation to Wales).
Inserted by the Anti-social Behaviour Act 2003, s 12(1).
Sub-ss (8), (8A): substituted for original sub-s (8) by the Police and Justice Act 2006, s 52, Sch 14, para 33, except in relation to any application for an injunction by a relevant landlord (other than a relevant Welsh landlord) made before 6 April 2007.

---

### 219  Directions as to certain charges by social landlords

(1)    The Secretary of State may give directions to social landlords about the making of service charges in respect of works of repair, maintenance or improvement—

    (a)    requiring or permitting the waiver or reduction of charges where relevant assistance is given by the Secretary of State, and

    (b)    permitting the waiver or reduction of charges in such other circumstances as may be specified in the directions.

(2)    A direction shall not require the waiver or reduction of charges by reference to assistance for which application was made before the date on which the direction was given, but subject to that directions may relate to past charges or works to such extent as appears to the Secretary of State to be appropriate.

(3)    Directions which require or permit the waiver or reduction of charges have corresponding effect—

    (a)    in relation to charges already demanded so as to require or permit the non-enforcement of the charges, and

    (b)    in relation to charges already paid so as to require or permit a refund.

(4)    For the purposes of this section "social landlord" means—

    (a)    an authority or body within section 80(1) of the Housing Act 1985 (the landlord condition for secure tenancies), other than [the Homes and Communities Agency, the Welsh Ministers and] a housing co-operative, or

    (b)    a registered social landlord.

(5)    In this section "assistance" means grant or other financial assistance of any kind; and directions may specify what assistance is relevant for the purposes of this section, and to what buildings or other land any assistance is to be regarded as relevant.

(6)    The provisions of section 220 supplement this section.

**[1113]**

**NOTES**

Sub-s (4): words in square brackets in para (a) inserted by the Housing and Regeneration Act 2008 (Consequential Provisions) Order 2008, SI 2008/3002, art 4, Sch 1, paras 45, 46.

## 220  Directions as to certain charges: supplementary provisions

(1)  Directions under section 219 may make different provision for different cases or descriptions of case.

This includes power to make—

(a)  different provision for different social landlords or descriptions of social landlords, and

(b)  different provision for different areas.

(2)  Directions under section 219 requiring the reduction of a service charge may specify the amount (or proportion) of the reduction or provide for its determination in such manner as may be specified.

(3)  Directions under section 219 permitting the waiver or reduction of a service charge may specify criteria to which the social landlord is to have regard in deciding whether to do so or to what extent.

(4)  The Secretary of State shall publish any direction under section 219 relating to all social landlords or any description of social landlords in such manner as he considers appropriate for bringing it to the notice of the landlords concerned.

(5)  For the purposes of section 219 "service charge" means an amount payable by a lessee of a dwelling—

(a)  which is payable, directly or indirectly, for repairs, maintenance or improvements, and

(b)  the whole or part of which varies or may vary according to the relevant costs.

(6)  The relevant costs are the costs or estimated costs incurred or to be incurred by or on behalf of the social landlord, or a superior landlord, in connection with the matters for which the service charge is payable.

For this purpose costs are relevant costs in relation to a service charge whether they are incurred, or to be incurred, in the period for which the service charge is payable or in an earlier or later period.

(7)  In this section—

"costs" includes overheads, and

"dwelling" means a building or part of a building occupied or intended to be occupied as a separate dwelling.

**[1114]**

**221, 222**	(*Outside the scope of this work.*)

*General*

**223–228**	(*Outside the scope of this work.*)

## 229  Meaning of "lease" and "tenancy" and related expressions

(1)  In this Act "lease" and "tenancy" have the same meaning.

(2)  Both expressions include—

(a)  a sub-lease or a sub-tenancy, and

(b)  an agreement for a lease or tenancy (or sub-lease or sub-tenancy).

(3)  The expressions "lessor" and "lessee" and "landlord" and "tenant", and references to letting, to the grant of a lease or to covenants or terms, shall be construed accordingly.

**[1115]**

## 230  Minor definitions: general

In this Act—

"assured tenancy", "assured shorthold tenancy" and "assured agricultural occupancy" have the same meaning as in Part I of the Housing Act 1988;

"enactment" includes an enactment comprised in subordinate legislation (within the meaning of the Interpretation Act 1978);

"housing action trust" has the same meaning as in the Housing Act 1988;

"housing association" has the same meaning as in the Housing Associations Act 1985;

"introductory tenancy" and "introductory tenant" have the same meaning as in Chapter I of Part V of this Act;

"local housing authority" has the same meaning as in the Housing Act 1985;

"registered social landlord" has the same meaning as in Part I of this Act;

"secure tenancy" and "secure tenant" have the same meaning as in Part IV of the Housing Act 1985.

[1116]

### Final provisions

## 231 Extent

(1)   The provisions of this Act extend to England and Wales, and only to England and Wales, subject as follows.

(2)   The following provisions also extend to Scotland—
Part IV (housing benefit and related matters), and
the provisions of this Part so far as relating to Part IV.

(3)   Section 226 (power to make corresponding provision for Northern Ireland) also extends to Northern Ireland.

(4)   Any amendment or repeal by this Act of an enactment has the same extent as the enactment amended or repealed, except that—

(a)   amendments or repeals of provisions of the Housing Associations Act 1985, other than in consequence of paragraph 1 of Schedule 18 to this Act (repeal of Part IV of the Housing Act 1988), do not extend to Scotland,

(b)   amendments or repeals of provisions of the Housing Act 1988 relating to registered housing associations do not extend to Scotland,

(c)   amendments or repeals of provisions of the Asylum and Immigration Appeals Act 1993 or the Asylum and Immigration Act 1996 do not extend to Scotland or Northern Ireland, and

(d)   repeals of the following provisions do not extend to Scotland—
(i)   section 24(5)(a) and (c) of the Local Government Act 1988,
(ii)   section 182 of the Local Government and Housing 1989,
(iii)   paragraph 21(3) of Schedule 6 to the Charities Act 1993, and
(iv)   provisions in Schedule 26 to the Local Government, Planning and Land Act 1980.

(5)   Any power conferred by this Act to make consequential amendments or repeals of enactments may be exercised in relation to enactments as they extend to any part of the United Kingdom.

[1117]

**NOTES**

Order the Housing Act 1996 (Consequential Provisions) Order 1996, SI 1996/2325 at **[3143]**.

## 232   Commencement

(1)   The following provisions of this Act come into force on Royal Assent—
section 110 (new leases: valuation principles),
section 120 (payment of housing benefit to third parties), and
sections 223 to 226 and 228 to 233 (general provisions).

(2)   The following provisions of this Act come into force at the end of the period of two months beginning with the date on which this Act is passed—
sections 81 and 82 (restriction on termination of tenancy for failure to pay service charge),
section 85 (appointment of manager by the court),
section 94 (provision of general legal advice about residential tenancies),
section 95 (jurisdiction of county courts),
section 221 (exercise of compulsory purchase powers in relation to Crown land),
paragraph 24 (powers of local housing authorities to acquire land for housing purposes), paragraph 26 (preserved right to buy) and paragraphs 27 to 29 of Schedule 18 (local authority assistance in connection with mortgages), and
sections 222 and 227, and Schedule 19 (consequential repeals), in so far as they relate to those paragraphs.

(3)   The other provisions of this Act come into force on a day appointed by order of the Secretary of State, and different days may be appointed for different areas and different purposes.

(4)   An order under subsection (3) shall be made by statutory instrument and may contain such transitional provisions and savings as appear to the Secretary of State to be appropriate.

[1118]

**NOTES**

Orders: the Housing Act 1996 (Commencement No 1) Order 1996, SI 1996/2048; the Housing Act 1996 (Commencement No 2 and Savings) Order 1996, SI 1996/2212; the Housing Act 1996 (Commencement No 3 and Transitional Provisions) Order 1996, SI 1996/2402; the Housing Act 1996 (Commencement No 4) Order 1996, SI 1996/2658; the Housing Act 1996 (Commencement No 5 and Transitional Provisions) Order 1996, SI 1996/2959; the Housing Act 1996 (Commencement No 6 and Savings) Order 1997, SI 1997/66;

the Housing Act 1996 (Commencement No 7 and Savings) Order 1997, SI 1997/225; the Housing Act 1996 (Commencement No 8) Order 1997, SI 1997/350; the Housing Act 1996 (Commencement No 9) Order 1997, SI 1997/596; the Housing Act 1996 (Commencement No 10 and Transitional Provisions) Order 1997, SI 1997/618; the Housing Act 1996 (Commencement No 11 and Savings) Order 1997, SI 1997/1851; the Housing Act 1996 (Commencement No 12 and Transitional Provisions) Order 1998, SI 1998/1768; the Housing Act 1996 (Commencement No 13) Order 2001, SI 2001/3164.

### 233 Short title

This Act may be cited as the Housing Act 1996.

**[1119]**

## SCHEDULES

(*Schs 1–3 outside the scope of this work.*)

## SCHEDULE 4
### RIGHTS EXERCISABLE BY SURVEYOR APPOINTED BY TENANTS' ASSOCIATION
Section 84

### *Introductory*

1.—(1)  A surveyor appointed for the purposes of section 84 has the rights conferred by this Schedule.

(2)  In this Schedule—
  (a)  "the tenants' association" means the association by whom the surveyor was appointed, and
  (b)  the surveyor's "functions" are his functions in connection with the matters in respect of which he was appointed.

### *Appointment of assistants*

2.—(1)  The surveyor may appoint such persons as he thinks fit to assist him in carrying out his functions.

(2)  References in this Schedule to the surveyor in the context of—
  (a)  being afforded any such facilities as are mentioned in paragraph 3, or
  (b)  carrying out an inspection under paragraph 4,
include a person so appointed.

### *Right to inspect documents, &c*

3.—(1)  The surveyor has a right to require the landlord or any other relevant person—
  (a)  to afford him reasonable facilities for inspecting any documents sight of which is reasonably required by him for the purposes of his functions, and
  (b)  to afford him reasonable facilities for taking copies of or extracts from any such documents.

(2)  In sub-paragraph (1) "other relevant person" means a person other than the landlord who is or, in relation to a future service charge, will be—
  (a)  responsible for applying the proceeds of the service charge, or
  (b)  under an obligation to a tenant who pays the service charge in respect of any matter to which the charge relates.

(3)  The rights conferred on the surveyor by this paragraph are extricable by him by notice in writing given by him to the landlord or other person concerned.

Where a notice is given to a person other than the landlord, the surveyor shall give a copy of the notice to the landlord.

(4)  The landlord or other person to whom notice is given shall, within the period of one week beginning with the date of the giving of the notice or as soon as reasonably practicable thereafter, either—
  (a)  afford the surveyor the facilities required by him for inspecting and taking copies or extracts of the documents to which the notice relates, or
  (b)  give the surveyor a notice stating that he objects to doing so for reasons specified in the notice.

(5)  Facilities for the inspection of any documents required under sub-paragraph (1)(a) shall be made available free of charge.

This does not mean that the landlord cannot treat as part of his costs of management any costs incurred by him in connection with making the facilities available.

(6)  A reasonable charge may be made for facilities for the taking of copies or extracts required under sub-paragraph (1)(b).

(7)  A notice is duly given under this paragraph to the landlord of a tenant if it is given to a person who receives on behalf of the landlord the rent payable by that tenant.

A person to whom such a notice is so given shall forward it as soon as may be to the landlord.

### *Right to inspect premises*

4.—(1)  The surveyor also has the right to inspect any common parts comprised in relevant premises or any appurtenant property.

(2)  In sub-paragraph (1)—

"common parts", in relation to a building or part of a building, includes the structure and exterior of the building or part and any common facilities within it;

"relevant premises" means so much of—

>  (i)  the building or buildings containing the dwellings let to members of the tenants' association, and
>  (ii)  any other building or buildings,

as constitute premises in relation to which management functions are discharged in respect of the costs of which service charges are payable by members of the association; and

"appurtenant property" means so much of any property not contained in relevant premises as constitutes property in relation to which any such management functions are discharged.

For the purposes of the above definitions "management functions" includes functions with respect to the provision of services, or the repair, maintenance[, improvement] or insurance of property.

(3)  On being requested to do so, the landlord shall afford the surveyor reasonable access for the purposes of carrying out an inspection under this paragraph.

(4)  Such reasonable access shall be afforded to the surveyor free of charge.

This does not mean that the landlord cannot treat as part of his costs of management any costs incurred by him in connection with affording reasonable access to the surveyor.

(5)  A request is duly made under this paragraph to the landlord of a tenant if it is made to a person appointed by the landlord to deal with such requests or, if no such person has been appointed, to a person who receives on behalf of the landlord the rent payable by that tenant.

A person to whom such a request is made shall notify the landlord of the request as soon as may be.

### *Enforcement of rights by the court*

5.—(1)  If the landlord or other person to whom notice was given under paragraph 3 has not, by the end of the period of one month beginning with the date on which notice was given, complied with the notice, the court may, on the application of the surveyor, make an order requiring him to do so within such period as is specified in the order.

(2)  If the landlord does not, within a reasonable period after the making of a request under paragraph 4, afford the surveyor reasonable access for the purposes of carrying out an inspection under that paragraph, the court may, on the application of the surveyor, make an order requiring the landlord to do so on such date as is specified in the order.

(3)  An application for an order under this paragraph must be made before the end of the period of four months beginning with the date on which notice was given under paragraph 3 or the request was made under paragraph 4.

(4)  An order under this paragraph may be made in general terms or may require the landlord or other person to do specific things, as the court thinks fit.

### *Documents held by superior landlord*

6.—(1)  Where a landlord is required by a notice under paragraph 3 to afford the surveyor facilities for inspection or taking copies or extracts in respect of any document which is in the custody or under the control of a superior landlord—

>  (a)  the landlord shall on receiving the notice inform the surveyor as soon as may be of that fact and of the name and address of the superior landlord, and
>  (b)  the surveyor may then give the superior landlord notice in writing requiring him to afford the facilities in question in respect of the document.

(2)  Paragraphs 3 and 5(1) and (3) have effect, with any necessary modifications, in relation to a notice given to a superior landlord under this paragraph.

*Effect of disposal by landlord*

7.—(1)  Where a notice under paragraph 3 has been given or a request under paragraph 4 has been made to a landlord, and at a time when any obligations arising out of the notice or request remain to be discharged by him—

    (a)    he disposes of the whole or part of his interest as landlord of any member of the tenants' association, and

    (b)    the person acquiring that interest ("the transferee") is in a position to discharge any of those obligations to any extent,

that person shall be responsible for discharging those obligations to that extent, as if he had been given the notice under paragraph 3 or had received the request under paragraph 4.

(2)  If the landlord is, despite the disposal, still in a position to discharge those obligations, he remains responsible for doing so.

Otherwise, the transferee is responsible for discharging them to the exclusion of the landlord.

(3)  In connection with the discharge of such obligations by the transferee, paragraphs 3 to 6 apply with the substitution for any reference to the date on which notice was given under paragraph 3 or the request was made under paragraph 4 of a reference to the date of the disposal.

(4)  In this paragraph "disposal" means a disposal whether by the creation or transfer of an estate or interest, and includes the surrender of a tenancy; and references to the transferee shall be construed accordingly.

*Effect of person ceasing to be a relevant person*

8.  Where a notice under paragraph 3 has been given to a person other than the landlord and, at a time when any obligations arising out of the notice remain to be discharged by him, he ceases to be such a person as is mentioned in paragraph 3(2), then, if he is still in a position to discharge those obligations to any extent he remains responsible for discharging those obligations, and the provisions of this Schedule continue to apply to him, to that extent.

**[1120]**

**NOTES**

    Para 4: word in square brackets inserted by the Commonhold and Leasehold Reform Act 2002, s 150, Sch 9, para 12.

    Modified, where the RTM company has acquired the right to manage, by the Commonhold and Leasehold Reform Act 2002, s 102, Sch 7, para 15 at **[1266]**, **[1306]**.

*(Sch 5 sets out the Landlord and Tenant Act 1987, Pt II at* **[681]** *et seq, as amended by this Act; Sch 6 amends the Landlord and Tenant Act 1987 at* **[644]** *et seq, and these amendments have been incorporated at the appropriate place in this work; Sch 7 sets out the Housing Act 1988, Sch 2A at* **[789]**; *Schs 8–11, 14 contain consequential amendments which, in so far as within the scope of this work, have been incorporated at the appropriate place; Schs 12, 13 outside the scope of this work.)*

SCHEDULE 15
ARREST FOR ANTI-SOCIAL BEHAVIOUR: POWERS OF HIGH COURT AND COUNTY
COURT TO REMAND
Section 155(6)

*Introductory*

1.—(1)  The provisions of this Schedule apply where the court has power to remand a person under section 155(2) or (5) (arrest for breach of injunction, &c).

(2)  In this Schedule "the court" means the High Court or a county court and includes—

    (a)    in relation to the High Court, a judge of that court, and

    (b)    in relation to a county court, a judge or district judge of that court.

*Remand in custody or on bail*

2.—(1)  The court may—

    (a)    remand him in custody, that is, commit him to custody to be brought before the court at the end of the period of remand or at such earlier time as the court may require, or

    (b)    remand him on bail, in accordance with the following provisions.

(2)  The court may remand him on bail—

    (a)    by taking from him a recognizance, with or without sureties, conditioned as provided in paragraph 3, or

    (b)    by fixing the amount of the recognizances with a view to their being taken subsequently, and in the meantime committing him to custody as mentioned in sub-paragraph (1)(a).

(3)  Where a person is brought before the court after remand, the court may further remand him.

3.—(1)  Where a person is remanded on bail, the court may direct that his recognizance be conditioned for his appearance—

    (a)    before that court at the end of the period of remand, or

    (b)    at every time and place to which during the course of the proceedings the hearing may from time to time be adjourned.

(2)    Where a recognizance is conditioned for a person's appearance as mentioned in sub-paragraph (1)(b), the fixing of any time for him next to appear shall be deemed to be a remand.

(3)    Nothing in this paragraph affects the power of the court at any subsequent hearing to remand him afresh.

4.—(1)    The court shall not remand a person for a period exceeding 8 clear days, except that—

    (a)    if the court remands him on bail, it may remand him for a longer period if he and the other party consent, and

    (b)    if the court adjourns a case under section 156(1) (remand for medical examination and report), the court may remand him for the period of the adjournment.

(2)    Where the court has power to remand a person in custody it may, if the remand is for a period not exceeding 3 clear days, commit him to the custody of a constable.

### Further remand

5.—(1)    If the court is satisfied that a person who has been remanded is unable by reason of illness or accident to appear or be brought before the court at the expiration of the period for which he was remanded, the court may, in his absence, remand him for a further time.

This power may, in the case of a person who was remanded on bail, be exercised by enlarging his recognizance and those of any sureties for him to a later time.

(2)    Where a person remanded on bail is bound to appear before the court at any time and the court has no power to remand him under sub-paragraph (1), the court may in his absence enlarge his recognizance and those of any sureties for him to a later time.

The enlargement of his recognizance shall be deemed to be a further remand.

(3)    Paragraph 4(1) (limit of period of demand) does not apply to the exercise of the powers conferred by this paragraph.

### Postponement of taking of recognizance

6.    Where under paragraph 2(2)(b) the court fixes the amount in which the principal and his sureties, if any, are to be bound, the recognizance may afterwards be taken by such a person as may be prescribed by rules of court, with the same consequences as if it had been entered into before the contract.

**[1121]**

*(Schs 16, 17, Sch 18, Pts III, IV contain consequential amendments which, in so far as within the scope of this work, have been incorporated at the appropriate place; Sch 18, Pts I, II outside the scope of this work; Sch 19 contains repeals only.)*

# HUMAN RIGHTS ACT 1998

### (1998 c 42)

### ARRANGEMENT OF SECTIONS

*An Act to give further effect to rights and freedoms guaranteed under the European Convention on Human Rights; to make provision with respect to holders of certain judicial offices who become judges of the European Court of Human Rights; and for connected purposes*

[9 November 1998]

*Introduction*

## 1 The Convention Rights

(1) In this Act "the Convention rights" means the rights and fundamental freedoms set out in—

    (a)    Articles 2 to 12 and 14 of the Convention,

    (b)    Articles 1 to 3 of the First Protocol, and

    (c)    [Article 1 of the Thirteenth Protocol],

as read with Articles 16 to 18 of the Convention.

(2) Those Articles are to have effect for the purposes of this Act subject to any designated derogation or reservation (as to which see sections 14 and 15).

(3) The Articles are set out in Schedule 1.

(4) The [Secretary of State] may by order make such amendments to this Act as he considers appropriate to reflect the effect, in relation to the United Kingdom, of a protocol.

(5) In subsection (4) "protocol" means a protocol to the Convention—

    (a)    which the United Kingdom has ratified; or

    (b)    which the United Kingdom has signed with a view to ratification.

(6) No amendment may be made by an order under subsection (4) so as to come into force before the protocol concerned is in force in relation to the United Kingdom.

**[1122]**

**NOTES**

Sub-s (1): words in square brackets in para (c) substituted by the Human Rights Act 1998 (Amendment) Order 2004, SI 2004/1574, art 2(1).

Sub-s (4): words in square brackets substituted by the Secretary of State for Constitutional Affairs Order 2003, SI 2003/1887, art 9, Sch 2, para 10(1).

## 2 Interpretation of Convention rights

(1) A court or tribunal determining a question which has arisen in connection with a Convention right must take into account any—

    (a)    judgment, decision, declaration or advisory opinion of the European Court of Human Rights,

    (b)    opinion of the Commission given in a report adopted under Article 31 of the Convention,

    (c)    decision of the Commission in connection with Article 26 or 27(2) of the Convention, or

    (d)    decision of the Committee of Ministers taken under Article 46 of the Convention,

whenever made or given, so far as, in the opinion of the court or tribunal, it is relevant to the proceedings in which that question has arisen.

(2) Evidence of any judgment, decision, declaration or opinion of which account may have to be taken under this section is to be given in proceedings before any court or tribunal in such manner as may be provided by rules.

(3) In this section "rules" means rules of court or, in the case of proceedings before a tribunal, rules made for the purposes of this section—

    (a)    by ... [the Lord Chancellor or] the Secretary of State, in relation to any proceedings outside Scotland;

    (b)    by the Secretary of State, in relation to proceedings in Scotland; or

    (c)    by a Northern Ireland department, in relation to proceedings before a tribunal in Northern Ireland—

        (i)    which deals with transferred matters; and

        (ii)    for which no rules made under paragraph (a) are in force.

**[1123]**

**NOTES**

Sub-s (3): words omitted from para (a) repealed by the Secretary of State for Constitutional Affairs Order 2003, SI 2003/1887, art 9, Sch 2, para 10(2); words in square brackets in para (a) inserted by the Transfer of Functions (Lord Chancellor and Secretary of State) Order 2005, SI 2005/3429, art 8, Schedule, para 3.

*Legislation*

## 3  Interpretation of legislation

(1)   So far as it is possible to do so, primary legislation and subordinate legislation must be read and given effect in a way which is compatible with the Convention rights.

(2)   This section—
  (a)   applies to primary legislation and subordinate legislation whenever enacted;
  (b)   does not affect the validity, continuing operation or enforcement of any incompatible primary legislation; and
  (c)   does not affect the validity, continuing operation or enforcement of any incompatible subordinate legislation if (disregarding any possibility of revocation) primary legislation prevents removal of the incompatibility.

**[1124]**

**4, 5**   (*Outside the scope of this work.*)

*Public authorities*

## 6  Acts of public authorities

(1)   It is unlawful for a public authority to act in a way which is incompatible with a Convention right.

(2)   Subsection (1) does not apply to an act if—
  (a)   as the result of one or more provisions of primary legislation, the authority could not have acted differently; or
  (b)   in the case of one or more provisions of, or made under, primary legislation which cannot be read or given effect in a way which is compatible with the Convention rights, the authority was acting so as to give effect to or enforce those provisions.

(3)   In this section "public authority" includes—
  (a)   a court or tribunal, and
  (b)   any person certain of whose functions are functions of a public nature,
but does not include either House of Parliament or a person exercising functions in connection with proceedings in Parliament.

(4)   …

(5)   In relation to a particular act, a person is not a public authority by virtue only of subsection (3)(b) if the nature of the act is private.

(6)   "An act" includes a failure to act but does not include a failure to—
  (a)   introduce in, or lay before, Parliament a proposal for legislation; or
  (b)   make any primary legislation or remedial order.

**[1125]**

NOTES

Sub-s (4): repealed by the Constitutional Reform Act 2005, ss 40(4), 146, Sch 9, Pt 1, para 66(1), (4), Sch 18, Pt 5.

## 7  Proceedings

(1)   A person who claims that a public authority has acted (or proposes to act) in a way which is made unlawful by section 6(1) may—
  (a)   bring proceedings against the authority under this Act in the appropriate court or tribunal, or
  (b)   rely on the Convention right or rights concerned in any legal proceedings,
but only if he is (or would be) a victim of the unlawful act.

(2)   In subsection (1)(a) "appropriate court or tribunal" means such court or tribunal as may be determined in accordance with rules; and proceedings against an authority include a counterclaim or similar proceeding.

(3)   If the proceedings are brought on an application for judicial review, the applicant is to be taken to have a sufficient interest in relation to the unlawful act only if he is, or would be, a victim of that act.

(4)   If the proceedings are made by way of a petition for judicial review in Scotland, the applicant shall be taken to have title and interest to sue in relation to the unlawful act only if he is, or would be, a victim of that act.

(5)   Proceedings under subsection (1)(a) must be brought before the end of—
  (a)   the period of one year beginning with the date on which the act complained of took place; or

    (b)   such longer period as the court or tribunal considers equitable having regard to all the circumstances,

but that is subject to any rule imposing a stricter time limit in relation to the procedure in question.

    (6)   In subsection (1)(b) "legal proceedings" includes—
    (a)   proceedings brought by or at the instigation of a public authority; and
    (b)   an appeal against the decision of a court or tribunal.

    (7)   For the purposes of this section, a person is a victim of an unlawful act only if he would be a victim for the purposes of Article 34 of the Convention if proceedings were brought in the European Court of Human Rights in respect of that act.

    (8)   Nothing in this Act creates a criminal offence.

    (9)   In this section "rules" means—
    (a)   in relation to proceedings before a court or tribunal outside Scotland, rules made by ... [the Lord Chancellor or] the Secretary of State for the purposes of this section or rules of court,
    (b)   in relation to proceedings before a court or tribunal in Scotland, rules made by the Secretary of State for those purposes,
    (c)   in relation to proceedings before a tribunal in Northern Ireland—
        (i)   which deals with transferred matters; and
        (ii)   for which no rules made under paragraph (a) are in force,
        rules made by a Northern Ireland department for those purposes,

and includes provision made by order under section 1 of the Courts and Legal Services Act 1990.

    (10)   In making rules, regard must be had to section 9.

    (11)   The Minister who has power to make rules in relation to a particular tribunal may, to the extent he considers it necessary to ensure that the tribunal can provide an appropriate remedy in relation to an act (or proposed act) of a public authority which is (or would be) unlawful as a result of section 6(1), by order add to—
    (a)   the relief or remedies which the tribunal may grant; or
    (b)   the grounds on which it may grant any of them.

    (12)   An order made under subsection (11) may contain such incidental, supplemental, consequential or transitional provision as the Minister making it considers appropriate.

    (13)   "The Minister" includes the Northern Ireland department concerned.

**[1126]**

---

**NOTES**

Sub-s (9): words omitted from para (a) repealed by the Secretary of State for Constitutional Affairs Order 2003, SI 2003/1887, art 9, Sch 2, para 10(2); words in square brackets in para (a) inserted by the Transfer of Functions (Lord Chancellor and Secretary of State) Order 2005, SI 2005/3429, art 8, Schedule, para 3.

Rules: the Proscribed Organisations Appeal Commission (Human Rights Act 1998 Proceedings) Rules 2006, SI 2006/2290.

---

## 8 Judicial remedies

    (1)   In relation to any act (or proposed act) of a public authority which the court finds is (or would be) unlawful, it may grant such relief or remedy, or make such order, within its powers as it considers just and appropriate.

    (2)   But damages may be awarded only by a court which has power to award damages, or to order the payment of compensation, in civil proceedings.

    (3)   No award of damages is to be made unless, taking account of all the circumstances of the case, including—
    (a)   any other relief or remedy granted, or order made, in relation to the act in question (by that or any other court), and
    (b)   the consequences of any decision (of that or any other court) in respect of that act,

the court is satisfied that the award is necessary to afford just satisfaction to the person in whose favour it is made.

    (4)   In determining—
    (a)   whether to award damages, or
    (b)   the amount of an award,

the court must take into account the principles applied by the European Court of Human Rights in relation to the award of compensation under Article 41 of the Convention.

    (5)   A public authority against which damages are awarded is to be treated—
    (a)   in Scotland, for the purposes of section 3 of the Law Reform (Miscellaneous Provisions) (Scotland) Act 1940 as if the award were made in an action of damages in which the authority has been found liable in respect of loss or damage to the person to whom the award is made;

(b)    for the purposes of the Civil Liability (Contribution) Act 1978 as liable in respect of damage suffered by the person to whom the award is made.

(6)    In this section—

"court" includes a tribunal;

"damages" means damages for an unlawful act of a public authority; and

"unlawful" means unlawful under section 6(1).

**[1127]**

## 9  Judicial acts

(1)    Proceedings under section 7(1)(a) in respect of a judicial act may be brought only—

(a)    by exercising a right of appeal;

(b)    on an application (in Scotland a petition) for judicial review; or

(c)    in such other forum as may be prescribed by rules.

(2)    That does not affect any rule of law which prevents a court from being the subject of judicial review.

(3)    In proceedings under this Act in respect of a judicial act done in good faith, damages may not be awarded otherwise than to compensate a person to the extent required by Article 5(5) of the Convention.

(4)    An award of damages permitted by subsection (3) is to be made against the Crown; but no award may be made unless the appropriate person, if not a party to the proceedings, is joined.

(5)    In this section—

"appropriate person" means the Minister responsible for the court concerned, or a person or government department nominated by him;

"court" includes a tribunal;

"judge" includes a member of a tribunal, a justice of the peace [(or, in Northern Ireland, a lay magistrate)] and a clerk or other officer entitled to exercise the jurisdiction of a court;

"judicial act" means a judicial act of a court and includes an act done on the instructions, or on behalf, of a judge; and

"rules" has the same meaning as in section 7(9).

**[1128]**

### NOTES

Sub-s (5): in definition "judge" words in square brackets inserted by the Justice (Northern Ireland) Act 2002, s 10(6), Sch 4, para 39.

---

**10–19**    (*Outside the scope of this work.*)

*Supplemental*

**20**    (*Outside the scope of this work.*)

## 21  Interpretation, etc

(1)    In this Act—

"amend" includes repeal and apply (with or without modifications);

"the appropriate Minister" means the Minister of the Crown having charge of the appropriate authorised government department (within the meaning of the Crown Proceedings Act 1947);

"the Commission" means the European Commission of Human Rights;

"the Convention" means the Convention for the Protection of Human Rights and Fundamental Freedoms, agreed by the Council of Europe at Rome on 4th November 1950 as it has effect for the time being in relation to the United Kingdom;

"declaration of incompatibility" means a declaration under section 4;

"Minister of the Crown" has the same meaning as in the Ministers of the Crown Act 1975;

"Northern Ireland Minister" includes the First Minister and the deputy First Minister in Northern Ireland;

"primary legislation" means any—

(a)    public general Act;

(b)    local and personal Act;

(c)    private Act;

(d)    Measure of the Church Assembly;

(e)    Measure of the General Synod of the Church of England;

(f)    Order in Council—

(i)    made in exercise of Her Majesty's Royal Prerogative;

(ii)    made under section 38(1)(a) of the Northern Ireland Constitution Act 1973 or the corresponding provision of the Northern Ireland Act 1998; or

(iii)    amending an Act of a kind mentioned in paragraph (a), (b) or (c);

and includes an order or other instrument made under primary legislation (otherwise than by the [Welsh Ministers, the First Minister for Wales, the Counsel General to the Welsh Assembly Government], a member of the Scottish Executive, a Northern Ireland Minister or a Northern Ireland department) to the extent to which it operates to bring one or more provisions of that legislation into force or amends any primary legislation;

"the First Protocol" means the protocol to the Convention agreed at Paris on 20th March 1952;

.....

"the Eleventh Protocol" means the protocol to the Convention (restructuring the control machinery established by the Convention) agreed at Strasbourg on 11th May 1994;

["the Thirteenth Protocol" means the protocol to the Convention (concerning the abolition of the death penalty in all circumstances) agreed at Vilnius on 3rd May 2002;]

"remedial order" means an order under section 10;

"subordinate legislation" means any—

    (a)    Order in Council other than one—

        (i)    made in exercise of Her Majesty's Royal Prerogative;

        (ii)    made under section 38(1)(a) of the Northern Ireland Constitution Act 1973 or the corresponding provision of the Northern Ireland Act 1998; or

        (iii)    amending an Act of a kind mentioned in the definition of primary legislation;

    (b)    Act of the Scottish Parliament;

    [(ba)    Measure of the National Assembly for Wales;

    (bb)    Act of the National Assembly for Wales;]

    (c)    Act of the Parliament of Northern Ireland;

    (d)    Measure of the Assembly established under section 1 of the Northern Ireland Assembly Act 1973;

    (e)    Act of the Northern Ireland Assembly;

    (f)    order, rules, regulations, scheme, warrant, byelaw or other instrument made under primary legislation (except to the extent to which it operates to bring one or more provisions of that legislation into force or amends any primary legislation);

    (g)    order, rules, regulations, scheme, warrant, byelaw or other instrument made under legislation mentioned in paragraph (b), (c), (d) or (e) or made under an Order in Council applying only to Northern Ireland;

    (h)    order, rules, regulations, scheme, warrant, byelaw or other instrument made by a member of the Scottish Executive[, Welsh Ministers, the First Minister for Wales, the Counsel General to the Welsh Assembly Government], a Northern Ireland Minister or a Northern Ireland department in exercise of prerogative or other executive functions of Her Majesty which are exercisable by such a person on behalf of Her Majesty;

"transferred matters" has the same meaning as in the Northern Ireland Act 1998; and

"tribunal" means any tribunal in which legal proceedings may be brought.

(2)    The references in paragraphs (b) and (c) of section 2(1) to Articles are to Articles of the Convention as they had effect immediately before the coming into force of the Eleventh Protocol.

(3)    The reference in paragraph (d) of section 2(1) to Article 46 includes a reference to Articles 32 and 54 of the Convention as they had effect immediately before the coming into force of the Eleventh Protocol.

(4)    The references in section 2(1) to a report or decision of the Commission or a decision of the Committee of Ministers include references to a report or decision made as provided by paragraphs 3, 4 and 6 of Article 5 of the Eleventh Protocol (transitional provisions).

(5)    ...

**[1129]**

---

**NOTES**

Sub-s (1): in definition "primary legislation" words in square brackets substituted, in definition "subordinate legislation" paras (ba), (bb) inserted and words in square brackets in para (h) inserted, by the Government of Wales Act 2006, s 160(1), Sch 10, para 56; definition "the Sixth Protocol" (omitted) repealed and definition "the Thirteenth Protocol" inserted by the Human Rights Act 1998 (Amendment) Order 2004, SI 2004/1574, art 2(2).

Sub-s (5): repealed by the Armed Forces Act 2006, s 378(2), Sch 17.

---

**22    Short title, commencement, application and extent**

(1)    This Act may be cited as the Human Rights Act 1998.

(2)    Sections 18, 20 and 21(5) and this section come into force on the passing of this Act.

(3)    The other provisions of this Act come into force on such day as the Secretary of State may by order appoint; and different days may be appointed for different purposes.

(4) Paragraph (b) of subsection (1) of section 7 applies to proceedings brought by or at the instigation of a public authority whenever the act in question took place; but otherwise that subsection does not apply to an act taking place before the coming into force of that section.

(5) This Act binds the Crown.

(6) This Act extends to Northern Ireland.

(7) ...

**[1130]**

**NOTES**
Sub-s (7): repealed by the Armed Forces Act 2006, s 378(2), Sch 17.
Orders: the Human Rights Act 1998 (Commencement) Order 1998, SI 1998/2882; the Human Rights Act 1998 (Commencement No 2) Order 2000, SI 2000/1851.

SCHEDULE 1
THE ARTICLES

Section 1(3)

PART I
THE CONVENTION

.....

*Article 6*
*Right to a fair trial*

1. In the determination of his civil rights and obligations or of any criminal charge against him, everyone is entitled to a fair and public hearing within a reasonable time by an independent and impartial tribunal established by law. Judgment shall be pronounced publicly but the press and public may be excluded from all or part of the trial in the interest of morals, public order or national security in a democratic society, where the interests of juveniles or the protection of the private life of the parties so require, or to the extent strictly necessary in the opinion of the court in special circumstances where publicity would prejudice the interests of justice.

2, 3. ...

.....

*Article 8*
*Right to respect for private and family life*

1. Everyone has the right to respect for his private and family life, his home and his correspondence.

2. There shall be no interference by a public authority with the exercise of this right except such as is in accordance with the law and is necessary in a democratic society in the interests of national security, public safety or the economic well-being of the country, for the prevention of disorder or crime, for the protection of health or morals, or for the protection of the rights and freedoms of others.

.....

**[1131]**

**NOTES**
Text omitted outside the scope of this work.

PART II
THE FIRST PROTOCOL

*Article 1*
*Protection of property*

Every natural or legal person is entitled to the peaceful enjoyment of his possessions. No one shall be deprived of his possessions except in the public interest and subject to the conditions provided for by law and by the general principles of international law.

The preceding provisions shall not, however, in any way impair the right of a State to enforce such laws as it deems necessary to control the use of property in accordance with the general interest or to secure the payment of taxes or other contributions or penalties.

.....

**[1132]**

**NOTES**
Text omitted outside the scope of this work.

*(Sch 1, Pt III, Schs 2–4 outside the scope of this work.)*

# CONTRACTS (RIGHTS OF THIRD PARTIES) ACT 1999

## (1999 c 31)

### ARRANGEMENT OF SECTIONS

*An Act to make provision for the enforcement of contractual terms by third parties.*

[11 November 1999]

## 1   Right of third party to enforce contractual term

(1)    Subject to the provisions of this Act, a person who is not a party to a contract (a "third party") may in his own right enforce a term of the contract if—
    (a)    the contract expressly provides that he may, or
    (b)    subject to subsection (2), the term purports to confer a benefit on him.

(2)    Subsection (1)(b) does not apply if on a proper construction of the contract it appears that the parties did not intend the term to be enforceable by the third party.

(3)    The third party must be expressly identified in the contract by name, as a member of a class or as answering a particular description but need not be in existence when the contract is entered into.

(4)    This section does not confer a right on a third party to enforce a term of a contract otherwise than subject to and in accordance with any other relevant terms of the contract.

(5)    For the purpose of exercising his right to enforce a term of the contract, there shall be available to the third party any remedy that would have been available to him in an action for breach of contract if he had been a party to the contract (and the rules relating to damages, injunctions, specific performance and other relief shall apply accordingly).

(6)    Where a term of a contract excludes or limits liability in relation to any matter references in this Act to the third party enforcing the term shall be construed as references to his availing himself of the exclusion or limitation.

(7)    In this Act, in relation to a term of a contract which is enforceable by a third party—
    "the promisor" means the party to the contract against whom the term is enforceable by the third party, and
    "the promisee" means the party to the contract by whom the term is enforceable against the promisor.

**[1133]**

## 2   Variation and rescission of contract

(1)    Subject to the provisions of this section, where a third party has a right under section 1 to enforce a term of the contract, the parties to the contract may not, by agreement, rescind the contract, or vary it in such a way as to extinguish or alter his entitlement under that right, without his consent if—
    (a)    the third party has communicated his assent to the term to the promisor,
    (b)    the promisor is aware that the third party has relied on the term, or
    (c)    the promisor can reasonably be expected to have foreseen that the third party would rely on the term and the third party has in fact relied on it.

(2)    The assent referred to in subsection (1)(a)—
    (a)    may be by words or conduct, and
    (b)    if sent to the promisor by post or other means, shall not be regarded as communicated to the promisor until received by him.

(3)    Subsection (1) is subject to any express term of the contract under which—
    (a)    the parties to the contract may by agreement rescind or vary the contract without the consent of the third party, or
    (b)    the consent of the third party is required in circumstances specified in the contract instead of those set out in subsection (1)(a) to (c).

(4)   Where the consent of a third party is required under subsection (1) or (3), the court or arbitral tribunal may, on the application of the parties to the contract, dispense with his consent if satisfied—

(a)   that his consent cannot be obtained because his whereabouts cannot reasonably be ascertained, or

(b)   that he is mentally incapable of giving his consent.

(5)   The court or arbitral tribunal may, on the application of the parties to a contract, dispense with any consent that may be required under subsection (1)(c) if satisfied that it cannot reasonably be ascertained whether or not the third party has in fact relied on the term.

(6)   If the court or arbitral tribunal dispenses with a third party's consent, it may impose such conditions as it thinks fit, including a condition requiring the payment of compensation to the third party.

(7)   The jurisdiction conferred on the court by subsections (4) to (6) is exercisable by both the High Court and a county court.

**[1134]**

## 3   Defences etc available to promisor

(1)   Subsections (2) to (5) apply where, in reliance on section 1, proceedings for the enforcement of a term of a contract are brought by a third party.

(2)   The promisor shall have available to him by way of defence or set-off any matter that—

(a)   arises from or in connection with the contract and is relevant to the term, and

(b)   would have been available to him by way of defence or set-off if the proceedings had been brought by the promisee.

(3)   The promisor shall also have available to him by way of defence or set-off any matter if—

(a)   an express term of the contract provides for it to be available to him in proceedings brought by the third party, and

(b)   it would have been available to him by way of defence or set-off if the proceedings had been brought by the promisee.

(4)   The promisor shall also have available to him—

(a)   by way of defence or set-off any matter, and

(b)   by way of counterclaim any matter not arising from the contract,

that would have been available to him by way of defence or set-off or, as the case may be, by way of counterclaim against the third party if the third party had been a party to the contract.

(5)   Subsections (2) and (4) are subject to any express term of the contract as to the matters that are not to be available to the promisor by way of defence, set-off or counterclaim.

(6)   Where in any proceedings brought against him a third party seeks in reliance on section 1 to enforce a term of a contract (including, in particular, a term purporting to exclude or limit liability), he may not do so if he could not have done so (whether by reason of any particular circumstances relating to him or otherwise) had he been a party to the contract.

**[1135]**

## 4   Enforcement of contract by promisee

Section 1 does not affect any right of the promisee to enforce any term of the contract.

**[1136]**

## 5   Protection of party promisor from double liability

Where under section 1 a term of a contract is enforceable by a third party, and the promisee has recovered from the promisor a sum in respect of—

(a)   the third party's loss in respect of the term, or

(b)   the expense to the promisee of making good to the third party the default of the promisor,

then, in any proceedings brought in reliance on that section by the third party, the court or arbitral tribunal shall reduce any award to the third party to such extent as it thinks appropriate to take account of the sum recovered by the promisee.

**[1137]**

## 6   Exceptions

(1)   Section 1 confers no rights on a third party in the case of a contract on a bill of exchange, promissory note or other negotiable instrument.

(2)   Section 1 confers no rights on a third party in the case of any contract binding on a company and its members under [section 33 of the Companies Act 2006 (effect of company's constitution)].

[(2A)   Section 1 confers no rights on a third party in the case of any incorporation document of a limited liability partnership [or any agreement (express or implied) between the members of a limited liability partnership, or between a limited liability partnership and its members, that determines the mutual rights and duties of the members and their rights and duties in relation to the limited liability partnership.].]

(3)     Section 1 confers no right on a third party to enforce—
    (a)     any term of a contract of employment against an employee,
    (b)     any term of a worker's contract against a worker (including a home worker), or
    (c)     any term of a relevant contract against an agency worker.

(4)     In subsection (3)—
    (a)     "contract of employment", "employee", "worker's contract", and "worker" have the meaning given by section 54 of the National Minimum Wage Act 1998,
    (b)     "home worker" has the meaning given by section 35(2) of that Act,
    (c)     "agency worker" has the same meaning as in section 34(1) of that Act, and
    (d)     "relevant contract" means a contract entered into, in a case where section 34 of that Act applies, by the agency worker as respects work falling within subsection (1)(a) of that section.

(5)     Section 1 confers no rights on a third party in the case of—
    (a)     a contract for the carriage of goods by sea, or
    (b)     a contract for the carriage of goods by rail or road, or for the carriage of cargo by air, which is subject to the rules of the appropriate international transport convention,

except that a third party may in reliance on that section avail himself of an exclusion or limitation of liability in such a contract.

(6)     In subsection (5) "contract for the carriage of goods by sea" means a contract of carriage—
    (a)     contained in or evidenced by a bill of lading, sea waybill or a corresponding electronic transaction, or
    (b)     under or for the purposes of which there is given an undertaking which is contained in a ship's delivery order or a corresponding electronic transaction.

(7)     For the purposes of subsection (6)—
    (a)     "bill of lading", "sea waybill" and "ship's delivery order" have the same meaning as in the Carriage of Goods by Sea Act 1992, and
    (b)     a corresponding electronic transaction is a transaction within section 1(5) of that Act which corresponds to the issue, indorsement, delivery or transfer of a bill of lading, sea waybill or ship's delivery order.

(8)     In subsection (5) "the appropriate international transport convention" means—
    (a)     in relation to a contract for the carriage of goods by rail, the Convention which has the force of law in the United Kingdom under [regulation 3 of the Railways (Convention on International Carriage by Rail) Regulations 2005],
    (b)     in relation to a contract for the carriage of goods by road, the Convention which has the force of law in the United Kingdom under section 1 of the Carriage of Goods by Road Act 1965, and
    (c)     in relation to a contract for the carriage of cargo by air—
        (i)     the Convention which has the force of law in the United Kingdom under section 1 of the Carriage by Air Act 1961, or
        (ii)     the Convention which has the force of law under section 1 of the Carriage by Air (Supplementary Provisions) Act 1962, or
        (iii)    either of the amended Conventions set out in Part B of Schedule 2 or 3 to the Carriage by Air Acts (Application of Provisions) Order 1967.

**[1138]**

---

**NOTES**

Sub-s (2): words in square brackets substituted by the Companies Act 2006 (Consequential Amendments, Transitional Provisions and Savings) Order 2009, SI 2009/1941, art 2(1), Sch 1, para 179(1), (2)(a).

Sub-s (2A): inserted by the Limited Liability Partnerships Regulations 2001, SI 2001/1090, reg 9(1), Sch 5, para 20; words in square brackets substituted by SI 2009/1941, art 2(1), Sch 1, para 179(1), (2)(b).

Sub-s (8): words in square brackets in para (a) substituted by the Railways (Convention on International Carriage by Rail) Regulations 2005, SI 2005/2092, reg 9(2), Sch 3, para 3, subject to transitional provisions in reg 9(3) thereof.

---

## 7     Supplementary provisions relating to third party

(1)     Section 1 does not affect any right or remedy of a third party that exists or is available apart from this Act.

(2)     Section 2(2) of the Unfair Contract Terms Act 1977 (restriction on exclusion etc of liability for negligence) shall not apply where the negligence consists of the breach of an obligation arising from a term of a contract and the person seeking to enforce it is a third party acting in reliance on section 1.

(3)   In sections 5 and 8 of the Limitation Act 1980 the references to an action founded on a simple contract and an action upon a specialty shall respectively include references to an action brought in reliance on section 1 relating to a simple contract and an action brought in reliance on that section relating to a specialty.

(4)   A third party shall not, by virtue of section 1(5) or 3(4) or (6), be treated as a party to the contract for the purposes of any other Act (or any instrument made under any other Act).

**[1139]**

## 8   Arbitration provisions

(1)   Where—
   (a)   a right under section 1 to enforce a term ("the substantive term") is subject to a term providing for the submission of disputes to arbitration ("the arbitration agreement"), and
   (b)   the arbitration agreement is an agreement in writing for the purposes of Part I of the Arbitration Act 1996,

the third party shall be treated for the purposes of that Act as a party to the arbitration agreement as regards disputes between himself and the promisor relating to the enforcement of the substantive term by the third party.

(2)   Where—
   (a)   a third party has a right under section 1 to enforce a term providing for one or more descriptions of dispute between the third party and the promisor to be submitted to arbitration ("the arbitration agreement"),
   (b)   the arbitration agreement is an agreement in writing for the purposes of Part I of the Arbitration Act 1996, and
   (c)   the third party does not fall to be treated under subsection (1) as a party to the arbitration agreement,

the third party shall, if he exercises the right, be treated for the purposes of that Act as a party to the arbitration agreement in relation to the matter with respect to which the right is exercised, and be treated as having been so immediately before the exercise of the right.

**[1140]**

## 9   Northern Ireland

(1)   In its application to Northern Ireland, this Act has effect with the modifications specified in subsections (2) and (3).

(2)   ...

(3)   In section 7, for subsection (3) there is substituted—

"(3)   In Articles 4(a) and 15 of the Limitation (Northern Ireland) Order 1989, the references to an action founded on a simple contract and an action upon an instrument under seal shall respectively include references to an action brought in reliance on section 1 relating to a simple contract and an action brought in reliance on that section relating to a contract under seal.".

(4)   ...

**[1141]**

---

**NOTES**

Sub-s (2): repealed by the Companies Act 2006 (Consequential Amendments, Transitional Provisions and Savings) Order 2009, SI 2009/1941, art 2(1), Sch 1, para 179(1), (3).

Sub-s (4): repeals the Law Reform (Husband and Wife) (Northern Ireland) Act 1964, s 5, and amends s 6 thereof.

---

## 10   Short title, commencement and extent

(1)   This Act may be cited as the Contracts (Rights of Third Parties) Act 1999.

(2)   This Act comes into force on the day on which it is passed but, subject to subsection (3), does not apply in relation to a contract entered into before the end of the period of six months beginning with that day.

(3)   The restriction in subsection (2) does not apply in relation to a contract which—
   (a)   is entered into on or after the day on which this Act is passed, and
   (b)   expressly provides for the application of this Act.

(4)   This Act extends as follows—
   (a)   section 9 extends to Northern Ireland only;
   (b)   the remaining provisions extend to England and Wales and Northern Ireland only.

**[1142]**

# LAND REGISTRATION ACT 2002

### (2002 c 9)

## ARRANGEMENT OF SECTIONS

### PART 1
### PRELIMINARY

### PART 2
### FIRST REGISTRATION OF TITLE

### CHAPTER 1
### FIRST REGISTRATION

*Voluntary registration*

*Compulsory registration*

*Classes of title*

*Effect of first registration*

### PART 3
### DISPOSITIONS OF REGISTERED LAND

*Registrable dispositions*

### PART 6
### REGISTRATION: GENERAL

*Registration as proprietor*

*Quality of title*

*Applications*

### PART 7
### SPECIAL CASES

*Miscellaneous*

### PART 12
### MISCELLANEOUS AND GENERAL

*Supplementary*

*Final provisions*

SCHEDULES:

*An Act to make provision about land registration; and for connected purposes*

[26 February 2002]

## PART 1
## PRELIMINARY

### 1 Register of title

(1) There is to continue to be a register of title kept by the registrar.

(2) Rules may make provision about how the register is to be kept and may, in particular, make provision about—

    (a) the information to be included in the register,

    (b) the form in which information included in the register is to be kept, and

    (c) the arrangement of that information.

**[1143]**

**NOTES**

Rules: the Land Registration Rules 2003, SI 2003/1417; the Land Registration (Electronic Conveyancing) Rules 2008, SI 2008/1750 at **[3782]**.

### 2 Scope of title registration

This Act makes provision about the registration of title to—

    (a) unregistered legal estates which are interests of any of the following kinds—

        (i) an estate in land,

        (ii) a rentcharge,

        (iii) a franchise,

        (iv) a profit a prendre in gross, and

        (v) any other interest or charge which subsists for the benefit of, or is a charge on, an interest the title to which is registered; and

    (b) interests capable of subsisting at law which are created by a disposition of an interest the title to which is registered.

**[1144]**

## PART 2
## FIRST REGISTRATION OF TITLE

### CHAPTER 1
### FIRST REGISTRATION

*Voluntary registration*

### 3 When title may be registered

(1) This section applies to any unregistered legal estate which is an interest of any of the following kinds—

    (a) an estate in land,

    (b) a rentcharge,

    (c) a franchise, and

    (d) a profit a prendre in gross.

(2) Subject to the following provisions, a person may apply to the registrar to be registered as the proprietor of an unregistered legal estate to which this section applies if—

    (a) the estate is vested in him, or

    (b) he is entitled to require the estate to be vested in him.

(3) Subject to subsection (4), an application under subsection (2) in respect of a leasehold estate may only be made if the estate was granted for a term of which more than seven years are unexpired.

(4) In the case of an estate in land, subsection (3) does not apply if the right to possession under the lease is discontinuous.

(5) A person may not make an application under subsection (2)(a) in respect of a leasehold estate vested in him as a mortgagee where there is a subsisting right of redemption.

(6) A person may not make an application under subsection (2)(b) if his entitlement is as a person who has contracted to buy under a contract.

(7) If a person holds in the same right both—
  (a) a lease in possession, and
  (b) a lease to take effect in possession on, or within a month of, the end of the lease in possession,

then, to the extent that they relate to the same land, they are to be treated for the purposes of this section as creating one continuous term.

**[1145]**

*Compulsory registration*

**4 When title must be registered**

(1) The requirement of registration applies on the occurrence of any of the following events—
  (a) the transfer of a qualifying estate—
    (i) for valuable or other consideration, by way of gift or in pursuance of an order of any court, ...
    (ii) by means of an assent (including a vesting assent);[ or
    (iii) giving effect to a partition of land subject to a trust of land;]
  [(aa) the transfer of a qualifying estate—
    (i) by a deed that appoints, or by virtue of section 83 of the Charities Act 1993 has effect as if it appointed, a new trustee or is made in consequence of the appointment of a new trustee, or
    (ii) by a vesting order under section 44 of the Trustee Act 1925 that is consequential on the appointment of a new trustee;]
  (b) the transfer of an unregistered legal estate in land in circumstances where section 171A of the Housing Act 1985 (c 68) applies (disposal by landlord which leads to a person no longer being a secure tenant);
  (c) the grant out of a qualifying estate of an estate in land—
    (i) for a term of years absolute of more than seven years from the date of the grant, and
    (ii) for valuable or other consideration, by way of gift or in pursuance of an order of any court;
  (d) the grant out of a qualifying estate of an estate in land for a term of years absolute to take effect in possession after the end of the period of three months beginning with the date of the grant;
  (e) the grant of a lease in pursuance of Part 5 of the Housing Act 1985 (the right to buy) out of an unregistered legal estate in land;
  (f) the grant of a lease out of an unregistered legal estate in land in such circumstances as are mentioned in paragraph (b);
  (g) the creation of a protected first legal mortgage of a qualifying estate.

(2) For the purposes of subsection (1), a qualifying estate is an unregistered legal estate which is—
  (a) a freehold estate in land, or
  (b) a leasehold estate in land for a term which, at the time of the transfer, grant or creation, has more than seven years to run.

(3) In subsection (1)(a), the reference to transfer does not include transfer by operation of law.

(4) Subsection (1)(a) does not apply to—
  (a) the assignment of a mortgage term, or
  (b) the assignment or surrender of a lease to the owner of the immediate reversion where the term is to merge in that reversion.

(5) Subsection (1)(c) does not apply to the grant of an estate to a person as a mortgagee.

(6) For the purposes of subsection (1)(a) and (c), if the estate transferred or granted has a negative value, it is to be regarded as transferred or granted for valuable or other consideration.

(7) In subsection (1)(a) and (c), references to transfer or grant by way of gift include transfer or grant for the purpose of—
  (a) constituting a trust under which the settlor does not retain the whole of the beneficial interest, or
  (b) uniting the bare legal title and the beneficial interest in property held under a trust under which the settlor did not, on constitution, retain the whole of the beneficial interest.

(8) For the purposes of subsection (1)(g)—
  (a) a legal mortgage is protected if it takes effect on its creation as a mortgage to be protected by the deposit of documents relating to the mortgaged estate, and
  (b) a first legal mortgage is one which, on its creation, ranks in priority ahead of any other mortgages then affecting the mortgaged estate.

(9) In this section—

"land" does not include mines and minerals held apart from the surface;
"vesting assent" has the same meaning as in the Settled Land Act 1925 (c 18).

**[1146]**

NOTES
Sub-s (1): word omitted from para (a)(i) repealed and paras (a)(iii) (and word immediately preceding it), (aa) inserted by the Land Registration Act 2002 (Amendment) Order 2008, SI 2008/2872, art 2(1)–(3).

## 5  Power to extend section 4

(1)  The Lord Chancellor may by order—

    (a)    amend section 4 so as to add to the events on the occurrence of which the requirement of registration applies such relevant event as he may specify in the order, and

    (b)    make such consequential amendments of any provision of, or having effect under, any Act as he thinks appropriate.

(2)  For the purposes of subsection (1)(a), a relevant event is an event relating to an unregistered legal estate which is an interest of any of the following kinds—

    (a)    an estate in land,

    (b)    a rentcharge,

    (c)    a franchise, and

    (d)    a profit a prendre in gross.

(3)  The power conferred by subsection (1) may not be exercised so as to require the title to an estate granted to a person as a mortgagee to be registered.

(4)  Before making an order under this section the Lord Chancellor must consult such persons as he considers appropriate.

**[1147]**

## 6  Duty to apply for registration of title

(1)  If the requirement of registration applies, the responsible estate owner, or his successor in title, must, before the end of the period for registration, apply to the registrar to be registered as the proprietor of the registrable estate.

(2)  If the requirement of registration applies because of section 4(1)(g)—

    (a)    the registrable estate is the estate charged by the mortgage, and

    (b)    the responsible estate owner is the owner of that estate.

(3)  If the requirement of registration applies otherwise than because of section 4(1)(g)—

    (a)    the registrable estate is the estate which is transferred or granted, and

    (b)    the responsible estate owner is the transferee or grantee of that estate.

(4)  The period for registration is 2 months beginning with the date on which the relevant event occurs, or such longer period as the registrar may provide under subsection (5).

(5)  If on the application of any interested person the registrar is satisfied that there is good reason for doing so, he may by order provide that the period for registration ends on such later date as he may specify in the order.

(6)  Rules may make provision enabling the mortgagee under any mortgage falling within section 4(1)(g) to require the estate charged by the mortgage to be registered whether or not the mortgagor consents.

**[1148]**

NOTES
Rules: the Land Registration Rules 2003, SI 2003/1417.

## 7  Effect of non-compliance with section 6

(1)  If the requirement of registration is not complied with, the transfer, grant or creation becomes void as regards the transfer, grant or creation of a legal estate.

(2)  On the application of subsection (1)—

    (a)    in a case falling within section 4(1)(a) or (b), the title to the legal estate reverts to the transferor who holds it on a bare trust for the transferee,

    [(aa)  in a case falling within section 4(1)(aa), the title to the legal estate reverts to the person in whom it was vested immediately before the transfer,] and

    (b)    in a case falling within section 4(1)(c) to (g), the grant or creation has effect as a contract made for valuable consideration to grant or create the legal estate concerned.

(3)  If an order under section 6(5) is made in a case where subsection (1) has already applied, that application of the subsection is to be treated as not having occurred.

(4) The possibility of reverter under subsection (1) is to be disregarded for the purposes of determining whether a fee simple is a fee simple absolute.

**[1149]**

**NOTES**
Sub-s (2): para (aa) inserted by the Land Registration Act 2002 (Amendment) Order 2008, SI 2008/2872, art 3.

### 8 Liability for making good void transfers etc

If a legal estate is retransferred, regranted or recreated because of a failure to comply with the requirement of registration, the transferee, grantee or, as the case may be, the mortgagor—

(a) is liable to the other party for all the proper costs of and incidental to the retransfer, regrant or recreation of the legal estate, and

(b) is liable to indemnify the other party in respect of any other liability reasonably incurred by him because of the failure to comply with the requirement of registration.

**[1150]**

*Classes of title*

### 9 (*Outside the scope of this work.*)

### 10 Titles to leasehold estates

(1) In the case of an application for registration under this Chapter of a leasehold estate, the classes of title with which the applicant may be registered as proprietor are—

(a) absolute title,
(b) good leasehold title,
(c) qualified title, and
(d) possessory title;

and the following provisions deal with when each of the classes of title is available.

(2) A person may be registered with absolute title if—

(a) the registrar is of the opinion that the person's title to the estate is such as a willing buyer could properly be advised by a competent professional adviser to accept, and

(b) the registrar approves the lessor's title to grant the lease.

(3) A person may be registered with good leasehold title if the registrar is of the opinion that the person's title to the estate is such as a willing buyer could properly be advised by a competent professional adviser to accept.

(4) In applying subsection (2) or (3), the registrar may disregard the fact that a person's title appears to him to be open to objection if he is of the opinion that the defect will not cause the holding under the title to be disturbed.

(5) A person may be registered with qualified title if the registrar is of the opinion that the person's title to the estate, or the lessor's title to the reversion, has been established only for a limited period or subject to certain reservations which cannot be disregarded under subsection (4).

(6) A person may be registered with possessory title if the registrar is of the opinion—

(a) that the person is in actual possession of the land, or in receipt of the rents and profits of the land, by virtue of the estate, and

(b) that there is no other class of title with which he may be registered.

**[1151]**

*Effect of first registration*

### 11 (*Outside the scope of this work.*)

### 12 Leasehold estates

(1) This section is concerned with the registration of a person under this Chapter as the proprietor of a leasehold estate.

(2) Registration with absolute title has the effect described in subsections (3) to (5).

(3) The estate is vested in the proprietor together with all interests subsisting for the benefit of the estate.

(4) The estate is vested subject only to the following interests affecting the estate at the time of registration—

(a) implied and express covenants, obligations and liabilities incident to the estate,
(b) interests which are the subject of an entry in the register in relation to the estate,
(c) unregistered interests which fall within any of the paragraphs of Schedule 1, and
(d) interests acquired under the Limitation Act 1980 (c 58) of which the proprietor has notice.

(5) If the proprietor is not entitled to the estate for his own benefit, or not entitled solely for his own benefit, then, as between himself and the persons beneficially entitled to the estate, the estate is vested in him subject to such of their interests as he has notice of.

(6) Registration with good leasehold title has the same effect as registration with absolute title, except that it does not affect the enforcement of any estate, right or interest affecting, or in derogation of, the title of the lessor to grant the lease.

(7) Registration with qualified title has the same effect as registration with absolute title except that it does not affect the enforcement of any estate, right or interest which appears from the register to be excepted from the effect of registration.

(8) Registration with possessory title has the same effect as registration with absolute title, except that it does not affect the enforcement of any estate, right or interest adverse to, or in derogation of, the proprietor's title subsisting at the time of registration or then capable of arising.

**[1152]**

**13–22** (*Outside the scope of this work.*)

## PART 3
## DISPOSITIONS OF REGISTERED LAND

**23–26** (*Outside the scope of this work.*)

*Registrable dispositions*

### 27 Dispositions required to be registered

(1) If a disposition of a registered estate or registered charge is required to be completed by registration, it does not operate at law until the relevant registration requirements are met.

(2) In the case of a registered estate, the following are the dispositions which are required to be completed by registration—

    (a) a transfer,

    (b) where the registered estate is an estate in land, the grant of a term of years absolute—

        (i) for a term of more than seven years from the date of the grant,

        (ii) to take effect in possession after the end of the period of three months beginning with the date of the grant,

        (iii) under which the right to possession is discontinuous,

        (iv) in pursuance of Part 5 of the Housing Act 1985 (c 68) (the right to buy), or

        (v) in circumstances where section 171A of that Act applies (disposal by landlord which leads to a person no longer being a secure tenant),

    (c) where the registered estate is a franchise or manor, the grant of a lease,

    (d) the express grant or reservation of an interest of a kind falling within section 1(2)(a) of the Law of Property Act 1925 (c 20), other than one which is capable of being registered under *the Commons Registration Act 1965 (c 64)*,

    (e) the express grant or reservation of an interest of a kind falling within section 1(2)(b) or (e) of the Law of Property Act 1925, and

    (f) the grant of a legal charge.

(3) In the case of a registered charge, the following are the dispositions which are required to be completed by registration—

    (a) a transfer, and

    (b) the grant of a sub-charge.

(4) Schedule 2 to this Act (which deals with the relevant registration requirements) has effect.

(5) This section applies to dispositions by operation of law as it applies to other dispositions, but with the exception of the following—

    (a) a transfer on the death or bankruptcy of an individual proprietor,

    (b) a transfer on the dissolution of a corporate proprietor, and

    (c) the creation of a legal charge which is a local land charge.

(6) Rules may make provision about applications to the registrar for the purpose of meeting registration requirements under this section.

(7) In subsection (2)(d), the reference to express grant does not include grant as a result of the operation of section 62 of the Law of Property Act 1925 (c 20).

**[1153]**

---

**NOTES**

Sub-s (2): for the words in italics in para (d) there are substituted the words "Part 1 of the Commons Act 2006" by the Commons Act 2006, s 52, Sch 5, para 8(1), (2), as from a day to be appointed.

Rules: the Land Registration Rules 2003, SI 2003/1417.

**28–57**    *(Ss 28–31, ss 32–57 (Pts 4, 5) outside the scope of this work.)*

### PART 6
### REGISTRATION: GENERAL
*Registration as proprietor*

### 58   Conclusiveness

(1)   If, on the entry of a person in the register as the proprietor of a legal estate, the legal estate would not otherwise be vested in him, it shall be deemed to be vested in him as a result of the registration.

(2)   Subsection (1) does not apply where the entry is made in pursuance of a registrable disposition in relation to which some other registration requirement remains to be met.

**[1154]**

**59–61**    *(Outside the scope of this work.)*

*Quality of title*

### 62   Power to upgrade title

(1)   Where the title to a freehold estate is entered in the register as possessory or qualified, the registrar may enter it as absolute if he is satisfied as to the title to the estate.

(2)   Where the title to a leasehold estate is entered in the register as good leasehold, the registrar may enter it as absolute if he is satisfied as to the superior title.

(3)   Where the title to a leasehold estate is entered in the register as possessory or qualified the registrar may—
    (a)   enter it as good leasehold if he is satisfied as to the title to the estate, and
    (b)   enter it as absolute if he is satisfied both as to the title to the estate and as to the superior title.

(4)   Where the title to a freehold estate in land has been entered in the register as possessory for at least twelve years, the registrar may enter it as absolute if he is satisfied that the proprietor is in possession of the land.

(5)   Where the title to a leasehold estate in land has been entered in the register as possessory for at least twelve years, the registrar may enter it as good leasehold if he is satisfied that the proprietor is in possession of the land.

(6)   None of the powers under subsections (1) to (5) is exercisable if there is outstanding any claim adverse to the title of the registered proprietor which is made by virtue of an estate, right or interest whose enforceability is preserved by virtue of the existing entry about the class of title.

(7)   The only persons who may apply to the registrar for the exercise of any of the powers under subsections (1) to (5) are—
    (a)   the proprietor of the estate to which the application relates,
    (b)   a person entitled to be registered as the proprietor of that estate,
    (c)   the proprietor of a registered charge affecting that estate, and
    (d)   a person interested in a registered estate which derives from that estate.

(8)   In determining for the purposes of this section whether he is satisfied as to any title, the registrar is to apply the same standards as those which apply under section 9 or 10 to first registration of title.

(9)   The Lord Chancellor may by order amend subsection (4) or (5) by substituting for the number of years for the time being specified in that subsection such number of years as the order may provide.

**[1155]**

### 63   Effect of upgrading title

(1)   On the title to a registered freehold or leasehold estate being entered under section 62 as absolute, the proprietor ceases to hold the estate subject to any estate, right or interest whose enforceability was preserved by virtue of the previous entry about the class of title.

(2)   Subsection (1) also applies on the title to a registered leasehold estate being entered under section 62 as good leasehold, except that the entry does not affect or prejudice the enforcement of any estate, right or interest affecting, or in derogation of, the title of the lessor to grant the lease.

**[1156]**

### 64   Use of register to record defects in title

(1)   If it appears to the registrar that a right to determine a registered estate in land is exercisable, he may enter the fact in the register.

(2)   Rules may make provision about entries under subsection (1) and may, in particular, make provision about—

    (a)   the circumstances in which there is a duty to exercise the power conferred by that subsection,

    (b)   how entries under that subsection are to be made, and

    (c)   the removal of such entries.

**[1157]**

**NOTES**
Rules: the Land Registration Rules 2003, SI 2003/1417.

**65–70**   (*Outside the scope of this work.*)

*Applications*

## 71   Duty to disclose unregistered interests

Where rules so provide—

    (a)   a person applying for registration under Chapter 1 of Part 2 must provide to the registrar such information as the rules may provide about any interest affecting the estate to which the application relates which—

        (i)   falls within any of the paragraphs of Schedule 1, and

        (ii)   is of a description specified by the rules;

    (b)   a person applying to register a registrable disposition of a registered estate must provide to the registrar such information as the rules may provide about any unregistered interest affecting the estate which—

        (i)   falls within any of the paragraphs of Schedule 3, and

        (ii)   is of description specified by the rules.

**[1158]**

**NOTES**
Rules: the Land Registration Rules 2003, SI 2003/1417; the Land Registration (Electronic Conveyancing) Rules 2008, SI 2008/1750 at **[3782]**.

**72–78**   (*Outside the scope of this work.*)

### PART 7
### SPECIAL CASES

**79–87**   (*Outside the scope of this work.*)

*Miscellaneous*

**88, 89**   (*Outside the scope of this work.*)

## 90   PPP leases relating to transport in London

(1)   No application for registration under section 3 may be made in respect of a leasehold estate in land under a PPP lease.

(2)   The requirement of registration does not apply on the grant or transfer of a leasehold estate in land under a PPP lease.

(3)   For the purposes of section 27, the following are not dispositions requiring to be completed by registration—

    (a)   the grant of a term of years absolute under a PPP lease;

    (b)   the express grant of an interest falling within section 1(2) of the Law of Property Act 1925 (c 20), where the interest is created for the benefit of a leasehold estate in land under a PPP lease.

(4)   No notice may be entered in the register in respect of an interest under a PPP lease.

(5)   Schedules 1 and 3 have effect as if they included a paragraph referring to a PPP lease.

(6)   In this section, "PPP lease" has the meaning given by section 218 of the Greater London Authority Act 1999 (c 29) (which makes provision about leases created for public-private partnerships relating to transport in London).

**[1159]**

**91–114**   ((*Pts 8–11*) *Outside the scope of this work.*)

PART 12
MISCELLANEOUS AND GENERAL

**115–127**    (*Outside the scope of this work.*)

*Supplementary*

**128–130**    (*Outside the scope of this work.*)

**131  "Proprietor in possession"**

(1)   For the purposes of this Act, land is in the possession of the proprietor of a registered estate in land if it is physically in his possession, or in that of a person who is entitled to be registered as the proprietor of the registered estate.

(2)   In the case of the following relationships, land which is (or is treated as being) in the possession of the second-mentioned person is to be treated for the purposes of subsection (1) as in the possession of the first-mentioned person—

    (a)    landlord and tenant;
    (b)    mortgagor and mortgagee;
    (c)    licensor and licensee;
    (d)    trustee and beneficiary.

(3)   In subsection (1), the reference to entitlement does not include entitlement under Schedule 6.

**[1160]**

**132**    (*Outside the scope of this work.*)

*Final provisions*

**133–135**    (*Outside the scope of this work.*)

**136  Short title, commencement and extent**

(1)   This Act may be cited as the Land Registration Act 2002.

(2)   This Act shall come into force on such day as the Lord Chancellor may by order appoint, and different days may be so appointed for different purposes.

(3)   Subject to subsection (4), this Act extends to England and Wales only.

(4)   Any amendment or repeal by this Act of an existing enactment, other than—

    (a)    section 37 of the Requisitioned Land and War Works Act 1945 (c 43), and
    (b)    Schedule 2A to the Building Societies Act 1986 (c 53),

has the same extent as the enactment amended or repealed.

**[1161]**

**NOTES**

Orders: the Land Registration Act 2002 (Commencement No 1) Order 2003, SI 2003/935; the Land Registration Act 2002 (Commencement No 2) Order 2003, SI 2003/1028; the Land Registration Act 2002 (Commencement No 3) Order 2003, SI 2003/1612; the Land Registration Act 2002 (Commencement No 4) Order 2003, SI 2003/1725.

SCHEDULE 1
UNREGISTERED INTERESTS WHICH OVERRIDE FIRST REGISTRATION
Sections 11 and 12

*Leasehold estates in land*

1.   A leasehold estate in land granted for a term not exceeding seven years from the date of the grant, except for a lease the grant of which falls within section 4(1) (d), (e) or (f).

*Interests of persons in actual occupation*

2.   An interest belonging to a person in actual occupation, so far as relating to land of which he is in actual occupation, except for an interest under a settlement under the Settled Land Act 1925 (c 18).

*Easements and profits a prendre*

3.   A legal easement or profit a prendre.

*Customary and public rights*

4.   A customary right.

5.   A public right.

*Local land charges*

6.   A local land charge.

*Mines and minerals*

7.   An interest in any coal or coal mine, the rights attached to any such interest and the rights of any person under section 38, 49 or 51 of the Coal Industry Act 1994 (c 21).

8.   In the case of land to which title was registered before 1898, rights to mines and minerals (and incidental rights) created before 1898.

9.   In the case of land to which title was registered between 1898 and 1925 inclusive, rights to mines and minerals (and incidental rights) created before the date of registration of the title.

*Miscellaneous*

10.   *A franchise.*

11.   *A manorial right.*

12.   *A right to rent which was reserved to the Crown on the granting of any freehold estate (whether or not the right is still vested in the Crown).*

13.   *A non-statutory right in respect of an embankment or sea or river wall.*

14.   *A right to payment in lieu of tithe.*

[15.   ... ]

[16.   A right in respect of the repair of a church chancel.]

**[1162]**

**NOTES**
   Paras 10–14: repealed by s 117(1) of this Act, as from 13 October 2013.
   Para 15: inserted by s 134(2) of, and Sch 12, para 7 to, this Act, with effect until 13 October 2006; now spent.
   Para 16: inserted by the Land Registration Act 2002 (Transitional Provisions) (No 2) Order 2003, SI 2003/2431, art 2(1), with effect until 13 October 2013.

SCHEDULE 2
REGISTRABLE DISPOSITIONS: REGISTRATION REQUIREMENTS

Section 27

PART 1
REGISTERED ESTATES

*Introductory*

1.   This Part deals with the registration requirements relating to those dispositions of registered estates which are required to be completed by registration.

*Transfer*

2.—(1)   In the case of a transfer of whole or part, the transferee, or his successor in title, must be entered in the register as the proprietor.

   (2)   In the case of a transfer of part, such details of the transfer as rules may provide must be entered in the register in relation to the registered estate out of which the transfer is made.

*Lease of estate in land*

3.—(1)   This paragraph applies to a disposition consisting of the grant out of an estate in land of a term of years absolute.

   (2)   In the case of a disposition to which this paragraph applies—
      (a)   the grantee, or his successor in title, must be entered in the register as the proprietor of the lease, and
      (b)   a notice in respect of the lease must be entered in the register.

*Lease of franchise or manor*

4.—(1)   This paragraph applies to a disposition consisting of the grant out of a franchise or manor of a lease for a term of more than seven years from the date of the grant.

   (2)   In the case of a disposition to which this paragraph applies—

PART I
STATUTES

(a)   the grantee, or his successor in title, must be entered in the register as the proprietor of the lease, and

(b)   a notice in respect of the lease must be entered in the register.

5.—(1)   This paragraph applies to a disposition consisting of the grant out of a franchise or manor of a lease for a term not exceeding seven years from the date of the grant.

(2)   In the case of a disposition to which this paragraph applies, a notice in respect of the lease must be entered in the register.

### Creation of independently registrable legal interest

6.—(1)   This paragraph applies to a disposition consisting of the creation of a legal rentcharge or profit a prendre in gross, other than one created for, or for an interest equivalent to, a term of years absolute not exceeding seven years from the date of creation.

(2)   In the case of a disposition to which this paragraph applies—

(a)   the grantee, or his successor in title, must be entered in the register as the proprietor of the interest created, and

(b)   a notice in respect of the interest created must be entered in the register.

(3)   In sub-paragraph (1), the reference to a legal rentcharge or profit a prendre in gross is to one falling within section 1(2) of the Law of Property Act 1925 (c 20).

### Creation of other legal interest

7.—(1)   This paragraph applies to a disposition which—

(a)   consists of the creation of an interest of a kind falling within section 1(2)(a), (b) or (e) of the Law of Property Act 1925, and

(b)   is not a disposition to which paragraph 4, 5 or 6 applies.

(2)   In the case of a disposition to which this paragraph applies—

(a)   a notice in respect of the interest created must be entered in the register, and

(b)   if the interest is created for the benefit of a registered estate, the proprietor of the registered estate must be entered in the register as its proprietor.

(3)   Rules may provide for sub-paragraph (2) to have effect with modifications in relation to a right of entry over or in respect of a term of years absolute.

### Creation of legal charge

8.   In the case of the creation of a charge, the chargee, or his successor in title, must be entered in the register as the proprietor of the charge.

**[1163]**

**NOTES**
Rules: the Land Registration Rules 2003, SI 2003/1417.

## PART 2
## REGISTERED CHARGES

### Introductory

9.   This Part deals with the registration requirements relating to those dispositions of registered charges which are required to be completed by registration.

### Transfer

10.   In the case of a transfer, the transferee, or his successor in title, must be entered in the register as the proprietor.

### Creation of sub-charge

11.   In the case of the creation of a sub-charge, the sub-chargee, or his successor in title, must be entered in the register as the proprietor of the sub-charge.

**[1164]**

*(Schs 3–13 outside the scope of this work.)*

# COMMONHOLD AND LEASEHOLD REFORM ACT 2002

(2002 c 15)

ARRANGEMENT OF SECTIONS

PART 1
COMMONHOLD

*Nature of commonhold*

*Registration*

*Effect of registration*

*Commonhold unit*

*Common parts*

*Commonhold community statement*

*Commonhold association*

*Operation of commonhold*

PART 2
LEASEHOLD REFORM

CHAPTER 1
RIGHT TO MANAGE

*Introductory*

*Qualifying rules*

*Claim to acquire right*

## CHAPTER 2
## COLLECTIVE ENFRANCHISEMENT BY TENANTS OF FLATS

*Introductory*

## CHAPTER 3
## NEW LEASES FOR TENANTS OF FLATS

*Introductory*

## CHAPTER 5
## OTHER PROVISIONS ABOUT LEASES

*Service charges, administration charges etc*

*Insurance*

*Ground rent*

*Forfeiture of leases of dwellings*

*Crown application*

*An Act to make provision about commonhold land and to amend the law about leasehold property*

[1 May 2002]

### PART 1
### COMMONHOLD

*Nature of commonhold*

**1   Commonhold land**

(1)   Land is commonhold land if—

(a)   the freehold estate in the land is registered as a freehold estate in commonhold land,

(b)   the land is specified in the [articles of association] of a commonhold association as the land in relation to which the association is to exercise functions, and

(c)   a commonhold community statement makes provision for rights and duties of the commonhold association and unit-holders (whether or not the statement has come into force).

(2)   In this Part a reference to a commonhold is a reference to land in relation to which a commonhold association exercises functions.

(3)   In this Part—

"commonhold association" has the meaning given by section 34,

"commonhold community statement" has the meaning given by section 31,

"commonhold unit" has the meaning given by section 11,

"common parts" has the meaning given by section 25, and

"unit-holder" has the meaning given by sections 12 and 13.

(4)   Sections 7 and 9 make provision for the vesting in the commonhold association of the fee simple in possession in the common parts of a commonhold.

**[1165]**

**NOTES**

   Sub-s (1): words in square brackets substituted by the Companies Act 2006 (Consequential Amendments, Transitional Provisions and Savings) Order 2009, SI 2009/1941, art 2(1), Sch 1, para 194(1), (2).

*Registration*

## 2 Application

(1) The Registrar shall register a freehold estate in land as a freehold estate in commonhold land if—

(a)   the registered freeholder of the land makes an application under this section, and

(b)   no part of the land is already commonhold land.

(2) An application under this section must be accompanied by the documents listed in Schedule 1.

(3) A person is the registered freeholder of land for the purposes of this Part if—

(a)   he is registered as the proprietor of a freehold estate in the land with absolute title, or

(b)   he has applied, and the Registrar is satisfied that he is entitled, to be registered as mentioned in paragraph (a).

**[1166]**

## 3 Consent

(1) An application under section 2 may not be made in respect of a freehold estate in land without the consent of anyone who—

(a)   is the registered proprietor of the freehold estate in the whole or part of the land,

(b)   is the registered proprietor of a leasehold estate in the whole or part of the land granted for a term of more than 21 years,

(c)   is the registered proprietor of a charge over the whole or part of the land, or

(d)   falls within any other class of person which may be prescribed.

(2) Regulations shall make provision about consent for the purposes of this section; in particular, the regulations may make provision—

(a)   prescribing the form of consent;

(b)   about the effect and duration of consent (including provision for consent to bind successors);

(c)   about withdrawal of consent (including provision preventing withdrawal in specified circumstances);

(d)   for consent given for the purpose of one application under section 2 to have effect for the purpose of another application;

(e)   for consent to be deemed to have been given in specified circumstances;

(f)   enabling a court to dispense with a requirement for consent in specified circumstances.

(3) An order under subsection (2)(f) dispensing with a requirement for consent—

(a)   may be absolute or conditional, and

(b)   may make such other provision as the court thinks appropriate.

**[1167]**

---

**NOTES**

Regulations: the Commonhold Regulations 2004, SI 2004/1829 at **[3379]**.

---

## 4 Land which may not be commonhold

Schedule 2 (which provides that an application under section 2 may not relate wholly or partly to land of certain kinds) shall have effect.

**[1168]**

## 5 Registered details

(1) The Registrar shall ensure that in respect of any commonhold land the following are kept in his custody and referred to in the register—

(a)   the prescribed details of the commonhold association;

(b)   the prescribed details of the registered freeholder of each commonhold unit;

(c)   a copy of the commonhold community statement;

(d)   a copy of the [articles of association] of the commonhold association.

(2) The Registrar may arrange for a document or information to be kept in his custody and referred to in the register in respect of commonhold land if the document or information—

(a)   is not mentioned in subsection (1), but

(b)   is submitted to the Registrar in accordance with a provision made by or by virtue of this Part.

(3) Subsection (1)(b) shall not apply during a transitional period within the meaning of section 8.

**[1169]**

PART I
STATUTES

**NOTES**

Sub-s (1): words in square brackets substituted by the Companies Act 2006 (Consequential Amendments, Transitional Provisions and Savings) Order 2009, SI 2009/1941, art 2(1), Sch 1, para 194(1), (3).

## 6   Registration in error

(1)   This section applies where a freehold estate in land is registered as a freehold estate in commonhold land and—

    (a)   the application for registration was not made in accordance with section 2,

    (b)   the certificate under paragraph 7 of Schedule 1 was inaccurate, or

    (c)   the registration contravened a provision made by or by virtue of this Part.

(2)   The register may not be altered by the Registrar under Schedule 4 to the Land Registration Act 2002 (c 9) (alteration of register).

(3)   The court may grant a declaration that the freehold estate should not have been registered as a freehold estate in commonhold land.

(4)   A declaration under subsection (3) may be granted only on the application of a person who claims to be adversely affected by the registration.

(5)   On granting a declaration under subsection (3) the court may make any order which appears to it to be appropriate.

(6)   An order under subsection (5) may, in particular—

    (a)   provide for the registration to be treated as valid for all purposes;

    (b)   provide for alteration of the register;

    (c)   provide for land to cease to be commonhold land;

    (d)   require a director or other specified officer of a commonhold association to take steps to alter or amend a document;

    (e)   require a director or other specified officer of a commonhold association to take specified steps;

    (f)   make an award of compensation (whether or not contingent upon the occurrence or non-occurrence of a specified event) to be paid by one specified person to another;

    (g)   apply, disapply or modify a provision of Schedule 8 to the Land Registration Act 2002 (c 9) (indemnity).

**[1170]**

*Effect of registration*

## 7   Registration without unit-holders

(1)   This section applies where—

    (a)   a freehold estate in land is registered as a freehold estate in commonhold land in pursuance of an application under section 2, and

    (b)   the application is not accompanied by a statement under section 9(1)(b).

(2)   On registration—

    (a)   the applicant shall continue to be registered as the proprietor of the freehold estate in the commonhold land, and

    (b)   the rights and duties conferred and imposed by the commonhold community statement shall not come into force (subject to section 8(2)(b)).

(3)   Where after registration a person other than the applicant becomes entitled to be registered as the proprietor of the freehold estate in one or more, but not all, of the commonhold units—

    (a)   the commonhold association shall be entitled to be registered as the proprietor of the freehold estate in the common parts,

    (b)   the Registrar shall register the commonhold association in accordance with paragraph (a) (without an application being made),

    (c)   the rights and duties conferred and imposed by the commonhold community statement shall come into force, and

    (d)   any lease of the whole or part of the commonhold land shall be extinguished by virtue of this section.

(4)   For the purpose of subsection (3)(d) "lease" means a lease which—

    (a)   is granted for any term, and

    (b)   is granted before the commonhold association becomes entitled to be registered as the proprietor of the freehold estate in the common parts.

**[1171]**

## 8   Transitional period

(1)   In this Part "transitional period" means the period between registration of the freehold estate in land as a freehold estate in commonhold land and the event mentioned in section 7(3).

(2)   Regulations may provide that during a transitional period a relevant provision—

(a)   shall not have effect, or
(b)   shall have effect with specified modifications.

(3)   In subsection (2) "relevant provision" means a provision made—
(a)   by or by virtue of this Part,
(b)   by a commonhold community statement, or
(c)   by the [articles] of the commonhold association.

(4)   The Registrar shall arrange for the freehold estate in land to cease to be registered as a freehold estate in commonhold land if the registered proprietor makes an application to the Registrar under this subsection during the transitional period.

(5)   The provisions about consent made by or under sections 2 and 3 and Schedule 1 shall apply in relation to an application under subsection (4) as they apply in relation to an application under section 2.

(6)   A reference in this Part to a commonhold association exercising functions in relation to commonhold land includes a reference to a case where a commonhold association would exercise functions in relation to commonhold land but for the fact that the time in question falls in a transitional period.

**[1172]**

**NOTES**
Sub-s (3): word in square brackets substituted by the Companies Act 2006 (Consequential Amendments, Transitional Provisions and Savings) Order 2009, SI 2009/1941, art 2(1), Sch 1, para 194(1), (4).

## 9   Registration with unit-holders

(1)   This section applies in relation to a freehold estate in commonhold land if—
(a)   it is registered as a freehold estate in commonhold land in pursuance of an application under section 2, and
(b)   the application is accompanied by a statement by the applicant requesting that this section should apply.

(2)   A statement under subsection (1)(b) must include a list of the commonhold units giving in relation to each one the prescribed details of the proposed initial unit-holder or joint unit-holders.

(3)   On registration—
(a)   the commonhold association shall be entitled to be registered as the proprietor of the freehold estate in the common parts,
(b)   a person specified by virtue of subsection (2) as the initial unit-holder of a commonhold unit shall be entitled to be registered as the proprietor of the freehold estate in the unit,
(c)   a person specified by virtue of subsection (2) as an initial joint unit-holder of a commonhold unit shall be entitled to be registered as one of the proprietors of the freehold estate in the unit,
(d)   the Registrar shall make entries in the register to reflect paragraphs (a) to (c) (without applications being made),
(e)   the rights and duties conferred and imposed by the commonhold community statement shall come into force, and
(f)   any lease of the whole or part of the commonhold land shall be extinguished by virtue of this section.

(4)   For the purpose of subsection (3)(f) "lease" means a lease which—
(a)   is granted for any term, and
(b)   is granted before the commonhold association becomes entitled to be registered as the proprietor of the freehold estate in the common parts.

**[1173]**

**NOTES**
Regulations: the Commonhold Regulations 2004, SI 2004/1829 at **[3379]**.

## 10   Extinguished lease: liability

(1)   This section applies where—
(a)   a lease is extinguished by virtue of section 7(3)(d) or 9(3)(f), and
(b)   the consent of the holder of that lease was not among the consents required by section 3 in respect of the application under section 2 for the land to become commonhold land.

(2)   If the holder of a lease superior to the extinguished lease gave consent under section 3, he shall be liable for loss suffered by the holder of the extinguished lease.

(3)   If the holders of a number of leases would be liable under subsection (2), liability shall attach only to the person whose lease was most proximate to the extinguished lease.

(4)   If no person is liable under subsection (2), the person who gave consent under section 3 as the holder of the freehold estate out of which the extinguished lease was granted shall be liable for loss suffered by the holder of the extinguished lease.

**[1174]**

PART 1<br>STATUTES

*Commonhold unit*

## 11   Definition

(1)   In this Part "commonhold unit" means a commonhold unit specified in a commonhold community statement in accordance with this section.

(2)   A commonhold community statement must—
- (a)   specify at least two parcels of land as commonhold units, and
- (b)   define the extent of each commonhold unit.

(3)   In defining the extent of a commonhold unit a commonhold community statement—
- (a)   must refer to a plan which is included in the statement and which complies with prescribed requirements,
- (b)   may refer to an area subject to the exclusion of specified structures, fittings, apparatus or appurtenances within the area,
- (c)   may exclude the structures which delineate an area referred to, and
- (d)   may refer to two or more areas (whether or not contiguous).

(4)   A commonhold unit need not contain all or any part of a building.

**[1175]**

**NOTES**

Regulations: the Commonhold Regulations 2004, SI 2004/1829 at **[3379]**.

## 12   Unit-holder

A person is the unit-holder of a commonhold unit if he is entitled to be registered as the proprietor of the freehold estate in the unit (whether or not he is registered).

**[1176]**

## 13   Joint unit-holders

(1)   Two or more persons are joint unit-holders of a commonhold unit if they are entitled to be registered as proprietors of the freehold estate in the unit (whether or not they are registered).

(2)   In the application of the following provisions to a unit with joint unit-holders a reference to a unit-holder is a reference to the joint unit-holders together—
- (a)   section 14(3),
- (b)   section 15(1) and (3),
- (c)   section 19(2) and (3),
- (d)   section 20(1),
- (e)   section 23(1),
- (f)   section 35(1)(b),
- (g)   section 38(1),
- (h)   section 39(2), and
- (i)   section 47(2).

(3)   In the application of the following provisions to a unit with joint unit-holders a reference to a unit-holder includes a reference to each joint unit-holder and to the joint unit-holders together—
- (a)   section 1(1)(c),
- (b)   section 16,
- (c)   section 31(1)(b), (3)(b), (5)(j) and (7),
- (d)   section 32(4)(a) and (c),
- (e)   section 35(1)(a), (2) and (3),
- (f)   section 37(2),
- (g)   section 40(1), and
- (h)   section 58(3)(a).

(4)   Regulations under this Part which refer to a unit-holder shall make provision for the construction of the reference in the case of joint unit-holders.

(5)   Regulations may amend subsection (2) or (3).

(6)   Regulations may make provision for the construction in the case of joint unit-holders of a reference to a unit-holder in—
- (a)   an enactment,
- (b)   a commonhold community statement,
- (c)   the [articles of association] of a commonhold association, or
- (d)   another document.

**[1177]**

**NOTES**

Sub-s (6): words in square brackets substituted by the Companies Act 2006 (Consequential Amendments, Transitional Provisions and Savings) Order 2009, SI 2009/1941, art 2(1), Sch 1, para 194(1), (5).

Regulations: the Commonhold Regulations 2004, SI 2004/1829 at **[3379]**.

## 14  Use and maintenance

(1)   A commonhold community statement must make provision regulating the use of commonhold units.

(2)   A commonhold community statement must make provision imposing duties in respect of the insurance, repair and maintenance of each commonhold unit.

(3)   A duty under subsection (2) may be imposed on the commonhold association or the unit-holder.

**[1178]**

## 15  Transfer

(1)   In this Part a reference to the transfer of a commonhold unit is a reference to the transfer of a unit-holder's freehold estate in a unit to another person—

   (a)   whether or not for consideration,

   (b)   whether or not subject to any reservation or other terms, and

   (c)   whether or not by operation of law.

(2)   A commonhold community statement may not prevent or restrict the transfer of a commonhold unit.

(3)   On the transfer of a commonhold unit the new unit-holder shall notify the commonhold association of the transfer.

(4)   Regulations may—

   (a)   prescribe the form and manner of notice under subsection (3);

   (b)   prescribe the time within which notice is to be given;

   (c)   make provision (including provision requiring the payment of money) about the effect of failure to give notice.

**[1179]**

## 16  Transfer: effect

(1)   A right or duty conferred or imposed—

   (a)   by a commonhold community statement, or

   (b)   in accordance with section 20,

shall affect a new unit-holder in the same way as it affected the former unit-holder.

(2)   A former unit-holder shall not incur a liability or acquire a right—

   (a)   under or by virtue of the commonhold community statement, or

   (b)   by virtue of anything done in accordance with section 20.

(3)   Subsection (2)—

   (a)   shall not be capable of being disapplied or varied by agreement, and

   (b)   is without prejudice to any liability or right incurred or acquired before a transfer takes effect.

(4)   In this section—

   "former unit-holder" means a person from whom a commonhold unit has been transferred (whether or not he has ceased to be the registered proprietor), and

   "new unit-holder" means a person to whom a commonhold unit is transferred (whether or not he has yet become the registered proprietor).

**[1180]**

## 17  Leasing: residential

(1)   It shall not be possible to create a term of years absolute in a residential commonhold unit unless the term satisfies prescribed conditions.

(2)   The conditions may relate to—

   (a)   length;

   (b)   the circumstances in which the term is granted;

   (c)   any other matter.

(3)   Subject to subsection (4), an instrument or agreement shall be of no effect to the extent that it purports to create a term of years in contravention of subsection (1).

(4)   Where an instrument or agreement purports to create a term of years in contravention of subsection (1) a party to the instrument or agreement may apply to the court for an order—

   (a)   providing for the instrument or agreement to have effect as if it provided for the creation of a term of years of a specified kind;

(b)    providing for the return or payment of money;

(c)    making such other provision as the court thinks appropriate.

(5)    A commonhold unit is residential if provision made in the commonhold community statement by virtue of section 14(1) requires it to be used only—

     (a)    for residential purposes, or

     (b)    for residential and other incidental purposes.

**[1181]**

**NOTES**

Regulations: the Commonhold Regulations 2004, SI 2004/1829 at **[3379]**.

## 18   Leasing: non-residential

An instrument or agreement which creates a term of years absolute in a commonhold unit which is not residential (within the meaning of section 17) shall have effect subject to any provision of the commonhold community statement.

**[1182]**

## 19   Leasing: supplementary

(1)    Regulations may—

     (a)    impose obligations on a tenant of a commonhold unit;

     (b)    enable a commonhold community statement to impose obligations on a tenant of a commonhold unit.

(2)    Regulations under subsection (1) may, in particular, require a tenant of a commonhold unit to make payments to the commonhold association or a unit-holder in discharge of payments which—

     (a)    are due in accordance with the commonhold community statement to be made by the unit-holder, or

     (b)    are due in accordance with the commonhold community statement to be made by another tenant of the unit.

(3)    Regulations under subsection (1) may, in particular, provide—

     (a)    for the amount of payments under subsection (2) to be set against sums owed by the tenant (whether to the person by whom the payments were due to be made or to some other person);

     (b)    for the amount of payments under subsection (2) to be recovered from the unit-holder or another tenant of the unit.

(4)    Regulations may modify a rule of law about leasehold estates (whether deriving from the common law or from an enactment) in its application to a term of years in a commonhold unit.

(5)    Regulations under this section—

     (a)    may make provision generally or in relation to specified circumstances, and

     (b)    may make different provision for different descriptions of commonhold land or commonhold unit.

**[1183]**

**NOTES**

Regulations: the Commonhold Regulations 2004, SI 2004/1829 at **[3379]**.

## 20   Other transactions

(1)    A commonhold community statement may not prevent or restrict the creation, grant or transfer by a unit-holder of—

     (a)    an interest in the whole or part of his unit, or

     (b)    a charge over his unit.

(2)    Subsection (1) is subject to sections 17 to 19 (which impose restrictions about leases).

(3)    It shall not be possible to create an interest of a prescribed kind in a commonhold unit unless the commonhold association—

     (a)    is a party to the creation of the interest, or

     (b)    consents in writing to the creation of the interest.

(4)    A commonhold association may act as described in subsection (3)(a) or (b) only if—

     (a)    the association passes a resolution to take the action, and

     (b)    at least 75 per cent of those who vote on the resolution vote in favour.

(5)    An instrument or agreement shall be of no effect to the extent that it purports to create an interest in contravention of subsection (3).

(6)    In this section "interest" does not include—

     (a)    a charge, or

**PART I
STATUTES**

(b)    an interest which arises by virtue of a charge.

**[1184]**

## 21  Part-unit: interests

(1)    It shall not be possible to create an interest in part only of a commonhold unit.

(2)    But subsection (1) shall not prevent—

(a)    the creation of a term of years absolute in part only of a residential commonhold unit where the term satisfies prescribed conditions,

(b)    the creation of a term of years absolute in part only of a non-residential commonhold unit, or

(c)    the transfer of the freehold estate in part only of a commonhold unit where the commonhold association consents in writing to the transfer.

(3)    An instrument or agreement shall be of no effect to the extent that it purports to create an interest in contravention of subsection (1).

(4)    Subsection (5) applies where—

(a)    land becomes commonhold land or is added to a commonhold unit, and

(b)    immediately before that event there is an interest in the land which could not be created after that event by reason of subsection (1).

(5)    The interest shall be extinguished by virtue of this subsection to the extent that it could not be created by reason of subsection (1).

(6)    Section 17(2) and (4) shall apply (with any necessary modifications) in relation to subsection (2)(a) and (b) above.

(7)    Where part only of a unit is held under a lease, regulations may modify the application of a provision which—

(a)    is made by or by virtue of this Part, and

(b)    applies to a unit-holder or a tenant or both.

(8)    Section 20(4) shall apply in relation to subsection (2)(c) above.

(9)    Where the freehold interest in part only of a commonhold unit is transferred, the part transferred—

(a)    becomes a new commonhold unit by virtue of this subsection, or

(b)    in a case where the request for consent under subsection (2)(c) states that this paragraph is to apply, becomes part of a commonhold unit specified in the request.

(10)    Regulations may make provision, or may require a commonhold community statement to make provision, about—

(a)    registration of units created by virtue of subsection (9);

(b)    the adaptation of provision made by or by virtue of this Part or by or by virtue of a commonhold community statement to a case where units are created or modified by virtue of subsection (9).

**[1185]**

---

**NOTES**

Commencement: 27 September 2004 (sub-ss (1)–(3), (6)–(10)); to be appointed (otherwise).

Regulations: the Commonhold Regulations 2004, SI 2004/1829 at **[3379]**.

---

## 22  Part-unit: charging

(1)    It shall not be possible to create a charge over part only of an interest in a commonhold unit.

(2)    An instrument or agreement shall be of no effect to the extent that it purports to create a charge in contravention of subsection (1).

(3)    Subsection (4) applies where—

(a)    land becomes commonhold land or is added to a commonhold unit, and

(b)    immediately before that event there is a charge over the land which could not be created after that event by reason of subsection (1).

(4)    The charge shall be extinguished by virtue of this subsection to the extent that it could not be created by reason of subsection (1).

**[1186]**

## 23  Changing size

(1)    An amendment of a commonhold community statement which redefines the extent of a commonhold unit may not be made unless the unit-holder consents—

(a)    in writing, and

(b)    before the amendment is made.

(2)   But regulations may enable a court to dispense with the requirement for consent on the application of a commonhold association in prescribed circumstances.

**[1187]**

### 24   Changing size: charged unit

(1)   This section applies to an amendment of a commonhold community statement which redefines the extent of a commonhold unit over which there is a registered charge.

(2)   The amendment may not be made unless the registered proprietor of the charge consents—
    (a)   in writing, and
    (b)   before the amendment is made.

(3)   But regulations may enable a court to dispense with the requirement for consent on the application of a commonhold association in prescribed circumstances.

(4)   If the amendment removes land from the commonhold unit, the charge shall by virtue of this subsection be extinguished to the extent that it relates to the land which is removed.

(5)   If the amendment adds land to the unit, the charge shall by virtue of this subsection be extended so as to relate to the land which is added.

(6)   Regulations may make provision—
    (a)   requiring notice to be given to the Registrar in circumstances to which this section applies;
    (b)   requiring the Registrar to alter the register to reflect the application of subsection (4) or (5).

**[1188]**

**NOTES**

Regulations: the Commonhold Regulations 2004, SI 2004/1829 at **[3379]**.

*Common parts*

### 25   Definition

(1)   In this Part "common parts" in relation to a commonhold means every part of the commonhold which is not for the time being a commonhold unit in accordance with the commonhold community statement.

(2)   A commonhold community statement may make provision in respect of a specified part of the common parts (a "limited use area") restricting—
    (a)   the classes of person who may use it;
    (b)   the kind of use to which it may be put.

(3)   A commonhold community statement—
    (a)   may make provision which has effect only in relation to a limited use area, and
    (b)   may make different provision for different limited use areas.

**[1189]**

### 26   Use and maintenance

A commonhold community statement must make provision—
    (a)   regulating the use of the common parts;
    (b)   requiring the commonhold association to insure the common parts;
    (c)   requiring the commonhold association to repair and maintain the common parts.

**[1190]**

### 27   Transactions

(1)   Nothing in a commonhold community statement shall prevent or restrict—
    (a)   the transfer by the commonhold association of its freehold estate in any part of the common parts, or
    (b)   the creation by the commonhold association of an interest in any part of the common parts.

(2)   In this section "interest" does not include—
    (a)   a charge, or
    (b)   an interest which arises by virtue of a charge.

**[1191]**

### 28   Charges: general prohibition

(1)   It shall not be possible to create a charge over common parts.

(2)   An instrument or agreement shall be of no effect to the extent that it purports to create a charge over common parts.

(3)    Where by virtue of section 7 or 9 a commonhold association is registered as the proprietor of common parts, a charge which relates wholly or partly to the common parts shall be extinguished by virtue of this subsection to the extent that it relates to the common parts.

(4)    Where by virtue of section 30 land vests in a commonhold association following an amendment to a commonhold community statement which has the effect of adding land to the common parts, a charge which relates wholly or partly to the land added shall be extinguished by virtue of this subsection to the extent that it relates to that land.

(5)    This section is subject to section 29 (which permits certain mortgages).

.    **[1192]**

### 29   New legal mortgages

(1)    Section 28 shall not apply in relation to a legal mortgage if the creation of the mortgage is approved by a resolution of the commonhold association.

(2)    A resolution for the purposes of subsection (1) must be passed—
    (a)    before the mortgage is created, and
    (b)    unanimously.

(3)    In this section "legal mortgage" has the meaning given by section 205(1)(xvi) of the Law of Property Act 1925 (c 20) (interpretation).

**[1193]**

### 30   Additions to common parts

(1)    This section applies where an amendment of a commonhold community statement—
    (a)    specifies land which forms part of a commonhold unit, and
    (b)    provides for that land (the "added land") to be added to the common parts.

(2)    The amendment may not be made unless the registered proprietor of any charge over the added land consents—
    (a)    in writing, and
    (b)    before the amendment is made.

(3)    But regulations may enable a court to dispense with the requirement for consent on the application of a commonhold association in specified circumstances.

(4)    On the filing of the amended statement under section 33—
    (a)    the commonhold association shall be entitled to be registered as the proprietor of the freehold estate in the added land, and
    (b)    the Registrar shall register the commonhold association in accordance with paragraph (a) (without an application being made).

**[1194]**

*Commonhold community statement*

### 31   Form and content: general

(1)    A commonhold community statement is a document which makes provision in relation to specified land for—
    (a)    the rights and duties of the commonhold association, and
    (b)    the rights and duties of the unit-holders.

(2)    A commonhold community statement must be in the prescribed form.

(3)    A commonhold community statement may—
    (a)    impose a duty on the commonhold association;
    (b)    impose a duty on a unit-holder;
    (c)    make provision about the taking of decisions in connection with the management of the commonhold or any other matter concerning it.

(4)    Subsection (3) is subject to—
    (a)    any provision made by or by virtue of this Part, and
    (b)    any provision of the [articles] of the commonhold association.

(5)    In subsection (3)(a) and (b) "duty" includes, in particular, a duty—
    (a)    to pay money;
    (b)    to undertake works;
    (c)    to grant access;
    (d)    to give notice;
    (e)    to refrain from entering into transactions of a specified kind in relation to a commonhold unit;
    (f)    to refrain from using the whole or part of a commonhold unit for a specified purpose or for anything other than a specified purpose;
    (g)    to refrain from undertaking works (including alterations) of a specified kind;
    (h)    to refrain from causing nuisance or annoyance;

  (i) to refrain from specified behaviour;

  (j) to indemnify the commonhold association or a unit-holder in respect of costs arising from the breach of a statutory requirement.

 (6) Provision in a commonhold community statement imposing a duty to pay money (whether in pursuance of subsection (5)(a) or any other provision made by or by virtue of this Part) may include provision for the payment of interest in the case of late payment.

 (7) A duty conferred by a commonhold community statement on a commonhold association or a unit-holder shall not require any other formality.

 (8) A commonhold community statement may not provide for the transfer or loss of an interest in land on the occurrence or non-occurrence of a specified event.

 (9) Provision made by a commonhold community statement shall be of no effect to the extent that—

  (a) it is prohibited by virtue of section 32,

  (b) it is inconsistent with any provision made by or by virtue of this Part,

  (c) it is inconsistent with anything which is treated as included in the statement by virtue of section 32, or

  (d) it is inconsistent with the [articles of association] of the commonhold association.

**[1195]**

**NOTES**

 Sub-s (4): word in square brackets substituted by the Companies Act 2006 (Consequential Amendments, Transitional Provisions and Savings) Order 2009, SI 2009/1941, art 2(1), Sch 1, para 194(1), (6)(a).

 Sub-s (9): words in square brackets substituted by SI 2009/1941, art 2(1), Sch 1, para 194(1), (6)(b).

 Regulations: the Commonhold Regulations 2004, SI 2004/1829 at **[3379]**.

## 32 Regulations

 (1) Regulations shall make provision about the content of a commonhold community statement.

 (2) The regulations may permit, require or prohibit the inclusion in a statement of—

  (a) specified provision, or

  (b) provision of a specified kind, for a specified purpose or about a specified matter.

 (3) The regulations may—

  (a) provide for a statement to be treated as including provision prescribed by or determined in accordance with the regulations;

  (b) permit a statement to make provision in place of provision which would otherwise be treated as included by virtue of paragraph (a).

 (4) The regulations may—

  (a) make different provision for different descriptions of commonhold association or unit-holder;

  (b) make different provision for different circumstances;

  (c) make provision about the extent to which a commonhold community statement may make different provision for different descriptions of unit-holder or common parts.

 (5) The matters to which regulations under this section may relate include, but are not limited to—

  (a) the matters mentioned in sections 11, 14, 15, 20, 21, 25, 26, 27, 38, 39 and 58, and

  (b) any matter for which regulations under section 37 may make provision.

**[1196]**

**NOTES**

 Regulations: the Commonhold Regulations 2004, SI 2004/1829 at **[3379]**.

## 33 Amendment

 (1) Regulations under section 32 shall require a commonhold community statement to make provision about how it can be amended.

 (2) The regulations shall, in particular, make provision under section 32(3)(a) (whether or not subject to provision under section 32(3)(b)).

 (3) An amendment of a commonhold community statement shall have no effect unless and until the amended statement is registered in accordance with this section.

 (4) If the commonhold association makes an application under this subsection the Registrar shall arrange for an amended commonhold community statement to be kept in his custody, and referred to in the register, in place of the unamended statement.

(5)　An application under subsection (4) must be accompanied by a certificate given by the directors of the commonhold association that the amended commonhold community statement satisfies the requirements of this Part.

(6)　Where an amendment of a commonhold community statement redefines the extent of a commonhold unit, an application under subsection (4) must be accompanied by any consent required by section 23(1) or 24(2) (or an order of a court dispensing with consent).

(7)　Where an amendment of a commonhold community statement has the effect of changing the extent of the common parts, an application under subsection (4) must be accompanied by any consent required by section 30(2) (or an order of a court dispensing with consent).

(8)　Where the Registrar amends the register on an application under subsection (4) he shall make any consequential amendments to the register which he thinks appropriate.

**[1197]**

*Commonhold association*

## 34　Constitution

[(1)　A commonhold association is a private company limited by guarantee—
- (a)　the articles of which state that an object of the company is to exercise the functions of a commonhold association in relation to specified commonhold land, and
- (b)　the statement of guarantee of which specifies £1 as the amount of the contribution required from each member in the event of the company being wound up.]

(2)　Schedule 3 (which makes provision about the constitution of a commonhold association) shall have effect.

**[1198]**

---

**NOTES**

Sub-s (1): substituted by the Companies Act 2006 (Consequential Amendments, Transitional Provisions and Savings) Order 2009, SI 2009/1941, art 2(1), Sch 1, para 194(1), (7).

---

## 35　Duty to manage

(1)　The directors of a commonhold association shall exercise their powers so as to permit or facilitate so far as possible—
- (a)　the exercise by each unit-holder of his rights, and
- (b)　the enjoyment by each unit-holder of the freehold estate in his unit.

(2)　The directors of a commonhold association shall, in particular, use any right, power or procedure conferred or created by virtue of section 37 for the purpose of preventing, remedying or curtailing a failure on the part of a unit-holder to comply with a requirement or duty imposed on him by virtue of the commonhold community statement or a provision of this Part.

(3)　But in respect of a particular failure on the part of a unit-holder (the "defaulter") the directors of a commonhold association—
- (a)　need not take action if they reasonably think that inaction is in the best interests of establishing or maintaining harmonious relationships between all the unit-holders, and that it will not cause any unit-holder (other than the defaulter) significant loss or significant disadvantage, and
- (b)　shall have regard to the desirability of using arbitration, mediation or conciliation procedures (including referral under a scheme approved under section 42) instead of legal proceedings wherever possible.

(4)　A reference in this section to a unit-holder includes a reference to a tenant of a unit.

**[1199]**

## 36　Voting

(1)　This section applies in relation to any provision of this Part (a "voting provision") which refers to the passing of a resolution by a commonhold association.

(2)　A voting provision is satisfied only if every member is given an opportunity to vote in accordance with any relevant provision of the [articles of association] or the commonhold community statement.

(3)　A vote is cast for the purposes of a voting provision whether it is cast in person or in accordance with a provision which—
- (a)　provides for voting by post, by proxy or in some other manner, and
- (b)　is contained in the [articles of association] or the commonhold community statement.

(4)　A resolution is passed unanimously if every member who casts a vote votes in favour.

**[1200]**

**NOTES**

Sub-ss (2), (3): words in square brackets substituted by the Companies Act 2006 (Consequential Amendments, Transitional Provisions and Savings) Order 2009, SI 2009/1941, art 2(1), Sch 1, para 194(1), (8).

*Operation of commonhold*

## 37 Enforcement and compensation

(1) Regulations may make provision (including provision conferring jurisdiction on a court) about the exercise or enforcement of a right or duty imposed or conferred by or by virtue of—

    (a) a commonhold community statement;

    (b) the [articles] of a commonhold association;

    (c) a provision made by or by virtue of this Part.

(2) The regulations may, in particular, make provision—

    (a) requiring compensation to be paid where a right is exercised in specified cases or circumstances;

    (b) requiring compensation to be paid where a duty is not complied with;

    (c) enabling recovery of costs where work is carried out for the purpose of enforcing a right or duty;

    (d) enabling recovery of costs where work is carried out in consequence of the failure to perform a duty;

    (e) permitting a unit-holder to enforce a duty imposed on another unit-holder, on a commonhold association or on a tenant;

    (f) permitting a commonhold association to enforce a duty imposed on a unit-holder or a tenant;

    (g) permitting a tenant to enforce a duty imposed on another tenant, a unit-holder or a commonhold association;

    (h) permitting the enforcement of terms or conditions to which a right is subject;

    (i) requiring the use of a specified form of arbitration, mediation or conciliation procedure before legal proceedings may be brought.

(3) Provision about compensation made by virtue of this section shall include—

    (a) provision (which may include provision conferring jurisdiction on a court) for determining the amount of compensation;

    (b) provision for the payment of interest in the case of late payment.

(4) Regulations under this section shall be subject to any provision included in a commonhold community statement in accordance with regulations made by virtue of section 32(5)(b).

**[1201]**

**NOTES**

Sub-s (1): word in square brackets substituted by the Companies Act 2006 (Consequential Amendments, Transitional Provisions and Savings) Order 2009, SI 2009/1941, art 2(1), Sch 1, para 194(1), (9).

Regulations: the Commonhold Regulations 2004, SI 2004/1829 at **[3379]**.

## 38 Commonhold assessment

(1) A commonhold community statement must make provision—

    (a) requiring the directors of the commonhold association to make an annual estimate of the income required to be raised from unit-holders to meet the expenses of the association,

    (b) enabling the directors of the commonhold association to make estimates from time to time of income required to be raised from unit-holders in addition to the annual estimate,

    (c) specifying the percentage of any estimate made under paragraph (a) or (b) which is to be allocated to each unit,

    (d) requiring each unit-holder to make payments in respect of the percentage of any estimate which is allocated to his unit, and

    (e) requiring the directors of the commonhold association to serve notices on unit-holders specifying payments required to be made by them and the date on which each payment is due.

(2) For the purpose of subsection (1)(c)—

    (a) the percentages allocated by a commonhold community statement to the commonhold units must amount in aggregate to 100;

    (b) a commonhold community statement may specify 0 per cent in relation to a unit.

**[1202]**

## 39 Reserve fund

(1) Regulations under section 32 may, in particular, require a commonhold community statement to make provision—

(a)  requiring the directors of the commonhold association to establish and maintain one or more funds to finance the repair and maintenance of common parts;

(b)  requiring the directors of the commonhold association to establish and maintain one or more funds to finance the repair and maintenance of commonhold units.

(2)  Where a commonhold community statement provides for the establishment and maintenance of a fund in accordance with subsection (1) it must also make provision—

(a)  requiring or enabling the directors of the commonhold association to set a levy from time to time,

(b)  specifying the percentage of any levy set under paragraph (a) which is to be allocated to each unit,

(c)  requiring each unit-holder to make payments in respect of the percentage of any levy set under paragraph (a) which is allocated to his unit, and

(d)  requiring the directors of the commonhold association to serve notices on unit-holders specifying payments required to be made by them and the date on which each payment is due.

(3)  For the purpose of subsection (2)(b)—

(a)  the percentages allocated by a commonhold community statement to the commonhold units must amount in aggregate to 100;

(b) .  a commonhold community statement may specify 0 per cent in relation to a unit.

(4)  The assets of a fund established and maintained by virtue of this section shall not be used for the purpose of enforcement of any debt except a judgment debt referable to a reserve fund activity.

(5)  For the purpose of subsection (4)—

(a)  "reserve fund activity" means an activity which in accordance with the commonhold community statement can or may be financed from a fund established and maintained by virtue of this section,

(b)  assets are used for the purpose of enforcement of a debt if, in particular, they are taken in execution or are made the subject of a charging order under section 1 of the Charging Orders Act 1979 (c 53), and

(c)  the reference to a judgment debt includes a reference to any interest payable on a judgment debt.

[1203]

## 40  Rectification of documents

(1)  A unit-holder may apply to the court for a declaration that—

(a)  the [articles of association] of the relevant commonhold association do not comply with regulations under paragraph 2(1) of Schedule 3;

(b)  the relevant commonhold community statement does not comply with a requirement imposed by or by virtue of this Part.

(2)  On granting a declaration under this section the court may make any order which appears to it to be appropriate.

(3)  An order under subsection (2) may, in particular—

(a)  require a director or other specified officer of a commonhold association to take steps to alter or amend a document;

(b)  require a director or other specified officer of a commonhold association to take specified steps;

(c)  make an award of compensation (whether or not contingent upon the occurrence or non-occurrence of a specified event) to be paid by the commonhold association to a specified person;

(d)  make provision for land to cease to be commonhold land.

(4)  An application under subsection (1) must be made—

(a)  within the period of three months beginning with the day on which the applicant became a unit-holder,

(b)  within three months of the commencement of the alleged failure to comply, or

(c)  with the permission of the court.

[1204]

**NOTES**

Sub-s (1): words in square brackets substituted by the Companies Act 2006 (Consequential Amendments, Transitional Provisions and Savings) Order 2009, SI 2009/1941, art 2(1), Sch 1, para 194(1), (10).

## 41  Enlargement

(1)  This section applies to an application under section 2 if the commonhold association for the purposes of the application already exercises functions in relation to commonhold land.

(2)  In this section—

(a) the application is referred to as an "application to add land", and

(b) the land to which the application relates is referred to as the "added land".

(3) An application to add land may not be made unless it is approved by a resolution of the commonhold association.

(4) A resolution for the purposes of subsection (3) must be passed—

(a) before the application to add land is made, and

(b) unanimously.

(5) Section 2(2) shall not apply to an application to add land; but the application must be accompanied by—

(a) the documents specified in paragraph 6 of Schedule 1,

(b) an application under section 33 for the registration of an amended commonhold community statement which makes provision for the existing commonhold and the added land, and

(c) a certificate given by the directors of the commonhold association that the application to add land satisfies Schedule 2 and subsection (3).

(6) Where sections 7 and 9 have effect following an application to add land—

(a) the references to "the commonhold land" in sections 7(2)(a) and (3)(d) and 9(3)(f) shall be treated as references to the added land, and

(b) the references in sections 7(2)(b) and (3)(c) and 9(3)(e) to the rights and duties conferred and imposed by the commonhold community statement shall be treated as a reference to rights and duties only in so far as they affect the added land.

(7) In the case of an application to add land where the whole of the added land is to form part of the common parts of a commonhold—

(a) section 7 shall not apply,

(b) on registration the commonhold association shall be entitled to be registered (if it is not already) as the proprietor of the freehold estate in the added land,

(c) the Registrar shall make any registration required by paragraph (b) (without an application being made), and

(d) the rights and duties conferred and imposed by the commonhold community statement shall, in so far as they affect the added land, come into force on registration.

**[1205]**

## 42 Ombudsman

(1) Regulations may provide that a commonhold association shall be a member of an approved ombudsman scheme.

(2) An "approved ombudsman scheme" is a scheme which is approved by the Lord Chancellor and which—

(a) provides for the appointment of one or more persons as ombudsman,

(b) provides for a person to be appointed as ombudsman only if the Lord Chancellor approves the appointment in advance,

(c) enables a unit-holder to refer to the ombudsman a dispute between the unit-holder and a commonhold association which is a member of the scheme,

(d) enables a commonhold association which is a member of the scheme to refer to the ombudsman a dispute between the association and a unit-holder,

(e) requires the ombudsman to investigate and determine a dispute referred to him,

(f) requires a commonhold association which is a member of the scheme to cooperate with the ombudsman in investigating or determining a dispute, and

(g) requires a commonhold association which is a member of the scheme to comply with any decision of the ombudsman (including any decision requiring the payment of money).

(3) In addition to the matters specified in subsection (2) an approved ombudsman scheme—

(a) may contain other provision, and

(b) shall contain such provision, or provision of such a kind, as may be prescribed.

(4) If a commonhold association fails to comply with regulations under subsection (1) a unit-holder may apply to the High Court for an order requiring the directors of the commonhold association to ensure that the association complies with the regulations.

(5) A reference in this section to a unit-holder includes a reference to a tenant of a unit.

**[1206]**

*Termination: voluntary winding-up*

## 43 Winding-up resolution

(1) A winding-up resolution in respect of a commonhold association shall be of no effect unless—

(a) the resolution is preceded by a declaration of solvency,

(b)    the commonhold association passes a termination-statement resolution before it passes the winding-up resolution, and

(c)    each resolution is passed with at least 80 per cent of the members of the association voting in favour.

(2)    In this Part—

"declaration of solvency" means a directors' statutory declaration made in accordance with section 89 of the Insolvency Act 1986 (c 45),

"termination-statement resolution" means a resolution approving the terms of a termination statement (within the meaning of section 47), and

"winding-up resolution" means a resolution for voluntary winding-up within the meaning of section 84 of that Act.

[1207]

## 44   100 per cent agreement

(1)    This section applies where a commonhold association—

(a)    has passed a winding-up resolution and a termination-statement resolution with 100 per cent of the members of the association voting in favour, and

(b)    has appointed a liquidator under section 91 of the Insolvency Act 1986 (c 45).

(2)    The liquidator shall make a termination application within the period of six months beginning with the day on which the winding-up resolution is passed.

(3)    If the liquidator fails to make a termination application within the period specified in subsection (2) a termination application may be made by—

(a)    a unit-holder, or

(b)    a person falling within a class prescribed for the purposes of this subsection.

[1208]

## 45   80 per cent agreement

(1)    This section applies where a commonhold association—

(a)    has passed a winding-up resolution and a termination-statement resolution with at least 80 per cent of the members of the association voting in favour, and

(b)    has appointed a liquidator under section 91 of the Insolvency Act 1986.

(2)    The liquidator shall within the prescribed period apply to the court for an order determining—

(a)    the terms and conditions on which a termination application may be made, and

(b)    the terms of the termination statement to accompany a termination application.

(3)    The liquidator shall make a termination application within the period of three months starting with the date on which an order under subsection (2) is made.

(4)    If the liquidator fails to make an application under subsection (2) or (3) within the period specified in that subsection an application of the same kind may be made by—

(a)    a unit-holder, or

(b)    a person falling within a class prescribed for the purposes of this subsection.

[1209]

**NOTES**

Regulations: the Commonhold Regulations 2004, SI 2004/1829 at **[3379]**.

## 46   Termination application

(1)    A "termination application" is an application to the Registrar that all the land in relation to which a particular commonhold association exercises functions should cease to be commonhold land.

(2)    A termination application must be accompanied by a termination statement.

(3)    On receipt of a termination application the Registrar shall note it in the register.

[1210]

## 47   Termination statement

(1)    A termination statement must specify—

(a)    the commonhold association's proposals for the transfer of the commonhold land following acquisition of the freehold estate in accordance with section 49(3), and

(b)    how the assets of the commonhold association will be distributed.

(2)    A commonhold community statement may make provision requiring any termination statement to make arrangements—

(a)    of a specified kind, or

(b)    determined in a specified manner,

PART I
STATUTES

about the rights of unit-holders in the event of all the land to which the statement relates ceasing to be commonhold land.

(3)   A termination statement must comply with a provision made by the commonhold community statement in reliance on subsection (2).

(4)   Subsection (3) may be disapplied by an order of the court—
    (a)   generally,
    (b)   in respect of specified matters, or
    (c)   for a specified purpose.

(5)   An application for an order under subsection (4) may be made by any member of the commonhold association.

**[1211]**

## 48   The liquidator

(1)   This section applies where a termination application has been made in respect of particular commonhold land.

(2)   The liquidator shall notify the Registrar of his appointment.

(3)   In the case of a termination application made under section 44 the liquidator shall either
    (a)   notify the Registrar that the liquidator is content with the termination statement submitted with the termination application, or
    (b)   apply to the court under section 112 of the Insolvency Act 1986 (c 45) to determine the terms of the termination statement.

(4)   The liquidator shall send to the Registrar a copy of a determination made by virtue of subsection (3)(b).

(5)   Subsection (4) is in addition to any requirement under section 112(3) of the Insolvency Act 1986.

(6)   A duty imposed on the liquidator by this section is to be performed as soon as possible.

(7)   In this section a reference to the liquidator is a reference—
    (a)   to the person who is appointed as liquidator under section 91 of the Insolvency Act 1986, or
    (b)   in the case of a members' voluntary winding up which becomes a creditors' voluntary winding up by virtue of sections 95 and 96 of that Act, to the person acting as liquidator in accordance with section 100 of that Act.

**[1212]**

## 49   Termination

(1)   This section applies where a termination application is made under section 44 and—
    (a)   a liquidator notifies the Registrar under section 48(3)(a) that he is content with a termination statement, or
    (b)   a determination is made under section 112 of the Insolvency Act 1986 (c 45) by virtue of section 48(3)(b).

(2)   This section also applies where a termination application is made under section 45.

(3)   The commonhold association shall by virtue of this subsection be entitled to be registered as the proprietor of the freehold estate in each commonhold unit.

(4)   The Registrar shall take such action as appears to him to be appropriate for the purpose of giving effect to the termination statement.

**[1213]**

*Termination: winding-up by court*

## 50   Introduction

(1)   Section 51 applies where a petition is presented under section 124 of the Insolvency Act 1986 for the winding up of a commonhold association by the court.

(2)   For the purposes of this Part—
    (a)   an "insolvent commonhold association" is one in relation to which a winding-up petition has been presented under section 124 of the Insolvency Act 1986,
    (b)   a commonhold association is the "successor commonhold association" to an insolvent commonhold association if the land specified for the purpose of section 34(1)(a) is the same for both associations, and
    (c)   a "winding-up order" is an order under section 125 of the Insolvency Act 1986 for the winding up of a commonhold association.

**[1214]**

## 51 Succession order

(1)   At the hearing of the winding-up petition an application may be made to the court for an order under this section (a "succession order") in relation to the insolvent commonhold association.

(2)   An application under subsection (1) may be made only by—
  (a)   the insolvent commonhold association,
  (b)   one or more members of the insolvent commonhold association, or
  (c)   a provisional liquidator for the insolvent commonhold association appointed under section 135 of the Insolvency Act 1986.

(3)   An application under subsection (1) must be accompanied by—
  (a)   prescribed evidence of the formation of a successor commonhold association, and
  (b)   a certificate given by the directors of the successor commonhold association that its [articles of association] comply with regulations under paragraph 2(1) of Schedule 3.

(4)   The court shall grant an application under subsection (1) unless it thinks that the circumstances of the insolvent commonhold association make a succession order inappropriate.

**[1215]**

---

**NOTES**

Sub-s (3): words in square brackets substituted by the Companies Act 2006 (Consequential Amendments, Transitional Provisions and Savings) Order 2009, SI 2009/1941, art 2(1), Sch 1, para 194(1), (11).
Regulations: the Commonhold Regulations 2004, SI 2004/1829 at **[3379]**.

---

## 52   Assets and liabilities

(1)   Where a succession order is made in relation to an insolvent commonhold association this section applies on the making of a winding-up order in respect of the association.

(2)   The successor commonhold association shall be entitled to be registered as the proprietor of the freehold estate in the common parts.

(3)   The insolvent commonhold association shall for all purposes cease to be treated as the proprietor of the freehold estate in the common parts.

(4)   The succession order—
  (a)   shall make provision as to the treatment of any charge over all or any part of the common parts;
  (b)   may require the Registrar to take action of a specified kind;
  (c)   may enable the liquidator to require the Registrar to take action of a specified kind;
  (d)   may make supplemental or incidental provision.

**[1216]**

## 53   Transfer of responsibility

(1)   Where a succession order is made in relation to an insolvent commonhold association this section applies on the making of a winding-up order in respect of the association.

(2)   The successor commonhold association shall be treated as the commonhold association for the commonhold in respect of any matter which relates to a time after the making of the winding-up order.

(3)   On the making of the winding-up order the court may make an order requiring the liquidator to make available to the successor commonhold association specified—
  (a)   records;
  (b)   copies of records;
  (c)   information.

(4)   An order under subsection (3) may include terms as to—
  (a)   timing;
  (b)   payment.

**[1217]**

## 54   Termination of commonhold

(1)   This section applies where the court—
  (a)   makes a winding-up order in respect of a commonhold association, and
  (b)   has not made a succession order in respect of the commonhold association.

(2)   The liquidator of a commonhold association shall as soon as possible notify the Registrar of—
  (a)   the fact that this section applies,
  (b)   any directions given under section 168 of the Insolvency Act 1986 (c 45) (liquidator: supplementary powers),
  (c)   any notice given to the court and the registrar of companies in accordance with section 172(8) of that Act (liquidator vacating office after final meeting),

(d)    any notice given to the Secretary of State under section 174(3) of that Act (completion of winding-up),

(e)    any application made to the registrar of companies under section 202(2) of that Act (insufficient assets: early dissolution),

(f)    any notice given to the registrar of companies under section 205(1)(b) of that Act (completion of winding-up), and

(g)    any other matter which in the liquidator's opinion is relevant to the Registrar.

(3)    Notification under subsection (2)(b) to (f) must be accompanied by a copy of the directions, notice or application concerned.

(4)    The Registrar shall—

(a)    make such arrangements as appear to him to be appropriate for ensuring that the freehold estate in land in respect of which a commonhold association exercises functions ceases to be registered as a freehold estate in commonhold land as soon as is reasonably practicable after he receives notification under subsection (2)(c) to (f), and

(b)    take such action as appears to him to be appropriate for the purpose of giving effect to a determination made by the liquidator in the exercise of his functions.

**[1218]**

*Termination: miscellaneous*

## 55 Termination by court

(1)    This section applies where the court makes an order by virtue of section 6(6)(c) or 40(3)(d) for all the land in relation to which a commonhold association exercises functions to cease to be commonhold land.

(2)    The court shall have the powers which it would have if it were making a winding-up order in respect of the commonhold association.

(3)    A person appointed as liquidator by virtue of subsection (2) shall have the powers and duties of a liquidator following the making of a winding-up order by the court in respect of a commonhold association.

(4)    But the order of the court by virtue of section 6(6)(c) or 40(3)(d) may—

(a)    require the liquidator to exercise his functions in a particular way;

(b)    impose additional rights or duties on the liquidator;

(c)    modify or remove a right or duty of the liquidator.

**[1219]**

## 56 Release of reserve fund

Section 39(4) shall cease to have effect in relation to a commonhold association (in respect of debts and liabilities accruing at any time) if—

(a)    the court makes a winding-up order in respect of the association,

(b)    the association passes a voluntary winding-up resolution, or

(c)    the court makes an order by virtue of section 6(6)(c) or 40(3)(d) for all the land in relation to which the association exercises functions to cease to be commonhold land.

**[1220]**

*Miscellaneous*

## 57 Multiple site commonholds

(1)    A commonhold may include two or more parcels of land, whether or not contiguous.

(2)    But section 1(1) of this Act is not satisfied in relation to land specified in the [articles of association] of a commonhold association unless a single commonhold community statement makes provision for all the land.

(3)    Regulations may make provision about an application under section 2 made jointly by two or more persons, each of whom is the registered freeholder of part of the land to which the application relates.

(4)    The regulations may, in particular—

(a)    modify the application of a provision made by or by virtue of this Part;

(b)    disapply the application of a provision made by or by virtue of this Part;

(c)    impose additional requirements.

**[1221]**

**NOTES**

Sub-s (2): words in square brackets substituted by the Companies Act 2006 (Consequential Amendments, Transitional Provisions and Savings) Order 2009, SI 2009/1941, art 2(1), Sch 1, para 194(1), (12).

Regulations: the Commonhold Regulations 2004, SI 2004/1829 at **[3379]**.

## 58  Development rights

(1)   In this Part—

"the developer" means a person who makes an application under section 2, and

"development business" has the meaning given by Schedule 4.

(2)   A commonhold community statement may confer rights on the developer which are designed—

    (a)    to permit him to undertake development business, or

    (b)    to facilitate his undertaking of development business.

(3)   Provision made by a commonhold community statement in reliance on subsection (2) may include provision—

    (a)    requiring the commonhold association or a unit-holder to co-operate with the developer for a specified purpose connected with development business;

    (b)    making the exercise of a right conferred by virtue of subsection (2) subject to terms and conditions specified in or to be determined in accordance with the commonhold community statement;

    (c)    making provision about the effect of breach of a requirement by virtue of paragraph (a) or a term or condition imposed by virtue of paragraph (b);

    (d)    disapplying section 41(2) and (3).

(4)   Subsection (2) is subject—

    (a)    to regulations under section 32, and

    (b)    in the case of development business of the kind referred to in paragraph 7 of Schedule 4, to the [articles of association] of the commonhold association.

(5)   Regulations may make provision regulating or restricting the exercise of rights conferred by virtue of subsection (2).

(6)   Where a right is conferred on a developer by virtue of subsection (2), if he sends to the Registrar a notice surrendering the right—

    (a)    the Registrar shall arrange for the notice to be kept in his custody and referred to in the register,

    (b)    the right shall cease to be exercisable from the time when the notice is registered under paragraph (a), and

    (c)    the Registrar shall inform the commonhold association as soon as is reasonably practicable.

**[1222]**

### NOTES

Sub-s (4): words in square brackets substituted by the Companies Act 2006 (Consequential Amendments, Transitional Provisions and Savings) Order 2009, SI 2009/1941, art 2(1), Sch 1, para 194(1), (13).

Regulations: the Commonhold Regulations 2004, SI 2004/1829 at **[3379]**.

## 59  Development rights: succession

(1)   If during a transitional period the developer transfers to another person the freehold estate in the whole of the commonhold, the successor in title shall be treated as the developer in relation to any matter arising after the transfer.

(2)   If during a transitional period the developer transfers to another person the freehold estate in part of the commonhold, the successor in title shall be treated as the developer for the purpose of any matter which—

    (a)    arises after the transfer, and

    (b)    affects the estate transferred.

(3)   If after a transitional period or in a case where there is no transitional period—

    (a)    the developer transfers to another person the freehold estate in the whole or part of the commonhold (other than by the transfer of the freehold estate in a single commonhold unit), and

    (b)    the transfer is expressed to be inclusive of development rights,

the successor in title shall be treated as the developer for the purpose of any matter which arises after the transfer and affects the estate transferred.

(4)   Other than during a transitional period, a person shall not be treated as the developer in relation to commonhold land for any purpose unless he—

    (a)    is, or has been at a particular time, the registered proprietor of the freehold estate in more than one of the commonhold units, and

    (b)    is the registered proprietor of the freehold estate in at least one of the commonhold units.

**[1223]**

**60 Compulsory purchase**

(1) Where a freehold estate in commonhold land is transferred to a compulsory purchaser the land shall cease to be commonhold land.

(2) But subsection (1) does not apply to a transfer if the Registrar is satisfied that the compulsory purchaser has indicated a desire for the land transferred to continue to be commonhold land.

(3) The requirement of consent under section 21(2)(c) shall not apply to transfer to a compulsory purchaser.

(4) Regulations may make provision about the transfer of a freehold estate in commonhold land to a compulsory purchaser.

(5) The regulations may, in particular—

    (a) make provision about the effect of subsections (1) and (2) (including provision about that part of the commonhold which is not transferred);

    (b) require the service of notice;

    (c) confer power on a court;

    (d) make provision about compensation;

    (e) make provision enabling a commonhold association to require a compulsory purchaser to acquire the freehold estate in the whole, or a particular part, of the commonhold;

    (f) provide for an enactment relating to compulsory purchase not to apply or to apply with modifications.

(6) Provision made by virtue of subsection (5)(a) in respect of land which is not transferred may include provision—

    (a) for some or all of the land to cease to be commonhold land;

    (b) for a provision of this Part to apply with specified modifications.

(7) In this section "compulsory purchaser" means—

    (a) a person acquiring land in respect of which he is authorised to exercise a power of compulsory purchase by virtue of an enactment, and

    (b) a person acquiring land which he is obliged to acquire by virtue of a prescribed enactment or in prescribed circumstances.

                                                      **[1224]**

**61 [Home] rights**

In the following provisions of this Part a reference to a tenant includes a reference to a person who has [home rights (within the meaning of section 30(2) of the Family Law Act 1996 (c 27) (rights in respect of matrimonial or civil partnership home))] in respect of a commonhold unit—

    (a) section 19,

    (b) section 35, and

    (c) section 37.

                                                      **[1225]**

**NOTES**

Words in square brackets substituted by the Civil Partnership Act 2004, s 82, Sch 9, Pt 2, para 24, subject to transitional provisions in s 82 of, and Sch 9, Pt 3 to, that Act at **[1324]**, **[1328]**.

**62 Advice [etc]**

(1) The Lord Chancellor may give financial assistance to a person in relation to the provision by that person of [information, training or] general advice [about, or a dispute resolution service in connection with—

    (a) any] aspect of the law of commonhold land, so far as relating to residential matters[, or

    (b) any other matter relating to commonhold land and residential matters].

(2) Financial assistance under this section may be given in such form and on such terms as the Lord Chancellor thinks appropriate.

(3) The terms may, in particular, require repayment in specified circumstances.

                                                      **[1226]**

**NOTES**

Section heading: word in square brackets inserted by the Housing and Regeneration Act 2008, s 319(2).

Sub-s (1): words in first and third pairs of square brackets inserted and words in second pair of square brackets substituted by the Housing and Regeneration Act 2008, s 319(1).

**63 The Crown**

This Part binds the Crown.

                                                      **[1227]**

*General*

## 64 Orders and regulations

(1)  In this Part "prescribed" means prescribed by regulations.

(2)  Regulations under this Part shall be made by the Lord Chancellor.

(3)  Regulations under this Part—
  (a)  shall be made by statutory instrument,
  (b)  may include incidental, supplemental, consequential and transitional provision,
  (c)  may make provision generally or only in relation to specified cases,
  (d)  may make different provision for different purposes, and
  (e)  shall be subject to annulment in pursuance of a resolution of either House of Parliament.

**[1228]**

## 65 Registration procedure

(1)  The Lord Chancellor may make rules about—
  (a)  the procedure to be followed on or in respect of commonhold registration documents, and
  (b)  the registration of freehold estates in commonhold land.

(2)  Rules under this section—
  (a)  shall be made by statutory instrument in the same manner as land registration rules within the meaning of the Land Registration Act 2002 (c 9),
  (b)  may make provision for any matter for which provision is or may be made by land registration rules, and
  (c)  may provide for land registration rules to have effect in relation to anything done by virtue of or for the purposes of this Part as they have effect in relation to anything done by virtue of or for the purposes of that Act.

(3)  Rules under this section may, in particular, make provision—
  (a)  about the form and content of a commonhold registration document;
  (b)  enabling the Registrar to cancel an application by virtue of this Part in specified circumstances;
  (c)  enabling the Registrar, in particular, to cancel an application by virtue of this Part if he thinks that plans submitted with it (whether as part of a commonhold community statement or otherwise) are insufficiently clear or accurate;
  (d)  about the order in which commonhold registration documents and general registration documents are to be dealt with by the Registrar;
  (e)  for registration to take effect (whether or not retrospectively) as from a date or time determined in accordance with the rules.

(4)  The rules may also make provision about satisfaction of a requirement for an application by virtue of this Part to be accompanied by a document; in particular the rules may—
  (a)  permit or require a copy of a document to be submitted in place of or in addition to the original;
  (b)  require a copy to be certified in a specified manner;
  (c)  permit or require the submission of a document in electronic form.

(5)  A commonhold registration document must be accompanied by such fee (if any) as is specified for that purpose by order under section 102 of the Land Registration Act 2002 (c 9)(fee orders).

(6)  In this section—
  "commonhold registration document" means an application or other document sent to the Registrar by virtue of this Part, and
  "general registration document" means a document sent to the Registrar under a provision of the Land Registration Act 2002.

**[1229]**

**NOTES**
Rules: the Commonhold (Land Registration) Rules 2004, SI 2004/1830 at **[3398]**.

## 66 Jurisdiction

(1)  In this Part "the court" means the High Court or a county court.

(2)  Provision made by or under this Part conferring jurisdiction on a court shall be subject to provision made under section 1 of the Courts and Legal Services Act 1990 (c 41) (allocation of business between High Court and county courts).

(3)  A power under this Part to confer jurisdiction on a court includes power to confer jurisdiction on a tribunal established under an enactment.

(4)   Rules of court or rules of procedure for a tribunal may make provision about proceedings brought—

(a)   under or by virtue of any provision of this Part, or

(b)   in relation to commonhold land.

**[1230]**

## 67   The register

(1)   In this Part—

"the register" means the register of title to freehold and leasehold land kept under section 1 of the Land Registration Act 2002,

"registered" means registered in the register, and

"the Registrar" means the Chief Land Registrar.

(2)   Regulations under any provision of this Part may confer functions on the Registrar (including discretionary functions).

(3)   The Registrar shall comply with any direction or requirement given to him or imposed on him under or by virtue of this Part.

(4)   Where the Registrar thinks it appropriate in consequence of or for the purpose of anything done or proposed to be done in connection with this Part, he may—

(a)   make or cancel an entry on the register;

(b)   take any other action.

(5)   Subsection (4) is subject to section 6(2).

**[1231]**

## 68   Amendments

Schedule 5 (consequential amendments) shall have effect.

**[1232]**

## 69   Interpretation

(1)   In this Part—

"instrument" includes any document, and

["object", in relation to a commonhold association, means an object stated in the association's articles of association (see section 31 of the Companies Act 2006);]

(2)   In this Part—

(a)   a reference to a duty to insure includes a reference to a duty to use the proceeds of insurance for the purpose of rebuilding or reinstating, and

(b)   a reference to maintaining property includes a reference to decorating it and to putting it into sound condition.

(3)   A provision of the Law of Property Act 1925 (c 20), [the Companies Act 2006] or the Land Registration Act 2002 (c 9) defining an expression shall apply to the use of the expression in this Part unless the contrary intention appears.

**[1233]**

---

**NOTES**

Sub-s (1): definition "object" substituted by the Companies Act 2006 (Consequential Amendments, Transitional Provisions and Savings) Order 2009, SI 2009/1941, art 2(1), Sch 1, para 194(1), (14)(a).

Sub-s (3): words in square brackets substituted by SI 2009/1941, art 2(1), Sch 1, para 194(1), (14)(b).

---

## 70   Index of defined expressions

In this Part the expressions listed below are defined by the provisions specified.

| *Expression* | *Interpretation provision* |
| --- | --- |
| Common parts | Section 25 |
| A commonhold | Section 1 |
| Commonhold association | Section 34 |
| Commonhold community statement | Section 31 |
| Commonhold land | Section 1 |
| Commonhold unit | Section 11 |
| Court | Section 66 |
| Declaration of solvency | Section 43 |

| Expression | Interpretation provision |
|---|---|
| Developer | Section 58 |
| Development business | Section 58 |
| Exercising functions | Section 8 |
| Insolvent commonhold association | Section 50 |
| Instrument | Section 69 |
| Insure | Section 69 |
| Joint unit-holder | Section 13 |
| Liquidator (sections 44 to 49) | Section 44 |
| Maintenance | Section 69 |
| Object | Section 69 |
| Prescribed | Section 64 |
| The register | Section 67 |
| Registered | Section 67 |
| Registered freeholder | Section 2 |
| The Registrar | Section 67 |
| Regulations | Section 64 |
| Residential commonhold unit | Section 17 |
| Succession order | Section 51 |
| Successor commonhold association | Section 50 |
| Termination application | Section 46 |
| Termination-statement resolution | Section 43 |
| Transfer (of unit) | Section 15 |
| Transitional period | Section 8 |
| Unit-holder | Section 12 |
| Winding-up resolution | Section 43 |

**[1234]**

# PART 2
## LEASEHOLD REFORM

### CHAPTER 1
### RIGHT TO MANAGE

*Introductory*

## 71 The right to manage

(1)   This Chapter makes provision for the acquisition and exercise of rights in relation to the management of premises to which this Chapter applies by a company which, in accordance with this Chapter, may acquire and exercise those rights (referred to in this Chapter as a RTM company).

(2)   The rights are to be acquired and exercised subject to and in accordance with this Chapter and are referred to in this Chapter as the right to manage.

**[1235]**

*Qualifying rules*

## 72 Premises to which Chapter applies

(1)   This Chapter applies to premises if—
  (a)   they consist of a self-contained building or part of a building, with or without appurtenant property,
  (b)   they contain two or more flats held by qualifying tenants, and
  (c)   the total number of flats held by such tenants is not less than two-thirds of the total number of flats contained in the premises.

(2)   A building is a self-contained building if it is structurally detached.

(3)	A part of a building is a self-contained part of the building if—
    (a)	it constitutes a vertical division of the building,
    (b)	the structure of the building is such that it could be redeveloped independently of the rest of the building, and
    (c)	subsection (4) applies in relation to it.

(4)	This subsection applies in relation to a part of a building if the relevant services provided for occupiers of it—
    (a)	are provided independently of the relevant services provided for occupiers of the rest of the building, or
    (b)	could be so provided without involving the carrying out of works likely to result in a significant interruption in the provision of any relevant services for occupiers of the rest of the building.

(5)	Relevant services are services provided by means of pipes, cables or other fixed installations.

(6)	Schedule 6 (premises excepted from this Chapter) has effect.

**[1236]**

## 73	RTM companies

(1)	This section specifies what is a RTM company.

(2)	A company is a RTM company in relation to premises if—
    (a)	it is a private company limited by guarantee, and
    (b)	its [articles of association state] that its object, or one of its objects, is the acquisition and exercise of the right to manage the premises.

(3)	But a company is not a RTM company if it is a commonhold association (within the meaning of Part 1).

(4)	And a company is not a RTM company in relation to premises if another company is already a RTM company in relation to the premises or to any premises containing or contained in the premises.

(5)	If the freehold of any premises is conveyed or transferred to a company which is a RTM company in relation to the premises, or any premises containing or contained in the premises, it ceases to be a RTM company when the conveyance or transfer is executed.

**[1237]**

**NOTES**
Sub-s (2): words in square brackets substituted by the Companies Act 2006 (Consequential Amendments, Transitional Provisions and Savings) Order 2009, SI 2009/1941, art 2(1), Sch 1, para 194(1), (15).

## 74	RTM companies: membership and regulations

(1)	The persons who are entitled to be members of a company which is a RTM company in relation to premises are—
    (a)	qualifying tenants of flats contained in the premises, and
    (b)	from the date on which it acquires the right to manage (referred to in this Chapter as the "acquisition date"), landlords under leases of the whole or any part of the premises.

(2)	The appropriate national authority shall make regulations about the content and form of the [articles of association] of RTM companies.

(3)	A RTM company may adopt provisions of the regulations for its [articles].

(4)	The regulations may include provision which is to have effect for a RTM company whether or not it is adopted by the company.

(5)	A provision of the [articles] of a RTM company has no effect to the extent that it is inconsistent with the regulations.

(6)	The regulations have effect in relation to [articles]—
    (a)	irrespective of the date of the [articles], but
    (b)	subject to any transitional provisions of the regulations.

[(7)	Section 20 of the Companies Act 2006 (default application of model articles) does not apply to a RTM company.]

**[1238]**

**NOTES**
Sub-ss (2), (3), (5), (6): words in square brackets substituted by the Companies Act 2006 (Consequential Amendments, Transitional Provisions and Savings) Order 2009, SI 2009/1941, art 2(1), Sch 1, para 194(1), (16)(a)–(c).
Sub-s (7): substituted by SI 2009/1941, art 2(1), Sch 1, para 194(1), (16)(d).

Regulations: the RTM Companies (Memorandum and Articles of Association) (England) Regulations 2003, SI 2003/2120 at **[3346]**; the RTM Companies (Memorandum and Articles of Association) (Wales) Regulations 2004, SI 2004/675 at **[3361]**; the RTM Companies (Model Articles) (England) Regulations 2009, SI 2009/2767 at **[3969]**.

## 75 Qualifying tenants

(1)   This section specifies whether there is a qualifying tenant of a flat for the purposes of this Chapter and, if so, who it is.

(2)   Subject as follows, a person is the qualifying tenant of a flat if he is tenant of the flat under a long lease.

(3)   Subsection (2) does not apply where the lease is a tenancy to which Part 2 of the Landlord and Tenant Act 1954 (c 56) (business tenancies) applies.

(4)   Subsection (2) does not apply where—
  (a)   the lease was granted by sub-demise out of a superior lease other than a long lease,
  (b)   the grant was made in breach of the terms of the superior lease, and
  (c)   there has been no waiver of the breach by the superior landlord.

(5)   No flat has more than one qualifying tenant at any one time; and subsections (6) and (7) apply accordingly.

(6)   Where a flat is being let under two or more long leases, a tenant under any of those leases which is superior to that held by another is not the qualifying tenant of the flat.

(7)   Where a flat is being let to joint tenants under a long lease, the joint tenants shall (subject to subsection (6)) be regarded as jointly being the qualifying tenant of the flat.

**[1239]**

## 76 Long leases

(1)   This section and section 77 specify what is a long lease for the purposes of this Chapter.

(2)   Subject to section 77, a lease is a long lease if—
  (a)   it is granted for a term of years certain exceeding 21 years, whether or not it is (or may become) terminable before the end of that term by notice given by or to the tenant, by re-entry or forfeiture or otherwise,
  (b)   it is for a term fixed by law under a grant with a covenant or obligation for perpetual renewal (but is not a lease by sub-demise from one which is not a long lease),
  (c)   it takes effect under section 149(6) of the Law of Property Act 1925 (c 20) (leases terminable after a death or marriage [or the formation of a civil partnership]),
  (d)   it was granted in pursuance of the right to buy conferred by Part 5 of the Housing Act 1985 (c 68) or in pursuance of the right to acquire on rent to mortgage terms conferred by that Part of that Act,
  (e)   it is a shared ownership lease, whether granted in pursuance of that Part of that Act or otherwise, where the tenant's total share is 100 per cent, or
  (f)   it was granted in pursuance of that Part of that Act as it has effect by virtue of section 17 of the Housing Act 1996 (c 52) (the right to acquire).

(3)   "Shared ownership lease" means a lease—
  (a)   granted on payment of a premium calculated by reference to a percentage of the value of the demised premises or the cost of providing them, or
  (b)   under which the tenant (or his personal representatives) will or may be entitled to a sum calculated by reference, directly or indirectly, to the value of those premises.

(4)   "Total share", in relation to the interest of a tenant under a shared ownership lease, means his initial share plus any additional share or shares in the demised premises which he has acquired.

**[1240]**

**NOTES**

Sub-s (2): words in square brackets in para (c) inserted by the Civil Partnership Act 2004, s 81, Sch 8, para 64.

## 77 Long leases: further provisions

(1)   A lease terminable by notice after [a death, a marriage or the formation of a civil partnership] is not a long lease if—
  (a)   the notice is capable of being given at any time after the death or marriage of[, or the formation of a civil partnership by,] the tenant,
  (b)   the length of the notice is not more than three months, and
  (c)   the terms of the lease preclude both its assignment otherwise than by virtue of section 92 of the Housing Act 1985 (assignments by way of exchange) and the sub-letting of the whole of the demised premises.

(2)   Where the tenant of any property under a long lease, on the coming to an end of the lease, becomes or has become tenant of the property or part of it under any subsequent tenancy (whether by express grant or by implication of law), that tenancy is a long lease irrespective of its terms.

(3)   A lease—

(a)   granted for a term of years certain not exceeding 21 years, but with a covenant or obligation for renewal without payment of a premium (but not for perpetual renewal), and

(b)   renewed on one or more occasions so as to bring to more than 21 years the total of the terms granted (including any interval between the end of a lease and the grant of a renewal),

is to be treated as if the term originally granted had been one exceeding 21 years.

(4)   Where a long lease—

(a)   is or was continued for any period under Part 1 of the Landlord and Tenant Act 1954 (c 56) or under Schedule 10 to the Local Government and Housing Act 1989 (c 42), or

(b)   was continued for any period under the Leasehold Property (Temporary Provisions) Act 1951 (c 38),

it remains a long lease during that period.

(5)   Where in the case of a flat there are at any time two or more separate leases, with the same landlord and the same tenant, and—

(a)   the property comprised in one of those leases consists of either the flat or a part of it (in either case with or without appurtenant property), and

(b)   the property comprised in every other lease consists of either a part of the flat (with or without appurtenant property) or appurtenant property only,

there shall be taken to be a single long lease of the property comprised in such of those leases as are long leases.

**[1241]**

**NOTES**

Sub-s (1): words in first pair of square brackets substituted and words in second pair of square brackets inserted by the Civil Partnership Act 2004, s 81, Sch 8, para 65.

*Claim to acquire right*

## 78   Notice inviting participation

(1)   Before making a claim to acquire the right to manage any premises, a RTM company must give notice to each person who at the time when the notice is given—

(a)   is the qualifying tenant of a flat contained in the premises, but

(b)   neither is nor has agreed to become a member of the RTM company.

(2)   A notice given under this section (referred to in this Chapter as a "notice of invitation to participate") must—

(a)   state that the RTM company intends to acquire the right to manage the premises,

(b)   state the names of the members of the RTM company,

(c)   invite the recipients of the notice to become members of the company, and

(d)   contain such other particulars (if any) as may be required to be contained in notices of invitation to participate by regulations made by the appropriate national authority.

(3)   A notice of invitation to participate must also comply with such requirements (if any) about the form of notices of invitation to participate as may be prescribed by regulations so made.

(4)   A notice of invitation to participate must either—

(a)   be accompanied by a copy of the [articles of association] of the RTM company, or

(b)   include a statement about inspection and copying of the [articles of association] of the RTM company.

(5)   A statement under subsection (4)(b) must—

(a)   specify a place (in England or Wales) at which the [articles of association] may be inspected,

(b)   specify as the times at which they may be inspected periods of at least two hours on each of at least three days (including a Saturday or Sunday or both) within the seven days beginning with the day following that on which the notice is given,

(c)   specify a place (in England or Wales) at which, at any time within those seven days, a copy of the [articles of association] may be ordered, and

(d)   specify a fee for the provision of an ordered copy, not exceeding the reasonable cost of providing it.

(6)   Where a notice given to a person includes a statement under subsection (4)(b), the notice is to be treated as not having been given to him if he is not allowed to undertake an inspection, or is not provided with a copy, in accordance with the statement.

(7)   A notice of invitation to participate is not invalidated by any inaccuracy in any of the particulars required by or by virtue of this section.

**[1242]**

---

**NOTES**
Sub-ss (4), (5): words in square brackets substituted by the Companies Act 2006 (Consequential Amendments, Transitional Provisions and Savings) Order 2009, SI 2009/1941, art 2(1), Sch 1, para 194(1), (17).
Regulations: the Right to Manage (Prescribed Particulars and Forms) (England) Regulations 2003, SI 2003/1988 at **[3299]**; the Right to Manage (Prescribed Particulars and Forms) (Wales) Regulations 2004, SI 2004/678.

---

## 79   Notice of claim to acquire right

(1)   A claim to acquire the right to manage any premises is made by giving notice of the claim (referred to in this Chapter as a "claim notice"); and in this Chapter the "relevant date", in relation to any claim to acquire the right to manage, means the date on which notice of the claim is given.

(2)   The claim notice may not be given unless each person required to be given a notice of invitation to participate has been given such a notice at least 14 days before.

(3)   The claim notice must be given by a RTM company which complies with subsection (4) or (5).

(4)   If on the relevant date there are only two qualifying tenants of flats contained in the premises, both must be members of the RTM company.

(5)   In any other case, the membership of the RTM company must on the relevant date include a number of qualifying tenants of flats contained in the premises which is not less than one-half of the total number of flats so contained.

(6)   The claim notice must be given to each person who on the relevant date is—
   (a)   landlord under a lease of the whole or any part of the premises,
   (b)   party to such a lease otherwise than as landlord or tenant, or
   (c)   a manager appointed under Part 2 of the Landlord and Tenant Act 1987 (c 31) (referred to in this Part as "the 1987 Act") to act in relation to the premises, or any premises containing or contained in the premises.

(7)   Subsection (6) does not require the claim notice to be given to a person who cannot be found or whose identity cannot be ascertained; but if this subsection means that the claim notice is not required to be given to anyone at all, section 85 applies.

(8)   A copy of the claim notice must be given to each person who on the relevant date is the qualifying tenant of a flat contained in the premises.

(9)   Where a manager has been appointed under Part 2 of the 1987 Act to act in relation to the premises, or any premises containing or contained in the premises, a copy of the claim notice must also be given to the leasehold valuation tribunal or court by which he was appointed.

**[1243]**

## 80   Contents of claim notice

(1)   The claim notice must comply with the following requirements.

(2)   It must specify the premises and contain a statement of the grounds on which it is claimed that they are premises to which this Chapter applies.

(3)   It must state the full name of each person who is both—
   (a)   the qualifying tenant of a flat contained in the premises, and
   (b)   a member of the RTM company,
and the address of his flat.

(4)   And it must contain, in relation to each such person, such particulars of his lease as are sufficient to identify it, including—
   (a)   the date on which it was entered into,
   (b)   the term for which it was granted, and
   (c)   the date of the commencement of the term.

(5)   It must state the name and registered office of the RTM company.

(6)   It must specify a date, not earlier than one month after the relevant date, by which each person who was given the notice under section 79(6) may respond to it by giving a counter-notice under section 84.

(7)   It must specify a date, at least three months after that specified under subsection (6), on which the RTM company intends to acquire the right to manage the premises.

(8)   It must also contain such other particulars (if any) as may be required to be contained in claim notices by regulations made by the appropriate national authority.

(9)    And it must comply with such requirements (if any) about the form of claim notices as may be prescribed by regulations so made.

**[1244]**

---

**NOTES**

Regulations: the Right to Manage (Prescribed Particulars and Forms) (England) Regulations 2003, SI 2003/1988 at **[3299]**; the Right to Manage (Prescribed Particulars and Forms) (Wales) Regulations 2004, SI 2004/678.

---

### 81   Claim notice: supplementary

(1)    A claim notice is not invalidated by any inaccuracy in any of the particulars required by or by virtue of section 80.

(2)    Where any of the members of the RTM company whose names are stated in the claim notice was not the qualifying tenant of a flat contained in the premises on the relevant date, the claim notice is not invalidated on that account, so long as a sufficient number of qualifying tenants of flats contained in the premises were members of the company on that date; and for this purpose a "sufficient number" is a number (greater than one) which is not less than one-half of the total number of flats contained in the premises on that date.

(3)    Where any premises have been specified in a claim notice, no subsequent claim notice which specifies—

(a)    the premises, or

(b)    any premises containing or contained in the premises,

may be given so long as the earlier claim notice continues in force.

(4)    Where a claim notice is given by a RTM company it continues in force from the relevant date until the right to manage is acquired by the company unless it has previously—

(a)    been withdrawn or deemed to be withdrawn by virtue of any provision of this Chapter, or

(b)    ceased to have effect by reason of any other provision of this Chapter.

**[1245]**

### 82   Right to obtain information

(1)    A company which is a RTM company in relation to any premises may give to any person a notice requiring him to provide the company with any information—

(a)    which is in his possession or control, and

(b)    which the company reasonably requires for ascertaining the particulars required by or by virtue of section 80 to be included in a claim notice for claiming to acquire the right to manage the premises.

(2)    Where the information is recorded in a document in the person's possession or control, the RTM company may give him a notice requiring him—

(a)    to permit any person authorised to act on behalf of the company at any reasonable time to inspect the document (or, if the information is recorded in the document in a form in which it is not readily intelligible, to give any such person access to it in a readily intelligible form), and

(b)    to supply the company with a copy of the document containing the information in a readily intelligible form on payment of a reasonable fee.

(3)    A person to whom a notice is given must comply with it within the period of 28 days beginning with the day on which it is given.

**[1246]**

### 83   Right of access

(1)    Where a RTM company has given a claim notice in relation to any premises, each of the persons specified in subsection (2) has a right of access to any part of the premises if that is reasonable in connection with any matter arising out of the claim to acquire the right to manage.

(2)    The persons referred to in subsection (1) are—

(a)    any person authorised to act on behalf of the RTM company,

(b)    any person who is landlord under a lease of the whole or any part of the premises and any person authorised to act on behalf of any such person,

(c)    any person who is party to such a lease otherwise than as landlord or tenant and any person authorised to act on behalf of any such person, and

(d)    any manager appointed under Part 2 of the 1987 Act to act in relation to the premises, or any premises containing or contained in the premises, and any person authorised to act on behalf of any such manager.

(3)    The right conferred by this section is exercisable, at any reasonable time, on giving not less than ten days' notice—

    (a)    to the occupier of any premises to which access is sought, or

    (b)    if those premises are unoccupied, to the person entitled to occupy them.

[1247]

## 84  Counter-notices

(1)    A person who is given a claim notice by a RTM company under section 79(6) may give a notice (referred to in this Chapter as a "counter-notice") to the company no later than the date specified in the claim notice under section 80(6).

(2)    A counter-notice is a notice containing a statement either—

    (a)    admitting that the RTM company was on the relevant date entitled to acquire the right to manage the premises specified in the claim notice, or

    (b)    alleging that, by reason of a specified provision of this Chapter, the RTM company was on that date not so entitled,

and containing such other particulars (if any) as may be required to be contained in counter-notices, and complying with such requirements (if any) about the form of counter-notices, as may be prescribed by regulations made by the appropriate national authority.

(3)    Where the RTM company has been given one or more counter-notices containing a statement such as is mentioned in subsection (2)(b), the company may apply to a leasehold valuation tribunal for a determination that it was on the relevant date entitled to acquire the right to manage the premises.

(4)    An application under subsection (3) must be made not later than the end of the period of two months beginning with the day on which the counter-notice (or, where more than one, the last of the counter-notices) was given.

(5)    Where the RTM company has been given one or more counter-notices containing a statement such as is mentioned in subsection (2)(b), the RTM company does not acquire the right to manage the premises unless—

    (a)    on an application under subsection (3) it is finally determined that the company was on the relevant date entitled to acquire the right to manage the premises, or

    (b)    the person by whom the counter-notice was given agrees, or the persons by whom the counter-notices were given agree, in writing that the company was so entitled.

(6)    If on an application under subsection (3) it is finally determined that the company was not on the relevant date entitled to acquire the right to manage the premises, the claim notice ceases to have effect.

(7)    A determination on an application under subsection (3) becomes final—

    (a)    if not appealed against, at the end of the period for bringing an appeal, or

    (b)    if appealed against, at the time when the appeal (or any further appeal) is disposed of.

(8)    An appeal is disposed of—

    (a)    if it is determined and the period for bringing any further appeal has ended, or

    (b)    if it is abandoned or otherwise ceases to have effect.

[1248]

**NOTES**

Regulations: the Right to Manage (Prescribed Particulars and Forms) (England) Regulations 2003, SI 2003/1988 at **[3299]**; the Right to Manage (Prescribed Particulars and Forms) (Wales) Regulations 2004, SI 2004/678.

## 85  Landlords etc not traceable

(1)    This section applies where a RTM company wishing to acquire the right to manage premises—

    (a)    complies with subsection (4) or (5) of section 79, and

    (b)    would not have been precluded from giving a valid notice under that section with respect to the premises,

but cannot find, or ascertain the identity of, any of the persons to whom the claim notice would be required to be given by subsection (6) of that section.

(2)    The RTM company may apply to a leasehold valuation tribunal for an order that the company is to acquire the right to manage the premises.

(3)    Such an order may be made only if the company has given notice of the application to each person who is the qualifying tenant of a flat contained in the premises.

(4)    Before an order is made the company may be required to take such further steps by way of advertisement or otherwise as is determined proper for the purpose of tracing the persons who are—

    (a)    landlords under leases of the whole or any part of the premises, or

    (b)    parties to such leases otherwise than as landlord or tenant.

(5)    If any of those persons is traced—

(a)    after an application for an order is made, but

(b)    before the making of an order,

no further proceedings shall be taken with a view to the making of an order.

(6)    Where that happens—

(a)    the rights and obligations of all persons concerned shall be determined as if the company had, at the date of the application, duly given notice under section 79 of its claim to acquire the right to manage the premises, and

(b)    the leasehold valuation tribunal may give such directions as it thinks fit as to the steps to be taken for giving effect to their rights and obligations, including directions modifying or dispensing with any of the requirements imposed by or by virtue of this Chapter.

(7)    An application for an order may be withdrawn at any time before an order is made and, after it is withdrawn, subsection (6)(a) does not apply.

(8)    But where any step is taken for the purpose of giving effect to subsection (6)(a) in the case of any application, the application shall not afterwards be withdrawn except—

(a)    with the consent of the person or persons traced, or

(b)    by permission of the leasehold valuation tribunal.

(9)    And permission shall be given only where it appears just that it should be given by reason of matters coming to the knowledge of the RTM company in consequence of the tracing of the person or persons traced.

**[1249]**

## 86    Withdrawal of claim notice

(1)    A RTM company which has given a claim notice in relation to any premises may, at any time before it acquires the right to manage the premises, withdraw the claim notice by giving a notice to that effect (referred to in this Chapter as a "notice of withdrawal").

(2)    A notice of withdrawal must be given to each person who is—

(a)    landlord under a lease of the whole or any part of the premises,

(b)    party to such a lease otherwise than as landlord or tenant,

(c)    a manager appointed under Part 2 of the 1987 Act to act in relation to the premises, or any premises containing or contained in the premises, or

(d)    the qualifying tenant of a flat contained in the premises.

**[1250]**

## 87    Deemed withdrawal

(1)    If a RTM company has been given one or more counter-notices containing a statement such as is mentioned in subsection (2)(b) of section 84 but either—

(a)    no application for a determination under subsection (3) of that section is made within the period specified in subsection (4) of that section, or

(b)    such an application is so made but is subsequently withdrawn,

the claim notice is deemed to be withdrawn.

(2)    The withdrawal shall be taken to occur—

(a)    if paragraph (a) of subsection (1) applies, at the end of the period specified in that paragraph, and

(b)    if paragraph (b) of that subsection applies, on the date of the withdrawal of the application.

(3)    Subsection (1) does not apply if the person by whom the counter-notice was given has, or the persons by whom the counter-notices were given have, (before the time when the withdrawal would be taken to occur) agreed in writing that the RTM company was on the relevant date entitled to acquire the right to manage the premises.

(4)    The claim notice is deemed to be withdrawn if—

(a)    a winding-up order … is made, or a resolution for voluntary winding-up is passed, with respect to the RTM company, [or the RTM company enters administration,]

(b)    a receiver or a manager of the RTM company's undertaking is duly appointed, or possession is taken, by or on behalf of the holders of any debentures secured by a floating charge, of any property of the RTM company comprised in or subject to the charge,

(c)    a voluntary arrangement proposed in the case of the RTM company for the purposes of Part 1 of the Insolvency Act 1986 (c 45) is approved under that Part of that Act, or

(d)    the RTM company's name is struck off the register under [section 1000, 1001 or 1003 of the Companies Act 2006].

**[1251]**

---

**NOTES**

Sub-s (4): in para (a), words omitted repealed and words in square brackets inserted by the Commonhold and Leasehold Reform Act 2002 (Commencement No 2 and Savings) (England) Order 2003, SI 2003/2096, art 4,

Schedule, Pt 1, paras 38, 39, except in relation to any case where a petition for an administration order was presented before 15 September 2003; words in square brackets in para (d) substituted by the Companies Act 2006 (Consequential Amendments, Transitional Provisions and Savings) Order 2009, SI 2009/1941, art 2(1), Sch 1, para 194(1), (18).

## 88  Costs: general

(1)   A RTM company is liable for reasonable costs incurred by a person who is—
  (a)   landlord under a lease of the whole or any part of any premises,
  (b)   party to such a lease otherwise than as landlord or tenant, or
  (c)   a manager appointed under Part 2 of the 1987 Act to act in relation to the premises, or any premises containing or contained in the premises,
in consequence of a claim notice given by the company in relation to the premises.

(2)   Any costs incurred by such a person in respect of professional services rendered to him by another are to be regarded as reasonable only if and to the extent that costs in respect of such services might reasonably be expected to have been incurred by him if the circumstances had been such that he was personally liable for all such costs.

(3)   A RTM company is liable for any costs which such a person incurs as party to any proceedings under this Chapter before a leasehold valuation tribunal only if the tribunal dismisses an application by the company for a determination that it is entitled to acquire the right to manage the premises.

(4)   Any question arising in relation to the amount of any costs payable by a RTM company shall, in default of agreement, be determined by a leasehold valuation tribunal.

[1252]

## 89  Costs where claim ceases

(1)   This section applies where a claim notice given by a RTM company—
  (a)   is at any time withdrawn or deemed to be withdrawn by virtue of any provision of this Chapter, or
  (b)   at any time ceases to have effect by reason of any other provision of this Chapter.

(2)   The liability of the RTM company under section 88 for costs incurred by any person is a liability for costs incurred by him down to that time.

(3)   Each person who is or has been a member of the RTM company is also liable for those costs (jointly and severally with the RTM company and each other person who is so liable).

(4)   But subsection (3) does not make a person liable if—
  (a)   the lease by virtue of which he was a qualifying tenant has been assigned to another person, and
  (b)   that other person has become a member of the RTM company.

(5)   The reference in subsection (4) to an assignment includes—
  (a)   an assent by personal representatives, and
  (b)   assignment by operation of law where the assignment is to a trustee in bankruptcy or to a mortgagee under section 89(2) of the Law of Property Act 1925 (c 20) (foreclosure of leasehold mortgage).

[1253]

*Acquisition of right*

## 90  The acquisition date

(1)   This section makes provision about the date which is the acquisition date where a RTM company acquires the right to manage any premises.

(2)   Where there is no dispute about entitlement, the acquisition date is the date specified in the claim notice under section 80(7).

(3)   For the purposes of this Chapter there is no dispute about entitlement if—
  (a)   no counter-notice is given under section 84, or
  (b)   the counter-notice given under that section, or (where more than one is so given) each of them, contains a statement such as is mentioned in subsection (2)(a) of that section.

(4)   Where the right to manage the premises is acquired by the company by virtue of a determination under section 84(5)(a), the acquisition date is the date three months after the determination becomes final.

(5)   Where the right to manage the premises is acquired by the company by virtue of subsection (5)(b) of section 84, the acquisition date is the date three months after the day on which the person (or the last person) by whom a counter-notice containing a statement such as is mentioned in subsection (2)(b) of that section was given agrees in writing that the company was on the relevant date entitled to acquire the right to manage the premises.

(6) Where an order is made under section 85, the acquisition date is (subject to any appeal) the date specified in the order.

**[1254]**

## 91 Notices relating to management contracts

(1) Section 92 applies where—

    (a) the right to manage premises is to be acquired by a RTM company (otherwise than by virtue of an order under section 85), and

    (b) there are one or more existing management contracts relating to the premises.

(2) A management contract is a contract between—

    (a) an existing manager of the premises (referred to in this Chapter as the "manager party"), and

    (b) another person (so referred to as the "contractor party"),

under which the contractor party agrees to provide services, or do any other thing, in connection with any matter relating to a function which will be a function of the RTM company once it acquires the right to manage.

(3) And in this Chapter "existing management contract" means a management contract which—

    (a) is subsisting immediately before the determination date, or

    (b) is entered into during the period beginning with the determination date and ending with the acquisition date.

(4) An existing manager of the premises is any person who is—

    (a) landlord under a lease relating to the whole or any part of the premises,

    (b) party to such a lease otherwise than as landlord or tenant, or

    (c) a manager appointed under Part 2 of the 1987 Act to act in relation to the premises, or any premises containing or contained in the premises.

(5) In this Chapter "determination date" means—

    (a) where there is no dispute about entitlement, the date specified in the claim notice under section 80(6),

    (b) where the right to manage the premises is acquired by the company by virtue of a determination under section 84(5)(a), the date when the determination becomes final, and

    (c) where the right to manage the premises is acquired by the company by virtue of subsection (5)(b) of section 84, the day on which the person (or the last person) by whom a counter-notice containing a statement such as is mentioned in subsection (2)(b) of that section was given agrees in writing that the company was on the relevant date entitled to acquire the right to manage the premises.

**[1255]**

## 92 Duties to give notice of contracts

(1) The person who is the manager party in relation to an existing management contract must give a notice in relation to the contract—

    (a) to the person who is the contractor party in relation to the contract (a "contractor notice"), and

    (b) to the RTM company (a "contract notice").

(2) A contractor notice and a contract notice must be given—

    (a) in the case of a contract subsisting immediately before the determination date, on that date or as soon after that date as is reasonably practicable, and

    (b) in the case of a contract entered into during the period beginning with the determination date and ending with the acquisition date, on the date on which it is entered into or as soon after that date as is reasonably practicable.

(3) A contractor notice must—

    (a) give details sufficient to identify the contract in relation to which it is given,

    (b) state that the right to manage the premises is to be acquired by a RTM company,

    (c) state the name and registered office of the RTM company,

    (d) specify the acquisition date, and

    (e) contain such other particulars (if any) as may be required to be contained in contractor notices by regulations made by the appropriate national authority,

and must also comply with such requirements (if any) about the form of contractor notices as may be prescribed by regulations so made.

(4) Where a person who receives a contractor notice (including one who receives a copy by virtue of this subsection) is party to an existing management sub-contract with another person (the "sub-contractor party"), the person who received the notice must—

    (a) send a copy of the contractor notice to the sub-contractor party, and

(b) give to the RTM company a contract notice in relation to the existing management sub-contract.

(5) An existing management sub-contract is a contract under which the sub-contractor party agrees to provide services, or do any other thing, in connection with any matter relating to a function which will be a function of the RTM company once it acquires the right to manage and which—

(a) is subsisting immediately before the determination date, or

(b) is entered into during the period beginning with the determination date and ending with the acquisition date.

(6) Subsection (4) must be complied with—

(a) in the case of a contract entered into before the contractor notice is received, on the date on which it is received or as soon after that date as is reasonably practicable, and

(b) in the case of a contract entered into after the contractor notice is received, on the date on which it is entered into or as soon after that date as is reasonably practicable.

(7) A contract notice must—

(a) give particulars of the contract in relation to which it is given and of the person who is the contractor party, or sub-contractor party, in relation to that contract, and

(b) contain such other particulars (if any) as may be required to be contained in contract notices by regulations made by the appropriate national authority,

and must also comply with such requirements (if any) about the form of contract notices as may be prescribed by such regulations so made.

[1256]

---

**NOTES**

Regulations: the Right to Manage (Prescribed Particulars and Forms) (England) Regulations 2003, SI 2003/1988 at **[3299]**; the Right to Manage (Prescribed Particulars and Forms) (Wales) Regulations 2004, SI 2004/678.

---

## 93 Duty to provide information

(1) Where the right to manage premises is to be acquired by a RTM company, the company may give notice to a person who is—

(a) landlord under a lease of the whole or any part of the premises,

(b) party to such a lease otherwise than as landlord or tenant, or

(c) a manager appointed under Part 2 of the 1987 Act to act in relation to the premises, or any premises containing or contained in the premises,

requiring him to provide the company with any information which is in his possession or control and which the company reasonably requires in connection with the exercise of the right to manage.

(2) Where the information is recorded in a document in his possession or control the notice may require him—

(a) to permit any person authorised to act on behalf of the company at any reasonable time to inspect the document (or, if the information is recorded in the document in a form in which it is not readily intelligible, to give any such person access to it in a readily intelligible form), and

(b) to supply the company with a copy of the document containing the information in a readily intelligible form.

(3) A notice may not require a person to do anything under this section before the acquisition date.

(4) But, subject to that, a person who is required by a notice to do anything under this section must do it within the period of 28 days beginning with the day on which the notice is given.

[1257]

## 94 Duty to pay accrued uncommitted service charges

(1) Where the right to manage premises is to be acquired by a RTM company, a person who is—

(a) landlord under a lease of the whole or any part of the premises,

(b) party to such a lease otherwise than as landlord or tenant, or

(c) a manager appointed under Part 2 of the 1987 Act to act in relation to the premises, or any premises containing or contained in the premises,

must make to the company a payment equal to the amount of any accrued uncommitted service charges held by him on the acquisition date.

(2) The amount of any accrued uncommitted service charges is the aggregate of—

(a) any sums which have been paid to the person by way of service charges in respect of the premises, and

(b) any investments which represent such sums (and any income which has accrued on them), less so much (if any) of that amount as is required to meet the costs incurred before the acquisition date in connection with the matters for which the service charges were payable.

(3)    He or the RTM company may make an application to a leasehold valuation tribunal to determine the amount of any payment which falls to be made under this section.

(4)    The duty imposed by this section must be complied with on the acquisition date or as soon after that date as is reasonably practicable.

**[1258]**

### *Exercising right*

### 95   Introductory

Sections 96 to 103 apply where the right to manage premises has been acquired by a RTM company (and has not ceased to be exercisable by it).

**[1259]**

### 96   Management functions under leases

(1)    This section and section 97 apply in relation to management functions relating to the whole or any part of the premises.

(2)    Management functions which a person who is landlord under a lease of the whole or any part of the premises has under the lease are instead functions of the RTM company.

(3)    And where a person is party to a lease of the whole or any part of the premises otherwise than as landlord or tenant, management functions of his under the lease are also instead functions of the RTM company.

(4)    Accordingly, any provisions of the lease making provision about the relationship of—
    (a)    a person who is landlord under the lease, and
    (b)    a person who is party to the lease otherwise than as landlord or tenant,
in relation to such functions do not have effect.

(5)    "Management functions" are functions with respect to services, repairs, maintenance, improvements, insurance and management.

(6)    But this section does not apply in relation to—
    (a)    functions with respect to a matter concerning only a part of the premises consisting of a flat or other unit not held under a lease by a qualifying tenant, or
    (b)    functions relating to re-entry or forfeiture.

(7)    An order amending subsection (5) or (6) may be made by the appropriate national authority.

**[1260]**

### 97   Management functions: supplementary

(1)    Any obligation owed by the RTM company by virtue of section 96 to a tenant under a lease of the whole or any part of the premises is also owed to each person who is landlord under the lease.

(2)    A person who is—
    (a)    landlord under a lease of the whole or any part of the premises,
    (b)    party to such a lease otherwise than as landlord or tenant, or
    (c)    a manager appointed under Part 2 of the 1987 Act to act in relation to the premises, or any premises containing or contained in the premises,
is not entitled to do anything which the RTM company is required or empowered to do under the lease by virtue of section 96, except in accordance with an agreement made by him and the RTM company.

(3)    But subsection (2) does not prevent any person from insuring the whole or any part of the premises at his own expense.

(4)    So far as any function of a tenant under a lease of the whole or any part of the premises—
    (a)    relates to the exercise of any function under the lease which is a function of the RTM company by virtue of section 96, and
    (b)    is exercisable in relation to a person who is landlord under the lease or party to the lease otherwise than as landlord or tenant,
it is instead exercisable in relation to the RTM company.

(5)    But subsection (4) does not require or permit the payment to the RTM company of so much of any service charges payable by a tenant under a lease of the whole or any part of the premises as is required to meet costs incurred before the right to manage was acquired by the RTM company in connection with matters for which the service charges are payable.

**[1261]**

## 98  Functions relating to approvals

(1)   This section and section 99 apply in relation to the grant of approvals under long leases of the whole or any part of the premises; but nothing in this section or section 99 applies in relation to an approval concerning only a part of the premises consisting of a flat or other unit not held under a lease by a qualifying tenant.

(2)   Where a person who is—
(a)   landlord under a long lease of the whole or any part of the premises, or
(b)   party to such a lease otherwise than as landlord or tenant,
has functions in relation to the grant of approvals to a tenant under the lease, the functions are instead functions of the RTM company.

(3)   Accordingly, any provisions of the lease making provision about the relationship of—
(a)   a person who is landlord under the lease, and
(b)   a person who is party to the lease otherwise than as landlord or tenant,
in relation to such functions do not have effect.

(4)   The RTM company must not grant an approval by virtue of subsection (2) without having given—
(a)   in the case of an approval relating to assignment, underletting, charging, parting with possession, the making of structural alterations or improvements or alterations of use, 30 days' notice, or
(b)   in any other case, 14 days' notice,
to the person who is, or each of the persons who are, landlord under the lease.

(5)   Regulations increasing the period of notice to be given under subsection (4)(b) in the case of any description of approval may be made by the appropriate national authority.

(6)   So far as any function of a tenant under a long lease of the whole or any part of the premises—
(a)   relates to the exercise of any function which is a function of the RTM company by virtue of this section, and
(b)   is exercisable in relation to a person who is landlord under the lease or party to the lease otherwise than as landlord or tenant,
it is instead exercisable in relation to the RTM company.

(7)   In this Chapter "approval" includes consent or licence and "approving" is to be construed accordingly; and an approval required to be obtained by virtue of a restriction entered on the register of title kept by the Chief Land Registrar is, so far as relating to a long lease of the whole or any part of any premises, to be treated for the purposes of this Chapter as an approval under the lease.

**[1262]**

## 99  Approvals: supplementary

(1)   If a person to whom notice is given under section 98(4) objects to the grant of the approval before the time when the RTM company would first be entitled to grant it, the RTM company may grant it only—
(a)   in accordance with the written agreement of the person who objected, or
(b)   in accordance with a determination of (or on an appeal from) a leasehold valuation tribunal.

(2)   An objection to the grant of the approval may not be made by a person unless he could withhold the approval if the function of granting it were exercisable by him (and not by the RTM company).

(3)   And a person may not make an objection operating only if a condition or requirement is not satisfied unless he could grant the approval subject to the condition or requirement being satisfied if the function of granting it were so exercisable.

(4)   An objection to the grant of the approval is made by giving notice of the objection (and of any condition or requirement which must be satisfied if it is not to operate) to—
(a)   the RTM company, and
(b)   the tenant,
and, if the approval is to a tenant approving an act of a sub-tenant, to the sub-tenant.

(5)   An application to a leasehold valuation tribunal for a determination under subsection (1)(b) may be made by—
(a)   the RTM company,
(b)   the tenant,
(c)   if the approval is to a tenant approving an act of a sub-tenant, the sub-tenant, or
(d)   any person who is landlord under the lease.

**[1263]**

**100 Enforcement of tenant covenants**

(1) This section applies in relation to the enforcement of untransferred tenant covenants of a lease of the whole or any part of the premises.

(2) Untransferred tenant covenants are enforceable by the RTM company, as well as by any other person by whom they are enforceable apart from this section, in the same manner as they are enforceable by any other such person.

(3) But the RTM company may not exercise any function of re-entry or forfeiture.

(4) In this Chapter "tenant covenant", in relation to a lease, means a covenant falling to be complied with by a tenant under the lease; and a tenant covenant is untransferred if, apart from this section, it would not be enforceable by the RTM company.

(5) Any power under a lease of a person who is—
(a) landlord under the lease, or
(b) party to the lease otherwise than as landlord or tenant,
to enter any part of the premises to determine whether a tenant is complying with any untransferred tenant covenant is exercisable by the RTM company (as well as by the landlord or party).

**[1264]**

**101 Tenant covenants: monitoring and reporting**

(1) This section applies in relation to failures to comply with tenant covenants of leases of the whole or any part of the premises.

(2) The RTM company must—
(a) keep under review whether tenant covenants of leases of the whole or any part of the premises are being complied with, and
(b) report to any person who is landlord under such a lease any failure to comply with any tenant covenant of the lease.

(3) The report must be made before the end of the period of three months beginning with the day on which the failure to comply comes to the attention of the RTM company.

(4) But the RTM company need not report to a landlord a failure to comply with a tenant covenant if—
(a) the failure has been remedied,
(b) reasonable compensation has been paid in respect of the failure, or
(c) the landlord has notified the RTM company that it need not report to him failures of the description of the failure concerned.

**[1265]**

**102 Statutory functions**

(1) Schedule 7 (provision for the operation of certain enactments with modifications) has effect.

(2) Other enactments relating to leases (including enactments contained in this Act or any Act passed after this Act) have effect with any such modifications as are prescribed by regulations made by the appropriate national authority.

**[1266]**

**103 Landlord contributions to service charges**

(1) This section applies where—
(a) the premises contain at least one flat or other unit not subject to a lease held by a qualifying tenant (an "excluded unit"),
(b) the service charges payable under leases of flats contained in the premises which are so subject fall to be calculated as a proportion of the relevant costs, and
(c) the proportions of the relevant costs so payable, when aggregated, amount to less than the whole of the relevant costs.

(2) Where the premises contain only one excluded unit, the person who is the appropriate person in relation to the excluded unit must pay to the RTM company the difference between—
(a) the relevant costs, and
(b) the aggregate amount payable in respect of the relevant costs under leases of flats contained in the premises which are held by qualifying tenants.

(3) Where the premises contain more than one excluded unit, each person who is the appropriate person in relation to an excluded unit must pay to the RTM company the appropriate proportion of that difference.

(4) And the appropriate proportion in the case of each such person is the proportion of the internal floor area of all of the excluded units which is internal floor area of the excluded unit in relation to which he is the appropriate person.

(5) The appropriate person in relation to an excluded unit—

(a) if it is subject to a lease, is the landlord under the lease,

(b) if it is subject to more than one lease, is the immediate landlord under whichever of the leases is inferior to all the others, and

(c) if it is not subject to any lease, is the freeholder.

**[1267]**

*Supplementary*

**104** (*Repealed by s 180 of, and Sch 14 to, this Act.*)

**105 Cessation of management**

(1) This section makes provision about the circumstances in which, after a RTM company has acquired the right to manage any premises, that right ceases to be exercisable by it.

(2) Provision may be made by an agreement made between—

(a) the RTM company, and

(b) each person who is landlord under a lease of the whole or any part of the premises,

for the right to manage the premises to cease to be exercisable by the RTM company.

(3) The right to manage the premises ceases to be exercisable by the RTM company if—

(a) a winding-up order ... is made, or a resolution for voluntary winding-up is passed, with respect to the RTM company, [or the RTM company enters administration,]

(b) a receiver or a manager of the RTM company's undertaking is duly appointed, or possession is taken, by or on behalf of the holders of any debentures secured by a floating charge, of any property of the RTM company comprised in or subject to the charge,

(c) a voluntary arrangement proposed in the case of the RTM company for the purposes of Part 1 of the Insolvency Act 1986 (c 45) is approved under that Part of that Act, or

(d) the RTM company's name is struck off the register under [section 1000, 1001 or 1003 of the Companies Act 2006].

(4) The right to manage the premises ceases to be exercisable by the RTM company if a manager appointed under Part 2 of the 1987 Act to act in relation to the premises, or any premises containing or contained in the premises, begins so to act or an order under that Part of that Act that the right to manage the premises is to cease to be exercisable by the RTM company takes effect.

(5) The right to manage the premises ceases to be exercisable by the RTM company if it ceases to be a RTM company in relation to the premises.

**[1268]**

**NOTES**

Sub-s (3): in para (a), words omitted repealed and words in square brackets inserted by the Commonhold and Leasehold Reform Act 2002 (Commencement No 2 and Savings) (England) Order 2003, SI 2003/2096, art 4, Schedule, Pt 1, paras 38, 40, except in relation to any case where a petition for an administration order was presented before 15 September 2003; words in square brackets in para (d) substituted by the Companies Act 2006 (Consequential Amendments, Transitional Provisions and Savings) Order 2009, SI 2009/1941, art 2(1), Sch 1, para 194(1), (19).

**106 Agreements excluding or modifying right**

Any agreement relating to a lease (whether contained in the instrument creating the lease or not and whether made before the creation of the lease or not) is void in so far as it—

(a) purports to exclude or modify the right of any person to be, or do any thing as, a member of a RTM company,

(b) provides for the termination or surrender of the lease if the tenant becomes, or does any thing as, a member of a RTM company or if a RTM company does any thing, or

(c) provides for the imposition of any penalty or disability if the tenant becomes, or does any thing as, a member of a RTM company or if a RTM company does any thing.

**[1269]**

**107 Enforcement of obligations**

(1) A county court may, on the application of any person interested, make an order requiring a person who has failed to comply with a requirement imposed on him by, under or by virtue of any provision of this Chapter to make good the default within such time as is specified in the order.

(2) An application shall not be made under subsection (1) unless—

(a) a notice has been previously given to the person in question requiring him to make good the default, and

(b) more than 14 days have elapsed since the date of the giving of that notice without his having done so.

**[1270]**

**108   Application to Crown**

(1)   This Chapter applies in relation to premises in which there is a Crown interest.

(2)   There is a Crown interest in premises if there is in the premises an interest or estate—
  (a)   which is comprised in the Crown Estate,
  (b)   which belongs to Her Majesty in right of the Duchy of Lancaster,
  (c)   which belongs to the Duchy of Cornwall, or
  (d)   which belongs to a government department or is held on behalf of Her Majesty for the purposes of a government department.

(3)   Any sum payable under this Chapter to a RTM company by the Chancellor of the Duchy of Lancaster may be raised and paid under section 25 of the Duchy of Lancaster Act 1817 (c 97) as an expense incurred in improvement of land belonging to Her Majesty in right of the Duchy.

(4)   Any sum payable under this Chapter to a RTM company by the Duke of Cornwall (or any other possessor for the time being of the Duchy of Cornwall) may be raised and paid under section 8 of the Duchy of Cornwall Management Act 1863 (c 49) as an expense incurred in permanently improving the possessions of the Duchy.

                                                                                          **[1271]**

**109   Powers of trustees in relation to right**

(1)   Where trustees are the qualifying tenant of a flat contained in any premises, their powers under the instrument regulating the trusts include power to be a member of a RTM company for the purpose of the acquisition and exercise of the right to manage the premises.

(2)   But subsection (1) does not apply where the instrument regulating the trusts contains an explicit direction to the contrary.

(3)   The power conferred by subsection (1) is exercisable with the same consent or on the same direction (if any) as may be required for the exercise of the trustees' powers (or ordinary powers) of investment.

(4)   The purposes—
  (a)   authorised for the application of capital money by section 73 of the Settled Land Act 1925 (c 18), and
  (b)   authorised by section 71 of that Act as purposes for which moneys may be raised by mortgage,

include the payment of any expenses incurred by a tenant for life or statutory owner as a member of a RTM company.

                                                                                          **[1272]**

**110   Power to prescribe procedure**

(1)   Where a claim to acquire the right to manage any premises is made by the giving of a claim notice, except as otherwise provided by this Chapter—
  (a)   the procedure for giving effect to the claim notice, and
  (b)   the rights and obligations of all parties in any matter arising in giving effect to the claim notice,

shall be such as may be prescribed by regulations made by the appropriate national authority.

(2)   Regulations under this section may, in particular, make provision for a person to be discharged from performing any obligations arising out of a claim notice by reason of the default or delay of some other person.

                                                                                          **[1273]**

**111   Notices**

(1)   Any notice under this Chapter—
  (a)   must be in writing, and
  (b)   may be sent by post.

(2)   A company which is a RTM company in relation to premises may give a notice under this Chapter to a person who is landlord under a lease of the whole or any part of the premises at the address specified in subsection (3) (but subject to subsection (4)).

(3)   That address is—
  (a)   the address last furnished to a member of the RTM company as the landlord's address for service in accordance with section 48 of the 1987 Act (notification of address for service of notices on landlord), or
  (b)   if no such address has been so furnished, the address last furnished to such a member as the landlord's address in accordance with section 47 of the 1987 Act (landlord's name and address to be contained in demands for rent).

(4)   But the RTM company may not give a notice under this Chapter to a person at the address specified in subsection (3) if it has been notified by him of a different address in England and Wales at which he wishes to be given any such notice.

PART I
STATUTES

(5)   A company which is a RTM company in relation to premises may give a notice under this Chapter to a person who is the qualifying tenant of a flat contained in the premises at the flat unless it has been notified by the qualifying tenant of a different address in England and Wales at which he wishes to be given any such notice.

**[1274]**

*Interpretation*

## 112   Definitions

(1)   In this Chapter—

"appurtenant property", in relation to a building or part of a building or a flat, means any garage, outhouse, garden, yard or appurtenances belonging to, or usually enjoyed with, the building or part or flat,

"copy", in relation to a document in which information is recorded, means anything onto which the information has been copied by whatever means and whether directly or indirectly,

"document" means anything in which information is recorded,

"dwelling" means a building or part of a building occupied or intended to be occupied as a separate dwelling,

"flat" means a separate set of premises (whether or not on the same floor)—
  (a)   which forms part of a building,
  (b)   which is constructed or adapted for use for the purposes of a dwelling, and
  (c)   either the whole or a material part of which lies above or below some other part of the building,

"relevant costs" has the meaning given by section 18 of the 1985 Act,

"service charge" has the meaning given by that section, and

"unit" means—
  (a)   a flat,
  (b)   any other separate set of premises which is constructed or adapted for use for the purposes of a dwelling, or
  (c)   a separate set of premises let, or intended for letting, on a tenancy to which Part 2 of the Landlord and Tenant Act 1954 (c 56) (business tenancies) applies.

(2)   In this Chapter "lease" and "tenancy" have the same meaning and both expressions include (where the context permits)—
  (a)   a sub-lease or sub-tenancy, and
  (b)   an agreement for a lease or tenancy (or for a sub-lease or sub-tenancy),
but do not include a tenancy at will or at sufferance.

(3)   The expressions "landlord" and "tenant", and references to letting, to the grant of a lease or to covenants or the terms of a lease, shall be construed accordingly.

(4)   In this Chapter any reference (however expressed) to the lease held by the qualifying tenant of a flat is a reference to a lease held by him under which the demised premises consist of or include the flat (whether with or without one or more other flats).

(5)   Where two or more persons jointly constitute either the landlord or the tenant or qualifying tenant in relation to a lease of a flat, any reference in this Chapter to the landlord or to the tenant or qualifying tenant is (unless the context otherwise requires) a reference to both or all of the persons who jointly constitute the landlord or the tenant or qualifying tenant, as the case may require.

(6)   In the case of a lease which derives (in accordance with section 77(5)) from two or more separate leases, any reference in this Chapter to the date of the commencement of the term for which the lease was granted shall, if the terms of the separate leases commenced at different dates, have effect as references to the date of the commencement of the term of the lease with the earliest date of commencement.

**[1275]**

## 113   Index of defined expressions

In this Chapter the expressions listed below are defined by the provisions specified.

| Expression | Interpretation provision |
| --- | --- |
| Approval (and approving) | Section 98(7) |
| Appurtenant property | Section 112(1) |
| Acquisition date | Sections 74(1)(b) and 90 |
| Claim notice | Section 79(1) |

| Expression | Interpretation provision |
|---|---|
| Contractor party | Section 91(2)(b) |
| Copy | Section 112(1) |
| Counter-notice | Section 84(1) |
| Date of the commencement of the term of a lease | Section 112(6) |
| Determination date | Section 91(5) |
| Document | Section 112(1) |
| Dwelling | Section 112(1) |
| Existing management contract | Section 91(3) |
| Flat | Section 112(1) |
| Landlord | Section 112(3) and (5) |
| Lease | Section 112(2) to (4) |
| Letting | Section 112(3) |
| Long lease | Sections 76 and 77 |
| Manager party | Section 91(2)(a) |
| No dispute about entitlement | Section 90(3) |
| Notice of invitation to participate | Section 78 |
| Notice of withdrawal | Section 86(1) |
| Premises to which this Chapter applies | Section 72 (and Schedule 6) |
| Qualifying tenant | Sections 75 and 112(4) and (5) |
| Relevant costs | Section 112(1) |
| Relevant date | Section 79(1) |
| Right to manage | Section 71(2) |
| RTM company | Sections 71(1) and 73 |
| Service charge | Section 112(1) |
| Tenancy | Section 112(2) |
| Tenant | Section 112(3) and (5) |
| Tenant covenant | Section 100(4) |
| Unit | Section 112(1) |

**[1276]**

## CHAPTER 2
## COLLECTIVE ENFRANCHISEMENT BY TENANTS OF FLATS

*Introductory*

### 114  Amendments of right to collective enfranchisement

This Chapter amends the right to collective enfranchisement which is conferred by Chapter 1 of Part 1 of the 1993 Act.

**[1277]**

**115–128**   (*Ss 115–123, 125-128 amend the Leasehold Reform, Housing and Urban Development Act 1993 at* **[803]** *et seq; these amendments have been incorporated at the appropriate place in this work; s 124 introduces Sch 8 to this Act.*)

## CHAPTER 3
## NEW LEASES FOR TENANTS OF FLATS

*Introductory*

**129 Amendments of right to acquire new lease**

This Chapter amends the right of tenants of flats to acquire new leases which is conferred by Chapter 2 of Part 1 of the 1993 Act.

**[1278]**

**130–136** (*Amend the Leasehold Reform, Housing and Urban Development Act 1993 at* **[803]** *et seq; these amendments have been incorporated at the appropriate place in this work.*)

## CHAPTER 4
## LEASEHOLD HOUSES

**137–149** (*S 137 introduces the Chapter; ss 138–149 amend the Leasehold Reform Act 1967 at* **[78]** *et seq; these amendments have been incorporated at the appropriate place in this work.*)

## CHAPTER 5
## OTHER PROVISIONS ABOUT LEASES

*Service charges, administration charges etc*

**150–157** (*S 150 introduces Sch 9; s 151 substitutes the Landlord and Tenant Act 1985, ss 20, 20ZA at* **[612]**, **[613]**; *s 152 substitutes ss 21, 21A of that Act at* **[617]**, **[618]**; *s 153 inserts s 21B of that Act at* **[619]**; *s 154 substitutes s 22 of that Act at* **[620]**; *s 155(1) inserts 27A of that Act at* **[627]**; *s 155(2), (3) amends ss 38, 39 of that Act at* **[640]**, **[641]**; *s 156(1) inserts the Landlord and Tenant Act 1987, ss 42A, 42B at* **[703]**, **[704]**; *s 156(2) amends s 53 of that Act at* **[710]**; *s 157 introduces Sch 10.*)

**158 Administration charges**

Schedule 11 (which makes provision about administration charges payable by tenants of dwellings) has effect.

**[1279]**

**159 Charges under estate management schemes**

(1) This section applies where a scheme under—

    (a) section 19 of the 1967 Act (estate management schemes in connection with enfranchisement under that Act),

    (b) Chapter 4 of Part 1 of the 1993 Act (estate management schemes in connection with enfranchisement under the 1967 Act or Chapter 1 of Part 1 of the 1993 Act), or

    (c) section 94(6) of the 1993 Act (corresponding schemes in relation to areas occupied under leases from Crown),

includes provision imposing on persons occupying or interested in property an obligation to make payments ("estate charges").

(2) A variable estate charge is payable only to the extent that the amount of the charge is reasonable; and "variable estate charge" means an estate charge which is neither—

    (a) specified in the scheme, nor

    (b) calculated in accordance with a formula specified in the scheme.

(3) Any person on whom an obligation to pay an estate charge is imposed by the scheme may apply to a leasehold valuation tribunal for an order varying the scheme in such manner as is specified in the application on the grounds that—

    (a) any estate charge specified in the scheme is unreasonable, or

    (b) any formula specified in the scheme in accordance with which any estate charge is calculated is unreasonable.

(4) If the grounds on which the application was made are established to the satisfaction of the tribunal, it may make an order varying the scheme in such manner as is specified in the order.

(5) The variation specified in the order may be—

    (a) the variation specified in the application, or

    (b) such other variation as the tribunal thinks fit.

(6) An application may be made to a leasehold valuation tribunal for a determination whether an estate charge is payable by a person and, if it is, as to—

    (a) the person by whom it is payable,

    (b) the person to whom it is payable,

(c)   the amount which is payable,

(d)   the date at or by which it is payable, and

(e)   the manner in which it is payable.

(7)   Subsection (6) applies whether or not any payment has been made.

(8)   The jurisdiction conferred on a leasehold valuation tribunal in respect of any matter by virtue of subsection (6) is in addition to any jurisdiction of a court in respect of the matter.

(9)   No application under subsection (6) may be made in respect of a matter which—

(a)   has been agreed or admitted by the person concerned,

(b)   has been, or is to be, referred to arbitration pursuant to a post-dispute arbitration agreement to which that person is a party,

(c)   has been the subject of determination by a court, or

(d)   has been the subject of determination by an arbitral tribunal pursuant to a post-dispute arbitration agreement.

(10)   But the person is not to be taken to have agreed or admitted any matter by reason only of having made any payment.

(11)   An agreement (other than a post-dispute arbitration agreement) is void in so far as it purports to provide for a determination—

(a)   in a particular manner, or

(b)   on particular evidence,

of any question which may be the subject matter of an application under subsection (6).

(12)   In this section—

"post-dispute arbitration agreement", in relation to any matter, means an arbitration agreement made after a dispute about the matter has arisen, and

"arbitration agreement" and "arbitral tribunal" have the same meanings as in Part 1 of the Arbitration Act 1996 (c 23).

**[1280]**

**160–163**   (*Amend the Landlord and Tenant Act 1987 at* **[644]** *et seq; these amendments have been incorporated at the appropriate place in this work.*)

*Insurance*

### 164  Insurance otherwise than with landlord's insurer

(1)   This section applies where a long lease of a house requires the tenant to insure the house with an insurer nominated or approved by the landlord ("the landlord's insurer").

(2)   The tenant is not required to effect the insurance with the landlord's insurer if—

(a)   the house is insured under a policy of insurance issued by an authorised insurer,

(b)   the policy covers the interests of both the landlord and the tenant,

(c)   the policy covers all the risks which the lease requires be covered by insurance provided by the landlord's insurer,

(d)   the amount of the cover is not less than that which the lease requires to be provided by such insurance, and

(e)   the tenant satisfies subsection (3).

(3)   To satisfy this subsection the tenant—

(a)   must have given a notice of cover to the landlord before the end of the period of fourteen days beginning with the relevant date, and

(b)   if (after that date) he has been requested to do so by a new landlord, must have given a notice of cover to him within the period of fourteen days beginning with the day on which the request was given.

(4)   For the purposes of subsection (3)—

(a)   if the policy has not been renewed the relevant date is the day on which it took effect and if it has been renewed it is the day from which it was last renewed, and

(b)   a person is a new landlord on any day if he acquired the interest of the previous landlord under the lease on a disposal made by him during the period of one month ending with that day.

(5)   A notice of cover is a notice specifying—

(a)   the name of the insurer,

(b)   the risks covered by the policy,

(c)   the amount and period of the cover, and

(d)   such further information as may be prescribed.

(6)   A notice of cover—

(a)   must be in the prescribed form, and

(b)   may be sent by post.

(7)    If a notice of cover is sent by post, it may be addressed to the landlord at the address specified in subsection (8).

(8)    That address is—

    (a)    the address last furnished to the tenant as the landlord's address for service in accordance with section 48 of the 1987 Act (notification of address for service of notices on landlord), or

    (b)    if no such address has been so furnished, the address last furnished to the tenant as the landlord's address in accordance with section 47 of the 1987 Act (landlord's name and address to be contained in demands for rent).

(9)    But the tenant may not give a notice of cover to the landlord at the address specified in subsection (8) if he has been notified by the landlord of a different address in England and Wales at which he wishes to be given any such notice.

(10)    In this section—

    "authorised insurer", in relation to a policy of insurance, means a person who may carry on in the United Kingdom the business of effecting or carrying out contracts of insurance of the sort provided under the policy without contravening the prohibition imposed by section 19 of the Financial Services and Markets Act 2000 (c 8),

    "house" has the same meaning as for the purposes of Part 1 of the 1967 Act,

    "landlord" and "tenant" have the same meanings as in Chapter 1 of this Part,

    "long lease" has the meaning given by sections 76 and 77 of this Act, and

    "prescribed" means prescribed by regulations made by the appropriate national authority.

**[1281]**

---

**NOTES**

Commencement: 26 July 2002 (in relation to England for the purpose of making regulations); 1 January 2003 (in relation to Wales for the purpose of making regulations); 28 February 2005 (in relation to England for remaining purposes); 31 May 2005 (in relation to Wales for remaining purposes).

Regulations: the Leasehold Houses (Notice of Insurance Cover) (England) Regulations 2004, SI 2004/3097 at **[3440]**; the Leasehold Houses (Notice of Insurance Cover) (Wales) Regulations 2005, SI 2005/1354 at **[3450]**.

---

**165**    *(Amends the Landlord and Tenant Act 1985, Schedule, para 8 at* **[643]**.*)*

*Ground rent*

**166    Requirement to notify long leaseholders that rent is due**

(1)    A tenant under a long lease of a dwelling is not liable to make a payment of rent under the lease unless the landlord has given him a notice relating to the payment; and the date on which he is liable to make the payment is that specified in the notice.

(2)    The notice must specify—

    (a)    the amount of the payment,

    (b)    the date on which the tenant is liable to make it, and

    (c)    if different from that date, the date on which he would have been liable to make it in accordance with the lease,

and shall contain any such further information as may be prescribed.

(3)    The date on which the tenant is liable to make the payment must not be—

    (a)    either less than 30 days or more than 60 days after the day on which the notice is given, or

    (b)    before that on which he would have been liable to make it in accordance with the lease.

(4)    If the date on which the tenant is liable to make the payment is after that on which he would have been liable to make it in accordance with the lease, any provisions of the lease relating to non-payment or late payment of rent have effect accordingly.

(5)    The notice—

    (a)    must be in the prescribed form, and

    (b)    may be sent by post.

(6)    If the notice is sent by post, it must be addressed to a tenant at the dwelling unless he has notified the landlord in writing of a different address in England and Wales at which he wishes to be given notices under this section (in which case it must be addressed to him there).

(7)    In this section "rent" does not include—

    (a)    a service charge (within the meaning of section 18(1) of the 1985 Act), or

    (b)    an administration charge (within the meaning of Part 1 of Schedule 11 to this Act).

(8)    In this section "long lease of a dwelling" does not include—

    (a)    a tenancy to which Part 2 of the Landlord and Tenant Act 1954 (c 56) (business tenancies) applies,

(b) a tenancy of an agricultural holding within the meaning of the Agricultural Holdings Act 1986 (c 5) in relation to which that Act applies, or

(c) a farm business tenancy within the meaning of the Agricultural Tenancies Act 1995 (c 8).

(9) In this section—

"dwelling" has the same meaning as in the 1985 Act,

"landlord" and "tenant" have the same meanings as in Chapter 1 of this Part,

"long lease" has the meaning given by sections 76 and 77 of this Act, and

"prescribed" means prescribed by regulations made by the appropriate national authority.

**[1282]**

**NOTES**

Commencement: 26 July 2002 (in relation to England for the purpose of making regulations); 1 January 2003 (in relation to Wales for the purpose of making regulations); 28 February 2005 (in relation to England for remaining purposes); 31 May 2005 (in relation to Wales for remaining purposes).

Regulations: the Landlord and Tenant (Notice of Rent) (England) Regulations 2004, SI 2004/3096 at **[3437]**; the Landlord and Tenant (Notice of Rent) (Wales) Regulations 2005, SI 2005/1355 at **[3451]**.

*Forfeiture of leases of dwellings*

## 167 Failure to pay small amount for short period

(1) A landlord under a long lease of a dwelling may not exercise a right of re-entry or forfeiture for failure by a tenant to pay an amount consisting of rent, service charges or administration charges (or a combination of them) ("the unpaid amount") unless the unpaid amount—

(a) exceeds the prescribed sum, or

(b) consists of or includes an amount which has been payable for more than a prescribed period.

(2) The sum prescribed under subsection (1)(a) must not exceed £500.

(3) If the unpaid amount includes a default charge, it is to be treated for the purposes of subsection (1)(a) as reduced by the amount of the charge; and for this purpose "default charge" means an administration charge payable in respect of the tenant's failure to pay any part of the unpaid amount.

(4) In this section "long lease of a dwelling" does not include—

(a) a tenancy to which Part 2 of the Landlord and Tenant Act 1954 (c 56) (business tenancies) applies,

(b) a tenancy of an agricultural holding within the meaning of the Agricultural Holdings Act 1986 (c 5) in relation to which that Act applies, or

(c) a farm business tenancy within the meaning of the Agricultural Tenancies Act 1995 (c 8).

(5) In this section—

"administration charge" has the same meaning as in Part 1 of Schedule 11,

"dwelling" has the same meaning as in the 1985 Act,

"landlord" and "tenant" have the same meaning as in Chapter 1 of this Part,

"long lease" has the meaning given by sections 76 and 77 of this Act, except that a shared ownership lease is a long lease whatever the tenant's total share,

"prescribed" means prescribed by regulations made by the appropriate national authority, and

"service charge" has the meaning given by section 18(1) of the 1985 Act.

**[1283]**

**NOTES**

Commencement: 26 July 2002 (in relation to England for the purpose of making regulations); 1 January 2003 (in relation to Wales for the purpose of making regulations); 28 February 2005 (in relation to England for remaining purposes); 31 May 2005 (in relation to Wales for remaining purposes).

Regulations: the Rights of Re-entry and Forfeiture (Prescribed Sum and Period) (England) Regulations 2004, SI 2004/3086 at **[3435]**; the Rights of Re-entry and Forfeiture (Prescribed Sum and Period) (Wales) Regulations 2005, SI 2005/1352 at **[3446]**.

## 168 No forfeiture notice before determination of breach

(1) A landlord under a long lease of a dwelling may not serve a notice under section 146(1) of the Law of Property Act 1925 (c 20) (restriction on forfeiture) in respect of a breach by a tenant of a covenant or condition in the lease unless subsection (2) is satisfied.

(2) This subsection is satisfied if—

(a) it has been finally determined on an application under subsection (4) that the breach has occurred,

(b) the tenant has admitted the breach, or

(c)   a court in any proceedings, or an arbitral tribunal in proceedings pursuant to a post-dispute arbitration agreement, has finally determined that the breach has occurred.

(3)   But a notice may not be served by virtue of subsection (2)(a) or (c) until after the end of the period of 14 days beginning with the day after that on which the final determination is made.

(4)   A landlord under a long lease of a dwelling may make an application to a leasehold valuation tribunal for a determination that a breach of a covenant or condition in the lease has occurred.

(5)   But a landlord may not make an application under subsection (4) in respect of a matter which—
(a)   has been, or is to be, referred to arbitration pursuant to a post-dispute arbitration agreement to which the tenant is a party,
(b)   has been the subject of determination by a court, or
(c)   has been the subject of determination by an arbitral tribunal pursuant to a post-dispute arbitration agreement.

**[1284]**

**NOTES**

Commencement: 28 February 2005 (in relation to England); 31 May 2005 (in relation to Wales).

## 169   Section 168: supplementary

(1)   An agreement by a tenant under a long lease of a dwelling (other than a post-dispute arbitration agreement) is void in so far as it purports to provide for a determination—
(a)   in a particular manner, or
(b)   on particular evidence,
of any question which may be the subject of an application under section 168(4).

(2)   For the purposes of section 168 it is finally determined that a breach of a covenant or condition in a lease has occurred—
(a)   if a decision that it has occurred is not appealed against or otherwise challenged, at the end of the period for bringing an appeal or other challenge, or
(b)   if such a decision is appealed against or otherwise challenged and not set aside in consequence of the appeal or other challenge, at the time specified in subsection (3).

(3)   The time referred to in subsection (2)(b) is the time when the appeal or other challenge is disposed of—
(a)   by the determination of the appeal or other challenge and the expiry of the time for bringing a subsequent appeal (if any), or
(b)   by its being abandoned or otherwise ceasing to have effect.

(4)   In section 168 and this section "long lease of a dwelling" does not include—
(a)   a tenancy to which Part 2 of the Landlord and Tenant Act 1954 (c 56) (business tenancies) applies,
(b)   a tenancy of an agricultural holding within the meaning of the Agricultural Holdings Act 1986 (c 5) in relation to which that Act applies, or
(c)   a farm business tenancy within the meaning of the Agricultural Tenancies Act 1995 (c 8).

(5)   In section 168 and this section—
"arbitration agreement" and "arbitral tribunal" have the same meaning as in Part 1 of the Arbitration Act 1996 (c 23) and "post-dispute arbitration agreement", in relation to any breach (or alleged breach), means an arbitration agreement made after the breach has occurred (or is alleged to have occurred),
"dwelling" has the same meaning as in the 1985 Act,
"landlord" and "tenant" have the same meaning as in Chapter 1 of this Part, and
"long lease" has the meaning given by sections 76 and 77 of this Act, except that a shared ownership lease is a long lease whatever the tenant's total share.

(6)   Section 146(7) of the Law of Property Act 1925 (c 20) applies for the purposes of section 168 and this section.

(7)   Nothing in section 168 affects the service of a notice under section 146(1) of the Law of Property Act 1925 in respect of a failure to pay—
(a)   a service charge (within the meaning of section 18(1) of the 1985 Act), or
(b)   an administration charge (within the meaning of Part 1 of Schedule 11 to this Act).

**[1285]**

**NOTES**

Commencement: 28 February 2005 (in relation to England); 31 May 2005 (in relation to Wales).

**170**    (*Amends the Housing Act 1996, s 81 at* **[1005]**.)

### 171    Power to prescribe additional or different requirements

(1)    The appropriate national authority may by regulations prescribe requirements which must be met before a right of re-entry or forfeiture may be exercised in relation to a breach of a covenant or condition in a long lease of an unmortgaged dwelling.

(2)    The regulations may specify that the requirements are to be in addition to, or instead of, requirements imposed otherwise than by the regulations.

(3)    In this section "long lease of a dwelling" does not include—

    (a)    a tenancy to which Part 2 of the Landlord and Tenant Act 1954 (c 56) (business tenancies) applies,

    (b)    a tenancy of an agricultural holding within the meaning of the Agricultural Holdings Act 1986 (c 5) in relation to which that Act applies, or

    (c)    a farm business tenancy within the meaning of the Agricultural Tenancies Act 1995 (c 8).

(4)    For the purposes of this section a dwelling is unmortgaged if it is not subject to a mortgage, charge or lien.

(5)    In this section—

"dwelling" has the same meaning as in the 1985 Act, and

"long lease" has the meaning given by sections 76 and 77 of this Act, except that a shared ownership lease is a long lease whatever the tenant's total share.

**[1286]**

**NOTES**

Commencement: 26 July 2002 (in relation to England for the purpose of making regulations); 1 January 2003 (in relation to Wales for the purpose of making regulations); 28 February 2005 (in relation to England for remaining purposes); 31 May 2005 (in relation to Wales for remaining purposes).

*Crown application*

### 172    Application to Crown

(1)    The following provisions apply in relation to Crown land (as in relation to other land)—

    (a)    sections 18 to 30B of (and the Schedule to) the 1985 Act (service charges, insurance and managing agents),

    (b)    Part 2 of the 1987 Act (appointment of manager by leasehold valuation tribunal),

    (c)    Part 4 of the 1987 Act (variation of leases),

    (d)    sections 46 to 49 of the 1987 Act (information to be furnished to tenants),

    (e)    Chapter 5 of Part 1 of the 1993 Act (management audit),

    (f)    section 81 of the Housing Act 1996 (c 52) (restriction on termination of tenancy for failure to pay service charge etc),

    (g)    section 84 of (and Schedule 4 to) that Act (right to appoint surveyor), and

    (h)    in this Chapter, the provisions relating to any of the provisions within paragraphs (a) to (g), Part 1 of Schedule 11 and sections 164 to 171.

(2)    Land is Crown land if there is or has at any time been an interest or estate in the land—

    (a)    comprised in the Crown Estate,

    (b)    belonging to Her Majesty in right of the Duchy of Lancaster,

    (c)    belonging to the Duchy of Cornwall, or

    (d)    belonging to a government department or held on behalf of Her Majesty for the purposes of a government department.

(3)    No failure by the Crown to perform a duty imposed by or by virtue of any of sections 21 to 23A of, or any of paragraphs 2 to 4A of the Schedule to, the 1985 Act makes the Crown criminally liable; but the High Court may declare any such failure without reasonable excuse to be unlawful.

(4)    Any sum payable under any of the provisions mentioned in subsection (1) by the Chancellor of the Duchy of Lancaster may be raised and paid under section 25 of the Duchy of Lancaster Act 1817 (c 97) as an expense incurred in improvement of land belonging to Her Majesty in right of the Duchy.

(5)    Any sum payable under any such provision by the Duke of Cornwall (or any other possessor for the time being of the Duchy of Cornwall) may be raised and paid under section 8 of the Duchy of Cornwall Management Act 1863 (c 49) as an expense incurred in permanently improving the possessions of the Duchy.

(6)    ...

**[1287]**

NOTES
Commencement: 30 September 2003 (sub-ss (1)–(5) in relation to England except in so far as they relate to the application to the Crown of ss 152–154, 164–171, sub-s (6) in relation to England for certain purposes); 30 March 2004 (sub-ss (1)–(5) in relation to Wales except in so far as they relate to the application to the Crown of ss 152–154, 164–171, sub-s (6) in relation to Wales for certain purposes); 28 February 2005 (sub-ss (1)–(5), in relation to England except in so far as they relate to the application to the Crown of the Landlord and Tenant Act 1985, ss 21, 21A, 21B, 22); 31 May 2005 (sub-ss (1)–(5), in relation to Wales except in so far as they relate to the application to the Crown of the Landlord and Tenant Act 1985, ss 21, 21A, 21B, 22); to be appointed (otherwise).
Sub-s (6): amends the Landlord and Tenant Act 1987, s 56 at [713].

## CHAPTER 6
## LEASEHOLD VALUATION TRIBUNALS

### 173 Leasehold valuation tribunals

(1)   Any jurisdiction conferred on a leasehold valuation tribunal by or under any enactment is exercisable by a rent assessment committee constituted in accordance with Schedule 10 to the Rent Act 1977 (c 42).

(2)   When so constituted for exercising any such jurisdiction a rent assessment committee is known as a leasehold valuation tribunal.

**[1288]**

### 174 Procedure

Schedule 12 (leasehold valuation tribunals: procedure) has effect.

**[1289]**

### 175 Appeals

(1)   A party to proceedings before a leasehold valuation tribunal may appeal to the [Upper Tribunal] from a decision of the leasehold valuation tribunal.

(2)   But the appeal may be made only with the permission of—
  (a)   the leasehold valuation tribunal, or
  (b)   the [Upper Tribunal].

(3)   …

(4)   On the appeal the [Upper Tribunal] may exercise any power which was available to the leasehold valuation tribunal.

(5)   And a decision of the [Upper Tribunal] on the appeal may be enforced in the same way as a decision of the leasehold valuation tribunal.

(6)   The [Upper Tribunal] may not order a party to the appeal to pay costs incurred by another party in connection with the appeal unless he has, in the opinion of the [Upper Tribunal], acted frivolously, vexatiously, abusively, disruptively or otherwise unreasonably in connection with the appeal.

(7)   In such a case the amount he may be ordered to pay shall not exceed the maximum amount which a party to proceedings before a leasehold valuation tribunal may be ordered to pay in the proceedings under or by virtue of paragraph 10(3) of Schedule 12.

(8)   No appeal lies from a decision of a leasehold valuation tribunal to the High Court by virtue of section 11(1) of the Tribunals and Inquiries Act 1992 (c 53).

(9)   And no case may be stated for the opinion of the High Court in respect of such a decision by virtue of that provision.

(10)   …

**[1290]**

NOTES
Sub-ss (1), (2), (4)–(6): words in square brackets substituted by the Transfer of Tribunal Functions (Lands Tribunal and Miscellaneous Amendments) Order 2009, SI 2009/1307, art 5(1), (2), Sch 1, para 269(a), subject to transitional provisions and savings in Sch 5 thereto.
Sub-ss (3), (10): repealed by SI 2009/1307, art 5(1), (2), Sch 1, para 269(b), subject to transitional provisions and savings in Sch 5 thereto.

### 176 Consequential amendments

Schedule 13 (minor and consequential amendments about leasehold valuation tribunals) has effect.

**[1291]**

**PART I
STATUTES**

**NOTES**
Commencement: 30 September 2003 (in relation to England for certain purposes); 30 March 2004 (in relation to Wales for certain purposes); 28 February 2005 (in relation to England for remaining purposes); 31 May 2005 (in relation to Wales for remaining purposes).

## CHAPTER 7
## GENERAL

### 177   Wales

The references to the 1985 Act, the 1987 Act and the 1993 Act in Schedule 1 to the National Assembly for Wales (Transfer of Functions) Order 1999 (SI 1999/672) are to be treated as referring to those Acts as amended by this Part.

**[1292]**

### 178   Orders and regulations

(1)   An order or regulations under any provision of this Part—
 (a)   may include incidental, supplementary, consequential and transitional provision,
 (b)   may make provision generally or only in relation to specified cases, and
 (c)   may make different provision for different purposes.

(2)   Regulations under Schedule 12 may make different provision for different areas.

(3)   Any power to make an order or regulations under this Part is exercisable by statutory instrument.

(4)   Regulations shall not be made by the Secretary of State under section 167 or 171 or paragraph 9(3)(b) or 10(3)(b) of Schedule 12 unless a draft of the instrument containing them has been laid before and approved by a resolution of each House of Parliament.

(5)   A statutory instrument containing an order or regulations made by the Secretary of State under this Part shall, if not so approved, be subject to annulment in pursuance of a resolution of either House of Parliament.

**[1293]**

**NOTES**
Regulations: Service Charges (Summary of Rights and Obligations, and Transitional Provision) (England) Regulations 2007, SI 2007/1257 at **[3759]**.

### 179   Interpretation

(1)   In this Part "the appropriate national authority" means—
 (a)   the Secretary of State (as respects England), and
 (b)   the National Assembly for Wales (as respects Wales).

(2)   In this Part—
"the 1967 Act" means the Leasehold Reform Act 1967 (c 88),
"the 1985 Act" means the Landlord and Tenant Act 1985 (c 70),
"the 1987 Act" means the Landlord and Tenant Act 1987 (c 31), and
"the 1993 Act" means the Leasehold Reform, Housing and Urban Development Act 1993
  (c 28).

**[1294]**

## PART 3
## SUPPLEMENTARY

### 180   Repeals

Schedule 14 (repeals) has effect.

**[1295]**

**NOTES**
Commencement: 26 July 2002 (in relation to England for certain purposes); 1 January 2003 (in relation to Wales for certain purposes); 30 September 2003 (in relation to England for certain purposes); 30 March 2004 (in relation to Wales for certain purposes); 17 November 2004 (certain purposes); 28 February 2005 (in relation to England for certain purposes); 31 May 2005 (in relation to Wales for certain purposes); to be appointed (otherwise).

### 181   Commencement etc

(1)   Apart from section 104 and sections 177 to 179, the preceding provisions (and the Schedules) come into force in accordance with provision made by order made by the appropriate authority.

(2)   The appropriate authority may by order make any transitional provisions or savings in connection with the coming into force of any provision in accordance with an order under subsection (1).

(3)   The power to make orders under subsections (1) and (2) is exercisable by statutory instrument.

(4)   In this section "the appropriate authority" means—

    (a)   in relation to any provision of Part 1 or section 180 and Schedule 14 so far as relating to section 104, the Lord Chancellor, and

    (b)   in relation to any provision of Part 2 or section 180 and Schedule 14 so far as otherwise relating, the Secretary of State (as respects England) and the National Assembly for Wales (as respects Wales).

**[1296]**

---

**NOTES**

Orders: the Commonhold and Leasehold Reform Act 2002 (Commencement No 1, Savings and Transitional Provisions) (England) Order 2002, SI 2002/1912 at **[3253]**; the Commonhold and Leasehold Reform Act 2002 (Commencement No 1, Savings and Transitional Provisions) (Wales) Order 2002, SI 2002/3012 at **[3265]**; the Commonhold and Leasehold Reform Act 2002 (Commencement No 2 and Savings) (England) Order 2003, SI 2003/1986 at **[3281]**; the Commonhold and Leasehold Reform Act 2002 (Commencement No 3) Order 2003, SI 2003/2377; the Commonhold and Leasehold Reform Act 2002 (Commencement No 2 and Savings) (Wales) Order 2004, SI 2004/669 at **[3356]**; the Commonhold and Leasehold Reform Act 2002 (Commencement No 4) Order 2004, SI 2004/1832; the Commonhold and Leasehold Reform Act 2002 (Commencement No 5 and Saving and Transitional Provision) Order 2004, SI 2004/3056 at **[3431]**; the Commonhold and Leasehold Reform Act 2002 Commencement No 5 and Saving and Transitional Provision) (Amendment) (England) Order 2005, SI 2005/193; the Commonhold and Leasehold Reform Act 2002 (Commencement No 3 and Saving and Transitional Provision) (Wales) Order 2005, SI 2005/1353 at **[3447]**; the Commonhold and Leasehold Reform Act 2002 (Commencement No 6) (England) Order 2007, SI 2007/1256; the Commonhold and Leasehold Reform Act 2002 (Commencement No 4) (Wales) Order 2007, SI 2007/3161.

---

**182   Extent**

This Act extends to England and Wales only.

**[1297]**

**183   Short title**

This Act may be cited as the Commonhold and Leasehold Reform Act 2002.

**[1298]**

## SCHEDULE 1
### APPLICATION FOR REGISTRATION: DOCUMENTS

Section 2

*Introduction*

1.   This Schedule lists the documents which are required by section 2 to accompany an application for the registration of a freehold estate as a freehold estate in commonhold land.

*Commonhold association documents*

2.   The commonhold association's [certificate of incorporation under section 15 of the Companies Act 2006].

3.   Any altered certificate of incorporation issued under [section 80 of that Act (change of name)].

4.   The [articles of association] of the commonhold association.

*Commonhold community statement*

5.   The commonhold community statement.

*Consent*

6.—(1)   Where consent is required under or by virtue of section 3—

    (a)   the consent,

    (b)   an order of a court by virtue of section 3(2)(f) dispensing with the requirement for consent, or

    (c)   evidence of deemed consent by virtue of section 3(2)(e).

(2)   In the case of a conditional order under section 3(2)(f), the order must be accompanied by evidence that the condition has been complied with.

*Certificate*

7.   A certificate given by the directors of the commonhold association that—

  (a)   the [articles of association] submitted with the application comply with regulations under paragraph 2(1) of Schedule 3,

  (b)   the commonhold community statement submitted with the application satisfies the requirements of this Part,

  (c)   the application satisfies Schedule 2,

  (d)   the commonhold association has not traded, and

  (e)   the commonhold association has not incurred any liability which has not been discharged.

**[1299]**

**NOTES**

   Paras 2–4, 7: words in square brackets substituted by the Companies Act 2006 (Consequential Amendments, Transitional Provisions and Savings) Order 2009, SI 2009/1941, art 2(1), Sch 1, para 194(1), (20).

## SCHEDULE 2
## LAND WHICH MAY NOT BE COMMONHOLD LAND

Section 4

*"Flying freehold"*

1.—(1)   Subject to sub-paragraph (2), an application may not be made under section 2 wholly or partly in relation to land above ground level ("raised land") unless all the land between the ground and the raised land is the subject of the same application.

   (2)   An application for the addition of land to a commonhold in accordance with section 41 may be made wholly or partly in relation to raised land if all the land between the ground and the raised land forms part of the commonhold to which the raised land is to be added.

*Agricultural land*

2.   An application may not be made under section 2 wholly or partly in relation to land if—

  (a)   it is agricultural land within the meaning of the Agriculture Act 1947 (c 48),

  (b)   it is comprised in a tenancy of an agricultural holding within the meaning of the Agricultural Holdings Act 1986 (c 5), or

  (c)   it is comprised in a farm business tenancy for the purposes of the Agricultural Tenancies Act 1995 (c 8).

*Contingent title*

3.—(1)   An application may not be made under section 2 if an estate in the whole or part of the land to which the application relates is a contingent estate.

   (2)   An estate is contingent for the purposes of this paragraph if (and only if)—

  (a)   it is liable to revert to or vest in a person other than the present registered proprietor on the occurrence or non-occurrence of a particular event, and

  (b)   the reverter or vesting would occur by operation of law as a result of an enactment listed in sub-paragraph (3).

   (3)   The enactments are—

  (a)   the School Sites Act 1841 (c 38) (conveyance for use as school),

  (b)   the Lands Clauses Acts (compulsory purchase),

  (c)   the Literary and Scientific Institutions Act 1854 (c 112) (sites for institutions), and

  (d)   the Places of Worship Sites Act 1873 (c 50) (sites for places of worship).

   (4)   Regulations may amend sub-paragraph (3) so as to—

  (a)   add an enactment to the list, or

  (b)   remove an enactment from the list.

**[1300]**

## SCHEDULE 3
## COMMONHOLD ASSOCIATION

Section 34

## PART 1
## [ARTICLES OF ASSOCIATION]

*Introduction*

[1.   In this Schedule "articles" means the articles of association of a commonhold association.]

*Form and content*

2.—(1)  Regulations shall make provision about the form and content of [the articles].

(2)  A commonhold association may adopt provisions of the regulations for its [articles].

(3)  The regulations may include provision which is to have effect for a commonhold association whether or not it is adopted under sub-paragraph (2).

(4)  A provision of the [articles] shall have no effect to the extent that it is inconsistent with the regulations.

(5)  Regulations under this paragraph shall have effect in relation to [articles]—
    (a)  irrespective of the date of the [articles], but
    (b)  subject to any transitional provision of the regulations.

[(6)  Section 20 of the Companies Act 2006 (default application of model articles) does not apply to a commonhold association.]

*Alteration*

3.—(1)  [Where a commonhold association alters its [articles] at a time when the land [specified in its articles] is commonhold land, the alteration] shall have no effect until the altered version is registered in accordance with this paragraph.

(2)  If the commonhold association makes an application under this sub-paragraph the Registrar shall arrange for an [altered articles] to be kept in his custody, and referred to in the register, in place of the unaltered version.

(3)  An application under sub-paragraph (2) must be accompanied by a certificate given by the directors of the commonhold association that the altered [articles] comply with regulations under paragraph 2(1).

(4)  Where the Registrar amends the register on an application under sub-paragraph (2) he shall make any consequential amendments to the register which he thinks appropriate.

4.  ...

[1301]

---

**NOTES**

Part heading: words in square brackets substituted by the Companies Act 2006 (Consequential Amendments, Transitional Provisions and Savings) Order 2009, SI 2009/1941, art 2(1), Sch 1, para 195(1), (2).

Para 1: substituted by SI 2009/1941, art 2(1), Sch 1, para 195(1), (3).

Para 2: words in square brackets substituted and sub-para (6) inserted by SI 2009/1941, art 2(1), Sch 1, para 195(1), (4).

Para 3: words in first (outer) pair of square brackets in sub-para (1) substituted by the Companies Act 2006, s 1283; other words in square brackets substituted by the Companies Act 2006 (Consequential Amendments, Transitional Provisions and Savings) Order 2009, SI 2009/1941, art 2(1), Sch 1, para 195(1), (5).

Para 4: repealed by SI 2009/1941, art 2(1), Sch 1, para 195(1), (6).

Regulations: the Commonhold Regulations 2004, SI 2004/1829 at **[3379]**.

---

PART 2
MEMBERSHIP

*Pre-commonhold period*

5.  During the period beginning with incorporation of a commonhold association and ending when [land specified in its articles] becomes commonhold land, the subscribers (or subscriber) to [the association's memorandum of association] shall be the sole members (or member) of the association.

*Transitional period*

6.—(1)  This paragraph applies to a commonhold association during a transitional period.

(2)  The subscribers (or subscriber) to [the association's memorandum of association] shall continue to be members (or the member) of the association.

(3)  A person who for the time being is the developer in respect of all or part of the commonhold is entitled to be entered in the register of members of the association.

*Unit-holders*

7.  A person is entitled to be entered in the register of members of a commonhold association if he becomes the unit-holder of a commonhold unit in relation to which the association exercises functions—
    (a)  on the unit becoming commonhold land by registration with unit-holders under section 9, or
    (b)  on the transfer of the unit.

*Joint unit-holders*

8.—(1)  This paragraph applies where two or more persons become joint unit-holders of a commonhold unit—

    (a)    on the unit becoming commonhold land by registration with unit-holders under section 9, or

    (b)    on the transfer of the unit.

(2)  If the joint unit-holders nominate one of themselves for the purpose of this sub-paragraph, he is entitled to be entered in the register of members of the commonhold association which exercises functions in relation to the unit.

(3)  A nomination under sub-paragraph (2) must—

    (a)    be made in writing to the commonhold association, and

    (b)    be received by the association before the end of the prescribed period.

(4)  If no nomination is received by the association before the end of the prescribed period the person whose name appears first in the proprietorship register is on the expiry of that period entitled to be entered in the register of members of the association.

(5)  On the application of a joint unit-holder the court may order that a joint unit-holder is entitled to be entered in the register of members of a commonhold association in place of a person who is or would be entitled to be registered by virtue of sub-paragraph (4).

(6)  If joint unit-holders nominate one of themselves for the purpose of this sub-paragraph, the nominated person is entitled to be entered in the register of members of the commonhold association in place of the person entered by virtue of—

    (a)    sub-paragraph (2),

    (b)    sub-paragraph (5), or

    (c)    this sub-paragraph.

*Self-membership*

9.  A commonhold association may not be a member of itself.

*No other members*

10.  A person may not become a member of a commonhold association otherwise than by virtue of a provision of this Schedule.

*Effect of registration*

11.  A person who is entitled to be entered in the register of members of a commonhold association becomes a member when the company registers him in pursuance of its duty under [section 113 of the Companies Act 2006] (duty to maintain register of members).

*Termination of membership*

12.  Where a member of a commonhold association ceases to be a unit-holder or joint unit-holder of a commonhold unit in relation to which the association exercises functions—

    (a)    he shall cease to be a member of the commonhold association, but

    (b)    paragraph (a) does not affect any right or liability already acquired or incurred in respect of a matter relating to a time when he was a unit-holder or joint unit-holder.

13.  A member of a commonhold association may resign by notice in writing to the association if (and only if) he is a member by virtue of paragraph 5 or 6 of this Schedule (and not also by virtue of any other paragraph).

*Register of members*

14.—(1)  Regulations may make provision about the performance by a commonhold association of its duty under [section 113 of the Companies Act 2006] (duty to maintain register of members) where a person—

    (a)    becomes entitled to be entered in the register by virtue of paragraphs 5 to 8, or

    (b)    ceases to be a member by virtue of paragraph 12 or on resignation.

(2)  The regulations may in particular require entries in the register to be made within a specified period.

(3)  A period specified under sub-paragraph (2) may be expressed to begin from—

    (a)    the date of a notification under section 15(3),

    (b)    the date on which the directors of the commonhold association first become aware of a specified matter, or

    (c)    some other time.

(4)  A requirement by virtue of this paragraph shall be treated as [a requirement of section 113 for the purposes of section 113(7) and (8) (offences)].

*[Supplementary provisions*

15.—(1)   Section 112(1) of the Companies Act 2006 (initial members of company) applies to a commonhold association subject to the provisions of this Schedule.

(2)   The following provisions of that Act do not apply to a commonhold association—
section 112(2) (new members);
section 136 (membership of holding company).]

**[1302]**

**NOTES**
Paras 5, 6, 11, 14: words in square brackets substituted by the Companies Act 2006 (Consequential Amendments, Transitional Provisions and Savings) Order 2009, SI 2009/1941, art 2(1), Sch 1, para 195(1), (7)–(10).
Para 15: substituted, together with preceding cross-heading by SI 2009/1941, art 2(1), Sch 1, para 195(1), (11).

## PART 3
## MISCELLANEOUS

*Name*

16.   Regulations may provide—
(a)   that the name by which a commonhold association is registered under the [Companies Act 2006] must satisfy specified requirements;
(b)   that the name by which a company other than a commonhold association is registered may not include a specified word or expression.

*[Statement of compliance]*

17.   For the purposes of [section 13 of the Companies Act 2006 (registration: statement of compliance)] as it applies to a commonhold association, a reference to the requirements of that Act shall be treated as including a reference to a provision of or made under this Schedule.

**[1303]**

**NOTES**
Paras 16, 17: words in square brackets substituted by the Companies Act 2006 (Consequential Amendments, Transitional Provisions and Savings) Order 2009, SI 2009/1941, art 2(1), Sch 1, para 195(1), (12), (13).
Regulations: the Commonhold Regulations 2004, SI 2004/1829 at **[3379]**.

## SCHEDULE 4
## DEVELOPMENT RIGHTS

Section 58

*Introductory*

1.   This Schedule sets out the matters which are development business for the purposes of section 58.

*Works*

2.   The completion or execution of works on—
(a)   a commonhold,
(b)   land which is or may be added to a commonhold, or
(c)   land which has been removed from a commonhold.

*Marketing*

3.—(1)   Transactions in commonhold units.

(2)   Advertising and other activities designed to promote transactions in commonhold units.

*Variation*

4.   The addition of land to a commonhold.

5.   The removal of land from a commonhold.

6.   Amendment of a commonhold community statement (including amendment to redefine the extent of a commonhold unit).

*Commonhold association*

7.   Appointment and removal of directors of a commonhold association.

**[1304]**

*(Sch 5 contains amendments which, in so far as within the scope of this work, have been incorporated at the appropriate place.)*

## SCHEDULE 6
### PREMISES EXCLUDED FROM RIGHT TO MANAGE
Section 72

*Buildings with substantial non-residential parts*

1.—(1)   This Chapter does not apply to premises falling within section 72(1) if the internal floor area—

(a)   of any non-residential part, or

(b)   (where there is more than one such part) of those parts (taken together),

exceeds 25 per cent of the internal floor area of the premises (taken as a whole).

(2)   A part of premises is a non-residential part if it is neither—

(a)   occupied, or intended to be occupied, for residential purposes, nor

(b)   comprised in any common parts of the premises.

(3)   Where in the case of any such premises any part of the premises (such as, for example, a garage, parking space or storage area) is used, or intended for use, in conjunction with a particular dwelling contained in the premises (and accordingly is not comprised in any common parts of the premises), it shall be taken to be occupied, or intended to be occupied, for residential purposes.

(4)   For the purpose of determining the internal floor area of a building or of any part of a building, the floor or floors of the building or part shall be taken to extend (without interruption) throughout the whole of the interior of the building or part, except that the area of any common parts of the building or part shall be disregarded.

*Buildings with self-contained parts in different ownership*

2.   Where different persons own the freehold of different parts of premises falling within section 72(1), this Chapter does not apply to the premises if any of those parts is a self-contained part of a building.

*Premises with resident landlord and no more than four units*

3.—(1)   This Chapter does not apply to premises falling within section 72(1) if the premises—

(a)   have a resident landlord, and

(b)   do not contain more than four units.

(2)   Premises have a resident landlord if—

(a)   the premises are not, and do not form part of, a purpose-built block of flats (that is, a building which, as constructed, contained two or more flats),

(b)   a relevant freeholder, or an adult member of a relevant freeholder's family, occupies a qualifying flat as his only or principal home, and

(c)   sub-paragraph (4) or (5) is satisfied.

(3)   A person is a relevant freeholder, in relation to any premises, if he owns the freehold of the whole or any part of the premises.

(4)   This sub-paragraph is satisfied if—

(a)   the relevant freeholder, or

(b)   the adult member of his family,

has throughout the last twelve months occupied the flat as his only or principal home.

(5)   This sub-paragraph is satisfied if—

(a)   immediately before the date when the relevant freeholder acquired his interest in the premises, the premises were premises with a resident landlord, and

(b)   he, or an adult member of his family, entered into occupation of the flat during the period of 28 days beginning with that date and has occupied the flat as his only or principal home ever since.

(6)   "Qualifying flat", in relation to any premises and a relevant freeholder or an adult member of his family, means a flat or other unit used as a dwelling—

(a)   which is contained in the premises, and

(b)   the freehold of the whole of which is owned by the relevant freeholder.

(7)   Where the interest of a relevant freeholder in any premises is held on trust, the references in sub-paragraphs (2), (4) and (5)(b) to a relevant freeholder are to a person having an interest under the trust (whether or not also a trustee).

(8)   A person is an adult member of another's family if he is—

(a)   the other's spouse [or civil partner],

(b)   a son, daughter, son-in-law or daughter-in-law of the other, or of the other's spouse [or civil partner], who has attained the age of 18, or

(c)  the father or mother of the other or of the other's spouse [or civil partner];
and "son" and "daughter" include stepson and stepdaughter ("son-in-law" and "daughter-in-law" being construed accordingly).

### Premises owned by local housing authority

4.—(1)  This Chapter does not apply to premises falling within section 72(1) if a local housing authority is the immediate landlord of any of the qualifying tenants of flats contained in the premises.

(2)  "Local housing authority" has the meaning given by section 1 of the Housing Act 1985 (c 68).

### Premises in relation to which rights previously exercised

5.—(1)  This Chapter does not apply to premises falling within section 72(1) at any time if—
  (a)  the right to manage the premises is at that time exercisable by a RTM company, or
  (b)  that right has been so exercisable but has ceased to be so exercisable less than four years before that time.

(2)  Sub-paragraph (1)(b) does not apply where the right to manage the premises ceased to be exercisable by virtue of section 73(5).

(3)  A leasehold valuation tribunal may, on an application made by a RTM company, determine that sub-paragraph (1)(b) is not to apply in any case if it considers that it would be unreasonable for it to apply in the circumstances of the case.

**[1305]**

### NOTES

Para 3: words in square brackets in sub-para (8) inserted by the Civil Partnership Act 2004, s 81, Sch 8, para 66.

## SCHEDULE 7
## RIGHT TO MANAGE: STATUTORY PROVISIONS

Section 102

### Covenants not to assign etc

1.—(1)  Section 19 of the Landlord and Tenant Act 1927 (c 36) (covenants not to assign without approval etc) has effect with the modifications provided by this paragraph.

(2)  Subsection (1) applies as if—
  (a)  the reference to the landlord, and
  (b)  the final reference to the lessor,
were to the RTM company.

(3)  Subsection (2) applies as if the reference to the payment of a reasonable sum in respect of any damage to or diminution in the value of the premises or neighbouring premises belonging to the landlord were omitted.

(4)  Subsection (3) applies as if—
  (a)  the first and final references to the landlord were to the RTM company, and
  (b)  the reference to the right of the landlord to require payment of a reasonable sum in respect of any damage to or diminution in the value of the premises or neighbouring premises belonging to him were omitted.

### Defective premises

2.—(1)  Section 4 of the Defective Premises Act 1972 (c 35) (landlord's duty of care by virtue of obligation or right to repair demised premises) has effect with the modifications provided by this paragraph.

(2)  References to the landlord (apart from the first reference in subsections (1) and (4)) are to the RTM company.

(3)  The reference to the material time is to the acquisition date.

### Repairing obligations

3.—(1)  The obligations imposed on a lessor by virtue of section 11 (repairing obligations in short leases) of the Landlord and Tenant Act 1985 (c 70) (referred to in this Part as "the 1985 Act") are, so far as relating to any lease of any flat or other unit contained in the premises, instead obligations of the RTM company.

(2)   The RTM company owes to any person who is in occupation of a flat or other unit contained in the premises otherwise than under a lease the same obligations as would be imposed on it by virtue of section 11 if that person were a lessee under a lease of the flat or other unit.

(3)   But sub-paragraphs (1) and (2) do not apply to an obligation to the extent that it relates to a matter concerning only the flat or other unit concerned.

(4)   The obligations imposed on the RTM company by virtue of sub-paragraph (1) in relation to any lease are owed to the lessor (as well as to the lessee).

(5)   Subsections (3A) to (5) of section 11 have effect with the modifications that are appropriate in consequence of sub-paragraphs (1) to (3).

(6)   The references in subsection (6) of section 11 to the lessor include the RTM company; and a person who is in occupation of a flat or other unit contained in the premises otherwise than under a lease has, in relation to the flat or other unit, the same obligation as that imposed on a lessee by virtue of that subsection.

(7)   The reference to the lessor in section 12(1)(a) of the 1985 Act (restriction on contracting out of section 11) includes the RTM company.

### Service charges

4.—(1)   Sections 18 to 30 of the 1985 Act (service charges) have effect with the modifications provided by this paragraph.

(2)   References to the landlord are to the RTM company.

(3)   References to a tenant of a dwelling include a person who is landlord under a lease of the whole or any part of the premises (so that sums paid by him in pursuance of section 103 of this Act are service charges).

(4)   Section 22(5) applies as if paragraph (a) were omitted and the person referred to in paragraph (b) were a person who receives service charges on behalf of the RTM company.

(5)   Section 26 does not apply.

### Right to request information on insurance

5.—(1)   Section 30A of, and the Schedule to, the 1985 Act (rights of tenants with respect to insurance) have effect with the modifications provided by this paragraph.

(2)   References to the landlord are to the RTM company.

(3)   References to a tenant include a person who is landlord under a lease of the whole or any part of the premises and has to make payments under section 103 of this Act.

(4)   Paragraphs 2(3) and 3(3) of the Schedule apply as if paragraph (a) were omitted and the person referred to in paragraph (b) were a person who receives service charges on behalf of the RTM company.

### Managing agents

6.   Section 30B of the 1985 Act (recognised tenants' associations to be consulted about landlord's managing agents) has effect as if references to the landlord were to the RTM company (and as if subsection (6) were omitted).

### Right of first refusal

7.   Where section 5 of the 1987 Act (right of first refusal: requirement that landlord serve offer notice on tenant) requires the landlord to serve an offer notice on the qualifying tenants of the flats contained in the premises, he must serve a copy of the offer notice on the RTM company.

### Appointment of manager

8.—(1)   Part 2 of the 1987 Act (appointment of manager by leasehold valuation tribunal) has effect with the modifications provided by this paragraph.

(2)   References to the landlord are to the RTM company.

(3)   References to a tenant of a flat contained in the premises include a person who is landlord under a lease of the whole or any part of the premises.

(4)   Section 21(3) (exception for premises where landlord is exempt or resident or where premises are functional land of a charity) does not apply.

(5)   The references in paragraph (a)(i) of subsection (2) of section 24 to any obligation owed by the RTM company to the tenant under his tenancy include any obligations of the RTM company under this Act.

(6)   And the circumstances in which a leasehold valuation tribunal may make an order under paragraph (b) of that subsection include any in which the RTM company no longer wishes the right to manage the premises to be exercisable by it.

(7)   The power in section 24 to make an order appointing a manager to carry out functions includes a power (in the circumstances specified in subsection (2) of that section) to make an order that the right to manage the premises is to cease to be exercisable by the RTM company.

(8)   And such an order may include provision with respect to incidental and ancillary matters (including, in particular, provision about contracts to which the RTM company is a party and the prosecution of claims in respect of causes of action, whether tortious or contractual, accruing before or after the right to manage ceases to be exercisable).

*Right to acquire landlord's interest*
9.   Part 3 of the 1987 Act (compulsory acquisition by tenants of landlord's interest) does not apply.

*Variation of leases*
10.   Sections 35, 36, 38 and 39 of the 1987 Act (variation of long leases relating to flats) have effect as if references to a party to a long lease (apart from those in section 38(8)) included the RTM company.

*Service charges to be held in trust*
11.—(1)   Sections 42 to 42B of the 1987 Act (service charge contributions to be held in trust and in designated account) have effect with the modifications provided by this paragraph.

(2)   References to the payee are to the RTM company.

(3)   The definition of "tenant" in section 42(1) does not apply.

(4)   References to a tenant of a dwelling include a person who is landlord under a lease of the whole or any part of the premises.

(5)   The reference in section 42(2) to sums paid to the payee by the contributing tenants by way of relevant service charges includes payments made to the RTM company under section 94 or 103 of this Act.

(6)   Section 42A(5) applies as if paragraph (a) were omitted and the person referred to in paragraph (b) were a person who receives service charges on behalf of the RTM company.

*Information to be furnished to tenants*
12.—(1)   Sections 46 to 48 of the 1987 Act (information to be furnished to tenants) have effect with the modifications provided by this paragraph.

(2)   References to the landlord include the RTM company.

(3)   References to a tenant include a person who is landlord under a lease of the whole or any part of the premises; and in relation to such a person the reference in section 47(4) to sums payable to the landlord under the terms of the tenancy are to sums paid by him under section 103 of this Act.

*Statutory duties relating to certain covenants*
13.—(1)   The Landlord and Tenant Act 1988 (c 26) (statutory duties in connection with covenants against assigning etc) has effect with the modifications provided by this paragraph.

(2)   The reference in section 1(2)(b) to the covenant is to the covenant as it has effect subject to section 98 of this Act.

(3)   References in section 3(2), (4) and (5) to the landlord are to the RTM company.

*Tenants' right to management audit*
14.—(1)   Chapter 5 of Part 1 (tenants' right to management audit by landlord) of the Leasehold Reform, Housing and Urban Development Act 1993 (c 28) (referred to in this Part as "the 1993 Act") has effect with the modifications provided by this paragraph.

(2)   References to the landlord (other than the references in section 76(1) and (2) to "the same landlord") are to the RTM company.

(3)   References to a tenant include a person who is landlord under a lease of the whole or any part of the premises and has to make payments under section 103 of this Act.

(4)   Section 80(5) applies as if the reference to a person who receives rent were to a person who receives service charges.

*Right to appoint surveyor*

15.—(1)   Section 84 of the Housing Act 1996 (c 52) and Schedule 4 to that Act (apart from paragraph 7) (right of recognised tenants' association to appoint surveyor to advise on matters relating to service charges) have effect as if references to the landlord were to the RTM company.

(2)   Section 84(5) and paragraph 4(5) of Schedule 4 apply as if the reference to a person who receives rent were to a person who receives service charges.

*Administration charges*

16.   Schedule 11 to this Act has effect as if references to the landlord (or a party to a lease) included the RTM company.

**[1306]**

(*Sch 8 amends the Land Compensation Act 1973, s 12A and the Leasehold Reform, Housing and Urban Development Act 1993 at* **[803]** *et seq.*)

## SCHEDULE 9
### MEANING OF SERVICE CHARGE AND MANAGEMENT
Section 150

1–12.   ...

*Power to amend certain provisions*

13.   An order amending—
    (a)   any of the provisions amended by paragraphs 7 to 12, or
    (b)   section 27A(3) of the 1985 Act (as inserted by section 155),
may be made by the appropriate national authority for or in connection with altering the meaning of "service charge", "management" or "management functions".

**[1307]**

**NOTES**
    Paras 1–12: amend the Housing Act 1985, ss 450A, 450B, 458, 459, and s 621A at **[570]**, the Landlord and Tenant Act 1985, s 18 at **[610]**, the Landlord and Tenant Act 1987, ss 24, 29 at **[684]**, **[689]**, the Leasehold Reform, Housing and Urban Development Act 1993, ss 84, 87(8) at **[887]**, **[888]**, and the Housing Act 1996, Sch 4 at **[1120]**.

(*Sch 10 substitutes the Landlord and Tenant Act 1985, ss 23, 24 at* **[621]**, **[623]**, *inserts s 23A of that Act at* **[622]**, *and amends ss 25–27, 28, 39 of, and the Schedule to, that Act at* **[624]**–**[626]**, **[628]**, **[641]**, **[643]**, *amends the Landlord and Tenant Act 1987, ss 24, 42 at* **[684]**, **[702]**, *and the Leasehold Reform, Housing and Urban Development Act 1993, ss 79–82 at* **[882]**–**[885]**.)

## SCHEDULE 11
### ADMINISTRATION CHARGES
Section 158

## PART 1
### REASONABLENESS OF ADMINISTRATION CHARGES

*Meaning of "administration charge"*

1.—(1)   In this Part of this Schedule "administration charge" means an amount payable by a tenant of a dwelling as part of or in addition to the rent which is payable, directly or indirectly—
    (a)   for or in connection with the grant of approvals under his lease, or applications for such approvals,
    (b)   for or in connection with the provision of information or documents by or on behalf of the landlord or a person who is party to his lease otherwise than as landlord or tenant,
    (c)   in respect of a failure by the tenant to make a payment by the due date to the landlord or a person who is party to his lease otherwise than as landlord or tenant, or
    (d)   in connection with a breach (or alleged breach) of a covenant or condition in his lease.

(2)   But an amount payable by the tenant of a dwelling the rent of which is registered under Part 4 of the Rent Act 1977 (c 42) is not an administration charge, unless the amount registered is entered as a variable amount in pursuance of section 71(4) of that Act.

(3)   In this Part of this Schedule "variable administration charge" means an administration charge payable by a tenant which is neither—
    (a)   specified in his lease, nor
    (b)   calculated in accordance with a formula specified in his lease.

(4)   An order amending sub-paragraph (1) may be made by the appropriate national authority.

*Reasonableness of administration charges*

2. A variable administration charge is payable only to the extent that the amount of the charge is reasonable.

3.—(1) Any party to a lease of a dwelling may apply to a leasehold valuation tribunal for an order varying the lease in such manner as is specified in the application on the grounds that—
    (a) any administration charge specified in the lease is unreasonable, or
    (b) any formula specified in the lease in accordance with which any administration charge is calculated is unreasonable.

(2) If the grounds on which the application was made are established to the satisfaction of the tribunal, it may make an order varying the lease in such manner as is specified in the order.

(3) The variation specified in the order may be—
    (a) the variation specified in the application, or
    (b) such other variation as the tribunal thinks fit.

(4) The tribunal may, instead of making an order varying the lease in such manner as is specified in the order, make an order directing the parties to the lease to vary it in such manner as is so specified.

(5) The tribunal may by order direct that a memorandum of any variation of a lease effected by virtue of this paragraph be endorsed on such documents as are specified in the order.

(6) Any such variation of a lease shall be binding not only on the parties to the lease for the time being but also on other persons (including any predecessors in title), whether or not they were parties to the proceedings in which the order was made.

*Notice in connection with demands for administration charges*

4.—(1) A demand for the payment of an administration charge must be accompanied by a summary of the rights and obligations of tenants of dwellings in relation to administration charges.

(2) The appropriate national authority may make regulations prescribing requirements as to the form and content of such summaries of rights and obligations.

(3) A tenant may withhold payment of an administration charge which has been demanded from him if sub-paragraph (1) is not complied with in relation to the demand.

(4) Where a tenant withholds an administration charge under this paragraph, any provisions of the lease relating to non-payment or late payment of administration charges do not have effect in relation to the period for which he so withholds it.

*Liability to pay administration charges*

5.—(1) An application may be made to a leasehold valuation tribunal for a determination whether an administration charge is payable and, if it is, as to—
    (a) the person by whom it is payable,
    (b) the person to whom it is payable,
    (c) the amount which is payable,
    (d) the date at or by which it is payable, and
    (e) the manner in which it is payable.

(2) Sub-paragraph (1) applies whether or not any payment has been made.

(3) The jurisdiction conferred on a leasehold valuation tribunal in respect of any matter by virtue of sub-paragraph (1) is in addition to any jurisdiction of a court in respect of the matter.

(4) No application under sub-paragraph (1) may be made in respect of a matter which—
    (a) has been agreed or admitted by the tenant,
    (b) has been, or is to be, referred to arbitration pursuant to a post-dispute arbitration agreement to which the tenant is a party,
    (c) has been the subject of determination by a court, or
    (d) has been the subject of determination by an arbitral tribunal pursuant to a post-dispute arbitration agreement.

(5) But the tenant is not to be taken to have agreed or admitted any matter by reason only of having made any payment.

(6) An agreement by the tenant of a dwelling (other than a post-dispute arbitration agreement) is void in so far as it purports to provide for a determination—
    (a) in a particular manner, or
    (b) on particular evidence,
of any question which may be the subject matter of an application under sub-paragraph (1).

*Interpretation*

6.—(1)   This paragraph applies for the purposes of this Part of this Schedule.

(2)   "Tenant" includes a statutory tenant.

(3)   "Dwelling" and "statutory tenant" (and "landlord" in relation to a statutory tenant) have the same meanings as in the 1985 Act.

(4)   "Post-dispute arbitration agreement", in relation to any matter, means an arbitration agreement made after a dispute about the matter has arisen.

(5)   "Arbitration agreement" and "arbitral tribunal" have the same meanings as in Part 1 of the Arbitration Act 1996 (c 23).

**[1308]**

**NOTES**
Modified, where the RTM company has acquired the right to manage, by the Commonhold and Leasehold Reform Act 2002, s 102, Sch 7, para 16 at **[1266]**, **[1306]**.
Regulations: the Administration Charges (Summary of Rights and Obligations) (England) Regulations 2007, SI 2007/1258 at **[3763]**; the Administration Charges (Summary of Rights and Obligations) (Wales) Regulations 2007, SI 2007/3162 at **[3777]**.

(*Pt 2 amends the Landlord and Tenant Act 1987, ss 24, 46–48 at* **[684]**, **[705]**–**[707]**.)

SCHEDULE 12
LEASEHOLD VALUATION TRIBUNALS: PROCEDURE
Section 174

*Procedure regulations*

1.   The appropriate national authority may make regulations about the procedure of leasehold valuation tribunals ("procedure regulations").

*Applications*

2.   Procedure regulations may include provision—
   (a)   about the form of applications to leasehold valuation tribunals,
   (b)   about the particulars that must be contained in such applications,
   (c)   requiring the service of notices of such applications, and
   (d)   for securing consistency where numerous applications are or may be brought in respect of the same or substantially the same matters.

*Transfers*

3.—(1)   Where in any proceedings before a court there falls for determination a question falling within the jurisdiction of a leasehold valuation tribunal, the court—
   (a)   may by order transfer to a leasehold valuation tribunal so much of the proceedings as relate to the determination of that question, and
   (b)   may then dispose of all or any remaining proceedings, or adjourn the disposal of all or any remaining proceedings pending the determination of that question by the leasehold valuation tribunal, as it thinks fit.

(2)   When the leasehold valuation tribunal has determined the question, the court may give effect to the determination in an order of the court.

(3)   Rules of court may prescribe the procedure to be followed in a court in connection with or in consequence of a transfer under this paragraph.

(4)   Procedure regulations may prescribe the procedure to be followed in a leasehold valuation tribunal consequent on a transfer under this paragraph.

*Information*

4.—(1)   A leasehold valuation tribunal may serve a notice requiring any party to proceedings before it to give to the leasehold valuation tribunal any information which the leasehold valuation tribunal may reasonably require.

(2)   The information shall be given to the leasehold valuation tribunal within such period (not being less than 14 days) from the service of the notice as is specified in the notice.

(3)   A person commits an offence if he fails, without reasonable excuse, to comply with a notice served on him under sub-paragraph (1).

(4)   A person guilty of an offence under sub-paragraph (3) is liable on summary conviction to a fine not exceeding level 3 on the standard scale.

*Pre-trial reviews*

5.—(1)   Procedure regulations may include provision for the holding of a pre-trial review (on the application of a party to proceedings or on the motion of a leasehold valuation tribunal).

(2)   Procedure regulations may provide for the exercise of the functions of a leasehold valuation tribunal in relation to, or at, a pre-trial review by a single member of the panel provided for in Schedule 10 to the Rent Act 1977 (c 42) who is qualified to exercise them.

(3)   A member is qualified to exercise the functions specified in sub-paragraph (2) if he was appointed to that panel by the Lord Chancellor.

*Parties*

6.   Procedure regulations may include provision enabling persons to be joined as parties to proceedings.

*Dismissal*

7.   Procedure regulations may include provision empowering leasehold valuation tribunals to dismiss applications or transferred proceedings, in whole or in part, on the ground that they are—
  (a)   frivolous or vexatious, or
  (b)   otherwise an abuse of process.

*Determination without hearing*

8.—(1)   Procedure regulations may include provision for the determination of applications or transferred proceedings without an oral hearing.

(2)   Procedure regulations may provide for the determinations without an oral hearing by a single member of the panel provided for in Schedule 10 to the Rent Act 1977.

*Fees*

9.—(1)   Procedure regulations may include provision requiring the payment of fees in respect of an application or transfer of proceedings to, or oral hearing by, a leasehold valuation tribunal in a case under—
  (a)   the 1985 Act (service charges and choice of insurers),
  (b)   Part 2 of the 1987 Act (managers),
  (c)   Part 4 of the 1987 Act (variation of leases),
  (d)   section 168(4) of this Act, or
  (e)   Schedule 11 to this Act.

(2)   Procedure regulations may empower a leasehold valuation tribunal to require a party to proceedings to reimburse any other party to the proceedings the whole or part of any fees paid by him.

(3)   The fees payable shall be such as are specified in or determined in accordance with procedure regulations; but the fee (or, where fees are payable in respect of both an application or transfer and an oral hearing, the aggregate of the fees) payable by a person in respect of any proceedings shall not exceed—
  (a)   £500, or
  (b)   such other amount as may be specified in procedure regulations.

(4)   Procedure regulations may provide for the reduction or waiver of fees by reference to the financial resources of the party by whom they are to be paid or met.

(5)   If they do so they may apply, subject to such modifications as may be specified in the regulations, any other statutory means-testing regime as it has effect from time to time.

*Costs*

10.—(1)   A leasehold valuation tribunal may determine that a party to proceedings shall pay the costs incurred by another party in connection with the proceedings in any circumstances falling within sub-paragraph (2).

(2)   The circumstances are where—
  (a)   he has made an application to the leasehold valuation tribunal which is dismissed in accordance with regulations made by virtue of paragraph 7, or
  (b)   he has, in the opinion of the leasehold valuation tribunal, acted frivolously, vexatiously, abusively, disruptively or otherwise unreasonably in connection with the proceedings.

(3)   The amount which a party to proceedings may be ordered to pay in the proceedings by a determination under this paragraph shall not exceed—
  (a)   £500, or
  (b)   such other amount as may be specified in procedure regulations.

(4)   A person shall not be required to pay costs incurred by another person in connection with proceedings before a leasehold valuation tribunal except by a determination under this paragraph or in accordance with provision made by any enactment other than this paragraph.

*Enforcement*

11.   Procedure regulations may provide for decisions of leasehold valuation tribunals to be enforceable, with the permission of a county court, in the same way as orders of such a court.

**[1309]**

**NOTES**
   Regulations: the Leasehold Valuation Tribunals (Fees) (England) Regulations 2003, SI 2003/2098 at **[3310]**; the Leasehold Valuation Tribunals (Procedure) (England) Regulations 2003, SI 2003/2099 at **[3319]**; the Leasehold Valuation Tribunals (Procedure) (Wales) Regulations 2004, SI 2004/681 at **[3363]**; the Leasehold Valuation Tribunals (Fees) (Wales) Regulations 2004, SI 2004/683 at **[3364]**.

*(Schs 13, 14 contain amendments and repeals which, in so far as within the scope of this work, have been incorporated at the appropriate place.)*

# FINANCE ACT 2003

## (2003 c 14)

### ARRANGEMENT OF SECTIONS

### PART 4
### STAMP DUTY LAND TAX

*Chargeable interests, chargeable transactions and chargeable consideration*

*Reliefs*

*Interpretation etc*

### PART 5
### STAMP DUTY

### PART 9
### MISCELLANEOUS AND SUPPLEMENTARY PROVISIONS

*Supplementary*

*An Act to grant certain duties, to alter other duties, and to amend the law relating to the National Debt and the Public Revenue, and to make further provision in connection with finance*

**[10 July 2003]**

**1–41**   *((Pts 1–3) outside the scope of this work.)*

PART 4
STAMP DUTY LAND TAX

**42–47**   (*Outside the scope of this work.*)

*Chargeable interests, chargeable transactions and chargeable consideration*

**48**   (*Outside the scope of this work.*)

### 49  Chargeable transactions

(1)   A land transaction is a chargeable transaction if it is not a transaction that is exempt from charge.

(2)   Schedule 3 provides for certain transactions to be exempt from charge.

Other transactions are exempt from charge under other provisions of this Part.

**[1310]**

**NOTES**

The date appointed as the implementation date for the purposes of stamp duty land tax is 1 December 2003: see the Stamp Duty Land Tax (Appointment of the Implementation Date) Order 2003, SI 2003/2899, art 2.

**50–56**   (*Outside the scope of this work.*)

*Reliefs*

**57–69**   (*Outside the scope of this work.*)

### 70  Right to buy transactions, shared ownership leases etc

Schedule 9 makes provision for relief in the case of right to buy transactions, shared ownership leases and certain related transactions.

**[1311]**

**NOTES**

The date appointed as the implementation date for the purposes of stamp duty land tax is 1 December 2003: see the Stamp Duty Land Tax (Appointment of the Implementation Date) Order 2003, SI 2003/2899, art 2.

### 71  Certain acquisitions by registered social landlord

[(A1)   A land transaction under which the purchaser is a profit-making registered provider of social housing is exempt from charge if the transaction is funded with the assistance of a public subsidy.]

(1)   A land transaction under which the purchaser is a *registered social landlord* is exempt from charge if—

(a)   the *registered social landlord* is controlled by its tenants,
(b)   the vendor is a qualifying body, or
(c)   the transaction is funded with the assistance of a public subsidy.

[(1A)   In this section "relevant housing provider" means—
(a)   a non-profit registered provider of social housing, or
(b)   a registered social landlord.]

(2)   The reference in subsection (1)(a) to a *registered social landlord* "controlled by its tenants" is to a *registered social landlord* the majority of whose board members are tenants occupying properties owned or managed by it.

"Board member", in relation to a *registered social landlord*, means—
(a)   if it is a company, a director of the company,
(b)   if it is a body corporate whose affairs are managed by its members, a member,
(c)   if it is body of trustees, a trustee,
(d)   if it is not within paragraphs (a) to (c), a member of the committee of management or other body to which is entrusted the direction of the affairs of the *registered social landlord*.

(3)   In subsection (1)(b) "qualifying body" means—
(a)   a *registered social landlord*,
(b)   a housing action trust established under Part 3 of the Housing Act 1988 (c 50),
(c)   a principal council within the meaning of the Local Government Act 1972 (c 70),
(d)   the Common Council of the City of London,
(e)   the Scottish Ministers,
(f)   a council constituted under section 2 of the Local Government etc (Scotland) Act 1994 (c 39),

    (g)    Scottish Homes,

    (h)    the Department for Social Development in Northern Ireland, or

    (i)    the Northern Ireland Housing Executive.

  (4)   In [this section] "public subsidy" means any grant or other financial assistance—

    (a)    made or given by way of a distribution pursuant to section 25 of the National Lottery etc Act 1993 (c 39) (application of money by distributing bodies),

    (b)    under section 18 of the Housing Act 1996 (c 52) (social housing grants),

    (c)    under section 126 of the Housing Grants, Construction and Regeneration Act 1996 (c 53) (financial assistance for regeneration and development),

    [(ca)    under section 19 of the Housing and Regeneration Act 2008 (financial assistance by the Homes and Communities Agency),]

    (d)    under section 2 of the Housing (Scotland) Act 1988 (c 43) (general functions of the Scottish Ministers), or

    (e)    under Article 33 [or 33A] of the Housing (Northern Ireland) Order 1992 (SI 1992/1725 (NI 15)).

**[1312]**

**NOTES**

Sub-s (A1): inserted by the Finance Act 2009, s 81(1)–(3), (8), with effect in relation to transactions with an effective date on or after 21 July 2009.

Sub-ss (1), (2), (3): for the words in italics in each place they appear, there are substituted the words "relevant housing provider" by the Housing and Regeneration Act 2008, s 277, Sch 9, paras 29, 30(1), (2), as from a day to be appointed.

Sub-s (1A): inserted by the Housing and Regeneration Act 2008, s 277, Sch 9, paras 29, 30(1), (3), as from a day to be appointed.

Sub-s (4): words in first pair of square brackets substituted by the Finance Act 2009, s 81(1), (2), (4), (8), with effect in relation to transactions with an effective date on or after 21 July 2009; para (ca) inserted by the Housing and Regeneration Act 2008, s 56, Sch 8, paras 78, 79, as from a day to be appointed; words in square brackets in para (e) inserted by the Housing (Amendment) (Northern Ireland) Order 2006, SI 2006/3337, art 3, Schedule, para 8.

The date appointed as the implementation date for the purposes of stamp duty land tax is 1 December 2003: see the Stamp Duty Land Tax (Appointment of the Implementation Date) Order 2003, SI 2003/2899, art 2.

---

**71A–73C**    *(Outside the scope of this work.)*

**[74    Exercise of collective rights by tenants of flats]**

  [(1)   This section applies where a chargeable transaction is entered into by a person or persons nominated or appointed by qualifying tenants of flats contained in premises in exercise of—

    (a)    a right under Part 1 of the Landlord and Tenant Act 1987 (right of first refusal), or

    (b)    a right under Chapter 1 of Part 1 of the Leasehold Reform, Housing and Urban Development Act 1993 (right to collective enfranchisement).]

  (2)   ... The rate of tax is determined by reference to the fraction of the relevant consideration produced by dividing the total amount of that consideration by the number of [qualifying flats contained in the premises].

  (3)   The tax chargeable is then determined by applying that rate to the chargeable consideration for the transaction.

  [(4)   In this section—

    "flat" and "qualifying tenant" have the same meaning as in the Chapter or Part of the Act conferring the right being exercised;

    "qualifying flat" means a flat that is held by a qualifying tenant who is participating in the exercise of the right.]

  (5)   References in this section to the relevant consideration have the same meaning as in section 55.

**[1313]**

---

**NOTES**

Section heading: substituted by the Finance Act 2009, s 80(1), (5), (7), with effect in relation to transactions with an effective date on or after 22 April 2009.

Sub-s (1): substituted by the Finance Act 2009, s 80(1), (2), (7), with effect in relation to transactions with an effective date on or after 22 April 2009.

Sub-s (2): words omitted repealed and words in square brackets substituted by the Finance Act 2009, s 80(1), (3), (7), with effect in relation to transactions with an effective date on or after 22 April 2009.

Sub-s (4): substituted by the Finance Act 2009, s 80(1), (4), (7), with effect in relation to transactions with an effective date on or after 22 April 2009.

The date appointed as the implementation date for the purposes of stamp duty land tax is 1 December 2003: see the Stamp Duty Land Tax (Appointment of the Implementation Date) Order 2003, SI 2003/2899, art 2.

---

**75–115**    *(Outside the scope of this work.)*

*Interpretation etc*

**116–120** (*Outside the scope of this work.*)

## 121 Minor definitions

In this Part—
"assignment", in Scotland, means assignation;
"completion", in Scotland, means—
    (a)   in relation to a lease, when it is executed by the parties (that is to say, by signing) or constituted by any means;
    (b)   in relation to any other transaction, the settlement of the transaction;
"employee" includes an office-holder and related expressions have a corresponding meaning;
["HMRC" means Her Majesty's Revenue and Customs;]
"jointly entitled" means—
    (a)   in England and Wales, beneficially entitled as joint tenants or tenants in common,
    (b)   in Scotland, entitled as joint owners or owners in common,
    (c)   in Northern Ireland, beneficially entitled as joint tenants, tenants in common or coparceners;
"land" includes—
    (a)   buildings and structures, and
    (b)   land covered by water;
"registered social landlord" means—
    (a)   in relation to England and Wales, a body registered as a social landlord in a register maintained under section 1(1) of the Housing Act 1996 (c 52);
    (b)   in relation to Scotland, a body registered in the register maintained under section 57 of the Housing (Scotland) Act 2001 (asp 10);
    (c)   in relation to Northern Ireland, a housing association registered in the register maintained under Article 14 of the Housing (Northern Ireland) Order 1992 (SI 1992/1725 (NI 15));
"standard security" has the meaning given by the Conveyancing and Feudal Reform (Scotland) Act 1970 (c 35);
"statutory provision" means any provision made by or under an Act of Parliament, an Act of the Scottish Parliament or any Northern Ireland legislation;
"surrender", in Scotland, means renunciation;
"tax", unless the context otherwise requires, means tax under this Part.
["tribunal" means the First-tier Tribunal or, where determined by or under Tribunal Procedure Rules, the Upper Tribunal].

**[1314]**

### NOTES
Definitions "HMRC" and "tribunal" inserted by the Transfer of Tribunal Functions and Revenue and Customs Appeals Order 2009, SI 2009/56, art 3(1), Sch 1, paras 359, 371, subject to transitional and savings provisions in Sch 3, paras 1, 6–8, 12, 13 thereto.
The date appointed as the implementation date for the purposes of stamp duty land tax is 1 December 2003: see the Stamp Duty Land Tax (Appointment of the Implementation Date) Order 2003, SI 2003/2899, art 2.

## 122 Index of defined expressions

In this Part the expressions listed below are defined or otherwise explained by the provisions indicated—

| | |
|---|---|
| acquisition relief | Schedule 7, paragraph 8(1) |
| assignment (in Scotland) | section 121 |
| bare trust | Schedule 16, paragraph 1(2) |
| the Board (in relation to the Inland Revenue) | section 42(3) |
| chargeable consideration | section 50 and Schedule 4 |
| chargeable interest | section 48(1) |
| chargeable transaction | section 49 |
| charities relief | Schedule 8, paragraph 1(1) |
| closure notice | Schedule 10, paragraph 23(1) (in relation to a land transaction return); … |

| | |
|---|---|
| company | section 100 (except as otherwise expressly provided) |
| completion (in Scotland) | section 121 |
| contingent (in relation to consideration) | section 51(3) |
| delivery (in relation to a land transaction return) | Schedule 10, paragraph 2(2) |
| discovery assessment | Schedule 10, paragraph 28(1) |
| effective date (in relation to a land transaction) | section 119 |
| employee | section 121 |
| exempt interest | section 48(2) to (5) |
| filing date (in relation to a land transaction return) | Schedule 10, paragraph 2(1) |
| implementation date | Schedule 19, paragraph 2(2) |
| the Inland Revenue | section 113 |
| jointly entitled | section 121 |
| land | section 121 |
| land transaction | section 43(1) |
| land transaction return | section 76(1) |
| lease (and related expressions) | [Schedule 17A] |
| linked transactions | section 108 |
| main subject-matter (in relation to a land transaction) | section 43(6) |
| major interest (in relation to land) | section 117 |
| market value | section 118 |
| notice of enquiry | Schedule 10, paragraph 12(1) (in relation to a land transaction return); ... |
| notifiable (in relation to a land transaction) | section 77 [(see too sections 71A(7) and 72A(7) [and paragraph 30 of Schedule 15])] |
| partnership (and related expressions) | Schedule 15, paragraphs 1 to 4 |
| purchaser | section 43(4) |
| rate of tax | section 55(7) |
| reconstruction relief | Schedule 7, paragraph 7(1) |
| registered social landlord | section 121 |
| residential property | section 116 |
| [Revenue certificate | section 79(3)(a)] |
| Revenue determination | Schedule 10, paragraph 25(1) |
| self-assessment | section 76(3)(a) |
| ... | ... |
| settlement | Schedule 16, paragraph 1(1) |
| standard security | section 121 |
| statutory provision | section 121 |
| subject-matter (in relation to a land transaction) | section 43(6) |
| substantial performance (in relation to a contract) | section 44(5) to (7) |
| surrender (in Scotland) | section 121 |
| tax | section 121 |
| [tribunal | section 121] |
| uncertain (in relation to consideration) | section 51(3) |

| unit holder | section 101(4) |
| unit trust scheme | section 101(4) |
| vendor | section 43(4) [(see too sections 45(5A) and 45A(9))] |

**[1315]**

---

**NOTES**

Words omitted from entries "closure notice" and "notice of enquiry" repealed and entry "self-certificate" (omitted) repealed by the Finance Act 2008, s 94(4), (5), Sch 30, paras 1, 5(1)–(3), (5), with effect in relation to transactions with an effective date on or after 12 March 2008.

In entry "lease (and related expressions)" words in square brackets substituted by the Finance Act 2004, s 296, Sch 39, Pt 2, para 22(7), in relation to any transaction of which the effective date is on or after 22 July 2004.

In entry "notifiable" words in first (outer) pair of square brackets inserted by the Finance Act 2005, s 94, Sch 8, paras 1, 6, with effect in any case where the effective date of the first transaction, within the meaning of ss 71A, 72A of this Act, falls on or after 7 April 2005; words in second (inner) pair of square brackets inserted by the Finance Act 2008, s 94(4), (5), Sch 30, paras 1, 5(1), (4), (5), with effect in relation to transactions with an effective date on or after 12 March 2008.

Entry "Revenue certificate" inserted by the Finance Act 2004, s 296, Sch 39, Pt 2, para 25(4), in relation to any transaction of which the effective date is on or after 22 July 2004.

Entry "tribunal" inserted by the Transfer of Tribunal Functions and Revenue and Customs Appeals Order 2009, SI 2009/56, art 3(1), Sch 1, paras 359, 372, subject to transitional and savings provisions in Sch 3, paras 1, 6–8, 12, 13 thereto.

In entry "vendor" words in square brackets inserted by the Finance Act 2004, s 296, Sch 39, Pt 1, paras 1, 5(1), (6), in relation to any transfer of rights occurring after 17 March 2004.

The date appointed as the implementation date for the purposes of stamp duty land tax is 1 December 2003: see the Stamp Duty Land Tax (Appointment of the Implementation Date) Order 2003, SI 2003/2899, art 2.

---

*Final provisions*

**123**   (*Outside the scope of this work.*)

**124   Commencement and transitional provisions**

Schedule 19 makes provision for and in connection with the coming into force of the provisions of this Part.

**[1316]**

PART 5
STAMP DUTY

**125–127**   (*Outside the scope of this work.*)

**128   Exemption of certain leases granted by registered social landlords**

(1)   No stamp duty is chargeable under Part 2 of Schedule 13 to the Finance Act 1999 (c 16) on a lease of a dwelling granted by a registered social landlord to one or more individuals in accordance with arrangements to which this section applies if the lease is for an indefinite term or is terminable by notice of a month or less.

(2)   "Registered social landlord" means—
   (a)   in relation to England and Wales, a body registered in the register maintained under section 1(1) of the Housing Act 1996 (c 52);
   (b)   in relation to Scotland, a body registered in the register maintained under section 57 of the Housing (Scotland) Act 2001 (asp 10);
   (c)   in relation to Northern Ireland, a housing association registered in the register maintained under Article 14 of the Housing (Northern Ireland) Order 1992 (SI 1992/1725 (NI 15)).

(3)   This section applies to arrangements between a registered social landlord and a housing authority under which the landlord provides, for individuals nominated by the authority in pursuance of its statutory housing functions, temporary rented accommodation which the landlord itself has obtained on a short-term basis.

The reference above to accommodation obtained by the landlord "on a short-term basis" is to accommodation leased to the landlord for a term of five years or less.

(4)   A "housing authority" means—
   (a)   in relation to England and Wales—
     (i)   a principal council within the meaning of the Local Government Act 1972 (c 70), or
     (ii)   the Common Council of the City of London;

(b)　in relation to Scotland, a council constituted under section 2 of the Local Government etc (Scotland) Act 1994 (c 39);

(c)　in relation to Northern Ireland—

(i)　the Department for Social Development in Northern Ireland, or

(ii)　the Northern Ireland Housing Executive.

(5)　An instrument on which stamp duty is not chargeable by virtue only of this section shall not be taken to be duly stamped unless—

(a)　it is stamped with the duty to which it would be liable but for this section, or

(b)　it has, in accordance with section 12 of the Stamp Act 1891 (c 39), been stamped with a particular stamp denoting that it is not chargeable with any duty.

(6)　This section shall be construed as one with the Stamp Act 1891.

(7)　This section applies to instruments executed after the day on which this Act is passed.

**[1317]**

### 129　Relief for certain leases granted before section 128 has effect

(1)　This section applies to instruments that—

(a)　are executed in the period beginning with 1 January 2000 and ending with the day on which this Act is passed, and

(b)　are instruments to which section 128 (exemption of certain leases granted by registered social landlords) would have applied if that provision had been in force when the instrument was executed.

(2)　If the instrument is not stamped until after the day on which this Act is passed, the law in force at the time of its execution shall be deemed for stamp duty purposes to be what it would have been if section 128 had been in force at that time.

(3)　If the Commissioners are satisfied that—

(a)　the instrument was stamped on or before the day on which this Act is passed,

(b)　stamp duty was chargeable in respect of it, and

(c)　had it been stamped after that day stamp duty would, by virtue of section 128, not have been chargeable,

they shall pay to such person as they consider appropriate an amount equal to the duty (and any interest or penalty) that would not have been payable if that section had been in force at the time the instrument was executed.

(4)　Any such payment must be claimed before 1st January 2004.

(5)　Entitlement to a payment is subject to compliance with such conditions as the Commissioners may determine with respect to the production of the instrument, to its being stamped so as to indicate that it has been produced under this section or to other matters.

(6)　For the purposes of [section 44 of the Commissioners for Revenue and Customs Act 2005 (payment into Consolidated Fund)] any amount paid under this section is a repayment.

(7)　This section shall be construed as one with the Stamp Act 1891.

(8)　For the purposes of this section as it applies in relation to instruments executed before the coming into force of section 57 of the Housing (Scotland) Act 2001 (asp 10), the references in section 128 to a registered social landlord shall be read in relation to Scotland as references to—

(a)　a housing association registered in the register maintained under section 3(1) of the Housing Associations Act 1985 (c 69) by Scottish Homes, or

(b)　a body corporate whose objects corresponded to those of a housing association and which, pursuant to a contract with Scottish Homes, was registered in a register kept for the purpose by Scottish Homes.

**[1318]**

**NOTES**

Sub-s (6): words in square brackets substituted by the Commissioners for Revenue and Customs Act 2005, s 50(6), Sch 4, paras 125, 126.

### 130　Registered social landlords: treatment of certain leases granted between 1st January 1990 and 27 March 2000

(1)　This section applies to a lease in relation to which the following conditions are met—

(a)　it is a lease of a dwelling to one or more individuals;

(b)　it is for an indefinite term or is terminable by notice of a month or less;

(c)　it was executed on or after 1st January 1990 and before 28th March 2000;

(d)　at the time it was executed the rate or average rate of the rent (whether reserved as a yearly rent or not) was £5,000 a year or less; and

(e)　the landlord's interest has at any time before 26th June 2003 been held by a registered social landlord.

(2)   A lease to which this section applies (whether or not presented for stamping) shall be treated—

    (a)    for the purposes of section 14 of the Stamp Act 1891 (c 39) (production of instrument in evidence) as it applies in relation to proceedings begun after the day on which this Act is passed, and

    (b)    for the purposes of section 17 of that Act (enrolment etc of instrument) as it applies to any act done after that day,

as if it had been duly stamped in accordance with the law in force at the time when it was executed.

(3)   If in the case of a lease to which this section applies the Commissioners are satisfied—

    (a)    that the instrument was stamped on or before the day on which this Act is passed, and

    (b)    that stamp duty was charged in respect of it,

they shall pay to such person as they consider appropriate an amount equal to the duty (and any interest or penalty) so charged.

(4)   Any such payment must be claimed before 1st January 2004.

(5)   Entitlement to a payment under subsection (3) is subject to compliance with such conditions as the Commissioners may determine with respect to the production of the instrument, to its being stamped so as to indicate that it has been produced under this section or to other matters.

(6)   For the purposes of [section 44 of the Commissioners for Revenue and Customs Act 2005 (payment into Consolidated Fund)] any amount paid under subsection (3) above is a repayment.

(7)   This section shall be construed as one with the Stamp Act 1891.

(8)   The reference in subsection (1) above to the landlord's interest being held by a "registered social landlord" is to its being held by a body that—

    (a)    is registered in a register maintained under—

        (i)    Article 124 of the Housing (Northern Ireland) Order 1981 (SI 1981/156 (NI 3)),

        (ii)    section 3(1) of the Housing Associations Act 1985 (c 69),

        (iii)    Article 14 of the Housing (Northern Ireland) Order 1992 (SI 1992/1725 (NI 15)),

        (iv)    section 1(1) of the Housing Act 1996 (c 52), or

        (v)    section 57 of the Housing (Scotland) Act 2001 (asp 10), or

    (b)    is a body corporate whose objects correspond to those of a housing association and which, pursuant to a contract with Scottish Homes, is registered in a register kept for the purposes by Scottish Homes.

(9)   Section 129 of this Act (relief for certain leases granted on or after 1st January 2000) does not apply to a lease to which this section applies.

**[1319]**

---

**NOTES**

Sub-s (6): words in square brackets substituted by the Commissioners for Revenue and Customs Act 2005, s 50(6), Sch 4, paras 125, 127.

---

**131–194**   ((*Pts 6–8*) *Outside the scope of this work.*)

## PART 9
## MISCELLANEOUS AND SUPPLEMENTARY PROVISIONS

**195–214**   (*Outside the scope of this work.*)

*Supplementary*

**215, 216**   (*Outside the scope of this work.*)

**217   Short title**

This Act may be cited as the Finance Act 2003.

**[1320]**

(*Schs 1, 2 outside the scope of this work.*)

## SCHEDULE 3
## STAMP DUTY LAND TAX: TRANSACTIONS EXEMPT FROM CHARGE

Section 49

1.   (*Outside the scope of this work.*)

*Grant of certain leases by registered social landlords*

2.—(1)   The grant of a lease of a dwelling is exempt from charge if the lease—

(a)    is granted by a *registered social landlord* to one or more individuals in accordance with arrangements to which this paragraph applies, and

(b)    is for an indefinite term or is terminable by notice of a month or less.

(2)    This paragraph applies to arrangements between a *registered social landlord* and a housing authority under which the *landlord* provides, for individuals nominated by the authority in pursuance of its statutory housing functions, temporary rented accommodation which the *landlord* itself has obtained on a short-term basis.

The reference above to accommodation obtained by the *landlord* "on a short-term basis" is to accommodation leased to the *landlord* for a term of five years or less.

[(2A)    A "relevant housing provider" means—
(a)    a non-profit registered provider of social housing, or
(b)    a registered social landlord.]

(3)    A "housing authority" means—
(a)    in relation to England and Wales—
(i)    a principal council within the meaning of the Local Government Act 1972 (c 70), or
(ii)    the Common Council of the City of London;
(b)    in relation to Scotland, a council constituted under section 2 of the Local Government etc (Scotland) Act 1994 (c 39);
(c)    in relation to Northern Ireland—
(i)    the Department for Social Development in Northern Ireland, or
(ii)    the Northern Ireland Housing Executive.

3–5.    (*Outside the scope of this work.*)

**[1321]**

## NOTES

Para 2: for the words in italics in each place they appear there are substituted the words "relevant housing provider" and sub-para (2A) inserted by the Housing and Regeneration Act 2008, s 277, Sch 9, paras 29, 31, as from a day to be appointed.

(*Schs 4–8 outside the scope of this work.*)

## SCHEDULE 9
### STAMP DUTY LAND TAX: RIGHT TO BUY, SHARED OWNERSHIP LEASES ETC
Section 70

*Right to buy transactions*

1.—(1)    In the case of a right to buy transaction—
(a)    section 51(1) (contingent consideration to be included in chargeable consideration on assumption that contingency will occur) does not apply, and
(b)    any consideration that would be payable only if a contingency were to occur, or that is payable only because a contingency has occurred, does not count as chargeable consideration.

(2)    A "right to buy transaction" means—
(a)    the sale of a dwelling at a discount, or the grant of a lease of a dwelling at a discount, by a relevant public sector body, or
(b)    the sale of a dwelling, or the grant of a lease of a dwelling, in pursuance of the preserved right to buy.

(3)    The following are relevant public sector bodies for the purposes of sub-paragraph (2)(a):

*Government*

A Minister of the Crown
The Scottish Ministers
A Northern Ireland department

*Local Government*

A local housing authority within the meaning of the Housing Act 1985 (c 68)
A county council in England
A council constituted under section 2 of the Local Government etc (Scotland) Act 1994 (c 39), the common good of such a council or any trust under its control
A district council within the meaning of the Local Government Act (Northern Ireland) 1972 (c 9 (NI))

*Social housing*

*The Housing Corporation*
Scottish Homes
The Northern Ireland Housing Executive
[A non-profit registered provider of social housing]

A registered social landlord

A housing action trust established under Part 3 of the Housing Act 1988 (c 50)

*New towns and development corporations [etc]*

The [Homes and Communities Agency]

A development corporation established by an order made, or having effect as if made, under the New Towns Act 1981 (c 64)

A development corporation established by an order made, or having effect as if made, under the New Towns (Scotland) Act 1968 (c 16)

A new town commission established under section 7 of the New Towns Act (Northern Ireland) 1965 (c 13 (NI))

An urban development corporation established by an order made under section 135 of the Local Government, Planning and Land Act 1980 (c 65)

...

*Police*

A police authority within the meaning of section 101(1) of the Police Act 1996 (c 16)

A police authority within the meaning of section 2(1) or 19(9)(b) of the Police (Scotland) Act 1967 (c 77)

The Northern Ireland Policing Board

*Miscellaneous*

An Education and Libraries Board within the meaning of the Education and Libraries (Northern Ireland) Order 1986 (SI 1986/594 (NI 3))

The United Kingdom Atomic Energy Authority

Any person mentioned in paragraphs (g), (k), (l) or (n) of section 61(11) of the Housing (Scotland) Act 1987 (c 26)

A body prescribed for the purposes of this sub-paragraph by Treasury order.

(4)    For the purposes of sub-paragraph (2)(b) the transfer of a dwelling, or the grant of a lease of a dwelling, is made in pursuance of the preserved right to buy if—

    (a)   the vendor is—

        (i)   in England and Wales, a person against whom the right to buy under Part 5 of the Housing Act 1985 (c 68) is exercisable by virtue of section 171A of that Act, or

        (ii)   in Scotland, a person against whom the right to buy under section 61 of the Housing (Scotland) Act 1987 is exercisable by virtue of section 81A of that Act, (which provide for the preservation of the right to buy on disposal to a private sector landlord),

    (b)   the purchaser is the qualifying person for the purposes of the preserved right to buy, and

    (c)   the dwelling is the qualifying dwelling-house in relation to the purchaser.

(5)    A grant under section 20 or 21 of the Housing Act 1996 (c 52) (purchase grants in respect of disposals at a discount by registered social landlords) does not count as part of the chargeable consideration for a right to buy transaction in relation to which the vendor is a registered social landlord [or registered provider of social housing].

[(6)    A grant under section 19 of the Housing and Regeneration Act 2008 which—

    (a)   is made by virtue of section 35 of that Act, or

    (b)   is otherwise made to a relevant provider of social housing (within the meaning of section 35 of that Act) in respect of discounts given by the provider on disposals of dwellings to tenants,

does not count as part of the chargeable consideration for a right to buy transaction to which the vendor is a relevant provider of social housing.]

*Shared ownership lease: election for market value treatment*

2.—(1)    This paragraph applies where—

    (a)   a lease is granted—

        (i)   by a qualifying body, or

        (ii)   in pursuance of the preserved right to buy,

    (b)   the conditions in sub-paragraph (2) are met, and

    (c)   the purchaser elects for tax to be charged in accordance with this paragraph.

(2)    The conditions are as follows—

    (a)   the lease must be of a dwelling;

    (b)   the lease must give the lessee or lessees exclusive use of the dwelling;

    (c)   the lease must provide for the lessee or lessees to acquire the reversion;

    (d)   the lease must be granted partly in consideration of rent and partly in consideration of a premium calculated by reference to—

        (i)   the market value of the dwelling, or

        (ii)   a sum calculated by reference to that value;

    (e)   the lease must contain a statement of—

        (i)   the market value of the dwelling, or

        (ii)   the sum calculated by reference to that value,

by reference to which the premium is calculated.

(3)    An election for tax to be charged in accordance with this paragraph must be included in the land transaction return made in respect of the grant of the lease, or in an amendment of that return, and is irrevocable, so that the return may not be amended so as to withdraw the election.

(4)    Where this paragraph applies the chargeable consideration for the grant of the lease shall be taken to be the amount stated in the lease in accordance with sub-paragraph (2)(e)(i) or (ii).

As to the tax treatment of the acquisition of the reversion in pursuance of the lease, see paragraph 3.

[(4A)    Where this paragraph applies no account shall be taken for the purposes of stamp duty land tax of the rent mentioned in sub-paragraph (2)(d).]

(5)    Section 118 (meaning of "market value") does not apply in relation to the reference in sub-paragraph (2)(e) above to the market value of the dwelling.

*Transfer of reversion under shared ownership lease where election made for market value treatment*

3.    The transfer of the reversion to the lessee or lessees under the terms of a lease to which paragraph 2 applies (shared ownership lease: election for market value treatment) is exempt from charge if—

    (a)    an election was made for tax to be charged in accordance with that paragraph, and

    (b)    any tax chargeable in respect of the grant of the lease has been paid.

*Shared ownership lease: election where staircasing allowed*

4.—(1)    This paragraph applies where—

    (a)    a lease is granted by a qualifying body or in pursuance of the preserved right to buy,

    (b)    the conditions in sub-paragraph (2) below are met, and

    (c)    the purchaser elects for tax to be charged in accordance with this paragraph.

(2)    The conditions are as follows—

    (a)    the lease must be of a dwelling;

    (b)    the lease must give the lessee or lessees exclusive use of the dwelling;

    (c)    the lease must provide that the lessee or lessees may, on the payment of a sum, require the terms of the lease to be altered so that the rent payable under it is reduced;

    (d)    the lease must be granted partly in consideration of rent and partly in consideration of a premium calculated by reference to—

        (i)    the premium obtainable on the open market for the grant of a lease containing the same terms as the lease but with the substitution of the minimum rent for the rent payable under the lease, or

        (ii)    a sum calculated by reference to that premium;

    (e)    the lease must contain a statement of the minimum rent and of—

        (i)    the premium obtainable on the open market, or

        (ii)    the sum calculated by reference to that premium,

    by reference to which the premium is calculated.

(3)    An election for tax to be charged in accordance with this paragraph must be included in the land transaction return made in respect of the grant of the lease, or in an amendment of that return, and is irrevocable, so that the return may not be amended so as to withdraw the election.

(4)    Where this paragraph applies—

    (a)    the rent in consideration of which the lease is granted shall be taken to be the minimum rent stated in the lease in accordance with sub-paragraph (2)(e), and

    (b)    the chargeable consideration for the grant other than rent shall be taken to be the amount stated in the lease in accordance with sub-paragraph (2)(e)(i) or (ii).

(5)    In this paragraph the "minimum rent" means the lowest rent which could become payable under the lease if it were altered as mentioned in sub-paragraph (2)(c) at the date when the lease is granted.

*[Shared ownership lease: treatment of staircasing transaction*

4A.—(1)    This paragraph applies where under a shared ownership lease—

    (a)    the lessee or lessees have the right, on the payment of a sum, to require the terms of the lease to be altered so that the rent payable under it is reduced, and

    (b)    by exercising that right the lessee or lessees acquire an interest, additional to one already held, calculated by reference to the market value of the dwelling and expressed as a percentage of the dwelling or its value (a "share of the dwelling").

(2)    Such an acquisition is exempt from charge if—

    (a)    an election was made for tax to be charged in accordance with paragraph 2 or, as the case may be, paragraph 4 and any tax chargeable in respect of the grant of the lease has been paid, or

(b)    immediately after the acquisition the total share of the dwelling held by the lessee or lessees does not exceed 80%.

(3)   In this paragraph "shared ownership lease" means a lease granted—
(a)    by a qualifying body, or
(b)    in pursuance of the preserved right to buy,
in relation to which the conditions in paragraph 2(2) or 4(2) are met.

(4)   Section 118 (meaning of "market value") does not apply in relation to the references in this paragraph to the market value of the dwelling.]

*[Shared ownership lease: grant not linked with staircasing transactions etc*

4B.—(1)   For the purpose of determining the rate of tax chargeable on the grant of a shared ownership lease of a dwelling, the grant shall be treated as if it were not linked to—
(a)    any acquisition of an interest in the dwelling to which paragraph 4A applies, or
(b)    a transfer of the reversion to the lessee or lessees under the terms of the lease.

(2)   In this paragraph "shared ownership lease" has the same meaning as in paragraph 4A.]

*Shared ownership leases: meaning of "qualifying body" and "preserved right to buy"*

5.—(1)   This paragraph has effect for the purposes of paragraphs [2, 4 and 4A] (shared ownership leases: election as to basis of taxation).

(2)   A "qualifying body" means—
(a)    a local housing authority within the meaning of the Housing Act 1985 (c 68);
(b)    a housing association within the meaning of—
    (i)   the Housing Associations Act 1985 (c 69), or
    (ii)  Part 2 of the Housing (Northern Ireland) Order 1992 (SI 1992/1725 (NI 15));
(c)    a housing action trust established under Part 3 of the Housing Act 1988 (c 50);
(d)    the Northern Ireland Housing Executive;
[(e)   the Homes and Communities Agency;]
(f)    a development corporation established by an order made, or having effect as if made, under the New Towns Act 1981 (c 64);
[(g)   a registered provider of social housing that is not within paragraph (b) (subject to sub-paragraph (2A))].

[(2A)   A registered provider of social housing within sub-paragraph (2)(g) ("R") is only a qualifying body in relation to a lease of premises if the following has been funded with the assistance of a grant or other financial assistance under section 19 of the Housing and Regeneration Act 2008—
(a)    the purchase or construction of the premises by R (or a person connected with R), or
(b)    the adaptation of the premises by R (or a person connected with R) for use as a dwelling.

(2B)   Section 839 of the Taxes Act 1988 (connected persons) has effect for the purposes of sub-paragraph (2A).]

(3)   A lease is granted "in pursuance of the preserved right to buy" if—
(a)    the vendor is a person against whom the right to buy under Part 5 of the Housing Act 1985 is exercisable by virtue of section 171A of that Act (preservation of right to buy on disposal to private sector landlord),
(b)    the lessee is, or lessees are, the qualifying person for the purposes of the preserved right to buy, and
(c)    the lease is of a dwelling that is the qualifying dwelling-house in relation to the purchaser.

*Rent to mortgage or rent to loan: chargeable consideration*

6.—(1)   The chargeable consideration for a rent to mortgage or rent to loan transaction is determined in accordance with this paragraph.

(2)   A "rent to mortgage transaction" means—
(a)    the transfer of a dwelling to a person, or
(b)    the grant of a lease of a dwelling to a person,
pursuant to the exercise by that person of the right to acquire on rent to mortgage terms under Part 5 of the Housing Act 1985 (c 68).

(3)   The chargeable consideration for such a transaction is equal to the price that, by virtue of section 126 of the Housing Act 1985, would be payable for—
(a)    a transfer of the dwelling to the person (where the rent to mortgage transaction is a transfer), or
(b)    the grant of a lease of the dwelling to the person (where the rent to mortgage transaction is the grant of a lease),
if the person were exercising the right to buy under Part 5 of that Act.

(4)    A "rent to loan transaction" means the execution of a heritable disposition in favour of a person pursuant to the exercise by that person of the right to purchase a house by way of the rent to loan scheme in Part 3 of the Housing (Scotland) Act 1987 (c 26).

(5)    The chargeable consideration for such a transaction is equal to the price that, by virtue of section 62 of the Housing (Scotland) Act 1987, would be payable for the house if the person were exercising the right to purchase under section 61 of that Act.

*[Shared ownership trust: introduction*

7.—(1)    In this Schedule "shared ownership trust" means a trust of land, within the meaning of section 1 of the Trusts of Land and Appointment of Trustees Act 1996, which satisfies the following conditions.

(2)    Condition 1 is that the trust property is—
- (a)    a dwelling, and
- (b)    in England or Wales.

(3)    Condition 2 is that one of the beneficiaries ("the social landlord") is a qualifying body ...

(4)    Condition 3 is that the terms of the trust—
- (a)    provide for one or more of the individual beneficiaries ("the purchaser") to have exclusive use of the trust property as the only or main residence of the purchaser,
- (b)    require the purchaser to make an initial payment to the social landlord ("the initial capital"),
- (c)    require the purchaser to make additional payments to the social landlord by way of compensation under section 13(6)(a) of the Trusts of Land and Appointment of Trustees Act 1996, ("rent-equivalent payments"),
- (d)    enable the purchaser to make other additional payments to the social landlord ("equity-acquisition payments"),
- (e)    determine the initial beneficial interests of the social landlord and of the purchaser by reference to the initial capital,
- (f)    specify a sum, equating or relating to the market value of the dwelling, by reference to which the initial capital was calculated, and
- (g)    provide for the purchaser's beneficial interest in the trust property to increase, and the social landlord's to diminish (or to be extinguished), as equity-acquisition payments are made.

(5)    Section 118 (meaning of "market value") does not apply to this paragraph.

(6)    In Condition 1 "dwelling" includes—
- (a)    a building which is being constructed or adapted for use as a dwelling,
- (b)    land which is to be used for the purpose of the construction of a dwelling, and
- (c)    land which is, or is to become, the garden or grounds of a dwelling.

[(7)    In Condition 2 "qualifying body" means—
- (a)    a qualifying body within the meaning of paragraph 5(2)(a) to (f), or
- (b)    a registered provider of social housing within paragraph 5(2)(g) (subject to sub-paragraph (8)).

(8)    A registered provider of social housing within paragraph 5(2)(g) ("R") is only a qualifying body in relation to a shared ownership trust if the following has been or is being funded with the assistance of a grant or other financial assistance under section 19 of the Housing and Regeneration Act 2008—
- (a)    the purchase or construction of the trust property by R (or a person connected with R), or
- (b)    the adaptation of the trust property by R (or a person connected with R) for use as a dwelling.

(9)    Section 839 of the Taxes Act 1988 (connected persons) has effect for the purposes of sub-paragraph (8).]

*Shared ownership trust: "purchaser"*

8.    For the purposes of the application of stamp duty land tax in relation to a shared ownership trust, the person (or persons) identified as the purchaser in accordance with paragraph 7, and not the social landlord or any other beneficiary, is (or are) to be treated as the purchaser of the trust property.

*Shared ownership trust: election for market value treatment*

9.—(1)    This paragraph applies where—
- (a)    a shared ownership trust is declared, and
- (b)    the purchaser elects for tax to be charged in accordance with this paragraph.

(2)    An election must be included in—
- (a)    the land transaction return for the declaration of the shared ownership trust, or
- (b)    an amendment of that return.

(3)   An election may not be revoked.

(4)   Where this paragraph applies—
  (a)   the chargeable consideration for the declaration of the shared ownership trust shall be taken to be the amount stated in accordance with paragraph 7(4)(f), and
  (b)   no account shall be taken for the purposes of stamp duty land tax of rent-equivalent payments.

(5)   The transfer to the purchaser of an interest in the trust property upon the termination of the trust is exempt from charge if—
  (a)   an election was made under this paragraph, and
  (b)   any tax chargeable in respect of the declaration of the shared ownership trust has been paid.

*Shared ownership trust: treatment of staircasing transaction*

10.—(1)   An equity-acquisition … payment under a shared ownership trust, and the consequent increase in the purchaser's beneficial interest, shall be exempt from charge if—
  (a)   an election was made under paragraph 9, and
  (b)   any tax chargeable in respect of the declaration of trust has been paid.

(2)   An equity-acquisition … payment under a shared ownership trust, and the consequent increase in the purchaser's beneficial interest, shall also be exempt from charge if following the increase the purchaser's beneficial interest does not exceed 80% of the total beneficial interest in the trust property.

*Shared ownership trust: treatment of additional payments where no election made*

11.   Where no election has been made under paragraph 9 in respect of a shared ownership trust—
  (a)   the initial capital shall be treated for the purposes of stamp duty land tax as chargeable consideration other than rent, and
  (b)   any rent-equivalent … payment by the purchaser shall be treated for the purposes of stamp duty land tax as a payment of rent.]

*[Shared ownership trust: declaration not linked with staircasing transactions etc*

12.   For the purpose of determining the rate of tax chargeable on the declaration of a shared ownership trust, the declaration shall be treated as if it were not linked to—
  (a)   any equity-acquisition payment under the trust or any consequent increase in the purchaser's beneficial interest in the trust property, or
  (b)   a transfer to the purchaser of an interest in the trust property upon the termination of the trust.]

*[Rent to shared ownership lease: charge to tax*

13.—(1)   The chargeable consideration for transactions forming part of a rent to shared ownership lease scheme is determined in accordance with this paragraph.

(2)   A "rent to shared ownership lease scheme" means a scheme or arrangement under which a qualifying body—
  (a)   grants an assured shorthold tenancy of a dwelling to a person ("the tenant") or persons ("the tenants"), and
  (b)   subsequently grants a shared ownership lease of the dwelling or another dwelling to the tenant or one or more of the tenants.

(3)   The following transactions are to be treated as if they were not linked to each other—
  (a)   the grant of the assured shorthold tenancy,
  (b)   the grant of the shared ownership lease, and
  (c)   any other land transaction between the qualifying body and the tenant, or any of the tenants, entered into as part of the scheme.

(4)   For the purpose of determining the effective date of the grant of the shared ownership lease, the possession of the dwelling by the tenant or tenants pursuant to the assured shorthold tenancy is to be disregarded.

(5)   In this paragraph—
  "assured shorthold tenancy" has the same meaning as in Part 1 of the Housing Act 1988;
  "qualifying body" has the same meaning as in paragraph 5;
  "shared ownership lease" has the same meaning as in paragraph 4A.

*Rent to shared ownership trust: charge to tax*

14.—(1)   The chargeable consideration for transactions forming part of a rent to shared ownership trust scheme is determined in accordance with this paragraph.

(2)   A "rent to shared ownership trust scheme" means a scheme or arrangement under which—

(a) a qualifying body grants an assured shorthold tenancy of a dwelling to a person ("the tenant") or persons ("the tenants"), and

(b) the tenant, or one or more of tenants, subsequently becomes the purchaser under a shared ownership trust of the dwelling, or another dwelling, under which the qualifying body is the social landlord.

(3) The following transactions are to be treated as if they were not linked to each other—

(a) the grant of the assured shorthold tenancy,

(b) the declaration of the shared ownership trust, and

(c) any other land transaction between the qualifying body and the tenant, or any of the tenants, entered into as part of the scheme.

(4) For the purpose of determining the effective date of the declaration of the shared ownership trust, the possession of the dwelling by the tenant or tenants pursuant to the assured shorthold tenancy is to be disregarded.

(5) In this paragraph—

"assured shorthold tenancy" has the same meaning as in Part 1 of the Housing Act 1988;

"qualifying body" has the same meaning as in paragraph 5;

"social landlord" and "purchaser", in relation to a shared ownership trust, have the same meaning as in paragraph 7.]

**[1322]**

---

**NOTES**

Para 1: in sub-para (3) under the heading "Social housing", for the entry "The Housing Corporation" in italics there is substituted the entry "The Regulator of Social Housing" and entry "A non-profit registered provider of social housing" inserted by the Housing and Regeneration Act 2008, s 277, Sch 9, paras 29, 32(1), (2), as from a day to be appointed; in sub-para (3) in the heading "New towns and development corporations" word in square brackets inserted and words in square brackets in entry "The Homes and Communities Agency" substituted by the Housing and Regeneration Act 2008, s 56, Sch 8, paras 78, 80(1), (2), subject to transitional provisions and savings in SI 2008/3068, arts 6–10 at **[3834B]**–**[3834F]**; entry "The Welsh Development Agency" (omitted) repealed by the Welsh Development Agency (Transfer of Functions to the National Assembly for Wales and Abolition) Order 2005, SI 2005/3226, art 7(1)(b), Sch 2, Pt 1, para 14, subject to transitional provisions in art 3 thereof; words in square brackets in sub-para (5), and sub-para (6) inserted by the Housing and Regeneration Act 2008, s 277, Sch 9, paras 29, 32(1), (3), (4), as from a day to be appointed.

Para 2: sub-para (4A) inserted by the Finance Act 2007, s 78.

Para 4A: inserted by the Finance Act 2004, s 303(1), in relation to an acquisition after 17 March 2004.

Para 4B: inserted by the Finance Act 2008, s 95(8), (13), in relation to transactions with an effective date on or after 12 March 2008.

Para 5: words in square brackets in sub-para (1) substituted by the Finance Act 2004, s 303(2), in relation to an acquisition after 17 March 2004; sub-para (2)(e) substituted by the Housing and Regeneration Act 2008, s 56, Sch 8, paras 78, 80(1), (3), subject to transitional provisions and savings in SI 2008/3068, arts 6–10 at **[3834B]**–**[3834F]**; sub-paras (2)(g), (2A), (2B) inserted by the Finance Act 2009, s 81(1), (5), (6), (8), in relation to transactions with an effective date on or after 21 July 2009.

Para 7: inserted by the Finance Act 2007, s 77, in relation to land transactions with an effective date on or after 19 July 2007; words omitted from sub-para (3) repealed and sub-paras (7)–(9) inserted by the Finance Act 2009, s 81(1), (5), (7), (8), in relation to transactions with an effective date on or after 21 July 2009.

Paras 8, 9: inserted by the Finance Act 2007, s 77, in relation to land transactions with an effective date on or after 19 July 2007.

Para 10: inserted by the Finance Act 2007, s 77, in relation to land transactions with an effective date on or after 19 July 2007; words omitted repealed by the Finance Act 2008, s 95(9), (13), in relation to transactions with an effective date on or after 12 March 2008.

Para 11: inserted by the Finance Act 2007, s 77, in relation to land transactions with an effective date on or after 19 July 2007; word omitted from sub-para (b) repealed by the Finance Act 2008, s 95(9), (13), in relation to transactions with an effective date on or after 12 March 2008.

Para 12: inserted by the Finance Act 2008, s 95(10), (13), in relation to transactions with an effective date on or after 12 March 2008.

Paras 13, 14: inserted by the Finance Act 2009, s 82, in relation to cases in which the effective date of the grant of the shared ownership lease or the declaration of the shared ownership trust is on or after 22 April 2009.

---

*(Schs 10–18 outside the scope of this work.)*

## SCHEDULE 19
### STAMP DUTY LAND TAX: COMMENCEMENT AND TRANSITIONAL PROVISIONS
Section 124

*Introduction*

1.—(1) Subject to the provisions of this Schedule, the provisions of this Part come into force on the passing of this Act.

(2) The following provisions have effect as regards what transactions are SDLT transactions, that is, are chargeable or notifiable or are transactions in relation to which section 79 (registration etc) applies.

(3)   Nothing in this Schedule shall be read as meaning that other transactions, whether effected before or after the passing of this Act, are to be disregarded in applying the provisions of this Part.

### The implementation date

2.—(1)   A transaction is not an SDLT transaction unless the effective date of the transaction is on or after the implementation date.

(2)   In this Part "the implementation date" means the date appointed by Treasury order as the implementation date for the purposes of stamp duty land tax.

### Contract entered into before first relevant date

3.—(1)   Subject to the following provisions of this paragraph, a transaction is not an SDLT transaction if it is effected in pursuance of a contract entered into before the first relevant date.

(2)   The "first relevant date" is the day after the passing of this Act.

(3)   The exclusion of transactions effected in pursuance of contracts entered into before the first relevant date does not apply—

   (a)   if there is any variation of the contract or assignment of rights under the contract on or after that date;
   (b)   if the transaction is effected in consequence of the exercise after that date of any option, right of pre-emption or similar right;
   [(c)   if on or after that date there is an assignment, subsale or other transaction (relating to the whole or part of the subject-matter of the contract) as a result of which a person other than the purchaser under the contract becomes entitled to call for a conveyance to him].

### Contract substantially performed before implementation date

4.—(1)   This paragraph applies where a transaction—

   (a)   is completed on or after the implementation date,
   (b)   is effected in pursuance of a contract entered into and substantially performed before that date, and
   (c)   is not excluded from being an SDLT transaction by paragraph 3.

(2)   The transaction is not an SDLT transaction if the contract was substantially performed before the first relevant date.

(3)   In any other case, the fact that the contract was substantially performed before the implementation date does not affect the matter.

Accordingly, the effective date of the transaction is the date of completion.

### [Contracts substantially performed after implementation date

4A.   Where—

   (a)   a transaction is effected in pursuance of a contract entered into before the first relevant date,
   (b)   the contract is substantially performed, without having been completed, after the implementation date, and
   (c)   there is subsequently an event within paragraph 3(3) by virtue of which the transaction is an SDLT transaction,

the effective date of the transaction shall be taken to be the date of the event referred to in paragraph (c) (and not the date of substantial performance).

### Application of provisions in case of transfer of rights

4B.—(1)   This paragraph applies where section 44 (contract and conveyance) has effect in accordance with section 45 (effect of transfer of rights).

(2)   Any reference in paragraph 3, 4 or 4A to the date when a contract was entered into (or made) shall be read, in relation to a contract deemed to exist by virtue of section 45(3) (deemed secondary contract with transferee), as a reference to the date of the assignment, subsale or other transaction in question.]

### Credit for ad valorem stamp duty paid

5.—(1)   Where a transaction chargeable to stamp duty land tax is effected in pursuance of a contract entered into before the implementation date, any *ad valorem* stamp duty paid on the contract shall go to reduce the amount of tax payable (but not so as to give rise to any repayment).

(2)   Where the application or operation of any exemption or relief from stamp duty land tax turns on whether tax was paid or payable in respect of an earlier transaction, that requirement is treated as met if *ad valorem* stamp duty was paid or (as the case may be) payable in respect of the instrument by which that transaction was effected.

*Effect for stamp duty purposes of stamp duty land tax being paid or chargeable*

6.—(1) …

(2) The references in section 111(1)(c) of, and paragraph 4(3) of Schedule 34 to, the Finance Act 2002 (c 23) (which relate to the circumstances in which stamp duty group relief is withdrawn) to a transfer at market value by a duly stamped instrument on which *ad valorem* duty was paid and in respect of which group relief was not claimed shall be read, on or after the implementation date, as including a reference to a transfer at market value by a chargeable transaction in respect of which relief under Part 1 of Schedule 7 to this Act was available but was not claimed.

(3) The references in section 113(1)(c) of, and in paragraph 3(3) or 4(3) of Schedule 35 to, the Finance Act 2002 (which relate to the circumstances in which stamp duty company acquisitions relief is withdrawn) to a transfer at market value by a duly stamped instrument on which *ad valorem* duty was paid and in respect of which section 76 relief was not claimed shall be read, on or after the implementation date, as including a reference to a transfer at market value by a chargeable transaction on which stamp duty land tax was chargeable and in respect of which relief under Part 2 of Schedule 7 to this Act was available but was not claimed.

*Earlier related transactions under stamp duty*

7.—(1) In relation to a transaction that is not an SDLT transaction but which is linked to an SDLT transaction and accordingly falls to be taken into account in determining the rate of stamp duty land tax chargeable on the latter transaction, any reference in this Part to the chargeable consideration for the first-mentioned transaction shall be read as a reference to the consideration by reference to which *ad valorem* stamp duty was payable in respect of the instrument by which that transaction was effected.

[(2) In paragraph 3 of Schedule 9 (relief for transfer of reversion under shared ownership lease where election made for market value treatment) and paragraph 4A of that Schedule (shared ownership lease: treatment of staircasing transaction) as they apply in a case where the original lease was granted before the implementation date—

 (a) a reference to a lease to which paragraph 2 of that Schedule applies shall be read as a reference to a lease to which section 97 of the Finance Act 1980 applied (which made provision for stamp duty corresponding to that paragraph), and

 (b) a reference to an election having been made for tax to be charged in accordance with paragraph 2 or 4 of that Schedule shall be read as a reference to the lease having contained a statement of the parties' intention such as is mentioned in section 97(2)(d) of the Finance Act 1980 or, as the case may be, paragraph (d) of section 108(5) of the Finance Act 1981 (which made provision for stamp duty corresponding to paragraph 4).]

(3) In section 54 (exceptions from deemed market value rule for transactions with connected company) the reference in subsection (4)(b) to group relief having been claimed in respect of a transaction shall be read in relation to a transaction carried out before the implementation date as a reference to relief having been claimed under section 42 of the Finance Act 1930 (c 28), section 11 of the Finance Act (Northern Ireland) 1954 (c 23 (N. I.)) or section 151 of the Finance Act 1995 (c 4) in respect of stamp duty on the instrument by which the transaction was effected.

[(4) For the purposes of paragraph 5 of Schedule 17A (treatment of successive linked leases) no account shall be taken of any transaction that is not an SDLT transaction.]

*[Stamping of contract where transaction on completion subject to stamp duty land tax*

7A.—(1) This paragraph applies where—

 (a) a contract that apart from paragraph 7 of Schedule 13 to the Finance Act 1999 (contracts chargeable as conveyances on sale) would not be chargeable with stamp duty is entered into before the implementation date,

 (b) a conveyance made in conformity with the contract is effected on or after the implementation date, and

 (c) the transaction effected on completion is an SDLT transaction or would be but for an exemption or relief from stamp duty land tax.

(2) If in those circumstances the contract is presented for stamping together with a Revenue certificate as to compliance with the provisions of this Part of this Act in relation to the transaction effected on completion—

 (a) the payment of stamp duty land tax on that transaction or, as the case may be, the fact that no such tax was payable shall be denoted on the contract by a particular stamp, and

 (b) the contract shall be deemed thereupon to be duly stamped.

(3) In this paragraph "conveyance" includes any instrument.]

*[Stamping of agreement for lease where grant of lease subject to stamp duty land tax]*

8.—(1) [This paragraph applies where—]

 (a) an agreement for a lease is entered into before the implementation date,

(b)    a lease giving effect to the agreement is executed on or after that date, and

(c)    the transaction effected on completion is an SDLT transaction or would be but for an exemption or relief from stamp duty land tax.

[(2)   If in those circumstances the agreement is presented for stamping together with a Revenue certificate as to compliance with the provisions of this Part of this Act in relation to the grant of the lease—

(a)    the payment of stamp duty land tax in respect of the grant of the lease or, as the case may be, the fact that no such tax was payable shall be denoted on the agreement by a particular stamp, and

(b)    the agreement shall be deemed thereupon to be duly stamped.]

(3)   For the purposes of this paragraph a lease gives effect to an agreement if the lease either is in conformity with the agreement or relates to substantially the same property and term as the agreement.

(4)   References in this paragraph to an agreement for a lease include missives of let in Scotland.

*Exercise of option or right of pre-emption acquired before implementation date*

9.—(1)   This paragraph applies where—

(a)    an option binding the grantor to enter into a land transaction, or

(b)    a right of pre-emption preventing the grantor from entering into, or restricting the right of the grantor to enter into, a land transaction,

is acquired before the implementation date and exercised on or after that date.

(2)   Where the option or right was acquired on or after 17th April 2003, any consideration for the acquisition is treated as part of the chargeable consideration for the transaction resulting from the exercise of the option or right.

(3)   Where the option or right was varied on or after 17th April 2003 and before the implementation date, any consideration for the variation is treated as part of the chargeable consideration for the transaction resulting from the exercise of the option or right.

(4)   Whether or not sub-paragraph (2) or (3) applies, the acquisition of the option or right and any variation of the option or right is treated as linked with the land transaction resulting from the exercise of the option or right.

But not so as to require the consideration for the acquisition or variation to be counted twice in determining the rate of tax chargeable on the land transaction resulting from the exercise of the option or right.

(5)   Where this paragraph applies any *ad valorem* stamp duty paid on the acquisition or variation of the option or right shall go to reduce the amount of tax payable on the transaction resulting from the exercise of the option or right (but not so as to give rise to any repayment).

*Supplementary*

10.   In this Schedule "contract" includes any agreement.

**[1323]**

**NOTES**

Para 3: sub-para (3)(c) substituted by the Finance Act 2004, s 296, Sch 39, Pt 1, paras 1, 12, in relation to any transaction effective after 17 March 2004.

Paras 4A, 4B: inserted by the Finance Act 2004, s 296, Sch 39, Pt 2, para 24, in relation to any transaction effective on or after 22 July 2004.

Para 6: sub-para (1) repealed by the Finance Act 2004, s 326, Sch 42, Pt 4(2), in relation to any transaction effective on or after 22 July 2004.

Para 7: sub-para (2) substituted by the Finance Act 2004, s 303(3); sub-para (4) inserted by the 2004 Act, s 296, Sch 39, Pt 2, para 22(8), in relation to any transaction effective on or after 22 July 2004.

Para 7A: inserted by the Finance Act 2004, s 296, Sch 39, Pt 2, para 25(1), in relation to any transaction effective on or after 22 July 2004.

Para 8: heading, words in square brackets in sub-para (1), and the whole of sub-para (2), substituted by the Finance Act 2004, s 296, Sch 39, Pt 2, para 25(2), in relation to any transaction of which the effective date is on or after 22 July 2004.

The date appointed as the implementation date for the purposes of stamp duty land tax is 1 December 2003: see the Stamp Duty Land Tax (Appointment of the Implementation Date) Order 2003, SI 2003/2899, art 2.

Orders: the Stamp Duty Land Tax (Appointment of the Implementation Date) Order 2003, SI 2003/2899.

(*Schs 20–43 outside the scope of this work.*)

# CIVIL PARTNERSHIP ACT 2004

(2004 c 33)

*An Act to make provision for and in connection with civil partnership*

[18 November 2004]

**1** ((*Pt 1*) *outside the scope of this work.*)

## PART 2
## CIVIL PARTNERSHIP: ENGLAND AND WALES

**2–79** ((*Chapters 1–5*) *outside the scope of this work.*)

## CHAPTER 6
## MISCELLANEOUS

**80, 81** (*Outside the scope of this work.*)

**82 Family homes and domestic violence**

Schedule 9 amends Part 4 of the Family Law Act 1996 (c 27) and related enactments so that they apply in relation to civil partnerships as they apply in relation to marriages.

**[1324]**

**NOTES**
Commencement: 5 December 2005.

**83–257** (*Ss 83, 84, ss 85–257 (Pts 3–7) outside the scope of this work.*)

## PART 8
## SUPPLEMENTARY

**258–261** (*Outside the scope of this work.*)

**262 Extent**

(1) Part 2 (civil partnership: England and Wales), excluding section 35 but including Schedules 1 to 9, extends to England and Wales only.

(2)–(9) (*Outside the scope of this work.*)

(10) Any amendment, repeal or revocation made by Schedules 24 to 27 and 30 has the same extent as the provision subject to the amendment, repeal or revocation.

**[1325]**

**263 Commencement**

(1) (*Outside the scope of this work.*)

(2) Part 2, including Schedules 1 to 9, comes into force in accordance with provision made by order by the Secretary of State.

(3)–(9) (*Outside the scope of this work.*)

(10) In this Part—
 (a) sections 258, 259, 260 and 262, this section and section 264 come into force on the day on which this Act is passed,
 (b)–(d) (*outside the scope of this work.*)

(11) The power to make an order under this section is exercisable by statutory instrument.

**[1326]**

**NOTES**
Orders: the Civil Partnership Act 2004 (Commencement No 1) Order 2005, SI 2005/1112; the Civil Partnership Act 2004 (Commencement No 1) (Northern Ireland) Order 2005, SI 2005/2399; the Civil Partnership Act 2004 (Commencement No 2) (Northern Ireland) Order 2005, SI 2005/3058; the Civil Partnership Act 2004 (Commencement No 2) Order 2005, SI 2005/3175; the Civil Partnership Act 2004 (Commencement No 3) (Northern Ireland) Order 2005, SI 2005/3255; the Civil Partnership Act 2004 (Commencement No 3) Order 2006, SI 2006/639; the Civil Partnership Act 2004 (Commencement No 4) (Northern Ireland) Order 2006, SI 2006/928.

**264 Short title**

This Act may be cited as the Civil Partnership Act 2004.

**[1327]**

*(Schs 1–8 outside the scope of this work.)*

## SCHEDULE 9
### FAMILY HOMES AND DOMESTIC VIOLENCE
Section 82

*(Pts 1, 2 outside the scope of this work.)*

### PART 3
### TRANSITIONAL PROVISION

25.—(1)   Any reference (however expressed) in any enactment, instrument or document (whether passed or made before or after the passing of this Act)—

    (a)   to rights of occupation under, or within the meaning of, the Matrimonial Homes Act 1983 (c 19), or

    (b)   to matrimonial home rights under, or within the meaning of, Part 4 of the Family Law Act 1996 (c 27),

is to be construed, so far as is required for continuing the effect of the enactment, instrument or document, as being or as the case requires including a reference to home rights under, or within the meaning of, Part 4 of the 1996 Act as amended by this Schedule.

(2)   Any reference (however expressed) in Part 4 of the 1996 Act or in any other enactment, instrument or document (including any enactment amended by this Schedule) to home rights under, or within the meaning of, Part 4 of the 1996 Act is to be construed as including, in relation to times, circumstances and purposes before the commencement of this Schedule, references to rights of occupation under, or within the meaning of, the 1983 Act and to matrimonial home rights under, or within the meaning of, Part 4 of the 1996 Act without the amendments made by this Schedule.

**[1328]**

**NOTES**

Commencement: 5 December 2005.

*(Schs 10–30 outside the scope of this work.)*

# HOUSING ACT 2004

## (2004 c 34)

### ARRANGEMENT OF SECTIONS

### PART 1
### HOUSING CONDITIONS

### CHAPTER 1
### ENFORCEMENT OF HOUSING STANDARDS: GENERAL

*New system for assessing housing conditions*

## CHAPTER 2
### IMPROVEMENT NOTICES, PROHIBITION ORDERS AND HAZARD AWARENESS NOTICES

*Improvement notices*

*Prohibition orders*

*Hazard awareness notices*

*Enforcement: improvement notices*

*Enforcement: prohibition orders*

*Enforcement: improvement notices and prohibition orders*

*Supplementary provisions*

## CHAPTER 3
### EMERGENCY MEASURES

*Emergency remedial action*

*Emergency prohibition orders*

*Appeals*

## CHAPTER 5
### GENERAL AND MISCELLANEOUS PROVISIONS RELATING TO ENFORCEMENT ACTION

*Recovery of expenses relating to enforcement action*

PART 4
ADDITIONAL CONTROL PROVISIONS IN RELATION TO RESIDENTIAL ACCOMMODATION

CHAPTER 1
INTERIM AND FINAL MANAGEMENT ORDERS

*An Act to make provision about housing conditions; to regulate houses in multiple occupation and certain other residential accommodation; to make provision for home information packs in connection with the sale of residential properties; to make provision about secure tenants and the right to buy; to make provision about mobile homes and the accommodation needs of gypsies and travellers; to make other provision about housing; and for connected purposes*

[18 November 2004]

PART 1
HOUSING CONDITIONS

CHAPTER 1
ENFORCEMENT OF HOUSING STANDARDS: GENERAL

*New system for assessing housing conditions*

## 1   New system for assessing housing conditions and enforcing housing standards

(1)   This Part provides—

   (a)   for a new system of assessing the condition of residential premises, and

   (b)   for that system to be used in the enforcement of housing standards in relation to such premises.

(2)   The new system—

   (a)   operates by reference to the existence of category 1 or category 2 hazards on residential premises (see section 2), and

   (b)   replaces the existing system based on the test of fitness for human habitation contained in section 604 of the Housing Act 1985 (c 68).

(3)   The kinds of enforcement action which are to involve the use of the new system are—

   (a)   the new kinds of enforcement action contained in Chapter 2 (improvement notices, prohibition orders and hazard awareness notices),

   (b)   the new emergency measures contained in Chapter 3 (emergency remedial action and emergency prohibition orders), and

   (c)   the existing kinds of enforcement action dealt with in Chapter 4 (demolition orders and slum clearance declarations).

(4)   In this Part "residential premises" means—

   (a)   a dwelling;

   (b)   an HMO;

   (c)   unoccupied HMO accommodation;

   (d)   any common parts of a building containing one or more flats.

(5)   In this Part—

"building containing one or more flats" does not include an HMO;

"common parts", in relation to a building containing one or more flats, includes—

   (a)   the structure and exterior of the building, and

   (b)   common facilities provided (whether or not in the building) for persons who include the occupiers of one or more of the flats;

"dwelling" means a building or part of a building occupied or intended to be occupied as a separate dwelling;

"external common parts", in relation to a building containing one or more flats, means common parts of the building which are outside it;

"flat" means a separate set of premises (whether or not on the same floor)—

   (a)   which forms part of a building,

   (b)   which is constructed or adapted for use for the purposes of a dwelling, and

   (c)   either the whole or a material part of which lies above or below some other part of the building;

"HMO" means a house in multiple occupation as defined by sections 254 to 259, as they have effect for the purposes of this Part (that is, without the exclusions contained in Schedule 14);

"unoccupied HMO accommodation" means a building or part of a building constructed or adapted for use as a house in multiple occupation but for the time being either unoccupied or only occupied by persons who form a single household.

(6)   In this Part any reference to a dwelling, an HMO or a building containing one or more flats includes (where the context permits) any yard, garden, outhouses and appurtenances belonging to, or usually enjoyed with, the dwelling, HMO or building (or any part of it).

(7)   The following indicates how this Part applies to flats—

   (a)   references to a dwelling or an HMO include a dwelling or HMO which is a flat (as defined by subsection (5)); and

   (b)   subsection (6) applies in relation to such a dwelling or HMO as it applies in relation to other dwellings or HMOs (but it is not to be taken as referring to any common parts of the building containing the flat).

(8)   This Part applies to unoccupied HMO accommodation as it applies to an HMO, and references to an HMO in subsections (6) and (7) and in the following provisions of this Part are to be read accordingly.

**NOTES**
Commencement: 6 April 2006 (in relation to England, subject to transitional provisions and savings in the Housing Act 2004 (Commencement No 5 and Transitional Provisions and Savings) (England) Order 2006, SI 2006/1060, art 3, Schedule at **[3700]**, **[3701]**); 16 June 2006 (in relation to Wales, subject to transitional provisions and savings in the Housing Act 2004 (Commencement No 3 and Transitional Provisions and Savings) (Wales) Order 2006, SI 2006/1535, art 3, Schedule at **[3714]**, **[3715]**).

## 2   Meaning of "category 1 hazard" and "category 2 hazard"

(1)   In this Act—

"category 1 hazard" means a hazard of a prescribed description which falls within a prescribed band as a result of achieving, under a prescribed method for calculating the seriousness of hazards of that description, a numerical score of or above a prescribed amount;

"category 2 hazard" means a hazard of a prescribed description which falls within a prescribed band as a result of achieving, under a prescribed method for calculating the seriousness of hazards of that description, a numerical score below the minimum amount prescribed for a category 1 hazard of that description; and

"hazard" means any risk of harm to the health or safety of an actual or potential occupier of a dwelling or HMO which arises from a deficiency in the dwelling or HMO or in any building or land in the vicinity (whether the deficiency arises as a result of the construction of any building, an absence of maintenance or repair, or otherwise).

(2)   In subsection (1)—

"prescribed" means prescribed by regulations made by the appropriate national authority (see section 261(1)); and

"prescribed band" means a band so prescribed for a category 1 hazard or a category 2 hazard, as the case may be.

(3)   Regulations under this section may, in particular, prescribe a method for calculating the seriousness of hazards which takes into account both the likelihood of the harm occurring and the severity of the harm if it were to occur.

(4)   In this section—

"building" includes part of a building;

"harm" includes temporary harm.

(5)   In this Act "health" includes mental health.

**[1330]**

**NOTES**
Regulations: the Housing Health and Safety Rating System (England) Regulations 2005, SI 2005/3208 at **[3584]**; the Housing Health and Safety Rating System (Wales) Regulations 2006, SI 2006/1702 at **[3719]**.

*Procedure for assessing housing conditions*

## 3   Local housing authorities to review housing conditions in their districts

(1)   A local housing authority must keep the housing conditions in their area under review with a view to identifying any action that may need to be taken by them under any of the provisions mentioned in subsection (2).

(2)   The provisions are—

(a)   the following provisions of this Act—

(i)   this Part,

(ii)   Part 2 (licensing of HMOs),

(iii)   Part 3 (selective licensing of other houses), and

(iv)   Chapters 1 and 2 of Part 4 (management orders);

(b)   Part 9 of the Housing Act 1985 (c 68) (demolition orders and slum clearance);

(c)   Part 7 of the Local Government and Housing Act 1989 (c 42) (renewal areas); and

(d)   article 3 of the Regulatory Reform (Housing Assistance) (England and Wales) Order 2002 (SI 2002/1860).

(3)   For the purpose of carrying out their duty under subsection (1) a local housing authority and their officers must—

(a)   comply with any directions that may be given by the appropriate national authority, and

(b)   keep such records, and supply the appropriate national authority with such information, as that authority may specify.

**[1331]**

**NOTES**
Commencement: 6 April 2006 (in relation to England, subject to transitional provisions and savings in the Housing Act 2004 (Commencement No 5 and Transitional Provisions and Savings) (England) Order 2006, SI 2006/1060, art 3, Schedule at **[3700]**, **[3701]**); 16 June 2006 (in relation to Wales, subject to transitional

provisions and savings in the Housing Act 2004 (Commencement No 3 and Transitional Provisions and Savings) (Wales) Order 2006, SI 2006/1535, art 3, Schedule at **[3714]**, **[3715]**).

## 4 Inspections by local housing authorities to see whether category 1 or 2 hazards exist

(1) If a local housing authority consider—

    (a) as a result of any matters of which they have become aware in carrying out their duty under section 3, or

    (b) for any other reason,

that it would be appropriate for any residential premises in their district to be inspected with a view to determining whether any category 1 or 2 hazard exists on those premises, the authority must arrange for such an inspection to be carried out.

(2) If an official complaint about the condition of any residential premises in the district of a local housing authority is made to the proper officer of the authority, and the circumstances complained of indicate—

    (a) that any category 1 or category 2 hazard may exist on those premises, or

    (b) that an area in the district should be dealt with as a clearance area,

the proper officer must inspect the premises or area.

(3) In this section "an official complaint" means a complaint in writing made by—

    (a) a justice of the peace having jurisdiction in any part of the district, or

    (b) the parish or community council for a parish or community within the district.

(4) An inspection of any premises under subsection (1) or (2)—

    (a) is to be carried out in accordance with regulations made by the appropriate national authority; and

    (b) is to extend to so much of the premises as the local housing authority or proper officer (as the case may be) consider appropriate in the circumstances having regard to any applicable provisions of the regulations.

(5) Regulations under subsection (4) may in particular make provision about—

    (a) the manner in which, and the extent to which, premises are to be inspected under subsection (1) or (2), and

    (b) the manner in which the assessment of hazards is to be carried out.

(6) Where an inspection under subsection (2) has been carried out and the proper officer of a local housing authority is of the opinion—

    (a) that a category 1 or 2 hazard exists on any residential premises in the authority's district, or

    (b) that an area in their district should be dealt with as a clearance area,

the officer must, without delay, make a report in writing to the authority which sets out his opinion together with the facts of the case.

(7) The authority must consider any report made to them under subsection (6) as soon as possible.

**[1332]**

**NOTES**

Commencement: 18 November 2004 (for the purpose of making orders or regulations); 25 November 2005 (in relation to Wales for remaining purposes); 6 April 2006 (in relation to England for remaining purposes, subject to transitional provisions and savings in the Housing Act 2004 (Commencement No 5 and Transitional Provisions and Savings) (England) Order 2006, SI 2006/1060, art 3, Schedule at **[3700]**, **[3701]**).

Regulations: the Housing Health and Safety Rating System (England) Regulations 2005, SI 2005/3208 at **[3584]**; the Housing Health and Safety Rating System (Wales) Regulations 2006, SI 2006/1702 at **[3719]**.

*Enforcement of housing standards*

## 5 Category 1 hazards: general duty to take enforcement action

(1) If a local housing authority consider that a category 1 hazard exists on any residential premises, they must take the appropriate enforcement action in relation to the hazard.

(2) In subsection (1) "the appropriate enforcement action" means whichever of the following courses of action is indicated by subsection (3) or (4)—

    (a) serving an improvement notice under section 11;

    (b) making a prohibition order under section 20;

    (c) serving a hazard awareness notice under section 28;

    (d) taking emergency remedial action under section 40;

    (e) making an emergency prohibition order under section 43;

    (f) making a demolition order under subsection (1) or (2) of section 265 of the Housing Act 1985 (c 68);

    (g) declaring the area in which the premises concerned are situated to be a clearance area by virtue of section 289(2) of that Act.

(3)   If only one course of action within subsection (2) is available to the authority in relation to the hazard, they must take that course of action.

(4)   If two or more courses of action within subsection (2) are available to the authority in relation to the hazard, they must take the course of action which they consider to be the most appropriate of those available to them.

(5)   The taking by the authority of a course of action within subsection (2) does not prevent subsection (1) from requiring them to take in relation to the same hazard—
- (a)   either the same course of action again or another such course of action, if they consider that the action taken by them so far has not proved satisfactory, or
- (b)   another such course of action, where the first course of action is that mentioned in subsection (2)(g) and their eventual decision under section 289(2F) of the Housing Act 1985 means that the premises concerned are not to be included in a clearance area.

(6)   To determine whether a course of action mentioned in any of paragraphs (a) to (g) of subsection (2) is "available" to the authority in relation to the hazard, see the provision mentioned in that paragraph.

(7)   Section 6 applies for the purposes of this section.

**[1333]**

**NOTES**
Commencement: 6 April 2006 (in relation to England, subject to transitional provisions and savings in the Housing Act 2004 (Commencement No 5 and Transitional Provisions and Savings) (England) Order 2006, SI 2006/1060, art 3, Schedule at **[3700]**, **[3701]**); 16 June 2006 (in relation to Wales, subject to transitional provisions and savings in the Housing Act 2004 (Commencement No 3 and Transitional Provisions and Savings) (Wales) Order 2006, SI 2006/1535, art 3, Schedule at **[3714]**, **[3715]**).

## 6   Category 1 hazards: how duty under section 5 operates in certain cases

(1)   This section explains the effect of provisions contained in subsection (2) of section 5.

(2)   In the case of paragraph (b) or (f) of that subsection, the reference to making an order such as is mentioned in that paragraph is to be read as a reference to making instead a determination under section 300(1) or (2) of the Housing Act 1985 (c 68) (power to purchase for temporary housing use) in a case where the authority consider the latter course of action to be the better alternative in the circumstances.

(3)   In the case of paragraph (d) of that subsection, the authority may regard the taking of emergency remedial action under section 40 followed by the service of an improvement notice under section 11 as a single course of action.

(4)   In the case of paragraph (e) of that subsection, the authority may regard the making of an emergency prohibition order under section 43 followed by the service of a prohibition order under section 20 as a single course of action.

(5)   In the case of paragraph (g) of that subsection—
- (a)   any duty to take the course of action mentioned in that paragraph is subject to the operation of subsections (2B) to (4) and (5B) of section 289 of the Housing Act 1985 (procedural and other restrictions relating to slum clearance declarations); and
- (b)   that paragraph does not apply in a case where the authority have already declared the area in which the premises concerned are situated to be a clearance area in accordance with section 289, but the premises have been excluded by virtue of section 289(2F)(b).

**[1334]**

**NOTES**
Commencement: 6 April 2006 (in relation to England, subject to transitional provisions and savings in the Housing Act 2004 (Commencement No 5 and Transitional Provisions and Savings) (England) Order 2006, SI 2006/1060, art 3, Schedule at **[3700]**, **[3701]**); 16 June 2006 (in relation to Wales, subject to transitional provisions and savings in the Housing Act 2004 (Commencement No 3 and Transitional Provisions and Savings) (Wales) Order 2006, SI 2006/1535, art 3, Schedule at **[3714]**, **[3715]**).

## 7   Category 2 hazards: powers to take enforcement action

(1)   The provisions mentioned in subsection (2) confer power on a local housing authority to take particular kinds of enforcement action in cases where they consider that a category 2 hazard exists on residential premises.

(2)   The provisions are—
- (a)   section 12 (power to serve an improvement notice),
- (b)   section 21 (power to make a prohibition order),
- (c)   section 29 (power to serve a hazard awareness notice),
- (d)   section 265(3) and (4) of the Housing Act 1985 (power to make a demolition order), and
- (e)   section 289(2ZB) of that Act (power to make a slum clearance declaration).

(3) The taking by the authority of one of those kinds of enforcement action in relation to a particular category 2 hazard does not prevent them from taking either—

(a) the same kind of action again, or

(b) a different kind of enforcement action,

in relation to the hazard, where they consider that the action taken by them so far has not proved satisfactory.

**[1335]**

**NOTES**

Commencement: 6 April 2006 (in relation to England, subject to transitional provisions and savings in the Housing Act 2004 (Commencement No 5 and Transitional Provisions and Savings) (England) Order 2006, SI 2006/1060, art 3, Schedule at **[3700]**, **[3701]**); 16 June 2006 (in relation to Wales, subject to transitional provisions and savings in the Housing Act 2004 (Commencement No 3 and Transitional Provisions and Savings) (Wales) Order 2006, SI 2006/1535, art 3, Schedule at **[3714]**, **[3715]**).

## 8 Reasons for decision to take enforcement action

(1) This section applies where a local housing authority decide to take one of the kinds of enforcement action mentioned in section 5(2) or 7(2) ("the relevant action").

(2) The authority must prepare a statement of the reasons for their decision to take the relevant action.

(3) Those reasons must include the reasons why the authority decided to take the relevant action rather than any other kind (or kinds) of enforcement action available to them under the provisions mentioned in section 5(2) or 7(2).

(4) A copy of the statement prepared under subsection (2) must accompany every notice, copy of a notice, or copy of an order which is served in accordance with—

(a) Part 1 of Schedule 1 to this Act (service of improvement notices etc),

(b) Part 1 of Schedule 2 to this Act (service of copies of prohibition orders etc), or

(c) section 268 of the Housing Act 1985 (service of copies of demolition orders),

in or in connection with the taking of the relevant action.

(5) In subsection (4)—

(a) the reference to Part 1 of Schedule 1 to this Act includes a reference to that Part as applied by section 28(7) or 29(7) (hazard awareness notices) or to section 40(7) (emergency remedial action); and

(b) the reference to Part 1 of Schedule 2 to this Act includes a reference to that Part as applied by section 43(4) (emergency prohibition orders).

(6) If the relevant action consists of declaring an area to be a clearance area, the statement prepared under subsection (2) must be published—

(a) as soon as possible after the relevant resolution is passed under section 289 of the Housing Act 1985, and

(b) in such manner as the authority consider appropriate.

**[1336]**

**NOTES**

Commencement: 6 April 2006 (in relation to England, subject to transitional provisions and savings in the Housing Act 2004 (Commencement No 5 and Transitional Provisions and Savings) (England) Order 2006, SI 2006/1060, art 3, Schedule at **[3700]**, **[3701]**); 16 June 2006 (in relation to Wales, subject to transitional provisions and savings in the Housing Act 2004 (Commencement No 3 and Transitional Provisions and Savings) (Wales) Order 2006, SI 2006/1535, art 3, Schedule at **[3714]**, **[3715]**).

## 9 Guidance about inspections and enforcement action

(1) The appropriate national authority may give guidance to local housing authorities about exercising—

(a) their functions under this Chapter in relation to the inspection of premises and the assessment of hazards,

(b) their functions under Chapter 2 of this Part in relation to improvement notices, prohibition orders or hazard awareness notices,

(c) their functions under Chapter 3 in relation to emergency remedial action and emergency prohibition orders, or

(d) their functions under Part 9 of the Housing Act 1985 (c 68) in relation to demolition orders and slum clearance.

(2) A local housing authority must have regard to any guidance for the time being given under this section.

(3) The appropriate national authority may give different guidance for different cases or descriptions of case or different purposes (including different guidance to different descriptions of local housing authority or to local housing authorities in different areas).

(4) Before giving guidance under this section, or revising guidance already given, the Secretary of State must lay a draft of the proposed guidance or alterations before each House of Parliament.

(5) The Secretary of State must not give or revise the guidance before the end of the period of 40 days beginning with the day on which the draft is laid before each House of Parliament (or, if copies are laid before each House of Parliament on different days, the later of those days).

(6) The Secretary of State must not proceed with the proposed guidance or alterations if, within the period of 40 days mentioned in subsection (5), either House resolves that the guidance or alterations be withdrawn.

(7) Subsection (6) is without prejudice to the possibility of laying a further draft of the guidance or alterations before each House of Parliament.

(8) In calculating the period of 40 days mentioned in subsection (5), no account is to be taken of any time during which Parliament is dissolved or prorogued or during which both Houses are adjourned for more than four days.

[1337]

## 10 Consultation with fire and rescue authorities in certain cases

(1) This section applies where a local housing authority—
  (a) are satisfied that a prescribed fire hazard exists in an HMO or in any common parts of a building containing one or more flats, and
  (b) intend to take in relation to the hazard one of the kinds of enforcement action mentioned in section 5(2) or section 7(2).

(2) Before taking the enforcement action in question, the authority must consult the fire and rescue authority for the area in which the HMO or building is situated.

(3) In the case of any proposed emergency measures, the authority's duty under subsection (2) is a duty to consult that fire and rescue authority so far as it is practicable to do so before taking those measures.

(4) In this section—
  "emergency measures" means emergency remedial action under section 40 or an emergency prohibition order under section 43;
  "fire and rescue authority" means a fire and rescue authority under the Fire and Rescue Services Act 2004 (c 21);
  "prescribed fire hazard" means a category 1 or 2 hazard which is prescribed as a fire hazard for the purposes of this section by regulations under section 2.

[1338]

**NOTES**
Commencement: 6 April 2006 (in relation to England, subject to transitional provisions and savings in the Housing Act 2004 (Commencement No 5 and Transitional Provisions and Savings) (England) Order 2006, SI 2006/1060, art 3, Schedule at **[3700]**, **[3701]**); 16 June 2006 (in relation to Wales, subject to transitional provisions and savings in the Housing Act 2004 (Commencement No 3 and Transitional Provisions and Savings) (Wales) Order 2006, SI 2006/1535, art 3, Schedule at **[3714]**, **[3715]**).

## CHAPTER 2
## IMPROVEMENT NOTICES, PROHIBITION ORDERS AND HAZARD AWARENESS NOTICES

*Improvement notices*

## 11 Improvement notices relating to category 1 hazards: duty of authority to serve notice

(1) If—
  (a) the local housing authority are satisfied that a category 1 hazard exists on any residential premises, and
  (b) no management order is in force in relation to the premises under Chapter 1 or 2 of Part 4,
serving an improvement notice under this section in respect of the hazard is a course of action available to the authority in relation to the hazard for the purposes of section 5 (category 1 hazards: general duty to take enforcement action).

(2) An improvement notice under this section is a notice requiring the person on whom it is served to take such remedial action in respect of the hazard concerned as is specified in the notice in accordance with subsections (3) to (5) and section 13.

(3) The notice may require remedial action to be taken in relation to the following premises—
  (a) if the residential premises on which the hazard exists are a dwelling or HMO which is not a flat, it may require such action to be taken in relation to the dwelling or HMO;

(b)    if those premises are one or more flats, it may require such action to be taken in relation to the building containing the flat or flats (or any part of the building) or any external common parts;

(c)    if those premises are the common parts of a building containing one or more flats, it may require such action to be taken in relation to the building (or any part of the building) or any external common parts.

Paragraphs (b) and (c) are subject to subsection (4).

(4)    The notice may not, by virtue of subsection (3)(b) or (c), require any remedial action to be taken in relation to any part of the building or its external common parts that is not included in any residential premises on which the hazard exists, unless the authority are satisfied—

(a)    that the deficiency from which the hazard arises is situated there, and

(b)    that it is necessary for the action to be so taken in order to protect the health or safety of any actual or potential occupiers of one or more of the flats.

(5)    The remedial action required to be taken by the notice—

(a)    must, as a minimum, be such as to ensure that the hazard ceases to be a category 1 hazard; but

(b)    may extend beyond such action.

(6)    An improvement notice under this section may relate to more than one category 1 hazard on the same premises or in the same building containing one or more flats.

(7)    The operation of an improvement notice under this section may be suspended in accordance with section 14.

(8)    In this Part "remedial action", in relation to a hazard, means action (whether in the form of carrying out works or otherwise) which, in the opinion of the local housing authority, will remove or reduce the hazard.

**[1339]**

**NOTES**

Commencement: 6 April 2006 (in relation to England, subject to transitional provisions and savings in the Housing Act 2004 (Commencement No 5 and Transitional Provisions and Savings) (England) Order 2006, SI 2006/1060, art 3, Schedule at **[3700]**, **[3701]**); 16 June 2006 (in relation to Wales, subject to transitional provisions and savings in the Housing Act 2004 (Commencement No 3 and Transitional Provisions and Savings) (Wales) Order 2006, SI 2006/1535, art 3, Schedule at **[3714]**, **[3715]**).

## 12   Improvement notices relating to category 2 hazards: power of authority to serve notice

(1)    If—

(a)    the local housing authority are satisfied that a category 2 hazard exists on any residential premises, and

(b)    no management order is in force in relation to the premises under Chapter 1 or 2 of Part 4,

the authority may serve an improvement notice under this section in respect of the hazard.

(2)    An improvement notice under this section is a notice requiring the person on whom it is served to take such remedial action in respect of the hazard concerned as is specified in the notice in accordance with subsection (3) and section 13.

(3)    Subsections (3) and (4) of section 11 apply to an improvement notice under this section as they apply to one under that section.

(4)    An improvement notice under this section may relate to more than one category 2 hazard on the same premises or in the same building containing one or more flats.

(5)    An improvement notice under this section may be combined in one document with a notice under section 11 where they require remedial action to be taken in relation to the same premises.

(6)    The operation of an improvement notice under this section may be suspended in accordance with section 14.

**[1340]**

**NOTES**

Commencement: 6 April 2006 (in relation to England, subject to transitional provisions and savings in the Housing Act 2004 (Commencement No 5 and Transitional Provisions and Savings) (England) Order 2006, SI 2006/1060, art 3, Schedule at **[3700]**, **[3701]**); 16 June 2006 (in relation to Wales, subject to transitional provisions and savings in the Housing Act 2004 (Commencement No 3 and Transitional Provisions and Savings) (Wales) Order 2006, SI 2006/1535, art 3, Schedule at **[3714]**, **[3715]**).

## 13   Contents of improvement notices

(1)    An improvement notice under section 11 or 12 must comply with the following provisions of this section.

(2)  The notice must specify, in relation to the hazard (or each of the hazards) to which it relates—

    (a)   whether the notice is served under section 11 or 12,

    (b)   the nature of the hazard and the residential premises on which it exists,

    (c)   the deficiency giving rise to the hazard,

    (d)   the premises in relation to which remedial action is to be taken in respect of the hazard and the nature of that remedial action,

    (e)   the date when the remedial action is to be started (see subsection (3)), and

    (f)   the period within which the remedial action is to be completed or the periods within which each part of it is to be completed.

(3)  The notice may not require any remedial action to be started earlier than the 28th day after that on which the notice is served.

(4)  The notice must contain information about—

    (a)   the right of appeal against the decision under Part 3 of Schedule 1, and

    (b)   the period within which an appeal may be made.

(5)  In this Part of this Act "specified premises", in relation to an improvement notice, means premises specified in the notice, in accordance with subsection (2)(d), as premises in relation to which remedial action is to be taken in respect of the hazard.

**[1341]**

**NOTES**

Commencement: 6 April 2006 (in relation to England, subject to transitional provisions and savings in the Housing Act 2004 (Commencement No 5 and Transitional Provisions and Savings) (England) Order 2006, SI 2006/1060, art 3, Schedule at **[3700]**, **[3701]**); 16 June 2006 (in relation to Wales, subject to transitional provisions and savings in the Housing Act 2004 (Commencement No 3 and Transitional Provisions and Savings) (Wales) Order 2006, SI 2006/1535, art 3, Schedule at **[3714]**, **[3715]**).

## 14  Suspension of improvement notices

(1)  An improvement notice may provide for the operation of the notice to be suspended until a time, or the occurrence of an event, specified in the notice.

(2)  The time so specified may, in particular, be the time when a person of a particular description begins, or ceases, to occupy any premises.

(3)  The event so specified may, in particular, be a notified breach of an undertaking accepted by the local housing authority for the purposes of this section from the person on whom the notice is served.

(4)  In subsection (3) a "notified breach", in relation to such an undertaking, means an act or omission by the person on whom the notice is served—

    (a)   which the local housing authority consider to be a breach of the undertaking, and

    (b)   which is notified to that person in accordance with the terms of the undertaking.

(5)  If an improvement notice does provide for the operation of the notice to be suspended under this section—

    (a)   any periods specified in the notice under section 13 are to be fixed by reference to the day when the suspension ends, and

    (b)   in subsection (3) of that section the reference to the 28th day after that on which the notice is served is to be read as referring to the 21st day after that on which the suspension ends.

**[1342]**

**NOTES**

Commencement: 6 April 2006 (in relation to England, subject to transitional provisions and savings in the Housing Act 2004 (Commencement No 5 and Transitional Provisions and Savings) (England) Order 2006, SI 2006/1060, art 3, Schedule at **[3700]**, **[3701]**); 16 June 2006 (in relation to Wales, subject to transitional provisions and savings in the Housing Act 2004 (Commencement No 3 and Transitional Provisions and Savings) (Wales) Order 2006, SI 2006/1535, art 3, Schedule at **[3714]**, **[3715]**).

## 15  Operation of improvement notices

(1)  This section deals with the time when an improvement notice becomes operative.

(2)  The general rule is that an improvement notice becomes operative at the end of the period of 21 days beginning with the day on which it is served under Part 1 of Schedule 1 (which is the period for appealing against the notice under Part 3 of that Schedule).

(3)  The general rule is subject to subsection (4) (suspended notices) and subsection (5) (appeals).

(4)  If the notice is suspended under section 14, the notice becomes operative at the time when the suspension ends.

This is subject to subsection (5).

(5)   If an appeal against the notice is made under Part 3 of Schedule 1, the notice does not become operative until such time (if any) as is the operative time for the purposes of this subsection under paragraph 19 of that Schedule (time when notice is confirmed on appeal, period for further appeal expires or suspension ends).

(6)   If no appeal against an improvement notice is made under that Part of that Schedule within the period for appealing against it, the notice is final and conclusive as to matters which could have been raised on an appeal.

**[1343]**

**NOTES**

Commencement: 6 April 2006 (in relation to England, subject to transitional provisions and savings in the Housing Act 2004 (Commencement No 5 and Transitional Provisions and Savings) (England) Order 2006, SI 2006/1060, art 3, Schedule at **[3700]**, **[3701]**); 16 June 2006 (in relation to Wales, subject to transitional provisions and savings in the Housing Act 2004 (Commencement No 3 and Transitional Provisions and Savings) (Wales) Order 2006, SI 2006/1535, art 3, Schedule at **[3714]**, **[3715]**).

### 16   Revocation and variation of improvement notices

(1)   The local housing authority must revoke an improvement notice if they are satisfied that the requirements of the notice have been complied with.

(2)   The local housing authority may revoke an improvement notice if—
    (a)   in the case of a notice served under section 11, they consider that there are any special circumstances making it appropriate to revoke the notice; or
    (b)   in the case of a notice served under section 12, they consider that it is appropriate to revoke the notice.

(3)   Where an improvement notice relates to a number of hazards—
    (a)   subsection (1) is to be read as applying separately in relation to each of those hazards, and
    (b)   if, as a result, the authority are required to revoke only part of the notice, they may vary the remainder as they consider appropriate.

(4)   The local housing authority may vary an improvement notice—
    (a)   with the agreement of the person on whom the notice was served, or
    (b)   in the case of a notice whose operation is suspended, so as to alter the time or events by reference to which the suspension is to come to an end.

(5)   A revocation under this section comes into force at the time when it is made.

(6)   If it is made with the agreement of the person on whom the improvement notice was served, a variation under this section comes into force at the time when it is made.

(7)   Otherwise a variation under this section does not come into force until such time (if any) as is the operative time for the purposes of this subsection under paragraph 20 of Schedule 1 (time when period for appealing expires without an appeal being made or when decision to vary is confirmed on appeal).

(8)   The power to revoke or vary an improvement notice under this section is exercisable by the authority either—
    (a)   on an application made by the person on whom the improvement notice was served, or
    (b)   on the authority's own initiative.

**[1344]**

**NOTES**

Commencement: 6 April 2006 (in relation to England, subject to transitional provisions and savings in the Housing Act 2004 (Commencement No 5 and Transitional Provisions and Savings) (England) Order 2006, SI 2006/1060, art 3, Schedule at **[3700]**, **[3701]**); 16 June 2006 (in relation to Wales, subject to transitional provisions and savings in the Housing Act 2004 (Commencement No 3 and Transitional Provisions and Savings) (Wales) Order 2006, SI 2006/1535, art 3, Schedule at **[3714]**, **[3715]**).

### 17   Review of suspended improvement notices

(1)   The local housing authority may at any time review an improvement notice whose operation is suspended.

(2)   The local housing authority must review an improvement notice whose operation is suspended not later than one year after the date of service of the notice and at subsequent intervals of not more than one year.

(3)   Copies of the authority's decision on a review under this section must be served—
    (a)   on the person on whom the improvement notice was served, and
    (b)   on every other person on whom a copy of the notice was required to be served.

**[1345]**

**NOTES**
Commencement: 6 April 2006 (in relation to England, subject to transitional provisions and savings in the Housing Act 2004 (Commencement No 5 and Transitional Provisions and Savings) (England) Order 2006, SI 2006/1060, art 3, Schedule at **[3700], [3701]**); 16 June 2006 (in relation to Wales, subject to transitional provisions and savings in the Housing Act 2004 (Commencement No 3 and Transitional Provisions and Savings) (Wales) Order 2006, SI 2006/1535, art 3, Schedule at **[3714], [3715]**).

## 18 Service of improvement notices etc and related appeals

Schedule 1 (which deals with the service of improvement notices, and notices relating to their revocation or variation, and with related appeals) has effect.

**[1346]**

**NOTES**
Commencement: 6 April 2006 (in relation to England, subject to transitional provisions and savings in the Housing Act 2004 (Commencement No 5 and Transitional Provisions and Savings) (England) Order 2006, SI 2006/1060, art 3, Schedule at **[3700], [3701]**); 16 June 2006 (in relation to Wales, subject to transitional provisions and savings in the Housing Act 2004 (Commencement No 3 and Transitional Provisions and Savings) (Wales) Order 2006, SI 2006/1535, art 3, Schedule at **[3714], [3715]**).

## 19 Change in person liable to comply with improvement notice

(1) This section applies where—
    (a) an improvement notice has been served on any person ("the original recipient") in respect of any premises, and
    (b) at a later date ("the changeover date") that person ceases to be a person of the relevant category in respect of the premises.

(2) In subsection (1) the reference to a person ceasing to be a "person of the relevant category" is a reference to his ceasing to fall within the description of person (such as, for example, the holder of a licence under Part 2 or 3 or the person managing a dwelling) by reference to which the improvement notice was served on him.

(3) As from the changeover date, the liable person in respect of the premises is to be in the same position as if—
    (a) the improvement notice had originally been served on him, and
    (b) he had taken all steps relevant for the purposes of this Part which the original recipient had taken.

(4) The effect of subsection (3) is that, in particular, any period for compliance with the notice or for bringing any appeal is unaffected.

(5) But where the original recipient has become subject to any liability arising by virtue of this Part before the changeover date, subsection (3) does not have the effect of—
    (a) relieving him of the liability, or
    (b) making the new liable person subject to it.

(6) Subsection (3) applies with any necessary modifications where a person to whom it applies (by virtue of any provision of this section) ceases to be the liable person in respect of the premises.

(7) Unless subsection (8) or (9) applies, the person who is at any time the "liable person" in respect of any premises is the person having control of the premises.

(8) If—
    (a) the original recipient was served as the person managing the premises, and
    (b) there is a new person managing the premises as from the changeover date,
that new person is the "liable person".

(9) If the original recipient was served as an owner of the premises, the "liable person" is the owner's successor in title on the changeover date.

**[1347]**

**NOTES**
Commencement: 6 April 2006 (in relation to England, subject to transitional provisions and savings in the Housing Act 2004 (Commencement No 5 and Transitional Provisions and Savings) (England) Order 2006, SI 2006/1060, art 3, Schedule at **[3700], [3701]**); 16 June 2006 (in relation to Wales, subject to transitional provisions and savings in the Housing Act 2004 (Commencement No 3 and Transitional Provisions and Savings) (Wales) Order 2006, SI 2006/1535, art 3, Schedule at **[3714], [3715]**).

*Prohibition orders*

## 20 Prohibition orders relating to category 1 hazards: duty of authority to make order

(1) If—
    (a) the local housing authority are satisfied that a category 1 hazard exists on any residential premises, and

(b)    no management order is in force in relation to the premises under Chapter 1 or 2 of Part 4,

making a prohibition order under this section in respect of the hazard is a course of action available to the authority in relation to the hazard for the purposes of section 5 (category 1 hazards: general duty to take enforcement action).

(2)    A prohibition order under this section is an order imposing such prohibition or prohibitions on the use of any premises as is or are specified in the order in accordance with subsections (3) and (4) and section 22.

(3)    The order may prohibit use of the following premises—
(a)    if the residential premises on which the hazard exists are a dwelling or HMO which is not a flat, it may prohibit use of the dwelling or HMO;
(b)    if those premises are one or more flats, it may prohibit use of the building containing the flat or flats (or any part of the building) or any external common parts;
(c)    if those premises are the common parts of a building containing one or more flats, it may prohibit use of the building (or any part of the building) or any external common parts.

Paragraphs (b) and (c) are subject to subsection (4).

(4)    The notice may not, by virtue of subsection (3)(b) or (c), prohibit use of any part of the building or its external common parts that is not included in any residential premises on which the hazard exists, unless the authority are satisfied—
(a)    that the deficiency from which the hazard arises is situated there, and
(b)    that it is necessary for such use to be prohibited in order to protect the health or safety of any actual or potential occupiers of one or more of the flats.

(5)    A prohibition order under this section may relate to more than one category 1 hazard on the same premises or in the same building containing one or more flats.

(6)    The operation of a prohibition order under this section may be suspended in accordance with section 23.

**[1348]**

**NOTES**

Commencement: 6 April 2006 (in relation to England, subject to transitional provisions and savings in the Housing Act 2004 (Commencement No 5 and Transitional Provisions and Savings) (England) Order 2006, SI 2006/1060, art 3, Schedule at **[3700]**, **[3701]**); 16 June 2006 (in relation to Wales, subject to transitional provisions and savings in the Housing Act 2004 (Commencement No 3 and Transitional Provisions and Savings) (Wales) Order 2006, SI 2006/1535, art 3, Schedule at **[3714]**, **[3715]**).

**21    Prohibition orders relating to category 2 hazards: power of authority to make order**

(1)    If—
(a)    the local housing authority are satisfied that a category 2 hazard exists on any residential premises, and
(b)    no management order is in force in relation to the premises under Chapter 1 or 2 of Part 4,

the authority may make a prohibition order under this section in respect of the hazard.

(2)    A prohibition order under this section is an order imposing such prohibition or prohibitions on the use of any premises as is or are specified in the order in accordance with subsection (3) and section 22.

(3)    Subsections (3) and (4) of section 20 apply to a prohibition order under this section as they apply to one under that section.

(4)    A prohibition order under this section may relate to more than one category 2 hazard on the same premises or in the same building containing one or more flats.

(5)    A prohibition order under this section may be combined in one document with an order under section 20 where they impose prohibitions on the use of the same premises or on the use of premises in the same building containing one or more flats.

(6)    The operation of a prohibition order under this section may be suspended in accordance with section 23.

**[1349]**

**NOTES**

Commencement: 6 April 2006 (in relation to England, subject to transitional provisions and savings in the Housing Act 2004 (Commencement No 5 and Transitional Provisions and Savings) (England) Order 2006, SI 2006/1060, art 3, Schedule at **[3700]**, **[3701]**); 16 June 2006 (in relation to Wales, subject to transitional provisions and savings in the Housing Act 2004 (Commencement No 3 and Transitional Provisions and Savings) (Wales) Order 2006, SI 2006/1535, art 3, Schedule at **[3714]**, **[3715]**).

**22 Contents of prohibition orders**

(1)   A prohibition order under section 20 or 21 must comply with the following provisions of this section.

(2)   The order must specify, in relation to the hazard (or each of the hazards) to which it relates—

(a)   whether the order is made under section 20 or 21,

(b)   the nature of the hazard concerned and the residential premises on which it exists,

(c)   the deficiency giving rise to the hazard,

(d)   the premises in relation to which prohibitions are imposed by the order (see subsections (3) and (4)), and

(e)   any remedial action which the authority consider would, if taken in relation to the hazard, result in their revoking the order under section 25.

(3)   The order may impose such prohibition or prohibitions on the use of any premises as—

(a)   comply with section 20(3) and (4), and

(b)   the local housing authority consider appropriate in view of the hazard or hazards in respect of which the order is made.

(4)   Any such prohibition may prohibit use of any specified premises, or of any part of those premises, either—

(a)   for all purposes, or

(b)   for any particular purpose,

except (in either case) to the extent to which any use of the premises or part is approved by the authority.

(5)   A prohibition imposed by virtue of subsection (4)(b) may, in particular, relate to—

(a)   occupation of the premises or part by more than a particular number of households or persons; or

(b)   occupation of the premises or part by particular descriptions of persons.

(6)   The order must also contain information about—

(a)   the right under Part 3 of Schedule 2 to appeal against the order, and

(b)   the period within which an appeal may be made,

and specify the date on which the order is made.

(7)   Any approval of the authority for the purposes of subsection (4) must not be unreasonably withheld.

(8)   If the authority do refuse to give any such approval, they must notify the person applying for the approval of—

(a)   their decision,

(b)   the reasons for it and the date on which it was made,

(c)   the right to appeal against the decision under subsection (9), and

(d)   the period within which an appeal may be made,

within the period of seven days beginning with the day on which the decision was made.

(9)   The person applying for the approval may appeal to a residential property tribunal against the decision within the period of 28 days beginning with the date specified in the notice as the date on which it was made.

(10)   In this Part of this Act "specified premises", in relation to a prohibition order, means premises specified in the order, in accordance with subsection (2)(d), as premises in relation to which prohibitions are imposed by the order.

**[1350]**

**NOTES**

Commencement: 6 April 2006 (in relation to England, subject to transitional provisions and savings in the Housing Act 2004 (Commencement No 5 and Transitional Provisions and Savings) (England) Order 2006, SI 2006/1060, art 3, Schedule at **[3700]**, **[3701]**); 16 June 2006 (in relation to Wales, subject to transitional provisions and savings in the Housing Act 2004 (Commencement No 3 and Transitional Provisions and Savings) (Wales) Order 2006, SI 2006/1535, art 3, Schedule at **[3714]**, **[3715]**).

**23 Suspension of prohibition orders**

(1)   A prohibition order may provide for the operation of the order to be suspended until a time, or the occurrence of an event, specified in the order.

(2)   The time so specified may, in particular, be the time when a person of a particular description begins, or ceases, to occupy any premises.

(3)   The event so specified may, in particular, be a notified breach of an undertaking accepted by the local housing authority for the purposes of this section from a person on whom a copy of the order is served.

(4)   In subsection (3) a "notified breach", in relation to such an undertaking, means an act or omission by such a person—

(a)   which the local housing authority consider to be a breach of the undertaking, and

(b)   which is notified to that person in accordance with the terms of the undertaking.

**[1351]**

**NOTES**

Commencement: 6 April 2006 (in relation to England, subject to transitional provisions and savings in the Housing Act 2004 (Commencement No 5 and Transitional Provisions and Savings) (England) Order 2006, SI 2006/1060, art 3, Schedule at **[3700]**, **[3701]**); 16 June 2006 (in relation to Wales, subject to transitional provisions and savings in the Housing Act 2004 (Commencement No 3 and Transitional Provisions and Savings) (Wales) Order 2006, SI 2006/1535, art 3, Schedule at **[3714]**, **[3715]**).

## 24  Operation of prohibition orders

(1)   This section deals with the time when a prohibition order becomes operative.

(2)   The general rule is that a prohibition order becomes operative at the end of the period of 28 days beginning with the date specified in the notice as the date on which it is made.

(3)   The general rule is subject to subsection (4) (suspended orders) and subsection (5) (appeals).

(4)   If the order is suspended under section 23, the order becomes operative at the time when the suspension ends.

This is subject to subsection (5).

(5)   If an appeal is brought against the order under Part 3 of Schedule 2, the order does not become operative until such time (if any) as is the operative time for the purposes of this subsection under paragraph 14 of that Schedule (time when order is confirmed on appeal, period for further appeal expires or suspension ends).

(6)   If no appeal against a prohibition order is made under that Part of that Schedule within the period for appealing against it, the order is final and conclusive as to matters which could have been raised on an appeal.

(7)   Sections 584A and 584B of the Housing Act 1985 (c 68) provide for the payment of compensation where certain prohibition orders become operative, and for the repayment of such compensation in certain circumstances.

**[1352]**

**NOTES**

Commencement: 6 April 2006 (in relation to England, subject to transitional provisions and savings in the Housing Act 2004 (Commencement No 5 and Transitional Provisions and Savings) (England) Order 2006, SI 2006/1060, art 3, Schedule at **[3700]**, **[3701]**); 16 June 2006 (in relation to Wales, subject to transitional provisions and savings in the Housing Act 2004 (Commencement No 3 and Transitional Provisions and Savings) (Wales) Order 2006, SI 2006/1535, art 3, Schedule at **[3714]**, **[3715]**).

## 25  Revocation and variation of prohibition orders

(1)   The local housing authority must revoke a prohibition order if at any time they are satisfied that the hazard in respect of which the order was made does not then exist on the residential premises specified in the order in accordance with section 22(2)(b).

(2)   The local housing authority may revoke a prohibition order if—

(a)   in the case of an order made under section 20, they consider that there are any special circumstances making it appropriate to revoke the order; or

(b)   in the case of an order made under section 21, they consider that it is appropriate to do so.

(3)   Where a prohibition order relates to a number of hazards—

(a)   subsection (1) is to be read as applying separately in relation to each of those hazards, and

(b)   if, as a result, the authority are required to revoke only part of the order, they may vary the remainder as they consider appropriate.

(4)   The local housing authority may vary a prohibition order—

(a)   with the agreement of every person on whom copies of the notice were required to be served under Part 1 of Schedule 2, or

(b)   in the case of an order whose operation is suspended, so as to alter the time or events by reference to which the suspension is to come to an end.

(5)   A revocation under this section comes into force at the time when it is made.

(6)   If it is made with the agreement of every person within subsection (4)(a), a variation under this section comes into force at the time when it is made.

(7)   Otherwise a variation under this section does not come into force until such time (if any) as is the operative time for the purposes of this subsection under paragraph 15 of Schedule 2 (time when period for appealing expires without an appeal being made or when decision to revoke or vary is confirmed on appeal).

(8)   The power to revoke or vary a prohibition order under this section is exercisable by the authority either—

(a)   on an application made by a person on whom a copy of the order was required to be served under Part 1 of Schedule 2, or

(b)   on the authority's own initiative.

**[1353]**

**NOTES**
Commencement: 6 April 2006 (in relation to England, subject to transitional provisions and savings in the Housing Act 2004 (Commencement No 5 and Transitional Provisions and Savings) (England) Order 2006, SI 2006/1060, art 3, Schedule at **[3700]**, **[3701]**); 16 June 2006 (in relation to Wales, subject to transitional provisions and savings in the Housing Act 2004 (Commencement No 3 and Transitional Provisions and Savings) (Wales) Order 2006, SI 2006/1535, art 3, Schedule at **[3714]**, **[3715]**).

## 26   Review of suspended prohibition orders

(1)   The local housing authority may at any time review a prohibition order whose operation is suspended.

(2)   The local housing authority must review a prohibition order whose operation is suspended not later than one year after the date on which the order was made and at subsequent intervals of not more than one year.

(3)   Copies of the authority's decision on a review under this section must be served on every person on whom a copy of the order was required to be served under Part 1 of Schedule 2.

**[1354]**

**NOTES**
Commencement: 6 April 2006 (in relation to England, subject to transitional provisions and savings in the Housing Act 2004 (Commencement No 5 and Transitional Provisions and Savings) (England) Order 2006, SI 2006/1060, art 3, Schedule at **[3700]**, **[3701]**); 16 June 2006 (in relation to Wales, subject to transitional provisions and savings in the Housing Act 2004 (Commencement No 3 and Transitional Provisions and Savings) (Wales) Order 2006, SI 2006/1535, art 3, Schedule at **[3714]**, **[3715]**).

## 27   Service of copies of prohibition orders etc and related appeals

Schedule 2 (which deals with the service of copies of prohibition orders, and notices relating to their revocation or variation, and with related appeals) has effect.

**[1355]**

**NOTES**
Commencement: 6 April 2006 (in relation to England, subject to transitional provisions and savings in the Housing Act 2004 (Commencement No 5 and Transitional Provisions and Savings) (England) Order 2006, SI 2006/1060, art 3, Schedule at **[3700]**, **[3701]**); 16 June 2006 (in relation to Wales, subject to transitional provisions and savings in the Housing Act 2004 (Commencement No 3 and Transitional Provisions and Savings) (Wales) Order 2006, SI 2006/1535, art 3, Schedule at **[3714]**, **[3715]**).

*Hazard awareness notices*

## 28   Hazard awareness notices relating to category 1 hazards: duty of authority to serve notice

(1)   If—

(a)   the local housing authority are satisfied that a category 1 hazard exists on any residential premises, and

(b)   no management order is in force in relation to the premises under Chapter 1 or 2 of Part 4,

serving a hazard awareness notice under this section in respect of the hazard is a course of action available to the authority in relation to the hazard for the purposes of section 5 (category 1 hazards: general duty to take enforcement action).

(2)   A hazard awareness notice under this section is a notice advising the person on whom it is served of the existence of a category 1 hazard on the residential premises concerned which arises as a result of a deficiency on the premises in respect of which the notice is served.

(3)   The notice may be served in respect of the following premises—

(a)   if the residential premises on which the hazard exists are a dwelling or HMO which is not a flat, it may be served in respect of the dwelling or HMO;

(b)   if those premises are one or more flats, it may be served in respect of the building containing the flat or flats (or any part of the building) or any external common parts;

    (c)    if those premises are the common parts of a building containing one or more flats, it may be served in respect of the building (or any part of the building) or any external common parts.

Paragraphs (b) and (c) are subject to subsection (4).

(4)    The notice may not, by virtue of subsection (3)(b) or (c), be served in respect of any part of the building or its external common parts that is not included in any residential premises on which the hazard exists, unless the authority are satisfied—

    (a)    that the deficiency from which the hazard arises is situated there, and

    (b)    that it is desirable for the notice to be so served in the interests of the health or safety of any actual or potential occupiers of one or more of the flats.

(5)    A notice under this section may relate to more than one category 1 hazard on the same premises or in the same building containing one or more flats.

(6)    A notice under this section must specify, in relation to the hazard (or each of the hazards) to which it relates—

    (a)    the nature of the hazard and the residential premises on which it exists,

    (b)    the deficiency giving rise to the hazard,

    (c)    the premises on which the deficiency exists,

    (d)    the authority's reasons for deciding to serve the notice, including their reasons for deciding that serving the notice is the most appropriate course of action, and

    (e)    details of the remedial action (if any) which the authority consider that it would be practicable and appropriate to take in relation to the hazard.

(7)    Part 1 of Schedule 1 (which relates to the service of improvement notices and copies of such notices) applies to a notice under this section as if it were an improvement notice.

(8)    For that purpose, any reference in that Part of that Schedule to "the specified premises" is, in relation to a hazard awareness notice under this section, a reference to the premises specified under subsection (6)(c).

**[1356]**

**NOTES**

    Commencement: 6 April 2006 (in relation to England, subject to transitional provisions and savings in the Housing Act 2004 (Commencement No 5 and Transitional Provisions and Savings) (England) Order 2006, SI 2006/1060, art 3, Schedule at **[3700]**, **[3701]**); 16 June 2006 (in relation to Wales, subject to transitional provisions and savings in the Housing Act 2004 (Commencement No 3 and Transitional Provisions and Savings) (Wales) Order 2006, SI 2006/1535, art 3, Schedule at **[3714]**, **[3715]**).

**29 Hazard awareness notices relating to category 2 hazards: power of authority to serve notice**

(1)    If—

    (a)    the local housing authority are satisfied that a category 2 hazard exists on any residential premises, and

    (b)    no management order is in force in relation to the premises under Chapter 1 or 2 of Part 4,

the authority may serve a hazard awareness notice under this section in respect of the hazard.

(2)    A hazard awareness notice under this section is a notice advising the person on whom it is served of the existence of a category 2 hazard on the residential premises concerned which arises as a result of a deficiency on the premises in respect of which the notice is served.

(3)    Subsections (3) and (4) of section 28 apply to a hazard awareness notice under this section as they apply to one under that section.

(4)    A notice under this section may relate to more than one category 2 hazard on the same premises or in the same building containing one or more flats.

(5)    A notice under this section must specify, in relation to the hazard (or each of the hazards) to which it relates—

    (a)    the nature of the hazard and the residential premises on which it exists,

    (b)    the deficiency giving rise to the hazard,

    (c)    the premises on which the deficiency exists,

    (d)    the authority's reasons for deciding to serve the notice, including their reasons for deciding that serving the notice is the most appropriate course of action, and

    (e)    details of the remedial action (if any) which the authority consider that it would be practicable and appropriate to take in relation to the hazard.

(6)    A notice under this section may be combined in one document with a notice under section 28 where they are served in respect of the same premises.

(7)    Part 1 of Schedule 1 (which relates to the service of improvement notices and copies of such notices) applies to a notice under this section as if it were an improvement notice.

(8)    For that purpose, any reference in that Part of that Schedule to "the specified premises" is, in relation to a hazard awareness notice under this section, a reference to the premises specified under subsection (5)(c).

**[1357]**

**NOTES**
    Commencement: 6 April 2006 (in relation to England, subject to transitional provisions and savings in the Housing Act 2004 (Commencement No 5 and Transitional Provisions and Savings) (England) Order 2006, SI 2006/1060, art 3, Schedule at **[3700]**, **[3701]**); 16 June 2006 (in relation to Wales, subject to transitional provisions and savings in the Housing Act 2004 (Commencement No 3 and Transitional Provisions and Savings) (Wales) Order 2006, SI 2006/1535, art 3, Schedule at **[3714]**, **[3715]**).

*Enforcement: improvement notices*

## 30  Offence of failing to comply with improvement notice

(1)    Where an improvement notice has become operative, the person on whom the notice was served commits an offence if he fails to comply with it.

(2)    For the purposes of this Chapter compliance with an improvement notice means, in relation to each hazard, beginning and completing any remedial action specified in the notice—
- (a)    (if no appeal is brought against the notice) not later than the date specified under section 13(2)(e) and within the period specified under section 13(2)(f);
- (b)    (if an appeal is brought against the notice and is not withdrawn) not later than such date and within such period as may be fixed by the tribunal determining the appeal; and
- (c)    (if an appeal brought against the notice is withdrawn) not later than the 21st day after the date on which the notice becomes operative and within the period (beginning on that 21st day) specified in the notice under section 13(2)(f).

(3)    A person who commits an offence under subsection (1) is liable on summary conviction to a fine not exceeding level 5 on the standard scale.

(4)    In proceedings against a person for an offence under subsection (1) it is a defence that he had a reasonable excuse for failing to comply with the notice.

(5)    The obligation to take any remedial action specified in the notice in relation to a hazard continues despite the fact that the period for completion of the action has expired.

(6)    In this section any reference to any remedial action specified in a notice includes a reference to any part of any remedial action which is required to be completed within a particular period specified in the notice.

**[1358]**

**NOTES**
    Commencement: 6 April 2006 (in relation to England, subject to transitional provisions and savings in the Housing Act 2004 (Commencement No 5 and Transitional Provisions and Savings) (England) Order 2006, SI 2006/1060, art 3, Schedule at **[3700]**, **[3701]**); 16 June 2006 (in relation to Wales, subject to transitional provisions and savings in the Housing Act 2004 (Commencement No 3 and Transitional Provisions and Savings) (Wales) Order 2006, SI 2006/1535, art 3, Schedule at **[3714]**, **[3715]**).

## 31  Enforcement action by local housing authorities

Schedule 3 (which enables enforcement action in respect of an improvement notice to be taken by local housing authorities either with or without agreement and which provides for the recovery of related expenses) has effect.

**[1359]**

**NOTES**
    Commencement: 6 April 2006 (in relation to England, subject to transitional provisions and savings in the Housing Act 2004 (Commencement No 5 and Transitional Provisions and Savings) (England) Order 2006, SI 2006/1060, art 3, Schedule at **[3700]**, **[3701]**); 16 June 2006 (in relation to Wales, subject to transitional provisions and savings in the Housing Act 2004 (Commencement No 3 and Transitional Provisions and Savings) (Wales) Order 2006, SI 2006/1535, art 3, Schedule at **[3714]**, **[3715]**).

*Enforcement: prohibition orders*

## 32  Offence of failing to comply with prohibition order etc

(1)    A person commits an offence if, knowing that a prohibition order has become operative in relation to any specified premises, he—
- (a)    uses the premises in contravention of the order, or
- (b)    permits the premises to be so used.

(2)    A person who commits an offence under subsection (1) is liable on summary conviction—
- (a)    to a fine not exceeding level 5 on the standard scale, and

(b)    to a further fine not exceeding £20 for every day or part of a day on which he so uses the premises, or permits them to be so used, after conviction.

(3)    In proceedings against a person for an offence under subsection (1) it is a defence that he had a reasonable excuse for using the premises, or (as the case may be) permitting them to be used, in contravention of the order.

**[1360]**

**NOTES**
    Commencement: 6 April 2006 (in relation to England, subject to transitional provisions and savings in the Housing Act 2004 (Commencement No 5 and Transitional Provisions and Savings) (England) Order 2006, SI 2006/1060, art 3, Schedule at **[3700]**, **[3701]**); 16 June 2006 (in relation to Wales, subject to transitional provisions and savings in the Housing Act 2004 (Commencement No 3 and Transitional Provisions and Savings) (Wales) Order 2006, SI 2006/1535, art 3, Schedule at **[3714]**, **[3715]**).

**33    Recovery of possession of premises in order to comply with order**
Nothing in—
    (a)    the Rent Act 1977 (c 42) or the Rent (Agriculture) Act 1976 (c 80), or
    (b)    Part 1 of the Housing Act 1988 (c 50),
prevents possession being obtained by the owner of any specified premises in relation to which a prohibition order is operative if possession of the premises is necessary for the purpose of complying with the order.

**[1361]**

**NOTES**
    Commencement: 6 April 2006 (in relation to England, subject to transitional provisions and savings in the Housing Act 2004 (Commencement No 5 and Transitional Provisions and Savings) (England) Order 2006, SI 2006/1060, art 3, Schedule at **[3700]**, **[3701]**); 16 June 2006 (in relation to Wales, subject to transitional provisions and savings in the Housing Act 2004 (Commencement No 3 and Transitional Provisions and Savings) (Wales) Order 2006, SI 2006/1535, art 3, Schedule at **[3714]**, **[3715]**).

**34    Power of tribunal to determine or vary lease**
    (1)    Subsection (2) applies where—
    (a)    a prohibition order has become operative, and
    (b)    the whole or part of any specified premises form the whole or part of the subject matter of a lease.

    (2)    The lessor or the lessee may apply to a residential property tribunal for an order determining or varying the lease.

    (3)    On such an application the tribunal may make an order determining or varying the lease, if it considers it appropriate to do so.

    (4)    Before making such an order, the tribunal must give any sub-lessee an opportunity of being heard.

    (5)    An order under this section may be unconditional or subject to such terms and conditions as the tribunal considers appropriate.

    (6)    The conditions may, in particular, include conditions about the payment of money by one party to the proceedings to another by way of compensation, damages or otherwise.

    (7)    In deciding what is appropriate for the purposes of this section, the tribunal must have regard to the respective rights, obligations and liabilities of the parties under the lease and to all the other circumstances of the case.

    (8)    In this section "lessor" and "lessee" include a person deriving title under a lessor or lessee.

**[1362]**

**NOTES**
    Commencement: 6 April 2006 (in relation to England, subject to transitional provisions and savings in the Housing Act 2004 (Commencement No 5 and Transitional Provisions and Savings) (England) Order 2006, SI 2006/1060, art 3, Schedule at **[3700]**, **[3701]**); 16 June 2006 (in relation to Wales, subject to transitional provisions and savings in the Housing Act 2004 (Commencement No 3 and Transitional Provisions and Savings) (Wales) Order 2006, SI 2006/1535, art 3, Schedule at **[3714]**, **[3715]**).

*Enforcement: improvement notices and prohibition orders*

**35    Power of court to order occupier or owner to allow action to be taken on premises**
    (1)    This section applies where an improvement notice or prohibition order has become operative.

    (2)    If the occupier of any specified premises—
    (a)    has received reasonable notice of any intended action in relation to the premises, but

    (b)   is preventing a relevant person, or any representative of a relevant person or of the local housing authority, from taking that action in relation to the premises,

a magistrates' court may order the occupier to permit to be done on the premises anything which the court considers is necessary or expedient for the purpose of enabling the intended action to be taken.

(3)   If a relevant person—

    (a)   has received reasonable notice of any intended action in relation to any specified premises, but

    (b)   is preventing a representative of the local housing authority from taking that action in relation to the premises,

a magistrates' court may order the relevant person to permit to be done on the premises anything which the court considers is necessary or expedient for the purpose of enabling the intended action to be taken.

(4)   A person who fails to comply with an order of the court under this section commits an offence.

(5)   In proceedings for an offence under subsection (4) it is a defence that the person had a reasonable excuse for failing to comply with the order.

(6)   A person who commits an offence under subsection (4) is liable on summary conviction to a fine not exceeding £20 in respect of each day or part of a day during which the failure continues.

(7)   In this section "intended action", in relation to any specified premises, means—

    (a)   where an improvement notice has become operative, any action which the person on whom that notice has been served is required by the notice to take in relation to the premises and which—

        (a)   (in the context of subsection (2)) is proposed to be taken by or on behalf of that person or on behalf of the local housing authority in pursuance of Schedule 3, or

        (b)   (in the context of subsection (3)) is proposed to be taken on behalf of the local housing authority in pursuance of Schedule 3;

    (b)   where a prohibition order has become operative, any action which is proposed to be taken and which either is necessary for the purpose of giving effect to the order or is remedial action specified in the order in accordance with section 22(2)(e).

(8)   In this section—

    "relevant person", in relation to any premises, means a person who is an owner of the premises, a person having control of or managing the premises, or the holder of any licence under Part 2 or 3 in respect of the premises;

    "representative" in relation to a relevant person or a local housing authority, means any officer, employee, agent or contractor of that person or authority.

**[1363]**

**NOTES**

Commencement: 6 April 2006 (in relation to England, subject to transitional provisions and savings in the Housing Act 2004 (Commencement No 5 and Transitional Provisions and Savings) (England) Order 2006, SI 2006/1060, art 3, Schedule at **[3700]**, **[3701]**); 16 June 2006 (in relation to Wales, subject to transitional provisions and savings in the Housing Act 2004 (Commencement No 3 and Transitional Provisions and Savings) (Wales) Order 2006, SI 2006/1535, art 3, Schedule at **[3714]**, **[3715]**).

### 36  Power of court to authorise action by one owner on behalf of another

(1)   Where an improvement notice or prohibition order has become operative, an owner of any specified premises may apply to a magistrates' court for an order under subsection (2).

(2)   A magistrates' court may, on an application under subsection (1), make an order enabling the applicant—

    (a)   immediately to enter on the premises, and

    (b)   to take any required action within a period fixed by the order.

(3)   In this section "required action" means—

    (a)   in the case of an improvement notice, any remedial action which is required to be taken by the notice;

    (b)   in the case of a prohibition order, any action necessary for the purpose of complying with the order or any remedial action specified in the order in accordance with section 22(2)(e).

(4)   No order may be made under subsection (2) unless the court is satisfied that the interests of the applicant will be prejudiced as a result of a failure by another person to take any required action.

(5)   No order may be made under subsection (2) unless notice of the application has been given to the local housing authority.

(6) If it considers that it is appropriate to do so, the court may make an order in favour of any other owner of the premises which is similar to the order that it is making in relation to the premises under subsection (2).

**[1364]**

**NOTES**

Commencement: 6 April 2006 (in relation to England, subject to transitional provisions and savings in the Housing Act 2004 (Commencement No 5 and Transitional Provisions and Savings) (England) Order 2006, SI 2006/1060, art 3, Schedule at **[3700]**, **[3701]**); 16 June 2006 (in relation to Wales, subject to transitional provisions and savings in the Housing Act 2004 (Commencement No 3 and Transitional Provisions and Savings) (Wales) Order 2006, SI 2006/1535, art 3, Schedule at **[3714]**, **[3715]**).

*Supplementary provisions*

**37 Effect of improvement notices and prohibition orders as local land charges**

(1) An improvement notice or a prohibition order under this Chapter is a local land charge if subsection (2), (3) or (4) applies.

(2) This subsection applies if the notice or order has become operative.

(3) This subsection applies if—
  (a) the notice or order is suspended under section 14 or 23, and
  (b) the period for appealing against it under Part 3 of Schedule 1 or 2 has expired without an appeal having been brought.

(4) This subsection applies if—
  (a) the notice or order is suspended under section 14 or 23,
  (b) an appeal has been brought against it under Part 3 of Schedule 1 or 2, and
  (c) were it not suspended—
    (i) the notice would have become operative under section 15(5) by virtue of paragraph 19(2) of Schedule 1 (improvement notices: confirmation on appeal or expiry of period for further appeal), or
    (ii) the order would have become operative under section 24(5) by virtue of paragraph 14(2) of Schedule 2 (prohibition orders: confirmation on appeal or expiry of period for further appeal).

**[1365]**

**NOTES**

Commencement: 6 April 2006 (in relation to England, subject to transitional provisions and savings in the Housing Act 2004 (Commencement No 5 and Transitional Provisions and Savings) (England) Order 2006, SI 2006/1060, art 3, Schedule at **[3700]**, **[3701]**); 16 June 2006 (in relation to Wales, subject to transitional provisions and savings in the Housing Act 2004 (Commencement No 3 and Transitional Provisions and Savings) (Wales) Order 2006, SI 2006/1535, art 3, Schedule at **[3714]**, **[3715]**).

**38 Savings for rights arising from breach of covenant etc**

(1) Nothing in this Chapter affects any remedy of an owner for breach of any covenant or contract entered into by a tenant in connection with any premises which are specified premises in relation to an improvement notice or prohibition order.

(2) If an owner is obliged to take possession of any premises in order to comply with an improvement notice or prohibition order, the taking of possession does not affect his right to take advantage of any such breach which occurred before he took possession.

(3) No action taken under this Chapter affects any remedy available to the tenant of any premises against his landlord (whether at common law or otherwise).

**[1366]**

**NOTES**

Commencement: 6 April 2006 (in relation to England, subject to transitional provisions and savings in the Housing Act 2004 (Commencement No 5 and Transitional Provisions and Savings) (England) Order 2006, SI 2006/1060, art 3, Schedule at **[3700]**, **[3701]**); 16 June 2006 (in relation to Wales, subject to transitional provisions and savings in the Housing Act 2004 (Commencement No 3 and Transitional Provisions and Savings) (Wales) Order 2006, SI 2006/1535, art 3, Schedule at **[3714]**, **[3715]**).

**39 Effect of Part 4 enforcement action and redevelopment proposals**

(1) Subsection (2) applies if—
  (a) an improvement notice or prohibition order has been served or made under this Chapter, and
  (b) a management order under Chapter 1 or 2 of Part 4 comes into force in relation to the specified premises.

(2) The improvement notice or prohibition order—

> (a) if operative at the time when the management order comes into force, ceases to have effect at that time, and
>
> (b) otherwise is to be treated as from that time as if it had not been served or made.

(3) Subsection (2)(a) does not affect any right acquired or liability (civil or criminal) incurred before the improvement notice or prohibition order ceases to have effect.

(4) Subsection (5) applies where, under section 308 of the Housing Act 1985 (c 68) (owner's re-development proposals), the local housing authority have approved proposals for the re-development of land.

(5) No action is to be taken under this Chapter in relation to the land if, and so long as, the re-development is being proceeded with (subject to any variation or extension approved by the authority)—

> (a) in accordance with the proposals; and
>
> (b) within the time limits specified by the local housing authority.

**[1367]**

**NOTES**

Commencement: 6 April 2006 (in relation to England, subject to transitional provisions and savings in the Housing Act 2004 (Commencement No 5 and Transitional Provisions and Savings) (England) Order 2006, SI 2006/1060, art 3, Schedule at **[3700]**, **[3701]**); 16 June 2006 (in relation to Wales, subject to transitional provisions and savings in the Housing Act 2004 (Commencement No 3 and Transitional Provisions and Savings) (Wales) Order 2006, SI 2006/1535, art 3, Schedule at **[3714]**, **[3715]**).

## CHAPTER 3
## EMERGENCY MEASURES

*Emergency remedial action*

### 40 Emergency remedial action

(1) If—

> (a) the local housing authority are satisfied that a category 1 hazard exists on any residential premises, and
>
> (b) they are further satisfied that the hazard involves an imminent risk of serious harm to the health or safety of any of the occupiers of those or any other residential premises, and
>
> (c) no management order is in force under Chapter 1 or 2 of Part 4 in relation to the premises mentioned in paragraph (a),

the taking by the authority of emergency remedial action under this section in respect of the hazard is a course of action available to the authority in relation to the hazard for the purposes of section 5 (category 1 hazards: general duty to take enforcement action).

(2) "Emergency remedial action" means such remedial action in respect of the hazard concerned as the authority consider immediately necessary in order to remove the imminent risk of serious harm within subsection (1)(b).

(3) Emergency remedial action under this section may be taken by the authority in relation to any premises in relation to which remedial action could be required to be taken by an improvement notice under section 11 (see subsections (3) and (4) of that section).

(4) Emergency remedial action under this section may be taken by the authority in respect of more than one category 1 hazard on the same premises or in the same building containing one or more flats.

(5) Paragraphs 3 to 5 of Schedule 3 (improvement notices: enforcement action by local authorities) apply in connection with the taking of emergency remedial action under this section as they apply in connection with the taking of the remedial action required by an improvement notice which has become operative but has not been complied with.

But those paragraphs so apply with the modifications set out in subsection (6).

(6) The modifications are as follows—

> (a) the right of entry conferred by paragraph 3(4) may be exercised at any time; and
>
> (b) the notice required by paragraph 4 (notice before entering premises) must (instead of being served in accordance with that paragraph) be served on every person, who to the authority's knowledge—
>
> > (i) is an occupier of the premises in relation to which the authority propose to take emergency remedial action, or
> >
> > (ii) if those premises are common parts of a building containing one or more flats, is an occupier of any part of the building; but
>
> (c) that notice is to be regarded as so served if a copy of it is fixed to some conspicuous part of the premises or building.

(7) Within the period of seven days beginning with the date when the authority start taking emergency remedial action, the authority must serve—

　　(a)　a notice under section 41, and
　　(b)　copies of such a notice,

on the persons on whom the authority would be required under Part 1 of Schedule 1 to serve an improvement notice and copies of it.

　(8)　Section 240 (warrant to authorise entry) applies for the purpose of enabling a local housing authority to enter any premises to take emergency remedial action under this section in relation to the premises, as if—

　　(a)　that purpose were mentioned in subsection (2) of that section, and
　　(b)　the circumstances as to which the justice of the peace must be satisfied under subsection (4) were that there are reasonable grounds for believing that the authority will not be able to gain admission to the premises without a warrant.

　(9)　For the purposes of the operation of any provision relating to improvement notices as it applies by virtue of this section in connection with emergency remedial action or a notice under section 41, any reference in that provision to the specified premises is to be read as a reference to the premises specified, in accordance with section 41(2)(c), as those in relation to which emergency remedial action has been (or is to be) taken.

**[1368]**

**NOTES**
　Commencement: 6 April 2006 (in relation to England, subject to transitional provisions and savings in the Housing Act 2004 (Commencement No 5 and Transitional Provisions and Savings) (England) Order 2006, SI 2006/1060, art 3, Schedule at **[3700]**, **[3701]**); 16 June 2006 (in relation to Wales, subject to transitional provisions and savings in the Housing Act 2004 (Commencement No 3 and Transitional Provisions and Savings) (Wales) Order 2006, SI 2006/1535, art 3, Schedule at **[3714]**, **[3715]**).

## 41　Notice of emergency remedial action

　(1)　The notice required by section 40(7) is a notice which complies with the following requirements of this section.

　(2)　The notice must specify, in relation to the hazard (or each of the hazards) to which it relates—

　　(a)　the nature of the hazard and the residential premises on which it exists,
　　(b)　the deficiency giving rise to the hazard,
　　(c)　the premises in relation to which emergency remedial action has been (or is to be) taken by the authority under section 40 and the nature of that remedial action,
　　(d)　the power under which that remedial action has been (or is to be) taken by the authority, and
　　(e)　the date when that remedial action was (or is to be) started.

　(3)　The notice must contain information about—

　　(a)　the right to appeal under section 45 against the decision of the authority to make the order, and
　　(b)　the period within which an appeal may be made.

**[1369]**

**NOTES**
　Commencement: 6 April 2006 (in relation to England, subject to transitional provisions and savings in the Housing Act 2004 (Commencement No 5 and Transitional Provisions and Savings) (England) Order 2006, SI 2006/1060, art 3, Schedule at **[3700]**, **[3701]**); 16 June 2006 (in relation to Wales, subject to transitional provisions and savings in the Housing Act 2004 (Commencement No 3 and Transitional Provisions and Savings) (Wales) Order 2006, SI 2006/1535, art 3, Schedule at **[3714]**, **[3715]**).

## 42　Recovery of expenses of taking emergency remedial action

　(1)　This section relates to the recovery by a local housing authority of expenses reasonably incurred in taking emergency remedial action under section 40 ("emergency expenses").

　(2)　Paragraphs 6 to 14 of Schedule 3 (improvement notices: enforcement action by local authorities) apply for the purpose of enabling a local housing authority to recover emergency expenses as they apply for the purpose of enabling such an authority to recover expenses incurred in taking remedial action under paragraph 3 of that Schedule.

But those paragraphs so apply with the modifications set out in subsection (3).

　(3)　The modifications are as follows—

　　(a)　any reference to the improvement notice is to be read as a reference to the notice under section 41; and
　　(b)　no amount is recoverable in respect of any emergency expenses until such time (if any) as is the operative time for the purposes of this subsection (see subsection (4)).

　(4)　This subsection gives the meaning of "the operative time" for the purposes of subsection (3)—

(a)   if no appeal against the authority's decision to take the emergency remedial action is made under section 45 before the end of the period of 28 days mentioned in subsection (3)(a) of that section, "the operative time" is the end of that period;

(b)   if an appeal is made under that section within that period and a decision is given on the appeal which confirms the authority's decision, "the operative time" is as follows—

    (i)   if the period within which an appeal to the [Upper Tribunal] may be brought expires without such an appeal having been brought, "the operative time" is the end of that period;

    (ii)  if an appeal to the [Upper Tribunal] is brought, "the operative time" is the time when a decision is given on the appeal which confirms the authority's decision.

(5)   For the purposes of subsection (4)—

(a)   the withdrawal of an appeal has the same effect as a decision which confirms the authority's decision, and

(b)   references to a decision which confirms the authority's decision are to a decision which confirms it with or without variation.

**[1370]**

**NOTES**

Commencement: 6 April 2006 (in relation to England, subject to transitional provisions and savings in the Housing Act 2004 (Commencement No 5 and Transitional Provisions and Savings) (England) Order 2006, SI 2006/1060, art 3, Schedule at **[3700]**, **[3701]**); 16 June 2006 (in relation to Wales, subject to transitional provisions and savings in the Housing Act 2004 (Commencement No 3 and Transitional Provisions and Savings) (Wales) Order 2006, SI 2006/1535, art 3, Schedule at **[3714]**, **[3715]**).

Sub-s (4): words in square brackets in para (b) substituted by the Transfer of Tribunal Functions (Lands Tribunal and Miscellaneous Amendments) Order 2009, SI 2009/1307, art 5(1), (2), Sch 1, paras 271, 272, subject to transitional and savings provisions in Sch 5 thereto.

*Emergency prohibition orders*

**43   Emergency prohibition orders**

(1)   If—

(a)   the local housing authority are satisfied that a category 1 hazard exists on any residential premises, and

(b)   they are further satisfied that the hazard involves an imminent risk of serious harm to the health or safety of any of the occupiers of those or any other residential premises, and

(c)   no management order is in force under Chapter 1 or 2 of Part 4 in relation to the premises mentioned in paragraph (a),

making an emergency prohibition order under this section in respect of the hazard is a course of action available to the authority in relation to the hazard for the purposes of section 5 (category 1 hazards: general duty to take enforcement action).

(2)   An emergency prohibition order under this section is an order imposing, with immediate effect, such prohibition or prohibitions on the use of any premises as are specified in the order in accordance with subsection (3) and section 44.

(3)   As regards the imposition of any such prohibition or prohibitions, the following provisions apply to an emergency prohibition order as they apply to a prohibition order under section 20—

(a)   subsections (3) to (5) of that section, and

(b)   subsections (3) to (5) and (7) to (9) of section 22.

(4)   Part 1 of Schedule 2 (service of copies of prohibition orders) applies in relation to an emergency prohibition order as it applies to a prohibition order, but any requirement to serve copies within a specified period of seven days is to be read as a reference to serve them on the day on which the emergency prohibition order is made (or, if that is not possible, as soon after that day as is possible).

(5)   The following provisions also apply to an emergency prohibition order as they apply to a prohibition order (or to a prohibition order which has become operative, as the case may be)—

(a)   section 25 (revocation and variation);

(b)   sections 32 to 36 (enforcement);

(c)   sections 37 to 39 (supplementary provisions); and

(d)   Part 2 of Schedule 2 (notices relating to revocation or variation);

(e)   Part 3 of that Schedule (appeals) so far as it relates to any decision to vary, or to refuse to revoke or vary, a prohibition order; and

(f)   sections 584A and 584B of the Housing Act 1985 (c 68) (payment, and repayment, of compensation).

(6)   For the purposes of the operation of any provision relating to prohibition orders as it applies in connection with emergency prohibition orders by virtue of this section or section 45, any

reference in that provision to the specified premises is to be read as a reference to the premises specified, in accordance with section 44(2)(c), as the premises in relation to which prohibitions are imposed by the order.

**[1371]**

**NOTES**
 Commencement: 6 April 2006 (in relation to England, subject to transitional provisions and savings in the Housing Act 2004 (Commencement No 5 and Transitional Provisions and Savings) (England) Order 2006, SI 2006/1060, art 3, Schedule at **[3700]**, **[3701]**); 16 June 2006 (in relation to Wales, subject to transitional provisions and savings in the Housing Act 2004 (Commencement No 3 and Transitional Provisions and Savings) (Wales) Order 2006, SI 2006/1535, art 3, Schedule at **[3714]**, **[3715]**).

## 44  Contents of emergency prohibition orders

(1)    An emergency prohibition order under section 43 must comply with the following requirements of this section.

(2)    The order must specify, in relation to the hazard (or each of the hazards) to which it relates—
 (a)    the nature of the hazard concerned and the residential premises on which it exists,
 (b)    the deficiency giving rise to the hazard,
 (c)    the premises in relation to which prohibitions are imposed by the order (see subsections (3) and (4) of section 22 as applied by section 43(3)), and
 (d)    any remedial action which the authority consider would, if taken in relation to the hazard, result in their revoking the order under section 25 (as applied by section 43(5)).

(3)    The order must contain information about—
 (a)    the right to appeal under section 45 against the order, and
 (b)    the period within which an appeal may be made,
and specify the date on which the order is made.

**[1372]**

**NOTES**
 Commencement: 6 April 2006 (in relation to England, subject to transitional provisions and savings in the Housing Act 2004 (Commencement No 5 and Transitional Provisions and Savings) (England) Order 2006, SI 2006/1060, art 3, Schedule at **[3700]**, **[3701]**); 16 June 2006 (in relation to Wales, subject to transitional provisions and savings in the Housing Act 2004 (Commencement No 3 and Transitional Provisions and Savings) (Wales) Order 2006, SI 2006/1535, art 3, Schedule at **[3714]**, **[3715]**).

*Appeals*

## 45  Appeals relating to emergency measures

(1)    A person on whom a notice under section 41 has been served in connection with the taking of emergency remedial action under section 40 may appeal to a residential property tribunal against the decision of the local housing authority to take that action.

(2)    A relevant person may appeal to a residential property tribunal against an emergency prohibition order.

(3)    An appeal under subsection (1) or (2) must be made within the period of 28 days beginning with—
 (a)    the date specified in the notice under section 41 as the date when the emergency remedial action was (or was to be) started, or
 (b)    the date specified in the emergency prohibition order as the date on which the order was made,
as the case may be.

(4)    A residential property tribunal may allow an appeal to be made to it after the end of that period if it is satisfied that there is a good reason for the failure to appeal before the end of that period (and for any delay since then in applying for permission to appeal out of time).

(5)    An appeal under subsection (1) or (2)—
 (a)    is to be by way of a re-hearing, but
 (b)    may be determined having regard to matters of which the authority were unaware.

(6)    The tribunal may—
 (a)    in the case of an appeal under subsection (1), confirm, reverse or vary the decision of the authority;
 (b)    in the case of an appeal under subsection (2), confirm or vary the emergency prohibition order or make an order revoking it as from a date specified in that order.

(7) Paragraph 16 of Schedule 2 applies for the purpose of identifying who is a relevant person for the purposes of subsection (2) in relation to an emergency prohibition order as it applies for the purpose of identifying who is a relevant person for the purposes of Part 3 of that Schedule in relation to a prohibition order.

**[1373]**

**NOTES**
Commencement: 6 April 2006 (in relation to England, subject to transitional provisions and savings in the Housing Act 2004 (Commencement No 5 and Transitional Provisions and Savings) (England) Order 2006, SI 2006/1060, art 3, Schedule at **[3700]**, **[3701]**); 16 June 2006 (in relation to Wales, subject to transitional provisions and savings in the Housing Act 2004 (Commencement No 3 and Transitional Provisions and Savings) (Wales) Order 2006, SI 2006/1535, art 3, Schedule at **[3714]**, **[3715]**).

## CHAPTER 4
## DEMOLITION ORDERS AND SLUM CLEARANCE DECLARATIONS

**46–48** (*S 46 substitutes the Housing Act 1985, s 265; ss 47, 48 amend ss 269, 289, 272, 317, 318 of that Act.*)

## CHAPTER 5
## GENERAL AND MISCELLANEOUS PROVISIONS RELATING TO ENFORCEMENT ACTION

*Recovery of expenses relating to enforcement action*

### 49 Power to charge for certain enforcement action

(1) A local housing authority may make such reasonable charge as they consider appropriate as a means of recovering certain administrative and other expenses incurred by them in—
  (a) serving an improvement notice under section 11 or 12;
  (b) making a prohibition order under section 20 or 21;
  (c) serving a hazard awareness notice under section 28 or 29;
  (d) taking emergency remedial action under section 40;
  (e) making an emergency prohibition order under section 43; or
  (f) making a demolition order under section 265 of the Housing Act 1985 (c 68).

(2) The expenses are, in the case of the service of an improvement notice or a hazard awareness notice, the expenses incurred in—
  (a) determining whether to serve the notice,
  (b) identifying any action to be specified in the notice, and
  (c) serving the notice.

(3) The expenses are, in the case of emergency remedial action under section 40, the expenses incurred in—
  (a) determining whether to take such action, and
  (b) serving the notice required by subsection (7) of that section.

(4) The expenses are, in the case of a prohibition order under section 20 or 21 of this Act, an emergency prohibition order under section 43 or a demolition order under section 265 of the Housing Act 1985, the expenses incurred in—
  (a) determining whether to make the order, and
  (b) serving copies of the order on persons as owners of premises.

(5) A local housing authority may make such reasonable charge as they consider appropriate as a means of recovering expenses incurred by them in—
  (a) carrying out any review under section 17 or 26, or
  (b) serving copies of the authority's decision on such a review.

(6) The amount of the charge may not exceed such amount as is specified by order of the appropriate national authority.

(7) Where a tribunal allows an appeal against the underlying notice or order mentioned in subsection (1), it may make such order as it considers appropriate reducing, quashing, or requiring the repayment of, any charge under this section made in respect of the notice or order.

**[1374]**

**NOTES**
Commencement: 6 April 2006 (in relation to England, subject to transitional provisions and savings in the Housing Act 2004 (Commencement No 5 and Transitional Provisions and Savings) (England) Order 2006, SI 2006/1060, art 3, Schedule at **[3700]**, **[3701]**); 16 June 2006 (in relation to Wales, subject to transitional provisions and savings in the Housing Act 2004 (Commencement No 3 and Transitional Provisions and Savings) (Wales) Order 2006, SI 2006/1535, art 3, Schedule at **[3714]**, **[3715]**).

**50 Recovery of charge under section 49**

(1) This section relates to the recovery by a local housing authority of a charge made by them under section 49.

(2) In the case of—
   (a) an improvement notice under section 11 or 12, or
   (b) a hazard awareness notice under section 28 or 29,

the charge may be recovered from the person on whom the notice is served.

(3) In the case of emergency remedial action under section 40, the charge may be recovered from the person served with the notice required by subsection (7) of that section.

(4) In the case of—
   (a) a prohibition order under section 20 or 21,
   (b) an emergency prohibition order under section 43, or
   (c) a demolition order under section 265 of the Housing Act 1985 (c 68),

the charge may be recovered from any person on whom a copy of the order is served as an owner of the premises.

(5) A demand for payment of the charge must be served on the person from whom the authority seek to recover it.

(6) The demand becomes operative, if no appeal is brought against the underlying notice or order, at the end of the period of 21 days beginning with the date of service of the demand.

(7) If such an appeal is brought and a decision is given on the appeal which confirms the underlying notice or order, the demand becomes operative at the time when—
   (a) the period within which an appeal to the [Upper Tribunal] may be brought expires without such an appeal having been brought, or
   (b) a decision is given on such an appeal which confirms the notice or order.

(8) For the purposes of subsection (7)—
   (a) the withdrawal of an appeal has the same effect as a decision which confirms the notice or order, and
   (b) references to a decision which confirms the notice or order are to a decision which confirms it with or without variation.

(9) As from the time when the demand becomes operative, the sum recoverable by the authority is, until recovered, a charge on the premises concerned.

(10) The charge takes effect at that time as a legal charge which is a local land charge.

(11) For the purpose of enforcing the charge the authority have the same powers and remedies under the Law of Property Act 1925 (c 20) and otherwise as if they were mortgagees by deed having powers of sale and lease, of accepting surrenders of leases and of appointing a receiver.

(12) The power of appointing a receiver is exercisable at any time after the end of the period of one month beginning with the date on which the charge takes effect.

(13) The appropriate national authority may by regulations prescribe the form of, and the particulars to be contained in, a demand for payment of any charge under section 49.

**[1375]**

---

**NOTES**

Commencement: 18 November 2004 (for the purpose of making orders or regulations); 6 April 2006 (in relation to England for remaining purposes, subject to transitional provisions and savings in the Housing Act 2004 (Commencement No 5 and Transitional Provisions and Savings) (England) Order 2006, SI 2006/1060, art 3, Schedule at **[3700]**, **[3701]**); 16 June 2006 (in relation to Wales for remaining purposes, subject to transitional provisions and savings in the Housing Act 2004 (Commencement No 3 and Transitional Provisions and Savings) (Wales) Order 2006, SI 2006/1535, art 3, Schedule at **[3714]**, **[3715]**).

Sub-s (7): words in square brackets in para (a) substituted by the Transfer of Tribunal Functions (Lands Tribunal and Miscellaneous Amendments) Order 2009, SI 2009/1307, art 5(1), (2), Sch 1, paras 271, 273, subject to transitional and savings provisions in Sch 5 thereto.

---

*Repeals*

**51–53** (*S 51 repeals the Housing Grants, Construction and Regeneration Act 1996, s 86; s 52 repeals the Housing Act 1985, ss 283–288; s 53 amends the London Building Acts (Amendment) Act 1939, ss 35–37, the Building Act 1984, s 72, the Leicestershire Act 1985, s 54 and repeals ss 48, 49(1), (2) of the 1984 Act.*)

*Index*

## 54 Index of defined expressions: Part 1

The following table shows where expressions used in this Part are defined or otherwise explained.

| Expression | Provision of this Act |
| --- | --- |
| Appropriate national authority | Section 261(1) |
| Building containing one or more flats | Section 1(5) |
| Category 1 hazard | Section 2(1) |
| Category 2 hazard | Section 2(1) |
| Common parts | Section 1(5) |
| Compliance with improvement notice | Section 30(2) |
| District of local housing authority | Section 261(6) |
| Dwelling | Section 1(5), (6) |
| External common parts | Section 1(5) |
| Flat | Section 1(5) to (7) |
| Hazard | Section 2(1) |
| Hazard awareness notice | Section 28(2) or 29(2) |
| Health | Section 2(5) |
| HMO | Section 1(5), (6) (and see also section 1(8)) |
| Improvement notice | Section 11(2) or 12(2) |
| Lease, lessee etc | Section 262(1) to (4) |
| Local housing authority | Section 261(2) to (5) |
| Occupier (and related expressions) | Section 262(6) |
| Owner | Section 262(7) |
| Person having control | Section 263(1) and (2) |
| Person managing | Section 263(3) and (4) |
| Prohibition order | Section 20(2) or 21(2) |
| Remedial action | Section 11(8) |
| Residential premises | Section 1(4) |
| Residential property tribunal | Section 229 |
| Specified premises, in relation to an improvement notice | Section 13(5) |
| Specified premises, in relation to a prohibition order | Section 22(10) |
| Tenancy, tenant | Section 262(1) to (5) |
| Unoccupied HMO accommodation | Section 1(5) (and see also section 1(8)). |

**[1376]**

NOTES

Commencement: 6 April 2006 (in relation to England, subject to transitional provisions and savings in the Housing Act 2004 (Commencement No 5 and Transitional Provisions and Savings) (England) Order 2006, SI 2006/1060, art 3, Schedule at **[3700]**, **[3701]**); 16 June 2006 (in relation to Wales, subject to transitional provisions and savings in the Housing Act 2004 (Commencement No 3 and Transitional Provisions and Savings) (Wales) Order 2006, SI 2006/1535, art 3, Schedule at **[3714]**, **[3715]**).

## PART 2
## LICENSING OF HOUSES IN MULTIPLE OCCUPATION

### *Introductory*

### 55   Licensing of HMOs to which this Part applies

(1)   This Part provides for HMOs to be licensed by local housing authorities where—

   (a)   they are HMOs to which this Part applies (see subsection (2)), and

   (b)   they are required to be licensed under this Part (see section 61(1)).

(2)   This Part applies to the following HMOs in the case of each local housing authority—

   (a)   any HMO in the authority's district which falls within any prescribed description of HMO, and

   (b)   if an area is for the time being designated by the authority under section 56 as subject to additional licensing, any HMO in that area which falls within any description of HMO specified in the designation.

(3)   The appropriate national authority may by order prescribe descriptions of HMOs for the purposes of subsection (2)(a).

(4)   The power conferred by subsection (3) may be exercised in such a way that this Part applies to all HMOs in the district of a local housing authority.

(5)   Every local housing authority have the following general duties—

   (a)   to make such arrangements as are necessary to secure the effective implementation in their district of the licensing regime provided for by this Part;

   (b)   to ensure that all applications for licences and other issues falling to be determined by them under this Part are determined within a reasonable time; and

   (c)   to satisfy themselves, as soon as is reasonably practicable, that there are no Part 1 functions that ought to be exercised by them in relation to the premises in respect of which such applications are made.

(6)   For the purposes of subsection (5)(c)—

   (a)   "Part 1 function" means any duty under section 5 to take any course of action to which that section applies or any power to take any course of action to which section 7 applies; and

   (b)   the authority may take such steps as they consider appropriate (whether or not involving an inspection) to comply with their duty under subsection (5)(c) in relation to each of the premises in question, but they must in any event comply with it within the period of 5 years beginning with the date of the application for a licence.

**[1377]**

**NOTES**

Commencement: 18 November 2004 (sub-ss (3), (4) for the purpose of making orders or regulations); 15 June 2005 (sub-ss (1), (2), (5)(a), (b) in relation to England); 25 November 2005 (sub-ss (1), (2), (5)(a), (b) in relation to Wales); 6 April 2006 (sub-ss (3), (4), (5)(c), (6) in relation to England for remaining purposes, subject to transitional provisions and savings in the Housing Act 2004 (Commencement No 5 and Transitional Provisions and Savings) (England) Order 2006, SI 2006/1060, art 3, Schedule at **[3700]**, **[3701]**); 16 June 2006 (sub-ss (3), (4), (5)(c), (6) in relation to Wales for remaining purposes, subject to transitional provisions and savings in the Housing Act 2004 (Commencement No 3 and Transitional Provisions and Savings) (Wales) Order 2006, SI 2006/1535, art 3, Schedule at **[3714]**, **[3715]**).

Orders: the Licensing of Houses in Multiple Occupation (Prescribed Descriptions) (England) Order 2006, SI 2006/371 at **[3609]**; the Licensing of Houses in Multiple Occupation (Prescribed Descriptions) (Wales) Order 2006, SI 2006/1712 at **[3722]**.

### *Designation of additional licensing areas*

### 56   Designation of areas subject to additional licensing

(1)   A local housing authority may designate either—

   (a)   the area of their district, or

   (b)   an area in their district,

as subject to additional licensing in relation to a description of HMOs specified in the designation, if the requirements of this section are met.

(2)   The authority must consider that a significant proportion of the HMOs of that description in the area are being managed sufficiently ineffectively as to give rise, or to be likely to give rise, to one or more particular problems either for those occupying the HMOs or for members of the public.

(3)   Before making a designation the authority must—

   (a)   take reasonable steps to consult persons who are likely to be affected by the designation; and

   (b)   consider any representations made in accordance with the consultation and not withdrawn.

(4)   The power to make a designation under this section may be exercised in such a way that this Part applies to all HMOs in the area in question.

(5)   In forming an opinion as to the matter mentioned in subsection (2), the authority must have regard to any information regarding the extent to which any codes of practice approved under section 233 have been complied with by persons managing HMOs in the area in question.

(6)   Section 57 applies for the purposes of this section.

[1378]

**NOTES**

Commencement: 15 June 2005 (in relation to England); 25 November 2005 (in relation to Wales).

Disapplication: as to the disapplication of sub-ss (2)–(6) above, and ss 57, 58, 59(1), (2) of this Act, see the Housing Act 2004 (Commencement No 5 and Transitional Provisions and Savings) (England) Order 2006, SI 2006/1060, art 3, Schedule, Pt 2, para 3 at **[3700]**, **[3702]**, and the Housing Act 2004 (Commencement No 3 and Transitional Provisions and Savings) (Wales) Order 2006, SI 2006/1535, art 3, Schedule, Pt 2, para 3 at **[3714]**, **[3716]**.

## 57   Designations under section 56: further considerations

(1)   This section applies to the power of a local housing authority to make designations under section 56.

(2)   The authority must ensure that any exercise of the power is consistent with the authority's overall housing strategy.

(3)   The authority must also seek to adopt a co-ordinated approach in connection with dealing with homelessness, empty properties and anti-social behaviour affecting the private rented sector, both—
   (a)   as regards combining licensing under this Part with other courses of action available to them, and
   (b)   as regards combining such licensing with measures taken by other persons.

(4)   The authority must not make a particular designation under section 56 unless—
   (a)   they have considered whether there are any other courses of action available to them (of whatever nature) that might provide an effective method of dealing with the problem or problems in question, and
   (b)   they consider that making the designation will significantly assist them to deal with the problem or problems (whether or not they take any other course of action as well).

(5)   In this Act "anti-social behaviour" means conduct on the part of occupiers of, or visitors to, residential premises—
   (a)   which causes or is likely to cause a nuisance or annoyance to persons residing, visiting or otherwise engaged in lawful activities in the vicinity of such premises, or
   (b)   which involves or is likely to involve the use of such premises for illegal purposes.

[1379]

**NOTES**

Commencement: 15 June 2005 (in relation to England); 25 November 2005 (in relation to Wales).

Disapplication: see the note to s 56 at **[1378]**.

## 58   Designation needs confirmation or general approval to be effective

(1)   A designation of an area as subject to additional licensing cannot come into force unless—
   (a)   it has been confirmed by the appropriate national authority; or
   (b)   it falls within a description of designations in relation to which that authority has given a general approval in accordance with subsection (6).

(2)   The appropriate national authority may either confirm, or refuse to confirm, a designation as it considers appropriate.

(3)   If the appropriate national authority confirms a designation, the designation comes into force on the date specified for this purpose by that authority.

(4)   That date must be no earlier than three months after the date on which the designation is confirmed.

(5)   A general approval may be given in relation to a description of designations framed by reference to any matters or circumstances.

(6)   Accordingly a general approval may (in particular) be given in relation to—
   (a)   designations made by a specified local housing authority;
   (b)   designations made by a local housing authority falling within a specified description of such authorities;
   (c)   designations relating to HMOs of a specified description.
   "Specified" means specified by the appropriate national authority in the approval.

(7) If, by virtue of a general approval, a designation does not need to be confirmed before it comes into force, the designation comes into force on the date specified for this purpose in the designation.

(8) That date must be no earlier than three months after the date on which the designation is made.

**[1380]**

**NOTES**
Commencement: 6 April 2006 (in relation to England, subject to transitional provisions and savings in the Housing Act 2004 (Commencement No 5 and Transitional Provisions and Savings) (England) Order 2006, SI 2006/1060, art 3, Schedule at **[3700]**, **[3701]**); 16 June 2006 (in relation to Wales, subject to transitional provisions and savings in the Housing Act 2004 (Commencement No 3 and Transitional Provisions and Savings) (Wales) Order 2006, SI 2006/1535, art 3, Schedule at **[3714]**, **[3715]**).
Disapplication: see the note to s 56 at **[1378]**.

## 59 Notification requirements relating to designations

(1) This section applies to a designation—
   (a) when it is confirmed under section 58, or
   (b) (if it is not required to be so confirmed) when it is made by the local housing authority.

(2) As soon as the designation is confirmed or made, the authority must publish in the prescribed manner a notice stating—
   (a) that the designation has been made,
   (b) whether or not the designation was required to be confirmed and either that it has been confirmed or that a general approval under section 58 applied to it (giving details of the approval in question),
   (c) the date on which the designation is to come into force, and
   (d) any other information which may be prescribed.

(3) After publication of a notice under subsection (2), and for as long as the designation is in force, the local housing authority must make available to the public in accordance with any prescribed requirements—
   (a) copies of the designation, and
   (b) such information relating to the designation as is prescribed.

(4) In this section "prescribed" means prescribed by regulations made by the appropriate national authority.

**[1381]**

**NOTES**
Commencement: 18 November 2004 (for the purpose of making orders or regulations); 6 April 2006 (in relation to England for remaining purposes, subject to transitional provisions and savings in the Housing Act 2004 (Commencement No 5 and Transitional Provisions and Savings) (England) Order 2006, SI 2006/1060, art 3, Schedule at **[3700]**, **[3701]**); 16 June 2006 (in relation to Wales for remaining purposes, subject to transitional provisions and savings in the Housing Act 2004 (Commencement No 3 and Transitional Provisions and Savings) (Wales) Order 2006, SI 2006/1535, art 3, Schedule at **[3714]**, **[3715]**).
Disapplication: see the note to s 56 at **[1378]**.
Regulations: the Licensing and Management of Houses in Multiple Occupation and Other Houses (Miscellaneous Provisions) (England) Regulations 2006, SI 2006/373 at **[3623]**; the Licensing and Management of Houses in Multiple Occupation and Other Houses (Miscellaneous Provisions) (Wales) Regulations 2006, SI 2006/1715 at **[3724]**.

## 60 Duration, review and revocation of designations

(1) Unless previously revoked under subsection (4), a designation ceases to have effect at the time that is specified for this purpose in the designation.

(2) That time must be no later than five years after the date on which the designation comes into force.

(3) A local housing authority must from time to time review the operation of any designation made by them.

(4) If following a review they consider it appropriate to do so, the authority may revoke the designation.

(5) If they do revoke the designation, the designation ceases to have effect at the time that is specified by the authority for this purpose.

(6) On revoking a designation the authority must publish notice of the revocation in such manner as is prescribed by regulations made by the appropriate national authority.

**[1382]**

**NOTES**
Commencement: 18 November 2004 (for the purpose of making orders or regulations); 6 April 2006 (in relation to England for remaining purposes, subject to transitional provisions and savings in the Housing Act 2004 (Commencement No 5 and Transitional Provisions and Savings) (England) Order 2006, SI 2006/1060, art 3, Schedule at **[3700]**, **[3701]**); 16 June 2006 (in relation to Wales for remaining purposes, subject to transitional provisions and savings in the Housing Act 2004 (Commencement No 3 and Transitional Provisions and Savings) (Wales) Order 2006, SI 2006/1535, art 3, Schedule at **[3714]**, **[3715]**).
Regulations: the Licensing and Management of Houses in Multiple Occupation and Other Houses (Miscellaneous Provisions) (England) Regulations 2006, SI 2006/373 at **[3623]**; the Licensing and Management of Houses in Multiple Occupation and Other Houses (Miscellaneous Provisions) (Wales) Regulations 2006, SI 2006/1715 at **[3724]**.

*HMOs required to be licensed*

### 61 Requirement for HMOs to be licensed

(1) Every HMO to which this Part applies must be licensed under this Part unless—
    (a) a temporary exemption notice is in force in relation to it under section 62, or
    (b) an interim or final management order is in force in relation to it under Chapter 1 of Part 4.

(2) A licence under this Part is a licence authorising occupation of the house concerned by not more than a maximum number of households or persons specified in the licence.

(3) Sections 63 to 67 deal with applications for licences, the granting or refusal of licences and the imposition of licence conditions.

(4) The local housing authority must take all reasonable steps to secure that applications for licences are made to them in respect of HMOs in their area which are required to be licensed under this Part but are not.

(5) The appropriate national authority may by regulations provide for—
    (a) any provision of this Part, or
    (b) section 263 (in its operation for the purposes of any such provision),
to have effect in relation to a section 257 HMO with such modifications as are prescribed by the regulations.

A "section 257 HMO" is an HMO which is a converted block of flats to which section 257 applies.

(6) In this Part (unless the context otherwise requires)—
    (a) references to a licence are to a licence under this Part,
    (b) references to a licence holder are to be read accordingly, and
    (c) references to an HMO being (or not being) licensed under this Part are to its being (or not being) an HMO in respect of which a licence is in force under this Part.

**[1383]**

**NOTES**
Commencement: 18 November 2004 (for the purpose of making orders or regulations); 6 April 2006 (in relation to England for remaining purposes, subject to transitional provisions and savings in the Housing Act 2004 (Commencement No 5 and Transitional Provisions and Savings) (England) Order 2006, SI 2006/1060, art 3, Schedule at **[3700]**, **[3701]**); 16 June 2006 (in relation to Wales for remaining purposes, subject to transitional provisions and savings in the Housing Act 2004 (Commencement No 3 and Transitional Provisions and Savings) (Wales) Order 2006, SI 2006/1535, art 3, Schedule at **[3714]**, **[3715]**).
Modification: this section, ss 64, 65, 67, 73, 75, 78 and Sch 4, are modified in relation to a house in multiple occupation to which s 257 of this Act applies, by the Houses in Multiple Occupation (Certain Converted Blocks of Flats) (Modifications to the Housing Act 2004 and Transitional Provisions for section 257 HMOs) (England) Regulations 2007, SI 2007/1904, regs 2–10, and the Housing Act 2004 and Transitional Provisions for section 257 HMOs) (Wales) Regulations 2007, SI 2007/3231, regs 2–10.
Regulations: the Houses in Multiple Occupation (Certain Converted Blocks of Flats) (Modifications to the Housing Act 2004 and Transitional Provisions for section 257 HMOs) (England) Regulations 2007, SI 2007/1904; the Houses in Multiple Occupation (Certain Blocks of Flats) (Modifications to the Housing Act 2004 and Transitional Provisions for section 257 HMOs) (Wales) Regulations 2007, SI 2007/3231.

### 62 Temporary exemption from licensing requirement

(1) This section applies where a person having control of or managing an HMO which is required to be licensed under this Part (see section 61(1)) but is not so licensed, notifies the local housing authority of his intention to take particular steps with a view to securing that the house is no longer required to be licensed.

(2) The authority may, if they think fit, serve on that person a notice under this section ("a temporary exemption notice") in respect of the house.

(3) If a temporary exemption notice is served under this section, the house is (in accordance with sections 61(1) and 85(1)) not required to be licensed either under this Part or under Part 3 during the period for which the notice is in force.

(4)    A temporary exemption notice under this section is in force—
  (a)    for the period of 3 months beginning with the date on which it is served, or
  (b)    (in the case of a notice served by virtue of subsection (5)) for the period of 3 months after the date when the first notice ceases to be in force.

(5)    If the authority—
  (a)    receive a further notification under subsection (1), and
  (b)    consider that there are exceptional circumstances that justify the service of a second temporary exemption notice in respect of the house that would take effect from the end of the period of 3 months applying to the first notice,
the authority may serve a second such notice on the person having control of or managing the house (but no further notice may be served by virtue of this subsection).

(6)    If the authority decide not to serve a temporary exemption notice in response to a notification under subsection (1), they must without delay serve on the person concerned a notice informing him of—
  (a)    the decision,
  (b)    the reasons for it and the date on which it was made,
  (c)    the right to appeal against the decision under subsection (7), and
  (d)    the period within which an appeal may be made under that subsection.

(7)    The person concerned may appeal to a residential property tribunal against the decision within the period of 28 days beginning with the date specified under subsection (6) as the date on which it was made.

(8)    Such an appeal—
  (a)    is to be by way of a re-hearing, but
  (b)    may be determined having regard to matters of which the authority were unaware.

(9)    The tribunal—
  (a)    may confirm or reverse the decision of the authority, and
  (b)    if it reverses the decision, must direct the authority to serve a temporary exemption notice that comes into force on such date as the tribunal directs.

**[1384]**

**NOTES**
Commencement: 6 April 2006 (in relation to England, subject to transitional provisions and savings in the Housing Act 2004 (Commencement No 5 and Transitional Provisions and Savings) (England) Order 2006, SI 2006/1060, art 3, Schedule at **[3700]**, **[3701]**); 16 June 2006 (in relation to Wales, subject to transitional provisions and savings in the Housing Act 2004 (Commencement No 3 and Transitional Provisions and Savings) (Wales) Order 2006, SI 2006/1535, art 3, Schedule at **[3714]**, **[3715]**).

*Grant or refusal of licences*

## 63    Applications for licences

(1)    An application for a licence must be made to the local housing authority.

(2)    The application must be made in accordance with such requirements as the authority may specify.

(3)    The authority may, in particular, require the application to be accompanied by a fee fixed by the authority.

(4)    The power of the authority to specify requirements under this section is subject to any regulations made under subsection (5).

(5)    The appropriate national authority may by regulations make provision about the making of applications under this section.

(6)    Such regulations may, in particular—
  (a)    specify the manner and form in which applications are to be made;
  (b)    require the applicant to give copies of the application, or information about it, to particular persons;
  (c)    specify the information which is to be supplied in connection with applications;
  (d)    specify the maximum fees which are to be charged (whether by specifying amounts or methods for calculating amounts);
  (e)    specify cases in which no fees are to be charged or fees are to be refunded.

(7)    When fixing fees under this section, the local housing authority may (subject to any regulations made under subsection (5)) take into account—
  (a)    all costs incurred by the authority in carrying out their functions under this Part, and
  (b)    all costs incurred by them in carrying out their functions under Chapter 1 of Part 4 in relation to HMOs (so far as they are not recoverable under or by virtue of any provision of that Chapter).

**[1385]**

**NOTES**

Commencement: 18 November 2004 (for the purpose of making orders or regulations); 6 April 2006 (in relation to England for remaining purposes, subject to transitional provisions and savings in the Housing Act 2004 (Commencement No 5 and Transitional Provisions and Savings) (England) Order 2006, SI 2006/1060, art 3, Schedule at [3700], [3701]); 16 June 2006 (in relation to Wales for remaining purposes, subject to transitional provisions and savings in the Housing Act 2004 (Commencement No 3 and Transitional Provisions and Savings) (Wales) Order 2006, SI 2006/1535, art 3, Schedule at [3714], [3715]).

Regulations: the Licensing and Management of Houses in Multiple Occupation and Other Houses (Miscellaneous Provisions) (England) Regulations 2006, SI 2006/373 at [3623]; the Licensing and Management of Houses in Multiple Occupation and Other Houses (Miscellaneous Provisions) (Wales) Regulations 2006, SI 2006/1715 at [3724]; the Licensing and Management of Houses in Multiple Occupation (Additional Provisions) (England) Regulations 2007, SI 2007/1903 at [3765]; the Licensing and Management of Houses in Multiple Occupation (Additional Provisions) (Wales) Regulations 2007, SI 2007/3229 at [3779].

## 64  Grant or refusal of licence

(1)    Where an application in respect of an HMO is made to the local housing authority under section 63, the authority must either—

    (a)    grant a licence in accordance with subsection (2), or

    (b)    refuse to grant a licence.

(2)    If the authority are satisfied as to the matters mentioned in subsection (3), they may grant a licence either—

    (a)    to the applicant, or

    (b)    to some other person, if both he and the applicant agree.

(3)    The matters are—

    (a)    that the house is reasonably suitable for occupation by not more than the maximum number of households or persons mentioned in subsection (4) or that it can be made so suitable by the imposition of conditions under section 67;

    (b)    that the proposed licence holder—

        (i)    is a fit and proper person to be the licence holder, and

        (ii)   is, out of all the persons reasonably available to be the licence holder in respect of the house, the most appropriate person to be the licence holder;

    (c)    that the proposed manager of the house is either—

        (i)    the person having control of the house, or

        (ii)   a person who is an agent or employee of the person having control of the house;

    (d)    that the proposed manager of the house is a fit and proper person to be the manager of the house; and

    (e)    that the proposed management arrangements for the house are otherwise satisfactory.

(4)    The maximum number of households or persons referred to in subsection (3)(a) is—

    (a)    the maximum number specified in the application, or

    (b)    some other maximum number decided by the authority.

(5)    Sections 65 and 66 apply for the purposes of this section.

**[1386]**

**NOTES**

Commencement: 6 April 2006 (in relation to England, subject to transitional provisions and savings in the Housing Act 2004 (Commencement No 5 and Transitional Provisions and Savings) (England) Order 2006, SI 2006/1060, art 3, Schedule at [3700], [3701]); 16 June 2006 (in relation to Wales, subject to transitional provisions and savings in the Housing Act 2004 (Commencement No 3 and Transitional Provisions and Savings) (Wales) Order 2006, SI 2006/1535, art 3, Schedule at [3714], [3715]).

Modification: see the note to s 61 at [1383].

## 65  Tests as to suitability for multiple occupation

(1)    The local housing authority cannot be satisfied for the purposes of section 64(3)(a) that the house is reasonably suitable for occupation by a particular maximum number of households or persons if they consider that it fails to meet prescribed standards for occupation by that number of households or persons.

(2)    But the authority may decide that the house is not reasonably suitable for occupation by a particular maximum number of households or persons even if it does meet prescribed standards for occupation by that number of households or persons.

(3)    In this section "prescribed standards" means standards prescribed by regulations made by the appropriate national authority.

(4)    The standards that may be so prescribed include—

    (a)    standards as to the number, type and quality of—

        (i)    bathrooms, toilets, washbasins and showers,

        (ii)   areas for food storage, preparation and cooking, and

        (iii)  laundry facilities,

(b)     standards as to the number, type and quality of other facilities or equipment which
        should be available in particular circumstances.

**[1387]**

**NOTES**
   Commencement: 18 November 2004 (for the purpose of making orders or regulations); 6 April 2006 (in
relation to England for remaining purposes, subject to transitional provisions and savings in the Housing
Act 2004 (Commencement No 5 and Transitional Provisions and Savings) (England) Order 2006, SI 2006/1060,
art 3, Schedule at **[3700]**, **[3701]**); 16 June 2006 (in relation to Wales for remaining purposes, subject to
transitional provisions and savings in the Housing Act 2004 (Commencement No 3 and Transitional Provisions
and Savings) (Wales) Order 2006, SI 2006/1535, art 3, Schedule at **[3714]**, **[3715]**).
   Modification: see the note to s 61 at **[1383]**.
   Regulations: the Licensing and Management of Houses in Multiple Occupation and Other Houses
(Miscellaneous Provisions) (England) Regulations 2006, SI 2006/373 at **[3623]**; the Licensing and Management
of Houses in Multiple Occupation and Other Houses (Miscellaneous Provisions) (Wales) Regulations 2006,
SI 2006/1715 at **[3724]**; the Licensing and Management of Houses in Multiple Occupation (Additional
Provisions) (England) Regulations 2007, SI 2007/1903 at **[3765]**; the Licensing and Management of Houses in
Multiple Occupation (Additional Provisions) (Wales) Regulations 2007, SI 2007/3229 at **[3779]**.

### 66   Tests for fitness etc and satisfactory management arrangements

   (1)   In deciding for the purposes of section 64(3)(b) or (d) whether a person ("P") is a fit and
proper person to be the licence holder or (as the case may be) the manager of the house, the local
housing authority must have regard (among other things) to any evidence within subsection (2)
or (3).

   (2)   Evidence is within this subsection if it shows that P has—
   (a)     committed any offence involving fraud or other dishonesty, or violence or drugs, or any
           offence listed in Schedule 3 to the Sexual Offences Act 2003 (c 42) (offences attracting
           notification requirements);
   (b)     practised unlawful discrimination on grounds of sex, colour, race, ethnic or national
           origins or disability in, or in connection with, the carrying on of any business;
   (c)     contravened any provision of the law relating to housing or of landlord and tenant law;
           or
   (d)     acted otherwise than in accordance with any applicable code of practice approved under
           section 233.

   (3)   Evidence is within this subsection if—
   (a)     it shows that any person associated or formerly associated with P (whether on a
           personal, work or other basis) has done any of the things set out in subsection (2)(a) to
           (d), and
   (b)     it appears to the authority that the evidence is relevant to the question whether P is a fit
           and proper person to be the licence holder or (as the case may be) the manager of the
           house.

   (4)   For the purposes of section 64(3)(b) the local housing authority must assume, unless the
contrary is shown, that the person having control of the house is a more appropriate person to be the
licence holder than a person not having control of it.

   (5)   In deciding for the purposes of section 64(3)(e) whether the proposed management
arrangements for the house are otherwise satisfactory, the local housing authority must have regard
(among other things) to the considerations mentioned in subsection (6).

   (6)   The considerations are—
   (a)     whether any person proposed to be involved in the management of the house has a
           sufficient level of competence to be so involved;
   (b)     whether any person proposed to be involved in the management of the house (other than
           the manager) is a fit and proper person to be so involved; and
   (c)     whether any proposed management structures and funding arrangements are suitable.

   (7)   Any reference in section 64(3)(c)(i) or (ii) or subsection (4) above to a person having
control of the house, or to being a person of any other description, includes a reference to a person
who is proposing to have control of the house, or (as the case may be) to be a person of that
description, at the time when the licence would come into force.

**[1388]**

**NOTES**
   Commencement: 6 April 2006 (in relation to England, subject to transitional provisions and savings in the
Housing Act 2004 (Commencement No 5 and Transitional Provisions and Savings) (England) Order 2006,
SI 2006/1060, art 3, Schedule at **[3700]**, **[3701]**); 16 June 2006 (in relation to Wales, subject to transitional
provisions and savings in the Housing Act 2004 (Commencement No 3 and Transitional Provisions and Savings)
(Wales) Order 2006, SI 2006/1535, art 3, Schedule at **[3714]**, **[3715]**).

## 67 Licence conditions

(1)   A licence may include such conditions as the local housing authority consider appropriate for regulating all or any of the following—

(a)   the management, use and occupation of the house concerned, and

(b)   its condition and contents.

(2)   Those conditions may, in particular, include (so far as appropriate in the circumstances)—

(a)   conditions imposing restrictions or prohibitions on the use or occupation of particular parts of the house by persons occupying it;

(b)   conditions requiring the taking of reasonable and practicable steps to prevent or reduce anti-social behaviour by persons occupying or visiting the house;

(c)   conditions requiring facilities and equipment to be made available in the house for the purpose of meeting standards prescribed under section 65;

(d)   conditions requiring such facilities and equipment to be kept in repair and proper working order;

(e)   conditions requiring, in the case of any works needed in order for any such facilities or equipment to be made available or to meet any such standards, that the works are carried out within such period or periods as may be specified in, or determined under, the licence;

(f)   conditions requiring the licence holder or the manager of the house to attend training courses in relation to any applicable code of practice approved under section 233.

(3)   A licence must include the conditions required by Schedule 4.

(4)   As regards the relationship between the authority's power to impose conditions under this section and functions exercisable by them under or for the purposes of Part 1 ("Part 1 functions")—

(a)   the authority must proceed on the basis that, in general, they should seek to identify, remove or reduce category 1 or category 2 hazards in the house by the exercise of Part 1 functions and not by means of licence conditions;

(b)   this does not, however, prevent the authority from imposing licence conditions relating to the installation or maintenance of facilities or equipment within subsection (2)(c) above, even if the same result could be achieved by the exercise of Part 1 functions;

(c)   the fact that licence conditions are imposed for a particular purpose that could be achieved by the exercise of Part 1 functions does not affect the way in which Part 1 functions can be subsequently exercised by the authority.

(5)   A licence may not include conditions imposing restrictions or obligations on a particular person other than the licence holder unless that person has consented to the imposition of the restrictions or obligations.

(6)   A licence may not include conditions requiring (or intended to secure) any alteration in the terms of any tenancy or licence under which any person occupies the house.

**[1389]**

**NOTES**

Commencement: 6 April 2006 (in relation to England, subject to transitional provisions and savings in the Housing Act 2004 (Commencement No 5 and Transitional Provisions and Savings) (England) Order 2006, SI 2006/1060, art 3, Schedule at **[3700]**, **[3701]**); 16 June 2006 (in relation to Wales, subject to transitional provisions and savings in the Housing Act 2004 (Commencement No 3 and Transitional Provisions and Savings) (Wales) Order 2006, SI 2006/1535, art 3, Schedule at **[3714]**, **[3715]**).

Modification: see the note to s 61 at **[1383]**.

## 68 Licences: general requirements and duration

(1)   A licence may not relate to more than one HMO.

(2)   A licence may be granted before the time when it is required by virtue of this Part but, if so, the licence cannot come into force until that time.

(3)   A licence—

(a)   comes into force at the time that is specified in or determined under the licence for this purpose, and

(b)   unless previously terminated by subsection (7) or revoked under section 70, continues in force for the period that is so specified or determined.

(4)   That period must not end more than 5 years after—

(a)   the date on which the licence was granted, or

(b)   if the licence was granted as mentioned in subsection (2), the date when the licence comes into force.

(5)   Subsection (3)(b) applies even if, at any time during that period, the HMO concerned subsequently ceases to be one to which this Part applies.

(6)   A licence may not be transferred to another person.

(7)  If the holder of the licence dies while the licence is in force, the licence ceases to be in force on his death.

(8)  However, during the period of 3 months beginning with the date of the licence holder's death, the house is to be treated for the purposes of this Part and Part 3 as if on that date a temporary exemption notice had been served in respect of the house under section 62.

(9)  If, at any time during that period ("the initial period"), the personal representatives of the licence holder request the local housing authority to do so, the authority may serve on them a notice which, during the period of 3 months after the date on which the initial period ends, has the same effect as a temporary exemption notice under section 62.

(10)  Subsections (6) to (8) of section 62 apply (with any necessary modifications) in relation to a decision by the authority not to serve such a notice as they apply in relation to a decision not to serve a temporary exemption notice.

**[1390]**

**NOTES**

Commencement: 6 April 2006 (in relation to England, subject to transitional provisions and savings in the Housing Act 2004 (Commencement No 5 and Transitional Provisions and Savings) (England) Order 2006, SI 2006/1060, art 3, Schedule at **[3700]**, **[3701]**); 16 June 2006 (in relation to Wales, subject to transitional provisions and savings in the Housing Act 2004 (Commencement No 3 and Transitional Provisions and Savings) (Wales) Order 2006, SI 2006/1535, art 3, Schedule at **[3714]**, **[3715]**).

*Variation and revocation of licences*

### 69  Variation of licences

(1)  The local housing authority may vary a licence—

    (a)  if they do so with the agreement of the licence holder, or

    (b)  if they consider that there has been a change of circumstances since the time when the licence was granted.

For this purpose "change of circumstances" includes any discovery of new information.

(2)  Subsection (3) applies where the authority—

    (a)  are considering whether to vary a licence under subsection (1)(b); and

    (b)  are considering—

        (i)  what number of households or persons is appropriate as the maximum number authorised to occupy the HMO to which the licence relates, or

        (ii)  the standards applicable to occupation by a particular number of households or persons.

(3)  The authority must apply the same standards in relation to the circumstances existing at the time when they are considering whether to vary the licence as were applicable at the time when it was granted.

This is subject to subsection (4).

(4)  If the standards—

    (a)  prescribed under section 65, and

    (b)  applicable at the time when the licence was granted,

have subsequently been revised or superseded by provisions of regulations under that section, the authority may apply the new standards.

(5)  A variation made with the agreement of the licence holder takes effect at the time when it is made.

(6)  Otherwise, a variation does not come into force until such time, if any, as is the operative time for the purposes of this subsection under paragraph 35 of Schedule 5 (time when period for appealing expires without an appeal being made or when decision to vary is confirmed on appeal).

(7)  The power to vary a licence under this section is exercisable by the authority either—

    (a)  on an application made by the licence holder or a relevant person, or

    (b)  on the authority's own initiative.

(8)  In subsection (7) "relevant person" means any person (other than the licence holder)—

    (a)  who has an estate or interest in the HMO concerned (but is not a tenant under a lease with an unexpired term of 3 years or less), or

    (b)  who is a person managing or having control of the house (and does not fall within paragraph (a)), or

    (c)  on whom any restriction or obligation is imposed by the licence in accordance with section 67(5).

**[1391]**

**NOTES**
Commencement: 6 April 2006 (in relation to England, subject to transitional provisions and savings in the Housing Act 2004 (Commencement No 5 and Transitional Provisions and Savings) (England) Order 2006, SI 2006/1060, art 3, Schedule at **[3700]**, **[3701]**); 16 June 2006 (in relation to Wales, subject to transitional provisions and savings in the Housing Act 2004 (Commencement No 3 and Transitional Provisions and Savings) (Wales) Order 2006, SI 2006/1535, art 3, Schedule at **[3714]**, **[3715]**).

## 70  Revocation of licences

(1)   The local housing authority may revoke a licence—
- (a)   if they do so with the agreement of the licence holder;
- (b)   in any of the cases mentioned in subsection (2) (circumstances relating to licence holder or other person);
- (c)   in any of the cases mentioned in subsection (3) (circumstances relating to HMO concerned); or
- (d)   in any other circumstances prescribed by regulations made by the appropriate national authority.

(2)   The cases referred to in subsection (1)(b) are as follows—
- (a)   where the authority consider that the licence holder or any other person has committed a serious breach of a condition of the licence or repeated breaches of such a condition;
- (b)   where the authority no longer consider that the licence holder is a fit and proper person to be the licence holder; and
- (c)   where the authority no longer consider that the management of the house is being carried on by persons who are in each case fit and proper persons to be involved in its management.

Section 66(1) applies in relation to paragraph (b) or (c) above as it applies in relation to section 64(3)(b) or (d).

(3)   The cases referred to in subsection (1)(c) are as follows—
- (a)   where the HMO to which the licence relates ceases to be an HMO to which this Part applies; and
- (b)   where the authority consider at any time that, were the licence to expire at that time, they would, for a particular reason relating to the structure of the HMO, refuse to grant a new licence to the licence holder on similar terms in respect of it.

(4)   Subsection (5) applies where the authority are considering whether to revoke a licence by virtue of subsection (3)(b) on the grounds that the HMO is not reasonably suitable for the number of households or persons specified in the licence as the maximum number authorised to occupy the house.

(5)   The authority must apply the same standards in relation to the circumstances existing at the time when they are considering whether to revoke the licence as were applicable at the time when it was granted.

This is subject to subsection (6).

(6)   If the standards—
- (a)   prescribed under section 65, and
- (b)   applicable at the time when the licence was granted,

have subsequently been revised or superseded by provisions of regulations under that section, the authority may apply the new standards.

(7)   A revocation made with the agreement of the licence holder takes effect at the time when it is made.

(8)   Otherwise, a revocation does not come into force until such time, if any, as is the operative time for the purposes of this subsection under paragraph 35 of Schedule 5 (time when period for appealing expires without an appeal being made or when decision to vary is confirmed on appeal).

(9)   The power to revoke a licence under this section is exercisable by the authority either—
- (a)   on an application made by the licence holder or a relevant person, or
- (b)   on the authority's own initiative.

(10)   In subsection (9) "relevant person" means any person (other than the licence holder)—
- (a)   who has an estate or interest in the HMO concerned (but is not a tenant under a lease with an unexpired term of 3 years or less), or
- (b)   who is a person managing or having control of that house (and does not fall within paragraph (a)), or
- (c)   on whom any restriction or obligation is imposed by the licence in accordance with section 67(5).

**NOTES**

Commencement: 18 November 2004 (for the purpose of making orders or regulations); 6 April 2006 (in relation to England for remaining purposes, subject to transitional provisions and savings in the Housing Act 2004 (Commencement No 5 and Transitional Provisions and Savings) (England) Order 2006, SI 2006/1060, art 3, Schedule at **[3700]**, **[3701]**); 16 June 2006 (in relation to Wales for remaining purposes, subject to transitional provisions and savings in the Housing Act 2004 (Commencement No 3 and Transitional Provisions and Savings) (Wales) Order 2006, SI 2006/1535, art 3, Schedule at **[3714]**, **[3715]**).

*Procedure and appeals*

### 71 Procedural requirements and appeals against licence decisions

Schedule 5 (which deals with procedural requirements relating to the grant, refusal, variation or revocation of licences and with appeals against licence decisions) has effect for the purposes of this Part.

**[1393]**

**NOTES**

Commencement: 6 April 2006 (in relation to England, subject to transitional provisions and savings in the Housing Act 2004 (Commencement No 5 and Transitional Provisions and Savings) (England) Order 2006, SI 2006/1060, art 3, Schedule at **[3700]**, **[3701]**); 16 June 2006 (in relation to Wales, subject to transitional provisions and savings in the Housing Act 2004 (Commencement No 3 and Transitional Provisions and Savings) (Wales) Order 2006, SI 2006/1535, art 3, Schedule at **[3714]**, **[3715]**).

*Enforcement*

### 72 Offences in relation to licensing of HMOs

(1)　A person commits an offence if he is a person having control of or managing an HMO which is required to be licensed under this Part (see section 61(1)) but is not so licensed.

(2)　A person commits an offence if—

(a)　he is a person having control of or managing an HMO which is licensed under this Part,

(b)　he knowingly permits another person to occupy the house, and

(c)　the other person's occupation results in the house being occupied by more households or persons than is authorised by the licence.

(3)　A person commits an offence if—

(a)　he is a licence holder or a person on whom restrictions or obligations under a licence are imposed in accordance with section 67(5), and

(b)　he fails to comply with any condition of the licence.

(4)　In proceedings against a person for an offence under subsection (1) it is a defence that, at the material time—

(a)　a notification had been duly given in respect of the house under section 62(1), or

(b)　an application for a licence had been duly made in respect of the house under section 63,

and that notification or application was still effective (see subsection (8)).

(5)　In proceedings against a person for an offence under subsection (1), (2) or (3) it is a defence that he had a reasonable excuse—

(a)　for having control of or managing the house in the circumstances mentioned in subsection (1), or

(b)　for permitting the person to occupy the house, or

(c)　for failing to comply with the condition,

as the case may be.

(6)　A person who commits an offence under subsection (1) or (2) is liable on summary conviction to a fine not exceeding £20,000.

(7)　A person who commits an offence under subsection (3) is liable on summary conviction to a fine not exceeding level 5 on the standard scale.

(8)　For the purposes of subsection (4) a notification or application is "effective" at a particular time if at that time it has not been withdrawn, and either—

(a)　the authority have not decided whether to serve a temporary exemption notice, or (as the case may be) grant a licence, in pursuance of the notification or application, or

(b)　if they have decided not to do so, one of the conditions set out in subsection (9) is met.

(9)　The conditions are—

(a)　that the period for appealing against the decision of the authority not to serve or grant such a notice or licence (or against any relevant decision of a residential property tribunal) has not expired, or

(b)　that an appeal has been brought against the authority's decision (or against any relevant decision of such a tribunal) and the appeal has not been determined or withdrawn.

PART I
STATUTES

(10) In subsection (9) "relevant decision" means a decision which is given on an appeal to the tribunal and confirms the authority's decision (with or without variation).

**[1394]**

**NOTES**
Commencement: 6 April 2006 (sub-ss (2), (3), (5)–(7), in relation to England, subject to transitional provisions and savings in the Housing Act 2004 (Commencement No 5 and Transitional Provisions and Savings) (England) Order 2006, SI 2006/1060, art 3, Schedule at **[3700]**, **[3701]**); 16 June 2006 (in relation to Wales, subject to transitional provisions and savings in the Housing Act 2004 (Commencement No 3 and Transitional Provisions and Savings) (Wales) Order 2006, SI 2006/1535, art 3, Schedule at **[3714]**, **[3715]**); 6 July 2006 (sub-ss (1), (4), (8)–(10) in relation to England, subject to transitional provisions and savings in SI 2006/1060, art 3, Schedule at **[3700]**, **[3701]**).

## 73 Other consequences of operating unlicensed HMOs: rent repayment orders

(1) For the purposes of this section an HMO is an "unlicensed HMO" if—
  (a) it is required to be licensed under this Part but is not so licensed, and
  (b) neither of the conditions in subsection (2) is satisfied.

(2) The conditions are—
  (a) that a notification has been duly given in respect of the HMO under section 62(1) and that notification is still effective (as defined by section 72(8));
  (b) that an application for a licence has been duly made in respect of the HMO under section 63 and that application is still effective (as so defined).

(3) No rule of law relating to the validity or enforceability of contracts in circumstances involving illegality is to affect the validity or enforceability of—
  (a) any provision requiring the payment of rent or the making of any other periodical payment in connection with any tenancy or licence of a part of an unlicensed HMO, or
  (b) any other provision of such a tenancy or licence.

(4) But amounts paid in respect of rent or other periodical payments payable in connection with such a tenancy or licence may be recovered in accordance with subsection (5) and section 74.

(5) If—
  (a) an application in respect of an HMO is made to a residential property tribunal by the local housing authority or an occupier of a part of the HMO, and
  (b) the tribunal is satisfied as to the matters mentioned in subsection (6) or (8),
the tribunal may make an order (a "rent repayment order") requiring the appropriate person to pay to the applicant such amount in respect of the housing benefit paid as mentioned in subsection (6)(b), or (as the case may be) the periodical payments paid as mentioned in subsection (8)(b), as is specified in the order (see section 74(2) to (8)).

(6) If the application is made by the local housing authority, the tribunal must be satisfied as to the following matters—
  (a) that, at any time within the period of 12 months ending with the date of the notice of intended proceedings required by subsection (7), the appropriate person has committed an offence under section 72(1) in relation to the HMO (whether or not he has been charged or convicted),
  (b) that housing benefit has been paid (to any person) in respect of periodical payments payable in connection with the occupation of a part or parts of the HMO during any period during which it appears to the tribunal that such an offence was being committed, and
  (c) that the requirements of subsection (7) have been complied with in relation to the application.

(7) Those requirements are as follows—
  (a) the authority must have served on the appropriate person a notice (a "notice of intended proceedings")—
    (i) informing him that the authority are proposing to make an application under subsection (5),
    (ii) setting out the reasons why they propose to do so,
    (iii) stating the amount that they will seek to recover under that subsection and how that amount is calculated, and
    (iv) inviting him to make representations to them within a period specified in the notice of not less than 28 days;
  (b) that period must have expired; and
  (c) the authority must have considered any representations made to them within that period by the appropriate person.

(8) If the application is made by an occupier of a part of the HMO, the tribunal must be satisfied as to the following matters—
  (a) that the appropriate person has been convicted of an offence under section 72(1) in

relation to the HMO, or has been required by a rent repayment order to make a payment in respect of housing benefit paid in connection with occupation of a part or parts of the HMO,

(b)    that the occupier paid, to a person having control of or managing the HMO, periodical payments in respect of occupation of part of the HMO during any period during which it appears to the tribunal that such an offence was being committed in relation to the HMO, and

(c)    that the application is made within the period of 12 months beginning with—

    (i)    the date of the conviction or order, or

    (ii)    if such a conviction was followed by such an order (or vice versa), the date of the later of them.

(9)    Where a local housing authority serve a notice of intended proceedings on any person under this section, they must ensure—

(a)    that a copy of the notice is received by the department of the authority responsible for administering the housing benefit to which the proceedings would relate; and

(b)    that that department is subsequently kept informed of any matters relating to the proceedings that are likely to be of interest to it in connection with the administration of housing benefit.

(10)    In this section—

"the appropriate person", in relation to any payment of housing benefit or periodical payment payable in connection with occupation of a part of an HMO, means the person who at the time of the payment was entitled to receive on his own account periodical payments payable in connection with such occupation;

"housing benefit" means housing benefit provided by virtue of a scheme under section 123 of the Social Security Contributions and Benefits Act 1992 (c 4);

"occupier", in relation to any periodical payment, means a person who was an occupier at the time of the payment, whether under a tenancy or licence or otherwise (and "occupation" has a corresponding meaning);

"periodical payments" means periodical payments in respect of which housing benefit may be paid by virtue of regulation 10 of the Housing Benefit (General) Regulations 1987 (SI 1987/1971) or any corresponding provision replacing that regulation.

(11)    For the purposes of this section an amount which—

(a)    is not actually paid by an occupier but is used by him to discharge the whole or part of his liability in respect of a periodical payment (for example, by offsetting the amount against any such liability), and

(b)    is not an amount of housing benefit,

is to be regarded as an amount paid by the occupier in respect of that periodical payment.

**[1395]**

---

**NOTES**

Commencement: 16 June 2006 (in relation to Wales, subject to transitional provisions and savings in the Housing Act 2004 (Commencement No 3 and Transitional Provisions and Savings) (Wales) Order 2006, SI 2006/1535, art 3, Schedule at **[3714]**, **[3715]**); 6 July 2006 (in relation to England, subject to transitional provisions and savings in the Housing Act 2004 (Commencement No 5 and Transitional Provisions and Savings) (England) Order 2006, SI 2006/1060, art 3, Schedule at **[3700]**, **[3701]**).

Modification: see the note to s 61 at **[1383]**.

---

### 74 Further provisions about rent repayment orders

(1)    This section applies in relation to rent repayment orders made by residential property tribunals under section 73(5).

(2)    Where, on an application by the local housing authority, the tribunal is satisfied—

(a)    that a person has been convicted of an offence under section 72(1) in relation to the HMO, and

(b)    that housing benefit was paid (whether or not to the appropriate person) in respect of periodical payments payable in connection with occupation of a part or parts of the HMO during any period during which it appears to the tribunal that such an offence was being committed in relation to the HMO,

the tribunal must make a rent repayment order requiring the appropriate person to pay to the authority an amount equal to the total amount of housing benefit paid as mentioned in paragraph (b).

This is subject to subsections (3), (4) and (8).

(3)    If the total of the amounts received by the appropriate person in respect of periodical payments payable as mentioned in paragraph (b) of subsection (2) ("the rent total") is less than the total amount of housing benefit paid as mentioned in that paragraph, the amount required to be paid by virtue of a rent repayment order made in accordance with that subsection is limited to the rent total.

PART I STATUTES

(4) A rent repayment order made in accordance with subsection (2) may not require the payment of any amount which the tribunal is satisfied that, by reason of any exceptional circumstances, it would be unreasonable for that person to be required to pay.

(5) In a case where subsection (2) does not apply, the amount required to be paid by virtue of a rent repayment order under section 73(5) is to be such amount as the tribunal considers reasonable in the circumstances.

This is subject to subsections (6) to (8).

(6) In such a case the tribunal must, in particular, take into account the following matters—

    (a) the total amount of relevant payments paid in connection with occupation of the HMO during any period during which it appears to the tribunal that an offence was being committed by the appropriate person in relation to the HMO under section 72(1);

    (b) the extent to which that total amount—

        (i) consisted of, or derived from, payments of housing benefit, and

        (ii) was actually received by the appropriate person;

    (c) whether the appropriate person has at any time been convicted of an offence under section 72(1) in relation to the HMO;

    (d) the conduct and financial circumstances of the appropriate person; and

    (e) where the application is made by an occupier, the conduct of the occupier.

(7) In subsection (6) "relevant payments" means—

    (a) in relation to an application by a local housing authority, payments of housing benefit or periodical payments payable by occupiers;

    (b) in relation to an application by an occupier, periodical payments payable by the occupier, less any amount of housing benefit payable in respect of occupation of the part of the HMO occupied by him during the period in question.

(8) A rent repayment order may not require the payment of any amount which—

    (a) (where the application is made by a local housing authority) is in respect of any time falling outside the period of 12 months mentioned in section 73(6)(a); or

    (b) (where the application is made by an occupier) is in respect of any time falling outside the period of 12 months ending with the date of the occupier's application under section 73(5);

and the period to be taken into account under subsection (6)(a) above is restricted accordingly.

(9) Any amount payable to a local housing authority under a rent repayment order—

    (a) does not, when recovered by the authority, constitute an amount of housing benefit recovered by them, and

    (b) until recovered by them, is a legal charge on the HMO which is a local land charge.

(10) For the purpose of enforcing that charge the authority have the same powers and remedies under the Law of Property Act 1925 (c 20) and otherwise as if they were mortgagees by deed having powers of sale and lease, and of accepting surrenders of leases and of appointing a receiver.

(11) The power of appointing a receiver is exercisable at any time after the end of the period of one month beginning with the date on which the charge takes effect.

(12) If the authority subsequently grant a licence under this Part or Part 3 in respect of the HMO to the appropriate person or any person acting on his behalf, the conditions contained in the licence may include a condition requiring the licence holder—

    (a) to pay to the authority any amount payable to them under the rent repayment order and not so far recovered by them; and

    (b) to do so in such instalments as are specified in the licence.

(13) If the authority subsequently make a management order under Chapter 1 of Part 4 in respect of the HMO, the order may contain such provisions as the authority consider appropriate for the recovery of any amount payable to them under the rent repayment order and not so far recovered by them.

(14) Any amount payable to an occupier by virtue of a rent repayment order is recoverable by the occupier as a debt due to him from the appropriate person.

(15) The appropriate national authority may by regulations make such provision as it considers appropriate for supplementing the provisions of this section and section 73, and in particular—

    (a) for securing that persons are not unfairly prejudiced by rent repayment orders (whether in cases where there have been over-payments of housing benefit or otherwise);

    (b) for requiring or authorising amounts received by local housing authorities by virtue of rent repayment orders to be dealt with in such manner as is specified in the regulations.

(16) Section 73(10) and (11) apply for the purposes of this section as they apply for the purposes of section 73.

**NOTES**
   Commencement: 18 November 2004 (for the purpose of making orders or regulations); 16 June 2006 (in relation to Wales for remaining purposes, subject to transitional provisions and savings in the Housing Act 2004 (Commencement No 3 and Transitional Provisions and Savings) (Wales) Order 2006, SI 2006/1535, art 3, Schedule at **[3714]**, **[3715]**); 6 July 2006 (in relation to England for remaining purposes, subject to transitional provisions and savings in the Housing Act 2004 (Commencement No 5 and Transitional Provisions and Savings) (England) Order 2006, SI 2006/1060, art 3, Schedule at **[3700]**, **[3701]**).
   Regulations: the Rent Repayment Orders (Supplementary Provisions) (England) Regulations 2007, SI 2007/572 at **[3749]**; the Rent Repayment Orders (Supplementary Provisions) (Wales) Regulations 2008, SI 2008/254 at **[3781]**.

**75   Other consequences of operating unlicensed HMOs: restriction on terminating tenancies**

   (1)   No section 21 notice may be given in relation to a shorthold tenancy of a part of an unlicensed HMO so long as it remains such an HMO.

   (2)   In this section—
      a "section 21 notice" means a notice under section 21(1)(b) or (4)(a) of the Housing Act 1988 (c 50) (recovery of possession on termination of shorthold tenancy);
      a "shorthold tenancy" means an assured shorthold tenancy within the meaning of Chapter 2 of Part 1 of that Act;
      "unlicensed HMO" has the same meaning as in section 73 of this Act.

**[1397]**

**NOTES**
   Commencement: 6 April 2006 (in relation to England, subject to transitional provisions and savings in the Housing Act 2004 (Commencement No 5 and Transitional Provisions and Savings) (England) Order 2006, SI 2006/1060, art 3, Schedule at **[3700]**, **[3701]**); 16 June 2006 (in relation to Wales, subject to transitional provisions and savings in the Housing Act 2004 (Commencement No 3 and Transitional Provisions and Savings) (Wales) Order 2006, SI 2006/1535, art 3, Schedule at **[3714]**, **[3715]**).
   Modification: see the note to s 61 at **[1383]**.

*Supplementary provisions*

**76   Transitional arrangements relating to introduction and termination of licensing**

   (1)   Subsection (2) applies where—
      (a)   an order under section 55(3) which prescribes a particular description of HMOs comes into force; or
      (b)   a designation under section 56 comes into force in relation to HMOs of a particular description.

   (2)   This Part applies in relation to the occupation by persons or households of such HMOs on or after the coming into force of the order or designation even if their occupation began before, or in pursuance of a contract made before, it came into force.

This is subject to subsections (3) to (5).

   (3)   Subsection (4) applies where—
      (a)   an HMO which is licensed under this Part, or a part of such an HMO, is occupied by more households or persons than the number permitted by the licence; and
      (b)   the occupation of all or any of those households or persons began before, or in pursuance of a contract made before, the licence came into force.

   (4)   In proceedings against a person for an offence under section 72(2) it is a defence that at the material time he was taking all reasonable steps to try to reduce the number of households or persons occupying the house to the number permitted by the licence.

   (5)   Subsection (4) does not apply if the licence came into force immediately after a previous licence in respect of the same HMO unless the occupation in question began before, or in pursuance of a contract made before, the coming into force of the original licence.

   (6)   An order under section 270 may make provision as regards the licensing under this Part of HMOs—
      (a)   which are registered immediately before the appointed day under a scheme to which section 347 (schemes containing control provisions) or 348B (schemes containing special control provisions) of the Housing Act 1985 (c 68) applies, or
      (b)   in respect of which applications for registration under such a scheme are then pending.

   (7)   In subsection (6) "the appointed day" means the day appointed for the coming into force of section 61.

**[1398]**

**NOTES**
   Commencement: 6 April 2006 (in relation to England, subject to transitional provisions and savings in the Housing Act 2004 (Commencement No 5 and Transitional Provisions and Savings) (England) Order 2006,

SI 2006/1060, art 3, Schedule at **[3700]**, **[3701]**); 16 June 2006 (in relation to Wales, subject to transitional provisions and savings in the Housing Act 2004 (Commencement No 3 and Transitional Provisions and Savings) (Wales) Order 2006, SI 2006/1535, art 3, Schedule at **[3714]**, **[3715]**).

Orders: the Housing Act 2004 (Commencement No 5 and Transitional Provisions and Savings) (England) Order 2006, SI 2006/1060 at **[3698]**; the Housing Act 2004 (Commencement No 3 and Transitional Provisions and Savings) (Wales) Order 2006, SI 2006/1535 at **[3712]**.

## 77 Meaning of "HMO"

In this Part—
    (a)   "HMO" means a house in multiple occupation as defined by sections 254 to 259, and
    (b)   references to an HMO include (where the context permits) any yard, garden, outhouses and appurtenances belonging to, or usually enjoyed with, it (or any part of it).

**[1399]**

**NOTES**
Commencement: 6 April 2006 (in relation to England, subject to transitional provisions and savings in the Housing Act 2004 (Commencement No 5 and Transitional Provisions and Savings) (England) Order 2006, SI 2006/1060, art 3, Schedule at **[3700]**, **[3701]**); 16 June 2006 (in relation to Wales, subject to transitional provisions and savings in the Housing Act 2004 (Commencement No 3 and Transitional Provisions and Savings) (Wales) Order 2006, SI 2006/1535, art 3, Schedule at **[3714]**, **[3715]**).

## 78 Index of defined expressions: Part 2

The following table shows where expressions used in this Part are defined or otherwise explained.

| *Expression* | *Provision of this Act* |
| --- | --- |
| Anti-social behaviour | Section 57(5) |
| Appropriate national authority | Section 261(1) |
| Category 1 hazard | Section 2(1) |
| Category 2 hazard | Section 2(1) |
| District of local housing authority | Section 261(6) |
| HMO | Section 77 |
| HMO to which this Part applies | Section 55(2) |
| Licence and licence holder | Section 61(6) |
| Licence (to occupy premises) | Section 262(9) |
| Local housing authority | Section 261(2) to (5) |
| Modifications | Section 250(7) |
| Occupier (and related expressions) | Section 262(6) |
| Person having control | Section 263(1) and (2) (and see also section 66(7)) |
| Person having estate or interest | Section 262(8) |
| Person managing | Section 263(3) |
| Person involved in management | Section 263(5) |
| Residential property tribunal | Section 229 |
| Tenant | Section 262(1) to (5). |

**[1400]**

**NOTES**
Commencement: 6 April 2006 (in relation to England, subject to transitional provisions and savings in the Housing Act 2004 (Commencement No 5 and Transitional Provisions and Savings) (England) Order 2006, SI 2006/1060, art 3, Schedule at **[3700]**, **[3701]**); 16 June 2006 (in relation to Wales, subject to transitional provisions and savings in the Housing Act 2004 (Commencement No 3 and Transitional Provisions and Savings) (Wales) Order 2006, SI 2006/1535, art 3, Schedule at **[3714]**, **[3715]**).

Modification: see the note to s 61 at **[1383]**.

## PART 3
## SELECTIVE LICENSING OF OTHER RESIDENTIAL ACCOMMODATION

*Introductory*

### 79 Licensing of houses to which this Part applies

(1)   This Part provides for houses to be licensed by local housing authorities where—
  (a)   they are houses to which this Part applies (see subsection (2)), and
  (b)   they are required to be licensed under this Part (see section 85(1)).

(2)   This Part applies to a house if—
  (a)   it is in an area that is for the time being designated under section 80 as subject to selective licensing, and
  (b)   the whole of it is occupied either—
    (i)   under a single tenancy or licence that is not an exempt tenancy or licence under subsection (3) or (4), or
    (ii)   under two or more tenancies or licences in respect of different dwellings contained in it, none of which is an exempt tenancy or licence under subsection (3) or (4).

(3)   A tenancy or licence is an exempt tenancy or licence if it is granted by a body which is registered as a social landlord under Part 1 of the Housing Act 1996 (c 52).

(4)   In addition, the appropriate national authority may by order provide for a tenancy or licence to be an exempt tenancy or licence—
  (a)   if it falls within any description of tenancy or licence specified in the order; or
  (b)   in any other circumstances so specified.

(5)   Every local housing authority have the following general duties—
  (a)   to make such arrangements as are necessary to secure the effective implementation in their district of the licensing regime provided for by this Part; and
  (b)   to ensure that all applications for licences and other issues falling to be determined by them under this Part are determined within a reasonable time.

**[1401]**

---

**NOTES**
Commencement: 18 November 2004 (for the purpose of making orders or regulations); 15 June 2005 (in relation to England for remaining purposes); 25 November 2005 (in relation to Wales for remaining purposes).
Orders: the Selective Licensing of Houses (Specified Exemptions) (England) Order 2006, SI 2006/370 at **[3607]**; the Selective Licensing of Houses (Specified Exemptions) (Wales) Order 2006, SI 2006/2824 at **[3743]**.

---

*Designation of selective licensing areas*

### 80 Designation of selective licensing areas

(1)   A local housing authority may designate either—
  (a)   the area of their district, or
  (b)   an area in their district,
as subject to selective licensing, if the requirements of subsections (2) and (9) are met.

(2)   The authority must consider that—
  (a)   the first or second set of general conditions mentioned in subsection (3) or (6), or
  (b)   any conditions specified in an order under subsection (7) as an additional set of conditions,
are satisfied in relation to the area.

(3)   The first set of general conditions are—
  (a)   that the area is, or is likely to become, an area of low housing demand; and
  (b)   that making a designation will, when combined with other measures taken in the area by the local housing authority, or by other persons together with the local housing authority, contribute to the improvement of the social or economic conditions in the area.

(4)   In deciding whether an area is, or is likely to become, an area of low housing demand a local housing authority must take into account (among other matters)—
  (a)   the value of residential premises in the area, in comparison to the value of similar premises in other areas which the authority consider to be comparable (whether in terms of types of housing, local amenities, availability of transport or otherwise);
  (b)   the turnover of occupiers of residential premises;
  (c)   the number of residential premises which are available to buy or rent and the length of time for which they remain unoccupied.

(5)   The appropriate national authority may by order amend subsection (4) by adding new matters to those for the time being mentioned in that subsection.

(6)   The second set of general conditions are—

(a)   that the area is experiencing a significant and persistent problem caused by anti-social behaviour;

(b)   that some or all of the private sector landlords who have let premises in the area (whether under leases or licences) are failing to take action to combat the problem that it would be appropriate for them to take; and

(c)   that making a designation will, when combined with other measures taken in the area by the local housing authority, or by other persons together with the local housing authority, lead to a reduction in, or the elimination of, the problem.

"Private sector landlord" does not include a registered social landlord within the meaning of Part 1 of the Housing Act 1996 (c 52).

(7)   The appropriate national authority may by order provide for any conditions specified in the order to apply as an additional set of conditions for the purposes of subsection (2).

(8)   The conditions that may be specified include, in particular, conditions intended to permit a local housing authority to make a designation for the purpose of dealing with one or more specified problems affecting persons occupying Part 3 houses in the area.

"Specified" means specified in an order under subsection (7).

(9)   Before making a designation the local housing authority must—

(a)   take reasonable steps to consult persons who are likely to be affected by the designation; and

(b)   consider any representations made in accordance with the consultation and not withdrawn.

(10)   Section 81 applies for the purposes of this section.

**[1402]**

**NOTES**
Commencement: 18 November 2004 (for the purpose of making orders or regulations); 15 June 2005 (in relation to England for remaining purposes); 25 November 2005 (in relation to Wales for remaining purposes).
Orders: the Selective Licensing of Houses (Additional Conditions) (Wales) Order 2006, SI 2006/2825 at **[3744]**.

## 81   Designations under section 80: further considerations

(1)   This section applies to the power of a local housing authority to make designations under section 80.

(2)   The authority must ensure that any exercise of the power is consistent with the authority's overall housing strategy.

(3)   The authority must also seek to adopt a co-ordinated approach in connection with dealing with homelessness, empty properties and anti-social behaviour, both—

(a)   as regards combining licensing under this Part with other courses of action available to them, and

(b)   as regards combining such licensing with measures taken by other persons.

(4)   The authority must not make a particular designation under section 80 unless—

(a)   they have considered whether there are any other courses of action available to them (of whatever nature) that might provide an effective method of achieving the objective or objectives that the designation would be intended to achieve, and

(b)   they consider that making the designation will significantly assist them to achieve the objective or objectives (whether or not they take any other course of action as well).

**[1403]**

**NOTES**
Commencement: 15 June 2005 (in relation to England); 25 November 2005 (in relation to Wales).

## 82   Designation needs confirmation or general approval to be effective

(1)   A designation of an area as subject to selective licensing cannot come into force unless—

(a)   it has been confirmed by the appropriate national authority; or

(b)   it falls within a description of designations in relation to which that authority has given a general approval in accordance with subsection (6).

(2)   The appropriate national authority may either confirm, or refuse to confirm, a designation as it considers appropriate.

(3)   If the appropriate national authority confirms a designation, the designation comes into force on a date specified for this purpose by that authority.

(4)   That date must be no earlier than three months after the date on which the designation is confirmed.

(5)   A general approval may be given in relation to a description of designations framed by reference to any matters or circumstances.

(6)    Accordingly a general approval may (in particular) be given in relation to—
  (a)    designations made by a specified local housing authority;
  (b)    designations made by a local housing authority falling within a specified description of such authorities;
  (c)    designations relating to Part 3 houses of a specified description.
  "Specified" means specified by the appropriate national authority in the approval.

(7)    If, by virtue of a general approval, a designation does not need to be confirmed before it comes into force, the designation comes into force on the date specified for this purpose in the designation.

(8)    That date must be no earlier than three months after the date on which the designation is made.

(9)    Where a designation comes into force, this Part applies in relation to the occupation by persons of houses in the area on or after the coming into force of the designation even if their occupation began before, or in pursuance of a contract made before, it came into force.

**[1404]**

**NOTES**
Commencement: 6 April 2006 (in relation to England, subject to transitional provisions and savings in the Housing Act 2004 (Commencement No 5 and Transitional Provisions and Savings) (England) Order 2006, SI 2006/1060, art 3, Schedule at **[3700]**, **[3701]**); 16 June 2006 (in relation to Wales, subject to transitional provisions and savings in the Housing Act 2004 (Commencement No 3 and Transitional Provisions and Savings) (Wales) Order 2006, SI 2006/1535, art 3, Schedule at **[3714]**, **[3715]**).

## 83    Notification requirements relating to designations

(1)    This section applies to a designation—
  (a)    when it is confirmed under section 82, or
  (b)    (if it is not required to be so confirmed) when it is made by the local housing authority.

(2)    As soon as the designation is confirmed or made, the authority must publish in the prescribed manner a notice stating—
  (a)    that the designation has been made,
  (b)    whether or not the designation was required to be confirmed and either that it has been confirmed or that a general approval under section 82 applied to it (giving details of the approval in question),
  (c)    the date on which the designation is to come into force, and
  (d)    any other information which may be prescribed.

(3)    After publication of a notice under subsection (2), and for as long as the designation is in force, the local housing authority must make available to the public in accordance with any prescribed requirements—
  (a)    copies of the designation, and
  (b)    such information relating to the designation as is prescribed.

(4)    In this section "prescribed" means prescribed by regulations made by the appropriate national authority.

**[1405]**

**NOTES**
Commencement: 18 November 2004 (for the purpose of making orders or regulations); 6 April 2006 (in relation to England for remaining purposes, subject to transitional provisions and savings in the Housing Act 2004 (Commencement No 5 and Transitional Provisions and Savings) (England) Order 2006, SI 2006/1060, art 3, Schedule at **[3700]**, **[3701]**); 16 June 2006 (in relation to Wales for remaining purposes, subject to transitional provisions and savings in the Housing Act 2004 (Commencement No 3 and Transitional Provisions and Savings) (Wales) Order 2006, SI 2006/1535, art 3, Schedule at **[3714]**, **[3715]**).
Regulations: the Licensing and Management of Houses in Multiple Occupation and Other Houses (Miscellaneous Provisions) (England) Regulations 2006, SI 2006/373 at **[3623]**; the Licensing and Management of Houses in Multiple Occupation and Other Houses (Miscellaneous Provisions) (Wales) Regulations 2006, SI 2006/1715 at **[3724]**.

## 84    Duration, review and revocation of designations

(1)    Unless previously revoked under subsection (4), a designation ceases to have effect at the time that is specified for this purpose in the designation.

(2)    That time must be no later than five years after the date on which the designation comes into force.

(3)    A local housing authority must from time to time review the operation of any designation made by them.

(4)    If following a review they consider it appropriate to do so, the authority may revoke the designation.

(5)   If they do revoke the designation, the designation ceases to have effect on the date that is specified by the authority for this purpose.

(6)   On revoking a designation, the authority must publish notice of the revocation in such manner as is prescribed by regulations made by the appropriate national authority.

**[1406]**

**NOTES**
Commencement: 18 November 2004 (for the purpose of making orders or regulations); 6 April 2006 (in relation to England for remaining purposes, subject to transitional provisions and savings in the Housing Act 2004 (Commencement No 5 and Transitional Provisions and Savings) (England) Order 2006, SI 2006/1060, art 3, Schedule at **[3700]**, **[3701]**); 16 June 2006 (in relation to Wales for remaining purposes, subject to transitional provisions and savings in the Housing Act 2004 (Commencement No 3 and Transitional Provisions and Savings) (Wales) Order 2006, SI 2006/1535, art 3, Schedule at **[3714]**, **[3715]**).
Regulations: the Licensing and Management of Houses in Multiple Occupation and Other Houses (Miscellaneous Provisions) (England) Regulations 2006, SI 2006/373 at **[3623]**; the Licensing and Management of Houses in Multiple Occupation and Other Houses (Miscellaneous Provisions) (Wales) Regulations 2006, SI 2006/1715 at **[3724]**.

*Houses required to be licensed*

**85   Requirement for Part 3 houses to be licensed**

(1)   Every Part 3 house must be licensed under this Part unless—
 (a)   it is an HMO to which Part 2 applies (see section 55(2)), or
 (b)   a temporary exemption notice is in force in relation to it under section 86, or
 (c)   a management order is in force in relation to it under Chapter 1 or 2 of Part 4.

(2)   A licence under this Part is a licence authorising occupation of the house concerned under one or more tenancies or licences within section 79(2)(b).

(3)   Sections 87 to 90 deal with applications for licences, the granting or refusal of licences and the imposition of licence conditions.

(4)   The local housing authority must take all reasonable steps to secure that applications for licences are made to them in respect of houses in their area which are required to be licensed under this Part but are not so licensed.

(5)   In this Part, unless the context otherwise requires—
 (a)   references to a Part 3 house are to a house to which this Part applies (see section 79(2)),
 (b)   references to a licence are to a licence under this Part,
 (c)   references to a licence holder are to be read accordingly, and
 (d)   references to a house being (or not being) licensed under this Part are to its being (or not being) a house in respect of which a licence is in force under this Part.

**[1407]**

**NOTES**
Commencement: 6 April 2006 (in relation to England, subject to transitional provisions and savings in the Housing Act 2004 (Commencement No 5 and Transitional Provisions and Savings) (England) Order 2006, SI 2006/1060, art 3, Schedule at **[3700]**, **[3701]**); 16 June 2006 (in relation to Wales, subject to transitional provisions and savings in the Housing Act 2004 (Commencement No 3 and Transitional Provisions and Savings) (Wales) Order 2006, SI 2006/1535, art 3, Schedule at **[3714]**, **[3715]**).

**86   Temporary exemption from licensing requirement**

(1)   This section applies where a person having control of or managing a Part 3 house which is required to be licensed under this Part (see section 85(1)) but is not so licensed, notifies the local housing authority of his intention to take particular steps with a view to securing that the house is no longer required to be licensed.

(2)   The authority may, if they think fit, serve on that person a notice under this section ("a temporary exemption notice") in respect of the house.

(3)   If a temporary exemption notice is served under this section, the house is (in accordance with section 85(1)) not required to be licensed under this Part during the period for which the notice is in force.

(4)   A temporary exemption notice under this section is in force—
 (a)   for the period of 3 months beginning with the date on which it is served, or
 (b)   (in the case of a notice served by virtue of subsection (5)) for the period of 3 months after the date when the first notice ceases to be in force.

(5)   If the authority—
 (a)   receive a further notification under subsection (1), and
 (b)   consider that there are exceptional circumstances that justify the service of a second temporary exemption notice in respect of the house that would take effect from the end of the period of 3 months applying to the first notice,

the authority may serve a second such notice on the person having control of or managing the house (but no further notice may be served by virtue of this subsection).

(6) If the authority decide not to serve a temporary exemption notice in response to a notification under subsection (1), they must without delay serve on the person concerned a notice informing him of—

    (a)   the decision,

    (b)   the reasons for it and the date on which it was made,

    (c)   the right to appeal against the decision under subsection (7), and

    (d)   the period within which an appeal may be made under that subsection.

(7) The person concerned may appeal to a residential property tribunal against the decision within the period of 28 days beginning with the date specified under subsection (6) as the date on which it was made.

(8) Such an appeal—

    (a)   is to be by way of a re-hearing, but

    (b)   may be determined having regard to matters of which the authority were unaware.

(9) The tribunal—

    (a)   may confirm or reverse the decision of the authority, and

    (b)   if it reverses the decision, must direct the authority to issue a temporary exemption notice with effect from such date as the tribunal directs.

**[1408]**

**NOTES**

Commencement: 6 April 2006 (in relation to England, subject to transitional provisions and savings in the Housing Act 2004 (Commencement No 5 and Transitional Provisions and Savings) (England) Order 2006, SI 2006/1060, art 3, Schedule at **[3700]**, **[3701]**); 16 June 2006 (in relation to Wales, subject to transitional provisions and savings in the Housing Act 2004 (Commencement No 3 and Transitional Provisions and Savings) (Wales) Order 2006, SI 2006/1535, art 3, Schedule at **[3714]**, **[3715]**).

*Grant or refusal of licences*

## 87 Applications for licences

(1) An application for a licence must be made to the local housing authority.

(2) The application must be made in accordance with such requirements as the authority may specify.

(3) The authority may, in particular, require the application to be accompanied by a fee fixed by the authority.

(4) The power of the authority to specify requirements under this section is subject to any regulations made under subsection (5).

(5) The appropriate national authority may by regulations make provision about the making of applications under this section.

(6) Such regulations may, in particular—

    (a)   specify the manner and form in which applications are to be made;

    (b)   require the applicant to give copies of the application, or information about it, to particular persons;

    (c)   specify the information which is to be supplied in connection with applications;

    (d)   specify the maximum fees which may be charged (whether by specifying amounts or methods for calculating amounts);

    (e)   specify cases in which no fees are to be charged or fees are to be refunded.

(7) When fixing fees under this section, the local housing authority may (subject to any regulations made under subsection (5)) take into account—

    (a)   all costs incurred by the authority in carrying out their functions under this Part, and

    (b)   all costs incurred by them in carrying out their functions under Chapter 1 of Part 4 in relation to Part 3 houses (so far as they are not recoverable under or by virtue of any provision of that Chapter).

**[1409]**

**NOTES**

Commencement: 18 November 2004 (for the purpose of making orders or regulations); 6 April 2006 (in relation to England for remaining purposes, subject to transitional provisions and savings in the Housing Act 2004 (Commencement No 5 and Transitional Provisions and Savings) (England) Order 2006, SI 2006/1060, art 3, Schedule at **[3700]**, **[3701]**); 16 June 2006 (in relation to Wales for remaining purposes, subject to transitional provisions and savings in the Housing Act 2004 (Commencement No 3 and Transitional Provisions and Savings) (Wales) Order 2006, SI 2006/1535, art 3, Schedule at **[3714]**, **[3715]**).

Regulations: the Licensing and Management of Houses in Multiple Occupation and Other Houses (Miscellaneous Provisions) (England) Regulations 2006, SI 2006/373 at **[3623]**; the Licensing and Management of Houses in Multiple Occupation and Other Houses (Miscellaneous Provisions) (Wales) Regulations 2006,

SI 2006/1715 at **[3724]**; the Licensing and Management of Houses in Multiple Occupation (Additional Provisions) (England) Regulations 2007, SI 2007/1903 at **[3765]**; the Licensing and Management of Houses in Multiple Occupation (Additional Provisions) (Wales) Regulations 2007, SI 2007/3229 at **[3779]**.

## 88 Grant or refusal of licence

(1) Where an application in respect of a house is made to the local housing authority under section 87, the authority must either—

    (a)    grant a licence in accordance with subsection (2), or

    (b)    refuse to grant a licence.

(2) If the authority are satisfied as to the matters mentioned in subsection (3), they may grant a licence either—

    (a)    to the applicant, or

    (b)    to some other person, if both he and the applicant agree.

(3) The matters are—

    (a)    that the proposed licence holder—

        (i)    is a fit and proper person to be the licence holder, and

        (ii)    is, out of all the persons reasonably available to be the licence holder in respect of the house, the most appropriate person to be the licence holder;

    (b)    that the proposed manager of the house is either—

        (i)    the person having control of the house, or

        (ii)    a person who is an agent or employee of the person having control of the house;

    (c)    that the proposed manager of the house is a fit and proper person to be the manager of the house; and

    (d)    that the proposed management arrangements for the house are otherwise satisfactory.

(4) Section 89 applies for the purposes of this section.

**[1410]**

**NOTES**

Commencement: 6 April 2006 (in relation to England, subject to transitional provisions and savings in the Housing Act 2004 (Commencement No 5 and Transitional Provisions and Savings) (England) Order 2006, SI 2006/1060, art 3, Schedule at **[3700]**, **[3701]**); 16 June 2006 (in relation to Wales, subject to transitional provisions and savings in the Housing Act 2004 (Commencement No 3 and Transitional Provisions and Savings) (Wales) Order 2006, SI 2006/1535, art 3, Schedule at **[3714]**, **[3715]**).

## 89 Tests for fitness etc and satisfactory management arrangements

(1) In deciding for the purposes of section 88(3)(a) or (c) whether a person ("P") is a fit and proper person to be the licence holder or (as the case may be) the manager of the house, the local housing authority must have regard (among other things) to any evidence within subsection (2) or (3).

(2) Evidence is within this subsection if it shows that P has—

    (a)    committed any offence involving fraud or other dishonesty, or violence or drugs, or any offence listed in Schedule 3 to the Sexual Offences Act 2003 (c 42) (offences attracting notification requirements);

    (b)    practised unlawful discrimination on grounds of sex, colour, race, ethnic or national origins or disability in, or in connection with, the carrying on of any business; or

    (c)    contravened any provision of the law relating to housing or of landlord and tenant law.

(3) Evidence is within this subsection if—

    (a)    it shows that any person associated or formerly associated with P (whether on a personal, work or other basis) has done any of the things set out in subsection (2)(a) to (c), and

    (b)    it appears to the authority that the evidence is relevant to the question whether P is a fit and proper person to be the licence holder or (as the case may be) the manager of the house.

(4) For the purposes of section 88(3)(a) the local housing authority must assume, unless the contrary is shown, that the person having control of the house is a more appropriate person to be the licence holder than a person not having control of it.

(5) In deciding for the purposes of section 88(3)(d) whether the proposed management arrangements for the house are otherwise satisfactory, the local housing authority must have regard (among other things) to the considerations mentioned in subsection (6).

(6) The considerations are—

    (a)    whether any person proposed to be involved in the management of the house has a sufficient level of competence to be so involved;

    (b)    whether any person proposed to be involved in the management of the house (other than the manager) is a fit and proper person to be so involved; and

    (c)    whether any proposed management structures and funding arrangements are suitable.

(7)　Any reference in section 88(3)(b)(i) or (ii) or subsection (4) above to a person having control of the house, or to being a person of any other description, includes a reference to a person who is proposing to have control of the house, or (as the case may be) to be a person of that description, at the time when the licence would come into force.

**[1411]**

**NOTES**

Commencement: 6 April 2006 (in relation to England, subject to transitional provisions and savings in the Housing Act 2004 (Commencement No 5 and Transitional Provisions and Savings) (England) Order 2006, SI 2006/1060, art 3, Schedule at **[3700]**, **[3701]**); 16 June 2006 (in relation to Wales, subject to transitional provisions and savings in the Housing Act 2004 (Commencement No 3 and Transitional Provisions and Savings) (Wales) Order 2006, SI 2006/1535, art 3, Schedule at **[3714]**, **[3715]**).

## 90　Licence conditions

(1)　A licence may include such conditions as the local housing authority consider appropriate for regulating the management, use or occupation of the house concerned.

(2)　Those conditions may, in particular, include (so far as appropriate in the circumstances)—
  (a)　conditions imposing restrictions or prohibitions on the use or occupation of particular parts of the house by persons occupying it;
  (b)　conditions requiring the taking of reasonable and practicable steps to prevent or reduce anti-social behaviour by persons occupying or visiting the house.

(3)　A licence may also include—
  (a)　conditions requiring facilities and equipment to be made available in the house for the purpose of meeting standards prescribed for the purposes of this section by regulations made by the appropriate national authority;
  (b)　conditions requiring such facilities and equipment to be kept in repair and proper working order;
  (c)　conditions requiring, in the case of any works needed in order for any such facilities or equipment to be made available or to meet any such standards, that the works are carried out within such period or periods as may be specified in, or determined under, the licence.

(4)　A licence must include the conditions required by Schedule 4.

(5)　As regards the relationship between the authority's power to impose conditions under this section and functions exercisable by them under or for the purposes of Part 1 ("Part 1 functions")—
  (a)　the authority must proceed on the basis that, in general, they should seek to identify, remove or reduce category 1 or category 2 hazards in the house by the exercise of Part 1 functions and not by means of licence conditions;
  (b)　this does not, however, prevent the authority from imposing (in accordance with subsection (3)) licence conditions relating to the installation or maintenance of facilities or equipment within subsection (3)(a) above, even if the same result could be achieved by the exercise of Part 1 functions;
  (c)　the fact that licence conditions are imposed for a particular purpose that could be achieved by the exercise of Part 1 functions does not affect the way in which Part 1 functions can be subsequently exercised by the authority.

(6)　A licence may not include conditions imposing restrictions or obligations on a particular person other than the licence holder unless that person has consented to the imposition of the restrictions or obligations.

(7)　A licence may not include conditions requiring (or intended to secure) any alteration in the terms of any tenancy or licence under which any person occupies the house.

**[1412]**

**NOTES**

Commencement: 18 November 2004 (for the purpose of making orders or regulations); 6 April 2006 (in relation to England for remaining purposes, subject to transitional provisions and savings in the Housing Act 2004 (Commencement No 5 and Transitional Provisions and Savings) (England) Order 2006, SI 2006/1060, art 3, Schedule at **[3700]**, **[3701]**); 16 June 2006 (in relation to Wales for remaining purposes, subject to transitional provisions and savings in the Housing Act 2004 (Commencement No 3 and Transitional Provisions and Savings) (Wales) Order 2006, SI 2006/1535, art 3, Schedule at **[3714]**, **[3715]**).

## 91　Licences: general requirements and duration

(1)　A licence may not relate to more than one Part 3 house.

(2)　A licence may be granted before the time when it is required by virtue of this Part but, if so, the licence cannot come into force until that time.

(3)　A licence—

(a) comes into force at the time that is specified in or determined under the licence for this purpose, and

(b) unless previously terminated by subsection (7) or revoked under section 93, continues in force for the period that is so specified or determined.

(4) That period must not end more than 5 years after—

(a) the date on which the licence was granted, or

(b) if the licence was granted as mentioned in subsection (2), the date when the licence comes into force.

(5) Subsection (3)(b) applies even if, at any time during that period, the house concerned subsequently ceases to be a Part 3 house or becomes an HMO to which Part 2 applies (see section 55(2)).

(6) A licence may not be transferred to another person.

(7) If the holder of the licence dies while the licence is in force, the licence ceases to be in force on his death.

(8) However, during the period of 3 months beginning with the date of the licence holder's death, the house is to be treated for the purposes of this Part as if on that date a temporary exemption notice had been served in respect of the house under section 86.

(9) If, at any time during that period ("the initial period"), the personal representatives of the licence holder request the local housing authority to do so, the authority may serve on them a notice which, during the period of 3 months after the date on which the initial period ends, has the same effect as a temporary exemption notice under section 86.

(10) Subsections (6) to (8) of section 86 apply (with any necessary modifications) in relation to a decision by the authority not to serve such a notice as they apply in relation to a decision not to serve a temporary exemption notice.

**[1413]**

---

**NOTES**

Commencement: 6 April 2006 (in relation to England, subject to transitional provisions and savings in the Housing Act 2004 (Commencement No 5 and Transitional Provisions and Savings) (England) Order 2006, SI 2006/1060, art 3, Schedule at **[3700]**, **[3701]**); 16 June 2006 (in relation to Wales, subject to transitional provisions and savings in the Housing Act 2004 (Commencement No 3 and Transitional Provisions and Savings) (Wales) Order 2006, SI 2006/1535, art 3, Schedule at **[3714]**, **[3715]**).

---

*Variation and revocation of licences*

**92 Variation of licences**

(1) The local housing authority may vary a licence—

(a) if they do so with the agreement of the licence holder, or

(b) if they consider that there has been a change of circumstances since the time when the licence was granted.

For this purpose "change of circumstances" includes any discovery of new information.

(2) A variation made with the agreement of the licence holder takes effect at the time when it is made.

(3) Otherwise, a variation does not come into force until such time, if any, as is the operative time for the purposes of this subsection under paragraph 35 of Schedule 5 (time when period for appealing expires without an appeal being made or when decision to vary is confirmed on appeal).

(4) The power to vary a licence under this section is exercisable by the authority either—

(a) on an application made by the licence holder or a relevant person, or

(b) on the authority's own initiative.

(5) In subsection (4) "relevant person" means any person (other than the licence holder)—

(a) who has an estate or interest in the house concerned (but is not a tenant under a lease with an unexpired term of 3 years or less), or

(b) who is a person managing or having control of the house (and does not fall within paragraph (a)), or

(c) on whom any restriction or obligation is imposed by the licence in accordance with section 90(6).

**[1414]**

---

**NOTES**

Commencement: 6 April 2006 (in relation to England, subject to transitional provisions and savings in the Housing Act 2004 (Commencement No 5 and Transitional Provisions and Savings) (England) Order 2006, SI 2006/1060, art 3, Schedule at **[3700]**, **[3701]**); 16 June 2006 (in relation to Wales, subject to transitional provisions and savings in the Housing Act 2004 (Commencement No 3 and Transitional Provisions and Savings) (Wales) Order 2006, SI 2006/1535, art 3, Schedule at **[3714]**, **[3715]**).

### 93   Revocation of licences

(1)   The local housing authority may revoke a licence—

   (a)   if they do so with the agreement of the licence holder,

   (b)   in any of the cases mentioned in subsection (2) (circumstances relating to licence holder or other person),

   (c)   in any of the cases mentioned in subsection (3) (circumstances relating to house concerned), or

   (d)   in any other circumstances prescribed by regulations made by the appropriate national authority.

(2)   The cases referred to in subsection (1)(b) are as follows—

   (a)   where the authority consider that the licence holder or any other person has committed a serious breach of a condition of the licence or repeated breaches of such a condition;

   (b)   where the authority no longer consider that the licence holder is a fit and proper person to be the licence holder; and

   (c)   where the authority no longer consider that the management of the house is being carried on by persons who are in each case fit and proper persons to be involved in its management.

Section 89(1) applies in relation to paragraph (b) or (c) above as it applies in relation to section 88(3)(a) or (c).

(3)   The cases referred to in subsection (1)(c) are as follows—

   (a)   where the house to which the licence relates ceases to be a Part 3 house;

   (b)   where a licence has been granted under Part 2 in respect of the house;

   (c)   where the authority consider at any time that, were the licence to expire at that time, they would, for a particular reason relating to the structure of the house, refuse to grant a new licence to the licence holder on similar terms in respect of it.

(4)   A revocation made with the agreement of the licence holder takes effect at the time when it is made.

(5)   Otherwise, a revocation does not come into force until such time, if any, as is the operative time for the purposes of this subsection under paragraph 35 of Schedule 5 (time when period for appealing expires without an appeal being made or when decision to vary is confirmed on appeal).

This is subject to subsection (6).

(6)   A revocation made in a case within subsection (3)(b) cannot come into force before such time as would be the operative time for the purposes of subsection (5) under paragraph 35 of Schedule 5 on the assumption that paragraph 35 applied—

   (a)   to an appeal against the Part 2 licence under paragraph 31 of the Schedule as it applies to an appeal under paragraph 32 of the Schedule, and

   (b)   to the period for appealing against the Part 2 licence mentioned in paragraph 33(1) of the Schedule as it applies to the period mentioned in paragraph 33(2) of the Schedule.

(7)   The power to revoke a licence under this section is exercisable by the authority either—

   (a)   on an application made by the licence holder or a relevant person, or

   (b)   on the authority's own initiative.

(8)   In subsection (7) "relevant person" means any person (other than the licence holder)—

   (a)   who has an estate or interest in the house concerned (but is not a tenant under a lease with an unexpired term of 3 years or less), or

   (b)   who is a person managing or having control of the house (and does not fall within paragraph (a)), or

   (c)   on whom any restriction or obligation is imposed by the licence in accordance with section 90(6).

**[1415]**

**NOTES**

Commencement: 18 November 2004 (for the purpose of making orders or regulations); 6 April 2006 (in relation to England for remaining purposes, subject to transitional provisions and savings in the Housing Act 2004 (Commencement No 5 and Transitional Provisions and Savings) (England) Order 2006, SI 2006/1060, art 3, Schedule at **[3700]**, **[3701]**); 16 June 2006 (in relation to Wales for remaining purposes, subject to transitional provisions and savings in the Housing Act 2004 (Commencement No 3 and Transitional Provisions and Savings) (Wales) Order 2006, SI 2006/1535, art 3, Schedule at **[3714]**, **[3715]**).

*Procedure and appeals*

### 94   Procedural requirements and appeals against licence decisions

Schedule 5 (which deals with procedural requirements relating to the grant, refusal, variation or revocation of licences and with appeals against licence decisions) has effect for the purposes of this Part.

**[1416]**

**NOTES**
Commencement: 6 April 2006 (in relation to England, subject to transitional provisions and savings in the Housing Act 2004 (Commencement No 5 and Transitional Provisions and Savings) (England) Order 2006, SI 2006/1060, art 3, Schedule at **[3700]**, **[3701]**); 16 June 2006 (in relation to Wales, subject to transitional provisions and savings in the Housing Act 2004 (Commencement No 3 and Transitional Provisions and Savings) (Wales) Order 2006, SI 2006/1535, art 3, Schedule at **[3714]**, **[3715]**).

*Enforcement*

## 95   Offences in relation to licensing of houses under this Part

(1)   A person commits an offence if he is a person having control of or managing a house which is required to be licensed under this Part (see section 85(1)) but is not so licensed.

(2)   A person commits an offence if—

   (a)   he is a licence holder or a person on whom restrictions or obligations under a licence are imposed in accordance with section 90(6), and

   (b)   he fails to comply with any condition of the licence.

(3)   In proceedings against a person for an offence under subsection (1) it is a defence that, at the material time—

   (a)   a notification had been duly given in respect of the house under section 62(1) or 86(1), or

   (b)   an application for a licence had been duly made in respect of the house under section 87, and that notification or application was still effective (see subsection (7)).

(4)   In proceedings against a person for an offence under subsection (1) or (2) it is a defence that he had a reasonable excuse—

   (a)   for having control of or managing the house in the circumstances mentioned in subsection (1), or

   (b)   for failing to comply with the condition,

as the case may be.

(5)   A person who commits an offence under subsection (1) is liable on summary conviction to a fine not exceeding £20,000.

(6)   A person who commits an offence under subsection (2) is liable on summary conviction to a fine not exceeding level 5 on the standard scale.

(7)   For the purposes of subsection (3) a notification or application is "effective" at a particular time if at that time it has not been withdrawn, and either—

   (a)   the authority have not decided whether to serve a temporary exemption notice, or (as the case may be) grant a licence, in pursuance of the notification or application, or

   (b)   if they have decided not to do so, one of the conditions set out in subsection (8) is met.

(8)   The conditions are—

   (a)   that the period for appealing against the decision of the authority not to serve or grant such a notice or licence (or against any relevant decision of a residential property tribunal) has not expired, or

   (b)   that an appeal has been brought against the authority's decision (or against any relevant decision of such a tribunal) and the appeal has not been determined or withdrawn.

(9)   In subsection (8) "relevant decision" means a decision which is given on an appeal to the tribunal and confirms the authority's decision (with or without variation).

**[1417]**

**NOTES**
Commencement: 6 April 2006 (sub-ss (2), (4), (6) in relation to England, subject to transitional provisions and savings in the Housing Act 2004 (Commencement No 5 and Transitional Provisions and Savings) (England) Order 2006, SI 2006/1060, art 3, Schedule at **[3700]**, **[3701]**); 16 June 2006 (in relation to Wales, subject to transitional provisions and savings in the Housing Act 2004 (Commencement No 3 and Transitional Provisions and Savings) (Wales) Order 2006, SI 2006/1535, art 3, Schedule at **[3714]**, **[3715]**); 6 July 2006 (sub-ss (1), (3), (5), (7)–(9) in relation to England, subject to transitional provisions and savings in SI 2006/1060, art 3, Schedule at **[3700]**, **[3701]**).

## 96   Other consequences of operating unlicensed houses: rent repayment orders

(1)   For the purposes of this section a house is an "unlicensed house" if—

   (a)   it is required to be licensed under this Part but is not so licensed, and

   (b)   neither of the conditions in subsection (2) is satisfied.

(2)   The conditions are—

   (a)   that a notification has been duly given in respect of the house under section 62(1) or 86(1) and that notification is still effective (as defined by section 95(7));

(b)    that an application for a licence has been duly made in respect of the house under section 87 and that application is still effective (as so defined).

(3)  No rule of law relating to the validity or enforceability of contracts in circumstances involving illegality is to affect the validity or enforceability of—

(a)    any provision requiring the payment of rent or the making of any other periodical payment in connection with any tenancy or licence of the whole or a part of an unlicensed house, or

(b)    any other provision of such a tenancy or licence.

(4)  But amounts paid in respect of rent or other periodical payments payable in connection with such a tenancy or licence may be recovered in accordance with subsection (5) and section 97.

(5)  If—

(a)    an application in respect of a house is made to a residential property tribunal by the local housing authority or an occupier of the whole or part of the house, and

(b)    the tribunal is satisfied as to the matters mentioned in subsection (6) or (8),

the tribunal may make an order (a "rent repayment order") requiring the appropriate person to pay to the applicant such amount in respect of the housing benefit paid as mentioned in subsection (6)(b), or (as the case may be) the periodical payments paid as mentioned in subsection (8)(b), as is specified in the order (see section 97(2) to (8)).

(6)  If the application is made by the local housing authority, the tribunal must be satisfied as to the following matters—

(a)    that, at any time within the period of 12 months ending with the date of the notice of intended proceedings required by subsection (7), the appropriate person has committed an offence under section 95(1) in relation to the house (whether or not he has been charged or convicted),

(b)    that housing benefit has been paid (to any person) in respect of periodical payments payable in connection with the occupation of the whole or any part or parts of the house during any period during which it appears to the tribunal that such an offence was being committed, and

(c)    that the requirements of subsection (7) have been complied with in relation to the

(7)  Those requirements are as follows—

(a)    the authority must have served on the appropriate person a notice (a "notice of intended proceedings")—

    (i)    informing him that the authority are proposing to make an application under subsection (5),

    (ii)    setting out the reasons why they propose to do so,

    (iii)    stating the amount that they will seek to recover under that subsection and how that amount is calculated, and

    (iv)    inviting him to make representations to them within a period specified in the notice of not less than 28 days;

(b)    that period must have expired; and

(c)    the authority must have considered any representations made to them within that period by the appropriate person.

(8)  If the application is made by an occupier of the whole or part of the house, the tribunal must be satisfied as to the following matters—

(a)    that the appropriate person has been convicted of an offence under section 95(1) in relation to the house, or has been required by a rent repayment order to make a payment in respect of housing benefit paid in connection with occupation of the whole or any part or parts of the house,

(b)    that the occupier paid, to a person having control of or managing the house, periodical payments in respect of occupation of the whole or part of the house during any period during which it appears to the tribunal that such an offence was being committed in relation to the house, and

(c)    that the application is made within the period of 12 months beginning with—

    (i)    the date of the conviction or order, or

    (ii)    if such a conviction was followed by such an order (or vice versa), the date of the later of them.

(9)  Where a local housing authority serve a notice of intended proceedings on any person under this section, they must ensure—

(a)    that a copy of the notice is received by the department of the authority responsible for administering the housing benefit to which the proceedings would relate; and

(b)    that that department is subsequently kept informed of any matters relating to the proceedings that are likely to be of interest to it in connection with the administration of housing benefit.

(10)  In this section—

"the appropriate person", in relation to any payment of housing benefit or periodical payment payable in connection with occupation of the whole or a part of a house, means the person who at the time of the payment was entitled to receive on his own account periodical payments payable in connection with such occupation;

"housing benefit" means housing benefit provided by virtue of a scheme under section 123 of the Social Security Contributions and Benefits Act 1992 (c 4);

"occupier", in relation to any periodical payment, means a person who was an occupier at the time of the payment, whether under a tenancy or licence (and "occupation" has a corresponding meaning);

"periodical payments" means periodical payments in respect of which housing benefit may be paid by virtue of regulation 10 of the Housing Benefit (General) Regulations 1987 (SI 1987/1971) or any corresponding provision replacing that regulation.

(11)  For the purposes of this section an amount which—

(a)  is not actually paid by an occupier but is used by him to discharge the whole or part of his liability in respect of a periodical payment (for example, by offsetting the amount against any such liability), and

(b)  is not an amount of housing benefit,

is to be regarded as an amount paid by the occupier in respect of that periodical payment.

**[1418]**

---

**NOTES**

Commencement: 16 June 2006 (in relation to Wales, subject to transitional provisions and savings in the Housing Act 2004 (Commencement No 3 and Transitional Provisions and Savings) (Wales) Order 2006, SI 2006/1535, art 3, Schedule at **[3714]**, **[3715]**); 6 July 2006 (in relation to England, subject to transitional provisions and savings in the Housing Act 2004 (Commencement No 5 and Transitional Provisions and Savings) (England) Order 2006, SI 2006/1060, art 3, Schedule at **[3700]**, **[3701]**).

---

**97  Further provisions about rent repayment orders**

(1)  This section applies in relation to orders made under section 96(5).

(2)  Where, on an application by the local housing authority, the tribunal is satisfied—

(a)  that a person has been convicted of an offence under section 95(1) in relation to the house, and

(b)  that housing benefit was paid (whether or not to the appropriate person) in respect of periodical payments payable in connection with occupation of the whole or any part or parts of the house during any period during which it appears to the tribunal that such an offence was being committed in relation to the house,

the tribunal must make a rent repayment order requiring the appropriate person to pay to the authority an amount equal to the total amount of housing benefit paid as mentioned in paragraph (b).

This is subject to subsections (3), (4) and (8).

(3)  If the total of the amounts received by the appropriate person in respect of periodical payments payable as mentioned in paragraph (b) of subsection (2) ("the rent total") is less than the total amount of housing benefit paid as mentioned in that paragraph, the amount required to be paid by virtue of a rent repayment order made in accordance with that subsection is limited to the rent total.

(4)  A rent repayment order made in accordance with subsection (2) may not require the payment of any amount which the tribunal is satisfied that, by reason of any exceptional circumstances, it would be unreasonable for that person to be required to pay.

(5)  In a case where subsection (2) does not apply, the amount required to be paid by virtue of a rent repayment order under section 96(5) is to be such amount as the tribunal considers reasonable in the circumstances.

This is subject to subsections (6) to (8).

(6)  In such a case the tribunal must, in particular, take into account the following matters—

(a)  the total amount of relevant payments paid in connection with occupation of the house during any period during which it appears to the tribunal that an offence was being committed by the appropriate person in relation to the house under section 95(1);

(b)  the extent to which that total amount—

(i)  consisted of, or derived from, payments of housing benefit, and

(ii)  was actually received by the appropriate person;

(c)  whether the appropriate person has at any time been convicted of an offence under section 95(1) in relation to the house;

(d)  the conduct and financial circumstances of the appropriate person; and

(e)  where the application is made by an occupier, the conduct of the occupier.

(7)    In subsection (6) "relevant payments" means—

    (a)    in relation to an application by a local housing authority, payments of housing benefit or periodical payments payable by occupiers;

    (b)    in relation to an application by an occupier, periodical payments payable by the occupier, less any amount of housing benefit payable in respect of occupation of the house, or (as the case may be) the part of it occupied by him, during the period in question.

(8)    A rent repayment order may not require the payment of an amount which—

    (a)    (where the application is made by a local housing authority) is in respect of any time falling outside the period of 12 months mentioned in section 96(6)(a); or

    (b)    (where the application is made by an occupier) is in respect of any time falling outside the period of 12 months ending with the date of the occupier's application under section 96(5);

and the period to be taken into account under subsection (6)(a) above is restricted accordingly.

(9)    Any amount payable to a local housing authority under a rent repayment order—

    (a)    does not, when recovered by the authority, constitute an amount of housing benefit recovered by them, and

    (b)    is, until recovered by them, a legal charge on the house which is a local land charge.

(10)    For the purpose of enforcing that charge the authority have the same powers and remedies under the Law of Property Act 1925 (c 20) and otherwise as if they were mortgagees by deed having powers of sale and lease, and of accepting surrenders of leases and of appointing a receiver.

(11)    The power of appointing a receiver is exercisable at any time after the end of the period of one month beginning with the date on which the charge takes effect.

(12)    If the authority subsequently grant a licence under Part 2 or this Part in respect of the house to the appropriate person or any person acting on his behalf, the conditions contained in the licence may include a condition requiring the licence holder—

    (a)    to pay to the authority any amount payable to them under the rent repayment order and not so far recovered by them; and

    (b)    to do so in such instalments as are specified in the licence.

(13)    If the authority subsequently make a management order under Chapter 1 of Part 4 in respect of the house, the order may contain such provisions as the authority consider appropriate for the recovery of any amount payable to them under the rent repayment order and not so far recovered by them.

(14)    Any amount payable to an occupier by virtue of a rent repayment order is recoverable by the occupier as a debt due to him from the appropriate person.

(15)    The appropriate national authority may by regulations make such provision as it considers appropriate for supplementing the provisions of this section and section 96, and in particular—

    (a)    for securing that persons are not unfairly prejudiced by rent repayment orders (whether in cases where there have been over-payments of housing benefit or otherwise);

    (b)    for requiring or authorising amounts received by local housing authorities by virtue of rent repayment orders to be dealt with in such manner as is specified in the regulations.

(16)    Section 96(10) and (11) apply for the purposes of this section as they apply for the purposes of section 96.

**[1419]**

---

**NOTES**

Commencement: 18 November 2004 (for the purpose of making orders or regulations); 16 June 2006 (in relation to Wales, subject to transitional provisions and savings in the Housing Act 2004 (Commencement No 3 and Transitional Provisions and Savings) (Wales) Order 2006, SI 2006/1535, art 3, Schedule at **[3714]**, **[3715]**); 6 July 2006 (in relation to England, subject to transitional provisions and savings in the Housing Act 2004 (Commencement No 5 and Transitional Provisions and Savings) (England) Order 2006, SI 2006/1060, art 3, Schedule at **[3700]**, **[3701]**).

Regulations: the Rent Repayment Orders (Supplementary Provisions) (England) Regulations 2007, SI 2007/572 at **[3749]**; the Rent Repayment Orders (Supplementary Provisions) (Wales) Regulations 2008, SI 2008/254 at **[3781]**.

---

**98   Other consequences of operating unlicensed houses: restriction on terminating tenancies**

(1)    No section 21 notice may be given in relation to a shorthold tenancy of the whole or part of an unlicensed house so long as it remains such a house.

(2)    In this section—

    a "section 21 notice" means a notice under section 21(1)(b) or (4)(a) of the Housing Act 1988 (c 50) (recovery of possession on termination of shorthold tenancy);

a "shorthold tenancy" means an assured shorthold tenancy within the meaning of Chapter 2 of Part 1 of that Act;

"unlicensed house" has the same meaning as in section 96 of this Act.

**[1420]**

**NOTES**
Commencement: 6 April 2006 (in relation to England, subject to transitional provisions and savings in the Housing Act 2004 (Commencement No 5 and Transitional Provisions and Savings) (England) Order 2006, SI 2006/1060, art 3, Schedule at **[3700]**, **[3701]**); 16 June 2006 (in relation to Wales, subject to transitional provisions and savings in the Housing Act 2004 (Commencement No 3 and Transitional Provisions and Savings) (Wales) Order 2006, SI 2006/1535, art 3, Schedule at **[3714]**, **[3715]**).

*Supplementary provisions*

**99 Meaning of "house" etc**

In this Part—

"dwelling" means a building or part of a building occupied or intended to be occupied as a separate dwelling;

"house" means a building or part of a building consisting of one or more dwellings;

and references to a house include (where the context permits) any yard, garden, outhouses and appurtenances belonging to, or usually enjoyed with, it (or any part of it).

**[1421]**

**NOTES**
Commencement: 6 April 2006 (in relation to England, subject to transitional provisions and savings in the Housing Act 2004 (Commencement No 5 and Transitional Provisions and Savings) (England) Order 2006, SI 2006/1060, art 3, Schedule at **[3700]**, **[3701]**); 16 June 2006 (in relation to Wales, subject to transitional provisions and savings in the Housing Act 2004 (Commencement No 3 and Transitional Provisions and Savings) (Wales) Order 2006, SI 2006/1535, art 3, Schedule at **[3714]**, **[3715]**).

**100 Index of defined expressions: Part 3**

The following table shows where expressions used in this Part are defined or otherwise explained.

| Expression | Provision of this Act |
|---|---|
| Anti-social behaviour | Section 57(5) |
| Appropriate national authority | Section 261(1) |
| Category 1 hazard | Section 2(1) |
| Category 2 hazard | Section 2(1) |
| District of local housing authority | Section 261(6) |
| Dwelling | Section 99 |
| House | Section 99 |
| Licence and licence holder | Section 85(5) |
| Licence (to occupy premises) | Section 262(9) |
| Local housing authority | Section 261(2) to (5) |
| Occupier (and related expressions) | Section 262(6) |
| Part 3 house | Section 85(5), together with section 79(2) |
| Person having control | Section 263(1) and (2) (and see also section 89(7)) |
| Person having estate or interest | Section 262(8) |
| Person managing | Section 263(3) |
| Person involved in management | Section 263(5) |
| Residential property tribunal | Section 229 |
| Tenant | Section 262(1) to (5) |

**[1422]**

**NOTES**
Commencement: 6 April 2006 (in relation to England, subject to transitional provisions and savings in the Housing Act 2004 (Commencement No 5 and Transitional Provisions and Savings) (England) Order 2006, SI 2006/1060, art 3, Schedule at **[3700]**, **[3701]**); 16 June 2006 (in relation to Wales, subject to transitional provisions and savings in the Housing Act 2004 (Commencement No 3 and Transitional Provisions and Savings) (Wales) Order 2006, SI 2006/1535, art 3, Schedule at **[3714]**, **[3715]**).

# PART 4
## ADDITIONAL CONTROL PROVISIONS IN RELATION TO RESIDENTIAL ACCOMMODATION

### CHAPTER 1
### INTERIM AND FINAL MANAGEMENT ORDERS

*Introductory*

**101 Interim and final management orders: introductory**

(1)  This Chapter deals with the making by a local housing authority of—

(a)  an interim management order (see section 102), or

(b)  a final management order (see section 113),

in respect of an HMO or a Part 3 house.

(2)  Section 103 deals with the making of an interim management order in respect of a house to which that section applies.

(3)  An interim management order is an order (expiring not more than 12 months after it is made) which is made for the purpose of securing that the following steps are taken in relation to the house—

(a)  any immediate steps which the authority consider necessary to protect the health, safety or welfare of persons occupying the house, or persons occupying or having an estate or interest in any premises in the vicinity, and

(b)  any other steps which the authority think appropriate with a view to the proper management of the house pending the grant of a licence under Part 2 or 3 in respect of the house or the making of a final management order in respect of it (or, if appropriate, the revocation of the interim management order).

(4)  A final management order is an order (expiring not more than 5 years after it is made) which is made for the purpose of securing the proper management of the house on a long-term basis in accordance with a management scheme contained in the order.

(5)  In this Chapter any reference to "the house", in relation to an interim or final management order (other than an order under section 102(7)), is a reference to the HMO or Part 3 house to which the order relates.

(6)  Subsection (5) has effect subject to sections 102(8) and 113(7) (exclusion of part occupied by resident landlord).

(7)  In this Chapter "third party", in relation to a house, means any person who has an estate or interest in the house (other than an immediate landlord and any person who is a tenant under a lease granted under section 107(3)(c) or 116(3)(c)).

**[1423]**

**NOTES**
Commencement: 6 April 2006 (in relation to England, subject to transitional provisions and savings in the Housing Act 2004 (Commencement No 5 and Transitional Provisions and Savings) (England) Order 2006, SI 2006/1060, art 3, Schedule at **[3700]**, **[3701]**); 16 June 2006 (in relation to Wales, subject to transitional provisions and savings in the Housing Act 2004 (Commencement No 3 and Transitional Provisions and Savings) (Wales) Order 2006, SI 2006/1535, art 3, Schedule at **[3714]**, **[3715]**).

*Interim management orders: making and operation of orders*

**102 Making of interim management orders**

(1)  A local housing authority—

(a)  are under a duty to make an interim management order in respect of a house in a case within subsection (2) or (3), and

(b)  have power to make an interim management order in respect of a house in a case within subsection (4) or (7).

(2)  The authority must make an interim management order in respect of a house if—

(a)  it is an HMO or a Part 3 house which is required to be licensed under Part 2 or Part 3 (see section 61(1) or 85(1)) but is not so licensed, and

(b)  they consider either—

(i)     that there is no reasonable prospect of its being so licensed in the near future, or

(ii)    that the health and safety condition is satisfied (see section 104).

(3)    The authority must make an interim management order in respect of a house if—

(a)    it is an HMO or a Part 3 house which is required to be licensed under Part 2 or Part 3 and is so licensed,

(b)    they have revoked the licence concerned but the revocation is not yet in force, and

(c)    they consider either—

    (i)    that, on the revocation coming into force, there will be no reasonable prospect of the house being so licensed in the near future, or

    (ii)   that, on the revocation coming into force, the health and safety condition will be satisfied (see section 104).

(4)    The authority may make an interim management order in respect of a house if—

(a)    it is an HMO other than one that is required to be licensed under Part 2, and

(b)    on an application by the authority to a residential property tribunal, the tribunal by order authorises them to make such an order, either in the terms of a draft order submitted by them or in those terms as varied by the tribunal;

and the authority may make such an order despite any pending appeal against the order of the tribunal (but this is without prejudice to any order that may be made on the disposal of any such appeal).

(5)    The tribunal may only authorise the authority to make an interim management order under subsection (4) if it considers that the health and safety condition is satisfied (see section 104).

(6)    In determining whether to authorise the authority to make an interim management order in respect of an HMO under subsection (4), the tribunal must have regard to the extent to which any applicable code of practice approved under section 233 has been complied with in respect of the HMO in the past.

(7)    The authority may make an interim management order in respect of a house if—

(a)    it is a house to which section 103 (special interim management orders) applies, and

(b)    on an application by the authority to a residential property tribunal, the tribunal by order authorises them to make such an order, either in the terms of a draft order submitted by them or in those terms as varied by the tribunal;

and the authority may make such an order despite any pending appeal against the order of the tribunal (but this is without prejudice to any order that may be made on the disposal of any such appeal).

Subsections (2) to (6) of section 103 apply in relation to the power of a residential property tribunal to authorise the making of an interim management order under this subsection.

(8)    The authority may make an interim management order which is expressed not to apply to a part of the house that is occupied by a person who has an estate or interest in the whole of the house.

In relation to such an order, a reference in this Chapter to "the house" does not include the part so excluded (unless the context requires otherwise, such as where the reference is to the house as an HMO or a Part 3 house).

(9)    Nothing in this section requires or authorises the making of an interim management order in respect of a house if—

(a)    an interim management order has been previously made in respect of it, and

(b)    the authority have not exercised any relevant function in respect of the house at any time after the making of the interim management order.

(10)   In subsection (9) "relevant function" means the function of—

(a)    granting a licence under Part 2 or 3,

(b)    serving a temporary exemption notice under section 62 or section 86, or

(c)    making a final management order under section 113.

**[1424]**

**NOTES**

Commencement: 6 April 2006 (in relation to England, subject to transitional provisions and savings in the Housing Act 2004 (Commencement No 5 and Transitional Provisions and Savings) (England) Order 2006, SI 2006/1060, art 3, Schedule at **[3700]**, **[3701]**); 16 June 2006 (in relation to Wales, subject to transitional provisions and savings in the Housing Act 2004 (Commencement No 3 and Transitional Provisions and Savings) (Wales) Order 2006, SI 2006/1535, art 3, Schedule at **[3714]**, **[3715]**).

**103   Special interim management orders**

(1)    This section applies to a house if the whole of it is occupied either—

(a)    under a single tenancy or licence that is not an exempt tenancy or licence under section 79(3) or (4), or

(b)    under two or more tenancies or licences in respect of different dwellings contained in it, none of which is an exempt tenancy or licence under section 79(3) or (4).

(2)    A residential property tribunal may only authorise the authority to make an interim management order in respect of such a house under section 102(7) if it considers that both of the following conditions are satisfied.

(3)    The first condition is that the circumstances relating to the house fall within any category of circumstances prescribed for the purposes of this subsection by an order under subsection (5).

(4)    The second condition is that the making of the order is necessary for the purpose of protecting the health, safety or welfare of persons occupying, visiting or otherwise engaging in lawful activities in the vicinity of the house.

(5)    The appropriate national authority may by order—

(a)    prescribe categories of circumstances for the purposes of subsection (3),

(b)    provide for any of the provisions of this Act to apply in relation to houses to which this section applies, or interim or final management orders made in respect of them, with any modifications specified in the order.

(6)    The categories prescribed by an order under subsection (5) are to reflect one or more of the following—

(a)    the first or second set of general conditions mentioned in subsection (3) or (6) of section 80, or

(b)    any additional set of conditions specified under subsection (7) of that section,

but (in each case) with such modifications as the appropriate national authority considers appropriate to adapt them to the circumstances of a single house.

(7)    In this section "house" has the same meaning as in Part 3 (see section 99).

(8)    In this Chapter—

(a)    any reference to "the house", in relation to an interim management order under section 102(7), is a reference to the house to which the order relates, and

(b)    any such reference includes (where the context permits) a reference to any yard, garden, outhouses and appurtenances belonging to, or usually enjoyed with, it (or any part of it).

**[1425]**

---

**NOTES**

Commencement: 18 November 2004 (for the purpose of making orders or regulations); 6 April 2006 (in relation to England for remaining purposes, subject to transitional provisions and savings in the Housing Act 2004 (Commencement No 5 and Transitional Provisions and Savings) (England) Order 2006, SI 2006/1060, art 3, Schedule at **[3700]**, **[3701]**); 16 June 2006 (in relation to Wales for remaining purposes, subject to transitional provisions and savings in the Housing Act 2004 (Commencement No 3 and Transitional Provisions and Savings) (Wales) Order 2006, SI 2006/1535, art 3, Schedule at **[3714]**, **[3715]**).

Orders: the Housing (Interim Management Orders) (Prescribed Circumstances) (England) Order 2006, SI 2006/369 at **[3605]**; the Housing (Interim Management Orders) (Prescribed Circumstances) (Wales) Order 2006, SI 2006/1706 at **[3720]**.

---

**104    The health and safety condition**

(1)    This section explains what "the health and safety condition" is for the purposes of section 102.

(2)    The health and safety condition is that the making of an interim management order is necessary for the purpose of protecting the health, safety or welfare of persons occupying the house, or persons occupying or having an estate or interest in any premises in the vicinity.

(3)    A threat to evict persons occupying a house in order to avoid the house being required to be licensed under Part 2 may constitute a threat to the welfare of those persons for the purposes of subsection (2).

This does not affect the generality of that subsection.

(4)    The health and safety condition is not to be regarded as satisfied for the purposes of section 102(2)(b)(ii) or (3)(c)(ii) where both of the conditions in subsections (5) and (6) are satisfied.

(5)    The first condition is that the local housing authority either—

(a)    (in a case within section 102(2)(b)(ii)) are required by section 5 (general duty to take enforcement action in respect of category 1 hazards) to take a course of action within subsection (2) of that section in relation to the house, or

(b)    (in a case within section 102(3)(c)(ii)) consider that on the revocation coming into force they will be required to take such a course of action.

(6)    The second condition is that the local housing authority consider that the health, safety or welfare of the persons in question would be adequately protected by taking that course of action.

**[1426]**

**NOTES**
Commencement: 6 April 2006 (in relation to England, subject to transitional provisions and savings in the Housing Act 2004 (Commencement No 5 and Transitional Provisions and Savings) (England) Order 2006, SI 2006/1060, art 3, Schedule at **[3700]**, **[3701]**); 16 June 2006 (in relation to Wales, subject to transitional provisions and savings in the Housing Act 2004 (Commencement No 3 and Transitional Provisions and Savings) (Wales) Order 2006, SI 2006/1535, art 3, Schedule at **[3714]**, **[3715]**).

## 105 Operation of interim management orders

(1)   This section deals with the time when an interim management order comes into force or ceases to have effect.

(2)   The order comes into force when it is made, unless it is made under section 102(3).

(3)   If the order is made under section 102(3), it comes into force when the revocation of the licence comes into force.

(4)   The order ceases to have effect at the end of the period of 12 months beginning with the date on which it is made, unless it ceases to have effect at some other time as mentioned below.

(5)   If the order provides that it is to cease to have effect on a date falling before the end of that period, it accordingly ceases to have effect on that date.

(6)   If the order is made under section 102(3)—
   (a)   it must include a provision for determining the date on which it will cease to have effect, and
   (b)   it accordingly ceases to have effect on the date so determined.

(7)   That date must be no later than 12 months after the date on which the order comes into force.

(8)   Subsections (9) and (10) apply where—
   (a)   a final management order ("the FMO") has been made under section 113 so as to replace the order ("the IMO"), but
   (b)   the FMO has not come into force because of an appeal to a residential property tribunal under paragraph 24 of Schedule 6 against the making of the FMO.

(9)   If—
   (a)   the house would (but for the IMO being in force) be required to be licensed under Part 2 or 3 of this Act (see section 61(1) or 85(1)), and
   (b)   the date on which—
      (i)    the FMO,
      (ii)   any licence under Part 2 or 3, or
      (iii)  another interim management order,
      comes into force in relation to the house (or part of it) following the disposal of the appeal is later than the date on which the IMO would cease to have effect apart from this subsection,
the IMO continues in force until that later date.

(10)   If, on the application of the authority, the tribunal makes an order providing for the IMO to continue in force, pending the disposal of the appeal, until a date later than that on which the IMO would cease to have effect apart from this subsection, the IMO accordingly continues in force until that later date.

(11)   This section has effect subject to sections 111 and 112 (variation or revocation of orders by authority) and to the power of revocation exercisable by a residential property tribunal on an appeal made under paragraph 24 or 28 of Schedule 6.

**[1427]**

**NOTES**
Commencement: 6 April 2006 (in relation to England, subject to transitional provisions and savings in the Housing Act 2004 (Commencement No 5 and Transitional Provisions and Savings) (England) Order 2006, SI 2006/1060, art 3, Schedule at **[3700]**, **[3701]**); 16 June 2006 (in relation to Wales, subject to transitional provisions and savings in the Housing Act 2004 (Commencement No 3 and Transitional Provisions and Savings) (Wales) Order 2006, SI 2006/1535, art 3, Schedule at **[3714]**, **[3715]**).

## 106 Local housing authority's duties once interim management order in force

(1)   A local housing authority who have made an interim management order in respect of a house must comply with the following provisions as soon as practicable after the order has come into force.

(2)   The authority must first take any immediate steps which they consider to be necessary for the purpose of protecting the health, safety or welfare of persons occupying the house, or persons occupying or having an estate or interest in any premises in the vicinity.

(3)    The authority must also take such other steps as they consider appropriate with a view to the proper management of the house pending—

(a)    the grant of a licence or the making of a final management order in respect of the house as mentioned in subsection (4) or (5), or

(b)    the revocation of the interim management order as mentioned in subsection (5).

(4)    If the house would (but for the order being in force) be required to be licensed under Part 2 or 3 of this Act (see section 61(1) or 85(1)), the authority must, after considering all the circumstances of the case, decide to take one of the following courses of action—

(a)    to grant a licence under that Part in respect of the house, or

(b)    to make a final management order in respect of it under section 113(1).

(5)    If subsection (4) does not apply to the house, the authority must, after considering all the circumstances of the case, decide to take one of the following courses of action—

(a)    to make a final management order in respect of the house under section 113(3), or

(b)    to revoke the order under section 112 without taking any further action.

(6)    In the following provisions, namely—

(a)    subsections (3) and (4), and

(b)    section 101(3)(b),

the reference to the grant of a licence under Part 2 or 3 in respect of the house includes a reference to serving a temporary exemption notice under section 62 or section 86 in respect of it (whether or not a notification is given under subsection (1) of that section).

(7)    For the avoidance of doubt, the authority's duty under subsection (3) includes taking such steps as are necessary to ensure that, while the order is in force, reasonable provision is made for insurance of the house against destruction or damage by fire or other causes.

**[1428]**

**NOTES**

Commencement: 6 April 2006 (in relation to England, subject to transitional provisions and savings in the Housing Act 2004 (Commencement No 5 and Transitional Provisions and Savings) (England) Order 2006, SI 2006/1060, art 3, Schedule at **[3700]**, **[3701]**); 16 June 2006 (in relation to Wales, subject to transitional provisions and savings in the Housing Act 2004 (Commencement No 3 and Transitional Provisions and Savings) (Wales) Order 2006, SI 2006/1535, art 3, Schedule at **[3714]**, **[3715]**).

**107    General effect of interim management orders**

(1)    This section applies while an interim management order is in force in relation to a house.

(2)    The rights and powers conferred by subsection (3) are exercisable by the authority in performing their duties under section 106(1) to (3) in respect of the house.

(3)    The authority—

(a)    have the right to possession of the house (subject to the rights of existing occupiers preserved by section 124(3));

(b)    have the right to do (and authorise a manager or other person to do) in relation to the house anything which a person having an estate or interest in the house would (but for the order) be entitled to do;

(c)    may create one or more of the following—

(i)    an interest in the house which, as far as possible, has all the incidents of a leasehold, or

(ii)    a right in the nature of a licence to occupy part of the house.

(4)    But the authority may not under subsection (3)(c) create any interest or right in the nature of a lease or licence unless consent in writing has been given by the person who (but for the order) would have power to create the lease or licence in question.

(5)    The authority—

(a)    do not under this section acquire any estate or interest in the house, and

(b)    accordingly are not entitled by virtue of this section to sell, lease, charge or make any other disposition of any such estate or interest;

but, where the immediate landlord of the house or part of it (within the meaning of section 109) is a lessee under a lease of the house or part, the authority is to be treated (subject to paragraph (a)) as if they were the lessee instead.

(6)    Any enactment or rule of law relating to landlords and tenants or leases applies in relation to—

(a)    a lease in relation to which the authority are to be treated as the lessee under subsection (5), or

(b)    a lease to which the authority become a party under section 124(4),

as if the authority were the legal owner of the premises (but this is subject to section 124(7) to (9)).

(7)    None of the following, namely—

(a)    the authority, or

(b)     any person authorised under subsection (3)(b),

is liable to any person having an estate or interest in the house for anything done or omitted to be done in the performance (or intended performance) of the authority's duties under section 106(1) to (3) unless the act or omission is due to the negligence of the authority or any such person.

(8)     References in any enactment to housing accommodation provided or managed by a local housing authority do not include a house in relation to which an interim management order is in force.

(9)     An interim management order which has come into force is a local land charge.

(10)     The authority may apply to the Chief Land Registrar for the entry of an appropriate restriction in the register of title in respect of such an order.

(11)     In this section "enactment" includes an enactment comprised in subordinate legislation (within the meaning of the Interpretation Act 1978 (c 30)).

**[1429]**

**NOTES**

Commencement: 6 April 2006 (in relation to England, subject to transitional provisions and savings in the Housing Act 2004 (Commencement No 5 and Transitional Provisions and Savings) (England) Order 2006, SI 2006/1060, art 3, Schedule at **[3700]**, **[3701]**); 16 June 2006 (in relation to Wales, subject to transitional provisions and savings in the Housing Act 2004 (Commencement No 3 and Transitional Provisions and Savings) (Wales) Order 2006, SI 2006/1535, art 3, Schedule at **[3714]**, **[3715]**).

**108     General effect of interim management orders: leases and licences granted by authority**

(1)     This section applies in relation to any interest or right created by the authority under section 107(3)(c).

(2)     For the purposes of any enactment or rule of law—
(a)     any interest created by the authority under section 107(3)(c)(i) is to be treated as if it were a legal lease, and
(b)     any right created by the authority under section 107(3)(c)(ii) is to be treated as if it were a licence to occupy granted by the legal owner of the premises,

despite the fact that the authority have no legal estate in the premises (see section 107(5)(a)).

(3)     Any enactment or rule of law relating to landlords and tenants or leases accordingly applies in relation to any interest created by the authority under section 107(3)(c)(i) as if the authority were the legal owner of the premises.

(4)     References to leases and licences—
(a)     in this Chapter, and
(b)     in any other enactment,

accordingly include (where the context permits) interests and rights created by the authority under section 107(3)(c).

(5)     The preceding provisions of this section have effect subject to—
(a)     section 124(7) to (9), and
(b)     any provision to the contrary contained in an order made by the appropriate national authority.

(6)     In section 107(5)(b) the reference to leasing does not include the creation of interests under section 107(3)(c)(i).

(7)     In this section—
"enactment" has the meaning given by section 107(11);
"legal lease" means a term of years absolute (within section 1(1)(b) of the Law of Property Act 1925 (c 20)).

**[1430]**

**NOTES**

Commencement: 18 November 2004 (for the purpose of making orders or regulations); 6 April 2006 (in relation to England for remaining purposes, subject to transitional provisions and savings in the Housing Act 2004 (Commencement No 5 and Transitional Provisions and Savings) (England) Order 2006, SI 2006/1060, art 3, Schedule at **[3700]**, **[3701]**); 16 June 2006 (in relation to Wales for remaining purposes, subject to transitional provisions and savings in the Housing Act 2004 (Commencement No 3 and Transitional Provisions and Savings) (Wales) Order 2006, SI 2006/1535, art 3, Schedule at **[3714]**, **[3715]**).

**109     General effect of interim management orders: immediate landlords, mortgagees etc**

(1)     This section applies in relation to—
(a)     immediate landlords, and
(b)     other persons with an estate or interest in the house,

while an interim management order is in force in relation to a house.

(2) A person who is an immediate landlord of the house or a part of it—
   (a)   is not entitled to receive—
      (i)   any rents or other payments from persons occupying the house or part which are payable to the local housing authority by virtue of section 124(4), or
      (ii)   any rents or other payments from persons occupying the house or part which are payable to the authority by virtue of any leases or licences granted by them under section 107(3)(c);
   (b)   may not exercise any rights or powers with respect to the management of the house or part; and
   (c)   may not create any of the following—
      (i)   any leasehold interest in the house or part (other than a lease of a reversion), or
      (ii)   any licence or other right to occupy it.

(3) However (subject to subsection (2)(c)) nothing in section 107 or this section affects the ability of a person having an estate or interest in the house to make any disposition of that estate or interest.

(4) Nothing in section 107 or this section affects—
   (a)   the validity of any mortgage relating to the house or any rights or remedies available to the mortgagee under such a mortgage, or
   (b)   the validity of any lease of the house or part of it under which the immediate landlord is a lessee, or any superior lease, or (subject to section 107(5)) any rights or remedies available to the lessor under such a lease,
except to the extent that any of those rights or remedies would prevent the local housing authority from exercising their power under section 107(3)(c).

(5) In proceedings for the enforcement of any such rights or remedies the court may make such order as it thinks fit as regards the operation of the interim management order (including an order quashing it).

(6) For the purposes of this Chapter, as it applies in relation to an interim management order, a person is an "immediate landlord" of the house or a part of it if—
   (a)   he is an owner or lessee of the house or part, and
   (b)   (but for the order) he would be entitled to receive the rents or other payments from persons occupying the house or part which are payable to the local housing authority by virtue of section 124(4).

**[1431]**

**NOTES**

Commencement: 6 April 2006 (in relation to England, subject to transitional provisions and savings in the Housing Act 2004 (Commencement No 5 and Transitional Provisions and Savings) (England) Order 2006, SI 2006/1060, art 3, Schedule at **[3700]**, **[3701]**); 16 June 2006 (in relation to Wales, subject to transitional provisions and savings in the Housing Act 2004 (Commencement No 3 and Transitional Provisions and Savings) (Wales) Order 2006, SI 2006/1535, art 3, Schedule at **[3714]**, **[3715]**).

## 110  Financial arrangements while order is in force

(1) This section applies to relevant expenditure of a local housing authority who have made an interim management order.

(2) "Relevant expenditure" means expenditure reasonably incurred by the authority in connection with performing their duties under section 106(1) to (3) in respect of the house (including any premiums paid for insurance of the premises).

(3) Rent or other payments which the authority have collected or recovered, by virtue of this Chapter, from persons occupying the house may be used by the authority to meet—
   (a)   relevant expenditure, and
   (b)   any amounts of compensation payable to a third party by virtue of a decision of the authority under section 128.

(4) The authority must pay to such relevant landlord, or to such relevant landlords in such proportions, as they consider appropriate—
   (a)   any amount of rent or other payments collected or recovered as mentioned in subsection (3) that remains after deductions to meet relevant expenditure and any amounts of compensation payable as mentioned in that subsection, and
   (b)   (where appropriate) interest on that amount at a reasonable rate fixed by the authority,
and such payments are to be made at such intervals as the authority consider appropriate.

(5) The interim management order may provide for—
   (a)   the rate of interest which is to apply for the purposes of paragraph (b) of subsection (4); and
   (b)   the intervals at which payments are to be made under that subsection.

Paragraph 24(3) of Schedule 6 enables an appeal to be brought where the order does not provide for both of those matters.

(6) The authority must—

    (a) keep full accounts of their income and expenditure in respect of the house; and

    (b) afford to each relevant landlord, and to any other person who has an estate or interest in the house, all reasonable facilities for inspecting, taking copies of and verifying those accounts.

(7) A relevant landlord may apply to a residential property tribunal for an order—

    (a) declaring that an amount shown in the accounts as expenditure of the authority does not constitute expenditure reasonably incurred by the authority as mentioned in subsection (2);

    (b) requiring the authority to make such financial adjustments (in the accounts and otherwise) as are necessary to reflect the tribunal's declaration.

(8) In this section—

"expenditure" includes administrative costs;

"relevant landlord" means any person who is an immediate landlord of the house or part of it;

"rent or other payments" means rents or other payments payable under leases or licences or in respect of furniture within section 126(1).

**[1432]**

**NOTES**

Commencement: 6 April 2006 (in relation to England, subject to transitional provisions and savings in the Housing Act 2004 (Commencement No 5 and Transitional Provisions and Savings) (England) Order 2006, SI 2006/1060, art 3, Schedule at **[3700]**, **[3701]**); 16 June 2006 (in relation to Wales, subject to transitional provisions and savings in the Housing Act 2004 (Commencement No 3 and Transitional Provisions and Savings) (Wales) Order 2006, SI 2006/1535, art 3, Schedule at **[3714]**, **[3715]**).

---

*Interim management orders: variation and revocation*

## 111 Variation of interim management orders

(1) The local housing authority may vary an interim management order if they consider it appropriate to do so.

(2) A variation does not come into force until such time, if any, as is the operative time for the purposes of this subsection under paragraph 31 of Schedule 6 (time when period for appealing expires without an appeal being made or when decision to vary is confirmed on appeal).

(3) The power to vary an order under this section is exercisable by the authority either—

    (a) on an application made by a relevant person, or

    (b) on the authority's own initiative.

(4) In this section "relevant person" means—

    (a) any person who has an estate or interest in the house or part of it (but is not a tenant under a lease with an unexpired term of 3 years or less), or

    (b) any other person who (but for the order) would be a person managing or having control of the house or part of it.

**[1433]**

---

**NOTES**

Commencement: 6 April 2006 (in relation to England, subject to transitional provisions and savings in the Housing Act 2004 (Commencement No 5 and Transitional Provisions and Savings) (England) Order 2006, SI 2006/1060, art 3, Schedule at **[3700]**, **[3701]**); 16 June 2006 (in relation to Wales, subject to transitional provisions and savings in the Housing Act 2004 (Commencement No 3 and Transitional Provisions and Savings) (Wales) Order 2006, SI 2006/1535, art 3, Schedule at **[3714]**, **[3715]**).

---

## 112 Revocation of interim management orders

(1) The local housing authority may revoke an interim management order in the following cases—

    (a) if the order was made under section 102(2) or (3) and the house has ceased to be an HMO to which Part 2 applies or a Part 3 house (as the case may be);

    (b) if the order was made under section 102(2) or (3) and a licence granted by them in respect of the house is due to come into force under Part 2 or Part 3 on the revocation of the order;

    (c) if a final management order has been made by them in respect of the house so as to replace the order;

    (d) if in any other circumstances the authority consider it appropriate to revoke the order.

(2) A revocation does not come into force until such time, if any, as is the operative time for the purposes of this subsection under paragraph 31 of Schedule 6 (time when period for appealing expires without an appeal being made or when decision to revoke is confirmed on appeal).

(3)   The power to revoke an order under this section is exercisable by the authority either—
- (a)   on an application made by a relevant person, or
- (b)   on the authority's own initiative.

(4)   In this section "relevant person" means—
- (a)   any person who has an estate or interest in the house or part of it (but is not a tenant under a lease with an unexpired term of 3 years or less), or
- (b)   any other person who (but for the order) would be a person managing or having control of the house or part of it.

**[1434]**

**NOTES**

**Commencement:** 6 April 2006 (in relation to England, subject to transitional provisions and savings in the Housing Act 2004 (Commencement No 5 and Transitional Provisions and Savings) (England) Order 2006, SI 2006/1060, art 3, Schedule at **[3700]**, **[3701]**); 16 June 2006 (in relation to Wales, subject to transitional provisions and savings in the Housing Act 2004 (Commencement No 3 and Transitional Provisions and Savings) (Wales) Order 2006, SI 2006/1535, art 3, Schedule at **[3714]**, **[3715]**).

*Final management orders: making and operation of orders*

## 113   Making of final management orders

(1)   A local housing authority who have made an interim management order in respect of a house under section 102 ("the IMO")—
- (a)   have a duty to make a final management order in respect of the house in a case within subsection (2), and
- (b)   have power to make such an order in a case within subsection (3).

(2)   The authority must make a final management order so as to replace the IMO as from its expiry date if—
- (a)   on that date the house would be required to be licensed under Part 2 or 3 of this Act (see section 61(1) or 85(1)), and
- (b)   the authority consider that they are unable to grant a licence under Part 2 or 3 in respect of the house that would replace the IMO as from that date.

(3)   The authority may make a final management order so as to replace the IMO as from its expiry date if—
- (a)   on that date the house will not be one that would be required to be licensed as mentioned in subsection (2)(a), and
- (b)   the authority consider that making the final management order is necessary for the purpose of protecting, on a long-term basis, the health, safety or welfare of persons occupying the house, or persons occupying or having an estate or interest in any premises in the vicinity.

(4)   A local housing authority who have made a final management order in respect of a house under this section ("the existing order")—
- (a)   have a duty to make a final management order in respect of the house in a case within subsection (5), and
- (b)   have power to make such an order in a case within subsection (6).

(5)   The authority must make a new final management order so as to replace the existing order as from its expiry date if—
- (a)   on that date the condition in subsection (2)(a) will be satisfied in relation to the house, and
- (b)   the authority consider that they are unable to grant a licence under Part 2 or 3 in respect of the house that would replace the existing order as from that date.

(6)   The authority may make a new final management order so as to replace the existing order as from its expiry date if—
- (a)   on that date the condition in subsection (3)(a) will be satisfied in relation to the house, and
- (b)   the authority consider that making the new order is necessary for the purpose of protecting, on a long-term basis, the health, safety or welfare of persons within subsection (3)(b).

(7)   The authority may make a final management order which is expressed not to apply to a part of the house that is occupied by a person who has an estate or interest in the whole of the house.

In relation to such an order, a reference in this Chapter to "the house" does not include the part so excluded (unless the context requires otherwise, such as where the reference is to the house as an HMO or a Part 3 house).

(8)   In this section "expiry date", in relation to an interim or final management order, means—
- (a)   where the order is revoked, the date as from which it is revoked, and
- (b)   otherwise the date on which the order ceases to have effect under section 105 or 114;

and nothing in this section applies in relation to an interim or final management order which has been revoked on an appeal under Part 3 of Schedule 6.

**[1435]**

NOTES
Commencement: 6 April 2006 (in relation to England, subject to transitional provisions and savings in the Housing Act 2004 (Commencement No 5 and Transitional Provisions and Savings) (England) Order 2006, SI 2006/1060, art 3, Schedule at **[3700]**, **[3701]**); 16 June 2006 (in relation to Wales, subject to transitional provisions and savings in the Housing Act 2004 (Commencement No 3 and Transitional Provisions and Savings) (Wales) Order 2006, SI 2006/1535, art 3, Schedule at **[3714]**, **[3715]**).

### 114 Operation of final management orders

(1)  This section deals with the time when a final management order comes into force or ceases to have effect.

(2)  The order does not come into force until such time (if any) as is the operative time for the purposes of this subsection under paragraph 27 of Schedule 6 (time when period for appealing expires without an appeal being made or when order is confirmed on appeal).

(3)  The order ceases to have effect at the end of the period of 5 years beginning with the date on which it comes into force, unless it ceases to have effect at some other time as mentioned below.

(4)  If the order provides that it is to cease to have effect on a date falling before the end of that period, it accordingly ceases to have effect on that date.

(5)  Subsections (6) and (7) apply where—
    (a)  a new final management order ("the new order") has been made so as to replace the order ("the existing order"), but
    (b)  the new order has not come into force because of an appeal to a residential property tribunal under paragraph 24 of Schedule 6 against the making of that order.

(6)  If—
    (a)  the house would (but for the existing order being in force) be required to be licensed under Part 2 or 3 of this Act (see section 61(1) or 85(1)), and
    (b)  the date on which—
        (i)   the new order, or
        (ii)  any licence under Part 2 or 3, or
        (iii) a temporary exemption notice under section 62 or 86,
        comes into force in relation to the house (or part of it) following the disposal of the appeal is later than the date on which the existing order would cease to have effect apart from this subsection,
the existing order continues in force until that later date.

(7)  If, on the application of the authority, the tribunal makes an order providing for the existing order to continue in force, pending the disposal of the appeal, until a date later than that on which it would cease to have effect apart from this subsection, the existing order accordingly continues in force until that later date.

(8)  This section has effect subject to sections 121 and 122 (variation or revocation of orders) and to the power of revocation exercisable by a residential property tribunal on an appeal made under paragraph 24 or 28 of Schedule 6.

**[1436]**

NOTES
Commencement: 6 April 2006 (in relation to England, subject to transitional provisions and savings in the Housing Act 2004 (Commencement No 5 and Transitional Provisions and Savings) (England) Order 2006, SI 2006/1060, art 3, Schedule at **[3700]**, **[3701]**); 16 June 2006 (in relation to Wales, subject to transitional provisions and savings in the Housing Act 2004 (Commencement No 3 and Transitional Provisions and Savings) (Wales) Order 2006, SI 2006/1535, art 3, Schedule at **[3714]**, **[3715]**).

### 115 Local housing authority's duties once final management order in force

(1)  A local housing authority who have made a final management order in respect of a house must comply with the following provisions once the order has come into force.

(2)  The local housing authority must take such steps as they consider appropriate with a view to the proper management of the house in accordance with the management scheme contained in the order (see section 119).

(3)  The local housing authority must from time to time review—
    (a)  the operation of the order and in particular the management scheme contained in it, and
    (b)  whether keeping the order in force in relation to the house (with or without making any variations under section 121) is the best alternative available to them.

(4)   If on a review the authority consider that any variations should be made under section 121, they must proceed to make those variations.

(5)   If on a review the authority consider that either—
  (a)   granting a licence under Part 2 or 3 in respect of the house, or
  (b)   revoking the order under section 122 and taking no further action,

is the best alternative available to them, the authority must grant such a licence or revoke the order (as the case may be).

(6)   For the avoidance of doubt, the authority's duty under subsection (2) includes taking such steps as are necessary to ensure that, while the order is in force, reasonable provision is made for insurance of the house against destruction or damage by fire or other causes.

**[1437]**

---

**NOTES**

Commencement: 6 April 2006 (in relation to England, subject to transitional provisions and savings in the Housing Act 2004 (Commencement No 5 and Transitional Provisions and Savings) (England) Order 2006, SI 2006/1060, art 3, Schedule at **[3700]**, **[3701]**); 16 June 2006 (in relation to Wales, subject to transitional provisions and savings in the Housing Act 2004 (Commencement No 3 and Transitional Provisions and Savings) (Wales) Order 2006, SI 2006/1535, art 3, Schedule at **[3714]**, **[3715]**).

## 116   General effect of final management orders

(1)   This section applies while a final management order is in force in relation to a house.

(2)   The rights and powers conferred by subsection (3) are exercisable by the authority in performing their duty under section 115(2) in respect of the house.

(3)   The authority—
  (a)   have the right to possession of the house (subject to the rights of existing and other occupiers preserved by section 124(3) and (6));
  (b)   have the right to do (and authorise a manager or other person to do) in relation to the house anything which a person having an estate or interest in the house would (but for the order) be entitled to do;
  (c)   may create one or more of the following—
    (i)   an interest in the house which, as far as possible, has all the incidents of a leasehold, or
    (ii)   a right in the nature of a licence to occupy part of the house.

(4)   The powers of the authority under subsection (3)(c) are restricted as follows—
  (a)   they may not create any interest or right in the nature of a lease or licence—
    (i)   which is for a fixed term expiring after the date on which the order is due to expire, or
    (ii)   (subject to paragraph (b)) which is terminable by notice to quit, or an equivalent notice, of more than 4 weeks,
    unless consent in writing has been given by the person who would (but for the order) have power to create the lease or licence in question;
  (b)   they may create an interest in the nature of an assured shorthold tenancy without any such consent so long as it is created before the beginning of the period of 6 months that ends with the date on which the order is due to expire.

(5)   The authority—
  (a)   do not under this section acquire any estate or interest in the house, and
  (b)   accordingly are not entitled by virtue of this section to sell, lease, charge or make any other disposition of any such estate or interest;

but, where the immediate landlord of the house or part of it (within the meaning of section 118) is a lessee under a lease of the house or part, the authority is to be treated (subject to paragraph (a)) as if they were the lessee instead.

(6)   Any enactment or rule of law relating to landlords and tenants or leases applies in relation to—
  (a)   a lease in relation to which the authority are to be treated as the lessee under subsection (5), or
  (b)   a lease to which the authority become a party under section 124(4),

as if the authority were the legal owner of the premises (but this is subject to section 124(7) to (9)).

(7)   None of the following, namely—
  (a)   the authority, or
  (b)   any person authorised under subsection (3)(b),

is liable to any person having an estate or interest in the house for anything done or omitted to be done in the performance (or intended performance) of the authority's duty under section 115(2) unless the act or omission is due to the negligence of the authority or any such person.

(8)   References in any enactment to housing accommodation provided or managed by a local housing authority do not include a house in relation to which a final management order is in force.

(9)   A final management order which has come into force is a local land charge.

(10)   The authority may apply to the Chief Land Registrar for the entry of an appropriate restriction in the register in respect of such an order.

(11)   In this section "enactment" includes an enactment comprised in subordinate legislation (within the meaning of the Interpretation Act 1978 (c 30)).

**[1438]**

**NOTES**
Commencement: 6 April 2006 (in relation to England, subject to transitional provisions and savings in the Housing Act 2004 (Commencement No 5 and Transitional Provisions and Savings) (England) Order 2006, SI 2006/1060, art 3, Schedule at **[3700]**, **[3701]**); 16 June 2006 (in relation to Wales, subject to transitional provisions and savings in the Housing Act 2004 (Commencement No 3 and Transitional Provisions and Savings) (Wales) Order 2006, SI 2006/1535, art 3, Schedule at **[3714]**, **[3715]**).

## 117   General effect of final management orders: leases and licences granted by authority

(1)   This section applies in relation to any interest or right created by the authority under section 116(3)(c).

(2)   For the purposes of any enactment or rule of law—
  (a)   any interest created by the authority under section 116(3)(c)(i) is to be treated as if it were a legal lease, and
  (b)   any right created by the authority under section 116(3)(c)(ii) is to be treated as if it were a licence to occupy granted by the legal owner of the premises,
despite the fact that the authority have no legal estate in the premises (see section 116(5)(a)).

(3)   Any enactment or rule of law relating to landlords and tenants or leases accordingly applies in relation to any interest created by the authority under section 116(3)(c)(i) as if the authority were the legal owner of the premises.

(4)   References to leases and licences—
  (a)   in this Chapter, and
  (b)   in any other enactment,
accordingly include (where the context permits) interests and rights created by the authority under section 116(3)(c).

(5)   The preceding provisions of this section have effect subject to—
  (a)   section 124(7) to (9), and
  (b)   any provision to the contrary contained in an order made by the appropriate national authority.

(6)   In section 116(5)(b) the reference to leasing does not include the creation of interests under section 116(3)(c)(i).

(7)   In this section—
  "enactment" has the meaning given by section 116(11);
  "legal lease" means a term of years absolute (within section 1(1)(b) of the Law of Property Act 1925 (c 20)).

**[1439]**

**NOTES**
Commencement: 18 November 2004 (for the purpose of making orders or regulations); 6 April 2006 (in relation to England for remaining purposes, subject to transitional provisions and savings in the Housing Act 2004 (Commencement No 5 and Transitional Provisions and Savings) (England) Order 2006, SI 2006/1060, art 3, Schedule at **[3700]**, **[3701]**); 16 June 2006 (in relation to Wales for remaining purposes, subject to transitional provisions and savings in the Housing Act 2004 (Commencement No 3 and Transitional Provisions and Savings) (Wales) Order 2006, SI 2006/1535, art 3, Schedule at **[3714]**, **[3715]**).

## 118   General effect of final management orders: immediate landlords, mortgagees etc

(1)   This section applies in relation to—
  (a)   immediate landlords, and
  (b)   other persons with an estate or interest in the house,
while a final management order is in force in relation to a house.

(2)   A person who is an immediate landlord of the house or a part of it—
  (a)   is not entitled to receive—
    (i)   any rents or other payments from persons occupying the house or part which are payable to the local housing authority by virtue of section 124(4), or

(ii) any rents or other payments from persons occupying the house or part which are payable to the authority by virtue of any leases or licences granted by them under section 107(3)(c) or 116(3)(c);

(b) may not exercise any rights or powers with respect to the management of the house or part; and

(c) may not create any of the following—

(i) any leasehold interest in the house or part (other than a lease of a reversion), or

(ii) any licence or other right to occupy it.

(3) However (subject to subsection (2)(c)) nothing in section 116 or this section affects the ability of a person having an estate or interest in the house to make any disposition of that estate or interest.

(4) Nothing in section 116 or this section affects—

(a) the validity of any mortgage relating to the house or any rights or remedies available to the mortgagee under such a mortgage, or

(b) the validity of any lease of the house or part of it under which the immediate landlord is a lessee, or any superior lease, or (subject to section 116(5)) any rights or remedies available to the lessor under such a lease,

except to the extent that any of those rights or remedies would prevent the local housing authority from exercising their power under section 116(3)(c).

(5) In proceedings for the enforcement of any such rights or remedies the court may make such order as it thinks fit as regards the operation of the final management order (including an order quashing it).

(6) For the purposes of this Chapter, as it applies in relation to a final management order, a person is an "immediate landlord" of the house or a part of it if—

(a) he is an owner or lessee of the house or part, and

(b) (but for the order) he would be entitled to receive the rents or other payments from persons occupying the house or part which are payable to the authority by virtue of section 124(4).

**[1440]**

---

**NOTES**

Commencement: 6 April 2006 (in relation to England, subject to transitional provisions and savings in the Housing Act 2004 (Commencement No 5 and Transitional Provisions and Savings) (England) Order 2006, SI 2006/1060, art 3, Schedule at **[3700]**, **[3701]**); 16 June 2006 (in relation to Wales, subject to transitional provisions and savings in the Housing Act 2004 (Commencement No 3 and Transitional Provisions and Savings) (Wales) Order 2006, SI 2006/1535, art 3, Schedule at **[3714]**, **[3715]**).

---

**119 Management schemes and accounts**

(1) A final management order must contain a management scheme.

(2) A "management scheme" is a scheme setting out how the local housing authority are to carry out their duty under section 115(2) as respects the management of the house.

(3) A management scheme is to be divided into two parts.

(4) Part 1 of the scheme is to contain a plan giving details of the way in which the authority propose to manage the house, which must (in particular) include—

(a) details of any works that the authority intend to carry out in connection with the house;

(b) an estimate of the capital and other expenditure to be incurred by the authority in respect of the house while the order is in force;

(c) the amount of rent or other payments that the authority will seek to obtain having regard to the condition or expected condition of the house at any time while the order is in force;

(d) the amount of any compensation that is payable to a third party by virtue of a decision of the authority under section 128 in respect of any interference in consequence of the final management order with the rights of that person;

(e) provision as to the payment of any such compensation;

(f) provision as to the payment by the authority to a relevant landlord, from time to time, of amounts of rent or other payments that remain after the deduction of—

(i) relevant expenditure, and

(ii) any amounts of compensation payable as mentioned in paragraph (d);

(g) provision as to the manner in which the authority are to pay to a relevant landlord, on the termination of the final management order, any amounts of rent or other payments that remain after the deduction of—

(i) relevant expenditure, and

(ii) any amounts of compensation payable as mentioned in paragraph (d);

(h)   provision as to the manner in which the authority are to pay, on the termination of the final management order, any outstanding balance of compensation payable to a third party.

(5)   Part 1 of the scheme may also state—

(a)   the authority's intentions as regards the use of rent or other payments to meet relevant expenditure;

(b)   the authority's intentions as regards the payment to a relevant landlord (where appropriate) of interest on amounts within subsection (4)(f) and (g);

(c)   that section 129(2) or (4) is not to apply in relation to an interim or (as the case may be) final management order that immediately preceded the final management order, and that instead the authority intend to use any balance or amount such as is mentioned in that subsection to meet—

(i)   relevant expenditure incurred during the currency of the final management order, and

(ii)   any compensation that may become payable to a third party;

(d)   that section 129(3) or (5) is not to apply in relation to an interim or (as the case may be) final management order that immediately preceded the final management order ("the order"), and that instead the authority intend to use rent or other payments collected during the currency of the order to reimburse the authority in respect of any deficit or amount such as is mentioned in that subsection;

(e)   the authority's intentions as regards the recovery from a relevant landlord, with or without interest, of any amount of relevant expenditure that cannot be reimbursed out of the total amount of rent or other payments.

(6)   Part 2 of the scheme is to describe in general terms how the authority intend to address the matters which caused them to make the final management order and may, for example, include—

(a)   descriptions of any steps that the authority intend to take to require persons occupying the house to comply with their obligations under any lease or licence or under the general law;

(b)   descriptions of any repairs that are needed to the property and an explanation as to why those repairs are necessary.

(7)   The authority must—

(a)   keep full accounts of their income and expenditure in respect of the house; and

(b)   afford to each relevant landlord, and to any other person who has an estate or interest in the house, all reasonable facilities for inspecting, taking copies of and verifying those accounts.

(8)   In this section—

"relevant expenditure" means expenditure reasonably incurred by the authority in connection with performing their duties under section 115(2) in respect of the house (including any reasonable administrative costs and any premiums paid for insurance of the premises);

"relevant landlord" means any person who is an immediate landlord of the house or part of it;

"rent or other payments" means rent or other payments—

(a)   which are payable under leases or licences or in respect of furniture within section 126(1), and

(b)   which the authority have collected or recovered by virtue of this Chapter.

(9)   In the provisions of this Chapter relating to varying, revoking or appealing against decisions relating to a final management order, any reference to such an order includes (where the context permits) a reference to the management scheme contained in it.

**[1441]**

**NOTES**

Commencement: 6 April 2006 (in relation to England, subject to transitional provisions and savings in the Housing Act 2004 (Commencement No 5 and Transitional Provisions and Savings) (England) Order 2006, SI 2006/1060, art 3, Schedule at **[3700]**, **[3701]**); 16 June 2006 (in relation to Wales, subject to transitional provisions and savings in the Housing Act 2004 (Commencement No 3 and Transitional Provisions and Savings) (Wales) Order 2006, SI 2006/1535, art 3, Schedule at **[3714]**, **[3715]**).

**120   Enforcement of management scheme by relevant landlord**

(1)   An affected person may apply to a residential property tribunal for an order requiring the local housing authority to manage the whole or part of a house in accordance with the management scheme contained in a final management order made in respect of the house.

(2)   On such an application the tribunal may, if it considers it appropriate to do so, make an order—

(a)   requiring the local housing authority to manage the whole or part of the house in accordance with the management scheme, or

(b)   revoking the final management order as from a date specified in the tribunal's order.

(3)   An order under subsection (2) may—
   (a)   specify the steps which the authority are to take to manage the whole or part of the house in accordance with the management scheme,
   (b)   include provision varying the final management order,
   (c)   require the payment of money to an affected person by way of damages.

(4)   In this section "affected person" means—
   (a)   a relevant landlord (within the meaning of section 119), and
   (b)   any third party to whom compensation is payable by virtue of a decision of the authority under section 128.

**[1442]**

**NOTES**

Commencement: 6 April 2006 (in relation to England, subject to transitional provisions and savings in the Housing Act 2004 (Commencement No 5 and Transitional Provisions and Savings) (England) Order 2006, SI 2006/1060, art 3, Schedule at **[3700]**, **[3701]**); 16 June 2006 (in relation to Wales, subject to transitional provisions and savings in the Housing Act 2004 (Commencement No 3 and Transitional Provisions and Savings) (Wales) Order 2006, SI 2006/1535, art 3, Schedule at **[3714]**, **[3715]**).

*Final management orders: variation and revocation*

### 121   Variation of final management orders

(1)   The local housing authority may vary a final management order if they consider it appropriate to do so.

(2)   A variation does not come into force until such time, if any, as is the operative time for the purposes of this subsection under paragraph 31 of Schedule 6 (time when period for appealing expires without an appeal being made or when decision to vary is confirmed on appeal).

(3)   The power to vary an order under this section is exercisable by the authority either—
   (a)   on an application made by a relevant person, or
   (b)   on the authority's own initiative.

(4)   In this section "relevant person" means—
   (a)   any person who has an estate or interest in the house or part of it (but is not a tenant under a lease with an unexpired term of 3 years or less), or
   (b)   any other person who (but for the order) would be a person managing or having control of the house or part of it.

**[1443]**

**NOTES**

Commencement: 6 April 2006 (in relation to England, subject to transitional provisions and savings in the Housing Act 2004 (Commencement No 5 and Transitional Provisions and Savings) (England) Order 2006, SI 2006/1060, art 3, Schedule at **[3700]**, **[3701]**); 16 June 2006 (in relation to Wales, subject to transitional provisions and savings in the Housing Act 2004 (Commencement No 3 and Transitional Provisions and Savings) (Wales) Order 2006, SI 2006/1535, art 3, Schedule at **[3714]**, **[3715]**).

### 122   Revocation of final management orders

(1)   The local housing authority may revoke a final management order in the following cases—
   (a)   if the order was made under section 113(2) or (5) and the house has ceased to be an HMO to which Part 2 applies or a Part 3 house (as the case may be);
   (b)   if the order was made under section 113(2) or (5) and a licence granted by them in respect of the house is due to come into force under Part 2 or Part 3 as from the revocation of the order;
   (c)   if a further final management order has been made by them in respect of the house so as to replace the order;
   (d)   if in any other circumstances the authority consider it appropriate to revoke the order.

(2)   A revocation does not come into force until such time, if any, as is the operative time for the purposes of this subsection under paragraph 31 of Schedule 6 (time when period for appealing expires without an appeal being made or when decision to vary is confirmed on appeal).

(3)   The power to revoke an order under this section is exercisable by the authority either—
   (a)   on an application made by a relevant person, or
   (b)   on the authority's own initiative.

(4)   In this section "relevant person" means—
   (a)   any person who has an estate or interest in the house or part of it (but is not a tenant under a lease with an unexpired term of 3 years or less), or
   (b)   any other person who (but for the order) would be a person managing or having control of the house or part of it.

**[1444]**

NOTES
Commencement: 6 April 2006 (in relation to England, subject to transitional provisions and savings in the Housing Act 2004 (Commencement No 5 and Transitional Provisions and Savings) (England) Order 2006, SI 2006/1060, art 3, Schedule at [3700], [3701]); 16 June 2006 (in relation to Wales, subject to transitional provisions and savings in the Housing Act 2004 (Commencement No 3 and Transitional Provisions and Savings) (Wales) Order 2006, SI 2006/1535, art 3, Schedule at [3714], [3715]).

*Interim and final management orders: procedure and appeals*

## 123 Procedural requirements and appeals

Schedule 6 (which deals with procedural requirements relating to the making, variation or revocation of interim and final management orders and with appeals against decisions relating to such orders) has effect.

**[1445]**

NOTES
Commencement: 6 April 2006 (in relation to England, subject to transitional provisions and savings in the Housing Act 2004 (Commencement No 5 and Transitional Provisions and Savings) (England) Order 2006, SI 2006/1060, art 3, Schedule at [3700], [3701]); 16 June 2006 (in relation to Wales, subject to transitional provisions and savings in the Housing Act 2004 (Commencement No 3 and Transitional Provisions and Savings) (Wales) Order 2006, SI 2006/1535, art 3, Schedule at [3714], [3715]).

*Interim and final management orders: other general provisions*

## 124 Effect of management orders: occupiers

(1)   This section applies to existing and new occupiers of a house in relation to which an interim or final management order is in force.

(2)   In this section—
"existing occupier" means a person who, at the time when the order comes into force, either—
    (a)    (in the case of an HMO or a Part 3 house) is occupying part of the house and does not have an estate or interest in the whole of the house, or
    (b)    (in the case of a Part 3 house) is occupying the whole of the house,
but is not a new occupier within subsection (6);
"new occupier" means a person who, at a time when the order is in force, is occupying the whole or part of the house under a lease or licence granted under section 107(3)(c) or 116(3)(c).

(3)   Sections 107 and 116 do not affect the rights or liabilities of an existing occupier under a lease or licence (whether in writing or not) under which he is occupying the whole or part of the house at the commencement date.

(4)   Where the lessor or licensor under such a lease or licence—
    (a)    has an estate or interest in the house, and
    (b)    is not an existing occupier,
the lease or licence has effect while the order is in force as if the local housing authority were substituted in it for the lessor or licensor.

(5)   Such a lease continues to have effect, as far as possible, as a lease despite the fact that the rights of the local housing authority, as substituted for the lessor, do not amount to an estate in law in the premises.

(6)   Section 116 does not affect the rights or liabilities of a new occupier who, in the case of a final management order, is occupying the whole or part of the house at the time when the order comes into force.

(7)   The provisions which exclude local authority lettings from the Rent Acts, namely—
    (a)    sections 14 to 16 of the Rent Act 1977 (c 42), and
    (b)    those sections as applied by Schedule 2 to the Rent (Agriculture) Act 1976 (c 80) and section 5(2) to (4) of that Act,
do not apply to a lease or agreement under which an existing or new occupier is occupying the whole or part of the house.

(8)   Section 1(2) of, and paragraph 12 of Part 1 of Schedule 1 to, the Housing Act 1988 (c 50) (which exclude local authority lettings from Part 1 of that Act) do not apply to a lease or agreement under which an existing or new occupier is occupying the whole or part of the house.

(9)   Nothing in this Chapter has the result that the authority are to be treated as the legal owner of any premises for the purposes of—
    (a)    section 80 of the Housing Act 1985 (c 68) (the landlord condition for secure tenancies); or
    (b)    section 124 of the Housing Act 1996 (c 52) (introductory tenancies).

(10)   If, immediately before the coming into force of an interim or final management order, an existing occupier was occupying the whole or part of the house under—

   (a)   a protected or statutory tenancy within the meaning of the Rent Act 1977 (c 42),

   (b)   a protected or statutory tenancy within the meaning of the Rent (Agriculture) Act 1976 (c 80), or

   (c)   an assured tenancy or assured agricultural occupancy within the meaning of Part 1 of the Housing Act 1988 (c 50),

nothing in this Chapter prevents the continuance of that tenancy or occupancy or affects the continued operation of any of those Acts in relation to the tenancy or occupancy after the coming into force of the order.

(11)   In this section "the commencement date" means the date on which the order came into force (or, if that order was preceded by one or more orders under this Chapter, the date when the first order came into force).

**[1446]**

**NOTES**

Commencement: 6 April 2006 (in relation to England, subject to transitional provisions and savings in the Housing Act 2004 (Commencement No 5 and Transitional Provisions and Savings) (England) Order 2006, SI 2006/1060, art 3, Schedule at **[3700]**, **[3701]**); 16 June 2006 (in relation to Wales, subject to transitional provisions and savings in the Housing Act 2004 (Commencement No 3 and Transitional Provisions and Savings) (Wales) Order 2006, SI 2006/1535, art 3, Schedule at **[3714]**, **[3715]**).

## 125   Effect of management orders: agreements and legal proceedings

(1)   An agreement or instrument within subsection (2) has effect, while an interim or final management order is in force, as if any rights or liabilities of the immediate landlord under the agreement or instrument were instead rights or liabilities of the local housing authority.

(2)   An agreement or instrument is within this subsection if—

   (a)   it is effective on the commencement date,

   (b)   one of the parties to it is a person who is the immediate landlord of the house or a part of the house ("the relevant premises"),

   (c)   it relates to the house, whether in connection with—

      (i)   any management activities with respect to the relevant premises, or

      (ii)   the provision of any services or facilities for persons occupying those premises, or otherwise,

   (d)   it is specified for the purposes of this subsection in the order or falls within a description of agreements or instruments so specified, and

   (e)   the authority serve a notice in writing on all the parties to it stating that subsection (1) is to apply to it.

(3)   An agreement or instrument is not within subsection (2) if—

   (a)   it is a lease within section 107(5) or 116(5), or

   (b)   it relates to any disposition by the immediate landlord which is not precluded by section 109(2) or 118(2), or

   (c)   it is within section 124(4).

(4)   Proceedings in respect of any cause of action within subsection (5) may, while an interim or final management order is in force, be instituted or continued by or against the local housing authority instead of by or against the immediate landlord.

(5)   A cause of action is within this subsection if—

   (a)   it is a cause of action (of any nature) which accrued to or against the immediate landlord of the house or a part of the house before the commencement date,

   (b)   it relates to the house as mentioned in subsection (2)(c),

   (c)   it is specified for the purposes of this subsection in the order or falls within a description of causes of action so specified, and

   (d)   the authority serve a notice in writing on all interested parties stating that subsection (4) is to apply to it.

(6)   If, by virtue of this section, the authority become subject to any liability to pay damages in respect of anything done (or omitted to be done) before the commencement date by or on behalf of the immediate landlord of the house or a part of it, the immediate landlord is liable to reimburse to the authority an amount equal to the amount of the damages paid by them.

(7)   In this section—

   "agreement" includes arrangement;

   "the commencement date" means the date on which the order comes into force (or, if that order was preceded by one or more orders under this Chapter, the date when the first order came into force);

   "management activities" includes repair, maintenance, improvement and insurance.

**[1447]**

**NOTES**

Commencement: 6 April 2006 (in relation to England, subject to transitional provisions and savings in the Housing Act 2004 (Commencement No 5 and Transitional Provisions and Savings) (England) Order 2006, SI 2006/1060, art 3, Schedule at **[3700]**, **[3701]**); 16 June 2006 (in relation to Wales, subject to transitional provisions and savings in the Housing Act 2004 (Commencement No 3 and Transitional Provisions and Savings) (Wales) Order 2006, SI 2006/1535, art 3, Schedule at **[3714]**, **[3715]**).

## 126 Effect of management orders: furniture

(1) Subsection (2) applies where, on the date on which an interim or final management order comes into force, there is furniture in the house which a person occupying the house has the right to use in consideration of periodical payments to a person who is an immediate landlord of the house or a part of it (whether the payments are included in the rent payable by the occupier or not).

(2) The right to possession of the furniture against all persons other than the occupier vests in the local housing authority on that date and remains vested in the authority while the order is in force.

(3) The local housing authority may renounce the right to possession of the furniture conferred by subsection (2) if—

(a) an application in writing has been made to them for the purpose by the person owning the furniture, and

(b) they renounce the right by notice in writing served on that person not less than two weeks before the notice takes effect.

(4) If the authority's right to possession of furniture conferred by subsection (2) is a right exercisable against more than one person interested in the furniture, any of those persons may apply to a residential property tribunal for an adjustment of their respective rights and liabilities as regards the furniture.

(5) On such an application the tribunal may make an order for such an adjustment of rights and liabilities, either unconditionally or subject to such terms and conditions, as it considers appropriate.

(6) The terms and conditions may, in particular, include terms and conditions about the payment of money by a party to the proceedings to another party to the proceedings by way of compensation, damages or otherwise.

(7) In this section "furniture" includes fittings and other articles.

**[1448]**

**NOTES**

Commencement: 6 April 2006 (in relation to England, subject to transitional provisions and savings in the Housing Act 2004 (Commencement No 5 and Transitional Provisions and Savings) (England) Order 2006, SI 2006/1060, art 3, Schedule at **[3700]**, **[3701]**); 16 June 2006 (in relation to Wales, subject to transitional provisions and savings in the Housing Act 2004 (Commencement No 3 and Transitional Provisions and Savings) (Wales) Order 2006, SI 2006/1535, art 3, Schedule at **[3714]**, **[3715]**).

## 127 Management orders: power to supply furniture

(1) The local housing authority may supply the house to which an interim or final management order relates with such furniture as they consider to be required.

(2) For the purposes of section 110 or a management scheme under section 119, any expenditure incurred by the authority under this section constitutes expenditure incurred by the authority in connection with performing their duty under section 106(3) or 115(2).

(3) In this section "furniture" includes fittings and other articles.

**[1449]**

**NOTES**

Commencement: 6 April 2006 (in relation to England, subject to transitional provisions and savings in the Housing Act 2004 (Commencement No 5 and Transitional Provisions and Savings) (England) Order 2006, SI 2006/1060, art 3, Schedule at **[3700]**, **[3701]**); 16 June 2006 (in relation to Wales, subject to transitional provisions and savings in the Housing Act 2004 (Commencement No 3 and Transitional Provisions and Savings) (Wales) Order 2006, SI 2006/1535, art 3, Schedule at **[3714]**, **[3715]**).

## 128 Compensation payable to third parties

(1) If a third party requests them to do so at any time, the local housing authority must consider whether an amount by way of compensation should be paid to him in respect of any interference with his rights in consequence of an interim or final management order.

(2) The authority must notify the third party of their decision as soon as practicable.

(3)   Where the local housing authority decide under subsection (1) that compensation ought to be paid to a third party in consequence of a final management order, they must vary the management scheme contained in the order so as to specify the amount of the compensation to be paid and to make provision as to its payment.

**[1450]**

**NOTES**

Commencement: 6 April 2006 (in relation to England, subject to transitional provisions and savings in the Housing Act 2004 (Commencement No 5 and Transitional Provisions and Savings) (England) Order 2006, SI 2006/1060, art 3, Schedule at **[3700]**, **[3701]**); 16 June 2006 (in relation to Wales, subject to transitional provisions and savings in the Housing Act 2004 (Commencement No 3 and Transitional Provisions and Savings) (Wales) Order 2006, SI 2006/1535, art 3, Schedule at **[3714]**, **[3715]**).

## 129   Termination of management orders: financial arrangements

(1)   This section applies where an interim or final management order ceases to have effect for any reason.

(2)   If, on the termination date for an interim management order, the total amount of rent or other payments collected or recovered as mentioned in section 110(3) exceeds the total amount of—
   (a)   the local housing authority's relevant expenditure, and
   (b)   any amounts of compensation payable to third parties by virtue of decisions of the authority under section 128,

the authority must, as soon as practicable after the termination date, pay the balance to such relevant landlord, or to such relevant landlords in such proportions, as they consider appropriate.

(3)   If, on the termination date for an interim management order, the total amount of rent or other payments collected or recovered as mentioned in section 110(3) is less than the total amount of—
   (a)   the authority's relevant expenditure, and
   (b)   any amounts of compensation payable as mentioned in subsection (2)(b),

the difference is recoverable by the authority from such relevant landlord, or such relevant landlords in such proportions, as they consider appropriate.

(4)   If, on the termination date for a final management order, any amount is payable to—
   (a)   a third party, or
   (b)   any relevant landlord in accordance with the management scheme under section 119,

that amount must be paid to that person by the local housing authority in the manner provided by the scheme.

(5)   If, on the termination date for a final management order, any amount is payable to the local housing authority in accordance with the management scheme, that amount is recoverable by the local housing authority—
   (a)   from such relevant landlord, or
   (b)   from such relevant landlords in such proportions,

as is provided by the scheme.

(6)   The provisions of any of subsections (2) to (5) do not, however, apply in relation to the order if—
   (a)   the order is followed by a final management order, and
   (b)   the management scheme contained in that final management order provides for that subsection not to apply in relation to the order (see section 119(5)(c) and (d)).

(7)   Any sum recoverable by the authority under subsection (3) or (5) is, until recovered, a charge on the house.

(8)   The charge takes effect on the termination date for the order as a legal charge which is a local land charge.

(9)   For the purpose of enforcing the charge the authority have the same powers and remedies under the Law of Property Act 1925 (c 20) and otherwise as if they were mortgagees by deed having powers of sale and lease, of accepting surrenders of leases and of appointing a receiver.

(10)   The power of appointing a receiver is exercisable at any time after the end of the period of one month beginning with the date on which the charge takes effect.

(11)   If the order is to be followed by a licence granted under Part 2 or 3 in respect of the house, the conditions contained in the licence may include a condition requiring the licence holder—
   (a)   to repay to the authority any amount recoverable by them under subsection (3) or (5), and
   (b)   to do so in such instalments as are specified in the licence.

(12)   In this section—
   "relevant expenditure" has the same meaning as in section 110;

"relevant landlord" means a person who was the immediate landlord of the house or part of it immediately before the termination date or his successor in title for the time being;

"rent or other payments" means rents or other payments payable under leases or licences or in respect of furniture within section 126(1);

"the termination date" means the date on which the order ceases to have effect.

**[1451]**

**NOTES**

Commencement: 6 April 2006 (in relation to England, subject to transitional provisions and savings in the Housing Act 2004 (Commencement No 5 and Transitional Provisions and Savings) (England) Order 2006, SI 2006/1060, art 3, Schedule at **[3700]**, **[3701]**); 16 June 2006 (in relation to Wales, subject to transitional provisions and savings in the Housing Act 2004 (Commencement No 3 and Transitional Provisions and Savings) (Wales) Order 2006, SI 2006/1535, art 3, Schedule at **[3714]**, **[3715]**).

## 130 Termination of management orders: leases, agreements and proceedings

(1) This section applies where—
  (a)  an interim or final management order ceases to have effect for any reason, and
  (b)  the order is not immediately followed by a further order under this Chapter.

(2) As from the termination date—
  (a)  a lease or licence in which the local housing authority was substituted for another party by virtue of section 124(4) has effect with the substitution of the original party, or his successor in title, for the authority; and
  (b)  an agreement which (in accordance with section 108 or 117) has effect as a lease or licence granted by the authority under section 107 or 116 has effect with the substitution of the relevant landlord for the authority.

(3) If the relevant landlord is a lessee, nothing in a superior lease imposes liability on him or any superior lessee in respect of anything done before the termination date in pursuance of the terms of an agreement to which subsection (2)(b) applies.

(4) If the condition in subsection (5) is met, any other agreement entered into by the authority in the performance of their duties under section 106(1) to (3) or 115(2) in respect of the house has effect, as from the termination date, with the substitution of the relevant landlord for the authority.

(5) The condition is that the authority serve a notice on the other party or parties to the agreement stating that subsection (4) applies to the agreement.

(6) If the condition in subsection (7) is met—
  (a)  any rights or liabilities that were rights or liabilities of the authority immediately before the termination date by virtue of any provision of this Chapter or under any agreement to which subsection (4) applies are rights or liabilities of the relevant landlord instead, and
  (b)  any proceedings instituted or continued by or against the authority by virtue of any such provision or agreement may be continued by or against the relevant landlord instead,

as from the termination date.

(7) The condition is that the authority serve a notice on all interested parties stating that subsection (6) applies to the rights or liabilities or (as the case may be) the proceedings.

(8) If by virtue of this section a relevant landlord becomes subject to any liability to pay damages in respect of anything done (or omitted to be done) before the termination date by or on behalf of the authority, the authority are liable to reimburse to the relevant landlord an amount equal to the amount of the damages paid by him.

(9) Where two or more persons are relevant landlords in relation to different parts of the house, any reference in this section to "the relevant landlord" is to be taken to refer to such one or more of them as is determined by agreement between them or (in default of agreement) by a residential property tribunal on an application made by any of them.

(10) This section applies to instruments as it applies to agreements.

(11) In this section—
  "agreement" includes arrangement;
  "relevant landlord" means a person who was the immediate landlord of the house immediately before the termination date or his successor in title for the time being;
  "the termination date" means the date on which the order ceases to have effect.

**[1452]**

**NOTES**

Commencement: 6 April 2006 (in relation to England, subject to transitional provisions and savings in the Housing Act 2004 (Commencement No 5 and Transitional Provisions and Savings) (England) Order 2006, SI 2006/1060, art 3, Schedule at **[3700]**, **[3701]**); 16 June 2006 (in relation to Wales, subject to transitional provisions and savings in the Housing Act 2004 (Commencement No 3 and Transitional Provisions and Savings) (Wales) Order 2006, SI 2006/1535, art 3, Schedule at **[3714]**, **[3715]**).

**131 Management orders: power of entry to carry out work**

(1)   The right mentioned in subsection (2) is exercisable by the local housing authority, or any person authorised in writing by them, at any time when an interim or final management order is in force.

(2)   That right is the right at all reasonable times to enter any part of the house for the purpose of carrying out works, and is exercisable as against any person having an estate or interest in the house.

(3)   Where part of a house is excluded from the provisions of an interim or final management order under section 102(8) or 113(7), the right conferred by subsection (1) is exercisable as respects that part so far as is reasonably required for the purpose of carrying out works in the part of the house which is subject to the order.

(4)   If, after receiving reasonable notice of the intended action, any occupier of the whole or part of the house prevents any officer, employee, agent or contractor of the local housing authority from carrying out work in the house, a magistrates' court may order him to permit to be done on the premises anything which the authority consider to be necessary.

(5)   A person who fails to comply with an order of the court under subsection (4) commits an offence.

(6)   A person who commits an offence under subsection (5) is liable on summary conviction to a fine not exceeding level 5 on the standard scale.

**[1453]**

**NOTES**

Commencement: 6 April 2006 (in relation to England, subject to transitional provisions and savings in the Housing Act 2004 (Commencement No 5 and Transitional Provisions and Savings) (England) Order 2006, SI 2006/1060, art 3, Schedule at **[3700], [3701]**); 16 June 2006 (in relation to Wales, subject to transitional provisions and savings in the Housing Act 2004 (Commencement No 3 and Transitional Provisions and Savings) (Wales) Order 2006, SI 2006/1535, art 3, Schedule at **[3714], [3715]**).

## CHAPTER 2
## INTERIM AND FINAL EMPTY DWELLING MANAGEMENT ORDERS

*Introductory*

**132 Empty dwelling management orders: introductory**

(1)   This Chapter deals with the making by a local housing authority of—
   (a)   an interim empty dwelling management order (an "interim EDMO"), or
   (b)   a final empty dwelling management order (a "final EDMO"),
in respect of a dwelling.

(2)   An interim EDMO is an order made to enable a local housing authority, with the consent of the relevant proprietor, to take steps for the purpose of securing that a dwelling becomes and continues to be occupied.

(3)   A final EDMO is an order made, in succession to an interim EDMO or a previous final EDMO, for the purpose of securing that a dwelling is occupied.

(4)   In this Chapter—
   (a)   "dwelling" means—
       (i)   a building intended to be occupied as a separate dwelling, or
       (ii)  a part of a building intended to be occupied as a separate dwelling which may be entered otherwise than through any non-residential accommodation in the building;
   (b)   any reference to "the dwelling", in relation to an interim EDMO or a final EDMO, is a reference to the dwelling to which the order relates;
   (c)   "relevant proprietor", in relation to a dwelling, means—
       (i)   if the dwelling is let under one or more leases with an unexpired term of 7 years or more, the lessee under whichever of those leases has the shortest unexpired term; or
       (ii)  in any other case, the person who has the freehold estate in the dwelling;
   (d)   "third party", in relation to a dwelling, means any person who has an estate or interest in the dwelling (other than the relevant proprietor and any person who is a tenant under a lease granted under paragraph 2(3)(c) or 10(3)(c) of Schedule 7); and
   (e)   any reference (however expressed) to rent or other payments in respect of occupation of a dwelling, includes any payments that the authority receive from persons in respect of unlawful occupation of the dwelling.

(5)   In subsection (4)(c), the reference to an unexpired term of 7 years or more of a lease of a dwelling is—
   (a)   in relation to a dwelling in respect of which the local housing authority are considering

    making an interim EDMO, a reference to the unexpired term of the lease at the time the authority begin taking steps under section 133(3),

(b)    in relation to a dwelling in respect of which an interim EDMO has been made, a reference to the unexpired term of the lease at the time the application for authorisation to make the interim EDMO was made under subsection (1) of that section, or

(c)    in relation to a dwelling in respect of which a local housing authority are considering making or have made a final EDMO, a reference to the unexpired term of the lease at the time the application for authorisation to make the preceding interim EDMO was made under subsection (1) of that section.

"Preceding interim EDMO", in relation to a final EDMO, means the interim EDMO that immediately preceded the final EDMO or, where there has been a succession of final EDMOs, the interim EDMO that immediately preceded the first of them.

(6)    Schedule 7 (which makes further provision regarding EDMOs) has effect.

**[1454]**

---

**NOTES**

Commencement: 18 November 2004 (sub-s (6), for the purpose of making orders or regulations); 6 April 2006 (sub-ss (1)–(5), (6) (for remaining purposes) in relation to England, subject to transitional provisions and savings in the Housing Act 2004 (Commencement No 5 and Transitional Provisions and Savings) (England) Order 2006, SI 2006/1060, art 3, Schedule at **[3700]**, **[3701]**); 16 June 2006 (sub-ss (1)–(5), (6) (for remaining purposes) in relation to Wales, subject to transitional provisions and savings in the Housing Act 2004 (Commencement No 3 and Transitional Provisions and Savings) (Wales) Order 2006, SI 2006/1535, art 3, Schedule at **[3714]**, **[3715]**).

---

*Interim empty dwelling management orders*

## 133  Making of interim EDMOs

(1)    A local housing authority may make an interim EDMO in respect of a dwelling if—

(a)    it is a dwelling to which this section applies, and

(b)    on an application by the authority to a residential property tribunal, the tribunal by order authorises them under section 134 to make such an order, either in the terms of a draft order submitted by them or in those terms as varied by the tribunal.

(2)    This section applies to a dwelling if—

(a)    the dwelling is wholly unoccupied, and

(b)    the relevant proprietor is not a public sector body.

"Wholly unoccupied" means that no part is occupied, whether lawfully or unlawfully.

(3)    Before determining whether to make an application to a residential property tribunal for an authorisation under section 134, the authority must make reasonable efforts—

(a)    to notify the relevant proprietor that they are considering making an interim EDMO in respect of the dwelling under this section, and

(b)    to ascertain what steps (if any) he is taking, or is intending to take, to secure that the dwelling is occupied.

(4)    In determining whether to make an application to a residential property tribunal for an authorisation under section 134, the authority must take into account the rights of the relevant proprietor of the dwelling and the interests of the wider community.

(5)    The authority may make an interim EDMO in respect of the dwelling despite any pending appeal against the order of the tribunal (but this is without prejudice to any order that may be made on the disposal of any such appeal).

(6)    An application to a residential property tribunal under this section for authorisation to make an interim EDMO in respect of a dwelling may include an application for an order under paragraph 22 of Schedule 7 determining a lease or licence of the dwelling.

(7)    In this section "public sector body" means a body mentioned in any of paragraphs (a) to (f) of paragraph 2(1) of Schedule 14.

(8)    Part 1 of Schedule 6 applies in relation to the making of an interim EDMO in respect of a dwelling as it applies in relation to the making of an interim management order in respect of a house, subject to the following modifications—

(a)    paragraph 7(2) does not apply;

(b)    paragraph 7(4)(c) is to be read as referring instead to the date on which the order is to cease to have effect in accordance with paragraph 1(3) and (4) or 9(3) to (5) of Schedule 7;

(c)    in paragraph 7(6)—

(i)    paragraph (a) is to be read as referring instead to Part 4 of Schedule 7; and

(ii)    paragraph (b) does not apply;

(d)    paragraph 8(4) is to be read as defining "relevant person" as any person who, to the knowledge of the local housing authority, is a person having an estate or interest in the dwelling (other than a person who is a tenant under a lease granted under paragraph 2(3)(c) of Schedule 7).

**[1455]**

**NOTES**

Commencement: 6 April 2006 (in relation to England, subject to transitional provisions and savings in the Housing Act 2004 (Commencement No 5 and Transitional Provisions and Savings) (England) Order 2006, SI 2006/1060, art 3, Schedule at **[3700]**, **[3701]**); 16 June 2006 (in relation to Wales, subject to transitional provisions and savings in the Housing Act 2004 (Commencement No 3 and Transitional Provisions and Savings) (Wales) Order 2006, SI 2006/1535, art 3, Schedule at **[3714]**, **[3715]**).

### 134  Authorisation to make interim EDMOs

(1)  A residential property tribunal may authorise a local housing authority to make an interim EDMO in respect of a dwelling to which section 133 applies if the tribunal—
- (a)  is satisfied as to the matters mentioned in subsection (2), and
- (b)  is not satisfied that the case falls within one of the prescribed exceptions.

(2)  The matters as to which the tribunal must be satisfied are—
- (a)  that the dwelling has been wholly unoccupied for at least 6 months or such longer period as may be prescribed,
- (b)  that there is no reasonable prospect that the dwelling will become occupied in the near future,
- (c)  that, if an interim order is made, there is a reasonable prospect that the dwelling will become occupied,
- (d)  that the authority have complied with section 133(3), and
- (e)  that any prescribed requirements have been complied with.

(3)  In deciding whether to authorise a local housing authority to make an interim EDMO in respect of a dwelling, the tribunal must take into account—
- (a)  the interests of the community, and
- (b)  the effect that the order will have on the rights of the relevant proprietor and may have on the rights of third parties.

(4)  On authorising a local housing authority to make an interim EDMO in respect of a dwelling, the tribunal may, if it thinks fit, make an order requiring the authority (if they make the EDMO) to pay to any third party specified in the order an amount of compensation in respect of any interference in consequence of the order with the rights of the third party.

(5)  The appropriate national authority may by order—
- (a)  prescribe exceptions for the purposes of subsection (1)(b),
- (b)  prescribe a period of time for the purposes of subsection (2)(a), and
- (c)  prescribe requirements for the purposes of subsection (2)(e).

(6)  An order under subsection (5)(a) may, in particular, include exceptions in relation to—
- (a)  dwellings that have been occupied solely or principally by the relevant proprietor who is at the material time temporarily resident elsewhere;
- (b)  dwellings that are holiday homes or that are otherwise occupied by the relevant proprietor or his guests on a temporary basis from time to time;
- (c)  dwellings undergoing repairs or renovation;
- (d)  dwellings in respect of which an application for planning permission or building control approval is outstanding;
- (e)  dwellings which are genuinely on the market for sale or letting;
- (f)  dwellings where the relevant proprietor has died not more than the prescribed number of months before the material time.

(7)  In this section—
"building control approval" means approval for the carrying out of any works under building regulations;
"planning permission" has the meaning given by section 336(1) of the Town and Country Planning Act 1990 (c 8);
"prescribed" means prescribed by an order under subsection (5);
"wholly unoccupied" means that no part is occupied, whether lawfully or unlawfully.

**[1456]**

**NOTES**

Commencement: 18 November 2004 (for the purpose of making orders or regulations); 16 June 2006 (in relation to Wales for remaining purposes, subject to transitional provisions and savings in the Housing Act 2004 (Commencement No 3 and Transitional Provisions and Savings) (Wales) Order 2006, SI 2006/1535, art 3, Schedule at **[3714]**, **[3715]**); 6 July 2006 (in relation to England for remaining purposes, subject to transitional provisions and savings in the Housing Act 2004 (Commencement No 5 and Transitional Provisions and Savings) (England) Order 2006, SI 2006/1060, art 3, Schedule at **[3700]**, **[3701]**).

Orders: the Housing (Empty Dwelling Management Orders) (Prescribed Exceptions and Requirements) (England) Order 2006, SI 2006/367 at **[3598]**; the Housing (Empty Dwelling Management Orders) (Prescribed Exceptions and Requirements) (Wales) Order 2006, SI 2006/2823 at **[3742]**.

## 135 Local housing authority's duties once interim EDMO in force

(1) A local housing authority who have made an interim EDMO in respect of a dwelling must comply with the following provisions as soon as practicable after the order has come into force (see paragraph 1 of Schedule 7).

(2) The authority must take such steps as they consider appropriate for the purpose of securing that the dwelling becomes and continues to be occupied.

(3) The authority must also take such other steps as they consider appropriate with a view to the proper management of the dwelling pending—

    (a)   the making of a final EDMO in respect of the dwelling under section 136, or

    (b)   the revocation of the interim EDMO.

(4) If the local housing authority conclude that there are no steps which they could appropriately take under the order for the purpose of securing that the dwelling becomes occupied, the authority must either—

    (a)   make a final EDMO in respect of the dwelling under section 136, or

    (b)   revoke the order under paragraph 7 of Schedule 7 without taking any further action.

(5) For the avoidance of doubt, the authority's duty under subsection (3) includes taking such steps as are necessary to ensure that, while the order is in force, reasonable provision is made for insurance of the dwelling against destruction or damage by fire or other causes.

**[1457]**

**NOTES**
Commencement: 6 April 2006 (in relation to England, subject to transitional provisions and savings in the Housing Act 2004 (Commencement No 5 and Transitional Provisions and Savings) (England) Order 2006, SI 2006/1060, art 3, Schedule at **[3700]**, **[3701]**); 16 June 2006 (in relation to Wales, subject to transitional provisions and savings in the Housing Act 2004 (Commencement No 3 and Transitional Provisions and Savings) (Wales) Order 2006, SI 2006/1535, art 3, Schedule at **[3714]**, **[3715]**).

*Final empty dwelling management orders*

## 136 Making of final EDMOs

(1) A local housing authority may make a final EDMO to replace an interim EDMO made under section 133 if—

    (a)   they consider that, unless a final EDMO is made in respect of the dwelling, the dwelling is likely to become or remain unoccupied;

    (b)   where the dwelling is unoccupied, they have taken all such steps as it was appropriate for them to take under the interim EDMO with a view to securing the occupation of the dwelling.

(2) A local housing authority may make a new final EDMO so as to replace a final EDMO made under this section if—

    (a)   they consider that unless a new final EDMO is made in respect of the dwelling, the dwelling is likely to become or remain unoccupied; and

    (b)   where the dwelling is unoccupied, they have taken all such steps as it was appropriate for them to take under the existing final EDMO with a view to securing the occupation of the dwelling.

(3) In deciding whether to make a final EDMO in respect of a dwelling, the authority must take into account—

    (a)   the interests of the community, and

    (b)   the effect that the order will have on the rights of the relevant proprietor and may have on the rights of third parties.

(4) Before making a final EDMO under this section, the authority must consider whether compensation should be paid by them to any third party in respect of any interference in consequence of the order with the rights of the third party.

(5) Part 1 of Schedule 6 applies in relation to the making of a final EDMO in respect of a dwelling as it applies in relation to the making of a final management order in respect of a house, subject to the following modifications—

    (a)   paragraph 7(2) does not apply;

    (b)   paragraph 7(4)(c) is to be read as referring instead to the date on which the order is to cease to have effect in accordance with paragraph 1(3) and (4) or 9(3) to (5) of Schedule 7;

    (c)   in paragraph 7(6)—

        (i)   paragraph (a) is to be read as referring to Part 4 of Schedule 7, and

      (ii)   paragraph (b) is to be read as referring instead to paragraph 27(2) of Schedule 7;
  (d)   paragraph 7(6) in addition is to be read as requiring the notice under paragraph 7(5) also
      to contain—
        (i)   the decision of the authority as to whether to pay compensation to any third party,
       (ii)   the amount of any such compensation to be paid, and
      (iii)   information about the right of appeal against the decision under paragraph 34 of
           Schedule 7;
  (e)   paragraph 8(4) is to be read as defining "relevant person" as any person who, to the
      knowledge of the local housing authority, is a person having an estate or interest in the
      dwelling (other than a person who is a tenant under a lease granted under
      paragraph 2(3)(c) or 10(3)(c) of Schedule 7).

**[1458]**

**NOTES**

Commencement: 6 April 2006 (in relation to England, subject to transitional provisions and savings in the Housing Act 2004 (Commencement No 5 and Transitional Provisions and Savings) (England) Order 2006, SI 2006/1060, art 3, Schedule at **[3700]**, **[3701]**); 16 June 2006 (in relation to Wales, subject to transitional provisions and savings in the Housing Act 2004 (Commencement No 3 and Transitional Provisions and Savings) (Wales) Order 2006, SI 2006/1535, art 3, Schedule at **[3714]**, **[3715]**).

### 137 Local housing authority's duties once final EDMO in force

(1)    A local housing authority who have made a final EDMO in respect of a dwelling must comply with the following provisions once the order has come into force (see paragraph 9 of Schedule 7).

(2)    The authority must take such steps as they consider appropriate for the purpose of securing that the dwelling is occupied.

(3)    The authority must also take such other steps as they consider appropriate with a view to the proper management of the dwelling in accordance with the management scheme contained in the order (see paragraph 13 of Schedule 7).

(4)    The authority must from time to time review—
  (a)   the operation of the order and in particular the management scheme contained in it,
  (b)   whether, if the dwelling is unoccupied, there are any steps which they could
      appropriately take under the order for the purpose of securing that the dwelling becomes
      occupied, and
  (c)   whether keeping the order in force in relation to the dwelling (with or without making
      any variations under paragraph 15 of Schedule 7) is necessary to secure that the dwelling
      becomes or remains occupied.

(5)    If on a review the authority consider that any variations should be made under paragraph 15 of Schedule 7, they must proceed to make those variations.

(6)    If the dwelling is unoccupied and on a review the authority conclude that either—
  (a)   there are no steps which they could appropriately take as mentioned in subsection (4)(b),
      or
  (b)   keeping the order in force is not necessary as mentioned in subsection (4)(c),
they must proceed to revoke the order.

(7)    For the avoidance of doubt, the authority's duty under subsection (3) includes taking such steps as are necessary to ensure that, while the order is in force, reasonable provision is made for insurance of the dwelling against destruction or damage by fire or other causes.

**[1459]**

**NOTES**

Commencement: 6 April 2006 (in relation to England, subject to transitional provisions and savings in the Housing Act 2004 (Commencement No 5 and Transitional Provisions and Savings) (England) Order 2006, SI 2006/1060, art 3, Schedule at **[3700]**, **[3701]**); 16 June 2006 (in relation to Wales, subject to transitional provisions and savings in the Housing Act 2004 (Commencement No 3 and Transitional Provisions and Savings) (Wales) Order 2006, SI 2006/1535, art 3, Schedule at **[3714]**, **[3715]**).

*Compensation*

### 138 Compensation payable to third parties

(1)    A third party may, while an interim EDMO is in force in respect of a dwelling, apply to a residential property tribunal for an order requiring the local housing authority to pay to him compensation in respect of any interference in consequence of the order with his rights in respect of the dwelling.

(2)    On such an application, the tribunal may, if it thinks fit, make an order requiring the authority to pay to the third party an amount by way of compensation in respect of any such interference.

(3)   If a third party requests them to do so at any time, the local housing authority must consider whether an amount by way of compensation should be paid to him in respect of any interference in consequence of a final EDMO with his rights.

(4)   The authority must notify the third party of their decision as soon as practicable.

(5)   Where the local housing authority decide under subsection (3) that compensation ought to be paid to a third party, they must vary the management scheme contained in the order so as to specify the amount of the compensation to be paid and to make provision as to its payment.

**[1460]**

**NOTES**

Commencement: 6 April 2006 (in relation to England, subject to transitional provisions and savings in the Housing Act 2004 (Commencement No 5 and Transitional Provisions and Savings) (England) Order 2006, SI 2006/1060, art 3, Schedule at **[3700]**, **[3701]**); 16 June 2006 (in relation to Wales, subject to transitional provisions and savings in the Housing Act 2004 (Commencement No 3 and Transitional Provisions and Savings) (Wales) Order 2006, SI 2006/1535, art 3, Schedule at **[3714]**, **[3715]**).

## CHAPTER 3
## OVERCROWDING NOTICES

### 139   Service of overcrowding notices

(1)   This Chapter applies to any HMO—
  (a)   in relation to which no interim or final management order is in force; and
  (b)   which is not required to be licensed under Part 2.

(2)   The local housing authority may serve an overcrowding notice on one or more relevant persons if, having regard to the rooms available, it considers that an excessive number of persons is being, or is likely to be, accommodated in the HMO concerned.

(3)   The authority must, at least 7 days before serving an overcrowding notice—
  (a)   inform in writing every relevant person (whether or not the person on whom the authority is to serve the notice) of their intention to serve the notice; and
  (b)   ensure that, so far as is reasonably possible, every occupier of the HMO concerned is informed of the authority's intention.

(4)   The authority must also give the persons informed under subsection (3) an opportunity of making representations about the proposal to serve an overcrowding notice.

(5)   An overcrowding notice becomes operative, if no appeal is brought under section 143, at the end of the period of 21 days from the date of service of the notice.

(6)   If no appeal is brought under section 143, an overcrowding notice is final and conclusive as to matters which could have been raised on such an appeal.

(7)   A person who contravenes an overcrowding notice commits an offence and is liable on summary conviction to a fine not exceeding level 4 on the standard scale.

(8)   In proceedings for an offence under subsection (7) it is a defence that the person had a reasonable excuse for contravening the notice.

(9)   In this section "relevant person" means a person who is, to the knowledge of the local housing authority—
  (a)   a person having an estate or interest in the HMO concerned, or
  (b)   a person managing or having control of it.

**[1461]**

**NOTES**

Commencement: 6 April 2006 (in relation to England, subject to transitional provisions and savings in the Housing Act 2004 (Commencement No 5 and Transitional Provisions and Savings) (England) Order 2006, SI 2006/1060, art 3, Schedule at **[3700]**, **[3701]**); 16 June 2006 (in relation to Wales, subject to transitional provisions and savings in the Housing Act 2004 (Commencement No 3 and Transitional Provisions and Savings) (Wales) Order 2006, SI 2006/1535, art 3, Schedule at **[3714]**, **[3715]**).

Modification: this section is modified in relation to a house in multiple occupation to which s 257 of this Act applies, by the Houses in Multiple Occupation (Certain Converted Blocks of Flats) (Modifications to the Housing Act 2004 and Transitional Provisions for section 257 HMOs) (England) Regulations 2007, SI 2007/1904, reg 11, and the Housing Act 2004 and Transitional Provisions for section 257 HMOs) (Wales) Regulations 2007, SI 2007/3231, reg 11.

### 140   Contents of overcrowding notices

(1)   An overcrowding notice must state in relation to each room in the HMO concerned—
  (a)   what the local housing authority consider to be the maximum number of persons by whom the room is suitable to be occupied as sleeping accommodation at any one time; or

(b)    that the local housing authority consider that the room is unsuitable to be occupied as sleeping accommodation.

(2)    An overcrowding notice may specify special maxima applicable where some or all of the persons occupying a room are under such age as may be specified in the notice.

(3)    An overcrowding notice must contain—

(a)    the requirement prescribed by section 141 (not to permit excessive number of persons to sleep in the house in multiple occupation); or

(b)    the requirement prescribed by section 142 (not to admit new residents if number of persons is excessive).

(4)    The local housing authority may at any time—

(a)    withdraw an overcrowding notice which has been served on any person and which contains the requirement prescribed by section 142, and

(b)    serve on him instead an overcrowding notice containing the requirement prescribed by section 141.

**[1462]**

**NOTES**

Commencement: 6 April 2006 (in relation to England, subject to transitional provisions and savings in the Housing Act 2004 (Commencement No 5 and Transitional Provisions and Savings) (England) Order 2006, SI 2006/1060, art 3, Schedule at **[3700]**, **[3701]**); 16 June 2006 (in relation to Wales, subject to transitional provisions and savings in the Housing Act 2004 (Commencement No 3 and Transitional Provisions and Savings) (Wales) Order 2006, SI 2006/1535, art 3, Schedule at **[3714]**, **[3715]**).

## 141  Requirement as to overcrowding generally

(1)    The requirement prescribed by this section is that the person on whom the notice is served must refrain from—

(a)    permitting a room to be occupied as sleeping accommodation otherwise than in accordance with the notice; or

(b)    permitting persons to occupy the HMO as sleeping accommodation in such numbers that it is not possible to avoid persons of opposite sexes who are not living together as husband and wife sleeping in the same room.

(2)    For the purposes of subsection (1)(b)—

(a)    children under the age of 10 are to be disregarded; and

(b)    it must be assumed that the persons occupying the HMO as sleeping accommodation sleep only in rooms for which a maximum is set by the notice and that the maximum set for each room is not exceeded.

**[1463]**

**NOTES**

Commencement: 18 November 2004 (for the purpose of making orders or regulations); 6 April 2006 (in relation to England for remaining purposes, subject to transitional provisions and savings in the Housing Act 2004 (Commencement No 5 and Transitional Provisions and Savings) (England) Order 2006, SI 2006/1060, art 3, Schedule at **[3700]**, **[3701]**); 16 June 2006 (in relation to Wales for remaining purposes, subject to transitional provisions and savings in the Housing Act 2004 (Commencement No 3 and Transitional Provisions and Savings) (Wales) Order 2006, SI 2006/1535, art 3, Schedule at **[3714]**, **[3715]**).

## 142  Requirement as to new residents

(1)    The requirement prescribed by this section is that the person on whom the notice is served must refrain from—

(a)    permitting a room to be occupied by a new resident as sleeping accommodation otherwise than in accordance with the notice; or

(b)    permitting a new resident to occupy any part of the HMO as sleeping accommodation if that is not possible without persons of opposite sexes who are not living together as husband and wife sleeping in the same room.

(2)    In subsection (1) "new resident" means a person who was not an occupier of the HMO immediately before the notice was served.

(3)    For the purposes of subsection (1)(b)—

(a)    children under the age of 10 are to be disregarded; and

(b)    it must be assumed that the persons occupying any part of the HMO as sleeping accommodation sleep only in rooms for which a maximum is set by the notice and that the maximum set for each room is not exceeded.

**[1464]**

**NOTES**

Commencement: 18 November 2004 (for the purpose of making orders or regulations); 6 April 2006 (in relation to England for remaining purposes, subject to transitional provisions and savings in the Housing

Act 2004 (Commencement No 5 and Transitional Provisions and Savings) (England) Order 2006, SI 2006/1060, art 3, Schedule at **[3700]**, **[3701]**); 16 June 2006 (in relation to Wales for remaining purposes, subject to transitional provisions and savings in the Housing Act 2004 (Commencement No 3 and Transitional Provisions and Savings) (Wales) Order 2006, SI 2006/1535, art 3, Schedule at **[3714]**, **[3715]**).

## 143 Appeals against overcrowding notices

(1) A person aggrieved by an overcrowding notice may appeal to a residential property tribunal within the period of 21 days beginning with the date of service of the notice.

(2) Such an appeal—
    (a)   is to be by way of a re-hearing, but
    (b)   may be determined having regard to matters of which the authority were unaware.

(3) On an appeal the tribunal may by order confirm, quash or vary the notice.

(4) If an appeal is brought, the notice does not become operative until—
    (a)   a decision is given on the appeal which confirms the notice and the period within which an appeal to the [Upper Tribunal] may be brought expires without any such appeal having been brought; or
    (b)   if an appeal is brought to the [Upper Tribunal], a decision is given on the appeal which confirms the notice.

(5) For the purposes of subsection (4)—
    (a)   the withdrawal of an appeal has the same effect as a decision which confirms the notice appealed against; and
    (b)   references to a decision which confirms the notice are to a decision which confirms it with or without variation.

(6) A residential property tribunal may allow an appeal to be made to it after the end of the period mentioned in subsection (1) if it is satisfied that there is good reason for the failure to appeal before the end of that period (and for any delay since then in applying for permission to appeal out of time).

**[1465]**

**NOTES**
Commencement: 6 April 2006 (in relation to England, subject to transitional provisions and savings in the Housing Act 2004 (Commencement No 5 and Transitional Provisions and Savings) (England) Order 2006, SI 2006/1060, art 3, Schedule at **[3700]**, **[3701]**); 16 June 2006 (in relation to Wales, subject to transitional provisions and savings in the Housing Act 2004 (Commencement No 3 and Transitional Provisions and Savings) (Wales) Order 2006, SI 2006/1535, art 3, Schedule at **[3714]**, **[3715]**).

Sub-s (4): words in square brackets substituted by the Transfer of Tribunal Functions (Lands Tribunal and Miscellaneous Amendments) Order 2009, SI 2009/1307, art 5(1), (2), Sch 1, paras 271, 274, subject to transitional and savings provisions in Sch 5 thereto.

## 144 Revocation and variation of overcrowding notices

(1) The local housing authority may at any time, on the application of a relevant person—
    (a)   revoke an overcrowding notice; or
    (b)   vary it so as to allow more people to be accommodated in the HMO concerned.

(2) The applicant may appeal to a residential property tribunal if the local housing authority—
    (a)   refuse an application under subsection (1); or
    (b)   do not notify the applicant of their decision within the period of 35 days beginning with the making of the application (or within such further period as the applicant may in writing allow).

(3) An appeal under subsection (2) must be made within—
    (a)   the period of 21 days beginning with the date when the applicant is notified by the authority of their decision to refuse the application, or
    (b)   the period of 21 days immediately following the end of the period (or further period) applying for the purposes of paragraph (b) of that subsection,
as the case may be.

(4) Section 143(2) applies to such an appeal as it applies to an appeal under that section.

(5) On an appeal the tribunal may revoke the notice or vary it in any manner in which it might have been varied by the local housing authority.

(6) A residential property tribunal may allow an appeal to be made to it after the end of the 21-day period mentioned in subsection (3)(a) or (b) if it is satisfied that there is good reason for the failure to appeal before the end of that period (and for any delay since then in applying for permission to appeal).

(7) In this section "relevant person" means—

(a)   any person who has an estate or interest in the HMO concerned, or
(b)   any other person who is a person managing or having control of it.

**[1466]**

**NOTES**
Commencement: 6 April 2006 (in relation to England, subject to transitional provisions and savings in the Housing Act 2004 (Commencement No 5 and Transitional Provisions and Savings) (England) Order 2006, SI 2006/1060, art 3, Schedule at **[3700]**, **[3701]**); 16 June 2006 (in relation to Wales, subject to transitional provisions and savings in the Housing Act 2004 (Commencement No 3 and Transitional Provisions and Savings) (Wales) Order 2006, SI 2006/1535, art 3, Schedule at **[3714]**, **[3715]**).

## CHAPTER 4
## SUPPLEMENTARY PROVISIONS

**145   Supplementary provisions**

(1)   The appropriate national authority may by regulations make such provision as it considers appropriate for supplementing the provisions of Chapter 1 or 2 in relation to cases where a local housing authority are to be treated as the lessee under a lease under—
(a)   section 107(5) or 116(5), or
(b)   paragraph 2(6) or 10(6) of Schedule 7.

(2)   Regulations under this section may, in particular, make provision—
(a)   as respects rights and liabilities in such cases of—
    (i)   the authority,
    (ii)   the person who (apart from the relevant provision mentioned in subsection (1)) is the lessee under the lease, or
    (iii)   other persons having an estate or interest in the premises demised under the lease;
(b)   requiring the authority to give copies to the person mentioned in paragraph (a)(ii) of notices and other documents served on them in connection with the lease;
(c)   for treating things done by or in relation to the authority as done by or in relation to that person, or vice versa.

**[1467]**

**NOTES**
Commencement: 18 November 2004 (for the purpose of making orders or regulations); 6 April 2006 (in relation to England for remaining purposes, subject to transitional provisions and savings in the Housing Act 2004 (Commencement No 5 and Transitional Provisions and Savings) (England) Order 2006, SI 2006/1060, art 3, Schedule at **[3700]**, **[3701]**); 16 June 2006 (in relation to Wales for remaining purposes, subject to transitional provisions and savings in the Housing Act 2004 (Commencement No 3 and Transitional Provisions and Savings) (Wales) Order 2006, SI 2006/1535, art 3, Schedule at **[3714]**, **[3715]**).
Regulations: the Housing (Management Orders and Empty Dwelling Management Orders) (Supplemental Provisions) (England) Regulations 2006, SI 2006/368 at **[3602]**; the Housing (Management Orders and Empty Dwelling Management Orders) (Supplemental Provisions) (Wales) Regulations 2006, SI 2006/2822 at **[3741]**.

**146   Interpretation and modification of this Part**

(1)   In this Part—
    "HMO" means a house in multiple occupation as defined by sections 254 to 259,
    "Part 3 house" means a house to which Part 3 of this Act applies (see section 79(2)),
and any reference to an HMO or Part 3 house includes (where the context permits) a reference to any yard, garden, outhouses and appurtenances belonging to, or usually enjoyed with, it (or any part of it).

(2)   For the purposes of this Part "mortgage" includes a charge or lien, and "mortgagee" is to be read accordingly.

(3)   The appropriate national authority may by regulations provide for—
(a)   any provision of this Part, or
(b)   section 263 (in its operation for the purposes of any such provision),
to have effect in relation to a section 257 HMO with such modifications as are prescribed by the regulations.

(4)   A "section 257 HMO" is an HMO which is a converted block of flats to which section 257 applies.

**[1468]**

**NOTES**
Commencement: 18 November 2004 (for the purpose of making orders or regulations); 6 April 2006 (in relation to England for remaining purposes, subject to transitional provisions and savings in the Housing Act 2004 (Commencement No 5 and Transitional Provisions and Savings) (England) Order 2006, SI 2006/1060, art 3, Schedule at **[3700]**, **[3701]**); 16 June 2006 (in relation to Wales for remaining purposes, subject to transitional provisions and savings in the Housing Act 2004 (Commencement No 3 and Transitional Provisions and Savings) (Wales) Order 2006, SI 2006/1535, art 3, Schedule at **[3714]**, **[3715]**).

Regulations: the Houses in Multiple Occupation (Certain Converted Blocks of Flats) (Modifications to the Housing Act 2004 and Transitional Provisions for section 257 HMOs) (England) Regulations 2007, SI 2007/1904; the Houses in Multiple Occupation (Certain Converted Blocks of Flats) (Modifications to the Housing Act 2004 and Transitional Provisions for section 257 HMOs) (Wales) Regulations 2007, SI 2007/3231.

## 147 Index of defined expressions: Part 4

The following table shows where expressions used in this Part are defined or otherwise explained.

| Expression | Provision of this Act |
|---|---|
| Appropriate national authority | Section 261(1) |
| Dwelling | Section 132(4)(a) and (b) |
| Final EDMO | Section 132(1)(b) |
| Final management order | Section 101(4) |
| Health | Section 2(5) |
| HMO | Section 146(1) |
| The house | Section 101(5) or 103(8) |
| Immediate landlord | Section 109(6) or 118(6) |
| Interim EDMO | Section 132(1)(a) |
| Interim management order | Section 101(3) |
| Landlord | Section 262(3) |
| Lease, lessee, etc | Section 262(1) to (4) |
| Licence (to occupy premises) | Section 262(9) |
| Local housing authority | Section 261(2) to (5) |
| Modifications | Section 250(7) |
| Mortgage, mortgagee | Section 146(2) |
| Occupier (and related expressions) | Section 262(6) |
| Owner | Section 262(7) |
| Part 3 house | Section 146(1) |
| Person having control | Section 263(1) and (2) |
| Person having estate or interest | Section 262(8) |
| Person managing | Section 263(3) |
| Relevant proprietor | Section 132(4)(c) and (5) |
| Rent or other payments (in Chapter 2) | Section 132(4)(e) |
| Residential property tribunal | Section 229 |
| Tenancy, tenant, etc | Section 262(1) to (5) |
| Third party (in Chapter 1) | Section 101(7) |
| Third party (in Chapter 2) | Section 132(4)(d). |

**[1469]**

**NOTES**

Commencement: 6 April 2006 (in relation to England, subject to transitional provisions and savings in the Housing Act 2004 (Commencement No 5 and Transitional Provisions and Savings) (England) Order 2006, SI 2006/1060, art 3, Schedule at **[3700]**, **[3701]**); 16 June 2006 (in relation to Wales, subject to transitional provisions and savings in the Housing Act 2004 (Commencement No 3 and Transitional Provisions and Savings) (Wales) Order 2006, SI 2006/1535, art 3, Schedule at **[3714]**, **[3715]**).

**148–178**   ((Pt 5) *Outside the scope of this work.*)

PART 6
OTHER PROVISIONS ABOUT HOUSING

CHAPTER 1
SECURE TENANCIES

**179**    (*Amends the Housing Act 1996, s 125 at* **[1010]** *and inserts ss 125A, 125B of that Act at* **[1011], [1012].**)

*Right to buy: when exercisable*

**180**    (*Amends the Housing Act 1985, ss 119, 129 at* **[462], [482].**)

**181   Exceptions to the right to buy: determination whether exception for dwelling-house suitable for elderly persons applies**

(1)–(3)   ...

(4)    Subsections (5) and (6) apply to any application under paragraph 11(4) in respect of a dwelling-house in England which—

     (a)    has been made to the Secretary of State before the day on which this section comes into force, and

     (b)    has not been determined by him before that day.

(5)    If the application was made more than 28 days before that day, it is to be determined by the Secretary of State as if the amendments made by this section had not come into force.

(6)    Otherwise—

     (a)    the application is to be determined by a residential property tribunal, and

     (b)    the Secretary of State must make all such arrangements as he considers necessary for the purpose of, or in connection with, enabling it to be so determined.

                                              **[1470]**

**NOTES**

Commencement: 4 July 2005 (in relation to England, subject to transitional provisions as noted below); to be appointed (otherwise).

Sub-ss (1)–(3): amend the Housing Act 1985, Sch 5, para 11 at **[584]**.

Transitional provisions: the Housing Act 2004 (Commencement No 4 and Transitional Provisions) (England) Order 2005, SI 2005/1729, art 2, appoints 4 July 2005 as the date (in relation to England) for the coming into force of this section, ss 230, 231, and s 229 and Sch 13 (so far as not already in force) subject to transitional provisions in art 3 thereof which provides that where an application made to the Secretary of State under the Housing Act 1985, Sch 5, para 11(4) at **[584]** on or after 6 June 2005 but before 4 July 2005 is determined by a residential property tribunal, the Residential Property Tribunal (Right to Buy Determinations) Procedure (England) Regulations 2005, SI 2005/1509 at **[3465]** shall apply to the proceedings of the residential property tribunal to determine that application, and where an application for the purpose mentioned in the Housing Act 1985, Sch 5, para 11(4) at **[584]** is made, on or after 4 July 2005 but before 29 August 2005, to the Secretary of State instead of to a residential property tribunal it shall be deemed to have been made to such a tribunal.

**182–184**    (*S 182 adds the Housing Act 1985, Sch 5, paras 13–16 at* **[584]**; *s 183 amends s 193 of that Act, inserts ss 138A–138C of that Act at* **[488]–[490]**, *and introduces Sch 9 to this Act; s 184 amends s 140 of that Act at* **[492].**)

*Right to buy: discounts*

**185   Repayment of discount: periods and amounts applicable**

(1)–(4)   ...

(5)    The amendments made by this section do not apply in any case where the tenant's notice under section 122 of the Act (notice claiming to exercise right to buy) was served before the day on which this section comes into force.

(6)    Subsection (7), however, applies in any such case if the first relevant disposal to which the covenant for repayment of discount applies takes place on or after the day on which this section comes into force.

(7)    In the following provisions—

     (a)    section 155(2) and (3) of the Housing Act 1985 (c 68) (as it has effect without the amendments made by this section), and

     (b)    any covenant for repayment of discount,

any reference (however expressed) to a person being liable to pay an amount to the landlord on demand is to be read as a reference to his being liable to pay to the landlord so much of that amount (if any) as the landlord may demand.

(8)  In subsections (6) and (7) "covenant for repayment of discount" means the covenant contained in a conveyance or grant in accordance with section 155 of that Act.

**[1471]**

**NOTES**
Commencement: 18 January 2005.
Sub-ss (1)–(4): amend the Housing Act 1985, s 155 at **[514]** and insert ss 155A, 155B of that Act at **[515]**, **[516]**.

**186, 187**    *(S 186 inserts the Housing Act 1985, s 155C at* **[517]** *and amends s 181 of that Act at* **[552]***; s 187 inserts s 163A of that Act at* **[527]***.)*

*Right to buy: landlord's right of first refusal*

**188  Right of first refusal for landlord etc**

(1)–(4)  ...

(5)  The amendments made by this section do not apply in relation to a conveyance of the freehold or grant of a lease in pursuance of Part 5 of that Act if the notice under section 122 of the Act (tenant's notice claiming to exercise right to buy) was served before the day on which this section comes into force.

(6)  Accordingly, nothing in this section affects—
  (a)  the operation of a limitation contained in such a conveyance or grant in accordance with section 157(4) of that Act, or
  (b)  the operation, in relation to such a limitation, of section 157(6) (so far as it renders a disposal in breach of covenant void) or section 158 (consideration payable) of that Act.

**[1472]**

**NOTES**
Commencement: 18 January 2005.
Sub-ss (1)–(4): insert the Housing Act 1985, s 156A at **[519]** and amend ss 157, 158, 162 of that Act, at **[520]**, **[521]**, **[525]**.

**189, 190**    *(S 189 inserts the Housing Act 1985, ss 121AA, 121B, at* **[466]**, **[467]** *and amends s 104 of that Act, at* **[445]***; s 190 inserts s 142A of that Act at* **[494]** *and amends ss 143, 144 of that Act at* **[495]**, **[498]***.)*

*Suspension of certain rights in connection with anti-social behaviour*

**191**    *(Inserts the Housing Act 1985, Sch 3, Ground 2A at* **[581]***.)*

**192  Right to buy: suspension by court order**

(1), (2)  ...

(3)  Regulations under—
  (a)  section 171C of that Act (modifications of Part 5 in relation to preserved right to buy), or
  (b)  section 17 of the Housing Act 1996 (c 52) (application of that Part in relation to right to acquire dwelling),
may make provision for continuing the effect of a suspension order where the secure tenancy in respect of which the order was made has been replaced by an assured tenancy.

**[1473]**

**NOTES**
Commencement: 6 June 2005 (in relation to England); 25 November 2005 (in relation to Wales).
Sub-s (1): amends the Housing Act 1985, s 121 at **[464]**.
Sub-s (2): inserts the Housing Act 1985, s 121A at **[465]**.

**193**    *(Amends the Housing Act 1985, s 138 at* **[487]***.)*

**194  Disclosure of information as to orders etc in respect of anti-social behaviour**

(1)  Any person may disclose relevant information to a landlord under a secure tenancy if the information is disclosed for the purpose of enabling the landlord—
  (a)  to decide whether either of the provisions of the Housing Act 1985 (c 68) mentioned in subsection (2) can be invoked in relation to the tenant under the tenancy; or
  (b)  to take any appropriate action in relation to the tenant in reliance on either of those provisions.

(2)  The provisions are—

(a)   Ground 2A in Schedule 3 (withholding of consent to mutual exchange where order in force or application pending in connection with anti-social behaviour), and

(b)   section 138(2B) (landlord's obligation to complete suspended while application pending in connection with such behaviour).

(3)  In this section—

(a)   "relevant information" means information relating to any order or application relevant for the purposes of either of the provisions mentioned in subsection (2), including (in particular) information identifying the person in respect of whom any such order or application has been made;

(b)   "secure tenancy" has the meaning given by section 79 of the Housing Act 1985; and

(c)   any reference to the tenant under a secure tenancy is, in relation to a joint tenancy, a reference to any of the joint tenants.

(4)  Regulations under—

(a)   section 171C of the Housing Act 1985 (modifications of Part 5 in relation to preserved right to buy), or

(b)   section 17 of the Housing Act 1996 (c 52) (application of that Part in relation to right to acquire dwelling),

may make provision corresponding to subsections (1) to (3) of this section so far as those subsections relate to section 138(2B) of the Housing Act 1985.

**[1474]**

**NOTES**

Commencement: 6 June 2005 (in relation to England); 25 November 2005 (in relation to Wales).

### CHAPTER 2
### DISPOSALS ATTRACTING DISCOUNTS OTHER THAN UNDER RIGHT TO BUY

**195–198**   (*S 195 amends the Housing Act 1985, s 35; s 196 inserts s 35A of that Act; s 197 inserts ss 36A, 36B of that Act and amends ss 33, 37, 41 of that Act; s 198 inserts s 39A of that Act.*)

*Disposals by registered social landlords*

**199–201**   (*S 199 substitutes the Housing Act 1996, s 11 and amends s 12 of that Act; s 200 inserts ss 12A, 12B of that Act and amends s 13 of that Act; s 201 inserts s 15A of that Act.*)

**202  Right of assured tenant to acquire dwelling not affected by collective enfranchisement**

(1), (2)  ...

(3)  The amendment made by subsection (2) applies in relation to the right conferred by section 16 as follows—

(a)   it applies for the purposes of any exercise of that right on or after the day on which this section comes into force, and

(b)   it so applies whether the lease granted in pursuance of paragraph 3 of Schedule 9 to the Leasehold Reform, Housing and Urban Development Act 1993 was granted on or after that day or before it.

**[1475]**

**NOTES**

Commencement: 18 January 2005.

Sub-ss (1), (2): amend the Housing Act 1996, s 16 at **[1002]**.

**203–205**   (*Amend the Housing Act 1988, Sch 11.*)

### CHAPTER 3
### MOBILE HOMES

**206–211**   (*S 206 substitutes the Mobile Homes Act 1983, s 1 at* **[395]** *and amends ss 2, 5 of that Act at* **[396]**, **[401]**; *s 207 amends Sch 1 to that Act at* **[403]**; *s 208 inserts s 2A of that Act* **[397]**; *ss 209–211 amend the Caravan Sites Act 1968, ss 1, 3, 4 at* **[135]**, **[137]**, **[138]**.)

### CHAPTER 4
### TENANCY DEPOSIT SCHEMES

**212  Tenancy deposit schemes**

(1)  The appropriate national authority must make arrangements for securing that one or more tenancy deposit schemes are available for the purpose of safeguarding tenancy deposits paid in connection with shorthold tenancies.

PART I STATUTES

(2)  For the purposes of this Chapter a "tenancy deposit scheme" is a scheme which—

    (a)   is made for the purpose of safeguarding tenancy deposits paid in connection with shorthold tenancies and facilitating the resolution of disputes arising in connection with such deposits, and

    (b)   complies with the requirements of Schedule 10.

(3)  Arrangements under subsection (1) must be arrangements made with any body or person under which the body or person ("the scheme administrator") undertakes to establish and maintain a tenancy deposit scheme of a description specified in the arrangements.

(4)  The appropriate national authority may—

    (a)   give financial assistance to the scheme administrator;

    (b)   make payments to the scheme administrator (otherwise than as financial assistance) in pursuance of arrangements under subsection (1).

(5)  The appropriate national authority may, in such manner and on such terms as it thinks fit, guarantee the discharge of any financial obligation incurred by the scheme administrator in connection with arrangements under subsection (1).

(6)  Arrangements under subsection (1) must require the scheme administrator to give the appropriate national authority, in such manner and at such times as it may specify, such information and facilities for obtaining information as it may specify.

(7)  The appropriate national authority may make regulations conferring or imposing—

    (a)   on scheme administrators, or

    (b)   on scheme administrators of any description specified in the regulations,

such powers or duties in connection with arrangements under subsection (1) as are so specified.

(8)  In this Chapter—

"authorised", in relation to a tenancy deposit scheme, means that the scheme is in force in accordance with arrangements under subsection (1);

"custodial scheme" and "insurance scheme" have the meaning given by paragraph 1(2) and (3) of Schedule 10;

"money" means money in the form of cash or otherwise;

"shorthold tenancy" means an assured shorthold tenancy within the meaning of Chapter 2 of Part 1 of the Housing Act 1988 (c 50);

"tenancy deposit", in relation to a shorthold tenancy, means any money intended to be held (by the landlord or otherwise) as security for—

    (a)   the performance of any obligations of the tenant, or

    (b)   the discharge of any liability of his,

arising under or in connection with the tenancy.

(9)  In this Chapter—

    (a)   references to a landlord or landlords in relation to any shorthold tenancy or tenancies include references to a person or persons acting on his or their behalf in relation to the tenancy or tenancies, and

    (b)   references to a tenancy deposit being held in accordance with a scheme include, in the case of a custodial scheme, references to an amount representing the deposit being held in accordance with the scheme.

**[1476]**

**NOTES**

Commencement: 18 November 2004 (for the purpose of making orders or regulations); 6 April 2007 (otherwise).

### 213  Requirements relating to tenancy deposits

(1)  Any tenancy deposit paid to a person in connection with a shorthold tenancy must, as from the time when it is received, be dealt with in accordance with an authorised scheme.

(2)  No person may require the payment of a tenancy deposit in connection with a shorthold tenancy which is not to be subject to the requirement in subsection (1).

(3)  Where a landlord receives a tenancy deposit in connection with a shorthold tenancy, the initial requirements of an authorised scheme must be complied with by the landlord in relation to the deposit within the period of 14 days beginning with the date on which it is received.

(4)  For the purposes of this section "the initial requirements" of an authorised scheme are such requirements imposed by the scheme as fall to be complied with by a landlord on receiving such a tenancy deposit.

(5)  A landlord who has received such a tenancy deposit must give the tenant and any relevant person such information relating to—

    (a)   the authorised scheme applying to the deposit,

PART 1
STATUTES

(b)    compliance by the landlord with the initial requirements of the scheme in relation to the deposit, and

(c)    the operation of provisions of this Chapter in relation to the deposit,

as may be prescribed.

(6)    The information required by subsection (5) must be given to the tenant and any relevant person—

(a)    in the prescribed form or in a form substantially to the same effect, and

(b)    within the period of 14 days beginning with the date on which the deposit is received by the landlord.

(7)    No person may, in connection with a shorthold tenancy, require a deposit which consists of property other than money.

(8)    In subsection (7) "deposit" means a transfer of property intended to be held (by the landlord or otherwise) as security for—

(a)    the performance of any obligations of the tenant, or

(b)    the discharge of any liability of his,

arising under or in connection with the tenancy.

(9)    The provisions of this section apply despite any agreement to the contrary.

(10)    In this section—

"prescribed" means prescribed by an order made by the appropriate national authority;

"property" means moveable property;

"relevant person" means any person who, in accordance with arrangements made with the tenant, paid the deposit on behalf of the tenant.

**[1477]**

**NOTES**

Commencement: 18 November 2004 (for the purpose of making orders or regulations); 6 April 2007 (otherwise).

Orders: the Housing (Tenancy Deposits) (Prescribed Information) Order 2007, SI 2007/797.

## 214    Proceedings relating to tenancy deposits

(1)    Where a tenancy deposit has been paid in connection with a shorthold tenancy, the tenant or any relevant person (as defined by section 213(10)) may make an application to a county court on the grounds—

(a)    that the initial requirements of an authorised scheme (see section 213(4)) have not, or section 213(6)(a) has not, been complied with in relation to the deposit; or

(b)    that he has been notified by the landlord that a particular authorised scheme applies to the deposit but has been unable to obtain confirmation from the scheme administrator that the deposit is being held in accordance with the scheme.

(2)    Subsections (3) and (4) apply if on such an application the court—

(a)    is satisfied that those requirements have not, or section 213(6)(a) has not, been complied with in relation to the deposit, or

(b)    is not satisfied that the deposit is being held in accordance with an authorised scheme,

as the case may be.

(3)    The court must, as it thinks fit, either—

(a)    order the person who appears to the court to be holding the deposit to repay it to the applicant, or

(b)    order that person to pay the deposit into the designated account held by the scheme administrator under an authorised custodial scheme,

within the period of 14 days beginning with the date of the making of the order.

(4)    The court must also order the landlord to pay to the applicant a sum of money equal to three times the amount of the deposit within the period of 14 days beginning with the date of the making of the order.

(5)    Where any deposit given in connection with a shorthold tenancy could not be lawfully required as a result of section 213(7), the property in question is recoverable from the person holding it by the person by whom it was given as a deposit.

(6)    In subsection (5) "deposit" has the meaning given by section 213(8).

**[1478]**

**NOTES**

Commencement: 6 April 2007.

## 215 Sanctions for non-compliance

(1) If a tenancy deposit has been paid in connection with a shorthold tenancy, no section 21 notice may be given in relation to the tenancy at a time when—

    (a)    the deposit is not being held in accordance with an authorised scheme, or

    (b)    the initial requirements of such a scheme (see section 213(4)) have not been complied with in relation to the deposit.

(2) If section 213(6) is not complied with in relation to a deposit given in connection with a shorthold tenancy, no section 21 notice may be given in relation to the tenancy until such time as section 213(6)(a) is complied with.

(3) If any deposit given in connection with a shorthold tenancy could not be lawfully required as a result of section 213(7), no section 21 notice may be given in relation to the tenancy until such time as the property in question is returned to the person by whom it was given as a deposit.

(4) In subsection (3) "deposit" has the meaning given by section 213(8).

(5) In this section a "section 21 notice" means a notice under section 21(1)(b) or (4)(a) of the Housing Act 1988 (recovery of possession on termination of shorthold tenancy).

**[1479]**

**NOTES**

Commencement: 6 April 2007.

## CHAPTER 5
## MISCELLANEOUS

*Overcrowding*

## 216 Overcrowding

(1) The appropriate national authority may by order make such provision as it considers appropriate for and in connection with—

    (a)    determining whether a dwelling is overcrowded for the purposes of Part 10 of the Housing Act 1985 (c 68) (overcrowding);

    (b)    introducing for the purposes of Chapter 3 of Part 4 of this Act a concept of overcrowding similar to that applying for the purposes of Part 10 (and accordingly removing the discretion of local housing authorities to decide particular issues arising under those sections);

    (c)    securing that overcrowding in premises to which Chapter 3 of Part 4 of this Act would otherwise apply, or any description of such premises, is regulated only by provisions of Part 10.

(2) An order under this section may, in particular, make provision for regulating the making by local housing authorities of determinations as to whether premises are overcrowded, including provision prescribing—

    (a)    factors that must be taken into account by such authorities when making such determinations;

    (b)    the procedure that is to be followed by them in connection with making such determinations.

(3) An order under this section may modify any enactment (including this Act).

(4) In this section—

    (a)    any reference to Part 10 of the Housing Act 1985 includes a reference to Part 10 as modified by an order under this section; and

    (b)    "enactment" includes an enactment comprised in subordinate legislation (within the meaning of the Interpretation Act 1978 (c 30)).

**[1480]**

*Energy efficiency*

## 217 Energy efficiency of residential accommodation: England

(1) The Secretary of State must take reasonable steps to ensure that by 2010 the general level of energy efficiency of residential accommodation in England has increased by at least 20 per cent compared with the general level of such energy efficiency in 2000.

(2) Nothing in this section affects the duties of the Secretary of State under section 2 of the Sustainable Energy Act 2003 (c 30) (energy efficiency aim in respect of residential accommodation in England).

(3) In this section "residential accommodation" has the meaning given by section 1 of the Home Energy Conservation Act 1995 (c 10).

**[1481]**

**NOTES**
Commencement: 18 January 2005.

*Registered social landlords*

## 218   Amendments relating to registered social landlords

Schedule 11 (which makes amendments relating to registered social landlords) has effect.

**[1482]**

**NOTES**
Commencement: 18 January 2005.

**219–224**   (*S 219 amends the Crime and Disorder Act 1998, s 115(2); s 220 inserts the Housing Act 1996, ss 27A, 27B; s 221 inserts s 16A of that Act at* **[1003]***; s 222 amends the Housing Act 1988, s 5 at* **[733]***; s 223 amends s 167 of the 1996 Act; s 224 amends the Housing Grants, Construction and Regeneration Act 1996, ss 1, 19, 22A, 23, 24, 29, 41, 57–59.)*

*Accommodation needs of gypsies and travellers*

## 225   Duties of local housing authorities: accommodation needs of gypsies and travellers

(1)   Every local housing authority must, when undertaking a review of housing needs in their district under section 8 of the Housing Act 1985 (c 68), carry out an assessment of the accommodation needs of gypsies and travellers residing in or resorting to their district.

(2)   Subsection (3) applies where a local housing authority are required under section 87 of the Local Government Act 2003 (c 26) to prepare a strategy in respect of the meeting of such accommodation needs.

(3)   The local authority who are that local housing authority must take the strategy into account in exercising their functions.
"Functions" includes functions exercisable otherwise than as a local housing authority.

(4)   A local housing authority must have regard to any guidance issued under section 226 in—
   (a)   carrying out such an assessment as mentioned in subsection (1), and
   (b)   preparing any strategy that they are required to prepare as mentioned in subsection (2).

(5)   In this section—
   (a)   "gypsies and travellers" has the meaning given by regulations made by the appropriate national authority;
   (b)   "accommodation needs" includes needs with respect to the provision of sites on which caravans can be stationed; and
   (c)   "caravan" has the same meaning as in Part 1 of the Caravan Sites and Control of Development Act 1960.

**[1483]**

**NOTES**
Commencement: 18 November 2004 (for the purpose of making orders or regulations); 2 January 2007 (in relation to England for remaining purposes); 13 December 2007 (in relation to Wales for remaining purposes).
Regulations: the Housing (Assessment of Accommodation Needs) (Meaning of Gypsies and Travellers) (England) Regulations 2006, SI 2006/3190 at **[3747]**; the Housing (Assessment of Accommodation Needs) (Meaning of Gypsies and Travellers) (Wales) Regulations 2007, SI 2007/3235 at **[3780]**.

## 226   Guidance in relation to section 225

(1)   The appropriate national authority may issue guidance to local housing authorities regarding—
   (a)   the carrying out of assessments under section 225(1), and
   (b)   the preparation of any strategies that local housing authorities are required to prepare as mentioned in section 225(2).

(2)   Before giving guidance under this section, or revising guidance already given, the Secretary of State must lay a draft of the proposed guidance or alterations before each House of Parliament.

(3)   The Secretary of State must not give or revise the guidance before the end of the period of 40 days beginning with the day on which the draft is laid before each House of Parliament (or, if copies are laid before each House of Parliament on different days, the later of those days).

(4)   The Secretary of State must not proceed with the proposed guidance or alterations if, within the period of 40 days mentioned in subsection (3), either House resolves that the guidance or alterations be withdrawn.

(5)   Subsection (4) is without prejudice to the possibility of laying a further draft of the guidance or alterations before each House of Parliament.

(6)   In calculating the period of 40 days mentioned in subsection (3), no account is to be taken of any time during which Parliament is dissolved or prorogued or during which both Houses are adjourned for more than four days.

[1484]

**NOTES**
Commencement: 2 January 2007 (in relation to England); 13 December 2007 (in relation to Wales).

**227, 228**   (*S 227 repeals the Local Government and Housing Act 1989, s 167; s 228 inserts the Housing Act 1996, ss 51(6), 51A–51C, introduces Sch 12 to this Act and amends the Local Government Act 1974, Sch 4.*)

## PART 7
### SUPPLEMENTARY AND FINAL PROVISIONS
*Residential property tribunals*

## 229   Residential property tribunals

(1)   Any jurisdiction conferred on a residential property tribunal by or under any enactment is exercisable by a rent assessment committee constituted in accordance with Schedule 10 to the Rent Act 1977 (c 42).

(2)   When so constituted for exercising any such jurisdiction a rent assessment committee is known as a residential property tribunal.

(3)   The appropriate national authority may by order make provision for and in connection with conferring on residential property tribunals, in relation to such matters as are specified in the order, such jurisdiction as is so specified.

(4)   An order under subsection (3) may modify an enactment (including this Act).

(5)   In this section "enactment" includes an enactment comprised in subordinate legislation (within the meaning of the Interpretation Act 1978 (c 30)).

[1485]

**NOTES**
Commencement: 18 November 2004 (for the purpose of making orders or regulations); 4 July 2005 (in relation to England for remaining purposes, subject to transitional provisions as noted to s 181 at [1470]); 16 June 2006 (in relation to Wales for remaining purposes, subject to transitional provisions and savings in the Housing Act 2004 (Commencement No 3 and Transitional Provisions and Savings) (Wales) Order 2006, SI 2006/1535, art 3, Schedule at [3714], [3715]).

## 230   Powers and procedure of residential property tribunals

(1)   A residential property tribunal exercising any jurisdiction by virtue of any enactment has, in addition to any specific powers exercisable by it in exercising that jurisdiction, the general power mentioned in subsection (2).

(2)   The tribunal's general power is a power by order to give such directions as the tribunal considers necessary or desirable for securing the just, expeditious and economical disposal of the proceedings or any issue raised in or in connection with them.

(3)   In deciding whether to give directions under its general power a tribunal must have regard to—

(a)   the matters falling to be determined in the proceedings,

(b)   any other circumstances appearing to the tribunal to be relevant, and

(c)   the provisions of the enactment by virtue of which it is exercising jurisdiction and of any other enactment appearing to it to be relevant.

(4)   A tribunal may give directions under its general power whether or not they were originally sought by a party to the proceedings.

(5)   When exercising jurisdiction under this Act, the directions which may be given by a tribunal under its general power include (where appropriate)—

(a)   directions requiring a licence to be granted under Part 2 or 3 of this Act;

(b)   directions requiring any licence so granted to contain such terms as are specified in the directions;

(c)   directions requiring any order made under Part 4 of this Act to contain such terms as are so specified;

(d)   directions that any building or part of a building so specified is to be treated as if an HMO declaration had been served in respect of it on such date as is so specified (without there being any right to appeal against it under section 255(9));

(e)   directions requiring the payment of money by one party to the proceedings to another by way of compensation, damages or otherwise.

(6) Nothing in any enactment conferring specific powers on a residential property tribunal is to be regarded as affecting the operation of the preceding provisions of this section.

(7) Schedule 13 (residential property tribunals: procedure) has effect.

(8) Section 229(5) applies also for the purposes of this section and Schedule 13.

**[1486]**

**NOTES**

Commencement: 18 November 2004 (sub-s (7), for the purpose of making orders or regulations); 4 July 2005 (sub-ss (1)–(6), (8), sub-s (7) for remaining purposes, in relation to England, subject to transitional provisions as noted to s 181 at **[1470]**); 16 June 2006 (sub-ss (1)–(6), (8), sub-s (7) for remaining purposes, in relation to Wales, subject to transitional provisions and savings in the Housing Act 2004 (Commencement No 3 and Transitional Provisions and Savings) (Wales) Order 2006, SI 2006/1535, art 3, Schedule at **[3714]**, **[3715]**).

### 231 Appeals from residential property tribunals

(1) A party to proceedings before a residential property tribunal may appeal to the [Upper Tribunal] from a decision of the residential property tribunal.

[(2) But the appeal may only be made with the permission of the residential property tribunal or the Upper Tribunal.]

(3) On the appeal—
(a) the [Upper Tribunal] may exercise any power which was available to the residential property tribunal, and
(b) a decision of the [Upper Tribunal] may be enforced in the same way as a decision of the residential property tribunal.

(4) Section 11(1) of the Tribunals and Inquiries Act 1992 (c 53) (appeals from certain tribunals to High Court) does not apply to any decision of a residential property tribunal.

(5) …

**[1487]**

**NOTES**

Commencement: 4 July 2005 (in relation to England, subject to transitional provisions as noted to s 181 at **[1470]**); 16 June 2006 (in relation to Wales, subject to transitional provisions and savings in the Housing Act 2004 (Commencement No 3 and Transitional Provisions and Savings) (Wales) Order 2006, SI 2006/1535, art 3, Schedule at **[3714]**, **[3715]**).

Sub-ss (1), (3): words in square brackets substituted by the Transfer of Tribunal Functions (Lands Tribunal and Miscellaneous Amendments) Order 2009, SI 2009/1307, art 5(1), (2), Sch 1, paras 271, 276(a), subject to transitional and savings provisions in Sch 5 thereto.

Sub-s (2): substituted by SI 2009/1307, art 5(1), (2), Sch 1, paras 271, 276(b), subject to transitional and savings provisions in Sch 5 thereto.

Sub-s (5): repealed by SI 2009/1307, art 5(1), (2), Sch 1, paras 271, 276(c), subject to transitional and savings provisions in Sch 5 thereto.

*Register of licences and management orders*

### 232 Register of licences and management orders

(1) Every local housing authority must establish and maintain a register of—
(a) all licences granted by them under Part 2 or 3 which are in force;
(b) all temporary exemption notices served by them under section 62 or section 86 which are in force; and
(c) all management orders made by them under Chapter 1 or 2 of Part 4 which are in force.

(2) The register may, subject to any requirements that may be prescribed, be in such form as the authority consider appropriate.

(3) Each entry in the register is to contain such particulars as may be prescribed.

(4) The authority must ensure that the contents of the register are available at the authority's head office for inspection by members of the public at all reasonable times.

(5) If requested by a person to do so and subject to payment of such reasonable fee (if any) as the authority may determine, a local housing authority must supply the person with a copy (certified to be true) of the register or of an extract from it.

(6) A copy so certified is prima facie evidence of the matters mentioned in it.

(7) In this section "prescribed" means prescribed by regulations made by the appropriate national authority.

**[1488]**

**NOTES**

Commencement: 18 November 2004 (for the purpose of making orders or regulations); 6 April 2006 (in relation to England for remaining purposes, subject to transitional provisions and savings in the Housing Act 2004 (Commencement No 5 and Transitional Provisions and Savings) (England) Order 2006, SI 2006/1060, art 3, Schedule at **[3700]**, **[3701]**); 16 June 2006 (in relation to Wales for remaining purposes, subject to transitional provisions and savings in the Housing Act 2004 (Commencement No 3 and Transitional Provisions and Savings) (Wales) Order 2006, SI 2006/1535, art 3, Schedule at **[3714]**, **[3715]**).

Regulations: the Licensing and Management of Houses in Multiple Occupation and Other Houses (Miscellaneous Provisions) (England) Regulations 2006, SI 2006/373 at **[3623]**; the Licensing and Management of Houses in Multiple Occupation and Other Houses (Miscellaneous Provisions) (Wales) Regulations 2006, SI 2006/1715 at **[3724]**; the Licensing and Management of Houses in Multiple Occupation (Additional Provisions) (England) Regulations 2007, SI 2007/1903 at **[3765]**; the Licensing and Management of Houses in Multiple Occupation (Additional Provisions) (Wales) Regulations 2007, SI 2007/3229 at **[3779]**.

*Codes of practice and management regulations relating to HMOs etc*

### 233 Approval of codes of practice with regard to the management of HMOs etc

(1)   The appropriate national authority may by order—

    (a)   approve a code of practice (whether prepared by that authority or another person) laying down standards of conduct and practice to be followed with regard to the management of houses in multiple occupation or of excepted accommodation;

    (b)   approve a modification of such a code; or

    (c)   withdraw the authority's approval of such a code or modification.

(2)   Before approving a code of practice or a modification of a code of practice under this section the appropriate national authority must take reasonable steps to consult—

    (a)   persons involved in the management of houses in multiple occupation or (as the case may be) excepted accommodation of the kind in question and persons occupying such houses or accommodation, or

    (b)   persons whom the authority considers to represent the interests of those persons.

(3)   The appropriate national authority may only approve a code of practice or a modification of a code if satisfied that—

    (a)   the code or modification has been published (whether by the authority or by another person) in a manner that the authority considers appropriate for the purpose of bringing the code or modification to the attention of those likely to be affected by it; or

    (b)   arrangements have been made for the code or modification to be so published.

(4)   The appropriate national authority may approve a code of practice which makes different provision in relation to different cases or descriptions of case (including different provision for different areas).

(5)   A failure to comply with a code of practice for the time being approved under this section does not of itself make a person liable to any civil or criminal proceedings.

(6)   In this section "excepted accommodation" means such description of living accommodation falling within any provision of Schedule 14 (buildings which are not HMOs for purposes of provisions other than Part 1) as is specified in an order under subsection (1).

**[1489]**

**NOTES**

Orders: the Housing (Approval of Codes of Management Practice) (Student Accommodation) (England) Order 2006, SI 2006/646, approving the following codes of practice for the purposes of this section: the Universities UK/Standing Conference Of Principals Code of Practice for the Management of Student Housing dated 20 February 2006, the Accreditation Network UK/Unipol Code of Standards for Larger Developments for Student Accommodation Managed and Controlled by Educational Establishments dated 20 February 2006, and the Accreditation Network UK/Unipol Code of Standards for Larger Developments for Student Accommodation Not Managed and Controlled by Educational Establishments dated 20 February 2006. The equivalent provisions for Wales are in the Housing (Approval of Codes of Management Practice) (Student Accommodation) (Wales) Order 2006, SI 2006/1709. See also the Housing (Approval of a Code of Management Practice) (Student Accommodation) (England) Order 2008, SI 2008/2345 at **[3789]**.

### 234 Management regulations in respect of HMOs

(1)   The appropriate national authority may by regulations make provision for the purpose of ensuring that, in respect of every house in multiple occupation of a description specified in the regulations—

    (a)   there are in place satisfactory management arrangements; and

    (b)   satisfactory standards of management are observed.

(2)   The regulations may, in particular—

    (a)   impose duties on the person managing a house in respect of the repair, maintenance, cleanliness and good order of the house and facilities and equipment in it;

    (b)   impose duties on persons occupying a house for the purpose of ensuring that the person managing the house can effectively carry out any duty imposed on him by the regulations.

(3)   A person commits an offence if he fails to comply with a regulation under this section.

(4) In proceedings against a person for an offence under subsection (3) it is a defence that he had a reasonable excuse for not complying with the regulation.

(5) A person who commits an offence under subsection (3) is liable on summary conviction to a fine not exceeding level 5 on the standard scale.

**[1490]**

**NOTES**

Regulations: the Management of Houses in Multiple Occupation (England) Regulations 2006, SI 2006/372 at **[3612]**; the Management of Houses in Multiple Occupation (Wales) Regulations 2006, SI 2006/1713 at **[3723]**; the Licensing and Management of Houses in Multiple Occupation (Additional Provisions) (England) Regulations 2007, SI 2007/1903 at **[3765]**; the Licensing and Management of Houses in Multiple Occupation (Additional Provisions) (Wales) Regulations 2007, SI 2007/3229 at **[3779]**; the Houses in Multiple Occupation (Management) (England) Regulations 2009, SI 2009/724; the Houses in Multiple Occupation (Management) (Wales) Regulations 2009, SI 2009/1915.

*Information provisions*

### 235 Power to require documents to be produced

(1) A person authorised in writing by a local housing authority may exercise the power conferred by subsection (2) in relation to documents reasonably required by the authority—

    (a) for any purpose connected with the exercise of any of the authority's functions under any of Parts 1 to 4 in relation to any premises, or

    (b) for the purpose of investigating whether any offence has been committed under any of those Parts in relation to any premises.

(2) A person so authorised may give a notice to a relevant person requiring him—

    (a) to produce any documents which—

        (i) are specified or described in the notice, or fall within a category of document which is specified or described in the notice, and

        (ii) are in his custody or under his control, and

    (b) to produce them at a time and place so specified and to a person so specified.

(3) The notice must include information about the possible consequences of not complying with the notice.

(4) The person to whom any document is produced in accordance with the notice may copy the document.

(5) No person may be required under this section to produce any document which he would be entitled to refuse to provide in proceedings in the High Court on grounds of legal professional privilege.

(6) In this section "document" includes information recorded otherwise than in legible form, and in relation to information so recorded, any reference to the production of a document is a reference to the production of a copy of the information in legible form.

(7) In this section "relevant person" means, in relation to any premises, a person within any of the following paragraphs—

    (a) a person who is, or is proposed to be, the holder of a licence under Part 2 or 3 in respect of the premises, or a person on whom any obligation or restriction under such a licence is, or is proposed to be, imposed,

    (b) a person who has an estate or interest in the premises,

    (c) a person who is, or is proposing to be, managing or having control of the premises,

    (d) a person who is, or is proposing to be, otherwise involved in the management of the premises,

    (e) a person who occupies the premises.

**[1491]**

**NOTES**

Commencement: 6 April 2006 (in relation to England, subject to transitional provisions and savings in the Housing Act 2004 (Commencement No 5 and Transitional Provisions and Savings) (England) Order 2006, SI 2006/1060, art 3, Schedule at **[3700]**, **[3701]**); 16 June 2006 (in relation to Wales, subject to transitional provisions and savings in the Housing Act 2004 (Commencement No 3 and Transitional Provisions and Savings) (Wales) Order 2006, SI 2006/1535, art 3, Schedule at **[3714]**, **[3715]**).

### 236 Enforcement of powers to obtain information

(1) A person commits an offence if he fails to do anything required of him by a notice under section 235.

(2) In proceedings against a person for an offence under subsection (1) it is a defence that he had a reasonable excuse for failing to comply with the notice.

(3) A person who commits an offence under subsection (1) is liable on summary conviction to a fine not exceeding level 5 on the standard scale.

(4)  A person commits an offence if he intentionally alters, suppresses or destroys any document which he has been required to produce by a notice under section 235.

(5)  A person who commits an offence under subsection (4) is liable—
(a)  on summary conviction, to a fine not exceeding the statutory maximum;
(b)  on conviction on indictment, to a fine.

(6)  In this section "document" includes information recorded otherwise than in legible form, and in relation to information so recorded—
(a)  the reference to the production of a document is a reference to the production of a copy of the information in legible form, and
(b)  the reference to suppressing a document includes a reference to destroying the means of reproducing the information.

**[1492]**

**NOTES**
Commencement: 6 April 2006 (in relation to England, subject to transitional provisions and savings in the Housing Act 2004 (Commencement No 5 and Transitional Provisions and Savings) (England) Order 2006, SI 2006/1060, art 3, Schedule at **[3700]**, **[3701]**); 16 June 2006 (in relation to Wales, subject to transitional provisions and savings in the Housing Act 2004 (Commencement No 3 and Transitional Provisions and Savings) (Wales) Order 2006, SI 2006/1535, art 3, Schedule at **[3714]**, **[3715]**).

**237  Use of information obtained for certain other statutory purposes**

(1)  A local housing authority may use any information to which this section applies—
(a)  for any purpose connected with the exercise of any of the authority's functions under any of Parts 1 to 4 in relation to any premises, or
(b)  for the purpose of investigating whether any offence has been committed under any of those Parts in relation to any premises.

(2)  This section applies to any information which has been obtained by the authority in the exercise of functions under—
(a)  section 134 of the Social Security Administration Act 1992 (c 5) (housing benefit), or
(b)  Part 1 of the Local Government Finance Act 1992 (c 14) (council tax).

**[1493]**

**NOTES**
Commencement: 15 June 2005 (in relation to England); 25 November 2005 (in relation to Wales).

**238  False or misleading information**

(1)  A person commits an offence if—
(a)  he supplies any information to a local housing authority in connection with any of their functions under any of Parts 1 to 4 or this Part,
(b)  the information is false or misleading, and
(c)  he knows that it is false or misleading or is reckless as to whether it is false or misleading.

(2)  A person commits an offence if—
(a)  he supplies any information to another person which is false or misleading,
(b)  he knows that it is false or misleading or is reckless as to whether it is false or misleading, and
(c)  he knows that the information is to be used for the purpose of supplying information to a local housing authority in connection with any of their functions under any of Parts 1 to 4 or this Part.

(3)  A person who commits an offence under subsection (1) or (2) is liable on summary conviction to a fine not exceeding level 5 on the standard scale.

(4)  In this section "false or misleading" means false or misleading in any material respect.

**[1494]**

**NOTES**
Commencement: 6 April 2006 (in relation to England, subject to transitional provisions and savings in the Housing Act 2004 (Commencement No 5 and Transitional Provisions and Savings) (England) Order 2006, SI 2006/1060, art 3, Schedule at **[3700]**, **[3701]**); 16 June 2006 (in relation to Wales, subject to transitional provisions and savings in the Housing Act 2004 (Commencement No 3 and Transitional Provisions and Savings) (Wales) Order 2006, SI 2006/1535, art 3, Schedule at **[3714]**, **[3715]**).

*Enforcement*

**239  Powers of entry**

(1)  Subsection (3) applies where the local housing authority consider that a survey or examination of any premises is necessary and any of the following conditions is met—

(a)      the authority consider that the survey or examination is necessary in order to carry out an inspection under section 4(1) or otherwise to determine whether any functions under any of Parts 1 to 4 or this Part should be exercised in relation to the premises;

(b)      the premises are (within the meaning of Part 1) specified premises in relation to an improvement notice or prohibition order;

(c)      a management order is in force under Chapter 1 or 2 of Part 4 in respect of the premises.

(2)    Subsection (3) also applies where the proper officer of the local housing authority considers that a survey or examination of any premises is necessary in order to carry out an inspection under section 4(2).

(3)    Where this subsection applies—

(a)      a person authorised by the local housing authority (in a case within subsection (1)), or

(b)      the proper officer (in a case within subsection (2)),

may enter the premises in question at any reasonable time for the purpose of carrying out a survey or examination of the premises.

(4)    If—

(a)      an interim or final management order is in force under Chapter 1 of Part 4 in respect of any premises consisting of part of a house ("the relevant premises"), and

(b)      another part of the house is excluded from the order by virtue of section 102(8) or 113(7),

the power of entry conferred by subsection (3) is exercisable in relation to any premises comprised in that other part so far as is necessary for the purpose of carrying out a survey or examination of the relevant premises.

(5)    Before entering any premises in exercise of the power conferred by subsection (3), the authorised person or proper officer must have given at least 24 hours' notice of his intention to do so—

(a)      to the owner of the premises (if known), and

(b)      to the occupier (if any).

(6)    Subsection (7) applies where the local housing authority consider that any premises need to be entered for the purpose of ascertaining whether an offence has been committed under section 72, 95 or 234(3).

(7)    A person authorised by the local housing authority may enter the premises for that purpose—

(a)      at any reasonable time, but

(b)      without giving any prior notice as mentioned in subsection (5).

(8)    A person exercising the power of entry conferred by subsection (3) or (7) may do such of the following as he thinks necessary for the purpose for which the power is being exercised—

(a)      take other persons with him;

(b)      take equipment or materials with him;

(c)      take measurements or photographs or make recordings;

(d)      leave recording equipment on the premises for later collection;

(e)      take samples of any articles or substances found on the premises.

(9)    An authorisation for the purposes of this section—

(a)      must be in writing; and

(b)      must state the particular purpose or purposes for which the entry is authorised.

(10)    A person authorised for the purposes of this section must, if required to do so, produce his authorisation for inspection by the owner or any occupier of the premises or anyone acting on his behalf.

(11)    If the premises are unoccupied or the occupier is temporarily absent, a person exercising the power of entry conferred by subsection (3) or (7) must leave the premises as effectively secured against trespassers as he found them.

(12)    In this section "occupier", in relation to premises, means a person who occupies the premises, whether for residential or other purposes.

**[1495]**

**NOTES**

Commencement: 6 April 2006 (in relation to England, subject to transitional provisions and savings in the Housing Act 2004 (Commencement No 5 and Transitional Provisions and Savings) (England) Order 2006, SI 2006/1060, art 3, Schedule at **[3700]**, **[3701]**); 16 June 2006 (in relation to Wales, subject to transitional provisions and savings in the Housing Act 2004 (Commencement No 3 and Transitional Provisions and Savings) (Wales) Order 2006, SI 2006/1535, art 3, Schedule at **[3714]**, **[3715]**).

## 240 Warrant to authorise entry

(1)   This section applies where a justice of the peace is satisfied, on a sworn information in writing, that admission to premises specified in the information is reasonably required for any of the purposes mentioned in subsection (2) by a person—

(a)   employed by, or

(b)   acting on the instructions of,

the local housing authority.

(2)   The purposes are—

(a)   surveying or examining premises in order to carry out an inspection under section 4(1) or (2) or otherwise to determine whether any functions under any of Parts 1 to 4 or this Part should be exercised in relation to the premises;

(b)   surveying or examining premises—

(i)   which are (within the meaning of Part 1) specified premises in relation to an improvement notice or prohibition order, or

(ii)   in respect of which a management order is in force under Chapter 1 or 2 of Part 4;

(c)   ascertaining whether an offence has been committed under section 72, 95 or 234(3).

(3)   The justice may by warrant under his hand authorise the person mentioned in subsection (1) to enter on the premises for such of those purposes as may be specified in the warrant.

(4)   But the justice must not grant the warrant unless he is satisfied—

(a)   that admission to the premises has been sought in accordance with section 239(5) or (7) but has been refused;

(b)   that the premises are unoccupied or that the occupier is temporarily absent and it might defeat the purpose of the entry to await his return; or

(c)   that application for admission would defeat the purpose of the entry.

(5)   The power of entry conferred by a warrant under this section includes power to enter by force (if necessary).

(6)   Subsection (8) of section 239 applies to the person on whom that power is conferred as it applies to a person exercising the power of entry conferred by subsection (3) or (7) of that section.

(7)   A warrant under this section must, if so required, be produced for inspection by the owner or any occupier of the premises or anyone acting on his behalf.

(8)   If the premises are unoccupied or the occupier is temporarily absent, a person entering under the authority of a warrant under this section must leave the premises as effectively secured against trespassers as he found them.

(9)   A warrant under this section continues in force until the purpose for which the entry is required is satisfied.

(10)   In a case within section 239(4)(a) and (b), the powers conferred by this section are exercisable in relation to premises comprised in the excluded part of the house as well as in relation to the relevant premises.

(11)   In this section "occupier", in relation to premises, means a person who occupies the premises, whether for residential or other purposes.

**[1496]**

**NOTES**

Commencement: 6 April 2006 (in relation to England, subject to transitional provisions and savings in the Housing Act 2004 (Commencement No 5 and Transitional Provisions and Savings) (England) Order 2006, SI 2006/1060, art 3, Schedule at **[3700]**, **[3701]**); 16 June 2006 (in relation to Wales, subject to transitional provisions and savings in the Housing Act 2004 (Commencement No 3 and Transitional Provisions and Savings) (Wales) Order 2006, SI 2006/1535, art 3, Schedule at **[3714]**, **[3715]**).

## 241 Penalty for obstruction

(1)   A person who obstructs a relevant person in the performance of anything which, by virtue of any of Parts 1 to 4 or this Part, that person is required or authorised to do commits an offence.

(2)   In proceedings against a person for an offence under subsection (1) it is a defence that he had a reasonable excuse for obstructing the relevant person.

(3)   A person who commits an offence under subsection (1) is liable on summary conviction to a fine not exceeding level 4 on the standard scale.

(4)   In this section "relevant person" means an officer of a local housing authority or any person authorised to enter premises by virtue of any of Parts 1 to 4 or section 239 or 240.

**[1497]**

**NOTES**

Commencement: 6 April 2006 (in relation to England, subject to transitional provisions and savings in the Housing Act 2004 (Commencement No 5 and Transitional Provisions and Savings) (England) Order 2006,

SI 2006/1060, art 3, Schedule at **[3700]**, **[3701]**); 16 June 2006 (in relation to Wales, subject to transitional provisions and savings in the Housing Act 2004 (Commencement No 3 and Transitional Provisions and Savings) (Wales) Order 2006, SI 2006/1535, art 3, Schedule at **[3714]**, **[3715]**).

### 242   Additional notice requirements for protection of owners

(1)   This section applies where an owner of premises gives a notice to the local housing authority for the purposes of this section informing them of his interest in the premises.

(2)   The authority must give him notice of any action taken by them under any of Parts 1 to 4 or this Part in relation to the premises.

**[1498]**

**NOTES**

Commencement: 6 April 2006 (in relation to England, subject to transitional provisions and savings in the Housing Act 2004 (Commencement No 5 and Transitional Provisions and Savings) (England) Order 2006, SI 2006/1060, art 3, Schedule at **[3700]**, **[3701]**); 16 June 2006 (in relation to Wales, subject to transitional provisions and savings in the Housing Act 2004 (Commencement No 3 and Transitional Provisions and Savings) (Wales) Order 2006, SI 2006/1535, art 3, Schedule at **[3714]**, **[3715]**).

*Authorisations*

### 243   Authorisations for enforcement purposes etc

(1)   This section applies to any authorisation given for the purposes of any of the following provisions—

    (a)   section 131 (management orders: power of entry to carry out work),

    (b)   section 235 (power to require documents to be produced),

    (c)   section 239 (powers of entry),

    (d)   paragraph 3(4) of Schedule 3 (improvement notices: power to enter to carry out work), and

    (e)   paragraph 25 of Schedule 7 (EDMOs: power of entry to carry out work).

(2)   Any such authorisation must be given by the appropriate officer of the local housing authority.

(3)   For the purposes of this section a person is an "appropriate officer" of a local housing authority, in relation to an authorisation given by the authority, if either—

    (a)   he is a deputy chief officer of the authority (within the meaning of section 2 of the Local Government and Housing Act 1989 (c 42)), and

    (b)   the duties of his post consist of or include duties relating to the exercise of the functions of the authority in connection with which the authorisation is given,

or he is an officer of the authority to whom such a deputy chief officer reports directly, or is directly accountable, as respects duties so relating.

**[1499]**

**NOTES**

Commencement: 6 April 2006 (in relation to England, subject to transitional provisions and savings in the Housing Act 2004 (Commencement No 5 and Transitional Provisions and Savings) (England) Order 2006, SI 2006/1060, art 3, Schedule at **[3700]**, **[3701]**); 16 June 2006 (in relation to Wales, subject to transitional provisions and savings in the Housing Act 2004 (Commencement No 3 and Transitional Provisions and Savings) (Wales) Order 2006, SI 2006/1535, art 3, Schedule at **[3714]**, **[3715]**).

*Documents*

### 244   Power to prescribe forms

(1)   The appropriate national authority may by regulations prescribe the form of any notice, statement or other document which is required or authorised to be used under, or for the purposes of, this Act.

(2)   The power conferred by this section is not exercisable where specific provision for prescribing the form of a document is made elsewhere in this Act.

**[1500]**

### 245   Power to dispense with notices

(1)   The appropriate national authority may dispense with the service of a notice which is required to be served by a local housing authority under this Act if satisfied that it is reasonable to do so.

(2)   A dispensation may be given either before or after the time at which the notice is required to be served.

(3)   A dispensation may be given either unconditionally or on such conditions (whether as to the service of other notices or otherwise) as the appropriate national authority considers appropriate.

(4)   Before giving a dispensation under this section, the appropriate national authority shall, in particular, have regard to the need to ensure, so far as possible, that the interests of any person are not prejudiced by the dispensation.

[1501]

**NOTES**
 Commencement: 18 January 2005.

### 246   Service of documents

(1)   Subsection (2) applies where the local housing authority is, by virtue of any provision of Parts 1 to 4 or this Part, under a duty to serve a document on a person who, to the knowledge of the authority, is—
  (a)   a person having control of premises,
  (b)   a person managing premises, or
  (c)   a person having an estate or interest in premises,
or a person who (but for an interim or final management order under Chapter 1 of Part 4) would fall within paragraph (a) or (b).

(2)   The local housing authority must take reasonable steps to identify the person or persons falling within the description in that provision.

(3)   A person having an estate or interest in premises may for the purposes of any provision to which subsections (1) and (2) apply give notice to the local housing authority of his interest in the premises.

(4)   The local housing authority must enter a notice under subsection (3) in its records.

(5)   A document required or authorised by any of Parts 1 to 4 or this Part to be served on a person as—
  (a)   a person having control of premises,
  (b)   a person managing premises,
  (c)   a person having an estate or interest in premises, or
  (d)   a person who (but for an interim or final management order under Chapter 1 of Part 4) would fall within paragraph (a) or (b),
may, if it is not practicable after reasonable enquiry to ascertain the name or address of that person, be served in accordance with subsection (6).

(6)   A person having such a connection with any premises as is mentioned in subsection (5)(a) to (d) is served in accordance with this subsection if—
  (a)   the document is addressed to him by describing his connection with the premises (naming them), and
  (b)   delivering the document to some person on the premises or, if there is no person on the premises to whom it can be delivered, by fixing it, or a copy of it, to some conspicuous part of the premises.

(7)   Subsection (1)(c) or (5)(c) applies whether the provision requiring or authorising service of the document refers in terms to a person having an estate or interest in premises or instead refers to a class of person having such an estate or interest (such as owners, lessees or mortgagees).

(8)   Where under any provision of Parts 1 to 4 or this Part a document is to be served on—
  (a)   the person having control of premises,
  (b)   the person managing premises, or
  (c)   the owner of premises,
and more than one person comes within the description in the provision, the document may be served on more than one of those persons.

(9)   Section 233 of the Local Government Act 1972 (c 70) (service of notices by local authorities) applies in relation to the service of documents for any purposes of this Act by the authorities mentioned in section 261(2)(d) and (e) of this Act as if they were local authorities within the meaning of section 233.

(10)   In this section—
  (a)   references to a person managing premises include references to a person authorised to permit persons to occupy premises; and
  (b)   references to serving include references to similar expressions (such as giving or sending).

(11)   *In this section—*
 "document" includes anything in writing;
 "premises" means premises however defined.

[1502]

PART I
STATUTES

**NOTES**

Commencement: 18 January 2005.

### 247 Licences and other documents in electronic form

(1) A local housing authority may, subject to subsection (3), issue a licence to a person under Part 2 or 3 by transmitting the text of the licence to him by electronic means, provided the text—

    (a)    is received by him in legible form, and

    (b)    is capable of being used for subsequent reference.

(2) A local housing authority may, subject to subsection (3), serve a relevant document on a person by transmitting the text of the document to him in the way mentioned in subsection (1).

(3) The recipient, or the person on whose behalf the recipient receives the document, must have indicated to the local housing authority the recipient's willingness to receive documents transmitted in the form and manner used.

(4) An indication for the purposes of subsection (3)—

    (a)    must be given to the local housing authority in such manner as they may require;

    (b)    may be a general indication or one that is limited to documents of a particular description;

    (c)    must state the address to be used and must be accompanied by such other information as the local housing authority require for the making of the transmission; and

    (d)    may be modified or withdrawn at any time by a notice given to the local housing authority in such manner as they may require.

(5) In this section any reference to serving includes a reference to similar expressions (such as giving or sending).

(6) In this section—

"document" includes anything in writing; and

"relevant document" means any document which a local housing authority are, by virtue of any provision of Parts 1 to 4 or this Part, under a duty to serve on any person.

**[1503]**

**NOTES**

Commencement: 18 January 2005.

### 248 Timing and location of things done electronically

(1) The Secretary of State may by regulations make provision specifying, for the purposes of any of Parts 1 to 4 or this Part, the manner of determining—

    (a)    the times at which things done under any of Parts 1 to 4 or this Part by means of electronic communications networks are done;

    (b)    the places at which things done under any of Parts 1 to 4 or this Part by means of such networks are done; and

    (c)    the places at which things transmitted by means of such networks are received.

(2) The Secretary of State may by regulations make provision about the manner of proving in any legal proceedings—

    (a)    that something done by means of an electronic communications network satisfies any requirements of any of Parts 1 to 4 or this Part for the doing of that thing; and

    (b)    the matters mentioned in subsection (1)(a) to (c).

(3) Regulations under this section may provide for such presumptions to apply (whether conclusive or not) as the Secretary of State considers appropriate.

(4) In this section "electronic communications network" has the meaning given by section 32 of the Communications Act 2003 (c 21).

**[1504]**

### 249 Proof of designations

(1) This subsection applies in respect of a copy of—

    (a)    a designation under section 56 (designation of an area as subject to additional licensing), or

    (b)    a designation under section 80 (designation of an area as subject to selective licensing),

which purports to be made by a local housing authority.

(2) A certificate endorsed on such a copy and purporting to be signed by the proper officer of the authority stating the matters set out in subsection (3) is prima facie evidence of the facts so stated without proof of the handwriting or official position of the person by whom it purports to be signed.

(3) Those matters are—

(a)    that the designation was made by the authority,

(b)    that the copy is a true copy of the designation, and

(c)    that the designation did not require confirmation by the confirming authority, or that on a specified date the designation was confirmed by the confirming authority.

**[1505]**

**NOTES**
Commencement: 18 January 2005.

*Other supplementary provisions*

## 250   Orders and regulations

(1)    Any power of the Secretary of State or the National Assembly for Wales to make an order or regulations under this Act is exercisable by statutory instrument.

(2)    Any power of the Secretary of State or the National Assembly for Wales to make an order or regulations under this Act—

(a)    may be exercised so as to make different provision for different cases or descriptions of case or different purposes or areas; and

(b)    includes power to make such incidental, supplementary, consequential, transitory, transitional or saving provision as the Secretary of State or (as the case may be) the National Assembly for Wales considers appropriate.

(3)    The Secretary of State must consult the National Assembly for Wales before making any regulations under Part 5 which relate to residential properties in Wales.

(4)    Subject to subsections (5) and (6), any order or regulations made by the Secretary of State under this Act are to be subject to annulment in pursuance of a resolution of either House of Parliament.

(5)    Subsection (4) does not apply to any order under section 270 or paragraph 3 of Schedule 10.

(6)    Subsection (4) also does not apply to—

(a)    any order under section 55(3) which makes the provision authorised by section 55(4),

(b)    any order under section 80(5) or (7),

(c)    any order under section 216 or 229(3),

(d)    any order under section 265(2) which modifies any provision of an Act,

(e)    any regulations under section 254(6),

(f)    any regulations under paragraph 3 of Schedule 4 or orders under paragraph 11 of Schedule 10, or

(g)    any regulations made by virtue of paragraph 11(3)(b) or 12(3)(b) of Schedule 13;

and no such order or regulations may be made by the Secretary of State (whether alone or with other provisions) unless a draft of the statutory instrument containing the order or regulations has been laid before, and approved by a resolution of, each House of Parliament.

(7)    In this Act "modify", in the context of a power to modify an enactment by order or regulations, includes repeal (and "modifications" has a corresponding meaning).

**[1506]**

## 251   Offences by bodies corporate

(1)    Where an offence under this Act committed by a body corporate is proved to have been committed with the consent or connivance of, or to be attributable to any neglect on the part of—

(a)    a director, manager, secretary or other similar officer of the body corporate, or

(b)    a person purporting to act in such a capacity,

he as well as the body corporate commits the offence and is liable to be proceeded against and punished accordingly.

(2)    Where the affairs of a body corporate are managed by its members, subsection (1) applies in relation to the acts and defaults of a member in connection with his functions of management as if he were a director of the body corporate.

**[1507]**

**NOTES**
Commencement: 18 January 2005.

## 252   Power to up-rate level of fines for certain offences

(1)    Subsection (2) applies if the Secretary of State considers that there has been a change in the value of money since the relevant date.

(2)    The Secretary of State may by order substitute for the sum or sums for the time being specified in any provision mentioned in subsection (3) such other sum or sums as he considers to be justified by the change.

(3)   The provisions are—
- (a)   section 32(2)(b);
- (b)   section 35(6);
- (c)   section 72(6); and
- (d)   section 95(5).

(4)   In subsection (1) "the relevant date" means—
- (a)   the date of the passing of this Act; or
- (b)   where the sums specified in a provision mentioned in subsection (3) have been substituted by an order under subsection (2), the date of that order.

(5)   Nothing in an order under subsection (2) affects the punishment for an offence committed before the order comes into force.

**[1508]**

### 253   Local inquiries

The appropriate national authority may, for the purposes of the execution of any of the authority's functions under this Act, cause such local inquiries to be held as the authority considers appropriate.

**[1509]**

**NOTES**
Commencement: 18 January 2005.

*Meaning of "house in multiple occupation"*

### 254   Meaning of "house in multiple occupation"

(1)   For the purposes of this Act a building or a part of a building is a "house in multiple occupation" if—
- (a)   it meets the conditions in subsection (2) ("the standard test");
- (b)   it meets the conditions in subsection (3) ("the self-contained flat test");
- (c)   it meets the conditions in subsection (4) ("the converted building test");
- (d)   an HMO declaration is in force in respect of it under section 255; or
- (e)   it is a converted block of flats to which section 257 applies.

(2)   A building or a part of a building meets the standard test if—
- (a)   it consists of one or more units of living accommodation not consisting of a self-contained flat or flats;
- (b)   the living accommodation is occupied by persons who do not form a single household (see section 258);
- (c)   the living accommodation is occupied by those persons as their only or main residence or they are to be treated as so occupying it (see section 259);
- (d)   their occupation of the living accommodation constitutes the only use of that accommodation;
- (e)   rents are payable or other consideration is to be provided in respect of at least one of those persons' occupation of the living accommodation; and
- (f)   two or more of the households who occupy the living accommodation share one or more basic amenities or the living accommodation is lacking in one or more basic amenities.

(3)   A part of a building meets the self-contained flat test if—
- (a)   it consists of a self-contained flat; and
- (b)   paragraphs (b) to (f) of subsection (2) apply (reading references to the living accommodation concerned as references to the flat).

(4)   A building or a part of a building meets the converted building test if—
- (a)   it is a converted building;
- (b)   it contains one or more units of living accommodation that do not consist of a self-contained flat or flats (whether or not it also contains any such flat or flats);
- (c)   the living accommodation is occupied by persons who do not form a single household (see section 258);
- (d)   the living accommodation is occupied by those persons as their only or main residence or they are to be treated as so occupying it (see section 259);
- (e)   their occupation of the living accommodation constitutes the only use of that accommodation; and
- (f)   rents are payable or other consideration is to be provided in respect of at least one of those persons' occupation of the living accommodation.

(5)   But for any purposes of this Act (other than those of Part 1) a building or part of a building within subsection (1) is not a house in multiple occupation if it is listed in Schedule 14.

(6)   The appropriate national authority may by regulations—
- (a)   make such amendments of this section and sections 255 to 259 as the authority considers

appropriate with a view to securing that any building or part of a building of a description specified in the regulations is or is not to be a house in multiple occupation for any specified purposes of this Act;

(b) provide for such amendments to have effect also for the purposes of definitions in other enactments that operate by reference to this Act;

(c) make such consequential amendments of any provision of this Act, or any other enactment, as the authority considers appropriate.

(7) Regulations under subsection (6) may frame any description by reference to any matters or circumstances whatever.

(8) In this section—

"basic amenities" means—

    (a) a toilet,

    (b) personal washing facilities, or

    (c) cooking facilities;

"converted building" means a building or part of a building consisting of living accommodation in which one or more units of such accommodation have been created since the building or part was constructed;

"enactment" includes an enactment comprised in subordinate legislation (within the meaning of the Interpretation Act 1978 (c 30);

"self-contained flat" means a separate set of premises (whether or not on the same floor)—

    (a) which forms part of a building;

    (b) either the whole or a material part of which lies above or below some other part of the building; and

    (c) in which all three basic amenities are available for the exclusive use of its occupants.

**[1510]**

**NOTES**

Commencement: 18 November 2004 (sub-s (5), for the purpose of making orders or regulations); 18 January 2005 (otherwise).

## 255 HMO declarations

(1) If a local housing authority are satisfied that subsection (2) applies to a building or part of a building in their area, they may serve a notice under this section (an "HMO declaration") declaring the building or part to be a house in multiple occupation.

(2) This subsection applies to a building or part of a building if the building or part meets any of the following tests (as it applies without the sole use condition)—

(a) the standard test (see section 254(2)),

(b) the self-contained flat test (see section 254(3)), or

(c) the converted building test (see section 254(4)),

and the occupation, by persons who do not form a single household, of the living accommodation or flat referred to in the test in question constitutes a significant use of that accommodation or flat.

(3) In subsection (2) "the sole use condition" means the condition contained in—

(a) section 254(2)(d) (as it applies for the purposes of the standard test or the self-contained flat test), or

(b) section 254(4)(e),

as the case may be.

(4) The notice must—

(a) state the date of the authority's decision to serve the notice,

(b) be served on each relevant person within the period of seven days beginning with the date of that decision,

(c) state the day on which it will come into force if no appeal is made under subsection (9) against the authority's decision, and

(d) set out the right to appeal against the decision under subsection (9) and the period within which an appeal may be made.

(5) The day stated in the notice under subsection (4)(c) must be not less than 28 days after the date of the authority's decision to serve the notice.

(6) If no appeal is made under subsection (9) before the end of that period of 28 days, the *notice comes into force on the day stated in the notice.*

(7) If such an appeal is made before the end of that period of 28 days, the notice does not come into force unless and until a decision is given on the appeal which confirms the notice and either—

(a) the period within which an appeal to the [Upper Tribunal] may be brought expires without such an appeal having been brought, or

(b)    if an appeal to the [Upper Tribunal] is brought, a decision is given on the appeal which confirms the notice.

(8)    For the purposes of subsection (7), the withdrawal of an appeal has the same effect as a decision which confirms the notice appealed against.

(9)    Any relevant person may appeal to a residential property tribunal against a decision of the local housing authority to serve an HMO declaration.

The appeal must be made within the period of 28 days beginning with the date of the authority's decision.

(10)    Such an appeal—
  (a)    is to be by way of a re-hearing, but
  (b)    may be determined having regard to matters of which the authority were unaware.

(11)    The tribunal may—
  (a)    confirm or reverse the decision of the authority, and
  (b)    if it reverses the decision, revoke the HMO declaration.

(12)    In this section and section 256 "relevant person", in relation to an HMO declaration, means any person who, to the knowledge of the local housing authority, is—
  (a)    a person having an estate or interest in the building or part of the building concerned (but is not a tenant under a lease with an unexpired term of 3 years of less), or
  (b)    a person managing or having control of that building or part (and not falling within paragraph (a)).

                                                                                            **[1511]**

**NOTES**
Commencement: 18 January 2005.
Sub-s (7): words in square brackets substituted by the Transfer of Tribunal Functions (Lands Tribunal and Miscellaneous Amendments) Order 2009, SI 2009/1307, art 5(1), (2), Sch 1, paras 271, 277, subject to transitional and savings provisions in Sch 5 thereto.

## 256    Revocation of HMO declarations

(1)    A local housing authority may revoke an HMO declaration served under section 255 at any time if they consider that subsection (2) of that section no longer applies to the building or part of the building in respect of which the declaration was served.

(2)    The power to revoke an HMO declaration is exercisable by the authority either—
  (a)    on an application made by a relevant person, or
  (b)    on the authority's own initiative.

(3)    If, on an application by such a person, the authority decide not to revoke the HMO declaration, they must without delay serve on him a notice informing him of—
  (a)    the decision,
  (b)    the reasons for it and the date on which it was made,
  (c)    the right to appeal against it under subsection (4), and
  (d)    the period within which an appeal may be made under that subsection.

(4)    A person who applies to a local housing authority for the revocation of an HMO declaration under subsection (1) may appeal to a residential property tribunal against a decision of the authority to refuse to revoke the notice.

The appeal must be made within the period of 28 days beginning with the date specified under subsection (3) as the date on which the decision was made.

(5)    Such an appeal—
  (a)    is to be by way of a re-hearing, but
  (b)    may be determined having regard to matters of which the authority were unaware.

(6)    The tribunal may—
  (a)    confirm or reverse the decision of the authority, and
  (b)    if it reverses the decision, revoke the HMO declaration.

                                                                                            **[1512]**

**NOTES**
Commencement: 18 January 2005.

## 257    HMOs: certain converted blocks of flats

(1)    For the purposes of this section a "converted block of flats" means a building or part of a building which—
  (a)    has been converted into, and
  (b)    consists of,
self-contained flats.

(2) This section applies to a converted block of flats if—

    (a) building work undertaken in connection with the conversion did not comply with the appropriate building standards and still does not comply with them; and

    (b) less than two-thirds of the self-contained flats are owner-occupied.

(3) In subsection (2) "appropriate building standards" means—

    (a) in the case of a converted block of flats—

        (i) on which building work was completed before 1st June 1992 or which is dealt with by regulation 20 of the Building Regulations 1991 (SI 1991/2768), and

        (ii) which would not have been exempt under those Regulations,

    building standards equivalent to those imposed, in relation to a building or part of a building to which those Regulations applied, by those Regulations as they had effect on 1st June 1992; and

    (b) in the case of any other converted block of flats, the requirements imposed at the time in relation to it by regulations under section 1 of the Building Act 1984 (c 55).

(4) For the purposes of subsection (2) a flat is "owner-occupied" if it is occupied—

    (a) by a person who has a lease of the flat which has been granted for a term of more than 21 years,

    (b) by a person who has the freehold estate in the converted block of flats, or

    (c) by a member of the household of a person within paragraph (a) or (b).

(5) The fact that this section applies to a converted block of flats (with the result that it is a house in multiple occupation under section 254(1)(e)), does not affect the status of any flat in the block as a house in multiple occupation.

(6) In this section "self-contained flat" has the same meaning as in section 254.

**[1513]**

**NOTES**

    Commencement: 18 January 2005.

## 258 HMOs: persons not forming a single household

(1) This section sets out when persons are to be regarded as not forming a single household for the purposes of section 254.

(2) Persons are to be regarded as not forming a single household unless—

    (a) they are all members of the same family, or

    (b) their circumstances are circumstances of a description specified for the purposes of this section in regulations made by the appropriate national authority.

(3) For the purposes of subsection (2)(a) a person is a member of the same family as another person if—

    (a) those persons are married to each other or live together as husband and wife (or in an equivalent relationship in the case of persons of the same sex);

    (b) one of them is a relative of the other; or

    (c) one of them is, or is a relative of, one member of a couple and the other is a relative of the other member of the couple.

(4) For those purposes—

    (a) a "couple" means two persons who are married to each other or otherwise fall within subsection (3)(a);

    (b) "relative" means parent, grandparent, child, grandchild, brother, sister, uncle, aunt, nephew, niece or cousin;

    (c) a relationship of the half-blood shall be treated as a relationship of the whole blood; and

    (d) the stepchild of a person shall be treated as his child.

(5) Regulations under subsection (2)(b) may, in particular, secure that a group of persons are to be regarded as forming a single household only where (as the regulations may require) each member of the group has a prescribed relationship, or at least one of a number of prescribed relationships, to any one or more of the others.

(6) In subsection (5) "prescribed relationship" means any relationship of a description specified in the regulations.

**[1514]**

**NOTES**

    *Commencement:* 18 November 2004 (for the purpose of making orders or regulations); 18 January 2005 (otherwise).

    Regulations: the Licensing and Management of Houses in Multiple Occupation and Other Houses (Miscellaneous Provisions) (England) Regulations 2006, SI 2006/373 at **[3623]**; the Licensing and Management of Houses in Multiple Occupation and Other Houses (Miscellaneous Provisions) (Wales) Regulations 2006, SI 2006/1715 at **[3724]**.

**259   HMOs: persons treated as occupying premises as only or main residence**

(1)   This section sets out when persons are to be treated for the purposes of section 254 as occupying a building or part of a building as their only or main residence.

(2)   A person is to be treated as so occupying a building or part of a building if it is occupied by the person—

    (a)     as the person's residence for the purpose of undertaking a full-time course of further or higher education;

    (b)     as a refuge, or

    (c)     in any other circumstances which are circumstances of a description specified for the purposes of this section in regulations made by the appropriate national authority.

(3)   In subsection (2)(b) "refuge" means a building or part of a building managed by a voluntary organisation and used wholly or mainly for the temporary accommodation of persons who have left their homes as a result of—

    (a)     physical violence or mental abuse, or

    (b)     threats of such violence or abuse,

from persons to whom they are or were married or with whom they are or were co-habiting.

**[1515]**

**NOTES**

Commencement: 18 November 2004 (for the purpose of making orders or regulations); 18 January 2005 (otherwise).

Regulations: the Licensing and Management of Houses in Multiple Occupation and Other Houses (Miscellaneous Provisions) (England) Regulations 2006, SI 2006/373 at **[3623]**; the Licensing and Management of Houses in Multiple Occupation and Other Houses (Miscellaneous Provisions) (Wales) Regulations 2006, SI 2006/1715 at **[3724]**.

**260   HMOs: presumption that sole use condition or significant use condition is met**

(1)   Where a question arises in any proceedings as to whether either of the following is met in respect of a building or part of a building—

    (a)     the sole use condition, or

    (b)     the significant use condition,

it shall be presumed, for the purposes of the proceedings, that the condition is met unless the contrary is shown.

(2)   In this section—

    (a)     "the sole use condition" means the condition contained in—

         (i)     section 254(2)(d) (as it applies for the purposes of the standard test or the self-contained flat test), or

         (ii)     section 254(4)(e),

       as the case may be; and

    (b)     "the significant use condition" means the condition contained in section 255(2) that the occupation of the living accommodation or flat referred to in that provision by persons who do not form a single household constitutes a significant use of that accommodation or flat.

**[1516]**

**NOTES**

Commencement: 18 January 2005.

*Other general interpretation provisions*

**261   Meaning of "appropriate national authority", "local housing authority" etc**

(1)   In this Act "the appropriate national authority" means—

    (a)     in relation to England, the Secretary of State; and

    (b)     in relation to Wales, the National Assembly for Wales.

(2)   In this Act "local housing authority" means, in relation to England—

    (a)     a unitary authority;

    (b)     a district council so far as it is not a unitary authority;

    (c)     a London borough council;

    (d)     the Common Council of the City of London (in its capacity as a local authority);

    (e)     the Sub-Treasurer of the Inner Temple or the Under-Treasurer of the Middle Temple (in his capacity as a local authority); and

    (f)     the Council of the Isles of Scilly.

(3)   In subsection (2) "unitary authority" means—

    (a)     the council of a county so far as it is the council for an area for which there are no district councils;

(b) the council of any district comprised in an area for which there is no county council.

(4) In this Act "local housing authority" means, in relation to Wales, a county council or a county borough council.

(5) References in this Act to "the local housing authority", in relation to land, are to the local housing authority in whose district the land is situated.

(6) References in this Act to the district of a local housing authority are to the area of the council concerned, that is to say—
(a) in the case of a unitary authority, the area or district;
(b) in the case of a district council so far as it is not a unitary authority, the district;
(c) in the case of an authority within subsection (2)(c) to (f), the London borough, the City of London, the Inner or Middle Temple or the Isles of Scilly (as the case may be); and
(d) in the case of a Welsh county council or a county borough council, the Welsh county or county borough.

(7) Section 618 of the Housing Act 1985 (c 68) (committees and members of Common Council of City of London) applies in relation to this Act as it applies in relation to that Act.

**[1517]**

**NOTES**
Commencement: 18 January 2005.

## 262 Meaning of "lease", "tenancy", "occupier" and "owner" etc

(1) In this Act "lease" and "tenancy" have the same meaning.

(2) Both expressions include—
(a) a sub-lease or sub-tenancy; and
(b) an agreement for a lease or tenancy (or sub-lease or sub-tenancy).

And see sections 108 and 117 and paragraphs 3 and 11 of Schedule 7 (which also extend the meaning of references to leases).

(3) The expressions "lessor" and "lessee" and "landlord" and "tenant" and references to letting, to the grant of a lease or to covenants or terms, are to be construed accordingly.

(4) In this Act "lessee" includes a statutory tenant of the premises; and references to a lease or to a person to whom premises are let are to be construed accordingly.

(5) In this Act any reference to a person who is a tenant under a lease with an unexpired term of 3 years or less includes a statutory tenant as well as a tenant under a yearly or other periodic tenancy.

(6) In this Act "occupier", in relation to premises, means a person who—
(a) occupies the premises as a residence, and
(b) (subject to the context) so occupies them whether as a tenant or other person having an estate or interest in the premises or as a licensee;

and related expressions are to be construed accordingly.

This subsection does not apply for the purposes of Part 5 and has effect subject to any other provision defining "occupier" for any purposes of this Act.

(7) In this Act "owner", in relation to premises—
(a) means a person (other than a mortgagee not in possession) who is for the time being entitled to dispose of the fee simple of the premises whether in possession or in reversion; and
(b) includes also a person holding or entitled to the rents and profits of the premises under a lease of which the unexpired term exceeds 3 years.

(8) In this Act "person having an estate or interest", in relation to premises, includes a statutory tenant of the premises.

(9) In this Act "licence", in the context of a licence to occupy premises—
(a) includes a licence which is not granted for a consideration, but
(b) excludes a licence granted as a temporary expedient to a person who entered the premises as a trespasser (whether or not, before the grant of the licence, another licence to occupy those or other premises had been granted to him);

and related expressions are to be construed accordingly.

And see sections 108 and 117 and paragraphs 3 and 11 of Schedule 7 (which also extend the meaning of references to licences).

**[1518]**

**NOTES**
Commencement: 18 January 2005.

### 263  Meaning of "person having control" and "person managing" etc

(1)  In this Act "person having control", in relation to premises, means (unless the context otherwise requires) the person who receives the rack-rent of the premises (whether on his own account or as agent or trustee of another person), or who would so receive it if the premises were let at a rack-rent.

(2)  In subsection (1) "rack-rent" means a rent which is not less than two-thirds of the full net annual value of the premises.

(3)  In this Act "person managing" means, in relation to premises, the person who, being an owner or lessee of the premises—

    (a)  receives (whether directly or through an agent or trustee) rents or other payments from—

        (i)  in the case of a house in multiple occupation, persons who are in occupation as tenants or licensees of parts of the premises; and

        (ii)  in the case of a house to which Part 3 applies (see section 79(2)), persons who are in occupation as tenants or licensees of parts of the premises, or of the whole of the premises; or

    (b)  would so receive those rents or other payments but for having entered into an arrangement (whether in pursuance of a court order or otherwise) with another person who is not an owner or lessee of the premises by virtue of which that other person receives the rents or other payments;

and includes, where those rents or other payments are received through another person as agent or trustee, that other person.

(4)  In its application to Part 1, subsection (3) has effect with the omission of paragraph (a)(ii).

(5)  References in this Act to any person involved in the management of a house in multiple occupation or a house to which Part 3 applies (see section 79(2)) include references to the person managing it.

**[1519]**

### NOTES

Commencement: 18 January 2005.

Modification: this section is modified in relation to a house in multiple occupation to which s 257 of this Act applies, by the Houses in Multiple Occupation (Certain Converted Blocks of Flats) (Modifications to the Housing Act 2004 and Transitional Provisions for section 257 HMOs) (England) Regulations 2007, SI 2007/1904, reg 12, and the Houses in Multiple Occupation (Certain Blocks of Flats) (Modifications to the Housing Act 2004 and Transitional Provisions for section 257 HMOs) (Wales) Regulations 2007, SI 2007/3231, reg 12.

### 264  Calculation of numbers of persons

(1)  The appropriate national authority may prescribe rules with respect to the calculation of numbers of persons for the purposes of—

    (a)  any provision made by or under this Act which is specified in the rules, or

    (b)  any order or licence made or granted under this Act of any description which is so specified.

(2)  The rules may provide—

    (a)  for persons under a particular age to be disregarded for the purposes of any such calculation;

    (b)  for persons under a particular age to be treated as constituting a fraction of a person for the purposes of any such calculation.

(3)  The rules may be prescribed by order or regulations.

**[1520]**

*Final provisions*

### 265  Minor and consequential amendments

(1)  Schedule 15 (which contains minor and consequential amendments) has effect.

(2)  The Secretary of State may by order make such supplementary, incidental or consequential provision as he considers appropriate—

    (a)  for the general purposes, or any particular purpose, of this Act; or

    (b)  in consequence of any provision made by or under this Act or for giving full effect to it.

(3)  An order under subsection (2) may modify any enactment (including this Act).

"Enactment" includes an enactment comprised in subordinate legislation (within the meaning of the Interpretation Act 1978 (c 30)).

(4)    The power conferred by subsection (2) is also exercisable by the National Assembly for Wales in relation to provision dealing with matters with respect to which functions are exercisable by the Assembly.

(5)    Nothing in this Act affects the generality of the power conferred by this section.

**[1521]**

**NOTES**
Commencement: 18 November 2004 (sub-ss (2)–(5)); 14 July 2005 (sub-s (1), in relation to Wales for certain purposes); 6 April 2006 (sub-s (1), in relation to England for certain purposes, subject to transitional provisions and savings in the Housing Act 2004 (Commencement No 5 and Transitional Provisions and Savings) (England) Order 2006, SI 2006/1060, art 3, Schedule at **[3700]**, **[3701]**); 16 June 2006 (sub-s (1), in relation to Wales for certain purposes, subject to transitional provisions and savings in the Housing Act 2004 (Commencement No 3 and Transitional Provisions and Savings) (Wales) Order 2006, SI 2006/1535, art 3, Schedule at **[3714]**, **[3715]**); 2 January 2007 (in relation to England for certain purposes); 13 December 2007 (sub-s (1), in relation to Wales for certain purposes); to be appointed (otherwise).

## 266   Repeals

Schedule 16 (which contains repeals) has effect.

**[1522]**

**NOTES**
Commencement: 17 February 2005 (in relation to England for certain purposes); 14 July 2005 (in relation to Wales for certain purposes); 6 April 2006 (in relation to England for certain purposes, subject to transitional provisions and savings in the Housing Act 2004 (Commencement No 5 and Transitional Provisions and Savings) (England) Order 2006, SI 2006/1060, art 3, Schedule at **[3700]**, **[3701]**); 16 June 2006 (in relation to Wales for certain purposes, subject to transitional provisions and savings in the Housing Act 2004 (Commencement No 3 and Transitional Provisions and Savings) (Wales) Order 2006, SI 2006/1535, art 3, Schedule at **[3714]**, **[3715]**); 6 April 2007 (in relation to England for certain purposes); to be appointed (otherwise).

## 267   Devolution: Wales

In Schedule 1 to the National Assembly for Wales (Transfer of Functions) Order 1999 (SI 1999/672) references to the following Acts are to be treated as references to those Acts as amended by virtue of this Act—
- (a)    the Housing Act 1985 (c 68);
- (b)    the Housing Act 1988 (c 50);
- (c)    the Housing Act 1996 (c 52).

**[1523]**

## 268   The Isles of Scilly

(1)    This Secretary of State may by order provide that, in its application to the Isles of Scilly, this Act is have effect with such modifications as are specified in the order.

(2)    Where a similar power is exercisable under another Act in relation to provisions of that Act which are amended by this Act, the power is exercisable in relation to those provisions as so amended.

**[1524]**

## 269   Expenses

There shall be paid out of money provided by Parliament—
- (a)    any expenditure incurred by the Secretary of State by virtue of this Act;
- (b)    any increase attributable to this Act in the sums payable out of money so provided under any other enactment.

**[1525]**

## 270   Short title, commencement and extent

(1)    This Act may be cited as the Housing Act 2004.

(2)    The following provisions come into force on the day on which this Act is passed—
- (a)    sections 2, 9, 161 to 164, 176, 190, 208, 216, 233, 234, 244, 248, 250, 252, 264, 265(2) to (5), 267 to 269 and this section, and
- (b)    any other provision of this Act so far as it confers any power to make an order or regulations which is exercisable by the Secretary of State or the National Assembly for Wales.

Subsections (3) to (7) have effect subject to paragraph (b).

(3)    The following provisions come into force at the end of the period of two months beginning with the day on which this Act is passed—
- (a)    sections 180, 182 to 189, 195 to 207, 209 to 211, 217, 218, 219, 222, 224, 245 to 247, 249, 251 and 253 to 263,
- (b)    Schedule 9,

(c)    Schedule 11, except paragraphs 15 and 16, and
(d)    Schedule 14.

(4)    The provisions listed in subsection (5) come into force—
(a)    where they are to come into force in relation only to Wales, on such day as the National Assembly for Wales may by order appoint, and
(b)    otherwise, on such day as the Secretary of State may by order appoint.

(5)    The provisions referred to in subsection (4) are—
(a)    Part 1 (other than sections 2 and 9),
(b)    Parts 2 to 4,
(c)    sections 179, 181, 191 to 194, 212 to 215, 220, 221, 223, 225, 226, 227, 229 to 232, 235 to 243, 265(1) and 266,
(d)    Schedule 10,
(e)    paragraphs 15 and 16 of Schedule 11, and
(f)    Schedules 13, 15 and 16.

(6)    Part 5 (other than sections 161 to 164 and 176) comes into force on such day as the Secretary of State may by order appoint.

(7)    Section 228 and Schedule 12 come into force on such day as the National Assembly for Wales may by order appoint.

(8)    Different days may be appointed for different purposes or different areas under subsection (4), (6) or (7).

(9)    The Secretary of State may by order make such provision as he considers necessary or expedient for transitory, transitional or saving purposes in connection with the coming into force of any provision of this Act.

(10)    The power conferred by subsection (9) is also exercisable by the National Assembly for Wales in relation to provision dealing with matters with respect to which functions are exercisable by the Assembly

(11)    Subject to subsections (12) and (13), this Act extends to England and Wales only.

(12)    Any amendment or repeal made by this Act has the same extent as the enactment to which it relates, except that any amendment or repeal in—
the Mobile Homes Act 1983 (c 34), or
the Crime and Disorder Act 1998 (c 37),
extends to England and Wales only.

(13)    This section extends to the whole of the United Kingdom.

**[1526]**

**NOTES**
Orders: the Housing Act 2004 (Commencement No 1) (England) Order 2005, SI 2005/326; the Housing Act 2004 (Commencement No 2) (England) Order 2005, SI 2005/1120; the Housing Act 2004 (Commencement No 3) (England) Order 2005, SI 2005/1451; the Housing Act 2004 (Commencement No 4 and Transitional Provisions) (England) Order 2005, SI 2005/1729; the Housing Act 2004 (Commencement No 1) (Wales) Order 2005, SI 2005/1814; the Housing Act 2004 (Commencement No 2) (Wales) Order 2005, SI 2005/3237; the Housing Act 2004 (Commencement No 5 and Transitional Provisions and Savings) (England) Order 2006, SI 2006/1060; the Housing Act 2004 (Commencement No 3 and Transitional Provisions and Savings) (Wales) Order 2006, SI 2006/1535; the Housing Act 2004 (Commencement No 6) (England) Order 2006, SI 2006/3191; the Housing Act 2004 (Commencement No 4) (Wales) Order 2007, SI 2007/305; the Housing Act 2004 (Commencement No 7) (England) Order 2007, SI 2007/1068; the Housing Act 2004 (Commencement No 8) (England and Wales) Order 2007, SI 2007/1668; the Housing Act 2004 (Commencement No 9) (England and Wales) Order 2007, SI 2007/2471; the Housing Act 2004 (Commencement No 5) (Wales) Order 2007, SI 2007/3232; the Housing Act 2004 (Commencement No 10) (England and Wales) Order 2007, SI 2007/3308; the Housing Act 2004 (Commencement No 11) (England and Wales) Order 2008, SI 2008/898.

## SCHEDULE 1
## PROCEDURE AND APPEALS RELATING TO IMPROVEMENT NOTICES
*Section 18*

## PART 1
## SERVICE OF IMPROVEMENT NOTICES

*Service of improvement notices: premises licensed under Part 2 or 3*

1.—(1)    This paragraph applies where the specified premises in the case of an improvement notice are—
(a)    a dwelling which is licensed under Part 3 of this Act, or
(b)    an HMO which is licensed under Part 2 or 3 of this Act.

(2)   The local housing authority must serve the notice on the holder of the licence under that Part.

*Service of improvement notices: premises which are neither licensed under Part 2 or 3 nor flats*

2.—(1)   This paragraph applies where the specified premises in the case of an improvement notice are—
  (a)   a dwelling which is not licensed under Part 3 of this Act, or
  (b)   an HMO which is not licensed under Part 2 or 3 of this Act,
and which (in either case) is not a flat.

  (2)   The local housing authority must serve the notice—
  (a)   (in the case of a dwelling) on the person having control of the dwelling;
  (b)   (in the case of an HMO) either on the person having control of the HMO or on the person managing it.

*Service of improvement notices: flats which are not licensed under Part 2 or 3*

3.—(1)   This paragraph applies where any specified premises in the case of an improvement notice are—
  (a)   a dwelling which is not licensed under Part 3 of this Act, or
  (b)   an HMO which is not licensed under Part 2 or 3 of this Act,
and which (in either case) is a flat.

  (2)   In the case of dwelling which is a flat, the local housing authority must serve the notice on a person who—
  (a)   is an owner of the flat, and
  (b)   in the authority's opinion ought to take the action specified in the notice.

  (3)   In the case of an HMO which is a flat, the local housing authority must serve the notice either on a person who—
  (a)   is an owner of the flat, and
  (b)   in the authority's opinion ought to take the action specified in the notice,
or on the person managing the flat.

*Service of improvement notices: common parts*

4.—(1)   This paragraph applies where any specified premises in the case of an improvement notice are—
  (a)   common parts of a building containing one or more flats; or
  (b)   any part of such a building which does not consist of residential premises.

  (2)   The local housing authority must serve the notice on a person who—
  (a)   is an owner of the specified premises concerned, and
  (b)   in the authority's opinion ought to take the action specified in the notice.

  (3)   For the purposes of this paragraph a person is an owner of any common parts of a building if he is an owner of the building or part of the building concerned, or (in the case of external common parts) of the particular premises in which the common parts are comprised.

*Service of copies of improvement notices*

5.—(1)   In addition to serving an improvement notice in accordance with any of paragraphs 1 to 4, the local housing authority must serve a copy of the notice on every other person who, to their knowledge—
  (a)   has a relevant interest in any specified premises, or
  (b)   is an occupier of any such premises.

  (2)   A "relevant interest" means an interest as freeholder, mortgagee or lessee.

  (3)   For the purposes of this paragraph a person has a relevant interest in any common parts of a building if he has a relevant interest in the building or part of the building concerned, or (in the case of external common parts) in the particular premises in which the common parts are comprised.

  (4)   The copies required to be served under sub-paragraph (1) must be served within the period of seven days beginning with the day on which the notice is served.

[1527]

**NOTES**

Commencement: 6 April 2006 (in relation to England, subject to transitional provisions and savings in the *Housing Act 2004 (Commencement No 5 and Transitional Provisions and Savings) (England) Order 2006*, SI 2006/1060, art 3, Schedule at [**3700**], [**3701**]); 16 June 2006 (in relation to Wales, subject to transitional provisions and savings in the Housing Act 2004 (Commencement No 3 and Transitional Provisions and Savings) (Wales) Order 2006, SI 2006/1535, art 3, Schedule at [**3714**], [**3715**]).

## PART 2
### SERVICE OF NOTICES RELATING TO REVOCATION OR VARIATION OF IMPROVEMENT NOTICES

*Notice of revocation or variation*

6.—(1) This paragraph applies where the local housing authority decide to revoke or vary an improvement notice.

(2) The authority must serve—
  (a) a notice under this paragraph, and
  (b) copies of that notice,

on the persons on whom they would be required under Part 1 of this Schedule to serve an improvement notice and copies of it in respect of the specified premises.

(3) Sub-paragraph (4) applies if, in so doing, the authority serve a notice under this paragraph on a person who is not the person on whom the improvement notice was served ("the original recipient").

(4) The authority must serve a copy of the notice under this paragraph on the original recipient unless they consider that it would not be appropriate to do so.

(5) The documents required to be served under sub-paragraph (2) must be served within the period of seven days beginning with the day on which the decision is made.

7. A notice under paragraph 6 must set out—
  (a) the authority's decision to revoke or vary the improvement notice;
  (b) the reasons for the decision and the date on which it was made;
  (c) if the decision is to vary the notice—
    (i) the right of appeal against the decision under Part 3 of this Schedule, and
    (ii) the period within which an appeal may be made (see paragraph 14(2)).

*Notice of refusal to revoke or vary notice*

8.—(1) This paragraph applies where the local housing authority refuse to revoke or vary an improvement notice.

(2) The authority must serve—
  (a) a notice under this paragraph, and
  (b) copies of that notice,

on the persons on whom they would be required to serve an improvement notice and copies of it under Part 1 of this Schedule.

(3) Sub-paragraph (4) applies if, in so doing, the authority serve a notice under this paragraph on a person who is not the person on whom the improvement notice was served ("the original recipient").

(4) The authority must serve a copy of the notice under this paragraph on the original recipient unless they consider that it would not be appropriate to do so.

(5) The documents required to be served under sub-paragraph (2) must be served within the period of seven days beginning with the day on which the decision is made.

9. A notice under paragraph 8 must set out—
  (a) the authority's decision not to revoke or vary the improvement notice;
  (b) the reasons for the decision and the date on which it was made;
  (c) the right of appeal against the decision under Part 3 of this Schedule; and
  (d) the period within which an appeal may be made (see paragraph 14(2)).

**[1528]**

**NOTES**

Commencement: 6 April 2006 (in relation to England, subject to transitional provisions and savings in the Housing Act 2004 (Commencement No 5 and Transitional Provisions and Savings) (England) Order 2006, SI 2006/1060, art 3, Schedule at **[3700]**, **[3701]**); 16 June 2006 (in relation to Wales, subject to transitional provisions and savings in the Housing Act 2004 (Commencement No 3 and Transitional Provisions and Savings) (Wales) Order 2006, SI 2006/1535, art 3, Schedule at **[3714]**, **[3715]**).

## PART 3
### APPEALS RELATING TO IMPROVEMENT NOTICES

*Appeal against improvement notice*

10.—(1) The person on whom an improvement notice is served may appeal to a residential property tribunal against the notice.

PART 1 STATUTES

(2)   Paragraphs 11 and 12 set out two specific grounds on which an appeal may be made under this paragraph, but they do not affect the generality of sub-paragraph (1).

11.—(1)   An appeal may be made by a person under paragraph 10 on the ground that one or more other persons, as an owner or owners of the specified premises, ought to—

    (a)   take the action concerned, or

    (b)   pay the whole or part of the cost of taking that action.

(2)   Where the grounds on which an appeal is made under paragraph 10 consist of or include the ground mentioned in sub-paragraph (1), the appellant must serve a copy of his notice of appeal on the other person or persons concerned.

12.—(1)   An appeal may be made by a person under paragraph 10 on the ground that one of the courses of action mentioned in sub-paragraph (2) is the best course of action in relation to the hazard in respect of which the notice was served.

(2)   The courses of action are—

    (a)   making a prohibition order under section 20 or 21 of this Act;

    (b)   serving a hazard awareness notice under section 28 or 29 of this Act; and

    (c)   making a demolition order under section 265 of the Housing Act 1985 (c 68).

*Appeal against decision relating to variation or revocation of improvement notice*

13.—(1)   The relevant person may appeal to a residential property tribunal against—

    (a)   a decision by the local housing authority to vary an improvement notice, or

    (b)   a decision by the authority to refuse to revoke or vary an improvement notice.

(2)   In sub-paragraph (1) "the relevant person" means—

    (a)   in relation to a decision within paragraph (a) of that provision, the person on whom the notice was served;

    (b)   in relation to a decision within paragraph (b) of that provision, the person who applied for the revocation or variation.

*Time limit for appeal*

14.—(1)   Any appeal under paragraph 10 must be made within the period of 21 days beginning with the date on which the improvement notice was served in accordance with Part 1 of this Schedule.

(2)   Any appeal under paragraph 13 must be made within the period of 28 days beginning with the date specified in the notice under paragraph 6 or 8 as the date on which the decision concerned was made.

(3)   A residential property tribunal may allow an appeal to be made to it after the end of the period mentioned in sub-paragraph (1) or (2) if it is satisfied that there is a good reason for the failure to appeal before the end of that period (and for any delay since then in applying for permission to appeal out of time).

*Powers of residential property tribunal on appeal under paragraph 10*

15.—(1)   This paragraph applies to an appeal to a residential property tribunal under paragraph 10.

(2)   The appeal—

    (a)   is to be by way of a re-hearing, but

    (b)   may be determined having regard to matters of which the authority were unaware.

(3)   The tribunal may by order confirm, quash or vary the improvement notice.

(4)   Paragraphs 16 and 17 make special provision in connection with the grounds of appeal set out in paragraphs 11 and 12.

16.—(1)   This paragraph applies where the grounds of appeal consist of or include that set out in paragraph 11.

(2)   On the hearing of the appeal the tribunal may—

    (a)   vary the improvement notice so as to require the action to be taken by any owner mentioned in the notice of appeal in accordance with paragraph 11; or

    (b)   make such order as it considers appropriate with respect to the payment to be made by any such owner to the appellant or, where the action is taken by the local housing authority, to the authority.

(3)   In the exercise of its powers under sub-paragraph (2), the tribunal must take into account, as between the appellant and any such owner—

    (a)   their relative interests in the premises concerned (considering both the nature of the interests and the rights and obligations arising under or by virtue of them);

    (b)   their relative responsibility for the state of the premises which gives rise to the need for the taking of the action concerned; and

    (c)   the relative degree of benefit to be derived from the taking of the action concerned.

(4)   Sub-paragraph (5) applies where, by virtue of the exercise of the tribunal's powers under sub-paragraph (2), a person other than the appellant is required to take the action specified in an improvement notice.

(5)   So long as that other person remains an owner of the premises to which the notice relates, he is to be regarded for the purposes of this Part as the person on whom the notice was served (in place of any other person).

17.—(1)   This paragraph applies where the grounds of appeal consist of or include that set out in paragraph 12.

(2)   When deciding whether one of the courses of action mentioned in paragraph 12(2) is the best course of action in relation to a particular hazard, the tribunal must have regard to any guidance given to the local housing authority under section 9.

(3)   Sub-paragraph (4) applies where—
    (a)   an appeal under paragraph 10 is allowed against an improvement notice in respect of a particular hazard; and
    (b)   the reason, or one of the reasons, for allowing the appeal is that one of the courses of action mentioned in paragraph 12(2) is the best course of action in relation to that hazard.

(4)   The tribunal must, if requested to do so by the appellant or the local housing authority, include in its decision a finding to that effect and identifying the course of action concerned.

*Powers of residential property tribunal on appeal under paragraph 13*

18.—(1)   This paragraph applies to an appeal to a residential property tribunal under paragraph 13.

(2)   Paragraph 15(2) applies to such an appeal as it applies to an appeal under paragraph 10.

(3)   The tribunal may by order confirm, reverse or vary the decision of the local housing authority.

(4)   If the appeal is against a decision of the authority to refuse to revoke an improvement notice, the tribunal may make an order revoking the notice as from a date specified in the order.

*"The operative time" for the purposes of section 15(5)*

19.—(1)   This paragraph defines "the operative time" for the purposes of section 15(5) (operation of improvement notices).

(2)   If an appeal is made under paragraph 10 against an improvement notice which is not suspended, and a decision on the appeal is given which confirms the notice, "the operative time" is as follows—
    (a)   if the period within which an appeal to the [Upper Tribunal] may be brought expires without such an appeal having been brought, "the operative time" is the end of that period;
    (b)   if an appeal to the [Upper Tribunal] is brought, "the operative time" is the time when a decision is given on the appeal which confirms the notice.

(3)   If an appeal is made under paragraph 10 against an improvement notice which is suspended, and a decision is given on the appeal which confirms the notice, "the operative time" is as follows—
    (a)   the time that would be the operative time under sub-paragraph (2) if the notice were not suspended, or
    (b)   if later, the time when the suspension ends.

(4)   For the purposes of sub-paragraph (2) or (3)—
    (a)   the withdrawal of an appeal has the same effect as a decision which confirms the notice, and
    (b)   references to a decision which confirms the notice are to a decision which confirms it with or without variation.

*"The operative time" for the purposes of section 16(7)*

20.—(1)   This paragraph defines "the operative time" for the purposes of section 16(7) (postponement of time when a variation of an improvement notice comes into force).

(2)   If no appeal is made under paragraph 13 before the end of the period of 28 days mentioned in paragraph 14(2), "the operative time" is the end of that period.

(3)   If an appeal is made under paragraph 13 before the end of that period and a decision is given on the appeal which confirms the variation, "the operative time" is as follows—
    (a)   if the period within which an appeal to the [Upper Tribunal] may be brought expires without such an appeal having been brought, "the operative time" is the end of that period;
    (b)   if an appeal to the [Upper Tribunal] is brought, "the operative time" is the time when a decision is given on the appeal which confirms the variation.

(4)   For the purposes of sub-paragraph (3)—
   (a)   the withdrawal of an appeal has the same effect as a decision which confirms the variation, and
   (b)   references to a decision which confirms the variation are to a decision which confirms it with or without variation.

**[1529]**

**NOTES**
Commencement: 6 April 2006 (in relation to England, subject to transitional provisions and savings in the Housing Act 2004 (Commencement No 5 and Transitional Provisions and Savings) (England) Order 2006, SI 2006/1060, art 3, Schedule at **[3700]**, **[3701]**); 16 June 2006 (in relation to Wales, subject to transitional provisions and savings in the Housing Act 2004 (Commencement No 3 and Transitional Provisions and Savings) (Wales) Order 2006, SI 2006/1535, art 3, Schedule at **[3714]**, **[3715]**).
Paras 19, 20: words in square brackets substituted by the Transfer of Tribunal Functions (Lands Tribunal and Miscellaneous Amendments) Order 2009, SI 2009/1307, art 5(1), (2), Sch 1, paras 271, 278, subject to transitional and savings provisions in Sch 5 thereto.

## SCHEDULE 2
## PROCEDURE AND APPEALS RELATING TO PROHIBITION ORDERS
Section 27

## PART 1
### SERVICE OF COPIES OF PROHIBITION ORDERS

*Service on owners and occupiers of dwelling or HMO which is not a flat*

1.—(1)   This paragraph applies to a prohibition order where the specified premises are a dwelling or HMO which is not a flat.

(2)   The authority must serve copies of the order on every person who, to their knowledge, is—
   (a)   an owner or occupier of the whole or part of the specified premises;
   (b)   authorised to permit persons to occupy the whole or part of those premises; or
   (c)   a mortgagee of the whole or part of those premises.

(3)   The copies required to be served under sub-paragraph (2) must be served within the period of seven days beginning with the day on which the order is made.

(4)   A copy of the order is to be regarded as having been served on every occupier in accordance with sub-paragraphs (2)(a) and (3) if a copy of the order is fixed to some conspicuous part of the specified premises within the period of seven days mentioned in sub-paragraph (3).

*Service on owners and occupiers of building containing flats etc*

2.—(1)   This paragraph applies to a prohibition order where the specified premises consist of or include the whole or any part of a building containing one or more flats or any common parts of such a building.

(2)   The authority must serve copies of the order on every person who, to their knowledge, is—
   (a)   an owner or occupier of the whole or part of the building;
   (b)   authorised to permit persons to occupy the whole or part of the building; or
   (c)   a mortgagee of the whole or part of the building.

(3)   Where the specified premises consist of or include any external common parts of such a building, the authority must, in addition to complying with sub-paragraph (2), serve copies of the order on every person who, to their knowledge, is an owner or mortgagee of the premises in which the common parts are comprised.

(4)   The copies required to be served under sub-paragraph (2) or (3) must be served within the period of seven days beginning with the day on which the order is made.

(5)   A copy of the order is to be regarded as having been served on every occupier in accordance with sub-paragraphs (2)(a) and (4) if a copy of the order is fixed to some conspicuous part of the building within the period of seven days mentioned in sub-paragraph (4).

**[1530]**

**NOTES**
Commencement: 6 April 2006 (in relation to England, subject to transitional provisions and savings in the Housing Act 2004 (Commencement No 5 and Transitional Provisions and Savings) (England) Order 2006, SI 2006/1060, art 3, Schedule at **[3700]**, **[3701]**); 16 June 2006 (in relation to Wales, subject to transitional provisions and savings in the Housing Act 2004 (Commencement No 3 and Transitional Provisions and Savings) (Wales) Order 2006, SI 2006/1535, art 3, Schedule at **[3714]**, **[3715]**).

## PART 2
## SERVICE OF NOTICES RELATING TO REVOCATION OR VARIATION OF PROHIBITION ORDERS

*Notice of revocation or variation*

3.—(1)  This paragraph applies where the local housing authority decide to revoke or vary a prohibition order.

(2)  The authority must serve a notice under this paragraph on each of the persons on whom they would be required under Part 1 of this Schedule to serve copies of a prohibition order in respect of the specified premises.

(3)  The notices required to be served under sub-paragraph (2) must be served within the period of seven days beginning with the day on which the decision is made.

(4)  Paragraph 1(4) applies in relation to the service of notices on occupiers in accordance with sub-paragraphs (2) and (3) as it applies in relation to the service on them of copies of a prohibition order in accordance with paragraph 1(2)(a) and (3).

4.  A notice under paragraph 3 must set out—
  (a)  the authority's decision to revoke or vary the order;
  (b)  the reasons for the decision and the date on which it was made;
  (c)  if the decision is to vary the order—
    (i)  the right of appeal against the decision under Part 3 of this Schedule; and
    (ii)  the period within which an appeal may be made (see paragraph 10(2)).

*Notice of refusal to revoke or vary order*

5.—(1)  This paragraph applies where the local housing authority refuse to revoke or vary a prohibition order.

(2)  The authority must serve a notice under this paragraph on each of the persons on whom they would be required under Part 1 of this Schedule to serve copies of a prohibition order in respect of the specified premises.

(3)  The notices required to be served under sub-paragraph (2) must be served within the period of seven days beginning with the day on which the decision is made.

(4)  Paragraph 1(4) applies in relation to the service of notices on occupiers in accordance with sub-paragraphs (2) and (3) as it applies in relation to the service on them of copies of a prohibition order in accordance with paragraph 1(2)(a) and (3).

6.  A notice under paragraph 5 must set out—
  (a)  the authority's decision not to revoke or vary the notice;
  (b)  the reasons for the decision and the date on which it was made;
  (c)  the right of appeal against the decision under Part 3 of this Schedule; and
  (c)  the period within which an appeal may be made (see paragraph 10(2)).

**[1531]**

**NOTES**
  Commencement: 6 April 2006 (in relation to England, subject to transitional provisions and savings in the Housing Act 2004 (Commencement No 5 and Transitional Provisions and Savings) (England) Order 2006, SI 2006/1060, art 3, Schedule at **[3700]**, **[3701]**); 16 June 2006 (in relation to Wales, subject to transitional provisions and savings in the Housing Act 2004 (Commencement No 3 and Transitional Provisions and Savings) (Wales) Order 2006, SI 2006/1535, art 3, Schedule at **[3714]**, **[3715]**).

## PART 3
## APPEALS RELATING TO PROHIBITION ORDERS

*Appeal against prohibition order*

7.—(1)  A relevant person may appeal to a residential property tribunal against a prohibition order.

(2)  Paragraph 8 sets out a specific ground on which an appeal may be made under this paragraph, but it does not affect the generality of sub-paragraph (1).

8.—(1)  An appeal may be made by a person under paragraph 7 on the ground that one of the courses of action mentioned in sub-paragraph (2) is the best course of action in relation to the hazard in respect of which the order was made.

(2)  The courses of action are—
  (a)  serving an improvement notice under section 11 or 12 of this Act;
  (b)  serving a hazard awareness notice under section 28 or 29 of this Act;
  (c)  making a demolition order under section 265 of the Housing Act 1985 (c 68).

*Appeal against decision relating to revocation or variation of prohibition order*

9. A relevant person may appeal to a residential property tribunal against—
    (a) a decision by the local housing authority to vary a prohibition order, or
    (b) a decision by the authority to refuse to revoke or vary a prohibition order.

*Time limit for appeal*

10.—(1) Any appeal under paragraph 7 must be made within the period of 28 days beginning with the date specified in the prohibition order as the date on which the order was made.

(2) Any appeal under paragraph 9 must be made within the period of 28 days beginning with the date specified in the notice under paragraph 3 or 5 as the date on which the decision concerned was made.

(3) A residential property tribunal may allow an appeal to be made to it after the end of the period mentioned in sub-paragraph (1) or (2) if it is satisfied that there is a good reason for the failure to appeal before the end of that period (and for any delay since then in applying for permission to appeal out of time).

*Powers of residential property tribunal on appeal under paragraph 7*

11.—(1) This paragraph applies to an appeal to a residential property tribunal under paragraph 7.

(2) The appeal—
    (a) is to be by way of a re-hearing, but
    (b) may be determined having regard to matters of which the authority were unaware.

(3) The tribunal may by order confirm, quash or vary the prohibition order.

(4) Paragraph 12 makes special provision in connection with the ground of appeal set out in paragraph 8.

12.—(1) This paragraph applies where the grounds of appeal consist of or include that set out in paragraph 8.

(2) When deciding whether one of the courses of action mentioned in paragraph 8(2) is the best course of action in relation to a particular hazard, the tribunal must have regard to any guidance given to the local housing authority under section 9.

(3) Sub-paragraph (4) applies where—
    (a) an appeal under paragraph 7 is allowed against a prohibition order made in respect of a particular hazard; and
    (b) the reason, or one of the reasons, for allowing the appeal is that one of the courses of action mentioned in paragraph 8(2) is the best course of action in relation to that hazard.

(4) The tribunal must, if requested to do so by the appellant or the local housing authority, include in its decision a finding to that effect and identifying the course of action concerned.

*Powers of residential property tribunal on appeal under paragraph 9*

13.—(1) This paragraph applies to an appeal to a residential property tribunal under paragraph 9.

(2) Paragraph 11(2) applies to such an appeal as it applies to an appeal under paragraph 7.

(3) The tribunal may by order confirm, reverse or vary the decision of the local housing authority.

(4) If the appeal is against a decision of the authority to refuse to revoke a prohibition order, the tribunal may make an order revoking the prohibition order as from a date specified in its order.

*"The operative time" for the purposes of section 24(5)*

14.—(1) This paragraph defines "the operative time" for the purposes of section 24(5) (operation of prohibition orders).

(2) If an appeal is made under paragraph 7 against a prohibition order which is not suspended, and a decision on the appeal is given which confirms the order, "the operative time" is as follows—
    (a) if the period within which an appeal to the [Upper Tribunal] may be brought expires without such an appeal having been brought, "the operative time" is the end of that period;
    (b) if an appeal to the [Upper Tribunal] is brought, "the operative time" is the time when a decision is given on the appeal which confirms the order.

(3) If an appeal is made under paragraph 7 against a prohibition order which is suspended, and a decision is given on the appeal which confirms the order, "the operative time" is as follows—
    (a) the time that would be the operative time under sub-paragraph (2) if the order were not suspended, or
    (b) if later, the time when the suspension ends.

(4) For the purposes of sub-paragraph (2) or (3)—

(a)  the withdrawal of an appeal has the same effect as a decision which confirms the notice, and

(b)  references to a decision which confirms the order are to a decision which confirms it with or without variation.

*"The operative time" for the purposes of section 25(7)*

15.—(1)  This paragraph defines "the operative time" for the purposes of section 25(7) (revocation or variation of prohibition orders).

(2)  If no appeal is made under paragraph 9 before the end of the period of 28 days mentioned in paragraph 10(2), "the operative time" is the end of that period.

(3)  If an appeal is made under paragraph 10 within that period and a decision is given on the appeal which confirms the variation, "the operative time" is as follows—

(a)  if the period within which an appeal to the [Upper Tribunal] may be brought expires without such an appeal having been brought, "the operative time" is the end of that period;

(b)  if an appeal to the [Upper Tribunal] is brought, "the operative time" is the time when a decision is given on the appeal which confirms the variation.

(4)  For the purposes of sub-paragraph (3)—

(a)  the withdrawal of an appeal has the same effect as a decision which confirms the variation, and

(b)  references to a decision which confirms the variation are to a decision which confirms it with or without variation.

*Meaning of "relevant person"*

16.—(1)  In this Part of this Schedule "relevant person", in relation to a prohibition order, means a person who is—

(a)  an owner or occupier of the whole or part of the specified premises,

(b)  authorised to permit persons to occupy the whole or part of those premises, or

(c)  a mortgagee of the whole or part of those premises.

(2)  If any specified premises are common parts of a building containing one or more flats, then in relation to those specified premises, "relevant person" means every person who is an owner or mortgagee of the premises in which the common parts are comprised.

**[1532]**

**NOTES**

Commencement: 6 April 2006 (in relation to England, subject to transitional provisions and savings in the Housing Act 2004 (Commencement No 5 and Transitional Provisions and Savings) (England) Order 2006, SI 2006/1060, art 3, Schedule at **[3700]**, **[3701]**); 16 June 2006 (in relation to Wales, subject to transitional provisions and savings in the Housing Act 2004 (Commencement No 3 and Transitional Provisions and Savings) (Wales) Order 2006, SI 2006/1535, art 3, Schedule at **[3714]**, **[3715]**).

Paras 14, 15: words in square brackets substituted by the Transfer of Tribunal Functions (Lands Tribunal and Miscellaneous Amendments) Order 2009, SI 2009/1307, art 5(1), (2), Sch 1, paras 271, 279, subject to transitional and savings provisions in Sch 5 thereto.

<hr/>

## SCHEDULE 3
### IMPROVEMENT NOTICES: ENFORCEMENT ACTION BY LOCAL HOUSING AUTHORITIES

Section 31

### PART 1
#### ACTION TAKEN BY AGREEMENT

*Power to take action by agreement*

1.—(1)  The local housing authority may, by agreement with the person on whom an improvement notice has been served, take any action which that person is required to take in relation to any premises in pursuance of the notice.

(2)  For that purpose the authority have all the rights which that person would have against any occupying tenant of, and any other person having an interest in, the premises (or any part of the premises).

(3)  In this paragraph—

"improvement notice" means an improvement notice which has become operative under Chapter 2 of Part 1 of this Act;

"occupying tenant", in relation to any premises, means a person (other than an owner-occupier) who—

(a)  occupies or is entitled to occupy the premises as a lessee;

    (b)    is a statutory tenant of the premises;
    (c)    occupies the premises under a restricted contract;
    (d)    is a protected occupier within the meaning of the Rent (Agriculture) Act 1976 (c 80); or
    (e)    is a licensee under an assured agricultural occupancy;
"owner-occupier", in relation to any premises, means the person who occupies or is entitled to occupy the premises as owner or lessee under a long tenancy (within the meaning of Part 1 of the Leasehold Reform Act 1967 (c 88)).

*Expenses of taking action by agreement*

2.    Any action taken by the local housing authority under paragraph 1 is to be taken at the expense of the person on whom the notice is served.

**[1533]**

**NOTES**
    Commencement: 6 April 2006 (in relation to England, subject to transitional provisions and savings in the Housing Act 2004 (Commencement No 5 and Transitional Provisions and Savings) (England) Order 2006, SI 2006/1060, art 3, Schedule at **[3700]**, **[3701]**); 16 June 2006 (in relation to Wales, subject to transitional provisions and savings in the Housing Act 2004 (Commencement No 3 and Transitional Provisions and Savings) (Wales) Order 2006, SI 2006/1535, art 3, Schedule at **[3714]**, **[3715]**).

PART 2
POWER TO TAKE ACTION WITHOUT AGREEMENT

*Power to take action without agreement*

3.—(1)    The local housing authority may themselves take the action required to be taken in relation to a hazard by an improvement notice if sub-paragraph (2) or (3) applies.

    (2)    This sub-paragraph applies if the notice is not complied with in relation to that hazard.

    (3)    This sub-paragraph applies if, before the end of the period which under section 30(2) is appropriate for completion of the action specified in the notice in relation to the hazard, they consider that reasonable progress is not being made towards compliance with the notice in relation to the hazard.

    (4)    Any person authorised in writing by the authority may enter any part of the specified premises for the purposes of the taking of any action which the authority are authorised to take under this paragraph.

    (5)    The right of entry conferred by sub-paragraph (4) may be exercised at any reasonable time.

    (6)    Any reference in this Part of this Schedule (of whatever nature) to a local housing authority entering any premises under this paragraph is a reference to their doing so in accordance with sub-paragraph (4).

    (7)    In this paragraph "improvement notice" means an improvement notice which has become operative under Chapter 2 of Part 1 of this Act.

*Notice requirements in relation to taking action without agreement*

4.—(1)    The local housing authority must serve a notice under this paragraph before they enter any premises under paragraph 3 for the purpose of taking action in relation to a hazard.

    (2)    The notice must identify the improvement notice to which it relates and state—
    (a)    the premises and hazard concerned;
    (b)    that the authority intend to enter the premises;
    (c)    the action which the authority intend to take on the premises; and
    (d)    the power under which the authority intend to enter the premises and take the action.

    (3)    The notice must be served on the person on whom the improvement notice was served, and a copy of the notice must be served on any other person who is an occupier of the premises.

    (4)    The notice and any such copy must be served sufficiently in advance of the time when the authority intend to enter the premises as to give the recipients reasonable notice of the intended entry.

    (5)    A copy of the notice may also be served on any owner of the premises.

*Obstruction of action taken without agreement*

5.—(1)    If, at any relevant time—
    (a)    the person on whom the notice under paragraph 4 was served is on the premises for the purpose of carrying out any works, or
    (b)    any workman employed by that person, or by any contractor employed by that person, is on the premises for such a purpose,

that person is to be taken to have committed an offence under section 241(1).

(2) In proceedings for such an offence it is a defence that there was an urgent necessity to carry out the works in order to prevent danger to persons occupying the premises.

(3) In sub-paragraph (1) "relevant time" means any time—
- (a) after the end of the period of 7 days beginning with the date of service of the notice under paragraph 4, and
- (b) when any workman or contractor employed by the local housing authority is taking action on the premises which has been mentioned in the notice in accordance with paragraph 4(2)(c).

*Expenses in relation to taking action without agreement*

6.—(1) Part 3 of this Schedule applies with respect to the recovery by the local housing authority of expenses incurred by them in taking action under paragraph 3.

(2) Sub-paragraph (3) applies where, after a local housing authority have given notice under paragraph 4 of their intention to enter premises and take action, the action is in fact taken by the person on whom the improvement notice is served.

(3) Any administrative and other expenses incurred by the authority with a view to themselves taking the action are to be treated for the purposes of Part 3 of this Schedule as expenses incurred by them in taking action under paragraph 3.

**[1534]**

**NOTES**

Commencement: 6 April 2006 (in relation to England, subject to transitional provisions and savings in the Housing Act 2004 (Commencement No 5 and Transitional Provisions and Savings) (England) Order 2006, SI 2006/1060, art 3, Schedule at **[3700]**, **[3701]**); 16 June 2006 (in relation to Wales, subject to transitional provisions and savings in the Housing Act 2004 (Commencement No 3 and Transitional Provisions and Savings) (Wales) Order 2006, SI 2006/1535, art 3, Schedule at **[3714]**, **[3715]**).

PART 3
RECOVERY OF CERTAIN EXPENSES

*Introductory*

7. This Part of this Schedule applies for the purpose of enabling a local housing authority to recover expenses reasonably incurred by them in taking action under paragraph 3.

*Recovery of expenses*

8.—(1) The expenses are recoverable by the local housing authority from the person on whom the improvement notice was served ("the relevant person").

(2) Where the relevant person receives the rent of the premises as agent or trustee for another person, the expenses are also recoverable by the local housing authority from the other person, or partly from him and partly from the relevant person.

(3) Sub-paragraph (4) applies where the relevant person proves in connection with a demand under paragraph 9—
- (a) that sub-paragraph (2) applies, and
- (b) that he has not, and since the date of the service on him of the demand has not had, in his hands on behalf of the other person sufficient money to discharge the whole demand of the local housing authority.

(4) The liability of the relevant person is limited to the total amount of the money which he has, or has had, in his hands as mentioned in sub-paragraph (3)(b).

(5) Expenses are not recoverable under this paragraph so far as they are, by any direction given by a residential property tribunal on an appeal to the tribunal under paragraph 11, recoverable under an order of the tribunal.

*Service of demand*

9.—(1) A demand for expenses recoverable under paragraph 8, together with interest in accordance with paragraph 10, must be served on each person from whom the local housing authority are seeking to recover them.

(2) If no appeal is brought, the demand becomes operative at the end of the period of 21 days beginning with the date of service of the demand.

(3) A demand which becomes operative under sub-paragraph (2) is final and conclusive as to matters which could have been raised on an appeal.

(4) Paragraph 11 deals with appeals against demands.

*Interest*

10.  Expenses in respect of which a demand is served carry interest, at such reasonable rate as the local housing authority may determine, from the date of service until payment of all sums due under the demand.

*Appeals*

11.—(1)  A person on whom a demand for the recovery of expenses has been served may appeal to a residential property tribunal against the demand.

(2)  An appeal must be made within the period of 21 days beginning with the date of service of the demand or copy of it under paragraph 9.

(3)  A residential property tribunal may allow an appeal to be made to it after the end of the period mentioned in sub-paragraph (2) if it is satisfied that there is a good reason for the failure to appeal before the end of that period (and for any delay since then in applying for permission to appeal out of time).

(4)  Where the demand relates to action taken by virtue of paragraph 3(3), an appeal may be brought on the ground that reasonable progress was being made towards compliance with the improvement notice when the local housing authority gave notice under paragraph 4 of their intention to enter and take the action.

This does not affect the generality of sub-paragraph (1).

(5)  The tribunal may, on an appeal, make such order confirming, quashing or varying the demand as it considers appropriate.

(6)  A demand against which an appeal is brought becomes operative as follows—
    (a)  if a decision is given on the appeal which confirms the demand and the period within which an appeal to the [Upper Tribunal] may be brought expires without such an appeal having been brought, the demand becomes operative at end of that period;
    (b)  if an appeal to the [Upper Tribunal] is brought and a decision is given on the appeal which confirms the demand, the demand becomes operative at the time of that decision.

(7)  For the purposes of sub-paragraph (6)—
    (a)  the withdrawal of an appeal has the same effect as a decision which confirms the demand, and
    (b)  references to a decision which confirms the demand are to a decision which confirms it with or without variation.

(8)  No question may be raised on appeal under this paragraph which might have been raised on an appeal against the improvement notice.

*Expenses and interest recoverable from occupiers*

12.—(1)  Where a demand becomes operative by virtue of paragraph 9(2) or 11(6), the local housing authority may serve a recovery notice on any person—
    (a)  who occupies the premises concerned, or part of those premises, as the tenant or licensee of the person on whom the demand was served under paragraph 9(1); and
    (b)  who, by virtue of his tenancy or licence, pays rent or any sum in the nature of rent to the person on whom the demand was served.

(2)  A recovery notice is a notice—
    (a)  stating the amount of expenses recoverable by the local housing authority; and
    (b)  requiring all future payments by the tenant or licensee of rent or sums in the nature of rent (whether already accrued due or not) to be made direct to the authority until the expenses recoverable by the authority, together with any accrued interest on them, have been duly paid.

(3)  In the case of a demand which was served on any person as agent or trustee for another person ("the principal"), sub-paragraph (1) has effect as if the references in paragraphs (a) and (b) to the person on whom the demand was served were references to that person or the principal.

(4)  The effect of a recovery notice, once served under sub-paragraph (1), is to transfer to the local housing authority the right to recover, receive and give a discharge for the rent or sums in the nature of rent.

(5)  This is subject to any direction to the contrary contained in a further notice served by the local housing authority on the tenant or licensee.

(6)  In addition, the right to recover, receive and give a discharge for any rent or sums in the nature of rent is postponed to any right in respect of that rent or those sums which may at any time be vested in a superior landlord by virtue of a notice under section 6 of the Law of Distress Amendment Act 1908 (c 53).

*Expenses and interest to be a charge on the premises*

13.—(1)   Until recovered, the expenses recoverable by the local housing authority, together with any accrued interest on them, are a charge on the premises to which the improvement notice related.

(2)   The charge takes effect when the demand for the expenses and interest becomes operative by virtue of paragraph 9(2) or 11(6).

(3)   For the purpose of enforcing the charge, the local housing authority have the same powers and remedies, under the Law of Property Act 1925 (c 20) and otherwise, as if they were mortgagees by deed having powers of sale and lease, of accepting surrenders of leases and of appointing a receiver.

(4)   The power of appointing a receiver is exercisable at any time after the end of one month beginning with the date when the charge takes effect.

*Recovery of expenses and interest from other persons profiting from taking of action*

14.—(1)   Sub-paragraph (2) applies if, on an application to a residential property tribunal, the local housing authority satisfy the tribunal that—
    (a)   the expenses and interest have not been and are unlikely to be recovered; and
    (b)   a person is profiting by the taking of the action under paragraph 3 in respect of which the expenses were incurred in that he is obtaining rents or other payments which would not have been obtainable if the number of persons living in the premises was limited to that appropriate for the premises in their state before the action was taken.

(2)   The tribunal may, if satisfied that the person concerned has had proper notice of the application, order him to make such payments to the local housing authority as the tribunal considers to be just.

**[1535]**

**NOTES**

Commencement: 6 April 2006 (in relation to England, subject to transitional provisions and savings in the Housing Act 2004 (Commencement No 5 and Transitional Provisions and Savings) (England) Order 2006, SI 2006/1060, art 3, Schedule at **[3700]**, **[3701]**); 16 June 2006 (in relation to Wales, subject to transitional provisions and savings in the Housing Act 2004 (Commencement No 3 and Transitional Provisions and Savings) (Wales) Order 2006, SI 2006/1535, art 3, Schedule at **[3714]**, **[3715]**).

Para 11: words in square brackets substituted by the Transfer of Tribunal Functions (Lands Tribunal and Miscellaneous Amendments) Order 2009, SI 2009/1307, art 5(1), (2), Sch 1, paras 271, 280, subject to transitional and savings provisions in Sch 5 thereto.

SCHEDULE 4
LICENCES UNDER PARTS 2 AND 3: MANDATORY CONDITIONS

Sections 67 and 90

*Conditions to be included in licences under Part 2 or 3*

1.—(1)   A licence under Part 2 or 3 must include the following conditions.

(2)   Conditions requiring the licence holder, if gas is supplied to the house, to produce to the local housing authority annually for their inspection a gas safety certificate obtained in respect of the house within the last 12 months.

(3)   Conditions requiring the licence holder—
    (a)   to keep electrical appliances and furniture made available by him in the house in a safe condition;
    (b)   to supply the authority, on demand, with a declaration by him as to the safety of such appliances and furniture.

(4)   Conditions requiring the licence holder—
    (a)   to ensure that smoke alarms are installed in the house and to keep them in proper working order;
    (b)   to supply the authority, on demand, with a declaration by him as to the condition and positioning of such alarms.

(5)   Conditions requiring the licence holder to supply to the occupiers of the house a written statement of the terms on which they occupy it.

*Additional conditions to be included in licences under Part 3*

2.   A licence under Part 3 must include conditions requiring the licence holder to demand references from persons who wish to occupy the house.

*Power to prescribe conditions*

3.   The appropriate national authority may by regulations amend this Schedule so as to alter (by the addition or removal of conditions) the conditions which must be included—

    (a)    in a licence under Part 2 or 3, or

    (b)    only in a licence under one of those Parts.

*Interpretation*

4.    In this Schedule "the house" means the HMO or Part 3 house in respect of which the licence is granted.

**[1536]**

**NOTES**

    Commencement: 18 November 2004 (for the purpose of making orders or regulations); 6 April 2006 (in relation to England for remaining purposes, subject to transitional provisions and savings in the Housing Act 2004 (Commencement No 5 and Transitional Provisions and Savings) (England) Order 2006, SI 2006/1060, art 3, Schedule at **[3700]**, **[3701]**); 16 June 2006 (in relation to Wales for remaining purposes, subject to transitional provisions and savings in the Housing Act 2004 (Commencement No 3 and Transitional Provisions and Savings) (Wales) Order 2006, SI 2006/1535, art 3, Schedule at **[3714]**, **[3715]**).

    Modification: see the note to s 61 at **[1383]**.

## SCHEDULE 5
## LICENCES UNDER PARTS 2 AND 3: PROCEDURE AND APPEALS
Sections 71 and 94

### PART 1
### PROCEDURE RELATING TO GRANT OR REFUSAL OF LICENCES

*Requirements before grant of licence*

1.    Before granting a licence, the local housing authority must—

    (a)    serve a notice under this paragraph, together with a copy of the proposed licence, on the applicant for the licence and each relevant person, and

    (b)    consider any representations made in accordance with the notice and not withdrawn.

2.    The notice under paragraph 1 must state that the authority are proposing to grant the licence and set out—

    (a)    the reasons for granting the licence,

    (b)    the main terms of the licence, and

    (c)    the end of the consultation period.

3.—(1)    This paragraph applies if, having considered representations made in accordance with a notice under paragraph 1 or this paragraph, the local housing authority propose to grant a licence with modifications.

    (2)    Before granting the licence the authority must—

    (a)    serve a notice under this paragraph on the applicant for the licence and each relevant person, and

    (b)    consider any representations made in accordance with the notice and not withdrawn.

4.    The notice under paragraph 3 must set out—

    (a)    the proposed modifications,

    (b)    the reasons for them, and

    (c)    the end of the consultation period.

*Requirements before refusal to grant licence*

5.    Before refusing to grant a licence, the local housing authority must—

    (a)    serve a notice under this paragraph on the applicant for the licence and each relevant person, and

    (b)    consider any representations made in accordance with the notice and not withdrawn.

6.    The notice under paragraph 5 must state that the local housing authority are proposing to refuse to grant the licence and set out—

    (a)    the reasons for refusing to grant the licence, and

    (b)    the end of the consultation period.

*Requirements following grant or refusal of licence*

7.—(1)    This paragraph applies where the local housing authority decide to grant a licence.

    (2)    The local housing authority must serve on the applicant for the licence (and, if different, the licence holder) and each relevant person—

    (a)    a copy of the licence, and

    (b)    a notice setting out—

        (i)    the reasons for deciding to grant the licence and the date on which the decision was made,

        (ii)    the right of appeal against the decision under Part 3 of this Schedule, and

    (iii)   the period within which an appeal may be made (see paragraph 33(1)).

(3)   The documents required to be served under sub-paragraph (2) must be served within the period of seven days beginning with the day on which the decision is made.

8.—(1)   This paragraph applies where the local housing authority refuse to grant a licence.

(2)   The local housing authority must serve on the applicant for the licence and each relevant person a notice setting out—

    (a)   the authority's decision not to grant the licence,
    (b)   the reasons for the decision and the date on which it was made,
    (c)   the right of appeal against the decision under Part 3 of this Schedule, and
    (d)   the period within which an appeal may be made (see paragraph 33(1)).

(3)   The notices required to be served under sub-paragraph (2) must be served within the period of seven days beginning with the day on which the decision is made.

### *Exceptions from requirements in relation to grant or refusal of licences*

9.   The requirements of paragraph 3 (and those of paragraph 1) do not apply if the local housing authority—

    (a)   have already served a notice under paragraph 1 but not paragraph 3 in relation to the proposed licence, and
    (b)   consider that the modifications which are now being proposed are not material in any respect.

10.   The requirements of paragraph 3 (and those of paragraph 1) do not apply if the local housing authority—

    (a)   have already served notices under paragraphs 1 and 3 in relation to the matter concerned, and
    (b)   consider that the further modifications which are now being proposed do not differ in any material respect from the modifications in relation to which a notice was last served under paragraph 3.

11.   Paragraphs 5, 6 and 8 do not apply to a refusal to grant a licence on particular terms if the local housing authority are proposing to grant the licence on different terms.

### *Meaning of "the end of the consultation period"*

12.—(1)   In this Part of this Schedule "the end of the consultation period" means the last day for making representations in respect of the matter in question.

(2)   The end of the consultation period must be—

    (a)   in the case of a notice under paragraph 1 or 5, a day which is at least 14 days after the date of service of the notice; and
    (b)   in the case of a notice under paragraph 3, a day which is at least 7 days after the date of service of the notice.

(3)   In sub-paragraph (2) "the date of service" of a notice means, in a case where more than one notice is served, the date on which the last of the notices is served.

### *Meaning of "licence" and "relevant person"*

13.—(1)   In this Part of this Schedule "licence" means a licence under Part 2 or 3 of this Act.

(2)   In this Part of this Schedule "relevant person", in relation to a licence under Part 2 or 3 of this Act, means any person (other than a person excluded by sub-paragraph (3))—

    (a)   who, to the knowledge of the local housing authority concerned, is—
       (i)   a person having an estate or interest in the HMO or Part 3 house in question, or
      (ii)   a person managing or having control of that HMO or Part 3 house (and not falling within sub-paragraph (i)), or
    (b)   on whom any restriction or obligation is or is to be imposed by the licence in accordance with section 67(5) or 90(6).

(3)   The persons excluded by this sub-paragraph are—

    (a)   the applicant for the licence and (if different) the licence holder, and
    (b)   any tenant under a lease with an unexpired term of 3 years or less.

                                                              **[1537]**

**NOTES**

Commencement: 6 April 2006 (in relation to England, subject to transitional provisions and savings in the Housing Act 2004 (Commencement No 5 and Transitional Provisions and Savings) (England) Order 2006, SI 2006/1060, art 3, Schedule at **[3700]**, **[3701]**); 16 June 2006 (in relation to Wales, subject to transitional provisions and savings in the Housing Act 2004 (Commencement No 3 and Transitional Provisions and Savings) (Wales) Order 2006, SI 2006/1535, art 3, Schedule at **[3714]**, **[3715]**).

PART 2
PROCEDURE RELATING TO VARIATION OR REVOCATION OF LICENCES

*Variation of licences*

14.   Before varying a licence, the local housing authority must—
(a)   serve a notice under this paragraph on the licence holder and each relevant person, and
(b)   consider any representations made in accordance with the notice and not withdrawn.

15.   The notice under paragraph 14 must state that the local housing authority are proposing to make the variation and set out—
(a)   the effect of the variation,
(b)   the reasons for the variation, and
(c)   the end of the consultation period.

16.—(1)   This paragraph applies where the local housing authority decide to vary a licence.

(2)   The local housing authority must serve on the licence holder and each relevant person—
(a)   a copy of the authority's decision to vary the licence, and
(b)   a notice setting out—
   (i)   the reasons for the decision and the date on which it was made,
   (ii)   the right of appeal against the decision under Part 3 of this Schedule, and
   (iii)   the period within which an appeal may be made (see paragraph 33(2)).

(3)   The documents required to be served under sub-paragraph (2) must be served within the period of seven days beginning with the day on which the decision is made.

*Exceptions from requirements of paragraph 14*

17.   The requirements of paragraph 14 do not apply if—
(a)   the local housing authority consider that the variation is not material, or
(b)   the variation is agreed by the licence holder and the local housing authority consider that it would not be appropriate to comply with the requirements of that paragraph.

18.   The requirements of paragraph 14 do not apply if the local housing authority—
(a)   have already served a notice under that paragraph in relation to a proposed variation, and
(b)   consider that the variation which is now being proposed is not materially different from the previous proposed variation.

*Refusal to vary a licence*

19.—   Before refusing to vary a licence, the local housing authority must—
(a)   serve a notice under this paragraph on the licence holder and each relevant person, and
(b)   consider any representations made in accordance with the notice and not withdrawn.

20.   The notice under paragraph 19 must state that the authority are proposing to refuse to vary the licence and set out—
(a)   the reasons for refusing to vary the licence, and
(b)   the end of the consultation period.

21.—(1)   This paragraph applies where the local housing authority refuse to vary a licence.

(2)   The authority must serve on the licence holder and each relevant person a notice setting out—
(a)   the authority's decision not to vary the licence,
(b)   the reasons for the decision and the date on which it was made,
(c)   the right of appeal against the decision under Part 3 of this Schedule, and
(d)   the period within which an appeal may be made (see paragraph 33(2)).

(3)   The documents required to be served under sub-paragraph (2) must be served within the period of seven days beginning with the day on which the decision is made.

*Revocation of licences*

22.   Before revoking a licence, the local housing authority must—
(a)   serve a notice on the licence holder under this paragraph and each relevant person, and
(b)   consider any representations made in accordance with the notice and not withdrawn.

23.   The notice under paragraph 22 must state that the authority are proposing to revoke the licence and set out—
(a)   the reasons for the revocation, and
(b)   the end of the consultation period.

24.—(1)   This paragraph applies where the local housing authority decide to revoke a licence.

(2)   The authority must serve on the licence holder and each relevant person—
(a)   a copy of the authority's decision to revoke the licence, and
(b)   a notice setting out—
   (i)   the reasons for the decision and the date on which it was made,

(ii)　the right of appeal against the decision under Part 3 of this Schedule, and
(iii)　the period within which an appeal may be made (see paragraph 33(2)).

(3)　The documents required to be served under sub-paragraph (2) must be served within the period of seven days beginning with the day on which the decision is made.

### Exception from requirements of paragraph 22

25.　The requirements of paragraph 22 do not apply if the revocation is agreed by the licence holder and the local housing authority consider that it would not be appropriate to comply with the requirements of that paragraph.

### Refusal to revoke a licence

26.　Before refusing to revoke a licence, the local housing authority must—
(a)　serve a notice under this paragraph on the licence holder and each relevant person, and
(b)　consider any representations made in accordance with the notice and not withdrawn.

27.　The notice under paragraph 26 must state that the authority are proposing to refuse to revoke the licence and set out—
(a)　the reasons for refusing to revoke the licence, and
(b)　the end of the consultation period.

28.—(1)　This paragraph applies where the local housing authority refuse to revoke a licence.

(2)　The authority must serve on the licence holder and each relevant person a notice setting out—
(a)　the authority's decision not to revoke the licence,
(b)　the reasons for the decision and the date on which it was made,
(c)　the right of appeal against the decision under Part 3 of this Schedule, and
(d)　the period within which an appeal may be made (see paragraph 33(2)).

(3)　The notices required to be served under sub-paragraph (2) must be served within the period of seven days beginning with the day on which the decision is made.

### Meaning of "the end of the consultation period"

29.—(1)　In this Part of this Schedule "the end of the consultation period" means the last day on which representations may be made in respect of the matter in question.

(2)　That date must be at least 14 days after the date of service of the notice in question.

(3)　In sub-paragraph (2) "the date of service" of a notice means, in a case where more than one notice is served, the date on which the last of the notices is served.

### Meaning of "licence" and "relevant person"

30.—(1)　In this Part of this Schedule "licence" means a licence under Part 2 or 3 of this Act.

(2)　In this Part of this Schedule "relevant person", in relation to a licence under Part 2 or 3 of this Act, means any person (other than a person excluded by sub-paragraph (3))—
(a)　who, to the knowledge of the local housing authority concerned, is—
(i)　a person having an estate or interest in the HMO or Part 3 house in question, or
(ii)　a person managing or having control of that HMO or Part 3 house (and not falling within sub-paragraph (i)), or
(b)　on whom any restriction or obligation is or is to be imposed by the licence in accordance with section 67(5) or 90(6).

(3)　The persons excluded by this sub-paragraph are—
(a)　the licence holder, and
(b)　any tenant under a lease with an unexpired term of 3 years or less.

**[1538]**

**NOTES**
Commencement: 6 April 2006 (in relation to England, subject to transitional provisions and savings in the Housing Act 2004 (Commencement No 5 and Transitional Provisions and Savings) (England) Order 2006, SI 2006/1060, art 3, Schedule at **[3700]**, **[3701]**); 16 June 2006 (in relation to Wales, subject to transitional provisions and savings in the Housing Act 2004 (Commencement No 3 and Transitional Provisions and Savings) (Wales) Order 2006, SI 2006/1535, art 3, Schedule at **[3714]**, **[3715]**).

## PART 3
### APPEALS AGAINST LICENCE DECISIONS

### Right to appeal against refusal or grant of licence

31.—(1)　The applicant or any relevant person may appeal to a residential property tribunal against a decision by the local housing authority on an application for a licence—

(a)   to refuse to grant the licence, or

(b)   to grant the licence.

(2)   An appeal under sub-paragraph (1)(b) may, in particular, relate to any of the terms of the licence.

### *Right to appeal against decision or refusal to vary or revoke licence*

32.—(1)   The licence holder or any relevant person may appeal to a residential property tribunal against a decision by the local housing authority—

(a)   to vary or revoke a licence, or

(b)   to refuse to vary or revoke a licence.

(2)   But this does not apply to the licence holder in a case where the decision to vary or revoke the licence was made with his agreement.

### *Time limits for appeals*

33.—(1)   Any appeal under paragraph 31 against a decision to grant, or (as the case may be) to refuse to grant, a licence must be made within the period of 28 days beginning with the date specified in the notice under paragraph 7 or 8 as the date on which the decision was made.

(2)   Any appeal under paragraph 32 against a decision to vary or revoke, or (as the case may be) to refuse to vary or revoke, a licence must be made within the period of 28 days beginning with the date specified in the notice under paragraph 16, 21, 24 or 28 as the date on which the decision was made.

(3)   A residential property tribunal may allow an appeal to be made to it after the end of the period mentioned in sub-paragraph (1) or (2) if it is satisfied that there is a good reason for the failure to appeal before the end of that period (and for any delay since then in applying for permission to appeal out of time).

### *Powers of residential property tribunal hearing appeal*

34.—(1)   This paragraph applies to appeals to a residential property tribunal under paragraph 31 or 32.

(2)   An appeal—

(a)   is to be by way of a re-hearing, but

(b)   may be determined having regard to matters of which the authority were unaware.

(3)   The tribunal may confirm, reverse or vary the decision of the local housing authority.

(4)   On an appeal under paragraph 31 the tribunal may direct the authority to grant a licence to the applicant for the licence on such terms as the tribunal may direct.

### *"The operative time" for the purposes of section 69(6), 70(8), 92(3) or 93(5)*

35.—(1)   This paragraph defines "the operative time" for the purposes of—

(a)   section 69(6) or 70(8) (variation or revocation of licence under Part 2 of this Act), or

(b)   section 92(3) or 93(5) (variation or revocation of licence under Part 3 of this Act).

(2)   If the period of 28 days mentioned in paragraph 33(2) has expired without an appeal having been made under paragraph 32, "the operative time" is the end of that period.

(3)   If an appeal is made under paragraph 32 within that period and a decision is given on the appeal which confirms the variation or revocation, "the operative time" is as follows—

(a)   if the period within which an appeal to the [Upper Tribunal] may be brought expires without such an appeal having been brought, "the operative time" is the end of that period;

(b)   if an appeal to the [Upper Tribunal] is brought, "the operative time" is the time when a decision is given on the appeal which confirms the variation or revocation.

(4)   For the purposes of sub-paragraph (3)—

(a)   the withdrawal of an appeal has the same effect as a decision confirming the variation or revocation appealed against; and

(b)   references to a decision which confirms a variation are to a decision which confirms it with or without variation.

### *Meaning of "licence" and "relevant person"*

36.—(1)   In this Part of this Schedule "licence" means a licence under Part 2 or 3 of this Act.

(2)   In this Part of this Schedule "relevant person", in relation to a licence under Part 2 or 3 of this Act, means any person (other than a person excluded by sub-paragraph (3))—

(a)   who is—

(i)   a person having an estate or interest in the HMO or Part 3 house concerned, or

  (ii) a person managing or having control of that HMO or Part 3 house (and not falling within sub-paragraph (i)), or

 (b) on whom any restriction or obligation is or is to be imposed by the licence in accordance with section 67(5) or 90(6).

(3) The persons excluded by this sub-paragraph are—

 (a) the applicant for the licence and (if different) the licence holder, and

 (b) any tenant under a lease with an unexpired term of 3 years or less.

**[1539]**

**NOTES**

 Commencement: 6 April 2006 (in relation to England, subject to transitional provisions and savings in the Housing Act 2004 (Commencement No 5 and Transitional Provisions and Savings) (England) Order 2006, SI 2006/1060, art 3, Schedule at **[3700]**, **[3701]**); 16 June 2006 (in relation to Wales, subject to transitional provisions and savings in the Housing Act 2004 (Commencement No 3 and Transitional Provisions and Savings) (Wales) Order 2006, SI 2006/1535, art 3, Schedule at **[3714]**, **[3715]**).

 Para 35: words in square brackets substituted by the Transfer of Tribunal Functions (Lands Tribunal and Miscellaneous Amendments) Order 2009, SI 2009/1307, art 5(1), (2), Sch 1, paras 271, 281, subject to transitional and savings provisions in Sch 5 thereto.

SCHEDULE 6

MANAGEMENT ORDERS: PROCEDURE AND APPEALS

Section 123

PART 1

PROCEDURE RELATING TO MAKING OF MANAGEMENT ORDERS

*Requirements before making final management order*

1. Before making a final management order, the local housing authority must—

 (a) serve a copy of the proposed order, together with a notice under this paragraph, on each relevant person; and

 (b) consider any representations made in accordance with the notice and not withdrawn.

2. The notice under paragraph 1 must state that the authority are proposing to make a final management order and set out—

 (a) the reasons for making the order;

 (b) the main terms of the proposed order (including those of the management scheme to be contained in it); and

 (c) the end of the consultation period.

3.—(1) This paragraph applies if, having considered representations made in accordance with a notice under paragraph 1 or this paragraph, the local housing authority propose to make a final management order with modifications.

 (2) Before making the order, the authority must—

 (a) serve a notice under this paragraph on each relevant person; and

 (b) consider any representations made in accordance with the notice and not withdrawn.

4. The notice under paragraph 3 must set out—

 (a) the proposed modifications;

 (b) the reasons for them; and

 (c) the end of the consultation period.

*Exceptions from requirements relating to making of final management order*

5. The requirements of paragraph 3 (and those of paragraph 1) do not apply if the local housing authority—

 (a) have already served notice under paragraph 1 but not paragraph 3 in relation to the proposed final management order; and

 (b) consider that the modifications which are now being proposed are not material in any respect.

6. The requirements of paragraph 3 (and those of paragraph 1) do not apply if the local housing authority—

 (a) have already served notices under paragraphs 1 and 3 in relation to the matter concerned; and

 (b) consider that the further modifications which are now being proposed do not differ in any material respect from the modifications in relation to which a notice was last served under paragraph 3.

*Requirements following making of interim or final management order*

7.—(1)   This paragraph applies where the local housing authority make an interim management order or a final management order.

(2)   As soon as practicable after the order is made, the authority must serve on the occupiers of the house—

(a)   a copy of the order, and

(b)   a notice under this sub-paragraph.

(3)   Those documents are to be regarded as having been served on the occupiers if they are fixed to a conspicuous part of the house.

(4)   The notice under sub-paragraph (2) must set out—

(a)   the reasons for making the order and the date on which it was made,

(b)   the general effect of the order, and

(c)   the date on which the order is to cease to have effect in accordance with section 105(4) and (5) or 114(3) and (4) (or, if applicable, how the date mentioned in section 105(6) is to be determined),

and (if it is a final management order) give a general description of the way in which the house is to be managed by the authority in accordance with the management scheme contained in the order.

(5)   The authority must also serve a copy of the order, together with a notice under this sub-paragraph, on each relevant person.

(6)   The notice under sub-paragraph (5) must comply with sub-paragraph (4) and also contain information about—

(a)   the right of appeal against the order under Part 3 of this Schedule, and

(b)   the period within which any such appeal may be made (see paragraph 25(2)).

(7)   The documents required to be served on each relevant person under sub-paragraph (5) must be served within the period of seven days beginning with the day on which the order is made.

*Meaning of "the end of the consultation period" and "relevant person"*

8.—(1)   In this Part of this Schedule "the end of the consultation period" means the last day for making representations in respect of the matter in question.

(2)   The end of the consultation period must be—

(a)   in the case of a notice under paragraph 1, a day which is at least 14 days after the date of service of the notice; and

(b)   in the case of a notice under paragraph 3, a day which is at least 7 days after the date of service of the notice.

(3)   In sub-paragraph (2) "the date of service" of a notice means, in a case where more than one notice is served, the date on which the last of the notices is served.

(4)   In this Part of this Schedule "relevant person" means any person who, to the knowledge of the local housing authority, is—

(a)   a person having an estate or interest in the house or part of it (but who is not a tenant under a lease with an unexpired term of 3 years or less), or

(b)   any other person who (but for the order) would be a person managing or having control of the house or part of it.

**[1540]**

**NOTES**

Commencement: 6 April 2006 (in relation to England, subject to transitional provisions and savings in the Housing Act 2004 (Commencement No 5 and Transitional Provisions and Savings) (England) Order 2006, SI 2006/1060, art 3, Schedule at **[3700]**, **[3701]**); 16 June 2006 (in relation to Wales, subject to transitional provisions and savings in the Housing Act 2004 (Commencement No 3 and Transitional Provisions and Savings) (Wales) Order 2006, SI 2006/1535, art 3, Schedule at **[3714]**, **[3715]**).

## PART 2
## PROCEDURE RELATING TO VARIATION OR REVOCATION OF MANAGEMENT ORDERS

*Variation of management orders*

9.   Before varying an interim or final management order, the local housing authority must—

(a)   serve a notice under this paragraph on each relevant person, and

(b)   consider any representations made in accordance with the notice and not withdrawn.

10.   The notice under paragraph 9 must state that the authority are proposing to make the variation and specify—

(a)   the effect of the variation,

(b)   the reasons for the variation, and

(c)   the end of the consultation period.

11.—(1)   This paragraph applies where the local housing authority decide to vary an interim or final management order.

(2)   The local housing authority must serve on each relevant person—
- (a)   a copy of the authority's decision to vary the order, and
- (b)   a notice setting out—
  - (i)   the reasons for the decision and the date on which it was made,
  - (ii)   the right of appeal against the decision under Part 3 of this Schedule, and
  - (iii)   the period within which an appeal may be made (see paragraph 29(2)).

(3)   The documents required to be served on each relevant person under sub-paragraph (2) must be served within the period of seven days beginning with the day on which the decision is made.

*Exceptions from requirements of paragraph 9*

12.   The requirements of paragraph 9 do not apply if the local housing authority consider that the variation is not material.

13.   The requirements of paragraph 9 do not apply if the local housing authority—
- (a)   have already served a notice under that paragraph in relation to a proposed variation; and
- (b)   consider that the variation which is now being proposed is not materially different from the previous proposed variation

*Refusal to vary interim or final management order*

14.   Before refusing to vary an interim or final management order, the local housing authority must—
- (a)   serve a notice under this paragraph on each relevant person, and
- (b)   consider any representations made in accordance with the notice and not withdrawn.

15.   The notice under paragraph 14 must state that the authority are proposing to refuse to make the variation and set out—
- (a)   the reasons for refusing to make the variation, and
- (b)   the end of the consultation period.

16.—(1)   This paragraph applies where the local housing authority refuse to vary an interim or final management order.

(2)   The authority must serve on each relevant person a notice setting out—
- (a)   the authority's decision not to vary the order;
- (b)   the reasons for the decision and the date on which it was made;
- (c)   the right of appeal against the decision under Part 3 of this Schedule; and
- (d)   the period within which an appeal may be made (see paragraph 29(2)).

(3)   The notices required to be served on each relevant person under sub-paragraph (2) must be served within the period of seven days beginning with the day on which the decision is made.

*Revocation of management orders*

17.   Before revoking an interim or final management order, the local housing authority must—
- (a)   serve a notice under this paragraph on each relevant person, and
- (b)   consider any representations made in accordance with the notice and not withdrawn.

18.   The notice under paragraph 17 must state that the authority are proposing to revoke the order and specify—
- (a)   the reasons for the revocation, and
- (b)   the end of the consultation period.

19.—(1)   This paragraph applies where the local housing authority decide to revoke an interim or final management order.

(2)   The authority must serve on each relevant person—
- (a)   a copy of the authority's decision to revoke the order; and
- (b)   a notice setting out—
  - (i)   the reasons for the decision and the date on which it was made;
  - (ii)   the right of appeal against the decision under Part 3 of this Schedule; and
  - (iii)   the period within which an appeal may be made (see paragraph 29(2)).

(3)   The documents required to be served on each relevant person under sub-paragraph (2) must be served within the period of seven days beginning with the day on which the decision is made.

*Refusal to revoke management order*

20.   Before refusing to revoke an interim or final management order, the local housing authority must—
- (a)   serve a notice under this paragraph on each relevant person; and
- (b)   consider any representations made in accordance with the notice and not withdrawn.

21.   The notice under paragraph 20 must state that the authority are proposing to refuse to revoke the order and set out—

    (a)    the reasons for refusing to revoke the order, and

    (b)    the end of the consultation period.

22.—(1)   This paragraph applies where the local housing authority refuse to revoke an interim or final management order.

    (2)   The authority must serve on each relevant person a notice setting out—

    (a)    the authority's decision not to revoke the order;

    (b)    the reasons for the decision and the date on which it was made;

    (c)    the right of appeal against the decision under Part 3 of this Schedule; and

    (d)    the period within which an appeal may be made (see paragraph 29(2)).

    (3)   The notices required to be served on each relevant person under sub-paragraph (2) must be served within the period of seven days beginning with the day on which the decision is made.

*Meaning of "the end of the consultation period" and "relevant person"*

23.—(1)   In this Part of this Schedule "the end of the consultation period" means the last day for making representations in respect of the matter in question.

    (2)   The end of the consultation period must be a day which is at least 14 days after the date of service of the notice.

    (3)   In sub-paragraph (2) "the date of service" of a notice means, in a case where more than one notice is served, the date on which the last of the notices is served.

    (4)   In this Part of this Schedule "relevant person" means any person who, to the knowledge of the local housing authority, is—

    (a)    a person having an estate or interest in the house or part of it (but who is not a tenant under a lease with an unexpired term of 3 years or less), or

    (b)    any other person who (but for the order) would be a person managing or having control of the house or part of it.

                                                        **[1541]**

**NOTES**

   Commencement: 6 April 2006 (in relation to England, subject to transitional provisions and savings in the Housing Act 2004 (Commencement No 5 and Transitional Provisions and Savings) (England) Order 2006, SI 2006/1060, art 3, Schedule at **[3700]**, **[3701]**); 16 June 2006 (in relation to Wales, subject to transitional provisions and savings in the Housing Act 2004 (Commencement No 3 and Transitional Provisions and Savings) (Wales) Order 2006, SI 2006/1535, art 3, Schedule at **[3714]**, **[3715]**).

PART 3

APPEALS AGAINST DECISIONS RELATING TO MANAGEMENT ORDERS

*Right to appeal against making of order etc*

24.—(1)   A relevant person may appeal to a residential property tribunal against—

    (a)    a decision of the local housing authority to make an interim or final management order, or

    (b)    the terms of such an order (including, if it is a final management order, those of the management scheme contained in it).

    (2)   Except to the extent that an appeal may be made in accordance with sub-paragraphs (3) and (4), sub-paragraph (1) does not apply to an interim management order made under section 102(4) or (7) or in accordance with a direction given under paragraph 26(5).

    (3)   An appeal may be made under sub-paragraph (1)(b) on the grounds that the terms of an interim management order do not provide for one or both of the matters mentioned in section 110(5)(a) and (b) (which relate to payments of surplus rent etc).

    (4)   Where an appeal is made under sub-paragraph (1)(b) only on those grounds—

    (a)    the appeal may be brought at any time while the order is in force (with the result that nothing in sub-paragraph (5) or paragraph 25 applies in relation to the appeal); and

    (b)    the powers of the residential property tribunal under paragraph 26 are limited to determining whether the order should be varied by the tribunal so as to include a term providing for the matter or matters in question, and (if so) what provision should be made by the term.

    (5)   If no appeal is brought against an interim or final management order under this paragraph within the time allowed by paragraph 25 for making such an appeal, the order is final and conclusive as to the matters which could have been raised on appeal.

*Time limits for appeals under paragraph 24*

25.—(1) This paragraph applies in relation to an appeal under paragraph 24 in respect of an interim or final management order.

(2) Any such appeal must be made within the period of 28 days beginning with the date specified in the notice under paragraph 7(5) as the date on which the order was made.

(3) A residential property tribunal may allow an appeal to be made to it after the end of the period mentioned in sub-paragraph (2) if it is satisfied that there is a good reason for the failure to appeal before the end of that period (and for any delay since then in applying for permission to appeal out of time).

*Powers of residential property tribunal on appeal under paragraph 24*

26.—(1) This paragraph applies to an appeal to a residential property tribunal under paragraph 24 in respect of an interim or final management order.

(2) The appeal—
    (a)    is to be by way of a re-hearing, but
    (b)    may be determined having regard to matters of which the authority were unaware.

(3) The tribunal may confirm or vary the order or revoke it—
    (a)    (in the case of an interim management order) as from a date specified in the tribunal's order, or
    (b)    (in the case of a final management order) as from the date of the tribunal's order.

(4) If—
    (a)    the tribunal revokes an interim or final management order,
    (b)    it appears to the tribunal that, on the revocation of the order, the house will be required to be licensed under Part 2 or 3 of this Act, and
    (c)    the tribunal does not give a direction under sub-paragraph (5) or (6),
the tribunal must direct the local housing authority to grant such a licence to such person and on such terms as the tribunal may direct.

(5) If the tribunal revokes a final management order, the tribunal may direct the local housing authority to make an interim management order in respect of the house or part of it on such terms as the tribunal may direct.

This applies despite section 102(9).

(6) If the tribunal revokes a final management order, the tribunal may direct the local housing authority to serve a temporary exemption notice under section 62 or 86 in respect of the house that comes into force on such date as the tribunal directs.

(7) The revocation of an interim management order by the tribunal does not affect the validity of anything previously done in pursuance of the order.

*"The operative time" for the purposes of section 114(2)*

27.—(1) This paragraph defines "the operative time" for the purposes of section 114(2).

(2) If no appeal is made under paragraph 24 before the end of the period of 28 days mentioned in paragraph 25(2), "the operative time" is the end of that period.

(3) If an appeal is made under paragraph 24 before the end of that period, and a decision is given on the appeal which confirms the order, "the operative time" is as follows—
    (a)    if the period within which an appeal to the [Upper Tribunal] may be brought expires without such an appeal having been brought, "the operative time" is the end of that period;
    (b)    if an appeal to the [Upper Tribunal] is brought, "the operative time" is the time when a decision is given on the appeal which confirms the order.

(4) For the purposes of sub-paragraph (3)—
    (a)    the withdrawal of an appeal has the same effect as a decision which confirms the order, and
    (b)    references to a decision which confirms the order are to a decision which confirms it with or without variation.

*Right to appeal against decision or refusal to vary or revoke interim management order*

28.    A relevant person may appeal to a residential property tribunal against—
    (a)    a decision of a local housing authority to vary or revoke an interim or final management order, or
    (b)    a refusal of a local housing authority to vary or revoke an interim or final management order.

*Time limits for appeals under paragraph 28*

29.—(1)   This paragraph applies in relation to an appeal under paragraph 28 against a decision to vary or revoke, or (as the case may be) to refuse to vary or revoke, an interim or final management order.

(2)   Any such appeal must be made before the end of the period of 28 days beginning with the date specified in the notice under paragraph 11, 16, 19 or 22 as the date on which the decision concerned was made.

(3)   A residential property tribunal may allow an appeal to be made to it after the end of the period mentioned in sub-paragraph (2) if it is satisfied that there is a good reason for the failure to appeal before the end of that period (and for any delay since then in applying for permission to appeal out of time).

*Powers of residential property tribunal on appeal under paragraph 28*

30.—(1)   This paragraph applies to an appeal to a residential property tribunal under paragraph 28 against a decision to vary or revoke, or (as the case may be) to refuse to vary or revoke, an interim or final management order.

(2)   Paragraph 26(2) applies to such an appeal as it applies to an appeal under paragraph 24.

(3)   The tribunal may confirm, reverse or vary the decision of the local housing authority.

(4)   If the appeal is against a decision of the authority to refuse to revoke the order, the tribunal may make an order revoking the order as from a date specified in its order.

*"The operative time" for the purposes of section 111(2), 112(2), 121(2) or 122(2)*

31.—(1)   This paragraph defines "the operative time" for the purposes of—
  (a)   section 111(2) or 112(2) (variation or revocation of interim management order), or
  (b)   section 121(2) or 122(2) (variation or revocation of final management order).

(2)   If no appeal is made under paragraph 28 before the end of the period of 28 days mentioned in paragraph 29(2), "the operative time" is the end of that period.

(3)   If an appeal is made under paragraph 28 within that period, and a decision is given on the appeal which confirms the variation or revocation, "the operative time" is as follows—
  (a)   if the period within which an appeal to the [Upper Tribunal] may be brought expires without such an appeal having been brought, "the operative time" is the end of that period;
  (b)   if an appeal to the [Upper Tribunal] is brought, "the operative time" is the time when a decision is given on the appeal which confirms the variation or revocation.

(4)   For the purposes of sub-paragraph (3)—
  (a)   the withdrawal of an appeal has the same effect as a decision which confirms the variation or revocation appealed against; and
  (b)   references to a decision which confirms a variation are to a decision which confirms it with or without variation.

*Right to appeal against decision in respect of compensation payable to third parties*

32.—(1)   This paragraph applies where a local housing authority have made a decision under section 128 as to whether compensation should be paid to a third party in respect of any interference with his rights in consequence of an interim or final management order.

(2)   The third party may appeal to a residential property tribunal against—
  (a)   a decision by the authority not to pay compensation to him, or
  (b)   a decision of the authority so far as relating to the amount of compensation that should be paid.

*Time limits for appeals under paragraph 32*

33.—(1)   This paragraph applies in relation to an appeal under paragraph 32 against a decision of a local housing authority not to pay compensation to a third party or as to the amount of compensation to be paid.

(2)   Any such appeal must be made within the period of 28 days beginning with the date the authority notifies the third party under section 128(2).

(3)   A residential property tribunal may allow an appeal to be made to it after the end of the period mentioned in sub-paragraph (2) if it is satisfied that there is good reason for the failure to appeal before the end of that period (and for any delay since then in applying for permission to appeal out of time).

*Powers of residential property tribunal on appeal under paragraph 32*

34.—(1)　This paragraph applies in relation to an appeal under paragraph 32 against a decision of a local housing authority not to pay compensation to a third party or as to the amount of compensation to be paid.

(2)　The appeal—
  (a)　is to be by way of re-hearing, but
  (b)　may be determined having regard to matters of which the authority were unaware.

(3)　The tribunal may confirm, reverse or vary the decision of the local housing authority.

(4)　Where the tribunal reverses or varies a decision of the authority in respect of a final management order, it must make an order varying the management scheme contained in the final management order accordingly.

*Meaning of "relevant person"*

35.　In this Part of this Schedule "relevant person" means—
  (a)　any person who has an estate or interest in the house or part of it (but is not a tenant under a lease with an unexpired term of 3 years or less), or
  (b)　any other person who (but for the order) would be a person managing or having control of the house or part of it.

**[1542]**

**NOTES**

Commencement: 6 April 2006 (in relation to England, subject to transitional provisions and savings in the Housing Act 2004 (Commencement No 5 and Transitional Provisions and Savings) (England) Order 2006, SI 2006/1060, art 3, Schedule at **[3700]**, **[3701]**); 16 June 2006 (in relation to Wales, subject to transitional provisions and savings in the Housing Act 2004 (Commencement No 3 and Transitional Provisions and Savings) (Wales) Order 2006, SI 2006/1535, art 3, Schedule at **[3714]**, **[3715]**).

Para 27: words in square brackets substituted by the Transfer of Tribunal Functions (Lands Tribunal and Miscellaneous Amendments) Order 2009, SI 2009/1307, art 5(1), (2), Sch 1, paras 271, 282, subject to transitional and savings provisions in Sch 5 thereto.

Para 31: words in square brackets substituted by SI 2009/1307, art 5(1), (2), Sch 1, paras 271, 282, subject to transitional and savings provisions in Sch 5 thereto.

## SCHEDULE 7
## FURTHER PROVISIONS REGARDING EMPTY DWELLING MANAGEMENT ORDERS
Section 132

## PART 1
### INTERIM EDMOS

*Operation of interim EDMOs*

1.—(1)　This paragraph deals with the time when an interim EDMO comes into force or ceases to have effect.

(2)　The order comes into force when it is made.

(3)　The order ceases to have effect at the end of the period of 12 months beginning with the date on which it is made, unless it ceases to have effect at some other time as mentioned below.

(4)　If the order provides that it is to cease to have effect on a date falling before the end of that period, it accordingly ceases to have effect on that date.

(5)　Sub-paragraphs (6) and (7) apply where—
  (a)　a final EDMO ("the final EDMO") has been made under section 136 so as to replace the order ("the interim EDMO"), but
  (b)　the final EDMO has not come into force because of an appeal to a residential property tribunal under paragraph 26 against the making of the final EDMO.

(6)　If the date on which the final EDMO comes into force in relation to the dwelling following the disposal of the appeal is later than the date on which the interim EDMO would cease to have effect apart from this sub-paragraph, the interim EDMO continues in force until that later date.

(7)　If, on the application of the authority, the tribunal makes an order providing for the interim EDMO to continue in force, pending the disposal of the appeal, until a date later than that on which the interim EDMO would cease to have effect apart from this sub-paragraph, the interim EDMO accordingly continues in force until that later date.

(8)　This paragraph has effect subject to paragraphs 6 and 7 (variation or revocation of orders by authority) and to the power of revocation exercisable by a residential property tribunal on an appeal made under paragraph 30.

*General effect of interim EDMOs*

2.—(1)   This paragraph applies while an interim EDMO is in force in relation to a dwelling.

(2)   The rights and powers conferred by sub-paragraph (3) are exercisable by the authority in performing their duties under section 135(1) to (3) in respect of the dwelling.

(3)   The authority—
 (a)   have the right to possession of the dwelling (subject to the rights of existing occupiers preserved by paragraph 18(3));
 (b)   have the right to do (and authorise a manager or other person to do) in relation to the dwelling anything which the relevant proprietor of the dwelling would (but for the order) be entitled to do;
 (c)   may create one or more of the following—
  (i)   an interest in the dwelling which, as far as possible, has all the incidents of a leasehold, or
  (ii)   a right in the nature of a licence to occupy part of the dwelling;
 (d)   may apply to a residential property tribunal for an order under paragraph 22 determining a lease or licence of the dwelling.

(4)   But the authority may not under sub-paragraph (3)(c) create any interest or right in the nature of a lease or licence unless—
 (a)   consent in writing has been given by the relevant proprietor of the dwelling, and
 (b)   where the relevant proprietor is a lessee under a lease of the dwelling, the interest or right is created for a term that is less than the term of that lease.

(5)   The authority—
 (a)   do not under this paragraph acquire any estate or interest in the dwelling, and
 (b)   accordingly are not entitled by virtue of this paragraph to sell, lease, charge or make any other disposition of any such estate or interest.

(6)   But, where the relevant proprietor of the dwelling is a lessee under a lease of the dwelling, the authority are to be treated (subject to sub-paragraph (5)(a)) as if they were the lessee instead.

(7)   Any enactment or rule of law relating to landlords and tenants or leases applies in relation to—
 (a)   a lease in relation to which the authority are to be treated as the lessee under sub-paragraph (6), or
 (b)   a lease to which the authority become a party under paragraph 4(2),
as if the authority were the legal owner of the premises (but this is subject to paragraph 4(4) to (6)).

(8)   None of the following, namely—
 (a)   the authority, or
 (b)   any person authorised under sub-paragraph (3)(b),
is liable to any person having an estate or interest in the dwelling for anything done or omitted to be done in the performance (or intended performance) of the authority's duties under section 135(1) to (3) unless the act or omission is due to negligence of the authority or any such person.

(9)   An interim EDMO which has come into force is a local land charge.

(10)   The authority may apply to the Chief Land Registrar for the entry of an appropriate restriction in the register of title in respect of such an order.

(11)   In this paragraph "enactment" includes an enactment comprised in subordinate legislation (within the meaning of the Interpretation Act 1978 (c 30)).

*General effect of interim EDMOs: leases and licences granted by authority*

3.—(1)   This paragraph applies in relation to any interest or right created by the authority under paragraph 2(3)(c).

(2)   For the purposes of any enactment or rule of law—
 (a)   any interest created by the authority under paragraph 2(3)(c)(i) is to be treated as if it were a legal lease, and
 (b)   any right created by the authority under paragraph 2(3)(c)(ii) is to be treated as if it were a licence to occupy granted by the legal owner of the dwelling,
despite the fact that the authority have no legal estate in the dwelling (see paragraph 2(5)(a)).

(3)   Any enactment or rule of law relating to landlords and tenants or leases accordingly applies in relation to any interest created by the authority under paragraph 2(3)(c)(i) as if the authority were the legal owner of the dwelling.

(4)   References to leases and licences—
 (a)   in this Chapter, and
 (b)   in any other enactment,
accordingly include (where the context permits) interests and rights created by the authority under paragraph 2(3)(c).

(5)    The preceding provisions of this paragraph have effect subject to—
     (a)    paragraph 4(4) to (6), and
     (b)    any provision to the contrary contained in an order made by the appropriate national authority.

(6)    In paragraph 2(5)(b) the reference to leasing does not include the creation of interests under paragraph 2(3)(c)(i).

(7)    In this paragraph—
     "enactment" has the meaning given by paragraph 2(11);
     "legal lease" means a term of years absolute (within section 1(1)(b) of the Law of Property Act 1925 (c 20)).

*General effect of interim EDMOs: relevant proprietor, mortgagees etc*

4.—(1)    This paragraph applies in relation to—
     (a)    the relevant proprietor, and
     (b)    other persons with an estate or interest in the dwelling,
while an interim EDMO is in force in relation to a dwelling.

(2)    Where the relevant proprietor is a lessor or licensor under a lease or licence of the dwelling, the lease or licence has effect while the order is in force as if the local housing authority were substituted in it for the lessor or licensor.

(3)    Such a lease continues to have effect, as far as possible, as a lease despite the fact that the rights of the local housing authority, as substituted for the lessor, do not amount to an estate in law in the dwelling.

(4)    The provisions mentioned in sub-paragraph (5) do not apply to a lease or licence within sub-paragraph (2).

(5)    The provisions are—
     (a)    the provisions which exclude local authority lettings from the Rent Acts, namely—
         (i)    sections 14 to 16 of the Rent Act 1977 (c 42), and
         (ii)    those sections as applied by Schedule 2 to the Rent (Agriculture) Act 1976 (c 80) and section 5(2) to (4) of that Act; and
     (b)    section 1(2) of, and paragraph 12 of Part 1 of Schedule 1 to, the Housing Act 1988 (c 50) (which exclude local authority lettings from Part 1 of that Act).

(6)    Nothing in this Chapter has the result that the authority are to be treated as the legal owner of any premises for the purposes of—
     (a)    section 80 of the Housing Act 1985 (c 68) (the landlord condition for secure tenancies); or
     (b)    section 124 of the Housing Act 1996 (c 52) (introductory tenancies).

(7)    The relevant proprietor of the dwelling—
     (a)    is not entitled to receive any rents or other payments made in respect of occupation of the dwelling;
     (b)    may not exercise any rights or powers with respect to the management of the dwelling; and
     (c)    may not create any of the following—
         (i)    any leasehold interest in the dwelling or a part of it (other than a lease of a reversion), or
         (ii)    any licence or other right to occupy it.

(8)    However (subject to sub-paragraph (7)(c)) nothing in paragraph 2 or this paragraph affects the ability of a person having an estate or interest in the dwelling to make any disposition of that estate or interest.

(9)    Nothing in paragraph 2 or this paragraph affects—
     (a)    the validity of any mortgage relating to the dwelling or any rights or remedies available to the mortgagee under such a mortgage, or
     (b)    the validity of any lease of the dwelling under which the relevant proprietor is a lessee, or any superior lease, or (subject to paragraph 2(6)) any rights or remedies available to the lessor under such a lease,
except to the extent that any of those rights or remedies would prevent the local housing authority from exercising their power under paragraph 2(3)(c).

(10)    In proceedings for the enforcement of any such rights or remedies the court may make such order as it thinks fit as regards the operation of the interim EDMO (including an order quashing it).

*Financial arrangements while order is in force*

5.—(1)    This paragraph applies to relevant expenditure of a local housing authority who have made an interim EDMO.

(2)   "Relevant expenditure" means—
    (a)   expenditure incurred by the authority with the consent of the relevant proprietor, or
    (b)   any other expenditure reasonably incurred by the authority,
in connection with performing their duties under section 135(1) to (3) in respect of the dwelling (including any premiums paid for insurance of the premises).

(3)   Rent or other payments which the authority have collected or recovered, by virtue of this Chapter, from persons occupying or having the right to occupy the dwelling may be used by the authority to meet—
    (a)   relevant expenditure, and
    (b)   any amounts of compensation payable to a third party by virtue of an order under section 134(4) or 138(2) or to a dispossessed landlord or tenant by virtue of an order under paragraph 22(5).

(4)   The authority must pay to the relevant proprietor—
    (a)   any amount of rent or other payments collected or recovered as mentioned in sub-paragraph (3) that remains after deductions to meet relevant expenditure and any amounts of compensation payable as mentioned in that sub-paragraph, and
    (b)   (where appropriate) interest on that amount at a reasonable rate fixed by the authority,
and such payments are to be made at such intervals as the authority consider appropriate.

(5)   The interim EDMO may provide for—
    (a)   the rate of interest which is to apply for the purposes of paragraph (b) of sub-paragraph (4); and
    (b)   the intervals at which payments are to be made under that sub-paragraph.
Paragraph 26(1)(c) enables an appeal to be brought where the order does not provide for both of those matters.

(6)   The authority must—
    (a)   keep full accounts of their income and expenditure in respect of the dwelling; and
    (b)   afford to the relevant proprietor, and to any other person who has an estate or interest in the dwelling, all reasonable facilities for inspecting, taking copies of and verifying those accounts.

(7)   The relevant proprietor may apply to a residential property tribunal for an order—
    (a)   declaring that an amount shown in the accounts as expenditure of the authority does not constitute relevant expenditure (see sub-paragraph (2));
    (b)   requiring the authority to make such financial adjustments (in the accounts and otherwise) as are necessary to reflect the tribunal's declaration.

(8)   In this paragraph—
"dispossessed landlord or tenant" means a person who was a lessor, lessee, licensor or licensee under a lease or licence determined by an order under paragraph 22;
"expenditure" includes administrative costs.

*Variation or revocation of interim EDMOs*
6.—(1)   The local housing authority may vary an interim EDMO if they consider it appropriate to do so.

(2)   A variation does not come into force until such time, if any, as is the operative time for the purposes of this sub-paragraph under paragraph 33 (time when period for appealing expires without an appeal being made or when decision to vary is confirmed on appeal).

(3)   The power to vary an order under this paragraph is exercisable by the authority either—
    (a)   on an application made by a relevant person, or
    (b)   on the authority's own initiative.

(4)   In this paragraph "relevant person" means any person who has an estate or interest in the dwelling (other than a person who is a tenant under a lease granted under paragraph 2(3)(c)).

7.—(1)   The local housing authority may revoke an interim EDMO in the following cases—
    (a)   where the authority conclude that there are no steps which they could appropriately take for the purpose of securing that the dwelling is occupied (see section 135(4));
    (b)   where the authority are satisfied that—
        (i)   the dwelling will either become or continue to be occupied, despite the order being revoked, or
        (ii)   that the dwelling is to be sold;
    (c)   where a final EDMO has been made by the authority in respect of the dwelling so as to replace the order;
    (d)   where the authority conclude that it would be appropriate to revoke the order in order to prevent or stop interference with the rights of a third party in consequence of the order; and
    (e)   where in any other circumstances the authority consider it appropriate to revoke the order.

(2) But, in a case where the dwelling is occupied, the local housing authority may not revoke an interim EDMO under sub-paragraph (1)(b), (d) or (e) unless the relevant proprietor consents.

(3) A revocation does not come into force until such time, if any, as is the operative time for the purposes of this sub-paragraph under paragraph 33 (time when period for appealing expires without an appeal being made or when decision to revoke is confirmed on appeal).

(4) The power to revoke an order under this paragraph is exercisable by the authority either—
     (a)    on an application made by a relevant person, or
     (b)    on the authority's own initiative.

(5) Where a relevant person applies to the authority for the revocation of an order under this paragraph, the authority may refuse to revoke the order unless the relevant proprietor (or some other person) agrees to pay to the authority any deficit such as is mentioned in paragraph 23(4).

(6) In this paragraph "relevant person" means any person who has an estate or interest in the dwelling (other than a person who is a tenant under a lease granted under paragraph 2(3)(c)).

8.—(1) Part 2 of Schedule 6 applies in relation to the variation or revocation of an interim EDMO as it applies in relation to the variation or revocation of an interim management order.

(2) But Part 2 of that Schedule so applies as if—
     (a)    references to the right of appeal under Part 3 of the Schedule and to paragraph 29(2) were to the right of appeal under Part 4 of this Schedule and to paragraph 31(2) of this Schedule, and
     (b)    paragraph 23(4) defined "relevant person" as any person who, to the knowledge of the local housing authority, is a person having an estate or interest in the dwelling (other than a person who is a tenant under a lease granted under paragraph 2(3)(c) of this Schedule).

**[1543]**

## NOTES

Commencement: 18 November 2004 (for the purpose of making orders or regulations); 6 April 2006 (in relation to England for remaining purposes, subject to transitional provisions and savings in the Housing Act 2004 (Commencement No 5 and Transitional Provisions and Savings) (England) Order 2006, SI 2006/1060, art 3, Schedule at **[3700]**, **[3701]**); 16 June 2006 (in relation to Wales for remaining purposes, subject to transitional provisions and savings in the Housing Act 2004 (Commencement No 3 and Transitional Provisions and Savings) (Wales) Order 2006, SI 2006/1535, art 3, Schedule at **[3714]**, **[3715]**).

## PART 2
## FINAL EDMOS

*Operation of final EDMOs*

9.—(1) This paragraph deals with the time when a final EDMO comes into force or ceases to have effect.

(2) The order does not come into force until such time (if any) as is the operative time for the purposes of this sub-paragraph under paragraph 29 (time when period for appealing expires without an appeal being made or when order is confirmed on appeal).

(3) The order ceases to have effect at the end of the period of 7 years beginning with the date on which it comes into force, unless it ceases to have effect at some other time as mentioned below.

(4) If the order provides that it is to cease to have effect on a date falling before the end of that period, it accordingly ceases to have effect on that date.

(5) If—
     (a)    the order provides that it is to cease to have effect on a date falling after the end of that period, and
     (b)    the relevant proprietor of the dwelling has consented to that provision,
the order accordingly ceases to have effect on that date.

(6) Sub-paragraphs (7) and (8) apply where—
     (a)    a new final EDMO ("the new order") has been made so as to replace the order ("the existing order"), but
     (b)    the new order has not come into force because of an appeal to a residential property tribunal under paragraph 26 against the making of that order.

(7) If the date on which the new order comes into force in relation to the dwelling following the disposal of the appeal is later than the date on which the existing order would cease to have effect apart from this sub-paragraph, the existing order continues in force until that later date.

(8) If, on the application of the authority, the tribunal makes an order providing for the existing order to continue in force, pending the disposal of the appeal, until a date later than that on which it would cease to have effect apart from this sub-paragraph, the existing order accordingly continues in force until that later date.

(9)   This paragraph has effect subject to paragraphs 15 and 16 (variation or revocation of orders) and to the power of revocation exercisable by a residential property tribunal on an appeal made under paragraph 26 or 30.

*General effect of final EDMOs*

10.—(1)   This paragraph applies while a final EDMO is in force in relation to a dwelling.

(2)   The rights and powers conferred by sub-paragraph (3) are exercisable by the authority in performing their duties under section 137(1) to (3) in respect of the dwelling.

(3)   The authority—
  (a)   have the right to possession of the dwelling (subject to the rights of existing and other occupiers preserved by paragraph 18(3) and (4));
  (b)   have the right to do (and authorise a manager or other person to do) in relation to the dwelling anything which the relevant proprietor of the dwelling would (but for the order) be entitled to do;
  (c)   may create one or more of the following—
    (i)   an interest in the dwelling which, as far as possible, has all the incidents of a leasehold, or
    (ii)   a right in the nature of a licence to occupy part of the dwelling;
  (d)   may apply to a residential property tribunal for an order under paragraph 22 determining a lease or licence of the dwelling.

(4)   The powers of the authority under sub-paragraph (3)(c) are restricted as follows—
  (a)   they may not create any interest or right in the nature of a lease or licence—
    (i)   which is for a fixed term expiring after the date on which the order is due to expire, or
    (ii)   (subject to paragraph (b)) which is terminable by notice to quit, or an equivalent notice, of more than 4 weeks,
    unless consent in writing has been given by the relevant proprietor;
  (b)   they may create an interest in the nature of an assured shorthold tenancy without any such consent so long as it is created before the beginning of the period of 6 months that ends with the date on which the order is due to expire.

(5)   The authority—
  (a)   do not under this paragraph acquire any estate or interest in the dwelling, and
  (b)   accordingly are not entitled by virtue of this paragraph to sell, lease, charge or make any other disposition of any such estate or interest.

(6)   But, where the relevant proprietor of the dwelling is a lessee under a lease of the dwelling, the authority are to be treated (subject to sub-paragraph (5)(a)) as if they were the lessee instead.

(7)   Any enactment or rule of law relating to landlords and tenants or leases applies in relation to—
  (a)   a lease in relation to which the authority are to be treated as the lessee under sub-paragraph (6), or
  (b)   a lease to which the authority become a party under paragraph 12(2),
as if the authority were the legal owner of the premises (but this is subject to paragraph 12(4) to (6)).

(8)   None of the following, namely—
  (a)   the authority, or
  (b)   any person authorised under sub-paragraph (3)(b),
is liable to any person having an estate or interest in the dwelling for anything done or omitted to be done in the performance (or intended performance) of the authority's duties under section 137(1) to (3) unless the act or omission is due to negligence of the authority or any such person.

(9)   A final EDMO which has come into force is a local land charge.

(10)   The authority may apply to the Chief Land Registrar for the entry of an appropriate restriction in the register in respect of such an order.

(11)   In this paragraph "enactment" includes an enactment comprised in subordinate legislation (within the meaning of the Interpretation Act 1978 (c 30)).

*General effect of final EDMOs: leases and licences granted by authority*

11.—(1)   This paragraph applies in relation to any interest or right created by the authority under paragraph 10(3)(c).

(2)   For the purposes of any enactment or rule of law—
  (a)   any interest created by the authority under paragraph 10(3)(c)(i) is to be treated as if it were a legal lease, and
  (b)   any right created by the authority under paragraph 10(3)(c)(ii) is to be treated as if it were a licence to occupy granted by the legal owner of the dwelling,
despite the fact that the authority have no legal estate in the dwelling (see paragraph 10(5)(a)).

(3)   Any enactment or rule of law relating to landlords and tenants or leases accordingly applies in relation to any interest created by the authority under paragraph 10(3)(c)(i) as if the authority were the legal owner of the dwelling.

(4)   References to leases and licences—
    (a)   in this Chapter, and
    (b)   in any other enactment,
accordingly include (where the context permits) interests and rights created by the authority under paragraph 10(3)(c).

(5)   The preceding provisions of this paragraph have effect subject to—
    (a)   paragraph 12(4) to (6), and
    (b)   any provision to the contrary contained in an order made by the appropriate national authority.

(6)   In paragraph 10(5)(b) the reference to leasing does not include the creation of interests under paragraph 10(3)(c)(i).

(7)   In this paragraph—
"enactment" has the meaning given by paragraph 10(11);
"legal lease" means a term of years absolute (within section 1(1)(b) of the Law of Property Act 1925 (c 20)).

*General effect of final EDMOs: relevant proprietor, mortgagees etc*

12.—(1)   This paragraph applies in relation to—
    (a)   the relevant proprietor, and
    (b)   other persons with an estate or interest in the dwelling,
while a final EDMO is in force in relation to a dwelling.

(2)   Where the relevant proprietor is a lessor or licensor under a lease or licence of the dwelling, the lease or licence has effect while the order is in force as if the local housing authority were substituted in it for the lessor or licensor.

(3)   Such a lease continues to have effect, as far as possible, as a lease despite the fact that the rights of the local housing authority, as substituted for the lessor, do not amount to an estate in law in the dwelling.

(4)   The provisions mentioned in sub-paragraph (5) do not apply to a lease or licence within sub-paragraph (2).

(5)   The provisions are—
    (a)   the provisions which exclude local authority lettings from the Rent Acts, namely—
        (i)   sections 14 to 16 of the Rent Act 1977 (c 42), and
        (ii)   those sections as applied by Schedule 2 to the Rent (Agriculture) Act 1976 (c 80) and section 5(2) to (4) of that Act; and
    (b)   section 1(2) of, and paragraph 12 of Part 1 of Schedule 1 to, the Housing Act 1988 (c 50) (which exclude local authority lettings from Part 1 of that Act).

(6)   Nothing in this Chapter has the result that the authority are to be treated as the legal owner of any premises for the purposes of—
    (a)   section 80 of the Housing Act 1985 (c 68) (the landlord condition for secure tenancies); or
    (b)   section 124 of the Housing Act 1996 (c 52) (introductory tenancies).

(7)   The relevant proprietor of the dwelling—
    (a)   is not entitled to receive any rents or other payments made in respect of occupation of the dwelling;
    (b)   may not exercise any rights or powers with respect to the management of the dwelling; and
    (c)   may not create any of the following—
        (i)   any leasehold interest in the dwelling or a part of it (other than a lease of a reversion), or
        (ii)   any licence or other right to occupy it.

(8)   However (subject to sub-paragraph (7)(c)) nothing in paragraph 10 or this paragraph affects the ability of a person having an estate or interest in the dwelling to make any disposition of that estate or interest.

(9)   Nothing in paragraph 10 or this paragraph affects—
    (a)   the validity of any mortgage relating to the dwelling or any rights or remedies available to the mortgagee under such a mortgage, or
    (b)   the validity of any lease of the dwelling under which the relevant proprietor is a lessee, or any superior lease, or (subject to paragraph 10(6)) any rights or remedies available to the lessor under such a lease;

except to the extent that any of those rights or remedies would prevent the local housing authority from exercising their power under paragraph 10(3)(c).

(10) In proceedings for the enforcement of any such rights or remedies the court may make such order as it thinks fit as regards the operation of the final EDMO (including an order quashing it).

*Management scheme and accounts*

13.—(1) A final EDMO must contain a management scheme.

(2) A "management scheme" is a scheme setting out how the local housing authority are to carry out their duties under section 137(1) to (3) as respects the dwelling.

(3) The scheme is to contain a plan giving details of the way in which the authority propose to manage the dwelling, which must (in particular) include—

(a) details of any works that the authority intend to carry out in connection with the dwelling;

(b) an estimate of the capital and other expenditure to be incurred by the authority in respect of the dwelling while the order is in force;

(c) the amount of rent which, in the opinion of the authority, the dwelling might reasonably be expected to fetch on the open market at the time the management scheme is made;

(d) the amount of rent or other payments that the authority will seek to obtain;

(e) the amount of any compensation that is payable to a third party by virtue of a decision of the authority under section 136(4) or 138(3) in respect of any interference in consequence of the final EDMO with the rights of that person;

(f) provision as to the payment of any such compensation and of any compensation payable to a dispossessed landlord or tenant by virtue of an order under paragraph 22(5);

(g) where the amount of rent payable to the authority in respect of the dwelling for a period is less than the amount of rent mentioned in paragraph (c) in respect of a period of the same length, provision as to the following—

    (i) the deduction from the difference of relevant expenditure and any amounts of compensation payable to a third party or dispossessed landlord or tenant;

    (ii) the payment of any remaining amount to the relevant proprietor;

    (iii) the deduction from time to time of any remaining amount from any amount that the authority are entitled to recover from the proprietor under paragraph 23(5) or (6);

(h) provision as to the payment by the authority to the relevant proprietor from time to time of amounts of rent or other payments that remain after the deduction of—

    (i) relevant expenditure, and

    (ii) any amount of compensation payable to a third party or dispossessed landlord or tenant;

(i) provision as to the manner in which the authority are to pay to the relevant proprietor, on the termination of the final EDMO, the balance of any amounts of rent or other payments that remain after the deduction of relevant expenditure and any amounts of compensation payable to a third party or dispossessed landlord or tenant;

(j) provision as to the manner in which the authority are to pay, on the termination of the final EDMO, any outstanding amount of compensation payable to a third party or dispossessed landlord or tenant.

(4) The scheme may also state—

(a) the authority's intentions as regards the use of rent or other payments to meet relevant expenditure;

(b) the authority's intentions as regards the payment to the relevant proprietor (where appropriate) of interest on amounts within sub-paragraph (3)(h) and (i);

(c) that paragraph 23(2) or, where the relevant proprietor consents, paragraph 23(3)(c) is not to apply in relation to an interim EDMO or (as the case may be) final EDMO that immediately preceded the final EDMO, and that instead the authority intend to use any balance such as is mentioned in that sub-paragraph to meet—

    (i) relevant expenditure incurred during the currency of that final EDMO, and

    (ii) any compensation that may become payable to a third party or a dispossessed landlord or tenant;

(d) that paragraph 23(4) to (6) are not to apply in relation to an interim EDMO or, where the relevant proprietor consents, a final EDMO that immediately preceded the final EDMO, and that instead the authority intend to use rent or other payments collected during the currency of that final EDMO to reimburse the authority in respect of any deficit such as is mentioned in paragraph 23(4);

(e) the authority's intentions as regards the recovery from the relevant proprietor, with or without interest, of any amount of relevant expenditure incurred under a previous interim EDMO or final EDMO that the authority are entitled to recover from the proprietor under paragraph 23(5) or (6).

(5) The authority must—

PART 1
STATUTES

(a)  keep full accounts of their income and expenditure in respect of the dwelling; and

(b)  afford to the relevant proprietor, and to any other person who has an estate or interest in the dwelling, all reasonable facilities for inspecting, taking copies of and verifying those accounts.

(6)  In this paragraph—

"dispossessed landlord or tenant" means a person who was a lessor, lessee, licensor or licensee under a lease or licence determined by an order under paragraph 22;

"relevant expenditure" means—

(a)  expenditure incurred by the authority with the consent of the relevant proprietor, or

(b)  any other expenditure reasonably incurred by the authority, in connection with performing their duties under section 135(1) to (3) or 137(1) to (3) in respect of the dwelling (including any reasonable administrative costs and any premiums paid for insurance of the premises);

"rent or other payments" means rent or other payments collected or recovered, by virtue of this Chapter, from persons occupying or having the right to occupy the dwelling.

(7)  In any provision of this Chapter relating to varying, revoking or appealing against decisions relating to a final EDMO, any reference to such an order includes (where the context permits) a reference to the management scheme contained in it.

### Application to residential property tribunal in respect of breach of management scheme

14.—(1)  An affected person may apply to a residential property tribunal for an order requiring the local housing authority to manage a dwelling in accordance with the management scheme contained in a final EDMO made in respect of the dwelling.

(2)  On such an application the tribunal may, if it considers it appropriate to do so, make an order—

(a)  requiring the authority to manage the dwelling in accordance with the management scheme, or

(b)  revoking the final EDMO as from a date specified in the tribunal's order.

(3)  An order under sub-paragraph (2) may—

(a)  set out the steps which the authority are to take to manage the dwelling in accordance with the management scheme,

(b)  include provision varying the final EDMO, and

(c)  require the payment of money to an affected person by way of damages.

(4)  In this paragraph "affected person" means—

(a)  the relevant proprietor, and

(b)  any third party to whom compensation is payable by virtue of an order under section 134(4) or 138(2) or a decision of the authority under section 136(4) or 138(3) or who was a lessor, lessee, licensor or licensee under a lease or licence determined by an order of the residential property tribunal under paragraph 22 and to whom compensation is payable by virtue of an order under sub-paragraph (5) of that paragraph.

### Variation or revocation of final EDMOs

15.—(1)  The local housing authority may vary a final EDMO if they consider it appropriate to do so.

(2)  A variation does not come into force until such time, if any, as is the operative time for the purposes of this sub-paragraph under paragraph 33 (time when period for appealing expires without an appeal being made or when decision to vary is confirmed on appeal).

(3)  The power to vary an order under this paragraph is exercisable by the authority either—

(a)  on an application made by a relevant person, or

(b)  on the authority's own initiative.

(4)  In this paragraph "relevant person" means any person who has an estate or interest in the dwelling (other than a person who is a tenant under a lease granted under paragraph 2(3)(c) or 10(3)(c)).

16.—(1)  The local housing authority may revoke a final EDMO in the following cases—

(a)  where the authority conclude that there are no steps which they could appropriately take as mentioned in section 137(4)(b) or that keeping the order in force is not necessary as mentioned in section 137(4)(c);

(b)  where the authority are satisfied that—

(i)  the dwelling will either become or continue to be occupied, despite the order being revoked, or

(ii)  that the dwelling is to be sold;

(c)  where a further final EDMO has been made by the authority in respect of the dwelling so as to replace the order;

(d)   where the authority conclude that it would be appropriate to revoke the order in order to prevent or stop interference with the rights of a third party in consequence of the order; and

(e)   where in any other circumstances the authority consider it appropriate to revoke the order.

(2)   But, in a case where the dwelling is occupied, the local housing authority may not revoke a final EDMO under sub-paragraph (1)(b), (d) or (e) unless the relevant proprietor consents.

(3)   A revocation does not come into force until such time, if any, as is the operative time for the purposes of this sub-paragraph under paragraph 33 (time when period for appealing expires without an appeal being made or when decision to revoke is confirmed on appeal).

(4)   The power to revoke an order under this paragraph is exercisable by the authority either—
(a)   on an application made by a relevant person, or
(b)   on the authority's own initiative.

(5)   Where a relevant person applies to the authority for the revocation of an order under this paragraph, the authority may refuse to revoke the order unless the relevant proprietor (or some other person) agrees to pay to the authority any deficit such as is mentioned in paragraph 23(4).

(6)   In this paragraph "relevant person" means any person who has an estate or interest in the dwelling (other than a person who is a tenant under a lease granted under paragraph 2(3)(c) or 10(3)(c)).

17.—(1)   Part 2 of Schedule 6 applies in relation to the variation or revocation of a final EDMO as it applies in relation to the variation or revocation of a final management order.

(2)   But Part 2 of that Schedule so applies as if—
(a)   references to the right of appeal under Part 3 of the Schedule and to paragraph 29(2) were to the right of appeal under Part 4 of this Schedule and to paragraph 31(2) of this Schedule, and
(b)   paragraph 23(4) defined "relevant person" as any person who, to the knowledge of the local housing authority, is a person having an estate or interest in the dwelling (other than a person who is a tenant under a lease granted under paragraph 2(3)(c) or 10(3)(c) of this Schedule).

**[1544]**

**NOTES**

Commencement: 18 November 2004 (for the purpose of making orders or regulations); 6 April 2006 (in relation to England for remaining purposes, subject to transitional provisions and savings in the Housing Act 2004 (Commencement No 5 and Transitional Provisions and Savings) (England) Order 2006, SI 2006/1060, art 3, Schedule at **[3700]**, **[3701]**); 16 June 2006 (in relation to Wales for remaining purposes, subject to transitional provisions and savings in the Housing Act 2004 (Commencement No 3 and Transitional Provisions and Savings) (Wales) Order 2006, SI 2006/1535, art 3, Schedule at **[3714]**, **[3715]**).

## PART 3
### INTERIM AND FINAL EDMOS: GENERAL PROVISIONS (OTHER THAN PROVISIONS RELATING TO APPEALS)

*Effect of EDMOs: persons occupying or having a right to occupy the dwelling*

18.—(1)   This paragraph applies to existing and new occupiers of a dwelling in relation to which an interim EDMO or final EDMO is in force.

(2)   In this paragraph—
"existing occupier" means a person other than the relevant proprietor who, at the time when the order comes into force—
(a)   has the right to occupy the dwelling, but
(b)   is not a new occupier within sub-paragraph (4);
"new occupier" means a person who, at a time when the order is in force, is occupying the dwelling under a lease or licence granted under paragraph 2(3)(c) or 10(3)(c).

(3)   Paragraphs 2 and 10 do not affect the rights or liabilities of an existing occupier under a lease or licence (whether in writing or not) under which he has the right to occupy the dwelling at the commencement date.

(4)   Paragraph 10 does not affect the rights and liabilities of a new occupier who, in the case of a final EDMO, is occupying the dwelling at the time when the order comes into force.

(5)   The provisions mentioned in sub-paragraph (6) do not apply to a lease or agreement under which a new occupier has the right to occupy or is occupying the dwelling.

(6)   The provisions are—
(a)   the provisions which exclude local authority lettings from the Rent Acts, namely—
(i)   sections 14 to 16 of the Rent Act 1977 (c 42), and

      (ii)    those sections as applied by Schedule 2 to the Rent (Agriculture) Act 1976 (c 80) and section 5(2) to (4) of that Act; and

    (b)    section 1(2) of, and paragraph 12 of Part 1 of Schedule 1 to, the Housing Act 1988 (c 50) (which exclude local authority lettings from Part 1 of that Act).

(7)   If, immediately before the coming into force of an interim EDMO or final EDMO, an existing occupier had the right to occupy the dwelling under—

    (a)    a protected or statutory tenancy within the meaning of the Rent Act 1977,

    (b)    a protected or statutory tenancy within the meaning of the Rent (Agriculture) Act 1976, or

    (c)    an assured tenancy or assured agricultural occupancy within the meaning of Part 1 of the Housing Act 1988,

nothing in this Chapter (except an order under paragraph 22 determining a lease or licence) prevents the continuance of that tenancy or occupancy or affects the continued operation of any of those Acts in relation to the tenancy or occupancy after the coming into force of the order.

(8)   In this paragraph "the commencement date" means the date on which the order came into force (or, if that order was preceded by one or more orders under this Chapter, the date when the first order came into force).

### Effect of EDMOs: agreements and legal proceedings

19.—(1)   An agreement or instrument within sub-paragraph (2) has effect, while an interim EDMO or final EDMO is in force, as if any rights or liabilities of the relevant proprietor under the agreement or instrument were instead rights or liabilities of the local housing authority.

(2)   An agreement or instrument is within this sub-paragraph if—

    (a)    it is effective on the commencement date,

    (b)    one of the parties to it is the relevant proprietor of the dwelling,

    (c)    it relates to the dwelling, whether in connection with any management activities with respect to it, or otherwise,

    (d)    it is specified for the purposes of this sub-paragraph in the order or falls within a description of agreements or instruments so specified, and

    (e)    the authority serve a notice in writing on all the parties to it stating that sub-paragraph (1) is to apply to it.

(3)   An agreement or instrument is not within sub-paragraph (2) if—

    (a)    it is a lease or licence within paragraph 2(6) or 10(6), or

    (b)    it relates to any disposition by the relevant proprietor which is not precluded by paragraph 4(7) or 12(7).

(4)   Proceedings in respect of any cause of action within sub-paragraph (5) may, while an interim EDMO or final EDMO is in force, be instituted or continued by or against the local housing authority instead of by or against the relevant proprietor.

(5)   A cause of action is within this sub-paragraph if—

    (a)    it is a cause of action (of any nature) which accrued to or against the relevant proprietor of the dwelling before the commencement date,

    (b)    it relates to the dwelling as mentioned in sub-paragraph (2)(c),

    (c)    it is specified for the purposes of this sub-paragraph in the order or falls within a description of causes of action so specified, and

    (d)    the authority serve a notice in writing on all interested parties stating that sub-paragraph (4) is to apply to it.

(6)   If, by virtue of this paragraph, the authority become subject to any liability to pay damages in respect of anything done (or omitted to be done) before the commencement date by or on behalf of the relevant proprietor of the dwelling, the relevant proprietor is liable to reimburse to the authority an amount equal to the amount of damages paid by them.

(7)   In this paragraph—

"agreement" includes arrangement;

"the commencement date" means the date on which the order comes into force (or, if that order was preceded by one or more orders under this Chapter, the date when the first order came into force);

"management activities" includes repair, maintenance, improvement and insurance.

### Effect of EDMOs: furniture

20.—(1)   Sub-paragraph (2) applies where, on the date on which an interim EDMO or final EDMO comes into force, there is furniture owned by the relevant proprietor in the dwelling.

(2)   Subject to sub-paragraphs (3) and (4), the right to possession of the furniture against all persons vests in the local housing authority on that date and remains vested in the authority while the order is in force.

PART I STATUTES

(3) The right of the local housing authority under sub-paragraph (2) to possession of the furniture is subject to the rights of any person who, on the date on which the interim EDMO or final EDMO comes into force, has the right to possession of the dwelling.

(4) Where—

    (a) the local housing authority have the right to possession of the furniture under sub-paragraph (2), and

    (b) they have not granted a right to possession of the furniture to any other person,

they must, on a request by the relevant proprietor, give up possession of the furniture to him.

(5) The local housing authority may renounce the right to possession of the furniture conferred by sub-paragraph (2) by serving notice on the relevant proprietor not less than two weeks before the renunciation is to have effect.

(6) Where the local housing authority renounce the right to possession of the furniture under sub-paragraph (5), they must make appropriate arrangements for storage of the furniture at their own cost.

(7) In this paragraph "furniture" includes fittings and other articles.

*EDMOs: power to supply furniture*

21.—(1) The local housing authority may supply the dwelling to which an interim EDMO or final EDMO relates with such furniture as they consider to be required.

(2) For the purposes of paragraph 5 or paragraph 13, any expenditure incurred by the authority under this paragraph constitutes expenditure incurred by the authority in connection with performing their duties under section 135(1) to (3) or 137(1) to (3).

(3) In this paragraph "furniture" includes fittings and other articles.

*Power of a residential property tribunal to determine certain leases and licences*

22.—(1) A residential property tribunal may make an order determining a lease or licence to which this paragraph applies if—

    (a) the case falls within sub-paragraph (3) or (4), and

    (b) the tribunal are satisfied that the dwelling is not being occupied and that the local housing authority need to have the right to possession of the dwelling in order to secure that the dwelling becomes occupied.

(2) This paragraph applies to the following leases and licences of a dwelling—

    (a) a lease of the dwelling in respect of which the relevant proprietor is the lessor,

    (b) a sub-lease of any such lease, and

    (c) a licence of the dwelling.

(3) A case falls within this sub-paragraph if—

    (a) an interim or final EDMO is in force in respect of the dwelling, and

    (b) the local housing authority have applied under paragraph 2(3)(d) or 10(3)(d) for an order determining the lease or licence.

(4) A case falls within this sub-paragraph if—

    (a) the local housing authority have applied to the residential property tribunal under section 133 for an order authorising them to make an interim EDMO in respect of the dwelling and an order determining the lease or licence, and

    (b) the residential property tribunal has decided to authorise the authority to make an interim EDMO in respect of the dwelling.

(5) An order under this paragraph may include provision requiring the local housing authority to pay such amount or amounts to one or more of the lessor, lessee, licensor or licensee by way of compensation in respect of the determination of the lease or licence as the tribunal determines.

(6) Where—

    (a) a final EDMO is in force in respect of a dwelling, and

    (b) the tribunal makes an order requiring the local housing authority to pay an amount of compensation to a lessor, lessee, licensor or licensee in respect of the determination of a lease or licence of the dwelling,

the tribunal must make an order varying the management scheme contained in the final EDMO so as to make provision as to the payment of that compensation.

*Termination of EDMOs: financial arrangements*

23.—(1) This paragraph applies where an interim EDMO or final EDMO ceases to have effect for any reason.

(2) If, on the termination date for an interim EDMO, the total amount of rent or other payments collected or recovered as mentioned in paragraph 5(3) exceeds the total amount of—

    (a) the authority's relevant expenditure, and

(3)   If no appeal is brought under this paragraph in respect of a final EDMO within the time allowed by paragraph 27 for making such an appeal, the order is final and conclusive as to the matters which could have been raised on appeal.

*Appeals: time limits for appeals under paragraph 26*

27.—(1)   This paragraph applies in relation to an appeal under paragraph 26 in respect of a final EDMO.

(2)   Any such appeal must be made within the period of 28 days beginning with the date specified in the notice under paragraph 7(5) of Schedule 6 (as applied by section 136(5)) as the date on which the order was made.

(3)   A residential property tribunal may allow an appeal to be made to it after the end of the period mentioned in sub-paragraph (2) if it is satisfied that there is a good reason for the failure to appeal before the end of that period (and for any delay since then in applying for permission to appeal out of time).

*Appeals: powers of residential property tribunal on appeal under paragraph 26*

28.—(1)   This paragraph applies to an appeal to a residential property tribunal under paragraph 26 in respect of an interim EDMO or a final EDMO.

(2)   The appeal—
    (a)   is to be by way of a re-hearing, but
    (b)   may be determined having regard to matters of which the authority were unaware.

(3)   The tribunal may—
    (a)   in the case of an interim EDMO, vary the order as mentioned in paragraph 26(2)(b), or
    (b)   in the case of a final EDMO, confirm or vary the order or revoke it as from the date of the tribunal's order.

*"The operative time" for the purposes of paragraph 9(2)*

29.—(1)   This paragraph defines "the operative time" for the purposes of paragraph 9(2).

(2)   If no appeal is made under paragraph 26 before the end of the period of 28 days mentioned in paragraph 27(2), "the operative time" is the end of that period.

(3)   If an appeal is made under paragraph 26 before the end of that period, and a decision is given on the appeal which confirms the order, "the operative time" is as follows—
    (a)   if the period within which an appeal to the [Upper Tribunal] may be brought expires without such an appeal having been brought, "the operative time" is the end of that period;
    (b)   if an appeal to the [Upper Tribunal] is brought, "the operative time" is the time when a decision is given on the appeal which confirms the order.

(4)   For the purposes of sub-paragraph (3)—
    (a)   the withdrawal of an appeal has the same effect as a decision which confirms the order, and
    (b)   references to a decision which confirms the order are to a decision which confirms it with or without variation.

*Right to appeal against decision or refusal to vary or revoke EDMO*

30.   A relevant person may appeal to a residential property tribunal against—
    (a)   a decision of a local housing authority to vary or revoke an interim EDMO or a final EDMO, or
    (b)   a refusal of a local housing authority to vary or revoke an interim EDMO or a final EDMO.

*Time limits for appeals under paragraph 30*

31.—(1)   This paragraph applies in relation to an appeal under paragraph 30 against a decision to vary or revoke, or (as the case may be) to refuse to vary or revoke, an interim EDMO or a final EDMO.

(2)   Any such appeal must be made before the end of the period of 28 days beginning with the date specified in the notice under paragraph 11, 16, 19 or 22 of Schedule 6 (as applied by paragraph 8 or 17 of this Schedule (as the case may be)) as the date on which the decision concerned was made.

(3)   A residential property tribunal may allow an appeal to be made to it after the end of the period mentioned in sub-paragraph (2) if it is satisfied that there is a good reason for the failure to appeal before the end of that period (and for any delay since then in applying for permission to appeal out of time).

*Powers of residential property tribunal on appeal under paragraph 30*

32.—(1)   This paragraph applies to an appeal to a residential property tribunal under paragraph 30 against a decision to vary or revoke, or (as the case may be) to refuse to vary or revoke, an interim EDMO or final EDMO.

(2)   The appeal—
   (a)   is to be by way of a re-hearing, but
   (b)   may be determined having regard to matters of which the authority were unaware.

(3)   The tribunal may confirm, reverse or vary the decision of the local housing authority.

(4)   If the appeal is against a decision of the authority to refuse to revoke the order, the tribunal may make an order revoking the order as from a date specified in its order.

*"The operative time" for the purposes of paragraphs 6, 7, 15 and 16*

33.—(1)   This paragraph defines "the operative time" for the purposes of—
   (a)   paragraph 6(2) or 7(3) (variation or revocation of interim EDMO), or
   (b)   paragraph 15(2) or 16(3) (variation or revocation of final EDMO).

(2)   If no appeal is made under paragraph 30 before the end of the period of 28 days mentioned in paragraph 31(2), "the operative time" is the end of that period.

(3)   If an appeal is made under paragraph 30 before the end of that period, and a decision is given on the appeal which confirms the variation or revocation, "the operative time" is as follows—
   (a)   if the period within which an appeal to the [Upper Tribunal] may be brought expires without such an appeal having been brought, "the operative time" is the end of that period;
   (b)   if an appeal to the [Upper Tribunal] is brought, "the operative time" is the time when a decision is given on the appeal which confirms the variation or revocation.

(4)   For the purposes of sub-paragraph (3)—
   (a)   the withdrawal of an appeal has the same effect as a decision which confirms the variation or revocation appealed against; and
   (b)   references to a decision which confirms a variation are to a decision which confirms it with or without variation.

*Right to appeal against decision in respect of compensation payable to third parties*

34.—(1)   This paragraph applies where a local housing authority have made a decision under section 136(4) or 138(3) as to whether compensation should be paid to a third party in respect of any interference with his rights in consequence of a final EDMO.

(2)   The third party may appeal to a residential property tribunal against—
   (a)   a decision by the authority not to pay compensation to him, or
   (b)   a decision of the authority so far as relating to the amount of compensation that should be paid.

*Time limits for appeals under paragraph 34*

35.—(1)   This paragraph applies in relation to an appeal under paragraph 34 against a decision of a local housing authority not to pay compensation to a third party or as to the amount of compensation to be paid.

(2)   Any such appeal must be made—
   (a)   where the decision is made before the final EDMO is made, within the period of 28 days beginning with the date specified in the notice under paragraph 7(5) of Schedule 6 (as applied by section 136(5)) as the date on which the order was made, or
   (b)   in any other case, within the period of 28 days beginning with the date the authority notifies the third party under section 138(4).

(3)   A residential property tribunal may allow an appeal to be made to it after the end of the period mentioned in sub-paragraph (2) if it is satisfied that there is good reason for the failure to appeal before the end of that period (and for any delay since then in applying for permission to appeal out of time).

*Powers of residential property tribunal on appeal under paragraph 34*

36.—(1)   This paragraph applies in relation to an appeal under paragraph 34 against a decision of a local housing authority not to pay compensation to a third party or as to the amount of compensation to be paid.

(2)   The appeal—
   (a)   is to be by way of re-hearing, but
   (b)   may be determined having regard to matters of which the authority were unaware.

(3)   The tribunal may confirm, reverse or vary the decision of the local housing authority.

(4)    Where the tribunal reverses or varies the decision of the authority, it must make an order varying the management scheme contained in the final EDMO accordingly.

*Meaning of "relevant person" for the purposes of this Part*

37.    In this Part of this Schedule "relevant person" means any person who has an estate or interest in the dwelling (other than a person who is a tenant under a lease granted under paragraph 2(3)(c) or 10(3)(c)).

**[1546]**

**NOTES**

Commencement: 6 April 2006 (in relation to England, subject to transitional provisions and savings in the Housing Act 2004 (Commencement No 5 and Transitional Provisions and Savings) (England) Order 2006, SI 2006/1060, art 3, Schedule at **[3700]**, **[3701]**); 16 June 2006 (in relation to Wales, subject to transitional provisions and savings in the Housing Act 2004 (Commencement No 3 and Transitional Provisions and Savings) (Wales) Order 2006, SI 2006/1535, art 3, Schedule at **[3714]**, **[3715]**).

Para 29: words in square brackets substituted by the Transfer of Tribunal Functions (Lands Tribunal and Miscellaneous Amendments) Order 2009, SI 2009/1307, art 5(1), (2), Sch 1, paras 271, 283, subject to transitional and savings provisions in Sch 5 thereto.

Para 33: words in square brackets substituted by SI 2009/1307, art 5(1), (2), Sch 1, paras 271, 283, subject to transitional and savings provisions in Sch 5 thereto.

*(Sch 8 outside the scope of this work; Sch 9 inserts the Housing Act 1985, Sch 5A at* **[585]**.*)*

# SCHEDULE 10
# PROVISIONS RELATING TO TENANCY DEPOSIT SCHEMES
Section 212

## Schemes to be custodial schemes or insurance schemes

1.—(1)    A tenancy deposit scheme must be either—
    (a)    a custodial scheme, or
    (b)    an insurance scheme.

(2)    A "custodial scheme" is a scheme under which—
    (a)    tenancy deposits in connection with shorthold tenancies are paid to the landlords under the tenancies,
    (b)    amounts representing the deposits are then paid by the landlords into a designated account held by the scheme administrator, and
    (c)    those amounts are kept by the scheme administrator in that account until such time as, in accordance with the scheme, they fall to be paid (wholly or in part) to the landlords or tenants under the tenancies.

(3)    An "insurance scheme" is a scheme under which—
    (a)    tenancy deposits in connection with shorthold tenancies are paid to the landlords under the tenancies,
    (b)    such deposits are retained by the landlords on the basis that, at the end of the tenancies—
        (i)    such amounts in respect of the deposits as are agreed between the tenants and the landlords will be repaid to the tenants, and
        (ii)    such amounts as the tenants request to be repaid to them and which are not so repaid will, in accordance with directions given by the scheme administrator, be paid into a designated account held by the scheme administrator,
    (c)    amounts paid into that account are kept by the scheme administrator in the account until such time as, in accordance with the scheme, they fall to be paid (wholly or in part) to the landlords or tenants under the tenancies,
    (d)    landlords undertake to reimburse the scheme administrator, in accordance with directions given by him, in respect of any amounts in respect of the deposits paid to the tenants by the scheme administrator (other than amounts paid to the tenants as mentioned in paragraph (c)), and
    (e)    insurance is maintained by the scheme administrator in respect of failures by landlords to comply with such directions.

## Provisions applying to custodial and insurance schemes

2.—(1)    A custodial scheme must conform with the following provisions—
    paragraphs 3 [to 4C], and
    paragraphs 9 [to 10C].

(2)    An insurance scheme must conform with the following provisions—
    paragraphs 5 to 8, and
    paragraphs 9 [to 10C].

*Custodial schemes: general*

3.—(1)   This paragraph applies to a custodial scheme.

(2)   The scheme must provide for any landlord who receives a tenancy deposit in connection with a shorthold tenancy to pay an amount equal to the deposit into a designated account held by the scheme administrator.

(3)   The designated account must not contain anything other than amounts paid into it as mentioned in sub-paragraph (2) and any interest accruing on such amounts.

(4)   Subject to sub-paragraph (5), the scheme administrator may retain any interest accruing on such amounts.

(5)   The relevant arrangements under section 212(1) may provide for any amount paid in accordance with paragraph 4 [or 4C] to be paid with interest—
    (a)   in respect of the period during which the relevant amount has remained in the designated account, and
    (b)   at such rate as the appropriate national authority may specify by order.

(6)   With the exception of any interest retained in accordance with sub-paragraph (4), nothing contained in the designated account may be used to fund the administration of the scheme.

(7)   In this paragraph "the relevant amount", in relation to a tenancy deposit, means the amount paid into the designated account in respect of the deposit.

*Custodial schemes: termination of tenancies*

4.—(1)   A custodial scheme must make provision—
    (a)   for enabling the tenant and the landlord under a shorthold tenancy in connection with which a tenancy deposit is held in accordance with the scheme to apply, at any time after the tenancy has ended, for the whole or part of the relevant amount to be paid to him, and
    (b)   for such an application to be dealt with by the scheme administrator in accordance with the following provisions of this paragraph.

(2)   Sub-paragraph (3) applies where the tenant and the landlord notify the scheme administrator that they have agreed that the relevant amount should be paid—
    (a)   wholly to one of them, or
    (b)   partly to the one and partly to the other.

(3)   If, having received such a notification, the scheme administrator is satisfied that the tenant and the landlord have so agreed, the scheme administrator must arrange for the relevant amount to be paid, in accordance with the agreement, within the period of 10 days beginning with the date on which the notification is received by the scheme administrator.

(4)   Sub-paragraph (5) applies where the tenant or the landlord notifies the scheme administrator that—
    (a)   a court has decided that the relevant amount is payable either wholly to one of them or partly to the one and partly to the other, and
    (b)   that decision has become final.

[(4A)   Sub-paragraph (5) also applies where the tenant or the landlord notifies the scheme administrator that a person acting as an adjudicator under the provision made under paragraph 10 has made a binding decision that the relevant amount is payable either wholly to one of them or partly to one and partly to the other.]

(5)   If, having received [a notification as mentioned in sub-paragraph (4) or (4A)], the scheme administrator is satisfied as to the matters mentioned in [that sub-paragraph], the scheme administrator must arrange for the relevant amount to be paid, in accordance with the decision, within the period of 10 days beginning with the date on which the notification is received by the scheme administrator.

(6)   For the purposes of this Schedule a decision becomes final—
    (a)   if not appealed against, at the end of the period for bringing an appeal, or
    (b)   if appealed against, at the time when the appeal (or any further appeal) is disposed of.

(7)   An appeal is disposed of—
    (a)   if it is determined and the period for bringing any further appeal has ended, or
    (b)   if it is abandoned or otherwise ceases to have effect.

(8)   In this paragraph "the relevant amount" has the meaning given by paragraph 3(7).

*[Custodial schemes: termination of tenancies—absent or un-cooperative landlord or tenant*

4A.—(1)   The provision made by a custodial scheme for the purposes of paragraph 4(1) in relation to the treatment of the relevant amount at the end of a tenancy must include provision—
    (a)   for enabling the landlord, if he considers that the conditions set out in sub-paragraph (2)

are met, to apply to the scheme administrator for the whole or a specified part of the relevant amount ("the amount claimed") to be paid to him; and

(b)    for such an application to be dealt with by the scheme administrator in accordance with the provisions of paragraph 4C

(2)    Such an application may be made if—

(a)    at least 14 days have elapsed since the day on which the tenancy ended;

(b)    the landlord and tenant have not reached an agreement under paragraph 4(2) with respect to the amount claimed;

(c)    either sub-paragraph (3) or sub-paragraph (4) applies; and

(d)    the landlord believes that he is entitled to be paid the amount claimed and that the amount claimed is referable to sums falling within sub-paragraph (5).

(3)    This sub-paragraph applies if the landlord has no current address for, or other means of contacting, the tenant.

(4)    This sub-paragraph applies if—

(a)    the tenant has, since the tenancy ended, received from the landlord a written notice asking whether the tenant accepts that the landlord should be paid the whole or a specified part of the relevant amount; and

(b)    the tenant has failed to respond to that notice within the period of 14 days beginning with the day on which he received the notice by indicating to the landlord whether he accepts that the landlord should be paid the relevant amount or the specified part of it (as the case may be).

(5)    The amount claimed must be referable to—

(a)    an amount of unpaid rent or any other sum due under the terms of the tenancy; or

(b)    a liability of the tenant to the landlord arising under or in connection with the tenancy in respect of—

     (i)    damage to the premises subject to the tenancy, or

     (ii)    loss of or damage to property on those premises,

other than damage caused by fair wear and tear.

(6)    If sub-paragraph (4) applies and the notice specifies part of the relevant amount, the amount claimed in the application must not exceed the specified part.

(7)    The application must be accompanied by a statutory declaration made by the landlord stating—

(a)    the date on which the tenancy ended;

(b)    that the landlord and the tenant have not reached any agreement under paragraph 4(2) with respect to the amount claimed, with details of any communications between them since that date (whether relating to the relevant amount or otherwise);

(c)    the basis on which the amount claimed is calculated, with particulars of any facts relied on to justify claiming that amount;

(d)    if the landlord relies on the condition in sub-paragraph (3), that he has no current address for, or other means of contacting, the tenant, giving particulars of any address (other than the premises subject to the tenancy) and other contact details (including telephone numbers or e mail addresses) which the landlord has had for the tenant;

(e)    if the landlord relies on the condition in sub-paragraph (4), that the condition is met, with particulars of the facts relied on to demonstrate that it is met and attaching a copy of the notice given to the tenant;

(f)    any information he has as to the whereabouts of the tenant;

(g)    that he gives his consent, in the event of the tenant disputing that the landlord should be paid the amount claimed, for the dispute to be resolved through the use of the dispute resolution service;

(h)    that he considers that he is entitled to be paid the amount claimed; and

(i)    that he makes the statutory declaration knowing that if he knowingly and wilfully makes a false declaration he may be liable to prosecution under the Perjury Act 1911.

4B.—(1)    The provision made by a custodial scheme for the purposes of paragraph 4(1) in relation to the treatment of the relevant amount at the end of a tenancy must include provision—

(a)    for enabling the tenant, if he considers that the conditions set out in sub-paragraph (2) are met, to apply to the scheme administrator for the whole or a specified part of the relevant amount ("the amount claimed") to be paid to him; and

(b)    for such an application to be dealt with by the scheme administrator in accordance with the provisions of paragraph 4C

(2)    Such an application may be made if—

(a)    at least 14 days have elapsed since the day on which the tenancy ended;

(b)    the landlord and tenant have not reached an agreement under paragraph 4(2) with respect to the amount claimed;

(c)    either sub-paragraph (3) or sub-paragraph (4) applies; and

(d)    the tenant believes that he is entitled to be paid the amount claimed.

(3) This sub-paragraph applies if the tenant has no current address for, or other means of contacting, the landlord.

(4) This sub-paragraph applies if—

    (a)    the landlord has, since the tenancy ended, received from the tenant a written notice asking whether the landlord accepts that the tenant should be paid the whole or a specified part of the relevant amount; and

    (b)    the landlord has failed to respond to that notice within the period of 14 days beginning with the day on which he received the notice by indicating to the tenant whether he accepts that the tenant should be paid the relevant amount or the specified part of it (as the case may be).

(5) If sub-paragraph (4) applies and the notice specifies part of the relevant amount, the amount claimed in the application must not exceed the specified part.

(6) The application must be accompanied by a statutory declaration made by the tenant stating—

    (a)    the date on which the tenancy ended;

    (b)    that the landlord and the tenant have not reached any agreement under paragraph 4(2) with respect to the amount claimed, with details of any communications between them since that date (whether relating to the relevant amount or otherwise);

    (c)    if the tenant relies on the condition in sub-paragraph (3), that he has no current address for, or other means of, contacting, the landlord, giving particulars of any address and other contact details (including telephone numbers or e mail addresses) which the tenant has had for the landlord;

    (d)    if the tenant relies on the condition in sub-paragraph (4), that the condition is met, with particulars of the facts relied on to demonstrate that it is met and attaching a copy of the notice given to the landlord;

    (e)    any information he has as to the whereabouts of the landlord;

    (f)    that he gives his consent, in the event of the landlord disputing that the tenant should be paid the amount claimed, for the dispute to be resolved through the use of the dispute resolution service;

    (g)    that he considers that he is entitled to be paid the amount claimed; and

    (h)    that he makes the statutory declaration knowing that if he knowingly and wilfully makes a false declaration he may be liable to prosecution under the Perjury Act 1911.

4C.—(1) Immediately upon receipt of—

    (a)    a duly completed application from the landlord, accompanied by a statutory declaration which appears to meet the requirements of paragraph 4A(7), or

    (b)    a duly completed application from the tenant, accompanied by a statutory declaration which appears to meet the requirements of paragraph 4B(6),

the scheme administrator must give to the tenant or, as the case may be, the landlord ("the other party") a copy of the application and accompanying statutory declaration and a notice under sub-paragraph (2).

(2) A notice under this sub-paragraph is a notice—

    (a)    asking the other party to indicate—

        (i)    whether he accepts that the applicant should be paid the whole or part of the amount claimed;

        (ii)    if he accepts that part of the amount claimed should be paid, the amount he accepts should be paid; and

        (iii)    if he does not accept that the applicant should be paid the whole of the amount claimed, whether he consents to the dispute being resolved through the use of the dispute resolution service; and

    (b)    warning the other party that—

        (i)    the amount claimed will be paid to the applicant unless, within the relevant period, the other party informs the scheme administrator that he does not accept that the whole of the amount claimed should be paid to the applicant; and

        (ii)    if the other party responds to the scheme administrator informing him that he does not accept that the whole of the amount claimed should be paid to the applicant, but fails to respond within the relevant period to the question mentioned in paragraph (a)(iii), he will be treated as having given his consent for the dispute to be resolved through the use of the dispute resolution service.

(3) If within the relevant period the scheme administrator receives a response from the other party to the effect that he accepts that the amount claimed should be paid to the applicant—

    (a)    the application must be granted; and

    (b)    the scheme administrator must arrange for the amount claimed to be paid to the applicant within the period of 10 days beginning with the day on which the scheme administrator receives that response.

(4) If within the relevant period the scheme administrator receives a response from the other party to the effect that he does not accept that the applicant should be paid any of the amount claimed—

  (a)   the application must be refused;
  (b)   the scheme administrator must not pay the amount claimed to either party except in accordance with the relevant provisions of paragraph 4; and
  (c)   the scheme administrator must inform the applicant of the other party's response to the questions asked in the notice under sub-paragraph (2).

(5) If within the relevant period the scheme administrator receives a response from the other party to the effect that he accepts that part of the amount claimed should be paid to the applicant—

  (a)   sub-paragraph (3) applies in relation to that part of the amount claimed; and
  (b)   sub-paragraph (4) applies to so much of the application as relates to the rest of the amount claimed.

(6) If the scheme administrator does not, within the relevant period, receive a response from the other party indicating whether he accepts that the whole or part of the amount claimed should be paid to the applicant, the scheme administrator must arrange for the amount claimed to be paid to the applicant within the period of 10 days beginning with the day after the last day of the relevant period.

(7) If within the relevant period the scheme administrator receives a response from the other party to the effect that he does not accept that the applicant should be paid the whole of the amount claimed but the other party fails within that period to indicate whether he consents to the dispute being resolved through the use of the dispute resolution service—

  (a)   the other party is to be treated as having given his consent to the use of that service; and
  (b)   the scheme administrator must inform the applicant that such consent is treated as having been given.

(8) In this paragraph "the relevant period", in relation to the application, means the period of 14 days beginning with the day on which the notice mentioned in sub-paragraph (2) is received by the other party.]

*Insurance schemes: general*

5.—(1)   This paragraph applies to an insurance scheme.

[(1A)   The scheme must make provision as to the requirements that fall to be complied with by the landlord or by the scheme administrator where—

  (a)   a landlord wishes to retain a tenancy deposit under the scheme; or
  (b)   a landlord retaining a tenancy deposit under the scheme (in relation to a tenancy that has not terminated) gives notice to the scheme administrator that he no longer wishes to retain the deposit under that scheme.]

(2)   The scheme must provide that any landlord by whom a tenancy deposit is retained under the scheme must give the scheme administrator an undertaking that, if the scheme administrator directs the landlord to pay him any amount in respect of the deposit in accordance with paragraph 6(3) or (7), the landlord will comply with such a direction.

(3)   The scheme must require the scheme administrator to effect, and maintain in force, adequate insurance in respect of failures by landlords by whom tenancy deposits are retained under the scheme to comply with such directions as are mentioned in sub-paragraph (2).

[(3A)   The scheme may make provision enabling the scheme administrator to determine that, by virtue of the landlord's failure to comply with a relevant obligation, a tenancy deposit which has previously been retained by a landlord under the scheme (and which relates to a tenancy which has not ended) is to cease to be retained under the scheme.

(3B)   Provision under sub-paragraph (3A) must require the scheme administrator, before making a determination, to give a notice to the landlord stating that the scheme administrator proposes to make such a determination and the reasons for the proposal.]

(4)   If the scheme provides for landlords participating in the scheme to be members of the scheme, the scheme may provide for a landlord's membership to be terminated by the scheme administrator in the event of any [failure by the landlord to comply with a relevant obligation].

[(4A)   Provision made under sub-paragraph (4) must require the scheme administrator, before determining that the landlord's membership be terminated, to give a notice to the landlord stating that the scheme administrator proposes to make such a determination and the reasons for the proposal.

(4B)   On the termination of a landlord's membership under sub-paragraph (4)—

  (a)   any tenancy deposits previously retained by the landlord under the scheme (in relation to tenancies which had not ended before the termination) cease to be retained under the scheme; but

(b)  the scheme continues to apply to a tenancy deposit retained by the landlord under the scheme in relation to a tenancy which ended before the termination as if the landlord were still a member.]

(5)  The scheme may provide for landlords participating in the scheme to pay to the scheme administrator—

(a)  fees in respect of the administration of the scheme, and

(b)  contributions in respect of the cost of the insurance referred to in sub-paragraph (3).

[(6)  Paragraph 5A makes further provision in relation to the procedure to be followed after a notice of the kind mentioned in sub-paragraph (1A)(b), (3B) or (4A) has been given in accordance with the scheme.

(7)  In this paragraph "relevant obligation" means—

(a)  the duty to comply with a direction mentioned in sub-paragraph (2); or

(b)  any obligation under the scheme which is specified in the scheme as a relevant obligation for the purposes of this paragraph.]

*[Requirements where deposit is to cease to be retained under an insurance scheme*

5A.—(1)  This paragraph applies in relation to—

(a)  a notice of the kind mentioned in paragraph 5(1A)(b) or (3B), or

(b)  a notice from the scheme administrator stating that he proposes to terminate a landlord's membership of the scheme under paragraph 5(4),

given in accordance with an insurance scheme.

(2)  The scheme must make provision for the scheme administrator, in the case of a notice of the kind mentioned in paragraph 5(1A)(b) which has not been not withdrawn—

(a)  to determine the date on which the tenancy deposit is to cease to be retained under the scheme; and

(b)  to give a notice under sub-paragraph (4) to the landlord and to the tenant.

(3)  The scheme must make provision for the scheme administrator, in the case of a notice of the kind mentioned in paragraph 5(3B), to take the following steps after the end of the period of 14 days beginning with the day on which that notice is received—

(a)  to determine whether the deposit should cease to be retained under the scheme and, if so, the date on which it is to cease to be so retained;

(b)  if the determination is that the deposit should continue to be retained under the scheme, to give a notice of the determination to the landlord;

(c)  if the determination is that the deposit should cease to be so retained, to give a notice under sub-paragraph (4) to the landlord and to the tenant.

(4)  A notice under this sub-paragraph is a notice—

(a)  identifying the tenancy deposit in question;

(b)  informing the recipients of the notice of the determination made by the scheme administrator and stating the date when the deposit ceases to be retained under the scheme; and

(c)  giving a general explanation of the continuing effect of sections 213 to 215 of this Act in relation to the deposit (including in particular the effect of section 213 as modified by sub-paragraph (9)).

(5)  The scheme must make provision for the scheme administrator, in the case of a notice of the kind mentioned in sub-paragraph (1)(b), to take the following steps after the end of the period of 14 days beginning with the day on which that notice is received—

(a)  to determine whether to terminate the landlord's membership and, if so, the date on which his membership is to terminate;

(b)  if the determination is that the landlord should continue as a member, to give a notice of the determination to the landlord; and

(c)  if the determination is that the membership should be terminated, to give a notice under sub-paragraph (6) to the landlord and to the tenant under any tenancy in relation to which a deposit affected by the determination is retained under the scheme.

(6)  A notice under this sub-paragraph is a notice—

(a)  informing the recipients of the notice of the determination by the scheme administrator that the landlord's membership of the scheme is to be terminated and stating the date on which his membership terminates;

(b)  giving a general explanation of the effect of the termination on any tenancy deposits retained by the landlord under the scheme; and

(c)  giving a general explanation of the continuing effect of sections 213 to 215 of this Act in relation to any tenancy deposits that cease to be retained under the scheme as a result of the termination of membership (including in particular the effect of section 213 as modified by sub-paragraph (9)).

(7)    The date determined under sub-paragraph (2)(a), (3)(a) or (5)(a) must not be within the period of three months beginning with the day on which the original notice mentioned in sub-paragraph (1) was received.

(8)    A notice under sub-paragraph (4) or (6) must be given at least two months before the date on which the deposit ceases to be retained under the scheme or the landlord's membership terminates (as the case may be).

(9)    In the application of section 213 to a tenancy deposit which ceases to be retained under an insurance scheme ("the old scheme") by virtue of a determination mentioned in this paragraph—

    (a)    references to receiving the deposit include a reference to ceasing to retain it under the terms of the old scheme;

    (b)    subsection (3) has effect as if for the words "within the period of 14 days beginning with the date on which it is received" there were substituted "before the deposit ceases to be retained under the old scheme"; and

    (c)    subsection (6)(b) has effect as if the reference to the date on which the landlord receives the deposit were a reference to the date on which the deposit ceases to be retained under the old scheme.]

*Insurance schemes: termination of tenancies*

6.—(1)    An insurance scheme must make provision in accordance with this paragraph and paragraphs [6A to] 8 in relation to the respective obligations of the landlord and the scheme administrator where—

    (a)    a tenancy deposit has been retained by the landlord under the scheme, and

    (b)    the tenancy has ended.

(2)    Sub-paragraphs (3) to (9) apply where the tenant notifies the scheme administrator that—

    (a)    the tenant has requested the landlord to repay to him the whole or any part of the deposit, and

    (b)    the amount in question ("the outstanding amount") has not been repaid to him within the period of 10 days beginning with the date on which the request was made.

[(2A)    When a tenant gives notice under sub-paragraph (2) he must also indicate whether he consents to any dispute as to the amount to be repaid to him being resolved through the use of the dispute resolution service.]

(3)    On receiving a notification in accordance with sub-paragraph (2), the scheme administrator must direct the landlord—

    (a)    to pay an amount equal to the outstanding amount into a designated account held by the scheme administrator, and

    (b)    to do so within the period of 10 days beginning with the date on which the direction is received by the landlord.

(4)    The following sub-paragraphs apply where the tenant or the landlord notifies the scheme administrator—

    (a)    that a court has decided that the outstanding amount is payable either wholly to one of them or partly to the one and partly to the other and the decision has become final (see paragraph 4(6) and (7)), ...

    (b)    that the tenant and landlord have agreed that such an amount is to be paid either wholly to one of them or partly to the one and partly to the other [or

    (c)    that a person acting as an adjudicator under the provision made under paragraph 10 has made a binding decision that the outstanding amount is payable either wholly to one of them or partly to one and partly to the other.]

(5)    If the scheme administrator is satisfied as to the matters mentioned in sub-paragraph (4)(a)[, (b) or (c)] (as the case may be), he must—

    (a)    pay to the tenant any amount due to him in accordance with the decision or agreement (and, to the extent possible, pay that amount out of any amount held by him by virtue of sub-paragraph (3)), and

    (b)    comply with sub-paragraph (6) or (7), as the case may be.

(6)    Where any amount held by the scheme administrator by virtue of sub-paragraph (3) is more than any amount due to the tenant in accordance with the decision or agreement, the scheme administrator must pay the balance to the landlord.

(7)    Where any amount so held by the scheme administrator is less than any amount so due to the tenant, the scheme administrator must direct the landlord to pay him the difference within the period of 10 days beginning with the date on which the direction is received by the landlord.

(8)    The scheme administrator must pay any amounts required to be paid to the tenant or the landlord as mentioned in sub-paragraph (5)(a) or (6) within 10 days beginning with the date on which the notification is received by the scheme administrator.

(9)    The landlord must comply with any direction given in accordance with sub-paragraph (3) or (7).

*[Notice to be sent to landlord when a direction under paragraph 6(3) is given*

6A.—(1)   This paragraph applies where the scheme administrator of an insurance scheme gives a direction under paragraph 6(3) to a landlord.

(2)   The scheme administrator must also send to the landlord a notice—
- (a) asking the landlord to indicate—
  - (i) whether he accepts that the tenant should be repaid the whole or part of the outstanding amount;
  - (ii) if he accepts that part of it should be repaid, the amount he accepts should be repaid; and
  - (iii) if he does not accept that the tenant should be repaid the whole of the outstanding amount, whether he consents to the dispute being resolved through the use of the dispute resolution service; and
- (b) warning the landlord that if he does not accept that the tenant should be repaid the whole of the outstanding amount but fails to respond within the relevant period to the question mentioned in paragraph (a)(iii), he will be treated as having given his consent for the dispute to be resolved through the use of that service.

(3)   If the scheme administrator does not, within the relevant period, receive a response from the landlord indicating whether he accepts that the whole or part of the outstanding amount should be paid to the tenant—
- (a) the scheme administrator must treat the lack of a response as an indication that the landlord does not accept that the tenant should be repaid any of the outstanding amount;
- (b) the scheme administrator must determine forthwith whether he is satisfied that the notice was received by the landlord;
- (c) if the scheme administrator determines that he is satisfied that it was so received, the landlord is to be treated as having given his consent for the dispute to be resolved through the use of the dispute resolution service; and
- (d) the scheme administrator must inform the tenant and the landlord whether or not such consent is to be treated as having been given.

(4)   If within the relevant period the scheme administrator receives a response to the notice under sub-paragraph (2) to the effect that the landlord does not accept that the tenant should be repaid the whole of the outstanding amount but the landlord fails within that period to indicate whether he consents to the dispute being resolved through the dispute resolution service—
- (a) the landlord is to be treated as having given his consent for the dispute to be resolved through the use of that service; and
- (b) the scheme administrator must inform the tenant and the landlord that such consent is to be treated as given.

(5)   In this paragraph—
"the outstanding amount" has the same meaning as in paragraph 6;
"the relevant period" means the period of 10 working days beginning with the day after that on which the notice referred to in sub-paragraph (2) is sent; and
"working days" shall be taken to exclude Saturdays, Sundays, Christmas Day, Good Friday and any day which, under the Banking and Financial Dealings Act 1971, is a bank holiday in England and Wales.]

*[Insurance schemes—supplementary provisions]*

7.—(1)   The designated account held by the scheme administrator must not contain anything other than amounts paid into it as mentioned in paragraph 6(3) and any interest accruing on such amounts.

(2)   Subject to sub-paragraph (3), the scheme administrator may retain any interest accruing on such amounts.

(3)   The relevant arrangements under section 212(1) may provide for any amount paid in accordance with paragraph 6(5)(a) or (6) to be paid with interest—
- (a) in respect of the period during which the relevant amount has remained in the designated account, and
- (b) at such rate as the appropriate national authority may specify for the purposes of paragraph 3(5)(b).

(4)   With the exception of any interest retained in accordance with sub-paragraph (2), nothing contained in the designated account may be used to fund the administration of the scheme.

(5)   In this paragraph "the relevant amount", in relation to a tenancy deposit, means the amount, in respect of the deposit, paid into the designated account by virtue of a direction given in accordance with paragraph 6(3).

8.—(1)   The scheme must make provision for preventing double recovery by a tenant in respect of the whole or part of the deposit, and may in that connection make provision—
- (a) for excluding or modifying any requirement imposed by the scheme in accordance with paragraph 6 or 7, and
- (b) for requiring the repayment of amounts paid to the tenant by the scheme administrator.

(2)   In this paragraph "double recovery", in relation to an amount of a tenancy deposit, means recovering that amount both from the scheme administrator and from the landlord.

*Notifications to tenants*

9.—(1)   Every custodial scheme or insurance scheme must provide for the scheme administrator to respond as soon as is practicable to any request within sub-paragraph (2) made by the tenant under a shorthold tenancy.

(2)   A request is within this sub-paragraph if it is a request by the tenant to receive confirmation that a deposit paid in connection with the tenancy is being held in accordance with the scheme.

*Dispute resolution procedures*

10.—(1)   Every custodial scheme or insurance scheme must provide for facilities to be available for enabling disputes relating to tenancy deposits subject to the scheme to be resolved without recourse to litigation.

(2)   The scheme must not, however, make the use of such facilities compulsory in the event of such a dispute.

[(3)   The provision made under this paragraph may confer power on a person acting as an adjudicator in relation to such a dispute to decline to proceed, or continue to proceed, with the case.

(4)   In this Schedule, in relation to a custodial scheme or an insurance scheme, "the dispute resolution service" means the facilities provided by the scheme in accordance with this paragraph.]

*[Service of documents: general*

10A   A tenancy deposit scheme may make provision as to the methods which may be used for giving or sending any direction, notice or other document which falls to be given or sent under the scheme.

*Service of documents by scheme administrator on landlords*

10B.—(1)   The provision made by a tenancy deposit scheme under paragraph 10A may include provision for any direction, notice or other document mentioned in this Schedule which is to be given or sent to a landlord by the scheme administrator to be treated as having been received on the second day after the day on which it is sent by first class post to the landlord at the address last provided by him to the scheme administrator as the postal address to which correspondence may be sent.

(2)   Sub-paragraph (1) does not apply to the notice mentioned in paragraph 6A(2).

(3)   Provision made under sub-paragraph (1) may require the scheme administrator—
   (a)   to send a document to an address other than that mentioned in that sub-paragraph; or
   (b)   to use or attempt to use any other available means of communication,
before sending a document which is to be treated as having been received as mentioned in that sub-paragraph.

*Service of documents by scheme administrator on tenants*

10C.—(1)   The provision made by a tenancy deposit scheme under paragraph 10A may include provision for any notice or other document mentioned in this Schedule which is to be given or sent to a tenant by the scheme administrator to be treated as having been received on the second day after the day on which it is sent by first class post to the tenant at the proper address.

(2)   In the case of a notice mentioned in paragraph 4C(2), the proper address is—
   (a)   the address (if any) last provided to the scheme administrator as the address to which correspondence may be sent; or
   (b)   if no such address has been provided, the address given in the landlord's statutory declaration as the tenant's last known address or, if the scheme administrator has a more recent address for the tenant, that address.

(3)   In the case of a notice of the kind mentioned in paragraph 5A(4) or (6), the proper address is the address of the premises subject to the tenancy in question.

(4)   Provision made under sub-paragraph (1) may require the scheme administrator—
   (a)   to send a document to an address other than the proper address, or
   (b)   to use or attempt to use any other available means of communication,
before sending a document which is to be treated as having been received as mentioned in that sub-paragraph.]

*Power to amend*

11.   The appropriate national authority may by order make such amendments of this Schedule as it considers appropriate.

*Interpretation*

12. In this Schedule references to tenants under shorthold tenancies include references to persons who, in accordance with arrangements made with such tenants, have paid tenancy deposits on behalf of the tenants.

**[1547]**

**NOTES**
Commencement: 18 November 2004 (for the purpose of making orders or regulations); 6 April 2007 (otherwise).
Para 2: words in square brackets substituted by the Housing (Tenancy Deposit Schemes) Order 2007, SI 2007/796, arts 2, 10.
Para 3: words in square brackets in sub-para (5) inserted by SI 2007/796, arts 2, 11.
Para 4: sub-para (4A) inserted and words in square brackets in sub-para (5) substituted, by SI 2007/796, arts 2, 3(1)–(3).
Paras 4A–4C: inserted, together with preceding cross-heading, by SI 2007/796, arts 2, 3(4).
Para 5: sub-paras (1A), (3A), (3B), (4A), (4B) inserted, words in square brackets in sub-para (4) substituted, and sub-paras (6), (7) added by SI 2007/796, arts 2, 4.
Paras 5A, 6A: inserted, together with preceding cross-headings, by SI 2007/796, arts 2, 5, 7.
Para 6: words in square brackets in sub-paras (1), (5) substituted, sub-para (2A) and words in square brackets in sub-para (4) inserted, and word omitted from sub-para (4) repealed by SI 2007/796, arts 2, 6.
Para 7: cross-heading inserted by SI 2007/796, arts 2, 12.
Para 10: sub-paras (3), (4) added by SI 2007/796, arts 2, 8.
Paras 10A–10C: inserted, together with preceding cross-headings, by SI 2007/796, arts 2, 9.
Orders: the Housing (Tenancy Deposit Schemes) Order 2007, SI 2007/796; the Housing (Tenancy Deposits) (Specified Interest Rate) Order 2007, SI 2007/798.

*(Sch 11 contains consequential amendments; Sch 12 repealed by the Public Services Ombudsman (Wales) Act 2005, s 39(2), Sch 7.)*

## SCHEDULE 13
## RESIDENTIAL PROPERTY TRIBUNALS: PROCEDURE
Section 230

*Procedure regulations*

1.—(1) The appropriate national authority may make regulations about the procedure of residential property tribunals.

(2) Nothing in the following provisions of this Schedule affects the generality of sub-paragraph (1).

(3) In those provisions—
"procedure regulations" means regulations under this paragraph;
"tribunal" means a residential property tribunal.

*Appeals*

2.—(1) Procedure regulations may include provision, in relation to applications to tribunals—
    (a) about the form of such applications and the particulars to be contained in them,
    (b) requiring the service of notices of such applications, and
    (c) in the case of applications under section 102(4) or (7) or 133(1), requiring the service of copies of the draft orders submitted with the applications.

(2) Procedure regulations may include provision, in relation to appeals to tribunals—
    (a) about the form of notices of appeal and the particulars to be contained in them, and
    (b) requiring the service of copies of such notices.

(3) Procedure regulations may include provision dispensing with the service of the notices or copies mentioned in sub-paragraph (1)(b) or (2)(b) in such cases of urgency as are specified in the regulations.

*Transfers*

3.—(1) This paragraph applies where, in any proceedings before a court, there falls for determination a question which a tribunal would have jurisdiction to determine on an application or appeal to the tribunal.

(2) The court—
    (a) may by order transfer to the tribunal so much of the proceedings as relate to the determination of that question, and
    (b) may then dispose of all or any remaining proceedings, or adjourn the disposal of all or any remaining proceedings pending the determination of that question by the tribunal, as it thinks fit.

(3) When the tribunal has determined the question, the court may give effect to the determination in an order of the court.

(4)    Rules of court may prescribe the procedure to be followed in a court in connection with or in consequence of a transfer under this paragraph.

(5)    Procedure regulations may prescribe the procedure to be followed in a tribunal consequent on a transfer under this paragraph.

(6)    Nothing in this Act affects any power of a court to make an order that could be made by a tribunal (such as an order quashing a licence granted or order made by a local housing authority) in a case where—

     (a)    the court has not made a transfer under this paragraph, and

     (b)    the order is made by the court in connection with disposing of any proceedings before it.

## Parties etc

4.—(1)    Procedure regulations may include provision enabling persons to be joined as parties to the proceedings.

(2)    Procedure regulations may include provision enabling persons who are not parties to proceedings before a tribunal to make oral or written representations to the tribunal.

## Information

5.—(1)    Procedure regulations may include—

     (a)    provision relating to the supply of information and documents by a party to the proceedings, and

     (b)    in particular any provision authorised by the following provisions of this paragraph.

(2)    The regulations may include provision for requiring, or empowering the tribunal to require, a party to proceedings before a tribunal—

     (a)    to supply to the tribunal information or documents specified, or of a description specified, in the regulations or in an order made by the tribunal;

     (b)    to supply to any other party copies of any information or documents supplied to the tribunal;

     (c)    to supply any such information, documents or copies by such time as is specified in or determined in accordance with the regulations or order.

(3)    The regulations may also include provision—

     (a)    for granting a party to the proceedings such disclosure or inspection of documents, or such right to further information, as might be granted by a county court;

     (b)    for requiring persons to attend to give evidence and produce documents;

     (c)    for authorising the administration of oaths to witnesses.

(4)    The regulations may include provision empowering a tribunal to dismiss, or allow, the whole or part of an appeal or application in a case where a party to the proceedings has failed to comply with—

     (a)    a requirement imposed by regulations made by virtue of this paragraph, or

     (b)    an order of the tribunal made by virtue of any such regulations.

## Pre-trial reviews etc

6.—(1)    Procedure regulations may include provision for the holding of a pre-trial review (on the application of a party to the proceedings or on the tribunal's own initiative).

(2)    Procedure regulations may provide for functions of a tribunal in relation to, or at, a pre-trial review to be exercised by a single qualified member of the panel.

(3)    Procedure regulations may provide for other functions as to preliminary or incidental matters to be exercised by a single qualified member of the panel.

(4)    For the purposes of this paragraph—

     (a)    a person is a qualified member of the panel if he was appointed to it by the Lord Chancellor; and

     (b)    "the panel" means the panel provided for in Schedule 10 to the Rent Act 1977 (c 42).

## Interim orders

7.    Procedure regulations may include provision empowering tribunals to make orders, on an interim basis—

     (a)    suspending, in whole or in part, the effect of any decision, notice, order or licence which is the subject matter of proceedings before them;

     (b)    granting any remedy which they would have had power to grant in their final decisions.

## Additional relief

8.—(1)    Procedure regulations may include provision as to—

     (a)    any additional relief which tribunals may grant in respect of proceedings before them; and

PART I
STATUTES

(b)    the grounds on which such relief may be granted.

(2)    In this paragraph "additional relief" means relief additional to any relief specifically authorised by any provision of Parts 1 to 4 of this Act.

## Dismissal

9.    Procedure regulations may include provision empowering tribunals to dismiss applications, appeals or transferred proceedings, in whole or in part, on the ground that they are—

    (a)    frivolous or vexatious, or

    (b)    otherwise an abuse of process.

## Determination without hearing

10.—(1)    Procedure regulations may include provision for the determination of applications, appeals or transferred proceedings without an oral hearing.

(2)    Procedure regulations may include provision enabling a single qualified member of the panel to decide whether an oral hearing is appropriate in a particular case.

(3)    Procedure regulations may provide for a single qualified member of the panel to make determinations without an oral hearing.

(4)    For the purposes of this paragraph—

    (a)    a person is a qualified member of the panel if he was appointed to it by the Lord Chancellor; and

    (b)    "the panel" means the panel provided for in Schedule 10 to the Rent Act 1977 (c 42).

## Fees

11.—(1)    Procedure regulations may include provision requiring the payment of fees in respect of applications, appeals or transfers of proceedings to, or oral hearings by, tribunals.

(2)    The fees payable shall be such as are specified in or determined in accordance with procedure regulations.

(3)    But the fee (or, where fees are payable in respect of both an application, appeal or transfer and an oral hearing, the aggregate of the fees) payable by a person in respect of any proceedings must not exceed—

    (a)    £500, or

    (b)    such other amount as may be specified in procedure regulations.

(4)    Procedure regulations may empower a tribunal to require a party to proceedings before it to reimburse another party to the proceedings the whole or any part of any fees paid by him.

(5)    Procedure regulations may provide for the reduction or waiver of fees by reference to the financial resources of the party by whom they are to be paid or met.

(6)    If they do so they may apply, subject to such modifications as may be specified in the regulations, any other statutory means-testing regime as it has effect from time to time.

## Costs

12.—(1)    A tribunal may determine that a party to proceedings before it is to pay the costs incurred by another party in connection with the proceedings in any circumstances falling within sub-paragraph (2).

(2)    The circumstances are where—

    (a)    he has failed to comply with an order made by the tribunal;

    (b)    in accordance with regulations made by virtue of paragraph 5(4), the tribunal dismisses, or allows, the whole or part of an application or appeal by reason of his failure to comply with a requirement imposed by regulations made by virtue of paragraph 5;

    (c)    in accordance with regulations made by virtue of paragraph 9, the tribunal dismisses the whole or part of an application or appeal made by him to the tribunal; or

    (d)    he has, in the opinion of the tribunal, acted frivolously, vexatiously, abusively, disruptively or otherwise unreasonably in connection with the proceedings.

(3)    The amount which a party to proceedings may be ordered to pay in the proceedings by a determination under this paragraph must not exceed—

    (a)    £500, or

    (b)    such other amount as may be specified in procedure regulations.

(4)    A person may not be required to pay costs incurred by another person in connection with proceedings before a tribunal, except—

    (a)    by a determination under this paragraph, or

    (b)    in accordance with provision made by any enactment other than this paragraph.

*Enforcement*

13. Procedure regulations may provide for decisions of tribunals to be enforceable, with the permission of a county court, in the same way as orders of such a court.

**[1548]**

**NOTES**

Commencement: 18 November 2004 (for the purpose of making orders or regulations); 4 July 2005 (in relation to England for remaining purposes, subject to transitional provisions as noted to s 181 at **[1470]**); 16 June 2006 (in relation to Wales for remaining purposes, subject to transitional provisions and savings in the Housing Act 2004 (Commencement No 3 and Transitional Provisions and Savings) (Wales) Order 2006, SI 2006/1535, art 3, Schedule at **[3714]**, **[3715]**).

Regulations: the Residential Property Tribunal (Right to Buy Determinations) Procedure (England) Regulations 2005, SI 2005/1509 at **[3465]**; the Residential Property Tribunal (Fees) (England) Regulations 2006, SI 2006/830 at **[3650]**; the Residential Property Tribunal Procedure (England) Regulations 2006, SI 2006/831 at **[3656]**; the Residential Property Tribunal Procedure (Wales) Regulations 2006, SI 2006/1641 at **[3717]**; the Residential Property Tribunal (Fees) (Wales) Regulations 2006, SI 2006/1642 at **[3718]**.

## SCHEDULE 14
## BUILDINGS WHICH ARE NOT HMOS FOR PURPOSES OF THIS ACT (EXCLUDING PART 1)

Section 254

*Introduction: buildings (or parts) which are not HMOs for purposes of this Act (excluding Part 1)*

1.—(1) The following paragraphs list buildings which are not houses in multiple occupation for any purposes of this Act other than those of Part 1.

(2) In this Schedule "building" includes a part of a building.

*Buildings controlled or managed by public sector bodies etc*

2.—(1) A building where the person managing or having control of it is—
  (a) a local housing authority,
  (b) a body which is registered as a social landlord under Part 1 of the Housing Act 1996 (c 52),
  (c) a police authority established under section 3 of the Police Act 1996 (c 16),
  (d) the Metropolitan Police Authority established under section 5B of that Act,
  (e) a fire and rescue authority, or
  (f) a health service body within the meaning of [section 9 of the National Health Service Act 2006].

(2) In sub-paragraph (1)(e) "fire and rescue authority" means a fire and rescue authority under the Fire and Rescue Services Act 2004 (c 21).

*Buildings regulated otherwise than under this Act*

3. Any building whose occupation is regulated otherwise than by or under this Act and which is of a description specified for the purposes of this paragraph in regulations made by the appropriate national authority.

*Buildings occupied by students*

4.—(1) Any building—
  (a) which is occupied solely or principally by persons who occupy it for the purpose of undertaking a full-time course of further or higher education at a specified educational establishment or at an educational establishment of a specified description, and
  (b) where the person managing or having control of it is the educational establishment in question or a specified person or a person of a specified description.

(2) In sub-paragraph (1) "specified" means specified for the purposes of this paragraph in regulations made by the appropriate national authority.

(3) Sub-paragraph (4) applies in connection with any decision by the appropriate national authority as to whether to make, or revoke, any regulations specifying—
  (a) a particular educational establishment, or
  (b) a particular description of educational establishments.

(4) The appropriate national authority may have regard to the extent to which, in its opinion—
  (a) the management by or on behalf of the establishment in question of any building or buildings occupied for connected educational purposes is in conformity with any code of practice for the time being approved under section 233 which appears to the authority to be relevant, or
  (b) the management of such buildings by or on behalf of establishments of the description in question is in general in conformity with any such code of practice,

as the case may be.

(5) In sub-paragraph (4) "occupied for connected educational purposes", in relation to a building managed by or on behalf of an educational establishment, means occupied solely or principally by persons who occupy it for the purpose of undertaking a full-time course of further or higher education at the establishment.

*Buildings occupied by religious communities*

5.—(1) Any building which is occupied principally for the purposes of a religious community whose principal occupation is prayer, contemplation, education or the relief of suffering.

(2) This paragraph does not apply in the case of a converted block of flats to which section 257 applies.

*Buildings occupied by owners*

6.—(1) Any building which is occupied only by persons within the following paragraphs—

   (a) one or more persons who have, whether in the whole or any part of it, either the freehold estate or a leasehold interest granted for a term of more than 21 years;
   (b) any member of the household of such a person or persons;
   (c) no more than such number of other persons as is specified for the purposes of this paragraph in regulations made by the appropriate national authority.

(2) This paragraph does not apply in the case of a converted block of flats to which section 257 applies, except for the purpose of determining the status of any flat in the block.

*Buildings occupied by two persons*

7. Any building which is occupied only by two persons who form two households.

**[1549]**

---

**NOTES**

Commencement: 18 November 2004 (for the purpose of making orders or regulations); 18 January 2005 (otherwise).

Para 2: words in square brackets substituted by the National Health Service (Consequential Provisions) Act 2006, s 2, Sch 1, paras 268, 269.

Regulations: the Licensing and Management of Houses in Multiple Occupation and Other Houses (Miscellaneous Provisions) (England) Regulations 2006, SI 2006/373 at **[3623]**; the Houses in Multiple Occupation (Specified Educational Establishments) (Wales) Regulations 2006, SI 2006/1707 at **[3721]**; the Licensing and Management of Houses in Multiple Occupation and Other Houses (Miscellaneous Provisions) (Wales) Regulations 2006, SI 2006/1715 at **[3724]**; the Houses in Multiple Occupation (Specified Educational Establishments) (England) (No 2) Regulations 2006, SI 2006/2280; the Houses in Multiple Occupation (Specified Educational Establishments) (England) Regulations 2007, SI 2007/708; the Houses in Multiple Occupation (Specified Educational Establishments) (England) Regulations 2009, SI 2009/2298 at **[3966]**.

---

(*Schs 15, 16 contain consequential amendments and repeals which, in so far as within the scope of this work, have been incorporated at the appropriate place.*)

# PUBLIC SERVICES OMBUDSMAN (WALES) ACT 2005

(2005 c 10)

ARRANGEMENT OF SECTIONS

PART 1
THE PUBLIC SERVICES OMBUDSMAN FOR WALES

PART 2
INVESTIGATION OF COMPLAINTS

POWER OF INVESTIGATION

COMPLAINTS

PART 1
STATUTES

*An Act to establish and make provision about the office of Public Services Ombudsman for Wales; to make provision about the functions of the Public Services Ombudsman for Wales; to make provision about compensation; to abolish the Commission for Local Administration in Wales and the offices of Welsh Administration Ombudsman, Health Service Commissioner for Wales and Social Housing Ombudsman for Wales; and for connected purposes.*

[7 April 2005]

## PART 1
## THE PUBLIC SERVICES OMBUDSMAN FOR WALES

**1   The Public Services Ombudsman for Wales**

(1)   There is to be a Public Services Ombudsman for Wales or Ombwdsmon Gwasanaethau Cyhoeddus Cymru (in this Act referred to as "the Ombudsman").

(2)   Schedule 1 makes further provision about the Ombudsman.

[1550]

**NOTES**

Commencement: 12 October 2005 (for the purposes of appointing the Ombudsmen); 1 April 2006 (for remaining purposes: for effect and transitional provisions see the Public Services Ombudsman (Wales) Act 2005 (Commencement No 1 and Transitional Provisions and Savings) Order 2005, SI 2005/2800, arts 6, 7 at [3580], [3581]).

## PART 2
## INVESTIGATION OF COMPLAINTS

*Power of investigation*

**2   Power of investigation**

(1)   The Ombudsman may investigate a complaint in respect of a matter if—
  (a)   the complaint has been duly made or referred to him, and
  (b)   the matter is one which he is entitled to investigate under sections 7 to 11.

(2)   A complaint is "duly made" to the Ombudsman if (but only if)—
  (a)   it is made by a person who is entitled under section 4 to make the complaint to the Ombudsman, and
  (b)   the requirements of section 5 are met in respect of it.

(3)   A complaint is "duly referred" to the Ombudsman if (but only if)—
  (a)   it is referred to him by a listed authority, and
  (b)   the requirements of section 6 are met in respect of it.

(4)   The Ombudsman may investigate a complaint in respect of a matter even if the requirements of section 5(1) or (as the case may be) section 6(1)(b) or (d) are not met in respect of the complaint, if—
  (a)   the matter is one which he is entitled to investigate under sections 7 to 11, and
  (b)   he thinks it reasonable to do so.

(5)   It is for the Ombudsman to decide whether to begin, continue or discontinue an investigation.

(6)   The Ombudsman may take any action which he thinks may assist in making a decision under subsection (5).

(7)   The Ombudsman may begin or continue an investigation into a complaint even if the complaint, or the referral of the complaint, has been withdrawn.

[1551]

**NOTES**

Commencement: 1 April 2006 (for effect and transitional provisions see the Public Services Ombudsman (Wales) Act 2005 (Commencement No 1 and Transitional Provisions and Savings) Order 2005, SI 2005/2800, arts 6, 7 at [3580], [3581]).

**3   Alternative resolution of complaints**

(1)   The Ombudsman may take any action he thinks appropriate with a view to resolving a complaint which he has power to investigate under section 2.

(2)    The Ombudsman may take action under this section in addition to or instead of conducting an investigation into the complaint.

(3)    Any action under this section must be taken in private.

**[1552]**

**NOTES**
Commencement: 1 April 2006 (for effect and transitional provisions see the Public Services Ombudsman (Wales) Act 2005 (Commencement No 1 and Transitional Provisions and Savings) Order 2005, SI 2005/2800, arts 6, 7 at **[3580]**, **[3581]**).

*Complaints*

## 4    Who can complain

(1)    The persons entitled to make a complaint to the Ombudsman are—
    (a)    a member of the public (in this Act referred to as "the person aggrieved") who claims or claimed to have sustained injustice or hardship in consequence of a matter which the Ombudsman is entitled to investigate under sections 7 to 11;
    (b)    a person authorised by the person aggrieved to act on his behalf;
    (c)    if the person aggrieved is not capable of authorising a person to act on his behalf (for example because he has died), a person who appears to the Ombudsman to be appropriate to act on behalf of the person aggrieved.

(2)    "Member of the public" means any person other than a listed authority acting in its capacity as such.

(3)    It is for the Ombudsman to determine any question of whether a person is entitled under this section to make a complaint to him.

**[1553]**

**NOTES**
Commencement: 1 April 2006 (for effect and transitional provisions see the Public Services Ombudsman (Wales) Act 2005 (Commencement No 1 and Transitional Provisions and Savings) Order 2005, SI 2005/2800, arts 6, 7 at **[3580]**, **[3581]**).

## 5    Requirements: complaints made to the Ombudsman

(1)    The requirements mentioned in section 2(2)(b) are that—
    (a)    the complaint must be made in writing;
    (b)    the complaint must be made to the Ombudsman before the end of the period of one year starting on the day on which the person aggrieved first has notice of the matters alleged in the complaint.

(2)    It is for the Ombudsman to determine any question of whether the requirements of subsection (1) are met in respect of a complaint.

**[1554]**

**NOTES**
Commencement: 1 April 2006 (for effect and transitional provisions see the Public Services Ombudsman (Wales) Act 2005 (Commencement No 1 and Transitional Provisions and Savings) Order 2005, SI 2005/2800, arts 6, 7 at **[3580]**, **[3581]**).

## 6    Requirements: complaints referred to the Ombudsman

(1)    The requirements mentioned in section 2(3)(b) are that—
    (a)    the complaint must have been made to the listed authority by a person who would have been entitled under section 4 to make the complaint to the Ombudsman;
    (b)    the complaint must have been made to the listed authority before the end of the period of one year starting on the day on which the person aggrieved first had notice of the matters alleged in the complaint;
    (c)    the complaint must be *referred to the Ombudsman* in writing;
    (d)    the complaint must be referred to the Ombudsman before the end of the period of one year starting on the day on which the complaint was made to the listed authority.

(2)    It is for the Ombudsman to determine any question of whether the requirements of subsection (1) are met in respect of a complaint.

**[1555]**

**NOTES**
Commencement: 1 April 2006 (for effect and transitional provisions see the Public Services Ombudsman (Wales) Act 2005 (Commencement No 1 and Transitional Provisions and Savings) Order 2005, SI 2005/2800, arts 6, 7 at **[3580]**, **[3581]**).

*Matters which may be investigated*

## 7 Matters which may be investigated

(1) The matters which the Ombudsman is entitled to investigate are—

    (a) alleged maladministration by a listed authority in connection with relevant action;

    (b) an alleged failure in a relevant service provided by a listed authority;

    (c) an alleged failure by a listed authority to provide a relevant service.

(2) Subsection (1) is subject to sections 8 to 11.

(3) Relevant action is—

    (a) in the case of a listed authority which is a family health service provider in Wales or an independent provider in Wales, action taken by the authority in connection with the provision of a relevant service;

    (b) in the case of a listed authority which is a social landlord in Wales or a Welsh health service body other than the [Welsh Ministers], action taken by the authority in the discharge of any of its functions;

    (c) in the case of a listed authority which is a person with functions conferred by regulations made under section 113(2) of the Health and Social Care (Community Health and Standards) Act 2003 (c 43), action taken by the authority in the discharge of any of those functions;

    (d) in the case of a listed authority which is a listed authority by virtue of an order under section 28(2) adding it to Schedule 3, action taken by the authority in the discharge of any of its specified functions;

    (e) in any other case, action taken by the authority in the discharge of any of its administrative functions.

(4) A relevant service is—

    (a) in the case of a listed authority which is a family health service provider in Wales, any of the family health services which the authority had, at the time of the action which is the subject of the complaint, entered into a contract, undertaken, or made arrangements, to provide;

    (b) in the case of a listed authority which is an independent provider in Wales, any service which the authority had, at that time, made arrangements with a Welsh health service body or a family health service provider in Wales to provide;

    (c) in the case of a listed authority falling within subsection (3)(c), any service which it was, at that time, the authority's function to provide in the discharge of any of the functions mentioned in that paragraph;

    (d) in the case of a listed authority falling within subsection (3)(d), any service which it was, at that time, the authority's function to provide in the discharge of any of its specified functions;

    (e) in any other case, any service which it was, at that time, the authority's function to provide.

(5) For the purposes of subsections (3)(d) and (4)(d), a listed authority's specified functions are the functions specified in relation to the authority in an order under section 28(2) as falling within the Ombudsman's remit.

(6) An administrative function which may be discharged by a person who is a member of the administrative staff of a relevant tribunal is to be treated as an administrative function of a listed authority for the purposes of subsection (3) if—

    (a) the person was appointed by the authority, or

    (b) the person was appointed with the consent of the authority (whether as to remuneration and other terms and conditions of service or otherwise).

[1556]

**NOTES**

Commencement: 1 April 2006 (for effect and transitional provisions see the Public Services Ombudsman (Wales) Act 2005 (Commencement No 1 and Transitional Provisions and Savings) Order 2005, SI 2005/2800, arts 6, 7 at [3580], [3581]).

Sub-s (3): words in square brackets substituted by the Government of Wales Act 2006, s 160(1), Sch 10, paras 67, 68.

## 8 Exclusion: matters not relating to Wales

(1) The Ombudsman may not investigate a matter arising in connection with the discharge by a listed authority of any of the authority's functions otherwise than in relation to Wales.

(2) Subsection (1) does not apply in relation to the [Welsh Assembly Government].

(3)   To the extent that a function of a listed authority is discharged in relation to the Welsh language or any other aspect of Welsh culture, it is to be regarded for the purposes of subsection (1) as discharged in relation to Wales.

**[1557]**

**NOTES**
   Commencement: 1 April 2006 (for effect and transitional provisions see the Public Services Ombudsman (Wales) Act 2005 (Commencement No 1 and Transitional Provisions and Savings) Order 2005, SI 2005/2800, arts 6, 7 at **[3580]**, **[3581]**).
   Sub-s (2): words in square brackets substituted by the Government of Wales Act 2006, s 160(1), Sch 10, paras 67, 69.

**9   Exclusion: other remedies**

(1)   The Ombudsman may not investigate a matter if the person aggrieved has or had—
- (a)   a right of appeal, reference or review to or before a tribunal constituted under an enactment or by virtue of Her Majesty's prerogative,
- (b)   a right of appeal to a Minister of the Crown[, the Welsh Ministers, the First Minister for Wales or the Counsel General to the Welsh Assembly Government], or
- (c)   a remedy by way of proceedings in a court of law.

(2)   But subsection (1) does not apply if the Ombudsman is satisfied that, in the particular circumstances, it is not reasonable to expect the person to resort, or to have resorted, to the right or remedy.

(3)   The Ombudsman may investigate a matter only if he is satisfied that—
- (a)   the matter has been brought to the attention of the listed authority to which it relates by or on behalf of the person aggrieved, and
- (b)   the authority has been given a reasonable opportunity to investigate and respond to it.

(4)   But subsection (3) does not prevent the Ombudsman from investigating a matter if he is satisfied that it is reasonable in the particular circumstances for him to investigate the matter despite the fact that the requirements of that subsection have not been met.

**[1558]**

**NOTES**
   Commencement: 1 April 2006 (for effect and transitional provisions see the Public Services Ombudsman (Wales) Act 2005 (Commencement No 1 and Transitional Provisions and Savings) Order 2005, SI 2005/2800, arts 6, 7 at **[3580]**, **[3581]**).
   Sub-s (1): words in square brackets substituted by the Government of Wales Act 2006, s 160(1), Sch 10, paras 67, 70.

**10   Other excluded matters**

(1)   The Ombudsman may not investigate a matter specified in Schedule 2.

(2)   The [Welsh Ministers] may by order amend Schedule 2 by—
- (a)   adding an entry;
- (b)   removing an entry;
- (c)   changing an entry.

(3)   Before making an order under subsection (2), the [Welsh Ministers] must consult the Ombudsman.

[(3A)   No order is to be made under subsection (2) unless a draft of the statutory instrument containing it has been laid before, and approved by a resolution of, the Assembly.]

(4)   Subsection (1) does not prevent the Ombudsman from investigating action of a listed authority in operating a procedure established to examine complaints or review decisions.

**[1559]**

**NOTES**
   Commencement: 12 October 2005 (for effect and transitional provisions see the Public Services Ombudsman (Wales) Act 2005 (Commencement No 1 and Transitional Provisions and Savings) Order 2005, SI 2005/2800, arts 6, 7 at **[3580]**, **[3581]**).
   Sub-ss (2), (3): words in square brackets substituted by the Government of Wales Act 2006, s 160(1), Sch 10, paras 67, 71(1), (2).
   Sub-s (3A): inserted by the Government of Wales Act 2006, s 160(1), Sch 10, paras 67, 71(1), (3).
   Order: the Public Services Ombudsman for Wales (Jurisdiction and Transitional Provisions and Savings) Order 2006, SI 2006/363.

**11   Decisions taken without maladministration**

(1)   The Ombudsman may not question the merits of a decision taken without maladministration by a listed authority in the exercise of a discretion.

(2)   Subsection (1) does not apply to the merits of a decision to the extent that the decision was taken in consequence of the exercise of professional judgement which appears to the Ombudsman to be exercisable in connection with the provision of health or social care.

**[1560]**

**NOTES**
Commencement: 1 April 2006 (for effect and transitional provisions see the Public Services Ombudsman (Wales) Act 2005 (Commencement No 1 and Transitional Provisions and Savings) Order 2005, SI 2005/2800, arts 6, 7 at **[3580]**, **[3581]**).

*Decisions not to investigate etc*

**12   Decisions not to investigate or to discontinue investigation**

(1)   If the Ombudsman decides under section 2(5)—
  (a)   not to begin an investigation into a complaint in respect of a listed authority, or
  (b)   to discontinue such an investigation,
he must prepare a statement of the reasons for his decision.

(2)   The Ombudsman must send a copy of the statement to—
  (a)   the person who made the complaint, and
  (b)   the listed authority.

(3)   The Ombudsman may send a copy of the statement to any other persons he thinks appropriate.

(4)   The Ombudsman may publish a statement under this section if, after taking account of the interests of the person aggrieved and any other persons he thinks appropriate, he considers it to be in the public interest to do so.

(5)   The Ombudsman may supply a copy of a statement published under subsection (4), or any part of such a statement, to any person who requests it.

(6)   The Ombudsman may charge a reasonable fee for supplying a copy of a statement, or part of a statement, under subsection (5).

(7)   If a statement prepared under subsection (1)—
  (a)   mentions the name of any person other than the listed authority in respect of which the complaint was made, or
  (b)   includes any particulars which, in the opinion of the Ombudsman, are likely to identify any such person and which, in his opinion, can be omitted without impairing the effectiveness of the statement,
that information must not be included in a version of the statement sent to a person under subsection (2) or (3) or published under subsection (4), subject to subsection (8).

(8)   Subsection (7) does not apply in relation to a version of the statement if, after taking account of the interests of the person aggrieved and any other persons he thinks appropriate, the Ombudsman considers it to be in the public interest to include that information in that version of the statement.

(9)   ...

**[1561]**

**NOTES**
Commencement: 1 April 2006 (for effect and transitional provisions see the Public Services Ombudsman (Wales) Act 2005 (Commencement No 1 and Transitional Provisions and Savings) Order 2005, SI 2005/2800, arts 6, 7 at **[3580]**, **[3581]**).
Sub-s (9): repealed by the Government of Wales Act 2006, ss 160(1), 163, Sch 10, paras 67, 72, Sch 12.

*Investigation procedure and evidence*

**13   Investigation procedure**

(1)   If the Ombudsman conducts an investigation into a complaint in respect of a listed authority, he must—
  (a)   give the listed authority an opportunity to comment on any allegations contained in the complaint;
  (b)   give any other person who is alleged in the complaint to have taken or authorised the action complained of an opportunity to comment on any allegations relating to that person.

(2)   An investigation must be conducted in private.

(3)   Subject to subsections (1) and (2), the procedure for conducting an investigation is to be such as the Ombudsman thinks appropriate in the circumstances of the case.

(4)   In particular, the Ombudsman may—

    (a)    make such inquiries as he thinks appropriate;

    (b)    determine whether any person may be represented in the investigation by *counsel, solicitor* or otherwise.

  [(4A)  In subsection (4) "authorised person" means a person who, for the purposes of the Legal Services Act 2007, is an authorised person in relation to an activity which constitutes the exercise of a right of audience or the conduct of litigation (within the meaning of that Act).]

  (5)   The Ombudsman may pay to the person who made the complaint and to any other person who attends or supplies information for the purposes of the investigation—

    (a)    such sums as he may determine in respect of expenses properly incurred by them, and

    (b)    such allowances as he may determine by way of compensation for the loss of their time,

subject to such conditions as he may determine.

  (6)   The conduct of an investigation in respect of a listed authority does not affect—

    (a)    the validity of any action taken by the listed authority, or

    (b)    any power or duty of the listed authority to take further action with respect to any matter under investigation.

**[1562]**

**NOTES**

  Commencement: 1 April 2006 (for effect and transitional provisions see the Public Services Ombudsman (Wales) Act 2005 (Commencement No 1 and Transitional Provisions and Savings) Order 2005, SI 2005/2800, arts 6, 7 at **[3580]**, **[3581]**).

  Sub-s (4): for the words in italics in para (b) there are substituted the words "an authorised person" by the Legal Services Act 2007, s 208(1), Sch 21, para 151(a), as from a day to be appointed.

  Sub-s (4A): inserted by the Legal Services Act 2007, s 208(1), Sch 21, para 151(b), as from a day to be appointed.

## 14  Information, documents, evidence and facilities

  (1)   For the purposes of an investigation the Ombudsman may require a person he thinks is able to supply information or produce a document relevant to the investigation to do so.

  (2)   For the purposes of an investigation the Ombudsman has the same powers as the High Court in respect of—

    (a)    the attendance and examination of witnesses (including the administration of oaths and affirmations and the examination of witnesses abroad), and

    (b)    the production of documents.

  (3)   For the purposes of an investigation the Ombudsman may require a person he thinks is able to supply information or produce a document relevant to the investigation to provide any facility he may reasonably require.

  (4)   Subject to subsection (6), no person is to be compelled for the purposes of an investigation to give any evidence or produce any document which he could not be compelled to give or produce in civil proceedings before the High Court.

  (5)   No obligation to maintain secrecy or other restriction on the disclosure of information obtained by or supplied to persons in Her Majesty's service, whether imposed by any enactment or rule of law, is to apply to the disclosure of information for the purposes of an investigation.

  (6)   The Crown is not entitled in relation to an investigation to any privilege in respect of the production of documents or the giving of evidence that would otherwise be allowed by law in legal proceedings.

**[1563]**

**NOTES**

  Commencement: 1 April 2006 (for effect and transitional provisions see the Public Services Ombudsman (Wales) Act 2005 (Commencement No 1 and Transitional Provisions and Savings) Order 2005, SI 2005/2800, arts 6, 7 at **[3580]**, **[3581]**).

## 15  Obstruction and contempt

  (1)   If the Ombudsman is satisfied that the condition in subsection (2) is met in relation to a person, he may issue a certificate to that effect to the High Court.

  (2)   The condition is that the person—

    (a)    without lawful excuse, has obstructed the discharge of any of the Ombudsman's functions under this Part, or

    (b)    has done an act in relation to an investigation which, if the investigation were proceedings in the High Court, would constitute contempt of court.

  (3)   But the condition in subsection (2) is not met in relation to a person merely because he has taken action such as is mentioned in section 13(6).

**PART I
STATUTES**

(4)   If the Ombudsman issues a certificate under subsection (1), the High Court may inquire into the matter.

(5)   If the High Court is satisfied that the condition in subsection (2) is met in relation to the person, it may deal with him in any manner in which it could have dealt with him if he had committed contempt in relation to the High Court.

**[1564]**

**NOTES**

Commencement: 1 April 2006 (for effect and transitional provisions see the Public Services Ombudsman (Wales) Act 2005 (Commencement No 1 and Transitional Provisions and Savings) Order 2005, SI 2005/2800, arts 6, 7 at **[3580]**, **[3581]**).

*Reports of investigations*

**16   Reports of investigations**

(1)   The Ombudsman must, after conducting an investigation into a complaint in respect of a listed authority—

(a)   prepare a report on his findings, and

(b)   send a copy of the report to all the appropriate persons.

This is subject to section 21.

(2)   The appropriate persons are—

(a)   the person who made the complaint;

(b)   the listed authority;

(c)   any other person who is alleged in the complaint to have taken or authorised the action complained of;

(d)   if the listed authority is a family health service provider in Wales—

(i)   any Local Health Board with whom the authority had, at the time of the action which is the subject of the complaint, entered into a contract to provide the family health services which are under investigation;

(ii)   any person to whom the authority had, at that time, undertaken to provide those services;

(iii)   any person with whom the authority had, at that time, made arrangements for the provision of those services;

(e)   if the listed authority is an independent provider in Wales—

(i)   any Welsh health service body with whom the authority had, at the time of the action which is the subject of the complaint, made arrangements for the provision of the services under investigation;

(ii)   any family health service provider in Wales with whom the authority had, at that time, made arrangements for the provision of those services;

(f)   the [First Minister for Wales] (unless the listed authority is itself the [Welsh Assembly Government] or is a local authority in Wales).

(3)   The Ombudsman may send a copy of the report to any other persons he thinks appropriate.

(4)   The Ombudsman may publish a report prepared under this section if, after taking account of the interests of the person aggrieved and any other persons he thinks appropriate, he considers it to be in the public interest to do so.

(5)   The Ombudsman may supply a copy of a report published under subsection (4), or any part of such a report, to any person who requests it.

(6)   The Ombudsman may charge a reasonable fee for supplying a copy of a report, or part of a report, under subsection (5).

(7)   If a report prepared under this section—

(a)   mentions the name of any person other than the listed authority in respect of which the complaint was made, or

(b)   includes any particulars which, in the opinion of the Ombudsman, are likely to identify any such person and which, in his opinion, can be omitted without impairing the effectiveness of the report,

that information must not be included in a version of the report sent to a person under subsection (1)(b) or (3) or published under subsection (4), subject to subsection (8).

(8)   Subsection (7) does not apply in relation to a version of the report if, after taking account of the interests of the person aggrieved and any other persons he thinks appropriate, the Ombudsman considers it to be in the public interest to include that information in that version of the report.

(9)   ...

**[1565]**

**NOTES**
Commencement: 1 April 2006 (for effect and transitional provisions, see the Public Services Ombudsman (Wales) Act 2005 (Commencement No 1 and Transitional Provisions and Savings) Order 2005, SI 2005/2800, arts 6, 7 at **[3580]**, **[3581]**).
Sub-s (2): words in square brackets in para (f) substituted by the Government of Wales Act 2006, s 160(1), Sch 10, paras 67, 73(1), (2).
Sub-s (9): repealed by the Government of Wales Act 2006, ss 160(1), 163, Sch 10, paras 67, 73(1), (3), Sch 12.

## 17   Publicising reports

(1)   If an investigation is conducted in respect of a listed authority and the authority receives a copy of a report under section 16(1)(b), the authority must make copies of that version of the report available for a period of at least three weeks—

(a)   at one or more of the authority's offices, and

(b)   if the authority has a website, on the website.

(2)   Throughout that period of three weeks, any person may—

(a)   inspect the copy of the report at the office or offices concerned at any reasonable time without payment;

(b)   make a copy of the report or any part of it at any reasonable time without payment;

(c)   require the authority to supply him with a copy of the report or any part of it, on payment of a reasonable sum if requested;

(d)   if the authority has a website, view the copy of the report on the website without payment.

(3)   Not later than two weeks after the copy of the report is received by the listed authority it must ensure that a notice is published in a newspaper circulating in the part of Wales in which the matter which is the subject of the report arose.

(4)   The notice must specify—

(a)   the date on which the period of three weeks referred to in subsection (1) will begin,

(b)   the office or offices at which a copy of the report can be inspected, and

(c)   the address of the authority's website (if any).

(5)   The Ombudsman may give directions to listed authorities with regard to the discharge of their functions under this section.

(6)   Directions under subsection (5) may relate—

(a)   to a particular listed authority in respect of a particular report, or

(b)   generally to the discharge of functions under this section by all or any listed authorities.

(7)   A person commits an offence if—

(a)   he wilfully obstructs a person in the exercise of a right conferred by subsection (2)(a), (b) or (d), or

(b)   he refuses to comply with a requirement under subsection (2)(c).

(8)   A person guilty of an offence under subsection (7) is liable on summary conviction to a fine not exceeding level 3 on the standard scale.

(9)   The Ombudsman may direct that subsections (1) to (4) are not to apply in relation to a particular report.

(10)   In deciding whether to give a direction under subsection (9), the Ombudsman must take into account—

(a)   the public interest,

(b)   the interests of the person aggrieved, and

(c)   the interests of any other persons he thinks appropriate.

**[1566]**

**NOTES**
Commencement: 1 April 2006 (for effect and transitional provisions see the Public Services Ombudsman (Wales) Act 2005 (Commencement No 1 and Transitional Provisions and Savings) Order 2005, SI 2005/2800, arts 6, 7 at **[3580]**, **[3581]**).

## 18   Publicising reports: health care providers

(1)   If an investigation is conducted in respect of a listed authority which is a family health service provider in Wales, section 17 has effect with the modifications specified in subsections (2) to (4).

(2)   For subsection (1) substitute—

"(1)   A person who has received a copy of a report under section 16 by virtue of section 16(2)(d) must make copies of the report available for a period of at least three weeks—

(a)   at one or more of the person's offices, and

(b)   if the person has a website, on the website."

(3)    The references to the listed authority are to be taken to be references to that person.

(4)    The references to listed authorities, or to a particular listed authority, are to be taken to be references to persons, or a particular person, of the same description as that person.

(5)    If an investigation is conducted in respect of a listed authority which is an independent provider in Wales, section 17 has effect with the modifications specified in subsections (6) to (8).

(6)    For subsection (1) substitute—

"(1)    A person who has received a copy of a report under section 16 by virtue of section 16(2)(e) must make copies of the report available for a period of at least three weeks—
(a)    at one or more of the person's offices, and
(b)    if the person has a website, on the website."

(7)    The references to the listed authority are to be taken to be references to that person.

(8)    The references to listed authorities, or to a particular listed authority, are to be taken to be references to persons, or a particular person, of the same description as that person.

**[1567]**

**NOTES**
Commencement: 1 April 2006 (for effect and transitional provisions see the Public Services Ombudsman (Wales) Act 2005 (Commencement No 1 and Transitional Provisions and Savings) Order 2005, SI 2005/2800, arts 6, 7 at **[3580]**, **[3581]**).

## 19    Action following receipt of a report

(1)    This section applies if, in a report under section 16 of an investigation in respect of a listed authority, the Ombudsman concludes that the person aggrieved has sustained injustice or hardship in consequence of the matter investigated.

(2)    The listed authority must consider the report and notify the Ombudsman before the end of the permitted period of—
(a)    the action it has taken or proposes to take in response to it, and
(b)    the period before the end of which it proposes to have taken that action (if it has not already done so).

(3)    The permitted period is—
(a)    the period of one month beginning on the date on which the authority receives the report, or
(b)    any longer period specified by the Ombudsman in writing.

**[1568]**

**NOTES**
Commencement: 1 April 2006 (for effect and transitional provisions see the Public Services Ombudsman (Wales) Act 2005 (Commencement No 1 and Transitional Provisions and Savings) Order 2005, SI 2005/2800, arts 6, 7 at **[3580]**, **[3581]**).

## 20    Non-action following receipt of a report

(1)    If the Ombudsman is satisfied that the condition in subsection (2) is met in relation to a listed authority, he may issue a certificate to that effect to the High Court.

(2)    The condition is that the listed authority has wilfully disregarded his report without lawful excuse.

**[1569]**

**NOTES**
Commencement: to be appointed.

## 21    Reports: alternative procedure

(1)    This section applies if, after the Ombudsman has conducted an investigation into a complaint in respect of a listed authority—
(a)    he concludes that the person aggrieved has not sustained injustice or hardship in consequence of the matter investigated, and
(b)    he is satisfied that the public interest does not require sections 16 to 19 to apply.

(2)    This section also applies if, after the Ombudsman has conducted an investigation into a complaint in respect of a listed authority—
(a)    he concludes that the person aggrieved has sustained injustice or hardship in consequence of the matter investigated,
(b)    the listed authority agrees to implement, before the end of the permitted period, any recommendations he makes, and
(c)    he is satisfied that the public interest does not require sections 16 to 19 to apply.

(3)   The permitted period is—
   (a)   a period agreed between the Ombudsman, the listed authority and the person who made the complaint, or
   (b)   if the Ombudsman thinks that no such agreement can be reached, the period specified by him in writing.

(4)   The Ombudsman may decide to prepare a report on his findings under this section instead of under section 16.

(5)   If the Ombudsman decides to prepare a report under this section—
   (a)   sections 16 to 19 do not apply;
   (b)   he must send a copy of the report to—
      (i)   the person who made the complaint;
      (ii)   the listed authority;
   (c)   he may send a copy of the report to any other persons he thinks appropriate.

(6)   The Ombudsman may publish a report prepared under this section if, after taking account of the interests of the person aggrieved and any other persons he thinks appropriate, he considers it to be in the public interest to do so.

(7)   The Ombudsman may supply a copy of a report published under subsection (6), or any part of such a report, to any person who requests it.

(8)   The Ombudsman may charge a reasonable fee for supplying a copy of a report, or part of a report, under subsection (7).

(9)   If a report prepared under this section—
   (a)   mentions the name of any person other than the listed authority in respect of which the complaint was made, or
   (b)   includes any particulars which, in the opinion of the Ombudsman, are likely to identify any such person and which, in his opinion, can be omitted without impairing the effectiveness of the report,

that information must not be included in a version of the report sent to a person under subsection (5) or published under subsection (6), subject to subsection (10).

(10)   Subsection (9) does not apply in relation to a version of the report if, after taking account of the interests of the person aggrieved and any other persons he thinks appropriate, the Ombudsman considers it to be in the public interest to include that information in that version of the report.

(11)   …

**[1570]**

---

**NOTES**

Commencement: 1 April 2006 (for effect and transitional provisions see the Public Services Ombudsman (Wales) Act 2005 (Commencement No 1 and Transitional Provisions and Savings) Order 2005, SI 2005/2800, arts 6, 7 at **[3580]**, **[3581]**).

Sub-s (11): repealed by the Government of Wales Act 2006, ss 160(1), 163, Sch 10, paras 67, 74, Sch 12.

---

*Special reports*

## 22   Special reports

(1)   The Ombudsman may prepare a report under this section (a "special report") if subsection (2), (4) or (6) applies.

(2)   This subsection applies if, in a report under section 16, the Ombudsman has concluded that the person aggrieved has sustained injustice or hardship in consequence of the matter investigated and—
   (a)   the Ombudsman has not received the notification required under section 19 before the end of the period permitted under that section,
   (b)   he has received that notification but he is not satisfied with—
      (i)   the action which the listed authority has taken or proposes to take, or
      (ii)   the period before the end of which it proposes to have taken that action, or
   (c)   he has received that notification but he is not satisfied that the listed authority has, before the end of the permitted period, taken the action it proposed to take.

(3)   The permitted period for the purposes of subsection (2)(c) is—
   (a)   the period referred to in section 19(2)(b), or
   (b)   any longer period specified by the Ombudsman in writing.

(4)   This subsection applies if the Ombudsman—
   (a)   has prepared a report under section 21 by virtue of subsection (2) of that section, and
   (b)   is not satisfied that the listed authority has implemented his recommendations before the end of the permitted period.

(5)   The permitted period for the purposes of subsection (4)(b) is—
   (a)   the period referred to in section 21(2)(b), or

PART I
STATUTES

(b)    any longer period specified by the Ombudsman in writing.

(6)    This subsection applies if—

(a)    a complaint in respect of a listed authority has been resolved under section 3,

(b)    in resolving the complaint, the Ombudsman has concluded that the person aggrieved has sustained injustice or hardship in consequence of the matter which is the subject of the complaint,

(c)    the listed authority has agreed to take particular action before the end of a particular period, and

(d)    the Ombudsman is not satisfied that the listed authority has taken that action before the end of the permitted period.

(7)    The permitted period for the purposes of subsection (6)(d) is—

(a)    the period referred to in subsection (6)(c), or

(b)    any longer period specified by the Ombudsman in writing.

(8)    A special report must—

(a)    set out the facts on the basis of which subsection (2), (4) or (6) applies, and

(b)    make such recommendations as the Ombudsman thinks fit with respect to the action which, in his opinion, should be taken—

(i)    to remedy the injustice or hardship to the person aggrieved, and

(ii)    to prevent similar injustice or hardship being caused in the future.

(9)    The Ombudsman must send a copy of a special report—

(a)    if the special report is prepared because subsection (2) applies, to each person to whom a copy of the report under section 16 was sent under section 16(1)(b);

(b)    if the special report is prepared because subsection (4) or (6) applies, to the person who made the complaint and the listed authority.

(10)    The Ombudsman may send a copy of a special report to any other persons he thinks appropriate.

[1571]

NOTES

Commencement: 1 April 2006 (for effect and transitional provisions see the Public Services Ombudsman (Wales) Act 2005 (Commencement No 1 and Transitional Provisions and Savings) Order 2005, SI 2005/2800, arts 6, 7 at [3580], [3581]).

## 23    Special reports: supplementary

(1)    The Ombudsman may—

(a)    publish a special report;

(b)    supply a copy of the published report or any part of it to any person who requests it.

(2)    The Ombudsman may charge a reasonable fee for supplying a copy of a report (or part of a report) under subsection (1)(b).

(3)    The listed authority in respect of which a special report is made must reimburse the Ombudsman for the cost of publishing a special report if requested to do so by the Ombudsman.

(4)    If a special report—

(a)    mentions the name of any person other than the listed authority in respect of which the complaint was made, or

(b)    includes any particulars which, in the opinion of the Ombudsman, are likely to identify any such person and which, in his opinion, can be omitted without impairing the effectiveness of the report,

that information must not be included in a version of the report sent to a person under section 22(9) or (10) or published under subsection (1) of this section, subject to subsection (5).

(5)    Subsection (4) does not apply in relation to a version of the special report if, after taking account of the interests of the person aggrieved and any other persons he thinks appropriate, the Ombudsman considers it to be in the public interest to include that information in that version of the special report.

(6)    ...

(7)    Sections 17 and 18 (publicising reports under section 16) apply in relation to a special report as they apply in relation to a report under section 16.

[1572]

NOTES

Commencement: 1 April 2006 (for effect and transitional provisions, see the Public Services Ombudsman (Wales) Act 2005 (Commencement No 1 and Transitional Provisions and Savings) Order 2005, SI 2005/2800, arts 6, 7 at [3580], [3581]).

Sub-s (6): repealed by the Government of Wales Act 2006, ss 160(1), 163, Sch 10, paras 67, 75, Sch 12.

**24    Special reports relating to the [Welsh Assembly Government etc]**

(1)    This section applies if a special report is made in a case where the complaint was made in respect of the [Welsh Assembly Government or the National Assembly for Wales Commission].

(2)    The [relevant person] must—
    (a)    lay a copy of the report before the Assembly, ...
    (b)    ...

[(2A)    In subsection (2) "the relevant person" means—
    (a)    if the complaint was made in respect of the Welsh Assembly Government, the First Minister for Wales, and
    (b)    if the complaint was made in respect of the National Assembly for Wales Commission, a member of that Commission.]

(3)    ...

                                                          **[1573]**

---

**NOTES**

Commencement: 1 April 2006 (for effect and transitional provisions, see the Public Services Ombudsman (Wales) Act 2005 (Commencement No 1 and Transitional Provisions and Savings) Order 2005, SI 2005/2800, arts 6, 7 at **[3580]**, **[3581]**).

Section heading: words in square brackets substituted by the Government of Wales Act 2006, s 160(1), Sch 10, paras 67, 76(1), (6).

Sub-s (1): words in square brackets substituted by the Government of Wales Act 2006, s 160(1), Sch 10, paras 67, 76(1), (2).

Sub-s (2): words in square brackets substituted and words omitted repealed by the Government of Wales Act 2006, ss 160(1), 163, Sch 10, paras 67, 76(1), (3), Sch 12.

Sub-s (2A): inserted by the Government of Wales Act 2006, s 160(1), Sch 10, paras 67, 76(1), (4).

Sub-s (3): repealed by the Government of Wales Act 2006, ss 160(1), 163, Sch 10, paras 67, 76(1), (5), Sch 12.

---

*Consultation and co-operation*

**25    Consultation and co-operation with other ombudsmen**

(1)    This section applies if, in making a decision under section 2(5) or conducting an investigation, the Ombudsman forms the opinion that any matter which is the subject of the complaint or investigation could be the subject of an investigation by an ombudsman mentioned in subsection (7).

(2)    The Ombudsman must consult that ombudsman about the matter.

(3)    The Ombudsman may co-operate with that ombudsman in relation to the matter.

(4)    Consultation under subsection (2), and co-operation under subsection (3), may extend to anything relating to any matter the subject of the complaint or investigation, including in particular—
    (a)    the conduct of an investigation into the complaint;
    (b)    the form, content and publication of a report of the investigation.

(5)    If the Ombudsman consults an ombudsman about a matter under subsection (2), the Ombudsman and that ombudsman may—
    (a)    conduct a joint investigation into the matter;
    (b)    prepare a joint report in relation to the investigation;
    (c)    publish the joint report.

(6)    Subsection (5) does not apply if the ombudsman consulted under subsection (2) is the Scottish Public Services Ombudsman.

(7)    The ombudsmen referred to in subsection (1) are—
    (a)    the Parliamentary Commissioner for Administration;
    (b)    the Health Service Commissioner for England;
    (c)    a Local Commissioner;
    (d)    the Scottish Public Services Ombudsman;
    (e)    a housing ombudsman appointed in accordance with a scheme approved under section 51 of the Housing Act 1996 (c 52);
    (f)    the Children's Commissioner for Wales.

(8)    The [Welsh Ministers] may by order amend subsection (7) by—
    (a)    adding a person;
    (b)    omitting a person;
    (c)    changing the description of a person.

(9)    An order under subsection (8) may add a person to subsection (7) only if the person appears to the [Welsh Ministers] to have functions relating to the investigation of complaints.

[(10)    No order is to be made under subsection (8) unless a draft of the statutory instrument containing it has been laid before, and approved by a resolution of, the Assembly.]

                                                          **[1574]**

NOTES
    Commencement: 12 October 2005 (sub-ss (7)–(9)); 1 April 2006 (sub-ss (1)–(6)). For effect and transitional provisions, see the Public Services Ombudsman (Wales) Act 2005 (Commencement No 1 and Transitional Provisions and Savings) Order 2005, SI 2005/2800, arts 6, 7 at **[3580]**, **[3581]**.
    Sub-ss (8), (9): words in square brackets substituted by the Government of Wales Act 2006, s 160(1), Sch 10, paras 67, 77(1), (2).
    Sub-s (10): inserted by the Government of Wales Act 2006, s 160(1), Sch 10, paras 67, 77(1), (3).

**[25A    Working jointly with the Commissioner for Older People in Wales**

(1)    This section applies where it appears to the Ombudsman that—
    (a)    there is a complaint in respect of a matter which he is entitled to investigate; and
    (b)    the matter is one which could also be the subject of an examination by the Commissioner for Older People in Wales (the 'Commissioner').

(2)    Where the Ombudsman considers it appropriate, he must—
    (a)    inform the Commissioner about the matter; and
    (b)    consult him in relation to it.

(3)    Where the Ombudsman consults the Commissioner under this section, he and the Commissioner may—
    (a)    co-operate with each other in relation to the matter;
    (b)    conduct a joint investigation into the matter;
    (c)    prepare and publish a joint report in relation to the investigation.]

**[1575]**

NOTES
    Commencement: 14 October 2006.
    Inserted, together with s 25B, by the Commissioner for Older People (Wales) Act 2006, s 22, Sch 4, para 2(1), (2).

**[25B    Working collaboratively with the Commissioner for Older People in Wales**

(1)    This section applies where it appears to the Ombudsman that a complaint relates to or raises a matter which could be the subject of an examination by the Commissioner (the 'connected matter').

(2)    Where the Ombudsman considers it appropriate, he must inform the Commissioner about the connected matter.

(3)    Where the Ombudsman considers that the complaint also relates to or raises a matter into which he is entitled to conduct an investigation himself ('the ombudsman matter'), he must also if he considers it appropriate—
    (a)    inform the Commissioner about the Ombudsman's proposals for conducting an investigation into the complaint; and
    (b)    consult the Commissioner about those proposals.

(4)    Where the Ombudsman and the Commissioner consider that they are entitled to investigate, respectively, the ombudsman matter and the connected matter they may—
    (a)    co-operate with each other in the separate investigation of each of those matters;
    (b)    act together in the investigation of those matters; and
    (c)    prepare and publish a joint report containing their respective conclusions in relation to the matters they have each investigated.

(5)    Where the Ombudsman considers—
    (a)    that the complaint does not relate to or raise a matter into which he is entitled to conduct an investigation himself, and
    (b)    that it is appropriate to do so,
he must inform the person who initiated the complaint about how to secure the referral of the connected matter to the Commissioner.

(6)    In this section 'Commissioner' has the meaning given in section 25A.]

**[1576]**

NOTES
    Commencement: 14 October 2006.
    Inserted as noted to s 25A at **[1575]**.

*Disclosure*

**26    Disclosure of information**

(1)    The information to which this section applies is—

(a)    information obtained by the Ombudsman, a member of his staff or another person acting on his behalf or assisting him in the discharge of any of his functions—
     (i)    in deciding whether to begin an investigation,
     (ii)    in the course of an investigation, or
     (iii)    in resolving a complaint under section 3;
(b)    information obtained from an ombudsman mentioned in section 25(7) by virtue of any provision of section 25 or a corresponding provision in an enactment relating to any of those ombudsmen;
[(ba)    information obtained from the Commissioner for Older People in Wales by virtue of any provision of section 25A or 25B of this Act or section 16 or 17 of the Commissioner for Older People (Wales) Act 2006;]
(c)    information obtained from the Information Commissioner by virtue of section 76 of the Freedom of Information Act 2000 (c 36) (disclosure between Information Commissioner and ombudsmen).

(2)    The information must not be disclosed except—
(a)    for the purposes of deciding whether to begin an investigation;
(b)    for the purposes of an investigation;
(c)    for the purposes of resolving a complaint under section 3;
(d)    for the purposes of a statement or report made in relation to a complaint or investigation;
(e)    for the purposes of any provision of section 25[, 25A or 25B];
(f)    for the purposes of proceedings for—
     (i)    an offence under the Official Secrets Acts 1911 to 1989 alleged to have been committed by the Ombudsman, a member of his staff or other person acting on his behalf or assisting him in the discharge of any of his functions;
     (ii)    an offence of perjury alleged to have been committed in the course of an investigation;
(g)    for the purposes of an inquiry with a view to the taking of proceedings mentioned in paragraph (f);
(h)    for the purposes of proceedings under section 15 (obstruction and contempt);
(i)    in the case of information to the effect that a person is likely to constitute a threat to the health or safety of one or more persons, to any person to whom the Ombudsman thinks it should be disclosed in the public interest;
(j)    in the case of information to which subsection (3) applies, to the Information Commissioner.

(3)    This subsection applies to information if it appears to the Ombudsman to relate to—
(a)    a matter in respect of which the Information Commissioner could exercise a power conferred by an enactment mentioned in subsection (4), or
(b)    the commission of an offence mentioned in subsection (5).

(4)    The enactments are—
(a)    Part 5 of the Data Protection Act 1998 (c 29) (enforcement);
(b)    section 48 of the Freedom of Information Act 2000 (c 36) (practice recommendations);
(c)    Part 4 of that Act (enforcement).

(5)    The offences are those under—
(a)    any provision of the Data Protection Act 1998 other than paragraph 12 of Schedule 9 to that Act (obstruction of execution of warrant);
(b)    section 77 of the Freedom of Information Act 2000 (offence of altering etc records with intent to prevent disclosure).

(6)    No person may be called upon to give evidence in any proceedings (other than proceedings mentioned in subsection (2)) of information obtained by him as mentioned in subsection (1)(a) or (b).

**[1577]**

**NOTES**

Commencement: 1 April 2006 (for effect and transitional provisions, see the Public Services Ombudsman (Wales) Act 2005 (Commencement No 1 and Transitional Provisions and Savings) Order 2005, SI 2005/2800, arts 6, 7 at **[3580]**, **[3581]**).

Sub-s (1): para (ba) inserted by the Commissioner for Older People (Wales) Act 2006, s 22, Sch 4, para 2(1), (3)(a).

Sub-s (2): words in square brackets in para (e) inserted by the Commissioner for Older People (Wales) Act 2006, s 22, Sch 4, para 2(1), (3)(b).

**27    Disclosure prejudicial to safety of State or contrary to public interest**

(1)    A Minister of the Crown may give notice to the Ombudsman with respect to—
(a)    any document or information specified in the notice, or
(b)    any class of document or information so specified,

that, in the opinion of the Minister, the disclosure of that document or information, or of documents or information of that class, would be prejudicial to the safety of the State or otherwise contrary to the public interest.

(2) If a notice is given under subsection (1), nothing in this Act is to be construed as authorising or requiring the Ombudsman, a member of his staff or another person acting on his behalf or assisting him in the discharge of any of his functions to disclose to any person or for any purpose any document or information, or class of document or information, specified in the notice.

**[1578]**

**NOTES**
Commencement: 1 April 2006 (for effect and transitional provisions, see the Public Services Ombudsman (Wales) Act 2005 (Commencement No 1 and Transitional Provisions and Savings) Order 2005, SI 2005/2800, arts 6, 7 at **[3580]**, **[3581]**).

*Listed authorities*

## 28 Listed authorities

(1) The persons specified in Schedule 3 are listed authorities for the purposes of this Act.

(2) The [Welsh Ministers] may by order amend Schedule 3 by—
    (a) adding a person;
    (b) omitting a person;
    (c) changing the description of a person.

(3) An order under subsection (2) adding a person to Schedule 3 may provide for this Act to apply to the person with the modifications specified in the order.

(4) Before making an order under subsection (2), the [Welsh Ministers] must consult the Ombudsman and any other persons it thinks appropriate.

[(4A) No order is to be made under subsection (2) unless a draft of the statutory instrument containing it has been laid before, and approved by a resolution of, the Assembly.]

(5) Sections 29 and 30 contain further restrictions on the power in subsection (2).

**[1579]**

**NOTES**
Commencement: 12 October 2005 (for effect and transitional provisions, see the Public Services Ombudsman (Wales) Act 2005 (Commencement No 1 and Transitional Provisions and Savings) Order 2005, SI 2005/2800, arts 6, 7 at **[3580]**, **[3581]**).
Sub-ss (2), (4): words in square brackets substituted by the Government of Wales Act 2006, s 160(1), Sch 10, paras 67, 78(1), (2).
Sub-s (4A): inserted by the Government of Wales Act 2006, s 160(1), Sch 10, paras 67, 78(1), (3).
Order: the Public Services Ombudsman for Wales (Jurisdiction and Transitional Provisions and Savings) Order 2006, SI 2006/363.

## 29 Restrictions on power to amend Schedule 3

(1) An order under section 28(2) may not omit the [Welsh Assembly Government or the National Assembly for Wales Commission] from Schedule 3.

(2) An order under section 28(2) may add a person to Schedule 3 only if—
    (a) the person has functions dischargeable in relation to Wales or a part of Wales (whether or not the functions are also dischargeable otherwise than in relation to Wales),
    (b) all or some of the person's functions are in a field in which the [Welsh Ministers have, or the First Minister for Wales or the Counsel General to the Welsh Assembly Government has,] functions, and
    (c) the person falls within subsection (3), (4) or (5).

(3) A person falls within this subsection if—
    (a) it is a body established by or under an enactment or by virtue of Her Majesty's prerogative or in any other way by a Minister of the Crown, a government department, the [Welsh Ministers, the First Minister for Wales, the Counsel General to the Welsh Assembly Government] or another listed authority,
    (b) it is a body wholly or partly constituted by appointment made by Her Majesty, a Minister of the Crown, a government department, the [Welsh Ministers, the First Minister for Wales, the Counsel General to the Welsh Assembly Government] or another listed authority, and
    (c) at least half of its expenditure on the discharge of its functions in relation to Wales is met [out of the Welsh Consolidated Fund or is met directly from payments made by other listed authorities].

(4) A person falls within this subsection if—
    (a) it is a body established by or under an enactment, and

 (b) it has power to issue a precept or a levy.

 (5) A person falls within this subsection if—

  (a) it appears to the [Welsh Ministers] that the person discharges functions of a public nature, and

  (b) at least half of the person's expenditure on the discharge of those functions in relation to Wales is met [out of the Welsh Consolidated Fund or directly or indirectly from payments made by other listed authorities].

 (6) An order under section 28(2) may not add to Schedule 3—

  (a) a Special Health Authority discharging functions only or mainly in England;

  (b) a person who carries on under national ownership an industry or undertaking or part of an industry or undertaking.

**[1580]**

**NOTES**

 Commencement: 12 October 2005 (for effect and transitional provisions, see the Public Services Ombudsman (Wales) Act 2005 (Commencement No 1 and Transitional Provisions and Savings) Order 2005, SI 2005/2800, arts 6, 7 at **[3580]**, **[3581]**).

 Sub-s (1): words in square brackets substituted by the Government of Wales Act 2006, s 160(1), Sch 10, paras 67, 79(1), (2).

 Sub-s (2): words in square brackets in para (b) substituted by the Government of Wales Act 2006, s 160(1), Sch 10, paras 67, 79(1), (3).

 Sub-s (3): words in square brackets substituted by the Government of Wales Act 2006, s 160(1), Sch 10, paras 67, 79(1), (4).

 Sub-s (5): words in square brackets substituted by the Government of Wales Act 2006, s 160(1), Sch 10, paras 67, 79(1), (5).

---

## 30 Provisions in orders adding persons to Schedule 3

 (1) If the [Welsh Ministers] propose to make an order under section 28(2) adding a person to Schedule 3, [they must] also specify in the order—

  (a) whether all or only some of the person's functions are to fall within the remit of the Ombudsman under this Part;

  (b) if only some of the person's functions are to fall within the remit of the Ombudsman under this Part, which those functions are.

 (2) If the person is to be added to Schedule 3 on the basis that the person falls within section 29(3) or (4), the order may specify a function under subsection (1) only if the function is in a field in which the [Welsh Ministers have, or the First Minister for Wales or the Counsel General to the Welsh Assembly Government has,] functions.

 (3) If the person is to be added to Schedule 3 on the basis that the person falls within section 29(5), the order may specify a function under subsection (1) only if—

  (a) the function is in a field in which the [Welsh Ministers have, or the First Minister for Wales or the Counsel General to the Welsh Assembly Government has,] functions, and

  (b) the function appears to the [Welsh Ministers] to be a function of a public nature.

 (4) The order may specify all a person's functions under subsection (1) only if all the person's functions satisfy the requirements of subsection (2) or (as the case may be) subsection (3).

**[1581]**

**NOTES**

 Commencement: 12 October 2005 (for effect and transitional provisions, see the Public Services Ombudsman (Wales) Act 2005 (Commencement No 1 and Transitional Provisions and Savings) Order 2005, SI 2005/2800, arts 6, 7 at **[3580]**, **[3581]**).

 Sub-ss (1)–(3): words in square brackets substituted by the Government of Wales Act 2006, s 160(1), Sch 10, paras 67, 80.

---

*Miscellaneous*

## 31 Power to issue guidance

 (1) The Ombudsman may issue to one or more listed authorities such guidance about good administrative practice as he thinks appropriate.

 (2) Before issuing guidance under this section the Ombudsman must consult such listed authorities, or persons appearing to him to represent them, as he thinks appropriate.

 (3) If guidance issued under this section is applicable to a listed authority, the authority must have regard to the guidance in discharging its functions.

 (4) In conducting an investigation in respect of a listed authority, the Ombudsman may have regard to the extent to which the authority has complied with any guidance issued under this section which is applicable to the authority.

(5)   The Ombudsman may publish any guidance issued under this section in any manner that he thinks appropriate, including in particular by putting the guidance in an annual or extraordinary report.

(6)   Guidance issued under this section may contain different provision for different purposes.

(7)   Subject to subsection (8), guidance issued under this section must not—

   (a)   mention the name of any person other than the listed authorities to which it is applicable or a listed authority in respect of which a complaint has been made or referred to the Ombudsman under this Act, or

   (b)   include any particulars which, in the opinion of the Ombudsman, are likely to identify any such person and which, in his opinion, can be omitted without impairing the effectiveness of the guidance.

(8)   Subsection (7) does not apply if, after taking account of the interests of any persons he thinks appropriate, the Ombudsman considers it to be in the public interest to include that information in the guidance.

**[1582]**

**NOTES**
   Commencement: 1 April 2006 (for effect and transitional provisions, see the Public Services Ombudsman (Wales) Act 2005 (Commencement No 1 and Transitional Provisions and Savings) Order 2005, SI 2005/2800, arts 6, 7 at **[3580]**, **[3581]**).

## 32   Protection from defamation claims

For the purposes of the law of defamation, the following are absolutely privileged—

   (a)   the publication of a matter by the Ombudsman, a member of his staff or another person acting on his behalf or assisting him in the discharge of any of his functions, in the discharge of any of the Ombudsman's functions under this Act;

   (b)   the publication of a matter by a person in the discharge of functions under section 17;

   (c)   the publication of a matter in connection with a complaint made or referred to the Ombudsman under this Part, in communications between—

      (i)   a listed authority, a member or co-opted member of a listed authority, an officer or member of the staff of a listed authority or another person acting on behalf of a listed authority or assisting it in the discharge of any of its functions, and

      (ii)   the Ombudsman, a member of his staff or another person acting on his behalf or assisting him in the discharge of any of his functions;

   (d)   the publication of any matter in connection with a complaint made or referred (or to be made or referred) by or on behalf of a person to the Ombudsman under this Part, in communications between a person and an Assembly member;

   (e)   the publication of any matter in connection with a complaint made or referred (or to be made or referred) by or on behalf of a person to the Ombudsman under this Part, in communications between the person and the Ombudsman, a member of his staff or another person acting on his behalf or assisting him in the discharge of any of his functions.

**[1583]**

**NOTES**
   Commencement: 1 April 2006 (for effect and transitional provisions, see the Public Services Ombudsman (Wales) Act 2005 (Commencement No 1 and Transitional Provisions and Savings) Order 2005, SI 2005/2800, arts 6, 7 at **[3580]**, **[3581]**).

## 33   Publicity for complaints procedures

(1)   A listed authority must take reasonable steps to provide information to the public about—

   (a)   the right to make a complaint to the Ombudsman in respect of the authority,

   (b)   the right of the authority to refer a complaint to the Ombudsman,

   (c)   the time limits for making and referring complaints to the Ombudsman, and

   (d)   how to contact the Ombudsman.

(2)   In particular, information about the matters specified in subsection (1) must be included in or provided with—

   (a)   any document published by the listed authority which contains information about—

      (i)   relevant services provided by the authority to members of the public, or

      (ii)   the procedures of the authority for dealing with complaints, and

   (b)   any document issued by the listed authority in responding to a complaint made to it by a person who might be entitled to make the complaint to the Ombudsman.

(3)   The Ombudsman may issue guidance to listed authorities with respect to the discharge of their functions under this section.

(4)　A listed authority must have regard to guidance given by the Ombudsman under subsection (3).

(5)　"Relevant service" has the meaning given in section 7.

**[1584]**

**NOTES**
Commencement: 1 April 2006 (for effect and transitional provisions, see the Public Services Ombudsman (Wales) Act 2005 (Commencement No 1 and Transitional Provisions and Savings) Order 2005, SI 2005/2800, arts 6, 7 at **[3580]**, **[3581]**).

### 34　Compensation for the person aggrieved

(1)　This section applies if—
    (a)　a complaint in respect of a matter is made or referred to the Ombudsman, and
    (b)　the complaint is one which the Ombudsman has power to investigate under section 2.

(2)　The listed authority in respect of which the complaint is made may make a payment to, or provide any other benefit for, the person aggrieved in respect of the matter which is the subject of the complaint.

(3)　It is immaterial for the purposes of this section that the Ombudsman has decided not to investigate the complaint, has discontinued an investigation of the complaint, has not yet completed an investigation of the complaint or has not upheld the complaint.

(4)　The power in subsection (2) does not affect any other power of the listed authority to make the payment or provide the benefit.

**[1585]**

**NOTES**
Commencement: 1 April 2006 (for effect and transitional provisions, see the Public Services Ombudsman (Wales) Act 2005 (Commencement No 1 and Transitional Provisions and Savings) Order 2005, SI 2005/2800, arts 6, 7 at **[3580]**, **[3581]**).

## PART 3
## MISCELLANEOUS AND GENERAL

**35**　(*Outside the scope of this work.*)

*Abolition of existing bodies and offices*

### 36　Abolition of existing bodies and offices

(1)　The Commission for Local Administration in Wales is abolished.

(2)　The office of Welsh Administration Ombudsman is abolished.

(3)　The office of Health Service Commissioner for Wales is abolished.

(4)　The office of Social Housing Ombudsman for Wales is abolished.

**[1586]**

**NOTES**
Commencement: 1 April 2006 (for effect and transitional provisions, see the Public Services Ombudsman (Wales) Act 2005 (Commencement No 1 and Transitional Provisions and Savings) Order 2005, SI 2005/2800, arts 6, 7 at **[3580]**, **[3581]**).

### 37　Transfer of property, staff etc

Schedule 5 (which provides for the transfer of property, staff etc to the Ombudsman) has effect.

**[1587]**

**NOTES**
Commencement: 1 April 2006 (for effect and transitional provisions, see the Public Services Ombudsman (Wales) Act 2005 (Commencement No 1 and Transitional Provisions and Savings) Order 2005, SI 2005/2800, arts 6, 7 at **[3580]**, **[3581]**).

### 38　Undetermined complaints

(1)　Subsection (2) applies if—
    (a)　a complaint has been made or referred to an existing Welsh ombudsman before the commencement date, and
    (b)　the complaint has not been determined by that ombudsman before that date.

(2)　On and after the commencement date, the relevant existing enactment continues to apply for the purposes of the complaint despite the other provisions of this Act.

(3)    Subsection (4) applies if—
    (a)    a complaint could (but for the other provisions of this Act) have been made or referred to an existing Welsh ombudsman, and
    (b)    the complaint relates to action taken by a person before the commencement date.

(4)    On and after the commencement date, the relevant existing enactment continues to apply for the purposes of enabling the complaint to be made or referred, and for the purposes of the complaint if made or referred, despite the other provisions of this Act.

(5)    As applied by subsections (2) and (4), the relevant existing enactment has effect as if for references to the existing Welsh ombudsman in relation to which that enactment applies there were substituted references to the Ombudsman.

(6)    In this section—
    "the commencement date" means the date on which this section comes into force;
    "existing Welsh ombudsman" means—
        (a)    the Welsh Administration Ombudsman;
        (b)    the Health Service Commissioner for Wales;
        (c)    a Local Commissioner who is a member of the Commission for Local Administration in Wales;
        (d)    the Social Housing Ombudsman for Wales;
    "the relevant existing enactment"—
        (a)    if the relevant existing Welsh ombudsman is the Welsh Administration Ombudsman, means Schedule 9 to the Government of Wales Act 1998 (c 38);
        (b)    if the relevant existing Welsh ombudsman is the Health Service Commissioner for Wales, means the Health Service Commissioners Act 1993 (c 46);
        (c)    if the relevant existing Welsh ombudsman is a Local Commissioner, means Part 3 of the Local Government Act 1974 (c 7);
        (d)    if the relevant existing Welsh ombudsman is the Social Housing Ombudsman for Wales, means Part 1 of the Housing Act 1996 (c 52);
    "the relevant existing Welsh ombudsman"—
        (a)    in relation to a complaint within subsection (1), means the existing Welsh ombudsman to whom the complaint was made or referred;
        (b)    in relation to a complaint within subsection (3), means the existing Welsh ombudsman to whom the complaint could have been made or referred.

**[1588]**

**NOTES**
Commencement: 1 April 2006 (for effect and transitional provisions, see the Public Services Ombudsman (Wales) Act 2005 (Commencement No 1 and Transitional Provisions and Savings) Order 2005, SI 2005/2800, arts 6, 7 at **[3580]**, **[3581]**).

*General*

## 39    Amendments and repeals

(1)    Schedule 6 (which contains amendments consequential on this Act) has effect.

(2)    Schedule 7 (which contains repeals) has effect.

**[1589]**

**NOTES**
Commencement: 12 October 2005 (for certain purposes); 1 April 2006 (for remaining purposes). For effect and transitional provisions, see the Public Services Ombudsman (Wales) Act 2005 (Commencement No 1 and Transitional Provisions and Savings) Order 2005, SI 2005/2800, arts 6, 7 at **[3580]**, **[3581]**.

## 40    Commencement

The preceding provisions of this Act come into force in accordance with provision made by the [Welsh Ministers] by order.

**[1590]**

**NOTES**
Commencement: 7 April 2005.
Words in square brackets substituted by the Government of Wales Act 2006, s 160(1), Sch 10, paras 67, 81.
Order: the Public Services Ombudsman (Wales) Act 2005 (Commencement No 1 and Transitional Provisions and Savings) Order 2005, SI 2005/2800.

## 41    Interpretation

(1)    In this Act—
    "act" and "action" include a failure to act (and related expressions must be construed accordingly);

"annual report" has the meaning given in paragraph 14 of Schedule 1;

...

"the Assembly" means the National Assembly for Wales;

"co-opted member", in relation to an authority, means a person who is not a member of the authority but who—

    (a)      is a member of a committee or sub-committee of the authority, or

    (b)      is a member of, and represents the authority on, a joint committee on which the authority is represented or a sub-committee of such a committee,

and who is entitled to vote on any question which falls to be decided at a meeting of the committee or sub-committee;

"extraordinary report" has the meaning given in paragraph 14 of Schedule 1;

"family health service provider in Wales" means—

    (a)      a person who, at the time of action which is the subject of a complaint under this Act, provided services under a contract entered into by that person with a Local Health Board under [section 42 or section 57 of the National Health Service (Wales) Act 2006];

    (b)      a person who, at that time, had undertaken to provide in Wales general ophthalmic services or pharmaceutical services under ... that Act;

    (c)      an individual who, at that time, provided in Wales [primary medical services or primary dental services] in accordance with arrangements made under [section 50 or 64] of that Act (except as an employee of, or otherwise on behalf of, a Welsh health service body or an independent provider in Wales);

    (d)      ...

"family health services" means services mentioned in any of paragraphs (a) to (d) of the definition of "family health service provider in Wales";

"financial year" means the 12 months ending on 31 March;

"independent provider in Wales" means a person who, at the time of action which is the subject of a complaint under this Act—

    (a)      provided services of any kind in Wales under arrangements with a Welsh health service body or a family health service provider in Wales, and

    (b)      was not a Welsh health service body or a family health service provider in Wales;

["investigation"—

    (a)      in relation to the Ombudsman, means an investigation under section 2 (and cognate expressions must be construed accordingly);

    (b)      in relation to another ombudsman or commissioner, includes an examination (and cognate expressions must be construed accordingly);]

"listed authority" has the meaning given in section 28;

"local authority in Wales" means a county council, county borough council or community council in Wales;

"Local Commissioner" has the meaning given in section 23(3) of the Local Government Act 1974 (c 7);

"NHS trust" has the same meaning as in [the National Health Service (Wales) Act 2006];

"the Ombudsman" has the meaning given in section 1;

"the person aggrieved" has the meaning given in section 4(1)(a);

"publicly-funded dwelling" means—

    (a)      a dwelling which was provided by means of a grant under—

        (i)      section 18 of the Housing Act 1996 (c 52) (social housing grant), or

        (ii)      section 50 of the Housing Act 1988 (c 50), section 41 of the Housing Associations Act 1985 (c 69), or section 29 or 29A of the Housing Act 1974 (c 44) (housing association grant);

    (b)      a dwelling which was acquired on a disposal by a public sector landlord (within the meaning of Part 1 of the Housing Act 1996);

"relevant tribunal" means a tribunal (including a tribunal consisting of only one person) specified by order made by the [Welsh Ministers];

"social landlord in Wales" means—

    (a)      a body which was at the time of action which is the subject of a complaint under this Act registered as a social landlord in the register maintained by the [Welsh Ministers] under section 1 of the Housing Act 1996 (or in the register previously maintained under that section by [the Assembly constituted by the Government of Wales Act 1998,] the Secretary of State or Housing for Wales);

    (b)      any other body which at the time of action which is the subject of a complaint under this Act was registered with Housing for Wales, the Secretary of State[, the Assembly constituted by the Government of Wales Act 1998 or the Welsh Ministers] and owned or managed publicly-funded dwellings;

"special report" has the meaning given in section 22;

"Wales" has the meaning given in section 155(1) of the Government of Wales Act 1998 (c 38);

"Welsh health service body" means—

(a)   the [Welsh Ministers];
(b)   a Local Health Board;
(c)   an NHS trust managing a hospital or other establishment or facility in Wales;
(d)   a Special Health Authority not discharging functions only or mainly in England.

(2)   For the purposes of the definition of "independent provider in Wales", arrangements with the [Welsh Ministers] are arrangements with a Welsh health service body only to the extent that they are made in the discharge of a function of the [Welsh Ministers] relating to the National Health Service.

[(2A)   A statutory instrument containing an order under subsection (1) is subject to annulment in pursuance of a resolution of the Assembly.]

(3)   The [Welsh Ministers] may by order amend the definitions of "family health service provider in Wales", "independent provider in Wales" and "social landlord in Wales".

(4)   Before making an order under subsection (3), the [Welsh Ministers] must consult such persons as [they think] appropriate.

[(4A)   No order is to be made under subsection (3) unless a draft of the statutory instrument containing it has been laid before, and approved by a resolution of, the Assembly.]

(5)   Section 13 of the National Audit Act 1983 (c 44) (interpretation of references to the Committee of Public Accounts) applies for the purposes of this Act as it applies for the purposes of that Act.

(6)   For the purposes of this Act, references to action taken by a listed authority include action taken by—
(a)   a member, co-opted member, committee or sub-committee of the authority acting in the discharge of functions of the authority;
(b)   an officer or member of staff of the authority, whether acting in the discharge of his own functions or the functions of the authority;
(c)   any other person acting on behalf of the authority.

**[1591]**

**NOTES**
Commencement: 7 April 2005.
Sub-s (1): definition "Assembly Cabinet" (omitted) repealed, words in square brackets in definitions "relevant tribunal" and "Welsh health service body" substituted, in definition "social landlord in Wales" words in first and third pairs of square brackets substituted and words in second pair of square brackets inserted by the Government of Wales Act 2006, ss 160(1), 163, Sch 10, paras 67, 82(1), (2), Sch 12; in definition "family health service provider in Wales" words in square brackets in para (a) and words in second pair of square brackets in para (c) substituted, and words omitted from para (b) repealed by the National Health Service (Consequential Provisions) Act 2006, s 2, Sch 1, paras 279, 280(a), words in first pair of square brackets in para (c) substituted and para (d) repealed by the Public Services Ombudsman for Wales (Jurisdiction and Transitional Provisions and Savings) Order 2006, SI 2006/363, art 4(b), (c), subject to transitional provisions and savings in arts 5–7 thereof; definition "investigation" substituted by the Commissioner for Older People (Wales) Act 2006, s 22, Sch 4, para 2(1), (4); in definition "NHS trust" words in square brackets substituted by the National Health Service (Consequential Provisions) Act 2006, s 2, Sch 1, paras 279, 280(b).
Sub-ss (2), (3), (4): words in square brackets substituted by the Government of Wales Act 2006, s 160(1), Sch 10, paras 67, 82(1), (3), (5), (6).
Sub-ss (2A), (4A): inserted by the Government of Wales Act 2006, s 160(1), Sch 10, paras 67, 82(1), (4), (7).

**42   Former health care providers and social landlords: modifications**

(1)   The [Welsh Ministers] may by regulations provide for this Act to apply with the modifications specified in the regulations to persons who are—
(a)   former family health service providers in Wales;
(b)   former independent providers in Wales;
(c)   former social landlords in Wales.

(2)   "Former family health service provider in Wales" means a person who—
(a)   at the relevant time, provided family health services of a particular description, and
(b)   subsequently ceased to provide services of that description (whether or not he has later started to provide them again).

(3)   "Former independent provider in Wales" means a person who—
(a)   at the relevant time, provided services of a particular description in Wales under arrangements with a Welsh health service body or a family health service provider in Wales,
(b)   was not a Welsh health service body or a family health service provider in Wales at that time, and
(c)   subsequently ceased to provide services of that description (whether or not he has later started to provide them again).

(4)   "Former social landlord in Wales" means a person who—
(a)   at the relevant time—

            (i)     was registered as a social landlord in the register maintained by the [Welsh Ministers] under section 1 of the Housing Act 1996 (c 52) (or in the register previously maintained under that section by [the Assembly constituted by the Government of Wales Act 1998,] the Secretary of State or Housing for Wales), or

          (ii)     was registered with Housing for Wales, the Secretary of State[, the Assembly constituted by the Government of Wales Act 1998 or the Welsh Ministers] and owned or managed publicly-funded dwellings, and

    (b)     subsequently—

            (i)     ceased to be registered as mentioned in paragraph (a)(i) or (ii) (whether or not he later became so registered again), or

          (ii)     ceased to own or manage publicly-funded dwellings (whether or not he later did so again).

    (5)     "The relevant time" is the time of action which is the subject of a complaint under this Act.

    [(6)     No regulations are to be made under this section unless a draft of the statutory instrument containing them has been laid before, and approved by a resolution of, the Assembly.]

                                                    **[1592]**

**NOTES**
Commencement: 7 April 2005.
Sub-s (1): words in square brackets substituted by the Government of Wales Act 2006, s 160(1), Sch 10, paras 67, 83(1), (2).
Sub-s (4): words in first and third pairs of square brackets substituted and words in second pair of square brackets inserted by the Government of Wales Act 2006, s 160(1), Sch 10, paras 67, 83(1), (3).
Sub-s (6): added by the Government of Wales Act 2006, s 160(1), Sch 10, paras 67, 83(1), (4).

### 43   Consequential, transitional provisions etc

    (1)     The [Welsh Ministers] may by order make—

    (a)     such consequential, incidental or supplemental provision, and

    (b)     such transitory, transitional or saving provision,

as [they think] necessary or expedient for the purposes of, in consequence of, or for giving full effect to, any provision of this Act.

    (2)     An order under subsection (1) may in particular amend, repeal or revoke any enactment other than one contained in an Act passed in a Session after that in which this Act is passed.

    (3)     The amendments that may be made by virtue of subsection (2) are in addition to those made by or under any other provision of this Act.

    [(4)     No order is to be made under subsection (1) unless a draft of the statutory instrument containing it has been laid before, and approved by a resolution of, the Assembly.]

                                                      **[1593]**

**NOTES**
Commencement: 7 April 2005.
Sub-s (1): words in square brackets substituted by the Government of Wales Act 2006, s 160(1), Sch 10, paras 67, 84(1), (2).
Sub-s (4): inserted by the Government of Wales Act 2006, s 160(1), Sch 10, paras 67, 84(1), (3).
Orders: the Public Services Ombudsman (Wales) Act 2005 (Commencement No 1 and Transitional Provisions and Savings) Order 2005, SI 2005/2800; the Public Services Ombudsman (Wales) Act 2005 (Transitional Provisions and Consequential Amendments) Order 2006, SI 2006/362; the Public Services Ombudsman for Wales (Jurisdiction and Transitional Provisions and Savings) Order 2006, SI 2006/363; the Public Services Ombudsman (Wales) Act 2005 (Consequential Amendments to the Local Government Pension Scheme Regulations 1997 and Transitional Provisions) Order 2006, SI 2006/1011.

### 44   Orders, regulations and directions

    (1)     A power of the [Welsh Ministers] to make an order or regulations under this Act is exercisable by statutory instrument.

    (2)     An order or regulations made by the [Welsh Ministers] under this Act may—

    (a)     make different provision for different purposes;

    (b)     make consequential, incidental, supplemental, transitory, transitional or saving provision.

    (3)     …

    (4)     A direction given under this Act—

    (a)     may be amended or revoked by the person who gave it;

    (b)     may make different provision for different purposes.

                                                       **[1594]**

**NOTES**
Commencement: 7 April 2005.

Sub-ss (1), (2): words in square brackets substituted by the Government of Wales Act 2006, s 160(1), Sch 10, paras 67, 85(1), (2).

Sub-s (3): repealed by the Government of Wales Act 2006, ss 160(1), 163, Sch 10, paras 67, 85(1), (3), Sch 12.

## 45 Extent

(1) Subject to subsection (2), this Act extends to England and Wales only.

(2) An amendment or repeal made by this Act has the same extent as the provision amended or repealed.

[1595]

**NOTES**

Commencement: 7 April 2005.

## 46 Short title

This Act may be cited as the Public Services Ombudsman (Wales) Act 2005.

[1596]

**NOTES**

Commencement: 7 April 2005.

## SCHEDULE 1
## PUBLIC SERVICES OMBUDSMAN FOR WALES: APPOINTMENT ETC

Section 1

*Appointment*

[1. The Ombudsman is to be appointed by Her Majesty on the nomination of the Assembly.]

*Status*

2.—(1) The Ombudsman is a corporation sole.

(2) The Ombudsman holds office under Her Majesty and discharges his functions on behalf of the Crown.

(3) The Ombudsman is a Crown servant for the purposes of the Official Secrets Act 1989 (c 6).

(4) But service as the Ombudsman is not service in the civil service of the Crown.

*Term of office*

3.—(1) A person's term of office as the Ombudsman is seven years (subject to sub-paragraphs (3) and (4) and paragraph 5).

(2) A person appointed as the Ombudsman is not eligible for re-appointment.

(3) Her Majesty may relieve a person of office as the Ombudsman—
    (a) at his request, or
    [(b) on Her Majesty being satisfied that the person is incapable for medical reasons of performing the duties of the office].

(4) Her Majesty may remove a person from office as the Ombudsman [on the making of a recommendation, on the ground of the person's misbehaviour, that Her Majesty should do so].

[(5) A recommendation for the removal of a person from office as the Ombudsman may not be made unless—
    (a) the Assembly has resolved that the recommendation should be made, and
    (b) the resolution of the Assembly is passed on a vote in which the number of Assembly members voting in favour of it is not less than two-thirds of the total number of Assembly seats.]

*Acting Public Services Ombudsman for Wales*

4.—[(1) If the office of the Ombudsman becomes vacant, Her Majesty may, on the nomination of the Assembly, appoint a person to act as the Ombudsman.]

(3) A person appointed to act as the Ombudsman ("an acting Ombudsman") may have held office as the Ombudsman.

(4) A person appointed as an acting Ombudsman is eligible for appointment as the Ombudsman (unless he has already held office as the Ombudsman).

(5) The power to appoint a person as an acting Ombudsman is not exercisable after the end of the period of two years starting with the date on which the vacancy arose.

(6) An acting Ombudsman holds office in accordance with the terms of his appointment, subject to sub-paragraph (7) (and paragraph 2, as applied by sub-paragraph (8)).

(7) An acting Ombudsman must not hold office after—

    (a) the appointment of a person as the Ombudsman, or

    (b) if sooner, the end of the period of two years starting with the date on which the vacancy arose.

(8) While an acting Ombudsman holds office he is to be regarded (except for the purposes of paragraphs 1, 3, 5 to 9 and this paragraph) as the Ombudsman.

### *Disqualification*

5.—(1) A person is disqualified from being the Ombudsman or an acting Ombudsman if any of the following applies—

    (a) he is a member of the House of Commons;

    (b) he is a listed authority;

    (c) he is a member, co-opted member, officer or member of staff of a listed authority;

    (d) he is disqualified from being a member of the Assembly (other than by virtue of paragraph 6 of this Schedule or [section 16(1)(d) of the Government of Wales Act 2006]);

    (e) he is disqualified from being a member of a local authority in Wales (other than by virtue of paragraph 6 of this Schedule).

(2) The appointment of a person as the Ombudsman or an acting Ombudsman is not valid if the person is disqualified under sub-paragraph (1).

(3) If a person who has been appointed as the Ombudsman or an acting Ombudsman becomes disqualified under sub-paragraph (1), he ceases to hold office on becoming so disqualified.

(4) But the validity of anything done by a person appointed as the Ombudsman or an acting Ombudsman is not affected by the fact that he is or becomes disqualified under sub-paragraph (1).

6.—(1) A person who holds office as the Ombudsman or an acting Ombudsman is disqualified from—

    (a) being a listed authority;

    (b) being a member, co-opted member, officer or member of staff of a listed authority;

    (c) holding a paid office to which appointment is by a listed authority.

(2) A person is not disqualified under sub-paragraph (1) from being a member of the Assembly.

7.—(1) A person who has ceased to hold office as the Ombudsman or as an acting Ombudsman is disqualified for the relevant period from—

    (a) holding an office which is a listed authority;

    (b) being a member, co-opted member, officer or member of staff of a listed authority;

    (c) holding a paid office to which appointment is by a listed authority.

(2) The relevant period is the period of three years starting on the date on which the person ceased to hold office as the Ombudsman or (as the case may be) as an acting Ombudsman.

(3) But sub-paragraph (1) does not disqualify a person from—

    (a) being a member of the Assembly [or the National Assembly for Wales Commission];

    (b) holding the office of presiding officer or deputy presiding officer of the Assembly or of [First Minister for Wales, Welsh Minister appointed under section 48 of the Government of Wales Act 2006, Counsel General to the Welsh Assembly Government or Deputy Welsh Minister];

    (c) being a member or co-opted member of a local authority in Wales;

    (d) holding the office of chairman, vice-chairman or elected mayor of a local authority in Wales.

8. The references in paragraphs 6 and 7 to a paid office include an office the holder of which is entitled only to the reimbursement of expenses.

### *Remuneration etc*

9.—(1) The Assembly must—

    (a) pay a person who is the Ombudsman or an acting Ombudsman such salary and allowances, and

    (b) make such payments towards the provision of superannuation benefits for or in respect of him,

as may be provided for by or under the terms of his appointment.

(2) The Assembly must pay to or in respect of a person who has ceased to hold office as the Ombudsman or an acting Ombudsman—

    (a) such amounts by way of pensions and gratuities, and

    (b) such amounts by way of provision for those benefits,

as may have been provided for by or under the terms of his appointment.

PART I
STATUTES

(3)   If a person ceases to be the Ombudsman or an acting Ombudsman and it appears to the Assembly that there are special circumstances which make it right that the person should receive compensation, the Assembly may pay to that person a sum of such amount as it thinks appropriate.

(4)   In Schedule 1 to the Superannuation Act 1972 (c 11) (offices etc to which section 1 of that Act applies) in the list of "Offices" at the appropriate places insert—
> "Public Services Ombudsman for Wales"
> "Acting Public Services Ombudsman for Wales".

(5)   The Assembly must pay to the Minister for the Civil Service, at such times as he may direct, such sums as he may determine in respect of any increase attributable to sub-paragraph (4) in the sums payable out of money provided by Parliament under the Superannuation Act 1972 (c 11).

[(6)   Sums required for the making of payments under sub-paragraphs (1), (2) and (5) are to be charged on the Welsh Consolidated Fund.]

*[Special financial provisions]*

10.—(1)   Any sums payable by the Ombudsman in consequence of a breach, in the performance of any of the Ombudsman's functions, of any contractual or other duty are to be charged on the Welsh Consolidated Fund.

(2)   And sub-paragraph (1) applies whether the breach occurs by reason of an act or omission of—
    (a)   the Ombudsman,
    (b)   a member of the Ombudsman's staff, or
    (c)   any other person acting on the Ombudsman's behalf or assisting the Ombudsman in the exercise of functions.

(3)   The Ombudsman may retain income derived from fees charged by virtue of sections 12(6), 16(6), 21(8) and 23(2) (rather than pay it into the Welsh Consolidated Fund) for use in connection with the exercise of the functions conferred or imposed by this Act.]

*Staff*

11.—(1)   The Ombudsman may appoint such staff as he thinks necessary for assisting him in the discharge of his functions, on such terms and conditions as he may determine.

(2)   No member of staff of the Ombudsman is to be regarded as holding office under Her Majesty or as discharging any functions on behalf of the Crown.

(3)   But each member of his staff is to be treated as being a Crown servant for the purposes of the Official Secrets Act 1989 (c 6).

(4)   In Schedule 1 to the Superannuation Act 1972 (offices etc to which section 1 of that Act applies) in the list of "other bodies" at the appropriate place insert—

> "Employment as a member of the staff of the Public Services Ombudsman for Wales."

(5)   The [Ombudsman] must pay to the Minister for the Civil Service, at such times as [the Minister] may direct, such sum as [the Minister] may determine in respect of any increase attributable to sub-paragraph (4) in the sums payable out of money provided by Parliament under the Superannuation Act 1972.

*Advisers*

12.—(1)   The Ombudsman may obtain advice from any person who, in his opinion, is qualified to give it, to assist him in the discharge of his functions.

(2)   The Ombudsman may pay to any person from whom he obtains advice under sub-paragraph (1) such fees or allowances as he may determine.

*Delegation*

13.—(1)   Any function of the Ombudsman may be discharged on his behalf—
    (a)   by any person authorised by the Ombudsman to do so, and
    (b)   to the extent so authorised.

(2)   Sub-paragraph (1) does not affect the responsibility of the Ombudsman for the discharge of any such function.

(3)   A person authorised by the Ombudsman under sub-paragraph (1) is to be treated as being a Crown servant for the purposes of the Official Secrets Act 1989 (c 6).

[(4)   No arrangements may be made between the Ombudsman, on the one hand, and the Welsh Ministers (or the First Minister for Wales or the Counsel General to the Welsh Assembly Government), on the other, for—
    (a)   any functions of one of them to be exercised by the other,

(b)     any functions of the Welsh Ministers (or the First Minister for Wales or the Counsel General to the Welsh Assembly Government) to be exercised by members of staff of the Ombudsman,

(c)     any functions of the Ombudsman to be exercised by members of the staff of the Welsh Assembly Government, or

(d)     the provision of administrative, professional or technical services by one of them for the other.]

(5)     Sub-paragraph (4) applies despite any provision that would otherwise permit such arrangements to be made.

#### Annual and extraordinary reports

14.—(1)     The Ombudsman—

(a)     must annually prepare a general report on the discharge of his functions (an "annual report");

(b)     may prepare any other report with respect to his functions that he thinks appropriate (an "extraordinary report").

(2)     A report prepared under this paragraph may include any general recommendations which the Ombudsman may have arising from the discharge of his functions.

(3)     The Ombudsman must lay a copy of each report prepared under this paragraph before the Assembly and at the same time [send a copy to the Welsh Assembly Government and] (if the report is an extraordinary report) must send a copy of it to any listed authorities (other [than the Welsh Assembly Government]) he thinks appropriate.

(4)     The Ombudsman may also send a copy of any report prepared under this paragraph to any other persons he thinks appropriate.

(5)     The Ombudsman must, and the Assembly may, publish any report laid before the Assembly under this paragraph.

(6)     The Ombudsman must comply with any directions given by the Assembly with respect to an annual report.

(7)     If a report prepared under this paragraph—

(a)     mentions the name of any person other than a listed authority in respect of which a complaint has been made or referred under this Act, or

(b)     includes any particulars which, in the opinion of the Ombudsman, are likely to identify any such person and which, in his opinion, can be omitted without impairing the effectiveness of the report,

that information must not be included in a version of the report laid before the Assembly under sub-paragraph (3), sent to a person under sub-paragraph (3) or (4) or published by the Ombudsman under sub-paragraph (5), subject to sub-paragraph (8).

(8)     Sub-paragraph (7) does not apply in relation to a version of the report if, after taking account of the interests of any persons he thinks appropriate, the Ombudsman considers it to be in the public interest to include that information in that version of the report.

#### Estimates

15.—(1)     For each financial year other than the first financial year, the Ombudsman must prepare an estimate of the income and expenses of his office.

(2)     The Ombudsman must submit the estimate [at least five months before the beginning of the financial year to which it relates to the committee or committees of the Assembly specified in the standing orders of the Assembly].

(3)     The [committee or committees] must examine an estimate submitted … in accordance with sub-paragraph (2) and must then lay the estimate before the Assembly with any modifications [thought] appropriate.

[(4)     Before laying before the Assembly with modifications an estimate submitted in accordance with sub-paragraph (2), the committee or committees must—

(a)     consult the Ombudsman, and

(b)     take into account any representations which the Ombudsman may make.]

(5)     The first financial year is the financial year during which the first person to be appointed as the Ombudsman is appointed.

#### Accounts

16.—(1)     The Ombudsman must—

(a)     keep proper accounting records; and

(b)     for each financial year, prepare accounts in accordance with directions given to him by the Treasury.

(2) The directions which the Treasury may give under sub-paragraph (1)(b) include, in particular, directions as to—
- (a) the information to be contained in the accounts and the manner in which it is to be presented;
- (b) the methods and principles in accordance with which the accounts are to be prepared;
- (c) the additional information (if any) that is to accompany the accounts.

### Audit

17.—(1) The accounts prepared by the Ombudsman for a financial year must be submitted by him to the Auditor General for Wales no later than 30 November in the following financial year.

(2) The Auditor General for Wales must—
- (a) examine, certify and report on each set of accounts submitted to him under this paragraph, and
- (b) no later than four months after the accounts are so submitted, lay before the Assembly a copy of them as certified by him together with his report on them.

(3) In examining accounts submitted to him under this paragraph the Auditor General for Wales must, in particular, satisfy himself that the expenditure to which the accounts relate has been incurred lawfully and in accordance with the authority which governs it.

### Accounting officer

18.—(1) The Ombudsman is the accounting officer for the office of the Ombudsman.

(2) If the Ombudsman is incapable of discharging his responsibilities as accounting officer, the [Audit Committee] may designate a member of his staff to be the accounting officer for as long as he is so incapable.

(3) If the office of the Ombudsman is vacant and there is no acting Ombudsman, the [Audit Committee] may designate a member of the Ombudsman's staff to be the accounting officer for as long as the office of the Ombudsman is vacant and there is no acting Ombudsman.

(4) The accounting officer has, in relation to the accounts and the finances of the Ombudsman, the responsibilities which are from time to time specified by the [Audit Committee].

(5) In this paragraph references to responsibilities include in particular—
- (a) responsibilities in relation to the signing of accounts,
- (b) responsibilities for the propriety and regularity of the finances of the Ombudsman, and
- (c) responsibilities for the economy, efficiency and effectiveness with which the resources of the Ombudsman are used.

(6) The responsibilities which may be specified under this paragraph include responsibilities owed to—
- (a) the Assembly, the [Welsh Ministers] or the Audit Committee, or
- (b) the House of Commons or its Committee of Public Accounts.

(7) If requested to do so by the House of Commons Committee of Public Accounts, the Audit Committee may—
- (a) on behalf of the Committee of Public Accounts take evidence from the accounting officer, and
- (b) report to the Committee of Public Accounts and transmit to that Committee any evidence so taken.

### Examinations into the use of resources

19.—(1) The Auditor General for Wales may carry out examinations into the economy, efficiency and effectiveness with which the Ombudsman has used his resources in discharging his functions.

(2) Sub-paragraph (1) is not to be construed as entitling the Auditor General for Wales to question the merits of the policy objectives of the Ombudsman.

(3) In determining how to discharge his functions under this paragraph, the Auditor General for Wales must take into account the views of the Audit Committee as to the examinations which he should carry out.

(4) The Auditor General for Wales may lay before the Assembly a report of the results of any examination carried out by him under this paragraph.

### Examinations by the Comptroller and Auditor General

20.—(1) For the purposes of enabling him to carry out examinations into, and report to Parliament on, the finances of the Ombudsman, the Comptroller and Auditor General—
- (a) has a right of access at all reasonable times to all such documents in the custody or under the control of the Ombudsman, or of the Auditor General for Wales, as he may reasonably require for that purpose, and

(b)    is entitled to require from any person holding or accountable for any of those documents any assistance, information or explanation which he reasonably thinks necessary for that purpose.

(2)    The Comptroller and Auditor General must—

(a)    consult the Auditor General for Wales, and

(b)    take account of any relevant work done or being done by the Auditor General for Wales,

before he acts in reliance on sub-paragraph (1) or carries out an examination in respect of the Ombudsman under section 7 of the National Audit Act 1983 (c 44) (economy etc examinations).

### *Supplementary powers*

21.    The Ombudsman may do anything (including acquire or dispose of any property or rights) which is calculated to facilitate, or is conducive or incidental to, the discharge of any of his functions.

**[1597]**

---

**NOTES**

Commencement: 12 October 2005 (paras 1–3, 5(1)–(3), 6, 8 (for the purposes of appointing the Ombudsman)); 1 April 2006 (paras 1–3, 5(1)–(3), 6, 8 (for remaining purposes), paras 4, 5(4), 7, 9–14, 15(1)–(4), 16–21). For effect and transitional provisions, see the Public Services Ombudsman (Wales) Act 2005 (Commencement No 1 and Transitional Provisions and Savings) Order 2005, SI 2005/2800, arts 6, 7 at **[3580]**, **[3581]**).

Para 1: substituted by the Government of Wales Act 2006, s 160(1), Sch 10, paras 67, 86(1), (2).

Para 3: sub-paras (3)(b), (5) and words in square brackets in sub-para (4) substituted by the Government of Wales Act 2006, s 160(1), Sch 10, paras 67, 86(1), (3).

Para 4: sub-para (1) substituted for original sub-paras (1), (2), by the Government of Wales Act 2006, s 160(1), Sch 10, paras 67, 86(1), (4).

Para 5: words in square brackets in sub-para (1)(d) substituted by the Government of Wales Act 2006, s 160(1), Sch 10, paras 67, 86(1), (5).

Para 7: in sub-para (3), words in first pair of square brackets inserted and words in second pair of square brackets substituted by the Government of Wales Act 2006, s 160(1), Sch 10, paras 67, 86(1), (6).

Para 9: sub-para (6) inserted by the Government of Wales Act 2006, s 160(1), Sch 10, paras 67, 86(1), (7).

Para 10: substituted. together with preceding cross-heading, by the Government of Wales Act 2006, s 160(1), Sch 10, paras 67, 86(1), (8).

Para 11: words in square brackets in sub-para (5) substituted by the Government of Wales Act 2006, s 160(1), Sch 10, paras 67, 86(1), (9).

Para 13: sub-para (4) substituted by the Government of Wales Act 2006, s 160(1), Sch 10, paras 67, 86(1), (10).

Para 14: in sub-para (3), words in first pair of square brackets inserted and words in second pair of square brackets substituted by the Government of Wales Act 2006, s 160(1), Sch 10, paras 67, 86(1), (11).

Para 15: words in square brackets in sub-paras (2), (3) substituted, words omitted from sub-para (3) repealed, and sub-para (4) substituted by the Government of Wales Act 2006, ss 160(1), 163, Sch 10, paras 67, 86(1), (12), Sch 12.

Para 18: words in square brackets substituted by the Government of Wales Act 2006, s 160(1), Sch 10, paras 67, 86(1), (13).

---

## SCHEDULE 2
## EXCLUDED MATTERS

Section 10

1.    Action taken by or with the authority of the [Welsh Ministers, the First Minister for Wales, the Counsel General to the Welsh Assembly Government] or a police authority for a police area in Wales for the purpose of—

(a)    the investigation or prevention of crime, or

(b)    the protection of the security of the State.

2.    The commencement or conduct of proceedings before a court of competent jurisdiction.

3.    Action taken by a member of the administrative staff of a relevant tribunal so far as taken at the direction, or on the authority (whether express or implied), of a person acting in his capacity as a member of the tribunal.

4.    Action taken in respect of appointments, removals, pay, discipline, superannuation or other personnel matters (apart from procedures for recruitment and appointment) in relation to—

(a)    service in an office or employment under the Crown or under a listed authority;

(b)    service in an office or employment, or under a contract for services, in respect of which power to take action in personnel matters, or to determine or approve action to be taken in personnel matters, is vested in Her Majesty or a listed authority.

5.    Action relating to the determination of the amount of rent.

6.—(1)    Action taken by an authority specified in sub-paragraph (2) and relating to—

(a)    the giving of instruction, or

(b)    conduct, curriculum, internal organisation, management or discipline,

in a school or other educational establishment maintained by a local authority in Wales.

(2)   The authorities are—
    (a)    a local authority in Wales;
    (b)    an admission appeal panel;
    (c)    the governing body of a community, foundation or voluntary school;
    (d)    an exclusion appeal panel.

7. ....

[8.   Action under—
    (a)    the National Health Service Act 1977,
    (b)    Part 1 of the National Health Service and Community Care Act 1990,
    (c)    Part 1 of the Health Act 1999 (with the exception of sections 33 to 38), or
    (d)    Part 1 of the Health and Social Care (Community Health and Standards) Act 2003,
where the action is or has been the subject of an inquiry under the Inquiries Act 2005.]

9.   Action taken by a Local Health Board in the discharge of its functions under—
    (a)    the National Health Service (Service Committees and Tribunal) Regulations 1992 or any
           instrument replacing those regulations;
    (b)    regulations made under section 38, 39, 41 or 42 of the National Health Service Act 1977
           by virtue of section 17 of the Health and Medicines Act 1988 (c 49) (investigations of
           matters relating to services).

10. ....

[1598]

---

**NOTES**
    Commencement: 12 October 2005 (for effect and transitional provisions, see the Public Services Ombudsman
(Wales) Act 2005 (Commencement No 1 and Transitional Provisions and Savings) Order 2005, SI 2005/2800,
arts 6, 7 at **[3580]**, **[3581]**).
    Para 1: words in square brackets substituted by the Government of Wales Act 2006, s 160(1), Sch 10, paras 67,
87.
    Para 7: repealed by the National Council for Education and Training for Wales (Transfer of Functions to the
National Assembly for Wales and Abolition) Order 2005, SI 2005/3238, art 9(1), Sch 1, paras 92, 93, subject to
transitional provisions in art 7 thereof.
    Para 8: substituted by the Public Services Ombudsman for Wales (Jurisdiction and Transitional Provisions and
Savings) Order 2006, SI 2006/363, art 2(a).
    Para 10: repealed by SI 2006/363, art 2(b).

---

# SCHEDULE 3
## LISTED AUTHORITIES
Section 28

.....

*Housing*
    A social landlord in Wales.

.....

[1599]

---

**NOTES**
    Commencement: 12 October 2005 (for effect and transitional provisions, see the Public Services Ombudsman
(Wales) Act 2005 (Commencement No 1 and Transitional Provisions and Savings) Order 2005, SI 2005/2800,
arts 6, 7 at **[3580]**, **[3581]**).
    Entries omitted outside the scope of this work.

---

(*Sch 4 contains consequential amendments outside the scope of this work.*)

# SCHEDULE 5
## TRANSFER OF STAFF, PROPERTY ETC
Section 37

*Interpretation*
1.   In this Schedule—
    "the commencement date" means the date on which this Schedule comes into force;
    "existing authority" means each of—
        (a)    the Welsh Administration Ombudsman;
        (b)    the Health Service Commissioner for Wales;
        (c)    the Commission for Local Administration in Wales;
        (d)    a Local Commissioner who is a member of the Commission for Local
               Administration in Wales;
        (e)    the Social Housing Ombudsman for Wales;
    "relevant employee" means a person who, immediately before the commencement date, was
    an officer or member of staff of an existing authority;

"the relevant existing authority", in relation to a relevant employee, means the existing authority of which he was an officer or member of staff immediately before the commencement date.

### Transfer of staff

2.    On the commencement date each relevant employee transfers to and becomes a member of the staff of the Ombudsman.

3.    The contract of employment of a relevant employee transferred under paragraph 2—
- (a)    is not terminated by the transfer;
- (b)    has effect on and after the commencement date as if originally made between the employee and the Ombudsman.

4.    Accordingly—
- (a)    all rights, powers, duties and liabilities of the relevant existing authority under or in connection with the contract of employment are transferred to the Ombudsman on the commencement date;
- (b)    anything done before that date by or in relation to the relevant existing authority in respect of that contract or the relevant employee is to be treated on and after that date as having been done by or in relation to the Ombudsman.

5.    But if a relevant employee informs the relevant existing authority or the Ombudsman before the commencement date that he objects to the transfer—
- (a)    paragraphs 2 to 4 do not apply; and
- (b)    the contract of employment is terminated immediately before the commencement date but the relevant employee is not to be treated, for any purpose, as having been dismissed by the relevant existing authority.

6.    Paragraph 5 does not affect any right of a relevant employee to terminate his contract of employment if (apart from the change of employer) a substantial change is made to his detriment in his working conditions.

### Transfer of property, rights and liabilities

7.    On the commencement date all property, rights and liabilities to which each existing authority was entitled or subject immediately before that date transfer to and vest in the Ombudsman.

8.    The reference in paragraph 7 to rights and liabilities does not include any rights and liabilities under a contract of employment transferred to the Ombudsman under paragraph 2.

9.    Paragraph 7 has effect in relation to any property, rights and liabilities to which it applies despite any provision (of whatever nature) which would otherwise prevent, penalise or restrict their transfer.

10.    Anything (including legal proceedings) which is in the process of being done by or in relation to an existing authority immediately before the commencement date and which relates to—
- (a)    any function of that existing authority, or
- (b)    any property, rights or liabilities of that existing authority transferred to the Ombudsman under paragraph 7,

may, on and after the commencement date, be continued by or in relation to the Ombudsman.

11.    Anything done by an existing authority for the purpose of, or in connection with—
- (a)    any function of that existing authority, or
- (b)    any property, rights or liabilities of that existing authority transferred to the Ombudsman under paragraph 7,

and which is in effect immediately before the commencement date is to have effect on and after the commencement date as if done by the Ombudsman.

12.    On and after the commencement date, the Ombudsman is to be substituted for each existing authority in any instruments, contracts or legal proceedings which relate to—
- (a)    any function of that existing authority, or
- (b)    any property, rights or liabilities of that existing authority transferred to the Ombudsman under paragraph 7,

and which are made or commenced before the commencement date.

**[1600]**

---

**NOTES**

Commencement: 1 April 2006 (for effect and transitional provisions, see the Public Services Ombudsman (Wales) Act 2005 (Commencement No 1 and Transitional Provisions and Savings) Order 2005, SI 2005/2800, arts 6, 7 at **[3580]**, **[3581]**).

---

*(Schs 6, 7 contain consequential amendments and repeals outside the scope of this work.)*

# HOUSING AND REGENERATION ACT 2008

## (2008 c 17)

### ARRANGEMENT OF SECTIONS

#### PART 1
#### THE HOMES AND COMMUNITIES AGENCY

##### CHAPTER 1
##### GENERAL

##### CHAPTER 2
##### LAND AND INFRASTRUCTURE

###### General

###### Powers to deal with land etc

###### Powers in relation to acquired land

###### Planning

###### Other powers etc in relation to land

##### CHAPTER 3
##### FINANCIAL PROVISION

###### Powers to give financial assistance

###### Borrowing powers of the HCA

###### Other

##### CHAPTER 4
##### OTHER FUNCTIONS OF THE HCA

###### General

## CHAPTER 4
## REGISTERED PROVIDERS

### General provisions

### Accounts

### Insolvency etc

### Restructuring and dissolution

## CHAPTER 5
## DISPOSAL OF PROPERTY

### Introductory

PART I
STATUTES

*An Act to establish the Homes and Communities Agency and make provision about it; to abolish the Urban Regeneration Agency and the Commission for the New Towns and make provision in connection with their abolition; to regulate social housing; to enable the abolition of the Housing Corporation; to make provision about sustainability certificates, landlord and tenant matters, building regulations and mobile homes; to make further provision about housing; and for connected purposes*

[22 July 2008]

PART 1
THE HOMES AND COMMUNITIES AGENCY

CHAPTER 1
GENERAL

### 1 Establishment and constitution

(1)   There shall be a body corporate known as the Homes and Communities Agency ("the HCA").

(2)   Schedule 1 (which makes further provision about the HCA) has effect.

**[1601]**

**NOTES**

Commencement: 8 September 2008.

### 2 Objects

(1)   The objects of the HCA are—

   (a)   to improve the supply and quality of housing in England,
   (b)   to secure the regeneration or development of land or infrastructure in England,
   (c)   to support in other ways the creation, regeneration or development of communities in England or their continued well-being, and
   (d)   to contribute to the achievement of sustainable development and good design in England.

with a view to meeting the needs of people living in England.

(2)   In subsection (1)—

   "good design" includes design which has due regard to the needs of elderly persons and disabled persons,
   "needs" includes future needs,

and the reference to improving the supply of housing includes a reference to improving the supply of particular kinds of housing.

(3)   In this Part—

   "building" means a building or other structure (including a house-boat or caravan),
   "caravan" has the meaning given by section 29(1) of the Caravan Sites and Control of Development Act 1960 (c 2),
   "housing" means a building, or part of a building, occupied or intended to be occupied as a dwelling or as more than one dwelling; and includes a hostel which provides temporary residential accommodation,
   "infrastructure" includes—

      (a)   water, electricity, gas, telecommunications, sewerage or other services,
      (b)   roads or other transport facilities,
      (c)   retail or other business facilities,
      (d)   health, educational, employment or training facilities,
      (e)   social, religious or recreational facilities,
      (f)   cremation or burial facilities, and
      (g)   community facilities not falling within paragraphs (a) to (f),

   "land" includes housing or other buildings (and see also the definition in Schedule 1 to the Interpretation Act 1978 (c 30)),

and references to housing include (where the context permits) any yard, garden, outhouses and appurtenances belonging to, or usually enjoyed with, the building or part of building concerned.

(4)   See also sections 19(5) (financial assistance), 44 (local government involvement) and 52 (role of the HCA in relation to certain former functions of the Commission for the New Towns).

**[1602]**

**NOTES**

Commencement: 8 September 2008.

### 3 Principal powers

The HCA may do anything it considers appropriate for the purposes of its objects or for purposes incidental to those purposes.

**[1603]**

**NOTES**

Commencement: 8 September 2008.

## 4 Powers: general

(1)    This Part contains various specific powers of the HCA.

(2)    The specific powers of the HCA (whether contained in this Part or elsewhere) are to be exercised for the purposes of its objects or for purposes incidental to those purposes.

(3)    Each power may be exercised separately or together with, or as part of, another power.

(4)    Each power does not limit the scope of another power.

(5)    Each power does not limit the scope of the powers conferred by section 3.

(6)    But—
    (a)    subsections (2) and (3) do not apply to the HCA in its capacity as a local planning authority by virtue of sections 13 and 14 or in its exercise of other functions by virtue of those sections, and
    (b)    the powers conferred by section 3 must not be used to override a restriction imposed on the exercise of a specific power.

**[1604]**

**NOTES**

Commencement: 8 September 2008 (for certain purposes); 1 December 2008 (for certain purposes, subject to transitional provisions and savings in SI 2008/3068, arts 6–10 at **[3834B]**–**[3834F]**); to be appointed (otherwise).

## CHAPTER 2
## LAND AND INFRASTRUCTURE
*General*

## 5 Powers to provide housing or other land

(1)    The HCA may provide housing or other land.

(2)    The HCA may facilitate the provision of housing or other land.

(3)    In this section "provide" includes provide by way of acquisition, construction, conversion, improvement or repair (and "provision" is to be read in the same way).

**[1605]**

**NOTES**

Commencement: 1 December 2008 (subject to transitional provisions and savings in SI 2008/3068, arts 6–10 at **[3834B]**–**[3834F]**).

## 6 Powers for regeneration, development or effective use of land

(1)    The HCA may regenerate or develop land.

(2)    The HCA may bring about the more effective use of land.

(3)    The HCA may facilitate—
    (a)    the regeneration or development of land, or
    (b)    the more effective use of land.

**[1606]**

**NOTES**

Commencement: 1 December 2008 (subject to transitional provisions and savings in SI 2008/3068, arts 6–10 at **[3834B]**–**[3834F]**).

## 7 Powers in relation to infrastructure

(1)    The HCA may provide infrastructure.

(2)    The HCA may facilitate the provision of infrastructure.

(3)    In this section "provide" includes provide by way of acquisition, construction, conversion, improvement or repair (and "provision" is to be read in the same way).

**[1607]**

**NOTES**

Commencement: 1 December 2008 (subject to transitional provisions and savings in SI 2008/3068, arts 6–10 at **[3834B]**–**[3834F]**).

*Powers to deal with land etc*

## 8 Powers to deal with land etc

The HCA may carry out, or facilitate the carrying out of, any of the following activities in relation to land—

(a)    acquiring, holding, improving, managing, reclaiming, repairing or disposing of housing,

(b)    acquiring, holding, improving, managing, reclaiming, repairing or disposing of other land, plant, machinery, equipment or other property, and

(c)    carrying out building and other operations (including converting or demolishing buildings).

**[1608]**

**NOTES**

Commencement: 1 December 2008 (subject to transitional provisions and savings in SI 2008/3068, arts 6–10 at **[3834B]**–**[3834F]**).

### 9   Acquisition of land

(1)    The HCA may acquire land by agreement.

(2)    The HCA may acquire land compulsorily if the Secretary of State authorises it to do so.

(3)    The power of acquiring land compulsorily under subsection (2) includes power to acquire new rights over land.

(4)    Subsection (5) applies where—

(a)    land or new rights over land are being acquired compulsorily under subsection (2), and

(b)    the land which is being acquired, or over which new rights are being acquired, forms part of a common, open space or allotment.

(5)    The power under subsection (2) to acquire land compulsorily includes the power to acquire land compulsorily for giving in exchange for the land or (as the case may be) new rights mentioned in subsection (4)(a).

(6)    Schedule 2 (which makes further provision in relation to the acquisition of land by the HCA) has effect.

(7)    In this Part—

"allotment" means a fuel or field garden allotment,

"common" has the meaning given by section 19(4) of the Acquisition of Land Act 1981 (c 67),

"open space" means any land which is—

(a)    laid out as a public garden,

(b)    used for the purposes of public recreation, or

(c)    a disused burial ground.

**[1609]**

**NOTES**

Commencement: 1 December 2008 (subject to transitional provisions and savings in SI 2008/3068, arts 6–10 at **[3834B]**–**[3834F]**).

### 10   Restrictions on disposal of land

(1)    The HCA may not dispose of land for less than the best consideration which can reasonably be obtained unless the Secretary of State consents.

(2)    Subsection (1) does not apply to a disposal by way of a short tenancy if the disposal consists of—

(a)    the grant of a term of not more than 7 years, or

(b)    the assignment of a term which, at the date of assignment, has not more than 7 years to run.

(3)    The HCA may not dispose of land which has been compulsorily acquired by it under this Part unless the Secretary of State consents.

(4)    Subject as above, the HCA may dispose of land held by it in any way it considers appropriate.

**[1610]**

**NOTES**

Commencement: 1 December 2008 (subject to transitional provisions and savings in SI 2008/3068, arts 6–10 at **[3834B]**–**[3834F]**).

*Powers in relation to acquired land*

### 11   Main powers in relation to acquired land

Schedule 3 (which makes provision about powers in relation to land of the HCA) has effect.

**[1611]**

**NOTES**

Commencement: 1 December 2008 (subject to transitional provisions and savings in SI 2008/3068, arts 6–10 at **[3834B]**–**[3834F]**).

## 12 Powers in relation to, and for, statutory undertakers

Schedule 4 (which provides for powers in relation to, and for, statutory undertakers) has effect.

**[1612]**

**NOTES**

Commencement: 1 December 2008 (subject to transitional provisions and savings in SI 2008/3068, arts 6–10 at **[3834B]**–**[3834F]**).

*Planning*

## 13 Power of Secretary of State to make designation orders

(1)   The Secretary of State may by order designate an area in England if the Secretary of State considers that—

(a)   the area is suitable for development, and

(b)   it is appropriate for the HCA to be the local planning authority for the whole or any part of the area—

(i)   for particular permitted purposes, and

(ii)   in relation to particular kinds of development.

(2)   In deciding whether it is appropriate for the HCA to be the local planning authority as mentioned in subsection (1)(b), the Secretary of State must, in particular, be satisfied that making the designation order is likely to improve the effectiveness with which the functions of the local planning authority for the area or part are discharged.

(3)   The Secretary of State must, before making a designation order—

(a)   publish—

(i)   a draft of the order, and

(ii)   the Secretary of State's reasons for making the order, and

(b)   consult the persons mentioned in subsection (4).

(4)   The persons are—

(a)   every local authority any part of whose area is intended to be included in the proposed designated area,

(b)   any person, other than a local authority, who is the local planning authority for the proposed designated area or any part of it,

(c)   such persons which appear to the Secretary of State to represent the interests of local authorities as the Secretary of State considers appropriate, and

(d)   persons who reside or carry on business in the proposed designated area.

(5)   In this Part—

"designated area" means an area designated by a designation order,

"designation order" means an order under this section,

"local planning authority", in relation to a designation order or proposed designation order, means—

(a)   so far as the order relates to permitted purposes under Part 2 of the Planning and Compulsory Purchase Act 2004 (c 5), the local planning authority within the meaning of that Part of that Act, and

(b)   in any other case, the local planning authority within the meaning of Part 1 of the Town and Country Planning Act 1990 (c 8),

"permitted purposes" means any purposes of—

(a)   the Town and Country Planning Act 1990 (other than section 137A, Parts 9 and 13, and sections 325A, 329A and 330A, of that Act),

(b)   the Planning (Listed Buildings and Conservation Areas) Act 1990 (c 9) (other than section 32A, Chapter 5 of Part 1, and sections 82A to 82F and 88C, of that Act), and

(c)   Part 2 of the Planning and Compulsory Purchase Act 2004, [and

(d)   Part 8 of the Planning Act 2008,]

and references to a designated area, in the case of an area whose boundaries have been amended by an order made under this section by virtue of section 14 of the Interpretation Act 1978 (c 30), are to be read as references to the designated area as so amended.

(6)   In this section "local authority" means a county council in England, a district council, a London borough council or the Common Council of the City of London.

**[1613]**

**NOTES**
Commencement: 1 December 2008 (subject to transitional provisions and savings in SI 2008/3068, arts 6–10 at **[3834B]**–**[3834F]**).
Sub-s (5): in definition "permitted purposes", para (d) and word immediately preceding it inserted by the Planning Act 2008, s 36, Sch 2, para 65, as from a day to be appointed.

## 14 Contents of designation orders

(1) A designation order may contain provisions of the following kind.

(2) The order may provide for the HCA to be the local planning authority for the whole or any part of the designated area—
(a) for specified permitted purposes, and
(b) in relation to specified kinds of development.

(3) The order may provide that where the HCA is the local planning authority for the whole or any part of the designated area it is to have—
(a) in relation to the whole or any part of the designated area, and
(b) subject to any specified modifications,
specified relevant functions conferred by or under specified planning-related provisions.

(4) An order which makes provision of the kind mentioned in subsection (2) may make provision about the application of enactments relating to local planning authorities to the HCA in its capacity as the local planning authority by virtue of the order.

(5) An order which makes provision of the kind mentioned in subsection (3)—
(a) may provide for the HCA to have the functions concerned instead of, or concurrently with, other persons who have them,
(b) may make provision about the application to the HCA of enactments relating to the functions concerned.

(6) Provision made by virtue of subsection (4) or (5), or section 320(1)(d) in its application to an order of a kind falling within this section, may, in particular, provide that any enactment—
(a) is to apply to the HCA without modification,
(b) is to apply to it subject to specified modifications.

(7) In this section—
"planning-related provisions" means—
(a) Chapter 1 of Part 6 (other than section 137A), and sections 188 and 330, of the Town and Country Planning Act 1990 (c 8),
(b) sections 32 and 33 to 37, 54 and 55 of the Planning (Listed Buildings and Conservation Areas) Act 1990 (c 9), and
(c) the Planning (Hazardous Substances) Act 1990 (c 10) (other than sections 30A to 31A and 36C of that Act),
"relevant functions" means functions of—
(a) a district council, a London borough council, the Common Council of the City of London, or any other body which is a local authority within the meaning of the Town and Country Planning Act 1990,
(b) a district planning authority (within the meaning of that Act), or
(c) a hazardous substances authority (within the meaning of the Planning (Hazardous Substances) Act 1990),
"specified", in relation to a designation order, means specified or described in the order.

**[1614]**

**NOTES**
Commencement: 1 December 2008 (subject to transitional provisions and savings in SI 2008/3068, arts 6–10 at **[3834B]**–**[3834F]**).

## 15 HCA as local planning authority: local involvement

(1) Subsections (2) to (6) apply where a designation order provides for the HCA to be the local planning authority for the whole or any part of the designated area.

(2) The HCA must prepare and publish a statement of local involvement.

(3) The statement of local involvement is a statement of the HCA's policy as to the extent to which it intends to involve persons mentioned in subsection (4) in relation to the exercise by the HCA of functions conferred on it by virtue of the designation order.

(4) The persons are—
(a) every local authority for the designated area or any part of the area in relation to which a function is to be exercised, and
(b) persons appearing to the HCA to have special knowledge or experience of matters relevant to functions to be exercised in relation to the area or part.

(5) The HCA must—
    (a) keep the statement under review, and
    (b) publish any revision of it.

(6) In deciding its policy about the extent of involvement of persons mentioned in subsection (4), the HCA must, in particular, have regard to—
    (a) the benefits that it might receive from their knowledge and experience, and
    (b) the nature of the functions concerned.

(7) Subsection (8) applies where—
    (a) the HCA establishes a committee for the purpose of exercising functions conferred on the HCA by virtue of a designation order,
    (b) such a committee establishes a sub-committee for such a purpose, or
    (c) a new or replacement member is to be appointed to such a committee or sub-committee.

(8) The HCA must—
    (a) inform every local authority for the designated area or any part of the area in relation to which the functions are to be, or are being, exercised of—
        (i) the establishment of the committee or sub-committee concerned, or
        (ii) (as the case may be) the proposed appointment, and
    (b) invite the authority to suggest one or more candidates for membership of the committee or (as the case may be) sub-committee.

(9) In this section "local authority" has the same meaning as in section 13.

**[1615]**

**NOTES**
Commencement: 1 December 2008 (subject to transitional provisions and savings in SI 2008/3068, arts 6–10 at **[3834B]–[3834F]**).

**16** (*Amends the Planning and Compulsory Purchase Act 2004, s 4.*)

*Other powers etc in relation to land*

## 17 Power to enter and survey land

(1) Any person authorised by the HCA may, at any reasonable time and subject as follows, enter any land for the purpose of surveying it, or estimating its value, in connection with—
    (a) any proposal for the HCA to acquire that land or any other land, or
    (b) any claim for compensation in respect of any such acquisition.

(2) A person authorised under subsection (1) to enter any land—
    (a) must, if required, produce evidence of the authority before entering the land, and
    (b) must not demand admission as of right to the land unless the HCA has served notice of the intended entry on every owner or occupier of the land not less than 28 days before the making of the demand.

(3) A notice under subsection (2)(b) must—
    (a) state the purpose for which entry is required, and
    (b) inform the person to whom it is given of the person's rights under this section and, if applicable, section 18.

(4) A person interested in any land may recover compensation from the HCA in respect of any damage done to the land—
    (a) in the exercise of a right of entry under this section, or
    (b) in making a survey under this section.

(5) Section 118 of the Town and Country Planning Act 1990 (c 8) (determination of claims for compensation) applies in relation to compensation under subsection (4) as it applies in relation to compensation under Part 4 of that Act.

(6) A person ("A") commits an offence if A intentionally obstructs another person ("B") in the exercise of B's powers under subsection (1) above.

(7) A person who commits an offence under subsection (6) is liable on summary conviction to a fine not exceeding level 2 on the standard scale.

(8) In subsection (2)(b) "owner" has the same meaning as in the Acquisition of Land Act 1981 (c 67).

(9) The references in subsections (4) and (6) to this section or subsection (1) include references to those provisions as extended by section 18.

**[1616]**

**NOTES**
Commencement: 1 December 2008 (subject to transitional provisions and savings in SI 2008/3068, arts 6–10 at **[3834B]–[3834F]**).

### 18 Section 17: supplementary

(1) The power to survey land conferred by section 17(1) includes power to search and bore for the purpose of ascertaining—

    (a)   the nature of the subsoil, or

    (b)   the presence of minerals in it.

(2) But this is subject to subsections (3) to (5).

(3) No person may carry out any works authorised by virtue of subsection (1) unless notice of the person's intention to do so was included in the notice required by section 17(2)(b).

(4) The authority of the appropriate Minister is required for the carrying out of any works authorised by virtue of subsection (1) if—

    (a)   the land concerned is held by statutory undertakers, and

    (b)   they object to the proposed works on the ground that the execution of the works would be seriously detrimental to carrying on their undertaking.

(5) The references in subsection (4) to the appropriate Minister, statutory undertakers and their undertaking have the same meanings as they have in section 325(9) of the Town and Country Planning Act 1990 (c 8) (supplementary provisions as to rights of entry).

**[1617]**

**NOTES**
Commencement: 1 December 2008 (subject to transitional provisions and savings in SI 2008/3068, arts 6–10 at **[3834B]–[3834F]**).

## CHAPTER 3
## FINANCIAL PROVISION

*Powers to give financial assistance*

### 19 Financial assistance

(1) The HCA may, with the consent of the Secretary of State, give financial assistance to any person.

(2) Financial assistance under this section may be given in any form.

(3) Financial assistance under this section may, in particular, be given by way of—

    (a)   grants,

    (b)   loans,

    (c)   guarantee or indemnity,

    (d)   investment, or

    (e)   incurring expenditure for the benefit of the person assisted.

(4) Financial assistance under this section may be given on such terms and conditions as the HCA considers appropriate (including provision for repayment, with or without interest).

(5) The objects of the HCA are not to be read as preventing the HCA from exercising functions in relation to financial assistance (whether under this section or otherwise) which—

    (a)   are transferred to the HCA from the Housing Corporation by virtue of this Act, or

    (b)   would supersede functions of the Housing Corporation,

in ways corresponding to those in which the Housing Corporation could have exercised its functions.

(6) See also sections 31 to 35 (further provision about certain types of financial assistance: social housing).

**[1618]**

**NOTES**
Commencement: 1 December 2008 (sub-ss (1)–(4) (except for the purpose of enabling the HCA to give financial assistance on condition that the recipient provides social housing), sub-s (5)); to be appointed (otherwise).

*Borrowing powers of the HCA*

### 20 Powers to borrow

(1) The HCA may, for the purpose of what it considers to be the short-term management of its finances, borrow from any person by way of overdraft or otherwise.

(2)    Subject to this, the HCA may only borrow from the Secretary of State or the European Investment Bank.

(3)    The HCA may not borrow in currencies other than sterling.

**[1619]**

**NOTES**

Commencement: 1 December 2008.

## 21   Loans by the Secretary of State

(1)    The Secretary of State may lend to the HCA any sums it has power to borrow from the Secretary of State under section 20.

(2)    Loans under subsection (1) may be made on such terms and conditions as the Secretary of State considers appropriate (including provision for repayment with or without interest).

**[1620]**

**NOTES**

Commencement: 1 December 2008.

## 22   Guarantees by the Secretary of State

(1)    The Secretary of State may guarantee—
  (a)    the repayment of the principal of any sums which the HCA borrows from a person other than the Secretary of State, and
  (b)    the payment of interest on such sums.

(2)    Such a guarantee is to be in such manner, and on such terms and conditions, as the Secretary of State considers appropriate.

(3)    The Secretary of State must lay a statement of any such guarantee before Parliament immediately after giving the guarantee.

(4)    The Secretary of State must lay before Parliament a statement relating to any sum issued for fulfilling such a guarantee.

(5)    A statement under subsection (4) must be laid as soon as possible after the end of each financial year—
  (a)    beginning with that in which the sum is issued, and
  (b)    ending with that in which all liability in respect of the principal of the sum guaranteed, and of interest on it, is finally discharged.

(6)    In respect of any sums issued in fulfilment of a guarantee given under this section, the HCA must make payments to the Secretary of State—
  (a)    of such amounts as the Secretary of State may direct in or towards repayment of those sums, and
  (b)    of interest on what is outstanding in respect of those sums, at such rates as the Secretary of State may direct.

(7)    Payments under subsection (6) must be made at such times, and in such manner, as the Secretary of State may direct.

**[1621]**

**NOTES**

Commencement: 1 December 2008.

## 23   Financial limits

(1)    The current borrowings of the HCA must not exceed £2,300 million.

(2)    The Secretary of State may by order amend subsection (1) so as to specify a greater amount than that for the time being specified there.

(3)    But an order under subsection (2) may not specify an amount of more than £3,000 million.

(4)    In this section "current borrowings of the HCA" means—
  (a)    the aggregate amount at any time of—
      (i)    sums borrowed by the HCA under section 20, and
      (ii)    sums borrowed by subsidiaries of the HCA (other than from the HCA), less
  (b)    repayments made, or treated as made, in respect of those sums.

(5)    In this Part "subsidiary" has the meaning given by section 1159 of the Companies Act 2006 (c 46).

**[1622]**

**NOTES**
Commencement: 1 December 2008.

*Other*

## 24 Power to charge for certain activities

(1) The HCA may impose charges for, or in connection with, anything done by it by virtue of section 38, 39 or 45

(2) Any such charges must be of such amounts as the HCA considers to be reasonable.

**[1623]**

**NOTES**
Commencement: 1 December 2008.

## 25 Directions as to surplus funds

(1) Subsection (2) applies if the Secretary of State considers that the HCA or any subsidiary of the HCA has a surplus, whether on capital or on revenue account, after making allowance by way of transfer to reserve or otherwise for its future requirements.

(2) The Secretary of State may give a direction to the HCA to pay to the Secretary of State such sum not exceeding the amount of the surplus as may be specified in the direction.

(3) The Secretary of State must consult the HCA before coming to a decision of the kind mentioned in subsection (1) or giving a direction as mentioned in subsection (2).

(4) The Secretary of State may decide to treat the whole or part of any payment under subsection (2) as made—

    (a) by way of repayment of such part of the principal of loans under section 21(1), and

    (b) in respect of the repayments due at such times,

as the Secretary of State may decide.

**[1624]**

**NOTES**
Commencement: 1 December 2008.

## 26 Duty to act as agent in respect of regeneration and development

(1) The Secretary of State may appoint the HCA to act as the agent of the Secretary of State in connection with such financial assistance functions as the Secretary of State may specify.

(2) In subsection (1) "financial assistance functions" means, so far as exercisable in relation to England, functions under sections 126 to 128 of the Housing Grants, Construction and Regeneration Act 1996 (c 53) (financial assistance for regeneration and development).

(3) An appointment under this section is to be on such terms as the Secretary of State may specify.

(4) The HCA must, if appointed, act as agent in accordance with the terms of its appointment.

**[1625]**

**NOTES**
Commencement: 1 December 2008.

## 27 Duty to act as agent in respect of derelict land etc

(1) The Secretary of State may appoint the HCA to act as the agent of the Secretary of State in connection with such derelict land functions as the Secretary of State may specify.

(2) In subsection (1) "derelict land functions" means functions under—

    (a) section 1 of the Derelict Land Act 1982 (c 42) (grants for reclaiming or improving land or bringing land into use), or

    (b) any enactment superseded by that section,

but excluding the powers to make orders under section 1(5) and (7) of that Act.

(3) An appointment under this section is to be on such terms as the Secretary of State may specify.

(4) The HCA must, if appointed, act as agent in accordance with the terms of its appointment.

**[1626]**

**NOTES**
Commencement: 1 December 2008.

## CHAPTER 4
## OTHER FUNCTIONS OF THE HCA

*General*

### 28 Business

(1) The HCA may carry on any business.

(2) In subsection (1) "business" includes undertaking.

[1627]

**NOTES**
Commencement: 1 December 2008.

### 29 Powers to form companies etc

The HCA may, with the consent of the Secretary of State, form, or acquire interests in, bodies corporate.

[1628]

**NOTES**
Commencement: 1 December 2008.

### 30 Community services

The HCA may provide such services for communities as it considers appropriate or facilitate the provision of such services.

[1629]

**NOTES**
Commencement: 1 December 2008.

*Social housing*

### 31 Duties in relation to social housing

(1) Subsection (2) applies if the HCA acquires, constructs or converts any housing or other land for use as low cost rental accommodation.

(2) The HCA must ensure that a relevant provider of low cost rental accommodation is the landlord of the accommodation when it is made available for rent.

(3) Subsection (4) applies if the HCA disposes of any housing or other land to a person on condition that the person provides low cost rental accommodation (whether in the same or different housing or other land).

(4) The HCA must impose a further condition that a relevant provider of low cost rental accommodation is the landlord of the accommodation when it is made available for rent.

(5) Subsection (6) applies if the HCA provides infrastructure to a person on condition that the person provides low cost rental accommodation.

(6) The HCA must impose a further condition ensuring that a relevant provider of low cost rental accommodation is the landlord of the accommodation when it is made available for rent.

(7) Subsection (8) applies if the HCA is proposing to give financial assistance on condition that the recipient provides low cost rental accommodation.

(8) The HCA must impose a further condition ensuring that a relevant provider of low cost rental accommodation is the landlord of the accommodation when it is made available for rent.

(9) Subsection (10) applies if the HCA is proposing to give financial assistance on condition that the recipient provides low cost home ownership accommodation.

(10) The HCA must consult the Regulator of Social Housing about the proposals.

(11) For the purposes of this section, a person provides low cost rental accommodation or low cost home ownership accommodation if (and only if) the person acquires, constructs or converts any housing or other land for use as low cost rental accommodation or (as the case may be) low cost home ownership accommodation or ensures such acquisition, construction or conversion by another.

(12) In this section—
"English local housing authority" means a local housing authority (within the meaning of *section 1 of the Housing Act 1985 (c 68)*) but excluding a Welsh county council or county borough council,
"low cost home ownership accommodation" has the meaning given by section 70,
"low cost rental accommodation" has the meaning given by section 69,
"relevant provider of low cost rental accommodation" means a registered provider of social housing, an English local housing authority, a county council in England or a person

controlled by an English local housing authority or county council in England (and regulations under subsections (5) and (6) of section 113 apply for the purposes of this definition as they apply for the purposes of subsection (4) of that section).

**[1630]**

**NOTES**

Commencement: to be appointed.

### 32 Recovery etc of social housing assistance

(1) The HCA may, in such events as it may determine, exercise the powers conferred by subsections (2) to (4) in relation to a person who has received social housing assistance.

(2) The HCA may reduce any grant payable by it or restrict any other social housing assistance due from it.

(3) The HCA may suspend or cancel any instalment of any grant payable by it or any aspect of any other social housing assistance due from it.

(4) The HCA may direct the recipient of any social housing assistance given by way of grant to—

    (a)    apply or appropriate for such purposes of the recipient as the HCA may specify, or

    (b)    pay to the HCA,

such amount as the HCA may specify.

(5) The HCA may not specify an amount which exceeds the recoverable amount.

(6) The recoverable amount is—

    (a)    the total amount of grant received by the person to whom the direction is given, less

    (b)    the total of any amounts applied, appropriated or paid in accordance with any previous directions given in respect of that grant under subsection (4),

and for the purposes of paragraph (b) any amounts provided for by virtue of section 33(1) are to be ignored.

(7) Subsection (5) is without prejudice to the power of the HCA under section 33(1).

(8) In exercising its powers under subsections (2) to (4) the HCA must act in accordance with such principles as it has determined.

(9) A person who has received social housing assistance must notify the HCA if an event of a kind determined by the HCA under subsection (1) occurs after the assistance has been given.

(10) Such a person must, if required by notice of the HCA, supply the HCA with such particulars of, and information relating to, the event as are specified in the notice.

(11) The HCA must notify the Regulator of Social Housing at least 14 days before exercising, in relation to a registered provider of social housing, any of the powers conferred by subsections (2) to (4).

(12) Events determined by the HCA under subsection (1), and principles determined by the HCA under subsection (8), must be determined on or before the time the HCA gives the social housing assistance concerned unless they are determined subsequently with the agreement of the recipient of the assistance.

(13) In this Part—

    "social housing" has the same meaning as in Part 2,

    "social housing assistance" means financial assistance given under section 19 on condition that the recipient provides social housing (whether by itself or as part of a wider project);

and, for the purposes of this Part, a person provides social housing if (and only if) the person acquires, constructs, converts, improves or repairs any housing or other land for use as social housing or ensures such acquisition, construction, conversion, improvement or repair by another.

**[1631]**

**NOTES**

Commencement: 1 April 2009 (for the purposes of enabling the HCA to make a determination under sub-ss (1) or (8)): to be appointed (otherwise).

### 33 Section 32: interest and successors in title

(1) A direction by the HCA under section 32(4) may require the application, appropriation or payment, in addition to the specified amount, of one or more of the following—

    (a)    interest on the specified amount,

    (b)    an amount calculated by reference to any increase in the market value of any housing or other land acquired, constructed, converted, improved or repaired as a result of the grant, and

    (c)    interest on the amount falling within paragraph (b).

(2) Any direction falling within subsection (1)(a) or (c) must specify—
  (a) the applicable rate or rates of interest (whether fixed or variable),
  (b) the date from which interest is payable, and
  (c) any provision for suspended or reduced interest which is applicable.

(3) The date specified under subsection (2)(b) must not be earlier than the date of the event giving rise to the power to give a direction.

(4) In subsection (2)(c)—
  (a) provision for suspended interest means provision to the effect that if the principal amount is applied, appropriated or paid before a date specified in the direction, no interest will be payable for any period after the date of the direction, and
  (b) provision for reduced interest means provision to the effect that if the principal amount is so applied, appropriated or paid, any interest payable will be payable at a rate or rates lower than the rate or rates which would otherwise be applicable.

(5) Any direction falling within subsection (1)(b) must specify—
  (a) the housing or other land concerned, and
  (b) the method of calculating the amount concerned.

(6) Subsection (7) applies if—
  (a) social housing assistance has been given to a person, and
  (b) at any time the social housing provided as a result of the assistance becomes vested in, or is leased for a term of years to, or reverts to, another person.

(7) Section 32 and this section (including this subsection) have effect in relation to periods after that time as if the assistance, or such element of it as may be determined by the HCA to be appropriate, had been given to that other person.

(8) The matters specified in a direction under subsection (2)(a) to (c) or (5), and the element mentioned in subsection (7), are to be—
  (a) such as the HCA, acting in accordance with such principles as it may determine, may specify as being appropriate, or
  (b) such as the HCA may determine to be appropriate in the particular case.

(9) Principles determined by the HCA under subsection (8)(a), and determinations by the HCA under subsection (8)(b), must be determined on or before the time the HCA gives the social housing assistance concerned unless they are determined subsequently with the agreement of the recipient of the assistance.

[1632]

---

**NOTES**
Commencement: 1 April 2009 (for the purposes of enabling the HCA to make a determination under sub-s (8)): to be appointed (otherwise).

---

## 34 Determinations under sections 32 and 33

(1) The HCA must not make a general determination under section 32 or 33 without the consent of the Secretary of State.

(2) Before making such a determination, the HCA must consult—
  (a) the Regulator of Social Housing, and
  (b) such other persons as it considers appropriate.

(3) Subsection (4) applies if a general determination under section 32 or 33 about relevant events relates to social housing assistance given to a registered provider of social housing.

(4) The HCA must, in particular, consult such bodies appearing to it to represent the interests of registered providers of social housing as it considers appropriate.

(5) The HCA must publish a general determination made under section 32 or 33 in such manner as it considers appropriate for bringing the determination to the attention of those affected by it.

(6) A general determination of the HCA under section 32 or 33 may make different provision for different cases or descriptions of case (including different provision for different areas).

(7) For the purposes of subsection (6) descriptions may be framed by reference to any matters whatever.

(8) A determination of the HCA under section 32 or 33 may be varied or revoked by it (subject to any provision as to the time by which such a determination must be made).

(9) In this section—
  "general determination" means a determination which does not relate solely to a particular case,
  "relevant event" means an event of a kind determined by the HCA under section 32(1).

[1633]

**NOTES**
Commencement: 1 April 2009.

### 35 Duty to give financial assistance in respect of certain disposals

(1)    The HCA must exercise its powers under section 19 to give financial assistance by way of grant to a relevant provider of social housing in respect of any discount given by the provider—
    (a)    to a person exercising the right to acquire conferred by section 180, or
    (b)    on a disposal of a dwelling in England by the provider to a qualifying tenant otherwise than in pursuance of the right conferred by that section.

(2)    In subsection (1)(b) "qualifying tenant" means a tenant who was entitled to exercise the right to acquire conferred by section 180, or by section 16 of the Housing Act 1996 (c 52), in relation to a dwelling of the relevant provider of social housing other than the dwelling being disposed of by the provider.

(3)    The amount of the grant given by virtue of subsection (1)(a) to a relevant provider of social housing for any year is to be the aggregate value of the discounts given by that provider in that year.

(4)    The amount of the grant given by virtue of subsection (1)(b) to a relevant provider of social housing must not exceed the amount of the discount to which the tenant would have been entitled in respect of the other dwelling.

(5)    The HCA must specify—
    (a)    the procedure to be followed in relation to applications for a grant by virtue of this section,
    (b)    in the case of a grant by virtue of subsection (1)(b), the method for calculating, and any other limitations on, the amount of the grant,
    (c)    the manner in which, and time or times at which, a grant by virtue of this section is to be paid,
    (d)    any other terms or conditions on which such a grant is given.

(6)    In this section—
"dwelling" has the same meaning as in Part 2,
"registered provider of social housing" includes a person falling within section 180(3),
"registered social landlord" has the same meaning as in Part 1 of the Housing Act 1996,
"relevant provider of social housing" means—
    (a)    a registered provider of social housing, or
    (b)    a registered social landlord,
"tenant" has the same meaning as in Part 2.

**[1634]**

**NOTES**
Commencement: to be appointed.

### 36 Information in relation to social housing

(1)    The Secretary of State may by order provide for the HCA to supply such information about—
    (a)    which accommodation provided directly or indirectly by it is to be social housing,
    (b)    the type of social housing to be so provided, and
    (c)    the consequences of it being social housing,
as may be specified or described in the order.

(2)    An order under this section may, in particular, provide for—
    (a)    the person or persons to whom the information is to be provided,
    (b)    the time at which, or period or frequency within which, the information is to be provided,
    (c)    the form and manner in which the information is to be provided.

**[1635]**

**NOTES**
Commencement: 1 April 2009.

### 37 Duty to co-operate with Regulator of Social Housing

(1)    The HCA must co-operate with the Regulator of Social Housing.

(2)    In particular, the HCA must consult the regulator on matters likely to interest the regulator.

**[1636]**

**NOTES**
Commencement: 8 September 2008.

PART I
STATUTES

*Information, education and guidance etc*

## 38 Information services

(1) The HCA may—
    (a) publish ideas or information, or
    (b) disseminate or promote ideas or information in other ways.

(2) The HCA may undertake research or experimentation.

(3) The HCA may provide other information services.

(4) The HCA may facilitate—
    (a) the publication or other dissemination or promotion of ideas or information,
    (b) research or experimentation, or
    (c) the provision of other information services.

**[1637]**

**NOTES**
Commencement: 1 December 2008.

## 39 Advice, education and training

(1) The HCA may provide—
    (a) advice, education or training, or
    (b) other advisory, education or training services.

(2) The HCA may facilitate the provision of—
    (a) advice, education or training, or
    (b) other advisory, education or training services.

**[1638]**

**NOTES**
Commencement: 1 December 2008.

## 40 Guidance

(1) The HCA may give guidance to such persons as it considers appropriate about any matters relating to its objects.

(2) Before giving guidance under this section, the HCA must consult such persons as it considers appropriate.

(3) As soon as reasonably practicable after giving guidance under this section, the HCA must take such steps as the HCA considers appropriate to bring it to the attention of those affected by it.

(4) The HCA may revoke guidance given under this section.

(5) The HCA—
    (a) must, before revoking guidance under this section, consult such persons as it considers appropriate, and
    (b) must, as soon as reasonably practicable after the revocation, take such steps as it considers appropriate to bring the revocation to the attention of those affected by it.

(6) References in this section to giving guidance include references to giving guidance by varying existing guidance.

**[1639]**

**NOTES**
Commencement: 1 December 2008.

*Functions in relation to companies and other persons*

## 41 Control of subsidiaries

(1) The HCA must ensure that no subsidiary of the HCA engages, without the consent of the Secretary of State, in an activity which the HCA would not be required or permitted to carry on.

(2) The HCA must ensure that no subsidiary of the HCA—
    (a) borrows from a person other than the HCA, or
    (b) raises money by the issue of shares or stock to a person other than the HCA,
without the consent of the Secretary of State.

**[1640]**

**NOTES**
Commencement: 1 December 2008.

**42 Agency arrangements with UDCs**

(1) The HCA may, with the consent of the Secretary of State, appoint an urban development corporation to act as its agent.

(2) The appointment—

(a) may be in connection with any of the functions of the HCA other than its functions in connection with Chapter 3, and

(b) is to be on such terms as may be agreed.

(3) The appointment must specify the functions in connection with which it is made.

(4) An urban development corporation must act as agent in accordance with the terms of its appointment.

(5) An urban development corporation may arrange for any of its property or staff to be made available to the HCA if—

(a) the purpose is to assist the HCA to exercise any of its functions, and

(b) the HCA asks the urban development corporation to make the property or staff available.

(6) The property or staff are to be made available for such period, and on such other terms, as the urban development corporation considers appropriate.

(7) In this Part "urban development corporation" means a corporation established by an order under section 135 of the Local Government, Planning and Land Act 1980 (c 65).

**[1641]**

**NOTES**

Commencement: 1 December 2008.

**43 Acting with, or for, other persons: general**

(1) The HCA may act with other persons (whether in partnership or otherwise).

(2) The HCA may act as agent for other persons.

**[1642]**

**NOTES**

Commencement: 1 December 2008.

**44 Local government involvement**

(1) The HCA must from time to time consult such representatives of local government as the HCA considers appropriate about how the HCA pursues its objects.

(2) The HCA must from time to time publish a statement about how it proposes to comply with subsection (1).

(3) Before publishing a statement the HCA must consult such persons as it considers appropriate.

**[1643]**

**NOTES**

Commencement: 8 September 2008.

*Other*

**45 Support services**

(1) The HCA may provide services in support of a project.

(2) The HCA may, in particular—

(a) second staff to the project,

(b) provide consultants or other manpower resources to the project on a temporary basis, or

(c) lend or otherwise provide technical, property or other resources to the project.

(3) The HCA may facilitate the provision of services in support of a project.

**[1644]**

**NOTES**

Commencement: 1 December 2008.

## CHAPTER 5
## SUPPLEMENTARY

*Certain supervisory powers of the Secretary of State*

### 46 Guidance by the Secretary of State

(1)    The Secretary of State may give guidance to the HCA as to the exercise of any of its functions.

(2)    Before giving guidance under this section, the Secretary of State must consult such persons as the Secretary of State considers appropriate.

(3)    The Secretary of State must publish any guidance given under this section as soon as reasonably practicable after giving it.

(4)    The Secretary of State may revoke guidance given under this section.

(5)    The Secretary of State must—
    (a)    consult, before revoking guidance under this section, such persons as the Secretary of State considers appropriate, and
    (b)    publish the fact that the guidance has been revoked as soon as reasonably practicable after the revocation.

(6)    The HCA must, in exercising its functions, have regard to any guidance for the time being in force under this section.

(7)    References in this section to giving guidance include references to giving guidance by varying existing guidance.

**[1645]**

**NOTES**

Commencement: 8 September 2008.

### 47 Directions by the Secretary of State

(1)    The Secretary of State may give the HCA general or specific directions as to the exercise of any of its functions.

(2)    The Secretary of State must publish any directions given by the Secretary of State under this Part as soon as reasonably practicable after giving them.

(3)    The Secretary of State—
    (a)    may revoke any directions given by the Secretary of State under this Part, and
    (b)    must publish the fact that the directions have been revoked as soon as reasonably practicable after the revocation.

(4)    The HCA must comply with any directions of the Secretary of State in force under this Part.

(5)    Subsections (2) and (3)(b) do not apply to directions given under section 22 or paragraph 7 of Schedule 1; and this section does not apply to directions given under Schedule 4.

(6)    References in this Part to the Secretary of State giving directions include references to the Secretary of State giving directions by varying existing directions.

**[1646]**

**NOTES**

Commencement: 8 September 2008.

### 48 Consents of the Secretary of State

(1)    Any consent of the Secretary of State required under this Part may be given—
    (a)    unconditionally or subject to conditions, and
    (b)    generally or specifically.

(2)    The Secretary of State may vary or revoke any such consent except in the case of anything already done, or agreed to be done, on the authority of it.

(3)    A variation or revocation under subsection (2) does not have effect until the Secretary of State has served notice of it on the HCA or (as the case may be) the other person to whom the consent is given.

**[1647]**

**NOTES**

Commencement: 1 December 2008.

*Abolition of existing bodies*

### 49  Abolition of Urban Regeneration Agency

The Urban Regeneration Agency shall cease to exist on such day as the Secretary of State may by order appoint.

**[1648]**

**NOTES**

Commencement: 8 September 2008.

Appointed Day: the Abolition of the Commission for the New Towns and the Urban Regeneration Agency (Appointed Day and Consequential Amendments) Order 2009, SI 2009/801, art 2 provides that 1 April 2009 is the day appointed for the purposes of this section.

### 50  Abolition of the Commission for the New Towns

(1)   The Commission for the New Towns shall cease to exist on such day as the Secretary of State may by order appoint.

(2)   Schedule 5 (which transfers Welsh functions of the Commission to the Welsh Ministers and makes other amendments of the New Towns Act 1981 (c 64)) has effect.

**[1649]**

**NOTES**

Commencement: 8 September 2008 (sub-s (1)); 1 December 2008 (sub-s (2), for certain purposes and subject to transitional provisions and savings in SI 2008/3068, arts 6–10 at **[3834B]–[3834F]**); 1 April 2009 (sub-s (2), for remaining purposes).

Appointed Day: the Abolition of the Commission for the New Towns and the Urban Regeneration Agency (Appointed Day and Consequential Amendments) Order 2009, SI 2009/801, art 2 provides that 1 April 2009 is the day appointed for the purposes of sub-s (1).

### 51  Property etc transfers to the HCA and the Welsh Ministers

(1)   The Secretary of State may make one or more schemes for—
  (a)   the transfer to the HCA of designated property, rights or liabilities of—
    (i)   the Urban Regeneration Agency,
    (ii)   the Commission for the New Towns,
    (iii)   a regional development agency (within the meaning of the Regional Development Agencies Act 1998 (c 45)), or
    (iv)   a Minister of the Crown, or
  (b)   the transfer to the Welsh Ministers of designated property, rights or liabilities of—
    (i)   the Urban Regeneration Agency, or
    (ii)   the Commission for the New Towns.

(2)   On the transfer date, the designated property, rights or liabilities are transferred and vest in accordance with the scheme.

(3)   Schedule 6 (which makes further provision about the making of schemes) has effect.

(4)   In this section and in Schedule 6—
  "designated" in relation to a scheme, means specified in, or determined in accordance with, the scheme,
  "Minister of the Crown" has the same meaning as in the Ministers of the Crown Act 1975 (c 26),
  "the transfer date" means a date specified by a scheme as the date on which the scheme is to have effect.

(5)   Schedule 7 makes provision about the tax implications of schemes under this section (and schemes under section 65).

**[1650]**

**NOTES**

Commencement: 8 September 2008.

### 52  Role of the HCA in relation to former CNT functions

(1)   The HCA must, so far as practicable, exercise its powers in relation to—
  (a)   any property, rights or liabilities of the Commission for the New Towns transferred to it by virtue of section 51 and Schedule 6,
  (b)   any property, rights or liabilities of a new town development corporation transferred to it by virtue of section 41 of, and Schedule 10 to, the New Towns Act 1981 (c 64),
  (c)   any undertaking, or part of an undertaking, of an urban development corporation transferred to it by virtue of an agreement under section 165 of the Local Government, Planning and Land Act 1980 (c 65), or

(d)    any property, rights or liabilities of an urban development corporation transferred to it by virtue of an order under section 165B of that Act,

for the purposes of the objects mentioned in section 2(1) or for purposes incidental to those purposes.

(2)    But subsection (1) does not apply if the HCA does not consider it appropriate to exercise its powers in this way having regard, in particular, to the purposes for which the transferred property was held by the Commission for the New Towns, the new town development corporation or (as the case may be) the urban development corporation.

(3)    In such a case, the HCA must exercise its powers in relation to the transferred property in such a way as it considers appropriate having regard, in particular, to—

(a)    the objects mentioned in section 2(1), and

(b)    the purposes for which the transferred property was held by the body concerned,

and the references in this Part to the objects of the HCA are to be read accordingly.

(4)    In this section—

"new town development corporation" means a development corporation established under section 3 of the New Towns Act 1981 (c 64),

"transferred property" means any property, rights or liabilities, or any undertaking or part of an undertaking, falling within paragraphs (a) to (d) of subsection (1) above.

**[1651]**

**NOTES**

Commencement: 8 September 2008.

## 53  Interim arrangements

(1)    The Secretary of State may by notice require the Urban Regeneration Agency or the Commission for the New Towns to provide staff, premises, facilities or other assistance on a temporary basis to—

(a)    the HCA, or

(b)    the Welsh Ministers.

(2)    *In paragraph 1(1) of Schedule 17 to the Leasehold Reform, Housing and Urban Development Act 1993 (c 28) (constitution of the Urban Regeneration Agency: number of members), for "six" substitute "two".*

(3)    This section is without prejudice to the power of the Secretary of State under section 322(1).

**[1652]**

**NOTES**

Commencement: 8 September 2008.

Sub-s (2): repealed by the Housing and Regeneration Act 2008, s 321(1), Sch 16, as from a day to be appointed.

*Other*

## 54  Validity of transactions

(1)    A transaction between a person and the HCA is not invalid merely because of a failure by the HCA to exercise its powers for the purposes mentioned in sections 3 and 4(2).

(2)    A transaction between a person and the HCA is not invalid merely because it was carried out in contravention of a direction under section 47.

(3)    A transaction between a person and a subsidiary of the HCA is not invalid merely because of a failure by the HCA to comply with section 41(1) or (2).

(4)    A person entering into a transaction with the HCA or a subsidiary of the HCA need not be concerned as to whether—

(a)    there has been a failure of the kind mentioned in subsection (1) or (3), or

(b)    a direction of the kind mentioned in subsection (2) has been given or complied with.

(5)    A disposal of land by the HCA is not invalid merely because any consent required by section 10(1) or (3) has not been given.

(6)    A person dealing with—

(a)    the HCA, or

(b)    a person claiming under the HCA,

in relation to any land need not be concerned as to whether any consent required by section 10(1) or (3) has been given.

**[1653]**

PART 1
STATUTES

**NOTES**
Commencement: 8 September 2008.

## 55 Notices

(1) Any notice required or authorised under this Part to be served on any person may be served by—

    (a)    delivering it to the person,

    (b)    leaving it at the person's proper address, or

    (c)    sending it by post to the person at that address.

(2) Any such notice may—

    (a)    in the case of a body corporate, be served in accordance with subsection (1) on an officer of the body, and

    (b)    in the case of a partnership, be served in accordance with subsection (1) on a partner or a person having the control or management of the partnership business.

(3) For the purposes of this section and section 7 of the Interpretation Act 1978 (c 30) (service of documents by post) in its application to this section, the proper address of any person on whom a notice is to be served is the person's last known address except as follows.

(4) For the purposes of this section and section 7 of the Act of 1978 in its application to this section, the proper address is—

    (a)    in the case of service on a body corporate or an officer of the body, the address of the registered or principal office of the body, and

    (b)    in the case of service on a partnership, a partner or a person having the control or management of the partnership business, the address of the principal office of the partnership.

(5) For the purposes of subsection (4) the principal office of a company registered outside the United Kingdom or of a partnership carrying on business outside the United Kingdom is its principal office within the United Kingdom.

(6) Subsection (7) applies if a person to be served under this Part with a notice has specified an address within the United Kingdom other than the person's proper address (as decided under subsections (3) and (4)) as the one at which the person, or someone on the person's behalf, will accept documents of the same description as the notice.

(7) The specified address is also to be treated for the purposes of this section and section 7 of the Act of 1978 in its application to this section as the person's proper address.

(8) Subsection (9) applies if the name or address of any owner, lessee or occupier of land on whom a notice is to be served under this Part cannot, after reasonable inquiry, be ascertained.

(9) The notice may be served by—

    (a)    leaving it in the hands of a person who is, or appears to be, resident or employed on the land, or

    (b)    leaving it conspicuously affixed to a building or object on the land.

(10) Any notice required or authorised under this Part to be served on any person may be served on the person by transmitting the text of the notice to the person by means of an electronic communications network or by other means but while in electronic form provided the text is received by the person in legible form and is capable of being used for subsequent reference.

(11) In this section—

    "body corporate" includes a limited liability partnership,

    "director", in relation to a body corporate whose affairs are managed by its members, means a member of the body corporate,

    "officer of a body corporate" means any director, manager, secretary or other similar officer of the body corporate,

    "partnership" does not include a limited liability partnership,

and references to serving include references to similar expressions (such as giving or sending).

**NOTES**
Commencement: 8 September 2008.

## 56 (*Introduces Sch 8 (consequential amendments) to this Act.*)

## 57 Interpretation: Part 1

(1) In this Part—

"conduit system" has the same meaning as in the electronic communications code; and references to providing a conduit system are to be read in accordance with paragraph 1(3A) of that code,

"develop" (and development), in relation to land or infrastructure, includes redevelop (and redevelopment),

"electronic communications apparatus" has the same meaning as in the electronic communications code,

"the electronic communications code" has the same meaning as in Chapter 1 of Part 2 of the Communications Act 2003 (c 21),

"electronic communications code network" means—

    (a)   so much of an electronic communications network or conduit system provided by an electronic communications code operator as is not excluded from the application of the electronic communications code by a direction under section 106 of the Act of 2003 (application of the electronic communications code), and

    (b)   an electronic communications network which the Secretary of State is providing or proposing to provide,

"electronic communications code operator" means a person in whose case the electronic communications code is applied by a direction under section 106 of the Act of 2003,

"electronic communications network" has the same meaning as in the Act of 2003,

"enactment" includes subordinate legislation (within the meaning of the Interpretation Act 1978 (c 30)),

"financial year" means—

    (a)   the period beginning with the day on which the HCA is established and ending with the next 31 March, and

    (b)   each subsequent period of 12 months ending with 31 March,

"improve", in relation to housing and other land, includes refurbish, equip and fit out,

"modifications" includes omissions,

"notice" means notice in writing,

"operator", in relation to an electronic communications code network means—

    (a)   the electronic communications code operator providing that network, or

    (b)   the Secretary of State, so far as the Secretary of State is providing or proposing to provide that network,

"provide" and related expressions, in relation to an electronic communications network, are to be read in accordance with section 32(4) of the Communications Act 2003 (c 21).

(2)   References in this Part to powers of the HCA do not include references to powers contained in duties imposed on the HCA.

**[1655]**

**NOTES**

Commencement: 8 September 2008 (for certain purposes); 1 December 2008 (for certain purposes); to be appointed (otherwise).

## 58 Index of defined expressions: Part 1

In this Part, the expressions listed in the left-hand column have the meaning given by, or are to be interpreted in accordance with, the provisions listed in the right-hand column.

| Expression | Provision |
| --- | --- |
| Allotment | Section 9(7) |
| Building | Section 2(3) |
| Caravan | Section 2(3) |
| Common | Section 9(7) |
| Conduit system (and providing such a system) | Section 57(1) |
| Designated area | Section 13(5) |
| Designation order | Section 13(5) |
| Develop (and development) | Section 57(1) |
| Electronic communications apparatus | Section 57(1) |
| Electronic communications code | Section 57(1) |
| Electronic communications code network | Section 57(1) |

| Expression | Provision |
|---|---|
| Electronic communications code operator | Section 57(1) |
| Electronic communications network | Section 57(1) |
| Enactment | Section 57(1) |
| Financial year | Section 57(1) |
| Giving directions | Section 47(6) |
| The HCA | Section 1(1) |
| Housing | Section 2(3) |
| Improve | Section 57(1) |
| Infrastructure | Section 2(3) |
| Land | Section 2(3) (and Schedule 1 to the Interpretation Act 1978 (c 30)) |
| Local planning authority (in relation to designation orders or proposed designation orders) | Section 13(5) |
| Modifications | Section 57(1) |
| Notice | Section 57(1) |
| Objects of the HCA | Sections 2, 19(5) and 52(3) |
| Open space | Section 9(7) |
| Operator (in relation to electronic communications code network) | Section 57(1) |
| Permitted purposes | Section 13(5) |
| Powers of the HCA | Section 57(2) |
| Provide (in relation to an electronic communications network) | Section 57(1) |
| Registered provider of social housing | Section 80(2)(a) |
| Regulator of Social Housing | Section 81(2)(a) |
| Social housing (and its provision) | Section 32(13) |
| Social housing assistance | Section 32(13) |
| Subsidiary | Section 23(5) |
| Urban development corporation | Section 42(7) |

**[1656]**

**NOTES**

Commencement: 8 September 2008 (for certain purposes); 1 December 2008 (for certain purposes); 1 April 2009 (for certain purposes); to be appointed (otherwise).

PART 2

REGULATION OF SOCIAL HOUSING

CHAPTER 1

INTRODUCTION

*Preliminary*

**59 Purpose**

The purpose of this Part is to regulate the provision of social housing (as defined in sections 68 to 77) by English bodies (as defined in section 79).

**[1657]**

**NOTES**

Commencement: 8 September 2008.

## 60 Structural overview

(1)   This Part replaces the system of "registered social landlords" under Part 1 of the Housing Act 1996 (c 52).

(2)   That Part will continue to apply in relation to Wales (see section 61).

(3)   Certain provisions of that Part—
    (a)   are applied in relation to England by this Part (see section 179), or
    (b)   are preserved although they apply to England only (see section 124).

(4)   The Table describes the content of this Part.

| Chapter | Sections | Topic | Contents |
|---|---|---|---|
| 1 | 59 to 80 | Introduction | (a) Preliminary<br>(b) Social housing<br>(c) Other key concepts |
| 2 | 81 to 109 | The Social Housing Regulator | (a) Constitution<br>(b) Proceedings<br>(c) Powers<br>(d) Money<br>(e) Relationship with other bodies<br>(f) Information |
| 3 | 110 to 121 | Registration | (a) Introduction<br>(b) Eligibility<br>(c) Procedure |
| 4 | 122 to 169 | Registered providers | (a) General provisions<br>(b) Accounts<br>(c) Insolvency etc<br>(d) Restructuring and dissolution |
| 5 | 170 to 191 | Disposal of property | (a) Introductory<br>(b) Regulator's consent<br>(c) Proceeds<br>(d) Tenants' rights and duties<br>(e) Miscellaneous<br>(f) Right to acquire<br>(g) Consents under other legislation |
| 6 | 192 to 217 | Regulatory powers | (a) Standards<br>(b) Monitoring<br>(c) Management and constitution<br>(d) Guidance<br>(e) Managers of social housing |
| 7 | 218 to 269 | Enforcement powers | (a) General<br>(b) Enforcement notice<br>(c) Penalty<br>(d) Compensation<br>(e) Management<br>(f) Restrictions on dealings<br>(g) Suspension and removal of officers |

| Chapter | Sections | Topic | Contents |
|---------|----------|-------|----------|
| 8 | 270 to 278 | General | (a) Interpretation<br>(b) Miscellaneous |

**[1658]**

PART I<br>STATUTES

---

**NOTES**

Commencement: to be appointed.

---

**61–63**     (*Amend the Housing Act 1996 at* **[1002]** *et seq and these amendments, in so far as relevant to this work, have been incorporated at the appropriate place.*)

### 64   Dissolution of Housing Corporation

(1)    The Secretary of State shall by order make provision for the dissolution of the Housing Corporation.

(2)    The Secretary of State may by order make consequential amendment of enactments referring to the Housing Corporation.

(3)    ...

**[1659]**

---

**NOTES**

Commencement: 16 February 2009 (sub-ss (1), (2)); to be appointed (sub-s (3)).
Sub-s (3): repeals the Housing Associations Act 1985, s 33A.
Order: the Housing Corporation (Dissolution) Order 2009, SI 2009/484.

---

### 65   Transfer schemes

(1)    The Secretary of State may make one or more schemes for the transfer of the Housing Corporation's property, rights or liabilities to—
    (a)    the regulator,
    (b)    the HCA, or
    (c)    the Secretary of State.

(2)    On the transfer date, the designated property, rights or liabilities are transferred and vest in accordance with the scheme.

(3)    Schedule 6 applies to a scheme under this section.

(4)    In this section—
    "designated", in relation to a scheme, means specified in or determined in accordance with the scheme;
    "the transfer date" means the date specified by a scheme as the date on which the scheme is to have effect.

(5)    Schedule 7 makes provision about the tax implications of schemes under this section (and schemes under section 51).

**[1660]**

---

**NOTES**

Commencement: 8 September 2008.

---

### 66   Interim arrangements

The Secretary of State may by notice require the Housing Corporation to provide staff, premises, facilities or other assistance to—
    (a)    the regulator, or
    (b)    the HCA.

**[1661]**

---

**NOTES**

Commencement: 8 September 2008.

---

### 67   Transitional arrangements

(1)    The Secretary of State may by order transfer functions of the Housing Corporation to—
    (a)    the regulator,
    (b)    the HCA, or
    (c)    the regulator and the HCA jointly or concurrently.

(2)   An order under subsection (1) may make provision in relation to English registered social landlords which is similar to any provision made by this Part in relation to registered providers.

(3)   "English registered social landlord" means a body—
  (a)   which is registered as a social landlord under Part 1 of the Housing Act 1996, and
  (b)   which does not fall within paragraphs (a) to (c) of section 56(2) of that Act (Welsh bodies).

(4)   The Secretary of State may by order make further provision in respect of a function transferred under this section (which may, in particular, include provision for the function to cease to be exercisable).

(5)   Provision made under this section, including provision made by virtue of section 320(1)(d), may modify an enactment.

(6)   Provision under section 322(1) in connection with the coming into force of a provision of this Act may, in particular, include transitional provision having regard to the effect of provision made under this section.

[1662]

**NOTES**
Commencement: 8 September 2008.
Orders: the Transfer of Housing Corporation Functions (Modifications and Transitional Provisions) Order 2008, SI 2008/2839; the Housing Corporation (Dissolution) Order 2009, SI 2009/484.

*Social housing*

## 68   Basic principle

(1)   In this Part "social housing" means—
  (a)   low cost rental accommodation (defined by section 69), and
  (b)   low cost home ownership accommodation (defined by section 70).

(2)   Accommodation which becomes "social housing" by satisfying subsection (1)(a) or (b) remains "social housing" for the purposes of this Part unless and until an event specified in sections 73 to 76 occurs.

(3)   Section 77 makes transitional provision as a result of which certain accommodation is to be treated as "social housing" whether or not it satisfies subsection (1)(a) or (b).

[1663]

**NOTES**
Commencement: 8 September 2008 (for certain purposes); to be appointed (otherwise).

## 69   Low cost rental

Accommodation is low cost rental accommodation if—
  (a)   it is made available for rent,
  (b)   the rent is below the market rate, and
  (c)   the accommodation is made available in accordance with rules designed to ensure that it is made available to people whose needs are not adequately served by the commercial housing market.

[1664]

**NOTES**
Commencement: 8 September 2008 (for certain purposes); to be appointed (otherwise).

## 70   Low cost home ownership

(1)   Accommodation is low cost home ownership accommodation if the following conditions are satisfied.

(2)   Condition 1 is that the accommodation is occupied, or made available for occupation, in accordance with—
  (a)   shared ownership arrangements,
  (b)   equity percentage arrangements, or
  (c)   shared ownership trusts.

(3)   Condition 2 is that the accommodation is made available in accordance with rules designed to ensure that it is made available to people whose needs are not adequately served by the commercial housing market.

(4)   "Shared ownership arrangements" means arrangements under a lease which—
  (a)   is granted on payment of a premium calculated by reference to a percentage of either the value of the accommodation or the cost of providing it, and

   (b)     provides that the tenant (or the tenant's personal representatives) will or may be entitled to a sum calculated by reference to the value of the accommodation.

   (5)     "Equity percentage arrangements" means arrangements under which—

   (a)     the owner of a freehold or leasehold interest in residential property ("the seller") conveys it to an individual ("the buyer"),

   (b)     the buyer, in consideration for the conveyance—

      (i)     pays the seller a sum (the "initial payment") expressed to represent a percentage of the value of the interest at the time of the conveyance, and

      (ii)     agrees to pay the seller other sums calculated by reference to a percentage of the value of the interest at the time when each sum is to be paid, and

   (c)     the liability to make any payment required by the arrangements (apart from the initial payment) is secured by a mortgage.

   (6)     Shared ownership trusts has the same meaning as in Schedule 9 to the Finance Act 2003 (c 14) (stamp duty land tax).

   (7)     The Secretary of State may make regulations amending—

   (a)     the definition of "low cost home ownership accommodation";

   (b)     the definition of any of the sub-categories specified in that definition.

**[1665]**

**NOTES**

Commencement: 8 September 2008 (for certain purposes); to be appointed (otherwise).

## 71   Shared ownership low cost rental

Accommodation which is both low cost rental accommodation and low cost home ownership accommodation is to be treated as the latter and not as the former.

**[1666]**

**NOTES**

Commencement: 8 September 2008 (for certain purposes); to be appointed (otherwise).

## 72   Regulations

   (1)     The Secretary of State may make regulations providing that specified property, or a specified class of property, is or is not to be treated as social housing for the purposes of this Part.

   (2)     The regulations may provide for property to be social housing despite not satisfying section 68(1)(a) or (b) where the Secretary of State thinks the property is of a kind, or is provided in circumstances, that serve the needs of a group whose needs are not adequately served by the commercial housing market.

   (3)     The regulations—

   (a)     may override section 68(2),

   (b)     are subject to sections 68(3) and 77, and

   (c)     are subject to sections 69 and 70 (but may clarify doubt about the application of those sections).

   (4)     The regulations—

   (a)     may make provision by reference to the opinion of the regulator or another specified person, and

   (b)     may make provision by reference to designation, agreement or other action by the regulator or another specified person.

**[1667]**

**NOTES**

Commencement: 8 September 2008.

## 73   Leaving the social housing stock: sale

   (1)     A dwelling ceases to be social housing if it is sold to the tenant.

   (2)     Low cost rental accommodation is "sold to the tenant" when the tenant exercises a statutory or contractual right and as a result becomes the owner of—

   (a)     the freehold interest in the property, or

   (b)     the leasehold interest previously owned by the person providing the social housing.

   (3)     Low cost home ownership accommodation of the shared ownership kind is "sold to the tenant" when the tenant exercises a statutory or contractual right and as a result becomes the owner of—

   (a)     the freehold interest in the property, or

   (b)     the leasehold interest previously owned by the person providing the social housing.

(4)   Low cost home ownership accommodation of the equity percentage kind is "sold to the tenant" when the "buyer" (see section 70(5)(a)) exercises a statutory or contractual right as a result of which the equity percentage arrangements (see section 70(5)) come to an end.

(5)   Low cost home ownership accommodation of the shared ownership trust kind comes to an end when the "purchaser" (see paragraph 7(4)(a) of Schedule 9 to the Finance Act 2003 (c 14)) exercises a statutory or contractual right as a result of which the trust comes to an end.

**[1668]**

**NOTES**
    Commencement: 8 September 2008 (for certain purposes); to be appointed (otherwise).

### 74   Leaving the social housing stock: expired lease

(1)   A dwelling ceases to be social housing if—
    (a)   the provider holds a leasehold interest in the dwelling, and
    (b)   the leasehold interest expires.

(2)   A lease from an associate or subsidiary of the provider is disregarded for the purposes of subsection (1).

**[1669]**

**NOTES**
    Commencement: 8 September 2008 (for certain purposes); to be appointed (otherwise).

### 75   Leaving the social housing stock: disposal with consent

(1)   A dwelling ceases to be social housing if it is disposed of with the regulator's consent in accordance with—
    (a)   Chapter 5,
    (b)   section 171D of the Housing Act 1985 (c 68) (consent to certain disposals of housing obtained subject to the preserved right to buy), or
    (c)   section 81 or 133 of the Housing Act 1988 (c 50) (consent to certain disposals of housing obtained from housing action trusts or local authorities).

(2)   Subsection (1) does not apply to a disposal in pursuance of shared ownership arrangements or equity percentage arrangements.

(3)   Subsection (1) does not apply if the consent is conditional upon the dwelling continuing to be low cost rental accommodation or low cost home ownership accommodation.

(4)   A condition of that kind shall include provision for determining when the dwelling ceases to be social housing.

**[1670]**

**NOTES**
    Commencement: 8 September 2008 (for certain purposes); to be appointed (otherwise).

### 76   Leaving the social housing stock: regulator's direction

(1)   The regulator may direct that a specified dwelling is to cease to be social housing.

(2)   The regulator may make a direction only on the application of the provider.

**[1671]**

**NOTES**
    Commencement: 8 September 2008 (for certain purposes); to be appointed (otherwise).

### 77   Housing stock under Housing Act 1996

(1)   This section applies to property owned by a registered social landlord within the meaning of Part 1 of the Housing Act 1996 (c 52) before the coming into force of section 61 of this Act.

(2)   Property to which this section applies is social housing—
    (a)   whether or not it satisfies section 68(1)(a) or (b), and
    (b)   unless and until an event specified in sections 73 to 76 occurs.

(3)   But property to which any of the exceptions below applies when section 61 comes into force is social housing only if the purchase, construction or renovation of the property was funded by means of a grant under—
    (a)   section 19 (financial assistance by the HCA),
    (b)   section 18 of the Housing Act 1996 (social housing grant), or
    (c)   section 50 of the Housing Act 1988, section 41 of the Housing Associations Act 1985 (c 69) or section 29 or 29A of the Housing Act 1974 (c 44) (housing association grant).

(4)   Exception 1 is accommodation let on the open market.

(5)    Exception 2 is accommodation made available only to students in full-time education or training.

(6)    Exception 3 is a care home (within the meaning of the Care Standards Act 2000 (c 14)) in which nursing is provided.

(7)    Exception 4 is accommodation provided in response to a request by the Secretary of State under section 100 of the Immigration and Asylum Act 1999 (c 33) (support for asylum seekers).

(8)    Exception 5 is property of a kind specified by regulations made by the Secretary of State.

**[1672]**

**NOTES**
   Commencement: 8 September 2008 (for certain purposes); to be appointed (otherwise).

### Other key concepts

## 78   Regulator of Social Housing

(1)    Section 81 establishes the Office referred to in this Part as "the regulator".

(2)    Chapter 2 makes provision for the regulator's constitution and general powers.

(3)    Other provisions of this Part confer functions on the regulator.

**[1673]**

**NOTES**
   Commencement: 8 September 2008 (for certain purposes); to be appointed (otherwise).

## 79   English bodies

(1)    In this Part "English body" means—
- (a)   a registered charity whose address for the purposes of registration by the Charity Commission is in England,
- (b)   an industrial and provident society whose registered office for the purposes of the Industrial and Provident Societies Act 1965 (c 12) is in England,
- (c)   a registered company which has its registered office in England,
- (d)   a community land trust which owns land in England, and
- (e)   any other person (whether or not a body corporate registered under the law of the United Kingdom) which—
  - (i)   is not a Welsh body within the meaning of section 1A of the Housing Act 1996 (c 52), and
  - (ii)   makes available, or intends to make available, accommodation in England.

(2)    In subsection (1)(d) "community land trust" means a body corporate which satisfies the conditions below.

(3)    In those conditions "local community" means the individuals who live or work, or want to live or work, in a specified area.

(4)    Condition 1 is that the body is established for the express purpose of furthering the social, economic and environmental interests of a local community by acquiring and managing land and other assets in order—
- (a)   to provide a benefit to the local community, and
- (b)   to ensure that the assets are not sold or developed except in a manner which the trust's members think benefits the local community.

(5)    Condition 2 is that the body is established under arrangements which are expressly designed to ensure that—
- (a)   any profits from its activities will be used to benefit the local community (otherwise than by being paid directly to members),
- (b)   individuals who live or work in the specified area have the opportunity to become members of the trust (whether or not others can also become members), and
- (c)   the members of the trust control it.

**[1674]**

**NOTES**
   Commencement: 8 September 2008 (for certain purposes); to be appointed (otherwise).

## 80   Provider of social housing

(1)    In this Chapter a reference to the provider of social housing is to be construed as follows.

| Type of social housing | Provider |
|---|---|
| Low cost rental accommodation | The landlord |
| Low cost home ownership accommodation: shared ownership | The landlord |
| Low cost home ownership accommodation: equity percentage | "The seller" within the meaning of section 70(5)(a) |
| Low cost home ownership accommodation: shared ownership trust | The "social landlord" within the meaning of paragraph 7(3) of Schedule 9 to the Finance Act 2003 |

(2) Chapter 3 provides for the establishment of a register of providers of social housing: persons listed in the register—

    (a) may be referred to in an enactment or other instrument as "registered providers of social housing", and

    (b) are referred to in this Part as "registered providers".

**[1675]**

**NOTES**

Commencement: 8 September 2008 (for certain purposes); to be appointed (otherwise).

CHAPTER 2

THE SOCIAL HOUSING REGULATOR

*Constitution*

**81 Establishment**

(1) There shall be a body corporate to be known as the Office for Tenants and Social Landlords.

(2) The Office—

    (a) may be referred to in an enactment or other instrument as "the Regulator of Social Housing", and

    (b) is referred to in this Part as "the regulator".

(3) The Office (and any member of the Office)—

    (a) is not the servant or agent of the Crown, and

    (b) does not share any immunity or privilege of the Crown.

**[1676]**

**NOTES**

Commencement: 8 September 2008.

**82 Membership**

(1) The regulator shall consist of—

    (a) a person appointed by the Secretary of State as chair,

    (b) neither less than 3 nor more than 10 other members appointed by the Secretary of State, and

    (c) the chief executive appointed under section 84.

(2) The Secretary of State must consult the chair before appointing other members.

(3) The Secretary of State may appoint a person under subsection (1) only if satisfied that the person has no financial or other personal interest in the performance of functions.

(4) Former membership of the Housing Corporation is not a bar to appointment.

(5) In this Part "appointed member" means—

    (a) the chair, or

    (b) a member appointed under subsection (1)(b).

(6) A vacancy for, or a defect in the appointment of, the chair, the chief executive or another member does not prevent or invalidate proceedings.

**[1677]**

**NOTES**

Commencement: 8 September 2008.

**83 Tenure**

(1) An appointed member holds and vacates office in accordance with the terms of appointment (subject to this section).

(2)    A period of appointment may not exceed 5 years (but a member may be reappointed).

(3)    An appointed member may resign by notice to the Secretary of State.

(4)    The Secretary of State may dismiss an appointed member if satisfied that any of the following cases applies—

    (a)    Case 1 is where a member has been absent from meetings of the regulator for a period of more than 6 months without its permission.

    (b)    Case 2 is where a member is subject to—

        (i)    a bankruptcy restrictions order, or

        (ii)    an interim bankruptcy restrictions order.

    (c)    Case 3 is where—

        (i)    a member's estate has been sequestrated by a court in Scotland, or

        (ii)    under the law of Scotland, a member has made a composition or arrangement with, or granted a trust deed for, creditors.

    (d)    Case 4 is where a member has a financial or other personal interest which is likely to influence the performance of functions.

    (e)    Case 5 is where a member has misbehaved or is for any other reason unable, unsuitable or unwilling to perform functions.

**[1678]**

**NOTES**
Commencement: 8 September 2008.

## 84   Chief executive

(1)    The regulator shall appoint a chief executive.

(2)    The regulator may appoint a person only if approved by the Secretary of State.

(3)    The first chief executive shall be appointed by the Secretary of State, having consulted the chair.

**[1679]**

**NOTES**
Commencement: 8 September 2008.

## 85   Other staff

The regulator may appoint employees (in addition to the chief executive).

**[1680]**

**NOTES**
Commencement: 8 September 2008.

*Proceedings*

## 86   Fundamental objectives

(1)    The regulator shall perform its functions with a view to achieving the following objectives so far as possible.

(2)    Objective 1 is to encourage and support a supply of well-managed social housing, of appropriate quality, sufficient to meet reasonable demands.

(3)    Objective 2 is to ensure that actual or potential tenants of social housing have an appropriate degree of—

    (a)    choice, and

    (b)    protection.

(4)    Objective 3 is to ensure that tenants of social housing have the opportunity to be involved in its management.

(5)    Objective 4 is to ensure that registered providers of social housing perform their functions efficiently, effectively and economically.

(6)    Objective 5 is to ensure that registered providers of social housing are financially viable and properly managed.

(7)    Objective 6 is to encourage registered providers of social housing to contribute to the environmental, social and economic well-being of the areas in which the housing is situated.

(8)    Objective 7 is to encourage investment in social housing (including by promoting the availability of financial services to registered providers of social housing).

(9)    Objective 8 is to avoid the imposition of an unreasonable burden (directly or indirectly) on public funds.

(10)    Objective 9 is to guard against the misuse of public funds.

(11) Objective 10 is to regulate in a manner which—
   (a) minimises interference, and
   (b) is proportionate, consistent, transparent and accountable.

(12) Pursuit of Objective 10 includes, but is not necessarily limited to, compliance with any duty of the regulator under section 22 of the Legislative and Regulatory Reform Act 2006 (c 51) (code of practice).

(13) The order in which the objectives are listed in this section is not significant; the regulator shall balance them as it thinks appropriate.

(14) The objectives are referred to in this Part as the regulator's fundamental objectives.

**[1681]**

**NOTES**
Commencement: 8 September 2008 (for certain purposes); to be appointed (otherwise).

## 87 Procedure

(1) The regulator may determine its own procedure (which may include provision about a quorum).

(2) The regulator shall make such arrangements as it thinks appropriate for publishing its procedure.

**[1682]**

**NOTES**
Commencement: 8 September 2008.

## 88 Conflict of interest

(1) The regulator's procedural arrangements under section 87 must include arrangements for dealing with any conflict of interest of—
   (a) members,
   (b) employees, or
   (c) members of committees and sub-committees.

(2) The arrangements must oblige a person—
   (a) to declare any financial or other personal interest relevant to the exercise of a function, and
   (b) to withdraw from the performance of that function unless the regulator directs otherwise, being satisfied that the interest will not influence performance of the function.

**[1683]**

**NOTES**
Commencement: 8 September 2008.

## 89 Committees

(1) The regulator may establish committees and sub-committees.

(2) A committee or sub-committee may include non-members (provided that it includes at least one member).

**[1684]**

**NOTES**
Commencement: 8 September 2008.

## 90 Delegation

The regulator may authorise any of the following to exercise a function—
   (a) a committee,
   (b) a sub-committee,
   (c) a member, and
   (d) an employee.

**[1685]**

**NOTES**
Commencement: 8 September 2008.

## 91 Seal

(1) The application of the regulator's seal shall be authenticated by a member or by some other person authorised (generally or specially) for that purpose.

(2) A document purporting to be duly executed under the seal—
    (a) shall be received in evidence, and
    (b) shall be treated as so executed unless the contrary is shown.

[1686]

**NOTES**
Commencement: 8 September 2008.

## 92 Annual report

(1) As soon as is reasonably practicable after the end of each financial year the regulator shall—
    (a) prepare a report on the performance of its functions during the year, and
    (b) send a copy to the Secretary of State.

(2) The report must, in particular—
    (a) include a statement of the regulator's accounts,
    (b) specify any direction given to the regulator by the Secretary of State in that year under section 197, and
    (c) contain a general description of complaints made to the regulator in that year about the performance of registered providers and of how those complaints have been dealt with.

(3) The Secretary of State shall lay a copy before Parliament.

[1687]

**NOTES**
Commencement: 8 September 2008.

*Powers*

## 93 General

(1) The regulator may do anything it thinks necessary or expedient for the purpose of or in connection with the performance of a function conferred on it by this Part or another enactment.

(2) In particular, the regulator may do anything it thinks appropriate for advancing its fundamental objectives.

[1688]

**NOTES**
Commencement: 8 September 2008 (for certain purposes); 1 April 2009 (for remaining purposes).

## 94 Studies

(1) The regulator may carry out or commission studies designed to improve the economy, effectiveness and efficiency of registered providers.

(2) The regulator may publish a report on a study.

[1689]

**NOTES**
Commencement: to be appointed.

## 95 Financial assistance

(1) The regulator may, where it thinks it advances a fundamental objective, give financial assistance to a person in connection with—
    (a) undertaking research,
    (b) preparing guidance,
    (c) developing and publicising best practice, or
    (d) facilitating the management of social housing by tenants.

(2) Financial assistance under subsection (1) may be given—
    (a) by way of grant,
    (b) by way of loan,
    (c) by defraying expenditure on behalf of a person, or
    (d) in any other way except purchasing loan or share capital of a body corporate or giving a guarantee or indemnity.

(3) The regulator may, where it thinks it advances a fundamental objective, give financial assistance to a registered provider by—
    (a) lending money to or in respect of the registered provider, or
    (b) giving a guarantee or indemnity in respect of the registered provider.

(4) Financial assistance may be given under subsection (3) only with the consent of the Secretary of State (given with the approval of the Treasury).

(5) Financial assistance under subsection (1) or (3) may be given on conditions (which may include provision for repayment, with or without interest).

**[1690]**

**NOTES**
Commencement: 8 September 2008 (sub-ss (1), (2), (5), for certain purposes); to be appointed (otherwise).

## 96 Evidence

In considering whether to exercise a power under this Part the regulator may have regard to information or opinions from any source including, in particular, from—

(a) tenants,
(b) bodies representing tenants,
(c) local housing authorities, or
(d) an ombudsman appointed by virtue of section 124.

**[1691]**

**NOTES**
Commencement: 8 September 2008 (for certain purposes); to be appointed (otherwise).

## 97 Information, advice etc

(1) The regulator may for the purpose of advancing its fundamental objectives—
(a) publish ideas or information;
(b) undertake research in relation to social housing;
(c) provide guidance, advice, education or training.

(2) The regulator may for that purpose—
(a) arrange for another person to do anything within subsection (1)(a) to (c);
(b) act jointly with, cooperate with or assist another person doing anything within subsection (1)(a) to (c).

(3) The persons to whom advice may be given under subsection (1) include—
(a) unregistered housing associations (as defined by section 2B of the Housing Associations Act 1985 (c 69)), and
(b) persons who may be forming a housing association (within the meaning of section 1(1) of that Act).

**[1692]**

**NOTES**
Commencement: 8 September 2008 (for certain purposes); to be appointed (otherwise).

## 98 Tenant involvement

(1) The regulator shall—
(a) promote awareness of the regulator's functions among tenants of social housing,
(b) where the regulator thinks it appropriate, consult them about the exercise of its functions (for example, by holding meetings), and
(c) where the regulator thinks it appropriate, involve them in the exercise of its functions (for example, by appointing them to committees or sub-committees).

(2) The regulator shall from time to time publish a statement about how it proposes to comply with subsection (1).

(3) Before publishing a statement the regulator must consult such persons as it thinks appropriate.

**[1693]**

**NOTES**
Commencement: 8 September 2008 (for certain purposes); to be appointed (otherwise).

*Money*

## 99 Remuneration

(1) The regulator may pay to or in respect of appointed members—
(a) remuneration,
(b) travelling and other allowances, and
(c) sums by way of or in respect of pensions and gratuities.

(2) The Secretary of State shall determine rates and eligibility criteria for payments under subsection (1).

(3)    If the Secretary of State thinks there are special circumstances that make it right to compensate a person on ceasing to be an appointed member, the regulator may pay compensation determined by the Secretary of State.

(4)    The regulator may pay to or in respect of employees—

(a)    remuneration,

(b)    travelling and other allowances, and

(c)    sums by way of or in respect of pensions and gratuities.

(5)    In this section a reference to a member or employee includes a reference to a former member or employee.

**[1694]**

**NOTES**

   Commencement: 8 September 2008.

## 100   Charging

The regulator may charge for giving advice, conducting research or providing other services.

**[1695]**

**NOTES**

   Commencement: 8 September 2008.

## 101   Assistance by Secretary of State

(1)    The Secretary of State may make payments to the regulator by way of grant or loan.

(2)    A grant or loan may be subject to conditions (which may include provision for repayment, with or without interest).

**[1696]**

**NOTES**

   Commencement: 8 September 2008.

## 102   Borrowing

(1)    The regulator may borrow—

(a)    by way of overdraft or otherwise, for the purpose of what it considers to be short-term management of its finances, or

(b)    from the Secretary of State.

(2)    The regulator may not borrow otherwise.

**[1697]**

**NOTES**

   Commencement: 8 September 2008.

## 103   Accounts

(1)    The regulator shall keep accounts (and records of its accounts).

(2)    As soon as is reasonably practicable after the end of each financial year the regulator shall prepare a statement of accounts in respect of that financial year.

(3)    The statement must be in such form as the Secretary of State may direct.

(4)    The regulator shall, within such period as the Secretary of State may direct, send a copy of the statement to—

(a)    the Secretary of State, and

(b)    the Comptroller and Auditor General.

(5)    The Comptroller and Auditor General shall—

(a)    examine, certify and report on the statement, and

(b)    lay a copy of the report before Parliament.

**[1698]**

**NOTES**

   Commencement: 8 September 2008.

## 104   Financial year

(1)    The regulator's financial year is each period of 12 months beginning with 1st April.

(2)    But the first financial year is the period—

(a) beginning with the day on which section 81 comes into force, and

(b) ending with the next 31st March.

**[1699]**

**NOTES**

Commencement: 8 September 2008.

*Relationship with other bodies*

## 105  Cooperation with the HCA

(1) The regulator shall cooperate with the HCA.

(2) In particular, the regulator shall consult the HCA on matters likely to interest it.

**[1700]**

**NOTES**

Commencement: 8 September 2008.

## 106  Direction to the HCA

(1) The regulator may direct the HCA not to give financial assistance to a specified registered provider—

(a) under section 19, and

(b) in connection with social housing.

(2) A direction may be given if—

(a) the regulator has decided to hold an inquiry into affairs of the registered provider under section 206 (and the inquiry is not concluded),

(b) the regulator has received notice in respect of the registered provider under section 145, or

(c) the regulator has appointed an officer of the registered provider under section 269 (and the person appointed has not vacated office).

(3) A direction may prohibit the HCA from giving assistance of a specified kind (whether or not in pursuance of a decision already taken and communicated to the registered provider).

(4) A direction may not prohibit grants to a registered provider in respect of discounts given by the provider on disposals of dwellings to tenants.

(5) A direction shall have effect until withdrawn.

**[1701]**

**NOTES**

Commencement: to be appointed.

*Information*

## 107  Collection

(1) The regulator may for a purpose connected with its functions require a person to provide documents or information which it has reason to believe is or may be in the person's possession and which relates to—

(a) the financial or other affairs of a registered provider;

(b) activities which are or may be carried out by a person who is, or who has applied to become, a registered provider.

(2) A requirement may be imposed on a person other than the body to which the document or information relates only if—

(a) the body has been required to provide the document or information but has failed to do so, or

(b) the regulator thinks that the body is unable to provide it.

(3) A requirement may specify—

(a) the form and manner in which a document or information is to be provided (which may include the provision of a legible copy of information stored electronically);

(b) when and where it is to be provided.

(4) The regulator may copy or record documents or information provided.

(5) Failure to comply with a requirement without reasonable excuse is an offence.

(6) Intentionally altering, suppressing or destroying a document or information to which a requirement relates is an offence.

(7) If a person fails to comply with a requirement the High Court may, on an application by the regulator, make an order for the purpose of remedying the failure.

**[1702]**

NOTES
Commencement: to be appointed.

## 108 Section 107: supplemental

(1) A requirement does not require a person to disclose anything which the person would be entitled to refuse to disclose on grounds of legal professional privilege in proceedings in the High Court.

(2) A requirement does not require a banker to breach a duty of confidentiality owed to a person who is not—

(a) the registered provider to whose affairs or activities the documents or information relates,

(b) a subsidiary of the registered provider, or

(c) an associate of the registered provider.

(3) A person guilty of an offence under section 107(5) is liable on summary conviction to a fine not exceeding level 5 on the standard scale.

(4) A person guilty of an offence under section 107(6) is liable—

(a) on summary conviction, to a fine not exceeding the statutory maximum;

(b) on conviction on indictment, to—

(i) imprisonment for a term not exceeding two years,

(ii) a fine, or

(iii) both.

(5) Proceedings for an offence under section 107(5) or (6) may be brought only by or with the consent of—

(a) the regulator, or

(b) the Director of Public Prosecutions.

(6) An order under section 107(7) may include provision about costs.

**[1703]**

NOTES
Commencement: to be appointed.

## 109 Disclosure

(1) A public authority may disclose information to the regulator if the authority thinks that the disclosure is necessary for a purpose connected with the regulator's functions.

(2) The regulator may disclose information to a public authority if the regulator thinks that the disclosure is necessary—

(a) for a purpose connected with the regulator's functions, or

(b) for a purpose connected with the authority's functions.

(3) The regulator may disclose information to a person acting on its behalf for a purpose connected with the regulator's functions.

(4) A disclosure may be subject to restrictions on further disclosure.

(5) The power to disclose information under this section is subject to any express restriction on disclosure imposed by another enactment (ignoring any restriction which allows disclosure if authorised by an enactment).

(6) Disclosure in contravention of a restriction under subsection (4) is an offence.

(7) A person guilty of an offence is liable on summary conviction to a fine not exceeding level 3 on the standard scale.

(8) "Public authority" means a person having functions of a public nature (whether or not in the United Kingdom).

**[1704]**

NOTES
Commencement: to be appointed.

## CHAPTER 3
## REGISTRATION

*Introduction*

## 110 Overview

This Chapter provides for the establishment of a register of providers of social housing.

**[1705]**

NOTES
Commencement: to be appointed.

## 111 The register

(1) The regulator shall maintain a register of providers of social housing.

(2) The regulator shall make the register available for inspection by the public.

**[1706]**

NOTES
Commencement: to be appointed.

*Eligibility*

## 112 Eligibility for registration

(1) An English body is eligible for registration if—
  (a) it satisfies the following conditions, and
  (b) it does not fall within the exceptions in section 113.

(2) Condition 1 is that the body—
  (a) is a provider of social housing in England, or
  (b) intends to become a provider of social housing in England.

(3) Condition 2 is that the body satisfies any relevant criteria set by the regulator as to—
  (a) its financial situation,
  (b) its constitution, and
  (c) other arrangements for its management.

(4) Before setting criteria the regulator must consult—
  (a) the HCA,
  (b) one or more bodies appearing to it to represent the interests of registered providers, and
  (c) one or more bodies appearing to it to represent the interests of tenants.

**[1707]**

NOTES
Commencement: 8 September 2008 (sub-ss (3), (4), for certain purposes, subject to transitional provisions in SI 2008/2358, art 3(3), (4), as noted below); to be appointed (otherwise).
Transitional provisions: the Housing and Regeneration Act 2008 (Commencement No 1 and Transitional Provision) Order 2008, SI 2008/2358, art 3(3), (4), provides as follows:
"(3) Paragraph (4) applies, for the purpose of giving effect to sections 112(4), 127(6), 174(5), 196(1), 197(4), and 216, until—
  (a) the regulator has set criteria for registration in exercise of the power conferred by section 112(3), and
  (b) a register of providers of social housing has been established in accordance with Chapter 3,
and in paragraph (4), the day when these conditions are satisfied is called the registration date.
(4) A requirement, in any of the provisions mentioned in paragraph (3), to consult one or more bodies appearing to the regulator (or, in the case of section 197(4), to the Secretary of State) to represent the interests of registered providers, may be satisfied instead by consulting one or more bodies so appearing to represent the interests of English bodies which may become eligible for registration on or after the registration date.".

## 113 Local authority non-registrable bodies

(1) This section sets out the exceptions to section 112(1).

(2) Exception 1 is a local housing authority.

(3) Exception 2 is a county council.

(4) Exception 3 is a person controlled by an authority within Exception 1 or 2.

(5) The Secretary of State may make regulations defining when a person is controlled by an authority for the purpose of Exception 3.

(6) The definition may be expressed by reference to a definition for the time being given in a document identified by regulations under section 21(2)(b) of the Local Government Act 2003 (c 26) (accounting practices for local authorities).

**[1708]**

NOTES
Commencement: 8 September 2008 (sub-ss (5), (6), for certain purposes); to be appointed (otherwise).

## 114 Registration of local authorities

(1) The Secretary of State may by order—

(a)    repeal section 113, or

(b)    amend it so as to permit the registration of specified classes of local authority.

(2)    The Secretary of State may by order require the regulator to register—

     (a)    a specified local authority, or

     (b)    a specified class of local authority.

(3)    Registration under subsection (2)—

     (a)    takes effect in accordance with any provision of the order about timing or other procedural or incidental matters,

     (b)    does not require an application for registration, and

     (c)    may apply to a local authority whether or not it is eligible for registration by virtue of subsection (1).

(4)    If the Secretary of State thinks it necessary or desirable in connection with the registration of local authorities, the Secretary of State may by order—

     (a)    provide for a provision of this Part or any other enactment not to apply in relation to registered local authorities;

     (b)    provide for a provision of this Part or any other enactment to apply with specified modifications in relation to registered local authorities;

     (c)    amend a provision of this Part or any other enactment.

(5)    In this section—

     (a)    "local authority" means an authority or person to whom section 113 applies or has applied, and

     (b)    "registered local authorities" means authorities or persons who are registered, registrable or to be registered as a result of an order under subsection (1) or (2) above.

(6)    Before making an order under this section the Secretary of State shall consult—

     (a)    any authority or person likely to be affected by it, and

     (b)    such other persons as the Secretary of State thinks fit.

**[1709]**

**NOTES**

Commencement: 8 September 2008 (for certain purposes); 7 September 2009 (for remaining purposes).

## 115   Profit-making and non-profit organisations

(1)    Each entry in the register shall designate the body registered as either—

     (a)    a non-profit organisation, or

     (b)    a profit-making organisation.

(2)    A body is a non-profit organisation if it is a registered or non-registrable charity.

(3)    A body is also a non-profit organisation if it satisfies the following conditions.

(4)    Condition 1 is that the body—

     (a)    does not trade for profit, or

     (b)    is prohibited by its constitution from issuing capital with interest or dividend at a rate exceeding that prescribed under section 1(1)(b) of the Housing Associations Act 1985 (c 69).

(5)    Condition 2 is that a purpose of the body is the provision or management of housing.

(6)    Condition 3 is that any other purposes of the body are connected with or incidental to the provision of housing.

(7)    The Secretary of State may make regulations providing that a specified purpose is to be, or not to be, treated as connected with or incidental to the provision of housing.

(8)    A body which is not a non-profit organisation under subsection (2) or (3) is a profit-making organisation.

(9)    If the regulator thinks that what was a profit-making organisation has become a non-profit organisation, the regulator must change the registered designation accordingly.

**[1710]**

**NOTES**

Commencement: to be appointed.

*Procedure*

## 116   Entry

(1)    The regulator shall register anyone who—

     (a)    is eligible for registration, and

     (b)    applies to be registered.

(2)    The regulator may make provision about—

    (a)   the form of an application;

    (b)   the information to be contained in it or provided with it;

    (c)   the manner in which an application is to submitted;

    (d)   the consequences of failure to comply with provision under paragraphs (a) to (c).

(3)   This section is subject to section 117 (fees).

(4)   Once entered a body remains registered unless and until removed under section 118 or 119.

(5)   It shall be presumed for all purposes that a person entered in the register is eligible for registration while the registration lasts (irrespective of whether and why the person is later removed from the register).

**[1711]**

**NOTES**

   Commencement: 8 September 2008 (sub-s (2)); to be appointed (otherwise).

## 117  Fees

(1)   The regulator may make initial registration conditional upon payment of a fee.

(2)   The regulator may make continued registration conditional upon payment of an annual fee.

(3)   The regulator shall—

    (a)   prescribe the amount of a fee, and

    (b)   make provision about the periods during which and in respect of which annual fees are payable.

(4)   The regulator may set different fees, and make different provision, for different cases or circumstances.

(5)   Fees must be set in accordance with principles which the regulator prepares and publishes and which are designed to ensure that so far as is reasonably practicable—

    (a)   fee income matches expenditure on the performance of functions,

    (b)   each fee is reasonable and proportionate to the costs to which it relates, and

    (c)   actual or potential registered providers can see the relationship between the amount of a fee and the costs to which it relates.

(6)   The principles—

    (a)   shall provide for section 95(3) to be disregarded for the purpose of subsection (5)(a), and

    (b)   may provide for specified expenditure or potential expenditure under section 95 or otherwise to be disregarded for the purpose of subsection (5)(a).

(7)   Principles do not have effect until approved by the Secretary of State.

(8)   In preparing (or revising) the principles the regulator shall consult persons appearing to the regulator to represent the interests of fee-payers.

(9)   The regulator's accounts shall show—

    (a)   fees received, and

    (b)   fees outstanding.

**[1712]**

**NOTES**

   Commencement: 8 September 2008 (for certain purposes); to be appointed (otherwise).

## 118  De-registration: compulsory

(1)   The regulator may remove from the register a body which the regulator thinks—

    (a)   is no longer eligible for registration,

    (b)   has ceased to carry out activities, or

    (c)   has ceased to exist.

(2)   Before removing a body under subsection (1)(a) or (b) the regulator must—

    (a)   take all reasonable steps to give the body at least 14 days' notice, and

    (b)   consider any representations it makes in that period.

(3)   After removing a body under subsection (1)(a) or (b) the regulator must take all reasonable steps to notify the body.

**[1713]**

**NOTES**

   *Commencement: to be appointed.*

## 119  De-registration: voluntary

(1)   A registered provider may ask the regulator to remove it from the register.

(2)   The regulator may comply with a request—

    (a)      on the grounds that the registered provider no longer is or intends to be a provider of social housing in England,

    (b)      on the grounds that the registered provider is subject to regulation by another authority whose control is likely to be sufficient, or

    (c)      on the grounds that the registered provider meets any relevant criteria for de-registration set by the regulator.

(3)     Before deciding whether or not to comply, the regulator must consult such local authorities in whose area the registered provider acts as it thinks appropriate.

(4)     The regulator shall not comply with a request by a non-profit registered provider if it thinks that removal is sought with a view to enabling the registered provider to distribute assets to members.

(5)     In deciding whether or not to comply, the regulator must (in particular) have regard to—

    (a)      any conditions imposed in connection with disposal consents given to the registered provider under Chapter 5, and

    (b)      any conditions imposed in connection with financial assistance given to the registered provider under any enactment.

(6)     Having decided whether or not to remove the registered provider the regulator must notify—

    (a)      the provider, and

    (b)      any authority consulted.

(7)     The regulator shall publish criteria set for the purposes of subsection (2)(c).

**[1714]**

**NOTES**

Commencement: 8 September 2008 (sub-ss (2), (7), for certain purposes); to be appointed (otherwise).

## 120   Notice

(1)     As soon as is reasonably practicable after registering or de-registering a body the regulator shall notify—

    (a)      in the case of a registered charity, the Charity Commission,

    (b)      in the case of an industrial and provident society, the Financial Services Authority, and

    (c)      in the case of a registered company (whether or not also a registered charity), the registrar of companies for England and Wales.

(2)     A notice of registration shall specify whether the person registered is designated as a non-profit or profit-making organisation.

(3)     If the designation changes, the regulator shall notify any person notified of the registration.

(4)     A person to whom notice is given under this section must keep a record of it.

**[1715]**

**NOTES**

Commencement: to be appointed.

## 121   Appeal

(1)     A body may appeal to the High Court against a decision of the regulator—

    (a)      to refuse to register it,

    (b)      to de-register it, or

    (c)      to refuse to de-register it.

(2)     The regulator shall not de-register a body while an appeal is pending.

(3)     The Secretary of State may by order provide for the First-tier Tribunal to have jurisdiction under this section instead of the High Court.

**[1716]**

**NOTES**

Commencement: to be appointed.

CHAPTER 4

REGISTERED PROVIDERS

*General provisions*

## 122   Payments to members etc

(1)     This section restricts the making of gifts, and the payment of dividends and bonuses, by a non-profit registered provider to—

    (a)   a member or former member of the registered provider,
    (b)   a member of the family of a member or former member,
    (c)   a company which has as a director a person within paragraph (a) or (b).

    (2)   A gift may be made, and a dividend or bonus may be paid, only if it falls within one of the following permitted classes.

    (3)   Class 1 is payments which—
    (a)   are in accordance with the constitution of the registered provider, and
    (b)   are due as interest on capital lent to the provider or subscribed in its shares.

    (4)   Class 2 is payments which—
    (a)   are paid by a fully mutual housing association (within the meaning of section 1(2) of the Housing Associations Act 1985 (c 69)),
    (b)   are paid to former members of the association, and
    (c)   are due under—
        (i)   tenancy agreements with the association, or
        (ii)   agreements under which the former members became members of the association.

    (5)   Class 3 is payments which—
    (a)   are in accordance with the constitution of the registered provider making the payment ("the payer"), and
    (b)   are made to a registered provider which is a subsidiary or associate of the payer.

    (6)   If a registered company or industrial and provident society contravenes this section—
    (a)   it may recover the wrongful gift or payment as a debt from the recipient, and
    (b)   the regulator may require it to take action to recover the gift or payment.

                                              **[1717]**

**NOTES**
Commencement: to be appointed.

## 123   Disposal of property

Chapter 5 makes provision about disposal of property.

                                            **[1718]**

**NOTES**
Commencement: to be appointed.

## 124   *(Amends the Housing Act 1996, s 51 and Sch 2.)*

## 125   Voluntary undertaking

    (1)   A registered provider may give the regulator an undertaking in respect of any matter concerning social housing.

    (2)   The regulator may prescribe a procedure to be followed in giving an undertaking.

    (3)   In exercising a power under Chapter 6 or 7 the regulator must have regard to any undertaking offered or given.

    (4)   The regulator may found a decision about whether to exercise a power under Chapter 6 or 7 wholly or partly on the extent to which an undertaking has been honoured.

                                            **[1719]**

**NOTES**
Commencement: to be appointed.

## 126   Sustainable community strategies

If invited by a local authority to participate in the preparation or modification of a sustainable community strategy under section 4 of the Local Government Act 2000 (c 22), a registered provider must co-operate with the local authority.

                                            **[1720]**

**NOTES**
Commencement: to be appointed.

*Accounts*

## 127   Directions

    (1)   The regulator may give directions to registered providers about the preparation of their accounts.

(2)　A direction may be given to a profit-making registered provider only in so far as its accounts relate to social housing activities.

(3)　The power must be exercised with a view to ensuring that accounts—
    (a)　are prepared in proper form, and
    (b)　present a true and fair view of—
        (i)　the state of affairs of each registered provider in relation to its social housing activities, and
        (ii)　the disposition of funds and assets which are, or have been, in its hands in connection with those activities.

(4)　A direction may require a registered charity to use a specified method for distinguishing in its accounts between—
    (a)　matters relating to its social housing activities, and
    (b)　other matters.

(5)　A direction—
    (a)　may make provision that applies generally or only to specified cases, circumstances or registered providers, and
    (b)　may make different provision for different cases, circumstances or registered providers.

(6)　A direction that relates to more than one registered provider may be given only after consulting one or more bodies appearing to the regulator to represent the interests of registered providers.

(7)　The regulator shall make arrangements for bringing a direction to the attention of every registered provider to which it applies.

**[1721]**

**NOTES**
Commencement: 8 September 2008 (sub-s (6), for certain purposes, subject to transitional provisions in SI 2008/2358, art 3(3), (4), as noted to s 112 at **[1707]**); to be appointed (otherwise).

## 128　Submission to regulator

(1)　Each registered provider shall send a copy of its accounts to the regulator within the period of 6 months beginning with the end of the period to which the accounts relate.

(2)　The accounts must be accompanied by—
    (a)　an auditor's report, or
    (b)　in the case of accounts that by virtue of an enactment are not subject to audit, any report that is required to be prepared in respect of the accounts by virtue of an enactment.

(3)　The report must specify whether the accounts comply with any relevant directions under section 127.

**[1722]**

**NOTES**
Commencement: to be appointed.

## 129　Companies exempt from audit

(1)　This section applies in relation to a registered provider which—
    (a)　is a registered company other than a charity, and
    (b)　is exempt from the audit requirements of the Companies Act 2006 (c 46) by virtue of section 477 of that Act (small companies' exemption).

(2)　The directors of the company shall cause a report to be prepared in accordance with section 130 and made to the company's members in respect of the company's individual accounts for any year in which the company takes advantage of its exemption from audit.

(3)　"Individual accounts" has the same meaning as in section 396 of the Companies Act 2006.

**[1723]**

**NOTES**
Commencement: to be appointed.

## 130　Exempt companies: accountant's report

(1)　The report required by section 129 must be prepared by a person ("the reporting accountant") who is eligible under section 131.

(2)　The report must state whether the individual accounts are in accordance with the company's accounting records kept under section 386 of the Companies Act 2006.

(3)　On the basis of the information contained in the accounting records the report must also state whether—

(a)    the accounts comply with Part 15 of the Companies Act 2006;

(b)    the company is entitled to exemption from audit under section 477 of that Act (small companies' exemption) for the year in question.

(4)    The report must give the name of the reporting accountant and be signed and dated.

(5)    The report must be signed—

(a)    where the reporting accountant is an individual, by that individual, and

(b)    where the reporting accountant is a firm, for and on behalf of the firm by an individual authorised to do so.

(6)    In this section and sections 131 and 132 "firm" has the meaning given by section 1173(1) of the Companies Act 2006.

**[1724]**

**NOTES**

Commencement: to be appointed.

**131    Exempt companies: reporting accountant**

(1)    A person is eligible for appointment by a company as a reporting accountant under section 130 if—

(a)    either of the following conditions is satisfied, and

(b)    the person would not be prohibited from acting as auditor of the company by virtue of section 1214 of the Companies Act 2006 (c 46).

(2)    Condition 1 is satisfied if the person is a member of a body listed in subsection (4) and under its rules—

(a)    the person is entitled to engage in public practice, and

(b)    is not ineligible for appointment as a reporting accountant.

(3)    Condition 2 is satisfied if the person—

(a)    is subject to the rules of a body listed in subsection (4) in seeking appointment or acting as a statutory auditor under Part 42 of the Companies Act 2006, and

(b)    under those rules, is eligible for appointment as a statutory auditor under that Part.

(4)    The bodies mentioned in subsections (2) and (3) are—

(a)    the Institute of Chartered Accountants in England and Wales,

(b)    the Institute of Chartered Accountants of Scotland,

(c)    the Institute of Chartered Accountants in Ireland,

(d)    the Association of Chartered Certified Accountants,

(e)    the Association of Authorised Public Accountants,

(f)    the Association of Accounting Technicians,

(g)    the Association of International Accountants,

(h)    the Chartered Institute of Management Accountants, and

(i)    the Institute of Chartered Secretaries and Administrators.

(5)    The Secretary of State may by order amend the list of bodies in subsection (4).

(6)    References in this section to the rules of a body are to rules (whether or not laid down by the body itself) which the body has power to enforce and which are relevant for the purposes of Part 42 of the Companies Act 2006 (statutory auditors) or this section; and this includes rules relating to the admission and expulsion of members of the body so far as relevant for the purposes of that Part or this section.

(7)    An individual or a firm may be appointed as a reporting accountant; and section 1216 of the Companies Act 2006 applies to the appointment of a partnership constituted under the law of—

(a)    England and Wales,

(b)    Northern Ireland, or

(c)    any other country or territory in which a partnership is not a legal person.

**[1725]**

**NOTES**

Commencement: 8 September 2008 (sub-s (5)); to be appointed (otherwise).

**132    Application of Companies Act**

(1)    The provisions of the Companies Act 2006 listed in subsection (2) apply to the reporting accountant and a reporting accountant's report as they apply to an auditor of the company and an auditor's report on the company's accounts (with any necessary modifications).

(2)    The provisions are—

(a)    sections 423 to 425 (duty to circulate copies of annual accounts),

(b)    sections 431 and 432 (right of member or debenture holder to demand copies of accounts),

- (c)    sections 434 to 436 (requirements in connection with publication of accounts),
- (d)    sections 441 to 444A (duty to file accounts with registrar of companies),
- (e)    section 454(4)(b) and regulations made under that provision (functions of auditor in relation to revised accounts),
- (f)    sections 499 to 502 (auditor's right to information), and
- (g)    sections 505 and 506 (name of auditor to be stated in published copies of report).

(3)    In sections 505 and 506 as they apply by virtue of this section in a case where the reporting accountant is a firm, any reference to the senior statutory auditor shall be read as a reference to the person who signed the report on behalf of the firm.

**[1726]**

---

**NOTES**

Commencement: to be appointed.

---

### 133   Exempt companies: extraordinary audit

(1)    This section applies where, in accordance with section 129, a company appoints a reporting accountant to prepare a report in respect of its accounts for any year.

(2)    The regulator may require the company to—
- (a)    cause a qualified auditor to audit its accounts and balance sheet for that year, and
- (b)    send a copy of the report to the regulator by a specified date.

(3)    A requirement may not be imposed before the end of the financial year to which it relates.

(4)    "Qualified auditor", in relation to a company, means a person who—
- (a)    is eligible for appointment as a statutory auditor of the company under Part 42 of the Companies Act 2006 (c 46) (statutory auditors), and
- (b)    is not prohibited from acting as statutory auditor of the company by virtue of section 1214 of that Act (independence requirement).

**[1727]**

---

**NOTES**

Commencement: to be appointed.

---

### 134   Non-audited industrial and provident society

(1)    This section applies to a registered provider which is an industrial and provident society.

(2)    Section 9A of the Friendly and Industrial and Provident Societies Act 1968 (c 55) applies to the society as if subsection (1)(b) were omitted (accountant's report required only where turnover exceeds specified sum).

(3)    The regulator may require the society to—
- (a)    appoint a qualified auditor to audit the society's accounts and balance sheet for any year of account in respect of which section 4 of the Friendly and Industrial and Provident Societies Act 1968 (audit requirements) has been disapplied (see section 4A of that Act), and
- (b)    send a copy of the auditor's report to the regulator by a specified date.

(4)    A requirement under subsection (3) may be imposed only during the year of account following the year to which the accounts relate.

(5)    In this section—
"qualified auditor" means a person who is a qualified auditor for the purposes of Friendly and Industrial and Provident Societies Act 1968 (c 55), and
"year of account" has the meaning given by section 21(1) of that Act.

**[1728]**

---

**NOTES**

Commencement: to be appointed.

---

### 135   Charity

(1)    This section applies to a non-profit registered provider which is a registered charity.

(2)    The charity shall—
- (a)    keep proper accounting records of its transactions and its assets and liabilities in relation to its housing activities, and
- (b)    maintain a satisfactory system of control of those records, its cash holdings and its receipts and remittances in relation to those activities.

(3)    For each period of account the charity shall prepare—
- (a)    a revenue account giving a true and fair view of the charity's income and expenditure during the period, so far as relating to its housing activities, and

    (b)    a balance sheet giving a true and fair view of the state of affairs of the charity as at the end of the period.

(4)    The revenue account and balance sheet must be signed by at least two directors or trustees.

(5)    "Period of account" means—
    (a)    a period of 12 months, or
    (b)    such other period not less than 6 months nor more than 18 as the charity may, with the consent of the regulator, determine.

(6)    This section does not affect any obligation under sections 41 to 45 of the Charities Act 1993 (c 10) (charity accounts).

**[1729]**

**NOTES**
Commencement: to be appointed.

## 136  Charity: audit

(1)    This section applies in relation to the accounts of a charity under section 135(3).

(2)    If Condition 1 or 2 is met, the charity shall cause a qualified person to audit the accounts and report on them in accordance with section 137.

(3)    If neither Condition is met, the charity shall cause a qualified person ("the reporting accountant") to report on the accounts in accordance with section 138.

(4)    Condition 1 is met if the accounts relate to a period during which the charity's gross income arising in connection with its housing activities was greater than the sum specified in section 43(1)(a) of the Charities Act 1993.

(5)    Condition 2 is met if—
    (a)    the accounts relate to a period during which the charity's gross income arising in connection with its housing activities was greater than the accounts threshold as defined by section 43(1) of the Charities Act 1993, and
    (b)    at the end of the period the aggregate value of its assets (before deduction of liabilities) in respect of its housing activities was greater than the sum specified in section 43(1)(b).

(6)    "Gross income" has the same meaning as in section 43 of the Charities Act 1993 (c 10).

(7)    "Qualified person" means a person professionally qualified as an accountant.

**[1730]**

**NOTES**
Commencement: to be appointed.

## 137  Charity: auditor's report

(1)    An auditor appointed for the purposes of section 136(2) or 139(2) in respect of a charity's accounts shall make a report to the charity in accordance with this section.

(2)    The report must state—
    (a)    whether the revenue account gives a true and fair view of the charity's income and expenditure, so far as relating to its housing activities, and
    (b)    whether the balance sheet gives a true and fair view of the state of affairs of the charity as at the end of the period to which the accounts relate.

(3)    The report must give the name of the auditor and be signed.

(4)    The auditor shall, in preparing the report, carry out such investigations as are necessary to form an opinion as to—
    (a)    whether the charity has complied with section 135(2) during the period to which the accounts relate, and
    (b)    whether the accounts are in accordance with accounting records kept under section 135(2)(a).

(5)    If the auditor thinks that the charity has not complied section 135(2) or that the accounts are not in accordance with its accounting records, that must be stated in the report.

(6)    If the auditor fails to obtain all the information and explanations which the auditor thinks necessary for the purposes of the audit, that must be stated in the report.

**[1731]**

**NOTES**
Commencement: to be appointed.

**138 Charity: accountant's report**

(1) A reporting accountant appointed for the purposes of section 136(3) in respect of a charity's accounts shall make a report to the charity in accordance with this section.

(2) The report must state whether the accounts are in accordance with accounting records kept under section 135(2)(a).

(3) On the basis of the information in the accounting records the report must also state whether—

    (a)    the accounts comply with the requirements of the Charities Act 1993;

    (b)    section 136(3) applied in respect of the accounts.

(4) The report must give the name of the reporting accountant and be signed.

(5) If the reporting accountant fails to obtain all the information and explanations which the reporting accountant thinks necessary for the purposes of preparing the report, that must be stated in the report.

**[1732]**

**NOTES**

Commencement: to be appointed.

**139 Charity: extraordinary audit**

(1) This section applies where, in accordance with section 136(3), a charity appoints a reporting accountant to prepare a report in respect of any accounts.

(2) The regulator may require the charity to—

    (a)    cause a qualified person to audit the accounts and prepare a report on them in accordance with section 137, and

    (b)    send a copy of the report to the regulator by a specified date.

(3) A requirement under subsection (2) may be imposed only during the period of account following the period to which the accounts relate.

(4) In this section—

    "period of account" has the meaning given by section 135(5), and

    "qualified person" has the meaning given by section 136(7).

**[1733]**

**NOTES**

Commencement: to be appointed.

**140 Charity: auditor's powers**

(1) This section applies to a person who is appointed by a charity for the purposes of section 136(2) or (3) or 139(2).

(2) The charity must grant the person access to its documents, if or in so far as they relate to its housing activities.

(3) An officer of the charity must provide such information or explanations as the person thinks necessary.

**[1734]**

**NOTES**

Commencement: to be appointed.

**141 Offences**

(1) A registered provider commits an offence if it fails, without reasonable excuse, to comply with—

    (a)    a direction under section 127,

    (b)    a provision listed in subsection (2), or

    (c)    a requirement imposed under a provision listed in subsection (3).

(2) The provisions referred to in subsection (1)(b) are—

    (a)    section 128;

    (b)    section 129;

    (c)    section 135;

    (d)    section 136.

(3) The provisions referred to in subsection (1)(c) are—

    (a)    section 133;

    (b)    section 134;

    (c)    section 139.

(4)   If a registered provider fails to comply with a direction, provision or requirement mentioned in subsection (1) every officer of the registered provider is guilty of an offence.

(5)   It is a defence for an officer to show that the officer did everything that could reasonably have been expected to ensure compliance by the registered provider.

(6)   A person guilty of an offence under this section is liable on summary conviction to a fine not exceeding level 5 on the standard scale.

(7)   Proceedings for an offence may be brought only by or with the consent of—
    (a)   the regulator, or
    (b)   the Director of Public Prosecutions.

[1735]

**NOTES**
Commencement: to be appointed.

## 142   High Court

(1)   If a registered provider fails to comply with a direction, provision or requirement mentioned in section 141(1), the High Court may on the application of the regulator make an order for the purpose of remedying the failure.

(2)   An order may include provision about costs.

[1736]

**NOTES**
Commencement: to be appointed.

## 143   Disclosure

(1)   This section applies to information that a person has received while acting—
    (a)   as auditor of a registered provider, or
    (b)   as a reporting accountant in relation to a registered provider.

(2)   The person may disclose the information to the regulator for a purpose connected with the regulator's functions—
    (a)   despite any duty of confidentiality, and
    (b)   whether or not the regulator requests the information.

(3)   The reference to disclosing information includes expressing an opinion on it.

(4)   "Reporting accountant" means a person who is appointed to prepare a report which, by virtue of any enactment, has to be prepared in respect of accounts that are not subject to audit.

[1737]

**NOTES**
Commencement: to be appointed.

*Insolvency etc*

## 144   Preparatory steps: notice

A step specified in the Table has effect only if the person specified has given the regulator notice.

| *Step* | *Person to give notice* |
| --- | --- |
| Any step, of a kind prescribed for the purposes of this section by the Secretary of State by order, to enforce a security over land held by a registered provider | The person taking the step |
| Presenting a petition for the winding up of a registered provider which is—<br><br>(a) a registered company, or<br><br>(b) an industrial and provident society<br><br>But not the presenting of a petition by the regulator under section 166 | The petitioner |
| Passing a resolution for the winding up of a registered provider which is— | The registered provider |

| Step | Person to give notice |
|---|---|
| (a) a registered company, or<br><br>(b) an industrial and provident society<br><br>But not the passing of a resolution for winding-up where the regulator's consent is required under section 162 or 164 | |
| Making an administration application in accordance with paragraph 12 of Schedule B1 to the Insolvency Act 1986 in respect of a registered provider which is a registered company | The applicant |
| Appointing an administrator under paragraph 14 or 22 of that Schedule in respect of a registered provider which is a registered company | The person making the appointment |
| Filing with the court a copy of a notice of intention to appoint a person under either of those paragraphs in respect of a registered provider which is a registered company | The person filing the notice |

**[1738]**

**NOTES**

Commencement: 1 April 2009 (for the purposes of enabling the Secretary of State to make an order); to be appointed (otherwise).

### 145 Moratorium

(1) If a step specified in the Table below is taken in respect of a registered provider, a moratorium on the disposal of land by the provider begins.

(2) Where a step specified in the Table is taken in respect of a registered provider, the person specified must give the regulator notice as soon as is reasonably practicable.

(3) If the notice is not given the step is not invalidated (but the end of the moratorium depends on the notice being given—see section 146(2)).

(4) The regulator shall give the HCA a copy of any notice received under this section.

| Step | Person |
|---|---|
| Any step, of a kind prescribed for the purposes of this section by the Secretary of State by order, to enforce a security over land held by a registered provider | The person taking the step |
| The presenting of a petition for winding up a registered provider which is—<br><br>(a) a registered company, or<br><br>(b) an industrial and provident society<br><br>But not the presenting of a petition by the directors or other governing body of the registered provider or by the regulator under section 166 | The petitioner |
| The passing of a resolution for the winding up of a registered provider which is—<br><br>(a) a registered company, or<br><br>(b) an industrial and provident society | The registered provider |

| Step | Person |
|------|--------|
| A decision by the directors or other governing body of a registered provider to present a petition for winding up where the registered provider is—<br><br>(a) a registered company, or<br><br>(b) an industrial and provident society | The directors or governing body |
| The making of an administration order in accordance with paragraph 13 of Schedule B1 to the Insolvency Act 1986 in respect of a registered provider which is a registered company | The person who applied for the order |
| The appointment of an administrator under paragraph 14 or 22 of that Schedule in respect of a registered provider which is a registered company | The person making the appointment |

**[1739]**

**NOTES**

Commencement: 1 April 2009 (sub-s (4), for the purposes of enabling the Secretary of State to make an order); to be appointed (otherwise).

## 146 Duration of moratorium

(1) The moratorium begins when the step specified in section 145 is taken.

(2) The moratorium ends (unless extended or cancelled) with the period of 28 working days beginning with the day on which the regulator receives notice under section 145(2).

(3) During a moratorium the regulator may extend it (or further extend it) for a specified period, with the consent of each secured creditor of the registered provider whom the regulator is able to locate after making reasonable enquiries.

(4) If the regulator extends a moratorium it shall notify—
 (a) the registered provider,
 (b) any liquidator, administrator, administrative receiver or receiver appointed in respect of the registered provider or its land, and
 (c) the HCA.

(5) During a moratorium the regulator may cancel it if satisfied that it is unnecessary to make proposals under section 152.

(6) Before cancelling a moratorium the regulator must consult the person who took the step that triggered it.

(7) When a moratorium ends the regulator shall give notice, and (except in the case of cancellation) an explanation of section 147, to—
 (a) the registered provider, and
 (b) such of its secured creditors as the regulator is able to locate after making reasonable enquiries.

(8) When a moratorium ends the regulator shall also give notice to the HCA.

(9) Taking a further step during a moratorium does not—
 (a) start a new moratorium, or
 (b) alter the existing moratorium's duration.

**[1740]**

**NOTES**

Commencement: to be appointed.

## 147 Further moratorium

(1) This section applies if—
 (a) a moratorium in respect of a registered provider ends otherwise than by cancellation, and
 (b) a further step specified in section 145 is taken in relation to the provider within the period of 3 years beginning with the end of the moratorium.

(2) The further step does not automatically trigger a further moratorium.

(3)   But the regulator may impose a further moratorium for a specified period, if each secured creditor of the registered provider whom the regulator is able to locate after making reasonable enquiries consents.

(4)   If the regulator imposes a new moratorium it shall notify—
  (a)   the registered provider,
  (b)   any liquidator, administrator, administrative receiver or receiver appointed in respect of the registered provider or any of its land, and
  (c)   the HCA.

(5)   This group of sections applies to a further moratorium as to a first moratorium (except for section 146(2)).

**[1741]**

**NOTES**
  Commencement: to be appointed.

## 148   Effect of moratorium

(1)   During a moratorium the HCA—
  (a)   may not give the registered provider a direction under section 32(4), and
  (b)   may not take steps to enforce such a direction against the registered provider.

(2)   During a moratorium a disposal of the registered provider's land requires the regulator's prior consent.

(3)   Section 149 sets out exceptions to subsection (2).

(4)   Consent—
  (a)   may be given before the moratorium begins, and
  (b)   may be subject to conditions.

(5)   This section does not prevent a liquidator from disclaiming land as onerous property during a moratorium.

(6)   In this section "land" includes a present or future interest in rent or other receipts arising from land.

**[1742]**

**NOTES**
  Commencement: to be appointed.

## 149   Exempted disposals

(1)   The regulator's consent is not required under section 148 for the following exceptions.

(2)   Exception 1 is a letting under—
  (a)   an assured tenancy, or
  (b)   an assured agricultural occupancy.

(3)   Exception 2 is a letting under what would be an assured tenancy or an assured agricultural occupancy but for any of paragraphs 4 to 8, 12(1)(h) and 12ZA to 12B of Schedule 1 to the Housing Act 1988 (c 50) (tenancies which cannot be assured tenancies).

(4)   Exception 3 is a letting under a secure tenancy.

(5)   Exception 4 is a letting under what would be a secure tenancy but for any of paragraphs 2 to 12 of Schedule 1 to the Housing Act 1985 (c 68) (tenancies which are not secure tenancies).

(6)   Exception 5 is a disposal for which consent is required under—
  (a)   section 81 or 133 of the Housing Act 1988 (c 50), or
  (b)   section 173 of the Local Government and Housing Act 1989 (c 42).

(7)   Exception 6 is a disposal under Part V of the Housing Act 1985 (right to buy).

(8)   Exception 7 is a disposal under the right conferred by—
  (a)   section 180, or
  (b)   section 16 of the Housing Act 1996 (c 52) (tenant's right to acquire social housing in Wales).

**[1743]**

**NOTES**
  Commencement: to be appointed.

## 150   Disposals without consent

(1)   A purported disposal by a registered provider is void if—
  (a)   it requires the regulator's consent under section 148, and
  (b)   the regulator has not given consent.

(2)   But subsection (1) does not apply to a disposal by a non-profit registered provider to one or more individuals ("the buyer") if—

(a)   the disposal is of a single dwelling, and

(b)   the registered provider reasonably believes at the time of the disposal that the buyer intends to use the property as the buyer's principal residence.

**[1744]**

**NOTES**

Commencement: to be appointed.

### 151   Interim manager

(1)   During a moratorium the regulator may appoint an interim manager of the registered provider.

(2)   An appointment may relate to the registered provider's affairs generally or to affairs specified in the appointment.

(3)   Appointment shall be on terms and conditions (including as to remuneration) specified in, or determined in accordance with, the appointment.

(4)   An appointment under this section shall come to an end with the earliest of the following—

(a)   the end of the moratorium,

(b)   the agreement of proposals under section 152, or

(c)   a date specified in the appointment.

(5)   An interim manager shall have—

(a)   any power specified in the appointment, and

(b)   any other power in relation to the registered provider's affairs required by the manager for the purposes specified in the appointment (including the power to enter into agreements and take other action on behalf of the registered provider).

(6)   But an interim manager may not—

(a)   dispose of land, or

(b)   grant security over land.

**[1745]**

**NOTES**

Commencement: to be appointed.

### 152   Proposals

(1)   During a moratorium the regulator may make proposals about the future ownership and management of the registered provider's land, with a view to ensuring that the property will be properly managed by a registered provider.

(2)   In making proposals the regulator shall—

(a)   have regard to the interests of the registered provider's creditors as a whole, and

(b)   so far as is reasonably practicable avoid worsening the position of unsecured creditors.

(3)   Proposals may provide for the appointment of a manager in accordance with section 155 to implement all or part of the proposals.

(4)   Proposals may not include anything which would result in—

(a)   a preferential debt being paid otherwise than in priority to a non-preferential debt, or

(b)   a preferential creditor (PC1) being paid a smaller proportion of a preferential debt than another preferential creditor (PC2) (unless PC1 consents).

(5)   Proposals relating to a registered provider which is a charity (C1)—

(a)   may not require it to act outside the terms of its trusts, and

(b)   may provide for the disposal of accommodation only to another charity whose objects the regulator thinks are similar to those of C1.

**[1746]**

**NOTES**

Commencement: to be appointed.

### 153   Proposals: procedure

*(1)   Before making proposals the regulator shall consult—*

(a)   the registered provider,

(b)   its tenants (so far as is reasonably practicable),

(c)   if the registered provider is an industrial and provident society, the Financial Services Authority, and

(d)   if the registered provider is a registered charity, the Charity Commission.

(2)    The regulator shall send a copy of proposals to—
- (a)    the registered provider and its officers,
- (b)    such of its secured creditors as the regulator is able to locate after making reasonable enquiries, and
- (c)    any liquidator, administrator, administrative receiver or receiver appointed in respect of the registered provider or any of its land.

(3)    The regulator shall also make arrangements for bringing proposals to the attention of—
- (a)    the registered provider's members,
- (b)    its tenants, and
- (c)    its unsecured creditors.

(4)    If each secured creditor to whom proposals were sent agrees to the proposals by notice to the regulator, the proposals have effect.

(5)    Proposals may be agreed with modifications if—
- (a)    each secured creditor to whom the proposals were sent consents by notice to the regulator, and
- (b)    the regulator consents.

(6)    The regulator shall send a copy of agreed proposals to—
- (a)    the registered provider and its officers,
- (b)    its secured creditors to whom the original proposals were sent,
- (c)    any liquidator, administrator, administrative receiver or receiver appointed in respect of the registered provider or any of its land,
- (d)    if the registered provider is an industrial and provident society, the Financial Services Authority, and
- (e)    if the registered provider is a registered charity, the Charity Commission.

(7)    The regulator shall also make arrangements for bringing agreed proposals to the attention of—
- (a)    the registered provider's members,
- (b)    its tenants, and
- (c)    its unsecured creditors.

(8)    Proposals may be amended by agreement between the secured creditors to whom the original proposals were sent and the regulator; and this section and section 152 apply to an amendment as to the original proposals.

**[1747]**

**NOTES**

Commencement: to be appointed.

## 154   Proposals: effect

(1)    The following are obliged to implement agreed proposals—
- (a)    the regulator,
- (b)    the registered provider,
- (c)    its creditors, and
- (d)    any liquidator, administrator, administrative receiver or receiver appointed in respect of the registered provider or any of its land.

(2)    The following shall co-operate with implementation of agreed proposals—
- (a)    in the case of a charitable trust, its trustees,
- (b)    in the case of an industrial and provident society, its committee members, and
- (c)    in the case of a registered company, its directors.

(3)    Subsection (2) does not require or permit a breach of a fiduciary or other duty.

**[1748]**

**NOTES**

Commencement: to be appointed.

## 155   Manager: appointment

(1)    This section applies where agreed proposals provide for the appointment of a manager.

(2)    The proposals must provide for the manager to be paid reasonable remuneration and expenses.

(3)    The regulator shall appoint a manager.

(4)    The regulator may give the manager directions (general or specific).

(5)    The manager may apply to the High Court for directions (and directions of the regulator are subject to directions of the High Court).

(6)   If the registered provider is a charity, the regulator must notify the Charity Commission that a manager has been appointed.

(7)   The regulator may appoint a new manager in place of a person who ceases to be manager (in accordance with terms of appointment specified in the proposals or determined by the regulator).

**[1749]**

**NOTES**
Commencement: to be appointed.

### 156   Manager: powers

(1)   A manager—
  (a)   may do anything necessary for the purpose of the appointment,
  (b)   acts as the registered provider's agent (and is not personally liable on a contract), and
  (c)   has ostensible authority to act for the registered provider (so that a person dealing with the manager in good faith and for value need not inquire into the manager's powers).

(2)   In particular, the terms of a manager's appointment may confer power—
  (a)   to sell or otherwise dispose of land by public auction or private contract;
  (b)   to raise or borrow money;
  (c)   to grant security over land;
  (d)   to grant or accept surrender of a lease;
  (e)   to take a lease;
  (f)   to take possession of property;
  (g)   to appoint a solicitor, accountant or other professional to assist the manager;
  (h)   to appoint agents and staff (and to dismiss them);
  (i)   to make payments;
  (j)   to bring or defend legal proceedings;
  (k)   to refer a question to arbitration;
  (l)   to make any arrangement or compromise;
  (m)   to carry on the business of the registered provider;
  (n)   to carry out works and do other things in connection with the management or transfer of land;
  (o)   to take out insurance;
  (p)   to use the registered body's seal;
  (q)   to execute in the name and on behalf of the registered provider any deed, receipt or other document;
  (r)   to do anything incidental to a power in paragraphs (a) to (q).

(3)   A manager shall so far as is reasonably practicable consult and inform the registered provider's tenants about an exercise of powers likely to affect them.

**[1750]**

**NOTES**
Commencement: to be appointed.

### 157   Manager of industrial and provident society: extra powers

(1)   This section applies to a manager appointed to implement proposals relating to an industrial and provident society.

(2)   The appointment may confer on the manager power to make and execute on behalf of the society—
  (a)   an instrument providing for the amalgamation of the society with another industrial and provident society, or
  (b)   an instrument transferring its engagements.

(3)   An instrument providing for the amalgamation of a society ("S1") with another has the same effect as a resolution by S1 under section 50 of the Industrial and Provident Societies Act 1965 (c 12) (amalgamation of societies by special resolution).

(4)   An instrument transferring engagements has the same effect as a transfer of engagements under sections 51 and 52 of the Industrial and Provident Societies Act 1965 (transfer by special resolution to another society or company).

(5)   A copy of the instrument shall be sent to and registered by the Financial Services Authority.

(6)   An instrument does not take effect until the copy is registered.

(7)   The copy must be sent for registration during the period of 14 days beginning with the date of execution; but a copy registered after that period is valid.

**[1751]**

**NOTES**
Commencement: to be appointed.

### 158   Assistance by regulator

(1)   The regulator may give financial or other assistance to a registered provider for the purpose of preserving its position pending the agreement of proposals.

(2)   The regulator may give financial or other assistance to a registered provider, or a manager appointed under section 155, to facilitate the implementation of agreed proposals.

(3)   In particular, the regulator may—
    (a)   lend staff;
    (b)   arrange payment of the manager's remuneration and expenses.

(4)   The regulator may do the following only with the Secretary of State's consent—
    (a)   make grants,
    (b)   make loans,
    (c)   indemnify a manager,
    (d)   make payments in connection with secured loans, and
    (e)   guarantee payments in connection with secured loans.

                                                         **[1752]**

**NOTES**
Commencement: to be appointed.

### 159   Applications to court

(1)   A registered provider may apply to the High Court where the registered provider thinks that action taken by a manager is not in accordance with the agreed proposals.

(2)   A creditor of a registered provider may apply to the High Court where the creditor thinks that action taken by a manager is not in accordance with the agreed proposals.

(3)   The High Court may—
    (a)   confirm, annul or modify an act of the manager;
    (b)   give the manager directions;
    (c)   make any other order.

(4)   If a person bound by agreed proposals (P1) thinks that action by another person (P2) breaches section 154, P1 may apply to the High Court.

(5)   The High Court may—
    (a)   confirm, annul or modify the action;
    (b)   grant relief by way of injunction, damages or otherwise.

                                                         **[1753]**

**NOTES**
Commencement: to be appointed.

*Restructuring and dissolution*

### 160   Company: arrangements and reconstructions

(1)   This section applies to a non-profit registered provider which is a registered company.

(2)   A voluntary arrangement under Part 1 of the Insolvency Act 1986 (c 45) in relation to the company is effective only if the regulator has first consented.

(3)   An order under section 899 of the Companies Act 2006 (c 46) (court sanction for compromise or arrangement)—
    (a)   is effective only if the regulator has first consented, and
    (b)   does not take effect until a copy of the consent is delivered to the registrar of companies.

(4)   An order under section 900 of the Companies Act 2006 (powers of court to facilitate reconstruction or amalgamation) is effective only if the regulator has first consented.

(5)   The requirement in section 900(6) of the Companies Act 2006 (sending copy of order to registrar) is satisfied only if the copy is accompanied by a copy of the regulator's consent.

                                                         **[1754]**

**NOTES**
Commencement: to be appointed.

### 161   Company: conversion into industrial and provident society

(1)   This section applies to a non-profit registered provider which is a registered company.

(2)    The registrar of companies may register a resolution under section 53 of the Industrial and Provident Societies Act 1965 (c 12) for converting the company into an industrial and provident society only if—

(a)    the regulator has consented to the resolution, and
(b)    a copy of the consent accompanies the resolution as sent to the registrar.

(3)    The regulator shall register the body created by the conversion and designate it as a non-profit organisation.

(4)    Pending registration the body shall be treated as if it were registered and designated as a non-profit organisation.

**[1755]**

**NOTES**
Commencement: to be appointed.

## 162    Company: winding up

(1)    This section applies to a non-profit registered provider which is a registered company.

(2)    A special resolution for the voluntary winding-up of the company under the Insolvency Act 1986 (c 45) is effective only if the regulator has first consented.

(3)    The requirement under section 30 of the Companies Act 2006 (c 46) (sending copy of resolution to registrar) is satisfied only if the copy is accompanied by a copy of the regulator's consent.

**[1756]**

**NOTES**
Commencement: to be appointed.

## 163    Industrial and provident society: restructuring

(1)    This section applies to a non-profit registered provider which is an industrial and provident society.

(2)    The Financial Services Authority may register a resolution passed by the society for the purposes of restructuring provisions listed in subsection (3) only if—

(a)    the regulator has consented to the resolution, and
(b)    a copy of the consent accompanies the resolution as sent to the Authority.

(3)    The following provisions of the Industrial and Provident Societies Act 1965 (c 12) are the restructuring provisions—

(a)    section 50 (amalgamation of societies),
(b)    section 51 (transfer of engagements between societies), and
(c)    section 52 of that Act (conversion into or amalgamation with registered company).

(4)    Where a resolution is registered in accordance with subsection (2), any body created or to whom engagements are transferred—

(a)    must be registered by the regulator and designated as a non-profit organisation, and
(b)    pending registration shall be treated as registered and designated as a non-profit organisation.

**[1757]**

**NOTES**
Commencement: to be appointed.

## 164    Industrial and provident society: winding up

(1)    This section applies to a non-profit registered provider which is an industrial and provident society.

(2)    A resolution for the voluntary winding-up of the society under the Insolvency Act 1986 is effective only if the regulator has first consented.

(3)    The requirement in section 30 of the Companies Act 2006 (c 46) (as applied by section 55 of the Industrial and Provident Societies Act 1965 and section 84(3) of the Insolvency Act 1986) (sending copy of resolution to FSA) is satisfied only if the copy is accompanied by a copy of the regulator's consent.

**[1758]**

**NOTES**
Commencement: to be appointed.

### 165   Industrial and provident society: dissolution

(1)   This section applies to a non-profit registered provider which is—

    (a)   an industrial and provident society, and

    (b)   to be dissolved by instrument of dissolution in accordance with section 58 of the Industrial and Provident Societies Act 1965.

(2)   The Financial Services Authority may register the instrument under section 58(5), or cause notice of the dissolution to be advertised under section 58(6), only if—

    (a)   the regulator has consented to the dissolution, and

    (b)   a copy of the consent accompanies the instrument as sent to the Authority.

**[1759]**

**NOTES**

Commencement: to be appointed.

### 166   Winding up petition by regulator

(1)   This section applies to a non-profit registered provider which is—

    (a)   a registered company, or

    (b)   an industrial and provident society.

(2)   The regulator may present a petition for the registered provider to be wound up under the Insolvency Act 1986 (c 45) on any of the following grounds.

(3)   Ground 1 is that the registered provider is failing properly to carry out its objects.

(4)   Ground 2 is that the registered provider is unable to pay its debts within the meaning of section 123 of the Insolvency Act 1986.

(5)   Ground 3 is that the regulator has directed the registered provider under section 253 to transfer all its land to another person.

**[1760]**

**NOTES**

Commencement: to be appointed.

### 167   Transfer of property

(1)   This section applies—

    (a)   where a non-profit registered provider which is an industrial and provident society is dissolved in accordance with section 55(a) or (b) of the Industrial and Provident Societies Act 1965 (c 12), and

    (b)   where a non-profit registered provider which is a registered company is wound up under the Insolvency Act 1986.

(2)   Any surplus property that is available after satisfying the registered provider's liabilities shall be transferred—

    (a)   to the regulator, or

    (b)   if the regulator directs, to a specified non-profit registered provider.

(3)   If land belonging to the registered provider needs to be sold to satisfy its liabilities, the regulator may discharge those liabilities so as to ensure that the land is instead transferred in accordance with subsection (2).

(4)   Where the registered provider dissolved or wound up is a charity, a registered provider may be specified under subsection (2)(b) only if it is a charity whose objects the regulator thinks are similar to those of the original charity.

(5)   This section has effect despite anything in—

    (a)   the Industrial and Provident Societies Act 1965,

    (b)   the Insolvency Act 1986,

    (c)   the Companies Act 2006 (c 46), or

    (d)   the constitution of a registered provider.

**[1761]**

**NOTES**

Commencement: to be appointed.

### 168   Section 167: supplemental

(1)   This section applies to property transferred to the regulator in accordance with section 167(2)(a).

(2)   The regulator may dispose of the property only to a non-profit registered provider.

(3)   Where the registered provider wound up or dissolved was a charity, the regulator may dispose of the property only to a registered provider—

    (a)    which is a charity, and

    (b)    whose objects the regulator thinks are similar to those of the original charity.

  (4)   If the property includes land subject to a mortgage or charge, the regulator may dispose of the land—

    (a)    subject to that mortgage or charge, or

    (b)    subject to a new mortgage or charge in favour of the regulator.

**[1762]**

**NOTES**

Commencement: to be appointed.

## 169 Extension of sections 167 and 168

The Secretary of State may by regulations provide for sections 167 and 168 to apply in relation to a registered provider which is a charity but not a registered company—

    (a)    in specified circumstances, and

    (b)    with specified modifications.

**[1763]**

**NOTES**

Commencement: to be appointed.

## CHAPTER 5
## DISPOSAL OF PROPERTY

*Introductory*

## 170 Overview

This Chapter makes provision about the disposal of property by registered providers.

**[1764]**

**NOTES**

Commencement: to be appointed.

## 171 Power to dispose

  (1)   A registered provider may dispose of land.

  (2)   But a non-profit registered provider may dispose of the landlord's interest under a secure tenancy only to another non-profit registered provider.

  (3)   Subsection (1) is subject to the following provisions of this Chapter (which include provisions requiring the regulator's consent for certain disposals).

**[1765]**

**NOTES**

Commencement: to be appointed.

*Regulator's consent*

## 172 Requirement of consent

  (1)   Disposal of a dwelling by a registered provider requires the regulator's consent if the dwelling is social housing.

  (2)   The regulator shall not consent to a disposal by a non-profit registered provider which it thinks is being made with a view to enabling the provider to distribute assets to members.

  (3)   Consent is not required under this section if the disposal falls within an exception listed in section 173.

**[1766]**

**NOTES**

Commencement: to be appointed.

## 173 Exceptions

  (1)   This section lists exceptions to the requirement of consent in section 172.

  (2)   Exception 1 is that consent is not required for disposal by a registered provider by way of—

    (a)    an assured tenancy,

    (b)    an assured agricultural occupancy,

    (c)    an arrangement that would be an assured tenancy or an assured agricultural occupancy but for any of paragraphs 4 to 8, 12(1)(h) and 12ZA to 12B of Schedule 1 to the Housing Act 1988 (c 50) (exclusions),

    (d)    a secure tenancy, or

    (e)    an arrangement that would be a secure tenancy but for any of paragraphs 2 to 12 of Schedule 1 to the Housing Act 1985 (c 68) (exclusions).

    (3)    Exception 2 is that consent is not required for a disposal for which consent is required under—

    (a)    section 81 or 133 of the Housing Act 1988, or

    (b)    section 173 of the Local Government and Housing Act 1989 (c 42).

    (4)    Exception 3 is that consent is not required for a disposal under Part V of the Housing Act 1985 (right to buy).

    (5)    Exception 4 is that consent is not required for a disposal in pursuance of a tenant's right to acquire under—

    (a)    section 180, or

    (b)    section 16 of the Housing Act 1996 (c 52) (tenant's right to acquire social housing in Wales).

[1767]

**NOTES**

Commencement: to be appointed.

---

## 174   Procedure

    (1)    Consent may be—

    (a)    general, or

    (b)    specific (whether as to particular registered providers, as to particular property, as to particular forms of disposal or in any other way).

    (2)    Consent may be retrospective.

    (3)    Consent may be expressed by reference to a policy for disposals submitted by a registered provider.

    (4)    Consent may be conditional.

    (5)    Before giving consent the regulator must consult—

    (a)    the HCA,

    (b)    one or more bodies appearing to it to represent the interests of registered providers, and

    (c)    one or more bodies appearing to it to represent the interests of tenants.

    (6)    Subsection (5) does not apply to specific consent relating only to one or more particular registered providers or properties.

[1768]

**NOTES**

Commencement: 8 September 2008 (sub-ss (5), (6), for certain purposes, subject to transitional provisions in SI 2008/2358, art 3(3), (4), as noted to s 112 at **[1707]**); to be appointed (otherwise).

---

## 175   Disposal without consent

    (1)    A purported disposal by a registered provider is void if—

    (a)    it requires the regulator's consent, and

    (b)    the regulator has not given consent.

    (2)    But subsection (1) does not apply to a disposal by a non-profit registered provider to one or more individuals ("the buyer") if—

    (a)    the disposal is of a single dwelling, and

    (b)    the registered provider reasonably believes at the time of the disposal that the buyer intends to use the property as the buyer's principal residence.

[1769]

**NOTES**

Commencement: to be appointed.

---

## 176   Notification where disposal consent not required

    (1)    If a non-profit registered provider disposes of land other than a dwelling which is social housing it shall notify the regulator as soon as is reasonably practicable.

    (2)    The regulator may give a direction dispensing with the notification requirement.

(3)  Section 174(1) and (3) to (6) applies to a direction under this section as it applies to consent under section 172.

[1770]

**NOTES**

Commencement: to be appointed.

*Proceeds*

**177  Separate accounting**

(1)  The accounts of a registered provider must show its net disposal proceeds, as a separate "disposal proceeds fund".

(2)  The following are net disposal proceeds—

    (a)    net proceeds of sale to a tenant in pursuance of the right to acquire conferred by section 180,

    (b)    net proceeds of sale to a tenant in pursuance of the right to acquire conferred by section 16 of the Housing Act 1996 (c 52),

    (c)    net proceeds of sale of property in respect of which a grant was made under section 21 of that Act,

    (d)    net proceeds of sale of property in respect of which a grant was made under section 19 of this Act in respect of discounts given by a registered provider on disposals of dwellings to tenants,

    (e)    grant received under section 20 or 21 of the 1996 Act,

    (f)    grant received under section 19 of this Act in respect of discounts given by a registered provider on disposals of dwellings to tenants,

    (g)    repayments of discount in respect of which grant was received under section 20 or 21 of the 1996 Act,

    (h)    repayments of discount in respect of which grant was received under section 19 of this Act in respect of discounts given by a registered provider on disposals of dwellings to tenants,

    (i)    other proceeds of sale specified by the regulator, and

    (j)    other grants specified by the regulator.

(3)  The regulator shall determine amounts to be deducted in determining net proceeds of sale.

(4)  The method of constituting the disposal proceeds fund and showing it in the accounts shall be in accordance with a direction of the regulator.

(5)  Subsections (5) to (7) of section 127 apply to a direction under this section as to a direction under that section.

(6)  Sections 141 and 142 apply in relation to a direction under this section as in relation to a direction under section 127.

(7)  Interest shall be added to the fund in accordance with a determination made by the regulator.

(8)  Where this section applies in relation to the proceeds of sale arising on a disposal, section 32 above, section 27 of the Housing Act 1996 (c 52) and section 52 of the Housing Act 1988 (c 50) do not apply.

[1771]

**NOTES**

Commencement: to be appointed.

**178  Use of proceeds**

(1)  Sums in a registered provider's disposal proceeds fund may be used or allocated only in accordance with a direction by the regulator.

(2)  The regulator may give a direction only with the Secretary of State's approval.

(3)  If at the end of a period specified by the regulator the disposal proceeds fund includes sums which have not been allocated in accordance with subsection (1), the regulator may require the registered provider to pay the sums to the HCA.

[1772]

**NOTES**

Commencement: to be appointed.

*Tenants' rights and duties*

### 179   Application of Housing Act 1996

(1)   The following provisions of the Housing Act 1996 apply in relation to disposals of social housing by registered providers, with the modifications set out below (and any other necessary modifications).

(2)   The provisions are—

   (a)   sections 11 to 12 (repayment of discount on disposal),

   (b)   sections 12A and 12B (landlord's right of first refusal),

   (c)   section 13 (disposal of property in National Park), and

   (d)   sections 14 and 15 (supplemental).

(3)   In those provisions—

   (a)   references to a registered social landlord shall be treated as references to a registered provider,

   (b)   references to consent given by the Welsh Ministers under section 9 of the 1996 Act shall be treated as references to consent given by the regulator under section 172 of this Act,

   (c)   references to the Welsh Ministers in connection with a power to make orders or regulations shall be treated as references to the Secretary of State,

   (d)   in section 12(5)(b) of the 1996 Act the reference to the Welsh Ministers shall be treated as a reference to the HCA, and

   (e)   references to a resolution of the National Assembly for Wales shall be treated as references to a resolution of either House of Parliament.

(4)   This section does not affect the continued application of the provisions listed in subsection (2) in relation to disposals made before this section comes into force.

**[1773]**

---

**NOTES**

Commencement: to be appointed.

---

*Right to acquire*

### 180   Right to acquire

(1)   The tenant of a dwelling in England has a right to acquire the dwelling if—

   (a)   the landlord is a registered provider or a registered social landlord,

   (b)   the tenancy is within subsection (2),

   (c)   the provision of the dwelling was publicly funded,

   (d)   the dwelling has remained in the social rented sector ever since that provision, and

   (e)   the tenant satisfies any qualifying conditions applicable under Part V of the Housing Act 1985 (c 68) (as it applies by virtue of section 184).

(2)   A tenancy is within this subsection if it is—

   (a)   an assured tenancy, other than an assured shorthold tenancy or a long tenancy, or

   (b)   a secure tenancy.

(3)   The reference in subsection (1)(a) to a registered provider includes—

   (a)   a person who provided the dwelling in fulfilment of a condition imposed by the HCA when giving assistance to the person;

   (b)   a person who provided the dwelling wholly or partly by means of a grant under section 27A of the Housing Act 1996 (c 52).

**[1774]**

---

**NOTES**

Commencement: to be appointed.

---

### 181   Interpretation: "publicly funded"

(1)   The provision of a dwelling was publicly funded if any of the following conditions is satisfied.

(2)   Condition 1 is that—

   (a)   the dwelling was provided by a person in fulfilment of a condition imposed by the HCA when giving assistance to the person, and

   (b)   before giving the assistance the HCA notified the person that if it did so the provision of the dwelling would be regarded as publicly funded.

(3)   Condition 2 is that the dwelling was provided wholly or partly by using sums in the disposal proceeds fund of—

   (a)   a registered provider, or

   (b)   a registered social landlord.

(4)   Condition 3 is that—

    (a)    the dwelling was acquired by a registered provider, or a registered social landlord, on a disposal by a public sector landlord,

    (b)    the disposal was made on or after 1st April 1997, and

    (c)    at the time of the disposal the dwelling was capable of being let as a separate dwelling.

(5)    Condition 3 is not satisfied if the dwelling was acquired in pursuance of a contract made, or option created, before 1st April 1997.

(6)    Condition 4 is that—

    (a)    the dwelling was provided wholly or partly by means of a grant under section 18 or 27A of the Housing Act 1996 (c 52), and

    (b)    when the grant was made the recipient was notified under section 16(4) of that Act that the dwelling was to be regarded as funded by means of such a grant.

**[1775]**

**NOTES**

Commencement: to be appointed.

## 182  Interpretation: "remained in the social rented sector"

(1)    This section applies for the purposes of determining whether a dwelling has remained in the social rented sector.

(2)    A dwelling shall be treated as having remained in the social rented sector for any period during which—

    (a)    the freeholder was a person within subsection (3), and

    (b)    each leaseholder was either a person within that subsection or an individual holding otherwise than under a long tenancy.

(3)    A person is within this subsection if the person is—

    (a)    a registered provider,

    (b)    a registered social landlord, or

    (c)    a public sector landlord.

(4)    A dwelling provided wholly or partly by means of a grant under section 27A of the Housing Act 1996 shall also be treated as having remained in the social rented sector for any period during which it was used exclusively for permitted purposes by—

    (a)    the recipient of the grant, or

    (b)    any person treated as the recipient by virtue of section 27B of that Act.

(5)    "Permitted purposes" are purposes for which the grant was made and any other purposes agreed by the Housing Corporation or the HCA.

(6)    Where a lease of a dwelling has been granted to a former freeholder in pursuance of paragraph 3 of Schedule 9 to the Leasehold Reform, Housing and Urban Development Act 1993 (c 28) (mandatory leaseback to former freeholder on collective enfranchisement) the reference in subsection (1)(a) above to the freeholder shall be construed as a reference to the leaseholder under that lease.

**[1776]**

**NOTES**

Commencement: to be appointed.

## 183  Interpretation: other expressions

(1)    The definitions in this section apply to sections 180 to 182.

(2)    The HCA gives "assistance" to a person if it—

    (a)    transfers housing or other land to the person,

    (b)    provides infrastructure to the person, or

    (c)    gives financial assistance to the person,

and for this purpose "infrastructure" has the same meaning as in Part 1.

(3)    References to a "registered social landlord" are to a body which, at the time to which the reference relates, was a registered social landlord within the meaning of Part 1 of the Housing Act 1996 (c 52) as it then had effect.

(4)    "Leaseholder" does not include a mortgagee.

(5)    "Long tenancy" has the same meaning as in Part V of the Housing Act 1985 (c 68).

(6)    A person provides a dwelling if the person—

    (a)    acquires, constructs, converts, improves or repairs housing or other land for use as a dwelling, or

    (b)    ensures such acquisition, construction, conversion, improvement or repair by another.

(7)   "Public sector landlord" means anyone falling within section 80(1) of the Housing Act 1985.

**[1777]**

PART I
STATUTES

**NOTES**
Commencement: to be appointed.

### 184   Right to acquire: supplemental

(1)   Section 17 of the Housing Act 1996 (right to acquire: supplemental) applies in relation to the right to acquire under section 180 of this Act with the modifications set out below.

(2)   The modifications are as follows—
  (a)   references to the right to acquire under section 16 of the 1996 Act shall be treated as references to the right to acquire under section 180 of this Act,
  (b)   references to the Welsh Ministers shall be treated as references to the Secretary of State,
  (c)   the reference to registered social landlords shall be treated as a reference to registered providers, and
  (d)   the reference to a resolution of the National Assembly for Wales shall be treated as a reference to a resolution of either House of Parliament.

**[1778]**

**NOTES**
Commencement: to be appointed.

### 185   (Amends the Housing Act 1996, ss 16, 16A at **[1002]**, **[1003]**, and ss 20, 21 thereof.)

*Miscellaneous*

### 186   Former registered providers

Where a person ceases to be a registered provider, sections 171 to 175 continue to apply in respect of any property owned by the person at any time when it was registered.

**[1779]**

**NOTES**
Commencement: to be appointed.

### 187   Change of use, etc

(1)   Where the regulator's consent is required for the disposal of a dwelling by a registered provider, sections 172 to 175 continue to apply in relation to a disposal of the land by the registered provider even if the land has ceased to be a dwelling.

(2)   Sections 172 to 175 also apply in relation to a disposal of land by a registered provider which would fall within Exception 2 or 3 of section 173 but for a change of use of the land by the registered provider.

**[1780]**

**NOTES**
Commencement: to be appointed.

### 188   Trustees

Section 39 of the Settled Land Act 1925 (c 18) (disposal by trustees: best price etc) shall not apply to the disposal of land by a registered provider.

**[1781]**

**NOTES**
Commencement: to be appointed.

### 189   Charities

Nothing in this Chapter authorises a charity to effect a disposal which it would not otherwise have power to effect.

**[1782]**

**NOTES**
Commencement: to be appointed.

*Consents under other legislation*

## 190 Consent to disposals under other legislation

The Secretary of State's functions under the following provisions are transferred to the regulator in so far as they relate to disposals by registered providers—

(a) section 171D of the Housing Act 1985 (c 68) (consent to certain disposals of housing subject to the preserved right to buy),

(b) sections 81 and 133 of the Housing Act 1988 (c 50) (consent to certain disposals of housing obtained from housing action trusts or local authorities), and

(c) section 173 of the Local Government and Housing Act 1989 (c 42) (consent to certain disposals of housing obtained from new town corporations).

**[1783]**

**NOTES**
Commencement: to be appointed.

191 (*Amends the Housing Act 1985, s 171D at* **[539]**, *the Housing Act 1988, ss 81, 133 and the Local Government and Housing Act 1989, s 173.*)

## CHAPTER 6
## REGULATORY POWERS

## 192 Overview

This Chapter—

(a) allows the regulator to set standards for the provision of social housing (sections 193 to 198),

(b) gives the regulator powers to monitor compliance (sections 199 to 210),

(c) gives the regulator a degree of control over the governance of non-profit registered providers (sections 211 to 214),

(d) requires the regulator to give guidance about complaints relating to registered providers and about the use of its powers under this Chapter and Chapter 7 (sections 215 and 216), and

(e) allows the regulator to arrange for the accreditation of managers of social housing (section 217).

**[1784]**

**NOTES**
Commencement: 8 September 2008.

*Standards*

## 193 Provision of social housing

(1) The regulator may set standards for registered providers as to the nature, extent and quality of accommodation, facilities or services provided by them in connection with social housing.

(2) Standards under subsection (1) may, in particular, require registered providers to comply with specified rules about—

(a) criteria for allocating accommodation,

(b) terms of tenancies,

(c) levels of rent (and the rules may, in particular, include provision for minimum or maximum levels of rent or levels of increase or decrease of rent),

(d) maintenance,

(e) procedures for addressing complaints by tenants against landlords,

(f) methods for consulting and informing tenants,

(g) methods of enabling tenants to influence or control the management of their accommodation and environment,

(h) policies and procedures required by section 218A of the Housing Act 1996 (c 52) in connection with anti-social behaviour,

(i) landlords' contribution to the environmental, social and economic well-being of the areas in which their property is situated, and

(j) estate management.

(3) In setting standards the regulator shall have regard to the desirability of registered providers being free to choose how to provide services and conduct business.

**[1785]**

**NOTES**
Commencement: 8 September 2008.

### 194 Management

(1) The regulator may set standards for registered providers in matters relating to the management of their financial and other affairs.

(2) In respect of profit-making registered providers, standards may be made in relation to the management of their affairs only so far as relating to the provision of social housing.

(3) In setting standards the regulator shall have regard to the desirability of registered providers being free to choose how to provide services and conduct business.

**[1786]**

**NOTES**
Commencement: 8 September 2008.

### 195 Code of practice

(1) The regulator may issue a code of practice which—
    (a) relates to a matter addressed by a standard, and
    (b) amplifies the standard.

(2) In considering whether standards have been met the regulator may have regard to a code of practice.

(3) The regulator may revise or withdraw a code of practice.

(4) The regulator shall make arrangements for bringing a code of practice to the attention of registered providers.

**[1787]**

**NOTES**
Commencement: 8 September 2008.

### 196 Consultation

(1) Before setting standards, or issuing, revising or withdrawing a code of practice, the regulator shall consult the following or ensure that they have been consulted—
    (a) one or more bodies appearing to it to represent the interests of registered providers,
    (b) one or more bodies appearing to it to represent the interests of secured creditors of registered providers,
    (c) one or more bodies appearing to it to represent the interests of tenants of social housing,
    (d) the Audit Commission for Local Authorities and the National Health Service in England,
    (e) one or more bodies appearing to it to represent the interests of local housing authorities,
    (f) the HCA, and
    (g) the Secretary of State.

(2) Before setting a standard which would apply to charities, or issuing, revising or withdrawing a code of practice which applies or would apply to charities, the regulator must consult the Charity Commission.

**[1788]**

**NOTES**
Commencement: 8 September 2008 (subject to transitional provisions in SI 2008/2358, art 3(3), (4), as noted to s 112 at **[1707]**).

### 197 Direction by Secretary of State

(1) The Secretary of State may direct the regulator—
    (a) to set a standard under section 193,
    (b) about the content of standards under section 193, or
    (c) to have regard to specified objectives when setting standards under section 193 or 194.

(2) The Secretary of State may give a direction under subsection (1)(a) or (b) only if it relates, in the Secretary of State's opinion, to—
    (a) quality of accommodation,
    (b) rent, or
    (c) involvement by tenants in the management by registered providers of accommodation.

(3) In deciding whether to give a direction the Secretary of State shall, in particular, have regard to the regulator's fundamental objectives.

(4) Before giving a direction the Secretary of State must consult—
    (a) the regulator,
    (b) the HCA,
    (c) the Audit Commission for Local Authorities and the National Health Service in England,

(d)    one or more bodies appearing to the Secretary of State to represent the interests of local housing authorities,

(e)    one or more bodies appearing to the Secretary of State to represent the interests of tenants of social housing, and

(f)    one or more bodies appearing to the Secretary of State to represent the interests of registered providers.

(5)    Before giving a direction about a standard which would apply to charities the Secretary of State must consult the Charity Commission.

(6)    A direction may disapply the requirement to consult under section 196 in relation to specified matters.

(7)    The regulator shall comply with any direction.

(8)    The Secretary of State shall publish—

    (a)    each proposed direction that is the subject of a consultation,

    (b)    each response to a consultation, and

    (c)    each direction.

**[1789]**

**NOTES**

Commencement: 8 September 2008 (subject to transitional provisions in SI 2008/2358, art 3(3), (4), as noted to s 112 at **[1707]**).

## 198  Supplemental

(1)    Failure to meet a standard is a ground for exercising a power in this Chapter or Chapter 7.

(2)    The regulator shall make arrangements for bringing standards to the attention of registered providers.

(3)    The regulator may revise or withdraw standards; and section 196 applies to revising or withdrawing standards as to setting standards.

(4)    Standards may be expressed by reference to documents prepared by others.

(5)    Standards—

    (a)    may make provision generally or only in relation to specified cases, circumstances or areas, and

    (b)    may make different provision for different cases, circumstances or areas.

**[1790]**

**NOTES**

Commencement: 8 September 2008 (sub-ss (2)–(5)); to be appointed (sub-s (1)).

*Monitoring*

## 199  Survey

(1)    This section applies where the regulator suspects that a registered provider may be failing to maintain premises in accordance with standards under section 193.

(2)    The regulator may arrange for a survey of the condition of the premises by an authorised person.

(3)    In subsection (2) "authorised person" means a member of the regulator's staff, or another person, authorised in writing by the regulator for the purposes of this section.

(4)    An authorised person may enter the premises at any reasonable time and carry out the survey.

(5)    Before carrying out the survey an authorised person must give the registered provider at least 28 days' notice.

(6)    A registered provider who receives notice of a survey must give each occupier of the premises at least 7 days' notice.

(7)    After carrying out a survey an authorised person must produce a written report.

(8)    The regulator must give the registered provider a copy of the report.

**[1791]**

**NOTES**

Commencement: to be appointed.

## 200  Survey: supplemental

(1)    An authorised person carrying out a survey, or seeking to enter premises in order to carry out a survey, must produce a copy of the authorisation on request by an occupier.

(2)    The regulator may require the registered provider to pay some or all of the costs of the survey and report.

(3)    A registered provider who fails without reasonable excuse to comply with section 199(6) commits an offence.

(4)    A registered provider, or an officer of a registered provider, who obstructs an authorised person in exercising a power under section 199 commits an offence.

(5)    A person guilty of an offence under this section is liable on summary conviction to a fine not exceeding level 3 on the standard scale.

(6)    Proceedings for an offence under this section may be brought only by or with the consent of—

   (a)    the regulator, or
   (b)    the Director of Public Prosecutions.

**[1792]**

**NOTES**
   Commencement: to be appointed.

## 201    Inspections

(1)    The regulator may arrange for a person to inspect—
   (a)    a registered provider's performance of its functions in relation to the provision of social housing, or
   (b)    the financial or other affairs of a registered provider.

(2)    The person must not be a member of the regulator's staff.

(3)    If the purpose (or main purpose) of an inspection is to assess a registered provider's performance by reference to standards under section 193 the regulator—
   (a)    shall invite the Audit Commission to carry out the inspection, and
   (b)    may arrange for another person to carry out the inspection only if the Audit Commission declines.

(4)    The regulator may direct a person carrying out an inspection to discontinue it.

(5)    An inspection may be general or specific.

(6)    The regulator shall reimburse costs incurred by the Audit Commission in carrying out an inspection.

(7)    If the regulator arranges for a person other than the Audit Commission to carry out an inspection the arrangements may include provision about payments.

(8)    In this section and sections 202 and 203 "the Audit Commission" means the Audit Commission for Local Authorities and the National Health Service in England.

**[1793]**

**NOTES**
   Commencement: to be appointed.

## 202    Inspections: supplemental

(1)    After carrying out an inspection under section 201 the person carrying out the inspection must produce a written report.

(2)    The regulator—
   (a)    must give the registered provider a copy of the report, and
   (b)    may publish the report and related information.

(3)    The person who carried out the inspection may publish the report and related information (whether or not the regulator has done so).

(4)    The Secretary of State may by order authorise the regulator to charge fees for inspections.

(5)    An inspected registered provider must pay any fee charged.

(6)    Before making an order the Secretary of State shall consult—
   (a)    the regulator,
   (b)    one or more bodies appearing to the Secretary of State to represent the interests of registered providers,
   (c)    the Audit Commission, and
   (d)    such other persons as the Secretary of State thinks appropriate.

(7)    The regulator shall prescribe a scale of fees for inspections, having consulted—
   (a)    the Secretary of State,

    (b)    one or more bodies appearing to the regulator to represent the interests of registered providers, and

    (c)    the Audit Commission.

**[1794]**

**NOTES**
Commencement: 8 September 2008 (sub-ss (4), (6), (7), for certain purposes); to be appointed (otherwise).

## 203 Inspector's powers

    (1)    An inspector may by notice require a person to provide specified documents or information.

    (2)    The power under subsection (1) may be exercised only in relation to documents and information of a kind in respect of which the regulator can impose a requirement under section 107.

    (3)    Sections 107(3) to (7) and 108 apply for the purposes of subsection (1) (with any necessary modifications).

    (4)    An inspector may at any reasonable time—
    (a)    enter premises occupied by the registered provider which is being inspected, and
    (b)    inspect, copy or take away documents found there.

    (5)    The reference to documents found on premises includes—
    (a)    documents stored on computers or electronic storage devices on the premises, and
    (b)    documents stored elsewhere which can be accessed by computers on the premises.

    (6)    The power to inspect documents includes the power to inspect any computer or electronic storage device on which they have been created or stored.

    (7)    An inspector may require any person on the premises to provide such facilities or assistance as the inspector reasonably requests.

    (8)    For the purposes of subsections (5) and (6) an inspector may require any person having charge of a computer to provide such assistance as the inspector reasonably requests.

    (9)    It is an offence for a person without reasonable excuse to obstruct an inspector exercising the powers conferred by subsections (4) to (8).

    (10)    A person guilty of an offence is liable on summary conviction to a fine not exceeding level 3 on the standard scale.

    (11)    Proceedings for an offence may be brought only by or with the consent of—
    (a)    the regulator, or
    (b)    the Director of Public Prosecutions.

    (12)    In this section "inspector" means—
    (a)    a person authorised in writing by the Audit Commission to exercise the powers under this section for the purpose of an inspection carried out by the Audit Commission under section 201, or
    (b)    a person authorised in writing by the regulator to exercise the powers under this section for the purpose of any other inspection under that section.

**[1795]**

**NOTES**
Commencement: to be appointed.

## 204 Performance information

    (1)    The regulator may require a registered provider—
    (a)    to prepare an annual report assessing the provider's performance by reference to standards under section 193 or 194, and
    (b)    to send the report to the regulator within a specified period.

    (2)    A requirement may specify matters to be covered by a report.

    (3)    Failure to comply with a requirement without reasonable excuse is an offence.

    (4)    A person guilty of an offence is liable on summary conviction to a fine not exceeding level 5 on the standard scale.

    (5)    Proceedings for an offence may be brought only by or with the consent of—
    (a)    the regulator, or
    (b)    the Director of Public Prosecutions.

**[1796]**

**NOTES**
Commencement: to be appointed.

### 205  Publication of performance information

(1)    The regulator shall publish, at least once a year, information about the performance of registered providers.

(2)    In particular, the regulator shall include information likely to be useful to—
(a)    tenants,
(b)    potential tenants, and
(c)    local authorities.

**[1797]**

**NOTES**
Commencement: to be appointed.

### 206  Inquiry

(1)    If the regulator suspects that the affairs of a registered provider may have been mismanaged, the regulator may hold an inquiry.

(2)    The regulator shall appoint one or more individuals to conduct the inquiry.

(3)    An individual is eligible for appointment only if the individual is independent of the regulator.

(4)    Individuals are independent of the regulator if they and the members of their family—
(a)    are not members, employees or consultants of the regulator, and
(b)    have not been members or employees of the regulator within the previous five years.

(5)    "Consultant" means an individual providing services to the regulator otherwise than by virtue of employment with the regulator or an appointment under this section.

**[1798]**

**NOTES**
Commencement: to be appointed.

### 207  Inquiry: supplemental

(1)    The individual or individuals conducting an inquiry ("the inquirer") shall determine its procedure.

(2)    The inquirer may consider the affairs of a profit-making registered provider only so far as relating to social housing.

(3)    The inquirer may consider affairs of a body which at the material time was a subsidiary or associate of the registered provider.

(4)    The inquirer may make interim reports.

(5)    The inquirer shall make a final report on matters specified by the regulator.

(6)    The regulator may arrange for the publication of all or part of an interim or final report.

(7)    A local authority may contribute to the regulator's expenses in connection with an inquiry.
**[1799]**

**NOTES**
Commencement: to be appointed.

### 208  Inquiry: evidence

(1)    The inquirer may by notice require a person to provide specified documents or information.

(2)    The notice may, in particular, require evidence to be given on oath (and the inquirer may administer oaths for that purpose).

(3)    The power under subsection (1) may be exercised only in relation to documents and information of a kind in respect of which the regulator can impose a requirement under section 107.

(4)    Sections 107(3) to (7) and 108 apply for the purposes of this section (with any necessary modifications).

**[1800]**

**NOTES**
Commencement: to be appointed.

### 209  Inquiry: charities

(1)    An inquiry may be held in relation to a registered charity only if it has received public assistance.

(2)   An inquiry in relation to a registered charity may only relate to its activities relating to housing.

(3)   If an inquiry is held in relation to a registered charity the regulator shall notify the Charity Commission.

**[1801]**

**NOTES**
Commencement: to be appointed.

## 210   Extraordinary audit

(1)   Where an inquiry in respect of a registered provider is being held, or has been held, under section 206, the regulator may require the registered provider to allow its accounts and balance sheet to be audited by a qualified auditor appointed by the regulator.

(2)   "Qualified auditor" means a person eligible for appointment as auditor of the registered provider's ordinary accounts.

(3)   On completion of the audit, the auditor shall report to the regulator about such matters and in such form as the regulator determines.

(4)   The revenue accounts of a registered charity may be audited under this section only insofar as they relate to its housing activities.

(5)   The registered provider shall pay the costs of the audit (including the auditor's remuneration).

**[1802]**

**NOTES**
Commencement: to be appointed.

*Management and constitution*

## 211   Non-profit providers only

This group of sections applies only to non-profit registered providers.

**[1803]**

**NOTES**
Commencement: to be appointed.

## 212   Industrial and provident society: change of rules

(1)   This section applies to an industrial and provident society.

(2)   An amendment of the society's rules requires consent if it—
  (a)   alters the society's objects,
  (b)   makes provision about the distribution of assets to members, or
  (c)   enables the society to become, or cease to be, a subsidiary or associate of another body.

(3)   An amendment of the rules which requires consent is effective only if the regulator has first consented.

(4)   The regulator may not consent to an amendment which it thinks would turn the society into a profit-making organisation.

(5)   The society must notify the regulator of an amendment of the rules which does not require consent.

(6)   In relation to an amendment which requires consent the requirement in section 10(1) of the Industrial and Provident Societies Act 1965 (c 12) (sending copies of amendment of rules to FSA) is satisfied only if the copies are accompanied by a copy of the regulator's consent.

(7)   The preceding provisions of this section shall be treated as if they formed part of that Act as well as of this Act.

(8)   The Secretary of State may by order amend the list in subsection (2).

**[1804]**

**NOTES**
Commencement: 8 September 2008 (sub-ss (2), (8)); to be appointed (otherwise).

## 213   Charity: change of objects

(1)   This section applies to a registered charity which is not a registered company.

(2) An amendment of the charity's objects is effective only if the Charity Commission has first consented.

(3) Before giving consent the Charity Commission must consult the regulator.

**[1805]**

**NOTES**
Commencement: to be appointed.

### 214 Companies: change of articles

(1) This section applies to a registered company.

(2) An amendment of the company's articles of association requires consent if it—
   (a) alters the company's objects,
   (b) makes provision about the distribution of assets to members, or
   (c) enables the company to become, or cease to be, a subsidiary or associate of another body.

(3) An amendment of the articles of association which requires consent is effective only if the regulator has first consented.

(4) The regulator may not consent to an amendment which it thinks would turn the company into a profit-making organisation.

(5) The company must notify the regulator—
   (a) of an amendment of the articles of association which does not require consent, or
   (b) of a change to its name or registered office.

(6) In relation to an amendment which requires consent the requirement in section 30 of the Companies Act 2006 (c 46) (sending copy of resolution to registrar) is satisfied only if the copy is accompanied by a copy of the regulator's consent.

(7) The Secretary of State may by order amend the list in subsection (2).

**[1806]**

**NOTES**
Commencement: 8 September 2008 (sub-ss (2), (7)); to be appointed (otherwise).

*Guidance*

### 215 Use of intervention powers

(1) The regulator shall publish—
   (a) guidance about complaints to the regulator about the performance of registered providers, and
   (b) guidance about how it uses and intends to use powers under this Chapter and Chapter 7.

(2) Guidance under subsection (1)(a) must, in particular, specify—
   (a) the procedure to be followed in making a complaint,
   (b) the criteria used by the regulator in deciding whether to investigate a complaint, and
   (c) periods within which the regulator aims to inform complainants of the result of complaints.

(3) The regulator shall have regard to guidance under this section.

**[1807]**

**NOTES**
Commencement: 8 September 2008 (sub-ss (1), (2)); to be appointed (sub-s (3)).

### 216 Consultation

Before giving guidance under section 215 the regulator must consult—
   (a) one or more bodies appearing to it to represent the interests of registered providers,
   (b) one or more bodies appearing to it to represent the interests of tenants,
   (c) one or more bodies appearing to it to represent the interests of local housing authorities,
   (d) the Audit Commission for Local Authorities and the National Health Service in England, and
   (e) the HCA.

**[1808]**

**NOTES**
Commencement: 8 September 2008 (subject to transitional provisions in SI 2008/2358, art 3(3), (4), as noted to s 112 at **[1707]**).

*Managers of social housing*

## 217  Accreditation

(1)  The regulator may operate a scheme for the purpose of accrediting persons who provide services in connection with the management of social housing.

(2)  The regulator may approve a scheme operated by someone else for that purpose.

(3)  Approval may be withdrawn.

(4)  A scheme may include provision about—
  (a)  eligibility for accreditation;
  (b)  standards to be met by accredited persons (which may operate by reference to standards under section 193);
  (c)  monitoring compliance;
  (d)  complaints against accredited persons;
  (e)  renewal, suspension and withdrawal of accreditation.

(5)  Accreditation, or continued accreditation, may be conditional on the payment of fees.

(6)  Standards under section 193 may refer to accreditation under this section.

**[1809]**

**NOTES**
Commencement: to be appointed.

CHAPTER 7
ENFORCEMENT POWERS

*General*

## 218  Exercise of enforcement powers

(1)  This section applies where the regulator is deciding—
  (a)  whether to exercise a power under this Chapter,
  (b)  which power under this Chapter to exercise, or
  (c)  how to exercise a power under this Chapter.

(2)  The regulator shall consider—
  (a)  the desirability of registered providers being free to choose how to provide services and conduct business;
  (b)  whether the failure or other problem concerned is serious or trivial;
  (c)  whether the failure or other problem is a recurrent or isolated incident;
  (d)  the speed with which the failure or other problem needs to be addressed.

**[1810]**

**NOTES**
Commencement: to be appointed.

*Enforcement notice*

## 219  Overview

This group of sections allows the regulator to require a registered provider to take specified action to resolve a specified failure or other problem.

**[1811]**

**NOTES**
Commencement: to be appointed.

## 220  Grounds for giving notice

(1)  The regulator may give an enforcement notice to a registered provider if the regulator is satisfied that—
  (a)  any of the following cases applies, and
  (b)  giving an enforcement notice is appropriate (whether it is likely to be sufficient in itself or a prelude to further action).

(2)  Case 1 is where the registered provider has failed to meet a standard under section 193 or 194.

(3)  Case 2 is where the affairs of the registered provider have been mismanaged.

(4)  Case 3 is where the registered provider has failed to comply with an earlier enforcement notice.

(5)    Case 4 is where the registered provider has failed to publish information in accordance with a requirement under section 228(3) or 240(3).

(6)    Case 5 is where the interests of tenants of the registered provider require protection.

(7)    Case 6 is where the assets of the registered provider require protection.

(8)    Case 7 is where the registered provider has given an undertaking under section 125 and failed to comply with it.

(9)    Case 8 is where the registered provider has failed to pay an annual fee under section 117(2).

(10)    Case 9 is where an offence under this Part has been committed by the registered provider.

(11)    Case 10 is where the registered provider has failed to comply with an order made by an ombudsman appointed by virtue of section 124.

(12)    Where the regulator is satisfied that an offence under this Part has been committed in respect of a registered provider but by another person (such as a member, employee or agent of the registered provider)—

    (a)    Case 9 applies,

    (b)    the regulator may give an enforcement notice to the other person, and

    (c)    this Chapter applies with the substitution of references to that other person for references to the registered provider.

**[1812]**

**NOTES**

Commencement: to be appointed.

### 221   Content

(1)    An enforcement notice must—

    (a)    specify the grounds on which it is given,

    (b)    specify the action the regulator wants the registered provider to take in response to the notice,

    (c)    specify when the action is to be taken (which may be immediately on receipt of the notice), and

    (d)    explain the effect of sections 223 to 225.

(2)    The action specified in an enforcement notice may include publishing the notice in a specified manner.

**[1813]**

**NOTES**

Commencement: to be appointed.

### 222   Notifying HCA

If the regulator gives an enforcement notice it must send a copy to the HCA.

**[1814]**

**NOTES**

Commencement: to be appointed.

### 223   Appeal

A registered provider who is given an enforcement notice may appeal to the High Court.

**[1815]**

**NOTES**

Commencement: to be appointed.

### 224   Withdrawal

The regulator may withdraw an enforcement notice by notice to the registered provider.

**[1816]**

**NOTES**

Commencement: to be appointed.

### 225   Sanction

(1)    If a registered provider does not comply with an enforcement notice the regulator shall consider exercising another power under Chapter 6 or this Chapter.

(2)    In the case of an enforcement notice given to a person other than the registered provider by virtue of section 220(12), the regulator may only—

(a) exercise the power to issue a penalty notice to the person in accordance with the next group of sections, or

(b) take steps to have the person prosecuted for the offence by reference to which the enforcement notice was given.

(3) A person to whom an enforcement notice is given on the ground in Case 9 of section 220 may not be prosecuted for the offence by reference to which the enforcement notice was given unless the person fails to comply with the enforcement notice.

**[1817]**

**NOTES**
Commencement: to be appointed.

*Penalty*

## 226 Overview

This group of sections allows the regulator to penalise failures on the part of registered providers by the imposition of fines.

**[1818]**

**NOTES**
Commencement: to be appointed.

## 227 Grounds for imposition

(1) The regulator may require a registered provider to pay a penalty if the regulator is satisfied that—

(a) any of the following cases applies, and

(b) the imposition of a penalty is appropriate (whether or not as part of a response including other action).

(2) Case 1 is where the registered provider has failed to meet a standard under section 193 or 194.

(3) Case 2 is where the affairs of the registered provider have been mismanaged.

(4) Case 3 is where the registered provider has failed to comply with an enforcement notice.

(5) Case 4 is where the registered provider has given an undertaking under section 125 and failed to comply with it.

(6) Case 5 is where the registered provider has failed to pay an annual fee under section 117(2).

(7) Case 6 is where an offence under this Part has been committed by the registered provider.

(8) Where the regulator is satisfied that an offence under this Part has been committed in respect of a registered provider but by another person (such as a member, employee or agent of the registered provider)—

(a) Case 6 applies,

(b) the regulator may require the other person to pay a penalty, and

(c) this Chapter applies with the substitution of references to that other person for references to the registered provider.

(9) In order to rely on Case 6 the regulator must be satisfied beyond reasonable doubt that it applies.

**[1819]**

**NOTES**
Commencement: to be appointed.

## 228 Imposition

(1) A penalty is imposed by the regulator giving notice (a "penalty notice") to the registered provider.

(2) The notice must specify—

(a) the grounds on which the penalty is imposed,

(b) the amount of the penalty,

(c) how the penalty must be paid,

(d) a period within which it must be paid, and

(e) *any interest or additional penalty which, by virtue of section 234(2), is payable in the event of late payment.*

(3) The notice may require the registered provider to publish information about the penalty in a specified manner.

(4) The notice must explain the effect of sections 234(1), (3) and (6) and 235.

(5)    The Secretary of State—

    (a)    shall make regulations about the period under subsection (2)(d),

    (b)    may make other regulations about the form and content of a penalty notice, and

    (c)    may make regulations about the manner in which a penalty notice is given.

**[1820]**

**NOTES**

Commencement: 1 April 2009 (sub-s (5), for the purpose of enabling the Secretary of State to make regulations); to be appointed (otherwise).

### 229   Amount

(1)    The amount of a penalty imposed on the ground specified in Case 6 of section 227 may not exceed the maximum amount of fine that a magistrates' court could impose for the relevant offence.

(2)    The amount of a penalty imposed on the ground specified in any other Case of that section may not exceed £5,000.

(3)    The Secretary of State may by order amend the amount specified in subsection (2).

**[1821]**

**NOTES**

Commencement: to be appointed.

### 230   Warning

(1)    Before giving a penalty notice to a registered provider the regulator must give the provider a notice (a "pre-penalty warning")—

    (a)    specifying grounds on which the regulator thinks a penalty could be imposed,

    (b)    warning the provider that the regulator is considering imposing a penalty,

    (c)    including any indication that the regulator is able to give of the likely amount of any penalty, and

    (d)    explaining the effect of sections 231, 234(1), (3) and (6) and 235.

(2)    If the regulator gives a pre-penalty warning it must send a copy to—

    (a)    the HCA, and

    (b)    any other persons it thinks appropriate.

(3)    For the purposes of subsection (2)(b) the regulator shall consider, in particular, any person who provided information as a result of which the pre-penalty warning is given.

(4)    A pre-penalty warning must—

    (a)    refer to section 125 (voluntary undertaking), and

    (b)    indicate whether or to what extent the regulator would accept a voluntary undertaking instead of, or in mitigation of, a penalty.

(5)    A pre-penalty warning may be combined with notice under one or more of sections 242, 248, 250 and 252.

**[1822]**

**NOTES**

Commencement: to be appointed.

### 231   Representations

(1)    A pre-penalty warning must specify a period during which the registered provider may make representations to the regulator.

(2)    The period must—

    (a)    be a period of at least 28 days, and

    (b)    begin with the date on which the registered provider receives the pre-penalty warning.

(3)    Representations may concern—

    (a)    whether a penalty should be imposed;

    (b)    the amount of any penalty that may be imposed.

(4)    After the end of the period specified under subsection (1) the regulator shall—

    (a)    consider any representations made, and

    (b)    decide whether to impose a penalty.

**[1823]**

**NOTES**

Commencement: to be appointed.

## 232  Notifying HCA

If the regulator imposes a penalty it must send a copy of the penalty notice to the HCA.

**[1824]**

**NOTES**

Commencement: to be appointed.

## 233  Destination

(1)  This section applies where the regulator receives money by way of penalty.

(2)  The regulator may deduct a sum which represents—
   (a)  the direct costs to the regulator of imposing and enforcing the penalty, and
   (b)  a reasonable share of expenditure by the regulator which is indirectly referable to the imposition and enforcement of the penalty.

(3)  Any excess shall be paid to the HCA, to be used for purposes which appear to it to amount to investment in social housing.

**[1825]**

**NOTES**

Commencement: to be appointed.

## 234  Enforcement

(1)  A penalty shall be treated as a debt owed to the regulator.

(2)  The Treasury may make regulations authorising the regulator—
   (a)  to charge interest on penalty not paid during the period specified under section 228(2)(d);
   (b)  to impose one or more additional penalties where a penalty is not paid during that period.

(3)  Interest and additional penalty shall be treated as penalty (and may have the effect of increasing the penalty above a limit set by section 229).

(4)  Regulations under subsection (2)(a) may provide for an interest rate to be—
   (a)  set by a specified person, or
   (b)  determined in accordance with the regulations.

(5)  A penalty notice may include provision allowing a discount if the penalty is paid on or before a date specified in the notice (falling within the period specified under section 228(2)(d)).

(6)  A person to whom a penalty notice is given on the ground in Case 6 of section 227 may not be prosecuted for the offence by reference to which the penalty notice was given.

**[1826]**

**NOTES**

Commencement: 1 April 2009 (sub-ss (2), (4), for the purpose of enabling the Treasury to make regulations); to be appointed (otherwise).

## 235  Appeal

A registered provider who is given a penalty notice may appeal to the High Court against—
   (a)  the imposition of the penalty,
   (b)  its amount, or
   (c)  both.

**[1827]**

**NOTES**

Commencement: to be appointed.

*Compensation*

## 236  Overview

This group of sections allows the regulator to award compensation to a victim of a failure on the part of a registered provider.

**[1828]**

**NOTES**

Commencement: to be appointed.

### 237　Grounds for award

(1)　The regulator may require a registered provider to pay compensation if the regulator is satisfied that—

    (a)　either of the following cases applies, and

    (b)　the award of compensation is appropriate (whether or not as part of a response including other action).

(2)　Case 1 is where the registered provider has failed to meet a standard under section 193 or 194.

(3)　Case 2 is where the registered provider has given an undertaking under section 125 and failed to comply with it.

**[1829]**

**NOTES**

    Commencement: to be appointed.

### 238　Nature

(1)　Compensation in respect of a failure may be awarded to one or more persons who have suffered as a result of the failure.

(2)　But an award may be made only to—

    (a)　a specified tenant of social housing provided by the registered provider,

    (b)　each member of a specified class of tenants of social housing provided by the registered provider, or

    (c)　each member of the class of tenants of social housing provided by the registered provider.

**[1830]**

**NOTES**

    Commencement: to be appointed.

### 239　Housing ombudsman compensation

(1)　The regulator may not award compensation to a person in respect of a matter if an ombudsman appointed by virtue of section 124 has awarded compensation to the person in respect of the matter.

(2)　But if compensation awarded by an ombudsman by virtue of section 124 has not been paid as required, the regulator may award compensation.

**[1831]**

**NOTES**

    Commencement: to be appointed.

### 240　Award

(1)　Compensation is awarded by the regulator giving notice (a "compensation notice") to—

    (a)　the registered provider, and

    (b)　the person to be compensated.

(2)　The notice must specify—

    (a)　the grounds on which the compensation is awarded,

    (b)　the amount of the compensation,

    (c)　the person to be compensated,

    (d)　any interest or additional compensation which, by virtue of section 244(2), is payable in the event of late payment, and

    (e)　a period within which it must be paid.

(3)　The notice may require the registered provider to publish information about the compensation award in a specified manner.

(4)　The notice must explain the effect of sections 244(1) and (3) and 245.

(5)　The Secretary of State—

    (a)　shall make regulations about the period under subsection (2)(e),

    (b)　may make other regulations about the form and content of a compensation notice, and

    (c)　may make regulations about the manner in which a compensation notice is given.

**[1832]**

**NOTES**

    Commencement: 1 April 2009 (sub-s (5), for the purpose of enabling the Secretary of State to make regulations); to be appointed (otherwise).

## 241 Impact

(1) This section applies when the regulator is considering—
  (a) whether to award compensation, or
  (b) the amount of compensation to award.

(2) The regulator must take account of any information available to it about the financial situation of the registered provider.

(3) The regulator must consider the likely impact of the compensation on the registered provider's ability to provide services.

(4) In particular, the regulator must aim to avoid—
  (a) jeopardising the financial viability of the registered provider,
  (b) preventing the registered provider from honouring financial commitments, or
  (c) preventing the registered provider from taking action to remedy the matters on the grounds of which the compensation might be awarded.

**[1833]**

**NOTES**
Commencement: to be appointed.

## 242 Warning

(1) Before giving a compensation notice to a registered provider the regulator must give the provider a notice (a "pre-compensation warning")—
  (a) specifying grounds on which the regulator thinks compensation could be awarded,
  (b) warning the provider that the regulator is considering awarding compensation to a specified person,
  (c) including any indication that the regulator is able to give of the likely amount of any compensation, and
  (d) explaining the effect of sections 243, 244(1) and (3) and 245.

(2) Before giving a pre-compensation warning the regulator must consult the person appointed by virtue of section 124 as the ombudsman for the scheme of which the registered provider is a member.

(3) If the regulator gives a pre-compensation warning it must send a copy to—
  (a) the HCA, and
  (b) any other persons it thinks appropriate.

(4) For the purposes of subsection (3)(b) the regulator shall consider, in particular, any person who provided information as a result of which the pre-compensation warning is given.

(5) A pre-compensation warning must—
  (a) refer to section 125 (voluntary undertaking), and
  (b) indicate whether or to what extent the regulator would accept a voluntary undertaking instead of, or in mitigation of, awarding compensation.

(6) A pre-compensation warning may be combined with notice under one or more of sections 230, 248, 250 and 252.

**[1834]**

**NOTES**
Commencement: to be appointed.

## 243 Representations

(1) A pre-compensation warning must specify a period during which the registered provider may make representations to the regulator.

(2) The period must—
  (a) be a period of at least 28 days, and
  (b) begin with the date on which the registered provider receives the pre-compensation warning.

(3) Representations may address—
  (a) whether compensation should be awarded;
  (b) the amount of any compensation that may be awarded.

(4) After the end of the period specified under subsection (1) the regulator shall—
  (a) consider any representations made, and
  (b) decide whether to award compensation.

**[1835]**

**NOTES**
Commencement: to be appointed.

## 244 Enforcement

(1) Compensation shall be treated as a debt owed to the person to whom it is awarded.

(2) The Treasury may make regulations authorising the regulator—
 (a) to award interest on compensation not paid during the period specified under section 240(2)(e);
 (b) to award additional compensation where compensation is not paid during that period.

(3) Interest and additional compensation shall be treated as compensation.

(4) Regulations under subsection (2)(a) may provide for an interest rate to be—
 (a) set by a specified person, or
 (b) determined in accordance with the regulations.

**[1836]**

**NOTES**
Commencement: 1 April 2009 (sub-ss (2), (4), for the purpose of enabling the Treasury to make regulations); to be appointed (otherwise).

## 245 Appeal

A registered provider who is given a compensation notice may appeal to the High Court against—
 (a) the award of compensation,
 (b) its amount, or
 (c) both.

**[1837]**

**NOTES**
Commencement: to be appointed.

*Management etc*

## 246 Overview

This group of sections gives the regulator various powers in relation to the management and constitution of registered providers.

**[1838]**

**NOTES**
Commencement: to be appointed.

## 247 Management tender

(1) This section applies if the regulator is satisfied that—
 (a) a registered provider has failed to meet a standard under section 193 or 194, or
 (b) the affairs of a registered provider have been mismanaged in relation to social housing.

(2) The regulator may require the registered provider to implement a process specified by the regulator for the purpose of—
 (a) inviting persons to apply to undertake management functions of the registered provider, and
 (b) selecting from the applications and making an appointment.

(3) A requirement may relate to—
 (a) the registered provider's affairs generally in so far as they relate to social housing, or
 (b) specified affairs relating to social housing.

(4) A requirement must include—
 (a) provision about the constitution of a selection panel (which must include provision for ensuring representation of tenants' interests),
 (b) provision for ensuring best procurement practice, and
 (c) provision about the terms and conditions on which the manager is to be appointed (including provision about—
  (i) setting, monitoring and enforcing performance standards, and
  (ii) resources).

**[1839]**

**NOTES**
Commencement: to be appointed.

**248  Section 247: supplemental**

(1)  Before acting under section 247(2) the regulator must give the registered provider a notice—
  (a)  specifying grounds on which action might be taken under that section,
  (b)  warning the provider that the regulator is considering action under that section, and
  (c)  explaining the effect of this section.

(2)  The notice must specify a period during which the registered provider may make representations to the regulator.

(3)  The period must—
  (a)  be a period of at least 28 days, and
  (b)  begin with the date on which the registered provider receives the notice.

(4)  The regulator must send a copy of a notice under subsection (1) to—
  (a)  the HCA, and
  (b)  any other persons it thinks appropriate (having regard, in particular, to any person who provided information as a result of which the notice is given).

(5)  A notice under subsection (1) must—
  (a)  refer to section 125 (voluntary undertaking), and
  (b)  indicate whether or to what extent the regulator would accept a voluntary undertaking instead of, or in mitigation of, action under section 247(2).

(6)  Notice under subsection (1) may be combined with notice under one or more of sections 230, 242, 250 and 252.

(7)  In imposing a requirement the regulator must have regard to views of—
  (a)  relevant tenants,
  (b)  the registered provider,
  (c)  the HCA, and
  (d)  if the regulator thinks it appropriate, any relevant local housing authority.

(8)  If the regulator imposes a requirement it must send a copy to the HCA.

(9)  A registered provider may appeal to the High Court against a requirement under section 247(2).

**[1840]**

**NOTES**
Commencement: to be appointed.

**249  Management transfer**

(1)  This section applies if as a result of an inquiry under section 206 or an audit under section 210 the regulator is satisfied that—
  (a)  the affairs of a registered provider have been mismanaged in relation to social housing, or
  (b)  a transfer of certain of a registered provider's management functions would be likely to improve the management of some or all of its social housing.

(2)  The regulator may require the registered provider to transfer management functions to a specified person.

(3)  A requirement to transfer management functions may be imposed only with the Secretary of State's consent (both as to the transfer and the terms).

(4)  A requirement may relate to—
  (a)  the registered provider's affairs generally in so far as they relate to social housing, or
  (b)  specified affairs relating to social housing.

(5)  Transfer shall be on terms and conditions (including as to remuneration) specified in, or determined in accordance with, the requirement.

(6)  A transferee manager shall have—
  (a)  any power specified in the requirement, and
  (b)  any other power in relation to the registered provider's affairs required by the manager for the purposes specified in the requirement (including the power to enter into agreements and take other action on behalf of the registered provider).

**[1841]**

**NOTES**
Commencement: to be appointed.

**250   Section 249: supplemental**

(1)   Before acting under section 249(2) the regulator must give the registered provider a notice—

    (a)   specifying grounds on which action might be taken under that section,

    (b)   warning the provider that the regulator is considering action under that section, and

    (c)   explaining the effect of this section.

(2)   The notice must specify a period during which the registered provider may make representations to the regulator.

(3)   The period must—

    (a)   be a period of at least 28 days, and

    (b)   begin with the date on which the registered provider receives the notice.

(4)   The regulator must send a copy of a notice under subsection (1) to—

    (a)   the HCA, and

    (b)   any other persons it thinks appropriate (having regard, in particular, to any person who provided information as a result of which the notice is given).

(5)   A notice under subsection (1) must—

    (a)   refer to section 125, and

    (b)   indicate whether or to what extent the regulator would accept a voluntary undertaking under that section instead of, or in mitigation of, action under section 249(2).

(6)   Notice under subsection (1) may be combined with notice under one or more of sections 230, 242, 248 and 252.

(7)   In imposing a requirement the regulator must have regard to views of—

    (a)   relevant tenants,

    (b)   the registered provider,

    (c)   the HCA, and

    (d)   if the regulator thinks it appropriate, any relevant local housing authority.

(8)   If the regulator imposes a requirement it must send a copy to the HCA.

(9)   A registered provider may appeal to the High Court against a requirement under section 249(2).

**[1842]**

**NOTES**

Commencement: to be appointed.

**251   Appointment of manager**

(1)   This section applies if the regulator is satisfied that—

    (a)   a registered provider has failed to meet a standard under section 193 or 194, or

    (b)   the affairs of a registered provider have been mismanaged in relation to social housing.

(2)   The regulator may—

    (a)   appoint an individual as a manager of the registered provider, or

    (b)   require the registered provider to appoint an individual as a manager.

(3)   An appointment or requirement may relate to a manager—

    (a)   of the registered provider's affairs generally in so far as they relate to social housing, or

    (b)   of specified affairs relating to social housing.

(4)   Appointment shall be on terms and conditions (including as to remuneration) specified in, or determined in accordance with, the appointment or requirement.

(5)   A manager shall have—

    (a)   any power specified in the appointment or requirement, and

    (b)   any other power in relation to the registered provider's affairs required by the manager for the purposes specified in the appointment or requirement (including the power to enter into agreements and take other action on behalf of the registered provider).

**[1843]**

**NOTES**

Commencement: to be appointed.

**252   Section 251: supplemental**

(1)   Before acting under section 251(2) the regulator must give the registered provider a notice—

    (a)   specifying grounds on which action might be taken under that section,

    (b)   warning the provider that the regulator is considering action under that section, and

    (c)   explaining the effect of this section.

(2) The notice must specify a period during which the registered provider may make representations to the regulator.

(3) The period must—
- (a) be a period of at least 28 days, and
- (b) begin with the date on which the registered provider receives the notice.

(4) The regulator must send a copy of a notice under subsection (1) to—
- (a) the HCA, and
- (b) any other persons it thinks appropriate (having regard, in particular, to any person who provided information as a result of which the notice is given).

(5) A notice under subsection (1) must—
- (a) refer to section 125 (voluntary undertaking), and
- (b) indicate whether or to what extent the regulator would accept a voluntary undertaking instead of, or in mitigation of, action under section 251(2).

(6) Notice under subsection (1) may be combined with notice under one or more of sections 230, 242, 248 and 250.

(7) The regulator must notify the HCA of an appointment or requirement under section 251(2).

(8) The regulator may require a manager to report to the regulator on the affairs specified in the appointment or requirement under section 251(3).

(9) A registered provider may appeal to the High Court against an appointment or requirement under section 251(2).

[1844]

---

**NOTES**

Commencement: to be appointed.

---

### 253 Transfer of land

(1) This section applies if as a result of an inquiry under section 206 or an audit under section 210 the regulator is satisfied that—
- (a) the affairs of a registered provider have been mismanaged in relation to social housing, or
- (b) a transfer of land by a registered provider would be likely to improve the management of the land.

(2) The regulator may require the registered provider to transfer specified land—
- (a) to the regulator, or
- (b) to another specified registered provider.

(3) A requirement may be imposed on a profit-making registered provider only in relation to its social housing and associated land.

(4) For the purposes of subsection (3) land is associated with social housing if the regulator thinks that it is used in connection with the social housing or its management.

(5) A requirement may not be imposed on a non-profit registered provider requiring it to transfer land to a profit-making registered provider.

(6) A requirement may not be imposed on a registered charity.

(7) A requirement may be imposed on a charity which is not registered (C1), but only for transfer to another charity (C2) whose objects the regulator thinks are similar to those of C1.

[1845]

---

**NOTES**

Commencement: to be appointed.

---

### 254 Section 253: supplemental

(1) A transfer under section 253 shall be on terms specified in, or determined in accordance with, the requirement.

(2) The price shall be not less than an amount certified by the district valuer as the amount the property would fetch if sold by a willing seller to another registered provider.

(3) The terms shall include provision as to the payment of any debts or liabilities in respect of the land (whether or not secured on it).

(4) A requirement to transfer land may be imposed only with the Secretary of State's consent (both as to the transfer and the terms).

(5) Where land is transferred to the regulator under section 253(2)(a)—
- (a) the regulator may dispose of it only to a registered provider, and

(b)    if it is transferred by a non-profit registered provider, the regulator may dispose of it only to a non-profit registered provider.

**[1846]**

**NOTES**

Commencement: to be appointed.

## 255   Amalgamation

(1)    This section applies if as a result of an inquiry under section 206 or an audit under section 210 the regulator is satisfied that—

     (a)    the affairs of a non-profit registered provider which is an industrial and provident society have been mismanaged in relation to social housing, or

     (b)    the management of social housing owned by a non-profit registered provider which is an industrial and provident society would be improved if the provider were amalgamated with another industrial and provident society.

(2)    The regulator may make and execute on behalf of the society an instrument providing for the amalgamation of the society with another industrial and provident society.

(3)    The regulator may act under subsection (2) only with the Secretary of State's consent.

(4)    An instrument providing for the amalgamation of a society ("S1") with another has the same effect as a resolution by S1 under section 50 of the Industrial and Provident Societies Act 1965 (c 12) (amalgamation of societies by special resolution).

(5)    A copy of an instrument shall be sent to and registered by the Financial Services Authority.

(6)    An instrument does not take effect until the copy is registered.

(7)    The copy must be sent for registration during the period of 14 days beginning with the date of execution; but a copy registered after that period is valid.

(8)    Any body created by virtue of an amalgamation—

     (a)    must be registered by the regulator and designated as a non-profit organisation, and

     (b)    pending registration shall be treated as registered and designated as a non-profit organisation.

**[1847]**

**NOTES**

Commencement: to be appointed.

*Restrictions on dealings*

## 256   Restrictions on dealings during inquiry

(1)    The regulator may make an order under this section if—

     (a)    an inquiry under section 206 is in progress in respect of a non-profit registered provider, and

     (b)    either of the following cases applies.

(2)    Case 1 applies if the regulator has reasonable grounds for believing—

     (a)    that the affairs of the registered provider have been mismanaged, and

     (b)    that the interests of tenants of the registered provider, or its assets, require protection.

(3)    Case 2 applies if as a result of an inquirer's interim report under section 207 the regulator is satisfied that the affairs of the registered provider have been mismanaged.

(4)    The regulator may order a bank or other person who holds money or securities on behalf of the registered provider not to part with the money or securities without the regulator's consent.

(5)    The regulator may make an order restricting—

     (a)    the transactions that may be entered into by the registered provider, or

     (b)    the nature and amounts of payments that may be made by it.

(6)    An order under subsection (5) may in particular provide that transactions may not be entered into or payments made without the regulator's consent.

(7)    The regulator may make an order in respect of a registered provider that is a registered charity only if it has received public assistance.

(8)    An order ceases to have effect at the end of the period of 6 months beginning with the day on which the inquirer's final report under section 207 is made.

(9)    But the regulator—

     (a)    may revoke the order before that time;

     (b)    may by order extend it for a specified period of up to 6 months.

**[1848]**

NOTES
Commencement: to be appointed.

### 257 Restrictions on dealings following inquiry

(1)    This section applies if as a result of an inquiry under section 206 or an audit under section 210 the regulator is satisfied that the affairs of a non-profit registered provider have been mismanaged.

(2)    The regulator may order a bank or other person who holds money or securities on behalf of the registered provider not to part with the money or securities without the regulator's consent.

(3)    The regulator may make an order restricting—
    (a)    the transactions that may be entered into by the registered provider, or
    (b)    the nature and amounts of payments that may be made by it.

(4)    An order under subsection (3) may in particular provide that transactions may not be entered into or payments made without the regulator's consent.

(5)    The regulator may make an order in respect of a registered provider that is a registered charity only if it has received public assistance.

(6)    An order under this section has effect until revoked by the regulator.

**[1849]**

NOTES
Commencement: to be appointed.

### 258 Restrictions on dealings: supplemental

(1)    Before making an order under section 256 or 257 the regulator must take all reasonable steps to give notice to—
    (a)    the registered provider, and
    (b)    in the case of an order under section 256(4) or 257(2), the person to whom the order is directed.

(2)    Contravention of an order under section 256(4) or 257(2) is an offence.

(3)    A person guilty of an offence is liable on summary conviction to a fine not exceeding level 5 on the standard scale.

(4)    Proceedings for an offence may be brought only by or with the consent of—
    (a)    the regulator, or
    (b)    the Director of Public Prosecutions.

**[1850]**

NOTES
Commencement: to be appointed.

*Suspension and removal of officers*

### 259 Suspension during inquiry

(1)    The regulator may make an order under this section if—
    (a)    an inquiry under section 206 is in progress in respect of a non-profit registered provider, and
    (b)    either of the following cases applies.

(2)    Case 1 applies if the regulator has reasonable grounds for believing—
    (a)    that the affairs of the registered provider have been mismanaged, and
    (b)    that the interests of tenants of the registered provider, or its assets, require protection.

(3)    Case 2 applies if as a result of an inquirer's interim report under section 207 the regulator is satisfied that the affairs of the registered provider have been mismanaged.

(4)    The regulator may by order suspend any officer, employee or agent of the registered provider who it thinks has contributed to the failure or mismanagement.

(5)    The regulator may suspend an officer, employee or agent of a registered charity only if the charity has received public assistance.

(6)    An order ceases to have effect at the end of the period of 6 months beginning with the day on which the inquirer's final report under section 207 is made.

(7)    But the regulator may revoke an order before the end of that period.

(8)    The regulator shall notify the Charity Commission if it suspends an officer, employee or agent of a registered charity.

**[1851]**

PART I
STATUTES

**NOTES**
Commencement: to be appointed.

### 260   Removal or suspension following inquiry

(1)   This section applies if as a result of an inquiry under section 206 or an audit under section 210 the regulator is satisfied that the affairs of a non-profit registered provider have been mismanaged.

(2)   The regulator may by order remove any officer, employee or agent of the registered provider who it thinks has contributed to the failure or mismanagement.

(3)   Pending a decision whether to remove an officer, employee or agent, the regulator may by order suspend the person for a specified period of up to 6 months.

(4)   The regulator may remove or suspend an officer, employee or agent of a registered charity only if the charity has received public assistance.

(5)   Before making an order the regulator must take all reasonable steps to give at least 14 days' notice to—
    (a)   the person, and
    (b)   the registered provider.

(6)   The regulator shall notify the Charity Commission if it removes or suspends an officer, employee or agent of a registered charity.

**[1852]**

**NOTES**
Commencement: to be appointed.

### 261   Suspension under section 259 or 260: supplemental

(1)   This section applies where the regulator suspends an officer, employee or agent of a registered provider under section 259 or 260.

(2)   The regulator may give directions to the registered provider about—
    (a)   the performance of the suspended person's functions, and
    (b)   any other matter arising from the suspension.

(3)   The regulator may appoint a person to perform the suspended person's functions.

**[1853]**

**NOTES**
Commencement: to be appointed.

### 262   Disqualification of removed person

(1)   A person is disqualified from acting as an officer of a registered provider if the person has been removed under—
    (a)   section 260, or
    (b)   paragraph 24(2)(a) of Schedule 1 to the Housing Act 1996 (c 52), section 30(1)(a) of the Housing Associations Act 1985 (c 69) or section 20(1)(a) of the Housing Act 1974 (c 44) (other similar provisions).

(2)   The regulator may waive a disqualification either generally or in relation to a particular registered provider or class of registered providers.

(3)   A waiver may be granted only on an application by the disqualified person.

(4)   The regulator shall notify a person whose disqualification is waived.

(5)   If a disqualified person acts as an officer of a registered provider, the person's acts are not invalid by reason only of the disqualification.

**[1854]**

**NOTES**
Commencement: to be appointed.

### 263   Register of disqualified persons

(1)   The regulator shall maintain a register of persons disqualified under section 262.

(2)   The register must show details of any waivers.

(3)   The regulator shall make the register available for inspection by the public.

**[1855]**

**NOTES**
Commencement: to be appointed.

## 264 Acting while disqualified: offence

(1)   It is an offence for a person to act as an officer of a registered provider in respect of which the person is disqualified under section 262.

(2)   A person guilty of an offence is liable—
   (a)   on summary conviction, to imprisonment for a term not exceeding 12 months or a fine not exceeding the statutory maximum or both;
   (b)   on conviction on indictment, to imprisonment for a term not exceeding two years or a fine or both.

(3)   Proceedings for an offence may be brought only by or with the consent of—
   (a)   the regulator, or
   (b)   the Director of Public Prosecutions.

(4)   In relation to an offence committed before the commencement of section 282 of the Criminal Justice Act 2003 (c 44) (short sentences) the reference in subsection (2)(a) to 12 months shall have effect as if it were a reference to 6 months.

**[1856]**

**NOTES**
Commencement: to be appointed.

## 265 Acting while disqualified: other consequences

(1)   This section applies where the regulator is satisfied that a person—
   (a)   has acted as an officer of a registered provider in respect of which the person is disqualified under section 262, and
   (b)   in doing so, has received payments or other benefits from the registered provider.

(2)   The regulator may require the person to repay the sum or, as the case may be, a specified amount representing the whole or part of the value of the benefit.

(3)   If a person fails to comply with a requirement the registered provider may recover the sum or specified amount as a debt.

**[1857]**

**NOTES**
Commencement: to be appointed.

## 266 Removal of officers

(1)   The regulator may by order remove an officer of a non-profit registered provider if a Case listed in this section applies to the officer.

(2)   Case 1 applies to a person who has been adjudged bankrupt.

(3)   Case 2 applies to a person who has made an arrangement with creditors.

(4)   Case 3 applies to a person who is subject to a disqualification order or a disqualification undertaking under the Company Directors Disqualification Act 1986 (c 46) or equivalent legislation in Northern Ireland.

(5)   Case 4 applies to a person who is subject to an order under section 429(2) of the Insolvency Act 1986 (c 45) (disabilities on revocation of county court administration order).

(6)   Case 5 applies to a person who is disqualified under section 72 of the Charities Act 1993 (c 10) from being a charity trustee.

(7)   Case 6 applies to a person who is incapable of acting by reason of mental disorder.

(8)   Case 7 applies to a person who is impeding the proper management of the registered provider by reason of absence or failure to act.

**[1858]**

**NOTES**
Commencement: to be appointed.

## 267 Section 266: supplemental

(1)   Before making an order under section 266 in respect of an officer the regulator must take all reasonable steps to give at least 14 days' notice to—
   (a)   the officer, and
   (b)   the registered provider.

(2)   An order may be made in respect of an officer of a registered charity only if the charity has received public assistance.

**[1859]**

**PART I
STATUTES**

**NOTES**
  Commencement: to be appointed.

### 268   Appeal against removal or suspension

A person removed or suspended under section 259, 260 or 266 may appeal to the High Court.

**[1860]**

**NOTES**
  Commencement: to be appointed.

### 269   Appointment of new officers

(1)   The regulator may by order appoint a person as an officer of a non-profit registered provider—

  (a)   to replace an officer removed by order under section 266,

  (b)   where there are no officers, or

  (c)   if the regulator thinks an additional officer is necessary for the proper management of the body's affairs.

(2)   The regulator may appoint more than a minority of the officers of a registered provider only if—

  (a)   the provider has fewer officers than required by its constitution, or

  (b)   its constitution does not specify a minimum number of officers.

(3)   Subsection (1) overrides any restriction on eligibility or numbers of officers imposed by the body's constitution.

(4)   An order appointing an officer shall specify the period for which, and the terms on which, the office is to be held; but—

  (a)   on expiry the regulator may by order renew the appointment, and

  (b)   the officer may resign or retire in accordance with the registered provider's constitution.

(5)   An officer appointed by order has the same rights, powers and obligations as an officer appointed under the registered provider's constitution.

(6)   The regulator may exercise the power in subsection (1) in respect of a registered charity only if—

  (a)   a condition in section 274 is satisfied, and

  (b)   the regulator has consulted the Charity Commission.

**[1861]**

**NOTES**
  Commencement: to be appointed.

CHAPTER 8
GENERAL

*Interpretation*

### 270   Officer

The Table gives the meaning of "officer" in relation to registered providers.

| *Registered provider* | *Meaning of "officer"* |
| --- | --- |
| Registered charity which is not a registered company | Trustee, secretary or treasurer |
| Industrial and provident society | "Officer" within the meaning given by section 74 of the Industrial and Provident Societies Act 1965 (including a person co-opted to serve on the society's committee) |
| Registered company | "Officer" within the meaning given by section 1173 of the Companies Act 2006 |

**[1862]**

**NOTES**
Commencement: to be appointed.

## 271 Subsidiary and associate

(1)   A company is a "subsidiary" of a person if any of the following conditions is satisfied.

(2)   Condition 1 is that the person—
  (a)   is a member of the company, and
  (b)   has power, independent of any other person, to appoint or remove all or a majority of the board of directors.

(3)   Condition 2 is that the person holds more than half in nominal value of the company's equity share capital.

(4)   Condition 3 is that the company is a subsidiary, within the meaning of the Companies Act 2006 (c 46) or the Friendly and Industrial and Provident Societies Act 1968 (c 55), of a company which is a subsidiary of the person by virtue of Condition 1 or 2.

(5)   In relation to a company which is an industrial and provident society a reference to the board of directors is a reference to the committee of management.

(6)   "Associate" of a provider means—
  (a)   a body of which the provider is a subsidiary, and
  (b)   any other subsidiary of that body.

[1863]

**NOTES**
Commencement: to be appointed.

## 272 Family

(1)   For the purposes of this Part one person is a member of the family of another if—
  (a)   they are, or live together as if they were, spouses or civil partners, or
  (b)   one is the parent, grandparent, child, grandchild, brother, sister, uncle, aunt, nephew or niece of the other.

(2)   For those purposes—
  (a)   a relationship by marriage or civil partnership shall be treated as a relationship by blood (and, in particular, P's stepchild shall be treated as P's child), and
  (b)   a relationship by half-blood shall be treated as a relationship by whole blood.

[1864]

**NOTES**
Commencement: to be appointed.

## 273 Disposal

(1)   In this Part a reference to disposing of property is a reference to—
  (a)   selling it,
  (b)   leasing it,
  (c)   mortgaging it,
  (d)   making it subject to a charge, and
  (e)   disposing of it, or of any interest in it, in any other way.

(2)   Granting an option to require a disposal shall be treated as making a disposal.

[1865]

**NOTES**
Commencement: to be appointed.

## 274 Charities that have "received public assistance"

(1)   For the purposes of this Part a registered charity has received public assistance if at least one of the following conditions is satisfied.

(2)   Condition 1 is that the charity has received financial assistance from the HCA under section 19.

(3)   Condition 2 is that the charity has received financial assistance under section 24 of the Local Government Act 1988 (c 9) (assistance for privately let housing accommodation).

(4)   Condition 3 is that the charity has had housing transferred to it pursuant to—
  (a)   a large scale disposal, within the meaning of section 34 of the Housing Act 1985 (c 68), for which consent was required under section 32 or 43 of that Act, or

(b)    a qualifying disposal that was made under section 135 of the Leasehold Reform, Housing and Urban Development Act 1993 (c 28).

(5)    Condition 4 is that the charity has received a grant or loan under—
- (a)    section 18 of the Housing Act 1996 (c 52) (social housing grants),
- (b)    section 22 of that Act (assistance from local authorities),
- (c)    section 58 of the Housing Associations Act 1985 (c 69) (grants or loans by local authorities),
- (d)    section 50 of the Housing Act 1988 (c 50), section 41 of the Housing Associations Act 1985 or any enactment replaced by that section (housing association grant),
- (e)    section 51 of the Housing Act 1988 (c 50) or section 54 or 55 of the Housing Associations Act 1985 (c 69) (revenue deficit grant or hostel deficit grant),
- (f)    section 79 of the Housing Associations Act 1985 (loans by Housing Corporation),
- (g)    section 31 of the Housing Act 1974 (c 44) (management grants), or
- (h)    any enactment mentioned in paragraph 2 or 3 of Schedule 1 to the Housing Associations Act 1985 (pre-1974 grants and certain loans).

**[1866]**

**NOTES**

Commencement: to be appointed.

## 275  General

In this Part, except where the context requires otherwise—

"action" includes inaction, proposed action and decision,

"assured agricultural occupancy" has the same meaning as in Part 1 of the Housing Act 1988,

"assured tenancy" has the same meaning as in that Part,

"the Charity Commission" means the Charity Commission for England and Wales,

"committee", in relation to an industrial and provident society, means the committee of management or other directing body of the society (including any person co-opted to serve on the committee, whether a member of the society or not),

"consent" means written consent,

"constitution" includes rules,

"conveyance" includes grant, assignment and any other instrument,

"district valuer" has the meaning given by section 622 of the Housing Act 1985 (c 68),

"dwelling"—
- (a)    means a house, flat or other building or part of a building occupied or intended to be occupied as a separate dwelling, and
- (b)    includes any garden, yard, outhouse or other appurtenance belonging to, or usually enjoyed with, the dwelling,

"the HCA" means the Homes and Communities Agency,

"industrial and provident society" means a society registered under the Industrial and Provident Societies Act 1965 (c 12),

"local authority" has the same meaning as in the Housing Associations Act 1985,

"local housing authority" has the same meaning as in the Housing Act 1985,

"maintenance" includes repair,

"mismanagement", in relation to the affairs of a registered provider, means—
- (a)    managed in contravention of a provision of this Part or of anything done under this Part, or
- (b)    otherwise conducted improperly or inappropriately,

"non-registrable charity" means a charity which is not required to be registered, in accordance with section 3A of the Charities Act 1993 (c 10),

"notice" means written notice (and to "notify" means to give written notice),

"preferential creditor" and "preferential debt" have the same meaning as in the Insolvency Act 1986 (c 45),

"price" includes premium,

"registered charity" means a charity registered under the Charities Act 1993 (c 10),

"registered company" means a company within the meaning of the Companies Act 2006 (c 46),

"rent" includes payments under a licence to occupy accommodation,

"representations" means written representations,

"secure tenancy" has the same meaning as in Part 4 of the Housing Act 1985 (c 68),

"secured creditor" means a creditor who holds a mortgage or charge (including a floating charge) over—
- (a)    land held by a registered provider, or
- (b)    a present or future interest of a registered provider in rents or other receipts from land,

"tenant" in relation to social housing includes other occupiers, and

"working day" means a day other than—

(a) a Saturday or Sunday,

(b) Christmas Day or Good Friday, or

(c) a day which is a bank holiday in England and Wales under the Banking and Financial Dealings Act 1971 (c 80).

**[1867]**

**NOTES**

Commencement: 8 September 2008 (for certain purposes); to be appointed (otherwise).

## 276 Index of defined terms

The Table lists expressions defined in this Part.

| Expression | Section |
| --- | --- |
| Appointed member | Section 82 |
| Associate | Section 271 |
| Assured agricultural occupancy | Section 275 |
| Assured tenancy | Section 275 |
| Charity Commission | Section 275 |
| Committee (industrial and provident society) | Section 275 |
| Compensation notice | Section 240 |
| Consent | Section 275 |
| Constitution | Section 275 |
| Conveyance | Section 275 |
| Disposal | Section 273 |
| District valuer | Section 275 |
| Dwelling | Section 275 |
| Enforcement notice | Sections 219 to 225 |
| Equity percentage arrangements | Section 70(5) |
| Family | Section 272 |
| Financial year | Section 104 |
| Fundamental objectives | Section 86 |
| The HCA | Section 275 |
| Industrial and provident society | Section 275 |
| Local authority | Section 275 |
| Local housing authority | Section 275 |
| Low cost home ownership accommodation | Section 70 |
| Low cost rental accommodation | Section 69 |
| Maintenance | Section 275 |
| Mismanagement | Section 275 |
| Non-profit organisation | Section 115 |
| Non-registrable charity | Section 275 |
| Notice | Section 275 |
| Officer | Section 270 |
| Penalty notice | Section 228 |
| Pre-compensation warning | Section 242 |
| Pre-penalty warning | Section 230 |
| Preferential creditor | Section 275 |
| Preferential debt | Section 275 |

| Expression | Section |
|---|---|
| Price | Section 275 |
| Profit-making organisation | Section 115 |
| Provider (of social housing) | Section 80 |
| Received public assistance (charities) | Section 274 |
| Registered charity | Section 275 |
| Registered company | Section 275 |
| Registered provider (of social housing) | Section 80 |
| The regulator | Section 81 |
| The Regulator of Social Housing | Section 81 |
| Rent | Section 275 |
| Representations | Section 275 |
| Secure tenancy | Section 275 |
| Secured creditor | Section 275 |
| Shared ownership arrangements | Section 70(4) |
| Shared ownership trust | Section 70(6) |
| Social housing | Section 68 |
| Subsidiary | Section 271 |
| Tenant | Section 275 |
| Working day | Section 275 |

**[1868]**

**NOTES**

Commencement: 8 September 2008 (for certain purposes); to be appointed (otherwise).

*Miscellaneous*

**277**    (*Introduces Sch 9 to this Act.*)

**278  Transitional**

(1)    The regulator shall include in the register under section 111 on its establishment anyone—

    (a)    who was registered under section 1 of the Housing Act 1996 (c 52) (register of social landlords) immediately before section 61 came into force, and

    (b)    in relation to whom the Relevant Authority was the Housing Corporation (in accordance with section 56 of that Act).

(2)    A person registered under this section shall be designated as a non-profit organisation.

**[1869]**

**NOTES**

Commencement: to be appointed.

**PART 3**
**OTHER PROVISIONS**

**279–293**    (*Outside the scope of this work.*)

**CHAPTER 2**
**LANDLORD AND TENANT MATTERS**

**294–296**    (*S 294 amends the Housing Act 1985, Sch 3A at* **[582]***; ss 295, 296 amend the Housing Act 1985, s 27AB and insert s 34A thereof.*)

*Family intervention tenancies*

**297**    (*Amends the Housing Act 1985, Sch 1 at* **[575]** *and the Housing Act 1988, Sch 1 at* **[782]**.)

## 298 Certain family intervention tenancies: termination

(1) A local housing authority must not serve a notice to quit on the tenant of a family intervention tenancy unless—
- (a) the authority has served a notice under subsection (2) on the tenant, and
- (b) either—
  - (i) the tenant has not requested a review of the kind mentioned in subsection (2)(e) within the period of 14 days beginning with the service of the notice,
  - (ii) any such request has been withdrawn, or
  - (iii) the authority has served a notice on the tenant under subsection (4)(b).

(2) A notice under this subsection is a notice in writing stating—
- (a) that the authority has decided to serve a notice to quit on the tenant,
- (b) the effect of serving a notice to quit,
- (c) the reasons for the authority's decision,
- (d) when the authority is intending to serve the notice to quit, and
- (e) that the tenant has the right to request, within the period of 14 days beginning with the service of the notice under this subsection, a review of the authority's decision.

(3) Subsection (4) applies if the tenant requests a review of the kind mentioned in subsection (2)(e) within the period of 14 days beginning with the service of the notice under subsection (2) and the request is not withdrawn.

(4) The local housing authority must—
- (a) review its decision to serve a notice to quit on the tenant, and
- (b) serve a notice on the tenant informing the tenant of the decision of the authority on the review and the reasons for it.

(5) The appropriate national authority may by regulations make provision about the procedure to be followed in connection with such a review.

(6) Regulations under subsection (5) may, in particular—
- (a) specify the description of person who is to make the decision on a review,
- (b) specify the circumstances in which the tenant is entitled to an oral hearing on a review,
- (c) specify whether, and by whom, the tenant is entitled to be represented at such a hearing.

(7) A notice under subsection (2), and a notice to quit, served by a local housing authority in respect of a family intervention tenancy must contain advice to the tenant as to how the tenant may be able to obtain assistance in relation to the notice.

(8) The appropriate national authority may by regulations make provision about the type of advice to be provided in such notices.

(9) In this section—
"appropriate national authority" means—
- (a) in relation to England, the Secretary of State, and
- (b) in relation to Wales, the Welsh Ministers,
"family intervention tenancy" has the same meaning as in paragraph 4ZA of Schedule 1 to the Housing Act 1985 (c 68),
and other expressions used in this section and in paragraph 4ZA of that Schedule have the same meaning as in that paragraph.

(10) This section does not apply to any tenancy granted before the coming into force of this section.

**[1870]**

**NOTES**
Commencement: 1 December 2008 (sub-ss (5), (6), (8), (9) (for the purpose of enabling the Secretary of State to make regulations)); 1 January 2009 (sub-ss (1)–(4), (7), (10) in relation to England, sub-ss (5), (6), (8), (9) (in relation to England for remaining purposes)); to be appointed (otherwise).
Regulations: the Family Intervention Tenancies (Review of Local Authority Decisions) (England) Regulations 2008, SI 2008/3111.

*Possession orders*

## 299 Possession orders relating to certain tenancies

Schedule 11 (which makes provision about possession orders and their effect on secure tenancies, assured tenancies, introductory tenancies and demoted tenancies including provision about the status of existing occupiers) has effect.

**[1871]**

**NOTES**
Commencement: 1 December 2008 (for the purpose of enabling the appropriate national authority to make orders); 20 May 2009 (otherwise).

**300–312**　(*S 300 amends the Leasehold Reform Act 1967, ss 1, 1A at* **[78]**, **[79]** *and repeals ss 1AA, 4A thereof at* **[80]**, **[85]**; *ss 301, 302 amend the Leasehold Reform Act 1967, Sch 4A at* **[133]**; *s 303 introduces Sch 12 to this Act; s 304 amends the Housing Act 1985, s 121 at* **[464]**; *s 305 introduces Sch 13 to this Act; s 306 inserts the Housing Act 1985, ss 128A, 128B at* **[480]**, **[481]** *and amends ss 125D, 128, 136, 140, 181 thereof at* **[475]**, **[479]**, **[485]**, **[492]**, **[552]**; *s 307 amends the Housing Act 1985, s 36, and ss 151B, 156, 622 thereof at* **[508]**, **[518]**, **[571]**, *the Housing Act 1988, Sch 11, and the Housing Act 1996, s 12; s 308 amends the Housing Act 1985, s 450C; s 309 inserts the Housing Act 1985, s 450D; s 310 amends the Housing Act 1985, Schs 5, 5A at* **[584]**, **[585]**; *s 311 introduces Sch 14 to this Act; s 312 amends the Housing Act 1996, s 94 at* **[1007]**.)

CHAPTER 3
HOUSING FINANCE AND OTHER PROVISIONS

**313–319**　(*S 313 inserts the Local Government and Housing Act 1989, s 80B and amends s 88 of, and Sch 4 to, that Act; s 314 introduces Sch 15 (amendments) to this Act; s 315 amends the Housing Act 1996, s 199 at* **[1091]**; *s 316 amends the Housing Act 1985, s 622 at* **[571]**; *s 317 amends the Building Act 1984, s 35A; s 318 amends the Mobile Homes Act 1983, s 5 at* **[401]**; *s 319 amends the Commonhold and Leasehold Reform Act 2002, s 62 at* **[1226]**.)

PART 4
SUPPLEMENTARY AND FINAL PROVISIONS

**320　Orders and regulations**

(1)　The power of the Secretary of State, the Treasury or the Welsh Ministers to make orders or regulations under this Act—

　(a)　is exercisable by statutory instrument,

　(b)　may be exercised so as to make provision generally or subject to exceptions or only in relation to specified cases or circumstances or descriptions of case,

　(c)　may be exercised so as to make different provision for different cases or descriptions of case, different circumstances, different purposes or different areas, and

　(d)　includes power to make supplementary, incidental, consequential, transitional, transitory or saving provision.

(2)　Subsection (1) does not apply to orders under—

　(a)　paragraph 3 of Schedule 3, or

　(b)　Schedule 4.

(3)　An instrument containing—

　(a)　an order under section 13, 114 or 229,

　(b)　an order of the Secretary of State under section 321,

　(c)　an order of the Secretary of State under paragraph 19(4), 21(2) or (4) or 24 of Schedule 11,

　(d)　regulations under section 70 or 72, or

　(e)　regulations of the Secretary of State under section 280(3) or 291,

may not be made unless a draft of the instrument has been laid before, and approved by a resolution of, each House of Parliament.

(4)　Subsection (3) does not apply to an instrument containing an order under section 321 if the order does not amend or repeal a provision of a public general Act.

(5)　If a draft of an instrument containing an order under section 13 would, apart from this subsection, be treated as a hybrid instrument for the purposes of the standing orders of either House of Parliament, it is to proceed in that House as if it were not a hybrid instrument.

(6)　An instrument containing an order under section 23 may not be made unless a draft of the instrument has been laid before, and approved by a resolution of, the House of Commons.

(7)　An instrument containing—

　(a)　an order under section 36 or Part 2 (excluding sections 114 and 229),

　(b)　an order of the Secretary of State under section 321 to which subsection (3) above does not apply,

　(c)　an order of the Secretary of State under paragraph 16(7), 18(4), 22(2) or 23(2) of Schedule 11,

　(d)　regulations under Part 2 (excluding sections 70 and 72),

　(e)　regulations of the Secretary of State under Chapter 1 of Part 3 (including Schedule 10 but excluding sections 280(3) and 291),

　(f)　regulations of the Secretary of State under section 298, or

　(g)　regulations under Part 3 of Schedule 3,

is subject to annulment in pursuance of a resolution of either House of Parliament.

(8)　An instrument containing—

　(a)　an order of the Welsh Ministers under section 321,

(b) an order of the Welsh Ministers under paragraph 19(4), 21(2) or (4) or 24 of Schedule 11, or

(c) regulations of the Welsh Ministers under section 280(3) or 291,

may not be made unless a draft of the instrument has been laid before, and approved by a resolution of, the National Assembly for Wales.

(9) Subsection (8) does not apply to an instrument containing an order under section 321 if the order does not amend or repeal a provision of a public general Act.

(10) An instrument containing—

(a) an order of the Welsh Ministers under section 321 to which subsection (8) above does not apply,

(b) an order of the Welsh Ministers under paragraph 16(7), 18(4), 22(2) or 23(2) of Schedule 11,

(c) regulations of the Welsh Ministers under Chapter 1 of Part 3 (including Schedule 10 but excluding section 280(3) or 291), or

(d) regulations of the Welsh Ministers under section 298,

is subject to annulment in pursuance of a resolution of the National Assembly for Wales.

**[1872]**

**NOTES**
Commencement: 22 July 2008.
Orders: the Housing and Regeneration Act 2008 (Commencement No 1 and Transitional Provision) Order 2008, SI 2008/2358; the Housing and Regeneration Act 2008 (Consequential Provisions) (No 2) Order 2008, SI 2008/2831; the Transfer of Housing Corporation Functions (Modifications and Transitional Provisions) Order 2008, SI 2008/2839; the Housing and Regeneration Act 2008 (Consequential Provisions) Order 2008, SI 2008/3002; the Housing Corporation (Dissolution) Order 2009, SI 2009/484; the Abolition of the Commission for the New Towns and the Urban Regeneration Agency (Appointed Day and Consequential Amendments) Order 2009, SI 2009/801.

### 321 Consequential amendments and repeals

(1) Schedule 16 (which contains repeals and revocations including repeals of spent enactments) has effect.

(2) The Secretary of State may by order make such supplementary, incidental or consequential provision as the Secretary of State considers appropriate for the general purposes, or any particular purpose, of this Act or in consequence of any provision made by or under this Act or for giving full effect to this Act or any such provision.

(3) The power conferred by subsection (2) may, in particular, be exercised by amending, repealing, revoking or otherwise modifying any provision made by or under an enactment (including this Act and any Act passed in the same Session as this Act).

(4) The power conferred by subsections (2) and (3) is also exercisable by the Welsh Ministers so far as it is exercisable in relation to matters with respect to which functions are exercisable by the Welsh Ministers.

**[1873]**

**NOTES**
Commencement: 22 July 2008.

### 322 Transitional, transitory or saving provision

(1) The Secretary of State may by order make such transitional, transitory or saving provision as the Secretary of State considers appropriate in connection with the coming into force of any provision of this Act other than a Welsh provision.

(2) The Welsh Ministers may by order make such transitional, transitory or saving provision as the Welsh Ministers consider appropriate in connection with the coming into force of any Welsh provision.

(3) In this section "Welsh provision" means any provision of this Act so far as it is to be brought into force by an order of the Welsh Ministers.

**[1874]**

**NOTES**
Commencement: 22 July 2008.

### 323 (*Outside the scope of this work.*)

### 324 Extent

(1) Subject as follows, Parts 1 to 3 (including Schedules 1 to 15) and Schedule 16 extend to England and Wales only.

(2)   Any amendment, repeal or revocation made by this Act, other than one falling within subsection (3), has the same extent as the provision to which it relates.

(3)   The following fall within this subsection—
   (a)   the repeal in section 5 of the Mobile Homes Act 1983 (c 34),
   (b)   the repeals of sections 50 and 51 of the Housing Act 1988 (c 50), and
   (c)   the amendments of sections 52 to 54 and 59 of that Act.

**[1875]**

**NOTES**
   Commencement: 22 July 2008.

### 325   Commencement

(1)   Subject as follows, this Act comes into force on such day as the Secretary of State may by order appoint; and different days may be appointed for different purposes or different areas.

(2)   The following provisions—
   (a)   sections 294, 304 to 307, 310, 312, 313 and 319 and Schedule 13, and
   (b)   section 321(1), and Schedule 16, so far as relating to the repeals in sections 125D(2), 128(2) and 136(2) of, and paragraph 13(5) of Schedule 5 to, the Housing Act 1985 (c 68),

come into force at the end of the period of 2 months beginning with the day on which this Act is passed.

(3)   Subsection (4) applies to the following provisions—
   (a)   Chapter 1 of Part 3 (including Schedule 10),
   (b)   sections 295 to 298, 300 to 303, 308, 309, 315 and 318 and Schedule 12, and
   (c)   section 321(1), and Schedule 16, so far as relating to repeals and revocations which are connected to the provisions mentioned in paragraph (b) above.

(4)   The provisions to which this subsection applies come into force—
   (a)   in relation to England, on such day as the Secretary of State may by order appoint; and different days may be appointed for different purposes or different areas, and
   (b)   in relation to Wales, on such day as the Welsh Ministers may by order appoint; and different days may be appointed for different purposes or different areas.

(5)   The Secretary of State must consult the Welsh Ministers before making an order under subsection (1) in relation to section 50(2) and Schedule 5 or section 299 and Schedule 11.

(6)   Subsection (1) does not apply to sections 320, 321(2) to (4), 322, 323 and 324, this section and section 326.

**[1876]**

**NOTES**
   Commencement: 22 July 2008.
   Orders: the Housing and Regeneration Act 2008 (Commencement No 1 and Transitional Provision) Order 2008, SI 2008/2358; the Housing and Regeneration Act 2008 (Commencement No 2 and Transitional, Saving and Transitory Provisions) Order 2008, SI 2008/3068; the Housing and Regeneration Act 2008 (Commencement No 3) Order 2009, SI 2009/363; the Housing and Regeneration Act 2008 (Commencement No 1 and Saving Provisions) Order 2009, SI 2009/415; the Housing and Regeneration Act 2008 (Commencement No 1) (Wales) Order 2009, SI 2009/773; the Housing and Regeneration Act 2008 (Commencement No 4 and Transitory Provisions) Order 2009, SI 2009/803; the Housing and Regeneration Act 2008 (Commencement No 5) Order 2009, SI 2009/1261; the Housing and Regeneration Act 2008 (Commencement No 6 and Transitional and Savings Provisions) Order 2009, SI 2009/2096.

### 326   Short title

This Act may be cited as the Housing and Regeneration Act 2008.

**[1877]**

**NOTES**
   Commencement: 22 July 2008.

## SCHEDULE 1
### THE HOMES AND COMMUNITIES AGENCY

Section 1

*Membership*

1.—(1)   The HCA is to consist of such number of members (being not less than six) as the Secretary of State may from time to time appoint.

(2)   The Secretary of State must appoint one of the members as the person with the function of chairing the HCA.

(3)   In appointing a person to be a member, the Secretary of State—
    (a)   must have regard to the desirability of appointing a person who has experience of, and has shown some capacity in, a matter relevant to the exercise of the functions of the HCA, and
    (b)   must be satisfied that the person will have no financial or other interest likely to affect prejudicially the exercise of the person's functions as a member.

(4)   The Secretary of State may require any person whom the Secretary of State proposes to appoint as a member to provide such information as the Secretary of State considers necessary for the purposes of sub-paragraph (3)(b).

## Terms of appointment of members

2.—(1)   Subject as follows, a member of the HCA holds and vacates office in accordance with the member's terms of appointment.

(2)   A member may resign by serving notice on the Secretary of State.

(3)   A person ceases to have the function of chairing the HCA if the person—
    (a)   resigns from exercising that function by serving notice on the Secretary of State, or
    (b)   ceases to be a member.

(4)   A person who—
    (a)   ceases to be a member, or
    (b)   ceases to have the function of chairing the HCA,
is eligible for reappointment.

(5)   The Secretary of State may remove a member who—
    (a)   has been absent from meetings of the HCA for a period of more than 6 months without the permission of the HCA,
    (b)   has become bankrupt or has made an arrangement with the member's creditors, or
    (c)   in the opinion of the Secretary of State, has failed to comply with the member's terms of appointment or is otherwise unable, unfit or unsuitable to exercise the member's functions as a member.

## Remuneration etc: members

3.—(1)   The HCA may pay to its members such remuneration and such allowances as the Secretary of State may decide.

(2)   The HCA may—
    (a)   pay such pensions, allowances or gratuities as the Secretary of State may decide to or in respect of any member or former member, or
    (b)   pay such sums as the Secretary of State may decide towards the provision for the payment of pensions, allowances or gratuities to or in respect of any member or former member.

(3)   Sub-paragraph (4) applies if—
    (a)   a person ceases to be a member of the HCA, and
    (b)   the Secretary of State considers that there are special circumstances which make it appropriate for the person to receive compensation.

(4)   The Secretary of State may require the HCA to pay the person such amount as the Secretary of State may decide.

## Staff

4.—(1)   The HCA must appoint a person to be chief executive but may only appoint a person who has been approved by the Secretary of State.

(2)   The chief executive is a member of staff of the HCA.

(3)   The HCA may appoint such number of other staff as the Secretary of State may approve.

(4)   The staff's terms and conditions of service are to be decided by the HCA with the approval of the Secretary of State.

(5)   The HCA may pay to its staff such remuneration and such allowances as it may, with the approval of the Secretary of State, decide.

(6)   The HCA may—
    (a)   pay such pensions, allowances or gratuities to or in respect of any member of staff or former member of staff, or
    (b)   pay such sums towards the provision for the payment of pensions, allowances or gratuities to or in respect of any member of staff or former member of staff,
as it may, with the approval of the Secretary of State, decide.

*Financial provision*

5.—(1)   The Secretary of State may make payments to the HCA by way of grant.

(2)   Such payments may be made on such terms and conditions as the Secretary of State considers appropriate.

*Committees*

6.—(1)   The HCA may establish one or more committees.

(2)   A committee may establish one or more sub-committees.

(3)   A member, or member of staff, of the HCA may be a member of a committee or sub-committee.

(4)   Other persons may be members of committees or sub-committees but only with the approval, in each case, of the Secretary of State.

(5)   No committee or sub-committee may consist exclusively of other persons.

(6)   The members of a sub-committee of a committee may include persons who are not members of the committee.

(7)   The HCA may pay such remuneration and such allowances as the Secretary of State may decide to any person who—
(a)   is a member of a committee or sub-committee, but
(b)   is neither a member nor member of staff of the HCA.

(8)   The HCA may dissolve a committee or sub-committee.

*Procedure and members' interests*

7.—(1)   The HCA may, subject to any directions given by the Secretary of State, decide—
(a)   its own procedure, and
(b)   the procedure of any of its committees or sub-committees.

(2)   Subject to this, a committee may decide the procedure of any of its sub-committees.

(3)   Subject as above, a committee or sub-committee may decide its own procedure.

(4)   In this paragraph "procedure" includes quorum.

8.   The validity of proceedings of the HCA, or of any of its committees or sub-committees, is not affected by—
(a)   any vacancy,
(b)   any defective appointment, or
(c)   any contravention of—
    (i)   directions given as mentioned in paragraph 7(1), or
    (ii)   paragraph 9.

9.—(1)   A member of the HCA who is directly or indirectly interested in any matter arising at a meeting of the HCA must disclose the nature of that interest to the meeting.

(2)   A member of a committee or sub-committee of the HCA who is directly or indirectly interested in any matter arising at a meeting of the committee or sub-committee must disclose the nature of that interest to the meeting.

(3)   In the case of a matter disclosed under this paragraph by a member of the HCA or of a committee or sub-committee, the member—
(a)   must not take part in any deliberation or decision about the matter if it is a contract or agreement of any description, but
(b)   may otherwise take part in any deliberation or decision about the matter unless at least one-third of the other members at the meeting decide that the interest disclosed might prejudicially affect the member's consideration of the matter.

*Delegation*

10.—(1)   The HCA may delegate any of its functions to any of its members, committees, sub-committees or staff.

(2)   Any such committee may delegate any function conferred on it to any sub-committee of the committee or to any staff of the HCA.

(3)   See also section 42 (agency arrangements of the HCA with urban development corporations).

*Reports, accounts etc*

11.—(1)   For each financial year, the HCA must—
(a)   prepare an annual report on how it has exercised its functions during the year, and

(b)   send a copy of the report to the Secretary of State within such period as the Secretary of State may direct.

(2)   The Secretary of State must lay before Parliament a copy of each report received under sub-paragraph (1).

12.—(1)   The HCA must keep proper accounts and proper records in relation to the accounts.

(2)   For each financial year, the HCA must—
(a)   prepare a statement of accounts in respect of that financial year, and
(b)   send copies of the statement to the Secretary of State and the Comptroller and Auditor General within such period as the Secretary of State may direct.

(3)   The statement must be in such form as the Secretary of State may direct.

(4)   The Comptroller and Auditor General must—
(a)   examine, certify and report on the statement, and
(b)   send a copy of the certified statement and of the report to the Secretary of State as soon as possible.

(5)   The Secretary of State must lay before Parliament a copy of each statement and report received under sub-paragraph (4).

13.—(1)   The HCA must provide the Secretary of State with such information as the Secretary of State may require relating to the HCA's property or to the exercise or proposed exercise of its functions.

(2)   The HCA must—
(a)   permit any person authorised by the Secretary of State to inspect and make copies of any accounts or other documents of the HCA, and
(b)   provide such explanation of them as that person or the Secretary of State may require.

*Supplementary and transitional provisions*

14.—(1)   The application of the seal of the HCA must be authenticated by the signature of—
(a)   a member of the HCA who is authorised (generally or specifically) for that purpose, or
(b)   a member of staff of the HCA who is so authorised.

(2)   A document purporting to be duly executed under the seal of the HCA, or signed on its behalf, is to be received in evidence and, unless the contrary is proved, is to be treated as so executed or signed.

15.   The HCA is not to be regarded—
(a)   as a servant or agent of the Crown, or
(b)   as enjoying any status, immunity or privilege of the Crown,
and its property is not to be regarded as property of, or held for or on behalf of, the Crown.

16.   The HCA is a public body for the purposes of the Prevention of Corruption Acts 1889 to 1916.

17.   The Secretary of State (instead of the HCA) may—
(a)   appoint the first chief executive, and
(b)   determine the terms and conditions of service as a member of staff of the HCA which are applicable to the first chief executive on appointment.

**[1878]**

**NOTES**
Commencement: 8 September 2008.

SCHEDULE 2
ACQUISITION OF LAND

Section 9(6)

PART 1
COMPULSORY ACQUISITION OF LAND

*Application of Acquisition of Land Act 1981 (c 67)*

1.—(1)   The Acquisition of Land Act 1981 applies to the compulsory acquisition of land under section 9 with the following modification.

(2)   The reference in section 17(3) of that Act (local authority and statutory undertakers' land) to statutory undertakers includes a reference to the HCA.

2.—(1)   Schedule 3 to the Act of 1981 applies to the compulsory acquisition of new rights under section 9 with the following modification.

(2)   The reference in paragraph 4(3) of that Schedule to statutory undertakers includes a reference to the HCA.

*Extinguishment of private rights of way etc*

3.—(1) Sub-paragraph (2) applies where the HCA completes the compulsory acquisition of land under this Part of this Act.

(2) On completion of the acquisition—
   (a) all private rights of way on, under or over the land are extinguished,
   (b) all rights of laying down, erecting, continuing or maintaining any apparatus on, under or over the land are extinguished, and
   (c) any such apparatus vests in the HCA.

(3) Sub-paragraph (2) is subject to paragraphs 4 to 6.

4. The HCA may give a direction before the completion of the acquisition that paragraph 3(2) is not to apply to any right or apparatus specified in the direction.

5. Paragraph 3(2) is subject to any agreement which may be made (whether before or after the completion of the acquisition) between—
   (a) the HCA, and
   (b) the person—
      (i) in whom the right or apparatus concerned is vested, or
      (ii) to whom it belongs.

6.—(1) Paragraph 3(2) does not apply to—
   (a) any right vested in statutory undertakers for the purpose of carrying on their undertaking,
   (b) any apparatus belonging to statutory undertakers for that purpose,
   (c) any right conferred by, or in accordance with, the electronic communications code on the operator of an electronic communications code network, or
   (d) any electronic communications apparatus kept installed for the purposes of any such network

(2) In sub-paragraph (1) "statutory undertakers" means persons who are, or are deemed to be, statutory undertakers for the purposes of any provision of Part 11 of the Town and Country Planning Act 1990 (c 8); and "statutory undertaking" is to be read in accordance with section 262 of that Act (meaning of "statutory undertakers").

7.(1) Any person who suffers loss by the extinguishment of a right, or the vesting of any apparatus, under paragraph 3 is entitled to compensation from the HCA.

(2) Any compensation payable under this paragraph is to be determined in accordance with the Land Compensation Act 1961 (c 33).

*New rights: Compulsory Purchase Act 1965 (c 56)*

8.—(1) The Compulsory Purchase Act 1965 applies, with the necessary modifications, to the compulsory acquisition of new rights under section 9 as it applies to the compulsory purchase of land.

(2) One result is that, in appropriate contexts, references in that Act to land are to be read as referring, or as including references, to—
   (a) the rights acquired or to be acquired, or
   (b) land over which the rights are, or are to be, exercisable,
according to the requirements of the particular context.

*New rights: specific adaptations of 1965 Act*

9.—(1) Part 1 of the Act of 1965 applies to the compulsory acquisition of new rights under section 9 with the modifications specified in paragraphs 10 to 15.

(2) Sub-paragraph (1) is without prejudice to the generality of paragraph 8.

10. Section 7 (measure of compensation) of the Act of 1965 is to be read as if for that section there were substituted—

"7.—(1) In assessing the compensation to be paid by the acquiring authority under this Act regard shall be had not only to the extent (if any) to which the value of the land over which the right is acquired is depreciated by the acquisition but also to the damage (if any) to be sustained by the owner of the land by reason of injurious affection of other land of the owner by the exercise of the right.

(2) The modifications subject to which subsection (1) of section 44 of the Land Compensation Act 1973 (compensation for injurious affection) is to have effect, as applied by subsection (2) of that section to compensation for injurious affection under this section, are that—
      (a) for "land is acquired or taken" there shall be substituted "a right over land is acquired"; and

(b)  for "acquired or taken from him" there shall be substituted "over which the right is exercisable"."

11.  Section 8 of the Act of 1965 (which relates to cases in which a vendor cannot be required to sell part only of a building or garden) is to be read as if for that section there were substituted—

"8.—(1)  Subsection (3) applies if—

(a)  a notice to treat in respect of a right over land consisting of a house, building or manufactory or of a park or garden belonging to a house ("the relevant land") has been served on a person in pursuance of section 5 of this Act; and

(b)  as a result—

(i)  a question of disputed compensation in respect of the purchase of the right would, apart from this section, fall to be determined by the [Upper Tribunal] ("the Tribunal"); and

(ii)  before the Tribunal has determined the question, the person satisfies the Tribunal as mentioned in subsection (2).

(2)  The person satisfies the Tribunal as mentioned in this subsection if the person satisfies the Tribunal that—

(a)  the person has an interest which the person is able and willing to sell in the whole of the relevant land; and

(b)  the right—

(i)  in the case of land consisting of a house, building or manufactory, cannot be purchased without material detriment to the land; or

(ii)  in the case of land consisting of a park or garden belonging to a house, cannot be purchased without seriously affecting the amenity or convenience of the house.

(3)  The compulsory purchase order to which the notice to treat relates, in relation to the person concerned—

(a)  ceases to authorise the purchase of the right; and

(b)  is deemed to authorise the purchase of the person's interest in the whole of the relevant land (including, in the case of land consisting of a park or garden belonging to a house, the house);

and the notice to treat is deemed to have been served in respect of that interest on such date as the Tribunal directs.

(4)  Any question as to the extent of the land in which a compulsory purchase order is deemed to authorise the purchase of an interest by virtue of subsection (3) is to be determined by the Tribunal.

(5)  Subsection (6) applies if, in consequence of a determination of the Tribunal that it is satisfied as mentioned in subsection (1)(b)(ii), a compulsory purchase order is deemed by virtue of subsection (3) to authorise the purchase of an interest in land.

(6)  The acquiring authority may, at any time within the period of six weeks beginning with the date of the determination, withdraw the notice to treat in consequence of which the determination was made.

(7)  Nothing in subsection (6) prejudices any other power of the authority to withdraw the notice.

(8)  The modifications subject to which subsection (1) of section 58 of the Land Compensation Act 1973 (determination of material detriment) is to have effect, as applied by subsection (2) of that section to the duty of the Tribunal in determining whether it is satisfied as mentioned in subsection (1)(b)(ii) above, are set out in subsection (9).

(9)  They are that—

(a)  at the beginning of paragraphs (a) and (b) there shall be inserted "a right over";

(b)  for "severance" there shall be substituted "right on the whole of the house, building or manufactory or of the house and the park or garden"; and

(c)  for "part proposed" and "part is" there shall be substituted respectively "right proposed" and "right is"."

12.—(1)  The provisions of the Act of 1965 mentioned in sub-paragraph (2) (which state the effect of a deed poll executed in various circumstances where there is no conveyance by persons with interests in the land) are to be read as if they were modified in accordance with sub-paragraph (3).

(2)  The provisions are—

(a)  section 9(4) (failure of owners to convey),

(b)  *paragraph 10(3) of Schedule 1* (owners under incapacity),

(c)  paragraph 2(3) of Schedule 2 (absent and untraced owners), and

(d)  paragraphs 2(3) and 7(2) of Schedule 4 (common land).

(3) The provisions are to be read as if they were modified so as to secure that, as against persons with interests in the land which are expressed to be overridden by the deed, the right which is to be acquired compulsorily is vested absolutely in the acquiring authority.

13.—(1) Section 11 of the Act of 1965 (powers of entry) is to be read as if it were modified so as to secure that, as from the date on which the acquiring authority has served notice to treat in respect of any right, the acquiring authority has power to enter for the purpose of exercising that right.

(2) For the purposes of sub-paragraph (1)—
- (a) the power to enter is to be exercisable in the same circumstances, and subject to the same conditions, as already contained in that section, and
- (b) the right is deemed to have been created on the date of service of the notice.

(3) Sections 12 (penalty for unauthorised entry) and 13 (entry on sheriff's warrant in the event of obstruction) of the Act of 1965 are to be read as if modified correspondingly.

14. Section 20 of the Act of 1965 (compensation for short-term tenants) is to be read as if it were modified so as to secure that persons with such interests as are mentioned in that section are compensated in a manner corresponding to that in which they would be compensated on a compulsory purchase of the interests but taking into account only the extent (if any) of such interference with such interests as is actually caused, or likely to be caused, by the exercise of the right concerned.

15. Section 22 of the Act of 1965 (protection of acquiring authority's possession of land where by inadvertence an interest in the land has not been purchased) is to be read as if it were modified so as to enable the acquiring authority, in circumstances corresponding to those referred to in that section, to continue to be entitled to exercise the right concerned, subject to compliance with that section as respects compensation.

*New rights: compensation*

16.—(1) The enactments relating to compensation for the compulsory purchase of land apply, with the necessary modifications, in relation to the acquisition of new rights under section 9 as they apply to compensation for the compulsory purchase of land.

(2) Sub-paragraph (1) is without prejudice to the generality of paragraph 8.

        **[1879]**

**NOTES**

Commencement: 1 December 2008, subject to transitional provisions and savings in SI 2008/3068, arts 6–10 at **[3834B]–[3834F]**.

Para 11: in the Compulsory Purchase Act 1965, s 8(1)(b)(i) (as set out), words in square brackets substituted by the Transfer of Tribunal Functions (Lands Tribunal and Miscellaneous Amendments) Order 2009, SI 2009/1307, art 5(1), (2), Sch 1, para 289, subject to transitional and savings provisions in Sch 5 thereto.

PART 2
ACQUISITION BY AGREEMENT

17.—(1) The provisions of Part 1 of the Compulsory Purchase Act 1965 (c 56) (other than section 31) apply, so far as applicable, to the acquisition by the HCA of land by agreement.

(2) In that Part as so applied "land" has the same meaning as in this Part of this Act.

        **[1880]**

**NOTES**

Commencement: 1 December 2008, subject to transitional provisions and savings in SI 2008/3068, arts 6–10 at **[3834B]–[3834F]**.

SCHEDULE 3
MAIN POWERS IN RELATION TO LAND OF THE HCA

Section 11

PART 1
POWERS TO OVERRIDE EASEMENTS ETC

*Powers to override easements etc in undertaking works or using land*

1.—(1) The HCA or any other person may undertake any construction or maintenance works on land of the HCA even if undertaking the works involves—
- (a) interference with a relevant right or interest, or
- (b) a breach of a restriction as to the user of land arising by virtue of a contract.

(2) But the construction or maintenance works must still be in accordance with planning permission.

(3)   The HCA or any other person may use any land of the HCA even if the use involves—
  (a)   interference with a relevant right or interest, or
  (b)   a breach of a restriction as to the user of land arising by virtue of a contract.

(4)   But the use of the land must be in accordance with planning permission.

(5)   Sub-paragraphs (1) to (4) do not authorise interference with—
  (a)   any right of way on, under or over land, or
  (b)   any right of laying down, erecting, continuing or maintaining apparatus on, under or over land,

if the right is a protected right.

(6)   In this paragraph—
  "construction or maintenance works" means the erection, construction, carrying out or maintenance of any building or work,
  "protected right" means—
    (a)   a right vested in, or belonging to, statutory undertakers for the purpose of carrying on their undertaking, or
    (b)   a right conferred by, or in accordance with, the electronic communications code on the operator of an electronic communications code network,
  "relevant right or interest" means any easement, liberty, privilege, right or advantage annexed to land and adversely affecting other land (including any natural right to support),
  "statutory undertakers" means persons who are, or are deemed to be, statutory undertakers for the purposes of any provision of Part 11 of the Town and Country Planning Act 1990 (c 8); and "statutory undertaking" is to be read in accordance with section 262 of that Act (meaning of "statutory undertakers").

*Compensation for overridden easements etc*

2.—(1)   Compensation is payable under section 7 or 10 of the Compulsory Purchase Act 1965 (c 56) in respect of any interference or breach made in pursuance of paragraph 1.

(2)   The compensation is to be assessed in the same manner, and subject to the same rules, as in the case of other compensation under those sections in respect of injurious affection where—
  (a)   the compensation is to be estimated in connection with a purchase by the HCA, or
  (b)   the injury arises from the execution of works on, or use of, land acquired by the HCA.

(3)   Sub-paragraph (4) applies if a person other than the HCA—
  (a)   is liable to pay compensation by virtue of sub-paragraphs (1) and (2), and
  (b)   fails to discharge that liability.

(4)   The liability is enforceable against the HCA.

(5)   But sub-paragraph (4) does not affect any agreement between the HCA and any other person for indemnifying the HCA against any liability under that sub-paragraph.

**[1881]**

**NOTES**
Commencement: 1 December 2008, subject to transitional provisions and savings in SI 2008/3068, arts 6–10 at **[3834B]–[3834F]**.

PART 2
POWERS TO EXTINGUISH PUBLIC RIGHTS OF WAY

*Powers of Secretary of State to extinguish public rights of way by order*

3.   The Secretary of State may by order extinguish any public right of way over land of the HCA if the Secretary of State is satisfied that—
  (a)   an alternative right of way has been, or will be, provided, or
  (b)   the provision of an alternative right of way is not required.

*Notification of proposal to make order*

4.—(1)   This paragraph applies if the Secretary of State is proposing to make an order under paragraph 3.

(2)   The Secretary of State must—
  (a)   publish a notice stating—
    (i)   the effect of the order,
    (ii)   the time (not less than 28 days starting with the date of publication of the notice) within which objections to the proposal may be made, and
    (iii)   the manner in which objections to the proposal may be made, and
  (b)   serve a copy of the notice on—
    (i)   the local planning authority in whose area the land is situated, and
    (ii)   the relevant highway authority.

(3)  In sub-paragraph (2) "the relevant highway authority" means any authority which is a highway authority in relation to the right of way which is proposed to be extinguished by the order.

(4)  Publication under sub-paragraph (2) must be in such manner as the Secretary of State considers appropriate.

*Duty to consider objections*

5.—(1)  The Secretary of State must proceed under paragraph 6 if—
   (a)  an objection to a proposal to make an order is properly made and not withdrawn, and
   (b)  the matter is not otherwise dealt with.

(2)  For the purposes of sub-paragraph (1) an objection is properly made if (and only if)—
   (a)  it is made—
      (i)  within the time, and
      (ii)  in the manner,
     stated in the notice under paragraph 4, and
   (b)  a written statement of the grounds of the objection is comprised in, or submitted with, the objection.

(3)  For the purposes of sub-paragraph (1) the matter is otherwise dealt with if (and only if) the Secretary of State—
   (a)  decides, irrespective of the objection, not to make the order, or
   (b)  decides to make a modification to the proposal which is agreed to by the objector as meeting the objection.

6.—(1)  The Secretary of State must, before making a final decision, consider the grounds of the objection as set out in the statement comprised in, or submitted with, the objection.

(2)  The Secretary of State may require the objector to submit within a particular period a further written statement as to any of the matters to which the objection relates.

*Duty to give opportunity to appear*

7.—(1)  The Secretary of State must, before making a final decision, give the objector an opportunity to appear before, and be heard by, a person appointed for the purpose by the Secretary of State.

(2)  Sub-paragraph (3) applies if the objector takes advantage of this opportunity.

(3)  The Secretary of State must give an opportunity of appearing and being heard on the same occasion as the objector to—
   (a)  the HCA, and
   (b)  any other persons whom the Secretary of State considers ought to be given the opportunity.

(4)  Sub-paragraphs (1) to (3) do not apply so far as the Secretary of State has the power to proceed under paragraph 8 or 9.

*Power to treat objection as irrelevant*

8.  The Secretary of State may treat the objection as irrelevant for the purpose of making a final decision—
   (a)  if the Secretary of State has considered the grounds of the objection as set out in the original statement and in any further statement, and
   (b)  so far as the Secretary of State is satisfied that the objection relates to a matter which can be dealt with in the assessment of compensation.

*Power to curtail decision-making process*

9.  The Secretary of State may make a final decision without further investigation as to the matters to which the objection relates if—
   (a)  the Secretary of State—
      (i)  has considered the grounds of the objection as set out in the original statement and in any further statement, and
      (ii)  is satisfied that, for the purpose of making a final decision, sufficient information is available as to the matters to which the objection relates, or
   (b)  a further statement has been required under paragraph 6(2) but is not submitted within the required period.

*Power to hold public local inquiry*

10.—(1)  The Secretary of State must cause a public local inquiry to be held in relation to an objection to a proposal to make an order under paragraph 3 if the Secretary of State considers that the matters to which the objection relates are such as to require investigation by such an inquiry before the Secretary of State makes a final decision.

(2)   The duty in sub-paragraph (1) is effective despite any other provisions of paragraphs 4 to 9.

(3)   The other provisions of those paragraphs are to be ignored if no effect has been given to them when the Secretary of State decides to cause an inquiry to be held.

*Orders relating to electronic communications apparatus: removal or abandonment of apparatus*

11.   Paragraphs 12 and 13 apply if—
  (a)   an order under paragraph 3 extinguishing a public right of way is made, and
  (b)   at the time of the publication of the notice required by paragraph 4 any electronic communications apparatus was kept installed for the purposes of an electronic communications code network under, in, on, over, along or across the land over which the right of way subsisted.

12.—(1)   The power of the operator of the network to remove the apparatus is exercisable, despite the order, at any time not later than the end of the period of 3 months beginning with the day on which the right of way is extinguished.

(2)   The power of the operator of the network to remove the whole or any part of the apparatus is exercisable after the end of that period if, before the end of the period, the operator has served notice on the HCA of the operator's intention to remove the apparatus or (as the case may be) part.

13.—(1)   The operator of the network may abandon the electronic communications apparatus, or any part of it, by serving notice to that effect on the HCA not later than the end of the period of 3 months beginning with the day on which the right of way is extinguished.

(2)   In the absence of such a notice, the operator of the network is to be treated at the end of the period of 3 months as having abandoned any part of the apparatus which, at that time, the operator has neither—
  (a)   removed, nor
  (b)   served notice of intention to remove.

14.—(1)   The operator of the network may recover from the HCA the expense of providing any substitute electronic communications apparatus in such other place as the operator may require.

(2)   In sub-paragraph (1) "substitute electronic communications apparatus" means electronic communications apparatus in substitution for—
  (a)   the electronic communications apparatus removed or abandoned, and
  (b)   any other electronic communications apparatus connected with the removed or abandoned apparatus which is made useless in consequence of the removal or abandonment.

15.   Electronic communications apparatus, or any part of it, abandoned by the operator of an electronic communications code network under paragraph 13—
  (a)   vests in the HCA, and
  (b)   is deemed, with its abandonment, to cease to be kept installed for the purposes of an electronic communications code network.

*Orders relating to electronic communications apparatus: notice requirements*

16.—(1)   The Secretary of State must serve notice on the operator of an electronic communications code network of the making of an order under paragraph 3 if the order extinguishes a public right of way in circumstances in which paragraphs 12 and 13 apply in relation to the operator.

(2)   The notice must be served as soon as practicable after the making of the order.

*Supplementary: Part 2*

17.   The power of the Secretary of State to make orders under paragraph 3 includes power to—
  (a)   vary or revoke such orders, and
  (b)   make supplementary, incidental, consequential, transitional, transitory or saving provision.

18.   In this Part of this Schedule, in relation to an order, any reference to making a final decision is a reference to deciding whether to make the order or what modification (if any) ought to be made.

**[1882]**

**NOTES**
  Commencement: 1 December 2008, subject to transitional provisions and savings in SI 2008/3068, arts 6–10 at **[3834B]–[3834F]**.

## PART 3
## POWERS IN RELATION TO BURIAL GROUNDS AND CONSECRATED LAND ETC

*Burial grounds*

19.—(1)   This paragraph applies in relation to any land of the HCA which consists in, or forms part of, a burial ground.

(2)   The HCA may use the land in any way which accords with planning permission despite—
  (a)   anything in any enactment relating to burial grounds, or
  (b)   any obligation or restriction imposed under ecclesiastical law or otherwise in respect of burial grounds.

(3)   But sub-paragraph (2) does not apply in relation to any land which has been used for the burial of the dead until prescribed requirements about the removal and reinterment of human remains and the disposal of monuments have been complied with in relation to the land.

*Consecrated land other than burial grounds*

20.—(1)   This paragraph applies in relation to any land of the HCA which—
  (a)   is consecrated land (whether or not including a building), and
  (b)   does not consist in, or form part of, a burial ground.

(2)   The HCA or any other person may use the land in any way which accords with planning permission despite any obligation or restriction imposed under ecclesiastical law or otherwise in respect of consecrated land.

(3)   But any such use of the land is subject to—
  (a)   prescribed requirements about the disposal of monuments, and
  (b)   prescribed provisions for prohibiting or restricting the use of the land while—
    (i)   any church or other building used, or formerly used, for religious worship remains on the land, or
    (ii)   any part of any such church or other building remains on the land.

(4)   Prohibitions or restrictions prescribed under sub-paragraph (3)(b) may be absolute or until a prescribed consent is obtained.

*Other land connected to religious worship*

21.—(1)   This paragraph applies in relation to any land of the HCA which—
  (a)   is neither consecrated land nor land which consists in, or forms part of, a burial ground, and
  (b)   at the time of acquisition included—
    (i)   a church or other building used, or formerly used, for religious worship, or
    (ii)   the site of such a church or other building.

(2)   Any use of the land is subject to prescribed requirements about the disposal of monuments.

*Regulations: general*

22.—(1)   Regulations under this Part of this Schedule must secure that any use of land which is subject to compliance with the regulations is (so far as possible) subject to an appropriate level of control.

(2)   For the purposes of sub-paragraph (1) an appropriate level of control is the same control—
  (a)   as imposed by law in relation to a similar use authorised by an enactment not contained in this Part of this Act,
  (b)   as imposed by a Measure, or
  (c)   as it would be proper to impose on a disposal of the land concerned otherwise than in pursuance of an enactment or Measure.

(3)   Regulations under this Part of this Schedule must impose such requirements in relation to the disposal of the land as the Secretary of State considers appropriate to secure that the requirements and other provisions in the regulations about the use of the land are complied with.

(4)   Regulations made for the purposes of paragraphs 19 to 21 may, in particular, include incidental or consequential provision about the closing of registers.

*Regulations about human remains and monuments*

23.—(1)   Regulations under this Part of this Schedule about the removal and reinterment of human remains and the disposal of monuments must require the persons in whom the land is vested to publish notice of their intention to carry out the removal and reinterment of any human remains or the disposal of any monuments.

(2)   Regulations under this Part of this Schedule about the removal and reinterment of human remains and the disposal of monuments must make provision for—

(a)   enabling the personal representatives or relatives of any deceased person themselves—
  (i)   to undertake the removal and reinterment of the remains of the deceased, and
  (ii)   the disposal of any monument commemorating the deceased, and
(b)   requiring the persons in whom the land is vested to meet the expenses of such removal, reinterment and disposal provided that they are not more than such amount as may be prescribed.

(3)   Regulations under this Part of this Schedule about the removal and reinterment of human remains and the disposal of monuments must require compliance with such reasonable conditions (if any) as may be imposed, in the case of consecrated land, by the bishop of the diocese, in relation to—
(a)   the manner of removal of any human remains,
(b)   the place and manner of reinterment of any human remains, and
(c)   the disposal of any monuments.

(4)   Regulations under this Part of this Schedule about the removal and reinterment of human remains must require compliance with any directions given in any case by the Secretary of State in relation to the removal and reinterment of any human remains.

*Disapplication of faculties*

24.—(1)   No faculty is required for—
(a)   the removal and reinterment of any human remains, or
(b)   the removal or disposal of any monuments,
in accordance with regulations under this Part of this Schedule.

(2)   Sub-paragraph (1) is subject to any provision to the contrary made by regulations under this Part of this Schedule.

*Disapplication of section 25 of the Burial Act 1857*

25.   Section 25 of the Burial Act 1857 (c 81) (which prohibits the removal of human remains without the licence of the Secretary of State except in certain cases) does not apply to a removal of human remains carried out in accordance with regulations under this Part of this Schedule.

*Interpretation: Part 3*

26.—(1)   In this Part of this Schedule—
  "burial ground" includes any churchyard, cemetery or other ground (whether or not consecrated) which has at any time been set apart for the purposes of interment,
  "monument" includes a tombstone or other memorial,
  "prescribed" means prescribed by regulations made by the Secretary of State.

(2)   Any power conferred by paragraph 19(2) or 20(2) to use land is to be read as a power to use the land, whether or not it involves—
(a)   the erection, construction or carrying out of any building or work, or
(b)   the maintenance of any building or work.

**[1883]**

**NOTES**
Commencement: 1 December 2008, subject to transitional provisions and savings in SI 2008/3068, arts 6–10 at [3834B]–[3834F].

## SCHEDULE 4
## POWERS IN RELATION TO, AND FOR, STATUTORY UNDERTAKERS
Section 12

## PART 1
## EXTINGUISHMENT OR REMOVAL POWERS FOR THE HCA

*Notice for extinguishment of rights of undertakers or for removal of their apparatus*

1.—(1)   Sub-paragraph (2) applies if—
(a)   a protected right subsists over land of the HCA and is vested in, or belongs to, statutory undertakers for the purpose of carrying on their undertaking, or
(b)   apparatus vested in, or belonging to, statutory undertakers for the purpose of carrying on their undertaking is on, under or over land of the HCA.

(2)   The HCA may serve a notice on the statutory undertakers.

(3)   The notice may, in the case of a protected right, state that, at the end of the relevant period, the right will be extinguished.

(4)   The notice may, in the case of apparatus, require that, before the end of the relevant period, the apparatus must be removed.

(5)    In this paragraph—
     "protected right" means—
        (a)     a right of way on, under or over land, or
        (b)     a right of laying down, erecting, continuing or maintaining apparatus on, under or over land,
     "relevant period" means—
        (a)     the period of 28 days beginning with the date of service of the notice, or
        (b)     any longer period beginning with that date and specified in the notice.

*Counter-notices*

2.—(1)    Sub-paragraph (2) applies if the HCA serves a notice under paragraph 1 on statutory undertakers.

(2)    The statutory undertakers may, before the end of the period of 28 days beginning with the date of the service of the notice, serve a counter-notice on the HCA.

(3)    The counter-notice is a notice stating that the statutory undertakers object to all or any provisions of the notice under paragraph 1.

(4)    The counter-notice must also specify the grounds of their objection.

*Effect of unopposed notice*

3.—(1)    This paragraph applies if—
        (a)     a notice is served under paragraph 1, and
        (b)     no counter-notice is served under paragraph 2.

(2)    Any right to which the notice under paragraph 1 relates is extinguished at the end of the period specified for that purpose in the notice.

(3)    The HCA may—
        (a)     remove any apparatus, and
        (b)     dispose of it as it considers appropriate,

if any requirement of the notice under paragraph 1 as to the removal of the apparatus has not been complied with by the end of the period specified for that purpose in the notice.

*Opposed notices and Ministerial orders*

4.—(1)    This paragraph applies if—
        (a)     a notice is served under paragraph 1, and
        (b)     a counter-notice is served under paragraph 2.

(2)    The HCA may—
        (a)     withdraw the notice served under paragraph 1, or
        (b)     apply to the Secretary of State and the appropriate Minister for an order under sub-paragraph (3).

(3)    The Secretary of State and the appropriate Minister may make an order embodying, with or without modifications, the provisions of the notice.

(4)    The fact that a notice has been withdrawn under sub-paragraph (2)(a) does not prejudice the service of a further notice.

5.—(1)    Before making an order under paragraph 4(3), the Secretary of State and the appropriate Minister must give the statutory undertakers on whom notice was served an opportunity to object to the application for the order.

(2)    The Secretary of State and the appropriate Minister—
        (a)     must consider any objections made by virtue of sub-paragraph (1), and
        (b)     must give—
            (i)     the statutory undertakers who made the objections, and
            (ii)     the HCA,
        an opportunity to appear before, and be heard by, a person appointed for this purpose by the Secretary of State and the appropriate Minister.

(3)    The Secretary of State and the appropriate Minister may then—
        (a)     decide not to make an order, or
        (b)     proceed to make an order in accordance with the application (with or without modifications).

6.—(1)    This paragraph applies if an order is made under paragraph 4(3).

(2)    Any right to which the order relates is extinguished at the end of the period specified for that purpose in the order.

(3)    The HCA may—
        (a)     remove any apparatus, and
        (b)     dispose of it as it considers appropriate,

if any requirement of the order as to the removal of the apparatus has not been complied with by the end of the period specified for that purpose in the order.

*Compensation*

7.—(1)   Statutory undertakers are entitled to compensation from the HCA if—
  (a)   any right vested in, or belonging to, the statutory undertakers is extinguished, or
  (b)   any requirement is imposed on the statutory undertakers,
by virtue of this Part of this Schedule.

  (2)   Sections 280 and 282 of the Town and Country Planning Act 1990 (c 8) (measure of compensation to statutory undertakers) apply to compensation under this paragraph as they apply to compensation under section 279(4) of that Act.

*Electronic communications*

8.—(1)   The reference in paragraph 1(1)(a) to a protected right vested in, or belonging to, statutory undertakers for the purpose of carrying on their undertaking includes a reference to a protected right conferred by, or in accordance with, the electronic communications code on the operator of an electronic communications code network.

  (2)   The reference in paragraph 1(1)(b) to apparatus vested in, or belonging to, statutory undertakers for the purpose of carrying on their undertaking includes a reference to electronic communications apparatus kept installed for the purposes of any such network.

  (3)   Sub-paragraphs (1) and (2) do not apply where paragraphs 12 and 13 of Part 2 of Schedule 3 apply (orders under paragraph 3 of that Schedule which relate to electronic communications apparatus).

  (4)   Where paragraph 1 has effect as mentioned in sub-paragraphs (1) and (2) above—
  (a)   any reference in this Part of this Schedule to statutory undertakers has effect as a reference to the operator of the electronic communications code network, and
  (b)   any reference in this Part of this Schedule to the appropriate Minister has effect as a reference to the Secretary of State for Business, Enterprise and Regulatory Reform.

**[1884]**

---

**NOTES**

Commencement: 1 December 2008, subject to transitional provisions and savings in SI 2008/3068, arts 6–10 at **[3834B]–[3834F]**.

---

PART 2
POWERS FOR UNDERTAKERS TO CARRY OUT WORKS

*Notices to carry out works*

9.—(1)   Sub-paragraph (2) applies if—
  (a)   apparatus vested in, or belonging to, statutory undertakers is on, under or over land of the HCA, and
  (b)   the statutory undertakers claim that development to be carried out on the land will require, on technical or other grounds connected with carrying on their undertaking, the removal or re-siting of the apparatus affected by the development.

  (2)   The statutory undertakers may serve on the HCA a notice claiming the right to—
  (a)   enter on the land, and
  (b)   carry out such works for the removal or re-siting of the apparatus or any part of it as may be specified in the notice.

  (3)   No notice may be served under sub-paragraph (2) more than 21 days after the beginning of the development on the land.

*Counter-notices*

10.—(1)   Sub-paragraph (2) applies if statutory undertakers serve a notice under paragraph 9 on the HCA.

  (2)   The HCA may, before the end of the period of 28 days beginning with the date of the service of the notice, serve a counter-notice on the statutory undertakers.

  (3)   The counter-notice is a notice stating that the HCA objects to all or any provisions of the notice under paragraph 9.

  (4)   The counter-notice must also specify the grounds of the HCA's objection.

*Effect of unopposed notice*

11.—(1)   This paragraph applies if—

    (a)    a notice is served under paragraph 9,

    (b)    no counter-notice is served under paragraph 10, and

    (c)    the period of 28 days beginning with the date of the service of the notice under paragraph 9 has ended.

    (2)    The statutory undertakers have the rights claimed in their notice under paragraph 9.

*Opposed notices and Ministerial orders*

12.—(1)    This paragraph applies if—

    (a)    a notice is served under paragraph 9, and

    (b)    a counter-notice is served under paragraph 10.

    (2)    The statutory undertakers may—

    (a)    withdraw the notice served under paragraph 9, or

    (b)    apply to the Secretary of State and the appropriate Minister for an order under sub-paragraph (3).

    (3)    The Secretary of State and the appropriate Minister may by order confer on the statutory undertakers—

    (a)    the rights claimed in the notice under paragraph 9, or

    (b)    such modified rights as the Secretary of State and the appropriate Minister consider it appropriate to confer on the statutory undertakers.

    (4)    The fact that a notice has been withdrawn under sub-paragraph (2)(a) does not prejudice the service of a further notice.

*Power to arrange for the works to be done by the HCA*

13.—(1)    Sub-paragraph (2) applies if statutory undertakers have the right to carry out works for the removal or re-siting of apparatus by virtue of this Part of this Schedule.

    (2)    The statutory undertakers may arrange with the HCA for the works to be carried out by the HCA, under the superintendence of the statutory undertakers, instead of by the statutory undertakers themselves.

*Compensation*

14.—(1)    Statutory undertakers are entitled to compensation from the HCA if works are carried out for the removal or re-siting of their apparatus which they have the right to carry out by virtue of this Part of this Schedule.

    (2)    Sections 280 and 282 of the Town and Country Planning Act 1990 (c 8) (measure of compensation to statutory undertakers) apply to compensation under this paragraph as they apply to compensation under section 279(4) of that Act.

*Electronic communications*

15.—(1)    The reference in paragraph 9(1)(a) to apparatus vested in, or belonging to, statutory undertakers includes a reference to electronic communications apparatus kept installed for the purposes of an electronic communications code network.

    (2)    Where paragraph 9(1)(a) has effect as mentioned in sub-paragraph (1) above—

    (a)    any reference in this Part of this Schedule to statutory undertakers has effect as a reference to the operator of the electronic communications code network, and

    (b)    any reference in this Part of this Schedule to the appropriate Minister has effect as a reference to the Secretary of State for Business, Enterprise and Regulatory Reform.

    **[1885]**

**NOTES**

Commencement: 1 December 2008, subject to transitional provisions and savings in SI 2008/3068, arts 6–10 at **[3834B]**–**[3834F]**.

## PART 3
### EXTENSION OR MODIFICATION OF FUNCTIONS OF UNDERTAKERS

*Ministerial order following representations by statutory undertakers*

16.—(1)    The Secretary of State and the appropriate Minister may by order provide for an extension or modification of the functions of particular statutory undertakers if conditions 1 and 2 are met.

    (2)    Condition 1 is that the statutory undertakers have made representations on the subject to the Secretary of State and the appropriate Minister.

(3)    Condition 2 is that the Secretary of State and the appropriate Minister consider it appropriate to extend or modify the functions of the statutory undertakers—
    (a)    to secure the provision of services which—
        (i)    would not otherwise be provided, or
        (ii)   would not otherwise be satisfactorily provided,
    in relation to relevant land, or
    (b)    to facilitate an adjustment of the carrying on of the undertaking necessitated by any of the acts and events mentioned in sub-paragraph (4).

(4)    The acts and events are—
    (a)    the acquisition by the HCA under this Part of this Act of any land—
        (i)    in which an interest was held for the purpose of carrying on the undertaking concerned, or
        (ii)   which was used for that purpose, and
    (b)    the extinguishment of a right, or the imposition of any requirement, by virtue of Part 1 of this Schedule.

(5)    In this Part of this Schedule "relevant land" means land in respect of which any of the functions of the HCA under this Part of this Act are being, or have been, exercised.

*Ministerial order following representations by the HCA*

17.—(1)    The Secretary of State and the appropriate Minister may by order provide for an extension or modification of the functions of particular statutory undertakers if conditions 1 and 2 are met.

(2)    Condition 1 is that the HCA has made representations on the subject to the Secretary of State and the appropriate Minister.

(3)    Condition 2 is that the Secretary of State and the appropriate Minister consider it appropriate to extend or modify the functions of the statutory undertakers to secure—
    (a)    the provision of new services in relation to relevant land, or
    (b)    the extension of existing services in relation to such land.

*Examples of contents of orders*

18.—(1)    An order under paragraph 16 or 17 may, in particular—
    (a)    give power to statutory undertakers—
        (i)    to acquire (whether compulsorily or by agreement) any land specified in the order, or
        (ii)   to erect or construct any buildings or works specified in the order,
    (b)    apply, in relation to the acquisition of any such land or the erection or construction of any such buildings or works, enactments relating to the acquisition of land or the erection or construction of buildings or works.

(2)    An order under paragraph 16 which is for the purposes mentioned in sub-paragraph (3)(a) of that paragraph or an order under paragraph 17 may, in particular, give effect to any financial arrangements—
    (a)    agreed between the HCA and the statutory undertakers, or
    (b)    in the absence of agreement, decided to be equitable in such manner, and by such tribunal, as may be specified in the order.

*Notification of proposal to make order*

19.—(1)    Statutory undertakers must, as soon as possible after making representations of the kind mentioned in paragraph 16(2), publish a notice—
    (a)    giving such particulars as the Secretary of State and the appropriate Minister may direct of the matters to which the representations relate,
    (b)    specifying the time within which objections to the making of an order as a result of the representations may be made, and
    (c)    specifying the manner in which objections to the making of such an order may be made.

(2)    The notice must be published in such form and manner as the Secretary of State and the appropriate Minister may direct.

(3)    The statutory undertakers must also serve a copy of the notice on such persons, or descriptions of persons, as the Secretary of State and the appropriate Minister may direct if the Secretary of State and the appropriate Minister direct that a copy is to be served.

20.—(1)    The HCA must, as soon as possible after making representations of the kind mentioned in paragraph 17(2), publish a notice—
    (a)    giving such particulars as the Secretary of State and the appropriate Minister may direct of the matters to which the representations relate,
    (b)    specifying the time within which objections to the making of an order as a result of the representations may be made, and

(c)    specifying the manner in which objections to the making of such an order may be made.

(2)    The notice must be published in such form and manner as the Secretary of State and the appropriate Minister may direct.

(3)    The HCA must also serve a copy of the notice on such persons, or descriptions of persons, as the Secretary of State and the appropriate Minister may direct if the Secretary of State and the appropriate Minister direct that a copy is to be served.

*Duty to consider objections*

21.—(1)    The Secretary of State and the appropriate Minister must proceed under paragraph 22 if—
    (a)    an objection to the making of an order under paragraph 16 or 17 is properly made and not withdrawn, and
    (b)    the matter is not otherwise dealt with.

(2)    For the purposes of sub-paragraph (1) an objection is properly made if (and only if)—
    (a)    it is made—
        (i)    within the time, and
        (ii)    in the manner,
    stated in the notice under paragraph 19(1) or (as the case may be) 20(1), and
    (b)    a written statement of the grounds of the objection is comprised in, or submitted with, the objection.

(3)    For the purposes of sub-paragraph (1) the matter is otherwise dealt with if (and only if) the Secretary of State and the appropriate Minister—
    (a)    decide, irrespective of the objection, not to make the order, or
    (b)    decide to make a modification which is agreed to by the objector as meeting the objection.

22.—(1)    The Secretary of State and the appropriate Minister must, before making a final decision, consider the grounds of the objection as set out in the statement comprised in, or submitted with, the objection.

(2)    The Secretary of State and the appropriate Minister may require the objector to submit within a specified period a further written statement as to any of the matters to which the objection relates.

*Duty to give opportunity to appear*

23.—(1)    The Secretary of State and the appropriate Minister must, before making a final decision, give the objector an opportunity to appear before, and be heard by, a person appointed for the purpose by the Secretary of State and the appropriate Minister.

(2)    The Secretary of State and the appropriate Minister must give an opportunity of appearing and being heard on the same occasion to—
    (a)    the statutory undertakers or (as the case may be) the HCA as a result of whose representations the order is proposed to be made, and
    (b)    any other persons whom the Secretary of State and the appropriate Minister consider ought to be given the opportunity,
if the objector takes advantage of the opportunity mentioned in sub-paragraph (1).

(3)    Sub-paragraphs (1) and (2) do not apply so far as the Secretary of State and the appropriate Minister have the power to proceed under paragraph 24 or 25.

*Power to treat objection as irrelevant*

24.    The Secretary of State and the appropriate Minister may treat the objection as irrelevant for the purpose of making a final decision—
    (a)    if the Secretary of State and the appropriate Minister have considered the grounds of the objection as set out in the original statement and in any further statement, and
    (b)    so far as the Secretary of State and the appropriate Minister are satisfied that the objection relates to a matter which can be dealt with in the assessment of compensation.

*Power to curtail decision-making process*

25.    The Secretary of State and the appropriate Minister may make a final decision without further investigation as to the matters to which the objection relates if—
    (a)    the Secretary of State and the appropriate Minister—
        (i)    have considered the grounds of the objection as set out in the original statement and in any further statement, and
        (ii)    are satisfied that, for the purpose of making a final decision, sufficient information is available as to the matters to which the objection relates, or
    (b)    a further statement has been required under paragraph 22(2) but is not submitted within the specified period.

*Power to hold public local inquiry*

26.—(1)   The Secretary of State and the appropriate Minister must cause a public local inquiry to be held in relation to an objection under this Part of this Schedule if the Secretary of State and the appropriate Minister consider that the matters to which the objection relates are such as to require investigation by such an inquiry before the Secretary of State and the appropriate Minister make a final decision.

(2)   The duty in sub-paragraph (1) is effective despite any other provisions of this Part of this Schedule.

(3)   The other provisions of this Part of this Schedule are to be ignored if, when the Secretary of State and the appropriate Minister decide to cause an inquiry to be held, effect has not been given to them.

*Special parliamentary procedure for orders*

27.   Orders under paragraph 16 or 17 are subject to special parliamentary procedure.

**[1886]**

**NOTES**

Commencement: 1 December 2008, subject to transitional provisions and savings in SI 2008/3068, arts 6–10 at **[3834B]**–**[3834F]**.

PART 4
## RELIEVING UNDERTAKERS OF OBLIGATIONS

*Orders to relieve obligations*

28.—(1)   The appropriate Minister may by order provide for statutory undertakers to be relieved (whether absolutely or so far as specified in the order) of the need to meet an obligation relating to the carrying on of their undertaking if conditions 1 and 2 are met.

(2)   Condition 1 is that the statutory undertakers have made representations on the subject to the appropriate Minister.

(3)   Condition 2 is that the appropriate Minister is satisfied that meeting some or all of the obligation has been made impracticable by any of the acts and events mentioned in sub-paragraph (4).

(4)   The acts and events are—
    (a)   the acquisition by the HCA under this Part of this Act of any land—
        (i)   in which an interest was held for the purpose of carrying on the undertaking concerned, or
        (ii)   which was used for that purpose, and
    (b)   the extinguishment of a right, or the imposition of any requirement, by virtue of Part 1 of this Schedule.

*Notification of proposal to make order*

29.—(1)   Statutory undertakers must, as soon as possible after making representations of the kind mentioned in paragraph 28(2), proceed as directed by the appropriate Minister.

(2)   The appropriate Minister may direct the statutory undertakers to do either or both of the following—
    (a)   publish a notice—
        (i)   giving such particulars as the appropriate Minister may direct of the matters to which the representations relate,
        (ii)   specifying the time within which objections to the making of an order as a result of the representations may be made, and
        (iii)   specifying the manner in which objections to the making of such an order may be made, and
    (b)   serve a corresponding notice on such persons, or descriptions of persons, as the appropriate Minister may direct.

(3)   Publication under sub-paragraph (2) must be in such form and manner as the appropriate Minister may direct.

*Duty to consider objections*

30.—(1)   The appropriate Minister must proceed under paragraph 31 if—
    (a)   an objection to the making of an order is properly made and not withdrawn, and
    (b)   the matter is not otherwise dealt with.

(2)   For the purposes of sub-paragraph (1) an objection is properly made if (and only if)—
    (a)   it is made—

    (i)   within the time, and

    (ii)  in the manner,

    stated in the notice under paragraph 29(2), and

  (b)   a written statement of the grounds of the objection is comprised in, or submitted with, the objection.

(3)   For the purposes of sub-paragraph (1) the matter is otherwise dealt with if (and only if) the appropriate Minister—

  (a)   decides, irrespective of the objection, not to make the order, or

  (b)   decides to make a modification which is agreed to by the objector as meeting the objection.

31.—(1)   The appropriate Minister must, before making a final decision, consider the grounds of the objection as set out in the statement comprised in, or submitted with, the objection.

(2)   The appropriate Minister may require the objector to submit within a specified period a further written statement as to any of the matters to which the objection relates.

*Duty to give opportunity to appear*

32.—(1)   The appropriate Minister must, before making a final decision, give the objector an opportunity to appear before, and be heard by, a person appointed for the purpose by the appropriate Minister.

(2)   The appropriate Minister must give an opportunity of appearing and being heard on the same occasion to—

  (a)   the statutory undertakers as a result of whose representations the order is proposed to be made, and

  (b)   any other persons whom the appropriate Minister considers ought to be given the opportunity,

if the objector takes advantage of the opportunity mentioned in sub-paragraph (1).

(3)   Sub-paragraphs (1) and (2) do not apply so far as the appropriate Minister has the power to proceed under paragraph 33 or 34.

*Power to treat objection as irrelevant*

33.   The appropriate Minister may treat the objection as irrelevant for the purpose of making a final decision—

  (a)   if the appropriate Minister has considered the grounds of the objection as set out in the original statement and in any further statement, and

  (b)   so far as the appropriate Minister is satisfied that the objection relates to a matter which can be dealt with in the assessment of compensation.

*Power to curtail decision-making process*

34.   The appropriate Minister may make a final decision without further investigation as to the matters to which the objection relates if—

  (a)   the appropriate Minister—

    (i)   has considered the grounds of the objection as set out in the original statement and in any further statement, and

    (ii)  is satisfied that, for the purpose of making a final decision, sufficient information is available as to the matters to which the objection relates, or

  (b)   a further statement has been required under paragraph 31(2) but is not submitted within the specified period.

*Power to hold public local inquiry*

35.—(1)   The appropriate Minister may cause a public local inquiry to be held in relation to an objection under this Part of this Schedule if the appropriate Minister considers that the matters to which the objection relates are such as to require investigation by such an inquiry before the appropriate Minister makes a final decision.

(2)   The power in sub-paragraph (1) is effective despite any other provisions of this Part of this Schedule.

(3)   The other provisions of this Part of this Schedule are to be ignored if, when the Secretary of State decides to cause an inquiry to be held, effect has not been given to them.

*Notification procedure after the making of an order*

36.—(1)   The appropriate Minister must, immediately after making an order under paragraph 28, proceed under sub-paragraphs (2) and (3).

(2)   The appropriate Minister must publish a notice stating—

  (a)   that the order has been made, and

(b)   a place where a copy of it may be seen at any reasonable hour.

(3)   The appropriate Minister must serve a copy of the notice on—
   (a)   any person who—
      (i)   duly made an objection to the order, and
      (ii)   has sent the appropriate Minister a written request for the notice with an address for service, and
   (b)   any other person whom the appropriate Minister considers appropriate.

*Operative date of orders*

37.   An order under paragraph 28 which is not subject to special parliamentary procedure becomes operative on the date on which the notice required by paragraph 36(2) is first published.

*Special parliamentary procedure for orders*

38.—(1)   An order under paragraph 28 is subject to special parliamentary procedure if any objection to the making of the order is properly made and not withdrawn before the order is made.

(2)   Sub-paragraph (2) of paragraph 30 applies for the purposes of sub-paragraph (1) above as it applies for the purposes of sub-paragraph (1) of that paragraph.

*Legal challenges to orders*

39.—(1)   Sub-paragraph (2) applies if a person aggrieved by an order under paragraph 28 wishes to question its validity on the ground that—
   (a)   it is not within the powers conferred by this Part of this Schedule, or
   (b)   any requirement of this Part of this Schedule has not been complied with in relation to the order.

(2)   The person may, within 6 weeks beginning with the date on which the notice required by paragraph 36(2) is first published, apply to the High Court.

(3)   The High Court may, on an application under sub-paragraph (2), make an interim order suspending (whether wholly or in part) the operation of the order under paragraph 28 until the final determination of the proceedings.

(4)   The operation of the order may be suspended generally or so far as affecting any property of the applicant.

(5)   The High Court may, on an application under sub-paragraph (2), quash (whether wholly or in part) the order under paragraph 28 if satisfied that—
   (a)   the order is wholly or to any extent outside the powers conferred by this Part of this Schedule, or
   (b)   the interests of the applicant have been substantially prejudiced by the failure to comply with any requirement of this Part of this Schedule.

(6)   The order under paragraph 28 may be quashed generally or so far as affecting any property of the applicant.

**[1887]**

**NOTES**

Commencement: 1 December 2008, subject to transitional provisions and savings in SI 2008/3068, arts 6–10 at **[3834B]–[3834F]**.

PART 5
SUPPLEMENTARY

*Orders and directions*

40.—(1)   The power of—
   (a)   the Secretary of State and the appropriate Minister,
   (b)   the Secretary of State and the Secretary of State for Business, Enterprise and Regulatory Reform, or
   (c)   the appropriate Minister,
to make orders under this Schedule includes power to vary or revoke such orders and to make supplementary, incidental, consequential, transitional, transitory or saving provision.

(2)   The power of—
   (a)   the Secretary of State and the appropriate Minister, or
   (b)   the appropriate Minister,
to give directions under this Schedule includes power to vary or revoke such directions and to make supplementary, incidental, consequential, transitional, transitory or saving provision.

*Interpretation*

41.—(1)   In this Schedule—

"the appropriate Minister" is to be read as if contained in Part 11 of the Town and Country Planning Act 1990 (c 8),

"the Secretary of State and the appropriate Minister" is to be read as if contained in Part 11 of the Town and Country Planning Act 1990 (and any references to the Secretary of State and the appropriate Minister are, in relation to anything done or to be done by them, to be read as references to them acting jointly),

"statutory undertakers" means persons who are or are deemed to be statutory undertakers for the purposes of any provision of Part 11 of the Town and Country Planning Act 1990; and "statutory undertaking" is to be read in accordance with section 262 of that Act (meaning of "statutory undertaker").

(2)   In this Schedule, in relation to an order, any reference to making a final decision is a reference to deciding whether to make the order or what modification (if any) ought to be made.

**[1888]**

---

**NOTES**

Commencement: 1 December 2008, subject to transitional provisions and savings in SI 2008/3068, arts 6–10 at **[3834B]–[3834F]**.

---

(*Sch 5 amends the New Towns Act 1981; outside the scope of this work.*)

<br>

## SCHEDULE 6
## TRANSFER SCHEMES

Sections 51(3) and 55(3)

*Creation and apportionment of property, rights and liabilities etc*

1.   A scheme may—

   (a)   create for the transferor interests in, or rights over, property transferred by virtue of the scheme,

   (b)   create for a transferee interests in, or rights over, property retained by the transferor or transferred to another transferee,

   (c)   create rights or liabilities between the transferor and a transferee or between transferees.

2.—(1)   A scheme may provide for the transfer of property, rights or liabilities that would not otherwise be capable of being transferred or assigned.

(2)   In particular, it may provide for the transfer to take effect regardless of a contravention, liability or interference with an interest or right that would otherwise exist by reason of a provision having effect in relation to the terms on which the transferor is entitled to the property or right, or subject to the liability, in question.

(3)   It does not matter whether the provision referred to in sub-paragraph (2) has effect under an enactment or an agreement or in any other way.

3.   A certificate by the Secretary of State that anything specified in the certificate has vested in any person by virtue of a scheme is conclusive evidence for all purposes of that fact.

*Employment contracts*

4.—(1)   This paragraph applies if rights and liabilities under a contract of employment are transferred by virtue of a scheme.

(2)   The contract of employment—

   (a)   is not terminated by the transfer, and

   (b)   has effect from the transfer date as if made between the employee and the transferee.

(3)   The rights, powers, duties and liabilities of the transferor under or in connection with the contract are transferred to the transferee on the transfer date.

(4)   Anything done before the transfer date by or in relation to the transferor in respect of the contract or the employee is to be treated from that date as having been done by or in relation to the transferee.

(5)   In particular, a period of employment with the transferor is to be treated as a period of employment with the transferee (and the transfer is not to be treated as interrupting the continuity of that employment).

(6)   This paragraph is subject to paragraph 5.

5.—(1)   Rights and liabilities under a contract of employment are not transferred by virtue of a scheme if the employee objects to the transfer and informs the transferor or transferee of that fact.

(2)   If the employee objects to the transfer and informs the transferor or transferee of that fact—

    (a)    the employee's contract of employment is terminated immediately before the transfer date, but

    (b)    the employee is not to be treated, for any purpose, as having been dismissed by the transferor.

6.   If (apart from the change of employer) a substantial detrimental change is made to a person's working conditions, nothing in this Schedule affects any right the person has to terminate the person's contract of employment.

*Civil servants treated as employed under a contract of employment etc*

7.—(1)   This Schedule applies with the following modifications in relation to employment in the civil service of the Crown on terms which do not constitute a contract of employment.

    (2)   An individual who holds employment in the civil service of the Crown immediately before the transfer date is to be treated as employed by virtue of a contract of employment.

    (3)   The terms of the employment in the civil service of the Crown are to be regarded as constituting the terms of the contract of employment.

    (4)   The reference in paragraph 5 to dismissal by the transferor is to termination of the employment in the civil service of the Crown.

*Compensation*

8.   A scheme may contain provision for the payment of compensation by the Secretary of State to any person whose interests are adversely affected by it.

*Continuity*

9.   A transfer by virtue of a scheme does not affect the validity of anything done by or in relation to the transferor before the transfer takes effect.

10.   Anything which—

    (a)    is done by the transferor for the purposes of, or otherwise in connection with, anything transferred by virtue of a scheme, and

    (b)    is in effect immediately before the transfer date,

is to be treated as done by the transferee.

11.   There may be continued by or in relation to the transferee anything (including legal proceedings)—

    (a)    which relates to anything transferred by virtue of a scheme, and

    (b)    which is in the process of being done by or in relation to the transferor immediately before the transfer date.

12.—(1)   This paragraph applies to any document—

    (a)    which relates to anything transferred by virtue of a scheme, and

    (b)    which is in effect immediately before the transfer date.

    (2)   Any references in the document to the transferor are to be read as references to the transferee.

*Supplementary etc provision*

13.   A scheme may include supplementary, incidental, transitional and consequential provision.

**[1889]**

---

**NOTES**

    Commencement: 8 September 2008.

---

## SCHEDULE 7
## TRANSFER SCHEMES: TAX

Sections 51(5), 65(5)

*Overview*

1.   This Schedule makes provision about the fiscal effect of transfers under schemes made under sections 51 and 65.

*Key concepts*

2.—(1)   In this Schedule—

    (a)    "transfer scheme" means a scheme under section 51 or 65, and

    (b)    "transfer" means a transfer under a transfer scheme.

    (2)   In this Schedule "transfer between bodies" means a transfer—

(a)   from the Urban Regeneration Agency, the Commission for the New Towns or the Housing Corporation, and

(b)   to the HCA or the Regulator of Social Housing.

(3)   In this Schedule "transfer to government" means a transfer to—

(a)   a Minister of the Crown, or

(b)   the Welsh Ministers.

*Other definitions*

3.—(1)   In this Schedule—

(a)   ICTA means the Income and Corporation Taxes Act 1988 (c 1),

(b)   TCGA means the Taxation of Chargeable Gains Act 1992 (c 12),

(c)   FA 1996 means the Finance Act 1996 (c 8),

(d)   FA 2002 means the Finance Act 2002 (c 23), and

(e)   HMRC means the Commissioners for Her Majesty's Revenue and Customs.

(2)   In this Schedule a reference to a trade includes a reference to part of a trade.

*Corporation tax: continuity of trade*

4.—(1)   This paragraph applies if as the result of a transfer scheme—

(a)   a transferor ceases a trade, and

(b)   a transferee commences it.

(2)   In connection with the computation of profits and losses for the purpose of corporation tax in respect of periods wholly or partly after the commencement of the transfer scheme—

(a)   the transferee shall be treated as having always carried on the trade, and

(b)   the trade shall be considered separately from any other trade of the transferee (with any necessary apportionment being made).

*Corporation tax: capital allowances*

5.—(1)   This paragraph applies in respect of property transferred under a transfer scheme from—

(a)   the Urban Regeneration Agency, or

(b)   the Commission for the New Towns.

(2)   Where the property was used by the transferor, and is to be used by the transferee, in connection with a trade, section 343(2) of ICTA (company reconstructions: capital allowances) shall apply.

6.   The following transfers shall be treated as giving rise to neither allowance nor charge for the purposes of capital allowances in respect of a trade (and allowances shall be calculated as if the transferee had always carried on the trade)—

(a)   a transfer from the Housing Corporation, and

(b)   a transfer to government.

*Corporation tax: capital gains*

7.—(1)   This paragraph applies in respect of property transferred under a transfer scheme from—

(a)   the Urban Regeneration Agency,

(b)   the Commission for the New Towns, or

(c)   the Housing Corporation.

(2)   Section 17 of TCGA (disposals and acquisitions treated as at market value) shall not apply.

(3)   For the purposes of TCGA the transfer (in relation to the transferor and the transferee) is to be taken as being a disposal for a consideration such that neither gain nor loss accrues.

8.   A transfer shall be disregarded for the purposes of section 30 of TCGA (value-shifting: tax-free benefits).

9.   …

*Corporation tax: intangible assets*

10.—(1)   This paragraph applies for the purposes of Schedule 29 to FA 2002 (intangible assets).

(2)   Expressions used in this paragraph have the same meaning as in that Schedule.

(3)   A transfer between bodies of a chargeable intangible asset is a tax-neutral transfer.

(4)   An intangible fixed asset which is an existing asset of the transferor at the time of a transfer between bodies is to be treated, on and after the transfer, as an existing asset of the transferee.

(5)   A transfer to government of a chargeable intangible asset is to be treated as not involving a realisation of the asset by the transferor.

*Corporation tax: loan relationships*

11.—(1)   If as a result of a transfer the transferee replaces the transferor as a party to a loan relationship, paragraph 12(2) of Schedule 9 to FA 1996 (transfer within group: continuity of treatment) shall apply (whether or not the transferor and transferee are bodies corporate).

(2)   Expressions used in this paragraph have the same meaning as in that Schedule.

*Stamp duty*

12.—(1)   Stamp duty shall not be chargeable on a transfer scheme.

(2)   Stamp duty shall not be chargeable on a document certified by HMRC as connected with a transfer scheme.

(3)   A document which is not chargeable by virtue of this paragraph must be stamped in accordance with section 12 of the Stamp Act 1891 (c 39) with a stamp denoting that it is not chargeable.

**[1890]**

**NOTES**
Commencement: 8 September 2008.
Para 9: repealed by the Housing and Regeneration Act 2008 (Consequential Provisions) Order 2008, SI 2008/3002, arts 4, 6, Sch 1, para 59, Sch 3. It is understood that the amendment originally set out in para 9 was drafted in error.

*(Schs 8, 9 contain amendments which, in so far as relevant to this work, have been incorporated at the appropriate place; Sch 10 outside the scope of this work.)*

## SCHEDULE 11
## POSSESSION ORDERS RELATING TO CERTAIN TENANCIES
Section 299

### PART 1
### AMENDMENTS TO THE HOUSING ACTS OF 1985, 1988 AND 1996
1–13.   …

*Transitional provisions*

14.—(1)   Subject as follows, this Part of this Schedule does not apply to any possession order made before the commencement date.

(2)   This Part of this Schedule does apply to a possession order made before the commencement date if the order applies to—
   (a)   a new tenancy by virtue of paragraph 20, or
   (b)   a tenancy which has not ended pursuant to the order before that date.

(3)   Paragraphs 3(3) and 8(3) apply to any possession order regardless of when it was made.

(4)   In determining for the purposes of sub-paragraph (2) whether a tenancy has ended, any ending which was temporary because the tenancy was restored in consequence of a court order is to be ignored.

(5)   In this paragraph "the commencement date" means the day on which section 299 comes into force for purposes other than the purposes of the Secretary of State or the Welsh Ministers making orders under Part 2 of this Schedule.

**[1891]**

**NOTES**
Commencement: 20 May 2009 (paras 1, 2, 3(1), (2), (4), 4–7, 8(1), (2), (4), 9–13, 14(1), (2), (4), (5)); to be appointed (otherwise).
Paras 1–4: amend the Housing Act 1985, ss 82, 85, Sch 3 at **[418]**, **[423]**, **[581]**.
Paras 5–9: amend the Housing Act 1988, ss 5, 7, 9, 21 at **[733]**, **[736]**, **[739]**, **[757]**.
Paras 10–13: amend the Housing Act 1996, ss 127, 130, 143D at **[1014]**, **[1017]**, **[1034]**.

### PART 2
### REPLACEMENT OF CERTAIN TERMINATED TENANCIES

*Circumstances in which replacement tenancies arise*

15.   In this Part of this Schedule "an original tenancy" means any secure tenancy, assured tenancy, introductory tenancy or demoted tenancy—
   (a)   in respect of which a possession order was made before the commencement date, and
   (b)   which ended before that date pursuant to the order but not on the execution of the order.

16.—(1)   A new tenancy of the dwelling-house which was let under the original tenancy is treated as arising on the commencement date between the ex-landlord and the ex-tenant if—
(a)   on that date—
  (i)   the home condition is met, and
  (ii)   the ex-landlord is entitled to let the dwelling-house, and
(b)   the ex-landlord and the ex-tenant have not entered into another tenancy after the date on which the original tenancy ended but before the commencement date.

(2)   The home condition is that the dwelling-house which was let under the original tenancy—
(a)   is, on the commencement date, the only or principal home of the ex-tenant, and
(b)   has been the only or principal home of the ex-tenant throughout the termination period.

(3)   In this Part of this Schedule "the termination period" means the period—
(a)   beginning with the end of the original tenancy, and
(b)   ending with the commencement date.

(4)   For the purposes of sub-paragraph (2)(a) the dwelling-house is the only or principal home of the ex-tenant on the commencement date even though the ex-tenant is then absent from the dwelling-house as a result of having been evicted in pursuance of a warrant if the warrant is subsequently set aside but the possession order under which it was granted remains in force.

(5)   In that case, the new tenancy is treated as arising on the first day (if any) on which the ex-tenant resumes occupation of the dwelling-house as that person's only or principal home.

(6)   For the purposes of sub-paragraph (2)(b) any period of time within the termination period is to be ignored if—
(a)   it is a period in which the ex-tenant was absent from the dwelling-house as a result of having been evicted in pursuance of a warrant which was then set aside although the possession order under which it was granted remained in force, and
(b)   the ex-tenant subsequently resumes occupation of the dwelling-house as the ex-tenant's only or principal home.

(7)   The appropriate national authority may by order provide for particular cases or descriptions of case, or particular circumstances, where the home condition is met where it would not otherwise be met.

*Nature of replacement tenancies*
17.   The new tenancy is to be—
(a)   a secure tenancy if—
  (i)   the original tenancy was a secure tenancy, or
  (ii)   the original tenancy was an introductory tenancy but no election by the ex-landlord under section 124 of the Housing Act 1996 (c 52) is in force on the day on which the new tenancy arises,
(b)   an assured shorthold tenancy if the original tenancy was an assured shorthold tenancy,
(c)   an assured tenancy which is not an assured shorthold tenancy if the original tenancy was a tenancy of that kind,
(d)   an introductory tenancy if the original tenancy was an introductory tenancy and an election by the ex-landlord under section 124 of the Housing Act 1996 is in force on the day on which the new tenancy arises,
(e)   a demoted tenancy to which section 20B of the Housing Act 1988 (c 50) applies if the original tenancy was a demoted tenancy of that kind, and
(f)   a demoted tenancy to which section 143A of the Housing Act 1996 applies if the original tenancy was a demoted tenancy of that kind.

18.—(1)   The new tenancy is, subject as follows, to have effect on the same terms and conditions as those applicable to the original tenancy immediately before it ended.

(2)   The terms and conditions of the new tenancy are to be treated as modified so as to reflect, so far as applicable, any changes made during the termination period to the level of payments for the ex-tenant's occupation of the dwelling-house or to the other terms and conditions of the occupation.

(3)   The terms and conditions of the new tenancy are to be treated as modified so that any outstanding liabilities owed by the ex-tenant to the ex-landlord in respect of payments for the ex-tenant's occupation of the dwelling-house during the termination period are liabilities in respect of rent under the new tenancy.

(4)   The appropriate national authority may by order provide for other modifications of the terms and conditions of the new tenancy.

(5)   Nothing in sub-paragraphs (2) to (4) is to be read as permitting modifications of the new tenancy which would not have been possible if the original tenancy had remained a tenancy throughout the termination period.

(6)   The terms and conditions of a new secure tenancy which arises by virtue of paragraph 17(a)(ii) are to be treated as modified so far as necessary to reflect the fact that the new tenancy is a secure tenancy and not an introductory tenancy.

19.—(1)   Any provision which is made by or under an enactment and relates to a secure tenancy, assured tenancy, introductory tenancy or demoted tenancy applies, subject as follows, to a new tenancy of a corresponding kind.

(2)   Any such provision which relates to an introductory tenancy applies to a new tenancy which is an introductory tenancy as if the trial period mentioned in section 125(2) of the Housing Act 1996 (c 52) were the period of one year beginning with the day on which the new tenancy arises.

(3)   Any such provision which relates to a demoted tenancy applies to a new tenancy which is a demoted tenancy as if the demotion period mentioned in section 20B(2) of the Housing Act 1988 (c 50) or section 143B(1) of the Housing Act 1996 were the period of one year beginning with the day on which the new tenancy arises.

(4)   The appropriate national authority may by order modify any provision made by or under an enactment in its application to a new tenancy.

### *Status of possession order and other court orders*

20.—(1)   The possession order in pursuance of which the original tenancy ended is to be treated, so far as practicable, as if it applies to the new tenancy.

(2)   Any court orders made before the commencement date which—
   (a)   are in force on that date,
   (b)   relate to the occupation of the dwelling-house, and
   (c)   were made in contemplation of, in consequence of or otherwise in connection with the possession order,
are to be treated, so far as practicable, as if they apply to the new tenancy.

### *Continuity of tenancies*

21.—(1)   The new tenancy and the original tenancy are to be treated for the relevant purposes as—
   (a)   the same tenancy, and
   (b)   a tenancy which continued uninterrupted throughout the termination period.

(2)   The relevant purposes are—
   (a)   determining whether the ex-tenant is a successor in relation to the new tenancy,
   (b)   calculating on or after the commencement date the period qualifying, or the aggregate of such periods, under Schedule 4 to the Housing Act 1985 (c 68) (qualifying period for right to buy and discount),
   (c)   determining on or after the commencement date whether the condition set out in paragraph (b) of Ground 8 of Schedule 2 to that Act is met, and
   (d)   any other purposes specified by the appropriate national authority by order.

(3)   In proceedings on a relevant claim the court concerned may order that the new tenancy and the original tenancy are to be treated for the purposes of the claim as—
   (a)   the same tenancy, and
   (b)   a tenancy which continued uninterrupted throughout the termination period.

(4)   The following are relevant claims—
   (a)   a claim by the ex-tenant or the ex-landlord against the other for breach of a term or condition of the original tenancy—
      (i)   in respect of which proceedings are brought on or after the commencement date, or
      (ii)   in respect of which proceedings were brought, but were not finally determined, before that date,
   (b)   a claim by the ex-tenant against the ex-landlord for breach of statutory duty in respect of which proceedings are or were brought as mentioned in paragraph (a)(i) or (ii), and
   (c)   any other claim of a description specified by the appropriate national authority by order.

(5)   For the purposes of sub-paragraph (4)(a) proceedings must be treated as finally determined if—
   (a)   they are withdrawn,
   (b)   any appeal is abandoned, or
   (c)   the time for appealing has expired without an appeal being brought.

### *Compliance with consultation requirements*

22.—(1)   The fact that—
   (a)   the views of the ex-tenant during the termination period were not sought or taken into account when they should have been sought or taken into account, or
   (b)   the views of the ex-tenant during that period were sought or taken into account when they should not have been sought or taken into account,
is not to be taken to mean that the consultation requirements were not complied with.

(2)   The consultation requirements are—
   (a)   the requirements under—

(i) section 105(1) of the Housing Act 1985 (c 68),

(ii) paragraphs 3 and 4 of Schedule 3A to that Act,

(iii) regulations made under section 27AB of that Act which relate to arranging for ballots or polls with respect to a proposal to enter into a management agreement, and

(iv) section 137(2) of the Housing Act 1996 (c 52), and

(b) any other requirements specified by the appropriate national authority by order.

*Joint tenancies*

23.—(1) In the application of this Part of this Schedule in relation to an original tenancy which was a joint tenancy, a reference to the dwelling-house being the only or principal home of the ex-tenant is to be treated as a reference to the dwelling-house being the only or principal home of at least one of the ex-tenants of the joint tenancy.

(2) The appropriate national authority may by order provide for this Part of this Schedule to apply in relation to an original tenancy which was a joint tenancy subject to such additional modifications as may be specified in the order.

*Successor landlords*

24.—(1) The appropriate national authority may by order provide for this Part of this Schedule to apply, subject to such modifications as may be specified in the order, to successor landlord cases.

(2) For the purposes of sub-paragraph (1) a successor landlord case is a case, in relation to an original tenancy, where the interest of the ex-landlord in the dwelling-house—

(a) has been transferred to another person after the end of the original tenancy and before the commencement date, and

(b) on the commencement date, belongs to the person to whom it has been transferred or a subsequent transferee.

*Supplementary*

25. In determining for the purposes of this Part of this Schedule whether a tenancy has ended, any ending which was temporary because the tenancy was restored in consequence of a court order is to be ignored.

26.—(1) In this Part of this Schedule—

"appropriate national authority" means—

(a) in relation to a dwelling-house in England, the Secretary of State, and

(b) in relation to a dwelling-house in Wales, the Welsh Ministers,

"assured shorthold tenancy" and "assured tenancy" have the same meanings as in Part 1 of the Housing Act 1988 (c 50) but do not include a demoted tenancy to which section 20B of that Act applies,

"the commencement date" means the day on which section 299 comes into force for purposes other than the purposes of the Secretary of State or the Welsh Ministers making orders under this Part of this Schedule,

"demoted tenancy" means a tenancy to which section 20B of the Act of 1988 or section 143A of the Housing Act 1996 (c 52) applies,

"dwelling-house"—

(a) in relation to an assured tenancy, or a tenancy to which section 20B of the Act of 1988 applies, has the same meaning as in Part 1 of that Act,

(b) in relation to a tenancy to which section 143A of the Act of 1996 applies, has the same meaning as in Chapter 1A of Part 5 of that Act,

(c) in relation to an introductory tenancy, has the meaning given by section 139 of the Act of 1996, and

(d) in relation to a secure tenancy, has the meaning given by section 112 of the Housing Act 1985 (c 68),

"ex-landlord" means the person who was the landlord under an original tenancy,

"ex-tenant" means the person who was the tenant under an original tenancy,

"introductory tenancy" has the same meaning as in Chapter 1 of Part 5 of the Act of 1996,

"modification" includes omission,

"new tenancy" means a tenancy which is treated as arising by virtue of paragraph 16,

"original tenancy" has the meaning given by paragraph 15,

"possession order", in relation to a tenancy, means a court order for the possession of the dwelling-house,

"secure tenancy" has the same meaning as in Part 4 of the Act of 1985,

"successor"—

(a) in relation to a new tenancy which is an assured tenancy or which is a demoted tenancy to which section 20B of the Act of 1988 applies, has the same meaning as in section 17 of that Act,

(b)    in relation to a new tenancy which is a demoted tenancy to which section 143A of the Act of 1996 applies, has the meaning given by section 143J of that Act,

(c)    in relation to a new tenancy which is an introductory tenancy, has the same meaning as in section 132 of the Act of 1996, and

(d)    in relation to a new tenancy which is a secure tenancy, has the same meaning as in section 88 of the Act of 1985.

"termination period" has the meaning given by paragraph 16(3).

(2)    For the purposes of the definition of "appropriate national authority" in sub-paragraph (1) a dwelling-house which is partly in England and partly in Wales is to be treated—

(a)    as being in England if it is treated as situated in the area of a billing authority in England by virtue of regulations under section 1(3) of the Local Government Finance Act 1992 (c 14) (council tax in respect of dwellings), and

(b)    as being in Wales if it is treated as situated in the area of a billing authority in Wales by virtue of regulations under that section.

**[1892]–[3000]**

---

**NOTES**

Commencement: 1 December 2008 (for the purpose of enabling the appropriate national authority to make orders); 20 May 2009 (for remaining purposes).

Modification: in relation to the application of paras 16–18, 21, 26 above, with modifications, in respect of successor landlord cases in England, see the Housing (Replacement of Terminated Tenancies) (Successor Landlords) (England) Order 2009, SI 2009/1262, arts 2–7 **[3838C]**–**[3838H]**; and in relation to Wales see the Housing (Replacement of Terminated Tenancies) (Successor Landlords) (Wales) Order 2009, SI 2009/1260 at **[3838A]**.

Orders: the Housing (Replacement of Terminated Tenancies) (Successor Landlords) (Wales) Order 2009, SI 2009/1260 at **[3838A]**; the Housing (Replacement of Terminated Tenancies) (Successor Landlords) (England) Order 2009, SI 2009/1262 at **[3838B]**.

---

(*Sch 12 substitutes the Landlord and Tenant Act 1985, s 21 at* **[617]**, *amends ss 21A, 22, 23, 23A, 26, 27, 39 thereof at* **[618]**, **[620]**, **[621]**, **[622]**, **[625]**, **[626]**, **[641]** *and repeals s 28 thereof, amends the Landlord and Tenant Act 1987, ss 42A, 53 at* **[703]**, **[710]** *and the Leasehold Reform, Housing and Urban Development Act 1993, ss 78, 79 at* **[881]**, **[882]**; *Sch 13 amends the Housing Act 1985, Schs 5, 5A at* **[584]**, **[585]**; *Sch 14 amends the Housing Act 1985, ss 34, 43, the Housing Act 1988, s 133, repeals the Leasehold Reform, Housing and Urban Development Act 1993, s 135 and amends ss 136, 137 thereof at* **[908]**, **[909]** *and amends the Housing Act 1996, s 51, Sch 1; Sch 15 makes amendments outside the scope of this work; Sch 16 contains repeals and revocations which in so far as relevant to this work have been incorporated at the appropriate place.*)

# PART II
## STATUTORY INSTRUMENTS

# LEASEHOLD REFORM (ENFRANCHISEMENT AND EXTENSION) REGULATIONS 1967

### (SI 1967/1879)

---

**NOTES**
Made: 15 December 1967.
Authority: Leasehold Reform Act 1967, s 22(2).
Commencement: 1 January 1968.

---

**1**—(1) These Regulations may be cited as the Leasehold Reform (Enfranchisement and Extension) Regulations 1967 and shall come into operation on 1st January 1968.

(2) In these Regulations and the conditions set out in the Schedule to them, unless the context otherwise requires:—

"the Act" means the Leasehold Reform Act 1967;

"conveyance" includes any conveyance, assignment, transfer or other assurance for giving effect to section 8 of the Act;

"landlord" means the estate owner in respect of the fee simple of the property to which the tenant's notice relates, or the reversioner within the meaning of Schedule 1 to the Act, or any other person who is conducting the proceedings arising out of the notice in accordance with the provisions of the Act or an order of the court;

"lease" means a lease to be granted to give effect to a tenant's notice;

"property" means the house and premises which are required to be granted to the tenant for an estate in fee simple, pursuant to section 8, or for a term of years pursuant to section 14 of the Act;

"tenant" means a tenant of a house who has given notice under Part I of the Act of his desire to have the freehold or an extended lease and includes his executors, administrators and assigns;

"tenant's notice" means in relation to Part I of the Schedule a notice given by a tenant under Part I of the Act of his desire to have a freehold, and in relation to Part 2 of the Schedule a notice given by a tenant under Part I of the Act of his desire to have an extended lease.

(3) The Interpretation Act 1889 shall apply to the interpretation of these Regulations as it applies to the interpretation of an Act of Parliament.

**[3001]**

---

**NOTES**
Interpretation Act 1889: see now the Interpretation Act 1978.

---

**2** In any transactions undertaken to give effect to a tenant's notice of his desire to have a freehold the landlord and the tenant shall, unless they otherwise agree, be bound by the conditions laid down in Part I of the Schedule to these Regulations as if the conditions formed part of a contract between them.

**[3002]**

**3** In any transactions undertaken to give effect to a tenant's notice of his desire to have an extended lease the landlord and the tenant shall, unless they otherwise agree, be bound by the conditions laid down in Part 2 of the Schedule to these Regulations as if the conditions formed part of a contract between them.

**[3003]**

**4** Where as a result of non-compliance with the conditions laid down in the Schedule to these Regulations, the landlord and the tenant are discharged from the performance of the obligations arising in giving effect to the tenant's notice, such obligations arising between the tenant and persons other than the landlord having an interest superior to the tenancy shall likewise be discharged.

**[3004]**

SCHEDULE

PART I
ENFRANCHISEMENT

*Payment of deposit*

1.   At any time after receipt of the tenant's notice the landlord may, by notice in writing given to the tenant, require a sum equal to three times the annual rent for the property payable under his tenancy (or, in the case of a notice given under section 34 of the Act, the former long tenancy) or £25, whichever is the greater, to be deposited with the landlord, or a person nominated by him in the notice as his agent or as stakeholder, on account of the price payable for the property and any other sums payable by a tenant in accordance with the provisions of the Act; and the tenant shall, within 14 days of the giving of the notice, pay the sum demanded to the landlord or person nominated by him.

*Evidence of tenant's right to enfranchise*

2.   At any time after receipt of the tenant's notice the landlord may, by notice in writing given to the tenant, require him to deduce his title to the tenancy and[, in a case to which paragraph 2A applies,] to furnish a statutory declaration as to the particulars of occupation of the property on which the tenant relies in the tenant's notice; and the tenant shall within 21 days of the giving of the landlord's notice comply with the requirement.

[2A.   This paragraph applies where—
   (a)   the tenancy in question is a business tenancy; or
   (b)   a flat forming part of the house is let to a person who is a qualifying tenant for the purposes of Chapter 1 or 2 of Part 1 of the Leasehold Reform, Housing and Urban Development Act 1993.]

*Delivery of proof of landlord's title*

3.—(1)   Where—
   (i)   a tenant has received no notice in reply to his tenant's notice within 2 months of giving it, or
   (ii)   a tenant has
      (a)   received a notice in reply stating that his right to have the freehold is admitted, or
      (b)   has received a notice in reply that his right is disputed but has established that right by agreement or an order of the court,
      and, in either case, the property to be conveyed has been established by agreement or an order of the court,
the tenant may by notice in writing given to the landlord require him to deduce his title by delivering:—
   (a)   in the case of land registered in the register of title kept at Her Majesty's Land Registry an authority to inspect the register together with all the particulars and information which pursuant to section 110 of the Land Registration Act 1925 have or may be required to be furnished on a sale of registered land,
   (b)   in the case of any other land, an abstract of his title to the property,
and the landlord shall not later than 4 weeks after receipt of the notice, comply with the requirement contained therein.

(2)   Where any landlord or the tenant has served notice under paragraph 5(2) of Schedule 1 to the Act, "landlord" in this condition includes a landlord who served the notice or upon whom such a notice has been served.

*Requisitions*

4.—(1)   The tenant shall within 14 days after delivery of the abstract or of the authority to inspect the register together with particulars and information (whether or not delivered within the time required) send to the landlord a statement in writing of all objections and requisitions (if any) to or on the title or the evidence of the title, and the abstract or the particulars and information.

(2)   All objections and requisitions, other than those going to the root of the title, not included in any statement sent within the aforesaid period shall be deemed waived, and any matters which could have been raised in such objections or requisitions, other than matters going to the root of the title, *shall be deemed not to form* a defect in the title for the purposes of section 9(2) of the Act.

(3)   The landlord shall give a written answer to any objections or requisitions within 14 days of their receipt, and any observations on the answer shall be made within 7 days of the receipt of the answer, and if they are not so made, the answer shall be considered satisfactory.

(4)    Any objections not included in any observations so made shall be deemed waived and any matter which could have been raised in any observations so made shall be deemed not to form a defect in the title for the purposes of section 9(2) of the Act.

## Particulars of rights of way and restrictions

5.—(1)    When or at any time after giving his notice in reply to the tenant's notice the landlord may by notice in writing given to the tenant require him within 4 weeks to state what rights of way and provisions concerning restrictive covenants he requires to be included in the conveyance in accordance with section 10 of the Act.

(2)    At any time when under condition 3 the tenant would be entitled to require the landlord to deduce his title he may by notice in writing given to the landlord require him within 4 weeks to state what rights of way over the property and provisions concerning restrictive covenants he requires to be included in the conveyance in accordance with the provisions of the Act.

(3)    A notice given under this condition shall contain a statement as to the rights of way and provisions concerning restrictive covenants required by the person giving the notice to be included in the conveyance.

(4)    If the tenant does not comply with a notice given under this condition within the time specified or, where no such notice has been given, does not communicate to the landlord a statement of the rights and provisions he requires to be included in the conveyance when or before serving a notice on the landlord under condition 3, the tenant shall be deemed to require no rights of way or provisions concerning restrictive covenants to be included in the conveyance.

(5)    If the landlord does not comply with a notice given under this condition within the time specified, or, where no such notice is given, does not communicate to the tenant a statement of the rights and provisions he requires to be included in the conveyance at or before the time fixed for compliance with a notice served on him under condition 3, the landlord shall be deemed to require no rights of way or provisions concerning restrictive covenants to be included in the conveyance.

## Completion

6.—(1)    After the expiration of one month after the price payable for the property under section 9 of the Act has been determined by agreement or otherwise, either the tenant or the landlord may give the other notice in writing requiring him to complete the conveyance of the property to the tenant, and thereupon the completion date shall be the first working day after the expiration of 4 weeks from giving of the notice.

(2)    Completion shall take place at the office of the landlord's solicitor or, if he so requires, at the office of the solicitor of his mortgagee.

## Apportionment of rent and outgoings

7.    The tenant shall (subject to the next following condition) pay rent up to the date when the conveyance is completed (whether on the completion date or subsequently) and shall as from that date pay all outgoings; and any current rent and all rates and other outgoings shall, if necessary, be apportioned as on that date (the date itself being apportioned to the landlord) and the balance be paid by or allowed to the tenant.

## Election for interest in lieu of rent

8.—(1)    If from any cause whatsoever (save as hereinafter mentioned) completion is delayed beyond the completion date, the rent shall continue to be payable under the tenancy until actual completion unless the landlord by notice in writing given to the tenant elects to receive interest on the price payable for the property in lieu of rent, in which event in lieu of the rent payable under the tenancy, the price payable (or if a deposit has been paid the balance thereof) shall bear interest at a rate per annum of 2 per cent above the bank rate from time to time in force as from the giving of the notice to the tenant until actual completion. Provided that, unless the delay in completion is attributable solely to the tenant's own act or default, the tenant may—
   (a)    at his own risk, deposit the price payable or, where a deposit has been paid, the balance thereof, at any bank in England or Wales, and
   (b)    forthwith give to the landlord or his solicitor notice in writing of the deposit,
and in that case the landlord shall (unless and until there is further delay in completion which is attributable solely to the tenant's own act or default) be bound to accept the interest, if any, allowed thereon, as from the date of such deposit, instead of the interest accruing after such date which would otherwise be payable to him under the foregoing provisions of this condition.

(2)    No interest under paragraph (1) of this condition shall become payable by a tenant if, and so long as, delay in completion is attributable to any act or default of the landlord or his mortgagee or Settled Land Act trustees.

*Preparation of conveyance*

9.—(1)   The conveyance shall be prepared by the tenant.

(2)   A draft of the conveyance shall be delivered at the office of the landlord's solicitor at least 14 days before the date fixed for completion in accordance with condition 6 and the engrossment of the conveyance for execution by the landlord and other parties, if any, shall be delivered at that office a reasonable time before the date for completion.

(3)   Where the conveyance is to contain restrictive covenants and the tenant intends contemporaneously with the conveyance to execute a mortgage or convey any interest in the property to a third party, he shall inform the landlord of his intention and, if necessary, allow the landlord time to give a priority notice for the registration of the intended covenants at least 14 days before the conveyance is completed.

(4)   Where a conveyance is to contain any covenant by the tenant or any grant or reservation of rights affecting other property of the landlord, the tenant shall, if the landlord so requires, execute and hand over to the landlord on completion as many duplicates of the conveyance as the landlord may reasonably require and the duplicates shall be prepared and engrossed by the tenant, and where any duplicate is executed the tenant shall, if so required by the landlord, produce the original duly stamped so as to enable the stamp on the duplicate to be denoted.

*Failure to comply with obligations*

10.—(1)   If either the landlord or the tenant shall neglect or fail to perform any of his obligations arising from the tenant's notice or arising out of any of these conditions, then the other party may give to the party in default at least 2 months' notice in writing referring to this condition, specifying the default and requiring him to make it good before the expiration of the notice.

(2)   If the tenant does not comply with such a notice given by the landlord then, without prejudice to any other rights or remedies available to the landlord under the Act or otherwise,
    (a)    the landlord and tenant shall thereupon be discharged from the further performance of their obligations, other than the tenant's obligation to pay the landlord's costs, and
    (b)    the deposit money, if any, shall be forfeited to the landlord,
but if the landlord recovers any sums in the exercise of any remedy he shall give credit for the deposit against any sums so recovered.

(3)   If the landlord does not comply with such a notice given by the tenant, then the tenant may require the deposit money, if any, to be returned to him forthwith and shall be discharged from the obligation to pay the landlord's reasonable costs imposed by section 9 of the Act, and thereupon the landlord and the tenant shall be discharged from the further performance of their obligations, but without prejudice to any other rights or remedies available to the tenant under the Act or otherwise.

*Cancellation of land charges etc*

11.   Where under section 5(5) of the Act a tenant's notice has been registered as a land charge or a notice or caution in respect thereof has been registered and either the tenant gives notice of withdrawal under section 9(3) or section 19(14) of the Act or the landlord is otherwise discharged from the obligations arising out of the notice, the tenant shall at the request of the landlord forthwith at his own cost procure the cancellation of the registration.

*Notices*

12.   Any notice to be given to any person in accordance with these conditions shall be deemed to be effectively given if served personally on that person, or left at his last known place of residence, or sent by post to him or his solicitor or other duly authorised agent at his last known address.

*Extension of time limits*

13.—(1)   These conditions shall have effect as if any period of time for the performance of any act or compliance with any notice (except a notice given under condition 10) by the landlord were twice the length of the period thereby laid down, where a person acting as reversioner under the provisions of Schedule 1 to the Act so requires by notice in writing given to the tenant at any time before the expiration of that period.

(2)   Any period when proceedings are pending in any court or tribunal with reference to any matter arising in giving effect to a tenant's notice shall be disregarded in computing any period of time laid down by these conditions or any notice served thereunder.

(3)   Any period of time laid down by these conditions or any notice served thereunder shall be extended for such further period as may be reasonable in all the circumstances if any party required to do any act within that period dies or becomes incapable of managing his affairs before the expiration of that period.

[3005]

**NOTES**

Para 2: words in square brackets inserted in relation to England by the Leasehold Reform (Enfranchisement and Extension) (Amendment) (England) Regulations 2003, SI 2003/1989, reg 3(a), in respect of cases where a notice under the National Council for Education and Training for Wales (Transfer of Functions to the National Assembly for Wales and Abolition) Order 2005, Pt 1, is given on or after 30 September 2003, and inserted in relation to Wales by the Leasehold Reform (Enfranchisement and Extension) (Amendment) (Wales) Regulations 2004, SI 2004/699, reg 3(a), in respect of cases where a notice under the Leasehold Reform Act 1967, Pt 1 at **[78]** et seq, is given on or after 31 March 2004.

Para 2A: inserted in relation to England by SI 2003/1989, reg 3(b) and inserted in relation to Wales by SI 2004/699, reg 3(b), subject to savings as noted above.

Modification: paras 6(2), 8(1)(b), 9(2), 12 are modified by the Solicitors' Incorporated Practices Order 1991, SI 1991/2684, arts 4, 5, Sch 1, such that any reference to a solicitor is to be construed as including a reference to a recognised body within the meaning of the Administration of Justice Act 1985, s 9.

PART 2

EXTENSION

*Evidence of tenant's right to have an extended lease*

1.  At any time after receipt of the tenant's notice the landlord may, by notice in writing given to the tenant, require him to deduce his title to the tenancy and[, in a case to which paragraph 1A applies,] to furnish a statutory declaration as to the particulars of occupation of the property on which the tenant relies in the tenant's notice; and the tenant shall within 21 days of the giving of the landlord's notice comply with the requirement.

[1A.   This paragraph applies where—
    (a)    the tenancy in question is a business tenancy; or
    (b)    a flat forming part of the house is let to a person who is a qualifying tenant for the purposes of Chapter 1 or 2 of Part 1 of the Leasehold Reform, Housing and Urban Development Act 1993.]

*Terms of new tenancy*

2.—(1)   Where—
    (a)    a tenant has received no notice in reply to his tenant's notice within 2 months of giving it, or
    (b)    a tenant has
        (i)    received a notice in reply stating that his right to have an extended lease is admitted, or
        (ii)    has received a notice in reply that his right is disputed but has established that right by agreement or an order of the court,
        and, in either case, the property to be leased has been established by agreement or an order of the court,

then the tenant may, by notice in writing given to the landlord, require him within 4 weeks to state what modifications in the terms of the existing tenancy, and what further provisions, other than as to payment of rent, are to be made by the terms of the new tenancy in accordance with section 15 of the Act.

(2)   Where the requirements of paragraph (1)(b) of this condition are satisfied the landlord may, by notice in writing given to the tenant, require him within four weeks to state what modifications in the terms of the existing tenancy and what further provisions other than as to payment of rent are to be made by the terms of the new tenancy, in accordance with section 15 of the Act.

(3)   A notice given under this condition shall contain a statement as to the modifications in the terms of the existing tenancy and the further provisions to be made by the terms of the new tenancy, required by the person giving the notice.

(4)   If either party does not comply with a notice given under this condition within the time specified or, where no such notice has been given, does not communicate to the other a statement of the modifications and provisions he requires to be made when or before serving a notice under this condition, he shall be deemed to require the new tenancy to be on the same terms as the existing tenancy and not to require any further provisions (other than as to payment of rent) to be made by the terms of the new tenancy in accordance with section 15 of the Act.

*Preparation of lease*

3.—(1)   Within eight weeks after the giving of a notice by either party under condition 2, a draft of the lease shall be submitted by the landlord to the tenant for approval, and the tenant shall approve the draft in writing with or without amendments within 21 days thereafter.

(2)   If the tenant does not approve the draft with any amendment required by him within the time laid down by this condition, he shall be deemed to have approved it in the form submitted by the landlord.

(3)   The lease and as many counterparts as the landlord may reasonably require shall be prepared by the landlord and the counterpart or counterparts shall be delivered to the tenant for execution a reasonable time before the completion date, and on completion (whether on the completion date or subsequently) the tenant shall deliver the counterpart or counterparts of the lease, duly executed, to the landlord and the landlord shall deliver the lease, duly executed, to the tenant.

*Completion*

4.—(1)   After the expiration of the time for approval of the draft lease by the tenant either the landlord or the tenant may give the other notice in writing requiring him to complete the grant of the lease, and thereupon the completion date shall be the first working day after the expiration of 4 weeks from the giving of the notice.

(2)   Completion shall take place at the office of the landlord's solicitor.

*Failure to comply with obligations*

5.—(1)   If either the landlord or the tenant shall neglect or fail to perform any of his obligations arising from the tenant's notice or arising out of any of these conditions, then the other party may give to the party in default at least 2 months' notice in writing referring to this condition, specifying the default and requiring him to make it good before the expiration of the notice.

(2)   If the tenant does not comply with such a notice given by the landlord, the landlord and the tenant shall be discharged from the further performance of their obligations, other than the tenant's obligation to pay the landlord's costs, but without prejudice to any other rights or remedies available to the landlord under the Act or otherwise.

(3)   If the landlord does not comply with such a notice given by the tenant, the tenant shall be discharged from the obligation to pay the landlord's reasonable costs imposed by section 14 of the Act, and thereupon the landlord and the tenant shall be discharged from the further performance of their obligations, but without prejudice to any other rights or remedies available to the tenant under the Act or otherwise.

*Cancellation of land charges etc*

6.   Where under section 5(5) of the Act a tenant's notice has been registered as a land charge or a notice or caution in respect thereof has been registered and the landlord is discharged from the obligations arising out of the notice, the tenant shall at the request of the landlord forthwith at his own cost procure the cancellation of the registration.

*Notices*

7.   Any notice to be given to any person in accordance with these conditions shall be deemed to be effectively given if served personally on that person, or left at his last known place of residence, or sent by post to him or his solicitor or other duly authorised agent at his last known address.

*Extension of time limits*

8.—(1)   These conditions shall have effect as if any period of time for the performance of any act or compliance with any notice (except a notice given under condition 5) by the landlord were twice the length of the period thereby laid down, where a person acting as reversioner under the provisions of Schedule 1 to the Act so requires by notice in writing given to the tenant at any time before the expiration of that period.

(2)   Any period when proceedings are pending in any court or tribunal with reference to any matter arising in giving effect to a tenant's notice shall be disregarded in computing any period of time laid down by these conditions or any notice served thereunder.

(3)   Any period of time laid down by these conditions or any notice served thereunder shall be extended for such further period as may be reasonable in all the circumstances if any party required to do any act within that period dies or becomes incapable of managing his affairs before the expiration of that period.

**[3006]**

**NOTES**

   Para 1: words in square brackets inserted in relation to England by the Leasehold Reform (Enfranchisement and Extension) (Amendment) (England) Regulations 2003, SI 2003/1989, reg 3(c), in respect of cases where a notice under the Leasehold Reform Act 1967, Pt 1 at **[78]** et seq, is given on or after 30 September 2003, and inserted in relation to Wales by the Leasehold Reform (Enfranchisement and Extension) (Amendment) (Wales) Regulations 2004, SI 2004/699, reg 3(c), in respect of cases where a notice under the Leasehold Reform Act 1967, Pt 1 at **[78]** et seq, is given on or after 31 March 2004.

   Para 1A: inserted in relation to England by SI 2003/1989, reg 3(d) and inserted in relation to Wales by SI 2004/699, reg 3(d), subject to savings as noted above.

Schedule 11 or under paragraph 9(1) of Schedule 12 to the Rent Act 1977 [or regulation 2A(2) of these regulations] as the date when the hearing would be held if a request to make oral representations were to be made.]

**[3010]**

**NOTES**

Para (1): words omitted revoked by the Tribunals, Courts and Enforcement Act 2007 (Transitional and Consequential Provisions) Order 2008, SI 2008/2683, art 6(1), Sch 1 para 2.

Para (3): substituted by the Rent Assessment Committees (England and Wales) (Amendment) Regulations 1980, SI 1980/1699, reg 3; words in square brackets substituted by the Rent Assessment Committees (England and Wales) (Amendment) Regulations 1981, SI 1981/1783, reg 4.

Para (4): added by SI 1981/1783, reg 4; words in square brackets inserted by the Rent Assessment Committees (England and Wales) (Amendment) Regulations 1988, SI 1988/2200, reg 2(4).

Rent Act 1977, Sch 11, paras 7, 11, Sch 12, paras 7, 9, 11: repealed (subject to savings) by the Housing Act 1988, s 140, Sch 17, Pt I, para 22, Sch 18.

**4**   At the hearing—
   (a)   the parties shall be heard in such order, and, subject to the provisions of these regulations, the procedure shall be such as the committee shall determine;
   (b)   a party may call witnesses, give evidence on his own behalf and cross-examine any witnesses called by the other party.

**[3011]**

**5**   **Documents, etc**

   (1)   The committee shall, where the reference is to be subject to a hearing, take all reasonable steps to ensure that there is supplied to each of the parties before the date of the hearing—
   (a)   a copy of, or sufficient extracts from or particulars of, any document relevant to the reference which has been received from the rent officer or from a party (other than a document which is in the possession of such party, or of which he has previously been supplied with a copy by the rent officer); and
   (b)   a copy of any document which embodies the results of any enquiries made by or for the committee for the purposes of that reference, or which contains relevant information in relation to fair rents previously determined for other dwelling-houses [or, as the case may be, to the terms (including rent) of assured tenancies or assured agricultural occupancies of other dwelling-houses where such tenancies or occupancies have been the subject of a reference to a committee and in either case] ... which has been prepared for the committee for the purposes of that reference.

   (2)   Where at any hearing—
   (i)   any document relevant to the reference is not in the possession of a party present at that hearing; and
   (ii)   that party has not been supplied with a copy of, or sufficient extracts from or particulars of, that document by the rent officer or by the committee in accordance with the provisions of paragraph (1) of this regulation,

then unless—
   (a)   that party consents to the continuation of the hearing; or
   (b)   the committee consider that that party has a sufficient opportunity of dealing with that document without an adjournment of the hearing,

the committee shall adjourn the hearing for a period which they consider will afford that party a sufficient opportunity of dealing with that document.

**[3012]**

**NOTES**

Para (1): in sub-para (b) words in square brackets inserted, and word omitted revoked, by the Rent Assessment Committees (England and Wales) (Amendment) Regulations 1988, SI 1988/2200, reg 2(5).

**6**   Where a reference is not to be subject to a hearing, the committee shall supply to each of the parties a copy of, or sufficient extracts from or particulars of, any such document as is mentioned in paragraph (1)(a) of regulation 5 of these regulations (other than a document excepted from that paragraph) and a copy of any such document as is mentioned in paragraph (1)(b) of that regulation, and they shall not reach their decision until they are satisfied that each party has been given a sufficient opportunity of commenting upon any document of which a copy, or from which extracts or of which particulars, has or have been so supplied, and upon the other's case.

**[3013]**

## 7 Inspection of dwelling-house

(1) The committee may of their own motion, and shall at the request of one of the parties (subject in either case to any necessary consent being obtained) inspect the dwelling-house which is the subject of the reference.

(2) An inspection may be made before, during or after the close of the hearing, or at such stage in relation to the consideration of the representations in writing, as the committee shall decide, and the committee shall give to the parties and their representatives an opportunity to attend.

(3) Notice of an inspection shall be given as though it were notice of a hearing, save that the requirements for such notice may be dispensed with or relaxed in so far as the committee are satisfied that the parties have received sufficient notice.

(4) Where an inspection is made after the close of a hearing, the committee shall, if they consider that it is expedient to do so on account of any matter arising from the inspection, reopen the hearing; and if the hearing is to be reopened paragraph (3) of regulation 3 of these regulations shall apply as it applied to the original hearing, save in so far as its requirements may be dispensed with or relaxed with the consent of the parties.

**[3014]**

## 8 Adjournment

The committee at their discretion may of their own motion, or at the request of the parties, or one of them, at any time and from time to time postpone or adjourn a hearing; but they shall not do so at the request of one party only unless, having regard to the grounds on which and the time at which such request is made and to the convenience of the parties, they deem it reasonable to do so. Such notice of any postponed or adjourned hearing as is reasonable in the circumstances shall be given to the parties by the committee.

**[3015]**

## 9 Non-appearance

If a party does not appear at a hearing the committee, on being satisfied that the requirements of these regulations regarding the giving of notice of hearings have been duly complied with, may proceed to deal with the reference upon the representations of any party present and upon the documents and information which they may properly consider.

**[3016]**

## 10 Decisions

(1) The decision of the committee upon a reference shall be recorded in a document signed by the chairman (or in the event of his absence or incapacity, by another member of the committee) which ... shall contain no reference to the decision being by a majority (if that be the case) or to any opinion of a minority.

(2) The chairman (or in the event of his absence or incapacity, either of the other members of the committee) shall have power, by certificate under his hand, to correct any clerical or accidental error or omission in the said document.

(3) A copy of the said document and of any such correction shall be sent by the committee to the parties and to the rent officer.

**[3017]**

**NOTES**

Para (1): words omitted revoked by the Rent Assessment Committees (England and Wales) (Amendment) Regulations 1981, SI 1981/1783, reg 4(3).

[**10A—(1)** Where the committee are requested, on or before the giving or notification of the decision, to state the reasons for the decision, those reasons shall be recorded in a document.

(2) Regulation 10 above shall apply to the document recording the reasons as it applies to the document recording the decision.]

**[3018]**

**NOTES**

Inserted by the Rent Assessment Committees (England and Wales) (Amendment) Regulations 1981, SI 1981/1783.

## 11 Giving of notices, etc

Where any notice or other written matter is required under the provisions of these regulations to be given or supplied by the committee (including any such matter to be supplied to a party for the purposes of a reference to which regulation 6 of these regulations applies) it shall be sufficient compliance with the regulations if such notice or matter is sent by post in a prepaid letter and addressed to the party for whom it is intended at his usual or last known address, or if that party has appointed an agent to act on his behalf in relation to the reference, to that agent at the address of the agent supplied to the committee.

**[3019]**

# HOUSING (RIGHT TO BUY) (DESIGNATED REGIONS) ORDER 1980 (NOTE)

## (SI 1980/1345)

**NOTES**

Made: 5 September 1980.

Authority: Housing Act 1980, ss 19(12), 151(1), (3). S 19 of the 1980 Act was repealed by the Housing (Consequential Provisions) Act 1985, s 3(1), Sch 1, Pt I; by virtue of s 2(2) thereof, this order now has effect as if made under the Housing Act 1985, s 157(3).

Commencement: 3 October 1980.

This order designates, for the purposes of the Housing Act 1985, s 157(3), in relation to a dwelling house in England which is situated in a National Park or an area of outstanding natural beauty, an area comprising:

(a) that Park or area of outstanding natural beauty;

(b) so much of the county in which the dwelling house is situated as is not within that Park or area.

Special provision is made for dwelling houses situated in the Wye Valley Area of Outstanding Natural Beauty and in the Isles of Scilly.

Further orders: The following orders (which were either made under the Housing Act 1980, ss 19(1), (12), 151(1), (3) (repealed), and now have effect under the Housing Act 1985, s 157(1), (3) (orders (a)–(d) below), or were made under the 1985 Act (orders (e)–(o) below), designate specified rural areas and regions for the purposes of s 157(1), (3):

(a) SI 1981/397 (in force on 14 April 1981), designating 18 rural areas in England and in respect of dwelling houses in those areas regions comprising the areas in which the dwelling house is situated and, so far as not situated in that area, the county in which it is situated;

(b) SI 1981/940 (in force on 31 July 1981), designating the District of Mid Devon with specified exceptions as a rural area and the County of Devon as the designated region in respect of any dwelling house situated in that rural area;

(c) SI 1982/21 (in force on 15 February 1982), designating the District of North Norfolk, with specified exceptions, as a rural area and the County of Norfolk as the designated region in respect of any dwelling house situated in that rural area;

(d) SI 1982/187 (in force on 22 March 1982), designating the District of Teignbridge, with specified exceptions, as a rural area and the County of Devon as the designated region in respect of any dwelling house situated in that rural area;

(e) SI 1986/1695 (made under s 157(1), (3) of the 1985 Act and in force on 29 October 1986), designating certain parishes in the Borough of Scarborough, with the exception of those parts which form part of the North York Moors National Park, as rural areas and providing that the County of North Yorkshire is the designated region for dwelling houses in those areas;

(f) SI 1988/2057 (made under s 157(1)(c), (3)(a) of the 1985 Act and in force on 22 December 1988), designating certain parishes in the District of Craven, with the exception of land which is part of the Yorkshire Dales National Park and land in an area of outstanding natural beauty in the Forest of Bowland, as rural areas and providing that the County of North Yorkshire is the designated region for dwelling houses in those areas;

(g) SI 1990/1282 (made under s 157(1)(c), (3)(a) of the 1985 Act and in force on 19 July 1990), designating the Borough of West Devon, with certain exceptions, as a rural area and providing that the County of Devon is the designated region for dwelling houses in those areas;

(h) SI 2002/1769 (made under s 157(1)(c), (3)(a) of the 1985 Act and in force on 6 August 2002), designating certain parishes in the Borough of Ribble Valley as rural areas for the purposes of s 157 of the 1985 Act, and providing that the Borough of Ribble Valley is the designated region for dwelling houses in those areas;

(i) SI 2003/54 (W 5), as amended by SI 2003/1147 (W 155) (made under s 157 of the 1985 Act and the Housing Act 1996, s 17 and in force on 7 February 2003), designating communities in Wales as rural areas for the purposes of s 157(1)(c) of the 1985 Act, and setting out the designated regions for dwelling houses in Wales. SI 2003/54 revokes the Housing (Right to Buy) (Designated Rural Areas and Designated Regions) (Wales) Order 1980, SI 1980/1375, and partly replaces SI 1997/685, noted to SI 1997/620; in so far as SI 2003/54 was made under s 17 of the 1996 Act and designates areas for the purposes of that section, see the note "Further orders" to SI 1997/620;

(j) SI 2003/1105 (made under s 157(1)(c), (3)(a) of the 1985 Act and in force on 14 May 2003), designating certain parishes in the District of Kennet as rural areas for the purposes of s 157 of the 1985 Act, and providing that the District of Kennet is the designated region for dwelling houses in those areas;

(k) SI 2004/418 (made under s 157(1)(c), (3)(a) of the 1985 Act and in force on 17 March 2004), designating certain parishes in the districts of Forest of Dean, Rochford, Rutland, and Kings Lynn and West Norfolk as rural areas for the purposes of s 157 of the 1985 Act, and providing that each of those districts is the designated region for dwelling houses in those areas;

(l) SI 2004/2681 (made under s 157(1)(c), (3)(a) of the 1985 Act and in force on 15 November 2004), designating certain parishes in the districts of Chester and Stratford-upon-Avon and the boroughs of Test Valley, Harrogate and Taunton Deane as rural areas for the purposes of s 157 of the 1985 Act, and providing that each of those districts and boroughs is the designated region for dwelling houses in those areas;

(m)  SI 2005/1995 (made under s 157(1)(c), (3) of the 1985 Act and in force on 15 August 2005), designating certain parishes in districts of Ryedale and Tendring as rural areas for the purposes of s 157 of the 1985 Act, and providing that each of those districts is the designated region for dwelling houses in those areas;

(n)  SI 2005/2908 (made under s 157(1)(c), (3) of the 1985 Act and in force on 16 November 2005), designating certain parishes in districts of Mole Valley and Richmondshire as rural areas for the purposes of s 157 of the 1985 Act, and providing that each of those districts is the designated region for dwelling houses in those areas;

(o)  SI 2006/1948 (made under s 157(1)(c), (3) of the 1985 Act and in force on 24 August 2006), designating certain parishes in the district of Hambleton as rural areas for the purposes of s 157 of the 1985 Act, and providing that the district of Hambleton is the designated region for dwelling houses in that area.

**[3020]**

# SECURE TENANCIES (DESIGNATED COURSES) REGULATIONS 1980

## (SI 1980/1407)

**NOTES**
Made: 17 September 1980.
Authority: Housing Act 1980, s 151, Sch 3, para 11 (repealed); now take effect under the Housing Act 1985, s 79, Sch 1, para 10(4).
Commencement: 3 October 1980.

## 1  Citation and Commencement

These Regulations may be cited as the Secure Tenancies (Designated Courses) Regulations 1980 and shall come into operation on 3rd October 1980.

**[3021]**

## 2  Designated Courses

There are hereby designated for the purposes of paragraph 11 of Schedule 3 to the Housing Act 1980—

(a)  any full-time course to which section 1 of the Education Act 1962 from time to time applies;

(b)  any full-time post-graduate course, that is to say, a course to which only students who hold a first degree of a university or an equivalent qualification are admitted; ...

(c)  any other full-time course provided by an establishment of further education which is maintained or assisted by a local education authority or in respect of the maintenance of which grants are for the time being paid in pursuance of Regulations made under section 100(1)(b) of the Education Act 1944.

[(d)  any full-time course at an establishment within the further education sector (within the meaning of section 91(3) of the Further and Higher Education Act 1992); and

(e)  any full-time course at an establishment within the higher education sector (within the meaning of section 91(5) of the Further and Higher Education Act 1992), other than a university.]

**[3022]**

**NOTES**
Words omitted from para (b) revoked and paras (d), (e) added by the Secure Tenancies (Designated Courses) (Amendment) Regulations 1993, SI 1993/931, reg 2.
Housing Act 1980, Sch 3, para 11: see now the Housing Act 1985, s 79, Sch 1, para 10.

# RENT ACT 1977 (FORMS ETC) REGULATIONS 1980

## (SI 1980/1697)

**NOTES**
Made: 30 October 1980.
Authority: Rent Act 1977, ss 49, 60, 66, 67, 73, 74, 77, 79, 81A, 84.
Commencement: 28 November 1980.

**1**  These regulations may be cited as the Rent Act 1977 (Forms etc) Regulations 1980 and shall come into operation on 28th November 1980.

**[3023]**

**2**—(1)   In these regulations the "1976 Act" means the Rent (Agriculture) Act 1976 and the "1977 Act" means the Rent Act 1977.

(2)   In these regulations any reference to a numbered form shall be construed as a reference to the form bearing that number in Schedule 1 hereto, or to a form substantially to the like effect.

**[3024]**

**3**—(1)   The forms prescribed for the purposes of notices of increase of rent under Part III of the 1977 Act shall be as follows:—

    [(a)   in the case of a notice under section 45(2) of the 1977 Act where the rent is not subject to the phasing provisions of Schedule 8 to the Act, form No 1;

    (b)   in the case of a notice under section 45(2) of the 1977 Act where a rent is subject to the phasing provisions of Schedule 8 to the Act, form No 2; and]

    (c)   in the case of a notice under section 46(2) of the 1977 Act, form No 4.

(2)   The forms prescribed for the purpose of Part IV of the 1977 Act, where an application is made to the rent officer, shall be as follows:—

    (a)   in the case of an application under section 67 of the Act—

       (i)   where a statutory tenancy arises at the end of a long tenancy under Part I of the Landlord and Tenant Act 1954, form No 6;

       (ii)   where the dwelling house is subject to a statutory tenancy as defined in the 1976 Act, form No 7; and

       (iii)   in any other case, form No 5;

    (b)   in the case of an application under section 69(1) of the 1977 Act for a certificate of fair rent, form No 8, and in the case of an application under section 69(4) for the registration of a rent in accordance with such a certificate, form No 9;

    [(bb)   in the case of an application under section 67A for an interim registration of rent, form No 9A;]

    (c)   in the case of an application under section 73 of the 1977 Act where the application is made by the landlord and the tenant jointly, form No 10, and in any other case, form No 11.

(3)   [Subject to paragraph (3A) below,] the form of notice to be served by a rent officer under paragraph 3(1) of Schedule 11 to the 1977 Act, as modified by the Regulated Tenancies (Procedure) Regulations 1980, shall be form No 13 if, in pursuance of section 67(2)(b) of the 1977 Act the application was accompanied by details of the landlord's expenditure in connection with the provision of services, and shall be form No 12 in any other case.

[(3A)   The form of notice to be served by a rent officer under paragraph 3(1) of Schedule 11 to the 1977 Act in the case of an application made under section 67A of that Act shall be form No 12A.]

(4)   The form of notice to be served by a rent assessment committee under paragraph 7 of Schedule 11 to the 1977 Act, shall be form No 14.

(5)   The form of an application under section 81A of the 1977 Act shall be form No 15.

**[3025]**

**NOTES**

Para (1): sub-paras (a), (b) substituted by the Rent Act 1977 (Forms etc) (Amendment) Regulations 1987, SI 1987/266, reg 2(i).

Paras (2), (3): words in square brackets inserted by the Rent Act 1977 (Forms etc) (Amendment) Regulations 1993, SI 1993/655, reg 2(a)(i), (ii).

Para (3A): inserted by SI 1993/655, reg 2(a)(iii).

Section 69(1), (4) of, Sch 8 to, the 1977 Act: repealed, subject to savings, by the Housing Act 1988, s 140, Sch 17, Pt I, paras 24, 27, Sch 18.

**4**   An application made under section 67, 69, 73 or 81A of the 1977 Act, as the case may be, shall contain the particulars specified in the relevant prescribed form.

**[3026]**

**NOTES**

Section 69 of the 1977 Act: see the note to reg 3 at **[3025]**.

**5**   The register kept for the purposes of Part IV of the 1977 Act under section 66(1) thereof shall contain the particulars with regard to a regulated tenancy or, as the case may be, housing association tenancy, specified in Schedule 2 hereto.

**[3027]**

**6**  The fee to be paid under section 66(4) of the 1977 Act for a copy of an entry in the register certified under the hand of the rent officer or person duly authorised by him shall be [£1.00].

**[3028]**

**NOTES**
Sum in square brackets substituted by the Rent Act 1977 (Forms etc) (Amendment) Regulations 1984, SI 1984/1391, reg 3.

**7**  The particulars relating to a restricted contract, referred to a rent tribunal, regarding which the lessor may be required by notice to give information reasonably required by the tribunal, are those specified in Schedule 3 hereto.

**[3029]**

**8**  The register kept for the purposes of Part V of the 1977 Act under section 79(1) thereof shall contain the particulars with regard to a restricted contract specified in Schedule 4 hereto.

**[3030]**

**9**  The fee to be paid under section 79(6) of the 1977 Act for a copy of an entry in the register certified under the hand of an officer duly authorised in that behalf by the president of the rent assessment panel concerned shall be [£1.00].

**[3031]**

**NOTES**
Sum in square brackets substituted by the Rent Act 1977 (Forms etc) (Amendment) Regulations 1984, SI 1984/1391, reg 3.

**10**  (*Revokes the Rent (Agriculture) (Rent Registration) Regulations 1978, SI 1978/494, and the Rent Regulation (Forms etc) Regulations 1978, SI 1978/495.*)

## SCHEDULES

## SCHEDULE 1

**NOTES**
This Schedule contains forms which are not themselves reproduced in this work, but their numbers and titles are listed below.

| Form No | Title |
| --- | --- |
| 1 | Notice of increase of rent under regulated tenancy where the increase is not subject to the phasing provisions of Schedule 8 to the Act (substituted by SI 1987/266; amended by SI 1993/655, SI 1997/2971) |
| 2 | Notice of increase of rent under regulated tenancy where the increase is subject to the phasing provisions of Schedule 8 to the Act (substituted by SI 1987/266; amended by SI 1993/655, SI 1997/2971) |
| 3 | Revoked by the Rent Act 1977 (Forms etc) (Amendment) Regulations 1987, SI 1987/266, reg 2(iii) |
| 4 | Notice of increase of unregistered rent under regulated Tenancy on account of increased rates |
| 5 | Application for registration of fair rent (substituted by SI 1984/1391; amended by SI 1993/655, SI 2008/2831; modified by SI 2008/2839) |
| 6 | Application for registration of fair rent in the case of a statutory tenancy arising at the end of a long tenancy under Part I of the Landlord and Tenant Act 1954 (substituted by SI 1984/1391; amended by SI 1993/655, SI 2008/2831; modified by SI 2008/2839) |
| 7 | Application for registration of fair rent where dwelling-house subject to a statutory tenancy under the Rent (Agriculture) Act 1976 (substituted by SI 1984/1391; amended by SI 1993/655) |
| 8 | Application for certificate of fair rent (substituted by SI 1984/1391; amended by SI 2008/2831; modified by SI 2008/2839) |

| *Form No* | *Title* |
|---|---|
| 9 | Application for registration of fair rent supported by certificate of fair rent (substituted by SI 1984/1391; amended by SI 2008/2831; modified by SI 2008/2839) |
| 9A | Application for an interim registration of fair rent in the case of increase on account of council tax (inserted by SI 1993/655; amended by SI 2008/2831; modified by SI 2008/2839) |
| 10 | Joint application for cancellation of a registered rent (substituted by SI 1984/1391) |
| 11 | Application for cancellation of registration of rent where there is no regulated tenancy |
| 12 | Notice by Rent Officer of application for registration of fair rent (substituted by SI 1984/1391) |
| 12A | Notification of application for an interim increase of registered rent on account of council tax (inserted by SI 1993/655) |
| 13 | Notice by Rent Officer of application for registration of fair rent where landlord includes an amount for services (substituted by SI 1984/1391) |
| 14 | Notice by Rent Assessment Committee requiring further information |
| 15 | Application for cancellation of a rent registered by a rent tribunal where the dwelling is not subject to a restricted contract (amended by SI 1988/2195) |

## SCHEDULE 2
### PARTICULARS WITH REGARD TO THE TENANCY TO BE REGISTERED IN THE REGISTER OF RENTS KEPT BY THE RENT OFFICER

Regulation 5

1. Address of premises.
2. Names and addresses of landlord and tenant.
3. If granted for a term, date of commencement of the tenancy and length of term.
4. The rental period.
5. Allocation between landlord and tenant of liabilities for repairs.
6. Details of services provided by the landlord or a superior landlord.
7. Details of furniture provided by the landlord or a superior landlord.
8. In the case of a statutory tenancy which has arisen by virtue of Part I of the Landlord and Tenant Act 1954, particulars of the initial repairs.
[8A. Liability for payment of council tax for the accommodation let to the tenant.]
9. Any other terms of the tenancy taken into consideration in determining the fair rent.

**[3032]**

---

**NOTES**

Para 8A: inserted by the Rent Act 1977 (Forms etc) (Amendment) Regulations 1993, SI 1993/655, reg 2(h).

---

## SCHEDULE 3
### PARTICULARS RELATING TO A RESTRICTED CONTRACT REGARDING WHICH LESSORS MAY BY NOTICE BE REQUIRED TO GIVE INFORMATION

Regulation 7

1. The name of the lessee.
2. A specification of the dwelling to which the contract relates.
3. Accommodation occupied or used by the lessee (a) exclusively, (b) in common with the lessor (c) in common with persons other than the lessor.
4. Furniture provided by the lessor for the use of the lessee.
5. Services provided by the lessor for the use of the lessee.
6. The rateable value of the accommodation occupied by the lessee, where this has been separately assessed, or, where it has not, the rateable value of the dwelling of which the accommodation forms part.
7. Responsibility for payment of the rates [and the council tax] for the accommodation occupied by the lessee.

8. Payments contracted to be made by the lessee to the lessor, and if separate payments are made in respect of occupation, furniture and services the separate payments in respect of each.

9. Whether board is supplied, and if so the nature and amount of the board.

10. The date the occupation of the accommodation began.

[3033]

**NOTES**
Para 7: words in square brackets inserted by the Rent Act 1977 (Forms etc) (Amendment) Regulations 1993, SI 1993/655, reg 2(i).

## SCHEDULE 4
### PARTICULARS WITH REGARD TO THE CONTRACT TO BE ENTERED IN THE REGISTER

Regulation 8

1. Names and addresses of parties to the restricted contract referred to the rent tribunal.

2.—(a) The accommodation of which the lessee is entitled to exclusive occupation;
   (b) the accommodation of which the lessee is entitled to the use in common with—
      (i) the lessor
      (ii) persons other than the lessor.

3. Details of any furniture provided by the lessor for the use of the lessee.

4. Details of any services provided by the lessor.

5. Whether board is supplied, and if so the nature and amount of the board.

[5A. Liability for payment of council tax for the accommodation occupied by the lessee.]

6. Any other terms of the contract taken into consideration in determining the rent.

[3034]

**NOTES**
Para 5A: inserted by the Rent Act 1977 (Forms etc) (Amendment) Regulations 1993, SI 1993/655, reg 2(j).

# RENT REGULATION (CANCELLATION OF REGISTRATION OF RENT) REGULATIONS 1980

### (SI 1980/1698)

**NOTES**
Made: 30 October 1980.
Authority: Rent Act 1977, s 74.
Commencement: 28 November 1980.

## 1 Citation and commencement

These regulations may be cited as the Rent Regulation (Cancellation of Registration of Rent) Regulations 1980 and shall come into operation on 28th November 1980.

[3035]

## 2 Interpretation

In these regulations—
   "the 1977 Act" means the Rent Act 1977;
   "a joint application" means an application for the cancellation of a fair rent under section 73(1) of the Rent Act 1977; and
   "relevant rent agreement" means the rent agreement, within the meaning of section 73(1)(a) of the 1977 Act, as the result of which a joint application is made.

[3036]

## 3 Procedures on joint application to rent officer

If, in the case of a joint application, after making such inquiry, if any, as he thinks fit and considering any information supplied to him, the rent officer is not satisfied that the rent, or the highest rent, payable under the relevant rent agreement does not exceed a fair rent for the dwelling-house, he shall serve a notice under regulation 4 below.

[3037]

**4**—(1)   A notice under this regulation shall be served on the landlord and on the tenant informing them that the rent officer proposes, at a time (which shall not be earlier than seven days after the service of the notice) and place specified in the notice to consider in consultation with the landlord and the tenant, or such of them as may appear at that time and place, whether the registration of the rent for the dwelling-house should be cancelled pursuant to section 73(4) of the 1977 Act.

(2)   At any such consultation the landlord and the tenant may each be represented by a person authorised by him in that behalf, whether or not that person is of counsel or a solicitor.

(3)   Where the rent officer is to consider, in accordance with paragraph (1) above, whether the registration of the rent for the dwelling-house should be cancelled, he shall not reach his decision until after such consideration.

(4)   The rent officer may, where he considers it appropriate, arrange for consultation in respect of more than one joint application to be held together with consultations in respect of one or more other joint applications.

**[3038]**

**5   Notices**

(1)   In the case of a joint application, any notices required to be served under regulation 4 above, and any notifications to be given under section 73(8) of the 1977 Act (notification of rent officer's decision) shall be sent by post in a prepaid letter or delivered—

    (a)   to the landlord and to the tenant at their respective addresses given in the application; or

    (b)   where the application is made on behalf of the landlord or of the tenant by an agent acting on his behalf, to that agent at the address of the agent given in the application.

(2)   In the case of an application under section 73(1A) of the 1977 Act, any notification to be given under section 73(8) of the 1977 Act shall be sent by post in a prepaid letter or delivered—

    (a)   to the applicant at the address given in the application; or

    (b)   where the application is made by an agent acting on behalf of the applicant, to that agent at the address of the agent given in the application.

**[3039]**

**6**   (*Revokes the Rent Regulation (Cancellation of Registration of Rent) Regulations 1972, SI 1972/1987.*)

# RENT ASSESSMENT COMMITTEES (ENGLAND AND WALES) (RENT TRIBUNAL) REGULATIONS 1980

## (SI 1980/1700)

**NOTES**
Made: 30 October 1980.
Authority: Rent Act 1977, s 74.
Commencement: 28 November 1980.

**1   Citation and Commencement**

These regulations may be cited as the Rent Assessment Committees (England and Wales) (Rent Tribunal) Regulations 1980 and shall come into operation on 28th November 1980.

**[3040]**

**2   Interpretation**

In these regulations, unless the context otherwise requires, "the Act" means the Rent Act 1977 and "Chairman" means the person acting as chairman of the rent tribunal.

**[3041]**

**3   Proceedings before rent tribunals**

Reference to a rent tribunal shall be by written notice. The notice shall specify the address of the house or part of a house to which the restricted contract relates, the names of the lessor and lessee, and the address of the lessor. The notice may be delivered at an office of the rent assessment panel, in which case it shall be deemed to have reached the rent tribunal on the day when it is so delivered, or may be posted to the rent assessment panel, in which case it shall be deemed to have reached the rent tribunal on the day when it would be delivered in the ordinary course of post.

**[3042]**

**4**   Where any reference is made to a rent tribunal, the rent tribunal shall give notice in writing to each party to the restricted contract informing him that he may within such time as the rent tribunal may allow (not being less than [7 days] from the date of the notice) give notice to the rent tribunal that he desires to be heard by them, or may send to the rent tribunal representations in writing:

Provided that the rent tribunal may extend the time stated in the notice.

**[3043]**

**NOTES**
Words in square brackets substituted by the Rent Assessment Committees (England and Wales) (Rent Tribunal) (Amendment) Regulations 1981, SI 1981/1493, reg 2, in relation to references to a rent tribunal made after 1 January 1982.

**5**—(1)   If any party to the restricted contract informs the rent tribunal that he desires to be heard, the rent tribunal shall give to each party not less than [7 clear days'] notice in writing of the time and place at which the parties will be heard.

(2)   If the house to which the reference relates is one the general management whereof is vested in and exercisable by the local authority as housing authority, the said local authority shall be given an opportunity of being heard, or if they so desire, of submitting representations in writing.

**[3044]**

**NOTES**
Para (1): words in square brackets substituted by the Rent Assessment Committees (England and Wales) (Rent Tribunal) (Amendment) Regulations 1981, SI 1981/1493, reg 2, in relation to references to a rent tribunal made after 1 January 1982.

**6**   At any hearing before a rent tribunal a party to the restricted contract may appear in person or by counsel or a solicitor or by any other representative or may be accompanied by any person whom he may wish to assist him thereat.

**[3045]**

**7**—(1)   Subject to the provisions of these regulations the procedure at a hearing shall be such as the rent tribunal may determine, and the rent tribunal may if they think fit, and at the request of either party shall, unless for some special reason they consider it undesirable, allow the hearing to be held in public …

(2)   The rent tribunal may postpone or adjourn the hearing from time to time as they think fit.

**[3046]**

**NOTES**
Para (1): words omitted revoked by the Tribunals, Courts and Enforcement Act 2007 (Transitional and Consequential Provisions) Order 2008, SI 2008/2683, art 6(1), Sch 1, para 17.

**8**—(1)   The decision of the majority of a rent tribunal shall be the decision of the tribunal. The decision shall be in writing, signed by the chairman, and shall be sent as soon as may be to the parties to the restricted contract, and to the local authority in cases where the restricted contract was referred to the rent tribunal by the authority.

(2)   The chairman shall have power, by certificate under his hand, to correct any clerical or accidental error or omission in the said decision.

**[3047]**

**9**   Where any notice is required or authorised by the Act or by these regulations to be given by the rent tribunal it shall be sufficient compliance with the Act or the regulations if the notice is sent by post in a pre-paid letter addressed to the party for whom it is intended at his usual or last known address.

**[3048]**

# ASSURED TENANCIES (NOTICE TO TENANT) REGULATIONS 1981

## (SI 1981/591)

**NOTES**
Made: 7 April 1981.
Authority: Housing Act 1980, ss 56(7), 151.
Commencement: 14 May 1981.

**1**   These regulations may be cited as the Assured Tenancies (Notice to Tenant) Regulations 1981 and shall come into operation on 14th May 1981.

**[3049]**

**2**   The requirements with which a notice is to comply in order to be valid for the purposes of section 56(6) of the Housing Act 1980 are that it shall be in the form set out in the Schedule to these regulations or in a form substantially to the like effect.

**[3050]**

### SCHEDULE

**NOTES**
This Schedule contains a notice which is not itself reproduced in this work, but its title is noted below.

Notice of the Grant of a Protected or Housing Association Tenancy by a Body Approved under section 56(4) of the Housing Act 1980 (amended by SI 1997/2971)

# RENT BOOK (FORMS OF NOTICE) REGULATIONS 1982

### (SI 1982/1474)

**NOTES**
Made: 15 October 1982.
Authority Landlord and Tenant Act 1962, ss 2(1), 6(1)(b) (repealed); now take effect under the Landlord and Tenant Act 1985, s 5.
Commencement: 1 January 1983.

**1**   These regulations may be cited as the Rent Book (Forms of Notice) Regulations 1982 and shall come into operation on 1st January 1983.

**[3051]**

**2**   In these regulations:—
    "the 1962 Act" means the Landlord and Tenant Act 1962;
    "the 1976 Act" means the Rent (Agriculture) Act 1976; and
    "the 1977 Act" means the Rent Act 1977 [and
    "the 1988 Act" means the Housing Act 1988.]

**[3052]**

**NOTES**
Words in square brackets added by the Rent Book (Forms of Notice) (Amendment) Regulations 1988, SI 1988/2198, reg 2(1).
Landlord and Tenant Act 1962: see now the Landlord and Tenant Act 1985.

**3**—(1)   The prescribed form in which, under section 2(1) of the 1962 Act, notice or particulars are required to be contained in a rent book or other similar document provided in pursuance of section 1 of the 1962 Act shall be as follows:—
  (a)  if the premises are occupied by virtue of a restricted contract within the meaning of the 1977 Act, the form set out in Part I of the Schedule to these regulations;
  (b)  if the premises are a dwelling house let on or subject to a protected or statutory tenancy within the meaning of the 1977 Act, the form set out in Part II of the Schedule to these regulations; and
  (c)  if the premises are a dwelling house subject to a statutory tenancy as defined in the 1976 Act, the form set out in Part III of the Schedule to these regulations
  [(d)  if the premises are a dwelling house let on an assured tenancy or an assured agricultural occupancy within the meaning of the 1988 Act, the form set out in Part IV of the Schedule to these regulations]
or, in each case, a form substantially to the same effect.

(2)   In the cases referred to in paragraphs [(a) to (d)] above, such rent book or similar document shall contain notice of the matters set out in the appropriate prescribed form, in addition to the name and address of the landlord and the particulars required by section 2(1) of the 1962 Act.

**[3053]**

PART II
STATUTORY INSTRUMENTS

**NOTES**
Para (1): sub-para (d) inserted by the Rent Book (Forms of Notice) (Amendment) Regulations 1988, SI 1988/2198, reg 2(2).
Para (2): words in square brackets substituted by SI 1988/2198, reg 2(3).

**4**   (*Revokes the Rent Book (Forms of Notice) Regulations 1976, SI 1976/378.*)

## SCHEDULE

**NOTES**
This Schedule contains forms which are not themselves reproduced in this work, but their numbers and titles are listed below.

| Form No | Title |
|---|---|
| I | Form for rent book for restricted contract (amended by SI 1988/2198, SI 1990/1067, SI 1993/656, SI 1997/2971) |
| II | Form for rent book for protected or statutory tenancy (amended by SI 1988/2198, SI 1990/1067, SI 1993/656, SI 1997/2971) |
| III | Form for rent book for tenancy under the Rent (Agriculture) Act 1976 (amended by SI 1988/2198, SI 1990/1067, SI 1993/656, SI 1997/2971) |
| IV | Form for rent book for assured tenancy or assured agricultural occupancy (added by SI 1988/2198; amended by SI 1990/1067, SI 1993/656, SI 1997/2971) |

# MOBILE HOMES (COMMISSIONS) ORDER 1983

## (SI 1983/748)

**NOTES**
Made: 16 May 1983.
Authority: Mobile Homes Act 1983, Sch 1, Pt I, para 8.
Commencement: 20 May 1983.

**1**   This order may be cited as the Mobile Homes (Commissions) Order 1983 and shall come into operation on 20th May 1983.

**[3054]**

**2**   The maximum rate of commission to which an owner shall be entitled, under the provisions of paragraph 8 of Part I of Schedule 1 to the Mobile Homes Act 1983, on the sale by an occupier of a mobile home shall be 10 per cent.

**[3055]**

# HOUSING (RIGHT TO BUY) (PRIORITY OF CHARGES) ORDER 1984 (NOTE)

## (SI 1984/1554)

**NOTES**
Made: 28 September 1984.
Authority: Housing Act 1980, s 8(5). S 8 repealed by the Housing (Consequential Provisions) Act 1985, s 3(1), Sch 1, Pt I; by virtue of s 2(2) thereof, this order now has effect under the Housing Act 1985, s 156(4).
Commencement: 20 October 1984.
Amended by: SI 2001/1149.
The bodies specified by this order are:
(a)   National Westminster Home Loans Limited;
(b)   the Bank of England; and
(c)   recognised banks and licensed institutions within the meaning of the Banking Act 1979 (largely repealed and replaced by the Banking Act 1987, which referred to "authorised institutions"; the 1987 Act has

itself been repealed by SI 2001/3649), other than any bank or institution falling within the Home Purchase Assistance and Housing Corporation Guarantee Act 1978, Schedule, para 7 (repealed).

Further orders: The following orders, all made under the Housing Act 1985, s 156(4) (except SI 1985/1979, which was made under the Housing Act 1980, s 8(5) and now takes effect under s 156(4) of the 1985 Act), specify further bodies for the purposes of s 156:

(a) SI 1985/1979 (amended by SI 1988/1726), specifying National Home Loans Corporation plc, Lombard Home Loans Limited and London and Manchester (Mortgages) (No 1) Limited;

(b) SI 1987/1203, specifying Yorkshire Bank Home Loans Limited, National Mutual Home Loans plc, Confederation Mortgage Services Limited, CL Mortgages Limited and Abbey Life Home Loans Limited;

(c) SI 1987/1810, specifying Abbey Life Executive Mortgages Limited and Abbey Life Funding Limited;

(d) SI 1988/85, specifying Abbey Life Home Service Limited, Abbey Life Mortgage Securities Limited, Abbey Life Residential Loans Limited, General Portfolio Finance Limited and Royal London Homebuy Limited;

(e) SI 1988/1726 (which amends SI 1985/1979), specifying Abbey Life Mortgage Finance Limited, Abbey Life Mortgage Loans Limited, CIS Mortgage Maker Limited and London and Manchester (Mortgages) (No 2) Limited;

(f) SI 1989/958, specifying HMC Group PLC, HMC First Home National PLC, Household Mortgage Bridging Limited, Household Mortgage Corporation PLC, London and Manchester (Mortgages) (No 3) Limited, London and Manchester (Mortgages) (No 4) Limited, Mortgage Express Limited and Wesleyan Home Loans Limited;

(g) SI 1989/2102, specifying Equity & Law Home Loans Limited, Credit Agricole Personal Finance plc, Credit Agricole Mortgage Company No 1 Limited, Credit Agricole Mortgage Company No 2 Limited, Credit Agricole Mortgage Company No 3 Limited, Providence Capitol Home Loans Limited, Providence Capitol Mortgage Services Limited, Providence Capitol Mortgage Services (No 2) Limited, Scotlife Home Loans (No 3) Limited, CIBC Mortgages plc, Mortgages plc, UCB Home Loans Corporation Limited, Secured Residential Funding plc and the Mortgage Corporation Limited;

(h) SI 1989/2329, specifying Halifax Loans Limited and BNP Mortgages Limited;

(i) SI 1990/1388, specifying Providence Capitol Mortgage Services (No 1) Limited, Sun Life of Canada Home Loans Limited, Halifax Loans (No 2) Limited, Halifax Loans (No 3) Limited and Halifax Loans (No 4) Limited;

(j) SI 1990/2390, specifying Capital Home Loans Limited, Paribas Lombard Mortgages Limited and Mortgage Funding Corporation PLC;

(k) SI 1991/619, specifying Legal and General Mortgage Services Limited, Leeds and Holbeck Mortgage Corporation Limited and Albion Home Loans Limited;

(l) SI 1991/2052 (amended by SI 1994/1762), specifying Barshelfco (No 16) Limited, Finance for Mortgages Limited, Gracechurch Mortgage Finance plc, Mortgage Services Funding plc, Mortgage Services Limited, Norwich Union Mortgage Finance Ltd, Scotlife Home Loans (No 2) Limited, the Consumer Loans Company Limited, the Mortgage Business Public Limited Company and Universal Credit Limited;

(m) SI 1992/2317, specifying Barshelfco (No 39) Limited, Barshelfco (No 40) Limited, Barshelfco (No 41) Limited, Bradford & Bingley Homeloans Limited, Bradford & Bingley Mortgages Limited, Bradford & Bingley Mortgage Management Limited, North Yorkshire Mortgage Management Limited, Northern Rock Mortgage Services Limited, London and Manchester (Mortgages) (No 5) Limited and London and Manchester (Mortgages) (No 6) Limited;

(n) SI 1993/303, specifying Derbyshire Home Loans Limited, Derbyshire Mortgages Limited, Norwich & Peterborough (AMC) Limited, Portman Financial and Mortgage Services Limited, Portman Land Services Limited, Portman Loans Limited and Portman Mortgage Services Limited;

(o) SI 1993/2757, specifying Alliance & Leicester Mortgage Loans Limited, CIS Home Loans Limited, CIS Mortgage Finance Limited and CIS Residential Mortgages Limited;

(p) SI 1994/1762 (which amends SI 1991/2052), specifying Alliance & Leicester Mortgage Loans (No 2) Limited, Alliance & Leicester Mortgage Loans (No 3) Limited, Alliance & Leicester Mortgage Loans (No 4) Limited, Britannia Mortgage Company Number One Limited, Britannia Mortgage Company Number Two Limited, Collateralised Mortgage Securities (No 16) PLC, Saffron Walden Mortgage Services Limited and Stroud and Swindon Mortgage Company (No 2) Limited;

(q) SI 1995/211, specifying Darlington Mortgage Services Limited, Furness Mortgage Services Limited, Gracechurch Mortgage Finance (No 5) Limited, Homeloans Direct Limited, Ipswich Mortgage Services Limited, LBS Insurance Services Limited, LBS Mortgage Services Limited, Leamington Mortgage Corporation Limited, Leeds and Holbeck Mortgage Funding Limited, N & P Mortgages Limited, N & P Mortgages Series A Limited, N & P Mortgages Series B Limited, N & P Mortgages Series C Limited and S A Mortgages No 1 Limited;

(r) SI 1995/2066, specifying Barshelfco (No 68) Limited, C L Mortgages Limited, Legal & General Mortgages Limited, Market Harborough Mortgages Limited, Newbury Mortgage Services Limited and West Bromwich Mortgage Company Limited;

(s) SI 1996/162, specifying Bradford & Bingley Loans Limited, Bradford & Bingley Management Limited, Bradford & Bingley Secured Loans Limited, Bradford & Bingley Secured Loans Management Limited, Chelsea Mortgage Services Limited, City Mortgage Corporation Limited, Pickering Finance Limited, Swift Advances Plc and Swift Securities Plc;

(t) SI 1997/945 (revoking SI 1996/2479), specifying Hanley Mortgage Services Limited, Hinckley and Rugby Mortgage Services Limited, Leek United Home Loans Limited, Mortgage Marque Limited, Preferred Mortgages Limited, Secondary Marketing Investment Conduit (No 3) Limited, Skipton Mortgage Corporation Limited, Skipton Mortgages Limited and Skipton Premier Mortgages Limited;

(u) SI 1997/2327, specifying Green Park Mortgage Funding Limited, HSMS, Hyde Park Mortgage Funding Limited, Regent's Park Mortgage Funding Limited, Silhouette Mortgages Limited, Southern Pacific Mortgage Limited, St James Park Mortgage Funding Limited and Transamerica Lending Company;

(v) SI 1998/320, specifying Mortgages PLC—Company No 03320975, The Money Store Limited—

Company No 03319091, The Money Store Company (No 1) Limited—Company No 3456337, The Money Store Company (No 2) Limited—Company No 3456341 and The Money Store Company (No 3) Limited—Company No 3456334;

(w) SI 1998/2015, specifying Capital Bank Mortgages Limited—Company No 2999410, Distinct Mortgages Limited—Company No 3138378, Future Mortgages 1 Limited—Company No 3300794, Ocwen Limited—Company No 3542994 and RFC Mortgage Services Limited—Company No 3489004;

(x) SI 1999/952, specifying Finsbury Park Mortgage Funding Limited—Company No 3437350;

(y) SI 1999/2919 (applying to England only) and SI 2000/349 (applying to Wales only), both specifying Mortgages 1 Limited—Company No 3186649, Mortgages 2 Limited—Company No 3587558 and Mortgages 4 Limited—Company No 3695068;

(z) SI 2001/205 (applying to England only) and SI 2001/1786 (applying to Wales only), both specifying Battersea Park Mortgage Funding Limited—Company No 3530410 and Richmond Park Mortgage Funding Limited—Company No 3597946;

(aa) SI 2001/3219 (applying to England only), specifying igroup Mortgages Limited—Company No 3770776, igroup UK Loans Limited—Company No 3749420, igroup 2 Limited—Company No 3610605, igroup 3 limited—Company No 3730890, igroup 4 limited—Company No 3797432, and igroup 5 limited—Company No 3770763;

(bb) SI 2001/3874 (applying to England only), specifying E-Mex Home Funding Limited—Company No 2124900;

(cc) SI 2002/763 (W 82) (applying to Wales only), specifying the same companies as SI 2001/3219 and SI 2001/3874 specify in relation to England;

(dd) SI 2003/1083 (applying to England only) and SI 2003/1853 (W 203) (applying to Wales only), both specifying Blemain Finance Limited—Company No 1185052;

(ee) SI 2004/1071 (applying to England only) and SI 2004/1806 (W194) (applying to Wales only) both specifying First National Home Finance Limited—Company No 592986;

(ff) SI 2005/92 (applying to England only) specifying London Scottish Finance Limited—Company No 233259 and Cheshire Mortgage Corporation Limited—Company No 2613335;

(gg) SI 2005/407 (applying to England only) specifying Money Partners Limited—Company No 4992438 and Money Partners Finance Limited—Company No 4992856;

(hh) SI 2005/1351 (W 99) (applying to Wales only) specifying Cheshire Mortgage Corporation Limited—Company No 02613335; London Scottish Finance Limited—Company No 00233259; Money Partners Limited—Company No 04992438; and Money Partners Finance Limited—Company No 05299032;

(ii) SI 2006/950 (W 99) (applying to Wales only) specifying Church House Trust plc—Company No 0980698;

(jj) SI 2006/1263 (applying to England only) specifying Cheval Property Finance plc—Company No 3131133 and Church House Trust plc—Company No 980698;

(kk) SI 2006/2563 (applying to England only) specifying Morgan Stanley Bank International Limited (Company No 3722571);

(ll) SI 2006/3242 (applying to England only) specifying Beacon Homeloans Limited (Company No 5304252) and Accord Mortgages Limited (Company No 2139881); and

(mm) SI 2008/371 (applying to Wales only) specifying Accord Mortgages Limited (Company No 2139881), Beacon Homeloans Limited (Company No 5304252) and Morgan Stanley Bank International Limited (Company No 3722571).

**[3056]**

# HOUSING (RIGHT TO BUY) (PRESCRIBED FORMS) REGULATIONS 1986

## (SI 1986/2194)

**NOTES**
Made: 12 December 1986.
Authority: Housing Act 1985, s 176(1), (5).
Commencement: 7 January 1987.

**1** These regulations may be cited as the Housing (Right to Buy) (Prescribed Forms) Regulations 1986 and shall come into operation on 7th January 1987.

**[3057]**

**2** The form set out in Schedule 1 to these regulations, or a form substantially to the like effect, shall be the form of notice to be used by a secure tenant in claiming to exercise the right to buy under section 122(1) of the Housing Act 1985.

**[3058]**

**3** The form set out in Schedule 2 to these regulations, or a form substantially to the like effect, shall be the form of notice to be used by the landlord in admitting or denying the tenant's right to buy under section 124(1) of the Housing Act 1985.

**[3059]**

**[3A** The form set out in Schedule 3 to these regulations, or a form substantially to the like effect, shall be the form of notice to be used by a secure tenant in claiming to exercise the right to acquire on rent to mortgage terms under section 144 of the Housing Act 1985.]

**[3060]**

**NOTES**
Inserted, together with reg 3B, by the Housing (Right to Buy) (Prescribed Forms) (Amendment) Regulations 1993, SI 1993/2246, reg 2(2).

**[3B** The form set out in Schedule 4 to these regulations, or a form substantially to the like effect, shall be the form of notice to be used by the landlord in admitting or denying the tenant's right to acquire on rent to mortgage terms under section 146 of the Housing Act 1985.]

**[3061]**

**NOTES**
Inserted as noted to reg 3A at **[3060]**.

**4** The particulars to be contained in any notice, the form of which is prescribed by regulation 2 or 3 above, shall be those required by that form.

**[3062]**

**5**—(1) ...

(2) Nothing in these regulations shall affect the validity of any notice served by a secure tenant under section 122(1) of the Housing Act 1985 before 7th March 1987 if the notice was in the form prescribed by the regulations mentioned in paragraph (1) above or in a form substantially to the like effect.

**[3063]**

**NOTES**
Para (1): revokes the Housing (Right to Buy) (Prescribed Forms) Regulations 1984, SI 1984/1175.

SCHEDULES 1–4

**NOTES**
These Schedules contain forms which are not themselves reproduced in this work, but their numbers are listed below.
The Housing (Right to Buy) (Prescribed Forms) (Welsh Forms) Regulations 1994, SI 1994/2932 prescribe Welsh language versions of the Forms RTB1, RTB2, RTB3 and RTB3A.

| *Form No* | *Title* |
|---|---|
| RTB 1 | Housing Act 1985: section 122—Notice claiming the right to buy (substituted in relation to England by SI 2007/784; amended by SI 2008/2831; modified by SI 2008/2839) |
| RTB 2 | Housing Act 1985: section 124—Notice in reply to tenant's right to buy claim (substituted in relation to England by SI 2005/1736) |
| RTB 3 | Housing Act 1985: section 144—Notice claiming the right to acquire on rent to mortgage terms (added by SI 1993/2246) |
| RTB 3A | Housing Act 1985: section 146—Notice in reply to tenant's notice claiming the right to acquire on rent to mortgage terms (added by SI 1993/2246) |

# SECURE TENANCIES (NOTICES) REGULATIONS 1987

(SI 1987/755)

**NOTES**
Made: 22 April 1987.
Authority: Housing Act 1985, s 83(2), (6).
Commencement: 13 May 1987.

PART II
STATUTORY INSTRUMENTS

**1** These Regulations may be cited as the Secure Tenancies (Notices) Regulations 1987 and shall come into force on 13th May 1987.

**[3064]**

**2**—(1) The notice to be served on a secure tenant under section 83 of the Housing Act 1985 before the court can entertain proceedings for possession of a dwelling-house let under a secure tenancy which is a periodic tenancy, shall be in the form specified in Part I of the Schedule to these Regulations, or in a form substantially to the same effect.

(2) The notice to be served on a secure tenant under section 83 of the Housing Act 1985 before the court can entertain proceedings for the termination of a secure tenancy which is a tenancy for a term certain, and for possession of the dwelling-house let under that tenancy, shall be in the form specified in Part II of the Schedule to these Regulations, or in a form substantially to the same effect.

(3) …

**[3065]**

**NOTES**

Para (3): revokes the Secure Tenancies (Notices) Regulations 1980, SI 1980/1339 and the Secure Tenancies (Notices) (Amendment) Regulations 1984, SI 1984/1224.

**[3** The notice to be served on a secure tenant under section 83 of the Housing Act 1985 before the court can entertain proceedings for a demotion order under section 82A of that Act, shall be in the form specified in Part III of the Schedule to these Regulations, or in a form substantially to the same effect.]

**[3066]**

**NOTES**

Commencement: 19 July 2004 (in relation to England); 30 April 2005 (in relation to Wales).

Inserted in relation to England by the Secure Tenancies (Notices) (Amendment) (England) Regulations 2004, SI 2004/1627, reg 2(1), (2), and in relation to Wales by the Secure Tenancies (Notices) (Amendment) (Wales) Regulations 2005, SI 2005/1226, reg 2(1), (2).

SCHEDULE

**NOTES**

This Schedule contains forms which are not reproduced in this work, but their numbers and titles are noted below.

| Form No | Title |
| --- | --- |
| I | Notice of seeking possession—Housing Act 1985, s 83 (amended by SI 1997/71, SI 1997/377; modified by SI 2008/2839) |
| II | Notice of seeking termination of tenancy and recovery of possession—Housing Act 1985, s 83 (modified by SI 2008/2839) |
| III | Notice before proceedings for a demotion order—Housing Act 1985, s 83 (added by SI 2004/1627 in relation to England and SI 2005/1226 in relation to Wales) |

# HOUSING ASSOCIATION SHARED OWNERSHIP LEASES (EXCLUSION FROM LEASEHOLD REFORM ACT 1967 AND RENT ACT 1977) REGULATIONS 1987

## (SI 1987/1940)

**NOTES**

Made: 13 November 1987.

Authority: Leasehold Reform Act 1967, Sch 4A, para 5; Rent Act 1977, s 5A(3).

Commencement: 11 December 1987.

These regulations supersede the Housing (Exclusion of Shared Ownership Tenancies from the Leasehold Reform Act 1967) Regulations 1982, SI 1982/62, which lapsed on the repeal of the enabling power.

**1**   These Regulations may be cited as the Housing Association Shared Ownership Leases (Exclusion from Leasehold Reform Act 1967 and Rent Act 1977) Regulations 1987 and shall come into force on 11th December 1987.

**[3067]**

**2**   The requirements or circumstances prescribed, for the purposes of the conditions in paragraph 3(2)(c), (e) and (f) of Schedule 4A ("Schedule 4A") to the Leasehold Reform Act 1967 and the conditions in section 5A(2)(c), (e) and (f) of the Rent Act 1977, are those set out in Schedule 1 to these Regulations.

**[3068]**

**3**   The matters prescribed for the purposes of paragraph 4 of Schedule 4A are those set out in Schedule 2.

**[3069]**

SCHEDULES

SCHEDULE 1
SHARED OWNERSHIP LEASES (GENERAL)

Article 2

*Definition*

1.   In this Schedule "market value price" means the amount agreed between or determined in a manner agreed between the parties or, in default of such agreement or determination, determined by an independent expert agreed between the parties or, in default of agreement, appointed on the application of either party by or on behalf of the President of the Royal Institution of Chartered Surveyors, as the amount which the interest of the tenant would fetch, if sold on the open market by a willing vendor, on the assumption that the tenant had previously purchased 100 per cent of the shares in the dwelling-house, disregarding the following matters—
- (i)   any mortgage of the tenant's interest;
- (ii)   any interest in or right over the dwelling-house created by the tenant;
- (iii)   any improvement made by the tenant or any predecessor in title of his;
- (iv)   any failure by the tenant or any predecessor in title to carry out any repairing obligations under the lease.

*Requirements relating to Condition (c)*

2.   The requirements as to the provision for the tenant to acquire additional shares in the dwelling-house are that—
- (a)   the tenant is to be entitled to acquire additional shares up to a maximum of 100 per cent, in instalments of 25 per cent or such lesser percentage, if any, as may be specified in the lease;
- (b)   the tenant is to be able to exercise this entitlement by serving notice in writing on the landlord at any time during the term of the lease, stating the additional shares he proposes to acquire;
- (c)   the price for the additional shares is to be an amount no greater than the same percentage of the market value price at the date of service of the tenant's notice under sub-paragraph (b) above, as the percentage of the additional shares;
- (d)   the rent payable by the tenant under the lease (excluding any amount payable, directly or indirectly, for services, repairs, maintenance, insurance or management costs) is to be reduced, upon the purchase of any additional shares, in the same proportion as the reduction in the percentage of shares remaining unpurchased by the tenant.

*Circumstances relating to Condition (e)*

3.—(1)   If the lease enables the landlord to require payment for the outstanding shares in the dwelling-house, the circumstances in which the landlord is entitled so to do shall be that—
- (a)   there has been a disposal, other than an exempt disposal, of any interest in the dwelling-house by the tenant;
- (b)   the amount payable by the tenant is an amount no greater than the same percentage of the market value price at the date of the disposal as the percentage of the shares in the dwelling-house remaining unpurchased by the tenant.

(2)   In sub-paragraph (1) above, "exempt disposal" means—
- (a)   a disposal under a will or intestacy;
- (b)   a disposal under section 24 of the Matrimonial Causes Act 1973 or section 2 of the Inheritance (Provision for Family and Dependants) Act 1975;
- (c)   a grant of a sub-tenancy in respect of which a notice has been given under

section 52(1)(b) of the Housing Act 1980 (notice that a tenancy is to be a protected shorthold tenancy) or of a kind mentioned in any of Cases 11 to 18 or 20 in Schedule 15 to the Rent Act 1977;

(d) a grant of a sub-tenancy of part of the dwelling-house, if any other part of the dwelling-house remains in the possession of the tenant;

(e) a grant of a mortgage.

*Requirements relating to Condition (f)*

4. The provision in the lease of a house for the tenant to acquire the landlord's interest shall—
    (a) be exercisable at any time by the tenant by giving notice in writing, to take effect not before he has acquired 100 per cent of the shares in the dwelling-house;
    (b) require the landlord's interest to be transferred, as soon as practicable after the coming into effect of the notice mentioned in sub-paragraph (a) above, to the tenant or to such other person as the tenant may direct;
    (c) not entitle the landlord to make any charge for the conveyance or assignment of his interest.

[3070]

## SCHEDULE 2
### LEASES FOR THE ELDERLY
Article 3

*Definition*

1. In paragraph 4 of Schedule 4A and in this Schedule, "lease for the elderly" means a lease to a person of or over the age of 55 at the date of the grant of the lease.

*Requirements as respects leases for the elderly*

2. The prescribed requirements for the purposes of the condition in paragraph 4(2)(b) of Schedule 4A are that a lease for the elderly—
    (a) shall contain a covenant by the landlord to provide the tenant with facilities which consist of or include access to the services of a warden and a system for calling him;
    (b) shall contain an absolute covenant by the tenant not to underlet the whole or part of the demised premises;
    (c) shall contain a covenant by the tenant not to assign or part with possession of the whole or part of the demised premises except—
        (i) subject to such conditions as the lease may specify, to a person of or over the age of 55 at the date of the assignment; or
        (ii) where the assignment is—
            (a) by an executor or administrator of a deceased tenant to that tenant's spouse if residing there at the date of the tenant's death, or to a person residing there with the tenant at that date who is of or over the age of 55 at the date of the assignment; or
            (b) if the lease so provides and subject to such conditions as the lease may specify, by a mortgagee or chargee exercising his power of sale;
    (d) shall not provide for the tenant to acquire the interest of the landlord under an option to purchase.

[3071]

# ASSURED TENANCIES AND AGRICULTURAL OCCUPANCIES (RENT INFORMATION) ORDER 1988

(SI 1988/2199)

NOTES
Made: 14 December 1988.
Authority: Housing Act 1988, s 42.
Commencement: 15 January 1989.

1 This Order may be cited as the Assured Tenancies and Agricultural Occupancies (Rent Information) Order 1988 and shall come into force on 15th January 1989.

[3072]

**2**   This Order applies to cases where the rent assessment committee for an area have made a determination [on an application] under section 13(4) or 22(1) of the Housing Act 1988 or are precluded from making a determination on an application under section 22(1) by reason of section 22(3) of that Act.

**[3073]**

**NOTES**
   Words in square brackets inserted by the Assured Tenancies and Agricultural Occupancies (Rent Information) (Amendment) Order 1990, SI 1990/1474, art 2.

**3**   The President of the rent assessment panel for the area concerned shall, as respects those cases, make available for public inspection under section 42 of the Housing Act 1988 the information specified in the Schedule to this Order.

**[3074]**

**4**   The President of each rent assessment panel shall keep the specified information available for public inspection without charge during usual office hours at the office or principal office of that panel.

**[3075]**

**5**   A person requiring a copy of any specified information certified under the hand of an officer duly authorised by the President of the rent assessment panel concerned shall be entitled to obtain it on payment of a fee of £1 for the specified information relating to each determination or, where no determination is made, each application.

**[3076]**

SCHEDULE
SPECIFIED INFORMATION

Article 3

1.   Address of premises.

2.   Description of premises.

3.   Names and addresses of landlord and tenant.

4.   If granted for a term, date of commencement of the tenancy and length of term.

5.   The rental period.

6.   Allocation between landlord and tenant of liabilities for repairs.

7.   Whether any [council tax or rates] are borne by the landlord or a superior landlord.

8.   Details of services provided by the landlord or a superior landlord.

9.   Details of furniture provided by the landlord or a superior landlord.

10.   Any other terms of the tenancy or notice relating to the tenancy taken into consideration in determining the rent.

11.   The rent determined, the date it was determined and the amount (if any) of the rent which, in the opinion of the committee, is fairly attributable to the provision of services, except where that amount is in their opinion negligible, or, in a case where the committee are precluded from making a determination by section 22(3) of the Housing Act 1988, the rent currently payable under the assured shorthold tenancy [and whether the committee are so precluded by paragraph (a) or paragraph (b) of that subsection].

**[3077]**

**NOTES**
   Para 7: words in square brackets substituted by the Assured Tenancies and Agricultural Occupancies (Rent Information) (Amendment) Order 1993, SI 1993/657, art 2.
   Para 11: words in square brackets added by the Assured Tenancies and Agricultural Occupancies (Rent Information) (Amendment) Order 1990, SI 1990/1474, art 2.

# NOTICES TO QUIT ETC (PRESCRIBED INFORMATION) REGULATIONS 1988

(SI 1988/2201)

**NOTES**
   Made: 14 December 1988.
   Authority: Protection from Eviction Act 1977, s 5.
   Commencement: 15 January 1989.

PART II
STATUTORY INSTRUMENTS

**1**  These Regulations may be cited as the Notices to Quit etc (Prescribed Information) Regulations 1988 and shall come into force on 15th January 1989.

**[3078]**

**2**  Where, on or after the date these Regulations come into force, a landlord gives a notice to quit any premises let as a dwelling, or a licensor gives a notice to determine a periodic licence to occupy premises as a dwelling (and the premises are not let or occupied as specified in section 5(1B) of the Protection from Eviction Act 1977), the information prescribed for the purposes of section 5 of the Protection from Eviction Act 1977 shall be that in the Schedule to these Regulations.

**[3079]**

**3**  *(Revokes the Notices to Quit (Prescribed Information) Regulations 1980, SI 1980/1624.)*

## SCHEDULE
## PRESCRIBED INFORMATION
Regulation 2

1.  If the tenant or licensee does not leave the dwelling, the landlord or licensor must get an order for possession from the court before the tenant or licensee can lawfully be evicted. The landlord or licensor cannot apply for such an order before the notice to quit or notice to determine has run out.

2.  A tenant or licensee who does not know if he has any right to remain in possession after a notice to quit or a notice to determine runs out can obtain advice from a solicitor. Help with all or part of the cost of legal advice and assistance may be available under the Legal Aid Scheme. He should also be able to obtain information from a Citizens' Advice Bureau, a Housing Aid Centre or a rent officer.

**[3080]**

# HOUSING (RIGHT TO BUY DELAY PROCEDURE) (PRESCRIBED FORMS) REGULATIONS 1989

(SI 1989/240)

**NOTES**
Made: 22 February 1989.
Authority: Housing Act 1985, s 176(1), (5).
Commencement: 10 March 1989.

**1**  These Regulations may be cited as the Housing (Right to Buy Delay Procedure) (Prescribed Forms) Regulations 1989 and come into force on 10th March 1989.

**[3081]**

**2**  There are set out in the Schedule to these Regulations—
    [(a)   the form (form RTB6) for an initial notice of delay under section 153A(1) of the Housing Act 1985;]
    (b)   the form (form RTB7) for a counter notice under section 153A(3)(b) of the Housing Act 1985.
    (c)   the form (form RTB8) for an operative notice of delay under section 153A(5) of the Housing Act 1985;

and each form, or a form substantially to the like effect, is prescribed for the purpose specified.

**[3082]**

**NOTES**
Para (a): substituted by the Housing (Right to Buy Delay Procedure) (Prescribed Forms) (Amendment) Regulations 1993, SI 1993/2245, reg 2(1), subject to savings in relation to cases where a notice under the Housing Act 1985, s 122 at **[468]**, was served before 11 October 1993, and in relation to cases served before 11 January 1994.

**3**  The prescribed particulars to be contained in any notice the form of which is prescribed by regulation 2 above are the particulars required by that form.

**[3083]**

## SCHEDULE

**NOTES**
This Schedule contains forms which are not reproduced in this work, but their numbers and titles are noted below.

The Housing (Right to Buy Delay Procedure) (Prescribed Forms) (Welsh Forms) Regulations 1994, SI 1994/2931 prescribe Welsh language versions of the Forms RTB6, RTB7 and RTB8.

| Form No | Title |
|---------|-------|
| RTB5 | Revoked by SI 1993/2245, subject to savings |
| RTB6 | Housing Act 1985: section 153A(1)—Initial notice of delay (amended by SI 1993/2245) |
| RTB7 | Housing Act 1985: section 153A(3)(b)—Landlord's counter notice (amended by SI 1993/2245) |
| RTB8 | Housing Act 1985: section 153A(5)—Operative notice of delay (amended by SI 1993/2245) |

# HIGH COURT AND COUNTY COURTS JURISDICTION ORDER 1991

## (SI 1991/724)

**NOTES**
Made: 19 March 1991.
Authority: Courts and Legal Services Act 1990, ss 1, 120.
Commencement: 1 July 1991.

## ARRANGEMENT OF ARTICLES

## 1  Title and commencement

This Order may be cited as the High Court and County Courts Jurisdiction Order 1991 and shall come into force on 1st July 1991.

**[3084]**

## [1A  Interpretation

In this Order—
- (a) "the EOP Regulation" means Regulation (EC) No 1896/2006 of the European Parliament and of the Council of 12 December 2006 creating a European order for payment procedure; and
- (b) "the ESCP Regulation" means Regulation (EC) No 861/2007 of the European Parliament and of the Council of 11 July 2007 establishing a European small claims procedure.]

**[3085]**

**NOTES**
Inserted by the High Court and County Courts Jurisdiction (Amendment) Order 2008, SI 2008/2934, art 3.

## 2  Jurisdiction

(1) A county court shall have jurisdiction under—
- (a) sections ... 146 and 147 of the Law of Property Act 1925,
- (b) ...
- (c) section 26 of the Arbitration Act 1950,
- (d) section 63(2) of the Landlord and Tenant Act 1954,

(e)    section 28(3) of the Mines and Quarries (Tips) Act 1969,

(f)    section 66 of the Taxes Management Act 1970,

(g)    section 41 of the Administration of Justice Act 1970,

(h)    ...

(i)    section 13 of the Torts (Interference with Goods) Act 1977,

(j)    section 87 of the Magistrates' Courts Act 1980,

[(k)    sections 17 and 18 of the Audit Commission Act 1998,]

(l)    sections 15, 16, 21, 25 and 139 of the County Courts Act 1984,

(m)    section 39(4) of, and paragraph 3(1) of Schedule 3 to, the Legal Aid Act 1988,

(n)    sections 99, 102(5), 114, 195, 204, 230, 231 and 235(5) of the Copyright, Designs and Patents Act 1988, ...

(o)    section 40 of the Housing Act 1988,

[(p)    sections 13 and 14 of the Trusts of Land and Appointment of Trustees Act 1996,]

[(q)    the EOP Regulation,

(r)    the ESCP Regulation,]

whatever the amount involved in the proceedings and whatever the value of any fund or asset connected with the proceedings.

(2)    A county court shall have jurisdiction under—

(a)    section 10 of the Local Land Charges Act 1975, and

(b)    section 10(4) of the Rentcharges Act 1977,

where the sum concerned or amount claimed does not exceed £5,000.

(3)    A county court shall have jurisdiction under the following provisions of the Law of Property Act 1925 where the capital value of the land or interest in land which is to be dealt with does not exceed £30,000:

(a)    sections 3, 49, 66, 181, and 188;

(b)    proviso (iii) to paragraph 3 of Part III of Schedule 1;

(c)    proviso (v) to paragraph 1(3) of Part IV of Schedule 1;

(d)    provisos (iii) and (iv) to paragraph 1(4) of Part IV of Schedule 1.

(4)    A county court shall have jurisdiction under sections 89, 90, 91 and 92 of the Law of Property Act 1925 where the amount owing in respect of the mortgage or charge at the commencement of the proceedings does not exceed £30,000.

(5)    A county court shall have jurisdiction under the proviso to section 136(1) of the Law of Property Act 1925 where the amount or value of the debt or thing in action does not exceed £30,000.

(6)    A county court shall have jurisdiction under section 1(6) of the Land Charges Act 1972—

(a)    in the case of a land charge of Class C(i), C(ii) or D(i), if the amount does not exceed £30,000;

(b)    in the case of a land charge of Class C(iii), if it is for a specified capital sum of money not exceeding £30,000 or, where it is not for a specified capital sum, if the capital value of the land affected does not exceed £30,000;

(c)    in the case of a land charge of Class A, Class B, Class C(iv), Class D(ii), Class D(iii) or Class E, if the capital value of the land affected does not exceed £30,000;

(d)    in the case of a land charge of Class F, if the land affected by it is the subject of an order made by the court under section 1 of the Matrimonial Homes Act 1983 or an application for an order under that section relating to that land has been made to the court;

(e)    in a case where an application under section 23 of the Deeds of Arrangement Act 1914 could be entertained by the court.

(7)    A county court shall have jurisdiction under sections 69, 70 and 71 of the Solicitors Act 1974 where a bill of costs relates wholly or partly to contentious business done in a county court and the amount of the bill does not exceed £5,000.

[(7A)    A patents county court and the county courts listed in paragraph (7B) shall have jurisdiction under the following provisions of the Trade Marks Act 1994—

(a)    sections 15, 16, 19, 23(5), 25(4)(b), 30, 31, 46, 47, 64, 73 and 74;

(b)    paragraph 12 of Schedule 1; and

(c)    paragraph 14 of Schedule 2,

to include jurisdiction to hear and determine any claims or matters ancillary to, or arising from proceedings brought under such provisions.

(7B)    For the purposes of paragraph (7A), the county courts at—

(a)    Birmingham;

(b)    Bristol;

(c)    Cardiff;

(d)    Leeds;

(e)    Liverpool;

(f)    Manchester; and

(g)    Newcastle upon Tyne,

shall have jurisdiction.]

(8)    The enactments and statutory instruments listed in the Schedule to this Order are amended as specified therein, being amendments which are consequential on the provisions of this article.

**[3086]**

**NOTES**

Para (1): in sub-para (a) number omitted revoked, in sub-para (n) word omitted revoked, and sub-para (p) inserted by the High Court and County Courts Jurisdiction (Amendment) Order 1996, SI 1996/3141, art 2; sub-para (b) revoked by the High Court and County Courts Jurisdiction (Amendment) Order 2005, SI 2005/587, art 3(a); sub-para (h) revoked by the High Court and County Courts Jurisdiction (Amendment) Order 2008, SI 2008/2934, art 1(5); sub-para (k) substituted by virtue of the Audit Commission Act 1998, s 54(2), Sch 4, para 4(1); sub-paras (q), (r) inserted by SI 2008/2934, art 5.

Paras (7A), (7B): inserted by SI 2005/587, art 3(b).

### 3 Injunctions

The High Court shall have jurisdiction to hear an application for an injunction made in the course of or in anticipation of proceedings in a county court where a county court may not, by virtue of regulations under section 38(3)(b) of the County Courts Act 1984 or otherwise, grant such an injunction.

**[3087]**

### 4 Allocation—Commencement of proceedings

Subject to articles [4A,] 5[, 6[, 6A and 6B]] proceedings in which both the county courts and the High Court have jurisdiction may be commenced either in a county court or in the High Court.

**[3088]**

**NOTES**

Reference in first pair of square brackets inserted by the High Court and County Courts Jurisdiction (Amendment) Order 1999, SI 1999/1014, art 4; reference in second (outer) pair of square brackets substituted by the Access to Neighbouring Land Act 1992, s 7(2); references in the third (inner) pair of square brackets substituted by the High Court and County Courts Jurisdiction (Amendment) Order 2008, SI 2008/2934, art 6.

**[4A**   Except for proceedings to which article 5 applies, a claim for money in which the county courts have jurisdiction may only be commenced in the High Court if the value of the claim is more than £25,000.]

**[3089]**

**NOTES**

Inserted by the High Court and County Courts Jurisdiction (Amendment) Order 1999, SI 1999/1014, art 5; substituted by the High Court and County Courts Jurisdiction (Amendment) Order 2009, SI 2009/577, art 2 (with effect in relation to proceedings issued on or after 6 April 2009: see SI 2009/577, arts 1(1), 8).

**5**—[(1)    Proceedings which include a claim for damages in respect of personal injuries may only be commenced in the High Court if the … value of the claim is £50,000 or more.]

(2)    In this article "personal injuries" means personal injuries to the [claimant] or any other person, and includes disease, impairment of physical or mental condition, and death.

[(3)    This article does not apply to proceedings which include a claim for damages in respect of an alleged breach of duty of care committed in the course of the provision of clinical or medical services (including dental or nursing services).]

**[3090]**

**NOTES**

Para (1): substituted by the High Court and County Courts Jurisdiction (Amendment) Order 1999, SI 1999/1014, art 6(a); word omitted revoked by the High Court and County Courts Jurisdiction (Amendment) Order 2009, SI 2009/577, art 3.

Para (2): word in square brackets substituted by SI 1999/1014, art 3.

Para (3): added by SI 1999/1014, art 6(b).

**6**    Applications [and appeals] under [section 17 of the Audit Commission Act 1998] and appeals under [section 18] of that Act shall be commenced in the High Court.

**[3091]**

**NOTES**

Words in first pair of square brackets inserted by the High Court and County Courts Jurisdiction (Amendment) Order 1993, SI 1993/1407, art 3; words in second and third pairs of square brackets substituted by virtue of the Audit Commission Act 1998, s 54(2), Sch 4, para 4(1).

**PART II**
**STATUTORY INSTRUMENTS**

**[6A** Applications under section 1 of the Access to Neighbouring Land Act 1992 shall be commenced in a county court.]

**[3092]**

NOTES
Inserted by the Access to Neighbouring Land Act 1992, s 7(2).

**[6B** Applications under article 4 of the ESCP Regulation must be commenced in a county court.]

**[3093]**

NOTES
Inserted by the High Court and County Courts Jurisdiction (Amendment) Order 2008, SI 2008/2934, art 7.

**7** (*Revoked by the High Court and County Courts Jurisdiction (Amendment) Order 1999, SI 1999/1014, art 7.*)

## 8 Enforcement

(1) [Subject to paragraph (1A)] a judgment or order of a county court for the payment of a sum of money which it is sought to enforce wholly or partially by execution against goods—

[(a) ... shall be enforced only in the High Court where the sum which it is sought to enforce is £5,000 or more;]

[(b) shall be enforced only in a county court where the sum which it is sought to enforce is less than [£600];]

(c) in any other case may be enforced in either the High Court or a county court.

[(1A) A judgment or order of a county court for the payment of a sum of money in proceedings arising out of an agreement regulated by the Consumer Credit Act 1974 shall be enforced only in a county court.]

(2) ...

[(2) Subject to paragraph (3), where—

(a) an enactment provides that a sum of money shall be or may be recoverable as if it were payable under a county court order; and

(b) the recovery of that sum is sought wholly or partially by execution against goods,

payment of that sum shall be enforced in accordance with paragraphs (1)(a) to (c).

(3) Paragraph (1)(b) does not apply to the enforcement of—

(a) a sum of money recoverable under section 15(1) of the Employment Tribunals Act 1996; or

(b) a compromise sum which is recoverable under section 19A(3) of that Act.]

**[3094]**

NOTES
Para (1): words in first pair of square brackets inserted, words omitted revoked, and sub-para (b) substituted by the High Court and County Courts Jurisdiction (Amendment) Order 1995, SI 1995/205, art 5; sub-para (a) substituted by the High Court and County Courts Jurisdiction (Amendment) Order 1993, SI 1993/1407, art 4; sum in square brackets in sub-para (b) substituted by the High Court and County Courts Jurisdiction (Amendment) Order 1999, SI 1999/1014, art 8.
Para (1A): inserted by SI 1995/205, art 5.
First para (2): amends the County Courts Act 1984, s 85(1).
Second para (2), para (3): inserted by the High Court and County Courts Jurisdiction (Amendment) Order 2009, SI 2009/577, art 4.

**[8A [Enforcement of traffic penalties]**

(1) Proceedings for the recovery of—

[(a) increased penalty charges provided for in charge certificates issued under—

(i) paragraph 6 of Schedule 6 to the 1991 Act; ...

(ii) paragraph 8 of Schedule 1 to the London Local Authorities Act 1996;

[(iii) regulation 17 of the Road User Charging (Enforcement and Adjudication) (London) Regulations 2001;

(iv) regulation 21 of the Civil Enforcement of Parking Contraventions (England) General Regulations 2007; and

(v) regulation 13 of the Civil Enforcement of Parking Contraventions (Penalty Charge Notices, Enforcement and Adjudication) (Wales) Regulations 2008;]]

(b) amounts payable by a person other than a [local] authority under an adjudication of a parking adjudicator pursuant to section 73 of the 1991 Act[; ...

[(c) amounts payable by a person other than a local authority under an adjudication pursuant to—

    (i)    the Road User Charging (Enforcement and Adjudication) (London) Regulations 2001;

    (ii)    the Civil Enforcement of Parking Contraventions (England) Representations and Appeals Regulations 2007; and

    (iii)    the Civil Enforcement of Parking Contraventions (Representations and Appeals) (Wales) Regulations 2008; and]]

  [(d)   increased fixed penalties referred to in—

    (i)    regulation 17(6) of the Road Traffic (Vehicle Emissions) (Fixed Penalty) (England) Regulations 2002; and

    (ii)    regulation 17(6) of the Road Traffic (Vehicle Emissions) (Fixed Penalty) (Wales) Regulations 2003,]

shall be taken in [Northampton] County Court.

    (2)   In this article, "the 1991 Act" means the Road Traffic Act 1991 ...

  [(3)   After paragraph (2) of article 8A, there shall be inserted the following:—

    (a)    in England, a [London borough council, the Common Council of the City of London, Transport for London], a county or district council or the Council of the Isles of Scilly; and

    (b)    in Wales, a county or county borough council.]]

**[3095]**

**NOTES**

Inserted by the High Court and County Courts Jurisdiction (Amendment) Order 1993, SI 1993/1407, art 5.

Heading: substituted by the High Court and County Courts Jurisdiction (Amendment) Order 2001, SI 2001/1387, arts 2, 3(a).

Para (1): sub-para (a) substituted by SI 2001/1387, arts 2, 3(b); word omitted from sub-para (a)(i) revoked by the High Court and County Courts Jurisdiction (Amendment) Order 2009, SI 2009/577, art 5(1)(a); sub-para (a)(iii)–(v) added by SI 2009/577, art 5(1)(b); in sub-para (b) word in square brackets substituted by the High Court and County Courts Jurisdiction (Amendment) Order 1996, SI 1996/3141, art 4(1), (2), word omitted revoked by SI 2009/577, art 5(1)(c); sub-para (c) inserted by SI 2001/1387, arts 2, 3(c), substituted by SI 2009/577, art 5(1)(d); sub-para (d) inserted by SI 2009/577, art 5(1)(e); final word in square brackets substituted by SI 1996/3141, art 4(1), (2).

Para (2): words omitted revoked by SI 2009/577, art 5(2).

Para (3): added by SI 1996/3141, art 4(1), (3); words in square brackets substituted by SI 2009/577, art 5(3).

## [8B   Enforcement of possession orders against trespassers

    (1)   A judgment or order of a county court for possession of land made in a possession claim against trespassers may be enforced in the High Court or a county court.

    (2)   In this article "a possession claim against trespassers" has the same meaning as in Part 55 of the Civil Procedure Rules 1998.]

**[3096]**

**NOTES**

Inserted by the High Court and County Courts Jurisdiction (Amendment No 2) Order 2001, SI 2001/2685, art 2.

## [9   ... [Value] of claim

For the purposes of Articles 4A and 5, the ... value of the claim shall be calculated in accordance with rule 16.3(6) of the Civil Procedure Rules 1998.]

**[3097]**

**NOTES**

Substituted by the High Court and County Courts Jurisdiction (Amendment) Order 1999, SI 1999/1014, art 9.

Words omitted revoked, and word in square brackets substituted by the High Court and County Courts Jurisdiction (Amendment) Order 2009, SI 2009/577, arts 6, 7.

**10**   (*Revoked by the High Court and County Courts Jurisdiction (Amendment) Order 1999, SI 1999/1014, art 10.*)

## 11   Crown proceedings—transitional provisions

For a period of two years from the date upon which this Order comes into force no order shall be made transferring proceedings in the High Court to which the Crown is a party to a county court, except—

    (a)    when the proceedings are set down to be tried or heard; or

    (b)    with the consent of the Crown.

**[3098]**

## 12 Savings

This Order shall not apply to:

(a)    family proceedings within the meaning of Part V of the Matrimonial and Family Proceedings Act 1984;

(b)    ...

**[3099]**

---

**NOTES**

Para (b) revoked by the High Court and County Courts Jurisdiction (Amendment) Order 1999, SI 1999/1014, art 11.

*(Schedule contains repeals and revocations only.)*

# LEASEHOLD REFORM (COLLECTIVE ENFRANCHISEMENT AND LEASE RENEWAL) REGULATIONS 1993

(SI 1993/2407)

---

**NOTES**

Made: 30 September 1993.
Authority: Leasehold Reform, Housing and Urban Development Act 1993, ss 98, 100(1).
Commencement: 1 November 1993.

## ARRANGEMENT OF REGULATIONS

## 1 Citation, commencement and interpretation

(1)    These Regulations may be cited as the Leasehold Reform (Collective Enfranchisement and Lease Renewal) Regulations 1993 and shall come into force on 1st November 1993.

(2)    In these Regulations references to sections and Schedules without more are references to sections of and Schedules to the Leasehold Reform, Housing and Urban Development Act 1993.

**[3100]**

## 2 Procedure for collective enfranchisement

In a transaction undertaken to give effect to an initial notice the nominee purchaser, the reversioner and any relevant landlord shall, unless they otherwise agree, be bound by Schedule 1 to these Regulations.

**[3101]**

## 3 Procedure for lease renewal

In a transaction undertaken to give effect to a tenant's notice, the landlord and the tenant shall, unless they otherwise agree, be bound by Schedule 2 to these Regulations.

**[3102]**

## 4 Notices

Any notice, statement, answer or document required or authorised to be given under these Regulations—

(a)    shall be in writing, and

(b)    may be sent by post.

**[3103]**

## SCHEDULES

## SCHEDULE 1
## COLLECTIVE ENFRANCHISEMENT

Regulation 2

*Interpretation*

1.    In this Schedule—

"counter-notice" means a notice given under section 21, and "further counter-notice" means a
     notice required by or by virtue of section 22(3) or section 23(5) or (6);
"qualifying tenant" shall be construed in accordance with section 5;
"the relevant date" has the meaning given by section 1(8);
"terms of acquisition" has the meaning given by section 24(8).

2. ....

### *Delivery of proof of title*

3.—(1)   Sub-paragraph (2) applies where the reversioner has given a counter-notice complying
with section 21(2)(a) (admitting the right to collective enfranchisement) or a further counter-notice,
or, if no such counter-notice or further counter-notice is given, the nominee purchaser has applied to
the court for an order under section 25(1) (applications where reversioner fails to give counter-notice
or further counter-notice).

(2)   Subject to paragraph 5, the nominee purchaser may require the reversioner to deduce title to
the interests proposed to be acquired in accordance with section 13(3)(a) and (c)(i) (matters
specified in the initial notice) and to any interest in relation to which the reversioner has made
proposals in accordance with section 21(3)(b) and (c) (matters specified in counter-notice), or to any
less extensive interest which it has been agreed or determined by a leasehold valuation tribunal will
be acquired, by giving him notice.

(3)   The reversioner shall comply with any such requirement by giving the nominee purchaser—
     (a)    in the case of an interest registered in the register of title kept at Her Majesty's Land
         Registry, all particulars and information which have to be given or may be required to be
         given on a sale of registered land pursuant to section 110 of the Land Registration
         Act 1925 (provisions as between vendor and purchaser), and
     (b)    in the case of any other interest, an epitome of title,
within the period of twenty-eight days beginning with the date the notice is given.

### *Requisitions*

4.—(1)   Subject to paragraph 5, the nominee purchaser shall give to the reversioner a statement of
any objections to or requisitions on the proof of title within the period of fourteen days beginning
with the date the proof is given (whether or not within the time required).

(2)   The reversioner shall give to the nominee purchaser an answer to any statement of
objections or requisitions within the period of fourteen days beginning with the date the statement is
given.

(3)   The nominee purchaser shall give to the reversioner a further statement of any objections to
or comments on the answer within the period of seven days beginning with the date the answer is
given.

(4)   Any objection or requisition not included in any statement given within the period referred
to in sub-paragraph (1) shall be deemed waived, and any matter which could have been raised in a
statement so given shall be deemed not to be a defect in title for the purposes of paragraph 3(3) of
Schedule 6 and as it is applied by paragraph 7(1) and by paragraph 11(1) of that Schedule (effect of
defect in title on valuation of interest to be acquired).

(5)   Any objection not included in any further statement given within the period specified in
sub-paragraph (3) shall be deemed waived and any matter which could have been raised in a further
statement so given shall be deemed not to be a defect in title for the purposes of paragraph 3(3) of
Schedule 6 and as it is applied as described in sub-paragraph (4).

(6)   If no further statement is given within the time specified in sub-paragraph (3), the
reversioner's answer shall be considered satisfactory.

### *Relevant landlords acting independently*

5.—(1)   Sub-paragraph (2) applies where—
     (a)    a relevant landlord has given notice in accordance with paragraph 7(1)(a) of Schedule 1
         (relevant landlord's entitlement to act independently of the reversioner) of his intention
         to deal directly with the nominee purchaser in connection with deducing, evidencing or
         verifying his title, or
     (b)    the nominee purchaser has given notice in accordance with paragraph 7(2) of Schedule 1
         (nominee purchaser's entitlement to require a relevant landlord to deal directly with him)
         to a relevant landlord.

(2)   Any notice, statement or further statement given—
     (a)    under paragraph 3 requiring proof of that relevant landlord's title, or
     (b)    under paragraph 4 raising requisitions, or making objections to or comments on that
         relevant landlord's title,

shall be given to him and not to the reversioner, and he will be under a duty to comply with any such notice or respond to any such statement instead of the reversioner.

*Preparation of contract*

6.—(1) The reversioner shall prepare the draft contract and give it to the nominee purchaser within the period of twenty-one days beginning with the date the terms of acquisition are agreed or determined by a leasehold valuation tribunal.

(2) The nominee purchaser shall give to the reversioner a statement of any proposals for amending the draft contract within the period of fourteen days beginning with the date the draft contract is given.

(3) If no statement is given by the nominee purchaser within the time specified in sub-paragraph (2) he shall be deemed to have approved the draft.

(4) The reversioner shall give to the nominee purchaser an answer, giving any objections to or comments on the proposals in the statement, within the period of fourteen days beginning with the date the statement is given.

(5) If no answer is given by the reversioner within the time specified in sub-paragraph (4), he shall be deemed to have agreed to the nominee purchaser's proposals for amendments to the draft contract.

*Payment of deposit*

7.—(1) The reversioner may require the nominee purchaser to pay a deposit on exchange of contracts in pursuance of the initial notice.

(2) The amount of the deposit required shall be £500, or 10 per cent of the purchase price agreed or determined by a leasehold valuation tribunal to be payable for the interests to be acquired, whichever is the greater.

(3) The nominee purchaser shall pay the deposit so required to the reversioner's solicitor or licensed conveyancer as stakeholder.

*Cancellation of land charges etc*

8. Where the initial notice has been registered as a land charge or a notice or caution has been registered in respect of it under section 97(1), and either it is withdrawn, deemed to have been withdrawn or otherwise ceases to have effect, the nominee purchaser shall at the request of the reversioner without delay take all steps necessary to procure cancellation of the registration.

**[3104]**

**NOTES**

Para 2: revoked in relation to England by the Leasehold Reform (Collective Enfranchisement and Lease Renewal) (Amendment) (England) Regulations 2003, SI 2003/1990, reg 3(a) in respect of cases where a notice under the Leasehold Reform, Housing and Urban Development Act 1993, s 13 or s 42 at **[817]**, **[848]**, is served on or after 30 September 2003, and revoked in relation to Wales by the Leasehold Reform (Collective Enfranchisement and Lease Renewal) (Amendment) (Wales) Regulations 2004, SI 2004/670, reg 3(a), in respect of cases where a notice under the Leasehold Reform, Housing and Urban Development Act 1993, s 13 or s 42 at **[817]**, **[848]**, is served on or after 31 March 2004.

## SCHEDULE 2
### LEASE RENEWAL

Regulation 3

*Interpretation*

1. In this Schedule—
   "counter-notice" means a notice given under section 45, and "further counter-notice" means a notice required by or by virtue of section 46(4) or section 47(4) or (5);
   "flat" shall be construed in accordance with section 62(2);
   "the landlord" has the meaning given by section 40(1);
   "lease" means a lease granted to give effect to a tenant's notice;
   "the relevant date" has the meaning given by section 39(8);
   "tenant" means a tenant who has given a tenant's notice;
   "terms of acquisition" has the meaning given by section 48(7).

*Payment of deposit*

2.—(1) The landlord may give to the tenant a notice requiring him to pay a deposit on account of the premium payable for the lease at any time when the tenant's notice continues in force under section 42(8).

(2)    The amount of the deposit shall be £250, or 10 per cent of the amount proposed in the tenant's notice as payable on the grant of the lease in accordance with Schedule 13 (premium and other amounts payable by tenant on grant of new lease), whichever is the greater.

(3)    The tenant shall pay the deposit so required to the landlord's solicitor or licensed conveyancer as stakeholder within the period of fourteen days beginning with the date the notice is given.

*Return of deposit*

3.—(1)    Subject to sub-paragraph (3), the tenant may give to the landlord a notice requiring him to procure the return of the deposit to the tenant at any time after the tenant's notice is withdrawn, deemed to have been withdrawn or otherwise ceases to have effect.

(2)    The landlord shall comply with any such requirement within the period of fourteen days beginning with the date the notice is given.

(3)    The landlord shall be entitled to have deducted from the deposit any amount due to him from the tenant in accordance with section 60 (tenant's liability for landlord's costs).

*Evidence of tenant's right to a lease*

4.—[(1)    The landlord may require the tenant to deduce his title to his tenancy, by giving him notice within the period of twenty one days beginning with the relevant date.]

(2)    The tenant shall comply with any such requirement within the period of twenty-one days beginning with the date the notice is given.

*Delivery of proof of title*

5.—(1)    Sub-paragraph (2) applies where the landlord has given a counter-notice complying with section 45(2)(a) (admitting the right to a new lease) or a further counter-notice, or, if no such counter-notice or further counter-notice is given, the tenant has applied to the court for an order under section 49(1) (applications where landlord fails to give counter-notice or further counter-notice).

(2)    The tenant may require the landlord to deduce title to his interest in the flat to which the tenant's notice relates by giving him notice.

(3)    The landlord shall comply with any such requirement by giving the tenant:—
   (a)    in the case of an interest registered in the register of title kept at Her Majesty's Land Registry, all particulars and information which have to be given or may be required to be given on a sale of registered land pursuant to section 110 of the Land Registration Act 1925 (provisions as between vendor and purchaser), and
   (b)    subject to sub-paragraph (4), in the case of any other interest, an epitome of title,
within the period of twenty-eight days beginning with the date the notice is given.

(4)    In a case where the landlord is not the freeholder, and the title to the freehold or any leasehold reversion to the landlord's title (if any) is not registered at Her Majesty's Land Registry, the landlord shall use his best endeavours to obtain an epitome of that title and shall also give it to the tenant.

*Requisitions*

6.—(1)    The tenant shall give to the landlord a statement of any objections to or requisitions on the proof of title within the period of fourteen days beginning with the date the proof is given (whether or not within the time required).

(2)    The landlord shall give to the tenant an answer to any statement of objections or requisitions within the period of fourteen days beginning with the date the statement is given.

(3)    The tenant shall give to the landlord a further statement of any objections to or comments on the answer within the period of seven days beginning with the date the answer is given.

(4)    Any objection or requisition not included in any statement given within the period referred to in sub-paragraph (1) shall be deemed waived, and any matter which could have been raised in a statement so given shall be deemed not to be a defect in title for the purposes of paragraph 3(5) of Schedule 13 and as it is applied by paragraph 8(1) of that Schedule (effect of defect in title on calculation of diminution in value of landlord's interest or any intermediate leasehold interest).

(5)    Any objection not included in any further statement given within the period specified in sub-paragraph (3) shall be deemed waived and any matter which could have been raised in a further statement so given shall be deemed not to form a defect in the title for the purposes of paragraph 3(5) of Schedule 13 and as it is applied as described in sub-paragraph (4).

(6)    If no further statement is given within the time specified in sub-paragraph (3), the landlord's answer shall be considered satisfactory.

*Preparation of lease*

7.—(1)  The landlord shall prepare a draft lease and give it to the tenant within the period of fourteen days beginning with the date the terms of acquisition are agreed or determined by a leasehold valuation tribunal.

(2)  The tenant shall give to the landlord a statement of any proposals for amending the draft lease within the period of fourteen days beginning with the date the draft lease is given.

(3)  If no statement is given by the tenant within the time specified in sub-paragraph (2), he shall be deemed to have approved the draft lease.

(4)  The landlord shall give to the tenant an answer giving any objections to or comments on the proposals in the statement within the period of fourteen days beginning with the date the statement is given.

(5)  If no answer is given by the landlord within the time specified in sub-paragraph (4), he shall be deemed to have approved the amendments to the draft lease proposed by the tenant.

(6)  The landlord shall prepare the lease and as many counterparts as he may reasonably require and shall give the counterpart or counterparts to the tenant for execution a reasonable time before the completion date.

(7)  The tenant shall give the counterpart or counterparts of the lease, duly executed, to the landlord and the landlord shall give the lease, duly executed, to the tenant, on the completion date or as soon as possible afterwards.

*Completion*

8.—(1)  Subject to sub-paragraph (2), after the draft lease is approved or deemed to have been approved, either the landlord or the tenant may give the other notice requiring him to complete the grant of the lease on the first working day after the expiration of twenty-one days beginning with the date the notice is given.

(2)  Sub-paragraph (1) shall not apply if the date for completion would fall after the expiry of the appropriate period specified for the purposes of section 48 or 49 (applications where terms in dispute or failure to enter into new lease, and applications where landlord fails to give counter-notice or further counter-notice), and in that event the date for completion shall be such day as the landlord and tenant agree in writing or the court orders under section 48(3) or 49(4) (order of the court on failure to enter into new lease).

(3)  The landlord shall by notice inform any other landlord who has given notice in accordance with paragraph 7(2) of Schedule 11 (other landlords acting independently) of the date for completion as soon as possible after notice has been given in accordance with sub-paragraph (1) or the date for completion agreed or ordered by the court in accordance with sub-paragraph (2).

(4)  Completion shall take place at the office of the landlord's solicitor or licensed conveyancer.

*Cancellation of land charges etc*

9.  Where a tenant's notice has been registered under section 97(1) as a land charge or a notice or caution has been registered in respect of it, and it is withdrawn, deemed to have been withdrawn or otherwise ceases to have effect, the tenant shall at the request of the landlord without delay take all steps necessary to procure cancellation of the registration.

**[3105]**

**NOTES**

Para 4: sub-para (1) substituted in relation to England by the Leasehold Reform (Collective Enfranchisement and Lease Renewal) (Amendment) (England) Regulations 2003, SI 2003/1990, reg 3(b) in respect of cases where a notice under the Leasehold Reform, Housing and Urban Development Act 1993, s 13 or s 42 at **[817]**, **[848]**, is served on or after 30 September 2003, and substituted in relation to Wales by the Leasehold Reform (Collective Enfranchisement and Lease Renewal) (Amendment) (Wales) Regulations 2004, SI 2004/670, reg 3(b), in respect of cases where a notice under the Leasehold Reform, Housing and Urban Development Act 1993, s 13 or s 42 at **[817]**, **[848]**, is served on or after 31 March 2004.

# SECURE TENANTS OF LOCAL HOUSING AUTHORITIES (RIGHT TO REPAIR) REGULATIONS 1994

(SI 1994/133)

**NOTES**

Made: 25 January 1994.
Authority: Housing Act 1985, s 96.
Commencement: 1 April 1994.

## 1   Citation and commencement

These Regulations may be cited as the Secure Tenants of Local Housing Authorities (Right to Repair) Regulations 1994 and shall come into force on 1st April 1994.

**[3106]**

## 2   Interpretation

In these Regulations—

"contractor" means a person prepared to carry out a qualifying repair and ... may include the landlord;

"first prescribed period" means (subject to regulation 11), in relation to repairing a defect described in column 1 of the Schedule, the period specified in column 2 opposite the description of that defect starting—

    (a)    in a case where the landlord considers it necessary to inspect the dwelling-house to satisfy itself that a repair is a qualifying repair—

         (i)    if the day the landlord issues the repair notice under regulation 5(1)(c) to the contractor is a working day, on the first working day after the day of issue, and

         (ii)    in any other case, on the second working day after the day of issue, and

    (b)    in any other case—

         (i)    if the day the landlord receives the application for the qualifying repair to be carried out is a working day, on the first working day after that day, and

         (ii)    in any other case, on the second working day after the day the application is received;

"second prescribed period" means (subject to regulation 11), in relation to repairing a defect described in column 1 of the Schedule, the period specified in column 2 opposite the description of that defect starting—

    (a)    if the day the landlord receives notification from the tenant that he requires another contractor to carry out the qualifying repair is a working day, on the first working day after that day; and

    (b)    in any other case, on the second working day after the day the notification is received; and

"working day" means a day which is not a public holiday, a Saturday or a Sunday.

**[3107]**

---

**NOTES**

Words omitted revoked by the Secure Tenants of Local Housing Authorities (Right to Repair) (Amendment) Regulations 1994, SI 1994/844, reg 2(a).

---

## 3   Entitlement

(1)   Subject to and in accordance with these Regulations, secure tenants [and introductory tenants] whose landlords are local housing authorities are entitled—

    (a)    to have qualifying repairs carried out, at their landlords' expense, to the dwelling-houses of which they are such tenants; and

    (b)    to receive compensation from their landlords if qualifying repairs are not carried out within a prescribed period.

(2)   Paragraph (1) and the subsequent provisions of these Regulations do not apply in a case where the landlord has less than 100 [relevant dwelling-houses] on the day it receives an application from the tenant to have a repair carried out. [In this paragraph "a relevant dwelling-house" means a dwelling-house let to a secure tenant or to an introductory tenant.]

(3)   Paragraph (1) and the subsequent provisions of these Regulations shall cease to apply in relation to a repair if—

    (a)    the tenant informs the landlord that he no longer wants the repair carried out, or

PART II
STATUTORY INSTRUMENTS

(b)    the tenant, although he has been given a reasonable opportunity, fails—

    (i)    to provide details of the arrangements for the contractor to obtain access to the dwelling-house, or

    (ii)    to provide access for an inspection or for the repair to be carried out.

**[3108]**

**NOTES**

Para (1): words in square brackets inserted by the Secure Tenants of Local Housing Authorities (Right to Repair) (Amendment) Regulations 1997, SI 1997/73, reg 2(a).

Para (2): words in first pair of square brackets substituted and words in second pair of square brackets inserted by SI 1997/73, reg 2(b).

## 4 Prescribed description of repair

A repair to a dwelling-house which—

    (a)    remedies a defect specified in column 1 of the Schedule, and

    (b)    will not, in the opinion of the landlord, cost more than £250 to carry out,

is a repair of a prescribed description for the purpose of the definition of a qualifying repair in section 96(6) of the Housing Act 1985.

**[3109]**

## 5 Repair notice

(1)    Where a secure tenant [or introductory tenant] of a local housing authority applies to his landlord for a repair to be carried out to the dwelling-house of which he is the secure tenant [or introductory tenant]—

    (a)    if the landlord considers it necessary to inspect the dwelling-house to satisfy itself that the repair is (or is not) a qualifying repair, the landlord shall forthwith inspect the dwelling-house;

    (b)    if the landlord is satisfied that the repair is not a qualifying repair, it shall notify the tenant of that and explain why it is so satisfied and give the tenant an explanation of the provisions of these Regulations; and

    (c)    if the landlord is satisfied that the repair is a qualifying repair, the landlord shall issue a repair notice to a contractor and give to the tenant a copy of the notice and an explanation of the provisions of these Regulations.

(2)    A repair notice shall contain a reference sufficient to identify the completed notice and shall specify—

    (a)    the name of the secure tenant [or introductory tenant];

    (b)    the address of the dwelling-house;

    (c)    the nature of the repair;

    (d)    the name, address and telephone number of the contractor who is to carry out the repair;

    (e)    the arrangements made for the contractor to obtain access to the dwelling-house; and

    (f)    the last day of the first prescribed period.

**[3110]**

**NOTES**

Paras (1), (2): words in square brackets inserted by the Secure Tenants of Local Housing Authorities (Right to Repair) (Amendment) Regulations 1997, SI 1997/73, reg 2(c).

## 6 Substitute Contractor

(1)    Subject to paragraph (3) and regulation 8, if—

    (a)    the qualifying repair has not been carried out within the first prescribed period, and

    (b)    the tenant notifies the landlord that he requires another contractor to carry out the qualifying repair,

the landlord, where it is reasonably practicable, shall issue a further repair notice to another contractor and give a copy of the notice to the tenant.

(2)    The further repair notice shall contain a reference sufficient to identify it and specify the matters referred to in regulation 5(2)(a) to (e) and the last day of the second prescribed period.

(3)    Paragraph (1) does not apply if compliance with that paragraph would infringe the terms of a guarantee for work done or materials supplied of which the landlord has the benefit.

**[3111]**

## 7 Compensation

(1)    Subject to regulation 8, the landlord shall pay the specified sum to the secure tenant [or introductory tenant] if the qualifying repair has not been carried out within the second prescribed period.

(2)    In paragraph (1), "specified sum" means the lesser of £50 and—

£10 + (£2 x N)

where N is the number of days (counting part of a day as a complete day) in the period starting on the day after the second prescribed period ends and ending on the day on which the qualifying repair is completed.

(3) The landlord may set off any sums owed to it by the secure tenant [or introductory tenant] against any compensation payable under this regulation.

**[3112]**

**NOTES**

Paras (1), (3): words in square brackets inserted by the Secure Tenants of Local Housing Authorities (Right to Repair) (Amendment) Regulations 1997, SI 1997/73, reg 2(c).

## 8 Suspension of Prescribed Period

The first prescribed period or, as the case may be, the second prescribed period, shall be suspended for so long as there are circumstances of an exceptional nature, beyond the control of the landlord or the contractor who is to carry out the qualifying repair, which prevent the repair being carried out.

**[3113]**

## 9 Notices

Any notice required to be issued or given by these Regulations may be issued or given by post.

**[3114]**

## 10 Disputes

Any questions arising under these Regulations may be determined by the county court.

**[3115]**

## [11 Transitional provision

In a case where a tenant applies to his landlord before 1st April 1996 for a qualifying repair to be carried out—

    (a)    if, on the date the tenant applies, there is in force a contract between the landlord and a contractor—

        (i)    which provides for the qualifying repair to be carried out by the contractor within a period which is longer than the first prescribed period, and

        (ii)    which was entered into before 1st April 1994, or

        (iii)    which was entered into on or after that date as a result of accepting an offer by the contractor which was made in response to an invitation to submit such an offer (and the invitation was given before 1st April 1994),

    the period provided for in the contract shall be substituted for the period specified in relation to the repair in column 2 of the Schedule;

    (b)    if paragraph (a) does not apply and—

        (i)    offers were invited before 1st April 1994 to undertake work which includes the qualifying repair,

        (ii)    the landlord's bid to undertake the work provided for the qualifying repair to be carried out within a period which is longer than the first prescribed period, and

        (iii)    the repair is to be carried out by the landlord in accordance with that bid, the period provided for in the bid shall be substituted for the period specified in relation to the repair in column 2 of the Schedule; and

    (c)    if paragraphs (a) and (b) do not apply and—

        (i)    offers were invited before 1st April 1994 to undertake work which includes the qualifying repair,

        (ii)    the conditions specified, or the specification prepared, for the purposes of the invitation provided for the qualifying repair to be carried out within a period which is longer than the first prescribed period, and

        (iii)    the repair is to be carried out by the landlord in accordance with those conditions or that specification,

    the period provided for in the conditions or specification shall be substituted for the period specified in relation to the repair in column 2 of the Schedule.]

**[3116]**

**NOTES**

Substituted by the Secure Tenants of Local Housing Authorities (Right to Repair) (Amendment) Regulations 1994, SI 1994/844, reg 2(b).

## SCHEDULE

Regulations 2, 4

| Defect | Prescribed period (in working days) |
| --- | --- |
| Total loss of electric power | 1 |
| Partial loss of electric power | 3 |
| Unsafe power or lighting socket, or electrical fitting | 1 |
| Total loss of water supply | 1 |
| Partial loss of water supply | 3 |
| Total or partial loss of gas supply | 1 |
| Blocked flue to open fire or boiler | 1 |
| Total or partial loss of space or water heating between 31st October and 1st May | 1 |
| Total or partial loss of space or water heating between 30th April and 1st November | 3 |
| Blocked or leaking foul drain, soil stack, or (where there is no other working toilet in the dwelling-house) toilet pan | 1 |
| Toilet not flushing (where there is no other working toilet in the dwelling-house) | 1 |
| Blocked sink, bath or basin | 3 |
| Tap which cannot be turned | 3 |
| Leaking from water or heating pipe, tank or cistern | 1 |
| Leaking roof | 7 |
| Insecure external window, door or lock | 1 |
| Loose or detached bannister or hand rail | 3 |
| Rotten timber flooring or stair tread | 3 |
| Door entryphone not working | 7 |
| Mechanical extractor fan in internal kitchen or bathroom not working | 7 |

[3117]

# SECURE TENANTS OF LOCAL AUTHORITIES (COMPENSATION FOR IMPROVEMENTS) REGULATIONS 1994

(SI 1994/613)

**NOTES**
Made: 5 March 1994.
Authority: Housing Act 1985, s 99A.
Commencement: 1 April 1994.

## ARRANGEMENT OF REGULATIONS

**1   Citation and commencement**

These Regulations may be cited as the Secure Tenants of Local Authorities (Compensation for Improvements) Regulations 1994 and shall come into force on 1st April 1994.

**[3118]**

**2   Interpretation**

In these Regulations—

    "qualifying improvement" means an improvement consisting of the installation or replacement of an item specified in column A of the Schedule to these Regulations;

    "notional life", in relation to a qualifying improvement, is the period in years specified in column B of the Schedule to these Regulations opposite the description of that improvement in column A of that Schedule; and

any reference to a section, Part or Schedule without more is a reference to a section or Part of or Schedule to the Housing Act 1985.

**[3119]**

**3   Entitlement**

(1)   Subject to and in accordance with the following provisions of these Regulations, in the cases described by section 99A(1) a qualifying person is entitled to be paid compensation by his landlord in respect of a qualifying improvement at the time when his tenancy comes to an end.

(2)   Paragraph (1) shall not apply where—

    (a)   the compensation which would otherwise be payable would be less than £50; or

    (b)   the tenancy comes to an end because—

        (i)   an order for possession was made on any of the grounds in Part I of Schedule 2;

        (ii)   the right to buy or the right to acquire on rent to mortgage terms in Part V of the Housing Act 1985 has been exercised;

        (iii)   the dwelling-house has been disposed of to the tenant or one of the joint tenants under section 32 or 43; or

        (iv)   a new tenancy of the same, or substantially the same, dwelling-house has been granted to the qualifying person (or, in the case of a joint tenancy, to all of the joint tenants) whether or not with anyone else.

**[3120]**

**4   Amount of compensation**

(1)   Subject to paragraphs (2) and (3), the amount of compensation payable for a qualifying improvement shall be—

$$C \times \left(1 - \frac{Y}{N}\right)$$

where—

    C = the cost of the improvement, which shall exclude the amount of any grant or minor works assistance under Part VIII of the Local Government and Housing Act 1989 or the Home Energy Efficiency Grants Regulations 1992 paid in respect of the improvement;

    N = the notional life of the improvement; and

    Y = the number of complete years, with part of a year being rounded up to a complete year, starting on the date the improvement was completed and ending on the date the compensation is claimed.

(2)   The landlord may deduct from and (in the case of sub-paragraph (c) below) add to the amount of compensation calculated in accordance with paragraph (1) such sum as is reasonable to take into account any of the following matters which applies (notwithstanding, in the case of sub-paragraph (c), that otherwise compensation would not be payable)—

    (a)   the cost of the improvement was excessive;

    (b)   the improvement is of a higher quality than it would have been had the landlord properly effected it;

    (c)   the improvement has deteriorated at a lesser rate than provided for in the notional life for that improvement; and

    (d)   the improvement has deteriorated at a greater rate than provided for in the notional life for that improvement.

(3)   Compensation shall not be payable to the extent that—

    (a)   the amount of compensation for a qualifying improvement would exceed £3,000; or

    (b)   compensation has been paid in relation to the improvement under section 100.

**[3121]**

PART II
STATUTORY INSTRUMENTS

**NOTES**
Local Government and Housing Act 1989, Pt VIII: see now the Housing Act 1996, Pt I.
Home Energy Efficiency Grants Regulations 1992: SI 1992/483 (revoked).

## 5 Deductions from payment

The landlord may set off against any compensation payable under these Regulations any sums owed
to it by the qualifying person.

[3122]

## 6 Claims for compensation

A claim for compensation—
- (a) shall contain sufficient information for the landlord to determine the claim;
- (b) shall be made in writing within the period starting 28 days before, and ending 14 days
after, the tenancy comes to an end; and
- (c) may be served by post.

[3123]

## 7 Disputes

Any question arising under these Regulations shall be determined by the county court.

[3124]

SCHEDULE
QUALIFYING IMPROVEMENTS AND NOTIONAL LIFE OF IMPROVEMENT
Regulation 2

| | A<br>Qualifying Improvement | B<br>Notional Life |
|---|---|---|
| 1 | Bath or shower | 12 |
| 2 | Wash-hand basin | 12 |
| 3 | Toilet | 12 |
| 4 | Kitchen sink | 10 |
| 5 | Storage cupboards in bathroom or kitchen | 10 |
| 6 | Work surfaces for food preparation | 10 |
| 7 | Space or water heating | 12 |
| 8 | Thermostatic radiator valves | 7 |
| 9 | Insulation of pipes, water tank or cylinder | 10 |
| 10 | Loft insulation | 20 |
| 11 | Cavity wall insulation | 20 |
| 12 | Draught proofing of external doors or windows | 8 |
| 13 | Double glazing or other external window replacement or<br>secondary glazing | 20 |
| 14 | Rewiring or the provision of power and lighting or other<br>electrical fittings (including smoke detectors) | 15 |
| 15 | Any object which improves the security of the dwelling-house,<br>but excluding burglar alarms | 10 |

[3125]

# HOUSING (RIGHT TO MANAGE) REGULATIONS 1994

(SI 1994/627)

**NOTES**
Made: 7 March 1994.
Authority: Housing Act 1985, ss 27(3), (7), 27AB.
Commencement: 1 April 1994.

ARRANGEMENT OF REGULATIONS

## 1  Citation, commencement and interpretation

(1)   These Regulations may be cited as the Housing (Right to Manage) Regulations 1994 and shall come into force on 1st April 1994.

(2)   In these Regulations—
   "approved person" means a member of a panel of persons approved by the Secretary of State for the purpose of conducting initial or full feasibility studies under these Regulations, and the Secretary of State may approve a person to act in a specified area only;
   "dwelling-house" has the same meaning as in section 112 of the Housing Act 1985;
   "full feasibility study" means, in relation to a particular proposal for a management agreement, a study carried out by an approved person to determine—
      (a)   whether it is reasonable to proceed with the agreement; and
      (b)   if so, the terms on which the agreement should be entered into;
   "initial feasibility study" means, in relation to a particular proposal for a management agreement, a study carried out by an approved person to determine whether it is reasonable to proceed with a full feasibility study;
   "proposal notice" means a notice served by a tenant management organisation on a local housing authority which complies with regulation 2 (and, in relation to a particular proposal for a management agreement, references to a proposal notice refer to the notice containing that proposal);
   "secure tenancy" has the same meaning as in section 79 of the Housing Act 1985;
   "tenant" means a person who holds a secure tenancy or other tenancy of a dwelling-house from a local housing authority.

(3)   For the purpose of these Regulations, two management agreements overlap when and to the extent that they contain provisions which relate to the exercise of the same management functions in relation to the same houses or land; and "overlapping provisions" shall be construed accordingly.

(4)   For the purpose of the definition of "tenant management organisation" in section 27AB(8) of the Housing Act 1985, the conditions which a body must satisfy are that its constitution—
      (a)   specifies an area as being the area of the organisation in relation to which it may serve a proposal notice;
      (b)   provides that any tenant of a dwelling-house in relation to which the organisation could serve a proposal notice may become a member of the organisation;
      (c)   provides that in conducting its affairs the organisation shall avoid discrimination against any person on grounds of racial origin, gender, sexuality, disability or religion; and
      (d)   provides either that the affairs of the organisation shall be conducted by the members of the organisation at general meeting, or that they shall be conducted by a committee or board of directors elected by the members of the organisation.

(5)   Where a matter is referred to an arbitrator under these Regulations, the arbitrator shall be chosen by agreement between the parties to the proposed arbitration, or, in default of agreement, appointed by the Secretary of State.

(6)   Subject to paragraph (7), where any person is required or permitted to exercise any function under these Regulations within a specified period, the tenant management organisation and local housing authority concerned may by agreement in writing before the expiry of that period extend the period for a further specified period.

(7)   Paragraph (6) shall not apply to the period specified in paragraph (16) of regulation 4.

(8)   Any ballot held under these Regulations shall be organised so that the vote cast by any individual is kept secret.

**[3126]**

PART II
STATUTORY INSTRUMENTS

## NOTES
Revoked, in relation to houses and local authorities in England, by the Housing (Right to Manage) (England) Regulations 2008, SI 2008/2361, reg 2, as from 1 October 2008, subject to transitional provisions in regs 1(1), 22–25 thereof.

## 2  Proposal notice

*(1)   Subject to paragraphs (2) and (4), a notice served by a tenant management organisation on a local housing authority complies with this regulation if it contains a proposal that the local housing authority should enter into a management agreement with the tenant management organisation in relation to such of the authority's houses, including not less than 25 dwelling-houses which at the time the notice is served are let under secure tenancies, and such other land held by the authority for a related purpose as are identified in the notice and—*

    *(a)   none of those houses or that land is outside the area of the tenant management organisation which has served the notice (as specified in the constitution of that organisation in accordance with regulation 1(4)); and*

    *(b)   none of those houses or that land is identified in any notice which complies with this regulation and which has previously been served on the authority and not withdrawn; and*

    *(c)   if any of those houses or that land is already included in a management agreement with a tenant management organisation, all of those houses or that land are so included, and either—*

        *(i)   the tenant management organisation which has served the notice is a party to that agreement; or*

        *(ii)   the number of dwelling-houses to which that agreement relates is greater than 2,500.*

*(2)   A local housing authority may decline to accept a notice (a "further notice") served on them by a tenant management organisation proposing a management agreement if that further notice contains a similar proposal to the proposal contained in a previous proposal notice which has been withdrawn within the two year period ending on the date on which the further notice is received, and where an authority decline to accept a further notice in accordance with this paragraph that notice shall not be treated as complying with this regulation.*

*(3)   For the purpose of paragraph (2), a further notice contains a similar proposal to the proposal contained in a previous proposal notice if at least half of the houses identified in it were also identified in the previous proposal notice.*

*(4)   Where paragraph (5) applies, the authority may decline to accept the notice, and where an authority decline to accept a notice in accordance with this paragraph, that notice shall not be treated as complying with this regulation.*

*(5)   This paragraph applies where a local housing authority has, within one month of receiving a notice served on them by a tenant management organisation proposing a management agreement, requested the organisation to demonstrate to the authority that—*

    *(a)   before the notice was served, the organisation had used its best endeavours to secure that a copy of the notice was delivered to every dwelling-house to which the notice relates; and*

    *(b)   before the notice was served, both a majority of tenants and a majority of secure tenants of the houses to which the notice relates who were at the time members of the organisation and who voted (either in a ballot or poll of all members, or on a resolution put before a properly constituted general meeting of the organisation) voted in favour of a proposal to serve the notice; and*

    *(c)   at the time the notice was served, the membership of the organisation included both at least 20% of the tenants and at least 20% of the secure tenants of the houses to which the notice relates; and*

*the organisation has failed within one month to comply with that request in relation to one or more of the matters described in sub-paragraphs (a) to (c).*

*(6)   An authority shall not be treated as having declined to accept a notice in accordance with paragraphs (2) or (4) unless they have, within the period specified in paragraph (7), informed the tenant management organisation concerned in writing that they have not accepted the notice and of the reason for their decision not to accept the notice.*

*(7)   The period referred to in paragraph (6) is, where paragraph (5) applies, six weeks from the date on which the authority made the request under paragraph (5), and, where paragraph (5) does not apply, one month from the date on which the notice was served.*

[3127]

## NOTES
Revoked, in relation to houses and local authorities in England, as noted to reg 1 at **[3126]**.

**3  Local authority support following proposal notice**

(1)  A tenant management organisation which has served a proposal notice on a local housing authority may, at any time after the service of the notice, request the authority to provide or finance the provision of such office accommodation and facilities, and such training, as the organisation reasonably requires at the time of the request for the purpose of pursuing the proposal contained in the notice.

(2)  A request under paragraph (1) shall be in writing and shall specify the provision which the tenant management organisation considers it reasonably requires at that time for that purpose.

(3)  On receipt of a request under paragraph (1), the authority shall—
    (a)  determine the provision which they consider the organisation reasonably requires at that time for that purpose; and
    (b)  notify the organisation of their determination within two months of receipt of the request.

(4)  Subject to paragraph (8), the authority shall provide support in accordance with the determination notified under paragraph (3)(b).

(5)  If a tenant management organisation is dissatisfied with an authority's determination under paragraph (3) it may, within 28 days of being notified of the determination, refer the request to an arbitrator.

(6)  A tenant management organisation which refers a request to an arbitrator under paragraph (5) shall, at the same time, give notice of that referral to the authority.

(7)  Where a request is referred to an arbitrator under paragraph (5), the arbitrator shall—
    (a)  determine the provision which he considers the organisation reasonably requires for the purpose of pursuing the proposal at the time of the request; and
    (b)  notify the authority and the organisation of his determination within two months of the request being referred to him.

(8)  Where a request has been referred to an arbitrator under paragraph (5), the authority shall provide support in accordance with the determination notified under paragraph (7)(b).

(9)  Where a proposal notice is withdrawn any requirement on an authority to make provision under this regulation shall cease.

**[3128]**

---

**NOTES**

Revoked, in relation to houses and local authorities in England, as noted to reg 1 at **[3126]**.

---

**4  Procedure following proposal notice**

(1)
    (a)  If a tenant management organisation has not, within three months of serving a proposal notice, appointed an approved person to carry out an initial feasibility study and notified the Secretary of State and the authority of the appointment, the proposal notice shall be deemed to have been withdrawn.
    (b)  The authority shall arrange for an initial feasibility study to be conducted by the approved person appointed under sub-paragraph (a).

(2)  The approved person appointed under paragraph (1) shall, within 9 months of his appointment, send a report of the study to the Secretary of State, the authority and the tenant management organisation, which shall include his conclusion as to whether or not it is reasonable to proceed with a full feasibility study.

(3)  Where the approved person concludes that it is not reasonable to proceed with a full feasibility study, the proposal notice shall be deemed to have been withdrawn.

(4)  Where the approved person concludes that it is reasonable to proceed with a full feasibility study, the authority shall, within one month of the approved person submitting his report to the authority under paragraph (2)—
    (a)  give to the tenants of each house identified in the proposal notice a description prepared by the approved person of the proposal; and
    (b)  arrange for a ballot or poll to be carried out within that period of those tenants with a view to establishing their opinion about the proposal.

(5)  If it appears from a ballot or poll carried out in accordance with paragraph (4)(b) that either a majority of the tenants or a majority of the secure tenants who, on that ballot or poll, express an opinion about the proposal are opposed to it, the authority shall notify the tenant management organisation accordingly, and the proposal notice shall be deemed to have been withdrawn.

(6)  If it does not appear as mentioned in paragraph (5), the authority shall notify the Secretary of State and the tenant management organisation accordingly.

(7)    Where all of the houses which are identified in a proposal notice are already included in a management agreement to which the tenant management organisation which has served the notice is a party, an approved person shall be deemed to have been appointed in accordance with paragraph (1)(a), and shall be deemed to have concluded that it is reasonable to proceed with a full feasibility study, and the authority shall be deemed to have complied with the requirements of sub-paragraphs (a) and (b) of paragraph (4), and with the requirements of paragraph (6).

(8)

(a)    If the tenant management organisation has not, within six months of receiving the notification mentioned in paragraph (6), or, where paragraph (7) applies, within six months of serving a proposal notice, appointed an approved person to carry out a full feasibility study and notified the Secretary of State and the authority of the appointment, the proposal notice shall be deemed to have been withdrawn.

(b)    The authority shall arrange for a full feasibility study to be conducted by the approved person appointed under sub-paragraph (a).

(9)    The approved person appointed under paragraph (8) shall, within two years of his appointment, submit a report of the full feasibility study to the Secretary of State, the authority and the tenant management organisation, which shall include his conclusion as to whether it is reasonable to proceed with the proposed management agreement and, if so, on what terms the agreement should be entered into.

(10)    The terms of a management agreement set out in a report submitted under paragraph (9) and the terms as modified in accordance with paragraph (14) shall be in such form as may be approved by the Secretary of State for the purpose of these Regulations.

(11)    Where the approved person concludes that it is not reasonable to proceed with the proposed agreement, and this conclusion is not referred to an arbitrator under regulation 5, the proposal notice shall be deemed to have been withdrawn.

(12)    Where the approved person concludes that it is reasonable to proceed with the proposed agreement, and neither this conclusion nor his conclusion as to the terms to be included in the agreement are referred to an arbitrator under regulation 5, the authority shall, within a period of two months beginning on the day on which the approved person submitted his report to the authority under paragraph (9)—

(a)    serve a notice prepared by the approved person on the tenants of each house identified in the proposal notice which—

(i)    summarises the terms of the proposed agreement set out in his report, and

(ii)    contains the address of a place within the locality of the identified houses at which a copy of that report, containing those terms, may be inspected; and

(b)    arrange for a ballot (using a ballot paper prepared by the approved person) to be carried out within such period of those tenants with a view to establishing their opinion about the proposal to enter into a management agreement on those terms.

(13)    If it does not appear from a ballot carried out in accordance with paragraph (12)(b) that both a majority of the tenants and a majority of the secure tenants are in favour of the proposal the authority shall notify the Secretary of State and the tenant management organisation and the proposal notice shall be deemed to have been withdrawn.

(14)    Subject to paragraph (15), if it does appear as mentioned in paragraph (13), the authority shall within one month notify the Secretary of State and the tenant management organisation, and within two months of that notification (or within one month of the registration of that organisation as mentioned in paragraph (15), if later) shall enter into a management agreement with the tenant management organisation on the terms made available for inspection pursuant to paragraph (12)(a)(ii), or on those terms subject to such modifications as may be agreed by the tenant management organisation.

(15)    An authority shall not enter into a management agreement under paragraph (14) unless the tenant management organisation is registered as an Industrial and Provident Society under the Industrial and Provident Societies Act 1965 or as a company under the Companies Act 1985; and where the organisation neither is so registered nor has applied to be so registered on the expiry of the two month period mentioned in that paragraph the proposal notice shall be deemed to have been withdrawn.

(16)    An authority shall, within fourteen days of entering into a management agreement under paragraph (14), submit a copy of the agreement to the Secretary of State.

**[3129]**

**NOTES**

Revoked, in relation to houses and local authorities in England, as noted to reg 1 at **[3126]**.

## 5   Determination of disputes under regulation 4

*(1)   Subject to paragraph (6), where an approved person submits a report under regulation 4(9), the local housing authority or the tenant management organisation may refer any of the conclusions set out in the report with which they disagree to an arbitrator within two months of the report being submitted to the body making the reference.*

*(2)   Where the approved person's conclusion as to whether it is reasonable to proceed with the proposed management agreement is referred to an arbitrator, the arbitrator shall decide whether it is reasonable so to proceed and notify the Secretary of State, the local housing authority, the tenant management organisation and the approved person of his decision within two months of the matter being referred to him.*

*(3)   Where the arbitrator decides that it is not reasonable to proceed with the agreement, the proposal notice shall be deemed to have been withdrawn.*

*(4)   Where the arbitrator decides that it is reasonable to proceed with the agreement, this decision accords with the approved person's conclusion, and the approved person's conclusion as to the terms on which the agreement should be entered into has not been referred to the arbitrator, the local authority shall comply with paragraphs (a) and (b) of regulation 4(12) within two months of being notified of the arbitrator's decision.*

*(5)   Where the arbitrator decides that it is reasonable to proceed with the agreement and that decision does not accord with the approved person's conclusion, the matter shall be referred back to the approved person, who shall, within three months of the matter being referred back to him, resubmit his report under regulation 4(9), which report shall be in accordance with the decision of the arbitrator and shall include the terms on which the agreement should be entered into.*

*(6)   Where a report is resubmitted in accordance with paragraph (5), the approved person's conclusion in the resubmitted report as to whether it is reasonable to proceed with the agreement shall not be referred to an arbitrator.*

*(7)   Where the approved person's conclusion as to the terms on which the agreement should be entered into is referred to an arbitrator, the arbitrator shall, within two months of the matter being referred to him (or, where he has given notice under paragraph (2) of his decision that it is reasonable to proceed with the agreement, within two months of giving that notice)—*

    *(a)   determine the terms on which the agreement should be entered into (which shall be in such form as may be approved by the Secretary of State for the purpose of these Regulations); and*

    *(b)   notify the Secretary of State, the local housing authority, the tenant management organisation and the approved person of his determination, setting out those terms in his notification.*

*(8)   Where an authority is notified of a determination under paragraph (7) it shall comply with paragraphs (a) and (b) of regulation 4(12) within two months of being so notified; and, for the purpose of such compliance, the reference in paragraph (a) of that regulation to the terms of the agreement as set out in the approved person's report and to that report shall be construed as a reference to the terms of the agreement as set out in the determination notified under paragraph (7) of this regulation and to that determination.*

**[3130]**

---

**NOTES**

Revoked, in relation to houses and local authorities in England, as noted to reg 1 at **[3126]**.

---

## 6   Withdrawal of proposal notice

*(1)   A tenant management organisation may by notice in writing to the local housing authority withdraw a proposal notice served by it at any time.*

*(2)   Where a proposal notice is withdrawn no further action shall be taken in relation to that notice under these Regulations.*

**[3131]**

---

**NOTES**

Revoked, in relation to houses and local authorities in England, as noted to reg 1 at **[3126]**.

---

## 7   Guidance by Secretary of State

*Any person exercising functions under these Regulations shall act in accordance with any guidance given by the Secretary of State.*

**[3132]**

---

**NOTES**

Revoked, in relation to houses and local authorities in England, as noted to reg 1 at **[3126]**.

## 8 Management agreements with tenant management organisations and other management agreements

*(1) A management agreement (other than an agreement with a tenant management organisation) entered into by a local housing authority after the entry into force of these Regulations shall contain a provision (a "break clause") enabling the authority to determine it to the extent that it overlaps with any subsequent management agreement entered into with a tenant management organisation.*

*(2) A break clause contained in a management agreement in accordance with paragraph (1) shall provide that the authority may exercise the rights conferred by it at different times in relation to different overlapping provisions and that it shall determine the provisions in relation to which it is exercised within three months of it being exercised.*

*(3) This paragraph applies where a local housing authority enter into a management agreement with a tenant management organisation in pursuance of these Regulations and—*

    *(a) at the time of entering into that agreement a previous agreement is in operation; and*

    *(b) either—*

        *(i) the two agreements overlap when the management agreement is entered into; or*

        *(ii) the two agreements subsequently overlap on the variation of either; and*

    *(c) the previous agreement contains provisions which allow the authority to determine the overlapping provisions (whether by determining the whole of that agreement or otherwise).*

*(4) Subject to paragraph (5), where paragraph (3) applies the local housing authority shall determine the overlapping provisions in the previous agreement (whether by determining the whole of that agreement or otherwise) as soon as possible after the two agreements overlap.*

*(5) Where paragraph (3) applies, if the tenant management organisation agrees in writing, the local housing authority may postpone the determination of the overlapping provisions (or some of them, if the previous agreement allows the authority to determine the provisions at different times) until such time as may be agreed.*

*(6) Nothing in this regulation requires an agreement (or any part of an agreement) to be determined otherwise than in accordance with provisions contained in that agreement.*

**[3133]**

**NOTES**

Revoked, in relation to houses and local authorities in England, as noted to reg 1 at **[3126]**.

## 9 Local housing authority participation in tenant management organisations

*A local housing authority may, if invited to do so by the organisation concerned, nominate one or more persons to be directors or other officers of any tenant management organisation with whom the authority have entered into, or propose to enter into, a management agreement.*

**[3134]**

**NOTES**

Revoked, in relation to houses and local authorities in England, as noted to reg 1 at **[3126]**.

## 10 Transitional provisions

*(1) Where any of the following paragraphs of this regulation apply the tenant management organisation shall be treated as having served on the day these Regulations come into force ("the commencement date") a proposal notice on the local housing authority in relation to the houses to which the study, ballot or poll relates.*

*(2) Where a study has been carried out during the period of twelve months ending on the commencement date or is being carried out immediately before the commencement date, which, if it had been carried out or were being carried out by an approved person for the purpose of paragraph (2) of regulation 4, would comply (or substantially comply) with the requirement in that paragraph to carry out an initial feasibility study ("a pre-commencement initial feasibility study") and none of the following paragraphs of this regulation applies, the study shall be treated, on and after the commencement date, as having been carried out or being carried out by an approved person for the purpose of complying with that requirement and—*

    *(a) if the study has been completed and a report of the study submitted to the Secretary of State, the authority and the tenant management organisation before that date, it shall be treated as having been submitted under regulation 4(2) on the commencement date;*

    *(b) if a report on the study has not been submitted to the Secretary of State, the authority and the tenant management organisation before that date, but is so submitted within nine months of that date, it shall be treated as having been submitted under regulation 4(2).*

(3)    Where a ballot or poll has been carried out during the period of twelve months ending on the commencement date or is being carried out immediately before the commencement date following a pre-commencement initial feasibility study which, if it had been carried out or were being carried out by an authority for the purpose of paragraph (4) of regulation 4, would comply (or substantially comply) with the requirement in that paragraph to carry out a ballot or poll, and none of the following paragraphs of this regulation apply—

(a)    if the ballot or poll has been completed before that date, it shall be treated as having been completed on that date for the purpose of regulation 4(4);

(b)    if the ballot or poll has not been completed before that date but is completed within one month of that date, it shall be treated as having been carried out for the purpose of regulation 4(4).

(4)    Where a study has been carried out during the period of twelve months ending on the commencement date or is being carried out immediately before the commencement date, which, if it had been carried out or were being carried out by an approved person for the purpose of paragraph (9) of regulation 4, would comply (or substantially comply) with the requirement in that paragraph to carry out a full feasibility study (a "pre-commencement full feasibility study"), and paragraph (5) of this regulation does not apply, the study shall be treated, on and after that date, as having been carried out or being carried out by an approved person for the purpose of complying with that requirement and—

(a)    if the study has been completed and a report on the study submitted to the Secretary of State, the authority and the tenant management organisation before that date, it shall be treated as having been submitted under regulation 4(9) on the commencement date;

(b)    if a report on the study has not been submitted to the Secretary of State, the authority and the tenant management organisation before that date, but is so submitted within two years of that date, it shall be treated as having been submitted under regulation 4(9).

(5)    Where a ballot has been carried out during the period of twelve months ending on the commencement date or is being carried out immediately before the commencement date following a pre-commencement full feasibility study, which, if it had been carried out or were being carried out for the purpose of paragraph (12) of regulation 4 by an authority, would comply (or substantially comply) with the requirement in that paragraph to carry out a ballot—

(a)    if the ballot has been completed before that date, it shall be treated as having been completed on that date for the purpose of regulation 4(12);

(b)    if the ballot has not been completed before that date, but is completed within one month of that date, it shall be treated as having been carried out for the purpose of regulation 4(12).

**[3135]**

**NOTES**
    Revoked, in relation to houses and local authorities in England, as noted to reg 1 at **[3126]**.

**11    Agreements entered into voluntarily**

A local housing authority may enter into a management agreement with a tenant management organisation otherwise than in pursuance of the foregoing regulations where that agreement is in such form as is approved by the Secretary of State for the purposes of these Regulations and the requirements of sections 27 and 27A of the Housing Act 1985 are satisfied.

**[3136]**

**NOTES**
    Revoked, in relation to houses and local authorities in England, as noted to reg 1 at **[3126]**.

# COLLECTIVE ENFRANCHISEMENT AND TENANTS' AUDIT (QUALIFIED SURVEYORS) REGULATIONS 1994

(SI 1994/1263)

**NOTES**
    Made: 7 May 1994.
    Authority: Leasehold Reform, Housing and Urban Development Act 1993, ss 13(7)(a), 78(5).
    Commencement: 7 June 1994.

**1    Citation and commencement**

These Regulations may be cited as the Collective Enfranchisement and Tenants' Audit (Qualified Surveyors) Regulations 1994 and shall come into force on 7th June 1994.

**[3137]**

## 2 Qualified surveyors

A requirement prescribed under sections 13(7) and 78(5) of the Leasehold Reform, Housing and Urban Development Act 1993 (meaning of "qualified surveyor") is that a person is a member or fellow of the Architects and Surveyors Institute.

**[3138]**

# LOCAL GOVERNMENT CHANGES (RENT ACT) REGULATIONS 1995

### (SI 1995/2451)

NOTES

Made: 18 September 1995.

Authority: Local Government Act 1992, ss 19, 26.

Commencement: 13 October 1995.

## 1 Citation and commencement

These Regulations may be cited as the Local Government Changes (Rent Act) Regulations 1995 and shall come into force on 13th October 1995.

**[3139]**

**2–7** *(Amend the Rent Act 1977, ss 62(1), 63(9), 83(1), 124(8), 149(2) at* **[239]**, **[240]**, **[264]**, **[294]**, **[312]**.*)*

## 8 Schemes for appointment of rent officers: transitional

(1)   Where the Secretary of State—

    (a)   has made a local government reorganisation order, and

    (b)   proposes in the interim period to make a scheme under section 63 of the Rent Act 1977 for an area which falls wholly or partly within a local government area affected by the order,

he shall, in making the scheme, take account of the provisions of the local government reorganisation order and of any supplementary order; and his obligation to consult under subsection (1) of that section shall apply subject to paragraphs (2) and (3) below.

(2)   Where the proposed scheme is to take effect before the reorganisation date, the Secretary of State's obligation to consult on the scheme under subsection (1) of section 63 of the 1977 Act shall include an obligation to consult any local authority—

    (a)   which he would be required to consult under that subsection if the scheme were made after the reorganisation date, and

    (b)   which will be in existence when the scheme is made.

(3)   Where the proposed scheme is to take effect on or after the reorganisation date, the Secretary of State's obligation to consult on the scheme under that subsection shall be read as an obligation to consult any local authority which he would be required to consult under that subsection if the scheme were made after the reorganisation date.

(4)   In this regulation—

    "interim period", in relation to a local government reorganisation order, means the period beginning with the date on which the order is made and ending with the reorganisation date;

    "local government reorganisation order" means an order under section 17 of the Local Government Act 1992 (local government reorganisation orders) which provides for a structural change or a boundary change within the meaning of Part II of that Act;

    "reorganisation date", in relation to a local government reorganisation order, has the meaning given in that order;

    "supplementary order" means, in relation to a local government reorganisation order, any order—

        (a)   which is made under section 17 of the Local Government Act 1992 after the local government reorganisation order; and

        (b)   which—

            (i)   makes provision relating to the structural or boundary change effected or to be effected by the local government reorganisation order; or

            (ii)   makes provision, in connection with the local government reorganisation order (or a later order made under section 17 of the 1992 Act in connection with the local government reorganisation order), which is equivalent to that which may be contained in regulations under section 19 of that Act.

**[3140]**

# LANDLORD AND TENANT (COVENANTS) ACT 1995 (NOTICES) REGULATIONS 1995

(SI 1995/2964)

**NOTES**
Made: 9 November 1995.
Authority: Landlord and Tenant (Covenants) Act 1995, s 27.
Commencement: 1 January 1996.

**1**—(1)  These Regulations may be cited as the Landlord and Tenant (Covenants) Act 1995 (Notices) Regulations 1995 and shall come into force on 1st January 1996.

(2)  In these Regulations, "the Act" means the Landlord and Tenant (Covenants) Act 1995, and a form referred to by number means the form so numbered in the Schedule to these Regulations.]

**[3141]**

**2**   The forms prescribed for the purposes of the Act shall be as follows, or in each case a form substantially to the like effect—

| PURPOSE OF NOTICE | FORM TO BE USED |
|---|---|
| (a)(i)   Landlord informing a former tenant or guarantor of such a tenant of an amount payable in respect of a fixed charge under a covenant of the tenancy which the landlord intends to recover from that person under section 17 of the Act | Form 1 |
| (ii)   Landlord informing a former tenant or guarantor of such a tenant of a revised, greater amount payable in respect of a fixed charge under a covenant of the tenancy which the landlord intends to recover from that person under section 17 of the Act | Form 2 |
| (b)(i)   Landlord applying to be released from all the landlord covenants of the tenancy on assignment of his entire interest under sections 6 and 8 of the Act | Whole of Form 3 (landlord to complete Part I only) |
| (ii)   Tenant objecting to the landlord's release under section 8 of the Act | Part II of Form 3 |
| (iii)   Tenant consenting to the landlord's release and withdrawing a notice objecting to such release under section 8 of the Act | Notice in writing stating that tenant is now consenting and that the notice of objection is withdrawn |
| (c)(i)   Landlord applying to be released from the landlord covenants of the tenancy to the appropriate extent on assignment of part only of his interest under sections 6 and 8 of the Act | Whole of Form 4 (landlord to complete Part I only) |
| (ii)   Tenant objecting to the landlord's release under section 8 of the Act | Part II of Form 4 |
| (iii)   Tenant consenting to the landlord's release and withdrawing a notice objecting to such release under section 8 of the Act | Notice in writing stating that tenant is now consenting and that the notice of objection is withdrawn |
| (d)(i)   Former landlord applying to be released from all the landlord covenants of the tenancy on a subsequent assignment of the landlord's interest under sections 7 and 8 of the Act | Whole of Form 5 (landlord to complete Part I only) |
| (ii)   Tenant objecting to the former landlord's release under section 8 of the Act | Part II of Form 5 |

PART II
STATUTORY INSTRUMENTS

| PURPOSE OF NOTICE | FORM TO BE USED |
|---|---|
| (iii) Tenant consenting to the former landlord's release and withdrawing a notice objecting to such release under section 8 of the Act | Notice in writing stating that tenant is now consenting and that the notice of objection is withdrawn |
| (e)(i) Former landlord who assigned part only of his interest applying to be released from the landlord covenants of the tenancy to the appropriate extent on a subsequent assignment of the landlord's interest under sections 7 and 8 of the Act | Whole of Form 6 (landlord to complete Part I only) |
| (ii) Tenant objecting to the former landlord's release under section 8 of the Act | Part II of Form 6 |
| (iii) Tenant consenting to the former landlord's release and withdrawing a notice objecting to such release under section 8 of the Act | Notice in writing stating that tenant is now consenting and that the notice of objection is withdrawn |
| (f)(i) Tenant and tenant's assignee jointly applying for an apportionment of liability under the covenants of the tenancy to become binding on the appropriate person under sections 9 and 10 of the Act | Whole of Form 7 (tenant and assignee to complete Part I only) |
| (ii) Appropriate person objecting to the apportionment becoming binding on that person under section 10 of the Act | Part II of Form 7 |
| (iii) Appropriate person consenting to the apportionment becoming binding on that person and withdrawing a notice objecting to the apportionment becoming so binding under section 10 of the Act | Notice in writing stating that appropriate person is now consenting and that the notice of objection is withdrawn |
| (g)(i) Landlord and landlord's assignee jointly applying for an apportionment of liability under the covenants of the tenancy to become binding on the appropriate person under sections 9 and 10 of the Act | Whole of Form 8 (landlord and assignee to complete Part I only) |
| (ii) Appropriate person objecting to the apportionment becoming binding on that person under section 10 of the Act | Part II of Form 8 |
| (iii) Appropriate person consenting to the apportionment becoming binding on that person and withdrawing a notice objecting to the apportionment becoming so binding under section 10 of the Act | Notice in writing stating that appropriate person is now consenting and that the notice of objection is withdrawn |

[3142]

**NOTES**

The Act: the Landlord and Tenant (Covenants) Act 1995.

## SCHEDULE

**NOTES**

This Schedule contains forms which are not reproduced in this work, but their titles are listed below. The forms can be found at www.opsi.gov.uk.

Form 1—Notice to Former Tenant or Guarantor of Intention to Recover Fixed Charge (Landlord and Tenant (Covenants) Act 1995, Section 17)

Form 2—Further Notice to former Tenant or Guarantor of Revised Amount due in Respect of a Fixed Charge (Landlord and Tenant (Covenants) Act 1995, section 17)

Form 3

Part I—Landlord's Notice Applying for Release from Landlord Covenants of a Tenancy on Assignment of Whole of Reversion (Landlord and Tenant (Covenants) Act 1995, Sections 6 and 8)

Part II—Tenant's Response to Landlord's Notice Applying for Release from Landlord Covenants of a Tenancy on Assignment of Whole of Reversion (Landlord and Tenant (Covenants) Act 1995, Section 8)

Form 4

Part I—Landlord's Notice Applying for Release from Landlord Covenants of a Tenancy on Assignment of Part of Reversion (Landlord and Tenant (Covenants) Act 1995, Sections 6 and 8)

Part II—Tenant's Response to Landlord's Notice Applying for Release from Landlord Covenants of a Tenancy on Assignment of Part of Reversion (Landlord and Tenant (Covenants) Act 1995, Section 8)

Form 5

Part I—Former Landlord's Notice Applying for Release from Landlord Covenants of a Tenancy (Landlord and Tenant (Covenants) Act 1995, Sections 7 and 8)

Part II—Tenant's Response to Former Landlord's Notice Applying for Release from Landlord Covenants of a Tenancy (Landlord and Tenant (Covenants) Act 1995, Section 8)

Form 6

Part I—Former Landlord's Notice Applying for Release from Landlord Covenants of a Tenancy (Former Landlord Having Assigned Part of Reversion) (Landlord and Tenant (Covenants) Act 1995, Sections 7 and 8)

Part II—Tenant's Response to Former Landlord's Notice Applying for Release from Landlord Covenants of a Tenancy (Former Landlord Having Assigned Part of Reversion) (Landlord and Tenant (Covenants) Act 1995, Section 8)

Form 7

Part I—Joint Notice by Tenant and Assignee for Binding Apportionment of Liability under Non-Attributable Tenant Covenants of a Tenancy on Assignment of Part of Property (Landlord and Tenant (Covenants) Act 1995, Sections 9 and 10)

Part II—Landlord's Response to Joint Notice by Tenant and Assignee Seeking Binding Apportionment of Liability under Non-Attributable Tenant Covenants of a Tenancy on Assignment of Part of Property (Landlord and Tenant (Covenants) Act 1995, Section 10)

Form 8

Part I—Joint Notice by Landlord and Assignee for Binding Apportionment of Liability under Non-Attributable Landlord Covenants of a Tenancy on Assignment of Part of Reversion (Landlord and Tenant (Covenants) Act 1995, Sections 9 and 10)

Part II—Tenant's Response to Joint Notice by Landlord and Assignee Seeking Binding Apportionment of Liability under Non-Attributable Landlord Covenants of a Tenancy on Assignment of Part of Reversion (Landlord and Tenant (Covenants) Act 1995, Section 10)

# HOUSING ACT 1996 (CONSEQUENTIAL PROVISIONS) ORDER 1996

## (SI 1996/2325)

**NOTES**

Made: 9 September 1996.

Authority: Housing Act 1996, ss 52, 55(2), (3), 231(5).

Commencement: 1 October 1996.

## ARRANGEMENT OF ARTICLES

**1  Citation and commencement**

(1)   This Order may be cited as the Housing Act 1996 (Consequential Provisions) Order 1996.

(2)   This Order comes into force on 1st October 1996.

**[3143]**

## 2  Interpretation

In this Order—

"subordinate legislation" has the meaning given in the Interpretation Act 1978;

"the 1985 Act" means the Housing Associations Act 1985; and

"the 1996 Act" means the Housing Act 1996.

**[3144]**

## 3  Continuity of the law

(1)   A reference (express or implied) in Part I of the 1996 Act or any other enactment, instrument or document to any provision of that Part shall, so far as the context permits, be construed as including, in relation to times, circumstances and purposes before the commencement of that provision, a reference to the corresponding provision of the 1985 Act or any corresponding earlier enactment.

(2)   Without prejudice to the generality of paragraph (1), a reference (express or implied) in Part I of the 1996 Act or any other enactment, instrument or document to registration as a social landlord shall, so far as the context permits, be construed as including, in relation to times, circumstances and purposes before the commencement of section 1 of the 1996 Act, a reference to registration under Part I of the 1985 Act or any corresponding earlier enactment.

(3)   Anything done (including subordinate legislation made), or having effect as done, under a provision of the 1985 Act repealed and re-enacted, with or without modifications, by or under Part I of the 1996 Act has effect as if done under the corresponding provision made by or under Part I of the 1996 Act.

(4)   A reference (express or implied) in an enactment, instrument or other document to a provision of the 1985 Act repealed and re-enacted, with or without modifications, by or under Part I of the 1996 Act shall be construed, so far as is required for continuing its effect and subject to any express amendment by or under that Part, as being, or as the case may require including, a reference to the corresponding provision made by or under that Part.

(5)   Without prejudice to the generality of paragraph (4), a reference (express or implied) in an enactment, instrument or other document to registration as a housing association shall, so far as the context permits, other than in relation to times, circumstances and purposes before the commencement of section 1 of the 1996 Act, be construed as being, or as the case may require including, a reference to registration as a social landlord.

(6)   This article is subject to any transitional provisions or savings made by or under the 1996 Act.

**[3145]**

**NOTES**

1985 Act: the Housing Associations Act 1985.
1996 Act: the Housing Act 1996.

## 4  Repeals

(1)   Subject to paragraphs (2) to (4), the enactments specified in Schedule 1 are repealed to the extent specified.

(2)   The repeal by this Order of an enactment which amends an enactment which is repealed by or under the 1996 Act subject to savings does not affect the operation of those savings.

(3)   The repeal of definitions or references to definitions in the 1985 Act does not affect their continued application in relation to enactments repealed subject to savings (whether previously or by or under Part I of the 1996 Act).

(4)   The repeal of the definition of "housing activities" in the 1985 Act does not affect its continued application in relation to sections 50 to 55 of the Housing Act 1988.

**[3146]**

**NOTES**

1985 Act: the Housing Associations Act 1985.
1996 Act: the Housing Act 1996.

## 5  Consequential amendments

(1)   Subject to paragraph (2), the enactments specified in Schedule 2 have effect with the amendments specified.

(2)   The amendment in paragraph 18(8)(b) of Schedule 2 does not apply in relation to periods ending on or before 30th September 1996.

**[3147]**

**6   Extent**

(1)   The provisions of this Order, other than Parts II and III of Schedule 1 and paragraphs 15(3) to (9), (11) to (18), (24)(a) and (35) and 18(9)(a) of Schedule 2, extend to England and Wales.

(2)   The following provisions of this Order extend to Scotland—
articles 1 to 6,
Part II of Schedule 1, and
paragraphs 2, 4, 10, 12, 15(1) to (19), (21), (24), (35) and (36), 18(1) and (9)(a) and 20 of Schedule 2.

(3)   The following provisions of this Order extend to Northern Ireland—
articles 1 to 6,
Part III of Schedule 1, and
paragraphs 2, 12 and 20 of Schedule 2.

**[3148]**

*(Schs 1, 2 contain repeals and amendments only.)*


# APPROVAL OF CODES OF MANAGEMENT PRACTICE (RESIDENTIAL PROPERTY) ORDER 1996

### (SI 1996/2839)

**NOTES**
Made: 11 November 1996.
Authority: Leasehold Reform, Housing and Urban Development Act 1993, ss 87, 100.
Commencement: 17 March 1997.

## 1   Citation and commencement

This Order may be cited as the Approval of Codes of Management Practice (Residential Property) Order 1996 and shall come into force on 17th March 1997.

**[3149]**

## 2   Approval of code of practice

"'Rent Only' Residential Management Code" (ISBN 0 85406 642 X) and "'Service Charge' Residential Management Code" (ISBN 0 85406 643 8), which were submitted for approval on 25th October 1996 by the Royal Institution of Chartered Surveyors and are to be published by RICS Business Services Limited, are approved.

**[3150]**

## 3   Transitional provision

Article 2 does not apply for the purposes of section 87(7)(a) and (b) of the Leasehold Reform, Housing and Urban Development Act 1993 (use of code in proceedings) in relation to an act or omission occurring before this Order comes into force.

**[3151]**


# HOMELESSNESS (SUITABILITY OF ACCOMMODATION) ORDER 1996

### (SI 1996/3204)

**NOTES**
Made: 19 December 1996.
Authority: Housing Act 1996, ss 177(3)(b), 210(2)(b).
Commencement: 20 January 1997.

## 1   Citation and commencement

This Order may be cited as the Homelessness (Suitability of Accommodation) Order 1996 and shall come into force on 20th January 1997.

**[3152]**

## 2  Matters to be taken into account

In determining whether it would be, or would have been, reasonable for a person to continue to occupy accommodation and in determining whether accommodation is suitable for a person there shall be taken into account whether or not the accommodation is affordable for that person and, in particular, the following matters—

   (a)    the financial resources available to that person, including, but not limited to,—

       (i)   salary, fees and other remuneration;

      (ii)   social security benefits;

    (iii)   payments due under a court order for the making of periodical payments to a spouse or a former spouse, or to, or for the benefit of, a child;

     (iv)   payments of child support maintenance due under the Child Support Act 1991;

      (v)   pensions;

     (vi)   contributions to the costs in respect of the accommodation which are or were made or which might reasonably be expected to be, or have been, made by other members of his household;

    (vii)   financial assistance towards the costs in respect of the accommodation, including loans, provided by a local authority, voluntary organisation or other body;

   (viii)   benefits derived from a policy of insurance;

     (ix)   savings and other capital sums;

   (b)    the costs in respect of the accommodation, including, but not limited to,—

       (i)   payments of, or by way of, rent;

      (ii)   payments in respect of a licence or permission to occupy the accommodation;

    (iii)   mortgage costs;

     (iv)   payments of, or by way of, service charges;

      (v)   mooring charges payable for a houseboat;

     (vi)   where the accommodation is a caravan or a mobile home, payments in respect of the site on which it stands;

    (vii)   the amount of council tax payable in respect of the accommodation;

   (viii)   payments by way of deposit or security in respect of the accommodation;

     (ix)   payments required by an accommodation agency;

   (c)    payments which that person is required to make under a court order for the making of periodical payments to a spouse or a former spouse, or to, or for the benefit of, a child and payments of child support maintenance required to be made under the Child Support Act 1991;

   (d)    that person's other reasonable living expenses.

                                                            **[3153]**

## [3  Circumstances in which accommodation is not to be regarded as suitable

For the purposes of section 197(1) of the Housing Act 1996 (duty where other suitable accommodation available), accommodation shall not be regarded as suitable unless the local housing authority are satisfied that it will be available for occupation by the applicant for at least two years beginning with the date on which he secures it.]

                                                            **[3154]**

**NOTES**

  Inserted by the Homelessness (Suitability of Accommodation) (Amendment) Order 1997, SI 1997/1741, art 2.

# LOCAL HOUSING AUTHORITIES (PRESCRIBED PRINCIPLES FOR ALLOCATION SCHEMES) (WALES) REGULATIONS 1997

### (SI 1997/45)

**NOTES**

  Made: 13 January 1997.
  Authority: Housing Act 1996, ss 167(5), 172(4).
  Commencement: 7 February 1997.

## 1  Citation, commencement and application

These Regulations may be cited as the Local Housing Authorities (Prescribed Principles for Allocation Schemes) (Wales) Regulations 1997 and shall come into force on 7th February 1997. They apply to Wales only.

                                                            **[3155]**

## 2   Interpretation

In these Regulations—

"the Act" means the Housing Act 1996;

"allocation decision" means a decision to allocate housing accommodation;

"allocation scheme" means an allocation scheme within the meaning of section 167(1) of the Act;

"authority" means a Welsh local housing authority;

"delegation arrangements" means arrangements made under section 101(1) or (2) of the Local Government Act 1972 for the discharge of an authority's function of making allocation decisions;

"officer delegation arrangements" means delegation arrangements which arrange for the discharge (in whole or in part) of an authority's function of making allocation decisions, by an officer or a description of officers of the authority; and

"qualifying person", in relation to an authority, means a person who is qualified to be allocated housing accommodation by that authority.

**[3156]**

## 3   Allocation scheme principles

As regards the procedure to be followed in allocating housing accommodation, the principles set out in the Schedule are prescribed as principles in accordance with which an authority's allocation scheme shall be framed.

**[3157]**

SCHEDULE
ALLOCATION SCHEME PRINCIPLES

Regulation 3

1.   In relation to an allocation decision where either—

    (a)    the housing accommodation in question is situated in the electoral division for which a member is elected, or

    (b)    the qualifying person in question has his sole or main residence in the electoral division for which a member is elected,

that member shall not be included in the persons or descriptions of persons by whom the allocation decision is to be taken.

2.   An officer or a description of officers of the authority shall be included in the persons or descriptions of persons by whom allocation decisions, or descriptions of allocation decisions, may be taken, except where the authority or a committee or sub-committee of the authority, as the case may be, has determined that no officer delegation arrangements shall be made.

**[3158]**

# INTRODUCTORY TENANTS (REVIEW) REGULATIONS 1997

(SI 1997/72)

**NOTES**

Made: 16 January 1997.

Authority: Housing Act 1996, ss 129, 142.

Commencement: 12 February 1997.

ARRANGEMENT OF REGULATIONS

## 1   Citation, commencement and interpretation

(1)   These Regulations may be cited as the Introductory Tenants (Review) Regulations 1997 and shall come into force on 12th February 1997.

(2)   In these Regulations references to—
  (a)   a tenant are to an introductory tenant; and
  (b)   a landlord are to a local authority or housing action trust which has elected to operate an introductory tenancy regime.

[3159]

## 2  Right to a hearing

The review under section 129 of the Housing Act 1996 of the decision to seek an order for possession of a dwelling-house let under an introductory tenancy shall not be by way of an oral hearing unless the tenant informs the landlord that he wishes to have such a hearing before the end of the time permitted under subsection (1) of that section to request a review of that decision.

[3160]

## 3  Who is to carry out the review

(1)   The review shall be carried out by a person who was not involved in the decision to apply for an order for possession.

(2)   Where the review of a decision made by an officer is also to be made by an officer, that officer shall be someone who is senior to the officer who made the original decision.

[3161]

## 4  Review without a hearing

If there is not to be a hearing the tenant may make representations in writing in connection with the review and such representations shall be considered by the landlord who shall inform the tenant of the date by which such representations must be received, which shall not be earlier than five clear days after receipt of this information by the tenant.

[3162]

## 5  Review by way of a hearing

(1)   Subject to the provisions of this regulation, the procedure in connection with a review by way of hearing shall be such as the person hearing the review shall determine.

(2)   A tenant who has requested a hearing has the right to—
  (a)   be heard and to be accompanied and may be represented by another person whether that person is professionally qualified or not, and for the purposes of the proceedings any representative shall have the rights and powers which the tenant has under these Regulations;
  (b)   call persons to give evidence;
  (c)   put questions to any person who gives evidence at the hearing; and
  (d)   make representations in writing.

[3163]

## 6  Notice of hearing

The landlord shall give the tenant notice of the date, time and place of the hearing, which shall be not less than five days after receipt of the request for a hearing and if the tenant has not been given such notice, the hearing may only proceed with the consent of the tenant or his representative.

[3164]

## 7  Absence of tenant at hearing

If any person shall fail to appear at the hearing, notice having been given to him in accordance with regulation 6, the person conducting the review may, having regard to all the circumstances including any explanation offered for the absence, proceed with the hearing notwithstanding his absence, or give such directions with a view to the conduct of the further review as that person may think proper.

[3165]

## 8  Postponement of hearing

A tenant may apply to the landlord requesting a postponement of the hearing and the landlord may grant or refuse the application as they see fit.

[3166]

## 9  Adjournment of hearing

A hearing may be adjourned by the person hearing the review at any time during the hearing on the application of the tenant, his representative, or at the motion of the person hearing the review and, if a hearing is adjourned part heard and after the adjournment the person or persons hearing the review differ from those at the first hearing, otherwise than through the operation of paragraph 7, proceedings shall be by way of a complete rehearing of the case.

[3167]

**10  Absence of person hearing the review**

Where more than one person is conducting the review, any hearing may, with the consent of the tenant or his representative but not otherwise, be proceeded with in the absence of one of the persons who is to determine the review.

**[3168]**

# ASSURED TENANCIES AND AGRICULTURAL OCCUPANCIES (FORMS) REGULATIONS 1997

## (SI 1997/194)

**NOTES**
Made: 29 January 1997.
Authority: Housing Act 1988, ss 6(2), (3), 8(3), 13(2), (4), 22(1), 41(2), 45(1), (5), Sch 2A, paras 7(2)(a), 9(2)(a)(i).
Commencement: 28 February 1997.

**1  Citation and commencement**

These Regulations may be cited as the Assured Tenancies and Agricultural Occupancies (Forms) Regulations 1997 and shall come into force on 28th February 1997.

**[3169]**

**2  Interpretation**

In these Regulations any reference to a section or Schedule is a reference to a section of, or Schedule to, the Housing Act 1988 and any reference to a numbered form is a reference to the form bearing that number in the Schedule to these Regulations, or to a form substantially to the same effect.

**[3170]**

**3  Prescribed forms**

The forms prescribed for the purposes of Part I (rented accommodation) of the Housing Act 1988 are—

- (a) for a notice under section 6(2) proposing terms of a statutory periodic tenancy different from the implied terms, Form No 1;
- (b) for an application under section 6(3) referring a notice under section 6(2) to a rent assessment committee, Form No 2;
- (c) for a notice under section 8 informing a tenant or licensee that the landlord intends to begin proceedings for possession of a dwelling-house let on an assured tenancy or an assured agricultural occupancy, Form No 3;
- (d) for a notice under section 13(2) proposing a new rent for an assured tenancy or an assured agricultural occupancy, Form No 4:
- [(d) for a notice under section 13(2) proposing a new rent for an assured tenancy of premises situated in England, Form No 4B;
- (da) for a notice under section 13(2) proposing a new rent or licence fee for an assured agricultural occupancy of premises situated in England, Form No 4C;]
- [(db) for a notice under section 13(2) proposing a new rent for an assured tenancy of premises situated in Wales, Form No 4D;
- (dc) for a notice under section 13(2) proposing a new rent or licence fee for an assured agricultural occupancy of premises situated in Wales, Form No 4E;]
- (e) for an application under section 13(4) referring to a rent assessment committee a notice under section 13(2) relating to an assured tenancy or an assured agricultural occupancy, Form No 5;
- (f) for an application under section 22(1) to a rent assessment committee for a determination of rent under an assured shorthold tenancy, Form No 6;
- (g) for a notice under section 41(2) requiring a landlord or tenant to give information to a rent assessment committee, Form No 7;
- (h) for a notice under paragraph 7 of Schedule 2A, by the tenant to the landlord proposing that an assured tenancy be replaced by an assured shorthold tenancy, Form No 8;
- (i) for a notice under paragraph 9 of Schedule 2A, by the landlord to the prospective tenant, proposing an assured shorthold tenancy where the tenancy meets the conditions for an assured agricultural occupancy, Form No 9.

**[3171]**

**NOTES**
Paras (d), (da) substituted for original para (d), in relation to England, by the Assured Tenancies and Agricultural Occupancies (Forms) (Amendment) (England) Regulations 2003, SI 2003/260, reg 2(a); paras (db),

(dc) inserted with savings in relation to Wales by the Assured Tenancies and Agricultural Occupancies (Forms) (Amendment) (Wales) Regulations 2003, SI 2003/307, reg 2(1), (2), for savings see reg 3(2) of those regulations.

## 4  Revocations and savings

(1) (*Revokes the Assured Tenancies and Agricultural Occupancies (Forms) Regulations 1988, SI 1988/2203, and the amending SI 1989/146, SI 1990/1532 and SI 1993/654.*)

(2) Nothing in paragraph (1) affects the validity of a notice served before the coming into force of these Regulations if, at the date of service of the notice, the notice was in the form then prescribed by the 1988 Regulations.

[3172]

## SCHEDULE

### NOTES

This Schedule contains forms which are not reproduced in this work, but their numbers and titles are noted below. The forms can be found at www.opsi.gov.uk.

| Form No | Title |
| --- | --- |
| 1 | Notice proposing different terms for a Statutory Periodic Tenancy (s 6(2)) |
| 2 | Application referring a Notice proposing different terms for a Statutory Periodic Tenancy to a Rent Assessment Committee (s 6(3)) |
| 3 | Notice seeking possession of a property let on an Assured Tenancy or an Assured Agricultural Occupancy (s 8, as amended by the Housing Act 1996, s 151) |
| 4 | Revoked in relation to England by SI 2002/337 and revoked in relation to Wales by SI 2003/307 |
| 4A | Inserted, in relation to England, by SI 2002/337; revoked by SI 2003/260 |
| 4B | Landlord's Notice proposing a new rent under an Assured Periodic Tenancy of premises situated in England (s 13(2), as amended by the Regulatory Reform (Assured Periodic Tenancies) (Rent Increases) Order 2003) (inserted, in relation to England, by SI 2003/260) |
| 4C | Landlord's or Licensor's Notice proposing a new rent or licence fee under an Assured Agricultural Occupancy of premises situated in England (s 13(2), as amended by the Regulatory Reform (Assured Periodic Tenancies) (Rent Increases) Order 2003) (inserted, in relation to England, by SI 2003/260) |
| 4D | Landlord's Notice proposing a new rent under an Assured Periodic Tenancy of premises situated in Wales (s 13(2), as amended by the Regulatory Reform (Assured Periodic Tenancies) (Rent Increases) Order 2003) (inserted, in relation to Wales, by SI 2003/307) |
| 4E | Landlord's or Licensor's Notice proposing a new rent or licence fee under an Assured Agricultural Occupancy of premises situated in Wales (s 13(2), as amended by the Regulatory Reform (Assured Periodic Tenancies) (Rent Increases) Order 2003) (inserted, in relation to Wales, by SI 2003/307) |
| 5 | Application referring a Notice proposing a new rent under an Assured Periodic Tenancy or Agricultural Occupancy to a Rent Assessment Committee (s 13(4)) |
| 6 | Application to a Rent Assessment Committee for a determination of a rent under an Assured Shorthold Tenancy (s 22(1), as amended by the Housing Act 1996, s 100) |
| 7 | Notice by Rent Assessment Committee requiring further information (s 41(2)) |
| 8 | Tenant's notice proposing that an Assured Tenancy be replaced by an Assured Shorthold Tenancy (Sch 2A, para 7(2), as inserted by the Housing Act 1996, Sch 7) |
| 9 | Landlord's notice proposing an Assured Shorthold Tenancy where the tenancy meets the conditions for an Assured Agricultural Occupancy (Sch 2A, para 9, as inserted by the Housing Act 1996, Sch 7) |

# ALLOCATION OF HOUSING (PROCEDURE) REGULATIONS 1997

### (SI 1997/483)

**NOTES**
Made: 26 February 1997.
Authority: Housing Act 1996, ss 167(5), 172(4).
Commencement: 1 April 1997.

## 1  Citation and commencement

These Regulations may be cited as the Allocation of Housing (Procedure) Regulations 1997 and shall come into force on 1st April 1997.

**[3173]**

## 2  Interpretation

In these Regulations—
"allocation decision" means a decision to allocate housing accommodation;
"authority" means a local housing authority in England;
"decision-making body" means an authority or a committee or sub-committee of an authority.

**[3174]**

## 3  Allocation scheme procedure

(1)  As regards the procedure to be followed, an authority's allocation scheme shall be framed in accordance with the principle prescribed in this regulation.

(2)  A member of an authority who has been elected for the electoral division or ward in which—

(a)  the housing accommodation in relation to which an allocation decision falls to be made is situated, or

(b)  the person in relation to whom that decision falls to be made has his sole or main residence,

shall not, at the time the allocation decision is made, be included in the persons constituting the decision-making body.

**[3175]**

# LEASEHOLD REFORM (NOTICES) REGULATIONS 1997

### (SI 1997/640)

**NOTES**
Made: 5 March 1997.
Authority: Landlord and Tenant Act 1954, s 66, as applied by the Leasehold Reform Act 1967, s 22(5).
Commencement: 1 April 1997.

## 1  Citation and commencement

These Regulations may be cited as the Leasehold Reform (Notices) Regulations 1997 and shall come into force on 1st April 1997.

**[3176]**

## 2  Interpretation

In these Regulations, unless the context otherwise requires—
"the Act" means the Leasehold Reform Act 1967;
any reference to a numbered section is a reference to the section so numbered in the Act; and
any reference to a numbered Form is a reference to the Form bearing that number in the Schedule to these Regulations or a form substantially to the same effect.

**[3177]**

## 3  Forms to be used by tenants and landlords

(1)  The form to be used by a tenant for the purpose of giving notice under Part I (enfranchisement and extension of long leaseholds) of the Act of his desire to have the freehold or an extended lease of a house and premises is Form 1.

(2)  The form to be used by a tenant for the purpose of giving notice under subsection (1)(b)(ii) of section 28 (retention or resumption of land required for public purposes) of his claim to be entitled to acquire the freehold or an extended lease of a house and premises is Form 2.

(3)   The form to be used by a landlord for the purpose of responding to a tenant's notice under paragraph (1) or (2) is Form 3.

**[3178]**

**NOTES**
    The Act: the Leasehold Reform Act 1967.

**4   Revocation, savings and transitional provision**

(1)   Subject to paragraph (2), the Leasehold Reform (Notices) Regulations 1967, the Leasehold Reform (Notices) Regulations 1969 and the Leasehold Reform (Notices) (Amendment) Regulations 1993 are hereby revoked.

(2)   The Regulations revoked by paragraph (1) shall continue to apply in a case where a notice under section 8, 14 or 28 (tenant's notice of desire to have or claim to be entitled to acquire the freehold or an extended lease) was given before the date these Regulations come into force.

**[3179]**

**NOTES**
    Sections 8, 14 or 28: the Leasehold Reform Act 1967, ss 8, 14 or 28.

SCHEDULE

**NOTES**
    This Schedule contains forms which are not reproduced in this work, but their titles are noted below; note that there is no prescribed form for claims made by flat leaseholders under the LRHUDA 1993. The forms can be found at www.opsi.gov.uk.

| Form No | Title |
|---|---|
| 1 | Notice of tenant's claim to acquire the freehold or an extended lease (substituted in relation to England by SI 2002/1715 and in relation to Wales by SI 2002/3187) |
| 2 | Notice of tenant's claim under section 28(1)(b)(ii) (substituted in relation to England by SI 2002/1715 and in relation to Wales by SI 2002/3187) |
| 3 | Notice in reply to tenant's claim (substituted in relation to England by SI 2002/3209 and in relation to Wales by SI 2003/991) |

# ALLOCATION OF HOUSING (REASONABLE AND ADDITIONAL PREFERENCE) REGULATIONS 1997

(SI 1997/1902)

**NOTES**
    Made: 30 July 1997.
    Authority: Housing Act 1996, s 167(3).
    Commencement: 1 November 1997.

**1   Citation and commencement**

These Regulations may be cited as the Allocation of Housing (Reasonable and Additional Preference) Regulations 1997 and shall come into force on 1st November 1997.

**[3180]**

**2   Further descriptions of people to whom reasonable preference is to be given**

The following are specified as further descriptions of people to whom reasonable preference is to be given in the allocation scheme of a local housing authority—

    (a)    people owed a duty by that authority under section 193 or 195(2) of the Housing Act 1996 ("the 1996 Act") or section 65(2) or 68(2) of the Housing Act 1985 (main housing duties owed to homeless persons),

    (b)    people in respect of whom that authority are exercising their power under section 194 of the 1996 Act (power to secure accommodation after minimum period of duty under section 193 of that Act), and

    (c)    people—

    (i)    who have within the previous two years been provided with advice and assistance by that authority under section 197(2) of the 1996 Act (duty where other suitable accommodation available) or

    (ii)    who are occupying accommodation secured with such advice and assistance.

**[3181]**

**3**    (*Amends the Housing Act 1996, s 167(2).*)

# RENT OFFICERS (HOUSING BENEFIT FUNCTIONS) ORDER 1997

## (SI 1997/1984)

**NOTES**

Made: 12 August 1997.

Authority: Housing Act 1996, s 122. S 122(3) has been repealed, and s 122(5) amended, by the Welfare Reform Act 2007, ss 40, 67, Sch 5, para 12, Sch 8, and consequential amendments have been made by the Rent Officers (Housing Benefit Functions) Amendment Order 2007, SI 2007/2871.

It should be noted that some amendments originally made by the Housing Benefit and Council Tax Benefit (Consequential Provisions) Regulations 2006, SI 2006/217 (made under, inter alia, the Housing Act 1996, s 122(3), (5)), which have ceased to have effect on the repeal of the said s 122(3) and consequent amendment of the said s 122(5), have been remade by SI 2007/2871 (made under the Housing Act 1996, s 122(1), (6)). See further the note "Modification" below.

Commencement: 18 August 1997 (arts 1, 8, 10(1)); 3 September 1997 (remainder).

Modification: This order was previously modified by the Rent Officers (Housing Benefit Functions) (Local Housing Allowance) Amendment Order 2003, SI 2003/2398 (amended by SI 2005/236), the Rent Officers (Housing Benefit Functions) (Local Housing Allowance) Amendment Order 2005, SI 2005/236, and SI 2006/217 in relation to the areas of pathfinder authorities, ie a local authority specified in the table in Pt II of Sch 3A to this order (revoked), as listed below: Blackpool, Brighton and Hove, Conwy, Coventry, East Riding of Yorkshire, Guildford, Leeds, Lewisham, North East Lincolnshire, Norwich, Pembrokeshire, St Helens, Salford, South Norfolk, Teignbridge and Wandsworth.

Sch 3A to this order has been revoked by the amending SI 2007/2871. By virtue of art 2 of SI 2007/2871, those provisions of this order which on 19 March 2008 applied only in relation to the area of the above local authorities now apply in the same way to the area of every other local authority in England and Wales. Modifications made by SI 2003/2398 in relation to the areas of pathfinder authorities which are still in force have accordingly now been noted as amendments which apply to all local authorities in England and Wales.

### ARRANGEMENT OF ARTICLES

**1   Citation and commencement**

(1)    This Order may be cited as the Rent Officers (Housing Benefit Functions) Order 1997.

(2)   This article and articles 8 and 10(1) shall come into force on 18th August 1997 and all the other articles shall come into force on 3rd September 1997.

## 2  Interpretation

(1)   In this Order, unless the context otherwise requires—

"assured tenancy" has the same meaning as in Part I of the Housing Act 1988, except that it includes a tenancy which would be an assured tenancy but for paragraph 2[, 8] or 10 of Schedule 1 to that Act and a licence which would be an assured tenancy (within the extended meaning given in this definition) were it a tenancy;

["board and attendance determination" means a determination made in accordance with article 4C;]

["broad rental market area" has the meaning specified in paragraph 4 of Schedule 3B;]

["broad rental market area determination" means a determination made in accordance with article 4B(1A);]

"child" means a person under the age of 16;

"determination" means a determination made in accordance with Part I or IV of Schedule 1 to this Order;

"dwelling" means any residential accommodation whether or not consisting of the whole or part of a building and whether or not comprising separate and self-contained premises;

["hostel" has the same meaning as in regulation 2(1) of the Housing Benefit Regulations or, as the case may be, regulation 2(1) of the Housing Benefit (State Pension Credit) Regulations;]

["the Housing Benefit Regulations" mean the Housing Benefit Regulations 2006;

"the Housing Benefit (State Pension Credit) Regulations" means the Housing Benefit (Persons who have attained the qualifying age for state pension credit) Regulations 2006;]

"local authority" has the same meaning as in the Social Security Administration Act 1992 in relation to England and in relation to Wales;

["local housing allowance determination" means a determination made in accordance with article 4B(2A);]

"occupier" means a person (whether or not identified by name) who is stated, in the application for the determination, to occupy the dwelling as his home;

[ ..... ]

"redetermination" means a redetermination made in accordance with article 4; "relevant time" means the time the application for the determination is made or, if earlier, the tenancy ends;

["relevant date" means the date specified by a local authority in an application for a local housing allowance determination made in accordance with regulation 13D(7)(a) of the Housing Benefit Regulations or, as the case may be, regulation 13D(7)(a) of the Housing Benefit (State Pension Credit) Regulations;]

["relevant period" means—

(a)   in relation to a determination, the period of five working days (or, where the determination does not relate to a prospective tenancy and the rent officer intends to inspect the dwelling before making the determination, 25 working days) beginning with—

(i)   where the rent officer requests further information under article 5, the date on which he receives the information; and

(ii)   in any other case, the date on which he receives the application for the determination; and

(b)   in relation to a redetermination, the period of 20 working days beginning with—

(i)   where the rent officer requests further information under article 5, the date on which he receives the information; and

(ii)   in any other case, the date on which he receives the application for that redetermination;]

"relevant time" means the time the application for the determination [or board and attendance determination] is made or, if earlier, the tenancy ends;

["rent" means any of the periodical payments referred to in regulation 12(1) of the Housing Benefit Regulations or, as the case may be, regulation 12(1) of the Housing Benefit (State Pension Credit) Regulations;]

"size criteria" means the standards relating to bedrooms and rooms suitable for living in specified in Schedule 2 to this Order;

"tenancy" includes—

(a)   a licence; and

(b)   a prospective tenancy or licence; and

references to a tenant, a landlord or any other expression appropriate to a tenancy shall be construed accordingly; and

.....

["working day" means any day other than a Saturday, a Sunday, Christmas Day, Good Friday or a day which is a bank holiday in England and Wales under the Banking and Financial Dealings Act 1971].

(2)    In this Order any reference to a notice or application is to a notice or application in writing, except in a case where the recipient consents (whether generally or specifically) to the notice or application being transmitted by electronic means.

**[3183]**

**NOTES**

Para (1) is amended as follows:

in definition "assured tenancy" reference in square brackets inserted by the Rent Officers (Housing Benefit Functions) (Student Accommodation) Amendment Order 2004, SI 2004/2101, art 2(1);

definition "board and attendance determination" inserted by the Rent Officers (Housing Benefit Functions) (Local Housing Allowance) Amendment Order 2003, SI 2003/2398, art 2;

definition "broad rental market area" inserted by SI 2003/2398, art 2; substituted by the Rent Officers (Housing Benefit Functions) Amendment Order 2007, SI 2007/2871, arts 3, 6(1), (2), (3)(a), as from 7 April 2008, for savings see the note below;

definition "broad rental market area determination" inserted by SI 2003/2398, art 2; substituted by SI 2007/2871, arts 3, 6(1), (2), (3)(b), as from 7 April 2008, for savings see the note below;

definitions "hostel" and "rent" substituted, definitions "the Housing Benefit Regulations", "the Housing Benefit (State Pension Credit) Regulations" and "working day" inserted, and definition "the 1987 Regulations" (omitted) revoked by SI 2007/2871, arts 3, 4(1)(d), 10(1)(a)–(d);

definition "local housing allowance determination" inserted by SI 2003/2398, art 2; substituted by SI 2007/2871, arts 3, 6(1), (2), (3)(c), as from 7 April 2008, for savings see the note below;

definition "pathfinder authority" inserted by SI 2003/2398, art 2; revoked by SI 2007/2871, arts 3, 6(1), (2), (3)(d), as from 7 April 2008, for savings see the note below;

definition "relevant date" inserted by SI 2003/2398, art 2; substituted by SI 2007/2871, arts 3, 6(1), (2), (3)(e), as from 7 April 2008, for savings see the note below;

definition "relevant period" inserted by the Rent Officers (Housing Benefit Functions) (Amendment) Order 2000, SI 2000/1, arts 2, 3;

words in square brackets in definition "relevant time" inserted by SI 2003/2398, art 2.

Modification: for the application of the amendments made by SI 2003/2398 to all local authorities in England and Wales, see the note "Modification" at the beginning of this order.

Savings: SI 2007/2871, art 6(1), (2) provides that the amendments to definitions "broad rental market area", "broad rental market area determination", "local housing allowance determination", "pathfinder authority" and "relevant date" by SI 2007/2871 shall not apply where:

(a)    a board and attendance determination, board and attendance redetermination, substitute board and attendance determination or substitute board and attendance redetermination is to be made and the application for the board and attendance determination or original board and attendance determination was made by virtue of the Housing Benefit Regulations 2006, SI 2006/213, reg 13A(6), or, as the case may be, the Housing Benefit (Persons who have attained the qualifying age for state pension credit) Regulations 2006, SI 2006/214, reg 13A(6), as in force immediately before 7 April 2008;

(b)    a local housing allowance determination is to be made and the application was made by virtue of reg 13A(4) or (5) of SI 2006/213, or, as the case may be, reg 13A(4) or (5) of SI 2006/214, as in force immediately before 7 April 2008; or

(c)    an error in relation to a broad rental market area determination, local housing allowance determination, board and attendance determination or a board and attendance redetermination is to be corrected and the original determination was made in accordance with this order as in force immediately before 7 April 2008. "Original determination" means the broad rental market area determination, local housing allowance determination, board and attendance determination or board and attendance redetermination to which the correction of an error relates.

## 3    Determinations

(1)    Subject to [articles 3A and 6], where a local authority, in accordance with regulations made under section 136(2) or (3) of the Social Security Administration Act 1992 [or section 122(5) of the Housing Act 1996], applies to a rent officer for determinations in respect of a tenancy of a dwelling, a rent officer shall—

    (a)    make the determinations in accordance with Part I of Schedule 1 (determinations);

    (b)    comply with Part II of Schedule 1 when making the determinations (assumptions etc); and

    (c)    give notice in accordance with Part III of Schedule 1 (notifications) [within the relevant period or as soon as is practicable after that period].

(2)    A rent officer for each registration area (within the meaning of section 62 of the Rent Act 1977), on the first working day of each month, shall—

    (a)    make determinations in accordance with Part IV of Schedule 1 (indicative rent levels) in relation to the area of each local authority[ … ] within the registration area;

    (b)    comply with paragraph 8(2) of Part II of Schedule 1 (assumptions etc) when making the determinations; and

    (c)    give to the local authority notice of the determinations relating to its area when they have been made.

**[3184]**

**NOTES**

Para (1): words in first pair of square brackets substituted by the Rent Officers (Housing Benefit Functions) (Amendment) Order 2001, SI 2001/1325, arts 2, 3(1); words in second and third pairs of square brackets inserted by the Rent Officers (Housing Benefit Functions) (Amendment) Order 2000, SI 2000/1, arts 2, 4(b), (c).

Para (2): words omitted inserted by the Rent Officers (Housing Benefit Functions) (Local Housing Allowance) Amendment Order 2003, SI 2003/2398, art 2(1), (4), and revoked by the Rent Officers (Housing Benefit Functions) Amendment Order 2007, SI 2007/2871, arts 3, 5(1).

Social Security Administration Act 1992, s 136: repealed by the Housing Act 1996, s 227, Sch 19, Pt VI, and replaced by ss 140A–140D of the 1992 Act (as inserted by s 121 of, and Sch 12, para 4 to, the 1996 Act). The Housing Act 1996, s 122(5), as amended by the Welfare Reform Act 2007, s 40, Sch 5, para 12, no longer provides for the making of regulations.

---

**[3A   Transitional arrangements for determination of Single Room Rents with effect from 2nd July 2001**

In a case where the rent officer has made and notified an authority of a determination of a single room rent pursuant to paragraph 5 of Schedule 1 in the period of 12 months before 2nd July 2001 that determination shall cease to have effect on … 2nd July 2001 and a rent officer shall—

   (a)   make a new determination of that single room rent in accordance with Part I of Schedule 1;

   (b)   comply with Part II of Schedule 1; and

   (c)   give notice in accordance with Part III of Schedule 1 within the relevant period or as soon as is practicable after that period;

without an application for a determination under [regulation 14 of the Housing Benefit Regulations or, as the case may be, regulation 14 of the Housing Benefit (State Pension Credit) Regulations] having been made.]

**[3185]**

---

**NOTES**

Inserted by the Rent Officers (Housing Benefit Functions) (Amendment) Order 2001, SI 2001/1325, arts 2, 3(2).

Words omitted revoked by the Rent Officers (Housing Benefit Functions) (Amendment) (No 2) Order 2001, SI 2001/2317, art 2(1), (2); words in square brackets substituted by the Rent Officers (Housing Benefit Functions) Amendment Order 2007, SI 2007/2871, arts 3, 10(2).

---

**[4   Redeterminations**

   [(1)   Subject to article 6, where the local authority applies to a rent officer for a redetermination of any determination or redetermination in respect of a tenancy of a dwelling the rent officer shall, in accordance with Schedule 3—

   (a)   make redeterminations of any effective determinations and any effective redeterminations in respect of that tenancy; and

   (b)   give notice within the relevant period or as soon as is practicable after that period.

   (2)   For the purposes of paragraph (1)—

   (a)   "effective determinations" means any determinations made in accordance with Part I of Schedule 1 which have effect at the date of the application for a redetermination of a determination or redetermination; and

   (b)   "effective redeterminations" means any redeterminations made in accordance with Schedule 3 which have effect at that date.

   (3)   A rent officer whose advice is sought as provided for in Schedule 3 shall give that advice.]

**[3186]**

---

**NOTES**

Substituted, together with art 4A, for original art 4, by the Rent Officers (Housing Benefit Functions) (Amendment) Order 2000, SI 2000/1, arts 2, 5.

---

**[4A   Substitute determinations and substitute redeterminations**

   (1)   Where a local authority applies to a rent officer for a substitute determination, in accordance with [regulation 17 of the Housing Benefit Regulations or, as the case may be, regulation 17 of the Housing Benefit (State Pension Credit) Regulations], the provisions of this Order shall apply to that substitute determination as they apply to a determination, but as if references to the relevant time were references to the date the application for the original determination was made or, if earlier, the date the tenancy ended.

   (2)   Where a local authority applies to a rent officer for a substitute redetermination, in accordance with that regulation, the provisions of this Order shall apply to that substitute redetermination as they apply to a redetermination.]

**[3187]**

**NOTES**
Substituted as noted to art 4 at **[3186]**.
Para (1): words in square brackets substituted by the Rent Officers (Housing Benefit Functions) Amendment Order 2007, SI 2007/2871, arts 3, 10(3).

### [4B  Broad rental market area determinations and local housing allowance determinations

(1)  …

[(1A)  On 20th March 2008 and so often thereafter as a rent officer considers appropriate, a rent officer shall, in relation to each local authority,—

    (a)    determine one or more broad rental market areas which will (during the month which next begins after the determination is made) fall, in whole or in part, within the area of the local authority so that every part of the area of that local authority falls within a broad rental market area and no part of the area of that authority falls within more than one broad rental market area; and

    (b)    give to that local authority a notice which—

        (i)    specifies the area contained within each broad rental market area as falls, in whole or in part, within the area of that authority, by reference to the postcodes for each such broad rental market area; and

        (ii)    identifies such of those postcodes as fall within the area of that authority.]

(2)  …

[(2A)  No more than 10 and not less than 8 working days before the end of each month a rent officer shall—

    (a)    for each broad rental market area determine, in accordance with the provisions of Schedule 3B—

        (i)    a local housing allowance for each of the categories of dwelling set out in paragraph 1 of Schedule 3B; and

        (ii)    local housing allowances for such other categories of dwelling of more than five bedrooms as a rent officer believes are likely to be required for the purpose of calculating housing benefit; and

    (b)    give to each local authority notice of the local housing allowance determination made in accordance with paragraph (a) for each broad rental market area falling within, in whole or in part, the area of that authority.]

(3)  …

[(3A)  Any broad rental market area determination made in accordance with paragraph (1A), or local housing allowance determination made in accordance with paragraph (2A) before 7th April 2008, shall take effect on 7th April 2008 and any subsequent determination shall take effect on the first … day of the month which begins after the day on which the determination is made.]

[(4)  Where a local authority makes an application in accordance with regulation 13D(7)(a) of the Housing Benefit Regulations or, as the case may be, regulation 13D(7)(a) of the Housing Benefit (State Pension Credit) Regulations, a rent officer shall determine, in accordance with the provisions of Schedule 3B and as soon as is reasonably practicable, the local housing allowance for that category of dwelling at the relevant date, for each broad rental market area falling within, in whole or in part, the area of the local authority that made the application, at the relevant date.

(4A)  Where a local authority makes an application in accordance with regulation 13D(8) of the Housing Benefit Regulations or, as the case may be, regulation 13D(8) of the Housing Benefit (State Pension Credit) Regulations, a rent officer shall determine in accordance with the provisions of Schedule 3B and as soon as is reasonably practicable, the local housing allowance for that category of dwelling for each broad rental market area falling within, in whole or in part, the areas of the local authority.]

(5)  Where a rent officer has made a local housing allowance determination in accordance with paragraph (4)—

    (a)    he shall give notice of the determination to the [local authority] that made the application;

    [(b)    any local housing allowance determination made in accordance with paragraph (4) shall take effect for the month in which the relevant date falls, except that no such determination can have effect before 7th April 2008; and

    (c)    any local housing allowance determination made in accordance with paragraph (4A) shall take effect for the month in which notice is given in accordance with sub-paragraph (a), except that no such determination can have effect before 7th April 2008].

[(6)  Where a rent officer has made a local housing allowance determination in accordance with paragraph (2A)[, (4) or (4A)] he shall—

    (a)    make an approximate monthly allowance determination in relation to that local housing allowance determination; and

(b)    give notice of the approximate monthly allowance determination to each authority to which he is required to give notice of the local housing allowance determination when he gives notice of that determination.]

**[3188]**

**NOTES**

Inserted, together with arts 4C–4E, by the Rent Officers (Housing Benefit Functions) (Local Housing Allowance) Amendment Order 2003, SI 2003/2398, art 2(1), (5).

Para (1): revoked by the Rent Officers (Housing Benefit Functions) Amendment Order 2007, SI 2007/2871, arts 3, 6(1), (2), (4)(a), as from 7 April 2008, for savings see the note below.

Para (1A): inserted by SI 2007/2871, arts 3, 4(2)(b).

Para (2): revoked by SI 2007/2871, arts 3, 6(1), (2), (4)(a), as from 7 April 2008, for savings see the note below.

Para (2A): inserted by SI 2007/2871, arts 3, 4(2)(c).

Para (3): revoked by SI 2007/2871, arts 3, 6(1), (2), (4)(a), as from 7 April 2008, for savings see the note below.

Para (3A): inserted by SI 2007/2871, arts 3, 4(2)(d) (amended by the Rent Officers (Housing Benefit Functions) Amendment Order 2008, SI 2008/587, art 2(1), (2)); word omitted revoked by the Rent Officers (Housing Benefit Functions) Amendment (No 2) Order 2008, SI 2008/3156, art 2(1), (2).

Paras (4), (4A): substituted, for para (4), by SI 2007/2871, arts 3, 6(1), (2), (4)(b), as from 7 April 2008, for savings see the note below.

Para (5): in sub-para (a) words in square brackets substituted by SI 2007/2871, arts 3, 6(1), (2), (4)(c)(i), as from 7 April 2008, for savings see the note below; sub-paras (b), (c) substituted by 2007/2871, arts 3, 6(1), (2), (4)(c)(ii) (amended by SI 2008/587, art 2(1), (3)(a)).

Para (6): inserted by SI 2007/2871, arts 3, 4(2)(e); words in square brackets inserted by SI 2007/2871, arts 3, 5(2).

Modification: for the application of the amendments made by SI 2003/2398 to all local authorities in England and Wales, see the note "Modification" at the beginning of this order.

Savings: SI 2007/2871, art 6(1), (2) provides that the revocations of paras (1), (2), (3), substitution of paras (4), (4A) and amendment of para (5) by SI 2007/2871 shall not apply in certain circumstances noted in the "Savings" note to art 2 at **[3183]**.

## [4C    Board and attendance determinations and notifications

[(1)    Where a relevant authority makes an application to a rent officer in accordance with regulation 13D(10) of the Housing Benefit Regulations or, as the case may be, regulation 13D(10) of the Housing Benefit (State Pension Credit) Regulations, a rent officer shall determine whether or not a substantial part of the rent under the tenancy at the relevant time is fairly attributable to board and attendance.

(2)    Where a rent officer determines that a substantial part of the rent under the tenancy at the relevant time is fairly attributable to board and attendance, he shall—

(a)    notify the relevant authority accordingly; and

(b)    treat the application as if it had been made in accordance with regulation 14(1) of the Housing Benefit Regulations or, as the case may be regulation 14(1) of the Housing Benefit (State Pension Credit) Regulations.]

(3)    Where a rent officer determines that a substantial part of the rent under the tenancy at the relevant time is not fairly attributable to board and attendance, he shall notify the pathfinder authority accordingly.

[(4)    Where an application for a board and attendance determination is treated as if it had been made in accordance with regulation 14(1) of the Housing Benefit Regulations or, as the case may be, regulation 14(1) of the Housing Benefit (State Pension Credit) Regulations, then, for the purposes of paragraph (a)(ii) of the definition of "relevant period" in article 2(1), it shall be treated as having been received on the day on which the further information provided in accordance with regulation 114A(4) of the Housing Benefit Regulations or regulation 95A(4) of the Housing Benefit (State Pension Credit) Regulations is received.]]

**[3189]**

**NOTES**

Inserted as noted to art 4B at **[3188]**.

Modification: for the application of the amendments made by the Rent Officers (Housing Benefit Functions) (Local Housing Allowance) Amendment Order 2003, SI 2003/2398 to all local authorities in England and Wales, see the note "Modification" at the beginning of this order.

Paras (1), (2): substituted by the Rent Officers (Housing Benefit Functions) Amendment Order 2007, SI 2007/2871, arts 3, 6(1), (2), (5), save for certain purposes as provided by art 6(1), (2) thereof, as noted in the "Savings" note to art 2 at **[3183]**.

Para (4): substituted by SI 2007/2871, arts 3, 7(1),(2), save for certain purposes as provided by art 7(1) thereof, where information is provided to the rent officer by virtue of regs 14 or 114 of SI 2006/213, or, as the case may be, regs 14 or 95 of SI 2006/214, as in force immediately before 7 April 2008.

**[4D   Board and attendance redeterminations**

(1)   Subject to article 6, where a [local authority] applies to a rent officer for a redetermination of a board and attendance determination or board and attendance redetermination, the rent officer shall, in accordance with paragraph (2)—

    (a)   make a redetermination of—

        (i)   the board and attendance determination, provided it was made in accordance with article 4C and had effect at the date of the application for it to be redetermined; or

        (ii)   the board and attendance redetermination provided it was made in accordance with head (i), and had effect at the date of the application for it to be redetermined; and

    (b)   notify the [local authority] of the redetermination.

(2)   When making a board and attendance redetermination under this article, the rent officer shall seek, and have regard to, the advice of one or two other rent officers in relation to the redetermination.

(3)   A rent officer whose advice is sought in accordance with paragraph (2) shall give that advice.

(4)   Article 4C shall apply in relation to a board and attendance redetermination but as if the references to the relevant time were references to the date on which the original application for a board and attendance determination was made, or if earlier, to the date on which the tenancy ended.]

**[3190]**

**NOTES**

Inserted as noted to art 4B at **[3188]**.

Modification: for the application of the amendments made by the Rent Officers (Housing Benefit Functions) (Local Housing Allowance) Amendment Order 2003, SI 2003/2398 to all local authorities in England and Wales, see the note "Modification" at the beginning of this order.

Para (1): words in square brackets substituted by the Rent Officers (Housing Benefit Functions) Amendment Order 2007, SI 2007/2871, arts 3, 6(1), (2), (6), save for certain purposes as provided by art 6(1), (2) thereof, as noted in the "Savings" note to art 2 at **[3183]**.

**[4E   Substitute   board   and   attendance   determinations   and   substitute   board   and attendance redeterminations**

(1)   Where a [local authority] applies to a rent officer for a substitute board and attendance determination in accordance with [regulation 17 of the Housing Benefit Regulations or, as the case may be, regulation 17 of the Housing Benefit (State Pension Credit) Regulations], the provisions of this Order shall apply to that substitute board and attendance determination as they apply to a board and attendance determination but as if references to the relevant time were references to the date on which the original application for a board and attendance determination was made or, if earlier, the date on which the tenancy ended.

(2)   Where a [local authority] applies to a rent officer for a substitute board and attendance redetermination in accordance with [regulation 17 of the Housing Benefit Regulations or, as the case may be, regulation 17 of the Housing Benefit (State Pension Credit) Regulations], the provisions of this Order shall apply to that substitute board and attendance redetermination as they apply to a board and attendance redetermination.]

**[3191]**

**NOTES**

Inserted as noted to art 4B at **[3188]**.

Modification: for the application of the amendments made by the Rent Officers (Housing Benefit Functions) (Local Housing Allowance) Amendment Order 2003, SI 2003/2398 to all local authorities in England and Wales, see the note "Modification" at the beginning of this order.

Para (1): words in first pair of square brackets substituted by the Rent Officers (Housing Benefit Functions) Amendment Order 2007, SI 2007/2871, arts 3, 6(1), (2), (6), as from 7 April 2008, for savings see the note below; words in second pair of square brackets substituted by SI 2007/2871, arts 3, 10(4).

Para (2): words in first pair of square brackets substituted by SI 2007/2871, arts 3, 6(1), (2), (6), as from 7 April 2008, for savings see the note below; words in second pair of square brackets substituted by SI 2007/2871, arts 3, 10(4).

Savings: SI 2007/2871, art 6(1), (2) provides that the substitution of the word "local authority" for "pathfinder authority" made by SI 2007/2871 shall not apply in certain circumstances as noted in the "Savings" note to art 2 at **[3183]**.

**5   Insufficient information**

If a rent officer needs further information in order to make a determination under article 3(1)[, a redetermination under article 4, a board and attendance determination under article 4C or a board and attendance redetermination under article 4D] [where the information supplied under regulation 114A of the Housing Benefit Regulations or regulation 95A of the Housing Benefit (State Pension Credit) Regulations was incomplete or incorrect, he shall serve notice on the local authority requesting it to supply the further information required under regulation 114A or regulation 95A, as the case may be, or to confirm whether the information already supplied is correct and, if it is not, to supply the correct information] …

**[3192]**

**NOTES**
Words in first pair of square brackets substituted by the Rent Officers (Housing Benefit Functions) (Local Housing Allowance) Amendment Order 2003, SI 2003/2398, art 2(1), (6); words in second pair of square brackets substituted by the Rent Officers (Housing Benefit Functions) Amendment Order 2007, SI 2007/2871, arts 3, 7(1), (3), as from 7 April 2008, for savings see the note below; words omitted revoked by the Rent Officers (Housing Benefit Functions) (Amendment) Order 2000, SI 2000/1, arts 2, 6.
Modification: for the application of the amendments made by SI 2003/2398 to all local authorities in England and Wales, see the note "Modification" at the beginning of this order.
Savings: SI 2007/2871, art 7(1), (3) provides that the substitution made by SI 2007/2871 shall not apply where information is provided to the rent officer by virtue of the Housing Benefit Regulations 2006, SI 2006/213, regs 14 or 114, or, as the case may be, the Housing Benefit (Persons who have attained the qualifying age for state pension credit) Regulations 2006, SI 2006/214, regs 14 or 95, as in force immediately before 7 April 2008.

## 6 Exceptions

(1)    No determination[, redetermination, board and attendance determination or board and attendance redetermination] shall be made if the application for it is withdrawn.

(2)    No determination shall be made under paragraph 3, 4 or 5 of Part I of Schedule 1 if the tenancy is of residential accommodation, within the meaning of [regulation 9(4) of the Housing Benefit Regulations or, as the case may be, regulation 9(4) of the Housing Benefit (State Pension Credit) Regulations] (registered homes etc), or in a hostel.

(3)    No determination shall be made under paragraph 5 of Part I of Schedule 1 unless the local authority states in the application that the claimant is, or may be, a young individual (which has the same meaning as in [the Housing Benefit Regulations and the Housing Benefit (State Pension Credit) Regulations]).

(4)    If the rent officer becomes aware that an application is not one which gives rise to a duty to make a determination[, redetermination, board and attendance determination or a board and attendance redetermination], the rent officer shall give the local authority notice to that effect.

**[3193]**

**NOTES**
Paras (1), (4): words in square brackets substituted by the Rent Officers (Housing Benefit Functions) (Local Housing Allowance) Amendment Order 2003, SI 2003/2398, art 2(1), (7).
Paras (2), (3): words in square brackets substituted by the Rent Officers (Housing Benefit Functions) Amendment Order 2007, SI 2007/2871, arts 3, 10(5)(a), (b).
Modification: for the application of the amendments made by SI 2003/2398 to all local authorities in England and Wales, see the note "Modification" at the beginning of this order.

## 7 Special cases

(1)    This Order shall apply as specified in Schedule 4 in relation to—
    (a)    mooring charges payable for a houseboat;
    (b)    payments in respect of the site on which a caravan or mobile home stands; or
    (c)    payments under a rental purchase agreement.

(2)    Terms used in paragraph (1) have the same meaning in this article and in Schedule 4 as they have in [regulation 12(1) of the Housing Benefit Regulations or, as the case may be, regulation 12(1) of the Housing Benefit (State Pension Credit) Regulations] (rents).

(3), (4)    …

**[3194]**

**NOTES**
Para (2): words in square brackets substituted by the Rent Officers (Housing Benefit Functions) Amendment Order 2007, SI 2007/2871, arts 3, 10(6).
Paras (3), (4): revoked by the Rent Officers (Housing Benefit Functions) (Amendment) Order 2000, SI 2000/1, arts 2, 7.

## [7A    Errors

[(1)]    If a rent officer is of the opinion that he has made an error (other than in the application of his professional judgement) in relation to a determination or redetermination, he shall notify the local authority which made the application for that determination or redetermination of the error as soon as practicable after he becomes aware of it.

[(2)    If a rent officer is of the opinion that he has made an error (other than in the application of his professional judgement) in relation to a board and attendance determination or board and attendance redetermination, he shall notify the [local authority] which made the application for that board and attendance determination or board and attendance redetermination of the error as soon as practicable after he becomes aware of it.

(3)　...]

[(4)　If a rent officer is of the opinion that he has made an error (other than in the application of his professional judgement) in relation to a broad rental market area determination determined in accordance with article 4B(1A) or a local housing allowance determination determined in accordance with article 4B(2A), he shall notify any local authority to which notification of that determination was sent of the error, and the amended determination, as soon as practicable after he becomes aware of it.]]

**[3195]**

**NOTES**

Inserted by the Rent Officers (Housing Benefit Functions) (Amendment) Order 2000, SI 2000/1, arts 2, 8.

Para (1): numbered as such by the Rent Officers (Housing Benefit Functions) (Local Housing Allowance) Amendment Order 2003, SI 2003/2398, art 2(1), (8).

Para (2): added by SI 2003/2398, art 2(1), (8); words in square brackets substituted by the Rent Officers (Housing Benefit Functions) Amendment Order 2007, SI 2007/2871, arts 3, 6(1), (2), (7)(a), as from 7 April 2008, for savings see the note below.

Para (3): added by SI 2003/2398, art 2(1), (8); revoked by SI 2007/2871, arts 3, 6(1), (2), (7)(b), as from 7 April 2008, for savings see the note below.

Para (4): added by SI 2007/2871, arts 3, 4(3)(b).

Modification: for the application of the amendments made by SI 2003/2398 to all local authorities in England and Wales, see the note "Modification" at the beginning of this order.

Savings: SI 2007/2871, art 6(1), (2) provides that the amendments to paras (2), (3) by SI 2007/2871 shall not apply in certain circumstances as noted in the "Savings" note to art 2 at **[3183]**.

**8, 9**　*(Art 8 amends the Rent Officers (Additional Functions) Order 1995, SI 1995/1642; art 9 revokes that order, and the amending SI 1995/2365, SI 1995/3148, SI 1996/959 and SI 1997/1000.)*

**10　Application**

(1)　The amendment made by article 8 does not have effect in a case where an application for a determination is made before the date that article comes into force.

(2)　The remaining articles of the Order (other than paragraph (1)) do not have effect in a case where an application is made for a determination before the date those articles come into force.

**[3196]**

## SCHEDULES

## SCHEDULE 1

Article 3(1)

## PART I
## DETERMINATIONS

Article 3(1)(a)

*Significantly high rents*

1.—(1)　The rent officer shall determine whether, in his opinion, the rent payable under the tenancy of the dwelling at the relevant time is significantly higher than the rent which the landlord might reasonably have been expected to obtain under the tenancy at that time.

(2)　If the rent officer determines under sub-paragraph (1) that the rent is significantly higher, the rent officer shall also determine the rent which the landlord might reasonably have been expected to obtain under the tenancy at the relevant time.

(3)　When making a determination under this paragraph, the rent officer shall have regard to the level of rent under similar tenancies of similar dwellings in the [vicinity] (or as similar as regards tenancy, dwelling and [vicinity] as is reasonably practicable) and shall assume that no one who would have been entitled to housing benefit had sought or is seeking the tenancy.

[(4)　For the purposes of this paragraph and paragraph 2 "vicinity" means—
　(a)　the area immediately surrounding the dwelling; or
　(b)　where, for the purposes of sub-paragraph (2)(c) of paragraph 2, there is no dwelling in the area immediately surrounding the dwelling which satisfies the description in heads (i), (ii) and (iii) of that sub-paragraph, the area nearest to the dwelling where there is such a dwelling.]

*Size and rent*

2.—(1)   The rent officer shall determine whether the dwelling, at the relevant time, exceeds the size criteria for the occupiers.

(2)   If the rent officer determines that the dwelling exceeds the size criteria, the rent officer shall also determine the rent which a landlord might reasonably have been expected to obtain, at the relevant time, for a tenancy which is—

- (a)   similar to the tenancy of the dwelling;
- (b)   on the same terms other than the term relating to the amount of rent; and
- (c)   of a dwelling which is in the same [vicinity] as the dwelling, but which—
  - (i)   accords with the size criteria for the occupiers;
  - (ii)   is in a reasonable state of repair; and
  - (iii)   corresponds in other respects, in the rent officer's opinion, as closely as is reasonably practicable to the dwelling.

(3)   When making a determination under sub-paragraph (2), the rent officer shall have regard to the same matter and make the same assumption as specified in paragraph 1(3), except that in judging the similarity of other tenancies and dwellings the comparison shall be with the tenancy of the second dwelling referred to in sub-paragraph (2) and shall assume that no one who would have been entitled to housing benefit had sought or is seeking that tenancy.

*Exceptionally high rents*

3.—(1)   The rent officer shall determine whether, in his opinion, the rent payable for the tenancy of the dwelling at the relevant time is exceptionally high.

(2)   In sub-paragraph (1) "rent payable for the tenancy" means—

- (a)   where a determination is made under sub-paragraph (2) of paragraph 2, the rent determined under that sub-paragraph;
- (b)   where no determination is so made and a determination is made under sub-paragraph (2) of paragraph 1, the rent determined under that sub-paragraph; and
- (c)   in any other case, the rent payable under the tenancy [at the relevant time].

(3)   If the rent officer determines under sub-paragraph (1) that the rent is exceptionally high, the rent officer shall also determine the highest rent, which is not an exceptionally high rent and which a landlord might reasonably have been expected to obtain at the relevant time (on the assumption that no one who would have been entitled to housing benefit had sought or is seeking the tenancy) for an assured tenancy of a dwelling which—

- (a)   is in the same [neighbourhood] as the dwelling;
- (b)   has the same number of bedrooms and rooms suitable for living in as the dwelling (or, where the dwelling exceeds the size criteria for the occupiers, accords with the size criteria); and
- (c)   is in a reasonable state of repair.

(4)   For the purpose of determining whether a rent is an exceptionally high rent under this paragraph, the rent officer shall have regard to the levels of rent under assured tenancies of dwellings which—

- (a)   are in the same [neighbourhood] as the dwelling (or in as similar a locality as is reasonably practicable); and
- (b)   have the same number of bedrooms and rooms suitable for living in as the dwelling (or, in a case where the dwelling exceeds the size criteria for the occupiers, accord with the size criteria).

[(5)   For the purposes of this paragraph and paragraph 4(6) "neighbourhood" means—

- (a)   where the dwelling is in a town or city, the part of that town or city where the dwelling is located which is a distinct area of residential accommodation; or
- (b)   where the dwelling is not in a town or city, the area surrounding the dwelling which is a distinct area of residential accommodation and where there are dwellings satisfying the description in sub-paragraph (4)(b).]

*Local reference rents*

4.—(1)   The rent officer shall make a determination of a local reference rent in accordance with the formula—

$$R = \frac{H+L}{2}$$

where—

   R is the local reference rent;
   H is the highest rent, in the rent officer's opinion,—
- (a)   which a landlord might reasonably have been expected to obtain, at the relevant time, for an assured tenancy of a dwelling which meets the criteria in sub-paragraph (2); and

      (b)    which is not an exceptionally high rent; and

L is the lowest rent, in the rent officer's opinion,—

      (a)    which a landlord might reasonably have been expected to obtain, at the relevant time, for an assured tenancy of a dwelling which meets the criteria in sub-paragraph (2); and

      (b)    which is not an exceptionally low rent.

  (2)    The criteria are—

    (a)    that the dwelling under the assured tenancy—

        (i)    is in the same [broad rental market area (local reference rent)] as the dwelling;

       (ii)    is in a reasonable state of repair; and

      (iii)    has the same number of bedrooms and rooms suitable for living in as the dwelling (or, in a case where the dwelling exceeds the size criteria for the occupiers, accords with the size criteria); and

    (b)    if the tenant does not have the use under the tenancy of the dwelling [at the relevant time] of more than one bedroom or room suitable for living in—

        (i)    that under the assured tenancy the tenant does not have the use of more than one bedroom or room suitable for living in;

       (ii)    if the rent under the tenancy [at the relevant time] includes payments for board and attendance and the rent officer considers the amount fairly attributable to board and attendance is a substantial part of the rent, that a substantial part of the rent under the assured tenancy is fairly attributable to board and attendance;

      (iii)    if sub-paragraph (ii) does not apply and the tenant shares a [kitchen, toilet, bathroom and room suitable for living in] with a person other than a member of his household, a non-dependant or a person who pays rent to the tenant, that the assured tenancy provides for the tenant to share a [kitchen, toilet, bathroom and room suitable for living in]; and

      (iv)    if sub-paragraphs (ii) and (iii) do not apply, that the circumstances described in sub-paragraphs (ii) and (iii) do not apply in relation to the assured tenancy.

  (3)    Where ascertaining H and L under sub-paragraph (1), the rent officer:

    (a)    shall assume that no one who would have been entitled to housing benefit had sought or is seeking the tenancy; and

    (b)    shall exclude the amount of any rent which, in the rent officer's opinion, is fairly attributable to the provision of services which are ineligible to be met by housing benefit[; ...

    (c)    ... ].

  (4)    In sub-paragraph (2)(b)—

"bedroom or room suitable for living in" does not include a room which the tenant shares with any person other than—

    (a)    a member of his household;

    (b)    a non-dependant (as defined in this sub-paragraph); or

    (c)    a person who pays rent to the tenant; and

["non-dependant" means a non-dependant of the tenant within the meaning of regulation 3 of the Housing Benefit Regulations or, as the case may be, regulation 3 of the Housing Benefit (State Pension Credit) Regulations].

  (5)    In sub-paragraph (3), "services" means services performed or facilities (including the use of furniture) provided for, or rights made available to, the tenant, but not[, in the case of a tenancy where a substantial part of the rent under the tenancy is fairly attributable to board and attendance, the provision of meals (including the preparation of meals or provision of unprepared food)].

  [(6)    For the purposes of this paragraph and paragraph 5 "broad rental market area (local reference rent)" means the area within which a tenant of the dwelling could reasonably be expected to live having regard to facilities and services for the purposes of health, education, recreation, personal banking and shopping, taking account of the distance of travel, by public and private transport, to and from those facilities and services.

  (7)    A broad rental market area (local reference rent) must contain—

    (a)    residential premises of a variety of types, including such premises held on a variety of tenures; and

    (b)    sufficient privately rented residential premises, to ensure that, in the rent officer's opinion, the local reference rents for tenancies in the area are representative of the rents that a landlord might reasonably be expected to obtain in that area.]

*Single room rents*

5.—(1)    The rent officer shall determine a single room rent in accordance with the following formula—

$$S = \frac{H+L}{2}$$

where—
S is the single room rent;
H is the highest rent, in the rent officer's opinion,—
    (a)    which a landlord might reasonably have been expected to obtain, at the relevant time, for an assured tenancy of a dwelling which meets the criteria in sub-paragraph (2); and
    (b)    which is not an exceptionally high rent; and
L is the lowest rent, in the rent officer's opinion,—
    (a)    which a landlord might reasonably have been expected to obtain, at the relevant time, for an assured tenancy of a dwelling which meets the criteria in sub-paragraph (2); and
    (b)    which is not an exceptionally low rent.

(2)    The criteria are—
    (a)    that the dwelling under the assured tenancy is in the same [broad rental market area (local reference rent)] as the dwelling and is in a reasonable state of repair;
    (b)    that, under the assured tenancy, the tenant—
        (i)    has the exclusive use of one bedroom;
        (ii)    does not have the use of any other bedroom ...;
        [(iia)  shares the use of a room suitable for living in;]
        (iii)  shares the use of a toilet [and bathroom]; and
        (iv)  shares the use of a kitchen and does not have the exclusive use of facilities for cooking food; and
    (c)    that the rent does not include any payment for board and attendance.

(3)    Sub-paragraphs [(3) and (5)] of paragraph 4 apply when ascertaining H and L under [this paragraph] as if the reference in those sub-paragraphs to H and L were to H and L under this paragraph.

*[Claim-related rent*

6.—[(1)    In this paragraph, and in paragraph 9, "claim-related rent" means the claim-related rent determined by the rent officer in accordance with paragraph (2A).]

(2)    ...

[(2A)    The rent officer shall determine that the claim-related rent is—
    (a)    where he makes a determination under sub-paragraph (2) of paragraph 1, sub-paragraph (2) of paragraph 2 and sub-paragraph (3) of paragraph 3, the lowest of the three rents determined under those sub-paragraphs;
    (b)    where he makes a determination under only two of the sub-paragraphs referred to in paragraph (a), the lower of the two rents determined under those sub-paragraphs;
    (c)    where he makes a determination under only one of the sub-paragraphs referred to in paragraph (a), the rent determined under that sub-paragraph;
    (d)    where he does not make a determination under any of the sub-paragraphs referred to in sub-paragraph (a), the rent payable under the tenancy of the dwelling at the relevant time.]

(3)    ... the rent officer shall also determine the total amount of ineligible charges, as defined in paragraph 7, which he has not included in the claim-related rent because of the assumptions made in accordance with that paragraph.]

**[3197]**

---

**NOTES**

Para 1: word "vicinity" in square brackets in each place it occurs substituted, and sub-para (4) added, by the Rent Officers (Housing Benefit Functions) (Amendment) Order 2001, SI 2001/3561, art 2(1), (2).

Para 2: word in square brackets substituted by SI 2001/3561, art 2(1), (3).

Para 3: words in square brackets in sub-para (2) added by the Rent Officers (Housing Benefit Functions) (Amendment) Order 2000, SI 2000/1, arts 2, 9; words in square brackets in sub-paras (3), (4) substituted and sub-para (5) added by SI 2001/3561, art 2(1), (4).

Para 4: words in square brackets in sub-para (2)(a) substituted by the Rent Officers (Housing Benefit Functions) Amendment (No 2) Order 2008, SI 2008/3156, art 2(1), (3)(a)(i); words in square brackets in sub-para (2)(b) and sub-para (2)(b)(ii) inserted and words in square brackets in sub-para (5) substituted by SI 2000/1, arts 2, 10(a), (c); words in square brackets in sub-para (2)(b)(iii) substituted by the Rent Officers (Housing Benefit Functions) (Amendment) (No 2) Order 2001, SI 2001/2317, art 2(1), (3); sub-para (3)(c) and the word (omitted) immediately preceding it inserted by SI 2000/1, arts 2, 10(b), and revoked by the Rent Officers (Housing Benefit Functions) Amendment Order 2003, SI 2003/478, art 2(1), (2); in sub-para (4), definition "non-dependant" substituted by the Rent Officers (Housing Benefit Functions) Amendment Order 2007, SI 2007/2871, arts 3, 10(7)(a); sub-paras (6), (7) substituted for para (6) (as added by SI 2001/3561, art 2(1), (5)) by SI 2008/3156, art 2(1), (3)(a)(ii).

Para 5: words in square brackets in sub-para (2)(a) substituted by SI 2008/3156, art 2(1), (3)(b); words omitted from sub-para (2)(b)(ii) revoked, sub-para (2)(b)(iia) inserted and words in square brackets in sub-para (2)(b)(iii) inserted by SI 2001/1325, arts 2, 4; words in square brackets in sub-para (3) substituted by the Rent Officers (Housing Benefit Functions) (Local Housing Allowance) Amendment Order 2005, SI 2005/236, art 3.

Para 6: substituted by SI 2000/1, arts 2, 11; sub-para (1) substituted, sub-para (2) revoked, sub-para (2A) inserted, and words in sub-para (3) omitted, by SI 2007/2871, arts 3, 9(1), (2), as from 7 April 2008, for savings see the note below.

Savings: SI 2007/2871, art 9(1) provides that the amendments to para 6 by SI 2007/2871 do not apply where the rent officer has made a determination under para 1, 2, 3, 4 or 5 above and that determination was made in relation to:

(a)  an application under:

    (i)  the Housing Benefit Regulations 2006, SI 2006/213, reg 14, as in force before the substitution of reg 14 by virtue of the Housing Benefit (Local Housing Allowance and Information Sharing) Amendment Regulations 2007, SI 2007/2868, reg 8; or

    (ii)  the Housing Benefit (Persons who have attained the qualifying age for state pension credit) Regulations 2006, SI 2006/214, reg 14, as in force before the substitution of reg 14 by virtue of the Housing Benefit (State Pension Credit) (Local Housing Allowance and Information Sharing) Amendment Regulations 2007, SI 2007/2869, reg 8; or

(b)  an application for a redetermination, substitute determination or substitute redetermination relating to a determination to which sub-paragraph (a) applies made under regs 15, 16 or 17 of the Regulations referred to in sub-paragraph (a)(i) or (ii).

---

## PART II
## ASSUMPTIONS ETC

Article 3(1)(b)

*[Ineligible charges and support charges*

7.—[(1)  "ineligible charges" means service charges which are ineligible to be met by housing benefit by virtue of regulation 12B(2) (rent) of and Schedule 1 (ineligible service charges) to the Housing Benefit Regulations or, as the case may be, regulation 12B(2) of and Schedule 1 to the Housing Benefit (State Pension Credit) Regulations except in the case of a tenancy where the rent includes payments for board and attendance, and the rent officer considers that a substantial part of the rent under the tenancy is fairly attributable to board and attendance, charges specified in paragraph 1(a)(i) of Schedule 1 to the Housing Benefit Regulations or, as the case may be, in paragraph 1(a)(i) of Schedule 1 to the Housing Benefit (State Pension Credit) Regulations (charges for meals).]

(2)  When making a determination under paragraph 1, 2 or 3 of this Schedule, the rent officer shall assume that-

    (a)  the items to which the ineligible charges relate; …

    (b)  …

were not to be provided or made available.

[(3)  For the purposes of paragraphs 1, 2, 3, and 6 of Part 1 of this Schedule, the rent officer shall assume that the rent payable under the tenancy at the relevant time is—

    (a)  where an amount is notified to the rent officer under regulation 114A(4)(b) of the Housing Benefit Regulations or, as the case may be, regulations 95A(4)(b) of the Housing Benefit (State Pension Credit) Regulations in respect of that tenancy, that notified amount less the total of any ineligible charges included in that amount; or

    (b)  in any other case, the total amount stated under regulation 114A(3)(d) of the Housing Benefit Regulations or, as the case may be regulation 95A(3)(d) of the Housing Benefit (State Pension Credit) Regulations less the total of any ineligible charges included in that stated amount.]

(4)  The total of any ineligible charges, referred to in sub-paragraph (3), shall be the total of the amounts (excluding any amount which he considers is negligible) of any charges included in the notified amount or the stated amount, as the case may be, which, in the rent officer's opinion, are at the relevant time fairly attributable to any items to which ineligible charges relate.]

*Housing associations etc*

8.—(1)  In a case where the local authority states in the application that the landlord is a housing association or a charity, the rent officer shall assume that the landlord is not such a body.

(2)  The rent officer shall not take into account the rent under any tenancy where the landlord is a housing association or where the landlord is a charity and the dwelling is provided by the landlord in the pursuit of its charitable purposes.

(3)  In this paragraph—

    "charity" has the same meaning as in the Charities Act 1993, except that it includes a Scottish charity (which has the same meaning as in section 1(7) of the Law Reform (Miscellaneous Provisions) (Scotland) Act 1990); and

    "housing association" has the same meaning as in the Housing Associations Act 1985.

**[3198]**

**NOTES**

Para 7: substituted by the Rent Officers (Housing Benefit Functions) (Amendment) Order 2000, SI 2000/1, arts 2, 12.

Para 7(1): substituted by the Rent Officers (Housing Benefit Functions) Amendment Order 2007, SI 2007/2871, arts 3, 8, save for certain purposes as provided by art 8(1) thereof, where the rent officer is required to make a determination under para 1, 2, 3, or 6 of Pt 1 of this Schedule by virtue of:

(a) an application made under:

    (i) the Housing Benefit Regulations 2006, SI 2006/213, reg 14, as in force before the substitution of reg 14 by virtue of the Housing Benefit (Local Housing Allowance and Information Sharing) Amendment Regulations 2007, SI 2007/2868, reg 8; or

    (ii) the Housing Benefit (Persons who have attained the qualifying age for state pension credit) Regulations 2006, SI 2006/214, reg 14, as in force before the substitution of reg 14 by virtue of the Housing Benefit (State Pension Credit) (Local Housing Allowance and Information Sharing) Amendment Regulations 2007, SI 2007/2869, reg 8; or

(b) an application for a redetermination, substitute determination or substitute redetermination relating to a determination to which sub-paragraph (a) applies made under regs 15, 16 or 17 of the Regulations referred to in sub-paragraph (a)(i) or (ii).

Para 7(2)(b): revoked, together with word "and" immediately preceding it, by the Rent Officers (Housing Benefit Functions) Amendment Order 2003, SI 2003/478, art 2(1), (3).

Para 7(3): substituted by SI 2007/2871, arts 3, 7(1), (4), save for certain purposes as provided by art 7(1) thereof, where information is provided to the rent officer by virtue of regs 14 or 114 of SI 2006/213, or, as the case may be, regs 14 or 95 of SI 2006/214, as in force immediately before 7 April 2008.

## PART III
### NOTIFICATIONS OF PART I DETERMINATIONS
Article 3(1)(c)

*Notifications*

9.—[(1) Subject to sub-paragraph (2), the rent officer shall give notice to the local authority of—

(a) the claim-related rent determined under Part I;

(b) where the dwelling is not in a hostel, the total amount of ineligible charges determined under paragraph 6(3) in relation to that claim-related rent;

[(c) where that claim-related rent includes an amount which would be ineligible for housing benefit under paragraph 1(a)(i) of Schedule 1 to the Housing Benefit Regulations or, as the case may be, paragraph 1(a)(i) of Schedule 1 to the Housing Benefit (State Pension Credit) Regulations (charges for meals), the inclusion of an ineligible amount in respect of meals;]

(d) any rent determined by the rent officer under paragraph 4 (local reference rents); and

[(da) where any rent determined under paragraph 4 includes an amount which would be ineligible for housing benefit under the provisions referred to in sub-paragraph (c), the inclusion of an ineligible amount in respect of meals; and]

(e) any rent determined by the rent officer under paragraph 5 (single room rents).]

(2) If the rent officer determines a rent under—

(a) paragraph 4 (local reference rents); or

(b) paragraph 5 (single room rents);

which is equal to or more than the [claim-related rent], the rent officer shall give notice to the local authority of this in place of giving notice of the determination made under paragraph 4 or, as the case may be, paragraph 5 …

(3) …

10. …

[3199]

**NOTES**

Para 9: sub-para (1) substituted, in sub-para (2) words in square brackets substituted and words omitted revoked, and sub-para (3) revoked by the Rent Officers (Housing Benefit Functions) (Amendment) Order 2000, SI 2000/1, arts 2, 13(1); sub-para (1)(c) substituted, and sub-para (1)(da) inserted, by the Rent Officers (Housing Benefit Functions) Amendment Order 2007, SI 2007/2871, arts 3, 9(1), (3)(a), (b), as from 7 April 2008, for savings see the note below.

Para 10: revoked by SI 2000/1, arts 2, 13(2).

Savings: SI 2007/2871, art 9(1) provides that the amendments to para 9 by SI 2007/2871 do not apply in the circumstances noted in the "Savings" note to Pt I of this Schedule at **[3197]**.

## PART IV
### INDICATIVE RENT LEVELS
Article 3(2)(a)

11.—(1) The rent officer shall determine the indicative rent level for each category described in sub-paragraph (3) in accordance with the following formula—

$$I = \frac{H + 3L}{4}$$

where—

I is the indicative rent level;

H is the highest rent, in the rent officer's opinion,—
- (a) which a landlord might reasonably be expected to obtain at the time the determination is being made for an assured tenancy of a dwelling meeting the criteria in sub-paragraph (2); and
- (b) which is not an exceptionally high rent; and

L is the lowest rent, in the rent officer's opinion,—
- (a) which a landlord might reasonably be expected to obtain at the time the determination is being made for an assured tenancy of a dwelling meeting the criteria in sub-paragraph (2); and
- (b) which is not an exceptionally low rent.

(2) The criteria are that—
- (a) the dwelling is in the area of the local authority;
- (b) the dwelling is in a reasonable state of repair; and
- (c) the dwelling and tenancy accord with the category to which the determination relates.

(3) The categories for the purposes of this paragraph are—
- (a) a dwelling where the tenant does not have use of more than one room where a substantial part of the rent under the tenancy is fairly attributable to board and attendance;
- (b) a dwelling where the tenant does not have use of more than one room, the tenancy provides for him to share a kitchen or toilet and paragraph (a) does not apply;
- (c) a dwelling where the tenant does not have use of more than one room and where paragraphs (a) and (b) do not apply;
- (d) a dwelling where the tenant does not have use of more than two rooms and where none of paragraphs (a) to (c) applies;
- (e) a dwelling where the tenant does not have use of more than three rooms and where none of paragraphs (a) to (d) applies;
- (f) a dwelling where the tenant does not have use of more than four rooms and where none of paragraphs (a) to (e) applies;
- (g) a dwelling where the tenant does not have use of more than five rooms and where none of paragraphs (a) to (f) applies; and
- (h) a dwelling where the tenant does not have use of more than six rooms and where none of paragraphs (a) to (g) applies.

(4) When ascertaining H and L under sub-paragraph (1), the rent officer:
- (a) shall assume that no one who would have been entitled to housing benefit had sought or is seeking the tenancy; and
- (b) shall exclude the amount of any rent which, in the rent officer's opinion, is fairly attributable to the provision of services which are ineligible to be met by housing benefit[ …
- (c) … ].

(5) In this paragraph—

"room" means a bedroom or room suitable for living in and in paragraphs (a), (b) and (c) of sub-paragraph (3) does not include a room which the tenant shares with any person other than—
- (a) a member of his household;
- (b) a non-dependant of the tenant (within the meaning of [regulation 3 of the Housing Benefit Regulations or, as the case may be, regulation 3 of the Housing Benefit (State Pension Credit) Regulations]); or
- (c) a person who pays rent to the tenant; and

"services" has the meaning given by paragraph 4(5).

**[3200]**

---

**NOTES**

Para 11: sub-para (4)(c) and word "and" immediately preceding it added by the Rent Officers (Housing Benefit Functions) (Amendment) Order 2000, SI 2000/1, arts 2, 14 and revoked by the Rent Officers (Housing Benefit Functions) Amendment Order 2003, SI 2003/478, art 2(1), (4); words in square brackets in sub-para (5)(b) substituted by the Rent Officers (Housing Benefit Functions) Amendment Order 2007, SI 2007/2871, arts 3, 10(7)(b).

PART II
STATUTORY INSTRUMENTS

## SCHEDULE 2
## SIZE CRITERIA

Article 2

1. One bedroom or room suitable for living in shall be allowed for each of the following categories of occupier (and each occupier shall come within only the first category for which he is eligible)—

    (a)    [a couple] (within the meaning of Part VII of the Social Security Contributions and Benefits Act 1992);

    (b)    a person who is not a child;

    (c)    two children of the same sex;

    (d)    two children who are less than ten years old;

    (e)    a child.

2. The number of rooms (excluding any allowed under paragraph 1) suitable for living in allowed are—

    (a)    if there are less than four occupiers, one;

    (b)    if there are more than three and less than seven occupiers, two; and

    (c)    in any other case, three.

**[3201]**

**NOTES**

Para 1: words in square brackets substituted by the Civil Partnership (Pensions, Social Security and Child Support) (Consequential, etc Provisions) Order 2005, SI 2005/2877, art 2(3), Sch 3, para 29.

## SCHEDULE 3
## REDETERMINATIONS

Article 4

[1. Schedules 1 and 2 shall apply in relation to a redetermination as they apply to a determination, but as if references in those Schedules to the relevant time were references to the date the application for the original determination was made or, if earlier, the date the tenancy ended.]

2. The rent officer making the redetermination shall seek and have regard to the advice of one or two other rent officers in relation to the redetermination.

**[3202]**

**NOTES**

Para 1: substituted by the Rent Officers (Housing Benefit Functions) (Amendment) Order 2000, SI 2000/1, arts 2, 15.

*(Sch 3A inserted by the Rent Officers (Housing Benefit Functions) (Local Housing Allowance) Amendment Order 2003, SI 2003/2398, art 2(1), (10), Sch 2; revoked by the Rent Officers (Housing Benefit Functions) Amendment Order 2007, SI 2007/2871, arts 3, 6(1), (2), (8), as from 7 April 2008, subject to savings for certain purposes as provided by art 6(1), (2) thereof (see the "Savings" note to art 2 at [3183]).)*

## [SCHEDULE 3B
## BROAD MARKET RENTAL AREA DETERMINATIONS AND LOCAL HOUSING ALLOWANCE DETERMINATIONS

Article 4B

*Categories of dwelling*

1.—(1) The categories of dwelling for which a rent officer is required to determine a local housing allowance in accordance with article 4B(2A)(a)(i) are—

    (a)    a dwelling where the tenant has the exclusive use of only one bedroom and where the tenancy provides for him to share the use of one or more of—

        (i)    a kitchen;

        (ii)    a bathroom;

        (iii)    a toilet; or

        (iv)    a room suitable for living in;

    (b)    a dwelling where the tenant (together with his partner where he has one) has the exclusive use of only one bedroom and exclusive use of a kitchen, a bathroom, a toilet and a room suitable for living in;

    (c)    a dwelling where the tenant has the use of only two bedrooms;

    (d)    a dwelling where the tenant has the use of only three bedrooms;

    (e)    a dwelling where the tenant has the use of only four bedrooms;

    (f)    a dwelling where the tenant has the use of only five bedrooms.

(2) In—

(a)  sub-paragraph (1)(b) "partner" has the same meaning as in regulation 2 of the Housing Benefit Regulations or, as the case may be, regulation 2 of the Housing Benefit (State Pension Credit) Regulations;

(b)  sub-paragraph (1)(c) to (f) "bedroom" means a bedroom, except for a bedroom which the tenant shares with any person other than—

    (i)  a member of his household;

    (ii)  a non-dependant of the tenant (within the meaning of regulation 3 of the Housing Benefit Regulations or, as the case may be, regulation 3 of the Housing Benefit (State Pension Credit) Regulations); or

    (iii)  a person who pays rent to the tenant.

*Local housing allowance for category of dwelling in paragraph 1*

2.—(1)  Subject to paragraph 3 (anomalous local housing allowances), the rent officer must determine a local housing allowance for each category of dwelling in paragraph 1 in accordance with the following sub-paragraphs.

(2)  The rent officer must compile a list of rents.

(3)  A list of rents means a list in ascending order of the rents which, in the rent officer's opinion, are payable at the date of the determination for a dwelling let under an assured tenancy which meets the criteria specified in sub-paragraph (5).

(4)  The list must include any rents which are of the same amount.

(5)  The criteria for including an assured tenancy on the list of rents in relation to each category of dwelling specified in paragraph 1 are—

(a)  that the dwelling let under the assured tenancy is in the broad rental market area for which the local housing allowance for that category of dwelling is being determined;

(b)  that the dwelling is in a reasonable state of repair; and

(c)  that the assured tenancy permits the tenant to use exclusively or share the use of, as the case may be, the same number and type of rooms as the category of dwelling in relation to which the list of rents is being compiled.

[(5A)  Where the rent officer is not satisfied that the list of rents in respect of any category of dwelling would contain sufficient rents, payable at the date of the determination for dwellings in the broad rental market area, to enable a local housing allowance to be determined which is representative of the rents that a landlord might reasonably be expected to obtain in that area, the rent officer may add to the list rents for dwellings in the same category in other areas in which a comparable market exists.]

(6)  Where rent is payable other than weekly the rent officer must use the figure which would be payable if the rent were to be payable weekly by—

(a)  multiplying the rent by an appropriate figure to obtain the rent for a year;

(b)  dividing the total in (a) by 365; and

(c)  multiplying the total in (b) by 7.

(7)  When compiling the list of rents for each category of dwelling, the rent officer must—

(a)  assume that no one who would have been entitled to housing benefit had sought or is seeking the tenancy; and

(b)  exclude the amount of any rent which, in the rent officer's opinion, is fairly attributable to the provision of services performed for, or facilities (including the use of furniture) provided for, or rights made available to, the tenant which are ineligible to be met by housing benefit.

(8)  ...

(9)  The local housing allowance for each category of dwelling specified in paragraph 1 is the amount of the median rent in the list of rents for that category of dwelling.

(10)  The median rent is determined as follows—

(a)  where there is an even number of rents on the list, the formula is—

$$\frac{\text{the amount of the rent at P + the amount of the rent at P1}}{2} = \text{the local housing allowance}$$

where P is the position on the list defined by dividing the number of rents on the list by 2 and P1 is the following position on the list.

(b)  where there is an odd number of rents on the list, the formula is—

$$\frac{\text{the number of rents on the list} + 1}{2} = L$$

where L is the position on the list in which the rent used to identify the local housing allowance lies.

(11) Where the median rent is not a whole number of pence, the rent must be rounded to the nearest whole penny by disregarding any amount less than half a penny and treating any amount of half a penny or more as a whole penny.

### Anomalous local housing allowances

3.—(1) Where—

   (a)   the rent officer has determined the local housing allowance for each of the categories of dwelling in paragraph 1(1) in accordance with the preceding paragraphs of this Schedule; and

   (b)   the local housing allowance for a category of dwelling in paragraph 1(1)(b) to (f) is lower than the local housing allowance for any of the categories of dwelling which precede it,

that local housing allowance shall be the same as the highest local housing allowance which precedes it.

(2) Where—

   (a)   the rent officer has determined a local housing allowance following an application made under article 4B(4); and

   (b)   that local housing allowance is lower than the local housing allowance for the category of dwelling in paragraph 1(1)(f),

that local housing allowance shall be the same as the local housing allowance for the category of dwelling in paragraph 1(1)(f).

### Broad rental market area

[4.   In this Schedule "broad rental market area" means an area within which a person could reasonably be expected to live having regard to facilities and services for the purposes of health, education, recreation, personal banking and shopping, taking account of the distance of travel, by public and private transport, to and from those facilities and services.

5.   A broad rental market area must contain—

   (a)   residential premises of a variety of types, including such premises held on a variety of tenures; and

   (b)   sufficient privately rented residential premises to ensure that, in the rent officer's opinion, the local housing allowance for the categories of dwelling in the area for which the rent officer is required to determine a local housing allowance is representative of the rents that a landlord might reasonably be expected to obtain in that area.]

**[3203]**

**NOTES**

Inserted by the Rent Officers (Housing Benefit Functions) Amendment Order 2007, SI 2007/2871, arts 3, 4(4).

Para 2: sub-para (5A) inserted by the Rent Officers (Housing Benefit Functions) Amendment Order 2009, SI 2009/2459, art 2; sub-para (8) revoked by the Rent Officers (Housing Benefit Functions) Amendment (No 2) Order 2008, SI 2008/3156, art 2(1), (4)(a).

Paras 4, 5: substituted for para 4 by SI 2008/3156, art 2(1), (4)(b).

### SCHEDULE 4
### SPECIAL CASES

Article 7

### Houseboats

1.   Where an application for a determination or a redetermination relates in whole or in part to mooring charges for a houseboat, this Order applies in relation to that application (or, as the case may be, to that part which relates to those charges) with the following modifications—

   (a)   references to a tenancy, a tenancy of a dwelling or an assured tenancy are references to an agreement under which those charges are payable (and references to a landlord and a tenant shall be construed accordingly); and

   (b)   no determination shall be made under paragraph 2 of Part I of Schedule 1 (size criteria) and references to the dwelling exceeding the size criteria shall not apply.

### Mobile homes

2.   Where an application for a determination or redetermination relates in whole or in part to payments in respect of the site on which a caravan or a mobile home stands, this Order applies in relation to that application (or, as the case may be, that part which relates to those payments) with the following modifications—

   (a)   references to a tenancy, a tenancy of a dwelling or an assured tenancy are references to an agreement under which those payments are payable (and references to a landlord and a tenant shall be construed accordingly); and

(b)     no determination shall be made under paragraph 2 of Part I of Schedule 1 (size criteria) and references to the dwelling exceeding the size criteria shall not apply.

*Rental purchase agreements*

3.     Where an application for a determination or a redetermination relates to a rental purchase agreement, the agreement is to be treated as if it were a tenancy.

**[3204]**

# LONG RESIDENTIAL TENANCIES (SUPPLEMENTAL FORMS) REGULATIONS 1997

## (SI 1997/3005)

**NOTES**

Made: 16 December 1997.
Authority: Landlord and Tenant Act 1954, ss 18, 66, Sch 5, para 5, as applied by the Local Government and Housing Act 1989, s 186(5), Sch 10, para 19.
Commencement: 15 January 1998.

### 1   Citation and commencement

These Regulations may be cited as the Long Residential Tenancies (Supplemental Forms) Regulations and shall come into force on 15th January 1998.

**[3205]**

### 2   Interpretation

In these Regulations—
    "the 1954 Act" means the Landlord and Tenant Act 1954;
    "the 1989 Act" means the Local Government and Housing Act 1989; and

any reference to a numbered form is a reference to the form bearing that number in the Schedule, or to a form substantially to the same effect.

**[3206]**

### 3   Forms

The forms prescribed for the purposes specified below shall be as follows—
    (a)     for a notice under section 18 of the 1954 Act (as applied by section 186(5) of the 1989 Act) requiring information about sub-tenancies, form 7;
    (b)     for a notice under paragraph 5 of Schedule 5 to the 1954 Act (as applied by paragraph 19 of Schedule 10 to the 1989 Act) requiring a landlord to consent to the giving of a notice under paragraph 4(1) of Schedule 10 to the 1989 Act terminating a long residential tenancy, form 8; and
    (c)     for a notice under paragraph 5 of Schedule 5 to the 1954 Act (as applied by paragraph 19 of Schedule 10 to the 1989 Act) requiring a landlord to consent to the making of an agreement with the tenant under Schedule 10 to the 1989 Act, form 9.

**[3207]**

**NOTES**

1954 Act: the Landlord and Tenant Act 1954.
1989 Act: the Local Government and Housing Act 1989.

### SCHEDULE

**NOTES**

    This Schedule contains forms which are not reproduced in this work, but their titles are noted below. The forms can be found at www.opsi.gov.uk.

| Form No | Table |
|---|---|
| 7 | Landlord's Notice Requiring Information about Sub-tenancies of Residential Property |
| 8 | Landlord's Notice Requiring Consent of Other Landlord to Notice Terminating Long Residential Tenancy |

| Form No | Table |
|---------|-------|
| 9 | Landlord's Notice Requiring Consent of Other Landlord to Agreement with Tenant under Schedule 10 to Local Government and Housing Act 1989 |

# LONG RESIDENTIAL TENANCIES (PRINCIPAL FORMS) REGULATIONS 1997

## (SI 1997/3008)

**NOTES**
Made: 16 December 1997.
Authority: Local Government and Housing Act 1989, Sch 10, paras 4(1), 6(1), 10, 12(1).
Commencement: 15 January 1998.

### 1  Citation and commencement

These Regulations may be cited as the Long Residential Tenancies (Principal Forms) Regulations and shall come into force on 15th January 1998.

**[3208]**

### 2  Interpretation

In these Regulations, any reference to a numbered form is a reference to the form bearing that number in the Schedule, or to a form substantially to the same effect.

**[3209]**

### 3  Forms

The forms prescribed for the purposes specified below shall be as follows—
- (a)  for a notice under paragraph 4(1) of Schedule 10 to the Local Government and Housing Act 1989 terminating a long residential tenancy and proposing an assured monthly periodic tenancy, form 1;
- (b)  for a notice under paragraph 4(1) of that Schedule terminating a long residential tenancy and proposing to apply to court for possession, form 2;
- (c)  for a notice under paragraph 6(1) of that Schedule proposing an interim monthly rent, form 3;
- (d)  for a notice under paragraph 10(1) of that Schedule proposing different rent or terms for an assured periodic tenancy, form 4;
- (e)  for a notice under paragraph 10(2) of that Schedule referring to a rent assessment committee a notice proposing different rent or terms for an assured periodic tenancy, form 5; and
- (f)  for a notice under section 41(2) of the Housing Act 1988, as applied by paragraph 12(1) of that Schedule, requiring a landlord or tenant to give information to a rent assessment committee, form 6.

**[3210]**

## SCHEDULE

**NOTES**
This Schedule contains forms which are not reproduced in this work, but their titles are noted below. The forms can be found at www.opsi.gov.uk.

| Form No | Title |
|---------|-------|
| 1 | Landlord's Notice Terminating Long Residential Tenancy and Proposing Assured Tenancy (amended by SI 2002/2227, SI 2003/233) |
| 2 | Landlord's Notice Terminating Long Residential Tenancy and Seeking Possession (amended by SI 2002/2227, SI 2003/233) |
| 3 | Landlord's Notice Proposing an Interim Monthly Rent after Notice Terminating Long Residential Tenancy |
| 4 | Tenant's Notice Proposing Different Terms or Rent for an Assured Tenancy |

| Form No | Title |
|---------|-------|
| 5 | Landlord's Application Referring Tenant's Notice Proposing Different Terms or Rent for a Proposed Assured Tenancy to a Rent Assessment Committee |
| 6 | Notice by Rent Assessment Committee Requiring Further Information |

# HOMELESSNESS (DECISIONS ON REFERRALS) ORDER 1998

(SI 1998/1578)

**NOTES**
Made: 25 June 1998.
Authority: Housing Act 1996, s 198(5), (6)(a).
Commencement: 20 July 1998.

## 1  Citation and commencement

This Order may be cited as the Homelessness (Decisions on Referrals) Order 1998 and shall come into force on the twenty eighth day after the day on which it is approved by resolution of each House of Parliament.

**[3211]**

## 2  Arrangements for deciding whether conditions for referral are satisfied

The arrangements set out in the Schedule to this Order are those agreed by the Local Government Association, the Welsh Local Government Association, the Association of London Government and the Convention of Scottish Local Authorities, and shall be the arrangements for the purposes of section 198(5) and (6)(a) of the Housing Act 1996.

**[3212]**

**3**    (*Revokes the Housing* (*Homeless Persons*) (*Appropriate Arrangements*) *Order 1978, SI 1978/69.*)

SCHEDULE
THE ARRANGEMENTS

Article 2

*Appointment of person by agreement between notifying authority and notified authority*

1.    Where the question whether the conditions for referral of a case are satisfied has not been decided by agreement between the notifying authority and the notified authority, the question shall be decided by a person appointed by those authorities.

*Appointment of person other than by agreement between notifying authority and notified authority*

2.    If within a period of 21 days commencing on the day on which the notified authority receives a notification under section 198(1) of the Housing Act 1996 a person has not been appointed in accordance with paragraph 1, the question shall be decided by a person—
    (a)    from the panel constituted in accordance with paragraph 3, and
    (b)    appointed in accordance with paragraph 4.

3.—(1)    Subject to sub-paragraph (2), the Local Government Association shall establish and maintain a panel of persons from which a person may be appointed to decide the question whether the conditions for referral of a case are satisfied.

    (2)    The Local Government Association shall consult such other associations of relevant authorities as they think appropriate before—
    (a)    establishing the panel,
    (b)    inviting a person to join the panel after it has been established, and
    (c)    removing a person from the panel.

4.—(1)    The notifying authority and the notified authority shall jointly request the Chairman of the Local Government Association or his nominee ("the proper officer") to appoint a person from the panel.

    (2)    If within a period of six weeks commencing on the day on which the notified authority receives a notification under section 198(1) of the Housing Act 1996 a person has not been appointed, the notifying authority shall request the proper officer to appoint a person from the panel.

## Procedural requirements

5.—(1)   Subject to the following provisions of this paragraph, the procedure for deciding whether the conditions for referral of a case are satisfied shall be determined by the appointed person.

(2)   The appointed person shall invite written representations from the notifying authority and the notified authority.

(3)   The appointed person may also invite—
(a)   further written representations from the notifying authority and the notified authority,
(b)   written representations from any other person, and
(c)   oral representations from any person.

(4)   If the appointed person invites representations from any person, those representations may be made by a person acting on his behalf, whether or not legally qualified.

## Notification of decision

6.   The appointed person shall notify his decision, and his reasons for it, in writing to the notifying authority and the notified authority.

## Costs

7.—(1)   The notifying authority and the notified authority shall pay their own costs incurred in connection with the arrangements set out in this Schedule.

(2)   Where a person has made oral representations, the appointed person may give directions as to the payment by the notifying authority or the notified authority or both authorities of any travelling expenses reasonably incurred by that person.

## Meaning of "appointed person"

8.   In this Schedule "appointed person" means a person appointed in accordance with paragraph 1 or 4.

[3213]

# ASSURED AND PROTECTED TENANCIES (LETTINGS TO STUDENTS) REGULATIONS 1998

## (SI 1998/1967)

**NOTES**
Made: 11 August 1998.
Authority: Rent Act 1977, s 8; Housing Act 1988, Sch 1, para 8.
Commencement: 1 September 1998.

**1**   These Regulations may be cited as the Assured and Protected Tenancies (Lettings to Students) Regulations 1998 and shall come into force on 1st September 1998.

[3214]

**2**   In these Regulations—
   "assisted" has the same meaning as in section 579(5) and (6) of the Education Act 1996;
   "further education" has the meaning assigned to it by section 2(3) and (5) of the Education Act 1996;
   "higher education" means education provided by means of a course of any description mentioned in Schedule 6 to the Education Reform Act 1988;
   "publicly funded" refers to an institution which is—
      (a)   provided or assisted by a local education authority;
      (b)   in receipt of grant under regulations made under section 485 of the Education Act 1996;
      (c)   within the higher education sector (within the meaning of section 91(5) of the Further and Higher Education Act 1992), other than a university; or
      (d)   within the further education sector (within the meaning of section 91(3) of the Further and Higher Education Act 1992), and
   "the relevant enactments" means section 8 of the Rent Act 1977 and paragraph 8 of Schedule 1 to the Housing Act 1988 (lettings to students).

[3215]

**3**   The following institutions are hereby specified as educational institutions for the purposes of the relevant enactments, that is to say—

(a)    any university or university college and any constituent college, school or hall or other institution of a university;

(b)    any other institution which provides further education or higher education or both and which is publicly funded;

(c)    the David Game Tutorial College, London.

**[3216]**

**4**    The following bodies of persons (whether unincorporated or bodies corporate) are hereby specified as bodies for the purposes of the relevant enactments, that is to say—

(a)    the governing body of any educational institution specified in regulation 3 above;

(b)    the body, other than a local education authority, providing any such educational institution; and

(c)    a body listed in Schedule 1 to these Regulations.

**[3217]**

**5**    The following bodies of persons (whether unincorporated or bodies corporate) are hereby specified as bodies for the purposes of paragraph 8 of Schedule 1 to the Housing Act 1988, that is to say—

(a)    any housing association (as defined in section 1 of the Housing Associations Act 1985) which is registered by the Housing Corporation or Housing for Wales in accordance with Part I of the Housing Associations Act 1985 and which is not listed in Schedule 1 to these Regulations; and

(b)    a body listed in Schedule 2 to these Regulations.

**[3218]**

**NOTES**

Modification: the reference to the Housing Corporation shall be treated as a reference to the Regulator of Social Housing: see the Transfer of Housing Corporation Functions (Modifications and Transitional Provisions) Order 2008, SI 2008/2839, arts 1(2), 3, 6, Schedule, para 7.

Transfer of functions: the functions of Housing for Wales were transferred, subject to transitional provisions, to the Secretary of State (for Wales) by the Government of Wales Act 1998, s 140, Sch 16, and Housing for Wales was abolished on 31 March 1999 by s 143 of the 1998 Act and the Housing for Wales (Abolition) Order 1999, SI 1999/781.

**6**    The Regulations specified in Schedule 3 to these Regulations are hereby revoked to the extent detailed in that Schedule.

**[3219]**

SCHEDULES

SCHEDULE 1
SPECIFIED BODIES UNDER REGULATION 4(C)

Regulation 4(c)

International Students House

The London Goodenough Trust for Overseas Graduates

**[3220]**

SCHEDULE 2
SPECIFIED BODIES UNDER REGULATION 5(B)

Regulation 5(b)

AFSIL Limited

[Beach General Partner Limited

Beach Nominee Limited]

[Campus Accommodation Ltd]

Derbyshire Student Residences Limited

Friendship Housing

Hull Student Welfare Association

International Lutheran Student Centre

International Students Club (Church of England) Limited

International Students' Club (Lee Abbey) Limited

International Students Housing Society

Oxford Brookes Housing Association Limited

Oxford Overseas Student Housing Association Limited

St Brigid's House Limited

St Thomas More Housing Society Limited

[SOAS Homes Limited]

The House of St Gregory and St Macrina Oxford Limited

The London Mission (West London) Circuit Meeting of the Methodist Church

The London School of Economics Housing Association

The Royal London Hospital Special Trustees

The Universities of Brighton and Sussex Catholic Chaplaincy Association

The Victoria League for Commonwealth Friendship

University of Leicester Students' Union

Wandsworth Students Housing Association Limited

[Willowbrook Properties Ltd]

York Housing Association Limited

**[3221]**

**NOTES**

Entries relating to "Beach General Partner Limited" and "Beach Nominee Limited" inserted, in relation to England, by the Assured and Protected Tenancies (Lettings to Students) (Amendment) (England) Regulations 2009, SI 2009/1825, reg 2; entry relating to "Campus Accommodation Ltd" inserted by the Assured and Protected Tenancies (Lettings to Students) (Amendment) Regulations 1999, SI 1999/1803, reg 2; entry "SOAS Homes Limited" inserted by the Assured and Protected Tenancies (Lettings to Students) (Amendment) (England) Regulations 2000, SI 2000/2706, reg 2; entry "Willowbrook Properties Ltd" inserted, in relation to England, by the Assured and Protected Tenancies (Lettings to Students) (Amendment) (No 2) (England) Regulations 1999, SI 1999/2268, reg 2.

*(Sch 3 contains revocations only.)*

# RENT ACTS (MAXIMUM FAIR RENT) ORDER 1999

(SI 1999/6)

**NOTES**

Made: 11 January 1999.
Authority: Landlord and Tenant Act 1985, s 31.
Commencement: 1 February 1999.

## 1 Citation, commencement and interpretation

(1)   This Order may be cited as the Rent Acts (Maximum Fair Rent) Order 1999 and shall come into force on 1st February 1999.

(2)   In this Order "the 1977 Act" means the Rent Act 1977.

**[3222]**

## 2 Maximum fair rent

(1)   Where this article applies, the amount to be registered as the rent of the dwelling-house under Part IV shall not, subject to paragraph (5), exceed the maximum fair rent calculated in accordance with the formula set out in paragraph (2).

(2)   The formula is—

$$MFR = LR \left[ 1 + \frac{(x-y)}{y} + P \right]$$

where—

MFR is the maximum fair rent;

LR is the amount of the existing registered rent for the dwelling-house;

x is the index published in the month immediately preceding the month in which the determination of a fair rent is made under Part IV;

y is the published index for the month in which the rent was last registered under Part IV before the date of the application for registration of a new rent; and

P is 0.075 for the first application for rent registration of the dwelling-house after this Order comes into force and 0.05 for every subsequent application.

(3)   Where the maximum fair rent calculated in accordance with paragraph (2) is not an integral multiple of 50 pence the maximum fair rent shall be that amount rounded up to the nearest integral multiple of 50 pence.

(4)   If $((x - y)/y) + P$ is less than zero the maximum fair rent shall be the existing registered rent.

(5)   In applying this article no account shall be taken of any variable sum to be included in the registered rent in accordance with section 71(4) of the 1977 Act.

(6)   Subject to paragraph (7), this article applies where an application for the registration of a new rent in respect of a dwelling-house is made after this Order comes into force and, on the date of that application, there is an existing registered rent under Part IV in respect of that dwelling-house.

(7)   This article does not apply in respect of a dwelling-house if because of a change in the condition of the dwelling-house or the common parts as a result of repairs or improvements (including the replacement of any fixture or fitting) carried out by the landlord or a superior landlord, the rent that is determined in response to an application for registration of a new rent under Part IV exceeds by at least 15% the previous rent registered or confirmed.

(8)   For the purposes of this article:
  (a)   references to Part IV are to Part IV of the 1977 Act;
  (b)   "common parts", in relation to a building, includes the structure and exterior of the building and common facilities provided for the occupiers of the dwelling-houses in the building;
  (c)   "index" means the monthly United Kingdom Index of Retail Prices (for all items) published by the Office for National Statistics.

**[3223]**

### 3   Modification

The 1977 Act shall be modified in accordance with the Schedule.

**[3224]**

(*Schedule inserts the Rent Act 1977, Sch 11, para 9B at* **[327]**.)

PART II
STATUTORY INSTRUMENTS

# ALLOCATION OF HOUSING AND HOMELESSNESS (REVIEW PROCEDURES) REGULATIONS 1999

## (SI 1999/71)

NOTES
Made: 14 January 1999.
Authority: Housing Act 1996, ss 165(1), (2), (5), 203(1), (2), (7).
Commencement: 11 February 1999.

## ARRANGEMENT OF REGULATIONS

### PART I
### GENERAL

### PART II
### THE HOUSING REGISTER

### PART III
### HOMELESSNESS

## PART I
## GENERAL

### 1 Citation, commencement and interpretation

(1) These Regulations may be cited as the Allocation of Housing and Homelessness (Review Procedures) Regulations 1999 and shall come into force on 11th February 1999.

(2) In these Regulations—

"the authority" means the local housing authority which has made the decision whose review under section 164 or 202 has been requested;

"the Decisions on Referrals Order" means the Homelessness (Decisions on Referrals) Order 1998;

"the reviewer" means—

(a) where the original decision falls within section 202(1)(a), (b), (c), (e) or (f), the authority;

(b) where the original decision falls within section 202(1)(d) (a decision under section 198(5) whether the conditions are met for referral of a case)—

(i) the notifying authority and the notified authority, where the review is carried out by those authorities;

(ii) the person appointed to carry out the review in accordance with regulation 7, where the case falls within that regulation.

(3) In these Regulations, references to sections are references to sections of the Housing Act 1996.

[3225]

### 2 Who is to make the decision on the review

Where the decision of the authority on a review of an original decision made by an officer of the authority is also to be made by an officer, that officer shall be someone who was not involved in the original decision and who is senior to the officer who made the original decision.

[3226]

## PART II
## THE HOUSING REGISTER

### 3 Notification of review procedure

Following a duly made request for a review under section 164, the authority shall—

(a) notify the person concerned that he, or someone acting on his behalf, may make representations in writing to the authority in connection with the review; and

(b) if they have not already done so, notify the person concerned of the procedure to be followed in connection with the review.

[3227]

### 4 Procedure on a review

The authority shall, subject to compliance with the provisions of regulation 5, consider any representations made under regulation 3.

[3228]

### 5 Notification of the decision on a review

The period within which the authority shall notify the person concerned of the decision on a review under section 164 is eight weeks from the day on which the request for a review is made to the authority or such longer period as the authority and the person concerned may agree in writing.

[3229]

## PART III
## HOMELESSNESS

### 6 Request for a review and notification of review procedure

(1) A request for a review under section 202 shall be made—

(a) to the authority, where the original decision falls within section 202(1)(a), (b), (c), (e) or (f);

(b) to the notifying authority, where the original decision falls within section 202(1)(d) (a decision under section 198(5) whether the conditions are met for referral of a case).

(2) Except where a case falls within regulation 7, the authority to whom a request for a review under section 202 has been made shall—

(a) notify the applicant that he, or someone acting on his behalf, may make representations in writing to the authority in connection with the review; and

(b) if they have not already done so, notify the applicant of the procedure to be followed in connection with the review.

(3)   Where a case falls within regulation 7, the person appointed in accordance with that regulation shall—

    (a)    notify the applicant that he, or someone acting on his behalf, may make representations in writing to that person in connection with the review; and

    (b)    notify the applicant of the procedure to be followed in connection with the review.

**[3230]**

## 7   Initial procedure where the original decision was made under the Decisions on Referrals Order

(1)   Where the original decision under section 198(5) (whether the conditions are met for the referral of the case) was made under the Decisions on Referrals Order, a review of that decision shall, subject to paragraph (2), be carried out by a person appointed by the notifying authority and the notified authority.

(2)   If a person is not appointed in accordance with paragraph (1) within five working days from the day on which the request for a review is made, the review shall be carried out by a person—

    (a)    from the panel constituted in accordance with paragraph 3 of the Schedule to the Decisions on Referrals Order ("the panel"), and

    (b)    appointed in accordance with paragraph (3) below.

(3)   The notifying authority shall within five working days from the end of the period specified in paragraph (2) request the chairman of the Local Government Association or his nominee ("the proper officer") to appoint a person from the panel and the proper officer shall do so within seven days of the request.

(4)   The notifying authority and the notified authority shall within five working days of the appointment of the person appointed ("the appointed person") provide him with the reasons for the original decision and the information and evidence on which that decision was based.

(5)   The appointed person shall—

    (a)    send to the notifying authority and the notified authority any representations made under regulation 6; and

    (b)    invite those authorities to respond to those representations.

(6)   The appointed person shall not be the same person as the person who made the original decision.

(7)   For the purposes of this regulation a working day is a day other than Saturday, Sunday, Christmas Day, Good Friday or a bank holiday.

**[3231]**

## 8   Procedure on a review

(1)   The reviewer shall, subject to compliance with the provisions of regulation 9, consider—

    (a)    any representations made under regulation 6 and, in a case falling within regulation 7, any responses to them; and

    (b)    any representations made under paragraph (2) below.

(2)   If the reviewer considers that there is a deficiency or irregularity in the original decision, or in the manner in which it was made, but is minded nonetheless to make a decision which is against the interests of the applicant on one or more issues, the reviewer shall notify the applicant—

    (a)    that the reviewer is so minded and the reasons why; and

    (b)    that the applicant, or someone acting on his behalf, may make representations to the reviewer orally or in writing or both orally and in writing.

**[3232]**

## 9   Notification of the decision on a review

(1)   The period within which notice of the decision on a review under section 202 shall be given under section 203(3) to the applicant shall be—

    (a)    eight weeks from the day on which the request for the review is made, where the original decision falls within section 202(1)(a), (b), (c), (e) or (f);

    (b)    ten weeks from the day on which the request for the review is made, where the original decision falls within section 202(1)(d) and the review is carried out by the notifying authority and the notified authority;

    (c)    twelve weeks from the day on which the request for the review is made in a case falling within regulation 7.

(2)   The period specified in paragraph (1) may be such longer period as the applicant and the reviewer may agree in writing.

(3)   In a case falling within paragraph (1)(c), the appointed person shall notify his decision on the review, and his reasons for it, in writing to the notifying authority and the notified authority

PART II
STATUTORY INSTRUMENTS

within a period of eleven weeks from the day on which the request for the review is made, or within a period commencing on that day which is one week shorter than that agreed in accordance with paragraph (2).

**[3233]**

*(Pt IV, reg 10 revokes the Allocation of Housing and Homelessness (Review Procedures and Amendment) Regulations 1996, SI 1996/3122, regs 2–8, amends the Allocation of Housing and Homelessness (Amendment) Regulations 1997, SI 1997/631, reg 1(3), and revokes reg 6 of those Regulations.)*

# UNFAIR TERMS IN CONSUMER CONTRACTS REGULATIONS 1999

(SI 1999/2083)

## NOTES
Made: 22 July 1999.
Authority: European Communities Act 1972, s 2(2).
Commencement: 1 October 1999.

### ARRANGEMENT OF REGULATIONS

## 1  Citation and commencement

These Regulations may be cited as the Unfair Terms in Consumer Contracts Regulations 1999 and shall come into force on 1st October 1999.

**[3234]**

**2**   *(Revokes the Unfair Terms in Consumer Contracts Regulations 1994, SI 1994/3159.)*

## 3  Interpretation

(1)   In these Regulations—

"the Community" means the European Community;

"consumer" means any natural person who, in contracts covered by these Regulations, is acting for purposes which are outside his trade, business or profession;

"court" in relation to England and Wales and Northern Ireland means a county court or the High Court, and in relation to Scotland, the Sheriff or the Court of Session;

"[OFT]" means [the Office of Fair Trading];

"EEA Agreement" means the Agreement on the European Economic Area signed at Oporto on 2nd May 1992 as adjusted by the protocol signed at Brussels on 17th March 1993;

"Member State" means a State which is a contracting party to the EEA Agreement;

"notified" means notified in writing;

"qualifying body" means a person specified in Schedule 1;

"seller or supplier" means any natural or legal person who, in contracts covered by these Regulations, is acting for purposes relating to his trade, business or profession, whether publicly owned or privately owned;

"unfair terms" means the contractual terms referred to in regulation 5.

[(1A)   The references—
    (a)   in regulation 4(1) to a seller or a supplier, and
    (b)   in regulation 8(1) to a seller or supplier,
include references to a distance supplier and to an intermediary.

   (1B)   In paragraph (1A) and regulation 5(6)—
    "distance supplier" means—
       (a)   a supplier under a distance contract within the meaning of the Financial Services (Distance Marketing) Regulations 2004, or
       (b)   a supplier of unsolicited financial services within regulation 15 of those Regulations; and
    "intermediary" has the same meaning as in those Regulations.]

   (2)   In the application of these Regulations to Scotland for references to an "injunction" or an "interim injunction" there shall be substituted references to an "interdict" or "interim interdict" respectively.

**[3235]**

**NOTES**
Para (1): words in square brackets substituted by virtue of the Enterprise Act 2002, s 2, subject to transitional provisions and savings in s 276 of, Sch 24, paras 2–6 to, that Act.
Paras (1A), (1B): inserted by the Financial Services (Distance Marketing) Regulations 2004, SI 2004/2095, reg 24(1), (2).

## 4  Terms to which these Regulations apply

   (1)   These Regulations apply in relation to unfair terms in contracts concluded between a seller or a supplier and a consumer.

   (2)   These Regulations do not apply to contractual terms which reflect—
    (a)   mandatory statutory or regulatory provisions (including such provisions under the law of any Member State or in Community legislation having effect in the United Kingdom without further enactment);
    (b)   the provisions or principles of international conventions to which the Member States or the Community are party.

**[3236]**

## 5  Unfair Terms

   (1)   A contractual term which has not been individually negotiated shall be regarded as unfair if, contrary to the requirement of good faith, it causes a significant imbalance in the parties' rights and obligations arising under the contract, to the detriment of the consumer.

   (2)   A term shall always be regarded as not having been individually negotiated where it has been drafted in advance and the consumer has therefore not been able to influence the substance of the term.

   (3)   Notwithstanding that a specific term or certain aspects of it in a contract has been individually negotiated, these Regulations shall apply to the rest of a contract if an overall assessment of it indicates that it is a pre-formulated standard contract.

   (4)   It shall be for any seller or supplier who claims that a term was individually negotiated to show that it was.

   (5)   Schedule 2 to these Regulations contains an indicative and non-exhaustive list of the terms which may be regarded as unfair.

   [(6)   Any contractual term providing that a consumer bears the burden of proof in respect of showing whether a distance supplier or an intermediary complied with any or all of the obligations placed upon him resulting from the Directive and any rule or enactment implementing it shall always be regarded as unfair.

   (7)   In paragraph (6)—
    "the Directive" means Directive 2002/65/EC of the European Parliament and of the Council of 23 September 2002 concerning the distance marketing of consumer financial services and amending Council Directive 90/619/EEC and Directives 97/7/EC and 98/27/EC; and
    "rule" means a rule made by the Financial Services Authority under the Financial Services and Markets Act 2000 or by a designated professional body within the meaning of section 326(2) of that Act.]

**[3237]**

**NOTES**
Paras (6), (7): added by the Financial Services (Distance Marketing) Regulations 2004, SI 2004/2095, reg 24(1), (3).

## 6 Assessment of unfair terms

(1)   Without prejudice to regulation 12, the unfairness of a contractual term shall be assessed, taking into account the nature of the goods or services for which the contract was concluded and by referring, at the time of conclusion of the contract, to all the circumstances attending the conclusion of the contract and to all the other terms of the contract or of another contract on which it is dependent.

(2)   In so far as it is in plain intelligible language, the assessment of fairness of a term shall not relate—

  (a)   to the definition of the main subject matter of the contract, or

  (b)   to the adequacy of the price or remuneration, as against the goods or services supplied in exchange.

[3238]

## 7 Written contracts

(1)   A seller or supplier shall ensure that any written term of a contract is expressed in plain, intelligible language.

(2)   If there is doubt about the meaning of a written term, the interpretation which is most favourable to the consumer shall prevail but this rule shall not apply in proceedings brought under regulation 12.

[3239]

## 8 Effect of unfair term

(1)   An unfair term in a contract concluded with a consumer by a seller or supplier shall not be binding on the consumer.

(2)   The contract shall continue to bind the parties if it is capable of continuing in existence without the unfair term.

[3240]

## 9 Choice of law clauses

These Regulations shall apply notwithstanding any contract term which applies or purports to apply the law of a non-Member State, if the contract has a close connection with the territory of the Member States.

[3241]

## 10 Complaints—consideration by [OFT]

(1)   It shall be the duty of the [OFT] to consider any complaint made to [it] that any contract term drawn up for general use is unfair, unless—

  (a)   the complaint appears to the [OFT] to be frivolous or vexatious; or

  (b)   a qualifying body has notified the [OFT] that it agrees to consider the complaint.

(2)   The [OFT] shall give reasons for [its] decision to apply or not to apply, as the case may be, for an injunction under regulation 12 in relation to any complaint which these Regulations require [it] to consider.

(3)   In deciding whether or not to apply for an injunction in respect of a term which the [OFT] considers to be unfair, [it] may, if [it] considers it appropriate to do so, have regard to any undertakings given to [it] by or on behalf of any person as to the continued use of such a term in contracts concluded with consumers.

[3242]

**NOTES**

  Words in square brackets substituted by virtue of the Enterprise Act 2002, s 2, subject to transitional provisions and savings in s 276 of, Sch 24, paras 2–6 to, that Act.

## 11 Complaints—consideration by qualifying bodies

(1)   If a qualifying body specified in Part One of Schedule 1 notifies the [OFT] that it agrees to consider a complaint that any contract term drawn up for general use is unfair, it shall be under a duty to consider that complaint.

(2)   Regulation 10(2) and (3) shall apply to a qualifying body which is under a duty to consider a complaint as they apply to the [OFT].

[3243]

**NOTES**

  Words in square brackets substituted by virtue of the Enterprise Act 2002, s 2, subject to transitional provisions and savings in s 276 of, Sch 24, paras 2–6 to, that Act.

**12   Injunctions to prevent continued use of unfair terms**

(1)   The [OFT] or, subject to paragraph (2), any qualifying body may apply for an injunction (including an interim injunction) against any person appearing to the [OFT] or that body to be using, or recommending use of, an unfair term drawn up for general use in contracts concluded with consumers.

(2)   A qualifying body may apply for an injunction only where—

    (a)   it has notified the [OFT] of its intention to apply at least fourteen days before the date on which the application is made, beginning with the date on which the notification was given; or

    (b)   the [OFT] consents to the application being made within a shorter period.

(3)   The court on an application under this regulation may grant an injunction on such terms as it thinks fit.

(4)   An injunction may relate not only to use of a particular contract term drawn up for general use but to any similar term, or a term having like effect, used or recommended for use by any person.

**[3244]**

**NOTES**

Words in square brackets substituted by virtue of the Enterprise Act 2002, s 2, subject to transitional provisions and savings in s 276 of, Sch 24, paras 2–6 to, that Act.

**13   Powers of the [OFT] and qualifying bodies to obtain documents and information**

(1)   The [OFT] may exercise the power conferred by this regulation for the purpose of—

    (a)   facilitating [its] consideration of a complaint that a contract term drawn up for general use is unfair; or

    (b)   ascertaining whether a person has complied with an undertaking or court order as to the continued use, or recommendation for use, of a term in contracts concluded with consumers.

(2)   A qualifying body specified in Part One of Schedule 1 may exercise the power conferred by this regulation for the purpose of—

    (a)   facilitating its consideration of a complaint that a contract term drawn up for general use is unfair; or

    (b)   ascertaining whether a person has complied with—

        (i)   an undertaking given to it or to the court following an application by that body, or

        (ii)   a court order made on an application by that body,

    as to the continued use, or recommendation for use, of a term in contracts concluded with consumers.

(3)   The [OFT] may require any person to supply to [it], and a qualifying body specified in Part One of Schedule 1 may require any person to supply to it—

    (a)   a copy of any document which that person has used or recommended for use, at the time the notice referred to in paragraph (4) below is given, as a pre-formulated standard contract in dealings with consumers;

    (b)   information about the use, or recommendation for use, by that person of that document or any other such document in dealings with consumers.

(4)   The power conferred by this regulation is to be exercised by a notice in writing which may—

    (a)   specify the way in which and the time within which it is to be complied with; and

    (b)   be varied or revoked by a subsequent notice.

(5)   Nothing in this regulation compels a person to supply any document or information which he would be entitled to refuse to produce or give in civil proceedings before the court.

(6)   If a person makes default in complying with a notice under this regulation, the court may, on the application of the [OFT] or of the qualifying body, make such order as the court thinks fit for requiring the default to be made good, and any such order may provide that all the costs or expenses of and incidental to the application shall be borne by the person in default or by any officers of a company or other association who are responsible for its default.

**[3245]**

**NOTES**

Words in square brackets substituted by virtue of the Enterprise Act 2002, s 2, subject to transitional provisions and savings in s 276 of, Sch 24, paras 2–6 to, that Act.

**14   Notification of undertakings and orders to [OFT]**

A qualifying body shall notify the [OFT]—

(a) of any undertaking given to it by or on behalf of any person as to the continued use of a term which that body considers to be unfair in contracts concluded with consumers;

(b) of the outcome of any application made by it under regulation 12, and of the terms of any undertaking given to, or order made by, the court;

(c) of the outcome of any application made by it to enforce a previous order of the court.

**[3246]**

**NOTES**

Words in square brackets substituted by virtue of the Enterprise Act 2002, s 2, subject to transitional provisions and savings in s 276 of, Sch 24, paras 2–6 to, that Act.

## 15 Publication, information and advice

(1) The [OFT] shall arrange for the publication in such form and manner as [it] considers appropriate, of—

(a) details of any undertaking or order notified to [it] under regulation 14;

(b) details of any undertaking given to [it] by or on behalf of any person as to the continued use of a term which the [OFT] considers to be unfair in contracts concluded with consumers;

(c) details of any application made by [it] under regulation 12, and of the terms of any undertaking given to, or order made by, the court;

(d) details of any application made by the [OFT] to enforce a previous order of the court.

(2) The [OFT] shall inform any person on request whether a particular term to which these Regulations apply has been—

(a) the subject of an undertaking given to the [OFT] or notified to [it] by a qualifying body; or

(b) the subject of an order of the court made upon application by [it] or notified to [it] by a qualifying body;

and shall give that person details of the undertaking or a copy of the order, as the case may be, together with a copy of any amendments which the person giving the undertaking has agreed to make to the term in question.

(3) The [OFT] may arrange for the dissemination in such form and manner as [it] considers appropriate of such information and advice concerning the operation of these Regulations as may appear to [it] to be expedient to give to the public and to all persons likely to be affected by these Regulations.

**[3247]**

**NOTES**

Words in square brackets substituted by virtue of the Enterprise Act 2002, s 2, subject to transitional provisions and savings in s 276 of, Sch 24, paras 2–6 to, that Act.

## [16 The functions of the Financial Services Authority

The functions of the Financial Services Authority under these Regulations shall be treated as functions of the Financial Services Authority under the [Financial Services and Markets Act 2000].]

**[3248]**

**NOTES**

Inserted by the Unfair Terms in Consumer Contracts (Amendment) Regulations 2001, SI 2001/1186, reg 2(a).

Words in square brackets substituted by the Financial Services and Markets Act 2000 (Consequential Amendments and Repeals) Order 2001, SI 2001/3649, art 583.

SCHEDULES

SCHEDULE 1
QUALIFYING BODIES

Regulation 3

PART ONE

[1. The Information Commissioner.

2. The Gas and Electricity Markets Authority.

3. The Director General of Electricity Supply for Northern Ireland.

4. The Director General of Gas for Northern Ireland.

5. [The Office of Communications].

6. [The Water Services Regulation Authority].

7. [The Office of Rail Regulation].

8. Every weights and measures authority in Great Britain.

9. The Department of Enterprise, Trade and Investment in Northern Ireland.

10. The Financial Services Authority.]

**[3249]**

---

**NOTES**

Substituted by the Unfair Terms in Consumer Contracts (Amendment) Regulations 2001, SI 2001/1186, reg 2(b).

Entry 5: words in square brackets substituted by the Communications Act 2003 (Consequential Amendments No 2) Order 2003, SI 2003/3182, art 2.

Entry 6: words in square brackets substituted by the Unfair Terms in Consumer Contracts (Amendment) and Water Act 2003 (Transitional Provision) Regulations 2006, SI 2006/523, reg 2, subject to transitional provisions in reg 3 thereof.

Entry 7: words in square brackets substituted by virtue of the Railways and Transport Safety Act 2003, s 16(4), (5), Sch 3, para 4.

---

## PART TWO

11. Consumers' Association

**[3250]**

## SCHEDULE 2
### INDICATIVE AND NON-EXHAUSTIVE LIST OF TERMS WHICH MAY BE REGARDED AS UNFAIR

Regulation 5(5)

1.    Terms which have the object or effect of—

    (a)    excluding or limiting the legal liability of a seller or supplier in the event of the death of a consumer or personal injury to the latter resulting from an act or omission of that seller or supplier;

    (b)    inappropriately excluding or limiting the legal rights of the consumer vis-à-vis the seller or supplier or another party in the event of total or partial non-performance or inadequate performance by the seller or supplier of any of the contractual obligations, including the option of offsetting a debt owed to the seller or supplier against any claim which the consumer may have against him;

    (c)    making an agreement binding on the consumer whereas provision of services by the seller or supplier is subject to a condition whose realisation depends on his own will alone;

    (d)    permitting the seller or supplier to retain sums paid by the consumer where the latter decides not to conclude or perform the contract, without providing for the consumer to receive compensation of an equivalent amount from the seller or supplier where the latter is the party cancelling the contract;

    (e)    requiring any consumer who fails to fulfil his obligation to pay a disproportionately high sum in compensation;

    (f)    authorising the seller or supplier to dissolve the contract on a discretionary basis where the same facility is not granted to the consumer, or permitting the seller or supplier to retain the sums paid for services not yet supplied by him where it is the seller or supplier himself who dissolves the contract;

    (g)    enabling the seller or supplier to terminate a contract of indeterminate duration without reasonable notice except where there are serious grounds for doing so;

    (h)    automatically extending a contract of fixed duration where the consumer does not indicate otherwise, when the deadline fixed for the consumer to express his desire not to extend the contract is unreasonably early;

    (i)    irrevocably binding the consumer to terms with which he had no real opportunity of becoming acquainted before the conclusion of the contract;

    (j)    enabling the seller or supplier to alter the terms of the contract unilaterally without a valid reason which is specified in the contract;

    (k)    enabling the seller or supplier to alter unilaterally without a valid reason any characteristics of the product or service to be provided;

    (l)    providing for the price of goods to be determined at the time of delivery or allowing a seller of goods or supplier of services to increase their price without in both cases giving the consumer the corresponding right to cancel the contract if the final price is too high in relation to the price agreed when the contract was concluded;

    (m)    giving the seller or supplier the right to determine whether the goods or services supplied are in conformity with the contract, or giving him the exclusive right to interpret any term of the contract;

    (n)    limiting the seller's or supplier's obligation to respect commitments undertaken by his agents or making his commitments subject to compliance with a particular formality;

    (o) obliging the consumer to fulfil all his obligations where the seller or supplier does not perform his;

    (p) giving the seller or supplier the possibility of transferring his rights and obligations under the contract, where this may serve to reduce the guarantees for the consumer, without the latter's agreement;

    (q) excluding or hindering the consumer's right to take legal action or exercise any other legal remedy, particularly by requiring the consumer to take disputes exclusively to arbitration not covered by legal provisions, unduly restricting the evidence available to him or imposing on him a burden of proof which, according to the applicable law, should lie with another party to the contract.

2. Scope of paragraphs 1(g), (j) and (l)

    (a) Paragraph 1(g) is without hindrance to terms by which a supplier of financial services reserves the right to terminate unilaterally a contract of indeterminate duration without notice where there is a valid reason, provided that the supplier is required to inform the other contracting party or parties thereof immediately.

    (b) Paragraph 1(j) is without hindrance to terms under which a supplier of financial services reserves the right to alter the rate of interest payable by the consumer or due to the latter, or the amount of other charges for financial services without notice where there is a valid reason, provided that the supplier is required to inform the other contracting party or parties thereof at the earliest opportunity and that the latter are free to dissolve the contract immediately.

    Paragraph 1(j) is also without hindrance to terms under which a seller or supplier reserves the right to alter unilaterally the conditions of a contract of indeterminate duration, provided that he is required to inform the consumer with reasonable notice and that the consumer is free to dissolve the contract.

    (c) Paragraphs 1(g), (j) and (l) do not apply to:

    —transactions in transferable securities, financial instruments and other products or services where the price is linked to fluctuations in a stock exchange quotation or index or a financial market rate that the seller or supplier does not control;

    —contracts for the purchase or sale of foreign currency, traveller's cheques or international money orders denominated in foreign currency.

    (d) Paragraph 1(1) is without hindrance to price indexation clauses, where lawful, provided that the method by which prices vary is explicitly described.

**[3251]**

# HOMELESS PERSONS (PRIORITY NEED) (WALES) ORDER 2001 (NOTE)

## (SI 2001/607 (W 30))

**NOTES**
Made: 27 February 2001.
Authority: Housing Act 1996, s 189(2).
Commencement: 1 March 2001.
Amended by: SI 2004/696.
This Order applies to Wales only. The equivalent provisions for England are in SI 2002/2051 at **[3259]** et seq.

**[3252]**

# COMMONHOLD AND LEASEHOLD REFORM ACT 2002 (COMMENCEMENT NO 1, SAVINGS AND TRANSITIONAL PROVISIONS) (ENGLAND) ORDER 2002

## (SI 2002/1912)

**NOTES**
Made: 17 July 2002.
Authority: Commonhold and Leasehold Reform Act 2002, s 181.

## 1 Citation, interpretation and extent

(1) This Order may be cited as the Commonhold and Leasehold Reform Act 2002 (Commencement No 1, Savings and Transitional Provisions) (England) Order 2002.

(2)    In this Order—

"the 1967 Act" means the Leasehold Reform Act 1967;

"the 1993 Act" means the Leasehold Reform, Housing and Urban Development Act 1993;

"the commencement date" means 26th July 2002 and

     references to sections and Schedules are, unless otherwise stated, references to sections of, and Schedules to, the Commonhold and Leasehold Reform Act 2002.

(3)    This Order extends to England only.

**[3253]**

## 2   Provisions coming into force on the commencement date

The following provisions shall come into force on the commencement date—

(a)     sections 114, 129, 132, 133, 137 and 142;

(b)     subject to the transitional provisions and savings in Schedule 2 to this Order—

     (i)     sections 115 to 120, 125, 127, 128, 130, 131, 134 to 136, 138 to 141, 143 to 147, 160 to 162, and;

     (ii)    section 180 in so far as it relates to those of the repeals in Schedule 14 which are set out in Schedule 1 to this Order;

(c)     sections 74, 78, 80, 84, 92, 110, 122, 151 to 153, 156, 164, 166, 167, 171, 174 and Schedule 12, in so far as they confer power to make regulations.

**[3254]**

SCHEDULES

SCHEDULE 1
REPEALS

Article 2(b)(ii)

PART 1

| Chapter | Short Title | Extent of Repeal |
|---|---|---|
| 1993 c 28 | Leasehold Reform, Housing and Urban Development Act 1993 | In section 5— |
| | |      in subsection (1), the words "which is at a low rent or for a particularly long term", and in subsection (2)(c), the words "at a low rent or for a particularly long term". |
| | | Section 6. |
| | | In section 7(3), the words "at a low rent". |
| | | Section 8. |
| | | Section 8A. |
| | | In section 10— |
| | |      subsections (2), (3) and (4A), and in subsection (6), the definition of "qualifying tenant". |
| | | In section 13— |
| | |      in subsection (2), sub-paragraph (i) of paragraph (b) and the words following that paragraph, and |
| | |      in subsection (3)(e), the words "the following particulars", the word "namely" and sub-paragraphs (ii) and (iii). |
| 1996 c 52. | Housing Act 1996 | Section 105(3). |
| | | Section 111. |
| | | In Schedule 9, paragraph 3 and sub-paragraphs 5(2) and (3). |
| | | In Schedule 10, paragraph 4. |

PART 2

| Chapter | Short Title | Extent of Repeal |
|---|---|---|
| 1993 c 28 | Leasehold Reform, Housing and Urban Development Act 1993 | In section 39— |
| | |     in subsection (2), paragraph (b) and the word "and" before it, |
| | |     subsections (2A) and (2B), |
| | |     subsection (3)(c) and (d), and subsections (4A) and (5). |
| | | Section 42(3)(b)(iii) and (iv) and (4). |
| | | In section 45(5), the words "and (b)". |
| | | Section 62(4). |
| | | In section 94— |
| | |     in subsections (3) and (4), the words "which is at a low rent or for a particularly long term", |
| | |     in subsection (12), the words "which is at a low rent or for a particularly long term" and the words ", 8 and 8A". |
| | | In Schedule 13, in paragraph 1, the definition of "the valuation date". |
| 1996 c 52. | Housing Act 1996 | Section 112. |
| | | In Schedule 9, paragraph 4. |

[3256]

PART 3

| Chapter | Short Title | Extent of Repeal |
|---|---|---|
| 1967 c 88 | Leasehold Reform Act 1967 | In section 1— |
| | |     in subsection (1), the words ", occupying the house as his residence," and the words ", and occupying it as his residence,", |
| | |     subsection (2), and |
| | |     in subsection (3)(a) the words "and occupied by". |
| | | In section 1AA— |
| | |     in subsection (1)(b), the words "falls within subsection (2) below and", and subsections (2) and (4). |
| | | In section 2— |
| | |     in subsection (3), the words "and occupied by" and the words from "and are occupied" to the end, and in subsection (4) the words "or a subletting". |
| | | In section 3(3) the words ", except section 1AA,". |
| | | In section 6— |

| Chapter | Short Title | Extent of Repeal |
|---|---|---|
| | | in subsection (2), the words "in respect of his occupation of the house", and in subsection (5) the words "or statutory owners, as the case may be," and the words "or them". |
| | | In section 7— |
| | | in subsection (1), the words "while occupying it as his residence", the words ", and occupying the house as his residence," and paragraph (b) and the word "and" before it, in subsection (4), the words "while so occupying the house" and the words "occupying in right of the tenancy", and subsection (6). |
| | | In section 9— |
| | | in subsection (1), the words "who reside in the house", |
| | | in subsection (1A)(a) the words "and where the tenancy has been extended under this Part of this Act, that the tenancy will terminate on the original term date" and |
| | | subsection (1C)(a). |
| | | In section 16— |
| | | subsection (1)(a), |
| | | in subsection (2), the words "or occupied", the words "(a) or" and the words "the freehold or", |
| | | in subsection (3), the words "the freehold or" and the proviso, and |
| | | in subsection (4) the words "the freehold or". |
| | | In section 37— |
| | | in subsection (4) the words ", except section 1AA,", and in subsection (5), the words from the beginning to "but". |
| | | In Schedule 3, in paragraph 6, sub-paragraph (1)(d) and, in sub-paragraph (2) the words "and (d)". |
| | | In Schedule 4A, in paragraph 3(2)(d), the word "assign,". |
| 1980 c 51 | Housing Act 1980 | In Schedule 21, paragraph 1. |
| 1989 c 42 | Local Government and Housing Act 1989 | Schedule 11, paragraph 10. |

## SCHEDULE 2
### TRANSITIONAL PROVISIONS AND SAVINGS

Article 2(b)(i)

*Collective enfranchisement by tenants of flats*

1.   The amendments made to the 1993 Act by sections 115 to 120, 125 and 127 to 128 and the repeals in Part 1 of Schedule 1 to this Order shall not have effect in relation to an application for collective enfranchisement in respect of which—

    (a)   a notice was given under section 13 of the 1993 Act; or

    (b)   an application was made for an order under section 26 of that Act before the commencement date.

2.    Until the coming into force of sections 121 to 124, in a case where there are only two qualifying tenants of flats contained in the premises, section 13(2)(b) of the 1993 Act as amended by section 119, shall not be satisfied unless both tenants are participating tenants as defined in section 14 of that Act.

3.    Sub-paragraph (2A) of paragraph 4 of Schedule 6 to the 1993 Act inserted by section 128, shall, until the coming into force of sections 121 to 124, have effect as if the reference to participating members were a reference to participating tenants as defined in section 14 of that Act.

### New leases for tenants of flats

4.    The amendments made to the 1993 Act by sections 130, 131 and 134 to 136, the repeals to sections 5, 7, 8 and 8A of that Act in Part 1 of Schedule 1 to this Order and the repeals in Part 2 of that Schedule shall not have effect in relation to an application for a new lease of a flat in respect of which—

(a)    a notice was given under section 42 of the 1993 Act, or

(b)    an application was made for an order under section 50 of that Act

before the commencement date.

### Enfranchisement and lease extensions for leasehold houses

5.    The amendments made to the 1967 Act by sections 138 to 141 and sections 143 to 147 and the repeals in Part 3 of Schedule 1 to this Order, shall not have effect in relation to an application for enfranchisement or an extended lease of a house in respect of which—

(a)    a notice was given under section 8 or 14 of the 1967 Act, or

(b)    an application was made under section 27 of that Act

before the commencement date.

### Managers appointed by leasehold valuation tribunal

6.    Amendments made to the Landlord and Tenant Act 1987 by sections 160 and 161 shall not have effect in relation to an application made under Part II of the Landlord and Tenant Act 1987 before the commencement date.

### Grounds for application to vary a lease

7.    The amendments made to the Landlord and Tenant Act 1987 by section 162 shall not have effect in respect of an application made under section 35 of the Landlord and Tenant Act 1987 before the commencement date.

**[3258]**

# HOMELESSNESS (PRIORITY NEED FOR ACCOMMODATION) (ENGLAND) ORDER 2002

(SI 2002/2051)

**NOTES**
Made: 30 July 2002.
Authority: Housing Act 1996, s 189(2).
Commencement: 31 July 2002.

## 1  Citation, commencement and interpretation

(1)    This Order may be cited as the Homelessness (Priority Need for Accommodation) (England) Order 2002 and shall come into force on the day after the day on which it is made.

(2)    This Order extends to England only.

(3)    In this Order—
"looked after, accommodated or fostered" has the meaning given by section 24(2) of the Children Act 1989; and
"relevant student" means a person to whom section 24B(3) of that Act applies—
(a)    who is in full-time further or higher education; and
(b)    whose term-time accommodation is not available to him during a vacation.

**[3259]**

## 2  Priority need for accommodation

The descriptions of person specified in the following articles have a priority need for accommodation for the purposes of Part 7 of the Housing Act 1996.

**[3260]**

**3   Children aged 16 or 17**

(1)   A person (other than a person to whom paragraph (2) below applies) aged sixteen or seventeen who is not a relevant child for the purposes of section 23A of the Children Act 1989.

(2)   This paragraph applies to a person to whom a local authority owe a duty to provide accommodation under section 20 of that Act (provision of accommodation for children in need).

**[3261]**

**4   Young people under 21**

(1)   A person (other than a relevant student) who—
(a)   is under twenty-one; and
(b)   at any time after reaching the age of sixteen, but while still under eighteen, was, but is no longer, looked after, accommodated or fostered.

**[3262]**

**5   Vulnerability: institutional backgrounds**

(1)   A person (other than a relevant student) who has reached the age of twenty-one and who is vulnerable as a result of having been looked after, accommodated or fostered.

(2)   A person who is vulnerable as a result of having been a member of Her Majesty's regular naval, military or air forces.

(3)   A person who is vulnerable as a result of—
(a)   having served a custodial sentence (within the meaning of section 76 of the Powers of Criminal Courts (Sentencing) Act 2000);
(b)   having been committed for contempt of court or any other kindred offence;
(c)   having been remanded in custody (within the meaning of paragraph (b), (c) or (d) of section 88(1) of that Act).

**[3263]**

**6   Vulnerability: fleeing violence or threats of violence**

A person who is vulnerable as a result of ceasing to occupy accommodation by reason of violence from another person or threats of violence from another person which are likely to be carried out.

**[3264]**

# COMMONHOLD AND LEASEHOLD REFORM ACT 2002 (COMMENCEMENT NO 1, SAVINGS AND TRANSITIONAL PROVISIONS) (WALES) ORDER 2002

## (SI 2002/3012 (W 284))

**NOTES**
Made: 4 December 2002.
Authority: Commonhold and Leasehold Reform Act 2002, s 181.

**1   Citation, interpretation and extent**

(1)   This Order may be cited as the Commonhold and Leasehold Reform Act 2002 (Commencement No 1, Savings and Transitional Provisions) (Wales) Order 2002.

(2)   In this Order—
"the 1967 Act" ("*Deddf 1967*") means the Leasehold Reform Act 1967;
"the 1993 Act" ("*Deddf 1993*") means the Leasehold Reform, Housing and Urban Development Act 1993;
"the commencement date" ("*y dyddiad cychwyn*") means 1st January 2003; and
references to sections and schedules are, unless otherwise stated, references to sections of, and Schedules to, the Commonhold and Leasehold Reform Act 2002.

(3)   This Order applies to Wales only.

**[3265]**

**2   Provisions coming into force on the commencement date**

The following provisions of the Commonhold and Leasehold Reform Act 2002 shall come into force on the commencement date—
(a)   sections 114, 129, 132, 133, 137 and 142;
(b)   subject to the transitional provisions and savings in Schedule 2 to this Order—
(i)   sections 115 to 120, 125, 127, 128, 130, 131, 134 to 136, 138 to 141, 143 to 147, 160 to 162; and

(ii)   section 180 in so far as it relates to those of the repeals in Schedule 14 which are set out in Schedule 1 to this Order;

(c)   sections 74, 78, 80, 84, 92, 110, 122, 151 to 153, 156, 164, 166, 167, 171, 174 and Schedule 12, in so far as they confer power to make regulations.

**[3266]**

## SCHEDULES

### SCHEDULE 1
### REPEALS

Article 2(b)(ii)

#### PART 1

| Chapter | Short Title | Extent of Repeal |
|---------|-------------|------------------|
| 1993 c 28 | Leasehold Reform, Housing and Urban Development Act 1993 | In section 5— |
| | | in subsection (1), the words "which is at a low rent or for a particularly long term", and in subsection (2)(c), the words "at a low rent or for a particularly long term". |
| | | Section 6. |
| | | In section 7(3), the words "at a low rent". |
| | | Section 8. |
| | | Section 8A. |
| | | In section 10— |
| | | subsections (2), (3) and (4A), and in subsection (6), the definition of "qualifying tenant". |
| | | In section 13— |
| | | in subsection (2), sub-paragraph (i) of paragraph (b) and the words following that paragraph, and in subsection (3)(e), the words "the following particulars", the word "namely" and sub-paragraphs (ii) and (iii). |
| 1996 c 52 | Housing Act 1996 | Section 105(3). |
| | | Section 111. |
| | | In Schedule 9, paragraph 3 and sub-paragraphs 5(2) and (3). |
| | | In Schedule 10, paragraph 4. |

**[3267]**

PART 2

| Chapter | Short Title | Extent of Repeal |
|---------|-------------|------------------|
| 1993 c 28 | Leasehold Reform, Housing and Urban Development Act 1993 | In section 39— |
| | | in subsection (2), paragraph (b) and the word "and" before it, |
| | | subsections (2A) and (2B), subsections (3)(c) and (d), and subsections (4A) and (5). |
| | | Section 42(3)(b)(iii) and (iv) and (4). |
| | | In section 45(5), the words "and (b)". |
| | | Section 62(4). |
| | | In section 94— |
| | | in subsections (3) and (4), the words "which is at a low rent or for a particularly long term", |
| | | in subsection (12), the words "which is at a low rent or for a particularly long term" and the words ", 8 and 8A". |
| | | In Schedule 13, in paragraph 1, the definition of "the valuation date". |
| 1996 c 52 | Housing Act 1996 | Section 112. |
| | | In Schedule 9, paragraph 4. |

**[3268]**

PART 3

| Chapter | Short Title | Extent of Repeal |
|---------|-------------|------------------|
| 1967 c 88 | Leasehold Reform Act 1967 | In section 1— |
| | | in subsection (1), the words ", occupying the house as his residence," and the words ", and occupying it as his residence,", |
| | | subsection (2), and in subsection (3)(a) the words "and occupied by". |
| | | In section 1AA— |
| | | in subsection (1)(b), the words "falls within subsection (2) below and", and subsections (2) and (4). |
| | | In section 2— |
| | | in subsection (3), the words "and occupied by" and the words from "and are occupied" to the end, and in subsection (4) the words "or a subletting". |
| | | In section 3(3) the words ", except section 1AA,". |
| | | In section 6— |
| | | in subsection (2), the words "in respect of his occupation of the house", and in subsection (5) the words "or statutory owners, as the case may be," and the words "or them". |

| Chapter | Short Title | Extent of Repeal |
|---|---|---|
| | | In section 7— |
| | | in subsection (1) the words "while occupying it as his residence", the words ", and occupying the house as his residence," and paragraph (b) and the word "and" before it, in subsection (4), the words "while so occupying the house" and the words "occupying in right of the tenancy", and subsection (6). |
| | | In section 9— |
| | | in subsection (1), the words "who reside in the house", |
| | | in subsection (1A)(a) the words "and where the tenancy has been extended under this Part of this Act that the tenancy will terminate on the original term date" and subsection (1C)(a). |
| | | In section 16— |
| | | subsection (1)(a), in subsection (2), the words "or occupied", the words "(a) or" and the words "the freehold or", |
| | | in subsection (3), the words "the freehold or" and the proviso, and |
| | | in subsection (4) the words "the freehold or". |
| | | In section 37— |
| | | in subsection (4) the words ", except section 1AA,", and in subsection (5), the words from the beginning to "but". |
| | | In Schedule 3, in paragraph 6, sub-paragraph (1)(d) and, in sub-paragraph (2) the words "and (d)". |
| | | In Schedule 4A, in paragraph 3(2)(d), the word "assign". |
| 1980 c 51 | Housing Act 1980 | In Schedule 21, paragraph 1. |
| 1989 c 42 | Local Government and Housing Act 1989 | Schedule 11, paragraph 10. |

[3269]

## SCHEDULE 2
### TRANSITIONAL PROVISIONS AND SAVINGS

Article 2(b)

*Collective enfranchisement by tenants of flats*

1.   The amendments made to the 1993 Act by sections 115 to 120, 125 and 127 to 128 and the repeals in Part 1 of Schedule 1 to this Order shall not have effect in relation to an application for collective enfranchisement in respect of which—

    (a)   a notice was given under section 13 of the 1993 Act; or

    (b)   an application was made for an order under section 26 of that Act before the commencement date.

2.   Until the coming into force of sections 121 to 124, in a case where there are only two qualifying tenants of flats contained in the premises, section 13(2)(b) of the 1993 Act as amended by section 119, shall not be satisfied unless both tenants are participating tenants as defined in section 14 of that Act.

3.   Sub-paragraph (2A) of paragraph 4 of Schedule 6 to the 1993 Act inserted by section 128, shall, until the coming into force of sections 121 to 124, have effect as if the reference to participating members were a reference to participating tenants as defined in section 14 of that Act.

*New leases for tenants of flats*

4. The amendments made to the 1993 Act by sections 130, 131 and 134 to 136, the repeals to sections 5, 7, 8 and 8A of that Act in Part 1 of Schedule 1 to this Order and the repeals in Part 2 of that Schedule shall not have effect in relation to an application for a new lease of a flat in respect of which—

   (a)    a notice was given under section 42 of the 1993 Act, or

   (b)    an application was made for an order under section 50 of that Act

before the commencement date.

*Enfranchisement and lease extensions for leasehold houses*

5. The amendments made to the 1967 Act by sections 138 to 141 and sections 143 to 147 and the repeals in Part 3 of Schedule 1 to this Order, shall not have effect in relation to an application for enfranchisement or an extended lease of a house in respect of which—

   (a)    a notice was given under section 8 or 14 of the 1967 Act, or

   (b)    an application was made under section 27 of that Act

before the commencement date.

*Managers appointed by leasehold valuation tribunal*

6. Amendments made to the Landlord and Tenant Act 1987 by sections 160 and 161 shall not have effect in relation to an application made under Part II of the Landlord and Tenant Act 1987 before the commencement date.

*Grounds for application to vary a lease*

7. The amendments made to the Landlord and Tenant Act 1987 by section 162 shall not have effect in respect of an application made under section 35 of the Landlord and Tenant Act 1987 before the commencement date.

**[3270]**

# LEASEHOLD REFORM (COLLECTIVE ENFRANCHISEMENT) (COUNTER-NOTICES) (ENGLAND) REGULATIONS 2002

(SI 2002/3208)

**NOTES**
   Made: 20 December 2002.
   Authority: Leasehold Reform, Housing and Urban Development Act 1993, s 99(6)(b).
   Commencement: 10 April 2003.

## 1   Citation, interpretation and extent

These Regulations may be cited as the Leasehold Reform (Collective Enfranchisement) (Counter-notices) (England) Regulations 2002 and shall come into force on 10th April 2003.

**[3271]**

**2**    These Regulations extend to England only.

**[3272]**

## 3   Interpretation

In these Regulations—

    "the 1993 Act" means the Leasehold Reform, Housing and Urban Development Act 1993;

    "the specified premises" has the same meaning as in section 13(12)(a) of the 1993 Act.

**[3273]**

## 4   Additional content of reversioner's counter-notice

A counter-notice given under section 21 (reversioner's counter-notice) of the 1993 Act shall contain (in addition to the particulars required by that section) a statement as to whether or not the specified premises are within the area of a scheme approved as an estate management scheme under section 70.

**[3274]**

## 5   Application

These Regulations shall apply to counter-notices given under section 21 on or after the date these Regulations come into force.

**[3275]**

# ALLOCATION OF HOUSING (ENGLAND) REGULATIONS 2002

## (SI 2002/3264)

**NOTES**
Made: 18 December 2002.
Authority: Housing Act 1996, ss 160(4), 160A(3), (5), 172(4).
Commencement: 31 January 2003.

## 1 Citation, commencement and application

(1)   These Regulations may be cited as the Allocation of Housing (England) Regulations 2002 and shall come into force on 31st January 2003.

(2)   These Regulations apply in England only.

**[3276]**

## 2 Interpretation

In these Regulations—

"the Act" means the Housing Act 1996;

"the Common Travel Area" means the United Kingdom, the Channel Islands, the Isle of Man and the Republic of Ireland collectively; and

["family intervention tenancy"—

(a)   in relation to a tenancy granted by a local housing authority, has the meaning given by paragraph 4ZA(3) of Schedule 1 to the Housing Act 1985;

(b)   in relation to a tenancy granted by a registered social landlord, has the meaning given by paragraph 12ZA(3) of Part 1 of Schedule 1 to the Housing Act 1988;]

"the immigration rules" means the rules laid down as mentioned in section 3(2) of the Immigration Act 1971 (general provisions for regulation and control).

**[3277]**

**NOTES**
Definition "family intervention tenancy": inserted by the Allocation of Housing (England) (Amendment) (Family Intervention Tenancies) Regulations 2008, SI 2008/3015, reg 2(1), (2).

## 3 Cases where the provisions of Part 6 of the Act do not apply

(1)   The provisions of Part 6 of the Act about the allocation of housing accommodation do not apply in the following cases.

(2)   They do not apply where a local housing authority secures the provision of suitable alternative accommodation under section 39 of the Land Compensation Act 1973 (duty to rehouse residential occupiers).

(3)   They do not apply in relation to the grant of a secure tenancy under sections 554 and 555 of the Housing Act 1985 (grant of tenancy to former owner-occupier or statutory tenant of defective dwelling-house).

[(4)   They do not apply in relation to the allocation of housing accommodation by a local housing authority to a person who lawfully occupies accommodation let on a family intervention tenancy.]

**[3278]**

**NOTES**
Para (4): inserted by the Allocation of Housing (England) (Amendment) (Family Intervention Tenancies) Regulations 2008, SI 2008/3015, reg 2(1), (3).

**4–6**   (*Regs 4, 5 revoked by the Allocation of Housing and Homelessness (Eligibility) (England) Regulations 2006, SI 2006/1294, reg 7, Schedule, as from 1 June 2006 (for transitional provisions see reg 8 of that regulation); reg 6 revokes the Allocation of Housing (England) Regulations 2000, SI 2000/702.*)

# ALLOCATION OF HOUSING (WALES) REGULATIONS 2003 (NOTE)

## (SI 2003/239 (W 36))

**NOTES**
Made: 28 January 2003.
Authority: Housing Act 1996, ss 160(4), 160A(3), (5), 215(2).

Commencement: 29 January 2003.
Amended by: SI 2006/2645 (subject to savings); SI 2009/393.
These Regulations apply to Wales only. The equivalent provisions for England are in SI 2002/3264 at **[3276]** et seq.

**[3279]**

# LEASEHOLD REFORM (COLLECTIVE ENFRANCHISEMENT) (COUNTER-NOTICES) (WALES) REGULATIONS 2003 (NOTE)

(SI 2003/990 (W 139))

**NOTES**
Made: 2 April 2003.
Authority: Leasehold Reform, Housing and Urban Development Act 1993, s 99(6)(b).
Commencement: 10 April 2003.
These Regulations apply to Wales only. The equivalent provisions for England are in SI 2002/3208 at **[3271]**.

**[3280]**

# COMMONHOLD AND LEASEHOLD REFORM ACT 2002 (COMMENCEMENT NO 2 AND SAVINGS) (ENGLAND) ORDER 2003

(SI 2003/1986)

**NOTES**
Made: 4 August 2003.
Authority: Commonhold and Leasehold Reform Act 2002, s 181.

## 1   Citation, interpretation and application

(1)   This Order may be cited as the Commonhold and Leasehold Reform Act 2002 (Commencement No 2 and Savings) (England) Order 2003.

(2)   In this Order—
"LVT" means a leasehold valuation tribunal;
"the 1967 Act" means the Leasehold Reform Act 1967;
"the 1985 Act" means the Landlord and Tenant Act 1985;
"the 1987 Act" means the Landlord and Tenant Act 1987;
"the 1993 Act" means the Leasehold Reform, Housing and Urban Development Act 1993;
"the 1996 Act" means the Housing Act 1996;
"the first commencement date" means 30 September 2003;
"the second commencement date" means 31 October 2003;
references to sections and Schedules are, unless otherwise stated, references to sections of, and
Schedules to, the Commonhold and Leasehold Reform Act 2002; and
any reference to a repeal is to a repeal made by section 180 and Schedule 14.

(3)   This Order applies to England only.

**[3281]**

## 2   Provisions coming into force on the first commencement date

The following provisions shall come into force on the first commencement date—
(a)   sections 71 to 73, 75 to 77, 79, 81 to 83 , 85 to 91, 93 to 103, 105 to 109, 111 to 113, 159, 163, 173, Schedules 6 and 7;
(b)   sections 74, 78, 80, 84, 92, 110, 174 and Schedule 12 to the extent that they are not already in force;
(c)   subject to the savings in Schedule 2 to this Order—
(i)   sections 148, 149, 150, 155, 157, 158, 175, 176, Schedule 9, paragraphs 8 to 13 of Schedule 10, Schedule 11 and paragraphs 1 to 15 of Schedule 13;
(ii)   subsections (1) to (5) of section 172 except in so far as they relate to the application to the Crown of sections 152 to 154, 164 to 171, paragraphs 1 to 7 of Schedule 10 and paragraph 16 of Schedule 13;
(iii)   subsection (6) of section 172 except in so far as the substitutions made by that subsection relate to sections 42A and 42B of the 1987 Act;

(iv)    to the extent that it is not already in force, section 180 in so far as it relates to the repeals in Schedule 14 which are set out in Schedule 1 to this Order.

**[3282]**

## 3  Provisions coming into force on the second commencement date

(1)    Subject to paragraphs (2) to (7), section 151, to the extent that it is not already in force, shall come into force on the second commencement date.

(2)    In relation to any case to which paragraph (3), (4), (5) or (7) applies, the amendment made by section 151 shall have no effect and the Service Charge (Estimates and Consultation) Order 1988 shall continue to apply.

(3)    This paragraph applies where qualifying works are begun before the second commencement date.

(4)    This paragraph applies where, in relation to qualifying works, the landlord has given or displayed the notice required under section 20 of the 1985 Act before the second commencement date.

(5)    This paragraph applies where, in relation to qualifying works to which paragraph (6) applies, the landlord has given notice in the Official Journal of the European Union in accordance with the Public Works Contracts Regulations 1991, the Public Services Contracts Regulations 1993 or the Public Supply Contracts Regulations 1995 before the second commencement date.

(6)    This paragraph applies to qualifying works which are carried out under a contract which—
   (a)    is to be entered into on or after the second commencement date; and
   (b)    is for a period of twelve months or less.

(7)    This paragraph applies where, under an agreement entered into, by or on behalf of the landlord or a superior landlord, before the second commencement date, qualifying works are carried out at any time in the period starting with the second commencement date and ending two months after that date.

**[3283]**

## SCHEDULES

## SCHEDULE 1
## REPEALS

Article 2(c)(iv)

## PART 1
## LEASEHOLD VALUATION TRIBUNALS

| Short title and chapter | Extent of repeal |
|---|---|
| Leasehold Reform Act 1967 (c 88) | Section 21(1A) and (3) to (4A). |
| Housing Act 1980 (c 51) | In section 142— |
| | subsection (2), and |
| | in subsection (3), the words from the beginning to "and". |
| | In Schedule 22— |
| | Part 1, and |
| | in Part 2, paragraph 8(4) to (6). |
| Landlord and Tenant Act 1985 (c 70) | Sections 31A to 31C. |
| | In the Schedule, paragraph 8(5). |
| Landlord and Tenant Act 1987 (c 31) | Section 23(2). |
| | Sections 24A and 24B. |
| | In section 38, in the sidenote, the words "by the court". |
| | Section 52A |
| | In section 53(2), the words "under section 52A(3) or". |
| Tribunals and Inquiries Act 1992 (c 53) | In Schedule 3, paragraph 13. |

| Short title and chapter | Extent of repeal |
|---|---|
| Leasehold Reform, Housing and Urban Development Act 1993 (c 28) | Section 75(4) and (5). |
| | In section 88— |
| |     in subsection (2)(b), the words "constituted for the purposes of that Part of that Act", and subsections (3) to (5) and (7). |
| | In section 91— |
| |     in subsection (1), the words from the beginning to "this section; and", |
| |     subsections (3) to (8), |
| |     subsection (10), and |
| |     in subsection (11), the words from "and the reference" to the end. |
| | In section 94, in subsection (10), the words from "and references in this subsection" to the end. |
| | In section 101(1), the definition of "rent assessment committee". |
| Housing Act 1996 (c 52) | Section 83(3). |
| | Section 86(4) and (5). |
| | Section 119. |
| | In Schedule 6, in Part 4, paragraphs 7 and 8. |

**[3284]**

## PART 2
## OTHER REPEALS

| Short title and chapter | Extent of repeal |
|---|---|
| Landlord and Tenant Act 1985 (c 70) | Section 19(2A) to (3). |
| | In section 39, the entry relating to the expression "flat". |
| | In the Schedule— |
| |     in the heading before paragraph 2, the words "Request for", |
| |     in the heading before paragraph 4, the words "Request relating to", |
| |     in the heading before paragraph 5, the words "on request". |
| Landlord and Tenant Act 1987 (c 31) | In section 29(2)(a), the words "repair, maintenance, insurance or". |
| | Section 56(2). |
| | In Schedule 2, paragraphs 3 and 7. |
| Housing Act 1996 (c 52) | Section 83(1). |
| | In Schedule 9, paragraph 2(3) and (7). |

PART II
STATUTORY INSTRUMENTS

## SCHEDULE 2
## SAVINGS

Article 2(c)

*Absent landlords—leasehold houses*

1.   The amendments made by sections 148 and 149 shall not have effect in relation to an application for enfranchisement made under section 27 of the 1967 Act before the first commencement date.

*Definition of service charges*

2.   The amendment made by paragraph 7 of Schedule 9 shall not apply to costs incurred before the first commencement date in connection with matters for which a service charge is payable.

*Meaning of "management" in section 24 of the 1987 Act*

3.   The amendment made by paragraph 8 of Schedule 9 shall not apply to an application made under section 24 of the 1987 Act before the first commencement date.

*Right to acquire landlord's interest*

4.   The amendment made by paragraph 9 of Schedule 9 and the repeal in section 29 of the 1987 Act shall not apply to an application made under section 29 of that Act before the first commencement date.

*Tenant's right to a management audit*

5.   The amendments made by paragraph 10 of Schedule 9 shall not apply to an application made under section 80 of the 1993 Act before the first commencement date.

*Liability to pay service charges*

6.   The amendment made by section 155 and the repeals of section 19(2A) to (3) of the 1985 Act and of section 83(1) of the 1996 Act shall not have effect in relation to—

   (a)   any application made to a LVT under section 19(2A) or (2B) of the 1985 Act; or
   (b)   any proceedings relating to a service charge transferred to a LVT by a county court,

before the first commencement date.

*Insurance*

7.   The amendments made by paragraphs 8 to 13 of Schedule 10 and the consequential repeals in the Schedule to the 1985 Act shall not apply to a request made under that Schedule before the first commencement date.

*Administration charges: reasonableness, demands and liability to pay*

8.   Paragraphs 2 to 5 of Schedule 11 shall not apply to an administration charge that was payable before the first commencement date.

*Administration charges: appointment of a manager*

9.   The amendments made by paragraph 8 of Schedule 11 shall not apply to an application made under section 24 of the 1987 Act before the first commencement date.

*Charges under estate management schemes*

10.   Section 159 shall not apply to a charge under an estate management scheme that was payable before the first commencement date.

*Variation of leases: transfer of jurisdiction*

11.   The amendments made by section 163 shall not have effect in relation to an application made to the court under Part 4 of the 1987 Act before the first commencement date.

*Crown land: variation of leases*

12.   A variation of any tenancy effected by or in pursuance of an order made before the first commencement date under section 38 of the 1987 Act shall not be treated as binding on the Crown, as predecessor in title under the tenancy, by virtue of section 39(1) of that Act.

*Leasehold valuation tribunals*

13.   Section 175, the amendments made by section 176 and Schedule 13 and the repeals in Part 1 of Schedule 1 to this Order shall not have effect in relation to—

(a)    any application made to a LVT; or
(b)    any proceedings transferred to a LVT by a county court,
before the first commencement date.

**[3286]**

# SERVICE CHARGES (CONSULTATION REQUIREMENTS) (ENGLAND) REGULATIONS 2003

## (SI 2003/1987)

**NOTES**
Made: 4 August 2003.
Authority: Landlord and Tenant Act 1985, ss 20(4), (5), 20ZA(3), (6).
Commencement: 31 October 2003.

## ARRANGEMENT OF REGULATIONS

## 1    Citation, commencement and application

(1)    These Regulations may be cited as the Service Charges (Consultation Requirements) (England) Regulations 2003 and shall come into force on 31st October 2003.

(2)    These Regulations apply in relation to England only.

(3)    These Regulations apply where a landlord—
(a)    intends to enter into a qualifying long term agreement to which section 20 of the Landlord and Tenant Act 1985 applies on or after the date on which these Regulations come into force; or
(b)    intends to carry out qualifying works to which that section applies on or after that date.

**[3287]**

## 2    Interpretation

(1)    In these Regulations—
"the 1985 Act" means the Landlord and Tenant Act 1985;
"close relative", in relation to a person, means a spouse or cohabitee, a parent, parent-in-law, son, son-in-law, daughter, daughter-in-law, brother, brother-in-law, sister, sister-in-law, step-parent, step-son or step-daughter of that person;
"cohabitee", in relation to a person, means—
(a)    a person of the opposite sex who is living with that person as husband or wife; or
(b)    a person of the same sex living with that person in a relationship which has the characteristics of the relationship between husband and wife;
"nominated person" means a person whose name is proposed in response to an invitation made as mentioned in paragraph 1(3) of Schedule 1 or paragraph 1(3) of Part 2 of Schedule 4; and "nomination" means any such proposal;
["public notice" means notice published in the Official Journal of the European Union pursuant to the Public Contracts Regulations 2006;]

"relevant period", in relation to a notice, means the period of 30 days beginning with the date of the notice;

"RTB tenancy" means the tenancy of an RTB tenant;

"RTB tenant", in relation to a landlord, means a person who has become a tenant of the landlord by virtue of section 138 of the Housing Act 1985 (duty of landlord to convey freehold or grant lease), section 171A of that Act (cases in which right to buy is preserved), or section 16 of the Housing Act 1996 (right of tenant to acquire dwelling) under a lease whose terms include a requirement that the tenant shall bear a reasonable part of such costs incurred by the landlord as are mentioned in paragraphs 16A to 16D of Schedule 6 to that Act (service charges and other contributions payable by the tenant);

"section 20" means section 20 (limitation of service charges: consultation requirements) of the 1985 Act;

"section 20ZA" means section 20ZA (consultation requirements: supplementary) of that Act;

"the relevant matters", in relation to a proposed agreement, means the goods or services to be provided or the works to be carried out (as the case may be) under the agreement.

(2)   For the purposes of any estimate required by any provision of these Regulations to be made by the landlord—

    (a)    value added tax shall be included where applicable; and

    (b)    where the estimate relates to a proposed agreement, it shall be assumed that the agreement will terminate only by effluxion of time.

**[3288]**

---

**NOTES**

Para (1): definition "public notice" substituted by the Public Contracts Regulations 2006, SI 2006/5, reg 48(a), Sch 7, Pt 1, para 3.

---

## 3   Agreements that are not qualifying long term agreements

(1)   An agreement is not a qualifying long term agreement—

    (a)    if it is a contract of employment; or

    (b)    if it is a management agreement made by a local housing authority and—

        (i)    a tenant management organisation; or

        (ii)    a body established under section 2 of the Local Government Act 2000;

    (c)    if the parties to the agreement are—

        (i)    a holding company and one or more of its subsidiaries; or

        (ii)    two or more subsidiaries of the same holding company;

    (d)    if—

        (i)    when the agreement is entered into, there are no tenants of the building or other premises to which the agreement relates; and

        (ii)    the agreement is for a term not exceeding five years.

(2)   An agreement entered into, by or on behalf of the landlord or a superior landlord—

    (a)    before the coming into force of these Regulations; and

    (b)    for a term of more than twelve months,

is not a qualifying long term agreement, notwithstanding that more than twelve months of the term remain unexpired on the coming into force of these Regulations.

(3)   An agreement for a term of more than twelve months entered into, by or on behalf of the landlord or a superior landlord, which provides for the carrying out of qualifying works for which public notice has been given before the date on which these Regulations come into force, is not a qualifying long term agreement.

(4)   In paragraph (1)—

"holding company" and "subsidiaries" have the same meaning as in the Companies Act 1985;

"management agreement" has the meaning given by section 27(2) of the Housing Act 1985; and

"tenant management organisation" has the meaning given by section 27AB(8) of the Housing Act 1985.

**[3289]**

## 4   Application of section 20 to qualifying long term agreements

(1)   Section 20 shall apply to a qualifying long term agreement if relevant costs incurred under the agreement in any accounting period exceed an amount which results in the relevant contribution of any tenant, in respect of that period, being more than £100.

(2)   In paragraph (1), "accounting period" means the period—

    (a)    beginning with the relevant date, and

    (b)    ending with the date that falls twelve months after the relevant date.

(3)   [Subject to paragraph (3A), in] the case of the first accounting period, the relevant date is—

(a)    if the relevant accounts are made up for periods of twelve months, the date on which the period that includes the date on which these Regulations come into force ends, or

(b)    if the accounts are not so made up, the date on which these Regulations come into force.

[(3A)    Where—

(a)    a landlord intends to enter into a qualifying long term agreement on or after 12th November 2004; and

(b)    he has not at any time between 31st October 2003 and 12th November 2004 made up accounts relating to service charges referable to a qualifying long term agreement and payable in respect of the dwellings to which the intended agreement is to relate,

the relevant date is the date on which begins the first period for which service charges referable to that intended agreement are payable under the terms of the leases of those dwellings.]

(4)    In the case of subsequent accounting periods, the relevant date is the date immediately following the end of the previous accounting period.

**[3290]**

---

**NOTES**

Para (3): words in square brackets substituted by the Service Charges (Consultation Requirements) (Amendment) (No 2) (England) Regulations 2004, SI 2004/2939, reg 2(a).

Para (3A): inserted by SI 2004/2939, reg 2(b).

---

## 5   The consultation requirements: qualifying long term agreements

(1)    Subject to paragraphs (2) and (3), in relation to qualifying long term agreements to which section 20 applies, the consultation requirements for the purposes of that section and section 20ZA are the requirements specified in Schedule 1.

(2)    Where public notice is required to be given of the relevant matters to which a qualifying long term agreement relates, the consultation requirements for the purposes of sections 20 and 20ZA, as regards the agreement, are the requirements specified in Schedule 2.

(3)    In relation to a RTB tenant and a particular qualifying long term agreement, nothing in paragraph (1) or (2) requires a landlord to comply with any of the consultation requirements applicable to that agreement that arise before the thirty-first day of the RTB tenancy.

**[3291]**

## 6   Application of section 20 to qualifying works

For the purposes of subsection (3) of section 20 the appropriate amount is an amount which results in the relevant contribution of any tenant being more than £250.

**[3292]**

## 7   The consultation requirements: qualifying works

(1)    Subject to paragraph (5), where qualifying works are the subject (whether alone or with other matters) of a qualifying long term agreement to which section 20 applies, the consultation requirements for the purposes of that section and section 20ZA, as regards those works, are the requirements specified in Schedule 3.

(2)    Subject to paragraph (5), in a case to which paragraph (3) applies the consultation requirements for the purposes of sections 20 and 20ZA, as regards qualifying works referred to in that paragraph, are those specified in Schedule 3.

(3)    This paragraph applies where—

(a)    under an agreement entered into, by or on behalf of the landlord or a superior landlord, before the coming into force of these Regulations, qualifying works are carried out at any time on or after the date that falls two months after the date on which these Regulations come into force; or

(b)    under an agreement for a term of more than twelve months entered into, by or on behalf of the landlord or a superior landlord, qualifying works for which public notice has been given before the date on which these Regulations come into force are carried out at any time on or after the date.

(4)    Except in a case to which paragraph (3) applies, and subject to paragraph (5), where qualifying works are not the subject of a qualifying long term agreement to which section 20 applies, the consultation requirements for the purposes of that section and section 20ZA, as regards those works—

(a)    in a case where public notice of those works is required to be given, are those specified in Part 1 of Schedule 4;

(b)    in any other case, are those specified in Part 2 of that Schedule.

(5)    In relation to a RTB tenant and particular qualifying works, nothing in paragraph (1), (2) or (4) requires a landlord to comply with any of the consultation requirements applicable to that agreement that arise before the thirty-first day of the RTB tenancy.

**[3293]**

# SCHEDULES

## SCHEDULE 1
### CONSULTATION REQUIREMENTS FOR QUALIFYING LONG TERM AGREEMENTS OTHER THAN THOSE FOR WHICH PUBLIC NOTICE IS REQUIRED

Regulation 5(1)

*Notice of intention*

1.—(1)  The landlord shall give notice in writing of his intention to enter into the agreement—
   (a)  to each tenant; and
   (b)  where a recognised tenants' association represents some or all of the tenants, to the association.

(2)  The notice shall—
   (a)  describe, in general terms, the relevant matters or specify the place and hours at which a description of the relevant matters may be inspected;
   (b)  state the landlord's reasons for considering it necessary to enter into the agreement;
   (c)  where the relevant matters consist of or include qualifying works, state the landlord's reasons for considering it necessary to carry out those works;
   (d)  invite the making, in writing, of observations in relation to the proposed agreement; and
   (e)  specify—
      (i)   the address to which such observations may be sent;
      (ii)  that they must be delivered within the relevant period; and
      (iii) the date on which the relevant period ends.

(3)  The notice shall also invite each tenant and the association (if any) to propose, within the relevant period, the name of a person from whom the landlord should try to obtain an estimate in respect of the relevant matters.

*Inspection of description of relevant matters*

2.—(1)  Where a notice under paragraph 1 specifies a place and hours for inspection—
   (a)  the place and hours so specified must be reasonable; and
   (b)  a description of the relevant matters must be available for inspection, free of charge, at that place and during those hours.

(2)  If facilities to enable copies to be taken are not made available at the times at which the description may be inspected, the landlord shall provide to any tenant, on request and free of charge, a copy of the description.

*Duty to have regard to observations in relation to proposed agreement*

3.  Where, within the relevant period, observations are made in relation to the proposed agreement by any tenant or recognised tenants' association, the landlord shall have regard to those observations.

*Estimates*

4.—(1)  Where, within the relevant period, a single nomination is made by a recognised tenants' association (whether or not a nomination is made by any tenant), the landlord shall try to obtain an estimate from the nominated person.

(2)  Where, within the relevant period, a single nomination is made by only one of the tenants (whether or not a nomination is made by a recognised tenants' association), the landlord shall try to obtain an estimate from the nominated person.

(3)  Where, within the relevant period, a single nomination is made by more than one tenant (whether or not a nomination is made by a recognised tenants' association), the landlord shall try to obtain an estimate—
   (a)  from the person who received the most nominations; or
   (b)  if there is no such person, but two (or more) persons received the same number of nominations, being a number in excess of the nominations received by any other person, from one of those two (or more) persons; or
   (c)  in any other case, from any nominated person.

(4)  Where, within the relevant period, more than one nomination is made by any tenant and more than one nomination is made by a recognised tenants' association, the landlord shall try to obtain an estimate—
   (a)  from at least one person nominated by a tenant; and
   (b)  from at least one person nominated by the association, other than a person from whom an estimate is sought as mentioned in paragraph (a).

*Preparation of landlord's proposals*

5.—(1)　The landlord shall prepare, in accordance with the following provisions of this paragraph, at least two proposals in respect of the relevant matters.

(2)　At least one of the proposals must propose that goods or services are provided, or works are carried out (as the case may be), by a person wholly unconnected with the landlord.

(3)　Where an estimate has been obtained from a nominated person, the landlord must prepare a proposal based on that estimate.

(4)　Each proposal shall contain a statement of the relevant matters.

(5)　Each proposal shall contain a statement, as regards each party to the proposed agreement other than the landlord—
- (a)　of the party's name and address; and
- (b)　of any connection (apart from the proposed agreement) between the party and the landlord.

(6)　For the purposes of sub-paragraphs (2) and (5)(b), it shall be assumed that there is a connection between a party (as the case may be) and the landlord—
- (a)　where the landlord is a company, if the party is, or is to be, a director or manager of the company or is a close relative of any such director or manager;
- (b)　where the landlord is a company, and the party is a partner in a partnership, if any partner in that partnership is, or is to be, a director or manager of the company or is a close relative of any such director or manager;
- (c)　where both the landlord and the party are companies, if any director or manager of one company is, or is to be, a director or manager of the other company;
- (d)　where the party is a company, if the landlord is a director or manager of the company or is a close relative of any such director or manager; or
- (e)　where the party is a company and the landlord is a partner in a partnership, if any partner in that partnership is a director or manager of the company or is a close relative of any such director or manager.

(7)　Where, as regards each tenant's unit of occupation and the relevant matters, it is reasonably practicable for the landlord to estimate the relevant contribution attributable to the relevant matters to which the proposed agreement relates, each proposal shall contain a statement of that estimated contribution.

(8)　Where—
- (a)　it is not reasonably practicable for the landlord to make the estimate mentioned in sub-paragraph (7); and
- (b)　it is reasonably practicable for the landlord to estimate, as regards the building or other premises to which the proposed agreement relates, the total amount of his expenditure under the proposed agreement,

each proposal shall contain a statement of that estimated expenditure.

(9)　Where—
- (a)　it is not reasonably practicable for the landlord to make the estimate mentioned in sub-paragraph (7) or (8)(b); and
- (b)　it is reasonably practicable for the landlord to ascertain the current unit cost or hourly or daily rate applicable to the relevant matters,

each proposal shall contain a statement of that cost or rate.

(10)　Where the relevant matters comprise or include the proposed appointment by the landlord of an agent to discharge any of the landlord's obligations to the tenants which relate to the management by him of premises to which the agreement relates, each proposal shall contain a statement—
- (a)　that the person whose appointment is proposed—
  - (i)　is or, as the case may be, is not, a member of a professional body or trade association; and
  - (ii)　subscribes or, as the case may be, does not subscribe, to any code of practice or voluntary accreditation scheme relevant to the functions of managing agents; and
- (b)　if the person is a member of a professional body trade association, of the name of the body or association.

(11)　Each proposal shall contain a statement as to the provisions (if any) for variation of any amount specified in, or to be determined under, the proposed agreement.

(12)　Each proposal shall contain a statement of the intended duration of the proposed agreement.

(13)　Where the landlord has received observations to which (in accordance with paragraph 3) he is required to have regard, each proposal shall contain a statement summarising the observations and setting out the landlord's response to them.

### Notification of landlord's proposals

6.—(1)  The landlord shall give notice in writing of proposals prepared under paragraph 5—
    (a)  to each tenant; and
    (b)  where a recognised tenants' association represents some or all of the tenants, to the association.

    (2)  The notice shall—
    (a)  be accompanied by a copy of each proposal or specify the place and hours at which the proposals may be inspected;
    (b)  invite the making, in writing, of observations in relation to the proposals; and
    (c)  specify—
        (i)  the address to which such observations may be sent;
        (ii)  that they must be delivered within the relevant period; and
        (iii)  the date on which the relevant period ends.

    (3)  Paragraph 2 shall apply to proposals made available for inspection under this paragraph as it applies to a description of the relevant matters made available for inspection under that paragraph.

### Duty to have regard to observations in relation to proposals

7.  Where, within the relevant period, observations are made in relation to the landlord's proposals by any tenant or recognised tenants' association, the landlord shall have regard to those observations.

### Duty on entering into agreement

8.—(1)  Subject to sub-paragraph (2), where the landlord enters into an agreement relating to relevant matters, he shall, within 21 days of entering into the agreement, by notice in writing to each tenant and the recognised tenants' association (if any)—
    (a)  state his reasons for making that agreement or specify the place and hours at which a statement of those reasons may be inspected; and
    (b)  where he has received observations to which (in accordance with paragraph 7) he is required to have regard, summarise the observations and respond to them or specify the place and hours at which that summary and response may be inspected.

    (2)  The requirements of sub-paragraph (1) do not apply where the person with whom the agreement is made is a nominated person or submitted the lowest estimate.

    (3)  Paragraph 2 shall apply to a statement, summary and response made available for inspection under this paragraph as it applies to a description of the relevant matters made available for inspection under that paragraph.

**[3294]**

### SCHEDULE 2
## CONSULTATION REQUIREMENTS FOR QUALIFYING LONG TERM AGREEMENTS FOR WHICH PUBLIC NOTICE IS REQUIRED
Regulation 5(2)

### Notice of intention

1.—(1)  The landlord shall give notice in writing of his intention to enter into the agreement—
    (a)  to each tenant; and
    (b)  where a recognised tenants' association represents some or all of the tenants, to the association.

    (2)  The notice shall—
    (a)  describe, in general terms, the relevant matters or specify the place and hours at which a description of the relevant matters may be inspected;
    (b)  state the landlord's reasons for considering it necessary to enter into the agreement;
    (c)  where the relevant matters consist of or include qualifying works, state the landlord's reasons for considering it necessary to carry out those works;
    (d)  state that the reason why the landlord is not inviting recipients of the notice to nominate persons from whom he should try to obtain an estimate for the relevant matters is that public notice of the relevant matters is to be given;
    (e)  invite the making, in writing, of observations in relation to the relevant matters; and
    (f)  specify—
        (i)  the address to which such observations may be sent;
        (ii)  that they must be delivered within the relevant period; and
        (iii)  the date on which the relevant period ends.

### Inspection of description of relevant matters

2.—(1)  Where a notice under paragraph 1 specifies a place and hours for inspection—
    (a)  the place and hours so specified must be reasonable; and

(b)   a description of the relevant matters must be available for inspection, free of charge, at that place and during those hours.

(2)   If facilities to enable copies to be taken are not made available at the times at which the description may be inspected, the landlord shall provide to any tenant, on request and free of charge, a copy of the description.

*Duty to have regard to observations in relation to relevant matters*

3.   Where, within the relevant period, observations are made, in relation to the relevant matters by any tenant or recognised tenants' association, the landlord shall have regard to those observations.

*Preparation of landlord's proposal*

4.—(1)   The landlord shall prepare, in accordance with the following provisions of this paragraph, a proposal in respect of the proposed agreement.

(2)   The proposal shall contain a statement—
   (a)   of the name and address of every party to the proposed agreement (other than the landlord); and
   (b)   of any connection (apart from the proposed agreement) between the landlord and any other party.

(3)   For the purpose of sub-paragraph (2)(b), it shall be assumed that there is a connection between the landlord and a party—
   (a)   where the landlord is a company, if the party is, or is to be, a director or manager of the company or is a close relative of any such director or manager;
   (b)   where the landlord is a company, and the party is a partner in a partnership, if any partner in that partnership is, or is to be, a director or manager of the company or is a close relative of any such director or manager;
   (c)   where both the landlord and the party are companies, if any director or manager of one company is, or is to be, a director or manager of the other company;
   (d)   where the party is a company, if the landlord is a director or manager of the company or is a close relative of any such director or manager; or.
   (e)   where the party is a company and the landlord is a partner in a partnership, if any partner in that partnership is a director or manager of the company or is a close relative of any such director or manager.

(4)   Where, as regards each tenant's unit of occupation, it is reasonably practicable for the landlord to estimate the relevant contribution to be incurred by the tenant attributable to the relevant matters to which the proposed agreement relates, the proposal shall contain a statement of that contribution.

(5)   Where—
   (a)   it is not reasonably practicable for the landlord to make the estimate mentioned in sub-paragraph (4); and
   (b)   it is reasonably practicable for the landlord to estimate, as regards the building or other premises to which the proposed agreement relates, the total amount of his expenditure under the proposed agreement,
the proposal shall contain a statement of the amount of that estimated expenditure.

(6)   Where—
   (a)   it is not reasonably practicable for the landlord to make the estimate mentioned in sub-paragraph (4) or (5)(b); and
   (b)   it is reasonably practicable for the landlord to ascertain the current unit cost or hourly or daily rate applicable to the relevant matters to which the proposed agreement relates,
the proposal shall contain a statement of that cost or rate.

(7)   Where it is not reasonably practicable for the landlord to make the estimate mentioned in sub-paragraph (6)(b), the proposal shall contain a statement of the reasons why he cannot comply and the date by which he expects to be able to provide an estimate, cost or rate.

(8)   Where the relevant matters comprise or include the proposed appointment by the landlord of an agent to discharge any of the landlord's obligations to the tenants which relate to the management by him of premises to which the agreement relates, each proposal shall contain a statement—
   (a)   that the person whose appointment is proposed—
      (i)   is or, as the case may be, is not, a member of a professional body or trade association; and
      (ii)   subscribes or, as the case may be, does not subscribe, to any code of practice or voluntary accreditation scheme relevant to the functions of managing agents; and
   (b)   if the person is a member of a professional body trade association, of the name of the body or association.

(9)   Each proposal shall contain a statement of the intended duration of the proposed agreement.

PART II
STATUTORY INSTRUMENTS

(10)   Where the landlord has received observations to which (in accordance with paragraph 3) he is required to have regard, the proposal shall contain a statement summarising the observations and setting out the landlord's response to them.

### Notification of landlord's proposal

5.—(1)   The landlord shall give notice in writing of the proposal prepared under paragraph 4—

   (a)   to each tenant; and
   (b)   where a recognised tenants' association represents some or all of the tenants, to the association.

   (2)   The notice shall—

   (a)   be accompanied by a copy of the proposal or specify the place and hours at which the proposal may be inspected;
   (b)   invite the making, in writing, of observations in relation to the proposal; and
   (c)   specify—
      (i)    the address to which such observations may be sent;
      (ii)   that they must be delivered within the relevant period; and
      (iii)  the date on which the relevant period ends.

   (3)   Paragraph 2 shall apply to a proposal made available for inspection under this paragraph as it applies to a description made available for inspection under that paragraph.

### Duty to have regard to observations in relation to proposal

6.   Where, within the relevant period, observations are made in relation to the landlord's proposal by any tenant or recognised tenants' association, the landlord shall have regard to those observations.

### Landlord's response to observations

7.   Where the landlord receives observations to which (in accordance with paragraph 6) he is required to have regard, he shall, within 21 days of their receipt, by notice in writing to the person by whom the observations were made, state his response to the observations.

### Supplementary information

8.   Where a proposal prepared under paragraph 4 contains such a statement as is mentioned in sub-paragraph (7) of that paragraph, the landlord shall, within 21 days of receiving sufficient information to enable him to estimate the amount, cost or rate referred to in sub-paragraph (4), (5) or (6) of that paragraph, give notice in writing of the estimated amount, cost or rate (as the case may be)—

   (a)   to each tenant; and
   (b)   where a recognised tenants' association represents some or all of the tenants, to the association.

**[3295]**

### SCHEDULE 3
### CONSULTATION REQUIREMENTS FOR QUALIFYING WORKS UNDER QUALIFYING LONG TERM AGREEMENTS AND AGREEMENTS TO WHICH REGULATION 7(3) APPLIES

Regulation 7(1) and (2)

### Notice of intention

1.—(1)   The landlord shall give notice in writing of his intention to carry out qualifying works—

   (a)   to each tenant; and
   (b)   where a recognised tenants' association represents some or all of the tenants, to the association.

   (2)   The notice shall—

   (a)   describe, in general terms, the works proposed to be carried out or specify the place and hours at which a description of the proposed works may be inspected;
   (b)   state the landlord's reasons for considering it necessary to carry out the proposed works;
   (c)   contain a statement of the total amount of the expenditure estimated by the landlord as likely to be incurred by him on and in connection with the proposed works;
   (d)   invite the making, in writing, of observations in relation to the proposed works or the landlord's estimated expenditure;
   (e)   specify—
      (i)    the address to which such observations may be sent;
      (ii)   that they must be delivered within the relevant period; and
      (iii)  the date on which the relevant period ends.

*Inspection of description of proposed works*

2.—(1)    Where a notice under paragraph 1 specifies a place and hours for inspection—

    (a)    the place and hours so specified must be reasonable; and

    (b)    a description of the proposed works must be available for inspection, free of charge, at that place and during those hours.

(2)    If facilities to enable copies to be taken are not made available at the times at which the description may be inspected, the landlord shall provide to any tenant, on request and free of charge, a copy of the description.

*Duty to have regard to observations in relation to proposed works and estimated expenditure*

3.    Where, within the relevant period, observations are made in relation to the proposed works or the landlord's estimated expenditure by any tenant or the recognised tenants' association, the landlord shall have regard to those observations.

*Landlord's response to observations*

4.    Where the landlord receives observations to which (in accordance with paragraph 3) he is required to have regard, he shall, within 21 days of their receipt, by notice in writing to the person by whom the observations were made, state his response to the observations.

**[3296]**

## SCHEDULE 4
### CONSULTATION REQUIREMENTS FOR QUALIFYING WORKS OTHER THAN WORKS UNDER QUALIFYING LONG TERM OR AGREEMENTS TO WHICH REGULATION 7(3) APPLIES

Regulation 7(4)

## PART 1
### CONSULTATION REQUIREMENTS FOR QUALIFYING WORKS FOR WHICH PUBLIC NOTICE IS REQUIRED

*Notice of intention*

1.—(1)    The landlord shall give notice in writing of his intention to carry out qualifying works—

    (a)    to each tenant; and

    (b)    where a recognised tenants' association represents some or all of the tenants, to the association.

(2)    The notice shall—

    (a)    describe, in general terms, the works proposed to be carried out or specify the place and hours at which a description of the proposed works may be inspected;

    (b)    state the landlord's reasons for considering it necessary to carry out the proposed works;

    (c)    state that the reason why the landlord is not inviting recipients of the notice to nominate persons from whom he should try to obtain an estimate for carrying out the works is that public notice of the works is to be given;

    (d)    invite the making, in writing, of observations in relation to the proposed works; and

    (e)    specify—

        (i)    the address to which such observations may be sent;

        (ii)    that they must be delivered within the relevant period; and

        (iii)    the date on which the relevant period ends.

*Inspection of description of proposed works*

2.—(1)    Where a notice under paragraph 1 specifies a place and hours for inspection—

    (a)    the place and hours so specified must be reasonable; and

    (b)    a description of the proposed works must be available for inspection, free of charge, at that place and during those hours.

(2)    If facilities to enable copies to be taken are not made available at the times at which the description may be inspected, the landlord shall provide to any tenant, on request and free of charge, a copy of the description.

*Duty to have regard to observations in relation to proposed works*

3.    Where, within the relevant period, observations are made in relation to the proposed works by any tenant or the recognised tenants' association, the landlord shall have regard to those observations.

### Preparation of landlord's contract statement

4.—(1)    The landlord shall prepare, in accordance with the following provisions of this paragraph, a statement in respect of the proposed contract under which the proposed works are to be carried out.

(2)    The statement shall set out—

    (a)    the name and address of the person with whom the landlord proposes to contract; and

    (b)    particulars of any connection between them (apart from the proposed contract).

(3)    For the purpose of sub-paragraph (2)(b) it shall be assumed that there is a connection between a person and the landlord—

    (a)    where the landlord is a company, if the person, or is to be, a director or manager of the company or is a close relative of any such director or manager;

    (b)    where the landlord is a company, and the person is a partner in a partnership, if any partner in that partnership is, or is to be, a director or manager of the company or is a close relative of any such director or manager;

    (c)    where both the landlord and the person are companies, if any director or manager of one company is, or is to be, a director or manager of the other company;

    (d)    where the person is a company, if the landlord is a director or manager of the company or is a close relative of any such director or manager; or

    (e)    where the person is a company and the landlord is a partner in a partnership, if any partner in that partnership is a director or manager of the company or is a close relative of any such director or manager.

(4)    Where, as regards each tenant's unit of occupation, it is reasonably practicable for the landlord to estimate the amount of the relevant contribution to be incurred by the tenant attributable to the works to which the proposed contract relates, that estimated amount shall be specified in the statement.

(5)    Where—

    (a)    it is not reasonably practicable for the landlord to make the estimate mentioned in sub-paragraph (4); and

    (b)    it is reasonably practicable for the landlord to estimate, as regards the building or other premises to which the proposed contract relates, the total amount of his expenditure under the proposed contract,

that estimated amount shall be specified in the statement.

(6)    Where—

    (a)    it is not reasonably practicable for the landlord to make the estimate mentioned in sub-paragraph (4) or (5)(b); and

    (b)    it is reasonably practicable for the landlord to ascertain the current unit cost or hourly or daily rate applicable to the works to which the proposed contract relates,

that cost or rate shall be specified in the statement.

(7)    Where it is not reasonably practicable for the landlord to make the estimate mentioned in sub-paragraph (6)(b), the reasons why he cannot comply and the date by which he expects to be able to provide an estimated amount, cost or rate shall be specified in the statement.

(8)    Where the landlord has received observations to which (in accordance with paragraph 3) he is required to have regard, the statement shall summarise the observations and set out his response to them.

### Notification of proposed contract

5.—(1)    The landlord shall give notice in writing of his intention to enter into the proposed contract—

    (a)    to each tenant; and

    (b)    where a recognised tenants' association represents some or all of the tenants, to the association.

(2)    The notice shall—

    (a)    comprise, or be accompanied by, the statement prepared in accordance with paragraph 4 ("the paragraph 4 statement") or specify the place and hours at which that statement may be inspected;

    (b)    invite the making, in writing, of observations in relation to any matter mentioned in the paragraph 4 statement;

    (c)    specify—

        (i)    the address to which such observations may be sent;

        (ii)    that they must be delivered within the relevant period; and

        (iii)    the date on which the relevant period ends.

(3)    Where the paragraph 4 statement is made available for inspection, paragraph 2 shall apply in relation to that statement as it applies in relation to a description of proposed works made available for inspection under that paragraph.

*Landlord's response to observations*

6.    Where, within the relevant period, the landlord receives observations in response to the invitation in the notice under paragraph 5, he shall, within 21 days of their receipt, by notice in writing to the person by whom the observations were made, state his response to the observations.

*Supplementary information*

7.    Where a statement prepared under paragraph 4 sets out the landlord's reasons for being unable to comply with sub-paragraph (6) of that paragraph, the landlord shall, within 21 days of receiving sufficient information to enable him to estimate the amount, cost or rate referred to in sub-paragraph (4), (5) or (6) of that paragraph, give notice in writing of the estimated amount, cost or rate (as the case may be)—

    (a)    to each tenant; and

    (b)    where a recognised tenants' association represents some or all of the tenants, to the association.

**[3297]**

## PART 2
### CONSULTATION REQUIREMENTS FOR QUALIFYING WORKS FOR WHICH PUBLIC NOTICE IS NOT REQUIRED

*Notice of intention*

8.—(1)    The landlord shall give notice in writing of his intention to carry out qualifying works—

    (a)    to each tenant; and

    (b)    where a recognised tenants' association represents some or all of the tenants, to the association.

    (2)    The notice shall—

    (a)    describe, in general terms, the works proposed to be carried out or specify the place and hours at which a description of the proposed works may be inspected;

    (b)    state the landlord's reasons for considering it necessary to carry out the proposed works;

    (c)    invite the making, in writing, of observations in relation to the proposed works; and

    (d)    specify—

        (i)    the address to which such observations may be sent;

        (ii)    that they must be delivered within the relevant period; and

        (iii)    the date on which the relevant period ends.

    (3)    The notice shall also invite each tenant and the association (if any) to propose, within the relevant period, the name of a person from whom the landlord should try to obtain an estimate for the carrying out of the proposed works.

*Inspection of description of proposed works*

9.—(1)    Where a notice under paragraph 1 specifies a place and hours for inspection—

    (a)    the place and hours so specified must be reasonable; and

    (b)    a description of the proposed works must be available for inspection, free of charge, at that place and during those hours.

    (2)    If facilities to enable copies to be taken are not made available at the times at which the description may be inspected, the landlord shall provide to any tenant, on request and free of charge, a copy of the description.

*Duty to have regard to observations in relation to proposed works*

10.    Where, within the relevant period, observations are made, in relation to the proposed works by any tenant or recognised tenants' association, the landlord shall have regard to those observations.

*Estimates and response to observations*

11.—(1)    Where, within the relevant period, a nomination is made by a recognised tenants' association (whether or not a nomination is made by any tenant), the landlord shall try to obtain an estimate from the nominated person.

    (2)    Where, within the relevant period, a nomination is made by only one of the tenants (whether or not a nomination is made by a recognised tenants' association), the landlord shall try to obtain an estimate from the nominated person.

    (3)    Where, within the relevant period, a single nomination is made by more than one tenant (whether or not a nomination is made by a recognised tenants' association), the landlord shall try to obtain an estimate—

    (a)    from the person who received the most nominations; or

    (b)    if there is no such person, but two (or more) persons received the same number of nominations, being a number in excess of the nominations received by any other person, from one of those two (or more) persons; or

(c)    in any other case, from any nominated person.

(4)    Where, within the relevant period, more than one nomination is made by any tenant and more than one nomination is made by a recognised tenants' association, the landlord shall try to obtain an estimate—

(a)    from at least one person nominated by a tenant; and

(b)    from at least one person nominated by the association, other than a person from whom an estimate is sought as mentioned in paragraph (a).

(5)    The landlord shall, in accordance with this sub-paragraph and sub-paragraphs (6) to (9)—

(a)    obtain estimates for the carrying out of the proposed works;

(b)    supply, free of charge, a statement ("the paragraph (b) statement") setting out—

    (i)    as regards at least two of the estimates, the amount specified in the estimate as the estimated cost of the proposed works; and

    (ii)    where the landlord has received observations to which (in accordance with paragraph 3) he is required to have regard, a summary of the observations and his response to them; and

(c)    make all of the estimates available for inspection.

(6)    At least one of the estimates must be that of a person wholly unconnected with the landlord.

(7)    For the purpose of paragraph (6), it shall be assumed that there is a connection between a person and the landlord—

(a)    where the landlord is a company, if the person is, or is to be, a director or manager of the company or is a close relative of any such director or manager;

(b)    where the landlord is a company, and the person is a partner in a partnership, if any partner in that partnership is, or is to be, a director or manager of the company or is a close relative of any such director or manager;

(c)    where both the landlord and the person are companies, if any director or manager of one company is, or is to be, a director or manager of the other company;

(d)    where the person is a company, if the landlord is a director or manager of the company or is a close relative of any such director or manager; or

(e)    where the person is a company and the landlord is a partner in a partnership, if any partner in that partnership is a director or manager of the company or is a close relative of any such director or manager.

(8)    Where the landlord has obtained an estimate from a nominated person, that estimate must be one of those to which the paragraph (b) statement relates.

(9)    The paragraph (b) statement shall be supplied to, and the estimates made available for inspection by—

(a)    each tenant; and

(b)    the secretary of the recognised tenants' association (if any).

(10)    The landlord shall, by notice in writing to each tenant and the association (if any)—

(a)    specify the place and hours at which the estimates may be inspected;

(b)    invite the making, in writing, of observations in relation to those estimates;

(c)    specify—

    (i)    the address to which such observations may be sent;

    (ii)    that they must be delivered within the relevant period; and

    (iii)    the date on which the relevant period ends.

(11)    Paragraph 2 shall apply to estimates made available for inspection under this paragraph as it applies to a description of proposed works made available for inspection under that paragraph.

*Duty to have regard to observations in relation to estimates*

12.    Where, within the relevant period, observations are made in relation to the estimates by a recognised tenants' association or, as the case may be, any tenant, the landlord shall have regard to those observations.

*Duty on entering into contract*

13.—(1)    Subject to sub-paragraph (2), where the landlord enters into a contract for the carrying out of qualifying works, he shall, within 21 days of entering into the contract, by notice in writing to each tenant and the recognised tenants' association (if any)—

(a)    state his reasons for awarding the contract or specify the place and hours at which a statement of those reasons may be inspected; and

(b)    there he received observations to which (in accordance with paragraph 5) he was required to have regard, summarise the observations and set out his response to them.

(2)    The requirements of sub-paragraph (1) do not apply where the person with whom the contract is made is a nominated person or submitted the lowest estimate.

(3)   Paragraph 2 shall apply to a statement made available for inspection under this paragraph as it applies to a description of proposed works made available for inspection under that paragraph.

**[3298]**

# RIGHT TO MANAGE (PRESCRIBED PARTICULARS AND FORMS) (ENGLAND) REGULATIONS 2003

## (SI 2003/1988)

**NOTES**

Made: 4 August 2003.

Authority: Commonhold and Leasehold Reform Act 2002, ss 78(2)(d), (3), 80(8), (9), 84(2), 92(3)(e), (7)(b), 178(1)(b), (c).

Commencement: 30 September 2003.

### ARRANGEMENT OF REGULATIONS

## 1   Citation, commencement and application

(1)   These Regulations may be cited as the Right to Manage (Prescribed Particulars and Forms) (England) Regulations 2003 and shall come into force on 30th September 2003.

(2)   These Regulations apply in relation to premises in England only.

**[3299]**

## 2   Interpretation

In these Regulations—

"the 2002 Act" means the Commonhold and Leasehold Reform Act 2002;

"landlord", in relation to RTM premises, means a person who is landlord under a lease of the whole or any part of the premises;

"RTM premises" means premises as regards which a RTM company intends to acquire the right to manage;

"third party", in relation to RTM premises, means a person who is party to a lease of the whole or any part of the premises otherwise than as landlord or tenant.

**[3300]**

## 3   Additional content of notice of invitation to participate

(1)   A notice of invitation to participate shall contain (in addition to the statements and invitation referred to in paragraphs (a) to (c) of subsection (2) of section 78 (notice inviting participation) of the 2002 Act), the particulars mentioned in paragraph (2).

(2)   The particulars referred to in paragraph (1) are—

(a)   the RTM company's registered number, the address of its registered office and the names of its directors and secretary;

(b)   the names of the landlord and any third party;

(c)   a statement that, subject to the exclusions mentioned in sub-paragraph (e), if the right to manage is acquired by the RTM company, the company will be responsible for—

(i)   the discharge of the landlord's duties under the lease; and

(ii)   the exercise of his powers under the lease,

with respect to services, repairs, maintenance, improvements, insurance and management;

(d)   a statement that, subject to the exclusion mentioned in sub-paragraph (e)(ii), if the right to manage is acquired by the RTM company, the company may enforce untransferred tenant covenants;

(e) a statement that, if the right to manage is acquired by the RTM company, the company will not be responsible for the discharge of the landlord's duties or the exercise of his powers under the lease—

    (i) with respect to a matter concerning only a part of the premises consisting of a flat or other unit not subject to a lease held by a qualifying tenant; or

    (ii) relating to re-entry or forfeiture;

(f) a statement that, if the right to manage is acquired by the RTM company, the company will have functions under the statutory provisions referred to in Schedule 7 to the 2002 Act;

(g) a statement that the RTM company intends or, as the case may be, does not intend, to appoint a managing agent within the meaning of section 30B(8) of the Landlord and Tenant Act 1985; and—

    (i) if it does so intend, a statement—

        (aa) of the name and address of the proposed managing agent (if known); and

        (bb) if it be the case, that the person is the landlord's managing agent; or

    (ii) if it does not so intend, the qualifications or experience (if any) of the existing members of the RTM company in relation to the management of residential property;

(h) a statement that, where the company gives a claim notice, a person who is or has been a member of the company may be liable for costs incurred by the landlord and others in consequence of the notice;

(i) a statement that, if the recipient of the notice (of invitation to participate) does not fully understand its purpose or implications, he is advised to seek professional help; and

(j) the information provided in the notes to the form set out in Schedule 1 to these Regulations.

**[3301]**

## 4 Additional content of claim notice

A claim notice shall contain (in addition to the particulars required by subsections (2) to (7) of section 80 (contents of claim notice) of the 2002 Act)—

(a) a statement that a person who—

    (i) does not dispute the RTM's company's entitlement to acquire the right to manage; and

    (ii) is the manager party under a management contract subsisting immediately before the date specified in the claim notice under section 80(6) of the 2002 Act,

    must, in accordance with section 92 (duties to give notice of contracts) of the 2002 Act, give a notice in relation to the contract to the person who is the contractor party in relation to the contract and to the RTM company;

(b) a statement that, from the acquisition date, landlords under leases of the whole or any part of the premises to which the claim notice relates are entitled to be members of the RTM company;

(c) a statement that the notice is not invalidated by any inaccuracy in any of the particulars required by section 80(2) to (7) of the 2002 Act or this regulation, but that a person who is of the opinion that any of the particulars contained in the claim notice are inaccurate may—

    (i) identify the particulars in question to the RTM company by which the notice was given; and

    (ii) indicate the respects in which they are considered to be inaccurate;

(d) a statement that a person who receives the notice but does not fully understand its purpose, is advised to seek professional help; and

(e) the information provided in the notes to the form set out in Schedule 2 to these Regulations.

**[3302]**

## 5 Additional content of counter-notice

A counter-notice shall contain (in addition to the statement referred to in paragraph (a) or (b) of subsection (2) of section 84 (counter-notices) of the 2002 Act)—

(a) a statement that, where the RTM company has been given one or more counter-notices containing such a statement as is mentioned in paragraph (b) of subsection (2) of section 84 of the 2002 Act, the company may apply to a leasehold valuation tribunal for a determination that, on the date on which notice of the claim was given, the company was entitled to acquire the right to manage the premises specified in the claim notice;

(b) a statement that, where the RTM company has been given one or more counter-notices containing such a statement as is mentioned in paragraph (b) of subsection (2) of section 84 of the 2002 Act, the company does not acquire the right to manage the premises specified in the claim notice unless—

    (i) on an application to a leasehold valuation tribunal, it is finally determined that the company was entitled to acquire the right to manage the premises; or

     (ii)    the person by whom the counter-notice was given agrees, or the persons by whom the counter-notices were given agree, in writing that the company was so entitled; and

  (c)    the information provided in the notes to the form set out in Schedule 3 to these Regulations.

**[3303]**

## 6   Additional content of contractor notice

A contractor notice shall contain (in addition to the particulars referred to in paragraphs (a) to (d) of subsection (3) of section 92 (duties to give notice of contracts) of the 2002 Act) the statement that, should the person to whom the notice is given wish to provide to the RTM company services which, as the contractor party, it has provided to the manager party under the contract of which details are given in the notice, it is advised to contact the RTM company at the address given in the notice.

**[3304]**

## 7   Additional content of contract notice

A contract notice shall contain (in addition to the particulars referred to in paragraph (a) of subsection (7) of section 92 of the 2002 Act)—

  (a)    the address of the person who is the contractor party, or sub-contractor party, under the contract of which particulars are given in the notice; and

  (b)    a statement that, should the RTM company wish to avail itself of the services which the contractor party, or sub-contractor party, has provided to the manager party under that contract, it is advised to contact the contractor party, or sub-contractor party, at the address given in the notice.

**[3305]**

## 8   Form of notices

  (1)    Notices of invitation to participate shall be in the form set out in Schedule 1 to these Regulations.

  (2)    Claim notices shall be in the form set out in Schedule 2 to these Regulations.

  (3)    Counter-notices shall be in the form set out in Schedule 3 to these Regulations.

**[3306]**

PART II
STATUTORY INSTRUMENTS

SCHEDULES

SCHEDULE 1
FORM OF NOTICE OF INVITATION TO PARTICIPATE

Regulations 3(2)(j) and 8(1)

COMMONHOLD AND LEASEHOLD REFORM ACT 2002

Notice of invitation to participate in right to manage

To *[name and address]* (**See Note 1 below**)

1.    *[name of RTM* company] ("the company"), a private company limited by guarantee, of *[address of registered office]*, and of which the registered number is *[number under Companies Act 1985]*, is authorised by its memorandum of association to acquire and exercise the right to manage *[name of premises to which notice relates]* ("the premises"). The company intends to acquire the right to manage the premises.

2.    *The company's memorandum of association, together with its articles of association, accompanies this notice.

*The company's memorandum of association, together with its articles of association, may be inspected at *[address for inspection]* between *[specify times]*. (**See Note 2 below**) At any time within the period of seven days beginning with the day after this notice is given, a copy of the memorandum of association and articles of association may be ordered from *[specify address]* on payment of *[specify fee]*. (**See Note 3 below**)

*Delete one of these statements, as the circumstances require.*

3.    The names of—

  (a)    the members of the company;

  (b)    the company's directors; and

  (c)    the company's secretary,

are set out in the Schedule below.

4.    The names of the landlord and of the person (if any) who is party to a lease of the whole or any part of the premises otherwise than as landlord or tenant are *[specify]*.

5.    Subject to the exclusions mentioned in paragraph 7, if the right to manage is acquired by the company, the company will be responsible for—

  (a)    the discharge of the landlord's duties under the lease; and

(b)   the exercise of his powers under the lease,

with respect to services, repairs, maintenance, improvements, insurance and management.

6.   Subject to the exclusion mentioned in paragraph 7(b), if the right to manage is acquired by the company, the company may enforce untransferred tenant covenants. (**See Note 4 below**)

7.   If the right to manage is acquired by the company, the company will not be responsible for the discharge of the landlord's duties or the exercise of his powers under the lease—

   (a)   with respect to a matter concerning only a part of the premises consisting of a flat or other unit not subject to a lease held by a qualifying tenant; or

   (b)   relating to re-entry or forfeiture.

8.   If the right to manage is acquired by the company, the company will have functions under the statutory provisions referred to in Schedule 7 to the Commonhold and Leasehold Reform Act 2002. (**See Note 5 below**)

9.   *The company intends to appoint a managing agent within the meaning of section 30B(8) of the Landlord and Tenant Act 1985. [If known, give the name and address of the proposed managing agent here. If that person is the current managing agent, that fact must also be stated here.]

*The company does not intend to appoint a managing agent within the meaning of section 30B(8) of the Landlord and Tenant Act 1985. [*If any existing member of the company has qualifications or experience in relation to the management of residential property, give details in the Schedule below.]*

*Delete one of these statements, as the circumstances require.*

10.   If the company gives notice of its claim to acquire the right to manage the premises (a "claim notice"), a person who is or has been a member of the company may be liable for costs incurred by the landlord and others in consequence of the claim notice. (**See Note 6 below**)

11.   You are invited to become a member of the company. (**See Note 7 below**)

12.   If you do not fully understand the purpose or implications of this notice you are advised to seek professional help.

SCHEDULE

The names of the members of the company are: [*state names of company members*]

The names of the company's directors are: [*state directors' names*]

The name of the company's secretary is: [*state company secretary's name*]

[*If applicable; see the second alternative in paragraph 9 above*] The following member[s] of the company [has][have] qualifications or experience in relation to the management of residential property: [*give details*]

Signed by authority of the company,

[*Signature of authorised member or officer*]

[*Insert date*]

## Notes

1.   The notice inviting participation must be sent to each person who is at the time the notice is given a qualifying tenant of a flat in the premises but who is not already, and has not agreed to become, a member of the company. A qualifying tenant is defined in section 75 of the Commonhold and Leasehold Reform Act 2002 ("the 2002 Act").

2.   The specified times must be periods of at least 2 hours on each of at least 3 days (including a Saturday or Sunday or both) within the 7 days beginning with the day following that on which the notice is given.

3.   The ordering facility must be available throughout the 7 day period referred to in Note 2. The fee must not exceed the reasonable cost of providing the ordered copy.

4.   An untransferred tenant covenant is a covenant in a tenant's lease that he must comply with, but which can be enforced by the company only by virtue of section 100 of the 2002 Act.

5.   The functions relate to matters such as repairing obligations, administration and service charges, and information to be furnished to tenants. Details may be obtained from the RTM company.

6.   If the claim notice is at any time withdrawn, deemed to be withdrawn or otherwise ceases to have effect, each person who is or has been a member of the company is liable (except in the circumstances mentioned at the end of this note) for reasonable costs incurred by—

   (a)   the landlord,

   (b)   any person who is party to a lease of the whole or any part of the premises otherwise than as landlord or tenant, or

   (c)   a manager appointed under Part 2 of the Landlord and Tenant Act 1987 to act in relation to the premises to which this notice relates, or any premises containing or contained in the premises to which this notice relates, in consequence of the claim notice.

A current or former member of the company is liable both jointly with the company and every other person who is or has been a member of the company, and individually. However, a former member is not liable if he has assigned the lease by virtue of which he was a qualifying tenant to another person and that other person has become a member of the company.

7.    All qualifying tenants of flats contained in the premises are entitled to be members. Landlords under leases of the whole or any part of the premises are also entitled to be members, but only once the right to manage has been acquired by the company. An application for membership may be made in accordance with the company's articles of association which, if they do not accompany this notice, may be inspected as mentioned in paragraph 2 of the notice.

8.    If the right to manage is acquired by the company, the company must report to any person who is landlord under a lease of the whole or any part of premises any failure to comply with any tenant covenant of the lease unless, within the period of three months beginning with the day on which the failure to comply comes to the attention of the company—
    (a)    the failure has been remedied,
    (b)    reasonable compensation has been paid in respect of the failure, or
    (c)    the landlord has notified the company that it need not report to him failures of the description of the failure concerned.

9.    If the right to manage is acquired by the company, management functions of a person who is party to a lease of the whole or any part of the premises otherwise than as landlord or tenant will become functions of the company. The company will be responsible for the discharge of that person's duties under the lease and the exercise of his powers under the lease, with respect to services, repairs, maintenance, improvements, insurance and management. However, the company will not be responsible for matters concerning only a part of the premises consisting of a flat or other unit not subject to a lease held by a qualifying tenant, or relating to re-entry or forfeiture.

10.    If the right to manage is acquired by the company, the company will be responsible for the exercise of the powers relating to the grant of approvals to a tenant under the lease, but will not be responsible for the exercise of those powers in relation to an approval concerning only a part of the premises consisting of a flat or other unit not subject to a lease held by a qualifying tenant.

**[3307]**

### SCHEDULE 2
### FORM OF CLAIM NOTICE

Regulations 4(e) and 8(2)

COMMONHOLD AND LEASEHOLD REFORM ACT 2002

Claim Notice

To *[name and address]* (**See Note 1 below**)

1.    *[Name of RTM company]* ("the company"), of *[address of registered office]*, and of which the registered number is *[number under Companies Act 1985]*, in accordance with Chapter 1 of Part 2 of the Commonhold and Leasehold Reform Act 2002 ("the 2002 Act") claims to acquire the right to manage *[name of premises to which notice relates]* ("the premises").

2.    The company claims that the premises are ones to which Chapter 1 of the 2002 Act applies on the grounds that *[state grounds]*. (**See Note 2 below**)

3.    The full names of each person who is both—
    (a)    the qualifying tenant of a flat contained in the premises, and
    (b)    a member of the company,
and the address of his flat are set out in Part 1 of the Schedule below.

4.    There are set out, in Part 2 of the Schedule, in relation to each person named in Part 1 of the Schedule—
    (a)    the date on which his lease was entered into,
    (b)    the term for which it was granted,
    (c)    the date of commencement of the term
    (d)    *such other particulars of his lease as are necessary to identify it.
*(d) may be ignored if no other particulars need to be given.*

5.    If you are—
    (a)    landlord under a lease of the whole or any part of the premises,
    (b)    party to such a lease otherwise than as landlord or tenant, or
    (c)    a manager appointed under Part 2 of the Landlord and Tenant Act 1987 to act in relation to the premises, or any premises containing or contained in the premises,
you may respond to this claim notice by giving a counter-notice under section 84 of the 2002 Act. A counter-notice must be in the form set out in Schedule 3 to the Right to Manage (Prescribed Particulars and Forms) (England) Regulations 2003. It must be given to the company, at the address

in paragraph 1, not later than [*specify date not earlier than one month after the date on which the claim notice is given*]. If you do not fully understand the purpose or implications of this notice you are advised to seek professional help.

6.   The company intends to acquire the right to manage the premises on [specify date, being at least three months after that specified in paragraph 5].

7.   If you are a person to whom paragraph 5 applies and—

    (a)   you do not dispute the company's entitlement to acquire the right to manage; and
    (b)   you are the manager party under a management contract subsisting immediately before the date specified in this notice,

you must, in accordance with section 92 (duties to give notice of contracts) of the 2002 Act, give a notice in relation to the contract to the person who is the contractor party in relation to the contract and to the company. (**See Note 3 below**).

8.   From the date on which the company acquires the right to manage the premises, landlords under leases of the whole or any part of the premises are entitled to be members of the company (**See Note 4 below**).

9.   This notice is not invalidated by any inaccuracy in any of the particulars required by section 80(2) to (7) of the 2002 Act or regulation 4 of the Right to Manage (Prescribed Particulars and Forms) (England) Regulations 2003. If you are of the opinion that any of the particulars contained in the claim notice are inaccurate you may notify the company of the particulars in question, indicating the respects in which you think that they are inaccurate.

SCHEDULE
PART 1
FULL NAMES AND ADDRESSES OF PERSONS WHO ARE BOTH QUALIFYING TENANTS AND MEMBERS OF THE COMPANY

[*set out here the particulars required by paragraph 3 above*]
PART 2
PARTICULARS OF LEASES OF PERSONS NAMED IN PART 1

[*set out here the particulars required by paragraph 4 above*]

Signed by authority of the company,

[*Signature of authorised member or officer*]

[*Insert date*]

## Notes

1.   A claim notice (a notice in the form set out in Schedule 2 to the Right to Manage (Prescribed Particulars and Forms) (England) Regulations 2003 of a claim to exercise the right to manage specified premises) must be given to each person who, on the date on which the notice is given, is—

    (a)   landlord under a lease of the whole or any part of the premises to which the notice relates,
    (b)   party to such a lease otherwise than as landlord or tenant, or
    (c)   a manager appointed under Part 2 of the Landlord and Tenant Act 1987 to act in relation to the premises, or any premises containing or contained in the premises.

But notice need not be given to such a person if he cannot be found, or if his identity cannot be ascertained. If that means that there is no one to whom the notice must be given, the company may apply to a leasehold valuation tribunal for an order that the company is to acquire the right to manage the premises. In that case, the procedures specified in section 85 of the 2002 Act (landlords etc not traceable) will apply.

2.   The relevant provisions are contained in section 72 of the 2002 Act (premises to which Chapter 1 applies). The company is advised to consider, in particular, Schedule 6 to the 2002 Act (premises excepted from Chapter 1).

3.   The terms "management contract", "manager party" and "contractor party" are defined in section 91(2) of the 2002 Act (notices relating to management contracts).

4.   Landlords under leases of the whole or any part of the premises are entitled to be members of the company, but only once the right to manage has been acquired by the company. An application for membership may be made in accordance with the company's articles of association, which may be inspected at the company's registered office, free of charge, at any reasonable time.

**[3308]**

SCHEDULE 3
FORM OF COUNTER-NOTICE
Regulations 5(c) and 8(3)

COMMONHOLD AND LEASEHOLD REFORM ACT 2002

Counter-notice

To *[name and address]* (**See Note 1 below**)

1.    *I admit that, on *[insert date on which claim notice was given]*, *[insert name of company by which claim notice was given]* ("the company") was entitled to acquire the right to manage the premises specified in the claim notice.

*I allege that, by reason of [specify provision of Chapter 1 of Part 2 of the Commonhold and Leasehold Reform Act 2002 relied on], on [insert date on which claim notice was given], [insert name of company by which claim notice was given] ("the company") was not entitled to acquire the right to manage the premises specified in the claim notice.

**Delete one of these statements, as the circumstances require.*

2.    If the company has been given one or more counter-notices containing such a statement as is mentioned in paragraph (b) of subsection (2) of section 84 of the Commonhold and Leasehold Reform Act 2002, the company may apply to a leasehold valuation tribunal for a determination that, on the date on which notice of the claim was given, the company was entitled to acquire the right to manage the premises specified in the claim notice (**See Note 2 below**).

3.    If the company has been given one or more counter-notices containing such a statement as is mentioned in paragraph (b) of subsection (2) of section 84 of the Commonhold and Leasehold Reform Act 2002, the company does not acquire the right to manage those premises unless—

    (a)   on an application to a leasehold valuation tribunal, it is finally determined that the company was entitled to acquire the right to manage the premises; or

    (b)   the person by whom the counter-notice was given agrees, or the persons by whom the counter-notices were given agree, in writing that the company was so entitled. (**See Note 3 below**)

Signed:

*[Signature of person on whom claim notice served, or of agent of such person. Where an agent signs, insert also "Duly authorised agent of [insert name of person on whom claim notice served]"]*

Address:

*[Give the address to which future communications relating to the subject-matter of the notice should be sent]*

Date:

*[Insert date]*

OR

Signed by authority of the company on whose behalf this notice is given

*[Signature of authorised member or officer and statement of position in company]*

Address:

*[Give the address to which future communications relating to the subject-matter of the notice should be sent]*

Date:

*[Insert date]*

**Notes**

1.    The counter-notice is to be given to the company that gave the claim notice (a notice in the form set out in Schedule 2 to the Right to Manage (Prescribed Particulars and Forms) (England) Regulations 2003 of a claim to exercise the right to manage specified premises). The company's name and address are given in that notice.

2.    An application to a leasehold valuation tribunal must be made within the period of two months beginning with the day on which the counter-notice (or, where more than one, the last of the counter-notices) was given.

3.    For the time at which an application is finally determined, see section 84(7) and (8) of the Commonhold and Leasehold Reform Act 2002.

**[3309]**

# LEASEHOLD VALUATION TRIBUNALS (FEES) (ENGLAND) REGULATIONS 2003

(SI 2003/2098)

**NOTES**
Made: 7 August 2003.
Authority: Commonhold and Leasehold Reform Act 2002, Sch 12, paras 1, 9.

Commencement: 30 September 2003 (regs 1, 2, 3(1), (2), (3)(b)–(d), (4), (5), 4–9); 31 October 2003 (reg 3(3)(a)).

ARRANGEMENT OF REGULATIONS

## 1   Citation, commencement and interpretation

(1)   These Regulations may be cited as the Leasehold Valuation Tribunals (Fees) (England) Regulations 2003.

(2)   These Regulations shall come into force—

(a)   for all purposes other than regulation 3(3)(a), on 30th September 2003; and

(b)   for the purposes of regulation 3(3)(a), on 31st October 2003.

(3)   In these Regulations—

"the 1985 Act" means the Landlord and Tenant Act 1985;

"the 1987 Act" means the Landlord and Tenant Act 1987;

"the 2002 Act" means the Commonhold and Leasehold Reform Act 2002;

"applicant" means—

(a)   the person making an application to a tribunal; or

(b)   the person who is the claimant or applicant in proceedings before a court which are transferred by order of the court to a tribunal;

"application" means an application made to the tribunal under—

(a)   section 20ZA of the 1985 Act (consultation requirements);

(b)   section 27A of the 1985 Act (service charges);

(c)   paragraph 8(2) of the Schedule to the 1985 Act (insurers);

(d)   section 24 of the 1987 Act (appointment of managers);

(e)   Part 4 of the 1987 Act (variation of leases);

(f)   paragraph 3 of Schedule 11 to the 2002 Act (administration charges); or

(g)   paragraph 5 of Schedule 11 to the 2002 Act;

"hearing" means a hearing before a tribunal to determine one or more of the following—

(a)   an application;

(b)   transferred proceedings; or

(c)   a representative application

but, for the purposes of the payment of a fee for a hearing, does not include—

(i)   a pre-trial review; or

(ii)   a hearing to consider dismissing an application as frivolous or vexatious;

"representative application" means an application dealt with as a representative application under regulation 8 of the Leasehold Valuation Tribunal (Procedure) (England) Regulations 2003;

"transferred proceedings" means proceedings which a court has transferred to a tribunal for determination; and

"tribunal" means a leasehold valuation tribunal.

**[3310]**

## 2   Application of Regulations

These Regulations shall apply—

(a)   in relation to any application (other than an application made under section 20ZA of the 1985 Act) made to a tribunal on or after 30th September 2003;

(b)   in relation to any proceedings transferred from a court to a tribunal on or after that date; and

(c)   in relation to an application under section 20ZA of the 1985 Act made to a tribunal on or after 31st October 2003,

in respect of premises in England.

**[3311]**

## 3   Fees: applications

(1)   Subject to regulation 8, a fee shall be payable for an application to a tribunal under—

(a)   section 27A of the 1985 Act (determination of liability to pay a service charge );

    (b)    paragraph 8(2)(b) of the Schedule to the 1985 Act (right to challenge the insurance premium);

    (c)    paragraph 3 of Schedule 11 to the 2002 Act (variation of lease because of administration charge); and

    (d)    paragraph 5 of Schedule 11 to the 2002 Act (determination of liability to pay an administration charge).

(2)    Subject to paragraph (5), the fee payable under paragraph (1), where the service charge, insurance premium or administration charge which is the subject of the application—

    (a)    is not more than £500, is £50;

    (b)    is more than £500 but not more than £1000, is £70;

    (c)    is more than £1000 but not more than £5000, is £100;

    (d)    is more than £5000 but not more than £15000, is £200; and

    (e)    is more than £15000, is £350.

(3)    Subject to regulation 8, a fee shall be payable for an application to a tribunal under—

    (a)    section 20ZA of the 1985 Act (determination to dispense with consultation requirements);

    (b)    paragraph 8(2)(a) of the Schedule to the 1985 Act (determination as to suitability of insurer);

    (c)    section 24 of the 1987 Act (appointment of managers); and

    (d)    Part 4 of the 1987 Act (variation of leases).

(4)    Subject to paragraph (5), the fee payable under paragraph (3)—

    (a)    where the application relates to 5 or fewer dwellings, is £150;

    (b)    where the application relates to between 6 and 10 dwellings, is £250; and

    (c)    where the application relates to more than 10 dwellings, is £350.

(5)    Where an application is made under—

    (a)    two or more of the provisions mentioned in paragraph (1);

    (b)    two or more of the provisions mentioned in paragraph (3); or

    (c)    one or more of the provisions mentioned in paragraph (1) and one or more of the provisions mentioned in paragraph (3),

the fee payable in respect of the application shall be the highest of the fees which would have been payable in accordance with paragraph (2) or (4) (as the case may be) if a separate application had been made under each of those provisions.

**[3312]**

### 4   Fees: applications transferred from court

(1)    Subject to paragraph (2) and regulation 8, where a court, by order, transfers to a tribunal so much of any proceedings as relate to the determination of a question falling within the jurisdiction of the tribunal by virtue of a provision mentioned in paragraph (1) or (3) of regulation 3, the fee payable to the tribunal shall be the fee which would have been payable under paragraph (2), (4) or (5) of that regulation (as the case may be) for an application less the total amount of any fees paid by the applicant to the court in respect of the proceedings on or before the date of that order.

(2)    Where the total amount of any fees paid to the court on or before the date of the order mentioned in paragraph (1) is equal to or more than the fee payable under that paragraph, no fee shall be payable to the tribunal under that paragraph.

**[3313]**

### 5   Fees: hearings

(1)    Subject to paragraph (2) and regulation 8, a fee of £150 shall be payable for a hearing.

(2)    Where part of an application or transferred proceedings is or will be determined at, or in accordance with, a hearing of a representative application and part is to be determined at a separate hearing, the fee for the part which is to be heard separately shall be £150 less the total amount of any fees paid by the applicant in accordance with regulation 7(5) for that part of the application or transferred proceedings which is to be determined at, or in accordance with, the representative application.

**[3314]**

### 6   Payment of fees

(1)    Any fee payable under regulation 3 shall accompany the application.

(2)    Any fee payable under regulation 4 or 5 shall be due within 14 days of a written request for payment by the tribunal and shall be sent to the address specified in that request.

(3)    The fee shall be paid by a cheque made payable to or postal order drawn in favour of the Office of the Deputy Prime Minister.

**[3315]**

PART II
STATUTORY INSTRUMENTS

**7  Liability to pay and apportionment of fees**

(1)    Subject to regulation 8 and the following paragraphs, the applicant shall be liable to pay any fee payable to a tribunal under these Regulations.

(2)    Subject to paragraph (3), where an application is made or transferred proceedings are brought by more than one person, any fee payable under regulations 3 or 4 for the application or transferred proceedings shall be apportioned equally between those persons and each person shall be liable to pay one portion.

(3)    Where—
    (a)    an application is made or transferred proceedings are brought by the tenant or the landlord of premises; and
    (b)    the tenant or landlord is more than one person,
those persons together shall be treated as one person for the purposes of paragraph (2).

(4)    Where two or more applications are heard together, other than applications which are heard with a representative application, any fee payable under regulation 5 for the hearing shall be apportioned equally between the applications and, subject to the provisions of paragraphs (2), (3) and (6) and regulation 8, the applicant in each application shall be liable to pay one portion.

(5)    Any fee payable under regulation 5 for the hearing of a representative application and any application heard with the representative application shall be apportioned equally between—
    (a)    the representative application;
    (b)    all other applications which, at the time of the request for payment of the fee, are to be determined in whole or in part in accordance with the representative application; and
    (c)    any application heard with the representative application,
and, subject to the provisions of paragraphs (2), (3) and (6) and regulation 8, the applicant in each application shall pay be liable to pay one portion of the fee.

(6)    The amount payable by any person in respect of a fee shall be calculated in accordance with the provisions of this article and by reference to the persons who are applicants on the date the application is made or the date of the request for payment issued by the tribunal.

(7)    In this regulation, "applicant" includes any person, whose request under regulation 6 of the Leasehold Valuation Tribunals (Procedure) (England) Regulations 2003 to be joined as a party to the proceedings and treated as an applicant, has been granted by the tribunal.

**[3316]**

**8  Waiver and reduction of fees**

(1)    A person shall not be liable to pay any fee due under these Regulations where on the relevant date, he or his partner is in receipt of—
    (a)    either of the following benefits under Part 7 of the Social Security Contributions and Benefits Act 1992—
        (i)    income support; or
        (ii)    housing benefit;
    (b)    an income-based jobseeker's allowance within the meaning of section 1 of the Jobseekers Act 1995;
    (c)    a tax credit to which paragraph (2) applies;
    (d)    guarantee credit under the State Pensions Credit Act 2002; ...
    (e)    a certificate—
        (i)    which has been issued under the Funding Code and which has not been revoked or discharged; and
        (ii)    which is in respect of the proceedings before the tribunal the whole or part of which have been transferred from the county court for determination by a tribunal; [or
    (f)    an income-related employment and support allowance payable under Part 1 of the Welfare Reform Act 2007.]

(2)    This paragraph applies to a working tax credit under Part 1 of the Tax Credits Act 2002, where—
    (a)    either—
        (i)    there is a disability element or severe disability element (or both) to the tax credit received by the person or his partner; or
        (ii)    the person or his partner is also in receipt of child tax credit; and
    (b)    the gross annual income taken into account for the calculation of the working tax credit is £14,213 or less;

(3)    Where a person is not liable to pay a fee by virtue of paragraph (1), the following provisions shall apply—
    (a)    where more than one person is the applicant and at least one of those persons is liable to pay a fee, the fee shall be reduced rateably in accordance with the number of persons who would have been liable but for paragraph (1); and

(b)  where more than one person is the applicant and at least one person is liable to pay a portion of a fee by virtue of regulation 7(2) to (5), such portion shall be reduced rateably in accordance with the number of persons who would have been liable but for paragraph (1).

(4)  In this regulation—

(a)  "applicant" includes any person, whose request under regulation 6 of the Leasehold Valuation Tribunals (Procedure)(England) Regulations 2003 to be joined as a party to the proceedings and treated as an applicant, has been granted by the tribunal;

(b)  "partner", in relation to a person, means—

   (i)  that person's spouse;

   (ii)  a person of the opposite sex who is living with that person as husband or wife; and

   (iii)  a person of the same sex living with that person in a relationship which has the characteristics of the relationship between husband and wife;

(c)  "relevant date" means—

   (i)  in the case of a fee payable under regulation 3, the date of the application;

   (ii)  in the case of a fee payable under regulation 4, the date of the court order transferring proceedings to the tribunal;

   (iii)  in the case of a fee payable under regulation 5, the date of the request for payment.

**[3317]**

**NOTES**

Para (1): in sub-para (d) word omitted revoked, and sub-para (f) inserted, by the Employment and Support Allowance (Consequential Provisions) (No 3) Regulations 2008, SI 2008/1879, reg 15.

## 9  Reimbursement of fees

(1)  Subject to paragraph (2), in relation to any proceedings in respect of which a fee is payable under these Regulations a tribunal may require any party to the proceedings to reimburse any other party to the proceedings for the whole or part of any fees paid by him in respect of the proceedings.

(2)  A tribunal shall not require a party to make such reimbursement if, at the time the tribunal is considering whether or not to do so, the tribunal is satisfied that the party is in receipt of any of the benefits, the allowance or a certificate mentioned in regulation 8(1).

**[3318]**

# LEASEHOLD VALUATION TRIBUNALS (PROCEDURE) (ENGLAND) REGULATIONS 2003

## (SI 2003/2099)

**NOTES**

Made: 7 August 2003.

Authority: Landlord and Tenant Act 1987, s 35(5); Commonhold and Leasehold Reform Act 2002, Sch 12.

Commencement: 30 September 2003 (for all purposes other than Sch 1, para 2(a)); 31 October 2003 (for purposes of Sch 1, para 2(a)).

In addition to revoking and replacing the Rent Assessment Committee (England and Wales) (Leasehold Valuation Tribunal) Regulations 1993, SI 1993/2408, these regulations also include provisions similar to those formerly contained in the Leasehold Valuation Tribunals (Service Charges, Insurance or Appointment of Managers Applications) Order 1997, SI 1997/1853.

## ARRANGEMENT OF REGULATIONS

## 1 Citation, commencement, and application

(1) These Regulations may be cited as the Leasehold Valuation Tribunals (Procedure) (England) Regulations 2003

(2) These Regulations shall come into force—

    (a) for all purposes other than paragraph 2(a) of Schedule 1, on 30th September 2003; and

    (b) for the purposes of paragraph 2(a) of Schedule 1, on 31st October 2003.

(3) These Regulations apply in relation to any application made, or proceedings transferred from a court, to a leasehold valuation tribunal in respect of premises in England on or after—

    (a) in the case of an application of the description specified in paragraph 2(a) of Schedule 1, 31st October 2003; and

    [(a) in the case of an application—

        (i) of the description specified in paragraph 2(a) of Schedule 1, 31st October 2003;

        (ii) of the description specified in paragraph 8 of that Schedule, 28th February 2005; and]

    (b) in any other case, 30th September 2003.

**[3319]**

**NOTES**

Para (3): sub-para (a) substituted by the Leasehold Valuation Tribunals (Procedure) (Amendment) (England) Regulations 2004, SI 2004/3098, regs 2, 3.

## 2 Interpretation

In these Regulations—

    "the 1985 Act" means the Landlord and Tenant Act 1985;

    "the 1987 Act" means the Landlord and Tenant Act 1987;

    "the 1993 Act" means the Leasehold Reform, Housing and Urban Development Act 1993;

    "the 2002 Act" means the Commonhold and Leasehold Reform Act 2002;

    "applicant" means—

        (a) the person making an application to a tribunal, or

        (b) the person who is the claimant or applicant in proceedings before a court which are transferred by order of the court to a tribunal;

    "application" means, other than for the purposes of regulations 1, 20 and 25—

        (a) an application to a tribunal of a description specified in Schedule 1, or

        (b) a transferred application;

    "recognised tenants' association" has the same meaning as in section 29 of the 1985 Act;

    "representative application" has the meaning given in regulation 8;

    "respondent" means—

        (a) the person against whom an applicant seeks an order or determination from a tribunal; or

        (b) the person who is the defendant or respondent in proceedings before a court which are transferred by order of the court to a tribunal;

    "transferred application" means so much of proceedings before a court as relate to a question falling within the jurisdiction of a tribunal as have been transferred to the tribunal for determination by order of the court; and

    "tribunal" means a leasehold valuation tribunal.

**[3320]**

## 3 Particulars of applications

(1) The particulars to be included with an application are—

    (a) the name and address of the applicant;

    (b) the name and address of the respondent;

(c)     the name and address of any landlord or tenant of the premises to which the application relates;

(d)     the address of the premises to which the application relates; and

(e)     a statement that the applicant believes that the facts stated in the application are true.

(2)     Where an application is of a description specified in paragraph 1 of Schedule 1 (enfranchisement and extended leases) the particulars and documents listed in paragraph 1 of Schedule 2 shall be included with the application.

(3)     Where an application is of a description specified in [any of sub-paragraphs (b) to (f) of paragraph 2] of Schedule 1 (service charges, administration charges and estate charges) the particulars and documents listed in paragraph 2 of Schedule 2 shall be included with the application.

(4)     Where an application is of a description specified in paragraph 3 of Schedule 1 (estate management schemes) the particulars and documents listed in paragraph 3 of Schedule 2 shall be included with the application.

(5)     Where an application is of a description specified in paragraph 4 of Schedule 1 (right to manage) the particulars and documents listed in paragraph 4 of Schedule 2 shall be included with the application.

(6)     Where an application is of a description specified in paragraph 5 of Schedule 1 (appointment of manager) the particulars and documents listed in paragraph 5 of Schedule 2 shall be included with the application.

(7)     Where an application is of a description specified in paragraph 6 of Schedule 1 (variation of leases) the particulars and documents listed in paragraph 6 of Schedule 2 shall be included with the application.

[(7A)     Where an application is of the description specified in paragraph 8 of Schedule 1 (determination as to breach of covenant or condition) the particulars and documents listed in paragraph 7 of Schedule 2 shall be included with the application.]

(8)     Any of the requirements in the preceding paragraphs may be dispensed with or relaxed if the tribunal is satisfied that—

(a)     the particulars and documents included with an application are sufficient to enable the application to be determined; and

(b)     no prejudice will, or is likely to, be caused to any party to the application.

**[3321]**

---

**NOTES**

Para (3): words in square brackets substituted by the Leasehold Valuation Tribunals (Procedure) (Amendment) (England) Regulations 2004, SI 2004/3098, regs 2, 4(a).

Para (7A): inserted by SI 2004/3098, regs 2, 4(b).

---

### 4   Notice of application under Part 4 of the 1987 Act

(1)     The applicant shall give notice of an application under Part 4 of the 1987 Act (variation of leases) to the respondent and to any person who the applicant knows, or has reason to believe, is likely to be affected by any variation specified in the application.

(2)     On receipt of the notice under paragraph (1) the respondent shall give notice of the application to any person not already notified under that paragraph, who the respondent knows, or has reason to believe, is likely to be affected by any variation specified in the application.

**[3322]**

### 5   Notice of application by tribunal

(1)     On receipt of an application, other than an application made under Part 4 of the 1987 Act, the tribunal shall send a copy of the application and each of the documents accompanying it to each person named in it as a respondent.

(2)     On receipt of an application of a description specified in paragraph 2 of Schedule 1 (service charges, administration charges and estate charges), the tribunal shall give notice of the application to—

(a)     the secretary of any recognised tenants' association mentioned in the particulars included in the application; and

(b)     any person, whose name and address the tribunal has, who the tribunal considers is likely to be significantly affected by the application.

(3)     On receipt of an application the tribunal may give notice to any other person it considers appropriate.

(4)     Any notice given under paragraph (2) or (3) shall include a statement that any person may make a request to the tribunal under regulation 6 to be joined as a party to the proceedings with details as to how such a request can be made.

(5)     Any notice given under paragraph (2) or (3) may be given by local advertisement.

(6)  In this regulation, "local advertisement" means publication of the notice in two newspapers (at least one of which should be a freely distributed newspaper) circulating in the locality in which the premises to which the application relates is situated.

[3323]

## 6  Request to be treated as an applicant or respondent

(1)  Any person may make a request to the tribunal to be joined as a party to the proceedings.

(2)  Any request under paragraph (1)—
  (a)  may be made without notice; and
  (b)  shall specify whether the person making the request wishes to be treated as—
     (i)  an applicant; or
     (ii)  a respondent
   to the application.

(3)  The tribunal may grant or refuse a request under paragraph (1).

(4)  As soon as possible after reaching its decision on a request under paragraph (1), the tribunal shall—
  (a)  notify the person making the request of the decision and the reasons for it; and
  (b)  send a copy of the notification to the applicant and the respondent.

(5)  Any person whose request under paragraph (1) is granted shall be treated as an applicant or respondent, as the case may be, for the purposes of regulations 8 to 18, 20 and 24.

(6)  In the regulations mentioned in paragraph (5) any reference to—
  (a)  an applicant, or
  (b)  a respondent
shall be construed as including a person treated as such under this regulation and any reference to a party shall be construed as including any such person.

[3324]

## 7  Non-payment of fees

(1)  In any case where a fee which is payable under regulation 4 or 5 of the Leasehold Valuation Tribunals (Fees) (England) Regulations 2003 is not paid in accordance with those Regulations, the tribunal shall not proceed further with the application to which the fee relates until the fee is paid.

(2)  Where a fee remains unpaid for a period of one month from the date on which it becomes due, the application shall be treated as withdrawn unless the tribunal is satisfied that there are reasonable grounds not to do so.

[3325]

## 8  Representative applications and other provisions for securing consistency

(1)  Where it appears to a tribunal that numerous applications—
  (a)  have been made in respect of the same or substantially the same matters; or
  (b)  include some matters which are the same or substantially the same,
the tribunal may propose to determine only one of those applications ("the representative application") as representative of all of the applications on those matters which are the same or substantially the same ("the common matters"), and shall give notice of the proposal to the parties to all such applications.

(2)  A notice under paragraph (1) shall—
  (a)  specify the common matters;
  (b)  specify the application which the tribunal proposes to determine as the representative application;
  (c)  explain that the tribunal's decision on the common matters in the representative application will apply to the common matters in any application made by a person to whom notice has been given under that paragraph;
  (d)  invite objections to the tribunal's proposal to determine the representative application; and
  (e)  specify the address to which objections may be sent and the date (being not less than 21 days after the date that the notice was sent) by which the objections must be received by the tribunal.

(3)  Where no objection is received on or before the date specified in the notice—
  (a)  the tribunal shall determine the representative application in accordance with these Regulations;
  (b)  the tribunal need not determine the matters mentioned in paragraph (1)(a) in any other application made by a person to whom a notice under paragraph (1) has been given; and
  (c)  the decision of the tribunal in respect of the representative application shall be recorded as the decision of the tribunal in respect of the common matters in any such other application.

(4)    Where an objection is received on or before the date specified in the notice—

    (a)    sub-paragraphs (a) to (c) of paragraph (3) shall apply only to those applications in respect of which no objection was made, and

    (b)    the application in respect of which an objection was made may be determined together with the representative application.

**[3326]**

## 9    Subsequent applications where notice of the representative application given

(1)    If, after a representative application has been determined, a subsequent application is made which includes any of the common matters on which the tribunal has made a decision in its determination of the representative application, and the applicant is a person to whom a notice under regulation 8(1) was given, the tribunal shall give notice to the parties to the subsequent application of—

    (a)    the matters which, in the opinion of the tribunal, are the common matters in the subsequent application and the representative application;

    (b)    the decision recorded in respect of the common matters in the representative application;

    (c)    the date on which notice under regulation 8(1) was given to the applicant;

    (d)    the tribunal's proposal to record the tribunal's decision on the common matters in the subsequent application in identical terms to the decision in the representative application;

    (e)    the address to which objections to the tribunal's proposal may be sent and the date (being not less than 21 days after the date that the notice was sent) by which such objections must be received by the tribunal; and

    (f)    a statement that any objection must include the grounds on which it is made and, in particular, whether it is alleged that the notice under regulation 8(1) was not received by the person making the objection.

(2)    Where no objection is received on or before the date specified in the notice—

    (a)    the tribunal need not determine the matters mentioned in paragraph 1(a); and

    (b)    the decision of the tribunal in respect of the common matters in the representative application shall be recorded as the decision of the tribunal in respect of the common matters in the subsequent application.

(3)    Where an objection is received to the tribunal's proposal on or before the date specified in the notice—

    (a)    the tribunal shall consider the objection when determining the subsequent application; and

    (b)    if the tribunal dismisses the objection, it may record the decision mentioned in paragraph (1)(b) as the decision of the tribunal in the subsequent application.

**[3327]**

## 10    Subsequent applications where notice of representative application not given

(1)    If, after a representative application has been determined, a subsequent application is made which includes any of the common matters on which the tribunal has made a decision in its determination of the representative application, and the applicant is not a person to whom a notice under regulation 8(1) was given, the tribunal shall give notice to the parties to the subsequent application of—

    (a)    the matters which, in the opinion of the tribunal, are the common matters in the subsequent application and the representative application;

    (b)    the decision recorded in respect of those common matters in the representative application;

    (c)    the tribunal's proposal to record its decision on the common matters in the subsequent application in identical terms to the decision in the representative application; and

    (d)    the address to which objections to the tribunal's proposal may be sent and the date (being not less than 21 days after the date that the notice was sent) by which such objections must be received by the tribunal.

(2)    Where no objection is received on or before the date specified in the notice—

    (a)    the tribunal need not determine the matters mentioned in paragraph (1)(a); and

    (b)    the decision of the tribunal in respect of the common matters in the representative application shall be recorded as the decision of the tribunal in respect of the common matters in the subsequent application.

(3)    Where an objection is received to the tribunal's proposal on or before the date specified in the notice the tribunal shall determine the application in accordance with the following provisions of these Regulations.

**[3328]**

## 11    Dismissal of frivolous etc applications

(1)    Subject to paragraph (2), where—

(a)   it appears to a tribunal that an application is frivolous or vexatious or otherwise an abuse
        of process of the tribunal; or
(b)   the respondent to an application makes a request to the tribunal to dismiss an application
        as frivolous or vexatious or otherwise an abuse of the process of the tribunal,

the tribunal may dismiss the application, in whole or in part.

(2)   Before dismissing an application under paragraph (1) the tribunal shall give notice to the
applicant in accordance with paragraph (3).

(3)   Any notice under paragraph (2) shall state—
(a)   that the tribunal is minded to dismiss the application;
(b)   the grounds on which it is minded to dismiss the application;
(c)   the date (being not less than 21 days after the date that the notice was sent) before which
        the applicant may request to appear before and be heard by the tribunal on the question
        whether the application should be dismissed.

(4)   An application may not be dismissed unless—
(a)   the applicant makes no request to the tribunal before the date mentioned in
        paragraph (3)(c); or
(b)   where the applicant makes such a request, the tribunal has heard the applicant and the
        respondent, or such of them as attend the hearing, on the question of the dismissal of the
        application.

                                                                                    **[3329]**

## 12   Pre-trial review

(1)   The tribunal may, whether on its own initiative or at the request of a party, hold a pre-trial
review in respect of an application.

(2)   The tribunal shall give the parties not less than 14 days notice (or such shorter notice as the
parties agree to) of the date, time and place of the pre-trial review.

(3)   At the pre-trial review the tribunal shall—
(a)   give any direction that appears to the tribunal necessary or desirable for securing the
        just, expeditious and economical disposal of proceedings;
(b)   endeavour to secure that the parties make all such admissions and agreements as ought
        reasonably to be made by them in relation to the proceedings; and
(c)   record in any order made at the pre-trial review any such admission or agreement or any
        refusal to make such admission or agreement.

(4)   The functions of the tribunal in relation to, or at, a pre-trial review may be exercised by any
single member of the panel provided for in Schedule 10 to the Rent Act 1977 who is qualified to
exercise them.

                                                                                    **[3330]**

## 13   Determination without a hearing

(1)   A tribunal may determine an application without an oral hearing, in accordance with the
following provisions of this regulation, if—
[(a)   it has given to both the applicant and the respondent not less than 28 days' notice in
        writing of its intention to proceed without an oral hearing; and
(b)   neither the applicant nor the respondent has made a request to the tribunal to be heard,
but this paragraph is without prejudice to paragraph (3).]

(2)   The tribunal shall—
(a)   notify the parties that the application is to be determined without an oral hearing;
(b)   invite written representations on the application;
(c)   set time limits for sending any written representations to the tribunal; and
(d)   set out how the tribunal intends to determine the matter without an oral hearing.

(3)   At any time before the application is determined—
(a)   the applicant or the respondent may make a request to the tribunal to be heard; or
(b)   the tribunal may give notice to the parties that it intends to determine the application at
        a hearing in accordance with regulation 14.

(4)   Where a request is made or a notice given under paragraph (3) the application shall be
determined in accordance with regulation 14.

(5)   The functions of the tribunal in relation to an application to be determined without an oral
hearing may be exercised by a single member of the panel provided for in Schedule 10 to the Rent
Act 1977, if he was appointed to that panel by the Lord Chancellor.

                                                                                    **[3331]**

_____

**NOTES**

Para (1): words in square brackets substituted for original sub-paras (a)–(c) by the Leasehold Valuation
Tribunals (Procedure) (Amendment) (England) Regulations 2004, SI 2004/3098, regs 2, 5.

**14  Hearings**

(1)   Subject to regulations 8(3), 9(2) and 10(2), a hearing shall be on the date and at the time and place appointed by the tribunal.

(2)   The tribunal shall give notice to the parties of the appointed date, time and place of the hearing.

(3)   Subject to paragraph (4), notice under paragraph (2) shall be given not less than 21 days (or such shorter period as the parties may agree) before the appointed date.

(4)   In exceptional circumstances the tribunal may, without the agreement of the parties, give less than 21 days notice of the appointed date, time and place of the hearing; but any such notice must be given as soon as possible before the appointed date and the notice must specify what the exceptional circumstances are.

(5)   The tribunal may arrange that an application shall be heard together with one or more other applications.

(6)   A hearing shall be in public unless, in the particular circumstances of the case, the tribunal decide that a hearing or part of a hearing shall be held in private.

(7)   At the hearing—
- (a)    the tribunal shall determine the procedure (subject to these Regulations) and the order in which the persons appearing before it are to be heard;
- (b)    a person appearing before the tribunal may do so either in person or by a representative authorised by him, whether or not that representative is a barrister or a solicitor; and
- (c)    a person appearing before the tribunal may give evidence on his own behalf, call witnesses, and cross-examine any witnesses called by any other person appearing.

(8)   If a party does not appear at a hearing, the tribunal may proceed with the hearing if it is satisfied that notice has been given to that party in accordance with these Regulations.

**[3332]**

**15  Postponement and adjournment**

(1)   Subject to paragraph (2) the tribunal may postpone or adjourn a hearing or pre-trial review either on its own initiative or at the request of a party.

(2)   Where a postponement or adjournment has been requested the tribunal shall not postpone or adjourn the hearing except where it considers it is reasonable to do so having regard to—
- (a)    the grounds for the request;
- (b)    the time at which the request is made; and
- (c)    the convenience of the other parties.

(3)   The tribunal shall give reasonable notice of any postponed or adjourned hearing to the parties.

**[3333]**

**16  Documents**

(1)   Before the date of the hearing, the tribunal shall take all reasonable steps to ensure that each of the parties is given—
- (a)    a copy of any document relevant to the proceedings (or sufficient extracts from or particulars of the document) which has been received from any other party (other than a document already in his possession or one of which he has previously been supplied with a copy); and
- (b)    a copy of any document which embodies the results of any relevant enquiries made by or for the tribunal for the purposes of the proceedings.

(2)   At a hearing, if a party has not previously received a relevant document or a copy of, or sufficient extracts from or particulars of, a relevant document, then unless—
- (a)    that person consents to the continuation of the hearing; or
- (b)    the tribunal considers that that person has a sufficient opportunity to deal with the matters to which the document relates without an adjournment of the hearing,

the tribunal shall adjourn the hearing for a period which it considers will give that person a sufficient opportunity to deal with those matters.

**[3334]**

**17  Inspections**

(1)   A tribunal may inspect—
- (a)    the house, premises or area which is the subject of the application; or
- (b)    any comparable house, premises or area to which its attention is directed.

(2)   Subject to paragraph (3), the tribunal shall give the parties an opportunity to attend an inspection.

(3) The making of, and attendance at, an inspection is subject to any necessary consent being obtained.

[(4) Where an inspection is to be made, the tribunal shall give notice to the parties.

(5) A notice under paragraph (4) shall—
   (a) state the date, time and place of the inspection; and
   (b) be given not less than 14 days before that date.]

(8) Where an inspection is made after the close of a hearing, the tribunal may reopen the hearing on account of any matter arising from the inspection.

(9) The tribunal shall give reasonable notice of the date, time and place of the reopened hearing to the parties.

(10) Any of the requirements for notice in the preceding paragraphs may be dispensed with or relaxed—
   (a) with the consent of the parties; or
   (b) if the tribunal is satisfied that the parties have received sufficient notice.

[3335]

---

**NOTES**

Paras (4), (5): substituted, for original paras (4)–(7), by the Leasehold Valuation Tribunals (Procedure) (Amendment) (England) Regulations 2004, SI 2004/3098, regs 2, 6.

## 18 Decisions

(1) This regulation applies to a decision on the determination of an application by—
   (a) a tribunal; or
   (b) a single member, as mentioned in regulation 13(5).

(2) If a hearing was held, the decision may be given orally at the end of the hearing.

(3) A decision shall, in every case, be recorded in a document as soon as possible after the decision has been made.

(4) A decision given or recorded in accordance with paragraph (2) or (3) need not record the reasons for the decision.

(5) Where the document mentioned in paragraph (3) does not record the reasons for the decision, they shall be recorded in a separate document as soon as possible after the decision has been recorded.

(6) A document recording a decision, or the reasons for a decision, shall be signed and dated by an appropriate person.

(7) An appropriate person may, by means of a certificate signed and dated by him, correct any clerical mistakes in a document or any errors arising in it from an accidental slip or omission.

(8) In this regulation, "appropriate person" means—
   (a) where an application was determined by a single member as mentioned in regulation 13(5)—
      (i) the single member; or
      (ii) in the event of his absence or incapacity, another member of the tribunal who was appointed by the Lord Chancellor;
   (b) in any other case—
      (i) the chairman of the tribunal; or
      (ii) in the event of his absence or incapacity, another member of the tribunal.

(9) A copy of any document recording a decision, or the reasons for a decision, and a copy of any correction certified under paragraph (7) shall be sent to each party.

[3336]

## 19 Enforcement

Any decision of the tribunal may, with the permission of the county court, be enforced in the same way as orders of such a court.

[3337]

## 20 Permission to appeal

Where a party makes an application to a tribunal for permission to appeal to the [Upper Tribunal]—
   (a) the application shall be made to the tribunal within the period of 21 days starting with the date on which the document which records the reasons for the decision under regulation 18 was sent to that party; and
   (b) a copy of the application shall be served by the tribunal on every other party.

[3338]

**NOTES**
Words in square brackets substituted by the Transfer of Tribunal Functions (Lands Tribunal and Miscellaneous Amendments) Order 2009, SI 2009/1307, art 5(1), (3), Sch 2, para 95, as from 1 June 2009, subject to savings and transitional provisions for the treatment of cases which would previously have been dealt with by the Lands Tribunal, and onward appeals from that Tribunal (see art 5(6), Sch 5 to that Order).

### [21   Attendance by member of Administrative Justice and Tribunals Council

A member of the Administrative Justice and Tribunals Council, who is acting in that capacity, may attend any inspection for which any necessary consent has been obtained.]

**[3339]**

**NOTES**
Substituted by the Tribunals, Courts and Enforcement Act 2007 (Transitional and Consequential Provisions) Order 2008, SI 2008/2683, art 6(1), Sch 1, para 238.
Administrative Justice and Tribunals Council: established by the Tribunals, Courts and Enforcement Act 2007, s 44, Sch 7 to replace the Council on Tribunals (abolished by s 45(1)(a) of the 2007 Act).

### 22   Information required by tribunal

Where a tribunal serves a notice requiring information to be given under paragraph 4 of Schedule 12 to the 2002 Act, the notice shall contain a statement to the effect that any person who fails without reasonable excuse to comply with the notice commits an offence and is liable on summary conviction to a fine not exceeding level 3 on the standard scale.

**[3340]**

### 23   Notices

(1)   Where any notice or other document is required under these Regulations to be given or sent to a person by the tribunal, it shall be sufficient compliance with the requirement if—
   (a)   it is delivered or sent by pre-paid post to that person at his usual or last known address;
   (b)   it is sent to that person by fax or other means of electronic communication which produces a text of the document;
   (c)   where that person has appointed an agent or representative to act on his behalf—
      (i)   it is delivered or sent by pre-paid post to the agent or representative at the address of the agent or representative supplied to the tribunal; or
      (ii)   it is sent to the agent or representative by fax or other means of electronic communication which produces a text of the document.

(2)   A notice or other document may be sent as mentioned in paragraphs (1) (b) or (c)(ii) only if that person or his agent has given his consent.

(3)   A notice or other document sent as mentioned in paragraphs (1) (b) or (c)(ii) shall be regarded as sent when the text of it is received in legible form.

(4)   This paragraph applies where—
   (a)   an intended recipient—
      (i)   cannot be found after all diligent enquiries have been made;
      (ii)   has died and has no personal representative; or
      (iii)   is out of the United Kingdom; or
   (b)   for any other reason a notice or other document cannot readily be given or sent in accordance with these Regulations.

(5)   Where paragraph (4) applies, the tribunal may—
   (a)   dispense with the giving or sending of the notice or other document; or
   (b)   may give directions for substituted service in such other form (whether by advertisement in a newspaper or otherwise) or manner as the tribunal think fit.

**[3341]**

### 24   Allowing further time

(1)   In a particular case, the tribunal may extend any period prescribed by these Regulations, or prescribed by a notice given under these Regulations, within which anything is required or authorised to be done.

(2)   A party may make a request to the tribunal to extend any such period but must do so before that period expires.

**[3342]**

### 25   Revocation and saving

(1)   Subject to paragraph (2) the Rent Assessment Committee (England and Wales) (Leasehold Valuation Tribunal) Regulations 1993 ("the 1993 Regulations") are hereby revoked in relation to England.

(2) The revocation in paragraph (1) shall not have effect in relation to any application made, or proceedings transferred from a court, to a tribunal before 30 September 2003.

**[3343]**

## SCHEDULES

## SCHEDULE 1
### DESCRIPTIONS OF APPLICATIONS

*Enfranchisement and extended leases*

1. Applications under—
   (a)  section 21 of the Leasehold Reform Act 1967;
   (b)  section 13 of the 1987 Act;
   (c)  section 31 of that Act;
   (d)  section 24 of the 1993 Act;
   (e)  section 25 of that Act;
   (f)  section 27 of that Act;
   (g)  section 48 of that Act;
   (h)  section 51 of that Act;
   (i)  section 88 of that Act;
   (j)  section 91 of that Act;
   (k)  section 94 of that Act; and
   (l)  paragraph 2 of Schedule 14 to that Act.

*Service Charges, administration charges and estate charges*

2. Applications under—
   (a)  section 20ZA of the 1985 Act;
   (b)  section 27A of that Act;
   (c)  paragraph 8 of the Schedule to that Act;
   (d)  section 159 of the 2002 Act;
   (e)  paragraph 3 of Schedule 11 to that Act; and
   (f)  paragraph 5 of Schedule 11 to that Act.

*Estate management schemes*

3. Applications under Chapter 4 of Part 1 to the 1993 Act.

*Right to manage*

4. Applications under—
   (a)  section 84 of the 2002 Act;
   (b)  section 85 of that Act;
   (c)  section 88 of that Act;
   (d)  section 94 of that Act;
   (e)  section 99 of that Act; and
   (f)  paragraph 5 of Schedule 6 to that Act.

*Appointment of a manager*

5. Applications under—
   (a)  section 22 of the Landlord and Tenant Act 1987; and
   (b)  section 24 of that Act.

*Variation of leases*

6. Applications under Part 4 of the 1987 Act.

*Cost of proceedings*

7. Applications under section 20C of the 1985 Act.

*[Determination as to breach of covenant or condition*

8. Applications under section 168(4) of the 2002 Act.]

**[3344]**

---

**NOTES**

Para 8: inserted by the Leasehold Valuation Tribunals (Procedure) (Amendment) (England) Regulations 2004, SI 2004/3098, regs 2, 7.

---

## SCHEDULE 2
## PARTICULARS OF APPLICATIONS

*Enfranchisement and extended leases*

1.—(1)   A copy of any notice served in relation to the enfranchisement.

(2)   The name and address of the freeholder and any intermediate landlord.

(3)   The name and address of any person having a mortgage or other charge over an interest in the premises the subject of the application held by the freeholder or other landlord.

(4)   Where an application is made under section 21(2) of the Leasehold Reform Act 1967, the name and address of the sub-tenant, and a copy of any agreement for the sub-tenancy.

(5)   Where an application is made under section 13 of the 1987 Act, the date on which the landlord acquired the property and the terms of acquisition including the sums paid.

[(6)   Except where an application is made under section 24, 25 or 27 of the 1993 Act, a copy of the lease.]

*Service charges, administration charges and estate charges*

2.—(1)   Where an application is made under section 27A of the 1985 Act, the name and address of the secretary of any recognised tenants' association.

(2)   Where an application is made under paragraph 3 of Schedule 11 to the 2002 Act, a draft of the proposed variation.

(3)   A copy of the lease or, where appropriate, a copy of the estate management scheme.

*Estate management charges*

3.—(1)   A copy of any estate management agreement or the proposed estate management scheme.

(2)   A statement that the applicant is either—
   (a)   a natural person;
   (b)   a representative body within the meaning of section 71(3) of the 1993 Act; or
   (c)   a relevant authority within the meaning of section 73(5) of that Act.

(3)   Where an application is made under section 70 of the 1993 Act, a copy of the notice given by the applicant under section 70(4) of that Act.

(4)   Where—
   (a)   approval is sought for a scheme;
   (b)   approval is sought to modify the area of an existing scheme; or
   (c)   approval is sought to vary an existing scheme
a description of the area of—
         (i)   the proposed scheme;
         (ii)   the proposed modification; or
         (iii)   the proposed variation,
including identification of the area by a map or plan.

(5)   Where an application is made under section 70 of the 1993 Act, a copy of any consent given by the Secretary of State under section 72(1) of that Act.

*Right to manage*

4.—(1)   The name and address for service of the RTM company (within the meaning of Chapter 1 of Part 2 of the 2002 Act).

(2)   The name and address of the freeholder, any intermediate landlord and any manager.

(3)   A copy of the memorandum and articles of association of the RTM company.

(4)   Where an application is made under section 84(3) of the 2002 Act, a copy of the claim notice and a copy of the counter notice received.

(5)   Where an application is made under section 85(2) of the 2002 Act—
   (a)   a statement that the requirements of sections 78 and 79 of the 2002 Act are fulfilled;
   (b)   a copy of the notice given under section 85(3) of the 2002 Act together with a statement that such notice has been served on all qualifying tenants;
   (c)   a statement describing the circumstances in which the landlord cannot be identified or traced.

(6)   Where an application is made under section 94(3) of the 2002 Act an estimate of the amount of the accrued uncommitted service charges.

(7)   Where an application is made under section 99(1) of the 2002 Act, a description of the approval sought and a copy of the relevant lease.

(8)   Where an application is made under paragraph 5 of Schedule 6 to the 2002 Act, the date and circumstances in which the right to exercise the right to manage has ceased within the past four years.

*Appointment of manager*

5.—(1)   Other than where an application is made under section 22(3) of the 1987 Act, a copy of the notice served under section 22 of that Act.

(2)   Where an application is made under section 24(9) of that Act, a copy of the management order.

*Variation of leases*

6.—(1)   The names and addresses of any person served with a notice in accordance with regulation 4 of these Regulations.

(2)   A draft of the variation sought.

[(3)   A copy of the lease.]

[*Determination of breach of covenant or condition*

7.—(1)   A statement giving particulars of the alleged breach of covenant or condition.

(2)   A copy of the lease concerned.]

**[3345]**

**NOTES**
   Para 1: sub-para (6) added by the Leasehold Valuation Tribunals (Procedure) (Amendment) (England) Regulations 2004, SI 2004/3098, regs 2, 8(a).
   Para 6: sub-para (3) added by SI 2004/3098, regs 2, 8(b).
   Para 7: added by SI 2004/3098, regs 2, 8(c).

# RTM COMPANIES (MEMORANDUM AND ARTICLES OF ASSOCIATION) (ENGLAND) REGULATIONS 2003

(SI 2003/2120)

**NOTES**
   Made: 7 August 2003.
   Authority: Commonhold and Leasehold Reform Act 2002, ss 74(2), (4), (6), 178(1).
   Commencement: 30 September 2003.

## 1  Citation, commencement and application

(*1*)   *These Regulations may be cited as the RTM Companies (Memorandum and Articles of Association) (England) Regulations 2003 and shall come into force on 30th September 2003.*

(*2*)   *These Regulations apply to RTM companies in relation to premises in England.*

**[3346]**

**NOTES**
   Revoked by the RTM Companies (Model Articles) (England) Regulations 2009, SI 2009/2767, reg 3(1), as from 9 November 2009 (for transitional provisions see below).
   Transitional provisions: the RTM Companies (Model Articles) (England) Regulations 2009, SI 2009/2767, reg 3(2), (3) at **[3971]** provides that RTM companies incorporated before 9 November 2009 can continue to operate under their existing constitutions until 30 September 2010. Alternatively, such companies can choose to adopt the articles of association prescribed by SI 2009/2767.

## 2  Form and content of memorandum and articles of association of RTM companies

(*1*)   *The memorandum of association of a RTM company shall take the form, and include the provisions, set out in Part 1 of the Schedule to these Regulations.*

(*2*)   *The articles of association of a RTM company shall take the form, and include the provisions, set out in Part 2 of that Schedule.*

(*3*)   *The provisions referred to in paragraphs (1) and (2) shall have effect for a RTM company whether or not they are adopted by the company.*

(*4*)   *Where—*

   (*a*)   *a RTM company has adopted a memorandum of association and articles of association before the coming into force of these Regulations; and*

(b)    the memorandum and the articles, or either of them, do not comply, as to content, with
the requirements of paragraphs (1) and (2),

the memorandum and articles shall be treated, on and after the coming into force of these
Regulations, as including such of the provisions set out in the Schedule as are required to secure
compliance with those requirements (whether in addition to or, as the circumstances require, in
substitution for their original content).

**[3347]**

## NOTES

Revoked, subject to transitional provisions, as noted to reg 1 at **[3346]**.

## SCHEDULE
## MEMORANDUM AND ARTICLES OF ASSOCIATION OF RTM COMPANIES
*Regulation 2*

### PART 1
### MEMORANDUM OF ASSOCIATION

### THE COMPANIES ACTS 1985 AND 1989

### COMPANY LIMITED BY GUARANTEE AND NOT HAVING A SHARE CAPITAL

### MEMORANDUM OF ASSOCIATION OF [NAME] RTM COMPANY LIMITED

1.    The name of the company is *"[name] RTM Company Limited"*.

2.    The registered office of the Company will be situated in [England and Wales] [Wales].

3.    The objects for which the Company is established are to acquire and exercise in accordance
with the Commonhold and Leasehold Reform Act 2002 ("the 2002 Act") the right to manage the
premises known as [name and address] ("the Premises"). These objects shall not be restrictively
construed but the widest interpretation shall be given to them.

4.    In furtherance of the objects, but not otherwise, the Company shall have power to do all such
things as may be authorised or required to be done by a RTM company by and under the 2002 Act,
and in particular (but without derogation from the generality of the foregoing)—

(a)    to prepare, make, pursue or withdraw a claim to acquire the right to manage the
Premises;

(b)    to exercise management functions under leases of the whole or any part of the Premises
in accordance with sections 96 and 97 of the 2002 Act;

(c)    to exercise functions in relation to the grant of approvals under long leases of the whole
or any part of the Premises in accordance with sections 98 and 99 of the 2002 Act;

(d)    in accordance with sections 100 and 101 of the 2002 Act, to monitor, keep under review,
report to the landlord, and procure or enforce the performance by any person of the
terms of any covenant, undertaking, duty or obligation in any way connected with or
affecting the Premises or any of its occupants;

(e)    to negotiate for and make applications for the variation of leases pursuant to Part 4 of
the Landlord and Tenant Act 1987 ("the 1987 Act");

(f)    to do such other things and to perform such other functions in relation to the Premises
or any leases of the whole or any part of the Premises as may be agreed from time to
time with the landlord or landlords or any other parties to the leases, as the case may
be;

(g)    to provide and maintain services and amenities of every description in relation to the
Premises; to maintain, repair, renew, redecorate, repaint and clean the Premises; and to
cultivate, maintain, landscape and plant any land, gardens and grounds comprised in
the Premises;

(h)    to enter into contracts with builders, decorators, cleaners, tenants, contractors,
gardeners, or any other person; to consult and retain any professional advisers and to
employ any staff and managing or other agents; and to pay, reward or remunerate in any
way any person supplying goods or services to the Company;

(i)    to make any appropriate or consequential agreements or arrangements for the right to
manage the Premises to cease to be exercisable by the Company;

(j)    to issue and receive any notice, counter-notice, consent or other communication and to
enter into any correspondence concerning or in any way affecting the Premises, the
management of the Premises, the occupants of the Premises, the Company, any of its
activities, or any of its members;

(k)    to commence, pursue, defend or participate in any application to, or other proceeding
before, any court or tribunal of any description;

(l)    to insure the Premises or any other property of the Company or in which it has an
interest against damage or destruction and such other risks as may be considered

necessary, appropriate or desirable and to insure the Company and its directors, officers or auditors against public liability and any other risks which it may consider prudent or desirable to insure against;

(m)  to collect in or receive monies from any person on account of service charges, administration charges and other charges in relation to the Premises and, where required by law to do so, to hold, invest and deal with the monies in accordance with the provisions of the 1987 Act and any regulations or orders made under that Act from time to time;

(n)  to establish, undertake and execute any trusts which may lawfully be, or which are required by law to be, established, undertaken or executed by the Company;

(o)  to establish and maintain capital reserves, management funds and any form of sinking fund in order to pay, or contribute towards, all fees, costs and other expenses incurred in the implementation of the Company's objects;

(p)  to invest any money of the Company in the United Kingdom by depositing it at interest with any financial institution with which a trust fund of service charge contributions might be held in accordance with the 1987 Act; or to invest it in such other manner (including the purchase of securities and other investments) as the Company in general meeting may authorise from time to time; and to hold, sell or otherwise dispose of any such investments;

(q)  subject to any limitations or conditions imposed by the Company in general meeting from time to time, to lend and advance money or give credit on any terms, with or without security to any person; to enter into guarantees, contracts of indemnity and suretyship of all kinds; to receive money on deposit or loan upon any terms; and to secure or guarantee in any manner and upon any terms the payment of any sum of money or the performance of any obligation by any person;

(r)  subject to any limitations or conditions imposed by the Company in general meeting from time to time, to borrow and raise money in any manner and to secure the repayment of any money borrowed, raised or owing by mortgage, charge, standard security, lien or other security upon the whole or part of the Company's property or assets (whether present or future) and also by a similar mortgage, charge, standard security, lien or security to secure and guarantee the performance by the Company of any obligation or liability it may undertake or which may become binding on it;

(s)  to operate bank accounts and to draw, make, accept, endorse, discount, negotiate, execute and issue cheques, bills of exchange, promissory notes, debentures and other negotiable or transferable instruments;

(t)  to pay all or any expenses incurred in connection with the promotion, formation and incorporation of the Company, or to contract with any person to pay such expenses;

(u)  with the consent of the Company in general meeting, to give or award pensions, annuities, gratuities, and superannuation or other allowances or benefits or charitable aid and generally to provide advantages, facilities and services for any persons who are or have been directors of, or who are or have been employed by, or who are serving or have served the Company and to the spouses, surviving spouses, children and other relatives and dependants of such persons; to make payments towards insurance; and to set up, establish, support and maintain superannuation and other funds or schemes (whether contributory or non-contributory) for the benefit of any such persons and of their spouses, surviving spouses, children and other relatives and dependants;

(v)  to monitor and determine for the purpose of voting, or for any other purpose, the physical dimensions of the Premises and any part or parts of the Premises and to take or obtain any appropriate measurements;

(w)  to enter into any agreements or arrangements with any government or authority (central, municipal, local, or otherwise) that may seem conducive to the attainment of the Company's objects, and to obtain from any such government or authority any charters, decrees, rights, privileges or concessions which the Company may think desirable, and to carry out, exercise, and comply with any such charters, decrees, rights, privileges, and concessions;

(x)  to do all things specified for the time being in the articles of association of the Company;

(y)  to do or procure or arrange for the doing of all or any of the things or matters mentioned above in any part of the world and either as principals, agents, contractors or otherwise, and by or through agents, brokers, sub-contractors or otherwise and either alone or in conjunction with others; and

(z)  to do all such other lawful things as may be incidental or conducive to the pursuit or attainment of the Company's objects.

5.   The income of the Company, from wherever derived, shall be applied solely in promoting the Company's objects, and, save on a winding up of the Company, no distribution shall be made to its members in cash or otherwise.

6.   The liability of the members is limited.

7.    *Every member of the Company undertakes to contribute such amount as may be required, not exceeding £1, to the assets of the Company in the event of the Company being wound up while he is a member, or within one year after he ceases to be a member, for payment of the debts and liabilities of the Company contracted before he ceases to be a member, and of the costs, charges, and expenses of winding up the Company, and for the adjustment of the rights of the contributories among themselves.*

8.    *If, on the winding up of the Company, there remains any surplus after the satisfaction of all its debts and liabilities, the surplus shall be paid to or distributed among the members of the Company.*

9.    *In this Memorandum, references to an Act include any statutory modification or re-enactment of the Act for the time being in force.*

*We, the subscribers to this memorandum of association, wish to be formed into a company pursuant to this memorandum.*

*Names and addresses of subscribers:*

*Dated*

*Witness to the above signatures*

**[3348]**

### NOTES

Revoked, subject to transitional provisions, as noted to reg 1 at **[3346]**.

### PART 2
### ARTICLES OF ASSOCIATION

### THE COMPANIES ACTS 1985 AND 1989

### COMPANY LIMITED BY GUARANTEE AND NOT HAVING A SHARE CAPITAL

### ARTICLES OF ASSOCIATION OF [NAME] RTM COMPANY LIMITED

### *INTERPRETATION*

1.    *In these articles—*
      *"the Companies Act" means the Companies Act 1985;*
      *"the 2002 Act" means the Commonhold and Leasehold Reform Act 2002;*
      *"address", in relation to electronic communications, includes any number or address used for the purposes of such communications;*
      *"clear days", in relation to a period of notice, means that period excluding the day when the notice is given or deemed to be given and the day for which it is given or on which it is to take effect;*
      *"communication" and "electronic communication" have the same meaning as in the Electronic Communications Act 2000;*
      *"the Company" means [name] RTM Company Limited;*
      *"immediate landlord", in relation to a unit in the Premises, means the person who—*
            *(a)    if the unit is subject to a lease, is the landlord under the lease; or*
            *(b)    if the unit is subject to two or more leases, is the landlord under whichever of the leases is inferior to the others;*
      *"the Premises" means [name and address];*
      *"residential unit" means a flat or any other separate set of premises which is constructed or adapted for use for the purposes of a dwelling;*
      *"registered office" means the registered office of the Company;*
      *"secretary" means the secretary of the Company or any other person appointed to perform the duties of the secretary of the Company, including a joint, assistant or deputy secretary.*

2.    *Unless the context otherwise requires, words or expressions contained in these articles bear the same meaning as in the Companies Act.*

3.    *In these articles, references to an Act shall include any statutory modification or re-enactment of the Act for the time being in force.*

### *MEMBERS*

4.    *Subject to the following articles, the subscribers to the Memorandum of Association of the Company, and such other persons as are admitted to membership in accordance with these articles shall be members of the Company. Membership of the Company shall not be transferable.*

5.    *No person shall be admitted to membership of the Company unless that person, whether alone or jointly with others, is—*
            *(a)    a qualifying tenant of a flat contained in the Premises as specified in section 75 of the 2002 Act; or*

    (b)   *from the date upon which the Company acquires the right to manage the Premises pursuant to the 2002 Act, a landlord under a lease of the whole or any part of the Premises.*

6.   *A person who, together with another or others, is to be regarded as jointly being the qualifying tenant of a flat, or as jointly constituting the landlord under a lease of the whole or any part of the Premises, shall, once admitted, be regarded as jointly being a member of the Company in respect of that flat or lease (as the case may be).*

7.   *Every person who is entitled to be, and who wishes to become a member of the Company, shall deliver to the Company an application for membership executed by him in the following form (or in a form as near to the following form as circumstances allow or in any other form which is usual or which the directors may approve)—*

        *To the Board of [name of Company]*
        *I, [name]*
        *of [address]*
        *am a qualifying tenant of [address of flat] and wish to become a member of [name of Company] subject to the provisions of the Memorandum and Articles of Association of the Company and to any Rules made under those Articles. I agree to pay to the Company an amount of up to £1 if the Company is wound up while I am a member or for up to 12 months after I have ceased to be a member.*
        *Signed ....................................................*
        *Dated ....................................................*

8.   *Applications for membership by persons who are to be regarded as jointly being the qualifying tenant of a flat, or who jointly constitute the landlord under a lease of the whole or any part of the Premises, shall state the names and addresses of all others who are jointly interested with them, and the order in which they wish to appear on the register of members in respect of such flat or lease (as the case may be).*

9.   *The directors shall, upon being satisfied as to a person's application and entitlement to membership, register such person as a member of the Company.*

10.   *Upon the Company becoming an RTM company in relation to the Premises, any of the subscribers to the Memorandum of Association who do not also satisfy the requirements for membership set out in article 5 above shall cease to be members of the Company with immediate effect. Any member who at any time ceases to satisfy those requirements shall also cease to be a member of the Company with immediate effect.*

11.   *If a member (or joint member) dies or becomes bankrupt, his personal representatives or trustee in bankruptcy will be entitled to be registered as a member (or joint member as the case may be) upon notice in writing to the Company.*

12.   *A member may withdraw from the Company and thereby cease to be a member by giving at least seven clear days' notice in writing to the Company. Any such notice shall not be effective if given in the period beginning with the date on which the Company gives notice of its claim to acquire the right to manage the Premises and ending with the date which is either—*

    (a)   *the acquisition date in accordance with section 90 of the 2002 Act; or*
    (b)   *the date of withdrawal or deemed withdrawal of that notice in accordance with sections 86 or 87 of that Act.*

13.   *If, for any reason—*

    (a)   *a person who is not a member of the Company becomes a qualifying tenant or landlord jointly with persons who are members of the Company, but fails to apply for membership within 28 days, or*
    (b)   *a member who is a qualifying tenant or landlord jointly with such persons dies or becomes bankrupt and his personal representatives or trustee in bankruptcy do not apply for membership within 56 days pursuant to article 11, or*
    (c)   *a member who is a qualifying tenant or landlord jointly with such persons resigns from membership pursuant to article 12,*

*those persons shall, unless they are otherwise entitled to be members of the Company by reason of their interest in some other flat or lease, also cease to be members of the Company with immediate effect. All such persons shall, however, be entitled to re-apply for membership in accordance with articles 7 to 9.*

### GENERAL MEETINGS

14.   *All general meetings, other than annual general meetings, shall be called extraordinary general meetings.*

15.   *The directors may call general meetings and, on the requisition of members pursuant to the provisions of the Companies Act, shall forthwith (and in any event within twenty-one days) proceed to convene an extraordinary general meeting for a date not more than twenty-eight days after the*

*date of the notice convening the meeting. If there are not within the United Kingdom sufficient directors to call a general meeting, any director or any member of the Company may call a general meeting.*

16.    *All general meetings shall be held at the Premises or at such other suitable place as is near to the Premises and reasonably accessible to all members.*

## NOTICE OF GENERAL MEETINGS

17.    *An annual general meeting and an extraordinary general meeting called for the passing of a special resolution or a resolution appointing a person as a director shall be called by at least twenty-one clear days' notice. All other extraordinary general meetings shall be called by at least fourteen clear days' notice but a general meeting may be called by shorter notice if it is so agreed,*

    (a)    *in the case of an annual general meeting, by all the members entitled to attend and vote; and*

    (b)    *in the case of any other meeting, by a majority in number of the members having a right to attend and vote, being a majority together holding not less than ninety-five per cent of the total voting rights at the meeting of all the members.*

18.    *The notice shall specify the time and place of the meeting and, in the case of an annual general meeting, shall specify the meeting as such.*

19.    *The notice shall also include or be accompanied by a statement and explanation of the general nature of the business to be transacted at the meeting.*

20.    *Subject to the provisions of these articles, the notice shall be given to all the members and to the directors and auditors.*

21.    *The accidental omission to give notice of a meeting to, or the non-receipt of notice of a meeting by, any person entitled to receive notice shall not invalidate the proceedings at that meeting.*

## PROCEEDINGS AT GENERAL MEETINGS

22.    *No business shall be transacted at any general meeting unless it was included in the notice convening the meeting in accordance with article 19.*

23.    *No business shall be transacted at any general meeting unless a quorum is present. The quorum for the meeting shall be 20 per cent of the members of the Company entitled to vote upon the business to be transacted, or two members of the Company so entitled (whichever is the greater) present in person or by proxy.*

24.    *If such a quorum is not present within half an hour from the time appointed for the meeting, or if during a meeting such a quorum ceases to be present, the meeting shall stand adjourned to the same day in the next week at the same time and place or to such time and place as the directors may determine.*

25.    *The chairman, if any, of the board of directors or in his absence some other director nominated by the directors shall preside as chairman of the meeting, but if neither the chairman nor such other director (if any) is present within fifteen minutes after the time appointed for holding the meeting and willing to act, the directors present shall elect one of their number to be chairman and, if there is only one director present and willing to act, he shall be chairman.*

26.    *If no director is willing to act as chairman, or if no director is present within fifteen minutes after the time appointed for holding the meeting, the members present and entitled to vote shall choose one of their number to be chairman.*

27.    *A director shall, notwithstanding that he is not a member, be entitled to attend, speak and propose (but, subject to article 33, not vote upon) a resolution at any general meeting of the Company.*

28.    *The chairman may, with the consent of a meeting at which a quorum is present (and shall if so directed by the meeting), adjourn the meeting from time to time and from place to place, but no business shall be transacted at an adjourned meeting other than business which might properly have been transacted at the meeting if the adjournment had not taken place. When a meeting is adjourned for fourteen days or more, at least seven clear days' notice shall be given specifying the time and place of the adjourned meeting and the general nature of the business to be transacted. Otherwise it shall not be necessary to give any such notice.*

29.    *A resolution put to the vote of a meeting shall be decided on a show of hands unless before, or on the declaration of the result of, the show of hands a poll is duly demanded. Subject to the provisions of the Companies Act, a poll may be demanded—*

    (a)    *by the chairman; or*

    (b)    *by at least two members having the right to vote at the meeting; or*

    (c)    *by a member or members representing not less than one-tenth of the total voting rights of all the members having the right to vote at the meeting;*

*and a demand by a person as proxy for a member shall be the same as a demand by the member.*

30.    *Unless a poll is duly demanded, a declaration by the chairman that a resolution has been carried or carried unanimously, or by a particular majority, or lost, or not carried by a particular majority and an entry to that effect in the minutes of the meeting shall be conclusive evidence of the fact without proof of the number or proportion of the votes recorded in favour of or against the resolution.*

31.    *The demand for a poll may, before the poll is taken, be withdrawn but only with the consent of the chairman and a demand so withdrawn shall not be taken to have invalidated the result of a show of hands declared before the demand was made.*

32.    *A poll shall be taken as the chairman directs and he may appoint scrutineers (who need not be members) and fix a time and place for declaring the result of the poll. The result of the poll shall be deemed to be the resolution of the meeting at which the poll was demanded.*

33.    *In the case of an equality of votes, whether on a show of hands or on a poll, the chairman shall be entitled to a casting vote in addition to any other vote he may have.*

34.    *A poll demanded on the election of a chairman or on a question of adjournment shall be taken forthwith. A poll demanded on any other question shall be taken either forthwith or at such time and place as the chairman directs, not being more than thirty days after the poll is demanded. The demand for a poll shall not prevent the continuance of a meeting for the transaction of any business other than the question on which the poll was demanded. If a poll is demanded before the declaration of the result of a show of hands and the demand is duly withdrawn, the meeting shall continue as if the demand had not been made.*

35.    *No notice need be given of a poll not taken forthwith if the time and place at which it is to be taken are announced at the meeting at which it is demanded. In any other case at least seven clear days' notice shall be given specifying the time and place at which the poll is to be taken.*

36.    *A resolution in writing executed by or on behalf of each member who would have been entitled to vote upon it if it had been proposed at a general meeting at which he was present shall be as effectual as if it had been passed at a general meeting duly convened and held and may consist of several instruments in the like form each executed by or on behalf of one or more members.*

## *VOTES OF MEMBERS*

37.    *On a show of hands every member who (being an individual) is present in person or (being a corporation) is present by a duly authorised representative, not being himself a member entitled to vote, shall have one vote and on a poll, each member shall have the number of votes determined in accordance with articles 38 to 40.*

38.    *If there are no landlords under leases of the whole or any part of the Premises who are members of the Company, then one vote shall be available to be cast in respect of each flat in the Premises. The vote shall be cast by the member who is the qualifying tenant of the flat.*

39.    *At any time at which there are any landlords under leases of the whole or any part of the Premises who are members of the Company, the votes available to be cast shall be determined as follows—*

  (a)    *there shall first be allocated to each residential unit in the Premises the same number of votes as equals the total number of members of the Company who are landlords under leases of the whole or any part of the Premises. Landlords under a lease who are regarded as jointly being a member of the Company shall be counted as one member for this purpose;*

  (b)    *if at any time the Premises includes any non-residential part, a total number of votes shall be allocated to that part as shall equal the total number of votes allocated to the residential units multiplied by a factor of A/B, where A is the total internal floor area of the non-residential parts and B is the total internal area of all the residential parts. Internal floor area shall be determined in accordance with paragraph 1(4) of Schedule 6 to the 2002 Act. Calculations of the internal floor area shall be measured in square metres, fractions of floor area of less than half a square metre shall be ignored and fractions of floor area in excess of half a square metre shall be counted as a whole square metre;*

  (c)    *the votes allocated to each residential unit shall be entitled to be cast by the member who is the qualifying tenant of that unit, or if there is no member who is a qualifying tenant of the unit, by the member who is the immediate landlord;*

  (d)    *the votes allocated to any non-residential part included in the Premises shall be entitled to be cast by the immediate landlord of that part, or where there is no lease of a non-residential part, by the freeholder. Where there is more than one such person, the total number of votes allocated to the non-residential part shall be divided between them in proportion to the internal floor area of their respective parts. Any resulting entitlement to a fraction of a vote shall be ignored;*

  (e)    *if a residential unit is not subject to any lease, no votes shall be entitled to be cast in respect of it;*

(f)     *any person who is a landlord under a lease or leases of the whole or any part of the Premises and who is a member of the Company but is not otherwise entitled to any votes, shall be entitled to one vote.*

40.     *In the case of any persons who are to be regarded as jointly being members of the Company, any such person may exercise the voting rights to which such members are jointly entitled, but where more than one such person tenders a vote, whether in person or by proxy, the vote of the senior shall be accepted to the exclusion of the votes of the others, and seniority shall be determined by the order in which the names of such persons appear in the register of members in respect of the flat or lease (as the case may be) in which they are interested.*

41.     *The Company shall maintain a register showing the respective entitlements of each of its members to vote on a poll at any meeting of the Company.*

42.     *Any objection to the qualification of any voter or to the computation of the number of votes to which he is entitled that is raised in due time at a meeting or adjourned meeting shall be referred to the chairman of the meeting, whose decision shall, for all purposes relating to that meeting or adjourned meeting, be final and conclusive. Subject to that, any dispute between any member and the Company or any other member, that arises out of the member's contract of membership and concerns the measurement of floor areas, shall be referred for determination by an independent chartered surveyor selected by agreement between the parties or, in default, by the President of the Royal Institution of Chartered Surveyors. Such independent chartered surveyor shall, in determining the measurements of the floor areas in question, act as an expert and not as an arbitrator and his decision shall be final and conclusive. The Company shall be responsible to such surveyor for payment of his fees and expenses, but he shall have the power, in his absolute discretion, to direct that some or all of such fees and expenses shall be reimbursed by the member(s) in question to the Company, in which event such monies shall be paid by the member(s) to the Company forthwith.*

43.     *A member in respect of whom an order has been made by any court having jurisdiction (whether in the United Kingdom or elsewhere) in matters concerning mental disorder may vote, whether on a show of hands or on a poll, by his receiver, curator bonis or other person, authorised in that behalf appointed by that court, and any such receiver, curator bonis or other person may, on a poll, vote by proxy. Evidence to the satisfaction of the directors of the authority of the person claiming to exercise the right to vote shall be deposited at the registered office, or at such other place as is specified in accordance with these articles for the deposit of instruments of proxy, not less than 48 hours before the time appointed for holding the meeting or adjourned meeting at which the right to vote is to be exercised and in default the right to vote shall not be exercisable.*

44.     *On a poll votes may be given either personally or by proxy. A member may appoint more than one proxy to attend on the same occasion.*

45.     *An instrument appointing a proxy shall be writing, executed by or on behalf of the appointor and shall be in the following form (or in a form as near to the following form as circumstances allow or in any other form which is usual or which the directors may approve)—*

*[Name of Company]*

      *[Name of member(s)], of [address], being a member/members of the above-named company, hereby appoint [name] of [address], or failing him, [name] of [address], as my/our proxy to vote in my/our name[s] and on my/our behalf at the annual/ extraordinary general meeting of the company to be held on [date], and at any adjournment of the meeting.*

*Signed on [date]*

46.     *Where it is desired to afford members an opportunity of instructing the proxy how he shall act, the instrument appointing a proxy shall be in the following form (or in a form as near to the following form as circumstances allow or in any other form which is usual or which the directors may approve)—*

*[Name of Company]*

      *[Name of member(s)], of [address], being a member/members of the above-named company, hereby appoint [name] of [address], or failing him [name] of [address], as my/our proxy to vote in my/our name[s] and on my/our behalf at the annual/ extraordinary general meeting of the company, to be held on [date], and at any adjournment of the meeting.*

      *This form is to be used in respect of the resolutions mentioned below as follows:*
      *Resolution No 1 [for] [against]*
      *Resolution No 2 [for] [against]*
      *[Strike out whichever is not desired]*
      *Unless otherwise instructed, the proxy may vote as he thinks fit or abstain from voting.*

*Signed on [date]*

47.     *The instrument appointing a proxy and any authority under which it is executed or a copy of such authority certified notarially or in some other way approved by the directors may—*

    (a)     *in the case of an instrument in writing, be deposited at the registered office or at such*

PART II
STATUTORY INSTRUMENTS

*other place within the United Kingdom as is specified in the notice convening the meeting or in any instrument of proxy sent out by the Company in relation to the meeting not less than 48 hours before the time for holding the meeting or adjourned meeting at which the person named in the instrument proposes to vote; or*

(b) *in the case of an appointment contained in an electronic communication, where an address has been specified for the purpose of receiving electronic communications—*

    (i) *in the notice convening the meeting, or*

    (ii) *in any instrument of proxy sent out by the Company in relation to the meeting, or*

    (iii) *in any invitation contained in an electronic communication to appoint a proxy issued by the Company in relation to the meeting,*

*be received at such address not less than 48 hours before the time for holding the meeting or adjourned meeting at which the person named in the appointment proposes to vote;*

(c) *in the case of a poll taken more than 48 hours after it is demanded, be deposited or received as mentioned in paragraph (a) or (b) after the poll has been demanded and not less than 24 hours before the time appointed for the taking of the poll; or*

(d) *where the poll is not taken forthwith but is taken not more than 48 hours after it was demanded, be delivered at the meeting at which the poll was demanded to the chairman or to the secretary or to any director;*

*and an instrument of proxy which is not deposited, delivered or received in a manner permitted by this article shall be invalid.*

48. *A vote given or poll demanded by proxy or by the duly authorised representative of a corporation shall be valid notwithstanding the previous termination of the authority of the person voting or demanding a poll unless notice of the termination was received by the Company at the registered office or at such other place at which the instrument of proxy was duly deposited or, where the appointment of the proxy was contained in an electronic communication, at the address at which such appointment was duly received before the commencement of the meeting or adjourned meeting at which the vote is given or the poll demanded or (in the case of a poll taken otherwise than on the same day as the meeting or adjourned meeting) the time appointed for taking the poll.*

## QUALIFICATION OF DIRECTORS

49. *A director need not be a member of the Company.*

## NUMBER OF DIRECTORS

50. *Unless otherwise determined by ordinary resolution, the number of directors (other than alternate directors) shall not be subject to any maximum but shall be not less than two.*

## APPOINTMENT AND REMOVAL OF DIRECTORS

51. *At the first annual general meeting, all of the directors shall retire from office, and at every subsequent annual general meeting one-third of the directors who are subject to retirement by rotation or, if their number is not three or a multiple of three, the number nearest to one-third shall retire from office; but if there is only one director who is subject to retirement by rotation, he shall retire.*

52. *Subject to the provisions of the Companies Act, the directors to retire by rotation shall be those who have been longest in office since their last appointment or reappointment, but as between persons who became or who were last reappointed directors on the same day those to retire shall (unless they otherwise agree among themselves) be determined by lot.*

53. *If the Company, at the meeting at which a director retires by rotation, does not fill the vacancy, the retiring director shall, if willing to act, be deemed to have been reappointed unless at the meeting it is resolved not to fill the vacancy or unless a resolution for the reappointment of the director is put to the meeting and lost.*

54. *A person other than a director retiring by rotation shall not be appointed or reappointed as a director at any general meeting unless—*

    (a) *he is recommended by the directors; or*

    (b) *not less than fourteen nor more than thirty-five clear days before the date appointed for the meeting, notice executed by a member qualified to vote at the meeting has been given to the Company of the intention to propose that person for appointment or reappointment stating the particulars which would, if he were so appointed or reappointed, be required to be included in the Company's register of directors together with notice executed by that person of his willingness to be appointed or reappointed.*

55. *Not less than seven nor more than twenty-eight clear days before the date appointed for holding a general meeting, notice shall be given to all who are entitled to receive notice of the meeting of any person who is recommended by the directors for appointment or reappointment as a director at the meeting or in respect of whom notice has been duly given to the Company of the intention to propose him at the meeting for appointment or reappointment as a director. The notice*

shall give the particulars of that person which would, if he were so appointed or reappointed, be required to be included in the Company's register of directors.

56.   Subject to articles 51 to 55, the Company may by ordinary resolution appoint a person who is willing to act to be a director either to fill a vacancy, or as an additional director and may also determine the rotation in which any additional directors are to retire.

57.   The directors may appoint a person who is willing to act to be a director, either to fill a vacancy or as an additional director, provided that the appointment does not cause the number of directors to exceed any number fixed by or in accordance with the articles as the maximum number of directors. A director so appointed shall hold office only until the next following annual general meeting. If not reappointed at such annual general meeting, he shall vacate office at the conclusion thereof.

58.   Subject to those articles, a director who retires at an annual general meeting may, if willing to act, be reappointed. If he is not reappointed, he shall retain office until the meeting appoints someone in his place, or if it does not do so, until the end of the meeting.

## ALTERNATE DIRECTORS

59.   Any director (other than an alternate director) may appoint any other director, or any other person approved by resolution of the directors and willing to act, to be an alternate director and may remove from office an alternate director so appointed by him.

60.   An alternate director shall be entitled to receive notice of all meetings of directors and of all meetings of committees of directors of which his appointor is a member, to attend and vote at any such meeting at which the director appointing him is not personally present and generally to perform all the functions of his appointor as a director in his absence but shall not be entitled to receive any remuneration from the Company for his service as an alternate director. It shall not be necessary to give notice of such a meeting to an alternate director who is absent from the United Kingdom unless he has given to the Company an address to which notices may be sent using electronic communications.

61.   An alternate director shall cease to be an alternate director if his appointor ceases to be a director. If a director retires but is reappointed or deemed to have been reappointed at the meeting at which he retires, any appointment of an alternate director made by him which was in force immediately prior to his retirement shall continue after his reappointment.

62.   Any appointment or removal of an alternate director shall be by notice to the Company signed by the director making or revoking the appointment or in any other manner approved by the directors.

63.   Except where otherwise provided in these articles, an alternate director shall be deemed for all purposes to be a director and shall alone be responsible for his own acts and defaults and he shall not be deemed to be the agent of the director appointing him.

## DISQUALIFICATION AND REMOVAL OF DIRECTORS

64.   The office of a director shall be vacated if—
   (a)   he ceases to be a director by virtue of any provision of the Companies Act or he becomes prohibited by law from being a director; or
   (b)   he becomes bankrupt and shall continue to be disqualified from acting as a director whilst he remains undischarged from his bankruptcy, or makes any arrangement or composition with his creditors generally; or
   (c)   he is, or may be, suffering from mental disorder and either—
       (i)   he is admitted to hospital in pursuance of an application for admission for treatment under the Mental Health Act 1983 or, in Scotland, an application for admission under the Mental Health (Scotland) Act 1960, or
       (ii)   an order is made by a court having jurisdiction (whether in the United Kingdom or elsewhere) in matters concerning mental disorder for his detention or for the appointment of a receiver, curator bonis or other person to exercise powers with respect to his property or affairs; or
   (d)   having been a member of the Company, he ceases to be a member of the Company; or
   (e)   he resigns his office by notice to the Company; or
   (f)   he shall for more than six consecutive months have been absent without permission of the directors from meetings of directors held during that period and the directors resolve that his office be vacated.

## POWERS OF DIRECTORS

65.   Subject to the provisions of the Companies Act, the memorandum and these articles and to any directions given by special resolution, the business of the Company shall be managed by the directors who may exercise all the powers of the Company. No alteration of the memorandum or articles and no such direction shall invalidate any prior act of the directors which would have been valid if that alteration had not been made or that direction had not been given. The powers given by

this article shall not be limited by any special power given to the directors by these articles and a meeting of directors at which a quorum is present may exercise all powers exercisable by the directors.

66. The directors may, by power of attorney or otherwise, appoint any person to be the agent of the Company for such purposes and on such conditions as they determine, including authority for the agent to delegate all or any of his powers.

## DELEGATION OF DIRECTORS' POWERS

67. The directors may delegate any of their powers to any committee consisting of one or more directors, members of the Company and others as they shall think fit. The majority of the members of any such committee from time to time shall be members of the Company. The directors may also delegate to any managing director, or any director holding any other executive office, such of their powers as they consider desirable to be exercised by him. Any such delegation may be made subject to any conditions the directors may impose, and either collaterally with or to the exclusion of their own powers and may be revoked or altered. Subject to any such conditions, the proceedings of a committee with two or more members shall be governed by the articles regulating the proceedings of directors so far as they are capable of applying.

## REMUNERATION OF DIRECTORS

68. Except with the consent of the Company in general meeting, the directors shall not be entitled to any remuneration. Any resolution giving such consent shall specify the amount of remuneration to be paid to the directors, and unless the resolution provides otherwise, the remuneration shall be deemed to accrue from day to day.

## DIRECTORS' EXPENSES

69. The directors may be paid all expenses properly incurred by them in connection with their attendance at meetings of directors or committees of directors or general meetings of the Company or otherwise in connection with the discharge of their duties.

## DIRECTORS' APPOINTMENTS AND INTERESTS

70. Subject to the provisions of the Companies Act, and provided that the terms of any such appointment, agreement or arrangement have been approved in advance by the Company, the directors may appoint one or more of their number to the office of managing director or to any other executive office under the Company and may enter into an agreement or arrangement with any director for his employment by the Company or for the provision by him of any services outside the scope of the ordinary duties of a director. Any appointment of a director to an executive office shall terminate if he ceases to be a director but without prejudice to any claim to damages for breach of the contract of service between the director and the Company.

71. Subject to the provisions of the Companies Act, and provided that he has disclosed to the directors the nature and extent of any material interest of his, a director notwithstanding his office—

(a)   may be a party to, or otherwise interested in, any transaction or arrangement with the Company or in which the Company is otherwise interested; and

(b)   may be a director or other officer of, or employed by, or a party to any transaction or arrangement with, or otherwise interested in, any body corporate promoted by the Company or in which the Company is otherwise interested; and

(c)   shall not, by reason of his office, be accountable to the Company for any benefit which he derives from any such office or employment or from any such transaction or arrangement or from any interest in any such body corporate and no such transaction or arrangement shall be liable to be avoided on the ground of any such interest or benefit.

72. For the purposes of article 71—

(a)   a general notice given to the directors that a director is to be regarded as having an interest of the nature and extent specified in the notice in any transaction or arrangement in which a specified person or class of persons is interested shall be deemed to be a disclosure that the director has an interest in any such transaction of the nature and extent so specified; and

(b)   an interest of which a director has no knowledge and of which it is unreasonable to expect him to have knowledge shall not be treated as an interest of his.

## DIRECTORS' GRATUITIES AND PENSIONS

73. The directors may provide benefits, whether by the payment of gratuities or pensions or by insurance or otherwise, for any director who has held but no longer holds any executive office or employment with the Company or with any body corporate which is or has been a subsidiary of the Company, and for any member of his family (including a spouse and a former spouse) or any person who is or was dependent on him, and may (as well before as after he ceases to hold such office or employment) contribute to any fund and pay premiums for the purchase or provision of any such benefit.

## PROCEEDINGS OF DIRECTORS

74.     *Subject to the provisions of these articles, the directors may regulate their proceedings as they think fit. A director may, and the secretary at the request of a director shall, call a meeting of the directors. It shall not be necessary to give notice of a meeting to a director who is absent from the United Kingdom unless he has given to the Company an address to which notices may be sent using electronic communications. Questions arising at a meeting shall be decided by a majority of votes. In the case of an equality of votes, the chairman shall have a second or casting vote. A director who is also an alternate director shall be entitled in the absence of his appointor to a separate vote on behalf of his appointor in addition to his own vote.*

75.     *The quorum for the transaction of the business of the directors may be fixed by the directors and, unless so fixed at any other greater number, shall be the greater of 50 per cent of the number of appointed directors for the time being, or two. A person who holds office only as an alternate director shall, if his appointor is not present, be counted in the quorum. A person who holds office both as a director and as an alternate director shall only be counted once in the quorum.*

76.     *The continuing directors or a sole continuing director may act notwithstanding any vacancies in their number, but, if the number of directors is less than the number fixed as the quorum, the continuing director may act only for the purpose of filling vacancies or of calling a general meeting.*

77.     *The directors may appoint one of their number to be the chairman of the board of directors and may at any time remove him from that office. Unless he is unwilling to do so, the director so appointed shall preside at every meeting of directors at which he is present. But if there is no director holding that office, or if the director holding it is unwilling to preside or is not present within fifteen minutes after the time appointed for the meeting, the directors present may appoint one of their number to be chairman of the meeting.*

78.     *All acts done by a meeting of directors, or of a committee of directors, or by a person acting as a director shall, notwithstanding that it be afterwards discovered that there was a defect in the appointment of any director or that any of them were disqualified from holding office, or had vacated office, or were not entitled to vote, be as valid as if every such person had been duly appointed and was qualified and had continued to be a director and had been entitled to vote.*

79.     *A resolution in writing signed by all the directors entitled to receive notice of a meeting of directors or of a committee of directors shall be as valid and effectual as if it had been passed at a meeting of directors or (as the case may be) a committee of directors duly convened and held and may consist of several documents in the like form each signed by one or more directors; but a resolution signed by an alternate director need not also be signed by his appointor and, if it is signed by a director who has appointed an alternate director, it need not be signed by the alternate director in that capacity.*

80.     *A director who is not a member of the Company shall not vote at a meeting of directors or of a committee of directors on any resolution concerning a matter in which he has, directly or indirectly, an interest or duty which is material and which conflicts or may conflict with the interests of the Company. For the purposes of this article, an interest of a person who is, for any purpose of the Companies Act, connected with a director shall be treated as an interest of the director and, in relation to an alternate director, an interest of his appointor shall be treated as an interest of the alternate director without prejudice to any interest which the alternate director has otherwise. A director shall not be counted in the quorum present at a meeting in relation to a resolution on which he is not entitled to vote.*

81.     *A director who is a member of the Company may vote at any meeting of directors or of any committee of directors of which he is a member notwithstanding that it in any way concerns or relates to a matter in which he has any interest whatsoever, directly or indirectly, and if he votes on such a resolution, his vote shall be counted; and, in relation to any such resolution, he shall (whether or not he votes on it) be taken into account in calculating the quorum present at the meeting.*

82.     *If a question arises at a meeting of directors or of a committee of directors as to the right of a director to vote, the question may, before the conclusion of the meeting, be referred to the chairman of the meeting and his ruling in relation to any director other than himself shall be final and conclusive.*

## SECRETARY

83.     *Subject to the provisions of the Companies Act, the secretary shall be appointed by the directors for such terms, at such remuneration and upon such conditions as they may think fit; and any secretary so appointed may be removed by them. The secretary may resign his office at any time by giving notice in writing to the Company.*

## MINUTES

84.     *The directors shall cause minutes to be made in books kept for the purpose—*
       *(a)    of all appointments of officers made by the directors; and*

(b)    of all proceedings at meetings of the Company, of members and of the directors, and of committees of directors, including the names of the directors present at each such meeting.

## NO DISTRIBUTION OF PROFITS

85.   Except in the case of a winding up, the Company shall not make any distribution to its members of its profits or assets, whether in cash or otherwise.

## WINDING UP

86.   If the Company is wound up, the liquidator may, with the sanction of [a special resolution] of the Company and any other sanction required by the Companies Act, divide among the members the whole or any part of the assets of the Company and may, for that purpose, value any assets and determine how the division shall be carried out as between the members or different classes of members. The liquidator may, with the like sanction, vest the whole or any part of the assets in trustees upon such trusts for the benefit of the members as he, with the like sanction, determines but no member shall be compelled to accept any asset upon which there is a liability.

## INSPECTION AND COPYING OF BOOKS AND RECORDS

87.   In addition to, and without derogation from, any right conferred by statute, any member shall have the right, on reasonable notice, at such time and place as shall be convenient to the Company, to inspect, and to be provided with a copy of, any book, minute, document or accounting record of the Company, upon payment of any reasonable charge for copying. Such rights shall be subject to any resolution of the Company in general meeting, and, in the case of any book, minute, document or accounting record which the directors reasonably consider contains confidential material, the disclosure of which would be contrary to the interests of the Company, to the exclusion or excision of such confidential material (the fact of such exclusion or excision being disclosed to the member), and to any other reasonable conditions that the directors may impose.

## NOTICES

88.   Any notice to be given to or by any person pursuant to these articles shall be in writing or shall be given using electronic communications to an address for the time being notified for that purpose to the person giving the notice. A notice calling a meeting of the directors need not be in writing or given using electronic communications if there is insufficient time to give such notice having regard to the urgency of the business to be conducted at the meeting.

89.   The Company may give any notice to a member either personally or by sending it by first class post in a prepaid envelope addressed to the member at his registered address or by leaving it at that address or by giving it using electronic communications in accordance with any of the methods described in subsections (4A)–(4D) of section 369 of the Companies Act. A member whose registered address is not within the United Kingdom and who gives to the Company an address within the United Kingdom at which notices may be given to him, or an address to which notices may be sent by electronic communications, shall be entitled to have notices given to him at that address, but otherwise no such member shall be entitled to receive any notice from the Company.

90.   A member present, either in person or by proxy, at any meeting of the Company shall be deemed to have received notice of the meeting and, where requisite, of the purposes for which it was called.

91.   Proof that an envelope containing a notice was properly addressed, prepaid and posted by fist class post shall be conclusive evidence that the notice was given. Proof that a notice contained in an electronic communication was sent in accordance with guidance issued by the Institute of Chartered Secretaries and Administrators shall be conclusive evidence that the notice was given.

92.   A notice sent by first class post shall be deemed to be given at the expiration of 48 hours after the envelope containing it was posted. A notice contained in an electronic communication sent in accordance with section 369(4A) of the Companies Act shall be deemed to be given at the expiration of 48 hours after the time it was sent. A notice contained in an electronic communication given in accordance with section 369(4B) of the Companies Act shall be deemed to be given when treated as having been so given in accordance with that subsection.

## INDEMNITY

93.   Subject to the provisions of the Companies Act, and in particular section 310 of that Act—
       (a)    without prejudice to any indemnity to which a director may otherwise be entitled, every director or other office or auditor of the Company shall be indemnified out of the assets of the Company against any losses or liabilities which he may sustain or incur in or about, or otherwise in relation to, the execution of the duties of his office, including any liability incurred by him in defending any proceedings, whether civil or criminal, in which judgment is given in his favour or in which he is acquitted or in connection with

any application in which relief is granted to him by the court from liability for negligence, default, breach of duty or breach of trust in relation to the affairs of the Company; and

(b)     no director or other officer shall be liable for any loss, damage or other misfortune which may happen to or be incurred by the Company in, or in relation to, the execution of the duties of his office.

94.     The directors shall have power to purchase and maintain for any director, officer or auditor of the Company, insurance against any such liability as is referred to in section 310(1) of the Companies Act.

### RULES OR BYE-LAWS

95.     The directors may from time to time make such rules or bye-laws as they may deem necessary or expedient or convenient for the proper conduct and management of the Company. Any such rules or bye-laws shall not be inconsistent with the Memorandum and these articles and may, in particular (but without prejudice to the generality of the directors' powers), regulate—

(a)     the conduct of the members of the Company in relation to one another and to the Company and the Company's servants;

(b)     the procedure at general meetings and meetings of the directors and committees of the directors of the Company in so far as such procedure is not regulated by these articles.

96.     The Company in general meeting shall have power to alter, repeal or add to any such rules or bye-laws and the directors shall adopt such means as they deem sufficient to bring to the notice of the members of the Company any such rules or bye-laws, which so long as they shall be in force, shall be binding on all members of the Company.

*Names and Addresses of Members:*

*[list names and addresses of members]*

**[3349]**

**NOTES**

Revoked, subject to transitional provisions, as noted to reg 1 at **[3346]**.

Article 86: words in square brackets substituted by the Companies Act 2006 (Commencement No 3, Consequential Amendments, Transitional Provisions and Savings) Order 2007, SI 2007/2194, art 10(1), (2), Sch 4, Pt 3, para 102(1), except in relation to company articles in which Article 86 is incorporated by virtue of having been adopted before 1 October 2007 or by virtue of the operation of the Commonhold and Leasehold Reform Act 2002, s 74(4) before that date (see SI 2007/2194, arts 1(3)(a), 10(1), (2), Sch 4, Pt 3, para 102(2); for further savings see art 12 thereof).

# LEASEHOLD VALUATION TRIBUNALS (FEES) (REVOCATION AND SAVING) (ENGLAND) ORDER 2003

## (SI 2003/2270)

**NOTES**

Made: 4 September 2003.
Authority: Landlord and Tenant Act 1985, s 31B; Landlord and Tenant Act 1987, s 24B.
Commencement: 30 September 2003.

### 1  Citation and commencement

This Order may be cited as the Leasehold Valuation Tribunals (Fees) (Revocation and Saving) (England) Order 2003 and shall come into force on 30th September 2003.

**[3350]**

### 2  Revocation and saving

(1)     Subject to paragraph (2), the Leasehold Valuation Tribunals (Fees) Order 1997 is hereby revoked in relation to England.

(2)     The revocation in paragraph (1) shall not have effect in relation to any application made, or proceedings transferred by a county court, to a leasehold valuation tribunal before 30th September 2003 in respect of premises in England.

**[3351]**

# HOMELESSNESS (SUITABILITY OF ACCOMMODATION) (ENGLAND) ORDER 2003

(SI 2003/3326)

**NOTES**
Made: 19 December 2003.
Authority: Housing Act 1996, ss 210(2)(a), 215(2).
Commencement: 1 April 2004.

## 1 Citation, commencement and application

(1)   This Order may be cited as the Homelessness (Suitability of Accommodation) (England) Order 2003 and shall come into force on 1st April 2004.

(2)   This Order applies in relation to the duties of local housing authorities in England to make accommodation available for occupation by applicants under Part 7 of the Housing Act 1996.

**[3352]**

## 2 Interpretation

In this Order—
  "applicant with family commitments" means an applicant—
   (a)   who is pregnant;
   (b)   with whom a pregnant woman resides or might reasonably be expected to reside; or
   (c)   with whom dependent children reside or might reasonably be expected to reside;
  "B&B accommodation" means accommodation (whether or not breakfast is included)—
   (a)   which is not separate and self-contained premises; and
   (b)   in which any one of the following amenities is shared by more than one household—

      (i)   a toilet;

      (ii)   personal washing facilities;

      (iii)   cooking facilities,

      but does not include accommodation which is owned or managed by a local housing authority, a registered social landlord or a voluntary organisation as defined in section 180(3) of the Housing Act 1996; and
  any reference to a numbered section is a reference to a section of the Housing Act 1996.

**[3353]**

## 3 Accommodation unsuitable where there is a family commitment

Subject to the exceptions contained in article 4, B&B accommodation is not to be regarded as suitable for an applicant with family commitments where accommodation is made available for occupation—
   (a)   under section 188(1), 190(2), 193(2) or 200(1); or
   (b)   under section 195(2), where the accommodation is other than that occupied by the applicant at the time of making his application.

**[3354]**

## 4 Exceptions

(1)   Article 3 does not apply—
   (a)   where no accommodation other than B&B accommodation is available for occupation by an applicant with family commitments; and
   (b)   the applicant occupies B&B accommodation for a period, or a total of periods, which does not exceed 6 weeks.

(2)   In calculating the period, or total period, of an applicant's occupation of B&B accommodation for the purposes of paragraph (1)(b), there shall be disregarded—
   (a)   any period before 1st April 2004; and
   (b)   where a local housing authority is subject to the duty under section 193 by virtue of section 200(4), any period before that authority became subject to that duty.

**[3355]**

# COMMONHOLD AND LEASEHOLD REFORM ACT 2002 (COMMENCEMENT NO 2 AND SAVINGS) (WALES) ORDER 2004

## (SI 2004/669 (W 62))

**NOTES**
Made: 9 March 2004.
Authority: Commonhold and Leasehold Reform Act 2002, s 181.

## 1  Citation, interpretation and application

(1)  This Order may be cited as the Commonhold and Leasehold Reform Act 2002 (Commencement No 2 and Savings) (Wales) Order 2004.

(2)  In this Order—
　　"LVT" ("*TPL*") means a leasehold valuation tribunal;
　　"the 1967 Act" ("*Deddf 1967*") means the Leasehold Reform Act 1967;
　　"the 1985 Act" ("*Deddf 1985*") means the Landlord and Tenant Act 1985;
　　"the 1987 Act" ("*Deddf 1987*") means the Landlord and Tenant Act 1987;
　　"the 1993 Act" ("*Deddf 1993*") means the Leasehold Reform, Housing and Urban
　　　　Development Act 1993;
　　"the 1996 Act" ("*Deddf 1996*") means the Housing Act 1996;
references to sections and Schedules are, unless otherwise stated, references to sections of, and Schedules to, the Commonhold and Leasehold Reform Act 2002; and
any reference to a repeal is to a repeal made by section 180 and Schedule 14.

(3)  This Order applies to Wales only.

**[3356]**

## 2  Provisions coming into force on 30th March 2004

The following provisions will come into force on 30th March 2004—

(a)　sections 71 to 73, 75 to 77, 79, 81 to 83 , 85 to 91, 93 to 103, 105 to 109, 111 to 113, 159, 163, 173, Schedules 6 and 7;

(b)　sections 74, 78, 80, 84, 92, 110, 174 and Schedule 12 to the extent that they are not already in force; and

(c)　subject to the savings in Schedule 2 to this Order—

　　(i)　sections 148, 149, 150, 155, 157 in so far as it relates to paragraphs 8 to 13 of Schedule 10, 158, 175, 176 in so far as it relates to paragraphs 1 to 15 of Schedule 13, Schedule 9, paragraphs 8 to 13 of Schedule 10, Schedule 11 and paragraphs 1 to 15 of Schedule 13;

　　(ii)　subsections (1) to (5) of section 172 except in so far as they relate to the application to the Crown of sections 152 to 154, 164 to 171, paragraphs 1 to 7 of Schedule 10 and paragraph 16 of Schedule 13;

　　(iii)　subsection (6) of section 172 except in so far as the substitutions made by that subsection relate to sections 42A and 42B of the 1987 Act;

　　(iv)　to the extent that it is not already in force, section 180 in so far as it relates to the repeals in Schedule 14 which are set out in Schedule 1 to this Order;

(d)　subject to subparagraphs (i) to (vi), section 151 to the extent that it is not already in force—

　　(i)　in relation to any case to which subparagraph (ii), (iii), (iv) or (vi) applies, the amendment made by section 151 shall have no effect and the Service Charge (Estimates and Consultation) Order 1988 will continue to apply;

　　(ii)　this subparagraph applies where qualifying works are begun before 31st March 2004;

　　(iii)　this subparagraph applies where, in relation to qualifying works, the landlord has given or displayed the notice required under section 20 of the 1985 Act before 31st March 2004;

　　(iv)　this subparagraph applies where, in relation to qualifying works to which subparagraph (v) applies, the landlord has given notice in the Official Journal of the European Union in accordance with the Public Works Contracts Regulations 1991, the Public Services Contracts Regulations 1993 or the Public Supply Contracts Regulations 1995 before 31st March 2004;

　　(v)　this subparagraph applies to qualifying works which are carried out under a contract which—

　　　　(a)　is to be entered into on or after 31st March 2004; and

　　　　(b)　is for a period of twelve months or less;

　　(vi)　this subparagraph applies where, under an agreement entered into, by or on behalf of the landlord or a superior landlord, before 31st March 2004, qualifying works are carried out at any time in the period starting with that date and ending two months after that date.

**[3357]**

## SCHEDULES

## SCHEDULE 1
## REPEALS

Article 2(c)(iv)

### PART 1
### LEASEHOLD VALUATION TRIBUNALS

| Short title and chapter | Extent of repeal |
| --- | --- |
| Leasehold Reform Act 1967 (c 88) | Section 21(1A) and (3) to (4A) |
| Housing Act 1980 (c 51) | In section 142— |
| | Subsection (2), and in subsection (3), the words from the beginning to "and". |
| | In Schedule 22— |
| | Part 1, and in Part 2, paragraph 8(4) to (6). |
| Landlord and Tenant Act 1985 (c 70) | Sections 31A to 31C. |
| | In the Schedule, paragraph 8(5). |
| Landlord and Tenant Act 1987 (c 31) | Section 23(2). |
| | Sections 24A and 24B. |
| | In section 38, in the sidenote, the words "by the court". |
| | Section 52A |
| | In section 53(2), the words "under section 52A(3) or". |
| Tribunals and Inquiries Act 1992 (c 53) | In Schedule 3, paragraph 13. |
| Leasehold Reform, Housing and Urban Development Act 1993 (c 28) | Section 75(4) and (5). |
| | In section 88— |
| | in subsection (2)(b), the words "constituted for the purposes of that Part of that Act", and subsections (3) to (5) and (7). |
| Leasehold Reform, Housing and Urban Development Act 1993 | In section 91— |
| | in subsection (2)(b), the words "constituted for the purposes of that Part of that Act", and subsections (3) to (5) and (7). |
| | In section 94, in subsection (10), the words from "and references in this subsection" to the end. |
| | In section 101(1), the definition of "rent assessment committee". |
| Housing Act 1996 (c 52) | Section 83(3). |
| | Section 86(4) and (5). |
| | Section 119. |
| | In Schedule 6, in Part 4, paragraphs 7 and 8. |

**[3358]**

PART 2
OTHER REPEALS

| Short title and chapter | Extent of repeal |
|---|---|
| Landlord and Tenant Act 1985 (c 70) | Section 19(2A) to (3). In section 39, the entry relating to the expression "flat". In the Schedule— in the heading before paragraph 2, the words "Request for", in the heading before paragraph 4, the words "Request relating to", in the heading before paragraph 5, the words "on request". |
| Landlord and Tenant Act 1987 (c 31) | In section 29(2)(a), the words "repair, maintenance, insurance or". Section 56(2). In Schedule 2, paragraphs and 7. |
| Housing Act 1996 (c 52) | Section 83(1). In Schedule 9, paragraph 2(3) and (7). |

**[3359]**

SCHEDULE 2
SAVINGS

Article 2(c)

*Absent landlords—leasehold houses*

1.   The amendments made by sections 148 and 149 will not have effect in relation to an application for enfranchisement made under section 27 of the 1967 Act before 31st March 2004.

*Definition of service charges*

2.   The amendment made by paragraph 7 of Schedule 9 will not apply to costs incurred before 31st March 2004 in connection with matters for which a service charge is payable.

*Meaning of "management" in section 24 of the 1987 Act*

3.   The amendment made by paragraph 8 of Schedule 9 will not apply to an application made under section 24 of the 1987 Act before 31st March 2004.

*Right to acquire landlord's interest*

4.   The amendment made by paragraph 9 of Schedule 9 and the repeal in section 29 of the 1987 Act will not apply to an application made under section 29 of that Act before 31st March 2004.

*Tenant's right to a management audit*

5.   The amendments made by paragraph 10 of Schedule 9 will not apply to an application made under section 80 of the 1993 Act before 31st March 2004.

*Liability to pay service charges*

6.   The amendment made by section 155 and the repeals of section 19(2A) to (3) of the 1985 Act and of section 83(1) of the 1996 Act will not have effect in relation to—
    (a)    any application made to a LVT under section 19(2A) or (2B) of the 1985 Act; or
    (b)    any proceedings relating to a service charge transferred to a LVT by a county court,
before 31st March 2004.

*Insurance*

7.   The amendments made by paragraphs 8 to 13 of Schedule 10 and the consequential repeals in the Schedule to the 1985 Act will not apply to a request made under that Schedule before 31st March 2004.

*Administration charges: reasonableness, demands and liability to pay*

8.   Paragraphs 2 to 5 of Schedule 11 will not apply to an administration charge that was payable before 31st March 2004.

*Administration charges: appointment of a manager*

9.   The amendments made by paragraph 8 of Schedule 11 will not apply to an application made under section 24 of the 1987 Act before 31st March 2004.

*Charges under estate management schemes*

10.   Section 159 will not apply to a charge under an estate management scheme that was payable before 31st March 2004.

*Variation of leases: transfer of jurisdiction*

11.   The amendments made by section 163 will not have effect in relation to an application made to the court under Part 4 of the 1987 Act before 31st March 2004.

*Crown land: variation of leases*

12.   A variation of any tenancy effected by or in pursuance of an order made before 31st March 2004 under section 38 of the 1987 Act will not be treated as binding on the Crown, as predecessor in title under the tenancy, by virtue of section 39(1) of that Act.

*Leasehold valuation tribunals*

13.   Section 175, the amendments made by section 176 and Schedule 13 and the repeals in Part 1 of Schedule 1 to this Order will not have effect in relation to—
    (a)    any application made to a LVT; or
    (b)    any proceedings transferred to a LVT by a county court,
before 31st March 2004.

**[3360]**

# RTM COMPANIES (MEMORANDUM AND ARTICLES OF ASSOCIATION) (WALES) REGULATIONS 2004 (NOTE)

## (SI 2004/675 (W 64))

**NOTES**
    Made: 9 March 2004.
    Authority: Welsh Language Act 1993, s 26(3); Commonhold and Leasehold Reform Act 2002, ss 74(2), (4), (6), 178(1).
    Commencement: 31 March 2004.
    Amended by: SI 2005/3302; SI 2007/2194.
    These Regulations apply to Wales only. The equivalent provisions for England are in SI 2003/2120 at **[3346]** et seq.

**[3361]**

# LEASEHOLD VALUATION TRIBUNALS (FEES) (REVOCATION AND SAVING) (WALES) ORDER 2004 (NOTE)

## (SI 2004/680 (W 68))

**NOTES**
    Made: 9 March 2004.
    Authority: Landlord and Tenant Act 1985, s 31B; Landlord and Tenant Act 1987, s 24B.
    Commencement: 31 March 2004.
    This Order applies to Wales only. The equivalent provisions for England are in SI 2003/2270 at **[3350]** et seq.

**[3362]**

# LEASEHOLD VALUATION TRIBUNALS (PROCEDURE) (WALES) REGULATIONS 2004 (NOTE)

(SI 2004/681 (W 69))

**NOTES**
Made: 9 March 2004.
Authority: Landlord and Tenant Act 1987, s 35(5); Commonhold and Leasehold Reform Act 2002, Sch 12.
Commencement: 31 March 2004.
Amended by: SI 2005/1356.
These Regulations apply to Wales only. The equivalent provisions for England are in SI 2003/2099 at **[3319]** et seq.

**[3363]**

# LEASEHOLD VALUATION TRIBUNALS (FEES) (WALES) REGULATIONS 2004 (NOTE)

(SI 2004/683 (W 71))

**NOTES**
Made: 9 March 2004.
Authority: Commonhold and Leasehold Reform Act 2002, Sch 12, paras 1, 9.
Commencement: 31 March 2004.
Amended by: SI 2005/3302; SI 2008/1879.
These Regulations apply to Wales only. The equivalent provisions for England are in SI 2003/2098 at **[3310]** et seq.

**[3364]**

# SERVICE CHARGES (CONSULTATION REQUIREMENTS) (WALES) REGULATIONS 2004 (NOTE)

(SI 2004/684 (W 72))

**NOTES**
Made: 9 March 2004.
Authority: Landlord and Tenant Act 1985, ss 20(4), (5), 20ZA(3)–(6).
Commencement: 31 March 2004.
Amended by: SI 2005/1357; SI 2005/3302; SI 2006/5.
These Regulations apply to Wales only. The equivalent provisions for England are in SI 2003/1987 at **[3287]** et seq.

**[3365]**

# DEMOTED TENANCIES (REVIEW OF DECISIONS) (ENGLAND) REGULATIONS 2004

(SI 2004/1679)

**NOTES**
Made: 1 July 2004.
Authority: Housing Act 1996, s 143F(3), (4).
Commencement: 30 July 2004.

## ARRANGEMENT OF REGULATIONS

PART II
STATUTORY INSTRUMENTS

## 1 Citation, commencement, and application

(1)    These Regulations may be cited as the Demoted Tenants (Review of Decisions) (England) Regulations 2004 and shall come into force on 30th July 2004.

(2)    These Regulations apply in relation to dwelling-houses in England only.

**[3366]**

## 2 Persons who may carry out reviews

(1)    A review under section 143F of the Housing Act 1996 of a decision to seek an order for possession of a dwelling-house let under a demoted tenancy ("the review") shall be carried out by a person who was not involved in that decision.

(2)    Where the review is of a decision made by an officer of the landlord and is to be carried out by an another officer, the officer reviewing the decision must occupy a more senior position within the organisation of the landlord.

**[3367]**

## 3 Notice of review

The landlord under the demoted tenancy shall give the tenant not less than five clear days' notice of the date of the review.

**[3368]**

## 4 Right to an oral hearing

(1)    Where the tenant so requests, the review shall be by way of an oral hearing.

(2)    Any such request must be made to the landlord before the end of the period mentioned in subsection (1) of section 143F of the Housing Act 1996 (time permitted for requesting a review).

(3)    If the tenant makes such a request the landlord shall, when giving the tenant notice of the date of the review in accordance with regulation 3, also inform the tenant of the time and place at which the review will be heard.

**[3369]**

## 5 Written representations

Whether or not the review is to be by way of an oral hearing—
    (a)    the tenant may make written representations to the landlord in connection with the review;
    (b)    such representations must be received by the landlord not less than two clear days before the date of the review; and
    (c)    the landlord shall consider any such representations which are received by that date.

**[3370]**

## 6 Review by way of an oral hearing

(1)    Where the review is to be by way of an oral hearing, the tenant shall have the right to be heard and to be accompanied or to be represented by another person (whether or not that person is professionally qualified).

(2)    The tenant or his representative may—
    (a)    call persons to give evidence at the hearing;
    (b)    put questions to any person who gives evidence at the hearing.

(3)    Subject to these Regulations, the procedure in connection with a review by way of an oral hearing shall be such as the person carrying out the review shall determine.

**[3371]**

## 7 Absence of tenant and representative from hearing

(1)    This paragraph applies where notice has been given to the tenant in accordance with regulations 3 and 4(3) and neither the tenant nor his representative appears at the hearing.

(2)    Where paragraph (1) applies, the person carrying out the review may, having regard to all the circumstances—
    (a)    proceed with the hearing, or
    (b)    give such directions with a view to the conduct of the review as he considers appropriate.

**[3372]**

## 8 Postponement of hearing

(1)    The tenant may request the landlord to postpone a hearing of which notice has been given in accordance with regulations 3 and 4(3) and the landlord may grant or refuse the request.

(2) In the application of the following provisions to a commonhold unit with joint unit-holders a reference to a unit-holder includes a reference to each joint unit-holder and to the joint unit-holders together—

    (a) regulations 11(1) and 18(2)(b);

    (b) [articles 9(d) and 75] in Schedule 2; and

    (c) all provisions in Schedule 3 except paragraphs 4.8.5 to 4.8.9.

(3) In section 13(2)—

    (a) omit paragraphs (a), (c), (g) and (h);

    (b) in paragraph (b) omit "and (3)"; and

    (c) in paragraph (f) after "section 35(1)(b)," insert "and".

(4) In section 13(3)—

    (a) after paragraph (a) insert—
        "(aa) section 14(3),
        (ab) section 15(3),";

    (b) after paragraph (b) insert—
        "(ba) section 19(2) and (3),"; and

    (c) after paragraph (f) insert—
        "(fa) section 38(1),
        (fb) section 39(2),".

**[3380]**

**NOTES**

Para (2): in sub-para (b) words in square brackets substituted by the Commonhold (Amendment) Regulations 2009, SI 2009/2363, regs 2, 3.

PART II

REGISTRATION

**3 Consents required prior to the creation of a commonhold additional to those required by section 3(1)(a) to (c)**

(1) An application under section 2 may not be made in respect of a freehold estate in land without the consent of anyone who is—

    (a) the estate owner of any unregistered freehold estate in the whole or part of the land;

    (b) the estate owner of any unregistered leasehold estate in the whole or part of the land granted for a term of more than 21 years;

    (c) the owner of any mortgage, charge or lien for securing money or money's worth over the whole or part of any unregistered land included in the application; or

    (d) subject to paragraph (2), the holder of a lease granted for a term of not more than 21 years which will be extinguished by virtue of section 7(3)(d) or 9(3)(f).

(2) An application under section 2 may be made without the consent of a person who would otherwise be required to consent by virtue of paragraph (1)(d) if—

    (a) the person is entitled to the grant of a term of years absolute—

        (i) of the same premises as are comprised in the extinguished lease;

        (ii) on the same terms as the extinguished lease, except to the extent necessary to comply with the Act and these Regulations and excluding any terms that are spent;

        (iii) at the same rent as the rent payable under, and including the same provisions for rent review as were included in, the extinguished lease as at the date on which it will be extinguished;

        (iv) for a term equivalent to the unexpired term of the lease which will be extinguished; and

        (v) to take effect immediately after the lease is extinguished by virtue of section 7(3)(d) or 9(3)(f); and

    (b) before the application under section 2 is made, the person's entitlement to the grant of a term of years absolute has been protected by a notice in the land register to the freehold title(s) for the land in the application or, in the case of unregistered land, by an entry in the land charges register in the name of the estate owner of the freehold title.

**[3381]**

**4 Details of consent**

(1) Consent to an application under—

    (a) section 2 must be given in Form CON 1; and

    (b) section 8(4) must be given in Form CON 2.

(2) Subject to paragraphs (3), (4) and (7), consent is binding on a person who gives consent or who is deemed to have given consent.

(3)    Consent may be given subject to conditions.

(4)    Subject to any condition imposing a shorter period, consent will lapse if no application is made within a period of 12 months beginning with the date on which consent was given.

(5)    Consent is deemed to have been given by—
    (a)    the person making the application where that person's consent would otherwise be required in accordance with section 3, but has not been expressly given; and
    (b)    a successor in title to a person who has given consent or who is deemed to have given consent.

(6)    Consent given for the purpose of one application has effect for the purpose of another application ("the new application") only where the new application is submitted—
    (a)    in place of a previous application which has been withdrawn by the applicant, or rejected or cancelled by the Registrar; and
    (b)    within a period of 12 months beginning with the date on which the consent was given.

(7)    Consent may be withdrawn at any time before the date on which any application is submitted to the Registrar.

(8)    In this regulation, "consent" means consent for the purposes of section 3.

**[3382]**

## 5  Dispensing with a requirement for consent

The court may dispense with the requirement for consent to an application under section 2 if a person whose consent is required—
    (a)    cannot be identified after all reasonable efforts have been made to ascertain his identity;
    (b)    has been identified but cannot be traced after all reasonable efforts have been made to trace him; or
    (c)    has been sent the request for consent and all reasonable efforts have been made to obtain a response but he has not responded.

**[3383]**

## 6  Statement under section 9(1)(b): Registration with unit-holders

A statement under section 9(1)(b) which accompanies an application under section 2 must, in relation to each commonhold unit, state—
    (a)    the full name of the proposed initial unit-holder or if there are proposed joint unit-holders the full name of each of them;
    (b)    the address for service of the proposed unit-holder or if there are proposed joint unit-holders the address for service of each of them;
    (c)    the unit number of the commonhold unit; and
    (d)    the postal address of the commonhold unit (if available).

**[3384]**

## 7  Multiple site commonholds

For the purposes of an application under section 2 made jointly by two or more persons, each of whom is the registered freeholder of part of the land to which the application relates ("a part site") section 11 is modified so that, in addition to complying with the requirements in section 11(3), in defining the extent of a commonhold unit, the commonhold community statement must provide for the extent of each commonhold unit to be situated wholly upon one part site, and not situated partly on one part site and partly on one or more other part sites.

**[3385]**

PART III
COMMONHOLD UNIT

## 8  Requirements of a plan defining the extent of a commonhold unit

A plan referred to in a commonhold community statement for the purposes of defining the extent of a commonhold unit must delineate the boundaries of the commonhold unit with any adjoining property.

**[3386]**

## 9  Definition of a commonhold unit

(1)    In defining the extent of a commonhold unit a commonhold community statement—
    (a)    may exclude, from the definition, the structure and exterior of a self-contained building, or of a self-contained part of a building, which only contains one commonhold unit or part of one commonhold unit; and
    (b)    must exclude, from the definition, the structure and exterior of a self-contained building, or of a self-contained part of a building, in any other case.

(2)    In this regulation—
"self-contained building" means a building which is structurally detached;

"self-contained part of a building" means a part of a building—

(a)   which constitutes a vertical division of the building;

(b)   the structure of which is such that it could be redeveloped independently of the rest of the building; and

(c)   in relation to which the relevant services provided for occupiers are provided independently of the relevant services provided for the occupiers of the rest of the building, or could be so provided without involving the carrying out of works likely to result in a significant interruption in the provision of any relevant services for occupiers of the rest of the building;

"relevant services" are services provided by the means of pipes, cables or other fixed installations; and

"structure and exterior" includes the relevant services in or to the building but does not include those which are within and exclusively to one commonhold unit.

**[3387]**

## 10   Requirement to notify Registrar

(1)   This regulation applies to an amendment of a commonhold community statement which redefines the extent of a commonhold unit over which there is a registered charge.

(2)   The unit-holder of a commonhold unit over which there is a registered charge must give notice of the amendment to the Registrar in Form COE.

(3)   On receipt of such notification the Registrar must alter the register to reflect the application of section 24(4) or (5).

**[3388]**

## 11   Leasing of a residential commonhold unit

(1)   A term of years absolute in a residential commonhold unit or part only of a residential commonhold unit must not—

(a)   be granted for a premium;

(b)   subject to paragraph (2), be granted for a term longer than 7 years;

(c)   be granted under an option or agreement if—

(i)    the person to take the new term of years absolute has an existing terms of years absolute of the premises to be let;

(ii)   the new term when added to the existing term will be more than 7 years; and

(iii)  the option or agreement was entered into before or at the same time as the existing term of years absolute;

(d)   contain an option or agreement to renew the term of years absolute which confers on the lessee or on the lessor an option or agreement for renewal for a further term which, together with the original term, amounts to more than 7 years;

(e)   contain an option or agreement to extend the term beyond 7 years; or

(f)   contain a provision requiring the lessee to make payments to the commonhold association in discharge of payments which are due, in accordance with the commonhold community statement, to be made by the unit-holder.

(2)   A term of years absolute in a residential commonhold unit or part only of a residential commonhold unit may be granted for a term of not more than 21 years to the holder of a lease which has been extinguished by virtue of section 7(3)(d) or 9(3)(f) if the term of years absolute—

(a)   is granted of the same premises as are comprised in the extinguished lease;

(b)   is granted on the same terms as the extinguished lease, except to the extent necessary to comply with the Act and these Regulations and excluding any terms that are spent;

(c)   is granted at the same rent as the rent payable under, and including the same provisions for rent review as were included in, the extinguished lease as at the date on which it was extinguished;

(d)   is granted for a term equivalent to the unexpired term of the lease immediately before it was extinguished or, if the unexpired term of the lease immediately before it was extinguished is more than 21 years, for a term of 21 years;

(e)   takes effect immediately after the lease was extinguished; and

(f)   does not include any option or agreement which—

(i)    may create a term or an extension to a term which, together with the term of the term of years absolute, would amount to more than 21 years; or

(ii)   may result in the grant of a term of years absolute containing an option or agreement to extend the term.

**[3389]**

## PART IV
## COMMONHOLD ASSOCIATION

**12 The name of the commonhold association**

(1) The name by which a commonhold association is registered under the [Companies Act 2006] must end with "commonhold association limited" or, [if the commonhold association is a Welsh company] those words or the Welsh equivalent ("Cymdeithas Cydradd-Ddaliad Cyfyngedig").

(2) The name by which a company other than a commonhold association is registered may not end with "commonhold association limited" or the Welsh equivalent "Cymdeithas Cydradd-Ddaliad Cyfyngedig".

(3) In this regulation references to the words "limited" and "cyfyngedig" include the abbreviations "ltd" and "cyf"[, and "Welsh company" has the meaning given by section 88 of the Companies Act 2006].

**[3390]**

**NOTES**

Para (1): words in square brackets substituted by the Commonhold (Amendment) Regulations 2009, SI 2009/2363, regs 2, 4(a).

Para (3): words in square brackets inserted by SI 2009/2363, regs 2, 4(b).

**13** (*Revoked by the Commonhold (Amendment) Regulations 2009, SI 2009/2363, regs 2, 5.*)

**14 Articles of association**

(1) The articles of association of a commonhold association must be in the form in Schedule 2 (articles of association) or a form to the same effect.

(2) Subject to the following paragraphs, the articles of association of a commonhold association must contain all the provisions in the form in Schedule 2 and each provision in that Schedule will have effect for a commonhold association whether or not it is adopted under paragraph 2(2) of Schedule 3 to the Act.

(3) In its articles of association a commonhold must include the name of the commonhold association on the front page.

[(4) The articles of association of a commonhold association may increase—
   (a) the proportion and number of members in article 16;
   (b) the notice periods in article 21;
   (c) the number of consecutive months and meetings in article 49(f); and
   (d) the proportion and number of directors in article 61.]

(5) ...

(6) A commonhold association may include additional provisions in its articles of association where each additional provision is immediately preceded by a heading which must include "additional provision specific to this commonhold association" and is identified with the numeral of the immediately preceding article followed by a capital letter, such letters to be allocated in alphabetical order in respect of each number.

(7) ...

(8) Where the commonhold community statement gives the developer the right to appoint and remove directors the following provisions have effect for a commonhold association whether or not they are adopted under paragraph 2(2) of Schedule 3 to the Act—
   (a) during the transitional period the developer may appoint up to two directors in addition to any directors appointed by the subscribers, and may remove or replace any director so appointed;
   (b) after the end of the transitional period and for so long as the developer is the unit-holder of more than one quarter of the total number of commonhold units in the commonhold, he may appoint up to one quarter of the directors of the commonhold association, and may remove or replace any director so appointed;
   (c) a director appointed by the developer pursuant to paragraph (a) or (b) is known as a "developer's director";
   (d) any appointment or removal of a developer's director made pursuant to paragraph (a) or (b) must be by notice in writing signed by or on behalf of the developer and will take effect immediately it is received at the office of the commonhold association or by the secretary, or as and from the date specified in the notice (if later);
   (e) if at any time the commonhold association resolves to specify or reduce the maximum number of directors, and as a consequence the number of developer's directors exceeds the number permitted under paragraph (b), the developer must immediately reduce the number of developer's directors accordingly and where such reduction has not been

effected by the start of the next directors' meeting, the longest in office of the developer's directors must cease to hold office immediately so as to achieve the required reduction in numbers;

(f)    if the developer ceases to be the unit-holder of more than one quarter of the total number of units in the commonhold, he may no longer appoint, replace or remove a director and any developer's directors previously appointed by him under this article will cease to hold office immediately;

(g)    a developer's director who is removed from office or who ceases to hold office under this article will not have any claim against the commonhold association in respect of such removal from, or cessation to hold, office;

(h)    at any time at which the developer is entitled to exercise the power to appoint and remove developer's directors, the developer is not entitled to vote upon a resolution fixing the number of directors of the commonhold association, or upon a resolution for the appointment or removal from office of any director not appointed by him, or upon any resolution concerning the remuneration of any director not appointed by him;

(i)    a developer's director may provide information to the developer that he receives by virtue of his being a director; and

(j)    the provisions in [articles 41, 42 and 56] do not apply to a developer's director.

(9)    Where the provisions in paragraph (8) have effect for a commonhold association—

(a)    [articles 46 and 47] are to have effect for a commonhold association but with "(other than a vacancy in respect of a developer's director)" inserted after "fill a vacancy"; and

(b)    article 61 is to have effect for a commonhold association but with "At least one of the persons present at the meeting must be a director other than a developer's director." inserted at the end.

(10)    In this regulation an article referred to by number alone means the article so numbered in Schedule 2.

**[3391]**

**NOTES**

Para (4): substituted by the Commonhold (Amendment) Regulations 2009, SI 2009/2363, regs 2, 6(a).
Paras (5), (7): revoked by SI 2009/2363, regs 2, 6(b).
Para (8): words in square brackets substituted by SI 2009/2363, regs 2, 6(c).
Para (9): words in square brackets substituted by SI 2009/2363, regs 2, 6(d).

## 15   Commonhold community statement

(1)    The commonhold community statement must be in the form in Schedule 3 (commonhold community statement) or a form to the same effect.

(2)    The commonhold community statement must contain all the provisions contained in the form in Schedule 3 and will be treated as including those provisions.

(3)    The commonhold community statement must include the name of the commonhold on the front page and signature page and must include the information relevant to the commonhold in the paragraphs in the Annexes.

(4)    The commonhold community statement must be signed at the end in the following form—

(a)    on application for registration under section 2—

"Signed [by] [on behalf of] the applicant: ...................................................................

Name: (please print) ...........................................................................................................

Title: ..............................................................................................................."; or

(b)    where an amended commonhold community statement is registered in accordance with section 33—

"Signed [by] [on behalf of] [the commonhold association] [the developer]:

...............................................................................................................................................

Name: (please print) ...........................................................................................................

Title: ..............................................................................................................."

(5)    The commonhold community statement must include information relevant to the commonhold in—

(a)    paragraph 2 of Annex 3 if the directors of the commonhold association have established funds to finance the repair and maintenance of the common parts or commonhold units; and

(b)    paragraph 5 of Annex 4 if there are other risks insured in addition to fire.

(6)    The commonhold community statement is treated as including "0 per cent" in paragraph 1 of Annex 4 unless different provision is made in its place.

(7) Where, by virtue of regulation 9(1)(b), in defining the extent of a commonhold unit, the commonhold community statement excludes the structure and exterior of a self-contained building, or of a self-contained part of a building, the commonhold community statement is treated as including provision which imposes a duty on the commonhold association to insure the whole of the self-contained building, or self-contained part of the building.

(8) Subject to paragraphs (9) to (12), the commonhold community statement may include further definitions and may include further numbered provisions relevant to the commonhold at the end of a Part or a Section or in an Annex.

(9) Where further definitions are included in the commonhold community statement each definition must be inserted in alphabetical order into paragraph 1.4.5 in the commonhold community statement.

(10) Where further provisions are included in the commonhold community statement which confer rights on the developer—

   (a)   the provisions must be inserted in an Annex headed "DEVELOPMENT RIGHTS", such Annex must be numbered and be the last Annex in the commonhold community statement and a reference to its heading must be included in the table of contents in the commonhold community statement;

   (b)   a paragraph containing "Annex [ ] specifies the rights of the developer which are designed to permit him to undertake development business or to facilitate his undertaking of development business." must be inserted in Section 1.3 in the commonhold community statement with the Annex number inserted in place of the brackets; and

   (c)   paragraph 4.8.14 in the commonhold community statement is treated as including "; or to remove any surrendered development rights" at the end.

(11) Where any other provisions are included in the commonhold community statement in a Part or Section—

   (a)   each additional provision must be inserted in numerical order continuing the numbers within the relevant Part or Section;

   (b)   each additional provision must be immediately preceded by a heading which must include "additional provision specific to this commonhold" in the relevant Part or Section; and

   (c)   a reference to the heading must be included in the table of contents in the commonhold community statement.

(12) Where any other provisions are included in the commonhold community statement in an Annex—

   (a)   a heading which must include "ADDITIONAL PROVISIONS SPECIFIC TO THIS COMMONHOLD" must be inserted at the end of Part 4 followed by a numbered paragraph which reads "Additional provisions are set out in Annex" followed by the number given to the Annex by the commonhold association;

   (b)   a paragraph must be inserted in Section 1.3 in the commonhold community statement giving the number of the Annex and details of its contents; and

   (c)   a reference to its heading must be included in the table of contents in the commonhold community statement.

(13) In this regulation "commonhold community statement" means the commonhold community statement of a commonhold and a reference to a Part, Section or Annex means a Part, Section or Annex in the commonhold community statement.

[3392]

## 16  Forms

The Forms contained in Schedule 4 (forms) or forms to the same effect must be used in accordance with the commonhold community statement of a commonhold.

[3393]

PART V
OPERATION OF A COMMONHOLD

## 17  Enforcement

Jurisdiction is conferred on the court to deal with the exercise or enforcement of a right conferred, or duty imposed, by or by virtue of—

   (a)   a commonhold *community statement*;

   (b)   these Regulations; or

   (c)   Part 1 of the Act.

[3394]

**18 Development Rights**

(1)   The rights (if any) conferred on the developer in a commonhold community statement are restricted or regulated in accordance with the following paragraphs.

(2)   The developer must not exercise development rights in such manner as to interfere unreasonably with—

(a)   the enjoyment by each unit-holder of the freehold estate in his unit; and

(b)   the exercise by any unit-holder or tenant of his rights under the commonhold community statement.

(3)   The developer may not remove land from the commonhold that has been transferred to a unit-holder unless the unit-holder consents in writing before the land is removed.

(4)   Any damage to the common parts or a commonhold unit caused by the developer in the course of undertaking development business must be put right by the developer as soon as reasonably practicable taking into account the future works required to complete the development and the degree of interference caused by the damage.

(5)   The developer must not exercise development rights if the works for which the development rights were conferred have been completed, save that any rights permitting or facilitating the undertaking of development business of the type referred to in paragraph 3 of Schedule 4 to the Act may be exercised for such further period as the developer continues to undertake that type of development business in relation to the whole or, as the case may be, the relevant part, of the commonhold.

(6)   In this regulation "developer" includes a person acting on his authority.

[3395]

PART VI
TERMINATION

**19 Termination**

(1)   The liquidator must, in accordance with section 45(2), apply to the court for an order determining—

(a)   the terms and conditions on which a termination application may be made; and

(b)   the terms of the termination statement to accompany a termination application

within the period of 3 months beginning with the date on which the liquidator was appointed.

(2)   An application under section 51(1) must be accompanied by the certificate of incorporation of the successor commonhold association given in accordance with [section 15 of the Companies Act 2006] and any altered certificates of incorporation issued under [section 80] of that Act.

[3396]

**NOTES**

Para (2): words in square brackets substituted by the Commonhold (Amendment) Regulations 2009, SI 2009/2363, regs 2, 7.

SCHEDULES

*(Schs 1, 2 outside the scope of this work.)*

SCHEDULE 3
COMMONHOLD COMMUNITY STATEMENT

Regulation 15

COMMONHOLD AND LEASEHOLD REFORM ACT 2002
COMMONHOLD COMMUNITY STATEMENT
OF
[ ]

**This document is important.**

**It creates legally binding rights and duties.**

**It is recommended that anyone affected by it should take appropriate advice.**

TABLE OF CONTENTS
*PART 1: INTRODUCTION*

*PART II STATUTORY INSTRUMENTS*

*ANNEX 1: IDENTITY OF THE COMMONHOLD AND THE COMMONHOLD ASSOCIATION*
1   NAME OF THE COMMONHOLD
2   NAME OF THE COMMONHOLD ASSOCIATION
3   COMPANY NUMBER OF THE COMMONHOLD ASSOCIATION

*ANNEX 2: DEFINITION OF THE PROPERTIES WITHIN THE COMMONHOLD*
1   LIST OF PLANS
2   DESCRIPTION OF THE LOCATION AND EXTENT OF COMMONHOLD LAND
3   TOTAL NUMBER OF COMMONHOLD UNITS IN THE COMMONHOLD
4   DESCRIPTION OF THE LOCATION AND EXTENT OF COMMONHOLD UNITS
5   FURTHER DESCRIPTION OF COMMONHOLD UNITS
6   RIGHTS FOR COMMONHOLD UNITS
7   RIGHTS OVER COMMONHOLD UNITS

*ANNEX 3: COMMONHOLD ALLOCATIONS*
1   ALLOCATION OF COMMONHOLD ASSESSMENT
2   ALLOCATION OF RESERVE FUND LEVY
3   ALLOCATION OF VOTES

*ANNEX 4: LOCAL RULES*
1   PRESCRIBED RATE OF INTEREST
2   PERMITTED USE OF COMMONHOLD UNITS
3   PERMITTED USE OF COMMON PARTS
4   LIMITED USE AREAS
5   INSURANCE OF COMMON PARTS—INSURED RISKS
6   INSURANCE OF COMMONHOLD UNITS—DUTIES
7   REPAIR AND MAINTENANCE OF COMMONHOLD UNITS—DUTIES
**SIGNATURE**

*PART 1: INTRODUCTION*

## 1.1  COMMONHOLD COMMUNITY STATEMENT

1.1.1   This document is a commonhold community statement ("CCS"). It defines the commonhold units and the common parts. It also specifies the rights and duties of the unit-holders and the commonhold association, and the procedure to be followed to enforce them.

1.1.2   This CCS imposes obligations on a tenant of a commonhold unit and specifies the procedure to be followed by a tenant to enforce a duty imposed on the commonhold association, a unit-holder, or another tenant.

1.1.3   These rights and duties are in addition to any rights and duties that may exist under the general law.

1.1.4   The provisions of this CCS are subject to the Act and regulations made under it. In particular, regulations may provide that a CCS is to be treated as including specified provisions or as including provisions of a specified kind, for a specified purpose or about a specified matter.

1.1.5   A provision of this CCS has no effect to the extent that it is—
    (a)   inconsistent with any provision made by or by virtue of the Act;
    (b)   inconsistent with anything which is treated as included in this CCS by regulations;
    (c)   inconsistent with the … articles of association; or
    (d)   prohibited by regulations.

## 1.2  THE COMMONHOLD AND COMMONHOLD ASSOCIATION

1.2.1   The name of the commonhold is in paragraph 1 of Annex 1.

1.2.2   The name and company number of the commonhold association are in paragraphs 2 and 3 of Annex 1.

## 1.3  STRUCTURE OF THIS DOCUMENT

1.3.1   This CCS is divided into numbered Parts and Annexes. Each of the Parts is divided into numbered Sections with numbered paragraphs. The Annexes are also divided into numbered paragraphs.

1.3.2   Part 1 contains general provisions. Annex 1 sets out the details of the commonhold and the commonhold association.

1.3.3    Part 2 and Annex 2 define the properties within the commonhold.

1.3.4    Part 3 and Annex 3 define the percentages allocated to each commonhold unit in respect of the commonhold assessment and any levy and the allocation of votes.

1.3.5    Part 4 and Annex 4 specify the rights and duties of the commonhold association and the unit-holders, the obligations imposed on tenants, and the procedures used for enforcement.

## 1.4   INTERPRETATION OF THIS DOCUMENT

1.4.1    In this CCS, references to a numbered Form are references to the Form so numbered in Schedule 4 to the Commonhold Regulations 2004. A requirement to use a numbered Form is satisfied by the use of a form to the same effect.

1.4.2    Unless otherwise stated, in the application of provisions in this CCS to a commonhold unit with joint unit-holders, a reference to a unit-holder is a reference to each joint unit-holder and to the joint unit-holders together.

1.4.3    Unless otherwise stated, in the application of provisions in this CCS, where two or more persons together hold a tenancy, a reference to a tenant is a reference to each tenant and to the tenants together.

1.4.4    Unless the contrary intention appears, words—
    (a)    referring to one gender include any other gender;
    (b)    in the singular include the plural; and
    (c)    in the plural include the singular.

1.4.5    Unless the contrary intention appears, the following definitions apply:
    "the Act" means Part 1 of the Commonhold and Leasehold Reform Act 2002 or any statutory modification or re-enactment of it for the time being in force;
    "articles of association" means the articles of association of the commonhold association;
    "common parts" means every part of the commonhold which is not for the time being a commonhold unit in accordance with this CCS (section 25(1) of the Act);
    "commonhold assessment" means the income required to be raised from unit-holders to meet the expenses of the commonhold association (section 38 of the Act);
    "commonhold association" means the commonhold association named in paragraph 2 of Annex 1;
    "commonhold land" means the land that is registered at Land Registry as a freehold estate in commonhold land and described in paragraph 2 of Annex 2;
    "commonhold unit" means a unit as defined in paragraphs 4 and 5 of Annex 2;
    "commonhold unit information certificate" means a certificate stating the debts owed to the commonhold association in respect of the commonhold assessment or levy allocated to a commonhold unit and any interest added in respect of late payment;
    "company number" means the number with which the commonhold association is registered under the [Companies Act 2006];
    "complaint notice" means a notice given in accordance with paragraph 4.11.5 or 4.11.27;
    "default notice" means a notice given in accordance with paragraph 4.11.13;
    "general meeting" means a meeting of the members of the commonhold association held in accordance with the articles of association of the commonhold association;
    "levy" means an amount set by the directors of the commonhold association from time to time to be raised from unit-holders for contribution to a reserve fund (section 39 of the Act);
    "limited use areas" means any part of the common parts that may only be used by authorised persons or in a manner consistent with the authorised use specified in paragraph 4 of Annex 4 (section 25(2) of the Act);
    "local rules" means provisions, including information contained in the Annexes, inserted by the developer or the commonhold association, that are not prescribed by regulations;
    "member" means a person whose name is entered as a member in the register of members of the commonhold association, but excludes any person who has ceased to be a unit-holder or joint unit-holder, or any person who has resigned as a member;

.....

    "ombudsman" means a person whose appointment has been approved in accordance with section 42 of the Act under an approved ombudsman scheme for commonhold;
    ["ordinary resolution" has the meaning given in section 282 (ordinary resolutions) of the Companies Act 2006;]
    "prescribed rate" means the rate of interest specified by the commonhold association in paragraph 1 of Annex 4;
    "regulations" means regulations made under the Act from time to time and for the time being in force;
    "*rent*" *means such monies as are defined as rent in the relevant tenancy agreement*;
    "reply notice" means a notice given in accordance with paragraph 4.11.6, 4.11.14 or 4.11.28;
    "reserve fund" means a fund set up by the directors of the commonhold association to which unit-holders contribute to finance the repair and maintenance of the common parts or commonhold units (section 39 of the Act);

"reserve study" means an inspection of the common parts to advise the directors whether or not it is appropriate to establish or maintain a reserve fund;

["special resolution" has the meaning given in section 283 (special resolutions) of the Companies Act 2006;]

"tenancy" means a term of years absolute in a commonhold unit or part only of a commonhold unit and includes "sub-tenancy"; and the term "tenant" should be interpreted accordingly;

"transfer" means a transfer of the freehold estate in a commonhold unit, whether or not for consideration, whether or not subject to any reservation or other terms, and whether or not by operation of law (section 15 of the Act);

"unanimous resolution" means a resolution passed by every member as (being entitled to do so) votes in person or, if proxies are allowed, by proxy, at a general meeting of the commonhold association of which notice specifying the intention to propose the resolution as a unanimous resolution has been given in accordance with the articles of association;

"unit-holder" means a person entitled to be registered at Land Registry as the proprietor of the freehold estate in a commonhold unit (whether or not he is registered).

## PART 2: THE COMMONHOLD

### 2.1 INTRODUCTION

2.1.1 This Part of this CCS defines the extent and location of the properties within the commonhold and the rights that exist over the commonhold land.

### 2.2 PLANS

2.2.1 A list of the plans incorporated in this CCS is set out in paragraph 1 of Annex 2.

### 2.3 COMMONHOLD LAND

2.3.1 The location and extent of the commonhold land are described in paragraph 2 of Annex 2.

### 2.4 COMMONHOLD UNITS

2.4.1 Number of units in the commonhold

The number of commonhold units in the commonhold is set out in paragraph 3 of Annex 2.

2.4.2 Location and extent of commonhold units

The commonhold units are defined in paragraphs 4 and 5 of Annex 2.

2.4.3 Rights for the benefit of commonhold units

Details of rights existing for the benefit of each commonhold unit over other commonhold units or over the common parts are set out in paragraph 6 of Annex 2.

2.4.4 Rights over commonhold units for the benefit of the common parts

Details of rights existing for the benefit of the common parts over one or more commonhold units are set out in paragraph 7 of Annex 2.

## PART 3: COMMONHOLD ALLOCATIONS

### 3.1 INTRODUCTION

3.1.1 This Part of this CCS defines the commonhold allocations.

### 3.2 ALLOCATION OF COMMONHOLD ASSESSMENT

3.2.1 The percentage allocated to each commonhold unit in respect of the commonhold assessment is specified in paragraph 1 of Annex 3.

### 3.3 ALLOCATION OF RESERVE FUND LEVY

3.3.1 The percentage allocated to each commonhold unit in respect of any levy to fund the repair and maintenance of the common parts or the commonhold units is specified in paragraph 2 of Annex 3.

### 3.4 ALLOCATION OF VOTES

3.4.1 The number of votes allocated to a member in respect of each commonhold unit is specified in paragraph 3 of Annex 3.

## PART 4: THE RULES OF THE COMMONHOLD

### 4.1 INTRODUCTION

4.1.1 This Part of this CCS sets out the rules regulating the affairs of the commonhold community and how they may be enforced.

4.1.2 The rules are for the benefit of, and bind, all unit-holders and the commonhold association. Where stated, rules also bind tenants.

## 4.2  FINANCIAL MATTERS

4.2.1   Commonhold Assessment—calculation and request for payment

The directors of the commonhold association must make an annual estimate of the income required to be raised from unit-holders to meet the expenses of the commonhold association, and may from time to time make estimates of income required to be raised from unit-holders in addition to the annual estimate.

4.2.2   Subject to paragraph 4.2.5, when the directors of the commonhold association consider that income is required to be raised from unit-holders they must give a notice containing details of the proposed commonhold assessment to each unit-holder. Form 1 [Notice of proposed commonhold assessment] must be used.

4.2.3   Within 1 month, beginning with the date on which the notice referred to in paragraph 4.2.2 is given, each unit-holder may make written representations to the commonhold association regarding the amount of the proposed commonhold assessment.

4.2.4   The directors must consider any representations made in accordance with paragraph 4.2.3 and must give a further notice to each unit-holder specifying the payments required to be made by that unit-holder and the date on which each payment is due. The notice must not specify a date for payment which is within 14 days, beginning with the date on which the notice is given. Form 2 [Request for payment of commonhold assessment] must be used.

4.2.5   Emergency commonhold assessment—request for payment

If the commonhold association requires income to meet its expenses in an emergency, then the directors of the commonhold association may give a notice to each unit-holder requiring payment of the commonhold assessment without seeking representations from unit-holders. Form 3 [Request for payment of emergency commonhold assessment] must be used.

4.2.6   Reserve Fund—establishment, calculation and request for payment

The directors of the commonhold association must consider whether to commission a reserve study by an appropriately qualified person in the first year in which the commonhold is registered.

4.2.7   The directors of the commonhold association must commission a reserve study by an appropriately qualified person at least once in every 10 years.

4.2.8   The directors of the commonhold association must consider the results of any reserve study to decide whether it is appropriate—
    (a)    to establish a reserve fund;
    (b)    to maintain any existing reserve fund; and
if it is appropriate to establish a reserve fund, or maintain an existing reserve fund, then the directors must do so.

4.2.9   The directors of the commonhold association must at appropriate intervals decide whether it is appropriate to establish one or more reserve funds or maintain any existing reserve fund; and, if they decide that it is appropriate to establish a reserve fund, or maintain an existing reserve fund, then the directors must do so.

4.2.10   The members may, by ordinary resolution, require the directors to establish a reserve fund.

4.2.11   If a reserve fund is established, then the directors of the commonhold association must set a levy from time to time; and in doing so must try to ensure that unnecessary reserves are not accumulated.

4.2.12   When the directors of the commonhold association set a levy they must give a notice containing details of the proposed levy to each unit-holder. Form 4 [Notice of proposed reserve fund levy] must be used.

4.2.13   Within 1 month, beginning with the date on which the notice referred to in paragraph 4.2.12 is given, each unit-holder may make written representations to the commonhold association regarding the amount of the levy.

4.2.14   The directors must consider any representations made in accordance with paragraph 4.2.13 and must give a further notice to each unit-holder specifying the payments required to be made by that unit-holder and the date on which each payment is due. The notice must not specify a date for payment which is within 14 days, beginning with the date on which the notice is given. Form 5 [Request for payment of reserve fund levy] must be used.

4.2.15   Commonhold assessment and reserve fund—payment

A unit-holder must pay to the commonhold association the amount that is allocated to his commonhold unit in accordance with a notice given under paragraphs 4.2.4, 4.2.5 or 4.2.14.

4.2.16   Commonhold assessment and reserve fund—late payment

If a payment required by paragraph 4.2.15 is not made by the date on which it is due, then the unit-holder must pay interest to the commonhold association at the prescribed rate for the period beginning with the date on which the payment is due and ending on the date on which the payment is made.

**4.2.17**   Commonhold assessment and reserve fund—unit-holder's failure to pay

In paragraphs 4.2.18 to 4.2.26—

"tenant" means only an immediate tenant of the unit-holder who has failed to pay; and

"diversion date" means the date on which a period of 14 days ends, beginning with the date on which the notice in paragraph 4.2.18 is given.

**4.2.18**   Diversion of rent from a tenant

If a unit-holder has not paid all or part of any payment due to the commonhold association under paragraphs 4.2.15 or 4.2.16, then the commonhold association may give a notice requiring a tenant to divert to the commonhold association all or part of the rent payable to the unit-holder from time to time under the tenancy agreement until the commonhold association has recovered from the tenant an equivalent sum to the amount due from the unit-holder. Form 6 [Notice to tenant of diversion of rent] must be used and the commonhold association must also give a copy to the unit-holder.

**4.2.19**   The commonhold association must specify in the notice the payments that the tenant is required to make. In any single payment, the commonhold association must not require the tenant to pay more rent than is due under the tenancy agreement, to pay rent earlier than is due under the tenancy agreement, or to pay rent earlier than the diversion date.

**4.2.20**   A tenant who receives a notice under paragraph 4.2.18 must make the payments required by the notice.

**4.2.21**   Unless the commonhold association specifies a later date in the notice, the tenant must make the first payment on the next date, after the diversion date, that rent is required to be paid under the tenancy agreement.

**4.2.22**   The commonhold association must, within a period of 14 days, beginning with the date on which all the payments required in the notice have been made, notify the tenant and the unit-holder that the diversion of rent has ended.

**4.2.23**   Diversion of rent from a tenant—no deduction

A tenant may not rely on any non-statutory right of deduction, set-off or counterclaim that he has against the unit-holder to reduce the amount to be paid to the commonhold association.

**4.2.24**   Diversion of rent from a tenant—discharge of liability

A payment made in accordance with paragraph 4.2.20 will discharge, to the extent of the payment, the liability of—

    (a)   the unit-holder for the amount he has failed to pay to the commonhold association; and

    (b)   the tenant for the payment of rent owed to the unit-holder.

**4.2.25**   A unit-holder is deemed to have received and accepted rent, for the purposes of the tenancy agreement, in an amount equal to the payment made in accordance with paragraph 4.2.20, and may not forfeit the tenancy for the non-payment of rent deemed to have been paid, or bring proceedings for breach of any covenant or condition in the tenancy agreement for the non-payment of the rent deemed to have been paid.

**4.2.26**   Diversion of rent from a tenant—late payment

If a payment required by paragraph 4.2.20 is not made by the date on which it is due, then the tenant must pay interest to the commonhold association at the prescribed rate for the period beginning with the date on which the payment is due and ending on the date on which the payment is made.

**4.2.27**   Commonhold assessment and reserve fund—tenant's failure to pay

In paragraphs 4.2.28 to 4.2.37—

"tenant" means only an immediate tenant of the unit-holder;

"sub-tenant" means only the immediate tenant of the tenant who has failed to pay; and

"diversion date" means the date on which a period of 14 days ends, beginning with the date on which the notice in paragraph 4.2.28 is given.

**4.2.28**   Diversion of rent from a sub-tenant

If a tenant has not paid all or part of any payment due to the commonhold association under paragraphs 4.2.20 or 4.2.26, then the commonhold association may give a notice requiring a sub-tenant to divert to the commonhold association all or part of the rent payable to the tenant from time to time under the sub-tenancy agreement until the commonhold association has recovered from the sub-tenant an equivalent sum to the amount due from the tenant. Form 7 [Notice to sub-tenant of diversion of rent] must be used and the commonhold association must also give copies to the unit-holder and the tenant.

**4.2.29**   The commonhold association must specify in the notice the payments that the sub-tenant is required to make and, in any single payment, the commonhold association must not require the sub-tenant to pay more rent than is due under the sub-tenancy agreement, to pay rent earlier than is due under the sub-tenancy agreement, or to pay rent earlier than the diversion date.

4.2.30    A sub-tenant who receives a notice under paragraph 4.2.28 must make the payments required by the notice.

4.2.31    Unless the commonhold association specifies a later date in the notice, the sub-tenant must make the first payment on the next date, after the diversion date, that rent is required to be paid under the sub-tenancy agreement.

4.2.32    The commonhold association must, within a period of 14 days, beginning with the date on which all the payments required in the notice have been made, notify the sub-tenant, the tenant and the unit-holder that the diversion of rent has ended.

4.2.33    Diversion of rent from a sub-tenant—no deduction

A sub-tenant may not rely on any non-statutory right of deduction, set off, or counterclaim that he has against the tenant to reduce the amount to be paid to the commonhold association.

4.2.34    Diversion of rent from a sub-tenant—discharge of liability

A payment made in accordance with paragraph 4.2.30 will discharge, to the extent of the payment, the liability of—

    (a)    the unit-holder for the amount he has failed to pay to the commonhold association;

    (b)    the tenant for the payment owed to the commonhold association in accordance with paragraph 4.2.20;

    (c)    the tenant for the payment of rent owed to the unit-holder; and

    (d)    the sub-tenant for the payment of rent owed to the tenant.

4.2.35    A unit-holder is deemed to have received and accepted rent, for the purposes of the tenancy agreement, in an amount equal to the payment made in accordance with paragraph 4.2.30, and may not forfeit the tenancy for the non-payment of rent deemed to have been paid, or bring proceedings for breach of any covenant or condition in the tenancy agreement for the non-payment of the rent deemed to have been paid.

4.2.36    A tenant is deemed to have received and accepted rent, for the purposes of the sub-tenancy agreement, in an amount equal to the payment made in accordance with paragraph 4.2.30, and may not forfeit the sub-tenancy for the non-payment of rent deemed to have been paid, or bring proceedings for breach of any covenant or condition in the sub-tenancy agreement for the non-payment of the rent deemed to have been paid.

4.2.37    Diversion of rent from a sub-tenant—late payment

If a payment required by paragraph 4.2.30 is not made by the date on which it is due, then the sub-tenant must pay interest to the commonhold association at the prescribed rate for the period beginning with the date on which the payment is due and ending on the date on which the payment is made.

4.2.38    Commonhold assessment and reserve fund—sub-tenant's failure to pay

If the sub-tenant fails to pay in accordance with paragraph 4.2.30, then paragraphs 4.2.28 to 4.2.37 may be applied with necessary modifications as against the immediate tenant of that sub-tenant and so on. The terms "tenant" and "sub-tenant" must be interpreted accordingly.

4.2.39    Reimbursement of tenant

If a tenant has suffered any loss as a result of a payment being made to the commonhold association in accordance with paragraph 4.2.20 or 4.2.30, then he may give a notice requiring the unit-holder to reimburse him for that loss.

4.2.40    Within 14 days, beginning with the date on which the notice referred to in paragraph 4.2.39 is given, the unit-holder must reimburse the tenant for the loss suffered.

4.2.41    Commonhold association's right to request details of tenancy

If a commonhold unit is let under a tenancy agreement, then the commonhold association may give a notice to one or all of the parties to the tenancy agreement requesting details of the length of the tenancy and the rent payable. Part A of Form 8 [Notice requesting further details about a tenancy] must be used.

4.2.42    Within 14 days, beginning with the date on which the notice referred to in paragraph 4.2.41 is given, the recipient must give a notice to the commonhold association providing the details requested. Part B of Form 8 [Notice requesting further details about a tenancy] must be used.

## 4.3    USE

4.3.1    A unit-holder or tenant must not use a commonhold unit other than in accordance with its permitted use as specified in paragraph 2 of Annex 4.

4.3.2    A *unit-holder or tenant* must not use the common parts other than in accordance with their permitted use as specified in paragraphs 3 or 4 of Annex 4, or other than in accordance with the rights specified in paragraph 6 of Annex 2.

### 4.4 INSURANCE

4.4.1    The commonhold association must insure the common parts to their full rebuilding and reinstatement costs against loss or damage by fire and such other risks as are specified in paragraph 5 of Annex 4.

4.4.2    The commonhold association must use the proceeds of any insurance taken out in accordance with paragraph 4.4.1 for the purpose of rebuilding or reinstating the common parts.

4.4.3    The commonhold association must keep details of common parts insurance and evidence of payment of the most recent premium at its registered office or such other place as the directors think fit.

4.4.4    A unit-holder may, on reasonable notice and at a reasonable time and place, inspect the common parts insurance policy taken out by the commonhold association and may also, upon payment of the commonhold association's reasonable charges, require the commonhold association to provide a copy of the insurance policy.

4.4.5    If a request is made by a unit-holder to provide a copy of the common parts insurance policy, the commonhold association must provide the copy to the unit-holder as soon as reasonably practicable upon payment of the charge.

4.4.6    The duties imposed by this CCS in respect of the insurance of the commonhold units are specified in paragraph 6 of Annex 4.

### 4.5 REPAIR AND MAINTENANCE

4.5.1    The commonhold association must repair and maintain the common parts. This includes decorating them and putting them into sound condition.

4.5.2    The duties imposed by this CCS in respect of the repair and maintenance of the commonhold units are specified in paragraph 7 of Annex 4.

### 4.6 ALTERATION OF THE COMMON PARTS

4.6.1    The commonhold association must not make any alterations to the common parts or cause or permit the common parts to be altered unless the proposed alteration is approved by ordinary resolution.

### 4.7 DEALINGS WITH THE LAND

4.7.1    Transfer of a commonhold unit—commonhold unit information certificate

A unit-holder may give a notice requiring the commonhold association to provide a commonhold unit information certificate in respect of his commonhold unit.

4.7.2    Within 14 days, beginning with the date on which the notice referred to in paragraph 4.7.1 is given, the commonhold association must provide a commonhold unit information certificate to the unit-holder and for the purposes of Section 4.9, a commonhold unit information certificate is a notice. Form 9 [Commonhold unit information certificate] must be used.

4.7.3    Transfer of a commonhold unit—new unit-holder's liability

Subject to paragraph 4.7.4, following a transfer of a commonhold unit, the commonhold association may give a notice requiring the new unit-holder to pay to the commonhold association the debts owed under paragraphs 4.2.15 and 4.2.16 by any former unit-holder in respect of that commonhold unit.

4.7.4    When the commonhold association has provided a commonhold unit information certificate the new unit-holder cannot be required to pay more than the amount specified in that certificate for the period up to and including the date of the certificate.

4.7.5    Within 14 days, beginning with the date on which the notice referred to in paragraph 4.7.3 is given, the new unit-holder must pay to the commonhold association the sum required by the notice.

4.7.6    If a payment required by paragraph 4.7.5 is not made by the date on which it is due, then the new unit-holder must pay interest to the commonhold association at the prescribed rate for the period beginning with the date on which the payment is due and ending on the date on which the payment is made.

4.7.7    When payment is made in accordance with paragraph 4.7.5 the commonhold association's right to enforce the payment of the sum paid against the former unit-holder is deemed to have been assigned to the new unit-holder.

4.7.8    Transfer of a commonhold unit—notification

Subject to paragraph 4.7.9, when a person becomes entitled to be registered as the proprietor of a freehold estate in a commonhold unit, he must notify the commonhold association within 14 days, beginning with the date on which he is entitled to be registered. Form 10 [Notice of transfer of a commonhold unit] or 11 [Notice of transfer of part of a commonhold unit] must be used.

4.7.9    When a person becomes entitled to be registered as the proprietor of a freehold estate in a commonhold unit by operation of law, he must notify the commonhold association within 14 days, beginning with the date on which he becomes aware of his entitlement. Form 12 [Notice of vesting of a commonhold unit by operation of law] must be used.

4.7.10   Application to add land

The commonhold association may not apply to Land Registry to add land to a commonhold unless the application is approved by a unanimous resolution.

4.7.11   Leasing—grant of a tenancy

A unit-holder or tenant may not grant a tenancy in a residential commonhold unit—

    (a)    for a premium;

    (b)    for a term of more than 7 years, unless regulation 11(2) of the Commonhold Regulations 2004 applies;

    (c)    under an option or agreement if—

        (i)    the person to take the new tenancy has an existing tenancy of the premises to be let;

        (ii)    the new term added to the existing term will be more than 7 years; and

        (iii)    the option or agreement was entered into before or at the same time as the existing tenancy;

    (d)    containing an option or agreement to renew which confers on either party to the tenancy an option or agreement for renewal for a further term which, together with the original term, amounts to more than 7 years;

    (e)    containing an option or agreement to extend the term beyond 7 years; or

    (f)    containing a provision requiring a tenant to make payments to the commonhold association in discharge of payments which are due, in accordance with this CCS, to be made by the unit-holder.

4.7.12   Before granting a tenancy in a commonhold unit, a prospective landlord must give the prospective tenant—

    (a)    a copy of this CCS, including such of the plans or parts of plans as are relevant to that commonhold unit; and

    (b)    a notice informing him that he will be required to comply with the paragraphs in the CCS that impose duties on him if he takes the tenancy. Form 13 [Notice to a prospective tenant] must be used.

4.7.13   If a landlord has not complied with paragraph 4.7.12 and a tenant has suffered loss as a result of an obligation in this CCS being enforced against him, then the tenant may give a notice requiring the landlord to reimburse him for that loss, unless the obligation is reproduced in the tenancy agreement.

4.7.14   Within 14 days, beginning with the date on which the notice referred to in paragraph 4.7.13 is given, the landlord must reimburse the tenant for the loss suffered.

4.7.15   Leasing—notification of the grant of a tenancy

Within 14 days, beginning with the date on which a tenancy is granted, the unit-holder or tenant who grants the tenancy must notify the commonhold association that the tenancy has been granted and must give a copy of any written tenancy agreement, or details of the terms of any oral tenancy, to the commonhold association. Form 14 [Notice of grant of a tenancy in a commonhold unit] must be used.

4.7.16   Leasing—assignment of a tenancy

Before assigning a tenancy in a commonhold unit a tenant must give the prospective assignee—

    (a)    a copy of this CCS, including such of the plans or parts of plans as are relevant to that commonhold unit; and

    (b)    a notice informing him that he will be required to comply with those paragraphs in the CCS that impose duties on him if he takes the assignment of the tenancy. Form 15 [Notice to a prospective assignee] must be used.

4.7.17   If a tenant has not complied with paragraph 4.7.16 and an assignee has suffered loss as a result of any obligation in this CCS being enforced against him, then the assignee may give a notice requiring the tenant to reimburse him for that loss, unless the obligation is reproduced in the tenancy agreement.

4.7.18   Within 14 days, beginning with the date on which the notice referred to in paragraph 4.7.17 is given, the tenant must reimburse the assignee for the loss suffered.

4.7.19   Leasing—notification of the assignment of a tenancy

Within 14 days, beginning with the date on which the tenancy is assigned, the new tenant must notify the commonhold association that the assignment has been completed. Form 16 [Notice of assignment of a tenancy in a commonhold unit] must be used.

4.7.20   Leasing—tenant's failure to comply with a duty

If the commonhold association has suffered loss because a tenant of a commonhold unit has not complied with a duty in this CCS, and the duty is one which must be complied with by both a unit-holder and a tenant, the commonhold association may give a notice requiring the unit-holder to reimburse it for that loss.

4.7.21   Within 14 days, beginning with the date on which the notice referred to in paragraph 4.7.20 is given, the unit-holder must reimburse the commonhold association for the loss.

## 4.8   AMENDMENT OF THE COMMONHOLD COMMUNITY STATEMENT

4.8.1   In the application of the provisions in paragraphs 4.8.5 to 4.8.9 to a commonhold unit with joint unit-holders, a reference to a unit-holder is a reference to the joint unit-holders together.

4.8.2   A paragraph in Parts 1 to 4 of this CCS cannot be amended unless it is a local rule.

4.8.3   Except where this CCS provides otherwise and subject to the [Companies Act 2006], local rules cannot be amended unless the proposed amendment is approved by ordinary resolution.

4.8.4   The format for paragraphs 1 to 3 of Annex 1, paragraphs 1 to 7 of Annex 2, paragraphs 1 to 3 of Annex 3 and paragraphs 1 to 7 of Annex 4 to this CCS cannot be amended.

4.8.5   An amendment to the rights for, or over, a commonhold unit specified in paragraphs 6 or 7 of Annex 2 cannot be made unless the unit-holder and the registered proprietor of any charge over that commonhold unit have consented in writing to the proposed amendment before it is made.

4.8.6   An amendment to remove a reference to a unit-holder in the column headed "Authorised users" in paragraph 4 of Annex 4 cannot be made unless the unit-holder and the registered proprietor of any charge over his commonhold unit have consented in writing to the proposed amendment before it is made.

4.8.7   An amendment to the permitted use of a commonhold unit specified in paragraph 2 of Annex 4 cannot be made unless the proposed amendment is approved by special resolution and the unit-holder has consented in writing to the proposed amendment before it is made.

4.8.8   An amendment to this CCS which redefines the extent of a commonhold unit cannot be made unless the unit-holder and the registered proprietor of any charge over that commonhold unit have consented in writing to the proposed amendment before it is made.

4.8.9   An amendment to this CCS which specifies that land which forms part of a commonhold unit is to be added to the common parts cannot be made unless the unit-holder and the registered proprietor of any charge over that land have consented in writing to the proposed amendment before it is made.

4.8.10   This CCS cannot be amended to record a change in the boundaries of the commonhold, a commonhold unit or the common parts following a transfer unless any consent required under paragraphs 4.8.8 and 4.8.9 has been given and the approval of the members by special resolution has been given.

4.8.11   An amendment to the following provisions cannot be made unless the proposed amendment is approved by special resolution—

   (a)   the percentage of the commonhold assessment or levy allocated to a commonhold unit in paragraphs 1 and 2 of Annex 3; and
   (b)   the number of votes allocated to a member in paragraph 3 of Annex 3.

4.8.12   A unit-holder has the right not to have the percentage of the commonhold assessment or levy allocated to his, or any other, commonhold unit altered if the effect of the alteration, taking into account all the circumstances of the case, would be to allocate a significantly disproportionate percentage of the commonhold assessment or levy to his commonhold unit.

4.8.13   A unit-holder who is a member has the right not to have the number of votes allocated to him, or any other member, in respect of a commonhold unit altered if the effect of the alteration, taking into account all the circumstances of the case, would be to allocate a significantly disproportionate number of votes to him.

4.8.14   The directors of the commonhold association may amend this CCS without any resolution of the members to include specified provisions, or provisions of a specified kind, for a specified purpose or about a specified matter required by the Act and regulations or to delete any provisions that are of no effect for the reasons set out in paragraph 1.1.5.

4.8.15   If this CCS has been amended, then the directors must apply, as soon as practicable, to Land Registry for the registration of the amended CCS.

4.8.16   Amendments to this CCS only take effect when the amended version is registered at Land Registry.

## 4.9   NOTICES

4.9.1   Any notice given by the commonhold association under this CCS must contain the name of the commonhold association, its company number, and an address for correspondence. If a notice does not specify an address for correspondence, it will be deemed to be the same address as the address of the registered office.

4.9.2   Any Form used in accordance with this CCS must be completed in full.

4.9.3   Within 14 days, beginning with the date on which a person becomes a unit-holder or tenant, he must give a notice to the commonhold association specifying a full postal address in the United Kingdom including postcode as his address for correspondence, unless notice of that address has already been given to the commonhold association under paragraphs 4.7.8, 4.7.9, 4.7.15 or 4.7.19.

4.9.4   A unit-holder or tenant may give a notice to the commonhold association specifying up to two more addresses for correspondence, which may be postal or electronic.

4.9.5   A unit-holder or tenant may give a notice to the commonhold association requesting that an address for correspondence held by the commonhold association is amended or removed, or requesting that an additional address for correspondence is to be held by the commonhold association, provided that the notice does not request the commonhold association to hold more than three addresses for the unit-holder or tenant at any time and that at least one of those addresses is, at all times, a full postal address in the United Kingdom including postcode.

4.9.6   When giving notice to a unit-holder or tenant, the commonhold association must give notice to each of the addresses for correspondence for that unit-holder or tenant held by the commonhold association in the register referred to in paragraph 4.10.1 or 4.10.2.

4.9.7   If a commonhold unit has joint unit-holders, then any notice to be given in accordance with this CCS must be addressed to all the joint unit-holders together.

4.9.8   Any notice to be given in accordance with this CCS must be in writing and given—
- (a)   personally;
- (b)   by leaving it at an address given as an address for correspondence;
- (c)   by sending it by first class post in a prepaid envelope properly addressed to an address given as an address for correspondence; or
- (d)   if an electronic address has been provided as an address for correspondence, by electronic communication to that address in accordance with any terms or conditions previously specified by the intended recipient.

4.9.9   Proof that an envelope containing a notice was properly addressed, prepaid and posted by first class post is conclusive evidence that it was given to a postal address. Electronic confirmation of receipt is conclusive evidence that a notice was given to an e-mail address.

4.9.10   A notice is deemed to have been given, unless proved otherwise—
- (a)   on the day it was handed to the recipient or left at the address for correspondence;
- (b)   on the second day after it was posted to the recipient; or
- (c)   on the day after it was transmitted by electronic communication.

## 4.10   COMMONHOLD REGISTERS AND DOCUMENTS

4.10.1   The commonhold association must maintain a register of unit-holders and their commonhold units and, within 14 days of receiving notice from a unit-holder under—
- (a)   paragraph 4.7.8, 4.7.9, 4.9.3 or 4.9.4, enter in the register the name and address for correspondence of the unit-holder; or
- (b)   paragraph 4.9.5, amend the register in accordance with the notice if, as a result of the amendment proposed, the commonhold association will hold in the register in respect of the unit-holder at least one full postal address in the United Kingdom including postcode and no more than three addresses in total.

4.10.2   The commonhold association must maintain a register of tenants and, within 14 days of receiving notice under—
- (a)   paragraph 4.7.15, 4.7.19, 4.9.3 or 4.9.4, enter in the register—
    - (i)   a description of the premises let;
    - (ii)   the name and address of the tenant; and
    - (iii)   the length of the tenancy; or
- (b)   paragraph 4.9.5, amend the register in accordance with the notice, if as a result of the amendment proposed, the commonhold association will hold in the register in respect of the tenant at least one full postal address in the United Kingdom including postcode and no more than three addresses in total.

4.10.3   The commonhold association must keep up-to-date copies of the CCS and the ... articles of association at the registered office of the commonhold association.

4.10.4   A unit-holder or tenant may, on reasonable notice and at a reasonable time and place, inspect the CCS or the ... articles of association, and may also, on payment of the commonhold association's reasonable charges, require the commonhold association to provide a copy of such documents.

## 4.11   DISPUTE RESOLUTION

4.11.1   The dispute resolution procedure contained in the following paragraphs applies only to the enforcement of rights and duties that arise from this CCS or from a provision made by or by virtue of the Act. References to enforcing a right include enforcing the terms and conditions to which a right is subject.

4.11.2　Procedure for enforcement by unit-holder or tenant against the commonhold association

Subject to paragraph 4.11.3, a unit-holder or tenant must use the dispute resolution procedure contained in paragraphs 4.11.4 to 4.11.9 when seeking to enforce against the commonhold association a right or duty contained in this CCS or a provision made by or by virtue of the Act.

4.11.3　A unit-holder or tenant, when seeking to enforce against the commonhold association a duty to pay money or a right or duty in an emergency, may—
- (a)　use the dispute resolution procedure contained in paragraphs 4.11.4 to 4.11.9;
- (b)　if the commonhold association is a member of an approved ombudsman scheme, refer a dispute directly to the ombudsman; or
- (c)　bring legal proceedings.

4.11.4　When seeking to enforce a right or duty a unit-holder or tenant (the "complainant") must first consider resolving the matter by—
- (a)　negotiating directly with the commonhold association; or
- (b)　using arbitration, mediation, conciliation, or any other form of dispute resolution procedure involving a third party, other than legal proceedings.

4.11.5　If the matter is not resolved in accordance with paragraph 4.11.4, then the complainant must, if he wishes to take further action to enforce the right or duty, give a complaint notice to the commonhold association. Form 17 [Complaint notice against commonhold association] must be used.

4.11.6　The commonhold association may respond to the complaint notice by giving a reply notice to the complainant. Form 18 [Reply to complaint notice against commonhold association] must be used.

4.11.7　Upon receipt of the reply notice or when 21 days have passed, beginning with the date on which the complaint notice is given, (whichever is earlier) the complainant must, if he wishes to take further action to enforce the right or duty, first reconsider whether the matter could be resolved—
- (a)　by negotiating directly with the commonhold association; or
- (b)　by using arbitration, mediation, conciliation, or any other form of dispute resolution procedure involving a third party, other than legal proceedings.

4.11.8　If the matter is not resolved in accordance with paragraph 4.11.7 and the complainant wishes to take further action to enforce the right or duty, then he must, if the commonhold association is a member of an approved ombudsman scheme, refer the matter to the ombudsman.

4.11.9　If the commonhold association is a member of an approved ombudsman scheme, then legal proceedings may only be brought once the ombudsman has investigated and determined the matter and he has notified the parties of his decision. If the commonhold association is not a member of an approved ombudsman scheme, then legal proceedings may be brought upon completion of the dispute resolution procedure contained in paragraphs 4.11.4 to 4.11.7.

4.11.10　Procedure for enforcement by commonhold association against a unit-holder or tenant

Subject to paragraph 4.11.11, the commonhold association must use the dispute resolution procedure contained in paragraphs 4.11.12 to 4.11.16 when seeking to enforce against a unit-holder or tenant a right or duty contained in this CCS or a provision made by or by virtue of the Act.

4.11.11　The commonhold association, when seeking to enforce against a unit-holder or tenant a duty to pay money or a right or duty in an emergency, may—
- (a)　use the dispute resolution procedure contained in paragraphs 4.11.12 to 4.11.16;
- (b)　if the commonhold association is a member of an approved ombudsman scheme, refer a dispute directly to the ombudsman; or
- (c)　bring legal proceedings.

4.11.12　When seeking to enforce a right or duty the commonhold association must first consider—
- (a)　resolving the matter by—
  - (i)　negotiating directly with the unit-holder or tenant (the "alleged defaulter"); or
  - (ii)　using arbitration, mediation, conciliation, or any other form of dispute resolution procedure involving a third party, other than legal proceedings; or
- (b)　taking no action if it reasonably thinks that inaction is in the best interests of establishing or maintaining harmonious relationships between all the unit-holders, and that it will not cause any unit-holder (other than the alleged defaulter) significant loss or significant disadvantage.

4.11.13　If the matter is not resolved in accordance with paragraph 4.11.12, then the commonhold association must, if it wishes to take further action to enforce the right or duty, give a default notice to the alleged defaulter. Form 19 [Default notice] must be used.

4.11.14　The alleged defaulter may respond to the default notice by giving a reply notice to the commonhold association. Form 20 [Reply to default notice] must be used.

4.11.15   Upon receipt of the reply notice or when 21 days have passed, beginning with the date on which the default notice is given, (whichever is earlier) the commonhold association must, if it wishes to take further action to enforce the right or duty, first reconsider whether the matter could be resolved—
  (a)   by negotiating directly with the alleged defaulter; or
  (b)   by using arbitration, mediation, conciliation, or any other form of dispute resolution procedure involving a third party, other than legal proceedings.

4.11.16   If the matter is not resolved in accordance with paragraph 4.11.15, then the commonhold association may either, if it is a member of an approved ombudsman scheme, refer the matter to the ombudsman, or, if it is satisfied that the interests of the commonhold require it, bring legal proceedings.

4.11.17   Procedure for enforcement by unit-holder or tenant against another unit-holder or tenant

Subject to paragraph 4.11.18, a unit-holder or tenant must use the dispute resolution procedure contained in paragraphs 4.11.19 to 4.11.30 when seeking to enforce against another unit-holder or tenant a right or duty contained in this CCS or a provision made by or by virtue of the Act.

4.11.18   A unit-holder or tenant, when seeking to enforce against another unit-holder or tenant a duty to pay money or a right or duty in an emergency, may—
  (a)   use the dispute resolution procedure contained in paragraphs 4.11.19 to 4.11.30; or
  (b)   bring legal proceedings.

4.11.19   When seeking to enforce a right or duty a unit-holder or tenant (the "complainant") must first consider resolving the matter by—
  (a)   negotiating directly with the other unit-holder or tenant (the "alleged defaulter"); or
  (b)   using arbitration, mediation, conciliation, or any other form of dispute resolution procedure involving a third party, other than legal proceedings.

4.11.20   If the matter is not resolved in accordance with paragraph 4.11.19, then the complainant must, if he wishes to take further action to enforce the right or duty, give a notice to the commonhold association requesting that the commonhold association take action to enforce the right or duty against the alleged defaulter. Form 21 [Request for action] must be used.

4.11.21   The commonhold association must consider the notice referred to in paragraph 4.11.20 and decide whether to—
  (a)   take action to enforce the right or duty against the alleged defaulter; and if it so decides, then to take action as soon as reasonably practicable using the dispute resolution procedure contained in paragraphs 4.11.12 to 4.11.16; or
  (b)   take no action in accordance with paragraph 4.11.22; and if it so decides, then to decide whether, in accordance with paragraph 4.11.23, to allow the complainant to enforce the right or duty against the alleged defaulter directly.

4.11.22   The commonhold association may decide to take no action in respect of the matters specified in the notice referred to in paragraph 4.11.20 if it reasonably thinks that inaction is in the best interests of establishing or maintaining harmonious relationships between all the unit-holders or tenants, and that it will not cause any unit-holder or tenant (other than the alleged defaulter) significant loss or significant disadvantage.

4.11.23   The commonhold association may refuse the complainant the right to take further action in relation to the matter specified in the notice referred to in paragraph 4.11.20, if the commonhold association reasonably thinks that the complaint—
  (a)   does not amount to a breach of a right enjoyed by, or a duty owed to, the complainant; or
  (b)   is vexatious, frivolous or trivial.

4.11.24   The commonhold association must, as soon as practicable after making a decision in accordance with paragraph 4.11.21, inform the complainant of outcome of its decision. Form 22 [Reply to request for action] must be used.

4.11.25   If the complainant wishes to challenge the decision made by the commonhold association under paragraph 4.11.21 he may use the dispute resolution procedure contained in paragraphs 4.11.4 to 4.11.9, save that for these purposes the time period mentioned in paragraph 4.11.7 is to be 7 days.

4.11.26   If the commonhold association fails to comply with paragraph 4.11.24 within 21 days, beginning with the date on which the notice referred to in paragraph 4.11.20 is given, the complainant may enforce the right or duty against the alleged defaulter directly, and if he does so, he must use the dispute resolution procedure in paragraphs 4.11.27 to 4.11.30.

4.11.27   If, by virtue of the notice referred to in paragraph 4.11.24, the complainant has the right to enforce the right or duty against the alleged defaulter directly then the complainant must, if he wishes to take further action to enforce the right or duty, give a complaint notice to the alleged defaulter. Form 23 [Complaint notice against unit-holder or tenant] must be used.

4.11.28   The alleged defaulter may respond to the complaint notice by giving a reply notice to the complainant. Form 24 [Reply to complaint notice against unit-holder or tenant] must be used.

4.11.29   Upon receipt of the reply notice or when 21 days have passed, beginning with the date on which the complaint notice is given, (whichever is earlier) the complainant must, if he wishes to take further action to enforce the right or duty, reconsider whether the matter could be resolved—
- (a)   by negotiating directly with the alleged defaulter; or
- (b)   by using arbitration, mediation, conciliation, or any other form of dispute resolution procedure involving a third party, other than legal proceedings.

4.11.30   If the matter is not resolved in accordance with paragraph 4.11.29 the complainant may bring legal proceedings against the alleged defaulter in respect of the complaint specified in the notice given under paragraph 4.11.20.

### ANNEX 1: IDENTITY OF THE COMMONHOLD AND THE COMMONHOLD ASSOCIATION

**1 Name of the commonhold**

|  |
|--|
|  |

**2 Name of the commonhold association**

|  |
|--|
|  |

**3 Company number of the commonhold association**

|  |
|--|
|  |

### ANNEX 2: DEFINITION OF THE PROPERTIES WITHIN THE COMMONHOLD

**1 List of plans**

| Plan Number | Plan reference number (if different) | Date of plan (if any) |
|-------------|--------------------------------------|------------------------|
|  |  |  |
|  |  |  |
|  |  |  |
|  |  |  |

**2 Description of the location and extent of commonhold land**

|  |
|--|
|  |

**3 Total number of commonhold units in the commonhold**

|  |
|--|
|  |

**4 Description of the location and extent of commonhold units**

| Commonhold unit number | Plan number | Details of how the commonhold unit is shown on the plan | Property description |
|------------------------|-------------|---------------------------------------------------------|----------------------|
|  |  |  |  |
|  |  |  |  |
|  |  |  |  |
|  |  |  |  |

**5 Further description of commonhold units**

**6 Rights for commonhold units**

**7 Rights over commonhold units**

## ANNEX 3: COMMONHOLD ALLOCATIONS

**1 Allocation of commonhold assessment**

| Commonhold unit number | Percentage allocation (total 100%) |
|---|---|
|  |  |
|  |  |
|  |  |

**2 Allocation of reserve fund levy**

| Name of reserve fund | Commonhold unit number | Percentage allocation (total 100%) |
|---|---|---|
|  |  |  |
|  |  |  |
|  |  |  |
|  |  |  |

**3 Allocation of votes**

| Commonhold unit number | Number of votes allocated to member |
|---|---|
|  |  |
|  |  |
|  |  |

## ANNEX 4: LOCAL RULES

**1 Prescribed rate of interest**

## 2 Permitted use of commonhold units

| Commonhold unit number | Permitted use |
|---|---|
|  |  |
|  |  |
|  |  |

## 3 Permitted use of common parts

|  |
|---|
|  |

## 4 Limited use areas

| Description of area | Plan number | Authorised users | Authorised use |
|---|---|---|---|
|  |  |  |  |
|  |  |  |  |
|  |  |  |  |

## 5 Insurance of common parts—inserted risks

|  |
|---|
|  |

## 6 Insurance of commonhold units—duties

|  |
|---|
|  |

## 7 Repair and maintenance of commonhold units—duties

|  |
|---|
|  |

## SIGNATURE

This is the commonhold community statement of [ ] commonhold signed in the form required by the Commonhold Regulations 2004.

[

]

Date

**NOTES**

Para 1.1.5: sub-para (c) words omitted revoked by the Commonhold (Amendment) Regulations 2009, SI 2009/2363, regs 2, 10(a).

Para 1.4.5: definition "company number" words in square brackets substituted by SI 2009/2363, regs 2, 10(b)(i); definition "memorandum" (omitted) revoked by SI 2009/2363, regs 2, 10(b)(ii); definitions "ordinary resolution" and "special resolution" substituted by SI 2009/2363, regs 2, 10(b)(iii), (iv).

Para 4.8.3: words in square brackets substituted by SI 2009/2363, regs 2, 10(c).

Para 4.10.3: words omitted revoked by SI 2009/2363, regs 2, 10(d).

Para 4.10.4: words omitted revoked by SI 2009/2363, regs 2, 10(e).

SCHEDULE 4

**NOTES**
This Schedule contains forms which are not reproduced in this work, but their titles are listed below. The forms can be found at www.opsi.gov.uk.

| Form No | Title |
|---|---|
| 1 | Notice of proposed commonhold assessment |
| 2 | Request for payment of commonhold assessment |
| 3 | Request for payment of emergency commonhold assessment |
| 4 | Notice of proposed reserve fund levy |
| 5 | Request for payment of reserve fund levy |
| 6 | Notice to tenant of diversion of rent |
| 7 | Notice to sub-tenant of diversion of rent |
| 8 | Notice requesting further details about a tenancy |
| 9 | Commonhold unit information certificate |
| 10 | Notice of transfer of a commonhold unit |
| 11 | Notice of transfer of part of a commonhold unit |
| 12 | Notice of vesting of a commonhold unit by operation of law |
| 13 | Notice to a prospective tenant |
| 14 | Notice of grant of a tenancy in a commonhold unit |
| 15 | Notice to a prospective assignee |
| 16 | Notice of assignment of a tenancy in a commonhold unit |
| 17 | Complaint notice against commonhold association |
| 18 | Reply to complaint notice against commonhold association |
| 19 | Default notice |
| 20 | Reply to default notice |
| 21 | Request for action |
| 22 | Reply to request for action |
| 23 | Complaint notice against unit-holder or tenant |
| 24 | Reply to complaint notice against unit-holder or tenant |

# COMMONHOLD (LAND REGISTRATION) RULES 2004

(SI 2004/1830)

**NOTES**
Made: 14 July 2004.
Authority: Commonhold and Leasehold Reform Act 2002, s 65.
Commencement: 27 September 2004 (see r 1 and the note thereto at **[3398]**).

ARRANGEMENT OF RULES

*General*

## 1 Citation and commencement

These rules may be cited as the Commonhold (Land Registration) Rules 2004 and shall come into force on the day that section 2 of the Act comes into force.

**[3398]**

---

**NOTES**

Commencement: 27 September 2004.

Section 2 of the Act: brought into force on 27 September 2004 by the Commonhold and Leasehold Reform Act 2002 (Commencement No 4) Order 2004, SI 2004/1832, art 2.

---

## 2 Interpretation

(1) In these rules—

"the Act" means Part 1 of the Commonhold and Leasehold Reform Act 2002,

"commonhold entries" means the entries referred to in paragraphs (a) to (c) of rule 28(1) and

"main rules" means the Land Registration Rules 2003.

(2) In these rules except where otherwise stated, a form referred to by letters or numbers means the form so designated in Schedule 1 to these rules.

**[3399]**

## 3 Land registration rules

(1) Land registration rules within the meaning of the Land Registration Act 2002 have effect in relation to anything done by virtue of or for the purposes of the Act as they have effect in relation to anything done by virtue of or for the purposes of the Land Registration Act 2002 subject to paragraphs (2) and (3).

(2) Rules 3(3)(a), 3(4)(a), 126, 127 and 214 of the main rules shall not apply to any application made under the Act.

(3) In its application to the Act—

(a) subject to paragraph (2), rule 3 of the main rules (individual registers and more than one registered estate, division and amalgamation) shall apply as if the words "and are vested in the same proprietor" in paragraph (1) and the words "and are vested in the same proprietor" in paragraph (4) were omitted,

(b) rule 54 of the main rules (outline applications) shall apply as if paragraph (6) of that rule referred to the forms in Schedule 1 to these rules,

(c) rules 136 to 138 of the main rules (exempt information documents) shall apply as if a commonhold community statement and a memorandum and articles of association of a commonhold association were excluded from the definition of a "relevant document" in rule 136(7),

(d) for the purposes of rule 208 of the main rules (Welsh language forms) the forms in Schedule 1 to these rules shall be treated as if they were scheduled forms within the meaning of the main rules,

(e) rules 210 and 211 of the main rules (documents in a Schedule 1 form and electronically produced forms) shall apply to the forms in Schedule 1 to these rules as they apply to the forms in Schedule 1 to the main rules, and

(f) Parts 3 and 4 of Schedule 6 to the main rules (information to be included in the results of certain official searches) shall apply as if the words "relevant pending application" included any application made under the Act.

**[3400]**

## *Applications*

## 4 Lodging a copy document

(1) This rule applies to—
(a) the commonhold association's certificate of incorporation,
(b) any altered certificate of incorporation,
(c) the [articles of association] of the commonhold association,
(d) any altered [articles of association] of the commonhold association,
(e) a commonhold community statement,
(f) any amended commonhold community statement,
(g) an order of the court under the Act, and
(h) a termination statement.

(2) Where the Act or these rules requires an application to be accompanied by a document referred to in paragraph (1), a certified copy of that document may be submitted in place of the original.

(3) Where the original document is lodged a certified copy must accompany it.

**[3401]**

**NOTES**
Para (1): words in square brackets substituted by the Commonhold (Land Registration) (Amendment) Rules 2009, SI 2009/2024, rr 2, 3(1), (2).

## 5 Application for registration

(1) An application to register a freehold estate in land as a freehold estate in commonhold land must be made in Form CM1 accompanied, where appropriate, by the statement required by section 9(1)(b) of the Act.

(2) The statement required by section 9(1)(b) of the Act shall be in Form COV.

(3) Unless the Registrar otherwise directs, the application must be accompanied by a [statement of truth] made by the applicant that complies with rule 6.

**[3402]**

**NOTES**
Para (3): words in square brackets substituted by the Commonhold (Land Registration) (Amendment) Rules 2008, SI 2008/1920, r 3.

## 6 [Statement of truth]

(1) The [statement of truth] referred to in rule 5(3) must comply with paragraphs (2) to (6).

(2) The [statement] must list the consents, or orders of court dispensing with consent, that have been obtained under or by virtue of section 3 of the Act.

(3) Where there is a restriction entered in any individual register affected by the application, the [statement] must confirm that either the restriction does not protect an interest in respect of which the consent of the holder is required or, if it does that the appropriate consent has been obtained.

(4) The [statement] must confirm that—
(a) no other consents are required under or by virtue of section 3 of the Act,
(b) no consent has lapsed or been withdrawn, and
(c) if a consent is subject to conditions, all conditions have been fully satisfied.

(5) Where the application involves the extinguishment under section 22 of the Act of a charge that is the subject of an entry in the register the [statement] must—
(a) identify the charge to be extinguished
(b) identify the title of the owner of the charge,
(c) give the name and address of the owner of the charge, and

(d)    confirm that the consent of the owner of the charge has been obtained.

(6)    The Registrar must accept the [statement of truth] as conclusive evidence that no additional consents are required under or by virtue of section 3 of the Act and must cancel any entry in the register relating to an interest that has been identified in the [statement of truth] to be extinguished.

**[3403]**

**NOTES**

Heading: substituted by the Commonhold (Land Registration) (Amendment) Rules 2008, SI 2008/1920, r 4(1).

Paras (1)–(6): words in square brackets substituted by SI 2008/1920, r 4(1), (2).

## 7   Form of consent

The form of consent required under or by virtue of sections 3 and 41 of the Act is Form CON 1.

**[3404]**

## 8   Rejection or cancellation of application

In addition to the Registrar's powers contained in rule 16 of the main rules, the Registrar may reject an application on delivery or he may cancel it at any time thereafter if plans submitted with it (whether as part of the commonhold community statement or otherwise) are insufficiently clear or accurate.

**[3405]**

## 9   Title to interests

(1)    Where a consent required under or by virtue of section 3 of the Act has been lodged relating to an interest which is unregistered or is the subject of only a notice, caution or restriction in the register, the applicant must also lodge sufficient evidence to satisfy the Registrar that the person whose consent has been lodged is the person who was entitled to that interest at the time the consent was given.

(2)    For the purposes of paragraph (1), the Registrar may accept as sufficient evidence of entitlement a conveyancer's certificate that he is satisfied that the person whose consent has been lodged in relation to that interest is the person who was entitled to it at the time the consent was given and that he holds evidence of this.

**[3406]**

## 10   Service of notice—extinguished leases

(1)    Subject to paragraph (3), where, as the result of an application under section 2 of the Act, a lease the title to which is registered is extinguished under section 9(3)(f) of the Act, the Registrar must give notice of the closure of the leasehold title to the following—

(a)    the registered proprietor of the leasehold title,

(b)    the registered proprietor of any charge affecting the leasehold title, and

(c)    the person entitled to the benefit of a notice, a restriction or a caution against dealings entered in the register of the leasehold title.

(2)    Subject to paragraph (3), where, as the result of an application under section 2 of the Act, an unregistered lease which is noted in the register of the freehold title is extinguished under section 9(3)(f) of the Act, the Registrar must give notice of the completion of the application to the holder of the leasehold estate that has been extinguished.

(3)    The Registrar is not obliged to give notice to a person referred to in paragraph (1) or (2) or in both if—

(a)    that person consented under section 3 of the Act to the application, or

(b)    that person's name and his address for service under rule 198 of the main rules are not set out in the relevant individual register.

**[3407]**

## 11   Service of notice at end of transitional period—extinguished leases

(1)    Subject to paragraph (3), where a lease the title to which is registered is extinguished under section 7(3)(d) of the Act and rule 29 (2) applies, the Registrar must give notice of the closure of the leasehold title to the following—

(a)    the registered proprietor of the leasehold title,

(b)    the registered proprietor of any charge affecting the leasehold title, and

(c)    the person entitled to the benefit of a notice, a restriction or a caution against dealings entered in the register of the leasehold title.

(2)    Subject to paragraph (3), where an unregistered lease which is noted in the register of the freehold title is extinguished under section 7(3)(d) and rule 29(2) applies, the Registrar must give notice of the completion of the application to the holder of the leasehold estate that has been extinguished.

PART II
STATUTORY INSTRUMENTS

(3)    The Registrar is not obliged to give notice to a person referred to in paragraph (1) if—

(a)    that person consented under section 3 of the Act to the application, or

(b)    that person's name and his address for service under rule 198 of the main rules are not set out in the relevant individual register.

**[3408]**

## 12   Court order

An application to give effect in the register to an order of the court under the Act, other than a succession order, must be made in Form AP1 of the main rules.

**[3409]**

## 13   Registration of an amended commonhold community statement

(1)    An application to register an amended commonhold community statement must be made in Form CM3.

(2)    The application must be accompanied by a new version of the commonhold community statement incorporating the amendments.

(3)    On completion of the application, the Registrar must enter a note of the amended commonhold community statement in the register of the title to the common parts in a manner that distinguishes it from previous versions of the commonhold community statement.

**[3410]**

## 14   Cessation of commonhold during the transitional period

(1)    An application for the freehold estate in land to cease to be registered as a freehold estate in commonhold land during the transitional period must be made in Form CM2.

(2)    When satisfied that the application is in order, the Registrar must cancel to the necessary extent the commonhold entries made in the register under rule 28(1)(a) to (c).

(3)    Unless the Registrar otherwise directs, the application must be accompanied by—

(a)    a [statement of truth] made by the applicant that complies with rule 6 to the extent necessary, and

(b)    all necessary consents in Form CON 2.

**[3411]**

**NOTES**
    Para (3): words in square brackets substituted by the Commonhold (Land Registration) (Amendment) Rules 2008, SI 2008/1920, r 5.

## 15   Transfer of part of a commonhold unit

(1)    An application to register a transfer of the freehold estate in part only of a commonhold unit must be accompanied by an application in Form CM3 to register the commonhold community statement that has been amended in relation to the transfer.

(2)    The Registrar may reject on delivery the application to register the transfer, or he may cancel it at any time thereafter, if it is not accompanied by an application to register the amended commonhold community statement.

**[3412]**

## 16   Transfer of part of the common parts

(1)    An application to register a transfer of the freehold estate in part of the common parts must be accompanied by an application in Form CM3 to register the commonhold community statement that has been amended in relation to the transfer.

(2)    The Registrar may reject on delivery the application to register the transfer, or he may cancel it at any time thereafter, if it is not accompanied by an application to register the amended commonhold community statement.

**[3413]**

## 17   Alteration of the extent of a commonhold unit

(1)    An application to register an amended commonhold community statement in Form CM3 which would have the effect of altering the extent of a commonhold unit (other than by removing the whole of the unit) must be accompanied by an application to register any relevant transfer.

(2)    Where there is a relevant transfer, the Registrar may reject on delivery the application to register the amended commonhold community statement, or he may cancel it at any time thereafter, if paragraph (1) is not complied with.

**[3414]**

**18 Alteration of the extent of the common parts**

(1) An application to register an amended commonhold community statement in Form CM3 which would have the effect of altering the extent of the common parts (unless section 30(4) of the Act applies) must be accompanied by an application to register any relevant transfer.

(2) Where there is a relevant transfer, the Registrar may reject on delivery the application to register the amended commonhold community statement, or he may cancel it at any time thereafter, if paragraph (1) is not complied with.

**[3415]**

**19 Registration of [altered articles of association]**

(1) An application to register [altered articles of association] must be made in Form CM3.

(2) The application must be accompanied by a new version of the [articles of association] of the commonhold association incorporating the amendments.

(3) On completion of the application, the Registrar must enter a note of the altered [articles of association] in the register of the title to the common parts in a manner that distinguishes them from previous versions of the [articles of association] of the commonhold association.

**[3416]**

**NOTES**
Heading: words in square brackets substituted by the Commonhold (Land Registration) (Amendment) Rules 2009, SI 2009/2024, rr 2, 4(1).
Para (1): words in square brackets substituted by SI 2009/2024, rr 2, 4(1).
Paras (2)–(3): words in square brackets substituted by SI 2009/2024, rr 2, 4(2).

**20 Application to add land**

(1) An application to add land within the meaning of section 41 of the Act must be made in Form CM4.

(2) Such an application must be accompanied by an application to register the amended commonhold community statement in Form CM3.

(3) The Registrar may reject on delivery the application to add land, or he may cancel it at any time thereafter, if it is not accompanied by an application to register the amended commonhold community statement.

(4) Unless the Registrar otherwise directs the application must be accompanied by a [statement of truth] by the applicant that complies with rule 6 to the extent necessary.

**[3417]**

**NOTES**
Para (4): words in square brackets substituted by the Commonhold (Land Registration) (Amendment) Rules 2008, SI 2008/1920, r 6.

**21 Termination application following a voluntary winding up**

(1) A termination application must be—
    (a) made in Form CM5, and
    (b) accompanied by the order, appointment by the Secretary of State or resolution under which the liquidator was appointed and such other evidence as the Registrar may require.

(2) Where a termination application is made and the liquidator notifies the Registrar that he is content with the termination statement, or sends to the Registrar a copy of the court's determination of the terms of the termination statement, the Registrar must—
    (a) enter the commonhold association as proprietor of the commonhold units, and
    (b) cancel the commonhold entries on every registered title affected.

**[3418]**

**22 Application to terminate a commonhold registration following the winding-up of a commonhold association by the court**

(1) An application to terminate a commonhold registration where the court has made a winding—up order in respect of a commonhold association and has not made a succession order must be made in Form CM5.

(2) When the Registrar has received notification under section 54(2)(c) to (f) of the Act, and is otherwise satisfied that the application is in order, he may cancel the commonhold entries on the registered titles affected.

**[3419]**

## 23   Registration of a successor commonhold association

(1)   Where a succession order is made, an application must be made to the Registrar to register the successor commonhold association in Form CM6.

(2)   Unless the Registrar otherwise directs, the application must be accompanied by—
- (a)   the succession order,
- (b)   the [articles of association] of the successor commonhold association, and
- (c)   the winding up order.

(3)   When satisfied that the application is in order, the Registrar must—
- (a)   cancel the note of the [articles of association] of the insolvent commonhold association in the property register of the registered title to the common parts,
- (b)   enter a note of the [articles of association] of the successor commonhold association in the property register of the registered title to the common parts, and
- (c)   give effect to the terms of the succession order in the individual registers of the registered titles affected.

(4)   Where a succession order includes provisions falling within section 52(4) of the Act, the successor commonhold association must make an application to give effect in the register to those provisions so far as necessary.

[3420]

**NOTES**

Paras (2), (3): words in square brackets substituted by the Commonhold (Land Registration) (Amendment) Rules 2009, SI 2009/2024, rr 2, 5.

## 24   Application to register surrender of a development right

(1)   An application to note the surrender of a right conferred by section 58(2) of the Act in the register must be accompanied by a notice in Form SR1.

(2)   When satisfied as to the application, the Registrar must complete it by entering the notice surrendering the right in the property register of the registered title to the common parts.

[3421]

## 25   Official copies

An application for official copies of the individual register and title plan of the common parts in relation to a commonhold must be made by inserting the following words in [panel 7] of Form OC1 in Schedule 1 of the main rules—

"official copy(ies) of the register and title plan of the common parts in a commonhold development."

[3422]

**NOTES**

Words in square brackets substituted by the Commonhold (Land Registration) (Amendment) Rules 2008, SI 2008/1920, r 7.

## 26   Searches of the index map

If a person who applies for a search of the index map requires the title numbers of the units in relation to a commonhold, he must insert the common parts title number followed by the words "common parts" in panel 2 of Form SIM in Schedule 1 of the main rules or supply a plan of the commonhold land showing sufficient detail to enable the land to be clearly identified on the Ordnance Survey map.

[3423]

*The Register*

## 27   Restrictions

To give effect to the terms of the Act the Registrar must—
- (a)   enter a restriction in Form CA in Schedule 2 in the individual register of the common parts title, and
- (b)   enter a restriction in Form CB in Schedule 2 in the individual register of each unit title.

[3424]

## 28   Completion of application for registration

(1)   When satisfied that an application under section 2 of the Act is in order, the Registrar must complete it by entering in the individual register of the affected registered titles—
- (a)   a note that the freehold estate is registered as a freehold estate in commonhold land,
- (b)   a note of the [articles of association] of the commonhold association and the commonhold community statement,
- (c)   where the application is not accompanied by Form COV, a note that the rights and duties

conferred and imposed by the commonhold community statement will not come into force until the end of the transitional period, and

    (d)    where the application is not accompanied by Form COV, the applicant as proprietor of the registered title to each of the units and as proprietor of the registered title to the common parts.

(2)   Where an application to register the freehold estate in land as the freehold estate in commonhold land is accompanied by Form COV, the Registrar must—

    (a)    cancel notice of any lease extinguished under section 9(3)(f) of the Act, and

    (b)    close the title if the lease is registered.

**[3425]**

**NOTES**

   Para (1): words in square brackets substituted by the Commonhold (Land Registration) (Amendment) Rules 2009, SI 2009/2024, rr 2, 6.

---

### 29   End of transitional period

(1)   This rule applies where an application has been made under section 2 of the Act and was not accompanied by Form COV.

(2)   Where the Registrar is aware that the transitional period has come to an end, he must—

    (a)    cancel the entries made in the register under rule 28(1)(c),

    (b)    cancel notice of any lease extinguished under section 7(3)(d) of the Act, and

    (c)    close the title to any such lease where the lease is registered.

**[3426]**

### 30   Leases of commonhold units

When a term of years absolute is created in a commonhold unit and the lease is registered, the Registrar must enter a note in the property register of the leasehold title that it is a lease of a commonhold unit.

**[3427]**

### 31   Changing size: charged unit

On an application to which rule 15 or rule 17 relates and where section 24(1) of the Act applies, on receipt of Form COE, the Registrar must give effect in the register to section 24(4) and (5) of the Act as appropriate.

**[3428]**

### 32   Charges over common parts

Where a charge is extinguished, in whole or in part, under section 28(3) or section 28(4) of the Act, the Registrar must cancel or alter as appropriate any entry of the charge in the register to the extent that it is extinguished.

**[3429]**

SCHEDULES

SCHEDULE 1

**NOTES**

  This Schedule contains forms which are not reproduced in this work, but their titles are listed below. The forms can be found at www.opsi.gov.uk.

---

| Form No | Title |
|---|---|
| CM1 | Application to register a freehold estate in commonhold land (substituted by SI 2008/1920; amended by SI 2009/2024) |
| CM2 | Application for the freehold estate to cease to be registered as a freehold estate in commonhold land during the transitional period (substituted by SI 2008/1920) |
| CM3 | Application for the registration of an amended commonhold community statement and/or altered memorandum and articles of association (amended by SI 2009/2024) |
| CM4 | Application to add land to a commonhold registration (substituted by SI 2008/1920) |
| CM5 | Application for the termination of a commonhold registration |

| Form No | Title |
|---------|-------|
| CM6 | Application for the registration of a successor commonhold association (amended by SI 2009/2024) |
| COE | Notification of change of extent of a commonhold unit over which there is a registered charge |
| CON1 | Consent to the registration of land as commonhold land |
| CON2 | Consent to an application for the freehold estate to cease to be registered as a freehold estate in commonhold land during the transitional period |
| COV | Application for registration with unit-holders (Section 9 Statement) |
| SR1 | Notice of surrender of development right(s) |

## SCHEDULE 2
## COMMONHOLD RESTRICTIONS

Rule 27

*Form CA (Restriction in common parts title)*

No charge by the proprietor of the registered estate is to be registered other than a legal mortgage which is accompanied by a certificate by a conveyancer or a director or secretary of the commonhold association that the creation of the mortgage was approved by a resolution complying with section 29(2) of the Commonhold and Leasehold Reform Act 2002.

*Form CB (Restriction in unit title)*

No disposition by the proprietor of the registered estate (other than a transfer or charge of the whole of the land in the title) is to be registered without a certificate by a conveyancer or a director or secretary of the commonhold association that the disposition is authorised by and made in accordance with the provisions of the Commonhold and Leasehold Reform Act 2002.

**[3430]**

# COMMONHOLD AND LEASEHOLD REFORM ACT 2002 (COMMENCEMENT NO 5 AND SAVING AND TRANSITIONAL PROVISION) ORDER 2004

(SI 2004/3056)

**NOTES**
Made: 16 November 2004.
Authority: Commonhold and Leasehold Reform Act 2002, s 181.

### 1  Citation and interpretation

(1)  This Order may be cited as the Commonhold and Leasehold Reform Act 2002 (Commencement No 5 and Saving and Transitional Provision) Order 2004.

(2)  In this Order, unless otherwise stated, references to sections and Schedules are references to sections of, and Schedules to, the Commonhold and Leasehold Reform Act 2002.

**[3431]**

### 2  Provision coming into force in England and Wales

Section 180, in so far as it relates to the repeal in Schedule 14 of section 104, shall come into force in England and Wales on the day after that on which this Order is made.

**[3432]**

### 3  Provisions coming into force in England on 28th February 2005

Subject to article 4, the following provisions shall come into force in England on 28th February 2005—

    (a)    section 126,
    (b)    section 157, in so far as it relates to paragraph 15 of Schedule 10,
    (c)    section 164, to the extent that it is not already in force,
    (d)    section 165,
    (e)    sections 166 and 167, to the extent that they are not already in force,

(f)  sections 168 to 170,
(g)  section 171, to the extent that it is not already in force,
(h)  in section 172, subsections (1) to (5), except to the extent that they relate to the application to the Crown of sections 21 to 22 of the Landlord and Tenant Act 1985, as substituted or inserted by sections 152 to 154,
(i)  section 176 and Schedule 13, to the extent that they are not already in force, and
(j)  section 180, in so far as it relates to the repeals in Schedule 14 of—
    (i)  the definition of "the valuation date" in paragraph 1(1) of Schedule 6 to the Leasehold Reform, Housing and Urban Development Act 1993;
    (ii)  section 82 of the Housing Act 1996; and
    (iii)  in paragraph 18(2) of Schedule 10 to that Act, paragraph (b) and the word "and" before it.

**[3433]**

### 4  Saving and transitional provision

(1)  During the period beginning with 28th February 2005 and ending on the date on which sections 121 to 124 come into force, paragraph 4(2) of Schedule 6 to the Leasehold Reform, Housing and Urban Development Act 1993 shall have effect as if, for "participating tenants", there were substituted "persons who are participating tenants immediately before a binding contract is entered into in pursuance of the initial notice".

[(1A)  Section 126 (valuation date) shall not have effect as regards—
    (a)  notices given before 28th February 2005 under section 13 of the Leasehold Reform, Housing and Urban Development Act 1993 (notice by qualifying tenants of claim to exercise right); or
    (b)  applications made before 28th February 2005 under section 26 of that Act (applications where relevant landlord cannot be found).]

(2)  Section 168 shall not have effect as regards notices served under section 146(1) of the Law of Property Act 1925 before 28th February 2005 in respect of a breach by a tenant of any covenant or condition.

(3)  The amendments made by section 170 shall not have effect as regards notices served under section 146(1) of the Law of Property Act 1925 (restriction on re-entry or forfeiture) before 28th February 2005.

**[3434]**

**NOTES**
Para (1A): inserted, in relation to England, by the Commonhold and Leasehold Reform Act 2002 (Commencement No 5 and Saving and Transitional Provision) (Amendment) (England) Order 2005, SI 2005/193, art 2.

# RIGHTS OF RE-ENTRY AND FORFEITURE (PRESCRIBED SUM AND PERIOD) (ENGLAND) REGULATIONS 2004

(SI 2004/3086)

**NOTES**
Made: 22 November 2004.
Authority: Commonhold and Leasehold Reform Act 2002, s 167(1).
Commencement: 23 November 2004.

### 1  Citation, commencement and application

(1)  These Regulations may be cited as the Rights of Re-entry and Forfeiture (Prescribed Sum and Period) (England) Regulations 2004 and shall come into force on the day after that on which they are made.

(2)  These Regulations apply in relation to dwellings in England that are occupied under a long lease.

**[3435]**

**NOTES**
Commencement: 23 November 2004.

## 2 Prescribed sum and period

(1) The sum prescribed for the purposes of subsection (1)(a) of section 167 (failure to pay small amount for short period) of the Commonhold and Leasehold Reform Act 2002 is £350.

(2) The period prescribed for the purposes of subsection (1)(b) of that section is three years.

**[3436]**

**NOTES**

Commencement: 23 November 2004.

# LANDLORD AND TENANT (NOTICE OF RENT) (ENGLAND) REGULATIONS 2004

## (SI 2004/3096)

**NOTES**

Made: 22 November 2004.
Authority: Commonhold and Leasehold Reform Act 2002, s 166.
Commencement: 28 February 2005.

## 1 Citation, commencement, application and interpretation

(1) These Regulations may be cited as the Landlord and Tenant (Notice of Rent) (England) Regulations 2004 and shall come into force on 28th February 2005.

(2) These Regulations apply in relation to dwellings in England only.

(3) In these Regulations, "the 2002 Act" means the Commonhold and Leasehold Reform Act 2002.

**[3437]**

**NOTES**

Commencement: 28 February 2005.

## 2 Additional content and form of notice of rent due

(1) A notice under subsection (1) of section 166 of the 2002 Act (requirement to notify long leaseholders that rent is due) shall contain (in addition to the information specified in accordance with paragraphs (a) and (b) of subsection (2) of that section and, if applicable, paragraph (c) of that subsection)—

    (a)    the name of the leaseholder to whom the notice is given;

    (b)    the period to which the rent demanded is attributable;

    (c)    the name of the person to whom payment is to be made, and the address for payment;

    (d)    the name of the landlord by whom the notice is given and, if not specified pursuant to sub-paragraph (c) above, his address; and

    (e)    the information provided in the notes to the form set out in the Schedule to these Regulations.

(2) A notice under subsection (1) of section 166 of the 2002 Act shall be in the form set out in the Schedule to these Regulations.

**[3438]**

**NOTES**

Commencement: 28 February 2005.

## SCHEDULE
### FORM OF RENT DEMAND NOTICE

Regulation 2

**Commonhold and Leasehold Reform Act 2002, Section 166**
**Notice to Long Leaseholders of Rent Due**

To (*insert name(s) of leaseholder(s)*):

.............................................................. (**note 1**)

This notice is given in respect of (*address of premises to which the long lease relates*)

.........................................................................

It requires you to pay rent of £ ......... on (*insert date*) ............. (**note 2**)

This rent is payable in respect of the period (*state period*) ...................

[In accordance with the terms of your lease the amount of £ ......... is/was due on ......... (*insert date on which rent due in accordance with the lease*).] **(note 3)**

Payment should be made to (*insert name of landlord(s) or, if payment to be made to an agent, name of agent*) at (*insert address*)

.......................................................................................

.......................................................................................

This notice is given by (*insert name of landlord(s) and, if not given above, address*)

NOTES FOR LEASEHOLDERS

**Read this notice carefully. It sets out the amount of rent due from you and the date by which you must pay it. You are advised to seek help immediately, if you cannot pay, or dispute the amount. Those who can help you include a citizens' advice bureau, a housing advice centre, a law centre and a solicitor. Show this notice and a copy of your lease to whoever helps you.**

The landlord may be able to claim additional sums from you if you do not pay by the date specified in this notice. You have the right to challenge the reasonableness of any additional sums at a leasehold valuation tribunal.

Section 167 of the Commonhold and Leasehold Reform Act 2002 and regulations made under it prevent your landlord from forfeiting your lease for non-payment of rent, service charges or administration charges (or a combination of them) if the amount owed is £350 or less, or none of the unpaid amount has been outstanding for more than three years.

NOTES FOR LANDLORDS

1.     If you send this notice by post, address it to the leaseholder at the dwelling in respect of which the payment is due, unless he has notified you in writing of a different address in England and Wales at which he wishes to be given notices under section 166 of the Commonhold and Leasehold Reform Act 2002.

2.     This date must not be *either* less than 30 days or more than 60 days after the day on which this notice is given *or* before that on which the leaseholder would have been liable to make the payment in accordance with the lease.

3.     Include this statement only if the date for payment is not the same as the date determined in accordance with the lease.

**[3439]**

NOTES
   Commencement: 28 February 2005.

PART II
STATUTORY INSTRUMENTS

# LEASEHOLD HOUSES (NOTICE OF INSURANCE COVER) (ENGLAND) REGULATIONS 2004

(SI 2004/3097)

NOTES
   Made: 23 November 2004.
   Authority: Commonhold and Leasehold Reform Act 2002, s 164(5)(d), (6)(a).
   Commencement: 28 February 2005.

**1   Citation and commencement**

These Regulations may be cited as the Leasehold Houses (Notice of Insurance Cover) (England) Regulations 2004 and shall come into force on 28th February 2005.

**[3440]**

NOTES
   Commencement: 28 February 2005.

**2   Application**

These Regulations apply in respect of houses in England only.

**[3441]**

NOTES
   Commencement: 28 February 2005.

**3   Additional content of notice of cover**

A notice of cover shall specify (in addition to the particulars referred to in paragraphs (a) to (c) of subsection (5) of section 164 (insurance otherwise that with the landlord's insurer) of the Commonhold and Leasehold Reform Act 2002)—

(a) the address of the house insured under the policy;

(b) the registered office of the authorised insurer or, if the authorised insurer has no registered office, its head office;

(c) the number of the policy;

(d) the frequency with which premiums are payable under the policy;

(e) the amount of any excess payable by the tenant under the policy;

(f) where an excess is payable, whether it is payable in respect of every claim made under the policy or only in particular circumstances and, if the latter, a brief description of those circumstances;

(g) whether the policy has been renewed and, if so, the date on which it was last renewed;

(h) if the policy has not been renewed, the date on which it took effect;

(i) that the tenant is satisfied that the policy covers his or her interests; and

(j) that the tenant has no reason to believe that the policy does not cover the interests of the landlord.

[3442]

**NOTES**

Commencement: 28 February 2005.

**4  Form of notice of cover**

A notice of cover shall be in the form set out in the Schedule to these Regulations, or a form substantially to the same effect.

[3443]

**NOTES**

Commencement: 28 February 2005.

SCHEDULE
FORM OF NOTICE OF COVER
COMMONHOLD AND LEASEHOLD REFORM ACT 2002

Regulation 4

**Notice of Cover**

To [*insert name and address of landlord*]

1    I am the tenant/We are the tenants of the house at [*insert address*].

2    The house is insured under an insurance policy issued by [*insert name of insurer and its registered office or, if the insurer has no registered office, its head office*] who is an authorised insurer within the meaning of section 164 of the Commonhold and Leasehold Reform Act 2002.

3    The policy number is [*insert number*].

4    * The risks covered by the policy are: [*list the risks covered*].

OR

* The risks covered by the policy are set out in the pages attached to this notice [*attach a copy of the relevant pages from your insurance documents*].

* Delete as appropriate.

5    The amount of the cover (the sum insured) is £ [*insert amount*] and it is provided for the period beginning on [*insert date on which cover begins*] and ending on [*insert date on which cover ends*].

6    Premiums are payable [*state how frequently premiums are payable e g annually, monthly*].

7    The amount of the excess under the policy is £ [*insert amount*]. [It is payable whenever the insurer makes a payment under the policy.] [It is payable in the following circumstances:]

(*Delete this paragraph if no excess is payable. If an excess is payable every time that the insurer meets a claim under the policy, delete the third sentence. If an excess is payable only in certain circumstances, delete the second sentence and specify the circumstances here. If different amounts are payable in different circumstances, give details here.*)

8    The policy has been renewed and was last renewed on [*insert date*].

OR

The policy has not been renewed and took effect on [*insert date*].

(*Delete the statement that does not apply.*)

**9**    I am/We are satisfied that the policy covers my/our interests.

**[10**    I/We have no reason to believe that the policy does not cover your interests.]
[*signature*]
[*insert date*]

**[3444]**

**NOTES**
Commencement: 28 February 2005.
Para 10: substituted by the Leasehold Houses (Notice of Insurance Cover) (England) (Amendment)
Regulations 2005, SI 2005/177, reg 2.

# DEMOTED TENANCIES (REVIEW OF DECISIONS) (WALES) REGULATIONS 2005 (NOTE)

(SI 2005/1228 (W 86))

**NOTES**
Made: 26 April 2005.
Authority: Housing Act 1996, s 143F(3), (4).
Commencement: 30 April 2005.
These Regulations apply to Wales only. The equivalent provisions for England are in SI 2004/1679 at **[3366]**
et seq.

**[3445]**

# RIGHTS OF RE-ENTRY AND FORFEITURE (PRESCRIBED SUM AND PERIOD) (WALES) REGULATIONS 2005 (NOTE)

(SI 2005/1352 (W 100))

**NOTES**
Made: 17 May 2005.
Authority: Commonhold and Leasehold Reform Act 2002, ss 167(1), (5), 179(1).
Commencement: 31 May 2005.
These Regulations apply to Wales only. The equivalent provisions for England are in SI 2004/3086 at **[3435]**
et seq.

**[3446]**

# COMMONHOLD AND LEASEHOLD REFORM ACT 2002 (COMMENCEMENT NO 3 AND SAVING AND TRANSITIONAL PROVISION) (WALES) ORDER 2005

(SI 2005/1353 (W 101))

**NOTES**
Made: 17 May 2005.
Authority: Commonhold and Leasehold Reform Act 2002, s 181.

**1    Name, interpretation and application**

(1)    The name of this Order is the Commonhold and Leasehold Reform Act 2002 (Commencement No 3 and Saving and Transitional Provision) (Wales) Order 2005.

(2)    In this Order, unless otherwise stated, references to sections and Schedules are references to sections of, and Schedules to, the Commonhold and Leasehold Reform Act 2002.

(3)    This Order applies to Wales.

**[3447]**

**2    Provisions coming into force in Wales on 31 May 2005**

Subject to article 3, the following provisions shall come into force in Wales on 31 May 2005—

(a)    section 126,
(b)    section 157, in so far as it relates to paragraph 15 of Schedule 10,
(c)    section 164, to the extent that it is not already in force,
(d)    section 165,
(e)    sections 166 and 167, to the extent that they are not already in force,
(f)    sections 168 to 170,
(g)    section 171, to the extent that it is not already in force,
(h)    in section 172, subsections (1) to (5), except to the extent that they relate to the application to the Crown of sections 21 to 22 of the Landlord and Tenant Act 1985, as substituted or inserted by sections 152 to 154,
(i)    section 176 and Schedule 13, to the extent that they are not already in force, and
(j)    section 180, in so far as it relates to the repeals in Schedule 14 of—
    (i)    the definition of "the valuation date" in paragraph 1(1) of Schedule 6 to the Leasehold Reform, Housing and Urban Development Act 1993;
    (ii)    section 82 of the Housing Act 1996; and
    (iii)    in paragraph 18(2) of Schedule 10 to that Act, paragraph (b) and the word "and" before it.

[3448]

### 3  Saving and transitional provision

(1)    During the period beginning with 31 May 2005 and ending on the date on which sections 121 to 124 come fully into force, paragraph 4(2) of Schedule 6 to the Leasehold Reform, Housing and Urban Development Act 1993 shall have effect as if, for "participating tenants", there were substituted "persons who are participating tenants immediately before a binding contract is entered into in pursuance of the initial notice".

(2)    Section 126 shall not have effect as regards—
  (a)    notices given before 31 May 2005 under section 13 of the Leasehold Reform, Housing and Urban Development Act 1993; or
  (b)    applications made before 31 May 2005 under section 26 of that Act.

(3)    Section 168 shall not have effect as regards notices served under section 146(1) of the Law of Property Act 1925 before 31 May 2005 in respect of a breach by a tenant of any covenant or condition.

(4)    The amendments made by section 170 shall not have effect as regards notices served under section 146(1) of the Law of Property Act 1925 before 31 May 2005.

[3449]

# LEASEHOLD HOUSES (NOTICE OF INSURANCE COVER) (WALES) REGULATIONS 2005 (NOTE)

### (SI 2005/1354 (W 102))

**NOTES**
Made: 17 May 2005.
Authority: Commonhold and Leasehold Reform Act 2002, s 164(5)(d).
Commencement: 31 May 2005.
These Regulations apply to Wales only. The equivalent provisions for England are in SI 2004/3097 at [3440] et seq.

[3450]

# LANDLORD AND TENANT (NOTICE OF RENT) (WALES) REGULATIONS 2005 (NOTE)

### (SI 2005/1355 (W 103))

**NOTES**
Made: 17 May 2005.
Authority: Commonhold and Leasehold Reform Act 2002, s 166.
Commencement: 31 May 2005.
These Regulations apply to Wales only. The equivalent provisions for England are in SI 2004/3096 at [3437] et seq.

[3451]

# DISPLACED PERSONS (TEMPORARY PROTECTION) REGULATIONS 2005

(SI 2005/1379)

**NOTES**
Made: 18 May 2005.
Authority: European Communities Act 1972, s 2(2).
Commencement: 15 June 2005.

## ARRANGEMENT OF REGULATIONS

## 1   Citation and commencement

These Regulations may be cited as the Displaced Persons (Temporary Protection) Regulations 2005 and shall come into force on 15th June 2005.

**[3452]**

**NOTES**
Commencement: 15 June 2005.

## 2   Interpretation

(1)   In these Regulations—
- (a)   "the 2002 Act" means the Nationality, Immigration and Asylum Act 2002;
- (b)   "claim for asylum" has the same meaning as in section 18 of the 2002 Act;
- (c)   "consular officer" has the same meaning as in article 2 of the Consular Fees (No 2) Order 1999;
- (d)   "entry clearance" has the same meaning as in article 2 of the Consular Fees (No 2) Order 1999;
- (e)   "local authority" means—
  - (i)    in England and Wales, a district council, a county council, a county borough council, a London borough council, the Common Council of the City of London or the Council of the Isles of Scilly; and
  - (ii)   in Scotland, a council constituted under section 2 of the Local Government etc (Scotland) Act 1994;
- (f)   "registered social landlord"—
  - (i)    in England and Wales, has the same meaning as in Part I of the Housing Act 1996; and
  - (ii)   in Scotland, means a body in the register maintained under section 57 of the Housing (Scotland) Act 2001;
- (g)   "registered housing association" has the same meaning, in relation to Northern Ireland, as in Part II of the Housing (Northern Ireland) Order 1992;
- (h)   "temporary protection" means limited leave to enter or remain granted pursuant to Part 11A of the Immigration Rules; and
- (i)   "Temporary Protection Directive" means Council Directive 2001/55/EC of 20 July 2001 on minimum standards for giving temporary protection in the event of a mass influx of displaced persons and on measures promoting a balance of efforts between member States in receiving such persons and bearing the consequences thereof.

**[3453]**

**NOTES**
Commencement: 15 June 2005.

**3, 4**   (*Outside the scope of this work.*)

## 5   Housing: provision of accommodation

(1)   The Secretary of State may provide, or arrange for the provision of, accommodation for any person granted temporary protection.

(2)   Subject to paragraph (3), paragraph (1) shall cease to apply on the date when the period of mass influx of displaced persons to which the grant of temporary protection relates ends in accordance with Chapter II of the Temporary Protection Directive.

(3)   Paragraph (1) shall continue to apply for a period not exceeding 28 days from the date referred to in paragraph (2) for as long as the conditions in paragraph (4) are satisfied and the person is in the United Kingdom.

(4)   Those conditions are—
    (a)   the person's grant of temporary protection has expired; and
    (b)   the person is taking all reasonable steps to leave the United Kingdom or place himself in a position in which he is able to leave the United Kingdom, which may include co-operating with a voluntary return programme.

**[3454]**

NOTES
Commencement: 15 June 2005.

**6**   A local authority or the Northern Ireland Housing Executive may provide accommodation for those granted temporary protection in accordance with arrangements made by the Secretary of State under regulation 5.

**[3455]**

NOTES
Commencement: 15 June 2005.

**7**   When exercising his power under regulation 5 to provide, or arrange for the provision of, accommodation, the Secretary of State—
    (a)   shall have regard to the desirability, in general, of providing, or arranging for the provision of, accommodation in areas in which there is a ready supply of accommodation; and
    (b)   shall not have regard to any preference that those who have been granted temporary protection or their dependants may have as to the locality in which the accommodation is to be provided.

**[3456]**

NOTES
Commencement: 15 June 2005.

**8  Housing: requests for assistance**

(1)   This regulation applies if the Secretary of State asks—
    (a)   a local authority;
    (b)   the Northern Ireland Housing Executive;
    (c)   a registered social landlord; or
    (d)   a registered housing association in Northern Ireland
to assist him in the exercise of his power under regulation 5 to provide, or arrange for the provision of, accommodation.

(2)   The body to whom the request is made shall co-operate in giving the Secretary of State such assistance in the exercise of that power as is reasonable in the circumstances.

(3)   This regulation does not require a registered social landlord to act beyond his powers.

(4)   The Secretary of State shall pay to a body listed in regulation 8(1) any costs reasonably incurred by that body in assisting the Secretary of State to provide, or arrange for the provision of, accommodation.

**[3457]**

NOTES
Commencement: 15 June 2005.

**9**   A local authority or the Northern Ireland Housing Executive shall supply to the Secretary of State such information about its housing accommodation (whether or not occupied) as the Secretary of State may request.

**[3458]**

NOTES
Commencement: 15 June 2005.

**10   Housing: direction by the Secretary of State**

(1)   If the Secretary of State considers that a local authority or the Northern Ireland Housing Executive has suitable housing accommodation, the Secretary of State may direct the authority or the Executive to make available such accommodation as may be specified in the direction for a period so specified to the Secretary of State for the purpose of providing accommodation under regulation 5.

(2)   The Secretary of State shall pay to a body to which a direction is given costs reasonably incurred by the body in complying with the direction.

(3)   Any such direction is enforceable, on an application made on behalf of the Secretary of State, by injunction or, in Scotland, by an order under section 45(b) of the Court of Session Act 1988.

**[3459]**

**NOTES**
Commencement: 15 June 2005.

**11**   Housing accommodation shall be suitable for the purposes of regulation 10 if it is—
   (a)   unoccupied;
   (b)   likely to remain unoccupied for the foreseeable future if not made available; and
   (c)   appropriate for the accommodation of persons with temporary protection or is capable of being made so with minor work.

**[3460]**

**NOTES**
Commencement: 15 June 2005.

**12**—(1)   If the housing accommodation specified in a direction under regulation 10 is not appropriate for the accommodation of persons with temporary protection but is capable of being made so with minor work, the Secretary of State may require the directed body to secure that the work is carried out without delay.

(2)   The Secretary of State shall meet the reasonable cost of carrying out the minor work.

**[3461]**

**NOTES**
Commencement: 15 June 2005.

**13**   Before giving a direction under regulation 10, the Secretary of State shall consult—
   (a)   such local authorities, local authority associations and other persons as he thinks appropriate in respect of a direction given to a local authority;
   (b)   the Northern Ireland Housing Executive in respect of a direction given to the Executive;
   (c)   the National Assembly of Wales in respect of a direction given to a local authority in Wales; and
   (d)   the Scottish Ministers in respect of a direction given to a local authority in Scotland.

**[3462]**

**NOTES**
Commencement: 15 June 2005.

**14   Housing: rent liability**

A person with temporary protection who is provided with accommodation under regulation 5 shall be liable to make periodical payments of, or by way of, rent in respect of the accommodation provided and, in relation to any claim for housing benefit by virtue of regulation 3, such payments shall be regarded as rent for the purposes of [14(1)(a) of the Housing Benefit Regulations 2006, regulation 12(1)(a) of the Housing Benefit (Persons who have attained the qualifying age for state pension credit) Regulations 2006] and regulation 10(1)(a) of the Housing Benefit (General) Regulations (Northern Ireland) 1987.

**[3463]**

**NOTES**
Commencement: 15 June 2005.
   Words in square brackets substituted by the Housing Benefit and Council Tax Benefit (Consequential Provisions) Regulations 2006, SI 2006/217, reg 5, Sch 2, para 26.

## 15   Housing: notice to vacate

(1)   A tenancy, licence or right of occupancy granted in order to provide accommodation under regulation 5 shall end on the date specified in a notice to vacate complying with paragraph (2) regardless of when the tenancy, licence or right of occupancy could otherwise be brought to an end.

(2)   A notice to vacate complies with this paragraph if it is in writing and it specifies as the notice period a period of at least 7 days from the date of service by post of the notice to vacate.

**[3464]**

**NOTES**
   Commencement: 15 June 2005.

**16, 17**   (*Outside the scope of this work.*)

(*The Schedule contains consequential amendments outside the scope of this work.*)

# RESIDENTIAL PROPERTY TRIBUNAL (RIGHT TO BUY DETERMINATIONS) PROCEDURE (ENGLAND) REGULATIONS 2005

(SI 2005/1509)

**NOTES**
   Made: 6 June 2005.
   Authority: Housing Act 2004, Sch 13.
   Commencement: 4 July 2005.

## ARRANGEMENT OF REGULATIONS

## 1   Citation, commencement and application

(1)   These Regulations may be cited as The Residential Property Tribunal (Right to Buy Determinations) Procedure (England) Regulations 2005.

(2)   These Regulations shall come into force on 4th July 2005.

(3)   These Regulations apply to proceedings of a residential property tribunal to determine applications made under paragraph 11(4) of Schedule 5 of the Housing Act 1985 on or after 4th July 2005 in relation to dwelling-houses in England.

**[3465]**

## 2 Interpretation

In these Regulations—
"the Act" means the Housing Act 1985;
"application" means an application under paragraph 11(4) of Schedule 5 to the Act;
"case management conference" means a pre-trial review or any other meeting held by a tribunal for the purpose of managing the proceedings in respect of an application;
"landlord" means the landlord of the property;
"participant" means a party or witness or other person taking part in proceedings relating to an application or to whom an order of the tribunal is addressed;
"the property" means the dwelling-house which is the subject of the application;
"tribunal" means a residential property tribunal, and "the tribunal" in relation to an application means the tribunal by which the application is to be determined.

**[3466]**

## 3 The overriding objective

(1)  When a tribunal—
    (a)  exercises any power under these Regulations; or
    (b)  interprets any regulation,
it shall seek to give effect to the overriding objective of dealing fairly and justly with applications which it is to determine.

(2)  Dealing with an application fairly and justly includes—
    (a)  dealing with it in ways which are proportionate to the complexity of the issues and to the resources of the parties;
    (b)  ensuring, so far as practicable, that the parties are on an equal footing procedurally and are able to participate fully in the proceedings;
    (c)  assisting any party in the presentation of his case without advocating the course he should take;
    (d)  using the tribunal's special expertise effectively; and
    (e)  avoiding delay, so far as is compatible with proper consideration of the issues.

**[3467]**

## 4 Particulars of application

(1)  An application shall be in writing and shall contain the following particulars—
    (a)  the name and address of the applicant;
    (b)  the name and address of the landlord;
    (c)  the address of the property if different from the applicant's address;
    (d)  a statement of reasons for disputing the landlord's decision that paragraph 11 of Schedule 5 to the Act applies to the property.

(2)  Any of the requirements in paragraph (1) may be dispensed with or relaxed if the tribunal is satisfied that—
    (a)  the particulars and documents included with an application are sufficient to enable the application to be determined; and
    (b)  no prejudice will, or is likely to, be caused to any party to the application.

(3)  A single qualified member of the panel may exercise the power conferred by paragraph (2).

**[3468]**

## 5 Acknowledgement of application by tribunal

(1)  Where an application has been made before the end of the period mentioned in paragraph 11(4) of Schedule 5 to the Act, the tribunal shall, as soon as practicable after receiving it, send—
    (a)  an acknowledgement of receipt to the applicant;
    (b)  a copy of the application and of each document accompanying it to the landlord; and

(c)    a notice to the landlord specifying the date by which the reply mentioned in regulation 6 shall be sent.

(2)    The date specified in paragraph (1)(c) shall not be less than 14 days after the date the notice was sent.

**[3469]**

NOTES

Commencement: 4 July 2005.

## 6  Reply by landlord

(1)    A landlord who receives the copy documents mentioned in regulation 5(1)(b) shall by the date specified in the notice mentioned in regulation 5(1)(c) send to the tribunal a written reply acknowledging receipt of the copies and stating—
(a)    whether or not the landlord intends to oppose the application; and
(b)    the address to which documents should be sent for the purposes of the application.

(2)    Subject to paragraph (3) where a landlord fails to reply in accordance with paragraph (1) the tribunal may determine the application on the basis of the information available to it at the time of making the determination.

(3)    Before proceeding to a determination in accordance with paragraph (2) the tribunal shall give to the landlord not less than 14 days' notice that a determination may be so made.

(4)    Where a reply in accordance with paragraph (1) is received from the landlord after the date specified in the notice mentioned in regulation 5(1)(c) but before a determination has been made, the tribunal shall take into account the information provided by the landlord.

**[3470]**

NOTES

Commencement: 4 July 2005.

## 7  Distribution of documents by tribunal

Before determining an application, a tribunal shall take all reasonable steps to ensure that each of the parties is given—
(a)    a copy of any document relevant to the proceedings (or sufficient extracts from or particulars of the document) which has been received from any other party (other than a document already in his possession or one of which he has previously been supplied with a copy); and
(b)    a copy of any document which embodies the results of any relevant enquiries made by or for the tribunal for the purposes of the proceedings.

**[3471]**

NOTES

Commencement: 4 July 2005.

## 8  Determination without a hearing

(1)    Subject to paragraph (2) a tribunal may determine an application without an oral hearing if it has given the parties not less than 28 days' notice in writing of its intention to proceed without an oral hearing.

(2)    At any time before the application is determined—
(a)    the applicant or the landlord may request an oral hearing; or
(b)    the tribunal may give notice to the parties that it intends to hold an oral hearing.

(3)    Where a request is made or a notice given under paragraph (2) the tribunal shall give notice of a hearing in accordance with regulation 15.

(4)    A single qualified member of the panel may—
(a)    determine an application without an oral hearing;
(b)    decide whether an oral hearing is appropriate to determine an application.

**[3472]**

NOTES

Commencement: 4 July 2005.

## 9  Directions

(1)    A party may request a tribunal to give directions by order under its general power in section 230(2) of the Housing Act 2004.

(2)    Any such request may be made—

(a)    orally at a case management conference or hearing;
(b)    in writing; or
(c)    by such other means as the tribunal may permit.

(3)    The party making the request shall specify the directions which are sought and the reasons for seeking them.

(4)    Before giving a direction addressed to a participant the tribunal shall take reasonable steps to give that participant an opportunity of objecting to, or making representations about, the direction.

(5)    Where a participant to whom a direction is addressed was given no such opportunity, he may apply to the tribunal to vary it or set it aside.

(6)    A single qualified member of the panel may give a direction as to any matter which is—
    (a)    preliminary to an oral hearing; or
    (b)    preliminary or incidental to a determination which is to be made by such a member without an oral hearing.

**[3473]**

**NOTES**
Commencement: 4 July 2005.

## 10  Supply of information and documents

(1)    Subject to paragraph (5), a tribunal may make an order requiring a party to supply to the tribunal any information or document specified, or of a description specified, in the order which it is in the power of that party to supply.

(2)    A tribunal may make an order requiring a party to supply to another party copies of any documents supplied to the tribunal under paragraph (1).

(3)    A party shall supply such information, documents or copies by such time as may be specified in, or determined in accordance with, an order made under paragraph (1) or (2).

(4)    Subject to paragraph (5) a tribunal may make an order requiring any person to attend an oral hearing to give evidence and produce any documents specified, or of a description specified, in the order which it is in the power of that person to produce.

(5)    Paragraphs (1) and (4) do not apply in relation to any document which a person could not be compelled to produce on the trial of an action in a court of law in England.

(6)    A single qualified member of the panel may make an order under paragraph (1), (2) or (4) which is—
    (a)    preliminary to an oral hearing; or
    (b)    preliminary or incidental to a determination which is to be made by such a member without an oral hearing.

**[3474]**

**NOTES**
Commencement: 4 July 2005.

## 11  Failure to comply with an order to supply information and documents

(1)    Where a party has failed to comply with an order made under regulation 10(1), (2) or (4) the tribunal may make an order dismissing or allowing the whole or part of the application.

(2)    Where an application is to be determined by a single qualified member of the panel an order under paragraph (1) may be made by such a member.

**[3475]**

**NOTES**
Commencement: 4 July 2005.

## 12  Inspection of property and neighbourhood

(1)    Subject to paragraph (3) a tribunal may inspect—
    (a)    the property;
    (b)    the approach to and neighbourhood of the property;
    (c)    local transport and shopping facilities.

(2)    Subject to paragraph (3)—
    (a)    the tribunal shall give the parties an opportunity to attend an inspection; and
    (b)    a member of the [Administrative Justice and Tribunals Council] who is acting in that capacity may attend any inspection.

(3)    The making of and attendance at an inspection is subject to any necessary consent being obtained.

(4)  Subject to paragraph (5), where an inspection is to be made—
  (a)  the tribunal shall give notice to the parties of the date, time and place of the inspection; and
  (b)  such notice shall be given not less than 14 days before that date.

(5)  Any of the requirements for notice in paragraph (4) may be dispensed with or relaxed with the consent of the parties, or if the tribunal is satisfied that the parties have received sufficient notice.

(6)  Where an application is to be determined by a single qualified member of the panel, the functions of the tribunal under this regulation may be exercised by that member.

**[3476]**

**NOTES**
Commencement: 4 July 2005.
Para (2): words in square brackets substituted by the Tribunals, Courts and Enforcement Act 2007 (Transitional and Consequential Provisions) Order 2008, SI 2008/2683, art 6(1), Sch 1, paras 296, 297.
Administrative Justice and Tribunals Council: established by the Tribunals, Courts and Enforcement Act 2007, s 44, Sch 7 to replace the Council on Tribunals (abolished by s 45(1)(a) of the 2007 Act).

## 13  Case management conference

(1)  A tribunal may hold a case management conference.

(2)  The tribunal shall give the parties not less than 14 days' notice, or a shorter notice period if the parties agree, of the date, time and place of the case management conference.

(3)  At the case management conference the tribunal may order the parties to take such steps or do such things as appear to it to be necessary or desirable for securing the just, expeditious and economical determination of the application.

(4)  The tribunal may postpone or adjourn a case management conference.

(5)  A party may be represented at a case management conference.

(6)  The functions of the tribunal under this regulation may be exercised by a single qualified member of the panel.

**[3477]**

**NOTES**
Commencement: 4 July 2005.

## 14  Other case management powers

(1)  Except where these Regulations provide otherwise a tribunal may—
  (a)  extend the time appointed by or under these Regulations for doing any act even if the time appointed has expired if—
    (i)  it would not be reasonable to expect the participant in question to comply or have complied within that time; or
    (ii)  not to extend the time would result in substantial injustice;
  (b)  permit the use of telephone, video link, or any other method of communication—
    (i)  to make representations to the tribunal;
    (ii)  for the purposes of a case management conference or hearing;.
  (c)  require any participant giving written evidence to include with that evidence a signed statement that he believes the facts stated in the evidence are true;
  (d)  take any other step or make any other decision which the tribunal considers necessary or desirable for the purpose of managing the case.

(2)  A tribunal may exercise its powers under these Regulations in response to a request to do so or on its own initiative.

(3)  Where a tribunal proposes to exercise a power on its own initiative it shall give any person likely to be affected an opportunity to make representations by such date and time and in such manner as the tribunal may specify.

(4)  A single qualified member of the panel may exercise the powers under this regulation as to any matter which is—
  (a)  preliminary to an oral hearing; or
  (b)  preliminary or incidental to a determination which is to be made by such a member without an oral hearing.

**[3478]**

**NOTES**
Commencement: 4 July 2005.

## 15  Notice of hearing

(1)  A hearing shall be on the date and at the time and place appointed by the tribunal.

(2)   The tribunal shall give notice to the parties of the appointed date, time and place of the hearing.

(3)   Subject to paragraph (4) notice under paragraph (2) shall be given not less than 21 days (or such shorter period as the parties may agree) before the appointed date.

(4)   In exceptional circumstances the tribunal may, without the agreement of the parties, give less than 21 days' notice of the appointed date, time and place of the hearing; but any such notice must be given as soon as practicable before the appointed date and the notice must specify what the exceptional circumstances are.

**[3479]**

**NOTES**
   Commencement: 4 July 2005.

### 16   Postponement of hearing

(1)   Subject to paragraph (3) a tribunal may postpone an oral hearing.

(2)   The tribunal shall give reasonable notice of any postponed hearing to the parties.

(3)   Where postponement has been requested by a party the tribunal shall not postpone the hearing except where it considers it is reasonable to do so having regard to—
   (a)   the grounds for the request;
   (b)   the time at which the request is made; and
   (c)   the convenience of the parties.

(4)   A single qualified member of the panel may exercise the tribunal's powers in this regulation.

**[3480]**

**NOTES**
   Commencement: 4 July 2005.

### 17   Hearing

(1)   At a hearing—
   (a)   the tribunal shall determine the procedure (subject to these regulations);
   (b)   any person appearing before the tribunal may do so either in person or by his representative;
   (c)   the parties shall be entitled to give evidence, to call witnesses, to question any witnesses, and to address the tribunal both on the evidence and generally on the subject matter of the application;
   (d)   the tribunal may receive evidence of any fact which seems to it to be relevant, even if the evidence would be inadmissible in proceedings before a court of law, and must not refuse to admit any evidence presented in due time which is admissible at law and is relevant and necessary and has not been improperly obtained; and
   (e)   the tribunal may limit the questioning of any witness.

(2)   At any hearing the tribunal may, if it is satisfied that it is just and reasonable to do so, permit a party to rely on reasons not previously stated, and to adduce any evidence not available at the time the landlord took the disputed decision.

(3)   A tribunal may require any witness to give evidence on oath and for that purpose may administer an oath.

(4)   A tribunal may adjourn a hearing but if this is done at the request of a party it must be satisfied it is reasonable to do so having regard to—
   (a)   the grounds for the request;
   (b)   the time at which the request is made; and
   (c)   the convenience of the parties.

**[3481]**

**NOTES**
   Commencement: 4 July 2005.

### 18   Hearing in public or private

(1)   A hearing shall be in public except—
   (a)   where the tribunal is satisfied that in the circumstances of the case and subject to the overriding objective the hearing should be held in private; or
   (b)   where a party has requested in writing that the hearing be in private and the Tribunal is satisfied that there is no important public interest consideration that calls for the public to be present.

(2)   The tribunal may decide under paragraph (1) that part only of the hearing shall be in private or that information about the proceedings before the tribunal, the names and identifying characteristics of persons concerned in the proceedings or specified evidence given in the proceedings shall not be made public.

[3482]

**NOTES**
Commencement: 4 July 2005.

## 19   Failure of a party to appear at a hearing

Where a party fails to appear at a hearing the tribunal may proceed with the hearing if it is satisfied that—

(a)   notice has been given to that party in accordance with these Regulations; and
(b)   there is no good reason for the failure to appear.

[3483]

**NOTES**
Commencement: 4 July 2005.

## 20   Decisions of the Tribunal

(1)   This regulation applies to a decision on the determination of an application by—

(a)   a tribunal; or
(b)   a single qualified member of the panel.

(2)   If a hearing was held, the decision may be given orally at the end of the hearing.

(3)   A decision shall, in every case, be recorded in a document as soon as practicable after the decision has been made.

(4)   A decision given or recorded in accordance with paragraphs (2) or (3) need not record the reasons for the decision.

(5)   Where the document mentioned in paragraph (3) does not record the reasons for the decision, they shall be recorded in a separate document as soon as practicable after the decision has been recorded.

(6)   A document recording a decision or the reasons for a decision ("a decision document"), shall be signed and dated by an appropriate person.

(7)   An appropriate person may, by means of a certificate signed and dated by him, correct any clerical mistakes in a decision document or any errors arising in it from an accidental slip or omission.

(8)   In this regulation "appropriate person" means—

(a)   where an application was determined by a single qualified member of the panel—
    (i)   that member; or
    (ii)   in the event of his absence or incapacity, another member of the panel who was appointed by the Lord Chancellor;
(b)   in any other case—
    (i)   the Chair of the tribunal; or
    (ii)   in the event of his absence or incapacity, another member of the tribunal.

(9)   A copy of any decision document, and a copy of any correction certified under paragraph (7) shall be sent to each party.

[3484]

**NOTES**
Commencement: 4 July 2005.

## 21   Costs

(1)   A tribunal shall not make a determination under paragraph 12 of Schedule 13 to the Housing Act 2004 ("a costs determination") in respect of a party without first giving that party an opportunity of making representations to the tribunal.

(2)   Where an application is determined by a single qualified member of the panel he may make a costs determination in respect of a party to the proceedings on the application.

[3485]

**NOTES**
Commencement: 4 July 2005.

## 22  Assistance to participants

(1)  If a participant is unable to read or speak or understand the English language, the tribunal shall make arrangements for him to be provided, free of charge, with the necessary translations and assistance of an interpreter to enable his effective participation in the proceedings.

(2)  If a participant is without hearing or speech, the tribunal shall make arrangements for him to be provided, free of charge, with the services of a sign language interpreter, lip speaker, or palantypist, to enable his effective participation in the proceedings.

(3)  A participant shall be entitled to assistance under this regulation whether or not he is represented.

(4)  A participant who requires assistance under this regulation shall at the earliest opportunity notify the requirement to the tribunal.

**[3486]**

**NOTES**
Commencement: 4 July 2005.

## 23  Notice and documents

(1)  Any document or notice required or authorised by these Regulations to be given or sent to any person shall be duly given or sent to that person—
- (a)   if it is sent to his proper address by first class post or by special delivery, or by recorded delivery;
- (b)   if it is sent by any other means to his proper address;
- (c)   subject to paragraph (2), if with his written consent it is sent to him—
  - (i)   by fax, email or other electronic communication which produces a text received in legible form;
  - (ii)   by a private document delivery service.

(2)  For the purposes of paragraph (1)(c) a legal representative of a participant shall be deemed to have given written consent if the reference or address for the means of fax or electronic communication or private document delivery system is shown on the legal representative's notepaper.

(3)  A person's proper address for the purposes of paragraph (1) is—
- (a)   in the case of a tribunal, the address of the office of the tribunal;
- (b)   in the case of an incorporated company or other body registered in the United Kingdom, the address of the registered or principal office of the company or body;
- (c)   in the case of any other person the usual or last known address of that person.

**[3487]**

**NOTES**
Commencement: 4 July 2005.

## 24  Time

Where the time specified by these Regulations for doing any act expires on a Saturday or Sunday or public holiday, it shall be treated as expiring on the next following day which is not a Saturday or Sunday or public holiday.

**[3488]**

**NOTES**
Commencement: 4 July 2005.

## 25  Frivolous and vexatious applications

(1)  Subject to paragraph (2), where it appears to a tribunal that an application is frivolous or vexatious or otherwise an abuse of process, the tribunal may dismiss the application in whole or in part.

(2)  Before dismissing an application under paragraph (1) the tribunal shall give notice to the applicant in accordance with paragraph (3).

(3)  Any notice under paragraph (2) shall state—
- (a)   that the tribunal is minded to dismiss the application;
- (b)   the grounds on which it is minded to dismiss the application;
- (c)   the date (being not less than 21 days after the date that the notice was sent) before which the applicant may request to appear before and be heard by the tribunal on the question whether the application should be dismissed.

(4)  An application may not be dismissed under paragraph (1) unless—

   (a)    the applicant makes no request to the tribunal before the date mentioned in paragraph (3)(c) or

   (b)    where the applicant makes such a request, the tribunal has heard the applicant and the landlord, or such of them as attend the hearing, on the question of the dismissal of the application.

**[3489]**

**NOTES**

Commencement: 4 July 2005.

## 26  Persons entitled to be present at a hearing held in private

(1)    Subject to paragraphs (2) and (3) the following persons shall be entitled to attend a hearing held in private and to be present at the tribunal's deliberations with respect to the determination of the application—

   (a)    a president or chair or other panel member not forming part of the tribunal for the purpose of the hearing;

   (b)    ...

   (c)    the staff of the Tribunal Service;

   (d)    any other person permitted by the tribunal with the consent of the parties.

(2)    None of the persons specified in paragraph (1) may take any part in the hearing or such deliberations.

(3)    The tribunal may admit persons to a hearing held in private on such terms and conditions as it considers appropriate.

**[3490]**

**NOTES**

Commencement: 4 July 2005.

Para (1): sub-para (b) revoked by the Tribunals, Courts and Enforcement Act 2007 (Transitional and Consequential Provisions) Order 2008, SI 2008/2683, art 6(1), Sch 1, paras 296, 298.

## 27  Irregularities

Any irregularity resulting from failure by a party to comply with any provision of these Regulations or of any direction of the tribunal before the tribunal has reached its decision shall not of itself render the proceedings void.

**[3491]**

**NOTES**

Commencement: 4 July 2005.

## 28  Signature of documents

Where these Regulations require a document to be signed, that requirement shall be satisfied—

   (a)    if the signature is either written or produced by computer or other mechanical means; and

   (b)    the name of the signatory appears beneath the signature in such a way that he may be identified.

**[3492]**

**NOTES**

Commencement: 4 July 2005.

# REGULATORY REFORM (FIRE SAFETY) ORDER 2005

(SI 2005/1541)

**NOTES**

Made: 7 June 2005.

Authority: Regulatory Reform Act 2001, s 1.

Commencement: 8 June 2005 (arts 1, 52(1)(a)); 1 October 2006 (otherwise): see art 1(1)–(3) at **[3493]**.

Transfer of Functions: as to the transfer of certain functions of the Secretary of State under this order, so far as they are exercisable in or as regards Wales, to the National Assembly for Wales, see the National Assembly for Wales (Transfer of Functions) Order 2006, SI 2006/1458, arts 2(b), 3.

## ARRANGEMENT OF ARTICLES

### PART I
### GENERAL

### PART 2
### FIRE SAFETY DUTIES

### PART 3
### ENFORCEMENT

### PART 4
### OFFENCES AND APPEALS

### PART 5
### MISCELLANEOUS

PART II
STATUTORY INSTRUMENTS

PART 1
GENERAL

## 1  Citation, commencement and extent

(1)    This Order may be cited as the Regulatory Reform (Fire Safety) Order 2005 and shall come into force in accordance with paragraphs (2) and (3).

(2)    This article and article 52(1)(a) shall come into force on the day after the day on which this Order is made.

(3)    The remaining provisions of this Order shall come into force on [1st October 2006].

(4)    This Order extends to England and Wales only.

**[3493]**

**NOTES**
    Commencement: 8 June 2005.
    Para (3): words in square brackets substituted by the Regulatory Reform (Fire Safety) Subordinate Provisions Order 2006, SI 2006/484, art 2.

## 2  Interpretation

In this Order—
    "alterations notice" has the meaning given by article 29;
    "approved classification and labelling guide" means the Approved Guide to the Classification and Labelling of Dangerous Substances and Dangerous Preparations (5th edition) approved by the Health and Safety Commission on 16th April 2002;
    "the CHIP Regulations" means the Chemicals (Hazard Information and Packaging for Supply) Regulations 2002;
    "child" means a person who is not over compulsory school age, construed in accordance with section 8 of the Education Act 1996;
    "dangerous substance" means—
        (a)    a substance or preparation which meets the criteria in the approved classification and labelling guide for classification as a substance or preparation which is explosive, oxidising, extremely flammable, highly flammable or flammable, whether or not that substance or preparation is classified under the CHIP Regulations;
        (b)    a substance or preparation which because of its physico-chemical or chemical properties and the way it is used or is present in or on premises creates a risk; and
        (c)    any dust, whether in the form of solid particles or fibrous materials or otherwise, which can form an explosive mixture with air or an explosive atmosphere;
    "domestic premises" means premises occupied as a private dwelling (including any garden, yard, garage, outhouse, or other appurtenance of such premises which is not used in common by the occupants of more than one such dwelling);
    "employee" means a person who is or is treated as an employee for the purposes of the Health and Safety at Work etc Act 1974 and related expressions are to be construed accordingly;
    "enforcement notice" has the meaning given by article 30;
    "enforcing authority" has the meaning given by article 25;
    "explosive atmosphere" means a mixture, under atmospheric conditions, of air and one or more dangerous substances in the form of gases, vapours, mists or dusts in which, after ignition has occurred, combustion spreads to the entire unburned mixture;
    "fire and rescue authority" means a fire and rescue authority under the Fire and Rescue Services Act 2004;
    "fire inspector" means an inspector or assistant inspector appointed under section 28 of the Fire and Rescue Services Act 2004;
    "general fire precautions" has the meaning given by article 4;
    "hazard", in relation to a dangerous substance, means the physico-chemical or chemical property of that substance which has the potential to give rise to fire affecting the safety of a person, and references in this Order to "hazardous" are to be construed accordingly;
    "inspector" means an inspector appointed under article 26 or a fire inspector;
    "licensing authority" has the meaning given by article 42(3);

"normal ship-board activities" include the repair of a ship, save repair when carried out in dry dock;

"owner" means the person for the time being receiving the rackrent of the premises in connection with which the word is used, whether on his own account or as agent or trustee for another person, or who would so receive the rackrent if the premises were let at a rackrent;

"personal protective equipment" means all equipment which is intended to be worn or held by a person in or on premises and which protects that person against one or more risks to his safety, and any addition or accessory designed to meet that objective;

"place of safety" in relation to premises, means a safe area beyond the premises.

"premises" includes any place and, in particular, includes—

    (a)      any workplace;

    (b)      any vehicle, vessel, aircraft or hovercraft;

    (c)      any installation on land (including the foreshore and other land intermittently covered by water), and any other installation (whether floating, or resting on the seabed or the subsoil thereof, or resting on other land covered with water or the subsoil thereof); and

    (d)      any tent or movable structure;

"preparation" means a mixture or solution of two or more substances;

"preventive and protective measures" means the measures which have been identified by the responsible person in consequence of a risk assessment as the general fire precautions he needs to take to comply with the requirements and prohibitions imposed on him by or under this Order;

"prohibition notice" has the meaning given by article 31;

"public road" means a highway maintainable at public expense within the meaning of section 329 of the Highways Act 1980;

"rackrent" in relation to premises, means a rent that is not less than two-thirds of the rent at which the property might reasonably be expected to be let from year to year, free from all usual tenant's rates and taxes, and deducting from it the probable average cost of the repairs, insurance and other expenses (if any) necessary to maintain the property in a state to command such rent;

"the relevant local authority", in relation to premises, means—

    (a)      if the premises are in Greater London but are not in the City of London, the London Borough in the area of which the premises are situated;

    (b)      if the premises are in the City of London, the Common Council of the City of London;

    (c)      if the premises are in England in a metropolitan county, the district council in the area of which the premises are situated;

    (d)      if the premises are in England but are not in Greater London or a metropolitan county—

        (i)      the county council in the area of which the premises are situated; or

        (ii)      if there is no county council in the area of which the premises are situated, the district council in that area;

    (e)      if the premises are in Wales, the county council or county borough council in the area of which the premises are situated;

"relevant persons" means—

    (a)      any person (including the responsible person) who is or may be lawfully on the premises; and

    (b)      any person in the immediate vicinity of the premises who is at risk from a fire on the premises,

but does not include a fire-fighter who is carrying out his duties in relation to a function of a fire and rescue authority under section 7, 8 or 9 of the Fire and Rescue Services Act 2004 (fire-fighting, road traffic accidents and other emergencies), other than in relation to a function under section 7(2)(d), 8(2)(d) or 9(3)(d) of that Act;

"responsible person" has the meaning given by article 3;

"risk" means the risk to the safety of persons from fire;

"risk assessment" means the assessment required by article 9(1);

"safety" means the safety of persons in respect of harm caused by fire; and "safe" shall be interpreted accordingly;

"safety data sheet" means a safety data sheet within the meaning of regulation 5 of the CHIP Regulations;

"ship" includes every description of vessel used in navigation;

"special, technical and organisational measures" include—

    (a)      technical means of supervision;

    (b)      connecting devices;

    (c)      control and protection systems;

    (d)      engineering controls and solutions;

    (e)    equipment;
    (f)    materials;
    (g)    protective systems; and
    (h)    warning and other communication systems;
"substance" means any natural or artificial substance whether in solid or liquid form or in the form of a gas or vapour;
"visiting force" means any such body, contingent, or detachment of the forces of any country as is a visiting force for the purposes of any of the provisions of the Visiting Forces Act 1952;
"workplace" means any premises or parts of premises, not being domestic premises, used for the purposes of an employer's undertaking and which are made available to an employee of the employer as a place of work and includes—
    (a)    any place within the premises to which such employee has access while at work; and
    (b)    any room, lobby, corridor, staircase, road, or other place—
        (i)    used as a means of access to or egress from that place of work; or
        (ii)    where facilities are provided for use in connection with that place of work, other than a public road;
"young person" means any person who has not attained the age of 18.

**[3494]**

**NOTES**
Commencement: 1 October 2006.

## 3  Meaning of "responsible person"

In this Order "responsible person" means—
    (a)    in relation to a workplace, the employer, if the workplace is to any extent under his control;
    (b)    in relation to any premises not falling within paragraph (a)—
        (i)    the person who has control of the premises (as occupier or otherwise) in connection with the carrying on by him of a trade, business or other undertaking (for profit or not); or
        (ii)    the owner, where the person in control of the premises does not have control in connection with the carrying on by that person of a trade, business or other undertaking.

**[3495]**

**NOTES**
Commencement: 1 October 2006.

## 4  Meaning of "general fire precautions"

(1)    In this Order "general fire precautions" in relation to premises means, subject to paragraph (2)—
    (a)    measures to reduce the risk of fire on the premises and the risk of the spread of fire on the premises;
    (b)    measures in relation to the means of escape from the premises;
    (c)    measures for securing that, at all material times, the means of escape can be safely and effectively used;
    (d)    measures in relation to the means for fighting fires on the premises;
    (e)    measures in relation to the means for detecting fire on the premises and giving warning in case of fire on the premises; and
    (f)    measures in relation to the arrangements for action to be taken in the event of fire on the premises, including—
        (i)    measures relating to the instruction and training of employees; and
        (ii)    measures to mitigate the effects of the fire.

(2)    The precautions referred to in paragraph (1) do not include special, technical or organisational measures required to be taken or observed in any workplace in connection with the carrying on of any work process, where those measures—
    (a)    are designed to prevent or reduce the likelihood of fire arising from such a work process or reduce its intensity; and
    (b)    are required to be taken or observed to ensure compliance with any requirement of the relevant statutory provisions within the meaning given by section 53(1) of the Health and Safety at Work etc 1974.

(3)    In paragraph (2) "work process" means all aspects of work involving, or in connection with—

(a)   the use of plant or machinery; or

(b)   the use or storage of any dangerous substance.

**[3496]**

**NOTES**
   Commencement: 1 October 2006.

## 5   Duties under this Order

(1)   Where the premises are a workplace, the responsible person must ensure that any duty imposed by articles 8 to 22 or by regulations made under article 24 is complied with in respect of those premises.

(2)   Where the premises are not a workplace, the responsible person must ensure that any duty imposed by articles 8 to 22 or by regulations made under article 24 is complied with in respect of those premises, so far as the requirements relate to matters within his control.

(3)   Any duty imposed by articles 8 to 22 or by regulations made under article 24 on the responsible person in respect of premises shall also be imposed on every person, other than the responsible person referred to in paragraphs (1) and (2), who has, to any extent, control of those premises so far as the requirements relate to matters within his control.

(4)   Where a person has, by virtue of any contract or tenancy, an obligation of any extent in relation to—

(a)   the maintenance or repair of any premises, including anything in or on premises; or

(b)   the safety of any premises,

that person is to be treated, for the purposes of paragraph (3), as being a person who has control of the premises to the extent that his obligation so extends.

(5)   Articles 8 to 22 and any regulations made under article 24 only require the taking or observance of general fire precautions in respect of relevant persons.

**[3497]**

**NOTES**
   Commencement: 1 October 2006.

## 6   Application to premises

(1)   This Order does not apply in relation to—

(a)   domestic premises, except to the extent mentioned in article 31(10);

(b)   an offshore installation within the meaning of regulation 3 of the Offshore Installation and Pipeline Works (Management and Administration) Regulations 1995;

(c)   a ship, in respect of the normal ship-board activities of a ship's crew which are carried out solely by the crew under the direction of the master;

(d)   fields, woods or other land forming part of an agricultural or forestry undertaking but which is not inside a building and is situated away from the undertaking's main buildings;

(e)   an aircraft, locomotive or rolling stock, trailer or semi-trailer used as a means of transport or a vehicle for which a licence is in force under the Vehicle Excise and Registration Act 1994 or a vehicle exempted from duty under that Act;

(f)   a mine within the meaning of section 180 of the Mines and Quarries Act 1954, other than any building on the surface at a mine;

(g)   a borehole site to which the Borehole Sites and Operations Regulations 1995 apply.

(2)   Subject to the preceding paragraph of this article, this Order applies in relation to any premises.

**[3498]**

**NOTES**
   Commencement: 1 October 2006.

## 7   Disapplication of certain provisions

(1)   Articles 9(4) and (5) and 19(2) do not apply in relation to occasional work or short-term work involving work regulated as not being harmful, damaging, or dangerous to young people in a family undertaking.

(2)   Articles 9(2), 12, 16, 19(3) and 22(2) do not apply in relation to the use of means of transport by land, water or air where the use of means of transport is regulated by international agreements and the European Community directives giving effect to them and in so far as the use of means of transport falls within the disapplication in article 1.2(e) of Council Directive 1999/92/EC

on minimum requirements for improving the safety and health of workers potentially at risk from explosive atmospheres, except for any means of transport intended for use in a potentially explosive atmosphere.

(3)   Articles 19 and 21 impose duties only on responsible persons who are employers.

(4)   The requirements of articles 8 to 23, or of any regulations made under article 24, do not have effect to the extent that they would prevent any of the following from carrying out their duties—

   (a)   any member of the armed forces of the Crown or of any visiting force;
   (b)   any constable or any member of a police force not being a constable;
   (c)   any member of any emergency service.

(5)   Without prejudice to paragraph (4), article 14(2)(f) does not apply to any premises constituting, or forming part of, a prison within the meaning of the Prison Act 1952 or constituting, or forming part of, a remand centre, detention centre or youth custody centre provided by the Secretary of State under section 43 of that Act or any part of any other premises used for keeping persons in lawful custody or detention.

(6)   Where paragraph (4) or (5) applies, the safety of relevant persons must nevertheless be ensured so far as is possible.

**[3499]**

**NOTES**
Commencement: 1 October 2006.

## PART 2
## FIRE SAFETY DUTIES

**8   Duty to take general fire precautions**

   (1)   The responsible person must—
   (a)   take such general fire precautions as will ensure, so far as is reasonably practicable, the safety of any of his employees; and
   (b)   in relation to relevant persons who are not his employees, take such general fire precautions as may reasonably be required in the circumstances of the case to ensure that the premises are safe.

**[3500]**

**NOTES**
Commencement: 1 October 2006.

**9   Risk assessment**

   (1)   The responsible person must make a suitable and sufficient assessment of the risks to which relevant persons are exposed for the purpose of identifying the general fire precautions he needs to take to comply with the requirements and prohibitions imposed on him by or under this Order.

   (2)   Where a dangerous substance is or is liable to be present in or on the premises, the risk assessment must include consideration of the matters set out in Part 1 of Schedule 1.

   (3)   Any such assessment must be reviewed by the responsible person regularly so as to keep it up to date and particularly if—
   (a)   there is reason to suspect that it is no longer valid; or
   (b)   there has been a significant change in the matters to which it relates including when the premises, special, technical and organisational measures, or organisation of the work undergo significant changes, extensions, or conversions,

and where changes to an assessment are required as a result of any such review, the responsible person must make them.

   (4)   The responsible person must not employ a young person unless he has, in relation to risks to young persons, made or reviewed an assessment in accordance with paragraphs (1) and (5).

   (5)   In making or reviewing the assessment, the responsible person who employs or is to employ a young person must take particular account of the matters set out in Part 2 of Schedule 1.

   (6)   As soon as practicable after the assessment is made or reviewed, the responsible person must record the information prescribed by paragraph (7) where—
   (a)   he employs five or more employees;
   (b)   a licence under an enactment is in force in relation to the premises; or
   (c)   an alterations notice requiring this is in force in relation to the premises.

   (7)   The prescribed information is—
   (a)   the significant findings of the assessment, including the measures which have been or will be taken by the responsible person pursuant to this Order; and

    (b)     any group of persons identified by the assessment as being especially at risk.

  (8)    No new work activity involving a dangerous substance may commence unless—
    (a)     the risk assessment has been made; and
    (b)     the measures required by or under this Order have been implemented.

                                                                  **[3501]**

**NOTES**
  Commencement: 1 October 2006.

## 10   Principles of prevention to be applied

Where the responsible person implements any preventive and protective measures he must do so on the basis of the principles specified in Part 3 of Schedule 1.

                                                                  **[3502]**

**NOTES**
  Commencement: 1 October 2006.

## 11   Fire safety arrangements

  (1)    The responsible person must make and give effect to such arrangements as are appropriate, having regard to the size of his undertaking and the nature of its activities, for the effective planning, organisation, control, monitoring and review of the preventive and protective measures.

  (2)    The responsible person must record the arrangements referred to in paragraph (1) where—
    (a)     he employs five or more employees;
    (b)     a licence under an enactment is in force in relation to the premises; or
    (c)     an alterations notice requiring a record to be made of those arrangements is in force in relation to the premises.

                                                                    **[3503]**

**NOTES**
  Commencement: 1 October 2006.

## 12   Elimination or reduction of risks from dangerous substances

  (1)    Where a dangerous substance is present in or on the premises, the responsible person must ensure that risk to relevant persons related to the presence of the substance is either eliminated or reduced so far as is reasonably practicable.

  (2)    In complying with his duty under paragraph (1), the responsible person must, so far as is reasonably practicable, replace a dangerous substance, or the use of a dangerous substance, with a substance or process which either eliminates or reduces the risk to relevant persons.

  (3)    Where it is not reasonably practicable to eliminate risk pursuant to paragraphs (1) and (2), the responsible person must, so far as is reasonably practicable, apply measures consistent with the risk assessment and appropriate to the nature of the activity or operation, including the measures specified in Part 4 of Schedule 1 to this Order to—
    (a)     control the risk, and
    (b)     mitigate the detrimental effects of a fire.

  (4)    The responsible person must—
    (a)     arrange for the safe handling, storage and transport of dangerous substances and waste containing dangerous substances; and
    (b)     ensure that any conditions necessary pursuant to this Order for ensuring the elimination or reduction of risk are maintained.

                                                                    **[3504]**

**NOTES**
  Commencement: 1 October 2006.

## 13   Fire-fighting and fire detection

  (1)    Where necessary (whether due to the features of the premises, the activity carried on there, any hazard present or any other relevant circumstances) in order to safeguard the safety of relevant persons, the responsible person must ensure that—
    (a)     the premises are, to the extent that it is appropriate, equipped with appropriate fire-fighting equipment and with fire detectors and alarms; and
    (b)     any non-automatic fire-fighting equipment so provided is easily accessible, simple to use and indicated by signs.

(2)   For the purposes of paragraph (1) what is appropriate is to be determined having regard to the dimensions and use of the premises, the equipment contained on the premises, the physical and chemical properties of the substances likely to be present and the maximum number of persons who may be present at any one time.

(3)   The responsible person must, where necessary—
(a)   take measures for fire-fighting in the premises, adapted to the nature of the activities carried on there and the size of the undertaking and of the premises concerned;
(b)   nominate competent persons to implement those measures and ensure that the number of such persons, their training and the equipment available to them are adequate, taking into account the size of, and the specific hazards involved in, the premises concerned; and
(c)   arrange any necessary contacts with external emergency services, particularly as regards fire-fighting, rescue work, first-aid and emergency medical care.

(4)   A person is to be regarded as competent for the purposes of paragraph (3)(b) where he has sufficient training and experience or knowledge and other qualities to enable him properly to implement the measures referred to in that paragraph.

**[3505]**

**NOTES**
Commencement: 1 October 2006.

## 14   Emergency routes and exits

(1)   Where necessary in order to safeguard the safety of relevant persons, the responsible person must ensure that routes to emergency exits from premises and the exits themselves are kept clear at all times.

(2)   The following requirements must be complied with in respect of premises where necessary (whether due to the features of the premises, the activity carried on there, any hazard present or any other relevant circumstances) in order to safeguard the safety of relevant persons—
(a)   emergency routes and exits must lead as directly as possible to a place of safety;
(b)   in the event of danger, it must be possible for persons to evacuate the premises as quickly and as safely as possible;
(c)   the number, distribution and dimensions of emergency routes and exits must be adequate having regard to the use, equipment and dimensions of the premises and the maximum number of persons who may be present there at any one time;
(d)   emergency doors must open in the direction of escape;
(e)   sliding or revolving doors must not be used for exits specifically intended as emergency exits;
(f)   emergency doors must not be so locked or fastened that they cannot be easily and immediately opened by any person who may require to use them in an emergency;
(g)   emergency routes and exits must be indicated by signs; and
(h)   emergency routes and exits requiring illumination must be provided with emergency lighting of adequate intensity in the case of failure of their normal lighting.

**[3506]**

**NOTES**
Commencement: 1 October 2006.

## 15   Procedures for serious and imminent danger and for danger areas

(1)   The responsible person must—
(a)   establish and, where necessary, give effect to appropriate procedures, including safety drills, to be followed in the event of serious and imminent danger to relevant persons;
(b)   nominate a sufficient number of competent persons to implement those procedures in so far as they relate to the evacuation of relevant persons from the premises; and
(c)   ensure that no relevant person has access to any area to which it is necessary to restrict access on grounds of safety, unless the person concerned has received adequate safety instruction.

(2)   Without prejudice to the generality of paragraph (1)(a), the procedures referred to in that sub-paragraph must—
(a)   so far as is practicable, require any relevant persons who are exposed to serious and imminent danger to be informed of the nature of the hazard and of the steps taken or to be taken to protect them from it;
(b)   enable the persons concerned (if necessary by taking appropriate steps in the absence of guidance or instruction and in the light of their knowledge and the technical means at their disposal) to stop work and immediately proceed to a place of safety in the event of their being exposed to serious, imminent and unavoidable danger; and

(c)    save in exceptional cases for reasons duly substantiated (which cases and reasons must be specified in those procedures), require the persons concerned to be prevented from resuming work in any situation where there is still a serious and imminent danger.

(3)    A person is to be regarded as competent for the purposes of paragraph (1) where he has sufficient training and experience or knowledge and other qualities to enable him properly to implement the evacuation procedures referred to in that paragraph.

**[3507]**

---

**NOTES**

Commencement: 1 October 2006.

## 16   Additional emergency measures in respect of dangerous substances

(1)    Subject to paragraph (4), in order to safeguard the safety of relevant persons arising from an accident, incident or emergency related to the presence of a dangerous substance in or on the premises, the responsible person must ensure that—
- (a)    information on emergency arrangements is available, including—
  - (i)    details of relevant work hazards and hazard identification arrangements; and
  - (ii)    specific hazards likely to arise at the time of an accident, incident or emergency;
- (b)    suitable warning and other communication systems are established to enable an appropriate response, including remedial actions and rescue operations, to be made immediately when such an event occurs;
- (c)    where necessary, before any explosion conditions are reached, visual or audible warnings are given and relevant persons withdrawn; and
- (d)    where the risk assessment indicates it is necessary, escape facilities are provided and maintained to ensure that, in the event of danger, relevant persons can leave endangered places promptly and safely.

(2)    Subject to paragraph (4), the responsible person must ensure that the information required by article 15(1)(a) and paragraph (1)(a) of this article, together with information on the matters referred to in paragraph (1)(b) and (d) is—
- (a)    made available to relevant accident and emergency services to enable those services, whether internal or external to the premises, to prepare their own response procedures and precautionary measures; and
- (b)    displayed at the premises, unless the results of the risk assessment make this unnecessary.

(3)    Subject to paragraph (4), in the event of a fire arising from an accident, incident or emergency related to the presence of a dangerous substance in or on the premises, the responsible person must ensure that—
- (a)    immediate steps are taken to—
  - (i)    mitigate the effects of the fire;
  - (ii)    restore the situation to normal; and
  - (iii)    inform those relevant persons who may be affected; and
- (b)    only those persons who are essential for the carrying out of repairs and other necessary work are permitted in the affected area and they are provided with—
  - (i)    appropriate personal protective equipment and protective clothing; and
  - (ii)    any necessary specialised safety equipment and plant,
  which must be used until the situation is restored to normal.

(4)    Paragraphs (1) to (3) do not apply where—
- (a)    the results of the risk assessment show that, because of the quantity of each dangerous substance in or on the premises, there is only a slight risk to relevant persons; and
- (b)    the measures taken by the responsible person to comply with his duty under article 12 are sufficient to control that risk.

**[3508]**

---

**NOTES**

Commencement: 1 October 2006.

## 17   Maintenance

(1)    Where necessary in order to safeguard the safety of relevant persons the responsible person must ensure that the premises and any facilities, equipment and devices provided in respect of the premises under this Order or, subject to paragraph (6), under any other enactment, including any enactment repealed or revoked by this Order, are subject to a suitable system of maintenance and are maintained in an efficient state, in efficient working order and in good repair.

(2)    Where the premises form part of a building, the responsible person may make arrangements with the occupier of any other premises forming part of the building for the purpose of ensuring that the requirements of paragraph (1) are met.

(3) Paragraph (2) applies even if the other premises are not premises to which this Order applies.

(4) The occupier of the other premises must co-operate with the responsible person for the purposes of paragraph (2).

(5) Where the occupier of the other premises is not also the owner of those premises, the references to the occupier in paragraphs (2) and (4) are to be taken to be references to both the occupier and the owner.

(6) Paragraph (1) only applies to facilities, equipment and devices provided under other enactments where they are provided in connection with general fire precautions.

**[3509]**

**NOTES**
Commencement: 1 October 2006.

## 18 Safety assistance

(1) The responsible person must, subject to paragraphs (6) and (7), appoint one or more competent persons to assist him in undertaking the preventive and protective measures.

(2) Where the responsible person appoints persons in accordance with paragraph (1), he must make arrangements for ensuring adequate co-operation between them.

(3) The responsible person must ensure that the number of persons appointed under paragraph (1), the time available for them to fulfil their functions and the means at their disposal are adequate having regard to the size of the premises, the risks to which relevant persons are exposed and the distribution of those risks throughout the premises.

(4) The responsible person must ensure that—
    (a) any person appointed by him in accordance with paragraph (1) who is not in his employment—
        (i) is informed of the factors known by him to affect, or suspected by him of affecting, the safety of any other person who may be affected by the conduct of his undertaking; and
        (ii) has access to the information referred to in article 19(3); and
    (b) any person appointed by him in accordance with paragraph (1) is given such information about any person working in his undertaking who is—
        (i) employed by him under a fixed-term contract of employment, or
        (ii) employed in an employment business,
    as is necessary to enable that person properly to carry out the function specified in that paragraph.

(5) A person is to be regarded as competent for the purposes of this article where he has sufficient training and experience or knowledge and other qualities to enable him properly to assist in undertaking the preventive and protective measures.

(6) Paragraph (1) does not apply to a self-employed employer who is not in partnership with any other person, where he has sufficient training and experience or knowledge and other qualities properly to assist in undertaking the preventive and protective measures.

(7) Paragraph (1) does not apply to individuals who are employers and who are together carrying on business in partnership, where at least one of the individuals concerned has sufficient training and experience or knowledge and other qualities—
    (a) properly to undertake the preventive and protective measures; and
    (b) properly to assist his fellow partners in undertaking those measures.

(8) Where there is a competent person in the responsible person's employment, that person must be appointed for the purposes of paragraph (1) in preference to a competent person not in his employment.

**[3510]**

**NOTES**
Commencement: 1 October 2006.

## 19 Provision of information to employees

(1) The responsible person must provide his employees with comprehensible and relevant information on—
    (a) the risks to them identified by the risk assessment;
    (b) the preventive and protective measures;
    (c) the procedures and the measures referred to in article 15(1)(a);
    (d) the identities of those persons nominated by him in accordance with article 13(3)(b) or appointed in accordance with article 15(1)(b); and

    (e)    the risks notified to him in accordance with article 22(1)(c).

(2) The responsible person must, before employing a child, provide a parent of the child with comprehensible and relevant information on—

    (a)    the risks to that child identified by the risk assessment;

    (b)    the preventive and protective measures; and

    (c)    the risks notified to him in accordance with article 22(1)(c),

and for the purposes of this paragraph, "parent of the child" includes a person who has parental responsibility, within the meaning of section 3 of the Children Act 1989, for the child.

(3) Where a dangerous substance is present in or on the premises, the responsible person must, in addition to the information provided under paragraph (1) provide his employees with—

    (a)    the details of any such substance including—

        (i)    the name of the substance and the risk which it presents;

        (ii)    access to any relevant safety data sheet; and

        (iii)    legislative provisions (concerning the hazardous properties of any such substance) which apply to the substance; and

    (b)    the significant findings of the risk assessment.

(4) The information required by paragraph (3) must be—

    (a)    adapted to take account of significant changes in the activity carried out or methods or work used by the responsible person; and

    (b)    provided in a manner appropriate to the risk identified by the risk assessment.

        **[3511]**

**NOTES**

Commencement: 1 October 2006.

**20 Provision of information to employers and the self-employed from outside undertakings**

(1) The responsible person must ensure that the employer of any employees from an outside undertaking who are working in or on the premises is provided with comprehensible and relevant information on—

    (a)    the risks to those employees; and

    (b)    the preventive and protective measures taken by the responsible person.

(2) The responsible person must ensure that any person working in his undertaking who is not his employee is provided with appropriate instructions and comprehensible and relevant information regarding any risks to that person.

(3) The responsible person must—

    (a)    ensure that the employer of any employees from an outside undertaking who are working in or on the premises is provided with sufficient information to enable that employer to identify any person nominated by the responsible person in accordance with article 15 (1)(b) to implement evacuation procedures as far as those employees are concerned; and

    (b)    take all reasonable steps to ensure that any person from an outside undertaking who is working in or on the premises receives sufficient information to enable that person to identify any person nominated by the responsible person in accordance with article 15 (1)(b) to implement evacuation procedures as far as they are concerned.

        **[3512]**

**NOTES**

Commencement: 1 October 2006.

**21 Training**

(1) The responsible person must ensure that his employees are provided with adequate safety training—

    (a)    at the time when they are first employed; and

    (b)    on their being exposed to new or increased risks because of—

        (i)    their being transferred or given a change of responsibilities within the responsible person's undertaking;

        (ii)    the introduction of new work equipment into, or a change respecting work equipment already in use within, the responsible person's undertaking;

        (iii)    the introduction of new technology into the responsible person's undertaking; or

        (iv)    the introduction of a new system of work into, or a change respecting a system of work already in use within, the responsible person's undertaking.

(2) The training referred to in paragraph (1) must—

    (a)    include suitable and sufficient instruction and training on the appropriate precautions and actions to be taken by the employee in order to safeguard himself and other relevant persons on the premises;

(b)    be repeated periodically where appropriate;
(c)    be adapted to take account of any new or changed risks to the safety of the employees concerned;
(d)    be provided in a manner appropriate to the risk identified by the risk assessment; and
(e)    take place during working hours.

**[3513]**

NOTES
Commencement: 1 October 2006.

## 22  Co-operation and co-ordination

(1)    Where two or more responsible persons share, or have duties in respect of, premises (whether on a temporary or a permanent basis) each such person must—
(a)    co-operate with the other responsible person concerned so far as is necessary to enable them to comply with the requirements and prohibitions imposed on them by or under this Order;
(b)    (taking into account the nature of his activities) take all reasonable steps to co-ordinate the measures he takes to comply with the requirements and prohibitions imposed on him by or under this Order with the measures the other responsible persons are taking to comply with the requirements and prohibitions imposed on them by or under this Order; and
(c)    take all reasonable steps to inform the other responsible persons concerned of the risks to relevant persons arising out of or in connection with the conduct by him of his undertaking.

(2)    Where two or more responsible persons share premises (whether on a temporary or a permanent basis) where an explosive atmosphere may occur, the responsible person who has overall responsibility for the premises must co-ordinate the implementation of all the measures required by this Part to be taken to protect relevant persons from any risk from the explosive atmosphere.

**[3514]**

NOTES
Commencement: 1 October 2006.

## 23  General duties of employees at work

(1)    Every employee must, while at work—
(a)    take reasonable care for the safety of himself and of other relevant persons who may be affected by his acts or omissions at work;
(b)    as regards any duty or requirement imposed on his employer by or under any provision of this Order, co-operate with him so far as is necessary to enable that duty or requirement to be performed or complied with; and
(c)    inform his employer or any other employee with specific responsibility for the safety of his fellow employees—
(i)    of any work situation which a person with the first-mentioned employee's training and instruction would reasonably consider represented a serious and immediate danger to safety; and
(ii)    of any matter which a person with the first-mentioned employee's training and instruction would reasonably consider represented a shortcoming in the employer's protection arrangements for safety,
in so far as that situation or matter either affects the safety of that first-mentioned employee or arises out of or in connection with his own activities at work, and has not previously been reported to his employer or to any other employee of that employer in accordance with this sub-paragraph.

**[3515]**

NOTES
Commencement: 1 October 2006.

## 24  Power to make regulations about fire precautions

(1)    The Secretary of State may by regulations make provision as to the precautions which are to be taken or observed in relation to the risk to relevant persons as regards premises in relation to which this Order applies.

(2)    Without prejudice to the generality of paragraph (1), regulations made by the Secretary of State may impose requirements—
(a)    as to the provision, maintenance and keeping free from obstruction of any means of escape in case of fire;

(b)    as to the provision and maintenance of means for securing that any means of escape can be safely and effectively used at all material times;

(c)    as to the provision and maintenance of means for fighting fire and means for giving warning in case of fire;

(d)    as to the internal construction of the premises and the materials used in that construction;

(e)    for prohibiting altogether the presence or use in the premises of furniture or equipment of any specified description, or prohibiting its presence or use unless specified standards or conditions are complied with;

(f)    for securing that persons employed to work in the premises receive appropriate instruction or training in what to do in case of fire;

(g)    for securing that, in specified circumstances, specified numbers of attendants are stationed in specified parts of the premises; and

(h)    as to the keeping of records of instruction or training given, or other things done, in pursuance of the regulations.

(3)    Regulations under this article—

(a)    may impose requirements on persons other than the responsible person; and

(b)    may, as regards any of their provisions, make provision as to the person or persons who is or are to be responsible for any contravention of that provision.

(4)    The Secretary of State must, before making any regulations under this article, consult with such persons or bodies of persons as appear to him to be appropriate.

(5)    The power of the Secretary of State to make regulations under this article—

(a)    is exercisable by statutory instrument, which is subject to annulment in pursuance of a resolution of either House of Parliament;

(b)    includes power to make different provision in relation to different circumstances; and

(c)    includes power to grant or provide for the granting of exemptions from any of the provisions of the regulations, either unconditionally or subject to conditions.

**[3516]**

**NOTES**

Commencement: 1 October 2006.

Regulations: the Fire Precautions (Sub-surface Railway Stations) (England) Regulations 2009, SI 2009/782.

PART 3
ENFORCEMENT

## 25   Enforcing authorities

For the purposes of this Order, "enforcing authority" means—

(a)    the fire and rescue authority for the area in which premises are, or are to be, situated, in any case not falling within any of sub-paragraphs (b) to (e);

(b)    the Health and Safety Executive in relation to—

     (i)    any premises for which a licence is required in accordance with section 1 of the Nuclear Installations Act 1965 or for which a permit is required in accordance with section 2 of that Act;

     (ii)    any premises which would, except for the fact that it is used by, or on behalf of, the Crown, be required to have a licence or permit in accordance with the provisions referred to in sub-paragraph (i);

     (iii)    a ship, including a ship belonging to Her Majesty which forms part of Her Majesty's Navy, which is in the course of construction, reconstruction or conversion or repair by persons who include persons other than the master and crew of the ship;

     (iv)    any workplace which is or is on a construction site within the meaning of regulation 2(1) of [the Construction (Design and Management) Regulations 2007] and to which those Regulations apply, other than construction sites referred to in regulation [46] of those Regulations.

(c)    the fire service maintained by the Secretary of State for Defence in relation to—

     (i)    premises, other than premises falling within paragraph (b)(iii), occupied solely for the purposes of the armed forces of the Crown;

     (ii)    premises occupied solely by any visiting force or an international headquarters or defence organisation designated for the purposes of the International Headquarters and Defence Organisations Act 1964;

     (iii)    premises, other than premises falling within paragraph (b)(iii), which are situated within premises occupied solely for the purposes of the armed forces of the Crown but which are not themselves so occupied;

(d)    the relevant local authority in relation to premises which consist of—

     (i)    a sports ground designated as requiring a safety certificate under section 1 of the Safety of Sports Grounds Act 1975 (safety certificates for large sports stadia);

PART II
STATUTORY INSTRUMENTS

(ii)  a regulated stand within the meaning of section 26(5) of the Fire Safety and Safety of Places of Sport Act 1987 (safety certificates for stands at sports grounds);

(e)  a fire inspector, or any person authorised by the Secretary of State to act for the purposes of this Order, in relation to—

(i)  premises owned or occupied by the Crown, other than premises falling within paragraph (b)(ii) and (c);

(ii)  premises in relation to which the United Kingdom Atomic Energy Authority is the responsible person, other than premises falling within paragraph (b)(ii).

**[3517]**

**NOTES**
Commencement: 1 October 2006.
Words and figure in square brackets in para (b)(iv) substituted by the Construction (Design and Management) Regulations 2007, SI 2007/320, reg 48(2), Sch 5.
See further, the National Assembly for Wales Commission (Crown Status) Order 2007, SI 2007/1118, art 8(1), (2)(a), and the Government of Wales Act 2006, s 161(1), which provide that as from 4 May 2007 immediately after the 2007 election, the reference to the Crown in para (e) above shall be treated as including a reference to the National Assembly for Wales Commission.

## 26  Enforcement of Order

(1)  Every enforcing authority must enforce the provisions of this Order and any regulations made under it in relation to premises for which it is the enforcing authority and for that purpose, except where a fire inspector or other person authorised by the Secretary of State is the enforcing authority, may appoint inspectors.

(2)  In performing the duty imposed by paragraph (1), the enforcing authority must have regard to such guidance as the Secretary of State may give it.

(3)  A fire and rescue authority has power to arrange with [the Health and Safety Executive] or the Office of Rail Regulation for such of the authority's functions under this Order as may be specified in the arrangements to be performed on its behalf by the Health and Safety Executive or the Office of Rail Regulation, as the case may be, (with or without payment) in relation to any particular workplace.

**[3518]**

**NOTES**
Commencement: 1 October 2006.
Para (3): words in square brackets substituted by the Legislative Reform (Health and Safety Executive) Order 2008, SI 2008/960, art 22, Sch 3, as from 1 April 2008; for transitional provisions see art 21, Sch 2 of that Order.

## 27  Powers of inspectors

(1)  Subject to the provisions of this article, an inspector may do anything necessary for the purpose of carrying out this Order and any regulations made under it into effect and in particular, so far as may be necessary for that purpose, shall have power to do at any reasonable time the following—

(a)  to enter any premises which he has reason to believe it is necessary for him to enter for the purpose mentioned above and to inspect the whole or part of the premises and anything in them, where such entry and inspection may be effected without the use of force;

(b)  to make such inquiry as may be necessary for any of the following purposes—

(i)  to ascertain, as regards any premises, whether the provisions of this Order or any regulations made under it apply or have been complied with; and

(ii)  to identify the responsible person in relation to the premises;

(c)  to require the production of, or where the information is recorded in computerised form, the furnishing of extracts from, any records (including plans)—

(i)  which are required to be kept by virtue of any provision of this Order or regulations made under it; or

(ii)  which it is necessary for him to see for the purposes of an examination or inspection under this article,

and to inspect and take copies of, or of any entry in, the records;

(d)  to require any person having responsibilities in relation to any premises (whether or not the responsible person) to give him such facilities and assistance with respect to any matters or things to which the responsibilities of that person extend as are necessary for the purpose of enabling the inspector to exercise any of the powers conferred on him by this article;

(e)  to take samples of any articles or substances found in any premises which he has power to enter for the purpose of ascertaining their fire resistance or flammability; and

(f)     in the case of any article or substance found in any premises which he has power to enter, being an article or substance which appears to him to have caused or to be likely to cause danger to the safety of relevant persons, to cause it to be dismantled or subjected to any process or test (but not so as to damage or destroy it unless this is, in the circumstances, necessary).

(2)     An inspector must, if so required when visiting any premises in the exercise of powers conferred by this article, produce to the occupier of the premises evidence of his authority.

(3)     Where an inspector proposes to exercise the power conferred by paragraph (1)(f) he must, if requested by a person who at the time is present in and has responsibilities in relation to those premises, cause anything which is to be done by virtue of that power to be done in the presence of that person.

(4)     Before exercising the power conferred by paragraph (1)(f) an inspector must consult such persons as appear to him appropriate for the purpose of ascertaining what dangers, if any, there may be in doing anything which he proposes to do under that power.

**[3519]**

**NOTES**

Commencement: 1 October 2006.

## 28   Exercise on behalf of fire inspectors etc of their powers by officers of fire brigades

(1)     The powers conferred by article 27 on a fire inspector, or any other person authorised by the Secretary of State under article 25(e), are also exercisable by an employee of the fire and rescue authority when authorised in writing by such an inspector for the purpose of reporting to him on any matter falling within his functions under this Order; and articles 27(2) and (3) and 32(2)(d) to (f), with the necessary modifications, apply accordingly.

(2)     A fire inspector, or other person authorised by the Secretary of State, must not authorise an employee of a fire and rescue authority under this article except with the consent of the fire and rescue authority.

**[3520]**

**NOTES**

Commencement: 1 October 2006.

## 29   Alterations notices

(1)     The enforcing authority may serve on the responsible person a notice (in this Order referred to as "an alterations notice") if the authority is of the opinion that the premises—

(a)     constitute a serious risk to relevant persons (whether due to the features of the premises, their use, any hazard present, or any other circumstances); or

(b)     may constitute such a risk if a change is made to them or the use to which they are put.

(2)     An alterations notice must—

(a)     state that the enforcing authority is of the opinion referred to in paragraph (1); and

(b)     specify the matters which in their opinion, constitute a risk to relevant persons or may constitute such a risk if a change is made to the premises or the use to which they are put.

(3)     Where an alterations notice has been served in respect of premises, the responsible person must, before making any of the changes specified in paragraph (4) which may result in a significant increase in risk, notify the enforcing authority of the proposed changes.

(4)     The changes referred to in paragraph (3) are—

(a)     a change to the premises;

(b)     a change to the services, fittings or equipment in or on the premises;

(c)     an increase in the quantities of dangerous substances which are present in or on the premises;

(d)     a change to the use of the premises.

(5)     An alterations notice may include a requirement that, in addition to the notification required by paragraph (3), the responsible person must—

(a)     take all reasonable steps to notify the terms of the notice to any other person who has duties under article 5(3) in respect of the premises;

(b)     record the information prescribed in article 9(7), in accordance with article 9(6);

(c)     record the arrangements required by article 11(1), in accordance with article 11(2); and

(d)     before making the changes referred to in paragraph (3), send the enforcing authority the following—

(i)     a copy of the risk assessment; and

(ii)     a summary of the changes he proposes to make to the existing general fire precautions.

PART II

STATUTORY INSTRUMENTS

(6)   An alterations notice served under paragraph (1) may be withdrawn at any time and, for the purposes of this article, the notice is deemed to be in force until such time as it is withdrawn or cancelled by the court under article 35(2).

(7)   Nothing in this article prevents an enforcing authority from serving an enforcement notice or a prohibition notice in respect of the premises.

**[3521]**

**NOTES**
Commencement: 1 October 2006.

## 30   Enforcement notices

(1)   If the enforcing authority is of the opinion that the responsible person or any other person mentioned in article 5(3) has failed to comply with any provision of this Order or of any regulations made under it, the authority may, subject to article 36, serve on that person a notice (in this Order referred to as "an enforcement notice").

(2)   An enforcement notice must—
- (a)   state that the enforcing authority is of the opinion referred to in paragraph (1) and why;
- (b)   specify the provisions which have not been complied with; and
- (c)   require that person to take steps to remedy the failure within such period from the date of service of the notice (not being less than 28 days) as may be specified in the notice.

(3)   An enforcement notice may, subject to article 36, include directions as to the measures which the enforcing authority consider are necessary to remedy the failure referred to in paragraph (1) and any such measures may be framed so as to afford the person on whom the notice is served a choice between different ways of remedying the contravention.

(4)   Where the enforcing authority is of the opinion that a person's failure to comply with this Order also extends to a workplace, or employees who work in a workplace, to which this Order applies but for which they are not the enforcing authority, the notice served by them under paragraph (1) may include requirements concerning that workplace or those employees; but before including any such requirements the enforcing authority must consult the enforcing authority for that workplace.

(5)   Before serving an enforcement notice which would oblige a person to make an alteration to premises, the enforcing authority must consult—
- (a)   in cases where the relevant local authority is not the enforcing authority, the relevant local authority;
- (b)   in the case of premises used as a workplace which are within the field of responsibility of one or more enforcing authorities within the meaning of Part 1 of the Health and Safety at Work etc Act 1974, that authority or those authorities; and section 18(7) of the Health and Safety at Work etc Act 1974 (meaning in Part I of that Act of "enforcing authority" and of such an authority's "field of responsibility") applies for the purposes of this article as it applies for the purposes of that Part;
- (c)   in the case of a building or structure in relation to all or any part of which an initial notice given under section 47 of the Building Act 1984 is in force, the approved inspector who gave that initial notice;
- (d)   in the case of premises which are, include, or form part of, a designated sports ground or a sports ground at which there is a regulated stand, the relevant local authority, where that authority is not the enforcing authority; and for the purposes of this sub-paragraph, "sports ground" and "designated sports ground" have the same meaning as in the Safety of Sports Grounds Act 1975 and "regulated stand" has the same meaning as in the Fire Safety and Safety of Places of Sport Act 1987;
- (e)   any other person whose consent to the alteration would be required by or under any enactment.

(6)   Without prejudice to the power of the court to cancel or modify an enforcement notice under article 35(2), no failure on the part of an enforcing authority to consult under paragraphs (4) or (5) makes an enforcement notice void.

(7)   Where an enforcement notice has been served under paragraph (1)—
- (a)   the enforcing authority may withdraw the notice at any time before the end of the period specified in the notice; and
- (b)   if an appeal against the notice is not pending, the enforcing authority may extend or further extend the period specified in the notice.

**[3522]**

**NOTES**
Commencement: 1 October 2006.

### 31   Prohibition notices

(1)   If the enforcing authority is of the opinion that use of premises involves or will involve a risk to relevant persons so serious that use of the premises ought to be prohibited or restricted, the authority may serve on the responsible person or any other person mentioned in article 5(3) a notice (in this Order referred to as "a prohibition notice").

(2)   The matters relevant to the assessment by the enforcing authority, for the purposes of paragraph (1), of the risk to relevant persons include anything affecting their escape from the premises in the event of fire.

(3)   A prohibition notice must—
   (a)   state that the enforcing authority is of the opinion referred to in paragraph (1);
   (b)   specify the matters which in their opinion give or, as the case may be, will give rise to that risk; and
   (c)   direct that the use to which the prohibition notice relates is prohibited or restricted to such extent as may be specified in the notice until the specified matters have been remedied.

(4)   A prohibition notice may include directions as to the measures which will have to be taken to remedy the matters specified in the notice and any such measures may be framed so as to afford the person on whom the notice is served a choice between different ways of remedying the matters.

(5)   A prohibition or restriction contained in a prohibition notice pursuant to paragraph (3)(c) takes effect immediately it is served if the enforcing authority is of the opinion, and so states in the notice, that the risk of serious personal injury is or, as the case may be, will be imminent, and in any other case takes effect at the end of the period specified in the prohibition notice.

(6)   Before serving a prohibition notice in relation to a house in multiple occupation, the enforcing authority shall, where practicable, notify the local housing authority of their intention and the use which they intend to prohibit or restrict.

(7)   For the purposes of paragraph (6)—
   "house in multiple occupation" means a house in multiple occupation as defined by sections 254 to 259 of the Housing Act 2004, as they have effect for the purposes of Part 1 of that Act (that is, without the exclusions contained in Schedule 14 to that Act); and
   "local housing authority" has the same meaning as in section 261(2) of the Housing Act 2004.

(8)   Without prejudice to the power of the court to cancel or modify a prohibition notice under article 35(2), no failure on the part of an enforcing authority to notify under paragraph (6) makes a prohibition notice void.

(9)   Where a prohibition notice has been served under paragraph (1) the enforcing authority may withdraw it at any time.

(10)   In this article, "premises" includes domestic premises other than premises consisting of or comprised in a house which is occupied as a single private dwelling and article 27 (powers of inspectors) shall be construed accordingly.

**[3523]**

### NOTES
   Commencement: 1 October 2006.

### PART 4
### OFFENCES AND APPEALS

### 32   Offences

(1)   It is an offence for any responsible person or any other person mentioned in article 5(3) to—
   (a)   fail to comply with any requirement or prohibition imposed by articles 8 to 22 and 38 (fire safety duties) where that failure places one or more relevant persons at risk of death or serious injury in case of fire;
   (b)   fail to comply with any requirement or prohibition imposed by regulations made, or having effect as if made, under article 24 where that failure places one or more relevant persons at risk of death or serious injury in case of fire;
   (c)   fail to comply with any requirement imposed by article 29(3) or (4) (alterations notices);
   (d)   fail to comply with any requirement imposed by an enforcement notice;
   (e)   fail, without reasonable excuse, in relation to apparatus to which article 37 applies (luminous tube signs)—
      (i)   to ensure that such apparatus which is installed in premises complies with article 37(3) and (4);
      (ii)   to give a notice required by article 37(6) or (8), unless he establishes that some other person duly gave the notice in question;
      (iii)   to comply with a notice served under article 37(9).

PART II
STATUTORY INSTRUMENTS

(2)   It is an offence for any person to—

(a)   fail to comply with article 23 (general duties of employees at work) where that failure places one or more relevant persons at risk of death or serious injury in case of fire;

(b)   make in any register, book, notice or other document required to be kept, served or given by or under, this Order, an entry which he knows to be false in a material particular;

(c)   give any information which he knows to be false in a material particular or recklessly give any information which is so false, in purported compliance with any obligation to give information to which he is subject under or by virtue of this Order, or in response to any inquiry made by virtue of article 27(1)(b);

(d)   obstruct, intentionally, an inspector in the exercise or performance of his powers or duties under this Order;

(e)   fail, without reasonable excuse, to comply with any requirements imposed by an inspector under article 27(1)(c) or (d);

(f)   pretend, with intent to deceive, to be an inspector;

(g)   fail to comply with the prohibition imposed by article 40 (duty not to charge employees);

(h)   fail to comply with any prohibition or restriction imposed by a prohibition notice.

(3)   Any person guilty of an offence under paragraph (1)(a) to (d) and (2)(h) is liable—

(a)   on summary conviction to a fine not exceeding the statutory maximum; or

(b)   on conviction on indictment, to a fine, or to imprisonment for a term not exceeding two years, or to both.

(4)   Any person guilty of an offence under paragraph (1)(e)(i) to (iii) is liable on summary conviction to a fine not exceeding level 3 on the standard scale.

(5)   Any person guilty of an offence under paragraph (2)(a) is liable—

(a)   on summary conviction to a fine not exceeding the statutory maximum; or

(b)   on conviction on indictment, to a fine.

(6)   Any person guilty of an offence under paragraph (2)(b), (c), (d) or (g) is liable on summary conviction to a fine not exceeding level 5 on the standard scale.

(7)   Any person guilty of an offence under paragraph (2)(e) or (f) is liable on summary conviction to a fine not exceeding level 3 on the standard scale.

(8)   Where an offence under this Order committed by a body corporate is proved to have been committed with the consent or connivance of, or to be attributable to any neglect on the part of, any director, manager, secretary or other similar officer of the body corporate, or any person purporting to act in any such capacity, he as well as the body corporate is guilty of that offence, and is liable to be proceeded against and punished accordingly.

(9)   Where the affairs of a body corporate are managed by its members, paragraph (8) applies in relation to the acts and defaults of a member in connection with his functions of management as if he were a director of the body corporate.

(10)   Where the commission by any person of an offence under this Order, is due to the act or default of some other person, that other person is guilty of the offence, and a person may be charged with and convicted of the offence by virtue of this paragraph whether or not proceedings are taken against the first-mentioned person.

(11)   Nothing in this Order operates so as to afford an employer a defence in any criminal proceedings for a contravention of those provisions by reason of any act or default of—

(a)   an employee of his; or

(b)   a person nominated under articles 13(3)(b) or 15(1)(b) or appointed under 18(1).

[3524]

**NOTES**

Commencement: 1 October 2006.

## 33   Defence

Subject to article 32(11), in any proceedings for an offence under this Order, except for a failure to comply with articles 8(1)(a) or 12, it is a defence for the person charged to prove that he took all reasonable precautions and exercised all due diligence to avoid the commission of such an offence.

[3525]

**NOTES**

Commencement: 1 October 2006.

## 34   Onus of proving limits of what is practicable or reasonably practicable

In any proceedings for an offence under this Order consisting of a failure to comply with a duty or requirement so far as is practicable or so far as is reasonably practicable, it is for the accused to prove that it was not practicable or reasonably practicable to do more than was in fact done to satisfy the duty or requirement.

**[3526]**

**NOTES**

Commencement: 1 October 2006.

## 35   Appeals

(1)   A person on whom an alterations notice, an enforcement notice, a prohibition notice or a notice given by the fire and rescue authority under article 37 (fire-fighters' switches for luminous tube signs) is served may, within 21 days from the day on which the notice is served, appeal to the court.

(2)   On an appeal under this article the court may either cancel or affirm the notice, and if it affirms it, may do so either in its original form or with such modifications as the court may in the circumstances think fit.

(3)   Where an appeal is brought against an alterations notice or an enforcement notice, the bringing of the appeal has the effect of suspending the operation of the notice until the appeal is finally disposed of or, if the appeal is withdrawn, until the withdrawal of the appeal.

(4)   Where an appeal is brought against a prohibition notice, the bringing of the appeal does not have the effect of suspending the operation of the notice, unless, on the application of the appellant, the court so directs (and then only from the giving of the direction).

(5)   In this article "the court" means a magistrates' court.

(6)   The procedure for an appeal under paragraph (1) is by way of complaint for an order, and—

    (a)   the Magistrates' Courts Act 1980 applies to the proceedings; and

    (b)   the making of the complaint is deemed to be the bringing of the appeal.

(7)   A person aggrieved by an order made by a magistrates' court on determining a complaint under this Order may appeal to the Crown Court; and for the avoidance of doubt, an enforcing authority may be a person aggrieved for the purposes of this paragraph.

**[3527]**

**NOTES**

Commencement: 1 October 2006.

## 36   Determination of disputes by Secretary of State

(1)   This article applies where—

    (a)   a responsible person or any other person mentioned in article 5(3) has failed to comply with any provision of this Order or of any regulations made under it; and

    (b)   the enforcing authority and that person cannot agree on the measures which are necessary to remedy the failure.

(2)   Where this article applies, the enforcing authority and the person referred to in paragraph (1)(a) may agree to refer the question as to what measures are necessary to remedy the failure referred to in paragraph (1)(a) to the Secretary of State for his determination.

(3)   The Secretary of State may, by notice in writing to both parties, require the provision of such further information, including plans, specified in the notice, within the period so specified, as the Secretary of State may require for the purpose of making a determination.

(4)   If the information required under paragraph (3) is not provided within the period specified, the Secretary of State may refuse to proceed with the determination.

(5)   Where the Secretary of State has made a determination under this article, the enforcing authority may not, subject to paragraph (6), take any enforcement action the effect of which would be to conflict with his determination; and in this article, "enforcement action" means the service of an enforcement notice or the inclusion of any directions in an enforcement notice.

(6)   Paragraph (5) does not apply where, since the date of the determination by the Secretary of State, there has been a change to the premises or the use to which they are put such that the risk to relevant persons has significantly changed.

**[3528]**

**NOTES**

Commencement: 1 October 2006.

## PART 5
## MISCELLANEOUS

### 37  Fire-fighters' switches for luminous tube signs etc

(1)  Subject to paragraph (11), this article applies to apparatus consisting of luminous tube signs designed to work at a voltage normally exceeding the prescribed voltage, or other equipment so designed, and references in this article to a cut-off switch are, in a case where a transformer is provided to raise the voltage to operate the apparatus, references to a cut-off switch on the low-voltage side of the transformer.

(2)  In paragraph (1) the "prescribed voltage" means—
  (a)  1000 volts AC or 1500 volts DC if measured between any two conductors; or
  (b)  600 volts AC or 900 volts DC if measured between a conductor and earth.

(3)  No apparatus to which this article applies is to be installed unless it is provided with a cut-off switch.

(4)  Subject to paragraph (5), the cut-off switch must be so placed, and coloured or marked as to satisfy such reasonable requirements as the fire and rescue authority may impose to secure that it must be readily recognisable by and accessible to fire-fighters.

(5)  If a cut-off switch complies in position, colour and marking with the current regulations of the Institution of Electrical Engineers for a fire-fighter's emergency switch, the fire and rescue authority may not impose any further requirements pursuant to paragraph (4).

(6)  Not less than 42 days before work is begun to install apparatus to which this article applies, the responsible person must give notice to the fire and rescue authority showing where the cut-off switch is to be placed and how it is to be coloured or marked.

(7)  Where notice has been given to the fire and rescue authority as required by paragraph (6), the proposed position, colouring or marking of the switch is deemed to satisfy the requirements of the fire authority unless, within 21 days from the date of the service of the notice, the fire and rescue authority has served on the responsible person a counter-notice stating that their requirements are not satisfied.

(8)  Where apparatus to which this article applies has been installed in or on premises before the day on which this article comes into force, the responsible person must, not more than 21 days after that day, give notice to the fire and rescue authority stating whether the apparatus is already provided with a cut-off switch and, if so, where the switch is placed and how it is coloured or marked.

(9)  Subject to paragraph (10), where apparatus to which this article applies has been installed in or on premises before the day on which this article comes into force, the fire and rescue authority may serve on the responsible person a notice—
  (a)  in the case of apparatus already provided with a cut-off switch, stating that they are not satisfied with the position, colouring or marking of the switch and requiring the responsible person, within such period as may be specified in the notice, to take such steps as will secure that the switch will be so placed or coloured or marked as to be readily recognisable by, and accessible to, fire-fighters in accordance with the reasonable requirements of the fire and rescue authority; or
  (b)  in the case of apparatus not already provided with a cut-off switch, requiring him, within such period as may be specified in the notice, to provide such a cut-off switch in such a position and so coloured or marked as to be readily recognisable by, and accessible to, fire-fighters in accordance with the reasonable requirements of the fire and rescue authority.

(10)  If a cut-off switch complies in position, colour and marking with the current regulations of the Institution of Electrical Engineers for a fire-fighter's emergency switch, the fire and rescue authority may not serve a notice in respect of it under paragraph (9).

(11)  This article does not apply to—
  (a)  apparatus installed or proposed to be installed in or on premises in respect of which a premises licence under the Licensing Act 2003 has effect authorising the use of premises for the exhibition of a film, within the meaning of paragraph 15 of Schedule 1 to that Act; or
  (b)  apparatus installed in or on premises before the day on which this article comes into force where, immediately before that date—
    (i)  the apparatus complied with section 10(2) and (3) (requirement to provide cut-off switch) of the Local Government (Miscellaneous Provisions) Act 1982; and
    (ii)  the owner or occupier of the premises, as the case may be, had complied with either subsection (5) or subsection (7) (notice of location and type of switch) of section 10 of that Act.

**NOTES**
Commencement: 1 October 2006.

### 38   Maintenance of measures provided for protection of fire-fighters

(1)   Where necessary in order to safeguard the safety of fire-fighters in the event of a fire, the responsible person must ensure that the premises and any facilities, equipment and devices provided in respect of the premises for the use by or protection of fire-fighters under this Order or under any other enactment, including any enactment repealed or revoked by this Order, are subject to a suitable system of maintenance and are maintained in an efficient state, in efficient working order and in good repair.

(2)   Where the premises form part of a building, the responsible person may make arrangements with the occupier of any premises forming part of the building for the purpose of ensuring that the requirements of paragraph (1) are met.

(3)   Paragraph (2) applies even if the other premises are not premises to which this Order applies.

(4)   The occupier of the other premises must co-operate with the responsible person for the purposes of paragraph (2).

(5)   Where the occupier of the other premises is not also the owner of those premises, the reference to the occupier in paragraphs (2) and (4) are to be taken to be references to both the occupier and the owner.

**[3530]**

**NOTES**
Commencement: 1 October 2006.

### 39   Civil liability for breach of statutory duty

(1)   Subject to paragraph (2), nothing in this Order is to be construed as conferring a right of action in any civil proceedings (other than proceedings for recovery of a fine).

(2)   Notwithstanding section 86 of the Fires Prevention (Metropolis) Act 1774, breach of a duty imposed on an employer by or under this Order, so far as it causes damage to an employee, confers a right of action on that employee in civil proceedings.

**[3531]**

**NOTES**
Commencement: 1 October 2006.

### 40   Duty not to charge employees for things done or provided

No employer may levy or permit to be levied on any employee of his any charge in respect of anything done or provided in pursuance of any requirement of this Order or of regulations made under it.

**[3532]**

**NOTES**
Commencement: 1 October 2006.

**41**   (*Amends the Safety Representatives and Safety Committees Regulations 1977, SI 1977/500, reg 4A, and the Health and Safety (Consultation with Employees) Regulations 1996, SI 1996/1513, reg 3.*)

### 42   Special provisions in respect of licensed etc premises

(1)   Subject to paragraph (2), where any enactment provides for the licensing of premises in relation to which this Order applies, or the licensing of persons in respect of any such premises—

   (a)   the licensing authority must ensure that the enforcing authority for the premises has the opportunity to make representations before issuing the licence; and

   (b)   the enforcing authority must notify the licensing authority of any action that the enforcing authority takes in relation to premises to which the licence relates; but no failure on the part of an enforcing authority to notify under this paragraph shall affect the validity of any such action taken.

(2)   Paragraph (1) does not apply where the licensing authority is also the enforcing authority.

(3)   In this article and article 43(1)(a)—

   (a)   "licensing authority" means the authority responsible for issuing the licence; and

   (b)   "licensing" includes certification and registration and "licence" is to be construed accordingly; and

(c)  references to the issue of licences include references to their renewal, transfer or variation.

[3533]

NOTES
Commencement: 1 October 2006.

## 43  Suspension of terms and conditions of licences dealing with same matters as this Order

(1)  Subject to paragraph (3), paragraph (2) applies if—
   (a)  an enactment provides for the licensing of premises in relation to which this Order applies, or the licensing of persons in respect of any such premises;
   (b)  a licence is issued in respect of the premises (whether before or after the coming into force of this Order); and
   (c)  the licensing authority is required or authorised to impose terms, conditions or restrictions in connection with the issue of the licences.

(2)  At any time when this Order applies in relation to the premises, any term, condition or restriction imposed by the licensing authority has no effect in so far as it relates to any matter in relation to which requirements or prohibitions are or could be imposed by or under this Order.

(3)  Paragraph (1) does not apply where the licensing authority is also the enforcing authority.

[3534]

NOTES
Commencement: 1 October 2006.

## 44  Suspension of byelaws dealing with same matters as this Order

Where any enactment provides for the making of byelaws in relation to premises to which this Order applies, then, so long as this Order continues to apply to the premises, any byelaw has no effect in so far as it relates to any matter in relation to which requirements or prohibitions are or could be imposed by or under this Order.

[3535]

NOTES
Commencement: 1 October 2006.

## 45  Duty to consult enforcing authority before passing plans

(1)  Where it is proposed to erect a building, or to make any extension of or structural alteration to a building and, in connection with the proposals, plans are, in accordance with building regulations, deposited with a local authority, the local authority must, subject to paragraph (3), consult the enforcing authority before passing those plans.

(2)  Where it is proposed to change the use to which a building or part of a building is put and, in connection with that proposal, plans are, in accordance with building regulations, deposited with a local authority, the authority must, subject to paragraph (3), consult with the enforcing authority before passing the plans.

(3)  The duty to consult imposed by paragraphs (1) and (2)—
   (a)  only applies in relation to buildings or parts of buildings to which this Order applies, or would apply following the erection, extension, structural alteration or change of use;
   (b)  does not apply where the local authority is also the enforcing authority.

[3536]

NOTES
Commencement: 1 October 2006.

## 46  Other consultation by authorities

(1)  Where a government department or other public authority intends to take any action in respect of premises which will or may result in changes to any of the measures required by or under this Order, that department or authority must consult the enforcing authority for the premises before taking that action.

(2)  Without prejudice to any power of the court to cancel or modify a notice served by a government department or other authority, no failure on the part of the department or authority to consult under paragraph (1) invalidates the action taken.

(3)  In paragraph (1), "public authority" includes an approved inspector within the meaning of section 49 of the Building Act 1984.

[3537]

**NOTES**
  Commencement: 1 October 2006.

## 47 Disapplication of the Health and Safety at Work etc Act 1974 in relation to general fire precautions

(1)   Subject to paragraph (2), the Health and Safety at Work etc Act 1974 and any regulations made under that Act shall not apply to premises to which this Order applies, in so far as that Act or any regulations made under it relate to any matter in relation to which requirements are or could be imposed by or under this Order.

(2)   Paragraph (1) does not apply—

  (a)   where the enforcing authority is also the enforcing authority within the meaning of the Health and Safety at Work etc Act 1974;

  (b)   in relation to the Control of Major Accident Hazards Regulations 1999.

                                                  **[3538]**

**NOTES**
  Commencement: 1 October 2006.

## 48 Service of notices etc

(1)   Any notice required or authorised by or by virtue of this Order to be served on any person may be served on him either by delivering it to him, or by leaving it at his proper address, or by sending it by post to him at that address.

(2)   Any such notice may—

  (a)   in the case of a body corporate, be served on or given to the secretary or clerk of that body; and

  (b)   in the case of a partnership, be served on or given to a partner or a person having control or management of the partnership business.

(3)   For the purposes of this article, and of section 7 of the Interpretation Act 1978 (service of documents by post) in its application to this Order, the proper address of any person is his last known address, except that—

  (a)   in the case of a body corporate or their secretary or clerk, it is the address of the registered or principal office of that body;

  (b)   in the case of a partnership or person having control or the management of the partnership business, it is the principal office of the partnership,

and for the purposes of this paragraph the principal office of a company registered outside the United Kingdom or of a partnership carrying on business outside the United Kingdom is their principal office within the United Kingdom.

(4)   If the person to be served with or given any such notice has specified an address in the United Kingdom other than his proper address as the one at which he or someone on his behalf will accept notices and other documents, that address is also to be treated for the purposes of this article and section 7 of the Interpretation Act 1978 as his proper address.

(5)   Without prejudice to any other provision of this article, any such notice required or authorised to be served on or given to the responsible person in respect of any premises (whether a body corporate or not) may be served or given by sending it by post to him at those premises, or by addressing it by name to the person on or to whom it is to be served or given and delivering it to some responsible individual who is or appears to be resident or employed in the premises.

(6)   If the name or the address of the responsible person on whom any such notice is to be served cannot after reasonable inquiry be ascertained by the person seeking to serve it, the document may be served by addressing it to the person on whom it is to be served by the description of "responsible person" for the premises (describing them) to which the notice relates, and by delivering it to some responsible individual resident or appearing to be resident on the premises or, if there is no such person to whom it can be delivered, by affixing it or a copy of it to some conspicuous part of the premises.

(7)   Any notice required or authorised to be given to or served on the responsible person or enforcing authority may be transmitted to that person or authority—

  (a)   by means of an electronic communications network (within the meaning given by section 32 of the Communications Act 2003); or

  (b)   by other means but in a form that nevertheless requires the use of apparatus by the recipient to render it intelligible.

(8)   Where the recipient of the transmission is the responsible person, the transmission has effect as a delivery of the notice to that person only if he has indicated to the enforcing authority on whose behalf the transmission is made his willingness to receive a notice transmitted in the form and manner used.

(9)    An indication to an enforcing authority for the purposes of paragraph (8)—

(a)    must be given to the authority in any manner it requires;

(b)    may be a general indication or one that is limited to notices of a particular description;

(c)    must state the address to be used and must be accompanied by any other information which the authority requires for the making of the transmission;

(d)    may be modified or withdrawn at any time by a notice given to the authority in any manner it requires.

(10)    Where the recipient of the transmission is the enforcing authority, the transmission has effect as a delivery of the notice only if the enforcing authority has indicated its willingness to receive a notice transmitted in the form and manner used.

(11)    An indication for the purposes of paragraph (10)—

(a)    may be given in any manner the enforcing authority thinks fit;

(b)    may be a general indication or one that is limited to notices of a particular description;

(c)    must state the address to be used and must be accompanied by any other information which the responsible person requires for the making of the transmission;

(d)    may be modified or withdrawn at any time in any manner the enforcing authority thinks fit.

(12)    If the making or receipt of the transmission has been recorded in the computer system of the enforcing authority, it must be presumed, unless the contrary is proved, that the transmission—

(a)    was made to the person recorded in that system as receiving it;

(b)    was made at the time recorded in that system as the time of delivery;

(c)    contained the information recorded on that system in respect of it.

(13)    For the purposes of this article—

"notice" includes any document or information; and

"transmission" means the transmission referred to in paragraph (7).

[3539]

**NOTES**

Commencement: 1 October 2006.

## 49   Application to the Crown and to the Houses of Parliament

(1)    Subject to paragraphs (2) to (4), this Order, except for articles 29, 30 and 32 to 36, binds the Crown.

(2)    Articles 27 and 31 only bind the Crown in so far as they apply in relation to premises owned by the Crown but not occupied by it.

(3)    For the purposes of this article—

(a)    the occupation of any premises by the Corporate Officer of the House of Lords for the purposes of that House, by the Corporate Officer of the House of Commons for the purpose of that House, or by those Corporate Officers acting jointly for the purposes of both Houses, is to be regarded as occupation by the Crown;

(b)    any premises in which either or both of those Corporate Officers has or have an interest which is that of an owner are to be regarded as premises owned by the Crown; and

(c)    in relation to premises specified in sub-paragraphs (a) and (b), the relevant Corporate Officer is the responsible person.

(4)    Nothing in this Order authorises the entry of any premises occupied by the Crown.

(5)    Nothing in this Order authorises proceedings to be brought against Her Majesty in her private capacity, and this paragraph shall be construed as if section 38(3) of the Crown Proceedings Act 1947 (interpretation of references in that Act to Her Majesty in her private capacity) were contained in this Order.

[3540]

**NOTES**

Commencement: 1 October 2006.

See further, the National Assembly for Wales Commission (Crown Status) Order 2007, SI 2007/1118, art 8(1), (2)(b), (3), and the Government of Wales Act 2006, s 161(1), which provide that as from 4 May 2007 immediately after the 2007 election, the reference to the Crown in paras (1), (2), (4) above shall be treated as including a reference to the National Assembly for Wales Commission and the occupation or ownership of any premises within the meaning of this Order by the Assembly Commission is to be regarded as occupation or ownership by the Crown.

## 50   Guidance

(1)    The Secretary of State must ensure that such guidance, as he considers appropriate, is available to assist responsible persons in the discharge of the duties imposed by articles 8 to 22 and by regulations made under article 24.

(2)    In relation to the duty in paragraph (1), the guidance may, from time to time, be revised.

(3)    The Secretary of State shall be treated as having discharged his duty under paragraph (1) where—

    (a)    guidance has been made available before this article comes into force; and

    (b)    he considers that the guidance is appropriate for the purpose mentioned in paragraph (1).

**[3541]**

**NOTES**

Commencement: 1 October 2006.

## 51   Application to visiting forces, etc

This Order applies to a visiting force or an international headquarters or defence organisation designated for the purposes of the International Headquarters and Defence Organisations Act 1964 only to the extent that it applies to the Crown.

**[3542]**

**NOTES**

Commencement: 1 October 2006.

## 52   Subordinate provisions

(1)    For the purposes of section 4(3) of the Regulatory Reform Act 2001 (subordinate provisions) the following are designated as subordinate provisions—

    (a)    article 1(3);

    (b)    in article 2, the definition of "relevant local authority";

    (c)    article 9(6) and (7);

    (d)    in article 10, the reference to "Part 3 of Schedule 1";

    (e)    article 11(2);

    (f)    article 14(2);

    (g)    article 16(1)(a) to (d);

    (h)    article 16(4);

    (i)    article 18(6) and (7);

    (j)    article 25;

    (k)    article 45(3);

    (l)    article 49; and

    (m)   Schedule 1.

(2)    A subordinate provisions order made in relation to article 1(3) shall be subject to annulment in pursuance of a resolution of either House of Parliament.

(3)    A subordinate provisions order made in relation to any of the provisions mentioned in article 52(1)(b) to (m) may not be made unless a draft of the instrument has been laid before, and approved by a resolution of, each House of Parliament.

**[3543]**

**NOTES**

Commencement: 8 June 2005 (para (1)(a)); 1 October 2006 (otherwise).

## 53   Repeals, revocations, amendments and transitional provisions

(1)    The enactments and instruments referred to in Schedules 2 and 3 are amended, repealed and revoked in accordance with those Schedules.

(2)    The enactments and instruments specified in column 1 of Schedules 4 and 5 are repealed or revoked, as the case may be, to the extent specified in the corresponding entry in column 3.

(3)    Any conditions imposed under section 20(2A) or (2C) of the London Building Acts (Amendment) Act 1939 before the date when this Order comes into force and which relate to maintenance, shall cease to have effect from that date.

**[3544]**

**NOTES**

Commencement: 1 October 2006.

# SCHEDULES

# SCHEDULE 1

## PART 1
### MATTERS TO BE CONSIDERED IN RISK ASSESSMENT IN RESPECT OF DANGEROUS SUBSTANCES

Article 9(2)

The matters are—

   (a)   the hazardous properties of the substance;

   (b)   information on safety provided by the supplier, including information contained in any relevant safety data sheet;

   (c)   the circumstances of the work including—

      (i)   the special, technical and organisational measures and the substances used and their possible interactions;

      (ii)   the amount of the substance involved;

      (iii)   where the work will involve more than one dangerous substance, the risk presented by such substances in combination; and

      (iv)   the arrangements for the safe handling, storage and transport of dangerous substances and of waste containing dangerous substances;

   (d)   activities, such as maintenance, where there is the potential for a high level of risk;

   (e)   the effect of measures which have been or will be taken pursuant to this Order;

   (f)   the likelihood that an explosive atmosphere will occur and its persistence;

   (g)   the likelihood that ignition sources, including electrostatic discharges, will be present and become active and effective;

   (h)   the scale of the anticipated effects;

   (i)   any places which are, or can be connected via openings to, places in which explosive atmospheres may occur; and

   (j)   such additional safety information as the responsible person may need in order to complete the assessment.

**[3545]**

**NOTES**

Commencement: 1 October 2006.

## PART 2
### MATTERS TO BE TAKEN INTO PARTICULAR ACCOUNT IN RISK ASSESSMENT IN RESPECT OF YOUNG PERSONS

Article 9(5)

The matters are—

   (a)   the inexperience, lack of awareness of risks and immaturity of young persons;

   (b)   the fitting-out and layout of the premises;

   (c)   the nature, degree and duration of exposure to physical and chemical agents;

   (d)   the form, range, and use of work equipment and the way in which it is handled;

   (e)   the organisation of processes and activities;

   (f)   the extent of the safety training provided or to be provided to young persons; and

   (g)   risks from agents, processes and work listed in the Annex to Council Directive 94/33/EC on the protection of young people at work.

**[3546]**

**NOTES**

Commencement: 1 October 2006.

## PART 3
### PRINCIPLES OF PREVENTION

Article 10

The principles are—

   (a)   avoiding risks;

   (b)   evaluating the risks which cannot be avoided;

   (c)   combating the risks at source;

   (d)   adapting to technical progress;

   (e)   *replacing the dangerous by the non-dangerous or less dangerous;*

   (f)   developing a coherent overall prevention policy which covers technology, organisation of work and the influence of factors relating to the working environment;

   (g)   giving collective protective measures priority over individual protective measures; and

   (h)   giving appropriate instructions to employees.

**[3547]**

**NOTES**

Commencement: 1 October 2006.

## PART 4
### MEASURES TO BE TAKEN IN RESPECT OF DANGEROUS SUBSTANCES
Article 12

1. In applying measures to control risks the responsible person must, in order of priority—
   - (a) reduce the quantity of dangerous substances to a minimum;
   - (b) avoid or minimise the release of a dangerous substance;
   - (c) control the release of a dangerous substance at source;
   - (d) prevent the formation of an explosive atmosphere, including the application of appropriate ventilation;
   - (e) ensure that any release of a dangerous substance which may give rise to risk is suitably collected, safely contained, removed to a safe place, or otherwise rendered safe, as appropriate;
   - (f) avoid—
     - (i) ignition sources including electrostatic discharges; and
     - (ii) such other adverse conditions as could result in harmful physical effects from a dangerous substance; and
   - (g) segregate incompatible dangerous substances.

2. The responsible person must ensure that mitigation measures applied in accordance with article 12(3)(b) include—
   - (a) reducing to a minimum the number of persons exposed;
   - (b) measures to avoid the propagation of fires or explosions;
   - (c) providing explosion pressure relief arrangements;
   - (d) providing explosion suppression equipment;
   - (e) providing plant which is constructed so as to withstand the pressure likely to be produced by an explosion; and
   - (f) providing suitable personal protective equipment.

3. The responsible person must—
   - (a) ensure that the premises are designed, constructed and maintained so as to reduce risk;
   - (b) ensure that suitable special, technical and organisational measures are designed, constructed, assembled, installed, provided and used so as to reduce risk;
   - (c) ensure that special, technical and organisational measures are maintained in an efficient state, in efficient working order and in good repair;
   - (d) ensure that equipment and protective systems meet the following requirements—
     - (i) where power failure can give rise to the spread of additional risk, equipment and protective systems must be able to be maintained in a safe state of operation independently of the rest of the plant in the event of power failure;
     - (ii) means for manual override must be possible, operated by employees competent to do so, for shutting down equipment and protective systems incorporated within automatic processes which deviate from the intended operating conditions, provided that the provision or use of such means does not compromise safety;
     - (iii) on operation of emergency shutdown, accumulated energy must be dissipated as quickly and as safely as possible or isolated so that it no longer constitutes a hazard; and
     - (iv) necessary measures must be taken to prevent confusion between connecting devices;
   - (e) where the work is carried out in hazardous places or involves hazardous activities, ensure that appropriate systems of work are applied including—
     - (i) the issuing of written instructions for the carrying out of work; and
     - (ii) a system of permits to work, with such permits being issued by a person with responsibility for this function prior to the commencement of the work concerned.

**[3548]**

**NOTES**

Commencement: 1 October 2006.

*(Schs 2–5 contain amendments, repeals and revocations.)*

PART II
STATUTORY INSTRUMENTS

# HOUSING (RIGHT TO BUY) (INFORMATION TO SECURE TENANTS) (ENGLAND) ORDER 2005

## (SI 2005/1735)

**NOTES**
Made: 29 June 2005.
Authority: Housing Act 1985, ss 121AA, 121B.
Commencement: 26 July 2005.

### ARRANGEMENT OF ARTICLES

## 1 Citation, commencement and application

(1) This Order may be cited as The Housing (Right to Buy) (Information to Secure Tenants) (England) Order 2005 and shall come into force on 26th July 2005.

(2) This Order applies in relation to England only.

**[3549]**

**NOTES**
Commencement: 26 July 2005.

## 2 Interpretation

In this Order—
    "the Act" means the Housing Act 1985;
    "the document" means the document prepared by a landlord in accordance with section 121AA of the Act;
    "landlord" means a body which lets dwelling-houses under secure tenancies.

**[3550]**

**NOTES**
Commencement: 26 July 2005.

## 3 Matters about which information is to be provided to secure tenants

The matters set out in the Schedule to this Order are specified for the purposes of section 121AA of the Act.

**[3551]**

**NOTES**
Commencement: 26 July 2005.

## 4 When the document must be published

(1) A landlord shall publish the document within two months of this Order coming into force.

(2) Where a landlord revises the document under section 121AA(4) of the Act it shall publish the document in its revised form within one month of the revision.

**[3552]**

**NOTES**
Commencement: 26 July 2005.

## 5 When the document must be supplied

(1) Following publication of the document in accordance with article 4(1) or (2) a landlord shall supply a copy of the document—
    (a)    as soon as is reasonably practicable to each of its secure tenants at that time; and
    (b)    to each subsequent new secure tenant at the time he signs his tenancy.

(2) A landlord shall supply each of its secure tenants with a copy of the current version of the document at least once in every period of 5 years beginning with the date on which the document was supplied pursuant to article 5(1)(a).

**[3553]**

**NOTES**
Commencement: 26 July 2005.

**SCHEDULE**
**MATTERS ABOUT WHICH INFORMATION SHALL BE GIVEN TO SECURE TENANTS**
Article 3

1.   An outline of the effect of the provisions of Part 5 of the Act relating to—
    (a)   the circumstances in which the right to buy can and cannot be exercised;
    (b)   the exceptions to the right to buy set out in Schedule 5 to the Act;
    (c)   the procedure for claiming to exercise the right to buy;
    (d)   the price payable for the dwelling-house by a tenant exercising the right to buy; and
    (e)   the delay notice procedures for landlords and tenants set out in section 140, 141, 153A and 153B of the Act.

2.—(1)   The fact that initial costs are likely to be incurred by a secure tenant exercising the right to buy.

  (2)   The reference in paragraph (1) to initial costs includes costs in respect of—
    (a)   stamp duty;
    (b)   legal and survey fees;
    (c)   valuation fees and costs associated with taking out a mortgage.

3.—(1)   The fact that a secure tenant will be likely to have to make regular payments as an owner of a dwelling-house.

  (2)   The reference in paragraph (1) to regular payments includes payments in respect of—
    (a)   any mortgage or charge on the dwelling-house;
    (b)   building insurance, life assurance, and mortgage payment protection insurance;
    (c)   council tax;
    (d)   water, sewerage, gas, electricity, or other utility services.

4.   The risk of repossession of the dwelling-house if regular mortgage payments are not made.

5.   The fact that in order to keep the property maintained and in good repair an owner of a dwelling-house will be likely to have to incur expenditure which may include payment of service charges in respect of major works.

**[3554]**

**NOTES**
Commencement: 26 July 2005.

# HOUSING (RIGHT OF FIRST REFUSAL) (ENGLAND) REGULATIONS 2005

(SI 2005/1917)

**NOTES**
Made: 12 July 2005.
Authority: Housing Act 1985, ss 36A, 156A, 171C; Housing Act 1988, Sch 11, para 2A; Housing Act 1996, ss 12A, 17(2)–(5).
Commencement: 10 August 2005.

## ARRANGEMENT OF REGULATIONS

PART II
STATUTORY INSTRUMENTS

## 1   Citation, commencement, interpretation and application

(1)   These Regulations may be cited as the Housing (Right of First Refusal) (England) Regulations 2005 and shall come into force on 10th August 2005.

(2)   In these Regulations—

"the 1985 Act" means the Housing Act 1985;

"acceptance notice" means a notice which complies with the requirements of regulation 12(2);

"former landlord" means the landlord which disposed of the property under Part 5 of the 1985 Act;

"local housing authority" means a district council, a London borough council, the Common Council of the City of London or the Council of the Isles of Scilly;

"offer notice" means a notice which complies with the requirements of regulation 12(1);

"owner" means the person who is the freehold or leasehold owner of a property and who is bound by a right of first refusal covenant imposed under section 156A of the 1985 Act;

"property" means a property which is subject to a right of first refusal covenant imposed under section 156A of the 1985 Act; and

"rejection notice" means a notice which complies with the requirements of regulation 12(3).

(3)   These Regulations apply where a right of first refusal covenant has been imposed in relation to a dwelling-house situated in England.

**[3555]**

**NOTES**

Commencement: 10 August 2005.

## 2   Operative provisions for leasehold and freehold properties

(1)   These Regulations apply where there is to be a relevant disposal, other than an exempted disposal, of the owner's interest in the property.

(2)   Where the owner has a leasehold interest he must comply with the requirements of regulation 3.

(3)   Where the owner has a freehold interest he must comply with the requirements of regulation 4.

**[3556]**

**NOTES**

Commencement: 10 August 2005.

## 3   Service of offer notice—leasehold property

The owner must serve an offer notice on—

     (a)    the former landlord, if it is still the landlord; or

     (b)    if the former landlord is not still the landlord, the person in which the reversionary interest is currently vested.

**[3557]**

**NOTES**

Commencement: 10 August 2005.

## 4   Service of offer notice—freehold property

The owner must serve an offer notice on—

     (a)    the former landlord (if that person is still in existence); or

     (b)    if the former landlord is not still in existence, the local housing authority for the area in which the property is situated.

**[3558]**

**NOTES**

Commencement: 10 August 2005.

## 5   Acknowledgement of receipt of offer notice

(1)   The recipient of an offer notice under either regulation 3 or 4 must send an acknowledgement of receipt to the owner as soon as reasonably practicable.

(2)	The acknowledgement of receipt must—
   (a)	specify the date of receipt of the offer notice; and
   (b)	explain the effect of regulations 6 to 10, in simple terms.

**[3559]**

**NOTES**
   Commencement: 10 August 2005.

## 6	Acceptance notices

(1)	Where the recipient of an offer notice wishes to accept the offer, it must do so within the period of 8 weeks beginning with the date of receipt of the notice.

(2)	Acceptance of an offer must be by acceptance notice, in which the recipient of the offer notice must either—
   (a)	itself accept the offer; or
   (b)	nominate another person to accept the offer in accordance with regulation 8.

(3)	The service of an acceptance notice by any person entitled to do so shall not confer any right on the owner of the property to require that person to purchase the property unless and until that person enters into a binding contract for sale in accordance with regulation 10.

**[3560]**

**NOTES**
   Commencement: 10 August 2005.

## 7	Rejection notices

(1)	The recipient of an offer notice must serve a rejection notice as soon as it has decided that it does not wish to either—
   (a)	accept the offer itself; or
   (b)	nominate another person to accept the offer in accordance with regulation 8.

(2)	The rejection notice must be served within 8 weeks from the date of receipt of the offer notice.

**[3561]**

**NOTES**
   Commencement: 10 August 2005.

## 8	Nomination of another person to accept an offer

(1)	The recipient of an offer notice may nominate another person to accept the offer.

(2)	The only persons who can be nominated to accept an offer are those who either—
   (a)	are registered as a social landlord under Part 1 of the Housing Act 1996; or
   (b)	fulfil the landlord condition in section 80 of the 1985 Act.

(3)	Before a person can be nominated to accept a particular offer, that person must have given an unequivocal indication in writing to the recipient of the offer notice that it wishes to be nominated to accept the offer.

(4)	For the purposes of this regulation, "in writing" includes a document transmitted by facsimile or other electronic means.

**[3562]**

**NOTES**
   Commencement: 10 August 2005.

## 9	Disposal of property and requirement for further offer notice

(1)	Where an owner has served an offer notice and the recipient—
   (a)	has not served either an acceptance notice or a rejection notice within 8 weeks from the date of receipt of the offer notice; or
   (b)	has served a rejection notice,
then, subject to paragraph (2), the owner may dispose of the property as he sees fit; and these Regulations shall not apply to any subsequent disposal of the property by him.

(2)	If after the expiry of the period of 12 months, as determined in accordance with paragraphs (3) or (4) as appropriate, the owner retains his interest in the property, these Regulations shall apply if there is to be a disposal of a kind described in regulation 2(1).

(3)	In the circumstances referred to in paragraph (1)(a), the 12 month period begins the day after the expiry of the 8 week period.

(4)   In the circumstances referred to in paragraph (1)(b), the 12 month period begins the day after that on which the rejection notice is served.

[3563]

**NOTES**
Commencement: 10 August 2005.

## 10   Time limit for completion of purchase

(1)   A person who accepts an offer must enter into a binding contract with the owner for the purchase of the property—
- (a)   not later than 12 weeks after the date on which the acceptance notice is served on the owner; or
- (b)   not later than 4 weeks after the date of receipt of written notification from the owner that he is ready to complete;

whichever is later.

(2)   If the time limit in paragraph (1) is not complied with, the owner may dispose of the property as he sees fit; and these Regulations shall not apply to any subsequent disposal of the property by him.

(3)   If either or both of the parties request that the District Valuer determine the value of the property in accordance with section 158 of the 1985 Act, the time from the date that the request is received by the District Valuer until the date that the determined value is notified to the parties shall be excluded from the calculation of the period in paragraph (1).

[3564]

**NOTES**
Commencement: 10 August 2005.

## 11   Computation of time

In calculating a period for any purpose of these Regulations, with the exception of the 12 month period in regulation 9, Christmas Day, Good Friday, or a day which under the Banking and Financial Dealings Act 1971 is a bank holiday, shall be excluded.

[3565]

**NOTES**
Commencement: 10 August 2005.

## 12   Contents of notices

(1)   An offer notice must—
- (a)   be in writing;
- (b)   state that the owner wishes to dispose of the property, giving its full postal address;
- (c)   state that there is a covenant requiring him to first offer the property to the recipient of the notice;
- (d)   in relation to the property to which the notice relates—
  - (i)   specify whether the property is a house, a flat or a maisonette;
  - (ii)   specify the number of bedrooms;
  - (iii)   give details of the heating system;
  - (iv)   specify any improvements or structural changes which have been made since the purchase; and
- (e)   state the address at which the recipient can serve notices upon the owner.

(2)   An acceptance notice must—
- (a)   be in writing;
- (b)   indicate clearly whether the person giving the notice is—
  - (i)   accepting the offer; or
  - (ii)   nominating another person to accept the offer; and
- (c)   provide the full postal address and telephone number of any nominee.

(3)   A rejection notice must—
- (a)   be in writing; and
- (b)   state that the person is rejecting the offer to purchase the property.

[3566]

**NOTES**
Commencement: 10 August 2005.

### 13  Service of notices

Notices under these Regulations may be served either by personal delivery, or by post.

**[3567]**

**NOTES**
   Commencement: 10 August 2005.

### 14  Disposal of property acquired under preserved right to buy

With the exception of regulations 15 to 18, these Regulations shall also apply if there is to be a relevant disposal, other than an exempted disposal, of the owner's interest in a property acquired in exercise of the right conferred by section 171A of the 1985 Act.

**[3568]**

**NOTES**
   Commencement: 10 August 2005.

### 15  Disposal of property acquired under right to acquire

With the exception of regulations 14 and 16 to 18 these Regulations shall also apply if there is to be a relevant disposal, other than an exempted disposal, of the owner's interest in a property acquired in exercise of the right conferred by section 16 of the Housing Act 1996.

**[3569]**

**NOTES**
   Commencement: 10 August 2005.

### 16  Disposal of property acquired on voluntary disposal at a discount by local authority

(1)   With the exception of regulations 14, 15, 17 and 18, these Regulations shall also apply if there is to be a relevant disposal, other than an exempted disposal, of the owner's interest in a property acquired at a discount from a local authority using its power to dispose of land in section 32 of the 1985 Act, subject to the following modifications.

(2)   In regulation 1—
  (a)   for the definition of "former landlord" substitute—
      ""former owner" means the local authority which disposed of the property under section 32 of the 1985 Act";
  (b)   for the definition of "owner" substitute—
      ""owner" means the person who is the freehold or leasehold owner of the property and who is bound by a right of first refusal covenant imposed under section 36A of the 1985 Act"; and
  (c)   for the definition of "property" substitute—
      ""property" means a property which is subject to a right of first refusal covenant imposed under section 36A of the 1985 Act".

(3)   For all occurrences of the term "former landlord" substitute "former owner".

(4)   In regulation 10(3), for "section 158" substitute "section 36B".

**[3570]**

**NOTES**
   Commencement: 10 August 2005.

### 17  Disposal of property acquired on voluntary disposal at a discount by registered social landlord

(1)   With the exception of regulations 14 to 16 and 18, these Regulations shall also apply if there is to be a relevant disposal, other than an exempted disposal, of the owner's interest in a property acquired at a discount from a registered social landlord using its power to dispose of land in section 9 of the Housing Act 1996, subject to the following modifications.

(2)   In regulation 1—
  (a)   for the definition of "former landlord" substitute—
      ""former owner" means the registered social landlord which disposed of the property under section 9 of the Housing Act 1996";
  (b)   for the definition of "owner" substitute—
      ""owner" means the person who is the freehold or leasehold owner of the property and who is bound by a right of first refusal covenant imposed under section 12A of the Housing Act 1996"; and
  (c)   for the definition of "property" substitute—

""property" means a property which is subject to a right of first refusal covenant imposed under section 12A of the Housing Act 1996".

(3)   In regulation 10(3), for "section 158 of the 1985 Act" substitute "section 12B of the Housing Act 1996".

(4)   For all occurrences of the term "former landlord" substitute "former owner".

**[3571]**

**NOTES**
Commencement: 10 August 2005.

## 18   Disposal of property acquired on voluntary disposals at a discount by housing action trust

(1)   With the exception of regulations 14 to 17, these Regulations shall also apply if there is to be a relevant disposal, other than an exempted disposal, of the owner's interest in a property acquired at a discount from a housing action trust using its power to dispose of land in section 79 of the Housing Act 1988, subject to the following modifications.

(2)   In regulation 1—
    (a)   for the definition of "former landlord" substitute—
       ""former owner" means the housing action trust which disposed of the property under section 79 of the Housing Act 1988";
    (b)   for the definition of "owner" substitute—
       ""owner" means the person who is the freehold or leasehold owner of the property and who is bound by a right of first refusal covenant imposed under paragraph 2A of Schedule 11 to the Housing Act 1988"; and
    (c)   for the definition of "property" substitute—
       ""property" means a property which is subject to a right of first refusal covenant imposed under paragraph 2A of Schedule 11 to the Housing Act 1988".

(3)   In regulation 10(3), for "section 158 of the 1985 Act" substitute "paragraph 2B of Schedule 11 to the Housing Act 1988".

(4)   For all occurrences of the term "former landlord" substitute "former owner".

**[3572]**

**NOTES**
Commencement: 10 August 2005.

# HOUSING (RIGHT OF FIRST REFUSAL) (WALES) REGULATIONS 2005 (NOTE)

## (SI 2005/2680 (W 186))

**NOTES**
Made: 27 September 2005.
Authority: Housing Act 1985, ss 36A, 156A, 171C; Housing Act 1996, ss 12A, 17(2)–(5).
Commencement: 28 September 2005.
These Regulations apply to Wales only. The equivalent provisions for England are in SI 2005/1917 at **[3555]** et seq.

**[3573]**

# HOUSING (RIGHT TO BUY) (INFORMATION TO SECURE TENANTS) (WALES) ORDER 2005 (NOTE)

## (SI 2005/2681 (W 187))

**NOTES**
*Made: 27 September 2005.*
Authority: Housing Act 1985, ss 121AA, 121B.
Commencement: 28 September 2005.
This Order applies to Wales only. The equivalent provisions for England are in SI 2005/1735 at **[3549]** et seq.

**[3574]**

# PUBLIC SERVICES OMBUDSMAN (WALES) ACT 2005 (COMMENCEMENT NO 1 AND TRANSITIONAL PROVISIONS AND SAVINGS) ORDER 2005

### (SI 2005/2800 (W 199))

**NOTES**
Made: 11 October 2005.
Authority: Public Services Ombudsman (Wales) Act 2005, ss 40, 43(1)(b), 44(1), (2).

### ARRANGEMENT OF ARTICLES

## 1   Title and interpretation

The name of this Order is the Public Services Ombudsman (Wales) Act 2005 (Commencement No 1 and Transitional Provisions and Savings) Order 2005.

**[3575]**

**2**—(1)   In this Order—
"a Local Commissioner in Wales" ("*Comisiynydd Lleol yng Nghymru*") means a Local Commissioner (within the meaning of Part 3 of the Local Government Act 1974) who is a member of the Commission,
"the Act" ("*y Ddeddf*") means the Public Services Ombudsman (Wales) Act 2005,
"the Commission" ("*Y Comisiwn*") means the Commission for Local Administration in Wales established by section 23(1)(b) of the Local Government Act 1974,
"the Ombudsman" ("*yr Ombwdsmon*") means the Public Services Ombudsman for Wales, and
"the 2000 Act" ("*Deddf 2000*") means the Local Government Act 2000.

(2)   In this Order references to sections and Schedules are, unless otherwise stated, references to sections of and Schedules to the Act.

**[3576]**

## 3   Provisions coming into force on 12 October 2005

The following provisions come into force on 12 October 2005 for the purposes referred to—
    (a)   the provisions specified in the first column of the Table in Part 1 of Schedule 1 to this Order come into force for the purposes specified in the second column of that Table, and
    (b)   the provisions specified in the first column of the Table in Part 2 of Schedule 1 to this Order come into force for the purposes specified in the second column of that Table.

**[3577]**

**4**—(1)   Section 35 and the following paragraphs of Schedule 4 come into force in accordance with paragraphs (2) and (3) below—
    (a)   1, 2, 4,
    (b)   11(a) and (c) to (e),
    (c)   14(a), and
    (d)   23.

(2)   Save as provided for in paragraph (3) below, the provisions referred to in paragraph (1) above come into force on 12 October 2005 for the purpose of making orders and regulations (as the case may be) relating to the functions of the Ombudsman under Part 3 of the 2000 Act.

(3)   Until 1 April 2006 the provisions referred to in sub-paragraph (a) below continue to have effect, for the purpose referred to in sub-paragraph (b) below, as if the amendments made by the provisions referred to in paragraph (1) above did not have effect—
    (a)   the provisions referred to above are the following sections of the 2000 Act—
        (i)   49,
        (ii)   53,
        (iii)   68(1), (3) and (4),
        (iv)   70(2)(b), and
        (v)   82.

(b)　the purpose referred to above is the purpose of making orders and regulations (as the case may be) relating to the functions of the Commission or a Local Commissioner in Wales under Part 3 of the 2000 Act.

**[3578]**

## 5　Provisions coming into force on 1 April 2006

(1)　Save as provided for in paragraph (2) below, and except as provided for in paragraph (3) below, the provisions of the Act, insofar as they are not already in force, come into force on 1 April 2006.

(2)　For the purposes of the financial year ending 31 March 2006—

(a)　subject to sub-paragraph (b) below and despite the coming into force of section 39 and Schedule 7, the provisions of the Acts referred to in the first column of the Table in Schedule 2 to this Order continue to have effect as if those provisions had not been repealed by the Act, and

(b)　those provisions continue to have effect in accordance with sub-paragraph (a) above subject to the modifications specified in the second column of the Table in Schedule 2 to this Order.

(3)　The following provisions do not come into force on 1 April 2006—

(a)　section 20, and

(b)　paragraph 15(5) of Schedule 1.

**[3579]**

## 6　Complaints spanning commencement date

(1)　Where this article applies the Ombudsman must consider the complaint in accordance with the provisions of Part 2 of the Act.

(2)　This article applies where—

(a)　a complaint has been duly made or referred to the Ombudsman in respect of a matter which relates to events that occurred before 1 April 2006 and events that occurred after that date, and

(b)　as regards the events that occurred before 1 April 2006 a complaint could (but for the other provisions of the Act) have been but has not been made to an existing Welsh Ombudsman under the relevant existing enactment.

(3)　For the purposes of this article the Ombudsman is not prevented from investigating a matter (or part of a matter) in accordance with Part 2 of the Act only because it relates to events that occurred before 1 April 2006.

(4)　For the purposes of paragraph (2) above—

(a)　"existing Welsh Ombudsman", and

(b)　"the relevant existing enactment",

have the same meanings as in section 38(6).

**[3580]**

## 7　Transitional Provision—estimates

(1)　The following provisions of this article apply to the Ombudsman in relation to the financial year ending 31 March 2007.

(2)　The Ombudsman must prepare an estimate of the income and expenses of that office for that financial year and submit it to the Assembly Cabinet not later than one month before the beginning of that financial year.

(3)　The Assembly Cabinet must examine the estimate and then lay it before the Assembly with any modifications it thinks appropriate.

(4)　If the Assembly Cabinet proposes to lay the estimate before the Assembly with modifications, it must first consult the Secretary of State.

**[3581]**

SCHEDULES

SCHEDULE 1
PROVISIONS COMING INTO FORCE ON 12 OCTOBER 2005

Article 3

PART 1

| Provisions | Purpose |
|---|---|
| Section 1 and paragraphs 1, 2, 3, 5(1) to (3), 6 and 8 of Schedule 1 | For the purpose of appointing the Ombudsman. |
| Section 10 and Schedule 2 | All purposes. |
| Subsections (7) to (9) of section 25 | All purposes. |
| Section 28 and Schedule 3 | All purposes. |
| Section 29 | All purposes. |
| Section 30 | All purposes. |
| Section 39 and paragraphs 61 to 63 of Schedule 6 | For the purpose of appointing the Ombudsman. |

PART 2

| Provisions | Purpose |
|---|---|
| Section 39 and paragraph 18(11) and (13) of Schedule 6 | For the purpose of removing the duty on the Commission for Local Administration in Wales to prepare and submit an estimate of the expenses it will incur in the financial year ending 31 March 2007. |
| Section 39 and the entry in Schedule 7 for the "Health Service Commissioners Act 1993" but only to effect the repeal of paragraph 9 of Schedule 1A to that Act | For the purpose of removing the duty on the Health Service Commissioner for Wales to prepare and submit an estimate of the income and expenses of his or her office for the financial year ending 31 March 2007. |
| Section 39 and the entry in Schedule 7 for the "Government of Wales Act 1998" but only to effect the repeal of paragraph 8 of Schedule 9 to that Act | For the purpose of removing the duty on the Welsh Administration Ombudsman to prepare and submit an estimate of the income and expenses of his office for the financial year ending 31 March 2007. |

**[3582]**

SCHEDULE 2
SAVINGS

Article 5

| Provisions | Modifications |
|---|---|
| Section 1(3) of and paragraphs 10 to 14 of Schedule 1A to the Health Service Commissioners Act 1993 | For the purposes of paragraph 12 of that Schedule to that Act, the Ombudsman shall be regarded as the accounting officer. |
| Section 111(2) of and paragraphs 9 to 13 of Schedule 9 to the Government of Wales Act 1998 | For the purposes of paragraph 11 of that Schedule to that Act, the Ombudsman shall be regarded as the accounting officer. |
| Section 51A(7) of and paragraphs 13 to 17 of Schedule 2A to the Housing Act 1996 | For the purposes of paragraph 15 of that Schedule to that Act, the Ombudsman shall be regarded as the accounting officer. |

**[3583]**

# HOUSING HEALTH AND SAFETY RATING SYSTEM (ENGLAND) REGULATIONS 2005

## (SI 2005/3208)

**NOTES**
Made: 17 November 2005.
Authority: Housing Act 2004, ss 2, 4, 250(2)(a).
Commencement: 6 April 2006.

### ARRANGEMENT OF REGULATIONS

## 1  Citation, commencement and application

(1)   These Regulations may be cited as the Housing Health and Safety Rating System (England) Regulations 2005 and shall come into force on 6th April 2006.

(2)   These Regulations apply in relation to residential premises in England only.

**[3584]**

**NOTES**
Commencement: 6 April 2006.

## 2  Interpretation

In these Regulations—
  "the Act" means the Housing Act 2004;
  "harm" means harm which is within any of Classes I to IV as set out in Schedule 2 to these Regulations;
  "inspector" means a person carrying out an inspection under section 4 of the Act (inspections by local housing authorities to see whether a category 1 or 2 hazard exists); and except in regulation 6(7)(e), "occupier" includes potential occupier.

**[3585]**

**NOTES**
Commencement: 6 April 2006.

## 3  Prescribed descriptions of hazard

(1)   A hazard is of a prescribed description for the purposes of the Act where the risk of harm is associated with the occurrence of any of the matters or circumstances listed in Schedule 1.

(2)   In Schedule 1, a reference to a matter or circumstance is, unless otherwise stated, to a matter or circumstance in or, as the case may be, at the dwelling or HMO in question, or in any building or land in the vicinity of the dwelling or HMO.

**[3586]**

**NOTES**
Commencement: 6 April 2006.

## 4  Prescribed fire hazard

For the purposes of section 10 of the Act a category 1 or 2 hazard is a prescribed fire hazard if the risk of harm is associated with exposure to uncontrolled fire and associated smoke.

**[3587]**

**NOTES**
Commencement: 6 April 2006.

## 5  Inspections

An inspector must—

   (a)   have regard to any guidance for the time being given under section 9 of the Act in relation to the inspection of residential premises;

   (b)   inspect any residential premises with a view to preparing an accurate record of their state and condition; and

   (c)   prepare and keep such a record in written or in electronic form.

**[3588]**

**NOTES**

Commencement: 6 April 2006.

## 6  Seriousness of hazards

(1)  Where, following an inspection of residential premises under section 4 of the Act, the inspector—

   (a)   determines that a hazard of a prescribed description exists; and

   (b)   considers, having regard to any guidance for the time being given under section 9 of the Act in relation to the assessment of hazards, that it is appropriate to calculate the seriousness of that hazard,

the seriousness of that hazard shall be calculated in accordance with paragraphs (2) to (4) of this regulation.

(2)  The inspector shall assess the likelihood, during the period of 12 months beginning with the date of the assessment, of a relevant occupier suffering any harm as a result of that hazard as falling within one of the range of ratios of likelihood set out in column 1 of Table 1.

**Table 1**

| Column 1<br>*Range of ratios of likelihood* | Column 2<br>*Representative scale point of range* |
|---|---|
| Less likely than 1 in 4200 | 5600 |
| 1 in 4200 to 1 in 2400 | 3200 |
| 1 in 2400 to 1 in 1300 | 1800 |
| 1 in 1300 to 1 in 750 | 1000 |
| 1 in 750 to 1 in 420 | 560 |
| 1 in 420 to 1 in 240 | 320 |
| 1 in 240 to 1 in 130 | 180 |
| 1 in 130 to 1 in 75 | 100 |
| 1 in 75 to 1 in 42 | 56 |
| 1 in 42 to 1 in 24 | 32 |
| 1 in 24 to 1 in 13 | 18 |
| 1 in 13 to 1 in 7.5 | 10 |
| 1 in 7.5 to 1 in 4 | 6 |
| 1 in 4 to 1 in 2.5 | 3 |
| 1 in 2.5 to 1 in 1.5 | 2 |
| More likely than 1 in 1.5 | 1 |

(3)  The inspector shall assess which of the four classes of harm (set out in Schedule 2) a relevant occupier is most likely to suffer during the period mentioned in paragraph (2).

(4)  The inspector shall—

   (a)   assess the possibility of each of the other classes of harm occurring as a result of that hazard, as falling within one of the range of percentages of possibility set out in column 1 of Table 2;

   (b)   record each possibility so assessed as the corresponding RSPRR set out in column 2 of Table 2; and

   (c)   record the possibility (which shall be known, for the purposes of the formula in paragraph (5), as the RSPPR) of the most likely class of harm occurring as a percentage calculated using the following formula—

$$100\% - (A + B + C)$$

Where—

A is the RSPPR recorded under sub paragraph (b) as the second most likely class of harm;

B is the RSPPR recorded under sub paragraph (b) as the third most likely class of harm; and

C is the RSPPR recorded under sub paragraph (b) as the fourth most likely class of harm.

**Table 2**

| Column 1<br>Range of percentages of possibility | Column 2<br>Representative scale point of the percentage range (RSPPR) |
|---|---|
| Below 0.05% | 0% |
| 0.05 to 0.15% | 0.1% |
| 0.15% to 0.3% | 0.2% |
| 0.3% to 0.7% | 0.5% |
| 0.7% to 1.5% | 1% |
| 1.5% to 3% | 2.2% |
| 3% to 7% | 4.6% |
| 7% to 15% | 10% |
| 15% to 26% | 21.5% |
| 26% to 38 % | 31.6% |
| Above 38% | 46.4% |

(5)   When the inspector has assessed likelihood under paragraph (2) and assessed the possibility of each harm occurring under paragraph (3), the seriousness of that hazard shall be expressed by a numerical score calculated using the following formula—

$$S1 + S2 + S3 + S4$$

Where—

$$S1 = 10000 \times (1 / L) \times O1$$
$$S2 = 1000 \times (1 / L) \times O2$$
$$S3 = 300 \times (1 / L) \times O3$$
$$S4 = 10 \times (1 / L) \times O4$$

(6)   For the purposes of the formula in paragraph (5)—

(a)   L is the representative scale point of range in column 2 of Table 1 corresponding to the range that has been recorded under paragraph (2);

(b)   O1 is the RSPPR recorded under paragraph (4) in relation to Class I harm;

(c)   O2 is the RSPPR recorded under paragraph (4) in relation to Class II harm;

(d)   O3 is the RSPPR recorded under paragraph (4) in relation to Class III harm;

(e)   O4 is the RSPPR recorded under paragraph (4) in relation to Class IV harm.

(7)   In this regulation—

"relevant occupier" means, where the risk of harm concerned is associated with the occurrence of any of the matters or circumstances listed in—

(a)   paragraph 1 of Schedule 1, an occupier under the age of 15 years;

(b)   paragraph 2, 3 or 6(a) of Schedule 1, an occupier aged 65 years or over;

(c)   paragraph 7 of Schedule 1, an occupier under the age of 3 years;

(d)   paragraph 8 of Schedule 1, an occupier aged 60 years or over who has been exposed to radon since birth;

(e)   paragraph 11 of Schedule 1, the actual occupier;

(f)   paragraph 17, 22, 23 or 25 of Schedule 1, an occupier under the age of 5 years;

(g)   paragraph 19, 20, 21, 24 or 28 of Schedule 1, an occupier aged 60 years or over;

(h)   paragraph 26—

(i)   except where a collision is with low architectural features, an occupier under the age of 5 years, and

(ii)   where a collision is with low architectural features, an occupier aged 16 years or over;

(i)   any other paragraph of Schedule 1, any occupier; and

"RSPPR" means the representative scale point of the percentage range.

(8)     In making assessments under this regulation, an inspector shall have regard to any guidance for the time being given under section 9 of the Act.

**[3589]**

**NOTES**
Commencement: 6 April 2006.

## 7   Prescribed bands

For the purposes of the Act a hazard falls within a band identified by a letter in column 1 of Table 3 where it achieves a numerical score calculated in accordance with regulation 6(5) which is within the range corresponding to that letter in column 2 of that Table.

**Table 3**

| Column 1 | Column 2 |
|----------|----------|
| *Band* | *Numerical Score Range* |
| A | 5000 or more |
| B | 2000 to 4999 |
| C | 1000 to 1999 |
| D | 500 to 999 |
| E | 200 to 499 |
| F | 100 to 199 |
| G | 50 to 99 |
| H | 20 to 49 |
| I | 10 to 19 |
| J | 9 or less |

**[3590]**

**NOTES**
Commencement: 6 April 2006.

## 8   Category of hazard

For the purposes of the Act—
    (a)     a hazard falling within band A, B or C of Table 3 is a category 1 hazard; and
    (b)     a hazard falling within any other band in that Table is a category 2 hazard.

**[3591]**

**NOTES**
Commencement: 6 April 2006.

SCHEDULES

SCHEDULE 1
MATTERS AND CIRCUMSTANCES
Regulation 3(1)

**1   Damp and mould growth**
Exposure to house dust mites, damp, mould or fungal growths.

**2   Excess cold**
Exposure to low temperatures.

**3   Excess heat**
Exposure to high temperatures.

**4   Asbestos and MMF**
Exposure to asbestos fibres or manufactured mineral fibres.

**5   Biocides**
Exposure to chemicals used to treat timber and mould growth.

**6  Carbon monoxide and fuel combustion products**

Exposure to—
- (a)    carbon monoxide;
- (b)    nitrogen dioxide;
- (c)    sulphur dioxide and smoke.

**7  Lead**

The ingestion of lead.

**8  Radiation**

Exposure to radiation.

**9  Uncombusted fuel gas**

Exposure to uncombusted fuel gas.

**10  Volatile organic compounds**

Exposure to volatile organic compounds.

**11  Crowding and space**

A lack of adequate space for living and sleeping.

**12  Entry by intruders**

Difficulties in keeping the dwelling or HMO secure against unauthorised entry.

**13  Lighting**

A lack of adequate lighting.

**14  Noise**

Exposure to noise.

**15  Domestic hygiene, pests and refuse**

(1)    Poor design, layout or construction such that the dwelling or HMO cannot readily be kept clean.

(2)    Exposure to pests.

(3)    An inadequate provision for the hygienic storage and disposal of household waste.

**16  Food safety**

An inadequate provision of facilities for the storage, preparation and cooking of food.

**17  Personal hygiene, sanitation and drainage**

An inadequate provision of—
- (a)    facilities for maintaining good personal hygiene;
- (b)    sanitation and drainage.

**18  Water supply**

An inadequate supply of water free from contamination, for drinking and other domestic purposes.

**19  Falls associated with baths etc**

Falls associated with toilets, baths, showers or other washing facilities.

**20  Falling on level surfaces etc**

Falling on any level surface or falling between surfaces where the change in level is less than 300 millimetres.

**21  Falling on stairs etc**

Falling on stairs, steps or ramps where the change in level is 300 millimetres or more.

**22  Falling between levels**

Falling between levels where the difference in levels is 300 millimetres or more.

**23  Electrical hazards**

Exposure to electricity.

**24  Fire**

Exposure to uncontrolled fire and associated smoke.

**25  Flames, hot surfaces etc**

Contact with—

    (a)   controlled fire or flames;
    (b)   hot objects, liquid or vapours.

**26  Collision and entrapment**

Collision with, or entrapment of body parts in, doors, windows or other architectural features.

**27  Explosions**

An explosion at the dwelling or HMO.

**28  Position and operability of amenities etc**

The position, location and operability of amenities, fittings and equipment.

**29  Structural collapse and falling elements**

The collapse of the whole or part of the dwelling or HMO.

**[3592]**

---

**NOTES**

Commencement: 6 April 2006.

---

SCHEDULE 2

CLASSES OF HARM

Regulation 2

**Class I**

1.   A Class I harm is such extreme harm as is reasonably foreseeable as a result of the hazard in question, including—
    (a)   death from any cause;
    (b)   lung cancer;
    (c)   mesothelioma and other malignant tumours;
    (d)   permanent paralysis below the neck;
    (e)   regular severe pneumonia;
    (f)   permanent loss of consciousness;
    (g)   80% burn injuries.

**Class II**

2.   A Class II harm is such severe harm as is reasonably foreseeable as a result of the hazard in question, including—
    (a)   cardio-respiratory disease;
    (b)   asthma;
    (c)   non-malignant respiratory diseases;
    (d)   lead poisoning;
    (e)   anaphylactic shock;
    (f)   cryptosporidiosis;
    (g)   legionnaires disease;
    (h)   myocardial infarction;
    (i)   mild stroke;
    (j)   chronic confusion;
    (k)   regular severe fever;
    (l)   loss of a hand or foot;
    (m)   serious fractures;
    (n)   serious burns;
    (o)   loss of consciousness for days.

**Class III**

3.   A Class III harm is such serious harm as is reasonably foreseeable as a result of the hazard in question, including—
    (a)   eye disorders;
    (b)   rhinitis;
    (c)   hypertension;
    (d)   sleep disturbance;
    (e)   neuropsychological impairment;
    (f)   sick building syndrome;
    (g)   regular and persistent dermatitis, including contact dermatitis;
    (h)   allergy;
    (i)   gastro-enteritis;
    (j)   diarrhoea;
    (k)   vomiting;

(l)     chronic severe stress;
(m)    mild heart attack;
(n)     malignant but treatable skin cancer;
(o)     loss of a finger;
(p)     fractured skull and severe concussion;
(q)     serious puncture wounds to head or body;
(r)     severe burns to hands;
(s)     serious strain or sprain injuries;
(t)     regular and severe migraine.

**Class IV**

4.    A Class IV harm is such moderate harm as is reasonably foreseeable as a result of the hazard in question, including—

(a)     pleural plaques;
(b)     occasional severe discomfort;
(c)     benign tumours;
(d)     occasional mild pneumonia;
(e)     broken finger;
(f)     slight concussion;
(g)     moderate cuts to face or body;
(h)     severe bruising to body;
(i)     regular serious coughs or colds.

**[3593]**

**NOTES**
Commencement: 6 April 2006.

# APPROVAL OF CODE OF MANAGEMENT PRACTICE (PRIVATE RETIREMENT HOUSING) (ENGLAND) ORDER 2005

(SI 2005/3307)

**NOTES**
Made: 29 November 2005.
Authority: Leasehold Reform, Housing and Urban Development Act 1993, ss 87, 100.
Commencement: 2 January 2006.

## 1   Citation, commencement and application

(1)    This Order may be cited as the Approval of Code of Management Practice (Private Retirement Housing) (England) Order 2005 and shall come into force on 2nd January 2006.

(2)    This Order applies in relation to the management of residential properties in England only.
**[3594]**

**NOTES**
Commencement: 2 January 2006.

## 2   Approval of code of practice

With the exception of Appendices 4 to 6, "The Code of Practice for Private Retirement Housing", (ISBN 0-9526691-2-9), which was submitted for approval on 13th October 2005 by the Association of Retirement Housing Managers and is to be published by Chain and Pyle, Unit 3, King James Court, King James Street, London, SE1 0DH, is approved.
**[3595]**

**NOTES**
Commencement: 2 January 2006.

## 3   Revocation of orders and withdrawal of approvals

The Approval of Codes of Management Practice (Residential Property) (No 2) Order 1995 and the Approval of Codes of Management Practice (Residential Property) Order 1998 are revoked; and the approvals given by those Orders are withdrawn.
**[3596]**

**NOTES**
  Commencement: 2 January 2006.

### 4   Saving and transitional provision

Articles 2 and 3 do not apply for the purposes of section 87(7)(a) and (b) of the Leasehold Reform, Housing and Urban Development Act 1993 (use of code in proceedings) in relation to an act or omission alleged to have occurred before this Order comes into force.

**[3597]**

**NOTES**
  Commencement: 2 January 2006.

# HOUSING (EMPTY DWELLING MANAGEMENT ORDERS) (PRESCRIBED EXCEPTIONS AND REQUIREMENTS) (ENGLAND) ORDER 2006

### (SI 2006/367)

**NOTES**
  Made: 15 February 2006.
  Authority: Housing Act 2004, s 134(5)(a), (c), (6).
  Commencement: 6 April 2006.

### 1   Citation, commencement and application

  (1)   This Order may be cited as The Housing (Empty Dwelling Management Orders) (Prescribed Exceptions and Requirements) (England) Order 2006 and shall come into force on 6th April 2006.

  (2)   This Order shall apply in England only.

**[3598]**

**NOTES**
  Commencement: 6 April 2006.

### 2   Interpretation

In this Order "the Act" means the Housing Act 2004.

**[3599]**

**NOTES**
  Commencement: 6 April 2006.

### 3   Prescribed exceptions

For the purposes of section 134(1)(b) of the Act a dwelling falls within a prescribed exception if—

  (a)   it has been occupied solely or principally by the relevant proprietor and is wholly unoccupied because—
      (i)   he is temporarily resident elsewhere;
      (ii)   he is absent from the dwelling for the purpose of receiving personal care by reason of old age, disablement, illness, past or present alcohol or drug dependence or past or present mental disorder;
      (iii)   he is absent from the dwelling for the purpose of providing, or better providing, personal care for a person who requires such care by reason of old age, disablement, illness, past or present alcohol or drug dependence or past or present mental disorder; or
      (iv)   he is a serving member of the armed forces and he is absent from the dwelling as a result of such service;
  (b)   it is used as a holiday home (whether or not it is let as such on a commercial basis) or is otherwise occupied by the relevant proprietor or his guests on a temporary basis from time to time;
  (c)   it is genuinely on the market for sale or letting;
  (d)   it is comprised in an agricultural holding within the meaning of the Agricultural Holdings Act 1986 or a farm business tenancy within the meaning of the Agricultural Tenancies Act 1995;

(e) it is usually occupied by an employee of the relevant proprietor in connection with the performance of his duties under the terms of his contract of employment;

(f) it is available for occupation by a minister of religion as a residence from which to perform the duties of his office;

(g) it is subject to a court order freezing the property of the relevant proprietor;

(h) it is prevented from being occupied as a result of a criminal investigation or criminal proceedings;

(i) it is mortgaged, where the mortgagee, in right of the mortgage, has entered into and is in possession of the dwelling; or

(j) the person who was the relevant proprietor of it has died and six months has not elapsed since the grant of representation was obtained in respect of such person.

**[3600]**

**NOTES**
Commencement: 6 April 2006.

**4 Prescribed requirements**

(1) For the purpose of section 134(2)(e) of the Act the prescribed requirements with which a local housing authority must comply are that—

(a) it must make reasonable efforts to establish from the relevant proprietor whether he considers that any of the exceptions contained in article 3 apply to the dwelling;

(b) it must provide to the residential property tribunal—

(i) details of the efforts they have made to notify the relevant proprietor that they are considering making an interim empty dwelling management order in respect of his dwelling, as required under section 133(3)(a) of the Act;

(ii) details of the enquiries they have made to ascertain what steps (if any) the relevant proprietor is taking, or is intending to take, to secure that the dwelling is occupied, as required under section 133(3)(b) of the Act;

(iii) details of any advice and assistance they have provided to the relevant proprietor with a view to the relevant proprietor securing that the dwelling is occupied;

(iv) all information they have that suggests that the dwelling may fall within one of the exceptions described in article 3, whether available from the authority's own enquiries or from representations made to it by the relevant proprietor; and

(v) the classification of the dwelling for council tax purposes under the Local Government Finance Act 1992; and

(c) where the relevant proprietor—

(i) has undertaken or is undertaking repairs, maintenance or improvement works; or

(ii) has applied to a local planning authority or other authority for permission to make structural alterations or additions to the dwelling and he awaits the decision of a relevant authority on the application,

it must give reasons to the tribunal why it considers that an empty dwelling management order is required to secure occupation of the dwelling.

(2) For the purpose of paragraph (1)(c)(ii) a relevant authority is—

(a) the authority to whom the relevant proprietor has made the application; or,

(b) where that authority has made a decision against which the relevant proprietor or another person has appealed, the person or body that determines the appeal.

**[3601]**

**NOTES**
Commencement: 6 April 2006.

# HOUSING (MANAGEMENT ORDERS AND EMPTY DWELLING MANAGEMENT ORDERS) (SUPPLEMENTAL PROVISIONS) (ENGLAND) REGULATIONS 2006

(SI 2006/368)

**NOTES**
Made: 15 February 2006.
Authority: Housing Act 2004, s 145.
Commencement: 6 April 2006.

**1  Citation, commencement and application**

(1)   These Regulations may be cited as The Housing (Management Orders and Empty Dwelling Management Orders) (Supplemental Provisions) (England) Regulations 2006 and shall come into force on 6th April 2006.

(2)   These Regulations apply in England only.

**[3602]**

**NOTES**
Commencement: 6 April 2006.

**2  Interpretation**

In these regulations—
- (a)   "the Act" means the Housing Act 2004;
- (b)   "order" means—
  - (i)   an interim management order;
  - (ii)   a final management order;
  - (iii)   an interim EDMO; or
  - (iv)   a final EDMO;
- (c)   "premises" means a house, to which Chapter 1 of part 4 of the Act applies or a dwelling to which Chapter 2 of Part 4 of the Act applies; and
- (d)   "the relevant person", in relation to a lease of premises (or part of premises), means the person who (apart from, as the case may be, section 107(5) or 116(5) of, or paragraph 2(6) or 10(6) of Schedule 7 to, the Act) is the lessee under the lease.

**[3603]**

**NOTES**
Commencement: 6 April 2006.

**3  Supplementary provisions**

(1)   Where, under—
- (a)   section 107(5) or 116(5) of the Act; or
- (b)   paragraph 2(6) or 10(6) of Schedule 7 to the Act,
a local housing authority are to be treated as a lessee of premises (or a part of premises) under a lease, the following paragraphs apply.

(2)   As soon as an order is made the local housing authority making the order must serve on the immediate lessor of the relevant person ("the lessor") a notice with the following details—
- (a)   the type of order by reference to the relevant provision of the Act under which it has been made;
- (b)   the date the order comes into force;
- (c)   a summary of the effect the order has on the validity of the lease, by reference to the relevant provision of the Act; and
- (d)   the name and address of the local housing authority or any person authorised to receive on their behalf any future demand for ground rent, service charges or other charges due, or any notices or other documents in respect of the premises.

(3)   From the date the order comes into force neither the local housing authority nor the relevant person shall be liable for the payment of ground rent, service charges or other charges due under the lease, whether due before or after the date of the order if—
- (a)   the notice described in paragraph (2) has been served on the lessor; and
- (b)   the lessor fails to send the demand for such payment to the local housing authority.

(4)   From the date the order comes into force the local housing authority—
- (a)   are liable to pay any ground rent, service charges or other charges demanded of them that fall due under the lease in respect of a period after such date;
- (b)   may pay any outstanding ground rent, service charges or other charges due in respect of a period before such date;
- (c)   may challenge the reasonableness of any demands for such payments referred to in sub-paragraphs (a) or (b), whether on their own behalf or on behalf of the relevant person; and
- (d)   must send a copy of any demand for payment of ground rent, service charges or other charges, or any other notice or other document they receive from the lessor, to the relevant person (if his whereabouts are known) within 10 days of receiving it.

(5)   Where the relevant person receiving a copy of a demand, notice or other document under paragraph (4)(d) wishes to dispute any matter contained in it the local housing authority must provide such information and assistance as he may reasonably require.

(6)    The relevant person may not require the local housing authority to delay payment of any ground rent, service charge or other charges that the local housing authority reasonably believe are due or outstanding under the lease, whether or not he disputes a demand for such payment.

**[3604]**

**NOTES**
Commencement: 6 April 2006.

# HOUSING (INTERIM MANAGEMENT ORDERS) (PRESCRIBED CIRCUMSTANCES) (ENGLAND) ORDER 2006

(SI 2006/369)

**NOTES**
Made: 15 February 2006.
Authority: Housing Act 2004, s 103(5)(a), (6).
Commencement: 6 April 2006.

## 1  Citation, commencement and application

(1)    This Order may be cited as The Housing (Interim Management Orders) (Prescribed Circumstances) (England) Order 2006 and shall come into force on 6th April 2006.

(2)    This Order applies to houses in England to which section 103 of the Housing Act 2004 ("the Act") applies.

**[3605]**

**NOTES**
Commencement: 6 April 2006.

## 2  Prescribed circumstances for authorisation of interim management orders to which this Order applies

(1)    The following circumstances are prescribed for the purposes of section 103(3) of the Act—
  (a)    the area in which the house is located is experiencing a significant and persistent problem caused by anti-social behaviour;
  (b)    that problem is attributable, in whole or in part, to the anti-social behaviour of an occupier of the house;
  (c)    the landlord of the house is a private sector landlord;
  (d)    the landlord of the house is failing to take action to combat that problem that it would be appropriate for him to take; and
  (e)    the making of an interim management order, when combined with other measures taken in the area by the local housing authority, or by other persons together with the local housing authority, will lead to a reduction in, or elimination of, that problem.

(2)    In this article "private sector landlord" does not include a registered social landlord within the meaning of Part 1 of the Housing Act 1996.

**[3606]**

**NOTES**
Commencement: 6 April 2006.

# SELECTIVE LICENSING OF HOUSES (SPECIFIED EXEMPTIONS) (ENGLAND) ORDER 2006

(SI 2006/370)

**NOTES**
Made: 15 February 2006.
Authority: Housing Act 2004, s 79(4).
Commencement: 6 April 2006.

## 1  Citation, commencement and application

(1)    This Order may be cited as The Selective Licensing of Houses (Specified Exemptions) (England) Order 2006 and shall come into force on 6th April 2006.

(2)    This Order applies to houses in England only.

**[3607]**

**NOTES**
  Commencement: 6 April 2006.

## 2  Exempt tenancies or licences for the purposes of Part 3 of the Housing Act 2004

(1)   A tenancy or licence of a house or a dwelling contained in a house is an exempt tenancy or licence for the purposes of Part 3 of the Housing Act 2004 ("the Act") if it falls within any of the following descriptions—

- (a)   a tenancy or licence of a house or dwelling that is subject to a prohibition order made under section 20 of the Act whose operation has not been suspended in accordance with section 23 of the Act;
- (b)   a tenancy described in any of the following provisions of Part 1 of Schedule 1 to the Housing Act 1988, which cannot be an assured tenancy by virtue of section 1(2) of that Act—
  - (i)   paragraph 4 (business tenancies);
  - (ii)   paragraph 5 (licensed premises);
  - (iii)   paragraph 6 (tenancies of agricultural land); or
  - (iv)   paragraph 7 (tenancies of agricultural holdings etc);
- (c)   a tenancy or licence of a house or a dwelling that is managed or controlled by—
  - (i)   a local housing authority;
  - (ii)   a police authority established under section 3 of the Police Act 1996;
  - (iii)   the Metropolitan Police Authority established under section 5B of the Police Act 1996;
  - (iv)   a fire and rescue authority under the Fire and Rescue Services Act 2004; or
  - (v)   a health service body within the meaning of section 4 of the National Health Service and Community Care Act 1990;
- (d)   a tenancy or licence of a house which is not a house in multiple occupation for any purposes of the Act (except Part 1) by virtue of—
  - (i)   paragraph 3 of Schedule 14 to the Act (buildings regulated otherwise than under the Act); or
  - (ii)   paragraph 4(1) of that Schedule (buildings occupied by students);
- (e)   a tenancy of a house or a dwelling where—
  - (i)   the full term of the tenancy is more than 21 years;
  - (ii)   the lease does not contain a provision enabling the landlord to determine the tenancy, other than by forfeiture, earlier than at end of the term; and
  - (iii)   the house or dwelling is occupied by a person to whom the tenancy was granted or his successor in title or any members of such person's family;
- (f)   a tenancy or licence of a house or a dwelling granted by a person to a person who is a member of his family where—
  - (i)   the person to whom the tenancy or licence is granted occupies the house or dwelling as his only or main residence;
  - (ii)   the person granting the tenancy or licence is the freeholder or the holder of a lease of the house or dwelling the full term of which is more than 21 years; and
  - (iii)   the lease referred to in sub-paragraph (ii) does not contain a provision enabling the landlord to determine the tenancy, other than by forfeiture, earlier than at end of the term;
- (g)   a tenancy or licence that is granted to a person in relation to his occupancy of a house or a dwelling as a holiday home; or
- (h)   a tenancy or licence under the terms of which the occupier shares any accommodation with the landlord or licensor or a member of the landlord's or licensor's family.

(2)   For the purposes of this article—

- (a)   a person is a member of the same family as another person if—
  - (i)   those persons live as a couple;
  - (ii)   one of them is the relative of the other; or
  - (iii)   one of them is, or is a relative of, one member of a couple and the other is a relative of the other member of the couple;
- (b)   "couple" means two persons who are married to each other or live together as husband and wife (or in an equivalent relationship in the case of persons of the same sex);
- (c)   "relative" means parent, grandparent, child, grandchild, brother, sister, uncle, aunt, nephew, niece or cousin;
- (d)   a relationship of the half-blood is to be treated as a relationship of the whole blood;
- (e)   a stepchild of a person is to be treated as his child;
- (f)   an occupier shares accommodation with another person if he has the use of an amenity in common with that person (whether or not also in common with others); and
- (g)   "amenity" includes a toilet, personal washing facilities, a kitchen or a living room but excludes any area used for storage, a staircase, corridor or other means of access.

**[3608]**

**NOTES**
Commencement: 6 April 2006.

# LICENSING OF HOUSES IN MULTIPLE OCCUPATION (PRESCRIBED DESCRIPTIONS) (ENGLAND) ORDER 2006

(SI 2006/371)

**NOTES**
Made: 15 February 2006.
Authority: Housing Act 2004, s 55(3).
Commencement: 6 April 2006.

## 1 Citation, commencement and application

(1) This Order may be cited as The Licensing of Houses in Multiple Occupation (Prescribed Descriptions) (England) Order 2006 and shall come into force on 6th April 2006.

(2) This Order applies to any HMO in England, other than a converted block of flats to which section 257 of the Act applies.

[3609]

**NOTES**
Commencement: 6 April 2006.

## 2 Interpretation

In this Order—
    (a)   "the Act" means the Housing Act 2004; and
    (b)   "business premises" means premises, or any part of premises, which are not, or are not used in connection with, and as an integral part of, living accommodation.

[3610]

**NOTES**
Commencement: 6 April 2006.

## 3 Description of HMOs prescribed by the Secretary of State

(1) An HMO is of a prescribed description for the purpose of section 55(2)(a) of the Act where it satisfies the conditions described in paragraph (2).

(2) The conditions referred to in paragraph (1) are that—
    (a)   the HMO or any part of it comprises three storeys or more;
    (b)   it is occupied by five or more persons; and
    (c)   it is occupied by persons living in two or more single households.

(3) The following storeys shall be taken into account when calculating whether the HMO or any part of it comprises three storeys or more—
    (a)   any basement if—
        (i)   it is used wholly or partly as living accommodation;
        (ii)  it has been constructed, converted or adapted for use wholly or partly as living accommodation;
        (iii) it is being used in connection with, and as an integral part of, the HMO; or
        (iv) it is the only or principal entry into the HMO from the street.
    (b)   any attic if—
        (i)   it is used wholly or partly as living accommodation;
        (ii)  it has been constructed, converted or adapted for use wholly or partly as living accommodation, or
        (iii) it is being used in connection with, and as an integral part of, the HMO;
    (c)   where the living accommodation is situated in a part of a building above business premises, each storey comprising the business premises;
    (d)   where the living accommodation is situated in a part of a building below business premises, each storey comprising the business premises;
    (e)   any mezzanine floor not used solely as a means of access between two adjoining floors if—
        (i)   it is used wholly or mainly as living accommodation; or
        (ii)  it is being used in connection with, and as an integral part of, the HMO; and

(f)     any other storey that is used wholly or partly as living accommodation or in connection with, and as an integral part of, the HMO.

**[3611]**

**NOTES**
Commencement: 6 April 2006.

# MANAGEMENT OF HOUSES IN MULTIPLE OCCUPATION (ENGLAND) REGULATIONS 2006

### (SI 2006/372)

**NOTES**
Made: 15 February 2006.
Authority: Housing Act 2004, s 234.
Commencement: 6 April 2006.

## ARRANGEMENT OF REGULATIONS

## 1   Citation, commencement and application

(1)   These Regulations may be cited as The Management of Houses in Multiple Occupation (England) Regulations 2006 and shall come into force on 6th April 2006.

(2)   These Regulations apply to any HMO in England other than a converted block of flats to which section 257 of the Act applies.

**[3612]**

**NOTES**
Commencement: 6 April 2006.

## 2   Interpretation

In these Regulations—
(a)     "the Act" means the Housing Act 2004;
(b)     "fixtures, fittings or appliances" are—
  (i)    lighting, space heating or water heating appliances;
  (ii)   toilets, baths, showers, sinks, or wash basins or any cupboards, shelving or fittings supplied in a bathroom or lavatory;
  (iii)  cupboards, shelving or appliances used for the storage, preparation or cooking of food; and
  (iv)   washing machines or other laundry appliances; and
(c)     "the manager", in relation to an HMO, means the person managing the HMO.

**[3613]**

**NOTES**
Commencement: 6 April 2006.

## 3   Duty of manager to provide information to occupier

The manager must ensure that—
(a)     his name, address and any telephone contact number are made available to each household in the HMO; and
(b)     such details are clearly displayed in a prominent position in the HMO.

**[3614]**

## 4  Duty of manager to take safety measures

(1)   The manager must ensure that all means of escape from fire in the HMO are—
(a)   kept free from obstruction; and
(b)   maintained in good order and repair.

(2)   The manager must ensure that any fire fighting equipment and fire alarms are maintained in good working order.

(3)   Subject to paragraph (6), the manager must ensure that all notices indicating the location of means of escape from fire are displayed in positions within the HMO that enable them to be clearly visible to the occupiers.

(4)   The manager must take all such measures as are reasonably required to protect the occupiers of the HMO from injury, having regard to—
(a)   the design of the HMO;
(b)   the structural conditions in the HMO; and
(c)   the number of occupiers in the HMO.

(5)   In performing the duty imposed by paragraph (4) the manager must in particular—
(a)   in relation to any roof or balcony that is unsafe, either ensure that it is made safe or take all reasonable measures to prevent access to it for so long as it remains unsafe; and
(b)   in relation to any window the sill of which is at or near floor level, ensure that bars or other such safeguards as may be necessary are provided to protect the occupiers against the danger of accidents which may be caused in connection with such windows.

(6)   The duty imposed by paragraph (3) does not apply where the HMO has four or fewer occupiers.

[3615]

## 5  Duty of manager to maintain water supply and drainage

(1)   The manager must ensure that the water supply and drainage system serving the HMO is maintained in good, clean and working condition and in particular he must ensure that—
(a)   any tank, cistern or similar receptacle used for the storage of water for drinking or other domestic purposes is kept in a good, clean and working condition, with a cover kept over it to keep the water in a clean and proper condition; and
(b)   any water fitting which is liable to damage by frost is protected from frost damage.

(2)   The manager must not unreasonably cause or permit the water or drainage supply that is used by any occupier at the HMO to be interrupted.

(3)   In this regulation "water fitting" means a pipe, tap, cock, valve, ferrule, meter, cistern, bath, water closet or soil pan used in connection with the supply or use of water, but the reference in this definition to a pipe does not include an overflow pipe or the mains supply pipe.

[3616]

## 6  Duty of manager to supply and maintain gas and electricity

(1)   The manager must supply to the local housing authority within 7 days of receiving a request in writing from that authority the latest gas appliance test certificate it has received in relation to the testing of any gas appliance at the HMO by a recognised engineer.

[(2)   In paragraph (1), "recognised engineer" means an engineer approved under regulation 3 of the Gas Safety (Installation and Use) Regulations 1998.]

(3)   The manager must—
(a)   ensure that every fixed electrical installation is inspected and tested at intervals not exceeding five years by a person qualified to undertake such inspection and testing;
(b)   obtain a certificate from the person conducting that test, specifying the results of the test; and
(c)   supply that certificate to the local housing authority within 7 days of receiving a request in writing for it from that authority.

(4)    The manager must not unreasonably cause the gas or electricity supply that is used by any occupier within the HMO to be interrupted.

**[3617]**

NOTES
Commencement: 6 April 2006.
Para (2): substituted by the Houses in Multiple Occupation (Management) (England) Regulations 2009, SI 2009/724, reg 2.

### 7    Duty of manager to maintain common parts, fixtures, fittings and appliances

(1)    The manager must ensure that all common parts of the HMO are—
   (a)    maintained in good and clean decorative repair;
   (b)    maintained in a safe and working condition; and
   (c)    kept reasonably clear from obstruction.

(2)    In performing the duty imposed by paragraph (1), the manager must in particular ensure that—
   (a)    all handrails and banisters are at all times kept in good repair;
   (b)    such additional handrails or banisters as are necessary for the safety of the occupiers of the HMO are provided;
   (c)    any stair coverings are safely fixed and kept in good repair;
   (d)    all windows and other means of ventilation within the common parts are kept in good repair;
   (e)    the common parts are fitted with adequate light fittings that are available for use at all times by every occupier of the HMO; and
   (f)    subject to paragraph (3), fixtures, fittings or appliances used in common by two or more households within the HMO are maintained in good and safe repair and in clean working order.

(3)    The duty imposed by paragraph (2)(f) does not apply in relation to fixtures, fittings or appliances that the occupier is entitled to remove from the HMO or which are otherwise outside the control of the manager.

(4)    The manager must ensure that—
   (a)    outbuildings, yards and forecourts which are used in common by two or more households living within the HMO are maintained in repair, clean condition and good order;
   (b)    any garden belonging to the HMO is kept in a safe and tidy condition; and
   (c)    boundary walls, fences and railings (including any basement area railings), in so far as they belong to the HMO, are kept and maintained in good and safe repair so as not to constitute a danger to occupiers.

(5)    If any part of the HMO is not in use the manager shall ensure that such part, including any passage and staircase directly giving access to it, is kept reasonably clean and free from refuse and litter.

(6)    In this regulation—
   (a)    "common parts" means—
      (i)    the entrance door to the HMO and the entrance doors leading to each unit of living accommodation within the HMO;
      (ii)    all such parts of the HMO as comprise staircases, passageways, corridors, halls, lobbies, entrances, balconies, porches and steps that are used by the occupiers of the units of living accommodation within the HMO to gain access to the entrance doors of their respective unit of living accommodation; and
      (iii)    any other part of an HMO the use of which is shared by two or more households living in the HMO, with the knowledge of the landlord.

**[3618]**

NOTES
Commencement: 6 April 2006.

### 8    Duty of manager to maintain living accommodation

(1)    Subject to paragraph (4), the manager must ensure that each unit of living accommodation within the HMO and any furniture supplied with it are in clean condition at the beginning of a person's occupation of it.

(2)    Subject to paragraphs (3) and (4), the manager must ensure, in relation to each part of the HMO that is used as living accommodation, that—
   (a)    the internal structure is maintained in good repair;
   (b)    any fixtures, fittings or appliances within the part are maintained in good repair and in clean working order; and

(c) every window and other means of ventilation are kept in good repair.

(3) The duties imposed under paragraph (2) do not require the manager to carry out any repair the need for which arises in consequence of use by the occupier of his living accommodation otherwise than in a tenant-like manner.

(4) The duties imposed under paragraphs (1) and (2) (b) do not apply in relation to furniture, fixtures, fittings or appliances that the occupier is entitled to remove from the HMO or which are otherwise outside the control of the manager.

(5) For the purpose of this regulation a person shall be regarded as using his living accommodation otherwise than in a tenant-like manner where he fails to treat the property in accordance with the covenants or conditions contained in his lease or licence or otherwise fails to conduct himself as a reasonable tenant or licensee would do.

[3619]

**NOTES**
Commencement: 6 April 2006.

## 9  Duty to provide waste disposal facilities

The manager must—
  (a) ensure that sufficient bins or other suitable receptacles are provided that are adequate for the requirements of each household occupying the HMO for the storage of refuse and litter pending their disposal; and
  (b) make such further arrangements for the disposal of refuse and litter from the HMO as may be necessary, having regard to any service for such disposal provided by the local authority.

[3620]

**NOTES**
Commencement: 6 April 2006.

## 10  Duties of occupiers of HMOs

Every occupier of the HMO must—
  (a) conduct himself in a way that will not hinder or frustrate the manager in the performance of his duties;
  (b) allow the manager, for any purpose connected with the carrying out of any duty imposed on him by these Regulations, at all reasonable times to enter any living accommodation or other place occupied by that person;
  (c) provide the manager, at his request, with any such information as he may reasonably require for the purpose of carrying out any such duty;
  (d) take reasonable care to avoid causing damage to anything which the manager is under a duty to supply, maintain or repair under these Regulations;
  (e) store and dispose of litter in accordance with the arrangements made by the manager under regulation 9; and
  (f) comply with the reasonable instructions of the manager in respect of any means of escape from fire, the prevention of fire and the use of fire equipment.

[3621]

**NOTES**
Commencement: 6 April 2006.

## 11  General

(1) Nothing in these Regulations shall—
  (a) require or authorise anything to be done in connection with the water supply or drainage or the supply of gas or electricity otherwise than in accordance with any enactment; or
  (b) oblige the manager to take, in connection with those matters, any action which is the responsibility of a local authority or any other person, other than such action as may be necessary to bring the matter promptly to the attention of the authority or person concerned.

(2) Any duty imposed by these Regulations to maintain or keep in repair are to be construed as requiring a standard of maintenance or repair that is reasonable in all the circumstances, taking account of the age, character and prospective life of the house and the locality in which it is situated.

[3622]

**NOTES**
Commencement: 6 April 2006.

# LICENSING AND MANAGEMENT OF HOUSES IN MULTIPLE OCCUPATION AND OTHER HOUSES (MISCELLANEOUS PROVISIONS) (ENGLAND) REGULATIONS 2006

## (SI 2006/373)

**NOTES**
Made: 15 February 2006.
Authority: Housing Act 2004, ss 59(2)–(4), 60(6), 63(5), (6), 65(3), (4), 83(2), (4), 84(6), 87(5), (6), 232(3), (7), 250(2), 258(2)(b), (5), (6), 259(2)(c), Sch 14, paras 3, 6(1)(c).
Commencement: 6 April 2006.

### ARRANGEMENT OF REGULATIONS

## 1   Citation, commencement and application

(1)   These Regulations may be cited as The Licensing and Management of Houses in Multiple Occupation and Other Houses (Miscellaneous Provisions) (England) Regulations 2006 and shall come into force on 6th April 2006.

(2)   These Regulations apply in relation to any HMO in England, ... and to any house in England to which Part 3 of the Act applies.

**[3623]**

**NOTES**
Commencement: 6 April 2006.
Para (2): words omitted revoked, in relation to any HMO in England to which the Housing Act 2004, Pt 2 applies, by the Licensing and Management of Houses in Multiple Occupation (Additional Provisions) (England) Regulations 2007, SI 2007/1903, reg 12(1), (2).

## 2   Interpretation

In these Regulations "the Act" means the Housing Act 2004[; and "section 257 HMO" means an HMO which is a converted block of flats to which section 257 of the Act applies].

**[3624]**

**NOTES**
Commencement: 6 April 2006.
Words in square brackets added, in relation to any HMO in England to which the Housing Act 2004, Pt 2 applies, by the Licensing and Management of Houses in Multiple Occupation (Additional Provisions) (England) Regulations 2007, SI 2007/1903, reg 12(1), (3).

## 3   Persons to be regarded as forming a single household for the purposes of section 254 of the Act: employees

(1)   Where—

(a) a person ("person A") occupies living accommodation in a building or part of a building; and

(b) another person ("person B") and any member of person B's family living with him occupy living accommodation in the same building or part,

those persons are only to be regarded as forming a single household for the purposes of section 254 of the Act if their circumstances are those described in paragraph (2).

(2) The circumstances are that—

(a) Person A carries out work or performs a service of an exclusively domestic nature for person B or such a member of person B's family;

(b) Person A's living accommodation is supplied to him by person B or by such a member of person B's family as part of the consideration for carrying out the work or performing the service; and

(c) person A does not pay any rent or other consideration in respect of his living accommodation (other than carrying out the work or performance of the service).

(3) Work or a service usually carried out or performed by any of the following is to be regarded as work or service of a domestic nature for the purpose of paragraph (2)(a)—

(a) au pair;
(b) nanny;
(c) nurse;
(d) carer;
(e) governess;
(f) servant, including maid, butler, cook or cleaner;
(g) chauffeur;
(h) gardener;
(i) secretary; or
(j) personal assistant.

(4) Where person A and person B are to be regarded as forming a single household under paragraph (1) any member of person A's family occupying the living accommodation with him is to be regarded as forming a single household with person A, person B and any member of person B's family living with him for the purpose of section 254 of the Act.

**[3625]**

**NOTES**

Commencement: 6 April 2006.

## 4 Other persons to be regarded as forming a single household for the purposes of section 254 of the Act

(1) Where a person receiving care and his carer occupy living accommodation in the same building or part of a building, they are to be regarded as forming a single household for the purposes of section 254 of the Act if—

(a) the carer is an adult placement carer approved under the Adult Placement Schemes (England) Regulations 2004; and

(b) the carer provides care in that living accommodation for not more than three service users under the terms of a scheme permitted by those Regulations.

(2) Where a person and his foster parent occupy living accommodation in the same building or part of a building, they are to be regarded as forming a single household for the purposes of section 254 of the Act if that person is placed with the foster parent under the provisions of the Fostering Services Regulations 2002.

(3) The terms "adult placement carer" and "service users" have the meanings given to those expressions in the regulations referred to in paragraph (1)(a).

**[3626]**

**NOTES**

Commencement: 6 April 2006.

## 5 Persons treated as occupying premises as their only or main residence for the purposes of section 254 of the Act

(1) A person is to be treated as occupying a building or part of a building as his only or main residence for the purposes of section 254 of the Act if he is—

(a) a migrant worker or a seasonal worker—

(i) whose occupation of the building or part is made partly in consideration of his employment within the United Kingdom, whether or not other charges are payable in respect of that occupation; and

(ii) where the building or part is provided by, or on behalf of, his employer or an agent or employee of his employer; or

    (b)    an asylum seeker or a dependent of an asylum seeker who has been provided with accommodation under section 95 of the Immigration and Asylum Act 1999 and which is funded partly or wholly by the National Asylum Support Service.

  (2)  In this regulation—
    (a)    "a migrant worker" is—
        (i)    a person who is a national of a member State of the European Economic Area or Switzerland who has taken up an activity as an employed person in the United Kingdom under Council Regulation (EEC) No 1612/68 on Freedom of Movement for Workers Within the Community, as extended by the EEA Agreement or the Switzerland Agreement; or
        (ii)    any person who has a permit indicating, in accordance with the immigration rules, that a person named in it is eligible, though not a British citizen, for entry into the United Kingdom for the purpose of taking employment;
    (b)    "EEA agreement" means the agreement on the European Economic Area signed at Oporto on 2nd May 1992, as adjusted by the Protocol signed at Brussels on 17th March 1993;
    (c)    "Switzerland agreement" means the agreement between the European Community and its Member States of the one part and the Swiss Confederation of the other on the Free Movement of Persons signed at Luxembourg on 21st June 1999 and which came into force on 1st June 2002;
    (d)    "seasonal worker" means a person who carries out for an employer or undertaking employment of a seasonal character—
        (i)    the nature of which depends on the cycle of the seasons and recurs automatically each year; and
        (ii)    the duration of which cannot exceed eight months;
    (e)    "immigration rules" means the rules for the time being laid down as mentioned in section 3(2) of the Immigration Act 1971 and
    (f)    "asylum seeker" has the meaning given to that expression in section 94 of Immigration and Asylum Act 1999.

**[3627]**

**NOTES**
Commencement: 6 April 2006.

## 6  Buildings that are not HMOs for the purposes of the Act (excluding Part 1)

  (1)  A building is of a description specified for the purposes of paragraph 3 of Schedule 14 to the Act (buildings regulated otherwise than under the Act which are not HMOs for purposes of the Act (excluding Part 1)) where its occupation is regulated by or under any of the enactments listed in Schedule 1.

  (2)  The number of persons specified for the purposes of paragraph 6(1)(c) of Schedule 14 to the Act is two.

**[3628]**

**NOTES**
Commencement: 6 April 2006.

## 7  Applications for licences under Part 2 or 3 of the Act

  (1)  An application for a licence under section 63 (application for HMO licence) or 87 (application for licence of Part 3 house) of the Act ("an application") must include a statement in the form specified in paragraph 1 of Schedule 2

  (2)  An applicant must supply as a part of his application—
    (a)    the information contained in paragraph 2 of Schedule 2; and
    (b)    the information relating to the proposed licence holder or proposed manager of the HMO or house specified in paragraph 3 of that Schedule.

  (3)  An applicant must—
    (a)    supply with the application completed and signed declarations in the form specified in paragraph 4 of Schedule 2; and
    (b)    sign the application.

  (4)  Where the applicant proposes that another person should be the licence holder, both the applicant and the proposed licence holder must comply with the requirements in paragraph (3).

  (5)  The applicant must give the following information about the application to every relevant person—
    (a)    the name, address, telephone number and any e-mail address or fax number of the applicant;

PART II
STATUTORY INSTRUMENTS

(b)    the name, address, telephone number and any e-mail address or fax number of the proposed licence holder (if he is not the applicant);

(c)    the type of application by reference to it being made in respect of an HMO that must be licensed under Part 2 or in respect of a house that must be licensed under Part 3 of the Act;

(d)    the address of the HMO or house to which the application relates;

(e)    the name and address of the local housing authority to which the application is made; and

(f)    the date on which the application is, or is to be, made.

(6)    Nothing in paragraph (5) precludes an applicant from supplying a copy of the application, or other information about the application, to a relevant person.

(7)    A local housing authority must refund an applicant in full any fee that he has paid in respect of an application as soon as reasonably practicable after it learns that at the time the fee was paid—

(a)    in the case of an application for a licence under Part 2 of the Act, the house was not an HMO, or was not an HMO that was required to be licensed; or

(b)    in the case of an application for a licence under Part 3 of the Act, the house was a house that was not required to be licensed under Part 2 or 3 of the Act.

(8)    Paragraph (7) applies whether or not the local housing authority, pursuant to the application, granted a licence for the HMO or house when it was not required to be licensed.

(9)    For the purposes of this regulation a "relevant person" is any person (other than a person to whom paragraph (10) applies)—

(a)    who, to the knowledge of the applicant, is—

    (i)    a person having an estate or interest in the HMO or house that is the subject of the application, or

    (ii)    a person managing or having control of that HMO or house (and not falling within paragraph (i)); or

(b)    where the applicant proposes in the application that conditions should be in the licence imposing a restrictions or obligation on any person (other than the licence holder, that person.

(10)    This paragraph applies to any tenant under a lease with an unexpired term of three years or less.

**[3629]**

---

**NOTES**

Commencement: 6 April 2006.

---

**[8  Prescribed standards for deciding the suitability of a house for multiple occupation by a particular maximum number of households or persons**

(1)    The standards prescribed for HMOs other than section 257 HMOs for the purpose of section 65 of the Act (tests as to suitability of HMO for multiple occupation) are those set out in Schedule 3.

(2)    The standards prescribed for section 257 HMOs for the purpose of section 65 of the Act are—

(a)    that all bathrooms and toilets contained in each flat must be of an adequate size and layout, and all wash-hand basins must be suitably located and be fit for purpose, having regard to the age and character of the HMO, the size and layout of each flat and its existing provision for wash-hand basins, toilets and bathrooms;

(b)    those standards set out in paragraph 4(1) of Schedule 3, in so far as it is reasonably practicable to comply with them; and

(c)    those standards set out in paragraph 5 of Schedule 3.]

**[3630]**

---

**NOTES**

Commencement: 6 April 2006.

Substituted, in relation to any HMO in England to which the Housing Act 2004, Pt 2 applies, by the Licensing and Management of Houses in Multiple Occupation (Additional Provisions) (England) Regulations 2007, SI 2007/1903, reg 12(1), (4).

---

**9  Publication requirements relating to designations under Part 2 or 3 of the Act**

(1)    A local housing authority that is required under section 59(2) or 83(2) of the Act to publish a notice of a designation of an area for the purpose of Part 2 or 3 of the Act must do so in the manner prescribed by paragraph (2).

(2)    Within 7 days after the date on which the designation was confirmed or made the local housing authority must—

(a)    place the notice on a public notice board at one or more municipal buildings within the

designated area, or if there are no such buildings within the designated area, at the closest of such buildings situated outside the designated area;
(b) publish the notice on the authority's internet site; and
(c) arrange for its publication in at least two local newspapers circulating in or around the designated area—
   (i) in the next edition of those newspapers; and
   (ii) five times in the editions of those newspapers following the edition in which it is first published, with the interval between each publication being no less than two weeks and no more than three weeks.

(3) Within 2 weeks after the designation was confirmed or made the local housing authority must send a copy of the notice to—
(a) any person who responded to the consultation conducted by it under section 56(3) or 80(9) of the Act;
(b) any organisation which, to the reasonable knowledge of the authority—
   (i) represents the interests of landlords or tenants within the designated area; or
   (ii) represents managing agents, estate agents or letting agents within the designated area; and
(c) every organisation within the local housing authority area that the local housing authority knows or believes provides advice on landlord and tenant matters, including—
   (i) law centres;
   (ii) citizens' advice bureaux;
   (iii) housing advice centres; and
   (iv) homeless persons' units.

(4) In addition to the information referred to in section 59(2)(a), (b) and(c) or 83(2)(a), (b) and(c), the notice must contain the following information—
(a) a brief description of the designated area;
(b) the name, address, telephone number and e-mail address of—
   (i) the local housing authority that made the designation;
   (ii) the premises where the designation may be inspected; and
   (iii) the premises where applications for licences and general advice may be obtained;
(c) a statement advising any landlord, person managing or tenant within the designated area to seek advice from the local housing authority on whether their property is affected by the designation; and
(d) a warning of the consequences of failing to licence a property that is required to be licensed, including the criminal sanctions.

**[3631]**

**NOTES**
Commencement: 6 April 2006.

**10 Publication requirements relating to the revocation of designations made under Part 2 or 3 of the Act**

(1) A local housing authority that is required under section 60(6) or 84(6) of the Act to publish a notice of revocation of a designation of an area for the purposes of Part 2 or 3 of the Act, must do so in the manner prescribed by paragraph (2).

(2) Within 7 days after revoking a designation the local housing authority must—
(a) place a notice on a public notice board at one or more municipal buildings within the designated area, or if there are no such buildings within the designated area, at the closest of such buildings situated outside the designated area;
(b) publish the notice on the authority's internet site; and
(c) arrange for the publication of the notice in at least two local newspapers circulating in or around the designated area in the next edition of those newspapers.

(3) The notice must contain the following information—
(a) a brief description of the area to which the designation being revoked relates;
(b) a summary of the reasons for the revocation;
(c) the date from which the revocation takes effect;
(d) the name, address, telephone number and e-mail address—
   (i) of the local housing authority that revoked the designation; and
   (ii) where the revocation may be inspected.

**[3632]**

**NOTES**
Commencement: 6 April 2006.

PART II STATUTORY INSTRUMENTS

## 11 Registers of Licences

(1) The following particulars are prescribed for each entry in a register established and maintained under section 232(1)(a) of the Act in respect of a licence granted under Part 2 (HMOs) or 3 (selective licensing) of the Act which is in force—

- (a) the name and address of the licence holder;
- (b) the name and address of the person managing the licensed HMO or house;
- (c) the address of the licensed HMO or house;
- (d) a short description of the licensed HMO or house;
- (e) a summary of the conditions of the licence;
- (f) the commencement date and duration of the licence;
- (g) summary information of any matter concerning the licensing of the HMO or house that has been referred to a residential property tribunal or to the [Upper Tribunal]; and
- (h) summary information of any decision of the tribunals referred to in sub-paragraph (g) that relate to the licensed HMO or house, together with the reference number allocated to the case by the tribunal.

(2) [Subject to paragraph (3), the] following additional particulars are prescribed for each entry in a register established and maintained under section 232(1)(a) of the Act in respect of a licence granted under Part 2 of the Act which is in force—

- (a) the number of storeys comprising the licensed HMO;
- (b) the number of rooms in the licensed HMO providing—
  - (i) sleeping accommodation; and
  - (ii) living accommodation;
- (c) in the case of a licensed HMO consisting of flats—
  - (i) the number of flats that are self contained; and
  - (ii) the number of flats that are not self contained;
- (d) a description of shared amenities including the numbers of each amenity; and
- (e) the maximum number of persons or households permitted to occupy the licensed HMO under the conditions of the licence.

[(3) The particulars mentioned in sub-paragraphs (b), (c)(ii), (d) and (e) of paragraph (2) are not prescribed for any entry in a register referred to in that paragraph in respect of a licence granted in relation to a section 257 HMO.]

[3633]

---

**NOTES**

Commencement: 6 April 2006.

Para (1): in sub-para (g) words in square brackets substituted by the Transfer of Tribunal Functions (Lands Tribunal and Miscellaneous Amendments) Order 2009, SI 2009/1307, art 5(1), (3), Sch 2, paras 108, 109, as from 1 June 2009, subject to savings and transitional provisions for the treatment of cases which would previously have been dealt with by the Lands Tribunal, and onward appeals from that Tribunal (see art 5(6), Sch 5 to that Order).

Para (2): words in square brackets substituted, in relation to any HMO in England to which the Housing Act 2004, Pt 2 applies, by the Licensing and Management of Houses in Multiple Occupation (Additional Provisions) (England) Regulations 2007, SI 2007/1903, reg 12(1), (5)(a).

Para (3): inserted, in relation to any HMO in England to which the Housing Act 2004, Pt 2 applies, by SI 2007/1903, reg 12(1), (5)(b).

## 12 Registers of temporary exemption notices

(1) The following particulars are prescribed for each entry in a register established and maintained under section 232(1)(b) of the Act in respect of a temporary exemption notice served under section 62 or 86 of the Act which is in force—

- (a) the name and address of the person notifying the local housing authority under section 62(1) or section 86(1) of the Act;
- (b) the address of the HMO or house in respect of which the local housing authority has served the temporary exemption notice and any reference number allocated to it by the authority;
- (c) a summary of the effect of the notice;
- (d) details of any previous temporary exemption notices that have been served in relation to the same HMO or house for a period immediately preceding the current temporary exemption notice;
- (e) a statement of the particular steps that the person referred to in sub-paragraph (a) intends to take with a view to securing that the HMO or house is no longer required to be licensed;
- (f) the date on which the local housing authority served the temporary exemption notice and the date on which it ceases to be in force;
- (g) summary information of any matter concerning the HMO or house that has been referred to a residential property tribunal or to the [Upper Tribunal]; and

(h)    summary information of any decision of the tribunals referred to in sub-paragraph (g) that relate to the HMO or house together with the reference number allocated to the case by the tribunal.

**[3634]**

**NOTES**
Commencement: 6 April 2006.
Para (1): in sub-para (g) words in square brackets substituted by the Transfer of Tribunal Functions (Lands Tribunal and Miscellaneous Amendments) Order 2009, SI 2009/1307, art 5(1), (3), Sch 2, paras 108, 110, as from 1 June 2009, subject to savings and transitional provisions for the treatment of cases which would previously have been dealt with by the Lands Tribunal, and onward appeals from that Tribunal (see art 5(6), Sch 5 to that Order).

### 13  Registers of management orders

(1)    The following particulars are prescribed for each entry in a register established and maintained under section 232(1)(c) of the Act in respect of a management order made under section 102(2), (3), (4) or (7) or 113(1) or (6) of the Act—

    (a)    the address of the HMO or house to which the order relates and any reference number allocated to it by the local housing authority;

    (b)    a short description of the HMO or house;

    (c)    the date on which the order comes into force;

    (d)    a summary of the reasons for making the order;

    (e)    a summary of the terms of the order and the type of order made;

    (f)    summary information of any application concerning the HMO or house that has been made to a residential property tribunal or to the [Upper Tribunal]; and

    (g)    summary information of any decision of the tribunals referred to in sub-paragraph (f) that relate to the HMO or house, together with the reference number allocated to the case by the tribunal.

(2)    [Subject to paragraph (4), the] following additional particulars are prescribed for each entry in a register established and maintained under section 232(1)(c) of the Act in respect of a management order made under section 102(2), (3), (4) or (7) or 113(1) or (6) of the Act which is in force—

    (a)    the number of storeys comprising the HMO;

    (b)    the number of rooms in the HMO providing—

        (i)    sleeping accommodation; and

        (ii)    living accommodation;

    (c)    in the case of an HMO consisting of flats—

        (i)    the number of flats that are self contained;

        (ii)    the number of flats that are not self contained;

        (iii)    a description of shared amenities including the numbers of each amenity;

        (iv)    the maximum number of households permitted to occupy the HMO; and

        (v)    the maximum number of persons permitted to occupy the HMO.

(3)    The following particulars are prescribed for each entry in a register established and maintained under section 232(1)(c) of the Act in respect of an empty dwelling management order made under section 133(1) or 136(1) or (2) of the Act—

    (a)    the address of the dwelling to which the order relates and any reference number allocated to it by the local housing authority;

    (b)    a short description of the dwelling;

    (c)    the date on which the order comes into force;

    (d)    a summary of the reasons for making the order;

    (e)    a summary of the terms of the order;

    (f)    summary information of any application concerning the dwelling that has been made to a residential property tribunal or to the Lands Tribunal; and

    (g)    summary information of any decision of the tribunals referred to in sub-paragraph (f) that relate to the dwelling, together with the reference number allocated to the case by the tribunal.

[(4)    The particulars mentioned in sub-paragraphs (b) and (c)(ii) to (v) of paragraph (2) are not prescribed for any entry referred to in that paragraph in respect of a management order made in relation to a section 257 HMO.]

**[3635]**

**NOTES**
Commencement: 6 April 2006.
Para (1): in sub-para (f) words in square brackets substituted by the Transfer of Tribunal Functions (Lands Tribunal and Miscellaneous Amendments) Order 2009, SI 2009/1307, art 5(1), (3), Sch 2, paras 108, 111, as from 1 June 2009, subject to savings and transitional provisions for the treatment of cases which would previously have been dealt with by the Lands Tribunal, and onward appeals from that Tribunal (see art 5(6), Sch 5 to that Order).

Para (2): words in square brackets substituted, in relation to any HMO in England to which the Housing Act 2004, Pt 2 applies, by the Licensing and Management of Houses in Multiple Occupation (Additional Provisions) (England) Regulations 2007, SI 2007/1903, reg 12(1), (6)(a).

Para (4): inserted, in relation to any HMO in England to which the Housing Act 2004, Pt 2 applies, by SI 2007/1903, reg 12(1), (6)(b).

## SCHEDULES

## SCHEDULE 1
## BUILDINGS WHICH ARE NOT HMOS FOR ANY PURPOSE OF THE ACT (EXCLUDING PART 1)

Regulation 6(1)

The enactments referred to in regulation 13(1) are—

- (h)    sections 87, 87A, 87B, 87C and 87D of the Children Act 1989;
- (i)    section 43(4) of the Prison Act 1952;
- (j)    section 34 of the Nationality, Immigration and Asylum Act 2002;
- (k)    The Secure Training Centre Rules 1998;
- (l)    The Prison Rules 1999;
- (m)    The Young Offender Institute Rules 2000;
- (n)    The Detention Centre Rules 2001;
- (o)    The Criminal Justice and Court Services Act 2000 (Approved Premises) Regulations 2001;
- (p)    The Care Homes Regulations 2001;
- (q)    The Children's Homes Regulations 2001; and
- (r)    The Residential Family Centres Regulations 2002;

[3636]

**NOTES**

Commencement: 6 April 2006.

## SCHEDULE 2
## CONTENT OF APPLICATIONS UNDER SECTIONS 63 AND 87 OF THE ACT

Regulation 7(1), (2) and (3)

1.    The form of statement mentioned in regulation 7(1) is:

"You must let certain persons know in writing that you have made this application or give them a copy of it. The persons who need to know about it are—

any mortgagee of the property to be licensed

any owner of the property to which the application relates (if that is not you) ie the freeholder and any head lessors who are known to you

any other person who is a tenant or long leaseholder of the property or any part of it (including any flat) who is known to you other than a statutory tenant or other tenant whose lease or tenancy is for less than three years (including a periodic tenancy)

the proposed licence holder (if that is not you)

the proposed managing agent (if any) (if that is not you)

any person who has agreed that he will be bound by any conditions in a licence if it is granted.

You must tell each of these persons—

your name, address telephone number and e-mail address or fax number (if any)

the name, address, telephone number and e-mail address or fax number (if any) of the proposed licence holder (if it will not be you)

whether this is an application for an HMO licence under Part 2 or for a house licence under Part 3 of the Housing Act 2004

the address of the property to which the application relates

the name and address of the local housing authority to which the application will be made

the date the application will be submitted"

2.—(1)    The information mentioned in regulation 7(2)(a) is—

- (a)    the name, address, telephone number and e-mail address of—
  - (i)    the applicant;
  - (ii)    the proposed licence holder;
  - (iii)    the person managing the HMO or house;
  - (iv)    the person having control of the HMO or house; and
  - (v)    any person who has agreed to be bound by a condition contained in the licence;
- (b)    the address of the HMO or house for which the application is being made;
- (c)    the approximate age of the original construction of the HMO or house (using the categories before 1919, 1919–45, 1945–64, 1965–80 and after 1980);

(d)    the type of HMO or house for which the application is being made, by reference to one of the following categories—
  (i)  house in single occupation;
  (ii)  house in multiple occupation;
  (iii)  flat in single occupation;
  (iv)  flat in multiple occupation;
  (v)  a house converted into and comprising only of self contained flats;
  (vi)  a purpose built block of flats; or
  (vii)  other;

(e)    details of other HMOs or houses that are licensed under Part 2 or 3 of the Act in respect of which the proposed licence holder is the licence holder, whether in the area of the local housing authority to which the application is made or in the area of any other local housing authority;

(f)    the following information about the HMO or house for which the application is being made[, except in respect of an application in respect of a section 257 HMO]—
  (i)  the number of storeys comprising the HMO or house and the levels on which those storeys are situated;
  (ii)  the number of separate letting units;
  (iii)  the number of habitable rooms (excluding kitchens);
  (iv)  the number of bathrooms and shower rooms;
  (v)  the number of toilets and wash basins;
  (vi)  the number of kitchens;
  (vii)  the number of sinks;
  (viii)  the number of households occupying the HMO or house;
  (ix)  the number of people occupying the HMO or house;
  (x)  details of fire precautions equipment, including the number and location of smoke alarms;
  (xi)  details of fire escape routes and other fire safety [information] provided to occupiers;
  (xii)  a declaration that the furniture in the HMO or house that is provided under the terms of any tenancy or licence meets any safety requirements contained in any enactment; and
  (xiii)  a declaration that any gas appliances in the HMO or house meet any safety requirements contained in any enactment;

[(g)    where the application is being made in respect of a section 257 HMO, the following information—
  (i)  the number of storeys comprising the HMO and the levels on which those storeys are situated;
  (ii)  the number of self-contained flats and, of those, the number—
    (aa)  that the applicant believes to be subject to a lease of over 21 years; and
    (bb)  over which he cannot reasonably be able to exercise control;
  (iii)  in relation to each self-contained flat that is not owner-occupied and which is under the control of or being managed by the proposed licence holder, and in relation to the common parts of the HMO—
    (aa)  details of fire precautions equipment, including the number and location of smoke alarms;
    (bb)  details of fire escape routes and other fire safety information provided to occupiers; and
    (cc)  a declaration that the furniture in the HMO or house that is provided under the terms of any tenancy or licence meets any safety requirements contained in any enactment; and
  (iv)  a declaration that any gas appliances in any parts of the HMO over which the proposed licence holder can reasonably be expected to exercise control meet any safety requirements contained in any enactment.]

3.    The information mentioned in regulation 7(2)(b) is—
  (a)  details of any unspent convictions that may be relevant to the proposed licence holder's fitness to hold a licence, or the proposed manager's fitness to manage the HMO or house, and, in particular any such conviction in respect of any offence involving fraud or other dishonesty, or violence or drugs or any offence listed in Schedule 3 to the Sexual Offences Act 2003;
  (b)  details of any finding by a court or tribunal against the proposed licence holder or manager that he has practised unlawful discrimination on grounds of sex, colour, race, ethnic or national origin or disability in, or in connection with, the carrying on of any business;
  (c)  details of any contravention on the part of the proposed licence holder or manager of any provision of any enactment relating to housing, public health, environmental health or landlord and tenant law which led to civil or criminal proceedings resulting in a judgement being made against him.

    (d)    information about any HMO or house the proposed licence holder or manager owns or manages or has owned or managed which has been the subject of—

        (i)    a control order under section 379 of the Housing Act 1985 in the five years preceding the date of the application; or

        (ii)    any appropriate enforcement action described in section 5(2) of the Act.

    (e)    information about any HMO or house the proposed licence holder or manager owns or manages or has owned or managed for which a local housing authority has refused to grant a licence under Part 2 or 3 of the Act, or has revoked a licence in consequence of the licence holder breaching the conditions of his licence; and

    (f)    information about any HMO or house the proposed licence holder or manager owns or manages or has owned or managed that has been the subject of an interim or final management order under the Act.

4.    The form of declaration mentioned in regulation 7(3)(a) is as follows—

    I/we declare that the information contained in this application is correct to the best of my/our knowledge. I/We understand that I/we commit an offence if I/we supply any information to a local housing authority in connection with any of their functions under any of Parts 1 to 4 of the Housing Act 2004 that is false or misleading and which I/we know is false or misleading or am/are are reckless as to whether it is false or misleading.

    Signed (all applicants)

    Dated

    I/We declare that I/We have served a notice of this application on the following persons who are the only persons known to me/us that are required to be informed that I/we have made this application:

| Name | Address | Description of the person's interest in the property or the application | Date of service |
|------|---------|------------------------------------------------------------------------|-----------------|
|      |         |                                                                        |                 |
|      |         |                                                                        |                 |

[3637]

**NOTES**

    Commencement: 6 April 2006.

    Para 2: sub-para (1)(f) words in square brackets inserted, sub-para (1)(f)(xi) word in square brackets substituted, and sub-para (1)(g) inserted, in relation to any HMO in England to which the Housing Act 2004, Pt 2 applies, by the Licensing and Management of Houses in Multiple Occupation (Additional Provisions) (England) Regulations 2007, SI 2007/1903, reg 12(1), (7)(a), (b).

## SCHEDULE 3
### PRESCRIBED STANDARDS FOR DECIDING THE SUITABILITY FOR OCCUPATION OF AN HMO BY A PARTICULAR MAXIMUM NUMBER OF HOUSEHOLDS OR PERSONS
Regulation 8

*Heating*

1.    Each unit of living accommodation in an HMO must be equipped with adequate means of space heating.

*Washing Facilities*

2.—[(1)    Where all or some of the units of living accommodation in an HMO do not contain bathing and toilet facilities for the exclusive use of each individual household—

    (a)    there must be an adequate number of bathrooms, toilets and wash-hand basins suitable for personal washing) for the number of persons sharing those facilities; and

    (b)    where reasonably practicable there must be a wash hand basin with appropriate splash back in each unit other than a unit in which a sink has been provided as mentioned in paragraph 4(1),

having regard to the age and character of the HMO, the size and layout of each flat and its existing provision for wash-hand basins, toilets and bathrooms.]

    (3)    All baths, showers and wash hand basins in an HMO must be equipped with taps providing an adequate supply of cold and constant hot water.

    (4)    All bathrooms in an HMO must be suitably and adequately heated and ventilated.

    (5)    All bathrooms and toilets in an HMO must be of an adequate size and layout.

    (6)    All baths, toilets and wash hand basins in an HMO must be fit for the purpose.

(7)   All bathrooms and toilets in an HMO must be suitably located in or in relation to the living accommodation in the HMO.

### Kitchens

3.   Where all or some of the units of accommodation within the HMO do not contain any facilities for the cooking of food—

    (a)   there must be a kitchen, suitably located in relation to the living accommodation, and of such layout and size and equipped with such facilities so as to adequately enable those sharing the facilities to store, prepare and cook food;

    (b)   the kitchen must be equipped with the following equipment, which must be fit for the purpose and supplied in a sufficient quantity for the number of those sharing the facilities—

        (i)    sinks with draining boards;

        (ii)   an adequate supply of cold and constant hot water to each sink supplied;

        (iii)  installations or equipment for the cooking of food;

        (iv)   electrical sockets;

        (v)    worktops for the preparation of food;

        (vi)   cupboards for the storage of food or kitchen and cooking utensils;

        (vii)  refrigerators with an adequate freezer compartment (or, where the freezer compartment is not adequate, adequate separate freezers);

        (viii) appropriate refuse disposal facilities; and

        (ix)   appropriate extractor fans, fire blankets and fire doors .

### Units of living accommodation without shared basic amenities

4.—(1)   Where a unit of living accommodation contains kitchen facilities for the exclusive use of the individual household, and there are no other kitchen facilities available for that household, that unit must be provided with—

    (a)   adequate appliances and equipment for the cooking of food;

    (b)   a sink with an adequate supply of cold and constant hot water;

    (c)   a work top for the preparation of food;

    (d)   sufficient electrical sockets;

    (e)   a cupboard for the storage of kitchen utensils and crockery; and

    (f)   a refrigerator.

  [(1A)   The standards referred to in paragraphs (a) and (f) of sub-paragraph (1) shall not apply in relation to a unit of accommodation where—

    (a)   the landlord is not contractually bound to provide such appliances or equipment;

    (b)   the occupier of the unit of accommodation is entitled to remove such appliances or equipment from the HMO; or

    (c)   the appliances or equipment are otherwise outside the control of the landlord.]

(2)   Where there are no adequate shared washing facilities provided for a unit of living accommodation as mentioned in paragraph 2, an enclosed and adequately laid out and ventilated room with a toilet and bath or fixed shower supplying adequate cold and constant hot water must be provided for the exclusive use of the occupiers of that unit either—

    (a)   within the living accommodation; or

    (b)   within reasonable proximity to the living accommodation

### Fire precautionary facilities

5.   Appropriate fire precaution facilities and equipment must be provided of such type, number and location as is considered necessary.

**[3638]**

**NOTES**

  Commencement: 6 April 2006.

  Para 2: sub-para (1) substituted, for original sub-paras (1), (2), in relation to any HMO in England to which the Housing Act 2004, Pt 2 applies, by the Licensing and Management of Houses in Multiple Occupation (Additional Provisions) (England) Regulations 2007, SI 2007/1903, reg 12(1), (8)(a).

  Para 4: sub-para (1A) inserted, in relation to any HMO in England to which the Housing Act 2004, Pt 2 applies, by SI 2007/1903, reg 12(1), (8)(b).

PART II
STATUTORY INSTRUMENTS

# HOMELESSNESS (SUITABILITY OF ACCOMMODATION) (WALES) ORDER 2006

## (SI 2006/650 (W 71))

**NOTES**
Made: 8 March 2006.
Authority: Housing Act 1996, ss 210(2), 215(2).
Commencement: 3 April 2006 (arts 1–3); 2 April 2007 (arts 4–6); 7 April 2008 (arts 7–10).

### ARRANGEMENT OF ARTICLES

## 1   Title, commencement and application

(1)   The title of this Order is the Homelessness (Suitability of Accommodation) (Wales) Order 2006.

(2)   Save as provided in paragraphs (3) and (4) of this Article, this Order comes into force on 3 April 2006.

(3)   Articles 4, 5 and 6 of, and the Schedule to this Order come into force on 2 April 2007.

(4)   Articles 7, 8, 9 and 10 of this Order come into force on 7 April 2008.

(5)   This Order applies in relation to the duties of local housing authorities in Wales under Part 7 of the Housing Act 1996 (homelessness).

**[3639]**

**NOTES**
Commencement: 3 April 2006.

## 2   Interpretation

In this Order—

"the 1996 Act" ("*Deddf 1996*") means the Housing Act 1996; and any reference to a numbered section is a reference to a section of the Housing Act 1996;

"B&B accommodation" ("*llety Gwely a Brecwast*") means commercially provided accommodation (whether or not breakfast is included)—

(a)   which is not separate and self-contained premises;

(b)   in which any of the following amenities is not available to the applicant or is shared by more than one household—

(i)    a toilet;

(ii)   personal washing facilities;

(iii)  cooking facilities;

(c)   which is not accommodation which is owned or managed by a local housing authority, a registered social landlord or a voluntary organisation as defined in section 180(3) of the Housing Act 1996; or

      (d)     which is not an establishment registered under the provisions of the Care Standards Act 2000;

and "B&B" ("*Gwely a Brecwast*") is to be construed accordingly;

"basic standard accommodation" ("*llety o safon sylfaenol*") means accommodation that—

      (a)     complies with all statutory requirements (such as requirements relating to fire and gas safety, planning and licences for houses in multiple occupation, where applicable); and

      (b)     has a manager deemed by the local housing authority to be a fit and proper person with the ability to manage B&B accommodation;

and "basic standard" ("*safon sylfaenol*") is to be construed accordingly;

"higher standard accommodation" ("*llety o safon uwch*") means accommodation that meets—

      (a)     the basic standard; and

      (b)     the standards contained in the Schedule to this Order,

and "higher standard" ("*safon uwch*") is to be construed accordingly;

"shared accommodation" ("*llety a rennir*") means accommodation—

      (a)     which is not separate and self-contained premises; or

      (b)     in which any of the following amenities is not available to the applicant or is shared by more than one household—

           (i)    a toilet;

           (ii)   personal washing facilities;

           (iii)  cooking facilities; or

      (c)     which is not an establishment registered under the provisions of the Care Standards Act 2000;

"small B&B" ("*llety Gwely a Brecwast bach*") means—

      B&B accommodation—

           (i)    where the manager resides on the premises; and

           (ii)   which has fewer than 7 bedrooms available for letting.

    **[3640]**

---

**NOTES**

Commencement: 3 April 2006.

# PART 1
## ADDITIONAL MATTERS TO BE TAKEN INTO ACCOUNT IN DETERMINING SUITABILITY

**3**   In determining for the purposes of Part 7 of the 1996 Act whether accommodation is suitable for a person in priority need there must be taken into account the following matters—

      (a)    the specific health needs of the person;

      (b)    the proximity and accessibility of social services;

      (c)    the proximity and accessibility of the support of the family or other support services; or

      (d)    any disability of the person.

    **[3641]**

---

**NOTES**

Commencement: 3 April 2006.

# PART 2
## CIRCUMSTANCES APPLYING FROM 2 APRIL 2007 IN WHICH ACCOMMODATION IS NOT TO BE REGARDED AS SUITABLE

### 4  B&B accommodation used for housing a homeless person to meet the basic standard

For the purposes of Part 7 of the 1996 Act, B&B accommodation is not to be regarded as suitable unless it meets at least the basic standard.

    **[3642]**

---

**NOTES**

Commencement: 2 April 2007.

### 5  B&B accommodation not to be regarded as suitable for a minor or a pregnant woman

For the purposes of Part 7 of the 1996 Act and subject to the exceptions contained in Article 6, B&B accommodation is not to be regarded as suitable for a person who is a minor or a pregnant woman.

    **[3643]**

---

**NOTES**

Commencement: 2 April 2007.

## 6  Exceptions

(1)    Article 5 does not apply where—

(a)    the person occupies a basic standard B&B for a period, or a total of periods, which does not exceed 2 weeks;

(b)    the person occupies a higher standard B&B for a period or a total of periods which does not exceed 6 weeks;

(c)    the person occupies a basic standard small B&B for a period or a total of periods which does not exceed 6 weeks, and the local housing authority has, before the expiry of the two-week period referred to in sub-paragraph (a), offered suitable alternative accommodation, but the person has chosen to remain in the said B&B;

(d)    the person occupies a basic standard small B&B after exercising the choice referred to in sub-paragraph (c) above, and the local housing authority has offered suitable alternative accommodation before the end of the six-week period referred to in sub-paragraph (c) above, but the person has chosen to remain in the said B&B; or

(e)    the person occupies a higher standard small B&B, and the local housing authority has offered suitable alternative accommodation, before the expiry of the six-week period referred to in sub-paragraph (b) above, but the person has chosen to remain in the said B&B.

(2)    If the suitable alternative accommodation offered for the purposes of paragraph (1) is shared, it must meet the higher standard.

(3)    In the case of households with dependant children or a pregnant woman, the offer made under sub-paragraphs (d) or (e) must be of suitable self-contained accommodation. In the case of an applicant who is a minor, the offer must be of suitable accommodation with support.

(4)    In calculating a period, or total period, of a person's occupation of B&B accommodation for the purposes of paragraph (1), there must be disregarded—

(a)    any period before 2 April 2007; and

(b)    where a local housing authority is subject to the duty under section 193 by virtue of section 200(4), any period before that authority became subject to that duty.

**[3644]**

**NOTES**
Commencement: 2 April 2007.

PART 3
EXTENSION FROM 7 APRIL 2008 TO ALL ACCOMMODATION PROVIDED IN
DISCHARGE OF HOMELESSNESS FUNCTIONS

## 7  B&B accommodation not to be regarded as suitable for a homeless person in priority need

For the purposes of Part 7 of the 1996 Act and subject to the exceptions contained in article 9, B&B accommodation is not to be regarded as suitable for a person who is in priority need.

**[3645]**

**NOTES**
Commencement: 7 April 2008.

## 8  Shared accommodation to meet the higher standard

For the purposes of Part 7 of the 1996 Act and subject to the exceptions contained in articles 9 and 10, shared accommodation is not to be regarded as suitable for a person who is in priority need unless it meets the higher standard.

**[3646]**

**NOTES**
Commencement: 7 April 2008.

## 9  Exceptions

(1)    Articles 7 and 8 do not apply where—

(a)    the person occupies basic standard B&B for a period, or a total of periods, which does not exceed 2 weeks;

(b)    the person occupies a higher standard B&B for a period or a total of periods which does not exceed 6 weeks;

(c)    the person occupies a basic standard small B&B for a period or a total of periods which does not exceed 6 weeks, and the local housing authority has, before the expiry of the two-week period referred to in sub-paragraph (a), offered suitable alternative accommodation, but the person has chosen to remain in the said B&B;

(d)    the person occupies a basic standard small B&B after exercising the choice referred to in sub-paragraph (c), and the local housing authority has offered suitable alternative accommodation before the end of the six-week period referred to in sub-paragraph (c) above, but the person has chosen to remain in the said B&B;

(e)    the person occupies a higher standard small B&B, the local housing authority has offered suitable alternative accommodation, before the expiry of the six-week period referred to in sub-paragraph (b), but the person has chosen to remain in the said B&B: or

(f)    the person occupies basic standard shared accommodation for a period, or a total of periods, which does not exceed 2 weeks;

(g)    the person occupies, for a period or a total of periods which does not exceed 6 weeks, basic standard shared accommodation owned by a local housing authority or registered social landlord, and the local housing authority has offered suitable alternative accommodation before the expiry of the two-week period referred to in sub-paragraph (f), but the person has chosen to remain in the said accommodation.

(2)    If the suitable alternative accommodation offered for the purposes of paragraph (1) is shared, it must meet the higher standard.

(3)    In the case of households with dependant children or a pregnant woman, the offer made under sub-paragraphs (d) or (e) must be of suitable self-contained accommodation. In the case of an applicant who is a minor, the offer must be of suitable accommodation with support.

(4)    In calculating a period, or total period, of a person's occupation of shared accommodation for the purposes of paragraph (1), there must be disregarded—

(a)    any period before 7 April 2008; and

(b)    where a local housing authority is subject to the duty under section 193 by virtue of section 200(4), any period before that authority became subject to that duty.

**[3647]**

**NOTES**
    Commencement: 7 April 2008.

## 10   Delayed application to Social Housing

Article 7 is not to apply until 4 April 2011 to any property owned or managed by a local authority or registered social landlord and used for the purposes of Part 7 of the 1996 Act on 7 April 2008.

**[3648]**

**NOTES**
    Commencement: 7 April 2008.

SCHEDULE
HIGHER STANDARD

## 1   Minimum Space Standards

Space standards for sleeping accommodation

*Room sizes where cooking facilities provided in a separate room or kitchen*

| Floor Area of Room | Maximum No of Persons |
| --- | --- |
| Not less than 6.5 square metres | 1 person |
| Not less than 10.2 square metres | 2 persons |
| Not less than 14.9 square metres | 3 persons |
| Not less than 19.6 square metres | 4 persons |

*Room sizes where cooking facilities provided within the room*

| Floor Area of Room | Maximum No of Persons |
| --- | --- |
| Not less than 10.2 square metres | 1 person |
| Not less than 13.9 square metres | 2 persons |
| Not less than 18.6 square metres | 3 persons |
| Not less than 23.2 square metres | 4 persons |

*For the purposes of the room size calculations above, a child less than 10 years old is treated as a half person.*

- (a)  No room to be occupied by more than 4 persons, except where the occupants consent.
- (b)  No sharing of rooms for those of opposite genders, aged 10 or above unless they are living together as partners and both are over the age of consent, or where a parent or guardian elects to share with an older child.
- (c)  All rooms must have a floor to ceiling height of at least 2.1 metres over not less than 75% of the room area. Any part of the room where the ceiling height is less than 1.5 metres must be disregarded when calculating the floor area.
- (d)  Separate kitchens and bathrooms are unsuitable for sleeping accommodation.

## 2  Installation for heating

The premises must have adequate provision for heating. All habitable rooms and bath- or shower-rooms must have a heating system capable of maintaining the room at a minimum temperature of 18°C when the outside temperature is minus 1°C.

## 3  Facilities for the storage, preparation and cooking of food within the unit

(1)  In a unit of accommodation accommodating more than one person, the food preparation area provided within the unit must include the following facilities:

- (a)  four burners or hobs, conventional oven and grill, or two burners or hobs and a microwave with a built in oven and grill,
- (b)  a sink and integral drainer, with a constant supply of hot water and cold drinking water,
- (c)  a storage cupboard of a minimum capacity 0.2 cubic metres excluding storage beneath the sink,
- (d)  a refrigerator,
- (e)  a minimum of four 13-amp sockets (single or double) situated over the worktop,
- (f)  a worktop for food preparation of minimum dimensions 1 metre x 0.6 metre, and
- (g)  a minimum of 1 metre circulation space from facilities to other furniture in the room.

(2)  In a unit of accommodation accommodating one person, the food preparation area provided within the unit of accommodation must include the following facilities:

As (a)–(g) above but (a) to have a minimum of two burners or hobs.

## 4  Storage, preparation and cooking of food in a shared facility

(1)  Where food preparation areas are shared between more than one household there must be one set of kitchen facilities for:

- (a)  every 3 family households or fewer;
- (b)  every 5 single-person households or fewer. (For between 6 and 9 single-person households an additional oven or microwave is required.)
- (c)  every 10 persons or fewer where there is a mixture of family and single-person households within the same premises.

(2)  Each set of shared facilities must provide the following facilities:

- (a)  as for unit accommodating more than one person except that cooking facilities must consist of 4 burners or hobs, conventional oven, grill and microwave,
- (b)  an electric kettle,
- (c)  a toaster.

The food preparation area used by the management may be included when calculating the ratio, provided it meets the criteria for storage, preparation and cooking of food in a shared facility.

Where residents have no access to kitchen facilities and the proprietor provides at least a breakfast and evening-meal for residents, the requirements for shared kitchen facilities will be deemed to have been met.

Additional facilities to be provided in each bedroom or within the total accommodation occupied exclusively by each household must include:

- (a)  a refrigerator; and
- (b)  lockable storage.

Alternatively, these may be provided elsewhere within the building.

## 5  Toilet and washing facilities

(1)  Facilities for the exclusive use of the occupant or household must include:

- (a)  bath or shower,
- (b)  a wash hand basin with a constant supply of hot and cold water, and
- (c)  a water-closet either en-suite or in a separate room reserved for the exclusive use of individuals or households.

(2)  Shared facilities must include:

- (a)  One water closet and wash hand basin with a constant supply of hot and cold water within the building for every five households or fewer. This must be located not more than one floor away from the intended users. For the first five households the water closet and wash hand basin may be in the shower or bathroom. All additional water closets and wash hand basins for occupancies of six households or more must be in a separate compartment.

(b)    One bathroom or shower-room to be provided for every five persons. This must be located not more than one floor away from the intended users.

(c)    In premises accommodating children under the age of 10, at least half of the bathing facilities must contain baths suitable for children.

The number of persons occupying a unit of accommodation with a water closet facility provided for their exclusive use is not to be included in the calculation for shared water closets.

## 6   Security

The entrance door to each unit of accommodation must be lockable and be capable of being unlocked from inside without the use of a key.

## 7   Common Room(s)

Every premises must have a common room of at least 12 square metres unless all households have a living area separate from their sleeping area that is available for their exclusive use or the premises are for single person households only.

## 8   Management Standard

(a)    Each household must be issued with written "house rules" which include details as to how sanctions will be applied. This document is to be approved by the local authority placing homeless households in the premises.

(b)    Each household must be issued with written information relating to the premises including how to operate all installations, for example heating and hot water appliances and fire fighting equipment.

(c)    Written information must be made available to residents relating to the local area including the location or contact details of local facilities, laundrettes, doctors' surgeries and schools.

(d)    Residents must have access to their rooms at all times except when rooms are being cleaned or otherwise maintained. Provision must be made to accommodate residents at these times.

(e)    Access is allowed for the appropriate officers of the local housing authority in whose area the premises are situated, and officers of any authority placing homeless households in the premises, to inspect the premises as and when they consider necessary, to ensure that the requirements are being complied with; and that the manager will allow such inspections to take place, if necessary without notice.

(f)    Access is allowed for the officers of the local authority and authorised health and community workers for the area in which the premises are situated, to visit the occupiers of the premises and interview them in private in the room(s) they occupy.

(g)    A manager with adequate day to day responsibility to ensure the good management of the property can be contacted at all times and that a notice giving the name, address and telephone number of the manager must be displayed in a readily visible position in the property.

(h)    A clear emergency evacuation plan is in place setting out action upon hearing the fire alarm, escape routes and safe assembly points. The managers must ensure that each person newly arriving at the premises is told what to do in the event of a fire and about fire precautions provided.

(i)    Each household must be issued with a complaints procedure which specifies how a complaint can be made. This information must also include where the complainant can obtain further advice and assistance.

**[3649]**

**NOTES**
Commencement: 2 April 2007.

# RESIDENTIAL PROPERTY TRIBUNAL (FEES) (ENGLAND) REGULATIONS 2006

(SI 2006/830)

**NOTES**
Made: 17 March 2006.
Authority: Housing Act 2004, Sch 13, paras 1, 11.
Commencement: 13 April 2006.

## 1  Citation, commencement and interpretation

(1)   These Regulations may be cited as the Residential Property Tribunal (Fees) (England) Regulations 2006 and shall come into force on 13th April 2006.

(2)   In these Regulations—
"the Act" means the Housing Act 2004;
"the 1985 Act" means the Housing Act 1985;
"tribunal" means a residential property tribunal.

**[3650]**

**NOTES**
Commencement: 13 April 2006.

## 2  Application

These Regulations apply in relation to appeals and applications of any of the descriptions specified in regulation 3 made after 6th April 2006 in respect of premises in England.

**[3651]**

**NOTES**
Commencement: 13 April 2006.

## 3  Fees

(1)   Subject to regulation 5(2), a fee of £150 shall be payable for—
(a)   an appeal to a tribunal under—
(i)   section 22(9) of the Act (refusal to approve use of premises subject to a prohibition order);
(ii)   paragraph 10 of Schedule 1 to the Act (improvement notice);
(iii)   paragraph 13 of Schedule 1 to the Act (refusal to revoke or vary an improvement notice);
(iv)   paragraph 7 of Schedule 2 to the Act (prohibition order);
(v)   paragraph 9 of Schedule 2 to the Act (refusal to revoke or vary a prohibition order);
(vi)   paragraph 11 of Schedule 3 to the Act (improvement notice: demand for recovery of expenses);
(vii)   paragraph 32 of Schedule 5 to the Act (HMO licensing: decision or refusal to vary or revoke licence);
(viii)   paragraph 32 of Schedule 6 to the Act (management order: third party compensation);
(ix)   paragraph 26(1)(a) and (b) of Schedule 7 to the Act (final EDMO);
(x)   paragraph 30 of Schedule 7 to the Act (decision or refusal to revoke or vary an interim or final EDMO);
(xi)   paragraph 34(2) of Schedule 7 to the Act (EDMO: third party compensation);
(xii)   section 269(1) of the 1985 Act (demolition orders);
(b)   an application to a tribunal under—
(i)   section 126(4) of the Act (effect of management orders: furniture);
(ii)   under section 138 of the Act (compensation payable to third parties);
(iii)   section 318(1) of the 1985 Act (power of the tribunal to authorise execution of works on unfit premises or for improvement).

(2)   Subject to paragraph (3) and regulation 5(2), a fee of £150 shall be payable for an appeal to a tribunal under one or more of the following provisions—
(a)   section 62(7) of the Act (HMO licensing: refusal to grant temporary exemption notice);
(b)   section 86(7) of the Act (selective licensing: refusal to grant temporary exemption notice);
(c)   paragraph 31 of Schedule 5 to the Act (grant or refusal of licence);
(d)   paragraph 24 of Schedule 6 to the Act (interim and final management order);
(e)   paragraph 28 of Schedule 6 to the Act (decision or refusal to vary or revoke a management order).

(3)   No fee is payable where an appeal under sub-paragraph (1)(b) of paragraph 24 of Schedule 6 to the Act is made on the grounds set out in sub-paragraph (4) of that paragraph.

**[3652]**

**NOTES**
Commencement: 13 April 2006.

## 4  Payment of fees

Any fee payable under regulation 3 must accompany the appeal or application and must be paid by a cheque made payable to, or postal order drawn in favour of, the Office of the Deputy Prime Minister.

**[3653]**

**NOTES**
Commencement: 13 April 2006.

## 5  Liability to pay fee and waiver of fees

(1)   The appellant or applicant shall be liable to pay any fee payable under regulation 3.

(2)   No fee is payable under regulation 3 where, on the date that the appeal or application is made, the appellant or applicant (as the case may be) or his partner is in receipt of—

    (a)   either of the following benefits under Part 7 of the Social Security Contributions and Benefits Act 1992—

        (i)   income support; or

        (ii)   housing benefit;

    (b)   an income-based jobseeker's allowance within the meaning of section 1 of the Jobseekers Act 1995;

    (c)   a working tax credit under Part 1 of the Tax Credits Act 2002 to which paragraph (3) applies;

    (d)   a guarantee credit under the State Pensions Credit Act 2002;

    [(e)   income-related employment and support allowance payable under Part 1 of the Welfare Reform Act 2007].

(3)   This paragraph applies where—

    (a)   either—

        (i)   there is a disability element or severe disability element (or both) to the tax credit received by the person or his partner; or

        (ii)   the person or his partner is also in receipt of child tax credit; and

    (b)   the gross annual income taken into account for the calculation of the working tax credit is £14, 213 or less.

(4)   In this regulation "partner", in relation to a person, means—

    (a)   where the person is a member of a couple, the other member of that couple; or

    (b)   where the person is polygamously married to two or more members of his household, any such member.

(5)   In paragraph (4), "couple" means—

    (a)   a man and woman who are married to each other and are members of the same household;

    (b)   a man and woman who are not married to each other but are living together as husband and wife;

    (c)   two people of the same sex who are civil partners of each other and are members of the same household; or

    (d)   two people of the same sex who are not civil partners of each other but are living together as if they were civil partners,

and for the purposes of sub-paragraph (d), two people of the same sex are to be regarded as living together as if they were civil partners if, but only if, they would be regarded as living together as husband and wife were they instead two people of the opposite sex.

**[3654]**

**NOTES**
Commencement: 13 April 2006.
Para (2): sub-para (e) inserted by the Employment and Support Allowance (Consequential Provisions) (No 3) Regulations 2008, SI 2008/1879, reg 17.

## 6 Reimbursement of fees

(1)   Subject to paragraph (2), in relation to any appeal or application in respect of which a fee is payable under regulation 3, a tribunal may require any party to the appeal or application to reimburse any other party to the extent of the whole or part of any fee paid by him in respect of the appeal or application.

(2)   A tribunal shall not require a party to make such reimbursement if, at the time the tribunal is considering whether or not to do so, the tribunal is satisfied that the party or his partner is in receipt of assistance of any description mentioned in regulation 5(2).

**[3655]**

**NOTES**

Commencement: 13 April 2006.

# RESIDENTIAL PROPERTY TRIBUNAL PROCEDURE (ENGLAND) REGULATIONS 2006

### (SI 2006/831)

**NOTES**

Made: 17 March 2006.
Authority: Housing Act 2004, s 250(2)(a), Sch 13.
Commencement: 13 April 2006.

## ARRANGEMENT OF REGULATIONS

## 1　Citation and commencement

(1)　These Regulations may be cited as the Residential Property Tribunal Procedure (England) Regulations 2006.

(2)　These Regulations shall come into force on 13th April 2006.

**[3656]**

---

**NOTES**

Commencement: 13 April 2006.

---

## 2　Interpretation

In these Regulations—

"the Act" means the Housing Act 2004;

"the 1985 Act" means the Housing Act 1985;

"application" means an application or appeal to a tribunal under the Act or Part 9 of the 1985 Act and "applicant" bears a corresponding meaning;

"case management conference" means a pre-trial review or any other meeting held by a tribunal for the purpose of managing the proceedings in respect of an application;

"the Fees Regulations" means the Residential Property Tribunals (Fees) (England) Regulations 2006;

"IMO authorisation application" means an application for authorisation to make an interim management order;

"interested person" means in relation to a particular application—

    (a)　a person other than the applicant who would have been entitled under the Act or the 1985 Act (as the case may be) to make the application;

    (b)　a person to whom notice of the application must be given by the applicant in accordance with the following provisions of the Act—

        (i)　section 73(7);

        (ii)　section 96(7);

        (iii)　paragraph 11(2) of Schedule 1; or

        (iv)　paragraph 14(2) of Schedule 3;

    (c)　a person to whom the tribunal must give the opportunity of being heard in accordance with the following provisions of the Act—

        (i)　section 34(4); or

        (ii)　section 317(2);

    (d)　the LHA where it is not a party to the application;

"LHA" means the local housing authority;

"premises" means the dwelling or building to which the application relates;

"the respondent" means, in respect of an application to which a paragraph of the Schedule to these Regulations applies, the person or persons, or one of the persons, specified in sub-paragraph (3) of that paragraph;

"statement of reasons" means a statement of reasons prepared by the LHA under section 8 of the Act (reasons for decision to take enforcement action); and

"tribunal" means a residential property tribunal, and "the tribunal" in relation to an application means the tribunal by which the application is to be determined.

**[3657]**

---

**NOTES**

Commencement: 13 April 2006.

---

## 3　Application

These Regulations apply to proceedings of residential property tribunals for determining applications in respect of premises in England made—

    (a)　under the Act;

    (b)　under section 318(1) of the 1985 Act in respect of applications made on or after 6th April 2006; or

    (c)　under any of sections 269(1), 272(1) or (2)(a), 272(2)(b), or 317(1) of the 1985 Act in respect of demolition orders made on or after 6th April 2006.

**[3658]**

---

**NOTES**

Commencement: 13 April 2006.

---

## 4  The overriding objective

(1)  When a tribunal—

    (a)    exercises any power under these Regulations; or

    (b)    interprets any regulation,

it must seek to give effect to the overriding objective of dealing fairly and justly with applications which it is to determine.

(2)  Dealing with an application fairly and justly includes—

    (a)    dealing with it in ways which are proportionate to the complexity of the issues and to the resources of the parties;

    (b)    ensuring, so far as practicable, that the parties are on an equal footing procedurally and are able to participate fully in the proceedings;

    (c)    assisting any party in the presentation of his case without advocating the course he should take;

    (d)    using the tribunal's special expertise effectively; and

    (e)    avoiding delay, so far as is compatible with proper consideration of the issues.

**[3659]**

**NOTES**

Commencement: 13 April 2006.

## 5  Request for extension of time to make an application

(1)  This regulation applies where a person makes a request to a tribunal for permission to make an application after the end of the period stipulated in the Act as the period within which the application must be made.

(2)  A request to which this regulation applies must—

    (a)    be in writing;

    (b)    give reasons for the failure to make the application before the end of that period and for any further delay since then;

    (c)    include a statement that the person making the request believes that the facts stated in it are true; and

    (d)    be dated and signed.

(3)  Where a request mentioned in paragraph (1) is made, the applicant must at the same time send the completed application to which the request relates to the tribunal.

**[3660]**

**NOTES**

Commencement: 13 April 2006.

## 6  Particulars of application

(1)  An application must be in writing and must include the following particulars—

    (a)    the applicant's name and address;

    (b)    the name and address of the respondent where known to the applicant, or where not known a description of the respondent's connection with the premises;

    (c)    the address of the premises;

    (d)    the applicant's connection with the premises;

    (e)    the applicant's reasons for making the application including the remedy sought;

    (f)    where known to the applicant, the name and address of any interested person;

    (g)    a statement that the applicant believes that the facts stated in the application are true; and

    (h)    in respect of each application to which a paragraph in the Schedule to these Regulations applies, the documents specified in sub-paragraph (2) of that paragraph.

(2)  Any of the particulars required by paragraph (1) may be dispensed with or relaxed if the tribunal is satisfied that—

    (a)    the particulars and documents included with an application are sufficient to establish that the application is one which may be made to a tribunal; and

    (b)    no prejudice will be, or is likely to be, caused to any party to the application.

(3)  A single qualified member of the panel may exercise the power conferred by paragraph (2).

**[3661]**

**NOTES**

Commencement: 13 April 2006.

## 7  Acknowledgement and notification of application by tribunal

(1)  As soon as practicable after receiving the application, the tribunal must—

    (a)    send an acknowledgement of receipt to the applicant; and

(b)    send a copy of the application and of each document accompanying it to the respondent.

(2)    Except in a case to which regulation 9 applies, the tribunal must also send to the respondent a notice specifying the date by which he must send the reply mentioned in regulation 8.

(3)    The date specified in the notice must not be less than 14 days after the date specified in the notice as the date on which it was made.

**[3662]**

**NOTES**
Commencement: 13 April 2006.

## 8    Reply by respondent

(1)    This regulation applies where a respondent receives the notice mentioned in regulation 7(2).

(2)    Where this regulation applies the respondent must by the date specified in that notice send to the tribunal a written reply acknowledging receipt of the copy documents sent in accordance with regulation 7(1)(b) and stating—
    (a)    whether or not he intends to oppose the application;
    (b)    where not already included in the application, the name and address of each interested person known to the respondent; and
    (c)    the address to which documents should be sent for the purposes of the proceedings.

**[3663]**

**NOTES**
Commencement: 13 April 2006.

## 9    Urgent IMO authorisation applications

(1)    This regulation applies where the LHA requests a tribunal to deal with an IMO authorisation application as a matter of urgency.

(2)    Where it appears to the tribunal, on the basis of information accompanying the application, that the exceptional circumstances mentioned in paragraph (3) exist, it may order that an oral hearing (an "urgent oral hearing") shall be held without complying with the notice requirements of regulation 25.

(3)    The exceptional circumstances are that—
    (a)    there is an immediate threat to the health and safety of the occupiers of the house or to persons occupying or having an estate or interest in any premises in the vicinity of the house; and
    (b)    by making the interim management order as soon as possible (together where applicable with such other measures as the LHA intends to take) the LHA will be able to take immediate appropriate steps to arrest or significantly reduce the threat.

(4)    The tribunal must as soon as practicable notify the parties and each interested person whose name and address have been notified to it—
    (a)    that the application is being dealt with as a matter of urgency under this regulation;
    (b)    of the reasons why it appears to the tribunal that the exceptional circumstances exist;
    (c)    of any requirement to be satisfied by a party before the hearing; and
    (d)    of the date on which the urgent oral hearing will be held.

(5)    The date of the hearing must be not less than 4 days after the date that notification of the urgent oral hearing is sent.

(6)    At the urgent oral hearing the tribunal must—
    (a)    if it is satisfied upon hearing evidence that the exceptional circumstance do exist, determine the application; or
    (b)    if it is not so satisfied—
        (i)    adjourn the hearing; and
        (ii)    give such directions as it considers appropriate.

(7)    A single qualified member of the panel may—
    (a)    exercise the power conferred by paragraph (2); and
    (b)    decide the date of the urgent oral hearing.

(8)    Where the tribunal orders an urgent oral hearing the notice provisions contained in the following regulations shall not apply to the application—
    (a)    regulation 21(5) (notice for an inspection); and
    (b)    regulation 25(3) and (4) (notice of hearing).

**[3664]**

**NOTES**
Commencement: 13 April 2006.

## 10 Request to be treated as an applicant or respondent

(1) A person ("the potential party") may make a request to the tribunal to be joined as a party to the proceedings.

(2) Any request under paragraph (1)—
(a) may be made without notice;
(b) must be in writing;
(c) must give reasons for the request; and
(d) must specify whether the potential party wishes to be treated as—
(i) an applicant; or
(ii) a respondent.

(3) As soon as practicable after reaching its decision whether to grant or refuse a request under paragraph (1), the tribunal must—
(a) notify the potential party of the decision and the reasons for it; and
(b) send a copy of the notification to the existing parties.

(4) Any potential party whose request under paragraph (1) is granted must be treated as an applicant or respondent for the purposes of regulations 4, 9, 11, 13 to 37 and 39 to 41.

(5) In the regulations mentioned in paragraph (4) any reference to an applicant or a respondent must be construed as including a person treated as such under this regulation, and any reference to a party must be construed as including any such person.

(6) A single qualified member of the panel may grant or refuse a request under paragraph (1).

**[3665]**

**NOTES**
Commencement: 13 April 2006.

## 11 Determining applications together

(1) This regulation applies where separate applications have been made which in the opinion of the tribunal—
(a) involve related issues concerning the same premises; or
(b) are made in respect of two or more premises in which the same parties have interests and as to which similar or related issues fall to be determined.

(2) Where paragraph (1) applies, the tribunal may order that—
(a) some or all of those applications; or
(b) particular issues or matters raised in the applications,

shall be determined together.

**[3666]**

**NOTES**
Commencement: 13 April 2006.

## 12 Payment of fees

Where a fee which is payable under the Fees Regulations is not paid within a period of 14 days from the date on which the application is received, the application shall be treated as withdrawn unless the tribunal is satisfied that there are reasonable grounds not to do so.

**[3667]**

**NOTES**
Commencement: 13 April 2006.

## 13 Representatives

(1) This regulation applies where a party or an interested person makes a request in writing to the tribunal for information or documents to be supplied to his representative.

(2) A request mentioned in paragraph (1) must contain the name and address of the representative.

(3) Where this regulation applies any duty of the tribunal under these Regulations to supply any information or document shall be satisfied by sending or giving it to the representative.

**[3668]**

**NOTES**
Commencement: 13 April 2006.

**14 Supply of information and documents to interested persons**

(1) Where the tribunal is notified of the name and address of an interested person, it must ensure that as soon as is practicable he is supplied with—

(a) a copy of the application;

(b) an explanation of the procedure for applying to be joined as an applicant or respondent; and

(c) any other information or document which the tribunal considers appropriate.

(2) The tribunal may ensure the supply of information or documents under paragraph (1) by—

(a) itself supplying the interested person with the information or documents; or

(b) requiring a party to do so by an order made under regulation 16(2).

(3) Where information and documents are supplied to an interested person in accordance with paragraph (1) but—

(a) he responds to the tribunal but is not joined as a party under regulation 10; or

(b) he does not so respond,

the tribunal shall not be under any further duty to ensure the supply of information or documents to that person.

**[3669]**

**NOTES**

Commencement: 13 April 2006.

**15 Supply of documents by tribunal**

(1) Before determining an application, the tribunal must take all reasonable steps to ensure that each of the parties is supplied with—

(a) a copy of any document relevant to the proceedings (or sufficient extracts from or particulars of the document) which has been received from any other party or from an interested person (other than a document already in his possession or one of which he has previously been supplied with a copy); and

(b) a copy of any document which embodies the results of any relevant enquiries made by or for the tribunal for the purposes of the proceedings.

(2) At a hearing, if a party has not previously received a relevant document or a copy of, or sufficient extracts from or particulars of, a relevant document, then unless—

(a) that person consents to the continuation of the hearing; or

(b) the tribunal considers that that person has a sufficient opportunity to deal with the matters to which the document relates without an adjournment of the hearing,

the tribunal must adjourn the hearing for a period which it considers will give that person a sufficient opportunity to deal with those matters.

**[3670]**

**NOTES**

Commencement: 13 April 2006.

**16 Supply of information and documents by parties**

(1) Subject to paragraph (5), the tribunal may make an order requiring a party to supply to the tribunal any information or document which it is in the power of that party to supply and which is specified, or of a description specified, in the order.

(2) The tribunal may make an order requiring a party to supply to another party or to an interested person copies of any documents supplied or to be supplied to the tribunal under paragraph (1).

(3) A party who is subject to an order made under paragraph (1) or (2) must supply such information, documents or copies by such time as may be specified in, or determined in accordance with, the order.

(4) Subject to paragraph (5) the tribunal may make an order requiring any person to attend an oral hearing to give evidence and produce any documents specified, or of a description specified, in the order which it is in the power of that person to produce.

(5) Paragraphs (1) and (4) do not apply in relation to any document which a person could not be compelled to produce on the trial of an action in a court of law in England.

(6) A single qualified member of the panel may make an order under paragraph(1), (2) or (4) which is—

(a) preliminary to an oral hearing; or

(b) preliminary or incidental to a determination.

**[3671]**

## 17 Failure to comply with an order to supply information and documents

Where a party has failed to comply with an order made under regulation 16(1), (2) or (4) the tribunal may make an order dismissing or allowing the whole or part of the application.

[3672]

## 18 Determination without a hearing

(1)   Subject to paragraphs (2) and (6) the tribunal may determine an application without an oral hearing if it has given the parties not less than 14 days' notice in writing of its intention to do so.

(2)   At any time before the application is determined—
    (a)   the applicant or the respondent may request an oral hearing; or
    (b)   the tribunal may give notice to the parties that it intends to hold an oral hearing.

(3)   Where a request is made or a notice given under paragraph (2) the tribunal must give notice of a hearing in accordance with regulation 25.

(4)   A determination without an oral hearing may be made in the absence of any representations by the respondent.

(5)   A single qualified member of the panel may decide whether an oral hearing is or is not appropriate to determine an application.

(6)   This regulation does not apply to an application to which regulation 9 (urgent IMO authorisation applications) applies.

[3673]

## 19 Interim orders

(1)   A tribunal may make an order on an interim basis (an "interim order")—
    (a)   suspending, in whole or in part, the effect of any decision, notice, order or licence which is the subject matter of proceedings before it; or
    (b)   for the time being granting any remedy which it would have had power to grant in its final decision.

(2)   Where the tribunal makes an interim order without first giving the parties the opportunity to make representations with regard to making it, a party may request that the interim order be varied or set aside.

(3)   Any such request may be made—
    (a)   orally at a case management conference or hearing;
    (b)   in writing; or
    (c)   by such other means as the tribunal may permit.

(4)   An interim order must be recorded as soon as possible in a document which, except in the case of an order made with the consent of all parties, must give reasons for the decision to make the order.

(5)   This regulation does not apply to an IMO authorisation application.

[3674]

## 20 Directions

(1)   A party may request the tribunal to give directions by order under its general power in section 230(2) of the Housing Act 2004.

(2)   A party to whom a direction is addressed may request the tribunal to vary it or set it aside.

(3)   A request referred to in paragraph (1) or (2) may be made—
    (a)   orally at a case management conference or hearing;
    (b)   in writing; or
    (c)   by such other means as the tribunal may permit.

(4)    The party making the request must specify the directions which are sought and the reasons for seeking them.

(5)    A single qualified member of the panel may give a procedural direction as to any matter which is—

    (a)    preliminary to an oral hearing; or

    (b)    preliminary or incidental to a determination.

(6)    In paragraph (5)(a), "procedural direction" means any direction other than one of those set out in paragraphs (a) to (e) of section 230(5) of the Act.

**[3675]**

**NOTES**
    Commencement: 13 April 2006.

## 21   Inspection of premises and neighbourhood

(1)    Subject to paragraph (3) the tribunal may inspect—

    (a)    the premises;

    (b)    any other premises inspection of which may assist the tribunal in determining the application;

    (c)    the locality of the premises.

(2)    Subject to paragraph (3)—

    (a)    the tribunal must give the parties an opportunity to attend an inspection; and

    (b)    a member of the [Administrative Justice and Tribunals Council] who is acting in that capacity may attend any inspection.

(3)    The making of and attendance at an inspection is subject to any necessary consent being obtained.

(4)    Where there is an oral hearing, an inspection may be carried out before, during, or after the hearing.

(5)    Subject to paragraph (6), the tribunal must give the parties not less than 14 days notice of the date, time and place of the inspection.

(6)    Any of the requirements for notice in paragraph (5) may be dispensed with or relaxed if the tribunal is satisfied that the parties have received sufficient notice.

(7)    Where an inspection is made after the close of an oral hearing, the tribunal may reopen the hearing on account of any matter arising from the inspection, after giving reasonable notice of the date, time and place of the reopened hearing to the parties.

**[3676]**

**NOTES**
    Commencement: 13 April 2006.
    Para (2): in sub-para (b) words in square brackets substituted by the Tribunals, Courts and Enforcement Act 2007 (Transitional and Consequential Provisions) Order 2008, SI 2008/2683, art 6(1), Sch 1, paras 315, 316.

## 22   Expert evidence

(1)    In this regulation "expert" means an independent expert who is not an employee of a party.

(2)    Subject to paragraph (4) a party may adduce expert evidence, and in doing so must—

    (a)    provide the tribunal with a written summary of the evidence; and

    (b)    supply a copy of that written summary to each other party at least 7 days before—

        (i)    the date of the relevant oral hearing notified in relation to the application under regulation 25; or

        (ii)    the date notified under regulation 18 upon which the application will be determined without an oral hearing.

(3)    An expert's written summary of his evidence must—

    (a)    be addressed to the tribunal;

    (b)    include details of the expert's qualifications;

    (c)    contain a statement that the expert understands and has complied with his duty to assist the tribunal on the matters within his expertise, overriding any obligation to the person from whom the expert has received instructions or by whom he is employed or paid.

(4)    Where the tribunal gives a direction, under its general power in section 230(2) of the Act, that a party may not adduce expert evidence without its permission, it may specify as a condition of that permission that—

    (a)    the expert's evidence must be limited to such matters as the tribunal directs;

    (b)    the expert must attend a hearing to give oral evidence; or

    (c)    the parties must jointly instruct the expert.

**[3677]**

NOTES

Commencement: 13 April 2006.

## 23 Case management conference

(1)    The tribunal may hold a case management conference.

(2)    The tribunal must give the parties not less than 7 days' notice of the date, time and place of the case management conference.

(3)    At the case management conference the tribunal may order the parties to take such steps or do such things as appear to it to be necessary or desirable for securing the just, expeditious and economical determination of the application.

(4)    The tribunal may postpone or adjourn a case management conference.

(5)    A party may be represented at a case management conference.

(6)    The functions of the tribunal under this regulation may be exercised by a single qualified member of the panel.

**[3678]**

NOTES

Commencement: 13 April 2006.

## 24 Other case management powers

(1)    The tribunal may—

(a)    reduce the time appointed by or under these Regulations for doing any act where all parties agree the reduction in question;

(b)    extend the time appointed by or under these Regulations for doing any act, even if the time appointed has expired, where—

(i)    it would not be reasonable to expect the person in question to comply or have complied within that time; or

(ii)    not to extend the time would result in substantial injustice;

(c)    permit the use of telephone, video link, or any other method of communication—

(i)    to make representations to the tribunal; or

(ii)    for the purposes of a case management conference or hearing;

(d)    require any person giving written evidence to include with that evidence a signed statement that he believes the facts stated in the evidence are true;

(e)    take any other step or make any other decision which the tribunal considers necessary or desirable for the purpose of managing the case.

(2)    The tribunal may exercise its powers under these Regulations in response to a request to do so or on its own initiative.

(3)    A single qualified member of the panel may exercise the powers under this regulation as to any matter which is preliminary to—

(a)    an oral hearing; or

(b)    a determination which is to be made without an oral hearing.

**[3679]**

NOTES

Commencement: 13 April 2006.

## 25 Notice of hearing

(1)    A hearing shall be on the date and at the time and place appointed by the tribunal.

(2)    The tribunal must give notice to the parties of the appointed date, time and place of the hearing.

(3)    Subject to paragraph (4) notice of the hearing must be given not less than 21 days before the appointed date.

(4)    In exceptional circumstances the tribunal may, without the agreement of the parties, give less than 21 days' notice of the appointed date, time and place of the hearing; but any such notice must be given as soon as practicable before the appointed date and the notice must specify what the *exceptional circumstances* are.

**[3680]**

NOTES

Commencement: 13 April 2006.

**26  Postponement of hearing**

(1)  Subject to paragraph (3) the tribunal may postpone an oral hearing.

(2)  The tribunal must give reasonable notice to the parties of the time and date to which a hearing is postponed

(3)  Where postponement has been requested by a party the tribunal must not postpone the hearing except where it considers it is reasonable to do so having regard to—
   (a)  the grounds for the request;
   (b)  the time at which the request is made; and
   (c)  the convenience of the parties.

**[3681]**

**NOTES**
Commencement: 13 April 2006.

**27  Hearing**

(1)  At a hearing—
   (a)  the tribunal shall (subject to these regulations) determine the procedure and conduct;
   (b)  any person appearing before the tribunal may do so either in person or by his representative;
   (c)  the parties shall be entitled to—
     (i)  give relevant evidence;
     (ii)  call witnesses;
     (iii)  question any witness; and
     (iv)  address the tribunal on the evidence and law and generally on the subject matter of the application; and
   (d)  the tribunal may receive evidence of any fact which seems to it to be relevant, even if the evidence would be inadmissible in proceedings before a court of law, and must not refuse to admit any evidence presented in due time which is admissible at law and is relevant and necessary and has not been improperly obtained.

(2)  At a hearing the tribunal may, if it is satisfied that it is just and reasonable to do so, permit a party to rely on reasons not previously stated and on evidence not previously available or not previously adduced.

(3)  The tribunal may adjourn a hearing, but if this is done at the request of a party it must consider that it is reasonable to do so having regard to—
   (a)  the grounds for the request;
   (b)  the time at which the request is made; and
   (c)  the convenience of the parties.

**[3682]**

**NOTES**
Commencement: 13 April 2006.

**28  Hearing in public or private**

(1)  A hearing must be in public except where the tribunal is satisfied that in the circumstances of the case and subject to the overriding objective the hearing should be held in private.

(2)  The tribunal may decide under paragraph (1) that—
   (a)  part only of the hearing must be in private; or
   (b)  any of the following matters must not be made public—
     (i)  information about the proceedings before the tribunal;
     (ii)  the names and identifying characteristics of persons concerned in the proceedings; or
     (iii)  specified evidence given in the proceedings.

**[3683]**

**NOTES**
Commencement: 13 April 2006.

**29  Persons entitled to be present at a hearing held in private**

(1)  Subject to paragraphs (2) and (3) the following persons shall be entitled to attend a hearing held in private and to be present at the tribunal's deliberations with respect to the determination of the application—
   (a)  a president or chair or other panel member not forming part of the tribunal for the purpose of the hearing;
   (b)  ...

    (c)    the staff of the Tribunal Service;

    (d)    any other person permitted by the tribunal with the consent of the parties.

(2)    None of the persons specified in paragraph (1) may take any part in the hearing or such deliberations.

(3)    The tribunal may admit persons to a hearing held in private on such terms and conditions as it considers appropriate.

**[3684]**

**NOTES**

Commencement: 13 April 2006.

Para (1): sub-para (b) revoked by the Tribunals, Courts and Enforcement Act 2007 (Transitional and Consequential Provisions) Order 2008, SI 2008/2683, art 6(1), Sch 1, paras 315, 317.

## 30  Failure of a party to appear at a hearing

Where a party fails to appear at a hearing the tribunal may proceed with the hearing if—

    (a)    it is satisfied that notice has been given to that party in accordance with these Regulations; and

    (b)    it is not satisfied that there is a good reason for the failure to appear.

**[3685]**

**NOTES**

Commencement: 13 April 2006.

## 31  Decisions of the Tribunal in determining applications

(1)    This regulation applies to the decision determining an application.

(2)    If a hearing was held, the decision may be given orally at the end of the hearing.

(3)    A decision must, in every case, be recorded in a document as soon as practicable after the decision has been made.

(4)    A decision given or recorded in accordance with paragraph (2) or (3) need not record the reasons for the decision.

(5)    The reasons for the decision must be recorded in a document as soon as practicable after the decision has been given or recorded.

(6)    A document recording a decision or the reasons for a decision (a "decision document"), must be signed and dated by an appropriate person.

(7)    An appropriate person may, by means of a certificate signed and dated by him, correct any clerical mistakes in a decision document or any errors arising in it from an accidental slip or omission.

(8)    In this regulation "appropriate person" means—

    (a)    the Chair of the tribunal; or

    (b)    in the event of his absence or incapacity, another member of the tribunal.

(9)    A copy of any decision document, and a copy of any correction certified under paragraph (7) must be sent to each party.

**[3686]**

**NOTES**

Commencement: 13 April 2006.

## 32  Costs

The tribunal must not make a determination under paragraph 12 of Schedule 13 to the Act in respect of a party without first giving that party an opportunity of making representations to the tribunal.

**[3687]**

**NOTES**

Commencement: 13 April 2006.

## 33  Withdrawal of application

(1)    Subject to paragraph (3) an applicant ("the withdrawing party") may withdraw the whole or part of his application in accordance with paragraph (2) at any time before determination of the application.

(2)    The withdrawing party must notify withdrawal of his application by a signed and dated notice supplied to the tribunal—

    (a)    sufficiently identifying the application or part of the application which is withdrawn;

(b)　stating whether any part of the application, and if so what, remains to be determined; and

(c)　confirming that a copy of the notice of the withdrawal has been supplied to all other parties and stating the date on which this was done.

(3)　In any of the circumstances set out in paragraph (4), withdrawal of the application shall not take effect until one of the courses of action in paragraph (5) has been carried out.

(4)　The circumstances mentioned in paragraph (3) are that—

(a)　an interim order in favour of a party has been made;

(b)　a party has given an undertaking to the tribunal;

(c)　payment to the withdrawing party has been ordered whether by way of compensation, damages, costs, reimbursement of fees or otherwise;

(d)　a party has requested an order for reimbursement of fees; or

(5)　The courses of action mentioned in paragraph (3) are that—

(a)　the withdrawing party has sent to the tribunal a written statement signed by all other parties setting out how any of the circumstances in sub-paragraphs (a) to (d) of paragraph (4) which apply to the case are to be dealt with; or

(b)　the withdrawing party has given notice of the intended withdrawal to all parties and—

(i)　the withdrawing party has requested the tribunal to give directions as to the conditions on which the withdrawal may be made; and

(ii)　the tribunal has given such directions.

(6)　In giving directions under paragraph (5)(b)(ii) the tribunal may impose such conditions as it considers appropriate.

(7)　A single qualified member may give directions under paragraph (5)(b)(ii).

**[3688]**

_____

**NOTES**

Commencement: 13 April 2006.

## 34　Enforcement

Any decision of the tribunal may, with the permission of the county court, be enforced in the same way as orders of such a court.

**[3689]**

_____

**NOTES**

Commencement: 13 April 2006.

## 35　Permission to appeal

(1)　In this regulation "to appeal" means to make an appeal from a decision of the tribunal to the [Upper Tribunal] and "appellant" bears a corresponding meaning.

(2)　Where a party makes a request to the tribunal for permission to appeal to the [Upper Tribunal] from a decision of the tribunal the request may be made—

(a)　orally at the hearing at which the decision is announced by the tribunal; or

(b)　subsequently in writing to the office of the tribunal.

(3)　A request for permission to appeal must be made within the period of 21 days starting with the date specified in the decision notice as the date on which reasons for the decision were given.

(4)　Where a request for permission to appeal is made in writing it must be signed by the appellant or the appellant's representative and must—

(a)　state the name and address of the appellant and of any representative of the appellant;

(b)　identify the decision and the tribunal to which the request for leave relates; and

(c)　state the grounds on which the appellant intends to rely in the appeal.

(5)　The decision of the tribunal on a request for permission to appeal must be recorded in writing together with the reasons for it, and the tribunal must send a copy of the decision and reasons to the appellant and to the other parties to the application which is the subject of the appeal.

(6)　A notification under paragraph (5) must, as appropriate, include a statement of any relevant statutory provision, rule or guidance relating to any further request to the [Upper Tribunal] for permission to appeal and of the time and place for making the further request or for giving notice of appeal.

**[3690]**

_____

**NOTES**

Commencement: 13 April 2006.

Paras (1), (2), (6): words in square brackets substituted by the Transfer of Tribunal Functions (Lands Tribunal and Miscellaneous Amendments) Order 2009, SI 2009/1307, art 5(1), (3), Sch 2, para 112, as from 1 June 2009, subject to savings and transitional provisions for the treatment of cases which would previously have been dealt with by the Lands Tribunal, and onward appeals from that Tribunal (see art 5(6), Sch 5 to that Order).

_____

**36  Assistance to participants**

(1)   In this regulation "participant" means a party or witness or other person taking part in proceedings relating to an application or to whom an order of the tribunal is addressed.

(2)   If a participant is unable to read or speak or understand the English language, the tribunal must make arrangements for him to be provided, free of charge, with the necessary translations and assistance of an interpreter to enable his effective participation in the proceedings.

(3)   If a participant is without hearing or speech, the tribunal must make arrangements for him to be provided, free of charge, with the services of a sign language interpreter, lip speaker, or palantypist, to enable his effective participation in the proceedings.

(4)   A participant shall be entitled to assistance under this regulation whether or not he is represented.

(5)   A participant who requires assistance under this regulation must at the earliest opportunity notify the requirement to the tribunal.

[3691]

NOTES
Commencement: 13 April 2006.

**37  Requirements for supply of notices and documents**

(1)   Any document or notice required or authorised by these Regulations to be supplied to any person, whether by the tribunal, a party, or any other person, shall be duly supplied to that person—
   (a)   if it is sent to his proper address by first class post or by special delivery, or by recorded delivery;
   (b)   if it is delivered by any other means to his proper address;
   (c)   subject to paragraph (2), if with his written consent it is sent to him—
       (i)   by fax, email or other electronic communication which produces a text received in legible form;
       (ii)   by a private document delivery service.

(2)   For the purposes of paragraph (1)(c) a person's legal representative shall be deemed to have given written consent if the reference or address for the means of fax or electronic communication or private document delivery system is shown on the legal representative's notepaper.

(3)   A person's proper address for the purposes of paragraph (1) is—
   (a)   in the case of the tribunal, the address of the office of the tribunal;
   (b)   in the case of an incorporated company or other body registered in the United Kingdom, the address of the registered or principal office of the company or body;
   (c)   in the case of any other person the usual or last known address of that person.

(4)   This paragraph applies where—
   (a)   an intended recipient of a document or notice—
       (i)   cannot be found after all diligent enquiries have been made;
       (ii)   has died and has no personal representative; or
       (iii)   is out of the United Kingdom; or
   (b)   for any other reason a notice or other document cannot readily be supplied in accordance with these Regulations.

(5)   Where paragraph (4) applies, the tribunal may—
   (a)   dispense with supplying the notice or other document; or
   (b)   give directions for substituted service in such other form (whether by advertisement in a newspaper or otherwise) or manner as the tribunal thinks fit.

(6)   Where it is required under the Act or these Regulations that a party must provide evidence that he has supplied any person with a document, a party may satisfy the requirement by providing a signed certificate confirming that the document was served in accordance with the requirements of this regulation.

[3692]

NOTES
Commencement: 13 April 2006.

**38  Time**

Where the time specified by these Regulations for doing any act expires on a Saturday or Sunday or public holiday, it shall be treated as expiring on the next following day which is not a Saturday or Sunday or public holiday.

[3693]

**NOTES**
Commencement: 13 April 2006.

**39   Frivolous and vexatious applications**

(1)   Subject to paragraph (2), where it appears to the tribunal that an application is frivolous or vexatious or otherwise an abuse of process, the tribunal may dismiss the application in whole or in part.

(2)   Before dismissing an application under paragraph (1) the tribunal must give notice of its intention to do so to the applicant in accordance with paragraph (3).

(3)   Any notice under paragraph (2) must state—
  (a)   that the tribunal is minded to dismiss the application;
  (b)   the grounds on which it is minded to dismiss the application;
  (c)   the date (being not less than 21 days after the date that the notice was sent) before which the applicant may be heard by the tribunal on the question of whether the application should be dismissed.

(4)   An application may not be dismissed under paragraph (1) unless—
  (a)   the applicant makes no request to the tribunal before the date mentioned in paragraph (3)(c) or
  (b)   where the applicant makes such a request, the tribunal has heard the applicant and the respondent, or such of them as attend the hearing, on the question of the dismissal of the application.

**[3694]**

**NOTES**
Commencement: 13 April 2006.

**40   Irregularities**

Any irregularity resulting from failure by a party to comply with any provision of these Regulations or of any direction of the tribunal before the tribunal has determined the application shall not of itself render the proceedings void.

**[3695]**

**NOTES**
Commencement: 13 April 2006.

**41   Signature of documents**

Where these Regulations require a document to be signed, that requirement shall be satisfied—
  (a)   if the signature is either written or produced by computer or other mechanical means; and
  (b)   the name of the signatory appears beneath the signature in such a way that he may be identified.

**[3696]**

**NOTES**
Commencement: 13 April 2006.

SCHEDULE
ADDITIONAL DETAILS WITH REGARD TO CERTAIN APPLICATIONS
Regulation 2 and 6

*Applications relating to improvement notices*

1.—(1)   This paragraph applies to an application under paragraph 10(1) of Schedule 1 to the Act (appeal against improvement notice) other than an application referred to in paragraph 2.

(2)   The specified documents are—
  (a)   a copy of the improvement notice (including any schedule to it);
  (b)   the statement of reasons; and
  (c)   where the ground or one of the grounds of the application is that one of the courses of action mentioned in paragraph 12(2) of Schedule 1 to the Act is the best course of action in relation to the hazard, a statement identifying that course of action with the applicant's reasons for considering it the best course.

(3)   The specified respondent is the LHA.

2.—(1)   This paragraph applies to an application under paragraph 10 of Schedule 1 to the Act which consists of or includes the ground set out in paragraph 11(1) of that Schedule (ground of appeal relating to other persons).

(2)   The specified documents are—
  (a)   a copy of the improvement notice (including any schedule to it);
  (b)   the statement of reasons;
  (c)   where one of the grounds of the application is that another course of action mentioned in paragraph 12(2) of Schedule 1 to the Act is the best course of action in relation to the hazard, a statement identifying that course of action with the applicant's reasons for considering it the best course;
  (d)   the name and address of any person who as an owner of the premises, in the applicant's opinion ought to take the action required by the improvement notice or pay the whole or part of the costs of taking that action("the other owner");
  (e)   proof of service of a copy of the application on the other owner; and
  (f)   a statement containing the following details—
    (i)    the nature of the other owner's interest in the premises;
    (ii)   the reason the applicant considers the other owner ought to take the action concerned or pay the whole or part of the cost of taking that action; and
    (iii)  where the ground of the application is that the other owner ought to pay the whole or part of the cost of taking the action, the estimated cost of taking the action and the proportion of that cost which the applicant considers the other owner ought to pay.
(3)   The specified respondent is the LHA.

3.—(1)   This paragraph applies to an application under paragraph 13(1) of Schedule 1 to the Act (appeal against LHA's decision to vary or refuse to vary or revoke an improvement notice).

(2)   The specified documents are—
  (a)   a copy of the improvement notice (including any schedule to it);
  (b)   the statement of reasons; and
  (c)   a copy of the LHA's decision to vary or refuse to vary or revoke (including any documentation issued by the LHA in connection with its notice of decision).
(3)   The specified respondent is the LHA.

4.—(1)   This paragraph applies to an application under—
  (a)   paragraph 11(1) of Schedule 3 to the Act (appeal against demand by the LHA for recovery of expenses incurred by LHA in taking action where improvement notice has been served); and
  (b)   that paragraph as applied with modifications by section 42 of the Act (an appeal against a demand by the LHA for recovery of expenses incurred by taking emergency remedial action).

(2)   The specified documents are—
  (a)   a copy of the improvement notice or (as the case may be) the notice of emergency remedial action (including any schedule to it);
  (b)   the statement of reasons notice;
  (c)   a copy of the notice served by the LHA under paragraph 4 of Schedule 3 to the Act (notice of LHA's intention to enter premises to carry out specified actions without agreement);
  (d)   a copy of the LHA's demand for expenses; and
  (e)   where the application is made on the ground mentioned in paragraph 11(4) of that Schedule, details of the progress relied upon as being made towards compliance with the notice.
(3)   The specified respondent is the LHA.

### Applications relating to prohibition orders

5.—(1)   This paragraph applies to an application under section 22(9) of the Act (appeal against LHA's refusal to give approval of particular use under section 22(4)).

(2)   The specified documents are—
  (a)   a copy of the prohibition order (including any schedule to it);
  (b)   the statement of reasons; and
  (c)   notice of the LHA's decision to refuse a particular use of the whole or part of the premises.
(3)   The specified respondent is the LHA.

6.—(1)   This paragraph applies to an application under section 34(2) of the Act (application by lessor or lessee for order determining or varying lease where a prohibition order has become operative).

(2)   The specified documents are—
  (a)   a copy of the prohibition order (including any schedule to it);
  (b)   the statement of reasons;
  (c)   a copy of the relevant lease; and

    (d)    a statement of the name and address of any other party to the lease and of any party to an inferior lease.

    (3)    The specified respondent is the other party to the lease.

7.—(1)    This paragraph applies to an application under paragraph 7(1) of Schedule 2 to the Act (appeal against prohibition order).

    (2)    The specified documents are—
      (a)    a copy of the prohibition order (including any schedule to it);
      (b)    the statement of reasons; and
      (c)    where one of the grounds of the application is that one of the courses of action mentioned in paragraph 8(2) of Schedule 2 to the Act is the best course of action in relation to the hazard, a statement identifying that course of action with the applicant's reasons for considering it the best course.

    (3)    The specified respondent is the LHA.

8.—(1)    This paragraph applies to an application under paragraph 9(1) of Schedule 2 to the Act (appeal against LHA's decision to vary or refuse to vary or revoke a prohibition order).

    (2)    The specified documents are—
      (a)    a copy of the prohibition order (including any schedule to it);
      (b)    the statement of reasons; and
      (c)    a copy of the LHA's decision to vary or refuse to vary or revoke (including any documentation issued by the LHA in connection with its notice of decision).

    (3)    The specified respondent is the LHA.

### *Applications relating to emergency remedial action*

9.—(1)    This paragraph applies to an application under section 45(1) of the Act (appeal by person upon whom a notice under section 41 of the Act has been served against LHA's decision to take emergency remedial action).

    (2)    The specified documents are—
      (a)    a copy of the notice of emergency remedial action (including any schedule to it); and
      (b)    the statement of reasons.

    (3)    The specified respondent is the LHA.

10.—(1)    This paragraph applies to an application under section 45(2) of the Act (appeal by relevant person against emergency prohibition order).

    (2)    The specified documents are—
      (a)    a copy of the notice of emergency prohibition order made under section 43 of the Act (including any schedule to it); and
      (b)    the statement of reasons.

    (3)    The specified respondent is the LHA.

11.—(1)    This paragraph applies to an application under—
      (a)    paragraph 14 of Schedule 3 to the Act (application by LHA for order for recovery of expenses and interest from person profiting from the taking of action without agreement); and
      (b)    that paragraph as applied with modifications by section 42 of the Act.

    (2)    The specified documents are—
      (a)    a copy of the notice of the improvement notice or, as the case may be, the notice of emergency remedial action (including any schedule to it);
      (b)    the statement of reasons;
      (c)    a copy of the demand for expenses served under paragraph 9 of that Schedule;
      (d)    a copy of any notice served under paragraph 12 of that Schedule; and
      (e)    proof of service of notice of the application on the person concerned as mentioned in paragraph 14(2) of that Schedule.

    (3)    The specified respondent is the person from whom the LHA seeks to recover expenses and interest.

### *Applications relating to demolition orders*

12.—(1)    This paragraph applies to an application under section 269(1) of the 1985 Act (appeal by person aggrieved by demolition order).

    (2)    The specified documents are—
      (a)    a copy of the demolition order made under section 265 of the 1985 Act (including any schedule to it); and
      (b)    the statement of reasons; and
      (c)    where the ground or one of the grounds of the application is that one of the courses of

action mentioned in section 269A(2) of the 1985 Act is the best course of action in relation to the hazard, a statement identifying that course of action with the applicant's reasons for considering it the best course.

(3)   The specified respondent is the LHA.

13.—(1)   This paragraph applies to an application under section 272(1) or (2)(a) of the 1985 Act (application in connection with recovery of LHA's expenses in executing demolition order under section 271 of the 1985 Act including determination of contributions by joint owners ).

(2)   The specified documents are—
   (a)   a copy of the demolition order made under section 265 of the 1985 Act (including any schedule to it);
   (b)   the statement of reasons; and
   (c)   a statement of—
      (i)   the expenses incurred by the LHA under section 271 of the 1985 Act (execution of demolition order);
      (ii)   the amount (if any) realised by the sale of materials; and
      (iii)   the amount the LHA seeks to recover from an owner of the premises.

(3)   The specified respondent is the owner of the premises.

14.—(1)   This paragraph applies to an application under section 272(2)(b) of the 1985 Act (application by owner of premises for determination of contribution to LHA's expenses to be paid by another owner).

(2)   The specified documents are—
   (a)   a copy of the demolition order made under section 265 of the 1985 Act (including any schedule to it);
   (b)   the statement of reasons; and
   (c)   a statement of—
      (i)   the owners' respective interests in the premises; and
      (ii)   their respective obligations and liabilities in respect of maintenance and repair under any covenant or agreement, whether express or implied.

(3)   The specified respondent is the owner from whom the applicant seeks a contribution to the LHA's expenses.

15.—(1)   This paragraph applies to an application under section 317(1) of the 1985 Act (application by lessor or lessee of premises in respect of which demolition order has become operative, for an order varying or determining lease).

(2)   The specified documents are—
   (a)   a copy of the demolition order made under section 265 of the 1985 Act (including any schedule to it);
   (b)   the statement of reasons;
   (c)   a copy of the relevant lease; and
   (d)   a statement of the name and address of any other party to the lease and of any party to an inferior lease.

(3)   The specified respondent is the other party to the lease.

### *Application relating to work on unfit premises*

16.—(1)   This paragraph applies to an application under section 318(1) of the 1985 Act (application by person with interest in premises for authorisation by tribunal of execution of works on unfit premises or for improvement).

(2)   The specified documents are—
   (a)   details of the work which the applicant proposes to carry out including—
      (i)   names and addresses of proposed contractors where relevant;
      (ii)   an estimate of the costs of the work; and
      (iii)   a timetable for starting and completing the work;
   (b)   where the application is made on the ground mentioned in section 318(1)(b) of the 1985 Act, details of—
      (i)   the scheme of improvement or reconstruction which the applicant wishes to carry out; and
      (ii)   the LHA's approval of the scheme.
   (c)   a statement of the financial standing of the applicant including disclosure of funds available to meet the estimated costs of the work;
   (d)   where the application includes a request for an order determining a lease held from the applicant or a derivative lease, a copy of that lease.

(3)   The specified respondents are—
   (a)   the person with a right to possession of the premises;
   (b)   the owner of the premises.

*Applications relating to HMO licensing*

17.—(1)   This paragraph applies to an application under section 62(7) of the Act (appeal against refusal by LHA to serve a temporary exemption notice).

(2)   The specified documents are—

   (a)   a copy of the notification to the LHA under section 62(1) of the Act; and

   (b)   a copy of the LHA's decision notice under section 62(6) of the Act.

(3)   The specified respondent is the LHA.

18.—(1)   This paragraph applies to an application under section 73(5) of the Act (application by LHA or occupier for rent repayment order).

(2)   The specified documents are—

   (a)   where the application is made by the LHA—

      (i)   a copy of the notice of intending proceedings under section 73(7);

      (ii)   a copy of any representation received in respect of the notice;

      (iii)   either—

          (aa)   a statement containing the details relied on in making the allegation that an offence under section 72(1) of the Act was committed; or

          (bb)   where the LHA relies on the provisions of section 74 of the Act, proof that the appropriate person has been convicted of an offence under section 72(1) of the Act; and

      (iv)   a document showing the housing benefit paid by the LHA in connection with occupation of the premises during the period in which it is alleged such an offence was committed; or

   (b)   where the application is made by an occupier—

      (i)   evidence that the appropriate person has been convicted of an offence under section 72(1) of the Act or has been required by a rent repayment order to make a payment in respect of housing benefit; and

      (ii)   evidence that the occupier has paid periodical payments in respect of occupation of the premises during a period which it is alleged that such an offence was being committed.

(3)   The specified respondent is the appropriate person.

19.—(1)   This paragraph applies to an application under section 255(9) of the Act (appeal against decision of LHA to serve an HMO declaration).

(2)   The specified document is a copy of the HMO declaration.

(3)   The specified respondent is the LHA.

20.—(1)   This paragraph applies to an application under section 256(4) of the Act (appeal against decision of LHA to refuse to revoke HMO declaration).

(2)   The specified documents are—

   (a)   a copy of the HMO declaration; and

   (b)   a copy of the LHA's notice of decision not to revoke the HMO declaration.

(3)   The specified respondent is the LHA.

21.—(1)   This paragraph applies to an application under paragraph 31(1) of Schedule 5 to the Act (appeal against decision by LHA to grant, or refuse to grant, a licence under Part 2 of the Act, or against any of the terms of the licence).

(2)   The specified documents are—

   (a)   where the application relates to the grant or terms of a licence—

      (i)   a copy of the LHA's notices under paragraphs 1 and 7 of Schedule 5, and of any notice under paragraph 3 of that Schedule; and

      (ii)   a copy of the licence; and

   (b)   where the application relates to a refusal to grant a licence, a copy of the LHA's notices under paragraphs 5 and 8 of that Schedule.

(3)   The specified respondent is the LHA.

22.—(1)   This paragraph applies to an application under paragraph 32(1) of Schedule 5 to the Act (appeal by licence holder or any relevant person against decision by LHA with regard to the variation or revocation of licence).

(2)   The specified documents are—

   (a)   where the application relates to a decision to vary a licence, a copy of the LHA's notices under paragraphs 14 and 16 of Schedule 5;

   (b)   where the application relates to refusal to vary a licence, a copy of the LHA's notices under paragraphs 19 and 21 of that Schedule;

   (c)   where the application relates to a decision to revoke a licence, a copy of the LHA's notices under paragraphs 22 and 24 of that Schedule;

   (d)   where the application relates to refusal to revoke a licence, a copy of the LHA's notices under paragraphs 26 and 28 of that Schedule; and

PART II
STATUTORY INSTRUMENTS

    (e)   in all cases a copy of the licence.

(3)   The specified respondent is the LHA.

*Applications relating to selective licensing of other residential accommodation*

23.—(1)   This paragraph applies to an application under section 86(7) of the Act (appeal against refusal by the LHA to serve a temporary exemption notice).

(2)   The specified documents are—
    (a)   a copy of the notification to the LHA under section 86(1) of the Act; and
    (b)   a copy of the LHA's decision notice under section 86(6) of the Act.

(3)   The specified respondent is the LHA.

24.—(1)   This paragraph applies to an application under section 96(5) of the Act (application by LHA or occupier for a rent repayment order).

(2)   The specified documents are—
    (a)   where the application is made by the LHA—
        (i)   a copy of the notice of intended proceedings under section 96(7);
        (ii)   a copy of any representation received in respect of the notice;
        (iii)   either—
            (aa)   a statement containing the details relied on in making the allegation that an offence under section 95(1) of the Act was committed; or
            (bb)   where the LHA relies on the provisions of section 97 of the Act, proof that the appropriate person has been convicted of an offence under section 95(1) of the Act; and
        (iv)   a document showing the housing benefit paid by the LHA in connection with occupation of the premises during the period in which it is alleged such an offence was committed; or
    (b)   where the application is made by an occupier—
        (i)   evidence that the appropriate person has been convicted of an offence under section 95(1) of the Act or has been required by a rent repayment order to make a payment in respect of housing benefit; and
        (ii)   evidence that the occupier has paid periodical payments in respect of occupation of the premises for a period during which it is alleged that such an offence was being committed.

(3)   The specified respondent is the appropriate person.

25.—(1)   This paragraph applies to an application under paragraph 31 of Schedule 5 to the Act (appeal against decision by LHA to grant or refuse licence under Part 3 or relating to terms of licence).

(2)   The specified documents are—
    (a)   where the application relates to the grant or terms of a licence—
        (i)   a copy of the LHA's notices under paragraphs 1 and 7 of Schedule 5, and of any notice under paragraph 3 of that Schedule; and
        (ii)   a copy of the licence; and
    (b)   where the application relates to a refusal to grant a licence, a copy of the LHA's notices under paragraphs 5 and 8 of that Schedule.

(3)   The specified respondent is the LHA.

26.—(1)   This paragraph applies to an application under paragraph 32(1) of Schedule 5 to the Act (appeal by licence holder or relevant person against decision by LHA relating to variation or revocation of licence).

(2)   The specified documents are—
    (a)   where the application relates to a decision to vary a licence, a copy of the LHA's notices under paragraphs 14 and 16 of Schedule 5;
    (b)   where the application relates to refusal to vary a licence, a copy of the LHA's notices under paragraphs 19 and 21 of that Schedule;
    (c)   where the application relates to a decision to revoke a licence, a copy of the LHA's notices under paragraphs 22 and 24 of that Schedule;
    (d)   where the application relates to refusal to revoke a licence, a copy of the LHA's notices under paragraphs 26 and 28 of that Schedule; and
    (e)   in any case a copy of the licence.

(3)   The specified respondent is the LHA.

*Applications relating to interim and final management orders*

27.—(1)   This paragraph applies to an application under section 102(4) of the Act (LHA application for authorisation to make an interim management order).

(2)   The specified documents are—

    (a)   a copy of the draft order;

    (b)   a statement of matters relevant to the tribunal's consideration of—

        (i)   whether the health and safety condition in section 104 of the Act is satisfied; and

        (ii)  the extent to which any applicable code of practice approved under section 233 of the Act has been complied with; and

        (iii)  where the LHA requests that the application be dealt with as a matter of urgency under regulation 9, a statement giving sufficient details to enable the tribunal to form an opinion as to whether the exceptional circumstances mentioned in paragraph (3) of that regulation appear to exist.

    (3)   The specified respondent is a relevant person as defined in paragraph 8(4) and paragraph 35 of the Act.

**28.**—(1)   This paragraph applies to an application under section 102(7) of the Act (LHA application for authorisation to make an interim management order in respect of a house to which section 103 of the Act applies).

    (2)   The specified documents are—

    (a)   a copy of the draft order;

    (b)   a statement of matters relevant to the tribunal's consideration as to whether the conditions in section 103(3) and (4) are satisfied; and

    (c)   where the LHA requests that the application be dealt with as a matter of urgency under regulation 9, a statement giving sufficient details to enable the tribunal to form an opinion as to whether the exceptional circumstances mentioned in paragraph (3) of that regulation appear to exist.

    (3)   The specified respondent is a relevant person as defined in paragraph 8(4) and paragraph 35 of Schedule 6 to the Act.

**29.**—(1)   This paragraph applies to an application under section 105(10) of the Act (LHA application for order that an interim management order continue in force pending disposal of appeal).

    (2)   The specified documents are—

    (a)   a copy of the interim management order; and

    (b)   a copy of the notice of appeal under paragraph 24 of Schedule 6 to the Act against the making of a final management order.

    (3)   The specified respondent is the applicant who has made the relevant appeal.

**30.**—(1)   This paragraph applies to an application under section 110(7) of the Act (application by relevant landlord for order regarding financial arrangements while interim management order in force).

    (2)   The specified documents are—

    (a)   a copy of the interim management order;

    (b)   a copy of the accounts kept by the LHA in accordance with section 110(6).

    (3)   The specified respondent is the LHA.

**31.**—(1)   This paragraph applies to an application under section 114(7) of the Act (LHA application for order that existing final management order continue in force pending disposal of appeal against new final management order).

    (2)   The specified documents are—

    (a)   a copy of the existing final management order;

    (b)   a copy of the new final management order made in order to replace it; and

    (c)   a copy of the notice of appeal under paragraph 24 of Schedule 6 to the Act against the making of the new final management order.

    (3)   The specified respondent is the applicant who has made the relevant appeal.

**32.**—(1)   This paragraph applies to an application under section 120(1) of the Act (application by an affected person for order that LHA manage in accordance with management scheme in final management order).

    (2)   The specified document is a copy of the final management order which contains the management scheme to which the application relates.

    (3)   The specified respondent is the LHA.

**33.**—(1)   This paragraph applies to an application under section 126(4) of the Act (application for adjustment of rights and liabilities with regard to furniture vested in LHA while management order in force).

    (2)   The specified documents are—

    (a)   a copy of the relevant management order; and

    (b)   a statement giving details of the respective rights and liabilities (including ownership) of the persons interested in the furniture.

    (3)   The specified respondent is the other person interested in the furniture.

34.—(1)   This paragraph applies to an application under section 130(9) of the Act (application to determine who is "the relevant landlord" for the purposes of section 130 on termination of management order).

(2)   The specified document is a copy of the management order.

(3)   The specified respondent is the other relevant landlord.

35.—(1)   This paragraph applies to an application under paragraph 24 of Schedule 6 to the Act (appeal against making of a management order, or against the terms of the order or of associated management scheme).

(2)   The specified documents are—
- (a)   a copy of the management order (including the management scheme);
- (b)   a copy of the notice served by the LHA under paragraph 7(2)(b) of Schedule 6 to the Act;
- (c)   where the application relates to the terms of the management order, a statement specifying each term to which objection is made, with reasons for the objection; and
- (d)   where the application is made on the ground specified in paragraph 24(3) of Schedule 6 to the Act, a statement of the matters in section 110(5) (which relates to payments of surplus rents etc) relevant to that ground.

(3)   The specified respondent is the LHA.

36.—(1)   This paragraph applies to an application under paragraph 28 of Schedule 6 to the Act (appeal against LHA's decision or refusal to vary or revoke management order).

(2)   The specified documents are—
- (a)   where the application relates to a decision to vary a management order, a copy of the LHA's notices under paragraphs 9 and 11 of Schedule 6;
- (b)   where the application relates to refusal to vary a management order, a copy of the LHA's notices under paragraphs 14 and 16 of that Schedule;
- (c)   where the application relates to a decision to revoke a management order, a copy of the LHA's notices under paragraphs 17 and 19 of that Schedule; and
- (d)   where the application relates to refusal to revoke a management order, a copy of the LHA's notices under paragraphs 20 and 22 of that Schedule; and
- (e)   in any case—
  - (i)   a copy of the management order; and
  - (ii)   a copy of the notice served by the LHA under paragraph 7(2)(b) of Schedule 6 to the Act.

(3)   The specified respondent is the LHA.

37.—(1)   This paragraph applies to an application under paragraph 32(2) of Schedule 6 to the Act (appeal by third party against LHA's decision under section 128 of the Act regarding compensation payable to third parties).

(2)   The specified documents are—
- (a)   a copy of the management order (including the management scheme);
- (b)   a copy of the LHA's notification of its decision to the third party in accordance with section 128(2) of the Act; and
- (c)   a statement giving full details of—
  - (i)   the rights in respect of which it is claimed that there has been interference in consequence of the management order; and
  - (ii)   the amount of compensation claimed in respect of that interference.

(3)   The specified respondent is the LHA.

*Applications in relation to empty dwelling management orders*

38.—(1)   This paragraph applies to an application under section 133(1) of the Act (LHA application for authorisation to make interim EDMO).

(2)   The specified documents are—
- (a)   a copy of the draft interim EDMO;
- (b)   a statement of evidence—
  - (i)   in respect of the matters as to which the tribunal must be satisfied under section 134(2) of the Act;
  - (ii)   of the LHA's consideration of the rights and interests specified in section 133(4) of the Act; and
- (c)   where the LHA in accordance with section 133(3) of the Act notified the relevant proprietor that it was considering making an interim EDMO, a copy of the notification.

(3)   The specified respondent is the relevant proprietor.

39.—(1)   This paragraph applies to an application under section 138(1) of the Act (application while interim EDMO in force for order that the LHA pay compensation to third party for interference with rights).

(2)　The specified documents are—
    (a)　a copy of the interim EDMO (including the management scheme);
    (b)　a copy of the LHA's notification of its decision to the third party in accordance with section 138(4) of the Act; and
    (c)　a statement giving full details of—
        (i)　the rights in respect of which it is claimed that there has been interference in consequence of the interim EDMO; and
        (ii)　the amount of compensation claimed in respect of that interference.

(3)　The specified respondent is the LHA.

**40.**—(1)　This paragraph applies to an application under paragraph 1(7) of Schedule 7 to the Act (LHA application for order that interim EDMO continue in force pending disposal of appeal under paragraph 26 of that Schedule).

(2)　The specified documents are—
    (a)　a copy of the interim EDMO; and
    (b)　a copy of the notice of appeal under paragraph 26 of Schedule 7 to the Act against the making of an interim EDMO.

(3)　The specified respondent is the applicant who has made the relevant appeal.

**41.**—(1)　This paragraph applies to an application under paragraph 2(3)(d) or paragraph 10(3)(d) of Schedule 7 to the Act (LHA's application for order under paragraph 22 of that Schedule determining a lease or licence while interim or final EDMO is in force).

(2)　The specified documents are—
    (a)　a copy of the interim or final EDMO (including any management scheme);
    (b)　a copy of the relevant lease or licence, or if not available evidence of the existence of the lease or licence; and
    (c)　a statement containing the following details—
        (i)　the name and address where known of any lessor, lessee, sub-lessor, sub-lessee or licensee;
        (ii)　evidence of matters in respect of which the tribunal must be satisfied under paragraph 22(1)(b) of Schedule 7 to the Act; and
        (iii)　the amount of compensation (if any) which the LHA is willing to pay in respect of the determination of the lease or licence, including details of how such compensation has been calculated.

(3)　The specified respondents are the parties to the lease or licence.

**42.**—(1)　This paragraph applies to an application under paragraph 5(7) of Schedule 7 to the Act (application by relevant proprietor for order in connection with financial arrangements while interim EDMO in force).

(2)　The specified documents are—
    (a)　a copy of the interim EDMO; and
    (b)　a copy of the accounts kept by the LHA in accordance with paragraph 5(6) of Schedule 7 to the Act.

(3)　The specified respondent is the LHA.

**43.**—(1)　This paragraph applies to an application under paragraph 9(8) of Schedule 7 to the Act (application by LHA for order that final EDMO should continue in force pending disposal of an appeal under paragraph 26).

(2)　The specified documents are—
    (a)　a copy of the interim EDMO; and
    (b)　a copy of the notice of appeal under paragraph 26 of Schedule 7 to the Act against the making of a final EDMO.

(3)　The specified respondent is the applicant who has made the relevant appeal.

**44.**—(1)　This paragraph applies to an application under paragraph 14(1) of Schedule 7 to the Act (application by a affected person for order that LHA manage dwelling in accordance with management scheme in final EDMO).

(2)　The specified document is a copy of the final EDMO (including the management scheme).

(3)　The specified respondent is the LHA.

**45.**—(1)　This paragraph applies to an application under paragraph 26(1) of Schedule 7 to the Act (appeal against LHA's decision to make final EDMO or against terms of the order or of associated management scheme).

(2)　The specified documents are—
    (a)　a copy of the final EDMO (including the management scheme);
    (b)　where the application relates to the terms of the management order, a statement specifying each term to which objection is made, with reasons for the objection; and
    (c)　where the application is made on the ground specified in paragraph 26(1)(c) of

Schedule 6 to the Act, a statement of the matters in paragraph 5(5)(a) and (b) (which relate to payments of surplus rents etc) relevant to that ground.

(3)   The specified respondent is the LHA.

46.—(1)   This paragraph applies to an application under paragraph 30 of Schedule 7 to the Act (appeal against LHA's decision or refusal to vary or revoke interim or final EDMO).

(2)   The specified documents are—
   (a)   where the application relates to a decision to vary an interim or final EDMO, a copy of the LHA's notices under paragraphs 9 and 11 of Schedule 6 to the Act (as applied by paragraph 17 of Schedule 7);
   (b)   where the application relates to refusal to vary an interim or final EDMO, a copy of the LHA's notices under paragraphs 14 and 16 of that Schedule;
   (c)   where the application relates to a decision to revoke an interim or final EDMO, a copy of the LHA's notices under paragraphs 17 and 19 of that Schedule; and
   (d)   where the application relates to refusal to revoke an interim or final EDMO, a copy of the LHA's notices under paragraphs 20 and 22 of that Schedule; and
   (e)   in any case a copy of the interim or final EDMO (as the case may be).

(3)   The specified respondent is the LHA.

47.—(1)   This paragraph applies to an application under paragraph 34(2) of Schedule 7 to the Act (appeal against LHA's decision under section 136(4) or 138(3) of the Act in respect of compensation payable to third parties for interference with rights in consequence of final EDMO).

(2)   The specified documents are—
   (a)   a copy of the final EDMO (including the management scheme);
   (b)   where the third party has requested compensation under section 138 of the Act, a copy of the LHA's notification of its decision to the third party in accordance with subsection (4) of that section; and
   (c)   a statement giving full details of—
       (i)   the rights in respect of which it is claimed that there has been interference in consequence of the final EDMO; and
       (ii)   the amount of compensation claimed in respect of that interference.

(3)   The specified respondent is the LHA.

### *Applications in relation to overcrowding notices*

48.—(1)   This paragraph applies to an application under section 143(1) of the Act (appeal by a person aggrieved by overcrowding notice).

(2)   The specified document is a copy of the overcrowding notice, or a statement by the applicant explaining the circumstances by reason of which he is not able to provide a copy of this notice.

(3)   The specified respondent is the LHA.

49.—(1)   This paragraph applies to an application under section 144(2) (appeal by relevant person against LHA's refusal to revoke or vary an overcrowding notice, or against failure by the LHA to respond in time to an application to revoke or vary it).

(2)   The specified documents are—
   (a)   a copy of the overcrowding notice;
   (b)   where the LHA refused to vary an overcrowding notice, a copy of the LHA's decision.

(3)   The specified respondent is the LHA.

**[3697]**

**NOTES**
Commencement: 13 April 2006.

# HOUSING ACT 2004 (COMMENCEMENT NO 5 AND TRANSITIONAL PROVISIONS AND SAVINGS) (ENGLAND) ORDER 2006

(SI 2006/1060)

**NOTES**
Made: 4 April 2006.
Authority: Housing Act 2004, ss 76(6), 250(2), 270(4), (5), (9).

**1 Citation, application and interpretation**

(1) This Order may be cited as the Housing Act 2004 (Commencement No 5 and Transitional Provisions and Savings) (England) Order 2006.

(2) This Order applies in relation to England only.

(3) In this Order—
- (a) "the 1985 Act" means the Housing Act 1985;
- (b) "the 2004 Act" means the Housing Act 2004;
- (c) "the first commencement date" means 6th April 2006;
- (d) "the second commencement date" means 6th July 2006; and
- (e) any reference to a repeal is to a repeal contained in Schedule 16 to the 2004 Act.

**[3698]**

**2 Commencement**

(1) The following provisions of the 2004 Act shall come into force on the first commencement date—
- (a) in so far as they are not already in force, sections 1, 3 to 8, 10 to 52, 54, 55, 58 to 71, 75 to 78, 82 to 94, 98 to 103, 135 to 147, 232, 235, 236, 238 to 243 and Schedules 1 to 7;
- (b) in section 72, subsections (2), (3), (5), (6) and (7);
- (c) in section 95, subsections (2), (4) and (6);
- (d) section 265(1) in so far as it relates to paragraphs 2 to 6, 8 to 36 and 38 to 44 of Schedule 15 (minor and consequential amendments);
- (e) section 266 in so far as it relates to the repeals in—
  - (i) the Friendly and Industrial and Provident Societies Act 1968;
  - (ii) the Land Compensation Act 1973;
  - (iii) the Civil Aviation Act 1982;
  - (iv) the Mobile Homes Act 1983;
  - (v) the 1985 Act;
  - (vi) the Housing Associations Act 1985;
  - (vii) the Housing (Consequential Provisions) Act 1985;
  - (viii) the Airports Act 1986;
  - (ix) the Housing Act 1988;
  - (x) the Electricity Act 1989;
  - (xi) the Local Government and Housing Act 1989;
  - (xii) the Housing Act 1996;
  - (xiii) the Housing Grants, Construction and Regeneration Act 1996; and
  - (xiv) the Transport Act 2000.

(2) The following provisions of the 2004 Act shall come into force on the second commencement date—
- (a) sections 73 and 96; and
- (b) in so far as they are not already in force, sections 72, 74, 95, 97 and 134.

**[3699]**

**3 Transitional provisions and savings**

The Schedule shall have effect for the purpose of making transitional provision and savings in connection with the coming into force of provisions mentioned in article 2.

**[3700]**

SCHEDULE

Article 3

PART 1
ACTION UNDER THE 1985 ACT RELATING TO UNFITNESS

*Repair notices*

1.—(1) A repair notice served under section 189 or 190 of the 1985 Act before the first commencement date shall cease to have effect on that date unless it is a notice to which sub-paragraph (2) applies.

(2) This sub-paragraph applies to a repair notice—
- (a) which has become operative as mentioned in section 189(4) or 190(4) of the 1985 Act before the first commencement date; or
- (b) in respect of which an appeal has been brought under section 191 of that Act before that date.

(3) During the period beginning on the first commencement date and ending on 5th April 2007, the repeal of sections 189 to 208, 345, 398, 604 and 604A of, and Schedule 10 to, the 1985 Act shall not have effect in relation to a repair notice to which sub-paragraph (2) applies.

(4) Where—

(a) an appeal in respect of a repair notice to which sub-paragraph (2) applies is allowed; and
(b) the judge includes in his judgment a finding such as is mentioned in section 191(3) of the 1985 Act,

the local housing authority shall take the finding into account if they subsequently consider taking action of a kind mentioned in section 5(2) or 7(2) of the 2004 Act in respect of the premises concerned.

(5) A repair notice to which sub-paragraph (2) applies shall cease to have effect on 6th April 2007 except in relation to anything done in connection with the notice before that date.

(6) The repeal of section 191(3A)(b) of the 1985 Act shall not have effect in relation to an order made by a court under that paragraph before that date.

(7) The amendment made by paragraph 4(2) of Schedule 15 to the 2004 Act (which amends the Land Compensation Act 1973) shall not have effect in relation to a repair notice to which sub-paragraph (2) applies.

### Closing orders

2.—(1) A closing order made under section 264 or 368(4) of the 1985 Act before the first commencement date shall cease to have effect on that date unless it is an order to which sub-paragraph (2) applies.

(2) This sub-paragraph applies to a closing order—
(a) which has become operative as mentioned in section 268(2) of the 1985 Act before the first commencement date; or
(b) in respect of which an appeal has been brought under section 269 of that Act before that date.

(3) During the period beginning on the first commencement date and ending on 5th April 2008, the following shall not have effect in relation to a closing order to which sub-paragraph (2) applies—
(a) the repeal of sections 264, 267(2) and (3), 269(2A) and (3A), 276 to 278, 368, 395, 396, 397, 604 and 604A of the 1985 Act;
(b) the repeals in sections 317, 319(1)(b) and 323 of that Act; and
(c) the amendments made by section 48(2) and (4) of, and paragraphs 13, 14, 22, 26, 27 and 33 of Schedule 15 to the 2004 Act.

(4) Where—
(a) an appeal in respect of a closing order to which sub-paragraph (2) applies is allowed; and
(b) the judge includes in his judgment a finding such as is mentioned in section 269(3A) of the 1985 Act,

the local housing authority shall take the finding into account if they subsequently consider taking action of a kind mentioned in section 5(2) or 7(2) of the 2004 Act in respect of the premises concerned.

(5) A closing order to which sub-paragraph (2) applies shall cease to have effect on 6th April 2008 except in relation to anything done in connection with the order before that date.

(6) The amendments made by—
(a) paragraphs 3, 4(3), 5 and 6 of Schedule 15 to the 2004 Act (which amend the Land Compensation Act 1973); and
(b) paragraphs 30 and 31 of that Schedule (which substitute compensation provisions of the Housing Act 1985),

shall not have effect in relation to a closing order to which sub-paragraph (2) applies.

### Demolition orders

3.—(1) A demolition order made under section 265 or 279 of the 1985 Act before the first commencement date shall cease to have effect on that date unless it is an order to which sub-paragraph (2) applies.

(2) This sub-paragraph applies to a demolition order—
(a) which has become operative as mentioned in section 268(2) of the 1985 Act before the first commencement date; or
(b) in respect of which an appeal has been brought under section 269 of that Act before that date.

(3) During the period beginning on the first commencement date and ending on 5th April 2008, the following shall not have effect in relation to a demolition order to which sub-paragraph (2) applies—
(a) the repeal of sections 269(2A) and (3A), 604 and 604A of the 1985 Act;
(b) the repeals in section 323 of that Act; and

(c)    the amendments made by sections 46 and 48(2) to (4) of, and paragraphs 13 to 18, 21, 22, 26, 27, and 33 of Schedule 15 to the 2004 Act.

(4)    Where—

(a)    an appeal in respect of a demolition order to which sub-paragraph (2) applies is allowed; and

(b)    the judge includes in his judgment a finding such as is mentioned in section 269(3A) of the 1985 Act,

the local housing authority shall take the finding into account if they subsequently consider taking action of a kind mentioned in section 5(2) or 7(2) of the 2004 Act in respect of the premises concerned.

(5)    During the period mentioned in sub-paragraph (3)—

(a)    section 275 of the 1985 Act (demolition orders: substitution of closing orders) shall have effect in relation to a demolition order to which sub-paragraph (2) applies as if—

(i)    in subsection (1) the words "and make a closing order as respects the premises" were omitted; and

(ii)    for subsection (2) there were substituted—

"(2)    The authority shall serve notice that the demolition order has been determined on every person on whom they would be required by section 268 to serve a copy of a demolition order as respects the premises."; and

(b)    subsection (2) of section 304 of the 1985 Act (closing order to be made in respect of listed building subject to section 265) shall have effect in relation to such an order as if for the words after "operative" there were substituted the words "and they shall serve notice that the demolition order has been determined on every person on whom they would be required by section 268 to serve a copy of a demolition order as respects the premises".

(6)    A demolition order to which sub-paragraph (2) applies shall cease to have effect on 6th April 2008 except in relation to anything done in connection with the order before that date.

(7)    The amendments made by—

(a)    paragraphs 3, 4(3), 5 and 6 of Schedule 15 to the 2004 Act; and

(b)    paragraphs 30 and 31 of that Schedule,

shall not have effect in relation to a demolition order to which sub-paragraph (2) applies.

### *Obstructive building orders*

4.    An obstructive building order served under section 284 of the 1985 Act before the first commencement date shall cease to have effect on that date except in relation to anything done in connection with the order before that date.

### *Clearance areas*

5.—(1)    The amendments made by section 47 of, and paragraphs 19, 22, 26 and 27 of Schedule 15 to, the 2004 Act shall not have effect in relation to an area declared to be a clearance area under section 289(3)(b) of the 1985 Act before the first commencement date.

(2)    This sub-paragraph applies where, before the first commencement date, a local housing authority—

(a)    have served notice under section 289(2B)(a) of the 1985 Act of intention to include a building in an area which is to be a clearance area; but

(b)    have not passed a resolution under section 289(3)(b) of that Act declaring the area to be a clearance area.

(3)    Where sub-paragraph (2) applies—

(a)    the notice mentioned in paragraph (a) of that sub-paragraph shall cease to have effect; and

(b)    the requirements of section 289(2B)(b) and (c) and (2F) shall cease to apply to the local housing authority.

### *Purchase of houses liable to be demolished or closed*

6.—(1)    A notice of determination to purchase premises served under section 300(2)(a) of the 1985 Act before the first commencement date shall cease to have effect on that date unless it is a notice to which sub-paragraph (2) applies.

(2)    This sub-paragraph applies to a notice of determination—

(a)    which has become operative under section 268(2) of the 1985 Act before the first commencement date; or

(b)    in respect of which an appeal has been brought under section 269 of that Act before that date.

(3)   The amendments made by section 48(2) of, and paragraphs 13, 14, 20, 21, 26 and 27 of Schedule 15 to, the 2004 Act shall not have effect in relation to a notice of determination to which sub-paragraph (2) applies.

### Owner's proposals for re-development

7.—(1)   This paragraph applies in relation to any proposals submitted to a local housing authority under subsection (1) of section 308 of the 1985 Act (approval of owner's proposals for re-development) before the first commencement date.

(2)   Where notice under subsection (2) of that section has not been given before that date, the authority shall cease to be subject to the requirements of that subsection on and after that date.

(3)   Subject to sub-paragraph (4), any notice given under that subsection before that date shall cease to have effect except in relation to anything done in connection with it before that date.

(4)   If the authority, on or after that date, consider taking action of a kind mentioned in section 5(2) or 7(2) of the 2004 Act in respect of the premises to which such a notice relates, the authority shall, when making their decision, take into account the notice and the extent to which re-development has been proceeded with in accordance with the proposals and within the time-limits specified in the notice (subject to any variation or extension approved by the authority before that date).

### Owner's proposals for improvement or alteration

8.—(1)   Subject to sub-paragraph (2), any proposals submitted by an owner, or certificate issued by a local housing authority, under section 310 of the 1985 Act (owner's improvements or alterations) before the first commencement date shall cease to have effect on that date except in relation to anything done in connection with them before that date.

(2)   The repeal of section 311(2) of the 1985 Act (proposals to be treated as objection to compulsory purchase order) shall not have effect in relation to proposals—
    (a)   submitted by an owner under section 310 of that Act; and
    (b)   transmitted by the local housing authority to the Secretary of State under section 311(1) of that Act,
before the first commencement date.

### Authorisation by court of execution of works on unfit premises etc

9.   The amendments made by section 48(5) of, and paragraphs 25 to 27 of Schedule 15 to, the 2004 Act shall not have effect in relation to an application made to the court under section 318 of the 1985 Act before the first commencement date.

### Deferred action notices etc

10.—(1)   Subject to sub-paragraph (3), a deferred action notice served under section 81 of the Housing Grants, Construction and Regeneration Act 1996 ("the 1996 Act") before the first commencement date shall cease to have effect on that date except in relation to anything done in connection with the notice before that date.

(2)   The repeal of section 86 of the 1996 Act (unfitness for human habitation etc: power to improve enforcement procedures) shall not have effect in relation to any appeal brought under section 191 (repair notices) or 269 (closing and demolition orders) of the 1985 Act before the first commencement date.

(3)   The repeal of sections 87 (unfitness for human habitation etc: power to charge for enforcement action) and 88 (recovery of charge for enforcement action) shall not have effect in relation to—
    (a)   any action of a kind mentioned in section 87(1) of that Act which has been taken before the first commencement date; or
    (b)   an appeal such as is mentioned in section 87(6) of that Act which has been brought before that date.

**[3701]**

### PART 2
### MEASURES RELATING TO HOUSES IN MULTIPLE OCCUPATION UNDER PART 11 OF THE HOUSING ACT 1985

### Interpretation of Part

1.—(1)   In this Part—
    (a)   "relevant converted block of flats" means a building or a part of a building which is—
        (i)   a converted block of flats to which section 257 of the 2004 Act applies; and
        (ii)   a house in multiple occupation for the purposes of Part 11 of the 1985 Act;

(b)     "prescribed HMO" means a HMO that falls within the description prescribed by the Licensing of Houses in Multiple Occupation (Prescribed Descriptions) (England) Order 2006; and

(c)     "relevant scheme" means. a registration scheme made under section 346 of the 1985 Act containing any of the control provisions or special control provisions described in section 347, 348, 348A, 348B, 348C, 348D, 348E or 348F of that Act.

(2)     The repeal of sections 345, 398, 399 and 400 of the 1985 Act (which give meanings of expressions used in Part 11 of the 1985 Act) shall not have effect in so far as those sections are relevant to the construction of any provision of this Part which refers to Part 11 of that Act or any provision of that Part 11.

### Registration Schemes

2.—(1)     Subject to sub-paragraph (2), during the period beginning on the first commencement date and ending on the date when regulations made by the Secretary of State under section 61(5) of the 2004 Act come into force, the repeal of sections 346, 346A, 346B, 347, 348, 348A to 348G, 350, 351 and 395 to 397 of the 1985 Act shall not have effect in relation to any registration scheme which—

(a)     conforms to a model scheme prepared by the Secretary of State under section 346B of the 1985 Act; or

(b)     is confirmed by the Secretary of State before the first commencement date,

in so far as such scheme applies to a relevant converted block of flats.

(2)     No new registration scheme may be made under section 346(1) on or after the first commencement date.

(3)     Notwithstanding the repeal of sections 346 and 347 of the 1985 Act, a local housing authority may use the information contained in any register it has compiled and maintained under section 346—

(a)     for any purpose connected with the exercise of any of the authority's functions under Parts 1 to 4 of the 2004 Act in relation to HMOs; or

(b)     for the purposes of investigating whether any offence has been committed under any of those Parts or under Part 11 of the 1985 Act in relation to HMOs.

### Areas deemed to be designated under section 56 of the 2004 Act

3.—(1)     This sub-paragraph applies to any area for which a local housing authority have made a relevant scheme.

(2)     On the first commencement date a local housing authority shall be deemed to have designated, under section 56(1) of the 2004 Act, each area to which sub-paragraph (1) applies as subject to additional licensing in relation to the HMOs registered under such a scheme.

(3)     A designation deemed to have been made under sub-paragraph (2) shall come into force on the first commencement date.

(4)     The requirements of sections 56(2) to (6), 57, 58 and 59(1) and (2) of the 2004 Act shall not apply in relation to designations that are deemed to have been made under sub-paragraph (2).

(5)     Sub-paragraphs (6), (7) and (8) apply to a designation deemed to have been made under sub-paragraph (2).

(6)     Within the period of three months beginning on the first commencement date the local housing authority shall publish a notice stating which areas in its district are designated areas as a result of being deemed to be designated areas under sub-paragraph (2) in the manner described in sub-paragraph (7).

(7)     The notice shall—

(a)     be published in accordance with paragraphs (a), (b) and (c) of regulation 2 of the Licensing and Management of Houses in Multiple Occupation and Other Houses (Miscellaneous Provisions) (England) Regulations 2006;

(b)     be sent to the organisations referred to in paragraphs (3)(b) and (c) of those regulations; and

(c)     contain the information described in paragraph (4) of those regulations.

(8)     Section 60 of the 2004 Act (duration, review and revocation of designation) shall apply to a designation deemed to have been made under subsection (2) and, for the purposes of subsection (2) of that section, the local housing authority shall be deemed to have specified 6th April 2009 as the time at which that designation ceases to have effect.

### HMOs registered under certain relevant schemes: transitional arrangements relating to introduction of licensing

4.—(1)     Subject to sub-paragraph (2), this paragraph applies to an HMO which immediately before the first commencement date is registered under a relevant scheme and is either—

PART II
STATUTORY INSTRUMENTS

    (a)   a prescribed HMO; or

    (b)   situated within an area in respect of which a designation is deemed to have been made under paragraph 3(2).

(2)   This paragraph does not apply to an HMO which is a converted block of flats to which section 257 of the 2004 Act applies.

(3)   A local housing authority shall be deemed to have granted a licence in respect of a HMO to which this paragraph applies to any person who, before the first commencement date, was recorded on the register authorised by the relevant scheme as the person managing the HMO.

(4)   Subject to the following sub-paragraphs, a licence deemed to have been granted under sub-paragraph (3) shall—

    (a)   be treated for all purposes of the 2004 Act as a licence under Part 2 of that Act;

    (b)   be deemed to specify in it the first commencement date as the date the licence comes into force;

    (c)   unless previously terminated by section 68(7) or revoked under section 70 of the 2004 Act, continue in force until the date that the HMO's registration under the relevant scheme would have expired; and

    (d)   be deemed to have been granted on the same conditions as those attached to the registration under the relevant scheme.

(5)   The conditions on which such a licence are deemed to have been granted do not include any conditions attaching to a HMO's registration under a relevant scheme which relates to—

    (a)   a repair notice served under sections 189 or 190 of the 1985 Act;

    (b)   a notice served under section 352 of that Act (power to require execution of works to render premises fit for number of occupants); or

    (c)   an occupancy direction made under section 348D of that Act which could not be imposed as a condition under section 67(2) of the 2004 Act.

(6)   Within the period of three months beginning on the first commencement date the local housing authority shall—

    (a)   send to the person to whom the licence is deemed to have been granted under sub-paragraph (3) ("the licence holder") particulars of the licence including—

        (i)   the conditions of the licence; and

        (ii)  the date of expiry of the licence; and

    (b)   if the licence expires less than 6 months after the first commencement date, send to the licence holder a notice informing him of the need to apply for a new licence on the expiry of the licence.

(7)   Schedule 4 (licences under Parts 2 and 3: mandatory conditions) and Part 1 of Schedule 5 (licences under Parts 2 and 3: procedure and appeals) to the 2004 Act shall not apply in relation to a licence deemed to have been granted under sub-paragraph (3).

(8)   Registration of an HMO under a relevant scheme in respect of which a licence is deemed to have been granted under sub-paragraph (3) shall cease to have effect on the first commencement date.

(9)   The licence holder shall not be charged for any costs incurred by the local housing authority taking any action under this paragraph.

*Applications for HMO registration outstanding on first commencement date:*
*transitional arrangements*

5.—(1)   This paragraph applies to an application for registration under a relevant scheme of a prescribed HMO or a HMO which is situated within an area in respect of which a designation is deemed to have been made under paragraph 3(2)—

    (a)   which has been made to a local housing authority before the first commencement date and not been withdrawn; and

    (b)   on which that authority has not made a decision before that date.

(2)   The authority must reach its decision on the application as it would have done if Part 11 of the 1985 Act had not been repealed.

(3)   Where the authority decides that the HMO satisfies the conditions for registration under a relevant scheme, it shall not register it but must instead grant a licence to the person specified in the application as the person managing the HMO—

    (a)   for a period of five years beginning on the first commencement date; and

    (b)   subject to the same conditions (other than any condition of a description mentioned in paragraph 4(5)(a), (b) or (c)) that it would have imposed if it had registered the HMO under the relevant scheme.

(4)   Where the authority decides that the HMO does not satisfy the conditions for registration under the scheme, it must—

    (a)   inform the applicant of the need to apply for a licence under section 63 of the 2004 Act; and

(b)    where the authority provides applicants for a licence with a form for making such an application, supply him with a copy of the form.

(5)   The licence holder shall not be charged for any costs incurred by the local housing authority taking any action under this paragraph.

(6)   Where an applicant to whom subsection (4) applies has paid a fee for his application for registration under a relevant scheme, he shall not be required to pay a fee for his application for a licence under section 63 of the 2004 Act.

### *Fitness of a house in multiple occupation for the number of occupants*

6.—(1)   During the period beginning on the first commencement date and ending on the date when regulations made by the Secretary of State under section 61(5) of the 2004 Act come into force, the repeal of sections 352, 352A or 353, shall not have effect in relation to a HMO which is a relevant converted block of flats.

(2)   During the period beginning on the first commencement date and ending on 5th April 2007—

    (a)    the repeal of sections 352, 352A and 353 of, and Schedule 10 to, the 1985 Act shall not have effect in relation to any notice served under section 352(1) of that Act before the first commencement date; and

    (b)    the repeal of sections 354, 355, 356, 395, 396 or 397 of the 1985 Act shall not have effect in relation to the commission of any offence committed before the first commencement date under—

       (i)    subsection (2) of section or 355 of that Act; or

       (ii)    subsection (2) of section 356 of that Act.

(3)   In relation to an appeal brought under subsection (2) of section 357 of the 1985 Act before the first commencement date a decision of a court to vary, or not to revoke, a direction under section 354 of that Act shall not have effect.

### *Overcrowding notices*

7.—(1)   A notice served under section 358(1) of the 1985 Act (service of overcrowding notice) before the first commencement date shall cease to have effect on that date unless it is a notice to which sub-paragraph (2) applies.

(2)   This sub-paragraph applies to a notice—

    (a)    which has become operative under section 358(3) of the 1985 Act before the first commencement date; or

    (b)    in respect of which an appeal has been brought under section 362 of that Act before that date.

(3)   During the period beginning on the first commencement date and ending on 5th April 2008 the repeal of sections 358 to 364, 395, 396 and 397 of the 1985 Act shall not have effect in relation to a notice served to which sub-paragraph (2) applies.

### *Means of escape from fire*

8.   During the period beginning on the first commencement date and ending on 5th April 2008 the repeal of sections 365, 368, 395, 396 or 397 of the 1985 Act shall not have effect in relation to an undertaking accepted by a local housing authority under subsection (2) of section 368 of that Act before the first commencement date.

### *Standards of Management*

9.—(1)   During the period beginning on the first commencement date and ending on the date when regulations made by the Secretary of State under section 61(5) of the 2004 Act come into force, the repeal of sections 369, 372, 373 and 378 of the 1985 Act shall not have effect in relation to a relevant converted block of flats.

(2)   During the period beginning on the first commencement date and ending on 5th April 2007—

    (a)    the repeal of sections 369, 395, 396 and 397 of the 1985 Act shall not have effect in relation to the commission of any offence under regulations made under section 369 of that Act before the first commencement date;

    (b)    the repeal of section 372 of the 1985 Act shall not have effect in relation to any notice served under subsection (1) of that section before that date; and

    (c)    the repeal of section 373 of the 1985 Act shall not have effect in relation to an appeal brought under subsection (1) of that section before that date.

*Works carried out by a local housing authority and enforcement*

10.—(1)  During the period beginning on the first commencement date and ending on the date when regulations made by the Secretary of State under section 61(5) of the 2004 Act come into force, the repeal of section 375 shall not have effect in relation a relevant converted block of flats.

(2)  During the period beginning on the first commencement date and ending on 5th April 2008 the repeal of sections 375, 376, 377, 377A and 378 of, and Schedule 10 to, the 1985 Act shall not have effect in relation to any notice served under section 352 or 372 of that Act before the first commencement date.

*Control Orders*

11.—(1)  This paragraph applies to a control order made under section 379(1) of the 1985 Act before the first commencement date.

(2)  The repeal of sections 379 to 397 of, and Schedule 13 to, the 1985 Act shall not have effect in relation to a control order to which this paragraph applies.

(3)  For so long as a control order to which this paragraph applies continues in force on and after the first commencement date, the provisions of Part 2 and 3 and Chapter 1 of Part 4 of the 2004 Act shall not have effect in relation to the house which is subject to the order.

(4)  This sub-paragraph applies to a house which is subject to a control order to which this paragraph applies if, on the date, or immediately before the date, the order expires or is revoked in accordance with section 392 of the 1985 Act, the house is—

(a)  a HMO which is required to be licensed under Part 2 or 3 of the 2004 Act but is not so licensed and the local housing authority consider either—
  (i)  that there is no reasonable prospect of it being so licensed in the near future, or
  (ii)  that the health and safety condition described in section 104 of the 2004 Act is satisfied; or
(b)  is a house other than one which is required to be licensed under Part 2 of the 2004 Act but in relation to which the local housing authority considers that that condition is satisfied.

(5)  The local housing authority shall not be required to make an interim management order under section 102 of the 2004 Act before making a final management order under section 113 of that Act in respect of a house to which sub-paragraph (4) applies.

(6)  Section 113 of the 2004 Act shall have effect for the purpose of the making of a final management order in respect of a house to which sub-paragraph (4) applies as if—

(a)  in subsection (1) the words "who have made an interim management order in respect of a house under section 102("the IMO")" were omitted; and
(b)  in subsections (2) and (3)—
  (i)  references to the IMO were construed as references to the control order to which this paragraph applies; and
  (ii)  references to the expiry date of the IMO were construed as references to the date mentioned in sub-paragraph (4).

(7)  Section 114 of the 2004 Act shall have effect for the purpose of the making of a final management order in respect of a house to which sub-paragraph (4) applies as if—

(a)  references to a "new final management order" were references to a final management order made under section 113 of that Act as modified by sub-paragraph (6); and
(b)  references to the "existing order" in subsections (5) to (7) were references to the control orders to which this paragraph applies.

(8)  A control order to which sub-paragraph 4 applies shall remain in force until—

(a)  an interim management order under section 102 of the 2004 Act is made;
(b)  a final management order under section 113 of the 2004 Act is made; or
(c)  the local housing authority decide that neither type of order described in paragraphs (a) or (b) of this sub-paragraph should be made.

**[3702]**

# ALLOCATION OF HOUSING AND HOMELESSNESS (ELIGIBILITY) (ENGLAND) REGULATIONS 2006

*(SI 2006/1294)*

---

**NOTES**

Made: 11 May 2006.

Authority: Housing Act 1996, ss 160A(3), (5), 172(4), 185(2), (3), 215(2).

Commencement: 1 June 2006.

---

## 1   Citation, commencement and application

(1)   These Regulations may be cited as the Allocation of Housing and Homelessness (Eligibility) (England) Regulations 2006 and shall come into force on 1st June 2006.

(2)   These Regulations apply to England only.

**[3703]**

**NOTES**

Commencement: 1 June 2006.

## 2   Interpretation

(1)   In these Regulations—

"the 1996 Act" means the Housing Act 1996;

["the Accession Regulations 2004" means the Accession (Immigration and Worker Registration) Regulations 2004;

"the Accession Regulations 2006" means the Accession (Immigration and Worker Authorisation) Regulations 2006;]

"the EEA Regulations" means the Immigration (European Economic Area) Regulations 2006;

"the Immigration Rules" means the rules laid down as mentioned in section 3(2) of the Immigration Act 1971 (general provisions for regulation and control);

"the Refugee Convention" means the Convention relating to the Status of Refugees done at Geneva on 28th July 1951, as extended by Article 1(2) of the Protocol relating to the Status of Refugees done at New York on 31st January 1967; and

"sponsor" means a person who has given an undertaking in writing for the purposes of the Immigration Rules to be responsible for the maintenance and accommodation of another person.

(2)   For the purposes of these Regulations—

(a)   "jobseeker", "self-employed person", and "worker" have the same meaning as for the purposes of the definition of a "qualified person" in regulation 6(1) of the EEA Regulations; and

(b)   subject to paragraph (3), references to the family member of a jobseeker, self-employed person or worker shall be construed in accordance with regulation 7 of those Regulations.

(3)   For the purposes of regulations 4(2)(d) and 6(2)(d) "family member" does not include a person who is treated as a family member by virtue of regulation 7(3) of the EEA Regulations.

[(4)   For the purposes of regulations 4(2)(h) and 6(2)(h), "the relevant period" means the period beginning at 4pm on 25th July 2006 and ending on 31st January 2007.]

**[3704]**

**NOTES**

Commencement: 1 June 2006.

Para (1): definitions "the Accession Regulations 2004" and "the Accession Regulations 2006" substituted, for original definition "the Accession Regulations", by the Allocation of Housing and Homelessness (Eligibility) (England) (Amendment) (No 2) Regulations 2006, SI 2006/3340, reg 2(1), (2) (except in relation to an applicant whose application for an allocation of housing accommodation under the Housing Act 1996, Pt 6, or housing assistance under Pt 7 of that Act, was made before 1 January 2007: see reg 3 of that regulation).

Para (4): inserted by the Allocation of Housing and Homelessness (Eligibility) (England) (Amendment) Regulations 2006, SI 2006/2007, reg 2(1), (2).

## 3   Persons subject to immigration control who are eligible for an allocation of housing accommodation

The following classes of persons subject to immigration control are persons who are eligible for an allocation of housing accommodation under Part 6 of the 1996 Act—

(a)　Class A—a person who is recorded by the Secretary of State as a refugee within the definition in Article 1 of the Refugee Convention and who has leave to enter or remain in the United Kingdom;

(b)　Class B—a person—
　　(i)　who has exceptional leave to enter or remain in the United Kingdom granted outside the provisions of the Immigration Rules; and
　　(ii)　who is not subject to a condition requiring him to maintain and accommodate himself, and any person who is dependent on him, without recourse to public funds;

(c)　Class C—a person who is habitually resident in the United Kingdom, the Channel Islands, the Isle of Man or the Republic of Ireland and whose leave to enter or remain in the United Kingdom is not subject to any limitation or condition, other than a person—
　　(i)　who has been given leave to enter or remain in the United Kingdom upon an undertaking given by his sponsor;
　　(ii)　who has been resident in the United Kingdom, the Channel Islands, the Isle of Man or the Republic of Ireland for less than five years beginning on the date of entry or the date on which his sponsor gave the undertaking in respect of him, whichever date is the later; and
　　(iii)　whose sponsor or, where there is more than one sponsor, at least one of whose sponsors, is still alive; and

[(d)　Class D—a person who has humanitarian protection granted under the Immigration Rules].

**[3705]**

**NOTES**

Commencement: 1 June 2006.

Para (d): substituted by the Allocation of Housing and Homelessness (Miscellaneous Provisions) (England) Regulations 2006, SI 2006/2527, reg 2(1), (2) (except in relation to an applicant whose application for an allocation of housing accommodation under the Housing Act 1996, Pt 6, or housing assistance under Pt 7 of that Act, was made before 9 October 2006: see reg 4 of that regulation at **[3735]**).

## 4　Other persons from abroad who are ineligible for an allocation of housing accommodation

(1)　A person who is not subject to immigration control is to be treated as a person from abroad who is ineligible for an allocation of housing accommodation under Part 6 of the 1996 Act if—

(a)　subject to paragraph (2), he is not habitually resident in the United Kingdom, the Channel Islands, the Isle of Man, or the Republic of Ireland;

(b)　his only right to reside in the United Kingdom—
　　(i)　is derived from his status as a jobseeker or the family member of a jobseeker; or
　　(ii)　is an initial right to reside for a period not exceeding three months under regulation 13 of the EEA Regulations; or

(c)　his only right to reside in the Channel Islands, the Isle of Man or the Republic of Ireland is a right equivalent to one of those mentioned in sub-paragraph (b) which is derived from the Treaty establishing the European Community.

(2)　The following are not to be treated as persons from abroad who are ineligible for an allocation of housing accommodation pursuant to paragraph (1)(a)—

(a)　a worker;

(b)　a self-employed person;

[(c)　a person who is treated as a worker for the purpose of the definition of "qualified person" in regulation 6(1) of the EEA Regulations pursuant to either—
　　(i)　regulation 5 of the Accession Regulations 2004 (application of the 2006 Regulations in relation to accession State worker requiring registration), or
　　(ii)　regulation 6 of the Accession Regulations 2006 (right of residence of an accession State national subject to worker authorisation);]

(d)　a person who is the family member of a person specified in sub-paragraphs (a)–(c);

(e)　a person with a right to reside permanently in the United Kingdom by virtue of regulation 15(c), (d) or (e) of the EEA Regulations;

(f)　a person who left the territory of Montserrat after 1st November 1995 because of the effect on that territory of a volcanic eruption; ...

(g)　a person who is in the United Kingdom as a result of his deportation, expulsion or other removal by compulsion of law from another country to the United Kingdom[; ... ]

[(h)　during the relevant period, a person who left Lebanon on or after 12th July 2006 because of the armed conflict there]; [and

(i)　a person who—
　　(i)　arrived in Great Britain on or after 28th February 2009 but before 18th March 2011;
　　(ii)　immediately before arriving in Great Britain had been resident in Zimbabwe; and

(iii) before leaving Zimbabwe, had accepted an offer, made by Her Majesty's Government, to assist that person to settle in the United Kingdom].

**[3706]**

**NOTES**

Commencement: 1 June 2006.

Para (2): sub-para (c) substituted by the Allocation of Housing and Homelessness (Eligibility) (England) (Amendment) (No 2) Regulations 2006, SI 2006/3340, reg 2(1), (3) (except in relation to an applicant whose application for an allocation of housing accommodation under the Housing Act 1996, Pt 6, or housing assistance under Pt 7 of that Act, was made before 1 January 2007: see reg 3 of that regulation); sub-para (f) word omitted revoked by the Allocation of Housing and Homelessness (Eligibility) (England) (Amendment) Regulations 2006, SI 2006/2007, reg 2(1), (3); sub-para (g) semi-colon and word omitted in square brackets inserted by SI 2006/2007, reg 2(1), (4), word omitted revoked by the Allocation of Housing and Homelessness (Eligibility) (England) (Amendment) Regulations 2009, SI 2009/358, reg 2(1), (2); sub-para (h) inserted by SI 2006/2007, reg 2(1), (5); sub-para (i) and word "and" immediately preceding it inserted by SI 2009/358, reg 2(1), (3).

## 5 Persons subject to immigration control who are eligible for housing assistance

(1) The following classes of persons subject to immigration control are persons who are eligible for housing assistance under Part 7 of the 1996 Act—

    (a) Class A—a person who is recorded by the Secretary of State as a refugee within the definition in Article 1 of the Refugee Convention and who has leave to enter or remain in the United Kingdom;

    (b) Class B—a person—

        (i) who has exceptional leave to enter or remain in the United Kingdom granted outside the provisions of the Immigration Rules; and

        (ii) whose leave to enter or remain is not subject to a condition requiring him to maintain and accommodate himself, and any person who is dependent on him, without recourse to public funds;

    (c) Class C—a person who is habitually resident in the United Kingdom, the Channel Islands, the Isle of Man or the Republic of Ireland and whose leave to enter or remain in the United Kingdom is not subject to any limitation or condition, other than a person—

        (i) who has been given leave to enter or remain in the United Kingdom upon an undertaking given by his sponsor;

        (ii) who has been resident in the United Kingdom, the Channel Islands, the Isle of Man or the Republic of Ireland for less than five years beginning on the date of entry or the date on which his sponsor gave the undertaking in respect of him, whichever date is the later; and

        (iii) whose sponsor or, where there is more than one sponsor, at least one of whose sponsors, is still alive;

    [(d) Class D—a person who has humanitarian protection granted under the Immigration Rules; and]

    (e) Class E—a person who is an asylum-seeker whose claim for asylum is recorded by the Secretary of State as having been made before 3rd April 2000 and in the circumstances mentioned in one of the following paragraphs—

        (i) on arrival (other than on his re-entry) in the United Kingdom from a country outside the United Kingdom, the Channel Islands, the Isle of Man or the Republic of Ireland;

        (ii) within three months from the day on which the Secretary of State made a relevant declaration, and the applicant was in Great Britain on the day on which the declaration was made; or

        (iii) on or before 4th February 1996 by an applicant who was on 4th February 1996 entitled to benefit under regulation 7A of the Housing Benefit (General) Regulations 1987 (persons from abroad).

(2) For the purpose of paragraph (1)(e)—

    (a) "asylum-seeker" means a person who is at least 18 years old, who is in the United Kingdom, and who has made a claim for asylum;

    (b) "claim for asylum" means a claim that it would be contrary to the United Kingdom's obligations under the Refugee Convention for the claimant to be removed from, or required to leave, the United Kingdom;

    (c) "relevant declaration" means a declaration to the effect that the country of which the applicant is a national is subject to such a fundamental change of circumstances that the Secretary of State would not normally order the return of a person to that country; and

    (d) subject to paragraph (3), a person ceases to be an asylum-seeker when his claim for asylum is recorded by the Secretary of State as having been decided (other than on appeal) or abandoned.

(3) For the purposes of paragraph (1)(e)(iii), a person does not cease to be an asylum-seeker as mentioned in paragraph (2)(d) while he is eligible for housing benefit by virtue of—

    (a) regulation 10(6) of the Housing Benefit Regulations 2006; or

(b)    regulation 10(6) of the Housing Benefit (Persons who have attained the qualifying age for state pension credit) Regulations 2006,

as modified in both cases by paragraph 6 of Schedule 3 to the Housing Benefit and Council Tax Benefit (Consequential Provisions) Regulations 2006.

[3707]

**NOTES**

Commencement: 1 June 2006.

Para (1): sub-para (d) substituted by the Allocation of Housing and Homelessness (Miscellaneous Provisions) (England) Regulations 2006, SI 2006/2527, reg 2(1), (3) (except in relation to an applicant whose application for an allocation of housing accommodation under the Housing Act 1996, Pt 6, or housing assistance under Pt 7 of that Act, was made before 9 October 2006: see reg 4 of that regulation at [3735]).

## 6   Other persons from abroad who are ineligible for housing assistance

(1)    A person who is not subject to immigration control is to be treated as a person from abroad who is ineligible for housing assistance under Part 7 of the 1996 Act if—

(a)    subject to paragraph (2), he is not habitually resident in the United Kingdom, the Channel Islands, the Isle of Man, or the Republic of Ireland;

(b)    his only right to reside in the United Kingdom—

(i)    is derived from his status as a jobseeker or the family member of a jobseeker; or

(ii)    is an initial right to reside for a period not exceeding three months under regulation 13 of the EEA Regulations; or

(c)    his only right to reside in the Channel Islands, the Isle of Man or the Republic of Ireland is a right equivalent to one of those mentioned in sub-paragraph (b) which is derived from the Treaty establishing the European Community.

(2)    The following are not to be treated as persons from abroad who are ineligible for housing assistance pursuant to paragraph (1)(a)—

(a)    a worker;

(b)    a self-employed person;

[(c)    a person who is treated as a worker for the purpose of the definition of "qualified person" in regulation 6(1) of the EEA Regulations pursuant to either—

(i)    regulation 5 of the Accession Regulations 2004 (application of the 2006 Regulations in relation to accession State worker requiring registration), or

(ii)    regulation 6 of the Accession Regulations 2006 (right of residence of an accession State national subject to worker authorisation);]

(d)    a person who is the family member of a person specified in sub-paragraphs (a)–(c);

(e)    a person with a right to reside permanently in the United Kingdom by virtue of regulation 15(c), (d) or (e) of the EEA Regulations;

(f)    a person who left the territory of Montserrat after 1st November 1995 because of the effect on that territory of a volcanic eruption; ...

(g)    a person who is in the United Kingdom as a result of his deportation, expulsion or other removal by compulsion of law from another country to the United Kingdom[; ... ]

[(h)    during the relevant period, a person who left Lebanon on or after 12th July 2006 because of the armed conflict there]; [and

(i)    a person who—

(i)    arrived in Great Britain on or after 28th February 2009 but before 18th March 2011;

(ii)    immediately before arriving in Great Britain had been resident in Zimbabwe; and

(iii)    before leaving Zimbabwe, had accepted an offer, made by Her Majesty's Government, to assist that person to settle in the United Kingdom].

[3708]

**NOTES**

Commencement: 1 June 2006.

Para (2): sub-para (c) substituted by the Allocation of Housing and Homelessness (Eligibility) (England) (Amendment) (No 2) Regulations 2006, SI 2006/3340, reg 2(1), (4) (except in relation to an applicant whose application for an allocation of housing accommodation under the Housing Act 1996, Pt 6, or housing assistance under Pt 7 of that Act, was made before 1 January 2007: see reg 3 of that regulation); sub-para (f) word omitted revoked by the Allocation of Housing and Homelessness (Eligibility) (England) (Amendment) Regulations 2006, SI 2006/2007, reg 2(1), (6); sub-para (g) semi-colon and word omitted in square brackets inserted by SI 2006/2007, reg 2(1), (7); word omitted revoked by the Allocation of Housing and Homelessness (Eligibility) (England) (Amendment) Regulations 2009, SI 2009/358, reg 2(1), (4); sub-para (h) inserted by SI 2006/2007, reg 2(1), (8); sub-para (i) and word "and" immediately preceding it inserted by SI 2009/358, reg 2(1), (5).

## 7   Revocation

Subject to regulation 8, the Regulations specified in column (1) of the Schedule are revoked to the extent mentioned in column (3) of the Schedule.

[3709]

**NOTES**
Commencement: 1 June 2006.

## 8  Transitional provisions

The revocations made by these Regulations shall not have effect in relation to an applicant whose application for—

(a)   an allocation of housing accommodation under Part 6 of the 1996 Act; or

(b)   housing assistance under Part 7 of the 1996 Act,

was made before 1st June 2006.

**[3710]**

**NOTES**
Commencement: 1 June 2006.

### SCHEDULE
Regulation 7

### Revocation schedule

| (1) Regulations Revoked | (2) References | (3) Extent of revocation |
|---|---|---|
| The Homelessness (England) Regulations 2000 | SI 2000/701 | The whole Regulations |
| The Allocation of Housing (England) Regulations 2002 | SI 2002/3264 | Regulations 4 and 5 |
| The Allocation of Housing and Homelessness (Amendment) (England) Regulations 2004 | SI 2004/1235 | The whole Regulations |
| The Allocation of Housing and Homelessness (Amendment) (England) Regulations 2006 | SI 2006/1093 | The whole Regulations |

**[3711]**

**NOTES**
Commencement: 1 June 2006.

# HOUSING ACT 2004 (COMMENCEMENT NO 3 AND TRANSITIONAL PROVISIONS AND SAVINGS) (WALES) ORDER 2006

### (SI 2006/1535 (W 152))

**NOTES**
Made: 13 June 2006.
Authority: Housing Act 2004, ss 76(6), 250(2), 270(4), (5), (10).

## 1  Title, interpretation and application

(1)   The title of this Order is the Housing Act 2004 (Commencement No 3 and Transitional Provisions and Savings) (Wales) Order 2006.

(2)   In this Order—

(a)   "the 1985 Act" ("*Deddf 1985*") means the Housing Act 1985;

(b)   "the 2004 Act" ("*Deddf 2004*") means the Housing Act 2004;

(c)   "the commencement date" ("*y dyddiad cychwyn*") means 16 June 2006; and

PART II
STATUTORY INSTRUMENTS

     (d)    any reference to a repeal is to a repeal contained in Schedule 16 to the 2004 Act.

  (3)   This Order applies in relation to Wales.

[3712]

## 2  Provisions coming into force on the commencement date

The following provisions of the 2004 Act come into force on the commencement date—
     (a)    in so far as they are not already in force, sections 1, 3, 5 to 8, 10 to 52, 54, 55, 58 to 78, 82 to 147, 229 to 232, 235, 236, 238 to 243, Schedules 1 to 7 and Schedule 13;
     (b)    section 265(1) in so far as it relates to paragraphs 2 to 6, 9 to 36 and 38 to 44 of Schedule 15 (minor and consequential amendments);
     (c)    section 266 in so far as it relates to the repeals in—
        (i)   the Friendly and Industrial and Provident Societies Act 1968;
        (ii)   the Land Compensation Act 1973;
       (iii)   the Civil Aviation Act 1982;
       (iv)   the Mobile Homes Act 1983;
        (v)   the 1985 Act;
       (vi)   the Housing Associations Act 1985;
      (vii)   the Housing (Consequential Provisions) Act 1985;
      (viii)   the Airports Act 1986;
       (ix)   the Housing Act 1988;
        (x)   the Electricity Act 1989);
       (xi)   the Local Government and Housing Act 1989);
      (xii)   the Housing Act 1996);
     (xiii)   the Housing Grants, Construction and Regeneration Act 1996); and
     (xiv)   the Transport Act 2000).

[3713]

## 3  Transitional provisions and savings

The Schedule has effect for the purpose of making transitional provisions and savings in connection with the coming into force of provisions mentioned in article 2.

[3714]

SCHEDULE

Article 3

PART 1
### ACTION UNDER THE 1985 ACT RELATING TO UNFITNESS

*Repair notices*

1.—(1)  A repair notice served under section 189 or 190 of the 1985 Act before the commencement date ceases to have effect on that date unless it is a notice to which sub-paragraph (2) applies.

  (2)   This sub-paragraph applies to a repair notice—
     (a)    which has become operative as mentioned in section 189(4) or 190(4) of the 1985 Act before the commencement date; or
     (b)    in respect of which an appeal has been brought under section 191 of that Act before that date.

  (3)   During the period beginning on the commencement date and ending on 15 June 2007, the repeal of sections 189 to 208, 345, 398, 604 and 604A of, and Schedule 10 to, the 1985 Act do not have effect in relation to a repair notice to which sub-paragraph (2) applies.

  (4)   Where—
     (a)    an appeal in respect of a repair notice to which sub-paragraph (2) applies is allowed; and
     (b)    the judge includes in the judgment a finding such as is mentioned in section 191(3) of the 1985 Act,
the local housing authority must take the finding into account if they subsequently consider taking action of a kind mentioned in section 5(2) or 7(2) of the 2004 Act in respect of the premises concerned.

  (5)   A repair notice to which sub-paragraph (2) applies ceases to have effect on 16 June 2007 except in relation to anything done in connection with the notice before that date.

  (6)   The repeal of section 191(3A)(b) of the 1985 Act does not have effect in relation to an order made by a court under that paragraph before that date.

  (7)   The amendment made by paragraph 4(2) of Schedule 15 to the 2004 Act (which amends the Land Compensation Act 1973) does not have effect in relation to a repair notice to which sub-paragraph (2) applies.

*Closing orders*

2.—(1) A closing order made under section 264 or 368(4) of the 1985 Act before the commencement date ceases to have effect on that date unless it is an order to which sub-paragraph (2) applies.

(2) This sub-paragraph applies to a closing order—
   (a) which has become operative as mentioned in section 268(2) of the 1985 Act before the commencement date; or
   (b) in respect of which an appeal has been brought under section 269 of that Act before that date.

(3) During the period beginning on the commencement date and ending on 15 June 2008, the following does not have effect in relation to a closing order to which sub-paragraph (2) applies—
   (a) the repeal of sections 264, 267(2) and (3), 269(2A) and (3A), 276 to 278, 368, 395, 396, 397, 604 and 604A of the 1985 Act;
   (b) the repeals in sections 317, 319(1)(b) and 323 of that Act; and
   (c) the amendments made by section 48(2) and (4) of, and paragraphs 13, 14, 22, 26, 27 and 33 of Schedule 15 to the 2004 Act.

(4) Where—
   (a) an appeal in respect of a closing order to which sub-paragraph (2) applies is allowed; and
   (b) the judge includes in the judgment a finding such as is mentioned in section 269(3A) of the 1985 Act,
the local housing authority must take the finding into account if they subsequently consider taking action of a kind mentioned in section 5(2) or 7(2) of the 2004 Act in respect of the premises concerned.

(5) A closing order to which sub-paragraph (2) applies ceases to have effect on 16 June 2008 except in relation to anything done in connection with the order before that date.

(6) The amendments made by—
   (a) paragraphs 3, 4(3), 5 and 6 of Schedule 15 to the 2004 Act (which amend the Land Compensation Act 1973); and
   (b) paragraphs 30 and 31 of that Schedule (which substitute compensation provisions of the Housing Act 1985),
do not have effect in relation to a closing order to which sub-paragraph (2) applies.

*Demolition orders*

3.—(1) A demolition order made under section 265 or 279 of the 1985 Act before the commencement date ceases to have effect on that date unless it is an order to which sub-paragraph (2) applies.

(2) This sub-paragraph applies to a demolition order—
   (a) which has become operative as mentioned in section 268(2) of the 1985 Act before the commencement date; or
   (b) in respect of which an appeal has been brought under section 269 of that Act before that date.

(3) During the period beginning on the commencement date and ending on 15 June 2008, the following do not have effect in relation to a demolition order to which sub-paragraph (2) applies—
   (a) the repeal of sections 269(2A) and (3A), 604 and 604A of the 1985 Act;
   (b) the repeals in section 323 of that Act; and
   (c) the amendments made by sections 46 and 48(2) to (4) of, and paragraphs 13 to 18, 21, 22, 26, 27, and 33 of Schedule 15 to the 2004 Act.

(4) Where—
   (a) an appeal in respect of a demolition order to which sub-paragraph (2) applies is allowed; and
   (b) the judge includes in the judgment a finding such as is mentioned in section 269(3A) of the 1985 Act,
the local housing authority must take the finding into account if they subsequently consider taking action of a kind mentioned in section 5(2) or 7(2) of the 2004 Act in respect of the premises concerned.

(5) During the period mentioned in sub-paragraph (3)—
   (a) section 275 of the 1985 Act (demolition orders: substitution of closing orders) has effect in relation to a demolition order to which sub-paragraph (2) applies as if—
      (i) in subsection (1) the words "and make a closing order as respects the premises" were omitted; and
      (ii) for subsection (2) there were substituted—

PART II
STATUTORY INSTRUMENTS

"(2)   The authority must serve notice that the demolition order has been determined on every person on whom they would be required by section 268 to serve a copy of a demolition order as respects the premises."; and

(b)   subsection (2) of section 304 of the 1985 Act (closing order to be made in respect of listed building subject to section 265) has effect in relation to such an order as if for the words after "operative" there were substituted the words "and they must serve notice that the demolition order has been determined on every person on whom they would be required by section 268 to serve a copy of a demolition order as respects the premises".

(6)   A demolition order to which sub-paragraph (2) applies cease to have effect on 16 June 2008 except in relation to anything done in connection with the order before that date.

(7)   The amendments made by—
(a)   paragraphs 3, 4(3), 5 and 6 of Schedule 15 to the 2004 Act; and
(b)   paragraphs 30 and 31 of that Schedule,
do not have effect in relation to a demolition order to which sub-paragraph (2) applies.

### Obstructive building orders

4.   An obstructive building order served under section 284 of the 1985 Act before the commencement date ceases to have effect on that date except in relation to anything done in connection with the order before that date.

### Clearance areas

5.—(1)   The amendments made by section 47 of, and paragraphs 19, 22, 26 and 27 of Schedule 15 to, the 2004 Act do not have effect in relation to an area declared to be a clearance area under section 289(3)(b) of the 1985 Act before the commencement date.

(2)   This sub-paragraph applies where, before the commencement date, a local housing authority—
(a)   have served notice under section 289(2B)(a) of the 1985 Act of intention to include a building in an area which is to be a clearance area; but
(b)   have not passed a resolution under section 289(3)(b) of that Act declaring the area to be a clearance area.

(3)   Where sub-paragraph (2) applies—
(a)   the notice mentioned in paragraph (a) of that sub-paragraph ceases to have effect; and
(b)   the requirements of section 289(2B)(b) and (c) and (2F) cease to apply to the local housing authority.

### Purchase of houses liable to be demolished or closed

6.—(1)   A notice of determination to purchase premises served under section 300(2)(a) of the 1985 Act before the commencement date ceases to have effect on that date unless it is a notice to which sub-paragraph (2) applies.

(2)   This sub-paragraph applies to a notice of determination—
(a)   which has become operative under section 268(2) of the 1985 Act before the commencement date; or
(b)   in respect of which an appeal has been brought under section 269 of that Act before that date.

(3)   The amendments made by section 48(2) of, and paragraphs 13, 14, 20, 21, 26 and 27 of Schedule 15 to, the 2004 Act do not have effect in relation to a notice of determination to which sub-paragraph (2) applies.

### Owner's proposals for re-development

7.—(1)   This paragraph applies in relation to any proposals submitted to a local housing authority under subsection (1) of section 308 of the 1985 Act (approval of owner's proposals for re-development) before the commencement date.

(2)   Where notice under subsection (2) of that section has not been given before that date, the authority ceases to be subject to the requirements of that subsection on and after that date.

(3)   Subject to sub-paragraph (4), any notice given under that subsection before that date ceases to have effect except in relation to anything done in connection with it before that date.

(4)   If the authority, on or after that date, consider taking action of a kind mentioned in section 5(2) or 7(2) of the 2004 Act in respect of the premises to which such a notice relates, the authority must, when making their decision, take into account the notice and the extent to which re-development has been proceeded with in accordance with the proposals and within the time-limits specified in the notice (subject to any variation or extension approved by the authority before that date).

*Owner's proposals for improvement or alteration*

8.—(1)    Subject to sub-paragraph (2), any proposals submitted by an owner, or certificate issued by a local housing authority, under section 310 of the 1985 Act (owner's improvements or alterations) before the commencement date cease to have effect on that date except in relation to anything done in connection with them before that date.

(2)    The repeal of section 311(2) of the 1985 Act (proposals to be treated as objection to compulsory purchase order) does not have effect in relation to proposals—

> (a)    submitted by an owner under section 310 of that Act; and
> (b)    transmitted by the local housing authority to the National Assembly for Wales under section 311(1) of that Act,

before the commencement date.

*Authorisation by court of execution of works on unfit premises etc*

9.    The amendments made by section 48(5) of, and paragraphs 25 to 27 of Schedule 15 to, the 2004 Act do not have effect in relation to an application made to the court under section 318 of the 1985 Act before the commencement date.

*Deferred action notices etc*

10.—(1)    Subject to sub-paragraph (3), a deferred action notice served under section 81 of the Housing Grants, Construction and Regeneration Act 1996 ("the 1996 Act") before the commencement date ceases to have effect on that date except in relation to anything done in connection with the notice before that date.

(2)    The repeal of section 86 of the 1996 Act (unfitness for human habitation etc: power to improve enforcement procedures) does not have effect in relation to any appeal brought under section 191 (repair notices) or 269 (closing and demolition orders) of the 1985 Act before the commencement date.

(3)    The repeal of sections 87 (unfitness for human habitation etc: power to charge for enforcement action) and 88 (recovery of charge for enforcement action) do not have effect in relation to—

> (a)    any action of a kind mentioned in section 87(1) of that Act which has been taken before the commencement date; or
> (b)    an appeal such as is mentioned in section 87(6) of that Act which has been brought before that date.

**[3715]**

PART 2
## MEASURES RELATING TO HOUSES IN MULTIPLE OCCUPATION UNDER PART 11 OF THE HOUSING ACT 1985

*Interpretation of Part*

1.—(1)    In this Part, "relevant converted block of flats" means a building or a part of a building which is—

> (i)    a converted block of flats to which section 257 of the 2004 Act applies; and
> (ii)    a house in multiple occupation for the purposes of Part 11 of the 1985 Act;
> (b)    "prescribed HMO" means a HMO that falls within the description prescribed by the National Assembly for Wales when an Order under section 55 of the 2004 Act comes into force; and
> (c)    "relevant scheme" means a registration scheme made under section 346 of the 1985 Act containing any of the control provisions or special control provisions described in section 347, 348, 348A, 348B, 348C, 348D, 348E or 348F of that Act.

(2)    The repeal of sections 345, 398, 399 and 400 of the 1985 Act (which give meanings of expressions used in Part 11 of the 1985 Act) do not have effect in so far as those sections are relevant to the construction of any provision of this Part which refers to Part 11 of that Act or any provision of that Part 11.

*Registration Schemes*

2.—(1)    Subject to sub-paragraph (2), during the period beginning on the commencement date and ending on the date when regulations made by the National Assembly for Wales under section 61(5) of the 2004 Act come into force, the repeal of sections 346, 346A, 346B, 347, 348, 348A to 348G, 350, 351 and 395 to 397 of the 1985 Act do not have effect in relation to any registration scheme which—

> (a)    conforms to a model scheme prepared by the National Assembly for Wales under section 346B of the 1985 Act; or
> (b)    is confirmed by the National Assembly for Wales before the commencement date,

(2) No new registration scheme may be made under section 346(1) on or after the commencement date.

(3) Notwithstanding the repeal of sections 346 and 347 of the 1985 Act, a local housing authority may use the information contained in any register it has compiled and maintained under section 346—

    (a)    for any purpose connected with the exercise of any of the authority's functions under Parts 1 to 4 of the 2004 Act in relation to HMOs; or

    (b)    for the purposes of investigating whether any offence has been committed under any of those Parts or under Part 11 of the 1985 Act in relation to HMOs.

*Areas deemed to be designated under section 56 of the 2004 Act*

3.—(1) This sub-paragraph applies to any area for which a local housing authority have made a relevant scheme.

(2) On the commencement date a local housing authority is deemed to have designated, under section 56(1) of the 2004 Act, each area to which sub-paragraph (1) applies as subject to additional licensing in relation to the HMOs registered under such a scheme.

(3) A designation deemed to have been made under sub-paragraph (2) comes into force on the commencement date.

(4) The requirements of sections 56(2) to (6), 57, 58 and 59(1) and (2) of the 2004 Act do not apply in relation to designations that are deemed to have been made under sub-paragraph (2).

(5) Sub-paragraphs (6), (7) and (8) apply to a designation deemed to have been made under sub-paragraph (2).

(6) Within the period of three months beginning on the commencement date the local housing authority must publish a notice stating which areas in its district are designated areas as a result of being deemed to be designated areas under sub-paragraph (2) in the manner described in sub-paragraph (7).

(7) The notice must be published in accordance with regulations made by the National Assembly for Wales under sections 59 and 60 of the 2004 Act.

(8) Section 60 of the 2004 Act (duration, review and revocation of designation) applies to a designation deemed to have been made under subsection (2) and, for the purposes of subsection (2) of that section, the local housing authority is deemed to have specified 16 June 2009 as the time at which that designation ceases to have effect.

*HMOs registered under certain relevant schemes: transitional arrangements relating to introduction of licensing*

4.—(1) Subject to sub-paragraph (2), this paragraph applies to an HMO which immediately before the commencement date is registered under a relevant scheme and is either—

    (a)    a prescribed HMO; or

    (b)    situated within an area in respect of which a designation is deemed to have been made under paragraph 3(2).

(2) This paragraph does not apply to an HMO which is a converted block of flats to which section 257 of the 2004 Act applies.

(3) A local housing authority is deemed to have granted a licence in respect of a HMO to which this paragraph applies to any person who, before the commencement date, was recorded on the register authorised by the relevant scheme as the person managing the HMO.

(4) Subject to the following sub-paragraphs, a licence deemed to have been granted under sub-paragraph (3) must—

    (a)    be treated for all purposes of the 2004 Act as a licence under Part 2 of that Act;

    (b)    be deemed to specify in it the commencement date as the date the licence comes into force;

    (c)    unless previously terminated by section 68(7) or revoked under section 70 of the 2004 Act, continue in force until the date that the HMO's registration under the relevant scheme would have expired; and

    (d)    be deemed to have been granted on the same conditions as those attached to the registration under the relevant scheme.

(5) The conditions on which such a licence are deemed to have been granted do not include any conditions attaching to a HMO's registration under a relevant scheme which relates to—

    (a)    a repair notice served under sections 189 or 190 of the 1985 Act;

    (b)    a notice served under section 352 of that Act (power to require execution of works to render premises fit for number of occupants); or

    (c)    an occupancy direction made under section 348D of that Act which could not be imposed as a condition under section 67(2) of the 2004 Act.

(6)    Within the period of three months beginning on the commencement date the local housing authority must—
- (a)    send to the person to whom the licence is deemed to have been granted under sub-paragraph (3) ("the licence holder") particulars of the licence including—
  - (i)    the conditions of the licence; and
  - (ii)    the date of expiry of the licence; and
- (b)    if the licence expires less than 6 months after the commencement date, send to the licence holder a notice informing the licence holder of the need to apply for a new licence on the expiry of the licence.

(7)    Schedule 4 (licences under Parts 2 and 3: mandatory conditions) and Part 1 of Schedule 5 (licences under Parts 2 and 3: procedure and appeals) to the 2004 Act do not apply in relation to a licence deemed to have been granted under sub-paragraph (3).

(8)    Registration of an HMO under a relevant scheme in respect of which a licence is deemed to have been granted under sub-paragraph (3) ceases to have effect on the commencement date.

(9)    The licence holder must not be charged for any costs incurred by the local housing authority taking any action under this paragraph.

*Applications for HMO registration outstanding on the commencement date: transitional arrangements*

5.—(1)    This paragraph applies to an application for registration under a relevant scheme of a prescribed HMO or a HMO which is situated within an area in respect of which a designation is deemed to have been made under paragraph 3(2)—
- (a)    which has been made to a local housing authority before the commencement date and not been withdrawn; and
- (b)    on which that authority has not made a decision before that date.

(2)    The authority must reach its decision on the application as it would have done if Part 11 of the 1985 Act had not been repealed.

(3)    Where the authority decides that the HMO satisfies the conditions for registration under a relevant scheme, it must not register it but must instead grant a licence to the person specified in the application as the person managing the HMO—
- (a)    for a period of five years beginning on the commencement date; and
- (b)    subject to the same conditions (other than any condition of a description mentioned in paragraph 4(5)(a), (b) or (c)) that it would have imposed if it had registered the HMO under the relevant scheme.

(4)    Where the authority decides that the HMO does not satisfy the conditions for registration under the scheme, it must—
- (a)    inform the applicant of the need to apply for a licence under section 63 of the 2004 Act; and
- (b)    where the authority provides applicants for a licence with a form for making such an application, supply the applicant with a copy of the form.

(5)    The licence holder must not be charged for any costs incurred by the local housing authority taking any action under this paragraph.

(6)    Where an applicant to whom sub-paragraph (4) applies has paid a fee for the application for registration under a relevant scheme, the applicant must not be required to pay a fee for the application for a licence under section 63 of the 2004 Act.

*Fitness of a house in multiple occupation for the number of occupants*

6.—(1)    During the period beginning on the commencement date and ending on the date when regulations made by the National Assembly for Wales under section 61(5) of the 2004 Act come into force, the repeal of sections 352, 352A or 353, do not have effect in relation to a HMO which is a relevant converted block of flats.

(2)    During the period beginning on the commencement date and ending on 15 June 2007—
- (a)    the repeal of sections 352, 352A and 353 of, and Schedule 10 to, the 1985 Act do not have effect in relation to any notice served under section 352(1) of that Act before the commencement date; and
- (b)    the repeal of sections 354, 355, 356, 395, 396 or 397 of the 1985 Act do not have effect in relation to the commission of any offence committed before the commencement date under—
  - (i)    subsection (2) of section 355 of that Act; or
  - (ii)    subsection (2) of section 356 of that Act.

(3)    In relation to an appeal brought under subsection (2) of section 357 of the 1985 Act before the commencement date a decision of a court to vary, or not to revoke, a direction under section 354 of that Act does not have effect.

## Overcrowding notices

7.—(1)   A notice served under section 358(1) of the 1985 Act (service of overcrowding notice) before the commencement date ceases to have effect on that date unless it is a notice to which sub-paragraph (2) applies.

(2)   This sub-paragraph applies to a notice—

  (a)   which has become operative under section 358(3) of the 1985 Act before the commencement date; or

  (b)   in respect of which an appeal has been brought under section 362 of that Act before that date.

(3)   During the period beginning on the commencement date and ending on 15 June 2008 the repeal of sections 358 to 364, 395, 396 and 397 of the 1985 Act will not have effect in relation to a notice served to which sub-paragraph (2) applies.

## Means of escape from fire

8.   During the period beginning on the commencement date and ending on 15 June 2008 the repeal of sections 365, 368, 395, 396 or 397 of the 1985 Act will not have effect in relation to an undertaking accepted by a local housing authority under subsection (2) of section 368 of that Act before the commencement date.

## Standards of Management

9.—(1)   During the period beginning on the commencement date and ending on the date when regulations made by the National Assembly for Wales under section 61(5) of the 2004 Act come into force, the repeal of sections 369, 372, 373 and 378 of the 1985 Act will not have effect in relation to a relevant converted block of flats.

(2)   During the period beginning on the commencement date and ending on 15 June 2007—

  (a)   the repeal of sections 369, 395, 396 and 397 of the 1985 Act will not have effect in relation to the commission of any offence under regulations made under section 369 of that Act before the commencement date;

  (b)   the repeal of section 372 of the 1985 Act does not have effect in relation to any notice served under subsection (1) of that section before that date; and

  (c)   the repeal of section 373 of the 1985 Act does not have effect in relation to an appeal brought under subsection (1) of that section before that date.

## Works carried out by a local housing authority and enforcement

10.—(1)   During the period beginning on the commencement date and ending on the date when regulations made by the National Assembly for Wales under section 61(5) of the 2004 Act come into force, the repeal of section 375 does not have effect in relation a relevant converted block of flats.

(2)   During the period beginning on the commencement date and ending on 15 June 2008 the repeal of sections 375, 376, 377, 377A and 378 of, and Schedule 10 to, the 1985 Act will not have effect in relation to any notice served under section 352 or 372 of that Act before the commencement date.

## Control Orders

11.—(1)   This paragraph applies to a control order made under section 379(1) of the 1985 Act before the commencement date.

(2)   The repeal of sections 379 to 397 of, and Schedule 13 to, the 1985 Act will not have effect in relation to a control order to which this paragraph applies.

(3)   For so long as a control order to which this paragraph applies continues in force on and after the commencement date, the provisions of Part 2 and 3 and Chapter 1 of Part 4 of the 2004 Act will not have effect in relation to the house which is subject to the order.

(4)   This sub-paragraph applies to a house which is subject to a control order to which this paragraph applies if, on the date, or immediately before the date, the order expires or is revoked in accordance with section 392 of the 1985 Act, the house is—

  (a)   a HMO which is required to be licensed under Part 2 or 3 of the 2004 Act but is not so licensed and the local housing authority consider either—

    (i)   that there is no reasonable prospect of it being so licensed in the near future, or

    (ii)   that the health and safety condition described in section 104 of the 2004 Act is satisfied; or

  (b)   is a house other than one which is required to be licensed under Part 2 of the 2004 Act but in relation to which the local housing authority considers that that condition is satisfied.

(5) The local housing authority is not required to make an interim management order under section 102 of the 2004 Act before making a final management order under section 113 of that Act in respect of a house to which sub-paragraph (4) applies.

(6) Section 113 of the 2004 Act has effect for the purpose of the making of a final management order in respect of a house to which sub-paragraph (4) applies as if-

   (a)    in subsection (1) the words "who have made an interim management order in respect of a house under section 102 ("the IMO")" were omitted; and

   (b)    in subsections (2) and (3)—

       (i)    references to the IMO were construed as references to the control order to which this paragraph applies; and

       (ii)    references to the expiry date of the IMO were construed as references to the date mentioned in sub-paragraph (4).

(7) Section 114 of the 2004 Act has effect for the purpose of the making of a final management order in respect of a house to which sub-paragraph (4) applies as if—

   (a)    references to a "new final management order" were references to a final management order made under section 113 of that Act as modified by sub-paragraph (6); and

   (b)    references to the "existing order" in subsections (5) to (7) were references to the control orders to which this paragraph applies.

(8) A control order to which sub-paragraph 4 applies remains in force until—

   (a)    an interim management order under section 102 of the 2004 Act is made;

   (b)    a final management order under section 113 of the 2004 Act is made; or

   (c)    the local housing authority decide that neither type of order described in paragraphs (a) or (b) of this sub-paragraph should be made.

**[3716]**

PART II
STATUTORY INSTRUMENTS

# RESIDENTIAL PROPERTY TRIBUNAL PROCEDURE (WALES) REGULATIONS 2006 (NOTE)

### (SI 2006/1641 (W 156))

**NOTES**

Made: 20 June 2006.

Authority: Housing Act 2004, s 250(2)(a), Sch 13.

Commencement: 23 June 2006.

These Regulations apply to Wales only. The equivalent provisions for England are in SI 2006/831 at **[3656]** et seq.

**[3717]**

# RESIDENTIAL PROPERTY TRIBUNAL (FEES) (WALES) REGULATIONS 2006 (NOTE)

### (SI 2006/1642 (W 157))

**NOTES**

Made: 20 June 2006.

Authority: Housing Act 2004, Sch 13, paras 1, 11.

Commencement: 23 June 2006.

Amended by: SI 2008/1879.

These Regulations apply to Wales only. The equivalent provisions for England are in SI 2006/830 at **[3650]** et seq.

**[3718]**

# HOUSING HEALTH AND SAFETY RATING SYSTEM (WALES) REGULATIONS 2006 (NOTE)

### (SI 2006/1702 (W 164))

**NOTES**

Made: 27 June 2006.

Authority: Housing Act 2004, ss 2, 4, 250(2)(a).

Commencement: 30 June 2006.

These Regulations apply to Wales only. The equivalent provisions for England are in SI 2005/3208 at **[3584]** et seq.

**[3719]**

# HOUSING (INTERIM MANAGEMENT ORDERS) (PRESCRIBED CIRCUMSTANCES) (WALES) ORDER 2006 (NOTE)

### (SI 2006/1706 (W 168))

**NOTES**
Made: 27 June 2006.
Authority: Housing Act 2004, s 103(5)(a), (6).
Commencement: 30 June 2006.
This Order applies to Wales only. The equivalent provisions for England are in SI 2006/369 at **[3605]** et seq.

**[3720]**

# HOUSES IN MULTIPLE OCCUPATION (SPECIFIED EDUCATIONAL ESTABLISHMENTS) (WALES) REGULATIONS 2006 (NOTE)

### (SI 2006/1707 (W 169))

**NOTES**
Made: 27 June 2006.
Authority: Housing Act 2004, Sch 14, para 4(2).
Commencement: 7 July 2006.
These Regulations apply to Wales only. The equivalent provisions for England are in SI 2009/2298 at **[3966]** et seq.

**[3721]**

# LICENSING OF HOUSES IN MULTIPLE OCCUPATION (PRESCRIBED DESCRIPTIONS) (WALES) ORDER 2006 (NOTE)

### (SI 2006/1712 (W 174))

**NOTES**
Made: 27 June 2006.
Authority: Housing Act 2004, s 55(3).
Commencement: 30 June 2006.
This Order applies to Wales only. The equivalent provisions for England are in SI 2006/371 at **[3609]** et seq.

**[3722]**

# MANAGEMENT OF HOUSES IN MULTIPLE OCCUPATION (WALES) REGULATIONS 2006 (NOTE)

### (SI 2006/1713 (W 175))

**NOTES**
Made: 27 June 2006.
Authority: Housing Act 2004, s 234(1).
Commencement: 30 June 2006.
Amended by: SI 2009/1915.
These Regulations apply to Wales only. The equivalent provisions for England are in SI 2006/372 at **[3612]** et seq.

**[3723]**

## LICENSING AND MANAGEMENT OF HOUSES IN MULTIPLE OCCUPATION AND OTHER HOUSES (MISCELLANEOUS PROVISIONS) (WALES) REGULATIONS 2006 (NOTE)

### (SI 2006/1715 (W 177))

**NOTES**
Made: 27 June 2006.
Authority: Housing Act 2004, ss 59(2)–(4), 60(6), 63(5), (6), 65(3), (4), 83(2)–(4), 84(6), 87(5), (6), 232(3), (7), 250(2), 258(2)(b), (5), (6), 259(2)(c), Sch 14, paras 3, 6(1)(c).
Commencement: 30 June 2006.
Amended by: SI 2007/3229.
These Regulations apply to Wales only. The equivalent provisions for England are in SI 2006/373 at **[3623]** et seq.

**[3724]**

## MOBILE HOMES (WRITTEN STATEMENT) (ENGLAND) REGULATIONS 2006

### (SI 2006/2275)

**NOTES**
Made: 22 August 2006.
Authority: Mobile Homes Act 1983, s 1(2)(e).
Commencement: 1 October 2006.

### 1   Citation, commencement, and application

(1) These Regulations may be cited as the Mobile Homes (Written Statement) (England) Regulations 2006 and shall come into force on 1st October 2006.

(2) These Regulations apply in relation to every written statement given after 1st October 2006 with respect to an agreement—

(a) for the stationing of a mobile home on a protected site, and

(b) to which the Mobile Homes Act 1983 will apply.

**[3725]**

**NOTES**
Commencement: 1 October 2006.

### 2   Interpretation

In these Regulations—

"the 1983 Act" means the Mobile Homes Act 1983;

"written statement" means the written statement that the owner of a protected site is required by section 1(2) of the 1983 Act to give to the proposed occupier.

**[3726]**

**NOTES**
Commencement: 1 October 2006.

### 3   Written statement: prescribed requirements

The requirements with which a written statement must comply for the purposes of section 1(2) of the 1983 Act (in addition to the requirements of section 1(2)(a) to (d) of the 1983 Act); are—

(a) that it shall contain—

(i) the note preceding Part 1 of the Schedule to these Regulations, and

(ii) the particulars mentioned in Part 1 of that Schedule (so far as not required by section 1(2)(a) to (d) of the 1983 Act) and Parts 2 and 4 of that Schedule; and

(b) that it shall be in the form set out in that Schedule or a form substantially to the same effect.

**[3727]**

**NOTES**
Commencement: 1 October 2006.

**4** (*Revokes the Mobile Homes (Written Statement) Regulations 1983 in relation to England.*)

SCHEDULE

WRITTEN STATEMENT UNDER MOBILE HOMES ACT 1983

Regulation 3

IMPORTANT—PLEASE READ THIS STATEMENT CAREFULLY AND KEEP IT IN A SAFE PLACE. IT SETS OUT THE TERMS ON WHICH YOU WILL BE ENTITLED TO KEEP YOUR MOBILE HOMES ON SITE AND TELLS YOU ABOUT THE RIGHTS WHICH WILL BE GIVEN TO YOU BY LAW IF THERE IS ANYTHING YOU DO NOT UNDERSTAND YOU SHOULD GET ADVICE (FOR EXAMPLE FROM A SOLICITOR OR A CITIZENS ADVICE BUREAU)

PART 1

INTRODUCTORY PROVISIONS AND EXPRESS TERMS (OTHER THAN THOSE SPECIFIED IN PART 5)

1. The Mobile Homes Act 1983 ("the 1983 Act"), as amended by the Housing Act 2004, will apply to the agreement.

**2 Parties to the agreement**

The parties to the agreement will be—

..................................................................................................................

(*name and address of mobile home occupier*)

..................................................................................................................

(*name and address of site owner*)

**3 Start date**

The agreement will begin on .................................................. (*insert date*)

**4 Particulars of the pitch**

The particulars of the land on which you will be entitled to station your mobile home are

..................................................................................................................

..................................................................................................................

..................................................................................................................

**5 Plan**

A plan showing—

    (a)    the size and location of the pitch;

    (b)    the size of the base on which the mobile home is to be stationed; and

    (c)    measurements between identifiable fixed points on the site and the pitch and base;

is attached to this statement.

**6 Site owner's interest**

The site owner's estate or interest in the land will end on ..................................

(*If this statement applies insert date*); or

The site owner's planning permission for the site will end on ........................

(*If this statement applies insert date*)

This means that your right to stay on the site will not continue after either of these dates unless the site owner's interest or planning permission is extended.

(*If only one of these statements apply, cross out the words that do not apply. If neither of these statements apply, delete this paragraph.*)

**7 Pitch fee**

The pitch fee will be payable from .................................................. (*insert date*)

The pitch fee will be payable weekly/monthly/quarterly/annually

(*cross out the words which do not apply*)

The pitch fee is ................................................

The following services are included in the pitch fee—

    Water

    Sewerage

    ....................

    ....................

(*Cross out the services which are not included and add any others which are included in the pitch fee*)

## 8   Review of pitch fee

The pitch fee will be reviewed on .................................................... (*insert date*)
This date is the review date.

## 9   Additional charges

An additional charge will be made for the following matters—

....................
....................
....................

(*List the matters for which an additional charge will be made*)

**[3728]**

**NOTES**

Commencement: 1 October 2006.

### PART 2
### INFORMATION ABOUT YOUR RIGHTS

## 1   The Mobile Homes Act 1983

Because you will have an agreement with a site owner which will entitle you to keep your mobile home on his site and live in it as your home, you will have certain rights under the Mobile Homes Act 1983, affecting in particular your security of tenure, the sale of your home and the review of the pitch fee.

## 2   Implied terms

These rights, which are contained in the implied terms set out in Part 3 of this statement, will apply automatically and cannot be overridden, so long as your agreement continues to be one to which the 1983 Act applies.

## 3   Express terms

If you are not happy with any of the express terms of your proposed agreement (as set out in Part 5 of this statement) you should discuss them with the site owner, who may agree to change them.

## 4   Right to challenge

If you enter into the agreement and subsequently become dissatisfied with the express terms of the agreement you can challenge them as explained in paragraphs 5–7. But you must do so within six months of the date on which you enter into the agreement or the date you received the written statement, whichever is the later. If you wish to challenge your agreement, you may wish to consult a solicitor or citizens' advice bureau.

**5.**   A challenge can be made either in the county court or before an arbitrator. You can—
   (a)   ask for any express terms of the agreement (those set out in Part 5 of this statement) to be changed or deleted; or
   (b)   ask for further terms to be included in the agreement concerning the matters set out in Part 2 of Schedule 1 to the 1983 Act (see paragraph 8).

  The site owner can also go to court or to an arbitrator to ask for the agreement to be changed in these two ways.

**6.**   The appointment of an arbitrator may be provided for in one of the express terms of the agreement. If not, you and the site owner can still agree in writing to appoint an arbitrator to settle a dispute between you.

**7.**   The court or arbitrator must make an order on terms they consider just and equitable in the circumstances.

## 8   Further terms

The matters set out in Part 2 of Schedule 1 to the 1983 Act are—
   (a)   the sums payable by the occupier in pursuance of the agreement and the times at which they are to be paid;
   (b)   the review at yearly intervals of the sums so payable;
   (c)   the provision or improvement of services available on the protected site, and the use by the occupier of such services; and
   (d)   the preservation of the amenity of the protected site.

### 9 Time limit

If no application to the court or an arbitrator is made within six months of the date on which you entered into the agreement or the date you received the written statement, which ever is the later, both you and the site owner will be bound by the terms of the agreement and will not be able to change them unless both parties agree.

### 10 Unfair terms

If you consider that any of the express terms of the proposed agreement (as set out in Part 5 of this statement) are unfair, you can, in accordance with the provisions of the Unfair Terms in Consumer Contracts Regulations 1999, complain to the Office of Fair Trading or any qualifying body.

**[3729]**

**NOTES**
Commencement: 1 October 2006.

PART 3
IMPLIED TERMS

*Under the 1983 Act, certain terms will be automatically included in your agreement. These implied terms are set out in Part 1 of Schedule 1 to the 1983 Act This is set out below and includes the amendments made to Schedule 1 by the Housing Act 2004 and the Mobile Homes Act 1983 (Amendment of Schedule 1) (England) Order 2006. The numbering follows that used in the 1983 Act as amended by the 2004 Act and the 2006 Order.*

"SCHEDULE 1
AGREEMENTS UNDER THE ACT

PART 1
TERMS IMPLIED BY ACT

### 1 Duration of agreement

Subject to paragraph 2 below, the right to station the mobile home on land forming part of the protected site shall subsist until the agreement is determined under paragraph 3, 4, 5 or 6 below.

### 2 Owner's estate or interest

(1) If the owner's estate or interest is insufficient to enable him to grant the right for an indefinite period, the period for which the right subsists shall not extend beyond the date when the owner's estate or interest determines.

(2) If planning permission for the use of the protected site as a site for mobile homes has been granted in terms such that it will expire at the end of a specified period, the period for which the right subsists shall not extend beyond the date when the planning permission expires.

(3) If before the end of a period determined by this paragraph there is a change in circumstances which allows a longer period, account shall be taken of that change.

### 3 Termination by occupier

The occupier shall be entitled to terminate the agreement by notice in writing given to the owner not less than four weeks before the date on which it is to take effect.

### 4 Termination by owner

The owner shall be entitled to terminate the agreement forthwith, if on the application of the owner, the court—

    (a)   is satisfied that the occupier has breached a term of the agreement and, after service of a notice to remedy the breach, has not complied with the notice within a reasonable time; and

    (b)   considers it reasonable for the agreement to be terminated.

**5.** The owner shall be entitled to terminate the agreement forthwith if, on the application of the owner, the court—

    (a)   is satisfied that the occupier is not occupying the mobile home as his only or main residence; and

    (a)   considers it reasonable for the agreement to be terminated.

**6.**—(1)   the owner shall be entitled to terminate the agreement forthwith if, on the application of the owner, the court is satisfied that, having regard to its condition, the mobile home—

    (a)   is having a detrimental effect on the amenity of the site; or

    (b)   the court considers it reasonable for the agreement to be terminated.

(2)    Sub-paragraphs (3) and (4) below apply if, on an application under sub-paragraph (1) above—

    (a)    the court considers that, having regard to the present condition of the mobile home, paragraph (a) of that sub-paragraph applies to it, but

    (b)    it also considers that it would be reasonably practicable for particular repairs to be carried out on the mobile home that would result in sub-paragraph (1)(a) not applying to it, and

    (c)    the occupier indicates that he intends to carry out those repairs.

(3)    In such a case the court may make an order adjourning proceedings on the application for such period specified in the order as the court considers reasonable to allow the repairs to be carried out.

The repairs must be set out in the order.

(4)    If the court makes such an order, the application shall not be further proceeded with unless the court is satisfied that the specified period has expired without the repairs having been carried out.

### 7   Recovery of overpayments by occupier

Where the agreement is terminated as mentioned in paragraph 3, 4, 5 or 6 above, the occupier shall be entitled to recover from the owner so much of any payment made by him in pursuance of the agreement as is attributable to a period beginning after the termination.

### 8   Sale of mobile home

(1)    The occupier shall be entitled to sell the mobile home, and to assign the agreement, to a person approved of by the owner, whose approval shall not be unreasonably withheld.

(1A)    The occupier may serve on the owner a request for the owner to approve a person for the purposes of sub-paragraph (1) above.

(1B)    Where the owner receives such a request, he must, within the period of 28 days beginning with the date on which he received the request—

    (a)    approve the person, unless it is reasonable for him not to do so, and

    (b)    serve on the occupier notice of his decision whether or not to approve the person.

(1C)    The owner may not give his approval subject to conditions.

(1D)    If the approval is withheld, the notice under sub-paragraph (1B) above must specify the reasons for withholding it.

(1E)    If the owner fails to notify the occupier as required by sub-paragraphs (1B) (and, if applicable, sub-paragraph (1D)) above, the occupier may apply to the court for an order declaring that the person is approved for the purposes of sub-paragraph (1) above; and the court may make such an order if it thinks fit.

(1F)    It is for the owner—

    (a)    if he served a notice as mentioned in sub-paragraph (1B) (and, if applicable, sub-paragraph (1D)) and the question arises whether he served the notice within the required period of 28 days, to show that he did;

    (b)    if he did not give his approval and the question arises whether it was reasonable for him not to do so, to show that it was reasonable.

(1G)    A request or notice under this paragraph—

    (a)    must be in writing, and

    (b)    may be served by post.

(2)    Where the occupier sells the mobile home, and assigns the agreement, as mentioned in sub-paragraph (1) above, the owner shall be entitled to receive a commission on the sale at a rate not exceeding such rate as may be specified by an order made by the appropriate national authority.

(2A)    Except to the extent mentioned in sub-paragraph (2) above, the owner may not require any payment to be made (whether to himself or otherwise) in connection with the sale of the mobile home, and the assignment of the agreement, as mentioned in sub-paragraph (1) above.

(3)    An order under this paragraph—

    (a)    shall be made by statutory instrument which (if made by the Secretary of State) shall be subject to annulment in pursuance of a resolution of either House of Parliament; and

    (b)    may make different provision for different areas or for sales at different prices.

*The maximum rate is currently fixed at 10% by the Mobile Homes (Commissions) Order 1983 (SI 1983/748)*

### 9   Gift of mobile home

(1)   The occupier shall be entitled to give the mobile home, and to assign the agreement, to a member of his family approved by the owner, whose approval shall not be unreasonably withheld.

(2)   Sub-paragraphs (1A) to (1G) of paragraph 8 above shall apply in relation to the approval of a person for the purposes of sub-paragraph (1) above as they apply in relation to the approval of a person for the purposes of sub-paragraph (1) of that paragraph.

(3)   The owner may not require any payment to be made (whether to himself or otherwise) in connection with the gift of the mobile home, and the assignment of the agreement, as mentioned in sub-paragraph (1) above.

### 10   Re-siting of mobile home

(1)   The owner shall be entitled to require that the occupier's right to station the mobile home is exercisable for any period in relation to another pitch forming part of the protected site ("the other pitch") if (and only if)—

   (a)   on the application of the owner, the court is satisfied that the other pitch is broadly comparable to the occupier's original pitch and that it is reasonable for the mobile home to be stationed on the other pitch for that period; or

   (b)   the owner needs to carry out essential repair or emergency works that can only be carried out if the mobile home is moved to the other pitch for that period, and the other pitch is broadly comparable to the occupier's original pitch.

(2)   If the owner requires the occupier to station the mobile home on the other pitch so that he can replace, or carry out repairs to, the base on which the mobile home is stationed, he must if the occupier so requires, or the court on the application of the occupier so orders, secure that the mobile home is returned to the original pitch on the completion of the replacement or repairs.

(3)   The owner shall pay all the costs and expenses incurred by the occupier in connection with his mobile home being moved to and from the other pitch.

(4)   In this paragraph and in paragraph 13 below, "essential repair or emergency works" means—

   (a)   repairs to the base on which the mobile home is stationed;

   (b)   works or repairs needed to comply with any relevant legal requirements; or

   (c)   works or repairs in connection with restoration following flood, landslide or other natural disaster.

### 11   Quiet enjoyment of the mobile home

The occupier shall be entitled to quiet enjoyment of the mobile home together with the pitch during the continuance of the agreement, subject to paragraphs 10, 12, 13 and 14.

### 12   Owner's right of entry to the pitch

The owner may enter the pitch without prior notice between the hours of 9am and 6pm—

   (a)   to deliver written communications, including post and notices, to the occupier; and

   (b)   to read any meter for gas, electricity, water, sewerage or other services supplied by the owner.

**13.**   The owner may enter the pitch to carry out essential repair or emergency works on giving as much notice to the occupier (whether in writing or otherwise) as is reasonably practicable in the circumstances.

**14.**   Unless the occupier has agreed otherwise, the owner may enter the pitch for a reason other than one specified in paragraph 12 or 13 only if he has given the occupier at least 14 clear days' written notice of the date, time and reason for his visit.

**15.**   The rights conferred by paragraphs 12 to 14 above do not extend to the mobile home.

### 16   The pitch fee

The pitch fee can only be changed in accordance with paragraph 17, either—

   (a)   with the agreement of the occupier, or

   (b)   if the court, on the application of the owner or the occupier, considers it reasonable for the pitch fee to be changed and makes an order determining the amount of the new pitch fee.

**17.**—(1)   The pitch fee shall be reviewed annually as at the review date.

(2)   At least 28 clear days before the review date the owner shall serve on the occupier a written notice setting out his proposals in respect of the new pitch fee.

(3)   If the occupier agrees to the proposed new pitch fee, it shall be payable as from the review date.

(4)   If the occupier does not agree to the proposed new pitch fee—

(a)    the owner may apply to the court for an order under paragraph 16(b) determining the amount of the new pitch fee;

(b)    the occupier shall continue to pay the current pitch fee to the owner until such time as the new pitch fee is agreed by the occupier or an order determining the amount of the new pitch fee is made by the court under paragraph 16(b); and

(c)    the new pitch fee shall be payable as from the review date but the occupier shall not be treated as being in arrears until the 28th day after the date on which the new pitch fee is agreed or, as the case may be, the 28th day after the date of the court order determining the amount of the new pitch fee.

(5)    An application under sub-paragraph (4)(a) may be made at any time after the end of the period of 28 days beginning with the review date.

(6)    Sub-paragraphs (7) to (10) apply if the owner—

(a)    has not served the notice required by sub-paragraph (2) by the time by which it was required to be served, but

(b)    at any time thereafter serves on the occupier a written notice setting out his proposals in respect of a new pitch fee.

(7)    If (at any time) the occupier agrees to the proposed pitch fee, it shall be payable as from the 28th day after the date on which the owner serves the notice under sub-paragraph (6)(b).

(8)    If the occupier has not agreed to the proposed pitch fee—

(a)    the owner may apply to the court for an order under paragraph 16(b) determining the amount of the new pitch fee;

(b)    the occupier shall continue to pay the current pitch fee to the owner until such time as the new pitch fee is agreed by the occupier or an order determining the amount of the new pitch fee is made by the court under paragraph 16(b); and

(c)    if the court makes such an order, the new pitch fee shall be payable as from the 28th day after the date on which the owner serves the notice under sub-paragraph (6)(b).

(9)    An application under sub-paragraph (8) may be made at any time after the end of the period of 56 days beginning with the date on which the owner serves the notice under sub-paragraph (6)(b).

(10)    The occupier shall not be treated as being in arrears—

(a)    where sub-paragraph (7) applies, until the 28th day after the date on which the new pitch fee is agreed; or

(b)    where sub-paragraph (8)(b) applies, until the 28th day after the date on which the new pitch fee is agreed or, as the case may be, the 28th day after the date of the court order determining the amount of the new pitch fee.

**18.**—(1)    When determining the amount of the new pitch fee particular regard shall be had to—

(a)    any sums expended by the owner since the last review date on improvements—

    (i)    which are for the benefit of the occupiers of mobile homes on the protected site;

    (ii)    which were the subject of consultation in accordance with paragraph 22(e) and (f) below; and

    (iii)    to which a majority of the occupiers have not disagreed in writing or which, in the case of such disagreement, the court, on the application of the owner, has ordered should be taken into account when determining the amount of the new pitch fee;

(b)    any decrease in the amenity of the protected site since the last review date; and

(c)    the effect of any enactment, other than an order made under paragraph 8(2) above, which has come into force since the last review date.

(2)    When calculating what constitutes a majority of the occupiers for the purposes of sub-paragraph (1)(a)(iii) each mobile home is to be taken to have only one occupier and, in the event of there being more than one occupier of a mobile home, its occupier is to be taken to be the occupier whose name first appears on the agreement.

(3)    In a case where the pitch fee has not been previously reviewed, references in this paragraph to the last review date are to be read as references to the date when the agreement commenced.

**19.**    When determining the amount of the new pitch fee, any costs incurred by the owner in connection with expanding the protected site shall not be taken into account.

**20.**—(1)    There is a presumption that the pitch fee shall increase or decrease by a percentage which is no more than any percentage increase or decrease in the retail prices index since the last review date, unless this would be unreasonable having regard to paragraph 18(1) above.

(2)    Paragraph 18(3) above applies for the purposes of this paragraph as it applies for the purposes of paragraph 18.

## 21   Occupier's obligations

The occupier shall—

(a)    pay the pitch fee to the owner;

(b)    pay to the owner all sums due under the agreement in respect of gas, electricity, water, sewerage or other services supplied by the owner;

(c)    keep the mobile home in a sound state of repair;

(d)    maintain—

    (i)    the outside of the mobile home, and

    (ii)    the pitch, including all fences and outbuildings belonging to, or enjoyed with, it and the mobile home,

in a clean and tidy condition; and

(e)    if requested by the owner, provide him with documentary evidence of any costs or expenses in respect of which the occupier seeks reimbursement.

## 22   Owner's obligations

The owner shall—

(a)    if requested by the occupier, and on payment by the occupier of a charge of not more than £30, provide accurate written details of—

    (i)    the size of the pitch and the base on which the mobile home is stationed; and

    (ii)    the location of the pitch and the base within the protected site;

and such details must include measurements between identifiable fixed points on the protected site and the pitch and the base;

(b)    if requested by the occupier, provide (free of charge) documentary evidence in support and explanation of—

    (i)    any new pitch fee;

    (ii)    any charges for gas, electricity, water, sewerage or other services payable by the occupier to the owner under the agreement; and

    (iii)    any other charges, costs or expenses payable by the occupier to the owner under the agreement;

(c)    be responsible for repairing the base on which the mobile home is stationed and for maintaining any gas, electricity, water, sewerage or other services supplied by the owner to the pitch or to the mobile home;

(d)    maintain in a clean and tidy condition those parts of the protected site, including access ways, site boundary fences and trees, which are not the responsibility of any occupier of a mobile home stationed on the protected site;

(e)    consult the occupier about improvements to the protected site in general, and in particular about those which the owner wishes to be taken into account when determining the amount of any new pitch fee; and

(f)    consult a qualifying residents' association, if there is one, about all matters which relate to the operation and management of, or improvements to, the protected site and may affect the occupiers either directly or indirectly.

**23.**    The owner shall not do or cause to be done anything which may adversely affect the ability of the occupier to perform his obligations under paragraph 21(c) and (d) above.

**24.**    For the purposes of paragraph 22(e) above, to "consult" the occupier means—

(a)    to give the occupier at least 28 clear days' notice in writing of the proposed improvements which—

    (i)    describes the proposed improvements and how they will benefit the occupier in the long and short term;

    (ii)    details how the pitch fee may be affected when it is next reviewed; and

    (iii)    states when and where the occupier can make representations about the proposed improvements; and

(b)    to take into account any representations made by the occupier about the proposed improvements, in accordance with paragraph (a)(iii), before undertaking them.

**25.**    For the purposes of paragraph 22(f) above, to "consult" a qualifying residents' association means—

(a)    to give the association at least 28 clear days' notice in writing of the matters referred to in paragraph 22(f) which—

    (i)    describes the matters and how they may affect the occupiers either directly or indirectly in the long and short term; and

    (ii)    states when and where the association can make representations about the matters; and

(b)    to take into account any representations made by the association, in accordance with paragraph (a)(ii), before proceeding with the matters.

**26 Owner's name and address**

(1)   The owner shall by notice inform the occupier and any qualifying residents' association of the address in England or Wales at which notices (including notices of proceedings) may be served on him by the occupier or a qualifying residents' association.

(2)   If the owner fails to comply with sub-paragraph (1), then (subject to sub-paragraph (5) below) any amount otherwise due from the occupier to the owner in respect of the pitch fee shall be treated for all purposes as not being due from the occupier to the owner at any time before the owner does so comply.

(3)   Where in accordance with the agreement the owner gives any written notice to the occupier or (as the case may be) a qualifying residents' association, the notice must contain the following information—

    (a)   the name and address of the owner; and

    (b)   if that address is not in England or Wales, an address in England or Wales at which notices (including notices of proceedings) may be served on the owner.

(4)   Subject to sub-paragraph (5) below, where—

    (a)   the occupier or a qualifying residents' association receives such a notice, but

    (b)   it does not contain the information required to be contained in it by virtue of sub-paragraph (3) above,

the notice shall be treated as not having been given until such time as the owner gives the information to the occupier or (as the case may be) the association in respect of the notice.

(5)   An amount or notice within sub-paragraph (2) or (4) (as the case may be) shall not be treated as mentioned in relation to any time when, by virtue of an order of any court or tribunal, there is in force an appointment of a receiver or manager whose functions include receiving from the occupier the pitch fee, payments for services supplied or other charges.

(6)   Nothing in sub-paragraphs (3) to (5) applies to any notice containing a demand to which paragraph 27(1) below applies.

**27.**—(1)   Where the owner makes any demand for payment by the occupier of the pitch fee, or in respect of services supplied or other charges, the demand must contain—

    (a)   the name and address of the owner; and

    (b)   if that address is not in England or Wales, an address in England or Wales at which notices (including notices of proceedings) may be served on the owner.

(2)   Subject to sub-paragraph (3) below, where—

    (a)   the occupier receives such a demand, but

    (b)   it does not contain the information required to be contained in it by virtue of sub-paragraph (1),

the amount demanded shall be treated for all purposes as not being due from the occupier to the owner at any time before the owner gives that information to the occupier in respect of the demand.

(3)   The amount demanded shall not be so treated in relation to any time when, by virtue of an order of any court or tribunal, there is in force an appointment of a receiver or manager whose functions include receiving from the occupier the pitch fee, payments for services supplied or other charges.

**28 Qualifying residents' association**

(1)   A residents' association is a qualifying residents' association in relation to a protected site if—

    (a)   it is an association representing the occupiers of mobile homes on that site;

    (b)   at least 50 per cent of the occupiers of the mobile homes on that site are members of the association;

    (c)   it is independent from the owner, who together with any agent or employee of his is excluded from membership;

    (d)   subject to paragraph (c) above, membership is open to all occupiers who own a mobile home on that site;

    (e)   it maintains a list of members which is open to public inspection together with the rules and constitution of the residents' association;

    (f)   it has a chairman, secretary and treasurer who are elected by and from among the members;

    (g)   with the exception of administrative decisions taken by the chairman, secretary and treasurer acting in their official capacities, decisions are taken by voting and there is only one vote for each mobile home; and

(2)   the owner has acknowledged in writing to the secretary that the association is a qualifying residents' association, or, in default of this, the court has so ordered.

PART II
STATUTORY INSTRUMENTS

(3)    When calculating the percentage of occupiers for the purpose of sub-paragraph (1)(b) above, each mobile home shall be taken to have only one occupier and, in the event of there being more than one occupier of a mobile home, its occupier is to be taken to be the occupier whose name first appears on the agreement.

### 29  Interpretation

In this Schedule—

"pitch" means the land, forming part of the protected site and including any garden area, on which the occupier is entitled to station the mobile home under the terms of the agreement;

"pitch fee" means the amount which the occupier is required by the agreement to pay to the owner for the right to station the mobile home on the pitch and for use of the common areas of the protected site and their maintenance, but does not include amounts due in respect of gas, electricity, water and sewerage or other services, unless the agreement expressly provides that the pitch fee includes such amounts;

"retail prices index" means the general index (for all items) published by the Office for National Statistics or, if that index is not published for a relevant month, any substituted index or index figures published by that Office;

"review date" means the date specified in the written statement as the date on which the pitch fee will be reviewed in each year, or if no such date is specified, each anniversary of the date the agreement commenced; and

"written statement" means the written statement that the owner of the protected site is required to give to the occupier by section 1(2) of this Act."

[3730]

Commencement: 1 October 2006.

PART 4
SUPPLEMENTARY PROVISIONS

*Part 3 of Schedule 1 to the 1983 Act sets out provisions which supplement those in Part 1 of Schedule 1. These are set out below.*

"SCHEDULE 1

PART 3
SUPPLEMENTARY PROVISIONS

### 1  Duty to forward requests under paragraph 8 or 9 of Part 1

(1)    This paragraph applies to—

(a)    a request by the occupier for the owner to approve a person for the purposes of paragraph 8(1) of Part 1 above (see paragraph 8(1A)), or

(b)    a request by the occupier for the owner to approve a person for the purposes of paragraph 9(1) of Part 1 above (see paragraph 8(1A) as applied by paragraph 9(2)).

(2)    If a person ("the recipient") receives such a request and he—

(a)    though not the owner, has an estate or interest in the protected site, and

(b)    believes that another person is the owner (and that the other person has not received such a request),

the recipient owes a duty to the occupier to take such steps as are reasonable to secure that the other person receives the request within the period of 28 days beginning with the date on which the recipient receives it.

(3)    In paragraph 8(1B) of Part III above (as it applies to any request within sub-paragraph (1) above) any reference to the owner receiving such a request includes a reference to his receiving it in accordance with sub-paragraph (2) above.

### 2  Action for breach of duty under paragraph 1

(1)    A claim that a person has broken the duty under paragraph 1(2) above may be made the subject of civil proceedings in like manner as any other claim in tort for breach of statutory duty.

(2)    The right conferred by sub-paragraph (1) is in addition to any right to bring proceedings, in respect of a breach of any implied term having effect by virtue of paragraph 8 or 9 of Part 1 above, against a person bound by that term."

[3731]

Commencement: 1 October 2006.

## PART 5
### EXPRESS TERMS OF THE AGREEMENT

*This part of the written statement sets out other terms of the agreement which may be agreed between you and the site owner in addition to the implied terms.(Terms to be inserted by site owner.)*

**[3732]**

**NOTES**
Commencement: 1 October 2006.

## ALLOCATION OF HOUSING AND HOMELESSNESS (MISCELLANEOUS PROVISIONS) (ENGLAND) REGULATIONS 2006

### (SI 2006/2527)

**NOTES**
Made: 14 September 2006.
Authority: Housing Act 1996, ss 160A(3), 172(4), 185(2), 198(4), 215(2).
Commencement: 9 October 2006.

PART II
STATUTORY INSTRUMENTS

### 1 Citation, commencement, interpretation and application

(1) These Regulations may be cited as the Allocation of Housing and Homelessness (Miscellaneous Provisions) (England) Regulations 2006 and shall come into force on 9th October 2006.

(2) In these Regulations, "the 1996 Act" means the Housing Act 1996.

(3) These Regulations apply to England only.

**[3733]**

**NOTES**
Commencement: 9 October 2006.

### 2 (*Amends the Allocation of Housing and Homelessness (Eligibility) (England) Regulations 2006, SI 2006/1294 at* **[3703]** *et seq.*)

### 3 Prescribed period for referral of case to another local housing authority

For the purposes of section 198(4)(b) of the 1996 Act (referral of case to another local housing authority), the prescribed period is the aggregate of—

(a) five years; and

(b) the period beginning on the date of the previous application and ending on the date on which the applicant was first placed in pursuance of that application in accommodation in the district of the authority to whom the application is now made.

**[3734]**

**NOTES**
Commencement: 9 October 2006.

### 4 Transitional provisions

The amendments made by these Regulations shall not have effect in relation to an applicant whose application for—

(a) an allocation of housing accommodation under Part 6 of the 1996 Act; or

(b) housing assistance under Part 7 of the 1996 Act,

was made before 9th October 2006.

**[3735]**

**NOTES**
Commencement: 9 October 2006.

# HOMELESSNESS (WALES) REGULATIONS 2006

(SI 2006/2646 (W 227))

**NOTES**
Made: 3 October 2006.
Authority: Housing Act 1996, s 185(2), (3).
Commencement: 9 October 2006.

## 1  Title, commencement and application

(1)    The title of these Regulations is the Homelessness (Wales) Regulations 2006 and they come into force on 9 October 2006.

(2)    These Regulations apply to Wales.

**[3736]**

**NOTES**
Commencement: 9 October 2006.

## 2  Interpretation

(1)    In these Regulations—
"the 1971 Act" ("*Deddf 1971*") means the Immigration Act 1971;
"the 1995 Act" ("*Deddf 1995*") means the Jobseekers Act 1995;
"the 1996 Act" ("*Deddf 1996*") means the Housing Act 1996;
"asylum-seeker" ("*ceisydd lloches*") means a person who is not under 18 and who made a claim for asylum which is recorded by the Secretary of State as having been made before 3 April 2000 but which has not been determined;
"claim for asylum" ("*hawliad lloches*") means a claim that it would be contrary to the United Kingdom's obligations under the Refugee Convention for the claimant to be removed from, or required to leave, the United Kingdom;
"the Common Travel Area" ("*Ardal Deithio Gyffredin*") means the United Kingdom, the Channel Islands, the Isle of Man and the Republic of Ireland collectively;
"the immigration rules" ("*y rheolau mewnfudo*") means the rules laid down as mentioned in section 3(2) of the 1971 Act (general provisions for regulation and control);
"limited leave" ("*caniatâd cyfyngedig*") means leave under the 1971 Act to enter or remain in the United Kingdom which is limited as to duration; and
"the Refugee Convention" ("*y Confensiwn ynglyn â Ffoaduriaid*") means the Convention relating to the Status of Refugees done at Geneva on 28 July 1951, as extended by Article 1(2) of the Protocol relating to the Status of Refugees done at New York on 31 January 1967.

(2)    For the purposes of the definition of "asylum-seeker", a claim for asylum is determined at the end of such period beginning—
(a)    on the day on which the Secretary of State notifies the claimant of the decision on the claim; or
(b)    if the claimant has appealed against the Secretary of State's decision, on the day on which the appeal is disposed of,
as may be prescribed under section 94(3) of the Immigration and Asylum Act 1999.

(3)    For the purposes of regulations 3(1)(i) (Class I)—
(a)    "an income-based jobseeker's allowance" ("*lwfans ceisio gwaith ar sail incwm*")means a jobseeker's allowance, payable under the 1995 Act, entitlement to which is based on the claimant satisfying conditions which include those set out in section 3 of the 1995 Act (the income-based conditions);
(b)    "income support" ("*cymhorthdal incwm*") has the same meaning as in section 124 of the Social Security Contributions and Benefits Act 1992 (income support); ...
(c)    a person is on an income-based jobseeker's allowance on any day in respect of which an income-based jobseeker's allowance is payable to that person and on any day—
(i)    in respect of which that person satisfies the conditions for entitlement to an income-based jobseeker's allowance but where the allowance is not paid in accordance with section 19 of the 1995 Act (circumstances in which jobseeker's allowance is not payable); or
(ii)    which is a waiting day for the purposes of paragraph 4 of Schedule 1 to the 1995 Act (waiting days) and which falls immediately before a day in respect of which an income-based jobseeker's allowance is payable to that person or would be payable to that person but for section 19 of the 1995 Act; [and
(d)    "an income-related employment and support allowance" means an employment and

support allowance payable under Part 1 of the Welfare Reform Act 2007 entitlement to which is based on the claimant satisfying conditions which include those set out in Part 2 of Schedule 1 to that Act].

**[3737]**

**NOTES**

Commencement: 9 October 2006.

Para (3): sub-para (b) word omitted revoked, and sub-para (d) and word "and" immediately preceding it inserted, by the Employment and Support Allowance (Consequential Provisions) (No 3) Regulations 2008, SI 2008/1879, reg 31(1), (2).

## 3   Classes of persons subject to immigration control who are eligible for housing assistance

(1)   The following are classes of persons prescribed for the purposes of section 185(2) of the 1996 Act (persons subject to immigration control who are eligible for housing assistance)—

(a)   Class A—a person recorded by the Secretary of State as a refugee within the definition in Article 1 of the Refugee Convention;

(b)   Class B—a person—

    (i)   who has been granted by the Secretary of State exceptional leave to enter or remain in the United Kingdom outside the provisions of the immigration rules; and

    (ii)   whose leave is not subject to a condition requiring that person to maintain and accommodate themselves, and any person who is dependent on that person, without recourse to public funds;

(c)   Class C—a person who has current leave to enter or remain in the United Kingdom which is not subject to any limitation or condition and who is habitually resident in the Common Travel Area other than a person—

    (i)   who has been given leave to enter or remain in the United Kingdom upon an undertaking given by another person (that person's "sponsor") in writing in pursuance of the immigration rules to be responsible for that person's maintenance and accommodation;

    (ii)   who has been resident in the United Kingdom for less than five years beginning on the date of entry or the date on which the undertaking was given in respect of that person, whichever date is the later; and

    (iii)   whose sponsor or, where there more than one sponsor, at least one of whose sponsors, is still alive;

(d)   Class D—a person who left the territory of Montserrat after 1 November 1995 because of the effect on that territory of a volcanic eruption;

(e)   Class E—a person who is habitually resident in the Common Travel Area and who—

    (i)   is a national of a state which has ratified the European Convention on Social and Medical Assistance done at Paris on 11 December 1953 or a state which has ratified the European Social Charter done at Turin on 18 October 1961 and is lawfully present in the United Kingdom; or

    (ii)   before 3 April 2000 was owed a duty by a housing authority under Part III of the Housing Act 1985 (housing and homeless) or Part VII of the 1996 Act (homelessness) which is extant, and who is a national of a state which is a signatory to the European Convention on Social and Medical Assistance done at Paris on 11 December 1953 or a state which is a signatory to the European Social Charter done at Turin on 18 October 1961;

(f)   Class F—a person who is an asylum-seeker and who made a claim for asylum—

    (i)   which is recorded by the Secretary of State as having been made on his arrival (other than on his re-entry) in the United Kingdom from a country outside the Common Travel Area; and

    (ii)   which has not been recorded by the Secretary of State as having been either decided (other than on appeal) or abandoned;

(g)   Class G—a person who is an asylum-seeker and—

    (i)   who was in Great Britain when the Secretary of State made a declaration to the effect that the country of which that person is a national is subject to such a fundamental change in circumstances that the Secretary of State would not normally order the return of a person to that country;

    (ii)   who made a claim for asylum which is recorded by the Secretary of State as having been made within a period of three months from the day on which that declaration was made; and

    (iii)   whose claim for asylum has not been recorded by the Secretary of State as having been either decided (other than on appeal) or abandoned;

(h)   Class H—a person who is an asylum-seeker and—

    (i)   who made a relevant claim for asylum on or before 4 February 1996; and

    (ii)  who was, on 4 February 1996, entitled to benefit under regulation 7A of the Housing Benefit (General) Regulations 1987 (persons from abroad);

  (i)  Class I—a person who is on an income-based jobseeker's allowance[, an income-related employment and support allowance] or in receipt of income support and is eligible for that benefit other than because—

    (i)  that person has limited leave to enter or remain in the United Kingdom which was given in accordance with the relevant immigration rules and that person is temporarily without funds because remittances to that person from abroad have been disrupted; or

    (ii)  that person has been deemed by regulation 3 of the Displaced Persons (Temporary Protection) Regulations 2005 to have been granted leave to enter or remain in the United Kingdom exceptionally for the purposes of the provision of means of subsistence; and

  (j)  Class J—a person who has humanitarian protection granted under the Immigration Rules.

(2)  In paragraph (1)(h)(i) (Class H), a relevant claim for asylum is a claim for asylum which—

  (a)  has not been recorded by the Secretary of State as having been either decided (other than on appeal) or abandoned; or

  (b)  has been recorded as having been decided (other than on appeal) on or before 4 February 1996 and in respect of which an appeal is pending which—

    (i)  was pending on 5 February 1996; or

    (ii)  was made within the time limits specified in the rules of procedure made under section 22 of the 1971 Act (procedure).

(3)  In paragraph (1)(i)(i) (Class I), "relevant immigration rules" ("*rheolau mewnfudo perthnasol*") means the immigration rules relating to—

  (a)  there being or there needing to be no recourse

  (b)  there being no charge on public funds.

(4)  In paragraph (1)(i) (Class I), "means of subsistence" ("*moddion byw*") has the same meaning as in regulation 4 of the Displaced Persons (Temporary Protection) Regulations 2005.

**[3738]**

**NOTES**

Commencement: 9 October 2006.

Para (1): sub-para (i) words in square brackets inserted by the Employment and Support Allowance (Consequential Provisions) (No 3) Regulations 2008, SI 2008/1879, reg 31(1), (3).

## 4 Description of persons who are to be treated as persons from abroad ineligible for housing assistance

(1)  The following are descriptions of persons, other than persons who are subject to immigration control, who are to be treated for the purposes of Part VII of the 1996 Act (homelessness) as persons from abroad who are ineligible for housing assistance—

  (a)  subject to paragraphs (2) and (3), a person who is not habitually resident in the United Kingdom, the Channel Islands, the Isle of Man or the Republic of Ireland;

  (b)  a person whose right to reside in the United Kingdom, the Channel Islands, the Isle of Man or the Republic of Ireland is derived solely from Council Directive No 90/364/EEC or Council Directive No 90/365/EEC

(2)  The following persons will not, however, be treated as persons from abroad who are ineligible pursuant to paragraph (1)(a)—

  (a)  a person who is a worker for the purposes of Council Regulation (EEC) No 1612/68 or (EEC) No 1251/70;

  (b)  a person who is an accession state worker requiring registration who is treated as a worker for the purpose of the definition of "qualified person" in regulation 6 of the Immigration (European Economic Area) Regulations 2006 pursuant to regulation 5 of the Accession (Immigration and Worker Registration) Regulations 2004;

  (c)  a person with a right to reside pursuant to the Immigration (European Economic Area) Regulations 2006, which is derived from Council Directive No 68/360/EEC, No 73/148/EEC or No 75/34/EEC;

  (d)  a person who left the territory of Montserrat after 1 November 1995 because of the effect on that territory of a volcanic eruption[;

  (e)  a person who—

    (i)  arrived in Great Britain on or after 28 February 2009 but before 18 March 2011;

    (ii)  immediately before arriving in Great Britain had been resident in Zimbabwe; and

    (iii)  before leaving Zimbabwe, had accepted an offer, made by Her Majesty's Government, to assist that person to settle in the United Kingdom].

(3)    A person will not be treated as habitually resident in the United Kingdom, the Channel Islands, the Isle of Man or the Republic of Ireland for the purposes of paragraph (1)(a) if he does not have a right to reside in the United Kingdom, the Channel Islands, the Isle of Man or the Republic of Ireland.

**[3739]**

**NOTES**
   Commencement: 9 October 2006.
   Para (2): sub-para (e) inserted by the Allocation of Housing and Homelessness (Eligibility) (Wales) Regulations 2009, SI 2009/393, reg 3.

**5   Transitional Provisions**

The amendments made by these Regulations do not have effect in relation to an applicant whose application for housing assistance under Part VII of the 1996 Act was made before 9 October 2006.

**[3740]**

**NOTES**
   Commencement: 9 October 2006.

**6**    (*Revokes the Homelessness (Wales) Regulations 2000, SI 2000/1079.*)

# HOUSING (MANAGEMENT ORDERS AND EMPTY DWELLING MANAGEMENT ORDERS) (SUPPLEMENTAL PROVISIONS) (WALES) REGULATIONS 2006 (NOTE)

(SI 2006/2822 (W 245))

**NOTES**
   Made: 25 October 2006.
   Authority: Housing Act 2004, s 145.
   Commencement: 26 October 2006.
   These Regulations apply to Wales only. The equivalent provisions for England are in SI 2006/368 at **[3602]** et seq.

**[3741]**

# HOUSING (EMPTY DWELLING MANAGEMENT ORDERS) (PRESCRIBED EXCEPTIONS AND REQUIREMENTS) (WALES) ORDER 2006 (NOTE)

(SI 2006/2823 (W 246))

**NOTES**
   Made: 25 October 2006.
   Authority: Housing Act 2004, s 134(5)(a), (c), (6).
   Commencement: 26 October 2006.
   This Order applies to Wales only. The equivalent provisions for England are in SI 2006/367 at **[3598]** et seq.

**[3742]**

# SELECTIVE LICENSING OF HOUSES (SPECIFIED EXEMPTIONS) (WALES) ORDER 2006 (NOTE)

(SI 2006/2824 (W 247))

**NOTES**
   Made: 25 October 2006.
   Authority: Housing Act 2004, s 79(4).
   Commencement: 26 October 2006.
   This Order applies to Wales only. The equivalent provisions for England are in SI 2006/370 at **[3607]** et seq.

**[3743]**

# SELECTIVE LICENSING OF HOUSES (ADDITIONAL CONDITIONS) (WALES) ORDER 2006

## (SI 2006/2825 (W 248))

**NOTES**
Made: 25 October 2006.
Authority: Housing Act 2004, s 80(7).
Commencement: 26 October 2006.

## 1 Title, commencement and application

(1) The title of this Order is The Selective Licensing of Houses (Additional Conditions) (Wales) Order 2006, and it comes into force on 26 October 2006.

(2) This Order applies to houses and dwellings to which Part 3 of the Act applies in relation to Wales.

**[3744]**

**NOTES**
Commencement: 26 October 2006.

## 2 Interpretation

In this Order—
    (a)    "the Act" ("*Y Ddeddf*") means the Housing Act 2004;
    (b)    "the 1989 Act" ("*Deddf 1989*") means the Local Government and Housing Act 1989; and
    (c)    "the 2002 Order" ("*Gorchymyn 2002*") means the Regulatory Reform (Housing Assistance) (England and Wales) Order 2002.

**[3745]**

**NOTES**
Commencement: 26 October 2006.

## 3 Additional Conditions

(1) Subject to paragraph (2), for the purposes of section 80(2)(b) of the Act either the first or second condition applies—
    (a)    the first condition is that, either
        (i)    a local housing authority has declared an area as a renewal area under section 89 of the 1989 Act; or
        (ii)    a local housing authority has provided assistance to any person in accordance with an adopted and published policy under articles 3 and 4 of the 2002 Order in that area (power of local housing authorities to provide assistance);
    (b)    The second condition is that the area of their district or area in their district comprises a minimum of 25% of housing stock let by private sector landlords.

(2) A local housing authority must be satisfied that either of the conditions set out under sub-paragraph (a) or (b) of paragraph (1) are met before designating an area of their district or in their district as subject to selective licensing.

**[3746]**

**NOTES**
Commencement: 26 October 2006.

# HOUSING (ASSESSMENT OF ACCOMMODATION NEEDS) (MEANING OF GYPSIES AND TRAVELLERS) (ENGLAND) REGULATIONS 2006

## (SI 2006/3190)

**NOTES**
Made: 27 November 2006.
Authority: Housing Act 2004, s 225(5)(a).
Commencement: 2 January 2007.

**1    Citation, commencement and application**

(1)    These Regulations may be cited as the Housing (Assessment of Accommodation Needs) (Meaning of Gypsies and Travellers) (England) Regulations 2006 and shall come into force on 2nd January 2007.

(2)    These Regulations apply where a local housing authority in England undertakes a review of housing needs in their district under section 8 of the Housing Act 1985.

**[3747]**

**NOTES**
Commencement: 2 January 2007.

**2    Meaning of Gypsies and Travellers for the Purposes of Section 225 of the Housing Act 2004**

For the purposes of section 225 of the Housing Act 2004 (duties of local housing authorities: accommodation needs of gypsies and travellers) "gypsies and travellers" means—

(a)    persons with a cultural tradition of nomadism or of living in a caravan; and

(b)    all other persons of a nomadic habit of life, whatever their race or origin, including—

(i)    such persons who, on grounds only of their own or their family's or dependant's educational or health needs or old age, have ceased to travel temporarily or permanently; and

(ii)    members of an organised group of travelling showpeople or circus people (whether or not travelling together as such).

**[3748]**

**NOTES**
Commencement: 2 January 2007.

# RENT REPAYMENT ORDERS (SUPPLEMENTARY PROVISIONS) (ENGLAND) REGULATIONS 2007

(SI 2007/572)

**NOTES**
Made: 27 February 2007.
Authority: Housing Act 2004, ss 74(15), 97(15).
Commencement: 6 April 2007.

**1    Citation, commencement, application and interpretation**

(1)    These Regulations may be cited as the Rent Repayment Orders (Supplementary Provisions) (England) Regulations 2007 and shall come into force on 6th April 2007.

(2)    These Regulations apply in relation to England only.

(3)    In these Regulations, "the Act" means the Housing Act 2004.

**[3749]**

**NOTES**
Commencement: 6 April 2007.

**2    Overpayments of housing benefit**

(1)    Paragraph (2) applies if, in the course of proceedings on an application under subsection (5) of section 73 of the Act (other consequences of operating unlicensed HMOs: rent repayment orders) or subsection (5) of section 96 of the Act (other consequences of operating unlicensed houses: rent repayment orders), it comes to the notice of the local housing authority that in respect of periodical payments payable in connection with occupation of the part or parts of the HMO or of the whole or part of the house to which the application applies there may have been a payment of housing benefit that was not properly payable.

(2)    A local housing authority may apply to the residential property tribunal for leave to amend their application by substituting for the total amount of housing benefit paid, such part of that amount as they believe is properly payable.

(3)    For the purposes of paragraphs (1) and (2)—

(a)    an amount of housing benefit is properly payable if the person to whom, or in respect of whom, it is paid is entitled to it under the Housing Benefit Regulations 2006 or the Housing Benefit (Persons who have attained the qualifying age for state pension credit)

Regulations 2006 (whether on the initial decision or as subsequently revised or superseded or further revised or superseded), and

(b) "overpayment of housing benefit" has the meaning given by regulation 99 of the Housing Benefit Regulations 2006 or, as the case may be, regulation 80 of the Housing Benefit (Persons who have obtained the qualifying age for state pension credit) Regulations 2006.

**[3750]**

---

**NOTES**
Commencement: 6 April 2007.

---

**3**—(1) Subject to paragraph (3), a local housing authority may apply an amount recovered under a rent repayment order for any of the purposes mentioned in paragraph (2).

(2) The purposes are the reimbursement of the authority's costs and expenses (whether administrative or legal) incurred in, or associated with—

(a) the making of the application under section 73(5) of the Act or, as the case may be, section 96(5) of the Act;

(b) the registration and enforcement of any legal charge under section 74(9)(b) or 97(9)(b) of the Act on the relevant property;

(c) dealing with any application for the grant of a licence in respect of the relevant property under Part 2 of the Act (licensing of HMOs) or, as the case may be, Part 3 of the Act (selective licensing of other residential accommodation);

(d) the prosecution of the appropriate person for an offence under section 72(1) of the Act or, as the case may be, section 95(1) of the Act, in relation to the relevant property (whether proceedings are instituted before or after the making of the order);

(e) the making of an interim or final management order under Chapter 1 of Part 4 of the Act (interim and final management orders) in respect of the relevant property (whether the management order is made before or after the making of the rent repayment order);

(f) the management of the relevant property while an interim or final management order is in force;

(g) the execution of works undertaken in relation to the relevant property while an interim management order is in force; and

(h) the preparation of, or execution of works under, a management scheme under section 119 of the Act (management schemes and accounts) while a final management order is in force.

(3) Nothing in paragraph (1) authorises the application of an amount by way of reimbursement of an authority's costs or expenses where a court or residential property tribunal has made an order with respect to all or some of those costs or expenses.

(4) In paragraph (2), "the relevant property" means the HMO or house to which the rent repayment order relates.

**[3751]**

---

**NOTES**
Commencement: 6 April 2007.

---

**4 Treatment of surpluses**

An amount recovered under a rent repayment order which is not applied for a purpose mentioned in regulation 3(2), shall be paid into the Consolidated Fund.

**[3752]**

---

**NOTES**
Commencement: 6 April 2007.

---

# APPROVAL OF CODE OF PRACTICE (PRIVATE RETIREMENT HOUSING) (WALES) ORDER 2007 (NOTE)

(SI 2007/578 (W 50))

---

**NOTES**
Made: 27 February 2007.
Authority: Leasehold Reform, Housing and Urban Development Act 1993, ss 87, 100.

Commencement: 2 March 2007.
This Order applies to Wales only. The equivalent provisions for England are in SI 2005/3307 at **[3594]** et seq.

**[3753]**

# SMOKE-FREE (EXEMPTIONS AND VEHICLES) REGULATIONS 2007

## (SI 2007/765)

**NOTES**
Made: 7 March 2007.
Authority: Health Act 2006, ss 3, 5 and 79(3).
Commencement: 1 July 2007.
These regulations, which apply in relation to England, provide exemptions from the smoke-free requirements of the Health Act 2006, s 2, and provide for most public and work vehicles to be smoke-free under s 5 thereof. In relation to the smoke-free requirements of Chapter 1 of Part 1 of the Health Act 2006, see also:
the Smoke-free (Penalties and Discounted Amounts) Regulations 2007, SI 2007/764 (made under ss 6(8), 7(6), 8(7), 79(3), Sch 1, paras 5, 8);
the Smoke-free (Premises and Enforcement) Regulations 2006, SI 2006/3368 (made under ss 2(5), 10(1), (2), 79(3));
the Smoke-free Premises etc (Wales) Regulations 2007, SI 2007/787 (made under ss 2(5), 3, 5(1), (2), 6, 8(3), 10, 79(3), Sch 1, para 4 and the Welsh Language Act 1993, s 26);
the Smoke-free (Signs) Regulations 2007, SI 2007/923 (made under ss 6(2)–(4), 79(3)); and
the Smoke-free (Vehicle Operators and Penalty Notices) Regulations 2007, SI 2007/760 (made under ss 8(3), 79(3), Sch 1, para 4).

## PART 1
## GENERAL

### 1   Citation, commencement and application

(1)   These Regulations which may be cited as the Smoke-free (Exemptions and Vehicles) Regulations 2007 shall come into force on 1st July 2007.

(2)   These Regulations apply in relation to England.

**[3754]**

**NOTES**
Commencement: 1 July 2007.

## PART 2
## EXEMPTIONS

### 2   Application of Part 2
The exemptions in this Part apply only to premises that would be smoke-free under section 2 of the Health Act 2006 if those exemptions had not been made.

**[3755]**

**NOTES**
Commencement: 1 July 2007.

### 3   Private accommodation

(1)   A private dwelling is not smoke-free except for any part of it which is—
   (a)   used in common in relation to more than one set of premises (including premises so used in relation to any other private dwelling or dwellings); or
   (b)   used solely as a place of work (other than work that is excluded by paragraph (2)) by—
      (i)     more than one person who does not live in the dwelling;
      (ii)    a person who does not live in the dwelling and any person who does live in the dwelling; or
      (iii)   a person (whether he lives in the dwelling or not) who in the course of his work invites persons who do not live or work in the dwelling to attend the part of it which is used solely for work.

(2)   There is excluded from paragraph (1)(b) all work that is undertaken solely—
   (a)   to provide personal care for a person living in the dwelling;
   (b)   to assist with the domestic work of the household in the dwelling;
   (c)   to maintain the structure or fabric of the dwelling; or

(d)   to install, maintain or remove any service provided to the dwelling for the benefit of persons living in it.

(3)   In this regulation, "private dwelling" includes self-contained residential accommodation for temporary or holiday use and any garage, outhouse or other structure for the exclusive use of persons living in the dwelling.

**[3756]**

**NOTES**
Commencement: 1 July 2007.

## 4  Accommodation for guests and club members

(1)   A designated bedroom in a hotel, guest house, inn, hostel or members' club is not smoke-free.

(2)   In this regulation "a designated bedroom" means a room which—
  (a)   is set apart exclusively for sleeping accommodation;
  (b)   has been designated in writing by the person having the charge of the premises in which the room is situated as being a room in which smoking is permitted;
  (c)   has a ceiling and, except for doors and windows, is completely enclosed on all sides by solid, floor-to-ceiling walls;
  (d)   does not have a ventilation system that ventilates into any other part of the premises (except any other designated bedrooms);
  (e)   does not have any door that opens onto smoke-free premises which is not mechanically closed immediately after use; and
  (f)   is clearly marked as a bedroom in which smoking is permitted.

(3)   In this regulation "bedroom" does not include any dormitory or other room that a person in charge of premises makes available under separate arrangements for persons to share at the same time.

**[3757]**

**NOTES**
Commencement: 1 July 2007.

## 5  Other residential accommodation

(1)   A designated room that is used as accommodation for persons aged 18 years or over in the premises specified in paragraph (2) is not smoke-free.

(2)   The specified premises are—
  (a)   care homes as defined in section 3 (care homes) of the Care Standards Act 2000;
  (b)   hospices which as their whole or main purpose provide palliative care for persons resident there who are suffering from progressive disease in its final stages; and
  (c)   prisons.

(3)   In this regulation "designated room" means a bedroom or a room used only for smoking which—
  (a)   has been designated in writing by the person having charge of the premises in which the room is situated as being a room in which smoking is permitted;
  (b)   has a ceiling and, except for doors and windows, is completely enclosed on all sides by solid, floor-to-ceiling walls;
  (c)   does not have a ventilation system that ventilates into any other part of the premises (except any other designated rooms);
  (d)   is clearly marked as a room in which smoking is permitted; and
  (e)   except where the room is in a prison, does not have any door that opens onto smoke-free premises which is not mechanically closed immediately after use.

**[3758]**

**NOTES**
Commencement: 1 July 2007.

**6–11**   *(Outside the scope of this work.)*

# SERVICE CHARGES (SUMMARY OF RIGHTS AND OBLIGATIONS, AND TRANSITIONAL PROVISION) (ENGLAND) REGULATIONS 2007

### (SI 2007/1257)

**NOTES**
  Made: 16 April 2007.
  Authority: Landlord and Tenant Act 1985, s 21B; Commonhold and Leasehold Reform Act 2002, s 178.
  Commencement: 1 October 2007.

## 1  Citation and commencement

These Regulations may be cited as the Service Charges (Summary of Rights and Obligations, and Transitional Provision) (England) Regulations 2007 and shall come into force on the 1st October 2007.

**[3759]**

**NOTES**
  Commencement: 1 October 2007.

## 2  Application

(1)  Subject to regulation 4, these Regulations apply where, on or after 1st October 2007, a demand for payment of a service charge is served in relation to a dwelling.

(2)  Subject to paragraph (3) these Regulations apply to dwellings in England which are subject to a lease.

(3)  These Regulations do not apply where—
  (a)  the lease is not a long lease within section 26 of the Landlord and Tenant Act 1985; and
  (b)  the landlord is a local authority, a National Park Authority or a new town corporation.

**[3760]**

**NOTES**
  Commencement: 1 October 2007.

## 3  Form and content of summary of rights and obligations of interest

Where these Regulations apply the summary of rights and obligations which must accompany a demand for the payment of a service charge must be legible in a typewritten or printed form of at least 10 point, and must contain—
  (a)  the title "Service Charges—Summary of tenants' rights and obligations"; and
  (b)  the following statement—

  "(1)  This summary, which briefly sets out your rights and obligations in relation to variable service charges, must by law accompany a demand for service charges. Unless a summary is sent to you with a demand, you may withhold the service charge. The summary does not give a full interpretation of the law and if you are in any doubt about your rights and obligations you should seek independent advice.

  (2)  Your lease sets out your obligations to pay service charges to your landlord in addition to your rent. Service charges are amounts payable for services, repairs, maintenance, improvements, insurance or the landlord's costs of management, to the extent that the costs have been reasonably incurred.

  (3)  You have the right to ask a leasehold valuation tribunal to determine whether you are liable to pay service charges for services, repairs, maintenance, improvements, insurance or management. You may make a request before or after you have paid the service charge. If the tribunal determines that the service charge is payable, the tribunal may also determine—
  who should pay the service charge and who it should be paid to;
  the amount;
  the date it should be paid by; and
  how it should be paid.

  However, you do not have these rights where—
  a matter has been agreed or admitted by you;
  a matter has already been, or is to be, referred to arbitration or has been determined by arbitration and you agreed to go to arbitration after the disagreement about the service charge or costs arose; or
  a matter has been decided by a court.

(4)   If your lease allows your landlord to recover costs incurred or that may be incurred in legal proceedings as service charges, you may ask the court or tribunal, before which those proceedings were brought, to rule that your landlord may not do so.

(5)   Where you seek a determination from a leasehold valuation tribunal, you will have to pay an application fee and, where the matter proceeds to a hearing, a hearing fee, unless you qualify for a waiver or reduction. The total fees payable will not exceed £500, but making an application may incur additional costs, such as professional fees, which you may also have to pay.

(6)   A leasehold valuation tribunal has the power to award costs, not exceeding £500, against a party to any proceedings where—

> it dismisses a matter because it is frivolous, vexatious or an abuse of process; or
> it considers a party has acted frivolously, vexatiously, abusively, disruptively or unreasonably.

The [Upper Tribunal] has similar powers when hearing an appeal against a decision of a leasehold valuation tribunal.

(7)   If your landlord—

> proposes works on a building or any other premises that will cost you or any other tenant more than £250, or
> proposes to enter into an agreement for works or services which will last for more than 12 months and will cost you or any other tenant more than £100 in any 12 month accounting period,
> your contribution will be limited to these amounts unless your landlord has properly consulted on the proposed works or agreement or a leasehold valuation tribunal has agreed that consultation is not required.

(8)   You have the right to apply to a leasehold valuation tribunal to ask it to determine whether your lease should be varied on the grounds that it does not make satisfactory provision in respect of the calculation of a service charge payable under the lease.

(9)   You have the right to write to your landlord to request a written summary of the costs which make up the service charges. The summary must—

> cover the last 12 month period used for making up the accounts relating to the service charge ending no later than the date of your request, where the accounts are made up for 12 month periods; or
> cover the 12 month period ending with the date of your request, where the accounts are not made up for 12 month periods.

The summary must be given to you within 1 month of your request or 6 months of the end of the period to which the summary relates whichever is the later.

(10)   You have the right, within 6 months of receiving a written summary of costs, to require the landlord to provide you with reasonable facilities to inspect the accounts, receipts and other documents supporting the summary and for taking copies or extracts from them.

(11)   You have the right to ask an accountant or surveyor to carry out an audit of the financial management of the premises containing your dwelling, to establish the obligations of your landlord and the extent to which the service charges you pay are being used efficiently. It will depend on your circumstances whether you can exercise this right alone or only with the support of others living in the premises. You are strongly advised to seek independent advice before exercising this right.

(12)   Your lease may give your landlord a right of re-entry or forfeiture where you have failed to pay charges which are properly due under the lease. However, to exercise this right, the landlord must meet all the legal requirements and obtain a court order. A court order will only be granted if you have admitted you are liable to pay the amount or it is finally determined by a court, tribunal or by arbitration that the amount is due. The court has a wide discretion in granting such an order and it will take into account all the circumstances of the case.".

**[3761]**

**NOTES**
Commencement: 1 October 2007.
Para (3): in sub-para (b) in para (6) of the statement words in square brackets substituted by the Transfer of Tribunal Functions (Lands Tribunal and Miscellaneous Amendments) Order 2009, SI 2009/1307, art 5(1), (3), Sch 2, para 119, as from 1 June 2009, subject to savings and transitional provisions for the treatment of cases which would previously have been dealt with by the Lands Tribunal, and onward appeals from that Tribunal (see art 5(6), Sch 5 to that Order).

**4   Transitional provision**

The following provisions apply where a demand ("the first demand") for the payment of service charges was served prior to 1st October 2007—

    (a)    the requirements of section 21B(3) and (4) of the Landlord and Tenant Act 1985, as inserted by section 153 of the Act, shall not apply to a further demand for the payment of service charges where the first demand was served before 1st October 2007 in respect of service charges due for payment before 1st October 2007; and

    (b)    section 21B of the Landlord and Tenant Act 1985 shall apply to a further demand for the payment of service charges where the first demand was served before 1st October 2007 in respect of service charges due for payment on or after 1st October 2007.

**[3762]**

---

**NOTES**
Commencement: 1 October 2007.

---

# ADMINISTRATION CHARGES (SUMMARY OF RIGHTS AND OBLIGATIONS) (ENGLAND) REGULATIONS 2007

## (SI 2007/1258)

---

**NOTES**
Made: 16 April 2007.
Authority: Commonhold and Leasehold Reform Act 2002, Sch 11, para 4(2).
Commencement: 1 October 2007.

**1   Citation, commencement and application**

    (1)   These Regulations may be cited as the Administration Charges (Summary of Rights and Obligations) (England) Regulations 2007 and shall come into force on 1st October 2007.

    (2)   These Regulations apply where, on or after 1st October 2007, a demand for payment of an administration charge is served in relation to a dwelling in England.

**[3763]**

---

**NOTES**
Commencement: 1 October 2007.

---

**2   Form and content of summary of rights and obligations**

The summary of rights and obligations which must accompany a demand for the payment of an administration charge must be legible in a typewritten or printed form of at least 10 point, and must contain—

    (a)    the title "Administration Charges–Summary of tenants' rights and obligations"; and

    (b)    the following statement—

"(1)   This summary, which briefly sets out your rights and obligations in relation to administration charges, must by law accompany a demand for administration charges. Unless a summary is sent to you with a demand, you may withhold the administration charge. The summary does not give a full interpretation of the law and if you are in any doubt about your rights and obligations you should seek independent advice.

(2)   An administration charge is an amount which may be payable by you as part of or in addition to the rent directly or indirectly—

    for or in connection with the grant of an approval under your lease, or an application for such approval;

    for or in connection with the provision of information or documents;

    in respect of your failure to make any payment due under your lease; or

    in connection with a breach of a covenant or condition of your lease.

If you are liable to pay an administration charge, it is payable only to the extent that the amount is reasonable.

(3)   Any provision contained in a grant of a lease under the right to buy under the Housing Act 1985, which claims to allow the landlord to charge a sum for consent or approval, is void.

(4)   You have the right to ask a leasehold valuation tribunal whether an administration charge is payable. You may make a request before or after you have paid the administration charge. If the tribunal determines the charge is payable, the tribunal may also determine—

    who should pay the administration charge and who it should be paid to;

    the amount;

the date it should be paid by; and
how it should be paid.

However, you do not have this right where—

a matter has been agreed to or admitted by you;

a matter has been, or is to be, referred to arbitration or has been determined by arbitration and you agreed to go to arbitration after the disagreement about the administration charge arose; or

a matter has been decided by a court.

(5)   You have the right to apply to a leasehold valuation tribunal for an order varying the lease on the grounds that any administration charge specified in the lease, or any formula specified in the lease for calculating an administration charge is unreasonable.

(6)   Where you seek a determination or order from a leasehold valuation tribunal, you will have to pay an application fee and, where the matter proceeds to a hearing, a hearing fee, unless you qualify for a waiver or reduction. The total fees payable to the tribunal will not exceed £500, but making an application may incur additional costs, such as professional fees, which you may have to pay.

(7)   A leasehold valuation tribunal has the power to award costs, not exceeding £500, against a party to any proceedings where—

it dismisses a matter because it is frivolous, vexatious or an abuse of process; or

it considers that a party has acted frivolously, vexatiously, abusively, disruptively or unreasonably.

The [Upper Tribunal] has similar powers when hearing an appeal against a decision of a leasehold valuation tribunal.

(8)   Your lease may give your landlord a right of re-entry or forfeiture where you have failed to pay charges which are properly due under the lease. However, to exercise this right, the landlord must meet all the legal requirements and obtain a court order. A court order will only be granted if you have admitted you are liable to pay the amount or it is finally determined by a court, a tribunal or by arbitration that the amount is due. The court has a wide discretion in granting such an order and it will take into account all the circumstances of the case.".

**[3764]**

**NOTES**
Commencement: 1 October 2007.
Para (b): in para (7) of the statement words in square brackets substituted by the Transfer of Tribunal Functions (Lands Tribunal and Miscellaneous Amendments) Order 2009, SI 2009/1307, art 5(1), (3), Sch 2, para 120, as from 1 June 2009, subject to savings and transitional provisions for the treatment of cases which would previously have been dealt with by the Lands Tribunal, and onward appeals from that Tribunal (see art 5(6), Sch 5 to that Order).

# LICENSING AND MANAGEMENT OF HOUSES IN MULTIPLE OCCUPATION (ADDITIONAL PROVISIONS) (ENGLAND) REGULATIONS 2007

## (SI 2007/1903)

**NOTES**
Made: 28 June 2007.
Authority: Housing Act 2004, ss 63(5), (6), 65(3), (4), 87(5), (6), 232(3), (7), 234.
Commencement: 1 October 2007.

### ARRANGEMENT OF REGULATIONS

## 1  Citation, commencement and application

(1)    These Regulations may be cited as the Licensing and Management of Houses in Multiple Occupation (Additional Provisions) (England) Regulations 2007 and shall come into force on 1st October 2007.

(2)    Regulations 2 to 11 apply to any HMO in England which is an HMO to which section 257 of the Housing Act 2004 applies and regulation 12 applies to any HMO in England to which Part 2 of that Act (licensing of houses in multiple occupation) applies.

**[3765]**

**NOTES**
Commencement: 1 October 2007.

## 2  Interpretation

In these Regulations—
    (a)    "the Act" means the Housing Act 2004;
    (b)    "fixtures, fittings or appliances" are—
        (i)    lighting, space heating or water heating appliances;
        (ii)    toilets, baths, showers, sinks, or wash basins or any cupboards, shelving or fittings supplied in a bathroom or lavatory;
        (iii)    cupboards, shelving or appliances used for the storage, preparation or cooking of food; and
        (iv)    washing machines or other laundry appliances; and
    (c)    "the manager", in relation to an HMO, means the person managing the HMO.

**[3766]**

**NOTES**
Commencement: 1 October 2007.

## 3  Manager's duties: general

(1)    Regulations 4 to 10 shall apply subject to the following limitations—
    (a)    the manager's duty shall only apply in relation to such parts of the HMO over which it would be reasonable to expect the licence holder, in all the circumstances, to exercise control; and
    (b)    the manager's duty to maintain or keep in repair is to be construed as requiring a standard of maintenance or repair that is reasonable in all the circumstances, taking account of the age, character and prospective life of the house and the locality in which it is situated.

(2)    Nothing in regulations 4 to 10 shall—
    (a)    require or authorise anything to be done in connection with the water supply or drainage or the supply of gas or electricity otherwise than in accordance with any enactment; or
    (b)    oblige the manager to take, in connection with those matters, any action which is the responsibility of a local authority or any other person, other than such action as may be necessary to bring the matter promptly to the attention of the authority or person concerned.

**[3767]**

**NOTES**
Commencement: 1 October 2007.

## 4  Duty of manager to provide information to occupier

The manager must ensure that his name, address and any telephone contact number are clearly displayed in a prominent position in the common parts of the HMO so that they may be seen by all occupiers.

**[3768]**

**NOTES**
Commencement: 1 October 2007.

## 5  Duty of manager to take safety measures

(1)    The manager must ensure that all means of escape from fire in the HMO are—
    (a)    kept free from obstruction; and
    (b)    maintained in good order and repair.

(2) The manager must ensure that any fire fighting equipment and fire alarms are maintained in good working order.

(3) The manager must ensure that all notices indicating the location of means of escape from fire are displayed in positions within the common parts of the HMO that enable them to be clearly visible to all the occupiers.

(4) The manager must take all such measures as are reasonably required to protect the occupiers of the HMO from injury, having regard to—

    (a) the design of the HMO;

    (b) the structural conditions in the HMO; and

    (c) the number of flats or occupiers in the HMO.

(5) In performing the duty imposed by paragraph (4) the manager must in particular—

    (a) in relation to any roof or balcony that is unsafe, either ensure that it is made safe or take all reasonable measures to prevent access to it for so long as it remains unsafe; and

    (b) in relation to any window the sill of which is at or near floor level, ensure that bars or other such safeguards as may be necessary are provided to protect the occupiers against the danger of accidents which may be caused in connection with such windows.

[3769]

**NOTES**
Commencement: 1 October 2007.

## 6 Duty of manager to maintain water supply and drainage

(1) The manager must ensure that the water supply and drainage system serving the HMO is maintained in good, clean and working condition and in particular he must ensure that—

    (a) any tank, cistern or similar receptacle used for the storage of water for drinking or other domestic purposes is kept in a good, clean and working condition, with a cover kept over it to keep the water in a clean and proper condition; and

    (b) any water fitting which is liable to damage by frost is protected from frost damage.

(2) The manager must not unreasonably cause or permit the water or drainage supply that is used by any occupier at the HMO to be interrupted.

(3) In this regulation "water fitting" means a pipe, tap, cock, valve, ferrule, meter, cistern, bath, water closet or soil pan used in connection with the supply or use of water, but the reference in this definition to a pipe does not include an overflow pipe or the mains supply pipe.

[3770]

**NOTES**
Commencement: 1 October 2007.

## 7 Duty of manager to supply and maintain gas and electricity

(1) The manager must supply to the local housing authority within 7 days of receiving a request in writing from that authority the latest gas appliance test certificate it has received in relation to the testing of any gas appliance at the HMO by a recognised engineer.

[(2) In paragraph (1), "recognised engineer" means an engineer approved under regulation 3 of the Gas Safety (Installation and Use) Regulations 1998.]

(3) The manager must—

    (a) ensure that every fixed electrical installation is inspected and tested at intervals not exceeding five years by a person qualified to undertake such inspection and testing;

    (b) obtain a certificate from the person conducting that test, specifying the results of the test; and

    (c) supply that certificate to the local housing authority within 7 days of receiving a request in writing for it from that authority.

(4) The manager must not unreasonably cause the gas or electricity supply that is used by any occupier within the HMO to be interrupted.

[3771]

**NOTES**
Commencement: 1 October 2007.
Para (2): substituted by the Houses in Multiple Occupation (Management) (England) Regulations 2009, SI 2009/724, reg 3.

## 8 Duty of manager to maintain common parts, fixtures, fittings and appliances

(1) The manager must ensure that all common parts of the HMO are—

    (a) maintained in good and clean decorative repair;

    (b) maintained in a safe and working condition; and

    (c)    kept reasonably clear from obstruction.

  (2)   In performing the duty imposed by paragraph (1), the manager must in particular ensure that—

    (a)    all handrails and banisters are at all times kept in good repair;

    (b)    such additional handrails or banisters as are necessary for the safety of the occupiers of the HMO are provided;

    (c)    any stair coverings are safely fixed and kept in good repair;

    (d)    all windows and other means of ventilation within the common parts are kept in good repair;

    (e)    the common parts are fitted with adequate light fittings that are available for use at all times by every occupier of the HMO; and

    (f)    subject to paragraph (3), fixtures, fittings or appliances used in common by two or more households within the HMO are maintained in good and safe repair and in clean working order.

  (3)   The duty imposed by paragraph (2)(f) does not apply in relation to fixtures, fittings or appliances that the occupier is entitled to remove from the HMO or which are otherwise outside the control of the manager.

  (4)   The manager must ensure that—

    (a)    outbuildings, yards and forecourts which are used in common by two or more households living within the HMO are maintained in repair, clean condition and good order;

    (b)    any garden belonging to the HMO is kept in a safe and tidy condition; and

    (c)    boundary walls, fences and railings (including any basement area railings), in so far as they belong to the HMO, are kept and maintained in good and safe repair so as not to constitute a danger to occupiers.

  (5)   If any part of the HMO is not in use the manager shall ensure that such part, including any passage and staircase directly giving access to it, is kept reasonably clean and free from refuse and litter.

  (6)   In this regulation—

    (a)    "common parts" means—

        (i)    the entrance door to the HMO and the entrance doors leading to each unit of living accommodation within the HMO; and

       (ii)    all such parts of the HMO as comprise staircases, lifts, passageways, corridors, halls, lobbies, entrances, balconies, porches and steps that are used by the occupiers of the units of living accommodation within the HMO to gain access to the entrance doors of their respective unit of living accommodation.

**[3772]**

**NOTES**

Commencement: 1 October 2007.

## 9  Duty of manager to maintain living accommodation

  (1)   Subject to paragraph (4), the manager must ensure that each unit of living accommodation within the HMO and any furniture supplied with it are in clean condition at the beginning of a person's occupation of it.

  (2)   Subject to paragraphs (3) and (4), the manager must ensure, in relation to each part of the HMO that is used as living accommodation, that—

    (a)    the internal structure is maintained in good repair;

    (b)    any fixtures, fittings or appliances within the part are maintained in good repair and in clean working order; and

    (c)    every window and other means of ventilation are kept in good repair.

  (3)   The duties imposed under paragraph (2) do not require the manager to carry out any repair the need for which arises in consequence of use by the occupier of his living accommodation otherwise than in a tenant-like manner.

  (4)   The duties imposed under paragraphs (1) and (2) do not apply in relation to furniture, fixtures, fittings or appliances that the occupier is entitled to remove from the HMO or which are otherwise outside the control of the manager.

  (5)   For the purpose of this regulation a person shall be regarded as using his living accommodation otherwise than in a tenant-like manner where he fails to treat the property in accordance with the covenants or conditions contained in his lease or licence or otherwise fails to conduct himself as a reasonable tenant or licensee would do.

**[3773]**

NOTES
Commencement: 1 October 2007.

**10 Duty to provide waste disposal facilities**

The manager must—
  (a)  ensure that sufficient bins or other suitable receptacles are provided that are adequate for the requirements of each household occupying the HMO for the storage of refuse and litter pending their disposal; and
  (b)  make such further arrangements for the disposal of refuse and litter from the HMO as may be necessary, having regard to any service for such disposal provided by the local authority.

**[3774]**

NOTES
Commencement: 1 October 2007.

**11 Duties of occupiers of HMOs**

Every occupier of the HMO must—
  (a)  conduct himself in a way that will not hinder or frustrate the manager in the performance of his duties;
  (b)  allow the manager, for any purpose connected with the carrying out of any duty imposed on him by these Regulations, at all reasonable times to enter any living accommodation or other place occupied by that person;
  (c)  provide the manager, at his request, with such information as he may reasonably require for the purpose of carrying out any such duty;
  (d)  take reasonable care to avoid causing damage to anything which the manager is under a duty to supply, maintain or repair under these Regulations;
  (e)  store and dispose of litter in accordance with the arrangements made by the manager under regulation 10; and
  (f)  comply with the reasonable instructions of the manager in respect of any means of escape from fire, the prevention of fire and the use of fire equipment.

**[3775]**

NOTES
Commencement: 1 October 2007.

**12**  (*Amends the Licensing and Management of Houses in Multiple Occupation and Other Houses (Miscellaneous Provisions) (England) Regulations 2006, SI 2006/373 at* **[3623]** *et seq.*)

# SERVICE CHARGES (SUMMARY OF RIGHTS AND OBLIGATIONS, AND TRANSITIONAL PROVISIONS) (WALES) REGULATIONS 2007 (NOTE)

## (SI 2007/3160 (W 271))

NOTES
Made: 5 November 2007.
Authority: Landlord and Tenant Act 1985, s 21B; Commonhold and Leasehold Reform Act 2002, s 178; Welsh Language Act 1993, s 26.
Commencement: 30 November 2007.
These Regulations apply to Wales only. The equivalent provisions for England are in SI 2007/1257 at **[3759]** et seq.

**[3776]**

# ADMINISTRATION CHARGES (SUMMARY OF RIGHTS AND OBLIGATIONS) (WALES) REGULATIONS 2007 (NOTE)

## (SI 2007/3162 (W 273))

NOTES
Made: 5 November 2007.
Authority: Commonhold and Leasehold Reform Act 2002, Sch 11, para 4(2); Welsh Language Act 1993, s 26.

Commencement: 30 November 2007.
These Regulations apply to Wales only. The equivalent provisions for England are in SI 2007/1258 at **[3763]** et seq.

**[3777]**

# MOBILE HOMES (WRITTEN STATEMENT) (WALES) REGULATIONS 2007 (NOTE)

### (SI 2007/3164 (W 275))

**NOTES**
Made: 5 November 2007.
Authority: Mobile Homes Act 1983, s 1(2)(e).
Commencement: 30 November 2007.
These Regulations apply to Wales only. The equivalent provisions for England are in SI 2006/2275 at **[3725]** et seq.

**[3778]**

# LICENSING AND MANAGEMENT OF HOUSES IN MULTIPLE OCCUPATION (ADDITIONAL PROVISIONS) (WALES) REGULATIONS 2007 (NOTE)

### (SI 2007/3229 (W 281))

**NOTES**
Made: 12 November 2007.
Authority: Housing Act 2004, ss 63(5), (6), 65(3), (4), 87(5), (6), 232(3), (7), 234.
Commencement: 5 December 2007.
Amended by: SI 2009/1915.
These Regulations apply to Wales only. The equivalent provisions for England are in SI 2007/1903 at **[3765]** et seq.

**[3779]**

# HOUSING (ASSESSMENT OF ACCOMMODATION NEEDS) (MEANING OF GYPSIES AND TRAVELLERS) (WALES) REGULATIONS 2007 (NOTE)

### (SI 2007/3235 (W 285))

**NOTES**
Made: 12 November 2007.
Authority: Housing Act 2004, s 225(5)(a).
Commencement: 14 December 2007.
These Regulations apply to Wales only. The equivalent provisions for England are in SI 2006/3190 at **[3747]**–**[3748]**.

**[3780]**

# RENT REPAYMENT ORDERS (SUPPLEMENTARY PROVISIONS) (WALES) REGULATIONS 2008 (NOTE)

### (SI 2008/254 (W 30))

**NOTES**
Made: 6 February 2008.
Authority: Housing Act 2004, ss 74(15), 97(15).
Commencement: 4 March 2008.

These Regulations apply to Wales only. The equivalent provisions for England are in SI 2007/572 at **[3749]** et seq.

**[3781]**

# LAND REGISTRATION (ELECTRONIC CONVEYANCING) RULES 2008

## (SI 2008/1750)

**NOTES**
Made: 2 July 2008.
Authority: Land Registration Act 2002, ss 1(2), 25(1), 66(2), 67(3), 71, 73(4), 91(2), (3)(d), 92(2), 95(b), 126, 128(1), Sch 5, para 5, Sch 10 paras 6(a), (b), (c), 8.
Commencement: 4 August 2008.

## 1 Citation and commencement

These rules may be cited as the Land Registration (Electronic Conveyancing) Rules 2008 and shall come into force on 4 August 2008.

**[3782]**

**NOTES**
Commencement: 4 August 2008.

## 2 Interpretation

(1)   In these rules—
"Borrower" means the person who charges the registered estate,
"E-MD reference" means a reference supplied by the registrar to the Lender which enables all or part of the wording of an electronic legal charge to be generated automatically,
"electronic legal charge" means a charge within rule 3(1),
"land registry network" means a network provided under section 92(1) of the Act,
"Lender" means the person to whom the registered estate is charged, and
"the principal rules" means the Land Registration Rules 2003.

(2)   Expressions used in these rules have the meaning that they bear in the principal rules, unless the contrary intention appears.

(3)   In Schedule 2, a reference to a rule by number is a reference to the rule so numbered in the principal rules.

**[3783]**

**NOTES**
Commencement: 4 August 2008.

## 3 Electronic legal charges

(1)   Subject to paragraphs (2) to (7), the grant of a legal charge of the whole of the registered estate in a single registered title is a disposition within section 91(2) of the Act.

(2)   Paragraph (1) does not apply to—
(a)   a disposition to which rule 38 of the principal rules applies,
(b)   the grant of a legal charge by a body corporate, whether the body corporate is the Borrower or a Joint Borrower, or
(c)   a charge which is authenticated by a person other than the Borrower.

(3)   Paragraph (1) only applies if at the time a person authenticates the charge as Borrower or Joint Borrower—
(a)   that person is entered in the register as proprietor or joint proprietor of the registered estate that is charged, or
(b)   there is entered in the day list notice of an application to register that person as proprietor or joint proprietor of the registered estate that is charged.

(4)   Paragraph (1) only applies if the Borrower authenticates the charge personally.

(5)   Paragraph (1) only applies if—
(a)   the charge is prepared using a procedure for doing so permitted by the land registry network, and
(b)   each electronic signature which the charge has, and the certification of each electronic signature, are in accordance with the provisions of a network access agreement.

(6)   A procedure within paragraph (5)(a) may, whether or not it is the only procedure within that sub-paragraph, require all or any of the provisions specified in Schedule 1 to be drafted automatically using an E-MD reference.

(7)   Schedule 1 (which makes provision about the contents of an electronic legal charge) has effect.

(8)   In this rule—

"Joint Borrower" means, where the Borrower comprises two or more persons, one of those persons, and

"joint proprietor" means, where the proprietor of a registered estate comprises two or more persons, one of those persons.

**[3784]**

**NOTES**

Commencement: 4 August 2008.

## 4   Registrar's acknowledgement of time and date that an electronic legal charge took effect

Following receipt of notification, in accordance with the provisions in the charge required by paragraph 1(b) and (c) of Schedule 1, that the charge is to take effect, the registrar must send to the person who notified the registrar an acknowledgement stating the time and date when the notification was received.

**[3785]**

**NOTES**

Commencement: 4 August 2008.

## 5   (*Amends the Land Registration Rules 2003, SI 2003/1417.*)

## 6   Disapplication of certain provisions in the principal rules

Provisions in the principal rules are disapplied as set out in Part 2 of Schedule 2.

**[3786]**

**NOTES**

Commencement: 4 August 2008.

## SCHEDULES

### SCHEDULE 1
### CONTENTS OF AN ELECTRONIC LEGAL CHARGE

Rule 3

1.   To be within rule 3(1), a charge must contain the following—

   (a)   the title number and description of the property that is charged,

   (b)   a provision that the charge takes effect when the registrar receives notification, using a procedure for doing so permitted by the land registry network and in accordance with the provision in the charge required by sub-paragraph (c), that the charge is to take effect,

   (c)   a provision that the Subscriber who prepared the charge under rule 3(5)(a) is the person who is to notify the registrar that the charge is to take effect,

   (d)   the Borrower's name,

   (e)   the E-MD reference, if any, applicable to the charge,

   (f)   the Lender's name and intended address for service for entry in the register,

   (g)   if the Lender is a company registered in any part of the United Kingdom under the Companies Acts or the Companies (Northern Ireland) Order 1986, the Lender's registered number,

   (h)   if the Lender is a limited liability partnership incorporated under the Limited Liability Partnerships Act 2000, the Lender's registered number,

   (i)   if the Lender is a corporation incorporated outside the United Kingdom, the territory in which the Lender is incorporated and the Lender's registered number, if any, in England and Wales,

   (j)   a statement to the effect that the Borrower (stating, if desired, whether with full or limited title guarantee) charges to the Lender the property referred to in sub-paragraph (a) by way of legal mortgage with payment of all money secured by the charge,

   (k)   a statement, if such be the case, that the Lender is under an obligation to make further advances and applies for the obligation to be entered in the register, and

   (l)   a statement, if such be the case, that the Borrower applies to enter a standard form of restriction in the proprietorship register of the registered estate that is charged and, if so, the wording of the standard form of restriction.

2.—(1) A charge within rule 3(1) may contain provisions additional to those in paragraph 1.

(2) For the purposes of registration of an electronic legal charge, if there is a conflict between any such additional provision and a provision contained in the charge in accordance with paragraph 1 the latter provision shall prevail.

(3) The registrar need make no entry in the register in respect of any matter contained in any such additional provisions.

3. In this Schedule—

"full network access agreement" has the same meaning as in the Land Registration (Network Access) Rules 2008, and

"Subscriber" means a person who has entered into a full network access agreement with the registrar.

[3787]

**NOTES**

Commencement: 4 August 2008.

## SCHEDULE 2
### PROVISIONS AFFECTING THE PRINCIPAL RULES

Rules 5 and 6

*(Pt 1 amends the Land Registration Rules 2003, SI 2003/1417.)*

### PART 2
### DISAPPLICATION OF PROVISIONS IN THE PRINCIPAL RULES

**1 Disapplication of Part 3 of the principal rules**

Part 3 of the principal rules (Applications: General Provisions) does not apply to applications for a network access agreement under paragraph 1(4) of Schedule 5 to the Act.

**2 Disapplication of rule 57**

Rule 57 does not apply to a person applying to register an electronic legal charge.

**3 Disapplication of rule 81(1)(b)**

Rule 81(1)(b) does not apply to an application for an agreed notice in respect of an electronic legal charge stored by the registrar, provided that the applicant gives sufficient details of the charge to enable the registrar to identify it.

**4 Disapplication of rule 203**

Rule 203 does not apply to an application made using the land registry network where the document delivered with the application is in electronic form but the registrar may retain the document and at any time thereafter delete it if satisfied that further retention is unnecessary.

[3788]

**NOTES**

Commencement: 4 August 2008.

# HOUSING (APPROVAL OF A CODE OF MANAGEMENT PRACTICE) (STUDENT ACCOMMODATION) (ENGLAND) ORDER 2008

(SI 2008/2345)

**NOTES**

Made: 2 September 2008.
Authority: Housing Act 2004, s 233(1), (3), (4).
Commencement: 1 October 2008.

## 1 Citation, commencement and application

(1) This Order may be cited as the Housing (Approval of a Code of Management Practice) (Student Accommodation) (England) Order 2008 and shall come into force on 1st October 2008.

(2) This Order shall apply in relation to premises in England only.

**[3789]**

**NOTES**
Commencement: 1 October 2008.

## 2 Approval of code of practice

The ANUK/Unipol Code of Standards for Larger Developments for Student Accommodation Managed and Controlled by Educational Establishments, which is dated 28th August 2008 and which lays down standards of conduct and practice to be followed with regard to the management of—

    (a) houses in multiple occupation that are occupied solely or principally by persons who occupy them for the purpose of undertaking a full-time course of further or higher education; or

    (b) buildings falling within paragraph 4 of Schedule 14 to the Housing Act 2004 (buildings occupied by students),

is approved for the purposes of section 233 of that Act.

**[3790]**

**NOTES**
Commencement: 1 October 2008.

## 3 Withdrawal of approval of code of practice

(1) The approval of the Accreditation Network UK/Unipol Code of Standards for Larger Developments for Student Accommodation Managed and Controlled by Educational Establishments dated 20th February 2006 ("the 2006 Code") is withdrawn.

(2) The Housing (Approval of Codes of Management Practice) (Student Accommodation) (England) Order 2006, which approved the 2006 Code, is amended by the omission of paragraph 2(2)(b).

**[3791]**

**NOTES**
Commencement: 1 October 2008.

# TRIBUNAL PROCEDURE (UPPER TRIBUNAL) RULES 2008

(SI 2008/2698 (L 15))

**NOTES**
Made: 9 October 2008.
Authority: Tribunals, Courts and Enforcement Act 2007, ss 10(3), 16(9), 22, 29(3), (4), Sch 5.
Commencement: 3 November 2008.

## ARRANGEMENT OF RULES

### PART 1
### INTRODUCTION

### PART 2
### GENERAL POWERS AND PROVISIONS

PART 3

PROCEDURE FOR CASES IN THE UPPER TRIBUNAL

PART 4

JUDICIAL REVIEW PROCEEDINGS IN THE UPPER TRIBUNAL

PART 5

HEARINGS

PART 6

DECISIONS

PART 7

CORRECTING, SETTING ASIDE, REVIEWING AND APPEALING DECISIONS OF THE UPPER TRIBUNAL

PART 1

INTRODUCTION

## 1 Citation, commencement, application and interpretation

(1)   These Rules may be cited as the Tribunal Procedure (Upper Tribunal) Rules 2008 and come into force on 3rd November 2008.

(2)   These Rules apply to proceedings before the Upper Tribunal [except proceedings in the Lands Chamber].

(3)   In these Rules—

"the 2007 Act" means the Tribunals, Courts and Enforcement Act 2007;

["appellant" means—

    (a)    a person who makes an appeal, or applies for permission to appeal, to the Upper Tribunal;

    (b)    in proceedings transferred or referred to the Upper Tribunal from the First-tier Tribunal, a person who started the proceedings in the First-tier Tribunal; or

(c)      a person substituted as an appellant under rule 9(1) (substitution and addition of parties);]

"applicant" means a person who applies for permission to bring, or does bring, judicial review proceedings before the Upper Tribunal and, in judicial review proceedings transferred to the Upper Tribunal from a court, includes a person who was a claimant or petitioner in the proceedings immediately before they were transferred;

["appropriate national authority" means, in relation to an appeal, the Secretary of State, the Scottish Ministers or the Welsh Ministers, as the case may be;]

["authorised person" means an examiner appointed by the Secretary of State under section 66A of the Road Traffic Act 1988, or a person acting under the direction of such an examiner, who has detained the vehicle to which an appeal relates;]

.....

"dispose of proceedings" includes, unless indicated otherwise, disposing of a part of the proceedings;

"document" means anything in which information is recorded in any form, and an obligation under these Rules or any practice direction or direction to provide or allow access to a document or a copy of a document for any purpose means, unless the Upper Tribunal directs otherwise, an obligation to provide or allow access to such document or copy in a legible form or in a form which can be readily made into a legible form;

"hearing" means an oral hearing and includes a hearing conducted in whole or in part by video link, telephone or other means of instantaneous two-way electronic communication;

"interested party" means—

(a)      a person who is directly affected by the outcome sought in judicial review proceedings, and has been named as an interested party under rule 28 or 29 (judicial review), or has been substituted or added as an interested party under rule 9 (substitution and addition of parties); and

(b)      in judicial review proceedings transferred to the Upper Tribunal under section 25A(2) or (3) of the Judicature (Northern Ireland) Act 1978 or section 31A(2) or (3) of the Supreme Court Act 1981, a person who was an interested party in the proceedings immediately before they were transferred to the Upper Tribunal;

"judicial review proceedings" means proceedings within the jurisdiction of the Upper Tribunal pursuant to section 15 or 21 of the 2007 Act, whether such proceedings are started in the Upper Tribunal or transferred to the Upper Tribunal;

.....

"mental health case" means proceedings before the Upper Tribunal on appeal against a decision in proceedings under the Mental Health Act 1983 or paragraph 5(2) of the Schedule to the Repatriation of Prisoners Act 1984;

"party" means a person who is an appellant, an applicant, a respondent or an interested party in proceedings before the Upper Tribunal, a person who has referred a question to the Upper Tribunal or, if the proceedings have been concluded, a person who was an appellant, an applicant, a respondent or an interested party when the Tribunal finally disposed of all issues in the proceedings;

"permission" includes leave in cases arising under the law of Northern Ireland;

"practice direction" means a direction given under section 23 of the 2007 Act;

"respondent" means—

(a)      in an appeal, or application for permission to appeal, against a decision of another tribunal, any person other than the appellant who—

     (i)      was a party before that other tribunal;

     (ii)      ...

     (iii)      otherwise has a right of appeal against the decision of the other tribunal and has given notice to the Upper Tribunal that they wish to be a party to the appeal;

(b)      in an appeal against any other decision [except a decision of a traffic commissioner], the person who made the decision;

(c)      in judicial review proceedings—

     (i)      in proceedings started in the Upper Tribunal, the person named by the applicant as the respondent;

     (ii)      in proceedings transferred to the Upper Tribunal under section 25A(2) or (3) of the Judicature (Northern Ireland) Act 1978 or section 31A(2) or (3) of the Supreme Court Act 1981, a person who was a defendant in the proceedings immediately before they were transferred;

     (iii)      in proceedings transferred to the Upper Tribunal under section 20(1) of the 2007 Act, a person to whom intimation of the petition was made before the proceedings were transferred, or to whom the Upper Tribunal has required intimation to be made;

[(ca) in proceedings transferred or referred to the Upper Tribunal from the First-tier Tribunal, a person who was a respondent in the proceedings in the First-tier Tribunal;]

(d) in a reference under the Forfeiture Act 1982, the person whose eligibility for a benefit or advantage is in issue; or

(e) a person substituted or added as a respondent under rule 9 (substitution and addition of parties);

.....

["tribunal" does not include a traffic commissioner;]

"working day" means any day except a Saturday or Sunday, Christmas Day, Good Friday or a bank holiday under section 1 of the Banking and Financial Dealings Act 1971.

**[3792]**

**NOTES**

Commencement: 3 November 2008.

Para (2): words in square brackets inserted by the Tribunal Procedure (Amendment No 2) Rules 2009, SI 2009/1975, rr 7, 8(a).

Para (3) is amended as follows:

definition "appellant": substituted by the Tribunal Procedure (Amendment) Rules 2009, SI 2009/274, rr 3, 5(a);

definition "appropriate national authority": inserted by SI 2009/1975, rr 7, 8(b)(i);

definition "authorised person": inserted by SI 2009/1975, rr 7, 8(b)(i);

definition "disability discrimination in schools case" (omitted): revoked by SI 2009/274, rr 3, 5(b);

definition "legal representative" (omitted): revoked by SI 2009/274, rr 3, 5(c);

definition "respondent": sub-para (a)(ii) revoked by SI 2009/274, rr 3, 5(d)(i); sub-para (b) words in square brackets inserted by SI 2009/1975, rr 7, 8(b)(ii); sub-para (ca) inserted by SI 2009/274, rr 3, 5(d)(ii);

definition "special educational needs case" (omitted): revoked by SI 2009/274, rr 3, 5(e);

definition "tribunal": inserted by SI 2009/1975, rr 7, 8(b)(iii).

## 2 Overriding objective and parties' obligation to co-operate with the Upper Tribunal

(1) The overriding objective of these Rules is to enable the Upper Tribunal to deal with cases fairly and justly.

(2) Dealing with a case fairly and justly includes—

(a) dealing with the case in ways which are proportionate to the importance of the case, the complexity of the issues, the anticipated costs and the resources of the parties;

(b) avoiding unnecessary formality and seeking flexibility in the proceedings;

(c) ensuring, so far as practicable, that the parties are able to participate fully in the proceedings;

(d) using any special expertise of the Upper Tribunal effectively; and

(e) avoiding delay, so far as compatible with proper consideration of the issues.

(3) The Upper Tribunal must seek to give effect to the overriding objective when it—

(a) exercises any power under these Rules; or

(b) interprets any rule or practice direction.

(4) Parties must—

(a) help the Upper Tribunal to further the overriding objective; and

(b) co-operate with the Upper Tribunal generally.

**[3793]**

**NOTES**

Commencement: 3 November 2008.

## 3 Alternative dispute resolution and arbitration

(1) The Upper Tribunal should seek, where appropriate—

(a) to bring to the attention of the parties the availability of any appropriate alternative procedure for the resolution of the dispute; and

(b) if the parties wish and provided that it is compatible with the overriding objective, to facilitate the use of the procedure.

(2) Part 1 of the Arbitration Act 1996 does not apply to proceedings before the Upper Tribunal.

**[3794]**

**NOTES**

Commencement: 3 November 2008.

## PART 2
## GENERAL POWERS AND PROVISIONS

### 4   Delegation to staff

(1)   Staff appointed under section 40(1) of the 2007 Act (tribunal staff and services) may, with the approval of the Senior President of Tribunals, carry out functions of a judicial nature permitted or required to be done by the Upper Tribunal.

(2)   The approval referred to at paragraph (1) may apply generally to the carrying out of specified functions by members of staff of a specified description in specified circumstances.

(3)   Within 14 days after the date on which the Upper Tribunal sends notice of a decision made by a member of staff under paragraph (1) to a party, that party may apply in writing to the Upper Tribunal for that decision to be considered afresh by a judge.

**[3795]**

### NOTES
Commencement: 3 November 2008.

### 5–7   (*Outside the scope of this work.*)

### 8   Striking out a party's case

(1)   The proceedings, or the appropriate part of them, will automatically be struck out if the appellant or applicant has failed to comply with a direction that stated that failure by the appellant or applicant to comply with the direction would lead to the striking out of the proceedings or that part of them.

(2)   The Upper Tribunal must strike out the whole or a part of the proceedings if the Upper Tribunal—

    (a)   does not have jurisdiction in relation to the proceedings or that part of them; and

    (b)   does not exercise its power under rule 5(3)(k)(i) (transfer to another court or tribunal) in relation to the proceedings or that part of them.

(3)   The Upper Tribunal may strike out the whole or a part of the proceedings if—

    (a)   the appellant or applicant has failed to comply with a direction which stated that failure by the appellant or applicant to comply with the direction could lead to the striking out of the proceedings or part of them;

    (b)   the appellant or applicant has failed to co-operate with the Upper Tribunal to such an extent that the Upper Tribunal cannot deal with the proceedings fairly and justly; or

    (c)   in proceedings which are not an appeal from the decision of another tribunal or judicial review proceedings, the Upper Tribunal considers there is no reasonable prospect of the appellant's or the applicant's case, or part of it, succeeding.

(4)   The Upper Tribunal may not strike out the whole or a part of the proceedings under paragraph (2) or (3)(b) or (c) without first giving the appellant or applicant an opportunity to make representations in relation to the proposed striking out.

(5)   If the proceedings have been struck out under paragraph (1) or (3)(a), the appellant or applicant may apply for the proceedings, or part of them, to be reinstated.

(6)   An application under paragraph (5) must be made in writing and received by the Upper Tribunal within 1 month after the date on which the Upper Tribunal sent notification of the striking out to the appellant or applicant.

(7)   This rule applies to a respondent [or an interested party] as it applies to an appellant or applicant except that—

    (a)   a reference to the striking out of the proceedings is to be read as a reference to the barring of the respondent [or interested party] from taking further part in the proceedings; and

    (b)   a reference to an application for the reinstatement of proceedings which have been struck out is to be read as a reference to an application for the lifting of the bar on the respondent [or interested party] ... taking further part in the proceedings.

(8)   If a respondent [or an interested party] has been barred from taking further part in proceedings under this rule and that bar has not been lifted, the Upper Tribunal need not consider any response or other submission made by that respondent [or interested party, and may summarily determine any or all issues against that respondent or interested party].

**[3796]**

NOTES
Commencement: 3 November 2008.
Para (7): words in square brackets inserted, and word omitted revoked, by the Tribunal Procedure
(Amendment) Rules 2009, SI 2009/274, rr 3, 6(1), (2).
Para (8): words in square brackets inserted by SI 2009/274, rr 3, 6(1), (3)(a), (b).

## [9 Addition, substitution and removal of parties

(1) The Upper Tribunal may give a direction adding, substituting or removing a party as an appellant, a respondent or an interested party.

(2) If the Upper Tribunal gives a direction under paragraph (1) it may give such consequential directions as it considers appropriate.

(3) A person who is not a party may apply to the Upper Tribunal to be added or substituted as a party.

(4) If a person who is entitled to be a party to proceedings by virtue of another enactment applies to be added as a party, and any conditions applicable to that entitlement have been satisfied, the Upper Tribunal must give a direction adding that person as a respondent or, if appropriate, as an appellant.]

[3797]

NOTES
Commencement: 1 September 2009.
Substituted by the Tribunal Procedure (Amendment No 2) Rules 2009, SI 2009/1975, rr 7, 10.

## [10 Orders for costs

(1) The Upper Tribunal may not make an order in respect of costs (or, in Scotland, expenses) in proceedings [transferred or referred by, or on appeal from,] another tribunal except—

(a) in proceedings [transferred by, or on appeal from,] the Tax Chamber of the First-tier Tribunal; or

(b) to the extent and in the circumstances that the other tribunal had the power to make an order in respect of costs (or, in Scotland, expenses).

(2) The Upper Tribunal may not make an order in respect of costs or expenses under section 4 of the Forfeiture Act 1982.

(3) In other proceedings, the Upper Tribunal may not make an order in respect of costs or expenses except—

(a) in judicial review proceedings;

(b) ...

(c) under section 29(4) of the 2007 Act (wasted costs); or

(d) if the Upper Tribunal considers that a party or its representative has acted unreasonably in bringing, defending or conducting the proceedings.

(4) The Upper Tribunal may make an order for costs (or, in Scotland, expenses) on an application or on its own initiative.

(5) A person making an application for an order for costs or expenses must—

(a) send or deliver a written application to the Upper Tribunal and to the person against whom it is proposed that the order be made; and

(b) send or deliver with the application a schedule of the costs or expenses claimed sufficient to allow summary assessment of such costs or expenses by the Upper Tribunal.

(6) An application for an order for costs or expenses may be made at any time during the proceedings but may not be made later than 1 month after the date on which the Upper Tribunal sends—

(a) a decision notice recording the decision which finally disposes of all issues in the proceedings; or

(b) notice of a withdrawal under rule 17 which ends the proceedings.

(7) The Upper Tribunal may not make an order for costs or expenses against a person (the "paying person") without first—

(a) giving that person an opportunity to make representations; and

(b) if the paying person is an individual and the order is to be made under paragraph (3)(a), (b) or (d), considering that person's financial means.

(8) The amount of costs or expenses to be paid under an order under this rule may be ascertained by—

(a) summary assessment by the Upper Tribunal;

(b) agreement of a specified sum by the paying person and the person entitled to receive the costs or expenses ("the receiving person"); or

    (c)    assessment of the whole or a specified part of the costs or expenses incurred by the receiving person, if not agreed.

(9)    Following an order for assessment under paragraph (8)(c), the paying person or the receiving person may apply—

    (a)    in England and Wales, to the High Court or the Costs Office of the Supreme Court (as specified in the order) for a detailed assessment of the costs on the standard basis or, if specified in the order, on the indemnity basis; and the Civil Procedure Rules 1998 shall apply, with necessary modifications, to that application and assessment as if the proceedings in the tribunal had been proceedings in a court to which the Civil Procedure Rules 1998 apply;

    (b)    in Scotland, to the Auditor of the Court of Session for the taxation of the expenses according to the fees payable in that court; or

    (c)    in Northern Ireland, to the Taxing Office of the High Court of Northern Ireland for taxation on the standard basis or, if specified in the order, on the indemnity basis.]

**[3798]**

---

**NOTES**

Commencement: 1 April 2009.

Substituted by the Tribunal Procedure (Amendment) Rules 2009, SI 2009/274, rr 3, 7.

Para (1): words in square brackets in both places substituted by the Tribunal Procedure (Amendment No 2) Rules 2009, SI 2009/1975, rr 7, 11(a)(i), (ii).

Para (3): sub-para (b) revoked by SI 2009/1975, rr 7, 11(b).

## 11  Representatives

(1)    A party may appoint a representative (whether a legal representative or not) to represent that party in the proceedings.

(2)    If a party appoints a representative, that party (or the representative if the representative is a legal representative) must send or deliver to the Upper Tribunal ... written notice of the representative's name and address.

[(2A)    If the Upper Tribunal receives notice that a party has appointed a representative under paragraph (2), it must send a copy of that notice to each other party.]

(3)    Anything permitted or required to be done by a party under these Rules, a practice direction or a direction may be done by the representative of that party, except signing a witness statement.

(4)    A person who receives due notice of the appointment of a representative—

    (a)    must provide to the representative any document which is required to be provided to the represented party, and need not provide that document to the represented party; and

    (b)    may assume that the representative is and remains authorised as such until they receive written notification that this is not so from the representative or the represented party.

(5)    At a hearing a party may be accompanied by another person whose name and address has not been notified under paragraph (2) but who, subject to paragraph (8) and with the permission of the Upper Tribunal, may act as a representative or otherwise assist in presenting the party's case at the hearing.

(6)    Paragraphs (2) to (4) do not apply to a person who accompanies a party under paragraph (5).

(7)    In a mental health case if the patient has not appointed a representative the Upper Tribunal may appoint a legal representative for the patient where—

    (a)    the patient has stated that they do not wish to conduct their own case or that they wish to be represented; or

    (b)    the patient lacks the capacity to appoint a representative but the Upper Tribunal believes that it is in the patient's best interests for the patient to be represented.

(8)    In a mental health case a party may not appoint as a representative, or be represented or assisted at a hearing by—

    (a)    a person liable to be detained or subject to guardianship or after-care under supervision, or who is a community patient, under the Mental Health Act 1983; or

    (b)    a person receiving treatment for mental disorder at the same hospital home as the patient.

[(9)    In this rule "legal representative" means an authorised advocate or authorised litigator as defined by section 119(1) of the Courts and Legal Services Act 1990, an advocate or solicitor in Scotland or a barrister or solicitor in Northern Ireland.]

**[3799]**

---

**NOTES**

Commencement: 3 November 2008.

Para (2): words omitted revoked by the Tribunal Procedure (Amendment) Rules 2009, SI 2009/274, rr 3, 8(a).

Para (2A): inserted by SI 2009/274, rr 3, 8(b).
Para (9): inserted by SI 2009/274, rr 3, 8(c).

## 12 Calculating time

(1) An act required by these Rules, a practice direction or a direction to be done on or by a particular day must be done by 5pm on that day.

(2) If the time specified by these Rules, a practice direction or a direction for doing any act ends on a day other than a working day, the act is done in time if it is done on the next working day.

(3) In a special educational needs case or a disability discrimination in schools case, the following days must not be counted when calculating the time by which an act must be done—

    (a)    25th December to 1st January inclusive; and

    (b)    any day in August.

(4) Paragraph (3) does not apply where the Upper Tribunal directs that an act must be done by or on a specified date.

[(5) In this rule—

    "disability discrimination in schools case" means proceedings concerning disability discrimination in the education of a child or related matters; and

    "special educational needs case" means proceedings concerning the education of a child who has or may have special educational needs.]

**[3800]**

**NOTES**

Commencement: 3 November 2008.

Para (5): inserted by the Tribunal Procedure (Amendment) Rules 2009, SI 2009/274, rr 3, 9.

## 13 Sending and delivery of documents

(1) Any document to be provided to the Upper Tribunal under these Rules, a practice direction or a direction must be—

    (a)    sent by pre-paid post or [by document exchange, or delivered by hand,] to the address specified for the proceedings;

    (b)    sent by fax to the number specified for the proceedings; or

    (c)    sent or delivered by such other method as the Upper Tribunal may permit or direct.

(2) Subject to paragraph (3), if a party provides a fax number, email address or other details for the electronic transmission of documents to them, that party must accept delivery of documents by that method.

(3) If a party informs the Upper Tribunal and all other parties that a particular form of communication, other than pre-paid post or delivery by hand, should not be used to provide documents to that party, that form of communication must not be so used.

(4) If the Upper Tribunal or a party sends a document to a party or the Upper Tribunal by email or any other electronic means of communication, the recipient may request that the sender provide a hard copy of the document to the recipient. The recipient must make such a request as soon as reasonably practicable after receiving the document electronically.

(5) The Upper Tribunal and each party may assume that the address provided by a party or its representative is and remains the address to which documents should be sent or delivered until receiving written notification to the contrary.

**[3801]**

**NOTES**

Commencement: 3 November 2008.

Para (1): sub-para (a) words in square brackets substituted by the Tribunal Procedure (Amendment) Rules 2009, SI 2009/274, rr 3, 10.

## 14 Use of documents and information

(1) The Upper Tribunal may make an order prohibiting the disclosure or publication of—

    (a)    specified documents or information relating to the proceedings; or

    (b)    any matter likely to lead members of the public to identify any person whom the Upper Tribunal considers should not be identified.

(2) The Upper Tribunal may give a direction prohibiting the disclosure of a document or information to a person if—

    (a)    the Upper Tribunal is satisfied that such disclosure would be likely to cause that person or some other person serious harm; and

    (b)    the Upper Tribunal is satisfied, having regard to the interests of justice, that it is proportionate to give such a direction.

(3)　If a party ("the first party") considers that the Upper Tribunal should give a direction under paragraph (2) prohibiting the disclosure of a document or information to another party ("the second party"), the first party must—

　　(a)　exclude the relevant document or information from any documents that will be provided to the second party; and

　　(b)　provide to the Upper Tribunal the excluded document or information, and the reason for its exclusion, so that the Upper Tribunal may decide whether the document or information should be disclosed to the second party or should be the subject of a direction under paragraph (2).

(4)　...

(5)　If the Upper Tribunal gives a direction under paragraph (2) which prevents disclosure to a party who has appointed a representative, the Upper Tribunal may give a direction that the documents or information be disclosed to that representative if the Upper Tribunal is satisfied that—

　　(a)　disclosure to the representative would be in the interests of the party; and

　　(b)　the representative will act in accordance with paragraph (6).

(6)　Documents or information disclosed to a representative in accordance with a direction under paragraph (5) must not be disclosed either directly or indirectly to any other person without the Upper Tribunal's consent.

(7)　Unless the Upper Tribunal gives a direction to the contrary, information about mental health cases and the names of any persons concerned in such cases must not be made public.

[(8)　The Upper Tribunal may, on its own initiative or on the application of a party, give a direction that certain documents or information must or may be disclosed to the Upper Tribunal on the basis that the Upper Tribunal will not disclose such documents or information to other persons, or specified other persons.

(9)　A party making an application for a direction under paragraph (8) may withhold the relevant documents or information from other parties until the Upper Tribunal has granted or refused the application.

(10)　In a case involving matters relating to national security, the Upper Tribunal must ensure that information is not disclosed contrary to the interests of national security.

(11)　The Upper Tribunal must conduct proceedings and record its decision and reasons appropriately so as not to undermine the effect of an order made under paragraph (1), a direction given under paragraph (2) or (8) or the duty imposed by paragraph (10).]

**[3802]**

---

**NOTES**

Commencement: 3 November 2008.
Para (4): revoked by the Tribunal Procedure (Amendment No 2) Rules 2009, SI 2009/1975, rr 7, 13(a).
Paras (8)–(11): inserted by SI 2009/1975, rr 7, 13(b).

---

## 15　Evidence and submissions

(1)　Without restriction on the general powers in rule 5(1) and (2) (case management powers), the Upper Tribunal may give directions as to—

　　(a)　issues on which it requires evidence or submissions;

　　(b)　the nature of the evidence or submissions it requires;

　　(c)　whether the parties are permitted or required to provide expert evidence, and if so whether the parties must jointly appoint a single expert to provide such evidence;

　　(d)　any limit on the number of witnesses whose evidence a party may put forward, whether in relation to a particular issue or generally;

　　(e)　the manner in which any evidence or submissions are to be provided, which may include a direction for them to be given—

　　　　(i)　orally at a hearing; or

　　　　(ii)　by written submissions or witness statement; and

　　(f)　the time at which any evidence or submissions are to be provided.

(2)　The Upper Tribunal may—

　　(a)　admit evidence whether or not—

　　　　(i)　the evidence would be admissible in a civil trial in the United Kingdom; or

　　　　(ii)　the evidence was available to a previous decision maker; or

　　(b)　exclude evidence that would otherwise be admissible where—

　　　　(i)　the evidence was not provided within the time allowed by a direction or a practice direction;

　　　　(ii)　the evidence was otherwise provided in a manner that did not comply with a direction or a practice direction; or

　　　　(iii)　it would otherwise be unfair to admit the evidence.

PART II
STATUTORY INSTRUMENTS

(3) The Upper Tribunal may consent to a witness giving, or require any witness to give, evidence on oath, and may administer an oath for that purpose.

**[3803]**

**NOTES**
Commencement: 3 November 2008.

## 16 Summoning or citation of witnesses and orders to answer questions or produce documents

(1) On the application of a party or on its own initiative, the Upper Tribunal may—
    (a) by summons (or, in Scotland, citation) require any person to attend as a witness at a hearing at the time and place specified in the summons or citation; or
    (b) order any person to answer any questions or produce any documents in that person's possession or control which relate to any issue in the proceedings.

(2) A summons or citation under paragraph (1)(a) must—
    (a) give the person required to attend 14 days' notice of the hearing or such shorter period as the Upper Tribunal may direct; and
    (b) where the person is not a party, make provision for the person's necessary expenses of attendance to be paid, and state who is to pay them.

(3) No person may be compelled to give any evidence or produce any document that the person could not be compelled to give or produce on a trial of an action in a court of law in the part of the United Kingdom where the proceedings are due to be determined.

[(4) A person who receives a summons, citation or order may apply to the Upper Tribunal for it to be varied or set aside if they did not have an opportunity to object to it before it was made or issued.

(5) A person making an application under paragraph (4) must do so as soon as reasonably practicable after receiving notice of the summons, citation or order.

(6) A summons, citation or order under this rule must—
    (a) state that the person on whom the requirement is imposed may apply to the Upper Tribunal to vary or set aside the summons, citation or order, if they did not have an opportunity to object to it before it was made or issued; and
    (b) state the consequences of failure to comply with the summons, citation or order.]

**[3804]**

**NOTES**
Commencement: 3 November 2008.
Paras (4)–(6): substituted, for original para (4), by the Tribunal Procedure (Amendment) Rules 2009, SI 2009/274, rr 3, 11.

## 17 Withdrawal

(1) Subject to paragraph (2), a party may give notice of the withdrawal of its case, or any part of it—
    (a) at any time before a hearing to consider the disposal of the proceedings (or, if the Upper Tribunal disposes of the proceedings without a hearing, before that disposal), by sending or delivering to the Upper Tribunal a written notice of withdrawal; or
    (b) orally at a hearing.

(2) Notice of withdrawal will not take effect unless the Upper Tribunal consents to the withdrawal except in relation to an application for permission to appeal.

(3) A party which has withdrawn its case may apply to the Upper Tribunal for the case to be reinstated.

(4) An application under paragraph (3) must be made in writing and be received by the Upper Tribunal within 1 month after—
    (a) the date on which the Upper Tribunal received the notice under paragraph (1)(a); or
    (b) the date of the hearing at which the case was withdrawn orally under paragraph (1)(b).

(5) The Upper Tribunal must notify each party in writing of a withdrawal under this rule.

**[3805]**

**NOTES**
Commencement: 3 November 2008.

### 18   Notice of funding of legal services

If a party is granted funding of legal services at any time, that party must as soon as practicable—
- (a)    (i)    if funding is granted by the Legal Services Commission or the Northern Ireland Legal Services Commission, send a copy of the funding notice to the Upper Tribunal; or
-        (ii)    if funding is granted by the Scottish Legal Aid Board, send a copy of the legal aid certificate to the Upper Tribunal; and
- (b)   notify every other party in writing that funding has been granted.

                                                                    **[3806]**

**NOTES**

Commencement: 3 November 2008.

### 19   (*Outside the scope of this work.*)

### 20   Power to pay expenses and allowances

(1)   In proceedings brought under section 4 of the Safeguarding Vulnerable Groups Act 2006 … , the Secretary of State may pay such allowances for the purpose of or in connection with the attendance of persons at hearings as the Secretary of State may, with the consent of the Treasury, determine.

(2)   Paragraph (3) applies to proceedings on appeal from a decision of—
- (a)   the First-tier Tribunal in proceedings under the Child Support Act 1991, section 12 of the Social Security Act 1998 or paragraph 6 of Schedule 7 to the Child Support, Pensions and Social Security Act 2000;
- (b)   the First-tier Tribunal in a war pensions and armed forces case (as defined in the Tribunal Procedure (First-tier Tribunal) (War Pensions and Armed Forces Compensation Chamber) Rules 2008); or
- (c)   a Pensions Appeal Tribunal for Scotland or Northern Ireland.

(3)   The Lord Chancellor (or, in Scotland, the Secretary of State) may pay to any person who attends any hearing such travelling and other allowances, including compensation for loss of remunerative time, as the Lord Chancellor (or, in Scotland, the Secretary of State) may determine.

                                                                    **[3807]**

**NOTES**

Commencement: 3 November 2008.

Para (1): words omitted revoked by the Tribunal Procedure (Amendment) Rules 2009, SI 2009/274, rr 3, 12.

### [20A   Procedure for applying for a stay of a decision pending an appeal

(1)   This rule applies where another enactment provides in any terms for the Upper Tribunal to stay or suspend, or to lift a stay or suspension of, a decision which is or may be the subject of an appeal to the Upper Tribunal ("the substantive decision") pending such appeal.

(2)   A person who wishes the Upper Tribunal to decide whether the substantive decision should be stayed or suspended must make a written application to the Upper Tribunal which must include—
- (a)   the name and address of the person making the application;
- (b)   the name and address of any representative of that person;
- (c)   the address to which documents for that person should be sent or delivered;
- (d)   the name and address of any person who will be a respondent to the appeal;
- (e)   details of the substantive decision and any decision as to when that decision is to take effect, and copies of any written record of, or reasons for, those decisions; and
- (f)   the grounds on which the person making the application relies.

(3)   In the case of an application under paragraph (2) for a stay of a decision of a traffic commissioner—
- (a)   the person making the application must notify the traffic commissioner when making the application;
- (b)   within 7 days of receiving notification of the application the traffic commissioner must send or deliver written reasons for refusing or withdrawing the stay—
  - (i)   to the Upper Tribunal; and
  - (ii)   to the person making the application, if the traffic commissioner has not already done so.

(4)   If the Upper Tribunal grants a stay or suspension following an application under this rule—
- (a)   the Upper Tribunal may give directions as to the conduct of the appeal of the substantive decision; and
- (b)   the Upper Tribunal may, where appropriate, grant the stay or suspension subject to conditions.

PART II
STATUTORY INSTRUMENTS

(5)   Unless the Upper Tribunal considers that there is good reason not to do so, the Upper Tribunal must send written notice of any decision made under this rule to each party.]

**[3808]**

**NOTES**
Inserted by the Tribunal Procedure (Amendment No 2) Rules 2009, SI 2009/1975, rr 7, 14.

### PART 3
### [PROCEDURE FOR CASES IN] THE UPPER TRIBUNAL

**21   Application to the Upper Tribunal for permission to appeal**

(1)   ...

(2)   A person may apply to the Upper Tribunal for permission to appeal to the Upper Tribunal against a decision of another tribunal only if—

    (a)   they have made an application for permission to appeal to the tribunal which made the decision challenged; and

    (b)   that application has been refused or has not been admitted.

(3)   An application for permission to appeal must be made in writing and received by the Upper Tribunal no later than—

    (a)   in the case of an application under section 4 of the Safeguarding Vulnerable Groups Act 2006, 3 months after the date on which written notice of the decision being challenged was sent to the appellant; or

    (b)   otherwise, a month after the date on which the tribunal that made the decision under challenge sent notice of its refusal of permission to appeal, or refusal to admit the application for permission to appeal, to the appellant.

(4)   The application must state—

    (a)   the name and address of the appellant;

    (b)   the name and address of the representative (if any) of the appellant;

    (c)   an address where documents for the appellant may be sent or delivered;

    (d)   details (including the full reference) of the decision challenged;

    (e)   the grounds on which the appellant relies; and

    (f)   whether the appellant wants the application to be dealt with at a hearing.

(5)   The appellant must provide with the application a copy of—

    (a)   any written record of the decision being challenged;

    (b)   any separate written statement of reasons for that decision; and

    (c)   if the application is for permission to appeal against a decision of another tribunal, the notice of refusal of permission to appeal, or notice of refusal to admit the application for permission to appeal, from that other tribunal.

(6)   If the appellant provides the application to the Upper Tribunal later than the time required by paragraph (3) or by an extension of time allowed under rule 5(3)(a) (power to extend time)—

    (a)   the application must include a request for an extension of time and the reason why the application was not provided in time; and

    (b)   unless the Upper Tribunal extends time for the application under rule 5(3)(a) (power to extend time) the Upper Tribunal must not admit the application.

(7)   If the appellant makes an application to the Upper Tribunal for permission to appeal against the decision of another tribunal, and that other tribunal refused to admit the appellant's application for permission to appeal because the application for permission or for a written statement of reasons was not made in time—

    (a)   the application to the Upper Tribunal for permission to appeal must include the reason why the application to the other tribunal for permission to appeal or for a written statement of reasons, as the case may be, was not made in time; and

    (b)   the Upper Tribunal must only admit the application if the Upper Tribunal considers that it is in the interests of justice for it to do so.

**[3809]**

**NOTES**
Commencement: 3 November 2008.

Part heading: words in square brackets substituted by the Tribunal Procedure (Amendment) Rules 2009, SI 2009/274, rr 3, 13.

Para (1): revoked by the Tribunal Procedure (Amendment No 2) Rules 2009, SI 2009/1975, rr 7, 15.

See further, for transitional provisions in relation to an appeal which lies to the Upper Tribunal by virtue of the Transfer of Tribunal Functions and Revenue and Customs Appeals Order 2009, SI 2009/56, Sch 3, para 11(2): the First-tier Tribunal and Upper Tribunal (Chambers) (Amendment) Order 2009, SI 2009/196, art 9.

**22  Decision in relation to permission to appeal**

(1)   If the Upper Tribunal refuses permission to appeal, it must send written notice of the refusal and of the reasons for the refusal to the appellant.

(2)   If the Upper Tribunal gives permission to appeal—

  (a)   the Upper Tribunal must send written notice of the permission, and of the reasons for any limitations or conditions on such permission, to each party;

  (b)   subject to any direction by the Upper Tribunal, the application for permission to appeal stands as the notice of appeal and the Upper Tribunal must send to each respondent a copy of the application for permission to appeal and any documents provided with it by the appellant; and

  (c)   the Upper Tribunal may, with the consent of the appellant and each respondent, determine the appeal without obtaining any further response.

[(3)   Paragraph (4) applies where the Upper Tribunal, without a hearing, determines an application for permission to appeal—

  (a)   against a decision of—

     (i)    the Tax Chamber of the First-tier Tribunal;

     (ii)   the Health, Education and Social Care Chamber of the First-tier Tribunal;

     [(iia)  the General Regulatory Chamber of the First-tier Tribunal;]

     (iii)  the Mental Health Review Tribunal for Wales; or

     (iv)   the Special Educational Needs Tribunal for Wales; or

  (b)   under section 4 of the Safeguarding Vulnerable Groups Act 2006.]

(4)   In the circumstances set out at paragraph (3) the appellant may apply for the decision to be reconsidered at a hearing if the Upper Tribunal—

  (a)   refuses permission to appeal; or

  (b)   gives permission to appeal on limited grounds or subject to conditions.

(5)   An application under paragraph (4) must be made in writing and received by the Upper Tribunal within 14 days after the date on which the Upper Tribunal sent written notice of its decision regarding the application to the appellant.

                                                                                      **[3810]**

**NOTES**

Commencement: 3 November 2008.

Para (3): substituted by the Tribunal Procedure (Amendment) Rules 2009, SI 2009/274, rr 3, 14; sub-para (a)(iia) inserted by the Tribunal Procedure (Amendment No 2) Rules 2009, SI 2009/1975, rr 7, 16.

**23  Notice of appeal**

[(1)   This rule applies—

  (a)   to proceedings on appeal to the Upper Tribunal for which permission to appeal is not required, except proceedings to which rule 26A applies;

  (b)   if another tribunal has given permission for a party to appeal to the Upper Tribunal; or

  (c)   subject to any other direction by the Upper Tribunal, if the Upper Tribunal has given permission to appeal and has given a direction that the application for permission to appeal does not stand as the notice of appeal.

(2)   The appellant must provide a notice of appeal to the Upper Tribunal so that it is received within 1 month after—

  (a)   the date that the tribunal that gave permission to appeal sent notice of such permission to the appellant; or

  (b)   if permission to appeal is not required, the date on which notice of decision to which the appeal relates was sent to the appellant.]

(3)   The notice of appeal must include the information listed in rule 21(4)(a) to (e) (content of the application for permission to appeal) and, where the Upper Tribunal has given permission to appeal, the Upper Tribunal's case reference.

(4)   If another tribunal has granted permission to appeal, the appellant must provide with the notice of appeal a copy of—

  (a)   any written record of the decision being challenged;

  (b)   any separate written statement of reasons for that decision; and

  (c)   the notice of permission to appeal.

(5)   If the appellant provides the notice of appeal to the Upper Tribunal later than the time required by paragraph (2) or by an extension of time allowed under rule 5(3)(a) (power to extend time)—

  (a)   the notice of appeal must include a request for an extension of time and the reason why the notice was not provided in time; and

  (b)   unless the Upper Tribunal extends time for the notice of appeal under rule 5(3)(a) (power to extend time) the Upper Tribunal must not admit the notice of appeal.

[(6) When the Upper Tribunal receives the notice of appeal it must send a copy of the notice and any accompanying documents—

    (a)    to each respondent; or

    (b)    in an appeal against the decision of a traffic commissioner, to—

        (i)    the traffic commissioner;

        (ii)    the appropriate national authority; and

        (iii)    in a case relating to the detention of a vehicle, the authorised person.]

**[3811]**

**NOTES**

Commencement: 3 November 2008.

Paras (1), (2): substituted by the Tribunal Procedure (Amendment No 2) Rules 2009, SI 2009/1975, rr 7, 17(a).

Para (6): substituted by SI 2009/1975, rr 7, 17(b).

## 24 Response to the notice of appeal

[(1) This rule and rule 25 do not apply to an appeal against a decision of a traffic commissioner, in respect of which Schedule 1 makes alternative provision.

(1A) Subject to any direction given by the Upper Tribunal, a respondent may provide a response to a notice of appeal.]

(2) Any response provided under paragraph (1) must be in writing and must be sent or delivered to the Upper Tribunal so that it is received—

    (a)    [if an application for permission to appeal] stands as the notice of appeal, no later than 1 month after the date on which the Upper Tribunal sent notice that it had granted permission to appeal to the respondent; or

    (b)    in any other case, no later than 1 month after the date on which the Upper Tribunal sent a copy of the notice of appeal to the respondent.

(3) The response must state—

    (a)    the name and address of the respondent;

    (b)    the name and address of the representative (if any) of the respondent;

    (c)    an address where documents for the respondent may be sent or delivered;

    (d)    whether the respondent opposes the appeal;

    (e)    the grounds on which the respondent relies, including [(in the case of an appeal against the decision of another tribunal)] any grounds on which the respondent was unsuccessful in the proceedings which are the subject of the appeal, but intends to rely in the appeal; and

    (f)    whether the respondent wants the case to be dealt with at a hearing.

(4) If the respondent provides the response to the Upper Tribunal later than the time required by paragraph (2) or by an extension of time allowed under rule 5(3)(a) (power to extend time), the response must include a request for an extension of time and the reason why the [response] was not provided in time.

(5) When the Upper Tribunal receives the response it must send a copy of the response and any accompanying documents to the appellant and each other party.

**[3812]**

**NOTES**

Commencement: 3 November 2008.

Paras (1), (1A): substituted, for original para (1), by the Tribunal Procedure (Amendment No 2) Rules 2009, SI 2009/1975, rr 7, 18(a).

Para (2): sub-para (a) words in square brackets substituted by SI 2009/1975, rr 7, 18(b).

Para (3): sub-para (e) words in square brackets inserted by SI 2009/1975, rr 7, 18(c).

Para (4): word in square brackets substituted by the Tribunal Procedure (Amendment) Rules 2009, SI 2009/274, rr 3, 15.

## 25 Appellant's reply

(1) Subject to any direction given by the Upper Tribunal, the appellant may provide a reply to any response provided under rule 24 (response to the notice of appeal).

(2) Any reply provided under paragraph (1) must be in writing and must be sent or delivered to the Upper Tribunal so that it is received within one month after the date on which the Upper Tribunal sent a copy of the response to the appellant.

(3) When the Upper Tribunal receives the reply it must send a copy of the reply and any accompanying documents to each respondent.

**[3813]**

**NOTES**

Commencement: 3 November 2008.

**26**    (*Outside the scope of this work.*)

**[26A   Cases transferred or referred to the Upper Tribunal, applications made directly to the Upper Tribunal and proceedings without notice to a respondent**

[(1)    Paragraphs (2) and (3) apply to—
- (a)    a case transferred or referred to the Upper Tribunal from the First-tier Tribunal; or
- (b)    a case, other than an appeal or a case to which rule 26 (references under the Forfeiture Act 1982) applies, which is started by an application made directly to the Upper Tribunal.]

(2)    In a case to which this paragraph applies—
- (a)    the Upper Tribunal must give directions as to the procedure to be followed in the consideration and disposal of the proceedings; and
- (b)    the preceding rules in this Part will only apply to the proceedings to the extent provided for by such directions.

(3)    If a case or matter to which this paragraph applies is to be determined without notice to or the involvement of a respondent—
- (a)    any provision in these Rules requiring a document to be provided by or to a respondent; and
- (b)    any other provision in these Rules permitting a respondent to participate in the proceedings

does not apply to that case or matter.]

                                                        **[3814]**

**NOTES**
Commencement: 1 April 2009.
Inserted by the Tribunal Procedure (Amendment) Rules 2009, SI 2009/274, rr 3, 16.
Para (1): substituted by the Tribunal Procedure (Amendment No 2) Rules 2009, SI 2009/1975, rr 7, 19.

**PART 4**
JUDICIAL REVIEW PROCEEDINGS IN THE UPPER TRIBUNAL

**27   Application of this Part to judicial review proceedings transferred to the Upper Tribunal**

(1)    When a court transfers judicial review proceedings to the Upper Tribunal, the Upper Tribunal—
- (a)    must notify each party in writing that the proceedings have been transferred to the Upper Tribunal; and
- (b)    must give directions as to the future conduct of the proceedings.

(2)    The directions given under paragraph (1)(b) may modify or disapply for the purposes of the proceedings any of the provisions of the following rules in this Part.

(3)    In proceedings transferred from the Court of Session under section 20(1) of the 2007 Act, the directions given under paragraph (1)(b) must—
- (a)    if the Court of Session did not make a first order specifying the required intimation, service and advertisement of the petition, state the Upper Tribunal's requirements in relation to those matters;
- (b)    state whether the Upper Tribunal will consider summary dismissal of the proceedings; and
- (c)    where necessary, modify or disapply provisions relating to permission in the following rules in this Part.

                                                        **[3815]**

**NOTES**
Commencement: 3 November 2008.

**28   Applications for permission to bring judicial review proceedings**

(1)    A person seeking permission to bring judicial review proceedings before the Upper Tribunal under section 16 of the 2007 Act must make a written application to the Upper Tribunal for such permission.

(2)    Subject to paragraph (3), an application under paragraph (1) must be made promptly and, unless any other enactment specifies a shorter time limit, must be sent or delivered to the Upper Tribunal so that it is received no later than 3 months after the date of the decision[, action or omission] to which the application relates.

(3)    An application for permission to bring judicial review proceedings challenging a decision of the First-tier Tribunal may be made later than the time required by paragraph (2) if it is made within 1 month after the date on which the First-tier Tribunal sent—
- (a)    written reasons for the decision; or

(b)    notification that an application for the decision to be set aside has been unsuccessful, provided that that application was made in time.

(4)   The application must state—
- (a)   the name and address of the applicant, the respondent and any other person whom the applicant considers to be an interested party;
- (b)   the name and address of the applicant's representative (if any);
- (c)   an address where documents for the applicant may be sent or delivered;
- (d)   details of the decision challenged (including the date, the full reference and the identity of the decision maker);
- (e)   that the application is for permission to bring judicial review proceedings;
- (f)   the outcome that the applicant is seeking; and
- (g)   the facts and grounds on which the applicant relies.

(5)   If the application relates to proceedings in a court or tribunal, the application must name as an interested party each party to those proceedings who is not the applicant or a respondent.

(6)   The applicant must send with the application—
- (a)   a copy of any written record of the decision in the applicant's possession or control; and
- (b)   copies of any other documents in the applicant's possession or control on which the applicant intends to rely.

(7)   If the applicant provides the application to the Upper Tribunal later than the time required by paragraph (2) or (3) or by an extension of time allowed under rule 5(3)(a) (power to extend time)—
- (a)   the application must include a request for an extension of time and the reason why the application was not provided in time; and
- (b)   unless the Upper Tribunal extends time for the application under rule 5(3)(a) (power to extend time) the Upper Tribunal must not admit the application.

(8)   When the Upper Tribunal receives the application it must send a copy of the application and any accompanying documents to each person named in the application as a respondent or interested party.

**[3816]**

**NOTES**
Commencement: 3 November 2008.
Para (2): words in square brackets inserted by the Tribunal Procedure (Amendment) Rules 2009, SI 2009/274, rr 3, 17.

## 29  Acknowledgment of service

(1)   A person who is sent a copy of an application for permission under rule 28(8) (application for permission to bring judicial review proceedings) and wishes to take part in the proceedings must send or deliver to the Upper Tribunal an acknowledgment of service so that it is received no later than 21 days after the date on which the Upper Tribunal sent a copy of the application to that person.

(2)   An acknowledgment of service under paragraph (1) must be in writing and state—
- (a)   whether the person intends to [support or] oppose the application for permission;
- (b)   their grounds for any [support or] opposition under sub-paragraph (a), or any other submission or information which they consider may assist the Upper Tribunal; and
- (c)   the name and address of any other person not named in the application as a respondent or interested party whom the person providing the acknowledgment considers to be an interested party.

(3)   A person who is sent a copy of an application for permission under rule 28(8) but does not provide an acknowledgment of service may not take part in the application for permission, but may take part in the subsequent proceedings if the application is successful.

**[3817]**

**NOTES**
Commencement: 3 November 2008.
Para (2): words in square brackets in both places inserted by the Tribunal Procedure (Amendment) Rules 2009, SI 2009/274, rr 3, 18(a), (b).

## 30  Decision on permission or summary dismissal, and reconsideration of permission or summary dismissal at a hearing

(1)   The Upper Tribunal must send to the applicant, each respondent and any other person who provided an acknowledgment of service to the Upper Tribunal, and may send to any other person who may have an interest in the proceedings, written notice of—
- (a)   its decision in relation to the application for permission; and
- (b)   the reasons for any refusal of the application, or any limitations or conditions on permission.

(2)    In proceedings transferred from the Court of Session under section 20(1) of the 2007 Act, where the Upper Tribunal has considered whether summarily to dismiss of the proceedings, the Upper Tribunal must send to the applicant and each respondent, and may send to any other person who may have an interest in the proceedings, written notice of—

(a)    its decision in relation to the summary dismissal of proceedings; and

(b)    the reasons for any decision summarily to dismiss part or all of the proceedings, or any limitations or conditions on the continuation of such proceedings.

(3)    Paragraph (4) applies where the Upper Tribunal, without a hearing—

(a)    determines an application for permission to bring judicial review proceedings and either refuses permission, or gives permission on limited grounds or subject to conditions; or

(b)    in proceedings transferred from the Court of Session, summarily dismisses part or all of the proceedings, or imposes any limitations or conditions on the continuation of such proceedings.

(4)    In the circumstances specified in paragraph (3) the applicant may apply for the decision to be reconsidered at a hearing.

(5)    An application under paragraph (4) must be made in writing and must be sent or delivered to the Upper Tribunal so that it is received within 14 days after the date on which the Upper Tribunal sent written notice of its decision regarding the application to the applicant.

**[3818]**

**NOTES**

Commencement: 3 November 2008.

## 31   Responses

(1)    Any person to whom the Upper Tribunal has sent notice of the grant of permission under rule 30(1) (notification of decision on permission), and who wishes to contest the application or support it on additional grounds, must provide detailed grounds for contesting or supporting the application to the Upper Tribunal.

(2)    Any detailed grounds must be provided in writing and must be sent or delivered to the Upper Tribunal so that they are received not more than 35 days after the Upper Tribunal sent notice of the grant of permission under rule 30(1).

**[3819]**

**NOTES**

Commencement: 3 November 2008.

## 32   Applicant seeking to rely on additional grounds

The applicant may not rely on any grounds, other than those grounds on which the applicant obtained permission for the judicial review proceedings, without the consent of the Upper Tribunal.

**[3820]**

**NOTES**

Commencement: 3 November 2008.

## 33   Right to make representations

Each party and, with the permission of the Upper Tribunal, any other person, may—

(a)    submit evidence, except at the hearing of an application for permission;

(b)    make representations at any hearing which they are entitled to attend; and

(c)    make written representations in relation to a decision to be made without a hearing.

**[3821]**

**NOTES**

Commencement: 3 November 2008.

## PART 5
### HEARINGS

## 34   Decision with or without a hearing

(1)    Subject to paragraph (2), the Upper Tribunal may make any decision without a hearing.

(2)    The Upper Tribunal must have regard to any view expressed by a party when deciding whether to hold a hearing to consider any matter, and the form of any such hearing.

**[3822]**

PART II
STATUTORY INSTRUMENTS

NOTES
Commencement: 3 November 2008.

## 35 Entitlement to attend a hearing

Subject to rule 37(4) (exclusion of a person from a hearing), each party is entitled to attend a hearing.

**[3823]**

NOTES
Commencement: 3 November 2008.

## 36 Notice of hearings

(1)   The Upper Tribunal must give each party entitled to attend a hearing reasonable notice of the time and place of the hearing (including any adjourned or postponed hearing) and any change to the time and place of the hearing.

(2)   The period of notice under paragraph (1) must be at least 14 days except that—
   (a)   in applications for permission to bring judicial review proceedings, the period of notice must be at least 2 working days; and
   (b)   the Upper Tribunal may give shorter notice—
      (i)   with the parties' consent; or
      (ii)   in urgent or exceptional cases.

**[3824]**

NOTES
Commencement: 3 November 2008.

## 37 Public and private hearings

(1)   Subject to the following paragraphs, all hearings must be held in public.

(2)   The Upper Tribunal may give a direction that a hearing, or part of it, is to be held in private.

(3)   Where a hearing, or part of it, is to be held in private, the Upper Tribunal may determine who is entitled to attend the hearing or part of it.

(4)   The Upper Tribunal may give a direction excluding from any hearing, or part of it—
   (a)   any person whose conduct the Upper Tribunal considers is disrupting or is likely to disrupt the hearing;
   (b)   any person whose presence the Upper Tribunal considers is likely to prevent another person from giving evidence or making submissions freely;
   (c)   any person who the Upper Tribunal considers should be excluded in order to give effect to [the requirement at rule 14(11) (prevention of disclosure or publication of documents and information)]; ...
   (d)   any person where the purpose of the hearing would be defeated by the attendance of that person[; or
   (e)   a person under the age of eighteen years].

(5)   The Upper Tribunal may give a direction excluding a witness from a hearing until that witness gives evidence.

**[3825]**

NOTES
Commencement: 3 November 2008.
Para (4): sub-para (c) words in square brackets substituted by the Tribunal Procedure (Amendment No 2) Rules 2009, SI 2009/1975, rr 7, 20, and word omitted revoked by the Tribunal Procedure (Amendment) Rules 2009, SI 2009/274, rr 3, 19(a); sub-para (e) and word immediately preceding it inserted by SI 2009/274, rr 3, 19(b).

## 38 Hearings in a party's absence

If a party fails to attend a hearing, the Upper Tribunal may proceed with the hearing if the Upper Tribunal—
   (a)   is satisfied that the party has been notified of the hearing or that reasonable steps have been taken to notify the party of the hearing; and
   (b)   considers that it is in the interests of justice to proceed with the hearing.

**[3826]**

NOTES
Commencement: 3 November 2008.

PART 6
DECISIONS

**39   Consent orders**

(1)   The Upper Tribunal may, at the request of the parties but only if it considers it appropriate, make a consent order disposing of the proceedings and making such other appropriate provision as the parties have agreed.

(2)   Notwithstanding any other provision of these Rules, the Tribunal need not hold a hearing before making an order under paragraph (1)…

**[3827]**

**NOTES**
Commencement: 3 November 2008.
Para (2): words omitted revoked by the Tribunal Procedure (Amendment) Rules 2009, SI 2009/274, rr 3, 20.

**40   Decisions**

(1)   The Upper Tribunal may give a decision orally at a hearing.

(2)   … the Upper Tribunal must provide to each party as soon as reasonably practicable after making a decision which finally disposes of all issues in the proceedings (except a decision under Part 7)—
    (a)   a decision notice stating the Tribunal's decision; and
    (b)   notification of any rights of review or appeal against the decision and the time and manner in which such rights of review or appeal may be exercised.

(3)   [Subject to rule [14(11) (prevention of disclosure or publication of documents and information)],] the Upper Tribunal must provide written reasons for its decision with a decision notice provided under paragraph (2)(a) unless—
    (a)   the decision was made with the consent of the parties; or
    (b)   the parties have consented to the Upper Tribunal not giving written reasons.

(4)   The [Upper] Tribunal may provide written reasons for any decision to which paragraph (2) does not apply.

**[3828]**

**NOTES**
Commencement: 3 November 2008.
Para (2): words omitted revoked by the Tribunal Procedure (Amendment) Rules 2009, SI 2009/274, rr 3, 21(a).
Para (3): words in outer pair of square brackets inserted by SI 2009/274, rr 3, 21(b); words in inner pair of square brackets substituted by the Tribunal Procedure (Amendment No 2) Rules 2009, SI 2009/1975, rr 7, 21(a).
Para (4): word in square brackets inserted by SI 2009/1975, rr 7, 21(b).

PART 7
CORRECTING, SETTING ASIDE, REVIEWING AND APPEALING DECISIONS OF THE
UPPER TRIBUNAL

**41   Interpretation**
In this Part—
    "appeal"[, except in rule 44(2) (application for permission to appeal),] means the exercise of a
    right of appeal under section 13 of the 2007 Act; and
    "review" means the review of a decision by the Upper Tribunal under section 10 of the 2007
    Act.

**[3829]**

**NOTES**
Commencement: 3 November 2008.
Definition "appeal": words in square brackets inserted by the Tribunal Procedure (Amendment) Rules 2009, SI 2009/274, rr 3, 22.

**42   Clerical mistakes and accidental slips or omissions**
The Upper Tribunal may at any time correct any clerical mistake or other accidental slip or omission in a decision or record of a decision by—
    (a)   sending notification of the amended decision, or a copy of the amended record, to all
    parties; and
    (b)   making any necessary amendment to any information published in relation to the
    decision or record.

**[3830]**

PART II
STATUTORY INSTRUMENTS

**NOTES**
Commencement: 3 November 2008.

### 43 Setting aside a decision which disposes of proceedings

(1)   The Upper Tribunal may set aside a decision which disposes of proceedings, or part of such a decision, and re-make the decision or the relevant part of it, if—
  (a)   the Upper Tribunal considers that it is in the interests of justice to do so; and
  (b)   one or more of the conditions in paragraph (2) are satisfied.

(2)   The conditions are—
  (a)   a document relating to the proceedings was not sent to, or was not received at an appropriate time by, a party or a party's representative;
  (b)   a document relating to the proceedings was not sent to the Upper Tribunal at an appropriate time;
  (c)   a party, or a party's representative, was not present at a hearing related to the proceedings; or
  (d)   there has been some other procedural irregularity in the proceedings.

(3)   A party applying for a decision, or part of a decision, to be set aside under paragraph (1) must make a written application to the Upper Tribunal so that it is received no later than 1 month after the date on which the Tribunal sent notice of the decision to the party.

**[3831]**

**NOTES**
Commencement: 3 November 2008.

### 44 Application for permission to appeal

(1)   A person seeking permission to appeal must make a written application to the Upper Tribunal for permission to appeal.

(2)   Paragraph (3) applies to an application under paragraph (1) in respect of a decision—
  (a)   on an appeal against a decision in a social security and child support case (as defined in the Tribunal Procedure (First-tier Tribunal) (Social Entitlement Chamber) Rules 2008);
  (b)   on an appeal against a decision in proceedings in the War Pensions and Armed Forces Compensation Chamber of the First-tier Tribunal; …
  [(ba)   on an appeal against a decision of a Pensions Appeal Tribunal for Scotland or Northern Ireland; or]
  (c)   in proceedings under the Forfeiture Act 1982.

(3)   Where this paragraph applies, the application must be sent or delivered to the Upper Tribunal so that it is received within 3 months after the date on which the Upper Tribunal sent to the person making the application—
  (a)   written notice of the decision;
  (b)   notification of amended reasons for, or correction of, the decision following a review; or
  (c)   notification that an application for the decision to be set aside has been unsuccessful.

(4)   Where paragraph (3) does not apply, an application under paragraph (1) must be sent or delivered to the Upper Tribunal so that it is received within 1 month after the latest of the dates on which the Upper Tribunal sent to the person making the application—
  (a)   written reasons for the decision;
  (b)   notification of amended reasons for, or correction of, the decision following a review; or
  (c)   notification that an application for the decision to be set aside has been unsuccessful.

(5)   The date in paragraph (3)(c) or (4)(c) applies only if the application for the decision to be set aside was made within the time stipulated in rule 43 (setting aside a decision which disposes of proceedings) or any extension of that time granted by the Upper Tribunal.

(6)   If the person seeking permission to appeal provides the application to the Upper Tribunal later than the time required by paragraph (3) or (4), or by any extension of time under rule 5(3)(a) (power to extend time)—
  (a)   the application must include a request for an extension of time and the reason why the application notice was not provided in time; and
  (b)   unless the Upper Tribunal extends time for the application under rule 5(3)(a) (power to extend time) the Upper Tribunal must refuse the application.

(7)   An application under paragraph (1) must—
  (a)   identify the decision of the Tribunal to which it relates;
  (b)   identify the alleged error or errors of law in the decision; and
  (c)   state the result the party making the application is seeking.

**[3832]**

**NOTES**
Commencement: 3 November 2008.
Para (2): sub-para (a) word omitted revoked by the Tribunal Procedure (Amendment) Rules 2009, SI 2009/274, rr 3, 23(a); sub-para (ba) inserted by SI 2009/274, rr 3, 23(b).

**45   Upper Tribunal's consideration of application for permission to appeal**

(1)   On receiving an application for permission to appeal the Upper Tribunal may review the decision in accordance with rule 46 (review of a decision), but may only do so if—

   (a)   when making the decision the Upper Tribunal overlooked a legislative provision or binding authority which could have had a material effect on the decision; or

   (b)   since the Upper Tribunal's decision, a court has made a decision which is binding on the Upper Tribunal and which, had it been made before the Upper Tribunal's decision, could have had a material effect on the decision.

(2)   If the Upper Tribunal decides not to review the decision, or reviews the decision and decides to take no action in relation to the decision or part of it, the Upper Tribunal must consider whether to give permission to appeal in relation to the decision or that part of it.

(3)   The Upper Tribunal must send a record of its decision to the parties as soon as practicable.

(4)   If the Upper Tribunal refuses permission to appeal it must send with the record of its decision—

   (a)   a statement of its reasons for such refusal; and

   (b)   notification of the right to make an application to the relevant appellate court for permission to appeal and the time within which, and the method by which, such application must be made.

(5)   The Upper Tribunal may give permission to appeal on limited grounds, but must comply with paragraph (4) in relation to any grounds on which it has refused permission.

**[3833]**

**NOTES**
Commencement: 3 November 2008.

**46   Review of a decision**

(1)   The Upper Tribunal may only undertake a review of a decision—

   (a)   pursuant to rule 45(1) (review on an application for permission to appeal); or

   (b)   pursuant to rule 47 (reviews of decisions in proceedings under the Forfeiture Act 1982).

(2)   The Upper Tribunal must notify the parties in writing of the outcome of any review and of any rights of review or appeal in relation to the outcome.

(3)   If the Upper Tribunal decides to take any action in relation to a decision following a review without first giving every party an opportunity to make representations, the notice under paragraph (2) must state that any party that did not have an opportunity to make representations may apply for such action to be set aside and for the decision to be reviewed again.

**[3834]**

**NOTES**
Commencement: 3 November 2008.

**47**   (*Outside the scope of this work.*)

# HOUSING AND REGENERATION ACT 2008 (COMMENCEMENT NO 2 AND TRANSITIONAL, SAVING AND TRANSITORY PROVISIONS) ORDER 2008

(SI 2008/3068)

**NOTES**
Made: 26 November 2008.
Authority: Housing and Regeneration Act 2008, ss 322, 325.

**1   Citation and interpretation**

(1)   This Order may be cited as the Housing and Regeneration Act 2008 (Commencement No 2 and Transitional, Saving and Transitory Provisions) Order 2008.

(2)    In this Order—
"the 1993 Act" means the Leasehold Reform, Housing and Urban Development Act 1993;
"the Act" means the Housing and Regeneration Act 2008;
"the CNT" means the Commission for the New Towns;
"the HCA" means the Homes and Communities Agency;
"the URA" means the Urban Regeneration Agency;
"the commencement date" means 1st December 2008.

[3834A]

**2–5**    (*Set out the provisions of the Housing and Regeneration Act 2008 brought into force by this Order; the effect of the commencement of those provisions is noted at the appropriate place in this work.*)

## 6    General saving provision

The amendments made by the provisions brought into force by this Order do not affect the validity of anything done (or having effect as if done) by or in relation to the URA or the CNT before the commencement date.

[3834B]

## 7    Transitional and saving provisions: functions transferred from the URA or the CNT to the HCA or the Welsh Ministers

(1)    Anything which, on the commencement date, is in the process of being done by or in relation to the transferor may, so far as it relates to any function transferred by a relevant enactment from the transferor to the transferee, be continued by or in relation to the transferee.

(2)    Anything done (or having effect as if done) by or in relation to the transferor for the purposes of or in connection with any function transferred by a relevant enactment from the transferor to the transferee shall, if in force or effective on the commencement date, have effect as if done by or in relation to the transferee so far as that is required for continuing its effect on or after the commencement date.

(3)    Any enactment, instrument or other document passed or made before the commencement date shall have effect, so far as necessary for the purposes of or in consequence of paragraph (1) or (2), as if any references (however expressed) to the transferor were references to the transferee.

(4)    The references in paragraphs (1) and (2) to things done include references to things omitted to be done.

(5)    In this article—
"relevant enactment" means—
(a)    in the case of a transfer from the URA to the HCA, paragraph 4 of Schedule 8 to the Act;
(b)    in the case of a transfer from the CNT to the HCA or the Welsh Ministers, paragraphs 8 and 31 of Schedule 5 to the Act and paragraphs 4 to 12, 17, 18, 36, 43, 61, 80 and 82 of Schedule 8 to the Act;
"the transferee"—
(a)    where the transferor is the URA, means the HCA;
(b)    where the transferor is the CNT, means the HCA or the Welsh Ministers;
"the transferor", except in the definition of "the transferee", means the URA or the CNT,
and the references in this paragraph to the HCA or the Welsh Ministers are to be read as including references to them acting in a particular capacity or in relation to particular matters.

[3834C]

## 8    Transitional provisions in relation to investigations under the Local Government Act 1974

An investigation may be begun in accordance with Part 3 of the Local Government Act 1974 ("the 1974 Act") on or after the commencement date in relation to actions or failures to act of the CNT or the URA before the commencement date, but in such a case the provisions of that Part shall have effect as if the actions or failures concerned were actions or failures of the HCA, and for this purpose and in particular—
(a)    section 26(7)(a) of the 1974 Act shall continue to have effect as though that subsection were not repealed by section 56 of, and paragraph 18 of Schedule 8 to, the Act; and
(b)    section 26(7)(ba) of the 1974 Act shall continue to have effect as though that subsection were not repealed in part and amended by section 56 of, and paragraph 18 of Schedule 8 to, the Act, but
(c)    the references to the CNT and the URA in each of those subsections respectively shall be construed as though they were references to the HCA.

[3834D]

## 9    Transitional provisions in relation to the acquisition of land etc.

(1)    This article is subject to article 10.

(2)   Anything which, on the commencement date, is in the process of being done by or in relation to the URA under a superseded enactment may be continued by or in relation to the HCA under the corresponding provision of the Act.

(3)   Any subordinate legislation or other thing done (or having effect as if done) by or in relation to the URA under or for the purposes of a superseded enactment shall, if in force or effective on the commencement date, have effect as if done by or in relation to the HCA under the corresponding provision of the Act so far as that is required for continuing its effect on and after the commencement date.

(4)   Any enactment, instrument or other document (including the Act) passed or made before the commencement date shall have effect, so far as necessary for the purposes of or in consequence of paragraph (2) or (3), as if—

(a)   any references (however expressed) to the HCA included, in relation to times, circumstances or purposes in relation to which any superseded enactment had effect, references to the URA;

(b)   any references (however expressed) to the corresponding provision of the Act included, in relation to times, circumstances or purposes in relation to which any superseded enactment had effect, references to the superseded enactment;

(c)   any references (however expressed) to the URA included, in relation to times, circumstances or purposes in relation to which any corresponding provision of the Act has effect, references to the HCA; and

(d)   any references (however expressed) to a superseded enactment included, in relation to times, circumstances or purposes in relation to which any corresponding provision of the Act has effect, references to the corresponding provision.

(5)   The references in paragraphs (2) and (3) to things done include references to things omitted to be done.

(6)   In this article "superseded enactment" means sections 162 and 169 of, and Schedule 20 to, the 1993 Act.

**[3834E]**

**10**—(1)   Paragraph (2) applies in relation to a compulsory purchase order which—

(a)   was made by the URA before the commencement date under section 162 of the 1993 Act but in respect of which the Secretary of State has not made a decision before that date; and

(b)   is treated by virtue of article 9 above as made by the HCA under section 9 of the Act.

(2)   Before the Secretary of State—

(a)   confirms the order under section 9 of, and Schedule 2 to, the Act on or after the commencement date; or

(b)   decides under the enactments applied by those provisions on or after that date to permit the HCA to exercise the power to confirm the order,

the Secretary of State must be satisfied that the acquisition of the land to which the order relates would have been within the powers of the URA when the order was made.

**[3834F]**

**11–13**   (*Outside the scope of this work.*)

(*The Schedule sets out provisions of the Housing and Regeneration Act 2008 brought into force by this Order; the effect of the commencement of those provisions is noted at the appropriate place in this work.*)

# APPROVAL OF CODE OF MANAGEMENT PRACTICE (RESIDENTIAL MANAGEMENT) (SERVICE CHARGES) (ENGLAND) ORDER 2009

(SI 2009/512)

**NOTES**

Made: 4 March 2009.

Authority: Leasehold Reform, Housing and Urban Development Act 1993, ss 87, 100.

Commencement: 6 April 2009.

**1   Citation, commencement and application**

(1)   This Order may be cited as the Approval of Code of Management Practice (Residential Management) (Service Charges) (England) Order 2009 and shall come into force on 6th April 2009.

(2)   This Order applies in relation to the management of residential properties in England only.

**[3835]**

**NOTES**
   Commencement: 6 April 2009.

## 2   Approval of code of practice

"Service Charge Residential Management Code" (ISBN 978 1 84219 168 2), which is to be published by the Royal Institution of Chartered Surveyors, is approved in relation to England.

**[3836]**

**NOTES**
   Commencement: 6 April 2009.

## 3   Withdrawal of approval

(1)   The Secretary of State withdraws approval of "Service Charge Residential Management Code" (ISBN 0 85406 643 8) in so far as it applies to the management of residential properties in England.

**[3837]**

**NOTES**
   Commencement: 6 April 2009.

## 4   Saving and transitional provision

Articles 2 and 3 do not apply for the purposes of section 87(7)(a) and (b) of the Leasehold Reform, Housing and Urban Development Act 1993 (use of code in proceedings) in relation to an act or omission alleged to have occurred before this Order comes into force.

**[3838]**

**NOTES**
   Commencement: 6 April 2009.

# HOUSING (REPLACEMENT OF TERMINATED TENANCIES) (SUCCESSOR LANDLORDS) (WALES) ORDER 2009 (NOTE)

## (SI 2009/1260 (W 112))

**NOTES**
   Made: 19 May 2009.
   Authority: Housing and Regeneration Act 2008, Sch 11, para 24.
   Commencement: 20 May 2009.
   This Order applies to Wales only. The equivalent provisions for England are in SI 2009/1262 at **[3838B]** et seq.

**[3838A]**

# HOUSING (REPLACEMENT OF TERMINATED TENANCIES) (SUCCESSOR LANDLORDS) (ENGLAND) ORDER 2009

## (SI 2009/1262)

**NOTES**
   Made: 19 May 2009.
   Authority: Housing and Regeneration Act 2008, Sch 11, para 24.
   Commencement: 20 May 2009.

## 1   Citation, commencement and application

(1)   This Order may be cited as the Housing (Replacement of Terminated Tenancies) (Successor Landlords) (England) Order 2009 and shall come into force on the day after it is made.

(2)   This Order applies in relation to dwelling-houses in England only.

**[3838B]**

**NOTES**
Commencement: 20 May 2009.

## 2   Replacement of terminated tenancies: successor landlord cases

Part 2 of Schedule 11 to the Housing and Regeneration Act 2008 (replacement of certain terminated tenancies) shall apply, subject to the modifications specified in articles 3 to 7, to successor landlord cases.

**[3838C]**

**NOTES**
Commencement: 20 May 2009.

## 3   Circumstances in which replacement tenancies arise

Paragraph 16 (circumstances in which replacement tenancies arise) applies as if in sub-paragraph (1)—
- (a)   for "ex-landlord", in the first and second places where that word occurs, "successor landlord" were substituted; and
- (b)   for paragraph (b) there were substituted—
  "(b)   the ex-tenant has not entered into another tenancy with—
    (i)   the successor landlord, or
    (ii)   any initial transferee or subsequent transferee who is not the successor landlord,
    after the date on which the original tenancy ended but before the commencement date.".

**[3838D]**

**NOTES**
Commencement: 20 May 2009.

## 4   Nature of replacement tenancies

Paragraph 17 applies as if there were substituted for it—

"**17.**   The new tenancy is to be—
- (a)   a secure tenancy if—
  - (i)   the original tenancy was—
    - (aa)   a secure tenancy,
    - (bb)   an assured tenancy (whether or not an assured shorthold tenancy),
    - (cc)   an introductory tenancy, or
    - (dd)   a demoted tenancy,
  - (ii)   the new tenancy satisfies the conditions for a secure tenancy in accordance with Part IV of the Housing Act 1985,
  - (iii)   the new tenancy is one which, by virtue of subsection (2) of section 1 of the Housing Act 1988, cannot be an assured tenancy,
  - (iv)   where the original tenancy was an assured shorthold tenancy or an introductory tenancy, no election by the successor landlord under section 124 of the Housing Act 1996 is in force on the day on which the new tenancy arises, and
  - (v)   where the original tenancy was a demoted tenancy, the successor landlord is not a person entitled to apply for an order of the court under section 82A of the Housing Act 1985 (a demotion order),
- (b)   an assured shorthold tenancy if—
  - (i)   the original tenancy was—
    - (aa)   an assured shorthold tenancy,
    - (bb)   an introductory tenancy, or
    - (cc)   a demoted tenancy,
  - (ii)   the new tenancy is not one which, by virtue of subsection (2) of section 1 of the Housing Act 1988, cannot be an assured tenancy,
  - (iii)   the new tenancy is not one which falls within any paragraph of Schedule 2A to the Housing Act 1988,
  - (iv)   the new tenancy does not satisfy the conditions for a secure tenancy in accordance with Part IV of the Housing Act 1985, and
  - (v)   where the original tenancy was a demoted tenancy, the successor landlord is not a registered social landlord,
- (c)   an assured tenancy which is not an assured shorthold tenancy if—
  - (i)   the original tenancy was—

(aa) an assured tenancy which was not an assured shorthold tenancy, or

(bb) a secure tenancy,

    (ii) the new tenancy is not one which, by virtue of subsection (2) of section 1 of the Housing Act 1988, cannot be an assured tenancy, and

    (iii) the new tenancy does not satisfy the conditions for a secure tenancy in accordance with Part IV of the Housing Act 1985,

  (d) an introductory tenancy if—

    (i) the original tenancy was—

(aa) an introductory tenancy, or

(bb) an assured shorthold tenancy,

    (ii) the new tenancy is one which, by virtue of subsection (2) of section 1 of the Housing Act 1988, cannot be an assured tenancy,

    (iii) an election by the successor landlord under section 124 of the Housing Act 1996 is in force on the day on which the new tenancy arises, and

    (iv) but for that election, the new tenancy would be a secure tenancy because it satisfies the conditions for a secure tenancy in accordance with Part IV of the Housing Act 1985,

  (e) a demoted tenancy to which section 20B of the Housing Act 1988 applies if—

    (i) the original tenancy was a demoted tenancy, and

    (ii) the successor landlord is a registered social landlord, or

  (f) a demoted tenancy to which section 143A of the Housing Act 1996 applies if—

    (i) the original tenancy was a demoted tenancy, and

    (ii) the new tenancy satisfies the first and second conditions in section 143A of the Housing Act 1996.".

**[3838E]**

**NOTES**

Commencement: 20 May 2009.

### 5  Nature of replacement tenancies—further provisions

Paragraph 18 applies as if—

  (a) in sub-paragraph (3) for "ex-landlord" there were substituted "successor landlord"; and

  (b) for sub-paragraph (6) there were substituted—

"(6) The terms and conditions of a new secure tenancy which arises by virtue of paragraph 17(a), where the original tenancy was—

    (a) an assured tenancy,

    (b) an introductory tenancy, or

    (c) a demoted tenancy

are to be treated as modified so far as necessary to reflect the fact that the new tenancy is a secure tenancy and not an assured tenancy, an introductory tenancy or a demoted tenancy (as the case may be).

(7) The terms and conditions of a new assured shorthold tenancy which arises by virtue of paragraph 17(b), where the original tenancy was—

    (a) an introductory tenancy, or

    (b) a demoted tenancy,

are to be treated as modified so far as necessary to reflect the fact that the new tenancy is an assured shorthold tenancy and not an introductory tenancy or a demoted tenancy (as the case may be).

(8) The terms and conditions of a new assured tenancy which arises by virtue of paragraph 17(c), where the original tenancy was a secure tenancy, are to be treated as modified so far as necessary to reflect the fact that the new tenancy is an assured tenancy and not a secure tenancy.

(9) The terms and conditions of a new introductory tenancy which arises by virtue of paragraph 17(d), where the original tenancy was an assured shorthold tenancy, are to be treated as modified so far as necessary to reflect the fact that the new tenancy is an introductory tenancy and not an assured shorthold tenancy.

(10) The terms and conditions of a new demoted tenancy which arises by virtue of paragraph 17(e), where the original tenancy was a demoted tenancy to which section 143A of the Housing Act 1996 applied, are to be treated as modified so far as necessary to reflect the fact that the new tenancy is a demoted tenancy to which section 20B of the Housing Act 1988 applies and not a demoted tenancy to which section 143A of the Housing Act 1996 applies.

(11) The terms and conditions of a new demoted tenancy which arises by virtue of paragraph 17(f), where the original tenancy was a demoted tenancy to which section 20B of the Housing Act 1988 applied, are to be treated as modified so far as necessary to reflect the

fact that the new tenancy is a demoted tenancy to which section 143A of the Housing Act 1996 applies and not a demoted tenancy to which section 20B of the Housing Act 1988 applies.".

**[3838F]**

---

## NOTES
Commencement: 20 May 2009.

---

## 6　Continuity of tenancies

Paragraph 21 (continuity of tenancies) applies as if—

(a)　paragraph (a) of sub-paragraph (2) were omitted;

(b)　after sub-paragraph (2) there were inserted—

"(2A)　Where the ex-tenant was a successor in relation to the original tenancy, the ex-tenant shall be treated as a successor in relation to the new tenancy."; and

(c)　for sub-paragraphs (3) to (5) there were substituted—

"(3)　In proceedings on a claim of a description specified in sub-paragraph (7), the court concerned may order that, for the purposes of the claim, the original tenancy is to be treated as having continued during the termination period until the relevant interest was transferred to the initial transferee.

(4)　In proceedings on a claim of a description specified in sub-paragraph (8), the court concerned may order that, for the purposes of the claim, the original tenancy is to be treated as having continued during the termination period until the relevant interest was transferred to the successor landlord.

(5)　In proceedings on a claim of a description specified in sub-paragraph (9), the court concerned may order that, for the purposes of the claim, the new tenancy is to be treated as having commenced when the relevant interest was transferred to the successor landlord.

(6)　In proceedings on a claim of a description specified in sub-paragraph (8) together with a claim of a description specified in sub-paragraph (9), where those claims relate to the same alleged breach, the court concerned may order that, for the purposes of the claims, the original tenancy and the new tenancy are to be treated as—

(a)　the same tenancy, and

(b)　a tenancy which continued uninterrupted throughout the termination period.

(7)　The following are claims specified for the purposes of sub-paragraph (3)—

(a)　a claim by the ex-tenant or the ex-landlord against the other for breach of a term or condition of the original tenancy—

(i)　in respect of which proceedings are brought on or after the commencement date, or

(ii)　in respect of which proceedings were brought, but were not finally determined, before that date, and

(b)　a claim by the ex-tenant against the ex-landlord for breach of statutory duty—

(i)　where the alleged breach occurred before the relevant interest was transferred to the initial transferee, and

(ii)　in respect of which proceedings are or were brought as mentioned in paragraph (a)(i) or (ii).

(8)　Where any rights or liabilities in relation to the original tenancy were transferred to the successor landlord, the following is a claim specified for the purposes of sub-paragraph (4): a claim by the ex-tenant or the successor landlord against the other for breach of a term or condition of the original tenancy in respect of which proceedings are or were brought as mentioned in sub-paragraph (7)(a)(i) or (ii).

(9)　The following are claims specified for the purposes of sub-paragraph (5)—

(a)　a claim by the ex-tenant or the successor landlord against the other for breach of a term or condition of the new tenancy, and

(b)　a claim by the ex-tenant against the successor landlord for breach of statutory duty, where the alleged breach occurred after the relevant interest was transferred to the successor landlord,

in respect of which proceedings are or were brought as mentioned in sub-paragraph (7)(a)(i) or (ii).

(10)　For the purposes of sub-paragraphs (7) to (9) proceedings must be treated as finally determined if—

(a)　they are withdrawn,

(b)　any appeal is abandoned, or

(c)　the time for appealing has expired without an appeal being brought.".

**[3838G]**

**NOTES**
Commencement: 20 May 2009.

## 7 Interpretation

Sub-paragraph (1) of paragraph 26 (supplementary) applies as if—

  (a)  after the definition of "ex-tenant" there were inserted—
        ""initial transferee" means the person to whom the relevant interest was transferred by the ex-landlord after the end of the original tenancy and before the commencement date,";

  (b)  after the definition of "possession order" there were inserted—
        ""registered social landlord" has the same meaning as in Part 1 of the Housing Act 1996, "relevant interest" means the interest of the ex-landlord in the dwelling-house which was let under an original tenancy,";

  (c)  after the definition of "secure tenancy" there were inserted—
        ""subsequent transferee" means any person to whom, before the commencement date, the relevant interest was transferred after the transfer from the ex-landlord to the initial transferee,";

  (d)  in the definition of "successor"—
        (i)   after ""successor"" there were inserted ", except in the expression "successor landlord"";
        (ii)  for "a new tenancy which is", in each place where those words occur, there were substituted "an original tenancy which was, or a new tenancy which is,"; and
        (iii) in paragraph (a), for "or which is a demoted tenancy" there were substituted ", or in relation to an original tenancy which was, or a new tenancy which is, a demoted tenancy"; and

  (e)  after the definition of "successor" there were inserted—
        ""successor landlord" means the initial transferee, or, as the case may be, a subsequent transferee, to whom the relevant interest belongs on the commencement date

**[3838H]**

**NOTES**
Commencement: 20 May 2009.

# HOUSING (SHARED OWNERSHIP LEASES) (EXCLUSION FROM LEASEHOLD REFORM ACT 1967) (ENGLAND) REGULATIONS 2009

## (SI 2009/2097)

**NOTES**
Made: 4 August 2009.
Authority: Leasehold Reform Act 1967, Sch 4A, paras 3A(1), (2), 4A(1), (2), 5.
Commencement: 7 September 2009.

### ARRANGEMENT OF REGULATIONS

## 1    Citation, commencement and application

(1)    These Regulations may be cited as the Housing (Shared Ownership Leases) (Exclusion from Leasehold Reform Act 1967) (England) Regulations 2009 and shall come into force on 7th September 2009.

(2)    These Regulations apply in relation to the granting of a long tenancy for a house in England at any time after the coming into force of these Regulations except where such tenancy arises from a written agreement for the grant of that tenancy made before the coming into force of these Regulations.

**[3839]**

**NOTES**

Commencement: 7 September 2009.

## 2    Interpretation

In these Regulations "the Act" means the Leasehold Reform Act 1967.

**[3840]**

**NOTES**

Commencement: 7 September 2009.

## 3    Meaning of "market value price", etc

(1)    For the purposes of these Regulations, "market value price" means the amount which the interest in the house of the tenant would fetch, if sold on the open market by a willing vendor, on the assumption that the tenant had previously purchased 100 per cent of the shares in the house, disregarding the following matters—

   (a)    any mortgage of the tenant's interest;

   (b)    any interest in or right over the house created by the tenant;

   (c)    any improvement made by the tenant or any predecessor in title of the tenant; and

   (d)    any failure by the tenant or any predecessor in title of the tenant to carry out any repairing obligations under the lease.

(2)    Subject to paragraph (3), the market value price shall be agreed between the landlord and the tenant, or determined in a manner agreed between them.

(3)    Where the landlord and tenant are unable to agree the manner in which the market value price should be determined they may appoint an independent expert to determine the price.

(4)    If the landlord and tenant are unable to agree on the person to be appointed, either party may apply to the President of the Royal Institution of Chartered Surveyors for the market value price to be determined by the President or such person as he may nominate.

**[3841]**

**NOTES**

Commencement: 7 September 2009.

## 4    Prescribed condition under paragraph 3A(1)(b) of Schedule 4A to the Act

The condition prescribed under paragraph 3A(1)(b) of Schedule 4A to the Act is that the lease must set out the amount of any rent payable and the basis for calculating or determining any increase in the rent payable.

**[3842]**

**NOTES**

Commencement: 7 September 2009.

## 5    Acquisition of additional shares in the house: requirements prescribed under paragraph 3A(2)(c) of Schedule 4A to the Act

(1)    The following requirements are prescribed under paragraph 3A(2)(c) of Schedule 4A to the Act for the purposes of paragraph 3A(1)(a) of that Schedule.

(2)    The tenant is to be entitled to acquire additional shares in the house, up to a maximum of 100 per cent, in instalments of 25 per cent or such lesser percentage as may be specified in the lease.

(3)    If the lease specifies the date after which the tenant may acquire additional shares in the house, such date must not be later than 12 months after the date the tenant first acquired shares in the house.

(4)    The tenant is to be able to exercise the entitlement to acquire additional shares in the house by serving notice in writing on the landlord at any time during the term of the lease, stating the additional shares the tenant proposes to acquire.

(5)   Where the tenant serves a notice under paragraph (4) the landlord must not act in a way that would unreasonably delay the acquisition by the tenant of the additional shares.

(6)   The price for the additional shares is to be an amount no greater than the same percentage of the market value price at the date of service of the tenant's notice under paragraph (4) as is represented by the percentage of the additional shares being acquired.

(7)   The rent payable by the tenant to the landlord under the lease (excluding amounts payable, directly or indirectly, for services, repairs, maintenance, insurance, or management costs) is to be reduced, on the tenant's acquisition of additional shares, in the same proportion as is represented by the reduction in the percentage of shares remaining un-acquired by the tenant.

**[3843]**

**NOTES**

Commencement: 7 September 2009.

## 6   Payment for outstanding shares in the house: circumstances prescribed under paragraph 3A(2)(e) of Schedule 4A to the Act

(1)   (1) The circumstances prescribed under paragraph 3A(2)(e) of Schedule 4A to the Act for the purposes of paragraph 3A(1)(a) of that Schedule are that the lease must provide—

   (a)   that there shall have been a disposal, other than an exempt disposal, of any interest in the house by the tenant; and

   (b)   that the amount payable by the tenant to the landlord is to be an amount no greater than the same percentage of the market value price at the date of the disposal as is represented by the percentage of the shares in the house remaining un-acquired by the tenant.

(2)   In paragraph (1) "exempt disposal" means—

   (a)   a disposal under a will or intestacy;

   (b)   a disposal under section 24 of the Matrimonial Causes Act 1973 or section 2 of the Inheritance (Provision for Family and Dependants) Act 1975;

   (c)   a grant of a sub-tenancy in respect of which a notice has been given under section 52(1)(b) of the Housing Act 1980 (notice that a tenancy is to be a protected shorthold tenancy) or of a kind mentioned in any of Cases 11 to 18 or 20 in Schedule 15 to the Rent Act 1977;

   (d)   a grant of a sub-tenancy of part of the house, if any other part of the house remains in the possession of the tenant; or

   (e)   a grant of a mortgage.

**[3844]**

**NOTES**

Commencement: 7 September 2009.

## 7   Acquisition of the landlord's interest in the house: requirements prescribed under paragraph 3A(2)(f) of Schedule 4A to the Act

(1)   The following requirements are prescribed under paragraph 3A(2)(f) of Schedule 4A to the Act for the purposes of paragraph 3A(1)(a) of that Schedule.

(2)   The lease must provide that the tenant may not acquire the landlord's interest until the tenant has acquired 100 per cent of the shares in the house.

(3)   If the lease specifies the date after which the tenant may acquire the landlord's interest, such date must not be later than 12 months after the date the tenant first acquired shares in the house.

(4)   Where the lease does not provide for the landlord's interest to be transferred automatically to the tenant once the tenant has acquired 100 per cent of the shares in the house, it must provide for the tenant to acquire the landlord's interest—

   (a)   by serving notice in writing on the landlord at any time during the term of the lease; and

   (b)   requiring the landlord's interest to be transferred to the tenant as soon as practicable after the coming into effect of the notice referred to in sub-paragraph (a).

(5)   The lease must not make provision entitling the landlord to make any charge for the conveyance or assignment of his interest in the house.

**[3845]**

**NOTES**

Commencement: 7 September 2009.

## 8   Protected areas: conditions prescribed under paragraph 4A(1)(c) of Schedule 4A to the Act

(1)   The following conditions are prescribed under paragraph 4A(1)(c) of Schedule 4A to the Act.

(2)   The lease must contain a condition enabling the tenant to acquire at least 80 per cent of the total shares in the house.

(3)   If the lease enables the tenant to acquire more than 80 per cent of the shares in the house the lease must also contain conditions to the effect that where the tenant holds more than 80 per cent of the shares and wants to sell those shares—

    (a)   except in the circumstances described in paragraph (4)(h), the tenant must sell the shares to the landlord, or to a housing association or registered social landlord nominated by the landlord; and

    (b)   on a sale of the shares the landlord, nominated housing association or nominated registered social landlord, as the case may be, must pay to the tenant an amount no greater than the same percentage of the market value price at the date of service of the tenant's notice under sub-paragraph (4)(e) as is represented by the percentage of the shares being sold.

(4)   Where the lease contains conditions to the effect specified in paragraph (3) the lease must also—

    (a)   specify the circumstances in which the tenant may notify the landlord of the tenant's intention to sell the shares in the house;

    (b)   require the tenant to notify the landlord that the tenant intends to sell those shares;

    (c)   specify the time by which the landlord must respond to the tenant's notice of intended sale, which must be no later than 3 months after the date of receipt by the landlord of the tenant's notice;

    (d)   specify that the landlord's response—

        (i)   will confirm that the landlord will purchase the shares; or

       (ii)   will state the name, address and contact details of the housing association or registered social landlord nominated by the landlord to purchase the shares;

    (e)   specify that the landlord, the nominated housing association or the registered social landlord will complete the purchase of the tenant's shares no later than 6 months after the date of receipt by the landlord, the nominated housing association or the nominated registered social landlord of the tenant's notice that the tenant is ready to sell the tenant's shares specified in the notice referred to in sub-paragraph (b);

    (f)   prohibit the tenant from giving the notice referred to in sub-paragraph (e) until the market value price has been ascertained in accordance with regulation 3;

    (g)   specify the manner in which notices referred to in this regulation may be served, including any circumstances in which service shall be deemed to have taken place; and

    (h)   specify the remedies available to the tenant in the event of a failure by the landlord, the nominated housing association or the nominated registered social landlord to complete the purchase of the tenant's shares in the house in accordance with the conditions of the lease, which must include enabling the tenant—

        (i)   to dispose of the shares as the tenant sees fit; and

       (ii)   to recover from the landlord compensation for any loss occasioned by the tenant as a result of delay or failure on the part of the landlord, the nominated housing association or the nominated registered social landlord to complete the purchase in accordance with the conditions of the lease.

(5)   The lease must contain conditions to the effect that—

    (a)   the landlord may not nominate a housing association or registered social landlord to purchase the tenant's shares unless that housing association or registered social landlord has confirmed in writing to the landlord that it wishes to be nominated to purchase the tenant's shares; and

    (b)   where a housing association or registered social landlord has been nominated by the landlord, the housing association or registered social landlord will be substituted for the landlord during the process of acquiring the tenant's shares (whether or not the tenant's shares are acquired by the nominated association or landlord) and, in particular, will be subject to the same conditions as would apply to the landlord if the landlord were purchasing the shares, with the exception of that referred to in paragraph (4)(h)(ii).

(6)   A lease granted by a person other than a housing association or registered social landlord must set out the amount of any rent payable and the basis for calculating or determining any increase in the rent payable.

(7)   In this regulation a "registered social landlord" is a landlord that is registered as a social landlord in England under Part 1 of the Housing Act 1996 .

**[3846]**

---

**NOTES**

Commencement: 7 September 2009.

PART II
STATUTORY INSTRUMENTS

**9 Protected areas: acquisition of additional shares in the house—requirements prescribed under paragraph 4A(2)(c) of Schedule 4A to the Act**

(1)   The following requirements are prescribed under paragraph 4A(2)(c) of Schedule 4A to the Act for the purposes of paragraph 4A(1)(a) of that Schedule.

(2)   The tenant is to be entitled to acquire additional shares in the house, up to the maximum specified in the lease (being not less than 80 per cent of the total shares in the house), in instalments of 25 per cent or such lesser percentage as may be specified in the lease.

(3)   If the lease specifies the date after which the tenant may acquire additional shares in the house, such date must not be later than 12 months after the date the tenant first acquired shares in the house.

(4)   The tenant is to be able to exercise the entitlement to acquire additional shares in the house by serving notice in writing on the landlord at any time during the term of the lease, stating the additional shares the tenant proposes to acquire.

(5)   Where the tenant serves a notice under paragraph (4) the landlord must not act in a way that would unreasonably delay the acquisition by the tenant of the additional shares.

(6)   The price for the additional shares is to be an amount no greater than the same percentage of the market value price at the date of service of the tenant's notice under paragraph (4) as is represented by the percentage of the additional shares being acquired.

(7)   The rent payable by the tenant to the landlord under the lease (excluding amounts payable, directly or indirectly, for services, repairs, maintenance, insurance, or management costs) is to be reduced, on the tenant's acquisition of additional shares, in the same proportion as is represented by the reduction in the percentage of shares remaining un-acquired by the tenant.

**[3847]**

**NOTES**
Commencement: 7 September 2009.

**10 Protected areas: payment for outstanding shares in the house—circumstances prescribed under paragraph 4A(2)(e) of Schedule 4A to the Act**

(1)   The circumstances prescribed under paragraph 4A(2)(e) of Schedule 4A to the Act for the purposes of paragraph 4A(1)(a) of that Schedule are that the lease must provide—
  (a)   that there shall have been a disposal, other than an exempt disposal, of any interest in the house by the tenant; and
  (b)   that the amount payable by the tenant to the landlord is to be an amount no greater than the same percentage of the market value price at the date of the disposal as is represented by the percentage of the shares in the house remaining un-acquired by the tenant.

(2)   In paragraph (1) "exempt disposal" means—
  (a)   a disposal under a will or intestacy;
  (b)   a disposal under section 24 of the Matrimonial Causes Act 1973 or section 2 of the Inheritance (Provision for Family and Dependants) Act 1975;
  (c)   a grant of a sub-tenancy in respect of which a notice has been given under section 52(1)(b) of the Housing Act 1980 (notice that a tenancy is to be a protected shorthold tenancy) or of a kind mentioned in any of Cases 11 to 18 or 20 in Schedule 15 to the Rent Act 1977;
  (d)   a grant of a sub-tenancy of part of the house, if any other part of the house remains in the possession of the tenant; or
  (e)   a grant of a mortgage.

**[3848]**

**NOTES**
Commencement: 7 September 2009.

# HOUSING (RIGHT TO ENFRANCHISE) (DESIGNATED PROTECTED AREAS) (ENGLAND) ORDER 2009

(SI 2009/2098)

**NOTES**
Made: 4 August 2009.
Authority: Leasehold Reform Act 1967, Sch 4A, para 4A(3).
Commencement: 7 September 2009.

## ARRANGEMENT OF ARTICLES

**1   Citation and commencement and interpretation**

(1)   This Order may be cited as the Housing (Right to Enfranchise) (Designated Protected Areas) (England) Order 2009 and shall come into force on 7th September 2009.

(2)   In this Order "the 1967 Act" means the Leasehold Reform Act 1967.

**[3849]**

**NOTES**
Commencement: 7 September 2009.

**2   Designated protected areas in the West Midlands**

The following areas in the West Midlands region are designated protected areas for the purposes of paragraph 4A(1) of Schedule 4A to the 1967 Act (certain leases in protected areas)—

(a)   those parishes in the district of Herefordshire and in the counties of Shropshire, Staffordshire, Warwickshire, West Midlands and Worcestershire specified in Schedule 1 to this Order; and

(b)   those areas in the parishes and the unparished areas in the district of Herefordshire and in the counties of Shropshire, Staffordshire, Warwickshire, West Midlands and Worcestershire specified in Schedule 2 to this Order each shown bounded with a black line and crossed hatched on one of the maps contained in the volume entitled "Maps of the Protected Areas in the West Midlands designated as protected areas by the Housing (Right to Enfranchise) (Designated Protected Areas) (England) Order 2009 (SI No: 2009/2098) and referred to in article 2(b) and Schedule 2 to the Order", which volume is—

(i)   signed by a member of the Senior Civil Service in the Department for Communities and Local Government; and

(ii)   deposited and available for inspection at the principal office of the Secretary of State for Communities and Local Government.

**[3850]**

**NOTES**
Commencement: 7 September 2009.

**3   Designated protected areas in the South West**

The following areas in the South West region are designated protected areas for the purposes of paragraph 4A(1) of Schedule 4A to the 1967 Act—

(a)   those parishes in the districts of Bath and North East Somerset, North Somerset and South Gloucestershire and in the counties of Cornwall, Devon, Dorset, Gloucestershire, Somerset and Wiltshire specified in Schedule 3 to this Order; and

(b)   those areas in the parishes and the unparished areas in the districts of Bath and North East Somerset, North Somerset and South Gloucestershire and in the counties of Cornwall, Devon, Dorset, Gloucestershire, Somerset and Wiltshire specified in Schedule 4 to this Order each shown bounded with a black line and cross hatched on one of the maps contained in the volume entitled "Maps of the Protected Areas in the South West designated as protected areas by the Housing (Right to Enfranchise) (Designated Protected Areas) (England) Order 2009 (SI No: 2009/2098) and referred to in article 3(b) and Schedule 4 to the Order", which volume is—

(i)   signed by a member of the Senior Civil Service in the Department for Communities and Local Government; and

(ii)   deposited and available for inspection at the principal office of the Secretary of State for Communities and Local Government.

**[3851]**

**NOTES**
Commencement: 7 September 2009.

**4   Designated protected areas in the North West**

The following areas in the North West region are designated protected areas for the purposes of paragraph 4A(1) of Schedule 4A to the 1967 Act—

(a)   those parishes in the districts of Cheshire East, Cheshire West and Chester, Halton and Warrington and in the counties of Cumbria, Greater Manchester, Lancashire and Merseyside specified in Schedule 5 to this Order; and

(b)   those areas in the parishes and the unparished areas in the districts of Cheshire East, Cheshire West and Chester and Warrington and in the counties of Cumbria, Greater Manchester, Lancashire and Merseyside specified in Schedule 6 to this Order each shown bounded with a black line and cross hatched on one of the maps contained in the volume entitled "Maps of the Protected Areas in the North West designated as protected

areas by the Housing (Right to Enfranchise) (Designated Protected Areas) (England) Order 2009 (SI No: 2009/2098) and referred to in article 4(b) and Schedule 6 to the Order", which volume is—
   (i)   signed by a member of the Senior Civil Service in the Department for Communities and Local Government; and
   (ii)  deposited and available for inspection at the principal office of the Secretary of State for Communities and Local Government.

**[3852]**

**NOTES**
Commencement: 7 September 2009.

## 5 Designated protected areas in the East of England

The following areas in the East of England region are designated protected areas for the purposes of paragraph 4A(1) of Schedule 4A to the 1967 Act—
   (a)   those parishes in the district of Bedford and in the counties of Cambridgeshire, Essex, Hertfordshire, Norfolk and Suffolk specified in Schedule 7 to this Order; and
   (b)   those areas in the parishes and the unparished areas in the district of Beford and in the counties of Cambridgeshire, Essex, Hertfordshire, Norfolk and Suffolk specified in Schedule 8 to this Order each shown bounded with a black line and cross hatched on one of the maps contained in the volume entitled "Maps of the Protected Areas in the East of England designated as protected areas by the Housing (Right to Enfranchise) (Designated Protected Areas) (England) Order 2009 (SI No: 2009/2098) and referred to in article 5(b) and Schedule 8 to the Order", which volume is—
      (i)   signed by a member of the Senior Civil Service in the Department for Communities and Local Government; and
      (ii)  deposited and available for inspection at the principal office of the Secretary of State for Communities and Local Government.

**[3853]**

**NOTES**
Commencement: 7 September 2009.

## 6 Designated protected areas in the North East

The following areas in the North East region are designated protected areas for the purposes of paragraph 4A(1) of Schedule 4A to the 1967 Act—
   (a)   the parishes in the districts of Hartlepool, Middlesborough, Redcar and Cleveland, and Stockton-on-Tees and in the counties of Durham, Northumberland and Tyne and Wear specified in Schedule 9 to this Order; and
   (b)   those areas in the parishes and the unparished areas in the districts of Hartlepool and Redcar and Cleveland and in the counties of Durham, Northumberland and Tyne and Wear specified in Schedule 10 to this Order each shown bounded with a black line and cross hatched on one of the maps contained in the volume entitled "Maps of the Protected Areas in the North East designated as protected areas by the Housing (Right to Enfranchise) (Designated Protected Areas) (England) Order 2009 (SI No: 2009/2098) and referred to in article 6(b) and Schedule 10 to the Order", which volume is—
      (i)   signed by a member of the Senior Civil Service in the Department for Communities and Local Government; and
      (ii)  deposited and available for inspection at the principal office of the Secretary of State for Communities and Local Government.

**[3854]**

**NOTES**
Commencement: 7 September 2009.

## 7 Designated protected areas in the South East

The following areas in the South East region are designated protected areas for the purposes of paragraph 4A(1) of Schedule 4A to the 1967 Act—
   (a)   those parishes and the unparished area in the district of West Berkshire and in the counties of Buckinghamshire, East Sussex, Hampshire, the Isle of Wight, Kent, Oxfordshire, Surrey and West Sussex specified in Schedule 11 to this Order; and
   (b)   those areas in the parishes and the unparished areas in the district of West Berkshire and in the counties of Buckinghamshire, East Sussex, Hampshire, the Isle of Wight, Kent, Oxfordshire, Surrey and West Sussex specified in Schedule 12 to this Order each shown bounded with a black line and cross hatched on one of the maps contained in the volume entitled "Maps of the Protected Areas in the South East designated as protected areas by

the Housing (Right to Enfranchise) (Designated Protected Areas) (England) Order 2009"
(SI No: 2009/2098) and referred to in article 7(b) and Schedule 12 to the Order, which
volume is—
- (i) signed by a member of the Senior Civil Service in the Department for
Communities and Local Government; and
- (ii) deposited and available for inspection at the principal office of the Secretary of
State for Communities and Local Government.

**[3855]**

**NOTES**
Commencement: 7 September 2009.

## 8 Designated protected areas in the East Midlands

The following areas in the East Midlands region are designated protected areas for the purposes of
paragraph 4A(1) of Schedule 4A to the 1967 Act—
- (a) those parishes in the counties of Derbyshire, Leicestershire, Lincolnshire,
Northamptonshire and Nottinghamshire specified in Schedule 13 to this Order; and
- (b) those areas in the parishes and the unparished areas in the counties of Derbyshire,
Leicestershire, Lincolnshire, Northamptonshire and Nottinghamshire specified in
Schedule 14 to this Order each shown bounded with a black line and crossed hatched on
one of the maps contained in the volume entitled "Maps of the Protected Areas in the
East Midlands designated as protected areas by the Housing (Right to Enfranchise)
(Designated Protected Areas) (England) Order 2009 " (SI No: 2009/2098) and referred
to in article 8(b) and Schedule 14 to the Order, which volume is—
  - (i) signed by a member of the Senior Civil Service in the Department for
Communities and Local Government; and
  - (ii) deposited and available for inspection at the principal office of the Secretary of
State for Communities and Local Government.

**[3856]**

**NOTES**
Commencement: 7 September 2009.

## 9 Designated protected areas in Yorkshire and the Humber

The following areas in Yorkshire and the Humber region are designated protected areas for the
purposes of paragraph 4A(1) of Schedule 4A to the 1967 Act—
- (a) those parishes in the districts of the East Riding of Yorkshire, North East Lincolnshire
and North Lincolnshire and in the counties of North Yorkshire, South Yorkshire and
West Yorkshire specified in Schedule 15 to this Order; and
- (b) those areas in the parishes and the unparished areas in the districts of the East Riding of
Yorkshire and North Lincolnshire and in the counties of North Yorkshire, South
Yorkshire and West Yorkshire specified in Schedule 16 to this Order each shown
bounded with a black line and crossed hatched on one of the maps contained in the
volume entitled "Maps of the Protected Areas in Yorkshire and the Humber designated
as protected areas by the Housing (Right to Enfranchise) (Designated Protected Areas)
(England) Order 2009 (SI No: 2009/2098) and referred to in article 9(b) and Schedule 16
to the Order", which volume is—
  - (i) signed by a member of the Senior Civil Service in the Department for
Communities and Local Government; and
  - (ii) deposited and available for inspection at the principal office of the Secretary of
State for Communities and Local Government.

**[3857]**

**NOTES**
Commencement: 7 September 2009.

**SCHEDULES**

**SCHEDULE 1**
**DESIGNATED PROTECTED AREAS IN THE WEST MIDLANDS—ENTIRE PARISHES**

Regulation 2(a)

**PART 1**
**HEREFORDSHIRE**

Abbey Dore, Aconbury, Acton Beauchamp, Adforton, Allensmore, Almeley, Ashperton, Aston
Ingham, Avenbury, Aylton, Aymestrey,

Bacton, Ballingham, Bartestree, Birley with Upper Hill, Bishops Frome, Bishopstone, Blakemere, Bodenham, Bolstone, Bosbury, Brampton Abbotts, Brampton Bryan, Bredenbury, Bredwardine, Breinton, Bridge Sollers, Bridstow, Brilley, Brimfield, Brinsop and Wormsley, Brobury with Monnington on Wye, Brockhampton, Brockhampton (in the district of South Herefordshire), Bromyard and Winslow, Buckton and Coxall, Burghill, Burrington, Byford, Byton,

Callow, Canon Frome, Canon Pyon, Castle Frome, Clehonger, Clifford, Coddington, Collington, Colwall, Combe, Cradley, Craswall, Credenhill, Croft and Yarpole, Cusop,

Dewsall, Dilwyn, Dinedor, Dinmore, Docklow and Hampton Wafer, Donnington, Dormington, Dorstone, Downton, Dulas,

Eardisland, Eardisley, Eastnor, Eaton Bishop, Edvin Loach and Saltmarshe, Edwyn Ralph, Eggleton, Elton, Evesbatch, Ewyas Harold, Eye Moreton and Ashton, Eyton,

Felton, Ford and Stoke Prior, Fownhope, Foy,

Ganarew, Garway, Goodrich, Grafton, Grendon Bishop,

Hampton Bishop, Hampton Charles, Harewood, Hatfield and Newhampton, Haywood, Hentland, Holme Lacy, Hope Mansell, Hope under Dinmore, How Caple, Humber,

Kenchester, Kenderchurch, Kentchurch, Kilpeck, Kimbolton, Kings Pyon, Kings Caple, Kingsland, Kingstone, Kington (in the district of Leominster), Kington Rural, Kinnersley, Kinsham, Knill,

Laysters, Lea, Leinthall Starkes, Leintwardine, Letton, Lingen, Linton, Linton (in the district of South Herefordshire), Little Birch, Little Cowarne, Little Dewchurch, Little Hereford, Little Marcle, Llancillo, Llandinabo, Llangarron, Llanrothal, Llanveynoe, Llanwarne, Longtown, Lower Harpton, Lucton, Lugwardine, Luston, Lyonshall,

Madley, Mansell Gamage, Mansell Lacy, Marden, Marstow, Mathon, Michaelchurch Escley, Middleton on the Hill, Moccas, Monkland and Stretford, Mordiford, Moreton Jeffries, Moreton on Lugg, Much Birch, Much Cowarne, Much Dewchurch, Much Marcle, Munsley,

Newton (in the district of South Herefordshire), Newton (in the district of Leominster), Norton Canon, Norton,

Ocle Pychard, Orcop, Orleton,

Pembridge, Pencombe with Grendon Warren, Pencoyd, Peterchurch, Peterstow, Pipe and Lyde, Pipe Aston, Pixley, Preston on Wye, Preston Wynne, Pudlestone, Putley,

Richards Castle (Hereford), Rodd, Nash & Little Brampton, Ross Rural, Rowlstone,

Sarnesfield, Sellack, Shobdon, Sollers Hope, St Devereux, St Margarets, St Weonards, Stanford Bishop, Stapleton, Staunton on Arrow, Staunton on Wye, Stoke Edith, Stoke Lacy, Stretton Grandison, Stretton Sugwas, Sutton,

Tarrington, Tedstone Delamere, Tedstone Wafer, Thornbury, Thruxton, Titley, Tretire with Michaelchurch, Treville, Turnastone, Tyberton,

Ullingswick, Upper Sapey, Upton Bishop,

Vowchurch,

Wacton, Walford, Letton and Newton, Walterstone, Wellington, Wellington Heath, Welsh Bicknor, Welsh Newton, Weobley, Westhide, Weston Beggard, Weston under Penyard, Whitbourne, Whitchurch, Whitney on Wye, Wigmore, Willersley and Winforton, Willey, Withington, Wolferlow, Woolhope, Wormbridge,

Yarkhill, Yatton, Yazor.

[3858]

**NOTES**
  Commencement: 7 September 2009.

PART 2
SHROPSHIRE

Abdon, Acton Burnell, Acton Round, Acton Scott, Adderley, Alberbury with Cardeston, All Stretton, Alveley, Ashford Bowdler, Ashford Carbonel, Astley Abbotts, Astley, Aston Botterell, Aston Eyre, Atcham,

Badger, Barrow, Baschurch, Beckbury, Bedstone, Berrington, Bettws y Crwyn, Bicton, Billingsley, Bishops Castle, Bitterley, Boningale, Boraston, Boscobel, Bromfield, Bucknell, Buildwas, Burford, Burwarton,

Cardington, Caynham, Chelmarsh, Cheswardine, Chetton, Chetwynd Aston & Woodcote, Chetwynd, Childs Ercall, Chirbury with Brompton, Church Preen, Church Pulverbatch, Claverley, Clee St Margaret, Cleobury Mortimer, Cleobury North, Clive, Clun, Clunbury, Clungunford, Cockshutt cum Petton, Colebatch, Condover, Coreley, Cound, Craven Arms, Cressage, Culmington,

Deuxhill, Diddlebury, Ditton Priors,

Eardington, Easthope, Eaton under Heywood, Edgemond, Edgton, Ellesmere Rural, Ercall Magna, Eyton upon the Weald Moors,

Farlow, Ford, Frodesley,

Glazeley, Great Hanwood, Great Ness, Greete, Grinshill,

Hadnall, Harley, Heath, Hinstock, Hodnet, Hope Bagot, Hope Bowdler, Hopesay, Hopton Cangeford, Hopton Castle, Hopton Wafers, Hordley, Hughley,

Ightfield,

Kemberton, Kenley, Kinlet, Kinnerley, Knockin, Kynnersley,

Lawley and Overdale, Leebotwood, Leighton & Eaton Constantine, Little Ness, Little Wenlock, Llanfair Waterdine, Llanyblodwel, Llanymynech and Pant, Longden, Longnor, Loppington, Ludford, Lydbury North, Lydham,

Mainstone, Melverley, Middleton Scriven, Milson, Minsterley, Monkhopton, Montford, More, Moreton Corbet and Lee Brockhurst, Moreton Say, Morville, Much Wenlock, Munslow, Myddle and Broughton, Myndtown,

Nash, Neen Savage, Neen Sollars, Neenton, Newcastle on Clun, Norbury, Norton in Hales,

Onibury, Oswestry Rural,

Pimhill, Pitchford, Pontesbury, Prees, Preston upon the Weald Moors,

Quatt Malvern,

Ratlinghope, Richards Castle, Rodington, Romsley, Ruckley and Langley, Rudge, Rushbury, Ruyton XI Towns, Ryton,

Selattyn and Gobowen, Shawbury, Sheinton, Sheriffhales, Shipton, Sibdon Carwood, Sidbury, Smethcott St Martins, Stanton Lacy, Stanton Long, Stanton upon Hine Heath, Stockton, Stoke St Milborough, Stoke upon Tern, Stottesdon, Stowe, Sutton Maddock, Sutton upon Tern,

Tasley, The Gorge, Tibberton and Cherrington, Tong,

Uffington, Upton Cressett, Upton Magna,

Waters Upton, Welshampton and Lyneal, Wem Rural, Wentnor, West Felton, Westbury, Weston Rhyn, Weston under Redcastle, Wheathill, Whitchurch Rural, Whittington, Whitton, Whixall, Wistanstow, Withington, Woolstaston, Woore, Worfield, Worthen with Shelve, Wrockwardine, Wroxeter and Uppington.

**[3859]**

**NOTES**

Commencement: 7 September 2009.

## PART 3
## STAFFORDSHIRE

Abbots Bromley, Acton Trussell and Bednall, Adbaston, Alrewas, Alstonefield, Alton, Anslow,

Bagnall, Balterley, Barlaston, Berkswich, Betley, Blithfield, Blore with Swinscoe, Blymhill and Weston under Lizard, Bobbington, Bradley, Bradnop, Branston, Brewood, Brindley Heath, Brocton, Butterton,

Cannock Wood, Castle Church, Caverswall, Chapel and Hill Chorlton, Chebsey, Checkley, Church Eaton, Clifton Campville, Colton, Colwich, Consall, Coppenhall, Cotton, Croxden, Curborough and Elmhurst,

Denstone, Dilhorne, Draycott in the Clay, Draycott in the Moors, Drayton Bassett, Dunstall, Dunston,

Eccleshall, Edingale, Elford, Ellastone, Ellenhall, Enville, Essington,

Farewell and Chorley, Farley, Fawfieldhead, Featherstone, Fisherwick, Forton, Fradley and Streethay, Fradswell,

Gayton, Grindon, Gnosall,

Hamstall Ridware, Hanbury, Harlaston, Hatherton, Haughton, Heathylee, Heaton, High Offley, Hilderstone, Hilton, Himley, Hints, Hoar Cross, Hollinsclough, Horton,

Ilam, Ingestre, Ipstones,

Keele, Kings Bromley, Kingsley, Kingstone,

Lapley Stretton and Wheaton Aston, Leekfrith, Leigh, Loggerheads, Longdon, Longnor, Longsdon, Lower Penn,

Madeley, Maer, Marchington, Marston, Mavesyn Ridware, Mayfield, Milwich,

PART II
STATUTORY INSTRUMENTS

Newborough, Norbury,

Oakamoor, Okeover, Onecote,

Pattingham and Patshull, Perton,

Quarnford,

Ramshorn, Ranton, Rocester, Rushton,

Salt and Enson, Sandon and Burston, Saredon, Shareshill, Sheen, Standon, Stanton, Stone Rural, Stowe, Swindon, Swinfen and Packington,

Tatenhill, Teddesley Hay, Thorpe Constantine, Tittesworth, Tixall, Trysull and Seisdon,

Uttoxeter Rural,

Wall, Warslow and Elkstones, Waterhouses, Weeford, Weston, Wetton, Whitgreave, Whitmore, Whittington, Wigginton, Wootton, Wychnor,

Yoxhall.

**[3860]**

**NOTES**

Commencement: 7 September 2009.

## PART 4
## WARWICKSHIRE

Admington, Alderminster, Ansley, Ansty, Arley, Arrow with Weethley, Ashow, Astley, Aston Cantlow, Atherstone on Stour, Austrey, Avon Dassett,

Baddesley Clinton, Baddesley Ensor, Baginton, Barcheston, Barford, Barton-on-the-Heath, Baxterley, Bearley, Beaudesert, Beausale, Haseley, Honiliey and Wroxall, Bentley, Billesley, Binley Woods, Binton, Birdingbury, Bishops Itchington, Bishops Tachbrook, Blackdown, Bourton and Draycote, Brailes, Brandon and Bretford, Brinklow, Bubbenhall, Budbrooke, Burmington, Burton Dassett, Burton Hastings, Bushwood, Butlers Marston,

Caldecote, Chadshunt, Chapel Ascote, Charlecote, Cherington, Chesterton and Kingston, Church Lawford, Churchover, Claverdon, Clifford Chambers and Milcote, Clifton upon Dunsmore, Combe Fields, Combrook, Compton Verney, Compton Wynyates, Copston Magna, Corley, Cosford, Coughton, Curdworth,

Dorsington, Dunchurch,

Easenhall, Eathorpe, Ettington, Exhall,

Farnborough, Fenny Compton, Fillongley, Frankton, Fulbrook,

Gaydon, Grandborough, Great Alne, Great Packington, Great Wolford, Grendon,

Halford, Hampton Lucy, Harborough Magna, Harbury, Haselor, Hatton, Henley-in-Arden, Hodnell and Wills Pastures, Honington, Hunningham,

Ildicote, Ilmington,

Kineton, Kings Newnham, Kinwarton,

Ladbroke, Langley, Lapworth, Lea Marston, Leamington Hastings, Leek Wootton and Guys Cliffe, Lighthorne, Little Compton, Little Lawford, Little Packington, Little Wolford, Long Compton, Long Itchington, Long Lawford, Long Marston, Loxley, Luddington,

Marton, Maxstoke, Merevale, Middleton, Monks Kirby, Moreton Morrell, Morton Bagot,

Napton on the Hill, Nether Whitacre, Newbold Pacey, Newton and Biggin, Newton Regis, Norton Lindsey,

Offchurch, Old Milverton, Old Stratford and Drayton, Oldberrow, Over Whitacre, Oxhill,

Pailton, Pillerton Hersey, Pillerton Priors, Preston Bagot, Preston on Stour, Princethorpe, Priors Hardwick, Priors Marston,

Quinton,

Radbourn, Radford Semele, Radway, Ratley and Upton, Rowington, Ryton-on-Dunsmore,

Salford Priors, Sambourne, Seckington, Sherbourne, Shilton, Shotteswell, Shrewley, Shustoke, Shuttington, Snitterfield, Spernall, Stockton, Stoneleigh, Stoneton, Stourton, Stretton on Fosse, Stretton Baskerville, Stretton under Fosse, Stretton-on-Dunsmore, Sutton-under-Brailes,

Tanworth-in-Arden, Temple Grafton, Thurlaston, Tidmington, Tredington, Tysoe,

Ufton, Ullenhall, Upper and Lower Shuckburgh,

Wappenbury, Warmington, Wasperton, Watergall, Welford-on-Avon, Weston under Wetherley, Weston on Avon, Whatcote, Whichford, Whitchurch, Wibtoft, Willey, Willoughby, Wishaw, Withybrook, Wixford, Wolfhampcote, Wolston, Wolverton, Wolvey, Wootton Wawden, Wormleighton.

**[3861]**

**NOTES**
Commencement: 7 September 2009.

## PART 5
## WEST MIDLANDS

Allesley,

Barston,

Hampton in Arden, Hockley Heath,

Keresley.

**[3862]**

**NOTES**
Commencement: 7 September 2009.

## PART 6
## WORCESTERSHIRE

Abberley, Abberton, Abbots Morton, Aldington, Alfrick, Ashton under Hill, Astley and Dunley, Aston Somerville,

Badsey, Bayton, Beckford, Belbroughton, Bentley Pauncefoot, Beoley, Berrow, Besford, Bickmarsh, Birlingham, Birtsmorton, Bishampton, Bockleton, Bransford, Bredicot, Bredon, Bredons Norton, Bretforton, Bricklehampton, Broadheath, Broadwas, Broadway, Broome, Broughton Hackett, Bushley,

Castlemorton, Chaddesley Corbett, Charlton, Childswickham, Church Lench, Churchill and Blakedown, Churchill, Cleeve Prior, Clifton upon Teme, Conderton, Cookhill, Cotheridge, Croome D'Abitot, Cropthorne, Crowle,

Defford, Doddenham, Dodderhill, Dodford with Grafton, Dormston, Doverdale, Drakes Broughton and Wadborough,

Earls Croome, Eastham, Eckington, Eldersfield, Elmbridge, Elmley Castle, Elmley Lovett,

Feckenham, Fladbury, Flyford Flavell,

Grafton Flyford, Great Comberton, Great Witley, Grimley, Guarlford,

Hadzor, Hallow, Hampton Lovett, Hanbury, Hanley Castle, Hanley, Hartlebury, Harvington, Hill and Moor, Hill Croome, Hillhampton, Himbleton, Hindlip, Hinton on the Green, Holdfast, Holt, Honeybourne, Huddington, Hunnington,

Inkberrow

Kemerton, Kempsey, Kenswick, Kidderminster Foreign, Kington (in the district of Wychavon), Knighton on Teme, Knightwick, Kyre,

Leigh, Lindridge, Little Comberton, Little Malvern, Little Witley, Longdon, Lower Sapey, Lulsley,

Madresfield, Malvern Wells, Mamble, Martin Hussingtree, Martley,

Naunton Beauchamp, Netherton, Newland, North and Middle Littleton, North Piddle, Norton Juxta Kempsey,

Oddingley, Offenham, Ombersley, Overbury,

Pebworth, Pendock, Pensax, Peopleton, Pinvin, Pirton, Powick,

Queenhill,

Ribbesford, Ripple, Rochford, Rock, Rous Lench, Rushock, Rushwick,

Salwarpe, Sedgebarrow, Severn Stoke, Shelsley Beauchamp, Shelsley Kings, Shelsley Walsh, Shrawley, South Littleton, Spetchley, St Peter the Great County, Stanford with Orleton, Stapleton, Stock and Bradley, Stockton on Teme, Stoke Bliss, Stone, Stoulton, Strensham, Suckley,

Tenbury, Throckmorton, Tibberton, Tutnall and Cobley,

Upper Arley, Upton upon Severn, Upton Snodsbury, Upton Warren,

Warndon, Welland, Westwood, White Ladies Aston, Whittington, Wichenford, Wick, Wickhamford, Wolverley and Cookley, Wyre Piddle.

**[3863]**

**NOTES**
Commencement: 7 September 2009.

## SCHEDULE 2
## DESIGNATED PROTECTED AREAS IN THE WEST MIDLANDS—BY MAPS
Regulation 2(b)

### PART 1
### HEREFORDSHIRE

The parishes of—
  Holmer,
  Ledbury, Leominster, Lower Bullingham,

**[3864]**

**NOTES**
Commencement: 7 September 2009.

### PART 2
### SHROPSHIRE

The parishes of—
  Bridgnorth,
  Church Aston, Church Stretton,
  Donington,
  Hadley,
  Lilleshall and Donnington,
  Shifnal,
  Whitchurch Urban.

**[3865]**

**NOTES**
Commencement: 7 September 2009.

### PART 3
### STAFFORDSHIRE

The parishes of—
  Audley Rural,
  Barton under Needwood, Biddulph, Bilbrook, Brown Edge,
  Cheadle, Cheddleton, Codsall, Creswell,
  Endon and Stanley,
  Forsbrook, Fulford,
  Hammerwich, Hopton and Coton,
  Kidsgrove, Kinver,
  Leek,
  Penkridge,
  Seighford, Shenstone, Swynnerton,
  Werrington.

**[3866]**

**NOTES**
Commencement: 7 September 2009.

### PART 4
### WARWICKSHIRE

The parishes of—
  Alcester,
  Bidford on Avon,
  Dordon,
  Hartshill,
  Kenilworth, Kingsbury,
  Mancetter,
  Polesworth,
  Stratford upon Avon, Studley.

**[3867]**

**NOTES**
Commencement: 7 September 2009.

PART 5
WEST MIDLANDS

The parishes of—
Balsall, Berkswell, Bickenhill.

**[3868]**

**NOTES**
Commencement: 7 September 2009.

PART 6
WORCESTERSHIRE

The parishes of—
Alvechurch,
Bewdley,
Clent,
Frankley,
North Claines, Norton and Lenchwick,
Pershore,
Romsley,
Stoke Prior,
Wythall.

The unparished area bounded by the parishes of Cofton Hackett, Alvechurch, Tutnall & Cobley, Stoke Prior, Dodford with Grafton, Belbroughton, Romsley; and by the borough constituency of Birmingham Northfield in the West Midlands.

The unparished area bounded by the parishes of Cookhill, Inkberrow, Feckenham, Bentley Pauncefoot, Tutnall & Cobley, Alvechurch, Beoley; and by the parishes of Studley and Sambourne in the county of Warwickshire.

**[3869]**

**NOTES**
Commencement: 7 September 2009.

SCHEDULE 3
DESIGNATED PROTECTED AREAS IN THE SOUTH WEST—ENTIRE PARISHES
Regulation 3(a)

PART 1
BATH AND NORTH EAST SOMERSET

Bathampton, Batheaston, Bathford,

Cameley, Camerton, Charlcombe, Chelwood, Chew Magna, Chew Stoke, Claverton, Clutton, Combe Hay, Compton Dando, Compton Martin, Corston,

Dunkerton,

East Harptree, Englishcombe,

Farmborough, Farrington Gurney, Freshford,

High Littleton, Hinton Blewett, Hinton Charterhouse,

Kelston,

Marksbury, Monkton Combe,

Nempnett Thrubwell, Newton St Loe, North Stoke, Norton Malreward,

Priston, Publow,

Shoscombe, Southstoke, St Catherine, Stanton Drew, Stowey-Sutton, Swainswick,

Timsbury,

Ubley,

Wellow, West Harptree, Whitchurch.

**[3870]**

PART II
STATUTORY INSTRUMENTS

**NOTES**
Commencement: 7 September 2009.

## PART 2
## CORNWALL

Advent, Altarnun, Antony,

Blisland, Boconnoc, Botusfleming, Boyton, Breage, Broadoak, Budock,

Calstock, Camelford, Cardinham, Carharrack, Carn Brea, Chacewater, Colan, Constantine, Crantock, Crowan, Cubert, Cuby, Cury,

Davidstow, Dobwalls and Trewidland, Duloe,

Egloshayle, Egloskerry,

Feock, Forrabury and Minster, Fowey,

Germoe, Gerrans, Grade Ruan, Grampound with Creed, Gunwalloe, Gweek, Gwennap, Gwinear, Gwithian,

Helland,

Jacobstow,

Kea, Kilkhampton,

Ladock, Landewednack, Landrake with St Erney, Landulph, Laneast, Lanhydrock, Lanivet, Lanlivery, Lanner, Lanreath, Lansallos, Lanteglos, Launcells, Lawhitton Rural, Lesnewth, Lewannick, Lezant, Linkinhorne, Lostwithiel, Ludgvan, Luxulyan,

Mabe, Madron, Maker with Rame, Manaccan, Marazion, Marhamchurch, Mawgan in Meneage, Mawgan in Pydar, Mawnan, Menheniot, Mevagissey, Michaelstow, Millbrook, Morvah, Morval, Morwenstow, Mullion, Mylor,

North Hill, North Petherwin, North Tamerton,

Otterham,

Padstow, Paul, Pelynt, Penryn, Perranarworthal, Perranuthnoe, Perranzabuloe, Philleigh, Pillaton, Porthleven, Portreath, Poundstock, Probus,

Quethiock,

Roche, Ruanlanihorne,

Sancreed, Sennan, Sheviock, Sithney, South Hill, South Petherwin, St Agnes, St Allen, St Anthony in Meneage, St Breock, St Breward, St Buryan, St Cleer, St Clement, St Clether, St Columb Major, St Day, St Dennis, St Dominick, St Endellion, St Enoder, St Erme, St Erth, St Ervan, St Eval, St Ewe, St Gennys, St Germans, St Gluvias, St Goran, St Hilary, St Issey, St Ive, St John, St Juliot, St Just, St Just in Roseland, St Keverne, St Kew, St Keyne, St Levan, St Mabyn, St Martin, St Martin in Meneage, St Mellion, St Merryn, St Mewan, St Michael Caerhays, St Michael Penkevil, St Michaels Mount, St Minver Highlands, St Minver Lowlands, St Neot, St Newlyn East, St Pinnock, St Sampson, St Stephen in Brannel, St Stephens by Launceston Rural, St Teath, St Thomas the Apostle Rural, St Tudy, St Veep, St Wenn, St Winnow, Stithians, Stokeclimsland,

Tintagel, Towednack, Tregoney, Tremaine, Treneglos, Tresmeer, Trevalga, Treverbyn, Trewen, Tywardreath,

Veryan,

Warbstow, Warleggan, Week St Mary, Wendron, Werrington, Whitstone, Withiel,

Zennor,

The Isles of Scilly.

**[3871]**

**NOTES**
Commencement: 7 September 2009.

## PART 3
## DEVON

Abbots Bickington, Abbotsham, Abbotskerswell, All Saints, Alverdiscott, Alwington, Arlington, Ashburton, Ashcombe, Ashford, Ashprington, Ashreigney, Ashton, Ashwater, Atherington, Aveton Gifford, Awliscombe, Axmouth, Aylesbeare,

Bampton, Beaford, Beaworthy, Belstone, Beer, Bere Ferrers, Berrynarbor, Bickington, Bickleigh (in the district of South Hams), Bickleigh (in the district of Mid Devon), Bicton, Bigbury, Bishops

Nympton, Bishops Tawton, Bishopsteignton, Bittadon, Black Torrington, Blackawton, Bondleigh, Bow, Bradford, Bradninch, Bradstone, Bradworthy, Brampford Speke, Branscombe, Bratton Clovelly, Bratton Fleming, Brayford, Brendon, Brentor, Bridestow, Bridford, Bridgerule, Brixton, Broad Clyst, Broadhembury, Broadhempston, Broadwoodkelly, Broadwoodwidger, Brushford, Buckerell, Buckfastleigh, Buckland Brewer, Buckland Filleigh, Buckland in the Moor, Buckland Monachorum, Buckland Tout Saints, Bulkworthy, Burlescombe, Burrington, Butterleigh,

Cadbury, Cadeleigh, Chagford, Challacombe, Chardstock, Charlton, Chawleigh, Cheriton Bishop, Cheriton Fitzpaine, Chittlehamholt, Chittlehampton, Chivelstone, Christow, Chulmleigh, Churchstow, Clannaborough, Clawton, Clayhanger, Clayhidon, Clovelly, Clyst Honiton, Clyst Hydon, Clyst St George, Clyst St Lawrence, Clyst St Mary, Coffinswell, Colaton Raleigh, Coldridge, Colebrooke, Colyton, Combe Martin, Combe Raleigh, Combpyne Rousdon, Cookbury, Copplestone, Cornwood, Cornworthy, Coryton, Cotleigh, Countisbury, Crediton, Crediton Hamlets, Cruwys Morchard, Culmstock,

Dalwood, Dartington, Dartmoor Forest, Dean Prior, Diptford, Dittisham, Doddiscombsleigh, Dolton, Dowland, Down St Mary, Drewsteighnton, Dunchideock, Dunkeswell, Dunsford, Dunterton,

East Allington, East and West Buckland, East Anstey, East Budleigh, East Down, East Portlemouth, East Putford, East Worlington, Eggesford, Ermington, Exbourne, Exminster,

Farringdon, Farway, Feniton, Filleigh, Frithelstock, Frogmore and Sherford,

George Nympton, Georgeham, Germansweek, Gidleigh, Gittisham, Goodleigh, Gulworthy,

Haccombe with Combe, Halberton, Halwell and Moreleigh, Halwill, Harberton, Harford, Hartland, Hatherleigh, Hawkchurch, Heanton Punchardon, Hemyock, Hennock, High Bickington, Highampton, Hittisleigh, Hockworthy, Holbeton, Holcombe Burnell, Holcombe Rogus, Hollacombe, Holne, Holsworthy, Holsworthy Hamlets, Horrabridge, Horwood, Lovacott and Newton Tracey, Huish, Huntsham, Huntshaw, Huxham,

Iddesleigh, Ide, Ideford, Ilsington, Instow, Inwardleigh, Ipplepen,

Jacobstowe,

Kelly, Kenn, Kennerleigh, Kentisbeare, Kentisbury, Kenton, Kilmington, Kings Nympton, Kingston, Kingswear, Knowstone,

Lamerton, Landcross, Landkey, Langtree, Lapford, Lewtrenchard, Lifton, Little Torrington, Littleham, Littlehempston, Loddiswell, Loxbeare, Loxhore, Luffincott, Luppitt, Lustleigh, Lydford, Lympstone, Lynton and Lynmouth,

Malborough, Mamhead, Manaton, Mariansleigh, Marldon, Martinhoe, Marwood, Mary Tavy, Marystow, Meavy, Meeth, Membury, Merton, Meshaw, Milton Abbot, Milton Damerel, Modbury, Molland, Monkleigh, Monkokehampton, Monkton, Morchard Bishop, Morebath, Moretonhampstead, Mortehoe, Musbury,

Nether Exe, Newton and Noss, Newton Poppleford and Harpford, Newton St Cyres, Newton St Petrock, North Bovey, North Huish, North Molton, North Tawton, Northcott, Northleigh, Northlew, Nymet Rowland,

Oakford, Offwell, Okehampton Hamlets, Otterton,

Pancrasweek, Parkham, Parracombe, Payhembury, Peter Tavy, Peters Marland, Petrockstow, Plymtree, Poltimore, Poughill, Powderham, Puddington, Pyworthy,

Queens Nympton,

Rackenford, Rattery, Rewe, Ringmore, Roborough, Rockbeare, Romansleigh, Rose Ash,

Sampford Courtenay, Sampford Peverell, Sampford Spiney, Sandford, Satterleigh and Warkleigh, Shaldon, Shaugh Prior, Shebbear, Sheepstor, Sheepwash, Sheldon, Shillingford St George, Shirwell, Shobrooke, Shute, Silverton, Slapton, Sourton, South Brent, South Huish, South Milton, South Pool, South Tawton, Southleigh, Sowton, Sparkwell, Spreyton, St Giles in the Wood, St Giles on the Heath, Starcross, Staverton, Sticklepath, Stockland, Stockleigh English, Stockleigh Pomeroy, Stoke Canon, Stoke Fleming, Stoke Gabriel, Stoke Rivers, Stokeinteignhead, Stokenham, Stoodleigh, Stowford, Strete, Sutcombe, Swimbridge, Sydenham Damerel,

Talaton, Tedburn St Mary, Teigngrace, Templeton, Tetcott, Thelbridge, Thornbury, Thorverton, Throwleigh, Thrushelton, Thurleston, Torbryan, Trentishoe, Trusham, Twitchen,

Uffculme, Ugborough, Uplowman, Uplyme, Upottery, Upton Hellions, Upton Pyne,

Virginstow,

Walkampton, Washfield, Washford Pyne, Weare Giffard, Welcombe, Wembury, Wembworthy, West Alvington, West Anstey, West Buckfastleigh, West Down, West Pilton, West Putford, Westleigh, Whimple, Whitchurch, Whitestone, Widecombe in the Moor, Widworthy, Willand, Winkleigh, Witheridge, Woodbury, Woodland, Woodleigh, Woolfardisworthy (in the Mid Devon district), Woolfardisworthy (in the district of Torridge),

Yarcombe, Yarnscombe, Yealmpton, Zeal Monachorum.

[3872]

**NOTES**
Commencement: 7 September 2009.

PART 4
DORSET

Abbotsbury, Affpuddle, Alderholt, Allington, Alton Pancras, Anderson, Arne, Ashmore, Askerswell, Athelhampton,

Batcombe, Beaminster, Beer Hackett, Bere Regis, Bettiscombe, Bincombe, Bishop's Caundle, Blandford St Mary, Bloxworth, Bothenhampton, Bourton, Bradford Abbas, Bradford Peverell, Broadmayne, Broadwindsor, Bryanston, Buckhorn Weston, Buckland Newton, Burleston, Burstock, Burton Bradstock, Burton,

Cann, Castleton, Catherston Leweston, Cattistock, Caundle Marsh, Cerne Abbas, Chalbury, Chaldon Herring, Charlton Marshall, Charminster, Charmouth, Chedington, Cheselbourne, Chetnole, Chettle, Chideock, Child Okeford, Chilcombe, Compton Valence, Chilfrome, Church Knowle, Clifton Maybank, Compton Abbas, Coombe Keynes, Corfe Castle, Corscombe, Cranborne, Crossways,

Dewlish, Durweston,

East Chelborough, East Holme, East Lulworth, East Orchard, East Stoke, East Stour, Edmondsham, Evershot,

Farnham, Fifehead Magdalene, Fifehead Neville, Fleet, Folke, Fontmell Magna, Frampton, Frome St Quintin, Frome Vauchurch,

Glanvilles Wootton, Goathill, Godmanstone, Gussage All Saints, Gussage St Michael,

Halstock, Hammoon, Hanford, Haydon, Hazelbury Bryan, Hermitage, Hilfield, Hilton, Hinton Martell, Hinton Parva, Hinton St Mary, Holnest, Holt, Holwell, Hooke, Horton, Hurn,

Ibberton, Iwerne Courtney or Shroton, Iwerne Minster, Iwerne Stepleton,

Kimmeridge, Kingston Russell, Kington Magna,

Langton Herring, Langton Long Blandford, Langton Matravers, Leigh, Leweston, Lillington, Littlebredy, Litton Cheney, Loders, Long Bredy, Long Crichel, Longburton, Lydlinch, Lytchett Matravers,

Maiden Newton, Manston, Mapperton, Mappowder, Margaret Marsh, Marnhull, Marshwood, Melbury Abbas, Melbury Bubb, Melbury Osmond, Melbury Sampford, Melcombe Horsey, Milborne St Andrew, Milton Abbas, Minterne Magna, Moor Crichel, Morden, Moreton, Mosterton, Motcombe,

Nether Cerne, Nether Compton, Netherbury, North Poorton, North Wootton,

Oborne, Okeford Fitzpaine, Osmington, Over Compton, Owermoigne,

Pamphill, Pentridge, Piddlehinton, Piddletrenthide, Pilsdon, Pimperne, Portesham, Portland, Powerstock, Poxwell, Poyntington, Puddletown, Pulham, Puncknowle, Purse Caundle,

Rampisham, Ryme Intrinseca,

Sandford Orcas, Seaborough, Shapwick, Shillingstone, Shipton Gorge, Silton, Sixpenny Handley, South Perrott, Spetisbury, Stalbridge, Stanton St Gabriel, Steeple, Stinsford, Stockwood, Stoke Abbott, Stoke Wake, Stour Provost, Stourpaine, Stourton Caundle, Stratton, Studland, Sturminster Marshall, Sturminster Newton, Sutton Waldron, Swyre, Sydling St Nicholas, Symondsbury,

Tarrant Crawford, Tarrant Gunville, Tarrant Hinton, Tarrant Keyneston, Tarrant Launceston, Tarrant Monkton, Tarrant Rawston, Tarrant Rushton, Thorncombe, Thornford, Tincleton, Todber, Toller Fratrum, Toller Porcorum, Tolpuddle, Trent, Turners Puddle, Turnworth, Tyneham,

Up Cerne,

Wareham St Martin, Warmwell, West Chelborough, West Compton, West Knighton, West Lulworth, West Orchard, West Stafford, West Stour, Whitcombe, Whitchurch Canonicorum, Wimborne St Giles, Winfrith Newburgh, Winterborne Came, Winterborne Clenston, Winterborne Herringston, Winterborne Houghton, Winterborne Kingston, Winterborne Monkton, Winter borne St Martin, Winterborne Stickland, Winterborne Whitechurch, Winterborne Zelston, Winterbourne Abbas, Winterbourne Steepleton, Witchampton, Woodlands, Woodsford, Wool, Wolland, Wootton Fitzpaine, Worth Matravers, Wraxall, Wynford Eagle,

Yetminster.

[3873]

PART II
STATUTORY INSTRUMENTS

**NOTES**
 Commencement: 7 September 2009.

## PART 5
## GLOUCESTERSHIRE

Adlestrop, Alderley, Alderton, Aldsworth, Alkington, Alvington, Ampney Crucis, Ampney St Mary, Ampney St Peter, Andoversford, Arlingham, Ashleworth, Ashley, Aston Subedge, Avening, Awre, Ayleburton,

Badgeworth, Bagendon, Barnsley, Barrington, Batsford, Baunton, Berkeley, Beverstone, Bibury, Bisley with Lypiatt, Blaisdon, Bledington, Blockley, Boddington, Bourton on the Hill, Bourton on the Water, Boxwell with Leighterton, Brimpsfield, Broadwell, Bromsberrow, Brookthorpe with Whaddon, Buckland,

Chaceley, Chedworth, Cherington, Chipping Campden, Churcham, Clapton, Coaley, Coates, Coberley, Cold Aston, Colesbourne, Coln St Aldwyns, Coln St Dennis, Compton Abdale, Condicote, Corse, Cowley, Cranham, Cutsdean,

Daglingworth, Deerhurst, Didmarton, Donnington, Dowdeswell, Down Ampney, Down Hatherley, Driffield, Drybrook, Dumbleton, Duntisbourne Abbots, Duntisbourne Rouse, Dymock,

Eastington, Eastleach, Ebrington, Edgeworth, Elkstone, Elmore, Elmstone Hardwicke, English Bicknor, Evenlode,

Fairford, Farmington, Forthampton, Frampton on Severn, Fretherne with Saul, Frocester,

Gotherington, Great Rissington, Great Witcombe, Guiting Power,

Ham and Stone, Hamfallow, Hampnett, Hardwicke, Harescombe, Haresfield, Hartpury, Hasfield, Hatherop, Hawling, Hazelton, Hewelsfield, Highnam, Hillesley and Tresham, Hinton, Horsley, Huntley,

Icomb,

Kemble, Kempley, Kempsford, Kings Stanley, Kingscote, Kingswood,

Lechlade, Leigh, Leonard Stanley, Little Rissington, Littledean, Long Newnton, Longborough, Longhope, Longney, Lower Slaughter, Lydbrook,

Maisemore, Maiseyhampton, Maugersbury, Mickleton, Minsterworth, Miserden, Mitcheldean, Moreton Valence, Moreton in Marsh,

Naunton, Newland, Newnham, North Cerney, North Nibley, Northleach with Eastington, Norton, Notgrove, Nympsfield,

Oddington, Owlpen, Oxenhall, Oxenton, Ozelworth,

Painswick, Pauntley, Pitchcombe, Poole Keynes, Poulton, Prescott, Preston,

Quenington,

Redmarley D'Abitot, Rendcomb, Rodmarton, Ruardean, Rudford and Highleadon, Ruspidge,

Saintbury, Sandhurst, Sapperton, Sevenhampton, Sezincote, Sherborne, Shipton, Shipton Moyne, Shurdington, Siddington, Slimbridge, Snowshill, Somerford Keynes, Southam, South Cerney, Southrop, St Briavels, Standish, Stanton, Stanway, Staunton Coleford, Staunton, Staverton, Stinchcombe, Stoke Orchard, Stow on the Wold, Sudeley, Swell, Syde,

Taynton, Teddington, Temple Guiting, Tibberton, Tidenham, Tirley, Toddington, Todenham, Turkdean, Twigworth, Twyning,

Uckington, Uley, Upleadon, Upper Slaughter,

Walton Cardiff, Westbury on Severn, Westcote, Weston Subedge, Westonbirt with Lasborough, Wheatpieces, Whiteshill and Ruscombe, Whitminster, Whittington, Wick Rissington, Willersey, Windrush, Winson, Winstone, Withington, Woodchester, Woodmancote, Woolaston,

Yanworth.

**[3874]**

**NOTES**
 Commencement: 7 September 2009.

## PART 6
## NORTH SOMERSET

Abbotts Leigh,

Banwell, Barrow Gurney, Blagdon, Bleadon, Brockley, Burrington, Butcombe,

Churchill, Clapton-in-Gordano, Cleeve,

Dundry,

Flax Bourton,

Hutton,

Kenn, Kewstoke, Kingston Seymour,

Locking, Loxton,

Portbury, Puxton,

Tickenham,

Walton-in-Gordano, Weston-in-Gordano, Wick St Lawrence, Winford, Wraxhall, Wrington.

**[3875]**

**NOTES**
Commencement: 7 September 2009.

PART 7
SOMERSET

Abbas and Templecombe, Alford, Aller, Ansford, Ash, Ash Priors, Ashbrittle, Ashcott, Ashill, Ashwick, Axbridge,

Babcary, Badgworth, Baltonsborough, Barrington, Barton St David, Barwick, Batcombe, Bathealton, Bawdrip, Beckington, Beercrocombe, Berkley, Berrow, Bickenhall, Bicknoller, Binegar, Bishops Lydeard, Bradford on Tone, Bratton Seymour, Brean, Brent Knoll, Brewham, Bridgewater Without, Broadway, Brompton Ralph, Brompton Regis, Broomfield, Brushford, Bruton, Buckland Dinham, Buckland St Mary, Burnham Without, Burrowbridge, Burtle, Butleigh,

Cannington, Carhampton, Castle Cary, Catcott, Chaffcombe, Chapel Allerton, Charlton Horethorne, Charlton Mackrell, Charlton Musgrove, Cheddon Fitzpaine, Chedzoy, Chewton Mendip, Chilcompton, Chillington, Chilthorne Domer, Chilton Cantelo, Chilton Polden, Chilton Trinity, Chipstable, Chiselborough, Churchstanton, Clatworthy, Closworth, Coleford, Combe Florey, Combe St Nicholas, Compton Bishop, Compton Dundon, Compton Pauncefoot, Corfe, Corton Denham, Cossington, Cothelstone, Cranmore, Creech St Michael, Cricket St Thomas, Croscombe, Crowcombe, Cucklington, Cudworth, Curland, Curry Mallet, Curry Rivel, Cutcombe,

Dinnington, Ditcheat, Donyatt, Doulting, Dowlish Wake, Downhead, Drayton, Dulverton, Dunster, Durston,

East Brent, East Chinnock, East Huntspill, East Pennard, East Quantoxhead, Edington, Elm, Elworthy, Emborough, Enmore, Evercreech, Exford, Exmoor, Exton,

Fiddington, Fitzhead, Fivehead,

Goathurst, Godney, Greinton,

Halse, Hambridge and Westport, Hardington Mandeville, Haselbury Plucknett, Hatch Beauchamp, Hemington, Henstridge, High Ham, Hinton St George, Holcombe, Holford, Holton, Horsington, Horton, Huish Champflower, Huish Episcopi,

Ilchester, Ilton, Isle Abbotts, Isle Brewers,

Keinton Mandeville, Kilmersdon, Kilve, Kingsbury Episcopi, Kingsdon, Kingston St Mary, Kingstone, Kingweston, Knowle St Giles,

Lamyat, Langford Budville, Langport, Leigh on Mendip, Limington, Litton, Long Load, Long Sutton, Lopen, Lovington, Luccombe, Lullington, Luxborough, Lydeard St Lawrence, Lydford on Fosse, Lympsham, Lyng,

Maperton, Mark, Marston Magna, Meare, Mells, Merriott, Middlezoy, Milborne Port, Milton Clevedon, Milverton, Minehead Without, Misterton, Monksilver, Montacute, Moorlinch, Muchelney, Mudford,

Nether Stowey, Nettlecombe, North Barrow, North Cadbury, North Cheriton, North Curry, North Perrott, North Wootton, Norton Fitzwarren, Norton St Phillip, Norton Sub Hamdon, Nunney, Nynehead,

Oake, Oare, Odcombe, Old Cleeve, Orchard Portman, Othery, Otterford, Otterhampton, Over Stowey,

Pawlett, Pen Selwood, Pilton, Pitcombe, Pitminster, Pitney, Porlock, Priddy, Puckington, Puriton, Pylle,

Queen Camel,

Rimpton, Rode, Rodney Stoke, Ruishton,

Sampford Arundel, Sampford Brett, Seavington St Mary, Seavington St Michael, Selwood, Selworthy, Shapwick, Sharpham, Shepton Beachamp, Shepton Montague, Shipham, Skilgate, South Barrow, South Cadbury, South Petherton, Sparkford, Spaxton, St Cuthbert Out, Staple Fitzpaine,

Staplegrove, Stawell, Stawley, Stockland Bristol, Stocklinch, Stogumber, Stogursey, Stoke St Gregory, Stoke St Mary, Stoke St Michael, Stoke Sub Hamdon, Stoke Trister, Ston Easton, Stratton on the Fosse, Stringston,

Tatworth and Forton, Tellisford, Thornfalcon, Thurloxton, Timberscombe, Tintinhull, Tolland, Treborough, Trudoxhill, Trull,

Upton, Upton Noble,

Walton, Wambrook, Wanstrow, Wayford, Weare, Wedmore, Wellington Without, Wembdon, West Bagborough, West Bradley, West Buckland, West Camel, West Chinnock, West Coker, West Crewkerne, West Hatch, West Huntspill, West Monkton, West Pennard, West Quantoxhead, Westbury, Westonzoyland, Whatley, Whitelackington, Whitestaunton, Williton, Winsford, Winsham, Witham Friary, Withycombe, Withypool, Wiveliscombe, Wookey, Woolavington, Wootton Courtenay,

Yarlington, Yeovilton.

**[3876]**

**NOTES**
Commencement: 7 September 2009.

## PART 8
## SOUTH GLOUCESTERSHIRE

Acton Turville, Alveston, Aust,

Badminton,

Charfield, Cold Ashton, Cromhall,

Doynton, Dyrham and Hinton,

Falfield,

Hawkesbury, Hill, Horton,

Iron Acton,

Little Sodbury,

Marshfield,

Oldbury-upon-Severn, Olveston,

Pilning and Severn Beach, Pucklechurch,

Rangeworthy, Rockhampton,

Tormarton, Tortworth, Tytherington,

Wick and Abson, Wickwar.

**[3877]**

**NOTES**
Commencement: 7 September 2009.

## PART 9
## WILTSHIRE

Aldbourne, Alderbury, Allcannings, Allington, Alton, Alvediston, Ansty, Ashton Keynes, Atworth, Avebury,

Barford St Martin, Baydon, Beechingstoke, Berwick Bassett, Berwick St James, Berwick St John, Berwick St Leonard, Biddestone, Bishopstone (in the district of Thamesdown), Bishopstone (in the district of Salisbury), Bishopstrow, Blunsdon St Andrew, Bower Chalke, Box, Boyton, Bratton, Braydon, Bremhill, Brinkworth, Britford, Brixton Deverill, Broad Chalke, Broad Hinton, Broad Town, Brokenborough, Bromham, Broughton Gifford, Bulkington, Burbage, Burcombe Without, Buttermere,

Calne Without, Castle Combe, Castle Eaton, Chapmanslade, Charlton (in the district of Kennet), Charlton (in the district of North Wiltshire), Cherhill, Cheverell Magna, Cheverell Parva, Chicklade, Chilmark, Chilton Foliat, Chirton, Chiseldon, Chitterne, Cholderton, Christian Malford, Chute, Chute Forest, Clarendon Park, Clyffe Pypard, Codford, Colerne, Collingbourne Ducis, Collingbourne Kingston, Compton Bassett, Compton, Chamberlayne, Coombe Bissett, Corsley, Coulston, Crudwell,

Dauntsey, Dilton Marsh, Dinton, Donhead St Andrew, Donhead St Mary, Downton, Durnford,

East Kennett, East Knoyle, Easterton, Easton Royal, Easton Grey, Ebbesborne Wake, Edington, Enford, Erlestoke, Etchilhampton, Everleigh,

Figheldean, Firsdown, Fittleton, Fonthill Bishop, Fonthill Gifford, Fovant, Froxfield, Fyfield,

Grafton, Great Bedwyn, Great Hinton, Great Somerford, Great Wishford, Grimstead, Grittleton,

Ham, Hankerton, Hannington, Heddington, Heytesbury, Heywood, Hilmarton, Hindon, Holt, Horningsham, Huish, Hullavington,

Idmiston, Inglesham,

Keevil, Kilmington, Kingston Deverill, Kington Langley, Kington St Michael, Knook,

Lacock, Landford, Langley Burrell Without, Latton, Lea and Cleverton, Leigh, Liddington, Limpley Stoke, Little Bedwyn, Little Somerford, Longbridge Deverill, Luckington, Lydiard Millicent, Lydiard Tregoze,

Maiden Bradley with Yarnfield, Manningford, Marden, Market Lavington, Marston, Marston Maisey, Melksham Without, Mere, Mildenhall, Milston, Milton Lilbourne, Minety, Monkton Farleigh,

Netheravon, Nettleton, Newton Toney, North Bradley, North Newnton, North Wraxall, Norton, Norton Bavant,

Oaksey, Odstock, Ogbourne St Andrew, Ogbourne St George, Orcheston,

Patney, Pewsey, Pitton and Farley, Potterne, Poulshot, Preshute,

Quidhampton,

Ramsbury, Redlynch, Rowde, Rushall,

Savernake, Seagry, Sedgehill and Semley, Seend, Semington, Shalbourne, Sherrington, Sherston, Shrewton, Sopworth, South Marston, South Newton, South Wraxhall, Southwick, Stanton Fitzwarren, Stanton St Bernard, Stanton St Quentin, Stapleford, Staverton, Steeple Ashton, Steeple Langford, Stert, Stockton, Stourton with Gasper, Stratford Toney, Sutton Benger, Sutton Mandeville, Sutton Veny, Swallowcliffe,

Teffont, Tidcombe and Fosbury, Tilshead, Tisbury, Tockenham, Tollard Royal,

Upavon, Upton Lovell, Upton Scudamore, Urchfont,

Wanborough, West Ashton, West Dean, West Knoyle, West Lavington, West Overton, West Tisbury, Westwood, Whiteparish, Wilcot, Wilsford, Wilsford cum Lake, Wingfield, Winsley, Winterbourne Bassett, Winterbourne, Winterbourne Monkton, Winterbourne Stoke, Winterslow, Woodborough, Woodford, Wootton Rivers, Worton, Wylye,

Yatton Keynell,

Zeals.

[3878]

**NOTES**
  Commencement: 7 September 2009.

---

## SCHEDULE 4
### DESIGNATED PROTECTED AREAS IN THE SOUTH WEST—BY MAPS
Regulation 3(b)

### PART 1
### BATH AND NORTH EAST SOMERSET

The parishes of—
  Norton Radstock,
  Peasedown St John.

The unparished area of the borough constituency of Bath.

[3879]

**NOTES**
  Commencement: 7 September 2009.

### PART 2
### CORNWALL

The parishes of—
  Bodmin, Bude Stratton,
  Callington, Camborne,
  Falmouth,
  Hayle,
  Illogan,
  Kenwyn,

Launceston, Liskeard, Looe,
Newquay,
Penzance,
Redruth,
Saltash, St Blaise, St Ives,
Wadebridge.

The unparished area bounded by the parishes of Treverbyn, St Blaise, Mevagissey, St Ewe and St Mewan.

**[3880]**

**NOTES**

Commencement: 7 September 2009.

PART 3
DEVON

The parishes of—

Ashburton, Axminster,
Berry Pomeroy, Bideford, Bovey Tracey, Braunton, Broad Clyst, Budleigh Salterton,
Chudleigh, Cullompton,
Dartmouth, Dawlish,
Fremington,
Honiton,
Ilfracombe,
Kingskerswell, Kingsteignton,
Newton Abbot,
Ogwell, Ottery St Mary,
Salcombe, Sidmouth, South Molton,
Tavistock, Tawstock, Tiverton.

The unparished area bounded by the parishes of Lympstone, East Budleigh, Budleigh Salterton, Dawlish and Starcross.

The unparished area bounded by the parishes of Stokeinteignhead, Shaldon, Kingswear, Dittisham, Stoke Gabriel, Berry Pomeroy, Marldon, Kingskerswell and Coffinswell.

**[3881]**

**NOTES**

Commencement: 7 September 2009.

PART 4
DORSET

The parishes of—

Bothenhampton, Bradpole,
Chickerell, Colehill, Corfe Mullen,
Ferndown Town,
Gillingham,
Lytchett Minster and Upton,
St Leonards and St Ives,
Verwood.

**[3882]**

**NOTES**

Commencement: 7 September 2009.

PART 5
GLOUCESTERSHIRE

The parishes of—

Ashchurch Rural,
Cam, Cinderford, Cirencester,
Lydney,
Minchinhampton,
Newent,
Northway,
Rodborough,
Siddington,
Tetbury Upton,

Tewksbury Town,
West Dean, Winchcombe, Wotton under Edge.

**[3883]**

**NOTES**
Commencement: 7 September 2009.

## PART 6
## NORTH SOMERSET

The parishes of—
  Backwell,
  Congresbury,
  Long Ashton,
  Nailsea,
  Winscombe and Sandford,
  Yatton.

**[3884]**

**NOTES**
Commencement: 7 September 2009.

## PART 7
## SOMERSET

The parishes of—
  Bishops Hull, Brympton,
  Cheddar,
  Durleigh,
  East Coker,
  Glastonbury,
  Martock,
  North Petherton,
  Shepton Mallet, Somerton,
  Wellington, Wincanton,
  Yeovil Without.

**[3885]**

**NOTES**
Commencement: 7 September 2009.

## PART 8
## SOUTH GLOUCESTERSHIRE

The parishes of—
  Almondsbury,
  Bitton,
  Dodington,
  Siston, Sodbury,
  Thornbury,
  Westerleigh, Winterbourne.

**[3886]**

**NOTES**
Commencement: 7 September 2009.

## PART 9
## WILTSHIRE

The parishes of—
  Amesbury,
  Bishops Cannings, Bulford,
  Chippenham Without, Corsham, Cricklade,
  Haydon Wick, Highworth, Hilperton,
  Laverstock, Lyneham,
  Marlborough,
  Netherhampton,
  Purton,
  Roundway,

St Paul Malmesbury Without,
Wroughton.

The area of North Tidworth (within the parish of Tidworth).

**[3887]**

Commencement: 7 September 2009.

## SCHEDULE 5
## DESIGNATED PROTECTED AREAS IN THE NORTH WEST—ENTIRE PARISHES
Regulation 4(a)

### PART 1
### CHESHIRE EAST

Acton, Adlington, Agden, Alpraham, Arclid, Ashley, Aston by Budworth, Aston juxta Mondrum, Audlem, Austerson

Baddiley, Baddington, Barthomley, Basford, Batherton, Betchton, Bexton, Bickerton, Blakenhall, Bosley, Bradwall, Brereton, Bridgemere, Brindley, Broomhall, Buerton, Bulkeley, Bunbury, Burland,

Calveley, Checkley cum Wrinehill, Chelford, Cholmondeley, Cholmondeston, Chorley (formerly Macclesfield Rural District), Chorley (formerly Nantwich Rural District), Chorlton, Church Lawton, Church Minshull, Coole Pilate, Cranage, Crewe by Farndon, Crewe Green,

Dodcott cum Wilkesley, Doddington,

Eaton, Edleston, Egerton,

Faddiley,

Gawsworth, Goostrey, Great Warford,

Hankelow, Hassall, Hatherton, Haughton, Henbury, Henhull, High Legh, Hough, Hulme Walfield, Hunsterson, Hurleston,

Kettleshulme,

Lea, Leighton, Little Bollington, Little Warford, Lower Withington, Lyme Handley,

Macclesfield Forest and Wildboarclough, Marbury cum Quoisley, Marthall, Marton, Mere, Millington, Minshull Vernon, Mobberley, Moreton cum Alcumlow, Moston, Mottram St Andrew,

Nether Alderley, Newbold Astbury, Newhall, Norbury, North Rode,

Odd Rode, Ollerton, Over Alderley,

Peckforton, Peover Inferior, Peover Superior, Pickmere, Plumley, Poole, Pott Shrigley,

Rainow, Ridley, Rostherne,

Siddington, Smallwood, Snelson, Somerford, Somerford Booths, Sound, Spurstow, Stapeley, Stoke, Sutton, Swettenham,

Tabley Inferior, Tabley Superior, Tatton, Toft, Twemlow,

Walgherton, Wardle, Warmingham, Weston, Wettenhall, Wincle, Wirswall, Woolstanwood, Worleston, Wrenbury cum Frith, Wybunbury.

**[3888]**

Commencement: 7 September 2009.

### PART 2
### CHESHIRE WEST AND CHESTER

Acton Bridge, Agden, Aldersey, Aldford, Allostock, Alvanley, Anderton with Marbury, Antrobus, Ashton Hayes, Aston,

Backford, Barrow, Barton, Beeston, Bickley, Bostock, Bradley, Bridge Trafford, Broxton, Bruen Stapleford, Buerton, Burton, Burwardsley, Byley,

Caldecote, Capenhurst, Carden, Chidlow, Chorlton, Chorlton by Backford, Chowley, Church Shocklach, Churton by Aldford, Churton by Farndon, Churton Heath, Claverton, Clotton Hoofield, Clutton, Coddington, Comberbach, Cotton Abbotts, Cotton Edmunds, Croughton, Crowton, Cuddington,

Darnhall, Delamere, Dodleston, Duckington, Duddon, Dunham-on-the-Hill, Dutton,

Eaton, Eccleston, Edge, Edgerley, Elton,

Farndon, Foulk Stapleford,

Golborne Bellow, Golborne David, Grafton, Great Budworth, Guilden Sutton,

Hampton, Handley, Hapsford, Harthill, Hatton, Hockenhull, Hoole Village, Horton by Malpas, Horton-cum-Peel, Huntington, Huxley,

Iddinshall, Ince,

Kelsall, Kings Marsh, Kingsley,

Lach Dennis, Larkton, Lea by Backford, Lea Newbold, Ledsham, Little Budworth, Little Leigh, Little Stanney, Littleton, Lower Kinnerton,

Macefen, Malpas, Manley, Marlston-cum-Lache, Marston, Mickle Trafford, Mollington, Mouldsworth, Moulton

Nether Peover, Newton by Malpas, Newton-by-Tattenhall, Norley,

Oakmere, Oldcastle, Overton,

Picton, Poulton, Prior's Heys, Puddington, Pulford,

Rowton, Rushton,

Saighton, Shocklach Oviatt, Shotwick, Shotwick Park, Sproston, Stanthorne, Stockton, Stoke, Stretton, Sutton,

Tarporley, Tarvin, Tattenhall, Thornton-le-Moors, Threapwood, Tilston, Tilstone Fearnall, Tiverton, Tushingham cum Grindley,

Utkinton,

Waverton, Wervin, Whitegate and Marton, Whitley, Wigland, Willington, Wimbolds Trafford, Wimboldsley, Wincham, Woodbank, Wychough.

**[3889]**

---
**NOTES**
Commencement: 7 September 2009.

---

PART 3
CUMBRIA

Above Derwent, Aikton, Ainstable, Aldingham, Allhallows, Allonby, Alston Moor, Angerton, Appleby-in-Westmorland, Arlecdon and Frizington, Arnside, Arthuret, Asby, Askam and Ireleth, Askerton, Askham, Aspatria,

Bampton, Barbon, Barton, Bassenthwaite, Beaumont, Beetham, Bewaldeth and Snittlegarth, Bewcastle, Blawith and Subberthwaite, Blennerhasset and Torpenhow, Blindbothel, Blindcrake, Bolton, Boltons, Bootle, Borrowdale, Bothel and Threapland, Bowness, Bridekirk, Brigham, Bromfield, Brough, Brough Sowerby, Brougham, Broughton, Broughton East, Broughton Moor, Broughton West, Burgh by Sands, Burtholme, Burton in Kendal, Buttermere,

Caldbeck, Camerton, Carlatton, Cartmel Fell, Casterton, Castle Carrock, Castle Sowerby, Catterlen, Claife, Cliburn, Clifton, Colby, Colton, Coniston, Crackenthorpe, Crook, Crosby Garrett, Crosby Ravensworth, Crosscanonby, Crosshwaite and Lyth, Culgaith, Cummersdale, Cumrew, Cumwhitton,

Dacre, Dalston, Dean, Dearham, Dent, Distington, Docker, Drigg and Carleton, Dufton, Dundraw, Dunnerdale with Seathwaite,

Egton with Newland, Embleton, Ennerdale and Kinniside, Eskdale,

Farlam, Fawcett Forest, Firbank,

Garsdale, Gilcrux, Glassonby, Gosforth, Grayrigg, Great Clifton, Great Salkeld, Great Strickland, Greysouthen, Greystoke,

Haile, Hartley, Haverthwaite, Hawkshead, Hayton and Mealo, Hayton, Helbeck, Helsington, Hesket, Hethersgill, Heversham, Hincaster, Hoff, Holme Abbey, Holme, Holme East Waver, Holme Low, Holme St Cuthbert, Hugill, Hunsonby, Hutton, Hutton Roof,

Ireby and Uldale, Irthington, Irton with Santon,

Kaber, Kentmere, Killington, Kings Meaburn, Kingmoor, Kingwater, Kirkandrews, Kirkbampton, Kirkbride, Kirkby Ireleth, Kirkby Lonsdale, Kirkby Stephen, Kirkby Thore, Kirklinton Middle, Kirkoswald,

Lakes, Lambrigg, Lamplugh, Langwathby, Lazonby, Levens, Lindal and Marton, Little Clifton, Little Strickland, Long Marton, Longsleddale, Lorton, Lowca, Lower Allithwaite, Lower Holker, Loweswater, Lowick, Lowside Quarter, Lowther, Lupton,

Mallerstang, Mansergh, Mansriggs, Martindale, Matterdale, Meathop and Ulpha, Middleton, Midgeholme, Milburn, Millom Without, Milnthorpe, Moresby, Morland, Muncaster, Mungrisdale, Murton, Musgrave,

Nateby, Natland, Nether Denton, Nether Staveley, Nether Wasdale, New Hutton, Newbiggin, Newby, Nicholforest,

Old Hutton and Holmescales, Ormside, Orton (in the district of Carlisle), Orton (in the district of Eden), Osmotherley, Oughterside and Allerby, Ousby, Over Staveley,

Papcastle, Parton, Patterdale, Pennington, Plumbland, Ponsonby, Preston Patrick, Preston Richard,

Ravenstonedale, Rockcliffe,

Satterthwaite, Scaleby, Scalthwaiterigg, Seascale, Sebergham, Sedbergh, Sedgwick, Setmurthy, Shap, Shap Rural, Silloth-on-Solway, Skelsmergh, Skelton, Skelwith, Sleagill, Sockbridge and Tirril, Solport, Soulby, St Bees, St Bridget Beckermet, St Cuthbert Without, St Johns Castlerigg and Wythburn, Stainmore, Stainton, Stanwix Rural, Stapleton, Staveley in Cartmel, Strickland Ketel, Strickland Roger,

Tebay, Temple Sowerby, Threlkeld, Thrimby, Thursby, Torver,

Ulpha, Ulverston, Underbarrow and Bradleyfield, Underskiddaw, Upper Allithwaite, Upper Denton, Urswick,

Waberthwaite, Waitby, Walton, Warcop, Waterhead, Waverton, Weddicar, Westlinton, Westnewton, Westward, Wetheral, Wharton, Whicham, Whinfell, Whitwell and Selside, Winscales, Winton, Witherslack, Woodside, Wythop,

Yanwath and Eamont Bridge.

**[3890]**

**NOTES**
Commencement: 7 September 2009.

## PART 4
## GREATER MANCHESTER

Dunham,

Massey,

Ringway,

Warburton, Worthington.

**[3891]**

**NOTES**
Commencement: 7 September 2009.

## PART 5
## HALTON

Daresbury,

Moore,

Preston Brook.

**[3892]**

**NOTES**
Commencement: 7 September 2009.

## PART 6
## LANCASHIRE

Aighton, Bailey and Chaigley, Altham, Anglezarke, Arkholme with Cawood,

Balderstone, Barley with Wheatley Booth, Barnacre with Bonds, Barton, Bashall Eaves, Bickerstaffe, Billington, Bispham, Blackco, Bleasdale, Bolton by Bowland, Borwick, Bowland Forest High, Bowland Forest Low, Bowland with Leagram, Bracewell and Brogden, Bretherton, Brindle, Broughton, Burrow with Burrow,

Cantsfield, Caton with Littledale, Catteral, Charnock Richard, Chatburn, Chipping, Claughton (in the district of Wyre), Claughton (in the district of Lancaster), Cliviger, Cockerham, Croston, Cuerdale, Cuerden,

Dalton, Dinckley, Downham, Down Holland, Dunnockshaw, Dutton,

Easington, Eccleshill, Ellel, Elswick,

Forton, Foulridge,

Gisburn, Gisburn Forest, Goldshaw Booth, Goosnarch, Great Altcar, Great Eccleston, Great Mitton, Greenhalgh with Thistleton, Gressingham, Grimsargh, Grindleton,

Haighton, Halsall, Halton with Aughton, Hambleton, Hapton, Heapey, Heath Charnock, Heaton with Oxcliffe, Heskin, Higham with West Close Booth, Hoghton, Hornby with Farleton, Horton, Hothersall, Hutton,

Ightenhill, Inskip with Sowerby, Ireby,

Kirkland,

Lathom, Leck, Little Hoole, Little Mitton, Little Eccleston with Larbreck, Longridge,

Mawdesley, Mearley, Melling with Wrayton, Mellor, Middleton, Middop, Much Hoole, Myerscough and Bilsborrow,

Nateby, Nether Kellet, Nether Wyersdale, Newburgh, Newsholme, Newton, Newton with Clifton, North Turton,

Old Laund Booth, Osbaldeston, Out Rawcliffe, Over Kellet, Over Wyresdale, Overton,

Parbold, Paythorne, Pendleton, Pilling, Pleasington, Priest Hutton,

Quernmore,

Read, Ribby with Rea, Ribchester, Rimington, Rivington, Roeburndale, Roughlee Booth Rufford,

Sabden, Salesbury, Salterforth, Samlesbury, Sawley, Scarisbrick, Scotforth, Silverdale, Simonstone, Singleton, Slaidburn, Staining, Stalmine with Staynall,

Tatham, Thornley with Wheatley, Thurnham, Tockholes, Trawden Forest, Treales, Roseacre and Wharles, Tunstall, Twiston,

Ulnes Walton, Upper Rawcliffe with Tarnacre,

Waddington, Warton, Weeton with Preese, Wenninghton, West Bradford, Westby with Plumptons, Whalley, Wheelton, Whittingham, Whittington, Winmarleigh, Wiswell, Withnell, Woodplumpton, Worsthorne with Hurstwood, Worston, Wray with Botton, Wrightington,

Yate and Pickup Bank, Yealand Coyners, Yealand Redmayne.

**[3893]**

**NOTES**
Commencement: 7 September 2009.

## PART 7
## MERSEYSIDE

Bold,

Cronton,

Ince Blundell,

Sefton, Simonswood,

Tarbock.

**[3894]**

**NOTES**
Commencement: 7 September 2009.

## PART 8
## WARRINGTON

Croft, Cuerdley,

Hatton,

Rixton and Glazebrook,

Stretton,

Winwick.

**[3895]**

**NOTES**
Commencement: 7 September 2009.

## SCHEDULE 6
## DESIGNATED PROTECTED AREAS IN THE NORTH WEST—BY MAPS
Regulation 4(b)

### PART 1
### CHESHIRE EAST

The parishes of—
  Bollington,
  Haslington,
  Prestbury,
  Willaston, Wistaston.

The unparished area bounded by the parishes of Warmingham, Moston, Haslington, Crewe Green, Weston, Basford, Savington cum Gresty, Rope, Wistaston, Woolstanwood, Leighton and Minshull Vernon.

The unparished area bounded by the parishes of Mottram St Andrew, Alderly Edge, Chorley, Mobberley and Ringway and by the borough constituencies of Cheadle and Manchester Wythenshawe.

**[3896]**

**NOTES**
  Commencement: 7 September 2009.

### PART 2
### CHESHIRE WEST AND CHESTER

The parishes of—
  Appleton,
  Culcheth and Glazebury,
  Davenham,
  Lostock Gralam, Lymm,
  Walton, Winsford.

The unparished area of the county constituency of Ellesmere Port and Neston excluding the parishes of Ince, Elton, Hapsford, Thornton-le-Moors, Dunham-on-the-Hill, Wimbolds Trafford, Bridge Trafford, Stoke, Wervin, Picton, Mickle Trafford, Hoole Village, Crought, Caughall, Moston, Mollington, Saughall, Shotwick Park, Woodbank, Shotwick, Charlton-by-Beckford, Little Stanley, Backford, Lea-by-Backford, Capenhurst, Ledsham and Puddington.

**[3897]**

**NOTES**
  Commencement: 7 September 2009.

### PART 3
### CUMBRIA

The parishes of—
  Brampton,
  Cleator Moor,
  Dalton Town and Newton,
  Egremont,
  Maryport, Millom,
  St John Beckermet,
  Windermere, Workington.

The unparished area bounded by the parishes of Askram and Ireleth, Dalton Town with Newton and Aldingham.

The unparished area bounded by the parishes of Lazonby, Great Salkeld, Langwathby, Brougham, Yanwath and Eamont Bridge, Dacre, Catterlen and Hesket.

The unparished area bounded by the parishes of Parton, Moresby, Weddicar and St Bees.

**[3898]**

**NOTES**
  Commencement: 7 September 2009.

PART II
STATUTORY INSTRUMENTS

## PART 4
## GREATER MANCHESTER

The parishes of—
 Haigh, Heywood and Middleton,
 Saddleworth,
 Westhoughton.

The unparished area of the borough constituency of Bury North.

The unparished area of the county constituency of Littleborough and Saddleworth excluding the parishes of Saddleworth and Shaw and Crompton.

The unparished area of the county constituency of Rochdale.

**[3899]**

**NOTES**
 Commencement: 7 September 2009.

## PART 5
## LANCASHIRE

The parishes of—
 Anderton, Aughton,
 Briercliffe, Brying with Warton, Burscough,
 Cabus, Clayton-Le-Dale,
 Euxton,
 Farington, Freckleton,
 Hesketh with Becconsall,
 Lea, Longton,
 Ramsgreave,
 Tarleton,
 Up Holland,
 Whitworth.

The unparished area bounded by the parishes of Trawden Forest, Reedley Hallows, Old Laund Booth, Barrowford, Blacko, Foulridge, Salterforth; the borough constituency of Burnley; and the parishes of Thornton in Craven and Lothersdale in North Yorkshire.

The unparished area bounded by the parishes of Cliviger, Whitworth, North Turton, Yate and Pickup Bank, Hyndburn, Hapton, Dunnockshaw, Habergham Eaves; the borough constituency of Hyndburn; the parish of Todmorden in West Yorkshire; the county constituency of Heywood and Middleton and the borough constituency of Bury North in Greater Manchester.

The unparished area bounded by the parishes of Latham, Newburgh, Dalton, Up Holland, Bickerstaffe, Aughton, Scarisbrick and Burscough.

The unparished area bounded by the parishes of Cuerdale, Salmesbury, Hoghton, Brindle, Clayton-le-Woods, Cuerden, Farington, Penwortham; and the borough constituency of Preston.

**[3900]**

**NOTES**
 Commencement: 7 September 2009.

## PART 6
## MERSEYSIDE

The parishes of—
 Knowsley,
 Melling,
 Rainford,
 Thornton.

The unparished area of the borough constituency of Crosby bounded by the parishes of Little Altcar, Ince Blundell, Thornton and Sefton and by the borough constituency of Bootle.

The unparished area of the county constituency of Wirral South.

**[3901]**

**NOTES**
 Commencement: 7 September 2009.

### PART 7
### WARRINGTON

Burtonwood and Westbrook.

**[3902]**

---

**NOTES**
Commencement: 7 September 2009.

### SCHEDULE 7
### DESIGNATED PROTECTED AREAS IN THE EAST OF ENGLAND—ENTIRE PARISHES
Regulation 5(a)

### PART 1
### BEDFORD

Aspley Heath, Astwick,

Battlesden, Biddenham, Billington, Bletsoe, Blunham, Bolnhurst and Keysoe, Brogborough,

Campton and Chicksands, Cardington, Carlton and Chellington, Chalgrave, Clifton, Clophill, Colmworth, Cople,

Dean and Shelton, Dunton,

Eastcotts, Edworth, Eggington, Elstow, Eversholt, Everton, Eyeworth,

Felmersham, Flitton and Greenfield,

Gravenhurst, Great Barford,

Harlington, Harrold, Haynes, Heath and Reach, Henlow, Hockliffe, Houghton Conquest, Hulcote and Salford, Husbourne Crawley, Hyde,

Kempston Rural, Kensworth, Knotting and Souldrop,

Lidlington, Little Barford, Little Staughton,

Maulden, Marston Moretaine, Melchbourne and Yielden, Meppershall, Millbrook, Milton Bryan, Milton Ernest, Mogerhanger,

Northill,

Oakley, Odell, Old Warden,

Pavenham, Pertenhall, Podington, Potsgrove, Potton, Pulloxhill,

Ravensden, Renhold, Ridgmont, Riseley, Roxton,

Silsoe, Sharnbrook, Shefford, Shillington, Southill, Stagsden, Stanbridge, Staploe, Steppingley, Stevington, Stewartby, Stondon, Streatley, Studham, Sundon, Sutton, Swineshead,

Tempsford, Thurleigh, Tilsworth, Tingrith, Totternhoe, Turvey,

Westoning, Whipsnade, Wilden, Willington, Wilshamstead, Woburn, Wrestlingworth and Cockayne Hatley, Wymington.

**[3903]**

---

**NOTES**
Commencement: 7 September 2009.

### PART 2
### CAMBRIDGESHIRE

Abbots Ripton, Abbotsley, Abington Pigotts, Ailsworth, Alconbury, Alconbury Weston, Alwalton, Arrington, Ashley,

Babraham, Bainton, Balsham, Barham and Woolley, Barnack, Barrington, Bartlow, Barton, Bassingbourn cum Kneesworth, Benwick, Bluntisham, Borough Fen, Bottisham, Bourn, Boxworth, Brington and Molesworth, Brinkley, Broughton, Buckden, Buckworth, Burrough Green, Bury, Bythorn and Keyston,

Caldecote, Carlton, Castle Camps, Castor, Catworth, Caxton, Chesterton, Cheveley, Childerley, Chippenham, Christchurch, Colne, Comberton, Connington (in the district of South Cambridgeshire), Connington (in the district of Huntingdonshire), Coton, Coveney, Covington, Croxton, Croydon,

Deeping Gate, Denton and Caldecote, Diddington, Doddington, Downham, Dry Drayton, Dullingham, Duxford,

Earith, Easton, Ellington, Elsworth, Eltisley, Elton, Etton, Eye, Eynesbury Hardwicke,

Farcet, Fen Ditton, Fen Drayton, Fenstanton, Folksworth and Washingley, Fordham, Fowlmere, Foxton,

Gamlingay, Glatton, Glinton, Grafham, Grantchester, Graveley, Great Abington, Great and Little Chishill, Great Eversden, Great Gidding, Great Gransden, Great Paxton, Great Staughton, Great Wilbarham, Guilden Morden,

Haddenham, Hail Weston, Hamerton and Steeple Gidding, Hardwick, Harlton, Harston, Haslingfield, Hatley, Hauxton, Helpston, Hemingford Abbotts, Hemingford Grey, Heydon, Hildesham, Hilton, Hinxton, Holme, Holywell cum Needingworth, Horningsea, Horseheath, Houghton and Wyton,

Ickleton, Isleham,

Kennett, Kimbolton, Kings Ripton, Kingston, Kirtling, Knapwell,

Landbeach, Leighton, Litlington, Little Abington, Little Eversden, Little Gidding, Little Gransden, Little Shelford, Little Wilbraham, Lode, Lolworth, Longstanton, Longstowe,

Madingley, Manea, Marholm, Maxey, Meldreth, Mepal, Morborne,

Newborough, Newton (in the district of Fenland), Newton (in the district of South Cambridgeshire), Northborough,

Oakington and Westwick, Offord Cluny and Offord D'Arcy, Old Hurst, Old Weston, Orwell, Over,

Pampisford, Papworth Everard, Papworth St Agnes, Parson Drove, Peakirk, Perry, Pidley cum Fenton,

Rampton, Reach,

Shepreth, Shingay cum Wendy, Shudy Camps, Sibson cum Stibbington, Snailwell, Southoe and Midloe, Southorpe, Spaldwick, St Martins Without, St Neots, Steeple Morden, Stetchworth, Stilton, Stow cum Quy, Stow Longa, Stretham, Sutton (in the district of East Cambridgeshire), Sutton (in the district of Peterborough) Swaffham Bulbeck, Swaffham Prior, Swavesey,

Tadlow, Teversham, The Stukeleys, Thetford, Thorney, Thornhaugh, Thriplow, Tilbrook, Toft, Toseland, Tydd St Giles,

Ufford, Upton and Coppingford, Upton, Upwood and the Raveleys,

Wansford, Warboys, Waresley cum Tetworth, Water Newton, Waterbeach, Wentworth, West Wickham, West Wratting, Westley Waterless, Weston Colville, Whaddon, Whittlesford, Wicken, Wilburton, Wimblington, Wimpole, Winwick, Wisbech St Mary, Wistow, Witcham, Witchford, Wittering, Wood Walton, Woodditton, Woodhurst, Wothorpe,

Yelling.

**[3904]**

---

NOTES
Commencement: 7 September 2009.

---

PART 3
ESSEX

Abberton, Abbess Beauchamp and Berners Roding, Aldham, Alphamstone, Alresford, Althorne, Ardleigh, Arkesden, Ashdon, Asheldham, Ashen, Aythorpe Roding,

Bardfield Sailing, Barling Magna, Barnston, Beaumont cum Moze, Belchamp Otten, Belchamp St Paul, Belchamp Walter, Berden, Birch, Birchanger, Birdbrook, Black Notley, Blackmore, Bobbingworth, Borley, Boxted, Bradfield, Bradwell, Bradwell on Sea, Broxted, Bulmer, Bures Hamlet,

Canewdon, Castle Hedingham, Chappel, Chickney, Chignall, Chrishall, Clavering, Cold Norton, Colne Engaine, Copford, Cressing,

Debden, Dedham, Dengie, Doddinghurst,

East Donyland, East Hanningfield, East Mersea, Eight Ash Green, Elmdon, Elsenham, Epping Upland,

Fairstead, Farnham, Faulkbourne, Feering, Felsted, Finchingfield, Fingrinhoe, Fordham, Foulness, Foxearth, Frating, Fyfield,

Gestingthorpe, Goldhanger, Good Easter, Gosfield, Great and Little Leighs, Great and Little Wigborough, Great Bardfield, Great Bentley, Great Braxted, Great Bromley, Great Canfield, Great Chesterford, Great Easton, Great Hallingbury, Great Henny, Great Horkesley, Great Maplestead, Great Oakley, Great Saling, Great Sampford, Great Tey, Great Totham, Great Waltham, Great Yeldham, Greenstead Green and Halstead Rural,

Hadstock, Hatfield Broad Oak, Hatfield Heath, Hazeleigh, Hellions Bumpstead, Hempstead, Henham, High Easter, High Laver, High Ongar, High Roothing, Highwood,

Kelvedon, Kelvedon Hatch,

Lamarsh, Lambourne, Langenhoe, Langford, Langham, Langley, Latchingdon, Layer Breton, Layer Marney, Layer de la Haye, Leaden Roding, Lindsell, Liston, Little Baddow, Little Bardfield, Little Bentley, Little Braxted, Little Bromley, Little Burstead, Little Canfield, Little Chesterford, Little Clacton, Little Dunmow, Little Easton, Little Hallingbury, Little Henny, Little Horkesley, Little Laver, Little Maplestead, Little Oakley, Little Sampford, Little Totham, Little Waltham, Little Yeldham, Littlebury,

Magden Laver, Manuden, Margaret Roding, Margaretting, Marshbury, Matching, Messing cum Inworth, Middleton, Mistley, Moreton, Mount Bures, Mountnessing, Mundon,

Navestock, Newport, North Fambridge, North Weald Basset,

Ovington,

Paglesham, Panfield, Pebmarsh, Peldon, Pentlow, Pleshey, Purleigh,

Quendon and Rickling,

Radwinter, Ramsden Bellhouse, Ramsden Crays, Ramsey and Parkeston, Rawreth, Rayne, Rettendon, Ridgewell, Rivenhall, Roxwell, Roydon,

Salcott, Sandon, Shalford, Sheering, South Hanningfield, St Lawrence, St Osyth, Stambourne, Stambridge, Stanford Rivers, Stapleford Abbotts, Stapleford Tawney, Stebbing, Steeple Bumpstead, Steeple, Stisted, Stock, Stondon Massey, Stow Maries, Strethall, Sturmer, Sutton,

Takeley, Tendring, Terling, Thaxted, Theydon Bois, Theydon Garnon, Theydon Mount, Thorrington, Thorpe le Soken, Tilbury Juxta Clare, Tillingham, Tilty, Tollesbury, Tolleshunt d'Arcy, Tolleshunt Knight, Tolleshunt Major, Toppesfield, Twinstead,

Ugley, Ulting,

Virley,

Wakes Colne, Weeley, Wenden Lofts, Wendens Ambo, West Hanningfield, Wethersfield, White Colne, White Notley, White Roothing, Wicken Bonhunt, Wickham Bishops, Wickham St Paul, Widdington, Willingale, Wimbish, Wix, Woodham Ferrers & Bicknare, Woodham Mortimer, Woodham Walter, Wormingford, Wrabnes.

**[3905]**

**NOTES**

Commencement: 7 September 2009.

PART 4

## HERTFORDSHIRE

Albury, Aldbury, Anstey, Ardeley, Ashwell, Aspenden, Aston, Ayot St Lawrence, Ayot St Peter,

Barkway, Barley, Bayford, Bengeo Rural, Benington, Bramfield, Braughing, Brent Pelham, Brickendon Liberty, Buckland, Bygrave,

Caldecote, Chipperfield, Clothall, Codicote, Cottered,

Datchworth,

Eastwick, Essendon,

Flamstead, Flaunden, Furneux Pelham,

Gilston, Graveley, Great Amwell, Great Gaddesden, Great Munden,

Harpenden Rural, Hertford Health, Hertingfordbury, Hexton, High Wych, Hinxworth, Holwell, Hormead, Hunsdon,

Ickleford,

Kelshall, Kimpton, Kings Walden,

Langley, Lilley, Little Berkhamsted, Little Gaddesden, Little Hadham, Little Munden,

Markyate, Meesden, Much Hadham,

Nettleden with Potten End, Newnham, Nuthampstead,

Offley,

Pirton, Preston,

Radwell, Reed, Ridge, Rushden,

Sacombe, Sandon, Sarratt, Shenley, St Pauls Walden, Standon, Stapleford, Stocking Pelham,

Tewin, Therfield, Thorley, Thundridge, Tring Rural,

Walkern, Wallington, Ware Rural, Watton at Stone, Westmill, Weston, Widford, Wiggington Wyddial, Wymondley.

**[3906]**

**NOTES**
Commencement: 7 September 2009.

PART 5
NORFOLK

Acle, Alburgh, Alby with Thwaite, Aldborough, Aldeby, Alderford, Alpington, Anmer, Antingham, Ashby St Mary, Ashby with Oby, Ashill, Ashmanhaugh, Ashwellthorpe, Aslacton, Attlebridge, Aylmerton,

Baconsthorpe, Bacton, Bagthorpe with Barmer, Banham, Barford, Barnham Broom, Barsham, Barton Bendish, Barton Turf, Barwick, Bawburgh, Bawdeswell, Bawsey, Beachamwell, Bedingham, Beeston Regis, Beeston St Andrew, Beeston with Bittering, Beetley, Beighton, Belaugh, Bergh Apton, Besthorpe, Billingford, Binham, Bintree, Bircham, Bixley, Blakeney, Blickling, Blo' Norton, Blofield, Bodham, Booton, Boughton, Bracon Ash, Bradenham, Bramerton, Brampton, Brancaster, Brandiston, Bressingham, Brettenham, Bridgham, Briningham, Brinton, Brisley, Briston, Brockdish, Brooke, Broome, Brumstead, Bunwell, Burgh and Tuttington, Burgh Castle, Burgh St Peter, Burnham Market, Burnham Norton, Burnham Overy, Burnham Thorpe, Burston and Shimpling, Buxton with Lammas, Bylaugh,

Caistor St Edmund, Cantley, Carbrooke, Carleton Rode, Carlton St Peter, Castle Acre, Castle Rising, Caston, Catfield, Cawston, Chedgrave, Choseley, Claxton, Clenchwarton, Cley Next the Sea, Cockley Cley, Colby, Colkirk, Colney, Coltishall, Congham, Corpusty, Cranwich, Cranworth, Crimplesham, Cringleford, Crostwick, Croxton,

Denton, Denver, Deopham, Dickleburgh and Rushall, Didlington, Dilham, Ditchingham, Docking, Downham West, Dunton,

Earsham, East Beckham, East Carleton, East Rudham, East Ruston, East Tuddenham, East Walton, East Winch, Easton, Edgefield, Ellingham, Elsing, Erpingham,

Felbrigg, Felmingham, Felthorpe, Feltwell, Field Dalling, Filby, Fincham, Fleggburgh, Flitcham with Appleton, Florden, Fordham, Forncett, Foulden, Foulsham, Foxley, Framingham Pigot, Fransham, Freethorpe, Frettenham, Fring, Fritton and St Olaves, Fulmodeston,

Garboldisham, Garvestone, Gateley, Gayton, Geldeston, Gillingham, Gimingham, Gissing, Gooderstone, Great and Little Plumstead, Great Cressingham, Great Dunham, Great Ellingham, Great Massingham, Great Melton, Great Moulton, Great Snoring, Great Witchingham, Gresham, Gressenhall, Grimston, Griston, Guestwick, Guist, Gunthorpe,

Haddiscoe, Hainford, Hales, Halvergate, Hanworth, Happisburgh, Hardingham, Harling, Harpley, Haveringland, Heckingham, Hedenham, Helhoughton, Hellington, Hemblington, Hempnall, Hempstead, Hempton, Hevingham, Heydon, Hickling, High Kelling, Hilborough, Hilgay, Hillington, Hindolveston, Hindringham, Hingham, Hockering, Hockham, Hockwold cum Wilton, Hoe, Holkham, Holme Hale, Holme next the Sea, Holverston, Holt, Honing, Honingham, Horning, Horningtoft, Horsey, Horsford, Horsham St Faith and Newton St Faith, Horstead with Stanninghall, Houghton, Howe,

Ickburgh, Ingham, Ingoldisthorpe, Ingworth, Itteringham,

Kelling, Kempstone, Kenninghall, Keswick, Ketteringham, Kettlestone, Kilverstone, Kimberley, Kirby Bedon, Kirby Cane, Kirstead, Knapton,

Langham, Langley with Hardley, Lessingham, Letheringsett with Glandford, Lexham, Leziate, Lingwood and Burlingham, Litcham, Little Barningham, Little Cressingham, Little Dunham, Little Ellingham, Little Massingham, Little Melton, Little Snoring, Little Witchingham, Loddon, Long Stratton, Longham, Ludham, Lynford, Lyng,

Marham, Marlingford, Marsham, Marshland St James, Martham, Matlask, Mattishall, Mautby, Melton Constable, Merton, Methwold, Middleton, Mileham, Moreley, Morning Thorpe, Morston, Morton on the Hill, Mulbarton, Mundesley, Mundford, Mundham,

Narborough, Narford, Neatishead, Necton, Needham, New Buckenham, Newton by Castle Acre, Newton Flotman, Nordelph, North Creake, North Elmham, North Lopham, North Pickenham, North Tuddenham, North Wootton, Northwold, Norton Subcourse,

Old Buckenham, Old Hunstanton, Ormesby St Michael, Ormesby St Margaret with Scatby, Oulton, Outwell, Overstrand, Ovington, Oxborough,

Paston, Pentney, Plumstead, Postwick, Potter Heigham, Pudding Norton, Pulham Market, Pulham St Mary,

Quidenham,

Rackheath, Raveningham, Raynham, Reedham, Reepham, Repps with Bastwick, Riddlesworth, Ringland, Ringstead, Rockland St Mary, Rocklands, Rollesby, Roudham, Rougham, Roughton, Roydon (in the Kings Lynn and West Norfolk district), Runcton Holme, Runhall, Runton, Ryburgh, Ryston,

Saham Toney, Salhouse, Sall, Salthouse, Sandringham, Saxlingham Nethergate, Scarning, Scole, Scottow, Scoulton, Sea Palling, Sedgeford, Seething, Shelfanger, Shelton, Shernborne, Shipdham, Shotesham, Shouldham, Shouldham Thorpe, Shropham, Sidestrand, Sisland, Skeyton, Sloley, Smallburgh, Snetterton, Snettisham, Somerton, South Acre, South Creake, South Lopham, South Pickenham, South Walsham, Southery, Southrepps, Sparham, Sporle with Palgrave, Stalham, Stanfield, Stanford, Stanhoe, Starston, Stibbard, Stiffkey, Stockton, Stody, Stoke Ferry, Stoke Holy Cross, Stokesby with Herringby, Stow Bardolph, Stow Bedon, Stradsett, Stratton Strawless, Strumpshaw, Sturston, Suffield, Surlingham, Sustead, Sutton, Swafield, Swainsthorpe, Swannington, Swanton Abbott, Swanton Morley, Swanton Novers, Swardeston, Syderstone,

Tacolneston, Tasburgh, Tattersett, Terrington St Clement, Terrington St John, Tharston, Themelthorpe, Thompson, Thornage, Thornham, Thorpe Market, Thurlton, Thurne, Thurning, Thursford, Thurton, Thwaite, Tibenham, Tilney All Saints, Tilney St Lawrence, Titchwell, Tittleshall, Tivetshall St Margaret, Tivetshall St Mary, Toft Monks, Topcroft, Tottenhill, Tottington, Trimingham, Trowse With Newton, Trunch, Tunstead, Twyford,

Upper Sheringham, Upton with Fishley, Upwell,

Wacton, Walpole, Walpole Cross Keys, Walpole Highway, Walsingham, Warham, Watlington, Weasenham All Saints, Weasenham St Peter, Weeting with Broomhill, Wellingham, Wells next the Sea, Welney, Wendling, Wereham, West Acre, West Beckham, West Caister, West Dereham, West Rudham, West Walton, West Winch, Weston Longville, Westwick, Weybourne, Wheatacre, Whinburgh, Whissonsett, Wicklewood, Wickmere, Wiggenhall St Germans, Wiggenhall St Mary Magdalen, Wighton, Wimbotsham, Winfarthing, Winterton on Sea, Witton, Wiveton, Wood Dalling, Wood Norton, Woodbastwick, Woodton, Wormegay, Worstead, Wortwell, Wramplingham, Wreningham, Wretham, Wretton,

Yaxham, Yelverton.

**[3907]**

**NOTES**
Commencement: 7 September 2009.

PART II
STATUTORY INSTRUMENTS

## PART 6
## SUFFOLK

Acton, Akenham, Aldeburgh, Alderton, Aldham, Aldringham cum Thorpe, All Saints and St Nicholas South Elmham, Alpheton, Ampton, Arwarton, Ashbocking, Ashfield cum Thorpe, Aspall, Assington, Athelington,

Bacton, Badingham, Badley, Badwell Ash, Bardwell, Barham, Barking, Barnardiston, Barnby, Barnham, Barningham, Barrow, Barsham, Barton Mills, Battisford, Bawdsey, Baylham, Bedfield, Bedingfield, Belstead, Benacre, Benhall, Bentley, Beyton, Bildeston, Blaxhall, Blundeston, Blyford, Blythburgh, Botesdale, Boulge, Boxford, Boxted, Boyton, Bradfield Comburst with Stanningfield, Bradfield St Clare, Bradfield St George, Braiseworth, Bramfield, Bramford, Brampton with Stoven, Brandeston, Brantham, Bredfield, Brent Eleigh, Brettenham, Brightwell, Brockley, Brome and Oakley, Bromeswell, Bruisyard, Brundish, Bucklesham, Bures St Mary, Burgate, Burgh, Burstall, Butley, Buxhall,

Campsey Ash, Capel St Andrew, Cavendish, Cavenham, Charsfield, Chattisham, Chedburgh, Chediston, Chelmodiston, Chelsworth, Chevington, Chillesford, Chilton, Clare, Claydon, Clopton, Cockfield, Coddenham, Combs, Coney Weston, Cookley, Copdock, Corton, Cotton, Covehithe, Cowlinge, Cransford, Cratfield, Creeting St Mary, Creeting St Peter or West Creeting, Cretingham, Crowfield, Culford, Culpho,

Dalham, Dallinghoo, Darsham, Debach, Debenham, Denham (in the district of mid Suffolk), Denham (in the district of St Edmundsbury), Dennington, Denston, Depden, Drinkstone, Dunwich,

Earl Soham, East Bergholt, Easton, Edwardstone, Ellough, Elmsett, Elmswell, Elveden, Eriswell, Euston, Eye, Eyke,

Fakenham Magna, Falkenham, Farnham, Felsham, Finningham, Flempton, Flixton (in the district of Waveney, Lothingland Ward), Flixton (in the district of Waveney, South Elmham Ward), Flowton, Fornham St Genevieve, Fornham St Martin, Foxhall, Framlingham, Framsden, Freckenham, Fressingfield, Freston, Friston, Frostenden,

Gazeley, Gedding, Gedgrave, Gipping, Gisleham, Gislingham, Glemsford, Gosbeck, Great Ashfield, Great Barton, Great Bealings, Great Blakenham, Great Bradley, Great Bricett, Great Finborough, Great Glemham, Great Livermere, Great Thurlow, Great Waldingfield, Great Whelnetham, Great Wratting, Groton, Grundisburgh,

Hacheston, Hargrave, Harkstead, Harleston, Hartest, Hasketon, Haughley, Hawkedon, Hawstead, Helmingham, Hemingstone, Hemley, Hengrave, Henley, Henstead with Hulver Street, Hepworth, Herringswell, Hessett, Heveningham, Higham (in the district of Babergh), Higham (in the district of Forest Heath), Hinderclay, Hintlesham, Hitcham, Holbrook, Hollesley, Holton, Holton St Mary, Honington, Hoo, Hopton, Horham, Horringer, Hoxne, Hundon, Hunston, Huntingfield,

Icklingham, Ickworth, Iken, Ingham, Ixworth, Ixworth Thorpe,

Kedington, Kelsale Cum Carlton, Kentford, Kenton, Kersey, Kettlebaston, Kettleburgh, Kirton, Knettishall, Knodishall,

Lackford, Langham, Lavenham, Lawshall, Laxfield, Layham, Leavenheath, Letheringham, Levington, Lidgate, Lindsey, Linstead Magna, Linstead Parva, Little Bealings, Little Blakenham, Little Bradley, Little Cornard, Little Finborough, Little Glemham, Little Livermere, Little Thurlow, Little Waldingfield, Little Whelnetham, Little Wratting, Lound,

Market Weston, Marlesford, Mellis, Mendham, Mendlesham, Metfield, Mettingham, Mickfield, Middleton, Milden, Monewden, Monk Soham, Monks Eleigh, Moulton, Mutford,

Nacton, Nayland with Wissington, Nedging with Naughton, Nettleshead, Newbourne, Newton, North Cove, Norton, Nowton,

Occold, Offton, Old Newton with Dagworth, Onehouse, Orford, Otley, Ouseden,

Pakenham, Palgrave, Parham, Peasenhall, Pettaugh, Pettistree, Playford, Polstead, Poslingford, Preston St Mary, Purdis Farm,

Ramsholt, Rattlesden, Raydon, Reydon, Red Lodge, Rede, Redgrave, Redisham, Redlingfield, Rendham, Rendlesham, Rickinghall Inferior, Rickinghall Superior, Ringsfield, Ringshall, Risby, Rishangles, Rumburgh, Rushbrooke with Rougham, Rushmere,

Santon Downham, Sapiston, Saxmundham, Saxtead, Semer, Shadingfield, Shelland, Shelly, Shimpling, Shipmeadow, Shotley, Shottisham, Sibton, Snape, Somerleyton, Ashby and Herringfleet, Somersham, Somerton, Sotherton, Sotterley, South Cove, Southolt, Spexhall, St Andrew Ilketshall, St Cross South Elmham, St James South Elmham, St John Ilketshall, St Lawrence Ilketshall, St Margaret Ilketshall, St Margaret South Elmham, St Mary South Elmham Otherwise Homersfield, St Michael South Elmham, St Peter South Elmham, Stansfield, Stanstead, Stanton, Sternfield, Stoke Ash, Stoke By Clare, Stoke By Nayland, Stoneham Aspal, Stoneham Earl, Stoneham Parva, Stowlangtoft, Stowupland, Stradbroke, Stradishall, Stratford St Andrew, Stratford St Mary, Stratton Hall, Stuston, Stutton, Sudbourne, Sutton, Swefling, Swilland, Syleham,

Tannington, Tattingstone, The Saxhams, Theberton, Thelnetham, Thorington, Thorndon, Thornham Magna, Thornham Parva, Thorpe Morieux, Thrandeston, Thurston, Thwaite, Timworth, Tostock, Troston, Tuddenham St Martin, Tunstall,

Ubbeston, Ufford, Uggeshall,

Walberswick, Waldringfield, Walpole, Walsham Le Willows, Wangford, Wangford with Henham, Wantisden, Washbrook, Wattisfield, Wattisham, Wenham Magna, Wenham Parva, Wenhaston with Mells Hamlet, West Stow, Westerfield, Westhall, Westhorpe, Westleton, Westley, Weston, Wetherden, Wetheringsett cum Brockford, Weybread, Whatfield, Whepstead, Wherstead, Whitton, Wickham Market, Wickham Skeith, Wickhambrook, Wilby, Willingham St Mary, Willisham, Wingfield, Winston, Wissett, Withersfield, Witnesham, Wixoe, Woolpit, Woolverston, Wordwell, Worlington, Worlingworth, Wortham, Wrentham, Wyverstone,

Yaxley, Yoxford.

**[3908]**

---

**NOTES**

Commencement: 7 September 2009.

---

SCHEDULE 8
DESIGNATED PROTECTED AREAS IN THE EAST OF ENGLAND—BY MAPS
Regulation 5(b)

PART 1
BEDFORD

The parishes of—
  Caddington and Slip End, Cranfield,
  Houghton Regis,
  Langford,
  Sandy,
  Toddington.

**[3909]**

**NOTES**
    Commencement: 7 September 2009.

## PART 2
## CAMBRIDGESHIRE

The parishes of—
    Elm, Ely,
    Leverington,
    March,
    Ramsey,
    Soham,
    Whittlesey.

The unparished area of Stanground North bounded by the parish of Thorney, the parish of Whittlesey in the District of Fenland and the unparished area of the city of Peterborough.

**[3910]**

**NOTES**
    Commencement: 7 September 2009.

## PART 3
## ESSEX

The parishes of—
    Ashingdon,
    Elmstead,
    Frinton and Walton,
    Ingatestone and Fryerning,
    Marks Tey,
    Nazeing,
    Ongar,
    Saffron Walden, Southminster, Stansted Mountfitchet, Stanway,
    Waltham Abbey, Writtle.

The unparished area of the county constituency of Billericay.

The unparished area bounded by the parishes of Gosfield, Sisted, Cressing, Black Notley, Felsted, Rayne, Panfield, Shalford and Wethersfield.

The unparished area of the county constituency of Brentwood and Ongar excluding the parishes of Matching, Abbess Beauchamp & Berners Roding, High Laver, Little Laver, Magdalen Laver, Moreton, Fyfield Willingdale, Bobbingworth, Ongar, High Ongar, Theydon Garnon, Theydon Mount, Stapleford Rowney, Stanford Rivers, Lambourne, Stapleford Abbots, Navestock, Kelvedon Hatch, Standon Massey, Blackmore, Ingatestone & Fryerning, Doddinghurst and Mountnessing.

The unparished area bounded by the parishes of Runwell, Rettendon, Hullbridge, Hockley, Hawkwell, Rochford, the borough constituency of Southend West, the borough constituency of Castle Point the borough constituency of Basildon and the county constituency of Billericay.

The unparished area of the borough constituency of Thurrock

**[3911]**

**NOTES**
    Commencement: 7 September 2009.

## PART 4
## HERTFORDSHIRE

The parishes of—
    Abbots Langley, Aldenham,
    Hatfield,
    Ippollitts,
    Knebworth,
    Northaw and Cuffley, Northchurch,
    St Michael, St Stephen,
    Tring,
    Wheathampstead.

The unparished area bounded by the parishes of Ridge, North Mymms, Northaw and Cuffley, the London borough of Enfield and the London Borough of Barnet.

The unparished area bounded by the parishes of Chorley Wood, Sarratt, Croxley Green and Watford Rural, the borough constituency of Watford, the London Borough of Hillingdon and the parishes of Chalfont St Peter and Denham in the county of Buckinghamshire.

**[3912]**

**NOTES**
Commencement: 7 September 2009.

## PART 5
## NORFOLK

The parishes of—
    Belton with Browston,
    East Dereham, Emneth,
    Hopton on Sea,
    North Runcton, Northrepps,
    Redenhall with Harleston, Roydon (in the district of South Norfolk),
    Sculthorpe,
    Wymondham.

**[3913]**

**NOTES**
Commencement: 7 September 2009.

## PART 6
## SUFFOLK

The parishes of—
    Fornham All Saints,
    Lakenheath, Leiston,
    Mildenhall,
    Oulton,
    Sproughton.

The unparished area bounded by the parish of Moulton and the parishes of Fordham, Snailwell, Cheveley, Wooditton and Burwell in Cambridgeshire.

**[3914]**

**NOTES**
Commencement: 7 September 2009.

## SCHEDULE 9
### DESIGNATED PROTECTED AREAS IN THE NORTH EAST—ENTIRE PARISHES
Regulation 6(a)

## PART 1
## DURHAM

Archdeacon Newton,

Barforth, Barmpton, Barningham, Bearpark, Bishop Middleham, Bishopton, Bolam, Boldron, Bournmoor, Bowes, Bradbury and the Isle, Brafferton, Brancepeth, Brignall,

Castle Eden, Cleatlam, Coatham Mundeville, Cockfield, Cornforth, Cornsay, Cotherstone, Coxhoe, Croxdale and Hett,

Denton,

Easington Village, East and West Newbiggin, Edmonbyers, Edmondsley, Eggleston, Eggleston Abbey, Esh, Etherley, Evenwood and Barony,

Fishburn, Forest and Frith,

Gainford, Gilmonby, Great Burdon, Great Stainton, Greencroft,

Hamsterley, Haswell, Hawthorn, Headlam, Healeyfield, Hedleyhope, Heighington, High Coniscliffe, Hilton, Holwick, Hope, Houghton le Side, Hunderthwaite, Hustanworth, Hutton Henry, Hutton Magna,

Ingleton,

Kelloe, Killerby,

Langley, Langleydale and Shotton, Langton, Lartington, Little Lumley, Little Stainton, Low Coniscliffe and Merrybent, Low Dinsdale, Lunedale, Lynesack and Softley,

Mickleton, Middleton in Teesdale, Middleton St George Middridge, Monk Heselden, Mordon, Morton Palms, Morton Tinmouth, Muggleswick,

Neasham, Nesbitt, Newbiggin,

Ovington,

Piercebridge, Pittington,

Raby with Keverstone, Rokeby, Romaldkirk,

Sadeberge, Satley, Scargill, Seaton with Slingley, Shadforth, Sheraton with Hulam, Sherburn, Shincliffe, Shotton, Sockburn, South Bedburn, South Hetton, Staindrop, Stanhope, Streatlam and Stainton, Summerhouse,

Thornley, Tow Law, Trimdon Foundry,

Wackerfield, Walworth, West Rainton, Westwick, Whessoe, Whitton Gilbert, Whorlton, Windlestone, Winston, Wolsingham, Woodland, Wycliffe with Thorpe.

**[3915]**

**NOTES**

Commencement: 7 September 2009.

## PART 2
## HARTLEPOOL

Brierton,

Claxton,

Dalton Piercy,

Elwick,

Greatham,

Hart,

Newton Bewley.

**[3916]**

**NOTES**

Commencement: 7 September 2009.

## PART 3
## MIDDLESBROUGH

Stainton and Thornton.

**[3917]**

**NOTES**

Commencement: 7 September 2009.

## PART 4
## NORTHUMBERLAND

Acklington, Acomb, Adderstone with Lucker, Akeld, Allendale, Alnham, Alnmouth, Alwinton, Ancroft,

Bamburgh, Bardon Mill, Bavington, Beadnell, Belford, Bellingham, Belsay, Bewick, Biddlestone, Birtley, Blanchland, Bowsden, Branxton, Brinkburn, Broomhaugh and Riding, Broomley and Stocksfield, Bywell,

Callaly, Capheaton, Carham, Cartington, Chatton, Chillingham, Chollerton, Coanwood, Cornhill on Tweed, Corsenside, Craster, Cresswell,

Denwick, Doddington, Duddo,

Earle, Easington, East Chevington, Edlingham, Eglingham, Ellingham, Ellington, Elsdon, Embleton, Ewart,

Falstone, Featherstone, Felton, Ford,

Glanton, Greenhead, Greystead,

Harbottle, Hartburn, Hartleyburn, Hauxley, Haydon, Healey, Hebron, Heddon on the Wall, Hedgeley, Hedley, Henshaw, Hepple, Hepscott, Hesleyhurst, Hexhamshire, Hexhamshire Low Quarter, Hollinghill, Holy Island, Horncliffe, Horsley, Humshaugh,

Ilderton, Ingram,

Kielder, Kilham, Kirknewton, Kirkwhelpington, Knaresdale with Kirkhaugh, Kyloe,

Lesbury, Lilburn, Longframlington, Longhirst, Longhorsley, Longhoughton, Lowick, Lynemouth, Matfen, Meldon, Melkridge, Middleton, Milfield, Mitford,

Netherton, Netherwitton, Newbrough, Newton by the Sea, Newton on the Moor, Norham, North Sunderland, Nunnykirk,

Otterburn, Ovington,

Plenmeller with Whitfield,

Rennington, Rochester, Roddam, Rothbury, Rothley,

Sandhoe, Shilbottle, Shoreswood, Shotley Low Quarter, Simonburn, Slaley, Snitter, Stamfordham, Stannington,

Tarset, Thirlwall, Thirston, Thropton, Togston, Tritlington,

Ulgham,

Wall, Wallington Demesne, Warden, Wark, West Allen, West Chevington, Whalton, Whittingham, Whittington, Whitton and Tosson, Widdrington, Widdrington Station and Stobswood, Wooler, Wylam.

**[3918]**

**NOTES**
Commencement: 7 September 2009.

## PART 5
## REDCAR AND CLEVELAND

Lockwood.

**[3919]**

**NOTES**
Commencement: 7 September 2009.

## PART 6
## STOCKTON-ON-TEES

Aislaby,

Carlton, Castlelevington,

Elton,

Grindon,

Hilton,

Ingleby Barwick,

Kirklevington,

Longnewton,

Maltby,

Newsham,

Redmarshall,

Stillington and Whitton,

Wolviston.

**[3920]**

**NOTES**
Commencement: 7 September 2009.

## PART 7
## TYNE AND WEAR

Burdon,

Dinnington,

Warden Law.

**[3921]**

**NOTES**
Commencement: 7 September 2009.

SCHEDULE 10
DESIGNATED PROTECTED AREAS IN THE NORTH EAST—BY MAPS
Regulation 6(b)

PART 1
DURHAM

The parishes of—
Brandon and Byshottles,
Cassop cum Quarrington,
Dalton le Dale,
Great Lumley,
Hurworth,
Kimblesworth and Plawsworth,
Lanchester,
Marwood,
Pelton,
Sedgefield, Shildon, Spennymoor, Startforth,
Trimdon,
Urpeth,
Waldridge.

The unparished area bounded by the parishes of Spennymoor, Windlestone, Shildon, Etherley, Evenwood and Barony and the borough constituency of North West Durham.

The unparished area bounded by the county constituency of North Durham, the borough constituency of Blaydon, and by the parishes of Greencroft, Lanchester and Healeyfield, and the parish of Shotley Low Quarter Northumberland County Council.

The unparished area bounded by the parishes of Urpeth, Edmondsley, the county constituency of North West Durham and the borough constituency of Blaydon.

The unparished area bounded by the county constituency of Bishop Auckland and the parishes of Wolsingham, Hedleythorpe, Brandon and Byshottles, Brancepeth and Spennymore.

**[3922]**

**NOTES**

Commencement: 7 September 2009.

PART 2
HARTLEPOOL

The unparished area of the borough constituency of Hartlepool.

**[3923]**

**NOTES**

Commencement: 7 September 2009.

PART 3
NORTHUMBERLAND

The parishes of—
Hexham,
Ord,
Ponteland, Prudhoe,
Warkworth.

The unparished area of the borough constituency of Blyth Valley.

The unparished area of the county constituency of Wansbeck excluding the parishes of Longhurst, Pegswood, Hepscott, Morpeth, Mitford and Hebron.

**[3924]**

**NOTES**

Commencement: 7 September 2009.

PART 4
REDCAR AND CLEVELAND

The parishes of—
Guisborough,
Loftus,

Skelton and Brotton.

The unparished area of the borough constituency of Redcar.

**[3925]**

**NOTES**

Commencement: 7 September 2009.

## PART 5
## TYNE AND WEAR

The parishes of—
Hetton,
Lamesley,
Woolsington.

The unparished area of the borough constituency of Blaydon excluding the parishes of Lamesley.

The unparished area of Birtley.

**[3926]**

**NOTES**

Commencement: 7 September 2009.

## SCHEDULE 11
## DESIGNATED PROTECTED AREAS IN THE SOUTH EAST—ENTIRE PARISHES
Regulation 7(a)

## PART 1
## BUCKINGHAMSHIRE

Addington, Adstock, Akeley, Ashendon, Ashley Green, Aston Abbotts, Aston Sandford, Astwood,

Barton Hartshorn, Beachampton, Biddlesden, Bierton with Broughton, Bledlow cum Saunderton, Boarstall, Bow Brickhill, Bradenham, Brill, Buckland,

Castlethorpe, Charndon, Chartridge, Chearsley, Cheddington, Chenies, Chetwode, Chicheley, Chilton, Cholesbury cum St Leonards, Clifton Reynes, Cold Brayfield, Coleshill, Creslow, Cublington, Cuddington,

Dinton with Ford and Upton, Dorney, Dorton, Drayton Beauchamp, Draton Parslow, Dunton,

East Claydon, Edgcott, Edlesborough, Ellesborough, Emberton,

Fawley, Fleet Marston, Foscott, Fulmer,

Gawcott with Lenborough, Gayhurst, Granborough, Great and Little Hampden, Great and Little Kimble, Great Brickhill, Great Horwood, Grendon Underwood,

Halton, Hambleden, Hanslope, Hardmead, Hardwick, Haversham cum Little Linford, Hedgerley, Hedsor, Hillesden, Hoggeston, Hogshaw, Hugheden, Hulcott,

Ibstone, Ickford, Ivinghoe,

Kingsey, Kingswood,

Lacy Green, Lane End, Lathbury, Latimer, Lavendon, Leckhampstead, Lillingstone-Dayrell with Luffield Abbey, Lillingstone-Lovell, Little Brickhill, Little Horwood, Little Marlow, Long Crendon, Longwick cum Ilmer, Lower Winchendon, Ludgershall,

Maids Moreton, Marsh Gibbon, Marsworth, Medmenham, Mentmore, Middle Claydon, Moulsoe, Mursley,

Nash, Newton Blossomville, Newton Longville, North Crawley, North Marston,

Oakley, Oving,

Padbury, Piddington and Wheeler End, Pitchcott, Pitstone, Poundon, Preston Bissett,

Quainton, Quarrendon,

Radclive cum Chackmore, Radnage, Ravenstone,

Seer Green, Shabbington, Shalstone, Sherington, Slapton, Soulbury, Steeple Claydon, Stewkley, Stoke Goldington, Stoke Hammond, Stone with Bishopstone and Hartwell, Stowe, Swanbourne,

Taplow, The Lee, Thorton, Thornborough, Tingewick, Turville, Turweston, Twyford,

Upper Winchendon,

Waddesdon, Warrington, Water Stratford, Weedon, West Wycombe, Westbury, Westcott, Weston Turville, Weston Underwood, Wexham, Whaddon, Whitchurch, Wing, Wingrave with Rowsham, Woodham, Worminghall, Wotton Underwood.

The unparished area bounded by the parishes of Olney, Emberton, Sherrington, Lathbury, Gayhurst, Stoke Goldington, Ravenstone and Weston Underwood.

**[3927]**

**NOTES**

Commencement: 7 September 2009.

## PART 2
## EAST SUSSEX

Alciston, Alfriston, Arlington, Ashburnham,

Barcombe, Beckley, Beddingham, Berwick, Bodiam, Brede, Brightling, Burwash, Buxted,

Camber, Catsfield, Chailey, Chalvington with Ripe, Chiddingly, Crowhurst, Cuckmere Valley,

Dallington, Danehill, Ditchling,

East Chillington, East Dean and Friston, East Guldeford, East Hoathly, Etchingham, Ewhurst,

Falmer, Fairlight, Firle, Fletching, Framfield, Frant,

Glynde, Guestling,

Hadlow Down, Hamsey, Hartfield, Hellingly, Herstmonceux, Hooe, Horam, Hurst Green,

Icklesham, Iden, Iford, Isfield,

Kingston Near Lewes,

Laughton, Little Horsted, Long Man,

Maresfield, Mayfield, Mountfield,

Newick, Ninfield, Northiam,

Peasmarsh, Penhurst, Pett, Pevensey, Piddinghoe, Playden, Plumpton,

Ringmer, Rodmell, Rotherfield, Rye Foreign,

Salehurst, Sedlescombe, Selmeston, South Heighton, Southease, St Ann (Without), St John (Without), Streat,

Tarring Neville, Ticehurst,

Udimore,

Wadhurst, Warbleton, Wartling, Westfield, Westham, Westmeston, Whatlington, Withyam, Wivelsfield.

**[3928]**

**NOTES**

Commencement: 7 September 2009.

## PART 3
## HAMPSHIRE

Ampfield, Amport, Appleshaw, Ashford Hill with Headley, Ashley, Ashmansworth, Ashurst and Colbury, Awbridge,

Barton Stacey, Baughurst, Beaulieu, Beauworth, Bentley, Bentworth, Bighton, Binsted, Bishops Sutton, Boarhunt, Boldre, Bossington, Bradley, Braishfield, Bramdean, Bramley, Bramshaw, Bramshill, Breamore, Brockenhurst, Broughton, Buckholt, Bullington, Burghclere, Buriton, Burley,

Candovers, Chawton, Cheriton, Chilbolton, Chilcomb, Cliddesden, Colden Common, Colemore and Priors Dean, Compton and Shawford, Copythorne, Corhampton and Meonstoke, Crawley, Crondall, Crookham Village, Curdridge,

Damerham, Deane, Denmead, Denny Lodge, Dogmersfield, Droxford, Dummer, Durley,

East Boldre, East Dean, East Tisted, East Tytherley, East Woodhay, Eastmeon, Ecchinswell and Sydmonton, Ellingham, Harbridge and Ibsley, Ellisfield, Eversley, Exbury and Lepe, Exton,

Faccombe, Farleigh Wallop, Farringdon, Four Marks, Frenchmoor, Froxfield, Froyle, Fyfield,

Goodworth Clatford, Grately, Grayshott, Greatham, Greywell,

Hale, Hambledon, Hannington, Hartley Wespall, Hawkley, Heckfield, Herriard, Highclere, Houghton, Hursley, Hurstbourne Priors, Hurstbourne Tarrant, Hyde,

Itchen Stoke and Ovington,

Kilmiston, Kimpton, Kings Somborne, Kingsley,

Langrish, Lasham, Laverstoke, Leckford, Lindford, Linkenholt, Litchfield and Woodcott, Little Somborne, Lockerley, Long Sutton, Longparish, Longstock, Lyndhurst,

Mapledurwell and Up Nately, Martin, Mattingley, Medstead, Melchet Park and Plaitford, Micheldever, Michelmersh, Minstead, Monk Sherborne, Monxton, Mortimer West End, Mottisfont,

Nether Wallop, Netley Marsh, Newnham, Newton Valence, Newtown, North Waltham, Northington, Nutley,

Odiham, Old Alresford, Otterbourne, Over Wallop, Owlesbury,

Penton Grafton, Penton Mewsey, Popham, Preston Candover,

Quarley,

Rockbourne, Romsey Extra, Ropley, Rotherwick, Rowlands Castle,

Sandleheath, Selborne, Shalden, Shedfield, Sherborne St John, Sherfield English, Sherfield on Loddon, Shipton Bellinger, Silchester, Smannell, Soberton, Sopley, South Warnborough, South Wonston, Southwick and Widley, Sparsholt, St Mary Bourne, Steep, Steventon, Stockbridge, Stratfield Saye, Stratfield Turgis, Stroud, Swanmore, Sway,

Tangley, Thruxton, Tichborne, Tunworth, Twyford,

Upham, Upper Clatford, Upton Grey,

Vernhams Dean,

Warnford, West Tisted, West Tytherley, Westmeon, Weston Corbett, Weston Patrick, Wherwell, Whitsbury, Wickham, Wield, Winchfield, Winslade, Wonston, Woodgreen, Wootton St Lawrence, Worldham.

**[3929]**

**NOTES**

Commencement: 7 September 2009.

PART 4
ISLE OF WIGHT

Arreton,

Brightstone,

Calbourne, Chale,

Gatcombe, Godshill, Gurnard,

Newchurch, Niton and Whitwell,

Rookley,

Shalfleet, Shorwell, St Helens,

Wroxall,

Yarmouth.

**[3930]**

**NOTES**

Commencement: 7 September 2009.

PART 5
KENT

Acol, Acrise, Addington, Adisham, Aldington, Alkham, Allhallows, Appledore, Ash,

Badlesmere, Barham, Bean, Bekesbourne with Patrixbourne, Benenden, Bethersden, Bicknor, Bidborough, Biddenden, Bilsington, Birling, Bishopsbourne, Bobbing, Bonnington, Borden, Borough Green, Boughton Aluph, Boughton in the Blean, Boughton Malherbe, Boughton Monchelsea, Boxley, Brabourne, Brasted, Bredgar, Bredhurst, Brenchley, Brenzett, Bridge, Brook, Brookland, Broomfield, Buckland, Norton and Stone, Burham, Burmarsh,

Capel, Capel le Fern, Challock, Charing, Chart Sutton, Chartham, Chiddingstone, Chilham, Chislet, Cliffe, Cobham, Cooling, Cowden, Crockenhill, Crundale, Cuxton,

Denton with Wootton, Detling, Doddington, Dunkirk,

East Farleigh, East Peckham, East Sutton, Eastchurch, Eastling, Eastry, Eastwell, Egerton, Elham, Elmsted, Eynsford, Eythorne,

Farningham, Fawkham, Fordwich, Frinsted, Frittenden,

Godmersham, Goodnestone, Goudhurst, Graveney with Goodenstone, Great Chart with Singleton, Guston,

Hackington, Halling, Halstead, Harrietsham, Hartlip, Hastingleigh, Headcorn, Hernhill, Hever, Higham, High Halden, High Halstow, Hoath, Hollingbourne, Horsmonden, Horton Kirby & South Darenth, Hothfield, Hougham Without, Hucking, Hunton,

Ickham and Well, Ightham, Isle of Grain, Ivychurch, Iwade,

Kenardington, Kingsnorth, Kingston, Knockholt,

Lamberhurst, Langdon, Langley, Leaveland, Leeds, Leigh, Lenham, Leybourne, Leysdown, Linton, Little Chart, Littlebourne, Lower Halstow, Lower Hardres, Luddenham, Luddesdown, Lydden, Lyminge, Lympne, Lynsted,

Manston, Marden, Meopham, Mereworth, Mersham, Milstead and Kingsdown, Molash, Monks Horton, Monkton,

Nettlestead, Newchurch, Newenden, Newington (in the district of Shepway), Newington (in the district of Swale) Newnham, Nonington, Northbourne,

Oare, Offham, Old Romney, Orlestone, Ospringe, Otham, Otterden,

Paddlesworth, Penshurst, Petham, Platt, Plaxtol, Pluckley, Postling, Preston,

Ringwould with Kingsdown, Ripple, Rodmersham, Rolvenden, Ruckinge, Ryarsh,

Saltwood, Sandhurst, Sarre, Seal, Sellindge, Selling, Sevenoaks Weald, Sevington, Shadoxhurst, Sheldwich, Shepherdswell with Coldred, Shipbourne, Sholden, Shoreham, Shorne, Smarden, Smeeth, Snargate, Southfleet, St Margarets at Cliffe, St Mary Hoo, St Nicholas at Wade, Stalisfield, Stanford, Stansted, Staple, Stelling Minnis, Stockbury, Stoke, Stone cum Ebony, Stourmouth, Stowting, Sundridge, Sutton, Sutton Valence, Swingfield,

Teston, Throwley, Thurnham, Tilmanstone, Tonge, Trottiscliffe,

Ulcombe, Upchurch, Upper Hardres,

Waltham, Warden, Warehorne, Wateringbury, West Farleigh, West Malling, West Peckham, Westbere, Westwell, Wichling, Wickhambreaux, Wingham, Wittersham, Womenswold, Woodchurch, Woodnesborough, Wormshill, Worth, Wouldham, Wrotham,

Yalding.

**[3931]**

---

**NOTES**

　Commencement: 7 September 2009.

---

PART 6
OXFORDSHIRE

Adderbury, Adwell, Alvescot, Ambrosden, Appleford, Appleton with Eaton, Ardington, Ardley, Arncott, Ascott under Wychwood, Ashbury, Asthal, Aston Rowant, Aston Tirrold, Aston Upthorpe, Aston, Cote, Shifford and Chimney,

Bampton, Barford St John and St Michael, Baulking, Beckley and Stowood, Begbroke, Benson, Berinsfield, Berrick Salome, Besselsleigh, Bix and Assendon, Black Bourton, Blackthorn, Bladon, Blenheim, Bletchingdon, Blewbury, Bloxham, Bodicote, Bourton (in the district of the Vale of the White Horse), Bourton (in the district of Cherwell), Brightwell, Baldwin, Brightwell cum Sotwell, Britwell Salome, Brize Norton, Broadwell, Broughton, Bruern, Buckland, Bucknell, Burford, Buscot,

Cassington, Caversfield, Chadlington, Chalgrove, Charlbury, Charlton on Otmoor, Charney Bassett, Chastleton, Checkenden, Chesterton, Childrey, Chilson, Chilton, Cholsey, Churchill, Clanfield, Claydon with Clattercot, Clifton Hampden, Coleshill, Combe, Compton Beauchamp, Cornbury and Wychwood, Cornwell, Cottisford, Crawley, Cropredy, Crowell, Crowmarsh, Cuddesdon and Denton, Culham, Curbridge, Cuxham with Easington,

Deddington, Denchworth, Dorchester, Drayton (in the district of the Vale of the White Horse), Drayton St Leonard, Ducklington, Duns Tew,

East Challow, East Hagbourne, East Hanney, East Hendred, Eaton Hastings, Elsfield, Enstone, Epwell, Ewelme, Eye and Dunsden, Eynsham,

Fawler, Fencott and Murcott, Fernham, Fifield, Filkins and Broughton Poggs, Finmere, Finstock, Forest Hill with Shotover, Freeland, Frilford, Fringford, Fritwell, Fulbrook, Fyfield and Tubney,

Garford, Garsington, Glympton, Godington, Goosey, Goring Heath, Grafton and Radcot, Great Coxwell, Great Haseley, Great Milton, Great Tew,

Hailey, Hampton Gay and Poyle, Hanborough, Hanwell, Hardwick with Tusmore, Hardwick with Yelford, Harpsden, Harwell, Hatford, Hethe, Heythrop, Highmoor, Hinton Waldrist, Holton, Holwell, Hook Norton, Horley, Hornton, Horspath, Horton cum Studley,

Idbury, Ipsden, Islip,

Kelmscott, Kencot, Kiddington with Asterleigh, Kidmore End, Kingham, Kingston Bagpuize with Southmoor, Kingston Lisle, Kirtlington,

Langford, Launton, Leafield, Letcombe Bassett, Letcombe Regis, Lew, Lewknor, Little Coxwell, Little Faringdon, Little Milton, Little Tew, Little Wittenham, Littleworth, Lockinge, Long Wittenham, Longcot, Longworth, Lower Heyford, Lyford, Lyneham,

Mapledurham, Marcham, Marsh Baldon, Merton, Middle Aston, Middleton Stoney, Milcombe, Milton (in the district of the Vale of the White Horse), Milton (in the district of Cherwell), Milton under Wychwood, Minster Lovell, Mixbury, Mollington, Moulsford,

Nettlebed, Newington, Newton Purcell with Shelswell, Noke, North Aston, North Leigh, North Moreton, North Newington, Northmoor, Nuffield, Nuneham Courtenay,

Oddington, Over Norton,

Piddington, Pishill with Stonor, Prescote, Pusey, Pyrton,

Radley, Ramsden, Rollright, Rotherfield Greys, Rotherfield Peppard, Rousham,

Salford, Sandford St Martin, Sandford on Thames, Sarsden, Shellingford, Shenington with Alkerton, Shilton, Shiplake, Shipton on Cherwell and Thrupp, Shipton under Wychwood, Shirburn, Shutford, Sibford Ferris, Sibford Gower, Somerton, Souldern, South Hinksey, South Leigh, South Moreton, South Newington, South Stoke, Sparsholt, Spelsbury, St Helen Without, Stadhampton, Standlake, Stanford in the Vale, Stanton Harcourt, Stanton St John, Steeple Aston, Steeple Barton, Steventon, Stoke Lyne, Stoke Row, Stoke Talmage, Stonesfield, Stratton Audley, Sunningwell, Sutton Courtenay, Swalcliffe, Swerford, Swinbrook and Widford, Swyncombe, Sydenham,

Tackley, Tadmarton, Taynton, Tetsworth, Tiddington and Albury, Toot Baldon, Towersey,

Uffington, Upper Heyford, Upton.

Warborough, Wardington, Watchfield, Waterperry, Waterstock, Watlington, Wendlebury, West Challow, West Hagbourne, West Hanney, West Hendred, Westcot Barton, Weston on the Green, Westwell, Wheatfield, Whitchurch, Wigginton, Woodcote, Woodeaton, Woodstock, Woolstone, Wootton (in the district of the Vale of the White Horse), Wootton (in the district of West Oxfordshire), Worton, Wroxton, Wytham,

Yarnton.

**[3932]**

**NOTES**
Commencement: 7 September 2009.

PART 7
SURREY

Abinger, Albury, Alfold,

Betchworth, Bletchingley, Bramley, Brockham, Buckland, Busbridge,

Capel, Charlwood, Chelsham and Farleigh, Chiddingfold, Compton, Crowhurst,

Dockenfield, Dunsfold,

East Clandon, Effingham, Elstead, Ewhurst,

Felbridge, Frensham,

Godstone,

Hambledon, Hascombe, Headley, Holmwood, Horne,

Leigh, Limpsfield, Lingfield,

Mickleham,

Newdigate, Normandy, Nutfield,

Ockham, Ockley,

Peper Harrow, Pirbright, Puttenham,

Ripley,

Seale and Sands, Shackleford, Shalford, Shere, St. Martha,

Tandridge, Tatsfield, Thursley, Tilford, Titsey,

Wanborough, West Clandon, Wisley, Wonersh, Wotton.

**[3933]**

**NOTES**
Commencement: 7 September 2009.

## PART 8
## WEST BERKSHIRE

Aldermaston, Aldworth, Arborfield and Newland, Ashampstead,

Barkham, Basildon, Beech Hill, Beedon, Beenham, Bisham, Boxford, Bradfield, Brightwalton, Brimpton, Bucklebury,

Catmore, Chaddleworth, Charvil, Chieveley, Cold Ash, Combe, Compton, Cookham,

East Garston, East Ilsley, Enborne, Englefield, Eton,

Farnborough, Fawley, Frilsham,

Great Shefford,

Hampstead Marshall, Hampstead Norreys, Hermitage, Horton, Hurley,

Inkpen,

Kintbury,

Lamboarn, Leckhampstead,

Midgeham,

Old Windsor,

Padworth, Pangbourne, Peasemore,

Remenham, Ruscombe,

Shottesbrooke, St. Nicholas Hurst, Stanford Dingley, Stratfield-Mortimer, Streatley, Sulham, Sulhamstead, Swallowfield,

Tidmarsh,

Ufton Nervet,

Waltham St. Lawrence, Warfield, Wasing, Welford, West Ilsley, West Woodhay, White Waltham, Winterbourne, Wokefield, Woolhampton, Wraysbury,

Yattendon.

**[3934]**

**NOTES**
Commencement: 7 September 2009.

## PART 9
## WEST SUSSEX

Albourne, Aldingbourne, Amberley, Appledram, Ardingly, Arundel, Ashurst,

Balcombe, Barlavington, Bepton, Bignor, Birdham, Bolney, Bosham, Boxgrove, Broadbridge Heath, Burpham, Bury,

Chidham, Clapham, Climping, Cocking, Coldwaltham, Colgate, Compton, Coombes, Cowfold, Cuckfield, Cuckfield Rural,

Duncton,

Earnley, Eartham, Easeborne, East Dean, East Lavington, Ebernoe, Elsted and Treyford,

Fernhurst, Findon, Fittleworth, Fishbourne, Ford, Fulking, Funtington,

Graffam,

Harting, Heyshott, Horsted Keynes, Houghton, Hunston,

Itchingfield,

Kirdford,

Linch, Linchmere, Lodsworth, Lower Beeding, Loxwood, Lurgashall, Lyminster,

Madehurst, Marden, Milland,

Newtimber, North Mundham, Northchapel, Nuthurst,

Oving,

Parham, Patching, Petworth, Plaistow, Poling, Poynings, Pyecombe,

Rogate, Rudgwick, Rusper,

Shermanbury, Shipley, Sidlesham, Singleton, Slaugham, Slindon, Slinfold, South Stoke, Steadham with Iping, Stopham, Stoughton, Sutton,

Tangmere, Tillington, Trotton with Chithurst, Turners Hill, Twineham,

Upwaltham,

Walberton, Warnham, Warningcamp, West Chiltington, West Dean, West Grinstead, West Hoathly, West Itchenor, West Lavington, West Thorney, Westbourne, Westhampnett, Wisborough Green, Wiston, Woodmancote, Woolbeding.

**[3935]**

**NOTES**
Commencement: 7 September 2009.

## SCHEDULE 12
### DESIGNATED PROTECTED AREAS IN THE SOUTH EAST—BY MAPS
Regulation 7(b)

### PART 1
### BUCKINGHAMSHIRE

The parishes of—
    Amersham, Aston Clinton,
    Beaconsfield, Bow Brickhill,
    Chesham,
    Edlesborough,
    Great Marlow, Great Missenden,
    Haddenham,
    Little Missenden,
    Penn,
    Stoke Poges, Stokenchurch,
    Wendover.

The unparished area bounded by the parishes of Castlethorpe, Haversham-cum-Little Linford, Stantonbury, Bradwell Abbey, Shenley Church End, Whaddon and Beachampton and the parishes of Deanshanger, Old Stratford and Cosgrove in Northamptonshire.

**[3936]**

**NOTES**
Commencement: 7 September 2009.

### PART 2
### EAST SUSSEX

The parishes of—
    Battle,
    Forest Row,
    Hailsham, Heathfield and Waldron,
    Polegate,
    Ringmer,
    Telscombe,
    Willingdon and Jevington.

The unparished area bounded by the parishes of Newhaven, South Heighton, Alfriston and Cuckmere Valley.

**[3937]**

**NOTES**
Commencement: 7 September 2009.

### PART 3
### HAMPSHIRE

The parishes of—
    Abbotts Ann, Alton,
    Bishops Waltham, Bramshott and Liphook, Bransgore,
    Chilworth, Clanfield,
    Fair Oak and Horton Heath, Fawley, Fordingbridge,
    Hartley Wintney, Headbourne Worthy, Headley, Hook, Hordle, Horndean, Hythe and Dibden,
    Itchen Valley,
    Kings Worthy,
    Liss, Littleton and Harestock, Lymington and Pennington,
    Milford on Sea,
    New Milton, Nursling and Rownhams,
    Oakley, Overton,
    Pamber, Petersfield,

Ringwood,
Totton and Eling,
Wellow, Whitchurch, Whitehill.

The unparished area bounded by the parishes of Smannell, St. Mary Bourne, Longparish, Goodworth Clatford, Upper Clatford, Abbotts Ann, Monxton, Penton Mewsey, Charlton and Tangley.

**[3938]**

NOTES
Commencement: 7 September 2009.

## PART 4
## ISLE OF WIGHT

The parishes of—
Bembridge, Brading,
Freshwater,
Shanklin,
Totland,
Ventnor.

The unparished area bounded by the parishes of Wootton Bridge, Nettlestone & Seaview, Brading, Newchurch, Arreton, Gatcombe, Shorwell, Brighstone, Calbourne, Gurnard and Cowes.

**[3939]**

NOTES
Commencement: 7 September 2009.

## PART 5
## KENT

The parishes of—
Ash Cum Ridley, Aylesford, Aylesham,
Chestfield, Chevening, Cranbrook,
Darenth, Dunton Green,
Edenbridge,
Frindsbury Extra,
Hadlow, Harbledown, Hawkhurst, Hawkinge, Hildenborough, Hoo St Werburgh, Hythe,
Lydd,
Manston, Minster,
Queenborough,
Sandwich, Speldhurst, St Cosmus and St Damian in the Blean, St Mary in the Marsh, Sturry,
    Sutton at Hone and Hawley, Swanley,
Tenterden, Teynham, Tunstall,
West Kingsdown, Westerham, Whitfield, Wye with Hinxhill.

The unparished area bounded by the parishes of Ringwould with Kingsdown, Ripple, Sutton, Northbourne and Sholden.

The unparished area bounded by the parishes of St Nicholas at Wade, Chislet, Hoath, Sturry, Hackington and Chestfield.

The unparished area bounded by the parishes of Chestfield, St Cosmus and St Damian in the Blean, Dunkirk, Hernhill, Graveney with Goodnestone and Leysdown.

**[3940]**

NOTES
Commencement: 7 September 2009.

## PART 6
## OXFORDSHIRE

The parishes of—
Chinnor, Cumnor,
Drayton (in the district of Cherwell),
Gosford and Water Eaton,
Thame.

**[3941]**

NOTES
Commencement: 7 September 2009.

## PART 7
## SURREY

The parishes of—
  Artington,
  Burstow,
  Chobham, Cranleigh,
  Salfords and Sidlow,
  West Horsley, Witley, Worplesdon.

The unparished area of the county constituency of Mole Valley excluding the parishes of Headley, Mickleham, Bickland, Betchworth, Leigh, Charlwood, Newdigate, Capel, Holmwood, Ockley, Wotton and Abinger.

The unparished area bounded by the parishes of Chelsham and Fairleigh, Oxted, Tandridge, Godstone, Bletchingley, the borough constituency of Reigate and the London borough of Croydon.

The unparished area of the county constituency of Woking excluding the parishes of Byfleet, Pirbright, Normandy and Ash.

**[3942]**

NOTES
Commencement: 7 September 2009.

## PART 8
## WEST BERKSHIRE

The parishes of—
  Bray, Burghfield,
  Greenham,
  Hungerford,
  Shaw cum Donnington, Shinfield, Speen, Sulhamstead,
  Thatcham, Theale,
  Wargrave, Winkfield, Wokingham Without.

**[3943]**

NOTES
Commencement: 7 September 2009.

## PART 9
## WEST SUSSEX

The parishes of—
  Ashington,
  Billingshurst, Bramber,
  Clayton,
  Donnington,
  East Grinstead,
  Henfield, Hurstpierpoint,
  Lavant, Lindfield Rural,
  Pagham, Pulborough,
  Selsey, Southwater, Storrington,
  Thakeham,
  Upper Beeding,
  Washington, West Wittering.

**[3944]**

NOTES
Commencement: 7 September 2009.

SCHEDULE 13
DESIGNATED PROTECTED AREAS IN THE EAST MIDLANDS—ENTIRE PARISHES
Regulation 8(a)

PART 1
DERBYSHIRE

Abney and Abney Grange, Aldercar and Langley Mill, Alderwasley, Aldwark, Alkmorton, Ash, Ashford in the Water, Ashleyhay, Ashover, Aston, Aston upon Trent, Atlow, Ault Hucknall,

Bakewell, Ballidon, Bamford, Barlborough, Barlow, Barrow upon Trent, Barton Blount, Baslow and Bubnell, Bearwardcote, Beeley, Biggin, Birchover, Blackwell, Blackwell in the Peak, Bonsall, Boylestone, Brackenfield, Bradbourne, Bradley, Bradwell, Brailsford, Brampton, Brassington, Breadsall, Bretby, Brough and Shatton, Brushfield, Burnaston, Buxworth and Brownside,

Calke, Callow, Calow, Calver, Carsington, Castle Gresley, Castleton, Catton, Cauldwell, Charlesworth, Chatsworth, Chelmorton, Chinley, Chisworth, Church Broughton, Clifton and Compton, Coton in the Elms, Crich, Cromford, Cubley, Curbar,

Dalbury Lees, Denby, Derwent, Dethick Lea and Holloway, Doveridge, Drakelow, Draycott and Church Wilne,

Eaton and Alsop, Edale, Edensor, Edlaston and Wyaston, Eggington, Elton, Elvaston, Etwall, Eyam, Fenny Bentley, Findern, Flagg, Foolow, Foremark, Foston and Scropton, Froggatt,

Glapwell, Grassmoor Hasland & Winsick, Gratton, Great Hucklow, Great Longstone, Green Fairfield, Grindleford, Grindlow,

Harthill, Hartington Middle Quarter, Hartington Nether Quarter, Hartington Town Quarter, Hartington Upper Quarter, Hartshone, Hathersage, Hassop, Hatton, Hayfield, Hazelwood, Hazelbadge, Heath and Holmewood, Highlow, Hilton, Hognaston, Holbrook, Hollington, Holmesfield, Holymoorside and Walton, Hoon, Hope, Hope Woodlands, Hopton, Hopwell, Horsley, Horsley Woodhouse, Hulland, Hulland Ward, Hungry Bentley,

Ible, Idridgehay and Alton, Ingleby, Ironville, Ivonbrook Grange,

Kedlesston, Killamarsh, King Sterndale, Kirk Ireton, Kirk Langley, Kniveton,

Lea Hall, Linton, Little Eaton, Little Hucklow, Little Longstone, Litton, Longford, Lullington,

Mackworth, Mapleton, Mapperley, Marston Montgomery, Marstone on Dove, Matlock Bath, Mercaston, Middleton, Middleton and Smerrill, Monyash, Morley, Morton,

Nether Haddon, Netherseal, Newton Grange, Newton Solney, Norbury and Roston, Northwood and Tinkersley,

Offcote and Underwood, Offerton, Osleston and Thurvaston, Osmaston, Outseats, Over Haddon, Overseal,

Parwich, Peak Forest, Pentrich, Pilsley (in the district of the Derbyshire Dales), Pilsley (in the district of North East Derbyshire), Pleaseley,

Quarndon,

Radbourne, Ravensdale Park, Repton, Risley, Rodsley, Rosliston, Rowland, Rowsley,

Shardlow and Great Wilne, Sheldon, Shipley, Shirland and Higham, Shirley, Shottle and Postern, Smalley, Smisby, Snelston, Somersal Herbert, South Darley, South Wingfield, Stanley, Stanton, Stanton by Bridge, Stanton by Dale, Stenson Fields, Stoney Middleton, Stretton, Sudbury, Sutton cum Duckmartonton, Sutton on the Hill, Swarkestone,

Taddington, Tansley, Temple Normanton, Thornhill, Thorpe, Ticknall, Tideswell, Tintwistle, Tissington, Trusley, Tupton, Turnditch, Twyford and Stenson,

Unstone,

Walton upon Trent, Wardlow, Wessington, West Hallam, Weston Underwood, Weston upon Trent, Wheston, Willington, Windley, Winster, Woodville, Wormhill,

Yeaveley, Yeldersley, Youlgreave.

**[3945]**

NOTES

Commencement: 7 September 2009.

PART 2
LEICESTERSHIRE

Ab Kettleby, Allexton, Appleby Magna, Arnesby, Ashby Woulds, Ashfordby, Ashby Magna, Ashby Parva, Aswell, Aston Flamville, Ayston,

PART II
STATUTORY INSTRUMENTS

Bagworth, Bardon, Barkby, Barkby Thorpe, Barlestone, Barleythorpe, Barrow, Barrowden, Beaumont Chase, Beeby, Belton, Belton in Rutland, Belvoir, Billesdon, Bisbrooke, Bittesby, Bitteswell, Blaby, Blaston, Bottesford, Braunston in Rutland, Breedon on the Hill, Bringhurst, Brooke, Broughton and Old Dalby, Bruntingthorpe, Buckminster, Burley, Burton and Dalby, Burton on the Wolds, Burton Overy,

Cadeby, Caldecott, Carlton, Carlton Curlieu, Catthorpe, Charley, Chilcote, Clawson, Hose and Harby, Claybrooke Magna, Claybrooke Parva, Clipsham, Cold Newton, Coleorton, Cossington, Cotes, Cotesbach, Cottesmore, Cranoe, Croft, Croxton Kerrial,

Drayton, Dunton Bassett,

East Langton, East Norton, Eaton, Edith Weston, Egleton, Elmesthorpe, Empingham, Essendine, Exton,

Foxton, Freeby, Frisby, Frisby on the Wreake, Frolesworth,

Gaddesby, Garthorpe, Gaulby, Gilmorton, Glaston, Glooston, Goadby, Great Casterton, Great Easton, Greetham, Grimston, Gumley, Gunthorpe,

Hallaton, Hambleton, Hathern, Heather, Higham on the Hill, Hoby with Rotherby, Horn, Horninghold, Hoton, Houghton on the Hill, Huncote, Hungarton, Husbands Bosworth,

Illston on the Hill, Isley cum Langley,

Ketton, Keyham, Kibworth Harcourt, Kilby, Kimcote and Walton, Kings Norton, Kirkby Bellars, Knaptoft, Knossington and Cold Overton,

Langham, Laughton, Launde, Leicester Forest West, Leighfield, Leire, Little Casterton, Little Stretton, Lockington-Hemington, Loddington, Long Whatton, Lowesby, Lubbesthorpe, Lubenham, Lyddington, Lyndon,

Manton, Marefield, Market Bosworth, Market Overton, Martinsthorpe, Medbourne, Misterton, Morcott, Mowsley,

Nailstone, Nevill Holt, Newton Linford, Normanton, Normanton le Heath, North Kilworth, North Luffenham, Noseley,

Oakthorpe and Donisthorpe, Osbaston, Osgathorpe, Owston and Newbold,

Packington, Peatling Magna, Peatling Parva, Peckleton, Pickworth, Pilton, Potters Marston, Preston, Prestwold,

Ratcliffe on the Wreake, Ravenstone with Snibstone, Rearsby, Redmile, Ridlington, Rolleston, Ryhall,

Saddington, Sapcote, Scalford, Scraptoft, Seagrave, Seaton, Shackerstone, Shangton, Sharnford, Shawell, Shearsby, Sheepy, Skeffington, Slawston, Smeeton Westerby, Snarestone, Somerby, South Croxton, South Kilworth, South Luffenham, Sproxton, Stanton under Bardon, Stathern, Staunton Harold, Stokerston, Stoke Dry, Stoke Golding, Stonton Wyville, Stoughton, Stretton, Stretton en le Field, Stretton Magna, Sutton Cheney, Swannington, Swepstone, Swinsford, Swithland,

Teigh, Theddingworth, Thisleton, Thorpe by Water, Thorpe Langton, Thussington, Thurcaston and Cropston, Thurlaston, Tickencote, Tilton, Tinwell, Tixover, Tugby and Keythorpe, Tur Langton, Twycross, Twyford and Thorpe,

Ullesthorpe, Ulverscroft,

Waltham, Walton on the Wolds, Wanlip, Wardley, Welham, West Langton, Westrill and Starmore, Whatborough, Whissendine, Whitwell, Wigston Parva, Willough by Waterleys, Wing, Wistow, Withcote, Witherley, Woodhouse, Worthington, Wymeswold, Wymondham.

**[3946]**

**NOTES**

Commencement: 7 September 2009.

## PART 3
## LINCOLNSHIRE

Aby with Greenfield, Addlethorpe, Aisthorpe, Alford, Algarkirk, Allington, Alvingham, Amber Hill, Ancaster, Anderby, Anwick, Apley, Asgarby and Howell, Ashby de Launde & Bloxholm, Ashby with Scremby, Aslackby and Laughton, Asterby, Aswarby and Swarby, Aswardby, Aubourn Haddington and South Hykeham, Aunsby and Dembleby, Authorpe,

Bardney, Barholm and Stow, Barkston, Barlings, Barrowby, Bassingham, Baston, Baumber, Beckingham, Beesby with Saleby, Belchford, Belleau, Belton with Manthorpe, Benington, Benniworth, Bicker, Bigby, Billingborough, Billinghay, Bilsby, Binbrook, Bishop Norton, Bitchfield and Bassingthorpe, Blankney, Blyborough, Blyton, Bolingbroke, Boothby Graffoe, Boothby Pagnell, Braceborough with Wilsthorpe, Braceby and Sapperton, Brackenborough with Little Grimsby, Brampton, Brant Broughton and Stragglethorpe, Bratoft, Brattleby, Brauncewell,

Brinkhill, Broadholme, Brocklesby, Broxholme, Bucknall, Bullington, Burgh le Marsh, Burgh on Bain, Burton, Burton Coggles, Burton Pedwardine, Burwell, Buslingthorpe, Butterwick,

Cabourne, Caenby, Caistor, Calcethorpe with Kelstern, Cammeringham, Candlesby with Gunby, Canwick, Careby Aunby and Holywell, Carlby, Carlton Scroop, Carlton le Moorland, Carrington, Castle Bytham, Caythorpe, Chapel St Leonards, Cherry Willingham, Claxby (in the district of West Lindsey), Claxby (in the district of East Lindsey), Claxby with Moorby, Claypole, Claythorpe, Cold Hanworth, Coleby, Colsterworth, Coningsby, Conisholme, Corby Glen, Corringham, Counthorpe and Creeton, Covenham St Bartholomew, Covenham St Mary, Cowbit, Cranwell and Byard's Leap, Croft, Crowland, Culverthorpe and Kelby, Cumberworth,

Dalby, Deeping St Nicholas, Denton, Digby, Doddington and Whisby, Dogdyke, Donington, Donington on Bain, Dorrington, Dowsby, Dunholme, Dunsby,

Eagle and Swinethorpe, East Barkwith, East Ferry, East Keal, East Kirkby, East Stockwith, Easton, Eastville, Edenham, Edlington with Wispington, Elkington, Ewerby and Evedon,

Faldingworth, Farlesthorpe, Fenton (in the district of West Lindsey), Fenton (in the district of South Kesteven), Fillingham, Firsby, Fiskerton, Folkingham, Fosdyke, Foston, Fotherby, Frampton, Freiston, Friesthorpe, Friskney, Frithville and Westville, Fulbeck, Fulletby, Fulnetby, Fulstow,

Gate Burton, Gautby, Gayton le Marsh, Gayton le Wold, Gedney, Gedney Hill, Glentham, Glentworth, Goltho, Gosberton, Goulceby, Grainsby, Grainthorpe, Grange de Lings, Grasby, Grayingham, Great Carlton, Great Gonerby, Great Hale, Great Limber, Great Ponton, Great Steeping, Great Sturton, Greatford, Greetham with Somersby, Greetwell, Grimoldby, Gunby with Stainby,

Hackthorn, Haconby, Hagworthingham, Hainton, Hallington, Haltham, Halton Holegate, Hameringham, Hannah cum Hagnaby, Hardwick, Harlaxton, Harmston, Harpswell, Harrington, Hatton, Haugh, Haugham, Haydor, Heapham, Heckington, Helpringham, Hemingby, Hemswell, High Toynton, Hogsthorpe, Holland Fen with Brothertoft, Holton cum Beckering, Holton le Moor, Honington, Horbling, Horsington, Hough on the Hill, Hougham, Hundleby, Huttoft,

Ingham, Ingoldmells, Ingoldsby, Irby in the Marsh, Irnham,

Keddington, Keelby, Kettlethorpe, Kexby, Kirkby la Thorpe, Kirkby on Bain, Kirkby Underwood, Kirmond le Mire, Kirton, Knaith,

Langriville, Langtoft, Langton by Spilsby, Langton by Wragby, Langton, Laughton, Leadenham, Leasingham, Legbourne, Legsby, Lenton, Lenton Keisby and Osgodby, Leverton, Linwood, Lissington, Little Bytham, Little Carlton, Little Cawthorpe, Little Hale, Little Ponton and Stroxton, Little Steeping, Little Sutton, Long Bennington, Low Toynton, Ludborough, Ludford, Lusby with Winceby, Lutton,

Maidenwell, Maltby le Marsh, Manby, Mareham le Fen, Mareham on the Hill, Markby, Market Rasen, Market Stainton, Marsh Chapel, Marston, Martin, Marton, Mavis Enderby, Metheringham, Middle Rasen, Midville, Minting, Morton (in the district of South Kesteven), Moulton, Muckton, Mumby,

Navenby, Nettleton, New Leake, Newball, Newton and Haceby, Newton on Trent, Nocton, Normanby by Spital, Normanby le Wold, Normanton, North Carlton, North Coates, North Cockerington, North Kelsey, North Kyme, North Ormsby, North Rauceby, North Scarle, North Somercotes, North Thoresby, North Willingham, North Witham, Northorpe, Norton Disney,

Old Leake, Old Somerby, Orby, Osbournby, Osgodby, Owersby, Owmby,

Partney, Pickworth, Pilham, Pointon and Sempringham, Potter Hanworth,

Quadring,

Raithby, Raithby cum Maltby, Ranby, Rand, Reepham, Reston, Revesby, Riby, Rigsby with Ailby, Rippingale, Riseholme, Ropsley and Humby, Rothwell, Roughton, Rowston, Roxholm,

Saltfleetby, Sausthorpe, Saxby, Saxilby with Ingleby, Scamblesby, Scampton, Scopwick, Scothern, Scotter, Scotton, Scredington, Scrivelsby, Searby cum Owmby, Sedgebrook, Sibsey, Silk Willoughby, Sixhills, Skendleby, Skidbrooke with Saltfleet Haven, Skillington, Snarford, Snelland, Snitterby, Somerby, Sotby, South Carlton, South Cockerington, South Kelsey, South Kyme, South Ormsby cum Ketsby, South Rauceby, South Somercotes, South Thoresby, South Willingham, South Witham, Spilsby, Spridlington, Springthorpe, Stainfield, Stainton by Langworth, Stainton le Vale, Stapleford, Stenigot, Stewton, Stickford, Stickney, Stixwould and Woodhall, Stoke Rochford, Stow, Strubby with Woodthorpe, Stubton, Sturton by Stow, Sudbrooke, Surfleet, Sutterton, Sutton Bridge, Sutton St Edmond, Sutton St James, Swaby, Swallow, Swaton, Swayfield, Swinderby, Swineshead, Swinhope, Swinstead, Syston,

Tallington, Tathwell, Tattershall, Tattershall Thorpe, Tealby, Temple Bruer with Temple High Grange, Tetford, Tetney, Theddlethorpe All Saints, Theddlethorpe St Helen, Thimbleby, Thonock, Thoresway, Thorganby, Thorton le Fen, Thorpe in the Fallows, Thorpe on the Hill, Thorpe St Peter, Threekingham, Thurlby (in the district of North Kesteven), Thurlby (in the district of South

Kesteven), Timberland, Toft Newton, Toft with Lound & Manthorpe, Torksey, Toynton All Saints, Toynton St Peter, Tumby, Tupholme, Tydd St Mary,

Uffington, Ulceby with Fordington, Upton, Utterby,

Waddingham, Waddington, Waddingworth, Wainfleet All Saints, Wainfleet St Mary, Waithe, Walcot Near Folkingham, Walcott, Walesby, Walkerith, Walmsgate, Welbourn, Welby, Well, Wellingore, Welton, Welton le Marsh, Welton le Wold, West Ashby, West Barkwith, West Deeping, West Fen, West Firsby, West Keal, West Rasen, West Torrington, Westborough and Dry Doddington, Weston, Whaplode, Wickenby, Wigtoft, Wildmore, Wildsworth, Willingham, Willoughby with Sloothby, Willoughton, Wilsford, Witham on the Hill, Withcall, Withern with Stain, Wood Enderby, Woodhall Spa, Woolsthorpe, Wragby, Wrangle, Wyberton, Wyham cum Cadeby, Wycliffe cum Hungerton, Yarburgh.

[3947]

**NOTES**
Commencement: 7 September 2009.

## PART 4
## NORTHAMPTONSHIRE

Abthorpe, Adstone, Aldwincle, Althorp, Apethorpe, Arthingworth, Ashby St Ledgers, Ashley, Ashton (in the district of East Northamptonshire), Ashton (in the district of South Northamptonshire), Aston le Walls, Aynho,

Badby, Barby, Barnwell, Benefield, Blakesley, Blatherwycke, Blisworth, Boddington, Boughton, Bozeat, Bradden, Brafield on the Green, Brampton Ash, Braunston, Braybrooke, Brigstock, Brington, Brockhall, Broughton, Bugbrooke, Bulwick, Byfield,

Canons Ashby, Castle Ashby, Catesby, Chacombe, Charwelton, Chelveston cum Caldecott, Chipping Warden, Church with Chapel Brampton, Clay Coton, Clipston, Clopton, Cogenhoe and Whiston, Cold Ashby, Cold Higham, Collingtree, Collyweston, Cosgrove, Cotterstock, Cottesbrooke, Cottingham, Courteenhall, Cranford, Cransley, Creaton, Crick, Croughton, Culworth,

Deanshanger, Deene, Deenethorpe, Denford, Denton, Dingley, Dodford, Draughton, Duddington with Fineshade,

East Carlton, East Farndon, East Haddon, Easton Maudit, Easton Neston, Easton on the Hill, Ecton, Edgcote, Elkington, Evenley, Everdon, Eydon,

Farthinghoe, Farthingstone, Fawsley, Flore, Fotheringhay,

Gayton, Geddington, Glapthorn, Grafton Regis, Grafton Underwood, Great Addington, Great Doddington, Great Harrowden, Great Houghton, Great Oxendon, Greatworth, Greens Norton, Grendon, Gretton, Guilsborough,

Hackleton, Hannington, Hardwick, Hargrave, Harlestone, Harpole, Harrington, Harringworth, Hartwell, Haselbech, Hellidon, Helmdon, Hemington, Hinton in the Hedges, Holcot, Holdenby, Hollowell,

Isham, Islip,

Kelmarsh, Kilsby, Kings Cliffe, King's Sutton, Kislingbury,

Lamport, Laxton, Lilbourne, Lilford cum Wigsthorpe, Litchborough, Little Addington, Little Harrowden, Little Houghton, Loddington, Lowick, Luddington, Lutton,

Maidford, Maidwell, Marston St Lawrence, Marston Trussell, Mears Ashby, Middleton, Milton Malsor, Moreton Pinkney,

Naseby, Nassington, Nether Heyford, Newbottle, Newnham, Newton Bromswold, Newton, Norton, Old, Old Stratford, Orlingbury, Orton, Overstone,

Pattishall, Paulerspury, Pilton, Pitsford, Polebrook, Potterspury, Preston Capes, Pytchley,

Quinton,

Radstone, Ravensthorpe, Ringstead, Roade, Rockingham, Rothersthorpe, Rushton,

Scaldwell, Shutlanger, Sibbertoft, Silverstone, Slapton, Southwick, Spratton, Stanford, Stanion, Staverton, Stoke Albany, Stoke Bruerne, Stoke Doyle, Stowe Nine Churches, Strixton, Sudborough, Sulby, Sulgrave, Sutton Bassett, Syresham, Sywell,

Tansor, Thenford, Thornby, Thorpe Achurch, Thorpe Malsor, Thorpe Mandeville, Thurning, Tiffield, Twywell,

Upper Heyford,

Wadenhoe, Wakerley, Walgrave, Wappenham, Warkton, Warkworth, Warmington, Watford, Weedon Bec, Weekley, Weldon, Welford, Welton, West Haddon, Weston and Weedon, Weston by Welland,

Whilton, Whitfield, Whittlebury, Wicken, Wilbarston, Wilby, Winwick, Wollaston, Woodend, Woodford, Woodford cum Membris, Woodnewton,

Yardley Gobion, Yardley Hastings, Yarwell, Yelvertoft.

**[3948]**

**NOTES**
Commencement: 7 September 2009.

## PART 5
## NOTTINGHAMSHIRE

Alverton, Annesley, Askham, Aslockton, Averham, Awsworth,

Babworth, Barnby in the Willows, Barnby Moor, Barton in Fabis, Bathley, Beckingham, Besthorpe, Bestwood St Albans, Bevercotes, Bilsthorpe, Bleasby, Blyth, Bole, Bothamsall, Bradmore, Brinsley, Bunny, Broadholme,

Car Colston, Carburton, Carlton on Trent, Caunton, Caythorpe, Clarborough, Clayworth, Clipston, Clipstone, Coddington, Collingham, Colston Bassett, Cossall, Costock, Cotham, Cottam, Cromwell, Cropwell Bishop, Cropwell Butler, Cuckney,

Darlton, Dunham on Trent,

Eakring, East Bridgeford, East Drayton, East Markham, East Stoke, Eaton, Edingley, Egmanton, Elkesley, Elston, Elton, Epperstone, Everton,

Farndon, Farnsfield, Felley, Fiskerton cum Morton, Flawborough, Fledborough, Flintham,

Gamston (in the district of Bassetlaw), Gainston (in the district of Rushcliffe), Girton, Gonalston, Gotham, Granby, Grassthorpe, Gringley on the Hill, Grove, Gunthorpe,

Halam, Halloughton, Harby, Haughton, Hawksworth, Hawton, Hayton, Headon cum Upton, Hickling, Hockerton, Hodsock, Holbeck, Holme, Holme Pierrepont, Hoveringham,

Kelham, Kersall, Kilvington, Kingstoon on Soar, Kinoulton, Kirklington, Kirton, Kneesall, Kneeton,

Lambley, Laneham, Langar cum Barnstone, Langford, Laxton and Moorhouse, Linby, Lindhurst, Lound, Lowdham,

Maplebeck, Marnham, Mattersey, Meering, Misson, Misterton,

Nether Langwith, Newstead, Normanton on Soar, Normanton on the Wolds, Normanton on Trent, North Clifton, North Leverton with Habblesthorpe, North Muskham, North Wheatley, Norton, Norwell,

Ompton, Orston, Ossington, Owthorpe, Oxton,

Papplewick, Perlethorpe cum Budby, Plumtree,

Ragnall, Rampton, Ranskill, Ratcliffe on Soar, Rempstone, Rhodesia, Rolleston, Rufford,

Saundby, Saxondale, Scaftworth, Scarrington, Screveton, Scrooby, Shelford and Newton, Shelton, Shireoaks, Sibthorpe, South Clifton, South Leverton, South Muskham, South Scarle, South Wheatley, Spalford, Stanford on Soar, Staunton, Staythorpe, Stoke Bardolph, Stokeham, Strelley, Sturton le Steeple, Styrrup with Oldcotes, Sutton Bonington, Sutton, Sutton on Trent, Syerston,

Thorney, Thoroton, Thorpe, Thorpe in the Glebe, Thrumpton, Thurgarton, Tithby, Tollerton, Torworth, Treswell, Trowell, Tuxford,

Upper Broughton, Upton,

Walesby, Walkeringham, Wallingwells, Welbeck, Wellow, West Burton, West Drayton, West Leake, West Markham, West Stockwith, Weston, Whatton, Widmerpool, Wigsley, Willoughby on the Wolds, Winkburn, Winthorpe, Wiseton, Wiverton Hall, Woodborough, Wysall.

**[3949]**

**NOTES**
Commencement: 7 September 2009.

## SCHEDULE 14
## DESIGNATED PROTECTED AREAS IN THE EAST MIDLANDS—BY MAPS
Regulation 8(b)

## PART 1
## DERBYSHIRE

The parishes of—
> Belper,
> Chapel en le Frith,

Dale Abbey, Darley Dale,
Eckington, Elmton,
Kilburn,
Matlock Town, Melbourne,
New Mills,
Ocbrook, Old Bolsover,
Ripley,
Scarcliffe, Staveley,
Whaley Bridge, Whitwell, Wirksworth.

The unparished area bounded by the parishes of Chapel en le Frith, Wormhill, Green Fairfield, King Sterndale and Hartington Upper Quarter.

The unparished area bounded by the parishes of Tintwhistle, Charlesworth and by the county constituency of Stalybridge and Hyde in Greater Manchester.

**[3950]**

**NOTES**
Commencement: 7 September 2009.

PART 2
LEICESTERSHIRE

The parishes of—
Ashby de la Zouch,
Desford,
Markfield,
Narborough,
Rothley.

The unparished area bounded by the parishes of Cotes, Prestwold, Burton on the Wolds, Walton on the Wolds, Quordon, Woodhouse, Charley, Shepshed, Hathern; and the parishes of Normanton on Soar and Stanford on Soar in Nottinghamshire.

The unparished area bounded by the parishes of Thorpe Langton, Weston by Welland, Sutton Bassett, Lubenham, Foxton and East Langton; and the parishes of Dingley, Braybrooke, Great Oxenden, East Farndon in Northamptonshire.

The unparished area bounded by the parishes of Thurlaston, Potters Marston, Elmesthorpe, Burbage, Higham on the Hill, Stoke Golding, Peckleton; and the county constituency of Nuneaton.

The unparished area bounded by the parishes of Belton, Charley, Bardon, Markfield, Stanton-under-Bardon, Ibstock, Ravenstone with Snibstone, Swannington and Osgathorpe.

**[3951]**

**NOTES**
Commencement: 7 September 2009.

PART 3
LINCOLNSHIRE

The parishes of—
Bourne, Branston and Mere,
Coningsby,
Fishtoft, Fleet,
Holbeach
Londonthorpe and Harrowby Without,
Mablethorpe and Sutton, Morton (in the district of West Lindsey),
Pinchbeck,
Sleaford,
Welton.

**[3952]**

**NOTES**
Commencement: 7 September 2009.

PART 4
NORTHAMPTONSHIRE

The parishes of—
Irchester,
Middleton Cheney,

Raunds,
Titchmarsh, Towcester,
Upton.

**[3953]**

NOTES
Commencement: 7 September 2009.

## PART 5
## NOTTINGHAMSHIRE

The parishes of—
Bulcote,
Greasley,
Hayton,
Selston, Southwell, Stanton on the Wolds,
Warsop.

The unparished area bounded by the parishes of Hayton, Clarborough, North Leverton with Habblesthorpe, South Leverton, Grove, Eaton, Babworth and Sutton.

The unparished area bounded by the parishes of Carlton in Lindrick, Barnby Moor, Babworth, Elkesley, Perlethorpe cum Budby, Carbuton, Welbeck, Shireoaks, Rhodesia; the parishes of Woodsets, North and South Anston in South Yorkshire; and the parish of Whitwell in Derbyshire.

The unparished area in the county constituency of Ashfield excluding the parishes of Annesley, Felley, Selston, Brinsley and Eastwood.

**[3954]**

NOTES
Commencement: 7 September 2009.

## SCHEDULE 15
## DESIGNATED PROTECTED AREAS IN YORKSHIRE AND THE HUMBER – ENTIRE PARISHES
Regulation 9(a)

## PART 1
## EAST RIDING OF YORKSHIRE

Airmyn, Aldbrough, Allerthorpe, Asselby, Atwick,

Bainton, Barmby Moor, Barmby on the Marsh, Barmston, Beeford, Bempton, Beswick, Bewholme, Bielby, Bilton, Bishop Burton, Bishop Wilton, Blacktoft, Boynton, Brandesburton, Brantingham, Broomfleet, Bubwith, Bugthorpe, Burstwick, Burton Agnes, Burton Constable, Burton Fleming, Burton Pidsea,

Carnaby, Catton, Catwick, Cherry Burton, Coniston, Cottam, Cottingwith,

Dalton Holme,

Easington, East Garton, Eastrington, Ellerby, Ellerker, Ellerton, Elstronwick, Etton, Everingham,

Fangfoss, Fimber, Flamborough, Foggathorpe, Foston, Fridaythorpe, Full Sutton,

Garton, Gilberdyke, Goodmanham, Goole Fields, Gowdall, Grindale,

Halsham, Harpham, Hatfield, Hayton, Hollym, Holme upon Spalding Moor, Holmpton, Hook, Hotham, Huggate, Humbleton, Hutton Cranswick,

Kelk, Keyingham, Kilham, Kilpin, Kirby Underdale, Kirkburn,

Langtoft, Laxton, Leconfield, Leven, Lockington, Londesborough, Lund,

Mappleton, Melbourne, Middleton, Millington,

Nafferton, Newbald, Newport, Newton on Derwent, North Cave, North Dalton, North Frodingham, Nunburnholme,

Ottringham,

Patrington, Paull, Pollington, Preston,

Rawcliffe, Reedness, Rimswell, Rise, Riston, Roos, Routh, Rowley, Rudston,

Sancton, Seaton, Seaton Ross, Shipton Thorpe, Sigglesthorne, Skeffling, Skerne and Wansford, Skidby, Skipsea, Skirlaugh, Skirpenbeck, Sledmere, Snaith and Cowick, South Cliffe, Spaldington, Sproatley, Stamford Bridge, Sunk Island, Sutton upon Derwent, Swine, Swinefleet,

Thorngumbald, Thornton, Thwing, Tibthorpe, Tickton, Twin Rivers,

Ulrome,

Walkington, Warter, Watton, Wawne, Welton, Welwick, Wetwang, Wilberfoss, Withernwick, Wold Newton (split between the District of Cleethorpes and the District of East Yorkshire), Wressle, Yapham.

**[3955]**

**NOTES**
Commencement: 7 September 2009.

## PART 2
## NORTH EAST LINCOLNSHIRE

Ashby cum Fenby, Aylesby,

Barnoldby le Beck, Beelsby, Bradley, Brigsley,

East Ravendale,

Habrough, Hatcliffe, Hawerby cum Beesby, Healing,

Irby,

Stallingborough,

West Ravendale, Wold Newton (split between Cleethorpes District and East Yorkshire District).

**[3956]**

**NOTES**
Commencement: 7 September 2009.

## PART 3
## NORTH LINCOLNSHIRE

Alkborough, Amcotts, Appleby, Aylesby,

Barnetby le Wold, Barrow upon Humber, Bonby, Burringham, Burton upon Stather,

Cadney, Crowle, Croxton,

East Butterwick, East Halton, Eastoft, Elsham, Epworth,

Flixborough,

Garthorpe and Fockerby, Goxhill, Gunness,

Haxey, Hibaldstow, Holme, Horkstow,

Keadby with Althorpe, Kirmington, Kirton in Lindsey,

Luddington and Haldenby,

Manton, Melton Ross, Messingham,

New Holland, North Killingholme,

Owston Ferry,

Redbourne, Roxby cum Risby,

Saxby all Saints, Scawby, South Ferriby, South Killingholme,

Thornton Curtis,

Ulceby,

West Butterwick, West Halton, Whitton, Winteringham, Wootton, Worlaby, Wrawby, Wroot.

**[3957]**

**NOTES**
Commencement: 7 September 2009.

## PART 4
## NORTH YORKSHIRE

Acaster Malbis, Acaster Selby, Acklam, Ainderby Mires with Holtby, Ainderby Quernhow, Ainderby Steeple, Airton, Aiskew, Aislaby (in the district of Scarborough), Aislaby (in the district of Ryedale), Akebar, Aldborough, Aldfield, Aldwark, Allerston, Allerton Mauleverer with Hopperton, Alne, Amotherby, Ampleforth, Angram Grange, Appleton East and West, Appleton Roebuck, Appleton Wiske, Appleton Le Moors, Appleton Le Street with Easthorpe, Appletreewick, Arkendale, Arkengarthdale, Arncliffe, Arrathorne, Asenby, Aske, Askham Bryan, Askham Richard, Askrigg, Askwith, Austwick, Aysgarth, Azerley,

Bagby, Bainbridge, Baldersby, Balk, Balne, Bank Newton, Barden (in the district of Richmondshire), Barden (in the district of Craven), Barkston Ash, Barlow, Barnby, Barton, Barton le Street, Barton le Willows, Barugh (Great and Little), Beadlam, Beal, Beamsley, Bedale, Bellerby, Beningbrough, Bentham, Bewerley, Biggin, Bilbrough, Bilsdale Midcable, Bilton in Ainsty with Bickerton, Birdforth, Birdsall, Birkby, Birkin, Birstwith, Bishop Monkton, Bishop Thornton, Bishopdale, Blubberhouses, Boltby, Bolton Abbey, Bolton Percy, Bolton on Swale, Bordley, Boroughbridge, Borrowby (in the district of Hambleton), Borrowby (in the district of Scarborough), Bradleys Both, Brafferton, Brandsby cum Stearsby, Bransdale, Brawby, Brearton, Bridge Hewick, Brompton (in the district of Scarborough), Brompton (in the district of Hambleton), Brompton on Swale, Brotherton, Brough with St Giles, Broughton (in the district of Ryedale), Broughton (in the district of Craven), Broxa cum Troutsdale, Buckden, Bulmer, Burn, Burneston, Burniston, Burnsall, Burrill with Cowling, Burton cum Walden, Burton in Lonsdale, Burton Leonard, Burton Salmon, Burton on Yore, Burythorpe, Buttercrambe with Bossall, Byland with Wass, Byram cum Sutton,

Caldbergh with East Scrafton, Caldwell, Calton, Camblesforth, Carleton, Carlton (in the district of Hambleton), Carlton (in the district of Selby), Carlton Highdale, Carlton Husthwaite, Carlton Miniott, Carlton Town, Carperby cum Thoresby, Carthorpe, Castle Bolton with East and West Bolton, Castley, Cattal, Catterick, Catton, Cawood, Cawton, Cayton, Chapel Haddlesey, Church Fenton, Clapham Cum Newby, Claxton, Cleasby, Cliffe (in the district of Richmond shire), Cliffe (in the district of Selby), Clifton on Yore, Clint, Cloughton, Colburn, Cold Kirby, Colsterdale, Colton, Commondale, Coneysthorpe, Coneythorpe and Clareton, Coniston Cold, Conistone with Kilnsey, Cononley, Constable Burton, Copgrove, Copmanthorpe, Copt Hewick, Cotcliffe, Coulton, Coverham with Agglethorpe, Cowcsby, Cowling, Coxwold, Cracoe, Crakehall, Crambe, Crathorne, Crayke, Cridling Stubbs, Croft on Tees, Cropton, Crosby, Cundall with Leckby,

Dacre, Dalby cum Skewsby, Dalton (in the district of Richmondshire), Dalton (in the district of Hambleton), Dalton on Tees, Danby, Danby Wiske and Lazenby, Darncome cum Langdale End, Deighton (in the district of Hambleton), Deighton (in the district of Selby), Denton, Dishforth, Downholme, Draughton, Drax, Dunsforths,

Earswick, Easby (in the district of Richmondshire), Easby (in the district of Hambleton), Easingwold, East Ayton, East Cowton, East Harlsey, East Hauxwell, East Layton, East Rounton, East Tanfield, East Witton, Eavestone, Ebberston and Yedingham, Edstone, Eggborough, Egton, Eldmire with Crakehill, Ellenthorpe, Ellerbeck, Ellerby, Ellerton Abbey, Ellerton on Swale, Ellingstring, Ellington High and Low, Elslack, Elvington, Embsay with Eastby, Eppleby, Eryholme, Escrick, Eshton, Eskdaleside cum Ugglebarnby, Exelby, Leeming and Newton,

Faceby, Fadmoor, Fairburn, Farlington, Farndale East, Farndale West, Farnham, Farnhill, Farnley, Fawdington, Fearby, Felixkirk, Felliscliffe, Ferrensby, Fewston, Finghall, Firby, Flasby with Winterburn, Flawith, Flaxby, Flaxton, Folkton, Follifoot, Forcett and Carkin, Foston, Fountains Earth, Foxholes, Fryton, Fulford, Fylingdales,

Ganton, Gargrave, Garriston, Gate Helmsley, Gateforth, Gatenby, Gayles, Giggleswick, Gillamoor, Gilling East, Gilling with Hartforth and Sedbury, Girsby, Givendale, Glaisdale, Glusburn, Goathland, Goldsborough, Grantley, Grassington, Great and Little Broughton, Great Busby, Great Langton, Great Ouseburn, Great Ribston with Walshford, Great Smeaton, Great Timble, Green Hammerton, Grewelthorpe, Grimston, Grimstone, Grinton, Gristhorpe, Grosmont,

Habton, Hackforth, Hackness, Halton East, Halton Gill, Halton West, Hambleton, Hampsthwaite, Hanlith, Harmby, Harome, Hartlington, Hartoft, Harton, Hartwith cum Winsley, Harwood Dale, Haverah Park, Hawes, Hawkswick, Hawnby, Hawsker cum Stainsacre, Hazelwood with Storiths, Healaugh, Healey, Hebden, Heck, Hellifield, Helmsley, Helperby, Hemingborough, Henderskelfe, Hensall, Heslerton, Hessay, Hetton, High Abbotside, High and Low Bishopside, High Worsall, Hillam, Hinderwell, Hipswell, Hirst Courtney, Holme, Holtby, Hood Grange, Hornby (in the district of Richmondshire), Hornby (in the district of Hambleton), Horton in Ribblesdale, Hovingham, Howe, Howgrave, Howsham, Huby, Huddleston with Newthorpe, Hudswell, Humberton, Hunsingore, Hunton, Husthwaite, Hutton Bonville, Hutton Buscel, Hutton Conyers, Hutton Hang, Hutton Mulgrave, Hutton Rudby, Hutton Le Hole, Hutton Sessay, Huttons Ambo,

Ilton cum Pott, Ingleby Arncliffe, Ingleby Greenhow, Ingleton, Irton,

Kearby with Netherby, Kelfield, Kellington, Kepwick, Kettlewell with Starbotton, Kexby, Kilburn High and Low, Kildale, Kildwick, Killerby, Killinghall, Kiplin, Kirby Grindalythe, Kirby Hall, Kirby Hill (in the district of Richmondshire), Kirby Hill (in the district of Harrogate), Kirby Knowle, Kirby Misperton, Kirby Sigston, Kirby Wiske, Kirk Deighton, Kirk Hammerton, Kirk Smeaton, Kirkby, Kirkby Fleetham with Fencote, Kirkby Malham, Kirkby Malzeard, Kirkby Overblow, Kirkby Wharfe with North Milford, Kirkbymoorside, Kirklington cum Upsland, Knayton with Brawith,

Landmoth cum Catto, Langcliffe, Langthorne, Langthorpe, Langton, Lastingham, Laverton, Lawkland, Lands common to the Parishes of Fylingdales and Hawsker cum Stainsacre, Lead, Leake, Leathley, Leavening, Lebberston, Levisham, Leyburn, Lillings Ambo, Lindley, Lindrick with Studley Royal and Fountains, Linton, Linton on Ouse, Little Ayton, Little Busby, Little Fenton, Little Langton, Little Ouseburn, Little Ribston, Little Smeaton (in the district of Hambleton), Little

Smeaton (in the district of Selby), Little Timble, Littlethorpe, Litton, Lockton, Long Drax, Long Marston, Long Preston, Lothersdale, Low Abbotside, Low Worsall, Luttons, Lythe,

Malham, Malham Moor, Manfield, Marishes, Markingfield Hall, Markington with Wallerthwaite, Marrick, Marske, Marton, Marton cum Grafton, Marton cum Moxby, Marton Le Moor, Martons Both, Masham, Maunby, Melbecks, Melmerby (in the district of Richmondshire), Melmerby (in the district of Harrogate), Melsonby, Menwith with Darley, Mickleby, Middleham, Middleton (in the district of Ryedale), Middleton (in the district of Harrogate), Middleton Quernhow, Middleton Tyas, Middleton on Leven, Milby, Monk Fryston, Moor Monkton, Morton on Swale, Moulton, Muker, Muston, Myton on Swale,

Naburn, Nappa, Nawton, Newfield with Langbar, Nether Poppleton, Nether Silton, New Forest, Newall with Clifton, Newbiggin, Newburgh, Newby, Newby Wiske, Newby with Mulwith, Newholme cum Dunsley, Newland, Newsham, Newsham with Breckenbrough, Newton, Newton Kyme cum Toulston, Newton Morrell, Newton Mulgrave, Newton Le Willows, Newton on Ouse, Nidd, Normanby, North Cowton, North Deighton, North Duffield, North Kilvington, North Otterington, North Rigton, North Stainley with Sleningford, Norton Conyers, Norton Le Clay, Norwood, Nun Monkton, Nunnington,

Old Byland and Scawton, Oldstead, Osgodby, Osmotherley, Oswaldkirk, Otterburn, Oulston, Over Dinsdale, Over Silton, Overton, Oxton,

Pannal, Patrick Brompton, Pickhill with Roxby, Picton, Plompton, Pockley, Potto, Preston under Scar,

Rainton with Newby, Rand Grange, Raskelf, Rathmell, Ravensworth, Redmire, Reeth Fremington & Healaugh, Reighton, Riccal, Rievaulx, Rillington, Ripley, Ripon, Roecliffe, Rookwith, Rosedale East Side, Rosedale West Side, Roxby, Rudby, Rufforth, Rylstone, Ryther cum Ossendyke,

Salton, Sand Hutton (in the district of Ryedale), Sandhutton (in the district of Hambleton), Sawley, Saxton with Scarthingwell, Scackleton, Scagglethorpe, Scampston, Scorton, Scosthrop, Scotton (in the district of Richmondshire), Scotton (in the district of Harrogate), Scrayingham, Scruton, Seamer (in the district of Scarborough), Seamer (in the district of Hambleton), Sessay, Settrington, Sexhow, Sharow, Sherburn, Sherburn in Elmet, Sheriff Hutton, Shipton, Sicklinghall, Silpho, Sinderby, Sinnington, Skeeby, Skelding, Skelton (in the district of Ryedale), Skelton (in the district of Harrogate), Skipton on Swale, Skipwith, Skutterskelfe, Slingsby, Snaiton, Snape with Thorp, Sneaton, South Cowton, South Holme, South Kilvington, South Milford, South Otterington, South Stainley with Cayton, Sowerby Under Cotcliffe, Spaunton, Spennithorne, Spofforth with Stockeld, Sproxton, Stainburn, Stainforth, Stainton, Stainton Dale, Stanwick St John, Stapleton (in the district of Richmondshire), Stapleton (in the district of Selby), Staveley, Steeton, Stillingfleet, Stillington, Stirton with Thorlby, St Martins, Stockton on the Forest, Stonebeck Down, Stonebeck Up, Stonegrave, Studley Roger, Suffield cum Everley, Sutton, Sutton on the Forest, Sutton under Whitestonecliffe, Sutton with Howgrave, Swainby with Allerthorpe, Swinden, Swinton, Swinton with Warthermarske,

Temple Hirst, Terrington, Theakston, Thimbleby, Thirkleby High and Low with Osgodby, Thirlby, Thirn, Thixendale, Tholthorpe, Thoralby, Thorganby, Thormanby, Thornbrough, Thornthwaite with Padside, Thornton Bridge, Thornton in Craven, Thornton in Lonsdale, Thornton Rust, Thornton Steward, Thornton Watlass, Thornton Le Beans, Thornton Le Clay, Thornton Le Dale, Thornton Le Moor, Thornton Le Street, Thornton on the Hill, Thornville, Thorpe Bassett, Thorpe, Thorpe Underwoods, Thorpe Willoughby, Threshfield, Thrintoft, Thruscross, Tockwith, Tollerton, Topcliffe, Towthorpe, Towton, Tunstall,

Uckerby, Ugthorpe, Ulleskelf, Upper Helmsley, Upper Poppleton, Upsall,

Walburn, Walden Stubbs, Walkingham Hill with Occaney, Warlaby, Warsill, Warthill, Wath, Weaverthorpe, Weeton, Welburn (Amotherby Ward in the district of Ryedale), Welburn (Kirkbymoorside Ward in the district of Ryedale), Welbury, Well, Wensley, West Ayton, West Haddlesey, West Harlsey, West Hauxwell, West Layton, West Rounton, West Scrafton, West Tanfield, West Witton, Westerdale, Weston, Westow, Westwick, Wharram, Whashton, Wheldrake, Whenby, Whitley, Whitwell, Whitwell on the Hill, Whixley, Whorlton, Wig glesworth, Wighill, Wildon Grange, Willerby, Wilstrop, Wilton, Winksley, Winton Stank and Hallikeld, Wintringham, Wistow, Wombleton, Womersley, Wrelton, Wykeham,

Yafforth, Yearsley, Youlton.

[3958]

**NOTES**

Commencement: 7 September 2009.

## PART 5
## SOUTH YORKSHIRE

Auckley, Austerfield,

Barnburgh, Bawtry, Billingley, Blaxton, Braithwell, Burghwallis,

Cadeby, Cantley, Cawthorne, Clayton with Frickley, Conisbrough Parks,

Denaby, Dunford,

Edenthorpe,

Fenwick, Finningley, Firbeck, Fishlake,

Gildingwells, Great Houghton, Gunthwaite and Ingbirchworth,

Hampole, Harthill with Woodall, Hickleton, High Hoyland, High Melton, Hooton Levitt, Hooton Pagnell, Hooton Roberts, Hunshelf,

Kirk Bramwith,

Langsett, Letwell, Little Houghton, Loversall,

Marr, Moss Norton,

Owston, Oxspring,

Ravenfield,

Shafton, Silkstone, Stainborough, Stainton, Stensall with Towthorpe Sykehouse,

Tankersley, Thorpe in Balne, Thorpe Salvin, Thurgoland, Todwick, Treeton,

Ulley,

Wadworth, Wentworth, Woodsetts, Wortley.

**[3959]**

**NOTES**

Commencement: 7 September 2009.

## PART 6
## WEST YORKSHIRE

Aberford, Addingham, Austhorpe,

Badsworth, Bardsey cum Rigton, Barwick in Elmet and Scholes, Blackshaw, Bramham cum Oglethorpe,

Carlton, Chevet, Clifford, Collingham, Crofton, Cullingworth,

Darrington, Denholme,

East Hardwick, East Keswick, Erringden,

Great and Little Preston,

Havercroft with Cold Hiendley, Heptonstall, Hessle and Hill Top, Huntwick with Foulby and Nostell,

Ledsham, Ledston, Lotherton cum Aberford,

Micklefield,

Newland with Woodhouse Moor, Notton,

Oxenhope,

Parlington, Pool,

Ripponden, Ryhill,

Scarcroft, Sharlston, Sitlington, South Hiendley, Steeton with Eastburn, Sturton Grange,

Thorner, Thorpe Audlin,

Wadsworth, Walton (in the district of Leeds), Walton (in the district of Wakefield), Warmfield cum Heath, West Bretton, West Hardwick, Wintersett, Woolley, Wothersome.

The unparished area of the borough of Pudsey excluding the settlements of Guisely and Yeadon, and the unparished area of the county constituency of Elmet, bounded by the county consituency of Pontefract and Castleford, the county constituency of Normanton and the parishes of Swillingon, Great and Little Preston, Austhorpe, Barwick in Elmet and Scholes, Parlington, Sturton Grange and Ledston excluding the settlements of Garforth, Great Preston and Kippax.

**[3960]**

**NOTES**

Commencement: 7 September 2009.

## SCHEDULE 16
## DESIGNATED PROTECTED AREAS IN YORKSHIRE AND THE HUMBER—BY MAPS
Regulation 9(b)

## PART 1
## EAST RIDING OF YORKSHIRE

The parishes of—
    Howden,
    Pocklington,
    South Cave,
    Woodmansey.

**[3961]**

**NOTES**
    Commencement: 7 September 2009.

## PART 2
## NORTH LINCOLNSHIRE

The parish of Bottesford.

**[3962]**

**NOTES**
    Commencement: 7 September 2009.

## PART 3
## NORTH YORKSHIRE

The parishes of—
    Barlby, Brayton,
    Dunnington,
    Filey,
    Great Ayton,
    Hunmanby, Huntington,
    Malton, Murton,
    Newby and Scalby, Northallerton, Norton on Derwent,
    Pickering,
    Scriven, Selby, Settle, Stutton with Hazlewood,
    Thirsk,
    Whitby.

The unparished area bounded by the parishes of Nida, Brearton, Scotton, Knaresborough, Plompton, Follifoot, Spofforth with Stockfield, Kirkby Overblow, North Rigton, Pannal and Killinghall.

**[3963]**

**NOTES**
    Commencement: 7 September 2009.

## PART 4
## SOUTH YORKSHIRE

The parishes of—
    Adwick Upon Dearne,
    Bradfield, Brampton Bierlow, Brierley, Brodsworth,
    Dinnington St John's,
    Edlington,
    North and South Anston,
    Penistone,
    Stocksbridge,
    Thurcroft,
    Whiston.

**[3964]**

**NOTES**
    Commencement: 7 September 2009.

(4)    In determining attendance at a general meeting, it is immaterial whether any two or more members attending it are in the same place as each other.

(5)    Two or more persons who are not in the same place as each other attend a general meeting if their circumstances are such that if they have (or were to have) rights to speak and vote at that meeting, they are (or would be) able to exercise them.

### 29   Quorum for general meetings

(1)    No business other than the appointment of the chairman of the meeting is to be transacted at a general meeting if the persons attending it do not constitute a quorum as set out at 29 paragraph (2).

(2)    The quorum for the meeting shall be 20 per cent of the members of the company entitled to vote upon the business to be transacted, or two members of the company so entitled (whichever is the greater) present in person or by proxy.

### 30   Chairing general meetings

(1)    If the directors have appointed a chairman, the chairman shall chair general meetings if present and willing to do so.

(2)    If the directors have not appointed a chairman, or if the chairman is unwilling to chair the meeting or is not present within ten minutes of the time at which a meeting was due to start—
    (a)    the directors present, or
    (b)    (if no directors are present), the meeting,
must appoint a director or member to chair the meeting, and the appointment of the chairman of the meeting must be the first business of the meeting.

(3)    The person chairing a meeting in accordance with this article is referred to as "the chairman of the meeting".

### 31   Attendance and speaking by directors and non-members

(1)    Directors may attend and speak at general meetings, whether or not they are members.

(2)    The chairman of the meeting may permit other persons who are not members of the company to attend and speak at a general meeting.

### 32   Adjournment

(1)    If the persons attending a general meeting within half an hour of the time at which the meeting was due to start do not constitute a quorum, or if during a meeting a quorum ceases to be present, the chairman of the meeting must adjourn it.

(2)    The chairman of the meeting may adjourn a general meeting at which a quorum is present if—
    (a)    the meeting consents to an adjournment, or
    (b)    it appears to the chairman of the meeting that an adjournment is necessary to protect the safety of any person attending the meeting or ensure that the business of the meeting is conducted in an orderly manner.

(3)    The chairman of the meeting must adjourn a general meeting if directed to do so by the meeting.

(4)    When adjourning a general meeting, the chairman of the meeting must—
    (a)    either specify the time and place to which it is adjourned or state that it is to continue at a time and place to be fixed by the directors, and
    (b)    have regard to any directions as to the time and place of any adjournment which have been given by the meeting.

(5)    If the continuation of an adjourned meeting is to take place more than 14 days after it was adjourned, the company must give at least 7 clear days' notice of it (that is, excluding the day of the adjourned meeting and the day on which the notice is given)—
    (a)    to the same persons to whom notice of the company's general meetings is required to be given, and
    (b)    containing the same information which such notice is required to contain.

(6)    No business may be transacted at an adjourned general meeting which could not properly have been transacted at the meeting if the adjournment had not taken place.

*Voting at General Meetings*

### 33   Voting: general

(1)    A resolution put to the vote of a general meeting must be decided on a show of hands unless a poll is duly demanded in accordance with the articles.

(2)    If there are no landlords under leases of the whole or any part of the Premises who are members of the company, then one vote shall be available to be cast in respect of each flat in the Premises. The vote shall be cast by the member who is the qualifying tenant of the flat.

(3)   At any time at which there are any landlords under leases of the whole or any part of the Premises who are members of the company, the votes available to be cast shall be determined as follows—

    (a)    there shall first be allocated to each residential unit in the Premises the same number of votes as equals the total number of members of the company who are landlords under leases of the whole or any part of the Premises. Landlords under a lease who are regarded as jointly being a member of the company shall be counted as one member for this purpose;

    (b)    if at any time the Premises includes any non-residential part, a total number of votes shall be allocated to that part as shall equal the total number of votes allocated to the residential units multiplied by a factor of A/B, where A is the total internal floor area of the non-residential parts and B is the total internal area of all the residential parts. Internal floor area shall be determined in accordance with paragraph 1(4) of Schedule 6 to the 2002 Act. Calculations of the internal floor area shall be measured in square metres, fractions of floor area of less than half a square metre shall be ignored and fractions of floor area in excess of half a square metre shall be counted as a whole square metre;

    (c)    the votes allocated to each residential unit shall be entitled to be cast by the member who is the qualifying tenant of that unit, or if there is no qualifying tenant of the unit, by the member who is the immediate landlord. The immediate landlord will not be entitled to the vote of a residential unit held by a qualifying tenant who is not a member of the RTM company;

    (d)    the votes allocated to any non-residential part included in the Premises shall be entitled to be cast by the immediate landlord of that part, or where there is no lease of a non-residential part, by the freeholder. Where there is more than one such person, the total number of votes allocated to the non-residential part shall be divided between them in proportion to the internal floor area of their respective parts. Any resulting entitlement to a fraction of a vote shall be ignored;

    (e)    if a residential unit is not subject to any lease, no votes shall be entitled to be cast in respect of it;

    (f)    any person who is a landlord under a lease or leases of the whole or any part of the Premises and who is a member of the company but is not otherwise entitled to any votes, shall be entitled to one vote.

(4)   In the case of any persons who are to be regarded as jointly being members of the company, any such person may exercise the voting rights to which such members are jointly entitled, but where more than one such person tenders a vote, whether in person or by proxy, the vote of the senior shall be accepted to the exclusion of the votes of the others, and seniority shall be determined by the order in which the names of such persons appear in the register of members in respect of the flat or lease (as the case may be) in which they are interested.

## 34   Errors and disputes

(1)   No objection may be raised to the qualification of any person voting at a general meeting except at the meeting or adjourned meeting at which the vote objected to is tendered, and every vote not disallowed at the meeting is valid.

(2)   Any such objection must be referred to the chairman of the meeting whose decision is final.

## 35   Poll votes

(1)   A poll on a resolution may be demanded—

    (a)    in advance of the general meeting where it is to be put to the vote, or

    (b)    at a general meeting, either before a show of hands on that resolution or immediately after the result of a show of hands on that resolution is declared.

(2)   A poll may be demanded by—

    (a)    the chairman of the meeting;

    (b)    the directors;

    (c)    two or more persons having the right to vote on the resolution; or

    (d)    a person or persons representing not less than one tenth of the total voting rights of all the members having the right to vote on the resolution.

(3)   A demand for a poll may be withdrawn if—

    (a)    the poll has not yet been taken, and

    (b)    the chairman of the meeting consents to the withdrawal.

(4)   Polls must be taken immediately and in such manner as the chairman of the meeting directs.

## 36   Content of proxy notices

(1)   Proxies may only validly be appointed by a notice in writing (a "proxy notice") which—

    (a)    states the name and address of the member appointing the proxy;

    (b)    identifies the person appointed to be that member's proxy and the general meeting in relation to which that person is appointed;

(c)    is signed by or on behalf of the member appointing the proxy, or is authenticated in such manner as the directors may determine; and

(d)    is delivered to the company in accordance with the articles and any instructions contained in the notice of the general meeting to which they relate.

(2)    The company may require proxy notices to be delivered in a particular form, and may specify different forms for different purposes.

(3)    Proxy notices may specify how the proxy appointed under them is to vote (or that the proxy is to abstain from voting) on one or more resolutions.

(4)    Unless a proxy notice indicates otherwise, it must be treated as—

(a)    allowing the person appointed under it as a proxy discretion as to how to vote on any ancillary or procedural resolutions put to the meeting, and

(b)    appointing that person as a proxy in relation to any adjournment of the general meeting to which it relates as well as the meeting itself.

## 37  Delivery of proxy notices

(1)    A person who is entitled to attend, speak or vote (either on a show of hands or on a poll) at a general meeting remains so entitled in respect of that meeting or any adjournment of it, even though a valid proxy notice has been delivered to the company by or on behalf of that person.

(2)    An appointment under a proxy notice may be revoked by delivering to the company a notice in writing given by or on behalf of the person by whom or on whose behalf the proxy notice was given.

(3)    A notice revoking a proxy appointment only takes effect if it is delivered before the start of the meeting or adjourned meeting to which it relates.

(4)    If a proxy notice is not executed by the person appointing the proxy, it must be accompanied by written evidence of the authority of the person who executed it to execute it on the appointor's behalf.

## 38  Amendments to resolutions

(1)    An ordinary resolution to be proposed at a general meeting may be amended by ordinary resolution if—

(a)    notice of the proposed amendment is given to the company in writing by a person entitled to vote at the general meeting at which it is to be proposed not less than 48 hours before the meeting is to take place (or such later time as the chairman of the meeting may determine), and

(b)    the proposed amendment does not, in the reasonable opinion of the chairman of the meeting, materially alter the scope of the resolution.

(2)    A special resolution to be proposed at a general meeting may be amended by ordinary resolution, if—

(a)    the chairman of the meeting proposes the amendment at the general meeting at which the resolution is to be proposed, and

(b)    the amendment does not go beyond what is necessary to correct a grammatical or other non-substantive error in the resolution.

(3)    If the chairman of the meeting, acting in good faith, wrongly decides that an amendment to a resolution is out of order, the chairman's error does not invalidate the vote on that resolution.

**[3975]**

## NOTES
Commencement: 9 November 2009.

## PART 5

*Administrative Arrangements*

## 39  Means of communication to be used

(1)    Subject to the articles, anything sent or supplied by or to the company under the articles may be sent or supplied in any way in which the Companies Acts provides for documents or information which are authorised or required by any provision of those Acts to be sent or supplied by or to the company.

(2)    Subject to the articles, any notice or document to be sent or supplied to a director in connection with the taking of decisions by directors may also be sent or supplied by the means by which that director has asked to be sent or supplied with such notices or documents for the time being.

(3)    A director may agree with the company that notices or documents sent to that director in a particular way are to be deemed to have been received within a specified time of their being sent, and for the specified time to be less than 48 hours.

## 40  Company seals

(1)    Any common seal may only be used by the authority of the directors.

(2)    The directors may decide by what means and in what form any common seal is to be used.

(3)    Unless otherwise decided by the directors, if the company has a common seal and it is affixed to a document, the document must also be signed by at least one authorised person in the presence of a witness who attests the signature.

(4)    For the purposes of this article, an authorised person is—

  (a)    any director of the company;

  (b)    the company secretary (if any); or

  (c)    any person authorised by the directors for the purpose of signing documents to which the common seal is applied.

## 41  Inspection and copying of accounts and other records

(1)    In addition to, and without derogation from, any right conferred by statute, any member shall have the right, on reasonable notice, at such time and place as shall be convenient to the company, to inspect, and to be provided with a copy of, any book, minute, document or accounting record of the company, upon payment of any reasonable charge for copying. Such rights shall be subject to any resolution of the company in general meeting.

(2)    In the case of any book, minute, document or accounting record which the directors reasonably consider contains confidential material, the disclosure of which would be contrary to the interests of the company, to the exclusion or excision of such confidential material (the fact of such exclusion or excision being disclosed to the member), and to any other reasonable conditions that the directors may impose.

## 42  Provision for employees on cessation of business

The directors may decide to make provision for the benefit of persons employed or formerly employed by the company or any of its subsidiaries (other than a director or former director or shadow director) in connection with the cessation or transfer to any person of the whole or part of the undertaking of the company or that subsidiary.

[3976]

**NOTES**
Commencement: 9 November 2009.

PART 6
*Directors' Indemnity and Insurance*

## 43  Indemnity

(1)    Subject to paragraph (2), a relevant director of the company or an associated company may be indemnified out of the company's assets against—

  (a)    any liability incurred by that director in connection with any negligence, default, breach of duty or breach of trust in relation to the company or an associated company,

  (b)    any liability incurred by that director in connection with the activities of the company or an associated company in its capacity as a trustee of an occupational pension scheme (as defined in section 235(6) of the Companies Act 2006),

  (c)    any other liability incurred by that director as an officer of the company or an associated company.

(2)    This article does not authorise any indemnity which would be prohibited or rendered void by any provision of the Companies Acts or by any other provision of law.

(3)    In this article—

  (a)    companies are associated if one is a subsidiary of the other or both are subsidiaries of the same body corporate, and

  (b)    a "relevant director" means any director or former director of the company or an associated company.

## 44  Insurance

(1)    The directors may decide to purchase and maintain insurance, at the expense of the company, for the benefit of any relevant director in respect of any relevant loss.

(2)    In this article—

  (a)    a "relevant director" means any director or former director of the company or an associated company,

  (b)    a "relevant loss" means any loss or liability which has been or may be incurred by a relevant director in connection with that director's duties or powers in relation to the company, any associated company or any pension fund or employees' share scheme of the company or associated company, and

(c)    companies are associated if one is a subsidiary of the other or both are subsidiaries of the same body corporate.

**[3977]–[5000]**

**NOTES**
  Commencement: 9 November 2009.

# PART III
## OTHER MATERIAL

# HOMELESSNESS CODE OF GUIDANCE FOR LOCAL AUTHORITIES

## OVERVIEW OF THE HOMELESSNESS LEGISLATION

*This overview provides a summary of the homelessness legislation and the duties, powers and obligations on housing authorities and others towards people who are homeless or at risk of homelessness. This overview does not form part of the statutory code of guidance and is not a legal commentary.*

### Introduction

**1.** The homelessness legislation – that is, Part 7 of *the Housing Act 1996* – provides the statutory under-pinning for action to tackle homelessness.

**2.** The Government's strategy for tackling homelessness is outlined in *Sustainable Communities: Homes for All* and *Sustainable Communities: settled homes; changing lives*, published in 2005. The strategy aims to expand housing opportunities, including for those who need additional support, and for disadvantaged sections of society by offering a wider range of preventative measures and increasing access to settled homes.

### The homelessness legislation

**3.** The homelessness legislation places a general duty on housing authorities to ensure that advice and information about homelessness, and preventing homelessness, is available to everyone in their district free of charge. The legislation also requires authorities to assist individuals and families who are homeless or threatened with homelessness and apply for help.

**4.** In 2002, the Government amended the homelessness legislation through *the Homelessness Act 2002* and the *Homelessness (Priority Need for Accommodation) (England) Order 2002* to:
- ensure a more strategic approach to tackling and preventing homelessness, in particular by requiring a homelessness strategy for every housing authority district, and
- strengthen the assistance available to people who are homeless or threatened with homelessness by extending the priority need categories to homeless 16 and 17 year olds; care leavers aged 18,19 and 20; people who are vulnerable as a result of time spent in care, the armed forces, prison or custody, and people who are vulnerable because they have fled their home because of violence.

**5.** The legislation places duties on housing authorities, and gives them powers, to meet these aims. But it also emphasises the need for joint working between housing authorities, social services and other statutory, voluntary and private sector partners in tackling homelessness more effectively.

**6.** The Government continues to supplement housing authorities' resources with specific programmes to help them deliver effective homelessness strategies and services, prevent homelessness, reduce use of temporary accommodation and end the worst manifestations of homelessness such as people sleeping rough and families with children living in bed and breakfast hotels.

### The homelessness review and strategy

**7.** Under the *Homelessness Act 2002* all housing authorities must have in place a homelessness strategy based on a review of all forms of homelessness in their district. The first strategy was required by July 2003 and it must be renewed at least every 5 years (unless this duty has been disapplied by the Local Authorities *Plans and Strategies (Disapplication) (England) Order 2005*). The social services authority must provide all reasonable assistance.

**8.** The strategy must set out the local authority's plans for the prevention of homelessness and for securing that sufficient accommodation and support are or will be available for people who become homeless or who are at risk of becoming so. Housing authorities will therefore need to ensure that all organisations, within all sectors, whose work can help to prevent homelessness and/or meet the needs of homeless people in their district are involved in the strategy. This will need to include not just housing providers (such as housing associations and private landlords) but also other statutory bodies such as social services, the probation service, the health service and the wide range of organisations in the private and voluntary sectors whose work helps prevent homelessness or meet the needs of people who have experienced homelessness.

**9.** Housing authorities will also need to give careful consideration to the scope for joint working between social services and the many other key players in the district who are working to meet the needs of people who are homeless or have experienced homelessness.

### General duty to provide advice on homelessness

**10.** The housing authority can provide advice and information about homelessness – and the prevention of homelessness – themselves or arrange for another agency to do it on their behalf.

Either way, the advice and assistance provided will need to be up to date and robust if it is to be effective and help achieve the housing authority's strategic aim of preventing homelessness. The service will need to be wide-ranging so that it offers advice and information about not only housing options but also the broad range of factors that can contribute to homelessness. This might include, for example, advice on social security benefits, household budgeting, tenancy support services and family mediation services. The advice provided should also act as a signpost to other, more specialist advice such as debt management, health care and coping with drug and alcohol misuse, where this is needed.

### The main homelessness duty

**11.** Under the legislation, certain categories of household, such as families with children and households that include someone who is vulnerable, for example because of pregnancy, old age, or physical or mental disability, have a priority need for accommodation. Housing authorities must ensure that suitable accommodation is available for people who have priority need, if they are eligible for assistance and unintentionally homeless (certain categories of persons from abroad are ineligible.) This is known as the main homelessness duty. The housing authority can provide accommodation in their own stock or arrange for it to be provided by another landlord, for example, a housing association or a landlord in the private rented sector.

**12.** If settled accommodation is not immediately available, accommodation must be made available in the short term until the applicant can find a settled home, or until some other circumstance brings the duty to an end, for example, where the household voluntarily leaves the temporary accommodation provided by the housing authority. A settled home to bring the homelessness duty to an end could include the offer of a suitable secure or introductory tenancy in a local authority's housing stock (or nomination for a housing association assured tenancy) allocated under Part 6 of the 1996 Act or the offer of a suitable tenancy from a private landlord made by arrangement with the local authority.

**13.** Under *the Homelessness (Suitability of Accommodation) (England) Order 2003*, housing authorities can no longer discharge a homelessness duty to secure suitable accommodation by placing families with children, and households that include a pregnant woman, in Bed & Breakfast accommodation for longer than six weeks – and then only if more suitable accommodation is not available.

### Applications and inquiries

**14.** Housing authorities must give proper consideration to all applications for housing assistance, and if they have reason to believe that an applicant may be homeless or threatened with homelessness, they must make inquiries to see whether they owe them any duty under Part 7 of the 1996 Act. This assessment process is important in enabling housing authorities to identify the assistance which an applicant may need either to prevent them from becoming homeless or to help them to find another home. In each case, the authority will need to decide whether the applicant is eligible for assistance, actually homeless, has a priority need, and whether the homelessness was intentional (see below). If they wish, housing authorities can also consider whether applicants have a local connection with the local district, or with another district. Certain applicants who are persons from abroad are not eligible for any assistance under Part 7 except free advice and information about homelessness and the prevention of homelessness.

### Interim duty to accommodate

**15.** If an authority have reason to believe that an applicant may be homeless or threatened with homelessness, they must also decide if they also have reason to believe that the applicant may be eligible for assistance and have a priority need for accommodation. They must do this even before they have completed their inquiries. If there is reason to believe the applicant meets these criteria, the housing authority have an immediate duty to ensure that suitable accommodation is available until they complete their inquiries and decide whether a substantive duty is owed under Part 7. This is an important part of the safety net for people who have a priority need for accommodation and are unintentionally homeless.

### When is someone homeless?

**16.** Broadly speaking, somebody is statutorily homeless if they do not have accommodation that they have a legal right to occupy, which is accessible and physically available to them (and their household) and which it would be reasonable for them to continue to live in. It would not be reasonable for someone to continue to live in their home, for example, if that was likely to lead to violence against them (or a member of their family).

### Intentional homelessness

**17.** A person would be homeless intentionally where homelessness was the consequence of a deliberate action or omission by that person (unless this was made in good faith in ignorance of a relevant fact). A deliberate act might be a decision to leave the previous accommodation even though it would have been reasonable for the person (and everyone in the person's household) to continue to live there. A deliberate omission might be non-payment of rent that led to rent arrears and eviction.

### Local connection and referrals to another authority

**18.** Broadly speaking, for the purpose of the homelessness legislation, people may have a local connection with a district because of residence, employment or family associations in the district, or because of special circumstances. (There are exceptions, for example residence in a district while serving a prison sentence there does not establish a local connection.) Where applicants are found to be eligible for assistance, unintentionally homeless and in priority need (i.e. they meet the criteria for the main homelessness duty) and the authority consider the applicant does not have a local connection with the district but does have one somewhere else, the housing authority dealing with the application can ask the housing authority in that other district to take responsibility for the case. However, applicants cannot be referred to another housing authority if they, or any member of their household, would be at risk of violence in the district of the other authority.

### Other homelessness duties

**19.** If applicants are homeless but do not have a priority need, or if they have brought homelessness on themselves, the housing authority must ensure that they are provided with advice and assistance to help them find accommodation for themselves – but the authority does not have to ensure that accommodation becomes available for them. The housing authority can provide advice and assistance itself or arrange for another agency to do this. The housing authority must ensure that this includes a proper assessment of their housing needs and information about where they are likely to find suitable accommodation. Again, it will be crucial that the advice and assistance is effective and up to date if the housing authority's strategic aim of preventing homelessness is to be achieved.

**20.** Where people have a priority need but have brought homelessness on themselves, the housing authority must also ensure they have suitable accommodation available for a period that will give them a reasonable chance of finding accommodation for themselves. Sometimes, this may be for only a few weeks.

### Intentionally homeless families with children

**21.** So, families with children who have been found intentionally homeless will not be owed a main homelessness duty; they will be entitled to advice and assistance and temporary accommodation for a short period only. If homelessness persists, any children in the family could be in need and the family could seek assistance from the social services authority under the *Children Act 1989*. It is therefore important that social services are made aware of such cases as soon as possible. Consequently, where a housing authority are dealing with a family that includes a child under 18 and they consider the family may be found intentionally homeless, they must make social services aware of the case. Where the family are found to be intentionally homeless by the housing authority, and social services decide the child's needs would best be met by helping the family to obtain accommodation, social services can ask the housing authority for reasonable assistance and the housing authority must respond.

### Notifications/reviews of decisions/appeals to county court

**22.** Where authorities have reason to believe an applicant may be homeless or threatened with homelessness and make inquiries into the case, they must give the applicant written notification of their decision on the case, and the reasons for it insofar as it goes against the applicant's interests. Applicants can ask the housing authority to review most aspects of their decisions, and, if still dissatisfied, can appeal to the county court on a point of law. The county court can confirm or quash a housing authority's decision.

### Power to accommodate pending a review or appeal

**23.** Housing authorities have the power to accommodate applicants pending a review or appeal to the county court, and they must consider whether to exercise this power in all cases. If the housing authority decide not to exercise this power pending a review, and the applicant wishes to appeal to the courts, he or she would need to seek permission to ask the High Court to judicially review the decision. If the housing authority decide not to exercise this power pending an appeal to the county court, the applicant can appeal to the county court to review the decision not to accommodate, and the court can require the housing authority to accommodate the applicant, pending the appeal on the substantive homelessness decision if the court considers this is necessary.

PART III
OTHER MATERIAL

# INTRODUCTION

## PURPOSE OF THE CODE

**1.** The Secretary of State for Communities and Local Government is issuing this Code of Guidance to local housing authorities (referred to as housing authorities) in England under s.182 of the *Housing Act 1996* ("the 1996 Act"). Under s.182(1) of the 1996 Act, housing authorities are required to have regard to this guidance in exercising their functions under Part 7 of the 1996 Act and under the *Homelessness Act 2002* ("the 2002 Act"). This Code of Guidance replaces the previous version published in 2002.

**2.** Under s.182(1), social services authorities in England are also required to have regard to the guidance when exercising their functions relating to homelessness and the prevention of homelessness. The guidance applicable to social services authorities is issued jointly with the Secretary of State for Health and the Secretary of State for Education and Skills.

**3.** The Code gives guidance on how local authorities should exercise their homelessness functions and apply the various statutory criteria in practice. It is not a substitute for legislation and in so far as it comments on the law can only reflect the Department's understanding at the time of issue. Local authorities will still need to keep up to date on any developments in the law in these areas.

**4.** In addition to this Code, there is issued a range of good practice publications to assist local authorities in exercising their functions relating to homelessness and the prevention of homelessness (see Annex 1).

## WHO IS THE CODE FOR?

**5.** The Code is issued specifically for local authority members and staff. It is also of direct relevance to registered social landlords (RSLs). RSLs have a duty under the 1996 Act to co-operate with housing authorities in exercising their homelessness functions. RSLs are subject to the Housing Corporation's Regulatory Code and guidance and they need to take this into account when assisting housing authorities. Many of the activities discussed in the Code require joint planning and operational co-operation between housing authorities and social services authorities, health authorities, other referral agencies, voluntary sector organisations and the diverse range of bodies working in the rented sectors – so the Code is also relevant to these agencies.

## THE HOMELESSNESS LEGISLATION

**6.** Part 7 of the 1996 Act sets out the powers and duties of housing authorities where people apply to them for accommodation or assistance in obtaining accommodation. The 2002 Act places a requirement on housing authorities to formulate and publish a homelessness strategy based on a review of homelessness in their district. The 2002 Act also amends a number of provisions in Part 7 of the 1996 Act to strengthen the safety net for vulnerable people.

## EQUALITY AND DIVERSITY

**7.** When exercising their functions relating to homelessness and the prevention of homelessness, local authorities are under a statutory duty to ensure that their polices and procedures do not discriminate, directly or indirectly, on grounds of race, sex or gender, or disability. Authorities should also ensure that their policies and procedures do not discriminate on the basis of any other ground which is not material to a person's housing application, including grounds of sexual orientation or religion or belief. Authorities should observe relevant codes of practice and adopt a formal equality and diversity policy relating to all aspects of their homelessness service, to ensure equality of access and treatment for all applicants. Appropriate provision will need to be made to ensure accessibility for people with particular needs, including those with mobility difficulties, sight or hearing loss and learning difficulties, as well as those for whom English is not their first language.

**8.** The Race Relations Act 1976 now places a general duty on local authorities to promote race equality. This means that they must have due regard to the need to:
- eliminate unlawful racial discrimination; and
- promote equality of opportunity and good relations between people of difference racial groups.

In practice, this means building racial equality considerations into the day-to-day work of policy-making, service delivery, employment practice and other functions. The duty is a positive rather than a reactive one.

**9.** There are also specific duties relating to policy and service delivery. One of these concerns publishing a Race Equality Scheme every three years. Authorities' Race Equality Schemes should include their arrangements for:
- assessing and consulting on the likely impact of homelessness strategies on the promotion of race equality;

PART 5
WEST YORKSHIRE

The parishes of—
Ackworth, Arthington,
Denby Dale,
Featherstone,
Harewood, Hebden Royd,
Kirkburton,
North Elmsall,
Swillington.

The unparished area of the county constituency of Keighly excluding the parishes of Seeton with Eastburn, Silsden, Addingham, Ilkley and Oxenhope.

The unparished area of the borough constituency of Leeds North East excluding the parish of Harewood.

The unparished area of the county constituency of Normanton excluding the parishes of Normanton, Newland with Woodhouse Moor, Warmfield cum Heath and Sharlston.

**[3965]**

**NOTES**
Commencement: 7 September 2009.

# HOUSES IN MULTIPLE OCCUPATION (SPECIFIED EDUCATIONAL ESTABLISHMENTS) (ENGLAND) REGULATIONS 2009

(SI 2009/2298)

**NOTES**
Made: 24 August 2009.
Authority: Housing Act 2004, Sch 14, para 4(2).
Commencement: 1 October 2009.

## 1   Citation, commencement and application

(1)   These Regulations may be cited as the Houses in Multiple Occupation (Specified Educational Establishments) (England) Regulations 2009 and shall come into force on 1st October 2009.

(2)   These Regulations apply in relation to England only.

**[3966]**

**NOTES**
Commencement: 1 October 2009.

## 2   Educational establishments specified for certain purposes of the Housing Act 2004

An educational establishment is specified for the purposes of paragraph 4 of Schedule 14 to the Housing Act 2004 where—
(a)   it is listed in the Schedule to these Regulations; and
(b)   it is listed as the relevant educational establishment in respect of a building—
 (i)   listed on or before 3rd July 2009 in the Schedule annexed to The Universities UK/Standing Conference of Principals Code of Practice for the Management of Student Housing dated 20th February 2006; or
 (ii)   listed on or before 30th April 2009 in the second column of Schedule 1 of Appendix VII to the ANUK/Unipol Code of Standards for Larger Developments for Student Accommodation Managed and Controlled by Educational Establishments dated 28th August 2008.

**[3967]**

**NOTES**
Commencement: 1 October 2009.

**3**   (*Revokes the Houses in Multiple Occupation (Specified Educational Establishments) (England) Regulations 2008, SI 2008/2346.*)

SCHEDULE
EDUCATIONAL ESTABLISHMENTS LISTED FOR THE PURPOSES OF PARAGRAPH 4 OF
SCHEDULE 14 TO THE HOUSING ACT 2004

Regulation 2(a)

Anglia Ruskin University
Aston University
Balliol College, University of Oxford
Bath Spa University
Birmingham City University
Bishop Grosseteste University College
Blackfriars Hall, University of Oxford
Blackpool and Fylde College
Bournemouth University
Bradford University
Brasenose College, University of Oxford
Brunel University
Buckinghamshire New University
Campion Hall, University of Oxford
Canterbury Christ Church University
Castle College, Nottingham
Chichester College
Christ Church, University of Oxford
City University London
Corpus Christi College, University of Oxford
Coventry University
Cranfield University
David Game College
De Montfort University
Edge Hill University
Exeter College, University of Oxford
Foundation for International Education
Goldsmiths, University of London
Green Templeton College, University of Oxford
Harper Adams University College
Harris Manchester College, University of Oxford
Hertford College, University of Oxford
Hillcroft College
Imperial College London
Institute of Education, University of London
Jesus College, University of Oxford
Keble College, University of Oxford
Keele University
Kellogg College, University of Oxford
King's College London
Kingston University
Lady Margaret Hall, University of Oxford
Lancaster University
Leeds Metropolitan University
Leeds Trinity & All Saints
Linacre College, University of Oxford
Lincoln College, University of Oxford
Liverpool Hope University

Liverpool John Moores University
London South Bank University
Loughborough College
Loughborough University
Magdalen College, University of Oxford
Manchester Metropolitan University
Mansfield College, University of Oxford
Merton College, University of Oxford
New College, University of Oxford
Newman University College, Birmingham
Norwich University College of the Arts
Northumbria University
Nottingham Trent University
Nuffield College, University of Oxford
Oriel College, University of Oxford
Oxford Brookes University
Pembroke College, University of Oxford
Queen Mary (University of London)
Regent's Park College, University of Oxford
Richmond, The American International University in London
Roehampton University
Royal Agricultural College
Royal College of Music
Royal Holloway, University of London
Ruskin College, Oxford
Scholarship and Christianity in Oxford
Sheffield Hallam University
Somerville College, University of Oxford
Southampton Solent University
St Anne's College, University of Oxford
St Antony's College, University of Oxford
St Benet's Hall, University of Oxford
St Catherine's College, University of Oxford
St Chad's College, University of Durham
St Cross College, University of Oxford
St Edmund's College, University of Cambridge
St Edmund Hall, University of Oxford
St George's, University of London
St Hilda's College, University of Oxford
St Hugh's College, University of Oxford
St John's College, Durham
St John's College, University of Oxford
St Mary's University College, Twickenham
St Peter's College, University of Oxford
St Stephen's House, University of Oxford
Staffordshire University
Stanfords College UK
Thames Valley University
The Arts Institute at Bournemouth
The Guildhall School of Music and Drama
The London School of Economics and Political Science (University of London)

The Queen's College, University of Oxford
The Royal Veterinary College
The University of Bolton
The University of Hull
The University of Liverpool
The University of Manchester
The University of Northampton
The University of Nottingham
The University of Reading
The University of Salford
The University of Sheffield
The University of Surrey
The University of Warwick
The University of Winchester
The University of York
Trinity College, University of Oxford
University College Birmingham
University College for the Creative Arts
University College London
University College, Falmouth
University College Plymouth St Mark & St John
University College, University of Oxford
University of Bath
University of Bedfordshire
University of Birmingham
University of Brighton
University of Bristol
University of Buckingham
University of Central Lancashire
University of Chester
University of Chichester
University of Cumbria
University of Derby
University of Durham
University of East Anglia
University of East London
University of Essex
University of Exeter
University of Gloucester
University of Greenwich
University of Hertfordshire
University of Kent
University of Leeds
University of Leicester
University of Lincoln
University of London
University of Newcastle
University of Oxford
University of Plymouth
University of Portsmouth
University of Southampton

University of Sunderland

University of Sussex

University of Teesside

University of the Arts London

University of the West of England, Bristol

University of Westminster

University of Wolverhampton

University of Worcester

Wadham College, University of Oxford

Wolfson College, University of Oxford

Worcester College, University of Oxford

Writtle College

Wycliffe Hall, University of Oxford

York St John University

**[3968]**

**NOTES**
Commencement: 1 October 2009.

# RTM COMPANIES (MODEL ARTICLES) (ENGLAND) REGULATIONS 2009

(SI 2009/2767)

**NOTES**
Made: 13 October 2009.
Authority: Commonhold and Leasehold Reform Act 2002, ss 74(2), (4), (6), 178(1).
Commencement: 9 November 2009.

## 1 Citation, commencement and application

(1) These Regulations may be cited as the RTM Companies (Model Articles) (England) Regulations 2009 and shall come into force on 9th November 2009.

(2) These Regulations apply to RTM companies which exercise the right to manage premises in England.

**[3969]**

**NOTES**
Commencement: 9 November 2009.

## 2 Form and content of articles of association of RTM companies

(1) The articles of association of a RTM company shall take the form, and include the provisions, set out in the Schedule to these Regulations.

(2) Subject to regulation 3(2), the provisions referred to in paragraph (1) shall have effect for a RTM company whether or not they are adopted by the company.

**[3970]**

**NOTES**
Commencement: 9 November 2009.

## 3 Revocation of instrument and transitional provisions

(1) The RTM Companies (Memorandum and Articles of Association) (England) Regulations 2003 ("the 2003 Regulations") are revoked.

(2) During the transitional period the 2003 Regulations shall continue to have effect in relation to RTM companies incorporated before 9th November 2009.

(3) The transitional period is the period beginning on 9th November 2009 and ending on 30th September 2010.

**[3971]**

**NOTES**

Commencement: 9 November 2009.

SCHEDULE

ARTICLES OF ASSOCIATION OF A RTM COMPANY

Regulation 2

THE COMPANIES ACT 2006

A COMPANY LIMITED BY GUARANTEE AND NOT HAVING A SHARE CAPITAL

ARTICLES OF ASSOCIATION OF [NAME] RTM COMPANY LIMITED

PART 1

*Interpretation, Names and Objects of RTM Company and Limitation of Liability*

## 1 Defined terms

(1)    In the articles, unless the context requires otherwise—

"articles" means the company's articles of association;

"bankruptcy" includes individual insolvency proceedings in a jurisdiction other than England and Wales or Northern Ireland which have an effect similar to that of bankruptcy;

"chairman" has the meaning given in article 17;

"chairman of the meeting" has the meaning given in article 30;

"Companies Acts" means the Companies Acts as defined in section 2 of the Companies Act 2006, in so far as they apply to the company;

"director" means a director of the company, and includes any person occupying the position of director, by whatever name called;

"document" includes, unless otherwise specified, any document sent or supplied in electronic form;

"electronic form" has the meaning given in section 1168 of the Companies Act 2006 ("the 2006 Act");

"immediate landlord" in relation to a unit in the Premises, means the person who—

(a)    if the unit is subject to a lease, is the landlord under the lease; or

(b)    if the unit is subject to two or more leases, is the landlord under whichever of the leases is inferior to the others;

"member" has the meaning given in section 112 of the 2006 Act;

"ordinary resolution" has the meaning given in section 282 of the 2006 Act;

"participate", in relation to a directors' meeting, has the meaning given in article 15;

"the Premises" means [*name and address*];

"proxy notice" has the meaning given in article 36;

"residential unit" means a flat or any other separate set of premises which is constructed or adapted for use for the purposes of a dwelling;

"RTM company" (Right to Manage Company) has the meaning given in section 73 of the Commonhold and Leasehold Reform Act 2002

"special resolution" has the meaning given in section 283 of the 2006 Act;

"subsidiary" has the meaning given in section 1159 of the 2006 Act;

"writing" means the representation or reproduction of words, symbols or other information in a visible form by any method or combination of methods, whether sent or supplied in electronic form or otherwise; and

"2002 Act" means the Commonhold and Leasehold Reform Act 2002.

(2)    Unless the context otherwise requires, other words or expressions contained in these articles bear the same meaning as in the Companies Act 2006 as in force on the date when the RTM Companies (Model Articles) (England) Regulations 2009 are made.

*Name and Objects of RTM Company*

2.    The name of the company is

[*name*]..............................................................................................................

RTM Company Limited.

3.    The registered office of the company will be situated at

[*address*]..............................................................................................................

4.    The objects for which the company is established are to acquire and exercise in accordance with the 2002 Act the right to manage the Premises.

5.    These objects shall not be restrictively construed but the widest interpretation shall be given to them. In furtherance of the objects, but not otherwise, the company shall have power to do all such

things as may be authorised or required to be done by a RTM company by and under the 2002 Act, and in particular (but without derogation from the generality of the foregoing)—

- (a) to prepare, make, pursue or withdraw a claim to acquire the right to manage the Premises;
- (b) to exercise management functions under leases of the whole or any part of the Premises in accordance with sections 96 and 97 of the 2002 Act;
- (c) to exercise functions in relation to the grant of approvals under long leases of the whole or any part of the Premises in accordance with sections 98 and 99 of the 2002 Act;
- (d) in accordance with sections 100 and 101 of the 2002 Act, to monitor, keep under review, report to the landlord, and procure or enforce the performance by any person of the terms of any covenant, undertaking, duty or obligation in any way connected with or affecting the Premises or any of its occupants;
- (e) to negotiate for and make applications for the variation of leases pursuant to Part 4 of the Landlord and Tenant Act 1987 ("the 1987 Act");
- (f) to do such other things and to perform such other functions in relation to the Premises or any leases of the whole or any part of the Premises as may be agreed from time to time with the landlord or landlords or any other parties to the leases, as the case may be;
- (g) to provide and maintain services and amenities of every description in relation to the Premises;
- (h) to maintain, redecorate, repair, renew, repaint and clean the Premises; and to cultivate, maintain, landscape and plant any gardens, grounds or land comprised in the Premises;
- (i) to enter into contracts with builders, cleaners, contractors, decorators, gardeners, tenants, or any other person;
- (j) to consult and retain any professional advisers;
- (k) to employ any staff and managing or other agents;
- (l) to pay, remunerate or reward in any way any person supplying goods or services to the company;
- (m) to make any appropriate or consequential agreements or arrangements for the right to manage the Premises to cease to be exercisable by the company;
- (n) to issue and receive any notice, counter-notice, consent or other communication and to enter into any correspondence concerning or in any way affecting the Premises, the management of the Premises, the occupants of the Premises, the company, any of its activities, or any of its members;
- (o) to commence, defend, participate in or pursue any application to, or other proceeding before, any court or tribunal of any description;
- (p) to insure the Premises or any other property of the company or in which it has an interest up to and including the full cost of rebuilding and reinstating the Premises, including VAT, architects', engineers', solicitors', surveyors', and all other professional persons' fees, the fees payable on any applications for planning permission or other permits or consents that may be required in relation to rebuilding or reinstating the Premises, the cost of preparation of the site including debris removal, demolition, shoring-up, site clearance and any works that may be required by statute, and incidental expenses, subject to such excesses, exclusions or limitations as are usual in the London insurance market. To insure the company and its directors, officers or auditors against public liability and any other risks which it may consider prudent or desirable to insure against;
- (q) to collect in or receive monies from any person on account of administration charges, service charges, or other charges in relation to the Premises and, where required by law to do so, to deal with, hold or invest the monies in accordance with the provisions of the 1987 Act and any orders or regulations made under that Act from time to time;
- (r) to establish, undertake and execute any trusts which may lawfully be, or which are required by law to be, established, executed or undertaken by the company;
- (s) to establish and maintain capital reserves, management funds and any form of sinking fund in order to pay, or contribute towards, all costs, fees, and other expenses incurred in the implementation of the company's objects;
- (t) to invest any money of the company in the United Kingdom by depositing it at interest with any financial institution with which a trust fund of service charge contributions might be held in accordance with the 1987 Act; or to invest it in such other manner (including the purchase of securities and other investments) as the company in general meeting may authorise from time to time; and to hold, sell or otherwise dispose of any such investments;
- (u) subject to any conditions or limitations imposed by the company in general meeting from time to time, and subject to the provision of adequate security and the payment of interest, to advance and lend money or give credit to any person; to enter into guarantees, contracts of indemnity and surety; to receive money on deposit or loan; and to secure or guarantee the payment of any sum of money or the performance of any obligation by any person;
- (v) subject to any limitations or conditions imposed by the company in general meeting from time to time, to borrow and raise money in any manner and to secure the repayment

of any money borrowed, raised or owing by mortgage, charge, standard security, lien or other security upon the whole or part of the company's property or assets (whether present or future);

(w)  to operate bank accounts and to draw, make, accept, endorse, discount, negotiate, execute and issue cheques, bills of exchange, debentures, promissory notes, and other negotiable or transferable instruments;

(x)  to pay all or any expenses incurred in connection with the promotion, formation and incorporation of the company, or to contract with any person to pay such expenses;

(y)  to monitor and determine for the purpose of voting, or for any other purpose, the physical dimensions of the Premises and any part or parts of the Premises and to take or obtain any appropriate measurements;

(z)  to enter into any agreements or arrangements with any Minister of the Crown, authority (central, municipal, local, or otherwise) that may seem conducive to the attainment of the company's objects, and to obtain from any such Minister of the Crown or authority any charters, decrees, rights, privileges or concessions which the company may think desirable, and to carry out, exercise, and comply with any such charters, decrees, rights, privileges and concessions;

(aa)  to do all things specified for the time being in the articles of association of the company;

(bb)  to do or procure or arrange for the doing of all or any of the things or matters mentioned above in any part of the world and either as principals, agents, contractors or otherwise, and by or through agents, brokers, sub-contractors or otherwise and either alone or in conjunction with others; and

(cc)  to do all such other lawful things as may be incidental or conducive to the pursuit or attainment of the company's objects.

**6.**  The income of the company, from wherever derived, shall be applied solely in promoting the company's objects, and, save on a winding up of the company, no distribution shall be made to its members in cash or otherwise.

*Limitation of Liability*

### 7  Liability of members

The liability of each member is limited to £1, being the amount that each member undertakes to contribute to the assets of the company in the event of its being wound up while he is a member or within one year after he ceases to be a member, for—

(a)  payment of the company's debts and liabilities contracted before he ceases to be a member,

(b)  payment of the costs, charges and expenses of winding up; and

(c)  adjustment of the rights of the contributories among themselves.

[3972]

---

**NOTES**
Commencement: 9 November 2009.

## PART 2
*Directors*

*Directors' Powers and Responsibilities*

### 8  Directors' general authority

Subject to the articles, the directors are responsible for the management of the company's business, for which purpose they may exercise all the powers of the company.

### 9  Members' reserve power

(1)  The members may, by special resolution, direct the directors to take, or refrain from taking, specified action.

(2)  No such special resolution invalidates anything which the directors have done before the passing of the resolution.

### 10  Directors may delegate

(1)  Subject to the articles, the directors may delegate any of the powers which are conferred on them under the articles—

(a)  to such person or committee;

(b)  by such means (including by power of attorney);

(c)  to such an extent;

(d)  in relation to such matters; and

(e)  on such terms and conditions;

as they think fit.

(2) If the directors so specify, any such delegation may authorise further delegation of the directors' powers by any person to whom they are delegated.

(3) The directors may revoke any delegation in whole or part, or alter its terms and conditions.

## 11 Committees

(1) Committees to which the directors delegate any of their powers must follow procedures which are based, so far as they are applicable, on those provisions of the articles which govern the taking of decisions by directors.

### *Decision-Making by Directors*

## 12 Directors to take decisions collectively

(1) The general rule about decision-making by directors is that any decision of the directors must be either a majority decision at a meeting or a decision taken in accordance with article 13.

(2) If—
    (a) the company only has one director, and
    (b) no provision of the articles requires it to have more than one director,
the general rule does not apply, and the director may take decisions without regard to any of the provisions of the articles relating to directors' decision-making.

## 13 Unanimous decisions

(1) A decision of the directors is taken in accordance with this article when all eligible directors indicate to each other by any means that they share a common view on a matter.

(2) Such a decision may take the form of a resolution in writing, copies of which have been signed by each eligible director or to which each eligible director has otherwise indicated agreement in writing.

(3) References in this article to eligible directors are to directors who would have been entitled to vote on the matter had it been proposed as a resolution at a directors' meeting.

(4) A decision may not be taken in accordance with this article if the eligible directors would not have formed a quorum at such a meeting.

## 14 Calling a directors' meeting

(1) Any director may call a directors' meeting by giving notice of the meeting to the directors or by authorising the company secretary (if any) to give such notice.

(2) Notice of any directors' meeting must indicate—
    (a) its proposed date and time;
    (b) where it is to take place; and
    (c) if it is anticipated that directors participating in the meeting will not be in the same place, how it is proposed that they should communicate with each other during the meeting.

(3) Notice of a directors' meeting must be given to each director, but need not be in writing.

(4) Notice of a directors' meeting need not be given to directors who waive their entitlement to notice of that meeting, by giving notice to that effect to the company not more than 7 days after the date on which the meeting is held. Where such notice is given after the meeting has been held, that does not affect the validity of the meeting, or of any business conducted at it.

## 15 Participation in directors' meetings

(1) Subject to the articles, directors participate in a directors' meeting, or part of a directors' meeting, when—
    (a) the meeting has been called and takes place in accordance with the articles, and
    (b) they can each communicate to the others any information or opinions they have on any particular item of the business of the meeting.

(2) In determining whether directors are participating in a directors' meeting, it is irrelevant where any director is or how they communicate with each other.

(3) If all the directors participating in a meeting are not in the same place, they may decide that the meeting is to be treated as taking place wherever any of them is.

## 16 Quorum for directors' meetings

(1) At a directors' meeting, unless a quorum is participating, no proposal is to be voted on, except a proposal to call another meeting.

(2) The quorum for directors' meetings may be fixed from time to time by a decision of the directors, but it must never be less than two, and unless otherwise fixed it is two.

PART II
STATUTORY INSTRUMENTS

(3)   If the total number of directors for the time being is less than the quorum required, the directors must not take any decision other than a decision—

    (a)    to appoint further directors, or

    (b)    to call a general meeting so as to enable the members to appoint further directors.

## 17  Chairing of directors' meetings

(1)   The directors may appoint a director to chair their meetings.

(2)   The person so appointed for the time being is known as the chairman.

(3)   The directors may terminate the chairman's appointment at any time.

(4)   If the chairman is not participating in a directors' meeting within ten minutes of the time at which it was to start, the participating directors must appoint one of themselves to chair it.

## 18  Casting vote

(1)   If the numbers of votes for and against a proposal are equal, the chairman or other director chairing the meeting has a casting vote.

(2)   But this does not apply if, in accordance with the articles, the chairman or other director is not to be counted as participating in the decision-making process for quorum or voting purposes.

## 19  Conflicts of interest

(1)   If a proposed decision of the directors is concerned with an actual or proposed transaction or arrangement with the company in which a director is interested, that director is not to be counted as participating in the decision-making process for quorum or voting purposes.

(2)   But if paragraph (3) applies, a director who is interested in an actual or proposed transaction or arrangement with the company is to be counted as participating in the decision-making process for quorum and voting purposes.

(3)   This paragraph applies when—

    (a)    the company by ordinary resolution disapplies the provision of the articles which would otherwise prevent a director from being counted as participating in the decision-making process;

    (b)    the director's interest cannot reasonably be regarded as likely to give rise to a conflict of interest; or

    (c)    the director's conflict of interest arises from a permitted cause.

(4)   For the purposes of this article, the following are permitted causes—

    (a)    a guarantee given, or to be given, by or to a director in respect of an obligation incurred by or on behalf of the company or any of its subsidiaries;

    (b)    subscription, or an agreement to subscribe, for securities of the company or any of its subsidiaries, or to underwrite, sub-underwrite, or guarantee subscription for any such securities; and

    (c)    arrangements pursuant to which benefits are made available to employees and directors or former employees and directors of the company or any of its subsidiaries which do not provide special benefits for directors or former directors.

(5)   For the purposes of this article, references to proposed decisions and decision-making processes include any directors' meeting or part of a directors' meeting.

(6)   Subject to paragraph (7), if a question arises at a meeting of directors or of a committee of directors as to the right of a director to participate in the meeting (or part of the meeting) for voting or quorum purposes, the question may, before the conclusion of the meeting, be referred to the chairman whose ruling in relation to any director other than the chairman is to be final and conclusive.

(7)   If any question as to the right to participate in the meeting (or part of the meeting) should arise in respect of the chairman, the question is to be decided by a decision of the directors at that meeting, for which purpose the chairman is not to be counted as participating in the meeting (or that part of the meeting) for voting or quorum purposes.

## 20  Records of decisions to be kept

The directors must ensure that the company keeps a record, in writing, for at least 10 years from the date of the decision recorded, of every unanimous or majority decision taken by the directors.

## 21  Directors' discretion to make further rules

Subject to the articles, the directors may make any rule which they think fit about how they take decisions, and about how such rules are to be recorded or communicated to directors.

*Appointment of Directors*

## 22  Methods of appointing directors

(1)   Any person who is willing to act as a director, and is permitted by law to do so, may be appointed to be a director—

    (a)   by ordinary resolution, or

    (b)   by a decision of the directors.

(2)   In any case where, as a result of death, the company has no members and no directors, the personal representatives of the last member to have died have the right, by notice in writing, to appoint a person to be a director.

(3)   For the purposes of paragraph (2), where 2 or more members die in circumstances rendering it uncertain who was the last to die, a younger member is deemed to have survived an older member.

## 23  Termination of director's appointment

A person ceases to be a director as soon as—

    (a)   that person ceases to be a director by virtue of any provision of the Companies Acts 2006 or is prohibited from being a director by law;

    (b)   a bankruptcy order is made against that person;

    (c)   a composition is made with that person's creditors generally in satisfaction of that person's debts;

    (d)   a registered medical practitioner who is treating that person gives a written opinion to the company stating that that person has become physically or mentally incapable of acting as a director and may remain so for more than three months;

    (e)   by reason of that person's mental health, a court makes an order which wholly or partly prevents that person from personally exercising any powers or rights which that person would otherwise have;

    (f)   notification is received by the company from the director that the director is resigning from office, and such resignation has taken effect in accordance with its terms.

## 24  Directors' remuneration

Except with the consent of the company in general meeting, the directors shall not be entitled to any remuneration. Any resolution giving such consent shall specify the amount of remuneration to be paid to the directors, and unless the resolution provides otherwise, the remuneration shall be deemed to accrue from day to day.

## 25  Directors' expenses

The company may pay any reasonable expenses which the directors properly incur in connection with their attendance at—

    (a)   meetings of directors or committees of directors,

    (b)   general meetings, or

    (c)   separate meetings of the holders of debentures of the company,

or otherwise in connection with the exercise of their powers and the discharge of their responsibilities in relation to the company.

**[3973]**

**NOTES**

Commencement: 9 November 2009.

PART 3

*Becoming and Ceasing to be a Member*

## 26  Becoming a member

(1)   Every person who is entitled to be, and who wishes to become, a member of the company shall deliver to the company an application for membership executed by him in the following form (or in a form as near to the following form as circumstances allow or in any other form which is usual or which the directors may approve:)

To the Board of [name of company] I, [name] of [address] am a qualifying tenant of [address of flat] and wish to become a member of [name of company] subject to the provisions of the Articles of Association of the company and to any rules made under those Articles. I agree to pay the company an amount of up to £1 if the company is wound up while I am a member or for up to 12 months after I have ceased to become a member. Signed Dated

(2)   No person shall be admitted to membership of the company unless that person, whether alone or jointly with others, is—

    (a)   a qualifying tenant of a flat contained in the Premises as specified in section 75 of the 2002 Act; or

    (b)    from the date upon which the company acquires the right to manage the Premises pursuant to the 2002 Act, a landlord under a lease of the whole or any part of the Premises.

(3)    Membership of the company shall not be transferable.

(4)    A person who, together with another or others, is to be regarded as jointly being the qualifying tenant of a flat, or as jointly constituting the landlord under a lease of the whole or any part of the Premises, shall, once admitted, be regarded as jointly being a member of the company in respect of that flat or lease (as the case may be).

(5)    Applications for membership by persons who are to be regarded as jointly being the qualifying tenant of a flat, or who jointly constitute the landlord under a lease of the whole or any part of the Premises, shall state the names and addresses of all others who are jointly interested with them, and the order in which they wish to appear on the register of members in respect of such flat or lease (as the case may be.)

(6)    The directors shall, upon being satisfied as to a person's application and entitlement to membership, register such person as a member of the company.

## 27  Ceasing to be a member

(1)    A member who at any time fails to satisfy the requirements for membership set out in article 26 shall cease to be a member of the company with immediate effect.

(2)    If a member (or joint member) dies or becomes bankrupt, his personal representatives or trustee in bankruptcy will be entitled to be registered as a member (or joint member as the case may be) upon notice in writing to the company.

(3)    A member may withdraw from the company and thereby cease to be a member by giving at least seven clear days' notice in writing to the company. Any such notice shall not be effective if given in the period beginning with the date on which the company gives notice of its claim to acquire the right to manage the Premises and ending with the date which is either—

    (a)    the acquisition date in accordance with section 90 of the 2002 Act; or

    (b)    the date of withdrawal or deemed withdrawal of that notice in accordance with sections 86 or 87 of that Act.

(4)    If, for any reason—

    (a)    a person who is not a member of the company becomes a qualifying tenant or landlord jointly with persons who are members of the company, but fails to apply for membership within 28 days, or

    (b)    a member who is a qualifying tenant or landlord jointly with such persons dies or becomes bankrupt and his personal representatives or trustee in bankruptcy do not apply for membership within 56 days, or

    (c)    a member who is a qualifying tenant or landlord jointly with such persons resigns from membership pursuant to article 27(3),

those persons shall, unless they are otherwise entitled to be members of the company by reason of their interest in some other flat or lease, also cease to be members of the company with immediate effect. All such persons shall, however, be entitled to re-apply for membership in accordance with article 26.

**[3974]**

---

**NOTES**

Commencement: 9 November 2009.

---

PART 4

*Decision-Making by Members*

*Organisation of General Meetings*

## 28  Attendance and speaking at general meetings

(1)    A person is able to exercise the right to speak at a general meeting when that person is in a position to communicate to all those attending the meeting, during the meeting, any information or opinions which that person has on the business of the meeting.

(2)    A person is able to exercise the right to vote at a general meeting when—

    (a)    that person is able to vote, during the meeting, on resolutions put to the vote at the meeting, and

    (b)    that person's vote can be taken into account in determining whether or not such resolutions are passed at the same time as the votes of all the other persons attending the meeting.

(3)    The directors may make whatever arrangements they consider appropriate to enable those attending a general meeting to exercise their rights to speak or vote at it.

- monitoring homelessness policies for any adverse impact on the promotion of race equality;
- publishing the results of assessments, consultations and monitoring;
- ensuring access to homelessness information, advice and services.

The Commission for Racial Equality will publish a statutory Code of Practice on Racial Equality in Housing later this year (see Annex 1).

**10.** People from ethnic minority groups are around three times more likely than other households to be accepted as unintentionally homeless and in priority need[1]. Housing authorities need to ensure that their homelessness strategies and homelessness services pay particular attention to the needs of the ethnic minority communities they serve, for example, by ensuring that advice and information about homelessness and the prevention of homelessness is available in a range of ethnic languages appropriate to the district. ODPM published a Development Guide for local authorities on *Tackling Homelessness Amongst Ethnic Minority Households* (see Annex 1).

---

[1]  Source: ODPM data based on the P1E statistical returns completed by local authorities.

**11.** Section 49A of the *Disability Discrimination Act 1995* (added by the *Disability Discrimination Act 2005*) introduces a new duty to promote equality for disabled people. It requires public authorities to exercise their functions with due regard to the need to:

- eliminate unlawful discrimination against disabled people;
- eliminate harassment of disabled people that is related to their disabilities;
- promote equality of opportunity between disabled people and other persons;
- take steps to take account of disabled people's disabilities (even where that involves treating disabled people more favourably than other persons);
- promote positive attitudes towards disabled people; and
- encourage participation by disabled people in public life.

Authorities will be required to publish a Disability Equality Scheme every three years setting out how they will implement the duty to promote equality in their own context.

As with the duty to promote race equality, this is a positive duty rather than a reactive one and authorities will need to consider the implications for the delivery of their homelessness services.

The Disability Rights Commission has published a statutory Code of Practice on the Duty to Promote Disability Equality which will come into force in December 2006 (see Annex 1).

**12.** Authorities should also inform themselves of the provisions of Council Directives 2000/43/EC (the Race Directive) and 2000 78/EC (the Equality Directive). Under the *Equalities Act 2006* the Commission for Equality and Human Rights (CEHR) will bring together the Disability Rights Commission and the Equal Opportunities Commission from October 2007. The Act imposes a positive duty on public authorities to promote equality of opportunity and the elimination of discrimination on grounds of: age; colour; race, nationality or ethnic origins; disability; family status; gender reassignment; marital status; pregnancy; religion or belief; sex; and sexual orientation. Discrimination on any such grounds in the carrying out by a public authority of its functions would be made unlawful. The *Gender Recognition Act 2004*, the *Employment Equality (Sexual Orientation) (Amendment) Regulations 2003* and the *Employment Equality (Religion or Belief) Regulations 2003* outlaw discrimination on the grounds of gender reassignment, sexual orientation or religion in the fields of employment and vocational training. In addition, the Employment Equality (Age) Regulations, which are due to come into force in October 2006, will outlaw discrimination on the grounds of age in the fields of employment and vocational training.

**13.** Housing authorities should ensure that their homelessness strategies and homelessness services comply with existing equality and diversity legislation and new legislation as it comes into force.

## DEFINITIONS

Throughout the Code,

"the 1996 Act" means the Housing Act 1996;

"the 2002 Act" means the Homelessness Act 2002;

"the housing authority" means the local housing authority.

**[5002]**

## CHAPTER 1: HOMELESSNESS REVIEWS & STRATEGIES

**This chapter provides guidance on housing authorities' duties to carry out a homelessness review and to formulate and publish a strategy based on the results of that review.**

# DUTY TO FORMULATE A HOMELESSNESS STRATEGY

**1.1.**  Section 1(1) of the Homelessness Act 2002 ("the 2002 Act") gives housing authorities the power to carry out a homelessness review for their district and formulate and publish a homelessness strategy based on the results of the review. This power can be exercised from time to time, however s.1(3) required housing authorities to publish their first homelessness strategy by 31 July 2003. Section 1(4) requires housing authorities to publish a new homelessness strategy, based on the results of a further homelessness review, within the period of five years beginning with the day on which their last homelessness strategy was published (there is an exemption from this requirement for local authorities categorised as an "excellent authority", see paragraph 1.42). However, it is open to a housing authority to conduct homelessness reviews and strategies more frequently, if they wish.

**1.2.**  For a homelessness strategy to be effective housing authorities need to ensure that it is consistent with other local plans and strategies and takes into account any wider relevant sub-regional or regional plans and strategies. There will be a lot of common ground between an authority's housing strategy (whether its own or a sub-regional one produced with neighbouring authorities) and its homelessness strategy. It is open to authorities to produce either separate housing and homelessness strategies or combine these in a single document where it is consistent to do so. It is also open to authorities, again where it would be consistent to do so, to consider producing a wider composite plan that includes not only the housing and homelessness strategies but also their Housing Revenue Account Business Plans and Home Energy Conservation Act report. The homelessness strategy should also link with other strategies and programmes that address the wide range of problems that can cause homelessness (see indicative list at Annex 2). It will be important to consider how these strategies and programmes can help achieve the objectives of the homelessness strategy and vice-versa.

**1.3.**  Housing authorities are encouraged to take a broad view and consider the benefits of cross-boundary, sub-regional and regional co-operation. A county-wide approach will be particularly important in non-unitary authorities, where housing and homelessness services are provided by the district authority whilst other key services, such as social services and Supporting People, are delivered at the county level. Housing authorities should ensure that the homelessness strategy for their district forms part of a coherent approach to tackling homelessness with neighbouring authorities. Authorities may wish to collaborate with neighbouring housing authorities to produce a joint homelessness strategy covering a sub-regional area. London boroughs are encouraged to work closely with the Greater London Authority when formulating their homelessness strategies.

**1.4.**  When carrying out a review and formulating a strategy, housing authorities are encouraged to refer to *Homelessness Strategies: A good practice handbook, Local Authorities' Homelessness Strategies: Evaluation and Good Practice* and other relevant good practice documents published by the Office of the Deputy Prime Minister (see list of publications at Annex 1).

**1.5.**  Housing authorities are reminded that when drawing up their strategies for preventing and tackling homelessness, they must consider the needs of all groups of people in their district who are homeless or likely to become homeless, including Gypsies and Travellers. Under s.225 of the *Housing Act 2004*, which supplements s.8 of the *Housing Act 1985*, when undertaking a review of housing needs in their district, local authorities are required to carry out an assessment of the accommodation needs of Gypsies and Travellers residing in or resorting to their district. Draft guidance on accommodation needs assessment for Gypsies and Travellers is available on the DCLG website, and will be finalised after further consultation in 2006.

*Assistance from social services*

**1.6.**  In non-unitary districts, where the social services authority and the housing authority are different authorities, section 1(2) of the 2002 Act requires the social services authority to give the housing authority such assistance as may be reasonably required in carrying out a homelessness review and formulating and publishing a homelessness strategy. **Since a number of people who are homeless or at risk of homelessness will require social services support, it is unlikely that it would be possible for a housing authority to formulate an effective homelessness strategy without assistance from the social services authority. It will be necessary therefore in all cases for housing authorities to seek assistance from the social services authority.** In unitary authorities the authority will need to ensure that the social services department assists the housing department in carrying out a homelessness review and formulating and publishing a homelessness strategy.

**1.7.**  The social services authority must comply with all requests for assistance from housing authorities within their district which are reasonable. Examples of the type of assistance that a housing authority may reasonably require from the social services authority when carrying out a review and formulating a strategy may include:

- information about current and likely future numbers of social services client groups who are likely to be homeless or at risk of homelessness e.g. young people in need, care leavers and those with community care needs;

- details of social services' current programme of activity, and the resources available to them, for meeting the accommodation needs of these groups;
- details of social services' current programme of activity, and the resources available to them, for providing support for vulnerable people who are homeless or likely to become homeless (and who may not currently be social services clients).

**1.8.**   Effective co-operation will benefit both housing and social services authorities. See Chapter 5 for guidance on joint working with other agencies and Chapter 13 for guidance on co-operation in cases involving children.

*Taking the strategy into account*

**1.9.**   Sections 1(5) and (6) of the 2002 Act require housing and social services authorities to take the homelessness strategy into account when exercising their functions.

**1.10.**   For a homelessness strategy to be effective it will need to be based on realistic assumptions about how it will be delivered in practice. Whilst this will apply in respect of all the agencies and organisations involved, the key players will be the housing authority and the social services authority. Both authorities will therefore need to ensure that, on the one hand, the assumptions in the strategy about their future activities are realistic and, on the other, that in practice these activities are actually delivered through the operation of their statutory functions. When the strategy is formulated, the social services authority (or social services department within a unitary authority) will need to work closely with the housing authority (or department) to ensure that this can be achieved. All contributors will need to take ownership of the strategy if it is to be effective. Again, because of its crucial role in delivering the strategy, this will be particularly important in the case of the social services authority (or department).

## Homelessness Reviews

**1.11.**   Under section 2(1) of the 2002 Act a homelessness review means a review by a housing authority of:

  a)      the levels, and likely future levels, of homelessness in their district;
  b)      the activities which are carried out for any the following purposes (or which contribute to achieving any of them):
      i)      preventing homelessness in the housing authority's district;
      ii)     securing that accommodation is or will be available for people in the district who are or may become homeless; and
      iii)    providing support for people in the district:
         –      who are or may become homeless; or
         –      who have been homeless and need support to prevent them becoming homeless again;
  c)      the resources available to the housing authority, the social services authority for the district, other public authorities, voluntary organisations and other persons for the activities outlined in (b) above.

**1.12.**   The purpose of the review is to establish the extent of homelessness in the district, assess its likely extent in the future, and identify what is currently being done, and by whom, and what level of resources are available, to prevent and tackle homelessness.

*a) current levels, and likely future levels, of homelessness*

**1.13.**   Homelessness is defined by sections 175 to 178 of the 1996 Act (see Chapter 8 for guidance). The review must take account of **all** forms of homelessness within the meaning of the 1996 Act, not just people who are unintentionally homeless and have a priority need for accommodation under Part 7. The review should therefore consider a wide population of households who are homeless or at risk of homelessness, including those who might be more difficult to identify, including people sleeping rough, or those whose accommodation circumstances make them more likely than others to become homeless or to resort to sleeping rough.

**1.14.**   The housing authority's own records of its activity under the homelessness legislation (Part 7 of the 1996 Act) will provide a baseline for assessing the number of people who are likely to become homeless and seek help directly from the housing authority. These records should give some indication as to why those accepted as statutorily homeless became homeless. Other useful sources of data on potential homelessness in the district may include:

- records on rough sleeping;
- estimates of people staying with friends/family on an insecure basis;
- court records on possession orders;
- records of evictions by the local authority and registered social landlords (RSLs);
- local advice service records on homelessness cases;
- hospital records of people homeless on discharge;
- armed forces records of those homeless on discharge;
- prison/probation service records of ex-prisoners homeless on discharge;
- social services records of homeless families with children;

- social services records of young people leaving care and children in need requiring accommodation;
- records of Supporting People clients;
- records available from hostels and refuges;
- voluntary sector records, e.g. day centres, advice services;
- records of asylum seekers being accommodated in the district by the National Asylum Support Service;
- data from the national population census and housing authorities' own household surveys.

**1.15.** Some groups of people are likely to be more at risk of homelessness than others. These may include:

- young people who have become estranged from their family; have been in care; have a history of abuse, running away or school exclusions; or whose parents have had mental health, alcohol or drug problems; (see chapter 12)
- people from ethnic minority groups;
- people with an institutionalised background, for example where they have spent time in prison or the armed forces;
- former asylum seekers who have been given permission to stay in the UK and are no longer being accommodated by the National Asylum Support Service;
- people who have experienced other problems that may increase the risk of homelessness including family/relationship breakdowns; domestic, racial or other violence; poor mental or physical health; drug and alcohol abuse; age-related problems and debt.

**1.16.** As part of the process of mapping and understanding the extent of current homelessness in the district, housing authorities may wish to develop a profile of those who have experienced homelessness. Elements within a profile may include:

- location of homelessness;
- reason(s) for homelessness;
- housing history including previous tenures and length of homelessness;
- ethnic background;
- other background (e.g. care provided by the local authority or other institution);
- age;
- gender and sexuality;
- disabilities;
- levels and types of debts;
- employment/benefits history;
- composition of household;
- vulnerability of applicant (or household members);
- support needs (housing-related or other);
- health/drug problems;
- immigration status;
- trends in any of these elements.

**1.17.** Housing authorities will also need to consider the range of factors which could affect future levels of homelessness in their district. Many of these will be similar to factors taken into account for the purpose of assessing housing needs in the district (e.g. as part of a broader housing strategy). Relevant factors in the district may include:

- the availability of affordable accommodation including housing provided by the housing authority and by RSLs;
- housing market analyses, including property prices and rent levels;
- the supply of accommodation in the private rented sector;
- the provision and effectiveness of housing advice;
- local voluntary and community sector services;
- the allocation policy of the housing authority;
- the lettings policies of RSLs;
- the effectiveness of nomination agreements between the housing authority and RSLs;
- the policy of the housing authority and RSLs on management of tenants' rent arrears and on seeking repossession;
- the efficiency of the housing authority's administration of housing benefit;
- the provision and effectiveness of housing-related support services;
- redevelopment and regeneration activity;
- unemployment;
- strength of the local economy;
- the local population (and demographic trends);
- the level of overcrowding;
- the rate of new household formation in the district;
- the level of inward migration (both national and international);
- the flow of itinerant population (i.e. Gypsies and Travellers) and availability of authorised sites;
- the number of people likely to be in housing need on leaving:
  - the armed forces,

|   | residential care, |
| --- | --- |
| – | local authority care, |
| – | prison, |
| – | hospital or |
| – | accommodation provided by the National Asylum Support Service. |

**1.18.** Individual cases of homelessness are often the result of a complex matrix of problems that may develop over time. In many cases homelessness may be triggered by individual circumstances (for example, relationship breakdown or unemployment) but it can also be the result of a failure in the housing market (for example, high rents in the private sector and a shortage of accommodation in the social sector) or a failure of the administrative system (for example, delays in the payment of housing benefit). In districts where the housing market and administrative systems are functioning well, the levels of homelessness are likely to be lower. All these factors will need to be taken into account when assessing the likely future levels of homelessness in the district.

*b) activities which are carried out*

**1.19.** The public, private and voluntary sectors can all contribute, directly or indirectly, to the prevention of homelessness, the provision of accommodation and the provision of support for homeless people. When reviewing the activities which are being carried out for these purposes, the housing authority should consider the activities of **all** the various agencies and organisations, across all sectors, which are providing, or contributing to the provision of accommodation, support or relevant services in the district (Annex 3 provides an indicative list).

**1.20.** Having mapped all the current activities, the housing authority should consider whether these are appropriate and adequate to meet the aims of the strategy, and whether any changes or additional provision are needed.

### Preventing homelessness

**1.21.** Gaining a good understanding of the causes of homelessness during the homelessness review process will help to inform the range of preventative measures that need to be put in place. Many statutory and non-statutory services can contribute to preventing homelessness. Housing authorities should adopt an open approach and recognise that there will be a broad range of organisations operating in fields other than housing, including, for example, health, education and employment, whose activities may help to prevent homelessness. Activities that contribute to preventing homelessness may include:

- advice services;
- mediation and reconciliation services;
- tenancy support schemes;
- proactive liaison with private sector landlords;
- rent deposit/guarantee schemes;
- management of social housing by the housing authority and by RSLs;
- debt counselling;
- Supporting People programme;
- social services support for vulnerable people;
- housing benefit administration;
- benefit liaison to young people delivered through Connexions;
- 'Sanctuary Schemes' to enable victims of domestic violence to stay in their homes;
- planning for the housing needs of people leaving institutions – e.g. local authority care, prison and the armed services.

Further guidance on preventing homelessness is provided in Chapter 2.

### Securing accommodation

**1.22.** Housing authorities need to consider that a range of accommodation is likely to be required for people who are, or may become, homeless. Landlords, accommodation providers and housing developers across all sectors can contribute to the provision of accommodation in the district. Activities that contribute to securing that accommodation will be available for people who are homeless, or at risk of becoming homeless, may include:

- initiatives to increase the supply of new affordable accommodation in the district (e.g.: affordable housing secured through the planning system);
- provision of new housing for owner occupation;
- initiatives to increase the supply of specialist and/or supported accommodation;
- provision of accommodation from the housing authority's own stock;
- the proportion of lettings RSLs make available to the housing authority and to homeless people generally;
- programmes for the provision of hostel, foyer and refuge spaces;
- initiatives for maximising use of the private rented sector (e.g. rent deposit guarantee schemes and landlord/tenant mediation services);
- schemes for maximising access to affordable accommodation (e.g. rent guarantee schemes);

PART III
OTHER MATERIAL

- local, regional and national mobility schemes (e.g. to assist tenants or homeless households to move to other areas, incentives to reduce under-occupation, and assistance to move into home ownership).

Further guidance on ensuring a sufficient supply of accommodation is provided in Chapter 3.

**Providing support**

**1.23.** As part of the review housing authorities should consider all the current activities which contribute to the provision of support for people in the district who are, or may become, homeless and people in the district who have been homeless and need support to prevent them becoming homeless again. The range of providers whose activities will be making a contribution to this area are likely to embrace the public, private and voluntary sectors.

**1.24.** As a starting point, the housing authority may wish to consider the level of services being provided under the Supporting People programme. Other activities which may be relevant are:
- social services support under the community care programme;
- social services support for children in need who require accommodation;
- social services support for young people at risk;
- housing advice services;
- tenancy support services;
- schemes which offer practical support for formerly homeless people (e.g. furniture schemes);
- day centres for homeless people;
- supported hostel provision;
- women's refuges;
- support for people to access health care services (e.g. registration with a GP practice);
- support for people with problems of alcohol or substance abuse;
- support for people with mental health problems;
- support for people with learning disabilities;
- support for people seeking employment, e.g. personal adviser through Connexions, Jobcentre Plus, voluntary sector organisations dealing with homelessness and worklessness;
- advocacy support.

Further guidance on securing support services is provided in Chapter 4.

*c) resources available for activities*

**1.25.** As part of the homelessness review, the housing authority should consider the resources available for the activities set out in paragraph 1.11. The housing authority should consider not only its own resources (i.e. housing funding whether provided by central government or from authorities' own sources) but also those available for these purposes to the social services authority for their district, other public authorities, voluntary organisations and other persons. Annex 3 provides an indicative list of other authorities, organisations and persons whose activities may contribute to preventing and tackling homelessness.

**Preventing homelessness**

**1.26.** Housing authorities should invest their own resources in prevention services and measures since these are likely to produce direct net savings for the authority, for example through reduced processing of repeat homelessness applications, lower use of temporary accommodation and fewer social services interventions. Resources allocated to preventing homelessness will also help to reduce pressures on wider services, such as housing, health and employment, in the longer-term.

**1.27.** Resources available for the prevention of homelessness may include:
- staff or administrative budgets and resources available to the housing authority (e.g. related to the homeless persons unit, the housing advice service, the Supporting People programme, tenancy support etc.);
- the resources allocated within the housing authority for rent guarantee schemes and other preventative measures;
- the availability and quality of housing and homelessness advice in the district (e.g. number and location of advice centres);
- staff or administrative budgets and resources within other public bodies (e.g. social services authority, Primary Care Trust, local education authority) dedicated to activities that help prevent/tackle homelessness; and
- staff or administrative budgets and resources available to other agencies working to prevent homelessness in the district (e.g. housing advice services in the voluntary sector and agencies working with young people).

**Securing accommodation**

**1.28.** Resources available for securing that accommodation is, or will be, available may include:
- initiatives to increase the supply of new affordable accommodation in the district (e.g.

bids for resources through the Regional Housing Strategy and Housing Corporation Approved Development Programme, cash incentive schemes, affordable housing secured through the planning system, other RSL developments, Private Finance Initiative or regeneration developments, self-funded developments, self build schemes, shared ownership schemes, Homebuy);

- initiatives to increase the supply of specialist and/or supported accommodation;
- staff or administrative budgets and resources to make better use of the existing social housing stock (e.g. working with RSLs, managing own housing stock, mobility schemes);
- staff or administrative budgets and resources for maximising use of the private rented sector (e.g. landlord fora and accreditation schemes, rent deposit/guarantee schemes);
- initiatives to enable people to remain in their homes (e.g. through housing renewal assistance and disabled facilities grants).

## Providing Support

**1.29.** Resources available for providing support may include:
- staff or administrative budgets and resources available through the Supporting People programme;
- other staff or administrative budgets and resources available to the housing authority, for example through general fund expenditure or the Housing Revenue Account;
- staff or administrative budgets and resources available to the social services authority (e.g. personnel working to meet the support needs of homeless people);
- staff or administrative budgets and resources available to other public authorities and voluntary and community sector agencies (e.g. Primary Care Trusts, Drug Action Teams, Sure Start, Connexions and others listed at Annex 3); and
- availability of supported accommodation units and floating support for homeless people.

### Results of the review

**1.30.** Having completed a homelessness review, housing authorities must arrange for a copy of the results of the review to be made available at their principal office; these must be available to the public for inspection at all reasonable hours without charge. A copy of the results must also be made available to any member of the public, on request (for which a reasonable charge can be made).

## HOMELESSNESS STRATEGIES

**1.31.** Having carried out a homelessness review the housing authority will be in a position to formulate its homelessness strategy based on the results of that review as required by s.1(1)(b) of the 2002 Act. In formulating its strategy a housing authority will need to consider the necessary levels of activity required to achieve the aims set out in the paragraph below and the sufficiency of the resources available to them as revealed by the review.

**1.32.** Under s.3(1) of the 2002 Act a homelessness strategy means a strategy for:
i)     preventing homelessness in the district (see Chapter 2 for further guidance);
ii)    securing that sufficient accommodation is and will be available for people in the district who are or may become homeless (see Chapter 3 for further guidance);
iii)    securing the satisfactory provision of support for people in the district who are or may become homeless or who have been homeless and need support to prevent them becoming homeless again (see Chapter 4 for further guidance).

### Specific objectives and actions for housing and social services authorities

**1.33.** A homelessness strategy may include specific objectives to be achieved and actions planned to be taken in the course of the exercise of the functions of the housing authority and the social services authority. This will apply equally in areas where the social services authority is not also the housing authority (for example, in district councils in county areas). Examples of specific objectives and actions for housing and social services authorities that might be included in a strategy are set out in Annex 4.

### Specific action by others

**1.34.** A homelessness strategy can also include specific action which the housing authority expects to be taken by:
i)     other public authorities;
ii)    voluntary organisations; and
iii)    other persons whose activities could contribute to achieving the strategy's objectives.

**1.35.** In all housing authority districts there will be a significant number of agencies whose activities address the wide range of needs and problems that can be linked to homelessness. These will be found across all sectors: public, private and voluntary. Housing authorities will need to seek the participation of all relevant agencies in the district in order to assist them in formulating and delivering an effective homelessness strategy that includes specific action that the housing authority expects to be taken by others.

PART III
OTHER MATERIAL

**1.36.** In particular, housing authorities should enter into constructive partnerships with RSLs operating in their district. See Annex 5 for guidance on co-operation between housing authorities and RSLs.

**1.37.** An indicative list of the other public authorities, voluntary organisations and persons whose activities could contribute to achieving the strategy's objectives is at Annex 3. However, s.3(4) provides that a housing authority cannot include in a homelessness strategy any specific action expected to be taken by another body or organisation without their approval.

**1.38.** Examples of specific action that the housing authority might expect to be taken by others are provided at Annex 6.

*Joint action*

**1.39.** Section 3(5) of the 2002 Act requires housing authorities, when formulating a homelessness strategy, to consider (among other things) the extent to which any of the strategy's objectives could be achieved through joint action involving two or more of the persons or other bodies tackling homelessness in the district. This could include the housing authority, the social services authority, neighbouring housing authorities and any other public bodies working to alleviate homelessness within the district, for example, the National Offender Management Service. It might also include any other organisation or person whose activities could contribute to achieving the objectives of the homelessness strategy, for example, voluntary sector organisations working with homeless people, registered social landlords, and private landlords. The most effective strategies will be those which harness the potential of all the organisations and persons working to prevent and alleviate homelessness in the district, and which ensure that all the activities concerned are consistent and complementary. It will be important for all such organisations to take ownership of the strategy if they strive to help meet its objectives. See Chapter 5 for guidance on joint working with other agencies.

*Action plans*

**1.40.** As part of the homelessness strategy housing authorities should develop effective action plans, to help ensure that the objectives set out in the homelessness strategy are achieved. Action plans could include, for example, targets, milestones and arrangements for monitoring and evaluation. Good practice guidance on developing action plans is provided in the ODPM publication *'Local Authorities' Homelessness Strategies: Evaluation and Good Practice (2004)'*.

*Need to consult on a strategy*

**1.41.** Housing authorities must consult such public or local authorities, voluntary organisations or other persons as they consider appropriate before adopting or modifying a homelessness strategy. For a strategy to be effective it will need to involve every organisation and partnership whose activities contribute, or could contribute, in some way to achieving its objectives. As a minimum, therefore, it will be appropriate for all such organisations to be consulted on the strategy before it is adopted. It will be important to consult service users and homeless people themselves, or organisations representing their interests. Consultation with ethnic minority and faith-based groups will also be important in addressing the disproportionate representation of people from ethnic minority communities amongst homeless households. Annex 3 provides an indicative list of the types of authorities, organisations and people that the housing authority may wish to consult about a strategy.

*Publishing a strategy*

**1.42.** Under s.1(3) of the 2002 Act, housing authorities were required to publish their first homelessness strategy by 31 July 2003. Section 1(4) requires housing authorities to publish a new homelessness strategy, based on the results of a further homelessness review, within the period of five years beginning with the day on which their last homelessness strategy was published. However, those authorities which are categorised as an "excellent authority" by the Secretary of State by virtue of the *Local Authorities' Plans and Strategies (Disapplication) (England) Order 2005* are exempt from this requirement. Housing authorities must make a copy of the strategy available to the public at their principal office, and this is to be available for inspection at all reasonable hours without charge. A copy must also be made available to any member of the public, on request (for which a reasonable charge can be made).

*Keeping a strategy under review and modifying it*

**1.43.** Housing authorities must keep their homelessness strategy under review and may modify it from time to time. Before modifying the strategy, they must consult on the same basis as required before adopting a strategy (see paragraph 1.41). If a strategy is modified, the housing authority must publish the modifications or the modified strategy and make copies available to the public on the same basis as required when adopting a strategy (see paragraph 1.42).

**1.44.** Circumstances that might prompt modification of a homelessness strategy include: transfer of the housing authority's housing stock to an RSL; the setting up of an Arms Length Management

Organisation; a review of other, relevant local plans or strategies; new data sources on homelessness becoming available; a significant change in the levels or causes of homelessness; changes in either housing/homelessness/social security policy or legislation, or new factors that could contribute to a change in the levels or nature of homelessness in the district such as significant changes to the local economy (e.g. housing markets or levels of employment).

**[5003]**

## CHAPTER 2: PREVENTING HOMELESSNESS

**2.1.   This chapter provides guidance on housing authorities' duties to have a strategy to prevent homelessness in their district and to ensure that advice and information about homelessness, and the prevention of homelessness, are available free of charge to anyone in their district. The chapter also provides some examples of the action housing authorities and their partners can take to tackle the more common causes of homelessness and to prevent homelessness recurring.**

**2.2.**   Preventing homelessness means providing people with the ways and means to meet their housing, and any housing-related support, needs in order to avoid experiencing homelessness. Effective prevention will enable a person to remain in their current home, where appropriate, to delay a need to move out of current accommodation so that a move into alternative accommodation can be planned in a timely way; to find alternative accommodation, or to sustain independent living.

**2.3.**   The prevention of homelessness should be a key strategic aim which housing authorities and other partners pursue through the homelessness strategy. It is vital that individuals are encouraged to seek assistance at the earliest possible time when experiencing difficulties which may lead to homelessness. In many cases early, effective intervention can prevent homelessness occurring. Housing authorities are reminded that they must not avoid their obligations under Part 7 of the 1996 Act (including the duty to make inquiries under s.184, if they have reason to believe that an applicant may be homeless or threatened with homelessness), but it is open to them to suggest alternative solutions in cases of potential homelessness where these would be appropriate and acceptable to the applicant.

**2.4.**   The Secretary of State considers that housing authorities should take steps to prevent homelessness wherever possible, offering a broad range of advice and assistance for those in housing need. It is also important that, where homelessness does occur and is being tackled, consideration is given to the factors which may cause repeat homelessness and action taken to prevent homelessness recurring.

**2.5.**   Homelessness can have significant negative consequences for the people who experience it. At a personal level, homelessness can have a profound impact on health, education and employment prospects. At a social level, homelessness can impact on social cohesion and economic participation. Early intervention to prevent homelessness can therefore bring benefits for those concerned, including being engaged with essential services and increasing the likelihood that children will live in a more secure environment. Investment in prevention services can also produce direct cost savings for local authorities, for example through lower use of temporary accommodation and fewer social services interventions. Furthermore, measures to prevent homelessness will also help to reduce longer-term pressures on wider services, such as health and employment.

**2.6.**   There are three stages where intervention can prevent homelessness:

**early identification** – by identifying categories of people who are at risk of homelessness and ensuring that accommodation and any necessary support are available to them in time to prevent homelessness. Early identification can target people who fall within known indicator groups (e.g. those leaving local authority care, prison, secure accommodation or the armed forces, or people at known or observed risk due to mental or physical health problems) even though they may not currently have a need for housing but for whom timely intervention can avoid homelessness when they leave their institutional environment and before they reach a crisis point;

**pre-crisis intervention** – this can take the form of: advice services and proactive intervention such as negotiation with landlords to enable people to retain their current tenancies. Such intervention is important even if it only delays the date when a person has to leave their home, as this may allow time to plan and manage a move to alternative accommodation;

**preventing recurring homelessness** – ensuring tenancy sustainment can be central to preventing repeat homelessness where there is an underlying need for support and the provision of accommodation by itself is insufficient to prevent homelessness.

## STRATEGY TO PREVENT HOMELESSNESS

**2.7.**   Under s.1 of the 2002 Act, local housing authorities must formulate and publish a homelessness strategy based on a review of homelessness for their district, and they must take the strategy into account when exercising their functions. (See Chapter 1 for guidance.) Under section 3(1)(a) of the 2002 Act a homelessness strategy must include, among other things, a strategy

**PART III**
**OTHER MATERIAL**

for preventing homelessness in the district. Gaining a thorough understanding of the causes of homelessness in a local area through the review process will help to inform the range of measures required to prevent homelessness. As part of the review, housing authorities must consider all the current activities in their area that contribute to the prevention of homelessness. They must also consider the resources available. Both activities and resources are likely to involve a wide range of providers working in the public, private and voluntary sectors.

**2.8.** In developing their homelessness strategies, housing authorities should consider the range of measures that need to be put in place to prevent homelessness. These will depend on local circumstances. Housing authorities are advised to adopt an open approach and recognise that there will be a broad range of organisations operating in fields other than housing, for example, in education, health and employment, whose activities may help to prevent homelessness. (See Chapter 1 for further guidance on carrying out a homelessness review and formulating a homelessness strategy).

## ADVICE AND INFORMATION ABOUT HOMELESSNESS AND THE PREVENTION OF HOMELESSNESS

**2.9.** Under s.179(1) of the 1996 Act, housing authorities have a duty to secure that advice and information about homelessness, and the prevention of homelessness, are available free of charge to **any person** in their district. The provision of comprehensive advice will play an important part in delivering the housing authority's strategy for preventing homelessness in their district.

**2.10.** There is an enormous variety of reasons why people become homeless or find themselves threatened with homelessness. And, in many cases, there can be multiple reasons, and a complex chain of circumstances, that lead to homelessness. Some of these may relate to the housing market, for example, high rents and a shortage of affordable accommodation in the area, or to administrative systems, for example delays in the payment of benefits. Others may relate to personal circumstances, for example, relationship breakdown, a bereavement, long-term or acute ill health or loss of employment. The provision of advice and information to those at risk of homelessness will need to reflect this. It will need to be wide-ranging and comprehensive in its coverage and may require a full multi-disciplinary assessment.

**2.11.** Many people who face the potential loss of their current home will be seeking practical advice and assistance to help them remain in their accommodation or secure alternative accommodation. Some may be seeking to apply for assistance under the homelessness legislation without being aware of other options that could help them to secure accommodation. Advice services should provide information on the range of housing options that are available in the district. This might include options to enable people to stay in their existing accommodation, delay homelessness for long enough to allow a planned move, or access alternative accommodation in the private or social sectors. This 'housing options' approach is central to addressing housing need as a means of preventing homelessness.

**2.12.** Advice on the following issues may help to prevent homelessness:

- tenants' rights and rights of occupation;
- leaseholders' rights and service charges;
- what to do about harassment and illegal eviction;
- how to deal with possession proceedings;
- rights to benefits (e.g. housing benefit) including assistance with making claims as required;
- current rent levels;
- how to retrieve rent deposits;
- rent and mortgage arrears;
- how to manage debt;
- grants available for housing repair and/or adaptation;
- how to obtain accommodation in the private rented sector – e.g. details of landlords and letting agents within the district, including any accreditation schemes, and information on rent guarantee and deposit schemes;
- how to apply for an allocation of accommodation through the social housing waiting list or choice-based lettings scheme;
- how to apply to other social landlords for accommodation.

The advisory service might also include an advocacy service, which may include providing legal representation for people facing the loss of their home.

**2.13.** Housing authorities will need to ensure that the implications and likely outcomes of the available housing options are made clear to all applicants, including the distinction between having priority need for accommodation under Part 7 and having priority for an allocation of social housing under Part 6.

**2.14.** Advice services will need to be effectively linked to other relevant statutory and non-statutory service providers. As noted in paragraph 2.10 above, it is often a combination of factors that lead to homelessness, and housing authorities are advised to ensure that people who require advice of a wider or more specialist nature, for example, to address family and relationship breakdown, mental or physical health problems, drug and alcohol abuse, or worklessness are directed to other agencies who can provide the service they need. In situations where there is a history of child abuse or where there are child protection concerns, homelessness and housing organisations will need to work closely with the Local Safeguarding Children Board (LSCB).

**2.15.** The effectiveness of authorities' housing advice in preventing homelessness or the threat of homelessness is measured by Best Value Performance Indicator BVPI 213. Guidance on BVPI 213 is available at www.communities.gov.uk.

*Accessibility*

**2.16.** It is recommended that advisory services are well publicised and accessible to everyone in the district. Appropriate provision will need to be made to ensure accessibility for people with particular needs, including those with mobility difficulties, sight or hearing loss and learning difficulties, as well as those for whom English is not their first language.

*Who provides the advice and information?*

**2.17.** The legislation does not specify how housing authorities should ensure that advice and information on homelessness and the prevention of homelessness are made available. They could do this in a number of ways, for example:
  i)     provide the service themselves;
  ii)    ensure that it is provided by another organisation; or
  iii)   ensure that it is provided in partnership with another organisation.

**2.18.** The housing authority must ensure that the service is free of charge and available and accessible to everyone in their district. Securing the provision of an independent advisory service may help to avoid conflicts of interest. Private sector tenants may not naturally look to the housing authority for advice. Some young people may be reluctant to approach a statutory authority for advice, but they may feel more at ease in dealing with a more informal advisory service provided by the voluntary sector. People from different ethnic minority groups might also find advice more accessible if it is delivered through community or faith organisations. (See Chapter 21 for guidance on contracting out homelessness functions).

**2.19.** Under s.179(2), housing authorities may give grants or loans to other persons who are providing advice and information about homelessness and the prevention of homelessness on behalf of the housing authority. Under s.179(3), housing authorities may also assist such persons (e.g. voluntary organisations) by:
  i)     allowing them to use premises belonging to the housing authority,
  ii)    making available furniture or other goods, by way of gift, loan or some other arrangement, and
  iii)   making available the services of staff employed by the housing authority.

*Standards of advice*

**2.20.** Housing authorities should ensure that information provided is current, accurate and appropriate to the individual's circumstances. To ensure they are providing an effective service to a high standard, housing authorities may wish to refer to the quality assurance systems applied by the National Association of Citizens Advice Bureaux, the Shelter network of housing advice centres, the National Disabled Housing Services Ltd (HoDis) accreditation scheme and the Community Legal Service Quality Mark. Housing authorities are also advised to monitor the provision of advisory services to ensure they continue to meet the needs of all sections of the community and help deliver the aims of their homelessness strategy.

## PREVENTING HOMELESSNESS IN SPECIFIC CIRCUMSTANCES

**2.21.** Some groups of people are likely to be more at risk of homelessness than others. These may include:
  • young people who have become estranged from their family; have been in care and/or secure accommodation; have a history of abuse, running away or school exclusions; or whose parents have had mental health, alcohol or drug problems (see Chapter 12 for further guidance on 16 and 17 year olds);
  • people from ethnic minority groups;
  • people with an institutionalised background, for example where they have spent time in care, in prison or in the armed forces;
  • former asylum seekers who have been given permission to stay in the UK and are no longer being accommodated by the National Asylum Support Service;
  • people who have experienced other problems that may increase the risk of homelessness including family/relationship breakdowns; domestic, racial or other violence; poor mental or physical health; drug and alcohol misuse; age-related problems and debt.

**2.22.** In many cases homelessness can be prevented by identifying people who are in circumstances which put them at risk of homelessness, and by providing services which can enable them to remain in their current home. Homelessness can also be prevented by ensuring assistance is available at known risk points such as discharge from prison or hospital. Table 2.1 below gives examples of some of the measures that may help tackle some of the more common causes of homelessness. More detailed guidance is provided in Annex 7.

**2.23.** Housing authorities should also work with housing providers to encourage them to seek to maintain and sustain tenancies by employing effective strategies for the prevention and management of rent arrears. Landlords should be encouraged to make early and personal contact with tenants in arrears and to assess whether there are any additional support needs and, where relevant, to establish that all benefits to which tenants are entitled are being claimed. Landlords should offer assistance and advice on welfare benefits and in making a claim, debt counselling and money advice either in-house or through a referral to an external agency and implement ways for recovering the money such as debt management plans or attachment to benefits or earnings orders. Possession action should only be taken as a last resort. See Annex 1 for ODPM guidance on *Improving the Effectiveness of Rent Arrears Management.*

## TABLE 2.1: TACKLING COMMON CAUSES OF HOMELESSNESS

| Cause | Action |
|---|---|
| Parents, relatives or friends not being able or willing to provide accommodation | Mediation services, usually contracted out by local authority to, for example, Relate, Youth Crime prevention and parenting programmes. |
| Relationship breakdown, including domestic violence | 'Sanctuary' schemes, which allow domestic violence victims to remain in their homes where they choose to do so once security measures are in place. |
| Discharge from an institutional situation e.g. hospital, custody, residential treatment/ care | Early planning for discharge between institutional staff and local housing providers, including assessing support needs. Proactive provision of advice by local housing authority on housing options (prior to discharge). |
| End of assured shorthold tenancy | Housing advice. Rent deposit or bond schemes to encourage landlords to let to potentially homeless people. Landlord-tenant mediation services, to resolve disputes about behaviour or repairs. |
| Mortgage and rent arrears | Debt counselling. Advocacy services in county court. Fast tracking housing benefit claims. |
| Person ill-equipped to sustain a tenancy | Advice and support under the Supporting People programme for vulnerable people at risk of homelessness, for example improving budgeting and 'life' skills. |
| Lack of information | Early and proactive intervention from local authority homelessness services to discuss options and offer assistance and advice. |

## PREVENTING HOMELESSNESS RECURRING

**2.24.** The underlying problems which led to homelessness in the first place have to be addressed in order to provide long-term solutions. Failure to address these root causes can lead to repeated episodes of homelessness. Recurring homelessness may be indicative of problems that are not being resolved by the provision of accommodation alone.

**2.25.** An effective approach to tackling recurring homelessness is likely to be based on:
- effective monitoring that identifies housing applicants who are homeless or threatened with homelessness and who have previously been secured accommodation under the homelessness legislation (either by the same authority or another authority in a different area);
- an analysis of the main causes of homelessness among housing applicants who have experienced homelessness more than once; and
- the existence of support services (and, in particular, strong links with the local Supporting People strategy and services) for housing applicants who have experienced homelessness more than once, which tackle these causes and help the applicants to sustain tenancies or other forms of settled accommodation in the longer term.

**2.26.** Tenancy sustainment is central to preventing repeat homelessness and can include a range of interventions. It is closely linked with good housing management and the Supporting People programme. See Chapter 4 for further guidance on securing support services and the housing-related support services that can be funded through Supporting People.

**2.27.** Whilst tenancy sustainment is the eventual objective, there are some individuals who may not be able to sustain accommodation due to personal circumstances, for example mental health or substance misuse difficulties. Support will need to be provided to progress towards the time when they are able to maintain accommodation.

**[5004]**

## CHAPTER 3: ENSURING A SUFFICIENT SUPPLY OF ACCOMMODATION

**3.1.** **This chapter provides guidance on options available to housing authorities to help increase the supply of new housing and maximise the use of the housing stock in their district.**

**3.2.** Section 3(1)(b) of the *Homelessness Act 2002* provides that a homelessness strategy is a strategy for, amongst other things, securing that sufficient accommodation is and will be available for people who are or may become homeless. Chapter 16 provides guidance on the different ways in which housing authorities can ensure that suitable accommodation is available for applicants, for example by providing the accommodation themselves or by securing it from a private landlord or a registered social landlord.

**3.3.** Homelessness is significantly influenced by the availability of housing, and in particular affordable housing. A shortage of affordable housing can lead to increasing numbers of people being accommodated in temporary accommodation whilst waiting for settled housing to bring the main homelessness duty to an end. 'Settled housing' in this context will primarily be social housing and good quality private sector accommodation (see chapter 14 for further guidance on bringing the main homelessness (s.193(2)) duty to an end.)

**3.4.** Although, in 2005, over 80% of people living in temporary accommodation were in self-contained homes they often lack certainty over how long they will live there. This can cause disruption to their lives, make it hard for them to put roots down in the community or to access important services. For example, they may face real difficulties in gaining access to a local GP or in enrolling their children in a local school. Many may already have faced disruption and become disconnected or moved away from existing services and support networks as a result of homelessness.

**3.5.** The Government's current target is to halve the number of households living in temporary accommodation by 2010. Increasing the supply of new affordable housing and making better use of existing social and private rented stock to provide settled homes will be critical for achieving this target, as will measures to prevent homelessness.

## INCREASE SUPPLY OF NEW HOUSING

**3.6.** The *Sustainable Communities Plan* and *Sustainable Communities: Homes for All* set out how the Government is creating new communities and expanding existing communities in four areas in the wider South East. Taken together, these areas are expected to deliver an extra 200,000 homes above current planning totals.

**3.7.** At a regional level, local authorities have a key role to play to identify the priorities for housing in their region, to ensure these are reflected in regional housing strategies and to secure funding for their plans. Housing authorities will also need to ensure that housing strategies are aligned with regional economic and planning strategies.

**3.8.** There are a number of ways housing authorities can increase the supply of new housing. The main source of funding for the provision of affordable housing is the Housing Corporation's national Affordable Housing Programme (AHP), known formerly as the Approved Development Programme (ADP). From the 2006–2008 biannual bidding round, the AHP is open to both registered social landlords and non-registered bodies (e.g. developers). Bids continue to be assessed against a range of criteria including housing quality and value for money, and against regional and local priorities. Housing authorities will need to work closely with RSLs and others to make best use of this funding.

**3.9.** Another important means of providing affordable housing is through planning obligations, which are usually negotiated in the context of granting planning permission for new housing development. Planning obligations are generally secured by agreements made between a local authority and a developer under s.106 of the *Town and Country Planning Act 1990* and they are commonly referred to as "s.106 agreements". Obligations may be appropriate where, for example, a planning objection to a proposed development cannot be overcome by the imposition of a condition. More detailed guidance on the use of s.106 agreements is contained in ODPM Circular 05/2005: Planning Obligations.

**3.10.** National guidance on planning and affordable housing is currently contained in Planning Policy Guidance Note 3 (PPG3): Housing, as supplemented by Circular 06/98. These documents provide advice to planning authorities about securing the provision of affordable housing either in kind or by financial contribution. They also remind local authorities when formulating local policy or determining planning applications to take account of the need to cater for a range of housing needs and to encourage the development of mixed and balanced communities in order to avoid areas of social exclusion.

**3.11.** PPG3 and Circular 06/98 are presently under review and a draft Planning Policy Statement 3 (PPS3): Housing was issued for consultation in December 2005. Following the publication of final PPS3, local planning authorities will be expected to ensure that policies in their Local Development Frameworks take into account the updated national planning policy framework for delivering the Government's housing objectives.

**3.12.** Planning authorities will need to ensure that their affordable housing policies are evidence-based, kept up to date over time, and applied consistently across developments to ensure that affordable housing is effectively and fairly delivered through this route.

## MAXIMISING THE USE OF EXISTING HOUSING STOCK

**3.13.** A number of options are discussed below for how housing authorities might maximise the use of current housing stock.

### The private rented sector

**3.14.** Some people living in the private rented sector can experience homelessness, but this sector can also provide solutions to homelessness. Homelessness statistics routinely show that the end of an assured shorthold tenancy (AST) is one of the top three reasons for loss of a settled home. Authorities are encouraged to work with landlords in their area to see how this can be addressed, for example, by offering mediation between landlord and tenant where relations have broken down, and negotiating to extend or renew ASTs where appropriate.

**3.15.** For many, renting in the private sector may offer a practical solution to their housing need (for example, it may offer more choice over location and type of property). Authorities are therefore encouraged to consider providing rent deposits, guarantees or rent in advance, to help households access this sector. They may also consider establishing Accreditation Schemes, whereby landlords voluntarily agree to a set of standards relating to the management or physical condition of privately rented accommodation to help increase the supply of private rented accommodation.

**3.16.** Many local authorities have used the private rented sector as a source of good quality, self-contained temporary accommodation. However, the private rented sector can also provide a source of settled accommodation, where qualifying offers of ASTs are accepted by households who are owed the main homelessness duty.

**3.17.** There is scope to make greater use of the private rented sector, either to help households avoid homelessness or to provide more settled homes for people living in temporary accommodation. Authorities are recommended to establish and maintain good relations with private sector landlords, for example through landlord fora. This can be effective in securing an improved supply of properties in the private rented sector for homeless, or potentially homeless, households.

**3.18.** It is also recommended that authorities review the extent to which qualifying offers of ASTs are being made to households in temporary accommodation in their area; whether there are any barriers to such offers being made or accepted and, if so, what additional steps would need to be taken to address those barriers.

### Social housing

**3.19.** The Secretary of State considers that, generally, it is inappropriate for general needs social housing to be used as temporary accommodation for long periods, especially where such properties are able to be let as settled homes.

**3.20.** It is important that housing authorities work effectively with RSLs to help them prevent and tackle homelessness in the district. RSLs have a key role to play in sustaining tenancies, reducing evictions and abandonment, and preventing homelessness through their housing management functions. To ensure effective collaboration between themselves and partner RSLs operating in their district housing authorities are advised to consider establishing a nominations agreement. This would include the proportion of lettings that will be made available, any conditions that will apply, and how any disputes about suitability or eligibility will be resolved. Housing authorities are also advised to aim for any exclusion criteria (that may be applied to nominees by the RSL) to be kept to a minimum. Further guidance on co-operation between RSLs and housing authorities is at Annex 5.

**3.21.** There are a number of schemes and policies that social housing providers can implement to facilitate the effective management and use of the existing housing stock and to keep voids and re-let times to a minimum.

- **Mobility:** 'moveUK' (formerly Housing Employment and Mobility Services) has been developed to offer social housing tenants and jobseekers more choice about where they live and work around the UK. Its services will open up new opportunities for people who wish to move. 'moveUK' will have three main service components:
    (i)     facilitated mobility services to social landlords and their tenants and applicants to help tenants and applicants to find new homes. This will continue and enhance the provision of the grant funded mobility previously provided by Housing Mobility and Exchange Services (HOMES) and LAWN (the Association of London Government scheme that helps tenants who want to, move out of London to areas of low demand);
    (ii)    'one stop shop' web-based information about available housing, neighbourhoods and job vacancies;
    (iii)   web access to information on vacancies in social housing.
- **Cash Incentive Scheme** (CIS): although there is no obligation for a housing authority to provide a scheme, the main objectives of the Cash Incentive Scheme (CIS) are to release local authority accommodation required for letting to those in housing need, and to encourage sustainable home ownership. This is achieved by the payment of a grant to a local authority tenant to assist them in buying a property in the private sector.
- **The new HomeBuy scheme**: this scheme, which commenced on 1st April 2006, provides people with the opportunity to own a home based on equity sharing, whilst protecting the supply of social housing. Existing social tenants are one of the priority groups helped under the scheme, and any rented housing association/local authority home vacated by them will then be made available to others in priority housing need. The Social HomeBuy option, which allows housing association and local authority tenants to purchase a share in their rented home, will be voluntary. Landlords will be able to reinvest the proceeds in replacement social homes.

**3.22.** The Secretary of State also considers that where local authority or RSL stock is provided as temporary accommodation to discharge a main homelessness duty (owed under section 193(2)) the housing authority should give very careful consideration to the scope for allocating the accommodation as a secure or assured tenancy, as appropriate, especially where a household has been living in a particular property for anything other than a short-term emergency stay.

*Choice-based Lettings schemes*

**3.23.** The expansion of choice-based lettings policy aims to achieve nationwide coverage by 2010. Local authorities are encouraged to work together, and with RSL partners, to develop sub-regional and regional choice-based lettings schemes which provide maximum choice and flexibility. Local authorities are encouraged to offer choice to homeless households, while ensuring that their schemes are designed so as not to provide a perverse incentive to applicants to make a homelessness application in order to increase their priority for housing. Housing authorities should also consider involving the private rented sector in their choice-based lettings schemes in order to maximise the housing options available.

*Empty homes*

**3.24.** Housing authorities are encouraged to adopt positive strategies for minimising empty homes, and other buildings that could provide residential accommodation, across all housing sectors and tenures within their district. A strategy for minimising empty homes might include schemes for tackling low demand social housing, bringing empty private sector properties back into use and bringing flats over shops into residential use.

**3.25.** Under the *Housing Act 2004* new provisions on Empty Dwelling Management Orders (EDMOs) are expected to be brought into force. EDMOs are a discretionary power for local authorities to use as part of their empty homes strategy. The new powers will allow local authorities to apply to a residential property tribunal for approval to make an interim EDMO lasting for up to 12 months. During this interim period, the authority may only place tenants in the house with the consent of the owner.

**3.26.** Local authorities also have the discretion to set the council tax discount on long term empty properties at any point between 50% and 0%, as well as at any point between 50% and 10% on second homes, taking into account local conditions.

*Housing renewal*

**3.27.** Housing renewal assistance can also assist in meeting the aims of the homelessness strategy. Under the *Regulatory Reform (Housing Assistance)(England and Wales) Order 2002*, local authorities have power to promote housing renewal assistance to landlords, private homeowners and others to increase the supply of a particular type of accommodation through converting under-utilised accommodation to meet identified housing need within the district. Empty homes, vacant accommodation above shops or commercial buildings can be targeted for assistance. Housing renewal assistance can also enable private homeowners to carry out essential repairs or improvements, and remain in their home.

*Disabled facilities grant*

**3.28.** Uptake of the Disabled Facilities Grant – a mandatory entitlement administered by housing authorities for eligible disabled people in all housing tenures – can enable homeowners to remain living an independent life at home, and should be considered as part of an effective homelessness strategy. Authorities are required to give a decision within six months of receiving an application. The grant is subject to a maximum limit and is means tested to ensure that funding goes to those most in need.

[5005]

## CHAPTER 4: SECURING SUPPORT SERVICES

**4.1.** **This chapter provides guidance on the importance of support services in preventing and tackling homelessness and outlines the types of housing-related and other support services that might be required.**

**4.2.** A homelessness strategy is defined in section 3(1)(c) of the 2002 Act as (among other things) a strategy for securing the satisfactory provision of support for people in their district:

i)      who are or may become homeless; or

ii)     who have been homeless and need support to prevent them from becoming homeless again.

**4.3.** In formulating their homelessness strategies, housing authorities need to recognise that for some households, homelessness cannot be tackled, or prevented, solely through the provision of accommodation. Some households will require a range of support services, which may include housing-related support to help them sustain their accommodation, as well as personal support relating to factors such as relationship breakdown, domestic violence, mental health problems, drug and alcohol addiction, poverty, debt and unemployment.

**4.4.** Support can help to prevent people who are at risk of homelessness from becoming homeless at all. In other cases, where people have experienced homelessness and been placed in temporary accommodation, the provision of support may be essential to ensure that they are able to continue to enjoy a reasonable quality of life and access the range of services they need to rebuild their lives. The provision of support can also be important in helping formerly homeless households to sustain settled housing and prevent homelessness from recurring.

**4.5.** Solutions to homelessness should be based on a thorough assessment of the household's needs, including support needs. Housing authorities will need to establish effective links with the Supporting People team, the social services authority and other agencies (for example, Primary Care Trusts, the Criminal Justice Service, and voluntary and community organisations) to ensure that a joint assessment of an applicant's housing and support needs can be made where necessary. Such assessments should inform decisions on intervention to enable a household to remain in their home, placements in temporary accommodation and options for the provision of more settled accommodation that will bring the main homelessness duty to an end.

**4.6.** Where children and young people are involved, it is important that any solutions to homelessness address the issues they are facing and do not undermine any support they may already be receiving. In particular, housing authorities will need to establish effective links with children's services authorities[1] and establish whether a Common Assessment Framework has been undertaken, and, if so, which agency will have relevant information about the child's or young person's needs.

---

[1]     All authorities should have a children's services authority, delivering through a children's trust, by April 2008. All Directors of Children's Services will be in post by 2008.

---

## STRATEGY TO SECURE PROVISION OF SUPPORT SERVICES

**4.7.** Section 1 of the 2002 Act requires housing authorities to carry out a homelessness review for their district. Gaining a thorough understanding of the causes of homelessness through the review process will help to inform the range of support provision required. As part of the review, housing authorities must consider all the current activities in their area which contribute to the provision of support for households who are, or may become, homeless, as well as people in the district who have been homeless and need support to prevent them becoming homeless again. They must also consider the resources available. Both activities and resources are likely to involve a range of providers working in the public, private and voluntary sectors. (See Chapter 1 for further guidance on carrying out a homelessness review and formulating a homelessness strategy).

**4.8.** In formulating their homelessness strategies housing authorities will need to consider the different types and level of support that households may require. Households who have experienced homelessness or who are at risk of homelessness may have diverse needs. Some households may only need information and advice in order to avoid experiencing homelessness, or becoming homeless again. Others, however, will need greater assistance including housing-related support and in some cases may require intensive support from a range of services.

## INDIVIDUALS AT RISK OF HOMELESSNESS

**4.9.** Housing authorities should be aware that some individuals may be at particular risk of homelessness, for example young people leaving care, ex-offenders, former members of the armed forces, refugees, people with mental health problems or individuals leaving hospital, and may require a broader package of resettlement support. When developing their homelessness strategies, housing authorities should consider carefully how to work effectively to prevent homelessness amongst these groups and ensure that appropriate support is available. Early identification of people at risk will be crucial to preventing homelessness. Housing authorities should consider agreeing protocols for joint action with local agencies in order to assist with early identification and prevention measures.

**4.10.** Individuals at risk of homelessness may also include those who have never experienced homelessness in the past and for whom, with the appropriate support, homelessness can be avoided. These individuals may be at risk of homelessness due to specific problems such as managing debt or accessing benefits and require specialist advice which may be delivered through partner agencies such as Citizens Advice Bureaux or Jobcentre Plus. See Chapter 2 for guidance on preventing homelessness.

## YOUNG PEOPLE

**4.11.** Many young people who have experienced homelessness may lack skills in managing their affairs and require help with managing a tenancy and operating a household budget. Those estranged from their family, particularly care leavers, may lack the advice and support normally available to young people from family, friends and other mentors. 16 and 17 year olds who are homeless and estranged from their family will be particularly vulnerable and in need of support. See Chapter 12 for further guidance on 16 and 17 year olds.

## HOUSING-RELATED SUPPORT SERVICES

**4.12.** Housing-related support services have a key role in preventing homelessness occurring or recurring. The types of housing-related support that households who have experienced homelessness may need include:

- *support in establishing a suitable home* – help, advice and support in finding and maintaining suitable accommodation for independent living in the community;
- *support with daily living skills* – help, advice and training in the day-to-day skills needed for living independently, such as budgeting and cooking;
- *support in accessing benefits, health and community care services* – information, advice and help in claiming benefits or accessing community care or health services;
- *help in establishing and maintaining social support* – help in rebuilding or establishing social networks that can help counter isolation and help support independent living.

**4.13.** Services might be delivered through:

- **floating support services** – using support workers who travel to clients' accommodation in order to provide support. These services can operate across all tenures and generally provide time-limited and low intensity support;
- **short and medium stay housing with support** – including direct access schemes, night shelters, hostels, transitional housing and supported lodgings. Some of these services may specialise in supporting particular groups of individuals at risk of homelessness, such as vulnerable young people;
- **long-stay supported housing services** – to provide ongoing support to those who are unable to live independently in the community.

**4.14.** Housing-related support can be funded through the Supporting People programme, and close co-operation between housing authorities and the Supporting People team will be essential for ensuring effective support for households who have experienced homelessness, particularly through the local Commissioning Body and Core Strategy Group. Further information on housing-related support services is provided in separate guidance, *Supporting People – Guide to Accommodation and Support Options for Homeless Households* (ODPM, 2003).

## OTHER SUPPORT SERVICES

**4.15.** Households who have experienced homelessness may need additional support services which are not directly housing-related and fall outside the scope of the Supporting People programme funding. Housing authorities will need to co-operate and work collaboratively with other departments within the authority and a wide range of statutory, voluntary and private sector agencies in order to ensure that the support which is required is provided. Joint working with commissioners/planners and providers of the following services will be particularly important:

- health services;
- drug/alcohol services including Drug Action Teams;
- social services;

- children's and young persons' services (e.g. Connexions, Sure Start children's centres, child care services);
- voluntary and community sector service providers;
- National Offender Management Service (incorporating the Prison Service and the Probation Service);
- Youth Offending Teams;
- Crime and Disorder Reduction Partnerships;
- the Police;
- education and training services;
- the Employment Service (Jobcentre Plus);
- grant making charities and trusts;
- local strategic partnerships.

## SUPPORT FOR HOUSEHOLDS IN TEMPORARY ACCOMMODATION

**4.16.** The provision of support to households placed in temporary accommodation is essential to ensure that they are able to continue to enjoy a reasonable quality of life and access the range of services they need. In formulating their homelessness strategies, housing authorities should consider what arrangements need to be in place to ensure that households placed in temporary accommodation, within their district or outside, are able to access relevant support services. In particular households will need to be able to access:

- primary care services such as health visitors and GPs;
- appropriate education services;
- relevant social services; and
- employment and training services.

**4.17.** Housing authorities will need to liaise and work collaboratively with the relevant service providers to ensure that appropriate arrangements are put in place and monitored. When households are placed in temporary accommodation, it is recommended that housing authorities offer to liaise with the relevant health, education and social services departments in the area in which the households are temporarily housed. Liaison will be particularly important in cases where households have to be accommodated in the district of another housing authority.

**4.18.** The Secretary of State recommends that housing authorities offer to liaise with the appropriate Primary Care Trust of all families with babies or young children who are placed in temporary accommodation, to ensure that they have the opportunity to receive health and developmental checks from health visitors and/or other primary health care professionals and can participate in vaccination programmes. It would be insufficient for an authority simply to provide such a family with details of health centres and GP practices in the area.

*Notify*

**4.19.** Authorities are encouraged to participate in any regional or sub-regional arrangements which facilitate the notification of other authorities and agencies about the location and support needs of households in temporary accommodation. When considering procedures for notifying the relevant agencies of placements in temporary accommodation, housing authorities may wish to have regard to NOTIFY – a web-based notification and information system administered by the Greater London Authority (GLA).

**4.20.** NOTIFY is designed to improve access to services for households placed in temporary accommodation. Its primary role is to notify relevant services of the placement or movement of households placed in temporary accommodation by London boroughs under the homelessness legislation. The system uses information provided by London borough housing departments to notify housing, education, social services and Primary Care Trusts about households placed in, moving between or leaving temporary accommodation. Information is contained in a database and updated weekly. Authorised users of the NOTIFY notifications website can view information held on NOTIFY at any time, by accessing that website. Relevant services receive a weekly email alert from NOTIFY, informing them of any unviewed notifications and reminding them to access the website. NOTIFY will also shortly provide access for each borough to its own operational management data. The system also has the capacity to analyse aggregated data both at borough and London level. For further information on NOTIFY see notifylondon.gov.uk or contact notify@london.gov.uk.

[5006]

## CHAPTER 5: WORKING WITH OTHERS

**5.1. This chapter provides guidance to housing authorities on working in partnership with other agencies to deliver co-ordinated and effective services to tackle homelessness. It considers the range of organisations and people that contribute to preventing and tackling homelessness and provides examples of types of joint working. It also sets out the statutory provisions that require co-operation between various authorities.**

**5.2.** Under s.3(5) of the 2002 Act, when formulating a homelessness strategy the housing authority must consider, among other things, the extent to which any of the strategy's objectives could be achieved through joint action involving two or more of the organisations tackling homelessness in the district. Whilst housing authorities are best placed to take the strategic lead in tackling homelessness, it is vital that as part of their homelessness strategies effective partnerships are developed with other organisations to deliver co-ordinated and more effective approaches to tackling homelessness locally that address not only housing need but all aspects of social need.

## WHY JOINT WORKING?

**5.3.** At its best, joint working can result in higher quality and more efficient and cost-effective services. Joint working can:

- expand the knowledge and expertise of partner agencies;
- help to provide higher quality integrated services to clients with multiple needs;
- help to ensure people who are homeless or at risk of homelessness do not fall through the net because no one agency can meet all their needs;
- reduce wasteful referrals and duplicated work between agencies. For example, common procedures for assessing clients and exchanging information mean homeless people do not have to be repeatedly assessed by different agencies.

## ORGANISATIONS/PEOPLE WORKING TO PREVENT AND TACKLE HOMELESSNESS

**5.4.** The most effective homelessness strategies will be those which harness the potential of all the organisations and persons working to prevent and tackle homelessness in the district, and which ensure that all the activities concerned are consistent and complementary. Joint working could involve the social services authority, the Primary Care Trust, other public bodies such as the National Offender Management Service, voluntary and community sector organisations, registered social landlords, private landlords, and any other relevant organisations. Housing authorities should also consider joint working with other agencies, for example, the Police and voluntary and community sector organisations, to tackle issues related to homelessness such as street drinking, begging, drug misuse and anti-social behaviour. Such collaborative working can help reduce the numbers of people sleeping rough and provide effective services targeted at those who are homeless or at risk of becoming homeless. Annex 3 provides an indicative list of other authorities, organisations and persons whose activities may contribute to preventing and tackling homelessness. Chapter 2 provides guidance on the range of activities that housing authorities might undertake in conjunction with other bodies in order to prevent homelessness.

**5.5.** Housing authorities should also consider developing cross-boundary partnerships to help tackle homelessness, for example with neighbouring local authorities and local strategic partnerships. Initiatives at regional, cross-regional and sub-regional level that address issues which cut across administrative boundaries may also be relevant – for example regional strategies for refugee integration or reducing re-offending.

## TYPES OF JOINT WORKING

**5.6.** Joint working can take many forms. Examples of types of collaborative working that could help to achieve the objectives of a homelessness strategy might include:

- establishment of a multi-agency forum for key practitioners and providers to share knowledge, information, ideas and complementary practices;
- clear links between the homelessness strategy and other key strategies such as Supporting People, and the NHS Local Delivery Plan;
- protocols for the referral of clients between services and sharing information between services – for example a joint protocol between hospital-based social workers and housing officers to address the housing needs of patients to be discharged from hospital;
- joint consideration of the needs of homeless people by housing and social services authorities under Part 7, the *Children Act 1989* and community care legislation;
- establishment of formal links with other services – for example with those provided by voluntary and community sector organisations;
- joint planning and commissioning of services;
- joint training;
- funding of joint posts, for example with the social services authority;
- senior housing representation on key corporate groups such as the Local Strategic Partnership (LSP) and the Crime and Disorder Reduction Partnership (CDRP);
- senior commitment from all stakeholders to joined-up working to ensure the homelessness strategy action plan is carried out;
- appropriate user involvement and consultation.

**5.7.** When offering housing advice and assistance, housing authorities should consider devising screening procedures that identify at an early stage those cases where there is a need for case-specific joint working. Authorities may also wish to encourage their partner agencies to develop similar procedures. Where there is a need for such an approach, authorities are encouraged to adopt agreed protocols to ensure that appropriate action can be quickly initiated. Early appraisal of all clients who may require multiple assessments, by whichever authority is first approached, with agreed triggers and procedures for further action, may help to prevent duplication of enquiries.

**5.8.** *Homelessness Strategies – A good practice handbook* (DTLR, March 2002) provides advice on successful joint working and the establishment of good links between different agencies and programmes that can prevent and alleviate homelessness. The handbook also signposts to other sources of guidance, for example, on joint protocols, joint commissioning and joint assessments.

## THE STATUTORY FRAMEWORK

**5.9.**  The need for co-operation between statutory authorities is recognised in legislation:
- s.213, s.213A and s.170 of the *Housing Act 1996;*
- s.1 of the *Homelessness Act 2002;*
- s.2 of the *Local Government Act 2000;*
- s.27 of the *Children Act 1989;*
- s.10, s.11 and s.13 of the *Children Act 2004;*
- s.47 of the *National Health Service* and *Community Care Act 1990;*
- s.27 and s.31 of the *Health Act 1999.*

These provisions are outlined in more detail below. However, the absence of a formal legal duty should not act as a barrier to joint working. Rather this should be predicated on meeting local needs and effectively implementing the homelessness strategy.

*Housing Act 1996*

### Section 213

**5.10.**  Where housing or inquiry duties arise under the 1996 Act a housing authority may seek co-operation from another relevant housing authority or body or a social services authority in England, Scotland or Wales. The authority or body to whom the request is made must co-operate to the extent that is reasonable in the circumstances. For this purpose, "relevant housing authority or body" will include:

  *in England and Wales*:

  – another housing authority,

  – a registered social landlord,

  – a housing action trust, and

  *in Scotland*:

  – a local authority,

  – a registered social landlord, and

  – Scottish Homes.

**5.11.**  The duty on the housing authority, body or social services authority receiving such a request to co-operate will depend on their other commitments and responsibilities. However, they cannot adopt a general policy of refusing such requests, and each case will need to be considered in the circumstances at the time.

**5.12.**  Section 170 of the 1996 Act also provides that where a registered social landlord (RSL) has been requested by a housing authority to offer accommodation to people with priority under its allocation scheme, the RSL must co-operate to such extent as is reasonable in the circumstances. RSLs have a key role to play in preventing and tackling homelessness. See Annex 5 for guidance on co-operation between RSLs and housing authorities.

### Section 213A

**5.13.**  Section 213A applies where the housing authority has reason to believe than an applicant with whom a person under the age of 18 resides, or might normally be expected to reside, may be ineligible for assistance, or homeless, or threatened with homelessness, intentionally. Housing authorities are required to have arrangements in place to ensure that all such applicants are invited to agree to the housing authority notifying the social services authority of the essential facts of their case. This will give social services the opportunity to consider the circumstances of the child(ren) and family and plan any response that may be deemed by them to be appropriate. See Chapter 13 for further guidance on s.213A.

*Local Government Acts*

**5.14.**  The promotion of well-being power contained in s.2 of the *Local Government Act 2000* gives local authorities substantial capacity for cross-boundary partnership working with other authorities and partners, such as the health and social services sectors. In particular, the power provides local authorities with increased scope to improve the social, economic and environmental well-being of their communities. Section 2(5) of the *Local Government Act 2000* makes it clear that local authorities may act in relation to and for the benefit of any person or area outside their own area if they consider that to do so is likely to promote or improve the social, economic or environmental well-being of their own area. This, therefore, provides scope for:

- co-operation between neighbouring local authorities and local strategic partnerships; and
- initiatives at regional, cross-regional and sub-regional level that address issues which cut across administrative boundaries.

It should be noted, however, that the s.2 power cannot be used by authorities to delegate, or contract out their functions. In order to do this, authorities will need to make use of specific powers such as those in s.101 of the *Local Government Act 1972* which provides for the joint exercise of functions between local authorities.

### Children Act 1989

**5.15.** Under s.27 of the *Children Act 1989* ("the 1989 Act"), a local authority can ask a range of other statutory authorities, including a housing authority, to help them in delivering services for children and families, under their functions in Part 3 of the 1989 Act. Authorities must comply with such a request to the extent that it is compatible with their own statutory duties and other obligations, and does not unduly prejudice the discharge of any of their own functions. They cannot adopt a general policy of refusing such requests, and each case will need to be considered according to the circumstances at the time.

**5.16.** Children and young people should not be sent to and fro between different authorities (or between different departments within authorities). To provide an effective safety net for vulnerable young people who are homeless or at risk of homelessness, housing and social services will need to work together. Effective collaborative working will require clear corporate policies and departmental procedures agreed between the relevant departments. These should make provision for speedy resolution of any dispute as to which department should take responsibility for a particular case. Joint agreements should cover not only the assessment of clients, but should also reflect the strategic planning and delivery of provision to be set out in the local Children and Young People's Plan. Local Safeguarding Children Boards, which will co-ordinate and ensure the effectiveness of local work to safeguard and promote the welfare of children, may also be involved in drawing up policies and procedures to ensure effective inter-agency co-operation (see also paragraphs 5.17–5.20 below) and Chapter 13.

**5.17.** Under the 1989 Act, young people leaving care and 16/17 year old children assessed as in need are owed duties which may extend to the provision of accommodation. Where social services approach a housing authority for assistance in housing a young person, the housing authority must co-operate subject to the conditions referred to above in para 5.16. Whether a young person is accommodated under the auspices of the social services authority or the housing authority is a matter for individual authorities to determine in each case. Ideally the relationship of the two authorities should be symbiotic, with jointly agreed protocols in place in respect of the assessment of needs. In many cases the social services authority will have a continuing responsibility for the welfare of vulnerable young people and for assisting them in the transition to adulthood and independent living. Under the 1989 Act, these responsibilities can extend until the young person is aged 18 and in the case of care leavers until the age of 21 (or beyond that age if they are in an agreed programme of education and training). Thus, social services authorities can request assistance from housing authorities in meeting their obligations to provide accommodation for a young person and housing authorities can look to social services authorities to provide the support that young homeless applicants may require. In some cases, housing and social services authorities will both have responsibilities towards young people and will need to work together in order to ensure that an appropriate combination of housing and support is arranged to help the young person to live independently successfully.

### Children Act 2004

**5.18.** The *Children Act 2004* ("the 2004 Act") provides the legislative support for the *Every Child Matters: Change for Children* programme which sets out a national framework for local change programmes to build services around the needs of children and young people. Improved outcomes for children will be driven by an analysis of local priorities and secured through more integrated front-line delivery such as multi-agency working, integrated processes such as the Common Assessment Framework, integrated strategy with joint planning and commissioning, and governance arrangements such as the creation of a Director of Children's Services and lead member for children's services.

**5.19.** To support the integration of systems to improve outcomes for children and young people by the creation of children's trusts, s.10 of the 2004 Act establishes a duty on county level and unitary authorities[1] to make arrangements to promote co-operation between the authority, relevant partners (including district councils) and other persons or bodies engaged in activities in relation to children, to improve the well-being of children and young people in the authority's area. Relevant partners are required to co-operate with the authority. Section 11 of the 2004 Act requires a range of agencies –

including county level and unitary authorities and district authorities where there are two tiers of local government – to make arrangements for ensuring that their functions are discharged having regard to the need to safeguard and promote the welfare of children. Section 13 of the 2004 Act requires county level and unitary authorities to set up a Local Safeguarding Children Board (LSCB) incorporating key organisations including district councils where relevant. As set out in s.14, the objective of the LSCB is to co-ordinate and ensure the effectiveness of what is done by each person or body represented on the board to safeguard and promote the welfare of children in that area.

---

1 Section 65 of the Children Act 2004 uses the term 'children's services authority' to define these authorities as: a county council in England; a metropolitan district council; a non-metropolitan district council for an area where there is no county council; a London borough council; the Common Council of the City of London and the Council of the Isles of Scilly.

---

**5.20.** The 2004 Act also makes provision for indexes containing basic information about children and young people to enable better sharing of information. In addition, each local authority is required to draw up a Children and Young People's Plan (CYPP) by April 2006. The CYPP will be a single, strategic, over-arching plan for all services affecting children and young people. The CYPP and the process of joint planning should support local authorities and their partners as they work together. An integrated inspection framework is also being created with Joint Area Reviews assessing local areas' progress in improving outcomes.

The Department for Education and Skills has produced statutory guidance on the *Children Act 2004* which is available from **www.everychildmatters.gov.uk.**

*National Health Service and Community Care Act 1990*

**5.21.** Under the National Health Service (NHS) and Community Care Act 1990 ("the 1990 Act"), social services authorities are required to carry out an assessment of any person who may have a need for community care services. The purpose of the legislation is to ensure that the planning and assessment processes identify a person's full range of needs, including housing needs. Section 47 of the 1990 Act requires social service authorities to notify the housing authority if there appears to be a housing need when the assessment is carried out. The "housing need", for example, may be for renovation or adaptation of the person's current accommodation or for alternative accommodation.

**5.22.** An assessment of vulnerability under the homelessness legislation will not necessarily mean that a client is eligible for social care services. Policy guidance on fair access to care services (FACS) was published on 2 June 2002 under guidance of local authority circular (LAC) (2002) 13. The guidance provides authorities with an eligibility framework for adult social care for them to use when setting and applying their eligibility criteria.

*Health Act 1999*

**5.23.** Section 27 of the *Health Act 1999* ("the 1999 Act") requires NHS bodies and local authorities to co-operate with one another in exercising their respective functions in order to secure and advance the health and welfare of the people of England and Wales.

**5.24.** Under s.31 of the 1999 Act, partnership arrangements can be designed to help break down the barriers between NHS and local authority services by removing existing constraints in the system and increasing flexibility in the provision and commissioning of services. The legislation introduces three flexibilities: pooled budgets, lead commissioning and integrated provision. Any health-related local authority function can be included in these partnerships, for example, housing, social services, education and leisure services.

*National Standards, Local Action: Health and Social Care Standards and Planning Framework 2005/06–2007/08*

**5.25.** This document sets out the framework for all NHS organisations and social services authorities to use in planning over the financial years 2005/06–2007/08. It looks to Primary Care Trusts (PCTs) and local authorities to lead community partnership by even closer joint working to take forward the NHS Improvement Plan. Building on joint work on Local Strategic Partnerships (LSPs), they will need to work in partnership with other NHS organisations in preparing Local Delivery Plans (LDPs) for the period 2005/06 to 2007/08.

*Mental health*

**5.26.** The Mental Health National Service Framework (NSF 30/09/1999) addresses the mental health needs of working age adults up to 65. It sets out national standards; national service models; local action and national underpinning programmes for implementation; and a series of national milestones to assure progress, with performance indicators to support effective performance management. An organisational framework for providing integrated services and for commissioning services across the spectrum is also included.

**5.27.** The Government wants to ensure that people suffering from mental illness receive appropriate care and assistance, particularly those whose illness is severe and enduring. Research has shown that provision of suitable, settled housing is essential to the well-being of this vulnerable group. A key element in the spectrum of care and support is the development of a care plan under the Care Programme Approach (CPA). The initial assessment and ongoing reviews under the CPA must include an assessment of an individual's housing needs. It is essential that housing authorities liaise closely with social services authorities so that any provision of housing is appropriate to the needs of the individual, and meshes with the social and health care support that may be an essential part of the person's care programme.

**5.28.** This is equally important for young people up to the age of 18. Chapter 9 of the National Service Framework for Children, Young People and Maternity Services published in 2004 makes clear that use of the CPA is also a key marker of good practice for child and adolescent mental health services working with young people with high levels of mental health need.

**[5007]**

## CHAPTER 6: APPLICATIONS, INQUIRIES, DECISIONS AND NOTIFICATIONS

**6.1. This chapter provides guidance on dealing with applications for accommodation or assistance in obtaining accommodation; a housing authority's duty to carry out inquiries (where it has reason to believe an applicant may be homeless or threatened with homelessness); and, following inquiries, an authority's duty to notify an applicant of its decision.**

## APPLICATIONS FOR ASSISTANCE

**6.2.** Under s.184 of the 1996 Act, if a housing authority has reason to believe that a person applying to the authority for accommodation or assistance in obtaining accommodation may be homeless or threatened with homelessness, the authority must make such inquiries as are necessary to satisfy itself whether the applicant is eligible for assistance and if so, whether any duty, and if so what duty, is owed to that person under Part 7 of the 1996 Act. The definitions of "homeless" and "threatened with homelessness" are discussed in Chapter 8.

*Preventing homelessness*

**6.3.** Under s.179, housing authorities have a duty to ensure that advice and information about homelessness and the prevention of homelessness are available free of charge to anyone in their district (see Chapter 2 for further guidance on providing advice and information to prevent homelessness). In many cases early, effective intervention can prevent homelessness occurring. Many people who face the potential loss of their current home will be seeking practical advice and assistance to help them remain in their accommodation or secure alternative accommodation. Some may be seeking to apply for assistance under the homelessness legislation without being aware of other options that could help them to secure accommodation. Authorities should explain the various housing options that are available. These might include:

- advice and assistance (e.g. legal advice or mediation with a landlord) to enable them to remain in their current home;
- assistance (e.g. rent deposit or guarantee) to obtain accommodation in the private rented sector;
- an application for an allocation of long term social housing accommodation through a social housing waiting list or choice-based lettings scheme; or
- advice on how to apply to another social landlord for accommodation.

**6.4.** Housing authorities should ensure that the implications and likely outcomes of the available housing options are made clear to all applicants, including the distinction between having a priority need for accommodation under Part 7 and being in a "reasonable preference" category for an allocation of housing under Part 6. Authorities must not avoid their obligations under Part 7 (especially the duty to make inquiries under s.184), but it is open to them to suggest alternative solutions in cases of potential homelessness where these would be appropriate and acceptable to the applicant.

*Interim duty to accommodate*

**6.5.** If a housing authority has reason to believe that an applicant may be eligible for assistance, homeless and have a priority need, the authority will have **an immediate duty under s.188 to ensure that suitable accommodation is available for the applicant** (and his or her household) pending the completion of the authority's inquiries and its decision as to what duty, if any, is owed to the applicant under Part 7 of the Act. Chapter 7 provides guidance on the interim duty to accommodate. Authorities are reminded that 'having reason to believe' is a lower test than 'being satisfied'.

*Form of the application*

**6.6.** Applications can be made by any adult to any department of the local authority and expressed in any particular form; they need not be expressed as explicitly seeking assistance under Part 7. Applications may also be made by a person acting on behalf of the applicant, for example, by a social worker or solicitor acting in a professional capacity, or by a relative or friend in circumstances where the applicant is unable to make an application themselves.

*Applications to more than one housing authority*

**6.7.** In some cases applicants may apply to more than one housing authority simultaneously and housing authorities will need to be alert to cases where an applicant is doing this. In such cases, where a housing authority has reason to believe that the applicant may be homeless or threatened with homelessness, it may wish to contact the other housing authorities involved, to agree which housing authority will take responsibility for conducting inquiries. Where another housing authority has previously made decisions about an applicant's circumstances, a housing authority considering a fresh application may wish to have regard to those decisions. However, housing authorities should not rely solely on decisions made by another housing authority and will need to make their own inquiries in order to reach an independent decision on whether any duty, and if so which duty, is owed under Part 7. Any arrangements for the discharge of any of their functions by another housing authority must comply with s.101 of the *Local Government Act 1972*.

*Service provision*

**6.8.** A need for accommodation or assistance in obtaining accommodation can arise at anytime. Housing authorities will therefore need to provide access to advice and assistance at all times during normal office hours, and have arrangements in place for 24-hour emergency cover, e.g. by enabling telephone access to an appropriate duty officer. The police and other relevant services should be provided with details of how to access the service outside normal office hours.

**6.9.** In the interests of good administration, it is recommended that housing authorities should give proper consideration to the location of, and accessibility to, advice and information about homelessness and the prevention of homelessness, including the need to ensure privacy during interviews. Details of the service including the opening hours, address, telephone numbers and the 24-hour emergency contact should be well publicised within the housing authority's district.

**6.10.** Housing authorities should provide applicants with a clear and simple explanation of their procedures for handling applications and making decisions. It is recommended that this is provided in written form, for example as a leaflet, as well as orally. In order to ensure advice and assistance are accessible to everyone in the district, it is recommended that information is made available in the main languages spoken in the area, and that for languages less frequently spoken there is access to interpreters. Applicants should be kept informed of the progress of their application and the timescales involved for making a decision on their case. They should also be given a realistic expectation of the assistance to which they may be entitled.

**6.11.** Under s.214, it is an offence for a person, knowingly or recklessly to make a false statement, or knowingly to withhold information, with intent to induce the authority to believe that he or she, or another person, is entitled to accommodation under Part 7. If, before the applicant receives notification of a decision, there is any change of facts material to his or her case, he or she must inform the housing authority of this as soon as possible. Housing authorities must ensure that all applicants are made aware of these obligations and that they are explained in ordinary language. Housing authorities are advised to ensure that the obligations are conveyed sensitively to avoid intimidating applicants.

## INQUIRIES

**6.12.** Under s.184, where a housing authority has reason to believe that an applicant may be homeless or threatened with homelessness, it must make inquiries to satisfy itself whether the applicant is eligible for assistance (see Chapter 9) and, if so, whether any duty and if so what duty is owed to him or her under Part 7. In order to determine this, the authority will need to establish whether the applicant is homeless or threatened with homelessness (see Chapter 8), whether he or she became homeless, or threatened with homelessness, intentionally (see Chapter 11) and whether he or she has a priority need for accommodation (see Chapter 10).

**6.13.** In addition to determining whether an applicant is owed any duty under Part 7, housing authorities are reminded that they have a **power** to provide further assistance to applicants who are eligible for assistance, homeless (or threatened with homelessness) unintentionally and do not have a priority need. Under s.192(3), housing authorities may secure that accommodation is available for applicants who are eligible, unintentionally homeless and do not have a priority need (see Chapter 15 for further guidance). Under s.195(9), housing authorities may take reasonable steps to secure that accommodation does not cease to be available for applicants who are eligible for assistance, unintentionally threatened with homelessness and do not have a priority need for accommodation (see paragraph 14.7 for guidance on steps to secure that accommodation does not cease to be available).

**6.14.** Under s.184(2), housing authorities may also make inquiries to decide whether the applicant has a local connection with another housing authority district in England, Wales or Scotland, but they are not required to do so. The possibility of a referral of an applicant to another housing authority can only arise where the applicant has been accepted as eligible for assistance, unintentionally homeless and having a priority need for accommodation (see Chapter 18 for guidance on local connection and referrals).

**6.15.** The obligation to make inquiries, and satisfy itself whether a duty is owed, rests with the housing authority and it is not for applicants to "prove their case". Applicants should always be given the opportunity to explain their circumstances fully, particularly on matters that could lead to a decision against their interests, for example, a decision that an applicant is intentionally homeless.

**6.16.** Housing authorities should deal with inquiries as quickly as possible, whilst ensuring that they are thorough and, in any particular case, sufficient to enable the housing authority to satisfy itself what duty, if any, is owed or what other assistance can be offered. Housing authorities are obliged to begin inquiries as soon as they have reason to believe that an applicant may be homeless or threatened with homelessness and should aim to carry out an initial interview and preliminary assessment on the day an application is received. An early assessment will be vital to determine whether the housing authority has an immediate duty to secure accommodation under s.188 (see Chapter 7 for guidance on the interim duty to accommodate). Wherever possible, it is recommended that housing authorities aim to complete their inquiries and notify the applicant of their decision within 33 working days of accepting a duty to make inquiries under s.184. In many cases it should be possible for authorities to complete the inquiries significantly earlier.

*Violence*

**6.17.** Under s.177, it is not reasonable for a person to continue to occupy accommodation if it is probable that this will lead to domestic or other violence against him or her, or against a person who normally resides with him or her as a member of his or her family, or any other person who might reasonably be expected to reside with him or her. Violence includes threats of violence from another person which are likely to be carried out. Inquiries into cases where violence is alleged will need careful handling. It is essential that inquiries do not provoke further violence. It is not advisable for the housing authority to approach the alleged perpetrator, since this could generate further violence, and may delay the assessment. Housing authorities may, however, wish to seek information from friends and relatives of the applicant, social services and the police, as appropriate. In some cases, corroborative evidence of actual or threatened violence may not be available, for example, because there were no adult witnesses and/or the applicant was too frightened or ashamed to report incidents to family, friends or the police. In many cases involving violence, the applicant may be in considerable distress and an officer trained in dealing with the particular circumstances should conduct the interview. Applicants should be given the option of being interviewed by an officer of the same sex if they so wish.

**6.18.** In cases where violence is a feature and the applicant may have a local connection elsewhere, the housing authority, in considering whether to notify another housing authority about a possible referral of the case, must be aware that s.198 provides that an applicant cannot be referred to another housing authority if he or she, or any person who might reasonably be expected to reside with him or her, would be at risk of violence in the district of the other housing authority (see Chapter 18 for guidance on referrals to another housing authority).

*Support needs*

**6.19.** 16 and 17 year olds (including lone parents) who apply for housing assistance may also have care and support needs that need to be assessed. The Secretary of State recommends that housing authorities and social services authorities (and the relevant departments within unitary authorities) have arrangements in place for joint consideration of such young people's needs, whether the application is made initially to the housing department or social services department. See Chapter 12 for further guidance on 16 and 17 year olds.

**Assistance from another authority or body**

**6.20.** Under s. 213, a housing authority may request another relevant housing authority or body to assist them in the discharge of their functions under Part 7. In such cases the authority or body must co-operate in rendering such assistance in the discharge of the functions to which the request relates as is reasonable in the circumstances. For example, a housing authority may request another housing authority to co-operate in providing information about a previous application. See paragraph 5.10 for further guidance on s.213.

**DECISIONS/NOTIFICATIONS**

**6.21.** When a housing authority has completed its inquiries under s.184 it must notify the applicant in writing of its decision on the case. Where the decision is against the applicant's interests, e.g. a decision that he or she is ineligible for assistance, not homeless, not in priority need or homeless intentionally, the notification must explain clearly and fully the reasons for the decision. If the housing authority has decided that the conditions for referring the applicant's homelessness case to another housing authority have been met, they must notify the applicant of this and give their reasons for doing so.

**6.22.** All notifications must inform applicants of their right to request a review of the housing authority's decision and the time within which such a request must be made. At this stage, it is also recommended that housing authorities explain the review procedures. (See Chapter 19 for guidance on reviews of decisions and appeals to the county court).

**6.23.** It will be important to ensure that the applicant fully understands the decision and the nature of any housing duty that is owed. In cases where the applicant may have difficulty understanding the implications of the decision, it is recommended that housing authorities consider arranging for a member of staff to provide and explain the notification in person.

**6.24.** Under s.193(3A), where the housing authority accepts a duty to secure accommodation for an applicant under s.193(2), they must give the applicant a copy of the statement included in their allocation scheme of the housing authority's policy on offering people a choice of housing or the opportunity to express their preferences about the accommodation to be allocated to them. This statement is required to be included in the allocation scheme under s.167(1A).

**6.25.** Section 184(6) provides that where a notification is not received by an applicant, it can be treated as having been given to him or her, if it is made available at the housing authority's office for a reasonable period that would allow it to be collected by the applicant or by someone acting on his or her behalf.

## WITHDRAWN APPLICATIONS

**6.26.** It is recommended that housing authorities have procedures in place for dealing with applications that are withdrawn or where someone fails to maintain contact with the housing authority after making an application. The Secretary of State considers that it would be reasonable to consider an application closed where there has been no contact with the applicant for three months or longer. Any further approach from the applicant after this time may need to be considered as a fresh application. Where an applicant renews contact within three months the housing authority will need to consider any change of circumstances that may affect the application.

## FURTHER APPLICATIONS

**6.27.** There is no period of disqualification if someone wants to make a fresh application. Where a person whose application has been previously considered and determined under Part 7 makes a fresh application, the authority will need to decide whether there are any new facts in the fresh application which render it different from the earlier application. If no new facts are revealed, or any new facts are of a trivial nature, the authority would not be required to consider the new application. However, where the fresh application does reveal substantive new facts, the authority must treat the fresh application in the same way as it would any other application for accommodation or assistance in obtaining accommodation. Therefore, if the authority has reason to believe that the person is homeless, or threatened with homelessness, the authority should make inquiries under s.184 and decide whether any duty is owed under s.188(1).

[5008]

## CHAPTER 7: INTERIM DUTY TO ACCOMMODATE

**7.1.** This chapter provides guidance on housing authorities' interim duty to secure that accommodation is available for an applicant if they have reason to believe that the applicant may be homeless, eligible for assistance and has a priority need.

**7.2.** Section 188(1) imposes an interim duty on housing authorities to secure that accommodation is available for an applicant (and his or her household) pending their decision as to what duty, if any, is owed to the applicant under Part 7 of the Act if they have reason to believe that the applicant may:
a)     be homeless,
b)     be eligible for assistance, and
c)     have a priority need.

**7.3.** The threshold for the duty is low as the local authority only has to have a reason to believe that the applicant **may** be homeless, eligible for assistance and have a priority need. (See paragraph 6.5 for guidance on the "reason to believe" test.)

**7.4.** The s.188(1) duty applies even where the authority considers the applicant may not have a local connection with their district and may have one with the district of another housing authority (s.188(2)). Applicants cannot be referred to another housing authority unless the housing authority dealing with the application is satisfied that s.193 applies (i.e. the applicant is eligible for assistance, unintentionally homeless and has a priority need). (See Chapter 18 for guidance on referrals to other housing authorities.)

## SUITABILITY OF ACCOMMODATION

**7.5.** The accommodation provided under s.188(1) must be suitable for the applicant and his or her household and the suitability requirements under s.206(1) and s.210(1) apply (see Chapter 17 for guidance on the suitability of accommodation). The applicant does not have the right to ask for a review of the housing authority's decision as to the suitability of accommodation secured under the interim duty, but housing authorities are reminded that such decisions could be subject to judicial review.

**7.6.** Housing authorities should avoid using Bed &Breakfast (B&B) accommodation wherever possible. Where B&B accommodation has been used in an emergency situation, applicants should be moved to more suitable accommodation as soon as possible. The *Homelessness (Suitability of Accommodation) (England) Order 2003* provides that B&B accommodation is not suitable accommodation for families with children and households that include a pregnant woman unless there is no alternative accommodation available and then only for a maximum of six weeks.

## DISCHARGING THE INTERIM DUTY

**7.7.** Where the s.188(1) interim duty is being discharged, inquiries should be completed as quickly as possible to minimise uncertainty for the applicant and the period for which accommodation needs to be secured by the housing authority. (See Chapter 6 for guidance on inquiries).

**7.8.** Housing authorities can discharge their interim duty to secure accommodation by providing their own accommodation or by arranging that it is provided by some other person, or by providing advice and assistance so that it will be provided by some other person. (See Chapter 16 for more information on discharging the duty to secure accommodation).

## ENDING THE INTERIM DUTY

**7.9.** The s.188(1) interim duty ends once the housing authority has notified the applicant of its decision as to what duty, if any, is owed to him or her under Part 7, even if the applicant requests a review of the decision.

**7.10.** Where, having completed their inquiries, the housing authority is satisfied that they are under no further duty to secure accommodation, they should give the applicant a reasonable period of notice to vacate the accommodation to enable him or her to make alternative accommodation arrangements for him/herself. The time allowed should be reasonable when judged against the circumstances of the applicant. Housing authorities should give the applicant time to consider whether to request a review of their decision and, if a review is requested, will need to consider whether to exercise their discretionary power under s.188(3) to secure that accommodation is available (see paragraph 7.13 below).

**7.11.** It has been established that, as a general rule, accommodation provided pending inquiries under s.184 does not create a tenancy or a licence under the *Protection from Eviction Act 1977*. The courts have applied this principle in cases where the accommodation provided was B&B accommodation in a hotel and where it was a self-contained flat. Consequently, where this general rule applies, housing authorities are required only to provide an applicant with reasonable notice to vacate accommodation provided under the interim duty, and do not need to apply for a possession order from the court. Authorities should note, however, that this general rule may be displaced by an agreement between the housing authority and the applicant, or if the occupation of the accommodation is allowed to continue on more than a transient basis.

**7.12.** In cases involving applicants who have children under 18 where the housing authority are satisfied that the applicant is ineligible for assistance, the housing authority must alert the social services authority, or social services department, as appropriate, to the case (see Chapter 13 for further guidance on co-operation with social services). Applicants should be invited to consent to social services being notified of the case, but in certain circumstances, for example where the housing authority are concerned about the welfare of the child, they should disclose information about the case even where consent has not been given.

## ACCOMMODATION PENDING A REVIEW

**7.13.** Where a review of a decision of a housing authority is requested under s.202, although there is no duty under s.188(1), under s.188(3) the housing authority has a discretionary power to provide accommodation pending the outcome of the review. Failure to consider exercising this discretionary power could be the subject of challenge by judicial review proceedings. Housing authorities are reminded that applicants have 21 days in which to request a review of a decision. (See Chapter 19 for guidance on review of decisions and Chapter 15 for guidance on powers to accommodate pending a review).

**[5009]**

## CHAPTER 8: HOMELESS OR THREATENED WITH HOMELESSNESS

**8.1.** This chapter provides guidance on how to determine whether a person is "homeless" or "threatened with homelessness" for the purposes of Part 7.

**8.2.** Under s.184 of the 1996 Act, if a housing authority has reason to believe that a person applying to the housing authority for accommodation, or assistance in obtaining accommodation, may be homeless or threatened with homelessness, the housing authority must make inquiries to satisfy itself whether the applicant is eligible for assistance and if so, whether a duty is owed to that person under Part 7 of the 1996 Act (see Chapter 6 for guidance on applications for assistance).

## THREATENED WITH HOMELESSNESS

**8.3.** Under s.175(4), a person is "threatened with homelessness" if he or she is likely to become homeless within 28 days. In many cases, effective intervention can enable homelessness to be prevented or the loss of the current home to be delayed sufficiently to allow for a planned move. The Secretary of State considers that housing authorities should take steps to prevent homelessness wherever possible, offering a broad range of advice and assistance for those in housing need. Authorities should not wait until homelessness is a likelihood or is imminent before providing advice and assistance. (See Chapter 2 for guidance on preventing homelessness).

## HOMELESS

**8.4.** There are a number of different factors that determine whether a person is homeless. Under s.175, a person is homeless if he or she has no accommodation in the UK or elsewhere which is available for his or her occupation and which that person has a legal right to occupy. A person is also homeless if he or she has accommodation but cannot secure entry to it, or the accommodation is a moveable structure, vehicle or vessel designed or adapted for human habitation (such as a caravan or house boat) and there is no place where it can be placed in order to provide accommodation. A person who has accommodation is to be treated as homeless where it would not be reasonable for him or her to continue to occupy that accommodation.

*Available for occupation*

**8.5.** Section 176 provides that accommodation shall be treated as available for a person's occupation only if it is available for occupation by him or her together with:
   i)    any other person who normally resides with him or her as a member of the family, or
   ii)   any other person who might reasonably be expected to reside with him or her.

The first group covers those members of the family who normally reside with the applicant. The phrase "as a member of the family" although not defined, will include those with close blood or marital relationships and cohabiting partners (including same sex partners), and, where such a person is an established member of the household, the accommodation must provide for him or her as well. The second group relates to any other person, and includes those who may not have been living as part of the household at the time of the application, but whom it would be reasonable to expect to live with the applicant as part of his or her household. Persons in the second group might include a companion for an elderly or disabled person, or children who are being fostered by the applicant or a member of his or her family. The second group will also include those members of the family who were not living as part of the household at the time of the application but who nonetheless might reasonably be expected to form part of it.

**8.6.** It is for the housing authority to assess whether any other person might reasonably be expected to live with the applicant and there will be a range of situations that the authority will need to consider. Persons who would normally live with the applicant but who are unable to do so because there is no accommodation in which they can all live together should be included in the assessment. When dealing with a family which has split up, housing authorities will need to take a decision as to which members of the family normally reside, or might be expected to reside, with the applicant. A court may have made a residence order indicating with whom the children are to live, but in many cases it will be a matter of agreement between the parents and a court will not have been involved.

*Legal right to occupy accommodation*

**8.7.** Under s.175(1), a person is homeless if he or she has no accommodation which he or she can legally occupy by virtue of:
   i)    an interest in it (e.g. as an owner, lessee or tenant) or by virtue of a court order;
   ii)   an express or implied licence to occupy it (e.g. as a lodger, as an employee with a service occupancy, or when living with a relative); or
   iii)  any enactment or rule of law giving him or her the right to remain in occupation or restricting the right of another person to recover possession (e.g. a person retaining possession as a statutory tenant under the Rent Acts where that person's contractual rights to occupy have expired or been terminated).

**8.8.** A person who has been occupying accommodation as a licensee whose licence has been terminated (and who does not have any other accommodation available for his or her occupation) is homeless because he or she no longer has a legal right to continue to occupy, despite the fact that that person may continue to occupy but as a trespasser. This may include, for example:
   i)    those required to leave hostels or hospitals; or

ii)  former employees occupying premises under a service occupancy which is dependent upon contracts of employment which have ended.

## People asked to leave accommodation by family or friends

**8.9.** Some applicants may have been asked to leave their current accommodation by family or friends with whom they have been living. In such cases, the housing authority will need to consider carefully whether the applicant's licence to occupy the accommodation has in fact been revoked. Housing authorities may need to interview the parents or friends to establish whether they are genuinely revoking the licence to occupy and rendering the applicants homeless. Authorities are encouraged to be sensitive to situations where parents or carers may have been providing a home for a family member with support needs (for example a person with learning difficulties) for a number of years and who are genuinely finding it difficult to continue with that arrangement, but are reluctant to revoke their licence to occupy formally until alternative accommodation can be secured.

**8.10.** In some cases the applicant may be unable to stay in his or her accommodation and in others there may be scope for preventing or postponing homelessness, and providing the applicant with an opportunity to plan their future accommodation and pursue various housing options with assistance from the housing authority. However, housing authorities will need to be sensitive to the possibility that for some applicants it may not be safe for them to remain in, or return to, their home because of a risk of violence or abuse.

**8.11.** In areas of high demand for affordable housing, people living with family and friends may have genuine difficulties in finding alternative accommodation that can lead to friction and disputes within their current home, culminating in a threat of homelessness. In some cases external support, or the promise of assistance with alternative housing, may help to reduce tension and prevent homelessness. The use of family mediation services may assist here.

**8.12.** Housing authorities will also need to be alert to the possibility of collusion where family or friends agree to revoke a licence to occupy accommodation as part of an arrangement whose purpose is to enable the applicant to be entitled to assistance under Part 7. Some parents and children, for example, may seek to take advantage of the fact that 16 and 17 year old applicants have a priority need for accommodation (see also Chapter 11 on intentional homelessness).

## 16 and 17 year olds

**8.13.** The Secretary of State considers that, generally, it will be in the best interests of 16 and 17 year olds to live in the family home, unless it would be unsafe or unsuitable for them to do so because they would be at risk of violence or abuse. See Chapter 12 for further guidance on 16 and 17 year olds.

## Tenant given notice

**8.14.** With certain exceptions, a person who has been occupying accommodation as a tenant and who has received a valid notice to quit, or notice that the landlord requires possession of the accommodation, would have the right to remain in occupation until a warrant for possession was executed (following the granting of an order for possession by the court). The exceptions are tenants with resident landlords and certain other tenants who do not benefit from the *Protection from Eviction Act 1977*. **However, authorities should note that the fact that a tenant has a right to remain in occupation does not necessarily mean that he or she is not homeless.** In assessing whether an applicant is homeless in cases where he or she is a tenant who has a right to remain in occupation pending execution of a warrant for possession, the housing authority will also need to consider whether it would be reasonable for him or her to continue to occupy the accommodation in the circumstances (see paragraphs 8.30–8.32 below).

**8.15.** Some tenants may face having to leave their accommodation because their landlord has defaulted on the mortgage of the property they rent. Where a mortgage lender starts possession proceedings, the lender is obliged to give written notice of the proceedings to the occupiers of the property before an order for possession is granted. The notice must be given after issue of the possession summons and at least 14 days before the court hearing. As for tenants given notice that the landlord requires possession of the accommodation (see paragraph 8.14 above), authorities will need to consider whether it would be reasonable for a tenant to continue to occupy the accommodation after receiving notice of possession proceedings from the lender.

*Inability to secure entry to accommodation*

**8.16.** Under s.175(2), a person is homeless if he or she has a legal entitlement to accommodation, but is unable to secure entry to it, for example:

- those who have been evicted illegally, or
- those whose accommodation is being occupied illegally by squatters.

Although legal remedies may be available to the applicant to regain possession of th accommodation, housing authorities cannot refuse to assist while he or she is actually hom

*Accommodation consisting of a moveable structure*

**8.17.** Section 175(2)(b) provides that a person is homeless if he or she has accommodation available for his or her occupation which is a moveable structure, vehicle or vessel designed or adapted for human habitation (e.g. a caravan or houseboat), and there is nowhere that he or she is entitled or permitted to place it and reside in it. The site or mooring for the moveable structure need not be permanent in order to avoid homelessness. In many cases the nature of the structure may reflect the itinerant lifestyle of the applicant, who may not be looking for a permanent site but somewhere to park or moor on a temporary basis.

*Reasonable to continue to occupy*

**8.18.** Section 175(3) provides that a person shall not be treated as having accommodation unless it is accommodation which it would be reasonable for him or her to continue to occupy. There are a number of provisions relating to whether or not it is reasonable for someone to continue to occupy accommodation and these are discussed below. There is no simple test of reasonableness. It is for the housing authority to make a judgement on the facts of each case, taking into account the circumstances of the applicant.

## Domestic violence or other violence

**8.19.** Section 177(1) provides that it is not reasonable for a person to continue to occupy accommodation if it is probable that this will lead to domestic violence or other violence against:

i)      the applicant;
ii)     a person who normally resides as a member of the applicant's family; or
iii)    any other person who might reasonably be expected to reside with the applicant.

Section 177(1A) provides that violence means violence from another person or threats of violence from another person which are likely to be carried out. Domestic violence is violence from a person who is associated with the victim and also includes threats of violence which are likely to be carried out. Domestic violence is not confined to instances within the home but extends to violence outside the home.

**8.20.** Section 178 provides that, for the purposes of defining domestic violence, a person is associated with another if:

(a)     they are, or have been, married to each other;
(b)     they are or have been civil partners of each other;
(c)     they are, or have been, cohabitants (including same sex partners);
(d)     they live, or have lived, in the same household;
(e)     they are relatives, i.e. father, mother, stepfather, stepmother, son, daughter, stepson, stepdaughter, grandmother, grandfather, grandson, granddaughter, brother, sister, uncle, aunt, niece or nephew (whether of full blood, half blood or by affinity) of that person or of that person's spouse or former spouse. A person is also included if he or she would fall into any of these categories in relation to cohabitees or former cohabitees if they were married to each other;
(f)     they have agreed to marry each other whether or not that agreement has been terminated;
(g)     they have entered into a civil partnership agreement between them whether or not that agreement has been terminated;
(h)     in relation to a child, each of them is a parent of the child or has, or has had, parental responsibility for the child (within the meaning of the Children Act 1989). A child is a person under 18 years of age;
(i)     if a child has been adopted or freed for adoption (s.16(1) *Adoption Act 1976*), two persons are also associated if one is the natural parent or grandparent of the child and the other is the child of a person who has become the parent by virtue of an adoption order (s.72(1) *Adoption Act 1976*) or has applied for an adoption order or someone with whom the child has been placed for adoption.

**8.21.** The Secretary of State considers that the term 'violence' should not be given a restrictive meaning, and that 'domestic violence' should be understood to include threatening behaviour, violence or abuse (psychological, physical, sexual, financial or emotional) between persons who are, or have been, intimate partners, family members or members of the same household, regardless of gender or sexuality.

**8.22.** An assessment of the likelihood of a threat of violence being carried out should not be based on whether there has been actual violence in the past. An assessment must be based on the facts of the case and devoid of any value judgements about what an applicant should or should not do, or should or should not have done, to mitigate the risk of any violence (e.g. seek police help or apply for an injunction against the perpetrator). Inquiries into cases where violence is alleged will need careful handling. See Chapter 6 for further guidance.

**8.23.** In cases involving violence, housing authorities may wish to inform applicants of the option of seeking an injunction, but should make clear that there is no obligation on the applicant to do so. Where applicants wish to pursue this option, it is advisable that they obtain independent advice as an injunction may be ill-advised in some circumstances. Housing authorities should recognise that injunctions ordering a person not to molest, or enter the home of, an applicant may not be effective in deterring perpetrators from carrying out further violence or incursions, and applicants may not have confidence in their effectiveness. Consequently, applicants should not be expected to return home on the strength of an injunction. To ensure applicants who have experienced actual or threatened violence get the support they need, authorities should inform them of appropriate organisations in the area such as agencies offering counselling and support as well as specialist advice.

**8.24.** When dealing with cases involving violence, or threat of violence, from outside the home, housing authorities should consider the option of improving the security of the applicant's home to enable him or her to continue to live there safely, where that is an option that the applicant wishes to pursue. In some cases, immediate action to improve security within the victim's home may prevent homelessness. A fast response combined with support from the housing authority, police and the voluntary sector may provide a victim with the confidence to remain in their home. When dealing with domestic violence within the home, where the authority is the landlord, housing authorities should consider the scope for evicting the perpetrator and allowing the victim to remain in their home. **However, where there would be a probability of violence if the applicant continued to occupy his or her present accommodation, the housing authority must treat the applicant as homeless and should not expect him or her to remain in, or return to, the accommodation. In all cases involving violence the safety of the applicant and his or her household should be the primary consideration at all stages of decision making as to whether or not the applicant remains in their own home.**

**8.25.** The effectiveness of housing authorities' services to assist victims of domestic violence and prevent further domestic violence is measured by Best Value Performance Indicator BVPI 225. Guidance on BVPI 225 is available at www.communities.gov.uk.

### General housing circumstances in the district

**8.26.** Section 177(2) provides that, in determining whether it is reasonable for a person to continue to occupy accommodation, housing authorities may have regard to the general housing circumstances prevailing in the housing authority's district.

**8.27.** This would apply, for example, where it was suggested that an applicant was homeless because of poor physical conditions in his or her current home. In such cases it would be open to the authority to consider whether the condition of the property was so bad in comparison with other accommodation in the district that it would not be reasonable to expect someone to continue to live there.

**8.28.** Circumstances where an applicant may be homeless as a result of his or her accommodation being overcrowded should also be considered in relation to the general housing circumstances in the district. Statutory overcrowding, within the meaning of Part 10 of the *Housing Act 1985*, may not by itself be sufficient to determine reasonableness, but it can be a contributory factor if there are other factors which suggest unreasonableness.

### Affordability

**8.29.** One factor that **must** be considered in all cases is affordability. The *Homelessness (Suitability of Accommodation) Order 1996* (SI 1996 No.3204) requires the housing authority to consider the affordability of the accommodation for the applicant. The Order specifies, among other things, that in determining whether it would be (or would have been) reasonable for a person to continue to occupy accommodation, a housing authority must take into account whether the accommodation is affordable for him or her and must, in particular, take account of:

    (a)     the financial resources available to him or her;
    (b)     the costs in respect of the accommodation;
    (c)     maintenance payments (to a spouse, former spouse or in respect of a child); and
    (d)     his or her reasonable living expenses.

### Tenant given notice of intention to recover possession

**8.30.** In cases where the applicant has been occupying accommodation as a tenant and has received a valid notice to quit, or a notice that the landlord intends to recover possession, housing authorities should consider the scope for preventing homelessness through consulting the landlord at an early stage to explore the possibility of the tenancy being allowed to continue or the tenant being allowed to remain for a reasonable period to provide an opportunity for alternative accommodation to be found. If the landlord is not persuaded to agree, the authority will need to consider whether it would be reasonable for the applicant to continue to occupy the accommodation once the valid notice has expired.

**8.31.** In determining whether it would be reasonable for an applicant to continue to occupy accommodation, the housing authority will need to consider all the factors relevant to the case and decide the weight that individual factors should attract. As well as the factors set out elsewhere in this chapter, other factors which may be relevant include the general cost to the housing authority, the position of the tenant, the position of the landlord, the likelihood that the landlord will actually proceed with possession proceedings, and the burden on the courts of unnecessary proceedings where there is no defence to a possession claim (see paragraphs 8.14 and 8.15 above for guidance on the right to occupy where notice of possession proceedings has been given).

**8.32.** Each case must be decided on its facts, so **housing authorities should not adopt a general policy of accepting – or refusing to accept – applicants as homeless or threatened with homelessness when they are threatened with eviction but a court has not yet made an order for possession or issued a warrant of execution**. In any case where a housing authority decides that it would be reasonable for an applicant to continue to occupy their accommodation after a valid notice has expired – and therefore decides that he or she is not yet homeless or threatened with homelessness – that decision will need to be based on sound reasons which should be made clear to the applicant in writing (see Chapter 6 for guidance on housing authorities' duties to inform applicants of their decisions). **The Secretary of State considers that where a person applies for accommodation or assistance in obtaining accommodation, and:**

(a)     **the person is an assured shorthold tenant who has received proper notice in accordance with s.21 of the** *Housing Act 1988*;
(b)     **the housing authority is satisfied that the landlord intends to seek possession; and**
(c)     **there would be no defence to an application for a possession order;**

**then it is unlikely to be reasonable for the applicant to continue to occupy the accommodation beyond the date given in the s.21 notice, unless the housing authority is taking steps to persuade the landlord to withdraw the notice or allow the tenant to continue to occupy the accommodation for a reasonable period to provide an opportunity for alternative accommodation to be found.**

**8.32a.** Authorities are reminded that an applicant cannot be treated as intentionally homeless unless it would have been reasonable for him or her to have continued to occupy the accommodation. Guidance on 'intentional homelessness' is provided in Chapter 11.

**Former armed forces personnel required to leave service accommodation**

**8.33.** The Ministry of Defence recognises that housing authorities will need to be satisfied that entitlement to occupy service accommodation will end on a certain date, in order to determine whether applicants who are service personnel and who are approaching their date of discharge may be homeless or threatened with homelessness. For this purpose, the MOD issues a *Certificate of Cessation of Entitlement to Occupy Service Living Accommodation* six months before discharge (see examples at Annexes 14 and 15). These certificates indicate the date on which entitlement to occupy service accommodation ends, and the Secretary of State considers that housing authorities should not insist upon a court order for possession to establish that entitlement to occupy has ended. Authorities should take advantage of the six-month period of notice of discharge to ensure that service personnel receive timely and comprehensive advice on the housing options available to them when they leave the armed forces.

**Other relevant factors**

**8.34.** Other factors which may be relevant in determining whether it would be reasonable for an applicant to continue to occupy accommodation include:

**physical characteristics**: it would not be reasonable for an applicant to continue to occupy accommodation if the physical characteristics of the accommodation were unsuitable for the applicant because, for example, he or she was a wheelchair user and access was limited.

**type of accommodation**: some types of accommodation, for example women's refuges, direct access hostels, and night shelters are intended to provide very short-term, temporary accommodation in a crisis and it should not be regarded as reasonable to continue to occupy such accommodation in the medium and longer-term.

**people fleeing harassment**: in some cases severe harassment may fall short of actual violence or threats of violence likely to be carried out. Housing authorities should consider carefully whether it would be, or would have been, reasonable for an applicant to continue to occupy accommodation in circumstances where they have fled, or are seeking to leave, their home because of non-violent forms of harassment, for example verbal abuse or damage to property. Careful consideration should be given to applicants who may be at risk of witness intimidation. In some criminal cases the police may provide alternative accommodation for witnesses, but usually this will apply for the duration of the trial only. Witnesses may have had to give up their home or may feel unable to return to it when the trial has finished.

This is not an exhaustive list and authorities will need to take account of all relevant factors when considering whether it is reasonable for an applicant to continue to occupy accommodation.

## CHAPTER 9: ELIGIBILITY FOR ASSISTANCE

### GENERAL

**9.1.** Part 7 of the 1996 Act includes provisions that make certain persons from abroad ineligible for housing assistance. Housing authorities will therefore need to satisfy themselves that applicants are eligible before providing housing assistance. The provisions on eligibility are complex and housing authorities will need to ensure that they have procedures in place to carry out appropriate checks on housing applicants.

**9.2.** Housing authorities should ensure that staff who are required to screen housing applicants about eligibility for assistance are given training in the complexities of the housing provisions, the housing authority's duties and responsibilities under the race relations legislation and how to deal with applicants in a sensitive manner.

**9.3.** Local authorities are reminded that Schedule 3 to the *Nationality, Immigration and Asylum Act 2002* provides that certain persons shall not be eligible for support or assistance provided through the exercise of local housing authorities' powers to secure accommodation pending a review (s.188(3)) or pending an appeal to the county court (s.204(4)). See paragraph 9.22 below.

### PERSONS FROM ABROAD

**9.4.** A person will not be eligible for assistance under Part 7 if he or she is a person from abroad who is ineligible for housing assistance under s.185 of the 1996 Act. There are two categories of 'person from abroad' for the purposes s.185:

(i)     *a person subject to immigration control* – such a person is not eligible for housing assistance unless he or she comes within a class prescribed in regulations made by the Secretary of State, and

(ii)    *a person from abroad other than a person subject to immigration control* – the Secretary of State can make regulations to provide for other descriptions of person from abroad who, although they are not subject to immigration control, are to be treated as ineligible for housing assistance.

**9.5.** The regulations that set out which classes of persons from abroad are eligible or ineligible for housing assistance are the *Allocation of Housing and Homelessness (Eligibility) (England) Regulations 2006* (SI 2006 No.1294) ("the Eligibility Regulations"). Persons subject to immigration control are not eligible for housing assistance unless they fall within a class of persons prescribed in **regulation 5** of the Eligibility Regulations. Persons who are not subject to immigration control will be eligible for housing assistance unless they fall within a description of persons who are to be treated as persons from abroad who are ineligible for assistance by virtue of **regulation 6** of the Eligibility Regulations.

### PERSONS SUBJECT TO IMMIGRATION CONTROL

**9.6.** The term 'person subject to immigration control' is defined in s.13(2) of the *Asylum and Immigration Act 1996* as a person who requires leave to enter or remain in the United Kingdom (whether or not such leave has been given).

**9.7.** Only the following categories of person do **not** require leave to enter or remain in the UK:

(i)     British citizens;

(ii)    certain Commonwealth citizens with a right of abode in the UK;

(iii)   citizens of an EEA country, ("EEA nationals") and their family members, who have a right to reside in the UK that derives from EC law. The question of whether an EEA national (or family member) has a particular right to reside in the UK (or in another Member State e.g. the Republic of Ireland) will depend on the circumstances, particularly the economic status of the EEA national (e.g. whether he or she is a worker, self-employed, a student, or economically inactive etc.). See Annex 12 for further guidance on rights to reside;

(iv)   persons who are exempt from immigration control under the Immigration Acts, including diplomats and their family members based in the United Kingdom, and some military personnel.

For the purposes of this guidance, "EEA nationals" means nationals of any of the EU member states (excluding the UK), and nationals of Iceland, Norway, Liechtenstein and Switzerland.

**9.8.** Any person who **does not** fall within one of the 4 categories in paragraph 9.7 above will be a person subject to immigration control and will be ineligible for housing assistance unless they fall within a class of persons prescribed by regulation 5 of the Eligibility Regulations (see paragraph 9.10 below).

**9.9.** If there is any uncertainty about an applicant's immigration status, it is recommended that authorities contact the Home Office Immigration and Nationality Directorate, using the procedures set out in Annex 8. In some circumstances, local authorities may be under a duty to contact the Immigration and Nationality Directorate (see paragraph 9.24).

*Persons subject to immigration control who are eligible for housing assistance*

**9.10.** Generally, persons subject to immigration control are not eligible for housing assistance. However, by virtue of regulation 5 of the Eligibility Regulations, the following classes of person subject to immigration control are eligible for housing assistance:

(i)     *a person granted refugee status*: a person is granted refugee status when his or her request for asylum is accepted. Persons granted refugee status are granted 5 years' limited leave to remain in the UK. (Prior to 30 August 2005, it was the policy to provide immediate settlement (indefinite leave to remain) for persons granted refugee status.)

(ii)    *a person granted exceptional leave to enter or remain in the UK without condition that they and any dependants should make no recourse to public funds*: this status is granted to persons, including some persons whose claim for asylum has been refused, for a limited period where there are compelling humanitarian and/or compassionate circumstances for allowing them to stay. However, if leave was granted on condition that the applicant and any dependants should not be a charge on public funds, the applicant will not be eligible for homelessness assistance. Since April 2003, exceptional leave to remain (which is granted at the Secretary of State's discretion outside the Immigration Rules) has taken the form of either humanitarian protection or discretionary leave.

(iii)   *a person with current leave to enter or remain in the UK with no condition or limitation, and who is habitually resident in the UK, the Channel Islands, the Isle of Man or the Republic of Ireland*: such a person will have indefinite leave to enter (ILE) or remain (ILR) and will be regarded as having settled status. However, where ILE or ILR status was granted as a result of an undertaking that a sponsor would be responsible for the applicant's maintenance and accommodation, the person must have been resident in the UK, the Channel Islands, the Isle of Man or the Republic of Ireland for five years since the date of entry – or the date of the sponsorship undertaking, whichever is later – for the applicant to be eligible. Where a sponsor has (or, if there was more than one sponsor, all of the sponsors have) died within the first five years, the applicant will be eligible for housing assistance;

(iv)    *a person who left the territory of Montserrat after 1 November 1995 because of the effect on that territory of a volcanic eruption.* (See paragraph 9.19 below.)

*Asylum seekers*

**9.11.** Asylum seekers will almost always be persons subject to immigration control.

**Asylum seekers who are persons subject to immigration control and whose claim for asylum was made after 2 April 2000 are not eligible for assistance under Part 7 of the 1996 Act.** Some asylum seekers whose claim for asylum was made before 3 April 2000 would be eligible for assistance under Part 7 in certain limited circumstances, but the number of persons who fall in these classes is likely to be very small (if any). Annex 9 provides guidance on the limited categories of asylum seekers eligible for assistance under Part 7 of the 1996 Act.

**9.12.** Under s.186 of the 1996 Act, an asylum seeker who would otherwise be eligible for assistance under the Eligibility Regulations, will be ineligible, if he or she has any accommodation available in the UK for his or her occupation, however temporary.

## OTHER PERSONS FROM ABROAD WHO MAY BE INELIGIBLE FOR ASSISTANCE

**9.13.** By virtue of regulation 6 of the Eligibility Regulations, a person who is not subject to immigration control and who falls within one of the following descriptions of persons is to be treated as a person from abroad who is ineligible for housing assistance:

(i)     a person who is not habitually resident in the UK, the Channel Islands, the Isle of Man or the Republic of Ireland (subject to certain exceptions – see paragraph 9.14 below);

(ii)    a person whose only right to reside in the UK is derived from his status as a jobseeker (or his status as the family member of a jobseeker). For this purpose, "jobseeker" has the same meaning as for the purpose of regulation 6(1)(a) of the *Immigration (European Economic Area) Regulations 2006* (SI 2006 No. 1003) ("the EEA Regulations");

(iii)   a person whose only right to reside in the UK is an initial right to reside for a period not exceeding three months under regulation 13 of the EEA Regulations;

(iv)    a person whose only right to reside in the Channel Islands, the Isle of Man or the Republic of Ireland is a right equivalent to one of the rights mentioned in (ii) or (iii) above and which is derived from the Treaty establishing the European Community ("the EC Treaty").

See Annex 12 for guidance on rights to reside in the UK derived from EC law.

*Persons exempted from the requirement to be habitually resident*

**9.14.** Certain persons from abroad (not being persons subject to immigration control) will be eligible for housing assistance even though they are not habitually resident in the UK, the Channel Islands, the Isle of Man or the Republic of Ireland. Such a person will be eligible for assistance even if not habitually resident, if he or she is:

(a)    an EEA national who is in the UK as a worker (which has the same meaning as it does for the purposes of regulation 6(1) of the EEA Regulations);

(b)    an EEA national who is in the UK as a self-employed person (which has the same meaning as it does for the purposes of regulation 6(1) of the EEA Regulations);

(c)    a person who is an accession state worker requiring registration who is treated as a worker for the purposes of regulation 6(1) of the EEA Regulations, pursuant to the *Accession (Immigration and Worker Registration) Regulations 2004*, as amended;

(d)    a person who is a family member of a person referred to in (a) to (c) above;

(e)    a person with a right to reside permanently in the UK by virtue of regulation 15(c), (d) or (e) of the EEA Regulations (see Annex 12);

(f)    a person who left Montserrat after 1 November 1995 because of the effect of volcanic activity there (see paragraph 9.19 below);

(g)    a person who is in the UK as a result of his or her deportation, expulsion or other removal by compulsion of law from another country to the UK (see paragraph 9.21 below).

On (a) and (b), authorities should note that a person who is no longer working or no longer in self-employment will retain his or her status as a worker or self-employed person in certain circumstances. (See Annex 12 for further guidance.) On (c), authorities should note that accession state workers requiring registration will generally only be treated as a worker when they are actually working and will not retain 'worker' status in the circumstances referred to above. (See annexes 12 and 13 for further guidance.) On (d), authorities should note that 'family member' does not include a person who is an extended family member who is treated as a family member by virtue of regulation 7(3) of the EEA Regulations (see Annex 12 for further guidance).

### The habitual residence test

**9.15.**    The term "habitual residence" is intended to convey a degree of permanence in the person's residence in the UK, the Channel Islands, the Isle of Man or the Republic of Ireland; it implies an association between the individual and the place of residence and relies substantially on fact.

**9.16.**    The Secretary of State considers that it is likely that applicants who have been resident in the UK, Channel Islands, the Isle of Man or the Republic of Ireland continuously during the 2-year period prior to their housing application will be habitually resident. In such cases, therefore, housing authorities may consider it unnecessary to make further enquiries to determine whether the person is habitually resident, unless there are other circumstances that need to be taken into account. A period of continuous residence in the UK, Channel Islands, the Isle of Man or the Republic of Ireland might include periods of temporary absence, e.g. visits abroad for holidays or to visit relatives. Where two years' continuous residency has not been established, housing authorities will need to conduct further enquiries to determine whether the applicant is habitually resident.

**9.17.**    A person will not generally be habitually resident anywhere unless he or she has taken up residence and lived there for a period. There will be cases where the person concerned is not coming to the UK for the first time, and is resuming a previous period of habitual residence.

**9.18.**    Annex 10 provides guidance on the factors that a housing authority should consider in determining whether an applicant is habitually resident.

### Persons from Montserrat

**9.19.**    The classes of persons (not being persons subject to immigration control) who are not required to be habitually resident in order to be eligible for assistance under Part 7 include a person who left Montserrat after 1 November 1995 because of the effect of volcanic activity there.

**9.20.**    On 21 May 2002 most British overseas territories citizens, including those from Montserrat, became British Citizens. Since their new EU-style passport will not identify that they are from Montserrat, it has been recommended that they should also retain their old British Overseas Citizen passport, to help them demonstrate eligibility for, among other things, housing assistance in the UK.

### Persons deported, expelled or removed to the UK from another country

**9.21.**    Persons who are in the UK as a result of their deportation, expulsion or other removal by compulsion of law from another country to the UK will generally be UK nationals. (However, such persons could include EEA nationals, where the UK immigration authorities were satisfied that the person was settled in the UK and exercising EC Treaty rights prior to deportation from the third country.) Where deportation occurs, most countries will signal this in the person's passport and provide them with reasons for their removal. This should enable such persons to identify their circumstances when making an application for housing assistance.

## PERSONS INELIGIBLE UNDER CERTAIN PROVISIONS BY VIRTUE OF SCHEDULE 3 TO THE NATIONALITY, IMMIGRATION AND ASYLUM ACT 2002

**9.22.**    Section 54 of, and Schedule 3 to, the *Nationality, Immigration and Asylum Act 2002* have the effect of making certain applicants for housing assistance ineligible for accommodation under s.188(3) (*power to accommodate pending a review*) or s.204(4) (*power to accommodate pending an appeal to the county court*) of the 1996 Act. The following classes of person will be ineligible for assistance under those powers:

(i) *a person who has refugee status abroad*, i.e. a person:
 – who does not have the nationality of an EEA State, and
 – who the government of an EEA State other than the UK has determined is entitled to protection as a refugee under the Refugee Convention;

(ii) *a person who has the nationality of an EEA State other than the UK* (but see paragraph 9.23 below);

(iii) *a person who was (but is no longer) an asylum seeker and who fails to cooperate with removal directions* issued in respect of him or her;

(iv) *a person who is in the UK in breach of the immigration laws* (within the meaning of s.11 of the *Nationality, Immigration and Asylum Act 2002*) *and is not an asylum seeker*;

(v) *certain persons who are failed asylum seekers with dependent children*, where the Secretary of State has certified that, in his opinion, such a person has failed without reasonable excuse to take reasonable steps to leave the UK voluntarily or place himself or herself in a position where he or she is able to leave the UK voluntarily, and that person has received the Secretary of State's certificate more than 14 days previously;

(vi) *a person who is the dependant of a person who falls within class (i), (ii), (iii) or (v) above.*

**9.23. However, s.54 and Schedule 3 do not prevent the exercise of an authority's powers under s.188(3) and s.204(4) of the 1996 Act to the extent that such exercise is necessary for the purpose of avoiding a breach of a person's rights under the European Convention of Human Rights or rights under the EC Treaties.** Among other things, this means that a local authority can exercise these powers to accommodate an EEA national who has a right to reside in the UK under EC law (see Annex 12).

**9.24.** Paragraph 14 of Schedule 3 provides, among other things, that authorities must inform the Secretary of State where the powers under s.188(3) or s.204(4) apply, or may apply, to a person who is, or may come, within classes (iii), (iv) or (v) in paragraph 9.22 (by contacting the Home Office Immigration and Nationality Directorate).

**9.25.** For further guidance, local authorities should refer to Guidance to Local Authorities and Housing Authorities about the *Nationality, Immigration and Asylum Act*, Section 54 and Schedule 3, and the *Withholding and Withdrawal of Support (Travel Assistance and Temporary Accommodation) Regulations 2002*, issued by the Home Office.

**ELIGIBILITY – LIST OF RELATED ANNEXES:**
 ANNEX 8—HOW TO CONTACT THE HOME OFFICE IMMIGRATION AND NATIONALITY DIRECTORATE
 ANNEX 9—ASYLUM SEEKERS
 ANNEX 10—THE HABITUAL RESIDENCE TEST
 ANNEX 11—EUROPEAN GROUPINGS (EU, A8, EEA, SWITZERLAND)
 ANNEX 12—RIGHTS TO RESIDE IN THE UK DERIVED FROM EC LAW
 ANNEX 13—WORKER REGISTRATION SCHEME

[5011]

# CHAPTER 10: PRIORITY NEED

**This chapter provides guidance on the categories of applicant who have a priority need for accommodation under the homelessness legislation.**

**10.1.** Under the homelessness legislation, housing authorities must have a strategy for preventing homelessness and ensuring that accommodation and support are available to anyone in their district who is homeless or at risk of homelessness. They must also provide advice and assistance on housing and homelessness prevention to anyone in their district, free of charge. Stronger duties to secure accommodation exist for households who have a priority need for accommodation. Since 2002, the priority need categories have embraced a wider range of people whose age or background puts them at greater risk when homeless, including more single people.

**10.2.** The main homelessness duties in s.193(2) and s.195(2) of the 1996 Act (to secure accommodation or take reasonable steps to prevent the loss of accommodation) apply only to applicants who have a priority need for accommodation. Section 189(1) and the *Homelessness (Priority Need for Accommodation) (England) Order 2002* provide that the following categories of applicant have a priority need for accommodation:

i) a pregnant woman or a person with whom she resides or might reasonably be expected to reside (see paragraph 10.5);

ii) a person with whom dependent children reside or might reasonably be expected to reside (see paragraphs 10.6–10.11);

iii) a person who is vulnerable as a result of old age, mental illness or handicap or physical disability or other special reason, or with whom such a person resides or might reasonably be expected to reside (see paragraphs 10.12–10.18);

iv)    a person aged 16 or 17 who is not a 'relevant child' or a child in need to whom a local authority owes a duty under section 20 of the *Children Act 1989* (see paragraphs 10.36–10.39);

v)    a person under 21 who was (but is no longer) looked after, accommodated or fostered between the ages of 16 and 18 (except a person who is a 'relevant student') (see paragraphs 10.40–10.41);

vi)    a person aged 21 or more who is vulnerable as a result of having been looked after, accommodated or fostered (except a person who is a 'relevant student') (see paragraphs 10.19–10.20);

vii)    a person who is vulnerable as a result of having been a member of Her Majesty's regular naval, military or air forces (see paragraphs 10.21–10.23);

viii)    a person who is vulnerable as a result of:
     (a)    having served a custodial sentence,
     (b)    having been committed for contempt of court or any other kindred offence, or
     (c)    having been remanded in custody; (see paragraphs 10.24–10.27)

ix)    a person who is vulnerable as a result of ceasing to occupy accommodation because of violence from another person or threats of violence from another person which are likely to be carried out (see paragraphs 10.28–10.29);

x)    a person who is vulnerable for any other special reason, or with whom such a person resides or might reasonably be expected to reside (see paragraphs 10.30–10.35);

xi)    a person who is homeless, or threatened with homelessness, as a result of an emergency such as flood, fire or other disaster (see paragraph 10.42).

**10.3.** Inquiries as to whether an applicant has a priority need must be carried out in all cases where the housing authority has reason to believe that an applicant may be homeless or threatened with homelessness, and is eligible for assistance (s.184). Moreover, where the housing authority has reason to believe that the applicant is homeless, eligible for assistance and in priority need, they will have an immediate duty to secure interim accommodation, pending a decision on the case (see Chapter 7).

**10.4.** Once a housing authority has notified an applicant that he or she has a priority need and has been accepted as owed the main homelessness duty (s.193(2)) it cannot – unless the decision is subject to a request for a review – change the decision if the applicant subsequently ceases to have a priority need (e.g. because a dependent child leaves home). Any change of circumstance prior to the decision on the homelessness application should be taken into account. However, once all the relevant inquiries are completed, the housing authority should not defer making a decision on the case in anticipation of a possible change of circumstance. (See Chapter 19 for guidance on reviews.)

## PREGNANT WOMEN

**10.5.** A pregnant woman, and anyone with whom she lives or might reasonably be expected to live, has a priority need for accommodation. This is regardless of the length of time that the woman has been pregnant. Housing authorities should seek normal confirmation of pregnancy, e.g. a letter from a medical professional, such as a midwife, should be adequate evidence of pregnancy. If a pregnant woman suffers a miscarriage or terminates her pregnancy during the assessment process the housing authority should consider whether she continues to have a priority need as a result of some other factor (e.g. she may be vulnerable as a result of an other special reason – see paragraph 10.30).

## DEPENDENT CHILDREN

**10.6.** Applicants have a priority need if they have one or more dependent children who normally live with them or who might reasonably be expected to live with them. There must be actual dependence on the applicant, although the child need not be wholly and exclusively dependent on him or her. There must also be actual residence (or a reasonable expectation of residence) with some degree of permanence or regularity, rather than a temporary arrangement whereby the children are merely staying with the applicant for a limited period (see paragraphs 10.9 and 10.10). Similarly, the child need not be wholly and exclusively resident (or expected to reside wholly and exclusively) with the applicant.

**10.7.** The 1996 Act does not define dependent children, but housing authorities may wish to treat as dependent all children under 16, and all children aged 16–18 who are in, or are about to begin, full-time education or training or who for other reasons are unable to support themselves and who live at home. The meaning of dependency is not, however, limited to financial dependency. Thus, while children aged 16 and over who are in full-time employment and are financially independent of their parents would not normally be considered to be dependants, housing authorities should remember that such children may not be sufficiently mature to live independently of their parents, and there may be sound reasons for considering them to be dependent. Each case will need to be carefully considered according to the circumstances.

**10.8.** Dependent children need not necessarily be the applicant's own children but could, for example, be related to the applicant or his or her partner or be adopted or fostered by the applicant. There must, however, be some form of parent/child relationship.

PART III
OTHER MATERIAL

**10.9.**  Housing authorities may receive applications from a parent who is separated from his or her former spouse or partner. In some cases where parents separate, the court may make a residence order indicating with which parent the child normally resides. In such cases, the child may be considered to reside with the parent named in the order, and would not normally be expected to reside with the other parent. However, in many cases the parents come to an agreement themselves as to how the child is to be cared for, and a court order will not be made or required.

**10.10.**  Residence does not have to be full-time and a child can be considered to reside with either parent even where he or she divides his or her time between both parents. However, as mentioned above, there must be some regularity to the arrangement. If the child is not currently residing with the applicant, the housing authority will need to decide whether, in the circumstances, it would be reasonable for the child to do so. An agreement between a child's parents, or a joint residence order by a court, may not automatically lead to a conclusion that it would be reasonable for the child to reside with the parent making the application, and housing authorities will need to consider each case individually. However, housing authorities should remember that where parents separate, it will often be in the best interests of the child to maintain a relationship with both parents.

**10.11.**  Where the applicant's children are being looked after by a social services authority – for example, they are subject to a care order or are being accommodated under a voluntary agreement – and they are not currently living with the applicant, liaison with the social services authority will be essential. Joint consideration with social services will ensure that the best interests of the applicant and the children are served. This may, for example, enable a family to be reunited subject to suitable accommodation being available.

## VULNERABILITY

**10.12.**  A person has a priority need for accommodation if he or she is vulnerable as a result of:

i)      old age;
ii)     mental illness or learning disability (mental handicap) or physical disability;
iii)    having been looked after, accommodated or fostered and is aged 21 or more;
iv)     having been a member of Her Majesty's regular naval, military or air forces;
v)      having been in custody or detention;
vi)     ceasing to occupy accommodation because of violence from another person or threats of violence from another person which are likely to be carried out; or
vii)    any other special reason.

In the case of i), ii) and vii) only, a person with whom a vulnerable person lives or might reasonably be expected to live also has a priority need for accommodation and can therefore make an application on behalf of themselves and that vulnerable person.

**10.13.**  **It is a matter of judgement whether the applicant's circumstances make him or her vulnerable. When determining whether an applicant in any of the categories set out in paragraph 10.12 is vulnerable, the local authority should consider whether, when homeless, the applicant would be less able to fend for him/herself than an ordinary homeless person so that he or she would suffer injury or detriment, in circumstances where a less vulnerable person would be able to cope without harmful effects.**

**10.14.**  **Some of the factors which may be relevant to determining whether a particular category of applicant is vulnerable are set out below. The assessment of an applicant's ability to cope is a composite one taking into account all of the circumstances. The applicant's vulnerability must be assessed on the basis that he or she is or will become homeless, and not on his or her ability to fend for him or herself while still housed.**

*Old age*

**10.15.**  Old age alone is not sufficient for the applicant to be deemed vulnerable. However, it may be that as a result of old age the applicant would be less able to fend for him or herself as provided in paragraph 10.13 above. All applications from people aged over 60 need to be considered carefully, particularly where the applicant is leaving tied accommodation. However, housing authorities should not use 60 (or any other age) as a fixed age beyond which vulnerability occurs automatically (or below which it can be ruled out); each case will need to be considered in the light of the individual circumstances.

*Mental illness or learning disability or physical disability*

**10.16.**  Housing authorities should have regard to any advice from medical professionals, social services or current providers of care and support. In cases where there is doubt as to the extent of any vulnerability authorities may also consider seeking a clinical opinion. However, the final decision on the question of vulnerability will rest with the housing authority. In considering whether such applicants are vulnerable, authorities will need to take account of all relevant factors including:

i)      the nature and extent of the illness and/or disability which may render the applicant vulnerable;
ii)     the relationship between the illness and/or disability and the individual's housing difficulties; and

iii)     the relationship between the illness and/or disability and other factors such as drug/
alcohol misuse, offending behaviour, challenging behaviours, age and personality
disorder.

**10.17.**     Assessment of vulnerability due to mental health will require close co-operation between
housing authorities, social services authorities and mental health agencies. Housing authorities
should consider carrying out joint assessments or using a trained mental health practitioner as part
of an assessment team. Mental Health NHS Trusts and local authorities have an express duty to
implement a specifically tailored care programme (the Care Programme Approach – CPA) for all
patients considered for discharge from psychiatric hospitals and all new patients accepted by the
specialist psychiatric services (see *Effective care co-ordination in mental health services:
modernising the care programme approach*, DH, 1999). **People discharged from psychiatric
hospitals and local authority hostels for people with mental health problems are likely to be
vulnerable.** Effective, timely, liaison between housing, social services and NHS Trusts will be
essential in such cases but authorities will also need to be sensitive to direct approaches from former
patients who have been discharged and may be homeless.

**10.18.**     Learning or physical disabilities or long-term acute illnesses, such as those defined by the
*Disability Discrimination Act 1995*, which impinge on the applicant's housing situation and give
rise to vulnerability may be readily discernible, but advice from health or social services staff should
be sought, wherever necessary.

*Having been looked after, accommodated or fostered and aged 21 or over*

**10.19.**     A person aged 21 or over who is vulnerable as a result of having been looked after,
accommodated or fostered has a priority need (other than a person who is a 'relevant student'). The
terms 'looked after, accommodated or fostered' are set out in the *Children Act 1989* (s.24) and
include any person who has been:

i)     looked after by a local authority (i.e. has been subject to a care order or accommodated
under a voluntary agreement);

ii)     accommodated by or on behalf of a voluntary organisation;

iii)     accommodated in a private children's home;

iv)     accommodated for a consecutive period of at least three months:

–     by a health authority, special health authority, primary care trust or local
education authority, or

–     in any care home or independent hospital or in any accommodation provided by a
National Health Service trust; or

v)     privately fostered.

A 'relevant student' means a care leaver under 24 to whom section 24B(3) of the *Children Act 1989*
applies, and who is in full-time further or higher education and whose term-time accommodation is
not available during a vacation. Under s.24B(5), where a social services authority is satisfied that a
person is someone to whom section 24B(3) applies and needs accommodation during a vacation
they must provide accommodation or the means to enable it to be secured.

**10.20.**     Housing authorities will need to make enquiries into an applicant's childhood history to
establish whether he or she has been looked after, accommodated or fostered in any of these ways.
If so, they will need to consider whether he or she is vulnerable as a result. In determining whether
there is vulnerability (as set out in paragraph 10.13 above), factors that a housing authority may
wish to consider are:

i)     the length of time that the applicant was looked after, accommodated or fostered;

ii)     the reasons why the applicant was looked after, accommodated or fostered;

iii)     the length of time since the applicant was looked after, accommodated or fostered, and
whether the applicant had been able to obtain and/or maintain accommodation during any
of that period;

iv)     whether the applicant has any existing support networks, particularly including family,
friends or mentor.

*Having been a member of the armed forces*

**10.21.**     A person who is vulnerable as a result of having been a member of Her Majesty's regular
armed forces has a priority need for accommodation. Former members of the armed forces will
include a person who was previously a member of the regular naval, military or air forces, including
a person who has been released following detention in a military corrective training centre.

**10.22.**     The principal responsibility for providing housing information and advice to Service
personnel lies with the armed forces up to the point of discharge and these services are delivered
through the Joint Service Housing Advice Office (telephone: 01722 436575). Some people, who
have served in the armed forces for a long period, and those who are medically discharged, may be
offered assistance with resettlement by Ministry of Defence (MOD) resettlement staff. The MOD
issues a *Certificate of Cessation of Entitlement to Occupy Service Living Accommodation* (see
examples at Annexes 14 and 15) six months before discharge. Applications from former members of
the armed forces will need to be considered carefully to assess whether the applicant is vulnerable as
a result of having served in the armed forces.

PART III
OTHER MATERIAL

**10.23.** In considering whether former members of the armed forces are vulnerable (as set out in paragraph 10.13 above) as a result of their time spent in the forces, a housing authority may wish to take into account the following factors:

i) the length of time the applicant spent in the armed forces (although authorities should not assume that vulnerability could not occur as a result of a short period of service);

ii) the type of service the applicant was engaged in (those on active service may find it more difficult to cope with civilian life);

iii) whether the applicant spent any time in a military hospital (this could be an indicator of a serious health problem or of post-traumatic stress);

iv) whether HM Forces' medical and welfare advisers have judged an individual to be particularly vulnerable in their view and have issued a Medical History Release Form (F Med 133) giving a summary of the circumstances causing that vulnerability;

v) the length of time since the applicant left the armed forces, and whether he or she had been able to obtain and/or maintain accommodation during that time;

vi) whether the applicant has any existing support networks, particularly by way of family or friends.

*Having been in custody or detention*

**10.24.** A person who is vulnerable as a result of having served a custodial sentence, been committed for contempt of court or remanded in custody has a priority need for accommodation. This category applies to applicants who are vulnerable as a result of having:

i) served a custodial sentence within the meaning of the *Powers of Criminal Courts (Sentences) Act 2000*, s.76. (This includes sentences of imprisonment for those aged 21 or over and detention for those aged under 21, including children.);

ii) been committed for contempt of court or any other kindred offence (kindred offence refers to statutory provisions for contempt as opposed to the inherent jurisdiction of the court, e.g. under the *Contempt of Court Act 1981*, s.12 (magistrates' court) and *County Court Act 1984*, s.118 (county court)). (Committal may arise, e.g. where an applicant has breached a civil injunction.);

iii) been remanded in custody within the meaning of the *Powers of Criminal Courts (Sentencing) Act 2000*, s.88(1)(b), (c) or (d), i.e. remanded in or committed to custody by an order of a court; remanded or committed to housing authority accommodation under the *Children and Young Persons Act 1969* and placed and kept in secure accommodation; or, remanded, admitted or removed to hospital under the *Mental Health Act 1983*, ss. 35, 36, 38 or 48.

**10.25.** Applicants have a priority need for accommodation only if they are vulnerable (see paragraph 10.13 above) as a result of having been in custody or detention. In determining whether applicants who fall within one of the descriptions in paragraph 10.24 are vulnerable as a result of their period in custody or detention, a housing authority may wish to take into account the following factors:

i) the length of time the applicant served in custody or detention (although authorities should not assume that vulnerability could not occur as a result of a short period in custody or detention);

ii) whether the applicant is receiving supervision from a criminal justice agency e.g. the Probation Service, Youth Offending Team or Drug Intervention Programme. Housing authorities should have regard to any advice from criminal justice agency staff regarding their view of the applicant's general vulnerability, but the final decision on the question of vulnerability for the purposes of the homelessness legislation will rest with the housing authority;

iii) the length of time since the applicant was released from custody or detention, and the extent to which the applicant had been able to obtain and/or maintain accommodation during that time;

iv) whether the applicant has any existing support networks, for example family or friends, and how much of a positive influence these networks are likely to be in the applicant's life.

**10.26.** In many cases a housing needs assessment may have been completed in respect of offenders by the Probation Service, Prison Services, Youth Offending Team, Criminal Justice Intervention Team or a voluntary organisation acting on behalf of one of these agencies. Where such an assessment identifies an individual as needing help in finding accommodation and judges the individual to be particularly vulnerable and the applicant makes an application for housing assistance, this information will be made available to the relevant housing authority.

**10.27.** In addition to the question of priority need, when assessing applicants in this client group difficult issues may arise as to whether the applicant has become homeless intentionally. Housing authorities must consider each case in the light of all the facts and circumstances. **Housing authorities are reminded that they cannot adopt a blanket policy of assuming that homelessness will be intentional or unintentional in any given circumstances** (see Chapter 11 for guidance on intentional homelessness).

*Having left accommodation because of violence*

**10.28.** A person has a priority need if he or she is vulnerable (as set out in paragraph 10.13 above) as a result of having to leave accommodation because of violence from another person, or threats of violence from another person that are likely to be carried out. It will usually be apparent from the assessment of the reason for homelessness whether the applicant has had to leave accommodation because of violence or threats of violence (see Chapter 8 for further guidance on whether it is reasonable to continue to occupy accommodation). **In cases involving violence, the safety of the applicant and ensuring confidentiality must be of paramount concern.** It is not only domestic violence that is relevant, but all forms of violence, including racially motivated violence or threats of violence likely to be carried out. Inquiries of the perpetrators of violence should not be made. In assessing whether it is likely that threats of violence are likely to be carried out, a housing authority should only take into account the probability of violence, and not actions which the applicant could take (such as injunctions against the perpetrators). See Chapter 6 for further guidance on dealing with cases involving violence.

**10.29.** In considering whether applicants are vulnerable as a result of leaving accommodation because of violence or threats of violence likely to be carried out, a housing authority may wish to take into account the following factors:

i)     the nature of the violence or threats of violence (there may have been a single but significant incident or a number of incidents over an extended period of time which have had a cumulative effect);

ii)    the impact and likely effects of the violence or threats of violence on the applicant's current and future well being;

iii)   whether the applicant has any existing support networks, particularly by way of family or friends.

*Other special reason*

**10.30.** Section 189(1)(c) provides that a person has a priority need for accommodation if he or she is vulnerable for any "other special reason". A person with whom such a vulnerable person normally lives or might reasonably be expected to live also has a priority need. The legislation envisages that vulnerability can arise because of factors that are not expressly provided for in statute. Each application must be considered in the light of the facts and circumstances of the case. Moreover, other special reasons giving rise to vulnerability are not restricted to the physical or mental characteristics of a person. Where applicants have a need for support but have no family or friends on whom they can depend they may be vulnerable as a result of another special reason.

**10.31. Housing authorities must keep an open mind and should avoid blanket policies that assume that particular groups of applicants will, or will not, be vulnerable for any "other special reason".** Where a housing authority considers that an applicant may be vulnerable, it will be important to make an in-depth assessment of the circumstances of the case. Guidance on certain categories of applicants who may be vulnerable as a result of any "other special reason" is given below. The list below is not exhaustive and housing authorities must ensure that they give proper consideration to every application on the basis of the individual circumstances. In addition, housing authorities will need to be aware that an applicant may be considered vulnerable for any "other special reason" because of a combination of factors which taken alone may not necessarily lead to a decision that they are vulnerable (e.g. drug and alcohol problems, common mental health problems, a history of sleeping rough, no previous experience of managing a tenancy).

**10.32.** *Chronically sick people, including people with AIDS and HIV-related illnesses.* People in this group may be vulnerable not only because their illness has progressed to the point of physical or mental disability (when they are likely to fall within one of the specified categories of priority need) but also because the manifestations or effects of their illness, or common attitudes to it, make it very difficult for them to find and maintain stable or suitable accommodation. Whilst this may be particularly true of people with AIDS, it could also apply in the case of people infected with HIV (who may not have any overt signs or symptoms) if the nature of their infection is known.

**10.33.** *Young people.* The 2002 Order makes specific provision for certain categories of young homeless people (see paragraph 10.2). However, there are many other young people who fall outside these categories but who could become homeless and be vulnerable in certain circumstances. When assessing applications from young people under 25 who do not fall within any of the specific categories of priority need, housing authorities should give careful consideration to the possibility of vulnerability. Most young people can expect a degree of support from families, friends or an institution (e.g. a college or university) with the practicalities and costs of finding, establishing, and managing a home for the first time. But some young people, particularly those who are forced to leave the parental home or who cannot remain there because they are being subjected to violence or sexual abuse, may lack this back-up network and be less able than others to establish and maintain a home for themselves. Moreover, a young person on the streets without adequate financial resources to live independently may be at risk of abuse or prostitution. See Chapter 12 for further guidance on 16 and 17 year olds.

**10.34.** *People fleeing harassment.* Authorities should consider whether harassment falls under the general definition of domestic violence (see definition in Chapter 8 and paragraphs 10.28–10.29 above which give guidance on vulnerability as a result of violence). In some cases, however, severe harassment may fall short of actual violence or threats of violence likely to be carried out. Housing authorities should consider carefully whether applicants who have fled their home because of non-violent forms of harassment, for example verbal abuse or damage to property, are vulnerable as a result. Careful consideration should be given to applicants who may be at risk of witness intimidation. In some criminal cases the police may provide alternative accommodation for witnesses, but usually this will apply for the duration of the trial only. Witnesses may have had to give up their home or may feel unable to return to it when the trial has finished.

**10.35.** *Former asylum seekers.* Former asylum seekers who have been granted refugee status or exceptional leave to remain, humanitarian protection, or discretionary leave will be eligible for homelessness assistance and may be at risk of homelessness as a result of having to leave accommodation that had been provided for them (e.g. by the National Asylum Support Service) in the period before a decision was reached on their asylum claim. They may well have experienced persecution or trauma in their country of origin or severe hardship in their efforts to reach the UK and may be vulnerable as a result. In assessing applications from this client group, housing authorities should give careful consideration to the possibility that they may be vulnerable as a result of another special reason. Authorities should be sensitive to the fact that former asylum seekers may be reluctant to discuss, or have difficulty discussing, their potential vulnerability, if, for example, they have experienced humiliating, painful or traumatic circumstances such as torture, rape or the killing of a family member.

## 16 AND 17 YEAR OLDS

**10.36.** All 16 and 17 year old homeless applicants have a priority need for accommodation except those who are:
  i)      a relevant child, or
  ii)     a child in need who is owed a duty under s.20 of the *Children Act 1989.*

*Relevant child or child in need owed a duty under s.20 of the 1989 Act*

**10.37.** A relevant child is a child aged 16 or 17 who has been looked after by a local authority for at least 13 weeks since the age of 14 and has been looked after at some time while 16 or 17 and who is not currently being looked after (i.e. an 'eligible child' for the purposes of paragraph 19B of Schedule 2 to the *Children Act 1989*). In addition, a child is also a relevant child if he or she would have been looked after by the local authority as an eligible child but for the fact that on his or her 16th birthday he or she was detained through the criminal justice system, or in hospital, or if he or she has returned home on family placement and that has broken down (see the *Children Act 1989*, s.23A and the *Children (Leaving Care) Regulations 2001* regulation 4).

**10.38.** The *Children Act 1989* (s.20(3)) places a duty on children's services authorities to provide accommodation for a child in need aged 16 or over whose welfare is otherwise likely to be seriously prejudiced if they do not provide accommodation; and s.20(1) places a duty on children's services authorities to provide accommodation for children in need in certain other circumstances.

**10.39.** Responsibility for providing suitable accommodation for a relevant child or a child in need to whom a local authority owes a duty under s.20 of the *Children Act 1989* rests with the children's services authority. In cases where a housing authority considers that a section 20 duty is owed, they should verify this with the relevant children's services authority. In all cases of uncertainty as to whether a 16 or 17 year old applicant may be a relevant child or a child in need, the housing authority should contact the relevant children's services authority and, where necessary, should provide interim accommodation under s.188, pending clarification. A framework for joint assessment of 16 and 17 year olds will need to be established by housing and children's services authorities (and housing and children's services departments within unitary authorities) to facilitate the seamless discharge of duties and appropriate services to this client group.

See Chapter 12 for more detailed guidance on 16 and 17 year olds.

## HAVING BEEN LOOKED AFTER, ACCOMMODATED OR FOSTERED AND AGED UNDER 21

**10.40.** A person under 21 who was (but is no longer) looked after, accommodated or fostered between the ages of 16 and 18 has a priority need for accommodation (other than a person who is a 'relevant student'). The terms 'looked after', 'accommodated' or 'fostered' are set out in the *Children Act 1989* (s.24) and include any person who has been:
  i)      looked after by a local authority (i.e. has been subject to a care order or accommodated under a voluntary agreement);
  ii)     accommodated by or on behalf of a voluntary organisation;
  iii)    accommodated in a private children's home;
  iv)     accommodated for a consecutive period of at least three months:

–    by a health authority, special health authority, primary care trust or local education authority, or

–    in any care home or independent hospital or in any accommodation provided by a National Health Service trust; or

v)    privately fostered.

A 'relevant student' means a care leaver under 24 to whom section 24B(3) of the *Children Act 1989* applies, and who is in full-time further or higher education and whose term-time accommodation is not available during a vacation. Under s.24B(5), where a social services authority is satisfied that a person is someone to whom s.24B(3) applies and needs accommodation during a vacation they must provide accommodation or the means to enable it to be secured.

**10.41.**    Housing authorities will need to liaise with the social services authority when dealing with homeless applicants who may fall within this category of priority need.

## HOMELESS AS A RESULT OF AN EMERGENCY

**10.42.**    Applicants have a priority need for accommodation if they are homeless or threatened with homelessness as a result of an emergency such as fire, flood or other disaster. To qualify as an "other disaster" the disaster must be in the nature of a flood or fire, and involve some form of physical damage or threat of damage. Applicants have a priority need by reason of such an emergency whether or not they have dependent children or are vulnerable for any reason.

**[5012]**

## CHAPTER 11: INTENTIONAL HOMELESSNESS

**11.1.    This chapter provides guidance on determining whether an applicant became homeless, or threatened with homelessness, *intentionally* or *unintentionally*.**

**11.2.**    The duty owed towards those who are homeless, or threatened with homelessness, and who have a priority need for accommodation will depend upon whether they became homeless, or threatened with homelessness, intentionally or unintentionally. Section 191 defines the circumstances in which an applicant is to be regarded as having become homeless intentionally. Section 196 frames the same definitions in regard to someone who is threatened with homelessness.

**11.3.**    The duty owed to applicants who have a priority need for accommodation but have become homeless, or threatened with homelessness, intentionally is less than the duty owed to those who have a priority need for accommodation and have become homeless, or threatened with homelessness, unintentionally. This recognises the general expectation that, wherever possible, people should take responsibility for their own accommodation needs and ensure that they do not behave in a way which might lead to the loss of their accommodation.

**11.4.**    Where a housing authority finds an applicant to be homeless, or threatened with homelessness, intentionally they have a duty to provide the applicant (or secure that the applicant is provided) with advice and assistance in any attempts he or she may make to secure that accommodation becomes available (or does not cease to be available) for his or her occupation. Before this advice and assistance is given, the authority must assess the applicant's housing needs. The advice and assistance must include information about the likely availability in the authority's district of types of accommodation appropriate to the applicant's housing needs (including, in particular, the location and sources of such types of accommodation). Authorities should consider what best advice and assistance the authoritiy could provide, for example, providing information about applying for social housing, local lettings in the private rented sector, rent deposit schemes or housing benefit eligibility – to help the applicant avoid homelessness or secure accommodation (see Chapter 2 for further guidance on preventing homelessness). Where such an applicant also has a priority need for accommodation the authority will also have a duty to secure accommodation for such period as will give the applicant a reasonable opportunity of securing accommodation for his or her occupation. See Chapter 14 for guidance on the main duties owed to applicants on completion of inquiries.

**11.5.**    It is for housing authorities to satisfy themselves in each individual case whether an applicant is homeless or threatened with homelessness intentionally. Generally, it is not for applicants to "prove their case". The exception is where an applicant seeks to establish that, as a member of a household previously found to be homeless intentionally, he or she did not acquiesce in the behaviour that led to homelessness. In such cases, the applicant will need to demonstrate that he or she was not involved in the acts or omissions that led to homelessness, and did not have control over them.

**11.6.    Housing authorities must not adopt general policies which seek to pre-define circumstances that do or do not amount to intentional homelessness or threatened homelessness (for example, intentional homelessness should not be assumed in cases where an application is made following a period in custody – see paragraph 11.14).** In each case, housing authorities must form a view in the light of all their inquiries about that particular case. Where the original incident of homelessness occurred some years earlier and the facts are unclear, it may not be possible for the housing authority to satisfy themselves that the applicant became homeless intentionally. In such cases, the applicant should be considered to be unintentionally homeless.

## DEFINITIONS OF INTENTIONAL HOMELESSNESS

**11.7.**  Sections 191(1) and 196(1) provide that a person becomes homeless, or threatened with homelessness, intentionally if:

i)  he or she deliberately does or fails to do anything in consequence of which he or she ceases to occupy accommodation (or the likely result of which is that he or she will be forced to leave accommodation),

ii)  the accommodation is available for his or her occupation, and

iii)  it would have been reasonable for him or her to continue to occupy the accommodation.

However, for this purpose, an act or omission made in good faith by someone who was unaware of any relevant fact must not be treated as deliberate (see paragraph 11.20).

**11.8.**  Sections 191(3) and 196(3) provide that a person must be treated as homeless, or threatened with homelessness, intentionally if:

i)  the person enters into an arrangement under which he or she is required to cease to occupy accommodation which it would have been reasonable for the person to continue to occupy,

ii)  the purpose of the arrangement is to enable the person to become entitled to assistance under Part 7, and

iii)  there is no other good reason why the person is homeless or threatened with homelessness.

## WHOSE CONDUCT RESULTS IN INTENTIONAL HOMELESSNESS?

**11.9.**  Every applicant is entitled to individual consideration of his or her application. This includes applicants where another member of their family or household has made, or is making, a separate application. It is the **applicant** who must deliberately have done or failed to do something which resulted in homelessness or threatened homelessness. Where a housing authority has found an applicant to be homeless intentionally, nothing in the 1996 Act prevents another member of his or her household from making a separate application. Situations may arise where one or more members of a household found to be intentionally homeless were not responsible for the actions or omissions that led to the homelessness. For example, a person may have deliberately failed to pay the rent or defaulted on the mortgage payments, which resulted in homelessness or threatened homelessness, against the wishes or without the knowledge of his or her partner. However, where applicants were not directly responsible for the act or omission which led to their family or household becoming homeless, but they acquiesced in that behaviour, then they may be treated as having become homeless intentionally themselves. In considering whether an applicant has acquiesced in certain behaviour, the Secretary of State recommends that the housing authority take into account whether the applicant could reasonably be expected to have taken that position through a fear of actual or probable violence.

## CESSATION OF OCCUPATION

**11.10.**  For intentional homelessness to be established there must have been actual occupation of accommodation which has ceased. However, occupation need not necessarily involve continuous occupation at all times, provided the accommodation was at the disposal of the applicant and available for his or her occupation. The accommodation which has been lost can be outside the UK.

## CONSEQUENCE OF A DELIBERATE ACT OR OMISSION

**11.11.**  For homelessness, or threatened homelessness, to be intentional it must be a consequence of a deliberate act or omission. Having established that there was a deliberate act or omission, the housing authority will need to decide whether the loss of the applicant's home, or the likelihood of its loss, is the reasonable result of that act or omission. This is a matter of cause and effect. An example would be where a person voluntarily gave up settled accommodation that it would have been reasonable for them to continue to occupy, moved into alternative accommodation of a temporary or unsettled nature and subsequently became homeless when required to leave the alternative accommodation. Housing authorities will, therefore, need to look back to the last period of settled accommodation and the reasons why the applicant left that accommodation, to determine whether the current incidence of homelessness is the result of a deliberate act or omission.

**11.12.**  Where a person becomes homeless intentionally, that condition may persist until the link between the causal act or omission and the intentional homelessness has been broken. It could be broken, for example, by a period in settled accommodation which follows the intentional homelessness. Whether accommodation is settled will depend on the circumstances of the particular case. Factors such as security of tenure and length of residence will be relevant. It has been established that a period in settled accommodation after an incidence of intentional homelessness would make the deliberate act or omission which led to that homelessness irrelevant in the event of a subsequent application for housing assistance. Conversely, occupation of accommodation that was merely temporary rather than settled, for example, staying with friends on an insecure basis, may not be sufficient to break the link with the earlier intentional homelessness. However, a period in settled accommodation is not necessarily the only way in which a link with the earlier intentional homelessness may be broken: some other event, such as the break-up of a marriage, may be sufficient.

*Probability of violence*

**11.13.**  In cases where there is a probability of violence against an applicant if they continue, or had continued, to occupy their accommodation, and the applicant was aware of measures that could have been taken to prevent or mitigate the risk of violence but decided not to take them, their decision cannot be taken as having caused the probability of violence, and thus, indirectly, having caused the homelessness. Authorities must not assume that measures which could have been taken to prevent actual or threatened violence would necessarily have been effective.

*Ex-offenders*

**11.14.**  Some ex-offenders may apply for accommodation or assistance in obtaining accommodation following a period in custody or detention because they have been unable to retain their previous accommodation, due to that period in custody or detention. In considering whether such an applicant is homeless intentionally, the housing authority will have to decide whether, taking into account all the circumstances, there was a likelihood that ceasing to occupy the accommodation could reasonably have been regarded at the time as a likely consequence of committing the offence.

*Former members of the armed forces*

**11.15.**  Where service personnel are required to vacate service quarters as a result of taking up an option to give notice to leave the service, and in so doing are acting in compliance with their contractural engagement, the Secretary of State considers that they should not be considered to have become homeless intentionally.

**DELIBERATE ACT OR OMISSION**

**11.16.**  For homelessness to be intentional, the act or omission that led to homelessness must have been deliberate, and applicants must always be given the opportunity to explain such behaviour. An act or omission should not generally be treated as deliberate, even where deliberately carried out, if it is forced upon the applicant through no fault of their own. Moreover, an act or omission made in good faith where someone is genuinely ignorant of a relevant fact must not be treated as deliberate (see paragraph 11.24).

**11.17.**  Generally, an act or omission should not be considered deliberate where:
   i)     the act or omission was non-payment of rent which was the result of housing benefit delays, or financial difficulties which were beyond the applicant's control;
   ii)    the housing authority has reason to believe the applicant is incapable of managing his or her affairs, for example, by reason of age, mental illness or disability;
   iii)   the act or omission was the result of limited mental capacity; or a temporary aberration or aberrations caused by mental illness, frailty, or an assessed substance abuse problem;
   iv)    the act or omission was made when the applicant was under duress;
   v)     imprudence or lack of foresight on the part of an applicant led to homelessness but the act or omission was in good faith.

**11.18.**  An applicant's actions would not amount to intentional homelessness where he or she has lost his or her home, or was obliged to sell it, because of rent or mortgage arrears resulting from significant financial difficulties, and the applicant was genuinely unable to keep up the rent or mortgage payments even after claiming benefits, and no further financial help was available.

**11.19.**  Where an applicant has lost a former home due to rent arrears, the reasons why the arrears accrued should be fully explored. Similarly, in cases which involve mortgagors, housing authorities will need to look at the reasons for mortgage arrears together with the applicant's ability to pay the mortgage commitment when it was taken on, given the applicant's financial circumstances at the time.

**11.20.**  Examples of acts or omissions which may be regarded as deliberate (unless any of the circumstances set out in paragraph 11.17 apply) include the following, where someone:
   i)     chooses to sell his or her home in circumstances where he or she is under no risk of losing it;
   ii)    has lost his or her home because of wilful and persistent refusal to pay rent or mortgage payments;
   iii)   could be said to have significantly neglected his or her affairs having disregarded sound advice from qualified persons;
   iv)    voluntarily surrenders adequate accommodation in this country or abroad which it would have been reasonable for the applicant to continue to occupy;

v)    is evicted because of his or her anti-social behaviour, for example by nuisance to neighbours, harassment etc.;

vi)   is evicted because of violence or threats of violence by them towards another person;

vii)  leaves a job with tied accommodation and the circumstances indicate that it would have been reasonable for him or her to continue in the employment and reasonable to continue to occupy the accommodation (but note paragraph 11.15).

## AVAILABILE FOR OCCUPATION

**11.21.** For homelessness to be intentional the accommodation must have been available for the applicant and anyone reasonably expected to live with him or her. Further guidance on "availability for occupation" is provided in Chapter 8.

## REASONABLE TO CONTINUE TO OCCUPY THE ACCOMMODATION

**11.22.** An applicant cannot be treated as intentionally homeless unless it would have been reasonable for him or her to have continued to occupy the accommodation. Guidance on "reasonable to continue to occupy" is provided in Chapter 8. It will be necessary for the housing authority to give careful consideration to the circumstances of the applicant and the household, in each case, and with particular care in cases where violence has been alleged.

**11.23.** Authorities are reminded that, where the applicant has fled his or her home because of violence or threats of violence likely to be carried out, and has failed to pursue legal remedies against the perpetrator(s) which might have prevented the violence or threat of violence, although these decisions (to leave the home and not pursue legal remedies) may be deliberate, the homelessness would not be intentional if it would not have been reasonable for the applicant to continue to occupy the home.

## ACTS OR OMISSIONS IN GOOD FAITH

**11.24.** Acts or omissions made in good faith where someone was genuinely unaware of a relevant fact must not be regarded as deliberate. Provided that the applicant has acted in good faith, there is no requirement that ignorance of the relevant fact be reasonable.

**11.25.** A general example of an act made in good faith would be a situation where someone gave up possession of accommodation in the belief that they had no legal right to continue to occupy the accommodation and, therefore, it would not be reasonable for them to continue to occupy it. This could apply where someone leaves rented accommodation in the private sector having received a valid notice to quit or notice that the assured shorthold tenancy has come to an end and the landlord requires possession of the property, and the former tenant was genuinely unaware that he or she had a right to remain until the court granted an order and warrant for possession.

**11.26.** Where there was dishonesty there could be no question of an act or omission having been made in good faith.

**11.27.** Other examples of acts or omissions that could be made in good faith might include situations where:

i)    a person gets into rent arrears, being unaware that he or she may be entitled to housing benefit or other social security benefits;

ii)   an owner-occupier faced with foreclosure or possession proceedings to which there is no defence, sells before the mortgagee recovers possession through the courts or surrenders the property to the lender; or

iii)  a tenant, faced with possession proceedings to which there would be no defence, and where the granting of a possession order would be mandatory, surrenders the property to the landlord.

In (iii) although the housing authority may consider that it would have been reasonable for the tenant to continue to occupy the accommodation, the act should not be regarded as deliberate if the tenant made the decision to leave the accommodation in ignorance of material facts, e.g. the general pressure on the authority for housing assistance.

## APPLICANT ENTERS INTO AN ARRANGEMENT

**11.28.** Housing authorities will need to be alert to the possibility of collusion by which a person may claim that he or she is obliged to leave accommodation in order to take advantage of the homelessness legislation. Some parents and children, for example, may seek to take advantage of the fact that 16 and 17 year old applicants have a priority need for accommodation. Collusion is not confined to those staying with friends or relatives but can also occur between landlords and tenants. Housing authorities, while relying on experience, nonetheless need to be satisfied that collusion exists, and must not rely on hearsay or unfounded suspicions. For collusion to amount to intentional homelessness, s.191(3) specifies that there should be no other good reason for the applicant's homelessness. Examples of other good reasons include overcrowding or an obvious breakdown in relations between the applicant and his or her host or landlord. In some cases involving collusion the applicant may not actually be homeless, if there is no genuine need for the applicant to leave the accommodation. See paragraphs 8.9–8.12 for further guidance on applicants asked to leave by family or friends.

## FAMILIES WITH CHILDREN UNDER 18

**11.29.** It is important that social services are alerted as quickly as possible to cases where the applicant has children under 18 and the housing authority considers the applicant may be homeless, or threatened with homelessness, intentionally. Section 213A(2) therefore requires housing authorities to have arrangements in place to ensure that all such applicants are invited to agree to the housing authority notifying the social services authority of the essential facts of their case. The arrangements must also provide that, where consent is given, the social services authority are made aware of the essential facts and, in due course, of the subsequent decision on the homelessness case. See Chapter 13 for further guidance on section 213A.

## FURTHER APPLICATIONS FOR ASSISTANCE

**11.30.** There is no period of disqualification if someone wants to make a fresh application after being found intentionally homeless. Where a person whose application has just been decided makes a fresh application, the authority will need to decide whether there are any new facts in the fresh application which render it different from the earlier application. If no new facts are revealed, or any new facts are of a trivial nature, the authority would not be required to consider the new application. However, where the fresh application does reveal substantive new facts, the authority must treat the fresh application in the same way as it would any other application for accommodation or assistance in obtaining accommodation. Therefore, if the authority have reason to believe that the person is homeless or threatened with homelessness, the authority must make inquiries under s.184 and decide whether any interim duty is owed under s.188(1). See Chapter 6 for guidance on inquiries and Chapter 7 for guidance on the interim duty.

**[5013]**

## CHAPTER 12: 16 & 17 YEAR OLDS

**12.1.** **This chapter provides guidance on specific duties towards 16 and 17 year old applicants.**

*Priority need*

**12.2.** All 16 and 17 year old homeless applicants have a priority need for accommodation except those who are:
  i) a relevant child, or
  ii) a child in need who is owed a duty under s.20 of the *Children Act 1989*.

See Chapter 10 for more detailed guidance on priority need.

*Relevant child or child in need owed a duty under s.20 of the 1989 Act*

**12.3.** A relevant child is a child aged 16 or 17 who has been looked after by a local authority for at least 13 weeks since the age of 14 and has been looked after at some time while 16 or 17 and who is not currently being looked after (i.e. an 'eligible child' for the purposes of paragraph 19B of Schedule 2 to the *Children Act 1989*). In addition, a child is also a relevant child if he or she would have been looked after by the local authority as an eligible child but for the fact that on his or her 16th birthday he or she was detained through the criminal justice system, or in hospital, or if he or she has returned home on family placement and that has broken down (see the *Children Act 1989*, s.23A and the *Children (Leaving Care) Regulations 2001*, Regulation 4).

**12.4.** The *Children Act 1989* (s.20(3)) places a duty on children's services authorities to provide accommodation for a child in need aged 16 or over whose welfare is otherwise likely to be seriously prejudiced if they do not provide accommodation; and s.20(1) places a duty on children's services authorities to provide accommodation for children in need in certain other circumstances.

**12.5.** Responsibility for providing suitable accommodation for a relevant child or a child in need to whom a local authority owes a duty under s.20 of the *Children Act 1989* rests with the children's services authority. In cases where a housing authority considers that a s.20 duty is owed, they should verify this with the relevant children's services authority.

**12.6.** In all cases of uncertainty as to whether a 16 or 17 year old applicant may be a relevant child or a child in need, the housing authority should contact the relevant children's services authority and, where necessary, should provide interim accommodation under s.188, pending clarification. A framework for joint assessment of 16 and 17 year olds will need to be established by housing and children's services authorities (and housing and children's services departments within unitary authorities) to facilitate the seamless discharge of duties and appropriate services to this client group.

*Family relationships*

**12.7.**  The Secretary of State considers that, generally, it will be in the best interests of 16 and 17 year olds to live in the family home, unless it would be unsafe or unsuitable for them to do so because they would be at risk of violence or abuse. It is not unusual for 16 and 17 year olds to have a turbulent relationship with their family and this can lead to temporary disagreements and even temporary estrangement. Where such disagreements look likely to lead to actual or threatened homelessness the housing authority should consider the possibility of reconciliation with the applicant's immediate family, where appropriate, or the possibility of him or her residing with another member of the wider family.

*Reconciliation*

**12.8.**  In all cases involving applicants who are 16 or 17 years of age a careful assessment of the young person's circumstances and any risk to them of remaining at home should be made at the first response. Some 16 and 17 year olds may be at risk of leaving home because of a temporary breakdown in their relationship with their family. In such cases, the housing authority may be able to effect a reconciliation with the family. In some cases, however, relationships may have broken down irretrievably, and in others it may not be safe or desirable for the applicant to remain in the family home, for example, in cases involving violence or abuse.

**12.9.**  Therefore, any mediation or reconciliation will need careful brokering and housing authorities may wish to seek the assistance of social services in all such cases.

*Collusion*

**12.10.**  Where homelessness can not be avoided, local authorities should work with 16 and 17 year olds, and their families where appropriate, to explore alternative housing options. Where the main homelessness duty is owed young people need to be given the chance to consider a range of housing options including but not limited to any accommodation to be offered under s.193. Clear and accurate information is essential to allow young people to identify the right housing solution for them.

**12.11.**  Some parents and children may seek to take advantage of the fact that 16 and 17 year old applicants have a priority need for accommodation. Housing authorities will therefore need to be alive to the possibility of collusion when assessing applications from this client group. Section 191(3) (intentional homelessness) will apply in cases where there is no genuine basis for homelessness and parents have colluded with a child and fabricated an arrangement under which the child has been asked to leave the family home (see Chapter 11 for guidance on intentional homelessness).

*Care and support needs*

**12.12.**  Where young people actually become homeless and are provided with accommodation, local authorities should consider whether they have any care or support needs. Many young people who have experienced homelessness may lack skills in managing their affairs and require help with managing a tenancy and operating a household budget. Those estranged from their family, particularly care leavers, may lack the advice and support normally available to young people from family, friends and other mentors. 16 and 17 year olds who are homeless and estranged from their family will be particularly vulnerable and in need of support.

**12.13.**  Housing authorities will need to recognise that accommodation solutions for this client group are likely to be unsuccessful if the necessary support is not provided. Close liaison with social services, the Supporting People team and agencies working with young people will be essential. Most 16 and 17 year old applicants are likely to benefit from a period in supported accommodation before moving on to a tenancy of their own, but housing authorities should consider the circumstances of each case.

**12.14.  Housing authorities are reminded that Bed and Breakfast (B&B) accommodation is unlikely to be suitable for 16 and 17 year olds who are in need of support. Where B&B accommodation is used for this group it ought to be as a last resort for the shortest time possible and housing authorities will need to ensure that appropriate support is provided where necessary.** See Chapter 17 on the suitability of accommodation for further guidance on the use of B&B accommodation.

**12.15.**  16 and 17 year olds (including lone parents) who apply for housing assistance may also have care and support needs that need to be assessed. **The Secretary of State recommends that housing authorities and social services authorities (and the relevant departments within unitary authorities) have arrangements in place for joint assessments of such young people's needs, whether the application is made initially to the housing department or social services department.** In all cases where an applicant may have care, health or other support needs, it is recommended that the housing authority liaise with the social services authority, the Supporting People team and other agencies (for example, the Primary Care Trust, Criminal Justice Services, and voluntary and community organisations), as appropriate, as part of their inquiries. A joint consideration of an applicant's housing and support needs may be crucial to assist the authority in establishing whether the applicant has a priority need for accommodation and any non-housing support needs (see Chapter 4 for guidance on securing support services and Chapter 5 for guidance on joint working).

*Lone teenage parents under 18*

**12.16.** The provision of suitable accommodation with support for lone parents under 18 is a key part of the Government's Teenage Pregnancy Strategy. Providing accommodation with support for 16 and 17 year old lone parents is important for a very vulnerable group at risk of social isolation. It increases the likelihood of them making a successful transition to an independent tenancy and reduces the risk of subsequent homelessness.

**12.17.** The Government's objective is that all 16 and 17 year old lone parents who cannot live with their parents or partner should be offered accommodation with support. Housing authorities should work with social services, RSLs, the local teenage pregnancy co-ordinator and relevant voluntary organisations in their district to ensure that the Government's objective is met. The allocation of appropriate housing and support should be based on consideration of the young person's housing and support needs, their individual circumstances and their views and preferences. Young parents under the age of 16 must always be referred to social services so that their social care needs may be assessed. Housing authorities may find it helpful to refer to *Guidelines for Good Practice in Supported Accommodation for Young Parents*, separate guidance published jointly by DTLR and the Teenage Pregnancy Unit in September 2001 (available from **www.teenagepregnancyunit.gov.uk**).

**[5014]**

# CHAPTER 13: CO-OPERATION IN CERTAIN CASES INVOLVING CHILDREN

**13.1.** **This chapter provides guidance on the duty housing authorities and social services authorities have to co-operate in certain cases involving children.**

**13.2.** Section 10 of the *Children Act 2004* establishes a duty on county level and unitary authorities[1] to make arrangements to promote co-operation between the authority, relevant partners (including district authorities) and other persons or bodies engaged in activities in relation to children, to improve the well-being of children and young people in the authority's area. Relevant partners are required to co-operate with the authority. Section 11 of the 2004 Act requires a range of agencies – including county level and unitary authorities and district authorities where there are two tiers of local government – to make arrangements for ensuring that their functions are discharged having regard to the need to safeguard and promote the welfare of children. See Chapter 5 for guidance on joint working.

---

> [1]    Section 65 of the *Children Act 2004* uses the term 'children's' services authority' to define these authorities as: a county council in England; a metropolitan district council; a non-metropolitan district council for an area where there is no county council; a London borough council; the Common Council of the City of London and the Council of the Isles of Scilly.

---

**13.3.** Where an applicant is eligible for assistance and unintentionally homeless, and has a priority need because there is one or more dependent child in his or her household, the housing authority will owe a main homelessness duty to secure that accommodation is available to them. However, not all applicants with dependent children will be owed a main homelessness duty. Applicants who are found to be ineligible for assistance are not entitled to homelessness assistance under Part 7 of the 1996 Act. Where an applicant with a priority need is found to be eligible but homeless intentionally, s.190(2) requires the housing authority to secure accommodation for such period as will give the applicant a reasonable opportunity to secure accommodation for him/herself and to ensure that the applicant is provided with advice and assistance in any attempts he or she may make to secure accommodation for his or her occupation. Where an applicant with a priority need is found to be eligible but threatened with homelessness intentionally, s.195(5) requires the housing authority to ensure that the applicant is provided with advice and assistance in any attempts he or she may make to secure that accommodation does not cease to be available for his or her occupation. See Chapter 14 for guidance on the main duties owed to applicants on completion of inquiries, including the duty to provide advice and assistance.

**13.4.** In each of the above cases, there is a possibility that situations could arise where families may find themselves without accommodation and any prospect of further assistance from the housing authority. This could give rise to a situation in which the children of such families might become children in need, within the meaning of the term as set out in s.17 of the *Children Act 1989*.

**13.5.** In such cases, it is important that local authority children's services are alerted as quickly as possible because the family may wish to seek assistance under Part 3 of the *Children Act 1989*, in circumstances in which they are owed no, or only limited, assistance under the homelessness legislation. This will give local authority children's services the opportunity to consider the circumstances of the child(ren) and family, and plan any response that may be deemed by them to be appropriate.

PART III
OTHER MATERIAL

**13.6.** Section 213A of the 1996 Act applies where a housing authority has reason to believe that an applicant for assistance under Part 7 with whom a person under the age of 18 normally resides, or might reasonably be expected to reside:

a)   may be ineligible for assistance;
b)   may be homeless and may have become so intentionally; or
c)   may be threatened with homelessness intentionally.

In these circumstances, a housing authority is required to have arrangements in place to ensure that the applicant is invited to consent to the referral of the essential facts of his or her case to the social services authority[2] for the district (or, in the case of a unitary authority, the social services department of the authority). The arrangements must also provide that, where consent is given, the social services authority or department is made aware of the essential facts and, in due course, of the subsequent decision in relation to the homelessness case.

---

2      "Social services authority" is the term used in S.213A of the *Housing Act 1996*, and defined in S.217 of the *Housing Act 1996*. Such authorities are often now referred to as "children's services authorities". See footnote 1.

---

**13.7.** The requirement to obtain the applicant's consent to the referral of the essential facts of his or her case under section 213A(2) or (3) does not affect any other power for the housing authority to disclose information about a homelessness case to the social services authority or department. For example, even where consent is withheld, the housing authority should disclose information about a homelessness case to the social services authority, if they have reason to believe that a child is, or may be, at risk of significant harm, as laid out in Chapter 5 of *Working Together to Safeguard Children: A guide to inter-agency working to safeguard and promote the welfare of children* (2006). *Working Together* was recently revised to reflect developments in legislation, policy and practice. It was published in April 2006 and can be found on the *Every Child Matters* website at http://www.everychildmatters.gov.uk/socialcare/safeguarding/workingtogether/

**13.8.** Where a family with one or more children has been found ineligible for assistance under Part 7 or homeless, or threatened with homelessness, intentionally and approaches the social services authority, that authority will need to decide whether the child is a 'child in need' under the terms of the *Children Act 1989*, by carrying out an assessment of their needs in accordance with the *Framework for the Assessment of Children in Need and their Families* (2000), Department of Health. The findings of the assessment should provide the basis for the decision as to whether the child is a 'child in need' and what, if any, services should be offered to the child in order to safeguard and promote his/her welfare. Section 17 of the *Children Act 1989* requires a local authority to promote the upbringing of children within their family, in so far as this is consistent with their general duty to safeguard and promote their welfare. The social services authority might wish to consider, for example, whether the best way of meeting the child's needs would be by assisting the family to obtain accommodation, for example by providing temporary accommodation or a rent deposit, as part of the exercise of its duty set out in s.17 of the Children Act 1989. *Local Authority Circular 2003(13): Guidance on accommodating children in need and their families* provides further guidance to social services authorities on the effect of s.17.

**13.9.** Where a social services authority has been made aware of a family found to be ineligible for assistance or homeless, or threatened with homelessness, intentionally by the housing authority, and they consider the needs of a child or children could best be met by helping the family to obtain accommodation, they can request the housing authority to provide them with such advice and assistance as is reasonable in the circumstances. Under s.213A(5), the housing authority must comply with such a request. Advice and assistance as is reasonable in the circumstances might include, for example, help with locating suitable accommodation and making an inspection of the property to ensure that it meets adequate standards of fitness and safety. However, the housing authority is not under a duty to provide accommodation for the family in these circumstances.

**13.10.** Section 213A(6) requires unitary authorities to have similar arrangements in place so that the housing department provide the social services department with such advice and assistance as they may reasonably request.

**13.11.** Housing authorities may also wish to consider alerting social services authorities to cases where an applicant whose household includes a child has refused an offer of accommodation which the authority is satisfied is suitable, and the authority has made a decision that it has discharged its homelessness duty under Part 7. In such cases the household could find itself without accommodation and any prospect of further assistance from the housing authority. The applicant would, however, need to consent to the housing authority notifying the social services authority of the essential facts of his or her case (unless the housing authority has any other powers to disclose the information without consent).

## CHAPTER 14: MAIN DUTIES OWED TO APPLICANTS ON COMPLETION OF INQUIRIES

**14.1.** This chapter provides guidance on the main duties owed to applicants where the housing authority has completed its inquiries and is satisfied that an applicant is eligible for assistance and homeless or threatened with homelessness. The chapter also provides guidance on the circumstances that will bring the s.193(2) duty ('the main homelessness duty') to an end.

**14.2.** In many cases early, effective intervention can prevent homelessness occurring. The Secretary of State considers that housing authorities should take steps to prevent homelessness wherever possible, and offer a broad range of advice and assistance to those who face the prospect of losing their current home. However, where a housing authority has completed inquiries made under s.184 (see Chapter 6 for guidance on applications) and is satisfied that an applicant is eligible for assistance and homeless or threatened with homelessness, then one or more of the duties outlined in this chapter will apply under Part 7.

**14.3.** No duty is owed under Part 7 to applicants who are ineligible for assistance or not homeless or threatened with homelessness. However, homelessness strategies should aim to prevent homelessness amongst all households in the district and under s.179 advice and information about homelessness and the prevention of homelessness must be available free of charge to any person in the district, including these applicants. Housing authorities may also choose to offer other assistance to help them obtain accommodation, such as a rent deposit.

## DUTIES TO PROVIDE ADVICE AND ASSISTANCE

**14.4.** Housing authorities have a duty to ensure that the applicant is provided with advice and assistance in a number of different circumstances, and these are dealt with below. These duties require an assessment to be made of the housing needs of the applicant before advice and assistance is provided. This assessment may need to range wider than the housing authority's inquiries into the applicant's homelessness carried out for the purpose of s.184, and should inform the provision of appropriate advice and assistance for that particular applicant. Among other things, the Secretary of State considers the assessment should identify any factors that may make it difficult for the applicant to secure accommodation for him or herself, for example, poverty, outstanding debt, health problems, disabilities and whether English is not a first language. In particular, housing authorities are advised to take account of the circumstances that led to the applicant's homelessness, or threatened homelessness, since these may impact on his or her ability to secure and maintain accommodation and may indicate what types of accommodation would be appropriate.

## DUTIES OWED TO APPLICANTS WHO ARE THREATENED WITH HOMELESSNESS

**14.5.** Under s.175(4), a person is "threatened with homelessness" if he or she is likely to become homeless within 28 days. However, the Secretary of State considers that housing authorities should not wait until homelessness is a likelihood or is imminent before providing advice and assistance. Early intervention may enable homelessness to be prevented, or delayed sufficiently to allow for a planned move to be arranged. However, where a housing authority has completed its inquiries under s.184 and is satisfied that an applicant is eligible for assistance and threatened with homelessness, then the specific duties outlined in paragraphs 14.6 – 14.9 below will apply.

*Unintentionally threatened with homelessness and has priority need (s.195(2))*

**14.6.** Where the authority are satisfied that an applicant is threatened with homelessness unintentionally, eligible for assistance and has a priority need for accommodation, it has a **duty** under s.195(2) *to take reasonable steps to secure that accommodation does not cease to be available for the applicant's occupation.*

**14.7.** Such reasonable steps may include for example, negotiation with the applicant's landlord or, in cases where the applicant has been asked to leave by family and friends, by exploring the scope for mediation and the provision of support to the household in order to ease any pressures that may have led to the applicant being asked to leave. Where a housing authority is able to identify the precise reasons why the applicant is being required to leave his or her current accommodation – for example, by interviewing the applicant and visiting his or her landlord or family or friends (as appropriate) – there may be specific actions that the housing authority or other organisations can take, for example, addressing rent arrears due to delays in housing benefit payments or providing mediation services through the voluntary sector, that can prevent the threat of homelessness being realised. See Chapter 2 for further guidance on preventing homelessness.

**14.8.** Under s.195(3A), as soon as an authority has become subject to a duty under s.195(2), the authority must give the applicant a copy of the statement included in their allocation scheme about their policy on offering choice to people allocated housing accommodation under Part 6. Authorities are required to include such a statement in their allocation scheme by virtue of s.167(1A) of the 1996 Act.

**14.9.**  Where the housing authority is under a duty under s.195(2) and they are unable to prevent the applicant losing his or her current accommodation, the authority will need to secure alternative suitable accommodation for the applicant. Authorities should not delay; arrangements to secure alternative accommodation should begin as soon as it becomes clear that it will not be possible to prevent the applicant from losing their current home. Section 195(4) provides that, where alternative suitable accommodation is secured, the provisions of s.193(3) to (9) will apply in relation to the duty under s.195(2) as they apply in relation to the duty under s.193(2) (see paragraphs 14.17 to 14.24 below).

*Unintentionally threatened with homelessness, no priority need (s.195(5) and s.195(9))*

**14.10.**  Where the housing authority are satisfied that an applicant is threatened with homelessness, eligible for assistance and does not have a priority need for accommodation, it has a **duty** under s.195(5) *to ensure that the applicant is provided with advice and assistance in any attempts he or she may make to secure that accommodation does not cease to be available for his or her occupation.*

**14.11.**  In addition, where the housing authority are satisfied that an applicant is threatened with homelessness unintentionally, it has a **power** under s.195(9) *to take reasonable steps to secure that accommodation does not cease to be available for the applicant's occupation.* See Chapter 2 for guidance on preventing homelessness and paragraph 14.7 above.

*Intentionally threatened with homelessness and has priority need (s.195(5))*

**14.12.**  Where the authority are satisfied that an applicant is threatened with homelessness intentionally, eligible for assistance and has a priority need for accommodation, the housing authority has a **duty** under s.195(5) *to ensure that the applicant is provided with advice and assistance in any attempts he or she may make to secure that accommodation does not cease to be available for his or her occupation.* See Chapter 2 for guidance on preventing homelessness.

## DUTIES OWED TO APPLICANTS WHO ARE HOMELESS

**14.13.**  Under s.175 a person is "homeless" if he or she has no accommodation in the UK or elsewhere which is available for his or her occupation and which that person has a legal right to occupy. Where a housing authority has completed its inquiries under s.184 and is satisfied that an applicant is eligible for assistance and homeless then the specific duties outlined below will apply.

*Unintentionally homeless and has priority need (s.193(2))*

**14.14.**  Where an applicant is unintentionally homeless, eligible for assistance and has a priority need for accommodation, the housing authority has a **duty** under s.193(2) *to secure that accommodation is available for occupation by the applicant* (unless it refers the application to another housing authority under s.198). This is commonly known as 'the main homelessness duty'. In all cases, the accommodation secured must be available for occupation by the applicant together with any other person who normally resides with him or her as a member of his or her family, or any other person who might reasonably be expected to reside, with him or her, and must be suitable for their occupation. See Chapter 16 for guidance on discharging the duty to secure accommodation and Chapter 17 for guidance on suitability of accommodation.

**14.15.**  Acceptance of a duty under s.193(2) does not prevent an immediate allocation of accommodation under Part 6 of the 1996 Act if the applicant has the necessary priority under the housing authority's allocation scheme. Under s.193(3A), as soon as an authority has become subject to a duty under s.193(2), the authority must give the applicant a copy of the statement included in their allocation scheme about their policy on offering choice to people allocated housing accommodation under Part 6. Authorities are required to include such a statement in their allocation scheme by virtue of s.167(1A) of the 1996 Act.

**14.16.**  If the housing authority has notified the applicant that it proposes to refer the case to another housing authority, the authority has a duty under s.200(1) to secure that accommodation is available for the applicant until he or she is notified of the decision whether the conditions for referral of his case are met. The duty under s.200(1) is therefore an interim duty only. Once it has been established whether or not the conditions for referral are met, a duty under s.193(2) will be owed by either the notified housing authority or the notifying housing authority. See Chapter 18 for guidance on referrals to another housing authority.

**How the s.193(2) duty ends (this also applies where alternative accommodation has been secured under s.195(2))**

**14.17.**  The housing authority will cease to be subject to the duty under s.193(2) (the main homelessness duty) in the following circumstances:

    i)    *the applicant accepts an offer of accommodation under Part 6 (an allocation of long term social housing)* (s.193(6)(c)): this would include an offer of an assured tenancy of a registered social landlord property via the housing authority's allocation scheme (see current guidance on the allocation of accommodation issued under s.169 of the 1996 Act);

ii)   the applicant accepts an offer of an assured tenancy (*other than an assured shorthold tenancy*) *from a private landlord* (s.193(6)(cc): this could include an offer of an assured tenancy made by a registered social landlord;

iii)  *the applicant accepts a qualifying offer of an assured shorthold tenancy from a private landlord* (s.193(7B)). The local authority must not approve an offer of an assured shorthold tenancy for the purposes of s.193(7B), unless they are satisfied that the accommodation is suitable and that it would be reasonable for the applicant to accept it (s.193(7F)) (see paragraph 14.25 below);

iv)   *the applicant refuses a final offer of accommodation under Part 6 (an allocation of long term social housing)*: the duty does not end unless the applicant is informed of the possible consequences of refusal and of his or her right to ask for a review of the suitability of the accommodation (s.193(7)), the offer is made in writing and states that it is a final offer (s.193(7A)), and the housing authority is satisfied that the accommodation is suitable and that it would be reasonable for the applicant to accept it (s.193(7F)) (see paragraph 14.25 below);

v)    *the applicant refuses an offer of accommodation to discharge the duty which the housing authority is satisfied is suitable for the applicant* (s.193(5)): the duty does not end unless the applicant is informed of the possible consequences of refusal and of his or her right to ask for a review of the suitability of the accommodation. The housing authority must also notify the applicant that it regards itself as having discharged its duty, before it can end;

vi)   *the applicant ceases to be eligible for assistance as defined in s.185 of the 1996 Act;*

vii)  *the applicant becomes homeless intentionally from accommodation made available to him or her under s.193 or s.195;* see Chapter 11 for guidance on determining whether an applicant became homeless intentionally;

viii) *the applicant otherwise voluntarily ceases to occupy as his or her principal home accommodation made available under s.193 or s.195.*

**14.18.**   The Secretary of State recommends that applicants are given the chance to view accommodation before being required to decide whether they accept or refuse an offer, and before being required to sign any written agreement relating to the accommodation (e.g. a tenancy agreement). Under s.202(1A), an applicant who is offered accommodation can request a review of its suitability whether or not he or she has accepted the offer. See Chapter 17 for guidance on suitability and Chapter 19 for guidance on reviews.

**Qualifying offer of an assured shorthold tenancy**

**14.19.**   An offer of an assured shorthold tenancy is a qualifying offer if:
i)    it is made, with the approval of the authority, in pursuance of arrangements made by the authority with the landlord with a view to bringing the authority's duty under s.193 to an end;

ii)   it is for a fixed term within the meaning of Part 1 of the *Housing Act 1988* (i.e. not a periodic tenancy) and

iii)  it is accompanied by a written statement that states the term of the tenancy being offered and explains in ordinary language that there is no obligation on the applicant to accept the offer, but if the offer is accepted the housing authority will cease to be subject to the s.193 duty.

**14.20.**   The s.193 duty will not end with acceptance of an offer of a qualifying tenancy unless the applicant signs a statement acknowledging that he or she has understood the written statement accompanying the offer.

**Reasonable to accept an offer**

**14.21.**   Housing authorities must not make a final offer under Part 6 or approve a qualifying offer of an assured shorthold tenancy unless they are satisfied that the accommodation is suitable for the applicant and that it is reasonable for him or her to accept the offer (s.193(7F)) (see Chapter 17 for guidance on suitability). Where an applicant has contractual or other obligations in respect of his or her existing accommodation (e.g. a tenancy agreement or lease), the housing authority can reasonably expect the offer to be taken up only if the applicant is able to bring those obligations to an end before he is required to take up the offer (s.193(8)).

**14.22.**   Housing authorities must allow applicants a reasonable period for considering offers of accommodation made under Part 6 that will bring the homelessness duty to an end whether accepted or refused. There is no set reasonable period; some applicants may require longer than others depending on their circumstances, whether they wish to seek advice in making their decision and whether they are already familiar with the property in question. Longer periods may be required where the applicant is in hospital or temporarily absent from the district. In deciding what is a reasonable period, housing authorities must take into account the applicant's circumstances in each case.

**Other circumstances that bring the s.193(2) duty to an end**

**14.23.**   Under s.193(6) the housing authority will also cease to be subject to the duty under s.193 in the following circumstances:

PART III
OTHER MATERIAL

i)    *the applicant ceases to be eligible for assistance as defined in s.185 of the 1996 Act;*

ii)   *the applicant becomes homeless intentionally from accommodation made available to him or her under s.193 or s.195*: see Chapter 11 for guidance on determining whether an applicant became homeless intentionally;

iii)  *the applicant otherwise voluntarily ceases to occupy as his or her only or principal home accommodation made available under s.193 or s.195.*

**Further applications**

**14.24.**  Under s.193(9) a person who ceases to be owed a duty under s.193(2) can make a fresh application for accommodation or assistance in obtaining accommodation (see Chapter 6 for guidance on applications).

*Unintentionally homeless and has no priority need (s.192(2) and s.192(3))*

**14.25.**  Where an applicant is unintentionally homeless, eligible for assistance and does not have a priority need for accommodation, the housing authority has a **duty** under s.192(2) *to ensure that the applicant is provided with advice and assistance in any attempts he or she may make to secure that accommodation becomes available for his or her occupation.* The housing authority might, for example, provide assistance with a rent deposit or guarantee to help the applicant to obtain accommodation in the private rented sector, or advice on applying for an allocation of accommodation through the social housing waiting list or through another social landlord (see Chapter 2 for guidance on advisory services).

**14.26.**  In addition, housing authorities have a **power** under s.192(3) *to secure that accommodation is available for occupation by the applicant.* Authorities should consider whether to use this power in all relevant cases.

*Intentionally homeless and has priority need (s.190(2))*

**14.27.**  Where an applicant is intentionally homeless, eligible for assistance and has a priority need for accommodation, the housing authority has a **duty** under s.190(2) to:

a)    *secure that accommodation is available for the applicant's occupation for such period as it considers will give him or her a reasonable opportunity of securing accommodation for his or her occupation (s.190(2)(a)); and*

b)    *provide the applicant, or secure that the applicant is provided with, advice and assistance in any attempts he or she may make to secure that accommodation becomes available for his or her occupation (s.190(2)(b)).*

**14.28.**  The accommodation secured must be suitable. Housing authorities must consider each case on its merits when determining the period for which accommodation will be secured. A few weeks may provide the applicant with a reasonable opportunity to secure accommodation for him or herself. However, some applicants might require longer, and others, particularly where the housing authority provides pro-active and effective advice and assistance, might require less time. In particular, housing authorities will need to take account of the housing circumstances in the local area, including how readily other accommodation is available in the district, and have regard to the particular circumstances of the applicant, including the resources available to him or her to provide rent in advance or a rent deposit where this may be required by private landlords.

**14.29.**  In addition to securing accommodation, the housing authority must ensure the applicant is provided with advice and assistance to help him or her secure accommodation for him/herself. This might include, for example, assistance with a rent deposit or guarantee to help the applicant to obtain accommodation in the private rented sector, or advice on applying for an allocation of long term social housing or accommodation through another social landlord. See Chapter 2 for guidance on advisory services.

*Intentionally homeless and has no priority need (s.190(3))*

**14.30.**  Where an applicant is intentionally homeless, eligible for assistance and does not have a priority need for accommodation, the housing authority has a **duty** under s.190(3) *to ensure that the applicant is provided with advice and assistance in any attempts he or she may make to secure that accommodation becomes available for his or her occupation.* This might include, for example, assistance with a rent deposit or guarantee to help the applicant to obtain accommodation in the private rented sector, or advice on applying for an allocation of long term social housing accommodation or through another social landlord. See Chapter 2 for guidance on advisory services.

[5016]

## CHAPTER 15: DISCRETIONARY POWERS TO SECURE ACCOMMODATION

**15.1.**  This chapter provides guidance on the discretionary *powers* housing authorities have to secure accommodation for a household where they do not have a *duty* to secure accommodation for that household (see Chapter 16 for guidance on discharge of duties to secure accommodation).

**15.2.**  Housing authorities have powers to secure accommodation for:
i)    applicants who are eligible for assistance, unintentionally homeless and do not have a priority need for accommodation;
ii)   applicants who request a review of the housing authority's decision on their case and who satisfy the relevant conditions, pending a decision on the review; and
iii)  applicants who appeal to the county court against the housing authority's decision and who satisfy the relevant conditions, pending the determination of the appeal.

**15.3.**  The fact that a housing authority has decided that an applicant is ineligible for housing assistance under Part 7 does not preclude it from exercising its powers to secure accommodation pending a review or appeal. However, housing authorities should note that s.54 of, and Schedule 3 to, the *Nationality, Immigration and Asylum Act 2002* prevent them from exercising their powers to accommodate an applicant pending a review or appeal to the county court, where the applicant is a person who falls within one of a number of classes of person specified in Schedule 3. See paragraphs 9.20 – 9.23 in Chapter 9 on eligibility for assistance for further details.

## WAYS OF SECURING ACCOMMODATION

**15.4.**  A housing authority may only discharge its housing functions under Part 7 in the following ways:
a)    by securing that suitable accommodation provided by them is available for the applicant (s.206(1)(a));
b)    by securing that the applicant obtains suitable accommodation from some other person (s.206(1)(b)); or
c)    by giving the applicant such advice and assistance as will secure that suitable accommodation is available from some other person (s.206(1)(c)).

See Chapter 17 for guidance on the suitability of accommodation and Chapter 8 for guidance on when accommodation is available for occupation. In so far as is reasonably practicable, accommodation should be secured within the authority's own district (s.208(1)).

## POWER TO SECURE ACCOMMODATION FOR APPLICANTS WHO ARE UNINTENTIONALLY HOMELESS AND DO NOT HAVE PRIORITY NEED

**15.5.**  Under s.192(3), housing authorities may secure that accommodation is made available for applicants who are eligible for assistance, unintentionally homeless and do not have a priority need for accommodation. Where a housing authority decides to exercise this power it will still have a duty under s.192(2) to provide advice and assistance to the applicant in any attempts that he or she may make to secure accommodation for him/herself. See Chapter 14 for guidance on this duty.

**15.6.**  By virtue of paragraph 4 of Schedule 1 to the *Housing Act 1985*, a tenancy granted under the power in s.192(3) will not be a secure tenancy. Housing authorities are reminded that all secure and introductory tenancies must be allocated in accordance with their allocation scheme, as framed under Part 6.

**15.7.**  Housing authorities should consider using this power in all relevant cases. Any exercise of, or decision not to exercise, a power may be open to challenge by way of judicial review. In considering the use of this power, housing authorities must have regard to the legitimate expectations of others in housing need who have applied for an allocation of housing under Part 6, and to any need for accommodation to meet their obligations under Part 7.

**15.8.**  Housing authorities should, in particular, consider exercising the s.192(3) power in circumstances where to do so would enable compliance with the obligations imposed on them by virtue of s.6 of the *Human Rights Act 1998* and where not doing so would mean acting in a way that may be incompatible with the applicant's Convention rights. The same is true of the power in s.195(8) (see paragraph 15.17 below).

**15.9.**  Housing authorities may also wish to consider exercising the s.192(3) power to provide accommodation for a limited period to applicants such as key workers who are unintentionally homeless but do not have priority need under Part 7, or priority for an allocation under Part 6. This would be particularly appropriate where it would be in the interests of the local community for such persons to be accommodated in the district.

**15.10.**  Non-secure tenancies will generally be suitable for a limited period only. They should be provided as part of a managed programme of accommodation to give the applicant an opportunity to secure a more settled housing solution in due course. This should be explained to the applicant from the outset and the housing authority should assist him or her to secure alternative accommodation. Reasonable notice should be given of a decision to stop exercising the power.

**15.11.**  Housing authorities should not provide accommodation under s.192(3) as an alternative to allocating accommodation under Part 6 and should not allow non-secure tenancies to continue over the long-term.

## POWERS TO ACCOMMODATE PENDING A REVIEW

**15.12.** Under s.202, applicants have the right to ask for a review of a housing authority's decision on a number of issues relating to their case (see Chapter 19 for guidance on reviews). Housing authorities have three powers to accommodate applicants pending a decision on the review. The relevant powers are found in s.188(3), s.195(8)(b) and s.200(5).

**15.13.** Under s.188(1), housing authorities must secure that accommodation is available for occupation by an applicant who they have reason to believe is:
(a)     homeless,
(b)     eligible for assistance, and
(c)     in priority need,

pending their decision as to what duty, if any, is owed to that applicant under Part 7. See Chapter 7 for further guidance on this interim duty. Under s.188(3), if the applicant requests a review of the housing authority's decision on the duty owed to them under Part 7, the authority has the power to secure that accommodation is available for the applicant's occupation pending a decision on the review.

**15.14.** Section 188(3) includes a power to secure that accommodation is available where the applicant was found to be intentionally homeless and in priority need and:
(a)     a duty was owed under s.190(2)(a);
(b)     the s.190(2)(a) duty has been fully discharged; and
(c)     the applicant is awaiting a decision on a review.

**15.15.** In considering whether to exercise their s.188(3) power, housing authorities will need to balance the objective of maintaining fairness between homeless persons in circumstances where they have decided that no duty is owed to them against proper consideration of the possibility that the applicant might be right. The Secretary of State is of the view that housing authorities should consider the following, although other factors may also be relevant:
(a)     the merits of the applicant's case that the original decision was flawed and the extent to which it can properly be said that the decision was one which was either contrary to the apparent merits or was one which involved a very fine balance of judgment;
(b)     whether any new material, information or argument has been put to them which could alter the original decision; and
(c)     the personal circumstances of the applicant and the consequences to him or her of a decision not to exercise the discretion to accommodate.

The Secretary of State considers that when determining the merits of the applicant's case that the original decision was flawed, housing authorities should take account of whether there may have been procedural irregularities in making the original decision which could have affected the decision taken.

**15.16.** Housing authorities should give applicants reasonable notice to vacate accommodation provided under s.188(3) following an unsuccessful s.202 review. The Secretary of State considers that reasonableness should be judged against the particular applicant's circumstances. The applicant will require time to enable him or her to make alternative accommodation arrangements and housing authorities should take account of the fact that this may be easier for some applicants than others. Housing authorities may also require time to consider whether they should exercise their discretion under s.204(4) where the applicant appeals to the county court under s.204(1) (see paragraph 15.21).

**15.17.** Under s.195(5)(b), where a housing authority is satisfied that an applicant is:
(a)     threatened with homelessness,
(b)     eligible for assistance,
(c)     has a priority need, but
(d)     became threatened with homelessness intentionally,

the authority is under a duty to provide the applicant (or secure that he or she is provided with) advice and assistance so that accommodation does not cease to be available for his or her occupation. Under s.195(8)(b), if the applicant requests a review of the housing authority's decision and, pending a decision on the review, becomes homeless, the housing authority may secure that accommodation is available for his or her occupation.

**15.18.** Under s.200(1), where a housing authority notifies another authority of its opinion that the conditions for the referral of an applicant's case to that authority are met, the authority has a duty to secure that accommodation is available for occupation by the applicant until a decision on the referral is reached. See Chapter 18 for guidance on local connection and referrals. If the applicant subsequently requests a review of the decision reached on the referral of his or her case, the notifying authority has the power under s.200(5) to secure that accommodation is available for the applicant's occupation pending the decision on that review.

**15.19.** Where, generally, only a small proportion of requests for a review are successful, it may be open to housing authorities to adopt a policy of deciding to exercise their powers to accommodate pending a review only in exceptional circumstances. However, such a policy would need to be applied flexibly and each case would need to be considered on its particular fact. whether there were exceptional circumstances, the housing authority would need to take all material considerations and disregard all those which were immaterial.

**15.20.** Where an applicant is refused accommodation pending a review, he or she may se challenge the decision by way of judicial review.

## POWER TO ACCOMMODATE PENDING AN APPEAL TO THE COUNTY COURT

**15.21.** Applicants have the right to appeal to the county court on a point of law against a housing authority's decision on a review or, if they are not notified of the review decision, against the original homelessness decision (see Chapter 19 for guidance on appeals). Under s.204(4), housing authorities have the power to accommodate certain applicants:

 (a)  during the period for making an appeal against their decision, and
 (b)  if an appeal is brought, until it and any subsequent appeals are finally determined.

This power may be exercised where the housing authority was previously under a duty to secure accommodation for the applicant's occupation under s.188 (interim duty pending initial inquiries), s.190 (duty owed to applicants intentionally homeless and in priority need), or s.200 (interim duty owed pending decision on a referral). The power may also be exercised in a case where the applicant was owed a duty under s.195(5)(b) (intentionally threatened with homelessness and in priority need), the applicant requested a review and subsequently become homeless, and, in consequence, the housing authority had a power under s.195(8)(b) to secure accommodation pending the decision on the review.

**15.22.** The power under s.204(4) may be exercised whether or not the housing authority has exercised its powers to accommodate the applicant pending a review.

**15.23.** In deciding whether to exercise this power, housing authorities will need to adopt the same approach, and consider the same factors, as for a decision whether to exercise their power to accommodate pending a review (see paragraph 15.12).

**15.24.** Under s.204A, applicants have a right to appeal to the county court against a decision not to secure accommodation for them pending their main appeal. In deciding a s.204A appeal, the court must apply the principles that would be applied by the High Court on an application for judicial review. The county court cannot substitute its own decision as such. However, where the court quashes the decision of the housing authority, it may order the housing authority to accommodate the applicant, but only where it is satisfied that failure to do so would substantially prejudice the applicant's ability to pursue the main appeal on the homelessness decision.

                               **[5017]**

## CHAPTER 16: SECURING ACCOMMODATION

**16.1. This chapter provides guidance on the different ways in which housing authorities can ensure that suitable accommodation is available for applicants. In the case of the main homelessness duty the obligation to secure such accommodation will continue until such time as the duty ends in accordance with s.193.**

## WAYS OF SECURING ACCOMMODATION

**16.2.** Section 206(1) provides that a housing authority may only discharge its housing functions under Part 7 in the following ways:

 (a)  by securing that suitable accommodation provided by them is available for the applicant (s.206(1)(a));
 (b)  by securing that the applicant obtains suitable accommodation from some other person (s.206(1)(b)); or
 (c)  by giving the applicant such advice and assistance as will secure that suitable accommodation is available from some other person (s.206(1)(c)).

**16.3.** Accommodation secured must be available for occupation by the applicant and any other person who normally resides with them as a member of their family, or might reasonably be expected to reside with them. The accommodation must also be suitable for their occupation. See Chapter 8 for guidance on when accommodation is available for occupation and Chapter 17 for guidance on the suitability of accommodation.

**16.4.** In deciding what accommodation needs to be secured housing authorities will need to consider whether the applicant has any support needs. Housing authorities will therefore need to make arrangements for effective links with the Supporting People team, the social services authority or other bodies (for example, Primary Care Trusts, Criminal Justice Services, RSLs and voluntary and community organisations) to ensure that a joint assessment of an applicant's housing and support needs can be made where necessary. See Chapter 4 for guidance on securing support services.

**16.5.** Where a housing authority has a duty under s.193(2) to secure accommodation for an applicant ('the main homelessness duty'), the Secretary of State recommends that the authority considers, where availability of suitable housing allows, securing settled (rather than temporary) accommodation that will bring the duty to an end in the immediate or short term. For example, an offer of accommodation under the housing authority's allocation scheme or a qualifying offer of an assured shorthold tenancy from a private landlord. See Chapter 14 for guidance on bringing the s.193(2) duty to an end.

**16.6.** The Secretary of State considers that, generally, it is inappropriate for social housing to be used as temporary accommodation for applicants other than for short periods (see paragraph 16.18 below). Except in limited circumstances where social housing is only going to be available for use for a short period, where an authority has placed a household in social housing as a temporary arrangement to fulfil a duty under s.193(2), the Secretary of State recommends that the authority considers offering the household a settled home under the terms of its allocation scheme as soon as possible.

## ACCOMMODATION SECURED OUT OF DISTRICT

**16.7.** Section 208(1) requires housing authorities to secure accommodation within their district, in so far as is reasonably practicable. Housing authorities should, therefore, aim to secure accommodation within their own district wherever possible, except where there are clear benefits for the applicant of being accommodated outside of the district. This could occur, for example, where the applicant, and/or a member of his or her household, would be at risk of domestic or other violence in the district and need to be accommodated elsewhere to reduce the risk of further contact with the perpetrator(s) or where ex-offenders or drug/alcohol users would benefit from being accommodated outside the district to help break links with previous contacts which could exert a negative influence.

**16.8.** Where it is not reasonably practicable for the applicant to be placed in accommodation within the housing authority's district, and the housing authority places the applicant in accommodation elsewhere, s.208(2) requires the housing authority to notify the housing authority in whose district the accommodation is situated of the following:

i)      the name of the applicant;
ii)     the number and description of other persons who normally reside with the applicant as a member of his or her family or might reasonably be expected to do so;
iii)    the address of the accommodation;
iv)     the date on which the accommodation was made available;
v)      which function the housing authority is discharging in securing the accommodation.

The notice must be given in writing within 14 days of the accommodation being made available to the applicant.

**16.9.** The Secretary of State considers that applicants whose household has a need for social services support or a need to maintain links with other essential services within the borough, for example specialist medical services or special schools, should be given priority for accommodation within the housing authority's own district. In particular, careful consideration should be given to applicants with a mental illness or learning disability who may have a particular need to remain in a specific area, for example to maintain links with health service professionals and/or a reliance on existing informal support networks and community links. Such applicants may be less able than others to adapt to any disruption caused by being placed in accommodation in another district.

## ACCESS TO SUPPORT SERVICES

**16.10.** The Secretary of State recommends that housing authorities consider what arrangements need to be in place to ensure that households placed in temporary accommodation, within their district or outside, are able to access relevant support services, including health, education and social services. The Secretary of State considers that all babies and young children placed in temporary accommodation, for example, should have the opportunity to receive health and developmental checks from health visitors and/or other primary health care professionals. See Chapter 4 for further guidance on securing support services.

## ACCOMMODATION PROVIDED BY THE HOUSING AUTHORITY

**16.11.** Housing authorities may secure accommodation by providing suitable accommodation for the applicant themselves (s.206(1)(a)), in which case the housing authority will be the immediate landlord of the applicant, for example, where the housing authority place the applicant in:

i)      a house or flat from its own stock (i.e. held under Part 2 of the *Housing Act 1985*);
ii)     a hostel owned by the housing authority; or
iii)    accommodation leased by the housing authority from another landlord (e.g. under a private sector leasing agreement) and sub-let to the applicant.

*Housing authority's own stock*

**16.12.** In considering whether to provide accommodation from their own stock, housing authorities will need to balance the requirements of applicants owed a duty under Part 7 against the need to provide accommodation for others who have priority for an allocation under Part 6 of the 1996 Act. **The Secretary of State considers that, generally, it is inappropriate for social housing to be used as temporary accommodation for applicants other than for short periods.**

**16.13.** Paragraph 4 of Schedule 1 to the *Housing Act 1985* provides that a tenancy granted by a housing authority in pursuance of any function under Part 7 is not a secure tenancy unless the housing authority notifies the tenant that it is such. Housing authorities are reminded that the allocation of secure and introductory tenancies must be made in accordance with their allocation scheme framed under the provisions of Part 6.

*Housing authority hostels*

**16.14.** Some housing authorities operate their own hostels and may wish to use these to accommodate certain applicants, particularly where they consider an applicant would benefit from a supported environment. See paragraphs 16.25 and 16.26 for further guidance on the use of hostel accommodation.

*Accommodation leased from a private landlord*

**16.15.** Accommodation leased from a private landlord can provide housing authorities with a source of good quality, self-contained accommodation which can be let to applicants. Where there is a need for temporary accommodation, housing authorities are encouraged to maximise their use of this type of leasing, in so far as they can secure cost-effective arrangements with landlords.

**16.16.** Under the prudential capital finance system (introduced by the *Local Government Act 2003* on 1 April 2004) local authorities are free to borrow without Government consent, provided that they can service the debts without extra Government support. The authority must determine how much it can afford to borrow. The new system ended the former financial disincentives to use leasing (and other forms of credit). Consequently, there is no longer any need for special concessions relating to leases of property owned by private landlords where that property is used to accommodate households owed a duty under Part 7. When entering into leases, as when borrowing, the capital finance rules simply require authorities to be satisfied that the associated liabilities are affordable.

## ACCOMMODATION SECURED FROM ANOTHER PERSON

**16.17.** Housing authorities may secure that the applicant obtains suitable accommodation from some other person (s.206(1)(b)). Housing authorities can make use of a wide range of accommodation, including housing in the private rented sector and accommodation held by RSLs. The following paragraphs outline a number of options for securing accommodation from another landlord, which are available to housing authorities.

*Registered social landlords*

**16.18.** As the proportion of housing stock in the social sector held by RSLs increases, housing authorities should ensure that they maximise the opportunities for securing housing from RSLs. Under s.213 of the 1996 Act, where requested by a housing authority, an RSL must assist the housing authority in carrying out their duties under the homelessness legislation by co-operating with them as far as is reasonable in the circumstances. Housing Corporation regulatory guidance, issued with the consent of the Secretary of State under s.36 of the 1996 Act, requires RSLs, on request, to provide a proportion of their stock for nominations and as temporary accommodation for people owed a homelessness duty under Part 7 of the 1996 Act – to such extent as is reasonable in the circumstances. **The Secretary of State considers that, generally, it is inappropriate for social housing to be used as temporary accommodation other than for short periods** (see paragraph 16.6 above). Where a longer-term stay occurs or seems likely, the authority and RSL should consider offering an assured tenancy to bring the main homelessness duty to an end. See Annex 5 for further guidance on RSL co-operation with housing authorities.

**16.19.** Housing authorities may wish to consider contracting with RSLs for assistance in discharging their housing functions under arrangements whereby the RSL lease and/or manage accommodation owned by private landlords, which can be let to households owed a homelessness duty and nominated by the housing authority. A general consent under s.25 of the *Local Government Act 1988* (*The General Consent under Section 25 of the Local Government Act 1988 for Financial Assistance to Registered Social Landlords or to Private Landlords to Relieve or Prevent Homelessness 2005*) allows housing authorities to provide RSLs with financial assistance in connection with such arrangements. Housing authorities must reserve the right to terminate such agreements, without penalty, after 3 years.

*Private lettings*

**16.20.** Housing authorities may seek the assistance of private sector landlords in providing suitable accommodation direct to applicants. A general consent under s.25 of the *Local Government Act 1988* (*The General Consent under Section 25 of the Local Government Act 1988 for Financial Assistance to Registered Social Landlords or to Private Landlords to Relieve or Prevent*

*Homelessness 2005*) allows housing authorities to provide financial assistance to private landlords in order to secure accommodation for people who are homeless or at risk of homelessness. This could involve, for example, the authority paying the costs of leases; making small one-off grants ("finders' fees") to landlords to encourage them to let dwellings to households owed a homelessness duty; paying rent deposits or indemnities to ensure accommodation is secured for such households; and making one-off grant payments which would prevent an eviction. There is no limit set on the amount of financial assistance that can be provided, however authorities are obliged to act reasonably and in accordance with their fiduciary duty to local tax and rent payers. Housing authorities may also make Discretionary Housing Payments (DHP) to a private landlord to meet a shortfall between the rent and the amount of housing benefit payable to a person who is homeless or at risk of homelessness. DHPs are intended to provide extra financial assistance where there is a shortfall in a person's eligible rent and the housing authority consider that the claimant is in need of further financial assistance. They are governed by the *Discretionary Housing Payment (Grant) Order 2001*. Housing authorities should also consider working with private landlords to arrange qualifying offers of assured shorthold tenancies which would bring the main homelessness duty to an end if accepted by the applicant. See paragraph 14.19 for guidance on qualifying offers.

*Tenancies granted by private landlords and registered social landlords to assist with interim duties*

**16.21.** Section 209 governs security of tenure where a private landlord provides accommodation to assist a housing authority discharge an **interim** duty, for example, a duty under s.188(1), s.190(2), s.200(1) or 204(4). Any such accommodation is exempt from statutory security of tenure until 12 months from the date on which the applicant is notified of the authority's decision under s.184(3) or s.198(5) or from the date on which the applicant is notified of the decision of any review under s.202 or an appeal under s.204, unless the landlord notifies the applicant that the tenancy is an assured or assured shorthold tenancy.

**16.22.** Where a private landlord or RSL lets accommodation directly to an applicant to assist a housing authority discharge any other homelessness duty, the tenancy granted will be an assured shorthold tenancy unless the tenant is notified that it is to be regarded as an assured tenancy.

*Other social landlords*

**16.23.** Under s.213 other social landlords, i.e. new town corporations and housing action trusts, have a duty to co-operate, as far as is reasonable in the circumstances, with a housing authority in carrying out their housing functions under Part 7 of the 1996 Act, if asked to do so.

*Lodgings*

**16.24.** Lodgings provided by householders may be suitable for some young and/or vulnerable single applicants. Housing authorities may wish to establish a network of such landlords in their district, and to liaise with social services who may operate supported lodgings schemes for people with support needs.

*Hostels*

**16.25.** Some applicants may benefit from the supportive environment which managed hostels can provide. Hostels can offer short-term support to people who are experiencing a temporary crisis, and provide an opportunity for them to regain their equilibrium and subsequently move on to live independently. Where an applicant appears to need support, particularly on-going support, and there is no social worker or support worker familiar with their case, the housing authority should request a community care assessment by the social services authority. However, housing authorities should not assume that a hostel will automatically be the most appropriate form of accommodation for vulnerable people, particularly in relation to young people, people with mental health problems and those who have experienced violence and/or abuse. In addition, where hostel accommodation is used to accommodate vulnerable young people or families with children, the Secretary of State considers that it would be inappropriate to accommodate these groups alongside adults with chaotic behavioural problems.

**16.26.** Housing authorities will need to take into account that some hostels are designed to meet short-term needs only. In addition to the question of whether the hostel accommodation would be suitable for the applicant for other than a short period, housing authorities should have regard to the need to ensure that bed spaces continue to be available in hostels for others who need them.

*Women's refuges*

**16.27.** Housing authorities should develop close links with women's refuges within their district, and neighbouring districts, to ensure they have access to emergency accommodation for women applicants who are fleeing domestic or other violence or who are at risk of such violence. However, housing authorities should recognise that placing an applicant in a refuge will generally be a temporary expedient only, and a prolonged stay could block a bed space that was urgently needed by someone else at risk. Refuges should be used to provide accommodation for the minimum period necessary before alternative suitable accommodation is secured elsewhere. Housing authorities should not delay in securing alternative accommodation in the hope that the applicant might return to her partner.

*Bed and breakfast accommodation*

**16.28.** Bed and Breakfast (B&B) accommodation caters for very short-term stays only and generally will afford residents only limited privacy and may lack certain important amenities, such as cooking and laundry facilities. Consequently, where possible, housing authorities should avoid using B&B hotels to discharge a duty to secure accommodation for applicants, unless, in the very limited circumstances where it is likely to be the case, it is the most appropriate option for an applicant. The Secretary of State considers B&B hotels as particularly unsuitable for accommodating applicants with family commitments and applicants aged 16 or 17 years who need support. See paragraphs 17.23 *et seq* in Chapter 17 for guidance on suitability and Chapter 12 for more detailed guidance on 16 and 17 year olds.

*Accommodation provided by other housing authorities*

**16.29.** Other housing authorities experiencing less demand for housing may be able to assist a housing authority by providing temporary or settled accommodation for homeless applicants. This could be particularly appropriate in the case of applicants who would be at risk of violence or serious harassment in the district of the housing authority to whom they have applied for assistance. Other housing authorities may also be able to provide accommodation in cases where the applicant has special housing needs and the other housing authority has accommodation available which is appropriate to those needs. Under s.213(1), where one housing authority requests another to help them discharge a function under Part 7, the other housing authority must co-operate in providing such assistance as is reasonable in the circumstances. Housing authorities are encouraged to consider entering into reciprocal and co-operative arrangements under these provisions. See Chapter 5 for guidance on the statutory provisions on co-operation between authorities.

*Mobile homes*

**16.30.** Although mobile homes may sometimes provide emergency or short-term accommodation, e.g. to discharge an interim duty, housing authorities will need to be satisfied that the accommodation is suitable for the applicant and his or her household, paying particular regard to their needs, requirements and circumstances and the conditions and facilities on the site. Caravans designed primarily for short-term holiday use should not be regarded as suitable as temporary accommodation for applicants.

*Tenancies for minors*

**16.31.** There are legal complications associated with the grant of a tenancy to a minor because a minor cannot hold a legal estate in land. However, if a tenancy is granted it is likely to be enforceable as a contract for necessaries (ie. the basic necessities of life) under common law. In some circumstances, social services authorities may consider it appropriate to underwrite a tenancy agreement for a homeless applicant who is under 18.

## ADVICE AND ASSISTANCE THAT WILL SECURE ACCOMMODATION FROM ANOTHER PERSON

**16.32.** Housing authorities may secure accommodation by giving advice and assistance to an applicant that will secure that accommodation becomes available for him or her from another person (s.206(1)(c)). However, where an authority has a duty to secure accommodation, they will need to ensure that the advice and assistance provided results in suitable accommodation actually being secured. Merely assisting the applicant in any efforts that he or she might make to find accommodation would not be sufficient if suitable accommodation did not actually become available.

**16.33.** One example of securing accommodation in this way is where house purchase is a possibility for the applicant. Advice on all options for financing house purchase should be made available, especially those financial packages which may be suited to people on lower incomes.

**16.34.** One option to help people into home ownership is shared equity schemes (e.g. part buy/part rent or equity loans to assist with purchase). These schemes are mainly funded by the Housing Corporation and generally offered by RSLs. The Housing Corporation publishes booklets (available from their publication section) giving further details of the existing shared ownership and Homebuy schemes. A new HomeBuy scheme offering further opportunities for home ownership and building on the current schemes commenced on 1st April 2006.

**16.35.** In other cases, applicants may have identified suitable accommodation but need practical advice and assistance to enable them to secure it, for example the applicant may require help with understanding a tenancy agreement or financial assistance with paying a rent deposit.

**16.36.** Housing authorities should bear in mind that the advice and assistance must result in suitable accommodation being secured, and that applicants who wish to pursue this option may need alternative accommodation until this result is achieved.

## APPLICANTS WHO NORMALLY OCCUPY MOVEABLE ACCOMMODATION (E.G. CARAVANS, HOUSEBOATS)

**16.37.** Under s.175(2) applicants are homeless if the accommodation available for their occupation is a caravan, houseboat, or other movable structure and they do not have a place where they are entitled, or permitted, to put it and live in it. If a duty to secure accommodation arises in such cases, the housing authority is not required to make equivalent accommodation available (or provide a site or berth for the applicant's own accommodation). However, the authority must consider whether such options are reasonably available, particularly where this would provide the most suitable solution to the applicant's accommodation needs.

### Gypsies and Travellers

**16.38.** The circumstances described in paragraph 16.37 will be particularly relevant in the case of Gypsies and Travellers. Where a duty to secure accommodation arises but an appropriate site is not immediately available, the housing authority may need to provide an alternative temporary solution until a suitable site, or some other suitable option, becomes available. Some Gypsies and Travellers may have a cultural aversion to the prospect of 'bricks and mortar' accommodation. In such cases, the authority should seek to provide an alternative solution. However, where the authority is satisfied that there is no prospect of a suitable site for the time being, there may be no alternative solution. Authorities must give consideration to the needs and lifestyle of applicants who are Gypsies and Travellers when considering their application and how best to discharge a duty to secure suitable accommodation, in line with their obligations to act consistently with the *Human Rights Act 1998*, and in particular the right to respect for private life, family and the home.

### Temporary to settled accommodation

**16.39.** Housing authorities are encouraged to test new approaches that would enable temporary accommodation to become settled accommodation. This would reduce the uncertainty and lack of security that households in temporary accommodation can face, and provide them with a settled home more quickly. Such approaches could be developed with housing associations through a range of "temporary to settled" housing initiatives.

**16.40.** Each year approximately a quarter to a third of all leases of private sector accommodation held by social landlords expire. This presents an opportunity for the leased accommodation to be converted from use as temporary accommodation to the provision of settled housing, through negotiation with the landlord and the tenant during the final months of the lease. Where the household would be content to remain in the accommodation when the lease ends if it could be provided on a more settled basis, and the landlord would be prepared to let directly to the household, the local authority may wish to arrange for the landlord to make a 'qualifying offer' of an assured shorthold tenancy, for the purposes of s.193(7B). See paragraph 14.19 for guidance on 'qualifying offer'.

**16.41.** Where scope for conversion of temporary accommodation to settled accommodation is explored, the interests of the household must take priority, and the household should not be pressured to accept offers of accommodation that would bring the homelessness duty to an end.

**16.42.** There may also be limited potential for converting temporary accommodation leased from the private sector to a qualifying offer of an assured shorthold tenancy at the beginning or mid-point of a lease. However, this would probably require the lease to include a break clause to facilitate early termination.

**16.43.** While the local authority holds the lease of accommodation owned by a private sector landlord, the accommodation would not be capable of being offered to a household as a qualifying offer of an assured shorthold tenancy under s.193(7B). However, where a registered social landlord held such a lease, the accommodation may be capable of being offered to a household as a qualifying offer of an assured shorthold tenancy under s.193(7B) during the period of the lease, if all the parties agreed and the qualifying offer met the terms of s.193(7D).

[5018]

## CHAPTER 17: SUITABILITY OF ACCOMMODATION

**17.1. This chapter provides guidance on the factors to be taken into account when determining the suitability of temporary accommodation secured under the homelessness legislation. Key factors include: the needs, requirements and circumstances of each household; space and arrangement; health and safety considerations; affordability, and location. Annex 16 sets out the statutory definition of overcrowding and Annex 17 sets out the minimum recommended standards for Bed and Breakfast accommodation.**

**17.2.** Section 206 provides that where a housing authority discharges its functions to secure that accommodation is available for an applicant the accommodation must be suitable. This applies in respect of all powers and duties to secure accommodation under Part 7, including interim duties such as those under s.188(1) and s.200(1). The accommodation must be suitable in relation to the applicant and to all members of his or her household who normally reside with him or her, or who might reasonably be expected to reside with him or her.

**17.3.** Suitability of accommodation is governed by s.210. Section 210(2) provides for the Secretary of State to specify by order the circumstances in which accommodation is or is not to be regarded as suitable for someone, and matters to be taken into account or disregarded in determining whether accommodation is suitable for someone.

**17.4.** Space and arrangement will be key factors in determining the suitability of accommodation. However, consideration of whether accommodation is suitable will require an assessment of all aspects of the accommodation in the light of the relevant needs, requirements and circumstances of the homeless person and his or her family. The location of the accommodation will always be a relevant factor (see paragraph 17.41).

**17.5.** Housing authorities will need to consider carefully the suitability of accommodation for applicants whose household has particular medical and/or physical needs. The Secretary of State recommends that physical access to and around the home, space, bathroom and kitchen facilities, access to a garden and modifications to assist sensory loss as well as mobility need are all taken into account. These factors will be especially relevant where a member of the household is disabled.

**17.6.** Account will need to be taken of any social considerations relating to the applicant and his or her household that might affect the suitability of accommodation. Any risk of violence or racial harassment in a particular locality must also be taken into account. Where domestic violence is involved and the applicant is not able to stay in the current home, housing authorities may need to consider the need for alternative accommodation whose location can be kept a secret and which has security measures and staffing to protect the occupants. For applicants who have suffered domestic violence who are accommodated temporarily in hostels or bed and breakfast accommodation, the accommodation may need to be gender-specific as well as have security measures.

**17.7.** Accommodation that is suitable for a short period, for example bed and breakfast or hostel accommodation used to discharge an interim duty pending inquiries under s.188, may not necessarily be suitable for a longer period, for example to discharge a duty under s.193(2).

**17.8.** As the duty to provide suitable accommodation is a continuing obligation, housing authorities must keep the issue of suitability of accommodation under review. If there is a change of circumstances of substance the authority is obliged to reconsider suitability in a specific case.

## STANDARDS OF ACCOMMODATION

**17.9.** Section 210(1) requires a housing authority to have regard to the following provisions when assessing the suitability of accommodation for an applicant:
- Parts 9 and 10 of the *Housing Act 1985* (the "1985 Act") (slum clearance and overcrowding), and
- Parts 1 to 4 of the *Housing Act 2004* (the "2004 Act") (housing conditions, licensing of houses in multiple occupation, selective licensing of other residential accommodation and additional control provisions in relation to residential accommodation.)

*Fitness for habitation*

**17.10.** Part 1 of the *Housing Act 2004* (the "2004 Act") contains provisions that replace the housing fitness regime in s.604 of the 1985 Act. From 6th April 2006, the fitness standard in the 1985 Act is replaced by a new evidence-based assessment of risks to health and safety in all residential premises (including HMOs), carried out using the Housing Health and Safety Rating System (HHSRS). Part 9 of the 1985 Act is retained, with amendments, to deal with hazards for which demolition or area clearance is the most appropriate option.

**Housing Health and Safety Rating System (HHSRS)**

**17.11.** Action by local authorities is based on a three-stage consideration: (a) the hazard rating determined under HHSRS; (b) whether the authority has a duty or power to act, determined by the presence of a hazard above or below a threshold prescribed by Regulations (Category 1 and Category 2 hazards); and (c) the authority's judgment as to the most appropriate course of action to deal with the hazard.

**17.12.** The purpose of the HHSRS assessment is to generate objective information in order to determine and inform enforcement decisions. HHSRS allows for the assessment of twenty nine categories of housing hazard and provides a method for rating each hazard. It does not provide a single rating for the dwelling as a whole or, in the case of HMOs, for the building as a whole. A hazard rating is expressed through a numerical score which falls within a band, ranging from Band A to J. Scores in Bands A to C are Category 1 hazards. Scores in Bands D to J are Category 2 hazards. If a housing authority considers that a Category 1 hazard exists on any residential premises, they have a duty under the 2004 Act to take appropriate enforcement action in relation to the hazard. They also have a power to take particular kinds of enforcement action in cases where they consider that a Category 2 hazard exists.

**17.13.** The HHSRS assessment is based on the risk to the *potential occupant who is most vulnerable to that hazard.* For example, stairs constitute a greater risk to the elderly, so for assessing hazards relating to stairs they are considered the most vulnerable group. The very young as well as the elderly are susceptible to low temperatures. A dwelling that is safe for those most vulnerable to a hazard is safe for all.

**17.14.** Housing authorities should be familiar with the principles of the HHSRS and with the operational guidance issued under s.9 of the 2004 Act.

**17.15. The Secretary of State recommends that when determining the suitability of accommodation secured under the homelessness legislation, local authorities should, as a minimum, ensure that all accommodation is free of Category 1 hazards.** In the case of an out of district placement it is the responsibility of the placing authority to ensure that accommodation is free of Category 1 hazards.

*Overcrowding*

**17.16.** Part 10 of the 1985 Act is intended to tackle the problems of overcrowding in dwellings. Section 324 provides a definition of overcrowding which in turn relies on the room standard specified in s.325 and the space standard in s.326 (the standards are set out in Annex 17).

**17.17.** A room provided within an HMO may be defined as a "dwelling" under Part 10 of the 1985 Act and the room and space standards will therefore apply. Housing authorities should also note that 'crowding and space' is one of the hazards assessed by the HHSRS. Any breach of the room and space standards under Part 10 is likely to constitute a Category 1 hazard.

*Houses in Multiple Occupation (HMOs)*

**17.18.** Parts 2, 3 and 4 of the 2004 Act – which came into force on 6 April 2006 – contain provisions to replace Part 11 of the 1985 Act which relates to HMOs.

**17.19.** The 2004 Act introduces a new definition of an HMO. A property is an HMO if it satisfies the conditions set out in sections 254(2) to (4), has been declared an HMO under s.255 or is a converted block of flats to which s.257 applies.

**17.20.** Privately owned Bed and Breakfast or hostel accommodation that is used to accommodate a household pursuant to a homelessness function, and which is the household's main residence, will fall within this definition of an HMO. Buildings managed or owned by a public body (such as the police or the NHS), local housing authority, registered social landlord or buildings which are already regulated under other legislation (such as care homes or bail hostels) will be exempt from the HMO definition. Buildings which are occupied entirely by freeholders or long leaseholders, those occupied by only two people, or by a resident landlord with up to two tenants will also be exempt. Most student accommodation (housing students undertaking a course in higher or further education) will also be exempt if it is managed and controlled by the establishment in accordance with a code of management practice.

**17.21.** From 6 April 2006, local authorities have been required to undertake the mandatory licensing of all privately rented HMOs (except converted blocks of flats to which s.257 applies) of three or more storeys and occupied by five or more people who form two or more households. Local authorities will also have discretionary powers to introduce additional licensing schemes covering smaller HMOs. In order to be a licence holder, a landlord will have to be a "fit and proper" person, as defined in s.89 of the Act and demonstrate that suitable management arrangements are in place in their properties.

**17.22.** In addition a local authority will have to be satisfied that the HMO is suitable for the number of occupants it is licensed for and meets statutory standards relating to shared amenities and facilities, e.g. that it has an adequate number, type and quality of shared bathrooms, toilets and cooking facilities. These standards are set out in Schedule 3 to the *Licensing and Management of Houses in Multiple Occupation and Other Houses (Miscellaneous Provisions) (England) Regulations 2006* (SI No 2006/373). These 'amenity standards' will run alongside the consideration of health and safety issues under HHSRS. *The Housing (Management of Houses in Multiple Occupation) Regulations 1990* are to be replaced by the *Management of Houses in Multiple Occupation (England) Regulations 2006* (SI 2006/372). Neither the amenity standards nor the new management regulations apply to HMOs that are converted blocks of flats to which s.257 applies. It is intended that separate regulations will be made by July 6th to modify Part 2 of the 2004 Act (which deals with mandatory licensing) in so far as it relates to these types of HMO, and to extend, with modifications, the application of the new amenity standards and management regulations to these types of HMO. Until then they will continue to be subject to the registration schemes made under Part 11 of the 1985 Act. Transitional arrangements have been in place since April 2006 so that most HMOs that are registered in a 1985 scheme will automatically be licensed under the 2004 Act.

**17.23.** Local authorities also have discretion to extend licensing to privately rented properties in all, or part of, their area to address particular problems, such as low housing demand or significant incidence of anti-social behaviour. However, licensing in these selective circumstances is concerned only with property management and not the condition of the property.

## BED AND BREAKFAST ACCOMMODATION

**17.24.** Bed and Breakfast (B&B) accommodation caters for very short-term stays only and generally will afford residents only limited privacy and may lack certain important amenities, such as cooking and laundry facilities. Consequently, where possible, housing authorities should avoid using B&B hotels to discharge a duty to secure accommodation for homeless applicants, unless, in the very limited circumstances where it is likely to be the case, it is the most appropriate option for the applicant.

**17.25.** Living in B&B accommodation can be particularly detrimental to the health and development of children. Under s.210(2), the Secretary of State has made the *Homelessness (Suitability of Accommodation) (England) Order 2003* (SI 2003 No. 3326) ("the Order"). The Order specifies that when accommodation is made available for occupation under certain functions in Part 7, B&B accommodation is not to be regarded as suitable for applicants with family commitments.

**17.26.** Housing authorities should, therefore, use B&B hotels to discharge a duty to secure accommodation for applicants with family commitments only as a last resort. Applicants with family commitments means an applicant -
    (a)    who is pregnant;
    (b)    with whom a pregnant woman resides or might reasonably be expected to reside; or
    (c)    with whom dependent children reside or might reasonably be expected to reside.

**17.27.** For the purpose of the Order, B&B accommodation means accommodation (whether or not breakfast is included):
    (a)    which is not separate and self-contained premises; and
    (b)    in which any of the following amenities is shared by more than one household:
              (i)     a toilet;
              (ii)    personal washing facilities;
              (iii)   cooking facilities.

B&B accommodation does not include accommodation which is owned or managed by a local housing authority, a registered social landlord or a voluntary organisation as defined in section 180(3) of the *Housing Act 1996*.

**17.28.** B&B accommodation is not to be regarded as suitable for applicants with family commitments (except as specified in paragraph 17.29 below) for the purpose of discharging a duty under the following duties:
    ●      section 188(1) (interim duty to accommodate in case of apparent priority need);
    ●      section 190(2)(a) (duties to persons becoming homeless intentionally);
    ●      section 193(2) (duty to persons with priority need who are not homeless intentionally);
    ●      section 200(1) (duty to applicant whose case is considered for referral or referred); and
    ●      section 195(2) (duties in cases of threatened homelessness) where the accommodation is other than that occupied by the applicant at the time of making his or her application.

**17.29.** The Order provides that if no alternative accommodation is available for the applicant the housing authority may accommodate the family in B&B for a period, or periods, not exceeding six weeks in result of a single homelessness application. **Where B&B accommodation is secured for an applicant with family commitments, the Secretary of State considers that the authority should notify the applicant of the effect of the Order, and, in particular, that the authority will be unable to continue to secure B&B accommodation for such applicants any longer than 6 weeks, after which they must secure alternative, suitable accommodation.**

**17.30.** When determining whether accommodation other than B&B accommodation is available for use, housing authorities will need to take into account, among other things, the cost to the authority of securing the accommodation, the affordability of the accommodation for the applicant and the location of the accommodation. An authority is under no obligation to include in its considerations accommodation which is to be allocated in accordance with its allocation scheme, published under s.167 of the 1996 Act.

**17.31.** If there is a significant change in an applicant's circumstances that would bring the applicant within the scope of the Order (e.g. a new pregnancy), the six week period should start from the date the authority was informed of the change of circumstances not the date the applicant was originally placed in B&B accommodation.

**17.32.** If the conditions for referring a case are met and another housing authority accepts responsibility for an applicant under s.200(4), any time spent in B&B accommodation before this acceptance should be disregarded in calculating the six week period.

**17.33.** B&B accommodation is also unlikely to be suitable for 16 and 17 year olds who are in need of support. Where B&B accommodation is used for this group it ought to be as a last resort for the shortest time possible and housing authorities will need to ensure that appropriate support is provided where necessary. See Chapter 12 for guidance on the use of B&B for 16 and 17 year olds.

**17.34.** The Secretary of State considers that the limited circumstances in which B&B hotels may provide suitable accommodation could include those where:

(a) emergency accommodation is required at very short notice (for example to discharge the interim duty to accommodate under s.188); or

(b) there is simply no better alternative accommodation available and the use of B&B accommodation is necessary as a last resort.

**17.35.** The Secretary of State considers that where housing authorities are unable to avoid using B&B hotels to accommodate applicants, they should ensure that such accommodation is of a good standard (see paragaphs 17.36–17.38 below) and is used for the shortest period possible. The Secretary of State considers that where a lengthy stay seems likely, the authority should consider other accommodation more appropriate to the applicant's needs.

*Standards of B&B accommodation*

**17.36.** Where housing authorities are unable to avoid using B&B hotels to accommodate applicants they should ensure that such accommodation is of a suitable standard. Where a B&B hotel is used to accommodate an applicant and is their main residence, it falls within the definition of an HMO. Paragraphs 17.18 – 17.23 above explain the legislation that applies to HMOs with regard to health and safety and overcrowding. Since April 2006, local authorities have a power under the 2004 Act to issue an HMO Declaration confirming HMO status where there is uncertainty about the status of a property.

**17.37.** The Government recognises that living conditions in HMOs should not only be healthy and safe but should also provide acceptable, decent standards for people who may be unrelated to each other and who are sharing basic facilities. As noted at paragraph 17.22 above, the Government has set out in regulation the minimum 'amenity standards' required for a property to be granted an HMO licence. These standards will only apply to 'high-risk' HMOs covered by mandatory licensing or those HMOs that will be subject to additional licensing, and will not apply to the majority of HMOs. However, housing authorities (or groups of authorities) can adopt their own local classification, amenity specification or minimum standards for B&B and other shared accommodation provided as temporary accommodation under Part 7. In London, for example, boroughs have, since 1988, had a code of practice on the use of B&B and other shared temporary accommodation used to accommodate households under Part 7. This establishes clear benchmarks for standards across the Capital. Under the code of practice, properties are graded from A to E, with the grading dependent upon a wide range of considerations and factors relating to the facilities and services provided by an establishment. Placements are expected to be made only in those properties that meet the required standard. Setting the Standard (STS), a new automated system administered by the Greater London Authority (GLA), assists boroughs to comply with the code of practice. It collects and collates information from environmental health officers' annual inspections of properties and then makes this easily accessible to relevant borough officers across London. For further information on STS contact STS@london.gov.uk. The Secretary of State welcomes these arrangements and encourages other housing authorities to consider adopting similar systems to support the exchange of information and improve standards of temporary accommodation.

**17.38.** The Government considers that the size and occupancy levels of rooms, the provision and location of cooking, toilet and bathing facilities, and management standards are particularly important factors for determining whether B&B accommodation is suitable for accommodating households under Part 7. The Secretary of State therefore recommends that housing authorities have regard to the recommended minimum standards set out in Annex 17 when assessing whether B&B accommodation is suitable.

## AFFORDABILITY

**17.39.** Under s.210(2), the Secretary of State has made the *Homelessness (Suitability of Accommodation) Order 1996* (SI 1996 No. 3204). The 1996 Order specifies that in determining whether it would be, or would have been, reasonable for a person to occupy accommodation that is considered suitable, a housing authority must take into account whether the accommodation is affordable by him or her, and in particular must take account of:

(a) the financial resources available to him or her (*i.e. all forms of income*), including, but not limited to:

    i) salary, fees and other remuneration (*from such sources as investments, grants, pensions, tax credits etc.*);

    ii) social security benefits (*such as housing benefit, income support, income-based Jobseekers Allowances or Council Tax benefit etc.*);

    iii) payments due under a court order for the making of periodical payments to a spouse or a former spouse, or to, or for the benefit of, a child;

iv)      payments of child support maintenance due under the *Child Support Act 1991*;

v)      pensions;

vi)      contributions to the costs in respect of the accommodation which are or were made or which might reasonably be expected to be, or have been, made by other members of his or her household (*most members can be assumed to contribute, but the amount depends on various factors including their age and income. Other influencing factors can be drawn from the parallels of their entitlement to housing benefit and income support in relation to housing costs. Current rates should be available from housing authority benefit sections*);

vii)      financial assistance towards the costs in respect of the accommodation, including loans, provided by a local authority, voluntary organisation or other body;

viii)      benefits derived from a policy of insurance (*such as cover against unemployment or sickness*);

ix)      savings and other capital sums (*which may be a source of income or might be available to meet accommodation expenses. However, it should be borne in mind that, again drawing from the parallel social securities assistance, capital savings below a threshold amount are disregarded for the purpose of assessing a claim*);

(b)      the costs in respect of the accommodation, including, but not limited to:

i)      payments of, or by way of, rent (*including rent default/property damage deposits*);

ii)      payments in respect of a licence or permission to occupy the accommodation;

iii)      mortgage costs (*including an assessment of entitlement to Income Support Mortgage Interest (ISMI)*);

iv)      payments of, or by way of, service charges (*e.g. maintenance or other costs required as a condition of occupation of the accommodation*);

v)      mooring charges payable for a houseboat;

vi)      where the accommodation is a caravan or a mobile home, payments in respect of the site on which it stands;

vii)      the amount of council tax payable in respect of the accommodation;

viii)      payments by way of deposit or security in respect of the accommodation;

ix)      payments required by an accommodation agency;

(c)      payments which that person is required to make under a court order for the making of periodical payments to a spouse or former spouse, or to, or for the benefit of, a child and payments of child support maintenance required to be made under the *Child Support Act 1991*; and

(d)      his or her other reasonable living expenses.

**17.40.** In considering an applicant's residual income after meeting the costs of the accommodation, the Secretary of State recommends that housing authorities regard accommodation as not being affordable if the applicant would be left with a residual income which would be less than the level of income support or income-based jobseekers allowance that is applicable in respect of the applicant, or would be applicable if he or she was entitled to claim such benefit. This amount will vary from case to case, according to the circumstances and composition of the applicant's household. A current tariff of applicable amounts in respect of such benefits should be available within the authority's housing benefit section. Housing authorities will need to consider whether the applicant can afford the housing costs without being deprived of basic essentials such as food, clothing, heating, transport and other essentials. The Secretary of State recommends that housing authorities avoid placing applicants who are in low paid employment in accommodation where they would need to resort to claiming benefit to meet the costs of that accommodation, and to consider opportunities to secure accommodation at affordable rent levels where this is likely to reduce perceived or actual disincentives to work.

## LOCATION OF ACCOMMODATION

**17.41.** The location of the accommodation will be relevant to suitability and the suitability of the location for all the members of the household will have to be considered. Where, for example, applicants are in paid employment account will need to be taken of their need to reach their normal workplace from the accommodation secured. The Secretary of State recommends that local authorities take into account the need to minimise disruption to the education of young people, particularly at critical points in time such as close to taking GCSE examinations. Housing authorities should avoid placing applicants in isolated accommodation away from public transport, shops and other facilities, and, wherever possible, secure accommodation that is as close as possible to where they were previously living, so they can retain established links with schools, doctors, social workers and other key services and support essential to the well-being of the household.

## HOUSEHOLDS WITH PETS

**17.42.** Housing authorities will need to be sensitive to the importance of pets to some applicants, particularly elderly people and rough sleepers who may rely on pets for companionship. Although it will not always be possible to make provision for pets, the Secretary of State recommends that housing authorities give careful consideration to this aspect when making provision for applicants who wish to retain their pet.

## ASYLUM SEEKERS

**17.43.** Since April 2000 the National Asylum Support Service (NASS) has had responsibility for providing support, including accommodation, to asylum seekers who would otherwise be destitute, whilst their claims and appeals are being considered. Some local authorities may still be providing accommodation to asylum seekers who applied for asylum prior to April 2000 and whose cases have not yet been resolved. However, the number of these cases, if any, will be small and declining.

**17.44.** Section 210(1A) provides that, in considering whether accommodation is suitable for an applicant who is an asylum seeker, housing authorities:

(a)     shall also have regard to the fact that the accommodation is to be temporary pending the determination of the applicant's claim for asylum; and

(b)     shall not have regard to any preference that the applicant, or any person who might reasonably be expected to reside with him or her, may have as to the locality of the accommodation secured.

## RIGHT TO REQUEST A REVIEW OF SUITABILITY

**17.45.** Applicants may ask for a review on request of the housing authority's decision that the accommodation offered to them is suitable under s.202(1)(f), although this right does not apply in the case of accommodation secured under s.188, the interim duty to accommodate pending inquiries, or s.200(1), the interim duty pending the decision on a referral. Under s.202(1A) an applicant may request a review as to suitability regardless of whether or not he or she accepts the accommodation. This applies equally to offers of accommodation made under s.193(5) to discharge the s.193(2) duty and to offers of an allocation of accommodation made under s.193(7) that would bring the s.193(2) duty to an end. This means that the applicant is able to ask for a review of suitability without inadvertently bringing the housing duty to an end (see Chapter 19 for guidance on reviews). Housing authorities should note that although there is no right of review of a decision on the suitability of accommodation secured under s.188 or s.200(1), such decisions could nevertheless be subject to judicial review in the High Court.

[5019]

## CHAPTER 18: LOCAL CONNECTION AND REFERRALS TO ANOTHER HOUSING AUTHORITY

**18.1.** This chapter provides guidance on the provisions relating to an applicant's "local connection" with an area and explains the conditions and procedures for referring an applicant to another housing authority.

**18.2.** Where a housing authority ("the notifying authority") decide that s.193 applies to an applicant (i.e. the applicant is eligible for assistance, unintentionally homeless and has a priority need) but it considers that the conditions for referral of the case to another housing authority are met, they may notify the other housing authority ("the notified authority") of their opinion.

**18.3.** Notwithstanding that the conditions for a referral are apparently met, it is the responsibility of the notifying authority to determine whether s.193 applies before making a reference. **Applicants can only be referred to another authority if the notifying authority is satisfied that the applicant is unintentionally homeless, eligible for assistance and has a priority need.** Applicants cannot be referred while they are owed only the interim duty under s.188, or any duty other than the s.193 duty (e.g. where they are threatened with homelessness or found to be homeless intentionally).

**18.4.** **Referrals are discretionary only: housing authorities are not required to refer applicants to other authorities. Nor are they, generally, required to make any inquiries as to whether an applicant has a local connection with an area.** However, by virtue of s.11 of the *Asylum and Immigration (Treatment of Claimants, etc.) Act 2004*, housing authorities will need to consider local connection in cases where the applicant is a former asylum seeker:

i)     who was provided with accommodation in Scotland under s.95 of the *Immigration and Asylum Act 1999*, and

ii)     whose accommodation was not provided in an accommodation centre by virtue of s.22 of the *Nationality, Immigration and Asylum Act 2002*.

In such cases, by virtue of s.11(2)(d) and (3) of the *Asylum and Immigration (Treatment of Claimants, etc) Act 2004*, local connection to a district in England, Wales or Scotland will be relevant to what duty is owed under s.193. (See paragraph 18.21 below.)

**18.5.** Housing authorities may have a policy about how they may exercise their discretion to refer a case. This must not, however, extend to deciding in advance that in all cases where there is a local connection to another district the case should be referred.

**18.6.** The Local Government Association (LGA) has issued guidelines for housing authorities about procedures for referring a case. These include guidance on issues such as local connection and invoking the disputes procedure when two housing authorities are unable to agree whether the conditions for referral are met. (A copy of the LGA guidelines is at Annex 18 for information).

## CONDITIONS FOR REFERRAL

**18.7.** Sections 198(2) and (2A) describe the conditions which must be satisfied before a referral may be made. A notifying authority may refer an applicant to whom s.193 applies to another housing authority if all of the following are met:

i)    neither the applicant nor any person who might reasonably be expected to live with him or her has a local connection with its district; and

ii)   at least one member of the applicant's household has a local connection with the district of the authority to be notified; and

iii)  none of them will be at risk of domestic or non-domestic violence, or threat of domestic or non-domestic violence which is likely to be carried out, in the district of the authority to be notified.

## LOCAL CONNECTION

**18.8.** When a housing authority makes inquiries to determine whether an applicant is eligible for assistance and owed a duty under Part 7, it may also make inquiries under s.184(2) to decide whether the applicant has a local connection with the district of another housing authority in England, Wales or Scotland.

**18.9.** Section 199(1) provides that a person has a local connection with the district of a housing authority if he or she has a connection with it:

i)    because he or she is, or was in the past, normally resident there, and that residence was of his or her own choice; or

ii)   because he or she is employed there; or

iii)  because of family associations there; or

iv)   because of any special circumstances.

**18.10.** For the purposes of (i), above, residence in temporary accommodation provided by a housing authority under s.188 can constitute normal residence of choice and therefore contribute towards a local connection. With regard to (ii) the applicant should actually work in the district: it would not be sufficient that his or her employers' head office was located there. For the purposes of (iii), where the applicant raises family associations, the Secretary of State considers that this may extend beyond parents, adult children or siblings. They may include associations with other family members such as step-parents, grandparents, grandchildren, aunts or uncles provided there are sufficiently close links in the form of frequent contact, commitment or dependency. Family associations may also extend to unmarried couples, provided that the relationship is sufficiently enduring, and to same sex couples. With regard to (iv), special circumstances might include the need to be near special medical or support services which are available only in a particular district.

**18.11.** The grounds in s.199(1) should be applied in order to establish whether the applicant has the required local connection. However, the fact that an applicant may satisfy one of these grounds will not necessarily mean that he or she has been able to establish a local connection. For example, an applicant may be "normally resident" in an area even though he or she does not intend to settle there permanently or indefinitely, and the local authority could therefore determine that he or she does not have a local connection. The overriding consideration should always be whether the applicant has a real local connection with an area – the specified grounds are subsidiary to that overriding consideration.

**18.12.** In assessing whether an applicant's household has a local connection with either its district or a district to which the case might be referred, a housing authority should also consider whether any person who might reasonably be expected to live with the applicant has such a connection.

**18.13.** A housing authority may not seek to transfer responsibility to another housing authority where the applicant has a local connection with their district but they consider there is a stronger local connection elsewhere. However, in such a case, it would be open to a housing authority to seek assistance from the other housing authority in securing accommodation, under s.213.

**18.14.** Where a person has a local connection with the districts of more than one other housing authority, the referring housing authority will wish to take account of the applicant's preference in deciding which housing authority to notify.

*Ex-service personnel*

**18.15.** Under s.199(2) and (3), serving members of the armed forces, and other persons who normally live with them as part of their household, do not establish a local connection with a district by virtue of serving, or having served, there while in the forces.

*Ex-prisoners and detainees under the Mental Health Act 1983*

**18.16.** Similarly, detention in prison (whether convicted or not) does not establish a local connection with the district the prison is in. However, any period of residence in accommodation prior to imprisonment may give rise to a local connection under s.199(1)(a). The same is true of those detained under the *Mental Health Act 1983.*

*Former asylum seekers*

**18.17.** Sections 199(6) and (7) were inserted by section 11 of the *Asylum and Immigration (Treatment of Claimants, etc.) Act 2004.* Section 199(6) provides that a person has a local connection with the district of a housing authority if he or she was (at any time) provided with accommodation there under s.95 of the *Immigration and Asylum Act 1999* ("s.95 accommodation").

**18.18.** Under s.199(7), however, a person does not have a local connection by virtue of s.199(6):
  (a)   if he or she has been subsequently provided with s.95 accommodation in a different area. Where a former asylum seeker has been provided with s.95 accommodation in more than one area, the local connection is with the area where such accommodation was last provided; or
  (b)   if they have been provided with s.95 accommodation in an accommodation centre in the district by virtue of s.22 of the *Nationality, Immigration and Asylum Act 2002.*

**18.19.** A local connection with a district by virtue of s.199(6) does not override a local connection by virtue of s.199(1). Thus, a former asylum seeker who has a local connection with a district because he or she was provided with accommodation there under s.95 may also have a local connection elsewhere for some other reason, for example, because of employment or family associations.

*Former asylum seekers provided with s.95 accommodation in Scotland*

**18.20.** Under Scottish legislation, a person does not establish a local connection with a district in Scotland if he or she is resident there in s.95 accommodation. Consequently, if such a person made a homelessness application to a housing authority in England, and he or she did not have a local connection with the district of that authority, the fact that he or she had been provided with s.95 accommodation in Scotland would not establish conditions for referral to the relevant local authority in Scotland.

**18.21.** Sections 11(2) and (3) of the *Asylum and Immigration (Treatment of Claimants, etc) Act 2004* provides that where a housing authority in England or Wales is satisfied that an applicant is eligible for assistance, unintentionally homeless and in priority need and:
  i)      the applicant has been provided with s.95 accommodation in Scotland at any time;
  ii)     the s.95 accommodation was not provided in an accommodation centre by virtue of s.22 of the *Nationality, Immigration and Asylum Act 2002*;
  iii)    the applicant does not have a local connection anywhere in England and Wales (within the meaning of s.199 of the 1996 Act); and
  iv)     the applicant does not have a local connection anywhere in Scotland (within the meaning of s.27 of the *Housing (Scotland) Act 1987*);

then the duty to the applicant under s.193 (the main homelessness duty) shall not apply. However, the authority:
  (a)   may secure that accommodation is available for occupation by the applicant for a period giving him or her a reasonable opportunity of securing accommodation for his or her occupation; and
  (b)   may provide the applicant (or secure that he or she is provided with) advice and assistance in any attempts he or she may make to secure accommodation for his or her occupation.

When dealing with an applicant in these circumstances, authorities will need to take into account the wishes of the applicant but should consider providing such advice and assistance as would enable the applicant to make an application for housing to the Scottish authority in the district where the s.95 accommodation was last provided, or to another Scottish authority of the applicant's choice. If such a person was unintentionally homeless and in priority need, it would be open to them to apply to any Scottish housing authority and a main homelessness duty would be owed to them.

*No local connection anywhere*

**18.22.** If an applicant, or any person who might reasonably be expected to live with the applicant, has no local connection with any district in Great Britain, the duty to secure accommodation will rest with the housing authority that has received the application.

## RISK OF VIOLENCE

**18.23.** A housing authority cannot refer an applicant to another housing authority if that person or any person who might reasonably be expected to reside with him or her would be at risk of violence.

The housing authority is under a positive duty to enquire whether the applicant would be at such a risk and, if he or she would, it should not be assumed that the applicant will take steps to deal with the threat.

**18.24.** Section 198(3) defines violence as violence from another person or threats of violence from another person which are likely to be carried out. This is the same definition as appears in s.177 in relation to whether it is reasonable to continue to occupy accommodation and the circumstances to be considered as to whether a person runs a risk of violence are the same.

**18.25.** Housing authorities should be alert to the deliberate distinction which is made in s.198(3) between actual violence and threatened violence. A high standard of proof of actual violence in the past should not be imposed. The threshold is that there must be:
(a)      no risk of domestic violence (actual or threatened) in the other district; and
(b)      no risk of non-domestic violence (actual or threatened) in the other district.

Nor should "domestic violence" be interpreted restrictively (see definitions in the introduction to this Code).

## DUTIES WHERE CASE REFERRED TO ANOTHER HOUSING AUTHORITY

**18.26.** If a housing authority decide to refer a case to another housing authority, they will need to notify the other housing authority that they believe the conditions for referral are met (s.198(1)). They must also notify the applicant that they have notified, or intend to notify, another housing authority that they consider that the conditions for referral are met (s.184(4)). At that point, the notifying authority would cease to be subject to the interim duty to accommodate under s.188(1) but will owe a duty under s.200(1) to secure that accommodation is available for the applicant until the question of whether the conditions for referral are met is decided.

**18.27.** Under s.200(4), if the referral is accepted by the notified authority they will be under a duty to secure accommodation for the applicant under s.193(2). Regardless of whether the notified authority had reached a different decision on a previous application, it is not open to it to re-assess the notifying authority's decision that the applicant is eligible, unintentionally homeless and in priority need. Nor may the notified authority rely on an offer of accommodation which was refused having been made in pursuance of a previous application to it.

**18.28.** Under s.200(3), if it is decided that the conditions for referral are not met, the notifying authority will be under a duty to secure accommodation for the applicant under s.193(2).

**18.29.** When the question of whether the conditions for referral to the notified authority are met has been decided, the notifying housing authority must notify the applicant of the decision and the reasons for it (s.200(2)). The notification must also advise the applicant of his or her right to request a review of the decision, and the timescale within which such a request must be made. The interim duty to accommodate under s.200(1) ends regardless of whether the applicant requests a review of the decision. However, where the applicant does request a review the notifying authority has a power under s.200(5) to secure that accommodation is available pending the review decision. (See Chapter 15 for guidance on powers to secure accommodation).

**18.30.** Notifications to the applicant must be provided in writing and copies made available at the housing authority's office for collection by the applicant, or his or her representative, for a reasonable period.

## DISPUTES

**18.31.** Applicants have the right to request a review of various decisions relating to local connection and referrals (see Chapter 19 for further guidance). There is not a right to request a review of a housing authority's decision not to refer a case, although a failure by a housing authority to consider whether it has the discretion to refer an applicant may be amenable to challenge by way of judicial review. The same is true of an unreasonable use of the discretion.

**18.32.** The question of whether the conditions for referral are met in a particular case should be decided by agreement between the housing authorities concerned. If they cannot agree, the decision should be made in accordance with such arrangements as may be directed by order of the Secretary of State (s.198(5)).

**18.33.** The *Homelessness (Decisions on Referrals) Order 1998* (SI 1998 No. 1578) directs that the arrangements to be followed in such a dispute are the arrangements agreed between the local authority associations (i.e. the Local Government Association, the Convention of Scottish Local Authorities, the Welsh Local Government Association and the Association of London Government).

**18.34.** The arrangements are set out in the Schedule to the Order. Broadly speaking, they provide that in the event of two housing authorities being unable to agree whether the conditions for referral are met, they must agree on a person to be appointed to make the decision for them. If unable to agree on that, they should agree to request the LGA to appoint someone. In default of this, the notifying housing authority must make such a request of the LGA. In all cases the appointed person must be drawn from a panel established by the LGA for the purpose. The Local Government Association has issued guidelines for housing authorities on invoking the disputes procedure (a copy is at Annex 18 for information).

**18.35.** The arrangements set out in the Schedule to SI 1998 No.1578 apply where a housing authority in England, Wales or Scotland seek to refer a homelessness case to another housing authority in England or Wales, and they are unable to agree whether the conditions for referral are met. A similar Order, the *Homelessness (Decisions on Referrals) (Scotland) Order 1998*, SI 1998 No.1603 applies under the Scottish homelessness legislation. The arrangements in the latter apply in cases where a housing authority in England, Wales or Scotland refer a homelessness case to a housing authority in Scotland, and they are unable to agree whether the conditions for referral are met.

**18.36.** Where an English or Welsh housing authority seek to refer a case to a Scottish housing authority, a request to the local authority association to appoint an arbitrator should be made to the Convention of Scottish Local Authorities.

**18.37.** A notified authority which wishes to refuse a referral because it disagrees on a finding as to the application of s.193 to the applicant must challenge the notifying authority's finding (for example as to intentionality) by way of judicial review.

**[5020]**

## CHAPTER 19: REVIEW OF DECISIONS AND APPEALS TO THE COUNTY COURT

**19.1. This chapter provides guidance on the procedures to be followed when an applicant requests the housing authority to review their decision on the homelessness case.**

### RIGHT TO REQUEST A REVIEW

**19.2.** Applicants have the right to request the housing authority to review their decisions on homelessness cases in some circumstances. If the request is made in accordance with s.202 the housing authority must review the relevant decision.

**19.3.** When a housing authority have completed their inquiries into the applicant's homelessness case they must notify the applicant of:
   (a)   their decision and, if any decision is against the applicant's interest, the reasons for it;
   (b)   the applicant's right to request a review; and
   (c)   the time within which such a request must be made.

Housing authorities should also advise the applicant of his or her right to request a review of the suitability of any accommodation offered as a discharge of a homelessness duty, whether or not the offer is accepted. Authorities should also advise the applicant of the review procedures.

**19.4.** Under s.202 an applicant has the right to request a review of:
   (a)   any decision of a housing authority about his or her eligibility for assistance (i.e. whether he or she is considered to be a person from abroad who is ineligible for assistance under Part 7);
   (b)   any decision of a housing authority as to what duty (if any) is owed to him or her under s.190, s.191, s.192, s.193, s.195 and s.196 (duties owed to applicants who are homeless or threatened with homelessness);
   (c)   any decision of a housing authority to notify another housing authority under s.198(1) (i.e. a decision to refer the applicant to another housing authority because they appear to have a local connection with that housing authority's district and not with the district where they have made the application);
   (d)   any decision under s.198(5) whether the conditions are met for the referral of the applicant's case (including a decision taken by a person appointed under the *Homelessness (Decisions on Referrals) Order 1998* (SI 1998 No.1578));
   (e)   any decision under s.200(3) or (4) (i.e a decision as to whether the notified housing authority or the notifying housing authority owe the duty to secure accommodation in a case considered for referral or referred);
   (f)   any decision of a housing authority as to the suitability of accommodation offered to the applicant under any of the provisions in (b) or (e) above or the suitability of accommodation offered under s.193(7) (allocation under Part 6). Under s.202(1A), applicants can request a review of the suitability of accommodation whether or not they have accepted the offer.

**19.5.** An applicant must request a review before the end of the period of 21 days beginning with the day on which he or she is notified of the housing authority's decision. The housing authority may specify, in writing, a longer period during which a review may be requested. Applicants do not have a right to request a review of a decision made on an earlier review.

**19.6.** In reviewing a decision, housing authorities will need to have regard to any information relevant to the period before the decision (even if only obtained afterwards) as well as any new relevant information obtained since the decision.

## THE REVIEW REGULATIONS

**19.7.** The *Allocation of Housing and Homelessness (Review Procedures) Regulations 1999* (SI 1999 No.71) set out the procedures to be followed by housing authorities in carrying out reviews under Part 7.

*Who may carry out the review*

**19.8.** A review may be carried out by the housing authority itself or by someone acting as an agent of the housing authority (see Chapter 21 on contracting out homelessness functions). Where the review is to be carried out by an officer of the housing authority, the officer must not have been involved in the original decision, and he or she must be senior to the officer (or officers) who took that decision. Seniority for these purposes means seniority in rank or grade within the housing authority's organisational structure. The seniority provision does not apply where a committee or sub-committee of elected members took the original decision.

**19.9.** Where the decision under review is a joint decision by the notifying housing authority and the notified housing authority as to whether the conditions of referral of the case are satisfied, s.202(4) requires that the review should be carried out jointly by the two housing authorities. Where the decision under review was taken by a person appointed pursuant to the arrangements set out in the Schedule to the *Homelessness (Decisions on Referrals) Order 1998* (SI 1998 No.1578), the review must be carried out by another person appointed under those arrangements (see paragraph 19.15).

*Written representations*

**19.10.** The applicant should be invited to make representations in writing in connection with his or her request for a review. The relevant provisions in Part 7 give a person an unfettered right to request a review of a decision, so he or she is not required to provide grounds for challenging the housing authority's decision. The purpose of the requirement is to invite the applicant to state his or her grounds for requesting a review (if he or she has not already done so) and to elicit any new information that the applicant may have in relation to his or her request for a review.

**19.11.** Regulation 6 requires the housing authority to notify the applicant that he or she, or someone acting on his or her behalf, may make written representations in connection with the request for a review. The notice should also advise the applicant of the procedure to be followed in connection with the review (if this information has not been provided earlier). Regulation 6 also provides that:

i) where the original decision was made jointly by the notifying and notified housing authorities under s.198(5), the notification should be made by the notifying housing authority; and

ii) where the original decision was made by a person appointed pursuant to the *Homelessness (Decisions on Referrals) Order 1998* (SI 1998 No.1578), the notification should be made by the person appointed to carry out the review.

*Oral hearings*

**19.12.** Regulation 8 provides that in cases where a review has been requested, if the housing authority, authorities or person carrying out the review consider that there is a deficiency or irregularity in the original decision, or in the manner in which it was made, but they are minded nonetheless to make a decision that is against the applicant's interests on one or more issues, they should notify the applicant:

(a) that they are so minded and the reasons why; and,

(b) that the applicant, or someone acting on his or her behalf, may, within a reasonable period, make oral representations, further written representations, or both oral and written representations.

**19.13.** Such deficiencies or irregularities would include:

i) failure to take into account relevant considerations and to ignore irrelevant ones;

ii) failure to base the decision on the facts;

iii) bad faith or dishonesty;

iv) mistake of law;

v) decisions that run contrary to the policy of the 1996 Act;

vi) irrationality or unreasonableness;

vii) procedural unfairness, e.g. where an applicant has not been given a chance to comment on matters relevant to a decision.

**19.14.** The reviewer must consider whether there is "something lacking" in the decision, i.e. were any significant issues not addressed or addressed inadequately, which could have led to unfairness.

*Period during which review must be completed*

**19.15.** Regulation 9 provides that the period within which the applicant must be notified of the decision on review is:

i)      eight weeks from the day of the request for a review, where the original decision was
        made by the housing authority;
ii)     ten weeks, where the decision was made jointly by two housing authorities under s.198(5)
        (a decision whether the conditions for referral are met);
iii)    twelve weeks, where the decision is taken by a person appointed pursuant to the Schedule
        to the *Homelessness (Decisions on Referrals) Order* (SI 1998 No.1578).

The regulations provide that in all of these cases it is open to the reviewer to seek the applicant's
agreement to an extension of the prescribed period; any such agreement must be given in writing.

*Late representations*

**19.16.**   The regulations require the reviewer(s) to consider any written representations received
subject to compliance with the requirement to notify the applicant of the decision on review within
the period of the review, i.e. the period prescribed in the regulations or any extended period agreed
in writing by the applicant. It may in some circumstances be necessary to make further enquiries of
the applicant about information he or she has provided. The reviewer(s) should be flexible about
allowing such further exchanges, having regard to the time limits for reviews prescribed in the
regulations. If this leads to significant delays, the applicant may be approached to agree an extension
in the period for the review. Similarly, if an applicant has been invited to make oral representations
and this requires additional time to arrange, the applicant should be asked to agree an appropriate
extension.

## PROCEDURES FOR REVIEW OF DECISIONS MADE UNDER THE DECISIONS ON REFERRALS ORDER

**19.17.**   Where the original decision under s.198(5) was made by a person appointed pursuant to the
Schedule to the *Homelessness (Decisions on Referrals) Order 1998* (SI 1998 No.1578), regulation 7
provides that a review should be carried out by another person appointed by the notifying housing
authority and the notified housing authority. This requirement applies even where the original
decision was carried out by a person appointed from the panel by the chairman of the Local
Government Association, or his or her nominee. If, however, the two housing authorities fail to
appoint a person to carry out the review within five working days of the date of the request for a
review, the notifying housing authority must request the chairman of the Local Government
Association to appoint a person from the panel. The chairman, in turn, must within seven working
days of that request appoint a person from the panel to undertake the review. The housing authorities
are required to provide the reviewer with the reasons for the original decision, and the information
on which that decision is based, within five working days of his or her appointment.

**19.18.**   Any person thus appointed must comply with the procedures set out in regulations 6, 7, 8
and 9. Specifically, he or she must invite written representations from the applicant and send copies
of these to the two housing authorities, inviting them to respond. The reviewer is also required to
notify in writing the two housing authorities of his or her decision on review and the reasons for it at
least a week before the end of the prescribed period of twelve weeks (or of any extended period
agreed by the applicant). This allows the housing authorities adequate time to notify the applicant of
the decision before expiry of the period.

## NOTIFICATION OF DECISION ON REVIEW

**19.19.**   Section 203 requires a housing authority to notify the applicant in writing of their decision
on the review. The authority must also notify the applicant of the reasons for their decision where it:

i)      confirms the original decision on any issue against the interests of the applicant;
ii)     confirms a previous decision to notify another housing authority under s.198; or,
iii)    confirms a previous decision that the conditions for referral in s.198 are met in the
        applicant's case.

Where the review is carried out jointly by two housing authorities under s.198(5), or by a person
appointed pursuant to the *Homelessness (Decisions on Referrals) Order 1998* (SI 1998 No.1578),
the notification may be made by either of the two housing authorities concerned.

At this stage, the authority making the notification should advise the applicant of his or her right to
appeal to the County Court against a review decision under s.204 and of the period in which to
appeal.

## POWERS TO ACCOMMODATE PENDING A REVIEW

**19.20.**   Sections 188(3) and 200(5) give housing authorities powers to secure accommodation for
certain applicants pending the decision on a review. See Chapter 15 for guidance on powers to
secure accommodation.

## APPEALS TO THE COUNTY COURT

**19.21.**   Section 204 provides an applicant with the right of appeal on a point of law to the County
Court if:

(a)      he or she is dissatisfied with the decision on a review; or

(b)      he or she is not notified of the decision on the review within the time prescribed in regulations made under s.203.

In the latter case, an applicant will be entitled to appeal against the original decision.

**19.22.**    An appeal must be brought by an applicant within 21 days of:

(a)      the date on which he or she is notified of the decision on review; or

(b)      the date on which he or she should have been notified (i.e. the date marking the end of the period for the review prescribed in the regulations, or any extended period agreed in writing by the applicant).

**19.23.**    The court may give permission for an appeal to be brought after 21 days, but only where it is satisfied that:

(a)      (where permission is sought within the 21-day period), there is good reason for the applicant to be unable to bring the appeal in time; or

(b)      (where permission is sought after the 21-day period has expired), there was a good reason for the applicant's failure to bring the appeal in time and for any delay in applying for permission.

**19.24.**    On an appeal, the County Court is empowered to make an order confirming, quashing or varying the housing authority's decision as it thinks fit. It is important, therefore, that housing authorities have in place review procedures that are robust, fair, and transparent.

## POWER TO ACCOMMODATE PENDING AN APPEAL TO THE COUNTY COURT

**19.25.**    Section 204(4) gives housing authorities the power to accommodate certain applicants during the period for making an appeal, and pending the appeal and any subsequent appeal. Applicants have a right to appeal against a housing authority's decision not to secure accommodation for them pending an appeal to the County Court (s.204A). Applicants can also appeal against a housing authority's decision to secure accommodation for them for only a limited period which ends before final determination of the appeal. See Chapter 15 for guidance on powers to secure accommodation.

## LOCAL GOVERNMENT OMBUDSMAN

**19.26.**    Applicants may complain to a Local Government Ombudsman if they consider that they have been caused injustice as a result of maladministration by a housing authority. The Ombudsman may investigate the way a decision has been made, but may not question the merits of a decision properly reached. For example, maladministration would occur where a housing authority:

i)      took too long to do something;

ii)      did not follow their own rules or the law;

iii)      broke their promises;

iv)      treated the applicant unfairly;

v)      gave the applicant the wrong information.

**19.27.**    There are some matters an Ombudsman cannot investigate. These include:

i)      matters the applicant knew about more than twelve months before he or she wrote to the Ombudsman or to a councillor, unless the Ombudsman considers it reasonable to investigate despite the delay;

ii)      matters about which the applicant has already taken court action against the housing authority, for example, an appeal to the County Court under s.204;

iii)      matters about which the applicant could go to court, unless the Ombudsman considers there are good reasons why the applicant could not reasonably be expected to do so.

**19.28.**    Where there is a right of review the Ombudsman would expect an applicant to pursue the right before making a complaint. If there is any doubt about whether the Ombudsman can look into a complaint, the applicant should seek advice from the Ombudsman's office.

**[5021]**

## CHAPTER 20: PROTECTION OF PERSONAL PROPERTY

**20.1.**    **This chapter provides guidance on the duty and powers housing authorities have to protect the personal property of an applicant.**

**20.2.**    Under s.211(1) and (2), where a housing authority has become subject to a duty to an applicant under specified provisions of Part 7 and it has reason to believe that:

i)      there is a danger of loss of, or damage to, the applicant's personal property because the applicant is unable to protect it or deal with it, and

ii)      no other suitable arrangements have been, or are being, made,

then, whether or not the housing authority is still subject to such a duty, it must take reasonable steps to prevent the loss of, or to prevent or mitigate damage to, any personal property of the applicant.

**20.3.**   The specified provisions are:
- s.188 (interim duty to accommodate);
- s.190, s.193 or s.195 (duties to persons found to be homeless or threatened with homelessness); or
- s.200 (duties to applicant whose case is considered for referral or referred).

**20.4.**   In all other circumstances, housing authorities have a power to take any steps they consider reasonable to protect in the same ways an applicant's personal property (s.211(3)).

**20.5.**   Section 212 makes provisions supplementing s.211. For the purposes of both s.211 and s.212, the personal property of an applicant includes the personal property of any person who might reasonably be expected to reside with him or her (s.211(5) and s.212(6)).

**20.6.**   A danger of loss or damage to personal property means that there is a likelihood of harm, not just that harm is a possibility. Applicants may be unable to protect their property if, for example, they are ill or are unable to afford to have it stored themselves.

**20.7.**   Under s.212(1), in order to protect an applicant's personal property, a housing authority can enter, at all reasonable times, the applicant's current or former home, and deal with the property in any way which seems reasonably necessary. In particular, it may store the property or arrange for it to be stored; this may be particularly appropriate where the applicant is accommodated by the housing authority in furnished accommodation for a period. In some cases, where the applicant's previous home is not to be occupied immediately, it may be possible for the property to remain there, if it can be adequately protected.

**20.8.**   Where a housing authority does take steps to protect personal property, whether by storing it or otherwise, it must take reasonable care of it and deliver it to the owner when reasonably requested to do so.

**20.9.**   The applicant can request the housing authority to move his or her property to a particular location. If the housing authority considers that the request is reasonable, they may discharge their responsibilities under s.211 by doing as the applicant asks. Where such a request is met, the housing authority will have no further duty or power to protect the applicant's property, and it must inform the applicant of this consequence before complying with the request (s.212(2)).

**20.10.**   Housing authorities may impose conditions on the assistance they provide where they consider these appropriate to the particular case. Conditions may include making a reasonable charge for storage of property and reserving the right to dispose of property in certain circumstances specified by the housing authority – e.g. if the applicant loses touch with them and cannot be traced after a certain period (s.211(4)).

**20.11.**   Where a request to move personal property to another location is either not made or not carried out, the duty or power to take any action under s.211 ends when the housing authority believes there is no longer any danger of loss or damage to the property because of the applicant's inability to deal with or protect it (s.212(3)). This may be the case, for example, where an applicant recovers from illness or finds accommodation where he or she is able to place his or her possessions, or becomes able to afford the storage costs him/herself. However, where the housing authority has discharged the duty under s.211 by placing property in storage, it has a discretionary power to continue to keep the property in storage. Where it does so, any conditions imposed by the housing authority continue to apply and may be modified as necessary.

**20.12.**   Where the housing authority ceases to be under a duty, or ceases to have a power, to protect an applicant's personal property under s.211, it must notify the applicant of this and give the reasons for it. The notification must be delivered to the applicant or sent to his or her last known address (s.212(5)).

[5022]

## CHAPTER 21: CONTRACTING OUT HOMELESSNESS FUNCTIONS

**21.1.   This chapter provides guidance on contracting out homelessness functions and housing authorities' statutory obligations with regard to the discharge of those functions.**

**21.2.**   The *Local Authorities (Contracting Out of Allocation of Housing and Homelessness Functions) Order 1996* (SI 1996 No. 3215) ("the Order") enables housing authorities to contract out certain functions under Parts 6 and 7 of the 1996 Act. The Order is made under s.70 of the *Deregulation and Contracting Out Act 1994* ("the 1994 Act"). In essence, the Order allows the contracting out of executive functions while leaving the responsibility for making strategic decisions with the housing authority.

**21.3.**   The Order provides that the majority of functions under Part 7 can be contracted out. These include:
- making arrangements to secure that advice and information about homelessness, and the prevention of homelessness, is available free of charge within the housing authority's district;

- making inquiries about and deciding a person's eligibility for assistance;
- making inquiries about and deciding whether any duty, and, if so, what duty is owed to a person under Part 7;
- making referrals to another housing authority;
- carrying out reviews of decisions;
- securing accommodation to discharge homelessness duties.

**21.4.** Where decision-making in homelessness cases is contracted out, authorities may wish to consider retaining the review function under s.202 of the 1996 Act. This may provide an additional degree of independence between the initial decision and the decision on review.

**21.5.** The 1994 Act provides that a contract made:
i) may authorise a contractor to carry out only part of the function concerned;
ii) may specify that the contractor is authorised to carry out functions only in certain cases or areas specified in the contract;
iii) may include conditions relating to the carrying out of the functions, e.g. prescribing standards of performance;
iv) shall be for a period not exceeding 10 years and may be revoked at any time by the Minister or the housing authority. Any subsisting contract is to be treated as having been repudiated in these circumstances;
v) shall not prevent the housing authority from exercising themselves the functions to which the contract relates.

**21.6.** Schedule 2 to the Order lists the homelessness functions in Part 7 that may **not** be contracted out. These are:
- s.179(2) and (3): the provision of various forms of assistance to anyone providing advice and information about homelessness and the prevention of homelessness to people in the district, on behalf of the housing authority;
- s.180: the provision of assistance to voluntary organisations concerned with homelessness; and
- s.213: co-operation with relevant housing authorities and bodies by rendering assistance in the discharge of their homelessness functions.

**21.7.** Local authorities also **cannot** contract out their functions under the *Homelessness Act 2002* which relate to homelessness reviews and strategies. Chapter 1 provides guidance on homelessness reviews and strategies and outlines the main functions. These include:
- s.1(1): carry out a homelessness review for the district, and formulate and publish a homelessness strategy based on the results of that review;
- s.1(4): publish a new homelessness strategy within 5 years from the day on which their last homelessness strategy was published; and
- 3(6): keep their homelessness strategy under review and modify it from time to time.

Reviews and the formulation of strategies can, however, be informed by research commissioned from external organisations.

**21.8.** The 1994 Act also provides that the housing authority is responsible for any act or omission of the contractor in exercising functions under the contract, except:
i) where the contractor fails to fulfil conditions specified in the contract relating to the exercise of the function; or,
ii) where criminal proceedings are brought in respect of the contractor's act or omission.

**21.9.** Where there is an arrangement in force under s.101 of the *Local Government Act 1972* by virtue of which one local authority exercises the functions of another, the 1994 Act provides that the authority exercising the function is not allowed to contract it out without the principal authority's consent.

**21.10. Where a housing authority has contracted out the operation of any homelessness functions the authority remains statutorily responsible and accountable for the discharge of those functions.** This is the case whether a housing authority contracts with a Large Scale Voluntary Transfer registered social landlord, an Arms Length Management Organisation or any other organisation. The authority will therefore need to ensure that the contract provides for delivery of the homelessness functions in accordance with both the statutory obligations and the authority's own policies on tackling and preventing homelessness. The performance of a housing authority's homelessness functions will continue to be part of its Comprehensive Performance Assessment and will need to be covered by Best Value reviews, whether or not it discharges the homelessness functions directly.

**21.11.** When contracting out homelessness functions, housing authorities will need to ensure that:
- proposed arrangements are consistent with their obligations under the 2002 Act to have a strategy for preventing homelessness and ensuring that accommodation and any necessary support will be available to everyone in their district who is homeless or at risk of homelessness;

- a high quality homelessness service will be provided, in particular the assessment of applicants and the provision of advice and assistance; and
- both short-term and settled accommodation services will be available for offer to all applicants owed the main homelessness duty.

**21.12.** Housing authorities should also ensure they have adequate contractual, monitoring and quality assurance mechanisms in place to ensure their statutory duties are being fully discharged.

**21.13.** In deciding whether to contract out homelessness functions, housing authorities are encouraged to undertake an options appraisal of each function to decide whether it would best be provided in-house or by another organisation. *Housing Allocation, Homelessness and Stock Transfer – A guide to key issues (ODPM 2004)* provides guidance on the key issues that housing authorities need to consider when deciding whether to retain or contract out the delivery of their homelessness functions.

**[5023]**

# ANNEX 1

## GOOD PRACTICE/GUIDANCE PUBLICATIONS

*DEPARTMENT FOR COMMUNITIES AND LOCAL GOVERNMENT*

*Homelessness prevention: a guide to good practice* (2006)

*OFFICE OF THE DEPUTY PRIME MINISTER*

**Homelessness publications**

**www.communities.gov.uk/index.asp?id=1162505**

*Sustainable Communities: settled homes, changing lives. A strategy for tackling homelessness* (2005)

*Tackling homelessness amongst ethnic minority households – a development guide* (2005)

*Resources for homeless ex-service personnel in London* (2004)

*Effective Co-operation in Tackling Homelessness: Nomination Agreements and Exclusions* (2004)

*Achieving Positive Shared Outcomes in Health and Homelessness* (2004)

*Local Authorities' Homelessness Strategies: Evaluation and Good Practice* (2004)

*Reducing B&B use and tackling homelessness – What's working: A Good Practice Handbook* (2003)

*Housing Associations and Homelessness Briefing* (2003)

*Achieving Positive Outcomes on Homelessness – A Homelessness Directorate Advice Note to Local Authorities* (2003)

*Addressing the health needs of rough sleepers* (2002)

*Care leaving strategies – a good practice handbook* (2002)

*Drugs services for homeless people – a good practice handbook* (2002)

*Homelessness Strategies: A Good Practice Handbook* (2002)

*More than a roof: a report into tackling* homelessness (2002)

*Helping rough sleepers off the streets: A report to the Homelessness Directorate* – Randall, G and Brown, S. (2002)

*Preventing tomorrow's rough sleepers* – Rough Sleepers Unit (2001)

*Blocking the fast track from prison to rough sleeping* – Rough Sleepers Unit (2000)

**Homelessness and Housing Support Directorate Policy Briefings**

Briefing 15: *Summary of Homelessness Good Practice Guidance* (June 2006)

Briefing 14: *Sustainable Communities: settled homes; changing lives – one year on* (March 2006)

Briefing 13: *Survey of English local authorities about homelessness* (December 2005)

Briefing 12: *Hostels Capital Improvement Programme (HCIP)* (September 2005)

Briefing 11: *Providing More Settled Homes* (June 2005)

Briefing 10: *Delivering on the Positive Outcomes* (December 2004)

Briefing 9: *Homelessness Strategies: Moving Forward* (November 2004)

Briefing 8: *Improving the Quality of Hostels and Other Forms of Temporary Accommodation* (June 2004)

Briefing 7: *Addressing the Health Needs of Homeless People Policy* (April 2004)

Briefing 6: *Repeat Homelessness Policy* (January 2004)

Briefing 5: *Improving Employment Options for Homeless People* (September 2003)

Briefing 4: *Prevention of Homelessness Policy* (June 2003)

Briefing 3: *Bed and Breakfast Policy* (March 2003)

Briefing 2: *Domestic Violence Policy* (December 2002)

Briefing 1: *Ethnicity and Homelessness Policy* (September 2002)

## Supporting People publications

**www.spkweb.org.uk**

*Supporting People: Guide to Accommodation and Support Options for People with Mental Health Problems* (2005)

*Guide to Housing and Housing Related Support Options for Offenders and People at Risk of Offending* (2005)

*Supporting People: Guide to Accommodation and Support Options for Homeless Households* (2003)

*Supporting People: The Support Needs of Homeless Households* (2003)

*Supporting People: Guide to Accommodation and Support Options for Households Experiencing Domestic Violence* (2002)

*Reflecting the Needs and Concerns of Black and Minority Ethnic Communities in Supporting People* (2002)

## Other ODPM publications

**www.communities.gov.uk**

*Sustainable Communities: Homes for All. A Five Year Plan* (2005)

*Improving the Effectiveness of Rent Arrears Management* (2005)

*Housing Allocation, Homelessness and Stock Transfer – A guide to key issues* (2004)

*Guidance on Arms Length Management of Local Authority Housing* (2004)

*Allocation of Accommodation – Code of Guidance for local housing authorities* (2002)

*Working together, Connexions and youth homelessness agencies,* London, Department for Transport, Local Government and the Regions (DTLR) and Connexions (2001)

*Other Government publications*

## Audit Commission

**www.audit-commission.gov.uk**

*Homelessness: Responding to the New Agenda* (2003)

*ALMO Inspections. The Delivery of Excellent Housing Management Services* (2003)

*Housing Services After Stock Transfer* (2002)

## Department for Education and Skills

**www.dfes.gov.uk**

*Safeguarding Children, The second joint Chief Inspectors' Report on arrangements to Safeguard Children,* Commission for Social Care Inspection (2005)

*Every Child Matters: Change for Children* (2004)

*Working with Voluntary and Community Organisations to Deliver Change for Children and Young People* (2004)

## Department of Health

**www.dh.gov.uk/Home/fs/en**

*Our health, our care, our say: a new direction for community* (2006)

*Working together to safeguard children* (2005)

*Government response to Hidden Harm: the Report of an inquiry by the Advisory Council on the Misuse of Drugs* (2005)

*Making a Difference: Reducing Bureaucracy in Children, Young People and Family Services* (2005)

*Independence, well-being and choice: Our vision for the future of social care for adults in England* (2005)

*Commissioning a patient-led NHS* (2005)

*Health reform in England: update and next steps* (2005)

*National service framework for mental health: modern standards and service models* (1999)

*National service framework for children, young people and maternity services* (2004)

*From Vision to Reality: Transforming Outcomes for Children and Families* (2004)

*What to do if you're worried a child is being abused* (2003)

*Tackling Health Inequalities: a programme for action* (2003)

*Guidance on accommodating children in need and their families – Local Authority Circular 13* (2003)

*Children Missing from Care and Home – a guide for good practice* published in tandem with the Social Exclusion Unit's report *Young Runaways* (2002)

*Getting it Right: good practice in leaving care resource pack* (2000)

*The framework for assessment of children in need and their families* (2000)

*Valuing People: A New Strategy for Learning Disability for the 21st Century* (2000)

*Working Together to Safeguard Children: a guide to interagency working to safeguard and promote the welfare of children* (1999) Department of Health, Home Office and Department for Education and Employment

## Home Office

**www.homeoffice.gov.uk**

*Advice note on accommodation for vulnerable young people* (2001)

## Housing Corporation

**www.housingcorp.gov.uk**

*Tenancy management: eligibility and evictions* (2004)

*Local Authority Nominations. Circular 02/03/Regulation* (2003)

*Non-Government publications*

## Centrepoint

**www.centrepoint.org.uk**

*Joint protocols between housing and social services departments: a good practice guide for the assessment and assistance of homeless young people aged 16 and 17 years*, Bellerby, N. London (2000)

## Chartered Institute of Housing

**www.cih.org**

*The Housing Manual* (2005)

*Housing and Support Services for asylum seekers and refugees: a good practice guide*, John Perry (2005)

*Strategic Approaches to Homelessness; Good Practice Briefing 24* (2002)

## Commission for Racial Equality

**www.cre.gov.uk**

*CRE Code of Practice on Racial Equality in Housing* (2006)

## Disability Rights Commission

**www.drc-gb.org/**

*The Duty to Promote Disability Equality: Statutory Code of Practice* (2005)

**National Housing Federation**

**www.housing.org.uk**

*Level threshold: towards equality in housing for disabled people: good practice guide* (2005)

*Flexible allocation and local letting schemes* (2000)

**Homeless Link**

**www.homeless.org.uk**

*Hospital admission and discharge: Guidelines for writing a protocol for the hospital admission and discharge of people who are homeless* (2006)

**Shelter**

**http://england.shelter.org.uk/home/index.cfm**

*Sexual exclusion: issues and best practice in lesbian, gay and bisexual housing and homelessness* (2005)

*Youth housing: a good practice guide* (2004)

*Local authorities and registered social landlords* – best practice on joint working (2002)

**[5024]**

## ANNEX 2

### OTHER STRATEGIES AND PROGRAMMES THAT MAY ADDRESS HOMELESSNESS

- Local and Regional Housing Strategy
- Regional Homelessness Strategy
- Regional Economic Development Plan
- Local Strategic Partnership and Community Strategy
- Local Area Agreements
- Supporting People Strategy
- Children and Young People's Plan
- Sure Start
- Connexions
- Education and Employment programmes (e.g. The Princes Trust, New Deal, The Careers Service)
- Progress2work, for drug misusers, and where available, Progress2work-LinkUp for alcohol misusers, offenders and homeless people
- Local health schools programme
- Quality Protects
- NHS Local Delivery Plan
- Teenage Pregnancy Strategy
- Drug Action Team Plan
- Crime and Disorder Strategy
- Regional Reducing Reoffending Strategy
- Domestic Violence Strategy
- Anti-Social Behaviour Strategy
- Anti-Poverty Strategy
- Social Inclusion Strategy
- Valuing People Plan
- Town Centre Management Strategy
- Voluntary and community sector plans
- Gypsy and Traveller Accommodation Strategy (where required by s. 225 *Housing Act 2004*)

**[5025]**

## ANNEX 3

### OTHER AUTHORITES, ORGANISATIONS AND PERSONS WHOSE ACTIVITIES MAY CONTRIBUTE TO PREVENTING/TACKLING HOMELESSNESS

- Registered social landlords
- Private landlords
- Lettings agencies
- Self build groups
- Housing Co-operatives
- Housing Corporation
- Supported housing providers
- Home improvement agencies

PART III
OTHER MATERIAL

- Primary Care Trusts, health centres and GP practices
- NHS Trusts – Acute and Mental Health
- Local mental health organisations (e.g. Mind)
- Local disability groups
- Care Services Improvement Partnership Regional Development Centres
- Learning Disability Partnership Boards
- Children's Trusts
- Youth Services and youth advice groups
- Education Welfare Services
- LEA Pupil Referral Units
- Schools
- Sure Start
- Connexions
- Youth Offending Team
- Police
- Crime and Disorder Reduction Partnerships
- Drug Action Teams
- National Offender Management Service (incorporating The Prison and Probation Services)
- Victim support groups
- Anti-Social Behaviour Team
- Street Wardens
- Jobcentre Plus
- Learning and Skills Councils
- Environmental Health Team
- Housing Management Team
- Housing Benefits Team
- Armed Forces resettlement services
- National Asylum Support Service
- Refugee Community Organisations
- Law Centres
- Advice/advocacy services (e.g. Citizens Advice Bureaux and Shelter)
- Local voluntary sector infrastructure bodies (e.g. CVS)
- Faith groups
- Women's groups
- Local domestic violence fora
- Ethnic minority groups
- Age groups (e.g. Age Concern, Help the Aged)
- Lesbian, gay and bisexual groups
- Emergency accommodation providers (such as the Salvation Army)
- Day centres for homeless people
- Refuges
- The Samaritans
- Mediation Services
- Local Strategic Partnerships
- Local businesses/Chambers of Commerce
- Regional Housing Board
- Regional planning bodies
- People living in insecure accommodation (and their representative bodies)
- Rough sleepers (and their representative bodies)
- Residents/tenants organisations
- Self help/user groups
- Services supporting sex workers

[5026]

## ANNEX 4

## SPECIFIC OBJECTIVES AND ACTIONS FOR LOCAL AUTHORITIES THAT MIGHT BE INCLUDED IN A HOMELESSNESS STRATEGY

This Annex provides suggestions for objectives and actions that local authorities may wish to consider including in their homelessness strategies.

*HOUSING AUTHORITY*
- **Facilitate the effective co-ordination of all service providers, across all sectors in the district, whose activities contribute to preventing homelessness and/or meeting the accommodation and support needs of people who are homeless or at risk of homelessness (objective).**

– establish a homelessness forum to co-ordinate the activities of all the key players, across all sectors, who are contributing to meeting the aims of the homelessness strategy.

– ensure the homelessness strategy is consistent with other relevant local plans and strategies and that all relevant stakeholders are aware of how they work together.

- **Ensure that people who are at risk of homelessness are aware of, and have access to, the services they may need to help them prevent homelessness (objective).**
  - provide comprehensive advice and information about homelessness and the prevention of homelessness, free to everyone in the district.
  - provide mediation and reconciliation services (e.g. to tackle neighbour disputes and family relationship breakdown).
  - implement an effective tenancy relations service (and good liaison with private landlords).
- **Ensure that the supply of accommodation, including affordable accommodation, in the district reflects estimated housing need (objective).**
  - in conjunction with RSLs operating in the district, maximise the number of social lettings available for people who have experienced homelessness or at risk of homelessness, consistent with the need to meet the reasonable aspirations of other groups in housing need.
  - ensure that provision of specialised and supported accommodation for people who have experienced homelessness or at risk of homelessness (e.g. refuges and wet hostels) reflects estimated need.
  - maximise the provision of affordable housing through planning requirements for new private developments.
- **Work with the social services authority to ensure that the needs of clients who have both housing and social services support needs are fully assessed and taken into account (objective)**
  - develop a framework for effective joint working with the social services authority, including screening procedures to identify at an early stage where there is a need for case specific joint working.
  - put in place arrangements for carrying out joint assessments of people with support needs who are homeless or have experienced homelessness.
  - establish a protocol for the referral of clients and the sharing information between services.

*SOCIAL SERVICES AUTHORITY*
- **Work with the housing authority to ensure that the needs of clients who have both housing and social services support needs are fully assessed and taken into account (objective)**
  - develop a framework for effective joint working with the housing authority, including screening procedures, to identify at an early stage where there is a need for case specific joint working.
  - put in place arrangements for carrying out joint assessments of people with support needs who are homeless or have experienced homelessness.
  - establish a protocol for the referral of clients and the sharing information between services.
- **Ensure that, subject to relevant eligibility criteria, vulnerable people who are homeless, or at risk of homelessness, receive the support they need to help them sustain a home and prevent homelessness recurring (objective).**
  - provide a reconciliation service for young people estranged from their families.
  - exercise powers under the *Children Act 1989* to make payments to assist young people who are homeless or at risk of homelessness to sustain/find accommodation.
  - operate a supported lodgings scheme for homeless 16 and 17 year olds who need a supportive environment.
  - provide assistance to enable families with children who have become homeless intentionally (or are ineligible for housing assistance) to secure accommodation for themselves (e.g. financial assistance with rent deposit/guarantees).

**[5027]**

# ANNEX 5

## CO-OPERATION BETWEEN REGISTERED SOCIAL LANDLORDS AND HOUSING AUTHORITIES

### HOUSING: THE STRATEGIC CONTEXT

**1.** Housing authorities have a statutory obligation to consider the housing needs of their district (s.8 *Housing Act 1985*). Under the *Homelessness Act 2002* ("the 2002 Act"), they also have a statutory duty to formulate a strategy for preventing homelessness and ensuring that accommodation and support are available for people who are homeless or at risk of homelessness in their district. A homelessness strategy may include actions which the authority expects to be taken by various other organisations, with their agreement.

**2.** Most social housing is provided by housing authorities and by Registered Social Landlords (RSLs). Virtually all provision of new social housing is delivered through RSLs and, under the transfer programme, ownership of a significant proportion of housing authority stock is being transferred from housing authorities to RSLs, subject to tenants' agreement. This means that, increasingly, RSLs will become the main providers of social housing. Consequently, it is essential that housing authorities work closely with RSLs, as well as all other housing providers, in order to meet the housing needs in their district and ensure that the aims and objectives of their homelessness strategy are achieved.

## STATUTORY FRAMEWORK FOR CO-OPERATION

**3.** Section 170 of the *Housing Act 1996* ("the 1996 Act") provides that where an RSL has been requested by a housing authority to offer accommodation to people with priority under its allocation scheme, the RSL must co-operate to such extent as is reasonable in the circumstances. Similarly, s.213 provides that where an RSL has been requested by a housing authority to assist them in the discharge of their homelessness functions under Part 7, it must also co-operate to the same extent. Section 3 of the 2002 Act requires housing authorities to consult appropriate bodies and organisations before publishing a homelessness strategy, and this will inevitably need to include RSLs.

## HOUSING CORPORATION REGULATORY GUIDANCE

**4.** RSLs are regulated by the Housing Corporation which, under s.36 of the 1996 Act, and with the approval of the Secretary of State, has issued guidance to RSLs with respect to their management of housing accommodation. The Housing Corporation's Regulatory Code and guidance requires housing associations to work with local authorities to enable them to fulfil their statutory duties to, among others, homeless people and people who have priority for an allocation of housing. In particular, RSLs must ensure that:

- their lettings policies are flexible, non-discriminatory and responsive to demand while contributing to inclusivity and sustainable communities;
- they can demonstrate their co-operation with local authorities on homelessness reviews, homelessness strategies and the delivery of authorities' homelessness functions;
- when requested, and to such extent as is reasonable in the circumstances, they provide a proportion of their stock (at least 50% – see paragraph 9 below) to housing authority nominations and as temporary accommodation for people owed a homelessness duty;
- following consultation with local authorities, criteria are adopted for accepting or rejecting nominees and other applicants for housing;
- applicants are excluded from consideration for housing only if their unacceptable behaviour is serious enough to make them unsuitable to be a tenant; and
- their lettings policies are responsive to authorities' housing duties, take account of the need to give reasonable priority to transfer applicants, are responsive to national, regional and local mobility and exchange schemes, and are demonstrably fair and effectively controlled.

**5.** Therefore, the overriding requirement for RSLs in relation to homelessness is to demonstrate that they are co-operating with local authorities to enable them to fulfil their statutory duties.

## CO-OPERATION AND PARTNERSHIPS

**6.** Housing authorities need to draw on these regulatory requirements to form constructive partnerships with RSLs. It is also recommended that authorities refer to the strategic document "A Framework for Partnership" published jointly by the Local Government Association, the National Housing Federation and the Housing Corporation and available at www.lga.gov.uk/Documents/Briefing/framework.pdf

**7.** Where RSLs participate in choice-based lettings schemes, the Corporation will expect any protocols for joint working with housing authorities to make proper provision to meet the needs of vulnerable groups, and ensure that support is available to enable tenants and applicants to exercise choice. Housing authorities should involve RSLs in the implementation of choice-based lettings schemes at an early stage.

## NOMINATION AGREEMENTS

**8.** Whilst legislation provides the framework for co-operation between housing authorities and RSLs, nomination agreements set out the way in which this co-operation is given effect. It is crucial that a housing authority has a comprehensive nomination agreement with each of its partner RSLs to ensure that both sides know what is expected of them. The need for a robust nomination agreement applies in all circumstances, but will be particularly important where the housing authority has transferred ownership of its housing stock and is reliant on the transfer RSL (and any other partner RSLs) to provide housing for their applicants. ODPM guidance on *Housing Allocation,*

*Homelessness and Stock Transfer – A Guide to Key Issues* (2004) sets out the policy and operational matters which the nomination agreement between the housing authority and their transfer RSL should cover.

**9.**　RSLs are required to offer at least 50% of vacancies in their stock (net of internal transfers) to housing authority nominations, unless some lower figure is agreed between the two bodies[1]. In some circumstances, they may agree a substantially higher figure. However, housing authorities should bear in mind that RSLs are required to retain their independence. They must honour their constitutional obligations under their diverse governing instruments, and will make the final decision on the allocation of their housing, within their regulatory framework.

---

[1]　Housing Corporation Regulatory Circular, 02/03 Regulation, February 2003.

---

**10.**　Where requested by a housing authority, RSLs should consider the possible use of a proportion of their own stock to provide temporary accommodation for people owed a homelessness duty under Part 7 of the 1996 Act. This may be necessary in some areas, particularly those where demand for housing is very high and there is a significant number of homeless families with children who need to be placed in temporary accommodation. RSLs and housing authorities will have joint responsibility for determining the appropriate use of settled housing stock for temporary lettings, taking into account that such use will reduce the volume of RSL housing stock available for nominations into long-term tenancies. Housing authorities should ensure that their partnerships take maximum advantage of the flexibility that such arrangements can provide. The Secretary of State expects that, wherever possible, social housing should be allocated on a settled basis rather than used to provide temporary accommodation in the medium to long term. Where medium to long term accommodation is required, the authority and RSL should consider whether it is possible to offer a secure or an assured tenancy under the terms of the authority's allocations scheme.

**11.**　Housing authorities should ensure that the details of nominated households given to RSLs are accurate and comprehensive. Details should include information about the applicant's priority status under the housing authority's policy, as well as indications of vulnerability, support needs and arrangements for support.

**12.**　The Corporation expects that RSLs' approach to exclusions and evictions will generally reflect the principles to which housing authorities work. Housing Corporation Circular 07/04 *Tenancy management: eligibility and evictions* sets out the Corporation's expectations of RSLs when assessing the eligibility of applicants and when working to prevent or respond to breaches of tenancy.

## EFFECTIVE COLLABORATION

**13.**　It is important that housing authorities foster good partnership working with RSLs, to help them prevent and tackle homelessness in the district. The housing management and care and support approaches undertaken by RSLs are key to sustaining tenancies, reducing evictions and abandonment, and preventing homelessness. To ensure effective collaboration between themselves and partner RSLs operating in their district, housing authorities should consider the following:

**nominations agreements**: housing authorities should ensure that they have a formal nominations agreement with all partner RSLs and that there are robust arrangements in place to monitor effective delivery of the terms of the agreement. These should be clearly set out, and should include the proportion of lettings that will be made available, any conditions that will apply, and how any disputes about suitability or eligibility will be resolved. Housing authorities should negotiate for the maximum number of lettings that will be required to enable them to discharge their housing functions and which would be reasonable for the RSL to deliver.

**exclusion criteria**: when negotiating nominations agreements housing authorities should aim for any exclusion criteria (that may be applied to nominees by the RSL) to be kept to a minimum. To prevent new tenancies from failing and to minimise the likelihood of exclusion, housing authorities should also ensure that adequate support packages are in place for vulnerable applicants before a nominee is expected to take up their tenancy.

**eviction policies:** to help prevent homelessness, housing authorities should encourage RSLs to seek to minimise any need for eviction of their tenants by employing preventative strategies and taking early positive action where breaches of tenancy agreement have occurred. Associations should act to support and sustain, rather than terminate, a tenancy.

In cases involving anti-social behaviour eviction should, where possible, be used as a last resort, although in particularly serious cases or where perpetrators refuse to co-operate it may be necessary. A number of measures have been introduced which may be used to tackle anti-social behaviour without removing the perpetrator from their home and moving the problem to somewhere else. These include Acceptable Behaviour Contracts, Anti-Social Behaviour Orders, housing injunctions and demotion. Further information on the tools and powers available to tackle anti-social behaviour can be found on the TOGETHER website, a resource for practitioners working to tackle anti-social behaviour (www.together.gov.uk).

Similarly, in cases involving rent arrears eviction should, where possible, be used as a last resort. RSLs should employ strategies to maximise their income and to prevent and manage rent arrears. Where arrears have accrued they should seek early intervention through personal contact with the tenant(s) offering support and advice. They should offer practical ways for recovering the arrears through debt management plans, referrals to debt advice agencies and ensuring that tenants are claiming all the benefits to which they are entitled. ODPM published guidance for local authorities and RSLs on *Improving the Effectiveness of Rent Arrears Management* (June 2005).

**Supporting People programme:** housing authorities should ensure they work closely with RSLs in implementing the Supporting People programme to ensure that housing-related support can be delivered, where appropriate, for people who would be at risk of homelessness without such support.

**mobility:** housing authorities should work with RSLs in considering the scope for mobility – including moves to other areas, moves to other tenures, and joint action to reduce under-occupation and over-crowding – in meeting housing need and reducing homelessness. Larger RSLs, which operate in a number of different areas, may be uniquely placed to facilitate cross-boundary moves, including voluntary moves from high demand areas to areas of lower demand.

ODPM, in conjunction with the Housing Corporation, National Housing Federation and Local Government Association, published a good practice guide for local authorities and housing associations on *Effective Co-operation in Tackling Homelessness: Nomination Agreements and Exclusions* (2004).

**[5028]**

## ANNEX 6

### HOMELESSNESS STRATEGY: SPECIFIC ACTION THAT MIGHT BE EXPECTED TO BE TAKEN BY OTHERS

*PUBLIC SECTOR*

**Registered social landlords**
- ensure allocation policies meet the needs of people accepted as homeless including specialist provision for vulnerable groups, e.g. drug misusers;
- ensure allocation policies are inclusive, defensible and do not operate 'blanket bans' for particular groups;
- ensure arrears policies take into account the aims of the homelessness strategy (and facilitate early access to money and housing advice).

**Primary Care Trusts**
- develop health services for homeless people, (e.g. Personal Medical Service pilots, walk-in centres, GP service that visits hostels and day centres);
- ensure access to primary health care for all homeless people including rough sleepers and those using emergency access accommodation;
- liaise with social services and special needs housing providers to ensure access to dependency and multiple needs services where needed;
- ensure that hospital discharge policies and protocols are developed and put in place for those leaving hospital who are in housing need;
- ensure access to mental health services, including counselling and therapy where needed.

**Children's Trusts**
- ensure children's services and housing strategies are integrated to achieve better outcomes for children.

**Youth and Community Services**
- develop peer support schemes;
- raise awareness of homelessness issues with young people at risk.

**National Offender Management Service**
- complete a basic housing needs assessment on entry to custody in all local establishments;
- share information with other agencies on risk of harm, potential homelessness and vulnerability;
- develop local protocols regarding dealing with potentially homeless offenders and information sharing;
- as part of the local Supporting People Commissioning bodies, provide specialist knowledge to help commission new services for vulnerable offender and victim groups.

**Regional Offender Managers**
- ensure regional strategic representation of the needs of offenders in custody and the community.

**Community Safety Team/Anti-social Behaviour Team**
- develop steps/interventions to reduce anti-social behaviour and therefore reduce the risk of evictions.

**Youth Offending Team**
- work with children and young people to prevent their offending, effectively integrate them and their families within the community and ultimately prevent evictions.

**Drug Action Team**
- consider the need to commission treatment for homeless people, or whether mainstream services can be extended to meet their needs;
- develop accommodation options for substance misusers including such provision as Rent Deposit Schemes;
- develop, in collaboration with Supporting People teams, specialist housing provision for substance misusers;
- ensure that the children of adults with substance misuse problems are taken into account when planning services.

**Jobcentre Plus**
- ensure that clients are helped to find and keep a job;
- ensure that clients claim and receive the benefits they are entitled to.

**Connexions Service**
- provide advice and information on housing and related benefits (or referral to other agencies where appropriate) to all 13 to 19 year olds who need it;
- ensure vulnerable young people have access to a personal adviser with the aim of preventing those young people becoming homeless.

**National Asylum Support Service (NASS)**
- ensure NASS accommodation providers notify local authorities of the planned withdrawal of NASS accommodation within two days of a positive asylum decision;
- encourage NASS accommodation providers to help prevent homelessness amongst new refugees (e.g. via tenancy conversion or delaying evictions);
- ensure that homelessness and housing pressures are taken into account by Regional Strategic Co-ordination Meetings when decisions are taken on future asylum seeker dispersal areas.

*VOLUNTARY SECTOR*
- Provision of a range of services including:
  - Rent in advance/deposit bond schemes;
  - Night stop schemes;
  - Supported lodgings schemes;
  - Homelessness awareness/preventative input to schools;
  - Advice services (housing/debt/benefits etc.);
  - Counselling, mediation, reconciliation services;
  - Provision of floating support;
  - Lay advocacy services;
  - Dependency services;
  - Hospital discharge services;
  - Women's refuges;
  - Day Centres;
  - Outreach to those sleeping rough;
  - Provision of emergency accommodation (e.g. night shelters);
  - Hostels;
  - Foyers;
  - Resettlement services (including pre-tenancy, move-on accommodation and tenancy sustainment);
  - Mental health services;
  - Peer support, self-help and user groups;
  - Meaningful occupation/personal development work/job training/skills for employment/ work placements;
  - Support for parents of young people at risk of homelessness;
  - Support for victims of crime.

*PRIVATE SECTOR*
- provision of hostels;
- making lettings available to people who are homeless or at risk of homelessness (e.g. through landlord accreditation schemes);
- working with tenants to address rent arrears.

PART III
OTHER MATERIAL

**[5029]**

# ANNEX 7

## TACKLING COMMON CAUSES OF HOMELESSNESS

**1.** This annex provides guidance on how authorities might tackle some of the more common causes of homelessness at an early stage.

*Parents, relatives or friends not being able to provide accommodation*

**2.** Housing authorities are advised to consider a range of approaches aimed at avoiding the crisis of homelessness, resolving problems in the long-term or providing respite and time for a planned, and often more sustainable move. Home visits and mediation services can play an important role in delaying or preventing homelessness by helping people find solutions and resolve difficulties.

**3.** Family tensions can make living conditions intolerable for young people and their parents. Housing authorities are advised to work closely with children's trusts at strategic level to ensure that housing need and homelessness prevention are included in the strategic planning process through the Children and Young People's Plan. They are also advised to work closely with children's trusts at delivery level as part of local multi-agency teams that provide joined up services focusing on improving outcomes for children and young people. As part of this work, they may consider developing partnerships with key agencies in the voluntary sector who work with young people at risk of homelessness. Trained staff and peer mentors can often help young people in difficult relationships restore some links to their families or supporters, resolve family conflict or facilitate planned moves into alternative accommodation.

*Relationship breakdown*

**4.** Relationships may often be strained or break down due to periods of separation, e.g. long-term hospital or drug treatment or because of the behaviour of family members, e.g. offending or violence. Local authorities should develop systems for assessing appropriate forms of intervention and the assessment of risks to vulnerable family members to inform decisions about intervention, e.g. where domestic violence or child safety is involved.

**5.** Local authorities should consider the use of home visits, mediation and counselling services to help couples and families reconcile their differences or facilitate planned moves to alternative accommodation.

**6.** Housing authorities are advised to consider the provision of specialist advice targeted at young people at risk of homelessness. Local Connexions services, for example, can play a key role in reaching vulnerable young people; helping them access information and advice, providing one-to-one support or brokering appropriate specialist support from key services such as welfare, health, substance and/or alcohol misuse services, education and employment. Housing authorities might also consider working with local schools in order to provide young people with information about the implications of leaving home and the housing choices available to them.

**Domestic violence**

**7.** As well as being a direct and underlying cause of homelessness, it is becoming increasingly apparent that domestic violence is a major factor among people who experience "repeat" homelessness. In many cases, the provision of advice and outreach services to support people who experience domestic violence before they reach crisis point, for example on ex-partner rent arrears, tenancy agreements and property rights, can help to prevent homelessness.

**8.** Housing authorities are encouraged to offer people who have experienced domestic violence a range of accommodation and support options. For some, escaping domestic violence will involve leaving their home, often as a last resort, and those who have experienced domestic violence may be placed in a refuge or another form of appropriate temporary accommodation where necessary. Many people who have experienced domestic violence would, however, prefer to remain in their own homes with their social and support networks around them. From 1 April 2005 local authorities have been strongly encouraged to develop, launch and promote a sanctuary type scheme in order to meet part of the revised domestic violence Best Value Performance Indicator 225. The scheme provides security measures to allow those experiencing domestic violence to remain in their own homes where they choose to do so, where safety can be assured and where the perpetrator no longer lives within the accommodation.

**9.** It is important that when developing policies, strategies and practice-based interventions, housing authorities work with all relevant bodies. For example, when considering the safety, security and confidentiality of people who have experienced domestic violence and their children, especially those children who may be vulnerable and/or at risk, housing authorities will need to work with Crime and Disorder Reduction Partnerships, the Local Domestic Violence Fora and with the Local Safeguarding Children Board. BVPI 225 encourages further work in this area.

*End of an assured shorthold tenancy*

**10.** The use of home visits, landlord-tenant mediation services and tenancy sustainment services may enable tenants who have been asked to leave their home to remain with their existing private landlords, through negotiation, mediation and the offer of practical solutions, such as clearing a debt, providing the tenant with advice on managing budgets or fast-tracking a Housing Benefit claim.

**11.**  Housing authorities should also establish services to provide tenants in housing difficulties with advice and information about available housing options and, where necessary, assistance to help them access alternative accommodation. Advice might include, for example, advice about private landlords and letting agents, including any accreditation schemes, within the district; the availability of rent guarantee or rent deposit schemes; or how to apply for social housing through the local authority housing waiting list or from other social landlords).

*Rent and mortgage arrears*

**12.**  Early intervention by the housing authority could help prevent difficulties with rent or mortgage arrears from triggering a homelessness crisis for tenants or home owners.

Options might include:

–        personal contact with tenants or homeowners to offer support and advice;
–        mediation with private landlords;
–        welfare benefits advice and assistance with making claims;
–        debt counselling and money advice (either in-house or through referrals to specialist advice agencies);
–        advice on practical ways of recovering rent arrears through debt management plans, attachment to earnings or benefits orders or by referrals to a debt advice agencies.

**13.**  Many approaches to the prevention and management of rent arrears among tenants can apply equally whether the landlord is a social sector or a private sector landlord. ODPM published guidance for local authorities and RSLs on *Improving the Effectiveness of Rent Arrears Management* (*June 2005*).

**14.**  In some cases rent arrears may be the result of an underlying problem such as alcohol or drug misuse, death of a partner, relationship breakdown, change in employment status, or physical or mental health problems. In such cases the housing authority may wish to contact the appropriate health and social services departments and other relevant agencies for advice, assistance and specialist support. The Secretary of State considers that housing authorities should always consult the Children's Trust before considering the eviction of a family with children. Vital work helping vulnerable children can be affected if families with children are forced to move out of the local area. Effective, ongoing liaison arrangements and collaborative working will be important in such instances.

**Housing Benefit administration**

**15.**  Rent arrears can arise from delays in the calculation and payment of housing benefit. It is therefore in housing authorities' interests to develop prompt and efficient systems for the payment of benefit in order to avoid a risk of homelessness arising as a result of such delays. Where the administration of housing benefit and the provision of housing assistance are dealt with by different departments of the local authority, it will be necessary for the authority to ensure that effective liaison arrangements are in place. Efficient housing benefit payments systems can also help to increase the confidence of private sector landlords in letting accommodation to tenants who may rely on benefits to meet their rent costs.

*Anti-Social Behaviour and Offending*

**16.**  Tenants may be at risk of becoming homeless as a result of their own or others' anti-social or offending behaviour. Housing authorities are urged to contact tenants in these circumstances at the earliest possible stage where they have received a complaint or where it has been brought to their attention that a tenant is causing a nuisance or annoyance. This will enable them to inform such tenants of the possible consequences of continuing with the reported behaviour and may prevent homelessness resulting in some instances. Authorities will need to be aware of the need for discretion about the source of any complaint, particularly where there is concern about threatening or aggressive behaviour.

**17.**  In cases where a housing authority is satisfied that there is a substantive complaint of anti-social behaviour they will need to consider a range of options to address the problem with the tenant before embarking on action to terminate the tenancy. Housing authorities are advised, where possible, to use eviction as a last resort, although in particularly serious cases or where perpetrators refuse to co-operate it may be necessary.

**18.**  Mediation services may help to resolve neighbour disputes which have led to complaints of anti-social behaviour. A number of measures have been introduced which may be used to tackle anti-social behaviour without removing the perpetrator from their home and simply moving the problem somewhere else. These include: Acceptable Behaviour Contracts, Anti-Social Behaviour Orders, housing injunctions and demotion. Further information can be found on the TOGETHER website, a resource for practitioners working to tackle anti-social behaviour (www.together.gov.uk).

**19.** Where local authority tenants are at risk of homelessness as a result of other tenants' anti-social behaviour, authorities should be aware of the powers they have to take action against the perpetrators and make urgent housing transfers to protect victims of violence or harassment, where requested.

**20.** Housing authorities will need to work closely with the National Offender Management Service (NOMS) and their partners in the voluntary and community sector to manage the housing arrangements of offenders in the community, and ensure they receive any support necessary to avoid a risk of homelessness. Where an authority may be considering the eviction of an offender, it will need to consult closely with NOMS to ensure this can be avoided wherever possible. This will also help reduce re-offending and promote community safety.

*Leaving an institutional environment*

**21.** People leaving an institutional environment can be particularly at risk of homelessness and may seek assistance from the housing authority to obtain accommodation when they move on. Authorities should have systems in place to ensure that they have advance notice of such people's needs for accommodation in such circumstances to allow them to take steps well in advance to ensure that arrangements are in place to enable a planned and timely move.

**Young people leaving care**

**22.** It is important that, wherever possible, the housing needs of care leavers are addressed before they leave care. All care leavers must have a pathway plan prepared by appropriate staff of the authority responsible for their care, setting out the support they will be provided with to enable them make a successful transition to a more independent lifestyle. Making arrangements for accommodation and ensuring that, where necessary, care leavers are provided with suitable housing support will be an essential aspect of the pathway plan. Where care leavers may require social housing, their housing and related support needs should be discussed with the appropriate agencies. Where necessary, arrangements will need to be made for joint assessment between social services and housing authorities, as part of a multi-agency assessment necessary to inform the pathway plan of individual young people.

**23.** Consideration of an individual care leaver's housing needs should take account of their need for support and reasonable access to places of education, employment, training and health care. As far as possible, pathway plans should include contingency plans in the event of any breakdown in the young person's accommodation arrangements. It is recommended that housing and social services authorities (and relevant departments within unitary authorities) develop joint protocols for meeting the needs of care leavers to ensure that each agency (or department) plays a full role in providing support to – and building trust with – this client group.

**Custody or detention**

**24.** Around a third of prisoners lose their housing on imprisonment, so it is important that prisoners receive effective advice and assistance about housing options, either prior to or when being remanded or sentenced to custody. Assessing an offender's housing needs at this point will help to identify those prisoners who may require assistance to bring to an end, sustain or transfer an existing tenancy, make a claim for Housing Benefit to meet rent costs while in prison, or to help a prisoner transfer or close down an existing tenancy appropriately. Local authorities are advised to assist the Prison Service in providing advice to prisoners and taking action to ensure they can sustain their accommodation while in custody.

**25.** It is recommended that housing advice be made available to offenders throughout the period of custody or detention to ensure that any housing needs are addressed. It is important that early planning takes place between prison staff and housing providers to identify housing options on release, to prevent homelessness and enable them to make a smooth transition from prison, or remand, to independent living.

**26.** All prisoners in local prisons and Category C prisons have access to housing advice. And, from April 2005 all local prisons have been required to carry out a housing needs assessment for every new prisoner, including those serving short sentences. Local authorities are advised to assist the Prison Service in delivering these services.

**27.** All Youth Offending Teams (YOTs) now have named accommodation officers. YOTs can offer both practical support to children, young people and their families and can increasingly play a key strategic role in ensuring that young offenders are effectively resettled through accessing mainstream provision and services.

**28.** Joint working between the National Offender Management Service/Youth Offending Teams and their local housing authorities is essential to help prevent homelessness amongst offenders, ex-offenders and others who have experience of the criminal justice system. Options might include:
- having a single contact point within the housing authority to provide housing advice and assistance for those who have experience of the criminal justice system;
- Probation staff offering information on securing or terminating tenancies prior to custody;

- running housing advice sessions in local prisons to further enable prisoners to access advice on housing options prior to their release;
- prisons granting prisoners Release On Temporary Licence to attend housing interviews with landlords;
- developing tenancy support services for those who have experienced the criminal justice system.

### Armed forces

**29.** Members of Her Majesty's regular naval, military and air forces are generally provided with accommodation by the Ministry of Defence (MOD), but are required to leave this when they are discharged from the service. The principal responsibility for providing housing information and advice to Service personnel lies with the armed forces up to the point of discharge and these services are delivered through the Joint Service Housing Advice Office (telephone: 01722 436575). Some people, who have served in the armed forces for a long period, and those who are medically discharged, may be offered assistance with resettlement by Ministry of Defence (MOD) resettlement staff. The MOD issues a *Certificate of Cessation of Entitlement to Occupy Service Living Accommodation* (see examples at Annexes 14 and 15) six months before discharge.

**30.** Housing authorities that have a significant number of service personnel stationed in their area will need to work closely with relevant partners, such as the Joint Service Housing Advice Office and MOD's resettlement services, to ascertain likely levels of need for housing assistance amongst people leaving the forces and plan their services accordingly. In particular, housing authorities are advised to take advantage of the six-month period of notice of discharge to ensure that service personnel receive timely and comprehensive advice on the housing options available to them when they leave the armed forces. Authorities may also wish to consider creating links with the employment and business communities to assist people leaving the armed forces to find work or meaningful occupation, enabling them further to make a successful transition to independent living in the community.

**31.** The Veterans Agency should be the first point of contact for all former armed forces personnel who require information about housing issues. The agency provide a free help line (telephone: 0800 169 2277) which offers former armed forces personnel advice and signposting to ex-Service benevolent organisations who may be able to offer assistance with housing matters.

### Hospital

**32.** Some people who are admitted to hospital – even for a short time – may be in housing need or at risk of homelessness. And some people who may not be in housing need when they are admitted may become at risk of losing their home during a protracted stay in hospital, for example, if they are unable to maintain their rent or mortgage payments. This can apply, in particular, to people admitted to hospital for mental health reasons and for whom family, tenancy or mortgage breakdown is an accompanying factor to the admission to hospital.

**33.** Housing authorities are advised to work closely with social services and NHS Trusts in order to establish good procedures for the discharge of patients, and to ensure that former patients are not homeless or at risk of homelessness on leaving hospital. This could involve agreeing joint protocols for hospital admissions and discharge of patients to ensure that the housing and support needs of inpatients are identified as early as possible after admission, and that arrangements are put in place to meet the needs of patients in good time prior to discharge. Measures might include, for example, setting up a multi-agency discharge team as part of the homelessness strategy action plan or funding a dedicated post to support patients who may be at risk of homelessness when discharged from hospital.

**34.** Further guidance is provided in Department of Health publications on *Achieving timely simple discharge from hospital: A toolkit for the multi-disciplinary team* (2004) and *Discharge from hospital: pathway, process and practice* (2003).

### Accommodation provided by National Asylum Support Service (NASS)

**35.** Asylum seekers who receive leave to remain in the UK must move on from their NASS accommodation within 28 days of the decision on their case. Former asylum seekers will therefore have little time to find alternative accommodation and are unlikely to have had any experience of renting or buying accommodation in the UK, or experience of related matters such as claiming benefits or arranging essential services such as gas, water and electricity. These difficulties are likely to be compounded by the fact that many former asylum seekers may face cultural barriers such as language.

**36.** In order to prevent these factors leading to homelessness amongst former asylum seekers, housing authorities are advised to develop protocols with NASS accommodation providers, refugee support services and NASS regional managers to ensure that, where possible, a planned and timely move to alternative accommodation or the sustainment of existing accommodation can take place. Housing benefit, rent deposits, homeless prevention loans and discretionary housing benefit payments can all help to fund temporary extensions of the NASS notice period or longer-term tenancy conversion through the establishment of assured shorthold tenancies.

**37.**  Former asylum seekers will need effective and timely advice on the range of housing options available. It is vital that housing authorities ensure that this advice and information can be readily translated into community languages and delivered in locations accessible to asylum seekers and refugees. Authorities are also advised to consider whether there may be a need for ongoing resettlement support in order to maximise the chances of tenancy sustainment. As standard, authorities are advised to ensure that new refugees are made fully aware of the steps that they need to take to maintain a UK tenancy.

**38.**  Authorities may wish to refer to *Housing and Support Services for asylum seekers and refugees: a good practice guide* (2005) published by the Chartered Institute of Housing.

*Ethnic minority populations*

**39.**  Statistics provided by local authorities show that people from ethnic minority backgrounds are around three times more likely to be accepted as owed a main homelessness duty than their White counterparts. This pattern is found across all regions in England and the reasons are varied and complex. It is therefore critical that housing authorities and their partner agencies develop comprehensive strategies to better prevent and respond to homelessness among people from ethnic minority communities.

**40.**  ODPM published *Tackling homelessness amongst ethnic minority households – a development guide* (2005) to assist local authorities and their partner agencies in the development of inclusive, evidence-based and cost-effective homelessness services for their local ethnic minority populations.

*Drug Users*

**41.**  Drug use can both precede and occur as a result of homelessness. Between half and three quarters of single homeless people have in the past been problematic drug misusers. Many have a wide range of support needs, which reinforce each other and heighten the risk of drug use and homelessness. For those who are engaging in drug treatment, or have stabilised their use, homelessness increases their chances of relapse and continued problematic drug use. Housing authorities are advised to work closely with Drug Action Teams (multi-agency partnerships who co-ordinate the drug strategy at the local level) to ensure that housing and homelessness strategies are aligned with DAT treatment plans and Supporting People strategies help address the needs of homeless drug users as a shared client group.

[5030]

## ANNEX 8

## HOW TO CONTACT THE HOME OFFICE IMMIGRATION AND NATIONALITY DIRECTORATE

**1.**  The Home Office's Immigration and Nationality Directorate (IND) will exchange information with housing authorities subject to relevant data protection and disclosure policy requirements being met and properly managed, provided that the information is required to assist with the carrying out of statutory functions or prevention and detection of fraud.

**2.**  The Evidence and Enquiries Unit (EEU) will provide a service to housing authorities to confirm the immigration status of an applicant from abroad (Non-Asylum Seekers). In order to take advantage of the service, housing authorities first need to register with the Evidence and Enquiries Unit, Immigration and Nationality Directorate, 12th Floor Lunar House, Croydon, CR9 2BY either by letter or **Fax: 020 8196 3049**

**3.**  Registration details required by the EEU's Local Authorities' Team are:
   (a)    Name of enquiring housing authority on headed paper;
   (b)    Job title/status of officer registering on behalf of the local housing authority; and
   (c)    Names of housing authority staff and their respective job titles/status who will be making enquiries on behalf of the housing authority.

**4.**  Once the housing authority is registered with the EEU, and this has been confirmed, then the authorised personnel can make individual enquiries by letter or fax, but replies will be returned by post.

**5.**  The EEU will not usually indicate that someone is an asylum seeker unless the applicant has signed a disclaimer and it is attached to the enquiry or if the enquirer has specifically asked about asylum.

**6.**  If a response indicates that the applicant has an outstanding asylum claim, or there are any queries regarding an ongoing asylum case, enquiries should be made to NASS LA Comms on 020 8760 4527. Local authorities will also need to be registered with this team before any information can be provided.

**7.** The Home Office (IND) can only advise whether an EEA/foreign national has a right of residence in the United Kingdom. IND does not decide whether an EEA/Foreign national qualifies for benefits or for local authority housing.

## ANNEX 9

## ASYLUM SEEKERS

### OVERVIEW

**1.** Generally, asylum seekers can be expected to be *persons subject to immigration control* who have been given *temporary admission* but have not been granted leave to enter or remain in the UK.

**2. Asylum seekers who are *persons subject to immigration control* and whose claim for asylum was made after 2 April 2000 are not eligible for assistance under Part 7.** However, some asylum seekers who are *persons subject to immigration control* and whose claim for asylum was made before 3 April 2000 may be eligible (see below).

**3.** Broadly speaking, an asylum seeker is a person claiming to have a well-founded fear of being persecuted for reasons of race, religion, nationality, membership of a particular social group, or political opinion, and who is unable or unwilling to avail him or her self of the protection of the authorities in his or her own country.

**4.** A person only becomes an asylum seeker when his or her claim for asylum has been recorded by the Home Secretary, and he or she remains an asylum seeker until such time as that application has been finally resolved (including the resolution of any appeal). The recording, consideration and resolution of such claims is a matter for the Home Office Immigration and Nationality Directorate (IND).

**5.** If there is any uncertainty about an applicant's immigration or asylum status, housing authorities should contact the Home Office Immigration and Nationality Directorate, using the procedures set out in Annex 8. Before doing so, the applicant should be advised that an inquiry will be made: if at this stage the applicant prefers to withdraw his or her application, no further action will be required

### ASYLUM SEEKERS WHO ARE ELIGIBLE FOR PART 7 ASSISTANCE

**6.** The *Allocation of Housing and Homelessness (Eligibility) (England) Regulations 2006* (SI 2006 No.1294) ("the Eligibility Regulations") provide that asylum seekers who are *persons subject to immigration control* and who claimed asylum before 3 April 2000 are eligible for assistance under Part 7 in certain circumstances (set out below). However, by virtue of s.186(1), an asylum seeker is not eligible for Part 7 assistance if he or she has any accommodation in the UK – however temporary – available for his or her occupation. This would include a place in a hostel or bed and breakfast hotel.

**7.** Subject to s.186(1), such asylum seekers are eligible for assistance under Part 7, if they claimed asylum before 3 April 2000, and:

    i)      the claim for asylum was made at the port on initial arrival in the UK (but not on re-entry) from a country outside the United Kingdom, the Channel Islands, the Isle of Man or the Republic of Ireland; **or**

    ii)      the claim for asylum was made within 3 months of a declaration by the Secretary of State that he would not normally order the return of a person to the country of which he or she is a national because of a fundamental change of circumstances in that country, and the asylum seeker was present in Great Britain on the date the declaration was made; **or**

    iii)      the claim for asylum was made on or before 4 February 1996 and the applicant was entitled to housing benefit on 4 February 1996 under regulation 7A of the *Housing Benefit (General) Regulations 1987*.

**8.** Generally, a person ceases to be an asylum seeker for the purposes of the Eligibility Regulations when his claim for asylum is recorded by the Secretary of State as having been decided (other than on appeal) or abandoned. However, a person does not cease to be an asylum seeker in these circumstances for the purposes of paragraph 7(iii) if he continues to be eligible for housing benefit by virtue of:

    –      regulation 10(6) of the *Housing Benefit Regulations 2006* (SI 2006 No. 213), or

    –      regulation 10(6) of the *Housing Benefit (persons who have attained the qualifying age for state pension credit) Regulations 2006* (SI 2006 No. 214).

as amended by the *Housing Benefit and Council Tax Benefit (Consequential Provisions) Regulations 2006* (SI 2006 No.217).

### FORMER ASYLUM SEEKERS

**9.** Where an asylum claim is successful – either initially or following an appeal – the claimant will normally be granted refugee status. If a claim is unsuccessful, leave to remain in the UK may still be granted, in accordance with published policies on Humanitarian Protection and Discretionary Leave. Former asylum seekers granted refugee status, or those granted Humanitarian Protection or Discretionary Leave which is not subject to a condition requiring him to maintain and accommodate himself without recourse to public funds will be eligible for homelessness assistance.

**10.** Prior to April 2003, Exceptional Leave to Remain was granted rather than Humanitarian Protection or Discretionary Leave. Those with Exceptional Leave to Remain which is not subject to a condition requiring him to maintain and accommodate himself without recourse to public funds will also be eligible for homelessness assistance.

## INFORMATION

**11.** Under s.187 of the *Housing Act 1996*, the Home Office Immigration and Nationality Directorate (IND) will, on request, provide local housing authorities with the information necessary to determine whether a particular housing applicant is an asylum seeker, or a dependant of an asylum seeker, and whether he or she is eligible for assistance under Part 7. In cases where it is confirmed that a housing applicant is an asylum seeker, or the dependant of an asylum seeker, any subsequent change in circumstances which affect the applicant's housing status (eg. a decision on the asylum claim) will be notified to the authority by the IND. The procedures for contacting the IND are set out in Annex 8.

**[5032]**

## ANNEX 10

### THE HABITUAL RESIDENCE TEST

**1.** In practice, when considering housing applications from persons who are subject to the habitual residence test, it is only necessary to investigate habitual residence if the applicant has arrived or returned to live in the UK during the two year period prior to making the application.

### DEFINITION OF HABITUALLY RESIDENT

**2.** The term 'habitually resident' is not defined in legislation. Local authorities should always consider the overall circumstances of a case to determine whether someone is habitually resident in the UK, the Channel Islands, the Isle of Man or the Republic of Ireland.

### GENERAL PRINCIPLES

**3.** When deciding whether a person is habitually resident in a place, consideration must be given to all the facts of each case in a common sense way. It should be remembered that:-
- the test focuses on the fact and nature of residence;
- a person who is not resident somewhere cannot be habitually resident there. Residence is a more settled state than mere physical presence in a country. To be resident a person must be seen to be making a home. It need not be the only home or a permanent home but it must be a genuine home for the time being. For example, a short stay visitor or a person receiving short term medical treatment is not resident;
- the most important factors for habitual residence are the length, continuity and general nature of actual residence rather than intention;
- the practicality of a person's arrangements for residence is a necessary part of determining whether it can be described as settled and habitual;
- established habitual residents who have periods of temporary or occasional absence of long or short duration may still be habitually resident during such absences.

### ACTION ON RECEIPT OF AN APPLICATION

#### Applicant came to live in the UK during the previous two years

**4.** If it appears that the applicant came to live in the UK during the previous two years, authorities should make further enquiries to decide if the applicant is habitually resident, or can be treated as such.

#### Factors to consider

**5.** The applicant's stated reasons and intentions for coming to the UK will be relevant to the question of whether he or she is habitually resident. If the applicant's stated intention is to live in the UK, and not return to the country from which they came, that intention must be consistent with their actions.

**6.** To decide whether an applicant is habitually resident in the UK, authorities should consider the factors set out below. However, these do not provide an exhaustive check list of the questions or factors that need to be considered. Further enquiries may be needed. The circumstances of each case will dictate what information is needed, and all relevant factors should be taken into account.

**Why has the applicant come to the UK?**

**7.**   If the applicant is returning to the UK after a period spent abroad, and it can be established that the applicant was previously habitually resident in the UK and is returning to resume his or her former period of habitual residence, **he or she will be immediately habitually resident.**

**8.**   In determining whether an applicant is returning to resume a former period of habitual residence authorities should consider:

- when did the applicant leave the UK?
- how long did the applicant live in the UK before leaving?
- why did the applicant leave the UK?
- how long did the applicant intend to remain abroad?
- why did the applicant return?
- did the applicant's partner and children, if any, also leave the UK?
- did the applicant keep accommodation in the UK?
- if the applicant owned property, was it let, and was the lease timed to coincide with the applicant's return to the UK?
- what links did the applicant keep with the UK?
- have there been other brief absences? If yes, obtain details
- why has the applicant come to the UK?

**9.**   If the applicant has arrived in the UK within the previous two years and is not resuming a period of habitual residence, consideration should be given to his or her reasons for coming to the UK, and in particular to the factors set out below.

**Applicant is joining family or friends**

**10.**   If the applicant has come to the UK to join or rejoin family or friends, authorities should consider:

- has the applicant sold or given up any property abroad?
- has the applicant bought or rented accommodation or is he or she staying with friends?
- is the move to the UK intended to be permanent?

**Applicant's plans**

**11.**   Authorities should consider the applicant's plans, e.g.:

- if the applicant plans to remain in the UK, is the applicant's stated plan consistent with his or her actions?
- were any arrangements made for employment and accommodation (even if unsuccessful) before the applicant arrived in the UK?
- did the applicant buy a one-way ticket?
- did the applicant bring all his or her belongings?
- is there any evidence of links with the UK, e g membership of clubs?

**12.**   The fact that a person may intend to live in the UK for the foreseeable future does not, of itself, mean that habitual residence has been established. However, the applicant's intentions along with other factors, for example the disposal of property abroad, may indicate that the applicant is habitually resident in the UK.

**13.**   An applicant who intends to reside in the UK for only a short period, for example for a holiday or to visit friends is unlikely to be habitually resident in the UK.

**Length of residence in another country**

**14.**   Authorities should consider the length and continuity of an applicant's residence in another country:

- how long did the applicant live in the previous country?
- does the applicant have any remaining ties with his or her former country of residence?
- has the applicant stayed in different countries outside the UK?

**15.**   It is possible that a person may own a property abroad but still be habitually resident in the UK. A person who has a home or close family in another country would normally retain habitual residence in that country. A person who has previously lived in several different countries but has now moved permanently to the UK may be habitually resident here.

**Centre of interest**

**16.**   An applicant is likely to be habitually resident in the UK, the Channel Islands, the Isle of Man or the Republic of Ireland, despite spending time abroad, if his or her centre of interest is located in one of these places.

**17.**   People who maintain their centre of interest in the UK, the Channel Islands, the Isle of Man or the Republic of Ireland, for example a home, a job, friends, membership of clubs, are likely to be habitually resident there. People who have retained their centre of interest in another country and have no particular ties with the UK, the Channel Islands, the Isle of Man or the Republic of Ireland, are unlikely to be habitually resident in the UK, the Channel Islands, the Isle of Man or the Republic of Ireland.

18.   Authorities should take the following into account when deciding the centre of interest:
- home;
- family ties;
- club memberships;
- finance accounts

19.   If the centre of interest appears to be in the UK, the Channel Islands, the Isle of Man or the Republic of Ireland but the applicant has a home somewhere else, authorities should consider the applicant's intentions regarding the property.

20.   In certain cultures, e.g. the Asian culture, it is quite common for a person to live in one country but have property abroad that they do not intend to sell. Where such a person has lived in the UK, the Channel Islands, the Isle of Man or the Republic of Ireland for many years, the fact that they have property elsewhere does not necessarily mean that they intend to leave, or that the applicant's centre of interest is elsewhere.

[5033]

## ANNEX 11

## EUROPEAN GROUPINGS
## (EU, A8, EEA, SWITZERLAND)

*THE EUROPEAN UNION (EU)*

Austria, Belgium, Cyprus, the Czech Republic, Denmark, Estonia, Finland, France, Germany, Greece, Hungary, Ireland, Italy, Latvia, Lithuania, Luxembourg, Malta, the Netherlands, Poland, Portugal, Slovakia, Slovenia, Spain, Sweden, the United Kingdom and the A8 or Accession States.

*THE "A8" OR "ACCESSION STATES"*

The 8 eastern European States that acceded to the EU in 2004 (and whose nationals may be subject to the UK Worker Registration Scheme for a transitional period):

   the Czech Republic, Estonia, Hungary, Latvia, Lithuania, Poland, Slovakia and Slovenia.

*THE EUROPEAN ECONOMIC AREA (EEA)*

All EU countries, plus: Iceland, Norway and Liechtenstein.

*SWITZERLAND*

**Note:** Although not an EEA State, Switzerland should be treated as an EEA State for the purpose of this guidance. (See the *Immigration (European Economic Area) Regulations 2006* (S.I. 2006 No. 1003), regulation 2(1))

[5034]

## ANNEX 12

## RIGHTS TO RESIDE IN THE UK DERIVED FROM EC LAW

1.   EEA nationals and their family members who have a right to reside in the UK that derives from EC law are not persons subject to immigration control. This means that they will be eligible for assistance under Part 7 of the *Housing Act 1996* ("housing assistance") unless they fall within one of the categories of persons to be treated as a person from abroad who is ineligible for assistance by virtue of regulation 6 of the *Allocation of Housing and Homelessness (Eligibility) (England) Regulations 2006* ("the Eligibility Regulations").

*GENERAL*

**Nationals of EU countries**

2.   Nationals of EU countries enjoy a number of different rights to reside in other Member States, including the UK. These rights derive from the EC Treaty, EC secondary legislation (in particular *Directive 2004/38/EC*), and the case law of the European Court of Justice.

3.   Whether an individual EU national has a right to reside in the UK will depend on his or her circumstances, particularly his or her economic status (e.g. whether employed, self-employed, seeking work, a student, or economically inactive etc.).

**The accession states**

**4.** A slightly different regime applies to EU nationals who are nationals of the accession states. For the purposes of this guidance, 'the accession states' are the 8 eastern European countries that acceded to the EU on 1 May 2004: Poland, Lithuania, Estonia, Latvia, Slovenia, Slovakia, Hungary and the Czech Republic.

*The* Immigration (European Economic Area) Regulations 2006

**5.** The *Immigration (European Economic Area) Regulations 2006* ("the EEA Regulations") implement into UK domestic law EC legislation conferring rights of residence on EU nationals. Broadly, the EEA Regulations provide that EU nationals have the right to reside in the UK without the requirement for leave to remain under the *Immigration Act 1971* for the first 3 months of their residence, and for longer, if they are a "qualified person" or they have acquired a permanent right of residence.

**Nationals of Iceland, Liechtenstein and Norway.**

**6.** The EEA Regulations extend the same rights to reside in the UK to nationals of Iceland, Liechtenstein and Norway as those afforded to EU nationals (The EU countries plus Iceland, Liechtenstein and Norway together comprise the EEA.)

**Nationals of Switzerland**

**7.** The EEA Regulations also extend the same rights to reside in the UK to nationals of Switzerland.

**8.** For the purposes of this guidance, "EEA nationals" means nationals of any of the EU member states (excluding the UK), and nationals of Iceland, Norway, Liechtenstein and Switzerland.

*INITIAL 3 MONTHS OF RESIDENCE*

**9.** Regulation 13 of the EEA Regulations provides that EEA nationals have the right to reside in the UK for a period of up to 3 months without any conditions or formalities other than holding a valid identity card or passport. Therefore, during their first 3 months of residence in the UK, EEA nationals will not be subject to immigration control (unless the right to reside is lost following a decision by an immigration officer in accordance with regulation 13(3) of the EEA Regulations).

**10.** However, regulations 6(1)(b)(i) and (c) of the Eligibility Regulations provide that a person who is not subject to immigration control is not eligible for housing assistance if:
   (i)    his or her **only** right to reside in the UK is an initial right to reside for a period not exceeding 3 months under regulation 13 of the EEA Regulations, or
   (ii)   his or her **only** right to reside in the Channel Islands, the Isle of Man or the Republic of Ireland is a right equivalent to the right mentioned in (i) above which is derived from the Treaty establishing the European Community.

On (ii), article 6 of *Directive 2004/38/EC* provides that EU citizens have the right of residence in the territory of another Member State (e.g. the Republic of Ireland) for a period of up to 3 months without any conditions or formalities other than holding a valid identity card or passport.

*RIGHTS OF RESIDENCE FOR 'QUALIFIED PERSONS'*

**11.** Regulation 14 of the EEA Regulations provides that 'qualified persons' have the right to reside in the UK so long as they remain a qualified person. Under regulation 6 of the EEA Regulations, 'qualified person' means:
   a)    a jobseeker,
   b)    a worker,
   c)    a self-employed person,
   d)    a self-sufficient person,
   e)    a student.

**Jobseekers**

**12.** For the purposes of regulation 6(1)(a) of the EEA Regulations, 'jobseeker' means a person who enters the UK in order to seek employment and can provide evidence that he or she is seeking employment and has a genuine chance of being employed.

**13.** Accession state nationals who need to register to work (see paragraph 20 below) do not have a right to reside in the UK as a jobseeker (see regulation 5(2) of the Accession Regulations, as amended). However, accession state nationals seeking work may have a right to reside by virtue of another status, e.g. as a self-sufficient person.

**14.** Although a person who is a jobseeker for the purposes of the definition of "qualified person" in regulation 6(1)(a) of the EEA Regulations is not subject to immigration control, regulation 6 of the Eligibility Regulations provides that a person is not eligible for housing assistance if:
   (i)    his or her only right to reside in the UK is derived from his status as a jobseeker or the family member of a jobseeker, or

(ii)   his or her only right to reside in the Channel Islands, the Isle of Man or the Republic of Ireland is a right equivalent to the right mentioned in (i) above which is derived from the Treaty establishing the European Community.

### Workers

**15.**  In order to be a worker for the purposes of the EEA Regulations, a person must be employed, that is, the person is obliged to provide services for another person in return for monetary reward and who is subject to the control of that other person as regards the way in which the work is to be done.

**16.**  Activity as an employed person may include part-time work, seasonal work and cross-border work (i.e. where a worker is established in another Member State and travels to work in the UK). However, the case law provides that the employment must be effective and genuine economic activity, and not on such a small scale as to be regarded as purely marginal and ancillary.

**17.**  Provided the employment is effective and genuine economic activity, the fact that a person's level of remuneration may be below the level of subsistence or below the national minimum wage, or the fact that a person may be receiving financial assistance from public benefits, would not exclude that person from being a 'worker'. Housing authorities should note that surprisingly small amounts of work can be regarded as effective and genuine economic activity.

**18.**  Applicants in the labour market should be able to confirm that they are, or have been, working in the UK by providing, for example:
–    payslips,
–    a contract of employment, or
–    a letter of employment.

### Retention of worker status

**19.**  A person who is no longer working does not cease to be treated as a 'worker' for the purpose of regulation 6(1)(b) of the EEA Regulations, if he or she:
(a)    is temporarily unable to work as the result of an illness or accident; or
(b)    is recorded as involuntarily unemployed after having being employed in the UK, provided that he or she has registered as a jobseeker with the relevant employment office, and:
    (i)    was employed for one year or more before becoming unemployed, or
    (ii)   has been unemployed for no more than 6 months, or
    (iii)  can provide evidence that he or she is seeking employment in the UK and has a genuine chance of being engaged; or
(c)    is involuntarily unemployed and has embarked on vocational training; or
(d)    has voluntarily ceased working and embarked on vocational training that is related to his or her previous employment.

### Accession state workers requiring registration who are treated as workers

**20.**  By virtue of the *Accession (Immigration and Worker Registration) Regulations 2004* (SI 2004/1219) ("the Accession Regulations"), accession state nationals (with certain exceptions) are required to register their employment in the UK until they have accrued a period of 12 months' continuous employment. The exceptions are set out in Annex 13.

**21.**  An accession state national requiring registration is only treated as a worker if he or she is actually working and:
(a)    has registered his or her employment and is working in the UK for an authorised employer (see regulation 5(2) of the Accession Regulations, as amended), or
(b)    is not registered for employment, but has been working for an employer for less than one month (regulation 7(3) of the Accession Regulations), or
(c)    has applied to register under the Worker Registration Scheme and is working for the employer with whom he or she has applied to register (regulation 7(2)(b) of the Accession Regulations).

**22.**  To demonstrate eligibility for housing assistance, accession state workers requiring registration should be able to:
(a)    provide a valid worker registration card, and a valid worker registration certificate showing their current employer (see Annex 13 for specimens of these documents), or
(b)    (where the accession state worker has applied to register but not yet received the registration certificate) provide a copy of their application to register, or
(c)    show they have been working for their current employer for less than one month.

**23.**  Authorities may need to contact the employer named in the registration certificate, to confirm that the applicant continues to be employed.

**24.**  See Annex 13 for guidance on the Worker Registration Scheme.

**25.**  A person who is a 'worker' for the purposes of the definition of a qualified person in regulation 6(1) of the EEA Regulations is not subject to immigration control, and is eligible for housing assistance whether or not he or she is habitually resident in the UK, the Channel Islands, the Isle of Man or the Republic of Ireland.

### Self-employed persons

**26.** 'Self-employed person' means a person who establishes himself in the UK in order to pursue activity as a self-employed person in accordance with Article 43 of the Treaty establishing the European Union.

**27.** A self-employed person should be able to confirm that he or she is pursuing activity as a self-employed person by providing documents relating to their business such as:

    a)      invoices,
    b)      tax accounts, or
    c)      utility bills.

**28.** A person who is no longer in self-employment does not cease to be treated as a self-employed person for the purposes of regulation 6(1)(c) of the EEA regulations, if he or she is temporarily unable to pursue his or her activity as a self-employed person as the result of an illness or accident.

**29.** Accession state nationals are not required to register in order to establish themselves in the UK as a self-employed person.

**30.** A person who is a self-employed person for the purposes of the definition of a qualified person in regulation 6(1) of the EEA Regulations is not subject to immigration control, and is eligible for housing assistance whether or not he or she is habitually resident in the UK, the Channel Islands, the Isle of Man or the Republic of Ireland.

### Self-sufficient persons

**31.** Regulation 4(1)(c) of the EEA regulations defines 'self-sufficient person' as a person who has:

    (i)    sufficient resources not to become a burden on the social assistance system of the UK during his or her period of residence, and
    (ii)   comprehensive sickness insurance cover in the UK.

**32.** By regulation 4(4) of the EEA Regulations, the resources of a person who is a self-sufficient person or a student (see below), and where applicable, any family members, are to be regarded as sufficient if they exceed the maximum level of resources which a UK national and his or her family members may possess if he or she is to become eligible for social assistance under the UK benefit system.

**33.** Where an EEA national applies for housing assistance as a self-sufficient person and does not appear to meet the conditions of regulation 4(1)(c), the housing authority will need to consider whether he or she may have some other right to reside in the UK.

**34.** Where the applicant does not meet the conditions of regulation 4(1)(c) but has previously done so during his or her residence in the UK, the case should be referred to the Home Office for clarification of their status.

**35.** A person who is a self-sufficient person for the purposes of the definition of a qualified person in regulation 6(1) of the EEA Regulations is not subject to immigration control, but must be habitually resident in the UK, the Channel Islands, the Isle of Man or the Republic of Ireland to be eligible for housing assistance.

### Students

**36.** Regulation 4(1)(d) of the EEA regulations defines 'student' as a person who:

    (a)    is enrolled at a private or public establishment included on the Department of Education and Skills' Register of Education and Training Providers, or is financed from public funds, for the principal purpose of following a course of study, including vocational training, and
    (b)    has comprehensive sickness insurance cover in the UK, and
    (c)    assures the Secretary of State, by means of a declaration or such equivalent means as the person may choose, that he or she (and if applicable his or her family members) has sufficient resources not to become a burden on the social assistance system of the UK during his or her period of residence.

**37.** A person who is a student for the purposes of the definition of a qualified person in regulation 6(1) of the EEA Regulations is not subject to immigration control. The eligibility of such a person for housing assistance should therefore be considered in accordance with regulation 6 of the Eligibility Regulations.

### PERMANENT RIGHT OF RESIDENCE

**38.** Regulation 15 of the EEA Regulations provides that the following persons shall acquire the right to reside in the UK permanently:

    (a)    an EEA national who has resided in the UK in accordance with the EEA regulations for a continuous period of 5 years;
    (b)    a non-EEA national who is a family member of an EEA national and who has resided in the UK with the EEA national in accordance with the EEA regulations for a continuous period of 5 years;

(c) a worker or self-employed person who has ceased activity (see regulation 5 of the EEA Regulations for the definition of worker or self-employed person who has ceased activity);

(d) the family member of a worker or self-employed person who has ceased activity;

(e) a person who was the family member of a worker or self-employed person who has died, where the family member resided with the worker or self-employed person immediately before the death and the worker or self-employed person had resided continuously in the UK for at least 2 years before the death (or the death was the result of an accident at work or an occupational disease);

(f) a person who has resided in the UK in accordance with the EEA regulations for a continuous period of 5 years, and at the end of that period was a family member who has retained the right of residence (see regulation 10 of the EEA Regulations for the definition of a family member who has retained the right of residence).

Once acquired, the right of permanent residence can be lost through absence from the UK for a period exceeding two consecutive years.

**39.** A person with a right to reside permanently in the UK arising from (c), (d) or (e) above is eligible for housing assistance whether or not he or she is habitually resident in the UK, the Channel Islands, the Isle of Man or the Republic of Ireland. Persons with a permanent right to reside by virtue of (a),(b), or (f) must be habitually resident to be eligible.

## RIGHTS OF RESIDENCE FOR CERTAIN FAMILY MEMBERS

### The right to reside

**40.** Regulation 14 of the EEA Regulations provides that the following family members are entitled to reside in the UK:

(i) a family member of a qualified person residing in the UK;

(ii) a family member of an EEA national with a permanent right of residence under regulation 15; and

(iii) a family member who has retained the right of residence (see regulation 10 of the EEA Regulations for the definition).

**41.** A person who has a right to reside in the UK as the family member of an EEA national under the EEA Regulations will not be subject to immigration control. The eligibility of such a person for housing assistance should therefore be considered in accordance with regulation 6 of the Eligibility Regulations.

**42.** When considering the eligibility of a family member, local authorities should consider whether the person has acquired a right to reside in their own right, for example a permanent right to reside under regulation 15 of the EEA Regulations (see paragraph 38 above).

### Who is a 'family member'?

**43.** Regulation 7 of the EEA regulations provides that the following persons are treated as the family members of another person (with certain exceptions for students – see below):

(a) the spouse of the person;

(b) the civil partner of the person (part of a registered partnership equivalent to marriage);

(c) a direct descendant of the person, or of the person's spouse or civil partner, who is under the age of 21;

(d) a direct descendant of the person, or of the person's spouse or civil partner, who is over 21 and dependent on the person, or the spouse or civil partner;

(e) an ascendant relative of the person, or of the person's spouse or civil partner, who is dependent on the person or the spouse or civil partner.

(f) a person who is an extended family member and is treated as a family member by virtue of regulation 7(3) of the EEA regulations (see below).

### Family members of students

**44.** Regulation 7(2) of the EEA regulations provides that a person who falls within (c), (d) or (e) above shall not be treated as a family member of a student residing in the UK after the period of 3 months beginning on the date the student is admitted to the UK unless:

(i) in the case of paragraph 43 (c) and (d) above, the person is the dependent child of the student, or of the spouse or civil partner, or

(ii) the student is also a qualified person (for the purposes of regulation 6(1) of the EEA regulations) other than as a student.

### Extended family members

**45.** Broadly, extended family members will be persons who:

(a) do not fall within any of the categories (a) to (e) in paragraph 43 above, and

(b) are either a relative of an EEA national (or of the EEA national's spouse or civil partner) or the partner of an EEA national, and

(c) have been issued with an EEA family permit, a registration certificate or a residence card which is valid and has not been revoked.

### Family members' eligibility for housing assistance
### Relationship with other rights to reside

**46.** This section concerns the eligibility of an applicant for housing assistance whose right to reside is derived from his or her status as the family member of an EEA national with a right to reside. In some cases, a family member will have acquired a right to reside in his or her own right. In particular, a person who arrived in the UK as the family member of an EEA national may have subsequently acquired a permanent right of residence under regulation 15 of the EEA Regulations, as outlined in paragraph 38(a) – (f) above. The eligibility for housing assistance of those with a permanent right of residence is discussed at paragraph 39.

### Family members who must be habitually resident

**47.** For family members with a right to reside under regulation 14 of the EEA Regulations, the following categories of persons must be habitually resident in the UK, the Channel Islands, the Isle of Man or the Republic of Ireland in order to be eligible for housing assistance:

     a)      a person whose right to reside derives from their status as a family member of an EEA national who is a self-sufficient person for the purposes of regulation 6(1)(d) of the EEA regulations;

     b)      a person whose right to reside derives from their status as a family member of an EEA national who is a student for the purposes of regulation 6(1)(e) of the EEA regulations;

     c)      a person whose right to reside is dependent on their status as a family member of an EEA national with a permanent right to reside;

     d)      a person whose right to reside is dependent on their status as a family member who has retained the right of residence.

### Family members who are exempt from the habitual residence requirement

**48.** A person with a right to reside under regulation 14 as a family member of an EEA national who is a worker or a self-employed person for the purposes of regulation 6(1) of the EEA regulations is exempted from the requirement to be habitually resident by regulation 6(2)(d) of the Eligibility Regulations. However, authorities should note that an extended family member (see above) is not counted as a family member for the purposes of regulation 6(2)(d) of the Eligibility Regulations (see regulation 2(3) of the Eligibility Regulations).

### Family members of UK nationals exercising rights under the EC Treaty

**49.** There are some limited cases in which the non-EEA family member of a UK national may have a right to reside under EU law. Under regulation 9 of the EEA Regulations, the family member of a UK national should be treated as an EEA family member where the following conditions are met:

     (i)      the UK national is residing in an EEA State as a worker or self-employed person, or was so residing before returning to the UK; and

     (ii)      if the family member of the UK national is his spouse or civil partner, the parties are living together in the EEA State, or had entered into a marriage or civil partnership and were living together in that State before the UK national returned to the UK.

**50.** Where the family member of a UK national is to be treated as an EEA family member by virtue of regulation 9 of the EEA Regulations, that person is not subject to immigration control, and his or her eligibility for housing assistance should therefore be determined in accordance with regulation 6 of the Eligibility Regulations.

**[5035]**

## ANNEX 13

## WORKER REGISTRATION SCHEME

*Introduction*

**1.** On 1 May 2004, 10 new countries acceded to the European Union: Cyprus, Malta, Poland, Lithuania, Estonia, Latvia, Slovenia, Slovakia, Hungary and the Czech Republic.

**2.** Nationals of all of these countries have the right to move freely among all member states. Nationals of 2 of the Accession countries – Malta and Cyprus – enjoyed full EU Treaty rights from 1 May 2004. These include the right to seek work and take up employment in another Member State.

**3.** However, under the EU Accession Treaties that apply to the other 8 Accession states ("the A8 Member States"), existing Member States can impose limitations on the rights of nationals of the A8 Member States to access their labour markets (and the associated rights of residence), for a transitional period. (The EU Accession Treaties do not allow existing Member States to restrict access to their labour markets by nationals of Malta or Cyprus.)

**4.** Under the *Accession (Immigration and Worker Registration) Regulations 2004* (SI 2004/1219) as amended ("the Accession Regulations"), nationals of the A8 Member States (with certain exceptions) are required to register with the Home Office if they work in the UK during the transitional period. While looking for work (or between jobs) their right to reside will be conditional on them being self-sufficient and not imposing an unreasonable burden on the UK social assistance system. These conditions cease to apply once they have worked in the UK continuously for 12 months.

*The Accession (Immigration and Worker Registration) Regulations 2004*

**5.** The *Accession (Immigration and Worker Registration) Regulations 2004* provide that, from 1 May 2004, nationals of the A8 Member States can take up employment in the UK provided they are authorised to work for their employer under the Worker Registration scheme.

**6.** The Accession Regulations also give workers from the A8 Member States the right to reside in the UK. Workers from the A8 Member States who are working lawfully have the same right to equal treatment as other EEA workers while they are working.

*The Worker Registration scheme*

**7.** The Worker Registration scheme applies only to nationals of: Poland, Lithuania, Estonia, Latvia, Slovenia, Slovakia, Hungary and the Czech Republic (the A8 Member States). It is a transitional scheme under which the UK Government allows nationals of the A8 Member States access to the UK labour market provided they comply with the registration scheme.

**8.** The derogation from EC law allowed by the Treaties of Accession does not apply to nationals of existing EEA states. Workers from those states, therefore, have an EC right to work and reside in the UK.

**9.** The Worker Registration scheme is a transitional measure. The *Accession (Immigration and Worker Registration) Regulations 2004* provide for the registration scheme to operate for up to five years from 1 May 2004 (i.e. until 30 April 2009). The Government reviewed the scheme within its first two years of operation and decided that the scheme will continue beyond 1 May 2006, and may continue throughout the second phase of the transitional arrangements. However, the need to retain the scheme during the whole of the second phase will be kept under review.

**10.** Nationals of A8 Member States who are self-employed are not required to register. (Under the Accession Treaties, there is no derogation from the right of EU citizens to establish themselves in another Member State (including the UK) as self-employed persons.) However, nationals of A8 Member States who are self-employed cannot take paid employment unless they register (unless they are exempt from registration, see below).

*Registration under the scheme*

**11.** Nationals of A8 Member States (except those who are exempt from the scheme, see below) must apply to register with the Home Office as soon as they start work in the UK, and within one month of taking up employment at the very latest. They will be issued with a **worker registration card** and a **worker registration certificate,** authorising them to work for the employer concerned.

**12.** If they change employers they will have to apply to for a new **registration certificate** authorising them to work for their new employer. They will then be provided with a new certificate for that employer. If they change employer or have a break in employment and resume working for the same employer, they must apply for a new registration certificate.

**13.** Workers from the A8 Member States have the same right to equal treatment as other EEA workers while they are working.

**14.** After 12 months' uninterrupted work in the UK, a worker from an A8 Member State will acquire full EU Treaty rights, and will be free from the requirement to register to work. At that stage, they will be able to apply to the Home Office for an EEA residence permit to confirm their right to equal treatment on the same basis as other EEA nationals.

**15.** The Worker Registration Team issues applicants with a secure **worker registration card** containing:
- Name;
- Date of Birth;
- Nationality;
- Date of issue;
- Unique identification number;
- A facial identifier (photograph);

and

a **certificate** (on secure paper) which states:
- Worker's name;
- Worker's Date of Birth;
- Nationality;
- Worker's unique identification number;

-     Name and address (head or main office) of employer;
-     Job title;
-     Start date;
-     Date of issue.

**16.** The **registration card** is a secure document that provides applicants with a unique identification reference number. This is valid for as long as the applicant requires registration under the scheme.

**17.** The **registration certificate** is specific to a particular employer. The certificate expires as soon as the person stops working for that employer. If the person changes employers or has a break in employment and resumes working for the same employer, he or she must apply for a new registration certificate.

**18.** Specimen copies of the registration card and registration certificate are provided at the end of this annex.

*12 months' uninterrupted work*

**19.** A worker from an A8 Member State (who is subject to the registration scheme) must not be out of wormore than a total of 30 days in a 12-month period, in order to establish "12 months' uninterrupted work".

**20.** If a national of an A8 Member State has worked for a period of less than 12 months when the employment comes to an end, he or she will need to find another job within 30 days to be able to count the first period of work towards accruing a period of 12 months' uninterrupted employment.

**21.** If the worker's second (or subsequent) employment comes to an end before he or she has accrued a period of 12 months' uninterrupted employment, he or she must ensure that there has been no more than a total of 30 days between all of the periods of employment. If more than 30 days between periods of employment occur before a 12-month period of uninterrupted employment is established, a fresh period of 12 months' uninterrupted employment would need to commence from that point.

**22.** The Worker Registration scheme is based on continuity of employment – there is no restriction on the number of different jobs (or employers) that a worker can have during a 12-month period of continuous employment.

**23.** When an A8 Member State worker has worked for 12 months without interruption he or she can apply to the Home Office for an EEA residence permit. Evidence of 12 months' uninterrupted employment would include the worker registration card, registration certificates for each of the jobs they have undertaken, letters from employers and pay slips.

**A8 nationals who must register**

**24.** The Worker Registration Scheme applies to nationals of the following accession states: Poland; Lithuania; Estonia; Latvia; Slovenia; Slovakia; Hungary; and the Czech Republic.

**25.** Nationals of A8 Member States need to apply for a registration certificate under the Worker Registration Scheme, if they are a citizen of one of the countries listed above and they:
- start a new job on or after 1 May 2004;
- have been working in the UK before 1 May 2004 without authorisation or in breach of their immigration conditions;
- are working on a short-term or temporary basis; or
- are a student who is also working.

**A8 nationals exempt from registration**

**26.** The following are the categories of nationals of an A8 Member State who are not required to register under the Worker Registration Scheme:
-     those working in a self-employed capacity;
-     those who have been working with permission in the UK for 12 months or more without interruption;
-     those who have been working with permission in the UK for their current employer since before 1 May 2004;
-     those who have leave to enter the UK under the *Immigration Act 1971* on 30 April 2004 and their leave was not subject to any condition restricting their employment;
-     those who are providing services in the UK on behalf of an employer who is not established in the UK;
-     those who are a citizen of the UK, another EEA state (other than an A8 state) or Switzerland;
-     those who are a family member (spouse, civil partner, or child under the age of 21 or dependant) of a Swiss or EEA national (other than an A8 national) who is working in the UK;

–  those who are a family member (spouse, civil partner or dependant child) of a Swiss or EEA national who is in the UK and is a student, self-employed, retired, or self-sufficient.

**[5036]**

**Home Office**
BUILDING A SAFE, JUST
AND TOLERANT SOCIETY

| | | |
|---|---|---|
| [First Name] [Surname] | DATE OF ISSUE | [Issue Date] |
| [House Number] [Street Name] | REFERENCE No : | [URN] |
| [Town] | WORK CARD SERIAL No : | ▉▉▉▉ |
| [County] | | |
| [Post Code] | TELEPHONE : | 0114 207 6022 |

### Accession State Worker Registration Scheme

Thank you for your application to register on the Accession State Worker Registration scheme. I am pleased to inform you that we have approved your application and that you are now registered.

Your worker registration card is attached below. If you have any queries about this document, then please contact Work Permits (UK) on the telephone number above.

----------------------------------------------------------------

## Accession State Worker Registration Scheme
### Registration Card

| | | |
|---|---|---|
| SURNAME | : | [Surname] |
| FORENAME(S) | : | [First Name] |
| DATE OF BIRTH | : | [Date of Birth] |
| NATIONALITY | : | [Nationality] |
| REFERENCE No | : | [URN] |
| DATE OF ISSUE | : | [Issue Date] |

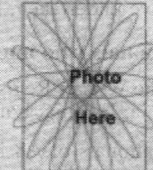

Photo
Here

This worker registration card should be retained as evidence of your registration with the Accession State Worker Registration Scheme.

PLEASE DO NOT LOSE - REPLACEMENTS MAY NOT BE ISSUED

WORK CARD SERIAL No ▉▉▉▉

Managed Migration
Home Office
PO Box 3468
Sheffield S3 8WA

www.workingintheuk.gov.uk

[First Name] [Surname]
[House Number] [Street]
[Town]
[County]
[Post Code]

Date of Issue: [Issue Date]

## ACCESSION STATE WORKER REGISTRATION SCHEME
## REGISTRATION CERTIFICATE

Thank you for your application to register on the Accession State Worker Registration Scheme. I am pleased to inform you that we have approved your application.

This is your worker registration certificate. It authorises you to work for the employer specified in this certificate.

This certificate ceases to be valid if you are no longer working for the employer specified in this certificate on the date on which it is issued.

This certificate expires on the date you cease working for the specified employer.

This certificate should be retained with your worker registration card.

Name                          : [First Name] [Surname]

Date of Birth                 : [Date of Birth]

Nationality                   : [Nationality]

Unique Reference Number: [URN]

Job start date                : [Date Started Employment]

Employer's Name               : [Employer Name]

Employer's Address            : [Unit Number] [Street Name]
                                [Town]
                                [County]
                                [Post Code]

PART III
OTHER MATERIAL

**ANNEX 14**

**MOD CERTIFICATE: CERTIFICATE OF CESSATION OF ENTITLEMENT FOR SINGLE PERSONNEL TO OCCUPY SERVICE LIVING ACCOMMODATION**

| | |
|---|---|
|  **MINISTRY OF DEFENCE** | MOD Form 1166<br>*Introduced 5/97*<br>*Revised 4/03* |

**CERTIFICATE OF CESSATION OF ENTITLEMENT FOR SINGLE PERSONNEL TO OCCUPY SERVICE LIVING ACCOMMODATION**

I certify that (Name)

(Rank & Number)

Of (Unit)

Will cease to be entitled (Address)
to occupy Service Living
Accommodation

(Date)
From

By reason of

An application for housing was made to ...................................Housing

Authority/Housing Association on ............................... (copy of letter attached)

The person has the following special circumstances ...........................................

.................................................................................................................

| Signed | UNIT STAMP |
|---|---|
| Name | |
| Position | |
| Date | |

1. This certificate provides evidence of cessation of entitlement to occupy Service Living Accommodation.

2. The certificate should be completed by the unit admin authority and sent at the earliest possible date to the Housing Authority/Association to which application for accommodation has been made, preferably as soon as it is known that entitlement to occupy Service Living Accommodation will cease.

3. Copies of this form are published in the Homelessness Code of Guidance For Local Authorities issued by DCLG, and in guidance issued by the Welsh Assembly and Scottish Executive.

## ANNEX 15

## CERTIFICATE OF CESSATION OF ENTITLEMENT TO OCCUPY SERVICE FAMILIES ACCOMMODATION OR SUBSTITUTE SERVICE FAMILIES ACCOMMODATE (SFA/SSFA)

| | | |
|---|---|---|
| | **MINISTRY OF DEFENCE** | MOD Form *Introduced 4/03* |

### CERTIFICATE OF CESSATION OF ENTITLEMENT TO OCCUPY SERVICE FAMILIES ACCOMMODATION OR SUBSTITUTE SERVICE FAMILIES ACCOMMODATION(SFA/SSFA)

I certify that        (Name)

(Rank & Number) #

Of             (Unit) #
(# Omit if only family involved)

Will cease to be entitled   (Address of SFA or
to occupy            SSFA)

From            (Date)
By reason of loss of entitlement to occupy Service Families Accommodation.

An application for housing was made to ................................Housing Authority/
Housing Association on ................................. (copy of letter attached)

The following special circumstances apply ................................................
................................................................................................
The household is as follows ....................................................
................................................................................................
................................................................................................

| | DHE STAMP |
|---|---|
| Signed | |
| Name | |
| Designation | |
| Date | |

1. **This certificate provides evidence of cessation of entitlement to occupy Service Families Accommodation or Substitute Service Families Accommodation. Authorities should not insist on a Court Order for possession to establish a threat of homelessness.**

2. The certificate should be completed by the Licences Officer of the Defence Housing Executive and sent at the earliest possible date to the Housing Authority/Association to which application for accommodation has been made, preferably as soon as it is known that entitlement to occupy Service Families Accommodation will cease.

3. A period of at least six months notice should normally be allowed so that the appropriate arrangements can be made.

4. Copies of this form are published in the Homelessness Code of Guidance For Local Authorities issued by DCLG, and in guidance issued by the Welsh Assembly and Scottish Executive.

**[5038]**

## ANNEX 16

## DEFINITION OF OVERCROWDING

Under s.324 of the *Housing Act 1985* a dwelling is overcrowded when the number of persons sleeping in the dwelling is such as to contravene –
(a)     the standard specified in s.325 (the room standard), or
(b)     the standard specified in s.326 (the space standard).

*a) The room standard*
(1)     The room standard is contravened when the number of persons sleeping in a dwelling and the number of rooms available as sleeping accommodation is such that two persons of opposite sexes who are not living together as husband and wife must sleep in the same room.
(2)     For this purpose –
(a)     children under the age of ten shall be left out of account, and
(b)     a room is available as sleeping accommodation if it is of a type normally used in the locality either as a bedroom or as a living room.

*b) The space standard*
(1)     The space standard is contravened when the number of persons sleeping in a dwelling is in excess of the permitted number, having regard to the number and floor area of the rooms of the dwelling available as sleeping accommodation.
(2)     For this purpose –
(a)     no account shall be taken of a child under the age of one and a child aged one or over but under ten shall be reckoned as one-half of a unit, and
(b)     a room is available as sleeping accommodation if it is of a type normally used in the locality either as a living room or as a bedroom.
(3)     The permitted number of persons in relation to a dwelling is whichever is the less of –
(a)     the number specified in Table I in relation to the number of rooms in the dwelling available as sleeping accommodation, and
(b)     the aggregate for all such rooms in the dwelling of the numbers specified in column 2 of Table II in relation to each room of the floor area specified in column 1.
No account shall be taken for the purposes of either Table of a room having a floor area of less than 50 square feet.

### TABLE I

| Number of rooms | Number of persons |
| --- | --- |
| 1 | 2 |
| 2 | 3 |
| 3 | 5 |
| 4 | 7½ |
| 5 or more | 2 for each room |

### TABLE II

| Floor area of room | Number of persons |
| --- | --- |
| 110 sq ft or more | 2 |
| 90 sq ft or more but less than 110 sq ft | 1½ |
| 70 sq ft or more but less than 90 sq ft | 1 |
| 50 sq ft or more but less than 70 sq ft | ½ |

(4)     The Secretary of State may by regulations prescribe the manner in which the floor area of a room is to be ascertained for the purposes of this section; and the regulations may provide for the exclusion from computation, or the bringing into computation at a reduced figure, of floor space in a part of the room which is of less than a specified height not exceeding eight feet.
(5)     Regulations under subsection (4) shall be made by statutory instrument which shall be subject to annulment in pursuance of a resolution of either House of Parliament.
(6)     A certificate of the local housing authority stating the number and floor areas of the rooms

in dwelling, and that the floor areas have been ascertained in the prescribed manner, is prima facie evidence for the purposes of legal proceedings of the facts stated in it.

**[5039]**

## ANNEX 17

### RECOMMENDED MINIMUM STANDARDS FOR BED AND BREAKFAST ACCOMMODATION

The Secretary of State recommends that housing authorities apply the standards set out below as minimum standards in deciding whether Bed and Breakfast accommodation is suitable for an applicant for the purposes of Part 7 of the Housing Act 1996 ('the homelessness legislation') in the very limited circumstances where an authority may use such accommodation for this purpose.

*Space Standards for Sleeping Accommodation*

1.  *Room sizes where cooking facilities provided in a separate room/kitchen*

| Floor Area of Room | Maximum No of Persons |
| --- | --- |
| Less than 70 sq ft (6.5 m²) | Nil persons |
| Not less than 70 sq ft (6.5 m²) | 1 person |
| Not less than 110 sq ft (10.2 m²) | 2 persons |
| Not less than 160 sq ft (14.9 m²) | 3 persons |
| Not less than 210 sq ft (19.6 m²) | 4 persons |
| Not less than 260 sq ft (24.2 m²) | 5 persons |

*Room sizes where cooking facilities provided within the room*

| Floor Area of Room | Maximum No of Persons |
| --- | --- |
| Less than 110 sq ft (10.2 m²) | Nil persons |
| Not less than 110 sq ft (10.2 m²) | 1 person |
| Not less than 150 sq ft (13.9 m²) | 2 persons |
| Not less than 200 sq ft (18.6 m²) | 3 persons |
| Not less than 250 sq ft (23.2 m²) | 4 persons |
| Not less than 300 sq ft (27.9 m²) | 5 persons |

2.  In no case should a room be occupied by more than 5 persons. The standard is to be applied irrespective of the age of the occupants. The sharing of rooms in bed and breakfast accommodation is not desirable, but it is accepted that where accommodation is not self-contained families may find it preferable to share.

3.  No persons of the opposite sex who are aged 12 and over should have to share a room unless they are living together as partners and both are above the age of consent or are lawfully married.

4.  All rooms must have a minimum floor to ceiling height of at least 7 feet (2.14 metres) over not less than 75% of the room area. Any floor area where the ceiling height is less than 5 feet (1.53 metres) should be disregarded.

5.  Separate kitchens, bathrooms, toilets, shower rooms, communal rooms and en-suite rooms are deemed unsuitable for sleeping accommodation.

*Installation for Heating*

6.  The premises should have adequate provision for heating. All habitable rooms and baths or shower rooms should be provided with a fixed space-heating appliance. The appliance must be capable of efficiently maintaining the room at a minimum temperature of 18°C when the outside temperature is −1°C. "Fixed space heating appliance" means fixed gas appliance, fixed electrical appliance or an adequate system of central heating, operable at all times.

*Facilities for the Storage, Preparation and Cooking of Food and Disposal of Waste Water*

7.  Wherever practicable, each household should have exclusive use of a full set of kitchen facilities including:

*   cooking facilities – a gas or electric cooker with a four-burner hob, oven and grill. In

single person lettings, a cooker with a minimum of two burners, oven and grill is permissible. Where the establishment caters for fewer than 6 persons, a small guest house for example, a microwave may be substituted for a gas or electric cooker for periods of stay not exceeding 6 weeks for any homeless household;

- sink and integral drainer – with a constant supply of hot and cold water and properly connected to the drainage system;
- storage cupboard, minimum capacity 0.4 m$^3$ (400 litres/15 ft$^3$). This provision is in addition to any base unit cupboards provided below the sink/drainer;
- refrigerator – minimum capacity 0.14 m$^3$ (140 litres/5 ft$^3$);
- electrical power sockets – minimum of two double 13 amp sockets situated at worktop height. These are in addition to electrical power sockets provided elsewhere in the letting;
- worktop – minimum surface area 1000 mm × 600 mm.

**8.** There may be circumstances where the housing authority is satisfied that the provision of kitchen facilities for exclusive use is not practicable or appropriate. These circumstances could, for example, include where a property is very small, no more than two or three letting rooms, or where the overall standard of the property is considered reasonable in all other respects and the costs of provision of exclusive use kitchens would be prohibitive or detrimentally affect the remaining amenity space. In circumstances such as these, the following standards for communal kitchens may be applied.

**9.** Kitchen facilities may be provided in the ratio of no less than one set for every 10 persons, irrespective of age. Such kitchen facilities should comprise a minimum of shared:

- gas or electric cooker with four burners, oven and grill. Where the establishment caters for fewer than 6 persons, a small guest house for example, a microwave may be substituted for a gas or electric cooker for periods of stay not exceeding 6 weeks for any homeless household;
- sink and integral drainer – with a constant supply of hot and cold water and properly connected to the drainage system;
- storage cupboard, minimum capacity 0.4 m$^3$ (400 litres/15 ft$^3$). This provision is in addition to any base unit cupboards provided below the sink/drainer;
- electrical power sockets – minimum of two double 13 amp sockets situated at worktop height. These are in addition to electrical power sockets provided elsewhere in the letting;
- worktop – minimum surface area 1000 mm × 600 mm;
- lockable storage cupboards, minimum capacity 0.14 m$^3$ (140 litres/5 ft$^3$) for each bedroom whose occupants use the kitchen. In calculating the required provision of storage cupboards, base unit cupboards below sinks/drainers should be discounted.

**10.** In addition, the following facilities should be provided within each bedroom, or within the total accommodation occupied exclusively by each household:

- worktop – minimum surface area 1000 mm × 600 mm;
- refrigerator – minimum capacity 0.14 m$^3$ (140 litres/5 ft$^3$);
- storage cupboard – minimum capacity 0.4 m$^3$ (400 litres/15 ft$^3$).

**11.** The kitchen used by management to provide breakfast may be included when calculating the one in ten ratio, unless it is not available, does not meet the conditions above or is deemed unsuitable for use by residents because:

- of the size of the kitchen and the equipment provided in it. In a commercial kitchen some equipment may be dangerous or unsatisfactory for use by residents; or
- the unsatisfactory location of the kitchen in relation to the accommodation it is supposed to serve.

**12.** In schemes providing a mix of kitchens for shared and exclusive use, one set of kitchen facilities should be provided for every 10 persons sharing. The number of persons who have kitchen facilities provided for their exclusive use should not be included in the calculations. Again, the kitchen used by management to provide breakfast may be included in the one in ten calculation subject to the above conditions.

**13.** Cooking facilities which are provided should be reasonably located in relation to the room(s) occupied by the person(s) for whom they are provided and in any event not more than one floor distant from these rooms. Please note the exception for smaller establishments described below.

**14.** In smaller establishments of not more than three storeys and not more than 30 bed spaces, communal cooking facilities may be provided in one area of the premises more than one floor distant from some bedrooms. In such cases, these kitchens must be provided in association with a suitable dining room or dining rooms of adequate size calculated on the basis of 1 m$^2$ per bed space. This should include one area of at least 15 m$^2$. Only effective usable space will be considered when calculating the areas for the purpose of this requirement. Dining room facilities should be provided with adequate seating provision.

**15.** Kitchen facilities should be made available for use 24 hours per day, subject to any representation from the owner/manager, which must be agreed by the receiving and placing authorities.

*Toilet and personal washing facilities*

**16.** One internal water closet should be provided for every five persons irrespective of age. The water closet must be within a reasonable distance from its users and not more than one floor distant and, where practicable, a water closet should not be situated within a bathroom. At least 50% of the water closets that are required to be provided should be situated in separate accommodation. The number of persons occupying a bedroom where this facility is provided for their exclusive use should not be included in the calculations.

**17.** A suitable wash hand basin (minimum dimensions 500 mm × 400 mm) with constant hot and cold water supplies, should be provided in every bedroom, except where an en suite bathroom is available, when the wash hand basin may be provided in that bathroom.

**18.** Each separate water closet compartment and bathroom should be provided with a suitable wash hand basin (minimum dimensions 500 mm × 400 mm), together with constant supplies of hot and cold running water. A tiled splashback (minimum 300 mm high) is to be provided to each wash hand basin.

**19.** One bath (minimum dimensions 1700 mm × 700 mm) or one shower (minimum dimensions 800 mm × 800 mm) should be provided for every eight persons, irrespective of age. These facilities must be within a reasonable distance of each user and not more than one floor distant. The number of persons having the exclusive use of a bath or shower should not be included in the calculations.

**20.** Where the operator chooses to provide showers for the exclusive use of each separate household or the majority of households, a minimum provision of baths, rather than showers will always be required. In such circumstances a minimum of one communal bath should be provided for every 20 persons, irrespective of age, with a minimum of one bath per property. These facilities must be within a reasonable distance of each user and ideally no more than one floor distant.

*Other facilities*

**21.** In the case of families with young children, the facilities should include a safe play area(s) that is located away from sleeping accommodation and cooking areas.

*Management Standards*

**22.** In any B&B accommodation, suitability for the purposes of Part 7 will depend upon the management standards operated within an establishment as well as the adequate provision of basic amenities. The minimum management standards set out below should apply and it is the responsibility of the housing authority to monitor the management of the property.

- Operators are required to ensure the property complies with all relevant statutory and regulatory requirements especially in relation to fire, gas and electrical safety. The supply of gas or electricity to any resident should never be interfered with.
- A clear emergency evacuation plan should be in place setting out action upon hearing the fire alarm, escape routes and safe assembly points. The manager must ensure that each person newly arriving at the premises is told what to do in the event of a fire and about the fire precautions provided.
- Residents should have access to their rooms at all times except when rooms are being cleaned. Provision should be made to accommodate residents at these times.
- Refuse and litter should be cleared from the property and not allowed to accumulate in, or in the curtilage, of the property, except in adequately sized and suitable bulk refuse container(s).
- All communal areas (including, hallways, kitchens, bathrooms/showers, WCs, dining areas, lounges if provided) should be regularly cleaned.
- Appropriate officers of the authority in whose area the premises are situated should have access to inspect the premises as and when they consider necessary, to ensure that the requirements are being complied with. The manager should allow such inspections to take place, if necessary without notice.
- Officers of the health authority, local authority and authorised community workers for the area in which the premises are situated should have acess to visit the occupiers of the premises and interview them in private in the room(s) they occupy.
- A manager with adequate day to day responsibility to ensure the good management of the property should be contactable at all times. A notice giving the name, address and telephone number of the manager should be displayed in a readily visible position in the property.
- Procedures should be in place to deal with any complaints relating to harassment on racial, sexual or other discriminatory grounds by either residents or staff.
- There should be a clear complaints procedure for the resolution of disputes between residents and/or staff.
- There should be available within the premises a working telephone available for use by the occupiers and a notice should be displayed by the telephone with information on the address and telephone numbers of: the local Environmental Health Department, Fire Brigade, Gas Company, Electricity Company, Police Station and local doctors.

## ANNEX 18

This is not guidance issued by the Secretaries of State.

## PROCEDURES FOR REFERRALS OF HOMELESS APPLICANTS ON THE GROUNDS OF LOCAL CONNECTON WITH ANOTHER LOCAL AUTHORITY

## GUIDELINES FOR LOCAL AUTHORITIES AND REFEREES

*AGREED BY*

---

**ASSOCIATION OF LONDON GOVERNMENT** (ALG)

**CONVENTION OF SCOTTISH LOCAL AUTHORITIES** (CoSLA)

**LOCAL GOVERNMENT ASSOCIATION** (LGA)

**WELSH LOCAL GOVERNMENT ASSOCIATION** (WLGA)

(*"the local authority associations"*)

---

### Index

## PROCEDURES FOR REFERRALS OF HOMELESS APPLICANTS ON THE GROUNDS OF LOCAL CONNECTON WITH ANOTHER LOCAL AUTHORITY

## GUIDELINES FOR LOCAL AUTHORITIES ON PROCEDURES FOR REFERRAL

*AGREED BY*

---

**ASSOCIATION OF LONDON GOVERNMENT** (ALG)

**CONVENTION OF SCOTTISH LOCAL AUTHORITIES** (CoSLA)

**LOCAL GOVERNMENT ASSOCIATION** (LGA)

**WELSH LOCAL GOVERNMENT ASSOCIATION** (WLGA)

(*"the local authority associations"*)

---

This procedure concerns the situation where, under Part 7 of the *Housing Act 1996*, a housing authority is satisfied that a housing applicant is eligible for assistance, homeless and has a priority need for accommodation, is not satisfied that the applicant is homeless intentionally and the authority consider that the conditions for referral of the case to another housing authority are met, and notifies the other housing authority of its opinion. Referrals are discretionary only. Housing authorities are not required to make inquiries as to whether an applicant has a local connection with another district, and where they decide to do so, there is no requirement to refer applicants to another authority, if the conditions for referral are met. Authorities may have a policy about how they may exercise their discretion. However, they cannot decide in advance that a referral will be made in all cases where an applicant who is eligible for assistance, unintentionally homeless and in priority need may have a local connection with another district.

## 1 PURPOSE OF THE GUIDELINES

**1.1** For English and Welsh authorities s.198 of the *Housing Act 1996* provides that:

"(5) The question whether the conditions for referral of a case are satisfied shall be determined by agreement between the notifying authority and the notified authority or, in default of agreement, in accordance with such arrangements as the Secretary of State may direct by order.

(6) An order may direct that the arrangements shall be:

(a) those agreed by any relevant authorities or associations of relevant authorities, or

(b) in default of such agreement, such arrangements as appear to the Secretary of State to be suitable, after consultation with such associations representing relevant authorities, and such other persons, as he thinks appropriate."

**1.2** Subsections 33(4) and (5) of the *Housing (Scotland) Act 1987* make the same provision for Scotland. However, s.8 of the *Homelessness (Scotland) Act 2003* gives Scottish ministers the power to suspend or vary the circumstances under which a homeless applicant may be referred by a Scottish local authority to another authority in Scotland. Please note any future orders made will need to be taken into account.

**1.3** The ALG, CoSLA, LGA and the WLGA, the local authority associations in England, Scotland and Wales, have agreed guidelines for referrals which they recommend to local housing authorities. Section 198 *Housing Act 1996* and s.33 *Housing (Scotland) Act 1987* lay down the general procedures to be followed where it appears that s.192(2) (England and Wales) or s.31 (Scotland) applies to the applicant and the applicant does not have a local connection with the area of the authority receiving the housing application but does have one with another area in England, Scotland or Wales. There are, however, considerable areas of possible disagreement and dispute in determining whether the conditions of referral are met in any particular case. Although, in the last resort, disagreements can only be resolved by the courts, the associations are anxious to avoid, as far as possible, legal disputes between local authorities. The associations therefore issue these agreed guidelines on the procedures and criteria to be followed, and recommend them for general adoption by all their members. **These Guidelines are without prejudice to the duty of local authorities to treat each case on its merits and to take into account existing and future case law.** Furthermore, these Guidelines only apply to the issues of local connection and whether the conditions for referral are met for the purposes of Part 7 of the *Housing Act 1996* (England and Wales) and s.33 of the *Housing (Scotland) Act 1987*.

**1.4** *In Re Betts (1983) the House of Lords considered the application of the referral arrangements agreed between the local authority associations. Their Lordships decided that a rigid application of the arrangements would constitute a fetter on an authority's discretion. The agreement could be taken into account, and applied as a guideline, provided its application to each case is given individual consideration.*

## 2 DEFINITIONS

**2.1** All references in this agreement to an "applicant" are to be taken as references to a housing applicant to whom s.193 of the *Housing Act 1996* (England and Wales) or s.28 *Housing (Scotland) Act 1987* or s.31 *Housing (Scotland) Act 1987* would apply but for the decision to refer the case to another authority. For the purposes of this agreement the 1996 Act and 1987 (Scotland) Act definitions apply.

**2.2** The authority to whom the applicant applies for accommodation or assistance (for the purposes of s.183 *Housing Act 1996* or s.28 *Housing (Scotland) Act 1987*) and which decides to refer the case to another authority is the *"notifying authority"*.

**2.3** Where the notifying authority consider that neither the applicant nor any person who might reasonably reside with the applicant, has a local connection with its district but does have one with another local authority district and notifies the other local authority of its opinion, the authority which they notify is known as the *"notified authority"*.

**2.4** Section 199 *Housing Act 1996* and s.27 *Housing (Scotland) Act 1987* set out the circumstances when a person may have a "local connection" with a district. These guidelines provide a framework within which the local connection referral procedures may be applied.

## 3 CRITERIA FOR NOTIFICATION

**3.1**   Before a local authority can consider referring an applicant to another local authority it must first be satisfied that the applicant is:

(i)     eligible for assistance
(ii)    homeless, and
(iii)   in priority need,
(iv)    not homeless intentionally.

**3.2**   Before making a referral the notifying authority must be satisfied that the conditions of referral are met. Broadly, the conditions for referral will be met if:

(a)     neither the applicant nor any person who might reasonably be expected to reside with the applicant has a local connection with the district of the authority receiving the application,

(b)     either the applicant or any person who might reasonably be expected to reside with the applicant has a local connection with the district of another authority in England, Scotland or Wales

(c)     neither the applicant nor any person who might reasonably be expected to reside with the applicant would run the risk of domestic violence/domestic abuse (Scotland) or face a probability of other violence in the district of the other authority (Refer to s.198 of the 1996 Act as amended by s.10 subsection (2&3) *Homelessness Act 2002* (England and Wales)). However, there are exceptions to these conditions, for example, where an applicant applies to an English or Welsh authority for assistance and has been provided with NASS support in Scotland

(d)     **For Welsh authorities only**, the conditions for referral to another authority will also be met if the applicant was placed in accommodation in the district of the notifying authority by the other authority as a discharge of a duty to secure accommodation under Part 7 of the 1996 Act following an application to the other authority made within the last five years. The period of 5 years is prescribed by the *Homelessness (Wales) Regulations 2000 SI 2000 No.1079.*)

**3.3**   3.2(a)(b) and (c) above apply to Scottish authorities. 3.2(d) above does not apply in Scotland.

**3.4**   In deciding whether or not to make a referral authorities should also consider the court judgment in the case of *R v LB Newham ex parte LB Tower Hamlets* (1990). The notifying authority should have regard to any decisions made by the notified authority that may have a bearing on the case in question (e.g. a previous decision that the applicant was intentionally homeless) as well as any other material considerations, which should include the general housing circumstances prevailing in the district of the notifying authority and in the district of the notified authority. The notifying authority should also consider whether it is in the public interest to accept a duty to secure accommodation under s.193(2) (England and Wales)

**3.5**   Should a local authority wish to accept a duty to secure accommodation for an applicant who does not have a local connection with its district, nothing in this agreement shall prevent the authority from providing such assistance. The decision to make a referral is discretionary and could be challenged if the discretion was considered to have been exercised unreasonably.

**3.6**   Under s.202 of the 1996 Act, housing applicants in England and Wales have the right to request a review of certain decisions made by the local authority about their application, including a decision to notify another authority under s.198 and a decision that the conditions are met for referral of the case. The equivalent right to review in Scotland is set out in s.4 of the *Housing (Scotland) Act 2001*.

## 4 LOCAL CONNECTION

**4.1**   The relevant date for deciding whether or not a local connection has been established is not the date when the application for housing assistance was made but the date of the decision or, if there is a review decision, the date of the review decision (cf. House of Lords' judgment in *Mohamed v Hammersmith and Fulham London Borough Council 2001*). Moreover, if inquiries prior to a decision have been prolonged, the notifying authority should also consider whether there may have been any material change in circumstances that might affect the question of whether a local connection has been established. A local connection may be established where the following grounds apply, subject to the exceptions outlined in paragraph 4.2:

(i)     the applicant or a person who might reasonably be expected to reside with the applicant is, or in the past was, normally resident in the district. It is suggested that a working definition of "normal residence" should be residence for at least 6 months in the area during the previous 12 months, or for not less than 3 years during the previous 5 year period. The period taken into account should be up to the date of the authority's decision. This should include any periods living in temporary accommodation secured by the authority under s.188 (interim duty pending inquiries);

(ii)    the applicant or a person who might reasonably be expected to reside with the applicant is at present employed in the district. The local authority should obtain confirmation from the employer that the person is in employment and that the employment is not of a casual nature;

(iii)    the applicant or a person who might reasonably be expected to reside with the applicant has family associations in the district. Family associations normally arise where an applicant or a person who might reasonably be expected to reside with the applicant has parents, adult children or brothers or sisters who have been resident in the district for a period of at least 5 years at the date of the decision, and the applicant indicates a wish to be near them. Only in exceptional circumstances would the residence of relatives other than those listed above be taken to establish a local connection. The residence of dependent children in a different district from their parents would not be residence of their own choice and therefore would not establish a local connection with that district. However, a referral should not be made to another local authority on the grounds of a local connection because of family associations if the applicant objects to those grounds. **NB:** A Scottish authority, when considering the application of this clause, is advised to bear in mind the definition of "family" in s.83 of the *Housing (Scotland) Act 1987* as amended.

(iv)    there are special circumstances which the authority considers establish a local connection with the district. This may be particularly relevant where the applicant has been in prison or hospital and his or her circumstances do not conform to the criteria in (i) – (iii) above. Where, for example, an applicant seeks to return to a district where he or she was brought up or lived for a considerable length of time in the past, there may be grounds for considering that the applicant has a local connection with that district because of special circumstances. An authority must exercise its discretion when considering whether special circumstances apply.

**4.2**    A notifying authority should not refer an applicant to another authority on grounds of a local connection because of special circumstances without the prior consent of the notified authority. Alternatively, authorities may come to an informal arrangement in such cases on a reciprocal basis, subject to the agreement of the applicants.

**4.3**    There are certain circumstances where a local connection is not established because of residence or employment in a district. For these purposes:

(i)    a person is not employed in a district if he or she is serving in the Regular Armed Forces of the Crown; and

(ii)    residence in a district is not of a person's own choice if he or she (or anyone who might reasonably be expected to reside with them) becomes resident there because he or she is serving in the Regular Armed Forces of the Crown or is detained under the authority of any Act of Parliament (e.g. held in prison, or a secure hospital).

**4.4    For Welsh authorities only** the conditions for referral to another authority are met if the applicant was placed in accommodation in the district of the notifying authority by the other authority as a discharge of a duty to secure accommodation under Part 7 of the 1996 Act following an application to the other authority made within the last five years. This is without prejudice to whether or not the applicant may have established a local connection with a particular district.

**4.5    Former asylum seekers (England and Wales).** Broadly, s.199(6) of the 1996 Act (inserted by s.11 of the *Asylum and Immigration (Treatment of Claimants, etc.) Act 2004* ("the 2004 Act")) (England and Wales) provides that a person has a local connection with the district of a local housing authority if that person was provided with accommodation there under s.95 of the *Immigration and Asylum Act 1999* (NASS accommodation). Where a person has been provided with NASS accommodation in more than one area, the local connection is with the area where accommodation was last provided. A local connection with a district by virtue of s.199(6) does not override a local connection by virtue of s.199(1). So, a former asylum seeker who has a local connection with a district because he or she was provided with NASS accommodation there could also have a local connection elsewhere for some other reason, for example, because of employment or family associations.

**4.6    Former asylum seekers (Scotland).** Under s.27(2)(a)(iii) of the *Housing (Scotland) Act 2001*, as inserted by s.7 of the *Homelessness etc (Scotland) Act 2003*, residence in accommodation provided in pursuance of s.95 of the *Immigration and Asylum Act 1999* does not constitute a local connection as it is deemed to be residence which is not of the applicant's own choice. A local connection could be formed for other reasons, such as family association.

**4.7    Former asylum seekers (cross-border arrangements).** If a former asylum seeker who was provided with asylum support in England or Wales seeks homelessness assistance in Scotland the Scottish local authority could refer the application to another area where a local connection is established, if there was no local connection with the authority applied to. However under Scottish legislation, a local connection would not be formed by virtue of residence in accommodation provided in pursuance of s.95 of the *Immigration and Asylum Act 1999*.

**4.8**    This paragraph explains the position where a former asylum seeker who was provided with asylum support in Scotland seeks homelessness assistance in England or Wales. The provisions of s.11(2) and (3) of the 2004 Act provide that where a local housing authority in England or Wales are satisfied that an applicant is eligible for assistance, unintentionally homeless and in priority need, the s.193 duty to secure accommodation does not apply if the authority are satisfied that the applicant: has been provided with s.95 accommodation in Scotland at any time and does not have a local connection anywhere in England and Wales (within the meaning of s.199(1) of the 1996 Act) or anywhere in Scotland (within the meaning of s.27 of the *Housing (Scotland) Act 1987*). However, the authority may secure that accommodation is available for the applicant for a period giving him a reasonable opportunity of securing accommodation for himself, and provide the applicant (or secure that he is provided with) advice and assistance in any attempts he may make to secure accommodation for himself.

**4.9**  Subject to paragraphs 4.6 to 4.9 above (former asylum seekers), once the local authority is satisfied that the applicant is eligible, unintentionally homeless, falls within a priority need category, and does not have a local connection with the district, the authority may notify another authority under s.198 *Housing Act 1996* or s.33 *Housing (Scotland) Act 1987*, provided it is satisfied that all the conditions for referral set out in paragraph 3.3 above are met.

**4.10**  Once the local authority has established that the applicant is eligible, homeless, in a priority need category, not intentionally homeless and does not have any local connection in its own area it may notify another authority under s.198 *Housing Act 1996* or s.33 *Housing (Scotland) Act 1987*, provided it has satisfied itself that a local connection with the notified authority exists and that no member of the household would be at risk of domestic violence or threat of domestic violence in returning to that area. In determining whether or not there is such a risk authorities should have regard, where relevant, to the advice in the Homelessness Code of Guidance.

**4.11**  The notifying authority must consider that neither the applicant nor any person who might reasonably be expected to reside with the applicant has **any** local connection with its own district but **does** have a local connection with another local authority district in England, Scotland or Wales, in accordance with the criteria and exceptions listed above. The strength of local connection is irrelevant except where an applicant has no local connection with the notifying authority's district but has a local connection with more than one other local authority district. In such a scenario, the notifying authority must weigh up all the relevant factors in deciding to which authority it would be appropriate to refer the applicant.

**4.12**  Any relevant changes in an applicant's circumstances, e.g. obtaining employment, will need to be taken into account in determining whether the applicant has a local connection. Authorities should always consider whether special circumstances may apply.

## 5 PROCEDURES PRIOR TO MAKING A REFERRAL

**5.1**  If an authority considers that the conditions for referral s.198 *Housing Act 1996* or s.33 *Housing (Scotland) Act 1987* are likely to be met in a particular case it should make any necessary enquiries in the area/s where there may be a local connection. This should be undertaken as soon as possible. An authority that is considering making a referral must investigate all the circumstances of the case with the same thoroughness as if it were not considering a referral.

**5.2**  The notifying authority has a duty under s.200(1)(England and Wales) or s.34 *Housing (Scotland) Act 1987* to ensure that suitable accommodation is available for occupation by the applicant until the question of whether the conditions for referral are met have been decided.

**5.3**  Under section 184(4) *Housing Act 1996* or s.34 *Housing (Scotland) Act 1987*, if a housing authority notify, or intend to notify another authority that they consider that the conditions for referral of a case are met, the authority must notify the applicant of this decision, and the reasons for it, at the same time. For English and Welsh authorities, under s.184(5) of the 1996 Act, the notice must also inform the applicant of his right, under s.202, to request a review of the decision and that any request must be made within 21 days (or such longer period as the authority allows in writing). Regulations made under s.203 of the 1996 Act set out the procedure to be followed when making a review and the period within which a request for review must be carried out and the decision made. The *Allocation of Housing and Homelessness (Review Procedures) Regulations 1999 (SI 1999 No. 71)* establishes for England and Wales the period within which the review must be carried out and the decision made. For England and Wales s.204 of the 1996 Act gives applicants the right to appeal to the county court on a point of law if dissatisfied with the decision on the review (or the initial decision, if a review decision is not made within the prescribed time limit).

**5.4**  Scottish local authorities have a duty to review homelessness decisions under s. 35A of the *Housing (Scotland) Act 1987* as amended by s. 4 of the *Housing (Scotland) Act 2001*. This process does not affect the rights of a homeless applicant to seek judicial review or to seek the redress of the Scottish Public Services Ombudsman.

**5.5**  Once the notifying authority is has decided that the applicant is eligible, unintentionally homeless, and in priority need, there is no provision for the notified authority to challenge the decision other than judicial review in the High Court. The local authority associations' disputes procedure should be used only where there is a disagreement over the question of whether the conditions for referral are met and not for resolving disagreement on any other matter.

## 6 MAKING THE NOTIFICATION

**6.1**  All notifications and arrangements concerning an applicant should be made by telephone and then confirmed in writing. A specimen standard notification form is attached, which authorities are advised to use. If telephone contact cannot be made a fax or e-mail should be sent. Where the notified authority accepts the conditions for referral are met, it should not wait for the receipt of written confirmation of notification before making appropriate arrangements to secure accommodation for the applicant and his or her household.

**6.2** Each authority should nominate an officer responsible for making decisions about applications notified by another authority. Appropriate arrangements should also be put in place to ensure cover during any absences of the designated officer.

**6.3** The notified authority should normally accept the facts of the case relating to residence, employment, family associations etc., as stated by the notifying authority, unless they have clear evidence to the contrary. It is the notifying authority's duty to make inquiries into the circumstances of homelessness with the same degree of care and thoroughness before referring a case to another authority as it would for any other case.

**6.4** Local authorities should try to avoid causing undue disruption to the applicant which could arise from the operation of the criteria and procedures set out above. For instance, where it is agreed that the conditions for referral are met two authorities involved could agree, subject to the applicants' consent, to enter into a reciprocal arrangement so as to avoid having to move a household which may already have made arrangements within the notifying authority's area for schooling, medical treatment etc. Such arrangements could involve provision via nominations to other social housing providers such as registered social landlords. Authorities are reminded that there is no requirement to refer applicants to another authority even where it is agreed that the conditions for referral are met.

**6.5** Once written confirmation of notification has been received the notified authority should, within 10 days, reply to the notifying authority. If, despite reminders, there is an unreasonable delay by the notified authority in formally responding to the notification, the notifying authority may ask its local authority association to intercede on its behalf.

## 7 ARRANGEMENTS FOR SECURING ACCOMMODATION

**7.1** As soon as the notifying authority has advised the applicant that it intends to notify, or has already notified, another authority that it considers that the conditions for referral are met, the notifying authority has a duty (under s.200 (1) of the 1996 Act) (England and Wales) and s.34 *Housing (Scotland) Act 1987* to secure accommodation until the applicant is informed of the decision whether the conditions for referral are met. During this period, the notifying authority also has a duty (under s.211) (England and Wales) and s.36 of the *Housing (Scotland) Act 1987* to take reasonable steps for the protection of property belonging to the applicant or anyone who might reasonably be expected to reside with the applicant.

**7.2.1** When it has been decided whether the conditions for referral are met the notifying authority must inform the applicant of the decision and the reason for it (s.200(2), England and Wales or s.34 of the *Housing (Scotland) Act 1987)*. The applicant must also be informed of his right to ask for a review of the decision and that any request must be made within 21 days or such longer period as the authority may allow in writing

**7.2.2** If it is decided that the conditions for referral are not met, under s.200(3) England and Wales or s.34(2) of the *Housing (Scotland) Act 1987* the notifying authority will be subject to the s.193 duty (England and Wales) or s.31 of the *Housing (Scotland) Act 1987* and must ensure that suitable accommodation is available for the applicant.

**7.2.3** If it is decided that the conditions for referral are met, under s.200(4) or s.34(2) of the *Housing (Scotland) Act 1987)*, the notified authority will be subject to the s.193 duty (England and Wales) s.31 of the *Housing (Scotland) Act 1987* and must ensure that suitable accommodation is available for the applicant.

**7.3** The local authority associations recommend that once a notified authority has accepted that the conditions of referral are met it shall reimburse the notifying authority for any expenses which may reasonably have been incurred in providing temporary accommodation, including protection of property. If the notifying authority unduly delays advising an authority of its intention to refer an applicant then the notified authority shall only be responsible for expenses incurred after the receipt of notification. In normal circumstances a period of more than 30 working days, commencing from the date when the notifying authority had reason to believe that the applicant may be homeless or threatened with homelessness and commenced inquiries under s.184, (England & Wales), s.28 of the *Housing (Scotland) Act 1987*, should be considered as constituting undue delay.

## 8. RIGHT OF REVIEW OF REFERRAL DECISIONS (ENGLAND AND WALES)

**8.1** Under s.202(1)(c) *Housing Act 1996*, applicants in England and Wales have the right to request a review of any decision by the authority to notify another authority of its opinion that the conditions for referral are met. And, under s.202(1)(d), applicants in England and Wales have the right to request a review of any decision whether the conditions for referral are met. In Scotland (under s.34(3A) and s.35A(2)(b) of the *Housing (Scotland) Act 1987*) as inserted by s.4 of the *Housing*

*Scotland Act 2001* the applicant must be notified that they can request a review of any decision to refer their case to another authority, any determination reached following referral and the time within which this request should be made – the authority should also notify the applicant of advice and assistance available to him in connection with this review. In both cases the request for review will be made to the notifying authority.

## 9 STATUTORY PROCEDURE ON REVIEW

**9.1  Review procedure for England** – The procedural requirements for a review are set out in the *Allocation of Housing and Homelessness (Review Procedures) Regulations 1999* (SI 1999 No.71).

**9.2**  The notifying authority shall notify the applicant:
- (i)  that the applicant, or someone acting on the applicant's behalf, may make written representations,
- (ii)  of the review procedures

**9.3**  If the reviewer acting for the notifying authority considers that there is an irregularity in the original decision, or in the manner in which it was made, but is nevertheless minded to make a decision which is against the interests of the applicant, the reviewer shall notify the applicant:
- (i)  that the reviewer is so minded, and the reasons why
- (ii)  that the applicant, or someone acting on the applicant's behalf, may make further written or oral representations.

**9.4**  In carrying out a review the reviewer shall:
- (i)  consider any representations made by, or on behalf of, the applicant,
- (ii)  consider any further written or oral representations made by, or on behalf of, the applicant in response to a notification referred to in paragraph 9.2 (b) above
- (iii)  make a decision on the basis of the facts known at the date of the review.

**9.5**  The applicant should be notified of the decision on a review within: eight weeks from the date on which a request for review was made under s.202(1)(c), ten weeks from the date on which a request for review was made under s.202(1)(d), or such longer period as the applicant may agree in writing.

**9.6  Review procedure for Scotland** – Procedures are set out in s.35A and s.35B of the *Housing (Scotland) Act 1987*. Good practice guidance on the procedures is set out in Chapter 11 of the Code of Guidance on Homelessness.

**9.7  Review Procedure for Wales.** The procedures are set out in *The Allocation of Housing and Homelessness (Review Procedures) Regulations 1999* (SI 1999 No 71).

**9.8**  Where the decision under review is a joint decision by the notifying housing authority and the notified housing authority s202 (4) requires that the review should be carried out jointly by the two housing authorities.

**9.9**  The notifying authority shall notify the applicant:
- (i)  that the applicant, or someone acting on the applicant's behalf, may make written representations,
- (ii)  of the review procedures

**9.10**  If the reviewer acting for the notifying authority considers that there is an irregularity in the original decision, or in the manner in which it was made, but is nevertheless minded to make a decision which is against the interests of the applicant, the reviewer shall notify the applicant:
- (i)  that the reviewer is so minded, and the reasons why
- (ii)  that the applicant, or someone acting on the applicant's behalf, may make further written and/or oral representations.

**9.11**  In carrying out a review the reviewer shall:
- (i)  consider any representations made by, or on behalf of, the applicant,
- (ii)  consider any further written or oral representations made by, or on behalf of, the applicant in response to a notification referred to in paragraph 9.9 (ii) above
- (iii)  make a decision on the basis of the facts known at the date of the review.

**9.12**  The applicant should be notified of the decision on a review within:
- (i)  eight weeks from the date on which a request for review was made, where the original decision was made by the housing authority,
- (ii)  ten weeks from the date on which a request for review was made where the decision was made jointly by two housing authorities
- (iii)  twelve weeks, where the decision is taken by a person appointed pursuant to the Schedule to the *Homelessness (Decisions on Referrals) Order 1998* (SI 1998 No.1578).

In all these cases it is open to the reviewer to seek the applicant's agreement to an extension of the proscribed period; any such agreement must be given in writing.

## 10 DISPUTES BETWEEN AUTHORITIES

**10.1** *The Homelessness (Decisions on Referrals (Scotland) Order 1998* and the *Homelessness (Decisions on Referrals) Order 1998* (SI 1998 No.1578) (England and Wales) set out the arrangements for determining whether the conditions for referral are met, should the notifying and the notified authority fail to agree. These arrangements allow the question to be decided either by a person agreed between the two authorities concerned or, in default of such agreement, by a person appointed from a panel established by the LGA.

**10.2** Where a notified authority considers the conditions for referral are not met it should write to the notifying authority giving its reasons in full, within 10 days. The letter should contain all the reasons for its opinion, to avoid delaying the appointment of a referee and to minimise any inconvenience for the applicant.

**10.3** Where two authorities cannot reach agreement on whether the conditions for referral are met they must seek to agree on a referee who will make the decision. CoSLA and the LGA have jointly established an independent panel of referees for this purpose. A referee should be appointed within 21 days of the notified authority receiving the notification.

**10.4** Authorities invoking the disputes procedure should, having first agreed on the proposed referee, establish that he or she is available and willing to accept the case. Each authority is then responsible for providing the referee with such information as he or she requires to reach a decision, making copies of the submission available to the applicant and ensuring prompt payment of fees and expenses. Sections 10–19 (Guidelines for Invoking the Disputes Procedure) set out in greater detail the requirements and timescale for the disputes procedure.

**10.5** Authorities invoking the disputes procedure should be bound by the decision of the referee, including the apportionment of fees and expenses, subject to a further decision by a referee where the applicant asks for a review of the initial decision.

**10.6** If the authorities are unable to agree on the choice of a referee, they must jointly request that CoSLA (for Scottish authorities) or the LGA (for English or Welsh authorities) appoint a referee on their behalf as outlined in paragraph 10.8 below.

**10.7** If a referee has not been appointed within six weeks of the notified authority receiving the referral the notifying authority may request CoSLA or the LGA, as appropriate, to appoint a referee as outlined in paragraph 10.8 below.

**10.8** Where two authorities fail to agree on the appointment of a referee CoSLA (if the dispute is between Scottish authorities) or the LGA (if the dispute is between English or Welsh authorities) may appoint a referee from the panel. Where the **notified** authority is Scottish then the local authority association responsible for appointing a referee will be CoSLA, even if the notifying authority is in England or Wales. The LGA will be the responsible association if the notified authority is English or Welsh.

**10.9** The local authority associations should only be involved in the direct appointment of referees as a last resort. Under normal circumstances authorities should jointly agree the arrangements between themselves in accordance with the Guidelines for Invoking the Disputes Procedure.

### PROCEDURES FOR REFERRALS OF HOMELESS APPLICANTS ON THE GROUNDS OF LOCAL CONNECTON WITH ANOTHER LOCAL AUTHORITY

### GUIDELINES FOR INVOKING THE DISPUTES PROCEDURE

*AGREED BY*

**ASSOCIATION OF LONDON GOVERNMENT (ALG)**

**CONVENTION OF SCOTTISH LOCAL AUTHORITIES (CoSLA)**

**LOCAL GOVERNMENT ASSOCIATION (LGA)**

**WELSH LOCAL GOVERNMENT ASSOCIATION (WLGA)**

("**the local authority associations**")

## 11 DETERMINING DISPUTES

**11.1** The local authority associations have been concerned to establish an inexpensive, simple, speedy, fair and consistent way of resolving disputes between authorities arising from the referral of homeless applicants under s.198 *Housing Act 1996* (England and Wales). In Scotland the provisions of s.33 *Housing (Scotland) Act 1987* apply.

**11.2** For the purpose of this Disputes procedure, arbitrators are referred to as "referees". Referees will not normally be entitled to apply the criteria set out in this agreed procedure without the consent of the local authorities involved in the dispute. Where the issues in the case are evenly balanced, referees may have regard to the wishes of the applicant.

**11.3** In determining disputes referees will need to have regard to:

a)  for English and Welsh authorities
- Part VII *Housing Act 1996*
- regulation 6 of the *Homelessness Regulations1996* (SI 1996 No. 2754) for Wales
- the *Homelessness (Decisions on Referrals) Order 1998* (SI 1998 No. 1578)
- the *Allocation of Housing and Homelessness (Review Procedures) Regulations 1999* (SI 1999 No.71)
- *Code of Guidance for Local Authorities on Allocation of Accommodation and Homelessness 2003 (Wales)* – currently under review
- *Homelessness Code of Guidance for Local Authorities 2006 (England)*

b)  for Scottish authorities
- *Housing (Scotland) Act 1987*
- the *Homelessness (Decisions on Referrals) (Scotland) Order 1998*
- the *Persons subject to Immigration Control (Housing Authority Accommodation and Homelessness) Order 2000* (SI 2000 706)
- *Homelessness etc (Scotland) Act 2003*
- *Code of Guidance on Homelessness: Guidance on legislation, policies and practices to prevent and resolve homelessness 2005 (Scotland)*

c)  for all authorities
- the *Procedures for s.198 (Local Connection) Homeless Referrals: Guidelines for Local Authorities and Referees* produced by the local authority associations
- *Asylum and Immigration (Treatment of Claimants, etc.) Act 2004*

**11.4** Where there is a cross border dispute between a Scottish authority and an English or Welsh authority then the legislation relevant to the location of the *notified* authority should be applied in determining whether the conditions for referral are met.

**11.5** Scottish authorities need to be aware of any orders exercised by s.8 of the *Homelessness (Scotland) Act 2003* that may effect referrals between Scottish authorities in the future.

## 12 ARRANGEMENTS FOR APPOINTING REFEREES

**12.1** Referees will be approached by the authorities in dispute, both of which must agree that the referee should be invited to accept the appointment, to establish whether they are willing and able to act in a particular dispute. The referee should be appointed within 21 days of the notified authority receiving the referral. If the local authorities are unable to agree on the choice of referee they should contact CoSLA or the LGA, as appropriate, in accordance with section 10 of the Guidelines for Local Authorities on Procedures for Referral.

**12.2** A referee will be given an initial indication of the reason for the dispute by the relevant authorities or the local authority association. The referee's jurisdiction is limited to the issue of whether the conditions for referral are met.

**12.3** A referee must not have any personal interest in the outcome of the dispute and should not accept the appointment if he or she is, or was, employed by, or is a council tax payer in, one of the disputing local authorities, or if he or she has any connection with the applicant.

## 13 PROCEDURES FOR DETERMINING THE DISPUTE

**13.1** The general procedures to be followed by a referee in determining a dispute are outlined in the Schedule to the *Homelessness (Decisions on Referrals) Order 1998* (SI 1998 No. 1578). (England and Wales) and SI 1998 No.1603 (*Scotland*). It is recommended that the following, more detailed, procedures are applied to *all* cases.

**13.2** Following appointment, the referee shall invite the notifying and notified authorities to submit written representations within a period of **fourteen** working days, specifying the closing date, and requiring them to send copies of their submission to the applicant and to the other authority involved in the dispute. Authorities must have the opportunity to see each other's written statements, and should be allowed a further period of **ten** working days to comment thereon before the referee proceeds to determine the issue. The referee may also invite further written representations from the authorities, if considered necessary.

**13.3** The homeless applicant to whom the dispute relates is not a direct party to the dispute but the referee may invite written or oral representations from the applicant, or any other person, which is proper and relevant to the issue. Where the referee invites representations from a person they may be made by another person acting on the person's behalf, whether or not the other person is legally qualified.

**13.4**   The disputing authorities should make copies of their submissions available to the applicant. The authorities should have the opportunity to comment on any information from the applicant (or any other source) upon which the referee intends to rely in reaching his/her decision.

**13.5**   Since the applicant's place of abode is in question, and temporary accommodation and property storage charges may be involved, it is important that a decision should be reached as quickly as possible – normally within *a month* of the receipt of the written representations and comments from the notifying and notified authority. This period will commence at the end of the process described in point 13.2. In the last resort, a referee may determine a dispute on the facts before him/her if one authority has, after reminders, failed to present its case without reasonable cause.

## 14 ORAL HEARINGS

**14.1**   Where an oral hearing is necessary or more convenient (e.g. where the applicant is illiterate, English is not his/her first language or further information is necessary to resolve issues in dispute), it is suggested that the notifying authority should be invited to present its case first, followed by the notified authority and any other persons whom the referee wishes to hear. The applicant may be invited to provide information on relevant matters. The authorities should then be given a right to reply to earlier submissions.

**14.2**   The referee's determination must be in writing even when there is an oral hearing. The referee will have to arrange the venue for the hearing and it is suggested that the offices of the notifying authority would often be the most convenient location.

**14.3**   Where a person has made oral representations the referee may direct either or both authorities to pay reasonable travelling expenses. The notifying and notified authorities will pay their own costs.

## 15 NOTIFICATION OF DETERMINATION

**15.1**   The written decision of the referee should set out:
    (a)    the issue(s) which he has been asked to determine
    (b)    the findings of fact which are relevant to the question(s) in issue
    (c)    the decision
    (d)    the reasons for the decision.

The referee's determination is binding upon the participating local authorities, subject to the applicant's right to ask for a review of the decision under s.202 of the 1996 Act (and possible right of appeal to the county court on a point of law under s.204). The statutory right to review does not apply to Scottish legislation.

## 16 COSTS OF DETERMINATION

**16.1**   Referees will be expected to provide their own secretarial services and to obtain their own advice on points of law. The cost of so doing, however, will be costs of the determination and recoverable as such.

## 17 CIRCULATION OF DETERMINATION

**17.1**   Referees should send copies of the determination to both disputing authorities and to the LGA. The LGA will circulate copies to other members of the Panel of Referees as an aid to settling future disputes and promoting consistency in decisions.

**17.2**   The notifying authority should inform the applicant of the outcome promptly.

## 18 PAYMENT OF FEES AND COSTS

**18.1**   The local authority associations recommend a flat rate fee of **£500** per determination (including determinations made on a review) which should be paid in full and as speedily as possible after the determination has been received. However, in exceptional cases where a dispute takes a disproportionate time to resolve, a referee may negotiate a higher fee. In addition, the referee may claim the actual cost of any travelling, secretarial or other incidental expenses which s/he has incurred, including any additional costs arising from the right of review or the right of appeal to a county court on a point of law.

**18.2**   The LGA will determine such additional fees as may be appropriate for any additional work which may subsequently arise should there be a further dispute or appeal after the initial determination has been made or should a referee be party to an appeal, under s.204 *Housing Act 1996*, to the county court on a point of law.

**18.3**   The referee's fees and expenses, and any third party costs, would normally be recovered from the unsuccessful party to the dispute, although a referee may choose to apportion expenses between the disputing authorities if he considers it warranted. Referees are advised, when issuing invoices to local authorities, to stipulate that payment be made within **28 days**.

## 19 REOPENING A DISPUTE

**19.1**   Once a determination on a dispute is made, a referee is not permitted to reopen the case, even though new facts may be presented to him or her, unless a fresh determination is required to rectify an error arising from a mistake or omission.

## 20 RIGHT OF REVIEW OF REFEREE'S DECISION

**20.1**   Section 202(1)(d) *Housing Act 1996* gives an applicant the right to request a review of any decision made under these procedures. The right to review does not apply to Scottish legislation.

**20.2**   If an applicant asks for a review of a referee's decision the notifying and notified authority must, within five working days, appoint another referee ("the reviewer") from the panel. This applies even if the original referee was appointed by the LGA. The reviewer must be a different referee from the referee who made the initial decision. If the two authorities fail to appoint a reviewer within this period then the notifying authority must, within five working days, request the LGA to appoint a reviewer and the LGA must do so within seven days of the request.

**20.3**   The authorities are required to provide the reviewer with the reasons for the initial decision, and the information on which the decision is based, within five working days of his or her appointment. The two authorities should decide between them who will be responsible for notifying the applicant of the reviewer's decision, once received.

## 21 STATUTORY PROCEDURE ON REVIEW

**21.1**   The procedural requirements for a review are set out in the *Allocation of Housing and Homelessness (Review Procedures) Regulations 1999* (SI 1999 No.71).

**21.2**   The reviewer is required to:
   (i)    notify the applicant that he or she, or someone acting on his or her behalf, may make written representations,
   (ii)   notify the applicant of the review procedures, and
   (iii)  send copies of the applicant's representations to the two authorities and invite them to respond.

**21.3**   If the reviewer considers that there is an irregularity in the original decision, or in the manner in which it was made, but is nevertheless minded to make a decision which is against the interests of the applicant, the reviewer shall notify the applicant:
   (a)   that the reviewer is so minded and the reasons why, and
   (b)   that the applicant, or someone acting on his behalf, may make further written or oral representations.

**21.4**   In carrying out a review, the reviewer is required to:
   (i)    consider any representations made by, or on behalf of, the applicant,
   (ii)   consider any responses to (i) above,
   (iii)  consider any further written or oral representations made by, or on behalf of, the applicant in response to a notification referred to in paragraph 21.3 (b), and
   (iv)  make a decision on the basis of the facts known at the date of the review.

**21.5**   The applicant should be notified of the decision on a review within twelve weeks from the date on which the request for the review was made, or such longer period as the applicant may agree in writing. The two authorities should be advised in writing of the decision on the review, and the reasons for it, **at least a week before the end of the period** in order to allow them adequate time to notify the applicant. Copies of the decision should also be sent to the LGA.

### PROCEDURES FOR REFERRALS OF HOMELESS APPLICANTS ON THE GROUNDS OF LOCAL CONNECTON WITH ANOTHER LOCAL AUTHORITY

**STANDARD NOTIFICATION FORM**

*AGREED BY*

---

**ASSOCIATION OF LONDON GOVERNMENT** (ALG)

**CONVENTION OF SCOTTISH LOCAL AUTHORITIES** (CoSLA)

**LOCAL GOVERNMENT ASSOCIATION** (LGA)

**WELSH LOCAL GOVERNMENT ASSOCIATION** (WLGA)

**("the local authority associations")**

---

## A  NOTIFYING AUTHORITY DETAILS

Contact Name _____

Authority _____

Telephone Number_____ Fax Number_____

E-mail _____

Address for Correspondence_____

_____

## B  APPLICANT DETAILS

Name of Main Applicant_____ Date of Birth _____

Current Address_____

_____

_____

_____

## C  FAMILY MEMBERS

Name                         Relationship          Date of Birth

_____   _____   _____

_____   _____   _____

_____   _____   _____

_____   _____   _____

_____   _____   _____

_____   _____   _____

_____   _____   _____

_____   _____   _____

## D  ADDRESSES IN LAST 5 YEARS (include dates and type of tenure)

_____

_____

_____

_____

_____

_____

_____

## E  PRESENT/PREVIOUS EMPLOYMENT DETAILS

Employer_____ Tel No_____

Address _____

Contact Name_____ Job Title _____

Previous Employer _____

Date from_____ Date to _____

Address _____

**F  REASONS FOR HOMELESSNESS**

_____
_____
_____
_____

**H  PRIORITY NEED CATEGORY**

_____
_____

**I  LOCAL CONNECTION DETAILS**

_____
_____
_____
_____
_____
_____

**J  WISHES OF THE APPLICANT(S) (in the context of the referral)**

_____
_____
_____
_____
_____

**K  THE NOTIFYING AUTHORITY CONSIDER THE CONDITIONS FOR REFERRAL ARE MET BECAUSE:**

_____
_____
_____
_____
_____
_____

**L  ANY SUPPLEMENTARY INFORMATION**
(attach supporting documentation if relevant)

I confirm that, in accordance with s.198 *Housing Act 1996,* this authority considers that neither the applicant nor any person who might reasonably be expected to reside with the applicant would run the risk of domestic violence or face a probability of other violence in the district of your authority, if this referral is made.

Signed_____ Date _____

[5041]

# HOMELESSNESS CODE OF GUIDANCE FOR LOCAL AUTHORITIES

## Supplementary Guidance on Intentional Homelessness

### APPLICANTS WHO FACE HOMELESSNESS FOLLOWING DIFFICULTIES IN MEETING MORTGAGE COMMITMENTS

In response to the current economic climate, and the robust framework of financial support the Government has put in place to help homeowners in financial difficulty[1], this note provides

**guidance on how local housing authorities should exercise their homelessness functions, and apply the various statutory criteria, when considering whether applicants who are homeless having lost their home because of difficulties in meeting mortgage commitments are intentionally or unintentionally homeless.**

---
<sup>1</sup>     The Mortgage Rescue Scheme and Homeowner Mortgage Support

## INTRODUCTION

**1.**   This guidance is issued by the Secretary of State under s.182 of the *Housing Act 1996* ("the 1996 Act"). Under s.182(1) of the 1996 Act, housing authorities are required to have regard to this guidance in exercising their functions under Part 7 of the 1996 Act.

**2.**   This statutory guidance supplements Chapter 11 of the *Homelessness Code of Guidance for Local Authorities* issued in July 2006 ("the 2006 Code"), and should be read in conjunction with that chapter.

## HOMELESSNESS FOLLOWING MORTGAGE DIFFICULTIES

**3.**   Homeowners may be at risk of homelessness if they experience difficulties in meeting their mortgage commitments, for example, because a member of the household loses their employment or suffers an income shock. Individual homeowners may respond in different ways when faced with such difficult circumstances.

**4.**   Some homeowners may voluntarily give up possession of the property (hand back the keys to the lender). Some homeowners may decide to sell the property. Others may seek help to remain in their home, including help under the Mortgage Rescue Scheme (MRS) or Homeowner Mortgage Support (HMS), but decide – if found eligible for the scheme – not to accept an offer because they consider that continuing with home ownership would be unsustainable or would entail unacceptable financial risk. Where homeowners who have experienced such circumstances become homeless or threatened with homelessness and apply to a local housing authority for assistance, the authority will need to give careful consideration to the substantive cause(s) of homelessness before coming to a decision on intentionality.

## DEFINITION OF INTENTIONAL HOMELESSNESS

**5.**   Authorities are reminded that by sections 191(1) and 196(1) of the 1996 Act, a person becomes homeless intentionally or threatened with homelessness intentionally, if:
  i)     the person deliberately does or fails to do anything in consequence of which the person ceases to occupy accommodation (or the likely result of which is that the person will be forced to leave accommodation);
  ii)    the accommodation is available for the person's occupation; and
  iii)   it would have been reasonable for the person to continue to occupy the accommodation.

However, an act or omission made in good faith by someone who was unaware of any relevant fact must not be treated as deliberate.

**6.**   Authorities are also reminded that they must not adopt general policies that seek to pre-define circumstances that do or do not amount to intentional homelessness or threatened homelessness (see paragraph 11.5 of the *Homelessness Code of Guidance for Local Authorities*).

## PRINCIPLES ESTABLISHED BY CASE LAW

**7.**   The broad thrust of section 191 is to ascribe intentional homelessness to a person who on the facts is responsible for his homelessness by virtue of his own act or omission. Whilst it is not part of the purpose of the legislation to require local authorities to house people whose homelessness is brought upon them by their own fault, equally, it is not part of the legislation that authorities should refuse to accommodate people whose homelessness has been brought upon them without fault on their part, for example, by an inability to make ends meet.

**8.**   Nobody may be presumed to be intentionally homeless; the local housing authority must be satisfied of intentionality and must ask and answer the questions set out in the legislation. The decision maker in the local authority must look for the substantive cause of the homelessness and the effective cause will not always be the most immediate proximate cause.

**9.**   Intentionality does not depend on whether applicants have behaved wisely or prudently or reasonably. Where an applicant's failure to seek help may have been foolish, imprudent or even unreasonable, this would not necessarily mean his or her conduct was not in good faith.

## SOME POSSIBLE SCENARIOS

**10.**   As mentioned above, some former homeowners may seek housing assistance from a local housing authority having lost their home in one of the following circumstances:

i)    having voluntarily surrendered the property (handed the keys back);
ii)   having sold the property;
iii)  where the property was repossessed after the applicant refused an offer under the MRS;
iv)   where the property was repossessed after the applicant refused an offer of HMS;
v)    where the property was repossessed and the applicant had not sought help.

There should be no general presumption that a homeowner will have brought homelessness on him or herself in any of the above scenarios. A person cannot be found to have become intentionally homeless from a property where he or she was already statutorily homeless: e.g. because it was not reasonable for him to continue to occupy the property (see paragraph 8.18 et seq of the *Homelessness Code of Guidance for Local Authorities*). Consequently, where someone was already homeless before surrendering or selling their home or refusing an offer under MRS or HMS, the 'acts' of surrender or sale, and the 'omission' of refusing an offer of MRS or HMS cannot be treated as the cause of homelessness.

**11.** In particular, authorities will need to satisfy themselves on two questions as applied at the point in time immediately before the applicant ceased to occupy accommodation (i.e. prior to the surrender, sale or refusal of help). First, was the applicant's home available as accommodation for the applicant, any other person who normally resides with him as a member of his family and any person who might reasonably be expected to reside with him? Second, did the applicant's home constitute accommodation that it would have been reasonable for him or her to continue to occupy? It would not have been reasonable for the applicant to continue to occupy his or her home, for example, if the home was not affordable, for example, because the applicant could not meet the cost of his or her mortgage commitments.

**12.** If the answer to either of the two questions above is in the negative, the applicant will have been homeless prior to the surrender or sale of the property or refusal of an offer of assistance under the MRS or HMS. In such a case, the authority may still consider whether the applicant's homelessness was intentional but will need to look at the substantive causes of that homelessness prior to surrender or sale of the property or refusal of an offer of assistance under the MRS or HMS.

Department for Communities and Local Government. © Crown copyright 2009.

Printed in the UK August 2009 on paper comprising no less than 75% post consumer waste.

Ref. Number: 09 PRH 06057 SG

ISBN: 978-1-4098-1750-5

[5042]

# Index